LAKE FOREST LIBRARY
3 1243 00295 5580

P9-BZW-458

the ENCYCLOPEDIA of the MUSICAL THEATRE

SECOND EDITION

the ENCYCLOPEDIA of the MUSICAL THEATRE

SECOND EDITION

2
GI–N

Kurt Gänzl

Schirmer Books
an imprint of the Gale Group
New York • Detroit • San Francisco • London • Boston • Woodbridge, CT

First edition published 1994 by Schirmer Books and in Great Britain by Blackwell Publishers

Schirmer Books
1633 Broadway
New York, NY 10019

Gale Group
27500 Drake Road
Farmington Hills, MI 48331

Library of Congress Cataloging-in-Publication Data

Gänzl, Kurt.
The encyclopedia of the musical theatre / Kurt Gänzl. — 2nd ed.
p. cm.
Includes bibliographical references and discographies.
ISBN 0-02-864970-2 (set)
1. Musicals—Encyclopedias. I. Title.

ML 102.M88 G3 2001
782.1'4'03—dc21 2001018361

Printed in the United States of America

Printing number
1 2 3 4 5 6 7 8 9 10

This book is printed on acid-free paper

FRONT COVER, CLOCKWISE: Japanese production of *Phantom of the Opéra*, *Babil and Bijou* sheet music cover, *Don Juan* poster, *The Pirates of Penzance* sheet music cover, *Faust Up-to-Date* sheet music cover.

Contents

Organization of the Encyclopedia

Alphabetization

Entries are arranged in a single alphabetical sequence, using a letter-by-letter system, as follows:

> **MANNEQUINS**
> **DER MANN MIT DEN DREI FRAUEN**
> **MANNSCHAFT AN BORD**
> **MANNSTADT, William**
> **MAN OF LA MANCHA**

For alphabetization purposes, the following conventions have been followed:

- the definite and indefinite articles A, The, L', Le, La, Les, Das, Der, Die, etc, are ignored where they appear at the beginning of show headwords;
- the Scots or Irish prefixes "Mac," "Mc" and "M" are alphabetized letter-by-letter rather than treated as if they were spelt out "Mac";
- and all accented letters are treated as English unaccented letters.

Cross references appear as follows:

> **MAYTIME** *see* WIE EINST IM MAI

with the capital letter indicating the letter under which the entry may be found.

Introductory and supplementary sections to people entries

The articles are written and ordered under the name in which their subject was active in the theatre. When that name is simply an easily shortened version of the subject's real full name, the rest of that real name is given in square brackets.

> **BROWN, Jon[athan Frederick]**

When the bold headword is not simply a shortened form of the real full name or when the nom de théâtre/nom de plume is not that with which the subject was born, the real full name (where known) is given separately, again in square brackets.

> **BROWN, John [BROWN, Jonathan Frederick]**
>
> **BROWN, John [BRAUNSTEIN, Johann Friedrich]**

The name is followed by the places and dates of birth and death, where known, in parentheses. If the date of death (or birth) is not known it is simply not included.

> (b London, 6 February 1933)

On a number of occasions, a birth year is included but is marked with a query. This is generally where a death certificate or obituary has given the subject's age at death, but a birth certificate and/or date has not been found to confirm that information.

> (b Paris, ?1946; d Nice, 10 August 1980).

The bibliographies given at the end of entries include a representative selection of biographies, autobiographies or other significant literature devoted to the subject. I have not attempted to list every published work—not least because many of the people who have the most works written about them are those whose principal activity was not the musical theatre.

Introductory and supplementary sections to show entries

The introductory sections to show entries give the title (and subtitle where relevant) under which the show was normally played, followed by any considerably used alternative title, then the credits as given on the playbill, and the date and place of the first production. As in the worklists that appear at the end of people articles (see below), this information refers to the first metropolitan performance. In the case of modern works, the date of the official "first night," rather than that of the first preview performance, is given. Out-of-town tryout dates are shown only when there is an appreciable gap between the initial out-of-town production and any later metropolitan production, or when the show failed to find its way to town at all.

NO, NO, NANETTE Musical comedy in 3 acts by Frank Mandel, Otto Harbach and Irving Caesar based on *My Lady Friends* by Mandel and Emil Nyitray (and *Oh, James!* by May Edgington). Music by Vincent Youmans. Garrick Theater, Detroit, 23 April 1923; Harris Theater, Chicago, 7 May 1923; Globe Theater, New York, 16 September 1925.

The supplementary sections at the end of the show entries consist of a record of the dates and places of the first productions of the show in what, for the purposes of this book, are treated as the "main centers" (Berlin, Budapest, London, Melbourne, New York, Paris, Sydney, Vienna) other than that in which it was first performed. When the show was, on these occasions, given in France, Austria, Britain, America, Australia, Hungary or Germany under a title other than its original, the altered or translated title is given, along with the date and place of the production.

Austria: Theater in der Josefstadt 15 May 1952; France: Theatre Marigny *Feu d'artifice* 1952; UK: Bristol Old Vic *Oh, My Papa!* 2 April, Garrick Theatre, London 17 July 1957

Recordings: selection (Ariola-Eurodisc), selection in English (Parlophone EP)

Mention is also made of films and recordings of, and books on, individual shows. I have made no attempt to give details of recordings, as labels and serial numbers of recordings vary from country to country and a complete list of all the show recordings in question would fill a vast volume. I have merely tried to indicate which of the shows dealt with can be found on record, at least some of the labels that have been responsible for those recordings, and whether "original cast" or foreign-language recordings are included amongst them. Similarly, I have mentioned books only in the rare instances where a book is wholly, or very largely, devoted to the show in question.

Authors' and composers' worklists

The worklists attached to the articles on librettists, lyricists and composers are intended to include all of each writer's credited works for the book musical theatre.

Works for which a writer was not credited on the playbills are not included, and neither are works written for such adjacent musical and theatrical areas as opera, ballet, pantomime and revue.

The original works in the list are given in chronological order of their first production.

When a show has been played under more than one title, the title in bold type is the title under which its main metropolitan run was given, with alternative titles in italic type in parentheses. Titles discarded in tryout are noted as "ex-."

1988 **Ain't Broadway Grand** (ex- *Mike*)

Post-metropolitan changes of title are indicated by the prefix "later-." Where the title change was part of a significant rewrite, the rewrite will have a separate entry as "revised version of [original title]."

The year and title of the piece are followed by the names of the writer's credited collaborators on the show in question, in the order: composer(s)/lyricist(s)/librettist(s). Writers who collaborated with the writer in his or her area are shown by a "w" indicating "with." Thus (Smith/w Brown/w Green) would mean that the person who is the subject of the article worked on the show's lyrics with Brown and its book with Green, and the music was by Smith. The names of the subject's collaborators are given in full on their first mention in a worklist, and thereafter by surname only except where a duplicated surname could lead to confusion, such as in the case of contemporaneous text-writers H B Smith, R B Smith and E Smith. Any variants occurring in a show's author/composer credits are included in square brackets. Major revisions of a show are credited separately in the worklist.

In the case of short works only, the names of the authors are followed by an indication such as "1 act" or "3 scenes." Otherwise all works are "full-length" pieces (in the loosest possible meaning of the term when some works from the 19th-century days of very long evenings are in question) in a minimum of two acts.

Each original work entry on the worklist ends with the place and date of the first metropolitan performance. In the case of modern works, the date of the official "first night" rather than that of the first preview performance is used. Out-of-town tryout dates are shown only when there is an appreciable gap between the initial out-of-town production and any later metropolitan production, or when the show failed to find its way to town at all. In the case of shows initially staged in other cities and subsequently remounted in what, for the purposes of this book, are accounted the "main centers" (Berlin, Budapest, London, Melbourne, New York, Paris, Sydney, Vienna), both dates are given. When the theatre in which the show's premiere is given is not based in the city that may be regarded as being/having been the writer's base, the name of the city is included alongside the theatre. So, for example, a Vienna-centered author will be credited with works at the Carltheater, the Theater an der Wien or the Raimundtheater without further elaboration, but for productions at the Theater am Gärtnerplatz, Munich, the Népszínház, Budapest, or the Thalia-Theater, Berlin, the cities would be specified.

1890 **Erminy** (*Erminie*) German version w Heinrich von Waldberg (Carltheater)

1890 **Der bleiche Gast** (Josef Hellmesberger, Zamara/w von Waldberg) Carl-Schultze Theater, Hamburg 6 September

Shows which are not the original work of the writer in question, but simply adaptations of a musical originally written and produced by other writers in another language, are listed under the year of their production in the version by the subject of the worklist. The year is followed by the title given to the piece in the subject's adaptation, followed in parentheses by the title of the original piece in its original language, a description of the nature of the adaptation (where applicable) and the theatre where the adaptation was first staged.

1889 **Capitän Wilson** (*The Yeomen of the Guard*) German version w Carl Lindau (Carltheater)

On the occasions where I have been unable to trace or to confirm that a show credited to a writer was in fact produced, rather than just being announced for production, I have listed the title at the end of the worklist under the heading "Other titles attributed." Conversely, shows which were definitely produced, but for which my details are incomplete, are included in the worklist, with their details as complete as I have been able to make them. Any dubious dates, places or credits are indicated with a question mark, thus, ?1849.

Occasionally circumstances arose which could not be adequately dealt with by the arrangements described above. In these cases, it has been my main care simply to make whatever the situation and credits might be as clear as possible without clinging too unbendingly to a "standard" layout.

Abbreviations

(X) ad (Y)	the work of (X) adapted by (Y), adapter
add	additional
aka	also known as
(X) arr (Y)	the work of (X) arranged by (Y), arranger
b	born
ch	choreographed by, choreographer
d	died
dir	directed by, director
Eng	English/England
fr	from
Fr	French/France
Frln	Fraulein
Ger	German/Germany
Hun	Hungarian/Hungary
ka	known as
jr	junior
Lat	Latin
lib	libretto
ly	lyric(s)
md	musical director
mus	music
nd	no date known
np	no place known
posth	posthumous
rev	revival
scr	screenplay
Sp	Spanish/Spain
sq/sqq	and that/those following
sr	senior
t/o	takeover (of a role)
UK	United Kingdom
u/s	understudy
USA	United States of America

GLAMOROUS NIGHT Musical play in 2 acts by Ivor Novello. Lyrics by Christopher Hassall. Music by Ivor Novello. Theatre Royal, Drury Lane, London, 2 May 1935.

The Theatre Royal, Drury Lane, had fallen into the doldrums since its great successes with American operettas in the late 1920 and early 1930s, but a lunchtime conversation between general manager Harry Tennent and actor-author-composer Ivor Novello provided the impetus that put the big theatre back on the right rails. Novello, who had not penned a musical play for some 14 years as he raced merrily on through several other successful careers, offered to write, compose and star in a suitably grandiose ''Drury Lane piece,'' and the piece he turned out, written to measure for the house and its audiences, was *Glamorous Night.*

The young inventor Anthony Allen (Novello) blows the money advanced to him to develop a television system on taking a Ruritanian cruise-ship holiday. When they stop at Krasnia he becomes involved in drama. An attempt is made on the life of prima donna Militza Hajós (Mary Ellis), the mistress of King Stefan (Barry Jones), during the course of her show, and Anthony is on hand to foil the killer. Pushed by the ambitious republican demagogue Lydyeff (Lyn Harding), Militza takes flight on the departing cruise ship, and love blossoms as the ''republicans'' pursue her and ultimately wreck the ship. Anthony and Militza escape, via a gypsy encampment and a gypsy wedding, back to Krasnia, where Lydyeff has almost got Stefan to abdicate. Anthony shoots the villain, but has finally to take his leave of Militza of whom the lonely King has the greater need in his struggle to continue to rule. Olive Gilbert of the Carl Rosa Opera played a contralto singer and veteran actress Minnie Rayner was Militza's ex-chorus-girl maid.

The production had a vast cast and lashings of scenery (including, of course, the shipwreck), but it also had a lush, romantic score—much of it represented as part of the operetta within the operetta—which produced several standards, the soprano/contralto duo ''Fold Your Wings,'' the soprano's soaring title song (also the title song of the internal show), the tenor's showtime arietta, ''Shine Through My Dreams,'' as well as a different kind of stand-up number, ''Shanty Town,'' purveyed by jazz vocalist Elisabeth Welch, in a tacked-in role as an entertaining stowaway in the shipboard scenes.

Glamorous Night was a huge success, but the directors of the Theatre Royal, Drury Lane, closed it after seven months, at the approach of Christmas, refusing to sacrifice the traditional (and traditionally profitable) Christmas pantomime. In spite of all Novello could do, his show was bundled out and ended up passing Christmas in Glasgow. Whilst Drury Lane's following productions bombed one after another, Prince Littler took over *Glamorous Night* and brought it back from 21 provincial weeks to the even more vast auditorium of the London Coliseum (28 May 1936) with Barry Sinclair and Muriel Barron now starred, and Miss Gilbert surprisingly doubling in the role of the stowaway. The impetus of the first run, however, was gone, and another 91 performances saw the end of the show's London career.

There was, however, plenty of life still left in *Glamorous Night.* It was produced at St Louis's Municipal Opera with Norma Terriss starred as Militza, Guy Robertson as Anthony and Florenz Ames as Stefan. Revived there in 1942, it was filmed, with Miss Ellis starred opposite Barry Mackay, and it was seen regularly (though with rather decreasing scenic means) in the British provinces for decades thereafter, as its favorite songs became ingrained in the repertoire of English sopranos.

USA: Municipal Opera, St Louis 24 August 1936

Film: Associated British 1937

Recordings: original cast assembly (WRC), selections (WRC, HMV, Columbia)

GLASER, Lulu [GLASER, Lilian] (b Allegheny City, Pa, 2 June 1874; d Norwalk, Conn, 5 September 1958).

At 17 the beautiful, lithe and sparky little Lulu Glaser landed her first theatrical job as a member of the chorus of Francis Wilson's company, playing in a butchered version of Lecocq's *Le Grand Casimir* (*The Lion Tamer*) at the Broadway Theater. When, six weeks later, she was called on to deputize for the ailing Marie Jansen in the starring role, opposite Wilson, she caused sufficient of a sensation for the manager-star immediately to promote her to larger roles in his established repertoire, playing the boy Lazuli in another massacred masterpiece called *The Merry Monarch* (ex- *L'Étoile*) and the maid, Javotte, in *Erminie.* During nine seasons with the company, she created roles in Wilson's productions of *The Devil's Deputy* (1894, Elverine), Sullivan's *The Chieftain* (1895, Rita), *Half a King* (1896, Pierrette), *The Little Corporal* (1898, Jacqueline) and *Cyrano de Bergerac* (1899, Roxane), providing the ever-broadening feminine comedy opposite the very low-jinks favored by Wilson.

She moved on to take top-billing in a couple of short-lived pieces, *Sweet Anne Page* (1900) and *The Prima Donna* (1901, Angela Chumpley), and then in *Dolly Varden* (1902), a Stanislaus Stange/Julian Edwards compound of bits of *Barnaby Rudge* and other English classics, which provided a fine vehicle for the new star in its title role. She next starred as Queen Mary of England opposite William Pruette's Henry VIII in version of the famous British comedy *When Knighthood Was in Flower* under the title A *Madcap Princess* (1904), appeared in the title roles of *Miss Dolly Dollars* (1905, Dor-

Plate 147. **Glamorous Night.** *The gypsy wedding between Anthony (Ivor Novello) and Militza (Mary Ellis).*

othy Gay) and—after an essay into non-musical comedy as the star of Sydney Rosenfeld's *The Aero Club*—of *Lola from Berlin* (1907, Lotchen von Breckenhaussett), and found a useful vehicle when she appeared at Joe Weber's as ''Fonia'' to Charles J Ross's ''Dandilo'' in a burlesque version of *The Merry Widow* (1908).

She was *Mlle Mischief* in an American version of the German *Ein tolles Mädel* in 1908 (Rosette), Daphne Dearborn who was *The Girl from the States* (until she walked out of the dying show on the road) and Cherry Winston who was *Just One of the Boys* in 1909. She featured as Pitti Sing in the all-star *Mikado* at the Casino Theater (1910), starred in two further Continental importations, *The Girl and the Kaiser* (*Die Förster-Christl,* 1910, Christl) and, sporting a sporran in Boston, *Miss Dudelsack* (1911), as well as in the operetta *First Love* (1912, Elaine Hampton) before turning her attentions to vaudeville (*First Love, A Captivating Capture,* etc) for the last part of a career which, for all its enduring charms, had not really brought her one top-class new role in a top-class new show.

Originally married (1907) to the musical-comedian Ralph Herz, in 1925 she married the 67-year-old De Wolf Hopper.

GLAWATSCH, Franz (b Graz, 16 December 1871; d Vienna, 22 June 1928).

A singing comedian in the old Vienna tradition, in line of descent from Karl Blasel, Glawatsch began his career as a juvenile light comedian, winning his first big role at Budweis when he appeared as Adam in *Der Vogelhändler.* He moved on to Marburg (1895) and then to Graz (1896), where he was resident comedian for four years, graduating there to the older roles in which he would specialize whilst still in his twenties.

In 1899 he was seen at Venedig in Wien, creating the role of Kampel in *Die Landstreicher,* and then, in 1900, he was engaged at the Carltheater. There he appeared in such important character parts as Ollendorf (*Bettelstudent*), Marquis Imari (*Die Geisha*) and Andredl (*Das verwunschene Schloss*) and created roles in *Die Diva* (General Menzel), *Die Primadonna* (Calignac), *Die drei Wünsche* (Fogosch) and the Viennese *Les Saltimbanques* and *Circus Malicorne* (Le Grand Pingouin). In 1902 he appeared at Danzers Orpheum in *Die beiden Blinde* and as Cosmos Bey in the Viennese version of the Gaiety Theatre's *The Messenger Boy,* and in 1903 he created the role of Maier in *Frühlingsluft* at Venedig in Wien before he moved to the Theater an der Wien. He made his first appearance there as Lespingot in *Venedig in Paris* (a version of Offenbach's *MM Dunanan*) and continued, under top comedians Girardi and Sigmund Natzler, as a character man/comic in *Der neue Bürgermeister* (Hulst), *Der Generalkonsul* (Giacomo di Ferrari), *Der Toreador* (Governor of Villaya), *Der Herr Professor* (Bruno Venarius), Clérice's *Ordre de l'Empereur* (Marquis de Bussière), *Der rothe Kosak* (Jorgu), *Das Garnisonsmädel* (Wenzel Placek), *Die Juxheirat* (Thomas Brodwiller) and *Pufferl* (Crispin).

After Girardi's departure from the Theater an der Wien company, he succeeded to some of the roles which might have been his—Thomas Plumpudding in *Prince Bob* (1905) and comic parts in *Der Rebell* (Cretinowitsch), *Peter und Paul reisen ins Schlaraffenland* (1906, Schlampamprius) and *Tip-Top* (1907, Colming)—taking over as director for the last-named piece. He both directed and created the role of John Couder in the original production of *Die Dollarprinzessin* (1907), directed and played in *Der Frauenjäger* (Sgrimazzi) and mounted the house productions of *Der schöne Gardist* and *Ihr Adjutant,* and later returned to play in in *Schneeglöckchen* (Fürst Timofei) and *Die schöne Risette* (Habakuk). He also succeeded to the role of Baron Zeta in the original run of *Die lustige Witwe* of which he played the 500th performance in 1911.

When Karczag took over the Raimundtheater in 1908, Glawatsch moved to that house, and there he worked for a number of years as both Oberregisseur and principal comedian. He played Zsupán—one of his best roles, in which he was also seen in Berlin—Ollendorf, Ko-Ko, Joschko in *Jabuka,* Couder, *Die Landstreicher,* Prosper Plewny in *Das süsse Mädel,* Lindoberer (*Der fidele Bauer*), Kagler (*Wiener Blut*), Colibrados (*Don Cesar*), Piffkow (*Der Feldprediger*), Offenbach's Jupiter, Ottokar (*Der lachende Ehemann*), Sigismund (*Prinz Methusalem*) and even the now rather young Adam (*Vogelhändler*), and created roles in *Liebeswalzer* (Leopold Führinger), *Die Sprudelfee* (Fürst Nepomuk Wrzbrzlicky), *Das Glückmädel* (Franz Mitterer), *Die keusche Barbara* (Pittifox), *Casimirs Himmelfahrt* (Peter Paul), *Mein Mäderl* (Franz Helmer), *Der Husarengeneral*

Plate 148. **Franz Glawatsch** *in* Die eiserne Jungfrau.

(Siegmund Weihrauch), *Die tolle Therese* (Damböck), *Die moderne Eva* (Kasimir Putschli), *Das Dreimäderlhaus* (a memorable old Christian Tschöll with his "Geh' alte, schau!"), *Zwölf Uhr nachts* (Maringer), *Hannerl* (Christian Tschöll), *Was Mädchen traumen* (Matthias Alsdorfer), *Der Tanz ins Glück* (top-billed as Sebastian Platzer), *Die Liebe geht um!* (1922), *Vierzehn Tage Arrest* (1923, Auguste Lämmermayer) and *Das Schwalbennest* (1926, Franz Rettenbacher), latterly making guest appearances at other theatres, to play in *Die Perlen der Cleopatra* (1923, Pampylos), *Auf Befehl der Kaiserin* (1925, Johann Weisskappel) as Dominik Grüber in *Der Mitternachtswalzer* (1926), in a revival of *Der Tanz ins Glück* (1927) at the Bürgertheater and, paired with Mizzi Zwerenz, as the comical Fridolin von Gumpendorf in *Die gold'ne Meisterin* (1927), at the Theater an der Wien, shortly before his death at the age of 56.

Amongst the new and nearly new shows which he directed at the Raimundtheater were included *Das Zirkuskind* (1911), *Die keusche Barbara* (1911), *Hoheit tanzt Walzer* (1912), *Mein Mäderl* (1913), *Der Husaren-*

general (1913), *Die tolle Therese* (1913) and *Die moderne Eva* (1914).

GLÜCKLICHE REISE Operette in 3 acts by Max Bertuch. Lyrics by Kurt Schwabach. Music by Eduard Künneke. Theater am Kurfürstendamm, Berlin, 23 November 1932.

Expatriate Berliners Robert von Hartenau (Walter Jankuhn) and Stefan Schwarzenberg (Ernst Verebes), tired of life on their unproductive farms in Brazil, work their way back to Germany and there Stefan goes in search of his pen-friend, the exciting-sounding Monika Brink (Lizzi Waldmüller). Actually, Monika and her friend Lona Vonderhoff (Hilde Wörner)—under whose name Monika has also been writing to Robert—work in a shipping office. Monika tries to keep up the pretence of being a society girl, Lona—who quickly falls for Robert—is mortified when Monika admits writing to him in her name, and when their boss (Kurt Lilienn) turns up the truth soon comes out. After a few more scenes, the shipping office issues four tickets back to Brazil.

Eduard Künneke's light, modern dance-based score—in another world from the pretty, winning melodies of his *Der Vetter aus Dingsda*—featured fox-trot, rumba, tango and blues rhythms in a lively combination in which the two boys' tango song ''Drüben in der Heimat,'' Monika's society-girl ''Jede Frau geht so gern mal zum Tanztee,'' Stefan's proposal of a married life in Brazil, ''Komm, mein kleines Farmerbräutchen'' and the marching ''Glückliche Reise'' were happy moments, alongside versions of such familiar musical-theatre sentiments as ''Das Leben ist ein Karussell'' (Monika) or Stefan's description of life ''Am Amazonas.''

A well-received success in Berlin, *Glückliche Reise* nevertheless had a career which was largely limited to Germany, where it has become accepted as the second most successful of Künneke's works, behind *Der Vetter aus Dingsda.* First filmed in 1933, the show was used again as the basis for a 1955 film which featured Paul Hubschmid, Inge Egger, Peer Schmidt and Ina Peters, swapped Brazil for a South-Sea Island called Formitosa and made Eva (Lona) into a doctor, but kept both the basic shape of the piece and (a revised version of) what were billed as Künneke's ''world-famous songs.''

Films: Alfred Abel 1933, Thomas Engel 1955

Recordings: selections (part-record) (Fontana, EMI, etc)

GO-BANG Musical farcical comedy in 2 acts by Adrian Ross. Music by F Osmond Carr. Trafalgar Square Theatre, London, 10 March 1894.

Produced by Fred Harris and C J Abud in the wake of the former's success with *Morocco Bound, Go-Bang* was another piece combining a colorful setting (Go-Bang is an oriental country), low to dudey comedy (John Shine, Harry Grattan, George Grossmith jr) and song and dance (Letty Lind as ''a prima ballerina assoluta, famous from St Petersburg to Utah,'' plus Jessie Bond and Frederick Rosse as the love interest, and Adelaide Astor as soubrette) with a rather more vertebrate story than its predecessor. It had a run of 159 performances and was accounted a success, was exported to some of the oriental and African circuits (it was played in Capetown by Hall's Juveniles), and its favorite number, Miss Lind's description of herself as ''Di, Di, Di'' was pilfered for inclusion in the American farce comedy *A Run on the Bank* and, in burlesqued form, in Eddie Foy's *Off the Earth,* but *Go Bang* itself did not linger nor leave much in the way of traces.

GODSPELL Musical in 2 acts by John Michael Tebelak based on the Gospel according to St Matthew. Music and lyrics by Stephen Schwartz. Cherry Lane Theater, New York, 17 May 1971; Promenade Theater, 10 August 1971; Broadhurst Theater, 22 June 1976.

Originally written by Tebelak as a college exercise, the text of *Godspell*—which, in spite of its claims, used as much material from the gospels of St Luke, St Mark and St John as from that of St Matthew—was a 1960s-style retelling of the last days of Christ, illustrated by re-enactments of some of his teachings, particularly as put over in the parables. The tone of the show was a young-teenage one, and the staging—an important element of the production, and done by the author himself—mixed styles and parodies from comic strips, television shows and circus, in a mélange aimed at that same age group.

The songs by Stephen Schwartz which illustrated the entertainment were in a suitably similar style, using the rock and country-and-western elements of the popular youth music of the time, and turning out several pieces which became popular: ''Day By Day,'' ''Prepare Ye the Way of the Lord,'' ''Turn Back, O Man.''

Tried first at La Mama, the show was then given an off-Broadway production by Edgar Lansbury, Stuart Duncan and Joseph Beruh at the Cherry Lane Theater where the cast of 10 was headed by Stephen Nathan in the role of ''Jesus.'' The show quickly proved to have a potential audience far beyond the lower-teens age-bracket, and it transferred to the Promenade Theater in 1971 and, soon after, whilst the off-Broadway production ran on, began its considerable international travels. H M Tennent Ltd's London production, with David Essex, Marti Webb, Julie Covington, Jeremy Irons and Verity-Ann Meldrum amongst the cast, started out at a well-chosen venue in the willfully fringe-y Roundhouse, but it quickly transferred into the thoroughly establishment

Plate 149. **Godspell.** *Jeremy Irons and the London cast.*

Wyndham's Theatre and there it compiled a run of 1,128 performances, prefatory to a long life on the British touring circuits, in British provincial houses where its small cast and staging demands made it particularly popular, and to several returns, often from such productions, for seasons in the West End (1975, 1977, 1978, 1985). Australia's Kenn Brodziak opened that country's first *Godspell* in Melbourne just days after London's opening and its initial 12-month season ran partly alongside another in Sydney (Richbrooke Theatre 10 April 1972), prior to repeated revivals.

Foreign-language adaptations followed in the next years. A German version (ad Robert Gilbert) was mounted in Hamburg with Heinz Ehrenfreund and Angelika Milster amongst the cast, and a French version (ad Bernard Giquel, Pierre Delanoë) was produced by Annie Fargue at Paris's Théâtre de la Porte-Saint-Martin, amongst a rush of productions, in all kinds of languages, worldwide.

In 1973 Victor Garber and Lynne Thigpen joined original cast members Dave Haskell, Joanne Jonas, Robin Lamont and Gilmer McCormick in a Columbia film version of the show made whilst the original production still ran on in its off-Broadway home. In 1976, after 2,124 performances off-Broadway, *Godspell* made the move up to Broadway's Broadhurst Theater (22 June), then to the Plymouth Theater (15 September) and to the Ambassador Theater (12 January 1977), winning, in the process, a total of 527 performances on Broadway to add to the continuing thousands played worldwide up to the present day. In 1988, when it might have been thought that its time and style were well and truly of the past, it nevertheless returned to New York's Lamb's Theater (12 June) and added yet another 225 performances to its remarkable on-and-around-Broadway tally. In 1995 it was still a part of the repertoire of Budapest's Várszínház, and in 1994, following an unfortunate resighting at London's

Barbican Hall (30 August), it was still to be seen walloping its way round the provinces of Britain.

UK: Roundhouse 17 November 1971, Wyndham's Theatre 26 January 1972; Australia: Playbox Theatre, Melbourne 15 November 1971; Germany: Hamburg 1972; France: Théâtre de la Porte-Saint-Martin 1973; Hungary: Ódry Színpad 19 December 1986

Film: Columbia 1973

Recordings: original cast (Bell), London cast (Bell), Australian casts (SFL, HMV, Etcetera), German casts (Reprise, Backstage), French cast (Philips), film soundtrack (Bell), Swedish cast (Aksent), South African casts (ACP, Cat), Netherlands cast (Polydor), Spanish cast (Noviola), Danish cast (Hamlet), Swedish cast (Metronome), British touring cast 1994 (Playback), studio cast (TER, etc), etc

GOETZ, E Ray (b Buffalo, NY, 12 June 1886; d Greenwich, Conn, 12 June 1954). Songwriter and producer of musicals and revues.

Goetz began a career as a songwriter in his teens, and he had his earliest theatre successes as the lyricist of occasional interpolated songs in Broadway musicals: ''When the Right Little Girl Comes Along'' in *The Earl and the Girl* (1905); ''Just the One I'm Looking For'' in *The Social Whirl* (1906); ''It's Lovely When Love Loves You'' in *The Lady's Maid* (1906); ''Don't Go in the Lion's Cage Tonight'' (mus: Gilroy) in *The Blue Moon* (1906); ''He Goes to Church on Sunday'' in *The Orchid* (mus: Vincent Bryan, 1907); ''I Think I Oughtn't Auto Anymore,'' ''Come and Float Me, Freddie Dear'' and ''Reincarnation'' (Bryan) in *The Ziegfeld Follies of 1907;* The Yankiana Rag (mus: Gideon) in *Miss Innocence,* etc. He provided his first full book of show-words for B E Forrester's production of the touring musical *In Africa,* with comedians Yorke and Adams starred, and his first Broadway set to Baldwin Sloane's score for the unsuccessful *The Prince of Bohemia* (1910) and, over the next few years, whilst still placing odd individual numbers (several of them written with Irving Berlin) in a variety of musicals and revues (*Hello, Paris, The Fascinating Widow, Watch Your Step*), followed up with several more scores—at first in collaboration with Sloane and then with some for which he provided both words and music himself. Most of these were for the musicals produced and/or performed by Lew Fields, either alone or in conjunction with his famous partner, Joe Weber, shows which became more and more like variety shows until they finally simply agreed to be honestly called revues rather than musicals.

Goetz himself turned to production with the 1917 revue *Hitchy-Koo* (w Raymond Hitchcock) in which his wife, Irene Bordoni, was featured. He subsequently coproduced the musical *Follow the Girl* (1918) and presented, solo, a series of other stage musical pieces including the much-rewritten French revue *As You Were,* the altogether less successful homemade revue *Here and There* (written w Glen MacDonough, 1920), and Armont and Gerbidon's musicalized comedy *Jeunes Filles de palaces* (*The French Doll*), Cole Porter's *Paris,* and several further rewritten Continental pieces—*Little Miss Bluebeard* (1924, *Der Gatte des Fräuleins*), *A Naughty Cinderella* (1925 w Charles Frohman, *Pouche*) and Sacha Guitry and Reynaldo Hahn's *Mozart*—each with Miss Bordoni starring, and often with some of his own work appearing in the score.

His other production credits in the musical theatre included the early George Gershwin flop *Our Nell* (ex- *The Hayseed*) (1922), Porter's *Fifty Million Frenchmen* (1929) and the musical *The New Yorkers* (1930) written by Herbert Fields, son of his old mentor, and were part of a highly active schedule which ranged from presenting the American seasons of the Spanish sensation vocalist Raquel Meller to operating New York's Club Mirador.

Goetz continued his songwriting activities throughout. He wrote the words to Finck's famous melody ''In the Shadows'' and had other song successes with such numbers as ''My Croony Melody'' (w Joe Goodwin), ''We'll Have a Jubilee in My Old Kentucky Home'' (mus: Walter Donaldson), ''For Me and My Gal'' (w Edgar Leslie, George Meyer) and ''Yaka Hula Hickey Dula'' (w Pete Wendling, Joe Young), sung by Jolson in *Robinson Crusoe Jr.* He also relyricked versions of several Continental song successes by Christiné (''Do I Love You?''), Kollo (''The Land of Going to Be''), Louis Alter and José Padilla (Raquel Meller's ''La Violetera'' for *Little Miss Bluebeard*), as well as creating a popular song by putting words to music by Puccini, more often than not to provide numbers to be performed by Miss Bordoni in her starring vehicles. He also contributed lyrics and/or music to the Shuberts' production of *Hands Up* and to *As You Were* and *George White's Scandals* (1922, 1923), and was credited (w Peter Arno) with the original story line for his last Broadway production *The New Yorkers.*

Goetz's sister was briefly the wife of Irving Berlin. She died a short time after her marriage (17 July 1912) at the age of 18.

1909 **In Africa** (Herbert Ingram/Aaron Hoffman) Yonkers, NY 21 August

1910 **The Prince of Bohemia** (A Baldwin Sloane/J Hartley Manners) Hackett Theater 14 January

1910 **A Matinée Idol** (Silvio Hein/w Seymour Brown/Armand, Barnard) Daly's Theater 28 April

1911 **The Hen Pecks** (Sloane/Glen MacDonough) Broadway Theater 4 February

1911 **The Never Homes** (Sloane/MacDonough) Broadway Theater 5 October

1912 **Hokey-Pokey** (Sloane, W T Francis, John Stromberg/w Edgar Smith/E Smith) Broadway Theater 8 February

1912 **Bunty Bulls and Strings** (Sloane, et al/E Smith) 2 scenes Broadway Theater 8 February

1912 **The June Bride** (*Johann der Zweite*) English lyrics (Majestic Theater, Boston)

1912 **Hanky Panky** (Sloane/E Smith) Broadway Theater 5 August

1912 **Roly Poly** (Sloane/E Smith) Weber and Fields' Music Hall 21 November

1912 **Without the Law** (Sloane/E Smith) 1 act Weber and Fields' Music Hall 21 November

1912 **The Sun Dodgers** (Sloane) Broadway Theater 30 November

1913 **All Aboard** (w Malvin Franklin/Mark Swan) 44th Street Theater Roof Garden 5 June

1913 **The Pleasure Seekers** (E Smith) Winter Garden 3 November

1915 **Hands Up** (Cole Porter, William Daly, et al/E Smith) Shubert Theater, New Haven 7 June; revised version (w Sigmund Romberg/w William Jerome/E Smith) 44th Street Theater 22 July

1916 **Step This Way** (w Bert Grant/E Smith) Shubert Theater 29 May

1917 **Words and Music** Fulton Theater 24 December

1921 **Phi-Phi** American lyrics (Globe Theater, Atlantic City)

GOETZE, Walter W[ilhelm] (b Berlin, 17 April 1883; d Berlin, 24 March 1961).

Goetze began his musical career as a bassoon player, worked as a theatre conductor in several German towns, and made his first mark as a musical-theatre writer when he set new music to a version of the play *Parkettsitz Nr 10* for Hermann Haller in Hamburg. The show went on to be played in Berlin and in Budapest (*Támlásszék* Vígszínház 23 August 1913) and, thereafter, Goetze composed regular Operette scores for Berlin and for other German theatres, winning some success with the vaudeville *Zwischen zwölf und eins,* played in Leipzig and at Vienna's Theater in der Josefstadt (29 March 1914), *Der liebe Pepi,* and the Hamburg Singspiel *Am Brunnen vor dem Tore,* but without any major results until the production of *Ihre Hoheit die Tänzerin* at the Bellevue-Theater, Stettin, in 1919. Produced soon after in Berlin, and subsequently at the Vienna Johann Strauss-Theater, it proved to be his biggest success and, in spite of good runs with such pieces as *Der goldene Pierrot, Adrienne* and *Die göttliche Jette,* played at Vienna's Raimundtheater in 1934, it was not topped during the 30 further years he devoted to the musical theatre.

1911 **Parkettsitz Nr 10** (Hermann Haller, Willy Wolff) Tivoli Theater, Hamburg 24 September

1912 **Nur nicht drängeln** (Richard Nessler, Willy Prager) Walhalla-Theater 13 July

1913 **Zwischen zwölf und eins** (Georg Okonkowski, Max Neal, M Ferner) Neues Operettentheater, Leipzig 9 February

1913 **Wenn Männer schwindeln** (Robert Pohl, Bruno Decker) Stadttheater, Halberstadt 2 November

1914 **Schürzenmanöver** (R von Gatti, August Neidhart ad Hans Brennert) Operettentheater, Leipzig 25 March

1914 **Der liebe Pepi** (*Der Bundesbruder*) (Decker, Otto Sprinzel) Montis Operettentheater 23 December

1917 **O schöne Zeit, o sel'ge Zeit** (Decker, Erich Platen) Deutsches Theater, Hanover 4 July

1918 **Am Brunnen vor dem Tore** (Oskar Felix) Deutsches Theater, Hanover 26 May

1919 **Ihre Hoheit die Tänzerin** (Richard Bars, Felix) Bellevue-Theater, Stettin 8 May; Thalia-Theater, Berlin 22 June 1920

1919 **Die—oder keine** (Bars) Walhalla-Theater, Halle am Saale 30 July

1920 **Amor auf Reisen** (Oskar Blumenthal, Gustav Kadelburg ad Decker) Thalia-Theater 15 April

1920 **Die Spitzenkönigin** (Felix, Bars) Bellevue-Theater, Stettin 16 June; Wallner-Theater, Berlin 22 December 1921

1922 **Die schwarze Rose** (Bars, Felix) Neues Operettentheater 5 October

1924 **Die vier Schlaumeier** (Decker, Bars) Residenztheater 11 September

1926 **[Die schöne] Adrienne** (Günter Bibo/Felix, Alexander Pordes-Milo) Carl-Schultze Theater, Hamburg 24 April; Komische Oper, Berlin

1928 **Die Männer von Manon** (Neidhart, Robert Gilbert) Kleines Haus, Düsseldorf 30 September

1929 **Henriette Sontag** (Bibo) Landestheater, Altenberg 20 January

1930 **Komödie in Venedig** (Bibo, Felix) Zentraltheater, Magdeburg 28 April

1931 **Für eine schöne Frau** (Leo Lenz ad Bibo, Felix) Operettentheater, Braunschweig 11 March

1931 **Hochzeit auf Japata** (Jan van Hern) Zentraltheater, Magdeburg 13 November

1931 **Die göttliche Jette** (revised *Henriette Sontag*) (Bibo, Emil Rameau) Schiller-Theater 31 December

1933 **Der Page des Königs** (Felix, I Rheinberg) Theater des Westens 21 February

1933 **Akrobaten des Glücks** (Emil Pohl ad Felix) Komische Oper 22 September

1934 **Der goldene Pierrot** (Felix, Otto Kleinert) Theater des Westens 31 March

1935 **Schach dem König!** (H A Schaufert, Paul Harms) Theater am Horst-Wessel-Platz 16 May

1936 **Sensation im Trocadero** (Felix) Stadttheater, Stettin 19 January

1936 **Der verliebte Wauwau** Stadttheater, Stettin

1939 **Die zwei Gesichter einer Königin** (Kurt Sauer) Städtische Bühnen, Frankfurt-am-Main 25 March

1940 **Kleopatra die zweite** (revised *Die zwei Gesichter einer Königin*) Künstlertheater 9 February

1940 **Der Tanz der Herren** (Felix) Stadttheater, Stettin 3 November

1950 **Liebe im Dreiklang** (w Emil F Malkowsky) Städtische Bühnen, Heidelberg 15 November

Other titles attributed: *Charlie* (1923), *Eine entzückende Frau, Schwarze Husaren* (1931)

GOING GREEK Musical show in 2 acts by Guy Bolton, Fred Thompson and Douglas Furber. Music and lyrics by Sam Lerner, Al Goodhart and Al Hoffmann. Gaiety Theatre, London, 16 September 1937.

The team, headed by star comic Leslie Henson, which had been successfully established at the Gaiety Theatre in the mid-1930s under the management of Firth Shephard, had done very nicely with *Seeing Stars* and *Swing Along,* and in 1937 Henson followed these up with his own production of *Going Greek* which utilized most of the same team on a show of a splendid zaniness.

Little, froglike Henson and vast Fred Emney (still sporting his trademark monocle and topper), decked out in Greek kilts, played a pair of incompetent banditti, whilst the third of the comic triumvirate, Richard Hearne, was an operatic hostage no one wants to ransom until it suddenly seems he has inherited a fortune. Juveniles Roy Royston and Louise Browne performed the song and dance routines, as in the earlier shows (''A Little Co-operation from You''), in a musical where the quality was in the devising and the performance of the extravagant comedy episodes rather than in an anodine made-for-dancing-and-forgetting score.

Going Greek ran for 303 performances at the Gaiety before being closed when Henson fell ill. It subsequently toured for a number of years with other artists in the made-to-measure roles, whilst Henson, Emney, Hearne and the Gaiety continued with more new shows of the same style.

GOING UP Musical comedy in 3 acts by Otto Harbach and James Montgomery based on *The Aviator* by James Montgomery. Lyrics by Otto Harbach. Music by Louis A Hirsch. Liberty Theater, New York, 25 December 1917.

James Montgomery's 1910 play *The Aviator* was put to musical use seven years on by its author and the now practiced manufacturer of musical comedy Otto Harbach, several of whose biggest successes to date (*Three Twins, Madame Sherry, High Jinks*) had been with adaptations. The music was allotted to Louis Hirsch, composer of two recent *Ziegfeld Follies* since his well-timed incursion into London revue, but whose record with book musicals was less impressive. *Going Up* changed that.

The libretto concerned one Robert Street (Frank Craven), the author of a popular book on flying called *Going Up*. When challenged to a flying race by the jealous French aviator Jules Gaillard (Joseph Lertora), whose girlfriend, Grace Douglas (Edith Day), he has attracted, he finds himself in a spot, for Robert's book is fiction and he has never handled an aeroplane. Grace, misunderstanding the situation, agrees to marry the winner of the challenge. Robert is given hurried flying lessons, and wins the contest, staying up in the sky longest simply because he is unable to land. When he does get down, he finds he is still a hero, and an affianced one. Frank Otto played Hopkinson (''Hoppy'') Brown, Robert's comical pal, whilst Marion Sunshine was Madeleine, Grace's chum, with whom Hoppy, inevitably, paired off.

Hirsch's songs included a delicious mixture of the lightest contemporary popular strains: the jaunty title-number led by the flying Frenchman, a dance speciality in which everyone was exhorted to do ''The Tickle Toe,'' Grace's graceful piece about the effect of ''The Touch of a Woman's Hand,'' Madeleine's march-time creed that ''I Want a Boy (who's determined to do what I say)'' and, above all, the two girls' delightful duo ''If You Look in Her Eyes.''

Sam Harris and George M Cohan's Broadway production of *Going Up* was a first-class success and remained 351 performances at the Liberty Theater before going on the road, but an even longer run awaited Joe Sacks's London mounting, produced under the reign of Alfred Butt at the Gaiety Theatre with Evelyn Laye (Madeleine), Marjorie Gordon (Grace), Joseph Coyne (Robert), Austin Melford (Hoppy) and Henry de Bray (Gaillard) leading the cast, and Arthur Chesney in the role of Grace's gambling-mad father. The show gave the Gaiety one of its greatest successes as wartime turned into celebration time, and it ran up 574 victory-year performances before going touring.

Australia, too, gave the show a strong welcome. Alfred Frith (Robert), Ethel Erskine (Grace), Cecil Bradley (Madeleine) and Jack Hooker (Gaillard) were featured in a very impressive 15-week run in Melbourne prior to an even more successful Sydney season of 17 weeks and 116 performances at the Criterion (23 August 1919), there was a return run in 1921, and for years half of urban Sydney was musically encouraging the other half to ''do the tickle-toe.''

In spite of its great initial success, *Going Up* was subsequently forgotten, whilst less successful shows and songs by more fashionable and/or well-plugged songwriters got the attention, but in 1976 it was revived in a revised version (which included the intake of other Hirsch songs, notably ''I'll Think of You'' from *The Rainbow Girl*) at the Goodspeed Opera House. Successful there, it did not survive a transfer to Broadway's John Golden Theatre (19 September) where it played but 49 performances.

A 1923 film version featured Douglas McLean as Robert Street, Hallam Cooley as Hoppy, Marjorie Daw and Edna Murphy as the girls, and Mervyn Le Roy in a supporting role.

UK: Gaiety Theatre 22 May 1918; Australia: His Majesty's Theatre, Melbourne 19 April 1919

Film: 1923

Plate 150. **Going Up.** *In a Goodspeed Opera House aeroplane.*

THE GOLDEN APPLE Musical in 2 acts by John Latouche. Music by Jerome Moross. Phoenix Theater, New York, 11 March 1954; Alvin Theater, 20 April 1954.

A virtual modern-day opéra-bouffe which used (or, rather, reused) parts of Homer's *Iliad* and *Odyssey* in a witty and topical tale of everyday American people-in-power, *The Golden Apple* has, in spite of its relative failure in the theatre, become a cult musical amongst those who make cults of such things.

Helen (Kaye Ballard) is no longer Homer's Helen, nor indeed Meilhac and Halévy's Helen, but the weak-willed wife of the small-town Sheriff Menelaus (Dean Michener) of Angel's Roost, Washington. And Paris (Jonathan Lucas), the Prince who wins her rather too easily away and starts the Trojan war, is nothing but a banal traveling salesman, even if he does travel by balloon. The pair elope to the seaside city of Rhododendron, pursued by Ulysses (Stephen Douglass) and the rest of Helen's former admirers, but the rescuers meet with stern opposition from the Mayor of Rhododendron, Hector (Jack Whiting). It is opposition of the insidious kind, and it takes the hero 10 whole years of resisting temptations which have nothing of the heroic to them, temptations that his friends fall prey to, before he beats Paris in a fist-fight and can traipse home to where the faithful Penelope (Priscilla Gillette) is waiting.

The show's score—virtually a series of sung scenas and with minimal dialogue—included a wide range of musical pieces in a selection of styles, from which ''Lazy Afternoon'' for Helen and ''Wind Flowers'' for Penelope proved the outstanding ballads, alongside the rich duo ''It's the Going Home Together,'' the comical ''Doomed, Doomed, Doomed'' sung by Portia Nelson in the role of Minerva, and the scena depicting the equivalent of the Judgement of Paris, in which the salesman is called upon to make his choice among three Washington matrons and selects Lovey Mars (Bibi Osterwald) and her promise of a good sex life.

First produced at the off-Broadway Phoenix Theater by Norris Houghton and T Edward Hambleton, *The Golden Apple* won some excited notices and the kind of attendances which encouraged Alfred de Liagre and Roger L Stevens to transfer the show (which many a Broadway producer had turned down prior to its production), after 48 performances, to Broadway's Alvin Theater. It managed only 125 performances there before closing. The show's reputation remained, however, amongst the cognoscenti, and it was given revivals, back in its off-Broadway element, in 1962 (York Playhouse 12 February 1962, 112 performances) and, most recently, by the York Theatre Company in 1990 (23 March). It was also televised in 1977.

Recording: original cast (RCA, Elektra)

GOLDEN BOY Musical in 2 acts by Clifford Odets and William Gibson based on the play of the same name by Odets. Lyrics by Lee Adams. Music by Charles Strouse. Majestic Theater, New York, 20 October 1964.

Odets's 1937 play told the story of an Italian-American slum boy who gives up music for prizefighting but, after a promising beginning in his search for a fist-won rise in social status, sees his life go sour professionally, when he kills an opponent, and personally, when he loses his girl. After a reconciliation they are killed in a car accident.

Some of the melodrama was squeezed out of the tale when it was made over into a musical, partly by Odets and, after his death, by Gibson, and the character of the young boxer was altered to allow him to belong to a more fashionable kind of seeker-after-social-status in a 1960s context. The Joe Wellington of the musical *Golden Boy* was a negro, and the cultural/physical dilemma of the original play was replaced by a simple go-getting attitude. Sammy Davis jr was Joe, Paula Wayne played the girl, Lorna, whom he wants, but who ultimately prefers his unprepossessing manager (Kenneth Tobey), Billy Daniels was the rival manager, Eddie Satin, and Joe met his death alone.

Davis had the bulk of the evening's music (''Night Song,'' ''Stick Around,'' ''Don't Forget 127th Street,'' ''Colorful,'' ''I Want to Be with You'' w Lorna, ''Can't You See It''), Lorna had the title song, Daniels delivered ''While the City Sleeps,'' and the boxing match which was the evening's highlight, and which resulted in the opponent's death, was a choreographed piece.

Hillard Elkins's production of *Golden Boy* played 569 performances on Broadway, and was subsequently mounted at the London Palladium with Davis repeating the performance which had encouraged much of the piece's popularity. London saw 118 performances.

A revised version with a libretto by Leslie Lee and an altered score was tested (1985, 1991) variously in Brooklyn, Florida and Connecticut without being launched on a wider scale, and a further revision (ad Keith Glover) was seen at Long Wharf, New Haven, 8 November 2000.

UK: London Palladium 4 June 1968
Recording: original cast (Capitol)

GOLDEN RAINBOW Musical in 2 acts by Ernest Kinoy based on *A Hole in the Head* by Arnold Shulman. Music and lyrics by Walter Marks. Shubert Theater, New York, 4 February 1968.

A vehicle for husband-and-wife singing team Steve Lawrence and Eydie Gorme, *Golden Rainbow* cast Lawrence as the unimpressive Larry Davis, a widower with a 10-year-old son, Ally (Scott Jacoby), and a rather seedy Las Vegas (rather than the play's original Florida) hotel, the Golden Rainbow, on which he is having a hard time keeping up the payments. His well-off sister-in-law, Judy Harris (Miss Gorme), who starts by trying to take the child into her care, ends up by marrying Larry and supplying the needed cash. The show's songs had of-the-period titles like ''We Got Us,'' ''He Needs Me Now,'' ''How Could I Be So Wrong?'' and, the most successful, Larry's cop-out excuse for everything, ''I've Gotta Be Me.'' Amongst the other players, only Joseph Sirola as a big-time hustler called Lou Garrity got a look-in musically, with a number about ''Taste.''

Golden Rainbow served Lawrence and Miss Gorme for 385 Broadway performances.

Recording: original cast (Calendar)

DIE GOLD'NE MEISTERIN Operette in 3 acts by Julius Brammer and Alfred Grünwald based on the play *Die goldene Eva* by Franz von Schönthan and Franz Koppel-Ellfeld. Music by Edmund Eysler. Theater an der Wien, Vienna, 13 September 1927.

Die gold'ne Meisterin was set in 16th-century Vienna, and the lady of the title was Margarete (Betty Fischer), the socially ambitious widow of a wealthy goldsmith. When she dances with an attractive stranger at a society ball, she is mortified to discover that he is only Christian (Hubert Marischka), her new goldsmith, and she petulantly permits the attentions of the gold-digging Count Jaromir von Greifenstein (Fritz Steiner) in retaliation. Christian exposes Greifenstein as a cheat and a married man, and the pair are finally brought together in the gardens of the monastery at Klosterneuburg under the guidance of the good Brother Ignatius (Richard Waldemar). Two veteran stars, Mizzi Zwerenz (Portschunkula) and Franz Glawatsch (Fridolin von Gumpendorf), provided the bulk of the comedy as Margarete's housekeeper and another penniless nobleman.

If Brammer and Grünwald's libretto was not, perhaps, their very best, the score with which Eysler illustrated it was one of his most outstanding. Margarete's dazzling entrance number (''Gräfin sein, Fürstin sein''), all excited by her success at the ball, Christian's waltz ''Du liebe, gold'ne Meisterin,'' their waltz-duo reminiscing over their dance together (''So tanzt man nur in Wien'') and the Danube-drenched little ''In Grinzing is' a Gasserl'' were all hits, whilst the comic pieces such as the duo for the two shabby noblemen, ''Jaromir von Greifenstein,'' Portschunkula's reminder to Fridolin of his tipsy proposal of marriage (''Portschunkula! Portschunkula!''), and Ignatius's little homily ''Jeder Mensch hat in der Brust,'' gave the traditional contrast.

Die gold'ne Meisterin turned out to be one of Eysler's most successful shows. A fine success at the Theater an der Wien, it ran past its 200th performance on 19 March 1928 and closed on 4 April, but, possibly because its Alt-Wienerisch tale and tunes seemed old-fashioned, with the coming of jazzier strains on the one hand and the dark romanticism of later Lehár on the other, its future was disproportionately limited. It was revived at the Raimundtheater just after the end of the Second World War (30 November 1945) with Waldemar repeating his original role, at the Volksbühne in May 1946, and again at the Raimundtheater in 1955 (29 April), but has been little seen, and, sadly, little heard, otherwise.

Recording: selection (Philips)

GOLDSMITH, Oliver (b Pallas, Co Longford, 10 November 1730; d London, 4 April 1774).

The two principal fictional works of novelist Oliver Goldsmith have served as the stuff of a number of musical plays. *The Vicar of Wakefield,* well-known in many versions on the straight stage, was burlesqued in Britain as *The Vicar of Wide-Awake-Field* (Gaiety Theatre, 1885) and treated more decorously in Thomas Dibdin's unsuccessful ''pastoral opera'' produced at the Theatre Royal, Haymarket in 1823 (27 September, mus: Sanderson), with Terry and Miss Chester featured, and the light opera composed by Liza Lehmann to a text by Laurence Housman (1906). *She Stoops to Conquer* became *The Two Roses* in Stanislaus Stange and Ludwig Englander's 1904 Broadway version, *O Marry Me* (Lola Pergament/Robert Kessler) at off-Broadway's Gate Theater (27 October 1961) and, updated into a wild western setting, *Liberty Ranch* in the hands of Caryl Brahms, Ned Sherrin, Dick Vosburgh and John Cameron (Greenwich Theatre 18 July 1972).

Goldsmith's 1765 *Mrs Margery Two Shoes* was the basis for many a Victorian pantomime, usually under the title of *Goody Two Shoes,* and his *The Hermit* became the musical *Edwin and Angelina, or the Banditti* (Victor Pellesier/Elihu Hubbard Smith) produced at Broadway's John Street Theater in 1796.

THE GONDOLIERS, or The King of Barataria Comic opera in 2 acts by W S Gilbert. Music by Arthur Sullivan. Savoy Theatre, London, 7 December 1889.

The last great success of the Gilbert and Sullivan partnership, *The Gondoliers* took the favorite comic-opera location of Venice for its setting, but ignored the Doge and his Council of Ten and the other usual elements of Venetian shows—even the usually inevitable last-act masked ball—and used the city of canals only as a picturesque background for a tale, made up of largely familiar elements (the main plot reeked largely of the recent *La Princesse des Canaries*) which might very well have taken place anywhere.

Foster-brothers Marco (Courtice Pounds) and Giuseppe (Rutland Barrington) Palmieri are a handsome pair of gondoliers, happily wedded before much of Act I has passed to local contadine Gianetta (Geraldine Ulmar) and Tessa (Jessie Bond). Then some disturbing news is delivered by the city's Grand Inquisitor (W H Denny). Casilda (Decima Moore), the teenaged daughter of the Duke (Frank Wyatt) and Duchess (Rosina Brandram) of Plaza Toro, was long ago betrothed to the infant King of Barataria. The little King was wet-nursed out during a revolution, but now the time has come for him—and that means one of the Palmieris—to be restored. Since it cannot be established which of Marco or Giuseppe is the apparently mislaid monarch, the two men, up to now staunch anti-royalists, go off to try to rule Barataria together, on egalitarian principles. Then the news about the wife is broken. One of them is a bigamist as well as a king. Fortunately, it turns out that the wet nurse did a double switch, and the real King is the drummer, Luiz (Wallace Brownlow), over whom Casilda has been mooning all night, and who has no nonsensically impractical ideas about the equality of all men.

The Gondoliers was full of typical and delightful Gilbert and Sullivan numbers, of which Marco's serenade ''Take a Pair of Sparkling Eyes'' proved to be the bonbon. The Ducal family were particularly well provided, with a series of numbers which were for the most Gilbert's superior variations on well-used themes, as they arrived in shabby style ''From the Sunny Spanish Shore,'' with the Duke clipping out the familiar tale of the accidental hero in ''In Enterprise of Martial Kind'' and trying to teach court manners to the unroyal Kings (''I am a Courtier Grave and Serious'') in the same way Robert Reece's characters had done in *Cattarina* more than a decade previously. The Duchess boomed out her recipe for falling in love with an aristocratic husband on command (''On the Day That I Was Wedded'') and joined with her husband in a clever piece on how to cash in on your nobility (''Small Titles and Orders''), whilst Casilda duetted forlornly with her Luis (''O Rapture!

When Alone Together,'' ''There Was a Time''). Tessa's best opportunity came in the lively ''When a Merry Maiden Marries'' and Gianetta's in ''Kind Sir, You Cannot Have the Heart,'' but, by and large, the four juveniles were less well served than the Inquisitor, who was featured in two bouncy basso expository tales (''I Stole the Prince,'' ''There Lived a King, As I've Been Told''). With its cachuca and gavotte, *The Gondoliers* also included a touch more in the way of dance than was usual in the Savoy operas.

The Gondoliers brought back the burlesque element to the Savoy after the more straight light-operatic tones of Gilbert and Sullivan's previous piece, *The Yeomen of the Guard,* and it was rewarded with excellent notices and a run of 554 performances before going on to become part of the hard core of the Gilbert and Sullivan repertoire. Carte opened his Broadway production whilst the London one ran on, importing George Temple (Duke), Kate Talby (Duchess), Esther Palliser (Gianetta), Richard Clarke (Marco) and Barrington to head a company through 103 nights at the Park and Palmer's Theatres, and *Gondoliers* productions quickly blossomed around the country as Koster and Bial's Music Hall accoladed the piece in burlesque (*The Chandeliers, or Venice in New York*).

In a Vienna still delighted over *Der Mikado, Die Gondoliere* (ad F Zell, Richard Genée) was produced at the Theater an der Wien in September. It did not, however, prove to have the same appeal to German-language audiences as its oriental predecessor, lasting only 18 performances before going on to Berlin in December. Link featured as Berlin's Duke, and Lili Lejo was Casilda.

In the English language, however, the piece did splendidly. J C Williamson's Australian production, with William Elton (Duke), Maggie Moore (Duchess), Jack Leumane (Marco), Charles Ryley (Giuseppe), Flora Graupner (Gianetta) and Florence Young (Casilda) proved as successful as the London version and, as in England, the show was regularly revived throughout Australia following its first showing there. The D'Oyly Carte company brought *The Gondoliers* back to London in 1898 (22 March) with Elton repeating his Australian performance as the Duke, Rosina Brandram still the Duchess, and the young Ethel Jackson—later to be America's *Merry Widow*—in the small but demanding role of Fiametta (125 performances); again in 1907 (22 January, 75 performances); and thereafter in the company's repertoire seasons. After the release of the Gilbert and Sullivan copyrights, the show was played by Scottish Opera (12 December 1968) and by the New Sadler's Wells company (9 February 1984), and it has remained a steady favorite amongst the Savoy canon.

Another *Die Gondoliere,* written by Arnoldo Bonometti and Willy Kissner, was produced at the Landshut Stadttheater in 1913 (28 January).

USA: Park Theater 7 January 1890; Austria: Theater an der Wien *Die Gondoliere* 20 December 1890; Australia: Princess Theatre, Melbourne 25 October 1890; Germany: Friedrich-Wilhelmstädtisches Theater *Die Gondoliere 20* December 1890

Recordings: complete (Decca, HMV), etc

Videos: CBC 1962, Brent-Walker 1982, Stratford Festival 1983, Australian Opera 1995

GONE WITH THE WIND Musical in 2 acts by Horton Foote based on the novel by Margaret Mitchell. Music and lyrics by Harold Rome. Theatre Royal, Drury Lane, London, 3 May 1972.

The original musical version of Margaret Mitchell's celebrated Civil War novel, *Gone With the Wind,* was put together under the aegis of American director and choreographer Joe Layton, and was produced in Japanese (lib: Kasuo Kikuta), under the title *Scarlett,* at Tokyo's Imperial Theatre on 3 January 1970. Layton then took it to Britain, where its original English-language version was produced under the management of Harold Fielding at London's Theatre Royal, Drury Lane with June Ritchie in the role of Scarlett O'Hara, Harve Presnell as Rhett Butler, Patricia Michael as Melanie, Robert Swann as Ashley Wilkes, and the very young Bonnie Langford as Bonnie. The opening night revealed a spectacular burning of Atlanta, a misbehaved horse and a classic over-the-top performance from the very young child, provoking Noël Coward to remark drily: ''If they'd shoved the little girl up the horse's arse, they'd have solved both problems.'' Horse and child both calmed down after opening night, and enough folk got used to seeing the well-known story interspersed with a long score of light musical theatre numbers for *Gone with the Wind* to turn into a distinct success (397 performances).

Fielding subsequently took the show to America, but alterations made for the Broadway-bound production, largely in an effort to try to top the big first-act ending of the famous fire with a second-act climax, proved ill-advised and, after a four-hour opening night, America's *Gone with the Wind,* with Lesley Ann Warren and Pernell Roberts featured, foundered in San Francisco.

The Japanese version was repeated in 1987 and in 1994 by the Takarazuka all-female company.

USA: Dorothy Chandler Pavilion, Los Angeles 28 August 1973

Recordings: original Japanese production *Scarlett* (Victor), original London cast (Columbia)

Literature: Rome, E: *The Scarlett Letters* (Colonial Press, Clinton, Mass, 1971)

GOODHART, Al (b New York, 26 January 1905; d New York, 30 November 1955).

Variously a vaudevillian, a radio announcer, a pianist and a theatrical agent, Goodhart also had some success as a songwriter, in tandem with the already-established Al Hoffman and others, turning out ''I Apologise'' (w Hoffman, Ed Nelson), ''Auf Wiederseh'n, My Dear'' (w Hoffman, Nelson, Milton Ager), ''Happy Go Lucky You and Broken Hearted Me'' (w Hoffman, John Murray), ''In the Dim Dawning'' (w Hoffman, Stanley Adams), ''Fit as a Fiddle'' (w Hoffman, Arthur Freed), later featured in *Singin' in the Rain* on screen and on stage, ''Who Walks In?'' (w Hoffman, Ralph Freed) and ''I Saw Stars'' (w Hoffman, Maurice Sigler) in the early 1930s.

In 1934, with the British fashion for American songwriters at its peak, he joined Hoffman and Sigler in Britain to supply songs for such early British Gaumont sound films as Jessie Matthews's *First a Girl* (''Everything's in Rhythm with My Heart''), Jack Buchanan's *Come Out of the Pantry* (''Everything Stops for Tea''), *She Shall Have Music* (''My First Thrill''), and then, with Sigler replaced by Sam Lerner, but still in the inevitable musical troilism, for Miss Matthews's *Gangway* (''Gangway''), etc.

During the same period the trios also supplied songs for Jack Buchanan's stage musical *This'll Make You Whistle* (''There Isn't Any Limit to My Love,'' ''I'm in a Dancing Mood,'' ''This'll Make You Whistle,'' ''You've Got the Wrong Rumba''), the Gaiety Theatre success *Going Greek* (''A Little Co-operation From You''), and the Cicely Courtneidge/Bobby Howes *Hide and Seek* (w Vivian Ellis). In 1938, when the vein of fashion ran out, the songwriters returned to America, after which, apart from the song ''I Ups to Her and She Ups to Me'' (w Hoffman, Manny Kurtz), Goodhart seems to have made no further impression on the international songwriting scene.

1936 **This'll Make You Whistle** (w Maurice Sigler, Al Hoffman/Guy Bolton, Fred Thompson) Palace Theatre 14 September

1937 **Going Greek** (w Sam Lerner, Hoffman/Bolton, Thompson, Douglas Furber) Gaiety Theatre 16 September

1937 **Hide and Seek** (w Vivian Ellis, Lerner, Hoffman/Bolton, Thompson, Furber) London Hippodrome 14 October

GOOD MORNING, DEARIE Musical comedy in 2 acts by Anne Caldwell. Music by Jerome Kern. Globe Theater, New York, 1 November 1921.

The libretto to *Good Morning Dearie* trod paths that were not quite as well-worn as many, in its details if not in its essence. The juvenile man was rich and social Billy van Cortlandt (Oscar Shaw), doomed to be wedded to equally rich and social Ruby Manners (Peggy Kurton). But his heart has gone astray, and the object of his sighing is the little milliner's errand girl, Rose-Marie (Louise Groody). Unfortunately, Rose-Marie does not have an unblemished past. She has been associated, in not the nicest possible way, with the very dubious Chesty Costello (Harland Dixon), to whom she is now beholden. Fortunately, Chesty's itchy fingers get the better of him. He is caught by hero and heroine in the act of stealing the jewels of a society lady and he is happy to swap his fiancée for his liberty.

Oscar Shaw drew the hit song of the show, in the pseudo-Hawaiian ''Ka-lu-a,'' as well as a ''Didn't You Believe?'' and a pair of watery duos with his heroine about ''Niagara Falls'' and ''The Blue Danube Blues,'' whilst she, in turn, called herself ''Rose-Marie'' and was given the title song of the evening. William Kent, in the role of detective Steve, had two numbers (''Sing Song Girl,'' ''Melican Papa''), but the accent was as much on dancing as it was on singing and there were Sixteen Sunshine Girls (Coolie Dance, ''Le Sport American''), Six Fan-Tan Girls, a dance soloist, Marie Callahan, to perform two routines with dance-specialist Dixon, as well as one of the novelty dances that characterized the period, ''The Teddy Toddle.''

Even though produced at a dicky moment in theatrical time, Charles Dillingham's production of *Good Morning, Dearie* proved a jolly, multi-colored piece of entertainment which ran through no less than 347 performances on Broadway. However, not everyone was happy with the show. First, City Hall got miffed at a lyric making fun of it and, waving its Big Brotherly fist, refused to issue new permits for the children in the show until the offending line was altered, and then poor, silly Fred Fisher, the composer of such hits as ''Peg o' my Heart,'' flew into court to prosecute Kern for lifting his ''Dardanella'' contrabass for ''Ka-lu-a.'' In one of those loony theatrical lawsuits, judged upon by judges who know nothing of theatre and of music, Fisher was given eventual winner and damages of $250.

Kern made rather more than that from his song and from his show, which followed its Broadway season with a good tour, and with a production in Australia which featured Josie Melville (Rose-Marie), George Vollaire (Billy), Percy Le Fre (Steve), George Crotty (Chesty) and Dan Agar. Hailed as ''a smart American piece . . . an eccentric dancing entertainment in excelsis set to daintily scored melodic numbers and with clever dialogue and lyrics,'' it ran for more than two months in Sydney, and played a Christmas season in Melbourne with Miss Melville paired with George Gee.

Australia: Theatre Royal, Sydney 5 July 1924

GOOD NEWS Musical comedy in 2 acts by Laurence Schwab and B G De Sylva. Lyrics by B G De Sylva and Lew Brown. Music by Ray Henderson. 46th Street Theater, New York, 6 September 1927.

What Bordman's *The American Musical Theatre* calls "probably the quintessential musical comedy of the era of wonderful nonsense," was a lively, ingenuous show about college kids, dating and footballing, much in the vein of the earlier *Leave It to Jane,* but without the element of smiling parody that would appear in its post-war equivalent, *Grease.* It used a problem which is still a contemporary American one for its main plot element—Tom Marlowe (John Price Jones), the not-very-academic pride of the Tait College football team, isn't going to be able to play in the Big Game if he doesn't pass his examinations. He gets both brain-help and a happy final curtain from fellow student Connie Lane (Mary Lawlor). Alongside the romantic line, there was the requisite amount of lighthearted comedy from fellow footballer and funster Bobby Randall (Gus Shy) and boisterous soubretting from an incidental lass called Flo (Zelma O'Neal), whilst Shirley Vernon played Patricia Bingham, the girl who is the hurdle Connie has to pass to get to Tom.

The plot of *Good News* was, however, much less important than its high-spirited production and its songs. Connie and Tom joined together to sing about being "Lucky in Love" and declared starrily that "The Best Things in Life Are Free," and Connie and her pals Patricia and Millie (Ruth Mayo) waxed dreamy in "Just Imagine," whilst Flo pelted out the "Good News," and George Olsen's band, which provided the accompaniment to the entertainment, joined in the fun in collegiate clothes. The highlight of the show, however, came with the performance of "The Varsity Drag" ("a kind of riotous cakewalk"), sung and danced, with legs aflying, by the young Miss O'Neal.

A joyful success alongside such pieces as *Rio Rita* and *Hit the Deck* and later *My Maryland, A Connecticut Yankee, Funny Face, The Three Musketeers* and *Show Boat* in the 1927–28 season, the Laurence Schwab/Frank Mandel production of *Good News* remained at the 46th Street Theater for a fine 557 performances.

Miss O'Neal repeated her famous dance when *Good News* was taken to London the following year, starring alongside Neil Collins (Tom), Evelyn Hoey (Connie) and Bobby Jarvis (Bobby) in a Clayton and Waller production at the Carlton Theatre. However, this very American show proved, in spite of its zingy collection of gramophonable songs, to have less to offer to the British and it closed after 132 performances. Australia's production, mounted by the Fullers in Melbourne and staged by Ernest Rolls, did no better. Sam Critcherson (Tom) headed the cast of a show which played a month-and-a-half at the Princess before going on to Sydney's St James Theatre (10 November 1928) where local stars Elsie Prince (Babe) and Jimmy Godden (Pooch) were brought in to give weight to the bill. Even with that favorite pair in place, the show did not manage to arouse any real enthusiasm.

A Budapest production (rechristened "student love, a tale of American college life" by adaptor Lázsló Szilágyi) was successfully staged at the Király Színház, the city's then home of operett, with Franziska Gaal and Kálmán Rózsahegyi starred, during Hungary's 1920s craze for musical comedy and for things American. Following on behind such highly successful pieces as the blockbusting *Mersz-e, Mary?* (*Mercenary Mary*), *Rose Marie* and *The Girl Friend* (*Kitty's Kisses)* and in the atmosphere of local pieces with titles like *Hullo Amerika!, Miss Amerika* and *Amerikai lányok, Good News* proved merrily à la mode.

In France, Jane Auber and Philippe Meyer introduced "La Chance en amour," "Avec un peu d'imagination" and "Tout ça, c'est pour tout le monde" and the chorus danced "Le Drag de l'université" in Albert Willemetz's version for a short season.

Two Hollywood film versions of *Good News* were made, the first in 1930 featuring original star Mary Lawlor, but utilizing only some of the show score (both "Just Imagine" and "Lucky in Love" were omitted) alongside some Hollywood interpolations, and the second in 1947 with Peter Lawford and June Allyson playing the young lovers and also heading the performance of "The Varsity Drag." This version used all the show hits (but not the rest of the score), supplemented by two in-house additions.

Following his success in bringing *No, No, Nanette* and *Irene* back to Broadway in the 1970s, Harry Rigby tried in 1974 to do the same with *Good News.* With a sizeable female film name—Alice Faye this time—again heading the bill, the new *Good News* (titivated with three numbers from *Follow Thru* and another half dozen from other shows) toured America for a year but Miss Faye, Stubby Kaye, Gene Nelson and their production stayed in New York (St James Theater 23 December 1974) for just 16 performances.

UK: Carlton Theatre 15 August 1928; Australia: Princess Theatre, Melbourne 16 June 1928; Hungary: Király Színház *Diákszerelem* 30 March 1929; France: Palace 20 December 1929

Films: MGM 1930, MGM 1947

Recordings: selection (part record) (World Records, Allegro), film soundtrack 1947 (MGM, Columbia), cast recording 1974 (private), Wichita cast recording 1993 (Jay)

GOODWIN, J[ohn] Cheever (b Boston, 14 July 1850; d New York, 19 December 1912). Free-flowing bricoleur of texts, many borrowed (or just pilfered) from the French, for Boston and for Broadway, who actually found his greatest successes not with these borrowings but with his few original pieces.

Born in Boston and educated at Harvard, Goodwin began his working life as a journalist on the *Boston Traveller.* He had his first experience in the theatre when he teamed with E E Rice on an imitation of the burlesques performed so successfully by Lydia Thompson's blondes, and came up with a flop called *Evangeline* (1874). He subsequently turned out some rather free ''adaptations'' required by Alice Oates to suit Continental and British musical plays to her company's sometimes outlandish needs (*La Jolie Parfumeuse, La Princesse de Trébizonde, Barbe-bleue, Giroflé-Girofla,* etc)—and he even played for a while with the lady's troupe—but struck success with a vengeance when a revised, revived and tricked-up version of his very first work, *Evangeline,* established itself as a long touring favorite.

In the years that followed, Goodwin continued to work in journalism, as a broker, as a secretary, as sometime press agent and playreader for New York's Park Theatre, and as a road agent for the Spanish Students while at the same time turning out a goodly list of musical theatre pieces. On the one hand, he adapted a further swatch of French opéras-bouffes and -comiques for the American stage, including some such as *La Gardeuse d'oies* (*A Normandy Wedding*), *Les Demoiselles de Saint-Cyriens* (*The Cadet Girl*), *Babolin* (*The Devil's Deputy*) and *Pervenche* (*Fleur de lis*) which—with their sources not always credited—were equipped with wholly or almost wholly new music. It was murmured quite loudly that his *Panjandrum,* presented as an original work, was in fact a rip-off of the French opérette *Miss Robinson,* and on the form there was every possibility it was true.

On the other hand, he turned out at first text (again, often, some form of adaptation) and lyrics, and later mostly lyrics only, for a series of native musical comedies and extravaganzas such as the Stella Belmore combination's production of *Greek Fire* on the New England circuit. Several of these loose-limbed pieces had extended lives around America, although they rarely traveled beyond. His greatest theatrical successes, apart from *Evangeline,* came with the ''comic opera'' *Wang* (1891), an apparently original echo of the oriental opéras-bouffes of the French and English stages written for the comedian De Wolf Hopper, and the burlesque *Cinderella at School* (1881), produced by Augustin Daly at his New York headquarters. He had his most popular single song hit with ''When Reuben Comes to Town.''

Several of Goodwin's works got showings beyond American shores. His musical version of the farce *Le Baptême du petit Oscar, Lost, Strayed or Stolen,* was played briefly at London's Duke of York's Theatre in 1897 and both his revamping of the French libretto to *L'Étoile* as *The Merry Monarch* (1891) and *Wang* (1901) were seen in Australia. *The Merry Monarch* was also used as part of the basis for another rehash of Chabrier's ill-treated opéra-comique, played at London's Savoy Theatre as *The Lucky Star,* with a score by Ivan Caryll. He also had a little (music-less) comedietta *Don Quixote Jr* (w John Howson) played as a forepiece during the London run of *Les Cloches de Corneville.*

A non-musical piece written in collaboration with Charles Bradley served as the basis for the musical comedy *The Regatta Girl* (14 March 1900), musicalized by Harry McLellan for Koster and Bial's Music Hall.

1874 **Evangeline, the Belle of Acadia** (E E Rice) Niblo's Garden 27 July

1874 **Giroflé-Girofla** American version w Harris (Boston Theater)

1877 **Le Petit Corsair** (American version of William Brough's *Conrad and Medora*) (Rice, John J Braham) Boston Museum 30 July

1877 **Pippins, or The First Go-week** (American version of Francis Talfourd's *Atalanta*) (J J Braham) Globe Theater, Boston 24 December; revised version Globe Theater, Boston 1 July 1878; Broadway Theater, New York 26 November 1890 with music by Woolson Morse

1879 **Le Petit Duc** American version (Bush Street Theater, Philadelphia)

1880 **Greek Fire** (J J Braham) Opera House, Providence, RI 24 November

1881 **Cinderella at School** (Morse) Daly's Theater 5 March

1883 **Virginia, or Ringing the Changes** revised version w John J Braham of Solomon and Stephens's comic opera (Bijou Theater, Boston)

1884 **Madam Piper** (Morse) Wallack's Theater 5 December

1887 **Jacquette** (*La Béarnaise*) American version (Wallack's Theater)

1889 **King Cole II** (Morse) (revised *Madam Piper*) Broad Street Theater, Philadelphia 24 April

1890 **The Merry Monarch** (*L'Étoile*) American version w new music by Morse (Broadway Theater)

1891 **Wang** (Morse) Broadway Theater 4 May

1891 **The Lion Tamer** (*Le Grand Casimir*) American version w new music by Richard Stahl (Broadway Theater)

1893 **Panjandrum** (Morse) Broadway Theater 1 May

1893 **Africa** (Randolph Cruger/w Clay Greene) Star Theater, San Francisco 25 December

1894 **Aladdin Jr** (W H Batchelder, Jesse Williams) Opera House, Chicago 14 June; Broadway Theater, New York 8 April 1895

1894 **Dr Syntax** (revised *Cinderella at School*) Broadway Theater 23 June

1894 **The Little Trooper** (*Les 28 Jours de Clairette*) American version w Clay Greene w new music by William Furst (Casino Theater)

1894 **The Devil's Deputy** (*Babolin*) American version w new music by Edward Jakobowski (Abbey's Theater)

1895 **A Daughter of the Regiment** (revised *1776,* English version) (Ludwig Englander) Broadway Theater 27 May

1895 **Fleur de lis** (*Pervenche*) American version w new music by Furst (Palmers Theater)

1896 **Lost, Strayed or Stolen** (aka *A Day in Paris*) (Morse) McVicker's Theater, Chicago 15 June; Fifth Avenue Theater 21 September

1897 **La Falote** English version (Casino Theater)

1897 **A Normandy Wedding** (ex- *Papa Gougou*) (*La Gardeuse d'oies*) American version w Charles A Byrne w new music by Furst (Opera House, Detroit; revised version Herald Square Theater, New York 21 February 1898)

1898 **Giroflé-Girofla** new American version (Tivoli, San Francisco)

1899 **An Arabian Girl and the Forty Thieves** revised *Ali Baba, or Morgiana and the Forty Thieves* (pasticcio) Herald Square Theater, New York 29 April

1899 **Around New York in Eighty Minutes** (Rice, J J Braham/ James T Waldron, Edward Fales Coward, Richard Carle) Koster and Bial's Music Hall 6 November

1899 **The Lady from Chicago** (Richard Henry Warren, Henry K Hadley, William F Peters, Melville Ellis/w Coward, Louis Fitzgerald jr, Rupert Hughes, Robert Sands, James Barnes) Strollers' Benefit, Waldorf Astoria 15 December

1900 **The Cadet Girl** (*Les Demoiselles de Saint-Cyriens*) (Englander [and Louis Varney]/H B Smith) American version w largely new score (Herald Square Theater)

1900 **The Monks of Malabar** (ex- *Booloo Boolboom*) (Englander) Knickerbocker Theater 14 September

1900 **The Rogers Brothers in Central Park** (Maurice Levi/J J McNally) Hammerstein's Victoria 17 September

1901 **The Sleeping Beauty and the Beast** American version w Fred Solomon Broadway Theater 4 November

1902 **The Rogers Brothers at Harvard** (Levi) Knickerbocker Theater 1 September

1903 **Mr Bluebeard** American version w Solomon (mus) Knickerbocker Theater 21 January

1904 **Baroness Fiddlesticks** revised libretto (Casino Theater)

GOODWIN, Nat [GOODWIN, Nathaniel Carl] (b Boston, 25 July 1857; d New York, 31 January 1919).

Goodwin began his career on stage at 17, in his native Boston, and he made his first notable Broadway appearance at Tony Pastor's burlesque house, playing the chief comedy role of Captain Crosstree in the celebrated burlesque version of *Black-Eyed Susan.* He played for a season with E E Rice and his Surprise Party company (Captain Dietrich in *Evangeline,* Yussef in *Le Petit Corsair,* Paidogogos in *Pippins,* etc) before breaking away, after an argument over a fine, and setting up a similar outfit of his own, the (or Eliza Weathersby's or Nat Goodwin's) Froliques (4 February 1878), playing farce-comedies (*Hobbies, Cruets, The Ramblers,* etc), with varying degrees of music, around the country.

Goodwin starred for long periods in specially made roles in musical-comedy vehicles such as Professor Pygmalion in Benjamin Woolf's *Hobbies* or Delaine in *The Skating Rink,* he appeared in burlesque (Matyas Irving in *Those Bells!, Cinderella in School,* Bottom in *Bottom's Dream*) and was also seen in literate comedy (Onesimus Epps in *The Member for Slocum*) and in comic opera (Lorenzo in *La Mascotte,* Sir Joseph in *HMS Pinafore,* Bunthorne in *Patience,* Duc des Ifs in *Olivette*). When he stopped in New York for seven months during the 1887–88 season, he presented his old *The Skating Rink;* Meyer Lutz's London Gaiety burlesque *Little Jack Sheppard,* in which Goodwin and Loie Fuller gave their versions of the roles created by Fred Leslie and Nellie Farren; a version of Mark Melford's English comedy *Turned Up,* plugged full of borrowed songs; and a standard musical farce-comedy *Big Pony, or The Gentlemanly Savage.*

In his buying-up of British successes around this time he is said (as are others) to have taken the rights to a new comic opera playing at the Comedy Theatre. But he let the rights lapse, and the record-breaking *Erminie* was instead produced by the Casino Theater and Rudolf Aronson. Goodwin's subsequent fame was made largely in comedy, the marriage registers and the newspaper scandal pages.

Amongst his wives were numbered the burlesque actress **ELIZA WEATHERSBY** (née SMITH; d New York, 24 March 1887), longtime of the Lydia Thompson troupe, and actress Maxine Elliott (1898).

Autobiography: *Nat Goodwin's Book* (R G Badger, Boston, 1914)

GORDON, Kitty [BLADES, Constance Minnie] (b Folkestone, 22 April 1878; d Brentwood, NY, 26 May 1974).

The daughter of Captain Joel Blades, a Lincolnshire-born army officer, long stationed in Guernsey, Miss Gordon was, thanks to her father's being subsequently posted to Melbourne, brought up largely in Australia. She first appeared on the stage at 23 in the chorus of a touring production of *San Toy* (1901), before going on to take over a chorus role in George Edwardes's provincial production of *Kitty Grey* (1901), two weeks prior to the end of the tour. She was retained when the show opened in town several months later and, at the end of the run, filled a similarly small but picturesque role in Edwardes's *The Girl from Kays* (1902, Mary Methuen). Her third Edwardes show was *The Duchess of Dantzic,* more demanding musically, and this time Miss Gordon's statuesque beauty and well-trained voice won her the supporting role of Princess Caroline Murat and the opportunity to substitute for Evie Greene in the star role on several occasions.

Edwardes then cast her as Agathe in London's *Véronique* (1904), a role she repeated on Broadway the following year, before she moved on to Charles Frohman's management to play the splendidly vicious Princess Rasslova, battling against Edna May's wansome *Nellie Neil* (1907) for a fair-to-poor West End run. After the quick failures of *The Three Kisses* (1907, Teresa) and *The Antelope* (1908, Speranza Derrick) she returned to Edwardes to play the cabaret vamp Olga Labinska in *The Dollar Princess,* before again crossing the Atlantic. In was in America that she finally moved from second leads to starring roles and it was in America that she spent the remainder of her career, boosted by publicity which claimed—with no obvious disparagement of her front—that she had "the most beautiful back in the world."

She appeared in the rollickingly comical *The Girl and the Wizard* (1909, Murietta) with Sam Bernard, playing a comic-opera prima donna to his temperamental tenor and getting to burlesque *Carmen,* and—with much-publicized success—as the slightly scandalous heroine of the hugely successful English-language production of *Alma, wo wohnst du?* (1910). She subsequently played in *La Belle Paree* (1911, Lady Guff Jordan, a society modiste) and capitalized on the reputation won as Alma to take star billing in the title role of *The Enchantress* (1911, Vivian). She toured *The Enchantress* long and mostly successfully, and latterly under her own management, but in 1913 her company playing that piece went bust out in California. Local producer Oliver Morosco came to Miss Gordon's rescue, and promptly mounted a production of *Alma, wo wohnst du?* Back in her most famous role the star was again a big hit. She played the vaudeville circuits in the suggestive *The Pink Nightgown* (1914) and a Jack Lait sketch, *Alma's Return* (Palace 7 October 1914), which featured her once again as Adolf Phillipp's inviting adventuress, and appeared in Morosco's *Pretty Mrs Smith* (1914) on Broadway, before switching her attentions to vaudeville, in which she was able, so it was reported, to command a salary of $1,500 per week.

Miss Gordon then turned her tracks to Hollywood and there she became a favorite "vampire" in such early silent movies as *The Beloved Adventuress, The Scar, The Wasp, The Divine Sacrifice, The Unveiling Hand* and *Adele* between 1916 and 1919. She was injured during the filming of a battlefield scene in *No Man's Land,* sued the company and won a week's salary ($1,250), but also effectively ended her film career.

She played in the revue *That's It* at San Francisco's Casino (1919), and several small venues in the less successful *Love for Sale* (1919) away from New York, and another attempt to return to the musical stage in 1920 with a vehicle called *Lady Kitty Inc* came to grief on the road after just five weeks of touring. However, although the starriest days were past, Miss Gordon continued to work and she was seen on American television as late as 1952, in *Life Begins at Eighty.*

Kitty Gordon's first husband was theatrical producer **Michael LEVENSTON** (b Glasgow, 19 July 1855; d London, 29 March 1904).

GORDON, Noele (b East Ham, 25 December 1919; d Birmingham, 14 April 1985).

A musical-comedy soubrette in the 1940s and 1950s, Miss Gordon was seen in London in *Let's Face It* (in place of Joyce Barbour), *The Lisbon Story,* in *Big Ben* (succeeding Gabrielle Brune) and in replacement of Julie Wilson in *Bet Your Life,* as well as introducing the role of Meg Brockie in London's version of *Brigadoon.*

Having established herself in the 1960s and 1970s as Britain's suppertime soap queen in the television series *Crossroads,* she was able to capitalize on that fame, after her summary removal from the screen, by appearing in the West End as Mrs Sally Adams (a role in which she had toured in earlier days) in a revival of *Call Me Madam.* She was in the throes of following up as Sue in *No, No, Nanette* when her final illness overtook her.

GOSSE DE RICHE Comédie musicale in 3 acts by Jacques Bousquet and Henri Falk. Music by Maurice Yvain. Théâtre Daunou, Paris, 2 May 1924.

A successful example of the Jazz Age Parisian musical, combining a lighthearted and smilingly lascivious libretto with lively up-to-date dance melodies, *Gosse de riche* ("rich kid") told the modern-day story of Colette (Alice Cocéa), the daughter of the parvenu Patarin (Vilbert), who sets her cap at the young artist André (Henri Defreyn), only to finally discover that he has a girl, Nane (Christiane Dor), who just happens also to be her father's petite amie. And it goes on from there to . . . well, just where you'd expect. But getting there is fun.

Vilbert's comedy was central to the piece, surfacing happily in the argot of his crooked "On biaise" or his blithe "Quand on est chic," whilst Mlle Cocéa identified herself as "gosse de riche" to fox-trot rhythm and duetted with Defreyn in waltz time ("Malgré moi") and in a java ("L'Invite à la Java"). *Ta bouche* star Jeanne Cheirel, as a jeweled Baroness without visible means of support, growled out a song in each act, detailing deliciously the advantanges of "Combine" (racketeering) in rather more open terms than *Gentleman Joe*'s Mrs Ralli Carr had done in the previous generation of shows. Yvain's score, unlike those for British and American shows of the same era, also included, alongside its dance melodies and comic songs, finely made concerted finales, a niftily harmonized septet and a quartet.

Parisian success was followed by a fine provincial life and an Hungarian production (ad Jenő Heltai) before the next Jazz Age musical comedy took its place.

Hungary: Fővárosi Operettszínház *A Párizsi lány* 24 August 1924

DER GÖTTERGATTE *see* DIE IDEALE GATTIN

GOUBLIER, Gustave [CONIN, Gustave] (b Paris, 15 January 1856; d Paris, 27 October 1926).

The young Goublier made his first musical steps as a pianist and accompanist before becoming a conductor, at first in spa resorts and then in Parisian music halls and cafés-concerts. At the same time, he began what was to be a successful career as a songwriter from which such numbers as ''L'Angelus de la mer'' and ''Le Crédo du paysan'' emerged as considerable hits. He spent six years as musical director at the Eldorado, where some of his earliest one-act stage compositions were produced, then moved to the Moulin-Rouge, where he conducted, amongst others, the Paris premiere of *La Belle de New-York,* and then to the Folies-Bergère. In 1915 his most substantial musical, *Mam'zelle Boy Scout,* was produced at the Théâtre de la Renaissance, and the following year he took the baton at the Variétés for a revival of *La Belle de New-York.*

1890 **Chanteur et Pipelot** (Gaston Marguery) 1 act Lille 7 October

1899 **Par-devant le notaire** (A L'Hoste) 1 act Eldorado 4 March

1899 **La Boule de neige** (E Verrier, G Fau) 1 act Galerie Vivienne 12 June

1899 **Le Sérum de l'amour** (H Darsay, A Trébitsch) 1 act Eldorado 7 October

1900 **Les Filles de la belle Hélène** (Gardel-Hervé) Eldorado 7 October

1909 **Ali-Bébé et les quarante voleuses** (Emil Codey, ''Trébla'' [ie, A Delvaille]) Parisiana 1 May

1909 **Lucette à la caserne** (Daniel Riche, Maurice Mareuil) Parisiana 8 June

1913 **Le Roi boîte** (Ernest Depré) 1 act Théâtre Impérial 7 February

1915 **Mam'zelle Boy Scout** (Paul Bonhomme) Théâtre de la Renaissance 3 April

1919 **Les Surprises d'une nuit d'amour** (Eugène Joullot) Orléans 25 April; Theatre Cluny, Paris 30 April 1920

1920 **Ah! Quelle nuit** (Bonhomme) Bouffes-du-Nord 19 November

Biography: Bru, J: *La Vie et la carrière de Gustave et Henri Goublier* (Priméra, Paris, 1976)

GOUBLIER, Henri (b Paris, 14 March 1888; d Paris, 23 May 1951).

The younger son of Gustave Goublier, Henri made his early career as an orchestral timpanist before scoring a considerable success as the composer of the patriotic wartime musical *La Cocarde de Mimi-Pinson,* one of the rare hits of the French musical stage of the period. Thereafter he had further, if not equivalent success with *Un Mariage parisien* (1919), a piece which actually predated *La Cocarde* in its writing, but which had not found a production until the young composer had made his name, and *Le Mariage d'un Tartarin* (1921), before devoting himself to management.

He set up the Nouveau Théâtre, at the center of a circuit of suburban theatres, to play opérette and opéra-comique, but the venture failed, as did his first attempt to return to the composing scene with *Billy-Bill* (1931). He worked as a conductor, both in France and abroad, on one occasion on a South American tour with a repertoire of French opérettes, but it was not until 1942 that he again found success as a composer with the show *Carnaval,* a collaboration with his daughter, Jeanette Bruno (''Jean Bru''), which had a 12-month run at the Théâtre de la Gaîté-Lyrique. His subsequent works included two radio pieces, *Jour de bal* and *Le Mariage de Chiffon* (23 May 1954), the latter of which was subsequently played on the stage.

1913 **Mam'zelle Vésuve** (Fabrice Lémon, Georges Vidès) Casino, Boulogne-sur-mer 14 August

1915 **La Cocarde de Mimi-Pinson** (Maurice Ordonneau, Francis Gally) Théâtre Apollo 25 November

1916 **La Demoiselle du Printemps** (Ordonneau, Gally) Théâtre Apollo 17 May

1917 **La Fiancée du lieutenant** (Gally) Théâtre Apollo 26 April

1919 **Un Mariage parisien** (Georges Léglise) Théâtre des Variétés 24 May

1920 **L'Heritière en loterie** (René Chavanne, Léglise) Theatre Royal, Liege 4 April

1920 **La Sirène, ou la baigneuse de minuit** (Léglise, Lémon) Théâtre Apollo 30 September

1921 **Le Mariage d'un Tartarin** (Léglise, Lémon) Eldorado 1 May

1931 **Billy-Bill** (Léglise, Max Dearly) Théâtre Scala 17 January

1935 **La Nuit est belle** (Albert Sablons) Théâtre Antoine 25 September

1942 **Carnaval** (R Holt, Jean Bru) Théâtre de la Gaîté-Lyrique

1950 **Les Folies de Mylord l'Arsouille** (Eugène Joullot, Rozet) Théâtre de l'Horloge, Lyon 16 October

GRAB ME A GONDOLA Musical comedy in 2 acts by Julian More. Lyrics by Julian More and James Gilbert. Music by James Gilbert. Theatre Royal, Windsor, 30 October 1956; Lyric, Hammersmith, 27 November 1956; Lyric Theatre, London, 26 December 1956.

One of the liveliest of the small-scale musicals to emerge from British repertory theatres in the mid-1950s, *Grab Me a Gondola* won its way, by stages, to the West End and a fine run of 673 performances. A burlesque of the film festival scene, it presented revue star Joan Heal in a virtuoso role as a busty blonde Diana Dors character with ambitions to become a Serious Actress (''Cravin' for the Avon'') and Denis Quilley as a young reporter whose search for a scoop leads him to neglect his girl (Jane Wenham) to the extent that, in a section satirizing the veracity and methods of the press, she fabricates a newspaper story which alters the course of the plot.

Some delightful light ballads, some showy material for Miss Heal and some fine burlesque (notably a zany harmonized ensemble declaring "The Motor Car is Treacherous"), teamed with a good helping of topical revusical satire, made *Grab Me a Gondola* a fine if ephemeral success on British and colonial stages.

Australia: Empire Theatre, Sydney 2 May 1959

Recording: original cast (HMV)

GRÄFIN DUBARRY *see* DIE DUBARRY

GRÄFIN MARIZA Operette in 3 acts by Julius Brammer and Alfred Grünwald. Music by Emmerich Kálmán. Theater an der Wien, Vienna, 28 February 1924.

One of the most successful of Kálmán's long list of successful Operetten, *Gräfin Mariza* has survived into the repertoire of the later years of the 20th century with marginally less strength than his *Die Csárdásfürstin* but, if it rates second of his works in general popularity, it has every claim to be the most satisfying musically.

Rich and lovely Countess Mariza (Betty Fischer) owns an estate in the Hungarian borderlands which is managed by the handsome Béla Török (Hubert Marischka). Török is, in fact, really the Count Tassilo Endrödy-Wittenburg, but he has been obliged to take an incognito and paid employment in order to pay off his family debts and to earn a dowry for his sister, Lisa (Elsie Altmann). Mariza pays an unaccustomed visit to the estate to announce her engagement but, in fact, the engagement is only a ruse to deter the perpetual string of proposals she has been subjected to, and she has chosen the phony name of her prospective bridegroom, Baron Koloman Zsupán, from the cast list of *Der Zigeunerbaron.* She gets a staggering surprise when a real Baron Zsupán (Max Hansen) turns up all ready to fulfill his "engagement." Tassilo, too, has some covering up to do when it turns out that Lisa is part of the house party. After two acts of fallings in love, misunderstandings and clearing up of the same misunderstandings, Mariza and Tassilo come together in a happy ending, alongside Lisa and the pig-farming Baron. Richard Waldemar played the interfering Fürst Moritz Dragomir Populescu, Hans Moser was the comical valet Penizek, and Poldi Eigner took the role of a gypsy girl with a solo.

The score of *Gräfin Mariza* was topped by a trio of contrasting numbers which would become Operette standards: the tenor's vibrant "Komm' Zigány!," the leading lady's csárdás "Höre ich Zigeunergeigen," and the comically dancing invitation offered by Zsupán, first to Mariza and later to Lisa, to "Komm mit nach Varasdin." These were, however, only the tip of a musical iceberg. Tassilo reminisced about his wild-oats days in Vienna to suitably waltzing rhythms ("Grüss mir die Süssen, die reizenden Frauen"), joined sweetly with Lisa in "Sonnenschein, hüll' dich ein," or with Mariza in the waltzing "Einmal möcht' ich wieder tanzen" and the wooing "Sag ja, mein Lieb, sag ja," whilst Mariza led the praises of "Braunes Mädel von der Puszta," Zsupán mused over his change of loyalties with Lisa in "Ich möchte träumen," and Manja opened the proceedings with her little gypsy song "Glück ist ein schöner Traum" in a score which was effective from end to end.

Plate 151. **Grab Me a Gondola.** *Joan Heal as the Diana Dors of a jolly parody of the world of film festivals.*

Marischka's production of *Gräfin Mariza* proved a triumph. It played for 374 consecutive performances at the Theater an der Wien, using up a long list of star players as the genuinely Hungarian Ernő Király and Emmi Kosáry took turns at the lead roles, Lea Seidl, Rosa Mittermardi, Lya Beyer and Carlotta Vanconi were seen as

Plate 152. **Gräfin Mariza.** *Glenys Fowles (Mariza), Anthony Warlow (Zsupán) and Gordon Wilcock (Popolescu) in the Australian Opera production of 1987.*

Mariza, Victor Flemming, Ludwig Herold, Karl Bachmann and Franz Galetta as Tassilo, and Walter Swoboda, Josef König and Josef Viktora took turns as Zsupán. Other productions quickly followed, with Budapest swiftly off the mark with a *Marica grófnő* (ad Zsolt Harsányi) with Juci Lábass (Mariza), Ferenc Kiss (Tassilo) and Márton Rátkai (Zsupán) starred which made its way firmly into the standard repertoire, and Berlin's Metropoltheater following, with a production featuring Adele Sandrock in the title role. The first English-language production (ad Harry B Smith) was mounted by the Shuberts in New York. Kálmán's score was given the usual Shubert treatment, and songwriters Sigmund Romberg and Al Goodman thus got their names on the bill and their tunes in the score of a *Countess Maritza* which featured Yvonne d'Arle, Walter Woolf, Vivian Hart and Carl Randall at the Shubert Theater. It played through a good run of 321 performances which established the show for an extended life on American soil.

Elsewhere, however, the show was slower to find promoters. *Comtesse Maritza* (ad Max Eddy, Jean Marietti) first saw the French stage in 1930, at Mulhouse, with Anna Martens, Louis Collet, Alphonse Massart and Fanély Revoil heading the cast, and it was taken up the following year for a Paris showing with Mary Lewis, Roger Bourdin, Janie Marèse and Paul Clerget featured. It found some success there, but it did not stick, in the way that *Princesse Csárdás* had, in the French repertoire. In London, where Kálmán's works by and large got a disappointing reception, what was now just called *Maritza* (ad Robert Layer-Parker, Eddie Garr, Arthur Stanley) did not improve matters. Mara Lossef, John Garrick, Douglas Byng and Patricia Leonard headed the cast of a version which managed only 68 performances, and it was 1983 before London again saw the show, in a new and very much more listenable version by Nigel Douglas, mounted at Sadler's Wells Theatre with Marilyn Hill Smith, Ramon Remedios and Tudor Davies featured. This version was subsequently played in Australia under the auspices of the Australian Opera.

In spite of its success, and its recognized position both as one of Kálmán's best works and as one of the best and most popular romantic musicals of its era, *Gräfin Mariza* seems to have done better with the recording companies and filmmakers than with the major theatres of central Europe in the years since its original productions, and sightings of the show are now at best intermittent. Except in Hungary. There, in its composer's homeland, it remains a central feature of the Operette repertoire, and it has been seen in a new production at Budapest's Fővárosi Operettszínház in 1992 and 1993 and again at the Városmajori Szabadtéri Színpad in 1997.

Filmed versions of *Gräfin Mariza* appeared in 1925 (w Vivian Gibson, Harry Liedtke), in 1932 (w Dorothea Wieck and Marischka in his original role), again in 1958 with Christine Görner and Rudolf Schock and with Hans Moser playing his typical servant part more than 30 years on, and in 1973 with René Kollo and Erzsébet Házy.

Hungary: Király Színház *Marica grófnő* 18 October 1924; Germany: Metropoltheater 1924; USA: Apollo Theater, Atlantic City, 29 March 1926, Shubert Theater *Countess Maritza* 18 September 1926; France: Mulhouse *Comtesse Maritza* 27 February 1930, Théâtre des Champs-Elysées, Paris 7 May 1931; UK: Palace Theatre *Maritza* 6 July 1938

Films: 1925, 1932, 1958, 1973

Recordings: complete (EMI, Bruno), complete in Russian (Melodiya), selections (Eurodisc, CBS, Philips, RCA, etc), English cast 1983 (TER), selection in Italian (EDM, Fonit Centra), selection in Hungarian (Qualiton, Muvesz-Haz, Electrecord, Marika), selection in Swedish (Telestar), selection in Czech (no label), selection in English (Reader's Digest), etc

GRAF TONI Singspiel in 2 acts by Rudolf Österreicher. Music by Edmund Eysler. Apollotheater, Vienna, 2 March 1917.

"A veritable variety-operetta, with many comical scenes and grateful rôles for the stars" was just the right kind of material for Vienna's Apollotheater which, like its Berlin namesake, had begun its life as a variety house before introducing first shorter and then longer opérettes as part of its programs. Mizzi Zwerenz starred as a Viennese cabaret star, alongside Fritz Werner and Oscar Sachs, in a production for which Eysler, who admitted to having written his score for the two acts of the show in a month, turned out a supply of joyous tunes from which one, the duo "So küsst nur eine Wienerin," as introduced by Zwerenz and Werner, became one of his greatest hits.

Graf Toni had a good initial run, and was revived at the Jantschtheater in 1922.

DER GRAF VON LUXEMBURG Operette in 3 acts by A M Willner and Robert Bodanzky based on Willner and Buchbinder's libretto *Die Göttin der Vernunft.* Music by Franz Lehár. Theater an der Wien, Vienna, 12 November 1909.

Die Göttin der Vernunft ("the goddess of reason") was the title of the libretto written by A M Willner and Bernard Buchbinder and set to music by Johann Strauss for an 1897 (13 March) production by Alexandrine von Schönerer at the Theater an der Wien. Annie Dirkens, Carl Streitmann, Josef Joseffy, Therese Biedermann, Julie Kopácsi-Karczag and Karl Blasel featured for a run of 32 performances and a handful of subsequent matinées; the piece was given a brief showing at Berlin's Theater Unter den Linden (20 January 1898), and then it was put away.

A decade on, Willner exhumed the *Göttin der Vernunft* libretto, had it legally divorced from its earlier

Plate 153. **Der Graf von Luxemburg.** *Angèle Didier weds René of Luxembourg in the Montmartre garret of the painter Brissac—which, in Wuppertal's production, actually looks like a garret and not the usual glamorous hotel suite.*

score, and rewrote it, in collaboration with Bodanzky, as *Der Graf von Luxemburg* (or, initially, Luxenberg, to avoid any protest from the touchy Grand Duchy). Musically set by Lehár and produced, again, at the Theater an der Wien, it proved this time a major success and went on from its Vienna premiere to become a worldwide favorite.

The plot of the piece was one well-beloved of, in particular, French comedy writers: the marriage of convenience which turns out to be more than that. The aristocratic Fürst Basil Basilowitsch (Max Pallenberg) wishes to marry the singer Angèle Didier (Annie von Ligety) but, unable for reasons of pedigree to wed an untitled lady, he arranges for her to go through a bought marriage with the penniless layabout René, Graf von Luxemburg (Otto Storm). The wedding is conducted in the studio of the artist Armand Brissard (Bernard Bötel), with the two parties hidden from each other by an easel. René breaks his bond not to return to Paris before the subsequent divorce is effected, the two wedded partners meet and fall in love, and Basil is cheated of his bride. Armand and his little Juliette (Luise Kartousch), having provided the soubrette moments of the show, paired off at the same curtain, whilst Basil was restored to his aristocratic fiancée.

Lehár's score, still in his champagne-days *Die lustige Witwe* style, was full of melody, the first act bringing a dazzling entry for Angèle (''Heut' noch werd' ich Ehefrau''), a delightfully loping admission from Basil that ''Ich bin verliebt'' and the famous marriage duet for tenor and soprano in which the pair wonder over a wedding after which ''Sie geht links, er geht rechts'' (''she goes left, he goes right'') as they build up into the big waltz tune of the first-act finale, ''Bist du's, lachendes Glück.'' The second act gave the soubrets the pretty waltz ''Mädel klein, Mädel fein,'' and René his big solo number ''Es duftet nach trèfle incarnat,'' in which he begins to realize that the woman with whom he has fallen in love is already his ''wife,'' whilst the final act brought the lively march trio ''Liebe, ach, du Sonnenschein'' (Basil, Juliette, Brissard).

Der Graf von Luxemburg ran 179 straight performances at the Theater an der Wien before moving out of the evening spot to give place to a visiting company from Berlin's Deutsches Theater, but it returned after the summer break and ran on through to its 226th performance on 7 October, before paying a brief visit to the Raimundtheater with Anny Mahrbach and Adolf Lutzmann featured. In 1911 Mizzi Günther and Louis Treumann gave their interpretations of Angèle and René between 10 and 30 September, and the show appeared intermittently in the house repertoire thereafter.

Germany's first *Graf von Luxemburg* was produced at the Neues Operettenhaus at Christmas of 1909, and Hungary got its first sight of *Luxemburg grófja* (ad Andor Gábor) in March 1910 with Ernő Király, Sári Petrass and Márton Rátkai (Basil) featured. It was a huge hit, passing its 200th performance at the Király Színház on 11 November, and going on to major revivals at the Revü Színház in 1921 (22 March), and at the Fővárosi Operettszínház in 1944 (12 May ad Kálmán Kovács), 1952 (28 November ad István Békeffy, Dezső Kéller), 1957 (8 February), 1963 (12 April) and 1997 (11 October).

Later the same year George Edwardes mounted an English-language production of *The Count of Luxembourg* (ad Basil Hood, Adrian Ross) at Daly's Theatre. Lily Elsie, London's Merry Widow, was cast as Angèle Didier, Bertram Wallis played René, W H Berry and May de Souza paired as the soubrets, and Huntley Wright followed Pallenberg's low-comedy interpretation of Basil although with a little more age behind him. If the show's 340 London performances were considerably less than the records set up at Daly's by *The Merry Widow* and *The Dollar Princess,* the show was nevertheless a firm success, but it faded from the repertoire thereafter and a production at Sadler's Wells Theatre in 1983 (24 January, ad Nigel Douglas, Eric Maschwitz) was its first London showing since Edwardes's production.

Paris first welcomed *Le Comte de Luxembourg* in German, as given by a touring company in 1911, but the following year Alphonse Frank produced Gaston de Caillavet and Robert de Flers's French version at the theatre which had housed *La Veuve joyeuse,* with that piece's leading man, Henri Defreyn, as René. A Parisian surgeon's wife making her stage debut under the name Brigitte Régent proved to be a surprisingly splendid Angèle, Angèle Gril (Juliette) and Félix Galipaux (Brissard) supported, and they all played the show through 149 performances, followed by a further 37 the next season. A few months later, New York finally got its production of the show when Klaw and Erlanger mounted a *The Count of Luxembourg* (ad Glen MacDonough from the English version) with a cast headed by Anne Swinburne (Angèle), George Lear Moore (René), Frances Cameron (Juliette), Frank Moulan (Basil) and Fred Walton (Brissard). The ''waltz on the stairs'' sung and danced by the romantic leads became the sensation of the moment, but the show had only a fair, rather than fabulous, run of 120 performances, sufficient nevertheless to establish it in such a way that it toured successfully and was remounted at the Jolson Theater in 1930 as part of the Shubert series of classic revivals (17 February).

Australia also took up the British version and J C Williamson Ltd mounted *The Count of Luxembourg* in Melbourne in 1913. Florence Young (Angèle), Talleur Andrews (René), Phil Smith (Brissac), W S Percy (Basil) and Sybil Arundale (Juliette) featured in a regular season in the comic-opera company's repertoire.

In 1937 Lehár made some alterations and additions to his piece for a new production at Berlin's Theater des Volkes (ex- Metropoltheater). Amongst these, the carnival opening was rearranged, and Basil's last-act fiancée, Gräfin Stosa Kokozew, was given something to sing. Hans-Heinz Bollmann and Elisa Illiard played the romantic leads, with Alfred Haase (Basil), Hans Hessling (Brissard) and Mara Jakisch (Juliette) in support. *Der Graf von Luxemburg,* usually in a version of this remade version, remains in repertoires in Europe, and it has regularly been produced at the Vienna Volksoper (1954, 1977, 1990). This ''official'' alteration was, however, nothing compared to the fate that the libretto which had once been accompanied by Strauss music, and which had won fame accompanied by Lehár music, would ultimately suffer. In New Brunswick, NJ, USA, in April of 1996, a musical by A R Gurney called *Let's Do It* was produced. The show's book was ''partially suggested by'' *Der Graf von Luxemburg,* and this time the score that was glued to it was a potpourri of . . . secondhand Cole Porter.

George Walsh starred in a 1926 American silent film version, but the piece has subsequently been filmed in both German—first for cinema with Gerd Riemann and Renate Holm, and later for television with Eberhard Wächter and Lilian Sukis—and also in Spanish with the young Plácido Domingo.

Germany: Neues Operettenhaus 23 December 1909; Hungary: Király Színház *Luxemburg grófja* 14 January 1910; UK: Daly's Theatre *The Count of Luxembourg* 20 May 1911; France: Théâtre du Vaudeville, Paris 1911, Théâtre Apollo *Le Comte de Luxembourg* 13 March 1912; USA: New Amsterdam Theater 16 September 1912; Australia: His Majesty's Theatre, Melbourne *The Count of Luxembourg* 5 April 1913

Films: Celebrity Pictures 1926, CCC 1957, TV Film (Mexican) 1963, (German) 1972

Recordings: complete (EMI), complete in Russian (Melodiya), selections (Decca, Eurodisc, Philips, Telefunken, etc), selection in English (TER, Columbia), selection in French (Decca, Adria, Pathé, Odéon), selection in Spanish (Montilla), selection in Italian (EDM), selection in Hungarian (Qualiton), selection in Swedish (Telestar), etc

GRAHAM, Harry [Joscelyn Clive] (b London, 23 December 1874; d London, 30 October 1936). One of the most successful lyricists of the British musical stage between the two World Wars.

The son of Sir Henry Graham KCB, and educated at Eton and the Royal Military College, Graham pursued a professional military career as an officer in the Coldstream Guards before giving up the army and becoming a journalist. He had his first play produced in 1914 and, in the same year, adapted the lyrics of Jean Gilbert's *Die Kino-Königin* for Robert Courtneidge's production as *The Cinema Star*. He then went on to collaborate on the successful musical *Tina* (1915), and, the following year, had his biggest success to date when Robert Evett hired him to write the songwords for Harold Fraser-Simson's music to *The Maid of the Mountains* (''Love Will Find a Way,'' ''Farewell'').

Graham became lyricist and, subsequently, librettist in chief to the Evett-Collins regime at Daly's Theatre (*A Southern Maid, Our Peg, Sybil*) and continued, after their deposition, to supply Daly's supremo, Jimmy White, with English books and lyrics for the series of Continental imports on which the inexperienced manager relied, with varying levels of success. His versions of *The Lady of the Rose* and *Madame Pompadour* were notable Daly's Theatre hits.

Although he contributed songwords and sometimes texts to several agreeable new musicals, Graham's forte was the adaptation of the colorful and musically expansive postwar Continental Operetten which were all the rage in the Britain of the 1920s and 1930s. His two most enduring successes in that area came in 1931 when he wrote the British version of *White Horse Inn,* including the English words for newly added ''Goodbye,'' and of Lehár's *Das Land des Lächelns,* for which he created the still-sung lyric to ''You Are My Heart's Delight.''

Apart from his principal musical-theatre credits, he also supplied additional lyrics for the musical plays *Sylvia's Lovers* (1919) and *Hold My Hand* (1931), and words for Richard Addinsell's songs to the stage adaptation of J B Priestly's *The Good Companions* (1931). He also adapted a number of plays from various Continental sources and languages, the most successful of which was Siegfried Geyer and Karl Farkas's *Bei Kerzenlicht* (*By Candlelight*), which later itself provided the basis for the musicals *You Never Know* (New York 1938) and *Romance in Candlelight* (London, 1955).

1914 **The Cinema Star** (*Die Kino-Königin*) English lyrics (Shaftesbury Theatre)

1915 **Tina** (Haydn Wood, Paul Rubens/w Rubens, Percy Greenbank) Adelphi Theatre 2 November

1917 **The Maid of the Mountains** (Harold Fraser-Simson/Frederick Lonsdale) Daly's Theatre 10 February

1917 **A Southern Maid** (Fraser-Simson/Harry Miller/w Dion Clayton Calthrop) Manchester 24 December; Daly's Theatre 15 May 1920

1919 **Our Peg** (Fraser-Simson/Edward Knoblock) Prince's Theatre, Manchester 24 December

1920 **The Little Dutch Girl** (*Das Hollandweibchen*) English book w Seymour Hicks and lyrics (Lyric Theatre)

1921 **Sybil** (*Szibill*) new English book and lyrics (Daly's Theatre)

1921 **Missy Jo** (Fraser-Simson/James Clive) Folkestone 4 July

1922 **The Lady of the Rose** (*Die Frau im Hermelin*) English lyrics (Daly's Theatre)

1922 **Whirled into Happiness** (*Der Tanz ins Glück*) English book and lyrics (Lyric Theatre)

1923 **Toni** (*Der Fürst von Pappenheim*) (Hugo Hirsch/w Douglas Furber) Hanley 6 August; Shaftesbury Theatre 12 May 1924

1923 **Head Over Heels** (Fraser-Simson/w Adrian Ross/Seymour Hicks) Adelphi Theatre 8 September

1923 **Madame Pompadour** English book w Lonsdale and lyrics (Daly's Theatre)

1924 **Our Nell** (revised *Our Peg*) (Fraser-Simson, Ivor Novello/Louis Parker, Reginald Arkell) Gaiety Theatre 16 April

1925 **Katja, the Dancer** (*Katja, die Tänzerin*) English book w Lonsdale and lyrics (Gaiety Theatre)

1925 **Cleopatra** (*Die Perlen der Cleopatra*) English lyrics (Daly's Theatre)

1925 **Cloclo** English book and lyrics w Furber (Shaftesbury Theatre)

1925 **Betty in Mayfair** (Fraser-Simson/J Hastings Turner) Adelphi Theatre 11 November

1925 **Riquette** English lyrics (King's Theatre, Glasgow)

1926 **My Son John** (revised *Riquette*) new book and lyrics w Graham John, Desmond Carter (Shaftesbury Theatre)

1926 **Merely Molly** (Herman Finck, Joseph Meyer/Hastings Turner) Adelphi Theatre 22 September

1927 **The Blue Mazurka** (*Die blaue Mazur*) English lyrics (Daly's Theatre)

1928 **Lady Mary** (Albert Szirmai/Lonsdale, Hastings Turner) Daly's Theatre 23 February

1931 **White Horse Inn** (*Im weissen Rössl*) English book and lyrics (London Coliseum)

1931 **The Land of Smiles** (*Das Land des Lächelns*) English book and lyrics (Theatre Royal, Drury Lane)

1931 **Viktoria and Her Hussar** (*Viktória*) English book and lyrics (Palace Theatre)

1932 **Casanova** English book and lyrics (London Coliseum)

1936 **Rise and Shine** (later *Darling You*) (Robert Stolz/ad w Desmond Carter, et al, later w Con West, Geoffrey Orme) Theatre Royal, Drury Lane 7 May

1946 **Yours is My Heart** (*Das Land des Lächelns*) revised version of his *The Land of Smiles* by Ira Cobb and Karl Farkas (Shubert Theater, New York)

GRAIN, [Richard] Corney (b Teversham, Cambs, 26 October 1844; d London, 16 March 1895).

A comic singer and entertainer at the piano, Grain effectively abandoned his four-year-old legal career at the age of 25 and joined the German Reeds' company at the Gallery of Illustration. His first appearance there was with the monologue *The School Feast* (16 May 1870), his first in a musical play was as Captain Bang, the pirate, in Gilbert and Clay's *Our Island Home,* and he appeared successively in comedy ''father'' roles in such pieces as *A Sensation Novel, Ages Ago, Charity Begins at Home, Happy Arcadia,* and each and every other of the several new short operettas presented annually at the Gallery and later at St George's Hall, for a number of which he also composed the music.

At the death of John Parry, whose solo performances at the piano had been a feature of the Gallery's programs, on the German Reeds'' bills, Grain took over his place and, from then on, he appeared additionally at the piano, a plump figure in tails, giving a musical monologue—inclusive of comic song(s)—usually between the two one-acters of the evening's entertainment. Grain remained with the St George's Hall company till his death, writing, composing, performing and, from 1877, with Alfred Reed, running the business, forming with the Reed family the continuing backbone of a company which was influential in the early development of musical comedy in Britain.

1879 **£100 Reward** (Arthur Law) 1 act St George's Hall 27 May

1880 **A Flying Visit** (Law) 1 act St George's Hall 31 May

1881 **All at Sea** (Law) 1 act St George's Hall 28 February

1882 **That Dreadful Boy** (Gilbert a' Beckett) 1 act St George's Hall 13 December

1884 **A Double Event** (Law, Alfred Reed) 1 act St George's Hall 18 February

1884 **A Terrible Fright** (Law) 1 act St George's Hall 18 June

1885 **A Night in Wales** (Herbert Gardner) 1 act St George's Hall 1 June

1890 **Carnival Time** (T Malcolm Watson) St George's Hall 7 April

1892 **The Barley Mow** (Walter Frith) St George's Hall 16 April

1893 **Box B** (Grain) 1 act St George's Hall 22 May

1893 **The Ugly Duckling** (Grain) 1 act St George's Hall 20 November

1894 **Walls Have Ears** (Grain) 1 act St George's Hall 26 March

1894 **That Fatal Menu** (Grain) 1 act St George's Hall 15 December

Autobiography: *Corney Grain: By Himself* (John Murray, London, 1883); Biography: in *The German Reeds and Corney Grain* (A D Innes & Co, London, 1895)

GRAINER, Ron[ald Erle] (b Atherton, Australia, 11 August 1922; d Cuckfield, 21 February 1981). Composer who had his main success in television, but who, in a rare venture into the musical theatre, provided the outstanding postwar light opera score of the British stage.

Musically educated in his native Australia, Grainer subsequently moved to Britain where his work as a composer for television produced several widely known pieces of title music (*Steptoe and Son, Maigret* and, above all, the theme for *Dr Who*). He made his entry into the theatre as a pianist and musical director (*The Pied Piper, Zuleika* 1957), and subsequently as a composer when he supplied two songs for the Ned Sherrin/Caryl Brahms musical *Cindy-Ella,* but he found significant success in 1964 when director Wendy Toye brought him in to write additional music for *The Third Kiss,* the American musical version of *The Barretts of Wimpole Street.*

Ultimately, all the show's original music was thrown out and Grainer composed the whole of the score for what became *Robert and Elizabeth.* Arguably the most successful and substantial light opera written in Britain since Edwardian days, the piece had a long London run followed by tours, overseas productions and two major revivals, but rather than pursue this kind of writing, Grainer and author Ronald Millar followed up with the modern, youthful *On the Level* (1966) which, in spite of many attractions, was a disappointing failure (118 performances). Grainer turned his attentions back to television and film (*The Moon Spinners,* etc) until failing sight led him to leave Britain to live in Portugal. His only further efforts for the theatre were songs for two more small-scale Ned Sherrin pieces, the Marie Lloyd story *Sing a Rude Song* (1970) and, in replacement for the Arthur Schwartz score originally scheduled, *Nickelby and Me* (1975).

1962 **Cindy-Ella** (pasticcio, w Peter Knight/Caryl Brahms, Ned Sherrin) Garrick Theatre 17 December

1964 **Robert and Elizabeth** (Ronald Millar) Lyric Theatre 20 October

1966 **On the Level** (Millar) Saville Theatre 19 April

1970 **Sing a Rude Song** (w pasticcio/Sherrin, Brahms) Garrick Theatre 26 May

1975 **Nickelby and Me** (Sherrin, Brahms) Theatre Royal, Stratford East 16 December

LE GRAND CASIMIR Opérette (vaudeville) in 3 acts by Jules Prével and Albert de Saint-Albin [and Edmond Gondinet uncredited]. Music by Charles Lecocq. Théâtre des Variétés, Paris, 11 January 1879.

The Great Casimir (José Dupuis) begins the show's story as an ordinary French provincial sous-préfet, but when he catches sight of the circus performer Angélina his world turns upside down and he ends by abandoning the sous-préfecture and becoming a wild-animal trainer and the director of her circus. Angélina weds her sous-préfet, but that doesn't stop her flirting as of yore with her past suitors, Gobson (Guyon) the régisseur, and Sothermann (Léonce) the juggler, and it seems that she is still ripe to be tempted by rich tent-flap Johnnies into some indiscretion. Casimir's company gets into financial difficulties, and in order that all should not be lost he decides to ''die'' and leave the circus to his wife. And so, he disappears into the depths of Corsica. A bad choice. There he gets unwittingly entangled with pretty local Ninetta (Mlle Baumaine) and her vendetta-making menfolk, and finds himself forcibly and bigamously remarried. But then Angélina arrives, her circus and suitors in tow, and after many a comical and farcical scene the marital status quo is reestablished in time for the final curtain.

The one and only José Dupuis, now much less of a tenor and more of a comic actor than a few years previously, added another fine creation to his impressive list as Casimir, with the lovely Céline Chaumont as his naughty wife, carrying on the series, begun and to be continued by Anna Judic, of vaudevillesque heroines who would be the stars of the Variétés in years to come. Léonce as the clown, and Baron as a burlesque of a nobleman on the ran-dan called simply Le Grand-Duc, were also featured in farcical roles. None of these popular stars was an outstanding vocalist, and Lecocq's score took heed of the fact whilst still producing some charming numbers.

Casimir declared (Couplets du dompteur) that while he might have tamed three bears, he could not tame his wife, joined with the lady in a duo in which she displayed how she would grieve were he killed in the ring, and indulged in some Couplets de la pêche (fishing song) during his ''dead'' period in Corsica. Angelina discovered, after Casimir's disappearance, that semi-widowhood was rather unsatisfactory, and searched for her husband through the accents of Europe in the rondeau: ''Il le savait bien, le perfide,'' then turned to waltz time with her Rondo des deux pigeons (''Deux piegons s'aimaient d'un amour tendre''). Léonce described his juggling skills merrily in the Couplets du jongleur (''Avec six balles je jonglais'').

The non-musical highlight of the show was, however, Mlle Chaumont's performance of the equestrian act of the Haute École of the Circus with a set of live horses, the result of four months of training under a circus master. She also juggled with knives and brass balls.

The show had a fine 113 consecutive performances in its first season at the Variétés, and was brought back the following year (12 April, 22 performances) with all its principal players in place, and again in 1884 (17 October) for further seasons, by which time *Le Grand Casimir* had already been picked up for other productions elsewhere. But unfortunately, no one else gave it much time.

Vienna's version, mounted under Franz Tewele at the Carltheater, opened just three months after the French premiere. It cast the manager as Casimir opposite the thoroughly billed and much-loved Josefine Gallmeyer (Angelina), supported by a royal cast including Josef Matras as the clown, Wilhelm Knaack (Prince Charles), Karl Blasel (Picasso) and Rosa Streitmann (whose brother, Carl, played a tiny role) as Ninetta. However *Der grosse Casimir*—musically expanded by Brandl for the occasion—proved no competition for the newly produced *Boccaccio* and folded in eight performances. In London, the Gaiety Theatre produced an H S Leigh version with a cast headed by the house's infallible stars Nellie Farren (Angelina), Edward Terry (Casimir) and Edward Royce (Grand Duke), the appelation ''vaudeville'' clearly attached, but met with little success. A production mounted in the British provinces in 1883 with Walter H Fisher and Lizzie Mulholland in the lead roles won little more attention. Budapest got *A hórihorgas Kazimir* (ad Lajos Evva) for three performances, and New York saw the piece performed by the Variétés company on tour and then, under the title *The Lion Tamer,* as a heftily rewritten vehicle for Francis Wilson and Marie Jansen. Lecocq's music had been squeezed into a corner by some local pieces by Richard Stahl. Another version (ad George H Lask) was produced at the San Francisco Tivoli in 1898 (20 October) as *The Circus Queen.* It interpolated ''My Honolulu Lady'' and ''On the Road to Mandalay'' into Lecocq's score, and seems to have been no more faithful to the original that the Wilson (per)version.

Producer Bertrand considered the piece, with its short score of 15 musical pieces, to be a virtual ''vaudeville à couplets'' and, as such, eminently suitable for his in-house team of star comedy performers, who tended to the category of actors-who-sing-a-bit, and the success of *Le Grand Casimir* confirmed him in the path which he was to follow at the Variétés in the next years. He followed *Le Grand Casimir* with such highlights of his celebrated series of Variétés vaudevilles as *Lili* and *Mam'zelle Nitouche,* and once again made his theatre one of the most flourishing centers of musical theatre in Paris.

Austria: Carltheater *Der grosse Casimir* 13 April 1879; UK: Gaiety Theatre *The Great Casimir* 27 September 1879; Hungary: Népszínház *A hórihorgas Kazimir* 25 October 1879; USA: Wallack's Theater (Fr) 10 October 1885, Broadway Theater *The Lion Tamer* 30 December 1891

THE GRAND DUKE, or The Statutory Duel Comic opera in 2 acts by W S Gilbert. Music by Arthur Sullivan. Savoy Theatre, London, 7 March 1896.

The last work of the Gilbert and Sullivan partnership, *The Grand Duke* was not a success. Gilbert's libretto was based on a Blackwood's magazine story, ''The Duke's Dilemma,'' which had already served as the source of Tito Mattei's comic opera *The Prima Donna,* but it moved away from the original in many ways as Gilbert developed and then redeveloped the piece to fit the needs of the Savoy company. The fact that the company was in rather a state of flux did not help, but the libretto ended up being far from Gilbert's best in construction or in dialogue.

Theatrical manager Ernest Dummkopf (Charles Kenningham) and his comedian Ludwig (Rutland Barrington) are both part of a plot to dethrone Grand Duke Rudolph (Walter Passmore), but the two plotters fall out and—after a statutory duel, done by drawing cards, in which Dummkopf is ''killed''—Ludwig persuades (by devious means) the Duke to allow himself also to be ''killed'' until the dueling law expires the next day. But when the deed is done, he then claims the throne and re-enacts the law. So the Duke is statutorily ''dead'' too. Further complications arrive when Ludwig's wife, Lisa (Florence Perry), leading lady Julia Jellicoe (Ilka Pálmay), the Baroness of Krakenfeldt (Rosina Brandram) and the Princess of Monte Carlo (Emmie Owen) all make marital claims on the new Duke, but all is resolved when it turns out that ace counts low, not high, and that, thus, Ludwig is ''dead'' and Dummkopf and Rudolph ''alive.''

Hungary's greatest Operette star, Ilka Pálmay (playing the English actress in a German court with her Hungarian accent to the standard English of the rest of the cast), had the showiest musical moments of the evening with her gamut-running ''The Grand Duke's Bride'' and her dramatic ''Broken Every Promise Plighted''; Passmore described himself as ''a broken-down crittur,'' Lisa had a pretty ''Take Care of Him,'' and there was a curious Herald's Song which drew some attention.

The Grand Duke played a meagre 123 performances at the Savoy and attracted little in the way of takers elsewhere, apart from a German production which was whipped on at Berlin's Neues Theater whilst the piece was only some two months old in London. An American production was announced when Ilka Pálmay visited New York in 1905, but in the event she stuck to performing in the German language and in *Heisses Blut.* The musical wins occasional performances to this day, more as a Gilbert and Sullivan curiosity than on any real merits.

Germany: Neues Theater *Der Grossherzog* 20 May 1896

Recordings: complete (Decca, Pearl), selection (Lyric Theater Company)

Plate 154. **La Grande-Duchesse de Gérolstein.** *Even the respected musician Sir Julian Benedict jumped on the Offenbach bandwagon and ended up playing piano for a tour of* La Grande-Duchesse. *At least the manager at Barnsley gave him bigger billing than Offenbach.*

LA GRANDE-DUCHESSE DE GÉROLSTEIN

Opéra-bouffe in 3 acts by Henri Meilhac and Ludovic Halévy. Music by Jacques Offenbach. Théâtre des Variétés, Paris, 12 April 1867.

Meilhac, Halévy and Offenbach's third great opéra-bouffe for the Théâtre des Variétés and for Paris's favorite diva, Hortense Schneider, *La Grande-Duchesse* followed the productions of *La Belle Hélène* and *Barbe-bleue,* and proved, if anything, the most sensational and worldwide hit of the group. Meilhac and Halévy chose to use things military and political as the main target of their fun this time round, and their heroine was the Grand Duchess of a fictional European state, who might or might not be a German, or a Luxembourgeoise (after all, the Grand Duchy?), but was—for the peace of mind of the French nobility—surely, but surely, not French.

The young Grande-Duchesse de Gérolstein (Hortense Schneider) is come of age, but her ministers, the Baron Puck (Kopp) and army chief General Boum (Couder), are not anxious to see their power diminished by an interfering girl, and are searching for a means to distract her interest from affairs of state. An attempt to wed her off to Prince Paul of Steis-Stein-Steis-Laper-Bottmoll-Schorstenburg (Grenier) has failed to occupy her attentions, so their next step is to try to enthrall their teenaged duchess with that collection of live dolls called the army. This works only too well. The Duchess takes an immediate shine to not the whole army, but to private

Fritz (Dupuis), whom she quickly promotes through the ranks until he replaces Boum at the head of the army. Fritz's wham-bam tactics actually win a battle and, when he returns, the Duchess fairly delicately tries to let him know of her interest in his person. But the dense soldier simply asks her permission to wed his Wanda (Élise Garait), and his piqued sovereign promptly changes sides and begins to plot with her ministers and Prince Paul's representative, Baron Grog (Baron), to bring the new Commander-in-Chief down. After some painful ups and downs the status quo is restored and the Duchess demurely agrees to marry Prince Paul.

The score to the show gave the prima donna superb opportunities, and the two principal hits from the show were her burlesque ceremonial ''Voici le sabre de mon père'' in which she hands over the sword of office to the rocketingly risen Fritz, and her winsome ''Dites-lui qu'on l'a remarqué, distingué'' as she relates to the boy how a certain friend of hers has developed an . . . interest in him. But there was more to the role than its two bonbons; there was a third dazzling soprano moment in the rippling Rondo Militaire (''Ah! Que j'aime les militaires''), a fourth in the regimental song, the ''Légende de la verre'' of the final act, and then still more. Amongst the men, Prince Paul had perhaps the finest and funniest moment with his dejected recital of the mockery that the scandal papers have been making of his inability to win the Duchess (Chronique de la Gazette de Hollande: ''Pour épouser une Princesse''), whilst Boum showed his credentials in the extravagantly martial ''Pif, Paf, Pouf!'' and Fritz shared numbers with Wanda and related his victory in battle (''Après la victoire'').

La Grande-Duchesse was pointed enough in its burlesque to attract some censorship. Mlle Schneider was forbidden to wear a splendid decoration she had had made as being too much like the real thing, the authors were obliged to remove a reference which seemed to point too acutely to the recent Austro-Prussian wars, and the ''Gérolstein'' was forcibly added to the original title (*La Grande-Duchesse*) to avoid offending Grand Duchesses in general and Luxembourg's in particular. However, neither the fun nor the éclat of the piece were in any way thus diminished and, after some heavy post-premiere cutting in the over-long third act and several other alterations, *La Grande-Duchesse,* having opened happily, indeed brilliantly for Mlle Schneider in particular, soon found itself the hit of the town.

In 1867 that meant something, for this was the year of the Paris Exposition and Europe, led by its crowned heads and high society, had descended upon Paris. *La Grande-Duchesse* became a must for the fashionables of the town and for any visitor of any social standing (even the Grand-Duchess of Mecklenburg-Schwerin was to be seen in the audience in June), and she sailed past her 100th night on 7 August, to box-office figures which outclassed even *La Vie parisienne* (''the fabulous sum of over 5,000 francs every night, the cashier requires an assistant to help him carry his bags of money''), and passed her 200th at top speed. When Mlle Schneider deserted the Variétés for a lucrative engagement at the Châtelet, first Élise Garait and then Lise Tautin succeded to the title role and *La Grande-Duchesse* played on until 4 December.

When Schneider returned to the Variétés, however, it was as *La Périchole,* and the sabre of the sovereign of Gérolstein was not taken up again until 1878, when Paola Marié starred at the Bouffes-Parisiens (5 October) in the first major revival of Offenbach's piece with Daubray (Boum), Emmanuel, Scipion, Jolly, Bonnet and Mlle Luce in support. Anna Judic appeared as the Duchess at the Variétés in 1887 (3 October), with Dupuis in his original role, Baron switching to Puck, and Christian as Boum; Jeanne Granier played the title role at the Gaîté in 1890; and Germaine Roger starred at her Gaîté-Lyrique in an unsatisfyingly readapted version (ad Albert Willemetz, André Mouëzy-Éon) in 1948.

A sensation to start with, and now a solid vertebra in the backbone of the French opéra-bouffe repertoire, the piece has returned in recent decades to the Marigny with Suzanne Lafaye (5 May 1966) and to the Châtelet where operatic diva Régine Crespin portrayed the teenaged Duchess in a rather different style from that used a century earlier by Mlle Schneider. In 1996 a so-called modern version was played at Théâtre Sylvia Montfort (19 March) by Opéra Éclaté.

In Vienna, Friedrich Strampfer's production of *Die Grossherzogin von Gérolstein* was again a major hit, with Marie Geistinger following in Schneider's footsteps, after her successes as Hélène and Boulotte, in taking the title role (the Duchess here acquired the christian name, Irene). Matthias Rott played General Boum, or, as he was now called, in double-barreled fashion, General Bum-Bum, Carl Adolf Friese was Baron Puck, Jani Szíka Fritz and Karl Blasel Prince Paul—his *Gazette de Hollande* now localized as the *Augsburger Allgemeine Zeitung* in Julius Hopp's adaptation—and the show, and its star (in spite of a high-heeled mishap in Act II of the opening night which meant she had to play part of Act III sitting down) confirmed the earlier successes dazzlingly. Geistinger returned regularly in her role—she was still playing it at the Theater an der Wien in 1879—and *Die Grossherzogin* proved a great favorite without quite outpointing *Die schöne Helena* in the Viennese public's favor. The same held true in Germany where Lina Mayr introduced the Duchess the following year at the Friedrich-Wilhelmstädtisches Theater. Extremely popular, it tucked in behind *Die schöne Helena, Pariser Leben* and

Orpheus in der Unterwelt in Offenbach's Germanic hit parade, joining those three pieces in a revivable repertoire which has lasted for more than a century-and-a-quarter. Phila Wolff played Irene at the Theater an der Wien in 1905–6, Vera Schwarz appeared at the Johann Strauss-Theater in 1911 and Fritzi Massary at Berlin's Metropoltheater in 1916 at the head of a long line of important Austrian and German Grossherzogins.

Hungary's first *Gérolsteini nagyhercegnő* (ad Károly Babos, Béla Erődi) was Antonia Hétenyi, who starred at the lesser Budai Népszínház in 1867 alongside János Timár (Bum-Bum) and with Vidor Kassai as Baron Grog, but the show got major revivals in later years both at the Népszínház, with Ilka Pálmay starred (6 December 1884, ad Lajos Evva, Béla J Fái), again at the Király Színház (13 September 1906) when Sári Fedák played the Duchess with Mihály Papp as Prince Paul and József Németh as Bum-Bum, and again at the Fővárosi Operettszínház (13 January 1950).

America actually saw *La Grande-Duchesse* whilst the Exposition and the Paris production still ran on. H L Bateman imported Lucille Tostée to America to play the piece in its original French and the production (notably its second-act finale in which the cancan was seen in all its glory for the first time in America) caused a sensation in New York, launching a craze for opéra-bouffe which would run for more than a decade, and establishing the show as 19th-century America's favorite amongst the Offenbach repertoire. Mlle Tostée's unreliability and a season by Ristori broke up the season somewhat, but *La Grande-Duchesse* played a remarkable 156 performances before Tostée switched to impersonating *La Belle Hélène,* with less thunderous effect. America's first home-bred Duchess (ad Owen Fawcett, "music arranged for full orchestra by Hassler") was on the stage within weeks, with Britain's visiting Mrs William Gomersal (née Maria Ribbon) winning the distinction of becoming the continent's first vernacular Offenbach prima donna (and the world's first English Duchess) by getting what seems to have been a slightly approximate version of the show, put together by herself and her husband, on to the stage at the Walnut Street Theater in Philadelphia. Mrs Gomersal didn't play New York, but soon the Grand Duchesses, English, French and German, were hustling each other down Broadway to grab some of the glory garnered by Tostée: Sophie Worrell was Broadway's first (if distinctly low-comic, and even more distinctly approximate) English Duchess (ad Benjamin A Baker) at the New York Theater (17 June 1868), Joseph Grau offered France's Rose Bell (5 October 1868), Mrs Howard Paul gave her classy version at the Théâtre Français (24 January 1870) to great admiration, and the all-embracing Marie Aimée (28 March 1871), the endlessly touring Alice Oates (13 October 1873) and Canada's Holman troupe (2 February 1874, potted, and with Fritz interpolating "La Marseillaise") soon arrived with their interpretations, followed shortly thereafter by England's Emily Soldene (30 November 1874) and the heroine of the Paris revival, Paola Marié (23 October 1879). Alongside these, the "only" Francis Leon scored a similar hit in his "Africanized opéra-bouffe" impersonation of *The Grand Dutch-S* at Kelly and Leon's minstrel theatre (3 February 1868). In this burlesque version "Le Sabre de mon père" became "the Cheeseknife of my Pa," Leon danced the cancan à la Tostée, and the whole piece ended with a bit of grand spectacle . . . a collision between two steamboats. Rival male prima donna Rollin Howard responded with *Grand Dutch-Us,* the San Francisco Minstrels gave *The Grand Dutch Cheese Opera,* and burlesque troupes ranging from the pretty downmarket Wallace Sisters and B F Whitman's company (trouping Little Falls, Rome and Lowell and points between and beyond) to the altogether more adept Canadian-based Holman family troupe (now unpotted), or J P Florence's combination with Jennie Kimball's competent Duchess at their head, took more-or-less versions of *La Grande-Duchesse* to every corner of the country. But there were less ostensible Duchesses as well. Some productions, such as Edmund Falconer's "original burlesque *Ye Grand Queen Bess* "at Broadway's Fifth Avenue Theatre (9 December 1867), simply helped themselves to as much of the show—music and text—as they wished, and in this one Elizabeth of England was seen presenting the sword of her fathers to the Earl of Essex. Over in Brooklyn, the sabre song became "The Wiper of My Ma" in a *Norwood* burlesque at Hooley's Opera House (December 1867) and down at Fox's American Theater in Philadelphia—where the previous hit had been "a hundred nights of the can-can"—the whole thing was turned into an "operatic ballet" (October 1868). Perhaps the most unlikely Grand Duchess, however, was seen at Baltimore in 1876 when the six-foot-plus, 225-pound George K Fortescue, a well-known dame specialist in burlesque, "dressed in the latest feminine fashion with a low neck and short sleeves" ventured the role at the city's New Central Theater.

La Grande-Duchesse was played throughout America for decades, and even when the fashion turned to newer shows it was still there, a regular part of the repertoire of comic opera seasons and touring troupes, until well past the turn of the century. New York got a fresh look at the show, too, when Lillian Russell starred in two Broadway revivals (Casino Theater 25 February 1890, Abbey's Theatre 8 December 1894) before America's taste for opéra-bouffe frittered away for the best part of a century, but the first opéra-bouffe to hit America between the eyes had remained forever its favorite.

London saw its first English-language *Grande-Duchesse* after Philadelphia, but before New York, when the ''operatic extravaganza'' was mounted at Covent Garden's Theatre Royal (ad Charles Lamb Kenney) with Australian prima donna Julia Mathews in the lead role, Thomas Aynsley Cook as Boum and William Harrison as Fritz. It was the first time that a full-length Offenbach opéra-bouffe had been given a fairly faithful British production, following hacked-up burlesquey stagings of *Orphée aux enfers, Barbe-bleue* and *La Belle Hélène,* and it was a distinct if rather over-staged hit. Tumbled out of the theatre after just 26 performances because of the all-important Christmas pantomime season, the show had, nevertheless, made its impression and, as John Russell's first-class production set off to tour Northern England and Scotland—with the publishers legally threatening the Gomersals who'd come home and were offering their version for sale—it quickly became the rage of the country. It returned briskly to London with Mrs Howard Paul now featured as the Duchess alongside Wilford Morgan as Fritz and Henri Drayton as Boum (Olympic Theatre 20 June 1868), only to find themselves in direct competition, a couple of nights after, with Mlle Schneider herself delivering her original Duchess for a short season to the French-speaking population (St James's Theatre 22 June), and the male prima donna Vestris playing *The Very Grand Dutch-S* in Charles Bernard's minstrel burlesque of the show. Miss Mathews touched London's suburban Standard Theatre a couple of times during her long touring life in the piece, then gave over her role to the rising Emily Soldene, but she was back again in 1871 to star in the Gaiety Theatre's version of a show which, along with *Geneviève de Brabant* and *Chilpéric,* proved itself to be one of the sensations and staples of the British opéra-bouffe stage. London subsequently saw Cornélie d'Anka as the Duchess in 1875 (Opera Comique 13 September) and 1878 (Alhambra 1 April), Mary Albert in a French version in 1886 (Her Majesty's 22 November) and 1888 (Royalty Theatre 7 January), whilst in 1897 Richard D'Oyly Carte mounted a new English version (ad C H E Brookfield, Adrian Ross) at the Savoy (4 December) with Florence St John starring alongside Charles Kenningham (Fritz) and Walter Passmore (Boum) for 104 performances. The piece was seen again at Daly's Theatre in 1937 with Enid Cruickshank starred, and London's most recent Duchess, Patricia Routledge, played a Camden Festival production in 1978 which has remained a fond memory with those who saw it.

La Grande-Duchesse was, in spite of all its success, slow to find its way to Australia. In fact, New Zealand saw the Duchess, as portrayed (in Dunedin, in a version by a local journalist) by Anna Forde to the Fritz of a Mr Whitworth, six months before the army of Gérolstein marched on to the stage on the other side of the Tasman sea. And when it did come, the first Australian *Duchess* was not a wholehearted success. William Lyster cast the finely singing (but not very funny) Fanny Simonsen as the Duchess alongside Armes Beaumont (Fritz), Georgia Hodson (Wanda) and Edward Farley (Boom) in Lyster and Smith's first production (''no attempt to grasp the spirit of the author . . . [the piece is] more fitted for a good singing burlesque company than for an opera company . . . they have made an utter mistake in producing it''), and *La Grande-Duchesse* turned out more opéra than bouffe. However the same journal completely reversed its opinion when England's Alice May, freshly arrived in the colonies, took over the part of the Duchess for Lyster the next season, and Australia later got a veritable pantheon of Duchesses when Emily Soldene brought her buxom British Duchess to the South Seas and Emilie Melville her incisively comic Jewish one, and the show, in spite of its slow beginnings, installed itself in its rightful place in the colonial repertoire.

Still a feature of the classic repertoire in France, *La Grande-Duchesse* has curiously (given its subject matter, and the 1970s and 1980s passion for turning defenseless classics into modern pseudosatire) faded from the repertoire elsewhere, whilst the ancient-world burlesques *Orphée aux enfers* and *La Belle Hélène* continue to prosper. However, for some reason France has now succumbed to a passion for cruiserweight (vocally) Duchesses, as witnessed by recordings with Régine Crespin (also video) and Jessye Norman. It would have given Hortense Schneider a sore throat just to listen.

Austria: Theater an der Wien *Die Grossherzogin von Gérolstein* 13 May 1867; USA: Théâtre Français (Fr) 24 September 1867, Walnut Street Theater, Philadelphia (Eng) 28 October 1867, New York Theater (Eng) 17 June 1868; Hungary: Budai Népszínház *Gérolsteini nagyhercegnő* 11 October 1867, Budai Színkör (Ger) 28 June 1868; UK: Theatre Royal, Covent Garden *The Grand Duchess* 18 November 1867; Germany: Friedrich-Wilhelmstädtisches Theater *Die Grossherzogin von Gérolstein* 10 January 1868; Australia: Princess Theatre, Melbourne 27 February 1871

Recordings: complete (CBS, Decca, Unique Opera Records, Urania, Gala, Dynamic), complete in German (Philips), etc

Video: Paris Opéra 1981

GRAND HOTEL Musical in 2 acts by Luther Davis. Music and lyrics by Robert Wright and George Forrest. Additional music and lyrics by Maury Yeston. Martin Beck Theater, New York, 12 November 1989.

Wright and Forrest's stage musical version of the Vicki Baum book and play *Menschen im Hotel,* and of its celebrated Barrymore/Garbo film offspring *Grand Hotel* (1932, Academy Award), was originally produced by California's Civic Light Opera (7 July 1958, Los Angeles) with Paul Muni starring, under the title *At the*

Grand. It failed to move east, but 30 years later it was revised and reproduced by a team made up of no less than nine credited producers with Liliane Montevecchi and David Carroll in its leading roles as the fading ballerina Grushinskaya and the aristocratic hotel thief Felix von Gaigern who brings the spring back to her fouetté.

In trouble on the road, the producers called in director Tommy Tune who solved their problem by coating the dislocated, and too often unintentionally funny piece in sufficient revusical glamor to please audiences, negate a poor critical reception, and, against the strongest opposition for a number of years, win himself two Tony Awards and a 1,018-performance run for the show. The two most popular items of the evening were a lively leg-mania comedy dance routine performed by Michael Jeeter (Tony Award) as the gentle, dying Otto Kringelein and an interpolated adagio dance in semi-darkness for two uncharacterized artists.

A German production was mounted at Berlin's Theater des Westens with Leslie Caron as Grushinskaya and Helmut Baumann as Kringelein (107 performances), whilst after a British production had been announced, advertised and abandoned, London instead got an underpatronized three-month (135-performance) season from an American touring company with Montevecchi and Brent Barrett featured. The show was subsequently seen in Hungarian (ad Gabriella Prekop) at Győr, and played by the all-women Takarazuka company in Japan (1993).

The same title was earlier used for the Viennese Posse with songs in three acts by Leopold Feldmann, music by Carl Millöcker, produced at the Theater an der Wien on 7 December 1870.

Germany: Theater des Westens 25 January 1991; UK: Dominion Theatre 5 July 1992; Hungary: Nemzeti Színház, Győr 5 February 1993

Recording: original cast (RCA Victor)

LE GRAND MOGOL Opéra-bouffe in 4 acts by Henri Chivot. Music by Edmond Audran. Théâtre du Gymnase, Marseille, 24 February 1877; Théâtre de la Gaîté, Paris, in a revised version by Chivot and Alfred Duru, 19 September 1884.

The libretto of *Le Grand Mogol* was entrusted to the comparatively inexperienced Audran by one of the most celebrated librettists of the French musical stage, largely because Chivot happened to be a friend of the composer's in-the-theatre-world family. The resultant opéra-bouffe, however, proved to be more than just the first step in Audran's long and successful career, for *Le Grand Mogol* was not only, on its own merits, a considerable success throughout France, where it was regularly revived and remained long in the standard repertoire, but also won a series of overseas productions.

The piece's plot centered on the young Indian Prince Mignapour who, in spite of the plottings of his Grand Vizier and the tempting Princess Bengaline, eventually succeeds in both hanging on to his Mogolship (which he would lose, should he fall from virginity before assuming his crown) and securing the hand of the pretty snake charmer, Irma, who has been coveted by another enemy, the Britisher Captain Crackson. Audran's score, highlighted by Irma's snake-charming song (''Allons, petit serpent'') and a lively Chanson du Vin de Suresnes, was in the bright, tuneful opérette style for which the composer would shortly become celebrated.

First produced in Audran's home town of Marseille with the young Jane Hading starring as Irma, it ran there for an astounding 60 nights but, strangely enough, it did not immediately head to Paris. Whilst the composer was swiftly signed up to write a fresh opérette for the Paris stage, *Le Grand Mogol* made its way instead to Milan (1879), and to New York (1881) where the young Lillian Russell charmed the snakes and Selina Dolaro sang the role of Mignapour en travesti. Produced with ''a flourish of trumpets'' it proved, however, ''a long way from setting the town astir,'' moved out of town after an unexceptional month-and-a-half, and fell apart in Brooklyn when Dolaro had the costumes attached in lieu of her unpaid wages. However, a fresh tour headed by Catherine Lewis (Mignapour) was sent out, and the piece returned to the Alcazar, with Dolaro teaming now with Lily Post the following season.

In 1884 Chivot and his partner of almost always, Alfred Duru, reworked *Le Grand Mogol* for a larger and more spectacular style of production, and this mega-*Mogol* was produced on the considerable Parisian stage of the Théâtre de la Gaîté with Mlle Thuillier-Leloir (Irma), Henri Cooper (Mignapour), Mesmaecker (Nicobar) and Marie Gélabert (Bengaline) starring. It was played there again in each of the three following seasons, and its success was prelude to further overseas productions.

In London Florence St John draped herself nightly in live snakes for two months, before Berlin (ad Eduard Jacobson), Antwerp, Mexico City, Zagreb and New York, yet again, welcomed the piece, but Austria waited until 1900 for its premiere when Louise Robinson (Irma) and Willy Bauer (Mignapour) played P Blumenreich's version at the Carltheater and the Theater an der Wien for three weeks. Paris, however, continued to be the friendliest, and hosted major revivals in 1895 with Mlle Bernaert as Irma and Paul Fugère playing Mignapour for comedy, in 1901, 1914–15, 1922 and 1949.

USA: Bijou Theater *The Snake Charmer* 29 October 1881; UK: Comedy Theatre 17 November 1884; Germany: Friedrich-Wilhelmstädtisches Theater 18 April 1885; Austria: Carltheater 29 September 1900

Recording: complete (Gaîté-Lyrique)

GRANICHSTAEDTEN, Bruno (b Vienna, 1 September 1879; d New York, 30 May 1944). Viennese writer and composer of the years between the World Wars, whose blend of traditional Operettic and modern dance and "jazz" music proved a particularly popular accompaniment to a series of successful musicals.

The young Granichstaedten worked at first as a songwriter and as a concert and Operette vocalist without causing much of a stir, but when his first attempt at the musical score for a full-scale Operette, the jaunty *Bub oder Mädel?,* was produced in 1908 at the recently opened Johann Strauss-Theater, the 29-year-old musician found himself with a real success on his hands. The show played over one hundred performances in Vienna, with Louis Treumann starring in its early performances, and went on to be played in Hungarian (*Fiu vagy lány*) in Budapest, and in English on Broadway (*The Rose Maid*) with such considerable success that the young writer was swiftly signed to a five-year publishing contract with Joseph Stern of New York. His *The Vagrant Princess* was announced for production in the 1913 season by *Rose Maid* producers Werba and Luescher, and Klaw and Erlanger announced the immediate staging of his *The Envious Butterfly.* Quite what these two pieces were (if they weren't just hot air) is a little hard to fathom.

Granichstaedten had indeed, by this time—five years on from *Bub oder Madel?*—followed up his initial hit with further successes: firstly the French-based musical comedy *Majestät Mimi* which, like *Bub oder Mädel?* was exported round Europe after its Vienna production (and could at a pinch have been a *Vagrant Princess*), and then *Casimirs Himmelfahrt,* which followed six weeks at the Raimundtheater with productions in Germany and Hungary (*Á brahám a mennyortszagban*) and doesn't seem to be related to butterflies. He had also made his large-stage debut as a librettist, with a collaboration on the text for the Robert Winterberg Operette *Madame Serafin,* which did better in its initial production at Hamburg than in a subsequent mounting at Vienna's Johann Strauss-Theater (two weeks). But, in the end, none of these pieces crossed the Atlantic.

From this time on, Granichstaedten often wrote or co-wrote the libretti as well as the music for his Operetten, and he found regular success with pieces such as the highly popular Theater an der Wien shows *Auf Befehl der Kaiserin* (189 performances) and *Die Bacchusnacht* (115 performances, *Bacchus-Éj* in Hungary), both of which were later given further productions around central Europe; *Die verbotene Stadt* (*Nadmé* in Hungary), first produced in Berlin; and two Operetten for the Vienna Apollotheater, before he scored the most substantial hit of his career, again at the Theater an der Wien, with the long-running 1925 piece *Der Orlow.*

He followed this success with others: *Das Schwalbennest,* which played 134 performances at the Raimundtheater before going on to Germany and Hungary (*A Fecskefészek*); *Die Königin,* on which he worked on the libretto for Oscar Straus; *Evelyne* which, after a strong Berlin start, was played for seven weeks at the Johann Strauss-Theater; and *Reklame,* which ran a fine 136 performances at the Theater an der Wien.

After devoting himself, in the early 1930s, to composing film scores, Granichstaedten surfaced again in the musical theatre in 1932 when he supplied the characterful song "Zuschau'n kann i net" to the score of *Im weissen Rössl,* but Nazi rule soon forced him from Germany and then from Austria. In 1939 he fled first to Luxembourg and from there to New York. Lacking a fashionable name and reputation in America, where the hit of *The Rose Maid* was now three decades old and Joseph Stern and his contract seemingly older, he found himself unable to get work. Projects such as *The Singing Caesar* and a Shubert *The Life of Mozart* failed to make it to the stage, and adaptations of his Continental successes fared no better. He ended up working as a bar pianist and died four years later without having contributed further to the musical stage.

- 1908 **Bub oder Mädel?** (Felix Dörmann, Adolf Altmann) Johann Strauss-Theater 13 November
- 1909 **Wein, Weib und Gesang** (Altmann) 1 act Hölle 1 October
- 1910 **Lolotte** (w Alfred Schick von Markenau) 1 act Apollotheater 30 July
- 1911 **Majestät Mimi** (Dörmann, Roda-Roda) Carltheater 17 February
- 1911 **Madame Serafin** (Robert Winterberg/w Georg Okonkowski) Neues Operettentheater, Hamburg 1 September
- 1911 **Casimirs Himmelfahrt** (A M Willner, Robert Bodanzky) Raimundtheater 25 December
- 1913 **Die verbotene Stadt** (w Carl Lindau) Montis Operettentheater, Berlin 23 December
- 1915 **Auf Befehl der Kaiserin** (aka *Auf Befehl der Herzogin*) (Leopold Jacobson, Bodanzky) Theater an der Wien 20 March
- 1916 **Der Glückspilz** (Josef Königsberg/w "Max Jungk") Carl-Schultze Theater, Hamburg 2 December
- 1918 **Walzerliebe** (w Bodanzky) Apollotheater 16 February
- 1918 **Das alte Lied** Raimundtheater 23 December
- 1921 **Indische Nächte** (Hardt-Warden, Bodanzky) Apollotheater 25 November
- 1923 **Die Bacchusnacht** (w Ernst Marischka) Theater an der Wien 18 May
- 1923 **Glück bei Frauen** (Victor Léon, Heinz Reichert) Carltheater 4 December
- 1925 **Der Orlow** (w E Marischka) Theater an der Wien 3 April
- 1926 **Das Schwalbennest** (w E Marischka) Raimundtheater 2 September
- 1927 **Die Königin** (Oscar Straus/w E Marischka) Theater an der Wien 4 February

1927 **Evelyne (Die Milliardärin)** (w Peter Herz/w Adolf Schütz) Deutsches Künstlertheater, Berlin 23 December

1930 **Reklame** (w E Marischka) Theater an der Wien 28 February

GRANIER, [Marie] Jeanne [Ernestine] (b Paris, 31 March 1852; d Paris, 18 December 1939). The brightest star of the Paris opérette stage, through a series of roles composed mostly to her measure by Charles Lecocq, in the 1870s and early 1880s.

The daughter of an actress, the young Mlle Granier was performing at Étretat in the summer of 1873 when she caught the eye and the ear of Jacques Offenbach. He had her hired for the company at the Théâtre de la Renaissance, and she was allotted a small role in *La Jolie Parfumeuse.* However, when she substituted for Louise Théo in the title role of Rose Michon, the 21-year-old Jeanne caused quite a stir, and it was not long before she was given a leading role of her own.

Her first star part in Paris was the showy double title role of *Giroflé-Girofla,* created in Belgium by Pauline Luigini, and Granier confirmed all the promise of her Rose Michon dazzlingly. The delighted Lecocq composed the role of Graziella, the heroine of *La Petite Mariée,* particularly for her and, following her triumph in that part, he molded the title role of *La Marjolaine* and the breeches part of the teenage Duc de Parthenay of *Le Petit Duc* around his new star. In this last role, paired with the pretty soubrette, Mily-Meyer, as the little Duchess, Granier made the biggest hit of her career and she reprised the ''little Duke'' many times over during the following decade. Her success led her to leave Paris for some lucrative foreign appearances and the star role of Lecocq's next Théâtre de la Renaissance opérette went instead to Zulma Bouffar, but Granier returned for another triumph in *La Petite Mademoiselle* (1879, Comtesse Cameroni) before Planquette's *Les Voltigeurs de la 32ème* (1880, Nicolette) put an end to the theatre's run of large successes. In 1881 she was seen in London with the Renaissance company in *Le Petit Duc, La Petite Marieé, Belle Lurette, Les Voltigeurs de la 32ème* and *Giroflé-Girofla.*

After a series of revivals of her big Lecocq hits, Granier again attempted some new roles, but *Janot* (1881, Janot), Raoul Pugno's *Ninetta* (1882, Ninetta), Serpette's *Madame le Diable* (1882, Flamma), *Fanfreluche* (1883, Brézette), a souped-up version of Offenbach's *Belle Lurette* (1883) and *Mam'zelle Gavroche* (1885, Gavroche) did not live up to her earlier pieces or roles. However, her reputation and value suffered not a whit: in 1883 Mlle Granier was whisked across to England to play a specially written opérette, *The Steeplechase,* at a private party given by Ferdinand de Rothschild. Her fee was a staggering £400 plus expenses.

Plate 155. **Jeanne Granier.** *The famous creator of* Le Petit Duc *and many of Lecocq's other opérettes.*

Although Messager's *La Béarnaise* (1885, Jacquette) and Audran's *La Cigale et la fourmi* (1886, Thérèse) gave her two further significant successes, Lacome's *Les Saturnales* (1887, Rosa) was another failure and, in the remaining eight years of her musical-theatre career, Granier, although appearing in such occasional new pieces as *La Fille à Cacolet* (1889, Rosette Cacolet), concentrated almost wholly on the tried and triumphant works of the classical repertoire, appearing in such pieces as *La Fille de Madame Angot* (Clairette, opposite Judic's Lange), *Barbe-bleue* (Boulotte), *La Grande-Duchesse* (Grande-Duchesse), *La Belle Hélène* (Hélène), *Orphée aux enfers* (Eurydice), *La Vie parisienne* (Gabrielle), *Le Petit Faust* (Marguerite), *Le Voyage dans la lune* (Prince Caprice) and *La Périchole* (Périchole).

In 1893 she starred as Asmodine, the titular lady of the Blum/Toché vaudeville *Madame Satan* at the Variétés, and two year later she moved her star name and singular stage abilities to the straight theatre, where she had a long and successful second career as a comedienne. That career stretched into her seventies, and she retired from performing only in 1926.

LA GRAN VÍA Zarzuela (revista madrileña comicalirica, fantastico-callejera) in 1 act and 5 scenes by Felipe

Perez y Gonzales. Music by Federico Chueca and Joaquín Valverde. Teatro Felipe, Madrid, 2 July 1886.

One of the most famous examples of the ''genero chico,'' the small-scale and topical Spanish musical play, *La gran vía,* did not, like most of these pieces, take a glimpse at a small slice of everyday city life, but was, rather, a revusical series of scenes set around a real-life town-planning decision, in which many of the characters were anthropomorphic streets.

La gran vía is the new main street which is planned for the center of Madrid, and its construction will involve the demolition of some old streets and affect others in various ways. The adjacent alley, the Caballero de Gracia (Joaquín Manini), is the least worried, as he will have a junction with the big new road. It is he who, in the second scene, sets out, in the company of a passerby to take a look at a few Madrilene scenes which may change—the poor district of La Prosperidad, where they meet the skivvy Menegilda (Lucia Pastor) and a team of rats; the Puerta del Sol, the great square which will lose its celebrated central fountain in the rebuilding, and which is the setting for the introduction of a group of singing sea cadets; a crossroad where the Lyceum dance hall is situated, where two newspapers, *Lidia* and *Uncle Jindama,* are found in vigorous discussion. The final scene shows the new road. It will be a fine road.

Chueca and Valverde's score employed the gamut of popular dance rhythms, amongst them the Caballero de Gracia's waltz (''Caballero de Gracia me llaman''), Menegilda's tango (''Pobre—chica, la que tiene que servir''), the sea cadets' mazurka (''Somos los maritanos que venimos a Madrid''), the schottische delivered by the Lyceum (''Yo soy el Elisedo'') and the jota trio of the rats (''Soy el rato primero . . .''), as well as two further numbers, a paso doble for a pair of Sergeants and a waltz for the Chief of Police, which were censored out of the show in later days.

La gran vía was a great success in Spanish-speaking territories, but unlike the great majority of other zarzuelas, it also attracted some attention further afield. Melio le Ghassi and P F Murro's Milan zarzuela troupe played the piece in its three-show repertoire at Vienna's Carltheater in 1894, and in 1902 another troupe played it, also in Spanish, as part of a season at Danzers Orpheum. In France, it was another variety house, L'Olympia, which mounted Maurice Ordonneau's French version, but in London the script was put aside and the music alone used as part of the score to a comic opera put together by Anglo-French performer Harry Fragson, called *Castles in Spain* (Royalty Theatre 18 April 1906). The Arcaraz Hermanes Grand Spanish Opera Company from Guatemala included the piece in their repertoire during an 1892 visit to America.

The piece was given a major revival at Madrid's Teatro de la Zarzuela in 1998.

USA: Orpheum Theater, San Francisco (Sp) 7 July 1892; Austria: Carltheater (Sp) 7 September 1894; France: L'Olympia 25 March 1896

Recordings: complete (Montilla, Hispavox, Columbia, Zafiro, etc)

GRAU, Maurice [GRAU, Moritz] (b Brünn, Austria, 1849; d Paris, 13 March 1907).

Brought up in America and intended for the law, Grau became involved in the theatre through his impresario uncle, **Jacob GRAU** (b Brünn, 1817; d New York, 14 December 1877), one of America's earliest importers of opéra-bouffe, with whom he worked from the age of 17. In 1872 he went into partnership with **Carlo A[quila] CHIZZOLA** (d Paris, 28 December 1891) and, on a joint capital of $1,500, the pair took a lease of Broadway's Lyceum Theater setting up a season of the newly popular French opéras-bouffes there with the Théâtre des Variétés' Marie Aimée at its bill-head. Under their management, Aimée became the most important and well-known performer of her kind in the country. Grau and Chizzola followed quickly up by presenting America with its first quality English opéra-bouffe, as played by London's Emily Soldene and her company, and with another fine French troupe top-billing Coralie Geoffory, and in good part due to their efforts opéra-bouffe and its successors and imitators became firmly fixed in the American theatre repertoire, laying the bases for much of future musical theatre in that part of the world.

The pair later diversified, separately or together, touring Salvini, Rossi, Ristori, Clara Louise Kellogg in opera, Rubinstein and others, and they were instrumental in taking Offenbach to America for a series of concerts in 1876, an exercise which left them $20,000 in the red. In 1879 Grau—now separatred from Chizzola—sponsored a new opéra-bouffe company, headed by Parisian star Paola Marié. This was the most significant of the latter-day French troupes to play throughout northern and southern America, although Grau continued successfully in the genre when he subsequently brought another French favorite, Louise Théo, to America.

Grau subsequently went into partnership with Henry E Abbey and, for a period, with John B Schoeffel, and they were responsible in the last years of the century for bringing to the American stage many Continental stars, including Bernhardt, Henry Irving, Réjane and Patti, as well as several musical companies. In 1890 they hosted a Broadway season by George Edwardes's Gaiety Theatre Company with *Faust Up-to-Date* and, in 1894, less successfully, they set up a British company, with Lillian Russell at its head, to bring Jakobowski's *Die Brillanten-Königin* from the Vienna Carltheater to America.

Grau was also, for more than a decade, co-director, with Abbey (and originally Schoeffel), of the Metropolitan Opera, New York, and at another stage became involved in the management of the Royal Opera House, Covent Garden.

A cousin, **Jules GRAU** (b Brünn 1853; d New York, 11 September 1905) who began similarly in the theatre under the tutelage of Jacob Grau, also toured comic opera companies around America for thirty years.

GRAVES, George [Windsor] (b London, 1 January 1876; d London, 2 April 1949). Highly popular but often destructive British comedian of the early 20th century, inclined to give his own stand-up performance regardless of the show.

Graves began his career touring in small comedy roles in *The Shop Girl* (1896, St Vaurien) with Wallace Erskine, *The Gay Grisette* (1898, t/o Janus), *Miss Chiquita* (1899, D'Arcy Davis) and *The Skirt Dancer* (1900, Captain Bunting) in his early twenties, and after five years of solid gagging in musical shows around the provinces, Russia and South Africa (*Kitty Grey, A Runaway Girl, The Geisha, Florodora,* etc) he made his first appearance in London as Marie Studholme's father in Edwardes and Frohman's production of *The School Girl* (1903, General Marchmont) at the Prince of Wales Theatre.

Edwardes next gave him the roles of MacSherry in *Madame Sherry* (1904) and Coquenard in *Véronique* (1904) and then took him to Daly's to succeed Willie Edouin as the comical father of the little heroines in *Les P'tites Michu.* Graves subsequently played this same part in the show's unsuccessful Broadway production (1907). However, it was his next role at Daly's which was his most famous: at 32 years of age he introduced his freely ad-libbed interpretation of *The Merry Widow*'s aging, buffo Baron Popoff and in that role he established himself as one of the town's favorite musical comedians.

He subsequently mixed theatre, music hall and pantomime engagements, appearing on the musical stage in *The Belle of Brittany* (1908, Marquis de St Gautier), *A Persian Princess* (1909, King Khayyam) as Bogumil in *Princess Caprice* (1912, *Der liebe Augustin*), in *Houp-La!* with Gertie Millar (1916, Marmaduke Bunn), *Maggie* (1919, Jim) and *Now and Then* (1921, George Gridd). He played with an increasing egoism, showing little concern for anything but his own performance and none for his fellow actors, and most of these later shows suffered sadly from such disruption.

In the later 1920s and 1930s he appeared as Tweedlepunch in *Florodora,* General von Spatz in *The Blue Mazurka* and Tabarie in *The Vagabond King* and, now the right age for the roles he had so long been playing, he found several congenial musical parts to which he returned regularly: Christian Veidt in *Lilac Time,* Popoff, and, from 1937, his one really significant original creation, the kindly Sir John Tremayne in *Me and My Girl,* a role which he played, in tandem with Lupino Lane, as late as 1945.

Autobiography: *Gaieties and Gravities* (Hutchinson, London, 1931)

GRAY, Dolores (b Chicago, 7 June 1924). Shapely, strong-voiced leading lady of American musicals, both in the United States and in Britain.

Miss Gray first appeared in musical comedy on Broadway at 21 in a little part in a pale blue musical called *Are You with It?* and, after a false start with the Vernon Duke book musical *Sweet Bye-and-Bye,* which closed on the road, moved up to the top of the bill when she took the Ethel Merman role of Annie Oakley in the London production of *Annie Get Your Gun* (1947).

She subsequently had lead roles on Broadway in the revue *Two on the Aisle,* the short-lived *Carnival in Flanders* (Tony Award) and as Frenchy—the tough out-west tart created by Marlene Dietrich on film—in the musical version of *Destry Rides Again* (1959). She appeared in the unsuccessful *Sherry* (1967), returned to London to briefly succeed Angela Lansbury in the star role of *Gypsy* (1973) and subsequently toured and played on Broadway as Dorothy Brock in *42nd Street.* In 1987 she again appeared in London, scoring a very personal success as Carlotta Campion in the revised version of *Follies,* performing ''I'm Still Here'' with lung-power that many a pre-microphone-era artist might have envied.

Amongst her screen appearances was numbered a lusciously blonde version of *Kismet*'s conniving Lalume.

GREASE New '50s rock 'n' roll musical by Jim Jacobs and Warren Casey. Eden Theater, New York, 14 February 1972; Broadhurst Theater, 7 June 1972.

A 1970s musical, set in the 1950s and making the most of ponytails and beehives, ducks'-arses and Vaseline tonic, *Grease* was the ingenuous and gently parodic successor to the equally ingenuous but scarcely parodic college musicals of the *Good News* and *Leave It to Jane* school of earlier years.

High-school slicky Danny Zuko (Barry Bostwick) has spent a sweetly romantic summer at the beach with toothpaste-clean Sandy Dumbrowksi (Carole Demas), but the version of the ''facts'' he gives his pals in the Burger Palace Boys gang when school is back in isn't quite as hand-holding as the truth. When it turns out Sandy has switched to the same school, he has to keep up his image with some double-talking and double-acting. He ends up not taking her to the school dance, catches up with an in-

Plate 156. **Grease**

vite to a drive-in movie, loses out when he gets too fresh, but finally gets his happy ending when Sandy swaps her Sandra Dee image for leather jacket, hoop earrings, chewing gum, cigarettes and all the other more attractive elements of 1950s sophistication.

The show's songs, a clever bunch of amusing 1950s pastiches, included a selection of teenage disaster songs—Danny's ''Alone at a Drive-In Movie,'' Sandy's ''It's Raining on Prom Night,'' and the piece sung to Frenchy (Marya Small), the girl who dropped out of high school to go to beauty school, but then dropped out there as well, by the Guardian Angel (Alan Paul) she doesn't have (''Beauty School Drop-Out'')—alongside a girl-group number ''Freddy, My Love,'' the two different tales of the ''Summer Nights'' as allegedly spent by Sandy and Danny, and the taunting ''Look at Me, I'm Sandra Dee'' sung by Betty Rizzo (Adrienne Barbeau), the head of the girls' gang, mocking Sandy's clean image. It was to Rizzo that the evening's only number which expressed any genuine feeling fell—her angry retort to Sandy that she'd rather be her unpretentious, slightly soiled self than something fresh out of a bubble-gum packet (''There Are Worse Things I Could Do'').

First produced at off-Broadway's Eden Theater under the management of Kenneth Waismann and Maxine Fox, *Grease* shifted to Broadway's Broadhurst Theater after less than four months, and there it began a remarkable run which was clearly due to more than just 1950s nostalgia. By the time that it had done, this refreshingly simple and silly tale of tongue-in-cheek collegiate hearts, flowers and pimples had become the then longest-running Broadway musical in history. When it closed in April 1980 after nearly eight years at the Broadhurst and Royale Theaters, it had played 3,388 performances, topping the records of *My Fair Lady, Hello, Dolly!* and *Fiddler on the Roof.*

Like other shows—from *Erminie, Adonis* and *Dorothy* to *A Chorus Line* and *Salad Days*—which have set up extraordinary runs in one country, *Grease* did not confirm that record in other productions. Produced 12 months after its Broadway transfer at London's New London Theatre, under the management of Triumph Theatre Productions, with Richard Gere (Danny), Stacey Gregg (Sandy) and Jacquie-Ann Carr (Rizzo) featured, *Grease* managed only a fair 236 performances, whilst Harry Miller's Australian production showed no signs of following the vast success of his *Jesus Christ Superstar* production and, after a disappointing Melbourne season, was not taken to Sydney. In Mexico, the show was called *Vaselina,* whilst in France François Wertheimer performed what can most kindly be called a rip-off by presenting his *Gomina*—which, in spite of appearances, was not Broadway's *Grease*—at the Théâtre de l'Europêen.

Grease ran on and on on Broadway, but was shunned by the rest of the world until 1978. In that year, Robert Stigwood released a film version. John Travolta, Olivia Newton-John and Stockard Channing featured, the score was enriched with the interpolated songs "You're the One That I Want" and "Hopelessly Devoted To You," some genuine 1950s numbers were also added to the score, the three-parts-sincere, one-part-parody feeling of the piece was caught to a nicety, and the result was a huge movie hit which prompted a fresh look at *Grease* in those countries which had rejected it before. London's Helen Montagu mounted a new production with Michael Howe and Jacqueline Reddin featured and the young Tracey Ullman as Frenchy, but once again London—which had rushed to the film—showed it had no interest in *Grease* on stage. The second coming of *Grease* did, however, win it a thorough round of the British provincial theatres which had ignored it originally. It also, ultimately, won it a showing in Sydney, Australia, when John Frost mounted a production at the Footbridge Theatre (26 September 1991).

However, *Grease* was to finally conquer all corners of the English-speaking world. In 1993 London got a third edition—a *Grease* mounted this time in the style of the recently successful London Palladium *Joseph and the Amazing Technicolor Dreamcoat:* large and soap-starry. Australian *Neighbours* TV-star Craig McLachlan top-billed in a production mounted at the vast Dominion Theatre (15 July 1993) and this time the show clicked. After three years plus at the Dominion, it shifted across to the more compact Cambridge Theatre (24 October 1996), running on until its lifespan reached a total of more than six years.

A Broadway revival cast in the same mold soon followed (11 May 1994), with Ricky Paull Goldin and Susan Wood starred as Danny and Sandy. It introduced some favorite players from the past—Micky Dolenz of Monkees fame (Vince), *Laugh-In* star Jo-Ann Worley (Miss Lynch), twister Chubby Checker (Teen Angel), Debby daughter of do-you-remember Pat Boone (Rizzo) and sometime British pop vocalist Sheena Easton—and a more recent "name" in Brooke Shields as a sometime Rizzo, as the show picked up where it had left off what seemed like no time at all before, confirming itself as Broadway's topmost tenant of all time. It racked up another 1,503 performances adding another record—the longest-running Broadway revival in history—to the show's already remarkable record.

In Australia, Frost followed up with an even bigger version—advertised as "Grease, the arena spectacular"—at Melbourne's Melbourne Park (24 April 1998) with McLachlan teamed with Jane Scali, Danni Minogue, and local star Anthony Warlow featured as Teen Angel. Following on behind Australia's hit arena *Superstar* production, *Grease* proved just as popular, and the production toured the large Entertainment Centres of Australia's principal cities, twice around and with enormous success.

The 1990s, however, didn't just bring *Grease* its English-language apotheosis. The reburgeoning European musical-theatre scene also turned its attentions to the 20-year-old show, and new-style *Grease* productions appeared in Germany (Munich, with songs in English and text in German ad Thorsten Schmidt, Hamburg ad Frank Thannhäuser, Capitol Theater, Düsseldorf, Theater des Westens), Hungary (ad Ákos Fodor), Austria (with German dialogue ad Michael Schittenberg and English lyrics) and Scandinavia as the London version of the show set off round the cities of Europe and *Grease* jived into its third decade, on the crest of a huge nostalgia boom, looking likely to stay around for at least three decades more.

Australia: Metro Theatre, Melbourne 9 September 1972; UK: New London Theatre 26 June 1973; Germany: Arri Studio, Munich 16 June 1990; Musiktheater an der Reeperbahn, Hamburg 24 February 1993; Hungary: Arany János Színház *Zselé—kend a hajadra* 18 June 1993; Austria: Raimundtheater 24 September 1994; France: Palais des Sports (Eng) 5 November 1999

Film: Paramount 1978

Recordings: original cast (MGM/Polygram), film soundtrack (RSO), Mexican cast (Orfeon, Raff), South African cast (EMI), London revival cast (CBS/Sony), Austrian cast, Hungarian cast (Polygram), German/Hamburg cast (Nice Music), Swedish cast (Four Leaf Clover), Swedish cast 1991 (Polydor), Danish cast, Australian cast, Broadway revival cast (RCA), Spanish studio cast (Universal PG), Czech cast *Pomada* (Mercury), etc

THE GREAT WALTZ *see* WALZER AUS WIEN

A GREEK SLAVE Musical comedy in 2 acts by Owen Hall. Lyrics by Harry Greenbank and Adrian Ross. Music by Sidney Jones. Additional music by Lionel Monckton. Daly's Theatre, London, 8 June 1898.

The authors of the vastly successful *The Geisha* swapped that piece's picturesque Orient setting for a pic-

Plate 157. **A Greek Slave.** *Hayden Coffin shows off his advantages in the title role.*

turesque Ancient Roman one for its successor on the stage of London's Daly's Theatre. Resident prima donna Marie Tempest was cast as Maia, daughter of the Persian soothsayer Heliodorus (Huntley Wright) to whom all matronly Rome runs for news of their future. *The Geisha*'s other stars were cast as their slaves: the pert Iris (Letty Lind), the sculptor Archias (H Scott Russell), and the exceedingly well-proportioned Diomed (Hayden Coffin) who has served as a model for his fellow slave's marble-chipping. One day, the Princess Antonia (Hilda Moody) comes to consult Heliodorus's oracle and, encouraged by the vengeful prefect Pomponius (Rutland Barrington) whom the princess has spurned, Maia announces to her customer that the God of Love has fallen in love with her. The God of Love is Archias's statue of Diomed, and the plan is to trick the cold (to Pomponius) Antonia into in her turn wasting her heart's sentiments on a piece of icy marble. But Heliodorus, determined to break up the love affair between his daughter and his handsome slave, substitutes the real man for the statue and so Diomed goes home with Antonia. It takes the entire second act—disguises, low comedy and much music and antics set during the festival of the Saturnalia—to unwind the complications thus entwined.

If the text of the piece got a little chaotic in its Saturnalic second half, as it indulged in an extended burlesque of *Cyrano de Bergerac* and a bevy of other topicalities, the score, on the other hand, never flagged. Miss Tempest had a delightful little piece about ''The Lost Pleiad'' and a romantic ballad ''The Golden Isle,'' Miss Lind followed her Tomtit and Parrot tales of the two previous Daly's shows with the Aristophanic fable of ''A Frog He Lived in a Pond-O,'' Wright described himself patteringly as ''The Wizard,'' and Barrington complained, with many a modern-day reference, that ''I Want to Be Popular,'' whilst Coffin heroically longed for ''Freedom'' in an extremely baritonic drawing-room solo, alongside some particularly attractive ensembles.

A Greek Slave, for all its attractions, could not equal the popularity of *The Geisha.* However, on its own terms, it did well enough. It played for a year at Daly's (349 performances), went into a second edition, with the usual bundle of fresh songs and scenes, toured lengthily, and was eagerly picked up by other countries where *The Geisha* had become a favorite. Budapest's Népszínház quickly mounted *A Görög rabszolga* (ad Emil Makai, Árpád Pásztor) with a fine cast headed by Aranka Hegyi, Klára Küry, Gabi Bárdy, Imre Szirmai and József Németh, and scored one of its biggest successes of the 1890s (79 performances); Vienna's Theater an der Wien followed suit with a localized version (ad Leo Stein), with Franz Tewele featured as Heliodorus, Joseffy as Pomponius (equipped with special topical lyrics for ''Populär'' provided by popular songwriter Alois Just) and Frln Reichsberg as Maia for 36 performances; and Berlin mounted C M Röhr and Georg Okonkowski's *Der griechische Sklave* with considerable success. On Broadway, however, Fred C Whitney's production with Dorothy Morton (Maia), Richard Carle (Heliodorus) and Herbert Sparling (Pomponius) featured, failed in just 29 performances.

In 1926 the new owner of Daly's Theatre, Jimmy White, decided to revive *A Greek Slave,* and mounted a London-bound production with José Collins starred as Maia. Dogged by squabbles and inefficiencies, the production folded without even getting to London.

Hungary: Népszínház *A Görög rabszolga* 4 March 1899; USA: Herald Square Theater 28 November 1899; Austria: Theater an der Wien *Der griechische Sklave* 16 December 1899; Germany: Centraltheater *Der grieschische Sklave* 15 September 1900

GREEN, Adolph (b New York, 2 December 1915). Originally a performer, Green teamed with a fellow member of the Revuers group, Betty Comden, to form the most enduring and successful lyric- and sometimes libretto-writing partnership in Broadway-cum-Hollywood history (see COMDEN, BETTY).

He has also continued an intermittent career as a performer since, featuring alongside Comden in their highly successful debut musical *On the Town* (1944), and coming to grief with their unsuccessful *Bonanza Bound* (1947). He appeared in the revue *A Party with Comden and Green* (1958, 1977) and also in the concert version and recording of *Follies.*

1944 **On the Town** (Leonard Bernstein/w Betty Comden) Adelphi Theater 28 December

1945 **Billion Dollar Baby** (Morton Gould/w Comden) Alvin Theater 21 December

1947 **Bonanza Bound** (Saul Chaplin/w Comden) Shubert Theater, Philadelphia 26 December

1953 **Wonderful Town** (Bernstein/w Comden/Jerome Chodorov, Joseph Fields) Winter Garden Theater 25 February

1954 **Peter Pan** (Jule Styne, Mark Charlap/w Comden, Carolyn Leigh/J M Barrie ad) Winter Garden Theater 20 October

1956 **Bells Are Ringing** (Styne/w Comden) Shubert Theater 29 November

1958 **Say, Darling** (Styne/w Comden/Richard Bissell, Marian Bissell) ANTA Theater 3 April

1960 **Do Re Mi** (Styne/w Comden/Garson Kanin) St James Theater 26 December

1961 **Subways Are for Sleeping** (Styne/w Comden) St James Theater 27 December

1964 **Fade Out—Fade In** (Styne/w Comden) Mark Hellinger Theater 26 May

1967 **Hallelujah, Baby!** (Styne/w Comden/Arthur Laurents) Martin Beck Theater 26 April

1970 **Applause** (Charles Strouse/Lee Adams) Palace Theater 30 March

1974 **Lorelei** revised *Gentlemen Prefer Blondes* (Palace Theater)

1978 **On the Twentieth Century** (Cy Coleman/w Comden) St James Theater 19 February

1982 **A Doll's Life** (Larry Grossman/w Comden) Mark Hellinger Theater 23 September

1985 **Singin' in the Rain** (pasticcio/w Comden) Gershwin Theater 2 July

1991 **The Will Rogers Follies** (Coleman/w Comden/Peter Stone) Palace Theater 1 May

1999 **Die Fledermaus** American version w Comden (Metropolitan Opera House)

GREEN, Marion (b Janesville, Iowa, 8 March 1890; d Rye, NY, 17 March 1956). American baritone who found several fine roles in a 25-year career.

Originally a concert vocalist in his native America, Green was selected to star opposite Maggie Teyte in the London premiere of Messager's *Monsieur Beaucaire* (''Red Rose''), a role he then repeated as his Broadway debut. He subsequently went no further than Philadelphia in the romantic lead of the Anna Nichols/Werner Janssen operetta *Love Dreams* (1921, Larry Pell), but returned to New York in the Spanish music-drama *The Wildcat* (1921, Juanillo) and, replacing Donald Brian who had walked out in tryout, in the demanding romantic tenor role of Achmed Bey in the American version of Fall's *The Rose of Stamboul* (1922).

He later appeared as the leading man of the Romberg/Kummer musical *Annie Dear* (1924, John Rawson), sang Captain Corcoran in the 1926 Winthrop Ames revival of *HMS Pinafore,* closed out-of-town in *Cherry Blossoms* (1927), featured in the American production of *The Dubarry* (1932, Louis XV), and appeared in musical-comedy character roles as the Secretary of State in *I'd Rather Be Right* (1937), in a revival of *Maytime,* and as the Magistrate in Kurt Weill's *The Firebrand of Florence* (1945).

GREEN, Martyn [MARTYN-GREEN, William] (b London, 22 April 1899; d Hollywood, Calif, 8 February 1975). Longtime chief comedian of the D'Oyly Carte Opera Company.

Green made his first appearances on the stage in the Daly's Theatre touring companies of *A Southern Maid, The Maid of the Mountains* and *Sybil,* playing at one stage the romantic tenor role of Petrov in the last named. He toured in *Shuffle Along* and then, in 1922, he joined the D'Oyly Carte Opera Company as a chorister and understudy, making his earliest appearances in named parts as Luiz, Major Murgatroyd, The Associate (*Trial by Jury*) and Cox. He was subsequently named understudy to Henry Lytton in the principal comedy roles and, between 1932–34, succeeded to those roles. With a break for war service, he remained at the comic head of the company until 1951, recording the repertoire on the first D'Oyly Carte sets of long-playing records of the Gilbert and Sullivan comic operas.

His subsequent career was in America where he repeated his well-known Savoy opera characterizations and lectured on and directed productions of the Gilbert and Sullivan comic operas. He appeared in regional productions of a number of plays, on television (voice of the Fox in *Pinocchio*) and, in spite of having lost a leg as a result of an accident in a lift in 1959, appeared as Chaucer in the Broadway production of the musical *The Canterbury Tales.* He was also, temporarily, director of the musical *Royal Flush.*

Autobiography: *Here's a How-de-Do* (Norton, New York, 1952)

GREEN, Stanley (b New York, 29 May 1923; d Brooklyn, NY, 12 December 1990).

One of the first and few writers on the American musical theatre to approach the subject with an historical and unpretentiously analytical eye, Stanley Green authored some 30 years of writings focusing on the area of 20th-century musical theatre and film in America: *The World of Musical Comedy* (1960 and regularly updated), *The Great Clowns of Broadway, The Rodgers and Hammerstein Story* (1963), *Ring Bells! Sing Songs!* (1971), *Starring Fred Astaire* (1973), *The Encyclopaedia of the Musical Theatre* (1976), *The Rodgers and Hammerstein Fact Book* and *Broadway Show by Show,* as well as an *Encyclopaedia of Musical Film* and, his final book, *Broadway Musicals Year by Year* (1990).

GREENBANK, Harry [GREENBANK, Henry Hewetson] (b London, 11 September 1865; d Boscombe, 26 February 1899). Short-lived lyricist to the influential British series of Daly's Theatre musicals.

The young Harry Greenbank had his introduction to the West End musical stage when his musical playlet *Captain Billy,* musically set by Frank Cellier, was staged at the Savoy Theatre as a curtain-raiser to *The Nautch Girl.* He continued to write the texts for such small-scale pieces over the following years, both for the Savoy and for the Lyric Theatre, until Lyric supremo Horace Sedger allotted him the job of supplying the English lyrics to F C Burnand's adaptation of the French opérette *Le Coeur et la main* (*Incognita*).

It was, thereafter, as a lyricist that Greenbank found his niche, and it was he whom George Edwardes chose to collaborate with composer Sidney Jones and librettist Owen Hall when, shortly after, he put together the team of neophytes from whom he commissioned the musical comedy *A Gaiety Girl.* After the enormous worldwide success of that piece, the three stayed together and they subsequently formed the backbone of the team which produced the famous turn-of-the-century series of Daly's Theatre musicals—*An Artist's Model, The Geisha, A Greek Slave* and *San Toy.*

Greenbank also provided lyrics for two of the most successful of the lighter brand of shows produced by Edwardes at the Gaiety Theatre—*The Circus Girl* and *A Runaway Girl*—and he ventured twice as a librettist-lyricist, once with an original musical, *Monte Carlo,* and once with an adaptation of Lecocq's *La Petite Mademoiselle* as *The Scarlet Feather.* His other assignments included additional lyrics for *The Bric à Brac Will* (1895) and, posthumously, a song for the London production of *A Chinese Honeymoon* (1901, "Roses Red and White").

Always extremely delicate of constitution, Greenbank was rarely seen in public and during the production of *A Greek Slave* moved, with his wife and son, to England's southern coast in an attempt to recruit his strength. He died there whilst engaged in writing the lyrics for *San Toy,* and the piece was completed by Adrian Ross, who, with Greenbank, was largely responsible for establishing the job of lyricist (as opposed to all-in writer, or co-writer) in the modern musical theatre.

1891 **Captain Billy** (François Cellier) 1 act Savoy Theatre 24 September

1892 **Incognita** (*Le Coeur et la main*) English lyrics (Lyric Theatre)

1892 **The Young Recruit** (*Le Dragon de la reine*) English lyrics w Adrian Ross, Harry Nicholls (Newcastle)

1892 **Beef Tea** (Wilfred Bendall) 1 act Lyric Theatre 22 October

1893 **Poor Jonathan** (*Der arme Jonathan*) English lyrics (Prince of Wales Theatre)

1893 **Mr Jericho** (Ernest Ford) 1 act Savoy Theatre 24 March

1893 **A Gaiety Girl** (Sidney Jones/Owen Hall) Prince of Wales Theatre 14 October

1894 **Mirette** (André Messager/Frederick E Weatherly) Savoy Theatre 3 July

1894 **The House of Lords** (Ford, George Byng) 1 act Lyric Theatre 6 July

1895 **An Artist's Model** (Jones/Hall) Daly's Theatre 2 February

1896 **The Geisha** (Jones/Hall) Daly's Theatre 25 April

1896 **Monte Carlo** (Howard Talbot) Avenue Theatre 27 August

1896 **The Circus Girl** (Ivan Caryll/w Adrian Ross/James T Tanner, Walter Palings) Gaiety Theatre 5 December

1897 **The Scarlet Feather** (*La Petite Mademoiselle*) English book and lyrics (Shaftesbury Theatre)

1897 **Old Sarah** (F Cellier) 1 act Savoy Theatre 17 June

1898 **A Runaway Girl** (Caryll, Monckton/w Aubrey Hopwood/Seymour Hicks, Harry Nicholls) Gaiety Theatre 21 May

1898 **A Greek Slave** (Jones/Hall) Daly's Theatre 8 June

1899 **San Toy** (Jones/w Adrian Ross/Edward Morton) Daly's Theatre 21 October

GREENBANK, [William] Percy (b Paddington, London, 24 January 1878; d Rickmansworth, 9 December 1968).

Harry Greenbank's younger brother, Percy, was originally intended to join his father in the legal profession, but instead he followed his celebrated brother's footsteps, via the world of journalism and contributions to such journals as *Punch, The Sketch* and *The Tatler,* into the theatre.

After Harry's death, George Edwardes offered the younger Greenbank the opportunity to collaborate with Adrian Ross on the lyrics for the new Gaiety show, *The Messenger Boy,* and also interpolated two of his lyrics into *San Toy,* when the score was reorganized to suit takeover Ada Reeve ("Somebody," "All I Want Is a Little Bit of Fun"). His *The Messenger Boy* contribution included one of the show's hits, its title number (and the rhyming of ''Rameses'' with ''clammy seas''), and won him a firm place in the Gaiety ''team'' along with composers Ivan Caryll and Lionel Monckton, Ross, and the deviser of the Gaiety show plots and outlines, James Tanner.

For the remaining 14 years of the ''Edwardes era'' Greenbank worked consistently for the producer, at the Gaiety, Daly's and later the Adelphi, contributing sometimes much and sometimes only a few lyrics to most of Edwardes's shows (although the frequent credit ''additional lyrics by . . .'' was often no guide to quantity) and being responsible for many a fairly ephemeral song hit.

After the end of the Edwardes era, he continued for a further decade to supply songwords and occasionally libretti to the musical stage, only rarely venturing into the world of revue (*Half Past Eight, Vanity Fair*). His last major work for the West End was the adaptation from the German of what was to become the book to the Jean Gilbert–Vernon Duke musical *Yvonne.* He subsequently did occasional work as a play doctor (*El Dorado,* et al) or an adaptor—he modernized *San Toy* with Percy Barrow for its 1931 revival—but basically settled into what proved to be a long retirement. Greenbank died at the age of 90 and, as a result, the Edwardian musical comedies to which he contributed remain in copyright well into the 21st century.

1900 **The Messenger Boy** (Lionel Monckton, Ivan Caryll/w Adrian Ross/James Tanner, Alfred Murray) Gaiety Theatre 3 February

1901 **The Toreador** (Monckton, Caryll/w Ross/Tanner, Harry Nicholls) Gaiety Theatre 17 June

1901 **The Gay Cadets** (Basil Davis/w Harold Simpson/Norman Prescott, J Thomson) Prince of Wales Theatre, Birmingham 24 June

1902 **A Country Girl** (Monckton/w Ross/Tanner) Daly's Theatre 18 January

1902 **Three Little Maids** (Paul Rubens/w Rubens/Rubens) Apollo Theatre 20 May

1903 **My Lady Molly** (Jones/w Charles H Taylor/George H Jessop) Terry's Theatre 14 March

1903 **The Orchid** (Monckton, Caryll/w Ross/Tanner) Gaiety Theatre 28 October

1903 **The Earl and the Girl** (Caryll/Seymour Hicks) Adelphi Theatre 10 December

1904 **The Lovebirds** (Raymond Roze/w George Grossmith/Grossmith) Savoy Theatre 10 February

1904 **The Blue Moon** (Talbot, Rubens/w Rubens/Harold Ellis) Northampton 29 February; Lyric Theatre, London 28 August 1905

1904 **The Cingalee** (Monckton/w Ross/Tanner) Daly's Theatre 5 March

1904 **Véronique** English lyrics w Lillian Eldee (Apollo Theatre)

1904 **Lady Madcap** (Rubens/w Rubens/N Newnham-Davis, Rubens) Prince of Wales Theatre 17 December

1905 **The Little Michus** (*Les P'tites Michu*) English lyrics (Daly's Theatre)

1905 **The Spring Chicken** (Monckton, Caryll/w Ross/George Grossmith) Gaiety Theatre 30 May

1906 **Two Naughty Boys** (Constance Tippett/Grossmith) Gaiety Theatre 8 January

1906 **The Girl Behind the Counter** (Talbot/w Anderson/Leedham Bantock, Arthur Anderson) Wyndham's Theatre 21 April

1906 **See See** (Jones/w Ross/C H E Brookfield) Prince of Wales Theatre 20 June

1906 **The New Aladdin** (Monckton, Caryll/w others/Tanner, W H Risque) Gaiety Theatre 29 September

1907 **The Three Kisses** (Talbot/w Bantock) Apollo Theatre 21 August

1908 **The Belle of Brittany** (Talbot/Bantock, P J Barrow) Queen's Theatre 24 October

1909 **Our Miss Gibbs** (Monckton, Caryll/w Ross/Tanner et al) Gaiety Theatre 23 January

1909 **A Persian Princess** (Jones/Barrow, Bantock) Queen's Theatre 27 April

1910 **The Quaker Girl** (Monckton/w Ross/Tanner) Adelphi Theatre 5 November

1911 **The Mousmé** (Talbot, Monckton/w Arthur Wimperis/Robert Courtneidge, Alexander M Thompson) Shaftesbury Theatre 9 September

1912 **Princess Caprice** (*Der liebe Augustin*) English lyrics w Scott Craven, C M Beswick (Shaftesbury Theatre)

1912 **Autumn Manoeuvres** (*Tatárjárás*) English lyrics (Adelphi Theatre)

1912 **The Dancing Mistress** (Monckton/w Ross/Tanner) Adelphi Theatre 19 October

1913 **The Girl from Utah** (Jones, Rubens/w Rubens/Tanner, Rubens) Adelphi Theatre 18 October

1914 **The Cinema Star** (*Die Kino-Königin*) additional English lyrics w Harry Graham (Shaftesbury Theatre)

1914 **After the Girl** (Rubens/w Rubens/Rubens) Gaiety Theatre 7 February

1914 **Tonight's the Night** (Rubens/w Rubens/Fred Thompson) Shubert Theatre, New York 24 December

1915 **Tina** (Rubens, Hadyn Wood/w Graham, Rubens) Adelphi Theatre 2 November

1915 **The Miller's Daughters** revised *Three Little Maids* (w Rubens) Prince's Theatre, Manchester 24 December; London Opera House 15 May 1916

1916 **Houp-La!** (Nat D Ayer/w Hugh E Wright/Wright, Thompson) St Martin's Theatre 23 November

1917 **The Boy** (Talbot, Monckton/w Ross/Thompson) Adelphi Theatre 14 September

1919 **The Girl for the Boy** (Howard Carr, Bernard Rolt/Austen Hurgon, George Arthurs) Duke of York's Theatre 23 September

1919 **The Kiss Call** (Caryll/w Ross, Clifford Grey/Thompson) Gaiety Theatre 8 October

1921 **My Nieces** (Talbot) Queen's Theatre 19 August

1922 **The Little Duchess** (G H Clutsam/w Bertrand Davis/Courtneidge, Davis) Glasgow 25 December

1924 **The Street Singer** (Fraser-Simson/Frederick Lonsdale) Lyric Theatre 27 June

1926 **Yvonne** (*Uschi, Zwei um Eine,* etc) English libretto and lyrics (Daly's Theatre)

1929 **Cupid and the Cutlets** (Patrick Barrow) 1 act Q Theatre 20 May

GREENE, Clay M[eredith] (b San Francisco, 12 March 1850; d San Francisco, 5 September 1933).

Greene was already established as a successful stockbroker in San Francisco when he first turned his hand to writing for the theatre and, from his early twenties when his first play was produced, for more than 20 years he turned out a stream of often highly popular and successful plays and libretti, mostly in a happily barnstorming style. He seems to have entered the musical theatre with a three-part remake of the Hanlon's famous *Le Voyage en Suisse* (the revised acts were introduced one at a time over a period of months), but his first attempt at an original musical pay was *Sybil* (1886), an Irish comedy-drama equipped with songs by John F Mitchell, composer of such famous Irishisms as ''An Exile's Lament'' and ''A Letter from Ireland,'' and toured by Frankie Kemble.

Hans the Boatman, a weepie comedy-drama with movable songs, constructed around the talents of Minnie Palmer's sometime leading man Charles Arnold, was the most widely successful of his musical pieces, whilst his Dutch sentimental melodrama with musical moments, *Struck Oil* (Salt Lake City, Utah 23 February 1874), was a longtime surefire vehicle for actor-producer J C Williamson and his wife Maggie Moore, in both America and Australia. On the romantic side, he adapted Longellow's *The Courtship of Miles Standish* as a comic opera for the Bostonians under the title *The Maid of Plymouth,* and put together a version of *Uncle Tom's Cabin* which he called *The Beautiful Slave* in which musical comedy actress Alice Harrison starred as Topsolina.

In his youthful days, Greene also varied the stockbroking with a dabble as a performer on the musical stage and in 1879, at the height of the *Pinafore* craze, he played Deadeye to the Josephine of Emilie Melville at San Francisco's Standard Theater.

In later years he turned out a series of burlesques and comical sketches for the vaudeville circuits and, after finally leaving the stage behind, he worked for a time as a ''photoplay author'' with the Lubin film company and spent considerable time authoring a memoir which, although it remained unpublished, is preserved in his local library.

1883 **Le Voyage en Suisse** revised version (Boston)

1886 **Sybil** (John F Mitchell, Max Maretzek) Poughkeepsie 24 January; Poole's Theater 14 February

1887 **Hans the Boatman** (pasticcio) Theatre Royal, Sheffield, England 7 March

1887 **Our Jennie** (Barney Fagan, Edward Harrigan, Harry Pepper, Willis Sweatnam, Jennie Yeamans) Pope's Theater, St Louis 27 August

1889 **Bluebeard Jr** (Fred Eustis, Richard Maddern) Opera House, Chicago 11 June; Niblo's Garden, New York 13 January 1890

1890 **Pete the Vagabond** Bush Street Theatre, San Francisco 25 August

1891 **Carl's Folly** (Charles Arnold) Theatre Royal, Hull 26 March

1891 **A High Roller** (credited to T Rosenfeld and Archibald Gordon) Bijou Theater 3 August

1893 **Africa** (Randolph Cruger/w J Cheever Goodwin) California Theater, San Francisco 12 June; Star Theatre, New York 25 December

1893 **The Maid of Plymouth** (Thomas Pearsall Thorne) Columbia Theater, Chicago 27 November; Broadway Theater 15 January 1894

1894 **The Little Trooper** (*Les 28 Jours de Clairette*) English version w music by William Furst (Casino Theater)

1897 **April Fool** (pasticcio) sketch Proctor's 18 April

1897 **A Musical Discord** (pasticcio) sketch Grand Theatre, Hull 14 May

1899 **In Gay Paree** (Ludwig Englander/Grant Stewart) Casino Theater 20 March

1899 **The Conspirators** (Humphrey J Green) Morosco's Grand Theatre, San Francisco 23 October

1899 **Sharp Becky** burlesque in *Round New York in 80 Minutes* Koster & Bial's Music Hall 6 November

1900 **[The Remarkable Pipe Dream of] Surelock Holmes** (various) Lamb's Gambol, then burlesque in *Around New York in 80 Minutes* January

1900 **Aunt Hannah** (A Baldwin Sloane/Matthew J Royal) Bijou Theater 22 February

1900 **The Regatta Girl** (Harry McLellan) Koster & Bial's Music Hall 14 March

1902 **Four Times Foiled, or The Marriage of Mamaronek Manor** Proctor's Fifth Avenue Music Hall February

1902 **The Gentle Mr Bellew of France** Proctor's Fifth Avenue Music Hall February

1902 **The Little Minister and His Mash, or A Very Hot Scotch** Proctor's Twenty-Third Street Music Hall 17 March

1902 **The Silver Slipper** revised American libretto (Broadway Theater)

GREENE, Evie [GREEN, Edith Elizabeth] (b Portsmouth, 14 January 1875; d Portsmouth, 11 September 1917). Dark, fine-voiced West End leading lady who created major roles in a number of highly successful musical shows.

After beginning her theatrical career as a dancer in a touring company of Slaughter's *Marjorie* as a young teenager, Evie Greene discovered a fine, growing soprano voice and she quickly progressed to principal singing roles, touring as Annabel in *Maid Marian* (*Robin Hood*), Ethel in *Morocco Bound* (1894), Norah in *The Gay Parisienne* (1895), Ethel Joy in *The New Barmaid,* Ethel in Bucalossi's *En Route* (1896) and opposite Little Tich as the heroine of *Billy* (1898).

At 24 she was hired by Tom Davis to play a leading part in his London production of Varney's *L'Amour mouillé.* She made a great personal success in the staunchly soprano breeches role of Prince Carlo, and Davis promptly cast her in the star role of his next new musical, *Florodora.* In the part of the darkly glamorous, mid-Pacific Dolores, she introduced "Silver Star of Love" and became, overnight, one of London's favorite musical stars. After *Florodora,* she was signed up by George Edwardes who starred her in a new version of *Les Fêtards, Kitty Grey* (1900), in which her portrayal of the sparkling actress of the title was contrasted with the demure, betrayed Baroness of Ethel Sydney (tour) and Edna May (town). Edwardes then moved her to Daly's Theatre where she created the role of Nan in *A Country Girl* ("Try Again Johnnie," "Molly the Marchioness"). After playing that role for most of the show's two-year run, she was next starred in the title role of Ivan Caryll's *The Duchess of Dantzic* (1903) as a light operatic *Madame Sans-Gêne,* scoring the greatest triumph of a career which had, since her first West End appearance, been nothing but high points.

She played Sans-Gêne through most of the London run, toured it and in 1905 repeated her performance on Broadway, before returning for new roles under Edwardes's management in *The Little Cherub* (1906, Molly Montrose), as the elegant, directoire heroine of Hugo Felix's *Les Merveilleuses* (1906, Lodoiska) and as another dark and dashing maiden in *Havana* (1908, Consuelo). After *Havana* she appeared in variety, featuring high on the bill at the Palladium, the Coliseum and the biggest provincial houses, and she returned only once to the musical stage, in a revival of *Florodora* in 1915, before her death at the age of 39.

Miss Greene's first husband was Richard W Temple, actor son of the Savoy baritone.

GREENWOOD, [Frances] Charlotte (b Philadelphia, 25 June 1892; d Beverly Hills, Calif, 18 January 1978).

A lanky, blonde comedienne with a talent for eccentric dance, Miss Greenwood made her first appearance on the stage as a dancer in *The White Cat* (1905). She subsequently played in a minor capacity in *The Rogers Brothers in Panama* (1907, Lola as "Lottie Greenwood") and *Nearly a Hero* (1908), toured in vaudeville and returned to Broadway to appear in *The Passing Show of 1912* and *of 1913,* and the Lehár musical *The Man with Three Wives* (1913, Sidonie). Following a tour in *The Tik-Tok Man of Oz* (1913), she won her best opportunity to date in the role of Letitia Proudfoot in the musical comedy *Pretty Mrs Smith* (1914). Her comical dancing and her song, "Long, Lean, Lanky Letty," won her particular notice and, as a result, the show's producer Oliver Morosco had a musical built around her talents and entitled, after her previous success, *So Long, Letty* (1915, Letty Robbins).

Letty became a running character name (though not a consistent character) through a series of musicals over the next half-dozen years which, if limited in their appeal to Broadway, proved highly successful on the road. Morosco followed *Linger Longer Letty* (1919) with *Let 'er Go, Letty* which had its title changed when Miss Greenwood abandoned it to go instead into *Letty Pepper* (1922), a musical revision of Charles Klein's successful vehicle for Rose Stahl, *Maggie Pepper.*

She played threafter in revue *(Music Box Revue, Ritz Revue,* her husband Martin Broones's *Rufus Le Maire's Affairs*) and comedy, and in 1930 she filmed *So Long, Letty,* but she did not return to the musical theatre until 1932, when she moved temporarily to London where her husband was establishing a career as a composer of musical-comedy songs. She played Auguste in the Drury Lane production of *Wild Violets* (*Wenn die kleinen Veilchen blühen*), Tiny Barbour in Jerome Kern's *Three Sisters* at the same house and had her best British role as the zany Aunt Isabel of *Gay Deceivers* (*Toi c'est moi*), a successful French musical for which Broones had largely replaced the original French score.

Back in America, she toured extensively in one more Letty show, *Leaning on Letty* (1935, a musical version of the play *The Post Road*), and, after a varying career including two years of *The Charlotte Greenwood Show* on radio and a trip to Australia with *Leaning on Letty,* made a final Broadway appearance as Juno in Cole Porter's *Out of This World* (1950).

A film performer from early on (she starred in Oliver Morosco's film of the famous comedy *Jane* in 1915), Miss Greenwood appeared on celluloid in her stage role in *So Long, Letty* in the filmed version of *Flying High* (Pansy), then later in such pieces as *Tall, Dark and Handsome, Down Argentina Way* and *Moon Over Miami* before, in 1956, delivering a memorable Aunt Eller in the film version of *Oklahoma!*

Miss Greenwood was married (1915) to film actor Cyril Ring, brother of Blanche Ring, and subsequently to songwriter Broones.

Autobiography: *Never Too Tall* (New York, 1947)

GREET, William (b River Thames, c1851; d Bournemouth, 25 April 1914).

At first an officer in the Royal Marines, then a farmer in Wimbledon, then, in the mid-1880s, business manager

Plate 158. **Charlotte Greenwood** *was ''Letty'' for the second time in* So Long, Letty, *a musical which got her mixed up in a touch of husband swapping.*

for Willie Edouin, Greet went on to become a highly successful manager of touring musical comedy. He had already made his West End debut with the fairly successful burlesque *Blue-Eyed Susan* produced at the Alhambra (w C J Abud) in 1892, when he picked up the second company rights of the touring musical *The Lady Slavey* from H Cecil Beryl (1893). *The Lady Slavey* turned out to be a touring phenomenon, and Greet's production toured virtually nonstop for a dozen years, soon sharing the circuits with companies of the producer's own hugely successful made-for-touring show *The Gay Parisienne.* Whilst leaving others to take the risks of the London and New York runs, Greet toured *The Gay Parisienne* and *The Lady Slavey* for more than a decade with great profit. He mounted *Dandy Dick Whittington* (aka *The Circus Boy,* 1895) in London and on the road, with limited success, but found another sturdy provincial annual with *The New Mephisto(pheles)* which accomplished eight years of touring from 1897 without ever venturing to the West End.

In 1901 he returned to London with a revival of the hardy *Morocco Bound* but also, on a rather different level, as the new lessee of the Savoy Theatre in succession to the widowed Helen D'Oyly Carte. Greet took over at the Savoy where the Cartes had left off, managing *The Emerald Isle* and producing *Ib and Little Christina, The Willow Pattern* (1901), *Merrie England* (1902) and *A Princess of Kensington* (1903), but, finding the revenues from comic opera to be rather less than from his tours of free-and-easy musicals, he switched the Savoy company to musical comedy and scored a fine hit first up with *The Earl and the Girl* (1903). The Christmas entertainment *Little Hans Andersen* (1903) and *The Talk of the Town* (1905) were less successful, however, and Greet's name disappeared thereafter from London bills.

He was, at various times, involved in the management of the Lyric, Garrick, Comedy and Adelphi Theatres.

His younger brother, **Ben Greet**, was also a well-known manager and actor, initially in touring musical comedy (*The Casino Girl,* etc) but later and principally in the Shakespearean field.

GREGH, Louis (b Philippeville, Algeria, 16 March 1843; d Saint-Mesme, 21 January 1915).

Conductor and composer, Gregh had his moments of success in the musical theatre with the very light musical accompaniments to the spicy *Un lycée de jeunes filles,* revived numerous times in Paris after its initial run and played in several other countries; the musical comedy *Le Présomptif,* produced with success in Belgium if not in France; and the vaudeville *Patart, Patart et cie,* which also won itself export to Vienna as *Kneisl & Co.* He also provided the music for a number of ballets and for Fernand Beissier's play *Arlette* (1891). Latterly he devoted himself to music publishing, establishing a firm which survived in his family for three generations.

1881 **Un lycée de jeunes filles** (Alexandre Bisson) Théâtre Cluny 28 December

1883 **Le Présomptif** (Albert Hennequin, Albin Valabrègue) Galeries-Saint Hubert, Brussels 12 December; Théâtre de la Renaissance 6 June 1884

1890 **Grande vitesse, port dû** (A Philibert) 1 act La Cigale 19 September

1893 **Patart, Patart et cie** (André Sylvane, Charles Clairville) Théâtre des Folies-Dramatiques 9 October

1895 **Le Capitaine Roland** (Armand Lafrique) Théâtre Mondaine 29 March

GREY, Clifford [DAVIS, Percival] (b Birmingham, 5 January 1887; d Ipswich, 25 September 1941).

Highly successful British lyricist who spent prolific periods working alternately for the London and New York musical stages.

"Clifford Grey" first worked in the entertainment business in concert parties, performing and contributing to the writing of his company's material, before Leslie Henson introduced him to the management of the Alhambra. There, in 1916, he was teamed with Nat Ayer to write lyrics for a few of the songs for the English version of the Paris revue *Les Fils Touffe sont à Paris* which that theatre had taken over from the schedule of the late George Edwardes. As *The Bing Boys Are Here* the show and its favorite songs were an enormous success ("If You Were the Only Girl in the World," "Another Little Drink") and Grey, who had quickly ended up supplying most of the songwords, including those for the two hit numbers, was launched on a series of revues which included *Pell Mell, The Bing Girls Are There* ("Let the Great Big World Keep Turning"), *The Bing Boys on Broadway* ("First Love, Last Love, Best Love"), *Hullo America, Johnny Jones* and George Gershwin's *The Rainbow,* and an even more substantial series of musical comedies.

The first of these book shows were the Gaiety Theatre's *Theodore & Co,* in which he combined with Jerome Kern to produce Leslie Henson's hit song "365 Days," and two adaptations, the London versions of the "Roderick Freeman/Ogden Hartley" Broadway musical *High Jinks,* and of the Belgian musical *Arlette,* into which Grey and Ivor Novello interpolated the comic song "On the Staff," with which Stanley Lupino scored his first major success.

During and after the First World War he supplied the songwords to some of the most successful and long-running musical plays in London, notably Leslie Henson's *Yes, Uncle!,* the Bill Berry comedy vehicle *Who's Hooper?* and the Winter Garden musical farce *A Night Out,* as well as one virtually British musical which made its first appearance on Broadway: Ivan Caryll's *The Girl Behind the Gun,* which would later become *Kissing Time* for its very successful London run.

Soon after the production of *Kissing Time,* Grey took what should have been a three-week holiday in America and, in spite of the fact that he completed commissions for several further London shows—*Phi-Phi, The Smith Family,* additional lyrics for the 1921 revival of *The Maid of the Mountains*—he ended up staying in the United States for most of the 1920s. One of his earliest jobs there was a fresh collaboration with Jerome Kern, as lyricist for *Sally,* and the result was a major hit and such songs as ''Sally'' and ''Wild Rose.'' In the years that followed, he provided lyrics, and on several occasions libretti as well, for a series of Broadway musicals and revues. Of the book musicals, many of which did not rise above the mediocre, *Hit the Deck* (''Hallelujah!,'' ''Sometimes I'm Happy'') and Rudolf Friml's *The Three Musketeers* were the two most notable successes but, amongst the other, less memorable productions, Grey also had individual song credits for an English version of Kálmán's ''Komm' Zigány!'' (*Gräfin Mariza*) and for José Padilla's hit song ''Valencia.''

During a spell in Hollywood he produced the lyrics for Victor Schertzinger's score to the 1929 film *The Love Parade* (''Nobody's Using It Now,'' ''My Love Parade,'' ''Paris, Stay the Same'' for Chevalier, ''Dream Lover'' for Jeanette MacDonald, ''March of the Grenadiers'') and for the unrecognizably botched versions of Lehár's *Zigeunerliebe* entitled *The Rogue Song* (Stothart's ''When I'm Looking at You,'' Lehár's ''The White Dove'' for Lawrence Tibbett) and of Oscar Straus's *Walzertraum,* Hollywoodized as *The Smiling Lieutenant,* before returning to Britain for the final years of his career.

Those years were as busy and successful as the others. After supplying lyrics to Kern's London show *Blue Eyes* (additional), he had major song hits in Vivian Ellis's *Mr Cinders* (''Spread a Little Happiness'') and Waller and Tunbridge's *For the Love of Mike* (''Got a Date With an Angel'' for Bobby Howes) as he mixed musical theatre work with a good number of films, collaborating on, amongst others, the screenplays for the film versions of the musicals *For the Love of Mike* (1932), *Hold My Hand* (1938), *Yes, Madam?* (1938), and *Me and My Girl* (*The Lambeth Walk,* 1939).

During the early part of the Second World War, Grey was engaged with ENSA organizing concerts for the troops, and a contribution to the revue *Black and Blue* was his last stage offering before his death.

1916 **Theodore & Co** (Jerome Kern, Ivor Novello/w Adrian Ross/H M Harwood, George Grossmith) Gaiety Theatre 19 September

1916 **The Kodak Girl** (Grace A Vernon/Harry M Vernon) 1 act Middlesex Music Hall 27 November

1917 **Arlette** English lyrics w Ross (Shaftesbury Theatre)

1917 **Yes, Uncle!** (Nat D Ayer/Austen Hurgon, George Arthurs) Prince of Wales Theatre 29 December

1918 **The Girl Behind the Gun** (aka *Kissing Time*) (Ivan Caryll/Guy Bolton, P G Wodehouse) New Amsterdam Theater 16 September

1919 **Who's Hooper?** (Howard Talbot, Novello/Fred Thompson) Adelphi Theatre 13 September

1919 **Baby Bunting** (Ayer/Thompson, Worton David) Shaftesbury Theatre 25 September

1919 **The Kiss Call** (Caryll/w Ross, Percy Greenbank/Thompson) Gaiety Theatre 8 October

1920 **A Night Out** (Willie Redstone/Grossmith, Arthur Miller) Winter Garden Theatre 19 September

1920 **Kissing Time** (Caryll/w Philander Johnson, Irving Caesar/George V Hobart) Lyric Theater, New York 11 October

1920 **Sally** (Kern/w Wodehouse/Bolton) New Amsterdam Theater, New York 21 December

1921 **Little Miss Raffles** (Caryll/Bolton) Stamford, Conn 1 December

1922 **The Hotel Mouse** revised *Little Miss Raffles* (Caryll, Armand Vecsey/Bolton) Shubert Theater, New York 13 March

1922 **Phi-Phi** English book and lyrics w Fred Thompson (London Pavilion)

1922 **The Smith Family** (Ayer/w Stanley Logan, Philip Page) Empire Theatre 6 September

1923 **Lady Butterfly** (Werner Janssen) Globe Theater, New York 22 January

1924 **Marjorie** (Sigmund Romberg, Herbert Stothart, Stephen Jones/w Harold Atteridge) Shubert Theater, New York 11 August

1924 **Annie Dear** (Romberg, Harry Tierney/Clare Kummer) Times Square Theater, New York 4 November

1925 **June Days** (ex- *The School Maid*) (J Fred Coots/Atteridge) Astor Theater, New York 6 August

1925 **Sky High** (*Der Tanz ins Gluck*) additional lyrics for American version (Casino Theater)

1925 **Mayflowers** (Eduard Künneke) Forrest Theater, New York 24 November

1926 **Patsy** (Isidore B Kornblum/w E Magnus Ingleton) Mason Theater, Los Angeles 8 March

1926 **Katja** (*Katja, die Tänzerin*) additional American lyrics to Harry Graham's English version (44th Street Theater, New York)

1926 **Bubbling Over** (Richard Myers/Leo Robin) Garrick Theater, Philadelphia 2 August

1927 **Hit the Deck** (Vincent Youmans/w Robin/Herbert Fields) Belasco Theater, New York 25 April

1928 **The Madcap** (Maurie Rubens, Coots, etc/Gladys Unger, Cosmo Hamilton [Gertrude Purcell]) Royale Theater, New York 31 January

1928 **Sunny Days** (Jean Schwartz/w William Cary Duncan) Imperial Theater, New York 8 February

1928 **The Three Musketeers** (Rudolf Friml/w Wodehouse/ William Anthony McGuire) Lyric Theater, New York 13 March

1928 **Mr Cinders** (Vivian Ellis, Richard Myers/w Greatrex Newman) Opera House, Blackpool 25 September; Adelphi Theatre 11 February 1929

1928 **Ups-a-Daisy** (Lewis Gensler) Shubert Theater, New York 8 October

1930 **Smiles** (*The One Girl*) (Youmans/w Harold Adamson, Ring Lardner) Ziegfeld Theater, New York 18 November and libretto revision for Britain w Frank Eyton and H M Sargent

1931 **For the Love of Mike** (Jack Waller, Joseph Tunbridge/w Sonny Miller/w H F Maltby) Saville Theatre 8 October

1932 **Out of the Bottle** (Ellis, Oscar Levant/w Thompson) London Hippodrome 11 June

1933 **He Wanted Adventure** (Waller, Tunbridge/w Weston, Lee) Saville Theatre 28 March

1933 **Command Performance** (Waller, Tunbridge/C Stafford Dickens) Saville Theatre 17 October

1933 **Mr Whittington** (Waller, Tunbridge, John Green/ Newman, Furber) Alahambra, Glasgow 30 November; London Hippodrome 1 March 1934

1935 **Jack o' Diamonds** (Noel Gay/w Maltby) Gaiety Theatre 25 February

1935 **Love Laughs—!** (ex- *Leave It to Love*) (Gay/w Newman) London Hippodrome 25 June

1936 **At the Silver Swan** (Edmond Samuels/Bolton, Percival Mackey) Palace Theatre 19 February

1937 **Oh! You Letty** (Paul Sharon/w Geoffrey Kerr, Lee) Palace Theatre 8 December

1938 **Bobby Get Your Gun** (Waller, Tunbridge/w Bolton, Thompson, Lee, Carter) Adelphi Theatre 7 October

1942 **Susie** revised *Jack o' Diamonds* (Oxford)

1942 **Wild Rose** revised *Sally* (Prince's Theatre, London)

GREY, Joel [KATZ, Joel] (b Cleveland, Ohio, 11 April 1932).

The son of comedian Mickey Katz, Grey made his musical comedy debut touring as Littlechap in *Stop the World—I Want to Get Off* and succeeded to the role created by Anthony Newley in the show's Broadway production in 1963. He later covered Tommy Steele in the starring role of *Half a Sixpence,* but came to fame with his creation of the role of the leering, epicene master of ceremonies in *Cabaret* (1966, ''Willkommen,'' ''Three Ladies,'' ''Money,'' etc) on the stage and again on film (Academy Award). He later appeared as George M Cohan in the biomusical *George M!* (1968), and with less success in the Joan of Arc musical *Goodtime Charley* (1975, Charley) and in the musicalization of *Jacobowsky and the Colonel* as *The Grand Tour* (1979, Jacobowsky). He was seen once again on Broadway in his celebrated role in *Cabaret* in a Broadway revival of 262 nights in 1987, followed by a tour, and in 1996 featured as Amos Hart in the highly successful remounting of *Chicago* in America and in Great Britain (1998 t/o).

Grey played Luisa's father in the 1995 film version of *The Fantasticks.*

GRIFFITH, Robert E (b Methuen, Mass, 1907; d Port Chester, NY, 7 June 1961).

Originally an actor and then, from 1935, a stage manager for George Abbott, Griffith found almost unmitigated success when he turned his hand to producing for the musical theatre. He teamed with Hal Prince (a stage-management colleague on *Touch and Go* and *Wonderful Town*) and Frederick Brisson to produce the musicals *The Pajama Game, Damn Yankees* and *New Girl in Town,* then with Prince only for *West Side Story, Fiorello!* and *Tenderloin.*

GRI-GRI Operette in 3 acts by Heinrich Bolten-Bäckers based on a play by Henriot [ie, Henri Maigrot] and Jules Chancel. Music by Paul Lincke. Metropoltheater, Cologne, 25 March 1911; Friedrich-Wilhelmstädtisches Theater, Berlin, 2 November 1912.

Gaston Deligny goes to equatorial Africa to purchase the land of the King Foulamer for France and, there, falls for the daughter of one of the monarch's two hundred wives, a lass who has, somehow, been born white. After a brief moment of ''married'' life with the charming Gri-Gri, however, he returns to the Quai d'Orsay and allies himself comfortably with the niece of his Minister. But Gri-Gri and her royal father make their way to Paris in search of the missing husband. The girl takes a very visible job in a music hall and scandal swirls around the internationally bigamous Gaston until, with the final curtain in sight, he returns to his equatorial bride.

The most successful of Lincke's latter-day Operetten, *Gri-Gri* was played for two seasons in Berlin during 1912–13, with Traute Rose starred; given as a wartime entertainment in Vienna (ad August Neidhart) with Susanne Bachrich in the title role of a localized version and Carl Pfann as the Viennese consul, Hans Heinz von Hoheneck (ex- Gaston); produced in Brussels in a version by Marcel Roels (Vieux-Bruxelles 28 April 1917); and in Amsterdam where Beppi de Vries starred as the light-skinned lass from darkest Africa; and ultimately made its way both to Paris—where its text was credited to Chancel, and Gaby Besset starred alongside Serjius and Bever, playing the King in blackface—and even to the German-language Yorkville Theater in New York. A production under the title *Mie-Mie* (ad Harry Graham) was announced for London's Adelphi Theatre in 1920 (variously under Grossmith and Laurillard, and then C B

Cochran), but since anti-German feeling was still strong in the wake of the war, the producer assured the press that American naturalized Englishman Howard Talbot would be redoing the music. Except perhaps for the ensembles. In the end, London didn't get *Gri-Gri* at all.

Austria: Wiener Stadttheater 12 February 1915; France: Gaîté-Rochechouart 6 December 1924; USA: Yorkville Theater (Ger) 26 January 1928

GRIMES, Tammy (b Lynn, Mass, 30 January 1934). Broadway soubrette of the straight and musical stages, who matured into an occasionally musical comedienne.

Miss Grimes stepped in as a stopgap in *Bus Stop,* made her regular Broadway debut in the play *Look After Lulu,* and subsequently mixed musical and straight theatre appearances. She had a false start on the musical scene when the 1955 musical *The Amazing Adele,* in which she played the title role, closed on the road, but she had happier times in the title role of *The Unsinkable Molly Brown* (1960, the first of two Tony Awards), as the ghostly Elvira in *High Spirits* (1964), as the original Dorothy Brock in *42nd Street* (1980) and, off-Broadway, in the one-performance *Sunset* (ex- *Platinum,* 1983) and in the top-billed role of *Mademoiselle Colombe* (1987, Madame Alexandra).

She also appeared in several televised musicals including the Elmer Rice *Holiday* (1956), *Sextuplets* (1956), *The Gift of the Magi* (1958) and the almost musical *The Borrowers* (1973).

GROBECKER, Anna [MEJO, Anna] (b Breslau, 27 July 1829; d Althofen, 27 September 1908).

The daughter of an opera singer and a member of a highly successful family of musical-theatre performers, Anna Mejo made her first stage appearances as a small child in Breslau (*Der Rattenfänger von Hameln*) in a childrens' company directed by her father. She had her first adult role at Magdeburg at the age of 15, and subsequently worked in Leipzig, Berlin, and in Budapest with Nestroy, before making her first appearances in Vienna aged 19, paired with her husband Philipp Grobecker in the Posse *Einmal hunderttausend Thaler* and *Benjamin, der seinen Vater sucht* at Nestroy's Carltheater. Her performances in those pieces led Karl Treumann to choose her to play one of the two gossipy neighbours in his production of *Hochzeit bei Laternenschein,* the first ever German-language performance of an Offenbach work, produced at the same house. She subsequently became a regular in Treumann's Offenbach productions, playing the first Viennese performances as Vasco in *Das Mädchen von Elisonzo,* Antoine in *Die Zaubergeige,* Lischen in *Die Savoyarden,* and as Öffentliche Meinung (L'Opinion Publique) in *Orpheus in der Unterwelt* (1860), in which her husband appeared as the original Orphée.

When Treumann established his own Theater am Franz-Josefs-Kai in late 1860, Grobecker joined him there and during the house's existence appeared as first ''boy'' as, amongst other roles, Daphnis in *Daphnis und Chloë,* Friquet in *Meister Fortunios Liebeslied,* Cascadetto in *Die Seufzerbrücke,* Frincke in Suppé's *Flotte Bursche* and, in skirts, as Martine in Caspers's *Ma Tante dort,* Beatrice in *Die Schwätzerin von Saragossa* (*Les Bavards*), the housekeeper Sidonia in *Zehn Mädchen und kein Mann,* Hedwig in *Die schöne Magellone* (*Geneviève de Brabant*) and Nanette in *Monsieur et Madame Denis.*

She returned to the Carltheater with Treumann in 1862, and appeared there in her most successful roles (Frincke, Friquet, Cascadetto, Daphnis), as well as introducing other opéra-bouffe roles (Pauline in *Pariser Leben,* Nani in *Les Géorgiennes,* Rigobert in *Der Regimentszauberer,* Croûte-au-Pot in *Die Damen der Halle*) and creating roles in several new local shows, including Ganymede in Suppé's *Die schöne Galathee* (1865), the title role in von Zaytz's *Fitzliputzli,* Max in his *Mannschaft an Bord* (1863) and Quint in his *Ein rendezvous in der Schweiz* (1867), Ludwig XV in *Herr von Papillon* and Der Herundhinlaufer in *Die Jungfrau von Dragant.* She retired momentarily in 1867 to wed her second husband, Count Vincente de la Rocca, son of Queen Christina, made a brief return to the stage in 1869–70, but retired definitively in 1871.

Grobecker's popularity and her skill at, in particular, travesty roles led her to be claimed as the ''perfect soubrette,'' ''the queen of the pants parts'' and the equal of the great French actress Déjazet. Offenbach, after hearing her perform, no longer complained at the ravages Treumann had worked on his opérettes in order to fabricate roles for her for, as the director quotably announced, ''wenn die Grobecker nicht dabei ist, ist es nicht lustig genug'' (''it isn't so funny when Grobecker isn't there''). The composer is even said to have tried to persuade the actress to join the Paris Palais-Royal company. In the earliest successful muiscal plays of the modern Austrian stage, Treumann and/or Suppé created the roles of Frincke, Sidonia and Ganymede in *Die schöne Galathee* especially to Anna Grobecker's measure, and she thus helped set the mold for what would be the soubrette of Viennese Operette.

In the Singspiel *Josefine Gallmeyer* (Wiener Bürgertheater, 1921) Grobecker was impersonated by Paula Back.

GROODY, Louise (b Waco, Tex, 26 March 1897; d Canadensis, Pa, 16 September 1961).

A vivacious dancing ingenue, Miss Groody appeared on Broadway first as a chorus dancer and then in supporting roles in *Around the Map* (1915, Gladiola, singing Louis Hirsch's "There's Only One Thing a Coon Can Do"), Jerome Kern's *Toot-Toot!* (1918, Mrs Walter Colt), *Fiddlers Three* (1918, Gilda Varelli) and again for Kern in *The Night Boat* (1920, Barbara) before taking leading parts as the Cinderella heroine with a Bill-Sykes fiancé in the same composer's *Good Morning, Dearie* (1921, Rose-Marie), in which she introduced the title song and joined Harlan Dixon in "Way Down Town" and Oscar Shaw in "Blue Danube Blues," and again in an adaptation of Yvain's *Ta Bouche* (*One Kiss,* 1923), as Eva, the girl who keeps on practicing for the action of her wedding night until parental assent can be obtained for the wedding.

Her major success came when she was brought in to replace Phyllis Cleveland in the title role of *No, No, Nanette* ("I Want to Be Happy," "No, No, Nanette," "Tea for Two") and, after fulfilling its Chicago run, came to Broadway in the title role of Youmans's hit show. She starred again in the composer's next piece, *Hit the Deck* ("Sometimes I'm Happy," "If He'll Come Back to Me"), before disappearing from the musical scene at little more than 30 years of age to reap her rewards in the greenbacked fields of vaudeville.

GROSSMITH, George (i) (b London, 9 December 1847; d Folkestone, 1 March 1912).

George Grossmith began performing in his early twenties, following the example of his father, as a solo entertainer at the piano, and he made his first regular professional appearance—whilst keeping up his day job as a court reporter and shorthand-writer—at the Polytechnic Hall in 1870. He played in London at the Polytechnic with such pieces as *Human Oddities, The Yellow Dwarf, The Silver Wedding, The Bunkum Penny Readings* and *Theatricals at Thespis Lodge,* and subsequently on the road—in tandem with his father, or occasionally with the Howard Pauls—performing *Jottings from the Jetty, Mrs Mayfair at Home, In the Stalls, The Christmas Pantomime, Seven Ages of Song, Our Choral Society* and others. In 1876 he toured a two-handed entertainment, *Entre Nous* in tandem with Florence Marryat, in which he featured a tiny musical duologue adapted from the French (Ernest d'Hervilly's *La Céramique*) as *Cups and Saucers.*

He first crossed paths with author W S Gilbert when he played the role of the Judge in a minor London performance of *Trial by Jury* and, as a result, he was, against considerable protest from the backers, given the leading comic part of John Wellington Wells, the sorcerer of *The Sorcerer,* when Gilbert and Sullivan's first full-length opera was staged at the Opera Comique. His tentativeness and nerves were forgiven by first-night critics who did not, at this time, expect to see anything like a finished performance at a premiere, and Grossmith worked up his part and his courage successfully enough through the run to be retained for the following piece. He created the role of Sir Joseph Porter KCB in *HMS Pinafore* ("When I Was a Lad," "Never Mind the Why and Wherefore") and played the Major General in the London version of *The Pirates of Penzance* ("I Am the Very Model of a Modern Major-General"), and thereafter, confirmed at the very top of the musical-comic profession, created the principal comedy roles in each of the Gilbert and Sullivan works of the next decade—Reginald Bunthorne (*Patience*), the Lord Chancellor (*Iolanthe,* "Nightmare Song," "The Law is the True Embodiment"), King Gama (*Princess Ida,* "If You Give Me Your Attention"), Ko-ko (*The Mikado,* "Tit Willow," "I've Got a Little List"), Robin/Ruthven (*Ruddigore*), and Jack Point (*The Yeomen of the Guard,* "I Have a Song to Sing, O," "A Private Buffoon"), confirming himself in the process as a comic-opera institution and a huge public favorite. Throughout this time he continued to write and perform his solo entertainments, and on several occasions pieces such as *Cups and Saucers, A Musical Nightmare* or *The Silver Wedding* were played as afterpieces on a Carte program.

After *The Yeomen of the Guard,* Grossmith retired from the stage and returned to his old form of entertaining at the piano, purveying such pieces as *Society Up-to-Date, Homburg, or Haunted by the Mikado, The Tide of Fashion* and *Do We Enjoy Our Holidays?* with lucrative results. He toured Britain with his entertainments and in 1892 visited America. On the few occasions where he allowed himself to be lured back to the theatre through family or financial considerations—with *His Excellency* (1894, Governor Griffenfeld), *His Majesty* (1897, Ferdinand V), *The Gay Pretenders* (1900, Lambert Simnel)—his natural nervousness and friability of memory, which he had largely conquered at the Opera Comique and the Savoy, got the better of him and each experience was less and less successful.

Having throughout his career as an entertainer provided himself with monologue material and songs, Grossmith also contributed the music to a number of little operettas of which the most successful was *Mr Guffin's Elopement,* played for many years by J L Toole and including the popular song "The Speakers Eye," and the most substantial a full score for W S Gilbert's unsuccessful musical version of *Un Chapeau de paille d'Italie* as *Haste to the Wedding.* He was also the author of several books, of which *The Diary of a Nobody,* written in collaboration with his brother, Weedon, was the most successful.

Grossmith has been portrayed in several one-man shows, most recently in 1998 at London's Covent Garden

Festival by Eric Roberts as *Gee-Gee* (2 June). **[Walter] Weedon GROSSMITH** (b London, 9 June 1852; d London, 14 June 1919) had a fine career as an actor, and briefly appeared on the musical stage as Leander Tweddle to the Venus of Rosina Vokes in *The Tinted Venus* (1885) and as Lord Arthur Pomeroy in the highly successful one-act musical *A Pantomime Rehearsal* (1891) in which his actress wife **May [Lever] PALFREY** (b 1 May 1873; d 31 October 1929) was also featured. He also authored an autobiography, *From Studio to Stage* (Lane, London, 1913).

1881 **Uncle Samuel** (Arthur Law) 1act Opera Comique 3 May

1882 **Mr Guffin's Elopement** (Law) 1 act Alexandra Theatre, Liverpool 29 September; Toole's Theatre 7 October

1883 **The Drama on Crutches** sketch Savoy Theatre 10 November

1884 **A Peculiar Case** (Law) 1 act St George's Hall 8 December

1885 **The Great Taykin** (Law) 1 act Toole's Theatre 30 April

1888 **The Real Case of Hide and Seekyll** Royalty Theatre 3 September

1892 **Haste to the Wedding** (Gilbert) Criterion Theatre 27 July

Memoirs: *A Society Clown* (J W Arrowsmith, Bristol, 1888), *Piano and I* (J W Arrowsmith, Bristol, 1910); Biography: Joseph, T: *George Grossmith: Biography of a Savoyard* (Arrowsmith/ Joseph, Bristol, 1982)

GROSSMITH, George (ii) (b Haverstock Hill, London, 11 May 1874; d London, 6 June 1935).

The son of the elder George, Grossmith (at this stage labeled, as his father had once been before him, as ''jr'') appeared on the London musical stage for the first time aged 18, in a small comic role in his father's musical *Haste to the Wedding* (1892, Cousin Foodle). He was seen in similarly foppish parts in *The Baroness* (1892, Hamilcar) and in the variety musical *Morocco Bound* (1893), where he built up the small role of Sir Percy Pimpleton with endless ad-libbing until it and he were one of the most prominent features of this most elastic of musical comedies. Similar, if slightly less elastic, roles followed in *Go-Bang* (1894, Hon Augustus Fitzpoop) and for George Edwardes in *A Gaiety Girl* (replacing Fred Kaye as Major Barclay), after which he was taken to the Gaiety Theatre to create the part of the gangling dude Bertie Boyd in *The Shop Girl* (1894). The 21-year-old actor, equipped with a fine song for which he had himself supplied the lyrics, describing himself as ''Beautiful, bountiful Bertie,'' made a considerable hit in both London and New York.

Much of his time in the next years was spent in the straight theatre, but he returned in 1898 to replace Lionel Mackinder in the musical *Little Miss Nobody* (t/o Gussie Stilton) and the following year one of the producers of that piece, Yorke Stephens, staged the burlesque, *Great Caesar,* which Grossmith had written with Paul Rubens and in which he appeared as Mark Antony. The failure of that piece did not deter him, and in his next musical as an author, *The Gay Pretenders* (1900, Prince Harry), he included roles for both himself and his famous father. The results were even less happy.

Grossmith returned to Edwardes's management to succeed G P Huntley in the lead comedy role of *Kitty Grey* on the road, and then moved into town with a part built to his measure in the Gaiety Theatre's *The Toreador* (1901,Sir Archibald Slackitt). Once again he supplied some of his own lyrics (''Archie''), but did best with Paul Rubens's song ''Everybody's Awfully Good to Me.'' He again succeeded Huntley in the comedy role of *The School Girl* (1903, Sir Orsmby St Leger) and subsequently toured America in that piece, but from now on he by and large remained at the Gaiety Theatre, a fixed part of the basic star team through the last decade of Edwardes's management, starring in *The Orchid* (1903, Hon Guy Scrymegour, rewriting Blanche Ring's ''Bedelia'' for himself), *The Spring Chicken* (1905, Gustave Babori), *The New Aladdin* (1906, Genie of the Lamp) , *The Girls of Gottenberg* (1907, Price Otto), *Our Miss Gibbs* (1909, Hon Hughie Pierpoint, interpolating a revised ''Yip-Ay-Addy-I-Ay''), *Peggy* (1911, Auberon Blow) and *The Sunshine Girl* (1912, Lord Bicester). When *Havana,* which he had co-written, was produced at the Gaiety in 1908, he moved to another parallel Edwardes production to play Count Lothar in *A Waltz Dream.*

Grossmith was credited with a hand in the authorship of some of the Gaiety pieces, but always, when it was not a case of a fairly straight adaptation from a French comedy, in collaboration, and it would seem his contribution was principally one of ''putting in the jokes.'' He adapted *Die Dollarprinzessin* for America (but not London) and also co-authored some of London's earliest modern revues, being named in the credits for such pieces as the Empire Theatre's 1908 *Oh! Indeed* (mus: Cuthbert Clarke, ly: CH Bovill), *Come Inside, Hullo . . . London! Everybody's Doing It, Kill That Fly!, Eightpence a Mile, Not Likely, The Bing Boys Are Here* and *The Bing Girls Are There,* in the 1910s.

He appeared on Broadway in the cartoon musical *Fluffy Ruffles* (1908, Hon Augustus Traddles) and in 1913 played in both London and America in *The Girl on the Film* (*Die Kino-Königin*) and, around this same time, went into partnership with producer Edward Laurillard, who had mounted his shortlived musical *The Lovebirds* many years earlier, to himself produce plays and musicals. The first of these latter was the *Pink Dominos* musical *Tonight's the Night,* staged initially in New York and then in London, where Grossmith moved back into ''his'' Gaiety Theatre (1915, Hon Dudley Mitten). The piece was a great success, and over the following years, at first in partnership with Laurillard and later with ex-Gaiety stage manager Pat Malone, Grossmith established himself as a major producing force in the London musical theatre.

He continued at the Gaiety Theatre with a second hit in *Theodore & Co* but, in the power struggles following Edwardes's death, found himself outmaneuvered by Alfred Butt, and was forced to move his operations elsewhere. Of three subsequent Grossmith-mounted successes which the Gaiety could well have done with, *Mr Manhattan* was produced at the Prince of Wales, *Arlette* at the Shaftesbury and *Yes, Uncle!* (1917) again, initially, at the Prince of Wales, before waltzing through three different theatres during its run, whilst the less successful *Oh! Joy* (*Oh, Boy!*) split its run between the Kingsway and the Apollo, before Grossmith completed the construction of his own theatre, the Winter Garden, on the site of the old Middlesex Music Hall in Drury Lane.

Grossmith and Laurillard opened the Winter Garden in 1919 with Grossmith and Leslie Henson starring in *Kissing Time* (Max Touquet), and the theatre established itself as a major West End musical venue with the Grossmith/Laurillard production of *A Night Out* (1920), and the Grossmith/Malone mountings of *Sally* (1921, Otis), *The Cabaret Girl* (1922, Mr Gripps), *The Beauty Prize* (1923, Flutey Warboy), a revival of *Tonight's the Night* (1924, Dudley Mitten), *Primrose* (1924), *Tell Me More!* (1925) and *Kid Boots* (1926) between 1920 and 1926, when diminishing returns led to the the operation being dissolved. *Eastward Ho!* (1919, Alhambra), *Baby Bunting* (1919, Shaftesbury) and *Faust on Toast* (Gaiety, 1921) were amongst the Grossmith/Laurillard productions staged in other venues during this period. Grossmith also had a hand in the writing of the new Winter Garden pieces, and directed many of his own productions.

His busy producing career in the early 1920s did not lessen his performing one and, whilst those shows in which he wasn't appearing were running at the Winter Garden, he played away from home in the London version of *La Reine s'amuse* (*The Naughty Princess*) and with great success as Billy Early in Joe Waller and Herbert Clayton's original British production of *No, No, Nanette* (1925). After the end of his producing days he continued to perform in musicals, playing King Christian II of Elyria in Szirmai's *Princess Charming* (*Alexandra*) for Robert Courtneidge (a role he repeated several years later in New York) and appearing in the same composer's *Lady Mary* (1928, Hatpin Pinge) and in *The Five o'Clock Girl* (1929) at the London Hippodrome. In New York in 1930 he played in Ralph Benatzky's *My Sister and I* (aka *Meet My Sister,* Marquis de Châtelard), which he subsequently persuaded his old partner, Laurillard, to bring to Britain. Grossmith directed and appeared in his New York role for a disastrous eight performances at the Shaftesbury, closing out his West End performing career on an unusual flop some 40 starry years after its beginning.

Plate 159. **George Grossmith** *the younger was ''beautiful, bountiful Bertie''—one of his most popular dude creations—in* The Shop Girl.

He was latterly involved in film productions, spent a brief and fairly hapless time at the head of the Theatre Royal, Drury Lane (*The Land of Smiles, Cavalcade*), and mainatined a connection with show business to his last days.

Grossmith's wife **Adelaide Astor**, one of the five sisters Rudge of whom the most celebrated was Letty Lind, had a good career in supporting roles in both new burlesque (*Carmen Up-to-Data, Ruy Blas and the Blasé Roué, Cinder-Ellen Up Too Late*) and in musical comedy (*The Lady Slavey, Go-Bang, The Shop Girl* [UK and USA], etc).

His younger brother **Lawrence [Randall] GROSSMITH** (b London, 29 March 1877; d Hollywood, Calif, 21 February 1944) followed George onto the stage, where he had a long and successful career, often in roles in the mold established by his brother. He first appeared in 1896 in *Nitouche,* and played in George's short-lived musical *The Lovebirds* (1904, Sir Billie Duffield) at the Savoy, before coming under the wing of George Edwardes for whom he appeared in dude roles in *The White Chrysanthemum* (1905, Lt Chippendale Bennett), *The Girl Behind the Counter* (1906, Viscount Gushington), *Havana* (1908, Don Adolfo) and in his brother's part in *The Girls of Gottenberg.* He also appeared in de Courville's unfortunate Leoncavallo musical *Are You There?* and on Broadway in the revue *About Town* (1906).

After a stint in straight theatre and an unfortunate attempt at management he returned to the musical theatre and appeared in *The Girl in the Taxi* and *The Joy Ride Lady* in London, and in America in the star role of Freddy Popple (created by G P Huntley) in *Nobody Home,* as Count Sergeiy Woronzeff in *Flora Bella* (1916), in *Love o' Mike* (1917, Capt Lord Michael Kildare), and in the revue *Hitchy Koo.* Latterly he played principally in plays and in films (including *The Girl in the Taxi*) as a character Englishman, but he appeared again on the musical stage in New York in *The Cat and the Fiddle* (1931, Major Sir George Wilfred Chatterly) and in London in *Command Performance* (1933, King of Vassau), paired in this last piece with Kate Cutler as the elderly monarchs of the piece.

Lawrence's wife, **Coralie [Maud] BLYTHE** (1880–1928), a sister of Vernon Castle (née Blyth), was a long-term Edwardes employee, mostly as a star understudy and sometimes in substantial soubrette roles in town (Susie in *The Girl Behind the Counter*) and on tour. Her best new metropolitan role was as Césarine in *The Dashing Little Duke.*

George's daughter, **Ena [Sylvia V] GROSSMITH** (b London, 14 August 1896; d London, 20 March 1944) worked largely as a straight actress, but appeared in London in the musicals *Dear Love* (1929, Marie), *Paulette* (1931, Muriel Hope) and *Tulip Time* (1935).

1899 **Great Caesar** (Paul Rubens, Walter Rubens/w Paul Rubens) Comedy Theatre 29 April

1900 **The Gay Pretenders** (Claude Nugent) Globe Theatre 10 November

1901 **Gulliver's Travels** (Augustus Barrett, Oscar Eve) Avenue Theatre 23 December

1904 **The Lovebirds** (Raymond Roze/w Percy Greenbank) Savoy Theatre 10 February

1905 **The Spring Chicken** (Ivan Caryll, Lionel Monckton/Adrian Ross, P Greenbank) Gaiety Theatre 30 May

1906 **Two Naughty Boys** (Constance Tippett/P Greenbank) Gaiety Theatre 8 January

1907 **The Girls of Gottenberg** (Caryll, Monckton/Ross, Basil Hood/w L E Berman) Gaiety Theatre 15 May

1908 **Havana** (Leslie Stuart/Ross/w Graham Hill) Gaiety Theatre 25 April

1908 **That Did It!** (Eustace Burnaby/w Ralph Roberts) 1 act Crouch End Hippodrome 11 May

1909 **The Dollar Princess** (*Die Dollarprinzessin*) American version (Knickerbocker Theater, New York)

1911 **Peggy** (Stuart/C H Bovill) Gaiety Theatre 4 March

1916 **Theodore & Co** (Jerome Kern, Ivor Novello/Ross, Clifford Grey/w H M Harwood) Gaiety Theatre 19 September

1920 **A Night Out** (Willie Redstone/Grey/w Arthur Miller) Winter Garden Theatre 19 September

1922 **The Cabaret Girl** (Kern/w P G Wodehouse) Winter Garden Theatre 19 September

1923 **The Beauty Prize** (Kern/w Wodehouse) Winter Garden Theatre 5 September

1924 **Primrose** (George Gershwin/Desmond Carter, Ira Gershwin/w Guy Bolton) Winter Garden Theatre 11 September

Autobiography: *GG* (Hutchinson, London, 1933); Biography: Naylor, S: *Gaiety and George Grossmith* (Stanley Paul, London, 1913)

GRÜN, Bernhard (b Starc, 11 February 1901; d London, 21 December 1972).

After early studies in law, Grün eventually became a theatre musical director in Prague, Vienna and Berlin. From 1924, for some five years, he held a conducting post at Prague's Deutches Theater and several of his earliest stage pieces were mounted in the small auditorium there. One of these, *Miss Chocolate,* got a subsequent showing at the Établissement Ronacher in Vienna (1 February 1929). His 1930 *Böhmische Musikanten* also made its way to Vienna (Bürgertheater 18 December 1931), as did *Musik um Susi* (Volksoper 2 May 1933), his first piece to be premiered in Berlin. In 1932 he arranged the score of *Freut euch das Lebens* from Johann and Josef Strauss music, and saw it progress from Leipzig to the Vienna Volksoper, whilst his 1934 Strauss pasticcio *Die Tänzerin Fanny Elssler* also found some success beyond Germany, notably in Italy.

He joined the exodus from Germany, and then from Austria, in the 1930s, and ended up in Britain, where he was involved in his one memorable success when he contributed some additional music to the score of George Posford's *Balalaika.* A second piece in the same vein, produced variously as *Paprika* and *Magyar Melody,* flopped utterly and twice, and his theatrical writing activity thereafter was largely limited to pasticcio work on such composers as Chopin for *Waltz without End* (1942), Offenbach for *Can-Can* (1943) and Dvořák for *Summer Song* (1956), or as the accomplice of Eric Maschwitz in "re-arrangements" of classic Operette scores designed for the amateur market.

He published a number of books, including several on the musical theatre—*Prince of Vienna: The Life of Oscar Straus* (1955), *Kulturgeschichte der Operette* (Munich, 1961) and *Gold und Silber: Franz Lehár und seine Zeit* (Munich, 1970), composed many radio and film scores and found a song success with the number "Broken Wings" (1952 w John Jerome).

1923 **Onkel Perl**

1924 **Der grosse David**

1926 **Mama vom Ballett** (ad Rudolf Stadler, Ernst Stadler) Deutsches Theater, Prague 20 February

1927 **Miss Chocolate** (Hans Regina Nack, R Stadler) Deutsches Theater, Prague 19 March

1928 **Olga von der Wolga** (Nack) Neues Deutsches Theater, Prague 28 January

1928 **Abenteuer in Schottland** (Paul Frank, Peter Herz) Neues Deutsches Theater, Prague 25 December

1930 **Böhmische Musikanten** (Herz, Julius Wilhelm) Neues Operettentheater, Leipzig 30 October

1931 **Amelie**

1932 **Freut euch das Lebens** (Johann Strauss, Josef Strauss arr/Nestroy ad Wilhelm, Herz) Neues Operettentheater, Leipzig 24 October

1932 **Musik um Susi** (Frank, Herz) Komische Oper, Berlin 12 November

1932 **Marlenes Brautfahrt** (Nack, Max Bertusch) Landestheater, Wiesbaden 26 December

1934 **Die Tänzerin Fanny Elssler** (Johann Strauss arr w Oskar Stalla/Hans Adler) Deutsches Theater, Berlin 22 December

1935 **Wo die liebe blüht** (Arnold Golz, Emil Golz) Wiener Komödienhaus 20 April

1935 **Gaby Deslys**

1936 **Balalaika** revised *The Gay Hussar* (w George Posford/Eric Maschwitz) Adelphi Theatre, London 22 December

1937 **Madame Sans-Gêne** (Hans Weigel) Theater an der Wien, Vienna 1 September

1938 **Paprika** (aka *Magyar Melody*) (w Posford/Maschwitz) His Majesty's Theatre, London 15 September

1942 **Waltz without End** (Frederic Chopin arr/Maschwitz) Cambridge Theatre 29 September

1943 **Old Chelsea** (w Richard Tauber/Fred Salo Tysh/Walter Ellis) Prince's Theatre 17 February

1946 **Can-Can** (Jacques Offenbach arr/Tysh/Max Catto) Adelphi Theatre 8 May

1956 **Summer Song** (Anton Dvořák arr/Maschwitz, Hy Kraft) Prince's Theatre 16 February

GRÜNBAUM, Fritz (b Brünn, 7 April 1880; d Dachau, 14 January 1941). Author for the Viennese silver-age theatre.

Grünbaum studied law in Vienna, but he soon switched his attentions to the theatrical world, working as a cabaret performer and stand-up comic, and writing for all areas of the stage. He scored an important success in the Operette world with his contribution to the text of *Die Dollarprinzessin* (1907), had a second success with the libretto and lyrics for Ziehrer's *Liebeswalzer,* and scored a third major hit with the Hungarian tale of *Der Zigeunerprimás* (1912) before becoming an army officer for the duration of the First World War. This commission did not, however, prevent him performing his *Humoristische Vorträge* on the bill at the Apollotheater at the height of the hostilities. He emerged from the War with a decoration and credits for both a number of patriotic war songs and a further handful of Operetten, which had been mounted in Berlin, Vienna and Budapest whilst he had been in uniform.

After the war, Grünbaum kept up his wide spread of theatrical activities. He spent a period running a cabaret in Berlin, supplied material for revues in Berlin and in Vienna—notably at the Apollotheater, teaming with composers including Benatzky, Richard Fall, Fritz Lehner and Rudolf Nelson (whose one prewar Operette hit, *Miss Dudelsack,* he had co-authored)—wrote cabaret material and lyrics for popular songs, and at the same time continued to produce a regular flow of Operetten. However, although pieces such as *Die Csikós-Baroness,* which made its way from Hamburg to Berlin and then further afield, the little *Dorine und der Zufall, Des Königs Nachbarin,* and the Revue-Operette *Journal der Liebe* found some success, he did not ever again approach the level of his two big prewar hits.

His name had ceased to appear on playbills by the Second World War, when the 60-year-old writer was imprisoned in Dachau. He died there.

1906 **Phryne** (Edmund Eysler/w Robert Bodanzky) 1 act Hölle 6 October

1906 **Peter und Paul reisen ins Schlaraffenland** (Franz Lehár/w Bodanzky) Theater an der Wien 1 December

1907 **Mitislaw der Moderne** (Lehár/w Bodanzky) 1 act Hölle 5 January

1907 **Brigantino** (Béla Lazsky) 1 act Hölle 19 April

1907 **Die Dollarprinzessin** (Leo Fall/w A M Willner) Theater an der Wien 2 November

1908 **Principessa** (Rudolf Nelson/w Georg Burghard) Residenztheater, Frankfurt-am-Main 1 May

1908 **Liebeswalzer** (Carl Michael Ziehrer/w Bodanzky) Raimundtheater 24 October

1908 **Madame Flirt** (Anselm Götzl/w Heinz Reichert) Neues Operettentheater, Hamburg 25 December

1909 **Miss Dudelsack** (Nelson/w Reichert) Neues Schauspielhaus, Berlin 3 August

1910 **Die teuerste Frau von Paris** (Leo Schottländer/w Reichert) 1 act Bellevue Theater, Stettin 13 November

1910 **Der ledige Gatte** (Gustav Wanda/w Reichert) Residenztheater, Dresden ?28 October

1910 **Don Quichotte** (Richard Heuberger/w Reichert) 1 act Hölle 1 December

1911 **Die weisse Fahne** (Josef Strauss arr Oskar Stalla) 1 act Hölle 18 November

1912 **Der Zigeunerprimás** (Emmerich Kálmán/w Julius Wilhelm) Johann Strauss-Theater 11 October

1912 **Der Frechling** (Carl Weinberger/w Reichert) Wiener Bürgertheater 21 December

1913 **Leute vom Stand** (Richard Fall/w Bodanzky) 1 act Hölle 1 March

1913 **Die Prinzenjagd** (Ludwig Friedmann/w Reichert) Residenztheater, Dresden 4 April

1914 **Anno 14, drei Bildern aus unsern Tagen** (Ralph Benatzky/w Benatzky) Kabarett Rideamus, Berlin 22 September

1914 **General Wutzikoff** (Benatzky) 1 act Budapester Orfeum 1 December

1916 **Der Favorit** (Robert Stolz/w Wilhelm Sterk) Komische Oper, Berlin 7 April

1916 **Mein Annerl** (Georg Jarno/w Sterk) Carltheater 7 October

1917 **Die Puppenbaronessen** (R Fall/w Alexander Engel) Apollotheater 1 September

1918 **Wenn Wien wieder walzt** (Fritz Lehner) February

1918 **Das Busserlschloss** (Stolz) 1 act Ronacher 1 August

1918 **Der rote Graf** (Paul Pallos) 1 act Ronacher 3 September

1918 **Eine einzige Rettung** (Gustav Benedict/w Reichert) Bellevue Theater, Stettin 30 July

1919 **Vox populi** (Otto Stransky) Ronacher 1 April

1919 **Die Csikós-Baroness** (Jarno) Neues Operettentheater, Hamburg 28 October

1921 **Der Frauenräuber** (Kurt Zorlig/w Herbert Steineck) Friedrich-Wilhelmstädtisches Theater, Berlin 23 December

1922 **Dorine und der Zufall** (Jean Gilbert/w Sterk) Neues Theater am Zoo, Berlin 15 September

1923 **Des Königs Nachbarin** (Leon Jessel/w Sterk) Wallner-Theater, Berlin 15 April

1926 **Journal der Liebe** (Egon Neumann/w Karl Farkas) Wiener Bürgertheater 29 January

1926 **Ich und Du** (Lamberto Pavanelli/w Sterk) Neues Deutsches Theater, Prague 28 November

1926 **Das tanzende Märchen** (K Steininger/w Farkas) 8 December

1927 **Meine Tochter Otto** (Jessel/w Sterk) Rolandbühne 5 May

1927 **Rosen aus Schiras** (Frank Stafford/w Sterk) Johann Strauss-Theater 24 June

1930 **Tschun-Tschi** (J Gardener, Anna May Wong/ad w Jacobson) Volksoper 14 August

1931 **Der Traum-Express** (Robert Katscher/w Farkas, Géza Herceg) Theater an der Wien 5 June

1937 **Sie, Johann . . . !** (P Weiss/w E Behrendt, Hans Lengsfelder, Siegfried Tisch) Volksoper 16 April

GRUNDY, Sydney (b Manchester, 23 March 1848; d London, 4 July 1914).

The son of a mayor of Manchester and a barrister in his native town until he was 28 years of age, Grundy made his first venture into theatrical writing with a version of Scribe and Duveyrier's *Oscar, ou le mari qui trompe sa femme* as *The Snowball* (1879) and subsequently became one of London's most popular playwrights with such pieces as *A Pair of Spectacles* (*Les Petits Oiseaux*), *Esther Sandraz* (*La Femme de glace*) and *The Bells of Hazelmere.*

In the early part of his career he also translated Meilhac and Millaud's text to *La Cosaque* for Kate Santley and collaborated on several musical theatre pieces with composer Edward Solomon. Following Solomon's success with *The Nautch Girl* at the Savoy, the most successful of these, *The Vicar of Bray,* was revived there by D'Oyly Carte. Grundy worked on the updating of the piece and found himself offered the next Savoy text—with Arthur Sullivan as his musical partner. The resulting *Haddon Hall,* more staid than usual Savoy fare, had a reasonable life but Grundy, after replying humorously to the critics who had in effect complained that he had not attempted to imitate Gilbert's style, was nevertheless not tempted to return again to the musical theatre.

Shortly before his death, however, he became, perhaps unwittingly, the author of another ''musical farcical comedy'' when Carrie Moore appeared in Melbourne, Australia, in *Much Married* (Bijou Theatre 5 July). Grundy's play was decorated with a long list of songs, including Eysler's *Bruder Straubinger* hit ''Kissing Is No Sin,'' ''The Chocolate Major,'' ''It Isn't Funny but It's True,'' ''Mr Shadow Man'' and an exasperated piece called ''Bury Alexander's Band!''

1880 **Popsy Wopsy** (Edward Solomon) 1 act Royalty Theatre 4 October

1882 **The Vicar of Bray** (Solomon) Globe Theatre 22 July

1884 **La Cosaque** English version (Royalty Theatre)

1884 **Pocahontas** (Solomon) Empire Theatre 26 December

1892 **Haddon Hall** (Arthur Sullivan) Savoy Theatre 24 September

GRÜNWALD, Alfred (b Vienna, 16 February 1884; d Forest Hills, NY, 24 February 1951). One of the most successful librettist/lyricists of the Viennese 20th-century stage.

Long a theatre critic on *Neues Wiener Journal,* Grünwald led parallel careers as a journalist and a theatrical writer. In a pairing, established from his early twenties, with actor-writer Julius Brammer, he at first worked on small musical and non-musical pieces for studio and variety theatres, but the pair had an immediate success when they moved into writing full-length musical plays, scoring initial hits with *Die Dame in Rot, Hoheit tanzt Walzer* and *Der lachende Ehemann,* continuing with the rewrite of Lehár's *Der Göttergatte* as *Die ideale Gattin,* and peaking with a collaboration with Leo Fall on *Die Kaiserin* and on the megahit of the war years, *Die Rose von Stambul* (1916).

The collaborators ran up an amazing series of hit or near-hit shows in the years that followed—*Der letzte Walzer, Die Bajadere, Die Perlen der Cleopatra, Gräfin Mariza, Die Zirkusprinzessin, Die gold'ne Meisterin, Das Veilchen vom Montmartre*—with Grünwald only rarely taking time out to collaborate with other authors, but there too finding success (*Mädi*), before the duo separated, after some 20 years of communal work, at the beginning of the 1930s. Grünwald went on to further success, at first adapting the Hungarian texts of Pál Ábrahám's most successsful Operetten, then providing him with original texts for his later pieces, and, most successfully, adapting Louis Verneuil's play *Le Fauteuil* (1923) as the libretto to Oscar Straus's *Eine Frau, die weiss, was sie will* for *Die Kaiserin* star Fritzi Massary.

In 1940 Grünwald fled the Second World War to America, and he ultimately became an American citizen, but although he worked there on much in the way of translation, notably Americanizing German wartime songs for the OWI, he got his name on only one Broadway show, an unfortunate attempt to produce a Johann Strauss biomusical without Strauss music called *Mr Strauss Goes to Boston,* for which he and Géza Herczeg were credited with ''based on an original story by.'' During the 1950s, however, he saw his name appear again on several fresh pieces on Continental playbills, first when Oscar Straus set the old libretto of *Bozena,* then when the Berne Stadttheater mounted Kálmán's ''American'' Operette *Arizona Lady* and, one last time, when Juan Cardona's *Fiesta,* like the previous piece written with fellow transatlantic exile Gustav Beer, was produced in Munich.

1907 **Fräulein Sherlock Holmes** (Georges Criketown/as ''A G Wald'' w Julius Brammer) Volkstheater, Munich 31 August

1908 **Die grüne Redoute** (Leo Ascher/w Brammer) 1 act Danzers Orpheum 26 March

1908 **Die lustigen Weiber von Wien** (Robert Stolz/w Brammer) 1 act Colosseum 16 November

1908 **Die kleine Manicure** (Ascher/ad w Brammer) 1 act Parisiana

1909 **Elektra** (Béla Laszky/w Brammer) 1 act Kabarett Fledermaus 1 December

1910 **Georgette** (Laszky/w Brammer) 1 act Kabarett Fledermaus 16 March

1910 **Vindobona, du herrliche Stadt** (Leo Ascher/w Brammer) Venedig in Wien 22 July

1911 **Das goldene Strumpfband** (Ascher/w Brammer) 1 act Ronacher 1 May

1911 **Die Dame in Rot** (Robert Winterberg/w Brammer) Theater des Westens, Berlin 16 September

1911 **Das Damenparadies** (Richard Fall/w Brammer) 1 act Wiener Colosseum 1 November

1912 **Hoheit tanzt Walzer** (Ascher/w Brammer) Raimundtheater 24 February

1912 **Eine vom Ballet** (*The Dancing Viennese*) (Oscar Straus/w Brammer) London Coliseum 2 June

1913 **Der lachende Ehemann** (Edmund Eysler/w Brammer) Bürgertheater 19 March

1913 **Die ideale Gattin** (Lehár/w Brammer) Theater an der Wien 11 October

1915 **Die schöne Schwedin** (Winterberg/w Brammer) Theater an der Wien 30 January

1915 **Die Kaiserin** (Leo Fall/w Brammer) Metropoltheater, Berlin 16 October

1916 **Fürstenliebe** revised *Die Kaiserin* Carltheater 1 February

1916 **Die Rose von Stambul** (Fall/w Brammer) Theater an der Wien 2 December

1917 **Bruder Leichtsinn** (Ascher/w Julius Brammer) Wiener Bürgertheater 28 December

1919 **Dichterliebe** (Mendelssohn arr Emil Stern/w Brammer) Komische Oper, Berlin 20 December

1920 **Der Sperrsechserl** (Stolz/w Robert Blum) Komödienhaus 1 April

1920 **Der letzte Walzer** (Straus/w Brammer) Berliner Theater, Berlin 12 February

1921 **Die Tangokönigin** revised *Die ideale Gattin* Apollotheater 9 September

1921 **Die Bajadere** (Kálmán/w Brammer) Carltheater 23 December

1923 **Mädi** (Stolz/w Leo Stein) Berliner Theater, Berlin 1 April

1923 **Die Perlen der Cleopatra** (Straus/w Brammer) Theater an der Wien 17 November

1924 **Gräfin Mariza** (Kálmán/w Brammer) Theater an der Wien 28 February

1926 **Die Zirkusprinzessin** (Kálmán/w Brammer) Theater an der Wien 26 March

1927 **Die gold'ne Meisterin** (Eysler/w Brammer) Theater an der Wien 13 September

1928 **Die Herzogin von Chicago** (Kálmán/w Brammer) Theater an der Wien 5 April

1929 **Marietta** German version (Theater an der Wien)

1930 **Das Veilchen vom Montmartre** (Kálmán/w Brammer) Johann Strauss-Theater 21 March

1930 **Viktoria und ihr Husar** (*Viktória*) German version w Fritz Löhner-Beda (Theater an der Wien)

1931 **Die Blume von Hawaii** (Pal Ábrahám/Imre Földes ad w Löhner-Beda) Neues Theater, Leipzig 24 July; Metropoltheater, Berlin 29 August

1932 **Eine Frau, die weiss, was sie will** (Straus) Metropoltheater, Berlin 1 September

1932 **Venus in Seide** (Stolz/w Ludwig Herzer) Stadttheater, Zürich 10 December

1932 **Ball im Savoy** (Ábrahám/w Löhner-Beda) Grosses Schauspielhaus, Berlin 23 December

1934 **Marchen im Grand-Hotel** (Ábrahám/w Löhner-Beda) Theater an der Wien 29 March

1934 **Die verliebte Königin** (*A szerelmes királynő*) German version w Löhner-Beda (Scala-Theater)

1935 **Das Walzerparadies** (Straus) Scala Theater 15 February

1935 **Dschainah, das Mädchen aus dem Tanzhaus** (Ábrahám/w Beda) Theater an der Wien 20 December

1937 **Roxy und ihr Wunderteam** (Ábrahám/László Szilágyi, Dezső Kellér ad w Hans Weigel) Theater an der Wien 25 March

1937 **Polnische Hochzeit** (Josef Beer/w Löhner-Beda) Stadttheater, Zürich 3 April

1952 **Bozena** (Oscar Straus/w Brammer) Theater am Gärtnerplatz, Munich 16 May

1954 **Arizona Lady** (Kálmán/w Gustav Beer) Stadttheater, Berne 14 February

1955 **Fiesta** (Juan Cardona/w Beer) Theater am Gärtnerplatz, Munich 11 February

Biography: Grünwald, H: *Ein Walzer muss es sein* (Überreuter, Vienna, 1991)

GUÉTARY, Georges [WORLOOU, Lambros] (b Alexandria, Egypt, 8 February 1915; d Mougins, 13 September 1997). Handsome tenor who created a number of successful musical theatre roles in nearly a half-century career in all media.

After an early working life as an accountant, Guétary made his first appearances as a vocalist with Jo Bouillon's orchestra and then worked, for a number of years, on the French music halls. His first stage performances were in revue, and in the isolated musical comedy *La Course d'amour* (1942), but although he starred in France in the film *Le Cavalier noir* (1945) he did not find theatrical fame until he went to London to feature as the romantic Frenchman who wooed Lizbeth Webb in *Bless the Bride* (1947, "This Is My Lovely Day," "A Table for Two," "Ma Belle Marguerite"). He next appeared, in Paris, in the title role of the successful Francis Lopez musical spectacular *Pour Don Carlos* (1950) at the Châtelet ("C'est l'amour," "Je suis un Bohémien") and subsequently went to America where he filmed *An American in Paris* (1950) and played on Broadway in a German role in the unsuccessful *Arms and the Girl* (1950, Franz).

On his return home, he teamed up with Bourvil and Annie Cordy for the enormously successful Parisian musical comedy *La Route fleurie* (1952, Jean-Pierre) and starred in the French version of the film of Strauss's *Der Zigeunerbaron* (1954), but another American visit, in 1958, ended with the three performances of *Portofino.* He had to return to France for further stage success, starring with Bourvil again in the unpretentious and long-running musical comedy *Pacifico* (1958), paired with Jean Richard in the *Some Like It Hot* musical *La Polka des Lampions* (1961), in Charles Aznavour's *Monsieur Carnaval* (1965), at the Mogador as *Monsieur Pompadour* (1971), and in a musical version of *Tom Jones* (1974, Squire Allworthy).

Thirty-three years after his first Francis Lopez creation he returned for two more—*Aventure à Monte-Carlo* (1981) and *L'Amour à Tahiti* (1983)—then starred in *Hourra Papa* (1984), in Lopez's *Carnaval aux Caraïbes* (1985) and his *Le Roi du Pacifique* (1986) before announcing his retirement in his 71st year on the grounds that "opérette is not what it was." Given the inexorably downward quality-curve of his vehicles, the comment was understandable.

GUITRY, Sacha [GUITRY, Alexandre Georges Pierre] (b St Petersburg, 21 February 1885; d Paris, 24 July 1957).

The celebrated "boulevardier" of the Paris theatre was the author, more often than not the star, and sometimes also the producer of a highly successful series of crisply literate and classy light comedies, revues and musical plays during nearly half a century in the theatre. The most significant of his musical pieces, musically illustrated by some of the most elegant composers of his time, were manufactured to feature the light comedy and outstanding soprano gifts of one of his five wives, the actress and vocalist Yvonne Printemps. *L'Amour masqué* (music by Messager), *Mozart* (Hahn) and *Mariette* (Oscar Straus) all won productions around the world after their Parisian successes, and his one rather atypical, straight-up opérette (without Mlle Printemps), the period piece *Florestan 1er,* with music by filmland's Werner Richard Heymann, also had a respectable Paris run.

Songs and incidental music were also inserted into others of his plays, in various amounts, mostly to permit Mlle Printemps to have a sing. Messager provided the music for his hit play *Deburau,* whilst the four-act comedy *Jean de la Fontaine* contained a musical program which took in three pieces by Lully and one by Gilles Durant, set with words by Guitry, as well as orchestral pieces by Glück, Haydn, Rameau and Lully. Guitry's wide-ranging musical theatre work also included revues, some written with Albert Willemetz, for the Palais-Royal, the Théâtre du Vaudeville, the Étoile, the Édouard VII and the Madeleine, as well as—at the other end of the scale of grandeur—a féerie, *Charles Lindbergh,* for the vast Théâtre du Châtelet (1928).

Guitry was, slightly improbably, portrayed on film in *Si Versailles m'etait conté* by the comedian Bourvil.

1902 **Le Page** (Ludo Ratz) 1 act Théâtre des Mathurins 15 April

1909 **Tell père, Tell fils** (Tiarko Richepin) 1 act Théâtre Mévisto 17 April

1923 **L'Amour masqué** (André Messager) Théâtre Édouard VII 15 February

1925 **Mozart** (Reynaldo Hahn) Théâtre Édouard VII 2 December

1928 **Mariette, ou comment écrire l'histoire** (Oscar Straus) Théâtre Édouard VII 1 October

1931 **La SADMP** (Louis Beydts) 1 act Théâtre Madeleine 4 November

1933 **O, mon bel inconnu** (Hahn) Théâtre des Bouffes-Parisiens 12 October

1933 **Florestan 1er, Prince de Monaco** (Werner Richard Heymann/Albert Willemetz) Théâtre des Variétés 8 December

Memoirs: *Souvenirs, ou si j'ai bonne mémoire* (1943), *Toutes réflexions faites* (1947); Biographies: Lorcey, J: *Sacha Guitry* (La Table Ronde, Paris, 1971), Benjamin, R: *Sacha Guitry, roi du théâtre* (1933), Madis, A: *Sacha* (1957), Harding, J: *Sacha*

Guitry, the Last Boulevardier (Methuen, London, 1968), Gidel, H: *Les deux Guitry* (Grandes Biographies Flammarion, Paris, 1995), Santi, D: *Sacha Guitry: 50 ans de spectacle* (Le Livre de Poche, Paris, 1982), etc

GÜL BABA Zenés színjáték (musical comedy) in 3 acts by Ferenc Martos. Music by Jenő Huszka. Király Színház, Budapest, 9 December 1905.

Jenő Huszka's third hit show, after *Bob herceg* and *Aranyvirág,* and one of the most successful Hungarian musical plays of its period, *Gül Baba* helped to give a further impetus to the then speeding-up Hungarian operett tradition. It has remained in the repertoire in its native country over the nearly a century since its initial showing, without making any impression beyond.

Gül Baba (József Németh), the saintly guardian of the sacred roses, goes to the Pasha, Kuksuk Ali (Ernő Mïhályi), to beg forgiveness for the young Gábor (Lenke Szentgyörgyi), who has been condemned to death. His crime was that, in order to meet and speak secretly with Gül Baba's daughter, Leila (Biri Kazal), he climbed the wall into the house and damaged the sacred flowers. His real crime, of course, is simply that he sought to see Leila, for the Pasha has his own eyes set on the daughter of the old guardian. Gül Baba tricks the overlord into himself destroying some of the plants and he is, thus, obliged both to withdraw the sentence on his young rival and permit a happy ending. Kornél Sziklai played the other principal role of Mujkó, Gábor's gypsy musician companion.

The largest part of Huszka's score fell to the leading juvenile man, originally played in travesty by a soprano but in modern times given to a tenor, with his opening song ''Rászállt a galambom a budai várra,'' a song on his conviction (''Az utolsó kívánságom''), a second-act drinking song (''A kulacsom kotyogós'') and the third-act ''Szállj, szállj, sóhajom'' being the featured solos. The heroine had a ''song of the Turkish woman's fate'' to add to her first-act entrance, Mujkó had numbers in each of the last two acts, and the Pasha a single spot, alongside a regulation amount of ensemble and dance music which took fine advantage of the Turkish settings.

After its original run, *Gül Baba* was revived regularly in Budapest, notably at the Fővárosi Operettszínház in 1941 (14 February) with Irma Patkós (Gábor), Kálmán Latabár (Mujkó), Biri Szondy (Leila) and György Solthy (Gül Baba), and in more recent times, televised.

Recording: selections (Qualiton)

GUNN, Michael [Ralph] (b Dublin, 1840; d London, 17 October 1901).

Originally partners in their father's Dublin music publishing firm of M Gunn & Sons, Michael Gunn and his brother, John (d 1877), built and from 1871 operated Dublin's Gaiety Theatre. From 1874 they also took over the running of the Theatre Royal in the same town. Whilst taking in the 1876 *Grande-Duchesse* and *Trial by Jury* tour sent out by Richard D'Oyly Carte, Gunn became firm friends with the young producer, and he subsequently went into a fairly silent partnership with him, providing much of the finance to produce the early Gilbert and Sullivan shows and, later, to build the Savoy Theatre and Hotel. On a couple of occasions Gunn himself ventured as a producer, buying up the rights to the works of Edward Solomon and Henry Pottinger Stephens with the hope of establishing a second Gilbert and Sullivan team, and staging Offenbach's *Belle Lurette* at the Avenue Theatre, in neither case with marked success. Gunn's connection with Carte was instrumental in his young cousin, George Edwardes, pursuing the early part of his theatrical career at the Opera Comique and Savoy Theatres.

Gunn's celebratedly beautiful wife, **Bessie SUDLOW** [Barbara Elizabeth JOHNSTONE] (b Liverpool, 22 July 1849; d Steyning, 28 January 1928), was a member of Lydia Thompson's blondes (1869), a prominent member of the Niblo's Garden company in New York (1870–73, Carline in *The Black Crook,* Fidelio in *Leo and Lotos,* Columbia/Queen Mab in *The Children in the Wood*), and an opéra-bouffe soprano in Britain (Césarine in *Fleur de thé* 1875, and a member of Carte's 1876 touring company playing Müller in *The Duke's Daughter,* Lange in *La Fille de Madame Angot,* Plaintiff in *Trial by Jury,* Paul in *La Grande-Duchesse* and the lead role of Carte's own *Happy Hampstead*) prior to her marriage and retirement. She maintained possession of the Gaiety Theatre, Dublin, until 1909.

Their elder daughter Haidée Gunn was an actress; whilst the elder John's son, **John [Francis] GUNN** (d Sydney, 19 October 1909), became the Gunn of the Australian musical-comedy producing firm of [Sir Rupert] Clarke, Gunn and [Claude] Meynell, married the musical-comedy actress **Hilda CORAL** [Hilda HALLECK], and was the father of Gladys Gunn, later to be the second Mrs Leslie Henson.

GUNNING, Louise (b Brooklyn, NY, 1 April 1879; d Sierra Madre, Calif, 24 July 1960). Attractive, red-haired soprano who played several important Broadway leads in the prewar years.

Miss Gunning, a pastor's daughter from Brooklyn, first appeared on the stage as a chorus singer, then as a Scots vocalist in concert and in variety programs. She made her earliest musical comedy appearances in *The Circus Girl* and in Hoyt's farce comedies *A Stranger in New York* (1898, Fairy Storey), *A Milk White Flag* (March 1898) and *A Day and a Night* (1898, Annette

Winner) and in a featured singing spot in *The Rogers Brothers in Wall Street* (1899, Patrice Rafferty), each time singing those same Scots songs, and as Violet in *The Chaperons* (with a song) before she moved up to more important roles. She played the principal juvenile part of Arabella in De Wolf Hopper's Broadway production of *Mr Pickwick* (1902), appeared opposite Frank Daniels in *The Office Boy* (1903, Euphemia), and subsequently featured alongside Ernestine Schumann-Heinck in the opera star's dip into the musical theatre in *Love's Lottery* (1904, Laura Skeffington), replaced Ruth Vincent in the title role of *Véronique,* and supplied the singing values in Kerker's *The White Hen* (1906–7, Pepi Glöckner).

In 1908 she took up another Ruth Vincent role, when she starred with Van Rensslaer Wheeler in Broadway production of Edward German's *Tom Jones* (Sophia), and followed this with the title role of the Luders/Pixley *Marcelle,* but she turned to another imported show for the kind of role which suited her best when she appeared opposite Robert Warwick as Princess Stephanie in *The Balkan Princess* (1911). Later the same year, she played alongside Henry Dixey, De Wolf Hopper, Eugene Cowles and Marie Cahill as Josephine in a starry revival of *HMS Pinafore* at the Casino Theater.

In 1913 she starred in Sousa's short-lived *The American Maid* (Annabel Vandeveer) but was seen just once more, in a revival of *Forty-Five Minutes from Broadway,* before quitting the stage.

GÜNTHER, Mizzi (b Warnsdorf, 8 February 1879; d Vienna, 18 March 1961). One of the most memorable stars of the 20th-century Viennese Operette stage.

Mizzi Günther began her stage career working in Brünn and came to notice in Vienna in 1901 when she appeared as O Mimosa San in a revival of *Die Geisha* at the Theater an der Wien and the Carltheater. Later the same year, she was star-billed as Lotti, the heroine of the Carltheater's *Die drei Wünsche* (1901), and she followed up as the hard-done-by circus waif, Suzon, in Louis Ganne's *Circus Malicorne* (1901), as the saucy Coralie in a revival of *Das verwunschene Schloss,* and as Nina Brunet, the wife who turns actress, in *Die Debutantin,* before scoring her first major hit in a new role as Lola Winter, the sweet maid of the title of Reinhardt's *Das süsse Mädel* (1901), introducing the tune of the year, ''Das ist das süsse Mädel.''

Günther had a second memorable new role when she created the juvenile lead role of Suza in Lehár's *Der Rastelbinder* (1902) alongside Louis Treumann, and, in the two following seasons, she played opposite Klára Küry as Katharina II in *Der kleine Gunstling,* in the 3 performances of *Der Glücklichste* (Fatime), co-starred with Treumann in a revival of *Apajune der Wassermann* (Natalitza), played the 13 performances of *Der Mameluck* (Miliora), Alkmene in *Der Göttergatte* (1904), Flora Stiebelli, the soubrette of the successful *Das Veilchenmädel,* and the 19 performances of the German Burlesque-Operette *'s Zuckersgoscherl* (Mary Parsley).

By now, after several years of sharing top roles with Marie Halton and Betty Stojan, she had established herself as the Carltheater's leading lady, and she had also established a regular partnership with light-comedy, light-baritone, leading man Treumann. They starred together in *Der Schätzmeister,* she as the singer, Mary Elliott, and he in the title role, in *Der Schnurrbart* (Countess Rolly von Gumpenburg) and in the short-lived *Kaisermanöver* (Jolán), and she also appeared, without him, for 21 nights in *Der Polizeichef* (Erminia) before the arrival of megastar Alexander Girardi at the Carltheater changed the house's production policy, and the Treumann-Günther partnership decamped to Girardi's old house, the Theater an der Wien.

They made their first appearances there in Ascher's *Vergeltsgott* (Jessie) and were then cast in the lead roles of its successor, *Die lustige Witwe* (1905). Günther's creation of the role of Hanna Glawari, the ''merry widow,'' turned her from a star into a superstar, and she carried that superstardom on through a whole series of creations in the years that followed, beginning with the self-made Mädel, Alice in *Die Dollarprinzessin* (1907), *Der Mann mit den drei Frauen* (1908, Lori) and *Der schöne Gardist* (Dorothea von Waldburghausen) at the Theater an der Wien. Günther and Treumann crossed to the Johann Strauss-Theater to create the lead roles of Lehár's *Das Fürstenkind* (1909, Mary Ann) and she followed up there as Melitta in *Das erste Weib* (1910), Lolotte Boncourt in *Die Sirene* (1911) and Ella in *Die romantische Frau,* before returning once more to the Theater an der Wien.

In her first season back, Günther appeared in *Die schöne Helena, Das Fürstenkind, Die schöne Risette,* passed the 500th performance of *Die lustige Witwe,* played Gabrielle in *Pariser Leben,* and created the role of Eva in the good run of Lehár's *Eva* (1911), once again playing alongside Treumann. The pair were again seen together in *Der blaue Held* (Helene) and *Der kleine König* (1912, Anita Montarini), but Günther starred opposite Otto Storm as Reinhardt's *Prinzess Gretl* (1913) and as Dolly in *Die ideale Gattin* (which she had previously sung as *Der Göttergatte*), and appeared as Dolly Doverland in *Endlich allein* (1914) opposite the more genuinely tenorizing Hubert Marischka.

In 1915 she moved again to the Johann Strauss-Theater to create the role of Sylva Varescu in *Die Csárdásfürstin* (1915) and, whilst Betty Fischer moved from the Raimundtheater to take up the prima-donna spot at the Theater an der Wien, Günther followed the long run of

Csárdásfürstin with *Liebe im Schnee* (1916, Gertrud), Straus's *Nachtfalter* (1917, Lona Valletti) and, back with Treumann, the little *Der Millionendieb* (1918, Rosannah) at Ronacher. She had a further success when she created Fürstin Alexandra Maria in *Die Faschingsfee* (1917) at the Johann Strauss-Theater, before returning to the Theater an der Wien to star as Die Fremde Dame in Hermann Dostal's version of the *Official Wife* tale, *Nimm mich mit!* (1919).

After 20 years as a leading lady, some Operette leading-lady roles were now not wholly suitable for the no-longer-juvenile star, but there were others which were. She added another fine creation to her remarkable list as Katja in *Katja, die Tänzerin* (1923) and appeared at the top of the bill in *Pusztaliebchen* (1923, Rosemarie), but, if the greatest part of her career as a star was now over, she was far from finished in the musical theatre. Mizzi Günther, like a number of the very greatest musical stars, subsequently began a second career as a character lady which was worth another quarter of a century's work on the musical stage.

In 1931 she played the Gräfin Fuchs in *Die Kaiserin* and in 1932 she appeared as Herzogin Marie Brankenhorst in *Schön ist die Welt,* paired with Gustav Charlé as the ''elders'' of the piece whilst her erstwhile leading man, Marischka, played the juvenile man, and she later joined the company at the Raimundtheater where she played in the wartime *Fremdenführer* (the written-in Excellenz Minna Freifrau von Eiseneck) and the prize ''komische Alte'' role of Palmatica in *Der Bettelstudent.* In the 1940s she was seen there in Pepöck's *Der Reiter der Kaiserin* (1941), as Frau Anna Strauss in *Die Straussbuben* (1946), and in Fred Raymond's *Die Perle von Tokay* (1948), whilst she also appeared at the Volksoper in roles such as the duenna, Zenobia, in *Gasparone* (1945), towards the end of one of the musical theatre's most remarkable careers.

Plate 160. **Mizzi Günther** *in* Das Fürstenkind.

GUTTMANN

The Operette comedian and singer **Alexander GUTTMANN** (b Budapest, 2 October 1851; d Meran, 15 February 1889), a member of the companies at the Theater an der Wien (Nakid in *Die Afrikareise,* Collinée in *Der schöne Nikolaus,* Delacqua in *Eine Nacht in Venedig,* Sindulfo in *Gasparone,* Sir Andrew Douglas in *Donna Juanita,* Dupont in *Der Marquis von Rivoli,* Bliemchen in *Der Feldprediger,* Graf Asinelli in *Pfingsten in Florenz,* Farigoul in *Zwillinge,* Cordonnier in *Gillette de Narbonne*) and at the Carltheater (Bobèche, Graf Propakoff in *Der Jagdjunker,* General Gregor Gregorovitch in *Der Vagabund,* etc), fathered three sons, all of whom would have important careers as actors and directors in the theatre, before his death at the age of 37.

Emil GUTTMANN (b 1879; Vienna, 26 March 1934) began his career as an actor-who-sings-very-little, and appeared at the Apollotheater in such pieces as *Der Gaukler* (1909), *Lumpus und Pumpus, Miss Exzentrik* (1910), *Das Frauenparlament* (1911) and *Der Natursänger* (1912); at the Theater in der Josefstadt in *Die Förster-Christl* (1907, Graf Gottfried von Leoben), *Das Wäschermädel* (Fürst Josef von Kleben), *Filmzauber* (Antonius Lichtenstädt), *Die Wundermühle* (Hans Leutenfeld) and *Die Patronesse vom Nachtcafé* (Peter Schlipp); and at the Johann Strauss-Theater as the principal baddie, Graf Lothar Mereditt, in *Die Faschingsfee* (1917).

He had, by this time, already established himself in a more important career as a director, notably when he both directed and played Scharntorff in the Raimundtheater's original production of *Das Dreimäderlhaus* (1916). He directed the musequel *Hannerl* (1918) and directed and took the lead comedy role of Poire in *Sybill* (1919) at the Stadttheater, before taking over from his brother, Paul, as regisseur-in-chief at the Theater an der Wien.

Amongst the shows which he directed and/or played in there over the next five years were *Nimm mich mit!* (1919), *Dorfmusikanten* (1919), *Die blaue Mazur* (1920, Klemens von Reiger), *Der letzte Walzer* (1921, t/o Paul), *Frasquita* (1922, Aristide Girot), *Die Bacchusnacht* (1923) and *Gräfin Mariza* (1924), whilst he simultaneously mounted pieces at the Johann Strauss-Theater (*Das Hollandweibchen* 1920, *Rinaldo* 1921, *Die Tanzgräfin* 1921, *Eine Sommernacht* 1921), the Apollotheater (*Die Tangokönigin,* 1921), the Bürgertheater (*Mädi,* 1923) and the Raimundtheater (*Zwölf Uhr Nachts, Der Tanz ins Glück* 1921), etc. His latter day credits included *Spiel um die Liebe* (1925, Fürst Leopold von Salmannsdorf, dir), *Das Schwalbennest* (1926, dir) and *Mädel aus Wien* (1931, Oberst Savigny, dir).

Paul GUTTMANN (b Vienna, 1 July 1877; d Minsk, ?1941) also began his career as an actor, and played at the Venedig in Wien summer theatre and/or Danzers Orpheum in *Die Eisjungfrau* (Scarlett, a pirate chief), *Die Ringstrassen-Prinzessin* (von Dembinsky), *Frau Luna* (Ferdinand Sküss), Eine vom ''Moulin Rouge'' (Schani), *Das Scheckbuch des Teufels* (Baron Cupido), etc. In 1911 he was hired as an actor and director at the Theater an der Wien, and over the next seven years he played in and/or directed a long list of productions including a *Pariser Leben* revival (1911, Gondremarck), *Eva* (1911, Prunelles, dir), *Der blaue Held* (1912, Regent, dir), *Der kleine König* (1912, dir), *Prinzess Gretl* (1913, Fürst Aloysius, dir), *Die ideale Gattin* (1913, Marquese Columbus, dir), *Die Ballkönigin* (ie, *The Catch of the Season,* 1913, Lord Dundreary), *Endlich allein* (1914, Graf Maximilian Splenningen, dir), *Leichte Kavallerie* revival (1914, dir), *Gold gab ich für Eisen* (1914, von Steinfeld), *Die schöne Schwedin* (1915, Axel, dir), *Der Opernball* revival (Beaubuisson, dir), *Auf Befehl der Herzogin* (1915, dir), *Wenn zwei sich lieben* (1915, von Varady, dir), *Die Winzerbraut* (dir), *Der Sterngucker* (1916, Nepomuk, dir), *Die Rose von Stambul* (1916, dir) and *Wo die Lerche singt* (1918, dir).

At the same time he directed several major hits at the Johann Strauss-Theater—*Der Zigeunerprimás* (1912), *Rund um die Liebe, Die Csárdásfürstin* (1915), *Die Faschingsfee* (1917)—and also staged Straus's *Nachtfalter* at Ronacher and subsequently at the Theater an der Wien. He was Oberregisseur and performer at the Apollotheater under Herbert Trau (*Der Pusztakavalier, Fürstenkind* revival, etc) and later staged *Faschingshochzeit* (1921) at the Carltheater. After quitting the Theater an der Wien, he continued thereafter both to appear on the stage and to direct, being seen at the Bürgertheater in *Yvette und ihre Freunde* (1927, Loriot) and *No, No, Nanette* (1927, George, the butler), and at the Johann Strauss-Theater in *Der Zarewitsch* (Ministerpräsident) which he also directed. He also directed Kálmán's *Das Veilchen vom Montmartre* (1930).

He was deported to Minsk during the Second World War and never seen again.

Arthur GUTTMANN (b Vienna, 1 July 1877; d Vienna, 3 June 1956) worked as a comedian in plays and musicals, his best musical roles being Lothar in *Ein Walzertraum* (1907), introducing ''Piccolo, piccolo, tsin, tsin, tsin'' with his wife, soubrette Mizzi Zwerenz, and Nazi, the comical waiter of *Frühlingsluft* (1903). His other musical appearances included *Fesche Geister, Der schöne Rigo,* and *Die Eisjungfrau* (ie, *The Girl from Up There,* 1904, Angesturia Pickles), all at Venedig in Wien, and Hippolit Zillinger in *Die Schützenliesel* (1905), Stanislaus Lämmermann in *Mutzi,* the marvelous dragon Schnidibumpfel in *Hugdietrichs Brautfahrt* (1906), Friedel in *Drei Musterweibchen,* Stieglitz in *Der Juxbaron* (1915), Dagobert in *Liebe im Schnee* (1916), Adolf Schmelkes in *Nachtfalter* (1917), Stepanowitsch in *Die Siegerin* (1922), Neljudow in *Das Weib im Purpur* (1924) and Jainkel in *Das Spiel um die Liebe* (1925).

He also directed musical productions at the Komödienhaus (*Der Liebesteufel*), the Neues Wiener Stadttheater (*Libellentanz*), Johann Strauss-Theater (*Ein Märchen aus Florenz, Das Weib im Purpur*), the Carltheater (*Hoheit Franzl*), etc.

GUYS AND DOLLS Musical fable of Broadway in 2 acts based on a story and characters by Damon Runyon. Book by Abe Burrows and Jo Swerling. Lyrics and music by Frank Loesser. 46th Street Theater, New York, 24 November 1950.

Producers Feuer and Martin were responsible for coming up with the idea that the New York short stories of Damon Runyon (1884–1946), with their strongly-defined and endearingly quirky characters and their colorful, made-to-measure jargon, might make up into a stage musical. Their first two commissions for a libretto proved unsatisfactory, but the second, written by Jo Swerling, got as far as being set with songs by Frank Loesser, the songwriter with whose *Where's Charley?* the producers had scored a fine success on their first venture into the Broadway musical sphere. When it was decided to junk book number two and replace it with a third, by Abe Burrows, the new librettist was obliged to build his tale—largely based on the story *The Idyll of Miss Sarah Brown,* but including incidents and characters from the earlier libretto—around the now-existing score. The work was so skillfully done that, in spite of this piecemeal creation, the book of *Guys and Dolls* stands out as one of the most remarkable musical plays in the English language.

Nathan Detroit (Sam Levene) runs the ''oldest established permanent floating crap game in New York.'' He has been promising to give it up, and to marry nightclub chantoosie, Adelaide (Vivian Blaine), his fiancée of 14 years standing, but the main chance always gets the better of him. This week he is in a pother, because the big-gambling Sky Masterson (Robert Alda) is coming to town, and Nathan hasn't got the stake money to launch a game. He tries to win it, by betting Masterson that he cannot get the holy-roller girl, Sarah Brown (Isabel Bigley), from the Save-a-Soul Mission to go with him on a day-trip to Havana. But Masterson promises Sarah to supply her enough ''souls'' to make her under-attended mission pass the test of a visiting General, and she goes. While she's away, the guys have their game in the mission house. But Masterson is as good as his promise. The next day he brings the crap-players, whom he has trounced in a game, to be Sarah's souls. The Mission is saved, Sky weds Sarah and seems, at the end of affairs, to have given up gambling to bang the big drum in her band. Adelaide's psychosomatic sniffles vanish for ever as she walks, in parallel, down the aisle with Nathan. The variegated selection of guys were headed by Stubby Kaye as Nicely-Nicely Johnson, Tom Pedi as Harry the Horse, Johnny Silver as Benny Southstreet, Douglas Deane as Rusty Charlie and B S Pully as Big Jule, whilst old time Irish star Pat Rooney (Arvide Abernathy) and Netta Packer (General Matilda B Cartwright) headed the forces of virtue.

The songs for *Guys and Dolls* were in a different class to those which Loesser had written for *Where's Charley?* Polite British pastiche was replaced by a richly individual set of thoroughly middle-to-low-life New York character songs in which even the one turn into a straight and sentimental love duet, ''I've Never Been in Love Before,'' seemed to take on the color of its surroundings. On the one hand, there were the songs for the guys: three of them opening the show talking racing tips in the harmonized ''Fugue for Tinhorns,'' the whole gang's hymn to ''The Oldest Established Permanent Floating Crap Game in New York,'' their celebration of a woman's influence in ''Guys and Dolls,'' Sky's baritonic gambling song, ''Luck Be a Lady,'' and the warmly philosophical ''My Time of Day,'' a solo for Nicely-Nicely, testifying before the mission in the ebullient ''Sit Down You're Rockin' the Boat,'' and the gem of the lot, Nathan's heartfelt cry, ''Sue Me,'' before Adelaide's charges of infidelity in the face of a deck of cards.

Then there were the dolls: Miss Adelaide pounding out her work-time numbers, ''A Bushel and a Peck'' and ''Take Back Your Mink,'' indulging in an orgy of post-nasal dripping as she described her fiancé's unconnubial tendencies in Adelaide's Lament or, in one of the show's most stunning numbers, joining with Sarah to decide that the answer to life is to ''Marry the Man Today'' and change his ways tomorrow; and Sarah insisting to Sky that ''I'll Know'' when the right man comes along, or tinkling tipsily through ''If I Were a Bell'' after too many Havana-style ''milk shakes.'' It was a score where there was barely a number which wasn't a stand-out.

Plate 161. **Guys and Dolls.** *Miss Adelaide (Vivian Blaine) keeps her Nathan (Sam Levene) up to the mark.*

Such was not necessarily the all-round opinion in 1950, but *Guys and Dolls* nevertheless took Tony Awards for best musical, book, score, direction (George S Kaufman) and choreography (Michael Kidd), as well as for Alda's performance, as Feuer and Martin's production settled in for 1,200 performances on Broadway. The first national tour was quickly on its way, with filmland's Allan Jones in the role of Masterson and Pamela Britton as Adelaide, but it was 1953 before Prince Littler and Arthur Lewis mounted a British production. Miss Blaine, Kaye, Levene, Pedi and Silver all repeated their original roles alongside Jerry Wayne (Masterson) and Lizbeth Webb (Sarah) through a fine London run of 555 performances. A film version followed, in 1955, in which Frank Sinatra (Nathan), Marlon Brando (Masterson), Jean Simmons (Sarah) and Miss Blaine featured, alongside three fresh numbers and a fair harvest of the original ones. Australia, however, waited very much longer for its first stage *Guys and Dolls.* It was 1974 before Liz Harris, Ken Lord, Judith Roberts and Barrie Hope were seen in a three-month season at Melbourne's Total Theatre, and more than another decade before Sydney (Her Majesty's Theatre 13 May 1986) saw the show.

Although *Guys and Dolls* found its way firmly into a prized place in the English-language repertoire, for some reason it did not attract attention further afield. And, similarly, given both its qualities and the laurels and the praise it had won, its subsequent career, even in America, was more than a little disappointing. Although it was given a cast-up revival at the City Center (20 April 1955) with Walter Matthau (Nathan), Helen Gallagher (Adelaide), Leila Martin (Sarah) and Ray Shaw (Sky) heading the players, it reappeared on Broadway only in a sorely rehashed version, performed by an uneven cast of black artists (Broadway Theater 21 July 1976), before a major revival was finally mounted in 1992 (Martin Beck Theater 14 April). Peter Gallagher (Sky), Nathan Lane (Nathan), Faith Prince (Adelaide) and Josie de Guzman (Sarah) featured in a production which won greater accolades for the piece than it had received first time around, but which didn't stay in town quite as long (1,144 performances). The show also made a modest European debut in a German version (ad Janne Furch) in Bremen, but was later given in Vienna in a version, subtitled *Strizzis und Mizzis* (ad Caroline Koczan, Dunja Sowinetz), in which the characters and language were localized and the action reset in Vienna. Karl-Heinz Hackl played Sigi Master (ie, Sky Masterson) and Ruth Brauer was Adelheid.

In Britain, where Laurence Olivier had earlier projected to bring the show back in the repertoire of the subsidized National Theatre, with himself featured as Nathan, it was eventually mounted by a later management of the National Theatre in 1982 (9 March). Julia McKenzie (Adelaide) and Bob Hoskins (Nathan) starred in an otherwise embarrassingly undersung, crudely orchestrated production which nevertheless won waves of praise from some newspaper critics, and was subsequently transferred to a commercial theatre for a run (Prince of Wales Theatre 19 June 1985, 354 performances), and revived in the theatre's repertoire in 1996 (Olivier Theatre 17 December).

UK: London Coliseum 28 May 1953; Australia: Total Theatre, Melbourne 27 July 1974; Germany: Theater der Hansestadt, Bremen 26 May 1969, Theater des Westens 14 December 1984; Austria: Landestheater, Linz

Film: Goldwyn 1955

Recordings: original cast (Decca), 1976 revival (revised version) (Motown), London 1982 revival (Chrysalis), 1992 revival (RCA Victor), Austrian cast (Reverso/BMG), Korean cast (Daewong/HMI), studio cast (TER), film soundtrack (Decca), etc

Literature: Wolf, M: *The Guys and Dolls Book* (Methuen, London, 1982)

GYPSY Musical in 2 acts by Arthur Laurents suggested by the memoirs of Gypsy Rose Lee. Lyrics by Stephen Sondheim. Music by Jule Styne. Broadway Theater, New York, 21 May 1959.

The musical based on the memoirs of the celebrated peeler Gypsy Rose Lee is rather less about the titular Gypsy, and rather more about Gypsy's grotesquely ambitious stage mother, a performer manquée, who apparently pushed her children towards careers in show business less for their own good or enjoyment, than for the vicarious thrill that she found in their performances and in their ultimate success. The reason for this re-angling of the story was a very valid one: *Gypsy* was built as a vehicle for the middle-aged Ethel Merman, and the role of mother Rose provided her with one of her best-devised parts ever.

Rose (Miss Merman) has her two daughters on stage from tot-talent time, performing an act devised by her which features the blonde and bubbling "Baby June" (the real-life June Havoc) as front kiddie. Brunette Louise supports discreetly. Stardom doesn't come, but Rose pushes on through stretches of minor engagements, with the girls and their support playing the same tatty act, decorated with any bits she can filch here and there, and twisted about to fit the latest fashions or mother's latest ideas. On the way, she wins the friendship and help of Herbie (Jack Klugman), but she loses June (Lane Bradbury) who only waits for the first twinges of puberty before running away with a boy from the act, Tulsa (Paul Wallace). Undaunted, Rose shifts her ambitions onto the previously unprized Louise (Sandra Church), who is tacked into June's place in the newest variation of the act. But one night, when they are booked into a burlesque house, the featured stripper doesn't show up. Rose shoves Louise into the spot and, within no time at all, the girl has found a métier. With the whiff of stardust up her nostrils, Rose abandons Herbie's proposal of marriage to follow "Gypsy Rose Lee." She can't understand that she isn't wanted—or even needed. She explodes in an agony of frustration, and Louise gives in. Momma has got at least some of what she wanted, yet again.

The score's favorite songs were Rose's raucously optimistic "Everything's Coming Up Roses" and a song-and-dance piece for Tulsa, practicing alone the double-handed routine he hopes will be his future, and announcing "All I Need Now Is the Girl." Three strippers turned out a grossly comical routine ("You Gotta Get a Gimmick") advising Louise on how to get on in the strip business, whilst the two little girls dreamed ungrammatically of escape from the vaudeville grind in ''If Momma Was Married,'' and made their way through the various stages of their careers to the ever-reorchestrated strains of the all-purpose ''Let Me Entertain You,'' a little song which began in Uncle Jocko's talent quest and culminated in Louise's starry strip routines. There were occasional gentler moments too—such as Louise's lonely song to her ''Little Lamb''—but the set piece of the evening was Rose's 11-o'clock number, ''Rose's Turn,'' the crazy ripping apart of a woman craving for recognition until it drives her round the bend.

David Merrick and Leland Hayward's Broadway production of *Gypsy* ran for 702 performances and, although Miss Merman had begun walking through her hugely demanding role before the end of the run, she nevertheless went on the road with it for the eight months of the national tour. A film version was made the following year, but it was made without the original star, whose role was taken by Rosalind Russell and the voice of Lisa Kirk. Natalie Wood was Louise and Karl Malden played Herbie.

The film was not a success, and when Miss Merman, who had agreed to go on to play her role in London, finally reneged, the production was shelved. It was 11 years before London saw *Gypsy,* and when it did it was Angela Lansbury who played Rose, in a production mounted by a team of American producers and London's H M Tennent Ltd, alongside Zan Charisse (Louise), Barrie Ingham (Herbie) and Bonnie Langford as a memorable Baby June. Miss Lansbury made a personal hit with a rather different reading of the role and, although the production folded soon after she left (300 performances), it was subsequently remounted back on Broadway with Rex Robbins (Herbie) replacing Ingham (23 September 1974). It played there for 120 performances. However, Angela Lansbury picked up the Tony Award that the show and Miss Merman had been denied first time round by *Fiorello!* and *The Sound of Music* (tied) and by Mary Martin's Maria von Trapp. Similarly, this production, although briefer in its run than the first, spawned others, including the first Australian showing. Gloria Dawn starred as Rose for four months in Melbourne and shared the role with Toni Lamond in a Sydney season. In Germany (ad Renate Axt) the show was given its first production at Munster in 1979.

In 1989 an American touring production (2 May 1989) with TV's *Cagney and Lacey* star Tyne Daly featured as Rose alongside Crista Moore (Louise) and Jonathan Hadary (Herbie), was brought to the St James Theater after some six months on the road to give Broadway its third helping of *Gypsy* in three decades (16 November 1989). It played there for 14 months, folding, as the previous revival had done, soon after the departure of its top-billed star, with whom later it returned briefly to bring its total to 582 performances. British and Australian revivals, announced off and on in its wake, didn't happen, but Hungary got its first taste of the show in 1993 (ad Tamás Ungvári) with Erszi Galambos as Rose and in 1997 a new German version (ad Frank Thannhäuser, Iris Schumacher) was produced at Augsburg with Beate Granzow as Rose, and subsequently played at Berlin's Theater des Westens with Angelika Milster starred.

Like that of a very select handful of shows, however, the popularity of *Gypsy* seems to have grown over the years since its good, but scarcely outstanding, first runs. Reviews such as the original ''[the] libretto is a touch commonplace and more than a touch repetitious . . . [and the star] cannot quite make the show's shortcomings seem negligible'' have become forgotten, as *Gypsy* has found extravagantly fervent followers amongst a group of musical-theatre fans, and amongst actresses of a certain age with an eye for a big, loud, virtuoso role. This new appraisal has prompted descriptions like ''one of the greatest musicals of our time'' from those fans, and, as a result, *Gypsy* has found itself productions in a number of regional houses in England and America, in South America, South Africa and eventually in other, non-English-speaking, venues.

Gypsy Rose Lee was also portrayed on stage in the musical *Ain't Broadway Grand* (1993, ex- *Mike*) by Debbie Shapiro.

UK: Piccadilly Theatre 29 May 1973; Australia: Her Majesty's Theatre, Melbourne 3 May 1975; Germany: Städtische Bühnen, Munster 9 March 1979, Theater des Westens 19 October 1997; Hungary: József Attila Színház 16 October 1993

Film: Warner Brothers 1962

Recordings: original cast (Columbia), London cast (RCA), South African cast (Philips), 1989 revival cast (Elektra-Nonsuch), film soundtrack (Warner Bros), TV soundtrack (East West, Atlantic), etc

THE GYPSY BARON *see* DER ZIGEUNERBARON

GYPSY LOVE *see* ZIGEUNERLIEBE

THE GYPSY PRINCESS *see* DIE CSÁRDÁSFÜRSTIN

H

HADDON HALL Light opera in 3 acts by Sydney Grundy. Music by Arthur Sullivan. Savoy Theatre, London, 24 September 1892.

One of the musical plays produced by D'Oyly Carte at the Savoy Theatre in the period post–*The Gondoliers,* in which W S Gilbert was no longer part of the theatre's creative team, *Haddon Hall* was written by the respected playwright Sydney Grundy, whose early comic opera, *The Vicar of Bray,* Carte had just revived with some success. Like *The Vicar of Bray, Haddon Hall* took an old English setting and a well-known subject, the 16th-century tale of the elopement of puritan's daughter Dorothy Vernon of Haddon Hall, Derbyshire. Grundy advanced the period to the picturesque days of Cavaliers and Roundheads, leavened the romantic-dramatic story with a certain amount of humor, but made no attempt—as George Dance had done with the Savoy's previous new show, *The Nautch Girl*—to catch the special opéra-bouffe flavor of the Savoy operas. *Haddon Hall* deserved its ''light opera'' description, particularly as Sullivan chose to set it musically in a style which was as near to his operatic *Ivanhoe* as to *The Yeomen of the Guard.*

Lucille Hill, the female star of *Ivanhoe,* played Dorothy, with Courtice Pounds as her romantic partner, John Manners. Rutland Barrington was the puritan Rupert Vernon and Rosina Brandram the uncomical Lady Vernon, whilst W H Denny had the most humorous moments as a Scots puritan called The McKrankie. The piece ran a respectable 204 performances in London before being taken on the road.

Recording: amateur cast recording (Pearl)

HADING, Jane [TRÉFOURET, Alfrédine Jeanne] (b Marseille, 26 November 1859; d Neuilly-sur-Seine, 30 January 1941).

A leading lady on the Paris musical stage who went on to a more famous career in the non-musical theatre.

Having first appeared on the stage as a three-year-old child in her native Marseille, Mlle Hading (the name was a variation on that of her natural father, Hadingue) attended the Conservatoire and, graduating at the age of 14, began her adult career in Algeria and in Cairo where she appeared in *La Fille de Madame Angot* and also in a number of plays. When she returned to Marseille, one of her engagements was for the leading role in a local opérette, *Le Grand Mogol,* staged at Théâtre du Gymnase. It turned out to be the first major work of Edmond Audran, who would go on to as many more successes as his teenaged star.

On going up to Paris, at the age of 18, she first worked at the Palais-Royal, where she made her debut in the central role in the vaudeville *La Chaste Suzanne* (1877), but then moved swiftly to the Théâtre de la Renaissance to take over from Jeanne Granier, at that time the reigning queen of Paris opérette, as Graziella in a revival of *La Petite Mariée.* She also played Héloïse in a reprise of Litolff's *Héloïse et Abélard* before, during Granier's absence from the French capital, creating her first leading role in Lecocq's *La Jolie Persane* (1879, Namouna). She also married the director of the theatre, Victor Koning. Mlle Hading starred in Offenbach's last work, *Belle Lurette* (1880, Lurette), in a role written to her measure, and appeared in several other revivals (*L'Oeil crevé,* 1881, ''she has little or no voice left''), but thereafter abandoned the musical theatre,and Koning, to move on to a notable career as a straight actress. In 1897, however, she was seen at the Porte-Saint-Martin playing Asitare in the fantastical musical play *La Montagne enchantée,* alongside Lassouche and Desclauzas.

HAGUE, Albert [MARCUSE, Albert] (b Berlin, 13 October 1920). Composer of two successful 1950s Broadway musicals.

Albert Hague studied in the United States of America, and served in the Air Force during the Second World War, before settling in New York and beginning a career as a songwriter. He had a musical produced in Cleveland in 1947, musicked a short television musical *The Mercer Girls* (1953), and placed such songs as ''One Is a Lonely Number'' (w Maurice Valency, *Dance Me a Song,* 1950), before scoring a considerable success with his first full Broadway show, *Plain and Fancy,* and its song hit ''Young and Foolish.'' A second success, the music-hall mystery musical *Redhead,* brought him a Tony Award for his score, but thereafter further wins eluded him. He supplied two numbers for *Ziegfeld Follies of 1956,* additional music for the revue *The Girls Against the Boys* (w Arnold Horwitt, 1959), and incidental music for the play *The Madwoman of Chaillot,* but his two musicals of the 1960s closed after only a few performances, and his 1974 musicalization of Emlyn Williams's *The Corn Is Green* (*Miss Moffat*) folded out of town. He subsequently had a second fine career as a character actor on television, notably in the role of Shorofsky in the series *Fame.*

1947 **Reluctant Lady** (Maurice Valency) Cain Park Theatre, Cleveland 26 July

1955 **Plain and Fancy** (Arnold Horwitt/Joseph Stein, Will Glickman) Mark Hellinger Theater 27 January

1959 **Redhead** (Dorothy Fields/Herbert Fields, Sidney Sheldon, David Shaw) 46th Street Theater 5 February

1964 **Café Crown** (Marty Brill/Hy Kraft) Martin Beck Theater 17 April

1969 **The Fig Leaves Are Falling** (Allan Sherman) Broadhurst Theater 2 January

1974 **Miss Moffat** (Emlyn Williams/Joshua Logan, Williams) Shubert Theater, Philadelphia 7 October

HAHN, Reynaldo (b Caracas, Venezuela, 9 August 1874; d Paris, 28 January 1947). Elegant, soigné composer whose work for the French stage, although much prized by his followers, produced only one enduring score.

A student at the Paris Conservatoire from an early age, the young and dashing Hahn made a name and a place for himself in Parisian fin de siècle society, playing and singing his settings of literary verse at fashionable salons. The songs found other and more famous interpreters, and Hahn many influential and important friends, as he expanded his musical horizons to take in theatre music, ballets for both the Opéra and Diaghilev (*Le Dieu bleu*), concert works and conducting. At the same time he both began what would be a long and highly considered career as a music critic, and, whilst still in his twenties, completed the composition of two substantial lyric stage works, the three-act, Pierre Loti–based ''idylle polynésienne'' *L'Île du rêve* (23 March 1898, lib: André Alexandre) and the four-act *La Carmélite* (16 December 1902), both of which were staged at the Opéra-Comique.

Other lyric works followed, amongst them the opera *Nausicaa* (Monte Carlo/Opéra-Comique) and the one-act ''conte lyrique japonais'' *La Colombe du Bouddha* (Cannes, 1921), whilst a pantomime composed to a rhythmic poem by Edmond Rostand, *Le Bois sacré,* was produced at the Théâtre Sarah Bernhardt (20 April 1910). He had a first brush with the light musical theatre when he contributed to *Miousic,* the unsuccessful revue-opérette by 10 composers fabricated for L'Olympia in 1914.

Hahn finally achieved an enduring popular theatrical success, as opposed to appreciation from artistic society, with the production of the pretty opérette *Ciboulette* at the Théâtre des Variétés in 1923. The songs which he provided for Yvonne Printemps in the musical play *Mozart,* also proved successful as an adjunct to the music of Wolfgang Amadeus and the sprightly comic romance of Sacha Guitry, and another pastel period piece with *Brummell* (1931) for its hero won fond friends, but further stage ventures in opérette and musical comedy with *Le Temps d'aimer* (1926), Guitry's *O, mon bel inconnu* (1933) and *Malvina* (1935), in opera (*Le Marchand de Venise,* 1935), and in revue (*Une revue,* 1926) had an often more limited appeal and shorter lives. Having in his middle age become a considerable and influential figure in Parisian musical circles, Hahn ultimately left the critic's chair at *Le Figaro,* which he had occupied for a decade, and became Director of the Paris Opéra in 1945, shortly before his death.

Hahn's refined, correct style of writing, with its tasteful shades, gentle charms and general absence of highly colored passion or obviously popular attractions, has always appealed to commentators, who are inclined to find alibis for the quick disappearance of each of his failed works or to blame public lack of good taste for his limited success. It is perhaps that very good taste in his writing which has rendered it more interesting to and appreciated by musicians than popular with the general public.

1923 **Ciboulette** (Robert de Flers, Francis de Croisset) Théâtre des Variétés 7 April

1925 **Mozart** (Sacha Guitry) Théâtre Édouard VII 2 December

1926 **Le Temps d'aimer** (Hugues Delorme/Pierre Wolff, Henri Duvernois) Théâtre de la Michodière 6 November

1931 **Brummell** (Rip, Robert Dieudonné) Folies Wagram 17 January

1933 **O, mon bel inconnu** (Guitry) Théâtre des Bouffes-Parisiens 12 October

1935 **Malvina** (Maurice Donnay, Duvernois) Théâtre de la Gaîté-Lyrique 23 March

1949 **Le ''Oui'' des jeunes filles** (René Fauchois) Opéra-Comique 21 June

Biography: Gavoty, B: *Reynaldo Hahn, le musicien de la Belle Époque* (Buchet/Chastel, Paris, 1976)

HAINES, Herbert E[dgar] (b Manchester, 8 November 1879; d Whitefield, Lancs, 21 April 1923).

The son of Alfred Haines, musical director at the Prince's Theatre in Manchester, Herbert Haines studied music in his native town and at the age of 17 composed the dance music for Robert Courtneidge's pantomime at the Prince's Theatre. At 20, he succeeded Ernest Vousden at the baton of Courtneidge's touring musical *The Gay Grisette* and went on from there to join George Edwardes's organization, acting as musical director for several of his road productions. He moved to London to succeed Howard Talbot as conductor of Edwardes's *Three Little Maids* and, thereafter, conducted shows at various London theatres over a period of 20 years.

Haines wrote his first musical comedy score, a vehicle for Ellaline Terriss and Seymour Hicks, for Charles Frohman in 1904. As *The Catch of the Season,* and with songs by other composers inserted freely into Haines's basic score, this piece ran for 17 months in London and went on to a series of overseas productions, whilst bringing him two individual song successes in ''The Church Parade'' and ''Cigarette.'' The same authorial team's *The Talk of the Town,* produced by William Greet the following year, had less success, but a second effort for Frohman, Seymour Hicks and Miss Terriss, *The Beauty of Bath,* produced a second London hit.

In 1907 Frohman set up a B-team in an attempt to duplicate the Hicks/Terriss successes, and he supplied them with a show by his A-team of writers: Hicks, Charles Taylor and Haines, who this time had also cornered a share in the book credit. *My Darling,* starring Henry Lytton and Marie Studholme, was not a success and, although he thereafter supplied some individual songs for interpolating in other people's scores, Haines wrote no more musical comedy scores of his own, concentrating on conducting, composing light orchestral music, and turning out such incidental scores as that for Courtneidge's production of *Paddy the Next Best Thing* (1920).

Haines won an extra Broadway credit when a Manchester Prince's Theatre pantomime to which he had supplied music was remade as a Broadway musical, *The Babes and the Baron,* and mounted at the New York Lyric Theater for Christmas 1905 (45 performances).

1904 **The Catch of the Season** (w Herbert Evelyn Baker/Charles H Taylor/Seymour Hicks, Cosmo Hamilton) Vaudeville Theatre 9 September

1905 **The Talk of the Town** (w Baker/Taylor/Hicks) Lyric Theatre 5 January

1905 **The Babes and the Baron** (w others/Taylor, Robert B Smith/A M Thompson, Robert Courtneidge) Lyric Theater, New York 25 December

1906 **The Beauty of Bath** (Taylor/Hicks, Hamilton) Aldwych Theatre 19 March

1907 **My Darling** (Taylor/Hicks) Hicks Theatre 2 March

1912 **Pebbles on the Beach** (Hicks) 1 act London Coliseum 16 December

HAIR American tribal love-rock musical in 2 acts by Gerome Ragni and James Rado. Music by Galt MacDermot. Anspacher Theater, New York, 17 October 1967; Biltmore Theater (revised version), 29 April 1968.

Less a musical, in the accepted sense, and more a semi-coherent celebration of the preoccupations of the make-love-not-war generation of the American 1960s, *Hair* moved from its off-Broadway beginnings in 50 performances at Joseph Papp's New York Shakespeare Festival (the connections with Shakespeare were not evident), via performances at the Cheetah nightclub (22 December 1967–28 January 1968), through revisions (mostly aimed at making the piece more aggressive and more strivingly shocking), to a berth on Broadway. There it established itself as one of the theatrical phenomena of its time, and found a fine 1,742-performance run prior to a long and often successful series of productions throughout the world.

Hair—or, rather, the fact of a male person wearing it long, like a girl—is a 1960s symbol of rebellious youngsters nose-thumbing at the values of their parents. Long-haired Claude (Walker Daniels/James Rado), Berger (Ragni) and Sheila (Jill O'Hara/ Lynn Kellogg), who share lodgings, Woof (Steve Dean/Steve Curry), Hud (Arnold Wilkerson/Lamont Washington) and Jeannie (Sally Eaton) are members of the hedonistic tribe of *Hair.* They want to be free. Free to reject responsibility, organization, and anyone or anything that stops them living a life of unspoiled pleasure. Pleasure means sleeping with whom you want, taking what drugs you like, having what you fancy and not doing anything you don't want to. Claude wants Sheila, who wants Berger, but she finally turns up the trick the night before Claude leaves the tribe to go into the real world. His hair cut short, he heads off for the draft and possibly the war in Vietnam.

The songs which illustrated the show—some of which were full-grown numbers, others merely fragments—underwent many changes during the period *Hair* spent off-, and on the way to, Broadway (the original 20 numbers rose to 31 between the Anspacher Theater and the Biltmore), but the score brought forth one hugely popular piece, ''Aquarius,'' which became the hymn of the 1960s people, with its astrologically disguised longings for the hedonistic life. ''Good Morning, Starshine'' followed it into popularity outside the show, whilst the girl-group comparison of ''White Boys/Black Boys,'' and the revusical ''Frank Mills,'' a number describing one tribal lassie's longings for a clean-cut American man, which was amongst the most skillful of the show's musical moments, registered and lasted much better than the trendier pieces and those which were merely catalogues of ''naughty'' words. It was notable that most of these, and particularly those with the carefully provocative titles

(''Hashish,'' ''Sodomy,'' ''Colored Spade'') were those which had been added following *Hair*'s original success.

Hair's career on Broadway was largely boosted not only by the success of its best songs, but also by some carefully nurtured publicity over the fact that it included some nudity, both male and female. This was nothing new: Ian Richardson's buttocks had recently been on display in the *Marat/Sade,* and varying nudities were visible in a half-dozen Broadway and off-Broadway shows in this season, not to mention in the burlesque houses. But *Hair*'s nudity was gratuitous and thus rated as much more daring.

The flashing first-act finale and the show's naughty words would have seemed to have ruled it out for a British production, but when a prospective producer submitted the script to the British censor, the results were surprising. Female nudity was not new on the London stage, but male nudity? It was the first time the censor had been asked. His office had been waiting for the point to be brought up for many years, and there was, a priori, nothing forbidding it. As for the naughty words, virtually the only objections he had were not on sexual grounds, but on religious ones. But the list of changes required was still enough to discourage an immediate production.

Robert Stigwood and his associates, however, took up a short-term gamble. They bought the British rights to *Hair* and waited for the imminently expected abolition of the censor's office. When it came, they were quick off the mark with their uncensored show, little glimpse of nudity and all, and all London—as well as much of Spain and Japan—rushed to experience the new freedoms on view at the Shaftesbury Theatre. Paul Nicholas (Claude), Oliver Tobias (Berger), Annabel Leventon (Sheila), Michael Feast (Woof), Peter Straker (Hud) and Linda Kendrick (Jeannie) headed the original cast of the show, which ran for 1,998 performances. It had reached the end of its tether by the time an accident to the roof of the theatre forced it to quit the Shaftesbury, but less than a year later it surfaced again, at the Queen's Theatre (25 June 1974), this time for 111 more performances.

In 1968 a German version (ad Walter Brandin) was premiered in Munich, whilst France, which rarely showed interest in transatlantic shows, followed remarkably swiftly with a production (ad Jacques Lanzmann) at the Théâtre de la Porte-Saint-Martin, with rising pop star Julien Clerc starred as Claude and some local topicalities slipped into the script. In Australia, Harry M Miller's production, profiting from even more publicity than had been lavished on the show's selling points elsewhere, was a major success, and *Hair* progressed on to Italy, the Netherlands, Mexico, Israel, Sweden, Japan and other usual and less usual corners of the theatrical and almost-theatrical world.

Hair returned to Broadway in 1977 (Biltmore Theater 5 October) with Randall Easterbrook, Michael Holt, Ellen Foley and Cleavant Derricks featured in its cast, but lasted this time only 43 performances in a rather different social and theatrical climate. Nevertheless, a film version, with a rearranged story line, was made in 1979 with John Savage, Treat Wilson, Beverley d'Angelo and Melba Moore amongst the cast.

If *Hair*'s time had now apparently passed in the main musical theatre centers, this did not, by any means, remain true further afield. The show has continued to be frequently produced regionally, and it toured Continental cities almost nonstop during the 1980s and 1990s, provoking the same responses from audiences comprising not only middle-aging children of the 1960s, and those who had just caught up with the 1960s, but also the young of later decades. An attempt to take the piece back to London, at the Old Vic in 1993 (14 September), foundered in 79 expensive performances; its 25th anniversary was celebrated by a starry showing back at the Public Theater; and *Hair* got another brief reshowing at Paris's Théâtre Mogador in 1998, and still, at the end of the century, the show—played not as a period novelty, or tongue-in-cheek but for real—was to be sighted trouping through the short-stands of Europe, with a permanently self-renewing audience still ready and eager to partake of its music and its attitudes.

UK: Shaftesbury Theatre 27 September 1968; Germany: Theater an der Brienner Strasse, Munich 24 October 1968; France: Théâtre de la Porte-Saint-Martin 31 May 1969; Australia: Metro Theatre, Sydney 5 June 1969; Austria: Stadthalle, Vienna, 1970; Hungary: Budai Színpad 27 August 1999

Film: United Artists 1979

Recordings: original cast (RCA), London cast (Polydor), Australian casts (Spin, Festival), Japanese cast (RCA), German cast (Polydor), Dutch cast (Polydor), Mexican cast (Orfeon), Israeli cast (CBS), London revival cast (EMI), Danish cast 1997 (Pomme/Sony), German cast 1993 (Polydor), Czech cast 1997 *Vlasy* (EMI-Prague), film soundtrack (RCA), etc

Literature: Davis, L, Gallagher, R: *Letting Down My Hair* (Paul Elek, London, 1973)

HAJOS, Mitzi [HAJÓS, Magdalena, aka Mizzi] (b Budapest, 27 April 1891; d New Preston, Conn, June 1970). A little, spitfiring soubrette who moved from Europe to America, and was there turned into a durable musical-comedy star.

After attending drama school in Budapest, Mizzi Hajós made her earliest appearances on the stage at the local Magyar Színház (*A Gyurkovics lányok,* 1908) and then in Vienna. She played in the Leo Ascher burlesque *Hut ab!* (1909, Lotte) at Venedig in Wien and starred as Mary Gibbs in the Viennese version of *Our Miss Gibbs* at the Établissement Ronacher before—at the age of 19—

being taken to America. She appeared there at first in vaudeville in an adaptation of the Ronacher burlesque of Rostand's *Chantecler* called *A Barnyard Romeo* (1910) playing a little white pheasant (''in coagulated English'') to Stella Mayhew's duck and William Morris's rooster, and moved on to play Fifi Montmartre in the Shuberts' revusical *La Belle Paree* (1911) at the Winter Garden, and to tour in Christie MacDonald's star role of Princess Bozena in Werba and Luescher's Broadway hit *The Spring Maid* (*Die Sprudelfee*), and had her first Broadway lead role in the same producers' production of De Koven's *Her Little Highness* (1913, Anna Victoria). That show, and the reduction of it, *Queen Ann,* played by the little singer on the vaudeville stage, disappeared quickly, but her next appearance, in the title role of the extremely Hungarian *Sári* (*Der Zigeunerprimás,* 1914) hoisted her briskly to star status. Over the following years, with the aid of *Sári* impresario Henry Savage, she staunchly maintained that status, billed as the ''baby star,'' ''the paprika prima donna'' and finally, from 1916, simply as ''Mitzi'' (''Americans don't know how to pronounce either of my names'') through a series of mostly unexceptional roles and shows which nevertheless packed in the audiences in the long series of tour dates she trouped year after year.

Anne Caldwell and Hugo Felix's *Pom-Pom* (1916, Paulette), a piece adapted for her benefit from the Hungarian operett *Csibészkirály,* had her cast as another Continental heroine, this time an actress mistaken for the pickpocket she plays on stage; *Head Over Heels* (1918, Mitzi Bambinetti) had her playing an acrobat to Jerome Kern music; while Zelda Sears and Harold Levey's *Lady Billy* (1920, Countess Antonio) cast her as an aristocrat disguised for much of the evening in boy's clothes. The same team of writers dipped into fantasy with a second vehicle for her in *The Magic Ring* (aka *Minnie an' Me,* 1923, Polly Church). A move to the Shubert management for Oscar Straus's *Naughty Riquette* (*Riquette,* 1926, Riquette Duval) gave her some worthwhile music and yet another long and successful tour, whilst *The Madcap* (1928, Chibi) cast the now 37-year-old star alongside Sidney Greenstreet as a teenager pretending to be 12 in a musical version of Régis Gignoux and Jacques Théry's Parisian play *Le Fruit vert.* She returned to Broadway for the last time as a star as *Sári* in a 1930 revival, and thereafter appeared only as a featured player on the nonmusical stage. In her retirement she worked in the offices of the Shubert organization, until she was firmly (and unwillingly) retired in 1952.

Mitzi was married to stage and screen actor Boyd Marshall (1885–1950) who played alongside her in *Lady Billy* (John Smith) and *The Magic Ring* (Tom Hammond).

HALE, J Robert [MONRO, John Robert] (b Newton Abbot, 25 March 1874; d Maidenhead, Berks, 18 April 1940). Musical theatre and revue comedian, and the father of two successful musical comedy and/or revue stars.

The son of a sometime grazier from Australia, the young Hale spent his first decade in the theatre on the road, in plays, variety musicals (title role in the Milton Rays's *Don Quixote,* etc), and then playing leading comic parts for Tom Davis in his touring companies of the musicals *Little Miss Nobody, Florodora* and *The Silver Slipper* (Twanks). He made his first appearance in London in the second comic role of Davis's *The Medal and the Maid* (1903, Simon Pentweazle). He joined George Dance in 1904 for the tour of *Madame Sherry* (1904, MacSherry) and George Edwardes in 1905 to tour in *Lady Madcap,* subsequently taking over the same number-two comic role in the show's London production, and he featured in the same producer's *Les Merveilleuses* at Daly's Theatre before Edwardes moved him to a resident spot in the Gaiety company, where he created good supporting comedy roles in *The Girls from Gottenberg* (1907, Allbrecht), *Havana* (1908, Frank Charteris), *Our Miss Gibbs* (1909, Slithers) and *Peggy* (1910, James Bendoyle).

Hale had a considerable success in London's early revues, and over the next eight years he played almost continuously in revue and in pantomime, returning to the musical comedy stage to play Madame Lucy in the British production of *Irene* (1920). He continued thereafter to appear frequently and successfully in revue, but other book musicals with which he was involved—*Faust on Toast* (1921, Mephistopheles), a touring musicalized version of the play *Biffy* (1923, Biffy), *Open Your Eyes* (1929, Inspector Merlin), *Sons o' Guns* (1930, Hobson), *The One Girl* (1933, Holy Joe) and *I Can Take It* (1939)—found little or no success. His film engagements included an appearance as Eberseder in the 1933 British film of the musical *Walzer aus Wien.*

His daughter **Binnie HALE** [Beatrice May MONRO] (b Liverpool, 22 May 1899; d Hastings, 10 January 1984) made her earliest stage appearance alongside her father in the revue *Follow the Crowd,* at the age of 17. She made her first musical comedy appearance the following year in a minor role in C B Cochran's *Houp-La!* (Annette) and, in between revue engagements, went on to take increasingly important roles in *The Kiss Call* (1920, Charlotte), *My Nieces* (1922, Betty Culverwell) and *Katinka* (1924, Helen Hopper). Her fame was made when she was cast in the title role of the London *No, No, Nanette* (1925), and she followed up in a trio of star ingenue roles in West End musical comedy productions: Sunny Peters in *Sunny* (1926), Jill Kemp in *Mr Cinders* (1929), introducing the song ''Spread a Little Happiness,'' and star-billed as the tea-house Nippy in *Nippy* (1930).

She toured in the much more vocally demanding role of *The Dubarry,* returned to town and the song-and-scene musical to succeed Evelyn Laye and Adèle Dixon as the ingenue of *Give Me a Ring* (1933, Peggy) and then paired with great success with her *Mr Cinders* partner, Bobby Howes, in the comedy musical *Yes, Madam?* (1934, Sally). *Rise and Shine* (1936, Anne) and *Magyar Melody* (1939, Roszi), both quick failures, were her last appearances on the musical stage, on which she had spent more than a decade as a major London favorite, although she appeared several times thereafter in revue, pantomime and children's shows during the 15 years remaining of her career.

Hale's son, **Sonnie HALE** [John Robert MONRO] (b London, 1 May 1902; d London, 9 June 1959), also began his stage career in revue, and made his first musical comedy appearance at the age of 21 in Cochran's London production of George M Cohan's *Little Nellie Kelly* (Sidney Potter). He subsequently had good juvenile roles in *Mercenary Mary* (1925, Jerry) and *Queen High* (1926, Richard Johns) before playing through four years of highly successful revues in various London theatres. He appeared in the revusical *Evergreen* (1930) and in *Hold My Hand* with Stanley Lupino at the Gaiety in 1931 (Pop Curry), but thereafter led an irregular stage and film career, returning to the musical stage to appear with his father and with his wife, the popular dancing soubrette Jessie Matthews, in their own production of *I Can Take It* (1939), which closed on the road; to play the comedy role of Tonio in a revival of *The Maid of the Mountains* (1942); to star in a flop musical version of *When Knight's Were Bold* (1943, Sir Guy de Vere); and as comedian in the short-lived *Rainbow Square* (1951, Peppi).

Hale appeared in or directed a number of musical films in the mid-1930s, including the cinema versions of the stage shows *Evergreen* and *Head Over Heels* (director) and *Gangway* (director). He was married successively to musical-theatre star, Evelyn Laye, and to Miss Matthews.

HALÉVY, Ludovic [aka Jules SERVIÈRES] (b Paris, 1 January 1834; d Paris, 8 May 1908). One half of the partnership of librettists and lyricists who supplied Jacques Offenbach with the texts for many of his greatest successes, and the author or co-author of a long series of hit plays and musical shows on the Paris and international stage in the second half of the 19th century.

The son of the author, playwright and occasional operatic librettist Léon Halévy (1802–1883), and the nephew of Fromenthal Halévy [Jacques Fromenthal Élie Lévy] (1799–1862), the composer of the celebrated opera *La Juive,* Ludovic began his working life in the Imperial civil service (Ministère d'État, 1852, Ministère de l'Algerie et des Colonies, 1858). However, from an early age he was taken by the theatre, and he soon began himself to write theatrical pieces. His opportunity to break into the musical theatre came when Jacques Offenbach, needing an introductory piece for the opening of his new Théâtre des Bouffes-Parisiens, and unable to find a suitable, established author with the immediate time available, offered the nephew of his old Conservatoire professor, Fromenthal Halévy, the chance to write a little libretto around some lyrics which had already been prepared by Jules Méry, the recent librettist of Reyer's first opera, and around the personnel of the Bouffes company. Thus constricted, Halévy confectioned the three-handed *Entrez Messieurs, Mesdames,* to be played as the first item on the four-part program which inaugurated the Bouffes. It was Jules Moinaux's *Les Deux Aveugles* which took the honors of the night, but the young civil servant, who had hidden his identity behind the pseudonym of ''Jules Servières'' in order not to sully his chances of promotion by a connection with the stage, was launched, and over the months that followed he became a regular supplier of little opérette texts to the Bouffes-Parisiens.

Halévy's first great success came with the chaotic chinoiserie *Ba-ta-clan,* written this time without the umbrella of a pseudonym, and amongst those that followed were an adaptation of Mozart's *Der Schauspieldirektor* as *L'Impresario* (1856), the prize libretto *Le Docteur Miracle,* which was set victoriously by Lecocq and by Bizet, and Léon Gastinel's little *L'Opéra aux fenêtres* (1857), which made itself an international career (*Das Singspiel am Fenster, A Suitable Villa,* etc) after its introduction at the Bouffes.

With the breaking down of the restrictions regarding the number of characters allowed in his shows, Offenbach was able to reach out into more substantial fields, and in 1858 Halévy and Hector Crémieux provided him with the libretto for his first major work, a burlesque on which they had begun work several years earlier, *Orphée aux enfers.* When the piece was mounted, however, Halévy was not named on the playbill. Again worried by the effect of a burlesque production on his prospects in his ''real'' job, he had withdrawn from the project, only to find himself dragged back in by Offenbach. But, at his insistence, anonymously. Thus, for the moment, he participated only privately in the triumph won by *Orphée.*

There were, however, plenty more triumphs to come, both in the musical theatre and in the world of the straight play. In the charming *La Chanson de Fortunio* and the burlesque *Le Pont des soupirs* he teamed again with Crémieux and with Offenbach, and the trio gave a helping hand to ''M de Saint-Rémy,'' otherwise the very royal Duc de Morny (whom Halévy had already provided with another little libretto), in his latest attempt at theatrical authorship with *M Choufleuri.* His cooperation helped to earn Halévy, by way of thanks, a post at the Corps Législatif. He put his hand to revue along with Eugène Grangé, Philippe Gille and Offenbach for the little *Le Carnaval des revues* (1860), but it was a further and new authorial collaboration which brought Halévy to the peak of his career, the collaboration with fellow playwright Henri Meilhac.

Meilhac, Halévy and Offenbach came together first when the composer provided one number for the authors' little Palais-Royal piece, *Le Brésilien* (1863), but they soon moved on to much more significant collaborations. Together, the soon famous pair provided Offenbach with the texts for the series of great musical plays which were to be the centerpiece of his oeuvre: the opéras-bouffes *La Belle Hélène, Barbe-bleue, La Grande-Duchesse de Gérolstein* and *Les Brigands,* the less burlesque *La Périchole,* and the vaudevillesque *La Vie parisienne,* as well as the almost successful, and textually delightful, *La Boulangère a des écus.* They also supplied Lecocq with the text for his charming and triumphant *Le Petit Duc, La Petite Mademoiselle* and, in collaboration with Albert Millaud, the internationally successful vaudeville *La Roussotte* (w Hervé). In addition, they scored huge successes in both the operatic world, with their adaptation of Prosper Merimée's novel as the libretto for *Carmen,* and in the straight theatre, with *Frou-Frou, Le Mari de la débutante, La Cigale, La Petite Marquise, La Boule, Le Réveillon, Toto chez Tata* and *Tricoche et Cacolet.*

The year 1881 saw the last original Halévy musical on the Paris stage, *La Roussotte,* ending a 25-year musical-theatre career which had produced some of the world's most loved and admired shows. ''He is forty-nine years old,'' a journalist reported a few years later, ''but does not look it. He is lean, grave, pale, taciturn, heavily and darkly bearded, and altogether morose and melancholy looking—in strange contrast to the wit and drollery of the pages to which he has affixed his signature. He has given up his former gay haunts and rollicking companions and lives quietly in the company of his children and his books.'' Halévy continued to write for the nonmusical stage, and found great success as a novelist, notably with *L'Abbé Constatin* (1882) as well as such pieces as *Un Mariage d'amour, Une Scandale* and *Princesse.* He was elected to the Académie Française, and became a Commander of the Legion of Honour.

Halévy's works have been the bases for a long list of musical plays from other, mostly Austrian, hands, the most famous being the adaptation of his play *Le Réveillon* (w Meilhac) as the libretto for Johann Strauss's *Die Fledermaus* (1874). *La Boule* (w Meilhac) became the Posse *Von Tisch und Bett,* written and composed by Julius Hopp (Theater an der Wien 7 September 1875), and *Tricoche et Cacolet* (w Meilhac) was given songs by Karl Treumann and Franz von Suppé (Carltheater 1876) and more liberally musicalized as *Ein toller Geschaft* by Kren and Schönfeld for the Berlin stage (Thalia Theater 7 September 1901, mus: Einödshofer) and as *Spitzbub et Cie* by Wilhelm Ascher and Robert Pohl, music by Josef Bayer, at the Vienna Lustspiel-Theater (5 July 1907). *La Cigale* (Variétés 6 October 1877 w Meilhac) was turned by J P Burnett into a disastrous *Good Luck* for London in 1885 and remade by H Osten and Julius Stern as a Viennese *Bum-Bum* (Carltheater 24 October 1896), whilst *La Petite Marquise* (w Meilhac) became Felix Albini's Operette *Madame Troubadour* (1907). *Le Mari de la débutante* was turned into two different Operetten at the Carltheater within eight months: Annie Dirkens played seven performances at both the home house and the Theater an der Wien in *Die Prima Donna* (Alfred Müller-Norden/Alexander Landesberg, Ludwig Fischl 31 January 1901) and Mizzi Günther played Nina in *Die Debutantin* (Alfred Zamara/A M Willner, Waldberg 4 October 1901) for 10 nights. *La Roussotte,* in one of its series of international remakings, was Germanned by Franz von Schönthan and given a new score by Carl Millöcker under the title of *Ein süsses Kind* (Theater an der Wien 1 April 1882) and the text of the Offenbach opérette *La Diva* was rewritten by Zell and Genée into a piece called *Die Theaterprinzessin* (Theater an der Wien 30 December 1872).

The 1938 French opérette *Les Petites Cardinal* (Honegger, Jacques Ibert/ad Willemetz, Paul Brach, Bouffes-Parisiens 12 February) was based on Halévy's series of sketches *M et Mme Cardinal, Les Petites Cardinal* and *La Famille Cardinal.*

1855 **Entrez Messieurs, Mesdames** (Jacques Offenbach/w Jules Méry) 1 act Théâtre des Bouffes-Parisiens 5 July

1855 **Une pleine eau** (Jules Costé/w d'Osmont) 1 act Théâtre des Bouffes-Parisiens 28 August

1855 **Madame Papillon** (Offenbach) 1 act Théâtre des Bouffes-Parisiens 3 October

1855 **Ba-ta-clan** (Offenbach) 1 act Théâtre des Bouffes-Parisiens 29 December

1856 **L'Imprésario** (*Der Schauspieldirektor*) French version w Léon Battu (Théâtre des Bouffes-Parisiens)

1857 **Le Docteur Miracle** (Charles Lecocq/w Battu) Théâtre des Bouffes-Parisiens 8 April

1857 **Le Docteur Miracle** (Georges Bizet/w Battu) Théâtre des Bouffes-Parisiens 8 April

1857 **L'Opéra aux fenêtres** (Léon Gastinel) 1 act Théâtre des Bouffes-Parisiens 5 October

1858 **Orphée aux enfers** (Offenbach/w Hector Crémieux) Théâtre des Bouffes-Parisiens 21 October

1859 **Voici le jour** (Jules Ward) 1 act Lyon

1860 **Titus et Bérénice** (Gastinel/w Édouard Fournier) 1 act Théâtre des Bouffes-Parisiens 11 May

1860 **Le Mari sans le savoir** (''Saint-Rémy,'' ie, Duc de Morny/w Léon Halévy) 1 act Théâtre des Bouffes-Parisiens 31 December

1861 **La Chanson de Fortunio** (Offenbach/w Crémieux) 1 act Théâtre des Bouffes-Parisiens 5 January

1861 **Les Deux Buveurs** (Léo Delibes/w Crémieux) 1 act Théâtre des Bouffes-Parisiens January

1861 **Le Pont des soupirs** (Offenbach/w Crémieux) Théâtre des Bouffes-Parisiens 23 March

1861 **M Choufleuri restera chez lui le . . .** (Offenbach/w ''Saint-Rémy,'' Crémieux) 1 act Présidence du Corps-legislatif 31 May; Théatre des Bouffes-Parisiens 14 September

1861 **La Baronne de San Francisco** (Henri Caspers/w Crémieux) 1 act Théâtre des Bouffes-Parisiens 27 November

1861 **Le Roman comique** (Offenbach/w Crémieux) Théâtre des Bouffes-Parisiens 10 December

1861 **Les Eaux d'Ems** (Delibes/w Crémieux) 1 act Bad Ems; Théâtre des Bouffes-Parisiens 9 April 1863

1862 **Un fin de bail** (Adolphe Varney/w Crémieux) 1 act Théâtre des Bouffes-Parisiens 29 January

1862 **Mon ami Pierrot** (Delibes/w Crémieux) 1 act Kursaal, Bad Ems July

1862 **Jacqueline** (Offenbach/w Crémieux) 1 act Théâtre des Bouffes-Parisiens 14 October

1864 **La Belle Hélène** (Offenbach/w Meilhac) Théâtre des Variétés 17 December

1866 **Barbe-bleue** (Offenbach/w Meilhac) Théâtre des Variétés 5 February

1866 **La Vie parisienne** (Offenbach/w Meilhac) Palais-Royal 31 October

1867 **La Grande-Duchesse de Gérolstein** (Offenbach/w Meilhac) Théâtre des Variétés 12 April

1868 **Le Château à Toto** (Offenbach/w Meilhac) Palais-Royal 6 May

1868 **La Périchole** (Offenbach/w Meilhac) Théâtre des Variétés 6 October

1869 **La Diva** (Offenbach/w Meilhac) Théâtre des Bouffes-Parisiens 22 March

1869 **Les Brigands** (Offenbach/w Meilhac) Théâtre des Variétés 10 December

1873 **Pomme d'api** (Offenbach/w William Busnach) 1 act Théâtre de la Renaissance 4 September

1875 **La Boulangère a des écus** (Offenbach/w Meilhac) Théâtre des Variétés 19 October

1878 **Le Petit Duc** (Lecocq/w Meilhac) Théâtre de la Renaissance 25 January

1879 **La Marocaine** (Offenbach/w Paul Ferrier) Théâtre des Bouffes-Parisiens 13 January

1879 **La Petite Mademoiselle** (Lecocq/w Meilhac) Théâtre de la Renaissance 12 April

1881 **Janot** (Lecocq/w Meilhac) Théâtre de la Renaissance 22 January

1881 **La Roussotte** (Hervé, Lecocq/w Meilhac, Millaud) Théâtre des Variétés 28 January

Memoirs: *L'Invasion, souvenirs et récits* (Boussod, Valadon & Cie, Paris, 1872), *Notes et Souvenirs, 1871–1872* (Calmann-Levy, Paris, 1889); Biography: Clarétie, J: *Ludovic Halévy* (Quantin, Paris, 1883)

HALEY, Jack [HALEY, John Joseph] (b Boston, 10 August 1897; d Los Angeles, 6 June 1979). Leading man for several song-and-dance shows of the 1920s and 1930s and for many a musical film.

Haley came from vaudeville to the musical stage via revue (*Round the Town* 1924, *Gay Paree* 1925–26), and made his mark starring as the quiet, wealthy and ever-so-attractive hero netted by soubrette Zelma O'Neal in De Sylva, Brown and Henderson's *Follow Thru* (1929, Jack Martin). The role in *Follow Thru* gave him the opportunity to introduce a hit song in ''Button Up Your Overcoat,'' but Richard Whiting and Oscar Hammerstein II gave him no equivalent chances in a similar part in the rather less successful *Free for All* (1931, Steve Potter). In *Take a Chance* (1932, Duke Stanley) he left the dashing hero's role to Jack Whiting, and appeared this time as a more dubious character who, nevertheless, got to sing the best number of the evening, Whiting's ''You're an Old Smoothie,'' with Ethel Merman.

Having already visited Hollywood for the film of *Follow Thru* (1930, Jack Martin), he now returned there for a series of more than 20 musical films including *Sitting Pretty* (1933, Peter Pendelton), *The Girl Friend* (1935, Henry), *Poor Little Rich Girl* (1936), *Alexander's Ragtime Band* (1938) and *The Wizard of Oz* (1939), in which he made a memorable appearance as the Tin Man. He made his only subsequent Broadway stage ventures in Rodgers and Hart's *Higher and Higher* (1940, film 1943, Mike O'Brien), the revusical *Show Time* (1942) and the revue *Inside USA* (1948) in the latter years of his career.

HALF A SIXPENCE Musical in 2 acts by Beverley Cross based on H G Wells's novel *Kipps*. Music and lyrics by David Heneker. Cambridge Theatre, London, 21 March 1963.

Commissioned by producer Harold Fielding as a vehicle for the rock 'n' roll singer Tommy Steele, whom he had successfully presented as the star of Rodgers and Hammerstein's *Cinderella, Half a Sixpence* was based on Wells's 1905 cautionary tale of a draper's boy who finds that money and social aspirations don't bring happiness.

Arthur Kipps (Steele) works in a lowly position in a Tunbridge Wells drapery, and has an ''understanding'' with the servant girl Ann Pornick (Marti Webb). But the extravagant actor Chitterlow (James Grout) arrives on the scene with the news that Kipps has inherited a fortune, and the foolish boy is soon flinging his wealth around and

Plate 162. **Half a Sixpence.** *James Grout (Chitterlow) knocks Tommy Steele (Kipps) flying with his bicycle.*

trying to mix with local highish society. The only society folk who pay any attention are those with something to gain, like the pretentious but poor Mrs Walsingham (Jessica James), her attractive daughter, Helen (Anna Barry), and her worthless son (Ian White), to whom, fatally, Kipps entrusts his money for investment. Bit by bit, the youngster comes to his senses. He renounces Helen and her kind and returns to Ann, and, when the money is lost, cashes in his assets and retires with his little wife to run a bookshop. Then Chitterlow arrives with the news that his play, in which Kipps had invested in his flush days, is a hit. Kipps has made a second fortune. He tells Chitterlow to keep it.

David Heneker's score for *Half a Sixpence* was one of the most warmly endearing to have appeared in the British theatre for decades. Kipps and Ann sealing their lover's pact by each taking ''Half a Sixpence'' as a lover's token instead of the split sovereign that better-off folk share, the boy mooning foolishly over the comparatively sophisticated Helen in ''She's Too Far Above Me,'' jubilating over his first date with the lady in ''If the Rain's Got to Fall,'' or, still in the thrall of what money can buy, insisting that ''I'll Build a Palace for My Girl'' whilst the practical Ann, in counterpoint, insists that ''I Only Want a Little House,'' were memorable moments for the star. Alongside these, there were fine pieces for Ann, stubbornly refusing to go posh (''I Know What I Am''), or blazing away at the unfaithful Artie (''I'm Talking to You!''); for Kipps's pals (Anthony Valentine, Colin Farrell, John Bull), leaping joyously about imagining what life would be like if they had ''Money to Burn''; for Chitterlow (''The One That Got Away''); and for the whole ensemble, celebrating an outing on ''The Grand Military Canal.'' Perhaps the greatest hit that came from the show, however, was a song which, like so many other show hits, was added to the score when the piece was already on its way to town: the crazy, music-hall-style wedding scena, ''Flash, Bang, Wallop!,'' the title of which has become a *Dictionary of Quotations* catchphrase as the song continues as a favorite 35 years on.

Half a Sixpence played for 677 performances in London, being closed down to allow Steele and Grout to lead a Broadway production, mounted by Fielding in collaboration with American associates. The ''I'll Build a Palace for My Girl'' sequence had to be cut when the scenery was lost en route from England, and trouble loomed as a whole series of other changes were instigated and then mostly abandoned along with the original American director before *Half a Sixpence* reached Broadway. There, with Polly James (Ann) teamed with Steele and Grout, it repeated its London success, playing in New York for 512 performances. The show toured in 1966–67, with Dick Kallman as Artie, and in 1967 Paramount mounted a film version in which Steele was teamed with Julia Foster (and the voice of Miss Webb) as Ann, Cyril Ritchard as Chitterlow, and some further alterations to the score. In spite of ending up as a pawn in a power-change at Paramount, which resulted in some clumsy cutting, the film proved an agreeable record of the show and of Steele's performance.

Australia saw *Half a Sixpence* in 1967 with Mark McManus (later of the National Theatre and TV's *Taggart*) as Artie and former Australian matinée idol Max Oldaker as Chitterlow. It ran for four months in Melbourne and three in Sydney (Theatre Royal 16 August 1967).

USA: Broadhurst Theater 25 April 1965; Australia: Comedy Theatre, Melbourne 11 March 1967

Film: Paramount 1967

Recordings: original cast (Decca), Broadway cast (RCA), Film soundtrack (RCA), etc

HALL, Juanita [LONG, Juanita] (b Keysport, NJ, 6 November 1901; d Bay Shore, NY, 28 February 1968).

Miss Hall appeared as a chorus singer in *Sing Out Sweet Land,* the 1946 *Show Boat* revival and *Street Scene,* and in a minor part in *St Louis Woman* before creating the role of Bloody Mary in *South Pacific.* In spite of the fact that she was, physically, wholly the opposite to the original character description—a short, squat and chunky black woman, where a tiny, wizened Asiatic was called for—she scored an enormous success (''Bali H'ai,'' ''Happy Talk'') and was signed to repeat her stage performance on film. On this occasion, however, her singing voice was dubbed. She later appeared on Broadway opposite Pearl Bailey in the Truman Capote/Harold Arlen musical *House of Flowers* (1954), as Madam Liang in Rodgers and Hammerstein's *Flower Drum Song* (1958) and at the Jones Beach Theater in the 1965 *Mardi Gras!* (Katie/Katherine/Marie Le Veau).

HALL, Natalie (b Providence, RI, 23 September 1904; d Wiscasset, Maine, 4 March 1994).

After a brief early career in opera, Miss Hall made her Broadway debut in the leading role of the Shuberts' imported Operette *Three Little Girls* (1930, Beate). She subsequently starred with Guy Robertson in another Continental piece, *Marching By* (1931, Anna), on the road, as Kathleen in Vincent Youmans's briefly seen musical version of *Smilin' Through, Through the Years* (1932), and as Roxane in the St Louis Muny *Cyrano de Bergerac* (1932) before she found her biggest success as the tempestuous prima donna Frieda Hatzfeld in Jerome Kern's Continental-style operetta *Music in the Air* (1932, ''The Song is You''). She visited London to take the lead role in the Theatre Royal, Drury Lane production of Ábrahám's *Ball at the Savoy* (1933), replaced Maria Jeritza in Friml's *Music Hath Charms* (1934) for its short time on Broadway, and played the role of Mrs Cynthia Bradley in the Gilbert and Sullivan tale *Knights of Song* (1938), performing *The Mikado*'s "The Moon and I," but thereafter her career in the musical theatre was limited to regional productions (Bertha in *The Red Mill,* 1940, etc).

Her sister **Bettina HALL** (b North Easton, Mass, 20 October 1906; d Maricopa, Arizona, 6 August 1997) had a parallel career, playing first in Gilbert and Sullivan, then in opera, and appearing alongside Natalie in *Three Little Girls* (1930, Marie). She appeared opposite Walter Slezak in the lead role of an Americanization of Benatzky's *Meine Schwester und ich* (*Meet My Sister,* 1930, Dolly) and starred alongside Georges Metaxa in the Harbach/Kern *The Cat and the Fiddle* (1931, Shirley Sheridan "She Didn't Say 'Yes,'" "Try to Forget"), with a success equivalent to that her sister would have the following year in *Music in the Air.* In 1934 she appeared in a souped-up Shubert revival of Herbert's *The Only Girl* (Ruth Wilson), which luckily lasted for a short enough time to allow her to take up the juvenile role of Hope Harcourt in the original production of *Anything Goes* (1934, "The Gypsy in Me"). Her subsequent career in the musical theatre did not include Broadway, although she appeared in New York in non-singing roles.

Both sisters married well and disappeared from the theatrical scene.

HALL, Owen [DAVIS, James] (b Dublin, 10 April 1853; d Harrogate, 9 April 1907). Style-setting librettist who authored some of the most successful musical plays of the 1890s and 1900s for the British stage.

The son of a Jewish artist, Hyman Davis, Jimmy Davis was aimed for a career as a solicitor and, from the age of 21, he busied himself in pursuit of a legal career from an office at Mayfair's 5 Albermarle Street. Like many another young and unenthusiastic solicitor of the period, however, he had a taste for the bottle, the pen and the sporting and bohemian lives, as well as an utter incapacity to control his indulgences and his outrageous bonhomie. As a result, at the age of 29, the young solicitor went bankrupt to the vast tune of £27,385. After a dozen years of ineffectual solicitoring, and an abortive attempt to take the Dundalk parliamentary seat for the Conservative Party, in 1886 he gave up the law and went full-time into journalism, where he exercised his trippingly caustic tongue as dramatic critic on *The Sporting Times* and for two years as editor of *The Bat* (1885–87). So caustic, indeed, was he that he was hauled into court by musical-comedy star Marius for what turned out to be £110 worth of rather too imaginatively libellous prose. He also continued his old way of life and, by 1888, ended up in the bankruptcy courts again.

Davis persevered both in his journalism and his vices—in which the musical theatre played a natural part—and was apparently not overly impressed when he saw George Edwardes's production of *In Town,* one of the heralds of what was to become accepted as the new-style musical comedy. Anecdote relates that, meeting Edwardes on the Brighton train, he told "the Guvnor" what he thought of the text of his new show, adding "I could do better myself." Edwardes's reply is said to have been "Then do."

The result of this conversation was a libretto which was entitled *A Gaiety Girl,* written under the pseudonym "Owen Hall" (said to be a reference to Davis's notorious propensity for alarming debts), which Edwardes accepted and entrusted to the young conductor and composer Sidney Jones, who had never written a full-sized musical before, and the neophyte lyricist Harry Greenbank for its songs. When it came to production time, Owen Hall's book had to undergo some changes. Not to the plot, for that was a simple little affair about a stolen comb and a few tangled romances, but to the dialogue. Hall had taken a slicingly satirical tone, and the little story with its pretty girls and songs was told in lines which jabbed here and there in the style of an upmarket and particularly vicious gossip columnist. Some of the jibes were so personal that Edwardes did not dare put them on the stage. But much of the smart society back-chat was still there on opening night, and it hit its marks with such effect that Edwardes received several requests from high places for alterations. The public, on the other hand, loved it, even when the Reverend Brierly, a character depicted as a man of doubtful moral rectitude, was demoted, after pressure from Lambeth Palace, to being just plain Dr Brierly.

A Gaiety Girl was a dazzling success and confirmed Edwardes in the way he was going. It also found a new career and a new source of money for Hall, who immediately went to work on a new show with Jones and Greenbank. *An Artist's Model* kept the snappy dialogue, but twinned it with a romantic plot, tacked in at the last minute when Edwardes managed to contract favorite prima donna, Marie Tempest, and needed a role for her. For the £850 he was being paid this time, Hall happily made the alterations and, by this lucky chance, set up the formula for a series of successes at Daly's Theatre.

An Artist's Model was succeeded by *The Geisha,* as Hall's price climbed to a dazzling £4,000 a script—sold outright, with no provision for royalties, for ready money was all the author cared about. Here Edwardes made a marvellous bargain, for *The Geisha* was to be the biggest international hit the British musical theatre had known, playing thousands of performances on the Continent (one source counts some 8,000 in Germany alone), America and the colonies and touring for decades in Britain.

Hall had now taken some of the more extremely spiced sauce off his style, and evolved a happy combination of sparky, up-to-date comedy and good old-fashioned (and sometimes new-fashioned) romance, into which he was never afraid to pop some general or particular parody when the opportunity arose. For the most part his subjects were modern, but he was by no means at a loss dealing with the citizens of Ancient Rome when he supplied Sidney Jones with the text for one of their finest works, *A Greek Slave.* They came out just like his Londoners. And all the time his honoraria were rising. He had earned £7,000 in the year *The Geisha* was produced, in the following year he netted £9,900. Astounding figures, but no less astounding was the £8,000 that he paid out to bookmakers in lost bets. A few weeks after the opening of *A Greek Slave,* Owen Hall was bankrupt again.

Given his continuing appetite for money, Hall did not confine himself to writing for Edwardes. He had already fleshed out a James Tanner plot line for ambitious touring manager Cissie Graham (*All Abroad,* £350) and when Edwardes found it a good idea to accept a libretto from the influential journalist ''E A Morton'' for his next show, Hall was happy to accept the proposition from up-and-coming producer Tom Davis and his associates to write a text for a first musical by successful songwriter Leslie Stuart. The result was *Florodora,* another international hit of huge proportions.

Hall turned out two more musicals for Davis: *The Silver Slipper* with Stuart, and his one and only genuine flop, a complicated piece of nonsense, nothing like his other works in tone, called *The Medal and the Maid,* in which he came back together with Sidney Jones. For Edwardes, on the other hand, he went back to the modern society tale to turn out perhaps the most delightful of all his libretti, the sweetly silly story of a misguided kiss told with the skill of a genuine farceur in *The Girl from Kays* (Hall did not initially admit he'd based it on Léon Gandillot's *La Mariée recalcitrante,* but he had to in the end when pinned down by just the kind of newspaper article he'd loved to write himself), and a semi-success in *The Little Cherub* (announcedly with the use of a bit of Meilhac's *Décoré*). For Frank Curzon he created a splendid character in the amorous copper *Sergeant Brue,* which Willie Edouin, who had already made *Florodora*'s Tweedlepunch and ''Piggy Hoggenheimer'' from *The Girl from Kays* into classic comic gentlemen of the theatre, turned into another memorable creation.

Life caught up with Jimmy Davis, at the age of 54, before the courts did again. His last show, the farcical comedy with music *King Silly,* apparently written without a commission, did not get to the stage, and his attempted launch of himself as a public company towards the end of 1906 with a capitalization of £12,000 did not take off. Perhaps investors knew. (Well, some did. After his death some sued to get their ''investment'' back.) When he died, with the credit for two of the world's most successful ever shows and a whole series of other hits to his name, with performances of his shows taking place every day all over the world, his assets came to just £200. But his long-serving coachman and valet attended his funeral.

Hall's non-theatrical writings included a successful novel, *The Track of a Storm* (1896), a mystery, *Jetsam* (1897), and *Hernando* (1902).

Hall's sister, Julia Frankau (b ?1859; d London, 17 March 1916) was a successful novelist under the name of ''Frank Danby,'' and the mother of author Gilbert Frankau and of the actor **Ronald Frankau** who appeared in London in *A Country Girl* (1914), *The Gay Princess* (1931) and a long run of 1930s and 1940s revues.

- 1893 **A Gaiety Girl** (Sidney Jones/Harry Greenbank) Prince of Wales Theatre 14 October
- 1895 **An Artist's Model** (Jones/Greenbank) Daly's Theatre 2 February
- 1895 **All Abroad** (Frederick Rosse/W H Risque/w James Tanner) Theatre Royal, Portsmouth 1 April; Criterion Theatre 8 August
- 1896 **The Geisha** (Jones/Greenbank) Daly's Theatre 25 April
- 1898 **A Greek Slave** (Jones/Greenbank) Daly's Theatre 8 June
- 1899 **Florodora** (Leslie Stuart/E Boyd-Jones) Lyric Theatre 11 November
- 1901 **The Silver Slipper** (Stuart/Risque) Lyric Theatre 1 June
- 1902 **The Girl from Kays** (Ivan Caryll, Cecil Cook/Adrian Ross, Claude Aveling) Apollo Theatre 15 November
- 1903 **The Medal and the Maid** (Jones/C H Taylor) Lyric Theatre 25 April
- 1904 **Sergeant Brue** (Liza Lehmann/J Hickory Wood) Strand Theatre 14 June
- 1905 **The Lady Bankrupt** (Frank Tours) 1 act Empress, Brixton 24 November; Oxford Music Hall 2 July 1906
- 1906 **The Little Cherub** (*The Girl on the Stage*) (Caryll/Ross) Prince of Wales Theatre 13 January

HALL, Pauline [SCHMIDGALL, Pauline Fredrika] (b Cincinnati, Ohio, 26 February 1860; d Yonkers, NY, 29 December 1919). Beautiful, shapely, dark-eyed vocalist who found stardom in the title role of the record-breaking *Erminie.*

Daughter of a Cincinnati druggist, Pauline Hall made a youthful start in the theatre as a dancer at the local Robinson's Opera House (1875), then moved on to tour in the front row of the chorus with Alice Oates's and Samuel Colville's companies in comic opera and extravaganza, and to appear in classic plays with Mary Anderson (Lady Capulet, Widow Melnotte). In the years that followed she played in small, and sometimes larger, roles with E E

Rice's company (1879–81, Sir Filbert Hazelnut in *Babes in the Wood,* Zissis in *Horrors,* St Denis of France in *Revels,* Hans Wagner and then Gabriel in *Evangeline,* Zidore in *Calino,* Honeydew in *Hiawatha,* etc), with J W Norcross and with Comley and Barton (1881, Christophe in *Les Cloches de Corneville*), appeared on Broadway in Haverley's productions of *The Merry War* (1882, in the fine role of Else) and *Patience* (1881, Lady Saphir), with Rice in *Orpheus in the Underworld* (1883, Venus), with what pretended to be Lila Clay's all-woman troupe in *An Adamless Eden* (1884) and as Venus—again—in Sydney Rosenfeld's (nearly) all-women adaptation of *Ixion.* She appeared regularly in burlesque where, given her fine figure, she was frequently put into tights in such boy's roles as Gabriel in *Evangeline,* Hassan in *Bluebeard* (1884), Lovesoul in the spectacular *The Seven Ravens* (1884), Ixion in *Ixion* (1885) or Oberon in *Bottom's Dream* (1885) with Nat Goodwin. She was a boy again when she appeared as Prince Orlofsky in *Die Fledermaus,* in her home tongue of German, at the Thalia Theater (1885).

In 1885 she took a firm step towards fame when she joined the Casino Theater company, with whom she appeared in the second-lead role of Ninon de l'Enclos in Genée's *Nanon,* as Angelo in *Amorita* (*Pfingsten in Florenz,* 1885) and as Sáffi in *The Gipsy Baron* (1885) before being allotted the title role of the first English musical to be staged at the Casino. *Erminie* created theatrical history and 26-year-old Miss Hall, in the role of Erminie de Pontvert—originated in London by Florence St John—found herself with the part of a lifetime. She played Mlle de Pontvert for most of the show's virtual two-year run at the Casino, and in the years to follow became identified nationwide not only with the part but also with Erminie's lullaby "Dear Mother, In Dreams I See Her" which, in spite of having gone for little in Britain, became a huge hit in America. She toured and toured again and yet again with this piece in the following years, and returned for further *Erminie* seasons at the Casino in 1889 and 1898.

Between repeated *Erminie* productions Miss Hall subsequently appeared on Broadway in the star role of a grossly rewritten version of *La Fille du tambour-major* (*The Drum Major*), in Chassaigne's *Nadgy* and as Prince Raphaël in Offenbach's *La Princesse de Trébizonde* (Harrigan's Theater, 1894), and toured as Offenbach's *Belle Hélène,* in breeches as Vivian Trevalyan in a comic opera vehicle called *Puritania* (1892) produced by her own comic opera company, and opposite Richard Golden in *The Honeymooners* (1893, Amadie). She was also seen in New York as *Madame Favart* and *La Belle Hélène,* in *Les Cloches de Corneville* and in the title role of Harry Paulton's *Dorcas* (1894, Dorcas/Lady Honoria) and made her well-paid debut in vaudeville (Chicago, January 1897), before she retired briefly to a new marriage.

Plate 163. **Pauline Hall.** *The beautiful American star of* Erminie.

She later returned to tour with Francis Wilson (Christian to his *Cyrano de Bergerac, Erminie* 1900) and with the touring Wilbur Opera Company (1901), and with her star rating now rather decreased, took *Dorcas* on the road again (1905–6), played summer season in *Erminie* (1908), toured in the role originally created for Lillian Russell in *Wildfire* (1909–10) and appeared in Chicago's *Love and Politics* with Joe Howard (1911). She was seen again on Broadway playing such character roles as Dame Durden in the 1912 revival of *Robin Hood* and as Lady Constance Wynne in an Arthur Hammerstein revival of *The Geisha* (1913), but she remained in the public mind inextricably connected with *Erminie* for the rest of her long career as a singer and an actress, a career which was closed by an appearance in David Belasco's play *The Gold Diggers* (1919), in which, shortly before her death, she appeared in the role of an aging comic-opera star.

Miss Hall's second husband was George B McLellan, theatrical manager and brother to librettist C M S McLellan.

A sister, Albertina, played in the chorus alongside Pauline in her earliest engagements as a singer, and a brother, Frederick, was a chorus member at the Casino up till his death aged just 26 (d New York, 4 January 1890).

HALLELUJAH, BABY! Musical in 2 acts by Arthur Laurents. Lyrics by Adolph Green and Betty Comden. Music by Jule Styne. Martin Beck Theater, New York, 26 April 1967.

A curiously tub-thumping piece written by three of Broadway's finest writers on one of their cloudier days, *Hallelujah, Baby!* took a conventional making-it-good-in-showbiz tale (with illustrations) and gave it the gimmick of an all-in leading character who did not age in her progress from beginning-of-the-century slavey-ing up through the some 80 or 90 years to present-day success, thus (allegedly) standing as a symbol of the ordinary black-maid-risen-to-showbiz-stardom in 20th-century American society.

Georgina (Leslie Uggams) opens proceedings as a poor, new-century black girl whose boyfriend, Pullman porter Clem (Robert Hooks), ruins her chance of a straightforward wedded life by losing their marriage money playing craps. So Georgina, with the surely not disinterested help of white man Harvey (Allen Case), goes into show business, and by the 1920s she has made her way into a New York cutie line. She sings for the troops in the War, gets to the glittering gowns and glitzy clubs (owned by white man Harvey) by the 1950s, and in the 1960s starts having 1960s-type qualms about her involvement with all these non-black people. So she drops helpful Harvey and goes back to Clem (who was a civil rights yeah-man in the 1950s) for a happy(?) and racially pure ending.

Laurents and Styne, authors of the recently successful *Gypsy,* once again built their story around show business and a large—though this time young—female leading role, in a piece which allowed 23-year-old Miss Uggams (instead of the originally intended Lena Horne) and the other performers/characters to present numbers written in the styles of the various periods that were passed through in the course of the evening. Harry Rigby, Albert Selden, Hal James and Jane C Nusbaum sponsored the production, which played 293 times on Broadway, and picked up the season's Tony Awards for best musical, best score and best actress (tied) after it had closed.

Recording: original cast (Columbia)

HALLER, Hermann [FREUND, Hermann] (b Berlin, 24 December 1871; d London, 5 May 1943). German producer and librettist who mounted some of Berlin's most successful musicals in the 1910s, and the city's glitziest revues in the 1920s.

In turn the director of the Olympia, Berlin (1894–96), the Haller-Ensemble (1896–1907), the Centraltheater, Leipzig (1907) and the Carl-Schultze Theater, Hamburg (from 1908), Haller during his Hamburg years followed up his first tentative ventures at authorship, and found some exportable success with the musical comedy *Parkettsitz Nr 10,* which launched the young composer, Walter Goetze, and with the Walter Kollo musical comedy *Der Juxbaron,* which went on from Hamburg to a fine career around central Europe.

Haller moved back to Berlin in 1914 to take over the Theater am Nollendorfplatz, and there he produced a series of new musicals, many of which were written to his own libretti. He began with a major hit when the patriotic wartime *Immer feste druff!* marked up a run of more than 650 performances, followed up with six months of *Blaue Jungens,* more than 200 nights of *Die Gulaschkanone* and nearly 500 of the *Quality Street* musical, *Drei alte Schachteln,* before beginning a series of collaborations with Eduard Künneke, of which the high point was the composer's most enduring work, the delightful *Der Vetter aus Dingsda.* When the last of these Künneke pieces, *Verliebte Leute,* disappointed in 138 performances, Haller switched to importing the proven *Ta bouche* from France with only average results, and *Die Königin von Montmartre* from the Netherlands (as *Die Königin der Strasse*) with decidedly poor ones.

He promptly divested himself of the Nollendorfplatz house, and resurfaced almost immediately at the Admiralspalast, which he opened in September 1923 with *Drunter und Druber,* the first of a series of spectacular revues on Parisian lines which would become famous in 1920s Berlin: *Noch und noch, Achtung! Welle 505!, An und Aus, Wann und Wo, Schön und Schick.* Haller's revues were concocted by their director-compiler after a careful examination of the best of what was on display in London, Paris and New York. He filched material freely from all three centers, but he hired top international talent, produced lavishly, and made his opening nights at the Admiralspalast into big, publicity-bearing social events. He also prospered, as he built himself a reputation as a first-class showman.

In 1930 Haller varied his programming by mounting an extravaganza-style production of *Die Csárdásfürstin.* It flopped, and once again he moved on. Soon, however, under Nazi threat, he was forced to move further and, having stuck it out in central Europe until 1936, ultimately emigrated to London, where he died before the war's end.

1902 **Cupido & Co** (*Le Carnet du diable*) German version w Maurice Rappaport (Belle-Alliance-Theater)

1911 **Parkettsitz Nr 10** (Walter Goetze/w Willy Wolff) Tivoli Theater, Hamburg 24 September

1913 **Der Juxbaron** (Walter Kollo/Wolff/w Alexander Pordes-Milo) Carl-Schultze Theater, Hamburg 14 November

- 1914 **Immer feste druff!** (aka *Gloria Viktoria*) (Kollo/w Wolff) Theater am Nollendorfplatz 1 October
- 1916 **Blaue Jungens** (Rudolf Nelson/Hermann Frey/w Kurt Kraatz) Theater am Nollendorfplatz 25 August
- 1917 **Die Gulaschkanone** (Kollo/w Wolff) Theater am Nollendorfplatz 23 February
- 1917 **Drei alte Schachteln** (Kollo/w ''Rideamus'' [ie, Fritz Oliven]) Theater am Nollendorfplatz 6 October
- 1919 **Der Vielgeliebte** (Eduard Künneke/w Rideamus) Theater am Nollendorfplatz 17 October
- 1920 **Wenn Liebe erwacht** (Künneke/w Rideamus) Theater am Nollendorfplatz 3 September
- 1921 **Der Vetter aus Dingsda** (Künneke/w Rideamus) Theater am Nollendorfplatz 15 April
- 1921 **Die Ehe im Kreise** (Künneke/w Rideamus) Theater am Nollendorfplatz 2 November
- 1922 **Verliebte Leute** (Künneke/w Rideamus) Theater am Nollendorfplatz 15 April
- 1922 **Dein Mund** (*Ta bouche*) German version w Rideamus (Theater am Nollendorfplatz)
- 1930 **Der doppelte Bräutigam** (Kollo/Wolff) Theater am Schiffbauerdamm 7 March
- 1937 **Herzklopfen** (Willi Rosen/w Max Bertuch) Johann Strauss-Theater, Vienna 4 June

HALLIDAY, Robert (b Loch Lomond, Scotland, 11 April 1891; d California, 31 October 1975). Scots baritone who created several memorable American operetta roles in the 1920s and 1930s.

Halliday moved to America at the age of 20 and toured as a chorister in musicals for several years before his earliest Broadway appearances in *The Rose Girl* (1921), *Springtime of Youth* (1922) and *Dew Drop Inn* (1923, Bobby Smith). He took over the hero's role in *Paradise Alley* (1924, Jack Harriman) at the Casino Theater, appeared alongside the Duncan Sisters in their curious *Uncle Tom's Cabin* musical, in which they starred jointly in the title roles of *Topsy and Eva* (1924, George Shelby), and spent the few performances of *Holka Polka* (*Frühling im Herbst*) at the Lyric Theatre (1925, Karel Boleslaw), before taking a supporting role in a rather more successful show, Gershwin's *Tip-Toes* (1925–26, Rollo), duetting ''Nice Baby'' with the young Jeanette MacDonald.

Later the same year he had his first major success when he created the part of Pierre Birabeau, the Red Shadow, in Romberg's *The Desert Song,* introducing ''The Desert Song,'' ''One Alone'' and ''The Riff Song,'' and he confirmed that success when he followed up as Robert Misson, the equally romantic hero of *The New Moon* (1928), introducing ''Stouthearted Men'' and, with his wife Evelyn Herbert, the famous duets ''Wanting You'' and ''Lover Come Back to Me.''

The pair were cast together again in Broadway's *Princess Charming* (*Alexandra,* 1930, Torelli) and in the London production of *Waltzes from Vienna* (*Walzer aus Wien,* 1931, Johann Strauss jr), and Halliday subsequently played opposite Natalie Hall in *Music Hath Charms* (1934, Charles Parker) and her sister, Bettina Hall, in a revival of *The Only Girl,* appeared as the romantic Donald Hutton (ie, Dr Siedler) in the American version of *Im weissen Rössl* (1936, *White Horse Inn*) on Broadway and went through another Red-Shadowy disguise to win Nancy McCord in the American premiere of *Beloved Rogue* (*Venus in Seide*) in St Louis (1935, The Stranger). He also appeared at the Muny in the American premiere of *Teresina* (Lavalette), *The Cat and the Fiddle* (Victor), *The Desert Song, Madame Sherry* and *The Chocolate Soldier.*

He toured Australia in 1937–38, appearing there in the baritone role of *Balalaika* and in his most famous role of the Red Shadow, and he made a final Broadway appearance, at almost 60, in a supporting role (but still with third billing) in *Three Wishes for Jamie* (1952). He was seen in 1954 as Archie Beaton in San Francisco Light Opera's *Brigadoon,* and finally settled into retirement with his wife at their ''New Moon Ranch'' in California. The couple died within months of each other in 1975.

HALTON, Marie [PRENDERGAST, Mary E] (b New York, 3 August ?1873). Although wholly forgotten today, the irrepressible Miss Halton had one of the most remarkable international careers of the turn-of-the-century musical theatre.

By all (her) accounts, this bloomingly blonde (most of the time) doctor's daughter from New York was brought up in Britain and began to study music in Paris ''under Madame La Grange, Sbriglian and Jacob Bouhy'' (and sometimes Marchesi was added to the list) at the age of 11, and was but 14 when she was cast as the little bride, Phyllis Tuppitt, in Broadway's production of *Dorothy* (1887). Other sources tack four years on to those ages, add that she performed as a teenager in Bordeaux, Lyon and elsewhere in the French provinces and suggest that is was on Aimée's advice that she returned to make a career in the land of her birth. On the post-Broadway tour she subbed for Lillian Russell in the show's title role. In 1889 she was seen at the Standard Theater in the co-starring role of Inez in *The Queen's Mate* (*La Princesse des Canaries*), and then at the Casino as the vivandière Claudine in *La Fille du tambour-major,* a role she abandoned to run off to Europe in the company of a South African diamond man. Four months and many a newspaper paragraph later she ran back, and was cast in the lead role of Babette in the Casino's new musical *The Brazilian,* in which part she rolled and smoked a cigarette whilst singing a song on the subject. *The New York Times* remarked with more venom than seemed objective that ''her acting is tiresome and her singing burdensome, and her gestures and poses are without significance, her reading of the lines is commonplace and dull, her voice is limited in compass and worn in quality and her method, like the earth before the creation, without form and void.'' Not for the last time the *New York Times* drama critic and the rest of the world saw things with wholly different eyes.

After the failure of *The Brazilian,* Miss Halton went on to play Clairette to the Lange of Camille D'Arville in *La Fille de Madame Angot,* but she quarreled newsworthily with her co-star, abandoned the Casino again, and headed off around America playing Clairette and the Grand-Duchess and as prima donna in *Poor Jonathan.* Part way into the tour, though, she announced her retirement, walked out and headed for Europe. Far from retiring, however, she soon (after having been ''specially coached by Audran in Paris'') appeared on the London stage, vice the recently married Geraldine Ulmar, as Marton in *La Cigale* (1891). She caused a small sensation, Ulmar came swiftly back, and Miss Halton was soon announced for other London starring engagements. However, in typical fashion, the job she accepted was in Australia, as prima donna of J C Williamson's Royal Comic Opera Company for the 1892 season. She appeared in Australia in more *La Cigale,* in the title role of *Dorothy* and as Bizet's *Carmen.* However, with the nonchalance which would characterize her extraordinarily mobile career, she cut short the successful run of *La Cigale* and sallied forth from Australia back to Britain. She arrived too late to take up the role for which she had been slated in Horace Sedger's production of *The Wedding Eve* and, whilst he muttered of suing, she instead took the Shaftesbury Theatre and presented herself in the soubrette role of the musical *La Rosière* (1893). The show was not successful, but Marie was well enough noticed quickly to be given leading roles first in Albéniz's comic opera *The Magic Ring* (Lolika, 1893), then opposite Arthur Roberts in a specially written-in role with written-up songs (''You've Never Seen Me Here Before,'' ''The Magic of Spring'') in the burlesque *Claude Du-val,* and to be signed to a three-year starring contract by no less a manager than George Edwardes.

Edwardes promptly announced that his new musical star would be launched in the title role of his new ''musical comedy'' *The Naughty Girl,* at the Gaiety Theatre. In the event, the landmark show at the Gaiety was called *The Shop Girl,* and Marie played the romantic juvenile role of the piece, leaving the soubrettery to Ada Reeve, whilst *A Naughty Girl* became Letty Lind's vehicle at Daly's, ultimately produced under the title *An Artist's Model.* Ill (well, absent anyway) on opening night, Marie missed the opportunity to introduce *The Shop Girl*'s soprano ballad ''Over the Hills and Far Away,'' which was left to her understudy, but she returned soon after and duly played her part in Edwardes's famous show.

Quite where she disappeared to for the next year or so one cannot tell, for—in spite of reports that she was ''shortly to go to South Africa for a couple of years as the principal singer of an opera company that George Edwardes is to send there''—she scuttled off from the Gaity soon after the show's opening, and the famous three-year contract certainly was not adhered to. But in 1896, having given birth (or whatever she was doing), she popped up in Paris, starring alongside Marguerite Deval in the Théâtre Marigny revue *Le Dernier des Marigny* (''a young American . . . who has a fine voice, but whose acting is rather too eccentric''), and before long she was back on Broadway again, appearing in Oscar Hammerstein's self-written comic opera *Santa Maria* and performing a musical monologue ''with six grinning darkies'' at Koster and Bial's Music Hall and at Proctor's (1897). However, it was not a long home-stop, and in the following year, now 24(?) years of age, she launched herself on the rest of the European Continent. In February 1898 she was starred at Vienna's Carltheater playing O Mimosa San in *Die Geisha* in German, after which she departed for Russia, and later the same year, after a return visit to Vienna, she was seen in the same role at Budapest's Magyar Színház, this time performing *A gésak* in Hungarian.

In 1899 the Vienna Carltheater cast her in the multiple lead role of *Adam und Eva* opposite no less a co-star than the great Alexander Girardi himself, and she played the roles of Eve, Madame Putiphar, Xantippe to his Sokrates, Dulcinea, and Signorina Roselli for the 52 performances of the run, before going on to star at the Theater an der Wien as Winifred Grey in *Ein durchgeganges Mädel* (*A Runaway Girl*). In February 1900 she created the title role of Hugo Felix's *Rhodope* at the Carltheater, repeated it at Berlin's Theater des Westens and Lessing-Theater (June 1900, ''she gained the favours of Berliners at once''), and next produced *San Toy,* for which she had purchased the German and Austrian rights from Edwardes, and which she played at the Carltheater in German and later at the Népszínház (December 1900) in Hungarian and at Berlin's Centraltheater (2 March 1901), again in German, whilst also—in between her regulation number of walkouts and no-shows—giving her O Mimosa San here and there in between times.

In October 1903 she returned to the Carltheater one more time to star as Jane MacSherry, alongside Karl Blasel and Louis Treumann, in the Vienna production of *Madame Sherry.* She had the top billing. And then, at the (admitted) age of 30, having starred for some of the greatest musical theatre managers in the greatest musical theatre centers, from one end of the world to the other, Marie Halton, now a slightly plumpish soubrette, just disappeared from the more obvious playbills of the world. I don't know what became of her. Given her record, she probably ended up starring in operetta in China.

HAMILTON, Cosmo [GIBBS, Henry Charles Hamilton] (b Norwood, 29 April 1870; d Guildford, 14 October 1942).

Author, journalist (sometime editor of *The World*), the writer of a dozen or so English plays and several more for America (amongst which a number which were taken from the French), Hamilton also collaborated on the texts for several musical comedies. He began with the libretto for the highly successful Cinderella musical, *The Catch of the Season,* built around Seymour Hicks and his wife, Ellaline Terriss, as a modern-day prince and his fireside waif, and he repeated the same task for another Hicks/Terriss vehicle, *The Beauty of Bath,* but he was involved in some controversy when his name appeared on the bill for *The Belle of Mayfair,* the show from which all theatreland knew that Basil Hood had recently withdrawn his name after his book had been unsatisfactorily altered by the producer.

He was at the source of an unlikely half-success when he tacked a new plot onto some songs from the zarzuela *La gran vía* and some more by the English-born Parisian music-hall star, Harry Fragson, to provide a stage vehicle for the latter as *Castles in Spain,* but thereafter, apart from a few adaptations, both while living in Britain and later in America, he worked very largely for the straight stage. A 1910 ''song play'' *The Iron King,* ''a heart story of the industrial world'' featuring an Irish baritone, Frank Adair, and singing German comic Charles A Loder, was toured in 1910 by Sidney B Ellis.

Hamilton's play *The Hoyden,* adapted from Tristan Bernard's French comedy *La Soeur,* was musicalized by Paul Rubens and Frank Tours in 1907 for Charles Dillingham and Charles Frohman as a Broadway vehicle for Elsie Janis.

Hamilton was married to actress **Beryl FABER** [Beryl Crossley SMITH] (d London, 1 May 1912), a sister of the actor-cricketer C Aubrey Smith, who appeared in the musicals *The Country Girl* (1902, Mrs Quinton Raikes) and *My Darling* (1907, Sylvaine of the Follies) during a career spent largely on the non-musical stage.

1904 **The Catch of the Season** (Herbert Haines, Herbert Evelyn Baker/Charles H Taylor/w Seymour Hicks) Vaudeville Theatre 9 September

1906 **The Beauty of Bath** (Haines/Taylor/w Hicks) Aldwych Theatre 19 March

1906 **The Belle of Mayfair** (Leslie Stuart/w Charles H E Brookfield) Vaudeville Theatre 11 April

1906 **Castles in Spain** (Federico Chueca, Joaquín Valverde, Harry Fragson/Eustace Ponsonby) Royalty Theatre 18 April

1907 **The Hoyden** (Paul Rubens, Frank E Tours) Knickerbocker Theater, New York 19 October

1909 **The Merry Peasant** (*Der fidele Bauer*) English version (Strand Theatre)

1910 **The Iron King** (Gerald Martin) Academy of Music, Baltimore 17 October

1916 **Flora Bella** English version w Dorothy Donnelly (Casino Theater, New York)

1917 **The Star Gazer** (*Der Sterngucker*) English version w Matthew C Woodward (Plymouth Theater, New York)

Autobiography: *Unwritten History* (Hutchinson, London, 1924)

HAMILTON, Henry (b Nunhead, Surrey, ?1853; d Sandgate, Kent, 4 September 1918).

At first an actor with J B Howard, Wilson Barrett, F Craven Robertson, the Pitt-Hamilton Company and others, Hamilton latterly had considerable success with his adaptation of Ouida, *Moths* (1882), and with a series of dramas written with Cecil Raleigh for the Theatre Royal, Drury Lane (*The Great Ruby, The Whip, White Heather, The Sins of Society, The Hope, Sealed Orders*).

His first attempt in the musical theatre was with the grandiose Venetian *The Lady of the Locket* (1885), but he made more of a mark with his lyrics for the song ''Private Tommy Atkins,'' originally written for actor Charles Arnold and played by him as part of a protean musical comedy-drama called *Captain Fritz,* which turned out to be the interpolated hit of the musical comedy *A Gaiety Girl* (1893). He supplied words for several other successful showsongs performed by baritone Hayden Coffin, including the wartime ''Hands Off!'' and the rolling drawing-room-ballad ''Freedom'' in *A Greek Slave,* and also had a number, ''Peek-a-Boo'' (mus: Meyer Lutz), sung by Minnie Palmer in *My Sweetheart,* but apart from collaborating with Raleigh and Augustus Harris on the text of a Drury Lane pantomime, he did not make any further inroads on the musical theatre until 1903, when he suddenly became very visible.

In one 12-month period his name appeared on the bills of the successful Leslie Stuart musical *The School Girl* (co-lib w Paul Potter); *The Duchess of Dantzic,* a piece which he had written with Ivan Caryll some years before, and which proved to be the most critically admired of all its composer's many works; and the West End production of Messager's *Véronique,* for which he had prepared the English libretto.

George Edwardes used him as adaptor for a second Messager musical, *Les P'tites Michu,* with equal success, but although he subsequently provided the English text for Edwardes's production of Kálmán's *Tatárjárás* (*Autumn Manoeuvres*), his brief but highly effective spasm of work for the musical theatre was otherwise done.

1885 **The Lady of the Locket** (William Fullerton) Empire Theatre 11 March

1903 **The School Girl** (Leslie Stuart/Charles H Taylor/w Paul Potter) Prince of Wales Theatre 9 May

1903 **The Duchess of Dantzic** (Ivan Caryll) Lyric Theatre 17 October

1904 **Véronique** English version (Apollo Theatre)

1905 **The Little Michus** (*Les P'tites Michu*) English version (Daly's Theatre)

1912 **Autumn Manoeuvres** (*Tatárjárás*) English version (Adelphi Theatre)

HAMLISCH, Marvin [Frederick] (b New York, 2 June 1944). Successful film composer who turned to the stage in the 1970s and launched two major international hits on a Broadway which was sadly thin on new composing stars.

Hamlisch studied originally as a classical pianist before moving on to a songwriting career which had its first landmark in 1965 when his song ''Sunshine, Lollipops and Roses'' made its way to the hit parades. He began his theatre work as a rehearsal pianist (*Funny Girl, Fade Out—Fade In*) and a dance-music arranger (*Golden Rainbow,* 1968), but a career as a composer of film songs intervened and, beginning with *The Swimmer* (1968), he provided songs for a series of movies including *Take the Money and Run, The April Fools* (1969), *Bananas, Kotch* (1971, ''Life Is What You Make It'') and *Save the Tiger* (1972), and peaking with the score (Academy Award) and title song to the Barbra Streisand film *The Way We Were* (1973, w Marilyn and Alan Bergman, Academy Award) and the complement to and adaptation of Scott Joplin's music as heard in *The Sting* (Academy Award).

His first venture into the musical theatre was a dazzling one. In 1975 he provided the musical score for the phenomenally long-lived *A Chorus Line* (''What I Did for Love,'' ''At the Ballet,'' ''Nothing,'' ''One,'' Tony Award), but, after this success, he once again concentrated on writing for television (*The Entertainer*) and film—*The Spy Who Loved Me* (1977, ''Nobody Does It Better''), *Same Time Next Year* (1978, ''The Last Time I Felt Like This''), *Starting Over, Ice Castles, The Champ* (1979), *Ordinary People* (1980)—and did not produce a second Broadway score until 1979.

They're Playing Our Song, a pop-music–based piece with a number of its songs presented as full-frontal pop singles (''I Still Believe in Love,'' ''Fallin','' ''When You're in My Arms''), recounted the ups and downs of the professional and personal association of a composer and his (female) lyricist, and was said to echo the real lives of Hamlisch and his lyricist Carole Bayer Sager. If this is indeed so, that makes it the first autobiographical musical after the long line of biographical ones. It was, autobiographical or not, a major international hit.

Hamlisch's subsequent ventures into the musical theatre did not have the same outstanding success as his first. A 1983 musical on the life of actress *Jean Seberg,* staged at London's National Theatre, was an undistinguished failure which seemed to have come from a different pen, the adaptation of the beauty-pageant screenplay, *Smile,* was a quick Broadway failure, and an attempt to musicalize *The Goodbye Girl* bombed in different versions on both sides of the Atlantic.

1975 **A Chorus Line** (Edward Kleban/James Kirkwood, Nicholas Dante) Public Theater 15 April; Shubert Theater 25 July

1979 **They're Playing Our Song** (Carole Bayer Sager/Neil Simon) Imperial Theater 11 February

1983 **Jean Seberg** (Christopher Adler/Julian Barry) National Theatre, London 15 November

1986 **Smile** (Howard Ashman) Lunt-Fontanne Theater 24 November

1993 **The Goodbye Girl** (David Zippel/Neil Simon) Marquis Theater 4 March; revised version Albery Theatre, London 1997

Autobiography: w Gardner, G: *The Way I Was* (Scribner, New York, 1992)

HAMMERSTEIN, Oscar (b Stettin, 8 May 1846; d New York, 1 August 1919). ''Proprietor, composer, inventor, librettist, scene-painter and architect all combined in one'' (*Era,* 1897).

Oscar Hammerstein moved into the theatre in 1888, having previously amassed a fortune in cigars, inventions (he sold some cigar-making machines he had invented for more than a million dollars) and real estate. He made his mark first as a theatre builder before turning producer, initially in the world of opera and later in the musical theatre.

In a career full of financial ups and downs, he constructed and/or ran first the Harlem Opera House (1888), then the Columbus Theater, the Manhattan Theater (1892, later Koster and Bial's), Hammerstein's Olympia (1895, with the ceiling lights arranged in red and white initials ''O H'') where he produced the Broadway version of *La Poupée* (1897) with the young Anna Held starred, Hammerstein's Victoria, and finally the Manhattan Opera House (1906). He operated this last named house with such social—if not exactly financial—success that the Metropolitan Opera, suffering in reputation and box office, was ultimately forced to buy him out of the operatic field (1910). He also attempted to launch a London Opera House in England.

At one stage, having already—amongst his multitude of other activities—tried his composing hand at grand opera, he struck a $1,000 wager with theatre composer Gustave Kerker that he could write and compose a light musical show in 24 hours. He was satisfied enough with his effort to put *Koh-I-Noor* on the stage, and it played two weeks at Koster and Bial's before moving on to its author-composer's Harlem Opera House. The event amused the town enough that Frank Dupree mounted a burlesque based on the episode, under the title *Hamm-in-Stein in Distress* (22 December) at the Imperial Theatre with Nick Burnham impersonating Oscar, and Anita Ellis playing a travesty Gustave Kerker. Hammerstein nevertheless followed this first effort with others. He wrote, composed, produced and staged a "spectacular opera and ballet" entitled *Marguerite* advertisedly based on the Faust legend but actually an extravaganza about a painter and his search for a nude model, on a bill at his variety house, and followed up with a comic opera *Santa Maria* whose three months' run encouraged him to dip further into the light musical theatre. He produced two more self-written pieces—*Mrs Radley Barton's Ball* ("a spectacular extravaganza") featuring George W Monroe, and a hotchpotch extravaganza called *War Bubbles,* which included in its music the *Il Trovatore* Miserere, "The Bowery" and a "Dewey March" composed by Hammerstein, and which sufficed to send the Olympia (by this stage rechristened the Lyric) into receivership.

When he started up operations again, at the Victoria, he also tried authorship again. He did poorly with *Sweet Marie* (1901) and better with a variety piece called *Punch and Judy & Co* (1903) and, in 1904, he wrote book, music and lyrics for a little piece called *Parsifallia* which burlesqued not Wagner's opera but the more than dubious methods employed by producer Hans Conried to pirate the opera for a New York production. Hammerstein's songs included "Lizzie O'Connor the Great Prima Donna," "When You Said Yes" and "Squirrels."

When the Victoria folded, Hammerstein confined his attentions to things operatic until 1910, when he brought Ganne's delightful French opérette *Hans, le joueur de flûte* to the Manhattan Opera House. It was after the unhappy end of his operation there, however, that he produced his one big musical-theatre hit, when he commissioned a vehicle for Emma Trentini, and the rest of the opera company whom he had hired for the Manhattan and still held under contract, from Victor Herbert, and got *Naughty Marietta.*

1892 **Koh-I-Noor** Koster and Bial's Music Hall 30 October

1896 **Marguerite** Hammerstein's Olympia 10 February

1896 **Santa Maria** Hammerstein's Olympia 24 September

1897 **Mrs Radley Barton's Ball in Greater New York** Hammerstein's Lyric 7 March

1898 **War Bubbles** (pasticcio) Hammerstein's Lyric 16 May

1901 **Sweet Marie** Hammerstein's Victoria 10 October

1903 **Punch and Judy & Co** 1 act Victoria Paradise Roof Garden 1 June

1904 **Parsifallia** 1 act Victoria Paradise Roof Gardens 12 June

Biography: Sheean, V: *Oscar Hammerstein I: The Life and Exploits of an Impresario* (Simon & Schuster, New York, 1956)

One of his sons, **Arthur HAMMERSTEIN** (b New York, 21 December 1875; d Palm Beach, Fla, 12 October 1955), followed his father into the production arena, taking up where the older Hammerstein had begun with *Naughty Marietta,* and producing the second Emma Trentini operetta, *The Firefly,* with considerable success. He thereafter mounted composer Friml's *High Jinks, Katinka, You're in Love, Sometime* and *The Blue Kitten,* to almost unalloyed good effect, but had rather less success when he put his faith in another neophyte composer, Herbert Stothart, in whose *Somebody's Sweetheart* he himself took credit for a couple of late additional songs, and whom he later teamed with his lyric-writing nephew, Oscar Hammerstein II, on *Always You, Tickle Me, Jimmie* and *Daffy Dill.*

When the producer put this, till now not particularly successful, pair together with composer Vincent Youmans for *Wildflower,* better times returned, but, when he teamed them with Friml, the result was the greatest success of his career as a producer: *Rose Marie.* It was a success which he did not really approach again. When the pair were put to work with a third prominent composer, George Gershwin, they produced the reasonably successful *Song of the Flame,* but Friml's *The Wild Rose,* Kálmán's *Golden Dawn, Good Boy, Polly,* Jerome Kern's nevertheless appreciable *Sweet Adeline,* Friml's South Seas musical *Luana* and the W C Fields flop *Ballyhoo* brought mostly diminishing returns, and Hammerstein withdrew from the last-named show and from Broadway musical producing in 1931.

HAMMERSTEIN, Oscar [Greeley Clendenning] II (b New York, 12 July 1895; d Doylestown, Pa, 23 August 1960).

The grandson of the first Oscar, and the son of William Hammerstein (d 10 June 1914), who had also worked as a theatre manager, Oscar II was sent to study law and graduated to work in a legal office. However, he left that office to work for his uncle, Arthur, as an assistant and then a full-blown stage manager. It was Arthur who produced his nephew's first and wholly unsuccessful attempt at playwriting, but his earliest experience of the musical theatre came with university and amateur shows, and it was only after several years of such an apprenticeship that Oscar II got his first shot at musical Broadway. Again, it was Uncle Arthur who mounted the piece which started out as *Joan of Ark-ansaw* but which finally made it to town as *Always You.* The show had a very limited amount of success, but it apparently showed sufficient signs of promise for Arthur to bring his nephew back to work with the experienced Otto Harbach and Frank Mandel on the just slightly more successful *Tickle Me* and the flop *Jimmie.*

A collaboration with Guy Bolton on *Daffy Dill* brought no credit to either of them, and the Nora Bayes vehicle *Queen o' Hearts* passed by in just 39 Broadway nights, but Uncle Arthur's continued patronage was finally rewarded when the younger Oscar and Otto Harbach first contributed materially to the success of *Wildflower* (''Bambalina'') and then supplied the book and lyrics for Arthur Hammerstein's biggest success, *Rose Marie* (''Rose Marie,'' ''Indian Love Call''). However, in true theatrical fashion, whilst the young man was enjoying his biggest success, he was also lending his name to a vast flop. A ''Musical Comedy Guild'' backed to the tune of $2 million by a Coca-Cola magnate, who had announced his intention to ''elevate American musical comedy,'' called Hammerstein in to doctor their opening show, *The Purple Cow*. It limped through engagements in Washington and Pittsburg and closed. Mr Coca-Cola withdrew his guarantee and Oscar went back to (if he had ever left) *Rose Marie*.

Now thoroughly launched to the upper strata of his profession, Hammerstein followed up this huge hit by providing lyrics and libretti, either alone or in collaboration, to a series of the most successful and enduring shows of the later 1920s, from which Jerome Kern's *Sunny* (1925, ''Who?,'' ''Sunny,'' ''Two Little Bluebirds'') and *Show Boat* (''Ol' Man River,'' ''Make Believe,'' ''Can't Help Lovin' Dat Man,'' etc), and Sigmund Romberg's *The Desert Song* (''One Alone,'' ''The Desert Song,'' etc) and *The New Moon* (''Lover, Come Back to Me,'' ''Softly, As in a Morning Sunrise,'' ''Stouthearted Men,'' ''One Kiss'') and their songs stand out as the most memorable and enduring examples. *The Desert Song, Show Boat* and *The New Moon* found Hammerstein the lyricist, in particular, showing enormous advances on the pretty banalities in which he and other lyric-writers had wallowed during the first part of the decade, turning out, in his best numbers, thoughtful and substantial romantic lyrics which have lasted through more than half a century with a surprising lack of visible aging.

Show Boat marked the debut of the author in another capacity, that of director, and following that splendid start he directed a large number of the 1920s and 1930s shows with which he was subsequently connected. The 1930s, however, brought little to equal his work of the 1920s. He wrote and directed two end-of-career flops for *New Moon* producer Mandel, provided one of his most unappetizing texts for Jerome Kern's kitsch-Mittel-European *Music in the Air* (but saved the affair by contributing the lyrics to ''I've Told Ev'ry Little Star'' and ''The Song Is You''), adapted the Continental hit *Ball im Savoy* for London's Theatre Royal, Drury Lane, and combined again with Kern for the short-lived *Three Sisters* and for *Very Warm for May* (''All the Things You Are''). He also ventured into films, working on such screen pieces as *The Night Is Young, Reckless, Give Us This Night, High, Wide and Handsome, Swing High, Swing Low, I'll Take Romance, The Lady Objects* and *The Great Waltz,* in which he turned the *Zigeunerbaron* Dompfaff duo into ''One Day When We Were Young'' and lyricked ''I'm in Love with Vienna'' etc, in a Hollywood where his stage successes of the 1920s were now being used as the bases for musical films.

The 1940s, however, relaunched Hammerstein on a second enormously successful era in the musical theatre. With the decline and demise of Larry Hart, he began a partnership with the late lyricist's partner of always, composer Richard Rodgers. Their first work together, *Oklahoma!* (''The Surrey with the Fringe On Top,'' ''People Will Say We're in Love,'' ''I Cain't Say 'No,''' ''Oh, What a Beautiful Mornin',''' etc), was a major international hit, and almost single-handedly it rekindled the fashion for the classic romantic operetta, which had frittered away somewhat in the 1930s, on the American stage. After Hammerstein had taken time out to write the book and lyrics to an updated rearrangement of Bizet's *Carmen* (*Carmen Jones*), the new partnership worked solidly together for the next 16 years, up until Hammerstein's death in 1960. Their works together included four which, with *Oklahoma!,* go to make up the principal part of the backbone of the surviving romantic musical play repertoire of the Broadway 1940s and 1950s—*Carousel, South Pacific, The King and I* and *The Sound of Music.*

In earlier days Rodgers had also operated as a producer, and after the production of their less than successful *Allegro* he and Hammerstein began to mount productions of their own. The plays *I Remember Mama,* Anita Loos's *Happy Birthday* (for which they supplied a song) and *John Loves Mary,* a revival of *Show Boat* and the mounting of the enormously successful *Annie Get Your Gun* started things off on the right foot, and they subsequently produced the last six of their own shows, from *South Pacific* to *The Sound of Music,* on Broadway and in London.

Hammerstein's remarkable double-peaked career resulted in an enduring contribution to the Broadway stage which no other lyricist-librettist has surpassed, with pieces from both his successful periods being the cornerstones of the most revived part of their respective eras of the American musical theatre repertoire. His work as a writer came to its first peak in the songs and texts for *The Desert Song, Show Boat* and for *The New Moon,* but he was ultimately best suited in the shows which he wrote with Rodgers, where his simple, often inspired, song ideas, his frequently sentimental but unhackneyed lyrics, and his tightly constructed libretti were popular models in Broadway's most successful years.

Two Rodgers and Hammerstein works originally written for other media were subsequently produced as stage musicals—the television version of the *Cinderella* tale, mounted at the London Coliseum with Tommy Steele as Buttons, and two rewrites of the film *State Fair,* the first staged at St Louis with Ron Husmann and Carol Richards as its young lead players, the second (lib: Tom Briggs, Louis Mattioli) produced by David Merrick at Broadway's Music Box in 1996 (27 March, 102 performances) with a cast including John Davidson and Kathryn Crosby.

Hammerstein's son, **Jamie HAMMERSTEIN** (d New York, 7 January 1999) directed a number of productions of his father's works in America (*State Fair,* etc), Britain and Australia during a career as a theatre director.

1920 **Always You** (ex- *Joan of Ark-ansaw*) (Herbert Stothart) Central Theater 5 January

1920 **Tickle Me** (Stothart/w Otto Harbach, Frank Mandel) Selwyn Theater 17 August

1920 **Jimmie** (Stothart/w Harbach/w Harbach, Mandel) Apollo Theater 17 November

1922 **Daffy Dill** (Stothart/w Guy Bolton) Apollo Theater 22 August

1922 **Queen o' Hearts** (Lewis Gensler, Dudley Wilkinson/w Mandel) Cohan Theater 10 October

1923 **Wildflower** (Vincent Youmans, Stothart/w Harbach) Casino Theater 7 February

1923 **Mary Jane McKane** (Youmans, Stothart/w William Cary Duncan) Imperial Theater 25 December

1924 **Rose Marie** (Rudolf Friml, Stothart/w Harbach) Imperial Theater 2 September

1925 **Sunny** (Kern/w Harbach) New Amsterdam Theater 22 September

1925 **Song of the Flame** (George Gershwin, Stothart/w Harbach) 44th Street Theater 30 December

1926 **The Wild Rose** (Friml/w Harbach) Martin Beck Theater 20 October

1926 **The Desert Song** (Romberg/w Harbach/w Harbach, Frank Mandel) Casino Theater 30 November

1927 **Golden Dawn** (Emmerich Kálmán, Stothart/w Harbach) Hammerstein's Theater 30 November

1927 **The New Moon** (Romberg/w Mandel, Laurence Schwab) Chestnut Street Opera House, Philadelphia 22 December 1927; Imperial Theater, New York (revised version) 19 September 1928

1927 **Show Boat** (Kern) Ziegfeld Theater 27 December

1928 **Good Boy** (Stothart, Bert Kalmar, Harry Ruby/w Harbach, Henry Meyers) Hammerstein's Theater 5 September

1928 **Rainbow** (Youmans/w Laurence Stallings) Gallo Theater 21 November

1929 **Sweet Adeline** (Kern) Hammerstein's Theater 3 September

1930 **Ballyhoo** (Louis Alter/w Harry Ruskin, Leighton Brill) Hammerstein's Theater 22 December

1931 **The Gang's All Here** (Gensler/w Russel Crouse, Morrie Ryskind) Imperial 18 February

1931 **Free for All** (Richard Whiting/w Schwab) Manhattan Theater 8 September

1931 **East Wind** (Romberg/w Mandel) Manhattan Theater 27 October

1932 **Music in the Air** (Kern) Alvin Theater 8 November

1933 **Ball at the Savoy** (*Ball im Savoy*) English version (Theatre Royal, Drury Lane, London)

1934 **Three Sisters** (Kern) Theatre Royal, Drury Lane, London 9 April

1935 **May Wine** (Romberg/Mandel) St James Theater 5 December

1938 **Gentlemen Unafraid** (Kern/w Harbach) Municipal Opera, St Louis 3 June

1939 **Very Warm for May** (Kern) Alvin Theater 17 November

1941 **Sunny River** (ex- *New Orleans*) (Romberg) St James Theater 4 December

1943 **Oklahoma!** (Richard Rodgers) St James Theater 31 March

1943 **Carmen Jones** (Bizet arr/Henri Meilhac, Ludovic Halévy ad) Broadway Theater 2 December

1945 **Carousel** (Rodgers) Majestic Theater 19 April

1947 **Allegro** (Rodgers) Majestic Theater 10 October

1949 **South Pacific** (Rodgers/w Joshua Logan) Majestic Theater 7 April

1951 **The King and I** (Rodgers) St James Theater 29 March

1953 **Me and Juliet** (Rodgers) Majestic Theater 28 May

1955 **Pipe Dream** (Rodgers) Shubert Theater 30 November

1958 **Flower Drum Song** (Rodgers/w Joseph Fields) St James Theater 1 December

1958 **Cinderella** (Rodgers) London Coliseum 18 December

1959 **The Sound of Music** (Rodgers/Crouse, Howard Lindsay) Lunt-Fontanne Theater 16 November

1969 **State Fair** (Rodgers/Lucille Kallen) Municipal Opera, St Louis 2 June

Literature: Green, S: *The Rodgers and Hammerstein Story* (Day, New York, 1963), Rodgers, R: *Musical Stages* (Random House, New York, 1975), Nolan, F: *The Sound of Their Music* (Dent, New York, 1978), Suskin, S: *Berlin, Kern, Rodgers, Hart, and Hammerstein: A Complete Song Catalogue* (McFarland, Jefferson, North Carolina, 1990), Mordden, E: *Rodgers and Hammerstein* (Abrams, New York, 1992), etc

Biographies: Taylor, D: *Some Enchanted Evenings* (Harpers, New York, 1953), Fordin, H: *Getting to Know Him* (Random House, New York, 1977), Citron, S: *The Wordsmiths* (OUP, New York, 1995)

HANNERL Singspiel in 3 acts by A M Willner and Heinz Reichert. Music from the works of Franz Schubert arranged by Karl Lafite. Raimundtheater, Vienna, 8 February 1918.

The unprecedented success of *Das Dreimäderlhaus* at Wilhelm Karczag's Raimundtheater unavoidably encouraged the theatre to try a musequel and the authors of the earlier hit were set to work on the tale of Hannerl, the daughter of Baron Schober and Hannerl Tschöll, the pair whose wedding at the end of the first piece had broken the heart of Franz Schubert. They provided a slim and conventional little tale which only the giving of the required secondhand names to the characters, and the very occasional reminiscence, gave *Hannerl* any connection at all with the earlier piece.

Anni Rainer, the Hannerl Tschöll of *Das Dreimäderlhaus,* now played her own daughter, grown up enough for her first ball and smitten with young Baron Hans von Gumpenberg (M de Taxi). As a result of a stone thrown at the wrong window, however, three acts of romantic complications occur and, at the ball, Hannerl ends up in tears when Hans seems to be attracted by Aranka (Klara Karry), the daughter of the Countess Clementine Oroszy (Mitzi Warbeck), whose window had received the pebble. But now papa Schober (Otto Langer) arrives back with the happy news that he has arranged for Hannerl's betrothal to the son of a friend. It is, of course, Hans. Fritz Neumann played Hannerl's brother, tactfully called Franz, who ran a secondary romance with her best friend, Helene (Gretl Martin), and one of the few, rather tacked in, echoes of the older piece came with the introduction of Franz Glawatsch in his original role of the now very old Christian Tschöll.

When it came to providing the music for *Hannerl,* Harry Berté—still smarting from having to arrange rather than compose the score for the earlier piece—refused to become involved. Karczag replaced him with Karl Lafite who duly provided the required ration of homogenized Schubert.

Like most musequels, *Hannerl* came nowhere near living up to its original, but it passed its 100th night at the Raimundtheater (15 May 1917), and it remained in the repertoire at the house until Karczag's management ended, and the musical content of the house's program shrank away. At the same time it also moved on to productions in other houses looking for a second *Dreimäderlhaus.* In Berlin it followed straight on behind the phenomenal run of *Das Dreimäderlhaus* at the Friedrich-Wilhelmstädtisches Theater, and the older piece actually played its 1,000th performance at a matinée during the run of *Hannerl* in the evening slot, giving the two ''episodes'' of the tale in one day. The show ran a good six months.

Hungary showed no more taste for *Médi* (ad Zsolt Harsányi) than Vienna had done, when the show was produced at the Vígszínház with Ilka Pálmay featured as Médi, the mother, and Erzsi Péchey as the daughter, again on the heels of their successful mounting of *Das Dreimäderlhaus.* Whereas the older piece had won a fine 155 performances, *Médi* made do with a milder 38.

An American performance was mounted for one night in Baltimore in 1924 under the management of the Johann Strauss-Theater Company, with a fine Austrian cast headed by Walter Jankuhn, Mizzi Delorm and Paul Dietz, playing in German. In spite of the vast success of *Blossom Time,* it did not persuade anyone to take up the show for Broadway.

Hungary: Vígszínház *Médi* 21 June 1918; Germany: Friedrich-Wilhelmstädtisches Theater 13 September 1918; USA: Lyric Theater, Baltimore 10 January 1924

HANS ANDERSEN Musical in 2 acts by Tommy Steele and Beverley Cross. Lyrics and music from the film score *Hans Christian Andersen* and other works by Frank Loesser. Additional numbers by Marvin Laird. London Palladium, 17 December 1974.

A musical put together around the well-loved score written by Frank Loesser for the 1952 film *Hans Christian Andersen* (''The Ugly Duckling,'' ''Wonderful Copenhagen,'' ''Inchworm,'' ''Thumbelina,'' etc), in which Danny Kaye had appeared as the Scandinavian poet and author of the title. Producer Harold Fielding, star Tommy Steele and librettist Beverley Cross, who had teamed a decade earlier on *Half a Sixpence,* came together again to construct and produce the piece as a vehicle for Steele, and they scored a fine success through a year's run at the Palladium, a national tour, and a subsequent return to the West End for a second season (17 December 1977), now starring Steele and Sally Ann Howes, before the show went on into regional and overseas productions.

Hans Andersen (Steele), the Odense cobbler who keeps the local children amused with his tales, has ambitions as a dramatic author, but his lack of education bars him from putting anything readable on paper. When a mysterious passerby, Otto (Milo O'Shea), takes him to the theatre, he meets the great soprano, Jenny Lind (Colette Gleeson), who encourages him to go back to school. It is she, again, years later who encourages him to put aside his attempts at ''serious'' writing, and to put his children's tales into book form. Hans wins fame and fortune, but not Jenny, whose interest has been friendly but not loving.

Steele sang the famous songs, Jenny Lind (rewritten at a late stage as the singer—the character was originally to have been a ballerina, and Gillian Lynne had been hired to choreograph) was given ''Truly Loved,'' taken from the score of Loesser's *Pleasures and Palaces,* and joined the star in ''No Two People (have ever been so in love),'' whilst several other un- or under-used Loesser pieces were topped off with some additional songs by Marvin Laird, of which a jolly piece for Steele, O'Shea (whose originally co-starring part shrank to nothing in rehearsals) and the chorus, ''Happy Days,'' and a spelling-song, ''Ecclesiasticus,'' proved lively interludes.

In spite of its success, the London version of *Hans Andersen* was prevented from playing in America, where

Plate 164. **Hans Andersen.** *Milo O'Shea as Otto in the London Palladium production. And hogging the spotlight, and the girl, at his feet . . . the author of this book.*

another version, under the title *Hans Christian Andersen,* was played regionally. Yet another version, written by Irene Mann, was produced in Germany and Austria (Raimundtheater 6 February 1986) and a further show entitled *Hans Christian Andersen,* composed by Knud Christiansen [''Sebastian''] was produced in 1996 at Copenhagen's Gladsaxe Theatre. The most recent *Hans Christian Andersen,* once again using Loesser's songs as a score (ad Richard Peaslee was produced by the American Conservatory Theater in San Francisco in 2000 (8 September). The allegedly all-new book was the work of Sebastian Barry, and Jon Glover (Hans) and Terri Dale Hansen (Jenny Lind) featured.

Recordings: original cast (Pye), London revival cast (Pye), Danish musical (Pladecompagniet/Sony), etc

HANSEN, Max (b Mannheim, 22 December 1897; d Copenhagen, 12 November 1961). Favorite tenor/light comedian of the German stage up until the Hitler era.

Hansen was born in Mannheim, the son of a Danish actress, and brought up in Munich, where, as a child, he made his first appearance on stage as a dwarf in *Snow White.* He went on to work as a singer in pubs, clubs and cabarets, appearing in Denmark and Norway during and after the First World War, and made his first Viennese appearances at the Établissement Ronacher before being taken up by the Theater an der Wien as a replacement for Josef König in the role of Metellus in *Die Bacchusnacht* (1923). He went on to create the role of the comical Baron Zsupán in *Gräfin Mariza* at the same house, but his name, and the best part of his career thereafter, was made in Berlin.

He played in Berlin's *No, No, Nanette* (1926) and *Die Zirkusprinzessin* (1927, Toni), appeared alongside Rita Georg in Granichstaedten's *Evelyne,* and then moved on to take part in some of the large-stage productions of Erik Charell, for whom he featured, alongside Fritzi Massary, as Camille in the souped-up *Die lustige Witwe,* as Aramis to the Porthos of Sig Arno and the D'Artagnan of Alfred Jerger in *Die drei Musketiere* and for whom, ultimately, in the most outstanding part of his career, he created the little waiter, Leopold, in *Im weissen Rössl* (1930).

Hansen subsequently appeared in the Berlin production of the unsuccessful *Hundert Meter Glück* (1932), paired with his wife, soubrette Lizzi Waldmüller, in the popular *Petite Chocolatière* musical comedy, *Bezauberndes Fräulein* (1933, Paul), in both Berlin and Vienna, and starred as the suddenly rich waiter Franz in Benatzky's *Das kleine Café* at Vienna's Deutsches Volkstheater. For a while, it seemed that his vast popularity on the German stage might outface his Jewishness. However, he took more and more engagements abroad, notably in Scandinavia, and ultimately quit Berlin, first for Vienna, where he scored a notable success starred opposite Zarah Leander in the Hollywooden musical comedy, *Axel an der Himmelstür* (1936, Axel Swift), and as Seppl Huber (''ski-teacher at Saint-Anton and Olympic champion''!) in *Herzen im Schnee* (1937, also director), and then for Sweden.

There he appeared on the stage in a number of the classic Operette roles of the tenor-comic repertoire (Menelaus, Calicot, Célestin), as well as in films, and he did not return to Germany until the beginning of the 1950s, celebrating his return with a repeat of his most famous role, the Leopold of *Im weissen Rössl,* in 1951. The latter part of his career was largely devoted to film appearances including a Danish *Belle Hélène* (1951).

His wife, **Lizzi WALDMÜLLER** (b Knittelfeld, Steiermark, 25 May 1904; d Vienna, 8 April 1945) was one of the most popular German musical comedy performers of her time, both on stage and film (*Lachende Erben, Bel Ami, Frau Luna,* etc). After an early career in juvenile roles in Austria, she made her mark when she appeared on the Berlin and Vienna stage as O Lia San in *Viktoria und ihr Husar* (1930), and she subsequently created the role of Monika in *Glückliche Reise* (1932) and the title role *in Bezauberndes Fräulein* (1933).

Autobiography: *Det máste vara underbart* (Copenhagen, 1955)

HANS, LE JOUEUR DE FLÛTE Opéra-comique in 3 acts by Maurice Vaucaire and Georges Mitchell. Music by Louis Ganne. Théâtre de Monte-Carlo, Monaco, 14 April 1906.

The most attractive of Ganne's limited output of musical plays, *Hans, le joueur de flûte,* a retelling of the tale of the pied piper of Hamelin with a difference, was first mounted in Monaco, where Ganne had made a considerable reputation at the head of the Concerts Louis Ganne.

The town of Milkatz is a prosperous one and its Burgomaster, Pippermann (Poudrier), and town council have only one preoccupation—the grain trade. All else—local traditions, arts, crafts, fetes—has been abandoned in the frantic pursuit of the benefits of commerce. Only the poet Yoris (Alberthal) yearns for the artistic past, and he has spent his time making one of the life-sized dolls with which the villagers used to compete for festival honors in days gone by. His doll shows where his heart is, for it is made in the image of Lisbeth (Mariette Sully), the burgomaster's daughter. When the strange, wandering Hans (Jean Périer) comes to town, only Yoris befriends him, and Hans takes his revenge on blinkered, profit-mad Milkatz by using his magic flute to lead all the town's cats to drown in the river, leaving the grain stores prey to a plague of mice. His price for stopping the mice is the restoration of, and a town subsidy for, the old festivals, and the doll competition. The townsfolk join in the doll-making and the fête as of yore and Yoris wins both the competition and Lisbeth before Hans, the flute-player, goes his way.

Ganne's score was full of charm and gentle parody as it brought on the bumbling town guard (''Un, deux, au pas, sacrebleu''), had Yoris apostrophizing the past in a passionate tenor (''Vous n'êtes plus, pauvres poupées'') or Lisbeth regretting her father's shopkeeper mentality (''Mon cher petit père est un commerçant''), but it rose to its heights in its first-act finale, a marvelously tongue-in-cheek piece in which, to a big, romantic melody, the massed citizens of Milkatz bewail the fate of their protective pussies (''Adieu, petits minets, petits minous''), and in Hans's two principal numbers, the mysterious ''Je viens d'un pays lointain'' and the memorable march, ''Cette flûte qui mena le monde.''

Following its Monégasque season, *Hans, le joueur de flûte* stagnated a while, but in 1910 Alphonse Franck, rich on *Veuve joyeuse* profits, decided to mount the show at his Parisian Théâtre Apollo. Périer and Poudrier took up their original roles with Gina Féraud as Lisbeth and Henri Defreyn as Yoris for a season of four weeks before Périer—the star and raison d'être of the production—had to move on to the Opéra-Comique. It was another 18 years before the piece was again seen in Paris, this time at the Gaîté-Lyrique with Gilbert Moryn starred. It was reproduced once more at the same house (17 February 1936), but, although still beloved by connoisseurs, it has not survived on the stage with the same vigor as its composer's more colorful but much less worthy *Les Saltimbanques.*

The Paris season, however, quickly won the piece overseas productions. Within months, Oscar Hammerstein mounted it (ad Algernon St John Brennan) at his Manhattan Opera House, with a cast headed by Georges Chadal (Hans), Sophie Brandt (Lisbeth), Frank Pollack (Yoris) and George W Callahan (Pippermann) for a season of 79 performances; *Hans, der Flötenspieler* (ad Felix Falzari) appeared in German in Breslau; and Budapest's Népopera mounted an Hungarian version (ad Miksa Bródy) early in 1912.

The pied piper of Hamelin, with variations on his theme, has been the subject of many stage pieces, of which Viktor Nessler's 1879 *Der Rattenfänger von Hameln,* first produced in Leipzig, and widely seen in German and in English over more than half a century, was the most successful. Adolf Neuendorff, conductor and sometime manager of the New York German theatres also produced his own German-language *Der Rattenfänger von Hameln* (lib: H Italianer, Germania Theater 14 December 1880), which was played again a decade later at the Amberg Theater and also visited other American cities, in both German and English versions, and the Kiralfy family produced a Niblo's Garden spectacular on the same tale (*The Ratcatcher, or The Pied Piper of Hamelin* 30 November 1885, mus: Selli Simonsen). In more recent times, a rock version of the tale written by Richard Jarboe, Harvey Shield and Matthew Wells under the title *Hamelin* was seen at New York's Circle in the Square Downtown (10 November 1985, 33 performances) and an hilariously awful children's entertainment in which the crippled child was characterized as an Aggressively Handicapped Person was mounted at London's National Theatre.

In 1908 De Wolf Hopper appeared on Broadway as the Piper in a sequel to the favorite tale, *The Pied Piper* (Manuel Klein/R H Burnside, Majestic Theater 3 December), which went inside the magic mountain to look at the descendents of the lost children, many years later. When the numbers of boys and girls is discovered to be unequal he has to import extra children to ensure suitable pairings, and the importation of "foreigners" soon brings problems to his City of Innocence.

France: Théâtre Apollo 31 May 1910; USA: Manhattan Opera House *Hans, the Fluteplayer* 20 September 1910; Germany: Schauspielhaus, Breslau *Hans der Flötenspieler* 17 December 1910; Hungary: Népopera *Furulyás Jancsi* 19 January 1912

Recordings: complete (Gaîté-Lyrique), selection (EMI-Pathé)

Plate 165. **Hans the Boatman**

HANS THE BOATMAN Musical play by Clay M Greene. Music from various sources. Theatre Royal, Sheffield, 7 March 1887.

Hans the Boatman was constructed to order by Clay Greene, in his home town of San Francisco, and then sent for its first production to Britain, there to showcase the American dialect actor Charles Arnold (b Lucerne, Switzerland, 25 December 1854; d London, 6 May 1905), who had endeared himself to British provincial audiences playing opposite Minnie Palmer as the ingenuously German-accented hero of *My Sweetheart*.

Arnold played Hans Bekel, the boatman of the title, equipped with a four-year-old child called May Hansen (playing a boy child called Fritz) and a trained St Bernard dog called Nord, in a sentimental comedy drama set on the shores of the Schroon Lake in the Adirondacks. Good-natured, lazy, dream-a-day Hans, who spends much of his time with his dog or singing songs with the country kiddies, elopes and marries Gladys (May Gurney) from the city instead of long-adoring local Jeffie (Jennie Rogers), the daughter of the old boatman Thursby (Robert Medlicott). Hans proves too unsupporting for words as a husband and, assisted by the unsavory Darrell Vincent (Robert Morgan), Gladys finally decides to go back to her father (Walter Russell). Thus, it is not his disillusioned wife but Jeffie who nurses Hans when an explosion renders him blind. However, by the final curtain both Hans's eyesight and his wife have been restored and Jeffie is happily tied up elsewhere. A long list of songs and dances of uncertain authorship, mostly for the star, included "The Boatman's Lullaby," "Pleasures Await You, My Boy," "Blind Man's Buff," "The Baby Coquette," "Little Gee-Gee," "Innocent Lilies," "The Spirit of the Lake and "The Daisy Chain." One provincial reviewer wrote, "it abounds in scenes and incidents of pure domestic pathos, it breathes of home and of child life, of fresh bracing mountain air and of sunny gardens."

Arnold toured Britain with great success for 46 weeks, played a season at London's Terry's Theatre (December 1887), and took his play, plus the all-important child (now his little daughter, Dora) and dog, on to Australia (1888), where they began with a splendid 50 nights in Melbourne, 37 in Sydney, and the biggest houses ever seen in Tasmania, as *Hans the Boatman* knocked up some 350 nights around the country. Arnold then proceeded to New Zealand (95 performances), India, China, Japan and, finally, to America, where *Hans* opened in Chicago and went on to notch up its 1,000th performance on 8 March 1890 in St Paul, Minnesota.

The show's popularity was such that Fred Reynolds (officially), the Stacy company and the Sillitoe-Palmer company (unofficially) all mounted versions of *Hans* on the Pacific circuits following Arnold's departure, but the show did not find the same favor in America and, when his three-year tour contract was canceled after one year, Arnold returned to Britain. He tried other vehicles with succeeding dogs and children (in one of which he gave an exhibition of sheep-shearing), including a *Captain Fritz,* in which he introduced Henry Hamilton's ''Tommy Atkins,'' but he always returned to *Hans,* which he toured in 1893 in a ''new version'' back to the South Pacific, where it and he had found such popularity. He died at the piano, in the middle of singing a song in a concert at London's Savage Club.

Australia: Bijou Theatre, Melbourne 5 May 1888; USA: McVickers Theater, Chicago 9 September 1889

THE HAPPY DAY Musical play in 2 acts by Seymour Hicks. Lyrics by Adrian Ross and Paul Rubens. Music by Sidney Jones and Paul Rubens. Daly's Theatre, London, 13 May 1916.

Left with a theatre in the red at the death of George Edwardes, Robert Evett began his attempts to keep Daly's going in the Edwardesian tradition with a Hicks/Ross/Rubens/Sidney Jones musical in the Ruritanian vein, into which the tried and still pretty true ingredients of the past decades of Daly's (et al) Theatre musicals were poured. The young soprano star Winifred Barnes and respected actor Arthur Wontner played a princess and prince in disguise, G P Huntley and Lauri de Frece were two comical villains straight out of *Erminie,* whilst soubrette Unity More from revue; Rosina Filippi, who had created a list of heart-tugging mother figures for Hicks; and concert vocalist Thorpe Bates, added for male vocal values, all had the opportunity to do what they did best. The mixture was topped off by a glamorous gypsy queen, played by young José Collins, brought back home from a budding career on Broadway.

There was plenty of value all-round in *The Happy Day,* but it was Miss Collins who dazzled the audiences with her evocation of Rubens's ''Bohemia,'' and Bates, with his handsome voice (Jones's ''Yours till the End''), who edged Miss Barnes for the vocal honors. 242 performances later (the shortest run at Daly's in years) the show went on tour, with the financial situation if anything worse than before, but Evett had laid the foundation of the company which would soon turn things round with *The Maid of the Mountains.*

The Happy Day marked Jones's farewell to the kind of English musical theatre he had largely helped to boost to international supremacy, for as the new rhythms began to enter theatre music he, resolutely of earlier days, simply stopped writing.

HAPPY END Musical play said to be ''by Elisabeth Hauptmann based on a story by Dorothy Lane. Songs by Kurt Weill, Bertolt Brecht and Elisabeth Hauptmann.'' Theater am Schiffbauerdamm, Berlin, 2 September 1929.

After the success of *Die Dreigroschenoper,* Hauptmann, Brecht and Weill came together on a second piece for the Theater am Schiffbauerdamm. An awkward, naive little tale about a Salvation Army girl called Lillian Holliday (Carola Neher) and a Chicago gangster called Bill Cracker (Oscar Homolka), pumped up with some equally naive and awkward political propaganda, and accompanied by a set of songs only intermittently attached to the play, it folded after three chaotic, unprofessional performances. In recent years the show has been exhumed several times in areas where its propaganda is popular, or where the incidental songs—including the slicing hymn to ''Surabaya Johnny,'' the ''Bilbao Song,'' the tango ''Matrosen Song'' and ''Der Song von Mandelay''—all subsequently made widely popular through their performance by Weill's wife, Lotte Lenya, have been adjudged to outweigh a libretto to which Brecht was, apparently, too canny to put his name.

London saw a version of *Happy End* (with the undoubtedly fictitious Dorothy Lane still in the credits) for a 37-performance run in 1975, and Broadway took in a Michael Feingold adaptation from the Brooklyn Academy of Music, with Meryl Streep and Bob Gunton in the principal roles, for 75 performances at the Martin Beck Theater two years later. In 1987 it was played at London's Camden Festival (The Place 7 April 1987) with Eric Roberts and Rosamund Shelley featured. However, if the piece has not been able to make itself a place on the non-aligned professional/commercial stage, the most popular of its songs have remained afloat, becoming often-featured standards in the repertoire of many a Lenya wannabe.

UK: Lyric Theatre 26 August 1975; USA: Brooklyn Academy of Music 8 March 1977; Martin Beck Theater 7 May 1977

Recordings: complete (DGG, Capriccio), selection by Lenya (CBS), etc

HAPPY HUNTING Musical comedy in 2 acts by Howard Lindsay and Russel Crouse. Lyrics by Matt Dubey. Music by Harold Karr. Majestic Theater, New York, 6 December 1956.

The combination of librettists Crouse and Lindsay and star Ethel Merman, which had been so successful in *Anything Goes* and *Call Me Madam* and not unsuccessful with *Red, Hot and Blue!,* came together yet again, along with Broadway newcomers Harold Karr and Matt Dubey, to bring *Happy Hunting* to the stage. In a plot which followed the *Call Me Madam* formula, Miss Merman was cast as Liz Livingstone, a brash and wealthy Philadelphia socialite, who is so cross at not being invited to the wedding of Prince Rainier and Grace Kelly that she heads right off for Monaco to outshine the mating of the princely couple by wedding her daughter Beth (Virginia Gibson) to a real, live Habsburg (Fernando Lamas). But the Habsburg, who clearly knows a star when he sees one, falls for mother instead.

The show's songs, topped by mother's and daughter's admission that they belong to a ''Mutual Admiration Society'' and ''A New Fangled Tango,'' did not manage to offer the star the kind of potential standards that Cole Porter and Irving Berlin had done in the earlier shows (she described them as ''jerry-built and shopworn''), but Jo Mielziner's production of *Happy Hunting* held the boards for a battling, but ultimately losing, 412 performances.

Recording: original cast (RCA Victor)

THE HAPPY TIME Musical in 2 acts by N Richard Nash suggested by a character in the stories of Robert L Fontaine. Lyrics by Fred Ebb. Music by John Kander. Broadway Theater, New York, 18 January 1968.

Rodgers and Hammerstein had a 614-performance success with their production of Samuel Taylor's adaptation of Fontaine's novel *The Happy Time* as a 1950 play. Richard Nash's musical adaptation, set with songs by John Kander and Fred Ebb, and produced by David Merrick, did not do as well, but it played for 286 performances on Broadway in 1968, and found both some fond fans and intermittent regional revival.

Michael Rupert played the French-Canadian boy Bibi Bonnard, whose growing-up is colored by the clash between his ordinary, decent father Philippe (George S Irving) and his showy photographer uncle Jacques (Robert Goulet, Tony Award), who descends from the big city on the little town of Saint-Pierre and upsets the family's unadventurous life there with his citifed ways. Grandpa Bonnard (David Wayne) succeeds in bringing back some balance between the two extremes, before dying at the approach of the final curtain, and allowing the other top-billed star, Goulet, to deliver the piece's perhaps rather dubious message—''get out and live.''

It was a message that the songwriters would deliver with more effect later the same year in their more successful and enduring *Zorba.* Here, their most winning musical moments came with Grandpa's old-fashioned assertions that he was once ''The Life of the Party,'' Bibi and Jacques's duet ''Please Stay'' and a lively ''Tomorrow Morning.'' The rest of the winning was done by director-choreographer Gower Champion, who picked up Tonys for both assignments.

A revised version of the show was mounted at the Goodspeed Opera House in 1980 (9 April).

Recording: original cast (RCA Victor)

HARBACH, Otto [HAUERBACH, Otto Abels] (b Salt Lake City, 18 August 1873; d New York, 24 January 1963). Broadway librettist and lyricist who collaborated on many of the most important musicals of his time.

The American-born son of a Danish family, Hauerbach began his working life as a teacher of English in Washington. He moved to New York in 1901 to attend Columbia University and, whilst studying, he worked at first in insurance, then in journalism, and as a copywriter in advertising. In 1902 he began working with the young musician Karl Hoschna on a musical play but, whilst others of Hoschna's earliest works found their way to the stage, their collaboration remained unproduced. His break came when Hoschna was asked by his employer, Isidore Witmark, to set Mrs Pacheco's play *Incog* as a musical. Hoschna recommended Hauerbach for the text part of the job, and when the resultant piece, *Three Twins,* proved a considerable success in the theatre and spawned a couple of successful songs, including Harbach's ''Cuddle Up a Little Closer,'' the team's future seemed assured. They teamed with Owen Davis on a musical farce, *Back Again,* for the Aborn Comic Opera Company's summer season of 1909 (old-time star Amelia Summerville featured) and, when they confirmed their first success with a major hit in the form of a remade version of the Continental musical comedy *Madame Sherry* (''Every Little Movement''), Hauerbach felt able to give up his advertising job to concentrate full time on a theatre career. The potentially fruitful Hoschna/Hauerbach collaboration was, however, cut short by the composer's early death.

Hauerbach was fortunate enough quickly to be paired with another rising young talent—a novice composer, working on his first Broadway show, a commission from Arthur Hammerstein for a vehicle for *Naughty Marietta* star Emma Trentini. The composer was Rudolf Friml, and the first musical which the pair turned out together was the neatly made star vehicle *The Firefly* (''Sympathy,'' ''Giannina Mia''). Although both writers worked intermittently with other collaborators, Harbach and Friml were associated in the years that followed on 10 further musical shows, including the highly successful adaptation of another French comedy as the widely popular *High Jinks* (1913) and Friml's most enduring romantic operetta, *Rose Marie* (1924). The librettist-lyricist (now billed, less Germanically, as ''Harbach'') had, however, the biggest international success of the early part of his career when he paired with composer Louis Hirsch on the adaptation of James Montgomery's *The Aviator* into the musical *Going Up* (1917, ''The Tickle Toe,'' ''If You Look in Her Eyes''), and the pair followed this hit with another in the every-Cinderella-day tale of *Mary* (1920, ''The Love Nest'').

Even before the production of *Mary,* however, Harbach had begun another collaboration which would lead him to further significant successes. Early in 1920 he started up what was to be a regular, though not exclusive, working partnership with fellow librettist and lyricist Oscar Hammerstein II. If their first work together, on two Herbert Stothart musicals, was less than distinguished, they rose several notches to turn out the pretty Mediterranean-romantic tale of *Wildflower* (1923), with a score by Vincent Youmans and Stothart, before topping all competition with *Rose Marie* (''Indian Love Call,'' ''Rose Marie,'' ''The Mounties,'' ''Totem Tom-Tom'') the following year.

In the meantime, however, the busy Harbach had been collecting the proceeds from another success, this one outside of New York. He had been the adapter and original lyricist for Harry H Frazee's production of the musical version of the play *My Lady Friends* as *No, No, Nanette* (''No, No, Nanette''). That piece, after having undergone some out-of-town changes at the hands of others, had been racking up a record run in Chicago since mid-1923, and when it finally came to New York Harbach had the distinction of being simultaneously involved in the authorship and the royalties of the two greatest hits the American musical theatre had known up to that time. It was estimated at the time by *Variety* that he was collecting something like half a million dollars of the period per annum from his stage works and songs.

Whilst this pair of hits went round the world, Harbach and Hammerstein pursued their collaboration on a run of further successes: *Sunny* for Jerome Kern (''Who?,'' ''Two Little Bluebirds''), the dashingly romantic *Song of the Flame* for George Gershwin and the inevitable Stothart (both 1925) and, in 1926, their other major romantic operetta hit, *The Desert Song* (1926), with its splendid *Sheik* of a book and its hit-filled Sigmund Romberg score (''The Desert Song,'' ''Romance,'' ''The Riff Song,'' ''One Alone''). Their final Broadway work together was on *Good Boy* (1928), after which Harbach authored the libretto for the lavish *Nina Rosa* for Romberg, and the altogether less than convincing books, but impressive lyrics, for Kern's *The Cat and the Fiddle* (''She Didn't Say 'Yes''') and *Roberta* (''Smoke Gets in Your Eyes,'' ''Yesterdays''), closing his Broadway record with another romantic piece, *Forbidden Melody,* again for Romberg, nearly 30 years after his first produced work. A final reunion with Hammerstein on a Civil War piece, *Gentlemen Unafraid,* musically set by Jerome Kern, played only regionally.

Alongside Harbach's successful productions there were, of course, also the failures, but the writer left very little of his work on the tryout trail, and his total of hit and near-hit shows was an impressive one, making it all the more surprising that his name has not lasted as a recognizable one in the public ear in the way that those of more fashionable and/or heavily publicized writers and composers, who achieved less in the same era, have done.

Many of Harbach's libretti, including most of his biggest hits, were original texts, but a good number were also adaptations from existing plays. Although *A kis gróf* (*Suzi*) was his only straight Operette adaptation, others of his libretti were based on Continental pieces, notably Maurice Ordonneau's original libretto for *Madame Sherry, Les Dragées d'Hercule,* which became *High Jinks, Le Chasseur de Chez Maxim,* the source of *The Blue Kitten,* and Hennequin and Veber's *La Présidente,* the basis for *Oh, Please!* Others, from the days of *Three Twins / Incog* onwards were adaptations of native works, including *Bright Eyes* (from Charles Dickson's *Mistakes Will Happen*), *Kitty Darlin'* (David Belasco's *Sweet Kitty Bellairs*), *Kitty's Kisses* (Bartholomae's *Little Miss Brown*), *Going Up* (James Montgomery's *The Aviator*), *Tumble In* (the Mary Roberts Rinehart/Avery Hopwood hit play *Seven Days*), *Roberta* (Alice Duer Miller's novel *Gowns by Roberta*), *June Love* (Charlotte Thompson's *In Search of a Sinner*), *Jack and Jill* (Frederick Isham's play *The Cherry Tree*), and the most famous, *No, No, Nanette* (*My Lady Friends*). He also—it would seem—had the novel distinction of being the first author to adapt a movie screenplay to the musical stage, when the silent screen's *Miss George Washington Jr* became the libretto to his 1919 musical *The Little Whopper.*

The reverse process occurred when an unproduced play-cum-screenplay of his (w Edgar McGregor) was adapted in England by Weston and Lee as the libretto for the musical comedy *Here Comes the Bride* (Piccadilly Theatre, London 20 February 1930).

1908 **Three Twins** (Karl Hoschna) Herald Square Theater 15 June

1909 **Back Again** (Hoschna/w Owen Davis) Olympic Park, Newark 7 June

1909 **Bright Eyes** (Hoschna/Charles Dickson) Grand Theater, New Haven 25 November; New York Theater 28 February 1910

1910 **Madame Sherry** (Hoschna) Colonial Theater, Chicago 10 April; New Amsterdam Theater 30 August

1910 **The Fascinating Widow** (Hoschna, later Percy Wenrich)

Apollo Theater, Atlantic City 14 November; Liberty Theater 11 September 1911

1910 **The Girl of My Dreams** (Hoschna/w Wilbur D Nesbit) Garrick Theater, Philadelphia 26 December; Criterion Theater 7 August

1911 **Dr Deluxe** (Hoschna) Knickerbocker Theater 17 April

1912 **The Firefly** (Rudolf Friml) Lyric Theater 2 December

1913 **High Jinks** (Friml) Lyric Theater 10 December

1914 **The Crinoline Girl** (Wenrich/Julian Eltinge) Knickerbocker Theater 16 March

1914 **Suzi** (*A kis gróf*) English version (Casino Theater)

1915 **Katinka** (Friml) 44th Street Theater 23 December

1917 **You're in Love** (Friml) Casino Theater 6 February

1917 **Kitty Darlin'** (Friml/w P G Wodehouse) Casino Theater 7 November

1917 **Going Up** (Louis Hirsch/w James Montgomery) Liberty Theater 25 December

1919 **Tumble In** (Friml) Selwyn Theater 24 March

1919 **The Little Whopper** (Friml/Bide Dudley) Casino Theater 13 October

1920 **Mary** (Hirsch/w Mandel) National Theater, Washington 31 March; Knickerbocker Theater 18 October

1920 **Tickle Me** (Stothart/w Hammerstein, Frank Mandel) Selwyn Theater 17 August

1920 **Jimmie** (Stothart/w Hammerstein/w Hammerstein, Mandel) Apollo Theater 17 November

1921 **June Love** (Friml/Brian Hooker/w W H Post) Knickerbocker Theater 25 April

1921 **The O'Brien Girl** (Hirsch/w Mandel) Liberty Theater 3 October

1922 **Molly Darling** (Tom Johnstone/Phil Cook/w William Cary Duncan) Liberty Theater 1 September

1922 **The Blue Kitten** (Friml) Selwyn Theater 13 January

1923 **Wildflower** (Vincent Youmans, Stothart/w Hammerstein) Casino Theater 7 February

1923 **Jack and Jill** (Augustus Barratt/w Barratt, John Murray Anderson) Globe Theater 22 March

1923 **No, No, Nanette** (Youmans/w Irving Caesar/w Mandel) Garrick Theater, Detroit 23 April; Palace Theatre, London 11 March 1925

1923 **Kid Boots** (Harry Tierney/Joseph McCarthy/w William Anthony McGuire) Earl Carroll Theater 31 December

1924 **Rose Marie** (Friml, Stothart/w Hammerstein) Imperial Theater 2 September

1924 **Betty Lee** (Hirsch, Conrad/w Caesar) 44th Street Theater 25 December

1925 **Sunny** (Kern/w Hammerstein) New Amsterdam Theater 22 September

1925 **Song of the Flame** (Gershwin, Stothart/w Hammerstein) 44th Street Theater 30 December

1926 **Kitty's Kisses** (Con Conrad/Gus Kahn/w Philip Bartholomae) Playhouse 6 May

1926 **Criss Cross** (Kern/Caldwell) Globe Theater 12 October

1926 **The Wild Rose** (Friml/w Hammerstein) Martin Beck Theater 20 October

1926 **The Desert Song** (Romberg/w Hammerstein/w Hammerstein, Frank Mandel) Casino Theater 30 November

1926 **Oh, Please!** (Youmans/w Anne Caldwell) Fulton Theater 17 December

1927 **Lucky** (Kern, Harry Ruby, Bert Kalmar) New Amsterdam Theater 22 March

1927 **Golden Dawn** (Emmerich Kálmán, Stothart/w Hammerstein) Hammerstein's Theater 30 November

1928 **Good Boy** (Stothart, Kalmar, Ruby/w Hammerstein, Henry Meyers) Hammerstein's Theater 5 September

1930 **Nina Rosa** (Romberg/Caesar) Majestic Theater 20 September

1931 **The Cat and the Fiddle** (Kern) Globe Theater 15 October

1933 **Roberta** (Kern) New Amsterdam Theater 18 November

1936 **Forbidden Melody** (Romberg) New Amsterdam Theater 2 November

1938 **Gentlemen Unafraid** (Kern/w Hammerstein) Municipal Light Opera, St Louis 3 June

HARBURG, E[dgar] Y ("Yip") [HOCHBURG, Isidore] (b New York, 8 April 1896; d Hollywood, Calif, 5 March 1981). Longtime lyricist whose film and revue work was ultimately more productive of enduring material than his book musicals.

As a collegian the young Harburg began contributing comic verse to magazines and to such newspapers as the *New York World* and the *New York Tribune* but, on graduating, he began an electrical appliance business, and it was not until that business went under in the depression that he began a full-time professional career as a lyricist.

Although he contributed the words for an interpolated number to *Queen High* (1926, "Brother, Just Laugh it Off" w Arthur Schwartz, Ralph Rainger) and for another in the film version of *Rio Rita* (1929, "Long Before You Came Along" w Harold Arlen), the significant part of Harburg's career began with lyrics for the revue stage, starting with *The Earl Carroll Sketch Book* (1929 w Jay Gorney, "Like Me Less, Love Me More") and continuing with contributions of more or less numbers to *Earl Carroll's Vanities of 1930* (w Gorney, Harold Arlen, Ted Koehler), *The Garrick Gaieties* (1930), *Americana* (1932, introducing Harburg's first major hit "Brother Can You Spare a Dime?"), *Ballyhoo of 1932* (w Lewis Gensler), *Ziegfeld Follies of 1931* (w Gorney) and *Ziegfeld Follies of 1934* (w Vernon Duke), *Walk a Little Faster* (1932, "April in Paris") *Life Begins at 8.40* (1934, w Harold Arlen) and *The Show Is On* (1936, w Arlen). He scored another stage song hit with "It's Only a Paper Moon" (w Arlen, Billy Rose), written for the play *The Great Magoo* and later used in the film *Take a Chance* (1933).

Over the following years Harburg wrote principally for the screen, supplying songwords notably for *Stage*

Struck (1936, Arlen), *At the Circus* (1939, Arlen) and for yet another Arlen score, *The Wizard of Oz,* which produced his best-remembered songs of all: ''Over the Rainbow'' (Academy Award), ''We're Off to See the Wizard,'' ''Follow the Yellow Brick Road,'' etc. ''God's Country,'' a song from Harburg's first stage book-musical *Hooray for What!,* which had run two hundred performances on Broadway in 1937–38 (''Moanin' in the Mornin,'' ''Down with Love''), was interpolated into the 1939 film of *Babes in Arms,* and he and Arlen also provided additional songs for the film versions of the musicals *Panama Hattie* and *Cabin in the Sky* (1943, ''Happiness is a Thing Called Joe''). In 1944 Harburg penned the words to Jerome Kern's music for the Deanna Durbin musical film *Can't Help Singing.*

The post-*Oklahoma!* period piece *Bloomer Girl* (1944) gave Harburg his first significant Broadway run with a book show, and *Finian's Rainbow* (1947), in which the lyricist paired with composer Burton Lane, was even more successful on its initial production. It was also subsequently seen overseas, and its prettiest song ''How Are Things in Glocca Morra?,'' written in the same pleasingly ingenuous strain as ''Over the Rainbow,'' gave lyricist and composer one of their most enduring hits. ''Old Devil Moon,'' ''When I'm Not Near the Girl I Love'' and ''If This Isn't Love'' were also amongst the lasting part of the *Finian's Rainbow* score.

Harburg co-produced his next musical, *Flahooley,* with *Finian's Rainbow* co-librettist Fred Saidy and Cheryl Crawford, but it and his subsequent stage musicals were less successful and/or productive, even though *Jamaica,* a custom-made Harold Arlen vehicle for Lena Horne, totted up a good Broadway run, materially thanks to its star's appeal. He continued to write for stage and screen through into the 1960s, providing the lyrics to the film cartoon *Gay Purree* (1962, w Arlen), relyricking Offenbach for the unsuccessful stage show *The Happiest Girl in the World* (97 performances) and making his farewell to Broadway with another short-lived show, *Darling of the Day* (which, yet again, had a song with a ''rainbow'' in it), in 1968 (31 performances). In 1973 he provided the lyrics to Earl Robinson's tunes for the television musical *The Great Man's Whiskers.*

A compilation show based on his work (w Saidy) was produced at the Studio Arena, Buffalo, as *I Got a Song* (26 September 1974), and another, *Look to the Rainbow,* in 1985 in London.

1937 **Hooray for What!** (Harold Arlen/Howard Lindsay, Russel Crouse) Winter Garden Theater 1 December

1940 **Hold on to Your Hats** (Burton Lane/Guy Bolton, Matt Brooks, Eddie Davis) Shubert Theater 11 September)

1942 **The Wizard of Oz** (with score from film and original stage versions) Muncipal Opera, St Louis

1944 **Bloomer Girl** (Arlen/Sig Herzig, Fred Saidy) Shubert Theater 5 October

1947 **Finian's Rainbow** (Lane/w Saidy) 46th Street Theater 10 January

1951 **Flahooley** (Sammy Fain/w Saidy) Broadhurst Theater 14 May

1952 **Jollyanna** revised *Flahooley* (w William Friml/w Saidy) Curran Theater, San Francisco 11 August

1957 **Jamaica** (Arlen/w Saidy) Imperial Theater 31 October

1961 **The Happiest Girl in the World** (Offenbach/arr Saidy, Henry Myers) Martin Beck Theater 3 April

1968 **Darling of the Day** (Styne/Nunnally Johnson, Keith Waterhouse, Willis Hall) George Abbott Theater 27 January

1971 **What a Day for a Miracle** (w Henry Myers/Larry Ornstein, Jeff Chandler) University of Vermont 29 April

Biography: Harburg, E, Meyeson, H: *Who Put the Rainbow in the Wizard of Oz* (University of Michigan, 1993)

HARDT-WARDEN, Bruno [WRADATSCH, Bruno] (b Drachenburg, 31 August 1883; d Vienna, 21 July 1954). Prolific writer for the German-language stage through three decades.

Bruno Hardt (his earliest work was done without the double-barrel) made his first attempts as a librettist in the operatic world, providing—most often in collaboration with Ignaz Welleminsky—the texts for such pieces as Max Oberleitner's *La Vallière* (1916) and *Der eiserne Heiland* (1917), *Das Heiderntor* and *Cäcilie* (1920), Jan Brandt-Buys's *Glockenspiel* (1913), *Der Schneider von Schonau* (1916), *Der Erober* (1918), *Mi-carême* and *Der Mann in der Mond* (1922) and Franz Schmidt's *Fredegundis* (1922). However, he soon made his way into the fields of musical comedy and revue, scoring an early success with the revusical Posse *Mädel, küsse mich!* which was set to music by Robert Stolz for Vienna and later played in Hungary as *Csókbakter* (Revü Színház 18 October 1919). Hardt subsequently supplied the text (w Otto Tumlitz) for Stolz's rare attempt at an opera, *Die Rosen der Madonna* (1920).

Revues such as *Hol's der Teufel* (1916), *Wie wird man Millionär* (1918), *Wie wird man jung?* (1920), *Wien, gib acht!* (1923), a mimodrama (w Welleminsky) *Todestarantelle,* set by Julius Bittner and produced at Zürich (29 April 1920) and several Operetten apparently premiered on the Hungarian stage in translation all made up part of Hardt's busy theatrical schedule, from which the first real Operette successes came in 1921 with the productions of Eysler's *Die schöne Mama* in Rome and then in Vienna, and of Stolz's comical musical play *Der Tanz ins Glück,* which followed its Vienna premiere with many musically varying, but textually solid-ish, versions in other countries.

In the 1920s Walter Kollo's *Marietta,* the good-old-days musical built around Fred Raymond's popular song *Ich hab' mein Herz in Heidelberg verloren,* and Straus's

Hochzeit in Hollywood gave him some further musical theatre successes, whilst in the 1930s he provided the texts for Stolz's *Wenn die kleinen Veilchen blühen* (turned into the spectacular *Wild Violets* in the British Empire), Kollo's *Drei arme kleine Mädels,* Pepöck's *Hofball in Schönbrunn,* and the piece which eventually became Kattnigg's *Balkanliebe.* Hardt continued to provide libretti and/or lyrics for the musical theatre into the 1940s, as well as authoring the text for Kattnigg's opera *Donna Miranda* as late as 1953, but although his list of works contained several pieces which had some degree of popularity in their time, none has survived into the revived repertoire.

1915 **A főnyeremény kisasszony** (Ludwig Grüber/w Ignaz M Welleminsky, ad Zsigmond Rajna) Pressburg, March; Hamburg 9 November 1920

1916 **Mädel, küsse mich!** (Robert Stolz/w Emil Schwarz) Lustspieltheater 29 April

1917 **Lang, lang ist's her** (Stolz) Lustspieltheater 18 March

1917 **Tavasz és szerelem** (*Lenz und Liebe*) (Heinrich Berté) Hungarian version Városi Színház 15 September; German version w Welleminsky Hamburg 1918

1918 **Li-i-San** (Wolfgang von Bartels/w Welleminsky) Königliches Theater, Kassel 1 October

1919 **Das Liebeslied** (Ludwig Uray/w Oskar Staudigl) 1 act Opernhaus, Graz 5 April

1919 **Amor in Kasernhof** (Uray) 1 act Opernhaus, Graz 19 November

1920 **Grossstadtmärchen** (Richard Fall/w Erwin Weill) Carltheater 10 January

1920 **Dienstmann Nr 16** (Károly Hajós/Otto Hein) Hölle 1 October

1920 **Der Tanz ins Glück** (later *Hallo, das ist die Liebe*) (Stolz/w Robert Bodanzky) Raimundtheater 23 December

1921 **Die schöne Mama** (*La bella mammina*) (Edmund Eysler/w Heinrich von Waldberg) Teatro Nazionale, Rome 9 April; Wiener Bürgertheater 17 September

1921 **A korhély gróf** (Grüber/w Welleminsky ad László Fodor) Budai Színkör, Budapest 18 June

1921 **Indische Nächte** (Bruno Granichstaedten/w Bodanzky) Apollotheater 25 November

1921 **Eine Sommernacht** (Stolz/w Bodanzky) Johann Strauss-Theater 23 December

1922 **Offenbach** (aka *Der Meister von Montmartre*) German version w Bodanzky (Neues Wiener Stadttheater)

1922 **Die Liebe geht um** (Stolz/w Bodanzky) Raimundtheater 22 June

1922 **Fräulein Frau** (Max Niederberger/w Waldberg) Wiener Bürgertheater 23 December

1923 **Marietta** (Walter Kollo/w Bodanzky, Willi Kollo) Metropoltheater, Berlin 22 December

1924 **Das Fräulein aus 1001 Nacht** (Stolz/w Karl Farkas, Fritz Rotter) Robert StolzBühne 6 October

1924 **Märchen der Liebe** (Emilie Wrana/ad Ernst Andress) Baden-bei-Wien 20 November

1926 **Das Amorettenhaus** (Leo Ascher/w Waldberg, Max Steiner-Kaiser) Carl-Schultze Theater, Hamburg January

1926 **Nur Du** (Walter Kollo/w Kollo) Berliner Theater, Berlin 23 December

1927 **Drei arme kleine Mädels** (Kollo/Willi Kollo/w Feiner) Theater am Nollendorfplatz, Berlin 2 April

1927 **Ich hab' mein Herz in Heidelberg verloren** (Fred Raymond/Ernst Neubach/w Löhner-Beda) Volksoper 29 April

1928 **Hochzeit in Hollywood** (Straus/w Jacobson) Johann Strauss-Theater 21 December

1928 **Eine Nacht in Kairo** (Jean Gilbert/w Leopold Jacobson) Centraltheater, Dresden 22 December

1929 **Die Frau in Gold** (Michael Krasznay-Krausz/w Jacobson) Neues Operettenhaus, Leipzig 28 February

1929 **Lebenslichter** (Hans Pero/w Welleminsky) Stadttheater, Hamburg 12 March

1929 **Das kleine Fräulein Li** (Martin Knopf/w Hermann Feiner) Thalia-Theater, Berlin 25 December

1930 **Mädel ade!** (August Pepöck) Operettenhaus, Leipzig 14 January; Wiener Bürgertheater 5 October

1930 **Das Herrgottslied** (Krazsnay-Kraus) Neues Wiener Schauspielhaus 21 November

1930 **Die Kleine vom Zirkus** (Heinrich Strecker/w Max Leo Deutsch) 30 December

1932 **Wenn die kleinen Veilchen blühen** (Stolz) Princess Theatre, The Hague 1 April

1933 **Rosen im Schnee** (Karl Löwe arr Oscar Jascha/w Löhner-Beda) Volksoper 20 January

1936 **Tausend Worte Liebe** (Walter Kollo/w Ritter) Theater im Europahaus 25 December

1937 **Mucki** (*Bub oder Mädel*) (Willy Engel-Berger) Stadttheater, Bremen 31 July

1937 **Hofball im Schönbrunn** (Pepöck/Josef Wentner) Theater des Volkes, Berlin 4 September

1937 **Die Gräfin von Durazzo** (aka *Balkanliebe*) (Rudolf Kattnigg) Neues Operetten-Theater, Lepizig 22 December

1938 **Der ewige Walzer** (Strecker/w Rudolf Köller) Staatsoper, Bremen 5 February; Volksoper, Vienna 10 May

1938 **Drei Wochen Sonne** (Pepöck) Städtische Bühnen, Nuremberg 15 November

1939 **Über alles siegt die Liebe** (Edmund Nick) Stadttheater, Troppau 25 November; Theater des Volkes, Berlin 1940

1940 **Aennchen von Thurau** (Strecker/w Spirk) Raimundtheater 8 February

1941 **Die Göttin der Liebe** (Franz Drdla/w Köller) Stadttheater, Brunn 17 May

1941 **Küsse in Mai** (Strecker)

1942 **Faschingstraum** (Michael Jary/w Köller) Theater des Volkes, Dresden 25 June

1942 **Eine kleine Liebelei** (Pepöck/w E A Iberer) ExlBühne, Vienna 3 July

1942 **Der liebe Augustin** (Josef Rixner/Köller) Theater des Volkes, Berlin 18 December

1944 **Frühlingsluft** revised version w Pepöck (Bürgertheater)

Other title attributed: *Die neue Mode* (1917, Aro van Leeuwen)

HARKER, Joseph C[unningham] (b Levenshulme, 17 October 1855; d London, 15 April 1927).

The doyen of London's scenic artists for many years, Harker, along with his studio, was responsible for designing and/or painting the sets for Irving's productions at the Lyceum and for Beerbohm Tree at His Majesty's Theatre. In 1898 he took over as the scenic supplier for George Edwardes and, beginning with *A Greek Slave* at Daly's and with *A Runaway Girl* at the Gaiety, designed and/or made the sets for all their productions, at home and usually abroad, up until Edwardes's death. In 1914 he turned out the spectacular settings for Oscar Asche's *Chu Chin Chow* and was subsequently responsible for the American productions of *Chu Chin Chow* and *Mecca* as well as the Comstock/Gest *Aphrodite,* which followed that management's success with their previous spectaculars.

In later years he was partnered with two of his five sons, Joseph [Cunningham] Harker and Phil Harker, who carried on the firm after his death. After Phil's death in 1933, Joseph jr continued the enterprise in partnership with the two other brothers, Roland and Colin.

Autobiography: *Studio and Stage* (Nisbet, London, 1924)

HARLAN, [W] Otis (b Zanesville, Ohio, 29 December 1865; d Martinsville, Ind, 20 January 1940).

Popular comedian who toured through a quarter of a century of starring roles in farce comedies and musicals, before transferring to the screen for a second quarter-century.

Chubby and cheerful Harlan took to the musical stage in Charles Hoyt's *A Hole in the Ground* in 1887 (The Romantic Young Man), toured with Frank Daniels in *Little Puck,* and rose quickly up the comic ladder to lead roles with Hoyt in *A Brass Monkey* (1888, Badger) and *A Texas Steer* (1890, Major Yell). He subsequently played in *Boys and Girls* (1892, Willie Tyre), Cheever Goodwin and Clay Greene's unsuccessful San Francisco musical *Africa* (1893, Mark Mansfield), in *Gloriana, The Isle of Champagne* and *Tabasco* (1894, Ben-Hidden), before returning to star with Hoyt in *A Black Sheep* (1896, Hot Stuff), *A Stranger in New York* (1897, Marble Hart) and *A Day and a Night* (1898, Marble Hart).

He introduced a slightly musicalized version of George R Sims's comedy *My Innocent Boy* in 1899, appeared on Broadway in the revusical *From Broadway to Tokio* (1900, Calcium Lightwayte) and *Star and Garter* (1900, Willie Tyre, ''Lady Bug''), in the extravaganza *The Girl from Up There* (1901, King Flush), and in *A Tin Soldier* (1901, Vilas Canby) and went on tour with the Bijou company in *Lost, Stolen or Strayed* (1902) and with Bulger and Matthews's well-used ''ragtime opera'' *By the Sad Sea Waves* (1902). He was lead comic with Elsie Janis in *The Vanderbilt Cup* (1906, Theodore Banting), teamed with the post-Fields Joe Weber in the double bill *Dream City* (1906, J Bilkington Holmes) and *The Magic Knight* (Frederick), toured with Anna Held in *A Parisian Model* (1907, Silas Goldfinch) and got two seasons of travel out of the farce comedy *A Broken Idol* (1908, Doc Whatt?).

He appeared as the Devil in *Hell* and Wiley Fox in *Gaby* at the Folies-Bergère, New York, toured in *The Girl and the Drummer* (1910), had another star comic role as Dupont, the detective in the successful Austrian musical play *Little Boy Blue* (1911), paired with Ada Lewis in the unsuccessful *The Dancing Duchess* (1914, Richter), and played in the pre-Broadway *Ninety in the Shade* (1914, Judge Splint), leaving the New York flop season to Fred Walton. His last musical comedy stage appearance seems to have been in 1915, featured opposite Australian swimmer Annette Kellerman in the brief tour of *The Model Maid.*

Harlan then closed down his stage career, and headed to where the sun shone, spending the rest of his life—to his last days—working as a film actor. Amongst his earliest vehicles were silent remakes of his great Hoyt successes—*A Black Sheep* (Selig 19 October 1915), *A Stranger in New York* (Selig 8 May 1916)—and his later credits included such pictures as *What Happened to Jones?* (1925), *Lightnin'* (1926), *The Hawk* (1932) and *Diamond Jim* (1935).

HARMATH, Imre (b Budapest, 1890; d Budapest, 15 September 1940).

A prolific and successful author and adapter for the Hungarian theatre, Harmath made the most important part of his career as a lyricist for the musical stage. He supplied the songwords for such Hungarian successes as Komjáti's *Pillangó főhadnagy,* the early works of Pál Ábrahám—beginning with *Zenebona* (*Spektakel*), *Az utolsó Verebély lány* and his jazz cabaret work, and continuing up to the internationally successful *Viktória* and *Die Blume von Hawaii* (originally presented in a German version)—and for Szabolcs Fényes's oft-revived *Maya* (book and lyrics), as well as turning out local versions of a long list of foreign hits. In March 1938 the Városi Színház presented a compilation show of his works for his ''25th anniversary'' in the theatre. His *A csúnya lány* also survived into productions in the 1990s.

Harmath died in a labor camp during the Second World War.

1916 **Fogadjunk!** (Dénes Buday) Budai Színkör 21 July

1918 **Pillangó főhadnagy** (Károly Komjáti/w Ferenc Martos) Király Színház 7 June

1918 **Hejehuja báró** (*Bruder Leichtsinn*) Hungarian version w Adorján Ötvös (Margitszigeti Színkör)

1918 **Aranykalitka** (Béla Zerkovitz) Royal Orfeum 1 December

1918 **A potferj** (*Der Aushilfsgatte*) Hungarian version

1919 **Beppo** (Zerkovitz) 1 act Royal Orfeum 1 February

1919 **Kalandor kisasszony** (Zerkovitz) Royal Orfeum 2 November

1920 **Csillagok csillaga** (Zerkovitz) Royal Orfeum 1 January

1920 **Zsuzsu** (Zerkovitz) Royal Orfeum 1 April

1920 **Lucia** (Zerkovitz) Royal Orfeum 1 September

1920 **Csalogánydal** (Zerkovitz) Royal Orfeum 1 November

1920 **Luna asszony** (*Frau Luna*) Hungarian version (Fővárosi Orfeum)

1921 **Kvitt** (Zerkovitz) Royal Orfeum 2 April

1921 **A bálkirálynő** (*Eine Ballnacht*) Hungarian version (Revü Színház)

1922 **Aranymadár** (Zerkovitz) 1 act Royal Orfeum September

1923 **A hattyúlovag** (Zerkovitz) Royal Orfeum 1 April

1924 **Szegény Jonathán** (*Der arme Jonathan*) Hungarian version (Fővárosi Operettszínház)

1924 **Póstás Katica** (Zerkovitz) Lujza Blaha Színház 19 December

1925 **Dolly** Hungarian version (Városi Színház)

1925 **A császárnő apródja** (Ákos Buttykay/w Jenő Faragó) Király Színház 24 March

1925 **A fiastyúk** (Lon Sandman, Fred Froman) Royal Orfeum 1 April

1925 **Az ártatlan özvegy** (Lajos Lajtai) Városi Színház 25 December

1926 **Az alvó feleség** (Lajtai/Mátyás Feld) Budapesti Színház 13 July

1926 **Ki a Tisza vizét issza** (Buday) Kisfaludy Színház 3 September

1927 **Zsiványkirály** (Zerkovitz) Royal Orfeum 1 January

1927 **A Schlesinger-fiu este Lefkovits Katovál** (A Red/Feld) 1 July

1927 **Az aranypók** (Zsigmond Vincze) Andrássy uti Színház 14 October

1927 **Mersz-e, Mary?** (*Mercenary Mary*) Hungarian lyrics (Király Színház)

1928 **Huzd rá Offenbach!** (Offenbach ad Dezső Losonczy) Andrássy uti Színház 29 February

1928 **Zenebona** (Pál Ábrahám/w István Bródy, László Lakatos) Fővárosi Operettszínház 2 March

1928 **Az utolsó Verebély lány** (Ábrahám/Gábor Drégely ad) Fővárosi Operettszínház 13 October

1928 **Rose Marie** Hungarian lyrics (Király Színház)

1928 **Yes** Hungarian lyrics (Magyar Színház)

1928 **Nizzai éjszaka** (*Lady X*) Hungarian version (Városi Színház)

1929 **Aranypáva** (Béla Neszmélyi/w László Békeffy) Városi Színház 20 April

1929 **Kikelet-utca 3** (Egon Kemény/w István Bródy) Fővárosi Operettszínház 27 April

1929 **Szökik az asszony** (Miklós Brodszky/Andor Kardos) Budai Színkör 14 June

1929 **Szeretem a feleségem** (Ábrahám/Adorján Stella) Magyar Színház 15 June

1929 **Strandszerelem** (pasticcio/Franz Arnold, Ernest Bach ad) Nyári Operettszínház 10 July

1929 **Diákszerelem a karzaton** (pasticcio) Andrássy uti Színház 30 August

1929 **Miss Europa** (Losonczy/László Bús Feketé) Andrássy uti Színház 30 August

1930 **A biarritzi Vénusz** (Dezső Szenkár/Andor Kardos) Városi Színház 30 January

1930 **A csúnya lány** (Alfréd Márkus/László Vadnai) Fővárosi Művesz Színház 7 February

1930 **Viktória** (Ábrahám/Imre Földes) Király Színház 21 February

1930 **Huszárfogás** (Vincze/w Rezső Török) Fővárosi Művesz Színház 4 April

1930 **Meluzina** (Zerkovitz/Harmath, Török) Városi Színház 12 April

1930 **Dunabár** (Otto Vincze) Bethlen-téri Színház 14 May

1930 **Sanyikát örökbe fogadják** (pasticcio) 1 act Andrássy uti Színház 29 May

1930 **Jobb, mint otthon** (arr Vincze/w Adorján Stella) Nyári Operettszínház 5 July

1930 **Az első tavasz** (Brodszky/Ernő Andai) Budai Színkör 16 June

1931 **Lámpaláz** (Kálmán Rozsnyai/Adorján Stella) Magyar Színház 24 January

1931 **Katóka** (*Peppina*) Hungarian version (Fővárosi Operettszínház)

1931 **Viharos nászéjszaka** (pasticcio/Albert Acrémant ad János Vaszary) Magyar Színház 4 April

1931 **Falu végén kurta kocsma** (Zerkovitz) Bethlen-téri Színház 10 April

1931 **A hárem** (Szabolcs Fényes/Ernő Vajda) Fővárosi Operettszínház 24 April

1931 **Die Blume von Hawaii** (*Hawaii Rószája*) original Hungarian lyrics (Neues Theater, Leipzig, in German; Király Színház 28 January 1932)

1931 **Maya** (Fényes) Fővárosi Operettszínház 10 December

1931 **A "Fehér Ló"** (*Im weissen Rössl*) Hungarian version w Adorján Stella, Király Színház

1932 **Nyiott áblak** (Imre Farkas/Károly Nóti) Fővárosi Operettszínház 6 February

1932 **Manolita** (Fényes) Fővárosi Operettszínház 24 September

1933 **A kék lampas** (Brodszky/w László Szilágyi) Király Színház 3 March

1933 **Dinom-dánom** (József Hajós) Pesti Színház 22 April

1934 **Vadvirág** (Mihály Eisemann/Ernő Andai) Andrássy uti Színház 24 March

1934 **Szeressen kedves** (Komjáthy/Ernő Andai) Fővárosi Operettszínház 1 April

1934 **Music Hall** (Fényes, Támás Bródy/Charles Méré) Fővárosi Operettszínház 13 October

1934 **Oh! Papa** Hungarian lyrics (Andrássy uti Színház)

1935 **Mimi** (Fényes/Endre Solt, Iván Tőrs) Royal Színház 13 February

1935 **Leányálom** (*La Madone du promenoir*) Hungarian version (Andrássy uti Színház)

1935 **Mariora** (Brodszky/László Bus Fekete)

1936 **Madame Bajazzo** (Ferenc Földes/Kardos) Kamara Színház 27 June

1936 **Sok hühó Emmiért** (Fényes/Károly Aszlányi) Kamara Színház 24 October

1936 **3:1 a szerelem javára** (Ábrahám/Szilágyi, Dezső Kellér) Royal Színház 18 December

1937 **A szerelmes királynő** (*Die verliebe Königin*) Hungarian lyrics (Városi Színház)

1937 **Antoinette** (Károly Komjáthy/Armand Szánthó, Mihály Szécsén) Művész Színház 23 December

1938 **Dinasztia** (Brodszky/w István Békeffy) Magyar Színház 16 April

1938 **Szomjas krokodil** (Márkus/Szilágyi) Márkuspark Színház 21 June

1938 **Kávé habbal** (Eisemann/Pál Barabás) Royal Színház 30 November

1938 **Fehér hattyú** (Ábrahám/Földes) Városi Színház 23 December

1939 **Egy bolond százat csinál** (László Walter/Mihály Szüle) Royal Színház 29 January

HARNICK, Sheldon [Mayer] (b Chicago, 27 December 1924). Lyricist for several Broadway successes and one oversized international hit.

Early on a violinist in a dance orchestra, then a songwriter (''The Boston Beguine''), Harnick did much of his first work as a writer for the theatre in the world of revue, contributing lyrics and/or music for songs in *New Faces of 1952, Two's Company* (1952), *John Murray Anderson's Almanac* (1953), *Shoestring Revue* (1955), *The Littlest Revue* (1956), *Shoestring '57* (1957), *Kaleidoscope* (1957), *Take Five* (1959) and *Vintage '60* (1960). During this time, he also made his first ventures into the world of the Broadway musical when he proffered some additional lyrics to the scores of the flop shows *The Amazing Adele* (1955) and *Shangri La* (1956). In 1958 he wrote the songs (w composer Jerry Bock) for the 60-performance musical *The Body Beautiful,* and shared the lyric-writing credit on the briefly seen *Portofino,* but he found his first considerable success soon after when he rejoined Bock to write the songs for the award-winning biomusical *Fiorello!* (''Little Tin Box'').

The two subsequently collaborated on the scores for five further stage musicals, each of which found at least some degree of success on Broadway, and the greatest of which, *Fiddler on the Roof* (''If I Were a Rich Man,'' ''Sunrise, Sunset,'' ''Do You Love Me?,'' ''Matchmaker, Matchmaker,'' etc), became one of the most important international hits of its era. Beyond Broadway, they also produced the score for the marionette show *The Man in the Moon* for Bill Baird's puppets (1963), the television musical *The Canterville Ghost* (ABC 2 November 1966) and, away from their own shows, supplied additional material to the score of *Her First Roman* (1968).

When Bock withdrew from the musical theatre scene in 1970 after *The Rothschilds,* Harnick continued with a variety of other projects, including a superior English adaptation of the libretto and lyrics of *Die lustige Witwe* and the English-language version of the widely acclaimed Parisian production of *La Tragédie de Carmen,* as well as an *Alice* (1975, w Joe Raposo) for the Baird puppets, for which he supplied not only the words but the voice of the White Rabbit. He also ventured into the operatic world, supplying the texts for the one-act operas *That Pig of a Molette* and *A Question of Faith,* with music by Thomas Z Shepard.

He has also returned intermittently to the musical theatre, most recently with a stage musical version of the Frank Capra film *A Wonderful Life,* again written with Raposo and produced in Washington, DC, in 1991.

1954 **Horatio** (David Baker/Ira Wallach) Theater 54, State Fair Park, Dallas 8 March

1958 **The Body Beautiful** (Jerry Bock/Joseph Stein, Will Glickman) Broadway Theater 23 January

1958 **Portofino** (Louis Bellson, Will Irwin/w Richard Ney/Ney) Adelphi Theater 21 February

1959 **Fiorello!** (Bock/Jerome Weidman, George Abbott) Broadhurst Theater 23 November

1960 **Tenderloin** (Bock/Abbott, Weidman) 46th Street Theater 17 October

1961 **Smiling, the Boy Fell Dead** (David Baker/Ira Wallach) Cherry Lane Theater 19 April

1963 **She Loves Me** (Bock/Joe Masteroff) Eugene O'Neill Theater 23 April

1964 **Fiddler on the Roof** (Bock/Stein) Imperial Theater 22 September

1966 **The Apple Tree** (Bock/w Bock, Jerome Coopersmith) Shubert Theater 16 October

1970 **The Rothschilds** (Bock/Sherman Yellen) Lunt-Fontanne Theater 19 October

1975 **Captain Jinks of the Horse Marines** (Jack Beeson) Kansas City 20 September

1976 **Rex** (Richard Rodgers/Yellen) Lunt-Fontanne Theater 25 April

1978 **The Merry Widow** (*Die lustige Witwe*) new English version (New York City Opera)

1979 **The Umbrellas of Cherbourg** (*Les Parapluies de Cherbourg*) English version (Public Theater)

1981 **Penny by Penny** (Michel Legrand) Playhouse, Wilmington 9 November

1982 **A Christmas Carol** revised *Penny by Penny* Stamford, Conn 10 December

1991 **A Wonderful Life** (Joe Raposo) Arena Stage, Washington, DC 15 November

HARRIGAN, Edward [Green] (b New York, 26 October 1843; d New York, 6 June 1911). Performer and author of a series of colorful and popular comedies with songs played on Broadway over a period of some 20 years.

After working for a couple of years in a shipyard and as a caulker, the young Ned Harrigan made his beginnings in show business on America's west coast, playing in minstrelsy and in variety, as he teamed up, first, in a double act with Master Alex O'Brien, then in 1869 with **Sam RICKEY** [Richard Thomas HIGGINS, b Providence, RI, 16 March 1848; d New York 10 September 1885), in whose company he made his first Broadway appearance in 1870 in Harrigan's sketches *The Little Fraud* and *The Mulcahy Twins,* and finally, from 1871, with the man who would be his partner through the largest part of his career, Tony Hart. This pair, performing more of such comic sketches—*The Caitucky Band,* a burlesque of *John Garth, The Big and the Little of It, The Day We Went West, You 'Spute Me,* as two quarreling Irishwomen in *Who Owns the Clothesline?,* as a couple of German immigrants in *Chicago, The Wonderful Doughnut, The Mulcahey Twins, The Cannibals, The Mixed Couple, The Mulligan Guard, After the War, Blackball Sailors, A Terrible Example* (featuring the song ''Was She Led or Did She Go Astray?''), *Who's Got the Flo?, The Italian Padrone,* etc—written to their measure by Harrigan, soon rose to a prominent and profitable place in their profession.

They joined John Stetson's Company at the Globe Theatre, New York, in October of 1871, played in 1872 with Arlington, Cotton and Kemble's company in Chicago, and the following year became a regular fixture at New York's Theatre Comique, performing an ever turning-over series of Harrigan's sketches and taking part in Josh Hart's little musical burlesque productions during the season, and traveling the country with much the same combination of attractions in the summer. Alongside and as part of his sketches, Harrigan also turned out a voluminous supply of songs amongst which the sextet ''The Regular Army-O!,'' first performed by Harrigan, Hart, John Wild, Diamond, Ryan and Bradley (4 May 1874), caused a sensation, and the comic song ''Hildebrandt Montrose'' became a nationwide favorite, interpolated by others into many a touring musical comedy.

In 1875–76 the pair took themselves out on their ''first starring tour'' with a three-act drama (''introducing their beautiful musical specialities''), *The Doyle Brothers,* written by Harrigan and by John Woodard and featuring such of their popular songs as ''The Mulligan Guard'' and ''The Skidmore Guards,'' plus such sketches as *The Blue and the Gray* and *The Green Above the Red,* and, at the end of this tour, in August 1876 they themselves took over the management of the old Theatre Comique as a permanent New York base. Their programs there, for the most part, eschewed the burlesques of Hart's days, and were made up of an olio, followed by one of their now rather extended comic and musical sketches, or a Harrigan-constructed Irish or ''local'' drama, the one and the other illustrated with numbers in which Harrigan's lyrics were set musically by his father-in-law and musical director, David Braham.

Plate 166. **Edward Harrigan**

Eventually, the olio was done away with and Harrigan's sketches were expanded to the size of a full-length musical comedy, filling the whole evening of Harrigan and Hart entertainment. The sketches and comedies purveyed by the team were aimed squarely at a variety-house audience. Harrigan's characters were European immigrants—particularly Irish or German—or blacks, and his plots often used the ridiculous rivalries and the comical mistrust that existed between these various over-exclusive bands of ''new Americans'' as the source of their fun. In those joyfully politically incorrect and liberated days, folk were still able to laugh at ''themselves'' and their foolishnesses and pretentiousnesses and, of course, at those of their neighbors.

Harrigan's own most popular character was that of Irishman Dan Mulligan, and he wrote a whole series of pieces in which he appeared as Dan, alongside his upwardly-striving wife Cordelia (Annie Yeamans), his son, Tommy (Hart) and their mouthy black maid, Mrs Rebecca Allup (also Hart). The Mulligans battled it out socially with the German Lochmüllers or physically with the black Skidmore Guards, the rival factions prancing up and down in uniform in pseudomilitary parades which made up for there being no real war to get all dressed up for, getting into a regular run of fistfights and barneys, all to the accompaniment of a series of songs which included a whole set of popular hits (''The Babies on the Block,'' ''The Mulligan Guards,'' ''Maggie Murphy's Home,'' ''Whist! the Bogie Man,'' ''McNally's Row of Flats,'' ''O, Never Drink Behind the Bar,'' etc).

The run of Harrigan and Hart shows, which is usually agreed to have reached its peak with *Cordelia's Aspirations* in 1884, ended soon after. In *Investigation,* Harrigan slipped from the genuine ''musical play'' format he had practiced so long by introducing for the first time a girlie chorus. And then, in what seemed like a judgment, the Theatre Comique was burned down. In the wake of the disaster, as the partners transferred their operations to the Park Theater, Harrigan and the increasingly unstable Hart fell out. After revivals of *The Major* and *Cordelia's Aspirations,* covering the dates which should have been used by Harrigan's newest piece, *McAllister's Legacy,* which, uncharacteristically, had failed, the partnership ended.

Harrigan continued on in the same vein, but not with quite the same élan. He suffered a one-week flop with *Are You Insured?,* in which he did not play, did slightly better when he appeared as a Civil War colonel in *The Grip,* and better again when he went back to his oldest formula and appeared as a comic Irishman, with Mrs Yeamans as ever his shrewish wife, in *The Leather Patch* (''Denny Grady's Hack,'' ''Baxter Avenue''). He remained Irish to appear as O'Reagan and McNooney in the next two pieces, and then tried himself out in blackface (with occasional lapses into Irish) as the servant of the title in *Pete. Pete* did well enough but, nevertheless, Harrigan stuck thereafter to the Googans and the Hogans and the Reillys, winning his last big success with *Reilly and the Four Hundred* in 1890. Latterly he reprised his old pieces, and in 1896 he was still playing his first Theatre Comique piece, *Old Lavender,* on one-night stands.

After this, however, things began to weaken seriously. The new and songless show Harrigan was preparing for Broadway, *My Son Dan,* was abandoned on the road, and he announced his retirement, only to return later the same year as *Marty Malone.* He reappeared from time to time thereafter, as a producer, a writer and a performer in stock and in comedy, and revisited the vaudeville circuits for the first time in years with the sketches *Larry Logan* (made up from bits of *My Son Dan* and *Investigation)* and *Sergeant Hickey,* but the 20-year series of Harrigan shows, which had won such vast and enthusiastic audiences for its genuinely popular brand of theatre, was over.

When Harrigan died, three years after his last stage appearance at the Lamb's Gambol in 1908, an obituary summed up his work: ''Harrigan's plays were intensely local; the types were true studies of New York life, but the story of the play was often extravagant and was intended to serve the purposes of character, drollery, comedy and song and dance. The social point of view, if it could be called a point of view, was democratic in the extreme. Harrigan's 'Four Hundred' was a conglomeration of all races, colors and creeds. The negro was a welcome guest in the parlours of the socially ambitious of the Fourth Ward. The incongruity of it finally became too much of a burden for the nimble feet and rollicking songs to carry. Harrigan himself, Tony Hart, Annie Yeamans, Collier, Quilter and others of the company were individually very clever and inimitable, but the plays as a whole meant nothing. True in character and details of life, often touching in incident and episode, they suddenly plunged into a whirlwind of social extravaganza. Harrigan was not a very good actor, but he had the genius of sympathy for poor, unlettered and odd people. He caught the passing types of the day and he knew how, as a stage manager, to reproduce them to the life in manners and dress and speech and thought. No adequate account can be given in print of his plays or, to speak with more accuracy, of his productions and performances, but they contained genius, some of which will remain in the music and songs of Braham.''

The obituarist was right. His description was inadequate. It tried to analyze what was little more than the appeal of a modern-day, working-class television comedy series: the joy of seeing familiar everyday folk, colorfully exaggerated, up there doing extravagantly silly and funny and foolish and sentimental and picturesque things. Whatever else, Harrigan knew his audiences, and he pleased them hugely for most of two happy decades. For that achievement, William Dean Howells gave him the rather curious soubriquet ''The American Dickens,'' and the description has been glibly quoted frequently since. I can think of no British dramatist—certainly not Dickens—who portrayed his everyday countrymen to themselves with such good-humored, pointed burlesquery, teetering somewhere between the satirical and the surreal and, almost always, the successful.

A biomusical on *Harrigan and Hart* was produced at the Goodspeed Opera House in 1984 and subsequently played for five performances at Broadway's Longacre Theater (31 January 1985). The score included a selection of Harrigan's songs, and the part of Harrigan was played by Harry Groener.

Harrigan's eldest son, **Edward Harrigan jr** (d 16 February 1895), appeared in several of his father's shows (*Old Lavender, Reilley and the 400, The Woolen Stocking,* Granville Bright in *The Major*) before his death, aged 18, from peritonitis.

1873 **The Mulligan Guard** (Braham) sketch, Chicago; Theatre Comique 8 September

1874 **[The St] Patrick's Day Parade** (Braham) sketch, Myer's Opera House, Chicago ?22 June; Theatre Comique 14 September

1876 **Sons of Temperance** (Braham) sketch Theatre Comique August

1876 **An Editor's Troubles** (Braham) sketch Theatre Comique September

1876 **Down Broadway, or the Gallant 69th** (Braham) sketch Theatre Comique September

1876 **The Terrible Example** (Braham) sketch Theatre Comique October

1876 **Walking for That Cake** (Braham) sketch Theatre Comique 23 October

1876 **Malone's Night Off, or The Turnverein Festival** (Braham) sketch 30 October

1876 **The Bold Hibernian Boys** (Braham) Theatre Comique October

1876 **The Bar Ber Ous** (Braham) sketch Theatre Comique

1876 **Darby and Lanty** (Braham) Theatre Comique 13 November

1876 **Lascaire** (Braham) Theatre Comique 20 November

1876 **Ireland vs Italy, or Who Owns the Clothes-Line?** (Braham) sketch Theatre Comique 18 December

1876 **Christmas Joys and Sorrows** (Braham) sketch Theatre Comique December

1877 **Callahan the Detective** (Braham) Theatre Comique 15 January

1877 **Mardi Gras** (Braham) sketch Theatre Comique February

1877 **The New York Hackman** (Braham) sketch Theatre Comique February

1877 **The Bradys** (Braham) sketch Theatre Comique February

1877 **Down in Dixie** (Braham) sketch Theatre Comique February

1877 **The Goats** (Braham) sketch Theatre Comique March

1877 **The Maguires Phoites** (Braham) sketch Theatre Comique March

1877 **Old Lavender** (Braham) Theatre Comique 3 September (revised version 22 April 1878)

1877 **The Rising Star** (Braham) 1 act Theatre Comique 22 October

1877 **The Pilsbury Muddle** (Braham) sketch Theatre Comique 17 December

1877 **Sullivan's Christmas** (Braham) 1 act Theatre Comique 24 December

1878 **A Celebrated Hard Case** burlesque (Braham) 1 act Theatre Comique 18 March

1878 **The Mulligan Guards' Pic-nic** (Braham) 1 act Theatre Comique 23 September

1878 **The Lorgaire, or the Murder at the Black Rock** (Braham) Theatre Comique 25 November

1879 **The Mulligan Guard Ball** (Braham) 1 act Theatre Comique 13 January

1879 **The Mulligan Guards' Chowder** (Braham) 1 act Theatre Comique 11 August

1879 **The Mulligan Guards' Christmas** (Braham) 1 act Theatre Comique 17 November

1880 **The Mulligan Guards' Surprise** (Braham) 1 act Theatre Comique 16 February

1880 **The Mulligan Guards' Nominee** (Braham) 1 act Theatre Comique 22 November

1881 **The Mulligans' Silver Wedding** (Braham) 1 act Theatre Comique 21 February

1881 **The Major** (Braham) Theatre Comique 29 August

1882 **Squatter Sovereignty** (Braham) Theatre Comique 9 January

1882 **The Blackbird** (Braham) Theatre Comique 26 August

1882 **Mordecai Lyons** (Braham) Theatre Comique 26 October

1882 **McSorley's Inflation** (Braham) Theatre Comique 27 November

1883 **The Muddy Day** (aka *Bunch o' Berries*) (Braham) Theatre Comique 2 April

1883 **Cordelia's Aspirations** (Braham) Theatre Comique 5 November

1884 **Dan's Tribulations** (Braham) Theatre Comique 7 April

1884 **Investigation** (Braham) Theatre Comique 1 September

1885 **McAllister's Legacy** (Braham) Park Theatre 5 January

1885 **Are You Insured?** (George F Braham) 14th Street Theater 11 May

1885 **The Grip** (Braham) Park Theater 30 November

1886 **The Leather Patch** (Braham) Park Theater 15 February

1886 **The O'Reagans** (Braham) Park Theater 11 October

1887 **McNooney's Visit** (Braham) Park Theater 31 January

1887 **Pete** (Braham) Park Theater 22 November

1888 **Waddy Googan** (Braham) Park Theater 3 September

1889 **4-11-44** (Braham) (revised *McNooney's Visit*) Park Theater 21 March

1890 **Reilly and the Four Hundred** (Braham) Harrigan's Theater 29 December

1891 **The Last of the Hogans** (Braham) Harrigan's Theater 21 December

1893 **The Woolen Stocking** (Braham) Harrigan's Theater 9 October

1894 **Notoriety** (Braham) Harrigan's Theater 10 December

1895 **My Son Dan** (Braham) Opera House, Paterson, NJ 21 October

1896 **Marty Malone** (Braham) Bijou Theater 31 August

1899 **Larry Logan** (Braham) sketch Proctor's Music Hall 27 February

1903 **Under Cover** (George L Braham) Smith's Theater, Bridgeport, Conn 26 August; Murray Hill Theater 28 November

Biographies: Kahn, E J: *The Merry Partners* (Random House, New York, 1955), Moody, R: *Ned Harrigan; From Corlear's Hook to Herald Square* (Nelson Hall, Chicago, 1980)

HARRIS, Charles [GLOSSOP, Charles Robert] (b London, 12 December 1853; d London, 23 February 1897).

The brother of **Augustus HARRIS** [Augustus Henry GLOSSOP] (b Paris, 18 March 1852; d Folkestone, 22 June 1896), third generation impresario, supremo of the Theatre Royal, Drury Lane, and a sometime writer of plays and libretti, ''Charley 'Arris'' found his theatrical niche as the most important and influential director in the English-language musical theatre of his time. He directed his first show at the age of 18—it was none other than the vastly proportioned Covent Garden pantomime, *Little Red Riding Hood*—initiated the Gilbert and Sullivan era, at the age of 22, with his direction of *The Sorcerer,* and went on to mount the original production of *HMS Pinafore* before Gilbert decided to take on the single-handed direction of his shows himself (''produced under the direction of the author and composer''). He later directed the show which would most seriously challenge the Carte productions, *Billee Taylor* (1880), and Broadway's *Iolanthe* (1882), mounted the record-breaking comedy opera *Dorothy* (1886) for George Edwardes, and set the ''new burlesque'' on its way to triumph at the Gaiety Theatre with his productions of *Monte Cristo Jr,* with its long-famous escape scene over the roofs of London, and *Miss Esmeralda,* before staging the high spots of the new burlesque era—*Faust Up-to-Date* and *Carmen Up-to-Data.* When Gilbert walked out of the Savoy Theatre, Harris returned to direct D'Oyly Carte's latter-day productions, including the two last Gilbert and Sullivan comic operas. He died at the age of 42, whilst directing the London production of the comic opera *His Majesty.*

Never an actor, Charlie Harris nevertheless appeared at Broadway's Standard Theatre, at a benefit, as the Judge in *Trial by Jury* (1882).

Harris was, without doubt, the outstanding British stager of musical plays of the 19th century, and he did more than any other ''stage manager'' in establishing the metier of director, as it later became known, as a separate and creative position, as opposed to the post of a stage manager, overseeing the day-to-day physical running of a show.

Amongst the shows which Harris directed, in an age when a ''stage manager'' or ''stage director'' was often not given a program credit, were *The Sorcerer* (1877), *The Spectre Knight* (1878), *Billee Taylor* (1880, USA 1881), *Claude Duval* (1881), *Patience* (USA), *Manteaux Noirs* (USA 1882), *Manola* (USA 1882), *Dorothy* (1886), *Monte Cristo Jr* (1886, USA 1888), *The Sultan of Mocha* (revival 1887), *Jack in-the-Box* (1887), *Miss Esmeralda* (1887), *Frankenstein* (1887), *Carina* (1888), *Faust Up-to-Date* (1888), *Doris* (1889), *The Red Hussar* (1889), *Captain Thérèse* (1890), *La Cigale* (1890), *Carmen Up-to-Data* (1890), *The Rose and the Ring* (1890), *The Nautch Girl* (1891), *The Vicar of Bray* (1892 revival), *Haddon Hall* (1892), *Jane Annie* (1893), *Utopia (Ltd)* (1893, USA 1894), *Mirette* (1894), *The Queen of Brilliants* (1894), *The Chieftain* (1894) and *The Grand Duke* (1896).

One of the Harris sisters, Patience Glossop [ka Harris] (b Brompton, 9 September 1857; d London, 26 December 1901), was for a number of turn-of-the-century years the costume firm ''Auguste et cie,'' which she took over shortly before the death of its founder, Augustus Harris sr (Augustus Harris Glossop, b Naples, 12 June 1826; d London, 19 April 1873), 27 years stage manager at the Royal Italian Opera, Covent Garden. It was thereafter run by his widow, Maria Ann (née Bone) (1828–1892). A second sister, Nellie, was the wife of producer Horace Sedger.

HARRIS, Sam[uel] H[enry] (b New York, 3 February 1872; d New York, 3 July 1941). Long successful Broadway producer and theatre owner.

After a variegated youthful life which included a stint in his teens running a steam laundry, Harris ended up becoming the manager of a prizefighter called Terry McGovern. When McGovern, like many boxers of his day, moved into a different area of show business, touring in the burlesque *The Gay Morning Glories,* Harris took a part share in the show, and thus began his career as a theatrical producer. He subsequently went into partnership with Paddy Sullivan and A H Woods staging slightly more substantial touring plays before, in 1904, he mounted the production of the young George M Cohan's musical comedy, *Little Johnny Jones.* Cohan and Harris subsequently formed a partnership which presented all of Cohan's later pieces, as well as a quantity of other musical shows and plays, over a period of some 16 years. Amongst the most successful of their revue and musical comedy productions were Cohan's own *Forty-Five Minutes from Broadway* (1912) and the international hit musical comedy *Going Up* (1917).

After the ending of his alliance with Cohan in 1920, Harris continued a lively production schedule in the straight theatre as well as staging both revues (notably *The Music Box Revue*s and the 1933 *As Thousands Cheer*) and musical comedy. He mounted the Marx Brothers' vehicles *The Cocoanuts* (1925) and *Animal Crackers* (1928), George Gershwin's *Of Thee I Sing*

(1931) and its sequel *Let 'em Eat Cake* (1933), Cole Porter's *Jubilee* (1935), Irving Berlin's *I'd Rather Be Right* (1937) and, just before his death, Moss Hart and Kurt Weill's *Lady in the Dark* (1941).

Harris built the Music Box Theater (w Irving Berlin), which housed his series of revues, and ran Sam H Harris Theaters in both New York and in Chicago.

HARSÁNYI, Zsolt (b Korompa, 27 January 1887; d Budapest, 29 November 1943).

Journalist, librettist and playwright, Harsányi adapted a vast number of foreign pieces for the Hungarian stage, including the long-surviving local versions of *Das Dreimäderlhaus, Das Land des Lächelns, Der Zigeunerprimás* and *Gräfin Mariza,* but he also contributed to several successful original works of the Hungarian musical stage—notably the libretto for the Zsigmond Vincze musical comedy *Limonádé ezredes,* and the lyrics for Huszka's *Nemtudomka,* both pieces which were seen beyond their country of origin.

Alongside his other musical theatre works he also provided Hungarian versions of Mozart's *Don Giovanni,* Rossini's *Il barbiere di Siviglia* and Strauss's *Ariadne auf Naxos,* and wrote the libretto for Kodály's *Háry János.*

1911 **Kreolvér** (*Kreolenblut*) Hungarian version (Budai Színkör)

1911 **A provanszi vándor** (Alfred Rieger/Franz Wolf) Hungarian version (Ujpesti Népszínház)

1911 **A nőtlen férj** (*Der ledige Gatte*) Hungarian version (Ujpesti Népszínház)

1912 **Limonádé ezredes** (Zsigmond Vincze) Király Színház 15 September

1913 **A cigányprimás** (*Der Zigeunerprimás*) Hungarian version (Király Színház)

1913 **Buksi** (*Puppchen*) Hungarian version (Király Színház)

1913 **A mozikirály** (*Filmzauber*) Hungarian version (Király Színház)

1913 **A tökéletes feleség** (*Die ideale Gattin*) Hungarian version (Király Színház)

1914 **Nemtudomka** (Jenő Huszka/Károly Bakonyi) Király Színház 14 January

1915 **Nad-Mé** (*Die verbotene Stadt*) Hungarian version (Király Színház)

1915 **A pirosruhás hölgy** (*Die Dame in Rot*) Hungarian version (Budai Színkör)

1915 **Link báró** (*Der Juxbaron*) Hungarian version (Royal Orfeum)

1915 **A költő éjzsakája** (*Die verschenkte Nacht*) Hungarian version (Royal Orfeum)

1915 **A bolondok háza** (*Der Narrenhaus*) Hungarian version (Royal Orfeum)

1915 **Végre egyedül** (*Endlich allein*) Hungarian version (Király Színház)

1916 **Vagy ő, vagy senki** (*Die, oder keine*) Hungarian version (Népopera)

1916 **Az artistabál** (''FG'') Royal Orfeum 1 April

1916 **Dicsőfalvi** (Miklós Balázs) 1 act Kolozsvár May

1916 **Egyszer volt** (*Wie einst im Mai*) Hungarian version (Fővárosi Nyári Színház)

1916 **Három a kislány** (*Das Dreimäderlhaus*) Hungarian version (Vígszínház)

1916 **Özvegy kisasszony** (*Toeff-Toeff*) Hungarian version with music by Adorján Ötvös (Budai Színkör)

1916 **A derék Fridolin** (*Der brave Hendrik*) Hungarian version (Budai Színkör)

1916 **A mecénás** (*Der Natursänger*) Hungarian version w Albert Kövessy (Royal Orfeum)

1916 **A világjaró** (*Der Weltenbummler*) Hungarian version (Budai Színkör)

1917 **Vandergold kisasszony** (Áladár Renyi/w Sándor Hevesi) Városi Színház 24 October

1917 **Ő, Teréz!** (*Das Fräulein von Amt*) Hungarian version (Vígszínház)

1917 **Milliomos Kati** (*Urschula*) Hungarian version (Budai Színkör)

1917 **A Favorit** (*Der Favorit*) Hungarian version (Budai Színkör)

1918 **Hóvirág** (*Liebe im Schnee*) Hungarian version (Városi Színház)

1918 **Csalni jó** Margitszigeti Színkör 18 May

1918 **Médi** (*Hannerl*) Hungarian version (Vígszínház)

1918 **A szép Saskia** (*Die schöne Saskia*) Hungarian version (Városi Színház)

1918 **Háztűznéző** (Béla Reinitz/w Gábor Drégely) 1 act Medgyaszayszínház 17 December

1920 **A kislány** (Károly Stefanides/w Emil Szomory) Revü Színház 20 March

1920 **Búcsúkeringő** (*Der letzte Walzer*) Hungarian version (Városi Színház)

1921 **Csókos asszony** (*Clary-Clara*) Hungarian version w new music by Béla Zerkovitz (Eskütéri Színház)

1921 **Az erénycsősz** (*Die keusche Barbara*) Hungarian version (Budai Színkör)

1923 **Marinka, a tancosnő** (*Katja, die Tänzerin*) Hungarian version (Fővárosi Operettszínház)

1923 **A diadalmas asszony** (*Die Siegerin*) Hungarian version (Városi Színház)

1923 **A három grácia** (*Libellentanz*) Hungarian version (Fővárosi Operettszínhaz)

1923 **Pompadour** (*Madame Pompadour*) Hungarian version (Fővárosi Operettszínház)

1924 **Amerika lánya** (László Kiszely/w Sándor Szilágyi) Városi Színház 17 May

1924 **Puszipajtások** (Tivadar Pallós/Ernst Marischka, Gustav Beer ad) 1 act Lujza Blaha Színház, Budapest 9 October

1924 **Apukám!** (*Cloclo*) Hungarian version (Fővárosi Operettszínház)

1924 **Dorina és a véletlen** (*Dorine und der Zufall*) Hungarian version (Renaissance Színház)

1924 **A párizsi lány** (*Gosse de riche*) Hungarian version (Fővárosi Operettszínház)

1924 **Marica grófnő** (*Gräfin Mariza*) Hungarian version (Király Színház)

1925 **Fraskita** (*Frasquita*) Hungarian version (Városi Színház)

1925 **Hármackskán** (*Quand on est trois*) Hungarian version (Vígszínház)

1925 **Az Orlov** (*Der Orlow*) Hungarian version (Fővárosi Operettszínház)

1925 **Terezina** (*Teresina*) Hungarian version (Fővárosi Operettszínház)

1926 **Párizsi kirakat** (*Mannequins*) Hungarian version (Magyar Színház)

1927 **Nachtmusik** (Mihály Nádor) 1 act Uj Színház 2 December

1928 **Szeretlek** (*J'aime*) Hungarian version (Király Színház)

1928 **Lulu** Hungarian lyrics (Fővárosi Operettszínház)

1928 **Jolly Joker** (*Le Petit Choc*) Hungarian version (Belvárosi Színház)

1929 **Libavásár** (*Le Renard chez les poules*) Hungarian version (Belvárosi Színház)

1929 **Volga-bar** Hungarian version of comedy with songs (Vígszínház)

1929 **Régen és most** (*Bitter-Sweet*) Hungarian version (Király Színház)

1930 **Csodabár** (*Die Wunder-Bar*) Hungarian version (Fővárosi Operettszínház)

1930 **A mosoly országa** (*Das Land des Lächelns*) Hungarian version (Magyar Királyi Operaház)

1933 **Ez a kislány nem eladó** (*Un soir de reveillon*) Hungarian version (Vígszínház)

1934 **Giuditta** Hungarian version (Magyar Királyi Operaház)

1937 **Szabó a kastélyban** Hungarian version of a play by Paul Armont and Leopold Marchand with songs by Alexander Steinbrecher (Vígszínház)

1940 **XIV-ik René** (Mihály Eisemann/w István Zágon) Vígszínház 14 September

1941 **A tizedik kérő** (pasticcio ad Támás Bródy/w Sándor Hunyady) Vígszínház 7 May

HART, Lorenz [Milton] (b New York, 2 May 1895; d New York, 22 November 1943). Lyricist half of the Rodgers and Hart team through two decades of successful musical comedies.

From his college days, lyricist Hart formed a songwriting partnership with composer Richard Rodgers and, after a struggling beginning, during which Hart worked as a translator for the German-language Irving Place Theater and for the Shuberts, the pair took their first Broadway steps under the wing of producer Lew Fields. They broke through with their songs for the revue *The Garrick Gaieties* (''Manhattan'') and became established, in the mid-1920s, as regular contributors to the Broadway musical stage. Beginning with the costume piece *Dearest Enemy* (''Here in My Arms''), they provided the scores for a sequence of musical comedies, of which a version of *The Girl Friend* (''The Blue Room''), *Peggy-Ann* and *A Connecticut Yankee* (''My Heart Stood Still,'' originally heard in the London revue *One Dam Thing After Another*) provoked productions beyond America, and which produced a number of individual songs that became popular: ''Mountain Greenery'' (*Garrick Gaieties 1926, The Girl Friend* UK), ''You Took Advantage of Me'' (*Present Arms*), ''With a Song in My Heart'' (*Spring Is Here*) and ''Ten Cents a Dance'' (*Simple Simon*).

After a not-so-productive spell in Hollywood the partners returned to Broadway, and in the eight years before the dissolution of their partnership and Hart's death, they turned out a flow of scores covering an eclectic range of established musical-comedy styles and, on some occasions, as in the dance-based *On Your Toes* (1936) and in their most remarkable and most retrospectively admired piece, the wryly misanthropic *Pal Joey,* taking altogether less usual tones. Alongside these two shows, a standard-studded let's-do-a-show show, *Babes in Arms,* the Hungarian fantasy *I Married an Angel,* and the classical burlesque *By Jupiter,* gave the partnership their best Broadway moments of a period which brought forth many of Hart's most enduring songs, including ''Where or When,'' ''My Funny Valentine,'' ''The Lady Is a Tramp,'' ''Johnny One Note,'' ''I Wish I Were in Love Again'' (all *Babes in Arms*), ''There's a Small Hotel,'' ''Glad to Be Unhappy'' (*On Your Toes*), ''Falling in Love With Love,'' ''This Can't Be Love'' (*The Boys from Syracuse*), ''I Could Write a Book'' and ''Bewitched'' (*Pal Joey*).

The Rodgers and Hart partnership broke down when the lyricist's erratic private life and drinking habits made him into an impossibly unreliable collaborator. Rodgers himself, in desperation, was forced anonymously to supply some of the lyrics which Hart was supposed to have written in their last days together. The composer, unable to rein in his energies to cope with his partner's failures to provide, joined Oscar Hammerstein II to write *Oklahoma!,* whilst producing a revival of a revised version of *A Connecticut Yankee,* for which Hart supplied some additional songs. The comically revusical ''To Keep My Love Alive'' proved the pick of what were to be his last theatre songs. Hart died later the same year, having survived long enough to see *Oklahoma!* become a bigger hit than anything he and Rodgers had written together.

At their best, Hart's songs were unusually attractive in their ideas, with lyrics that were unostentatiously clever and complex, easy and pleasantly ingenious in their rhyming, and sufficiently general to allow them a life away from the shows in which they were introduced.

His brother, **Teddy HART** appeared in vaudeville, comedy and on the musical stage as Dromio of Ephesus in *The Boys from Syracuse* (1938) and as Taxi Black in *One Touch of Venus* (1943).

Like many of his brethren, Larry Hart and his work suffered being posthumously potted into a compilation show. This one was called *Larry—This Funny World* and was produced in Amsterdam in 1998. Lou Landré impersonated Hart.

1920 **Poor Little Ritz Girl** (Richard Rodgers, Sigmund Romberg/Lew Fields, George Campbell) Central Theater 28 July

1925 **Dearest Enemy** (Rodgers/Herbert Fields) Knickerbocker Theater 18 September

1926 **The Girl Friend** (Rodgers/H Fields) Vanderbilt Theater 17 March

1926 **Lido Lady** (Rodgers/Guy Bolton, Bert Kalmar, Harry Ruby) Gaiety Theatre, London 1 December

1926 **Peggy-Ann** (Rodgers/ad H Fields) Vanderbilt Theater 27 December

1926 **Betsy** (Rodgers/Irving Caesar, David Freedman) New Amsterdam Theater 28 December

1927 **A Connecticut Yankee** (Rodgers/H Fields) Vanderbilt Theater 3 November

1928 **She's My Baby** (Rodgers/Kalmar, Ruby) Globe Theater 3 January

1928 **Present Arms** (Rodgers/H Fields) Lew Fields Mansfield Theater 26 April

1928 **Chee-Chee** (Rodgers/H Fields) Lew Fields Mansfield Theater 25 September

1929 **Spring Is Here** (Rodgers/Owen Davis) Alvin Theater 11 March

1929 **Heads Up!** (Rodgers/John McGowan, Paul Gerard Smith) Alvin Theater 11 November

1930 **Simple Simon** (Rodgers/Bolton, Ed Wynn) Ziegfeld Theater 18 February

1931 **America's Sweetheart** (Rodgers/H Fields) Broadhurst Theater 10 February

1935 **Jumbo** (Rodgers/Ben Hecht, Charles MacArthur) Hippodrome Theater 16 November

1936 **On Your Toes** (Rodgers/w Rodgers, George Abbott) Imperial Theater 11 April

1937 **Babes in Arms** (Rodgers/w Rodgers) Shubert Theater 14 April

1937 **I'd Rather Be Right** (Rodgers/Moss Hart, George S Kaufman) Alvin Theater 2 November

1938 **I Married an Angel** (Rodgers/ad w Rodgers) Shubert Theater 11 May

1938 **The Boys from Syracuse** (Rodgers/Abbott) Alvin Theater 23 November

1939 **Too Many Girls** (Rodgers/George Marion jr) Imperial Theater 18 October

1940 **Higher and Higher** (Rodgers/Gladys Hurlbut, Joshua Logan) Shubert Theater 4 April

1940 **Pal Joey** (Rodgers/John O'Hara) Ethel Barrymore Theater 25 December

1942 **By Jupiter** (Rodgers/w Rodgers) Shubert Theater 3 June

Literature: Hart, D, Kimball, R: *Complete Lyrics of Lorenz Hart* (Knopf, New York, 1986), Rodgers, R: *Musical Stages* (Random House, New York, 1975), Suskind, S: *Berlin, Kern, Rodgers, Hart, and Hammerstein: A Complete Song Catalogue* (MacFarland, Jefferson, North Carolina, 1990), Marx, S, Clayton, J: *Rodgers & Hart: Bewitched, Bothered and Bedevilled* (Putnam, New York, 1976), Hart, D: *Thou Swell, Thou Witty: the Life and Lyrics of Lorenz Hart* (Harper & Row, New York, 1976)

HART, Moss (b New York, 24 October 1904; d Palm Springs, Calif, 20 December 1961).

The winningly comical author of such highly successful plays as *Once in a Lifetime, Merrily We Roll Along, You Can't Take It with You, The Man Who Came To Dinner* (all w George S Kaufman) and *Light Up the Sky,* and of what is arguably the best theatrical autobiography of the postwar period (*Act One*), Hart had a rather less memorable career as an author in the musical theatre. His first and rather untypical work, *Jonica,* was a quick flop, collaborations with Irving Berlin (165 performances), Cole Porter (169 performances) and Rodgers and Hart (290 performances) gave him respectable rather than fine results, and he hit the jackpot only with his final work, the libretto for *Lady in the Dark,* in which an up-to-date skin of psychoanalysis was cleverly used to give an appearance of modernity to an old-fashioned romantic tale, decorated here with some particularly fine sung-through dream sequences by Ira Gershwin and Kurt Weill.

Hart supplied sketches for Berlin's successful revue *As Thousands Cheer* (1933) and for the 1938 *Sing Out the News* (w Kaufman), a Music Box Theater revue which he also co-produced and which was played for 105 performances, but, in the end, his memorable success in the musical theatre came not as a writer, but as a director: the original stager of *My Fair Lady* (1956) and of *Camelot* (1960, also co-producer). His only other venture as a producer of musical theatre was on the Irving Berlin *Miss Liberty* (1949, also director).

Musicals have been made from several of the plays which Hart wrote with Kaufman, *Merrily We Roll Along* (*Merrily We Roll Along* Stephen Sondheim/George Furth 1981, 16 performances) and *The Man Who Came to Dinner* (*Sherry!* Laurence Rosenthal/James Lipton 1967, 72 performances) being musicalized for brief Broadway stays, and *You Can't Take It with You* (*Igy élni . . . Ő!*, mus: Charles Bradley, Magyar Színház, Budapest 26 June 1948) for the Hungarian stage.

Hart was married to musical leading lady **Kitty CARLISLE** [Catharine CONN] (b New Orleans, 3 September 1914), who played on Broadway as Prince Orlofsky in *Champagne Sec* (1933), opposite William Gaxton as Katarina [ie, Josefa] in *White Horse Inn* (1936), in the triple star role of *Three Waltzes* (1938) and in *Walk with Music* (1940, Pamela Gibson). She also appeared on film in the 1930s in *Murder at the Vanities, A Night at the Opera, Hollywood Canteen,* etc. Latterly she was seen in Boston as *The Merry Widow* (1943) and in New York in *Kiss Me, Kate* (1955) in a career more orientated towards music-less theatre.

1930 **Jonica** (Joseph Meyer, William Friedlander/William Moll/w Dorothy Heyward) Craig Theater 7 April

1932 **Face the Music** (Irving Berlin/w Berlin) New Amsterdam Theater 17 February

1934 **The Great Waltz** (*Walzer aus Wien*) American version (Center Theater)

1935 **Jubilee** (Cole Porter) Imperial Theater 12 October

1937 **I'd Rather Be Right** (Richard Rodgers/Lorenz Hart/w George S Kaufman) Alvin Theater 2 November

1941 **Lady in the Dark** (Kurt Weill/Ira Gershwin) Alvin Theater 23 January

Literature: Hart, K C: *Kitty* (Doubleday, New York, 1988)

Autobiography: *Act One* (Random House, New York, 1959)

HART, Tony [CANNON, Anthony J] (b Worcester, Mass, 25 July 1855; d Worcester, Mass, 4 November 1891). Half of the celebrated musical-comedy team of Harrigan and Hart.

The young Hart worked in a circus and in minstrel troupes in his early youth before, at the age of 16, joining forces with Ned Harrigan in what was to become the famous double act of Harrigan and Hart. The pair worked at first in variety, and then, when Harrigan expanded their sketches into full-sized variety-based musical comedies, in a decade of mostly successful theatre shows. Hart starred opposite Harrigan's Dan Mulligan in blackface as the big-mouthed maid Rebecca Allup or, on occasions, as the Mulligan family's son, Tommy or, on yet other occasions, as both in the course of the same evening, and, in the later non-Mulligan shows, mostly as a selection of tough-talking little Irish dames such as Widow Nolan (*Squatter Sovereignty*), Mrs Bridget McSorley (*McSorley's Inflation*), Mary Ann O'Leary (*The Muddy Day*) and Molly McGouldrich (*McAllister's Legacy*). It was the sassy Rebecca, however, who remained the public's favorite amongst his creations.

When the partnership broke up, soon after the destruction by fire of their Theatre Comique base, Hart went on to appear in the farce-comedies *Buttons* (1885, six roles including two female) and *The Toy Pistol* (1886, Isaac Roost), opposite Lillian Russell in the Charles Hoyt/Edward Solomon musical comedy *The Maid and the Moonshiner* (1886, Upton O Dodge), and in the slightly musical comedy *Donnybrook* (1886, Con O'Grady), but none of these pieces succeeded, and his increasingly unstable behaviour finally led him to be committed. He died, insane, at the age of 36.

Hart was married to soubrette **Gertie GRANVILLE** (Gertrude Evelyn MONA[G]HAN, b England, 1850; d New York, 13 March 1890), a former circus and vaudeville artist who appeared in Harrigan's *The Major* (1881, Henrietta), *Squatter Sovereignty* (1882, Nellie Nolan), *The Blackbird* (1882, Mona), *Mordecai Lyons* (1882, Mary Radcliffe), *McSorley's Inflation* (1882, Annie Dempsey), *The Mulligan Guard Ball* (1883, Kitty Lochmuller), *The Mulligan Guard Pic-nic* (1883, Jenny), *Cordelia's Aspirations* (1883, Diana McFudd), *The Major* (1884, Henrietta) and *Are You Insured?* (1885) and with her husband in *Buttons.*

Biography: Kahn, E J: *The Merry Partners* (Random House, New York, 1955)

HASSALL, Christopher [Vernon] (b London, 24 March 1912; d Rochester, Kent, 25 April 1963). Lyricist to the Ivor Novello canon.

At first an actor, Hassall supplied some lyrics to his Oxford University revue (*The Oxford Blazers*), but only made his professional debut as a musical comedy writer when Ivor Novello, to whom he had acted as understudy, and with whom he was then appearing in *Murder in Mayfair,* gave him the opportunity to write the lyrics for his Drury Lane commission *Glamorous Night* (''Glamorous Night,'' ''Fold Your Wings,'' ''Shine Through My Dreams,'' ''Shanty Town''). He subsequently worked on Novello's *Careless Rapture* (''Music in May''), Crest of the Wave (''Rose of England''), *The Dancing Years* (''Waltz of My Heart,'' ''The Wings of Sleep,'' ''I Can Give You the Starlight,'' ''My Dearest Dear''), *Arc de Triomphe* (''Dark Music'') and *King's Rhapsody* (''Some Day My Heart Will Awake,'' ''Fly Home, Little Heart,'' ''The Mayor of Perpignan'').

In 1950 he adapted J M Barrie's *Quality Street* as the libretto for the successful musical play *Dear Miss Phoebe* (''I Leave My Heart in an English Garden''). His film work included the screenplay of the 1955 film version of *King's Rhapsody.*

Hassall committed suicide at the age of 51.

1935 **Glamorous Night** (Ivor Novello/Novello) Theatre Royal, Drury Lane 2 May

1936 **Careless Rapture** (Novello/Novello) Theatre Royal, Drury Lane 11 September

1937 **Crest of the Wave** (Novello/Novello) Theatre Royal, Drury Lane 1 September

1939 **The Dancing Years** (Novello/Novello) Theatre Royal, Drury Lane 23 March

1943 **Arc de Triomphe** (Novello/Novello) Phoenix Theatre 9 November

1949 **King's Rhapsody** (Novello/Novello) Palace Theatre 15 September

1950 **Dear Miss Phoebe** (Harry Parr Davies) Phoenix Theatre 13 October

HAVANA Musical comedy in 3 acts by George Grossmith jr and Graham Hill. Lyrics by Adrian Ross and George Arthurs. Music by Leslie Stuart. Gaiety Theatre, London, 25 April 1908.

When George Edwardes decided that it was time for a change of policy at the Gaiety Theatre he contracted Leslie Stuart of *Florodora* fame to compose the theatre's new musical in the place of the Ivan Caryll/Lionel Monckton team, which had served him so well for more than a decade. *Havana* had a mite more substance to it than some of the earlier Gaiety shows, and it had no made-to-measure role for the theatre's usual star, Gertie Millar (Mrs Monckton). Evie Greene starred in the substantial leading soprano role of Cuban Consuelo, in a fairly traditional tale in which the heroine, due to marry her influential cousin, Don Adolfo (Lawrence Grossmith, in a role tailored for his brother, co-author George), spends her last day of freedom romancing steam-yacht captain Jackson Villiers (Leonard Mackay) with predictable results. The comedy came from Villiers's crew, especially the bosun Nix (Alfred Lester) and the ship's boy, Reginald Brown (W H Berry). Nix had unwisely ''married'' a Cuban girl on an earlier trip, and is now faced by the gorgonic Isabelita (Gladys Homfrey), claiming her rights. Fortunately, pretty Anita (Jean Aylwin) turns out to be the real bride.

Stuart's score—which boasted an amount of ensemble music and concerted finales of a kind not seen for many years at the Gaiety—did not have the kind of hit numbers that *Florodora* had had, but Evie Greene scored with a weightless piece called ''Little Miquette,'' Grossmith had his best moment with a jolly ''Hello, People!,'' contralto Jessie Broughton sang of ''Zara,'' Bill Berry had a topical ''How Did the Bird Know That?,'' and there was a cautionary comical quartet which warned ''It's a Bomb!''

Havana had a good, if not outstanding, 221-performance run at the Gaiety before going on the road with the young Dorothy Ward featured at the head of one of the two companies, and then round the world. It had a notable success in America, where James T Powers had the text rearranged to corner all of the comedy in the role of Nix. The Shubert brothers' production, with Edith Decker as Consuelo, William Pruette (Diego) and Eva Davenport (Isabelita) caused a sensation in its Philadelphia tryout, and *Mr Hamlet of Broadway,* then currently on show at the Casino, was bundled brutally out to allow the piece to move swiftly to Broadway, where it was anticipated that it would out-*Florodora* its famous predecessor. It didn't, but it turned out nevertheless to be one of the biggest hits of its time, playing 236 Broadway performances (with a short summer break), and ''Hello, People!'' and ''How Did the Bird Know That?'' became decided hits. Stuart, a fanatical fighter against the interpolation habit had, however, no chance with the inveterately interpolating Shuberts, and he had to listen to ''My Little Deutscher Girl'' and other such ''improvements'' sung alongside his numbers.

Havana exported well. Berlin saw the show at the Belle-Alliance Theatre, J C Williamson mounted an Australian production with Florence Young (Consuelo), Victor Gouriet (Nix), W S Percy (Reginald, restored to his British-sized role), Fanny Dango (Anita) and Susie Vaughan (Isabelita) featured, and it was toured in repertoire in South Africa, but, in spite of the show's international popularity, Edwardes did not pursue the new line he had announced. For his next Gaiety show he returned to Monckton and Miss Millar and scored one of his biggest ever hits with *Our Miss Gibbs.*

Germany: Belle-Alliance-Theater 17 October 1908; USA: Casino Theater 11 February 1909; Australia: Her Majesty's Theatre, Sydney 13 March 1909

HAYDON, Ethel [Haydon] (b Melbourne, 13 June 1878; d Bosham, January 1954). Australian soubrette who played several important roles for George Edwardes in a very short stage career.

After a youthful career in Australia, where she moved from being the star of the local amateur group to playing professionally in pantomime at Melbourne's Princess Theatre with Robert Courtneidge, and in Arthur Garner's comedy company alongside Jennie Lee in *Jo* and in *The Morals of Marcus,* Miss Haydon traveled to Britain. There, at the age of 17, she made her first West End appearance, under the management of William Greet, as the juvenile heroine of the comic opera *Dandy Dick Whittington* (1895), opposite May Yohé's Dick. George Edwardes then took her to the Gaiety, to succeed Ellaline Terriss as the fifth heroine of the long run of *The Shop Girl,* and subsequently cast her as second girl alongside Miss Terriss in *My Girl* and in *The Circus Girl* (1896, La Favorita, the circus girl), in which she succeeded to the star role during the show's run. She subsequently created the role of Dorothy in *A Runaway Girl,* introducing one of the Gaiety's most famous songs of all, ''Soldiers in the Park.'' To all intents and purposes she terminated what looked like becoming a significant career before her 21st birthday, but she continued for several years to appear occasionally in pantomime and variety, sometimes alongside her then husband, star comedian George Robey [né George Edward Wade].

HAYWARD, Leland (b Nebraska City, Nebr, 13 September 1902; d Yorktown Heights, NY, 18 March 1971).

After spells in film and as a theatrical agent, Hayward turned theatrical producer in 1944 and, over the next two decades, had a high profile career in both the musical and straight theatre.

His first venture into the musical theatre was as co-producer with Rodgers, Hammerstein and Joshua Logan of the enormously successful *South Pacific,* and he followed up with further successes in *Call Me Madam, Wish You Were Here* (w Logan), *Gypsy* (w David Merrick) and *The Sound of Music* (w Rodgers, Hammerstein, Richard Halliday), before ending this remarkable run of hits on a less successful note with his final venture, *Mr President* (1962).

Biography: Hayward, B: *Haywire* (Knopf, New York, 1977)

HAZELL, Hy [O'HIGGINS, Hyacinth Hazel] (b London, 4 October 1921; d London, 10 May 1970). Favorite character actress of the London musical stage of the 1950s and 1960s.

Hy Hazell made her first appearance on the London stage in the chorus of *On Your Toes* (1937), and her first mark as a noticeably lush and glamorous principal boy in a long series of pantomimes. She subsequently played Penelope in the short-lived tryout of *By Jupiter* (1944) and won notice in her first major West End musical role as the middle-aging film star, Dixie Collins, in *Expresso Bongo* (1958), introducing the sultry ''Time'' and the revusical ''We Bought It,'' and confirmed largely the following year when she created the part of another sexually ravenous dame, Mrs Squeezum, in *Lock Up Your Daughters* (''When Does the Ravishing Begin,'' ''I'll Be There'') at the Mermaid Theatre. She repeated this role in America, in Australia, and in London's West End, but subsequent engagements in *Innocent as Hell* (1960, Inez Packard) and *No Strings* (1962, Mollie Plummer) in Britain and in the Broadway-bound *Pleasures and Palaces* (1965, Catherine) in America were short lived.

She created in 1965 the role of the brash American Kay Connor opposite Anna Neagle in the long-running *Charlie Girl,* in 1968 was seen as Mrs Peachum in a revival of *The Beggar's Opera,* and in 1969 played the role of Miss Miniver in the musicalization of H G Wells's *Anne Veronica.* She succeeded to the role of Golde in London's *Fiddler on the Roof* later the same year, and was playing that part when her accidental death occurred.

HAZZARD, John E[dward] (b New York, 22 February 1881; d Great Neck, NJ, 2 December 1935). Popular Broadway musical comedian of the 1910s and 1920s.

John Hazzard pergormed in both plays and musicals in the earliest part of his career (1901 ssq) and he appeared in New York in a return season of *The Yankee Consul* in 1905 (Herr Gebubler) and as Gerald MacSweeney in May Irwin's ''comedy with songs'' (for her) *Mrs Wilson That's All* (1906) before landing his first original Broadway musical engagement when he appeared at the Knickerbocker Theater in a comic role in *The Hurdy Gurdy Girl* (1907, Judge van Coover). He took a supporting role in the American production of *The Girls of Gottenberg* (1908, Sergeant Brittlbottl), a larger one in the less successful *The Echo* (1910, Rudolph W Sylvester) and gave out further prominent helpings of dialect comedy in *The Red Rose* (1911, Ludwig Spiegel), Victor Herbert's *The Duchess* (1911, Adolphe de Paravente), Luders and Pixley's *The Gypsy* (1912, Count von Sternberg), and *Miss Princess* (1912, t/o). In *The Lilac Domino* (1914) he appeared without the accent as Prosper Woodhouse, and in 1915 he took the principal low-comic role in Kern's *Very Good Eddie* (Al Cleveland) at the Princess Theater.

Thereafter Hazzard filled a whole series of fine starring comedy roles in major musical shows, appearing in the Americanization of Kálmán's *Zsuzsi kisasszony* (*Miss Springtime,* 1916, Michael Robin), in Ivan Caryll's *The Girl Behind the Gun* (1918, Paul Bréval) and in George Gershwin's debut show *La La Lucille* (1919, John Smith), and taking the central (if not very musical) role of Kern's *The Night Boat* (1920, Bob White) and, with considerable success, the principal comedy role of the colorful *Tangerine* (1921). He was top-billed over the up-and-coming Astaires in *For Goodness' Sake* (1922, Perry Reynolds), and appeared as Pas de Vis in the American version of Yvain's slickly comical *Ta bouche* (*One Kiss,* 1923) before his musical appearances largely gave way to straight comic roles. However, he later appeared as Sir Joseph Porter in Winthrop Ames's 1926 revival of *HMS Pinafore* and as Frosch in the version of *Die Fledermaus* presented in 1933 as *Champagne Sec.*

In 1916, following his success in *Very Good Eddie* (to which he had, with Herbert Reynolds, supplied a pair of songwords), Hazzard collaborated with Anne Caldwell and John Golden on an unsuccessful rewrite of Charles Hoyt's *A Milk White Flag,* produced by F Ray Comstock at the Princess Theater as *Go to It,* and he later ventured again as an author with the musical *The Houseboat on the Styx* in which he played Captain William Kidd (''An Irate Pirate Am I'') alongside Blanche Ring's Queen Elizabeth I for 103 performances. He did, however, have some success as a stage author, notably with the comedy *Turn to the Right!* (w Winchell Smith, 18 August 1916), and with the songs ''Ain't It Awful, Mabel?'' and ''Queenie Was There with Her Hair in a Braid.'' He also wrote and published books of poetry and vaudeville material.

Hazzard was married to star ingenue **Alice DOVEY** (b Plattsmouth, Nebr, 28 August 1884; d Tarzana, Calif, 11 January 1969) who played lead juvenile roles in *A Stubborn Cinderalla* (1909, Lois, ''Don't Be Anybody's Moon But Mine''), *Old Dutch* (1909, Lisa Streusand),

The Summer Widowers (1910, Celia Carew), *The Pink Lady* (1911, Angèle), *The Queen of the Movies* (1914, Anne Clutterbuck), *Papa's Darling* (1914, Germaine Petipas), *Nobody Home* (1915, Violet Brinton, ''You Know and I Know), *Hands Up* (1915, Helene Fudge) and *Very Good Eddie* (1915, Elsie Darling).

1916 **Go to It!** (A Baldwin Sloane/w John Golden, Anne Caldwell) Princess Theater 24 October

1928 **The Houseboat on the Styx** (Monte Carlo, Alma Sanders/w Kenneth Webb) Liberty Theater 25 December

HEADS UP! Musical comedy in 2 acts by John McGowan and Paul Gerard Smith. Lyrics by Lorenz Hart. Music by Richard Rodgers. Alvin Theater, New York, 11 November 1929.

In spite of the indifferent run of *Spring Is Here* (1929), producers Aarons and Freedley again teamed librettist Owen Davis and songwriters Rodgers and Hart as the authors of their next production, prematurely titled *Me for You.* Davis's text cast loveable comedian Victor Moore as a bootlegger who puts his daughter (Betty Starbuck) under the control of his partner-in-booze (Jack Whiting) to get her away from her legal-eagle boyfriend (John Hundley). As in *Spring Is Here,* Daddy won out and Hundley lost the girl, but this time he did not have the compensation of a song like the earlier piece's ''With a Song in My Heart.''

Produced out-of-town in Detroit, *Me for You* showed up unmistakeably as a potential flop. The producers closed the show, called in John McGowan, who had given them the text for the successful De Sylva, Brown and Henderson musical *Hold Everything!* the previous year, and Paul Gerard Smith, who had doctored *Funny Face* into a hit for them a couple of seasons back, and set them to writing a new libretto around the same sets, costumes and songs. The result was *Heads Up!,* which had Whiting as a coastguard chasing the yacht belonging to socialite Mrs Trumbell (Janet Velie), which is apparently running bootleg liquor. He proves his point and also wins Miss Mary Trumbell (Barbara Newberry). Moore played the yacht's cook, Skippy Dugan, a nervous fellow who is given to tinkering about with inventions. In a scene set in ''Skippy's galley aboard the Silver Lady,'' he was able to go through a kitchen routine, in the vein of the traditional British pantomime, before arriving at a happy ending, when one of his inventions finally came good.

Miss Starbuck became incidental to the plot and sang ''The Lass Who Loved a Sailor'' and half the old title song, while Hundley was left with nothing to sing at all. Additions to the cast included Ray Bolger, who sang about being a ''Play Boy'' and, with Alice Boulden, about ''Knees'' in the role of Georgie, and the dance team of Atlas and La Mar who did a speciality just before each finale, the second with the Reynolds Sisters (who'd already done their own speciality in the first act). Whiting got the best musical moment, ''A Ship without a Sail,'' and also the most plugged, his duet with Mary, ''Why Do You Suppose?''

Heads Up! opened in the earliest weeks of the depression, but was voted ''a lively diversion'' and managed to run up a total of 144 Broadway performances before moving on to the touring circuits. A London production, however, mounted under the management of Lee Ephraim, with Sydney Howard in Moore's role supported by Louise Browne, Clarice Hardwicke, Jack Hobbs and Arthur Margetson, was mildly noticed by one newspaper as ''not the best America has sent us'' and folded in 19 performances.

UK: Palace Theatre 1 May 1930

Plate 167. **George Hearn**

HEARN, George (b St Louis, Mo, 18 June 1934). Rich-voiced baritone and actor who has rarely found Broadway roles to allow him to display his talents.

In a career which has regularly mixed musical roles with non-musical engagements (*An Almost Perfect Person, The Changing Room*), Hearn had early musical-theatre parts in *1776, Camelot,* and *Wonderful Town* (w Lauren Bacall) on the road, and in *A Time for Singing* (1966), a musical based on *How Green Is My Valley* and featuring Ivor Emmanuel and Tessie O'Shea, in New York. His first high-billed role in a Broadway musical was as Papa to the Mama of Liv Ullman in Richard Rodgers's musical version of *I Remember Mama* (1979), and he subsequently succeeded to the title role of *Sweeney Todd,* following his Broadway performances with the national tour and with the made-for-television film of the show.

In the musical portion of a subsequent career which also saw him on Broadway in Lillian Hellman's *Watch on the Rhine,* the short-lived *Whodunnit,* and *Ghetto* at the Circle in the Square, he appeared as Torvald in the short-lived Ibsen musequel *A Doll's Life* (1982), created the role of the female impersonator Albin in the musical version of *La Cage aux Folles* (1983, Tony Award), introducing "I Am Who I Am" in both New York and London, played Hajj (*Kismet,* 1985) for the New York City Opera, appeared as Long John Silver in an unsuccessful musical version of *Treasure Island* in Canada, was seen as Alonzo Smith, the father of the family, in *Meet Me in St Louis* (1989), and featured as Max von Mayerling in the Broadway version of *Sunset Boulevard* (1994, Tony Award).

Hearn also appeared as Ben in the celebrity concert of *Follies* and its subsequent recording.

HEARNE, Richard [Lewis] (b Norwich, 30 January 1908; d Bearstead, Kent, 25 August 1979). Acrobatic comedian who had a successful career of nearly 20 years in West End musicals.

Hearne began his life on the stage as a child and worked in circus, variety, revue and pantomime before moving into musical comedy in the farcical *Nice Goings On* (1933, Lehmann) and *Lucky Break* (1934, Wilkins), alongside Leslie Henson. He went to the Alhambra to appear in the unsuccessful circus musical *The Flying Trapeze* (1935, Clown) with Jack Buchanan, but soon returned to join Henson at the head of comical affairs at the Gaiety Theatre. There, the gangling, long-faced, acrobatic comedian formed a comically contrasting team with obese Fred Emney and frog-like Henson through a series of successful musicals (Stefan in *Seeing Stars,* Alphonse in *Swing Along,* Mogolini in *Going Greek,* Burkinshaw in *Running Riot*), introducing with singular success a comedy routine in which he danced the lancers, alone, in a variety of characters.

He subsequently appeared in revue, but returned to the musical stage to play Maxie in a revised version of *Sally* (for which he took a share in the book credit) under the title *Wild Rose,* as Loppy in the London production of *Panama Hattie* (1943), and alongside his old teammate, Emney, as Mr Pastry in *Big Boy* (1945), creating a character whose name would remain with him for the rest of his life. He appeared with Emney again in the long-running *Blue for a Boy* (1950, Dickie Skippett), but thereafter left the musical stage, although he remained active as a performer in variety and in television (still performing the old lancers routine) until his death.

HEDLEY, H[erbert] B [arber] [BARBER, Herbert Hedley] (b London, 28 February 1890; d Brixton, 2 June 1931).

Originally a P&O steward, Hedley subsequently worked as a pianist in concert parties (notably with the celebrated Co-Optimists) and touring revue, and he composed music for some of Harry Day's provincial revues and for the music halls before he made his first metropolitan appearance as a composer—as one part of the songwriting team put together by producers Laddie Cliff and Firth Shephard when they ventured into the musical theatre with *Dear Little Billie* (1925). He teamed again with lyricist Desmond Carter and co-composer Jack Strachey on Cliff's next venture, *Lady Luck* (1927), and also appeared personally in the show heading a trio of speciality pianists, but he was forced to hide under a pseudonym (along with his composing colleagues) for *So This Is Love,* Cliff's biggest success to date, when the producer guessed—apparently with some justice—that the public would come to hear music by even an unknown composer as long as he was given out to be fashionably American, rather than the work of a handful of local boys. "Hal Brody" lasted only two shows, as Cliff could not resist triumphantly unveiling his trick, and Hedley went back to being himself for Cliff's following shows—*So Long, Letty!* (1928, additional songs), *Darling, I Love You* (1930), *The Love Race* (1931, additional songs) and *The Millionaire Kid* (1931, additional song)—before a premature death at the age of 41.

1920 **Fruit Salad** (Ernest Melvin) 1 act Penge Empire 29 November

1925 **Dear Little Billie** (w Jack Strachey/Desmond Carter/Firth Shephard) Shaftesbury Theatre 25 August

1927 **Lady Luck** (w Strachey/Carter/Shephard) Carlton Theatre 27 April

1928 **So This Is Love** (as part of "Hal Brody"/Carter/Stanley Lupino, Arthur Rigby) Winter Garden Theatre 25 April

1929 **Love Lies** (as part of "Hal Brody"/Carter/Lupino, Rigby) Gaiety Theatre 20 March

1930 **Darling, I Love You** (w Harry Acres/Carter/Stanley Brightman, Rigby) Gaiety Theatre 22 January

HEESTERS, Johannes [VAN HEESTERS, Jan] (b Amersfoort, Netherlands, 5 December 1903). Matinée and movie idol, longtime star of the German-language musical stage and screen, and Lehár's "ideal Danilo."

Heesters began his working life in a bank before becoming an actor and singer in the Dutch theatre. He appeared in Amsterdam, Rotterdam and The Hague in a mixture of classics and new productions (*Ein Walzertraum, Die Glocken von Corneville, Der Zarewitsch, Das Milliardensouper, Die Bajadere, Susi, Die blaue Mazur, Gräfin Mariza, Der liebe Augustin, Die Teresina, Das Veilchen vom Montmartre* [*Violetta*], Hirsch's *Dolly*) and original works (*Die Königin von Montmartre, Feminola, Der blaue Mantel, Seppl, Roszi der Zigeuner*) as well as such enterprising productions as the Hungarian *Éjféli tangó* and Friml's *De Vagebondkönig.*

In 1934 he joined the company at the Vienna Volksoper for a season (*Der Bettelstudent, Das Hollandweibchen, Wiener G'schichten, Polenblut, Die erste Liebelei, Orpheus in der Unterwelt, Valentino*) before going on to the Scala to appear—still as Jan Heesters—as film director Karl Hell in Robert Stolz's *Servus! Servus!* (1935) and to play in his first German-language film *Die Leuchter des Kaisers.* He made his first appearance in Berlin in the Operette *Tatanja* at the Theater am Nollendorfplatz at the end of 1935, and thereafter his career was centered in Berlin, where he became a major film and stage star in musical shows.

His stage shows in the late 1930s and early 1940s included Stolz's *Der süsseste Schwindel der Welt* (1937), Benatzky's *Meine Schwester und ich,* and his first performances in the role with which he would become so very identified: Danilo in *Die lustige Witwe.* He also created the part of tennis-playing Ulrich, the bridegroom of *Hochzeitsnacht im Paradies* (1942). His film credits in the same period included *Der Bettelstudent, Das Hofkonzert* (1936), *Wenn Frauen schweigen, Gasparone* (1937), *Manon, Das Abenteuer geht weiter* (1938), *Hallo Janine, Meine Tante, deine Tante* (1939), *Liebesschule, Die lustigen Vagabunden, Rosen in Tirol* (1940), *Immer nur du, Jenny und der Herr in Frack, Illusion* (1941), *Karneval der Liebe* (1942), *Glück bei Frauen, Es lebe die Liebe* (1943), *Es fing so harmlos an, Frech und verliebt* (1944) and *Die Fledermaus* (1945).

He moved to Vienna in 1948, and in 1949 he created another new part: the title role of Kattnigg's *Bel Ami* at the Raimundtheater. In 1950 he repeated *Hochzeitsnacht im Paradies* in Vienna, in Frankfurt and on both the film and television screens, and in the years that followed he returned to the role of Ulrich frequently throughout Europe, along with his other favorite parts and shows—*Die lustige Witwe, Der Graf von Luxemburg, Meine Schwester und ich* (also television)—whilst keeping up a regular schedule of films including versions of the stage musicals *Die Csárdásfürstin* (1951) with Marika Rökk, *Der Tanz ins Glück* (1951), *Im weissen Rössl* (1952), *Die geschiedene Frau* (1953) and *Der Opernball* (1956). He also starred in a German version of *The Moon Is Blue* in the role simultaneously taken by David Niven in the English version, and in the 1957 remake of *Viktor und Viktoria.*

In 1956 he appeared in *Kiss Me, Kate* in Munich, in 1959 in a revival of *Der Orlow* at the Raimundtheater, and in 1960 in a second *Bel Ami,* this one by Kreuder, at the same house. Thereafter he mixed straight and musical roles, the latter including a Dutch version of *The Sound of Music* in Amsterdam, further *Hochzeitsnacht im Paradies* and *Die lustige Witwe* performances, and a *Viktoria und ihr Husar* (1973) at the Mörbisch lake-theatre. He scored one final success when he took on the role created on screen by Maurice Chevalier in the stage adaptation of *Gigi* in Vienna, Berlin, Hamburg and Munich.

Autobiography: *Es kommt auf die Sekunde an* (Blanvalet Verlag, Munich, 1978); Biography: Dombrowski, I, Borchert, R: *Johannes Heesters* (Lübbe, Bergisch Gladbach, 1978)

HÉGOBURU, Loulou [HÉGOBURU, Marie Louise] (b Bordeaux, 6 August 1898; d La-Celle-Saint-Cloud, 20 December 1947).

A popular singing, dancing-revue and musical-comedy ingenue of the French années folles.

Pop-eyed, pop-cheeked Loulou Hégoburu began her career singing at Paris's Concert Mayol at the age of 22, but came to fame when she made a major hit as Nanette in the Théâtre Mogador's *No, No, Nanette* (''Heureux, tous les deux,'' ''Thé pour deux,'' ''No, no, Nanette''). Thereafter she was seen starred with Fernand Graavey in *L'Eau à la bouche* (1928, ''Ce n'est qu'un mannequin''), as the Parisian star of Gershwin's *Tip-Toes* (1929, ''Petit Boby,'' ie, ''Looking for a Boy,'' ''Le Petit Capitaine,'' ie, ''Virginia''), and alongside Edmée Favart, Bach and Géo Bury in the spectacular Théâtre du Châtelet *Sidonie Panache* (1931, ''C'est Rosalie,'' ''La cantinière''). Later in her career, she appeared in *Un petit bout de femme* (1936) and *Ma petite amie* (1937) before ceasing to be an ingenue.

Mlle Hégoburu was seen on Broadway in 1926, singing and dancing in *A Night in Paris* at the Casino de Paris, and on the singing screen alongside Fernandel in *Ça colle.*

HEGYI, Aranka (b Pest, 25 May 1855; d Pest, 9 June 1906).

One of the outstanding performers of the Hungarian musical theatre of the last two decades of the 19th century, soprano Aranka Hegyi shared the limelight and the star roles—particularly those which required the strongest vocal skills—at Budapest's Népszínház with Lujza Blaha and Ilka Pálmay, without following the former to a vaster celebrity, or the latter to fame abroad.

The daughter of a gypsy musician, she lived her early life in the wilds before, after her father's death, being

Plate 168. **Aranka Hegyi.** *The Nepszínház's most skillful soprano swapped happily between male roles (left) and such feminine parts as the title role of* Katalin *(right) in a long and dazzling career.*

adopted and brought up first by his fellow musician Sándor Herczenberger and then by the famous gypsy musician and composer Ferenc Sárközi. She appeared early on as a dancer at the Nemzeti Színház, but her singing talents soon became evident and in 1880 Jenő Rákosi hired her for the Népszínház, where she made her debut in the title role of *La Jolie Persane.* Amongst the other pieces which she introduced in the following decades were local versions of *Les Dragons de Villars* (Rose Friquet), *La Marquise des rues, Les Noces d'Olivette* (Bathilde), *Les Poupées de l'Infante, Le Jour et la nuit* (Béatrix), the enormously successful *Lili* (Lili), *Der Bettelstudent* (Laura, with Blaha as Symon and Pálmay as Bronislawa), *Der lustige Krieg* (Violetta), *Gasparone, Les Contes d'Hoffman* (Antonia, a particular success for her), *Les Pilules du Diable, Le Fils prodigue* (Pierrot), *Der Zigeunerbaron* (Sáffi), *La Fille de Madame Angot* (Lange), *The Mikado* (Nanki Poo), *Der arme Jonathan* (Harriet), *The Geisha* (O Mimosa San), *A Runaway Girl* and *Bruder Straubinger,* and she also reprised roles originally played by Blaha and others, including Rosalinde, Serpolette and Boccaccio, in the Népszínház repertoire. The arrival of the new wave of Hungarian musical stars, Sári Fedak and Klára Küry at their head, still found her firmly entrenched at the top of the tree, and whilst younger stars came and went she remained to the fore until after the turn of the century, retiring in 1903 at nearly 50 years of age.

Hegyi created leading roles in a number of Hungarian operetts, including Lajos Serly's *Világszép asszony Marica* (Marica), *Peking rózsája,* the title role of Verő's successful *A szultán, Virágcsata, A libapásztor,* Konti's *A Talmi hercegnő,* József Bokor's *A kis alamuszi* (Vicomte Renaud) and, in one of her last appearances, the title role in the record-breaking *Katalin.*

HEGYI, Béla (b Pápa, 1858; d Budapest, 19 April 1922).

Conductor and composer, Hegyi was trained at the Budapest Zeneakadémia and thereafter wrote a number of orchestral and instrumental works which, like his stage pieces, and unlike the operetts of some of his contemporaries, had a distinct Hungarian flavor to them. His stage opus comprised six operetts and a one-act opera (*Yvonne és Loïc,* aka *A falu csúfja* 27 March 1893), as well as incidental music and songs to the play *Az árendás zsidó* (1884). The two most successful of his lighter musical theatre works, both composed in collaboration with Szidor Bátor, were a remusicked version of Leterrier and Vanloo's libretto for *L'Étoile,* produced at the Népszínház as *Uff Király* (King Ouf), and *A titkos csók,* a musical adaptation of Bayard and Dumanoir's French play *La Vicomtesse Lolotte. Pepita,* composed alone, was a version of another French original, *Ne touchez pas à la reine.*

1886 **A milliomosnő** (w Szidor Bátor/Ferenc Rajna) 1 act Népszínház 27 December

1887 **Uff Király** (w Bátor/Vanloo, Leterrier ad Jenő Rákosi) Népszínház 21 May

1888 **A titkos csók** (w Bátor/Sándor Lukácsy) Népszínház 7 December

1890 **Pepita** (Rajna, Antal Radó) Népszínház 21 January

1899 **A liliputi hercegnő** (József Márkus) Magyar Színház 25 March

1904 **Boris Király** (Zsigmond Szőllősi) Király Színház 18 March

HEIMLICHE LIEBE Operette in 3 acts by Julius Bauer. Music by Paul Ottenheimer. Johann Strauss-Theater, Vienna, 13 October 1911.

The most successful work of the composer Ottenheimer, *Heimliche Liebe* was mounted in Vienna under the management of Leopold Müller, with Alexander Girardi and Gerda Walde starred for a run of two hundred consecutive performances. This first run record outdid that of the much more famous *Der Zigeunerprimás,* in which the same two stars followed up the following year, and was as good or better than anything yet produced at the three-year-old Johann Strauss-Theater, or anything that followed until the house's long-running production of *Rund um die Liebe* in 1914–15. Like the latter piece, however, and unlike *Zigeunerprimás, Heimliche Liebe* did not prove to have much of an afterlife following its fine initial run.

The piece was set in a Viennese fashion factory, ''Zur schöne Wienerin,'' run by Madame Grüber. The heroine, her niece Toni (Gerda Walde), profits from her aunt's profession, disguising herself as a boy on her way to discovering the ''heimliche Liebe'' of the title.

The center of attraction, however, was not the plot but Girardi who played Der Profoss equipped with a Basteilied, which slipped from march-time into his preferred waltz refrain (''Was jetzt die Mäderln machen''), and a little Vogellied at the top of the final act which took in some twittering bird imitations. The military Egon von Romberg supplied a Gondellied (''Lieblich leuchtet das Himmelszelt'') and a women-and-war piece (''Nur durch die Liebe kamen wir ums Paradies''), while the dancer Rositta (''from the Opera at Milan'') made her entrances to the showy strains of a mazurka and the waltz ''Wie sie alle mich umschmachten.'' Toni culled a little Veilchenlied in the first act and a Trommellied in the second (''Ich ging in Männerkleiden'') in a musically well-furnished evening which served its purposes admirably and was then forgotten.

HEIN, Silvio (b New York, 15 March 1879; d Saranac Lake, NY, 19 December 1928).

A pleasant, popular and prolific member of the Broadway establishment in the early years of the 20th century, Hein worked widely as a musical director whilst also turning his hand to a steady stream of straightforward and prettily functional scores, written over a period of some 15 years. He provided the songs for solid comedy touring vehicles for such stars as Marie Cahill, for whom he musicked *Nancy Brown, Moonshine, Marrying Mary* (''The Hottentot Love Song,'' ''He's a Cousin of Mine''), *Judy Forgot* and *The Boys and Betty* (''Marie Cahill's Arab Love Song''), De Wolf Hopper (*A Matinée Idol*), Blanche Ring (*The Yankee Girl*), Joseph Santley (*When Dreams Come True,* featuring a song called ''Dear World'' and another advising ''Come Along to the Movies'') and for the popular touring team of Cecil Lean and Cleo Mayfield (*Look Who's Here*). He won his longest Broadway run, however, with the 1917 musical comedy surprise *Flo-Flo* (220 performances), which boasted no such starry aid.

Outside his principal scores he also wrote for a number of revues from *The Ziegfeld Follies of 1907* (''I Want to Be a Drummer Boy'') to *Some Party* (1922), composed various scores of incidental music, ranging from that for the 1917 Park Theater revival of Shakespeare's *The Merry Wives of Windsor* to ''music and cabaret songs'' for George Hobart's play *Experience* (27 October 1914), and interpolated isolated songs into a range of musicals. Amongst these last were found some of his more successful numbers, such as ''Some Little Bug Is Going to Find You Someday'' (w Benjamin Hapgood Burt, Roy Attwood), introduced in Broadway's version of Lehár's *Endlich allein,* and ''All Dressed Up and No Place to Go'' (w Burt), which was performed by Raymond Hitchcock in Broadway's *The Beauty Shop* and in London's *Mr Manhattan.*

1903 **Nancy Brown** (w Henry Hadley/Frederick Ranken, George Broadhurst) Bijou Theater 16 February

1905 **Moonshine** (Benjamin Hapgood Burt/George V Hobart) Liberty Theater 30 October

1906 **Marrying Mary** (Burt/Edward Milton Royle) Daly's Theater 27 August

1908 **The Boys and Betty** (Hobart) Wallack's Theater 2 November

1910 **The Yankee Girl** (Hobart) Herald Square Theater 10 February

1910 **A Matinée Idol** (Seymour Brown, E Ray Goetz/Armand, Barnard) Daly's Theater 28 April

1910 **Judy Forgot** (Avery Hopwood) Broadway Theater 6 October

1910 **He Loved a Lassie** (George Arliss) remusicked version of 1909 Chicago musical, Van Curler Opera House, Schenectady 21 November

1913 **When Dreams Come True** (Philip H Bartholomae) Garrick Theater, Chicago 7 April; Lyric Theater, New York 18 August

1913 **Over the Garden Wall** (Hobart) sketch Proctor's, Newark 29 September

1913 **Glorianna** (Hobart/Bartholomae) Cort Theater, Chicago 12 October

1914 **Rita's Romance** (Burt/Leo Ditrichtein) Burbank Theater, Los Angeles 8 March

1914 **The Model Maid** (Bartholomae) Opera House, Providence 17 August; Majestic Theater Boston 24 August

1914 **Miss Daisy** (revised *The Model Maid*) (Bartholomae) Shubert Theater 9 September

1914 **At the Ball** (revised *Miss Daisy*) (Bartholomae, Alice Emery Gerstenberg) Van Curler Opera House, Schenectady 12 December; American Music Hall, Chicago 25 December

1915 **All Over Town** (Harry B Smith) Shubert Theater, New Haven 26 April; Garrick Theater, Chicago 30 April

1915 **One of the Boys** (Bartholomae) Palace Theater 24 May

1917 **The Red Clock** (Schuyler Greene/Val Crawford) Buffalo 24 September

1917 **Furs and Frills** (Edward Clark) Casino Theater 9 October

1917 **Flo-Flo** (Edward A Paulton/Fred de Grésac) Cort Theater 20 December

1917 **The Golden Goose** (Herbert Reynolds, Schuyler Greene/ Edgar Smith) Apollo Theater, Atlantic City 29 November

1918 **The Bride Shop** (w Walter Rosemont/de Grésac)

1918 **He Didn't Want to Do It** (George H Broadhurst) Broadhurst Theater 20 August

1918 **Miss Blue Eyes** (Hobart) Apollo Theater, Atlantic City 3 October

1920 **Look Who's Here** (E A Paulton/Frank Mandel) 44th Street Theater 2 March

1920 **The Girl from Home** (ex- *The New Dictator*) (Frank Craven) Globe Theater 3 May

HEISSES BLUT Posse mit Gesang in 3 acts and 7 scenes by Carl Lindau and Leopold Krenn. Music by Heinrich Schenk. Theater an der Wien, Vienna, 17 April 1892.

A highly successful musical play, built as a showpiece for its central female character, *Heisses Blut* allowed the winsome Ilona (Ilka Pálmay) to partake of a multiplicity of disguises as she runs away from her country home on her wedding day, through a series of adventures, including a spectacular duel, before, inevitably, ending her cavalcade by becoming a theatre star in Vienna. At the end, it proves all to have been a dream of what might have been, and she goes sweetly off to get married to her Miklós. Her dreams were accompanied by a bright score, much of it in 3/4 time, from which the waltz ''Schön sind die Veilchen'' proved to be the favorite musical moment.

Vienna's original production of *Heisses Blut* was a decided success. It played from Easter through to the summer break, was taken to Berlin for a season at the Thomas-Theater, and was brought back again to reopen the new season in the autumn, playing through until 14 October. It was kept in the house's repertoire until 1895, and ended up totaling one hundred performances in all at the Theater an der Wien.

The show was subsequently widely reprised in other German-language houses, but it proved particularly popular in America where Sydney Rosenfeld's English-language adaptation, under the title *A Dangerous Maid* (add ly Louis Harrison, add mus Fred J Eustis), was produced by George Lederer and George B McLellan at the Casino Theatre for a run of 65 performances in 1898. Madge Lessing was Ilona, Sam Bernard played the comical hairdresser Schmaltz who is her principal ally, and the rather loose-jointed proceedings included Cissie Loftus in her famous impersonations and Parisian leading lady Clara Lardinois performing a couple of her French songs. The show surfaced on Broadway again in 1905 in a much more comedy-orientated version (still credited to Rosenfeld), with new music by W T Francis and others (one Edmund Eysler song was featured). Hattie Williams starred as *The Rollicking Girl,* still called Ilona, alongside Sam Bernard as Schmaltz, and Joe Coyne as Panagl. Charles Frohman's production played a splendid 169 performances at the Herald Square Theater. Shortly after this Ilka Pálmay appeared at the city's German-speaking theatre, playing the original version of *Heisses Blut* (7 December 1905).

A film under this title, starring Marika Rökk, was produced by George Jacoby in 1936.

Germany: Thomas-Theater ?13 June 1892; USA: Casino Theater *A Dangerous Maid* 12 November 1898, Herald Square Theater *The Rollicking Girl* 1 May 1905

HELD, Anna (b ?Warsaw, 18 March 1873; d New York, 13 August 1918). Broadway's favorite ''parisienne'' of the turn-of-the-century years.

After beginning her career as a music-hall performer in Europe, the apparently Polish-born—or, at the least, partly Polish descended—pretty, 23-year-old Miss Held was whipped away from a contract binding her to Marchand of the Folies-Bergère (she was sued by the management and fined whackingly) and taken to America.

She first appeared on the American musical stage doing her act as known, tacked into Evans and Hoey's aged touring farce-comedy *A Parlor Match,* and went on to star for Oscar Hammerstein as the girl-doll in a version of Audran's *La Poupée* (1897, 46 performance); to appear in vaudeville at Koster and Bial's (1897), singing ''I Want Them Presents Back'' with a personalized version of the popular ''human music sheet'' behind her; on the road in the farce-comedy *The Gay Deceivers* (1898); in the title role of *The French Maid* (1898–99, Suzette); and then, under Florenz Ziegfeld's management, in a compote of two shows made famous by Anna Judic, *Mam'zelle Nitouche* and *La Femme à papa,* which called itself *Papa's Wife* (1899). In the process, she established herself prettily in the eyes of New York theatregoers as the epitome of all that was invitingly French. She also (although it has been suggested that the official deed might have been overlooked) apparently married Ziegfeld (''in Paris in the spring of 1901'').

Quickly publicized into a solid above-the-title name, she starred in a series of Broadway musicals in the space of a decade: a made-over version of another Anna Judic vehicle, *Niniche,* called *The Little Duchess* (1901, Claire de Brion), a musical allegedly custom-made from a Jean Richepin play and entitled *Mam'selle Napoléon* (1903, Mlle Mars), Joe Weber's variety musical *Higgledy-Piggledy* (1904, Mimi de Chartreuse), as *A Parisian Model* (1906, Anna, ''It's Delightful to Be Married,'' ''I Just Can't Make My Eyes Behave'') and as *Miss Innocence* (1908, Anna, ''I Wonder What's the Matter with My Eyes''). The star's ''naughty'' Continental charm and a good deal of expensive staging were, in each case, the main ingredients of what became known as ''an Anna Held show.'' Acting and singing and such details as plot and character were lesser considerations.

Her marriage to Ziegfeld ended and, although she subsequently appeared in New York in revue (*Anna Held's All-Star Variété Jubilee* [1913] for John Cort, including the one-act musical *Le Soir de fantaisie*), Miss Held's Broadway career had just one further musical comedy chapter. In 1916, she appeared for the Shuberts in a piece that had once been a Leo Ascher musical but was now a potpourri called *Follow Me* (Clair La Tour), singing ''I Want to Be Good But My Eyes Won't Let Me,'' the last of the parade of ''eyes'' songs she had featured during her American stage life. ''Anna Held, same as ever, with the rolling eyes and the shrugging of the shoulders.''

Anna Held was portrayed on film in *The Great Ziegfeld* (1936) by Luise Rainer, and on the musical stage in the London extravaganza *Ziegfeld* (1988) by French actress and singer Fabienne Guyon, as well as in a number of revues in her heyday.

A biography, *Une Étoile française au ciel de l'Amérique,* was published in 1954. Although the cover and first-person narration give the impression that this is an autobiography, it was apparently written by Held's daughter. That daughter, **Liane Carrera,** worked largely in vaudeville but she also briefly ventured into musical farce in 1915 as the heroine of the Anatole Friedland/Alexandre/Marcel Janvier show *Too Near Paris* (National Theater, Washington, DC 27 September). It died on the road to town.

Plate 169. **Heisses Blut**

Biographies: Carrera, L [as ''Anna Held'']: *Une Étoile française au ciel de l'Amérique* (La Nef de Paris, Paris, 1954) [translated as *Anna Held and Flo Ziegfeld* (Exposition Press, Hicksville, NY, 1979)], Golden, E: *Anna Held and the Birth of Ziefeld's Broadway* (University Press of Kentucky, Lexington, 2000)

HELD, Ludwig (b Regensberg, 14 April 1837; d Vienna, 2 March 1900).

The author of a number of successful comedies, Held had a memorable hit on the musical stage with his Posse *Die Näherin,* in which Marie Geistinger scored as the chatterbox seamstress of the title. He later joined with Moritz West to provide three libretti for Karl Zeller—including the composer's two most successful pieces, the inimitable *Der Vogelhändler* and *Der Obersteiger*—and co-wrote three texts for Suppé, of which *Bellman* and *Das Modell* both found some success.

Although *Die Näherin* and *Der Obersteiger* were both original creations, many of Held's libretti were, in fact, adaptations from French originals. *Der Vagabund* was taken from an original by Émile Souvestre, *Der Vogelhändler* from Charles Varin and de Biéville's *Ce qui deviennent les roses, Der Cognac-König* from Eugène Scribe and Bayard's *La Frontière de Savoie, Der Schlosserkönig* similarly from Scribe, whilst *Die Stiefmama* was a German musical version of the famous Hennequin and Millaud vaudeville *La Femme à papa.*

Plate 170. **Anna Held.** *Florenz Ziegfeld promoted the pretty soubrette as the epitome of Paris and also—according to all the evidence—married her.*

His son, **Leo HELD** (b Vienna, 1874; d Vienna, 16 May 1903) was the composer of several short-lived Operetten, and the music for a number of Possen, including the successful *Die Goldtante* at the Theater an der Wien (1897). He also composed additional pieces for the Vienna version of the German hit *Eine tolle Nacht,* and one short opera, *Gina, die Ziegunerin.* He committed suicide before the age of 30.

1880 **Die Näherin** (Carl Millöcker) Theater an der Wien 13 March

1884 **Gefundenes Geld** (Julius Stern) Theater an der Wien 18 October

1886 **Der Vagabund** (Karl Zeller/w Moritz West) Carltheater 30 October

1887 **Bellman** (Franz von Suppé/w West) Theater an der Wien 26 February

1889 **Der Schlosserkönig** (Eduard Kremser/w Benjamin Schier) Theater an der Wien 12 January

1891 **Der Vogelhändler** (Zeller/w West) Theater an der Wien 10 January

1894 **Der Obersteiger** (Zeller/w West) Theater an der Wien 5 January

1895 **Der Schnuffler** (Leo Held) Raimundtheater 1 February

1895 **Das Modell** (Suppé/w Victor Léon) Carltheater 4 October

1897 **Die Schwalben** (Leo Held/w West) Theater an der Wien 12 February

1897 **Der Cognac-König** (Franz Wagner/w Léon) Carltheater 20 February

1898 **Die Pariserin** (Suppé/w Léon) Carltheater 26 January

1900 **Die Stiefmama** (Leo Held) Theater an der Wien 20 February

HELDEN, HELDEN Musical comedy in 2 acts by Hans Gmür based on *Arms and the Man* by George Bernard Shaw. Lyrics by Eckart Hachfeld, Walter Brandin and Gmür. Music by Udo Jürgens. Theater an der Wien, Vienna, 27 October 1972.

After the success of *My Fair Lady* in Vienna, the Theater an der Wien leaped, as so many others did, on the idea of making another musical out of a Shaw play. Any Shaw play. In spite of the existence of *Der tapfere Soldat,* Rolf Kutschera and his team selected an existing German-language version of *Arms and the Man* written by Peter Goldbaum, which was subsequently revised textually by Hans Gmür. The score to this piece, the work of Udo Jürgens—best known for his Eurovision song ''Warum nur, warum,'' which had been taken to number four in the English charts by Matt Monro—was reworked over by its composer, and *Helden, Helden* (''Heroes, heroes'') was produced in 1972 with Michael Heltau as Bluntschli and Gabriele Jacoby (Vienna's Eliza Doolittle and the daughter of Marika Rökk) as Raina. Amongst the rest of the cast were opera star Irmgard Seefried as Catherine and the rising Julia Migenes as Louka. *Helden, Helden* was played 130 times in Vienna in 1972–73, and later also appeared in Hamburg with Frln Jacoby and Paul Hubschmid featured, and in Leipzig (10 October 1975).

Germany: Operettenhaus, Hamburg 23 February 1973

Recording: original cast (Ariola)

HELLMESBERGER, Josef (b Vienna, 9 April 1855; d Vienna, 26 April 1907). Viennese composer of the turn-of-the-century years.

A descendant of a celebrated Viennese musical family, Josef (known as ''Pepi'') was the son of the elder Josef Hellmesberger, longtime director of the Vienna Konservatorium, and famous for his 40 years at the head of the Hellmesberger quartet. Josef the younger played the violin and performed, often with his father's groups, from an early age, appearing in popular concerts and with dance groups, and becoming in the process a personality on the Vienna music scene. His career as a violinist took him, in his early twenties, to solo work and also to a teaching post at the Vienna Konservatorium, and it was while he was engaged there that he began to compose more substantial work than the small dance pieces which had been his first efforts as a writer.

His earliest Operetten were produced by Adolf Grünwald at the then-titled Ronachers Operetten-Theater im KK Prater, and one of them, *Der Graf von Gleichen,* proved sufficiently successful there to be later staged in both Germany and in Hungary (*A kétnejű gróf*). However, during the 1880s and 1890s it was as a conductor that Hellmesberger made his principal career, working first at the Carltheater, then at the Hofoper, as well as at the head of the Philharmonic society. He nevertheless produced a considerable amount of theatre music, including a lyric-dance-drama, *Fata Morgana,* played at the Hofoper, the ballets *Meissner Porzellan, Das Licht* and *Der Blumen rachen,* incidental music and arrangements of such pieces as Grisar's *Gute Nacht, Herr Pantalon* and London's *Manteaux Noirs* for the Carltheater, and several Operette scores, without finding any one particular success. One Operette, *Das Orakel,* was, however, given a brief production at New York's Casino Theater, following its Viennese run, under the title *Apollo.*

Hellmesberger lost his position in the royal music establishment through an amorous misdemeanour and was forced to leave town. He found a post at the Stuttgart Hoftheater, but the timely Carltheater success of his Operette *Das Veilchenmädel* (1904) and of the popular Posse (''ein Episode aus der Grossstadt'') *Wien bei Nacht* later the same year salvaged him both financially and professionally, and he was soon back in Vienna. Although *Das Veilchenmädel* was taken up by Berlin's Apollotheater (1905, with Willi Bauer and Robert Steidl featured) and his ''phantastiches Operette'' *Der Triumph des Weibes* followed its month's run in Vienna with a mounting (with considerable additional music by Lincke) at the same house, Hellmesberger was unable to repeat the success of *Das Veilchenmädel* in a list of subsequent works for the Operette stage. *Mutzi* flopped in seven performances at the Carltheater, and his last years were spent mostly supplying piece-work music to Gabor Steiner at his two Viennese houses and in increasingly less prominent positions in musical society, before his death at the age of 52.

A well-regarded piece called *Letzter Fasching,* arranged from Hellmesberger's musical leavings, was later mounted in Graz, and a second posthumous piece, a soi-disant sequel to *Das Veilchenmädel* entitled *Der Veilchenkavalier,* was played at Ronacher in Vienna. Many years later his work was used as the basis for a third made-up piece, *Wiener G'schichten,* played at the Volksoper in 1934.

1880 **Kapitän Ahlström** (Albert Hofmann) Ronachers Operetten-Theater 15 May

1880 **Der Graf von Gleichen [und seine beiden Frauen]** (Alois Just) Ronachers Operetten-Theater 31 July

1886 **Der schöne Kurfürst** (Böhrmann-Riegen) Theater am Gärtnerplatz, Munich 15 May

1887 **Rikiki** (Richard Genée, Wilhelm Mannstädt) Carltheater 28 September

1889 **Das Orakel** (Ignaz Schnitzer) Theater an der Wien 30 November

1890 **Der bleiche Gast** (w Alfred Zamara/Victor Léon, Heinrich von Waldberg) Carl-Schultze Theater, Hamburg 6 September

1895 **Die Doppelhochzeit** (Léon, Waldberg) Theater in der Josefstadt 21 September

1904 **Das Veilchenmädel** (Leopold Krenn, Carl Lindau) Carltheater 27 February

1904 **Die Eisjungfrau** revised version of *The Girl from Up There* (w Gustave Kerker/M Band, Lindau, Julius Wilhelm) Venedig in Wien 3 June

1904 **Wien bei Nacht** (Lindau, Wilhelm) 1 act Danzers Orpheum 28 October

1906 **Die drei Engel** (ad Lindau, F Antony) Venedig in Wien 4 May

1906 **Mutzi** (Wilhelm, Robert Pohl) Carltheater 15 September

1906 **Der Triumph des Weibes** (August Neidhart) Danzers Orpheum 16 November

1906 **Eine vom ''Moulin-Rouge''** (Leopold Krenn) Danzers Orpheum 21 December

1909 **Letzter Fasching** (arr Ludwig Prechtl/Louis Windhopp) Stadttheater, Graz 10 February

1911 **Der Veilchenkavalier** (Krenn) Ronacher 16 April

1934 **Wiener G'schichten** (arr Oskar Jascha/Wilhelm Sterk) Volksoper 27 October

Other title attributed: *Der Wunderkaftan* (1902)

Biography: Prosl, R M: *Die Hellmesberger* (Gerlach & Wiedling, Vienna, 1947)

HELLO, DOLLY! Musical in 2 acts by Michael Stewart based on Thornton Wilder's *The Matchmaker.* Music and lyrics by Jerry Herman. St James Theater, New York, 16 January 1964.

Thornton Wilder's successful play *The Matchmaker* (Royale Theater 1955, 486 performances) was a rewritten version of his unsuccessful 1938 piece *The Merchant of Yonkers,* but it had a much longer pedigree than that, being a linear descendant of the classic Viennese musical comedy *Einen Jux will er sich machen* by Johann Nestroy (Theater in der Leopoldtsadt 15 January 1842), itself apparently taken from an earlier, English musical play, John Oxenford's *A Day Well Spent, or Three Adventures* (English Opera House 4 April 1836). This newest and Americanized musical version of the tale followed the reshaping done by Wilder in making Mrs Dolly Levi, the matchmaker, the central character of the piece.

Widowed Mrs Levi (Carol Channing) of Yonkers, NY, is a ''woman who arranges things'' in the best tradition of such musical-theatre ladies as the commission-hunting Mrs Ralli-Carr of *Gentleman Joe.* Employed to find a suitable wife for rich shopowner Horace Vandergelder (David Burns), she comes to the decision that the most suitable candidate is not, after all, her pretty milliner client Irene Molloy (Eileen Brennan), but herself. She succeeds in turning Vandergelder both from thoughts of Mrs Molloy and an exasperated dislike of her bossy, managing self, to a frame of mind which brings a proposal, all in the space of two comedy-packed acts. When Vandergelder heads for New York for the day out which will change his life, his young employees Cornelius Hackl (Charles Nelson Reilly) and Barnaby Tucker (Jerry Dodge) take the opportunity to skive off for a jaunt to town themselves. They fall in with Irene and her assistant Minnie Fay (Sondra Lee) and, after a farcical series of events which peaks in a night out at the ritzy Harmonia Gardens (a scene echoing closely the famous centerpiece of the 19th-century American musical comedy *A Trip to Chinatown*) and ends up with all the characters hauled up in court, everyone heads back to Yonkers and a happy—or at least matrimonial—ending.

Jerry Herman's score did more than just illustrate the farcical incidents of the play, for it turned out a whole set of numbers which would become favorites, topped by the extravagant welcome proffered to Mrs Levi on her ''return'' to the Harmonia Gardens after many years of widowly absence. ''Hello, Dolly!,'' with a certain amount of help from Louis Armstrong's hugely popular broken-glass-voiced recording, became one of the most popular Broadway songs of its era. The two boys excitedly planned their day out in ''Put on Your Sunday Clothes'' and joined with their girls pretending to know what ''Elegance'' is, Irene primped prettily through her plans for the summer in ''I'll Be Wearing Ribbons Down My Back,'' and Cornelius pleaded, in an incoherent defence in a semi-surreal court, that ''It Only Takes a Moment'' to fall in love. Mrs Levi led a bewildering march in praise of ''Motherhood, [America and a hot lunch for orphans],'' squalled out her determination to get something more out of life ''Before the Parade Passes By'' (whilst *Funny Girl,* up the street, was simultaneously instructing the world ''Don't Rain on My Parade''), and closed her talons around Vandergelder with a succulent ''Goodbye, Dearie'' which had no intention of meaning ''goodbye.''

David Merrick's production of *Hello, Dolly!* scored a triumph on Broadway, with Carol Channing—in the role originally designed for Ethel Merman—shooting back to and even beyond the level of fame she had achieved many years earlier in *Gentlemen Prefer Blondes.* She shared the accolades with director-choreographer Gower Champion, whose arangement of the Harmonia Gardens scene with its soon-to-be famous Waiter's Galop and its splendid display of traditional dinner-table and dance-floor low comedy, was the high-point of the evening.

Hello, Dolly! broke America's musical comedy long-run record with a stay of no less than 2,844 performances in its first run on Broadway. Miss Channing was succeeded by a parade of often well-known names in the title role as the performances and the years passed by—Ginger Rogers, Martha Raye, Betty Grable, Bibi Osterwald, Pearl Bailey at the head of a wholly recast all-black version, Phyllis Diller and, in 1970, Miss Merman, who finally got to play the role she had originally been offered. For the occasion, two additional songs were added, but they did not succeed in impinging on the public consciousness in the way that virtually the entire original score had. Not for the first time, however, a major hit show and a major hit song brought forth a plagiarism lawsuit. This time it was ''Hello, Dolly!'' which was the subject of the accusations, songwriter Mack David claiming that the main theme had been lifted from his ''Sunflower.'' As in so many past cases, the challenge proved worth his while, to the tune of a quarter of a million dollars, when Herman found it advisable to settle rather than face the kind of costly litigation which has scared so many folk away from properly defending themselves in a Broadway court.

Fifteen months after the show's opening, the first touring company of *Hello, Dolly!* went out in America with Mary Martin in the role of Mrs Levi, and it was Miss Martin who went on to head H M Tennent Ltd's London production at the Theatre Royal, Drury Lane, later the same year. London, for some reason, did not display the same enthusiasm for *Hello, Dolly!* that Broadway had done, and after some five months the musical was on the verge of being closed. However, when (at Miss Martin's suggestion) local favorite Dora Bryan took over the part of Mrs Levi, the show picked up well enough to remain in the West End for 794 performances, after which Miss Bryan took it on tour. Before Britain had welcomed Dolly, however, the first overseas production had already been launched, in Australia, with rather more positive reactions. Carole Cook starred as Dolly alongside Jill Perryman (Eileen) and Bill Mulliken (Cornelius) for 10 months in Sydney and Melbourne (Her Majesty's Theatre 27 August 1965) prior to a tour of New Zealand and a long series of other dates.

A German-language version of the show (ad Robert Gilbert) was produced in Düsseldorf in 1966 with Tatania Iwanow starring, and the show went on to establish itself as a firm favorite in German-speaking countries, with Marika Rökk appearing in the title role in Berlin and at

Vienna's Theater an der Wien, and Gisela May leading the company in East Germany's production. The first French-language performance (ad Marc-Cab, André Hornez) was played in Liège, Belgium (26 March 1971), but the piece was brought to Paris the following year with Jacques Collard's name added to the adaptation credit and with Annie Cordy starring as a Dolly more adorable and less abrasive than some and Jacques Mareuil as Vandergelder. The Paris season was not a whole-hearted success, but the show nevertheless won a number of regional productions in France in the years that followed. Its only return to Paris, however, was in a season by one of the American touring companies which took to the European roads in the 1980s and 1990s, playing the show in English. French jazz-singer Nicole Croisille took the role of Mrs Levi (Théâtre du Châtelet 12 November 1992). *Hello, Dolly!* continues, however, to be one of a small handful of anglophone musicals regularly played in France.

A film version, produced in 1969, with Barbra Streisand playing a much younger-seeming and altogether rather different (but more dramatically valid) Dolly alongside Walter Matthau (Vandergelder) and the young Michael Crawford (Cornelius), made some alterations to the show's score, adding two numbers which had been cut prior to the show's Broadway opening and slimming out some others. It did not ever become as popular as the stage show, which has continued to be a worldwide favorite, but which has nevertheless not made anything like the impression made in its record-breaking original run in several returns to the main centers. Broadway had a second black-cast version, again with Pearl Bailey starred, in 1975 (Minskoff Theater 6 November, 42 performances), whilst Miss Channing played 147 more performances in her famous role at the Lunt-Fontanne Theater in 1978 (5 March) before going on to a disappointingly tatty London reproduction at the Shaftesbury Theatre (21 September 1979, 170 performances), and she took another roll round with the piece as late as 1994 when it pitched tent for 118 nights on Broadway (Lunt-Fontanne Theater 19 October 1995). The most recent London production perhaps provided the answer to this apparent droop in the show's favor when it showed the way that the role of Dolly Levi and, by extension, the show, had gone. At the Prince of Wales Theatre in 1984 (3 January), female impersonator Danny La Rue appeared briefly as a travesty Dolly. Around the same time, London's National Theatre was triumphing with a new and trippingly legitimate version of *Einen Jux* (*On the Razzle* ad Tom Stoppard).

Australia: Her Majesty's Theatre, Sydney 27 March 1965; UK: Theatre Royal, Drury Lane 2 December 1965; Germany: Schauspielhaus, Düsseldorf 26 November 1966; Hungary: Fővárosi Operettszínház 23 February 1968; Austria: Theater an der Wien 10 September 1968; France: Théâtre de Nancy 3 March 1972, Théâtre Mogador 29 September 1972

Film: Twentieth Century Fox 1969

Recordings: original cast (RCA), London cast (RCA Victor), London cast replacement stars (HMV), Broadway black cast (RCA), film soundtrack (Twentieth Century Fox), German cast (Columbia), French cast (CBS), Israeli cast (CBS), Austrian cast (Metronome), East German cast (Amiga), Russian cast (Melodiya), Mexican cast (RCA Victor), 1994 revival cast (Varese Sarabande), Dutch cast (MarlStone), Czech cast (EMI), Mexican cast *Que tal Dolly* (no label), etc

HELOÏSE ET ABÉLARD Opérette in 3 acts by Clairville and William Busnach. Music by Henry Litolff. Théâtre des Folies-Dramatiques, Paris, 19 October 1872.

Coralie Geoffroy appeared as Heloïse, alongside an Abélard (Luce) who remained intact at the final curtain, in an opérettic version of the famous tale which gave all the discomfort to the villain. The villain in Clairville and Busnach's text was Chanoine Fulbert (Milher), Heloïse's clerical uncle, a nasty, worldly fellow who is proposing to make free with the wife of his tenant in retaliation for his being behind with the rent, but who nevertheless has no intentions of allowing his bluestocking niece to cast sweet glances at her teacher. When Heloïse arranges for Abélard to carry her off, the Chanoine summons his men to kidnap and . . . er . . . chastise the ''ravisher.'' Unfortunately for him, they get the wrong man. Paola Marié as the heroin's maid, Bertrase, and Verdelet featured alongside the principals in the painful story.

Cantin of the Folies-Dramatiques provided a weighty production—two prima donnas, two tenors, considerably enlarged choruses and an enlarged orchestra—which helped support a fine score by opérettic novice Litolff which ranged alongside its more conventional items a clever quartette, a declaration of love made in Latin, and a polka-accompanied scene in pantomime for Milher. The show was an instant hit, the Folies-Dramatiques was taken by assault by the Paris public, and the box office gathered in the vast sum of 5,000 francs a night—but the censor was watching, and Cantin found himself obliged to make an alteration to his show. Fulbert was not allowed to be a clergyman, nor to wear clerical robes. Similarly, the cast were forbidden to deviate from the text—introduced gags (for which there were, evidently, too many salacious possibilities) were forbidden. As usual, the censoring rebounded on the censor rather than the censored, and the fine, scandalous new show ran happily on through a Parisian run of over one hundred nights, being withdrawn only when both Milher and Luce (who never recovered) fell ill simultanously. In gratitude for their success the authors and composers paid for the tomb of the famous lovers in Père Lachaise cemetery to have a nice new railing.

However, if Paris took *Heloïse et Abélard* in good humor and with thorough enjoyment, the show provoked different reactions elsewhere—in Lyon (not normally noted for any particular prudery) it was hissed off the stage for its extravagantly near-the-groin dialogue.

The show was subsequently given an Austrian production (ad Richard Genée) with Irma Nittinger and Jani Szika in the title roles and Matthias Rott as Fulbert, and revived at the Folies-Dramatiques in 1874, following the failure of Litolff's subsequent *La Fiancée du Roi de Garbe,* this time with Marie Desclauzas as the heroine and Anna van Ghell taking the role of Bertrase. It returned again at the Théâtre de la Renaissance in 1879 with Jane Hading, Vauthier and Urbain featured, but doesn't seem ever to have made it across the water.

Since those delicate days a whole series of (mostly rather less delicate) Abelardian musicals have been mooted for production without one yet finding consummation in the theatre.

Austria: Theater an der Wien 27 September 1873

HELTAI, Jenő (b Budapest, 11 August 1871; d Budapest, 3 September 1957).

Journalist Heltai had his first short play staged when he was 23, and he passed on through jobs at the Paris Exposition and as secretary at the Vígszínház, as well as in various capacities in the newspaper world, as his theatrical career as a writer and, most particularly, as an adaptor began to flourish. He subsequently worked as a dramaturg, directed the Belvárosi Színház, and held a number of other theatrical posts over the nearly 40 years in which he turned out a vast amount of writing for the Hungarian stage.

Heltai's original works included only a few for the musical stage, but he was responsible for the lyrics for the most important original Hungarian work of the early 20th century, *János vitéz,* and his early operett *Egyptom gyöngye* was sufficiently successful to be adapted and played in Germany under the title *Das heilige Krokodil* (Elberfeld 28 February 1911). A wide-ranging and very lengthy list of adaptation credits, most particularly from the French, but including *Abie's Irish Rose, The Constant Wife, Le Mariage de Mlle Beulemans, Coralie et Cie, Romance, Pillangókisasszony* (*Madame Butterfly*), *La Petite Chocolatière* and Xavier Leroux's *Le Chemineau* also included a varying selection of musical pieces, ranging from Gaiety musical comedy and French opéra-bouffe to postwar French Jazz Age musicals and a number of ''comedies with songs.''

Heltai had two posthumous musical theatre credits. Ernő Innocent Vincze adapted one of his works as the libretto for Albert Szirmai's *A tündérlaki lányok* (Fővárosi Operettszínház 29 January 1964), and his translation of Léon Gandillot's *Ferdinand le noceur* was musicalized (ly: Iván Szenes, mus: Szabolc Fényes) for the Székesfehérvári Nyári Színház in 1985 (24 June).

1898 **A bibliás asszony** (*Les Fêtards*) Hungarian version (Népszínház)

1899 **Egyptom gyöngye** (Miklós Forrai) Magyar Színház 17 February

1900 **El Párizsba!** (pasticcio/w Emil Makai) Magyar Színház 16 May

1902 **Az aranyos** (*The Casino Girl*) Hungarian version (Népszínház)

1902 **A sötét kamra** (*Joli sport*) Hungarian version of comedy with added songs (Magyar Színház)

1902 **Soh'se halunk meg!** Hungarian version of Horst/Stein comedy with added songs (Városligeti Nyári Színkör)

1902 **Az izé** (*Das gewiss etwas*) Hungarian version w Miska Márton (Népszínház)

1904 **A királynő férje** (*Le Prince Consort*) Hungarian version with songs by László Kun Vígszínház 8 April

1904 **János vitéz** (Pongrac Kacsoh/Károly Bakonyi) Király Színház 18 November

1904 **Az ezüstpapucs** (*The Silver Slipper*) Hungarian version (Népszínház)

1904 **Én, te, ő** (*Le Sire de Vergy*) Hungarian version (Király Színház)

1904 **A szalmaözvegy** (*Les Vacances de mariage*) Hungarian version of comedy with added songs (Népszínház)

1904 **A rátartós Királykisasszony** (*Der var en Gang*) Hungarian version with songs by Viktor Jacobi (Népszínház)

1904 **Muki** Hungarian version of Pierre Wolff comedy with songs by Géza Chorin (Budai Színkör)

1905 **Mulató istenek** (*Der Göttergatte*) Hungarian version (Magyar Színház)

1905 **A kedves bácsi** (*The Wrong Mr Wright*) Hungarian version of comedy with added songs (Magyar Színház)

1905 **Danzigi hercegnő** (*The Duchess of Dantzic*) Hungarian version (Király Színház)

1905 **Bohémszerelem** (*La Petite Bohème*) Hungarian version (Magyar Színház)

1905 **A férjhezment kisasszony** (*Le Voyage de la mariée*) Hungarian version (Magyar Színház)

1906 **A Tengerszem tündére** (Victor Jacobi/Zoltán Thury) Magyar Színház 7 November

1906 **A császárné legyezője** (*Les Dragons de l'imperatrice*) Hungarian version (Népszínház)

1907 **Miciszlav** (*Mitislaw der moderne*) Hungarian version (Király Színház)

1907 **Bernát** (Imre Kálmán) Vígszínház 1 June

1907 **A bálkirálynő** (*The Catch of the Season*) Hungarian version (Népszínház)

1908 **Naftalin** (Albert Szirmai) Vígszínház 6 June

1909 **Édes teher** (various) Vígszínház 5 June

1911 **A ferencvárosi angyal** (Szirmai/w Ferenc Molnár) Royal Orfeum 31 December

1911 **As ezred apja** (*Le Papa du régiment*) Hungarian version of comedy with songs by Károly Stephanides (Vígszínház)

1912 **Ábrahám a mennyorszagban** (*Casimirs Himmelfahrt*) Hungarian version w Molnár (Budai Színkör)

1914 **Napsugár kisasszony** (*The Sunshine Girl*) Hungarian version (Király Színház)

1914 **Léni néni** (*Le Portait de ma tante*) Hungarian version of comedy, with songs by Zsigmond Vincze (Magyar Színház)

1917 **A márványmenyasszony** (*Niobe*) Hungarian version (Vígszínház)

1917 **Tavasz és szerelem** (*Liebe und Lenz*) Hungarian version (Városi Színház)

1921 **Fi-fi** (*Phi-Phi*) Hungarian version (Lujza Blaha Színház)

1922 **Cserebere** (*Ta bouche*) Hungarian version (Vígszínház)

1923 **Dédé** Hungarian version (Lujza Blaha Színház)

1924 **A párizsi lány** (*Gosse de riche*) Hungarian version (Fővárosi Operettszínház)

1927 **Csókrol-csókra** (*Pas sur la bouche*) Hungarian version (Magyar Színház)

1928 **Enyém az első csók** (Szirmai) Andrássy uti Színház 16 May

1933 **Bál a Savoyban** (*Ball im Savoy*) Hungarian version (Magyar Színház)

1934 **A csodadoktor** (*Encore cinquante centimes*) Hungarian version (Magyar Színház)

HENDERSON, Alexander (b Hutton Soil, Hesket-in-the-Forest, Cumberland, christened there 20 January 1828; d Cannes, 1 February 1886). Highly successful London producer of burlesque, opéra-bouffe and opéra-comique.

Alexander Henderson began his working life as a station manager in the post office, but he quit postage under a financial cloud and fled to the Australian colonies. It was there that he made his first significant steps as a theatre manager when he became briefly lessee of Melbourne's Princess Theatre for an unprofitable season by peripatetic opera star Anna Bishop in 1857, and subsequently of the Theatre Royal in the goldmining town of Sandhurst and of "the principal circuit on the goldfields." In 1861 he returned to Britain, and took over Liverpool's Clayton Hall, reconstructing it as the Prince of Wales Theatre (26 December 1861, "a charming bijou theatre") with considerable success. He also for a time extended his activities to Birkenhead (1864). He remained several years in Liverpool at the helm of one or another of the city's theatres, winning much kudos for bringing first-rate London productions and performers to the city. He was subsequently manager (w Samuel Colville) and sometime stage director for Lydia Thompson's famous company of touring burlesque actresses and actors in America and in Britain, and in 1873 the fair and widowed Lydia actually became his (some said second, some said fourth, others said all sorts of things) wife.

Henderson had his first major success as a West End manager when, after the Lydia Thompson company had played a season at the Folly Theatre with the burlesques *Blubeard, Robinson Crusoe* (1876) and *Oxygen* (1877), he retained the not-very-loved theatre and mounted a triple-bill of French opérettes: *Up the River, La Créole* and *Sea Nymphs/Shooting Stars* (1877). They did well enough for him to venture again into the French, this time with a contemporary Paris hit, *Les Cloches de Corneville* (1878). Planquette's opéra-comique turned out the longest-running musical show in London theatre history, and Henderson's career as a manager was made. Part way through the show's record-breaking run he transferred out of the Folly to the slightly better and bigger Globe Theatre, leaving the smaller house to Selina Dolaro and her attempts to capitalize on the place's new reputation as a home for opérette, whilst he collected the extra coin produced by the move.

Over the next few years Henderson became omnipresent in the London musical theatre. He announced plans to build an Alcazar Theatre in Leicester Square to house his opérette productions, but ultimately, whilst *Les Cloches* gave way at the Globe to an unsuccessful *The Naval Cadets,* then more *Cloches, Les Mousquetaires au couvent* (1880), six weeks of *La Belle Normande* (*La Famille Trouillat,* 1881), *La Boulangère* (*a des écus*) (1881, 40 performances) and another *Cloches* revival (1881), he subleased the existing Strand Theatre, for so long the home of classic burlesque under the management of the Swanborough family, to be his principal arena of operations. There, with his loved/hated friend Henry Brougham Farnie alongside him as adaptor, director and artistic advisor, he launched a series of highly successful productions of opéras-comiques and opérettes, beginning with the 1879 *Madame Favart,* another triumphant production which gave him a second hit to run alongside the seemingly inexhaustible *Les Cloches de Corneville,* succeeded by another huge hit in *Olivette* (1880, 466 performances), then *Manola* (1882, three months) and a *La Mascotte* revival, before he returned the theatre to the Swanboroughs and again moved on.

In 1881 he took on another unloved little theatre, the Royalty, in order to mount his latest French opérette, but the new Comedy Theatre was completed sooner than scheduled and, in spite of having the bills already out, Henderson (now "lessee and manager" of the Comedy) mounted his newest French adaptation, *La Mascotte,* there. It turned out to be yet another vast hit. That hit was succeeded by another in *Boccaccio* (1882, 129 performances), then by Henderson's one real homemade hit, the remarkable *Rip van Winkle* (1882, 328 performances), by the amazingly successful *Falka* (1883, 157 performances), a transfer of *Nell Gwynne* (1884) from the

Avenue, *The Grand Mogul* (1884), and a revival of *Barbe-bleue* (1885). As for the Royalty, he got himself shot of it as quickly as he could.

In spite of a slight stroke, he subsequently took over the direction of the Avenue where his last production, the Farnie-Reece burlesque *Kenilworth* (1885) was running at his death. He died after a fall on the pier at Calais. As an obituary, a lady columnist in *The New York Dramatic Mirror* devoted a column and a half of abuse to his memory and that of the vast list of women that this apparently heartless Don Juan of the theatre had seduced and ruined. But he left much of his fortune to his children, and the bulk to Lydia Thomspon, the woman who, by pawning her jewels, had provided the finance to set him up for the great triumphs that had been the beginnings of his fortune.

Henderson's biggest successes were a year or two behind him when he died, still in the saddle, still the owner of the Avenue Theatre and the repurchased Liverpool Prince of Wales, of a string of racehorses and some splendid artworks (he commissioned major pieces from Burne-Jones and his colleagues) and by and large enormously and ostentatiously rich. With Farnie's aid and expertise as a potent arm, and a largely wise choice of the biggest Continental hits as material, he had given himself half a dozen years at the very top of the managerial tree. However, his record as an instigator of original material was a very short one, and only his version of *Rip van Winkle,* manufactured on his commission to the measure of its star, Fred Leslie, turned out to be an enduring item in the opérette repertoire.

One of Henderson's illegitimate sons, **Alexander F HENDERSON** [Alexander Francis Vere CUTTER, 1866–1933], worked as general manager for Charles Wyndham, and subsequently became a well-known suburban London theatre manager while one of his illegitimate daughters, Mrs Effie Adelaide ROWLANDS (née HENDERSON b Australia ?1859; d England, 1936), at first the wife of the playwright ''Cecil Raleigh,'' became a well-known novelist and the mother, by her second marriage, of Meggie Albanesi (1899–1923), a young actress who ensured herself a fond place in many memories by dying at a very early age. Effie's full sister **Carrie Hope HENDERSON** [Caroline HENDERSON] (b Heathcote, Vic, Australia, 9 January 1855; d London, 19 October 1887) had a good stage career before an early death. Her daughter **May HALLATT** (Marie Effie HULLATT, b Scarborough, 1 May 1878) carried the connection with the theatre into a further generation. Carrie and Effie were the daughters of actress and singer **Marie NELSON** (aka Marie SIDNEY), daughter of songwriter Sydney Nelson (1800–1862) and sister to the internationally successful burlesque actresses Carrie, Sara and Eliza Nelson.

HENDERSON, Ray [BROST, Raymond] (b Buffalo, NY, 1 December 1896; d Greenwich, Conn, 31 December 1970). One-third of the famous songwriting team of De Sylva-Brown-'n'-Henderson.

The son of a musician, and set from early on for a musical career, Henderson studied in Chicago and made his first money as a piano player in a dance band, as an accompanist in variety, and as a publisher's arranger. He worked as a song-plugger and pianist for several publishers and, at the same time, turned out a number of songs of which ''Humming'' (ly: Louis Breau), which was interpolated into *Tip Top* on Broadway for the Duncan Sisters and then found its way into the short-lived London musical *Faust on Toast,* got the most exposure.

Henderson first collaborated with lyricist Lew Brown (no relation to Lou Breau) in 1922 on a song called ''Georgette,'' which was sung with success in the *Greenwich Village Follies,* and the two continued to turn out songs together in the years that followed (''Why Did I Kiss That Girl?,'' ''Don't Bring Lulu,'' ''If You Hadn't Gone Away'' w Billy Rose). Both continued, however, also to work with other writers, and in 1923 Henderson had a success with ''That Old Gang of Mine,'' written with Billy Rose and Mort Dixon, with whom he also wrote ''Follow the Swallow'' for the *Ziegfeld Follies of 1924.* He followed up with such pieces as ''’Bam, ’Bam, ’Bammy Shore'' and ''Bye, Bye, Blackbird'' with Dixon, ''Five Foot Two, Eyes of Blue'' and ''I'm Sitting on Top of the World'' (both 1926 w Joe Young, Sam Lewis) and ''Keep Your Skirts Down, Mary Ann'' (w Andrew Sterling, Robert King). In 1925 he had a first success in a collaboration with Buddy De Sylva, when the pair put their names alongside each other's and the title of the song ''Alabamy Bound'' (w Bud Green).

The songwriting team that was to become famous to a generation as ''De Sylva-Brown-'n'-Henderson'' came wholly together for the first time on Broadway with a contribution to Al Jolson's *Big Boy* (1925, ''It All Depends on You'') and went on from there to find substantial theatrical success with their score for the 1926 edition of the revue *George White's Scandals.* The one hit of the previous edition, for which they had also written the score, had been Irving Berlin's secondhand ''All Alone,'' but the 1926 show included a Blues section in which several famous blues numbers, Gershwin's ''Rhapsody in Blue'' and bits of Schubert and Schumann were all topped by De Sylva, Brown and Henderson's new ''The Birth of the Blues,'' and Ann Pennington danced frenetically to their charlestonny ''The Black Bottom.'' ''The Girl Is You and the Boy Is Me,'' from the same score, went on to become a London hit when played, along with their ''Tweet Tweet,'' in the musical *Up with the Lark* in 1927.

Song successes continued apace (''I Wonder How I Look When I'm Asleep,'' ''Magnolia,'' etc), and it was not long before the trio turned out their first Broadway score for a book musical, the college show *Good News* (1927, ''The Best Things in Life Are Free,'' ''The Varsity Drag''). *Good News* was a major hit, and over the next four years, whilst continuing to supply the *George White Scandals* with annual material (some of which, such as ''I'm On the Crest of a Wave'' [*Love Lies*], was pilfered for London musicals and for the voracious Paris revue stage), they turned out four further book shows. They were a quartet of variable value, but all of them proved popular through good Broadway runs and were mostly exported—with uneven results—to London, and on several occasions to France, where the team's up-to-date musical style had become decidedly popular.

Manhattan Mary, a vehicle for comedian Ed Wynn, was short on song hits but long on personality; *Hold Everything!* invaded the world of boxing, introduced ''You're the Cream in My Coffee,'' and made a star of Bert Lahr; *Follow Thru* turned to golf and produced ''Button Up Your Overcoat''; whilst *Flying High* gave Lahr the opportunity to take comically to the skies, if without any songs as durable as the best of those in the earlier shows.

What had now become the hottest songwriting team on Broadway was naturally courted by Hollywood, and the trio moved west, where they quickly scored outstanding filmland successes with songs for such early sound pieces as *The Singing Fool* (1928, ''Sonny Boy'') and *Sunny Side Up* (1929, ''If I Had a Talking Picture of You,'' ''Sunny Side Up''). However, the combination broke up when De Sylva moved on to an executive position in the film industry and Brown and Henderson returned to Broadway. The pair turned out a score for the *Scandals of 1931,* in which ''Life Is Just a Bowl of Cherries'' was the take-away tune, but they did not succeed in producing anything of the same kind of lasting value for either of the subsequent revusical book shows to which they contributed scores: *Hot-Cha,* even with Bert Lahr, was a 15 week semi-flop, and *Strike Me Pink,* which Brown and Henderson produced themselves, had Jimmy Durante, a lot of limp material and an unimpressive life.

Brown then followed De Sylva back to Hollywood, but Henderson remained in the theatre to compose and co-produce one more musical, the short-lived *Say When,* on which he collaborated with Ted Koehler, and to contribute the score to one more edition of *George White's Scandals* (1935). His most successful individual number from this period came, however, from a film—''Animal Crackers in my Soup'' (1935, w Koehler, Irving Caesar) as performed by top tot Shirley Temple in *Curly Top.*

Henderson continued to write songs through the 1940s, including the score of the *Ziegfeld Follies of 1943* (w Jack Yellen), before he retired to Connecticut, where he devoted himself to some more serious composition in his later days.

A 1956 Hollywood biopic of the threesome, *The Best Things in Life Are Free,* had Henderson portrayed by Dan Dailey.

1927 **Good News** (Lew Brown, B G De Sylva/Laurence Schwab, De Sylva) 46th Street Theater 6 September
1927 **Manhattan Mary** (Brown, De Sylva/William K Wells, George White) Apollo Theater 26 September
1928 **Hold Everything!** (Brown, De Sylva/Jack McGowan, De Sylva) Broadhurst Theater 10 October
1929 **Follow Thru** (Brown, De Sylva/Schwab, De Sylva) 46th Street Theater 9 Janaury
1930 **Flying High** (Brown, De Sylva/McGowan) Apollo Theater 3 March
1932 **Hot-Cha!** (Brown, Hy S Kraft, Mark Hellinger) Ziegfeld Theater 8 March
1933 **Strike Me Pink** (ex- *Forward March*) (McGowan, Mack Gordon) Majestic Theater 4 March
1934 **Say When** (Ted Koehler/McGowan) Imperial Theater 8 November

HENEKER, David [William] (b Southsea, 31 March 1906; d Llechryd, nr Cardigan, Wales, 30 January 2001). Songwriter who turned out some of the most delightful work of the British 1950s and 1960s, and who kept at it even when his style had been made to seem outdated by the fashion for large-scale spectaculars.

A brigadier in the regular army, Heneker found sufficient success as a popular songwriter (''There Goes My Dream,'' etc) to encourage him to resign his commission and take up a job as a club pianist to allow himself to concentrate on writing. He provided material for several revues (*Scoop,* etc) prior to combining with lyricist Julian More and singer-songwriter Monty Norman to turn out the music and lyrics for *Expresso Bongo* (1958), the best of the British wave of ''realistic'' musicals of the 1950s (''Time,'' ''The Shrine on the Second Floor''). The team won a wider success with their remarkably characterful English adaptation of the French low-life slang of the Paris hit *Irma la Douce* (1958), and Heneker and Norman had a third successive hit with a second show with *Expresso Bongo* author, Wolf Mankowitz, in *Make Me an Offer,* before Heneker went solo on a commission to turn H G Wells's *Kipps* into a stage musical for rock star Tommy Steele. As *Half a Sixpence,* the show gave its songwriter his greatest success (''Half a Sixpence,'' ''She's Too Far Above Me,'' ''If the Rain's Got to Fall,'' ''Flash, Bang, Wallop'') and put the phrase ''Flash, Bang, Wallop'' into the world's dictionaries.

His 1965 show *Charlie Girl* was a very long-running West End hit, but the fox-hunting tale of R G Surtees's

Jorrocks, a Percy French biomusical, for which he supplemented the Irish songwriter's popular numbers with others mostly more plot-worthy (''They Don't Make Them Like That Any More'') and a musicalized version of the Ben Travers farce *Rookery Nook* (*Popkiss*) did not find extended success. After a gap of some eight years, Heneker returned to the West End with the songs for the small-scale history of soundless Hollywood, *The Biograph Girl,* and at the age of 78 he provided one final score, for a musical version of J Hartley Manners's *Peg o'My Heart* (''When a Woman Has to Choose''). Once again, these failed to find the success of his early work, in a theatrical world where his combination of unambitious musical elegance and precise lyrical charm were no longer the order of the day.

1958 **Expresso Bongo** (w Monty Norman/w Norman, Julian More/More, Wolf Mankowitz) Saville Theatre 23 April

1958 **Irma la Douce** English version w Norman, More (Lyric Theatre)

1959 **Make Me an Offer** (w Norman/Mankowitz) Theatre Royal, Stratford East 17 October; New Theatre 16 December

1963 **Half a Sixpence** (Beverley Cross) Cambridge Theatre 21 March

1965 **Charlie Girl** (w John Taylor/Hugh & Margaret Williams, Ray Cooney) Adelphi Theatre 15 December

1966 **Jorrocks** (Cross) New Theatre 22 September

1969 **Phil the Fluter** (w Percy French/Cross, Donal Giltinan) Palace Theatre 15 November

1971 **The Amazons** (John Addison/Michael Stewart) Playhouse, Nottingham, UK 7 April

1972 **Popkiss** (w John Addison/Michael Ashton) Globe Theatre 22 August

1980 **The Biograph Girl** (Warner Brown) Phoenix Theatre 19 November

1984 **Peg** (Robin Miller, Ronald Millar) Phoenix Theatre 8 March

HENNEQUIN, [Néocles] Alfred (b Liège, Belgium, 3 January 1842; d Épinay, 7 August 1887). Prominent author of comedies and vaudevilles for the French 1870s and 1880s stage.

Son of a Liégois lawyer, Hennequin studied for a career in civil engineering, and he was employed on the Belgian state railways when, at the age of 25, he began writing for the theatre. His first play, *J'attends mon oncle,* was produced at Brussels's Galeries Saint-Hubert in 1869 and, when Hennequin moved on to Paris, as the manager of a tramway company, he soon found notable success as a playwright there, with his contributions to such pieces as *Le Procès Veauradieux,* the celebrated *Les Dominos roses, Bébé* and *La Poudre de l'escampette.* He did not, however, write for the musical stage until 1878 when he began a collaboration with Albert Millaud which produced the internationally successful vaudevilles *Niniche, La Femme à papa* and *Lili* for Anna Judic and the Théâtre des Variétés. The other few libretti which he helped pen did not find the same success, and his last contributions to the musical stage were in the form of French adaptations of a couple of the most successful Viennese Operetten of the time. Both, however, proved less successful on the French-language stage than they had at home. In 1886 Hennequin suffered a breakdown, said to have been caused by overwork, and he died, insane and blind, the following year when he fell from a window of the asylum where he had been confined.

Hennequin's comedies subsequently proved fertile ground for adaptors. *Les Dominos roses* (Théâtre du Vaudeville 17 April 1876, w Alfred Delacour) became *Tonight's the Night* in America and Britain, *Der Opernball* in Vienna, and *Három légyott* (text and music by József Bokor 22 October 1897 Népszínház) in Budapest and—apparently, though without credit—*The Wager, or the Mask Ball* (E R Mollenhauer/Charles Barnard Park Theater, Philadelphia 18 May 1879) in America. *Bébé* (Théâtre du Gymnase 10 March 1877 w de Najac, known in its hit English translation as *Betsy*) was the source for the British musical *Oh, Don't, Dolly!* (1919) and for Hungary's *Kis fiu* (Áladár Váradi/Hugó Ilosvai Népszínház 30 January 1895), and *Les Petites Correspondences* (Théâtre du Gymnase 2 July 1878) became *Kleine Anzeigen* in a musicalized German-language form (mus: Josef Brandl, Carltheater 22 April 1880). Vienna's Theater an der Wien admitted that F Zell's 1885 musical play *Die Kindsfrau,* subsequently played in America by Geistinger, was based on ''Hennequin'' without identifying which Hennequin or which play, and *Niniche* and *La Femme à papa* also underwent all kinds of transsubstantiations, attached to all sorts of scores, notably those by the same Brandl, in several languages.

1878 **Niniche** (Marius Boullard/w Albert Millaud) Théâtre des Variétés 15 February

1878 **Fleur d'Oranger** (Auguste Coedès/w Victor Bernard) Théâtre des Nouveautés 7 December

1879 **La Femme à papa** (Hervé/w Millaud) Théâtre des Variétés 3 December

1882 **Lili** (Hervé/w Millaud, Ernest Blum) Théâtre des Variétés 10 January

1882 **Ninetta** (Raoul Pugno/w Alexandre Bisson) Théâtre de la Renaissance 26 December

1883 **L'Étudiant pauvre** (*Der Bettelstudent*) French version w Albin Valabrègue (Galeries Saint-Hubert, Brussels)

1883 **Le Présomptif** (Louis Gregh/w Valabrègue) Galeries Saint-Hubert, Brussels 12 December; Théâtre de la Renaissance 6 June 1884

1884 **Les Trois Devins** (Édouard Okolowicz/w Valabrègue) Théâtre de l'Ambigu-Comique 11 June

1885 **La Guerre joyeuse** (*Der lustige Krieg*) French version w Maurice Hennequin (Brussels)

HENNEQUIN, [Charles] Maurice [Néocles] (b Liège, Belgium, 10 December 1863; d Montreux, Switzerland, 3 September 1926).

The son of Alfred Hennequin, Maurice made his debut as a writer modestly refusing to capitalize on his father's name, and his first piece, the one-act comédie-vaudeville *L'Oiseau bleu,* was put out at the Théâtre de la Renaissance in 1882 under his mother's maiden name as "Maurice Debrun." He soon abandoned this pseudonym and, from 1886, under his own name, turned out a long list of highly successful comedies and vaudevilles in collaborations with such authors as Paul Bilhaud, Georges Duval, Georges Feydeau, Pierre Veber and Antony Mars. That list included such durable favorites as *Vous n'avez rien à declarer?, La Présidente, Le Système Ribadier* and *Madame et son filleul.*

Hennequin ventured intermittently into the musical theatre, scoring a major international success in 1897 with the uproarious musical comedy *Les Fêtards*—which went on to become the basis for successful musicals in Britain (*Kitty Grey*) and America (*The Rounders*), whilst conquering central Europe in its original form—and a second appreciable success, with the same partners, in *La Poule blanche.* Thereafter he concentrated almost entirely on the non-musical stage, but in 1926 he returned to collaborate on the libretto for the highly successful André Messager musical comedy *Passionnément.*

Hennequin's comedies and vaudevilles proved widely popular as the bases for musical shows by other hands, *Coralie et Cie* (Palais-Royal 30 November 1899 w Valabrègue) being made into a musical for Lottie Collins in Britain (*The Dressmaker*), *Les Dragées d'Hercule* (1904) turning into Rudolf Friml and Otto Harbach's international hit *High Jinks, Madame et son filleul* (Palais-Royal 12 September 1916, w Veber) becoming *The Girl Behind the Gun* on Broadway and then, to enormous effect, *Kissing Time* (1919) in Britain and English-speaking areas beyond. *Le Monsieur de cinq heures* (Palais-Royal 1 October 1924 w Veber) was the source for the American play *A Kiss in a Taxi* and for the musical comedy *Sunny Days* developed therefrom, the farce *Aimé des femmes* (Palais-Royal 2 May 1911 w Georges Mitchell) was taken as the source for Broadway's Henry Blossom/Alfred Robyn *All for the Ladies,* and an earlier Palais-Royal piece, *Place aux femmes!* (8 October 1898 w Valabrègue), made it to the German musical stage as *Die moderne Eva* (1911), with a score by Jean Gilbert.

Elsewhere, in a gust of nebulous credits, such as "from the French" or "based partly on a play by . . . ," both *Oh, Please!* and *Oh, Kay!* were claimed at one stage to be based on *La Présidente* (Bouffes-Parisiens 12 September 1902 w Veber), which Italy's *La Presidentessa* (a Robert Stolz pasticcio made by Carlo Lombardo) certainly was, whilst Vienna's *Fräulein Präsident,* perversely, had a heroine called Nelly Rozier, but doesn't seem to have any more to do with Hennequin's popular play of that name (w Bilhaud) than with *La Présidente.* The Frankfurt musical *Angst vor der Ehe* (Emil Reznicek/Erich Urban, Louis Taufstein, 28 November 1913) was announced as based on a Hennequin and Veber play known in German as *Der Taubenschlag* (*Le Colombier*), Italy also borrowed something of Hennequin's—presumably *Le Paradis* (w Bilhaud, Barre)—for a 1924 Mario Ferrarese musical called *Paradiso,* and in Hungary, Jenő Heltai adapted what seems to have been Hennequin's *Les Vacances du Mariage* (Menus-Plaisirs 12 February 1887 w Valabrègue) as a musical comedy under the title *A szalmaözvegy* (Népszínház 10 June 1904). Back home, *Le Système Ribadier* was set to music in 1994 (Théâtre Daniel Sorano, Vincennes 25 November) by Michael Frantz and Jean-Marie Pelabrat.

1885 **La Guerre joyeuse** (*Der lustige Krieg*) French version w Alfred Hennequin (Brussels)

1891 **La Petite Poucette** (Raoul Pugno/w Maurice Ordonneau) Théâtre de la Renaissance 5 March

1893 **Les Cousins de Nanette** (P Rougnon/w V Meusy) tour

1894 **Le Troisième Hussards** (Justin Clérice/w Antony Mars) Théâtre de la Gaîté 14 March

1894 **Le Régiment qui passe** (Lucien & Paul Hillemacher)1 act Royan 11 September

1896 **Sa majesté l'amour** (Victor Roger/w Mars) Eldorado 24 December

1897 **Les Fêtards** (Roger/w Mars) Palais-Royal 28 October

1899 **La Poule blanche** (Roger/w Mars) Théâtre Cluny 13 January

1907 **Betty, ou L'entente cordiale** (Eustache de Lorey/w Paul Bilhaud) Théâtre des Nouveautés (Olympia), Brussels 4 October

1914 **La Fille de Figaro** (Xavier Leroux/w Hugues Delorme) Théâtre Apollo 10 March

1916 **Le Poilu** (Maurice Jacquet/w Pierre Veber) Palais-Royal 14 January

1916 **Cyprien, ôte ta main d'là** (André Messager) 1 act Concert Mayol

1917 **La Petite Dactylo** (Jacquet/w Georges Mitchell) Gymnase 19 October

1926 **Passionnément** (Messager/w Albert Willemetz) Théâtre de la Michodière 15 January

HENSON, Leslie [Lincoln] (b London, 3 August 1891; d Harrow Weald, 2 December 1957). Frog-featured star comedian, long one of the reigning favorites of the West End musical stage.

Henson worked initially in concert party and in pantomime (Binbad in *Sinbad the Sailor,* Dalston 1910, etc) before landing his first musical comedy role, at the age

Plate 171. **Leslie Henson** *and the girls of the Gaiety Theatre in* Seeing Stars.

of 21, touring as Jeremiah in *The Quaker Girl* for George Dance. Two years later he had a minor role in Grossmith and Laurillard's New York company of *Tonight's the Night,* a part he enlarged sufficiently successfully to be given a larger one when the show was produced at London's Gaiety Theatre the following year.

Grossmith subsequently hired him for the star soubret role of *Theodore & Co* (1916, Pony Twitchin), a part which was increased to even greater size when the manager-star departed the show to join the war effort, and in the company's next and equally successful piece, *Yes, Uncle!* (1917, Bobby Summers), Henson showed up as the top comic of the evening. He had, however, an odd contract: wishing himself to join up, he agreed to go into the show just to create the role and its comical stage business before departing with a royalty in his pocket to find a uniform.

After the war Henson returned to Grossmith and Laurillard's (later Grossmith and Malone's) management for a seven-year series of mostly successful musicals at the Winter Garden Theatre, taking star comic roles in *Kissing Time* (1919, Bibi St Pol), *A Night Out* (1920, Pinglet), as the shorn Grand Duke Connie in *Sally* (1921), *The Cabaret Girl* (1923, Mr Gravvins), *The Beauty Prize* (1923, Odo Philpotts), a revival of *Tonight's the Night, Primrose* (1924, Tony Mopham), *Tell Me More!* (1925, Monte Sipkin) and *Kid Boots* (1926, Kid Boots), making up a comical team with slim, dudey Grossmith and big Davy Burnaby, which equaled any musical comedy combination in town. When the Winter Garden series terminated he appeared as the star of *Lady Luck* at the new Carlton Theatre (1927, Windy Bleugh), with the Astaires in *Funny Face* (1928, Dugsie Gibbs), and in *Follow Through* (1929, Jack Martin) at the Dominion Theatre. He then left the musical stage temporarily to appear in the comedies *It's a Boy* (*Hurra! Eine Junge!*) and *It's a Girl* under his own management, on London's ''comedy corner.''

Henson took up afresh his long run of musical comedy successes in the musical farces *Nice Goings On* (1933, Olaf Henscuttle) and *Lucky Break* (1934, Tommy Turtle), and then began at the Gaiety Theatre what turned out to be a new series of shows, a series which teamed him this time with bulky, monocled Fred Emney, acrobatic Richard Hearne, and dance-and-song juveniles Louise Browne and Roy Royston: *Seeing Stars* (1935, Jimmy Swing), *Swing Along* (1936, Maxie Mumm), *Going Greek* (1937, Alexander Saggappopolous) and *Running Riot* (1938, Cornelius Crumpet). In each of these he took a share of the direction, as he had, credited or uncredited, in all his own shows since Winter Garden days and several others besides (*So This Is Love, On Your Toes,* etc).

This Gaiety Theatre series came to an end with the Second World War, and although Henson came back once more with success in the postwar *Bob's Your Uncle* (1948), it was to a world where tastes had changed. They had not changed sufficiently, however, for audiences to allow their favorite, free-wheeling, frog-faced little comedian of the interwar years to change his coat and, when he attempted the role of Samuel Pepys in a well-made musical version of *And So to Bed* (1951), playing the script and just the script without his usual ad-libbing and antics, his public could not accept it. His last appearance on the musical stage was in 1955, when he played the role of Eccles in a musical version of *Caste* at the Theatre Royal, Windsor.

Henson was married first to the musical comedy ingenue **Madge SAUNDERS** (b Johannesburg, 25 August 1894; d 5 March 1967) who appeared in *Tonight's the Night* in New York and London (1915, Daisy de Menthe), *Theodore and Co* (1916, Lady Pansy), in London's *Very Good Eddie* (1918, Elsie Grey) and *Going Up* (1918, Grace Douglas), the Gaiety's *The Kiss Call* (1919, t/o Pauline Deare), and later mostly in comedy. His second wife was Gladys Gunn of the famous Dublin theatrical family.

His son, **Nicky HENSON** (b London, 12 May 1945), has had a successful career as an actor in musical and non-musical shows, appearing in his young days as Mordred in London's *Camelot,* in *Passion Flower Hotel,* as the original juvenile man of *Canterbury Tales,* as Toad in *Toad of Toad Hall* and as Jack Sheppard in *Stand and Deliver.* He returned to the musical stage in 1990 in the short-lived *Matador* (El Panama) and again in *Enter the Guardsman* (1997, The Playwright) as part of a later career angled towards the non-musical stage.

Autobiographies: *My Laugh Story* (Hodder & Stoughton, London, 1926), *Yours Faithfully* (John Long, London, 1948)

HENTSCHKE, Heinz (b Berlin, 20 February 1895; d Berlin, 3 July 1970).

After an early career spent in and with all kinds of theatre-related organizations, Hentschke made good as a theatre-ticket broker. At the same time, he won his way into the confidence of the Rotter brothers, who were then in control of most of Berlin's musical theatre, rising to be their managing director during the 1920s. When the brothers fell into, first, financial difficulties and then, in 1933, Nazi difficulties, Hentschke—who had made a fortune from his brokering activities—moved in to take over their holdings and their position in the Berlin theatre. He was the manager of Berlin's Metropoltheater from 1934, directing and also writing the libretti for the shows played there during the era of National Socialism. His term at the Metropoltheater came to an end in 1944, and his subsequent theatrical activities were on a less prominent scale.

Amongst his writings, he found greatest success with the banal but surprisingly enduring *Maske in Blau,* and with the rather more adeptly constructed *Hochzeitsnacht im Paradies,* two from a group of pieces of mostly very limited value, cobbled together as isn't-life-jolly type entertainments for the Hitlerian years.

1934 **Lauf ins Glück** (Fred Raymond/Paul Beyer) Metropoltheater 24 September

1935 **Ball der Nationen** (Raymond/Beyer) Metropoltheater 27 September

1936 **Auf grosser Fahrt** (Raymond/Günther Schwenn) Metropoltheater 21 August

1936 **Marielu** (Raymond/Schwenn/w Theo Halton) Centraltheater, Dresden 19 December

1937 **Maske in Blau** (Raymond/Schwenn) Metropoltheater 27 September

1938 **Melodie der Nacht** (Ludwig Schmidseder/Schwenn) Metropoltheater 21 September

1939 **Die, oder keine** (Schmidseder/Schwenn) Metropoltheater 20 September

1940 **Frauen im Metropol** (Schmidseder) Metropoltheater 27 September

1942 **Hochzeitsnacht im Paradies** (Friedrich Schröder/Schwenn) Metropoltheater 24 September

1943 **Der goldene Käfig** (Theo Mackeben/Schwenn) Admiralspalast 23 September

HERBERT, (Sir) A[lan] P[atrick] (b Elstead, Surrey, 24 September 1890; d London, 11 November 1971). British librettist and lyricist whose reputation for fine writing was not always upheld by his musical-theatre work.

Lawyer, journalist, novelist and longtime Member of Parliament, Herbert began writing for the stage in his thirties whilst working for *Punch* magazine. His earliest pieces, all written for the Lyric Theatre, Hammersmith, included a short operetta, the revue *Riverside Nights,* and what cannot strictly be called an adaptation of, but rather a new show loosely based on bits of, Offenbach's *La Vie parisienne*. He combined with Sir Thomas Dunhill to write the original musical *Tantivy Towers* (1931) and with Alfred Reynolds on the pompous *Derby Day* (1932) for the same theatre, and did an almost as devastating hatchet job on *La Belle Hélène* as he had done on *La Vie parisienne* for a spectacular C B Cochran production, based on a German Max Reinhardt remake and staging, called *Helen!*

He successfully, and much less drastically, adapted Oscar Straus's *Eine Frau, die weiss, was sie will* (*Mother of Pearl*, ''Every Woman Thinks She Wants to Wander'') for the English stage, Englished Franz Lehár's *Paganini* less fortunately for London and, in 1934, he collaborated for the first time in the theatre with composer Vivian Ellis to turn out the successful C B Cochran revue *Streamline* (''Other People's Babies''). That collaboration with Ellis was restarted after the war, when Ellis composed the scores to Herbert's texts for the effortfully political *Big Ben* (1946), and for his least ''meaningful'' and by far most successful musical, the period piece *Bless the Bride* (1947, ''This Is My Lovely Day,'' ''Ma Belle Marguerite,'' ''I Was Never Kissed Before''), for *Tough at the Top* (1949) and for *The Water Gipsies* (1955), the last of these based on Herbert's own novel and screenplay.

1927 **Plain Jane** (Richard Austin) 1 act Greyhound Theatre, Croydon 26 December

1929 **La Vie parisienne** rewritten English version (Lyric Theatre, Hammersmith)

1931 **Tantivy Towers** (Thomas Dunhill) Lyric Theatre, Hammersmith 16 January

1931 **The Gay Princess** (Robert Katscher/Siegfried Geyer) English lyrics (Kingsway Theatre)

1932 **Helen!** rewritten English version of *La Belle Hélène* (Adelphi Theatre)

1932 **Derby Day** (Alfred Reynolds) Lyric Theatre, Hammersmith 24 February

1933 **Mother of Pearl** (*Eine Frau, die weiss, was sie will*) English version (Gaiety Theatre)

1937 **Paganini** English version w Reginald Arkell (Lyceum)

1946 **Big Ben** (Vivian Ellis) Adelphi Theatre 17 July

1947 **Bless the Bride** (Ellis) Adelphi Theatre 26 April

1949 **Tough at the Top** (Ellis) Adelphi Theatre 15 July

1955 **The Water Gipsies** (Ellis) Winter Garden 31 August

Autobiography: *A.P.H.: His Life and Times* (Heinemann, London, 1970)

HERBERT, Evelyn [HOUSTELLIER, Evelyn Herbert] (b Philadelphia, 18 March 1898; d California, March 1975). Soprano star of several Broadway musicals of the 1920s and 1930s.

After a brief attempt at an operatic career (Mimi with the Chicago Grand Opera Company, etc), Miss Herbert lost her voice, and when she returned to the stage she switched to the musical theatre where her fine, and now less overworked, soprano quickly won her leading roles. Her first Broadway appearance was in support (with two solos and several ensembles to sing) of Fred and Dorothy Stone in Charles Dillingham's production *Stepping Stones* (1923, Lupina); her second, after the withdrawal of Marguerite Namara, was in the Hungarian Offenbach pasticcio, *The Love Song* (1925, Herminie), playing the role of Mrs Offenbach. In the same year, following a second rehearsal-time flit by Miss Namara, and an out-of-town interlude by Mary Mellish, she took up the title role in *Princess Flavia*, the musical version of *The Prisoner of Zenda*, for Broadway, and confirmed herself as one of the most impressive vocalists in the musical theatre of her time.

She appeared in revue for Charles Dillingham, and then created further operettic leading roles in Sigmund Romberg's *My Maryland* (1927), in which she appeared as a young and glamorized Barbara Frietchie, and in *The New Moon* (1928) where, in the role of Marianne, she introduced ''One Kiss,'' ''Lover, Come Back to Me'' and ''Wanting You,'' the last in partnership with her husband, Robert Halliday, cast opposite her in the role of Robert Misson.

She followed up, again paired with Halliday, in the title role of Szirmai's *Princess Charming* (*Alexandra*, Princess Elaine) and in London's large-scale presentation of the Strauss pasticcio *Waltzes from Vienna* (*Walzer aus Wien*), and she essayed another Romberg score in *Melody* (1933), with rather less return than on previous occasions. Her final appearance on the New York stage was in the leading role of Noël Coward's *Bitter-Sweet* on the occasion of a short Shubert revival at the 44th Street Theater in 1934. In 1935 she starred at the St Louis Municipal Opera as *Rio Rita*, and in the title role of the American premiere of *Teresina*.

Mr and Mrs Halliday ultimately went into retirement in California, and died there, within six months of each other, at their home, named ''New Moon Farm'' after their greatest success together.

HERBERT, Joseph W[illiam] (b Liverpool, 27 November 1863; d New York, 18 February 1923). A tall, gangling, comic actor, who had a considerable career in the Broadway theatre both as a performer and as a writer.

The young Joe Herbert emigrated to America at the age of 13 and settled in Chicago where, during his college days, he joined the local Church Choir Company as an amateur chorister. He deputized for a professional comedian who failed to show to play the Lord Chancellor in the company's production of *Iolanthe* and when C D Hess reformed the company as the Acme Opera Company and sent it on the road (1884) as a professional musical stock company, Herbert went with it. He subsequently played the Lord Chancellor, Gobo in *Cloches de Corneville, Fatinitza, HMS Pinafore, Pirates of Penzance, Patience,* Népomuc in *La Grande-Duchesse,* etc, through the tour and, following the Acme troupe's collapse, with a stuck-together season of a stuck-together company in New Orleans. He played with Sydney Rosenfeld's company as Chicago's first ever Ko-Ko in *The Mikado* (1885), with John Stetson's ''Mammoth *Mikado* Company'' (t/o more Ko-Ko 1885), at St Paul (Ko-Ko, Sir Joseph Porter), with the ''California Opera Company'' at Schnaider's Garden St Louis (*The Brigands*), as King Gama in Stetson's *Princess Ida* company (1887), Sosoriki in the Bijou Theater's *The Pearl of Pekin* (1888), in summer season (1889), on tour in the farce-comedy *A Stuffed Dog* (1889, Daguerrotype B Jones), as Christopher Columbus in *The World's Fair* with Rice's Surprise Party (1890), The Baron in Chicago's *Babes in the Wood* (1890), in *Iolanthe* (1890) in Boston, etc, and, in a long subsequent career as a comedian, he mixed appearances in classic plays (*The Merry Wives of Windsor,* Tranio in *The Taming of the Shrew,* etc) and modern comedy with a vast range of roles in the musical theatre.

In 30 years of comic musical roles, his credits included E E Rice's *The Pearl of Pekin* (1888), Carillon in *The King's Fool* (1890), The Duke of Plaza Toro in *The Gondoliers* (t/o 1890), Bacarel in *Miss Helyett* (1891), Prince Gregory of Montenegro in *The Algerian* (1893) with Marie Tempest, Sandy McSherey in *Rob Roy* (1894), Count Giulio Cesario in *La Tzigane* with Lillian Russell, Ki-Yi in the Chicago extravaganza *Aladdin Jr* (1895), Butter-Scotch in his own *Thrilby* (1895), Timiski in *The Goddess of Truth* (1896) and Frimousse in *Le Petit Duc,* both with Lillian Russell, Courte-Botte de Roquencourt in the Cheever Goodwin/Woolson Morse success *Lost, Strayed or Stolen* (1896), Auguste Pompier in *The Girl from Paris* (1896), Lorémois in Daly's revival of *La Poupée* (1898), Ringmaster Drivelli in his revival of *The Circus Girl* (1898), Marquis Imari in his revival of *The Geisha* (1898), Count Berezowski in Alice Nielsen's production of *The Fortune Teller* (USA and London) and Prince Pumpernickel in her *The Singing Girl* (1899). The new century found him as replacement for Dan Daly in *The Rounders* (1900, Duke of Paty de Clam); in Chicago's *The Explorers* (1901), for which he rewrote for himself the character of Burdock Root when taking over part way through the run; in *The Little Duchess* (1901, Maurice), *Mam'selle Napoléon* (1903, Miche), *The West Point Cadet* (1904, Washington Graft) with Della Fox, and Victor Herbert's *It Happened in Nordland* (1904, Duke of Toxen); as Harry Canting in his own *Music Master* burlesque for Lew Fields (1905), Captain Carmona of the Mexican army in *Mexicana* (1906), The Laird o'Finnan Haddock in his own *About Town* alongside his son, Joseph W Herbert jr (1906) and as Toby Blockett in *The Orchid* (1907); in *Fascinating Flora* (1907 t/o), as Lothar in *A Waltz Dream* (1908), pre-Broadway in *The Balkan Princess* (1911), as the Marquis d'Aucuneterre in *Baron Trenck* (1912), in the road-closing *Half Way to Paris* (1912), as Count Buzot in *Oh, I Say!* (1913), in *Lady Luxury* (t/o) and as The Duke of Crowborough (ex-Cambridge) in *Betty* (1916)—before, in 1919, he turned for the last years of his life to acting in films.

Herbert's first work for the stage as an author was a comedy, *After the Ball* (Allentown, Pa, 11 September 1893), which he got produced—with R E Graham and later Dan Daly in the lead—by pretending it was ''from the French,'' and his first as a musical-theatre writer was the text for a piece called *The Birth of Venus* (1895) on which he collaborated with *Erminie* composer Jakobowski. Grace Golden and Cora Tanner starred, but after playing just Baltimore and Philadelphia the piece was shut down to be rewritten by someone else. It never was. He did much better with a *Trilby* burlesque *Thrilby,* which was produced on Broadway in 1895, and he went on to supply a string of burlesques to the Chicago stage and several to the brand new Weber & Fields Broadway house, where his *Geisha* parody topped a hundred nights in 1896–97. Perhaps his most original was an early filmland burlesque, *The Lobsterscope,* ''a new invention in the moving picture line'' produced there in 1897.

He authored a musical play *The Prince of Borneo,* which was staged in three different versions in three different continents under three different titles in search of a ration of success; was lyricist and co-librettist for the Casino Theater's *The Social Whirl* and the revusical *About Town;* wrote adaptations of several Continental Operetten, including *Ein Walzertraum* and the successful Broadway version of *Endlich Allein;* and supplied the text for the Al Jolson vehicle *Honeymoon Express,* whilst also turning out pieces—such as a successful English version of Léon Gandillot's *La Tortue* for Sadie Martinot (1898), for the non-musical stage.

In his later days Herbert also worked as a director, and his credits include the staging of *The Red Feather* (1903, w Max Figman), *Mam'selle Napoléon* (1903), *The West Point* Cadet (1904), the Broadway production of the *King of Cadonia,* the 1910 revival of *The Mikado* and his own adaptation of Albini's *Madame Troubadour* (1910) for the Shuberts, and of the Jerome Kern musicals *The Red Petticoat* (1912) and *Nobody Home* (1915).

He was also seen in several silent films.

Joseph Herbert jr was also seen in the American musical theatre as Count Sherri in *About Town,* Ah Chew in *The Belle of the West* (1905), Lon Anderson in *The Great Decide* (1906), Daniel Frohman in *The Gay White*

Way (1907), Reggie Brewster in *The Echo* (1910), in *Mutt and Jeff* (1912), as Phil Faraday in *The Beauty Shop* (1914), Mr Brewster in *Yes, Yes Yvette* (1927), etc.

1895 **The Birth of Venus, or The Mole and the Model** (Edward Jakobowski) Albaugh's Lyceum Theater, Baltimore 13 February

1895 **Thrilby** (Charles Puerner) Garrick Theater 3 June

1896 **The Art of Maryland** (John Stromberg) 1 act Weber & Fields' Music Hall 5 September

1896 **The Geezer** (Stromberg) 1 act Weber & Fields Music Hall 8 October

1897 **Zenda's King, or The Merry Maidens and the Lords** (W T Francis, W H Glover) Gaiety Theater, Chicago 4 January

1897 **Under the Red Globe** (Stromberg) 1 act Weber & Fields Music Hall 18 February

1897 **The Isle of Gold** (Herman Perlet/Charles A Byrne ad) Olympia Theater 26 April

1897 **Mr New York Esq** (Stromberg, Francis) Weber & Fields's Music Hall 27 April

1898 **Le Rêve** (Max Gabriel) 1 act Koster & Bial's Music Hall 23 May

1898 **Cook's Tour** (Gabriel) Koster & Bial's Music Hall 6 June

1898 **In Gotham** (Gabriel) Koster & Bial's Music Hall 19 September

1899 **The Prince of Borneo** (Edward Jones) Strand Theatre, London 5 October

1901 **The Land of Delft** (Arthur Weld) 1 act Lamb's Gambol, Garrick Theater 29 December; played in *The London Follies* Weber's Theater 17 April 1911

1902 **Tommy Rot** (Safford Waters/w Rupert Hughes, Paul West, Kirk La Shelle) Mrs Osborn's Playhouse 21 October

1902 **Cryris** (Henry Waller) burlesque in *Tommy Rot* Mrs Osborn's Playhouse 21 October

1903 **Mam'selle Napoléon** (Gustave Luders/w Charles Doty) Knickerbocker Theater 8 December

1905 **The Music Master** (burlesque) 1 act in *It Happened in Nordland* (Hans Siegfried Linne) Lew Fields Theater 21 September

1906 **The Social Whirl** (Gustave Kerker/w Doty) Casino Theater 7 April

1906 **About Town** (Melville Ellis, Raymond Hubbell) Herald Square Theater 30 August

1906 **Footlight Favorites** (Alfred Solman/Arthur Lamb) sketch Family Theater, Scranton, Pa 8 October

1907 **Fascinating Flora** (Kerker/w R H Burnside) Casino Theater 20 May

1907 **The Orchid** American adaptation (Herald Square Theater)

1908 **A Waltz Dream** (*Ein Walzertraum*) American version (Broadway Theater)

1908 **Morning, Noon and Night** (Jean Schwartz/William Jerome) Opera House, Hartford, Conn 31 August; Yorkville Theater 5 October

1909 **The Beauty Spot** revised *The Prince of Borneo* with music by Reginald De Koven Herald Square Theater 10 April

1909 **The Golden Widow** (Melville Gideon, Louis A Hirsch, Jerome D Kern/ad Glen MacDonough) Belasco Theater, Washington, DC 26 October

1910 **Madame Troubadour** English version (Lyric Theater)

1911 **The Duchess** (ex- *The Rose Shop, Mlle Rosita*) (Victor Herbert/w H B Smith) Shubert Theater, Boston 20 March; Lyric Theater 16 October

1913 **The Honeymoon Express** (Schwartz/w Harold Atteridge) Winter Garden 6 February

1915 **Nobody's Home** (*Mr Popple of Ippleton*) American adaptation of English libretto (Princess Theater)

1915 **Alone at Last** (*Endlich allein*) English version w Edgar Smith (Shubert Theater)

1916 **Husbands Guaranteed** (August Kleinecke) Rochester, NY 30 November

1920 **Honeydew** (aka *What's the Odds*) (Ephraim Zimbalist) Casino Theater 6 September

1922 **Sue Dear** (Frank Grey/Bide Dudley/w Dudley, C S Montayne) Times Square Theater 10 July

HERBERT, Victor [August] (b Dublin, 1 February 1859; d New York, 24 May 1924). The most substantial and versatile composer for the Broadway musical stage of the early 20th century.

The grandson of Samuel Lover, the novelist, portrait painter and author of such Irish songs as "The Low-backed Car," "Rory O'More" and "Molly Bawn" and of several pieces of musical theatre (*The Happy Man, Il Paddy Whack in Italia*), Herbert was born in Dublin, but brought up and educated in Germany. He began his musical career as an orchestral 'cellist, and became a member of the Court Orchestra in Stuttgart, but in 1886 he left Germany for America, where his wife, vocalist Therese Förster, had secured a contract at the Metropolitan Opera House. Herbert worked in New York as a 'cellist at first at the Metropolitan and then elsewhere, as musical director at Koster & Bial's (1887) and with Locke's American Opera Company (1887), before making himself a place in the musical world as a popular conductor of classical works and a bandmaster. In 1894 he became Regimental Bandmaster of the 22nd Regiment Band, New York.

Herbert's earliest compositions were in the form of classical and light classical orchestral and instrumental works, and, although he contributed pieces of music to Charles Hoyt's musical play *The Midnight Bell* and other such shows, it was some time before he turned his attentions to the musical theatre. His first extended lyric work was, in fact, an oratorio, *The Captive.* His initial full score for the musical theatre, the comic opera *La Vivandière,* was submitted to Lillian Russell, but it was rejected and never performed. Thus it was the composer's second effort, *Prince Ananias,* produced in 1894 by the Boston Ideal Opera Company and played in their repertoire in that Broadway season (55 performances) that introduced him to the New York stage. Having arrived on Broadway, Herbert and his music were rarely long away from its theatres during the rest of his considerable career.

Over the next 30 years Herbert composed a long list of musical scores for the theatre, scores ranging from burlesque to romantic operetta and to the lighthearted dance-and-song pieces that subsequently became the popular musical theatre fodder. He scored a number of fine successes, but also a large number of flops—flops which were, it must be emphasized, not always such because of any lack in their musical content. In the process (and also in hindsight) he became regarded as the most important figure in Broadway's composing fraternity in the first decades of the 20th century.

After the modest beginnings made with *Prince Ananias* (which nevertheless remained three seasons in The Bostonians repertoire and was given more than 300 performances in all) Herbert quickly found success when his next work, the burlesque comic opera *The Wizard of the Nile* (''Star Light, Star Bright''), was given a fine 105 performances on Broadway. It went on to productions in Britain and on the Continent—a rare thing for an American work of the period—and to a revival in New York. It was an impressive beginning, but the international record compiled by *The Wizard of the Nile* was one which, amazingly, none of Herbert's later shows would ever equal. In spite of occasional showings abroad, even his greatest successes in the musical theatre were successes only within the United States.

A farcical piece called *The Gold Bug* foundered in a week on Broadway, and favorite soprano Camille D'Arville's self-starring production of his *Peg Woffington* failed to make it that far, collapsing in Philadelphia before its scheduled opening, but in the same year, 1897, Herbert scored his second important success with the romantic comic opera *The Serenade* (''I Love Thee, I Adore Thee''), again produced by the Bostonians. This more musically substantial work was followed by two further pieces which had good lives—another burlesquey vehicle for *The Wizard of the Nile* star, Frank Daniels, called *The Idol's Eye* (''The Tattooed Man''), and a piece commissioned by *Serenade* star, Alice Nielsen, with which to launch her own company. *The Fortune Teller* (''Slumber On, My Little Gypsy Sweetheart'') served Miss Nielsen well in America and in a season in London's West End, and confirmed its composer's now pre-eminent position in American comic opera.

Herbert's rate of writing thereafter became demential. In a period of little more than seven months in 1899–1900 he had four new works premiered. It was, perhaps, a salutory warning that none came near the best of his earliest pieces in popularity. An attempt to wed comic opera and burlesque in a version of *Cyrano de Bergerac* for Francis Wilson and Lulu Glaser was a 28-performance flop, but another piece for Miss Nielsen, *The Singing Girl,* while not coming up to the standard of

Plate 172. **Victor Herbert**

The Serenade or *The Fortune Teller,* served its star for a while in New York (77 performances) and on the road. A fresh work for Daniels, this time cast as *The Ameer,* did better on tour than in New York, and *The Viceroy,* another piece written for the Bostonians, also had an indifferent life.

After this burst of composing activity Herbert disappeared from the bills for a while, fulfilling a three-season contract as conductor of the Pittsburgh Symphony Orchestra and of a season at Chicago's Grand Opera House. He did not return to Broadway until 1903, when he was commissioned to provide the score for a grandiose musical extravaganza produced by Julian Mitchell and Fred Hamlin. *Babes in Toyland* was a fairy-tale spectacular which was designed specifically as a Broadway entertainment and not, like virtually every other one of Herbert's works to date, as a vehicle for a touring company or star. Lavishly staged, as a successor to the producers' previous *The Wizard of Oz,* it turned out to be a splendid success, and Herbert's score rendered up several pieces which have long remained popular in America (The March of the Toys, ''I Can't Do the Sum,'' ''Toyland'').

The comic opera *Babette,* with ex-opera star Fritzi Scheff starred in its title role, won only 55 Broadway performances, but Herbert scored a fresh success the following year with another commission from Hamlin and Mitchell (teamed this time with producer-star Lew Fields), when he composed the score for the Ruritanian musical comedy *It Happened in Nordland* (''Absinthe frappé''). It ran long into 1905, joined by two further Herbert shows, *Miss Dolly Dollars* and another fairytale piece which had started out in Chicago as *Alice and the Eight Princesses* but which reached Broadway, with Alice having been excised from the action and seven new songs shoved in, as *Wonderland* (73 performances). Both of these had only a moderate New York run, but a regular touring life. This time the high rate of activity to which he had returned did not seem to have any adverse effect on the quality of Herbert's scores. His third new work of 1905, again a vehicle for Fritzi Scheff, cast her as *Mlle Modiste* (''Kiss Me Again,'' ''I Want What I Want When I Want It'') with great success, whilst his first score of 1906, written for a blatantly low comedy musical, as opposed to the Frenchified light opérette of the previous show, brought him an equally fine success in *The Red Mill* (''Moonbeams,'' ''The Streets of New York,'' ''Every Day Is Ladies' Day with Me''). Each of these two very differently flavored pieces remained a favorite for decades in America, and the two proved themselves to be amongst the most durable of Herbert's works.

It was, however, a few years and rather more shows before such success came again. Herbert continued to turn out scores of all kinds, ranging through a rather classy burlesque on *Lohengrin* (*The Magic Knight*) for Joe Weber, a free-wheeling bit of low comedy for Daniels (*The Tattooed Man*), a farce comedy starring Emma Carus (*Too Near Home*), a spectacular children's show based on the comic strip *Little Nemo,* a fine romantic musical score (''Rose of the World'') to the underloved comic opera *Algeria* (later *The Rose of Algeria*), a disappointing *The Prima Donna* for Fritzi Scheff, and a short-lived Lew Fields dialect comedy show, *Old Dutch,* without notching up another major hit. In 1910, however, he hit the heights once more when he provided a score for another refugee from the world of opera, Emma Trentini, as *Naughty Marietta.* The show scored a fine success in America, and its title and songs (''Ah! Sweet Mystery of Life,'' '''Neath the Southern Moon,'' ''I'm Falling in Love with Someone,'' ''Tramp! Tramp! Tramp!,'' etc) later won worldwide recognition with the aid of the cinema.

Herbert kept up a resolute and regular output through the 1910s. The light musical comedy *When Sweet Sixteen* proved to be more to the taste of the provinces than the city, but *The Duchess,* another piece modeled around Fritzi Scheff, and of which enough was expected to have it tried out in a copyright performance at London's Ladbroke Hall (as *The Rose Shop*), went through out-of-town agonies as its star abandoned ship before Broadway proffered its thumbs down. *The Enchantress* (''The Land of My Own Romance,'' ''I Want to Be a Prima Donna'') also played only a medium season on Broadway (72 performances) but, like several other Herbert shows with similar metropolitan records, it lived out a good and highly profitable life on the touring circuits, where in most years several of the composer's works could be seen and heard, going round the country for the first, second, third or umpteenth time.

The composer's voluminous and ever-rebounding career soon brought forth a number of further successes. Montgomery and Stone, whom Herbert had served so well in *The Red Mill,* had a fine run with the Cinderella tale of *The Lady of the Slipper,* and another Ruritanian operetta, *Sweethearts* (''Sweethearts''), in spite of a cute, confused and confusing libretto, played 136 performances in New York and proved to have more staying power than some of Herbert's other and better pieces in the same vein. *The Madcap Duchess,* accounted a little too musically ambitious by some, failed to catch on, but the musical comedy *The Only Girl,* composed to an adaptation of Ludwig Fulda's *Jugendfreude* done by Herbert's most appreciable collaborator, Henry Blossom, gave him one of the longest Broadway runs of his career (240 performances) as well as one of his rare British productions.

Herbert paired with Blossom again for the pretty *The Princess Pat* (''Love Is Best of All''), the Ziegfeld revue *The Century Girl* (w Irving Berlin), the Irish light opera *Eileen,* and a version of a Frederick Jackson farce, *A Full House,* which had started out in Boston with a score by Uda Waldrop and the title *She Took a Chance,* but ultimately arrived in New York as Herbert's *The Velvet Lady.* From this group *Eileen* brought him the most praise, for its pretty Irishy melodies and superior concerted music. He worked on a second Ziegfeld revue, *Miss 1917,* but several other pieces to which he provided music proved poor stuff, and the resultant shows had short Broadway lives. In 1920, for only the second time in nearly 30 years of composing, a Victor Herbert show closed on the road. The small-scale *Oui, Madame,* announced as the show which would revive the George Edwardes kind of musical, underwent some last-minute efforts to gussy it up to more conventional proportions with Ned Wayburn girls, glitz and dances when its producers lost their ''small-scale'' nerve, but it still went under without making Broadway.

His 1919 *Angel Face,* a curious modern musical comedy with a plot about monkey glands, had to fight its way to some kind of success through strikes and lockouts, but there was a real disappointment when Fred de Grésac made over her elegant play *La Passerelle* as what should have been an ideal Herbert libretto. *Orange Blossoms* (1922, ''A Kiss in the Dark''), the last Herbert musical produced in his lifetime, played only 95 times in New York. The composer was represented once more, posthumously, on Broadway when *The Dream Girl,* a musical version of the reincarnation play *The Road to Yesterday,* played 117 performances for the Shuberts without establishing itself or its songs amongst Herbert's best.

Amongst Herbert's other dramatic compositions were two operas, *Natoma* (1911) and *Madeleine* (1914), and incidental music for the accompaniment of silent films.

The popularity ultimately won throughout the English-speaking world by the songs from *Naughty Marietta* would seem to indicate that Herbert's music should have had an appeal reaching beyond America, but apart from *The Wizard of the Nile,* Miss Nielsen's touring season of *The Serenade,* two unsuccessful attempts at *The Red Mill,* a production of *The Only Girl* and a handful of performances of *Angel Face,* the only Victor Herbert score to have been heard in London's West End was a musical mélange of *The Serenade* and *The Fortune Teller,* originally produced on America's west coast as *Gypsy Lady* (George Forrest, Robert Wright/Henry Myers, Century Theater 17 September 1946), which briefly played on Broadway, and in Britain as *Romany Love.*

Australia proved no more enthusiastic—although *The Fortune Teller* was given a brief showing there—and only *The Wizard of the Nile* seems to have penetrated into Europe. It must remain a mystery why Broadway's acknowledgedly most appreciable, versatile and prolific composer of the turn-of-the century years failed to ''travel,'' leaving what overseas laurels there were to be won and the position of international flagbearer for the era's American musical stage to the less appreciable Gustave Kerker and his loose-limbed *Belle of New York.*

A Hollywood film, *The Great Victor Herbert* (1939), which had little or nothing to do with the composer or his life story, had Walter Connolly starred as Herbert.

1894 **Prince Ananias** (Francis Neilson) Broadway Theater 20 November

1895 **The Wizard of the Nile** (H B Smith) Casino Theater 4 November

1896 **The Gold Bug** (Glen MacDonough) Casino Theater 21 September

1897 **The Serenade** (H B Smith) Knickerbocker Theater 16 March

1897 **Peg Woffington** (H B Smith) Lyceum, Scranton, Pa, 18 October

1897 **The Idol's Eye** (H B Smith) Broadway Theater 25 October

1898 **The Fortune Teller** (H B Smith) Wallack's Theater 26 September

1899 **Hula-Lula** (L J B Lincoln) 1 act Fifth Avenue Theatre (Lamb's Club Gambol) May

1899 **Cyrano de Bergerac** (H B Smith/Stuart Reed) Knickerbocker Theater 18 September

1899 **The Ameer** (Frederick Ranken/Kirk La Shelle) Scranton, Pa 9 October; Wallack's Theater 4 December

1899 **The Singing Girl** (H B Smith/Stanislaus Stange) Casino Theater 23 October

1900 **The Viceroy** (H B Smith) Columbia Theater, San Francisco 12 February; Knickerbocker Theater 13 March

1903 **Babes in Toyland** (MacDonough) Majestic Theater 13 October

1903 **Babette** (H B Smith) Broadway Theater 16 November

1904 **It Happened in Nordland** (MacDonough) Lew Fields Theater 5 December

1905 **Miss Dolly Dollars** (H B Smith) Knickerbocker Theater 4 September

1905 **Alice and the Eight Dancing Princesses** (MacDonough) Star Theater, Buffalo 14 September; Grand Opera House, Chicago 18 September

1905 **Wonderland** (revised *Alice and the Eight Dancing Princesses*) (MacDonough) Majestic Theater 24 October

1905 **Mlle Modiste** (Henry Blossom) Knickerbocker Theater 25 December

1906 **The Red Mill** (Blossom) Knickerbocker Theater 24 September

1906 **The Dream City** (Edgar Smith) Weber's Music Hall 25 December

1906 **The Magic Knight** (E Smith) Weber's Music Hall 25 December

1907 **Too Near Home** (MacDonough) Walnut Street Theater, Philadelphia 7 January

1907 **The Tattooed Man** (H B Smith, A N C Fowler) Criterion Theater 18 February

1907 **The Song Birds** (George V Hobart) 1 act Lambs' Club; New York Theater in *The Land of Nod* 1 April; Alhambra 2 September

1907 **Miss Camille** (Hobart) 1 act Lamb's Club 14 April; Shubert Theater, Newark 21 October

1908 **Algeria** (MacDonough) Broadway Theater 31 August

1908 **Little Nemo** (H B Smith) New Amsterdam Theater 20 October

1908 **The Prima Donna** (Blossom) Studebaker Theater, Chicago 5 October; Knickerbocker Theater 30 November

1909 **The Rose of Algeria** (revised *Algeria*) Herald Square Theater 20 September

1909 **Old Dutch** (E Smith/Hobart) Herald Square Theater 22 November

1910 **Naughty Marietta** (Rida Johnson Young) New York Theater 7 November

1910 **When Sweet Sixteen** (Hobart) Court Square, Springfield, Mass 28 November; Daly's Theater, New York 14 September 1911

1911 **The Duchess** (Joseph Herbert/H B Smith) Shubert Theater, Boston 20 March; Lyric Theater 16 October

1911 **The Enchantress** (H B Smith/Fred de Gresac) New York Theater 19 October

1912 **The Lady of the Slipper** (James O'Dea/Anne Caldwell, Lawrence McCarthy) Globe Theater 28 October

1912 **The Village Blacksmith** (Hobart) 1 act Lambs' Club 29 December

1913 **Sweethearts** (R B Smith/de Gresac, H B Smith) Academy of Music, Baltimore 24 March; New Amsterdam Theater, New York 8 September

1913 **The Madcap Duchess** (Justin Huntly McCarthy, David Stevens) Pittsburgh, Pa 15 September (as *The Coquette*); Globe Theater 11 November

1914 **The Only Girl** (Blossom) 39th Street Theater 2 November

1914 **The Débutante** (R B Smith, H B Smith) New Nixon Theater, Atlantic City 21 September; Knickerbocker Theater 7 December

1915 **The Princess Pat** (Blossom) Cort Theater 29 September

1917 **Eileen** (ex- *Hearts of Erin*) (Blossom) Shubert Theater 19 March

1917 **Her Regiment** (William Le Baron) Broadhurst Theater 12 November

1919 **The Velvet Lady** (Blossom) New Amsterdam Theater 3 February

1919 **Angel Face** (R B Smith/H B Smith) Knickerbocker Theater 30 December

1920 **My Golden Girl** (Frederic Arnold Kummer) Nora Bayes Theater 2 February

1920 **Oui, Madame** (R B Smith/''G M Wright'') Little Theater, Philadelphia 22 March

1920 **The Girl in the Spotlight** (ex- *The Miracle Maid*) (''Richard Bruce,'' ie, R B Smith) Knickerbocker Theater 12 July

1922 **Orange Blossoms** (B G de Sylva/de Grésac) Fulton Theater 19 September

1924 **The Dream Girl** (Young, Harold Atteridge) Ambassadors Theater 20 August

Biographies: Waters, E N: *Victor Herbert: A Life in Music* (Macmillan, New York, 1955), Kaye, J: *Victor Herbert* (G Howard Watt, New York, 1931)

HERE COMES THE BRIDE Musical farcical comedy in 2 acts by Robert P Weston and Bert Lee adapted from an original by Otto Harbach and Edgar McGregor. Lyrics by Desmond Carter. Music by Arthur Schwartz. Opera House, Blackpool, 7 October 1929; Piccadilly Theatre, London, 20 February 1930.

Here Comes the Bride was producer Julian Wylie's attempt—in the wake of the British success of his botched American musical comedy *Merry, Merry*—to manufacture his own American musical in the British provinces. He purchased an unproduced (American) screenplay which had been turned into an unproduced (American) play (but which had strong reminiscences of a certain French musical comedy) from American writers Otto Harbach and Edgar McGregor, had it turned into a libretto by the English adaptors of *Merry, Merry,* and equipped it with a set of new and nearly new songs composed by the young American songwriter Arthur Schwartz.

Rich Mexican Maria (Maria Minetti) will inherit even more money if she is still Mrs Tile at the end of a certain period. Having split with her husband, she pays well to wed impoverished and dejected Frederick Tile (Clifford Mollison) who has, apparently irrevocably, been forbidden to wed his beloved Kitty (Jean Colin). But Kitty defies her daddy, turns up in time to take part in a lot of farcical now-you-wed-me-now-you-don't action, and everything ends up being resolved when the original Mr Tile turns up to claim back his wife. The songs which lightly accompanied all the action included one, ''High and Low,'' sung by Miss Colin and Mollison, which would remain one of its composer's popular favorites.

After a four-month tour Wylie's production was taken to London, where it lasted a reasonable to good 175 performances at the Piccadilly Theatre and the Lyceum (26 May).

A different musical, entitled with less comprehensible grammar *Here Goes the Bride,* written by Peter Arno and with music by Edward Heyman, John W Green and Richard Myers, was a quick fold at Broadway's 46th Street Theater in 1931 (3 November).

HERE'S HOWE Musical comedy in 2 acts by Fred Thompson and Paul Gerard Smith. Lyrics by Irving Caesar. Music by Roger Wolfe Kahn and Joseph Meyer. Broadhurst Theater, New York, 1 May 1928.

Aarons and Freedley sponsored the production of this slightly unusual piece, which told the tale of one Joyce (Irene Delroy), a secretary who is encouraged by her boyfriend (Allen Kearns) to accept her boss's offer to accompany him on a world trip. When Joyce gets to Havana, she finds her Billy is there having lots of luck as a gambler. The two of them ultimately end up back where they started, still dreaming of a rosy future, but with a bit of colorful past behind them.

The one bit of *Here's Howe* which lasted beyond its 71 Broadway performances was the song ''Crazy Rhythm,'' introduced by June O'Dea, Peggy Chamberlain and Ben Bernie. The rest of the show did not make London, but the song did, interpolated into the 1928 show *Lucky Girl.*

HERE'S LOVE Musical in 2 acts by Meredith Willson based on *Miracle on 34th Street* by Valentine Davies and the screenplay therefrom by George Seaton. Shubert Theater, New York, 3 October 1963.

What happens when Macy's department-store Santa Claus falls down, incapable, just before the big parade, and personnel's Doris Walker (Janis Paige) hires an ideal looking replacement (Laurence Naismith) who just happens to be . . . Santa Claus? He spreads goodwill more extravagantly than seems real, helps get rid of the store's impossible surplus stock of plastic alligators by pure bonhomie, gets into all sorts of modern mix-ups and ends up besting a prosecuting District Attorney (Larry Douglas) who doesn't believe in Santa Claus, but whose little boy does. Valerie Hall played little Susan Walker, daughter of the personnel lady, who befriends lawyer Fred Gailly (Craig Stevens), who defends Santa and wins Doris.

Santa and the little girl sang of "Pine Trees and Holly Berries," Susan and her mum got on "Arm in Arm," and R H Macy (Paul Reed) sang a eulogy to the jolly man in red in "That Man Over There" in a score and show which mixed warmth and spectacle in well-judged doses for 338 performances.

The show was revived at the Goodspeed Opera House in 1991 (2 October).

Santa Claus was also the hero of the English musical *The Merry Gentleman* (Julian Slade/Dorothy Reynolds, Theatre Royal, Bristol 24 December 1953) and of the German musical *Santa Claus* (Bernd Stromberg, Stadthalle, Rostock 5 December 1996).

Recording: original cast (Columbia)

HERMAN, Jerry [HERMAN, Gerald] (b New York, 10 July 1933). Highly successful Broadway songwriter with a winningly popular touch.

Born in New York, brought up in Jersey City and schooled in Florida, Herman was at first orientated towards a career as a designer and architect but, whilst studying at New York's Parsons School of Design, he changed direction and moved on to take a theatre course at the University of Miami. There he wrote several stage shows, one of which, the revue *I Feel Wonderful,* gave him his first professional credit when it was reproduced at the off-Broadway Theater de Lys for a run of 49 performances.

In the years that followed, Herman wrote special material and individual songs for artists including Jane Froman and Hermione Gingold and for Tallulah Bankhead's *Welcome Darlings,* as well as supplying the songs for two further off-Broadway revues, *Nightcap* (1958) and *Parade* (1960, also director). The latter was produced by Lawrence Kasha, who simultaneously announced that he would produce Herman's first full-scale Broadway musical, *Spirit of the Chase. Spirit of the Chase* did not eventuate, but the following year Herman's first Broadway show did appear, under the banner of producer Gerald Oestreicher. *Milk and Honey* had an upbeat modern Israeli setting, a story about middle-aged love, and a warmly attractive and effective score, and it proved a fine first-up success for its composer. Whilst it built up a 543-performance run on Broadway, another Herman musical, the off-Broadway *Madame Aphrodite,* came and went in an unobtrusive 13 performances.

In 1964 Herman's second Broadway musical was produced, and it easily outran his not negligible first. In fact, *Hello, Dolly!,* Michael Stewart's musicalized version of *The Matchmaker* with Carol Channing starring as Mrs Dolly Levi, easily outran any and every Broadway musical up to that time in a first run of 2,844 performances. It also walked off with the season's Tony Award, and spread itself around the world to become one of the half-dozen major international classics of the modern Broadway stage, while its title song became first a hit and then a standard.

One extravagant leading lady followed another as Dolly Levi was succeeded on to the musical stage, with further great success, by *Mame.* Angela Lansbury personified the musical version of Patrick Dennis's much-portrayed Auntie at the top of a long Broadway run prior to Ginger Rogers taking up the relay at London's Theatre Royal, Drury Lane, and before *Mame* ("Mame," "If He Walked into My Life," "My Best Girl," "Bosom Buddies") went on to several other international productions.

After three fine hits in a row, things went rather less well for Herman for a number of years. An attempt to turn the winsomely unworldly old heroine of Giraudoux's *The Madwoman of Chaillot* into a further starring role for Lansbury saw Herman reaching out beyond the effectively straightforward songwriting of his earlier scores towards some characterful solos and interesting ensemble writing, but the public did not take to the more complex central character of *Dear World* as they had to the straightforwardly out-front ladies of the earlier shows, and the show lasted only 132 Broadway performances. *Mack and Mabel,* the filmland story of the unpleasant Mack Sennett and the foolish Mabel Normand, lasted even less time (66 performances) but, unlike *Dear World,* it left behind several numbers which, after some diligent plugging, became popular with theatrical folk, in particular ("I Won't Send Roses," "Look What Happened to Mabel," "Time Heals Everything," "Wherever He Ain't"), and resulted in several attempts at reviving the show. *The Grand Tour,* a musical *Jacobowsky and the Colonel* proved the shortest lived of all its composer's Broadway shows (61 performances) and left no reusable parts behind.

Following this run of by no means unmitigated (commercial) failures, Herman again connected with success when he contributed some additional numbers to the score of the British revue-musical *A Day in Hollywood—A Night in the Ukraine* (as he had earlier done for the 1964 *Ben Franklin in Paris*), and even more extensively in 1983 with a musical version of the popular French play and film *La Cage aux Folles* (Tony Award, "I Am Who I Am," "Song on the Sand"). Gene Barry and George Hearn played out the crises which sweep down upon the ménage who run and perform in the Riviera nightclub "La Cage aux Folles" through a Broadway run of 1,761 performances, and the show went on to win more overseas productions than virtually any other Broadway musical of its period, running up a record second, of the composer's works, only—for the moment—to the inexhaustible *Hello, Dolly!*

In 1996 he composed the songs for the television musical show *Mrs Santa Claus* (CBS 8 December 1996).

Herman's shows have produced a good number of take-out songs which have become popular material in the cabaret and concert world, and many of these, with the notable exception of "Hello, Dolly," which was growled and gurgled up the charts by Louis Armstrong, have been habitually performed (if not necessarily written) in the one, same late-night idiom. "If He Walked into My Life," "Time Heals Everything," "Wherever He Ain't" and their fellows and, most recently and extravagantly, *La Cage aux Folles*'s "I Am Who I Am" have been blazed into liberally by ladies no longer young but still strong-lunged. It was no surprise, given this, that when a compilation show made up of numbers from Herman's works was produced in 1985, its cast was entirely feminine. *Jerry's Girls* ran 141 performances at New York's St James Theater, had several successful productions, under the management of John Frost, in Australia, and was later also seen on the Continent. A second compilation, *An Evening with Jerry Herman*—a version of Herman's nightclub act—was played at Booth's Theater (28 July 1998) with the songwriter taking part for 28 performances, and a third *The Best of Times* was played in London in the same year (Bridewell Theater, Vaudeville Theatre).

1961 **Milk and Honey** (Don Appell) Martin Beck Theater 10 October

1961 **Madame Aphrodite** (Tad Mosel) Orpheum Theater 29 December

1964 **Hello, Dolly!** (Michael Stewart) St James Theater 16 January

1966 **Mame** (Jerome Lawrence, Robert E Lee) Winter Garden Theater 24 May

1969 **Dear World** (Lawrence, Lee) Mark Hellinger Theater 6 February

1974 **Mack and Mabel** (Stewart) Majestic Theater 6 October

1979 **The Grand Tour** (Stewart, Mark Bramble) Palace Theater 11 January

1983 **La Cage aux Folles** (Harvey Fierstein) Palace Theater 21 August

Autobiography: (w Stasio) *Showtune* (DIF Books, New York, 1996)

HERMECKE, Hermann (b Magdeburg, 29 May 1892; d Oberaudorf, 15 October 1961).

At first an actor, Dresden-based Hermecke then became a stage writer, scoring his first success with the musical comedy *Liebe in der Lerchengasse,* produced in Magdeburg in 1936. He subsequently paired with composer Nico Dostal to turn out five pieces, including the prewar *Monika* and *Die ungarische Hochzeit,* and *Doktor Eisenbart,* written after Hermecke's return to (East) Germany after the War, each of which found some success, principally in Germany.

1934 **Venezia** (Arno Vetterling) Deutsches Grenzland Theater, Görlitz 18 November

1936 **Die Dorothee** (Vetterling) Stadttheater, Fürth 18 April

1936 **Liebe in der Lerchengasse** (Vetterling, Heinrich Strecker) Magdeburg 31 December

1937 **Monika** (Nico Dostal) Staatstheater, Stuttgart 3 October

1939 **Die ungarische Hochzeit** (Dostal) Staatstheater, Stuttgart 4 February

1939 **Das Mädchen aus der Fremde** (Vetterling) Opernhaus, Nuremberg 23 October

1940 **Die Flucht ins Glück** (Dostal) Staatstheater, Stuttgart 22 December

1942 **Die Erntebraut** (new version) Opernhaus, Chemnitz 3 May

1949 **Die Rosenhochzeit** (Eva Engelhardt) Stadttheater, Bautzen 3 June

1950 **Zirkusblut** (Dostal) Volksbühne, Leipzig 3 March

1952 **Doktor Eisenbart** (Dostal) Opernhaus, Nuremberg 29 March

1957 **Der ideale Geliebte** (Gerhard Winkler) Städtische Bühne, Nuremberg-Fürth 5 March

HERVÉ [RONGER, Louis Auguste Joseph Florimond] (b Houdain, 30 June 1825; d Paris, 3 November 1892).

Florimond Ronger, known to the musical and theatrical world simply as Hervé, was one of the great characters in, and one of the moving influencers and inspirers of the course of, the French and world musical theatre in the 19th century. It was he who was at the root of the tradition of opéra-bouffe which developed in France in the mid-19th century, as an author, a composer, as a theatre manager and even, on a variety of occasions, as a performer. And, in a career which included more than the regulation amounts of ups and downs, he was still around more than 30 years on to take a significant part in an important wave of wholly different musical plays, the vaudevilles or musical comedies produced at the Théâtre des Variétés in the late 1870s and early 1880s, a series which gave their composer a second and highly popular "tour du monde" of successes.

Born in the Pas de Calais near Arras, the son of a French gendarme and his Spanish wife, Hervé lost his father at the age of 10. His mother moved to Paris, and there the child became a choirboy at Saint-Roch whilst following a regular course of musical studies, which allowed him, as a young teenager, to become organist at the chapel of the mental asylum at Bicêtre. During his time in this post he began to work musically with the asylum's inmates, setting up an orchestra and, in 1842, writing a little opérette, *L'Ours et le pacha,* based on the popular vaudeville by Scribe and Saintine, for his pupils to perform. He subsequently became organist at Saint-Eustache and also, around the same time, made his first appearances on the professional stage, working as a comedian and vocalist in several of Paris's suburban theatres.

In 1848 Hervé the performer, the writer and the composer concurrently made their first notable appearance on the Parisian stage when the young man wrote, composed and played in a little two-handed saynète devised as an occasional piece for the short, stout actor Désiré, and his tall, gangling self in the roles of a burlesque Sancho Panza and Don Quixote. *Don Quichotte et Sancho Pança,* played subsequently for a run at Adolphe Adam's Théâtre National, has been generally quoted, in retrospect, as being the starting point for the new French musical theatre tradition.

Hervé, still doubling as church organist and theatrical writer and performer, went on to appointments as chef d'orchestre at, respectively, the Odéon and the Palais-Royal. There he duly turned out a number of other little musical playlets—variously described in such terms as vaudeville-opérette, parodie-opérette or opérette-bouffe—and of wordless pantomimes to be played on the composite programs which made up the habitual bills at those houses. It was, however, his burlesque (''fantaisie bouffe'') *Les Folies dramatiques,* an extravagant five-act parody of all things theatrical which had a strong flavor of the topical revue about it, which gave him his first important impetus. The show aroused the interest of the powerful and stage-struck Duc de Morny, and in consequence Hervé was offered a position under royal patronage. He asked, instead, for permission to operate a theatre, and as a result the Folies-Concertantes (soon renamed the Folies-Nouvelles) was opened under his management in the Faubourg du Temple in 1854.

Hervé himself was the main supplier of the quickly turning-over repertoire played at his little theatre, writing and/or composing more than 30 short musical playlets, pochades, vaudevilles and pantomimes during the first three years of his operation. However, he also encouraged and mounted works by other composers, amongst whom the young Jacques Offenbach—in whose early *Oyayaye* Hervé took the travesty title role—and Léo Delibes, whose music the manager interpreted in such pieces as the little two-hander *Deux sous de charbon* (Bigarreau), were prominent. Hervé took part, in fact, in a large number of his own productions, playing opposite Joseph Kelm in the title role of the ''autobiographical'' *Le Compositeur toqué* (Fignolet), and in such other little pieces as *La Belle Espagnole* and *La Fine Fleur de l'Andalousie.*

Plate 173. **Hervé.** *The man who started the whole thing.*

In 1858 the multiple workload became too much for the producer-house author-star performer of the Folies-Nouvelles. Hervé fell ill and had to leave his theatre. He went abroad, touring around, taking employment where he could and would, and spending some time as musical director to the theatre in Cairo, before finally returning to Paris to take up posts first as musical director at the Eldorado, where he turned his hand to supplying the vast number of songs needed for the ever-changing programs of a café-concert, and then at the Délassements-Comiques, for which he composed a further run of the musical playlets and scenes which he had favored at the Folies-Nouvelles.

During Hervé's absence, however, the musical theatre in Paris had taken strides ahead. Offenbach had produced his famous full-length opéra-bouffe, *Orphée aux enfers,* and in 1864, whilst the Théâtre des Variétés mounted Hervé's winning one-act *Le Joueur de flûte,* they also premiered Offenbach's sensational three-act *La Belle Hélène.* Hervé, whilst still continuing his parallel career as a performer, soon followed Offenbach into the field of the full-length opéra-bouffe. His mock-Arthurian *Les Chevaliers de la table ronde,* composed to a text by Chivot and Duru, eased him into the genre with a medium ration of success, and the following year he topped it with a loopy burlesque of *William Tell, Robin Hood* and of anything else in flight, for which he himself supplied the text. *L'Oeil crevé* scored a major success in Paris and was soon exported around the world.

Chilpéric, the next year, saw Hervé, the librettist and the composer, in his very top form. This burlesque of things medieval won him a second triumph, compounded this time by a triumph as a performer, for Hervé himself starred in the title role of his thoroughly crazy opéra-bouffe, introducing the famous horseback Chanson du Jambon and the dippily echanting Butterfly Song in his character as the mad Merovingian monarch. His third major work, *Le Petit Faust,* came out only months later. Once more, Hervé the composer and Hervé the actor—appearing here in the dual role of the young and the aged Faust—scored a major hit, and *Le Petit Faust* proved to be internationally the most popular of all his pieces to date. Offenbach—who had turned out *Barbe-bleue, La Vie parisienne* and *La Grande-Duchesse de Gérolstein* in the same period—and Hervé were now at the peak of their glory, and the Parisian stage was the center of the musical-theatre world.

Adolphe Jaime and Hector Crémieux, the librettists of *Le Petit Faust,* supplied Hervé with the text for the less successful *Les Turcs,* but this time Hervé did not appear in his show, for he made his way across the Channel to Britain and there, as the Franco-Prussian war raged at home, he introduced London to English versions of, first, *Chilpéric* and then *Le Petit Faust.* London was stunned by *Chilpéric* (with Hervé starred), rather less by *Le Petit Faust* (in which he decided not to play), and opéra-bouffe in its genuine shape and form was launched on the English-language stage.

Hervé stayed several years in Britain, during which time he not only appeared as Roland in London's performances of *Le Chevalier de la table* ronde (Gaiety, 1871), in *Le Compositeur toqué* and eventually as Faust in a production of *Le Petit Faust,* but also turned his composing talents to supplying the emerging British opéra-bouffe with one of its earliest substantial scores in the Gaiety Theatre's parody of the Aladdin tale, *Aladdin II.* He also contributed musically to the vast spectacle that was Dion Boucicault's *Babil and Bijou* at Covent Garden, and to the Covent Garden pantomime of 1870, *The Sleeping Beauty, or Harlequin and the Spiteful Fairy* (w Betjemann/Gilbert a' Beckett, C H Ross). At the same time, however, the indefatigable writer continued to hold up a presence in Paris, where another extravagantly burlesque piece, the Scottish saga *Le Trône d'Écosse (et la difficulté de s'asseoir dessus),* had a fairly successful run.

After Hervé's postwar return to Paris, things went, at first, rather less well. The end of the Empire had more or less spelled the end of opéra-bouffe and its crazy follies, and Hervé's surreal, imaginative style was no longer what the public demanded. His *La Veuve du Malabar,* with Hortense Schneider starred, and *Alice de Nevers,* in which he himself took the role of the Prince de Ferrare alongside Milher, Marie Périer and Marie Desclauzas, were not successes, and if Hortense Schneider's impersonation of *La Belle Poule* and *La Marquise des rues* (68 Paris performances and an Hungarian showing as *Az utszéli grófkisasszony*) did a little better, it seemed that the composer had now passed his most popular days. When he again took to the stage as an actor in one of someone else's shows, it was in a prewar piece, in the role of Jupiter in Offenbach's revival of his early *Orphée aux enfers* (Gaîté, 1878).

However, renewed success arrived before the end of the decade. The Théâtre des Variétés had enjoyed a great triumph with the vaudeville-opérette *Niniche,* with Anna Judic starred in its oversized title role and a ''pont neuf'' score put together by Marius Boullard. Manager Bertrand decided to continue with more productions in the same vein, and it was Hervé to whom he went for the scores for the three subsequent pieces (and a share in the fourth, *La Roussotte*), conceived and written in a similar vein, with which the star and the theatre triumphed in the years that followed. *La Femme à papa,* with its famous ''Chanson du Colonel,'' *Lili* and the enduring *Mam'zelle Nitouche* brought Hervé three of the biggest successes of his long career, with the last two pieces, in particular, surviving into revivals long after virtually all of his rather more special opéras-bouffes had virtually vanished from the repertoire.

With *La Cosaque,* the vogue for vaudeville-opérette passed, but Hervé continued to write for the musical stage. There were, however, no further hits, and several echoing flops, after the last of which the composer put down his pen, left Paris and returned to England, where he became musical director and conductor at the Empire Theatre. He rarely returned to France in his last years, and although he composed several ballets for his London house and possibly a three-act comic opera called *Frivoli* (1886)—staged at London's Theatre Royal, Drury Lane, under the name ''Louis Hervé'' (which may, perhaps, actually have been the work of his son), with a fine cast but a short run—only a small handful of further Hervé compositions, the last posthumously, were produced in Paris. It was in Paris, however, that he died at the age of 67 after an asthmatic attack.

His son Louis Emmanuel Florimond RONGER (b Paris, 28 January 1847; d nr Paris, 18 July 1926), professionally known as **GARDEL[-Hervé],** had an eclectic career in the theatre. He worked as a performer, playing Médor in his father's *Les Chevaliers de la table ronde* and opposite Hervé in the little *Le Compositeur toqué* in both Paris and London (1871), and featuring in the Paris production of *Le nouvel Aladin* (1893, Roi Lallali), as Raab in *La Timbale d'argent,* Le Rougeaud in *L'Auberge du Tohu-bohu,* etc. He also worked in management (for a period as director of the Menus-Plaisirs), as a stage director (notably at the Théâtre de la Gaîté and at the Eldorado) and as an intermittent author and composer. He wrote and/or composed several small musical playlets (*Un Choriste amoureux* [Folies-Nouvelles 23 December 1871], *Dans le bain* [w Hermil, Eldorado 7 April 1873], *Le Roi Topino* [Excelsior 18 November 1898], *Le Brasseur* [Variétés 18 April 1896], *La Demoiselle de chez Maxim* [Parisiana 2 March 1899], *Les Aventures de Télémaque* [w Hervé, Scala 9 March 1900], *Les Filles de la belle Hélène* [w Goublier, Eldorado 6 January 1900], *La Môme Grenouille, Le Voyage d'amour,* etc), burlesques, revues, ballet scenarii, sketches, vaudevilles and even dramas.

1842 **L'Ours et le pacha** (Eugène Scribe, ''Saintine'' [ie, Xavier Boniface] ad), Bicêtre, March

1848 **Don Quichotte et Sancho Pança** (Hervé) 1 act Théâtre National 5 March

1849 **Les Gardes françaises** (Hervé) 1 act Théâtre de l'Odéon 16 December

1849 **Planètes et Satellites** 1 act Théâtre de l'Odéon

1851 **Passiflor et Cactus** (Hervé) Palais-Royal 6 May

1852 **L'Enseignement mutuel** (Théodore Barrière, Adrien Decourcelle) 1 act Palais-Royal 20 January

1852 **Roméo et Mariette** (Philippe Dumanoir) 1 act Palais-Royal

1853 **Les Folies dramatiques** (Dumanoir, Clairville) Tuileries 1 March; Palais-Royal 2 March

1854 **Prologue d'ouverture** (Charles Bridault) Folies-Concertantes 8 February

1854 **La Perle d'Alsace** (Hervé) 1 act Folies-Concertantes 8 February

1854 **Le Compositeur toqué** (Hervé) 1 act Folies-Concertantes 11 April

1854 **Amour, poésie et turlupinade** (revised *Passiflore et cactus*) 1 act Folies-Concertantes 20 June

1854 **La Fine Fleur de l'Andalousie** (Hervé) 1 act Folies-Nouvelles 21 October

1854 **La Caravane d'amour** (Théodore de Banville) 1 act Folies-Nouvelles 10 December

1855 **La Belle Créature** (Bridault) 1 act Folies-Nouvelles 8 January

1855 **Vadé au cabaret!** (Henri de Kock) 1 act Folies-Nouvelles 20 January

1855 **L'Intrigue espagnole** (Hervé) 1 act Folies-Nouvelles 22 January

1855 **Le Sergent Laramée** (Émile Durandeau) 1 act Folies-Nouvelles 3 February

1855 **Un Drame de 1779** (Hervé) 1 act Folies-Nouvelles 21 April

1855 **Latrouillat et Truffaldini** (Jules Petit, Ernest Blum) 1 act Folies-Nouvelles 10 May

1855 **Un Ténor très léger** (René Lordereau) 1 act Folies-Nouvelles 27 July

1855 **Le Testament de Polichinelle** (Armand Montjoie) 1 act Folies-Nouvelles 17 November

1855 **Le Trio d'enfoncés** (Hervé) 1 act Folies-Nouvelles 27 December

1856 **Fifi et Nini** (Albert Monnier) 1 act Folies-Nouvelles 15 January

1856 **Agamemnon, ou le chameau à deux bosses** (Hervé) 1 act Folies-Nouvelles 24 April

1856 **Toinette et son carabinier** (Michel Delaporte) 1 act Folies-Nouvelles 15 September

1856 **Femme à vendre** (Paul de Kock) 1 act Folies-Nouvelles 4 October

1857 **La Dent de sagesse** (Édouard Morin) 1 act Folies-Nouvelles 25 April

1857 **Le Pommier ensorcelé** (Morin) 1 act Folies-Nouvelles 28 April

1857 **Brin d'amour** (Achille Eyraud) 1 act Folies-Nouvelles 23 September

1857 **Phosphorus** (Hervé) 1 act Folies-Nouvelles 21 November

1858 **Le Voiturier** (Hervé) 1 act Bouffes-Deburau 3 September

1858 **La Belle Espagnole** 1 act Bouffes-Deburau 22 September

1858 **Simple Histoire** (Hervé) 1 act Bouffes-Deburau 10 October

1858 **Les Noces de Bigaro** (Hervé) 1 act Délassements-Comiques 24 December

1860 **La Belle Nini** (Hervé) Palais-Royal 28 January

1862 **L'Alchimiste** (Hervé) 1 act Délassements-Comiques 22 February

1862 **Le Hussard persecuté** (Blum) 1 act Délassements-Comiques 30 May

1862 **La Fanfare de Saint-Cloud** (Blum, Paul Siraudin) 1 act Délassements-Comiques 30 May

1862 **Le Retour d'Ulysse** (Édouard Montagne) 1 act Délassements-Comiques 21 August

1863 **Les Toréadors de Grenade** (Hervé) 1 act Palais-Royal 15 June

1863 **Les Troyens en Champagne** (w Jules Renard) 1 act Palais-Royal 30 December

1864 **Moldave et Circassiènne** (Hervé) 1 act Eldorado

1864 **Le Joueur de flûte** (Jules Moinaux) 1 act Théâtre des Variétés 16 April

1864 **La Liberté des Theatres** (Clairville) Théâtre des Variétés 10 August

1864 **La Revue pour rire /Roland à Rongeveau** (Clairville, Siraudin, Blum) 1 act Théâtre des Bouffes-Parisiens 27 December

1865 **Une Fantasia** (Nuitter, Nérée Desarb[r]es) 1 act Théâtre des Variétés 12 November

1866 **Les Chevaliers de la table ronde** (Chivot, Duru) Théâtre des Bouffes-Parisiens 17 November

1867 **La [Nouvelle] Biche au bois** (w Jean-Jacques de Billemont, Amédée Artus/Cogniard frères) Théâtre de la Porte-Saint-Martin 15 June

1867 **Le Pédicure** (Hippolyte Bédeau) 1 act Eldorado 14 July

1867 **L'Oeil crevé** (Hervé) Théâtre des Folies-Dramatiques 12 October

1867 **L'Enfant de la troupe** (Félix Baumaine, Charles Blondelet) 1 act Eldorado December

1867 **Clodoche et Normande** (Hervé) 1 act Eldorado 16 December

1868 **Le Gardien de sérail** (Hervé) 1 act Théâtre des Variétés 8 March

1868 **Trombolino** (Paul Renard, Charles de St Piat) 1 act Eldorado 9 May

1868 **Chilpéric** (Hervé) Théâtre des Folies-Dramatiques 24 October

1868 **Le Roi Amatibou** (Eugène Labiche, Edmond Cottinet) Palais-Royal 27 November

1868 **Entre deux vins** (René Lugot) 1 act Eldorado

1868 **Nini c'est fini** (Taratte) 1 act Théâtre Molière

1868 **Chilméric** (Renard, de Saint-Piat) 1 act Eldorado 10 December

1868 **Juliette et Dupiton** (Hervé) 1 act Comédie-Parisien

1869 **Deux portières pour un cordon** (w Jules Lecoq, Isidore Legouix, G Martin/''Lucian'') 1 act Palais-Royal 15 March

1869 **Les Metamorphoses de Tartempion** (Léon Quentin) 1 act Comédie-Parisien 8 April

1869 **Le Petit Faust** (Hector Crémieux, Adolphe Jaime) Théâtre des Folies-Dramatiques 28 April

1869 **Faust passementier** (Hervé) 1 act Eldorado 4 June

1869 **Une giboulée d'amoureux** (Hippolyte Lefèbvre) 1 act Grand Comédie-Parisien 8 August

1869 **Les Turcs** (Crémieux, Jaime) Théâtre des Folies-Dramatiques 23 December

1870 **Aladdin II** (Alfred Thompson) Gaiety Theatre, London, 23 December

1871 **Les Contes de fées** (w G Raspail, Maximilien Graziani/Oswald François, E Bloch) Délassements-Comiques 5 March

1871 **Le Trône d'Écosse** (Crémieux, Jaime) Théâtre des Variétés 17 November

1872 **Les Griffes du diable** (w Auguste Coedès/Clairville, Charles Gabet) Théâtre des Menus-Plaisirs 18 April

1872 **Babil and Bijou** (w Frederic Clay, Jules Rivière, et al/Dion Boucicault) Covent Garden Theatre, London 29 August

1872 **La Cocotte aux oeufs d'or** (w Coedès, Raspail/Clairville, Grangé, Victor Koning) Théâtre des Menus-Plaisirs 31 December

1873 **La Veuve du Malabar** (Crémieux, Delacour) Théâtre des Variétés 26 April

1873 **Le Hussard persecuté** revised 2-act version (Palais-Royal)

1874 **La France et la chanson** (Hippolyte Bideau) 1 act Eldorado 28 February

1874 **La Noce à Briochet** (Hermil [ie, Ange Milher]) Délassements-Comiques 26 April

1875 **Alice de Nevers** (Hervé) Théâtre des Folies-Dramatiques 22 April

1875 **Dagobert** (arr/Frank W Green/''R Sellman'' [ie, Richard Mansell]) Charing Cross Theater, London 30 August

1875 **La Belle Poule** (Crémieux, Saint-Albin) Théâtre des Folies-Dramatiques 29 December

1876 **Estelle et Némorin** (Amédée de Jallais, Gardel-Hervé) Théâtre des Menus-Plaisirs 2 September

1877 **Up the River, or The Strict Kew-Tea** (H B Farnie, Robert Reece) 1 act Folly Theatre, London 15 September

1879 **La Marquise des rues** (Siraudin, Gaston Hirsch) Théâtre des Bouffes-Parisiens 22 February

1879 **Les Sphinx** (Hervé) Folies-Bergère 29 April

1879 **Panurge** (Clairville, Octave Gastineau) Théâtre des Bouffes-Parisiens 10 September

1879 **La Femme à papa** (Alfred Hennequin, Albert Millaud) Théâtre des Variétés 3 December

1880 **Le Voyage en Amérique** (Maxime Boucheron, Hippolyte Raymond) Théâtre des Nouveautés 16 September

1880 **La Mère des compagnons** (Chivot, Duru) Théâtre des Folies-Dramatiques 15 December

1881 **La Roussotte** (w Charles Lecocq, Marius Boullard/Henri Meilhac, Ludovic Halévy, Millaud) Théâtre des Variétés 28 January

1881 **Les Deux Roses** (Clairville, Victor Bernard, Eugène Grangé) Théâtre des Folies-Dramatiques 20 October

1882 **Lili** (Millaud, Hennequin, Blum) Théâtre des Variétés 10 January

1883 **Mam'zelle Nitouche** (Meilhac, Millaud) Théâtre des Variétés 26 January

1883 **Le Vertigo** (Henri Bocage, Henri Crisafulli) Théâtre de la Renaissance 29 September

1884 **La Cosaque** (Meilhac, Millaud) Théâtre des Variétés 1 February

1884 **La Nuit aux soufflets** (Paul Ferrier, Adolphe d'Ennery) Théâtre des Nouveautés 18 September

1885 **Mam'zelle Gavroche** (Edmond Gondinet, Blum, Saint-Albin) Théâtre des Variétés 24 January

1886 **Fla-Fla** (Hirsch, Siraudin) Théâtre des Menus-Plaisirs 4 September

1887 **La Noce à Nini** (Émile de Najac, Millaud) Théâtre des Variétés 19 March

1890 **Les Bagatelles de la porte** (Baer) 1 act Théâtre des Menus-Plaisirs 14 August

1892 **Bacchanale** (Georges Bertal, Julien Lecocq) Théâtre des Menus-Plaisirs 22 October

1897 **Le Cabinet Piperlin** (Hippolyte Raymond, Paul Burani) Théâtre de l'Athénée-Comique 17 September

1900 **Les Aventures de Télémaque** (arr Gardel-Hervé) 1 act Scala 9 March

Biographies: Schneider, L: *Les Maîtres de l'Opérette Française: Hervé, Charles Lecocq* (Perrin, Paris, 1924), Cariven-Galharret, R, Ghesquière, D: *Hervé, un musicien paradoxale* (Édition des Cendres, Paris, 1992), Rouchouse, J: *Hervé, le père de l'opérette* (Michel de Maule, Paris, 1992)

HERZER, Ludwig [HERZL, Ludwig] (b Vienna, 18 March 1872; d St Gallen, 17 April 1939).

Gynecologist, author and playwright, Herzer apparently owed at least one production amongst his earlier works to a quid pro quo: having treated gratis the daughter-in-law of theatre director Oskar Fronz, he effectively put him in obligation to mount his *Der dunkle Schatz. Der dunkle Schatz* was Herzer's third collaboration with Oskar Friedmann and Edmund Eysler, and it did rather less well than their *Der Aushilfsgatte,* which had topped one hundred nights at the Apollotheater in 1917–18 and was subsequently played in Hungary as *A potférj* (ad Imre Harmath).

Herzer also wrote texts for Miska Herczel, leader of the Budapest Opera orchestra, who composed under the pseudonym of ''Max J Milian'' and whose *Die goldene Tochter* was seen in Germany, Austria (Wiener Bürgertheater 22 April 1916, 55 performances) and Hungary (*Az aranyos,* Budai Színkör 14 June 1918), and for Louis Grünberg, a composer who showed the color of his ambitions in the musical theatre by calling himself ''George Edwards'' and whose *Lady X,* similarly, won plays throughout central Europe (*Nizzai éjszaka* in its Hungarian production). However, the aspiring librettist had his first real success when he worked, with Fritz Löhner-Beda, on the text to the Singspiel *Friederike,* Lehár's setting-to-music of Goethe's putative love life. The pair subsequently provided Lehár with the rewrites which turned *Die gelbe Jacke* into *Das Land des Lächelns,* and *Endlich allein* into *Schön ist die Welt.*

A Strauss pasticcio for the Berlin Metropoltheater and Richard Tauber, and an attempt, with composer Ernst Steffan, to repeat the success of the remade *Die Dubarry* with a *Catherine the Great* musical, *Katharina,* were not in the same class, and the swashbuckling, romantic *Venus in Seide,* musically set by Robert Stolz, proved the best of Herzer's later pieces.

1913 **Gräfin Fifi** (Albert Chantrier/w Oskar Friedmann) Theater des Westens, Berlin 20 September

1914 **Die weisse Gefahr** (Max J Milian/w Friedmann) Wilhelm Theater, Stuttgart 1 July

1914 **Die goldene Tochter** (Milian/w Friedmann) Wilhelm Theater, Stuttgart 15 July; Wiener Bürgertheater 22 April 1916

1915 **Das Zimmer der Pompadour** (Edmund Eysler/w Friedmann) 1 act Hölle 1 December

1917 **Der Aushilfsgatte** (Eysler/w Friedmann) Apollotheater 7 November

1918 **Der dunkle Schatz** (Eysler/w Friedmann) Wiener Bürgertheater 14 November

1926 **Lady X** (George Edwards) Apollotheater 17 September

1927 **Cagliostro in Wien** revised text (Bürgertheater)

1928 **Friederike** (Lehár/w Löhner-Beda) Metropoltheater, Berlin 4 October

1929 **Das Land des Lächelns** revised *Die gelbe Jacke* (Lehár/w Löhner-Beda) Metropoltheater, Berlin 10 October

1930 **Hallo Tommy** (Edwards) Kleines Haus, Düsseldorf 4 October

1930 **Schön ist die Welt** revised *Endlich allein* (Lehár/Löhner-Beda) Metropoltheater, Berlin 3 December

1931 **Das Lied der Liebe** (Johann Strauss arr Erich Wolfgang Korngold) Metropoltheater, Berlin 23 December

1932 **Katharina** (Ernst Steffan) Admiralspalast, Berlin 22 August

1932 **Venus in Seide** (Robert Stolz/w Alfred Grünwald) Stadttheater, Zürich 10 December

1934 **Der Prinz von Schiras** (Josef Beer/w Löhner-Beda) Theater an der Wien 20 November

1937 **Verzeih' das ich dich lieb'** (*Esö után köpönyeg*) German version w Karl Farkas (Scala Theater)

Also credited: *Der geliebte Dieb* (Victor Reinshagen/Robert Gilbert)

DIE HERZOGIN VON CHICAGO Operette in 2 acts, a Vorspiel and Nachspiel, by Julius Brammer and Alfred Grünwald. Music by Emmerich Kálmán. Theater an der Wien, Vienna, 5 April 1928.

The ''Duchess of Chicago'' is the wealthy Mary Lloyd (Rita Georg) who, during a visit to a Budapest dance hall, throws a public tantrum when the Crown Prince Sándor of the Ruritanian kingdom of Sylvarien requests that the band play a waltz when she wants only the Charleston and a ''heisses Jazzband.'' She buys up the band to get her own way, then invades Sylvarien and promptly proceeds to buy up not only the royal family's castle but the Crown Prince (Hubert Marischka) himself. Hans Moser (King Pankraz XXVII) and Hans Thimig (Benjamin Lloyd) were, respectively, the poor royal and wealthy hot-dog-selling fathers. Elsie Altmann as the Sylvarien Princess Rosemarie Sonjuschka von Morenien and Fritz Steiner as Mary's secretary, James Jacques Bondy, provided the soubret part of the entertainment. The Nachspiel to the show, set in the ''Grill American'' in Budapest, was, naturally, entitled ''Happy End!'' If you call being married to a woman like that ''happy.''

As the tale suggested, the score was a mixture of traditional Austro-Hungarian music and American-style dance music. The evening opened with the chorus demanding that everyone ''Charleston! Charleston!,'' and the Prince responded with a Viennese song ''In Grinzing steht ein kleines Haus.'' By the time things come to a

Plate 174. **Die Herzogin von Chicago** *at the Light Opera Works, Evanston, Ill, 1998.*

peak he has convinced her that ''Den Walzer hat der Herrgott für verliebte nur gemacht,'' and she has convinced him of the interest of ''Ein kleiner Slow-Fox mit Mary'' and his father of the virtues of a brisker fox-trot (''Voulez-vous, Papachen?'').

Hubert Marischka produced and directed, and although the musical mixture provoked such comments as ''has Kálmán sold Austria's musical birthright for a mess of bad American jazz pottage?'' the show found plenty of takers. Anny Coty and Juci Lábass succeeded to the role of Mary, Harry Bauer, as usual, succeeded Marischka, and was in turn suceeded by Willy Thunis and Willy Degner, as the show ran past its 200th performance (28 September) and, with only a brief pause for a visiting company's season, ran on to 21 February 1929 (287 performances).

Die Herzogin von Chicago followed Kálmán's other successes abroad, but it did not make a significant mark. Budapest's Király Színház mounted a season of an Hungarian version (ad Adorján Stella, Ernő Kulinyi), whilst an American production (ad Edward Eliscu), staged under the Shubert management with Lilian Taiz and Walter Woolf in the starring roles, started out from Newark in the 1929 season but did not make it to Broadway.

Hungary: Király Színház *Csikágói hercegnő* 21 December 1928; USA: Shubert Theater, Newark *The Duchess of Chicago* 11 November 1929

Recording: complete (Decca)

HEUBERGER, Richard [Franz Joseph] (b Graz, 18 June 1850; d Vienna, 28 October 1914). Austrian composer who scored a major hit with his first venture into the Operette world.

Originally an engineer, Heuberger abandoned that career in his mid-twenties to become a professional musician. His subsequent working life combined a notable career as a music critic on the *Allgemeine Zeitung* and the *Neue freie Presse,* and wide work as a choral conductor and as a music teacher, with the composition of a variety of works including six Operetten and several operas (*Abenteuer ein Neujahresnacht / Prinz Bummler* [Leipzig 13 January 1886], *Manuel Benegas* [Leipzig 27 March 1889], *Maienacht* 1894, *Mirjam* 1894).

His first Operette, *Der Opernball,* produced at the Theater an der Wien when its composer was nearly 50, was a musical version of the hugely successful French comedy *Les Dominos roses.* It proved to be an enormous favorite at home, threw up an all-time hit in ''Im Chambre separée,'' and was freely exported, establishing Heuberger, on its strength alone, amongst the most in-view composers of his time. The Theater an der Wien hosted two further works which Heuberger and his librettists again based on solidly successful French stage pieces—Hennequin and Millaud's *Niniche* (already set with success by Marius Boullard, not to mention Brandl, 20 years earlier) was remade as *Ihre Excellenz* (1900, 48 performances), and Henri Meilhac's *Decoré* musicalized as *Der Sechsuhrzug* (1900, 25 performances)—and in 1902 he turned to British comedy with a musical, *Das Baby,* based on Pinero's *The Magistrate.* However, none of these well-made musicals, in spite of reasonable runs, approached the success of his first work.

Heuberger was, apparently, the originally intended composer for another French derivative, Léon and Stein's *Die lustige Witwe* libretto, but the job eventually went to Lehár with the well-known happy results, and Heuberger's only subsequent light musical pieces came nowhere near the success of his first. An original Operette, *Der Fürst von Düsterstein,* mounted at the new Johann Strauss-Theater, flopped in 13 performances, whilst his folk opera, *Barfüssele,* first produced at the Dresden Königliches Operntheater (11 March 1905, lib: Victor Léon) and posthumously played at the Vienna Volksoper (22 December 1915), left no mark.

1898 **Der Opernball** (Victor Léon, Heinrich von Waldberg) Theater an der Wien 5 January

1899 **Ihre Excellenz** (aka *Die kleine Excellenz*) (Léon, Waldberg) Centraltheater, Berlin 17 January

1900 **Der Sechsuhrzug** (Léon, Leo Stein) Centraltheater, Berlin 17 January

1902 **Das Baby** (Waldberg, A M Willner) Carltheater 3 October

1909 **Der Fürst von Düsterstein** (Gaudeamus) Johann Strauss-Theater 3 March

1910 **Don Quichotte** (Heinz Reichert, Fritz Grünbaum) 1 act Hölle 1 December

HE WANTED ADVENTURE Musical fantasy in 3 acts by Robert P Weston and Bert Lee based on *Ambrose Applejohn's Adventure* by Walter Hackett. Additional lyrics by Clifford Grey. Music by Jack Waller and Joseph Tunbridge. Saville Theatre, London, 28 March 1933.

After their successful adaptation of *Nothing But the Truth* as *Tell Her the Truth,* the Jack Waller team put together another musical comedy based on a well-liked play for comedian Bobby Howes and the Saville Theatre company. Walter Hackett's 1921 piece *Ambrose Applejohn's Adventure* was adapted to Howes's measure, and the usual short order of musical pieces (seven songs, two choruses and a finale) added.

Howes played Bobby Bramstone (ex- Ambrose Applejohn), a rich chappie who longs for picture-book adventure and who gets it, first in a dream in which he is a pirate chief, and then in real life when jewel-robbers get at a treasure hidden in his stately home. Darkly dramatic Marie Burke and villainous Raymond Newell were a harem girl and a mutineer in the pirate scenes and a pair of Russian crooks in the home ones, and Abraham Sofaer and Winifred Izard imitated, in turn, a pair of phony psychics and a couple of Indian mystics, whilst Wylie Watson, a slave-master at sea, became a bumbling scoutmaster, Eustace Didcott, on land, and scored the musical hit of the evening with the tongue-in-cheek boy-scout song "Smile and Be Bright." The show played 152 West End performances, toured well, and was remounted on the road in 1934 as *Smile and Be Bright.*

HICKMAN, Charles[John] (b Snaresbrook, Essex, 18 January 1905; d London, 3 April 1983).

At first an actor, Hickman found success as a director from the 1930s, notably with the *Sweet and Low* series of revues, and he went on to direct a number of West End musicals, including the local editions of *Song of Norway, The Red Mill* (revival) and *Annie Get Your Gun,* and the mostly successful British musicals *Cage Me a Peacock* (1948), *Dear Miss Phoebe* (1950), *Zip Goes a Million* (1951), *Love from Judy* (1952), *Wedding in Paris* (1954), *The Water Gipsies* (1955) and the pasticcio *Summer Song* (1956) for the London stage. He subsquently went on to direct musicals in both Australia (*The Sound of Music,* etc) and South Africa.

Autobiography: *Directed By . . .* (New Horizon, London, 1981)

HICKS, [Edward George] Seymour (Sir) (b St Helier, Jersey, 30 January 1871; d Fleet, Hampshire, 6 April 1949). Suave, light comedy leading man of the British musical stage.

An actor from the age of 16, Hicks played in the British provinces and appeared with the Kendals in their Broadway season with *The Squire* and *The Queen's Shilling* before his performance as a kind of comical Dr Watson to the Sherlock Holmes of C H E Brookfield in their revue *Under the Clock* (25 December 1893, mus: Edward Jones) at the Court Theatre brought him to the attention of George Edwardes. Hicks was hired to star in a Gaiety Theatre revival of *Little Jack Sheppard,* in the role famously created by Fred Leslie, and he put sufficient individuality into his part to win himself fine reviews, popularity and—after a quick trip to Broadway to play Ugly Sister to his wife's *Cinderella* (1894)—the lead juvenile role, opposite Ada Reeve, in Edwardes's next production, the musical comedy *The Shop Girl* (1894, Charlie Appleby). The pair, comedy players both, gave an unaccustomed lighthearted air to the show's juvenile roles (until that time, sentimentality rather than fun had been de rigueur in such parts) and Hicks scored a hit with

Plate 175. **Seymour Hicks** *as the young, lighthearted hero of* The Shop Girl.

the first of the many secondhand songs he would perform in shows over the years, Felix McGlennon's ''Her Golden Hair Was Hanging Down Her Back.'' The emphasis on charming light comedy was increased when Hicks's wife, Ellaline Terriss, took over as ''the shop girl,'' and together this attractive, bright pair of young performers helped materially to seal the fate of the drooping/sighing, tenor/soprano lovers in London musical plays.

Hicks repeated his *Shop Girl* role on Broadway, but refused the ''unsuitable'' juvenile part of Edwardes's *My Girl* (1895), a refusal which drove the angry manager to court to bar Hicks from breaking his contract by appearing anywhere else. However, all was back in order in time for him to join his wife in the starring juvenile roles of the next Gaiety show, *The Circus Girl* (1896, Dick Capel). It was Hicks's last appearance at the Gaiety, but he maintained sufficiently good relations with Edwardes to work as co-author on one of the house's most successful shows, *A Runaway Girl,* in which Miss Terriss played the lass of the title.

A Runaway Girl was, in fact, Hicks's second venture into authorship. He had ''adapted'' an Armenian operetta, *Leblébidji Horhor* (which had caused a slightly censorable sensation in Constantinople) for the London stage as *The Yashmak* the previous year. The adaptation seemed (to those who could understand Armenian) more like a total rewrite, and the piece was, in any case, not a success.

The Hickses then joined forces with producer Charles Frohman and, under his management, over a period of some seven years, they played in a series of musicals written by Hicks and designed as vehicles for them: *Bluebell in Fairyland* (1901, Dicky), *The Cherry Girl* (1903, Moonshine), *The Catch of the Season* (1904, Duke of St Jermyns), *The Beauty of Bath* (1906, Richard Alington), which opened the Frohman-sponsored Hicks Theatre, and *The Gay Gordons* (1907, Angus Graeme). Hicks, as author, also ventured further pieces on similar lines. For William Greet he wrote the highly successful *The Earl and the Girl* and the indifferent *The Talk of the Town;* for Frohman, *My Darling,* a piece destined, unsuccessfully, to be played by a B-team headed by would-be Terriss and Hicks clones.

Hicks and Miss Terriss established themselves, during this period, not only as the town's favorite musical comedy hero and heroine, but also as the theatre's ''ideal couple.'' As with most such ''ideal'' couples, the ideal was a pretty fictional one, but Miss Terriss tactfully ignored Hicks's repeated trips to the ladies' chorus, and their charming public image lasted happily and long, to the great good of their public popularity.

An attempt to put Miss Terriss into breeches as the hero of The *Dashing Little Duke* did only fairly, but gave place to an interesting incident when Hicks played some performances for his indisposed wife (surely the only case in the history of the musical where a husband succeeded to his wife's role), and the 1910 *Captain Kidd,* a version of the American comedy, *The Dictator,* adapted by Hicks, was a smart flop, marking the end of the Hicks/Terriss era of musical-theatre supremacy in what was now post–*Merry Widow* London. Hicks put his hand to several more not unsuccessful libretti, and the pair appeared together on the halls in the little musical piece *Pebbles on the Beach,* singing and dancing ''Alexander's Ragtime Band,'' and in the Palace Theatre musical *Cash on Delivery,* but, although Hicks remained a respected theatrical figure and, indeed, was awarded a knighthood in 1935, he did not appear further on the musical stage.

Amongst a limited list of film appearances, Hicks starred as Sir John Tremayne in the 1939 *The Lambeth Walk,* the film based on the stage musical *Me and My Girl.*

Hicks's brother, **Stanley BRETT** [Stanley F HICKS] (b St Helier, Jersey, 1879; d 9 November 1923), and his wife, **Maie ASH** (b Clapton, 31 May 1888; d December 1923), both appeared in number of Hicks's musical productions.

1895 **Papa's Wife** (Ellaline Terriss/w F C Phillips) 1 act Lyric Theatre 26 January

1897 **The Yashmak** (Napoléon Lambelet/w Cecil Raleigh) Shaftesbury Theatre 31 March

1898 **The Lady Wrangler** (Terriss) 1 act Duke of York's Theatre 4 March

1898 **A Runaway Girl** (Ivan Caryll, Lionel Monckton/Aubrey Hopwood, Harry Greenbank/w Harry Nicholls) Gaiety Theatre 21 May

1901 **Bluebell in Fairyland** (Walter Slaughter/Hopwood, C H Taylor) Vaudeville Theatre 18 December

1902 **An English Daisy** (Walter Slaughter) Royal County Theatre, Kingston, 11 August; Casino Theater, New York 18 January 1904

1903 **The Earl and the Girl** (Caryll/Greenbank) Adelphi Theatre 10 December

1903 **The Cherry Girl** (Caryll/Hopwood, et al) Vaudeville Theatre 21 December

1904 **The Catch of the Season** (Herbert Haines, Evelyn Baker/Taylor/w Cosmo Hamilton) Vaudeville Theatre 9 September

1905 **The Talk of the Town** (Haines, Baker/Taylor) Lyric Theatre 5 January

1906 **The Beauty of Bath** (Haines/Taylor/w Hamilton) Aldwych Theatre 19 March

1907 **My Darling** (Haines, Baker/Taylor, P G Wodehouse) Hicks Theatre 2 March

1907 **The Gay Gordons** (Guy Jones/several) Aldwych Theatre 11 September

1907 **A Dress Rehearsal** (Frank E Tours, ''A Lotte''/w A C Robatt) 1 act Tivoli 2 December

1909 **The Dashing Little Duke** (Tours/Adrian Ross) Hicks Theatre 17 February

1910 **Captain Kidd** (Leslie Stuart/Ross) Wyndhams Theatre 12 January

1910 **Cook's Man** (Tours) 1 act London Coliseum 4 April

1910 **The Model and the Man** (Tours/C H Bovill) 1 act King's Theatre, Southsea 15 August; London Hippodrome 22 August

1910 **Lady at Large** (Tours) 1 act King's Theatre, Southsea 10 October

1912 **O-Mi-Iy** (Tours, Herman Finck) 1 act London Hippodrome 25 March

1912 **Pebbles on the Beach** (Haines) 1 act London Coliseum 16 December

1914 **England Expects** (Edward Jones/w Edward Knoblock) 1 act London Opera House 17 September

1916 **The Happy Day** (Sidney Jones, Rubens/Ross) Daly's Theatre 13 May

1917 **Cash on Delivery** (Haydn Wood/H E Wright, Davy Burnaby, James Heard) Palace Theatre 13 October

1918 **Jolly Jack Tar** (Herman Darewski/Burnaby, Heard, J Harrington/w Arthur Shirley) Princes Theatre 29 November

1920 **The Little Dutch Girl** (*Das Hollandweibchen*) English version w Harry Graham (Lyric Theatre)

1923 **Head Over Heels** (Harold Fraser-Simson/Ross, Graham) Adelphi Theatre 8 September

Autobiographies: *Seymour Hicks: 24 Years of an Actor's Life* (Alston Rivers, London, 1910), *Between Ourselves* (Cassell, London, 1930), *Me and My Missus* (Cassell, London, 1939), etc

HIDE AND SEEK Musical play in 2 acts by Guy Bolton, Fred Thompson and Douglas Furber. Lyrics and music by Vivian Ellis, and Sam Lerner, Al Goodhart and Al Hoffman. London Hippodrome, 14 October 1937.

Lee Ephraim's production of *Hide and Seek* teamed comedians Cicely Courtneidge, returning to the theatre after having remade her dented name in movies, and Bobby Howes in a slightly confusing piece in which they played both themselves and their respective parents. The parents were a jockey and a barmaid, and the jockey wins some shares in a wager on the Derby before the pair run away to Montana together, and he finally walks out on her. The children—her daughter and his son—are a pair of seaside pierrots, before the daughter becomes a cabaret star. In the course of the evening—when not performing their routines—they outwit some Yankee gangsters and finally get hold of those ''worthless'' shares . . . in the original ''horseless carriage.''

Hide and Seek was a piece designed to get in the maximum of opportunities for the two stars—plus such currently over-fashionable elements as cabaret stars and American gangsters—and the filmland team of Lerner, Goodhart and Hoffman turned out some suitably functional songs as musical relief. However, the score leaped onto a different level when Howes delivered a song by co-composer Vivian Ellis. ''She's My Lovely'' was the little comedian's greatest ever hit. Ellis also supplied Miss Courtneidge with her best opportunity, the stand-up solo for her cabaret act, ''I Follow the Bride.'' The two hit songs, and the two favorite stars—not an ideal match, and it was not repeated—ensured two hundred West End performances for *Hide and Seek* prior to two seasons touring with other players in the made-to-measure star roles.

HIGH BUTTON SHOES Musical in 2 acts by Stephen Longstreet based on his *The Sisters Liked Them Handsome.* Lyrics by Sammy Cahn. Music by Jule Styne. New Century Theater, New York, 9 October 1947.

Stephen Longstreet's tales of his youth in pre–First World War New Brunswick, NJ, made up prettily into a period picture-postcard musical play in which comedian Phil Silvers appeared as Harrison Floy, a hometown boy made small-time bad. Returning to New Brunswick he befriends the Longstreet family—Mama Sara (Nanette Fabray), Papa Henry (Jack McCauley), maiden Auntie Fran (Lois Lee), and young Stevie (Johnny Stewart)—and gets them involved in a scheme to sell a piece of swampland they own, intending to decamp with the cash.

A jolly picnic is the scene of the sale, after which Floy, his helper, Mr Pontdue (Joey Faye), and the bewitched Fran run off to Atlantic City with the loot. After ups and downs which lead, via a football match, to an attempt to sell the swampland clay as mud-packs, Floy judges it safer to leave town, while the wiser and not much sadder Fran goes back to her first love, local footballer Hubert ''Oggle'' Ogglethorpe (Mark Dawson).

The highlight of the piece was the second-act scene in Atlantic City in which the chase after the stolen money—involving all the principals plus the police and a chorus of seaside holidaymakers—was set by choreographer Jerome Robbins as a dance routine performed in a frenetic Keystone Kops style. The favorite moments of the score fell to Mama and Papa, she persuading him to come and dance with her at the picnic (''Papa, Won't You Dance With Me?'') and he, looking sideways at Floy, reminding her that after years of happy marriage ''I Still Get Jealous.'' The star, too, had his musical moments. Silvers flashed out ''There's Nothing Like a Model 'T,' '' sang about ''Sunday by the Sea,'' and tried to get the local team to throw their football match in ''Nobody Ever Died for Dear Old Rutgers.''

Indifferently received by the critics, *High Button Shoes* nevertheless proved to be friendly and colorfully enjoyable entertainment and, in a period in which the musical theatre was flourishing brightly on Broadway, it drew for no less than 727 performances, before being sent on the road with Eddie Foy jr starring as Floy. It was also mounted in London under the management of Jack Hylton with Lew Parker (Floy), Kay Kimber (Mama), Sid James (Papa) and Hermene French (Fran) featured, for a run of 291 performances. It was recorded for American television in 1956 with Miss Fabray and Faye teamed with Hal March and Don Ameche, and again in 1966 with Jack Cassidy, Carol Lawrence and Maureen O'Hara, and has reappeared on the stage in a number of regional productions, including one at the Goodspeed Opera House (16 June 1982).

The Keystone Kops sequence was seen again on Broadway when it was recreated as part of the compilation show, *Jerome Robbins' Broadway.*

UK: London Hippodrome 22 December 1948

Recording: original cast (RCA)

HIGH JINKS Musical farce (musical jollity) in 3 acts by Leo Ditrichstein and Otto Harbach based on *Les Dragées d'Hercule* by Maurice Hennequin and Paul Bilhaud. Lyrics by Otto Harbach. Music by Rudolf Friml. Lyric Theater, New York, 10 December 1913.

Harbach and Friml followed up their success with the comic operetta *The Firefly* by writing a piece for producer Arthur Hammerstein which was wholly different in tone. *High Jinks* was based on Leo Ditrichstein's *Before and After* (1905), an adaptation of the 1904 French comedy *Les Dragées d'Hercule,* and used the famous ''magic potion'' element so beloved of the old fairy-tale spectaculars, and of W S Gilbert, as the basis of its plot. The ''lozenge'' in this case was a perfume which, supposed to cure ''all kinds of spiritual distempers,'' instead has strange effects on people, and it is in the hands not of a sorcerer, but of Dr Gaston Thorne (Robert Pitkin), a fashionable Parisian neurologist. It has effects on explorer Dick Wayne (Burrell Barbaretto), his girlfriend Sylvia Dale (Mana Zucca), a Spanish couple called M et Mme Rabelais (Ignacio Martinetti, Edith Gardiner), American Lumber King Mr J J Jeffreys (Tom Lewis) and runaway wife Adelaide Fontaine (Elizabeth Murray), as a crisscross of romances gets bundled up with rumors of a long-lost daughter through three acts.

Friml's score had moments when it launched into the lyrical, but they were mainly moments of gentle burlesque, and the score of *High Jinks* was almost entirely a dancing one. Dick described the symptoms of the ''high jinks'' in ''Something Seems Tingle-ingle-ingling'' and joined with Sylvia to waltz about ''Love's Own Kiss'' in the two most often repeated numbers of the score, Adelaide mooned over her big, Irish ''Jim'' and got come-hitherish with Mr J J Jeffreys in ''She Says It with Her Eyes'' (aka ''Come Hither Eyes'') and, with little care for the setting, encouraged ''All Aboard for Dixie!'' in Cobb and Yellen's interpolation, whilst the inevitable femme du demi-monde, Chi-Chi (Emilie Lea), sang of ''The Bubble.''

High Jinks had a sticky start. When it was produced in Syracuse on 29 October, Elizabeth Murray's self-written ''No Roaming Roamers For Me'' was the only song to get any attention, and the only bit of interest the trades could find in the production was the debut of Elaine Hammerstein, daughter of. The show looked far from promising as it set out on the road and Hammerstein toyed with the idea of abandoning it. Ultimately, however, in December, he took it in, to Broadway's Lyric Theater, and found himself with the season's most successful new show on his hands. *High Jinks* ran for 213 performances on Broadway, and it was swiftly taken up by J C Williamson for Australia, and by Alfred Butt for a London production as a vehicle for comedian W H Berry in the role of Dr Thorne. It was wartime and London was touchy about foreign-sounding names, so Butt tried a little dissembling. He masked the largely central European creative team of the piece under the credit ''by Ogden Hartley and Roderick Freeman'' and then—as if that were not enough—wiped them right off the bill, declaring simply that the French play was ''adapted by Frederick Lonsdale.'' He also inserted five Howard Talbot numbers, and other pieces by Paul Rubens, Jerome Kern, Jimmy Tate, et al into the score. Maisie Gay (Adelaide), Marie Blanche (Mrs Thorne), Peter Gawthorne (Dick), Nellie Taylor (Sylvia), Saffo Arnay (Chi-Chi) and W H Rawlins (Jeffreys) supported the star, and the production turned out a major hit which lasted 383 performances in wartime London before touring in 1917 and 1918 (2 companies).

Australia gave an equally warm and even longer welcome to the show (UK version and further fiddled with). Williamson's initial production featured Field Fisher (Thorne), Dorothy Brunton (Sylvia), C H Workman (Dick), W H Rawlins (Jeffreys), Gertrude Glyn (Chi-Chi) and Florence Vie (Adelaide) through 6 weeks in Sydney and 10 in Melbourne, but that was far from the end of *High Jinks*'s career in Australia. It was played again in Sydney in September of the same year, and thereafter was revived regularly for many years as one of the handful of staple musical comedies of which there never seemed to be too many performances for Australian audiences. Local favorites Cyril Ritchard and Madge Elliott were featured in a major revival as late as 1935 (Theatre Royal, Sydney 18 May).

Australia: Her Majesty's Theatre, Sydney 6 February 1915; UK: Adelphi Theatre 24 August 1916

HIGH SPIRITS Musical comedy in 2 acts by Hugh Martin and Timothy Gray based on Noël Coward's play *Blithe Spirit.* Alvin Theater, New York, 7 April 1964.

Any attempt to make a musical play out of Noël Coward's *Blithe Spirit* would appear to be an unnecessary exercise—there seems little that songs, extra scenes and choruses of singers and dancers prancing through the play's living-room set could add to the piece—and, indeed, the musical that was produced proved the point precisely. It was a distorted version of the original which was little more than a vehicle for revue star Beatrice Lillie in which to display her comic talents. In the now heavily featured role of the zany spiritualist Madame Arcati, arriving on the traditional bicycle (''Bicycle Song''), touching filmland parody with a scene in which she advised a chorus to ''Go into Your Trance,'' calling up her ouija board (''Talking to You'') and frothing with excitement over the prospect of meeting a real, live spirit in ''Something Is Coming to Tea,'' Miss Lillie made the most of the many opportunities with which her once supporting role was now endowed. Edward Woodward appeared as Charles Condomine, whose marriage to Ruth (Louise Troy) is disrupted when Madame Arcati raises the ghost of his first wife, the extravagant Elvira (Tammy Grimes). Coward himself directed Lester Osterman, Robert Fletcher and Richard Horner's production which played 375 performances on Broadway.

Elsewhere, Lillie-less, things went less well. A London production, mounted by Geoffrey Russell, featured Cicely Courtneidge as a rather more traditional Madame Arcati alongside Denis Quilley (Charles), Jan Waters (Ruth) and Marti Stevens (Elvira) and played 93 times, whilst an Australian production, a few months later, did even less well. Stuart Wagstaff, Amanda Fox, Dossie Hollingsworth and Betty Kean played a month and a half in Melbourne before the show was shuttered.

UK: Savoy Theatre 3 November 1964; Australia: Princess Theatre, Melbourne 13 March 1965

Recordings: original cast (ABC-Paramount), London cast (Pye)

THE HIGHWAYMAN Comic opera in 2 acts by H B Smith. Music by Reginald de Koven. Hyperion Theater, New Haven, Conn 28 October 1897; Broadway Theater 13 December 1897.

One of Smith and de Koven's most successful comic operas, *The Highwayman,* like their other two big hits, *Robin Hood* and *Rob Roy,* was written round an olde Englishe subject. Using once more the comic-chases-hero-through-many-disguises layout of *Robin Hood,* Smith introduced as his hero one Dick Fitzgerald (Joseph O'Mara), a gentleman who has turned highwayman to restore his family fortunes, while his chief comic was the policeman Foxy Quiller (Jerome Sykes), out to net the £1,000 reward for the thief's capture. The ration of mistaken identities was a hefty one—no less than three other characters took turns at disguising themselves as the highwayman: Toby Winkle (Harry McDonough) does so to impress his Doll Primrose (Nellie Braggins), Captain Rodney (van Rensslaer Wheeler) does so as part of a plot to rescue his beloved Pamela (Maud Williams) from an unwanted marriage, and Lady Constance Sinclair (Hilda Clarke, prima donna) dons male attire in order to wrest the highwayman's pardon from his horrid enemy, Sir John Hawkhurst (H W Berrill), at roadside pistolpoint. All three end up, in turn, in prison, but everyones escapes in time to pair off for the traditional happy ending.

A standard comic opera score had Dick singing about ''The Highwayman,'' saying ''Farewell to the King's Highway'' and duetting ''Do You Remember, Love?'' with his Constance, while the lady balladed ''For This'' and got into livelier strain with ''Vive la bagatelle.'' There was a nautical song for young Rodney (''While the Four Winds Blow''), Quiller sang about being ''On the Track'' and the soubrets went on about ''Bread and Cheese and Kisses'' in traditional style.

Produced by Andrew A McCormick's Broadway Theater Opera Company it was hailed as ''a real comic opera,'' ran through 126 Broadway performances ''turning people away at every performance'' and prompted Weber and Fields to poke a 15-minute burlesque *The*

Plate 176. **Rudy Hirigoyen.** *And he had a marvelous tenor voice, too.*

Way-High-Man into the middle of their already-running *Pousse-Café,* before going on the road, with Camille D'Arville as Constance alongside O'Mara and Sykes, for an extended tour. The show was frequently seen around America thereafter, in repertoire and in comic opera seasons, and it returned to Broadway in a Shubert production in 1917 (44th Street Theater 2 May) with John Charles Thomas and Jeff de Angelis starred (22 performances).

In 1900 Klaw and Erlanger mounted a musequel, *Foxy Quiller* (Broadway Theater 5 November), built around comedian Jerome Sykes, which found some favor around the country without winning the same kind of life as the original show.

HIRCHMANN, Henri *see* HIRSCHMANN, HENRI

HIRIGOYEN, Rudy (b Mendionde, 29 August 1919; d Buc, Yvelines, 24 October 2000). Heroically voiced French tenor of the postwar romantic musical.

Having worked as a hotel page and envisaged a career in hairdressing, the young Hirigoyen, who had won several singing competitions, ultimately went into the theatre. He was obliged to wait until after the war, however, to begin his stage career as a chorister and second understudy in *Valses de Vienne.* He appeared at the Casino de Paris in revue, in the musical comedy *La Concièrge est dans l'escalier* and in *Le Pays du sourire* at the Gaîté-Lyrique (1949), created the leading role of Louis Gasté's *La Rose de Bengale* (1948) out of town, then toured in the star tenor roles originally created by Luis Mariano in *La Belle de Cadix* and in *Andalousie,* as well as making several visits to Canada.

He subsequently created roles in *Le Brigand d'amour* (Lyon, 1951) and *Les Caprices de Vichnou* (1952) and made his first film appearance in *Musique en fête* (1951) before succeeding Mariano in the star role of *Le Chanteur de Mexico* at the Châtelet. The presence of the idolized Mariano and Rossi in Paris kept Hirigoyen largely to reproducing their roles in the provinces, but he starred in revivals of *Andalousie* and of *Méditerranée* and introduced the leading tenor role of *Maria Flora* at the Châtelet in 1957. Out of town, he created the star role of Georges Dherain's *Pour toi* (1955), as well as those of *Farandole d'amour* (1962) and *Rendezvous à Paris* (1968), neither of which was to brave Paris, but he finally got his metropolitan reward with the grand dual lead role of the Francis Lopez opérette *Viva Napoli* (1969), in which he appeared as Napoléon (and his double) to the stirring strains of ''Soldats, je suis content de vous.'' Hirigoyen appeared in Paris in some of the latter-day Lopez productions, and continued to tour, mostly in the Mariano/Rossi/Lopez repertoire, well into his sixties, before retiring from the stage.

Over the years, Hirigoyen recorded many of the French postwar shows, proving, in a remarkable display of rash and vibrant singing, that it was certainly not any lack of vocal capacities, but presumably merely name value that kept him largely in the provinces whilst Mariano and Rossi triumphed in Paris.

HIRSCH, Hugo (b Birnbaum, 12 March 1884; d Berlin, 16 August 1961). Prolific composer for the Berlin stage of the 1920s.

Hirsch studied medicine in Breslau before switching his attentions to music. He moved to Berlin in 1906 to pursue his new career, and in 1911 he began writing for the theatre. He had his first success with the Revue-Posse *Gehn Sie bloss nicht nach Berlin!,* but his consecration as a part of the Berlin composing world did not come until after the war, when Victor Barnowski produced his vaudeville *Die Scheidungsreise* at the Deutsches Künstlertheater. *Die Scheidungsreise,* from which the song ''Wer wird denn weinen, wenn man auseinander geht'' became quickly popular, went on from Berlin to be seen in Vienna, with Annie Dirkens and Otto Storm starred, for six weeks at the Bürgertheater (30 March 1922).

Other successes followed, and at the peak of his activities in the mid-1920s Hirsch was turning out four or five musical comedy and revue scores a season, a good number of which proved successful throughout Germany and occasionally even won exposure further afield. The musical Schwank *Die tolle Lola* went from Berlin to a guest season at Vienna's Raimundtheater (2 August 1924), to an American production, under the management of F C Coppicus, as *Lola in Love* (ad Irving Caesar, Scranton 25 December 1922), then to a revival as *Die Bolero-Prinzessin* in Vienna in 1945 and onto film in 1954, whilst *Dolly* (Johann Strauss-Theater 1 October 1924) and the vaudeville *Der Fürst von Pappenheim* (Bürgertheater 5 September 1924, ''Eine Frau wie ich ist ne Sache für sich'') also got Vienna showings, within two months of *Die tolle Lola.* At the same time, his music was heard on the London stage when, after a tour in which the entire score had been his, five Hirsch numbers were eventually combined with some by Broadway composer Stephen Jones to make up the score of Jack Buchanan's *Toni* (Shaftesbury Theatre 12 May 1924), a piece which seems to have been an uncredited variant on *Der Fürst von Pappenheim.* A Shubert production of *Bummelmädels* mooted for the American stage in 1915–16, under the title *The Broadway Girl,* apparently did not make it.

Hirsch's flush of fame was largely over when he joined the exodus from Berlin in 1933, and moved first to Belgium and then to Paris, where he lived until well after the war, returning in 1950 to settle in Wiesbaden and, later, Berlin. However, although still active as a musician, he never succeeded in making a comeback to the songwriting and stage-musical popularity that had been his in the 1920s.

1912 **Die Broadway-Girls** 1 act Viktoria Theater, Breslau 1 July

1912 **Eine kitzliche Geschichte** (Rudolf Schanzer/Erich Urban) Lustspielhaus, Düsseldorf 31 October

1913 **Die Hoflieranten** (Leo Walther Stein/Rudolf Presber) Deutsches Theater, Hannover 1 May

1913 **Bummelmädels** (w Schreyer/Max Heye) Berlin Pratertheater 11 May

1914 **Tanzfieber** [*Tangofieber*] (Schanzer, Theo Halton, Heye/Urban) Walhalla-Theater 15 January

1916 **'ne feine Familie** (Alfred Müller-Forster) Metropoltheater, Cologne 10 December

1918 **Die Scheidungsreise, oder Wer wird denn weinen..!** (L W Stein) Deutsches Künstlertheater

?1919 **Die tolle Lola** (Gustav Kadelburg, Arthur Rebner) Neues Operetten-Theater

1921 **Die ewige Braut** (Robert Liebmann/Alexander Engel, Ernst Gettke) Volkstheater, Munich 2 March

1922 **Die erste Nacht** (Heye/Urban, Hans Hellmut Zerlett) Deutsches Künstlertheater 1 June

1922 **Señora** (Alfred Berg/Presber)

1923 **Der Fürst von Pappenheim** (Berg, Willi Kollo/Franz Arnold, Ernst Bach) Deutsches Künstlertheater 16 February

1923 **Dolly** (Rudolf Bernauer/Arnold, Bach) Deutsches Künstlertheater 16 October

Plate 177. *One of the swathe of* **Hugo Hirsch** *songs which flooded on to Berlin's stages between the wars.*

1925 **Komm doch endlich** (Richard Kessler, Rebner) Operettenhaus am Schiffbauerdamm 27 February

1925 **Der blonde Traum** (Kessler, Rebner) Theater am Schiffbauerdamm 5 March

1925 **Monsieur Trulala** (Kessler) Deutsches Künstlertheater 1 May

1925 **Wenn man verliebt ist** (Rebner, Martin Zickel) Theater in der Kommandantenstrasse 1 November

1925 **[Das Abenteuer des Herrn] Maiermax** (Rudolf Österreicher, Leopold Jacobson) Lessing-Theater 31 December

1925 **Der Weg zu Hölle** (Rebner)

1926 **Yvonne** (August Neidhart, Rebner) Theater am Kurfürstendamm 1 August

1928 **Fräulein Mama** (Willi Kollo/Kessler) Deutsches Schauspielhaus, Hamburg 1 July

Other titles attributed: *Pippin der kleine, Die vertauschte Braut, Charleys Tante* (1925), *Kyritz-Pyritz* (1926)

HIRSCH, Louis A[chille] (b New York, 28 November 1881; d New York, 13 May 1924). One of the most happily light-fingered of the group of Broadway composers who carried the popular dance rhythms of the 1910s into the musical theatre and revue.

Hirsch, apparently at first self-taught as a musician, studied classical piano in New York and in Berlin, but on his return to America in 1906 he devoted himself to popular music, becoming a vaudeville accompanist (with Camille D'Arville, 1908, etc), and a pianist and arranger with the Tin Pan Alley music publishing houses of Gus Edwards and, subsequently, of Shapiro-Bernstein. At the same time, he began to place the songs he was writing, and he became a regular purveyor of material to the Lew Dockstader Minstrels whilst interpolating numbers into such Broadway shows as *The Gay White Way* (1907), *The Soul Kiss* (1908), *Nearly a Hero* (1908), *Miss Innocence* (1908), the Sam Bernard show *The Girl and the Wizard* (1909 w Edward Madden) and *Up and Down Broadway* (1910). He collaborated with his neighbor Jerome Kern and with Melville Gideon on the score for a misbegotten Shubert production called *The Golden Widow* (ex- *The Girl from the States*) which folded on the road and, as a result, he had to wait two years further for his first representation as a full-blown show composer on Broadway. This came when he collaborated with Ben Jerome on the music for the Shubert brothers' *He Came from Milwaukee,* another successful vehicle for comedy star Sam Bernard.

Hirsch joined the Shubert staff in 1911 and, over the nearly two years which he spent as a musical pieceworker on their large turnout of shows, he contributed songs to a variety of musicals, including interpolations for the imported *Vera Violetta* (''The Gaby Glide'' w Harry Pilcer), *The Siren* and *The Kiss Waltz* (''Elevation''), pieces for such revues as *The Revue of Revues* (''Pittsburgh, Pa,'' ''The Boardwalk Crawl'') and two editions of *The Passing Show,* and the composite program that made up the 1912 *Whirl of Society* (''My Sumurun Girl,'' ''How Do You Do, Miss Ragtime?''). When Hirsch abandoned his place in the musical production line at the Shubert organization in the later part of 1912 he was replaced by the young Sigmund Romberg.

Hirsch then moved to London, where he immediately scored a significant hit with his score to the London Hippodrome revue *Hullo, Ragtime!,* one of the earliest shows to emphasize the ''new'' American dance rhythms before the British public. He supplied much of the music (w J Rosamond Johnson) for *Come Over Here* at the London Opera House, the music for *Hullo, Ragtime!*'s successor *Hullo, Tango* and for a further revue, *Honeymoon Express,* at the Oxford, as well as composing scores and interpolated numbers for various variety house musical playlets, establishing himself as the most visible supplier of the now hugely fashionable American kind of dance/stage music to the London revue and variety theatre, before the outbreak of war sent him back to America.

Hirsch's first years back home saw him still concentrating largely on revue work, supplying songs for such pieces as Klaw and Erlanger's Broadway production of the London revue *Around the Map* (1915, ''There's Only One Thing a Coon Can Do''), the variety-house revue *Safety First* (1915), the *Ziegfeld Follies of 1915* (''Hello, Frisco!'' and ''My Radium Girl,'' both w Gene Buck; ''A Girl for Each Month in the Year,'' and ''Marie Odile,'' both w Channing Pollock, Rennold Wolf) and the *Ziegfeld Follies of 1916,* whilst also taking a turn back to the musical play. His first efforts in that field were not, however, successful. Neither Chicago's *Molly and I,* in which Lina Abarbanell starred, nor *My Home Town Girl,* a vehicle for popular touring stars John Hyams and Leila McIntyre produced by Perry J Kelly, ventured to Broadway, while *The Grass Widow,* a musicalization of the French comedy *Le Péril jaune* produced by Madison Corey with Howard Marsh, George Marion and Natalie Alt featured, which did, stayed there for only six weeks.

The kind of success Hirsch had enjoyed in his time in London, and in revue, was, nevertheless, soon to come. Whilst *The Grass Widow* was stumbling through its Broadway run, a second Hirsch score got its first airing on Broadway. *Going Up,* a musical version of James Montgomery's play *The Aviator,* scored a splendid success and the dance song ''The Tickle Toe,'' the pretty ballad ''If You Look in Her Eyes'' and the lively title number were swiftly added to the composer's growing list of song successes. Whilst *Going Up* went on to international success, its composer's hometown triumph was consolidated by Klaw and Erlanger's production of *The Rainbow Girl.* Based on Jerome K Jerome's play *Lady Fanny and the Servant Problem,* this musical featured another delightfully tuneful and rhythmic score from which the lilting ''I'll Think of You'' proved the stand-out number. *The Rainbow Girl* had a good Broadway run and a subsequent life on the road, though without winning *Going Up*'s popularity outside America.

This vein of success, however, soon faded temporarily out. Of his next three book musicals, one—a ragtimey reunion show for Weber and Fields—failed to make it to Broadway, whilst the other two left no mark. *Oh, My Dear!,* a small-scale piece constructed for the Princess Theater, on which Hirsch deputized for his old friend Jerome Kern in a collaboration with P G Wodehouse and Guy Bolton, was a disappointment. The show survived but six months in its little auditorium. This was more than the life garnered by the indifferent *See-Saw,* a piece originally intended as a vehicle for the irrepressible Mitzi, but ultimately played with a starless cast for 11 Broadway weeks.

The composer continued with a heavy schedule of new work—revue (*Ziegfeld Follies of 1918*), a musical show for the Friars' Club (*The Hit of the Season* 17 December 1917)—but it was again a musical comedy which gave him his next major hit. *Mary,* produced by George M Cohan, followed *Irene* and preceded *Sally* in the hit parade of poor, pretty ''Cinderella'' girls of the 1920s American musical theatre who made good to the accompaniment of the catchy, lighthearted melodies of the period. Hirsch turned out ''The Love Nest,'' ''Anything You Want to Do, Dear'' and ''We'll Have a Wonderful Party,'' and both the show, which racked up 217 performances on Broadway, and its songs, became widespread favorites. The same team of writers and producer Cohan attempted to repeat *Mary*'s success with *The O'Brien Girl,* a piece built rather transparently on the same lines, the following year. It found a fair degree of popularity, but did not bring forth the same kind of enduring response which had been evoked by *Mary.*

Hirsch then turned back to revue to write for *The Ziegfeld Follies of 1922* and *The Greenwich Village Follies of 1922* and *of 1923* (w Con Conrad), and he was to return only once more to the musical theatre, with the score for a version of Paul Armstrong and Rex Beach's comedy *Going Some,* produced in 1924 under the title *Betty Lee.* Like *The O'Brien Girl,* it won its due measure of success at home and as an export to Australia, but Hirsch was not around to accept its rewards. He died that year, at the age of 42, and *Betty Lee*'s Broadway season was played posthumously.

The composer of some of the most infectiously attractive theatre melodies of his era, Hirsch has suffered an eclipse under the shadow of the big, well-plugged names of, mostly, a slightly later period, but his *Going Up* was revived by the Goodspeed Opera House in 1976 and his favorite songs are still occasionally heard. Historically, he holds a firmer position in the British theatre where, in spite of his brief stay, he was an important figure in encouraging the spread of modern American popular dance and song music on the eve of the First World War.

1909 **The Golden Widow** (ex- *The Girl From the States*) (w Jerome Kern, Melville Gideon/Edward Madden/Glen MacDonough, Joseph Herbert) Belasco Theater, Washington, DC 26 October

1910 **He Came from Milwaukee** (w Ben Jerome/Madden/Mark Swan, Edgar Smith) Casino Theater 21 September

1912 **Whirl of Society** (Harold Atteridge/Harrison Rhodes) in *Whirl of Society* 1 act Winter Garden 5 March

1912 **A Night with the Pierrots** (Al Jolson, et al) in *Whirl of Society* 1 act Winter Garden 5 March

1914 **Dora's Doze** (George Arthurs) 1 act London Palladium 6 July

1915 **The Magic Touch** (w Leon Bassett, Maxwell Brunell/Arthurs, Charles Danvers) 1 act Walthamstow Palace, London 18 January

1915 **Go to Jericho** (w Fred Godfrey/Arthurs) 1 act Oxford Theatre, London 22 February

1915 **Molly and I** (Frank R Adams) La Salle Theater, Chicago 31 August

1915 **My Home Town Girl** (Frank M Stammers) Empire Theater, Syracuse 15 November

1917 **The Grass Widow** (Channing Pollock, Rennold Wolf) Liberty Theater 3 December

1917 **Going Up** (Otto Harbach) Liberty Theater 25 December

1918 **The Rainbow Girl** (Jerome K Jerome ad Wolf) New Amsterdam Theater 1 April

1918 **Back Again** (George V Hobart, Stammers) Chestnut Street Theater, Philadelphia 29 April

1918 **Oh, My Dear!** (ex- *Ask Dad*) (P G Wodehouse, Guy Bolton) Princess Theatre 26 November

1919 **See-Saw** (Earl Derr Biggers) George M Cohan Theater 23 September

1920 **Mary** (ex- *The House That Jack Built*) (Harbach, Frank Mandel) National Theater, Washington, DC 31 March; Knickerbocker Theater 18 October

1921 **The O'Brien Girl** (Mandel, Harbach) Liberty Theater 3 October

1924 **Betty Lee** (Harbach, Irving Caesar) 44th Street Theater 25 December

[CHARLES]-HIRSCH, Karoline [HIRSCH, Karoline] (b Vienna, 28 August 1848; d Vienna, 13 March 1932). Viennese operatic soprano, who created Strauss's Adele on an infrequent visit to the Operette stage.

After graduating with the top award from the Vienna Konservatorium, Karoline Charles-Hirsch performed coloratura soprano roles at Graz, Dresden, Budapest and at the Vienna Hofoper, where she made her debut in the role of Mozart's Queen of the Night. She broke her Viennese contract to go off to sing in Leipzig, and made her Operette debut at the Theater an der Wien, where she created the roles of Gräfin Falconi in Strauss's *Carneval in Rom* (1873) and Adele in *Die Fledermaus* (1874), introducing the famous laughing song (''Mein Herr Marquis'') and its companion audition song ''Spiel' ich die Unschuld vom Lande.'' She subsequently returned to operatic roles, playing throughout central Europe, before retiring and becoming a singing teacher.

HIRSCHMANN, Henri [Louis] [aka HERBLAY, Henri] (b St Mandé, 30 April 1872; d Paris, 3 November 1961). French composer of opéra-comique and musical comedy scores.

Hirschmann began his composing life with operatic ambitions, and he placed a short piece, *Amour à la Bastille,* at the Opéra-Comique at the age of 25. A more ambitious opéra-comique, *Lovelace,* was staged briefly at the Théâtre des Variétés, but before long the composer was purveying short musical scenes and ballet and pantomime music to such light music venues as the Olympia (*Néron, Les Sept Péchés capitaux,* etc) and the Boîte à Musique (*Le Siècle, Le Retour*). His first success came in that lighter musical theatre when his opérette *Les Hirondelles* was produced in Berlin in 1904. The piece went on to be played in Budapest (*Fecskefészek* 1904 Magyar Színház), in Vienna (*Das Schwalbennest* 1905 Venedig in Wien) and in Brussels before it finally made its way to Paris in 1907. By that time Hirschmann had already made himself a home reputation with the successful production of his *La Petite Bohème,* a musical comedy variant on the Murger/Puccini tale, mounted at the Théâtre des Variétés.

In the years that followed he continued to write scores for lyric drama (*Rolande* 1905, *Hernani* 1908, *La Danseuse de Tanagra* 1911), and was considered one of the country's great musical theatre hopes by those to whom the line of French opérette represented by Messager and *Ciboulette* was the legitimate one. Hirschmann lived up neither to their hopes nor to his early promise. Lightening his musical style to approach that of the fashionable and potentially lucrative dance-rhythmed shows of the wartime and postwar years, he supplied some agreeable music to a series of further musical shows in the next 20 years without achieving either a standard repertoire piece or, in spite of reasonable home success with such pretty pieces as *Pouche* (its foreign versions were given new scores), any particularly long runs.

He was represented briefly on Broadway in 1912 when the Léon Pavi mimodrama *Seostrata,* for which he had composed the music, was played on the bill at the Winter Garden with *The Whirl of Society.*

1897 **Amour à la Bastille** (Lucien Augé de Lassus) 1 act Opéra-Comique 14 December

1898 **Les Favorites** (Octave Pradels) 1 act Olympia 28 May

1898 **Folles amours** (w Oscar de Lagoanère/Max Maurey) 1 act Olympia 11 September

1898 **Lovelace** (Jules Barbier, Paul de Choudens) Théâtre des Variétés 15 September

1904 **Les Hirondelles** (Maurice Ordonneau ad Maurice Rappaport) Centraltheater, Berlin 9 January

1905 **La Petite Bohème** (Paul Ferrier) Théâtre des Variétés 19 January

1907 **La Feuille de vigne** (Ferrier) Théâtre du Moulin-Rouge 24 February

1910 **Mam'zelle Don Juan** (Antoine Yvan) Théâtre Grévin 26 January

1910 **La Vie joyeuse** (Antony Mars, Albert Barré) Théâtre Molière, Brussels 10 March

1911 **La Danseuse de Tanagra** (Ferrier, Felicien Champsaur) Opéra, Nice 10 February

1911 **Les Petites Étoiles** (Pierre Veber, Léon Xanrof) Théâtre Apollo 23 December

1913 **La Petite Manon** (Ordonneau, Henze) Théâtre Royal, Ghent 15 March

1916 **La Charmante Rosalie** (Veber) 1 act Opéra-Comique 18 February

1920 **La Princesse Carnaval** (Maurice Desvallières, Paul Moncousin) Théâtre Apollo 24 January

1923 **Epouse-la!** (Veber) Théâtre Fémina 15 February

1924 **La Dame du Pesage** (André Leroy) Théâtre Michel 24 May

1925 **Pouche** (René Peter, Henri Falk ad Alphonse Franck) Théâtre de l'Étoile 18 February

1927 **La Dame au domino** (Henri de Gorsse, Victor Darlay) Théâtre de la Gaîté-Lyrique 28 October

HIS LITTLE WIDOWS Musical comedy in 3 acts by Rida Johnson Young and William Cary Duncan. Music by William Schroeder. Astor Theater, New York, 30 April 1917.

Rida Johnson Young, recently successful with her adaptation of the Hungarian *Az obsitos* as *Her Soldier Boy,* and her collaborator William Cary Duncan took up a much older tale, which had served for a number of earlier musicals, as the plot for their 1917 musical, *His Little Widows.* However, whereas 19th-century pieces like *The Terrible Turk* and *Black and White* had used Eastern harems to supply the bevy of ''wives'' necessary to the story line, Mrs Young and her partner went more local and, following the line used by the French vaudeville *Les Douze Femmes de Japhet,* set their piece in the Mormon center, Salt Lake City.

Robert Emmett Keane played Jack Grayson, a member of the brokerage firm of Lloyd (Carter de Haven), Grayson and Hale (Harry Tighe), who has inherited from his uncle. The conditions of the will, however, state that Jack must marry the dead man's widows. There are eight of them, for Uncle was a Mormon. They are, after three acts of comic convolutions, eventually disposed of to Harry Jolson (Charles Prince), who runs a revue company, and each fellow pairs off with the girl he has been singing duets with most of the night—Pete Lloyd with Blanche (Frances Cameron), Biff Hale with Annabelle (Flora Parker) and Jack with Marilla (Hattie Burks). Frank Lalor featured as a Mormon called Abijah Smith, and the better songs included a song-and-dance quartet ''I'm Crazy About the Way You Dance with Me,'' and a trio led by Abijah about ''A Wife for Each Day in the Week.''

His Little Widows had an indifferent Broadway run of 72 performances and changed its title to a less funereal one before being shown to the rest of the country (*Some Little Girl* Empire, Syracuse 14 March 1918), but London's Bernard Hishin took it up and mounted it (ad Firth Shephard) at Wyndham's Theatre with its original title and a cast headed by Gene Gerrard (Jack), Eric Blore (Biff), Laddie Cliff (Pete), Joan Hay (Blanche) and Mabel Green (Annabelle) and the show achieved a thoroughly respectable 172 London performances before going on the road. Shephard and Cliff were clearly amongst those who remembered it fondly for, a few years later, they lifted the show's libretto, even more blatantly than its authors had lifted the earlier pieces for theirs, and attaching it to a fresh score, under the title *Lady Luck,* scored a 324-performance West End hit.

The first English version of *His Little Widows* also got a showing in Australia, produced on the Tivoli circuit with William Valentine (Jack), Muriel Cathcart (Marilla), Hugh Steyne (Biff), Marie La Varre (Annabelle), Rex London (Pete) and Vera Pearce, then Minnie Love (Blanche). It ran for around six weeks in Melbourne, and was then seen in Sydney (17 July 1920).

UK: Wyndham's Theatre 16 June 1919; Australia: Tivoli, Melbourne 24 April 1920

HITCHCOCK, Raymond (b Auburn, NY, 22 October 1871; d Beverly Hills, Calif, 24 November 1929). Popular star comedian of the Broadway musical stage in the early years of the 20th century.

Hitchcock began his professional career as a comic actor playing comic opera in repertoire and summer season: with the ''Casino Opera Co'' at Atlantic City 1891, at Boston's Palace (Flapper in *Billee Taylor,* etc). In 1894 he toured with George W Monroe in *My Aunt Bridget* (Alton McVeigh), in 1895 he toured with Peter Dailey in *The Night Clerk* (Owen's chum), and in 1896 he took part in the premiere of an original comic opera, *The Mandarin Zune,* at Providence (29 June). He subsequently played with the stock company at Philadelphia's Grand Opera House, on the road with May Irwin in *Courted into Court* (1896, Worthington Best), toured with W T Carleton's company in *Les Brigands* and *The Golden Wedding,* and then moved up to take leading comedy roles in the Castle Square Opera Company: Bicoquet in Planquette's *Paul Jones,* the Lord Chancellor (*Iolanthe*), Don Alhambra (*Gondoliers*), Ko-Ko (*Mikado*), Bunthorne (*Patience*), Flapper (*Billee Taylor*), Baron Puck (*La Grande-Duchesse*), Lambertuccio (*Boccaccio*), Duc de Ifs (*Les Noces d'Olivette*), Lurcher (*Dorothy*), Nicola (*Sinbad*), Enterich (*Der Bettelstudent*), Fanfani Pasha (*Die Afrikareise*), Corrigan (*Lily of Killarney*) and even Antonio (*Mignon*). He continued this musical line in summer season at the Louisville Auditorium (1899, Fay-Camp Opera Co, Sir Joseph Porter, Laurent in *La Mascotte,* Gaspard in *The Chimes of Normandy, Falka, The Mikado,* etc) and in the George Lederer production of the German musical comedy *A Dangerous Maid* (1899); teamed with Marie Cahill as one of the crooked protaganists of the revamped Boston musical *Three Little Lambs* (1899, David Tooke); appeared in *The Belle of Bridgeport* (1900, Bokhara Skitbolliski); and toured again with the Fay Opera Company (1900, *Trial by Jury, The Princess of Trébizonde,* etc), in Luders and Pixley's successful Chicago musical *The Burgomaster* (E Booth Talkington), and in *Miss Bob White,* establishing himself by the age of 30 as a solid principal musical comedian and a touring name.

He appeared on Broadway in the American version of the Strauss pasticcio *Wiener Blut,* playing the merry-go-round proprietor, Kagler, and then won his first Broadway starring role when he displaced William Norris in the title role of the newest Luders/Pixley piece, *King Dodo* (1902). *King Dodo* confirmed the young man as a top musical comedy name. When the great success of that piece was at last exhausted, producer Henry Savage starred Hitchcock as the comical Abijah Booze, American consul in Puerto Plata, in the even more successful musical comedy *The Yankee Consul* (1904, ''Ain't It Funny What a Difference Just a Few Hours Makes,'' ''In the Days of Old,'' ''In Old New York'').

He subsequently toured with his wife, Flora Zabelle, in the play (with three songs for him and one for her) *Easy Dawson* (1905, Ripley Royal Dawson also Wallack's Theater) and in De Koven's *The Student King* (1906, Rudolph) before the authors of *The Yankee Consul* came up with another useful Broadway vehicle for him in *The Yankee Tourist* (1907, Copeland Schuyler). He missed a few performances of this piece when, after a run-in with some blackmailers, he was sent to jail, and found himself arrested and declared insane by the superintendant of the State Hopital for Criminal Lunatics. He was deputized for during this publicity-worthy absence by one Wallace Beery, aged 22.

In 1908 Hitchcock appeared in the unexceptional *The Merrygoround* (t/o Hen Stubbs) and he then switched back to the French opérette of his early days on the stage to play Laurent in a revival of *La Mascotte* (1909) and to summer engagements playing his best-known roles and in such pieces as *The Mikado* (1909, Ko-Ko). He returned to Broadway in the star comic roles of *The Man Who Owns Broadway* (1909, Sydney Lyons), *The Red Widow* (1911, Cicero Hannibal Butts) and *The Beauty Shop* (1914, Dr Arbutus Budd). In 1915 he made his screen debut in *The Ring-Tailed Rhinoceros,* and played alongside Mabel Normand and Mack Sennett in *Stolen Magic* but although he appeared intermittently on the screen he continued to work largely on the stage.

He won a personal success when he appeared in London in the title role of the custom-made *Mr Manhattan* (1916, ''All Dressed Up and No Place to Go'') before coming back to one more musical in New York—the British piece *Betty* (1916), in which he gave his version of the role of Lord Playne created by G P Huntley. Thereafter his musical stage appearances were largely in revue—notably his own series of *Hitchy-Koo* shows—although he returned once more, a decade later, to the musical theatre to play a minor role in *Just Fancy* (1927) at the Casino Theater.

His (second) wife, **Flora ZABELLE** [Zabelle MANGASARIAN] (b Armenia, 1 April 1880; d New York, 7 October 1968), having begun her career in the chorus of the Castle Square Opera Company in Chicago, graduated to second soubrettes on the Broadway stage, appearing as Poppy, and covering the title role, in *San Toy* for Daniel Frohman and singing ''Maisie'' in *The Messenger Boy* (1901, Isabel Blythe) for Nixon and Zimmerman. She took the principal juvenile roles opposite Hitchcock in *King Dodo* (Annette), *The Yankee Consul* (1904, Bonita), *Easy Dawson* (1905, Sadie Collins) and *The Yankee Tourist* (1907, Grace Whitney) and starred alongside him in The *Merrygoround* (1908) and as Bettina in his *La Mascotte* (1909), as well as playing in burlesque (Banana in *The Squawman's Girl of the Golden West*), revue and straight theatre. Later musical appearances included *The Man Who Owns Broadway* (1909, Sylvia Bridwell), the Viennese Operette *The Kiss Waltz* (1911, Nella), *The Pearl Maiden* (1912, Nadine), *The Wedding Trip* (1912, tour), *The Red Widow* (1912, t/o Anna Varvara tour), *Have a Heart* (tour 1917), *Toot Toot* (1918, Mrs James Wellington), the short-lived *The Girl from Home* (1920, Juanita Arguilla) and a tour of *The Rose Girl.* She collapsed during this last engagement and was taken to hospital, reportedly dying. However, although she then retired from the stage, she lasted for nearly half a century more. After her husband's death she pursued a career as a designer.

HIT THE DECK Musical comedy in 2 acts by Herbert Fields based on the play *Shore Leave* by Hubert Osborne. Lyrics by Leo Robin and Clifford Grey. Music by Vincent Youmans. Belasco Theater, New York, 25 April 1927.

In 1927 Vincent Youmans, miffed at what he considered a lack of consideration from his latest producer, decided to mount his next show himself. He went into partnership with Lew Fields, optioned the 1922 play *Shore Leave,* and gave it to Fields's son, Herbert, to adapt. Young Fields turned the plain, demure heroine of the original into a bouncy stunner, shifted the action from seaside New England to the much more picturesque venues of a battleship and far-off China, and christened the piece with the rather more jazzy title of *Hit the Deck.*

Looloo Martin (Louise Groody), who runs a dockside cafe, takes an enduring shine to sailor Bilge Smith (Charles King), who has spent one of his evenings ashore romancing her. When Bilge goes back to sea, Looloo waits until she can wait no more and then, since she has come into some money, sets out to find the forgetful gob. She invites all the Smiths in the navy to a party on board a battleship, and then chases up Bilge's trail all the way to colorful China. This impresses him quite a lot, but her money doesn't, and he will only say ''yes'' when he thinks she is poor again.

Youmans supplied a score full of happy songs, topped by Looloo and Bilge's duo ''Sometimes I'm Happy'' and ''Hallelujah,'' a decidedly tacked-in revivalist number for Looloo's negro pal, Lavinia (Stella Mayhew in blackface), both of which became lasting hits. Neither, however, was precisely a new number: the former had already gone unappreciated in the composer's rewrite of the London hit *A Night Out,* which had folded on the American road, and the latter was also a melody he had composed some years earlier, although not previously used. Looloo also duetted through ''The Harbor of My Heart'' and ''If He'll Come Back to Me,'' Lavinia had a second spot with the comical ''Lucky Bird,'' and three supporting characters (Bobbie Perkins, Madeleine Cameron, John McCauley) sang and danced their way through ''What's a Little Kiss Between Friends?''

Hit the Deck was a fine Broadway success, running for 352 performances as its first touring company headed by Queenie Smith and Charles Purcell set out to cover the country. The show made its London debut under the management of Britain's *No, No, Nanette* producers Clayton and Waller and the Moss' Empires organization in a version adapted, and with two interpolated songs, by R P Weston and Bert Lee, which more politely rechristened Bilge Smith as Bill (Stanley Holloway). Ivy Tresmand played Looloo, Alice Morley was Lavinia, and the show was again a thorough success through 277 London performances, prior to going on tour in triplicate the following season. It was, perhaps, fortunate for Youmans that the British production of *Two Little Girls in Blue* had folded on the road a few months earlier—otherwise some further pieces of the show's reorganized musical score might have been rather too readily recognized as secondhand.

Australia followed close behind with its edition of the show, presenting the musically ''improved'' English version with English ingenue Annie Croft cast as Looloo alongside comic Gus Bluett (Battling), Lance Fairfax (weeks away from becoming the country's favorite Red Shadow) as Bill, and comedienne May Beatty blacked up to play Lavinia. It played seven weeks in Melbourne, and rather more the following season in Sydney (Theatre Royal 26 January 1929) without becoming a real hit.

The Parisian success of *No, No, Nanette* and, to a lesser extent, of subsequent American shows, encouraged the Isola brothers to mount a version of *Hit the Deck* at the Théâtre Mogador. Adapted by Roger Ferréol and Saint-Granier as *Hallelujah,* the piece was produced with local *Rose-Marie* star Coecilia Navarre as Looloo, Géo

Plate 178. **Hit the Deck.** *Stanley Holloway (Bill) chats up Ivy Tresmand (Looloo).*

Bury as Bilge and Gesky belting out ''Hallelujah!,'' with a male chorus of a hundred, a vast battleship, and the Borah Minevitch musical comedians and an acrobatic danseuse, Olympe Bradna, tacked in as extra attractions. However, in spite of the decided effect made by Minevitch's harmonica-playing team, *Hallelujah* didn't take, and after a month the management took it off and replaced it with a reprise of the reliable *Rose-Marie.*

Two film versions of *Hit the Deck* appeared, the first in 1930, with Polly Walker and Jack Oakie in the lead roles, the second in 1955 with Debbie Reynolds, Jane Powell and Tony Martin in a version which used more of the show's score (7 of 10 numbers, complemented by several other Youmans numbers and ''Ciribiribin''!) than its story. The show was also televised in 1950, but in spite of its original popularity, it has been rarely seen on the stage since. Characteristic revivals were seen at the Jones Beach Marine Theater in 1960 (23 June) and at the Goodspeed Opera House in 1977.

UK: London Hippodrome 3 November 1927; Australia: Her Majesty's Theatre, Melbourne 28 July 1828; France: Théâtre Mogador *Hallelujah* 15 December 1929

Films: RKO 1930, MGM 1955

Recordings: London cast recordings assembled (WRC), selection (HMV, Fontana), film soundtrack 1955 (MGM)

HMS PINAFORE, or The Lass That Loved a Sailor Comic opera in 2 acts by W S Gilbert. Music by Arthur Sullivan. Opera Comique, London, 25 May 1878.

Following the success of his Comedy Opera Company production of *The Sorcerer,* Richard D'Oyly Carte mounted a second comic opera written by W S Gilbert and Arthur Sullivan. The new piece abandoned the familiar English rustics and rural nobles of its predecessor and, instead, devoted itself to having some burlesque fun at the expense of things nautical and more specifically theatrical-nautical, much as F C Burnand had done with such felicity a decade or so earlier in his hugely successful bur-

Plate 179a. **HMS Pinafore.** *A Broadway production of the early part of the century.*

lesque *Black-Eyed Susan.* Gilbert's libretto, which recycled many ideas and elements first used in his comic poetry, had much more of the flavor of the Gallery of Illustration and of English operetta to it than Burnand's combination of low comedy, puns and panty hose, and the text of *HMS Pinafore* wittily mocked the conventions of the nautical melodrama in an altogether more sophisticated manner than the celebrated burlesque had done, following naturally, but more joyously, in the path rather politely set out by the English comic tale of *The Sorcerer.*

Extremely able seaman Ralph Rackstraw (George Power) is in love with Josephine (Emma Howson), the daughter of his Captain (Rutland Barrington), but she is intended as a bride for the Admiral, Sir Joseph Porter KCB (George Grossmith), a curious gentleman who has—shades of the van Ostebal of *Le Canard à trois becs*— never been to sea and who has trendy liberal ideas about all men been equal. Himself, of course, excepted. Josephine is not long able to mask her reciprocal yearnings for the pretty tar, and the two plan to elope. Alas, they are betrayed by the standard villain of melodrama, the hunchbacked sailor Dick Deadeye (Richard Temple). But the bumboat woman, Little Buttercup (Harriet Everard), comes to the rescue. Once, years ago, wet-nurse to Captain Corcoran and Ralph, she culpably mixed the two babes up, and thus—she is bound to admit—Ralph is Corcoran and Corcoran is Ralph. Since birth is the all-important consideration in such things, the lowborn Corcoran is stripped of his rank, and Ralph is promptly promoted to Captain. The new captain is quite able to wed the daughter of his inferior, now disdained by the Admiral, for love and liberalism (trendy or otherwise) certainly do not level all ranks quite that much.

The score of *HMS Pinafore* was in every way the equal of its libretto. On one hand, Sullivan clipped through the pattering notes of Sir Joseph's comical curriculum vitae (''When I was a lad I served a term . . .'') as the Admiral told of how he had ''polished up the handle of the big, front door'' on his way to becoming ''ruler of the Queen's Navee,'' and of Corcoran's jolly self-introduction (''I Am the Captain of the Pinafore'') claiming that he was ''never, never sick at sea.'' On the other, he turned out some soaringly romantic, but sufficiently twinkle-in-the-eyed, pieces for the romantic and dramatic moments: Josephine's prima donna soliloquy over giving up riches and rank for the sake of a lowly born sailor (''The Hours Creep on Apace''), Ralph's lyrical praises of ''A Maiden Fair to See'' for whom he is prepared to blow his brains out, their sub-operatic confrontation, with the lady not yet willing to drop her pretence of indiffer-

Plate 179b. **HMS Pinafore.** *An Irish-brought-to-London production of the 1980s. And the good ship Pinafore has as much wind in her sails in the year 2000 as she ever did.*

ence (''Refrain, Audacious Tar''), and their last farewell (''Farewell, My Own'') which, of course, turns out not to be the last. Captain Corcoran had his lyrical moment, too, serenading the moon in not quite traditional style (''Fair Moon, to Thee I Sing''), before joining in one of the show's lighthearted highlights, the trio song-and-dance ''Never Mind the Why and Wherefore,'' which introduced the most famous theatrical dance in years in Johnny D'Auban's tripping little routine for Grossmith, Temple and Miss Howson. Little Buttercup had her musical moment in her entry song (''I'm Called Little Buttercup''), whilst memories of many a nautical night in the theatre were echoed in the glee which Sullivan composed for a quartet of sailors, a piece presented as the philanthropic work of the Admiral, who intends it as a morale-boosting piece for the lower ranks—''A British Tar.''

After a mediocre beginning, *HMS Pinafore* soon established itself as a major hit and, in spite of managerial problems and a broken run, it ended by playing a total of 571 performances at the Opera Comique, a record for a British musical to that time, even though the London production of *Les Cloches de Corneville* was at the same time notching up an even longer run. At one stage there were two *Pinafore*s playing in the West End for, when Carte successfully outmaneuvered and outbattled his backers for control of the show, those gentlemen set up a rival production of *HMS Pinafore* at the Imperial Theatre. It lasted 12 weeks before they were obliged to give best, but the suings and countersuings continued for a long time.

Two concurrent productions was, however, nothing compared to what happened when *HMS Pinafore* hit Broadway. R M Field of Boston (with a female Ralph), the endlessly touring Mrs Alice Oates (with an interpolated role for her principal tenor—to make up for the fact she played Ralph—and several interpolated songs) and

John T Ford of Baltimore all got versions of the copyright-free show onto the stage before the end of 1878, and in January 1879 James C Duff mounted New York's first production. British baritone Thomas Whiffen played Sir Joseph, local soprano Eva Mills and Henri Laurent (ex-of the London Gaiety) the lovers, and Eugene Clarke the Captain, and Duff's production ran for a fine 175 nights in the metropolis, as a perfect tidal wave of royalty-free *Pinafores* began to sweep the stages of New York and the rest of the country. There was Edward Rice's *Pinafore* with George Fortescue playing a travesty Buttercup; the Holman Opera Company's version in which Bob Beckett sang ''Nancy Lee,'' Bobstay did a concertina solo and a character called Tom Bowling got ''La Marseillaise'' into the proceedings; there was Gorman's Philadelphia Church Choir Company with a cast of church vocalists; there was the Coloured Opera Troupe's negro version, a juvenile version with a cast of little Philadelphians, another children's troupe in which the young Minnie Maddern appeared as Ralph, an all-women one, a German-language version (*Ihre Majestats Schiff Pinafore*) and a Pennsylvania Dutch version (*HMS Pinafore, oder das Mädel und ihr Sailor Kerl* ad Alfred Charles Moss); and there was the Boston Ideal Opera Company's impeccably vocal version, which was set up to be the ''ideal'' production. At one stage, in 1879, there were said to be 150 companies playing the show throughout America, although it is a fair bet that some of these productions were very far from the original in both text and in music, and were largely cashing in on what had become the most famous stage title in decades. Finally, Carte himself brought a company to Broadway to show America how superior a faithful version of the piece, complete with director Charley Harris's original stage business, was, but his company was largely there to launch his next show and it played only four weeks of *Pinafore* in New York.

The rest of the English-speaking world followed Britain's, and America's, lead. Australia and New Zealand saw several approximate and pirated productions before J C Williamson's officially licensed production was mounted there; venues as far apart as India, China and Hong Kong (thanks to Australia's Victoria Loftus burlesque troupe) and Cuba saw the show before 1879 was out; and everywhere the response was the same: *HMS Pinafore* was unchallengedly the most successful English-language musical play ever—everything from *The Beggar's Opera* to *Maritana* had to fight only for second place.

American stages quickly got out a whole series of burlesques, among them the San Francisco Minstrels' *His-Mud-Scow Pinafore* (10 February 1879) with Charles Stevens as ''Little Buttertub'' and ''with the original music''; a *TPS Canal Boat Pinafore*—followed by an original *HBS Venus, or the Blessings of a Popular Government* (Thomas Hindley/William N Griffith, 19 May 1897), which owed more than a little to Gilbert's *The Happy Land*—at Tony Pastor's with Gus Williams as ''Sir Joseph Lager,'' a chorus of 40 and 12 clog dancers; the same Mr Williams's *New Orleans Schooner Pinafore* (with the comedian now as ''Joseph Weiss Beer''); Boston's Frank Nelson *Boston Museum Schooner Pinafore;* a piece called *The Admiral* with a low-Deutscher Sir Joseph; and even an exasperated *No Pinafore* which ended up with the whole cast hung from the yardarm. In fact, half the vaudeville houses on the Continent in mid-1879 featured some sort of a potted or parodied or just plain extremely approximate *Pinafore* piece on their program. As late as 1911 the *Ziegfeld Follies* burlesqued the show with Leon Errol as Bebe and Fannie Brice as Becky Butternut. Australia (*HMS Pinbehind, Pin-A-4,* etc) followed suit, with pieces largely designed to allow the company to give the show's famous music whilst escaping the copyright rules which banned them from producing the real show. Britain, however, satisfied itself with the real thing until a down-under piece called *The Wreck of the Pinafore* (Dunedin, New Zealand 29 November 1880) was mounted on the London stage in 1882 (Opera Comique 27 May). It lasted but four nights. Another sequel, *Sir Joseph at Sea,* was mounted by the Kelly and Leon minstrels after the Australian courts had prevented them continuing their popular but pirated performances of the real show, but it too sank quickly.

It was, perhaps, the difficulty involved in adapting Gilbert's humor to other tongues which led to such a great hit being largely ignored in Europe. Ernst Dohm's German-language version, *Amor am Bord,* was mounted in Berlin in 1881, and Budapest saw four performances of Jenő Rákosi's Hungarian version the same year, but there seems to have been little else in the way of Continental takers except for a one-act sainete called *Ensayo General* (dress rehearsal), with a libretto by Antonio Llanos, produced at the Teatro Apolo, Madrid, in 1887. In true Spanish fashion, the author helped himself to the music of *HMS Pinafore* to make up his score. If the show's popularity and influence was small in Europe, however, it was enormous in the English-speaking theatre. *HMS Pinafore* set the style and standard for English-language comic opera in the decades to come, and gave an impetus to the musical theatre in Britain and America at least equivalent to that given by *Orphée aux enfers* in France, or by *Die Fledermaus* in Vienna. Like those two shows, it has remained a staple in the English-language repertoire, and one of the most popular amongst the Gilbert and Sullivan shows.

In Britain, with the D'Oyly Carte company holding mainmise over the production of the show up till the expiry of the copyright, *HMS Pinafore* was seen only in that company's progressively more sterile mountings. In America, however, the show was seen both in the Carte organization's versions, during regular visits, but also in a number of other mountings, the most memorable of which was undoubtedly the 1911 ''all-star'' revival mounted by William Brady and the Shuberts with Henry Dixey (Sir Joseph), Louise Gunning (Josephine), Marie Cahill (Little Buttercup), De Wolf Hopper (Deadeye) and Eugene Cowles (Bill) featured. It played 48 performances on Broadway before going round the country.

Whilst other Gilbert and Sullivan shows—notably *The Mikado* and *The Pirates of Penzance*—have been staged in more or less gimmicky productions or ''versions'' in the 20th century, *HMS Pinafore* has proved remarkably resistant to such treatment. An attempt in America, in the wake of the first flush of souped-up *Mikado*s in the 1930s, resulted in a *Tropical Pinafore* being unsuccessfully mounted in Chicago in the 1939–40 season, and there were two simultaneous Broadway flops on the same lines in 1945: a black-cast *Memphis Bound!* (Broadway Theater 24 May) and a filmland burlesque *Hollywood Pinafore* (Alvin Theater 31 May). Much later, following the great success of the enlivened American *Pirates of Penzance,* London, in its turn, proffered a slightly modern *Pinafore* at the Collegiate Theatre, with Alec McCowen as Corcoran. The most successful such production, however, was one mounted in Dublin and subsequently played at London's Old Vic (22 April 1986), which took few liberties with the text, but swapped the 19th-century burlesque idiom for a vigorously hyperactive 20th-century one.

USA: Boston Museum 25 November 1878, Standard Theater, New York 15 January 1879, Germania Theater *IMS Pinafore* 22 March 1879; Australia: School of Arts, Sydney 3 May 1879; Hungary: Népszínház *A Pannifor kapitánya* 21 June 1881; Germany: Friedrich-Wilhelmstädtisches Theater 1881; France: St Edmund's College, Douai January 1901

Recordings: complete (Decca, HMV), selections (ALP, TER), selection in Danish (Polyphon), etc

HOBART, George V [PHILPOTT, George Vere Hobart] (b Cape Breton, Nova Scotia, 16 January 1867; d Cumberland, Md, 23 January 1926). A prolific supplier of texts of all kinds to the Broadway stage over some 25 years.

Telegraph operator, PA journalist, amateur actor and sometime baseball manager, George Hobart settled down eventually in the newspaper world, becoming managing editor of the Cumberland *Scimitar* in 1895 and then, during a period living and working in Baltimore, a contributor of verses, jokes and stories to the local *American, News* and *The Morning Journal*—in which he distinguished himself with a series of Dutch comedy yarns known as the ''Dinkelspiel Papers''—whilst also acting as editor of the Baltimore *Life.* He made his debut as a dramatist in 1897 when he adapted the successful Philadelphia piece *Miss Philadelphia* as *Miss Manhattan* for New York audiences, and for more than a quarter of a century thereafter he engaged himself in turning out the texts for a string of plays, revues, burlesques and musicals, directing all kinds of productions in all kinds of theatres and also turning out both newspaper copy and books, in a busy career which, whilst it ensured him a constant presence in the theatres of the time, did not in the end produce anything that might have become an enduring success.

On the revue front he provided material for six editions of the *Ziegfeld Follies* between 1911 and 1917, as well as for the *Music Box Revues*, *The Greenwich Village Follies, Hitchy Koo of 1919* and others; on the straight stage *Wildfire* (1908) and *Experience* (1914) gave him the most success from a considerable list of plays, whilst his musical shows—for which he wrote sometimes book and lyrics, and at other times just one or the other—ranged through the whole spectrum of current styles. The fairly traditional musical-play mode of pieces such as *The Wild Rose, The Jersey Lily* or *Glorianna* however, seemed to suit him less well than the frankly musical-comic genre, in which he turned out texts for all kinds of loose-limbed entertainments—vehicles for such stars as May Irwin or Marie Cahill, such broadly low-brow entertainments as the Rogers Brothers shows, Hippodrome spectacular and Broadway burlesque—as well as American adaptations of such German pieces as Jean Kren's Posse *Im Himmelshof* (*Hodge, Podge & Co*), the Viennese hit musical *Der Frauenfresser* and the spicily farcical and extremely successful *Alma, wo wohnst du?,* and rewrites of Adolf Phillip and Edward Paulton's musical comedy *Mimi* as the libretto for Ivan Caryll's *Kissing Time* and of the Charles Klein play *Maggie Pepper* as *Letty Pepper* for Charlotte Greenwood. At one stage, he even combined with Gitz Rice in writing miniature radio musical comedies plugging Goodrich Silverton Cord.

Several of Hobart's shows found a solid popularity on the American circuits, but probably the most generally successful amongst them was the sentimental postwar-time musical tale of *Buddies,* which provoked its author to a kind of musequel in *Sonny.*

A number of Hobart's non-musical works were subsequently turned into musical plays by his own or other hands. His farce *What's Your Husband Doing?* became *Miss Blue Eyes,* a piece with a Silvio Hein score which folded on the road to Broadway in 1918, as did the 1920 musical *Dearie* (Malvin Franklin/John Wilson, Detroit 5 September), based on the horse-racing play *Wildfire* written by Hobart and George Broadhurst. Hobart's book *Up the Line, John Henry,* initially dramatized (w E E Rose) for Dan Daly (Hyperion Theater, New Haven, Conn 14 May 1903), subsequently became the source for the musicals *It's Up to You, John Henry* and *All for You* (Mason Opera House, Los Angeles 24 October 1925, mus: Arthur Freed), and in a potted form the mini-musical *Peaches* played on the variety circuits by William Courtleigh.

1897 **Miss Manhattan** (Ferdinand Puehringer, Herman Perlet, et al/Edgar Smith ad) Wallack's Theater 23 March

1900 **Broadway to Tokio** (Reginald De Koven, A Baldwin Sloane/w Louis Harrison) New York Theater 23 January

1900 **A Million Dollars** (Sloane/w Harrison) New York Theater 27 September

1900 **The Military Maid** (Alfred E Aarons) Savoy Theater 8 October

1900 **Hodge, Podge & Co** (John Bratton/Walter Ford) Madison Square Theater 23 October

1900 **Nell-Go-In** (Sloane) burlesque 1 act New York Theater 31 October

1900 **Miss Prinnt** (John Golden) Albany 5 November, Victoria Theater 25 December

1900 **After Office Hours** (Sloane) burlesque in *The Giddy Throng* New York Theater 24 December

1901 **Fun on the Beach** (Sloane) 1 act Cherry Blossom Grove 3 May

1901 **The King's Carnival** (Sloane/w Sydney Rosenfeld/Rosenfeld) New York Theater 13 May

1901 **Supper at Sherry's** (Sloane) burlesque in *The King's Carnival* New York Theater September

1901 **The New Yorkers** (Ludwig Englander/Glen MacDonough) Herald Square Theater 7 October

1902 **The Hall of Fame** (Sloane/Rosenfeld) New York Theater 3 February

1902 **The Belle of Broadway** (Sloane, et al/W H Post) 1 scene Winter Garden Theater 17 March

1902 **The Wild Rose** (Englander/w H B Smith) Knickerbocker Theater 5 May

1902 **Sally in Our Alley** (Englander) Broadway Theater 29 August

1902 **Mr O'Reilly** (Sloane) Lyceum Theater, Elmira 29 September

1903 **The Darling of the Gallery Gods** (Ben Jerome/Matt C Woodward, John Gilroy) burlesque 1 act Crystal Gardens 22 June

1903 **Dress Parade** (B Jerome/Woodward, Gilroy) 1 act Crystal Gardens 22 June

1903 **Lifting the Cup** (B Jerome/Matt Woodward, Nicholas H Biddle) 1 act Crystal Gardens 27 July

1903 **The Rogers Brothers in London** (Max Hoffman, Max Ellis, Melville Ellis/w Edward Gardenier/J J McNally) Knickerbocker Theater 7 September

1903 **The Jersey Lily** (De Koven) Victoria Theater 14 September

1903 **The Sleepy King** (G E Conterno) Metropolitan Opera House, St Paul, Minn 24 September

1903 **Mother Goose** (Fred Solomon/McNally) New Amsterdam Theater 2 December

1904 **The Rogers Brothers in Paris** (Hoffman/McNally) New Amsterdam Theater 5 September

1904 **Mrs Black is Back** (several) Waterbury, Conn 29 September, Bijou Theater 7 November

1904 **The Smiling Island** (Albert von Tilzer, J Sebastian Hiller, K S Clark) Casino Theater, Philadelphia 15 December

1905 **The Athletic Girl** (Jean Schwartz) 1 act Colonial Music Hall 15 February

1905 **A Yankee Circus on Mars** (Manuel Klein, Schwartz/Harry Williams) New York Hippodrome 12 April

1905 **Comin' Thro' the Rye** (Sloane, J Sebastian/Hiller) Casino Theater, Philadelphia 25 May; Herald Square Theater 9 January 1906

1905 **The Ham Tree** (Schwartz/William Jerome) Lyceum Theater, Rochester 17 August; New York Theater 28 August

1905 **The Rogers Brothers in Ireland** (Hoffman/McNally) Liberty Theater 4 September

1905 **It's Up to You, John Henry** (various) Alvin Theater, Pittsburgh 24 September; Grand Opera House 23 October

1905 **Moonshine** (Silvio Hein/Edward Milton Royle) Detroit Theater, Detroit 24 September; Illinois Theater, Chicago 2 October; Liberty Theater 30 October

1906 **Mrs Wilson That's All** (various) Plainfield, NJ 21 September; Bijou Theater 5 November

1907 **The Land of Nod** (Joseph E Howard/Frank Adams, Will Hough) adaptation for New York (New York Theater)

1907 **The Song Birds** (Victor Herbert) 1 act Lamb's Club; New York Theater in *The Land of Nod* 1 April; Alhambra 2 September

1907 **Miss Camille** (V Herbert) 1 act Lamb's Club 14 April; Shubert Theater, Newark 21 October

1907 **Peaches** (various) potted *It's Up To You John Henry* Colonial Theater 3 June

1907 **The Big Stick** (uncredited) Norfolk, Va 9 September; West End Theater 24 February 1909

1908 **The Merry Widow burlesque** (Lehár arr) Weber's Music Hall 2 January

1908 **The Boys and Betty** (Hein) Wallack's Theater 2 November

1908 **The Merry Widow and the Devil** West End Theater 16 November

1909 **The Candy Shop** (Golden) Knickerbocker Theater 27 April

1909 **Old Dutch** (V Herbert/Edgar Smith) Herald Square Theater 22 November

1910 **The Yankee Girl** (Hein) Herald Square Theater 10 February

1910 **Girlies** (Egbert van Alstyne/Williams) New Amsterdam Theater 13 June

1910 **Alma, Where Do You Live?** (*Alma, wo wohnst du?*) English version (Weber's Theater)

1910 **When Sweet Sixteen** (V Herbert) Court Square, Springfield, Mass 28 November; Daly's Theater 14 September 1911

1911 **Little Miss Fix-It** (Jack Norworth, Nora Bayes, et al/w William J Hurlbutt) Globe Theater, New York 3 April

1911 **HMS Vaudeveel** (arr Maurice Levi) burlesque in *The Follies of 1911* New York Roof (Jardin de Paris) 26 June

1912 **Over the River** (Schwartz, John Golden/w H A du Souchet) Globe Theater 8 January

1912 **A Polish Wedding** (*Polnische Wirtschaft*) English version (Empire Theater, Syracuse)

1912 **The Woman Haters [Club]** (*Der Frauenfresser*) English version (Astor Theater)

1912 **The Village Blacksmith** (V Herbert) 1 act Lamb's Club 29 December

1913 **Over the Garden Wall** (Hein) sketch Proctor's, Newark 29 September

1913 **Glorianna** (Hein/Philip Bartholomae) Cort Theater, Chicago 12 October

1918 **Back Again** (Louis Hirsch/w Frank Stammers) Chestnut Street Theater, Philadelphia 29 April

1918 **Just Around the Corner** (various/w Herbert Hall Winslow) Apollo Theater, Atlantic City 9 May; Longacre Theater, New York 5 February 1919

1918 **Miss Blue Eyes** (Hein) Apollo Theater, Atlantic City 3 October

1919 **Buddies** (B C Hilliam) Selwyn Theater 27 October

1920 **Kissing Time** (Ivan Caryll/Philander Johnson, Clifford Grey, Irving Caesar) Lyric Theater 11 October

1921 **Sonny** (Raymond Hubbell) Cort Theater 16 August

1922 **Letty Pepper** (Werner Janssen/Leo Wood, Irving Bibo/w Oliver Morosco) Vanderbilt Theater 10 April

1923 **That Casey Girl** (Schwartz/Jerome/w Willard Mack) Lyceum Theater, Paterson, NJ 22 October

HOCHZEITSNACHT IM PARADIES Operette in 6 scenes by Heinz Hentschke. Lyrics by Günther Schwenn. Music by Friedrich Schröder. Metropoltheater, Berlin, 24 September 1942.

On the day of her wedding to tennis-playing Ulrich Hansen (Johannes Heesters), Regine (Hilde Seipp) succumbs to a fit of jealousy over a piece of his past, the extravagant Spanish dancer Doña Dolores, otherwise known as Dodo (Gretl Schörg), and the resulting tantrum ends with the bridegroom going off to spend what should have been his wedding night at the Hotel Paradies. The soon repentant Regine follows, but when she arrives and sees Ulrich with a woman—of whom she does not see enough to know it is her innocent friend Veronika (Ingeborg von Kusserow)—she promptly floods out again. So Ulrich takes Veronika on what should have been his honeymoon to Venice. There, amid the picturesque accoutrements of a gondoliers' festival, all is finally sorted out. Walter Müller played Poldi, who ends up with Veronika, whilst Paul Westermaier took the part of friend Felix, who pairs off with the harmful Dodo.

A little less feeble than most of Hentschke's libretti, *Hochzeitsnacht im Paradies* had the advantage of a delightful, dancing score by Schröder, a score which was topped by matinée idol Heesters's rendition of the joyful, pre-wedding ''Es kommt auf die Sekunde an,'' a number which subsequently became his theme song and even the title for his autobiography. In fact, *Hochzeitsnacht im Paradies* and the role of Ulrich became one of the actor's staple shows and parts. He repeated it over and over for nearly 30 years all around Germany and Austria as well as playing it on both film and television and almost single-handedly ensured its survival in the repertoire.

The first film version was made in 1950, with Heesters—now playing the drearily inevitable ''film-und-revuenstar'' of contemporary German films rather than a sportsman—alongside Claude Farell (Clarisse, the wife) and Frln Schorg (Rosita, now ''eine revusängerin''), and in the same year the matinée idol of the day introduced his show to Vienna, where he was now headquartered. Franz Stoss's mounting at the Bürgertheater featured Heesters alongside Friedl Loor (Regine), Herta Staal (Veronika), Hedy Fassler (Dodo), Fritz Imhoff (Felix) and Josef Menschik (Poldi). Heesters played Berlin with his show again in 1952 (Titaniapalast w Ilse Hülper, Paul Westermeier and Frln Staal), during which time the show passed what was announced as its 1,000th performance, and Frln Loor and Imhoff took up their roles again alongside Heesters when the show was revived at the Raimundtheater in 1957 with Rószi Bársony playing Dodo. The same theatre repeated the piece with Heesters, Raoul Retzer and Eleanore Bauer in 1961, and in 1971 when the now rather aged but still dashing star teamed with Inge Karstens, Peter Gerhard and Ossy Kolomon. When, in 1962, a second film version was put out, Heesters had terminated his film career and it was Peter Alexander, who had had a tiny role in the 1950 Vienna revival, who played the hard-done-by tennis player, starred alongside Waltraut Haas and Marika Rökk (Ilonka Davarosch, eine of course revuesängerin).

And so, with more than a little help from the always popular Heesters, *Hochzeitsnacht im Paradies* has remained one of the favorite German-language shows of its period, and has won the honors of recordings as well as revivals and films.

Austria: Wiener Bürgertheater 8 December 1950

Films: International Films 1950, Sascha Films 1962

Recordings: selection (part-record) (EMI Electrola, Polydor, SMS, Telefunken)

HOCKRIDGE, Edmund (b Vancouver, BC, 9 August 1919). Baritone leading man of the British editions of several Broadway musicals in the 1950s.

At first a concert and radio vocalist, Hockridge came to the theatrical fore when he succeeded Stephen Douglass in the role of Billy Bigelow in London's *Carousel.*

He subsequently took over as Sky Masterson in *Guys and Dolls,* and then appeared as London's Aristide Forrestier in *Can-Can* and as Sid Sorokin in *Pajama Game.* Thereafter seen largely in revue, variety and pantomime, he latterly played in musicals in the British provinces and made his last West End appearance in the role of Buffalo Bill in a revival of *Annie Get Your Gun.* He has, however, continued to appear in concert.

HOEY, Iris [HASBACH, Wilhelmina Iris Winifred] (b London, 17 July 1885; d London, 13 May 1979). Leading ingenue of the prewar and wartime British stage.

In the early part of her career Miss Hoey alternated appearances in straight theatre with Beerbohm Tree and in musical comedy with George Edwardes, appearing musically in minor roles in *Les P'tites Michu* and the 1906 revival of *The Geisha* (O Hana San). She had her first major part in the musical theatre as the ingenue of *Butterflies* (1908, Elsie Podmore), alongside Ada Reeve and Hayden Coffin, and subsequently appeared as juvenile lady in the unfortunate *The Pigeon House* (1911, Leontine), before taking a run of lead roles in West End musicals: Anna in *Princess Caprice* (1912), Delphine in Ivan Caryll's *Oh! Oh! Delphine* (1913), Miranda Peploe in *The Pearl Girl* (1913), Beatrice in the English company of *Tonight's the Night* which played on Broadway (1914), Peggy in *The Miller's Daughters* (1915), Lolotte in *Mr Manhattan* (1916) with Raymond Hitchcock, and Edna May's famous role in a revival of *The Belle of New York* (1916 revival). After the war, she concentrated her work in a long career in the straight theatre.

HOFFMAN, Al (b Minsk, 25 September 1902; d New York, 21 July 1960). Successful songwriter who supplied material to both theatre and film during a brief stay in Britain.

Seattle-bred and -based Hoffman went to New York to try to break into the songwriting world, and he soon managed to get his first songs published, finding successes with a series of writing partners and such numbers as ''Heartaches'' (1930, w John Klenner), ''I Apologize'' (w Al Goodhart, Ed Nelson), ''Auf Wiederseh'n, My Dear'' (w Goodhart, Nelson, Milton Ager), ''Happy Go Lucky You and Broken Hearted Me'' (w Goodhart, John Murray), ''In the Dim Dawning'' (w Goodhart, Stanley Adams), ''Little Man, You've Had a Busy Day'' (w Maurice Sigler, Mabel Wayne), ''Fit as a Fiddle'' (w Goodhart, Arthur Freed), later featured in *Singin' in the Rain* on screen and stage, ''Who Walks In?'' (w Goodhart, Ralph Freed) and ''I Saw Stars'' (w Goodhart, Sigler).

In 1934 he left America for Britain, when he was hired by Gaumont-British pictures to write songs for their musical films. His film credits over the following years included *Squibs, Jack of All Trades,* Jessie Matthews's *First a Girl* (''Everything's in Rhythm with My Heart''), Jack Buchanan's *Come Out of the Pantry* (''Everything Stops for Tea,'' *When Knights Were Bold, She Shall Have Music* (''My First Thrill'') and Miss Matthews's *Gangway* (''Gangway'').

During the same period he and his collaborators also supplied songs for Jack Buchanan's stage musical *This'll Make You Whistle* (''There Isn't Any Limit to My Love,'' ''I'm in a Dancing Mood,'' ''This'll Make You Whistle,'' ''You've Got the Wrong Rumba''), the Gaiety Theatre success *Going Greek* (''A Little Co-operation from You''), and the Cicely Courtneidge/Bobby Howes *Hide and Seek.*

He returned to America in 1937, and thereafter severed his connection with the musical theatre, but continued to turn out rather more characterful numbers than those he had contributed to the stage for some 20 further years: ''Story of a Starry Night,'' ''Mairzy Doats and Dozy Dotes,'' ''If I Knew You Were Comin' I'd've Baked a Cake,'' ''Hot Diggity,'' ''Me and My Imagination,'' ''Gilly Gilly Ossenfeffer Katzenelenbogen-by-the-Sea,'' ''I Can't Tell a Waltz from a Tango,'' ''Papa Loves Mambo,'' ''Where Will the Dimple Be,'' ''You Can't Be True to Two,'' ''Allegheny Moon,'' ''My House Is Your House'' and the score of Walt Disney's cartoon *Cinderella* (''Bibbidi-Bobbidi-Boo!,'' ''A Dream Is a Wish Your Heart Makes'' w Jerry Livingston, Mack David).

1936 **This'll Make You Whistle** (w Maurice Sigler, Al Goodhart/Guy Bolton, Fred Thompson) Palace Theatre 14 September

1937 **Going Greek** (w Sam Lerner, Goodhart/Bolton, Thompson, Douglas Furber) Gaiety Theatre 16 September

1937 **Hide and Seek** (w Vivian Ellis, Lerner, Goodhart/Bolton, Thompson, Furber) London Hippodrome 14 October

DER HOFNARR Romantic comic opera in 3 acts by Hugo Wittmann and Julius Bauer. Music by Adolf Müller jr, Theater an der Wien, Vienna, 20 November 1886.

Camillo Walzel's 1886–87 season at Vienna's Theater an der Wien saw the production of new works by Millöcker (*Der Viceadmiral*), Suppé (*Bellman*) and Brandl (*Der liebe Augustin*), but the theatre's young conductor, Adolf Müller, topped all their efforts with the most important Operette of his career, *Der Hofnarr.*

The ''royal fool'' of Wittmann and Bauer's 16th-century story is Carillon (Alexander Girardi), and like his more famous operatic counterpart, Rigoletto, he vows a fine revengeful hatred for his employer, the usurping Philip, King of Navarre (Carl Adolf Friese). But Philip is actually a no-holds-barred Bad King, who is unlovingly known simply as ''Philip the Bad,'' and the Jester is not the only one plotting to unseat him. Both the army, headed by Oberst Graf Rivarol (Josef Joseffy) and Lieutenant Archibald de Zornoza (Siegmund Stelzer), and the Home Office, under the manipulation of Der Protonotarius (Franz Eppich) and Der Kanzler (Carl Lindau), are intent on winkling out the hiding place of the legal heir to the crown of Navarre, Prince Julius (Karl Streitmann), so that they may rid themselves of rotten Philip. Baby Julius was hurried away from long-ago danger by the Gräfin Corisdanda von Pompignan (Antonie Hartmann) in good comic-opera fashion, and has been brought up, disguised as a girl, equipped with a gold chain bearing the star of Navarre, against the day when he was going to need to be refound. The diplomats get the right Prince, the Military—trusting the chain, which the homegoing Prince has left with his beloved Felisa d'Amores (Ottilie Collin) and her soubrette foster-sister Yvonne (Regina Stein)—get the wrong one, but, after an act-and-a half of ins-and-outs, and largely thanks to the machinations of the Jester, Philip gets his lot and the juveniles their throne in time for the final curtain.

Müller illustrated the largely comico-romantic, but also, occasionally, dramatic tale with a score which was more substantial but none the less melodious than those he had turned out for such pieces as his other hit of the season, *Die Wienerstadt in Wort und Bild,* and Walzel provided a fine production with ''neuen Dekorationen'' by Hoftheatermalern Carlo Brioschi and Burghart, ''neuen Kostüme'' by M Czibak and B Grünbaum, and a much-admired dance speciality of ''Grand Assauts'' for eight danseuses in the second-act setting of ''a military Camp near Pampeluna.''

Der Hofnarr won a fine reception from press and public and was played for an excellent 51 performances on its first run. It was brought back for a few additional performances in the Theater an der Wien repertoire in most of the next dozen or so seasons (85 performances to 1900) as it went on to be seen in Berlin, St Petersburg (7 February 1887), Budapest, Prague (24 May 1887), at Munich's Theater am Gärtnerplatz (10 September 1887) and throughout central Europe. It continued to find productions into the 20th century, and in 1920 Sigmund Eibenschütz mounted a major Vienna revival at the Carltheater (1 April), with director Louis Treumann in the role of Carillon supported by Grete Sedlitz (Felisa), Mizzi Egerth (Yvonne) and Victor Norbert (Julius), through 53 successive nights.

Although the show does not seem to have had a German-language production in New York, America did get to see *Der Hofnarr* when Heinrich Conried mounted an English-language version of the piece in Chicago and toured it extensively around America, ultimately bringing it to New York's Niblo's Gardens. His casting, however, did add one more string to the skein of the intrigue, for to play Julius—the boy disguised temporarily as a girl—he hired burlesque actress Helen Bertram. J P McGovern (Philip of Navarre), Della Fox (Yvonne), Ada Glasca (Felice), Jennie Reiffarth (Constantia) and Joseph W Herbert (Carillon) took the other principal roles in a production which moved off Broadway and back to the road after two weeks.

Plate 180. **Hoheit tanzt Walzer.** *Otto Storm as Peperl in Ascher's pretty musical play.*

Germany: Friedrich-Wilhelmstädtisches Theater 7 January 1887; Hungary: Király Színház *Az udvari bolond* 26 March 1887; USA: Columbia Theater, Chicago *The King's Fool* 24 December 1888, Niblo's Garden *The King's Fool* 17 February 1890

HOHEIT TANZT WALZER Operette in 3 acts by Julius Brammer and Alfred Grünwald. Music by Leo Ascher. Raimundtheater, Vienna, 24 February 1912.

The librarian Dominik Gaudenzdorf (Otto Langer) wants his daughter Lisi (Mimi Marlow) to wed the rich hotelier Plunderer (Anton Matschegg) of the ''Zum Goldenen Ochsen.'' Lisi, however, is in love with Plunderer's poor but striving rival, Aloisius Strampfl (Bernhard Bötel), who has been unable to save enough cash to purchase the lease on an inn. The girl's music-teacher Peperl Gschwandner (Otto Storm) comes to the rescue. He is about to be named a Hofkapellmeister, with all that means financially, so he gives his savings to the young pair to allow them to lease the ''Zur silbernen Bretze'' inn, and to be wed. Alas, the horrid Plunderer devotes himself to their ruin, and all looks black for the Strampfls until one day two pretty ladies stop off at their inn. Peperl, whose appointment never came through, and who now works as a waiter for his friends, takes a shine to one of them, and a jolly, dancing hour is had by all. Even Plunderer's big drawcard, the famous Lanner quartet, deserts his hotel to join in the merry music-making across the road. But the joyous session has to end when a coach draws up at the door. It has come to take the Princess Marie (Betty Fischer) and her Hofdame (Luise Lichten) back to court. In that hour, however, the name and fame of the ''Zur silbernen Bretze'' have been made, and the Strampfls are saved. Back at the castle, the Princess, preparing for her state wedding, thinks longingly of her carefree waltz at the inn and of sweet, happy Peperl. But all she can do is ensure that he, at last, gets his Hofkapellmeister's post.

Brammer and Grünwald's pretty, alt-Wienerisch story was illustrated by suitably Viennese music, in which waltz tempo reigned supreme. Peperl's first act ''Drunten am blauen Donaustrand,'' the duo for Lisi and Strampfl (''Erst zog ich bloss galant den Hut''), Lisi's second act ''Man preist in tausend Liedern dich,'' Marie's regretful ''Das ist die Prinzessin Tralala,'' and the key duo for the Princess and Peperl, at the heart of their happy hour, ''Das Lercherl von Hernals,'' were amongst the waltz-time features of a score in which most of what was not in 3/4 time was, give or take a moment or two of 9/8 or a gavotte, in the form of march music.

Hoheit tanzt Walzer had a fine Viennese run on its initial production. It was played for a month at the Raimundtheater before swapping theatres for a few performances with the Theater an der Wien's *Eva.* The run was broken again for the brief life of *Die liebe Unschuld,* and yet again for the summer recess, but the show continued on undiminished to pass its 100th night on 10 September, then, with the management now fully aware they had a hit, its 200th on 20 December, finally ending its first run 11 months after its premiere with 230 performances to its credit.

The show went on to become Ascher's most successful piece in Germany, outstripping even his big Berlin hit of a few years later, *Der Soldat der Marie,* and it was also mounted at Budapest's Népopera in 1913 in an Hungarian version (ad Adolf Mérei). An American adaptation was produced by Andreas Dippel under the title of *Princess Tralala* (ad Matthew Woodward) with Phyllis Partington starred as the Princess, and Vienna's Angelo Lippich and Berlin's Emmy Nicklass amongst the supporting cast, but it was not brought to New York, which saw *Hoheit tanzt Walzer* only at the Irving Place Theater in its original German. Hans Unterkirchner played Peperl for the occasion and Mady Christians was the Princess. In Europe, the piece was played regularly for many years. It was given a libretto-lift in 1937 for a production in Zürich under the title *Hochzeitswalzer,* returned to Vienna in 1945 and again at the Rextheater in 1946, and it still wins occasional performances when a ''Biedermeier-era'' Operette is chosen for revival.

A film version, which used some of Ascher's music, but also a bit of Beethoven, made the hero a handsome young waltz composer in a libretto which was very different from, and altogether less charming than, the stage book. Hans Jaray played him and Irene Agay was the Princess who danced the waltz and sang ''Das Lercherl von Hernals.''

Hungary: Népopéra *Budagyöngye* 5 September 1913; Germany: Friedrich-Wilhelmstädtisches Theater ?1920; USA: Irving Place Theater (Ger) 5 November 1915, Newark Theater, Newark, NJ *Princess Tralala* 7 February 1916

Film: Max Neufeld 1935

HOLD EVERYTHING! Musical comedy in 2 acts by B G De Sylva and John McGowan. Lyrics by Lew Brown and B G De Sylva. Music by Ray Henderson. Broadhurst Theater, New York, 10 October 1928.

In 1928 Aarons and Freedley, whose productions in the musical theatre up to that time had been almost all from the pen of George Gershwin, ventured with a show from the De Sylva/Brown/Henderson combination, a team at the top of the theatrical tree since their hit with *Good News. Hold Everything!* took the fashionable world of boxing as its venue, and its little tale told of the ups and downs of the love match between stalwart young boxer ''Sonny Jim'' Brooks (Jack Whiting), who is punching his way through college, and a tiresome little lady called Sue (Ona Munson), who keeps telling him how to fight his matches. Betty Compton played the rich (and therefore threatening and undesirable—only rich men were theatrically OK at this time, girls had to be poor and virtuous) Norine Lloyd, who gets after Sonny Jim whilst Sue is sulking over the boxer's preference for taking orders from his trainer. The comedy was provided by Victor Moore as boxing-camp cook Nosey Bartlett, equipped with a surefire drunk scene, and Bert Lahr as a punch-drunk and ever overweight boxer called Gink Schiner. In spite of bribery, corruption and the women battling over him, Jim punches his way through, pulling out the knock-down blow when the champ (understandably?) casts aspersions at his sulky Sue.

The show's score brought up one De Sylva, Brown and Henderson standard in Whiting and Miss Munson's ''You're the Cream in My Coffee,'' alongside a sort of anti-title song, in which Alice Boulden as an incidental person called Betty Dunn insisted ''Don't Hold Everything,'' and a number of pieces with reference to boxing (''Footwork'') or, more frequently, lovemaking (''An Outdoor Man for My Indoor Sports,'' ''When I Love, I Love,'' ''To Know You Is to Love You''). There was also ''much breathless dancing.''

Hold Everything! had the longest Broadway life of any Aarons and Freedley production, running up a splendid 413 performances at the Broadhurst Theater before going on the road. Even before that happened, however, a British production had already been opened in London, where Clayton and Waller's production of a version which had been anglicized by R P Weston and Bert Lee was mounted at the Palace Theatre. Owen Nares was the boxer, Mamie Watson the pouting beloved, Pamela Carne the opposition, and George Gee headed the comedy as Spike Skinner for a run of 173 performances. The anglicized version also put in an appearance on the J C Williamson Ltd Australian circuits, where speciality dancers Terry and Patricia Kendall starred as Sonny Jim and Sue, with Mary Lawson (Toots) as the feminine rival, and Alfred Frith (Gink), Cecil Kellaway (Chubby) and Pop Cory heading the comedy. It played a month in Sydney and nearly two in Melbourne (Theatre Royal 2 November 1929).

A film version produced in 1930 with 35-year-old former world light-heavyweight boxing champion Georges Carpentier starred alongside Winnie Lightener, Joe E Brown and Sally O'Neil used only three numbers from the original score, topped up by five by Al Dubin and Johnny Burke.

UK: Palace Theatre 12 June 1929; Australia: Her Majesty's Theatre, Sydney 28 September 1929

Film: Warner Brothers 1930

HOLLAND, Fanny (b St George's in the East, London, 14 September 1847; d Bournemouth, 18 June 1931). Soprano with the German Reed company through their most prosperous period.

Londoner Fanny Holland studied at the Royal Academy of Music, made her first appearance in concert in 1868, and quickly established herself as a new vocalist of more than usual liveliness (speciality, the *Faust* Jewel Song). However, she renounced what seemed like a first-class concert and classical career to join the German Reed company at the Gallery of Illustration in 1869 and thereafter created almost all the soprano roles in the Reeds' drawing room operettas, beginning with the ingenue, Rose, in Clay and Gilbert's *Ages Ago* and continuing in the librettist's *Our Island Home, A Sensation Novel* and *Happy Arcadia,* Cellier's *Charity Begins at Home* and *Dora's Dream,* Burnand's *Very Catching* and *Mildred's Well,* and many others. She left the group to play in the ''real'' theatre in Gilbert's *Topseyturveydom* (Tipto) and *Normandy Pipins* (Lina) at the Criterion in 1874, temporarily leaving her place at the Reeds' establishment to Leonora Braham, and departed a second time when, having married Arthur Law, actor and author for the organization, the couple toured with a drawing room entertainment. She also, briefly, took over the role of Josephine in the original *HMS Pinafore.* However, the very largest part of her career was devoted to drawing room musical plays, in which she was seen performing as late as 1895, when she took up the role of Daphne in *Happy Arcadia* during Rutland Barrington's attempt to revive the German Reed entertainments at the St George's Hall.

A charming and dignified young woman with a fine, uncomplicated soprano voice, her characters and performances at the Gallery can be considered the prototype for the English comic-opera heroines created by Gilbert at the Opera Comique and the Savoy.

HOLLÄNDER, Viktor (b Leobschütz, 20 April 1866; d Hollywood, Calif, 24 October 1940). Widely traveled all-purpose German theatre composer, more prolific than memorable.

After an early career conducting at, and intermittently composing for, several theatres in and around Germany, the young Viktor Holländer went to America to act as ''director of operettas and musical comedies'' at the German stock theatre in Milwaukee (1890, Deutsches Stadt Theater). After a brief time back in Berlin, some of it spent working at the Wallner-Theater where he provided the music for the successful Posse *König Krause,* he tried his luck abroad again, first in Chicago, then in London. He has been credited (by himself?) with being musical director of the so-called Royal Opera Comique during his six-years' stay in Britain, and with having at least two shows produced there (*The Bey of Morocco* [Karl Norden] 1894, *Double Dealings* [Fred Vigay] 1898). However, he conducted no musical at the run-down and very unroyal old Opera Comique theatre—although he was, for a period, musical director for Richard Mansell at the suburban Coronet Theatre—and he certainly had no work produced for a run in the London theatre.

On his return from England in 1901, however, he landed the post of musical director and house composer at Berlin's busy Metropoltheater. There he provided the music for a highly successful series of revues (*Ein tolles Jahr, Auf ins Metropol, Der Teufel lacht dazu, Das muss man seh'n!, Hurra! Wir leben noch!, Die Nacht von Berlin,* etc) and Possen for several years before succeeding Paul Lincke in the same position at the Thalia-Theater (1908–9). This second experience was not a success, and he was soon replaced by Jean Gilbert. He continued to supply scores for revues and musical plays not only to German theatres but also, occasionally, to houses abroad for another decade, providing the music for George Lederer's Broadway flop *The Charity Girl* and, in a small tit-for-tat for his replacement at the Thalia, almost an entire replacement score for the American production of Gilbert's *Die moderne Eva.* However, Lederer's announced productions of his *The Girl and the Canary* and *The Clairvoyant* never came to pass.

Holländer's attempts at musical plays were, by and large, not very successful. A little piece called *San Lin,* set in Chinese San Francisco and based on the popular play *The Cat and the Canary,* won productions in Berlin (Stadttheater 1899) and in Britain, his musical of H G Wells's *The Time Machine, Der Sonnenvogel,* was toured through Europe, his *Der rothe Kosak* (''Katzerl und Kater'') was seen in Berlin and Vienna, his 1915 *Die Schöne vom Strand* turned up as *A korzó szépe* at Budapest's Vígszínház (4 September 1915) and as *The Belle of the Beach* at New York's Yorkville Theater, and his 1915 piece *Die Prinzessin vom Nil,* probably the most successful of his Operetten, was played at New York's Irving Place Theater (31 March 1916). None of them, however, went as far afield as his incidental music for the oriental pantomime *Sumurun* (Kammerspiele, Berlin 1910), which was played in Budapest, in New York and around Europe, indeed everywhere Max Reinhardt's much admired spectacular traveled.

His son **Frederick M HOLLÄNDER** (b London, 18 October 1896; d Munich, 18 January 1976), originally a theatre conductor, became a successful film composer in Germany and in America (1933–56). His principal screen credits included *Der blaue Engel / The Blue Angel* (1930, ''Ich bin vom Kopf bis Fuss auf Liebe eingestellt'' aka ''Falling in Love Again''), *Die grosse Sehnsucht* (1930), Deanna Durbin's *One Hundred Men and a Girl* (1937), *Destry Rides Again* (1939, ''The Boys in the Backroom''), *The Man Who Came to Dinner* (1942), *A Foreign Affair* (''Black Marke'') and *Das Spukschloss im Spessart* (1962). In his early European days he also composed revues, Possen, vaudevilles and Operetten, including the 1929 *Ich tanze um die Welt mit dir* (Darmstadt 26 December, Deutsches Künstlertheater w Marcellus Schiffer, etc) and *Hetärengespräche* and the 1930 *Höchste Eisenbahn* (w Schiffer). A later Operette, written after his eventual return to Germany, *Das Blaue von Himmel* (Per Schwenzen), was produced at the Nuremberg-Fürth Städtische Bühnen in 1959 (14 November).

His brother Gustav Holländer (d Berlin, 5 December 1915) also worked as a musical director and composer.

1882 **Der Gesangvereinsprobe** (Holländer) 1 act Cologne July

1885 **Primanerliebe** 1 act

?1885 **Schloss Calliano** (Gustav Kadelburg) Carl-Schultze Theater, Hamburg 8 September

1887 **Carmosinella** (Rudolf Hirschsohn) Saalbau, Frankfurt-am-Main December

?1888 **Striese in Kamerun, oder Ein schwarzer Götze** (w Hirschson) 1 act

?1888 **E.Z.40, oder Schöne Geister treffen sich** 1 act

1891 **[König] Rhampsinit** (Leopold Winternitz) Stadttheater, Milwaukee 19 April; Residenztheater, Breslau 24 June 1893

1891 **The Dwarf's Wedding at the Court of King Peter the Great** (w Fritz Krause/Hans Gross) Milwaukee, Thalia Theater 6 July

1892 **König Krause** (Julius Keller, Louis Herrmann) Wallner-Theater January

1892 **Der berühmte Mitburger** (Karl Laufs, Wilhelm Jacoby) 1 act Wallner-Theater 10 February

1892 **Yvette** (Laufs, Max Krämer) Wallner-Theater 10 February

1897 **The Fair in Midgetown** (Robert Breitenbach) Star Theater, New York 20 September

1898 **San Lin** (Holbrook Blinn) 1 act Breslau 28 January

1901 **Schön war's doch** (Julius Freund) Metropoltheater 24 August

1901 **Der rothe Kosak** (Hermann, Hermann Hirschel) Friedrich-Wilhelmstädtisches Theater 21 December

1901 **'ne feine Nummer** (w Leo Fall/Freund) Metropoltheater 26 December

1902 **Die zwölf Frauen des Japhet** (*Les Douze Femmes de Japhet*) German version by Freund w new score (Metropoltheater)

1903 **Der Sonnenvogel** (aka *Der Phönix*) (Rudolf Schanzer, Georg Okonkowski) St Petersburg (Wiener Operetten Ensemble) 22 August; Centraltheater, Berlin April 1904

1903 **Durchlaucht Radieschen** (Freund) Metropoltheater 31 October

1904 **Die Herren von Maxim** (ad Freund) Metropoltheater 29 October

1906 **Kadettenstreiche** (Heinrich Bolten-Bäckers) Eden-Theater, Aachen 19 July

1906 **La Plus Belle** (Léon Xanrof, Pierre Veber) 1 act Casino de Paris, Paris 29 October

1907 **Die schöne Vestalin** revised *La Plus Belle* by Bolten-Bäckers 1 act Apollotheater 31 October

1908 **Das Mitternachtsmädchen** (Jean Kren, Arthur Lippschitz) Thalia-Theater 14 August

1908 **Schneider Fips** (Kotzebue ad Hans von Wentzel) 1 act Hoftheater, Weimar 17 November

1909 **Der Jockeyklub** (Robert Misch) Neues Operetten-Theater, Mannheim 8 January; Theater des Westens 27 March

1909 **Meister Tutti** (Alfred Schönfeld/Kren) Thalia-Theater 15 January

1909 **Wo wohnt sie denn?** (Kren, Okonkowski) Thalia-Theater 12 February

1909 **Prinz Bussi** (Schönfeld/Kren) Thalia-Theater 13 August

1909 **Revanche** (Louis Windhopp, Loebel) 1 act Hölle, Vienna 31 October

1909 **Die süsse Cora** (Kren, Lippschitz) Thalia-Theater 11 December

1910 **Hupf mein Mäderl!** (Krenn, Lindau) Ronacher, Vienna 13 August

1912 **The Charity Girl** (Edward Peple) Studebaker Theater, Chicago 29 July; Globe Theater, New York 2 October

1913 **Die Königin der Nacht** (Arnold Golz, Emil Golz) 1 act Apollotheater, Vienna 1 February

1914 **Der Regimentspapa** (Richard Kessler, Heinrich Stobitzer) Residenztheater 4 March

1914 **Und Michel lacht dazu** (Ely, Otto) Nationaltheater 2 November

1914 **Freiwillige vor** (Louis Taufstein) Kristallpalast, Leipzig 1 December

1915 **Die schöne vom Strand** (Oskar Blumenthal, Kadelburg) Reisdenztheater 5 February

1915 **Die Prinzessin vom Nil** (Franz Cornelius, Arthur Landsberger) Residenztheater 18 September

1916 **Loge nr 7** (Kurt Kraatz, Theo Halton) Residenztheater 28 January

1916 **Fliegende Blätter aus dem Jahrgang 1850** (Hans Gaus, Theo Halton/Gaus) Residenztheater, 12 May

1916 **Der Patentküss** (Stein-Wildegans) Stadttheater, Schweidnitz 20 October

1917 **Die Liebesgeige** Theater an der Westfront 17 May

1917 **Der Zigeuner** (Liszt arr/Ferdinand Bonn) Walhalla-Theater 31 May

1919 **Der Jäger von der Kurpfalz** (Bonn) Walhalla-Theater 2 April

1920 **Der Schwan von Siam** (Bruno Decker, Robert Pohl) Olympia-Theater, Dortmund 25 December

1921 **Der Marmorgraf** (Kessler, Gerhard Schätzler-Perasini) Residenztheater, Wiesbaden 12 March

Other titles attributed: *Die Rosiere, Tulipan von Panama* (1891), *Der Kerzverführer, Bitte recht freundlich, Die Blumenkönigin, An der schönen blauen Donau*

Autobiography (F Holländer): *Von Kopf bis Fuss, mein Leben mit Text und Musik* (Munich, 1965)

DAS HOLLANDWEIBCHEN Operette in 3 acts by Leo Stein and Béla Jenbach. Music by Emmerich Kálmán. Johann Strauss-Theater, Vienna, 30 January 1920.

Quite what decided Kálmán, the most Austro-Hungarian of composers, to put his music to a demi-semi-Dutch tale is a mystery, but the resultant piece, if a slightly curious variation on the usual Ruritanian Operette (the few moments of Dutch music sound rather Tyrolean, and the Dutch-accented dialogue as if it were burlesque) nevertheless provided the composer and his librettists, Stein and Jenbach, with a distinct success. *Das Hollandweibchen* ran up no fewer than 362 performances in its first run of over a year at Vienna's Johann Strauss-Theater, returning later in 1921 for several further weeks of performances. It also played some performances in between times at the Raimundtheater.

The Princess Jutta of Sonnenburg-Glücksburg (Ida Russka) is all ready to be married to Crown Prince Paul Roderich of Usingen (Karl Bachmann), but on the day of the ceremony only an envoy, Dr Udo von Sterzel (Fritz Werner), turns up. The Prince has apparently no intention of losing his freedom. The charming persuadings of the Baroness Elly von der Weyde (Steffi Walidt) convince Sterzel to stand proxy for his Prince, and it is only after the wedding that Jutta discovers that her bridegroom is not truly indisposed, he is just indisposed to getting wed, and is actually off yachting around Holland. She swears her revenge, heads for Holland in disguise as a little Dutch girl, hooks and catches her Prince, then dumps him, and makes him wait till the very end of the third act for a reconciliation and a happy, waltzing ending. Kálmán's score proved that Sonnenburg-Glücksburg was not too far from Vienna and that, most certainly, waltzes were in favor there but, given that the piece was set in 1920, there was also space for such modern (if again not very Dutch) musical moments as a tango.

Das Hollandweibchen quickly found its way from Vienna to Berlin's Metropoltheater, where, with Claire Dux starring, it had a fine run of more than six months up to March 1921, before being replaced by Lehár's *Die blaue Mazur,* by which time Seymour Hicks and Joe Sacks had brought an English version (ad Seymour Hicks, Harry Graham) to the stage in London. *A Little Dutch Girl* featured no less a star than opera diva Maggie Teyte as Princess Julia of Sylvania alongside Martin Iredale (Paul), Jack Hulbert (Posch), Cicely Debenham (Eloise) and Lauri de Frece (Bomba) for a run of 215 performances. That English version was also seen in Australia, where, after a tryout in Adelaide with Sheila Gale and J Roland Hogue featured, the piece was recast for Sydney (Her Majesty's Theatre 15 April 1922) with René Maxwell and Savoy veteran Claude Flemming. Its six weeks there were followed by a respectable seven in Melbourne (Her Majesty's Theatre 3 June 1922). In Hungary a local adaptation (ad Ernő Kulinyi), *Hollandi menyeckske,* was mounted at the Budapest Király Színház, but in America the show flopped, when a different English version (ad Guy Bragdon, Joe Burrows) got no closer to Broadway than Boston's Majestic Theater.

Germany: Metropoltheater 4 September 1920; UK: Lyric Theatre *A Little Dutch Girl* 1 December 1920; Hungary: Király Színház *Hollandi menyeckske* 21 October 1921; Australia: Theatre Royal, Adelaide *A Little Dutch Girl* 25 March 1922; USA: Majestic Theater, Boston *The Dutch Girl* 22 January 1925

HOLLIDAY, Judy [TUVIM, Judith] (b New York, 21 June 1922; d New York, 7 June 1965). Very blonde star of one Broadway musical whose performance won a Tony Award and, with the help of its film, some cult following.

A member of the night-club act "The Revuers" with Adolph Green and Betty Comden, in which capacity she was briefly a member of the cast of *My Dear Public,* Miss Holliday appeared in several films (including the screen version of *Something for the Boys*) before making her Broadway bow in the 1945 *Kiss Them for Me.* She hit the headlines with her dumb blonde performance in the play *Born Yesterday* and its subsequent film, for which she won an Academy Award and, after other successful films, returned to the musical theatre to star in the comical *Bells Are Ringing,* written by her revue-days partners. She scored a second oversized hit as the ministering angel of the ''ansaphone'' service who was the piece's heroine and introduced ''The Party's Over'' and ''Just in Time.'' She filmed *Bells are Ringing* in 1960 but returned to the theatre for just one further musical, *Hot Spot* (Sally Hopwinder), in 1963, before her early death.

Biographies: Holtzman, W: *Judy Holliday* (Putnam, New York, 1982), Carey, G: *Judy Holliday* (Seaview Books, New York, 1982)

HOLLINGSHEAD, John (b Hoxton, 9 September 1827; d Fulham, London, 10 October 1904). The man who made the London Gaiety Theatre.

The young Hollingshead began his working life as a clerk, and spent periods as a rent collector, a printer's devil and a commercial traveler before settling into a career as a journalist. He worked on *Household Words* and *All the Year Round* under Charles Dickens, for Thackeray on the *Cornhill Magazine* and for a period as dramatic critic of Dickens's *Daily News* before he switched from writing to the theatre, initially as house-manager at the Alhambra. He moved from there, and further into management, when he applied for and was given the tenancy of the newly built Gaiety Theatre.

Hollingshead opened the Gaiety in December 1868 and ran it for 17 years, making it into one of London's most popular and famous houses. From the start he put a particular accent on musical pieces, and he proved himself to be, through his whole career, one of the most enterprising producers in the English-language musical theatre, mounting fine productions of French opéra-bouffe as well as some of the earliest important musical shows of the modern British tradition—*Aladdin II, Thespis, Cinderella the Younger*—and a long and substantial run of superior burlesque, notably as played by J L Toole and Nellie Farren, and then by the famous quartet of Farren, Edward Terry, Edward Royce and Kate Vaughan. Hollingshead also mounted opéra-comique, classic British comic- and ballad-opera, and even operatic productions, as well as taking in visiting, mostly French, companies, both musical and dramatic, during the summer months. In 1885, following an illness, he took George Edwardes into partnership and, soon after, left the Gaiety to develop into the home of Victorian musical comedy in the younger man's hands.

In collaboration with the financier Henry Osborne O'Hagan and the actor John L Shine, Hollingshead also for a time ran the Empire Theatre in Leicester Square, but success proved difficult to find there, and ultimately he gave up that house, and returned his attentions to the Gaiety. He met with similarly bad results when he tried to run theatres in Manchester and in Liverpool (Palace of Amusement, 1897). After leaving the Gaiety, however, everything seemed to go wrong for Hollingshead. He lost all the money that he had made over the years, was forced to turn back to the journalism of his youngest days, and was eventually reduced to being given a benefit by the profession.

Hollingshead published two volumes of memoirs, and three volumes of collected stories and essays (*Miscellanies,* 1874).

Autobiographies: *My Lifetime* (Law, Marston, London, 1895), *Gaiety Chronicles* (Archibald Constable, London, 1898)

HOLLOWAY, Stanley [Augustus] (b West Ham, London, 1 October 1890; d Littlehampton, 1 October 1982). Comic stage and film actor who played in musicals at each end of his career, and made his biggest hit in his sixties.

Holloway spent most of his early career as a concert-party performer, and he made the first of his few widely spaced appearances in musical comedy at the Winter Garden under George Grossmith, appearing in supporting roles in *Kissing Time* (1919, Captain Wentworth) and *A Night Out* (1920, René). For the next decade he was an important member of the celebrated Co-Optimists concert party, taking time out to play leading roles in the London productions of *Hit the Deck* (Bill Smith) and *The Song of the Sea* (*Lady Hamilton,* Lieutenant Manners), but thereafter he interrupted his revue and film successes only for the chief comic role in Jerome Kern's short-lived *Three Sisters* (1934). It was 22 years after this flop before he returned to the musical stage, at the age of 65, to create the role for which he is now mostly remembered, the cockney dustman Alfred P Doolittle in *My Fair Lady,* introducing ''With a Little Bit o' Luck'' and ''I'm Getting Married in the Morning.'' He made, thereafter, just one further incursion on the musical stage, in 1964, in a *Faust*-based musical *Cool Off!,* which folded at Philadelphia.

Holloway also performed and recorded a series of comic monologues (''Albert and the Lion,'' ''Sam, Pick Up Thy Musket,'' etc) which remained long popular in Britain, and appeared in a vast number of films over more than 40 years, notably in his original role in *My Fair Lady* (1964), as Lockit in the 1952 film of *The Beggar's Opera* and in the filmed *The Co-Optimists* (1929) and *The Lily of Killarney* (1934). He also appeared on television as one of the fathers in a version of *The Fantasticks* (1964).

In 1993 his son, **Julian Holloway,** better known as an actor without music, took his father's original role in an American revival of *My Fair Lady.*

Autobiography: *Wiv a Little Bit o' Luck* (Stein & Day, New York, 1967)

HOLM, Celeste (b New York, 29 April 1919).

In a career in which the musical theatre played but a small part, Miss Holm achieved celebrity when she created the role of Ado Annie in *Oklahoma!* (1943), introducing "I Cain't Say No" and "All er Nuthin'." As a result, she was starred as Evelina, the titular lady of *Bloomer Girl,* the following year. Later in her career as a stage and film comedienne and dramatic actress she made intermittent musical theatre appearances, stepping in briefly to play Anna in Broadway's *The King and I,* touring as *Mame* (1967), starring in an attempt to make a musical out of *I Remember Mama* (*Mama,* Buffalo, NY, 1972) and in the short-lived *The Utter Glory of Morrissey Hall,* and playing the role of Liza Elliott in Britain's first performances of *Lady in the Dark* (Nottingham, 1981). In a film career which cast her mainly as smart ladies, she was given a rare musical moment in *High Society* (1956), introducing "Who Wants to Be a Millionaire" with Frank Sinatra.

HOLM, Grete (b c1882). Operette leading lady of two Viennese decades who created several important roles for Straus, Lehár and Kálmán.

Grete Holm made her first appearances in the musical theatre at Brünn, where, at the age of 23, she created the leading role in Robert Stolz's *Manöverliebe* (1906). Both she and the musician (to whom she was later, if briefly, married) were subsequently hired for the Theater an der Wien, but it was the lady who did the better out of the engagement. She had her first major success in Vienna when she created the role of Nadina in Oscar Straus's *Der tapfere Soldat* (1908), introducing "Held meiner Träume," the song which was to become internationally known as "My Hero" in Stanislaus Stange's English version. She then took the principal soprano role in the highly successful Vienna production of Kálmán's *Tatárjárás* (*Ein Herbstmanöver,* 1909) and played Risette/Jeanette in Fall's popular *Die schöne Risette* (1910), but she had her two most important new parts when she moved across to the Carltheater and there created the musically and dramatically substantial star role of Zorika in Lehár's *Zigeunerliebe* (1910) and that of Juliska in Kálmán's *Der Zigeunerprimás* (1912).

She appeared at the Theater an der Wien as Tatjana von Nadaschkin in *Schneeglöckchen* (1910) and as Erna von Hardenstein in *Ihr Adjutant* (1911); at the Johann Strauss-Theater in a revival of *Der lustige Krieg* (1911, Violetta); at the Venedig in Wien summer theatre in *Eine Nacht in Venedig* (1912); and, after spending several years in Germany, at Vienna's Bürgertheater in 1916. She was seen there as Coralie (*Das verwunschene Schloss*), as the star of *Der Soldat der Marie* (1917), as Laura in *Der Bettelstudent* and Heiderose in *Die Glocken von Corneville,* and subsequently created roles in Eysler's *Der fidele Geiger* (1919), in *Hasard* (1920, Steffi) and in *Drei arme Teufel* (1923, Nelly Wolfgang), as well as appearing as Titania in *Afrikareise,* in her most famous role of Zorika and in a repeat of *Herbstmanöver* in 1924.

Plate 181. **Grete Holm** *as the Marie of Ascher's* Der Soldat der Marie.

HOLM, Hanya [ECKERT, Johanna] (b Worms, Germany, 3 March 1893; d New York, 3 November 1992). Dancer, teacher and choreographer in all areas of stage and screen performance.

Miss Holm had several major successes as a choreographer for the musical theatre in the years following her emigration from Germany to America in 1931, beginning, after a contribution to the 1948 *Broadway Ballads,* with the dances for *Kiss Me, Kate* (''Too Darn Hot,'' New York 1948 and London 1951) and continuing, most notably, with those for *My Fair Lady* (The Ascot Gavotte, ''The Rain in Spain,'' New York 1956, London 1958) and for *Camelot.* Other credits included *Out of This World* (1950), *My Darlin' Aïda* (1952), *The Golden Apple* (1954), *Reuben, Reuben* (1955), *Where's Charley?* (London, 1958), *Christine* (1960) and *Anya* (1965).

Biography: Sorrell, W: *Hanya Holm: The Biography of an Artist* (Wesleyan University, Middletown, Conn, 1969)

HOMFREY, Gladys [née BEARD, Alice] (b Cardiff, 7 March 1848; d Kingston-on-Thames, 10 March 1932). Tall, imposing actress who became one of Victorian London's favorite musical comedy dragons.

The daughter of a Welsh cooper, and the wife of a striving bank manager called Samuel Arthur Humphries (''of 54 Lombard Street''), Miss Homfrey came to the theatre at the age of 34, presenting herself at a Gaiety matinée as Romeo and as Juliana in *The Honeymoon.* She won a number of amazed sneers (''an Amazon in stature, of proportions altogether such as we rarely witness in the heroines of modern comedy the masculine perfomers hardly reached the lady's shoulders we are unable to speak of the performance in terms of commendation''), but also a career. And she lost a husband, for a wife on the stage was more than the bank manager could take, and he walked out on her. He died in 1890, and *The Era* reported snarkily ''she is, of course, quite overwhelmed with sorrow.''

Miss Homfrey made her first musical theatre appearance in London as the Princess Badoura in Jakobowski's *Dick* (1884) but thereafter, apart from stints with Minnie Palmer's company in *My Sweetheart* and *My Brother's Sister,* she played mainly in the straight theatre for more than a decade. Then, in 1897, George Edwardes contracted her to succeed Maud Hobson in the important, if barely sung, role of Lady Constance Wynne in *The Geisha,* and Miss Homfrey went on from there to become the reigning heavy lady of the West End musical theatre, creating the roles of Melanopis (*A Greek Slave*), Wun-Lung (*San Toy*), Isabelita (*Havana*), the Duchess of Minster (*Our Miss Gibbs*) and Countess Kokozeff (*The Count of Luxembourg,* London and New York) and appearing at the Gaiety in *The Messenger Boy* (1902, t/o Lady Punchestown) for Edwardes, and playing the formidable Martha Sliggs in *Naughty Nancy* (1902) at the Savoy Theatre. She continued in the musical theatre under George Grossmith, playing dragonistic ladies in *Tonight's the Night* (1914, Angela Lovitt-Lovitt) on Broadway and then in London, in *Theodore & Co* (1916, Lady Theresa Wye), *Yes, Uncle!* (1917, Bébé) and in *The Shop Girl* revival (1920, Lady Appleby), into her seventies.

HONEYMOON LANE Musical comedy in 2 acts by Eddie Dowling. Lyrics by Eddie Dowling and Irving Caesar. Music by James T Hanley. Knickerbocker Theater, New York, 20 September 1926.

An ingenuous Irishy musical with songs with titles like ''The Little White House (at the end of Honeymoon Lane),'' and a cutesy-pie hero (author Dowling) and heroine (Pauline Mason) who dream that they encounter the horrid temptations of the big world outside—including the ghastly possibility that little Mary might make a career in show business—but wake up at the end of the nightmare, heading for their cosy love nest for two. The evil world was represented by the son of the owner of the pickle factory where our hero works, a wicked fellow who plans to hamstring the lead dancer of a show to allow Mary to have her big chance for stardom, thus entrenching her deep in the mire of beastly Broadway.

The real raison d'être of the show was a lavish production, heavily featuring Bobby Connolly's dancers and a series of variety acts which included 250-lb coon shouter Kate Smith and tiny pratfalling Gordon Dooley. Bernard Randall played the manager of the Broadway theatre which belonged to the dream-plot, made up to resemble Florenz Ziegfeld. The combination provided entertainment for Broadway audiences for a highly satisfactory 364 performances.

HONTHY, Hanna [HÜGEL, Hajnalka] (aka HAJNAL, Hajnalka) (b Budapest, 21 February 1893; d Budapest, 30 December 1978). The most important musical comedy star on the Hungarian stage in the years between the wars.

Hanna Honthy worked in the theatre as a child before going on to such roles as Juliette in *Der Graf von Luxemburg,* Gonda van der Loo in *Elvált asszony* (*Die geschiedene Frau*), and the soubrette role of *Tengerész Kató* (*Die Marinen-Gustl*) during her teenage years. She made a big success in the lead role of Hungary's version of *Das Dreimäderlhaus* (Médi), and in her twenties played in a wide range of classic pieces, including *Ein Walzertraum, Az obsitos, Mam'zelle Nitouche, Leányvásár, Der letzte Walzer,* as Adele in *Die Fledermaus* and, most particularly, in the title role of *Die Csárdásfürstin,* as well as the less enduring *Niobe, Rund um die Liebe,* Kollo's *Der selige Balduin,* etc.

She appeared at the Budapest Orfeum in *Frau Luna* and *Lysistrata* and in several original operetts, and scored a major hit as Aspasie in Hungary's version of *Fi-fi,* before joining the Király Színház as leading lady in 1922. There she starred in a series of musical shows, including Komjáti's *Három a tánc* (Maca), the local operett on the life and love of *Offenbach, Die Bajadere* (Mariette), *Die gelbe Jacke* (Mi), Nádor's *Fanny Elssler* (Fanny), Szirmai's *Mézeskálacs* (Queen), *Mädi,* Buttykay's *A császárnő apródja* and a revival of *Szibill,* before moving to the Budai Színkör to star in *A nóta vége,* and then, in 1925, to the Fővárosi Operettszínház, where she was starred in Jacobi's *Miami* and Straus's *Teresina* at the top of an extended association of nearly a quarter of a century with what by then was Budapest's principal musical house.

Amongst the Hungarian operetts in which she subsequently created leading roles were *Csókos asszony, Muzsikus Ferkó, A királyné papucsa, Asszonykám, Kiss és Kis, Mesék az írógepről, A régi nyár, Szökik az asszony, Lámpaláz, A balerina, Pillangó,* Fényes's highly successful *Maya, Egy csók és más semmi, Sárga Liliom, Aki mer, az nyer, Csárdás, Hulló falevél, Romantikus asszony, Julia, Zimberi Zombori szép asszony, Sárgarigo fészek, Fityfiritty, Száz piros rózsa, Mária főhadnagy, Egy boldog pesti nyár* and *Cserebogár, sárga cserebogár.*

She played the Hungarian versions of Lehár's *Die lustige Witwe* and *Zigeunerliebe* and, in the mid-1940s, she still appeared in such roles as the ''víg özvegy,'' or merry widow, in *Das Dreimäderlhaus,* as *Szibill* or the *Grande-Duchesse de Gérolstein,* whilst adding ever more new roles in local pieces such as *Barbara* (1948), and *Bécsi diákok* (1949). When age crept on, a special star-sized role, that of Cecilia, the ex-chorine mother of Prince Edwin, was created for her in a new libretto for *Die Csárdásfürstin,* and a similar one, as Madame Fleury, gardedame to Angèle Didier, in a new version of *Der Graf von Luxemburg* (1952). Eventually, like all the best Hungarian senior stars, she began to play Lujza Blaha's famous ''grandmother'' role in the musical version of Csiky's *Nagymama,* in the twilight of a long and memorable career in the musical theatre.

Biography: Molnár Gál, P: *Honthy Hanna és kora* (Színháztudományi Intézet, Budapest 1967), Gál, G S: *Honthy Hanna* (Zeneműkiadó, Budapest, 1973)

HOOD, Basil [Charles] (b Croydon, 5 April 1864; d London, 7 August 1917). Librettist and lyricist acclaimed as the ''new Gilbert,'' but who turned out to have a much wider range than his famous predecessor at the Savoy.

The younger son of Sir Charles Hood, Basil Hood was educated at Wellington and Sandhurst and joined the army at the age of 19, rising to be a Captain (1893) in the Prince of Wales's Own Regiment of Yorkshire. He began writing for the theatre in his mid-twenties, and a first little piece, *The Gypsies,* was mounted as a curtain-raiser at the Prince of Wales Theatre in 1890. He provided the lyrics to Lionel Monckton's song ''What Will You Have to Drink?,'' interpolated into the Gaiety burlesque *Cinder-Ellen Up Too Late,* and wrote two other short operettas before authoring his first full-scale musical comedy, *Gentleman Joe,* as a vehicle for comedian Arthur Roberts.

Gentleman Joe was a serious hit, and when his army duties threatened to take him away from London just when the time had come to enjoy his success, Hood promptly handed in his commission. He followed up his first winner with another major nationwide hit in the musical comedy *The French Maid,* and a second successful vehicle for Roberts, *Dandy Dan, the Lifeguardsman,* but then swapped the kind of popular musical comedy at which he had proven himself so adept for light opera, becoming the partner of Sir Arthur Sullivan, in the place of the estranged W S Gilbert, at the Savoy Theatre. The pair had a fine success with their first collaboration on *The Rose of Persia,* and the literate and intelligent librettist-lyricist was hailed as a worthy successor to Gilbert, but their second work together was interrupted by the composer's death, and Hood completed *The Emerald Isle* with Edward German. The new Savoy pairing was continued and together Hood and German turned out two more fine comic operas, *Merrie England* and *A Princess of Kensington,* before the new Savoy producer William Greet moved out of the light operatic area, effectively ending what looked like becoming a memorable collaboration.

Hood next set to work on a musical comedy based on *Romeo and Juliet,* but when producer Charles Frohman started chopping up his work to suit casting considerations he withdrew his name from the libretto of the piece which was ultimately produced as *The Belle of Mayfair.* He adapted Sardou's Directoire play as the libretto for George Edwardes's Daly's Theatre musical *Les Merveilleuses,* supplied the Gaiety Theatre with lyrics for *The Girls of Gottenberg,* and found himself a new area of expertise when, with the onset of the fashion for the Continental Operette, Edwardes hired him to do the English versions of what became *The Merry Widow, A Waltz Dream, The Dollar Princess, The Count of Luxembourg* and *Gipsy Love.*

His original works were few in these years of Continental domination, but in 1913 he authored a superior but only half-successful musical comedy, *The Pearl Girl,* for Robert Courtneidge. It turned out to be his last work: four years later he was found dead one morning in his bachelor chambers in St James Street, his death brought on, so it was said, ''from overwork at the War Office coupled with an indifference to eating.''

Hood directed a number of his own short and provincial pieces.

1890 **The Gypsies** (Wilfred Bendall) 1 act Prince of Wales Theatre 18 October

1892 **Donna Luiza** (Walter Slaughter) 1 act Prince of Wales Theatre 23 March

1893 **The Crossing Sweeper** (Slaughter) 1 act Gaiety Theatre 8 April

1895 **Gentleman Joe** (Slaughter) Prince of Wales Theatre 2 March

1896 **The French Maid** (Slaughter) Bath 4 April; Terry's Theatre, London 24 April 1897

1896 **Belinda** (Slaughter/w B C Stephenson) Prince's Theatre, Manchester 5 October

1897 **The Duchess of Dijon** (Slaughter) Theatre Royal, Portsmouth 20 September

1897 **Dandy Dan, the Lifeguardsman** (Slaughter) Lyric Theatre 4 December

1897 **Hans Andersen's Fairytales** (Slaughter) Terry's Theatre 23 December

1898 **Orlando Dando** (Slaughter) Grand Theatre, Fulham 1 August

1898 **Her Royal Highness** (Slaughter) Vaudeville Theatre 3 September

1899 **The Rose of Persia** (Arthur Sullivan) Savoy Theatre 29 November

1900 **Pretty Polly** (François Cellier) 1 act Savoy Theatre 8 December

1901 **The Emerald Isle** (Sullivan, Edward German) Savoy Theatre 27 April

1901 **The Willow Pattern** (Cecil Cook) 1 act Savoy Theatre 14 November

1901 **Ib and Little Christina** (Franco Leoni) 1 act Savoy Theatre 14 November

1902 **Merrie England** (German) Savoy Theatre 2 April

1903 **A Princess of Kensington** (German) Savoy Theatre 22 January

1903 **Little Hans Andersen** revised *Hans Andersen's Fairytales* Adelphi Theatre 23 December

1905 **The Golden Girl** (Hamish MacCunn) Prince of Wales Theatre, Birmingham 5 August

1906 **The Belle of Mayfair** (Leslie Stuart/w C H E Brookfield) Vaudeville Theatre 11 April

1906 **Les Merveilleuses** (Hugo Felix/Victorien Sardou ad) Daly's Theatre 27 October

1907 **The Girls of Gottenberg** (Ivan Caryll, Lionel Monckton/w Adrian Ross/L E Berman, George Grossmith) Gaiety Theatre 15 May

1907 **The Merry Widow** (*Die lustige Witwe*) English version (Daly's Theatre)

1908 **The Dollar Princess** (*Die Dollarprinzessin*) English version (Prince's Theatre, Manchester)

1911 **A Waltz Dream** (*Ein Walzertraum*) new English version (Daly's Theatre)

1911 **The Count of Luxembourg** (*Der Graf von Luxemburg*) English version (Daly's Theatre)

1912 **Gipsy Love** (*Zigeunerliebe*) English version (Daly's Theatre)

1913 **The Pearl Girl** (Felix, Howard Talbot) Shaftesbury Theatre 25 September

HOOD, Marion [ISAAC, Sarah Ann] (b Liverpool, 1 April 1854; d Thanet, 14 August 1912). Leading lady of the Savoy and Gaiety Theatres in the 1880s, playing star roles in comic opera or burlesque with equal facility.

''The elegant, blonde, 22-year-old Miss Hood was studying at the Royal Academy of Music when she accompanied Harriet Coveney to a rehearsal at the Opera Comique and was given the opportunity to audition for Gilbert and D'Oyly Carte. She sang the Shadow Song from *Dinorah,* and found herself cast, for her 'first appearance on any stage,' as the original Mabel of London's production of *The Pirates of Penzance.*'' That was the story handed out by Richard D'Oyly Carte when he put his new leading lady before the public. It was—like so many of his cast biographies—so much rhubarb. Sarah Ann Hunt was knocking 26, a wife and already a widow of several months, and she'd been earning her bread as a soprano vocalist by that time for 14 years.

''Marion Isaac,'' daughter of a Liverpool shipwright called George James Isaac and his wife Mary Rawlinson (''one of the Rawlinsons of Lynn,'' though she signed her daughter's birth certificate with an illiterate ''X'') made her first appearance on the stage at the age of 12, singing and dancing the role of Irish Moll in the ballet *The Rigs of Donnybrook Fair* (May 1866, ''nightly encored'') at the Rotunda in her native Liverpool. She took her remarkably fine, agile soprano voice into public as a stand-up vocalist for the first time at the same venue the following month with enormous success. Thereafter, she traveled Britain endlessly, performing ambitious soprano music in the country's better music halls and venturing come Christmastime on to the pantomime stage (Genie in *Aladdin,* Leeds, 1871, etc). The ''exquisite youthful soprano'' was seen particularly frequently at Hull's Alhambra Music Hall (manager, Charles Henry Hunt), and at the age of 17 she became Mrs Hunt. She continued to cover the halls of the British provinces, and occasionally of London, with regular success until, in 1879, Carte came into the picture and Sarah Ann stopped being ''Marion Isaac'' and became the less semitic and more British ''Marion Hood.'' And Arthur Sullivan was able to let himself go on the ''farmyard noises'' in ''Poor Wandering One'' for his experienced and skilled ''novice'' of a Mabel.

At the end of her noticeably successful engagement in *The Pirates of Penzance* Marion remarried and announced her retirement from the stage, but she returned after just six months' absence and was seen as Constance to the *Claude Duval* of Frank Celli in Solomon's comic opera (1881), starred as Casquette in *The Golden Ring* (1883) and as Laura in the first London production of *The Beggar Student* at the Alhambra, and took Florence St John's role of Girola in a revival of *Manteaux Noirs* (1885).

Having attempted Gounod's Marguerite at the Crystal Palace and found its operatic demands too strenuous, she returned to the musical theatre, beginning by playing principal girl in a revival of *Billee Taylor* (Phoebe) at the Gaiety. She followed up at the same house in her first burlesque role as Winifred Wood in *Little Jack Sheppard* (1885) and then, when Edwardes switched genres temporarily, created the title role in Cellier's *Dorothy* (1886). However, when that show transferred to the Prince of Wales for what would be the most famous part of its vast run, she remained behind to become the leading lady of the Gaiety new burlesques. She took over as Mercedes in *Monte Cristo Jr* (1887), created the roles of Tartina in *Frankenstein* (1887), Esmeralda in *Miss Esmeralda* (1887) and the Queen of Spain in *Ruy Blas and the Blasé Roué* (1889) alongside Nellie Farren and Fred Leslie, and she toured with the Gaiety's two megastars through Britain, to America and Australia.

She later took over the title role of the burlesque *Joan of Arc* in London, and in 1892 made another trip to Australia with the Gaiety company, playing Carmen (*Carmen Up-to-Data*), Marguerite (*Faust Up-to-Date*) and *Joan of Arc* for George Musgrove. On her return she took over the title role of Alma Somerset in Edwardes's tour of *A Gaiety Girl,* but then went into retirement as a comfortably-heeled stockbroker's wife, bringing to an end a dozen years as a leading lady in the musical theatre in which she had been at the front end of all the most active elements in the theatre of the time—Gilbert and Sullivan, the Alhambra Operettes, the record-breaking *Dorothy,* the Gaiety new burlesque and the new-style musical comedy.

HOOKER, [William] Brian (b New York, 2 November 1880; d New London, Conn, 28 December 1946).

A university English professor, Hooker served up English versions of such classics as *Cyrano de Bergerac* and *Ruy Blas* for the Broadway stage whilst also writing libretti and/or lyrics for a series of musicals in the 1920s and the early 1930s. His first musical ventures included the lyrics for Rudolf Friml's music in the adaptation of *In Search of a Sinner* as *June Love* (1921) and for Mrs Cushing's *Pomander Walk* musical, *Marjolaine* (1922), and he also collaborated with A E Thomas on the burlesque melodrama of *Our Nell,* this time having his words set by George Gershwin.

In 1925 he compiled a pastiche score for a musical version of W S Gilbert's play *Engaged,* before scoring his one memorable success with an adaptation of Justin Huntly McCarthy's *If I Were King* as the libretto for Friml's *The Vagabond King* (''Song of the Vagabonds,'' ''Only a Rose''). Musical versions of two further plays, *The Squaw Man* (*The White Eagle*) and *Smiling Through* (*Through the Years*), did not confirm that success, and another attempt at a swashbuckler, *The O'Flynn,* was a quick flop, ultimately leaving *The Vagabond King* as Hooker's one claim to musical theatre fame.

An opera entitled *Der weisse Vogel* (which may or may not have been *The White Eagle*) credited to Hooker and Ernest Carter was produced at Osnabrück, Germany, in 1927 (15 November).

1921 **June Love** (Rudolf Friml/W H Post, Otto Harbach) Knickerbocker Theater 25 April

1922 **Marjolaine** (Hugo Felix/Catherine Cushing) Broadhurst Theater 24 January

1922 **Our Nell** (ex- *The Hayseed*) (George Gershwin, William Daly/w A E Thomas) Bayes Theater 4 December

1925 **Engaged** (pasticcio) 52nd Street Theater 18 June

1925 **The Vagabond King** (Friml/w Post) Casino Theater 21 September

1927 **The White Eagle** (Friml/w Post) Casino Theater 26 December

1932 **Through the Years** (Vincent Youmans/Edward Heyman) Manhattan Theater 28 November

1934 **The O'Flynn** (Franklin Hauser/w Russell Janney) Broadway Theater 27 December

HOPE, Bob [HOPE, Leslie Towns] (Sir) (b Eltham, London, 26 May 1903). Celebrated film comedian whose early career included a rising curve of musical comedy roles.

Originally a performer in vaudeville, the young Hope appeared in the chorus of the musical *The Ramblers* (1926), in *The Sidewalks of New York* (1927, Monk), *Ups-a-Daisy* (1928, Screeves), *Smiles* (1930, chorus) and in the revue *Ballyhoo of 1932,* whilst working his way to the top in variety. When he returned to the musical theatre, in *Roberta* in 1933, it was in the lead comic role of Huck Haines, and he followed up in a similar capacity in *Say When* (1934, Jimmy Blake), in the *Ziegfeld Follies* and as Bob Hale in *Red, Hot and Blue!* (1936), introducing ''It's De-Lovely,'' before definitively abandoning the musical stage to make his fame in films.

Amongst those films—from *The Big Broadcast of 1938* and *Thanks for the Memory* through the celebrated series of *Road to . . .* films with Bing Crosby and Dorothy Lamour—were included many in which music was a part of the entertainment, and in 1941 he played the role of Jim Taylor in the film adaptation of Irving Berlin's stage musical *Louisiana Purchase.*

Autobiographies: *Have Tux Will Travel* (Simon and Schuster, New York, 1954), (w Thomas, B) *The Road to Hollywood* (Doubleday, Garden City, 1977); Biographies: Morella, J, Epstein, E, Clarke, E: *The Amazing Careers of Bob Hope* (Arlington House, New Rochelle, 1973), Marx, A: *The Secret Life of Bob Hope* (Barricade, New York, 1993)

HOPP, Julius (b Graz, 18 May 1819; d Vienna, 28 August 1885). Versatile and prolific author of texts and scores for the mid-19th-century Vienna stage.

From his teenage years, Hopp composed incidental music and songs for the Viennese theatre, beginning with scores for a half-dozen Possen written by his father, the actor and author Friedrich Hopp (1789–1869), for the Theater an der Wien, and continuing for some 40 years with incidental music and songs for most of the principal Vienna houses. Apart from regular scores for Possen, Volksstücke, Lebensbilder and other musical-comedy variants, a list that included Johann Grün's *Die letzte Fahrt* and Anton Langer's *Zwei Mann von Hess,* both of which would find later revivals, he also wrote and/or composed a number of more substantial musical pieces of his own. These included the popular five-act burlesque of the Faust legend *(Fäustling und) Margarethl* (the second of its title) which won productions throughout central Europe (Debrecen 1870, Budai Színkör 26 May 1872 ad Emil Follinusz), and the Operette *Morilla,* for which he wrote both text and music, and which was staged in Austria, Germany, Hungary and in America. However, his most notable contribution to the musical stage was his adaptation into German of many of the most important works of the French opéra-bouffe stage during the 1860s and 1870s, at a time when they dominated and influenced the development of the Viennese musical theatre.

Later works from more than 150 included:

1863 **Ein Deutschmeister** (*Der Köchin ihr Schatz*) (Karl Elmar) 1 act Fürsts Singspiel-Halle 6 April

1863 **Kein Taschentuch** 1 act Carltheater 7 May

1863 **Der Tugendpreis** (*Flotte Mädchen*) (Berger) Theater an der Wien 6 June

1863 **Zehntausend Gulden** (Karl Bayer) 1 act Fürsts Singspiel-Halle 11 August

1863 **Aurora's Geheimnis** (Julius Megerle) Theater an der Wien 27 August

1863 **Novara** (Therese Megerle) Thalia-Theater 13 September

1863 **Eine leichte Person** (O F Berg) Theater an der Wien 10 November

1864 **Er nimmt auf seine Frau Geld auf** (Franz Biringer) 1 act Theater an der Wien 18 January

1864 **Herr Arthur Gareissl** (Adolf Bahn) Theater an der Wien 1 June

1864 **Der halbe Mensch** (Berg) Theater an der Wien 17 June

1864 **Ein Matrose von der Fregatte Schwarzenberg** (Kies) 1 act Theater an der Wien 30 August

1864 **Der Postillion von Langenlois** (Anton Bittner) Theater an der Wien 20 September

1864 **(Fäustling und) Margarethl** (later *Mefeles*) (Julius Sixtus) Strampfertheater 20 September

1864 **Ein Wiener Findelkind** (Megerle) Theater an der Wien 19 November

1864 **Herr Maier** (ad Alois Blank) Theater an der Wien 26 December

1865 **Die verwandelete Katze** (*La Chatte métamorphosée en femme*) German version w music by Hopp (Theater an der Wien)

1865 **Der geheimnisvolle Dudelsack** (O F Berg) 1 act Theater an der Wien 27 May

1865 **Die fesche Godel** (Ferdinand Hein) Theater an der Wien 3 June

1865 **Die schöne Helena** (*La Belle Hélène*) German lyrics w F Zell (Theater an der Wien)

1866 **Coscoletto** German version (Theater an der Wien)

1866 **Die Schäfer** (*Les Bergers*) German version (Theater an der Wien)

1866 **Das Donauweibchen und der Ritter vom Kahlenberg** (w Paul Krone) Theater an der Wien 14 April

1866 **Ein dutzend Naturkind** (*Les Douze Innocents*) German version (Theater an der Wien)

1866 **Blaubart** (*Barbe-bleue*) German version (Theater an der Wien)

1867 **Auf einem Vulkan** (Alois Berla) Theater an der Wien 22 March

1867 **Die Ohren des Midas** (*Les Oreilles de Midas*) German version (Theater an der Wien)

1867 **Dorfschönheiten** (Poly Henrion) 1 act Theater an der Wien 6 April

1867 **Die Piraten von Savanna** (pasticcio) Theater an der Wien 18 June

1867 **Die Grossherzogin von Gérolstein** (*La Grande-Duchesse*) German version (Theater an der Wien)

1867 **Der Freischütz** (burlesque) Theater an der Wien 13 August

1868 **Genovefa von Brabant** (*Geneviève de Brabant*) German version (Theater an der Wien)

1868 **Morilla** Theater an der Wien 13 November

1868 **Der Pfeil im Auge** (*L'Oeil crevé*) German version (Theater an der Wien)

1869 **Toto** (*Le Château à Toto*) German version (Carltheater)

1869 **Tulipatan** (*L'Île de Tulipatan*) German version (Carltheater)

1869 **Nach Mitternacht** 1 act Fürsts Singspiel-Halle 10 July

1869 **In der Sackgasse** (aka *In der Kramergasse*) 1 act Carltheater 27 November

1869 **Einer von der Südbahn** (L Meier) 1 act

1870 **Kakadu** (*Vert-Vert*) German version (Carltheater)

1871 **Die Ente mit den drei Schnäbeln** (*Le Canard à trois becs*) German version (Strampfertheater)

1871 **Die Prinzessin von Trapezunt** (*La Princesse de Trébizonde*) German version (Carltheater)

1872 **Javotte, das neue Aschenbrödel** (*Cinderella the Younger*) German version (Strampfertheater)

1872 **Schneeball** (*Boule de Neige*) German version (Carltheater)

1872 **Confusius IX** (*La Cour du Roi Pétaud*) German version (Carltheater)

1872 **Am Fasching Dienstag** (w Franz Roth) Strampfertheater 30 January

1873 **Der Goldchignon** (*Chignon d'or*) German version (Strampfertheater)

1873 **Wiener Blut** (Bittner) Strampfertheater 3 October

1874 **Hammlet** (burlesque) Strampfertheater 29 January

1875 **Madame "Herzog"** (*Madame l'Archiduc*) German version (Theater an der Wien)

1875 **Die Perle die Wäscherinnen** (*La Blanchisseuse de Berg-op-Zoom*) German version (Theater an der Wien)
1875 **Von Tisch und Bett** German version of *LaBoule* with songs, Theater an der Wien 7 September
1876 **Die Creolin** (*La Créole*) German version (Theater an der Wien)
1876 **Seit Mittag vermählt** (*Mariée depuis midi*) German version (Carltheater)
1876 **König Carotte** (*Le Roi Carotte*) German version (Theater an der Wien)
1876 **Die Reise in den Mond** (*Le Voyage dans la lune*) German version (Theater an der Wien)
1877 **Der Jahrmarkt von St Laurent** (*La Foire St Laurent*) German version (Theater an der Wien)
1877 **Dorothea** (*Jacqueline*) German version (Theater an der Wien)
1878 **Der Teufel auf Erden** (Suppé/w Carl Juin) Carltheater 5 January
1878 **Hotel Klingebusch** (w C F Conradin/Rudolf Kneisl, Eduard Jacobson) Carltheater 16 March
1878 **Jeanne, Jeannette, Jeanneton** German version (Carltheater)
1878 **Atlantic-Pacific-Company** (M V Kautsky) Theater an der Wien 30 August
1879 **Unruhige Nachbarn** 1 act Ronacher 23 August
1879 **Der Abenteuer des Seekapitäns** (Arendorf) Theater in der Josefstadt 28 September
1879 **König Wenzel in Wien** (Franz von Radler) Theater in der Josefstadt 23 October
1879 **Die letzte Fee im Orient** (Carl Elmar) Theater in der Josefstadt 8 November
1879 **In China** 1 act Theater in der Josefstadt 29 November
1880 **Eine ruhige Partei** (Friedrich Wimmer) 1 act Theater in der Josefstadt 1 January
1880 **Die lieben Schwiegereltern** (Wimmer) 1 act Theater in der Josefstadt 24 January
1880 **Tausend und eine Nacht** (Renard) Theater in der Josefstadt 25 January
1880 **Eine Parforcejagd durch Europa** (Bruno Zappert) Theater in der Josefstadt 14 February
1880 **Doktor und Friseur** (Friedrich Kaiser) Theater in der Josefstadt 28 March
1881 **[Die] Musketiere in Damenstift** (*Les Mousquetaires au couvent*) German version w Eduard Mautner (Theater an der Wien)
1883 **Der Prinz Gemahl** (Ludwig Engländer/w Bohrmann-Riegen) Thalia Theater, New York 11 April
1884 **In der Einöd** (Karl Gründorf) Theater in Rudolsheim 15 March

HOPPER, De Wolf [HOPPER, William d'Wolf] (b New York, 30 March 1858; d Kansas City, 23 September 1935). Tall (very), slim (fairly) and deep-voiced (very) comedy star who spent 40 years on the American musical stage, many of them as a well-loved star.

The young Hopper toured with F F Mackay and Louise Sylvester in the musical farce–comedy *Freaks* (1880, Dr Ketchum), played at New York's Theatre Comique with Harrigan (Redmond Darcy in *The Blackbird* 1882) and, on the proceeds of a legacy from his father, attemped a theatrical career as a small-circuit actor-manager (*One Hundred Wives, Hazel Kirke,* etc). However, he soon found his niche in comedy and—with the help of a basso voice which led him (and his mother) to momentarily consider his training for an operatic career—in musical comedy.

His first significant job in the musical theatre was with John A McCaull. Hired as a lead romantic baritone, to replace no less a vocalist than W T Carleton, he was—thanks to McCaull's untiring shuffling of performers between one and another of his multiple companies—found to be de trop, and in consequence made his first appearance on the musical stage at Philadelphia in the company's production of J P Sousa's *Désirée* (10 November 1884), not as the Count de Courville, the fine singing hero, but in the comic part of Pomeret. Although the show was quickly dropped from the repertoire, Hopper's performance was adjudged a success (''he steps at once into the front rank of buffo comedians''), and McCaull promptly cast him in the star role of Ollendorf in the revival of *The Beggar Student* which replaced the flop piece. Thereafter he appeared in leading comedy roles in the long series of mostly imported comic operas which McCaull toured around America. Between 1884 and 1890 he was seen as Ollendorf in *Der Bettelstudent,* Sigismund in *Prinz Methusalem,* in which he introduced (à propos of nothing) his famous recitation of E L Thayer's poem ''Casey at the Bat,'' Frank in *Die Fledermaus,* Theophil Hackenback in *The Black Hussar* (*Der Feldprediger*), Gaspard in *Lorraine,* Lambertuccio in *Boccaccio,* Lord Middleditch in Czibulka's *The May Queen* (*Der Glücksritter*), Folbach in *Falka,* Elvegaard in *Bellman,* Jeremiah Hackett in *Chatter* (*Die Näherin*), Gavadeau in *The Crowing Hen* (*Serment d'amour*), Onofrio in *Don Cesar,* Alfred Pharaon Pasha in *Joséphine vendue pas ses soeurs,* Pomponio in *Jacquette* (*La Béarnaise*), Casimir in Suppé's *Clover* (*Die Jagd nach dem Glück*) and Captain Modesto Fracasse in Dellinger's *Capitän Fracasse*—but also in some of the earliest American comic operas (Howja-Dhu in *The Begum,* Pausanias in *The Lady or the Tiger*).

He left McCaull in 1890 to star as Filacoudre in Kerker's *Castles in the Air,* and was by now sufficient of a draw for the company to go under the title of the De Wolf Hopper Comic Opera Company. It was under that same banner that he appeared in the most successful of his new pieces to date, as the comical regent of a very Ruratasian Siam in *Wang* (1891). The revived *The Lady*

Plate 182. **De Wolf Hopper** *(center) as Colonel Popoff to the Bumerli of Donald Brian (right) in* The Chocolate Soldier.

and the Tiger (1892, Pausanias), *Panjandrum* (1893, Pedro) and *Dr Syntax* (1894, Dr Syntax) provided him with further vehicles, but neither could approach the effectiveness of *Wang* or of Klein and Sousa's comic opera *El Capitan* (1896, Don Errico Medigua), in which, in the part of the South American regent who disguises himself as his own enemy, Hopper found the best original role of his career. He repeated *El Capitan* and another useful vehicle, Sousa's *The Charlatan* (1898, Demidoff) as *The Mystical Miss,* in London in 1899.

Thereafter he appeared on Broadway and on the American road with a regular series of new pieces—Weber and Fields's revusical *Fiddle-Dee-Dee* (1900, Hoffman Barr/Petrolius) and *Hoity-Toity* (1901, General Steele, an ADT from Mars in *A Message from Mars* burlesque), as Dickens's *Mr Pickwick* (1903), in *Happyland* (1905, King Ecstaticus), *The Pied Piper* (1908, Piper) and in a soi-disant musical adaptation of *Le Medecin malgré lui* called *A Matinée Idol* (1910, Medford Griffin)—as well as reprising his former successes, most particularly and frequently *El Capitan* and *Wang.*

In his fifties he ceased this town-to-country routine, and appeared in New York as Dick Deadeye in the All-Star *HMS Pinafore* at the Casino (1911) before essaying a whole series of Gilbert and Sullivan roles (Bunthorne, Sergeant, Ko-Ko, Lord Chancellor, Jack Point, John Wellington Wells) and appearing once more in the role of General Ollendorf in *Der Bettelstudent,* which he had first played 30 years earlier at the Casino. He also appeared as Bogumil in the American version of Fall's *Der liebe Augustin* (1913), in the festive show *Hop o' my Thumb* (1913, King Mnemonica) at Oscar Hammerstein's Manhattan Opera House, toured in Gilbert and Sullivan (1914) and appeared both in revue in *The Passing Show of 1917* and in Hippodrome spectacular (*Everything,* 1918). In 1919 he succeeded Charles Coburn as Old Bill in the British wartime musical *The Better 'Ole* and, in his sixties, paired with Francis Wilson as Ravannes in a revival of Wilson's enduring vehicle *Erminie,* whilst continuing to tour successfully both in his old successes and in a selection of operettas. His last appearances in the Broadway musical theatre were as a takeover in *The Student Prince* (Lutz) and, at the age of 70, in the 1928 musical *White Lilacs* (Debusson), although he continued to perform, in roles of decreasing size, almost up to his death.

Hopper also appeared on film, notably as a memorable Don Quixote (1915), and in a filmed version of the baseball tale ''Casey at the Bat.''

Hopper's third wife (of six), the diminutive **Edna Wallace HOPPER** (b San Francisco, 17 January 1864; d New York, 14 December 1959), began a stage career as an actress in Boston and with Frohman, and joined Hopper's company to take over as Paquita in *Panjandrum.* She subsequently teamed her bright little singing voice with his comic basso as Merope Mallow in *Dr Syntax* (1894) and Estrelda in *El Capitan* before the marriage was over. After their divorce in 1898, she appeared in the extravaganza *Yankee Doodle Dandy* (1898, Tommy Twoshoes), as Orestes in the Casino Theater's revival of *La Belle Hélène* (1899), and took the title role in *Chris and the Wonderful Lamp* (1900) before being cast in Ada Reeve's role of Lady Holyrood (''Tact,'' ''When I Leave Town'') for the Broadway production of *Florodora.* Her personal success in this enormous hit was followed over the next decade by more roles in musical comedies British (Wrenne in *The Silver Slipper, My Lady's Maid,* ie, *Lady Madcap,* Betty in *The White Chrysanthemum, The School Girl*) and American—Fannie Frivol/Duchess of Ehwhattington in *About Town,* Sadie Woodis in *Fifty Miles from Boston* (1908), Chicago's *The Three Graces* (1906), Connie Curtis in *Jumping Jupiter* (1910–11)—before she turned her activities mostly to vaudeville. In 1918 she appeared at Broadway's Bijou Theater in a final musical, *Girl o'Mine* (Lulu), prior to retiring from the stage in 1920. She subsequently decided on a facelift, had the operation filmed, and went touring with the resultant film for eight years. She then retired to play the stockmarket into her nineties.

Hopper's last wife, wed when he was in his sixties, was another musical-theatre star, Lulu Glaser.

Autobiography (w Winan-Stout, W): *Once a Clown, Always a Clown* (Little, Brown, Boston, 1927)

HORST, Julius [HOSTASCH, Josef] (b Innsbrück, 12 November 1864; d Vienna, 12 May 1943).

Playwright and librettist Horst combined on a careerful of plays, mostly written in collaboration with Alexander Engel, but also with Arthur Lippschitz, Leo Stein and other successful writers. The most notable of these was the internationally played 1908 comedy *Die blaue Maus* (w Engel), and other successes included the 1900 Posse *Man lebt ja nur einmal* originally played by Girardi, *Der g'rade Michl* (w Engel) and *Der Schrei nach dem Kinde* (w Engel). He also provided the texts for a long list of pieces for the musical stage, both Possen and Operette libretti, of which *Der Pumpmajor,* a piece based on Gogol's *Der Revisor* and played in both Vienna and Berlin (Theater Unter den Linden 24 October 1896), and two pieces written with Ralph Benatzky (*Pipsi, Adieu Mimi*) were amongst the more successful. None of these, however, proved to be an international piece on a par with his most famous play.

Die blaue Maus was made over as a musical play with a score by Ludwig Grüber, and also became the American musical comedy *The Little Blue Devil* (Harry

Carroll/Harold Atteridge, Central Theater 3 November 1919), whilst *Der Schrei nach der Kinde* was later used as the basis for Lehár's musical comedy *Cloclo, Glück bei Frauen* became Martin Knopf's *Pariser Luft* (1912) and *Der Himmel auf Erden* was remade as the musical *Unser Frauchen* (Georg & Emil Pipping/ad Victor & Julius Pipping, Stadttheater, Katowice) in 1914 and, under its original title, again in 1943. Two other, unidentified, plays, one written with Arthur Lippschitz and the other with Engel, were musicalized for the Hungarian stage as the highly successful *Limonádé ezredes* (mus: Zsigmond Vincze, Király Színház 15 September 1912) and *Marci* (mus: Alfred Márkus, Fővárosi Nyári Színház 17 June 1916) respectively.

1885 **Die Pechvogel** (Paul Mestrozzi/w Fritz Waldau) Theater in der Josefstadt 14 November

1886 **Der Pascha von Podiebrad** (Franz Roth/w Waldau) 1 act Fürsttheater 2 June

1886 **Pfingsten in Wien** (F Roth/w Waldau) 1 act Fürsttheater 12 June

1887 **Münchhausen** (Hanns Krenn/w Waldau) Theater in der Josefstadt 10 April

1890 **Angelor** (Carl Weinberger) 1 act Troppau 15 January

1892 **Lachende Erben** (Weinberger/w Leo Stein) Carltheater 24 October

1896 **Der Pumpmajor** (Alexander Neumann/w Stein) Theater in der Josefstadt 11 January

1896 **Der Pfiffikus** (Adolf Müller jr/w Stein) 1 act Raimundtheater 18 April

1897 **Der Sergeant** (Friedrich von Thul/Charles Berger ad) Theater in der Josefstadt 2 April

1898 **Frau Reklame** (Louis Roth/w Stein) Venedig in Wien 6 August

1898 **Lolas Cousin** (*Le Papa de Francine*) German version (Theater in der Josefstadt)

1898 **Der Blondin von Namur** (A Müller jr/w Stein) Theater an der Wien 15 October

1899 **Die wahre Liebe ist das nicht** (Fritz Skallitzky/w Stein) Raimundtheater 9 November

1900 **Der Wundertrank** (Weinberger/w Benjamin Schier) 1 act Hotel Continental 17 March

1900 **Ein besserer Herr** (Ludwig Gothov-Grüneke/w Eduard Lunzer) Jantschtheater 19 October

1900 **Man lebt nur einmal** (w Stein) Raimundtheater 14 November

1902 **Ninettens Hochzeit** (von Thul) Jantschtheater 21 February

1902 **Der Mann ohne Kopf** (Heinrich Müller/w Lunzer) Jantschtheater 5 July

1902 **Die kleine Witwe** (Julius Eibenschütz) Stadttheater, Magdeburg 10 December

1904 **Der Polizeichef** (Josef Bayer/w Robert Pohl) Theater am Gärtnerplatz, Munich 12 November

1904 **Der Schätzmeister** (Carl Michael Ziehrer/w Alexander Engel) Carltheater 10 December

1905 **Uns gehört die Welt** (Karl Josef Fromm) Jantschtheater 20 January

1905 **Der Strohwitwer** (Rudolf Ehrich/w Emil Norini) Stadttheater, Brünn 7 March; Theater des Westens 1 June

1905 **Champagner** (Ehrich) Raimundtheater 14 November

1906 **Der blaue Klub** (Karl Kappeller/w Engel) Theater am Gärtnerplatz, Munich 24 November

1906 **Das Mädchen für Alles** (Karl F Adolfi) 1 act Wiener Colosseum November

1909 **Der Rodelbaron** (Fritz Fürst/w Engel) 2 scenes Apollotheater 1 January

1909 **Der Liebeskongress** (arr Wilhelm Eckstein) 1 act Apollotheater 1 December

1910 **Der Schwimmlehrer** (Josef Heller) 1 act Wiener Colosseum 1 September

1911 **Im Frauenparlament** (Rudolf Raimann) Apollotheater 1 March

1911 **Die Mumien** (von Thul) 1 act Wiener Colosseum 1 March

1912 **Der Lockvogel** (Leo Ascher/w Engel) Walhalla-Theater, Wiesbaden 11 January

1913 **Die blaue Maus** (Ludwig Grüber/w Engel) Graben Kino 11 November

1918 **Eheurlaub** (Jean Gilbert/w Horst Bachwitz) Liebich-Theater, Breslau 1 August; Apollotheater, Vienna 1 May 1919

1919 **Der Künstlerpreis** (Ascher/w Rudolf Österreicher) Apollotheater 1 October

1920 **Glück bei Frauen** (Knopf/w Oskar Engel) Neues Operetten-Theater, Munich 14 August

1920 **Die Witwe aus Indien** (Arthur M Werau/w Ernst Wengraf) 1 act Künstlerspiele Pan 1 November

1921 **Im Alpenhotel** (Richard Fall/w Wengraf) 1 act Apollotheater 6 August

1921 **Pipsi** (Ralph Benatzky/w Engel) Wiener Bürgertheater 30 December

1923 **Vierzehn Tage Arrest** (Edmund Eysler/w Österreicher) Raimundtheater 16 June

1926 **Adieu Mimi** (Benatzky/w Engel) Johann Strauss-Theater 9 June

1927 **Glück in der Liebe** (Michael Krasznay-Krausz/w Peter Herz) Johann Strauss-Theater 25 February

1929 **Aber Otty** (Egon Baderle/w Erwin Spahn) Kleine Bühne, Deutsches Theater, Prague 10 March

1931 **Frau, für die man schwärmt** (Camillo Faust/w Spahn) Stadttheater, Troppau 17 October

1931 **Die göttliche Jette** (revised *Henriette Sontag*) (Walter Goetze/Günther Bibo, Emil Rameau ad) Schillertheater, Berlin 31 December

1936 **Gloria und der Clown** (Robert Stolz/w Robert Gilbert) Stadttheater, Aussig 31 December

1941 **Immer sind die Männer schuld** (Hans Lang) Residenz-Bühne 13 June

1943 **Der Himmel auf Erden** (Nowosad-Nissen/w Josef Petrak) Zur Neuen Welt 6 July

HOSCHNA, Karl L (b Kuschwarda, 16 August 1876; d New York, 22 December 1911). Composer for the

Broadway stage whose few years of activity, before an early death, produced two hit shows.

Born in Bohemia and trained musically at the Vienna Konservatorium, Hoschna was originally an oboist in an Austrian army band. He moved to America at the age of 19 and worked initially as an instrumentalist, notably in Victor Herbert's celebrated orchestra, but he became quickly convinced that the continual pressure on the brain involved in playing the oboe was damaging his health, and he wrote to Isidore Witmark of the music publishing firm of Witmark Brothers asking for any kind of employment, no matter how menial or poorly paid, which would permit him to give up playing. Witmark employed him on arranging, copying and preparing piano reductions of show music for publication, and it was during his time in this employment that Hoschna began himself composing for the theatre.

In 1902 he met would-be lyricist and librettist Otto Hauerbach (later Harbach), then working in advertising, and the two men began to collaborate on a comic opera which, although finished, was never staged. Several other of Hoschna's attempts, however, did make the stage, but they were made-for-traveling pieces of little pretension—B F Forrester's production of the musical comedy melodrama *The Belle of the West* featuring Florence Bindley in the title role, *The Girl from Broadway* sent out in the fall of 1906 by Aubrey Mittenthal and Samuel E Rork's mounting of *Prince Humbug* with Frank Lalor starred (''Googly-Oo,'' ''The Two Pigeons'')—as were the pieces like *Captain Careless* (1907), to which he contributed additional numbers under Witmark's umbrella. It was not until Witmark commissioned his in-house employee—who had risen inexorably from over-qualified copyist to the position of friend, confidant and adviser—to provide the songs for a musical version of the play *Incog,* which he had himself adapted into a libretto (w Charles Dickson), that one of Hoschna's scores finally reached Broadway. *Three Twins* turned out to be a fine success, gave Hoschna his first song hits in ''Cuddle Up a Little Closer'' (ly: Hauerbach) and ''The Yama Yama Man'' (ly: George Collin Davis), and was seen on the American touring circuits for many seasons.

Hoschna subsequently teamed with Harbach and with melodramatist Owen Davis on the musical farce *Back Again* for the Aborn Comic Opera Company (''fifteen swing-y tunes''), contributed to the score for the Adeline Genée musical *The Silver Star,* and followed up with a fresh collaboration with Hauerbach and Dickson on a musical version of Dickson's play *Mistakes Will Happen,* entitled *Bright Eyes. Bright Eyes* was a one-month Broadway failure which nonetheless went on to a reasonable life on the road, but Joseph Gaites's production of the next Hoschna musical, *Katie Did,* a musical version of *My Friend from India* with Louis H Simon and May Vokes top-billed and sporting some lively songs (''Nobody Loves Me,'' ''I John, Take Thee Matilda,'' ''Dear Old Homeland''), did not succeed in crossing the continent. However, six months later Hoschna and Harbach came up with what would be their most successful piece as a team when they revamped the Berlin hit *Madame Sherry* for an American production. Hoschna replaced the whole of Hugo Felix's score with music of his own, came up with an agreeable set of songs which included one genuine hit number in ''Every Little Movement [Has A Meaning All Its Own],'' and, with its score filled out with one or two interpolated numbers, *Madame Sherry* proved both a singular Broadway success and a long-lived touring proposition.

The rash of Hoschna shows which followed over the next 12 months—vehicles for Richard Carle, Ralph Herz (star of *Madame Sherry*), variety performer Leila McIntyre, and female impersonator Julian Eltinge as The *Fascinating Widow*—did not produce anything which looked like equaling the success of their two earlier winners and Hoschna's one remaining show, *The Wall Street Girl,* produced in Pennsylvania by Frederick McKay only weeks before the composer's death at the age of 34, did little better, in spite of Blanche Ring's presence at the top of the bill and that of Will Rogers (''who did the most extraordinary lassoing feats'') lower down.

1905 **The Belle of the West** (Harry B Smith) Lyceum Theater, Harrisburg, Pa 28 August; Great Northern Theater, Chicago 29 October; Grand Opera House 13 November

1906 **The Girl from Broadway** (Chas Noel Douglas/Herbert Hall Winslow) York, Pa 10 September; 14th Street Theater 14 January 1907

1908 **Three Twins** (Otto Harbach/Charles Dickson, Isidore Witmark) Herald Square Theater 15 June

1908 **Prince Humbug** (Mark Swan) Court Square, Springfield, Mass 31 August; Park Theater, Boston 7 September

1909 **Back Again** (Harbach, Owen Davis) Olympic Park, Newark 7 June

1909 **Bright Eyes** (Harbach/Dickson) Grand Theater, New Haven 25 November; New York Theater 28 February 1910

1910 **Katie Did** (William Cary Duncan, Frank Smithson) Colonial Theater, Chicago 18 February

1910 **Madame Sherry** (Harbach/Maurice Ordonneau ad Harbach) Colonial Theater, Chicago 12 April; New Amsterdam Theater, New York 30 August

1910 **Jumping Jupiter** (Richard Carle, Sydney Rosenfeld) Cort Theater, Chicago 4 August; Criterion Theater 6 March 1911

1910 **The Fascinating Widow** (Harbach) Apollo Theater, Atlantic City 14 November; Liberty Theater, New York 11 September 1911

1910 **The Girl of My Dreams** (Harbach, Wilbur Nesbit) Garrick Theater, Philadelphia 26 December; Criterion Theater 7 August 1911

1911 **Dr Deluxe** (Harbach) Knickerbocker Theater 17 April

1911 **The Wall Street Girl** (Benjamin Hapgood Burt/Margaret Mayo, Edgar Selwyn) Grand Opera House, Wilkes-Barre 2 October; George M Cohan Theater 15 April 1912

HOTEL STADT LEMBERG Musical play [musikalisches Schauspiel] in 3 acts and an epilogue adapted from Lajos Biró's novel and the play by Ernst Neubach. Music by Jean Gilbert. Deutsches Schauspielhaus, Hamburg, 1 July 1929.

Set in Galicia during the First World War, *Hotel Stadt Lemberg* centered on the attempts of Anna, housemaid at the Hotel of the title, to stave off the attentions of, and otherwise outwit, the Russian General Juschkiewitsch and, at the same time, to help the Austrian hussar lieutenant Almasy to safety and a happy ending. The lighter moments were provided by the General's adjutant, Sascha Suchalow, and his wife Zinotschka, and the spectacle by the insertion of an ''original-russische-Tanz-und-Balalaika-Truppe'' into the proceedings. Jean Gilbert's score of dance-based songs featured the waltz duet ''Du liebst mich'' (Anna/Almasy), the fox-trot duo ''Hab' heut' die Sternlein am Himmel gezählt'' (Sascha/Zinotschka), Anna's opening slow-fox ''Bin nichts und hab' nichts,'' and the General and Anna's duo ''Nur diese Nacht.''

First mounted in Hamburg, the show was later played for two months at Vienna's Johann Strauss-Theater, with Anny Ahlers (Anna), Walter Jankuhn (Almasy), Franz Höbling (General), Victor Colani (Sascha) and Mimi Gyenes (Zinotschka) featured, and for 101 nights at Berlin's Theater des Westens, whilst an Hungarian version (ad Ernő Andai, István Zágon) was subsequently played at Budapest's Király Színház. An American version (ad Ernest Clarke, H B Smith, add songs Mack Gordon, Harry Revel) featuring the Continental star Emmi Kosáry was mounted in Philadelphia in 1930. It did not progress from there, but the piece was done over and produced by the Shuberts a year later, rechristened *Marching By* (ad Harry Clarke, Harry B Smith, Edward Eliscu, George Hirst). It got fine initial notices and played a good Chicago season, with Natalie Hall and Guy Robertson in the leading roles, but it lasted only 12 nights when it moved to Broadway.

Austria: Johann Strauss-Theater 13 September 1929; Germany: Theater des Westens 25 December 1929; Hungary: Király Színház *Hotel Lemberg* 6 June 1930, USA: Chestnut Street Opera House, Philadelphia *Arms and the Maid* 1 December 1930, 46th Street Theater *Marching By* 3 March 1932

HOUGH, Will M (b Chicago, 23 August 1882; d Carmel, Calif, 20 November 1962).

Hough collaborated with Frank Adams, his contemporary at the University of Chicago, and with Joe Howard on a series of musicals, the earliest of which had outstanding runs in Chicago, and helped to make that city for a period a strong center of musical theatre production. The Hough/Adams/Howard shows toured long and successfully, but, in spite of inherent values often as (or sometimes more) worthwhile as those the current East Coast shows had to offer, they were not accepted by New York's critics and public, and had limited Broadway runs. Hough and Adams split with Howard in 1910 and, shortly after, the vein of Chicago musical hits ran out. Hough turned to writing scenarios for the Selig film company (1913, *The Flower of Faith* 1914, etc), but he continued to work for another decade in the musical theatre, writing three pieces with composer William B Friedlander, the last of which, a musical adaptation of the William Collier comedy *Caught in the Rain,* had a fair run on Broadway under the title *Pitter Patter.*

1904 **His Highness the Bey** (Howard/w Adams) La Salle Theater, Chicago 21 November

1905 **The Isle of Bong-Bong** (Howard/w Adams) La Salle Theater, Chicago 14 March

1905 **The Land of Nod** (Howard/w Adams) Opera House, Chicago 17 June; New York Theater, New York 1 April 1907

1905 **The Umpire** (Howard/w Adams) La Salle Theater, Chicago 2 December

1906 **The Time, the Place and the Girl** (Howard/w Adams) La Salle Theater, Chicago 20 August; Wallack's Theater, New York 5 August 1907

1907 **The Girl Question** (Howard/w Adams) La Salle Theater, Chicago 24 August; Wallack's Theater, New York 3 August 1908

1908 **The Honeymoon Trail** (Howard/w Adams) La Salle Theater, Chicago 23 March

1908 **A Stubborn Cinderella** (Howard/w Adams) Princess Theater, Chicago 31 May; Broadway Theater, New York 25 January 1909

1909 **The Prince of Tonight** (Howard/w Adams) Princess Theater, Chicago 9 March

1909 **The Golden Girl** (Howard/w Adams) La Salle Theater, Chicago 16 March

1909 **The Goddess of Liberty** (Howard/w Adams) Princess Theater, Chicago 15 August; Weber's Theater, New York 22 December

1909 **The Flirting Princess** (Harold Orlob, Howard/w Adams) Princess Theater, Chicago 1 November

1910 **Miss Nobody from Starland** (Howard/w Adams/Howard Johnstone Mitchell) Princess Theater, Chicago 31 January

1911 **The Heartbreakers** (Orlob, Melville Gideon) Princess Theater, Chicago 30 May

1912 **The Girl at the Gate** (Ben Jerome/w Frederick Donaghey) La Salle Theater, Chicago 1 September

1914 **Lonesome Lasses** (R A Rolfe) Prospect, Brooklyn 5 October; Royal, New York 12 October

1915 **A Modern Eve** (*Die moderne Eva*) English version w Benjamin Hapgood Burt (Casino Theater)

1916 **Tickets Please** (William B Friedlander) Victoria Theater, Wheeling, Va 3 April

1917 **The Naughty Princess** (Friedlander) Palace Theater 24 September

1919 **Honeymoon Town** (Byron Gay, Felix Rice) La Salle Theater, Chicago 17 June

1920 **Pitter Patter** (Friedlander) Longacre Theater 28 September

HOUSE OF FLOWERS Musical in 2 acts by Truman Capote based on his story of the same title. Lyrics by Truman Capote and Harold Arlen. Music by Harold Arlen. Alvin Theater, New York, 30 December 1954.

Set under the hot sun of the West Indies, *House of Flowers* told the tale of two rival brothel-keepers, Madame Tango (Juanita Hall) and Madame Fleur (Pearl Bailey), proprietor of the titular ''House of Flowers.'' Madame Fleur's establishment is temporarily knocked out of commission by a mumps epidemic, and she has to put her hopes of regaining supremacy in taking under her management the saleable attractions of pretty, unmumped Ottilie (Diahann Carroll). Ottilie ends up marrying her young man, Royal (Rawn Spearman), instead, but Madame Tango's triumph is cut short when she, too, is put out of action: her girls are all whisked away on a world cruise by a passing ocean liner and its obliging captain.

Harold Arlen's score included some attractive numbers, both Caribbean-lively (''Two Ladies in de Shade of de Banana Tree'') and Caribbean-gentle (''A Sleeping Bee,'' ''I Never Has Seen Snow,'' both for Ottilie), which won more praise and popularity than the show as a whole. After a rocky ride in from Philadelphia, where—in obeisance to the star's demands—some cuts (to other folk's roles) had been, perhaps unwisely, introduced, Saint Subber's original Broadway production ran for only 165 performances. *House of Flowers,* however, lingered. In 1968 Subber mounted a revised version, with five new songs, and with Novella Nelson (Tango), Josephine Premice (Fleur) and Yolande Bavan (Ottilie) featured, at off-Broadway's Theater de Lys (28 January), but the show failed a second time in 57 performances. Its score and its subject nevertheless continued to encourage repeated attempts to bring it back to the stage, and in the early 1990s the piece was still to be seen regionally in America.

Recordings: original cast (Columbia), revival cast (United Artists), composer's demo recording (Mark 56)

HOWARD, Joseph E[dgar] (b New York, 12 February 1867; d Chicago, 19 May 1961). Lifelong performer and songwriter who spent a while in the musical comedy spotlight in Chicago.

A vaudeville performer as a child soprano, then as a teenager, and later a burlesque-house player in a team with his wife, Ida Emerson (Howard and Emerson's Own), Joe Howard began writing songs not only for his own use, but to supplement his uncertain stage income. He composed a rash of cheerfully rhythmic and down-to-earth numbers in the later years of the 19th century, from which ''Goodbye, My Lady Love'' (1904, initially heard in Howard's Trocadero summer show and reused by Jerome Kern as a period number in *Show Boat*) and ''Hello, Ma Baby'' (ly: Emerson) have survived the most strongly.

Howard entered the musical theatre in Chicago when he supplied first some additional songs for Raymond Hubbell's score to the burlesque *Chow Chow* (1902, also director) for the Orpheon Music Hall and then two full scores, written in collaboration with lyricist Raymond Peck, for *The Paraders* (1902, ''Coney Isle'') and *Tom Tom* (1903, ''The Ragtime Chinaman'') at the same house, now rechristened the La Salle. Howard and Emerson also appeared in the shows. Real success, however, came when he joined two young local writers, Will Hough and Frank Adams, to write the musical comedy *His Highness the Bey* (1904), for what was still then the quiescent Chicago theatre. The show was distinctly successful, the La Salle dropped its vaudeville-house tag and went theatre-straight, and the trio followed up with a whole series of lucrative hit musicals which were largely responsible for putting the city on the map as a producing center. These shows toured long and extensively with popular road performers and some rising stars in the main roles (the young John Barrymore played juvenile in *A Stubborn Cinderella*), but they were, not unexpectedly, sneered at by determinedly parochial New York, in spite of being as tuneful, as amiably foolish and, occasionally, more original than the bulk of East Coast musicals of the time.

Howard, in the meanwhile, continued his own career as a performer, expending an attractive tenor voice and an appealing personality on a variety of vehicles, including several musical comedy-dramas of his own writing and/or composing (Jack Dunning in *The District Leader,* Jack Farnum in *The Flower of the Ranch,* etc). At one stage, in 1907, when he was making his official debut as a star (ie, billed above the title) in Chicago, he had his name showing on the bills of three of the city's theatres at once—for his appearance in his musical comedy melodrama *The Flower of the Ranch,* and for his scores for *A Stubborn Cinderella* (Princess Theater) and *Honeymoon Trail* (La Salle Theater). However, when he was declared bankrupt in Iowa Falls in 1912, the performer declared that he had lost $100,000 in producing his shows over the four years preceeding.

Although Howard's songs, topped by *The Time, The Place and the Girl*'s ''The Waning Honeymoon,'' were whistled for a decade throughout Chicago, the nearest thing to a single hit song, on a wider basis, which he produced during the years of his Chicago collaborations was ''What's the Use of Dreaming?'' This did not, in fact, come from one of the team's shows, and when the Adams/Hough/Howard series finally did come up with a real hit, in *The Prince of Tonight,* the first of their shows not to be enthusiastically received by Chicago, it finally ended up as the subject of a lawsuit. It eventuated that Howard—in a manner not uncommon at the time—had bought the tune of ''I Wonder Who's Kissing Her Now'' from the penniless Harold Orlob and had put his name to it. Orlob was brought in as part of the writing team the following year and, soon after, Howard split away. After a couple of further Chicago successes with *The Sweetest Girl in Paris* and the 13-week run of *Lower Berth Thirteen,* he went back to writing and performing in his old style, both on the stage and in vaudeville. He did so for another 50 years, right up till his death in his nineties, and finished his days literally on the stage, collapsing and dying during a performance.

Howard was first married to performer-songwriter Ida Emerson, who after their burlesque years played in the early La Salle shows. His second wife was another musical-theatre player, **Mabel BARRISON** [Eva FARRANCE] (b Toronto c1882; d Toronto, 31 October 1912), who played a small part in Broadway's original *Florodora* (1900), in *The Little Duchess* (1901), suceeded Lotta Faust in *The Wizard of Oz,* was one of the original ''babes'' of *Babes in Toyland,* and starred alongside her husband in several of his stage shows (*The Flower of the Ranch,* etc) and in vaudeville (*My Big Sister's Beau,* etc). A third Mrs Howard, daughter of a wealthy steel manufacturer and previously the Countess Mauritio de Beaufort, shot herself in Omaha four weeks after their marriage and one subsequent meeting.

A film of his life, rather unfortunately (given the facts) entitled *I Wonder Who's Kissing Her Now,* was produced in 1947. Mark Stevens played the part of Howard, with his singing voice being provided by Buddy Clark.

1899 **An Alderman's Election** (Ida Emerson) burlesque Dewey Theater 2 January

1901 **Fol-de-Rol** (Emerson) burlesque Dewey Theater 30 September

1902 **The Paraders** (Raymond Peck) La Salle Theater, Chicago 21 December

1903 **Tom Tom** (Peck) La Salle Theater, Chicago 1 February

1904 **His Highness the Bey** (Hough, Adams) La Salle Theater, Chicago 21 November

1905 **The Isle of Bong-Bong** (Hough, Adams) La Salle Theater, Chicago 14 March

1905 **The Land of Nod** (Adams, Hough ad Hobart) Opera House, Chicago 17 June; New York Theater, New York 1 April 1907

1905 **The Umpire** (Hough, Adams) La Salle Theater, Chicago 2 December

1906 **The Time, the Place and the Girl** (Hough, Adams) La Salle Theater, Chicago 20 August; Wallack's Theater, New York 5 August 1907

1906 **The District Leader** (w George Collin Davis, Arthur Gillespie) Wallack's Theater 30 April

1907 **The Girl Question** (Hough, Adams) La Salle Theater, Chicago 24 August; Wallack's Theater, New York 3 August 1908

1907 **The Flower of the Ranch** Kansas City 15 September; Majestic Theater, New York, 20 April 1908

1908 **Honeymoon Trail** (Hough, Adams) La Salle Theater, Chicago 23 March

1908 **A Stubborn Cinderella** (Hough, Adams) Princess Theater, Chicago 31 May; Broadway Theater, New York 25 January 1909

1909 **The Prince of Tonight** (Hough, Adams) Princess Theater, Chicago 9 March

1909 **The Golden Girl** (Hough, Adams) La Salle Theater, Chicago 16 March

1909 **The Goddess of Liberty** (Hough, Adams) Princess Theater, Chicago 15 August; Weber's Theater, New York 22 December

1909 **The Flirting Princess** (w Orlob/Hough, Adams) Princess Theater, Chicago 1 November

1910 **Miss Nobody from Starland** (Hough, Adams/Howard Johnstone Mitchell) Princess Theater, Chicago 31 January

1910 **The Sweetest Girl in Paris** (w Gus Sohlke/Collin Davis, Addison Burkhart) La Salle Theater, Chicago 28 August

1910 **Lower Berth Thirteen** (w Gus Sohlke/Davis, Arthur Gillespie) Whitney Opera House, Chicago 16 October

1911 **Love and Politics** revised *The District Leader* Cort Theater, Chicago 3 April

1912 **Frivolous Geraldine** (w Herbert Stothart/Theodore Stempfel) Olympic Theater, Chicago 21 December

1913 A **Broadway Honeymoon** (w Stothart/Collin Davis/Collin Davis, Thomas T Reilley) Joe Howard's Theater, Chicago 3 October

1914 **The Manicure Shop** (ex- *All for the Girl*) (w Stothart/Stempfeldt) Suburban Garden, St Louis 29 June

1915 **The Girl of Tomorrow** (Stothart/w Joseph Knowles) La Salle Theater, Chicago 18 October

1917 **What Is Love?** National Theater, Washington, DC 2 July

1918 **In and Out** (Davis) ?22 January

1920 **Chin Toy** (Isidore Benjamin Kornblum)

HOWARD, Sydney (b Yeadon, 7 August 1885; d London, 12 June 1946). Plump comedian of the British revue and musical-comedy stage between the wars.

Howard began his performing career in his late twenties in the concert-party world, and was seen in London for the first time in the revue *Box o' Tricks.* After more than a decade of revue and variety work, he made his first appearance in the musical theatre when he played the role of Battling Smith in the London production of *Hit the*

Deck (1927). He followed up in *Funny Face* (1928, Herbert), *The Co-Optimists, Dear Love* (1930, Maurice Gerard) and *Heads Up* (1930, Skippy Dugan) and, after a period playing in farce and in films, returned to the musical stage to feature as Moonface Mooney in London's production of *Anything Goes* (1935). He subsequently appeared in leading comedy roles in Firth Shephard's productions of *Oh! You Letty* (1937, Mr Simmons), *Wild Oats* (1938, Samuel Cloppitt) and *Sitting Pretty* (1939, Wilberforce Tuttle), and in several of the same producer's wartime revues.

Howard also appeared in a regular schedule of films in the 1930s and 1940s, most of which were straight comedies, but some of which—such as the Gracie Fields movie *Shipyard Sally* (1939)—contained a musical element.

HOWARD, Willie [LEVKOWITZ, Wilhelm] (b Neustadt, Germany, 13 April ?1886; d New York, 12 January 1949). Popular vaudeville comedian who featured in a handful of Broadway musicals.

After an early career as a boy singer, Willie Howard found success in a vaudeville comedy act with his brother, **Eugene HOWARD** (b 1880; d 1965), and the pair appeared together in several editions of *The Passing Show* and in more than two decades of subsequent revues on Broadway. In 1925 Willie was cast in the star comedy role of Jimmy, the theatre usher, in *Sky High* (*Der Tanz ins Glück*), and he subsequently returned to the musical stage for a second fine role when he created the part of the comical taxi driver, Gieber Goldfarb, in *Girl Crazy* (1930). After his brother's retirement from the stage, he again returned to the musical theatre, appearing in the short-lived *My Dear Public* (1943, Barney) and as Connie in a 1948 revival of *Sally*.

HOWES, Bobby [HOWES, Charles Robert William] (b London, 4 August 1895; d London, 27 April 1972). Brash little comedian who became a star of the London musical stage between the wars.

Howes made his earliest appearances in variety and in concert parties, and was first seen in London in revue before moving on to take roles in the London productions of *The Blue Kitten* (1925, Octave) and *The Blue Train* (1927, *Mädi,* Freddie Royce). He established himself as a rising comic star with his performance in the musical melodrama *The Yellow Mask* (1928, Sam Slider), and took off thoroughly when he created the title role of the long-running musical comedy *Mr Cinders* (1929, Jim, ''On the Amazon''). He played in the London edition of *Sons o' Guns* (1930, Jimmy Canfield) and the Drury Lane spectacular *The Song of the Drum* (1931, Chips Wilcox), and scored a series of starring successes in three musical-

Plate 183. **Bobby Howes** *(right) gets mixed up with pirates Marie Burke and Raymond Newell in* He Wanted Adventure.

ized comedies written to his measure and mounted at the Saville Theatre by Jack Waller: *For the Love of Mike* (1931, Bobby Seymour), in which he introduced ''Got a Date with an Angel,'' *Tell Her the Truth* (1932, Bobby) and *He Wanted Adventure* (1933, Bobby Bramstone).

Howes had another major success when he paired again with his *Mr Cinders* co-star, Binnie Hale, in *Yes, Madam?* (1934, Bill Quinton), and yet another as the comical little hero of *Please, Teacher!* (1935, Tommy Deacon), and if *Big Business* (1937, Jimmy Rackstraw) proved less successful than its predecessors, he nevertheless came back to the top with a good run and a hit song (''She's My Lovely'') in *Hide and Seek* (1937), in which he was paired for a single occasion with comedienne Cicely Courtneidge.

Howes subsequently appeared in *Bobby Get Your Gun* (1938, Bobby Lockwood); took over from the ailing Stanley Lupino in *Lady Behave* (1941, Tony Meyrick) and then toured the show; played Jerry Walker in London's production of *Let's Face It* (1942); and took part in several revues. He had an unusual taste of failure in the quick 1949 flop *Roundabout,* and his resultant haranguing of the unappreciative audience left him for several years out of favor in London. He toured in *Good Night Vienna* (1952), and made his last London appearance in the musical theatre as Ben Rumson, alongside his daughter, Sally Ann, in the London version of *Paint Your Wagon* (1953). In 1960 he appeared as Og in a short-lived New York revival of *Finian's Rainbow,* a role he repeated in 1964 in the flop Australian production of the show.

Howes appeared in film versions of several of his stage successes—*For the Love of Mike* (1932), *Please, Teacher!* (1937) and *Yes, Madam?* (1938).

Sally Ann HOWES (b London, 20 July 1930) began her career on stage and film as a child, and appeared in leading ingenue roles in *Caprice* (1950, Joan), *Bet Your Life* (1952, Jane), *Paint Your Wagon* (1953, Jennifer), *Romance in Candlelight* (1955, Margaret) and *Summer Song* (1956, Karolka), before going to America to take over the role of Eliza Doolittle in *My Fair Lady.* She remained in America to take leading roles in *Kwamina* (1961) and *What Makes Sammy Run?* (1964), and was subsequently seen in England as Anna in a revival of *The King and I* (1973) and as Jenny Lind in *Hans Andersen* (1976). In 1991 she appeared in New York as Désirée in a revival of *A Little Night Music* and she has appeared with the New York City Opera as Fairy Godmother in *Cinderella* on several occasions.

She was for a period married to songwriter and producer Richard Adler.

HOWSON, John [Jerome] (b Hobart, Tasmania, 17 November 1842; d Troy, NJ, 16 December 1887).

After youthful days spent fighting with the British legion in the Spanish Carlist wars, and others working in various capacities in the musical theatres of Britain, **Francis HOWSON** (b London, 1817; d Omaha, Nebr, 16 September 1869), his wife Emma (née Richardson) (d New York, 7 December 1869), and brother John (b London, 1819; d Launceston, 19 September 1869) were taken out to Australia in 1842 by Mrs Clarke to perform in the recently established theatre in Hobart. Thereafter, following in the family tradition established by the Howson brothers' father, ''who taught Michael Balfe thorough bass and counterpoint,'' and Frank's celebrated sister, opera star Emma Albertazzi (1814–1847), the sometime queen of the Milanese (1832) and Parisian (1835) opera stage, the family was involved in some of Tasmania's (and Australia's) earliest theatricals, working on the stage when there was a stage to work on and giving dance and music lessons when there was not. Frank was star and stage director at Mrs Clarke's Royal Victoria Theatre whilst it existed (dancer Emma was, at the time, mostly giving birth to children in rapid succession), whilst John sr worked as vocalist, violinist, tenor trombonist, composer, actor and recitalist as required. Their children were given a full theatrical upbringing, and went forth, eventually, from their home island to win fame in the most competitive of musical-theatre arenas.

As professional theatrical activity came and went somewhat in Tasmania, Frank's son—the young John J Howson—worked in a lawyer's office, in a chandlers', as assistant to a dance-master, as an operatic chorister, as a violinist and, with the members of his family, took part in a concert party with which they visited the Australian goldfields, before Frank took his family to the metropolitan theatres of the Australian mainland to deliver a substantial program of English operas. Many such operas got their first Australian performances in this way, and the young John featured in these productions alongside his sisters, Emma and Clelia, and their stage director-cum-performer father, who thus earned the later soubriquet: ''the father of the opera in Australia.''

In 1866 the Howsons left Australia for America, pausing in Tahiti to give the island their repertoire. They began their American career as ''The Howson Family'' in San Francisco, joining the company at the Metropolitan Theater where they took part in all kinds of entertainments from opera to drama, concerts and oratorios, burlesque, spectaculars and opéra-bouffe, often with the support of other passing Australian theatrical adventurers. The productions of opéra-bouffe in which they played at San Francisco's Temple of Music and Alhambra in 1868 were some of the earliest to be seen on the western seabord, and included *La Grand-Duchesse, La Belle Hélène* and America's first English *Barbe-bleue* (Emma was Boulotte, John Popolani and Clelia Fleurette).

After three years of this sometimes thin-pickings life (May 1869), they left the West Coast and headed east playing *La Grande-Duchesse* as a meal ticket. However, the family did not make it to the East Coast. Father Frank died of cancer of the mouth in Omaha, and mother Emma soon after their arrival in New York. Whilst Emma jr got herself work with Caroline Richings, as an alternate leading lady in what was at the time America's most important English opera troupe, John and Clelia made their Broadway debut at Wood's Museum in the burlesque *Aladdin.* John worked subsequently in stock and as an orchestral player at the Grand Opera House, played with Mark Smith's company, took comic roles at the Variétés in New Orleans and returned to San Francisco in opéra-bouffe with Susie Galton, comedy at Maguire's Opera House with Jennie Lee (1873–74, Puck, Panatellas, Bobèche, Choufleuri, John Smith in *Po-co-han-tas,* Eily in *Eily O'Connor,* Cox in *Cox and Box, The Doctor of Al-*

Plate 184. *Baritone* **John Howson**—*London's first Marquis de Corneville—and his sister Emma, the creator of* HMS Pinafore'*s Josephine, pictured in their early days in the Australian theatre.*

cantara, Ching-Chow-Hi, etc) and in comedy and drama with Horace Lingard (Smalley in *Charity,* Marquis in *Alixe,* Dennis in *Naval Engagements, Creatures of Impulse,* etc). He spent a season with Alice Oates's company (America's first Judge in *Trial by Jury,* Bombastes Brag in Jesse Williams's *Mignonette,* Boléro in *Giroflé-Girofla,* etc) and appeared at the Boston Museum as La Cocardière in *La Jolie Parfumeuse,* before in 1877 moving on to see what London had to offer. There luck at last struck, and with a vengeance, for after being cast at the unfashionable Folly Theatre in productions of *La Créole* (Commodore) and *L'Oeil crevé* (Chamberlain), he was given the main baritone role in that house's next show: London's premiere of its most enormous hit to date, *Les Cloches de Corneville* (Henri). When the piece later went on the road, however, he dropped the star singing role to take up the showy character part of Gaspard the miser.

Howson subsequently played Escamillo in Lydia Thompson's West End season with the burlesque of *Carmen,* but in 1880 he returned to America. He appeared on Broadway as Cornwallis Algernon Prout in the indifferent *Lawn Tennis* and in some classic plays, revisited Britain for the disastrous *Gibraltar* (1881, *La Reine des Halles,* Major), and then definitively settled in America. Now thoroughly established as a leading musical-comedy player, he starred as John Wellington Wells in *The Sorcerer,* as Bunthorne (made up as Oscar Wilde) to the *Patience* of Lillian Russell, in *Olivette* for Comley and Barton, in *Madame Favart* and in *Manola,* but ultimately he performed less and less as a singer, returning more frequently to the comedy stage. In his last years he appeared musically as King Cole in the musical comedy *Madame Piper* (1884), alongside Mathilde Cottrelly as Jeremiah Hackett in *The Seamstress* (*Die Näherin*), as Folbach in John McCaull's production of *Falka* (1885), as John Whidden (with volin solo) in his own unsuccessful musical adaptation of Labiche and Martin's *La Poudre aux yeux* as *Putting on Style* (Opera House, Paterson, NJ 10 September 1885, mus: Frank Howson, Fred J Eustis), in Boston as Gavaudan in *Love's Vow* (1886, *Serment d'amour*) and on the road in *The Bat (Die Fledermaus,* 1887). He died in harness, whilst still in his forties, during a tour with Lotta.

John's sister **Emma HOWSON** (b Hobart, Tasmania, 28 March 1844; d New York, June 1928), who crossed from Australia to San Francisco and then New York with her brother, who introduced *Barbe-bleue*'s Boulotte to the West Coast, and who took the title role in the family tour of *Grande-Duchesse,* first used her fine soprano on the New York stage (20 November 1869) as a member of the Caroline Richings troupe (1869–71) in roles ranging from Maritana and Arline, Susanna (*Le nozze di Figaro*) and Rezia (*Oberon*) to Adalgisa to the manageresses' Norma. She appeared on Broadway at Niblo's in the musical drama *Paul Clifford* (1871, Lucy Brandon) and as Eily in *The Colleen Bawn* (1871), played with Rose Hersee's English Opera Company as Lenora (*Il Trovatore*), Susanna, Martha, Agathe (*Die Freischütz*) and Arline and was featured in the star role of J M Loretz's new opera *The Pearl of Baghdad* (Brooklyn, 1872), before returning to opéra-bouffe as Princess Cunégonde in Augustin Daly's starry production *King Carrot* and in the spectacular vaudeville *Round the Clock* (1872, Ernesta Hardacre).

She quit America in June 1873 to go to study with Lamberti in Milan, and she subsequently sang in opera in Malta (1875), before moving on to Britain. It was there that, like her brother, Emma Howson found her greatest success, when she was cast as the original Josephine in *HMS Pinafore* (1878, ''The Hours Creep On Apace,'' ''Never Mind the Why and Wherefore,'' etc). She scored a thorough prima donna's success in this epoch-making production but, oddly, she did not follow that success up, and although she toured with Sims Reeves in the little operetta *The Gay Cavalier,* she was little seen in Britain thereafter. In 1881 she was back in America, playing in the title role of *Madame Favart* and touring in *La Mascotte,* and in 1883 she was to be seen playing alongside John in *Olivette* through America, but thereafter her voice and her career thinned down, and she was seen only episodically in the theatre. She subsequently became a singing teacher in Brooklyn.

John and Emma's brother, **Frank A[lfred] HOWSON** (b Hobart, 8 June 1845; d Hollis, Long Island, 29 June 1926), who had been on the stage from the age of three, when he played Cupid to his father's Silenus in a ''mythological ballet'' at the Royal Victoria, later worked as a musical director in America and in Britain. He conducted the family tour of *La Grande-Duchesse,* Alice Oates's company and The English Opera Troupe (1874) in early days, later worked as musical director at Madison Square (1884) and with Irving at the Lyceum in London and ended up as musical supervisor for Charles Frohman. Amongst his composing credits were the incidental music for America's first production of the play *Im weissen Rössl* (*At the White Horse Tavern,* 1899) and for Daniel Frohman's 1902 *Notre Dame,* and the musical comedies *Putting on Style* (lib: John Howson, mus w Fred J Eustis Opera House, Paterson, NJ 10 September 1885) and *The Baron* (lib: H M Pitt Grand Opera House, Brooklyn 7 June 1886).

A third brother, **Charles E[dwin] Howson,** forsaking an early career as a performer, became the long-serving treasurer for Henry Irving. His two daughters, **Clelia Howson** and **Amy Howson,** both carried on the family tradition by going on the stage, the former with the Irving-Terry company, the latter with D'Oyly Carte.

Clelia HOWSON (b Hobart, 8 June 1845; d Brooklyn, 14 April 1908), who had also worked alongside Frank, John and Emma, in Australia and in America, soon retired to marriage. In later life, when Emma's singing career was done, she moved in with her sister and her husband and spent her later years keeping house for them whilst giving occasional voice lessons at Carnegie Hall.

One further member of the Howson family also had a brilliant career in the musical theatre. [**Maria Carolina] Clélia ALBERTAZZI** (b Milan, 6 December 1832; d Stockton-on-Tees, 24 November 1887) was the daughter of the operatic Emma and a cousin to Emma and John. She made herself a fine career in English opera and opéra-bouffe in the 1860s and 1870s under the name ''Mdlle Albertazzi,'' whilst running a parallel career as one of the music hall's most skilled soprano vocalists, purveying operatic arias and ballads of all kinds to London and provincial audiences under her married name of Madame Valckeneare. In line with the family tradition, she mothered two daughters, **Eugénie [Léonide Marie] VALCKENEARE** (b Boulogne-sur-mer, 1 January 1858) and **Marie [Athenais Clélia] VALCKENEARE** (b Bruges, 28 May 1856), who both went on to the musical stage from a very early age.

HOW TO SUCCEED IN BUSINESS WITHOUT REALLY TRYING Musical in 2 acts by Abe Burrows, Jack Weinstock and Willie Gilbert based on the book by Shepherd Mead. Music and lyrics by Frank Loesser. 46th Street Theater, New York, 14 October 1961.

Producers Feuer and Martin, songwriter Frank Loesser and librettist Abe Burrows, who had all worked together to such outstanding effect on *Guys and Dolls* a decade earlier, came together for a second time with a very different style of musical comedy in *How to Succeed in Business without Really Trying,* and scored a second major hit.

Whereas *Guys and Dolls* had wallowed wonderfully in its very special period downtown atmosphere and lingo, *How to Succeed* was a here-and-now musical, a brisk, bristling, big-business affair which drew its unbitter fun from the game of city office politics, and how to play it. Robert Morse appeared as J Pierrepont Finch, an ambitious window-cleaner who, equipped with a manual on ''How to Succeed in Business . . . ,'' sets out to make his way to the top of the corporate steeple. The firm on which he clips his pitons is World Wide Wickets and with a little help from a gentle distortion of the truth he gets a foot-in-the-door job in the mail room. From there, in spite of the rivalry and enmity of boss's nephew, Bud Frump (Charles Nelson Reilly), and aided by his all-foreseeing manual, ''Ponty'' quickly begins to rise through the echelons of management, springboarding with innocently smiling guile off the faces of his superiors as he leapfrogs over their superiors. By the end of the first act, having carefully spiked a handful of rivals for the good opinion of big boss Biggley (Rudy Vallee), he is Vice-President in Charge of Advertising, with his own office and his own secretary, the very Rosemary (Bonnie Scott) who has been his admiring supportrice from the start. Trouble arrives, however, when a televised advertising stunt featuring Biggley's bit-on-the-side, Hedy la Rue (Virginia Martin), goes horribly wrong, compromising not only Finch but big boss Biggley. But, summoned before even Bigger Boss Womper, our hero somehow pulls out of it all shining-white, and before Biggley knows it, Womper has disappeared off into the sunset with Hedy, and Finch has leapfrogged him into the position of biggest boss of all. Biggley is going to telegraph to the President of the United States to look out for his job.

The tale was illustrated with a scoreful of bright and funny songs. The office setting brought forth some—the retiring head of the mail room sang a hymn to ''The Company Way,'' the men and girls of the office insisted, some with more conviction than others, that ''A Secretary is Not a Toy''—but the happiest musical moments of the evening came in Finch's self-admiratory ''I Believe in You,'' Rosemary's vision of suburban bliss as Mrs Finch, ''Happy to Keep His Dinner Warm,'' and the after-hours song ''Been a Long Day,'' in which the two young folk mutter going-home platitudes at each other whilst the older secretary, Miss Jones (Ruth Kobart), interprets the real, longing thoughts behind their words.

How to Succeed in Business without Really Trying was a first-rate hit on Broadway. It walked away with the Tony Award for best musical of its season, as well as the awards for libretto, lyrics, Burrows's direction and Morse's performance, and garnered a handful of other awards (including a pre-devaluation Pulitzer Prize) as it settled in to the 46th Street Theater for a grand run of 1,417 performances. The other main centers, even those which had not picked up on *Guys and Dolls,* moved in cohort to stage *How to Succeed.* As the first American tour company took to the road, with Dick Kallman as Finch and Dyan Cannon as Rosemary, Arthur Lewis opened the first foreign production, in London. Warren Berlinger was seen as Finch, alongside Patricia Michael (Rosemary), Billy de Wolfe (Biggley), Eileen Gourlay (Hedy) and David Knight (Frump), the piece was again directed by Burrows, and it again scored a fine success with a West End run of 520 performances.

Plate 185. **How to Succeed in Business without Really Trying.** *Billy de Wolfe happily belies the maxim that ''a secretary is not a toy.'' Carole Buck and Monte Amundsen are the toys in this St Louis Muny production, 1966.*

Australia's production of the show, with Len Gochman, Edwin Steffe, Jay Gerber, Betty McGuire and Annabelle Adams featured, played some five months in Melbourne and more than six months further in Sydney (Her Majesty's Theatre 15 February 1964), and then the foreign-language mountings began. Paris got its *Comment réussir dans les affaires sans vraiment se fatiguer* (ad Raymond Castans), under the management of Elvire Popesco, Hubert de Malet and Lars Schmidt in 1964, with Jacques Duby (Finch), André Luguet (Biggley), Evelyne Dandry (Rosemary) and such countable-with names as Jacqueline Mille, Roger Tréville and Arlette Didier amongst the supporting cast. The following year Vienna saw a German-language adaptation (ad Robert Gilbert, Gerhard Bronner), with Harald Juhnke starred as Hannibal Fink, veteran character actor Theo Lingen as Biggley, Inge Brück as Rosemary and Franco Steinberg as Fred Strunk (ex- Bud Frump), through 62 performances at the Theater an der Wien.

The show was seen at New York's City Center in 1966, and in 1967 a film version was made, with Morse, Vallee and Miss Kobart repeating their original roles alongside Broadway takeover Michelle Lee as Rosemary, as *How to Succeed* made itself a regular home in regional theatres. Perhaps surprisingly, given its recognized merits, and its continued topicality in a world where office practices and big-to-medium business haven't changed that much (give or take a computer or two), it took nearly a quarter of a century for *How to Succeed* to return to one of the major musical theatre centers, in a full first-class production. In 1993 Australia got a fresh production of the piece, mounted under the management of John Frost (Footbridge Theatre, Sydney 9 January) with Tom Burlinson starred as Ponty alongside a high-energy selection of local veterans—Noel Ferrier (Biggley), Johnny Lockwood (Twimble), ballet star Garth Welch (Bratt) and June Bronhill (Miss Jones)—and soap star Georgie Parker (Rosemary). Then, in 1995 a fresh production was brought to Broadway from California's La Jolla Playhouse. Matthew Broderick was the Ponty of the occasion, alongside the Biggley of Ronn Carroll and the Rosemary of Megan Mullaly. The revival (Richard Rodgers Theater 23 March 1995) stayed around for a respectable 548 performances before hitting the road again, with its place among the classics of the American musical comedy repertoire thoroughly confirmed.

UK: Shaftesbury Theatre 28 March 1963; Australia: Her Majesty's Theatre, Melbourne 16 August 1963; France: Théâtre de Paris *Comment réussir dans les affaires sans vraiment se fatiguer* 1964, Austria: Theater an der Wien *Wie man was wird im Leben, ohne sich anzustrengen* 21 December 1965; Germany: Theater der Stadt, Trier 17 December 1968

Film: United Artists 1967

Recordings: original cast (RCA), London cast (RCA), French cast (Philips), Austrian cast (Ariola-Eurodisc), film soundtrack (United Artists), revival cast recording 1995 (RCA), Japanese cast recording (Takarazuka) (TCAC), etc

HOYT, Charles [Hale] (b Concord, NH, 26 July 1860; d New York, 20 November 1900). Author of some of the soundest and most successful farce-comedies of the American musical stage during the 1890s.

For five years the drama and music editor of the *Boston Post,* Hoyt made his first attempt as a dramatist when he cobbled up a one-act sketch, *Gifford's Luck,* for Frank Wright to help fill a bill at the local vaudeville house, the Boston Athenaeum (March 1881). He subsequently had a four-act comedy, *Cezalia,* produced in Boston (Globe Theater 28 May), did a rewrite on another, *Mrs Partington* (1882) for dame comedian Charles Fostelle, and turned out a piece called *Queen of Bohemia* (1882) for Kate Castleton. He got his first musical theatre credit when he worked over the text for Willie Edouin's mixture of low comedy and a patchwork of new and borrowed (and ever-changing) songs, *Dreams,* in a ''new version'' for the 1882 season. The famous farce-comedian was happy enough with his efforts to commission a second piece, and he got a second exceptionally long-lived touring show built on pretty much the same principles: the knock-about variety farce *A Bunch of Keys.*

In 1884 the playwright joined with Eugene Tomkins, owner of the Boston Theater, and Charles W Thomas to himself present his next musical play, the ''roaring farce'' *A Rag Baby,* starring the young Frank Daniels and Jennie Yeamans. Tomkins dropped out of the partnership after two seasons, but Thomas remained with Hoyt, co-producing his series of musically mobile farce comedies for extended tours, until his death in 1894, after which Frank McKee, nine years the general manager for the partners, took his place. During this period Hoyt had his greatest success, scoring a huge and international hit with his 1891 piece *A Trip to Chinatown,* notching up 10 consecutive years of touring with comedians Hoey and Evans's *A Parlor Match* (developed for them by Hoyt from an 1882 Frank Dumont sketch) and further multiple-year tours with such pieces as *A Milk White Flag* and *A Texas Steer.* In spite of getting himelf elected, like his father, to the New Hampshire legislature, on a Democratic ticket, he continued to turn out regular new works in the years that followed, scoring a fresh success with *A Black Sheep,* as his companies of ''Hoyt's Comedians'' toured his plays as far afield as Australia. In 1895 he put together a vehicle for baseball star Adrian C Anson, under the title *A Runaway Colt,* but an announced comic-opera version of the Helen of Troy tale, with a score by Safford Waters, did not eventuate. His later shows began to show signs of a mental disorder, brought on by venereal disease, and in 1899 McKee had his partner committed to an asylum. The wealthy Hoyt soon let himself out and tried to return to the theatre, but he died shortly after.

Hoyt's appeal was largely to American playgoers, and most particularly to the touring circuits rather than more sophisticated venues. Apart from *A Trip to Chinatown* (Toole's Theatre 29 September 1894), which held up its popularity throughout Britain for many years, his pieces did not go down well in London. Willie Edouin's production of *A Bunch of Keys* (Avenue Theatre, 25 August 1883, ''pitiful trash . . . decidedly more of a pantomime than anything else'') was a quick failure, and *A Stranger in New York* (Duke of York's Theatre 21 June 1898) and *A Parlor Match* (Terry's Theatre 4 October 1900, ''old music-hall jokes . . . stale and puerile . . . two hours of nothing in particular disguised as an excuse for presenting entertainment more or less humorous'') were no more happy, counting their runs in a few weeks. However, the former was later seen in the British provinces, remade under the more saleable title *In Gay Paree.*

Australia was rather more welcoming, and Hoyt was well represented on the colonial stages by his own productions of *A Trip to Chinatown* (Lyceum, Sydney 27 June 1896) and *A Milk White Flag* (1896), female impersonator Francis Leon and the Coghill brothers' version of *A Parlor Match* (St Georges Hall, Melbourne 23 January 1886), followed by a fresh production by Frank Clark in 1894, Harry Rickards's mounting of *A Bunch of Keys* (Opera House, Brisbane 18 September 1897) and J C Williamson's production of *A Rag Baby* (Theatre Royal, Adelaide 22 September 1899).

When long years of touring popularity finally wore them a touch thin, several of Hoyt's shows were later remade by other hands, with a more regular musical content. *A Texas Steer* became *A Trip to Washington* (La Salle Theater, Chicago 24 August 1913) and later, under the management of Elisabeth Marbury and Frederick McCay, *We Should Worry* (Apollo, Atlantic City 25 October 1917, A Baldwin Sloane/Henry Blossom); *A Trip to Chinatown* was remade and remounted by Florenz Ziegfeld as *A Winsome Widow* (Moulin Rouge 11 April 1912); and *A Milk White Flag* was turned with equal lack of success into *Go to It* (Princess Theater 24 October 1916, ad Anne Caldwell, John E Hazzard, John L Golden). His *A Contented Woman* became *Ladies First* (Broadhurst Theater 24 October 1918) in the hands of adapter Harry B Smith and composer A Baldwin Sloane, whilst *Dreams* also underwent many further alterations, and Edouin presented a version of some of its elements on the English and Australian stage under the title of *Binks, the Downy Photographer.*

Several of Hoyt's musical plays were filmed as silent films, beginning in 1913 with Selig Films two-reel feature of *A Midnight Bell* (5 May 1913) with Frank Weed and Lillian Leighton. Amongst those which followed it to celluloid were *A Texas Steer* (Selig 26 July 1915), with Tyrone Power, *A Bunch of Keys* (Essanay, 1915), *A Black Sheep* (Selig 19 October 1915) with Otis Harlan, and *A Stranger in New York* (Selig 8 May 1916) with Otis Harlan.

Hoyt was married to two farce-comedy actresses. The first **Flora WALSH** (b San Francisco, 25 July 1871; d Boston, 22 January 1893), began her career as Josephine in a juvenile *HMS Pinafore* and traveled with Rice's Surprise Party (1880, Cock Robin in *Babes in the Wood*), but spent almost her whole career playing for Hoyt in *A Rag Baby* (Clairette), *A Tin Soldier* (Carrie Story), *A Bunch of Keys, A Hole in the Ground* (Lady at the Lunch Counter), *A Brass Monkey* (Baggage), *A Texas Steer* (Bossy) and *A Temperance Town.* The second, **Caroline MISKEL** [née SCALES] (b Covington, Ky, 15 September 1873; d New York, 2 October 1898), played Ruth in *A Temperance Town* and the star role of Grace Holmes in *A Contented Woman.*

1882 **Dreams** "new edition" Gaiety Theater, Boston 27 February

1882 **A Bunch of Keys** (various) Park Theater, Newark, NJ 13 December; San Francisco Minstrels' Opera House, New York 26 March 1883

1884 **A Rag Baby** (Napier Lothian) Opera House, New Bedford, Mass 17 March; Tony Pastor's Theater, New York 14 April

1884 **A Parlor Match, or Turning a Crank** (revised *The Book Agent*) (pasticcio) Asbury Park 4 September; Tony Pastor's Theater, New York 22 September

1884 **A Case of Wine** (pasticcio) Millet's Opera House, Austin, Tex 10 November

1885 **A Tin Soldier** (Percy Gaunt, Hoyt and pasticcio) Opera House, New Bedford, Mass 30 March; Standard Theater, New York 3 May

1885 **Lend Me a Dollar** (pasticcio/credited to "John Harrison") Opera House, Newport, RI 4 April

1886 **The Maid and the Moonshiner** (Edward Solomon) Standard Theater 16 August

1887 **A Hole in the Ground** (Charles Zimmerman) Columbus, Ohio 21 February; 14th Street Theater, New York 12 September

1888 **A Midnight Bell** (various) Alcazar, San Francisco 4 April; Bijou Theater 5 March 1889

1888 **A Brass Monkey** (various) Opera House, New Bedford, Mass 15 May; Bijou Theater, New York 15 October

1890 **A Texas Steer, or Money Makes the Mare** (various) New Bedford, Mass 28 April; Bijou Theater 10 November

1890 **A Trip to Chinatown** (Gaunt, et al) Powers' Grand Opera House, Decatur, Ill 18 September; Harlem Opera House 8 December; Madison Square Theater 9 November 1891

1892 **A Temperance Town** (various) Academy of Music, Buffalo 14 March; Madison Square Theater 18 September 1893

1893 **A Milk White Flag, and Its Battle-Scarred Followers on the Field of Mars and in the Court of Venus** (Gaunt) Academy of Music, Buffalo 23 December; Boston Theater, Boston 5 February; Hoyt's Theater, New York 8 October 1894

1894 **A Black Sheep, and How It Came out in the Wash** (Richard Stahl) Academy of Music, Buffalo 10 September; Hoyt's Theater, New York 6 January 1896

1895 **A Contented Woman** (Stahl) Star Theater, Buffalo 2 September; Hoyt's Theater, New York 4 January 1897

1895 **A Runaway Colt** (various) Wieting Opera House, Syracuse 12 November; American Theater 2 December

1897 **A Stranger in New York** (various) Star Theater, Buffalo 15 February; Garrick Theater, New York 13 September

1898 **A Day and a Night in New York** (Stahl) Hyperion Theater, New Haven 18 April; Garrick Theater, New York 30 August

1899 **A Dog in the Manger** (various) Lafayette Square Theater, Washington, DC 30 January

Biography: Hunt, D L: *The Life and Work of Charles H Hoyt* (Joint University Libraries, Nashville, 1945)

HUBBELL, [John] Raymond (b Urbana, Ohio, 1 June 1879; d Miami, Fla, 13 December 1954). Composer of two decades of functional rather than memorable scores for the American theatre.

Hubbell moved to Chicago from his native Ohio to study, and he first entered the music world there as a dance-band conductor and songwriter and as an employee of the music publishing house of Charles K Harris. At the age of 23 he composed his first score for the musical theatre, a Chicago extravaganza called *Chow Chow* which mixed comedy, songs (not all by Hubbell) and a South Seas setting in traditional style with sufficient success for the show to be transported to Broadway the following season. Played there as *The Runaways,* under the management of Sam Shubert and Nixon and Zimmerman, it was scorned by sophisticated critics, ran up 167 metropolitan performances, and toured thereafter for five years. Hubbell had a second success with the score for another Sam Shubert piece on similar, but slightly more substantial, lines in *Fantana* (1905). He subsequently became a prolific composer of show music both for the Shubert management and for other producers through 20 years of occasionally attractive if utilitarian writing which, if it produced no memorable music or enduring shows, kept many a Broadway theatre musicked for considerable periods.

Hubbell was principal composer on five editions of the *Ziegfeld Follies* (1911 to 1914, 1917) and composed the scores for six of the Hippodrome spectaculars produced by Charles Dillingham (*Hip! Hip! Hooray!, The Big Show, Cheer Up, Happy Days, Good Times, Better Times*), the second of which produced his most successful single song, ''Poor Butterfly'' (ly: R H Burnside), a number written as a vehicle for a Japanese soprano who ultimately did not join the cast. He also composed the music for a number of vaudeville sketches, such as Bessie Clayton's Fenimore Cooper playlet *Spiritland* (1909).

In the realm of the book musical he rarely equaled the success of his earliest pieces. Sam Shubert failed to repeat *Fantana*'s run with *Mexicana,* but although John C Fisher's starring vehicle for Sallie Fisher was rejected as *Mam'selle Sallie,* it rebounded a season later as *A Knight for a Day* and ran for 176 nights on Broadway, prior to a healthy life on the road and an export to Australia. Hubbell suffered a couple of quick failures with *The Girl from the States,* which was totally rewritten (without his music) yet still folded out of town, and *The Air King,* which opened at Buffalo and got only as far as Chicago before collapsing, whilst *The Girl at the Helm* pleased Chicago for a five-month run in the wake of the Howard, Hough and Adams shows, but went no further. However, a collaboration with Glen MacDonough on a piece for Lew Fields, *The Midnight Sons,* won a fine success as a summer musical—that traditionally loose-limbed and undemanding form of entertainment which was played during the hot months of the year when people didn't feel like concentrating on anything but the lightest and most frivolous of entertainments.

Fields's follow-up production of the same team's *The Jolly Bachelors* starred Nora Bayes (instead of last time's Blanche Ring), who brought her own successful songs with her, whilst *The Bachelor Belles* featured another artist, Adeline Genée, who was also inclined to bring her own music with her, to the detriment of the show's nominal composer. Hubbell shared the score on a further indifferent Lew Fields vehicle, *The Never Homes,* and had little joy with the equally indifferent *Three Romeos* and with Ziegfeld's attempt to update the old hit *A Trip to Chinatown* as *A Winsome Widow.* Another summer musical, the allegedly French-farce-based *The Man from Cook's,* had some success in the hot part of 1912.

After several years of writing only for revue (*Fads and Fancies, Hitchy-Koo, Ziegfeld Follies* and the Hippodrome), Hubbell essayed a handful more musicals. *The Kiss Burglar* used a smidgin of a wartime theme in its Frenchified farce book and won a respectable run, but a piece written to launch swimming star Annette Kellerman as a musical performer and a tiny musical called *Miss Millions,* written with his Hippodrome colleague R H Burnside, both failed, as did a sentimental wartime piece called *Sonny,* which attempted too blatantly to cash in on the success of its author's previous Franco-weepie, *Buddies.* Hubbell's music was by now regarded more as an appendage to a show than an advantage, but he persevered with a respectable Leon Errol comedy vehicle, *Yours Truly* (127 performances), and a show for the slightly fading Fred Stone, *Three Cheers.* He also saw quite a bit of his music tacked in alongside some bits of Jean Gilbert in an R H Burnside concoction, apparently partially remade from *The Man from Cook's,* called *The Girl from Cook's,* mounted briefly at London's Gaiety Theatre, before he quit the theatre and moved to Miami in retirement.

Hubbell was married to musical-comedy player **Helen LORD** (b Hornell, NY, 12 December 1878; d Hornell, NY, 2 January 1911), who appeared prior to her marriage in the Casino productions of *The Belle of New York, The American Beauty, The Whirl of the Town, Miss Simplicity* and *The Runaways.*

1902 **Chow Chow** (Addison Burkhart) New Orpheon Theater, Chicago 4 October

1903 **The Runaways** revised *Chow Chow* Casino Theater 11 May

1904 **Fantana** (Robert B Smith) Garrick Theater, Chicago 9 October; Lyric Theater 14 January 1905

1906 **Mexicana** (Clara Driscoll, R B Smith) Lyric Theater 29 January

1906 **Mam'selle Sallie** (R B Smith) Poli's Theater, Waterbury, Conn 15 October; Grand Opera House 26 November

1907 **A Knight for a Day** revised *Mam'selle Sallie* Wallack's Theater 16 December

1908 **The Girl at the Helm** (R B Smith) La Salle Theater, Chicago 5 September

1908 **The Girl of the Great Divide** (R B Smith) burlesque in *Western Life* 125th Street Theater October

1909 **Spirit Land** 1 act Fifth Avenue Theater 8 February

1909 **The Midnight Sons** (Glen MacDonough) Broadway Theater 22 May

1909 **The Girl from the States** (w A Baldwin Sloane/MacDonough) Adelphi Theater, Philadelphia 11 October

1909 **The (Hot) Air King** (Harry B Smith) Star Theater, Buffalo 22 November; Colonial Theater, Chicago 28 November

1910 **The Jolly Bachelors** (MacDonough) Broadway Theater 6 January

1910 **The Bachelor Belles** (H B Smith) Globe Theater 7 November

1911 **The Never Homes** (w Sloane/E Ray Goetz/MacDonough) Broadway Theater 5 October

1911 **The Three Romeos** (R H Burnside) Globe Theater 13 November

1912 **The Man from Cook's** (Henry Blossom) New Amsterdam Theater 25 March

1912 **A Winsome Widow** (Charles Hoyt ad) Moulin Rouge 11 April

1915 **The Model Maid** (Anne Caldwell) Apollo Theater, Atlantic City 26 January

1916 **Come to Bohemia** (w Kenneth M Murchison/George S Chappell, MacDonough/Chappell) Maxine Elliott Theater 27 April

1918 **The Kiss Burglar** (MacDonough) George M Cohan Theater 9 May

1919 **Among the Girls** (Blossom, MacDonough/Blossom, Roi Cooper Megrue) Shubert Theater, New Haven 9 May; Park Square Theater, Boston 19 May

1919 **Miss Millions** (R H Burnside) Punch and Judy Theater 9 December

1921 **Sonny** (George V Hobart) Cort Theater 16 August

1922 **The Elusive Lady** (MacDonough) Ford's Theater, Baltimore 2 October

1927 **Yours Truly** (Caldwell/Clyde North) Shubert Theater 25 January

1927 **The Girl from Cook's** (w Jean Gilbert/Burnside, Greatrex Newman) Gaiety Theatre, London 1 November

1928 **Three Cheers** (Caldwell, Burnside) Globe Theater 15 October

HUGDIETRICHS BRAUTFAHRT Komische Märchen-Operette in 3 acts by ''Rideamus.'' Music by Oscar Straus. Carltheater, Vienna, 10 March 1906.

The second collaboration of ''Rideamus'' (Fritz Oliven) and the rising Oscar Straus, following their joyous burlesque on things legendary in *Die lustigen Nibelungen, Hugdietrichs Brautfahrt* was an imaginative fairy-tale piece, told with genuine burlesque wit and humor.

Hugdietrich (Mizzi Zwerenz), the ruler of Byzantium, is in need of a wealthy wife, as the expenses of running his country and his court and the upkeep on the royal mistresses are proving burdensome. A Royal Commission is set under way to solve the problem, but before it can lay an answer, Hugdietrich gets an unexpected hand from an out-of-favor fairy, Belladonna (Betti Seidl). Belladonna has been semi-seduced by the neighboring and seriously rich King Ladislaus (Karl Blasel), and she has sworn to be revenged on him. This she intends to do through his daughter, Miki (Helene Merviola). Ladislaus has engaged Miki, against her will, to the pillocky but profitable Prince Kakerlack (Ferdinand Pagin), and he has locked her up in a tower, guarded by a perpetually hungry dragon called Schnidibumpfl (Arthur Guttmann), until she can be duly thus wed. Belladonna magically disguises Hugdietrich as a girl, Hughlinde, who attracts lascivious Ladislaus's attention to the extent that ''she'' is made lady-in-waiting to Miki. Tower-bound Miki is delighted to have a lady-in-waiting who will share a cigarette with her and even more delighted when ''she'' reveals her manhood. Of course, the inevitable happens, and when the friendly and helpful Schnidibumpfl gets fearsomely rid of the local League of Virtue and devours the unwanted Kakerlack, everything can come to a happy, if slightly messy end.

The score included some jolly numbers especially for the dragon, reminiscing smokily over an unfaithful girlfriend, and for Miki, whose wistful sighings for romance and a knight (''Prinzesschen sass träumend auf duftiger Halde'') gave way to a whoop of joyous 4/4 (''Er ist ein Mann'') on Hugdietrich's self-exposure, whilst Belladonna made her fairy appearance to the waltzing strains of ''Sorgloser Schläfer,'' in one of the evening's prettiest, but nonetheless amusing, moments.

Mounted, like *Die lustigen Nibelungen,* at Vienna's Carltheater under the management of Andreas Aman, *Hugdietrichs Brautfahrt* started rather more promisingly than its predecessor, running for 53 straight performances (to 4 May), being brought swiftly back after the brief run of Kobler's *Der Rosenjungling* to play out the last weeks of the season, and then again to open the new one in the autumn (75th performance, 16 September). It remained in the repertoire in 1907, but was overwhelmed by the theatre's big hit of that year, Straus's own *Ein Walzertraum,* and disappeared from the schedules as the Carltheater switched to running the big new hit unbrokenly.

The show was afterwards seen in Germany, where it was played at the Rudolstadt Thüringisches Landestheater as recently as 1992 (28 November), but it does not seem to have traveled any further, nor to have returned to the Viennese stage. In the flush of the success of *The Merry Widow* in America, its producer Henry Savage announced that his version of *Prince Hugo's Honeymoon* was "in preparation," but sadly it doesn't ever seem to have made it beyond the announcement stage.

Germany: ?1907

HUGO, Victor [Marie] (b Besançon, 26 February 1802; d Paris, 22 May 1885).

Apart from supplying the verses for no less than three operatic versions of *Notre Dame de Paris,* composed by Louise Bertin (1836), Dargomysky (1847) and Lebeau (1857), the famous French novelist and dramatist did not actually dip his own pen into the musical theatre, but his works have proved the inspiration for other writers, of all degrees and kinds, to do so. At first this was in the operatic field, and Verdi's 1844 opera *Ernani* (*Hernani,* 1830), his *Rigoletto* (*Le Roi s'amuse,* 1832), Donizetti's *Lucrezia Borgia* (*Lucrèce Borgia,* 1833), Mercadante's *Il Guiramento* and Ponchielli's *La Gioconda* (both *Angelo,* 1835), and many other less-celebrated operas were based on Hugo's bulgingly dramatic works. These operas, in their turn, prompted burlesques, and London saw revamped Hugo in such pieces as the *Ernani* by William Brough (Alexandra Theatre, 1859), Henry Byron's *Handsome Hernani, or The Fatal Penny Whistle* (Gaiety Theatre, 1879), Lester Buckingham's *Lucrezia Borgia!, at Home and All Abroad* (St James's Theatre, 1860), Sydney French's *Lucrezia Borgia* (Marylebone Theatre, 1867) and Byron's *Lucrezia Borgia MD or the Grand Doctoress* (Holborn Theatre 28 October 1868). By far the most popular of Hugo's works amongst the burlesquers, however, was *Notre Dame.* Many times operaticized from 1836 onwards without a standard opera emerging, it was parodied as *Esmeralda* (Adelphi Theatre 5 June 1850), *Esmeralda, or The Sensation Goat* (Strand Theatre 28 September 1861), *Quasimodo, the Deformed, or The Man with the Hump and the Belle of Notre Dame* (Grecian Saloon 18 April 1870), *Pretty Esmeralda, and Captain Phoebus of Ours* (Gaiety Theatre 2 April 1879), pantomimed in *Mother Bunch and the Man with the Hunch, or The Reeds the Weeds, the Prest, the Swell, the Gipsy Girl and the Big Dumb Bell* (Surrey Theatre 26 December 1881 with G H MacDemott as Claude Frollico) and new-burlesqued in the highly successful Gaiety Theatre *Miss Esmeralda* (1887). *Ruy Blas* also came under the hands of both operatic and burlesque-writers and parodies appeared in London as *Ruy Blas Righted* (Vaudeville Theatre 3 January 1874) and as *Ruy Blas and the Blasé Roué* (Gaiety Theatre 21 September 1889). Paris gave a *Ruy Blas d'en-face* (Folies Dramatiques 13 April 1872) which had to be removed when the mob invaded the gallery and hissed and booed through the night to prevent the work of well-known conservative, Alfred Saint-Albin, being heard.

Quatre-vingt-treize became *Los hijos del batallón* in the hands of Spain's Ruperto Chapí and Guillermo Fernández Shaw as early as 1898, but it was nearly a century more before Hugo's most successful moment in the non-operatic musical theatre arrived. With the fashion for dramatic and sentimental musical plays replacing that for the comic in the 1980s, Hugo finally moved, unparodied, into the English-language musical theatre when *Les Misérables* was musicalized by Claude-Michel Schönberg, Alain Boublil and Jean-Marc Natel with vast international success. It was a success which, perhaps surprisingly in the new era of the copycat show, did not immediately produce a huge flood of musical Hugo from other sources. *Hernani* and *Ruy Blas, Le Roi s'amuse* and *Angelo* were left unmolested. However, the most obvious piece of Hugo was not. A whole bundle of musical versions of *Notre Dame* invaded the world's stages, beginning with a French and a German one (Charles Kálmán/ Maria Caleita, Mariello Momm, Schauspielbühne, Munich, 1988), both entitled *Quasimodo,* an Hungarian one (Hevesi Sándor Színház, Zalaegerszeg, Gábor Kemény/Peter Tömöry, 1989), subsequently mounted in Bruchsal, Germany, as *Der Glöckner von Notre Dame* (ad Franz Csiky, 1992), a British one by Mark Bramble and Callum McLeod (Oxford, 1991), an Argentinian one—*El jorobado de Paris* (Angel Mahler/ Pepe Cibrian, Luna Park, Buenos Aires 6 April 1993)—and an American one, which still subscribed to the old heroines-are-upfront-as-titles theory and called itself *Esmeralda* (Steven Lutvak/Kathryn Plazek, David Schechter, Repertory Theater, St Louis 24 March 1995). However serious success struck only when a French *Notre Dame de Paris* (Riccardo Cocciante/Luc Plamondon, Palais des Congrès 18 September 1998) was added to the already vast list of hunchbacked musicals of former years. The French musical turned out to be the biggest homemade hit since the same author's *Starmania.* Disney joined in the festival with an animated movie featuring a cutesy-pie Quasimodo, and this too was subsequently adapted to the musical stage (Alan Menken/Stephen Schwartz/James Lapine ad Michael Kunze, Theater des Westens, Berlin 5 June 1999).

Victor Hugo, who had originally refused, in 1884, to allow the production in Europe of the most successful *Notre Dame* musical, the *Esmeralda* composed by Arthur Goring Thomas (Drury Lane 26 March 1883), which would go on to wipe his own efforts of the repertoire, would doubtless not have been pleased.

HULBERT, Jack [HULBERT, John Norman] (b Ely, 24 April 1892; d London, 25 March 1978). A light-comic actor, singer and dancer with a well-known shovel-chin whose biggest successes as a performer were made in partnership with his wife, Cicely Courtneidge.

Hulbert moved into the professional musical theatre direct from his Cambridge University show *Cheer-Oh!*

Cambridge (also author), which was given a West End showing at the Queen's Theatre (12 June 1913) after its local performances. He joined Robert Courtneidge's company to play a light comedy supporting role in *The Pearl Girl* (1913, Robert Jaffray), and appeared consecutively in the same producer's *The Cinema Star* (Billy), *The Arcadians* revival (Bobby) and the disastrous *The Light Blues* (Arthur Hobbs), another Cambridge musical, for which the young man collaborated on the book.

He played in several revues, took the soubret role of Posch in the London version of *Das Hollandweibchen* (1920), made an appearance on Broadway with Miss Courtneidge in their successful London revue *By the Way* (1925), and then, following his managerial ambitions, joined with Paul Murray to commission and produce the musical comedy *Lido Lady* with a score by the young Rodgers and Hart. Both he (Harry Bassett) and his wife appeared in the piece, which Hulbert also directed with a fair degree of success. Thereafter he co-produced and occasionally appeared in several revues (*Clowns in Clover, The House That Jack Built, Folly to Be Wise, On with the Show*), whilst directing (*The Blue Train, Song of the Sea*) and choreographing (*Lady Mary*) musicals for other producers. Hulbert produced only one musical play himself, the Sophie Tucker vehicle *Follow a Star,* a virtual cabaret show in which he appeared opposite his star in the role of Bobby Hillary whilst also directing and choreographing the entertainment.

When his producing ventures finally sent him broke, Hulbert turned to the film world to help himself recuperate, and he starred in a number of successful musical movies (*Sunshine Susie, Jack's the Boy,* etc), returning to the theatre first to direct and choreograph his wife in *Hide and Seek* and then to team up with her on stage in a successful trio of musicals, *Under Your Hat* (1938, film 1940, Jack Millett), *Full Swing* (1942) and *Something in the Air* (1943), which he also co-wrote, directed and co-choreographed. He then distanced himself once more from performing, but he continued to direct Miss Courtneidge's musicals (*Under the Counter, Her Excellency* also co-producer w Val Parnell, *Gay's the Word, Star Maker*) and her revue *Over the Moon,* as well as such other musical plays as *Sweet Yesterday, The Nightingale* and a stage version of the radio series *Life with the Lyons,* mounted as a Blackpool holiday entertainment.

He made a late return to the stage to appear with his wife in a compilation entertainment based on their lives at the Yvonne Arnaud Theatre, Guildford (*Words and Music*).

His brother, **Claude [Noel] HULBERT** (b London, 25 December 1900; d Sydney, Australia, 23 January 1964), also had a career as a light-comic actor in musicals, appearing in London in *Primrose* (1924, Freddy Falls), *Tell Me More!* (1925, Billy), *Kid Boots* (1926, Menlo Melville), *Sunny* (1926, Harold), *Oh, Kay!* (1927, Duke of Datchet), *Song of the Sea* (1928, Bob Blake), *Dear Love* (1929, Peter Twigley), *Follow a Star* (1930, Snitch), *Panama Hattie* (1945, Vivian Budd) and as the Cowardly Lion in Britain's first production of *The Wizard of Oz* (1946). He also made a small contribution to the songs of *Under Your Hat.*

1914 **The Cinema Star** (*Die Kino-Königin*) English libretto (Shaftesbury Theatre)

1915 **The Light Blues** (Howard Talbot, Herman Finck/Adrian Ross/w Max Pemberton) Prince of Wales Theatre, Birmingham 13 September; Shaftesbury Theatre, London 14 September 1916

1919 **Too Many Girls** (Arthur Wood/G Hartley Milburn/w Harold Simpson, Robert Courtneidge) Hippodrome, Liverpool 22 December

1938 **Under Your Hat** (Vivian Ellis/w Archie Menzies, Arthur Macrae) Palace Theatre 24 November

1942 **Full Swing** (George Posford, Harry Parr Davies/w Menzies, Macrae) Palace Theatre 16 April

1943 **Something in the Air** (Manning Sherwin/Max Kester, Harold Purcell/w Macrae, Menzies) Palace Theatre 23 September

1952 **Life with the Lyons** (w others) Hippodrome, Blackpool 28 June

Autobiography: *The Little Woman's Always Right* (W H Allen, London, 1975)

HUMBERT, [Louis] Eugène (b Paris, 27 March 1836; d c12 May 1886).

For many years the hugely enthusiastic director and stage director of Brussels's Théâtre des Fantaisies-Parisiennes (later known as the Théâtre Alcazar), Humbert brought himself, for a period of several years, to the very center of the international world of the musical theatre by a diligent choice of premire productions.

His first major success came as a result of the siege of Paris and the period of the Commune. With Paris a dubiously healthy place to be, a number of writers and composers had gone to Britain or elsewhere away from the capital. Charles Lecocq, whose first full-scale success, *Fleur de thé,* had recently been staged at the Théâtre de l'Athénée, was amongst these, and when his latest collaboration with librettists Chivot and Duru (and, this time, also Clairville) was complete, it was offered not to Paris but to the respected and reliable Humbert in Brussels. Humbert produced and directed Lecocq's *Les Cent Vierges* in 1872 with great success, and the piece was subsequently played and revived throughout the world. However, even before this had happened, Humbert had started on the work which would be his greatest triumph. A dinner with wheeler-dealer Victor Koning brought forth the suggestion of a libretto set in the Directoire period and—so one version of the tale goes—when, three months later, the libretto was brought to Humbert he handed it on to ''his'' composer for a musical setting. *La Fille de Madame Angot* was to turn out to be one of the greatest and most enduring musicals of its century. From its rapturous reception in Brussels it went on to Paris and to the rest of the world with unalloyed success, spreading the fame of Humbert and his theatre. In 1878 the old Parisian Théâtre Beaumarchais, altered by director Debruyère into a musical house, was christened the ''Fantaisies-Parisiennes'' in imitation of Humbert's theatre.

During the summer recess of 1873, whilst his theatre was being redecorated, Humbert took his company to Britain, where they played *La Fille de Madame Angot, Les Cent Vierges, La Belle Hélène, Les Brigands* and Britain's only ever performances of *Les Braconniers.* On his return home, he then followed up *La Fille de Madame Angot* at the Fantaisies-Parisiennes with another outstanding Lecocq work, *Giroflé-Girofla,* and caused a sensation when he took the piece (still unseen in Paris) to London's Opera Comique. The Brussels company's season there had to be ended when Humbert and Lecocq sold the English rights to the piece, but the experience had been a paying one, and the Fantaisies-Parisiennes company returned to London in 1875 with their new piece, Vogel's *La Filleule du roi,* and in 1876 with *La Petite Mariée* and, again, *Giroflé-Girofla.*

La Filleule du roi was one of the new pieces, often by newer (but not always younger) composers, with which Humbert attempted to keep up the high profile won all around the world by his three Lecocq productions. It failed in Paris, whilst *Le Chignon d'or* by the better-known Jonas, Grangé and Tréfeu, produced in 1874, went to Vienna but not Paris. Apart from a triumphant French version of Suppé's *Fatinitza,* it was Vasseur's *Le Roi d'Yvetôt* (1873) which proved the best of Humbert's other productions—a group which included such pieces as *Rien qu'un jour* (Hubans/Dupin 25 November 1876) and *La Princesse Marmotte* (de Rillé) prior to his departure from the management of the Fantaisies-Parisiennes in 1880. His successor, Darcy, followed up with *La Petite Reinette* (Varney, 1882), and the far from unsuccessful *Les Beignets du roi* (Bernicat, 1882) and *Le Présomptif* (Gregh, 1883), but none of the later pieces came up to the expectations fulfilled and fueled by those first enormous hits.

With the production of *Les Beignets du roi,* the Fantaisies-Parisiennes gave a first significant opportunity to the long-striving young composer Bernicat, and Humbert took part in supplying the promising young man with his next libretto, *François les bas-bleus.* I suspect that Humbert actually wrote no more of the text of *François* than Victor Koning did of *La Fille de Madame Angot,* but he had seen, from Koning's example, how a producer's name on the authorial credits of a piece ensured him a continuing financial interest in the show. Humbert co-produced and directed his new opérette, however, not this time in Belgium, but at the house to which *Angot* had progressed: Paris's Théâtre des Folies-Dramatiques. It proved to be the success that he had not again found in Brussels. *François les bas-bleus* went round the world. Bernicat's death, prior to the completion of the show's score, had meant that Humbert and his partner, Dubreuil, had had to find someone to complete the music and their choice (at the urging of publishers Enoch) had fallen on another promising young man, André Messager. When Messager proved to be a real find they commissioned him to write his own first full-length work, *La Fauvette du Temple,* as a follow-up, and Humbert, who had already experienced a notable first ''co-authorial'' success with the libretto for *François,* again ''collaborated'' on the text, winning himself a second strong credit as an ''author.'' He was, however, not to see the extent of the show's success. Illness prevented him from taking an active part in the show's production, or from effectively running the new Brussels Bourse Théâtre to which he had been appointed in 1884, before his death intervened.

1867 **Une Croyance bretonne** 1 act (Balthazar-Florence/w Tourti) Théater de la Monnaie, Brussels 3 April

1883 **François les bas-bleus** (Firmin Bernicat, André Messager/w Ernest Dubreuil, Paul Burani) Théâtre des Folies-Dramatiques 8 November

1885 **La Fauvette du Temple** (Messager/w Burani) Théâtre des Folies-Dramatiques 17 November

HUNTINGTON, Agnes B (b Kalamazoo, Mich, 14 November 1864; d New York, 10 March 1953). Statuesque American contralto who briefly became a huge star in Victorian London.

The young (and apparently well-connected) Agnes Huntington studied voice in Germany and made early appearances on the concert stage in Baltimore (1883, alto to Amy Sherwin's soprano in *Elijah*), Boston (1884 billed as being ''of Worcester, Mass''), Washington (1885), Dresden, London, at the Paris Trocadero and with the New York Philharmonic. She was first seen on the American musical stage at Carll's Opera House, New Haven, in 1885 playing the Gipsy Queen in *The Bohemian Girl,* the Princess in *Giralda* and Célestine in *François les bas-bleus* with the Boston Ideal Comic Opera Company. She played several seasons with the Boston company, appearing with them in the contralto roles of their light operatic repertoire and in the untried *Alidor* at the St Paul Opera House (1887). She then crossed the Atlantic once more, and starred at London's Prince of Wales Theatre with the newly formed Carl Rosa Light

Opera Company, in the travesty title role of Planquette's *Paul Jones* (1889), a part which had been created in the provinces by baritone Michael Dwyer. She caused a sensation as Paul Jones, and *The Era* reported "a more brilliant debut has not been known in connection with comic opera." George Edwardes was amongst those dazzled by the lady and her performance, and he announced plans to build the Agnes Huntington Theatre, where he would feature Miss Huntington at the center of her own company.

At the end of the run of *Paul Jones* she was cast by the Carl Rosa to play another male role, Wilfred, in the medieval comic opera *Marjorie* (1890), a role again played in tryout by a male performer. After one week of performances, however, she walked out and, when taken to court by theatre-owner Henry Leslie, claimed that the role was unsuited to her voice. Since she refused to go on tour with *Paul Jones* as an alternative, Leslie was granted an injunction that prevented her from singing. Ultimately she was fined £1,000 and costs, and she then announced she was returning to America to play *Paul Jones.* When news filtered back to Britain that she was being paid a salary of $7,500 a week to do so, the degree of "unsuitability" of *Marjorie* became evident.

The "stately, handsome American girl" caused something of a stir back in America as well, but a touch less in singing circles than in social ones. It was noted that the President himself came to her Washington first night of *Paul Jones.* She appeared on Broadway both as Paul Jones and in the title role of *Captain Thérèse,* the new Planquette piece that had been commissioned by Carl Rosa especially to highlight her talents before her contract-breaking act, and then in 1892 she vanished from the world of the light musical theatre as suddenly as she had come, into marriage as the exceedingly wealthy Mrs Paul Drennan Cravath, wife of a rich, social and distinguished lawyer and patron of the arts. In the 60 years of her retirement, however, she maintained an interest in musical theatre, founding the Little Theater Opera Company and encouraging young singers.

Edwardes built his theatre, but its first leading lady was Ada Rehan, and it was called after his American partner in the venture, Augustin Daly.

HUNTLEY, G[eorge] P[atrick] (b Fermoy, Co Cork, 13 July 1868; d London, 21 September 1927). Warmly dotty star comedian of the British 1900s and 1910s.

Huntley had been 13 busy years on the stage before he appeared in the musical theatre for the first time, touring in *The Circus Boy* (ex- *Dandy Dick Whittington*) in the travesty role of Lady Fitzwarren, created by the celebrated dame-comic, John F Sheridan. He was then hired for George Edwardes's touring company of *The Circus Girl* (1897, Sir Titus) and was subsequently brought to the Gaiety by his manager to succeed Harry Monkhouse as Brother Tamarind in *A Runaway Girl.* This he did with such success that Edwardes gave him the top comic role of Lord Plantaganet in his new musical *Kitty Grey,* both for its original touring production and its London season.

Kitty Grey established Huntley as one of the best and most endearing comedians of the British musical stage. His subsequent creations in *Three Little Maids* (1902, Lord Cheyne), *The School Girl* (1903, Sir Ormesby St Leger) and *Lady Madcap* (1904, Trooper Smith)—each of which he repeated in America and Australia—and, above all, of *Mr Popple of Ippleton* (1905, Freddy Popple) and *Miss Hook of Holland* (1907, Mr Hook) thoroughly confirmed his position. *My Mimosa Maid* (1908, Victor Guilbert), the successor to *Miss Hook,* was not successful and neither was Huntley's venture into actor-authorship in *The Hon'ble Phil* (1908, Phil Giffard), but success returned when he took up his old role in *Kitty Grey* for a season on Broadway.

Huntley stayed in America for several non-musical engagements, and on returning home appeared in several musical playlets (including Fall's *Arms and the Girl*) in variety before his next musical theatre successes in Edwardes's production of Jacobi's *The Marriage Market* (*Leányvásár,* 1913, Lord Hurlingham) and *Betty* (1914, Lord Playne). He subsequently appeared in *The Happy Day* (1916, Captain), *Pamela* (1917, Toby Woodhouse) and *The Kiss Call* (1919, Allsop Bibby), until the pre-show tippling which had long aided his amiable, laid-back comedy style rose to a level that rendered him unemployable.

He subsequently appeared in America in the revue *Hitchy-Koo* with Raymond Hitchcock, as Alaric in the musicalized *Peg o' my Dreams* (1923), and in the musical comedy *Be Yourself* (1924, Joseph Peabody Prescott), and created the role of *Gentlemen Prefer Blondes*'s Sir Francis Beekman in the non-musical theatre version of Anita Loos's novel (1926), but he did not again return to the London musical stage.

His American-born wife **Eva KELLY** (b Lockhaven, Pa, 18 September 1880; d Los Angeles, 16 March 1948), who began her musical career in the chorus of the Alice Nielsen opera company and at the Casino Theater (Jolivet in *The Rounders,* 1899, etc), went to Britain and the Continent with the Casino company, playing in *An American Beauty* and *The Casino Girl* in London, and *The Belle of New York* (Mamie Clancy) through Europe, and she remained in Britain to take over from Florence Collingbourne as Nancy in *The Toreador.* She appeared as Nephele Noggs in *Naughty Nancy,* and then, with Huntley, in soubrette roles of varying sizes in the London *Kitty Grey* (Sadie), *Three Little Maids* (t/o Venetia), *The School Girl* (t/o Mrs Marchmont), *Mr Popple* (t/o Louise), *Miss Hook of Holland* (Gretchen), *My Mimosa Maid* (Mme de Pilaine), *The Hon'ble Phil* (Didine), Lady Binfield in *Kitty Grey* in America, *Betty* (Rawlins) and *The Happy Day* (Luna d'Étoile).

Their son, G P Huntley jr, was also an actor, who made occasional appearances on the musical stage (*The Golden Moth, Gay Divorce,* etc).

1897 **Turpin à la Mode** (H C Barry/w George H Grey) Royalty Theatre, Chester 29 March

1908 **The Hon'ble Phil** (Harold Samuel/Harold Lawson, Bertrand Davis, Claude Aveling/w Herbert Clayton) Hicks Theatre 12 December

HURGON, Austen A [HORGAN, Richard Cornelius] (b Netherlands, ?1867; d Folkestone, 24 June 1942). Director and librettist for several successful West End musicals of the 1900s and 1910s.

Hurgon began his career as an actor and appeared in improving roles in the touring *Dandy Dick Whittington* (1895, Chanta Buree), *Little Christopher Columbus* (1898, Mrs Block), the musical play *The Showman's Sweetheart* (1898, Ben Odger) and *Punch and Judy* (1900, Ben Odger), then in the West End in *Miss Wingrove* (1905, Alberto), which he also produced and directed in conjunction with Frank Curzon. Curzon subsequently employed him to direct *The White Chrysanthemum* (1905) and *The Girl Behind the Counter* (1906), and then engaged him as resident stage director at the Prince of Wales Theatre. When Paul Rubens fell ill during the preparation of *Miss Hook of Holland,* Curzon got Hurgon to complete the writing of the part-written piece, and the success that the show, which Hurgon also directed, achieved, led to his collaborating with Rubens on its successor, *My Mimosa Maid.* However, both *The Three Kisses* (1907) and *My Mimosa Maid* (1908), which he directed for Curzon, were failures, and the alliance ended.

Hurgon directed *The Hon'ble Phil* (1908) for *Miss Hook* star G P Huntley, and then made another attempt at producing when he took on the management of the failing musical *Two Merry Monarchs* (1909), which he had also directed. His management lasted four performances.

Hurgon subsequently went to the London Hippodrome, where he directed the famous revue *Hullo, Ragtime!* and its sequels for Albert de Courville, and he wrote both revue books and the libretti for the one-act operettas which were included in those revues for a period. He also penned a travesty of his own revue hit in the Chiswick Empire revue *What Ho! Ragtime.* At the same time, he found himself in demand as a director in New York, and in 1910 he mounted two musicals with British connections, Ivan Caryll's *Marriage à la Carte* and Leslie Stuart's *The Slim Princess,* on Broadway.

In 1915 he began an association with producers Grossmith and Laurillard, directing *Tonight's the Night* for Broadway and London, and following up with *Theodore & Co* and with *Yes, Uncle!,* both, like the first, considerable successes. He also continued to write, in collaboration with George Arthurs, and their musicals *Suzette,* the English version of *Arlette, Yes, Uncle!* (taken from Armont and Nancey's *Le Truc du Brésilien*), and *The Girl for the Boy,* adapted from Paul Gavault's *La Petite Chocolatière* as a vehicle for Gina Palerme, all had good to fine runs.

He tried production-direction again with Ivor Novello's comic opera *The Golden Moth* (1921), and with his own musical *His Girl* (1922), but although they suceeded better than his first attempts, neither was a *Miss Hook* or a *Hullo, Ragtime!* and, thereafter, he retired from the musical-theatre scene.

1907 **Miss Hook of Holland** (Paul Rubens/w Rubens) Prince of Wales Theatre 31 January

1908 **My Mimosa Maid** (Rubens/w Rubens) Prince of Wales Theatre 21 April

1911 **The Eternal Waltz** (Leo Fall) 1 act London Hippodrome 22 December

1912 **Arms and the Girl** (Richard Fall) 1 act London Hippodrome 29 April

1912 **The Blue House** (Emmerich Kálmán) 1 act London Hippodrome 28 October

1916 **Girl Wanted** (w Herbert C Sargent) 1 act

1917 **Suzette** (Max Darewski, George Arthurs) Globe Theatre 29 March

1917 **Arlette** (Jane Vieu, Novello, Guy Lefeuvre/w Arthurs) English version (Shaftesbury Theatre)

1917 **Yes, Uncle!** (Nat D Ayer/Clifford Grey/w Arthurs) Prince of Wales Theatre 29 December

1919 **The Girl for the Boy** (Howard Carr, Bernard Rolt/Percy Greenbank/w Arthurs) Duke of York's Theatre 23 September

1922 **His Girl** (M Darewski, Ernest Longstaffe/C E Burton/w F W Thomas) Gaiety Theatre 1 April

HUSZKA, Jenő (b Szeged, 24 April 1875; d Budapest, 2 February 1960). One of the earliest, most successful and longest active composers of Hungarian musical theatre.

Huszka studied music in Budapest and Paris and worked originally as a violinist. He was later employed at the Hungarian Ministry of Culture, and it was there that he first made contact with the playwright and librettist Ferenc Martos, who would be his most fruitful collaborator.

He made his first contribution as a theatre composer at the age of 24, when he supplied the songs and incidental music for Adolf Mérei's short musical play *Tilos a bemenet* at the Magyar Színház, and his first full-scale operett, *Bob herceg,* with a libretto by Martos and another established writer, Károly Bakonyi, was staged three years later at the Népszínház. *Bob herceg* proved to be the most successful Hungarian operett produced to date, and Huszka went on to compose several other major successes—*Aranyvirág, Gül Baba, Nemtudomka* (played in Vienna as *Die Patronesse vom Nachtcafé,* and in America by the Shuberts as *Miss I-Don't-Know* 1918), *Lili bárónő* and, 40 years after his first great success, *Mária főhadnagy*—many of which have remained in the repertoire in Hungary up to the present day, without being heard further afield.

1899 **Tilos a bemenet** (Adolf Mérei) 1 act Magyar Színház 2 September

1902 **Bob herceg** (Károly Bakonyi, Ferenc Martos) Népszínház 20 December

1903 **Aranyvirág** (Martos) Király Színház 6 November

1905 **Gül Baba** (Martos) Király Színház 9 December

1907 **Tündérszerelem** (Martos) Népszínház 20 December

1909 **Rébusz báró** (Ferenc Herczeg) Király Színház 20 November

1914 **Nemtudomka** (Zsolt Harsányi/Bakonyi) Király Színház 14 January

1919 **Lili bárónő** (Martos) Városi Színház 7 March

1926 **Hajtóvadászat** (Martos) Városi Színház 22 October

1939 **Erzsébet** (László Szilágyi) Magyar Színház 5 January

1941 **Gyergyói bál** (Szilágyi) Magyar Színház 4 January

1942 **Mária főhadnagy** (Szilágyi) Fővárosi Operettszínház 23 September

1955 **Szép juhászné** (Károly Kristóf) Nemzeti Színház, Szeged 8 May

1955 **Szabadság, szerelem** (Mór Jokai ad Gyula Háy) Fővárosi Operettszínház 1 April

Biography: Huszka, A M: *Szellő szárnyán* (Zenemükiadó, Budapest, 1977)

HYLTON, Jack [HILTON, William Jackson] (b Great Lever, Lancs, 2 July 1892; d London, 29 January 1965). Busy, canny producer in all areas of the postwar London theatre.

Originally a pianist and subsequently one of Britain's most popular dance-band leaders of the 1930s, Hylton gave up his band in 1940 and switched to theatrical production for a second, and equally successful, career. His first musical theatre production was the popular wartime musical comedy *Lady Behave* (1941), and he followed up with a mass of both musical and straight theatre productions, including revivals of *The Merry Widow, The Lilac Domino* and *Irene, Follow the Girls,* the pasticcii *Can-Can* and *Romany Love,* and London's productions of *High Button Shoes, Kiss Me, Kate, Call Me Madam, Paint Your Wagon, Wish You Were Here, Pal Joey, Wonderful Town, Kismet, Oh, My Papa!, Simply Heavenly* and *When in Rome,* as well as a mass of revue and variety productions, notably those of the Crazy Gang at the Victoria Palace.

Most of his musical productions were reproductions of proven, usually imported, material and he mounted very few original pieces (*Bet Your Life, Happy as a King, School*). Even his most successful single show, the British musical *Salad Days,* was brought in from an independent production in Bristol, in collaboration with the firm of Linnit and Dunfee.

In earlier days Hylton also composed the music for a musical play *Mutt and Jeff,* written by Bud Fisher and Con West and produced by Alexander Loftus and Wilfred Jessop at the King's Theatre in Hammersmith.

HYLTON, Millie *see* LIND, LETTY

I

I CAN GET IT FOR YOU WHOLESALE Musical in 2 acts by Jerome Weidman based on his novel of the same name. Music and lyrics by Harold Rome. Shubert Theater, New York, 22 March 1962.

Weidman wrote the novel *I Can Get It for You Wholesale* (1937) at the age of 22, basing it on a real-life character, a bankrupt young dress manufacturer who had gone astray in the unreal world of paper finance in the 1930s, and whom he had encountered during his teen years working as an accountant's clerk.

The charming Harry Bogen (Elliott Gould) of the musical-comedy version of the book is an unprincipled, egoistic go-getter. He makes his way up the money ladder by wickedly taking advantage of a labor strike to provide privately the services the strikers refuse, backed by cash wooed from rich and loving Ruthie (Marilyn Cooper). He does down his best friend (James Hickman) by selling him a half of what he knows will soon be a worthless company, and he woos away the designer (Ken LeRoy), salesman (Harold Lang) and secretary (Barbra Streisand) from his old boss to start his own nastily competitive dress firm. He throws money about to set his business going, acquires a Broadway showgirl (Sheree North), then proceeds to milk the company's bank accounts whilst making sure that someone else is lined up for the blame. When everything goes bust, Harry is theoretically clean, and he goes back to his first employer to await a fresh start with the money won from marrying Ruthie.

Harold Rome's score, which made no concessions to the 1930s, included few obvious numbers. Harry expounded his uncompromising business creed in ''The Way Things Are,'' his reasonably perspicacious Momma (Lillian Roth) warned Ruthie not to expect too much ''Too Soon,'' and the girl hinted at a first-act marriage in ''Who Knows?,'' but the number which proved the show's solo highlight was the lament of the taken-for-functional secretary ''Miss Marmelstein.'' As sung by the 19-year-old Barbra Streisand, wife-to-be to the leading man and, like him, making her Broadway debut in a principal role, it marked the beginning of what was to be a notable career.

David Merrick's production of *I Can Get It for You Wholesale* played three hundred performances on Broadway, but the show did not establish itself as the kind of success which would go on to productions in other centers. It was, however, revived in 1991 by New York's American Jewish Theater (Susan Bloch Theater 23 February).

Recording: original cast (Columbia)

ICH HAB' MEIN HERZ IN HEIDELBERG VERLOREN Singspiel in 3 acts by Bruno Hardt-Warden and Fritz Löhner-Beda. Lyrics by Ernst Neubach. Music by Fredy Raymond. Volksoper, Vienna, 29 April 1927.

Ich hab' mein Herz in Heidelberg verloren was a musical christened after Fred(y) Raymond's successful 1925 song of the same title, a song which became an international hit as ''I Left My Heart in Heidelberg.'' The number in question was used as the keystone of the show's score, much of the rest of which was made up of arrangements of existing folk tunes and student songs, in the fashion practiced in the days of Zaytz and his contemporaries, 60 or 70 years earlier.

The story into which the famous song was slipped was a fairly conventional operettic one, with more than a touch of *Hoheit tanzt Walzer* and other such well-known pieces to its outline. Max Schneckenroither (Heinz Kroegler), philosophy student and poet, and Karl Wilhelmi (Otto Glaser), law student, share rooms whilst they attend Heidelberg University in the year of 1825. Max is beloved by the innkeeper, Veronika Laubenthaler (Steffi Walidt), but he dreams romantically over a picture of the Princess Auguste (Paula Bäck), daughter of the local duke. When the Duke (Geacute;za Brand) and his court visit the University, Auguste, her lady Christiane (Vally Frank) and their company are freed to spend some time with the students. The young folk gather at Veronika's inn, and when a song contest is proposed, the starry-eyed Max wins himself a kiss from his dreamgirl with his rendition of ''I Left My Heart. . . .'' But the royal afternoon of freedom is soon over, and if at the end of things Christiane and Karl can harbor the hope that they may see each other again, Max knows he will be left with only the memory of the kiss. But his heart will remain in Heidelberg all his days. The supporting role of Hieronymus Strudelmayer was played by former star juvenile Josef König.

Directed by Rainer Simons, conducted by Oskar Jascha, and choreographed with a ballet ''Reigen'' in the second act by Grete Führer, the show proved to be well liked in its first run at the Volksoper. It was filmed in 1927 with Werner Futterer and Dorothea Wieck starred, and seen again first at the Bürgertheater (30 March 1928), where it passed its 300th Viennese performance, and then, briefly, at the Carltheater (2 July 1928), with Mimi Vesely and Otto Storm featured. It was finally revived in Vienna in 1946.

Warden, Beda and the Volksoper were not the only, nor even the first, to capitalize on the title of the hit song. The Leipzig Kleines Theater came out with a Thilo Schmidt Volksstuck of the same name in September 1926.

DIE IDEALE GATTIN Operette in 3 acts by Julius Brammer and Alfred Grünwald. Music by Franz Lehár. Theater an der Wien, Vienna, 11 October 1913.

Die ideale Gattin was the second, and probably the most successful, of the three Operetten produced to more or less the same Franz Lehár score, a score which had begun its life as an appendage to *Der Göttergatte* (Operette in a Vorspiel and two acts, Carltheater 20 January 1904). *Der Göttergatte,* which followed on behind Lehár's first real success with *Der Rastelbinder,* was set in Ancient Greece, and Victor Léon and Leo Stein's libretto was a version of the Amphytrion legend purposely written ''in the style of the Offenbachiade.'' Working on the Boccaccio principle that the best way to find a tale is to live it oneself, Jupiter (Willy Bauer) and Mercury (Friderich Becker) go down to earth to find themselves the subject matter for a new Olympian Operette. Juno (Mizzi Günther) is wise to her husband's antics, however, and when the two Olympian mashers disguise themself as Amphytrion (Karl Streitmann) and his valet Sosias (Louis Treumann), she takes the place of Alcmene, Amphytrion's wife, and allows herself to be seduced by her own husband. While the book had something of the frothy foolery of opéra-bouffe about it, Lehár's score was not a burlesque one, and it was this apparent failure on the composer's part to adapt his style to the intended kind of humor that, later, made Léon doubt whether the man who had composed *Der Rastelbinder* was the right collaborator for him on *Die lustige Witwe.*

Der Göttergatte proved something of a disappointment, and it played only 37 consecutive performances on its first run, A German production and a Hungarian version (*Mulató istenek* ad Jenő Heltai, Magyar Színház 10 February 1905) followed, but neither did anything to boost its popularity to the level attained by *Der Rastelbinder.* However, a revised version was remounted on 25 March 1905, and the show remained in the repertoire at the Carltheater until as late as 1913, when Lehár reclaimed and reused this first of the many ''wasted'' scores which he would, during his career, recycle to a different libretto. His revised music was attached to a new book by Brammer and Grünwald which, although it was now set in Spain, retained the same premise as the Göttergatte book of the wife winning her own husband (an almost tiresomely popular theme, added notably—and gratuitously—by the Viennese librettist or *Die Fledermaus* in its conversion from *Le Réveillon*).

With the Theater an der Wien's new star tenor, Hubert Marischka, in the role of the Visconde Pablo de Cavaletti, supported by a top-line cast including soubrette Luise Kartousch (Carmen), comic Ernst Tautenhayn (Don Gil de Tenorio de Sevilla), Otto Storm (Sergius Sartrewsky-Goifrin) and Mizzi Günther, who had played in the original *Göttergatte* nearly a decade earlier once again in the principal soprano role of Elvira, the ''perfect'' wife, *Die ideale Gattin* was played for 105 consecutive performances. It was a respectable rather than a good run (*Eva,* two years earlier, had run twice as long), and although the show was subsequently played at the Raimundtheater for a few performances with Ludwig Herold, Rosa Mittermardi, Therese Tautenhayn and Anton Matscheg, then in Hungary (*Tökéletes feleség* [later *A tökéletes asszony*], Király Színház 26 November 1913) and, with some considerable success, in Germany with Else Adler featured in its title role, it did not establish itself as an enduring repertoire piece.

The second metamorphosis of the show took place another eight years on. Brammer and Grünwald's libretto was amended to take Lehár to the Argentine and the then fashionable world of the tango—a Hispanic-to-Hispanic shift of venue which meant that the names of some of the characters did not even have to be changed. Produced by Herbert Trau at the Apollo-Künstlertheater, *Die Tangokönigin* (Operette in 3 acts, 9 September 1921, advertised as being ''mit teilweiser Benützung von Motiven aus der *Idealen Gatten*'') again followed the same basic plot to which the score had always been attached. Manolita (Ida Russka) needs to sprighten the failing ardor of her husband, Graf Leandro de Cavaletti (Robert Nästlberger), so, like *Quality Street*'s Phoebe, she pretends to be her own, highly seductive, sister, and by woman's wiles reawakens her husband's lust. Josef König (Don Gil di Tenorio), Eugen Günther (Marquese Columbus de Serranti), Willi Strehl (Sergius Sartrewski) and Mme

Olga Bartos-Trau (Coletta) completed the principal cast, and Lehár himself conducted a performance which showed novelty films in the interval, in the variety tradition of the Apollo. After two-and-a-half months the piece gave way to Granichstaedten's *Indische Nächte* and, whilst Hungary braved the third version of Lehár's score (*Tangokirálynő* ad Ernő Kulinyi 23 July 1923), Germany this time passed.

I DO! I DO! Story of a marriage in 2 acts by Tom Jones based on Jan de Hartog's play *The Fourposter.* Music by Harvey Schmidt. 46th Street Theater, New York, 5 December 1966.

A two-handed musical play set in the bedroom of the home of Michael (Robert Preston) and Agnes (Mary Martin), *I Do! I Do!* followed the pair through half a century of married life. Starting with their youthful wedding night and passing through two doses of childbirth (off-stage—this was 1966), professional success, brief infidelity for him and difficulties and fury for her, it included all the other little ups and downs of everyday life in a picture of a marriage which is, for all that we see here largely just its most colorful moments, based on a real affection. The children get married, Michael and Agnes are brought closer together by being once again on their own, and ultimately they leave their big house and the four-poster bed, in which they have spent 50 years together, for the use of the next generation.

Schmidt and Jones's songs and duets illustrated happily what was, in its essence, a warmly simple tale, with the couple's loving duet ''My Cup Runneth Over'' proving the highlight of the score. Michael sang and danced a tipsily barefoot, night-shirted wedding-night ''I Love My Wife,'' Agnes had a showy moment threatening, with the help of a garish hat, to become ''Flaming Agnes,'' the pair bickered in ''Nobody's Perfect,'' and contrasted dreams (''When the Kids Get Married'') and reality (''The Father of the Bride,'' ''What Is a Woman'') before finally bidding farewell to ''This House.''

David Merrick's Broadway production of *I Do! I Do!* ran for 561 performances, and, as it ran on, a London production was mounted by H M Tennent with Anne Rogers and Ian Carmichael featured. It ran for 115 performances. The show's one-set, two-star-character dimensions helped to make it a popular piece in regional houses, and London saw it for a second time when Rock Hudson and Juliet Prowse appeared in a brief season at the Phoenix Theatre in 1976. Australia saw the musical first in 1969, for a three months' Sydney season followed by a similar run in Melbourne (Her Majesty's Theatre 21 June 1969) with Stephen Douglass and Jill Perryman starred, and later, for a second time, in a 1976 revival at the Marian Street Theatre, Sydney (21 July 1976). A German-languge version (ad Peter Goldbaum, Walter Brandin) was produced initially in Düsseldorf in 1968.

In 1982 *I Do! I Do!* was filmed for American television with Lee Remick and Hal Linden in its roles, and it was seen again in New York, off-Broadway this time, in 1996 (Lamb's Theater 28 March, 68 performances) played in a truly small-scale edition with Karen Ziemba and David Garrison on the stage and two pianos supporting.

UK: Lyric Theatre 16 May 1968; Germany: Schauspielhaus, Düsseldorf *Das musikalische Himmelbett* 24 August 1968; Australia: Theatre Royal, Sydney 15 February 1969

Recordings: original cast (RCA), London cast (RCA), Japanese cast (Toshiba), German cast (Ariola), 1996 cast recording (Varese Sarabande)

I'D RATHER BE RIGHT Musical show in 2 acts by George S Kaufman and Moss Hart. Lyrics by Lorenz Hart. Music by Richard Rodgers. Alvin Theater, New York, 2 November 1937.

One of the run of 1930s American musicals (this one called itself successively ''a revue'' and ''a musical show'') written and staged by men who had apparently decided that the field of national politics was a fertile one for musical-comedy subject matter, *I'd Rather Be Right* went so far as to present on stage (''with merriment rather than vicious satire'') a character who represented the current President of the United States, Franklin D Roosevelt. Any real sting that might have been intended in this lampoon of the New Deal was, however, removed by the casting of George M Cohan, the aging musical-comedy megastar and former business partner of producer Sam H Harris, in the role of the President of the United States in a story which had two young lovers (Austin Marshall, Joy Hodges) petitioning the President to balance the budget (well, it was fiction) so that the boy can have a raise in wages (!) and they can get married. The President's comical efforts to find ways to raise money, beginning with a call to women to give up cosmetics and ending with a broadcast White House Jamboree Hour, made up much of the evening's revusical entertainment.

Although the show's four writers were all Roosevelt supporters, they had unfortunately chosen a man to impersonate him who, although in many ways an inspired choice, was not. He was, likewise, not at home with 1930s musical-comedy styles in songwriting, which were far from the driving ditties which he had written for his own greatest shows. On the run-in to Broadway, Cohan not only edged in as much as he could of the old-style Cohan, he also decided, unilaterally, to rewrite some lines in one of his songs (''Off the Record'') to his own political color, assuring, via an audience aside, that his lines were known to be his own. The writers exploded, but the

Plate 186. **I Do! I Do!** *Carol Burnett and Rock Hudson say the words that bind in the St Louis Muny's production of Schmidt and Jones's musical comedy of marriage.*

newspapers, who were covering every step in the development of this well-publicized show—which was doing what no other country would ever think of doing, in showing its leader in mildly critical song and dance—had a field day.

I'd Rather Be Right was ultimately met on Broadway with modified rapture. It was almost entirely political and topical in its text and songs, and thus of limited interest to many theatregoers, and, in any case, the subject matter had not propelled the composers to some of their easiest efforts. ''Have You Met Miss Jones?,'' the nearest thing to a purposeless number in the piece, was, perhaps not surprisingly, also the nearest to being a success. Cohan himself, who ''aroused wild applause with each new song and each familiar and beloved step'' had ''Off the Record'' and ''Tune Up, Bluebird'' in which to score, and also joined in the title trio with the two young people. Other actors were recognizable as members of Congress, notably Taylor Holmes as Treasurer Morgenthau crooning out a plea to the nation to buy ''A Baby Bond,'' whilst the Supreme Court, headed by Chief Justice Johnny Cherry, disported themselves in ''Not Such Innocent Fun.'' *I'd Rather Be Right* played five-and-a-half months at the Alvin Theater before transferring to the little Music Box to run out the last of its 290 performances.

The singing-dancing President idea was, it has to be said, far from something new on the American stage. As early as June 1868 Pittsburgh's Thomas R Hann produced a musical spectacular burlesque called *The Great Rebellion, or The Last Ditch* at the Pittsburgh Opera House. Mr C W Felton represented James Buchanan, 15th President of the United States, alongside the John Bull of Mr Lascelles and the Louis Napoléon of W J Ferguson, while Mrs Marble gave forth operatically as Columbia and the feminine chorus marched about leggily as American(?) zouaves. In more recent years, an avuncular President Roosevelt helped *Annie* on her way to finding a family, and *JFK—the Rock Opera* was inflicted on the patrons of the Münster Jovel Music Hall (30 March 1993). As for *The Fix,* it didn't actually say who the president was who was portrayed in its black burlesque book, any more than had done *Of Thee I Sing* or *Mr President,* but this time no one had much trouble guessing.

Plate 187. **Ignace** *is Fernandel.*

IGNACE Opérette in 3 acts by Jean Manse. Music by Roger Dumas. Théâtre des Variétés, Marseille, 1935; Théâtre de la Porte-Saint-Martin, Paris, 4 February 1936.

Ignace was a vaudevillesque piece written as a stage vehicle for the music-hall and film star Fernandel by his brother-in-law Jean Manse, who had previously written lyrics for a number of the films in which the comedian had appeared. It was produced at Marseille in 1935, with Fernandel cast in the military-vaudeville character so popular on the French stage: an exorbitantly innocent and foolish private soldier—here mixed up in a network of marital/sexual fidelities and, mostly only attempted, infidelities. Colonel Durozier looks sideways at the danseuse Loulette, his boomingly authoritarian wife attracts the comical Baron des Orfraies, his niece Monique (Simone Rouvière) sighs after the young lawyer Serge de Montroc but is being tied up with Captain Boisdelisle, whilst little Ignace himself gets friendly with their maid Annette.

Dumas's suitably music-hally score consisted largely of dance-rhythmed ballads (the fox-trot/blues ''Un mari,'' the waltz ''Lequel des deux?,'' the letter song ''Je vous écris ces quelques mots''), and of comical numbers for the star (Java des p'tits galons, the one-step ''Quelle famille!,'' two duets with his Annette, a reprise of Monique's waltz and a last-act waltz of his own). There was also a love duet for the principal girl, a one-step for Mlle Loulette and a dance called La Mexicana.

Originally intended for the Théâtre Mogador, the piece was forced by circumstances to move from Marseille to the big Théâtre de la Porte-Saint-Martin instead, but there, largely thanks to the appeal of the popular young comedian, it scored an undeniable success through a run of almost a year. Fernandel subsequently filmed the show with Andrex and Nita Raya as support, and returned to Paris in 1947 to star in a revival of a revised two-act version at the Théâtre de l'Étoile.

Film: Pierre Colombier 1937

Recording: complete w Fernandel (Decca)

IHRE HOHEIT DIE TÄNZERIN Operette in 3 acts by Richard Bars and Oskar Felix. Music by Walter Goetze. Bellevue Theater, Stettin, 8 May 1919.

The 18th-century Herzogin von Tyllberg disguises herself as a Spanish dancer called Marietta and, in that disguise, wins and tests the love of the officer Hans von Mayburg. In parallel to this main romantic plot, her steward's nephew Bolko von Wellhofen falls in love with a girl he thinks is the Countess's maid, only to find out in the end that she is really the Baroness Helma. Goetze's score and the star role of the Countess were highlighted by the song ''Im Rausch des Glücks'' and the duo ''Dich hat Frau Venus geboren,'' and the show gave the composer his first and most considerable stage success.

After a fine reception in Stettin and in Hanover, *Ihre Hoheit die Tänzerin* was taken to Berlin and mounted at the Thalia-Theater (22 June 1920). It transferred to the Friedrich-Wilhelmstädtisches Theater before passing its 100th night (29 September), and ran on there until 13 May, totaling nearly 300 performances. A Viennese production at Erich Müller's Johann Strauss-Theater with Elly Kreith as the Countess, Gisa Kolbe as Helma, Georg Kober as Hans and Fritz Imhoff as Bolko, played for 86 performances in 1922.

The show continued thereafter to appear intermittently in German theatres, and a revised version was produced in 1952.

Austria: Johann Strauss-Theater 7 July 1922

L'ÎLE DE TULIPATAN Opéra-bouffe in 1 act by Henri Chivot and Alfred Duru. Music by Jacques Offenbach. Théâtre des Bouffes-Parisiens, Paris, 30 September 1868.

Even after the success of his full-length opéras-bouffes and the disappearance of the constrictions which had limited him in earlier days to writing and producing one-act pieces with tiny casts, Offenbach continued to turn out musical playlets of the kind with which he had originally made his fame. Of those few written in the last dozen years of his life, the most widely successful was the mini opéra-bouffe *L'Île de Tulipatan.*

Chivot and Duru's libretto was a full-strength, crazy burlesque based on that favorite theme, that things are seldom what they seem, a libretto which overflowed with sexual ambiguity, treated, as was usual at this time, with a laughing freedom rather than the pink-lipped purposefulness of a century later. The action was extravagantly set on the island of Tulipatan, ''25,000 sea-kilometres from Nanterre, 473 years before the invention of the spittoon.'' Alexis (Mlle Castello), son and heir of King Cacatois XXII (Berthelier), is actually a girl, whom the seneschal, Romboïdal (Bonnet), has had brought up as a boy for dynastic reasons. Hermosa (Victor), Romboïdal's daughter, on the other hand, is a boy whom his mother, Théodorine (Mme Thierret), has brought up as a girl to avoid military service. Bouffe bit by bouffe bit, sexes and things get sorted out and, by the end, the two can be wed.

L'Île de Tulipatan was musically more substantial than some of the very shortest Offenbach pieces, with a score of a dozen numbers that included Cacatois's zany and incidental burlesque barcarolle (''Dans Venezia la belle'') and the Couplets du canard (''Prince doux et fort débonnaire''), in which the monarch denies the bad press he has been getting, Théodorine's nonsensically important-sounding excuse for an exit (''Je vais chercher les petites cuillières''), a lively piece for the ''girl'' (''Vive le tintamarre''), and a pretty one for the ''boy'' (''J'ai perdu mon ami''), as well as three duets.

Tulipatan was a success first up in Paris, and it was seen the following year in Germany (ad Emil Pohl), in Hungary (ad Emil Follinusz) and in Austria (ad Julius Hopp), where it was staged on double bills with *Die schöne Galathee* or *Flotte Bursche* with a royal cast featuring Josef Matras (Cactus), Hermine Meyerhoff (Oleander), Karl Blasel (Ficus) and Therese Schäfer (Aloe) for the earliest of its 35 performances in four years in the repertoire at the Carltheater. It also made its way to Britain, where it was played first, as *King Kokatoo* (ad F C Burnand), as an afterpiece to a touring production of W S Gilbert's *Pygmalion and Galatea,* with Anetta Scasi/Marion Inch, Amy Burnett, T B Appleby, Edward Perrini and Helen Maxse featured, then in Edinburgh adapted by Charles Horsman as *Charmian and Badoura, or The King of the Conjugal Islands* (19 May), and then at the Opera Comique, as an afterpiece to *Le Canard à trois becs,* remade and retitled *Kissi-Kissi* (ad F C Burnand), described as ''a Persian operatic bouffonerie,'' and with Pattie Laverne appearing in the title role. Largely helped by a staging which scandalously equated the Shah of the piece with the recently visiting Shah of Persia, it was ''better received by the audience than anything ever produced at the Opera Comique,'' maintained on the bill when the main piece was withdrawn, and brought back later in the year. Out on the road, opéra-bouffe star Julia Mathews junked her whole touring repertoire of shows and took to playing nothing but this topical and hot *Kissi-Kissi.*

In Australia, when the piece was finally shown there, it was in a different version, entitled *Alexis,* played by Amy Horton's burlesque company with the lady as Alexis and John L Hall as Cactus. America, on the other hand, seems—unless the piece was played under some unrecognizable title—to have passed it by. Which may be why the plot of the piece was, apparently, largely lifted for Richard F Carroll's fin de siècle Boston musical *Kismet.*

In Europe, *L'Île de Tulipatan* won numerous revivals over the years, including one at the Carltheater, by Franz

Steiner (24 January 1889) with a cast including Karl Streitmann (Azalea/Hermosa), Wilhelm Knaack (Ficus/Romboïdal) and Frln Seebold (Oléander/Alexis), and others at the Berlin Opera in 1917 and the Vienna Staatsoper in 1918. In Hungary it appeared under a different title (*XII Cactus*) in 1891, but apparently in the same Follinusz translation in which it had been originally played 20 years earlier in Arad. The piece was most recently played in Paris in 1982, originally at the Festival du Marais and subsequently at the Théâtre de la Gaîté-Montparnasse (16 July), with Christian Pernot, Kay Fender and Pierre Jacquemont in the cast.

Germany: Friedrich-Wilhelmstädtisches Theater 21 July 1869; Austria: Carltheater *Tulipatan* 5 May 1869; UK: Theatre Royal, Leeds *King Kokatoo, or Who Is Who and Which Is Which?* 4 March 1872, Opera Comique *Kissi-Kissi* 12 July 1873; Hungary: Arad 1869, Budai Színkör *Tulipatan szigete* 6 June 1872, *XII Cactus (herceg)* 1891; Australia: St George's Hall, Melbourne *Alexis* 3 June 1886

Recordings: complete (TLP), selection (Golden Age of Opera)

ILLYA DARLING Musical in 2 acts by Jules Dassin based on his film screenplay *Never on Sunday.* Lyrics by Joe Darion. Music by Manos Hadjidakis. Mark Hellinger Theater, New York, 11 April 1967.

The enormous success of the film *Never on Sunday,* from which Melina Mercouri's performance as a Greek prostitute and Manos Hadjidakis's hit-parade-worthy title song emerged memorably, prompted author Jules Dassin and United Artists to bring a fully musicalized version of the show to Broadway. Mercouri starred in her film role as the free-living and paid-loving Illya of the title (which had nothing to do with Russian spies, as British *Man from Uncle* watchers might have thought), who is lit upon by a well-meaning American teacher called Homer Thrace (Orson Bean) who attempts to turn her into a virtuous creature. It is soon obvious that a conventionally ''virtuous'' life does not come naturally to Illya and, ultimately, even Homer has to admit that it is right for the unhappy harlot to go uncomplicatedly back to her old job.

Hadjidakis supplemented his film song with four more for the star, two of which used the word ''love'' in the title, a couple for the leading man (''Golden Land,'' ''I Think She Needs Me'') and some lively Greek pieces for the lively Greek characters who peopled the rest of a sex-centered story which began to the sound of bouzouki music and ended to a massed ''Ya chara.'' Titos Vandis performed a title song which did not make up for the loss of the better known *Never on Sunday* as the show's title.

As they had in the film, the now widely popular ''Never on Sunday'' and the performance of Miss Mercouri proved the highlights and the drawcards of the musical, aided a little by the fairly sustained (political) newsworthiness of composer Hadjidakis. The colorful Kermit Bloomgarden/United Artists production held the stage for 320 Broadway performances, but the musical did not ever succeed in obliterating memories of a film version which was perhaps a little too close in the recent past. A German version (ad Robert Gilbert) was staged at Düsseldorf in 1969, and Mexico hosted a Spanish-language version which helped itself to a vernacular version of the more famous title, *Nunca en Domingo.*

Germany: Schauspielhaus, Düsseldorf 24 May 1969

Recordings: original cast (United Artists), Mexican cast (Private label)

I LOVE MY WIFE Musical in 2 acts by Michael Stewart based on the play *Viens chez moi, j'habite chez une copine* by Luis Rego. Music by Cy Coleman. Ethel Barrymore Theater, New York, 17 April 1977.

Purchased by Stewart, who had seen it on stage in Paris, the play which became the basis of the Broadway musical *I Love My Wife* was metamorphosed by him into a likeable, almost four-handed, comic story which gently mocked the permissive age in its tale of attempted wife-sharing in Trenton, New Jersey. The ''almost'' part of the four-handed came about because author Stewart conceived the idea of involving the orchestra in the action, along with the four actors. Thus, the four distinctly oddball musicians who made up the accompanying band wandered in and out of, and commented on, the story in which the endearing and not awfully bright Alvin (Lenny Baker) and his old pal Wally (James Naughton) tentatively set up a festive-season foursome. Their mini-orgy collapses under the weight of inexpertness, an intrusive banana cream pie and the ultimate admission that ''I Love My Wife.''

Coleman's lively and catchy score was at is best when able to escape the naively sexual subjects imposed by the plot (''Love Revolution,'' ''Sexually Free,'' ''Everybody Today Is Turning On,'' ''Married Couple Seeks Married Couple''). It turned out moments both infectiously swinging, as in the chorused ''Hey There, Good Times'' and country-fied, as in the duet for the two wives (Joanna Gleason, Ilene Graff) wondering if there was ''Someone Wonderful I Missed'' in Nashvillistic harmonies, both gently lilting, as in Alvin's explanation that ''I Love My Wife,'' and lugubriously comic as in the musicians' whimsical description of ''A Mover's Life.''

Harry Rigby and Terry Allen Kramer's Broadway production was well received, with the lanky, comical Baker winning particular kudos for his portrayal of eager-beaver Alvin, and the show settled down for an 857-performance run. Baker and Naughton were succeeded during the run by the television comedy duo the Smothers Brothers. The show was still on Broadway when Harold

Fielding opened a London version, with television sitcom star Richard Beckinsale (Alvin) and Ben Cross (Wally) featured alongside Deborah Fallender (Cleo) and Liz Robertson (Monica). If the show did not catch on quite as it had in America, it nevertheless ran profitably until Beckinsale left. With Robin (*Confessions of a Window-cleaner*) Asquith replacing, the atmosphere became more panting than endearing and the production closed after 410 performances.

The fact that both Baker and Beckinsale died very prematurely, shortly after their starring spells in *I Love My Wife,* did not deter other producers and actors, and the show's success and its economic proportions won it further English-language showings, including productions in both South Africa, and later (disastrously) in Australia, under the management of Louis Burke, and also several productions in a German version (ad Michael Kunze).

UK: Prince of Wales Theatre 6 October 1977; Germany: Theater Oberhausen *Ich liebe meine Frau* 12 September 1980; Australia: Her Majesty's Theatre, Sydney 22 September 1982

Recordings: original cast (Atlantic/DRG), South African cast (EMI), Australian cast (Festival)

I MARRIED AN ANGEL Musical comedy in 2 acts by Richard Rodgers and Lorenz Hart adapted from the play *Angyalt vettem feleségül* by János Vaszary. Shubert Theater, New York, 11 May 1938.

Richard Rodgers and Lorenz Hart were first introduced to the Hungarian musical play *Angyalt vettem feleségül* (Király Színház 23 April 1932, ly: Andor Szenes, mus: Dawies), which was to become *I Married an Angel,* in 1933, during their second period as Hollywood screen songwriters at MGM. Following their success with *Love Me Tonight,* Irving Thalberg set the pair to work with playwright Moss Hart to turn the piece, which had been purchased by the studio, into a musical film in which Jeanette MacDonald would play the angel who comes to earth to be the wife of a Budapest banker and shows him that perfection is not always something devoutly to be wished for in a wife. The score was written, but the film was canceled at the last moment.

Some years later, Dwight Deere Wiman, the co-producer of Rodgers and Hart's *On Your Toes* and *Babes in Arms,* succeeded in winkling the stage rights for the piece out of MGM. The songwriters, who had done well enough as self-librettists on *Babes in Arms,* adapted the piece from scratch (it was subsequently given a going over by director Josh Logan), and the resultant show was produced with Dennis King playing the role of Walter Palaffi, the banker, and Vera Zorina (who had played in *On Your Toes* in London) appearing as the angel. Since Miss Zorina danced more than she sang, the show contained a solid dance element. She danced gracefully to Balanchine's ballet ''The Modiste'' and in a Honeymoon Ballet in the first act, drew comedy from the second-act ''Angel without Wings,'' and fooled about in a sea nymph's costume with the rest of the girls in a burlesque piece which, apropos of nothing at all, sang about what goes on ''At the Roxy Music Hall.''

The short ration of songs went mostly to King, to Vivienne Segal in the role of his worldly wise sister, Countess Peggy Palaffi, who knocks some of the dust off the angel's wings, and to Audrey Christie as Walter's rejected girlfriend, Anna Murphy. King had the pick of the numbers in the flowing title song, and joined Miss Segal in ''Spring Is Here'' (a number which had nothing to do with the songwriters' earlier musical of the same name), whilst he and she and Charles Walters queried comically of one another ''Did You Ever Get Stung?''

I Married an Angel's Broadway life of 338 performances gave Rodgers and Hart their longest New York run since *A Connecticut Yankee*—better than *Babes in Arms* or *On Your Toes*—and the musical went on to tour America through 1939. Perhaps because of the failure there of *On Your Toes,* it was not taken up for London. However, Ernest C Rolls, who had recently come to the top spot in Australia's all-powerful J C Williamson Ltd, gave the show a lavish production in Melbourne with Jack Arthur (Willy), Helen Denizon (Angel) and Bernice Claire (Peggy) in the starring roles. It was a spectacular and utter four-week failure. A Sydney season was nevertheless persevered with (Theatre Royal 13 May 1939), with Katrin Rosselle taking over as the angel, and its equivalent failure—one of the most dire in Australian musical-theatre history—shook the foundations of the famous old firm of Williamson badly.

The tale went back to source when Vaszary produced and directed *I Married an Angel* under its original title (ly: Mihály Szécsén) at his Budapest Andrássy Színház whilst the show still ran on Broadway, but otherwise the show's export came only in film form. The film version starred Miss MacDonald and Nelson Eddy, and primped up the score with three new studio-made numbers by Herbert Stothart, a piece called ''Little Work-a-Day World'' which Rodgers had written for a play, and a barrage of fresh lyrics from the studio's Wright and Forrest. Rodgers didn't like it, and neither did many other people.

Hungary: Andrássy Színház *Angyalt vettem feleségül* 17 September 1938; Australia: Her Majesty's Theatre, Melbourne 26 November 1938

Film: MGM 1942

Recordings: original cast (AEI), film soundtrack (Pelican), etc

I'M GETTING MY ACT TOGETHER AND TAKING IT ON THE ROAD Musical by Gretchen Cryer. Music by Nancy Ford. Anspacher (Public) Theater, New

York, 14 June 1978; Circle in the Square, 16 December 1978.

The title of Gretchen Cryer and Nancy Ford's five-handed musical largely summed up its content. The central character was Heather Jones (Miss Cryer), 39 years old, a TV afternoon-soap actress and singer-songwriter who once made number 89 on the charts. She is putting together a program of new songs with which to go on tour, accompanied by her Liberated Man's Band and her backing singers Cheryl (Betty Aberlin) and Alice (Margot Rose). Heather's new songs are different from the ones she used to sing. They are tougher and less obviously attractive, and they reflect her own life as an obviously strong, intelligent and independent woman whose personal life has been unsatisfying. By the time she has said her strong, intelligent and independent say and done her thing, during the course of the evening, even her old friend and manager, Joe (Joel Fabiani), is alienated—just another man running away from commitment is the way Heather sees it—but she thinks there may be hope for the future and for that enduring relationship, in the young guitarist, Jake (Don Scardino). If, that is, Heather can ever sustain a one-to-one relationship.

Many of the songs of the show were the songs of Heather's act (''Natural High,'' ''Miss America,'' ''Old Friend,'' ''Feel the Love,'' ''Lonely Lady''), others illustrated events in her earlier life, but were equally presented as songs written by her. Of these the lightly attractive ''In a Simple Way I Love You,'' sung here by Jake and representing Heather's younger and more optimistic style of writing and thinking—a style which is for the moment his—proved the pick.

Produced by the New York Shakespeare Festival at the Public Theater, the show was shifted to off-Broadway's Circle in the Square after its initial season and remained there for 1,165 performances, during which time composer Nancy Ford, Carol Hall (composer of the score to *The Best Little Whorehouse in Texas*), and Betty Buckley each took a turn at the role of Heather. The handily sized piece got a wide showing at home and abroad, but largely fared less well outside America. A London version, which showed a number of textual alterations since the original American performances, was sponsored by Celia Bogan Ltd and Richard Denning, with Diane Langton as Heather and Ben Cross as Joe, and failed in 62 performances, whilst an Australian production was mounted by the Sydney Theatre Company with Nancye Hayes featured. A German version (ad Erika Gesell, Helmut Baumann) was produced at Berlin's Schlossparktheater in 1980, and was followed by other German-language productions on other smaller stages, whilst other adaptations were seen from Scandinavia to the Orient.

Australia: Recording Hall (Opera House) April 1980; Germany: Schlossparktheater *Ich steig aus und mach 'ne eigne Show* 18 October 1980; UK: Apollo Theatre 31 March 1981

Recordings: original cast (CBS), London cast (TER), Japanese cast (Sony), Norwegian cast *Det er jo mitt show!* (DNS), Swedish cast *Det av ju min show!* (Europa), Danish cast *I Morgen er jes påkej . . .* (Wilhem Hansen), etc

IM REICHE DES INDRA Operette in 1 act by Heinrich Bolten-Bäckers and Leopold Ely. Music by Paul Lincke. Apollotheater, Berlin, 18 December 1899.

Im Reiche des Indra was a piece made to order for the specific and spectacular needs of the Berlin Apollotheater, the variety house where the Lincke/Bolten-Bäckers *Frau Luna* had been such a splendid success. This time, instead of going to the moon like the hero of *Frau Luna,* the ordinary Berliner central to these pieces—in this tale reporter Gustave Steinbock—turned up in the almost as far-away kingdom of Brahmaputra, and became mixed up in the affairs of King Menelek and his Queen, Sita. Steinbock helps out the little page, Bhimo, who has been caught out sighing over his mistress, there incurs the King's wrath when he photographs Sita in her bath—but ends up improving matters between the ill-matched royal spouses, with the help of some magic rings, before heading back home to his newspaper. The plot was mainly an opportunity for some often revusical songs and some spectacular dance and costume scenes, and *Im Reiche des Indra,* with its three scenes and ''Schlussapotheose'' of oriental splendor, fulfilled its purpose on the Apollo program almost as well as its famous predecessor had done. Lincke's seductive invitation to ''Nimm mich mit in dein Kämmerlein'' proved the favorite piece of the score.

In 1903 the Apollotheater company played *Im Reiche des Indra* in their season at Vienna's Danzers Orpheum with Müller (Steinbock), Lucie Medlon (Sita) and Harnisch (Menelek) in the leading roles, and with the ''electric ballet'' ''Leuchtende Brillanten'' interpolated into the first act, and in 1906 an Hungarian version was played at Budapest's equivalent of the Apollo, the Royal Orfeum, where Lincke's *Luna asszony, Nakiri* and *Vénus a földön* had already been featured.

The show was later readapted by Hans Brennecke into a two-act version on the lines of the enlarged *Frau Luna,* but without the same enduring success. Another ''Neufassung'' was mounted at Chemnitz in 1938.

Austria: Danzers Orpheum 14 March 1903; Hungary: Royal Orfeum *Indra* 31 January 1906

Recording: selection (EMI)

IM WEISSEN RÖSSL Singspiel (Revue-Operette) in 3 acts by Hans Müller based on the play of the same name by Oscar Blumenthal and Gustav Kadelburg. Lyrics by Robert Gilbert. Music by Ralph Benatzky. Additional songs by Robert Stolz, Bruno Granichstaedten, Robert Gilbert, et al. Grosses Schauspielhaus, Berlin, 8 November 1930.

The Schwank *Im weissen Rössl,* originally produced in 1897 at Berlin's Lessing-Theater (30 December), was a highly successful comico-romantic play which was revived frequently on German-language stages following its first production. The story is told that director Erik Charell was given the idea of turning it into a musical spectacular when the actor Emil Jannings, who had appeared in Berlin in the piece's starring comic role of Giesecke, took the occasion of a luncheon with the director on the lakeside terrace of the real Weisses Rössl hotel in St Wolfgang, in the Austrian Salzkammergut, to lurch into some jokey backchat from the show with a waiter.

The book for the musical *Im weissen Rössl* was reorganized by Charell and rewritten by Hans Müller to fit Charell's and the Grosses Schauspielhaus's large-stage Revue-Operette requirements, the score was composed and collected by Ralph Benatzky, the theatre's house composer, with additional songs from Bruno Granichstaedten, Robert Stolz, lyricist Robert Gilbert and others tacked in, in the then and there accepted fashion (but to Benatzky's annoyance), and the piece was staged with even more than usual in the way of the spectacular accoutrements (if, given the subject, altogether less of the glitter) for which the Schauspielhaus had become famous.

Camilla Spira played Josefa Vogelhuber, the landlady of the Zum weissen Rössl, whose amorous sights are, much to the distress of her adoring headwaiter, Leopold (Max Hansen), set on the handsome city lawyer Otto Siedler (Walter Jankuhn). When Siedler comes to stay at the hotel, Josefa does everything to make his stay comfortable, but Leopold does just the opposite, and ends up getting himself sacked. However, Siedler is unaware of Josefa's attachment and he is soon sighing behind the cowshed with Ottilie (Trude Lieske), the daughter of the belligerent ladies' underwear manufacturer, Giesecke (Otto Wallburg). A commercial marriage has been proposed between Ottilie and Sigismund (Sig Arno), the son of Giesecke's business competitor, but in the end bald and beautiful Sigismund falls for little, stuttering Klärchen, Siedler gets his Ottilie, and, after some homespun truth from the lips of no less a guest than the Emperor Franz Josef (Paul Hörbiger) himself, Josefa sees the sense in marrying the adoring Leopold. The musical realigned the emphasis of the piece towards the Josefa/Leopold relationship rather than, as originally, towards Giesecke and his commercial and family problems, and Leopold, a role built in the good, old Girardi mold, became the principal comic character of the piece. There was also a small stand-out comic role for a little hotel busboy—something of a mini Hans Moser part—in which Gustl Stark Gstettenbauer pulled the notices in the original production.

The score was a friendly, catchy one, from its yodeling overture and a buzzing opening, with Leopold organizing crowds of tourists in and out of the hotel, to its final waltzing happily-ever-after finale. Leopold serenaded his employer with "Es muss was Wunderbares sein" and stood his amorous ground, in the face of dismissal, in Granichstaedten's delightful "Zuschau'n kann i net," whilst Josefa welcomed Siedler "Im weissen Rössl am Wolfgangsee" in waltz time and urged Giesecke into good temper with the thigh-slapping rhythms of "Im Salzkammergut." Sigismund wondered over his unobvious (to everyone else) good looks in Gilbert's "Was kann der Sigismund dafür," the romantic pair wallowed in the tuneful sentimentality of Stolz's "Die ganze Welt ist himmelblau" and the waltzing "Mein Liebeslied muss ein Walzer sein," and the Emperor delivered rich philosophy in the Sprechgesang of "Es ist einmal in Leben so."

The lavish production, designed by Ernst Stern to include anything and everything Salzkammerguttish that moved, included a boat, a train, a veritable arkful of live animals, a vast cast and real rain. All this, added to the charming music and the homely, countrified and familiar tale, made up a combination which was irresistible to Berliners of the depression years ("Stern catches the gaiety of the country, and the Schuhplattler is a breath of fresh air after all that dreary revue dancing"), and *Im weissen Rössl* scored a huge success through a first run of more than 400 performances.

The Berlin production was still at its peak when the foreign versions of the show started to come thick and fast. The first of these was mounted in London, where Oswald Stoll imported Charell to stage an English adaptation of the show (ad Harry Graham, with plot variations) at the vast London Coliseum. Clifford Mollison (Leopold) and Vienna's Lea Seidl (Josefa) starred, with Bruce Carfax (here anglicized from Otto Siedler into Valentine Sutton) and Rita Page (now the daughter of an English north-country businessman) providing the romantic music, and comedian George Gee as Sigismund. The London version of *White Horse Inn* boosted the popular musical content of the show by adding another song for Mollison. Declaring that, having been sacked, he would go off and join the Foreign Legion, he delivered Graham's version of Robert Stolz's already familiar march song "Adieu, mein kleiner Gardeoffizier," borrowed from the film score *Das Lied ist aus* (1930). As "Goodbye" the new/old song scored, with the title song, the hit of the evening. Another Stolz number, "You Too"

(''Auch du wirst mich einmal betrügen''), taken from the film score for *Zwei Herzen im Dreivierteltakt* (1930), was also added, and Stolz's contribution, which had now mounted to four numbers, was judged sufficient by the British publishers of the show to give him a co-composer's credit with Benatzky. The picturesque lashings of Tyrolean scenery, largely reproduced from Stern's Berlin designs, the dancing and the yodeling, the happy score and the happy story proved equally as popular in London as in Berlin. The show remained in London just over a year and played 650 twice-daily performances in its king-sized home. It was revived at the same theatre during the war with Derek Oldham and Nita Croft (20 March 1940) in the lead roles.

The London version and staging, with its great revolving stage and all, was subsequently produced in Australia. Popular prima donna Strella Wilson starred as Josefa and palliated the part's lack of music by introducing Ivor Novello's song ''Lend Me a Dream.'' Arthur Stigant (Giesecke), Charles Norman (Leopold) and Sydney Burchall (Valentine) supported, and the piece was, yet again, a vast hit, playing nearly four months in Sydney and four in Melbourne (Her Majesty's Theatre/King's Theatre 28 July 1934) before being sent out to tour Australia. The cast traveled by one train—the revolve went on ahead on a second.

In Vienna the show was staged at the Stadttheater with Hubert Marischka and Paula Brosig in the leading roles and Fritz Imhoff as Giesecke. The ''Blue-Boys'' jazz band was heavily featured, there was a ''Wäschentanzer'' scene, a ''Schützenfest am Wolfgangsee,'' a scene on the Bad Ischl esplanade (how did we get there?) featuring a song called ''Ischl'' (Anton Paulik/Karl Farkas) and a ''Quodlibet'' by the same pair, and there was a second contribution from Granichstaedten (''Ich hab' es fünfzigmal geschworen'') to swell the decidedly in-and-out score. Again—in spite of some mumbles about the propriety of representing Franz Josef on the musical stage—the show was a huge hit, which ended up alternating no fewer than three Josefas and two Emperors, and it returned two seasons later to pass its 700th Viennese performance during a week's stand at the Theater an der Wien. It has returned most recently at the Volksoper where it was remounted in 1993 (15 May) with Adolf Dallapozza as Leopold and Elisabeth Kales as Josepha.

Adorján Stella and Imre Harmath's Hungarian version also scored the show's now habitual fine success when it was mounted at Budapest's Király Színház with Márton Rátkai (Giesecke), Emmi Kosáry (Ottilie), Erzi Pechy (Josefa), Jenő Nádor (Siedler), Dezső Kertész (Leopold), Teri Féjes (Klärchen) and Gyula Kabos (Sigismund) featured, and Josef Jarno, longtime head of Vienna's Theater in der Josefstadt, stealing the show in the role of the Emperor.

Strangely enough, it was several years before *White Horse Inn* arrived in New York. When it did it was mounted at the enormous Center Theater (ad David Freeman, Irving Caesar) with Kitty Carlisle and William Gaxton starred, with Robert Halliday providing the romance, and with a bundle of the most un-Austrian numbers ever inserted into the ravaged score: Will Irwin and Norman Zeno's ''In a Little Swiss Chalet'' (Swiss????!), ''White Souls,'' Jara Benes's ''Leave It to Katarina'' and the Irving Caesar/Gerald Marks/Sam Lerner ''I Would Love to Have You Love Me,'' as well as a different ''Goodbye'' number credited to Eric Coates. It nevertheless pleased New York for 223 performances.

Meanwhile, however, the Paris production had given the show one of its most successful outings of all. As Stoll had done in London, the Isola Brothers imported Charell to supervise the staging of a version of his singular hit, on the rather less vast stage of the Théâtre Mogador (ad Lucien Besnard, René Dorin). Again, like Stoll, they used a version of Stern's designs, which had, like the show itself, been once again adapted. As far as the score was concerned, ''Goodbye'' had been retained from the London version, but ''You Too'' was replaced by a delicious duet ''Je vous emmènerai dans mon joli bateau,'' a piece gallicized from a 1929 song, ''Am Sonntag will mein Süsser mit mir segeln gehn,'' written by Robert Gilbert and composed by Anton Profès, which gave the score yet one more highlight. Several numbers from the original score, including Granichstaedten's lovely song, had, however, vanished. The comedians Milton (Léopold) and Charpin (Bistagne/Giesecke) and Gabrielle Ristori (Josépha) headed the cast, with André Goavec (Guy Florès/Siedler) and Rose Carday (Sylvabelle/Ottilie) as a pair of sweethearts here turned as French as the British production had made them British. Paris gave *L'Auberge du Cheval Blanc* its longest run of all, with a first series of over 700 performances, during which Hélène Régelly and Lucien Dorval replaced the original stars, and France also proved to be the show's most appreciative foreign home thereafter.

L'Auberge du Cheval Blanc returned to Paris and the Mogador in 1935. It then migrated to the Châtelet under Maurice Lehmann, where Luc Barney famously took possession of the role of Léopold, which he played again in the 1948 and 1953 revivals. The show returned once more in 1960, and in 1968 the Châtelet presented a revised version (ad Marcel Lamy, Jean Valmy) which raked up and replaced in the show the bits of the German score that had got dropped on the way to the definitive French version. Granichstaedten's song went back in, along with a heurige song by Hans Frankowski which had become part of the German show in the meantime, and two ''lost'' Benatzky pieces. In 1979 the Mogador repeated the show they had introduced nearly half a century earlier, and in 1987 the considerably smaller Eldorado mounted *L'Auberge du Cheval Blanc* with the aging Barney now playing Bistagne. Paris still welcomes the show into the 21st century.

In Vienna, *Im weissen Rössl* was reintroduced at the Volksoper in 1976 (1 March, w Christiane Hörbiger, Peter Minich), where its spectacular side was well catered for but, although Berlin's *Im weissen Rössl* was conceived as a spectacle, and owed much of its original success to its elaborate visual side, it has been often and successfully played, since its establishment as an international hit, in much smaller and virtually scenery-free productions without suffering—largely thanks to the positive charm of its Leopold/Josefa tale and the popularity of its well-known score.

Im weissen Rössl has been several times filmed, the first in 1934 with Christl Mardayn, Hermann Thimig and Theo Lingen, the second in 1952 with Hannerl Matz, Walter Müller and Johannes Heesters. The third, a distinctly up-to-date one with Peter Alexander, Waltraud Haus, Adrian Hoven, Günther Philipp and Karin Dor, is still played daily as a tourist attraction at the cinema in St Wolfgang, just along from the real Weisses Rössl on the Wolfgangsee. An Argentinian film of 1948 which borrowed the famous title told a rather different story, but a Danish one, featuring Dirch Passer and Susse Wold, dropped the title in favor of *Sommer i Tyrol* (1964).

UK: London Coliseum *White Horse Inn* 8 April 1931; Hungary: Király Színház *A ''Fehér Ló''* 20 October 1931; Austria: Wiener Stadttheater 25 September 1931, France: Théâtre Mogador *L'Auberge du Cheval Blanc* 1 October 1932; USA: Center Theater *White Horse Inn* 1 October 1936, Australia: Theatre Royal, Sydney *White Horse Inn* 31 May 1934.

Films: Carl Lamac 1934, Willi Först 1952, Tobik/Jupiter Films 1960, Erik Balling *Sommer i Tyrol* 1964

Recordings: complete (various versions) (Amadeo, Eurodisc, HMV), complete French version (EMI, Festival), selections (Telefunken, etc), selections in French (CBS, Barclay, Philips, etc), selections in English (MFP, etc), selections in Italian (EDM, RCA), selections in Danish (Philips, Telefunken), etc

IN DAHOMEY Negro musical comedy in a prologue and 2 acts by Jesse A Shipp. Lyrics by Paul Laurence Dunbar and others. Music by Will Marion Cook and others. Grand Opera House, Stamford, Conn, 8 September 1902; New York Theater, New York, 18 February 1903.

In Dahomey was the first American musical comedy written almost entirely by black writers and played entirely by black artists to be presented at a regular Broadway house, rather than the more fringe establishments which normally catered to such shows and their particular audiences. Conceived specifically to feature the popular vaudeville team of Bert Williams and George Walker, its delightfully free-wheeling libretto portrayed the two comedians as the comical Shylock Homestead, known as ''Shy'' to his friends (Williams), and Rareback Pinkerton, his buddy and adviser (Walker). The two get involved with the Get-the-Coin Syndicate, led by Hustling Charley (played by author Shipp), which is raising cash to back the Dahomey Colonisation Society set up by Hamilton Lightfoot (Peter Hampton) and his brother Moses (William Barker). The idea is to export all the down-and-out blacks of America to a promised land on the African continent. Rareback swindles the money out of the simple Shy, and puts most of it on his own slick back before Nemesis starts to tweak his coattails.

The original basic songs of the piece, the majority written by the respected poet Paul Dunbar and composed by Will Marion Cook, featured such pieces as ''Emancipation Day'' (on which ''white folk try to pass fo' coons''), ''The Czar'' and a song called ''Society,'' with lyrics that sounded like Victorian parlor words, and a well-liked ''All Goin Out, Nothin' Comin' In,'' but these soon proved insufficient and the score developed as *In Dahomey* developed out of town. With the help of lyricist Cecil Mack, Cook made over his earlier ''The Little Gipsy Maid'' to the only barely more colored-sounding ''Brown-skinned Baby Mine,'' wrote a waltz song ''Molly Green,'' and teamed up with James W Johnson on a piece about the ''Leader of the Colored Aristocracy.'' The most effective numbers, however, came from other sources: cast member J Leubrie Hill and Frank B Williams's ''My Dahomian Queen,'' Hill's later addition explaining catchily ''That's How the Cake Walk's Done,'' another cast member, Alex Rogers's ''I'm a Jonah Man'' for Williams (added in Chicago four months after opening), and Harry von Tilzer's infectious ''I Wants to Be an Actor Lady'' (sung by Aida Overton Walker) and ''Chocolate Drops'' cakewalk. Williams himself supplied the music for a jig.

The show had, in fact, been originally constructed to tour those variety houses which had specifically black audiences, and an eyebrow or two was raised when producers Jules Hurtig and Harry Seamon took the unusual step of opening their show on Broadway. Their gamble did not come off. Williams and Walker were appreciated, but *In Dahomey*—the lingoistic fun of which seemed altogether on a happier level than much of the music and lyrics—was not considered up to very much as a piece, and the producers could not hold it up in New York for more than 53 performances.

A second gamble, however, did work. The whole cast and production of *In Dahomey* was promptly shipped to London, where the show opened less than three months after its Broadway premiere to a very different reaction. There, where the nearest thing to a black show ever seen was the Christy Minstrels, *In Dahomey* was a genuine novelty, if nothing else in the unbridled energy with which the black artists played (''its vitality, quaint comedians, catchy music, and its unique environment should make it one of the dramatic sensations of the London season''). The show settled in nicely and—boosted very usefully by a command performance at Buckingham Palace for the young Prince's birthday celebration (which got the whole royal family up trying the cakewalk which was the raison d'être of the invitation)—swelled. Fifteen extra American blacks were brought across to London to expand the line of the cakewalk dancers, and the cast tasted a kind of theatrical and social success they had never before had through the 251 performances between May and the Boxing Day closure. Later the piece went on tour in Britain, but ultimately the *In Dahomey* folk had to go home, and the bubble burst. The show had no tomorrow, and not until the coming of the fashion for ragtime and revue to the international stage did black artists, once more Americans, again win such wide attention, either in Britain or America.

UK: Shaftesbury Theatre 16 May 1903

INDIANA Comic opera in 3 acts by H B Farnie. Music by Edmond Audran. Avenue Theatre, London, 11 October 1886.

After the enormous successes he had won working with Planquette, both on the original *Rip van Winkle* and then with the transformation of *Les Voltigeurs de la 32ème* and *Surcouf* into the long-lived moneymakers *The Old Guard* and *Paul Jones,* the oft-(critically)-despised librettist and director H B Farnie was anything but despised by the French musical establishment. It was announced that he had been signed to write four musicals with no less a composer than Edmond Audran and, eventually, *Indiana* appeared. It was, allegedly, based on a French vaudeville—the title was not disclosed, but the show had been originally announced in mid-1884 as *The Miller of Dee,* which didn't sound very French—which made up into a passable, but not terribly original, comic-opera book.

American Indiana Grayfaunt (American Mathilde Wadman) comes to Civil War England, disguised as a cavalier, secretly to look over her unknown fiancé, cavalier Philip Jervaulx (W T Hemsley). Jervaulx, under the pressure of current events, is also at this time disguised, hiding as a servant in the house of his cousin (Phyllis Broughton), whose foolish husband, Sir Mulberry Mullitt (Henry Ashley) is actually in charge of finding him. The principal comedy role was that of Matt o' the Mill (Arthur Roberts), whose mill Indiana uses as her headquarters—which Mullitt attacks, thinking she is Jervaulx. There was also a sexy subplot concerning the designing, lubricious Lord Dayrell (Charles Ryley) and the miller's young wife (Mary Duggan).

Audran wrote an attractive score to the piece, but one which was less obviously popular than the Planquette scores had been, and after the out-of-town tryout the piece was given a going-over to try to make it more catchily colorful. The up-and-coming comic Roberts was given his head, and had some extra material—including a song ''The Plain Potato,'' composed by musical director John Crook—added to his role. He added more himself, but even his popular low comedy efforts failed to make *Indiana* better than a half-success, and it closed after 70 performances. It returned to London briefly (with extra songs again) as a stopgap when a revival of *Madame Favart* was forced to close through star illness. It was also given two tours, as well as a brief showing (32 performances) and a briefer return season (16 performances, 11 July 1888 Wallack's Theater) on Broadway, where it was produced under John McCaull's management with Digby Bell and Lilly Post/Marion Manola starred. It was still to be seen intermittently on the American touring circuits a decade later (Jules Grau Opera Co, 1897), but it never reached the degree of success achieved by Farnie's collaborations with Planquette, and the other three musicals did not eventuate.

Audran, however, did not waste his score. He recycled it for the French stage, to a new libretto, under the title *La Fiancée des verts poteaux* (Théâtre des Menus-Plaisirs 8 November 1887). The French libretto of Maurice Ordonneau proved, however, even less well-liked than the British one. It was, in its turn, rewritten and the show reproduced in a largely slimmed version (Menus-Plaisirs 1 August 1888), but although the resultant show got seen as far afield as Budapest (*A kölcsönkért vőlegény*) it did not ever establish itself amongst Audran's more favored works.

USA: Star Theater 18 January 1887

INDIGO UND DIE VIERZIG RÄUBER Comic Operette in 3 acts ''by Maximilian Steiner.'' Music by Johann Strauss. Theater an der Wien, Vienna, 10 February 1871.

In the early 1870s Johann Strauss, widely famed for his popular orchestral music, was persuaded by his wife and by Maximilian Steiner of the Theater an der Wien to make an attempt to write for the stage. With some guidance from the Theater an der Wien's multi-talented and experienced in-house playwright-lyricist-composer Richard Genée, he at length completed the score for his first Operette, a score which was written to a libretto ultimately cobbled up from the Arabian Nights' tale of Ali Baba by Steiner himself, after several uncredited collaborators and play doctors had failed to get the piece into satisfactory order.

The book of *Indigo und die vierzig Räuber* was flavored liberally with Offenbachian elements. The heroine, Fantasca (Marie Geistinger), was a Viennese-born maiden, shipwrecked as a child on Macassar's shores, and now become the monarch's favorite bajadere. The country's High Priest, Romadour (Carl Adolf Friese), is another Viennese risen to high place with the help of his native wits, and a third Viennese, the young voyager Janio (né Schani, Albin Swoboda), who is to be the ''hero'' and love interest of the piece, makes up the *Ba-ta-clan*ish total of strayed Austrians.

The land ruled over by Indigo (Matthias) is in a shabby state, and practically run—or run down—by his ministers' wives. The court is also threatened by a robber band, and Indigo offers Fantasca as a prize to whomsoever shall rid him of these worrisome intruders. It is Fantasca herself, however, who discovers the secret of the robbers' cave and its ''sesame'' key word, and she resolves to lead the ladies of the harem to the cave, stack up the donkey of the donkeyman, Ali Baba (Jani Szíka), with as many sacks of riches as it can carry, and flee. In the event, she finally does her fleeing with Janio, leaving the harem in a drugged sleep in the cave of the robbers (who are never seen in this ''version'' of the tale!), and after an extra act of quiproquos and a great deal of dancing (Sclaven-Tanz, Mohren-Tanz, Mulatten-Tanz, Tanz-Finale), the pair head off back to the city of their birth.

The most successful single number in the evening's score was a waltz trio for Fantasca, Janio and Romadour, ''Ja, so singt man in der Stadt wo ich geboren,'' but there was a selection of attractive music to fit all the styles of the Theater an der Wien's lead players. The romantic pair, Fantasca and Janio, were particularly well-equipped with some virtuoso vocal pieces, including a vast, showy duo, ''Wir haben uns schön gern g'habt,'' Fantasca's first-act finale aria ''In des Harems Heiligthume'' and second-act military number ''Folget eures Ruf und Gebot,'' and a waltz song for Janio. Toffana, Ali Baba's wife (Frln Stauber), was endowed with an ariette and a romanze in the soubrette style, whilst Ali, at the head of the comical side of things, had several numbers, beginning with his first-act entrance song, and including a duettino with Janio. Elsewhere, the large score of music ran from a bacchanale and valse-brindisi, full of ornaments and runs, to a soldiers' chorus and back, two or three times.

The opening night of the first Operette by the beloved Viennese waltz king was quite an occasion, but the reaction to *Indigo* was at best mixed. The music was admired as music, if not necessarily as theatrical music, but the text came in for heavy criticism. The show was played 46 times at the Theater an der Wien before being withdrawn. Strauss's reputation, however, ensured that it had far more future than most shows with such a track record. Later the same year *Indigo* was played in Graz, and then appeared in Berlin, with its libretto revised by Ernst Dohm, over the next decade it was seen, in various revisions, in Prague, Pressburg, Magdeburg and several other European cities, resurfacing at Berlin's Theater Unter den Linden as late as 1897 (24 February) in yet another revised version (ad Eduard Jacobson).

In Paris, the unfancied libretto was given more than its usual cosmetic overhaul, and the piece produced as *La Reine Indigo* at the Théâtre de la Renaissance sported a largely different book written by Victor Wilder and Adolphe Jaime. Zulma Bouffar played Fantasca, Vauthier was Romadour, Daniel played Babazouk, Félix Puget was Janio and Madame Alphonsine played the queen of the title, a jealous creature who has vowed to sell off her late husband's harem, a job lot which includes Fantasca. She also has her eyes on Fantasca's beloved Janio. The lad proves of sufficient mettle, however, to duck the Queen's passion, and to reach a happy ending in time for the final curtain. The score of the original *Indigo* was not taken note for note into the new show, and the composer was on hand to provide extra numbers, especially in view of the libretto's introduction of another major feminine character. The bonbons were there, of course: ''So singt man'' even kept its sentiments, letting forth curiously (given the new plot) in joyous trio about the Danube and the joys of Vienna, but Babazouk's ''Ronde du marchand des quatre saisons'' replaced Miraka's Auftrittslied, ''Geschmiedet fest an starre Felsenwand'' gave way to the ''Couplets du merle blanc,'' Toffana's aria and Janio's waltz song both disappeared, and Fantasca was given a little youp-la! tyrolienne which wasn't familiar. The Queen's role was supplied with a new number and, in the final act of the French show, non-*Indigo* music came thick and fast.

Paris did not take with any great vigor to the waltzing Viennese Operette, nor to the book which the French librettists had patched around Strauss's score. Not even a luxurious production could persuade them to favor *La Reine Indigo* for more than 80 performances, although it was brought back for 18 further performances as a compliment to Strauss when the composer visited Paris to conduct, and to negotiate the production of *Die Fledermaus* with the Théâtre de la Renaissance management. Léa Silly was the Queen. In 1878 it was tried again when Koning put the out-of-work Renaissance actors into a summer production at the Bouffes-Parisiens with Mlle Bouffar now teamed with Mme Dharville and Urbain. If Parisians didn't care overly for *La Reine Indigo,* however, Strauss and his partners clearly did, for a revised German-language version, translated from Wilder and Jaime's French was subsequently produced at the Theater an der Wien as *Königin Indigo* (ad Josef Braun 9 October 1877) with Marie Stolle (Indigo), Jenny Heisler (Fantasca) Alexander Girardi (Ali Baba), Felix Schweighofer (Romadour) and Josef Eisenbach (Janio) in the lead roles. Two weeks and 15 performances saw it out again. America, too, had a chance to see the alternative *Indigo* when Marie Aimée introduced it briefly into her ever-touring repertoire (Lyceum Theater 14 December 1877). The piece was later included in the repertoire of the English-singing Carleton Opera Co and advertised in 1889–90 by Robert Grau (the jailable black sheep of the Grau family), who bannered "500 nights in Paris, two consecutive years in Vienna" in typical mendacious style and then failed to produce.

The first English-language performance of *Indigo* was played at London's Alhambra Theatre in a version which, like the French one, kept the principals' names but advertised "an entirely new libretto" by F C Burnand. It nevertheless seemed to have some bones of the Viennese *Indigo* left in it. Selina Dolaro (Fantasca, a young Hungarian wrecked on the Indigonian Isles and made chief Maid of Honour), Harry Paulton (King Indigo), J H Ryley (Babazouk, a descendant of Ali Baba), Guillaume Loredan (Janio, the King's Private Musician), Adelaide Newton (Princess Radamanta) and Emma Chambers (Zoë) were featured in a show whose text ran to no less than 40 pages of printed libretto, and that included a Hungarian ballet and a bayadère divertissement, but which still (after being chopped down to two-and-a-half hours after opening night) shared the evening program with a farce and a full-length ballet. It also managed to fit in an arrangement of the Blue Danube waltz. Like all its fellow makes and remakes, it failed, closing in just seven weeks.

America hosted its first performances of the show in German, when Lina Mayr starred as Fantasca alongside Witt (Indigo), Merten (Ali Baba) and Ferdinand Schütz (Janio) at the Germania Theater in 1875, and the piece was also seen in New York in its French alternative version, and in an 1891 revival at the Terrace Garten (30 July), before the Casino Theater finally tried an *Indigo* in English (ad Max Freeman, Edgar Smith), 20 years after the original production. Jefferson de Angelis (Ali), Pauline L'Allemand (Fantasca), Louise Beaudet (Toffana), Ferdinand Schütz (Janio) and Edwin Stevens (Indigo) starred, and it ran five weeks. It was subsequently toured by the William T Carleton Opera Company.

Hungary saw its first brief production in 1874 (ad Jenő Rákosi) and the Népszínház brought the show back nearly 20 years later in a revised version without notable success. Russia, Italy, Poland, Spain, South America and even Malta all had a go with *Indigo* over 20 years of bootless efforts to make a success out of it, and Berlin's Friedrich-Wilhelmstädtisches Theater tried it again in 1887 (9 April), but the sole real successes which emerged from the piece were Strauss's own arrangements of some of his melodies as dance music ("Tausend und eine Nacht," "Indigo-Marsch," etc).

The attempts to reuse Strauss's *Indigo* music (and, not coincidentally, his saleable name) continued after his death. In 1906 the score was largely borrowed to be set by Ernst Reiterer to a wholly different libretto by Leo Stein and Carl Lindau, albeit one which maintained the Middle Eastern flavor, under the title *Tausend und eine Nacht* (fantastic Operette in a prologue and two acts, Venedig in Wien 15 June). An extremely indifferent tale about a fisherman (Rauch) and a Prince (Willy Bauer) who take each other's places, and the Leila (Phila Wolff) they both love, it made place in its action for a Viennese soubrette (Fella Schreiter) who was able to make reasonable sense of singing "Ja so singt man" without changing the lyrics. In spite of a libretto which did not seem even as convincing as the original, *Tausend und eine Nacht* did better than *Indigo*. It was picked up by the Volksoper for the following season, and was subsequently given there as late as the 1970s. It was played in several mid-European countries and became a favorite (probably partly because of its opportunity for water-based scenes) at the lakeside theatre at Bregenz (1949, 1959, 1978). The revamping continued, however, and in 1936 *Tausend und eine Nacht* was itself given a reworking as *Eine Nacht am Bosporus* (ad G Heidrich, Ernst Schliepe, Nuremberg 30 August).

Germany: Viktoria-Theater, Berlin 1 September 1871; Hungary: Budai Színkör *Indigo* (Ger) 12 September 1874, Népszínház *Indigo és a nagyven rabló* 28 April 1893; France: Théâtre de la Renaissance *La Reine Indigo* 27 April 1875; USA: Germania Theater (Ger) 7 April 1875, Casino Theater *Indigo* 25 August 1891; UK: Alhambra *King Indigo* 24 September 1877

Recordings: selection (Fox), *Tausend und eine Nacht* complete (Urania)

INTO THE WOODS Musical in 2 acts by James Lapine. Music and lyrics by Stephen Sondheim. Martin Beck Theater, New York, 5 November 1987.

A piece in the vein of the fairy-tale burlesques of Victorian times, *Into the Woods* brought together some familiar nursery-tale characters—along with some other less familiar ones—in a jolly adventure of the Quest variety which didn't stop at its happy ending.

The quest is one imposed upon the Baker (Chip Zien) and his wife (Joanna Gleason) by their neighboring witch (Bernadette Peters), who cursed their family with childlessness after the Baker's naughty father (Tom Aldredge) stole her magic beans. The Baker sets out to get his hands on the cow of Jack the Giantkiller (Ben Wright), the golden slipper of Cinderella (Kim Crosby), the hair of Rapunzel (Pamela Winslow) and the hood of Little Red Riding-Hood (Danielle Ferland). Several dead bodies and a lot of lying and cheating later, the magic is concocted and everyone gets what they wanted—the Baker's Wife gets pregnancy, the Witch gets youth and beauty, Jack a fortune, Rapunzel and Cinderella a Prince apiece (Chuck Wagner, Robert Westenberg), and Cinderella's Ugly Sisters some self-improvement. Unfortunately for them, however, there is another act to go. Happiness cannot be ever-after. One of Jack's beanstalks produces a fresh giant (Merle Louise), the spouse of the last one killed, and as everyone heads off into the woods again, under the pressures of a few more deaths, more lying and more cheating, the happy ending starts to crack up. A little cooperation between Jack and the Baker eventually finishes off Mrs Giant, and at the end of the act the depleted band are left to mull over their experiences and the lessons they have (or ought to have) learned.

The score of the piece included some fine comic moments, topped by a duo for the two Princes suffering egoistic ''Agony'' as they lust over Rapunzel and Cinderella in Act I, and then over the Sleeping Beauty and Snow White in Act II; Little Red Riding-Hood's encounter with an X-rated wolf (''Hello, Little Girl''); Cinderella's Prince's polished line of seduction as practiced on the Baker's Wife (''Any Moment''); and Cinderella's monologue over the same Prince's dirty trick of laying pitch on the palace steps to stop her running away at midnight as per literary tradition. Little Red Riding-Hood headed a lively title song, and the Baker's Wife and the Witch performed the more contemplative and lyrical pieces, of which the Witch's melodious waltz, ''The Last Midnight,'' stood out.

Although the show had moral and social points to make, it stood up—particularly in its first act—perfectly well as a face-value fairy story and, helped by this double-level possibility of appreciation, Broadway's production (which billed six producers above its title) played for almost two years (764 performances), during which time (November 1988) the show went out into the regions. The touring cast included Cleo Laine (Witch), Charlotte Rae (Jack's mother), Kathleen Rowe McAllen (Cinderella), Ray Gill (Baker) and Mary Gordon Murray (Baker's Wife).

David Mirvisch's British production, with Julia McKenzie (Witch), Ian Bartholomew (Baker), Imelda Staunton (Baker's Wife), Mark Tinkler and Clive Carter (Princes) and Jacqueline Dankworth (Cinderella) featured was not given the kind of breath-for-breath restaging usual in the later years of the 20th century. However, it fared less well than its American counterpart, lasting only 186 performances at the Phoenix Theatre. After a German version (ad Michael Kunze) was first seen in Heilbronn in 1990 with Tom Zahner (Baker), Thea Schnering (Baker's Wife) and Esther Stein (Witch), and then at Munich's Theater am Gärtnerplatz (14 April 1991) with Erich Hallhuber, Noemi Nadelmann and Marianne Larsen featured, several other German houses showed interest in the piece, which seems to have found its most appreciative theatre directors in the land of the Brothers Grimm. *Into the Woods* was also taken up for regional production both in America and in Britain, appeared on stage and television in Denmark as *Langt ud i Skoven,* in New Zealand and—after a disastrous saga of walkouts, breakdowns amongst actors and the mechanical scenery, and postponements—in Sydney, where Philip Quast, Tony Sheldon, Judi Connelli and Geraldine Turner featured in a truncated season. It continued on to make itself one of the more frequently produced amongst the musicals of its era, largely in the subsidized theatre. In 1998 it was given a brief return season in London at the Donmar Warehouse (16 November), and another by Australia's Melbourne Theatre Company (17 January).

Germany: Stadttheater, Heilbronn *Ab in den Wald* 31 March 1990; UK: Phoenix Theatre 25 September 1990; Australia: Drama Theatre, Opera House, Sydney 18 March 1993

Recordings: original cast (RCA Victor), London cast (RCA Victor)

IN TOWN Musical farce in 2 acts by Adrian Ross and James Leader (ie, James T Tanner). Music by F Osmond Carr. Prince of Wales Theatre, London, 15 October 1892.

In Town, one of the several shows quoted loosely in the past as being ''the first musical comedy,'' may not have been precisely that, but it was indeed a show which marked a change in policy on the part of George Edwardes, at that time the most powerful and perspicacious producer in a London theatre which had been successfully producing exportable pieces for a number of years. Edwardes and his Gaiety Theatre company, headed by Nellie Farren and Fred Leslie, had run through the heyday of the ''new burlesque'' genre which he and they had initiated, but already, although Leslie was still pulling them in for *Cinder-Ellen Up Too Late* at the Gaiety (without Miss Farren, who was ill), Edwardes's antennae told him that the appeal of the new burlesque—which was no real burlesque, but simply a series of songs, dances and comic scenes played in fantastical costume—was faltering.

He decided on a shift of gear and, in the Prince of Wales Theatre production of *In Town,* he simply presented comic Arthur Roberts and star soprano Florence St John, two solid top-of-the-bill names featured large above the title, in a piece which made no pretense of being a parody or burlesque of anything. It merely presented the same kind of songs and dances as were used in the burlesques in the loose, revusical framework of a little tale peopled by contemporary folk, costumed not in fantastic or period clothes but in smart and attractive modern dress. Roberts was Captain Arthur Coddington, an easy-going man-about-town whose jokey charm is his passe-partout. In the style of a meneur de revue, he leads the young Lord Clanside (Phyllis Broughton in breeches) around the backstage of the Ambiguity Theatre and other important holes of London (mostly night-) life, in spite of the restrictions imposed by the lad's suspicious mother, the Duchess of Duffshire (Maria Davis). Miss St John played Kitty Hetherton, former governess to the Duchess's daughter, who has become an actress after being sacked for attracting the attention of the Duke (Eric Lewis). The second act brought everyone together backstage at the Ambiguity for a barrage of traditional disguises and mistakes, illustrated by the usual parade of songs and dances, before Coddington and Kitty were safely united in time for the final curtain. There was still sufficient real burlesque for those who liked it, for the second act managed to squeeze in a parody of *Romeo and Juliet* as performed on the stage of the Ambiguity Theatre.

The contemporary text joined up the songs and dances at least as well as, if not better than, the old burlesque libretti had done, and it had the advantage of taking in the large topical element of both the comedian's dialogue and of the song lyrics much more comfortably than the old type of book had done. Roberts described himself as a ''Typical Man About Town'' in an Adrian Ross lyric which wholly fitted his character, and dilated over the effects of alcohol in ''Drinks of the Day,'' as well as going through all the extravagances as a Scots Friar Lawrence (''Friar Larry'') in the burlesque and parodying the balcony scene with his co-star. She, as usual, stuck largely to ballads, scoring best with Osmond Carr's pretty ''Dreamless Rest.'' Lewis, too, had a character number, describing his unfortunate penchant for serving girls (''My Propensities Are All the Other Way'') and a topical number about ''The House of Lords''—a pair of pieces which pretty well exemplified the range of entertainment the show had to offer.

In Town was far from being a finished musical farce. It had some defined characters, with some songs and scenes which matched their characterizations, but at other times it leaned strongly towards being as much of a variety show as the later burlesques had been. This tendency was not diminished by Roberts who, often tipsy and almost always unbridled in his performances, ad libbed and interpolated fairly fresh and frankly old material freely. One of his additions was his own version of Vesta Victoria's music-hall hit ''Daddy Wouldn't Buy Me a Bow-Wow,'' to which he added topical verses, often of his own making. Later, in an openly revusical manner, Edwardes added some specialities into the theatrical scenes of the second act. Amongst these were included skirt-dancer Loie Fuller and 17-year-old impressionist Cissie Loftus.

The new mixture confused and displeased some of the critics, but it pleased the public, who were also pleased by the display of up-to-date fashion in which both the beautiful girls and the men of the cast were displayed. The clothes were from London fashion houses, and thus the stalls audience, at least, could, if they wished, purchase copies of the models worn by their favorite performers.

The death of Leslie precipitated the end of the new burlesque and, more immediately, the closure of *Cinder-Ellen* at the Gaiety Theatre. Edwardes had planned his all-important Gaiety Christmas show around his biggest star, and now he was stuck. So he transferred *In Town* from the Prince of Wales to the Gaiety, where it broke the line of burlesques which had held the stage there since *Dorothy* and where it played happily through till the summer (292 performances) before being sent on the road in two companies. Its success encouraged the producer to continue the modern-dress style of show—although he persisted with burlesque, in parallel, a little longer—and it was his second and rather more vertebrate musical comedy, *A Gaiety Girl,* with a score by *In Town*'s conductor, Sidney Jones, again produced at the Prince of Wales Theatre, which confirmed the way that he would go in his later productions.

In Town's out-of-town assignments soon took in the colonies, notably with Edwardes's own tour of 1895 which, having played *A Gaiety Girl* in America, continued to Australia with a repertoire including *In Town.* Louis Bradfield, who had succeeded Roberts at the Gaiety, starred alongside Gilbert and Sullivan's Casilda, Decima Moore. Two years later Edwardes put together another company to take the show to America, with Bradfield sharing top billing with Minnie Hunt. It played two weeks in London, then crossed the Atlantic, but Edwardes himself had by now shown Broadway his later pieces and *In Town* seemed already démodé. It played only 40 Broadway performances.

Australia: Princess Theatre, Melbourne 4 May 1895; USA: Knickerbocker Theater 6 September 1897

IOLANTHE, or The Peer and the Peri Comic (fairy) opera in 2 acts by W S Gilbert. Music by Arthur Sullivan. Savoy Theatre, London, 25 November 1882.

The first new Gilbert and Sullivan opera to be produced at Richard D'Oyly Carte's freshly built Savoy

Theatre, *Iolanthe* came along behind the team's great run of international successes with *HMS Pinafore, The Pirates of Penzance* and *Patience,* and, if it did not prove (to start with, anyway) quite as extravagantly exportable as they had done, it certainly became every bit as popular as its predecessors in the English-speaking theatres of the world. Following the nautical, melodramatic and aesthetic burlesques of the previous three shows, Gilbert decided on a burlesque of faërie, an area to which he had always shown a particular attachment (*The Wicked World, The Palace of Truth, Creatures of Impulse*), and—with a little reuse of some of the conceits from his older fairy-cum-politics burlesque *The Happy Land*—he built his characters and his plot around the now fairly settled core of D'Oyly Carte's Savoy Theatre company.

Jessie Bond played Iolanthe, a well-loved fairy who had, some years previously, married a mortal and borne him a son. This sort of thing being against fairy law, the Queen (Alice Barnett) was reluctantly forced to banish her from fairyland, but after a quarter of a century she feels able to relent and Iolanthe is summoned home, still looking not a fairy day over the age of 16. This causes a problem when Phyllis (Leonora Braham), an Arcadian shepherdess and ward-in-chancery beloved by Iolanthe's Arcadian shepherd son, Strephon (Richard Temple), as well as by the entire British House of Lords, sees the pair embracing. The distraught Phyllis, believing Strephon unfaithful, agrees to marry the House of Lords, and, in revenge for this mortal insult to a semi-fairy, the Fairy Queen calls upon her magic powers to put Strephon into the House of Commons, there to wreak havoc amongst British Institutions with the use of fairy logic. However, when the Lord Chancellor of England (George Grossmith) finally decides that it is commensurate with his position to marry Phyllis himself, Iolanthe can be quiet no longer, for the Chancellor is her long-lost husband and Strephon's father. Alas, by breaking her silence she has again broken fairy law and this time her Queen must doom her to die. However, it seems that all her fairy sisters have been busy, during Act II, breaking fairy law with the House of Lords as well. A swift redrafting of the fairy law in question by that experienced legal juggler, the Chancellor, serves to avert wholesale slaughter in fairyland and to legalize the tie-up of peers and peris for a happy ending.

Grossmith had one of his best roles as the Lord Chancellor, equipped with some of Gilbert and Sullivan's nippiest patter songs: his self-explanatory "The Law Is the True Embodiment," his declaration of principle "When I Went to the Bar (as a very young man)" and, most memorably, his nonsensical Nightmare Song, a cacophony of images of a sleepless, love-racked night. The imposing Alice Barnett as the booming Queen of the Fairies was also equipped with some of the Gilbert and Sullivan canon's best contralto moments, powering down her fairy thunders on the naughty peers ("bearded by these puny mortals") or giving her girls a lesson in sexual self-control ("O Foolish Fay"). Baritone Temple, used to playing fathers, and the Captain Corcoran, Pirate King and Colonel Calverley of the last three musicals, found himself unusually cast as the juvenile lead, since tenor Durward Lely and Rutland Barrington took the parts of the most forward members of the House of Lords, a group burlesqued with the green vigor that Gilbert always applied to the inherited position he clearly envied bitterly. In an unusual step, however, Gilbert wrote just one of his characters in this show in an entirely unburlesque manner. Iolanthe herself was presented as a wholly sentimental character with genuine rather than parodied emotions, and her love was presented in a wholly different way to that of the randy peers, the skittish fairies and even of the ever-so-Arcadian juveniles. And yet, such was the skill of the writer that neither her character nor her sentiments seemed out of place in the show's inherently comical tale.

Carte's production of *Iolanthe* was a splendid one, and the settings of Arcadia and, particularly, of the Thames Embankment and the Houses of Parliament, Johnnie D'Auban's show-stopping dance routine to the three peers' trio "Nothing Venture, Nothing Win," and the little electric lights which glittered in the hair of the fairies, all added materially to the success of the show. This success, however, did not stop some post-production alterations. Temple and Barrington both lost solos in the aftermath of opening night as the piece was trimmed to svelter proportions, preparatory to an initial run of 13 months and 398 performances at the Savoy.

As part of his continuing battle against theatrical piracy, Carte opened *Iolanthe* simultaneously in Britain and America. On Broadway J H Ryley added another Grossmith role to his list as the Chancellor and several other British artists, Lyn Cadwaladr (Tolloller), Augusta Roche (Queen) and Arthur Wilkinson (Mountararat), were joined by Americans Marie Jansen (Iolanthe), Sallie Reber (Phyllis) and the expatriate William T Carleton (Strephon) at the head of the cast under the imported-for-the-occasion direction of Charles Harris and baton of Alfred Cellier. The show was well received, the burlesque houses leaped into action with such perversions as the San Francisco Minstrels' *Hide-and-Lengthy, or The Steer and the Peri* (W S Mullaly/Frank Dumont, 9 January 1883), Philadelphia, Boston and the other main theatrical centers of the country quickly had their "by permission" *Iolanthe*s on the boards—Carte went quickly to court to stop any that weren't "by permission"—and *Iolanthe* was confirmed as a thorough winner. However, even though the welcome in other parts of the country was swingeingly enthusiastic, the opéra-bouffe fairies and the parody of the British Parliament did not raise quite the same merriment amongst New Yorkers that the lustier burlesque of *Pinafore* and *Pirates* or the particular parody of *Patience* had done, even when, half a dozen weeks into the run, the electric lights (up to then held in reserve!) were added to the fairies' coiffures. And so, rather than totting up a vast run, *Iolanthe* played just a respectable 105 increased-prices performances at the Standard Theater, plus a return season at the Fifth Avenue, whilst the Boston Bijou's superior mounting soared on towards its 150th night and the British production continued on past its 200th. In later years, however, *Iolanthe*'s New York popularity was eventually given its imprimatur. The show was brought back several times to Broadway, being produced by the Shuberts and William Brady at the Casino (12 May 1913) with De Wolf Hopper as the Chancellor (40 performances) and then, with the length of run that it had not been allowed first time round, by Winthrop Ames at the Plymouth Theater (19 April 1926), when it notched up a stretch of 355 performances—a run rarely bettered by a Gilbert and Sullivan production on Broadway.

Iolanthe quickly became and remained a favorite in the Gilbert and Sullivan repertoire in the British provinces and in the colonies. It was particularly successful in Australia, where a largely imported cast featuring Robert Brough (Chancellor), his wife Florence Trevallyan (Queen), returned Australian star Emma Chambers (Iolanthe) and W H Woodfield (Mountararat), with local heroine Nellie Stewart as Phyllis, set the piece rolling in 1885. Over the next half-century J C Williamson and his associates played the piece regularly, with both Alice Barnett and Leonora Braham repeating their original roles in different seasons as the piece established itself as one of the most popular of all comic operas on the Australian stage.

Following the release of the Gilbert and Sullivan copyrights in Britain, *Iolanthe* was the first of the Savoy canon to be given a major London production, when the Sadler's Wells Opera staged a production (24 January 1962) featuring Eric Shilling (Chancellor), Heather Begg (Queen) and Elizabeth Harwood (Phyllis), and *Iolanthe* hoisted another first when it was selected to open the initial season of the reformed D'Oyly Carte Opera Company in 1987, subsequently becoming the most effective part of the new company's repertoire.

USA: Standard Theater 25 November 1882; Australia: Theatre Royal, Melbourne 9 May 1885

Recordings: complete (Decca, Angel, HMV, TER), Sadlers Wells 1962 (HMV), etc

Videos: Brent-Walker 1982, CBC 1984

IRENE Musical comedy in 2 acts by James Montgomery based on his play *Irene O'Dare.* Lyrics by Joseph McCarthy. Music by Harry Tierney. Vanderbilt Theater, New York, 18 November 1919.

The most successful American musical comedy of its time, *Irene* was a powerful force in setting in motion the fashion for the ingenuous, modern-day Cinderella shows (poor-girl-wins-rich-boy) which inundated Broadway in the early and middle 1920s, and from which *Sally* and *Mary* emerged as some of the other happiest examples.

The show was evolved from a James Montgomery play, *Irene O'Dare,* which had foundered on the road to Broadway in 1916 but which, like many another contemporaneous play of limited success, was nevertheless picked up to be made into a musical. The picking up was done by producer Carle Carleton, whose lady friend, ingenue Edith Day, had been appearing in the highly successful musical version of another Montgomery play, *Going Up,* and the author remolded his play into a libretto with the young performer in mind. Miss Day was also instrumental in the choice of the show's songwriters, for it was her friend Anna Held who suggested—and she suggested to Carleton—that an opportunity be given to the little-tried composer Harry Tierney, who had provided Miss Held with a bundle of songs for her 1916 vehicle, *Follow Me,* and his newest lyric-writing partner, Joseph McCarthy.

Irene O'Dare (Miss Day) is an unmoneyed New York Irish lass from Ninth Avenue who attracts the attentions of the wealthy Donald Marshall (Walter Regan) when she is sent to his Long Island mansion on an upholstering job. Donald arranges for Irene and her friends Helen (Eva Puck) and Eleanor (Bernice McCabe) to go to work as models in the fashion house run by Madame Lucy (Bobbie Watson), and the girls are obliged to pass themselves off as ladies at a society party as part of Donald's efforts to launch the couturier. The upwardly striving J P Bowden (Arthur Burckly) pursues Irene, but when the truth of her origins emerges he wriggles away, leaving her to a happy ending with Donald. Dorothy Walters played Irene's canny Irish mother and Florence Hills was the aristocratic Mrs Marshall.

The highlight of *Irene*'s pretty score was the heroine's description of her "Alice-Blue Gown" (alice-blue was a shade of pale blue, allegedly linked to Alice Roosevelt), a sweet little piece which became an enduring favorite, whilst a lilting title song, the remake of a bit of Chopin's Minute Waltz as "Castle of Dreams," the jolly determination of the girls to be "The Talk of the Town" and a neat variation on the party type of song, "The Last Part of Every Party," were other popular musical items.

Carleton's production of *Irene* played for 670 performances at the little Vanderbilt Theater, setting up a long-run record on Broadway as Edith Day was succeeded first by Adele Rowland and then by Patti Harrold in the title role. Miss Day, in the meanwhile, crossed to London and there starred in Joe Sacks's production of her show, at the Empire Theatre, alongside Pat Somerset (Donald), Robert Hale (Mme Lucy), Robert Michaelis (Bowden), Margaret Campbell (Helen) and Daisy Hancox (Eleanor). It was another successful production, which played for over a year in the West End (399 performances) before it went on the road.

Even before this, *Irene* had made her way into Europe, where Budapest's Lujza Blaha Színház mounted what sounded like a rather unfamiliar version of the show. It was entitled *A tündérek cselédje* (''the fairy-like servant-girl,'' ad Ernő Kulinyi), and advertised as a ''latvanyos amerikai operett'' (spectacular American operetta). However, although the show was also, and much later, played in Vienna, it was in the English language that it made and maintained its greatest popularity.

In Sydney, where *Irene* was produced by the Tait brothers with Dorothy South as its heroine, Chester Clute as Lucy and Robert Jewett as Donald, the show was hit by an opening-night chorus strike. The handful of the chorus who went on were lustily cheered, the evening was an enormous hit and the production went on to pass its 100th night (1 November) before moving on in December to the rest of the country, and to a Melbourne season (Her Majesty's Theatre 9 April 1921) under the J C Williamson banner.

In spite of being followed onto the Broadway and British stages by a regular band of like shows, *Irene* survived as the most appealing of her kind, and she returned to the main English-speaking centers on a number of occasions. London impresario Jack Hylton followed in Carleton's steps when he mounted a revival of *Irene* in London in 1945 with his girlfriend Pat Taylor starred in the title role and, although the show ran less long this time, he had better luck than Carleton on the personal front. In spite of marrying Miss Day, her producer had quickly (if briefly) lost her to her West End leading man, Pat Somerset, in a shower of newspaper paragraphs. Hylton was already married . . . to someone else.

More than 50 years after its original production, the show had a second success, equal to that of its first run, when, encouraged by Montgomery's widow, Harry Rigby, Albert Selden and Jerome Minskoff mounted a revised version of *Irene* on Broadway in 1973 (Minskoff Theater 13 March). The libretto had been adapted by Rigby, Hugh Wheeler and Joseph Stein, with boring old J P Bowden disappearing completely from a story which was otherwise largely the same, and the score had been enlarged from its original 13 pieces (6 of which vanished) with the addition of a number of other songs to which lyricist McCarthy had contributed (''What Do You Want to Make Those Eyes at Me For?,'' ''They Go Wild, Simply Wild Over Me,'' ''You Made Me Love You,'' and another Chopin derivative ''I'm Always Chasing Rainbows'') plus several pieces by Charles Gaynor and Otis Clements and other modern hands.

Debbie Reynolds starred as Irene (now a piano tuner rather than an upholsterer), alongside Monte Markham (Donald), George S Irving (Mme Lucy) and Patsy Kelly (Mrs O'Dare), and the colorful production of this new version of the show played 605 Broadway performances, with Jane Powell succeeding Miss Reynolds in the later part of the run. The new *Irene* underwent further revisions before it was produced in Australia (Her Majesty's Theatre, Sydney 25 May 1974) with Julie Anthony (Irene), Noel Ferrier (Mme Lucy) and Robert Colman (Donald) featured, and with very considerable success. After a two months' Sydney season, it toured, played seven months in Melbourne (Her Majesty's Theatre 14 September 1974), and ultimately returned for a second Sydney season (2 May 1975), this time of five months. Further revisions to this version set in prior to Harold Fielding's production being mounted in London, with Miss Anthony repeating her down-under role in the West End alongside Jon Pertwee (Mme Lucy) and Eric Flynn (Donald). Patricia Michael succeeded to the title role as the show ran out the 974 performances which gave *Irene* its longest-ever run.

Irene was filmed in 1926 by First National with Colleen Moore as a silent Irene and George K Arthur as a silent Madame Lucy, and again in 1940 with Anna Neagle starred alongside Ray Milland, Alan Marshal and Roland Young.

UK: Empire Theatre 7 April 1920; Hungary: Lujza Blaha Színház *A tündérek cselédje* 23 October 1921; Austria: Rextheater 24 June 1946; Australia: Criterion Theatre, Sydney 7 August 1920

Films: First National 1926, RKO 1940

Recordings: original London cast (Monmouth-Evergreen), 1973 revival cast (Columbia), London revival cast (EMI)

IRMA LA DOUCE Musical play in 2 acts by Alexandre Breffort based on his story of the same name. Music by Marguerite Monnot. Théâtre Gramont, Paris, 12 November 1956.

The tale of *Irma la Douce,* the ultimate tart with the heart of gold, began as a short story written by Alexandre Breffort (d Paris, 23 February 1971) for the strivingly satirical French newspaper *Le Canard enchaîné.* Breffort subsequently adapted the piece as a sketch, and then finally as a stage musical illustrated with songs by Marguerite Monnot, whose only previous venture into the domain had been with a scoreful of songs for Edith Piaf's musical-comedy venture *La P'tite Lili.*

Plate 188. **Irma La Douce.** *A bunch of ''mecs'' get into the ''argot.''*

The show is narrated by Bob le Hotu (René Dupuy, also director), the patron of the Bar des Inquiets in the back streets of Pigalle, the hangout of the folk of the ''milieu,'' the ''poules'' (whores) and their flashy ''mecs'' (chaps/pimps). Nestor-le-Fripé (Michel Roux), a law student studying the milieu, comes to the bar one day and, before he leaves, finds he has, in the nicest possible way, become the mec of a little poule called Irma la Douce (Colette Renard). The lovers settle down together, but Irma does not give up her lucrative employment. Nestor tries not to be niggled, but he is. Finally, he disguises himself behind a beard as an elderly gent called Oscar and books Irma exclusively, paying her 10,000 francs a visit, 10,000 francs which go from Oscar, to Irma, to Nestor, to Oscar, and then round again. He has to take a job cleaning floors to bring in the money Irma thinks she is bringing in, and finally the double schedule becomes too much for him. He decides to kill Oscar off. It all goes wrong. Nestor is arrested for murder, tried in a surreal court and finally sentenced to Devil's Island along with all the other mecs. They escape, paddle across the seas to Paris, and reach home. But since they had no razors on their raft, Nestor gets home bearded, and Irma greets him . . . as Oscar! If Oscar is alive, then Nestor has been wrongly condemned. When he is pardoned, the razor comes out and Oscar can disappear once more. The happy ending is crowned by Irma giving birth to twins, one for each father.

Monnot's songs were a characterful, winning lot in the pure tradition of the French chanson which she had exploited so brilliantly in her work with Piaf. Irma fell in love over ''Me v'là, te v'là'' and ''Avec les anges'' (both w Nestor), bounced out a joyous ''Ah! Dis-donc, dis-donc'' at finding her rich protector, and came to the imprisoned Nestor in his dreams with ''Irma la Douce.'' Nestor looked at his overworked double self in ''La cave à Irma'' and bemoaned his imprisonment in ''L'aventure est morte,'' and the mecs indulged in the ''Valse milieu,'' doubled as Irma's admiring customers with ''Elle a du chien,'' chorused their admiration of her working-girl's success in ''To Be or Not to Be'' and of her double giving birth in ''Il est né, le môme à Irma,'' and longed for home in ''Y'a que Paris pour ça.''

Irma la Douce proved a singular hit at the little Théâtre Gramont, band singer Colette Renard became a star in short time, the show's songs became the rage and, as *Irma la Douce* ran through its more than two years of Parisian performances, shifting up to the larger Théâtre de l'Athénée part way through the run, it was taken up by overseas producers in a way that few French shows had been since the passing of the Jazz Age musical comedy.

A year-and-a-half into the Paris run, an English-language version of *Irma la Douce* opened in London. Bandleader Henry Hall had seen the show in Paris and snapped up the English rights, and he sublet them to Donald Albery's Donmar Productions and to H M Tennent Ltd, who mounted the piece at the West End's Lyric Theatre. The very special argot which gave the French *Irma la Douce* so much of its character had seemed almost impossible to reproduce in another language, but David Heneker, Julian More and Monty Norman not only succeeded in this tricky task, they succeeded so well that eventually the English-language *Irma* went on to become even more popular than the original French one. Britain's *Irma,* directed by Peter Brook, featured Elizabeth Seal in its title role, with Keith Michell as Nestor, Clive Revill as Bob and Ronnie Barker, Frank Olegario, Julian Orchard and Gary Raymond amongst the mecs, ''Avec les anges'' became ''Our Language of Love,'' and the show proved a copper-bottomed hit through 1,512 performances in the West End before going around Britain.

The London production was remounted (with a handful of alterations, including some more Broadwayish orchestrations) in America, with Michell, Revill and Miss Seal repeating their roles in a cast which also included George S Irving, Elliott Gould and Stuart Damon, under the management of David Merrick. The London success was repeated, Miss Seal took the year's Tony Award (in a season which included *Bye Bye Birdie, Camelot* and *Carnival*) and *Irma la Douce* graced Broadway for 524 performances before going on the road, with Taina Elg and Denis Quilley in the starring roles.

Australia's *Irma la Douce* underwent a postponement when leading lady Judith Bruce fell ill, but show and star both proved worth waiting for, and when *Irma* opened, with Kevin Colson (Nestor) and Noel Ferrier (Bob) sharing top billing, at Sydney's Theatre Royal, it ran 12 weeks before moving on to Melbourne's Comedy Theatre (17 June 1961) and to cities beyond.

Translation eventually proved to be no problem at all, and the English language was not the only one to have its *Irma* adaptation. In 1961 a German-language version (ad Ivo Kohorte, Hanns Bernhardt) was produced at Baden-Baden, with Margit Saad as Irma, and Harald Juhnke as Nestor then, the following year, at Munich's Theater die kleine Freiheit (14 February 1962) with Hanne Wieder and Harald Leipnitz, and at Berlin's Theater des Westens under the management of Rolf Kutschera with Violetta Ferrari in the title role. In 1964 an Hungarian *Irma, te édes* (ad Erzsébet Mágori, Tamás Ungvári, Tamás Blum) was produced in Budapest, and in 1966 the Theater an der Wien hosted a 45-performance season of the German production with Ferrari and Ernst Stankovsky (Nestor).

After widespread regional productions all round the world through a decade, *Irma* made reappearances in several main centers. Colette Renard took up her old role, alongside Dupuy and Franck Fernandel as Nestor, in a revival at the Théâtre de l'Athénée in 1967 which brought *Irma*'s Parisian total up to 932 performances. This total which was further increased by another mounting, at the Théâtre Fontaine, in 1977 (18 June, 69 performances), in which Joëlle Vauthier and Georges Belier teamed with the still present Dupuy, and again by one in 2000 (19 April), when Clotilde Courau, Arnaud Giovannineti and Patrick Rocca featured in a season at the Théâtre Nationale de Chaillot.

Sydney saw the piece again when it was staged at the Marian Street Theatre in 1975 (31 January), and London witnessed a brief second showing in 1979 when an underpar production featuring Helen Gelzer, Charles Dance and Bernard Spear was mounted at the Shaftesbury Theatre (27 November). Although the show has not appeared subsequently in London or New York, it continues to be played regionally, and was the subject of a major provincial revival in France in 1992, with Sophie Destaing and Eric Boucher in the leading roles, of a Budapest revival in 1991 (Józsefvárosi Színház) with Éva Vándor as Irma and Imre Harmath as Nestor, of a Vienna showing in 1998 (Volkstheater 2 April) and of regular revival seasons in German theatres.

A film version of *Irma la Douce,* which featured Shirley MacLaine and Jack Lemmon as Irma and Nestor, dropped both the concept of the stage piece and the songs.

UK: Lyric Theatre 17 July 1958; USA: Plymouth Theater 29 September 1960; Australia: Theatre Royal, Sydney 25 February 1961; Germany: Theater der Stadt, Baden-Baden 24 January 1961, Theater des Westens, Berlin 6 March 1962; Hungary: Fővárosi Operettszínház *Irma, te édes* 4 November 1964; Austria: Theater an der Wien 9 March 1966

Recordings: original cast star, French revival cast, complete w dialogue (Vega), London cast (Philips), Broadway cast (Columbia), South African cast (Plum), Israeli cast (CBS), Dutch cast (Artone), etc

IRVING, Ethel [IRVING, Frances Emily] (b Greenwich, 5 September 1869; d Bexhill, 3 May 1963). Dancer and soubrette in turn-of-the-century musicals who went on to a fine career in plays.

''Birdie'' Irving was the daughter of Joseph Henry Irving (d Greenwich, 6 September 1870) of the Strand, Haymarket, Surrey, Drury Lane and Olympic Theatres, a popular young actor whose greatest success had come in his portrayal of *David Copperfield*'s Uriah Heep. His death, a year after her birth, provoked a flood of friendly subscriptions from the profession to help support his destitute widow, soubrette Eunice IRVING (b 1840), and their young children. However, the family's future was assured when the eldest daughter of that family, Eunice McLewee IRVING (b Edinburgh, c1858), became in her mid-teens the de facto wife of the celebrated music-hall performer ''The Great'' VANCE [Alfred Peck STEVENS] (b London, c1838; d London, 26 December 1888), herself performing on the music-hall stage and later in musicals (Kitty Kettleby in *Little Jack Sheppard* 1884, Régina in *La Princesse de Trébizonde* 1892, *Little Puck* USA, Paquita in *The Voyage of Suzette* USA, etc) under the name **Eunice VANCE.** Another sister, Elsie, worked successfully as a dancer.

''Birdie'' began her career touring with her sister, and with Vance, in his musical comedy *Flirting* (1884) before going on to join the chorus at the Gaiety Theatre, where she appeared in *Little Jack Sheppard* (1886, Kitty, t/o Winifred Wood), and in the dancing roles of Valentine and Victorine in *Monte Cristo Jr* (1886). She took over the small dance role of Lady Betty in *Dorothy* at the Prince of Wales, played in Ivan Caryll's supporting operetta *Jubilation* (1888) and appeared for George Edwardes as principal dancer in *Ruy Blas and the Blasé Roué* (1889) and for Henry Leslie in *The Red Hussar* (1890), both in London and then on Broadway. She remained in America for six years, but the only evidence of her appearing on stage comes in July 1892 when she appeared on the Casino Roof Garden, now billed as Ethel Irving, playing alongside her now thoroughly established music-hall sister.

On returning to Britain, ''Ethel'' returned to the management of George Edwardes, who sent her on tour in Letty Lind's role of Molly in *The Geisha,* and then brought her to Daly's to replace Gracie Leigh in the comedy role of Dudley in *San Toy.* Edwardes then featured her as Sophie in *A Country Girl* (1902, ''Two Little Chicks'') and in the title role of *The Girl from Kays* (1902, Winnie Harborough), and she starred opposite Willie Edouin in *Sergeant Brue* (1904, Lady Bickenhall) for Frank Curzon before being inveigled into an amateurish flop called *Ladyland* (1904, Alma Molyneux). At this stage she began to mix plays with her musicals and, after playing the leading lady part of the tempting actress La Boléro in *Mr Popple of Ippleton* (1905) opposite G P Huntley, and the Contessa di Ravolgi in Curzon's unsuccessful *The Three Kisses* (1907), she was cast in a part which, legend insists, nobody wanted: the startling title role of Somerset Maugham's *Lady Frederick.* The sensation which she caused in this role set her on a major career as a straight actress, and she did not return to the musical theatre.

Miss Irving was married to vocalist **Gilbert [James] PORTEOUS** (b London, 19 May 1868; d London, 6 September 1928) who appeared on the British stage in *Nanon* (1888, Lucien), *La Cigale* (1891, William), in minor roles the original casts of *A Gaiety Girl* (1893, Lance) and *An Artist's Model* (1895, Apthorpe), in *The Geisha* (tour 1897, Imari), *The Ballet Girl* (1897, Eugene Taradelle), *A Runaway Girl* (1899, tour Brother Tamarind), *San Toy* (1900, tour Yen How), in the original production of *A Country Girl* (1902 t/o Douglas Verity), *The School Girl* (1903, Corner) and *Sergeant Brue* (1904, Mr Crank), and latterly in nonsinging roles.

IRVING, George S [SHELASKY, George Irving] (b Springfield, Mass, 1 November 1922). Versatile Broadway character man who compiled the kind of substantial musical-theatre career which has become rare in an era of long runs and shy (''I-can't-possibly-sign-for-six-months—there-just-might-be-a-film-offer'') actors.

After working in musical shows on the road, at the St Louis Muny (The Foreign Gentleman in America's premiere of *Glamorous Night,* etc) and at New Jersey's Paper Mill Playhouse, Irving first played in New York in the choruses of *Oklahoma!* and *Lady in the Dark.* After the Second World War he appeared in London and Paris with the company playing Menotti's *The Telephone* and *The Medium,* and he subsequently mixed revue and musical appearances, appearing in a multiple role in the fantasy *That's the Ticket* (1948), creating the roles of Roger Gage in *Gentlemen Prefer Blondes* (1949) and Dario in *Me and Juliet* (1953), taking over from Hans Conried as Boris in *Can-Can,* and introducing the role of the producer, Larry Hastings, in *Bells Are Ringing* (1956).

He subsequently appeared in *The Beggar's Opera* (Peachum), *Shinbone Alley* (Big Bill), *Lock Up Your Daughters* (Sotmore), the 1960 revival of *Oh, Kay!* (t/o McGee), *Irma la Douce* (Inspector), *Tovarich* (Charles Davis), *Bravo Giovanni* (Bellardi), *Street Scene* (Carl Olsen), and in *Anya* (Chernov), as well as in the road-closed *Comedy* (Captain Cockalorum) and a number of plays. He made a hit within a hit when he played the principal comedy role of Madame Lucy in the long-running revival of *Irene* (1973, Tony Award), and appeared in the short-lived *So Long, 174th Street* (1976) before going on to star alongside Liv Ullmann in Richard Rodgers's *I Remember Mama* (1979, Uncle Chris). He succeeded to the role of the Major-General in *The Pirates of Penzance* (1981) and played Mr Micawber in the short-lived *Copperfield* (1981) on Broadway, appeared at the New York City Opera in *Regina, The Good Soldier Schweik, Street Scene* and *The Ballad of Baby Doe,* and was then featured as Sergei Alexandrovitch in the 1983 revival of *On Your Toes* and as Sir John Tremayne in Broadway's *Me and My Girl* (1986–88). He has also appeared regionally in a number of other musicals, including a 1990 production of *Fanny* at the Paper Mill Playhouse. He played the King in *Cinderella* (1993) and Baron Zeta in *The Merry Widow* (1994) with the New York City Opera, and appeared in a concert performance of *Louisiana Purchase* at Carnegie Hall (Sentaor Oliver P Loganberry) in 1996.

Irving is married to actress and dancer Maria Karnilova.

IRWIN, May [CAMPBELL, Georgia] (b Whitby, Ontario, 27 June 1862; d New York, 22 October 1938). Top-notch coon-shouter and comedienne, the energetic Miss Irwin spent a decade of stardom touring in custom-made vehicles.

May Irwin began performing at the age of 12, in a vaudeville act with her sister, Flo IRWIN [Ada May CAMPBELL] (b Whitby, Ontario, 21 March, ?1863; d Los Angeles, 20 December 1930), and the pair joined Tony Pastor's burlesque company two years later. They remained with Pastor for six years, singing and dancing (and with May occasionally playing the cornet) in such pieces as Jacques Kruger's *Duno's Picnic* (1881), the burlesque *The Pie-Rats of Penn Yan* (May was Ruthie and Flo played Little Freddie), and the house burlesques of *School* (1881, May was stupid Sally Smithers, Flo was demure Jennie Roberts), of *Olivette* (1881, May was Bathilde and Flora played Valentine), of *Patience* (1882, May as Jane Jemima, Flo as Grosvenor) and of *La Mascotte* (May was Bettina and Flo played Pippo) and other current hits.

May moved on from Pastor's to spend the next three years playing comic soubrettes with Augustin Daly's famous dramatic company (Popham in *The Magistrate,* Susan in *A Night Off,* Becky in *Nancy and Co,* Caroline in *Needles and Pins,* etc). In the years that followed she mixed farce-comedy and vaudeville engagements, touring with Flo in the farce-comedy *Fashions* (1888) and J J McNally's sketch *Army Tactics* (1889), with Richard Golden in *Old Jed Prouty* (1889, Martha ''Last Thursday Night''), again alongside Flo in *The City Directory* (1890, Prima Donna Gaiety) and *Boys and Girls* (1891, Madame Alert, ''Oh What a Difference in the Morning''), featuring as Ophelia (singing ''Daddy Wouldn't Buy Me a Bow-Wow'') in the British Oscar Wilde burlesque *The Poet and the Puppets* (1893, Ophelia) and appearing in the play *The Junior Partner* (1892, ie, Bisson's *La Souricière*) before becoming a top-of-the-bill name in Rich and Harris's production of *A Country Sport* (1893, Elizabeth Alwright, singing her own ''Mamie, Come and Kiss Your Honey Boy'').

However, it was as Beatrice Byke in *The Widow Jones,* played at the Bijou Theater in 1895, that May truly made her name, notably with the huge hit made with the splendidly vigorous coon song known as the—or very quickly, as May Irwin's—Bully Song. She followed up in a string of like vehicles, playing in *Courted into Court* (1896) and the title roles in *The Swell Miss Fitzswell* (1897, Countess de Cagiac), *Kate Kip, Buyer* (1898 ''Ef Yo' Ain't Got No Money Yo' Needn't Come Around,'' ''Since My Hair Turned Red''), *Sister Mary* (1899), *Madge Smith, Attorney* (1900), *Mrs Black Is Back* (1904 and silent film 1914) and *Mrs Wilson That's All* (1906, ''Moonshine''), all played at Broadway's Bijou Theater and toured under her own management, and all of which gave further opportunities to the plump and popular comedienne to supply her public with the lusty, loud and low-comic mixture expected from her.

When her most popular days as a star-billed singing comedienne were over, she continued to play in comedy and vaudeville, and toured lengthily in such pieces as *Getting a Polish* (1910, Mrs Jim Griggs delivering ''Teaching McFadyen to Waltz'' and ''That Opera Rag'') and *Widow by Proxy* (1913, ''The Kellys Are at It Again''). She returned to New York in *Number 33 Washington Square* in 1915—and, in the course of its Broadway run, infiltrated ''Araby,'' ''I've Been Floating Down the Old Green River'' and ''Picture Me Down Home in Tennessee'' into what was originally a straight comedy—and, after her 1919 vehicle *Raising the Aunty* (Alicia Penn) closed prematurely in the country, in 1922 fulfilled a last Broadway engagement in a musical in *The 49ers.*

In 1896 May filmed ''The Kiss'' for Edison Vitascope. Her osculatory encounter with John C Rice proved an eye-opener to the public, who patronized ''May Irwin's Kiss'' in such a way as to make it one of the most popular of all early filmlets.

Flo Irwin, too, continued a useful career as a topliner in musical-theatre entertainments, going on from burlesque to appear in operetta (Fritellini in *La Mascotte* with Nat Goodwin), farce comedy—*The City Directory* (1890, Minerva Flats), *Boys and Girls* (1891, Mollie Fyer), *A Good Thing* (1896, Sadie Bradbury), etc—as a vaudeville topliner (Totty Shortribs in *Gayest Manhattan, The Gay Miss Con,* etc), and in such character roles in musical comedy as Lalage Potts in *Gentleman Joe* (1896), her sister's part in *The Widow Jones, The Swell Miss Fitzswell,* the title role in *Miss Kidder* (1901, ''That's Nothing'') and Catherine in *Madame Sherry* (1911), etc.

ISIDORA Comic opera in 3 acts by Carmini Morley (?). Music by Luscombe Searelle. Bijou Theatre, Melbourne, 7 July 1885.

A dramatic-comic spectacular light opera apparently from the pen of New Zealand's Carmini Morley (ex-tenor, ex-of San Francisco, at that time a Dunedin singing teacher) and with music by Luscombe Searelle, *Isidora* was first seen in Australia at the beginning of a career which would take it first to New Zealand, then to South Africa, and finally to the West End of London, under the guidance and promotion of its extravagant author. The story of the piece was a hotchpotch of operatic elements from *Lucia di Lammermoor* to *The Flying Dutchman.* Set in Cuba in the year 1550, it had for its heroine Isidora, the supposed daughter of estate owner Patronio, who is in love with fisherman Felix but is intended by her father for a wealthy nobleman. Felix and chief comedian Jacob set out on a get-rich-quick search for the legendary treasure of the Black Rover, but the mysterious Rover appears and carries everyone off to his ship for what threatens to be a sticky end. Then Isidora opportunely remembers a song she's been trying to remember all night. It is the lullaby her mother sang to her before she sank to her death under the prow of the Black Rover's ship, and its singing breaks the spell which binds the Rover to earth. He comes back in the third act, however—after Isidora's mad scene (with aria)—to protect her from a local revolution, before all ultimately ends happily.

Australian producers Majeroni and Wilson produced *Isidora* in Melbourne with Gracie Plaisted in the title role, Edwin Kelly (once of Kelly and Leon's ministrels) as the Black Rover, Charles Harding as Felix, Kelly's son, Edwin Lester as Jacob and the composer at the baton. It won some praise and went on to be played alongside such pieces as *La Périchole* and *Maritana* in the Majeroni/Wilson company's repertoire in Sydney (New Opera House 23 August), before Searelle pushed on with further productions, mostly under his own management. He ultimately got the piece to the stage in London in 1890 under the title *The Black Rover.* London proved less attracted to the melodramatic fate of Isidora as played by Mrs Searelle (Blanche Fenton) and William Ludwig (The Rover), and after six weeks the production folded.

UK: Globe Theatre *The Black Rover* 23 September 1890

ISOLA, Émile (b Blida, Algeria, 1860; d Paris, 17 May 1945).

ISOLA, Vincent (b Blida, Algeria, 1862; d Paris, September 1947). Parisian impresarii of the first half of the 20th century.

Originally illusionists on the music-hall stage, the Isola brothers went into management in 1892, presenting their own program at the little Théâtre des Capucines, which they rechristened the Théâtre Isola for the occasion. They moved on from there to take over the Parisiana, and it was there, amongst their music-hall programs, that they first dipped into the musical theatre, producing a number of opérettes and revues, from which the spectacular *Madame Méphisto* proved perhaps the most successful. They subsequently extended their control to the Olympia—where, following the trend of the Viennese day, they mounted, with some success, a series of imported musicals that included America's *The Prince of Pilsen* and *The Belle of New York,* Berlin's *Frau Luna* and Britain's *The Country Girl*—and also to the Folies-Bergère.

In 1903 they moved to more legitimate areas when they took over the big Théâtre de la Gaîté-Lyrique from Debruyère and, in the following decade, they mounted many productions of classic operas and opérettes before again moving up the ladder and taking over the control of the Opéra-Comique, in a team with the playwright Pierre-Barthélmy Gheusi. Their most notable period as producers of musical theatre came, however, in the decade 1926–36 when they managed the Théâtre Mogador, sponsoring Paris's productions of *Die Bajadere, No, No, Nanette, Rose-Marie, The Desert Song, Hit the Deck, Im weissen Rössl* and the original opérette *Mandrin.*

When the ever-rising pair eventually stopped rising and fell on hard times, largely thanks to their attempts at staging ''prestigious'' pieces at the Théâtre Sarah Bernhardt, they took up once more the illusion act of their young days and, at nearly 80 years of age, played engagements in theatres and casinos in France and Switzerland. Both died at the age of 85.

Biography: Andrieu, P: *Souvenirs des Frères Isola: cinquante ans de vie parisienne* (Flammarion, Paris, 1943)

IT HAPPENED IN NORDLAND Musical comedy in a prologue and 2 acts by Glen MacDonough. Music by Victor Herbert. Lew Fields Theater, New York, 5 December 1904.

Lew Fields's first production following his split from the Weber and Fields partnership had all the right ingredients. His producing associates were Fred R Hamlin and Julian Mitchell, the men behind *The Wizard of Oz* and *Babes in Toyland* spectaculars of the two previous seasons, and the authors were those of the second-named piece, librettist and lyricist Glen MacDonough and composer Victor Herbert. As far as its book was concerned, *It Happened in Nordland* was a marginally more adult piece than *Babes in Toyland,* but it relied, like its predecessor, on plenty of comedy and a glamorous and spectacular production rather than on anything else. Herbert's attractive score came, as it had in *Babes in Toyland,* as the lace on the hankie.

Queen Elsa of Nordland is to be wed against her royal will to the Czar's choice, Prince George of Nebula (Harry Davenport), and she takes the obvious way out: she runs away. Nordland's face is saved when the new American ambassadress, Kätherine Peepfogle (Marie

Cahill), turns out to be the queen's double, and she is corralled into standing in for the missing monarch for the length of the evening's entertainment. Fields himself played Hubert, Katherine's brother, who surfaces unexpectedly during her impersonation to cause considerable embarrassment to the new ''queen,'' with Joseph Herbert in the supporting comic role of the Duke of Toxen, May Robson as the Queen's comical aunt and Pauline Frederick in the small part of a lady-in-waiting.

Herbert supplied one of his musical-comedy style of scores for the show, with Prince George's hymn to ''Absinthe frappé'' proving the favorite number of the evening, but Miss Cahill had a fine *Grande-Duchesse de Gérolstein* finale to the first act, proclaiming herself ''Comanderess in Chief'' as well as a coon-song routine that included ''Bandana Land'' and ''The Coon Banshee,'' which gave her some unaccustomed coloratura moments. May Naudain, as an incidental Marchioness, sang in waltz time about ''The Knot of Blue,'' the Prince flirted with a maid (Bessie Clayton), threatening to sail her away on ''My Catamaran,'' and a pretty second-act opening entitled ''Al Fresco'' proved popular enough later to become an orchestral favorite. There was also an Indian Squaws' chorus, which (given the Czar bit of the plot) raised a few questions as to where precisely Nordland was supposed to be situated.

It Happened in Nordland opened at Harrisburg on 21 November 1904, but its New York opening was delayed a few days when producer Hamlin died. When it did open, as the first entertainment at the new Lew Fields Theater, it won pleased notices, and settled in for what looked like being a trouble-free run. In her usual style, however, Miss Cahill soon began to bring in her own material to interpolate into the musical part of the show. When—after getting ''by permission'' for a couple of songs—she finally overstepped the mark, there was a showdown with Herbert and, after Lew Fields backed up his composer, Miss Cahill walked out of the show. Miss Frederick stepped in for five weeks and caught enough eyes and ears to help set in motion what would be a notable career before, incomprehensibly, Fields went and hired Blanche Ring as a star replacement. If there was one leading lady on Broadway more famous for her interpolations than Marie Cahill, it was Blanche Ring. She naturally went ahead and interpolated, and she too was effectively fired. Amongst all this brouhaha *It Happened in Nordland* managed 154 successful Broadway performances, followed by a summer-break tour (with Jeannette Lowrie playing Katherine) and a return to New York (31 August 1905) for a further 100 nights. During this second season, the show got its biggest interpolation of all when an entire burlesque scena, taking the mickey out of David Warfield's performance in *The Music Master,* was added to the program (21 September). Fields impersonated Warfield as Herr Barewig whilst Blanche Ring as ''Helen Canting'' gave out with ''Hiram Green, Good-By'' and ''Little Houston Street'' and Georgie Lawrence got in Hough, Howard and Adams's Chicago number ''Same Old Moon.'' The original *It Happened in Nordland* had to be ''condensed'' to allow breathing space for the burlesque, but no one seems to have minded.

Recording: selection (part record) (AEI)

IT'S TIME TO DANCE Musical play (musical show) in 2 acts by Douglas Furber and L Arthur Rose. Lyrics by Harry Roy, Gaby Rogers, Harry Phillips and James Dyrenforth. Music by Kenneth Leslie-Smith, Roy, Rogers and Phillips. Winter Garden Theatre, London, 22 July 1943.

Jack Buchanan and Elsie Randolph returned, six years after their previous London musical together, with a piece whose title summed up the essence not of the era they were then in, but of that in which they had known their greatest success. *Me and My Girl* authors Rose and Furber supplied them with a conventional gangstery plot in which Buchanan played one Willmott Brown who, assisted by bulky comedian Fred Emney, infiltrates a gang of baddies and pops in and out of a series of melodramatic-comic situations until the inevitable missing jewels are saved and the girl (Miss Randolph) won. The light, dancing score was topped by the star pair's ''I'm Looking for a Melody,'' and the all-important choreographic content of the show was given variety by the inclusion of both American dancer Buddy Bradley and adagio pair Daria Luna and Nevill Astor, who were featured in their specialities alongside the more characterful dances of Randolph and Buchanan and the massed effects of the dancing chorus.

It's Time to Dance played three wartime months out of town, 259 performances in London, and then returned to the road. It played one more week in London in 1944 when a Manchester date had to be canceled because of bombing, and that return week represented Buchanan and Randolph's last London dance-and-comedy appearance as a West End pair.

IXION, or The Man at the Wheel Burlesque in 1 prologue, 4 scenes and ever so many tableaux by F C Burnand. Music selected and arranged by Theodore Herman. Royalty Theatre, London, 28 September 1863.

One of the most successful of all the vast output of musical burlesques that visited British and world stages in the 1860s, *Ixion* brought its young author firmly to the forefront amongst burlesque writers, a position he would maintain for a quarter of a century. The story he chose to parody here was the classical tale of Ixion, King of the Lapiths and the father of the Centaurs, who drew down Zeus' wrath upon himself by trying to imitate his thunders, and by paying court to the goddess Hera, and who was in consequence condemned to turn forever on a burning wheel in the depths of Hades.

Burnand's *Ixion* was a pretty, if inefficient, fellow (''though a King with a prefix of an (X,) it does not alphabetically follow that he has a *wise head* on his shoulders'') who was played in travesty by Jenny Willmore. Bumped from his throne by his disloyal spouse, Queen Dia (Mrs Charles Selby), and a trio of conspiring Thessalian democrats, he nevertheless wins the favor of the Olympian family. Particularly its feminine part. He flirts with Venus, almost elopes with Juno, but gets caught at his amours—as per mythology—and prettily wheeled. Much of the evening's entertainment was found in the burlesqued qualities of the Roman gods—Mercury, ''the celestial telegraph boy'' (David James), Apollo, ''secretary to the Imperial 'Sun' Light and Fire Insurance Co (Ltd)'' (Lydia Maitland), Minerva (''a quiet lady, though appearing with an 'owl''') (Felix Rogers), Bacchus (''promoter and chief director of the Celestial Light Wine Association''), the central Jupiter (Harriet Pelham), Juno (Blanche Elliston) and Venus (Amy Sheridan) and the mischievous Cupid (Marie Langford), this last a short-tunicked travesty role reserved for the prettiest young actress of the company. The role of Minerva was also played in travesty, by the company's chief comedian, as was that of the leg-displaying Apollo. Jupiter's pretty cupbearer, Ganymede, however, was played as a fat ''buttons'' of a boy, by comic Joe Robins. In the original production, Mercury was played by David James, later to be famous as one of the record-breaking *Our Boys.*

The scenic highlights of the production were Ixion's ascent from earth to Olympus, a ballet danced in Juno's drawing room, a salon ''commanding a fine view of the starry firmament and the milky way,'' Apollo's Private Room, Cupid's Château en Espagne, and its final tableau representing Fame, aided by Fact and Fiction, publishing Lemprière's famous classical dictionary, including the tale of Ixion, so that posterity might profit from the moral of his adventures, that Pride Comes Before a Fall. Theodore Herman's arranged music stretched from popular melodies to a song manufactured from a chunk of Verdi's *Un ballo in maschera.*

Staged at the little, unloved Royalty Theatre under the management of Mrs Selby (fronting for her former pupils, the well-off Pelham Sisters), *Ixion* was an instant hit, and went on to be played for a remarkable 153 consecutive nights. The next season, when the Misses Pelham dropped Mrs Selby (who had taken them to court to try to get her hands on some of the unexpected profits) and took over the theatre in their own names, they reprised the show (5 September 1864), themselves playing Ixion and Mercury, and provincial theatres were quick off the mark with their productions of what quickly proved to be the hottest burlesque in years. Burnand supplied the Royalty with a musequel, *Pirithous, Son of Ixion,* which played there, with Harriet Pelham in the title role, whilst the original piece played a season at the New Theatre, Greenwich (17 April 1865), with Florence Johnson as Ixion and the young Harriet Everard as Queen Dia. Then Miss Pelham brought it back to the Royalty (5 August 1865) for a third successive season, with Ada Cavendish playing Venus and Harriet Pelham back as Jupiter. The Alexandra Theatre mounted its production with Eliza Hamilton as Ixion (21 October 1865) and the Pelhams' production was played at Astley's (9 October 1865), whilst in Nottingham the demand for seats was such that the local producer was obliged to play the show twice daily.

Amongst the companies which toured *Ixion* in 1865 was one headed by the planturous Lydia Thompson. Although not the first to play the piece in America (visiting British burlesque actor Edward Warden had failed to make anyone notice it or him—as Jupiter—two years earlier), it was she who, after making her Broadway debut in the show (28 September 1868), ended by spreading her Americanized and topicalized version of *Ixion* throughout the continent. Supported by her famous troupe of British Blondes (several of whom were neither British nor blonde), she materially helped the show to win the same kind of popularity throughout America that it had won at home. In the wake of Lydia's appearance on the American stage, virtually every troupe of leggy burlesquers in the country toted a production of *Ixion* around the one- and two-night stands of inner and nether America, and they did it for years. Amongst the more durable were Alice Oates, the Chapman sisters (Blanche and Ella), the Willmore Sisters (in what Jennie, at least, claimed with uncommon justification as ''their original parts'') and the Zavistowski sisters (two sisters and mama) who took the roles of Ixion, Jupiter and Mercury in a version which was transported as far afield as Australia. Soon after Lydia Thompson's explosion on to the scene, Tony Pastor's variety house mounted a burlesque *Ixion in the Bowery* (Tony Pastor's Opera House 2 December 1868) written by John F Poole and ''borrowing'' virtually the whole score of the Burnand piece. Female impersonator T H Riggs pranced about in a wig of blonded hemp being Lydia whilst Pastor himself took off fellow blonde Lisa Weber. Fox's Theatre in Philadelphia followed suit (5 April 1869), actually playing their burlesque of the burlesque (and of the ''Blondes'' in general), opposite the Willmore's mounting of the real show. Miss L Robinson was ''Ixion in a blonde wig'' and the degrees of blondeness of the other characters were attached to their character name. A latter-day version of *Ixion* was remounted on Broadway in 1885 (Comedy Theater 11 February) with Alice Harrison as its star, it was produced again at Koster & Bial's Music Hall later the same season and it was featured on the bill at the San Franisco Tivoli as late as 1895 (23 December, ad John P Wilson, mus arr Adolf Bauer) and for the opening of the new theatre in 1903 (23 December, ad Ferris Hartmann as *Ixion the Wheelman*).

In Britain, as in America, the piece held its place in the provinces for many years, in spite of the deluge of burlesques which competed for attention in the 1870s, and it returned to London for further seasons at the Alexandra (March 1866), Sadlers Wells (2 April 1866) with Lizzie Willmore, at the Charing Cross Theatre (1870) with Emily Fowler starred, at the Court Theatre in 1872 (5 February) with Rose Evelyn, and in a revised version by Burnand as *Ixion Re-Wheeled* at the Opera Comique (21 November 1874). W H Swanborough also took round a reduced-size version entitled *The King of Thessaly, or A Pocket Edition of Ixion.* A last West End revival took place back at the Royalty Theatre in 1881 (16 July) with Jennie Willmore (Ixion) and Bella Goodall (Jupiter) featured.

The rest of the English-speaking world took to *Ixion* with equal vigor, and it became one of the half-dozen principal standards in the repertoires of burlesque companies throughout the globe. In Australia it seems to have been mounted for the first time by John Hall, in Melbourne, with his then wife Emily Wiseman as Ixion, supported by Julia Edouin (Venus), Tilly Earl (Cupid), Hall (Minerva) and William Gill (Mercury). In spite of being done by an unfashionable company, it proved ''the most successful burlesque ever done in Melbourne'' through a run of 44 consecutive nights, and it was later played there again by Bland Holt and his wife Lina Edwin (1870), by the Zavistowski family (1871) and by many other lesser burlesque companies.

USA: Washington Hall, Williamsburgh 21 June 1866, Wood's Museum, New York 28 September 1868; Australia: Princess's Theatre, Melbourne 21 September 1866

J

JABUKA, or Das Apfelfest Operette in 3 acts by Max Kalbeck and Gustav Davis. Music by Johann Strauss. Theater an der Wien, Vienna, 12 October 1894.

One of the series of essentially disappointing Operetten for which Johann Strauss composed the music in the later years of his career, *Jabuka* was nevertheless mounted throughout central Europe following its original run at the Theater an der Wien. The choice of a libretto set in Serbian Hungary, not the most obvious for the celebrated composer of Viennese waltzes, was apparently dictated by Strauss's admiration for Smetana's *Prodaná nevsta* (*The Bartered Bride*), which had been played for a season at the Theater an der Wien in 1893, but the tale concocted by the neophyte librettists Gustav Davis and Max Kalbeck was a comico-amorous affair, of an inherently different flavor from that of the Smetana piece.

Farmer's daughter Jelka (Jenny Pohlner) is heading for the local marriage market, the Apfelfest, dolled up in her finest and riding in an over-grand carriage, when she gets stuck in the mud. She is rescued by the less-than-wealthy but instantly lovestruck Count Mirko von Gradinaz (Karl Streitmann) whom she haughtily spurns, but she reacts more favorably to Mirko's pal, the comical bailiff Joschko (Alexander Girardi), who fools her into believing that he is a wealthy nobleman. Joschko whisks her off in Mirko's coach, but instead of delivering her to the city where the Apfelfest is taking place, he takes her to Mirko's castle and, indeed, to the gentleman's very bedroom. The lady's reaction when she discovers that she's been abducted is as predictable as is her ultimate winning over. Mirko's brother, Vasil (Herr Felix) and Annita (Therese Biedermann), daughter of the starch-manufacturing Bambora (Josef Joseffy), were the evening's number-two pair, whose amours reached their apotheosis at the same time as those of the number-one pair.

The three principal characters had the bulk of the music, with Girardi topping his first-act ''Im ganzen Land bin ich bekannt,'' and his comical description of Mirko's ancestral portraits, ''Alle uns're Ahnen waren, so zusagen, Gospodars,'' with the third-act ''Das Comität geht in die Höh,'' and Streitmann and Frln Pohlner leading the romantic numbers. The second pair had a pair of duets.

Jabuka was played 45 times before being removed in favor of a version of the French vaudeville *Patatart, Patatart et Cie.* When that flopped in a week, the standard repertoire was brought back and, amongst the *Der arme Jonathans* and *Bettelstudent*s, a handful of *Jabuka* performances helped it to pass its 50th performance (an important figure in rights and publishing contracts) on 18 December. It was a disappointing record, well below that achieved by such recent Theater an der Wien successes as *Heisses Blut, Ein armes Mädel* and *Der Obersteiger,* and even less than Strauss's last and already disappointing work, *Fürstin Ninetta,* the previous year. But the composer's reputation and name ensured *Jabuka* productions in Berlin, where Ottilie Collin appeared as Jelka alongside Steiner (Mirko) and Wellhof (Joschko), in Hamburg (Stadttheater 17 January 1895), in Prague, Poland and in Budapest (ad Dezső Megyeri, 8 performances), before it returned for a week of further performances (13 November 1895) in another Theater an der Wien repertoire period, following the flop of Louis Roth's *Der goldene Kamarad.*

The piece proved to have a little more subsequent appeal than *Fürstin Ninetta* amongst the minor Strauss works. In 1909 it was seen again in Vienna, at the Raimundtheater, with Franz Glawatsch as Joschko, Carl Streitmann as Mirko and Marthe Dorda-Winternitz as Jelka, and in 1942 a revised version, under the title *Das Apfelfest* (ad Karl Schleifer) was mounted at the Stadttheater in Kassel (22 September).

Germany: Friedrich-Wilhelmstädtisches Theater 7 November 1894; Hungary: Népszínház 21 September 1895

JACK O' LANTERN Musical comedy (musical extravaganza) in 2 acts by Anne Caldwell and R H Burnside. Music by Ivan Caryll. Globe Theater, New York, 16 October 1917.

After the splendid success of his version of *Aladdin* (*Chin-Chin*), producer Charles Dillingham ordered another vehicle on similar lines for comedians Montgomery and Stone from the same team of author Caldwell, author/director Burnside and composer Ivan Caryll. He got a piece which was, if anything, an even better prospect than his previous hit. *Jack o' Lantern* was another fairy-tale-based piece, leaning largely on the tale of *The Babes in the Wood,* with Montgomery and Stone cast in the famous British pantomime roles of the two murderers and robbers—the nasty one and the kindhearted one—who are hired by a beastly uncle to do away with his young wards.

The show was all prepared to go into rehearsal when Montgomery died. The authors hurriedly reorganized their piece, cutting down the two star roles and making them up into one, and Stone starred in the resulting piece as Jack o' Lantern, a whimsical little fellow who is mistaken for the hired assassin by wicked Uncle George (Oscar Ragland) and who, thereafter, helps the threatened children to escape from Appledale Farm, through a series of pretty pantomime-extravaganza places, until safety is assured and Uncle George reformed and repentant. The trio passed by the Banquet Hall in Jack's villa (scenery: Homer Emens, mechanical properties by Charles T Aldrich), and traveled to the Cave of Dreams, to Candyland and to a place Outside the Lines (all by Joseph Urban), to Camp Nowhere for an army scene in which Allene Crater as Villainessa led a Signal Corps March (Emens), to Clowntown (Urban), where the Six Brown Brothers did their speciality, and finally to an Ice Carnival, designed by Ernest Albert, where Misses Ellen Dallerup and Katie Smith were able to get in their ice-skating speciality and Stone to give his impersonation of the skater, Charlotte, prior to the happy ending.

Caryll's score illustrated the fun and spectacle in the gay vein that he had so successfully practiced at London's Gaiety Theatre, and he came up with several songs which became highly popular, and one which was a patent hit. The hit, oddly enough, did not fall to Stone, but to Helen Falconer and Douglas Stevenson, as they jauntily sang and danced their way through ''Wait Till the Cows Come Home.'' Miss Falconer also had another success with ''A Sweetheart of My Own''; Harold West and Kathleen Robinson as the two kiddies, Bobbie and Babbie, advised ''Take a Trip to Candyland''; whilst Stone had his jolliest musical moment with the comical ''Follow the Girls Around.'' The show used little in the way of interpolated songs, but Stone and Tessa Valerio performed one piece, ''I'll Take You Back to Italy,'' credited to the recently risen Irving Berlin.

Jack o' Lantern played 265 performances on Broadway before Stone went off to cash in on a lucrative engagement out west, but he returned to Dillingham in time to relaunch *Jack o' Lantern* at Boston's Colonial Theater for Christmas 1918 (''America's greatest entertainer in the incomparable musical extravaganza . . .'') prior to a long and successful tour. In later days, when Stone had moved on to his next show with Dillingham, *Jack o' Lantern* continued to be a favorite on the touring circuits in a version which restored the script to its original state and featured two ''murderers'' rather than one.

JACKSON, Ethel (b New York, 3 February 1877; d East Islip, NY, 23 November 1957). Broadway's *Merry Widow,* who never found another worthwhile vehicle.

A descendant of the painter Henry Inman, Miss Jackson studied piano in America and in Vienna, but went on the stage at the age of 20 as a vocalist in the chorus of the D'Oyly Carte company at London's Savoy Theatre, appearing in a chorus role in *The Beauty Stone,* in the 1898 revival of *The Gondoliers* as Fiametta and understudying Emmie Owen as Gianetta, and then covering Florence Perry (Wanda) in *The Grand Duchess.* She was taken back to America by Charles Frohman to play the title role in the British musical *Little Miss Nobody,* which closed on the road, but thereafter she made several appearances in New York, taking over from Virginia Earle in *A Runaway Girl,* appearing as *Little Red Riding-Hood* (1899) in the Casino Theater's piece of that title, as Cécile in *Hotel Topsy-Turvy* and as Gabriele in *Wiener Blut.* She also played in Philadelphia in the successful *Miss Bob White,* on tour as Suzette in *The French Maid,* with Henry Dixey in an umpteenth revival of *Adonis* (1900) and as Flo Honeydew in *The Lady Slavey* (1900) before retiring from the stage after what had been a fairly unremarkable career.

Four years later, however, she returned to Broadway in the role of the Indian singing-girl Chandra Nil, created by London's Florence Smithson, in a Broadway version of *The Blue Moon,* and the following year she won the title role in the American production of *The Merry Widow.* With its success she made a name for herself. She did not, however, go on to genuine stardom but, in a career which stretched to some 40 years, appeared spasmodically on the musical stage playing in another Philadelphai musical, *The Wild Goose* (1912, Princess Violetta), walking out of the role of Empress Josephine in *The Purple Road* (1913) as ''too insignificant,'' and never again finding a role to equal her one big success. She worked latterly in the non-musical theatre, making her last Broadway appearance in 1939 in *Key Largo.*

Miss Jackson married, and later divorced, producer J Fred Zimmerman. She then married the lawyer who had represented her in the divorce. When she subsequently divorced him, too, she doubtless used a different lawyer.

JACOBI, Georges (b Berlin, 13 February 1840; d London, 13 September 1906). Famed conductor and sometime director and composer for the British Victorian theatre.

Jacobi studied music in Brussels, attending the Conservatoire from the age of 9, and then in Paris, where he later played in the orchestra at the Opéra before becoming, at the age of 29, a conductor at the Théâtre des Bouffes-Parisiens. In that post he conducted a number of important Offenbach premieres. There, also, his one-act opérettes *Le Feu aux poudres, La Nuit du 15 Octobre* and *Mariée depuis midi* were played. The last of these—starring Anna Judic—had sufficient success to be later shown at London's Princess's Theatre and at Vienna's Carltheater (*Seit mittag vermählt*), whilst the second was seen as *The Fifteenth of October* at London's Alhambra (1875) and Prince of Wales (1891) Theatres.

Jacobi moved to London during the Franco-Prussian War and, in 1871, he was appointed musical director of the Alhambra Theatre under John Baum. There he composed and arranged a vast amount of music for the spectacular shows of which the Alhambra made a speciality: full and part-scores, single songs, short operettas and, above all, over a hundred ballets and dance interludes. He also organized and arranged the pasticcio and part-pasticcio scores which for a long time made up the musical part of the Alhambra book-musical shows. Before he had been long at the Alhambra, Jacobi also took over the stage direction of these shows, and many of the most spectacular of London's opéra-bouffe productions with their vast cohorts of extras and dancers and their monumental scenery were, in fact, staged by their musical director.

Amongst the shows which, apart from his own compositions and concoctions, he conducted during more than 16 years at the head of the Alhambra's orchestra were the London productions of many of Offenbach's works, including the original production of his London piece, *Whittington,* and other large-scale French opéras-bouffes, Clay's *Don Quixote* and the grand opéra-bouffe féerie *La Poule aux oeufs d'or* (for both of which he also supplied the dance music) and the aggrandized revival of Burnand's *Black-Eyed Susan* (1884).

Jacobi appeared occasionally as a conductor in other theatres (St James's Theatre *Le Voyage dans la lune,* Avenue Theatre *La Vie, Nell Gwynne,* etc) but the largest part of his career was spent in the service of the Alhambra until he departed from that theatre, the functions of which had severely altered, in 1897. He subsequently directed the orchestra at the Crystal Palace.

As a composer, he provided only two full scores to the lyric stage, one—*The Demon's Bride*—for London, the other, *Le Clairon,* for Lyon and Paris. He was also commissioned to compose a piece called *The Queen of Spain* (lib: George Sims) for the New York Casino, but before it could happen Casino supremo Aronson lost his theatre and *The Queen of Spain* never made it to the stage.

1869 **Le Feu aux poudres** (N Fournier, Élie Frébault) 1 act concert performance 21 March; Théâtre des Bouffes-Parisiens, Paris 11 April

1869 **La Nuit du 15 Octobre** (Eugène Leterrier, Albert Vanloo) 1 act Théâtre des Bouffes-Parisiens, Paris 15 October

1872 **[The] Black Crook** (w Frederic Clay/Harry Paulton, Joseph Paulton) Alhambra Theatre 23 December

1873 **Mariée depuis midi** (William Busnach, Armand Liorat) 1 act Marseille 20 August; Princess's Theatre 15 July 1873; Théâtre des Bouffes-Parisiens 6 March 1874

1874 **The Demon's Bride** (Leterrier, Vanloo ad H J Byron) Alhambra Theatre 7 September

1876 **Le Ruy Blas des Batignolles** (Clerc brothers) Fantaisies-Parisiennes, Paris 4 April

1879 **Rothomago** (w Edward Solomon, Procida Bucalossi, Gaston Serpette/H B Farnie) Alhambra Theatre 22 December

1882 **Le Clairon** (Gaston Marot, Frébault, Édouard Philippe) Lyon; Théâtre de la Renaissance, Paris 7 November 1883

1885 **Chirruper's Fortune** (US: *A Paper Doll*) (w others/Arthur Law) New Theatre Royal, Portsmouth 31 August

1886 **The Two Pros** (Frederick Bowyer) 1 act Prince of Wales Theatre 4 December

1886 **Vetah** arranged and supplemented the late Firmin Bernicat's score (Theatre Royal, Portsmouth)

1895 **The Newest Woman** (H Chance Newton) 1 act Avenue Theatre 4 April

JACOBI, Viktor [JAKABFI, Viktor] (b Budapest, 22 October 1883; d New York, 10 December 1921). One of the group of successful Hungarian composers who dominated the European musical stage in the early 20th century, but who lost his way when he left his native country.

Jacobi studied at the Budapest Zeneakadémia, alongside Kálmán and Szirmai, and was still a student when his first work was produced at no less a venue than the Budapest Népszínház (as Jakabfi). *A rátartós királykisasszony* (''the proud princess''), described as a mesejáték (fable, fairytale) in five scenes, and based on Holger Drachmann's *Der var en Gang* (''once upon a time'') was written by Jenő Heltai, the lyricist of the recently produced *János vitéz.* It was played a respectable 33 times with Klára Küry in its title role.

Still in his early twenties, Jacobi collaborated for the first time with librettist Ferenc Martos on *A legvitézebb huszár* (''the bravest hussar''), in which Ákos Ráthonyi appeared with great success at the Magyar Színház, and he also set Heltai's lyrics for the fairy play *A tengerszem tündére* (''the sea fairy'') (''Ha én rózsa volnék,'' ''Ki vagy te gyönyörüségem,'' ''Be sokat igér s ki tudja mier?''), in which Ráthonyi and Olga Turchányi featured

Plate 189. **Viktor Jacobi's** *earliest works were in the fairy-tale vein popularized by the success of* János vitéz.

at the same house. He subsequently gained a considerable success with his score to Martos's musicalization of Mór Jókai's poetic fairy tale *Az istenhegyi székeley leány,* produced at the Király Színház under the title *Tüskerózsa* (''prickly rose'') with a top-class cast including Sári Fedák, Márton Rátkai, József Németh and Kornél Sziklai.

In 1908 Jacobi supplied the accompanying music for Martos's 10-scene *100 év mulva* (''100 years after''), and the Király Színház also mounted his Operette *Van, de nincs* (''there is, but there isn't'') in which Vilma Medgyaszay scored a hit with the gavotte ''Szökellő keskeny ici-pici láb,'' as well as another Martos fairy-tale Operette, *Jánoska,* again with Fedák featured (''Tul, tul, tul az óperencian''), which initially ran rather less long than its predecessors, but which was brought back as late as 1925 for a revival at the Király Színház (24 October).

In spite of the fact that he had been collaborating with some of the finest writers in the Hungarian theatre, the breakthrough into wider success only came when Jacobi moved purposefully on from the *János vitéz*-influenced type of mythical/fairy-tale subject which these early works had used, and into something more attractive to the strivingly up-to-date theatres of the outside world. That success was accomplished with *Leányvásár,* a piece which took the American west as its setting, and the well-used fair-wedding plot, most famously used in Flotow's *Martha,* as its basic element. The composer filled his score to the brim with the kind of dancing melodies the English-speaking theatre currently favored, melodies that were, however, colored with an individual and, above all to the foreigner, exotic Hungarian tint. A major hit on its production in Hungary, *Leányvásár* went on to become a worldwide property, a veritable smash in London, and it remains a solid element of the basic Hungarian repertoire up to the present day.

The musical-comedy–styled *Leányvásár* was followed up by an even bigger success when Martos, Miksa Bródy and Jacobi collaborated on a second outward-looking piece, but this time one which had more of the romantic operetta element mixed with its lively dances and songs and its comic moments. Even in the face of the competition coming from Vienna, in particular, on the eve of the First World War, *Szibill* proved to be one of the outstanding musical plays of its time, and Jacobi's newly established international reputation was well and truly confirmed.

The composer was not slow to follow up this success and, in 1914, he was to be found in London, where *The Marriage Market* (*Leányvásár*) was still running, and where it was rumored that he would write the score for George Edwardes's next piece, when the war broke out. There was no question of Edwardes or anyone else employing any central European composer whilst Britain was at war with central Europe, and people like gossip columnist and aspiring composer Jimmy Glover were busy rooting anyone with a remotely Germanic name out of every seaside band in Britain. Jacobi's British prospects went down the drain along with those of Jean Gilbert who, like him, had recently become a West End favorite. When another rumor was spread to the effect that Jacobi had perhaps composed some music for Edwardes already, and that Paul Rubens had accommodatingly put his name to it, Rubens took the rumor-monger to court, and won.

Jacobi, in the meantime, moved on to America, where it was still possible for an Hungarian composer with a few hits to his name to find work. He quickly became naturalized as an American citizen, and his name soon appeared on a Broadway bill, as the composer of *Rambler Rose* (1917). Broadway's *Szibill* star Julia Sanderson featured, but Harry B Smith's book was a now-you-marry-money-now-you-don't sort of piece, far from the colorful romance of the Hungarian show, and *Rambler Rose* lasted only 72 performances on Broadway. *Apple Blossoms,* two seasons later, was based on a similarly slight tale of the road to marriage. This time, Jacobi shared the composing credit with Fritz Kreisler, but it was his ''You Are Free'' and ''Little Girls, Goodbye'' which proved the pick of the score through the show's seven months of Broadway run and subsequent life on the road.

This taste of almost-success apparently encouraged Jacobi to stick with the marriage-and-money type of libretto (and with routine librettist Le Baron) which seemed so alien to his style of composition, and it proved a mistake. *The Half Moon* was a quick flop in spite of a cast headed by Joseph Cawthorn, Joseph Santley and Ivy Sawyer, and an attempt by Dillingham to give the composer an opportunity to work in his Hungarian element also failed. Le Baron's emasculation of Molnár's *A Farkas* as *The Love Letter* did not inspire the now extremely nerve-racked composer to the heights of a *Szibill* and the show was again a quick flop (31 performances).

Jacobi's American episode had been an almost unmitigated failure. In the few years since his departure from Budapest he had fallen from a preeminent place, on a par with Fall, Lehár, Kálmán and Gilbert, in the European musical theatre, and at the same time he had destroyed his health. He died shortly after the failure of *The Love Letter.*

An operett called *Miámi,* with Jacobi music arranged by Zsigmond Vincze, and attached to an Hungarian-authored libretto set in Florida, was mounted in Budapest several years after the composer's death. A top-flight trio of local performers in Sári Petráss, Hanna Honthy and Teri Féjes featured, but the local opinion was that Jacobi's ''American'' music was only a shadow of that of his prewar works. A few weeks later the Theater an der Wien in Vienna mounted a half-dozen performances of a version of *Jánoska* as a children's Christmas entertainment, as one of the most promising careers of the 20th-century musical theatre went sadly out on the proverbial whimper.

1904 **A rátartós Királykisasszony** (Jenő Heltai) Népszínház 17 December

1905 **A legvitézebb huszár** (Ferenc Martos) Magyar Színház 30 December

1906 **A tengerszem tündére** (Heltai/Zoltán Thury) Magyar Színház 7 November

1907 **Tüskerózsa** (Martos) Király Színház 23 March

1908 **Van, de nincs** (Martos) Király Színház 30 October

1909 **Jánoska** (Martos) Király Színház 7 May

1911 **Leányvásár** (Martos, Miksa Bródy) Király Színház 14 November

1914 **Szibill** (Martos, M Bródy) Király Színház 27 February

1917 **Rambler Rose** (Harry B Smith) Empire Theater, New York 10 September

1919 **Apple Blossoms** (w Fritz Kreisler/William Le Baron) Globe Theater, New York 7 October

1920 **The Half Moon** (Le Baron) Liberty Theater, New York 1 November

1921 **The Love Letter** (Le Baron) Globe Theater, New York 4 October

1925 **Miámi** (pasticcio/István Bródy, László Vajda) Fővárosi Operettszínház 27 November

JACOBSON, Leopold (b Czernowitz, 30 June 1878; d Theresienstadt, 23 February 1943).

Theatre critic, chief editor of the *Neues Wiener Journal,* dramatist and operettic librettist, Jacobson began his career as a writer for the musical theatre with a fine series of successes: Oscar Straus's *Ein Walzertraum* and *Der tapfere Soldat,* Nedbal's *Die keusche Barbara* and Granichstaedten's *Auf Befehl der Herzogin.* If his first great success with Straus remained his most memorable, he nevertheless worked with the composer later on such long-running pieces as *Eine Ballnacht* and *Dorfmusikanten,* teamed profitably with Robert Stolz on *Die Tanzgräfin* and with Künneke on *Lady Hamilton,* and had a particularly fruitful alliance with Jean Gilbert, for whom he supplied the texts for *Katja, die Tänzerin* and *Das Weib im Purpur.*

His many-highlighted career in the theatre was over well before the Second World War, in which he was deported and then murdered.

1907 **Ein Walzertraum** (Oscar Straus/w Felix Dörmann) Carltheater 2 March

1908 **Der tapfere Soldat** (Straus/w Rudolf Bernauer) Theater an der Wien 14 November

1910 **Die keusche Barbara** (Oskar Nedbal/w Bernauer) Theater Weinberge, Prague 14 September; Raimundtheater 7 October 1911

1912 **Adam und Eva** (Schweiger) 1 act Ronacher 1 March

1913 **Fürst Ypsilon** (Friedrich Bermann/Somerset Maugham ad) Schauburg, Hannover 15 March

1913 **Der lachende Dreibund** (Ralph Benatzky) Theater am Nollendorfplatz, Berlin 31 October

1915 **Die schöne Unbekannte** (Straus/w Leo Stein) Carltheater 15 January

1915 **Auf Befehl der Herzogin** (Bruno Granichstaedten/w Robert Bodanzky) Theater an der Wien 20 March

1916 **Warum geht's denn jetzt?** (Edmund Eysler/w Bodanzky) Bundestheater 5 July

1917 **Nachtfalter** (Straus/w Bodanzky) Ronacher 13 March

1918 **Eine Ballnacht** (Straus/w Bodanzky) Johann Strauss-Theater 11 October

1919 **Der Liebesteufel** (Julius Bistron/w Bodanzky) Wiener Komödienhaus 17 October

1919 **Dorfmusikanten** (Straus/w Bodanzky) Theater an der Wien 29 November

1919 **Was Mädchen träumen** (Leo Ascher/w Bodanzky) Raimundtheater 6 December

1920 **Yuschi tanzt** (Benatzky/w Bodanzky) Wiener Bürgertheater 3 April

1921 **Die Tanzgräfin** (Robert Stolz/w Bodanzky) Wallner-Theater, Berlin 18 February

1923 **Katja, die Tänzerin** (Jean Gilbert/w Rudolf Österreicher) Johann Strauss-Theater 5 January

1923 **Das Weib im Purpur** (Gilbert/w Österreicher) Wiener Stadttheater 21 December

1924 **Der Tanz um die Liebe** (Straus/w Heinz Saltenburg) Deutsches Künstlertheater, Berlin 25 September

1924 **Zwei um Eine** (Gilbert)

1925 **[Das Abenteur des Herrn] Maiermax** (Hugo Hirsch/w Österreicher) Lessing-Theater, Berlin 31 December

1926 **Lady Hamilton** (Eduard Künneke/w Richard Bars) Schauspielhaus, Breslau 25 September

1927 **Eine einzige Nacht** (Stolz/w Österreicher) Carltheater 23 December

1928 **Hochzeit in Hollywood** (Straus/w Hardt-Warden) Johann Strauss-Theater 21 December

1928 **Eine Nacht in Kairo** (Gilbert/w Bruno Hardt-Warden) Centraltheater, Dresden 22 December

1929 **Die Frau in Gold** (Michael Krasznay-Krausz/w Hardt-Warden) Neues Operetten-Theater, Leipzig 28 February

1930 **Tschun-Tschi** (W Cliffords/John Gardener, Anna May Wong ad w Grünbaum) Neues Wiener Schauspielhaus 14 August

1930 **Peppina** (Stolz/w Österreicher) Komische Oper, Berlin 22 December

DIE JAGD NACH DEM GLÜCK Comic Operette in a Vorspiel and 3 acts by Richard Genée and Bruno Zappert. Music by Franz von Suppé. Carltheater, Vienna, 27 October 1888.

Suppé's *Die Jagd nach dem Glück* had only a fair introduction to Vienna, with a run of little more than a month at the Carltheater, but its more substantial than usual musical content won it praise from the critics and it was given a number of productions abroad, going through some curious permutations on the way.

Genée and Zappert's original text told of the ''chase after happiness'' of Bavarian Rudolf, the foster son of Graf Wilfried. Rudolf (Karl Streitmann) is engaged to be wed to Wilfried's daughter Stella (Frln Seebold), but he suddenly decides that he is not ready for marriage, and, with his servant Casimir (Herr Wittels) in supportive tow, quits his home town and heads off to Paris in search of fame and fortune. Stella, a wise lass, follows him in the disguise of a street singer, accompanied by Casimir's sweetheart Fanny (Frln Augustin). In Paris, Rudolf squanders his money and falls ruinously under the spell of the danseuse Florinde (Frln Tischler). In a last impoverished stroke he gambles all but the fare home, and loses. Unfortunately, in the meanwhile, Casimir has been robbed of the fare money by a highwayman. Deserted by all his fairweather French friends, Rudolf joins the Swedish army and leads them to a fine victory over the Danes, but the old Swedish king dies and he wins no reward. Venice in carnival time sees him fall once again into feminine webs and Rudolf—finally convinced that the ''chase after happiness'' in the form of money and fame is a vain one—returns home. Stella, who has watched over him all the way, will be there to welcome him.

In Germany Suppé's score was detached from its text and tacked on to another libretto by Hermann Hirschel under the title *Die Brautjagd,* and the resultant piece was produced at the Friedrich-Wilhelmstädtisches Theater (16 February 1894), whilst in America the show was produced by John McCaull under the meaningless title of *Clover.* The reason for this was that librettist Harry B Smith had promised the members of New York's Clover Club that he would give them a plug, and this was his way of doing so. Perhaps the club's members repaid Smith by attending Palmer's Theatre in bulk, for *Clover,* with a cast headed by De Wolf Hopper (Casimir), Jeff de Angelis (Don Cristoval), Eugene Oudin (Rudolf), Marion Manola (Stella) and Mathilde Cottrelly (Petronella) became a solid hit, unmarred by a row between Oudin and Miss Manola which caused them both to walk out. McCaull got a splendid run of 173 Broadway performances from the show, a success which encouraged the Amberg Theater to try the original German version. With original star Streitmann (Rudolf), Carl Friese jr (Casimir), Guste Zimmermann (Stella) and Carola Engländer featured, it ran for an initial week and was reprised later in the season. *Clover* was seen all round America in the years that followed, in repertoire companies and summer seasons.

Another show of the same title, composed by Leo Fall, was produced at the Carl Weiss-Theater, Berlin, 1 February 1900.

USA: Palmer's Theater *Clover* 8 May 1889, Amberg Theater (Ger) 10 April 1890

J'AIME Opérette in 3 acts by Albert Willemetz and Saint-Granier. Music by Henri Christiné. Théâtre des Bouffes-Parisiens, Paris, 22 December 1926.

The Théâtre des Bouffes-Parisiens and producers Gustave Quinson and Edmond Roze (also director) staged Willemetz and Christiné's *J'aime* at the continuing height of the vogue for the up-to-date musical comedy which had been inaugurated at the same theatre, and by the same authors, eight years previously. Now there were other writers and composers on the same wagon—the Bouffes itself had just had an enormous success with Raoul Moretti's *Trois jeunes filles . . . nues!* written to a libretto by Yves Mirande and the inevitable Willemetz—but Christiné and Willemetz proved surefire winners once again with their new piece, one which reused many of the creative team from the previous show.

The penniless Baron (Le Gallo) and Baroness (Nina Myral) de Malassis de la Panouille inherit a vast fortune from his late and disgraced sister who ran away to become a circus rider. But—horror!—they can touch the money only when they have spent a year and a day working in a circus. They become comically incompetent jugglers, but they win through with the aid of the little blackbottom dancing dog of the lawyer (Koval) who is overseeing their calvary. Of course, the sister (Marguerite Peuget) is not dead at all; she has married a duke and is merely wreaking her revenge on her snooty relatives before helping them out. Pretty Sim-Viva, baritone Géo Bury, soubrette Christiane Dor and Gustave Nellson, all from the *Trois jeunes filles . . . nues!* cast, were the singing and dancing younger generation, whilst Gabin père as a comical General completed the star line up.

Christiné's score was in his inexhaustibly lively, tuneful and modern style, ranging from Koval's description of ''L'Inventeur du Charleston,'' which comically detailed the alleged origins of the dance, and his syncopated song of the soundless ''Biniou,'' to lightsome ballads and the music of the circus. Sim-Viva described the joys of the telephone for long-distance lovemaking in spite of the hazards of intrusive operators, whilst Le Gallo and Myral, in roles made on the Dranem and Jeanne Cheirel format, sang in an embarrassed and brisk pianissimo of what to do ''Quand on n'a pas d'argent'' and made a middle-aged attempt to dance the polka. Bury discovered the aristocratic delight of having a ''de'' in his name and romanced over ''Djibouti,'' Myral comically demanded that her marriageable daughter choose between Ale Rolls Royce, les chapeaux d'Lewis, l'château en Anjou, la villa à Nice, l'hiver en Tunis'' or the pawnshop and her sweetheart, and whooped out the surprising joys of circus life as opposed to aristocratic leisure (''Quand on en a goûté''), whilst Mlle Dor swooped saucily through ''J'attends'' and ''Pour faire son trou,'' in a score which also boasted real concerted finales and some delightful ensembles.

A good Paris life, a longer touring one, and a production as far afield as Budapest (ad Zsolt Harsányi, Adorján Stella) all went to help add *J'aime* to Christiné and Willemetz's list of hit shows.

Hungary: Király Színház *Szeretlek* 26 May 1928

JAIME, Adolphe [GEM, Louis Adolphe] (b Paris, 1824; d Asnières, 4 March 1901).

A prolific author of vaudevilles and opérettes, Adolphe Jaime had his name attached—along with those of some of the most imaginative comic writers of the time—to a good number of important musical-theatre pieces of the second half of the 19th century and, posthumously, to one or two 20th-century adaptations of his work.

Jaime's earliest little pieces for the musical stage (a number of which—such as Delibes' *Maître Griffard* and *M de Bonne-Étoile* and Jonas's *Le Manoir des Larenardière*—he did not sign) included Offenbach's *Croquefe* r and *Une demoiselle en loterie,* Jonas's most successful short piece *Les Petits Prodiges* and, above all, *Six Demoiselles à marier,* originally set with some success by Delibes but later and memorably reset in a German translation by von Suppé as his highly successful *Zehn Mädchen und kein Mann.*

The playwright's entry into the full-length opéra-bouffe was equally as successful, his earliest works being collaborations with Philippe Gille on the text for Delibes' *La Cour du Roi Pétaud;* with Hector Crémieux on the libretti and lyrics for Hervé's extravagant burlesque *Le Petit Faust,* the parody of *Bajazet, Les Turcs,* and the Scots highjinks of *La Trône d'Écosse;* and with Jules Noriac, on the sweetly scabrous and hugely successful *La Timbale d'argent.*

In latter years his success rate in the musical—if not the comic—theatre fell somewhat, as the burlesque style of prewar years gave way to a more moderate comic-opera variety of libretto, and the most played of Jaime's latter-day musical-theatre pieces proved to be his Gaston Serpette musical *La Branche cassée* (1874); the remade libretto, *La Reine Indigo,* for Johann Strauss's *Indigo und die vierzig Räuber* score; and a new and enlarged remake of Étienne Tréfeu's *Geneviève de Brabant* text for an 1875 revival.

Several of his vaudevilles and comedies were later adapted to the musical stage elsewhere, the most notable being his *Coquin de printemps* (Folies-Dramatiques 13 June 1888 w Georges Duval), which was made into London's *The Spring Chicken* and Vienna's *Frühlingsluft,* both highly successful pieces. His vaudeville *Cent mille francs et ma fille* (w Gille) was later musicalized for a revival in Paris (1874) and again as *100,000 Gulden und meine Tochter* by Edvard Dorn, music by Ludwig Gothov-Grüneke, for Vienna's Theater in der Josefstadt (18 January 1879).

- 1856 **Six Demoiselles à marier** (Léo Delibes/w Adolphe Choler) 1 act Théâtre des Bouffes-Parisiens 12 November
- 1857 **Croquefer** (Offenbach/w Tréfeu) 1 act Théâtre des Bouffes-Parisiens 12 February
- 1857 **Le Roi boît** (Émile Jonas/w Eugène Mestépès) 1 act Théâtre des Bouffes-Parisiens 9 April
- 1857 **Dragonette** (Offenbach/w Mestépès) 1 act Théâtre des Bouffes-Parisiens 30 April
- 1857 **Une demoiselle en loterie** (Offenbach/w Hector Crémieux) 1 act Théâtre des Bouffes-Parisiens 27 July
- 1857 **Maître Griffard** (Delibes/ uncredited w Eugène Mestépès) 1 act Théâtre Lyrique 3 October
- 1857 **Les Petits Prodiges** (Jonas/w Étienne Tréfeu) 1 act Théâtre des Bouffes-Parisiens 19 November
- 1858 **La Harpe d'or** (Félix Godefroid/w Ernest Dubreuil) Théâtre Lyrique 8 September

1859 **Les Vivandières de la grande armée** (Offenbach/w Pittaud de Forges) 1 act Théâtre des Bouffes-Parisiens 6 July

1860 **Monsieur de Bonne-Étoile** (Delibes/ uncredited w Philippe Gille) 1 act Théâtre des Bouffes-Parisiens 4 February

1862 **Zehn Mädchen und kein Mann** (*Six Demoiselles à marier*) (Franz von Suppé/w Choler tr Karl Treumann) 1 act Theater am Franz-Josefs-Kai 25 October

1863 **L'Argent et l'amour** (Eugène Déjazet/w Colin, Auguste Polo) Théâtre Déjazet 5 February

1863 **La Mère de la débutante** (Eugène Moniot) 1 act Théâtre des Folies-Dramatiques 13 July

1869 **L'Écossais de Chatou** (Delibes/w Philippe Gille) 1 act Théâtre des Bouffes-Parisiens 16 January

1869 **La Cour du Roi Pétaud** (Delibes/w Gille) Théâtre des Variétés 24 April

1869 **Le Petit Faust** (Hervé/w Crémieux) Théâtre des Folies-Dramatiques 28 April

1870 **Les Turcs** (Hervé/w Crémieux) Théâtre des Folies-Dramatiques 23 December

1871 **Le Barbier de Trouville** (Charles Lecocq/w Jules Noriac) 1 act Théâtre des Bouffes-Parisiens 19 November

1871 **Le Trône d'Écosse** (Hervé/w Crémieux) Théâtre des Variétés 17 November

1872 **Un fi, deux fi, trois figurants** (Léon Vasseur) 1 act Alcazar 1 April

1872 **La Timbale d'argent** (Vasseur/w Noriac) Théâtre des Bouffes-Parisiens 9 April

1872 **Mon mouchoir** (Vasseur) 1 act Théâtre des Bouffes-Parisiens 9 May

1873 **L'Exemple** (Moniot) 1 act Théâtre des Bouffes-Parisiens 1 January

1873 **La Petite Reine** (Vasseur/w Noriac) Théâtre des Bouffes-Parisiens 9 January

1873 **La Casque de Thémistocle** (Fouqué) la Théâtre du Tivoli 18 April

1873 **Le Mouton enragé** (Lacome/w Noriac) 1 act Théâtre des Bouffes-Parisiens 27 May

1873 **Les Amours d'un pierrot** (Georges Rose) 1 act Délassements-Comiques 6 October

1874 **La Branche cassée** (Gaston Serpette/w Noriac) Théâtre des Bouffes-Parisiens 23 January

1874 **Madame de Rabucor** (Mme de Ste Croix) 1 act Théâtre des Bouffes-Parisiens 5 February

1874 **Paille d'avoine** (Robert Planquette/w Adolphe Lemonnier, Rozale) 1 act Délassements-Comiques 12 March

1874 **Cent Mille Francs et ma fille** (Jules Costé/w Gille) Théâtre des Menus-Plaisirs 27 April

1875 **Geneviève de Brabant** revised version w Tréfeu (Théâtre de la Gaîté)

1875 **La Reine Indigo** (Johann Strauss/w Victor Wilder) Théâtre de la Renaissance 27 April

1886 **Il était une fois . . .** (Oscar de Lagoanère/Doré-Simiane) Théâtre des Menus-Plaisirs 1 May

1888 **Mam'zelle Crénom** (Vasseur/w Georges Duval) Théâtre des Bouffes-Parisiens 19 January

1888 **Le Mariage avant la lettre** (Olivier Métra/w Duval) Théâtre des Bouffes-Parisiens 5 December

1889 **Le Diable à quatre** (Monteux-Brissac) 1 act La Cigale 4 October

1892 **Éros** (Paul Vidal/w Noriac, Maurice Bouchor) Théâtre des Bouffes-Parisiens 22 April

1893 **Les Colles des femmes** (Louis Ganne/w Henri Kéroul) Théâtre des Menus-Plaisirs 29 September

JAKOBOWSKI, Edward [aka BELLEVILLE, Edward or Édouard] (b Islington, London, 17 April 1856; d Friern Barnet, 29 April 1929). The composer of the score for one vast international hit, which was never confirmed.

Born in Hanover Street, Islington, the son of a Polish-born commercial traveler, Israel Jakobowski, and his Viennese wife, Fanny Schenheit, Jakobowski spent his youth in Vienna where he studied music under Hellmesberger and saw his first small operetta, *Le Réveil* (1873), played privately. He moved on first to Paris, and then back to Britain, where a showcase production of a burlesque *Little Carmen* (1884), written with another novice, Alfred Murray, attracted the attention of Gaiety Theatre manager John Hollingshead who, as a result, cocommissioned and staged the collaborators' comic-opera version of the Dick Whittington tale, *Dick* (1884), at the Globe Theatre.

The following year, Jakobowski leapt to fame with his score for Violet Melnotte's production of *Erminie. Erminie* proved to be one of the outstanding shows of its era. The most successful of all comic operas on the 19th-century American stage, it also toured incessantly in Britain for many years, won a variety of overseas productions, and its Lullaby (''Dear Mother, In Dreams I See Her'') became a popular American hit.

The celebrity Jakobowski found, particularly in America, as ''the composer of *Erminie*'' gradually frittered away as he failed to come up with another winner. A well-made piece built by and for the *Erminie* team, *Mynheer Jan* (1887), went under amidst backstage squabbles; a bandit musical called *Paola* (1889) found a limited success touring in Britain and America; a Broadway score for *Erminie* star Francis Wilson, *The Devil's Deputy* (1894), written to the libretto of the French opérette *Babolin,* was played 72 times in New York before touring; *The Birth of Venus* produced in Baltimore with Grace Golden as its star was adjudged ''more a play than an opera'' and in any case foundered swiftly; and a musical comedy for comedian Arthur Roberts, *Milord Sir Smith* (1898), based on another borrowed Continental text, had only an average success.

Jakobowski had, perhaps, his most satisfying result of the post-*Erminie* period with the well-considered *Die*

Brillanten-Königin. Written for the Vienna Carltheater, it was played there for 34 performances in 1894 before going on to Prague (1 July 1894) and then being heavily rewritten for London and New York. However, the composer's affairs were by this stage in a sad state. His *La Tarentella,* produced in Chicago by the Castle Square Opera Company (which had just done hugely well with *Erminie*) boasted ''house-record-breaking business'' but was never heard of again. Jacob Bier's promised mounting of *The Burgomaster's Ward* and Frank Perley's announced production of *Miss Walker of Woolloomoolloo* to a new libretto by Paulton never happened, and a much-touted commission for another musical for Wilson, to be composed to an unproduced Chivot and Duru text, *La Carême de Titine,* suffered the same fate. In 1902 Jakobowski was declared bankrupt, and a final attempt for the American stage ended in embarrassment. His score for *Winsome Winnie* was largely abandoned on the road in favor of some routine music by Kerker (5 numbers of 23 were kept), as the man who had been the toast of Broadway in the late 1880s vanished into professional oblivion. In the summer of 1906 *The Pet of Paris,* ''a new comic opera by H and E Paulton, music by Jakobowski and Alfred Moulton,'' was paragraphed by the New York press, but like almost all his later projects, it came to nothing.

Several other compositions from his pen did appear over the following decade or so, but they were played by provincial amateurs and did not get a professional performance.

Amongst his minor credits is included some music for the British touring show *Pat,* whilst his name appears, along with that of André Messager, as the composer of the incidental music for a production of the Eugène Grangé/Victor Bernard play *Az eltévedt bárányka* (*La Brebis égarée*) at the Budapest Népszínház in 1887.

1883 **The Three Beggars** (Sinclair Dunn) 1 act Royal Academy of Music 28 July

1884 **Little Carmen** (Alfred Murray) Globe Theatre 7 February

1884 **Dick** (Murray) Globe Theatre 17 April

1885 **Erminie** (Harry Paulton, Claxson Bellamy) Comedy Theatre 9 November

1886 **Mass-en-yell-oh** (Paulton, Mostyn Tedde) Comedy Theatre 23 March

1886 **The Palace of Pearl** (w Frederic Stanislaus/Murray, Willie Younge) Empire Theatre 12 June

1887 **Mynheer Jan** (Paulton, Mostyn Tedde) Comedy Theatre 14 February

1889 **Paola** (Paulton, Mostyn Tedde) Grand Opera House, Philadelphia 14 May; Fifth Avenue Theater, New York 26 August

1892 **Pat** (revised version w add mus by Jakobowski) (John Crook, Alfred Lee, Edward Solomon, Fred Eplett/Mark Ambient, Frederic Wood/George Roberts) Aquarium, Yarmouth 1 August

1893 **La Rosière** (Harry Monkhouse) Shaftesbury Theatre 14 January

1893 **The Venetian Singer** (B C Stephenson) 1 act Court Theatre 25 November

1894 **Die Brillanten-Königin** (Theodore Taube, Isidore Fuchs) Carltheater, Vienna 25 March

1894 **The Queen of Brilliants** (Brandon Thomas, new version of *Die Brillanten-Königin*) Lyceum 8 September

1894 **The Devil's Deputy** (J Cheever Goodwin) Abbey's Theater, New York 10 September

1895 **The Birth of Venus, or The Mole and the Model** (Joseph W Herbert) Albaugh's Lyceum Theater, Baltimore 13 February; Hooley's Theater, Chicago 19 May

1898 **Milord Sir Smith** (ex- *Campano*) (George Day, Adrian Ross) Comedy Theatre 15 December

1899 **La Tarantella** (Alfred Murray) Studebaker Theater, Chicago 17 July

1903 **Winsome Winnie** (Paulton) Academy of Music, Baltimore 28 September

1912 **The Myrtle Maiden, or The Girl of Granada** (O'Reilly) Ladbroke Hall (copyright performance) 13 July

JAMAICA Musical in 2 acts by E Y Harburg and Fred Saidy. Lyrics by Harburg. Music by Harold Arlen. Imperial Theater, New York, 31 October 1957.

Jamaica was a slice of Caribbean romance originally conceived as a vehicle for Harry Belafonte (as *Pigeon Island*) but subsequently reinvented as a vehicle for singing star Lena Horne, in the role of luscious Miss Savannah from the said Pigeon Island. For most of the evening Savannah refused to make do with the equally luscious local fisherman Koli (Ricardo Montalban), for she had her eye firmly fixed on getting out of Pigeon Island and up to New York. The get-rich-quick slicker, Joe Nashua (Joe Adams), seems like her ticket north but, thanks to a timely hurricane, she comes to her senses, stays home and marries the fisherman. A good half of the show's songs, both romantic (''Cocoanut Sweet'') and comic (''Push de Button,'' ''Ain't It the Truth,'' ''Napoleon'') were devoted to the star, with Montalban (''Monkey in the Mango Tree,'' ''Savannah''), Josephine Premice (''Leave the Atom Alone'') and Adelaide Hall (''For Every Fish'') sharing the remainder, but none of the numbers found the favor that Arlen's greatest and best songs had done.

The piece, however, served its star and its purpose well enough for David Merrick's shrewdly publicized production to run for 558 performances on Broadway.

Recording: original cast (RCA)

JANIS, Elsie [BIERBOWER, Elsie] (b Columbus, Ohio, 16 March 1889; d Los Angeles, 26 February 1956). Revue and musical comedy soubrette, specializing in impersonations.

Miss Janis began her career as ''Little Elsie'' or sometimes ''La Petite Elsie,'' a child performer, in vaudeville. With one of the most famous stage mothers of all time (''Mrs Jessie Bierbower, former Methodist Sunday School teacher'') behind and beside her, she made her first move into the legitimate theatre at the age of 10 as a member of the Neill stock company in Cincinatti (*The Charity Ball,* etc), and she made her earliest adult appearances in musical comedy in the Aborn Opera Company's touring productions of *Jack and the Beanstalk* (1903, Little Miss Muffett), *The Belle of New York* (1903, Fifi), *The Fortune Teller* (1904, Mlle Pom Pom) and *The Little Duchess* (1904). She was seen on Broadway for the first time in the burlesque *When We Were Forty-One* (1905, Columbia Barnard), performing the impersonations which were her speciality act, and touted as America's answer to Cissie Loftus. She also managed to squeeze this ''spot'' into the more legitimate musical comedy *The Vanderbilt Cup* (1906, Dorothy Willetts), in which she was cast as the juvenile heroine, in her book-musical debut on Broadway the following season.

A musical-comedy version of Tristam Bernard's *La Soeur* produced on Broadway as *The Hoyden* (1907, Joan Talbot); a piece which cast her as *The Fair Co-Ed* (1909, Cynthia Bright); Leslie Stuart's *The Slim Princess* (1910-11, Princess Kalora); and the role of Cinderella in Victor Herbert's *The Lady of the Slipper* alongside Montgomery and Stone (1912) provided further and similarly above-the-title opportunities. In 1914 she appeared in London in *The Passing Show* before returning home to play her last Broadway musical role in *Miss Information* (1915). Thereafter she appeared widely in revue in both America and Britain, latterly performing much material of her own making, and was seen again in musical comedy only when she toured America in the latter stages of her career, playing the title role in *Oh, Kay!*

During the war she was prominent amongst the troops' entertainers, taking for herself the soubriquet ''The Sweetheart of the AEF,'' and after the hostilities were over she trouped with a group of ex-servicemen in a variety show entitled *Elsie Janis and Her Gang* (1919). She retired from the stage in 1929 and for some years worked in the film industry—where she had been seen as early as 1915 in *The Caprices of Kitty* and as author, director and star of a Paramount five-parter called *'Twas Ever Thus*—as a writer (*Betty in Search of a Thrill, Close Harmony, Madam Satan*) and production supervisor (*Paramount on Parade*). She also fulfilled such occasional stage assignments as the ''supervision'' of Dillingham's *New Faces of 1934.*

During her time on the stage Miss Janis penned a number of songs including ''For I Love Only You'' (mus: Herman Darewski in *The Slim Princess*) and ''For de Lawd's Sake, Play a Waltz,'' as heard in *Over the River.*

Autobiographies: *So Far, So Good!* (Dutton, New York, 1932), *The Big Show, My Six Months with the American Expeditionary Forces* (Cosmopolitan, New York, 1919)

JÁNOS VITÉZ A play with songs (daljáték) in 3 acts by Károly Bakonyi based on the dramatic poem by Sándor Petőfi. Lyrics by Jenő Heltai. Music by Pongrác Kacsoh. Király Színház, Budapest, 18 November 1904.

János vitéz (''brave John''), the most celebrated and loved of all Hungarian musical plays, has been revived regularly and widely in its country of origin in the nearly one hundred years since its first production, and it has become regarded virtually as the Hungarian national show, without attracting the attention of the rest of the world.

The shepherd, János (Sári Fedák), is in love with the orphaned Iluska (Vilma Medgyaszay) and, to the despair of the devoted Bagó (Mihály Papp), she returns his love. Iluska's cruel stepmother (Janka Csatay) causes János's flock to stray whilst he is playing his pipes to his beloved, and the disgraced shepherd has to leave the village. He joins the army in the hope of winning fame and fortune, rises to command, comes to the aid of the beleaguered French King (József Németh) and leads his army to victory over the Turks, but he turns down the prize of half the French kingdom and the hand of the French Princess (Elza Szamosi) in order to return home, only to learn from Bagó that Iluska is dead, murdered by her jealous stepmother. With Bagó as his companion, János sets out for the afterworld and the Lake of Life, determined to find his love. Defeating the witch—for that indeed was what the stepmother was—he succeeds in calling up Iluska from her place, deep in the lake, as the queen of fairyland. She would have him stay there, to rule by her side, but Bagó insists that János belongs to the real world and, ultimately, Iluska leaves the fairy realms to return to the mortal world at János's side.

Kacsoh's score illustrated the tale with a warm, rich simplicity, producing some beautiful folk-toned melodies for his leading characters, with János's entrance song ''Én a pásztorok Királya'' and Iluska's introductory ''Van egy szegény kis árva lány'' being amongst the gems of the score. The French characters, the only ''foreigners'' of the piece, are pointedly given music of a different type. The Princess has a stylized showpiece of a waltz (the only one in the score), ''O, csak ne volnék gyönge leányka,'' whilst the King, traditionally played as a croaking ancient, wheezes through his two numbers in a depiction of decadent foreignness.

József Bokor's mounting of *János vitéz* at the Király Színház was a huge success. The piece was played one hundred times by 17 February 1905, passed its 200th performance on 10 June 1905, its 300th on 6 April 1906, its 400th on 23 May 1913, its 500th on 22 January 1920 and its 600th on 19 October 1921. A burlesque, *Kukorica Jónás* (Géza Vágó, Adolf Mérei) was seen at the Városligeti Színkör (21 June 1905), and the show was produced in Helsinki (4 January 1913) in Finnish, and played in Vienna, with Fedák and Csatay in their original roles, by the Király Színház company (Carltheater 6 May 1913).

Played, in all, 689 times at Király Színház, it has since been seen at the Népopera, the Városi Színház and, after many other productions and performances, most recently in the repertoire at Budapest's Erkel Színház, at Miskolc (1995) and at Kecskemét (1997).

In 1985 a souped-up version, *János a vitez,* subtitled a ''pop-dal-játék'' with Kacsoh's music rearranged by Maté Victor, was produced at Szeged (9 August).

The piece has been filmed both in a silent version (1917), and a highly successful sound version (1938). It was also the basis for a 1973 animated film.

Austria: Carltheater 6 May 1913

Films: Jenő Illés 1917, Béla Gaal 1938

Recordings: complete, selections (Qualiton), 1985 version (Hungaraton)

Literature: Bódis, M: *Két Színházi siker a századelőn* (Magyar Színházi Intézet, Budapest, 1984)

Plate 190. **János vitéz.** *Bagó (Miska Papp) encourages János, the hero (Sári Fedák), to seek out his lost love.*

JANSEN, Marie [JOHNSON, Harriet Mary] (b Boston, 1856; d Milford, Mass, 20 March 1914). Broadway musical leading lady of the 1880s and 1890s.

Miss Jansen (''shapely figure . . . delightful insouciance'') made her first Broadway appearance in the underpowered musical comedy *Lawn Tennis* in 1881 before going on to join the Comley-Barton company, with whom she took a small role in *Olivette* (Veloutine) at the Bijou Theater (though she was promoted to the principal soprano part of Bathilde when the show moved to Boston) and, alongside Catherine Lewis, the second lead as Béatrice in *Manola* (*Le Jour et la nuit*). She subsequently played leading ingenue roles in *Madame Favart* (Suzanne), *The Vicar of Bray* (Dorothy) and *Billee Taylor* (Phoebe), and appeared as Leila in *Satanella,* Patience in *Patience* and as Iolanthe in Broadway's *Iolanthe* (1882), before in 1883 she joined John McCaull's comic opera company to appear in *Der Bettelstudent* (Bronislawa). After a trip to London with a play called *Featherbrain* (1884), she returned to McCaull to play Fantine in *François les bas-bleus* and Rosetta in *The Black Hussar* (1884) and also ultimately the star role in the successful *Nadgy,* a role which fell to her lot when Sadie Martinot walked out in rehearsals.

In 1889 she joined Francis Wilson's comic-opera company and appeared as leading lady opposite the comedian in the American remakes of three French opérettes, *La Jolie Persane* / *The Oolah* (1889, Tourouloupi), *L'Étoile* / *The Merry Monarch* (1890, Lazuli) and *Le Grand Casimir* / *The Lion Tamer* (1891, Colombe), before taking advantage of her now considerable popularity to go out as the top-billed star of Glen MacDonough's play with songs, *Miss Dynamite* (1894, Georgia Day). She subsequently top-billed as the Countess in *The Merry Countess* (ie, *Niniche,* 1895), in the flop play *A Florida Enchantment,* then in the farce *The Nancy Hanks* in which, in the role of a music-hall artist, she interpolated several songs, and in *A Stranger in New York.* She played thereafter in vaudeville, and toured at the head of her own company until after the turn of the century, before tactfully retiring when her ventures proved that, although still a drawing favorite, she had begun to wane in public favor.

JARNO, Georg [KOHNER, György] (b Budapest, 3 June 1868; d Breslau, 25 May 1920). Composer for turn-of-the-century central European stages who scored one major hit amongst a grand average of lesser ones.

In the first part of his life in the musical theatre, Jarno led parallel careers as a conductor and a composer. He worked in the former capacity in Bremen, Gera, Halle, Metz, Liegnitz, Chemnitz and Magdeburg, and then as regisseur at Kissingen, whilst his early composing work included the music for a piece called *Die schwarze Kaschka* (lib: Viktor Blüthgen, Breslau 27 May 1895, Theater des Westens 5 June 1898, 3 performances), the incidental music for a comedy produced at Ischl, and an Operette, *Juno von Tarent,* which does not seem to have been staged. His *Der Richter von Zalamea/A zalameai biró* (lib based on Calderon by Blüthgen), at first described as an opera, was seen in Posen and at the Breslau Stadttheater (14 March) in 1899, and his first genuine Operette, *Der zerbrochene Krug,* based on the play by Heinrich von Kleist, although it took some while to find a producer, was ultimately mounted at Hamburg four years later. He had some success with the Operette *Der Goldfisch,* which went on from Breslau to be seen in Nagyvárad and other mid-European centers, but he was just short of his 40th birthday before he broke through to significant success with the score for the 1907 musical play *Die Förster-Christl,* mounted with extraordinary success at Vienna's Theater in der Josefstadt by his brother Josef Jarno, with his sister-in-law, star soubrette Hansi Niese, in the title role.

He repeated the *Förster-Christl* formula with *Das Musikantenmädel* and *Die Marinen-Gustl*—both vehicles for the hugely popular Niese and both produced with success (57 performances, 30 performances) at the Theater in der Josefstadt before going on to productions in Germany and in Hungary (*A Muzsikuslány* Budai Színkör 4 June 1911, *Tengerész Kató* Népopera 21 September 1912)—and with a Berlin wild-Western piece, *Das Farmermädchen.* He won a further ration of success with a wartime piece, *Mein Annerl,* mounted by Sigmund Eibenschütz at the Vienna Carltheater, with Alexander Girardi in the starring role, for a five months' run.

Jungfer Sonnenschein, with no Girardi to assist the box office, was, nevertheless, another Carltheater success before going on to a fine 140-performance run at Berlin's Thalia-Theater (5 July 1919), and his last work, *Die Csikós-Baroness,* a piece based on a Sándor Petőfi tale, kept up the composer's fine latter-day record, playing 50 nights in Hamburg and in Breslau before going on to Munich, Leipzig and to Berlin's Neues Theater (28 August 1919) for 112 performances—playing there whilst his previous piece still filled the Thalia, and subsequently being made into a film (J & L Fleck, 1930). Jarno was still at the peak of his late-found success when he died at the age of 51.

His brother, the actor and theatre director **Josef JARNO** [József KOHNER] (b Budapest, 24 August 1866; d Vienna, 11 January 1932) was the manager of Vienna's Theater in der Josefstadt from 1899. During his management, he premiered a number of musical plays, including a German version of the French vaudeville-opérette *La Dot de Brigitte, Auch so eine!, Das Wäschermädl, Der Schusterbub, Die Förster-Christl, Paula macht alles, Das Musikantenmädel, Die Frau Gretl, Die Marinen-Gustl, Die Wundermühle* and *Botschafterin Leni.* He also, for a period, concurrently ran the Lustspieltheater (*Tolle Wirtschaft, Alma, wo wohnst du?,* etc). Jarno made an enormously successful appearance as an actor on the musical stage when he appeared in his native Budapest, in his sixties, as the Emperor in the Hungarian premiere of *Im weissen Rössl.*

1903 **Der zerbrochene Krug** (Heinrich Lee) Stadttheater, Hamburg 15 January

1907 **Der Goldfisch** (Richard Jäger) Schauspielhaus, Breslau 20 January

1907 **Die Förster-Christl** (Bernhard Buchbinder) Theater in der Josefstadt 17 December

1910 **Das Musikantenmädel** (Buchbinder) Theater in der Josefstadt 18 February

1912 **Die Marinen-Gustl** (Buchbinder) Theater in der Josefstadt 22 March

1913 **Das Farmermädchen** (Georg Okonkowski) Gross-Berlin Operetten-Theater, Berlin 22 March

1916 **Mein Annerl** (Fritz Grünbaum, Wilhelm Sterk) Carltheater 7 October

1918 **Jungfer Sonnenschein** (Buchbinder) Volksoper, Hamburg 16 February; Carltheater, Vienna 18 May

1919 **Die Csikós-Baroness** (Grünbaum) Neues Operetten-Theater, Hamburg 28 October

JAUNER, Franz (b Vienna, 14 November 1832; d Vienna, 23 February 1900). Important Vienna producer of the last decades of the 19th century.

At first an actor of some repute, Jauner turned to production when he took over the management of the Carltheater from Anton Ascher in 1872. He continued the theatre's traditional programming policy of local musical comedies and imported opéras-bouffes and -comiques, bringing Vienna such pieces as German versions of *La Cour du Roi Pétaud* (*Confusius IX*), *Les Cent Vierges* (*Hundert Jungfrauen*), *La Fille de Madame Angot* (*Angot die Tochter der Halle*), *La Permission de dix heures* (*Urlaub nach Zapfenstreich*), *La Jolie Parfumeuse* (*Schönroschen*), *La Belle Bourbonnaise* (*Die schöne Bourbonnaise*), *Les Prés Saint-Gervais* (*Prinz Conti*), *La Petite Mariée* (*Graziella*), *Giroflé-Girofla* and Verne's spectacular *Die Reise um die Erde in 80 Tagen,* as well as Suppé's homemade *Cannebas, Die Frau Meisterin,* his reorganized *Banditenstreiche* and, above all, the premiere of his *Fatinitza,* and a number of short new native pieces by such composers as Löw, Zaytz and Brandl.

After five seasons, Jauner moved on to take over the management of the Vienna Hofoper (1877-80), which he left, in turn, in 1881 to go to the Ringtheater. He had been in charge there but a short time when the destruction of the theatre by fire occurred, during the course of a performance, in December 1881. This deathly disaster put a frost on Jauner's ostensible activities for a number of years and, although, during the management of Franz Steiner at the Theater an der Wien in the early 1880s, it was actually Jauner who was the owner of that famous house, he was little in evidence personally. In 1884 he sold the bricks and mortar to Alexandrine von Schönerer, but he remained an active co-director of the Theater an der Wien with her, through the artistic managements of Camillo Walzel and of Schönerer herself, for more than another decade, until the lady took over the theatre alone in 1895.

At that same time, Jauner returned to take over again the management of the Carltheater. In the five years that followed, however, he did not find a great deal of good fortune. He survived largely on revivals of repertoire pieces, as none of his wide selection of new works—Suppé's *Das Modell,* Victor Herbert's *Der Zauberer von Nil* (*The Wizard of the Nile*), the new German version of *König Chilperich,* the attempt to make a musical of *La Cigale* as *Bum-Bum* for Girardi, Ludwig and Leon Held's *Der Cognac-König,* Ferron's *Das Krokodil,* Suppé's *Die Pariserin,* Weinberger's *Adam und Eva,* a German version of *Les P'tites Michu,* Englander's American comic opera *Die kleine Corporal* and Gilbert and Osmond Carr's *Der Herr Gouverneur* (*His Excellency*)—proved to be the kind of hit he had housed in his first period at the theatre. Even *Wiener Blut,* a Johann Strauss pasticcio, which would later find its way into the revivable repertoire, was a failure on its first showing at Jauner's house.

Jauner committed suicide at his desk in the Carltheater in February of 1900.

Willi Först's film *Operette* used Jauner as its central character. As played by Först himself, he was depicted as the ''König der Wiener Operette'' leading a battle from the Carltheater for supremacy over Marie Geistinger and the Theater an der Wien.

JAVOTTE *see* CINDERELLA THE YOUNGER

JAY, Isabel [Emily] (b Wandsworth, London, 17 October 1877; d Monte Carlo, 26 February 1927). Star soprano of the London comic opera and musical comedy stage.

Miss Jay joined D'Oyly Carte's company at the age of 20 and made her first important appearance deputizing for Ilka Pálmay, as Elsie in *The Yeomen of the Guard,* before being sent out as principal with the Carte touring companies. She returned to the Savoy the following year, playing the Plaintiff in *Trial by Jury,* understudying Ruth Vincent and Emmie Owen, and then appearing as Aloès in *The Lucky Star* (1899). In the following production, *The Rose of Persia,* she was cast in the supporting role of Blush-of-Morning, but when the American vocalist Ellen Beach Yaw proved insufficient in the star role of the piece, she was promoted to leading lady, and she maintained that position at the Savoy for two years (Mabel, Patience, Phyllis, Lady Rosie Pippin in *The Emerald Isle,* Gipsy in *Ib and Little Christina*) before retiring to a brief first marriage to the African explorer Henry Shepperd Hart Cavendish.

She returned less than two years later, under the management of George Edwardes, to take over Lillian Eldée's role of Marjory Joy in *A Country Girl* for the final part of that show's long London run, and she remained with Edwardes to play the lead soprano role of *The Cingalee* (1904, Lady Patricia Vane) and to succeed Miss Vincent as *Véronique,* before moving to the management of Frank Curzon for the leading roles in a series of musicals between 1906 and her retirement in 1911, after becoming (1910) Mrs, later to be Lady, Curzon.

Amongst the musicals which she created under Curzon's management were *The White Chrysanthemum* (1905, Sybil Cunningham), *The Girl Behind the Counter* (1906, Winnie Willoughby), *Miss Hook of Holland* (1907, Sally Hook), *My Mimosa Maid* (1908, Paulette), *King of Cadonia* (1908, Princess Marie), *Dear Little Denmark* (1909, Christine) and *The Balkan Princess* (1910, Princess Stephanie). She also appeared with great critical success as Olivia in the Liza Lehmann/Laurence Housman musicalization of *The Vicar of Wakefield* (1906).

JEAN DE PARIS Opéra-comique in 2 acts by C Godard d'Aucour de Saint-Just. Music by Adrien Boïeldieu. Opéra-Comique, Paris, 1 April 1812.

The opéra-comique *Jean de Paris,* written and composed at a time when the beginnings of the modern musical theatre were still some half a century in the future, is a fine example of a work which might easily have belonged to a later generation. Even given the style and substance of its musical part, its relationship to the opéras-comiques of the late nineteenth-century and, indeed, to even later musical comedy is, in retrospect, clearly visible.

The action is set in a country inn, which, to its owner's exaggerated delight, has been reserved by the traveling Princesse de Navarre. But, before the Princess arrives, one Jean de Paris turns up, with a great retinue, and takes over the whole accommodation. Whilst the innkeeper suffers agonies, Jean then invites the Princess to partake of his hospitality. Her Chamberlain is horrified, but the Princess is pre-warned—Jean de Paris is none other than the disguised Prince of France, the friend of her childhood, whom her brother, the King, hopes she will wed and who has come to try to win her heart in disguise. Whilst the comical antics of their servants and the inn folks buzz on around them, the Princess leads her suitor on, and only after she has made him suffer for his trickery does she admit that she always had every intention of wedding him.

Long a favorite amongst Boïeldieu's works, and amongst French opéras-comiques of the early 19th century, *Jean de Paris* was given regular revivals in Paris and further productions around the world, both in opera houses and also in regular musical theatres. Following its earliest Viennese showings (ad Johann von Seyfried) at the Hoftheater, it was seen at the Theater an der Wien (ad Castelli) and the Theater in der Josefstadt and, as late as 1879, returned for a fresh showing at the Hofoper. London's and New York's first *John of Paris* (ad I Pocock) was a botched affair to which Henry Bishop added some music of his own, whilst the Australians, half a century on, presented a lively English version which also went in for a touch of botching, as it allowed the final curtain to come down on a rondo for the Princess ''composed expressly by A Reiff.'' The piece was played in London at all the principal theatres—Covent Garden, Drury Lane, the Haymarket—and reappeared as late as 1869, as part of an opera-in-English season at the Olympic Theatre (31 July), in a version topped up with ''several solos and concerted pieces by W F Taylor.''

Italian, Spanish, Russian, Hungarian (ad E Pály), Czech and Scandinavian adaptations and productions were all also seen in the decades following the show's first productions.

Austria: Hoftheater *Johann von Paris* 28 August 1812 Germany: Stuttgart *Johann von Paris* 28 September 1812, Berlin 25 March 1813; UK: Theatre Royal, Covent Garden *John of Paris* 14 November 1814; USA: Park Theater 25 November 1816 (Eng); Australia: Melbourne 1862

Recording: complete (Gaîté-Lyrique)

JEANNE, JEANNETTE ET JEANNETON Opéra-comique in 3 acts by Clairville and Alfred Delacour. Music by Paul Lacome. Théâtre des Folies-Dramatiques, Paris, 27 October 1876.

Lacome's most successful work, *Jeanne, Jeannette et Jeanneton* was a welcome hit at the Folies-Dramatiques, which had suffered through several previous years of flops prior to its production. It was played for 104 successive performances at Louis Cantin's theatre before being forcibly and unwillingly withdrawn in order to fulfill the theatre's contract to produce Offenbach's *La Foire Saint-Laurent.* Clairville and Delacour's fine libretto, however, sat long on Cantin's desk without being set. The manager originally offered it to Offenbach, who thought it might work well, but that it would require three top-of-the-bill prima donnas in the triple title role. The idea of Judic, Théo and Granier together in one show gave Cantin sufficient of a turn (doubtless both financially and in anticipation of the backstage dramas involved) to back off, and Offenbach returned *Jeanne, Jeannette et Jeanneton* unset. Thereafter, Cantin used the text as an audition piece for aspiring composers, doling them out three or four numbers to set as a trial. When he did this to Lacome, the neophyte composer instead set almost the whole piece in record time, and won himself a production.

The three poor girls of the title meet on a coach on their way to Paris, and make a promise to meet up again in five years time, on 3 June 1765. Jeanneton (Marie Gélabert) works at, and then inherits, her godfather's restaurant, and there she is courted by the soldier Laramée, who is none other than the Marquis de Nocé (Ernest Vois) in disguise. She fixes her marriage for the night of the reunion, but marriage is not what de Nocé had in mind, and though Jeannette (Berthe Stuart) and Jeanne (Mlle Prelly) turn up for the big night, the bridegroom doesn't—there is just a letter, saying his colonel has forbidden the marriage. But Jeannette is now the famous dancer, La Guimard, and Jeanne has become the Comtesse du Barry, the king's famous mistress, and they have influence. Moreover, it eventuates that they both have reason to be interested in Colonel de Nocé. He has been courting Jeannette under his real name, and now Jeanne finds herself in trouble with the King when a newspaper accuses her of a rendezvous galant with the same nobleman at Jeanneton's inn. So now the faithless De Nocé has the vengeance of all three to cope with. The girls manage things so that he gets his desserts. While Jeanneton ends up in the arms of faithful little Briolet (Simon-Max), who has managed to turn up in a different guise in each act, Jeannette makes peace with her principal protector, the Prince de Soubise (Ange Milher), and Jeanne sets the King's mind at rest, the Marquis de Nocé is bundled royally off to prove himself at the womanless battlefront.

The three girls shared the finale of the prologue (''Jeanne, Jeannette et Jeanneton, nous commençons un grand voyage avec un bien léger bagage ''), and thereafter also shared the show's main musical moments. Jeanneton had a romance (''Depuis longtemps'') and a duo with de Nocé in the first act, before Jeanne and Jeannette entered to join in a series of reunion Couplets. A second series of Couplets followed on their departure, when, in a neat piece of theatre, the announcement of each lady's carriage gives away, for the first time, her new station in life. In the second act, at her home, Jeannette sang of her double life (''On sait que j'ai deux amoureux''), and Jeanne bewailed the depredations of the gutter press (''La chronique médisante''), whilst in the third, at Jeanne's headquarters at Versailles, she delivered the air ''Oui, c'en est fait, me voilà reine!,'' Jeanneton the Couplets ''Je suis femme et cabaretière'' and Jeanette faced up to the slimy Marquis with ''Ah! tu prêtes l'oreille.''

The men were less largely served, though Briolet, having opened the prologue, turns up as a chef de cuisine at the Cabaret de Bancelin, with some jolly Act I moments, then as Jeannette's cook, equipped with a sorry romance (''Dieu! quelle faiblesse est le nôtre'') in the second part, and as a soldier in the third when Édouard Maugé, in the role of his Sergeant La Grenade, joined him in the comic duo ''Obéissance à la consigne'' and a quartet. The Marquis rendered the couplets ''En jeune et galant militaire'' in Act I, and the rondeau of excuses AVous allez comprendre peut-être'' in Act II.

Following its Paris success, the show was seen throughout Europe. Brussels's Théâtre des Fantaisies-Parisiennes played nothing else for two months, and a German version (ad Georg Friedrich Reiss) was played in Hamburg, then in Berlin, with considerable success, and subsequently in Vienna, where Hermine Meyerhoff (Jeanne), Rosa Streitmann (Jeannette) and Frln Schindler (Jeanneton) were paired with Franz Eppich (de Nocé), Karl Blasel (Briolet) and Grün (Prince). The piece failed to appeal to the Viennese and was dropped after 10 performances, but it continued on to be played in Graz, Nuremberg and elsewhere, and Italian and Spanish versions were also mounted.

The first English version (ad Robert Reece) was produced in Britain, where Alice May, Lizzie St Quinten and Constance Loseby appeared as the three ladies of the title, W S Penley was the Prince, W H Woodfield the Marquis and Fred Leslie was Briolet, and a ''grand mythological ballet'' called *Endymion,* music by Georges Jacobi, was pasted into the second act for ''the renowned Alhambra corps de ballet.'' It played a respectable three months in the big Alhambra auditorium. In America, where the piece was first seen in 1878 in French with Rosina Stani and Zélie Weil heading the cast, Reece's adaptation, re-adapted by Max Freeman, was produced in 1887 under the retitle *The Marquis.* The girls were now Mae (Isabelle Urquhart), Marie (Bertha Ricci) and Marion (Lucie Grubb), Mark Smith played the Marquis, James T Powers was Briolet and Courtice Pounds the Prince de Soubise, through some 70 performances.

In Hungary, a version by ''Imre Ukki'' (Mrs Csepreghy) was mounted at the Népszínház in 1885 for five performances.

Another opérette, in one act (Julien Nargeot/Émile Abraham, Marc Constantin), was produced under the same title at the Folies-Marigny on 31 October 1876.

Germany: Carl-Schultze Theater, Hamburg 30 September 1877, Friedrich-Wilhelmstädtisches Theater, Berlin 9 October 1877; Austria: Carltheater 24 February 1878; USA: Booth's Theater (Fr) 28 October 1878, Casino Theater *The Marquis* 19 September 1887; UK: Alhambra Theatre 28 March 1881; Hungary: Népszínház 20 February 1885

JEANNE QUI PLEURE ET JEAN QUI RIT Opérette in 1 act by Charles Nuitter and Étienne Tréfeu. Music by Jacques Offenbach. Ems, 19 July 1864; Théâtre des Bouffes-Parisiens, Paris, 3 November 1865.

The Jeanne who snivels (Zulma Bouffar) is actually a lively little miller's daughter, and the Jean who is jolly is also her, in disguise. It is all part of a plot to dissuade the local viticulteur, Cabochon (Désiré), from purchasing the mill which she has inherited and the new owner of which she must marry, so that her own boyfriend can become both boss and spouse. Jean-Paul, as Cabochon's offspring, and Pelva completed the cast as the two young men.

First produced, like a number of other one-act Offenbach pieces, in the spa resort of Ems, the little four-hander reached Vienna before it reached Paris, and with positive results. It became particularly popular in its German-language version (ad uncredited) and Vienna's Carltheater played *Hanni weint und Hansi lacht* in its repertoire regularly for 5 years, and intermittently for another ten, with Karl Blasel making the most of the role of the outwitted Sebastian Mosthuber (ex- Cabochon) with its grotesque leap into feminine clothes. The German version was seen in Hungary and in America, and an Hungarian version (ad Jenő Rákosi) was also later played in Budapest.

An English version, mounted at London's Adelphi Theatre with Johnny Toole as Popinoff (ex- Cabochon), Mrs Mellon as Jenny and Johnny, Theresa Furtado as Jocrisse (the son), and William H Eburne as the favored Jollibois was killed by undersungness, and had less of an afterlife.

Austria: Carltheater *Hanni weint und Hansi lacht* 4 February 1865; UK: Adelphi Theatre *Crying Jenny and Laughing Johnny* 16 April 1866; Hungary: Budai Színkör *Die Hanni weint, der Hansi lacht* 26 September 1869, Népszínház *Ancsi sir, Jancsi nevet* 18 January 1878; USA: Terrace Garten *Hanni weint, Hansi lacht* 17 May 1872

JEKYLL AND HYDE Musical in 2 acts by Leslie Bricusse based on the story *The Strange Case of Dr Jekyll and Mr Hyde* by Robert Louis Stevenson. Music by Frank Wildhorn. Alley Theater, Houston, 25 May 1990, Plymouth Theater, New York, 28 April 1997.

Stevenson's 1886 story has been adapted many time for the stage. Within two years of its publication, four different versions appeared in London alone, and a whole series sprouted up on the American road, easily the most successful of which was T Russell Sullivan's American version (Madison Square 12 September 1887) produced at the Lyceum (4 August 1888) with Richard Mansfield in the bravura double title role. Another successful version was that produced by H B Irving in 1910 (29 January). Both these plays elaborated the original tale heavily in acordance with the taste of the times, and both introduced a feminine element: Sullivan gave Jekyll a love interest (played by Beatrice Cameron, ie, Mrs Mansfield), Carr went so far as to give him a wife (played by Dorothea Baird, ie, Mrs Irving) blinded by the doctor in one of his earlier experiments, and an ex-mistress around whom the non-Stevensonian plot was evolved. Sullivan's version provoked the first musical Jekyll and Hyde in the shape of an Edward Kidder burlesque *Dr Freckle and Mr Snide.* What seem to have been the first full-sized musical *Dr Jekyll and Mr Hyde,* written by Oscar Dane and produced at the Orpheum, St Joseph, 23 April 1905, also emphasized the love story and ''concluded with an allegorical vision of the planet Venus where Dr Jekyll and his sweetheart meet in the spirit world.''

In more modern times, the Goodspeed Opera House produced a musical *After You, Mr Hyde* (Norman Sachs/Mel Mandel/Lee Thuna, 24 June 1968) which won continuing performances for more than 20 years thereafter, and NBC mounted a television *Dr Jekyll and Mr Hyde* (7 March 1973) with a libretto by Sherman Yellen, songs from Lionel Bart, Mel Mandel and Norman Sachs and Kirk Douglas starred as Jekyll and Hyde.

In the wake of the vast success of *The Phantom of the Opéra,* with disfigured and/or psychopathic and/or melodramatic heroes from Dracula to Jack the Ripper to Vampires being all the rage, the modern musical theatre's most persistent remaker of classic literature, Leslie Bricusse, had his go at this one, in collaboration with pop songwriter Frank Wildhorn (''Where Does a Broken Heart Go?''). Originally launched as a concept album, it was given its first stage production (''underwritten by AT&T'') at the Alley Theater, Houston in 1990 with Chuck Wagner as Jekyll/Hyde without creating too much positive interest: the local press found it ''lumpy, derivative and uninspired'' in its book (''jarring inconsistencies . . . forced humor'') and its ''marshmallow-soft-rock score'' (''colorless, pitter-patter recitative'' ''obvious hooks and synthesized orchestrations''). ''The creative team must disguise *Jekyll's* shameless legacy from earlier shows'' summed up another paper. However, a second recording followed, then a second, more extravagant Houston mounting, and ultimately, some seven years after its first production, the show made its way to Broadway's Plymouth Theatre.

Bricusse's version of the tale went as far and further than Sullivan's and Carr's in remaking the original. Little more than the characters of the leading man remained. This Hyde had a fiancée called Emma who sang the ingenue bits, and a music-hally tart, Lucy, who sang the brassy bits and supplied the bits of for-frustrated-housewives-style sex, and he rampaged through the evening as a purposeful serial killer (the original tale sports one, virtually accidental death) out to knock off the recalcitrant folk who won't let him use the local paupers as guinea pigs for his concoctions. There was also an invented chief nasty called Simon Stride.

The tart got the most effective number, ''A New Life,'' in a score which sported a bundle of poppish ballads with titles such as ''Someone Like You'' or ''Once Upon a Dream,'' whilst the leading man had his main moment in the tunefully take-awayable ''This Is the Moment.''

Robert Cuccioli, long in possession of the lead role, introduced it to Broadway with Linda Eder, who had been attached to the project since its inception, as Lucy. The piece was still as reminiscent as ever of bits of half a dozen or more other shows, the reviews were poor (''makes *Sunset Boulevard* sound like *Parsifal;* . . . like having the television and the radio [set to a 'lite' station] on at the same time''), the award givers ignored it, and yet *Jekyll and Hyde* made itself a fine career on Broadway (1,543 performances), while moving on to an afterlife in the American regions and in a Europe avid, in spite of its own burgeoning new musicals industry, for fresh hits from overseas.

Jekyll and Hyde had its European premiere at Antwerp on 26 September 1997 before going on to be seen in Germany (ad Melitta Edith) with Ethan Freeman in the title role and in Scandinavia (Norrköping 17 September 1999).

Following another mode started by *The Phantom of the Opéra, Jekyll and Hyde* inspired the copycats to action. One such piece, with book and lyrics by David Levy and Leslie Eberhard, began its life in Massachussetts and ended it in New Jersey, whilst England too fell into the sad fin de siècle fashion for unoriginality and put out a *Jekyll* by Tony Rees and Gary Young at Bromley. Denmark's Gladsaxe Theater, Copenhagen, a lively producer of new musicals almost always on other people's subjects followed suit in 1999 (17 October).

Germany: Musical-Theater, Bremen 19 February 1999

Recordings: pre-production Album (RCA Victor), original cast (Warner Atlantic), German cast selection (Polydor), Levy/Everhard (TER)

JENBACH, Béla [JAKOBOVITS, Béla] (b Miskolcz, 1 April 1871; d Vienna, 21 January 1943). Successful librettist/lyricist to, in particular, Kálmán, Eysler and Lehár in the 1910s and 1920s.

Originally an actor, the Vienna-based Jenbach was nearly 40 before he made his first attempts as a librettist, and he did well enough with his second text for an Operette *Die Liebesschule,* which was taken up for productions in Hungary (*Don Juan hadnagy* Városligeti Színkör 4 November 1910) and, under the Shubert management, in America (*The Love School* ad Howard Jacott, Wilkes-Barre, closed pre-Broadway) following its German premiere. His next Operette, *Die romantische Frau* (1911), written with Carl Weinberger and Carl Lindau, ran for 73 performances at the Johann Strauss-Theater, but the following year Jenbach notched up his first substantial success with the libretto to the Charles Cuvillier piece *Der lila Domino*—a show which would go on to a considerable life in, in particular, Britain. In 1913 he scored his first real Vienna hit, in collaboration with Leo Stein, with the libretto for Edmund Eysler's *Ein Tag im Paradies* (1913). *Ein Tag im Paradies* went on from considerable Vienna success to considerable Broadway success, attached to a botched score, as *The Blue Paradise.* However, Jenbach and Stein topped that record two seasons later when they supplied the libretto for Kálmán's enormously popular *Die Csárdásfürstin,* and they continued on to further successes with the same composer's *Das Hollandweibchen* and with Lehár's *Die blaue Mazur.*

Jenbach later continued the association with Lehár when he adapted Horst and Engel's play *Der Schrei nach der Kinde* as the libretto for his *Cloclo,* revised Paul Knepler's original *Paganini* libretto into its definitive version, and turned Gabryela Zapolska's play *A Cárevics* into the libretto for *Der Zarewitsch.* Like this piece, his other late works were also largely in the line of adaptations from the Hungarian.

1909 **Biribi** (Fritz Korolanyi/w Robert Pohl) Neues Operettentheater, Mannheim 5 February

1909 **Die Liebesschule** (Korolanyi/w R Pohl) Stadttheater, Leipzig 13 March

1911 **Die romantische Frau** (Carl Weinberger/w Carl Lindau) Johann Strauss-Theater 17 March

1911 **Der Natursänger** (Edmund Eysler/w Leo Stein) 1 act Apollotheater 22 December

1912 **Der lila Domino** (Charles Cuvillier/w Emmerich von Gatti) Stadttheater, Leipzig 3 February

1912 **Die Première** (J G Hart/w Stein) 1 act Apollotheater 10 August

1912 **Der tolle Kosak** (Siegwart Ehrlich/w Hans Hall) Neues Operetten-Theater, Leipzig 28 September

1912 **Der fliegende Rittmeister** (Hermann Dostal/w Stein) Apollotheater 5 October

1913 **Ein Tag im Paradies** (Eysler/w Stein) Wiener Bürgertheater 23 December

1915 **Liebesgeister** (Ernst Steffan/w Rudolf Österreicher) 1 act Apollotheater 1 March

1915 **Die—oder keine** (Eysler/w Stein) Wiener Bürgertheater 9 October

1915 **Die Csárdásfürstin** (Emmerich Kálmán/w Stein) Johann Strauss-Theater 17 November

1916 **Urschula** (H Dostal/w Julius Wilhelm) Apollotheater 1 September

1920 **Das Hollandweibchen** (Kálmán/w Stein) Johann Strauss-Theater 31 January

1920 **Die blaue Mazur** (Lehár/w Stein) Theater an der Wien 28 May

1921 **Rinaldo** (*Gróf Rinaldo*) German version w Österreicher (Johann Strauss-Theater)

1922 **Die Siegerin** (Tchaikovsky arr Josef Klein/w Oskar Friedmann, Fritz Lunzer) Neues Wiener Stadttheater 7 November

1923 **Die Ballkönigin** (Karl Stigler/w von Gatti) Löwingerbühne 21 September

1924 **Cloclo** (Lehár) Wiener Bürgertheater 8 March

1925 **Paganini** (Lehár/w Paul Knepler) Johann Strauss-Theater 30 October

1927 **Der Zarewitsch** (Lehár/w Heinz Reichert) Deutsches Künstlertheater, Berlin 21 February

1930 **Sisters** German version (Johann Strauss-Theater)

1931 **Die kluge Mama** (*Az okos mama*) German version (Volksoper)

1933 **Die Fahrt in die Jugend** (Eduard Künneke/w Ludwig Hirschfeld) Stadttheater, Zürich 26 March

JEROME, Ben[jamin M] (b New York, 6 April 1882; d Huntingdon Station [Brightwater], NY, 27 March 1938). The conductor at Chicago's La Salle Theater for some years, Ben Jerome was also one of the chief purveyors of music to the Chicago theatre during its heyday as a home of original musicals in the early years of the 20th century.

Jerome first came to the fore as a songwriter when he and lyricist Matt Woodward had the song "Blooming Lize" interpolated into the Broadway musical *The Chaperons* (1902). Since the score of *The Chaperons* was written by publisher Isidore Witmark, and he had ensured that his contract with the producer specifically forbade interpolations, the song had to be withdrawn, and the furious Jerome took vast advertisements in the trade press damning the "jealous" publisher and his work, and boosting and promoting himself and his work. "Blooming Lize" turned up in the touring version of *Mam'selle 'Awkins* (1902) instead. Thoroughly noticed, as a result of the brouhaha and his subsequent bannered boast of an $1,100 advance for the song "Let Us Swear by the Pale Moonlight," Jerome went on to interpolate songs into *The Wizard of Oz* (1902, "For I'm the Wizard of Oz"), *The Rogers Brothers in Harvard* (1902, "Ain't It Tough to Be so Absent-Minded"), *Weary Willie Walker* (1902, "A Soldier in the Ranks, That's All"), *Huckleberry Finn* ("When Little Tommy Sawyer Saw the Circus"), *When*

Reuben Comes to Town (''At the Ball Tonight''), *The Girl from Dixie* (1903, ''Love in an Orchard,'' ''Emelie Lou'') and into several of Gus Hill's fifty-cent circuit shows, including no less than eight numbers amongst those used in the cartoon musical *Alphonse and Gaston* (1902). Three additional songs for a revised revision of the musical comedy *The Defender* (1903) got him a co-composer credit. He also wrote some material for the vaudeville programs at New York's Crystal Gardens, but a burlesque, *The Queen of Ballyhoo Bey,* written for the Cherry Blossom Grove got canceled at the last minute when Jerome got into a barney with the management.

His first full-scale musical, written after his engagement in Chicago, was *The Isle of Spice.* It had a fine run of 143 performances in its little theatre, another good season in Boston and took in 80 performances on Broadway as part of a considerable touring life and, although others of his Chicago pieces did less well on the East Coast, they also had extraordinarily extended lives on the touring circuits. *The Royal Chef* played no less than 38 weeks in its initial Chicago run, followed by 9 in St Louis before going on to the first of its many tours, whilst *The Yankee Regent* (''entire production under the direction of . . .'') notched up 20 weeks at home base before taking a similar route. In November 1905, however, after another set-to with more-powerful-than-he, Jerome ''severed his connection'' with the La Salle and headed east to make his headquarters in New York.

From 1908 Jerome provided music for several shows at New York's Casino Theater, including the 1908 revue *The Mimic World, Mr Hamlet of Broadway* (54 performances) and the successful Sam Bernard piece *He Came from Milwaukee* (117 performances), but he returned west, and to the La Salle, in 1911. Of one of his latter day pieces there, *Louisiana Lou,* featuring the young Sophie Tucker, an East Coast journal remarked, in what was clearly intended as a compliment, that it ''comes closer to Broadway standards of glitter and girls than anything that has worn the trademark of Chicago in recent memory.'' But it did not have the kind of life that *The Isle of Spice* and *The Royal Chef* had had.

Jerome subsequently provided individual songs to the scores of several new and several made-over shows, including the German *A Modern Eve* (''A Quiet Evening at Home'') and the local *Queen High* (''My Lady''), but he returned only once more to Broadway in a more substantial way when he collaborated on the music for H H Frazee's production of *Yes, Yes, Yvette.*

Jerome's most popular individual songs included ''By the Pale Moonlight,'' ''Melancholy Mose,'' ''Take Me Back to Chicago,'' ''The Gumshoe Man'' and ''Lamb, Lamb, Lamb.''

1902 **Alphonse and Gaston** (w others/Matt Woodward, et al) Bridgeton, NJ 14 October; Metropolis Theater 27 December

1903 **The Darling of the Gallery Gods** (Matt C Woodward, John Gilroy/George Hobart) 1 act Crystal Gardens 22 June

1903 **Dress Parade** (Woodward, Gilroy/Hobart) 1 act Crystal Gardens 22 June

1903 **Lifting the Cup** (Woodward, Nicholas H Biddle/Hobart) 1 act Crystal Gardens 27 July

1903 **The Isle of Spice, or His Majesty of Nicobar** (w Paul Schindler/Allen Lowe, George E Stoddard) La Salle Theater, Chicago 12 September; Majestic Theater, New York 23 August 1904

1903 **The Belle of Newport** (revised *The Defenders*) (w Charles F Dennee/Allen Lowe) La Salle Theater, Chicago 21 December

1904 **The Royal Chef** (Stoddard, Charles S Taylor) La Salle Theater, Chicago 28 March

1905 **The Yankee Regent** (Charles S Adelman, Irving Lee Blumenstock) La Salle Theater, Chicago 19 August

1906 **Thebe** (George Siler, Blumenstock) 1 act Forest Park Highlands, St Louis; Majestic Theater, Chicago July; Proctors 23rd Street, New York 3 September

1908 **Mr Hamlet of Broadway** (Edward Madden/Edgar Smith) Casino Theater 23 December

1910 **He Came from Milwaukee** (w Louis Hirsch/Madden/Mark Swan [Edgar Smith]) Casino Theater 21 September

1911 **Louisiana Lou** (Addison Burkhardt, Frederick Donaghey) La Salle Theater, Chicago 3 September

1912 **The Girl at the Gate** (Will Hough, Donaghey) La Salle Theater, Chicago 1 September

1913 **A Trip to Washington** (Henry Blossom) La Salle Theater, Chicago 24 August

1927 **Yes, Yes, Yvette** (w Phil Charig/Irving Caesar/James Montgomery) Harris Theater 3 October

JEROME, Jerome K[lapka] (b Walsall, 2 May 1859; d Northampton, 14 June 1927).

The author of *Three Men in a Boat* had a number of successes as a playwright, but not in the musical-comedy field. His *(John Jenkins in) Biarritz,* written as a vehicle for Arthur Roberts, was a failure, in spite of the popular comedian's name on the bill. Subsequently, several musicals based on Jerome's works made their way to the stage, amongst them the pretty Broadway piece *The Rainbow Girl* and a curious German musical called *Lady Fanny* with a score by Theo Mackeben, both based on *Fanny and the Servant Problem* (1908, US: *The New Lady Bantock*). His name also appeared on the credits for the very short-lived *I Love a Lassie* (Shubert Theater, New Haven 15 May 1919), as the author of an unspecified original piece adapted by one Erwin Connelly with songs by its producer-star, Scottish-American actor Clifton Crawford.

1896 **Biarritz** (F Osmond Carr/Adrian Ross) Prince of Wales Theatre 11 April

Memoirs: *On the Stage and Off: The Brief Career of a Would-be Actor* (Holt, New York, 1891), *My Life and Times* (Harper, New York, 1926), etc

JEROME, William [FLANNERY, William Jerome] (b Cornwall-on-Hudson, NY, 30 September 1865; d New York, 25 June 1932). Highly successful songwriter of the earliest part of the 20th century, who also had some notable successes in the theatre.

Renouncing law studies, the young Billy Jerome became at first a minstrel man, with Howorth's Hibernica (1885) and with Wilson and Rankin's Minstrels, and then a farce-comedy player (*A Paper Doll, The Fakir, US Mail, Grimes' Cellar Door, Excitement*) and a vaudevillian (Charles and William Jerome in *Playmates* [1893] and in *The Prodigal Father* [1894], William Jerome's Herald Square Comedians in *Town Talk* [1895], in *McFadden's Flats* [1896–97] and in *A Jay in New York* [1898–99], etc). He concurrently worked as a facile lyricist, turning out a series of parodies and comic songs (''I'm Old Enough to Know,'' ''He's on the Police Force Now,'' ''I'm not Baby McKee,'' ''I Got It,'' ''Dead to Me,'' ''Take Your Time Gentlemen,'' ''He Never Came Back,'' ''His Sweet Face She Never Saw More'' ''He Didn't Split the Wood'' in *Hoss and Hoss,* 1892, etc) and latterly forming a team with composer Jean Schwartz which led them to a long run of song hits in the earliest years of the 20th century. Their songs, fresh and/or slightly used, were liberally interpolated into both Broadway and West End shows—although it was rumored that publishers Shapiro, Bernstein initially paid producers for the privilege—the same song being, on a number of occasions, used in more than one show. ''Rip van Winkle was a Lucky Man'' appeared in Broadway's *The Sleeping Beauty and the Beast* and in London's *The Cherry Girl,* ''Mr Dooley'' in America's *A Chinese Honeymoon, The Wizard of* Oz and *The Defender,* and in London's *The Toreador,* ''Bedelia'' was sung by Blanche Ring in *The Jersey Lily* (1903) and *When Claudia Smiles* (1914) in America and by George Grossmith in *The Orchid* in Britain, and ''Cordalia Malone,'' heard in *Glittering Gloria* on Broadway, was also put into *The Orchid* in London. All four were considerable hits in both countries.

The pair interpolated numbers into other shows such as *San Toy, An English Daisy, In Spotless Town* (''The Gambling Man,'' ''When the Stars Are Shining Bright'') *The Show Girl* (''In Spotless Town'' again), *The Wild Rose* (Eddie Foy's ''I'm Unlucky''), *Mr Bluebeard* (Foy's ''I'm a Poor Unhappy Maid,'' ''Julie''), *Beauty and the Beast* (''Dear Sing Sing''), *The Echo* (''The Newport Glide''), the Rays' *Down in the Pike, The Little Cherub* (''My Irish Rose''), *Over the River, Bunty Bulls and Strings* (''If It Wasn't for the Irish and the Jews''), *A Winsome Widow* (''String a Ring of Roses'') and several editions of the *Ziegfeld Follies;* provided seven numbers to soup up the Drury Lane pantomime *The White Cat* (1905) for Broadway; and had further show song hits with ''When Mr Shakespeare Comes to Town'' (*Hoity-Toity*), ''Hamlet Was a Melancholy Dane'' (*Mr Bluebeard*), ''My Irish Molly O'' (*Sergeant Brue*) and ''Any Old Time at All'' (*The Rich Mr Hoggenheimer*). From 1903, when they supplied the songs for the Elinore Sisters vehicle *Mrs Delaney of Newport,* they also supplied the full scores for a series of Broadway shows, of which the comical *Piff! Paff! Pouf!* was a long-running hit, composed the songs for two shows for blackface comedians McIntyre and Heath (*The Ham Tree, In Hayti*) and for the 1910 revue *Up and Down Broadway* (''Chinatown, My Chinatown''), and founded their own music publishing company to publish both their own and other folks' work.

Jerome also had song hits in his collaborations with other composers, scoring with such numbers as ''Row, Row, Row'' (*Ziegfeld Follies of 1912* w Jimmy Monaco), ''Back Home in Tennessee'' (w Walter Donaldson) and ''Get Out and Get under the Moon'' (w Larry Shay, Charles Tobias), and provided non-Schwartz interpolated numbers for such shows as *Whirl of Society* (''And the Villain Still Pursued Her'' w Harry von Tilzer for Al Jolson), *Betty* (''Sometime'' w Harry Tierney) and *Step This Way* (1916), where another Chinatown lyric encouraged the world to ''Take me down to blinky, winky, Chinky Chinatown.''

Jerome's wives, performer Maude Nugent and Leona Fontainebleau (née Wade) ''of the original Fontainebleaus,'' both also penned the odd song.

1899 **Hoddy Dotty** (Frank David, et al) burlesque Theatre Comique 11 December

1903 **Mrs Delaney of Newport** (Jean Schwartz) Collingwood Opera House, Poughkeepsie, NY 15 September; Grand Opera House 3 November

1904 **Piff! Paff! Pouf!** (Schwartz/Stanislaus Stange) Casino Theater 2 April

1905 **Lifting the Lid** (Schwartz/J J McNally) Aerial Gardens, New Amsterdam Theater 5 June

1905 **The Ham Tree** (Schwartz/George V Hobart) Lyceum Theater, Rochester 17 August; New York Theater 28 August

1905 **Fritz in Tammany Hall** (Schwartz/McNally) Herald Square Theater 16 October

1907 **Lola from Berlin** (Schwartz/McNally) Liberty Theater 16 September

1908 **Morning, Noon and Night** (Schwartz/Joseph Herbert) Opera House, Hartford, Conn 31 August; Yorkville Theater 5 October

1909 **In Hayti** (Schwartz/McNally) Circle Theater 30 August

1913 **When Claudia Smiles** (Jerome/ Leo Ditrichstein) Illinois Theater, Chicago 13 April

1914 **When Claudia Smiles** (revised version by Anne Caldwell) 39th Street Theater 2 February

1915 **Hands Up** (Sigmund Romberg, Goetz, et al/w E Ray Goetz/Edgar Smith) 44th Street Theater 22 July

1923 **That Casey Girl** (Schwartz/Hobart, Willard Mack) Lyceum, Paterson, NJ 22 October

JESSEL, Leon (b Stettin, 22 January 1871; d Berlin, 4 January 1942). Composer of one of Germany's most enduring Operetten.

A conductor from the age of 20 in such locales as Gelsenkirchen (1891), Mühlheim (1892) and Celle (1894), where his first short stage piece was produced, then later in Freiberg (1899) and at Stettin's important Bellevue-Theater, Chemnitz's Stadttheater and Lübeck's Wilhelm-Theater, Jessel concurrently won some considerable success as a composer of piano and instrumental music, producing, in particular, a little orchestral piece called ''Die Parade der Zinnsoldaten'' (''the parade of the tin-soldiers'') which would go round the world. It was heard in the Russian revue *Chauve-Souris,* in Charell's Berlin revue *An Alle,* recorded by the Andrews Sisters (the soldiers became ''wooden'' in Ballard McDonald's lyric) and remains the composer's single best-known piece of work internationally.

Jessel did not make any headway as an Operette composer until after he settled in Berlin in 1911. There, after contributing two numbers to the successful Posse *Grosse Rosinen,* he had his first full-sized piece, *Die beiden Husaren,* produced at the Theater des Westens (56 performances). It did well enough to go on to be seen in other German houses and in an Hungarian version in Budapest (*Ikrek a táborban* Fővárosi Nyári Színház 24 July 1915). It was, however, the enormously successful wartime Operette *Das Schwarzwaldmädel* produced at the Komische Oper two years later which gave Jessel the theatrical hit of his life and the basis and impetus for a career in the musical theatre.

In the 15 years that followed this singular hit Jessel turned out a regular stream of musical plays; finding, in the wake of the triumph of *Schwarzwaldmädel,* a willing acceptance for his works. Several of these shows had fine careers, but a second major success was not forthcoming. *Die närrische Liebe* had a 127-performance run at the Berlin Thalia-Theater; *Die Postmeisterin,* another collaboration with *Schwarzwaldmädel* librettist Neidhart, was played for over one hundred nights in Berlin and is generally regarded as the composer's best work after his big hit; *Das Detektivmädel,* which followed it, played some 60 nights and went on to be *Detektiv kisasszony* (Budai Színkör 15 September 1922 ad Ernő Kulinyi) in Hungary; whilst *Des Königs Nachbarin* played two months in Berlin and 88 performances at Vienna's Johann Strauss-Theater (6 June 1924).

Of his later pieces, *Meine Tochter Otto* did the best when it was played for 50 nights at Vienna's Rolandbühne, but in 1933, with the coming of National Socialism, the Jewish composer found his music banned. Although he stuck it out in Germany, his last Operette, *Die goldene Mühle,* was produced in Switzerland. It went on to a production at the Vienna Volksoper and a guest season at the Johann Strauss-Theater (21 April 1937), but it was not seen in his native land.

Jessel died in 1942 after having been knocked about by the Gestapo.

1894 **Die Brautwerburg** (Else Gehrke) 1 act Schlosstheater, Celle 1 August

1896 **Kruschke am Nordpol** (Max Reichardt) 1 act Tivoli Theater, Kiel 18 August

1911 **Die grosse Rosinen** (w Willi Bredschneider, Bogumil Zepler, et al/Rudolf Bernauer, Rudolf Schanzer) Berliner Theater 31 December

1913 **Die beiden Husaren** (Wilhelm Jacoby, Schanzer) Theater des Westens 6 February

1914 **Wer zuletzt lacht** (Arthur Lippschitz, A Bernstein-Sawersky) Deutsches Schauspielhaus 31 December

1917 **Schwarzwaldmädel** (August Neidhart) Komische Oper 25 August

1918 **Ein modernes Mädel** (Neidhart) Volkstheater, Munich 28 June

1918 **Ohne Mann kein Vergnügen** (Neidhart) Komische Oper, Berlin

1919 **Die närrische Liebe** (Jean Kren) Thalia Theater 28 November

1920 **Verliebte Frauen** (Alexander Pordes-Milo) Thalia Theater, Königsberg

1921 **Schwalbenhochzeit** (Pordes-Milo) Theater des Westens 28 January

1921 **Die Postmeisterin** (Neidhart) Centraltheater, Berlin 3 February

1921 **Das Detektivmädel** (*Miss Nobody*) (Neidhart) Centraltheater, Berlin 28 October

1923 **Des Königs Nachbarin** (Fritz Grünbaum, Wilhelm Sterk) Wallner-Theater, Berlin 15 April

1923 **Der keusche Benjamin** (Max Steiner-Kaiser, Hans Bodenstädt) Carl-Schultze Theater, Hamburg 1 September

1925 **Prinzessin Husch** (Neidhart) Operettenhaus, Hamburg, 22 December; Theater des Westens, Berlin 11 March 1926

1926 **Die kleine Studenten** (Leo Kastner, Alfred Möller) Bellevue Theater, Stettin 22 December

1927 **Mädels, die man liebt** (Kastner, Möller) Volksoper, Hamburg 17 April

1927 **Meine Tochter Otto** (Grünbaum, Sterk) Rolandbühne, Vienna 5 May

1929 **Die Luxuskabine** (Neidhart) Neues Operetten-Theater, Leipzig 20 October

1933 **Junger Wein** (Neidhart) Theater des Westens 1 September

1936 **Die goldene Mühle** (Hugo Wiener, Carl Costa ad Sterk) Städtebundtheater, Olten, Switzerland 29 October; Volksoper, Vienna 2 March 1937

Biography: Dümling, A: *Die verweigerte Heimat* (Die kleine Verlag, Düsseldorf, 1992)

JESSOP, George H[enry] (b Ireland, ?1851; d Swiss Cottage, London, 21 March 1915). Popular dramatist for America's country circuits who later produced two successful musicals for the London stage.

The apparently Irish-born Jessop moved to the western American seaboard on the proceeds of an inheritance in 1873, and there, over some 20 years, he wrote mostly plays of a colorfully basic but highly effective kind for the touring circuits. Several, written either alone or with such collaborators as William Gill or Brander Matthews, had long, profitable careers (*Sam'l of Posen, Nora, A Gold Mine, Stolen Money, The Power of the Press*). Some—notably the farce comedy *A Bottle of Ink,* which was played in America and Britain, Aimée's plays *Mam'zelle* and *Barnes's Daughters,* Scanlan's Irish vehicles *Myles Aroon* and *Mavourneen,* and *An Irish Artist,* written for Scanlan's successor at the head of the stage-Irish circuits, Chauncey Olcott—also included varying amounts of musical illustration and songs. At the other end of the scale, he ventured a stage adaptation of Dumas's *Edmund Kean.*

In the 1890s Jessop returned to Ireland, where he had in 1891 inherited an estate, and his first work for the British stage was the fine libretto for C V Stanford's light opera *Shamus O'Brien,* which the authors and Stanford's publisher, Boosey & Co, produced at the Opera Comique, with the young Louise Kirkby Lunn and Denis O'Sullivan starring and with some success.

A later collaboration with Sidney Jones produced the highly successful comedy opera *My Lady Molly,* which was, like *Shamus O'Brien,* a piece more substantial and play-like in its libretto than many of the musical comedies of its time, and vastly more vertebrate than the mish-mashes of burlesque, low comedy and extravaganza elements that Jessop had concocted in his earlier days. Although not ultimately credited, he is also said to have had a hand in the writing of a musical version of *The Scarlet Letter,* composed by Walter Damrosch with a text in the end credited only to George P Lathrop.

Jessop also wrote a number of novels (*Check and Counter Check, Judge Lynch, A Tale of the Californian Vineyards, Gerald Ffrench's Friends*).

- 1882 **All At Sea** (pasticcio) Academy of Music, Jersey City, NJ 27 February; San Francisco Minstrels Opera House 17 April
- 1884 **Mam'zelle, or The Little Milliner** (various/w William B Gill) Sampson's Opera House, Kingston, NY 11 September; Fifth Avenue Theater, New York 15 December
- 1885 **A Bottle of Ink** (w Gill) Bijou Theater, Boston 3 November; Comedy Theater, New York 6 January
- 1887 **Barnes's Daughters** (aka *Deceived*) (various) Los Angeles 21 January
- 1888 **Myles Aroon** (various/w Horace Townsend) Walnut Street Theater, Philadelphia 24 December; 4th Street Theater 21 January 1889
- 1891 **Mavourneen** (w Townsend) Springfield, Mass 7 September; 14th Street Theater 28 September
- 1894 **An Irish Artist** Boston Museum 3 September, 14th Street Theater 1 October
- 1896 **Shamus O'Brien** (Charles Villiers Stanford) Opera Comique, London 2 March
- 1902 **My Lady Molly** (Sidney Jones/w Percy Greenbank, C H Taylor) Theatre Royal, Brighton 11 August; Terry's Theatre, London 14 March 1903

JESUS CHRIST SUPERSTAR Rock opera in 2 acts with lyrics by Tim Rice. Music by Andrew Lloyd Webber. Mark Hellinger Theater, New York, 12 October 1971.

The first musical by Rice and Lloyd Webber to be produced on the professional stage, following their happy beginning with the children's cantata *Joseph and the Amazing Technicolor Dreamcoat, Jesus Christ Superstar* made its way into the theatre by stages. The first part of it to be heard was the title song, ''Superstar,'' which was issued as a record single. Then, after a search for a producer who was interested in putting a cantata-form sung-through biomusical of Jesus Christ, with a pop/rock music score, on to the stage had, perhaps not surprisingly, failed, David Land, the representative of the piece, instead settled for the offer by MCA Records' Brian Brolly to put the score of the show on record instead. The two-record album, costing £20,000 to produce, and starring Murray Head (Judas), Ian Gillam (Jesus) and Yvonne Elliman (Mary Magdalene) in its central roles, encouraged producer Harold Fielding to take the piece up, but whilst Land was dealing with Fielding, the young producer and pop music man, Robert Stigwood, had approached the authors direct. From having no producer, *Jesus Christ Superstar* suddenly had two. It also had a growing success, for the recording had caught on, particularly in the United States, and the double album three times topped the American album charts. In Britain, the response was more mitigated, but the titular ''superstar'' and Mary Magdalene's ''I Don't Know How to Love Him'' both made it into the British top 50 as singles.

It was Stigwood who eventually got *Superstar,* but MCA had covered their big investment well, and he had to share his producer's credit with the recording firm whose contract stipulated their right to first option on any staged version. The producers chose, given the record sales, to mount the show in America rather than in Britain, where there were, in any case, more worries over the tender subject matter. But there was still another stage to pass through before *Jesus Christ Superstar* was seen in a full theatrical production. The popularity of the recording had resulted in concert performances of the show's music—some authorized through ASCAP, others simply pirated—springing up around America. To protect their investment, Stigwood and MCA launched their own concert series, and whilst the music of *Superstar* was sung round the country, they took the final steps towards getting the show into the theatre.

Broadway's *Jesus Christ Superstar,* directed by Tom O'Horgan of *Hair* celebrity, featured Ben Vereen (Judas), Jeff Fenholt (Jesus) and Miss Elliman in the middle of a wildly extravagant and gimmicky production which did almost as much as the subject matter to arouse the not unexpected howls of disapproval which emanated from some prejudiced quarters. However, as had happened in the case of the recording, the show found a large number of enthusiastic fans and, as this initial production ran on towards a 711-performance Broadway record, it was clear that the stage version of *Jesus Christ Superstar* was a success equal to that of *Jesus Christ Superstar* on record.

The text of the show dealt with the last days of the life of Jesus Christ, as seen through the eyes of his disciple, Judas. Not the two-dimensional Judas of mythology, the archetypical betrayer, but a man, a follower of Christ who has become severely worried by the hysterical behaviour of his fellow followers and also by the effect of all this adulation on Christ himself, and on his clear seeing of the way events are going. He disapproves of Jesus's consorting so familiarly with the whore, Magdalene, but, more seriously, he sees a real and growing danger of a lashback, a civil disturbance which may destroy them all, and what they all believe in. As Christ sweeps into Jerusalem to the hosannas of the crowd, routs the moneylenders from the temple, and quails from the hordes of out-of-control cripples and beggars, crying out for the eternal something for nothing, for magic, Judas sees not a messiah or a magician but an overstretched and tiring man who is losing control. So, rather than let Jesus drag their whole enterprise down, he goes to the priests, Caiaphas (Bob Bingham) and Annas (Phil Jethro), and informs. Christ is taken prisoner by the soldiers of the state in the Garden of Gethsemane, and brought first before Pontius Pilate (Barry Dennen), who refuses to judge him, and then before a sybaritic, mocking King Herod (Paul Ainsley). As the ''king of the Jews'' heads on towards conviction and crucifixion, Judas, shattered by the part the designs of God have had him play in the whole affair, hangs himself.

The score, part pop, part rock, and withal, based in many of its parts firmly on classical tenets and styles, had already seen its favorite numbers climb the charts, but alongside the urging ''superstar'' and the plangent country melody of ''I Don't Know How to Love Him'' (originally written, to a different lyric, as a country song), there were other memorable moments, most particularly Jesus's nighttime monologue in the garden of Gethsemane, Pilate's puzzled relation of his dream, some dramatically effectively wide voice part-writing for a menacing counter-tenor and basso profundo pair of priests, and the searing moments of Judas's evening-long dilemma. Amongst all the drama, only Herod's sneeringly epicene interrogation, of all the score, loaned itself to an exaggerated comic staging, and that was what it would ever get.

The British representative of Australia's *Hair* producer, Harry M Miller, was a London colleague of Fielding, and even before the opening of *Superstar* on Broadway, he had secured the show for Miller in Australia. Thus, six months after the Broadway premiere, it was Australia which was first off the mark with another English-language production of the show. This was a very different production. In Jim Sharman's staging, the colorful, tricksy trimmings of Broadway's production were banished in favor of an almost spartan, space-age production, with stark, clear plastic pieces of scenery, spare, galactic costumes, and an altogether more essentially reverent style. Launched, after a concert series, at Sydney's big Capitol Theatre, *Superstar* style two, with Jon English (Judas), Trevor White (Jesus) and Michele Fawdon (Magdalene) featured, proved an even bigger success than it had on Broadway. It stayed for nine months in Sydney before moving on to another and even larger house, Melbourne's St Kilda Palais (30 March 1973), where it proved not a whit affected by a local attempt to preempt it with a piece called *Jesus Christ Revolution* (Comedy Theatre 8 January 1972). After going to the rest of the country, the show was soon back in both main centers, for a second showing, as early as 1976.

Productions soon began to sprout in all corners of the world. A German version (ad Anja Hauptmann) made its way from Munster to Berlin, a French adaptation (ad Pierre Delanoë) with Farid Dali (Judas), Daniel Beretta (Jesus) and Anne-Marie David (Mary) starred was played in Paris, and Scandinavia saw its first versions, but London still held back. Finally, however, the West End version came. The stylishness and success of the Australian production had not gone unnoticed, and it was Sharman who was called upon to mount the piece for London. This time there was, however, not even any plastic: the British *Superstar* was, by order, pictorially traditional and both sensitive and dramatic in its mood. The judgment which ensured this uncluttered, serious style of direction proved to be wholly sound. London's *Jesus Christ Superstar,* with Stephen Tate (Judas), Paul Nicholas (Jesus) and Dana Gillespie (Mary) as its original stars, was the most successful version of all. By the time it closed, after some eight years and 3,358 performances, it had become the longest running musical in West End history.

Whilst the London *Superstar* ran on, Broadway, like Australia, took in a second season (Longacre Theater 23

November 1977, 96 performances), and a filmed version, with Ted Neely (Jesus), Carl Anderson (Judas) and Miss Elliman again as Mary, was also produced, as the show spread itself to the regions and touring circuits and to just about every country where musical-theatre is played—Japan, Brazil, Mexico, Spain, Hungary—except for South Africa. There it was banned as irreligious.

Jesus Christ Superstar has been reproduced regularly, all around the world, in the quarter of a century since its first appearance and in the 1990s it returned to several principal musical-theatre centers. In Australia a series of vastly successful staged concerts of the show mounted by original producer Harry M Miller with local megastar Johnny Farnham in the role of Jesus, led to a full-scale stage production done in modern pop-music styles (and with modern pop-electric arrangements) which covered Australia and New Zealand to singular success.

In America, a touring production featuring the stars of the now slightly aged movie version, Neely and Anderson, popped into Broadway for a fortnight at Madison Square Garden (17 January 1995) with amazing box-office results, while in London Lloyd Webber's Really Useful Company mounted a major revival at the newly refurbished Lyceum Theatre (19 November 1996). Steve Balsamo (Jesus), Zubin Varla (Judas) and Joanna Ampil (Mary) featured in a production which went neither for the modern pop kind of staging seen in Australia, nor for nostalgia, but instead opted for the darkly dramatic. The new production played for nearly 18 months, before going on tour round Britain, America and Europe. It also revisited Broadway for a season at the Ford Center (16 April 2000, 161 performances) with Glenn Carter (Jesus), Tony Vincent (Judas) and Maya Days (Mary Magdalene) in the leading roles.

Australia: Capitol Theatre, Sydney 4 May 1972; Germany: Munsterlandhalle, Munster 18 February 1972, Deutschlandhalle, Berlin 31 March 1972; France: Théâtre National du Palais de Chaillot, 1972; UK: Palace Theatre 9 August 1972; Austria: Theater an der Wien 1981; Hungary: Open Air Theatre, Szeged 25 June 1986

Film: Universal 1973

Recordings: original concept recording, 2 records (MCA), original cast (MCA), London cast (MCA), Australian cast (MCA), French cast (Philips), German cast (Decca), Spanish cast (Pronto/Ariola), film soundtrack, 2 records (MCA), Japanese cast (Express), Swedish cast (Sonet), Hungarian cast (Qualiton), Czech cast (EMI-Monitor), Mexican cast (Orfeon), London revival cast (Polydor), etc

JE T'VEUX Opérette-revue in 3 acts by Wilned and Marcel Grandjean. Lyrics by Battaille-Henri. Music by Gaston Gabaroche, Fred Pearly, Albert Valsien and René Mercier. Théâtre Marigny, Paris, 12 February 1923.

Madeleine (Jane Pyrac) is obliged, for political reasons, to sell her successful couture business, the Maison Tapin, before wedding the rising young sous-préfet, Pierre Vignac (Adrien Lamy). However, her first husband, Tapin, demands that his name be removed from the firm on its sale, and that demand is a deal-breaker with Madeleine's American buyers. To get round the problem she temporarily marries an available and jolly little china-mender, who is also called Tapin (Milton), thus extending her claim to the name. But then Tapin number two falls for his temporary wife, and decides that he doesn't want to divorce her, until just before the final curtain.

The bright comedy of the piece was supported by a score by four popular songwriters which threw up several lively pieces in varying up-to-date dance rhythms—Gabaroche and Pearly combined on ''La Java-Javi-Java,'' sung and danced by Milton and Denise Grey as his rejected girlfriend; Adrien Lamy performed Valsien's ''schimmy oriental'' ''Là-bas''; and Marguerite Pierry, as a seamstress called Zou-zou, who tries to snaffle the temporarily available Pierre once Madeleine is apparently inextricably rewed, got tipsy to the tango strains of Mercier's ''C' coquin d'porto''—alongside a selection of more regular waltzes, fox-trots and one-steps.

Je t'veux proved a decided hit for producer Abel Deval and for the Théâtre Marigny. It ran there through to the summer, then reappeared at the Ba-ta-clan for a further run in the autumn, with Marthe Ferrare now playing Madeleine, as well as being sent on the road under the experienced eye of Charles Montcharmont, with Lerner, Pastore and Gaby Dargelle in the lead roles. In the year following its first production it was seen as far afield as Budapest's Lujza Blaha Színház (ad István Zágon).

Hungary: Lujza Blaha Színház *Gyere be rózsam* 24 April 1924

JILL DARLING Musical comedy (''all musical to tell a tale of laughter'') in 2 acts by Marriott Edgar. Additional scenes and lyrics by Desmond Carter. Music by Vivian Ellis. Alhambra Theatre, Glasgow (as *Jack and Jill*), 23 December 1933; Saville Theatre, London, 19 December 1934.

Produced by the Moss' Empires and Howard and Wyndham's touring organization to help fill their chain of provincial theatres, *Jack and Jill* was a swiftly written light comedy piece which starred Arthur Riscoe in a dual role as a prohibitionist parliamentary candidate and his gormless double who steps in for him when he gets prohibitively merry before a speech. Vivian Ellis provided a score including one song, the dancing ''I'm on a See-Saw'' (introduced by Marjery Wyn and Roy Royston), which would become an enduring hit.

Jack and Jill was a fine success on the road, and Riscoe determined to bring ''his'' show to town. Both he and Ellis were intent on using Riscoe's *Out of the Bottle* co-star, Frances Day, as leading lady and, with the help of

Plate 191. **Jill Darling.** *Juveniles John Mills and Louis Browne set out to confirm ''I'm on a See-Saw'' with the assistance of 16 Saville chorus girls.*

lyricist Desmond Carter, they changed the leading role into a vehicle for the unusual Miss Day as a flapper masquerading as an Hungarian chanteuse, equipped her with four made-to-measure new numbers (including ''Pardon My English'' and ''Dancing with a Ghost''), and dug up their own producer in the person of rich South African, Jack Eggar, who had a singing and dancing wife. The wife joined the cast alongside American dancer Louise Browne, Viola Tree and the young John Mills and Eddie Molloy, the piece was produced at the downmarket Saville Theatre, and it promptly became a hit. Mills and Miss Browne's ''I'm on a See-Saw,'' Riscoe's comedy and Miss Day's Hungarian version of Minnie Mouse were the highlights of a show which ran strongly till Miss Day flitted off to make a film and a bit of inept recasting (real Hungarian star Irene Palasty as the phony Hungarian!) closed the show after 242 performances.

Jill Darling returned to the provinces, where it toured for four years, but in 1944 Riscoe (in partnership with Alfred Zeitlin and Paul Murray) brought a revamped version (ad Caswell Garth) of the show back to London. This time Riscoe directed and starred opposite Carole Lynne, but the moment for *Jill Darling* was past and its revival folded in 67 performances.

Australia saw *Jill Darling* in 1936 with Nellie Barnes and Leo Franklyn featured alongside Frank Leighton, Diana du Cane, Marie La Varre and Cecil Kellaway for five weeks in Melbourne and seven at Sydney's Theatre Royal (11 April 1936).

Australia: Her Majesty's Theatre, Melbourne 22 February 1936

Recording: original cast recordings (WRC)

JOAN OF ARC

The historical tragedy of Jeanne d'Arc has been the subject of a number of serious stage pieces, including Schiller's 1801 play (*Die Jungfrau von Orleans*), the operas of Hovens and Volkert which were based on it, a Drury Lane opera of 1837 (30 November) with a score by Balfe, and more recently Honegger's well-known *Jeanne d'Arc au bûcher* (1938/1950). G B Shaw's *Saint Joan* drew some humor from the tale, but even the play of this most promising of musical-comedy librettists has never seemed likely source material for the musical theatre. Nevertheless, Joan has served as the subject of a handful of musical shows, of which the first, and the nearest to successful, were burlesques: an early Olympic Theatre piece *Joan of Arc, or The Maid of all Hell'uns* by Thomas Mildenhall (5 April 1847), a William Brough *Joan of Arc* staged at the Strand Theatre (29 March 1869) in which Thomas Thorne starred as Joan at the head of an Amazon ballet of soldiers, and another *Joan of Arc* produced by George Edwardes at the Opera Comique (17 January 1891).

Authored by the newfound writing team of Adrian Ross and composer F Osmond Carr in collaboration with the comedian John L Shine, this last piece had a Joan (Emma Chambers) from the village of Do-ré-mi pursued by the King (Shine) to use her talent for visions to find a winning system for him to use at the Monte Carlo roulette tables. Joan and her boyfriend de Richemont (Arthur Roberts) go off to war equipped with the great sword of Charlemagne, but Joan is captured and condemned to the stake only to be saved when the British troops succumb to their national malady and go on strike. The coster number ''Round the Town'' performed by Roberts and Charles Danby as Joan's father, and Roberts's burlesque of a solar-topeed Stanley, describing how ''I Went to Find Emin,'' were high spots of the evening. Neither of them, of course, had anything more to do with Joan of Arc than did an episode in which the whole French court crept up on the English, disguised in blackface, to sing a coon chorus ''De Mountains ob de Moon,'' but all three songs became hits. The show enjoyed some scandalous moments, firstly when the ''strike'' part of the plot ''offended'' some loud (and allegedly planted) members of the first-night audience, and then through the fact that shapely Alma Stanley wore no trunks over her tights. Politics proved more powerful than propriety. The tights stayed, the strikes were cut, and the show became a jolly, anodine and successful entertainment until the ''new edition'' alterations went in. This time it was Roberts's new hit song ''Randy, Pandy O'' which was seen as being offensive—to Randolph Churchill (which it was undoubtedly intended to be). The words were changed to ''Jack the Dandy, O'' and no one was fooled. The show had a fine run at the Opera Comique (181 performances) and subsequently moved to the Gaiety Theatre for another 101 nights, prior to a strong career in the provinces and in the colonies.

After this rather undignified treatment, Joan was left alone by the musical theatre for a good, long time, but she showed up on Broadway in 1975 as the heroine of what seemed to be a new burlesque, *Goodtime Charley* (Palace Theater 3 March), in which Joan was portrayed by the leggy, glamorous dancer Ann Reinking and the Dauphin by Joel Grey, and then surfaced again, in the era of ''serious'' musical plays, in both Ireland and in England. Graínne Renihan was Ireland's Joan to ''the witness'' of Colm Wilkinson in the musical *Visions* (T C Doherty, Olympia Theatre, Dublin 24 May 1984), whilst first Siobhan McCarthy and then Rebecca Storm went to the stake along with England's unfortunate *Jeanne* (Shirlie Roden, Birmingham Repertory Theatre 16 September 1985, Sadler's Wells Theatre 22 February 1986). And if France left its serious heroine seriously alone, French-speaking Canada did not. A *Jeanne la Pucelle* (Peter Sipos/Vincent de Tourdonnet) was mounted at Montreal's Place des Arts in 1997 (7 February). Denmark followed suit in 1998 with what assuredly and sadly will not be the last attempt to foist a seriously singing Maid of Orléans on to musical-theatregoers.

JOHN, Graham [COLMER, Graham John] (b London, 13 July 1887; d London, 16 January 1957). Librettist, lyricist and adapter for the British musical stage between the wars.

Educated at Rugby and Corpus Christi, John worked on the Stock Exchange for a number of years, and during this time he began writing material for the revue stage. Amongst his early musical-theatre assignments, he interpolated a number for George Grossmith and Leslie Henson into *Tonight's the Night,* provided the lyrics for Vivian Ellis's songs in the revue *By the Way,* additional dialogue for the London production of *Mercenary Mary* and lyrics for London's *Just a Kiss* (*Pas sur la bouche*), as well as the complete lyrics for the English version of Bruno Granichstaedten's Viennese hit *Der Orlow* (*Hearts and Diamonds*).

He subsequently rewrote the book of Oscar Straus's *Riquette* as *My Son John* for comedian Billy Merson, and collaborated with Guy Bolton on the book and lyrics of *Blue Eyes,* the romantic tale of how Evelyn Laye saved Scotland. He then shifted to America, where he supplied the lyrics for Busby Berkeley's Broadway musical *The Street Singer* (1929) and the Fred Stone vehicle *Ripples* (1930), and spent several years working in Hollywood.

On his return to Britain he collaborated with Hollywood's Martin Broones on the scores for *Give Me a Ring, Seeing Stars* and *Swing Along,* and adapted Robert Stolz's romantic *Venus in Seide* as a vehicle for Carl Brisson, before taking up an administrative entertainments post through the length of the war. He subsequently wrote material for several more revues, but not for the book musical.

1924 **Mamzelle Kiki** (Max Darewski/w Douglas Hoare/Hoare, Sydney Blow) Hippodrome, Portsmouth 25 August

1926 **Hearts and Diamonds** (*Der Orlow*) English lyrics (Strand Theatre)

1926 **Just a Kiss** (*Pas sur la bouche*) English lyrics w Desmond Carter, Vivian Ellis (Shaftesbury Theatre)

1928 **Blue Eyes** (Jerome Kern/w Guy Bolton) Piccadilly Theatre 27 April

1929 **The Street Singer** (Niclas Kempner, Sam Timberg/Edgar Smith) Shubert Theater, New York 17 September

1930 **Ripples** (Albert Szirmai, Oscar Levant/w Irving Caesar/ William Anthony McGuire) New Amsterdam Theater, New York 11 February

1933 **Give Me a Ring** (Martin Broones/Bolton, R P Weston, Bert Lee) London Hippodrome 22 June

1935 **Seeing Stars** (Broones/Bolton, Fred Thompson) Gaiety Theatre 31 October

1936 **Swing Along** (Broones/Bolton, Thompson, Douglas Furber) Gaiety Theatre 2 September

1937 **Venus in Silk** (*Venus in Seide*) English version w J Hastings Turner (Alhambra Theatre, Glasgow)

JOHNSON, Bill (b Baltimore, Md, 22 March 1918; d Flemington, NJ, 6 March 1957). Short-lived American leading man who starred in two major imported hits in Britain.

After an early career in stock, Johnson first appeared on Broadway in revue (*Two for the Show, All in Fun*) and in the musical comedy *Banjo Eyes* (1941, Charlie). He moved up the bill to feature opposite Ethel Merman in *Something for the Boys* (1943, Rocky Fulton), and to play a leading role in Lerner and Loewe's *The Day Before Spring* (1945) before going to London to play the part of Frank Butler in *Annie Get Your Gun* (1947). He played this role throughout the show's long West End run, and remained in Britain to star as Fred/Petruchio in *Kiss Me, Kate* (1951). Back in America he toured as Hajj in *Kismet,* and appeared once more on Broadway, as Doc in *Pipe Dream* (1955), before an accidental death at the age of 38.

Johnson was married to actress and vocalist **Shirl CONWAY** [Shirley Elizabeth CROSMAN] (b Franklinville, NY, 13 June 1916), a descendant of the well-known actress Henrietta Crosman, who featured on Broadway in *Plain and Fancy* and in London in *Carissima.*

JOHNSON, J[ohn] Rosamund (b Jacksonville, Fla, 11 August 1873; d New York, 11 November 1954).

The son of a Florida minister, Jack Johnson studied music at the New England conservatory before going on tour with John Isham's Oriental America troupe in 1896. His first attempt at writing for the musical stage was a piece called *Toloso,* written in collaboration with his brother James W Johnson, but when the pair went to New York to try to sell their work, they were unsuccessful. In 1902 Johnson (''baritone and pianist'') joined up with song-and-dance man Bob Cole (''comedian''), performing a vaudeville act for which they wrote their own material, and the three men began to make themselves known as a characterful songwriting team, interpolating numbers—sometimes several, sometimes just one—often of the imitation-negro coon-song variety, into such shows as *The Belle of Bridgeport, Humpty Dumpty, In Newport, The Little Duchess, The Rogers Brothers in Central Park, Sally in Our Alley* (''Under the Bamboo Tree''), *Sleeping Beauty and the Beast, Zig-Zag Alley* (''Under the Bamboo Tree'' again), *The Girl from Dixie, Mr Bluebeard, Nancy Brown, Mother Goose,* Peter Dailey's *Hello, My Lulu* and *An English Daisy* in the first years of the 20th century.

Cole and Johnson supplied the basic scores for two all-negro musical comedies, *The Shoo-fly Regiment* (1906, Edward Jackson, ''they are noted as songwriters but will hardly be famed as actors'') and A L Wilbur's mounting of *The Red Moon* (1908, Plunk Green), and Johnson also contributed material to F Ray Comstock's production of *Mr Lode of Koal* (40 performances), but all of these pieces were unsuccessful in finding a general audience and the pair returned to performing in vaudeville. After Cole's death Johnson held several musical directorial posts, and continued to compose and arrange and to perform, sometimes for the theatre (Alice Lloyd's ''If You'll Be My Eve, I'll Build an Eden for You,'' etc), but mostly in other areas. Some of Johnson's music was used, along with that of Louis Hirsch, to compile the score of the London revue *Come Over Here* (London Opera House 19 April 1913) at the dawning of the fashion for ''new'' American dance rhythms on the budding London variety-revue stage, and as late as 1930 he had a song featured in the score of *Brown Buddies.*

Amongst his other activities, Johnson authored a volume on negro song, compiled a collection of spirituals and wrote both dance and vocal music. He also appeared on the stage as a performer in *Porgy and Bess* (1935 and 1942, Frazier) and *Cabin in the Sky* (1940, Brother Green).

His brother, **James W[eldon] JOHNSON** (b Jacksonville, Fla, 17 June 1871; d Wiscasset, Maine, 26 June 1938), was trained as a lawyer and later became a diplomat and author (*Black Manhattan* 1930, *Along this Way* 1933). He joined his brother and Cole in their songwriting during their most successful years (''Mandy, Won't You Let Me Be Your Beau,'' ''The Maiden with the Dreamy Eyes,'' ''Nobody's Looking But the Owl and the Moon,'' etc) before going to Venezuela on a consular posting in 1906, a posting which did not, however, stop him from continuing to partner his brother in the manufacture of popular songs. He was killed in an accident in Maine in 1938. He was posthumously represented at off-Broadway's Astor Place Playhouse in 1963 by a Vinette Carroll compilation of sermons and gospel music under the title *God's Trombone* (21 December, 160 performances), repeated at the New Federal Theater in 1989 (4 October, 45 performances).

1900 **The Belle of Bridgeport** (w Accoe, Bob Cole, James William Jefferson, Cissie Loftus, etc/Glen MacDonough) Bijou Theater 29 October

1906 **The Shoofly Regiment** (James Weldon Johnson/Cole) Washington, DC 20 August; Bijou Theater 6 August 1907

1908 **The Red Moon** (Cole) Wilmington, Del 31 August; Majestic Theater 3 May 1909

1909 **Mr Lode of Koal** (Jesse A Shipp, Alexander Rogers) Casino, Toledo, Ohio 20 August; Majestic Theater 1 November

1911 **Hello, Paris!** (J Leubrie Hill/Edgar Allen Woolf) Folies Bergère 15 August

LA JOLIE PARFUMEUSE Opéra-comique in 3 acts by Hector Crémieux and Ernest Blum. Music by Jacques Offenbach. Théâtre de la Renaissance, Paris, 29 November 1873.

The tale of the pretty perfumeress, and her struggles to hold on to her virtue in the face of the worst the operettic world could fling at her, brought Offenbach his first genuine success in the two years since the Franco-Prussian War and the end of the Empire. To win this success, however, the composer and his authors had had to change their ways. Crémieux, the co-author of the fantastical burlesque texts of *Orphée aux enfers* and *Le Pont des soupirs,* abandoned the grotesqueries of the opéra-bouffe for a bright little farcical libretto of sexual quiproquos, and Offenbach went with him in illustrating a tale that seemed to owe more than a little to Sauvage and Grisar's 1850 opéra-comique *Les Porcherons* and others of its kind. Some of the success of *La Jolie Parfumeuse* was, however, due to one of the composer's other talents—that of discovering new leading ladies. This opérette served to launch charming, teenaged, pretty-voiced Louise Théo, previously seen only in the one-act *Pomme d'api,* who scored a huge personal success as the parfumeuse of the title.

Rose Michon (Théo), the pretty perfumeress, has to pass by some of the wickedest spots and folk in Paris on her way from her wedding to her nuptial bedding. As part of a surprise arranged by her new husband, she is whisked from her wedding reception amid the dizzy gaiety of the unbuttoned part of town known as les Porcherons by the wealthy financier and uncle of the groom, La Cocardière (Daubray). La Cocardière leads her to her old home, newly done up by her husband as a wedding gift, but once they are there, the naughty uncle, who all the time has had a bit of brisk, instant adultery on his mind, switches out the lights and pretends to be the new husband. Next, he leads the little bride to his own luxurious mansion, where the more usual company are such abandoned women as the danseuse Clorinde (Mlle Fonti), and lays siege to her again. When her unwealthy, unlubricious and uncomprehending little husband, Bavolet (Mlle Laurence Grivot), turns up inopportunely, the far from unskilled Rose salves his hurt by pretending to be his wife's double, a dancer called Dorothée Bruscambille. Clorinde helps in

Plate 192. *One of* **Jack Johnson's** *collaborations with Bob Cole.*

the deception and, the next morning, she uses the fact that the real Bruscambille is 50 and a mother of several, to pin down the still hopefully prowling La Cocardière, whilst the two newlyweds go their way, the cunning little wife still in one piece and the innocent little husband none the wiser.

Much of the appeal of *La Jolie Parfumeuse* was in its highjinks: the country-wedding-style first act, the sexual fencing of the second act, Rose's impersonation of the dancer, and the farcical japes of the final act with the persistent La Cocardière trying to rendezvous with Rose in her perfumery and subjected to all sorts of pretences, indignities and sudden exits. But the music played its part.

Théo had, as intended, the best moments of the score, topped by the pretty Couplets de la vertue, with their message that a girl loses nothing by waiting to lose her virtue, a tickling number, and the jolly Chanson de la Bruscambille in her disguise as the Opéra danseuse ("À Toulouse en Toulousain"). One of the other favorite moments fell to the supporting comedy character of Poirot, La Cocardière's accomplice in foolery in the first act, who finally falls for Rose after everyone else has been doing so for two acts, and delivers up his feelings in a comical letter-song.

La Jolie Parfumeuse was a grand success, playing for more than two hundred nights under the management of Hostein at the Théâtre de la Renaissance on its first run. In 1875 Charles Comte revived the piece at the Bouffes-Parisiens, where Théo and Daubray triumphed all over again, and the now well-known show appeared in Paris yet again in 1876, as it simultaneously spread itself around the world. In 1882 a now rather stouter Théo took up her role once more, in 1892 *La Jolie Parfumeuse* was given another revival at the Renaissance with Juliette Simon-Girard as Rose Michon, and in 1898 Mariette Sully played the title role in a production at the Théâtre de la Gaîté, but, in spite of its early popularity, *La Jolie Parfumeuse,* like almost all Offenbach's shows of the postwar 1870s, did not survive into the 20th century as part of the standard repertoire.

London's Alhambra Theatre was the first overseas house to snap up the latest Offenbach hit (ad H J Byron). In a program shared with the ballet *Flick and Flock,* Kate Santley starred as Rose Michon to the Clorinde of Rose Bell, the La Cocardière of Harry Paulton and the Bavolet of Lennox Grey, through a good run of 94 straight performances, and the following year Emily Soldene took the piece on the British road. America was slower to take up an English version, and the first performances that were seen in New York were in the original French, with Marie Aimée leading her company as a particularly successful Rose Michon. She kept the work in her repertoire for four seasons, and during that time the show made its first appearance as *The Pretty Perfumer,* in English, in the repertoire of the ever-anglicizing Alice Oates. In 1883 (17 March) New York got the original pretty perfumeress, when a now slightly older Louise Théo repeated her most famous role, expanded for the occasion with a rendition of Judic's famous song "Piii-ouit!," on Broadway, and, like Aimée, she subsequently kept the show as a feature of her repertoire through her several seasons of performances through America.

Australia swiftly welcomed the English *Jolie Parfumeuse* when Clara Thompson introduced Rose Michon first to Melbourne and then (23 May 1876) to Sydney, with Jeannie Winston as her Bavolet, and the colonies later got a variant version when Kelly and Leon's minstrel troupe introduced their *Rose Michon, or The Little Bride* (School of Arts, Sydney, 1879) with Leon impersonating Rose Michon in a version where the quiproquos took on rather a different flavor.

Austria, too, took to *Schönröschen* (ad Carl Treumann, add mus Brandl) with a will. Produced by Franz Jauner at the Carltheater with Hermine Meyerhoff (Rose), Wilhelm Knaack (La Cocardière), Frln Wiedermann (Clorinde), Karl Blasel (Persiflage) and Antonie Link (Bavolet) featured, the piece was played 22 times en suite, 40 times in its first 12 months in the repertoire, and 63 times (with Rosa Streitmann taking over the lead role) before Jauner quit the house in 1878. The new manager, Tewele, immediately mounted a fresh production (4 December 1878), and *Schönröschen* reappeared in Vienna as late as 1907, when Kurt von Lessen starred himself briefly alongside Frln Blank at the Lustspieltheater. In Berlin Mila Roeder took the starring role alongside Ernestine Wagner (Bavolet) and Helmerding (La Cocardière), with local composer Bial credited this time with the "new couplets."

In spite of its general success, however, Hungary seems curiously to have largely ignored the show, and a version mounted as late as 1886 at the Népszínház (ad György Verő, Béla J Fái) was played just four times.

UK: Alhambra Theatre 18 May 1874; Austria: Carltheater *Schönröschen* 6 November 1874; Germany: Wallner Theater *Schönröschen* 16 January 1875; USA: Lyceum Theater (Fr) 31 March 1875, Brooklyn Theater *The Pretty Perfumer* 5 October 1876; Australia: Prince of Wales Opera House, Melbourne 17 November 1875; Hungary: Népszínház *Százszorszép* 22 May 1886

LA JOLIE PERSANE Opérette in 3 acts by Eugène Leterrier and Albert Vanloo. Music by Charles Lecocq. Théâtre de la Renaissance, Paris, 28 October 1879.

Nadir (Lary) and Namouna (Jane Hading), who have only just wed, quarrel and promptly get themselves divorced by Moka (Vauthier), the Cadi. The local Prince (Marie Gélabert) is anxious to marry Namouna himself, but the hasty young pair have already made up their differences and decided that they prefer to be married to each other after all. Unfortunately for them, the law of the land says they can only rewed after having, in between, been wed elsewhere. As in most countries with silly laws, there is an equally silly traditional way of subverting this one. The hulla, old Broudoudour (Ismaël), is available, for the 115th time, to go through a marriage of convenience with Namouna prior to a quick divorce. The Prince, however, determines to take the hulla's place. There are plenty of comings and goings before the youngsters get back together, with the Prince ultimately switching his affections to Moka's wife (obliging the Cadi to hastily divorce) and Broudoudour, who had been momentarily determined to have and hold Namouna as well, ending up with the buxom Babouche (Marie Desclauzas), the orange-seller.

Lecocq's score had some attractive moments, including Moka's suggestive Couplets des pêches ("L'été, quand la pêche est mure"), Namouna's Rondeau du petit ange, a lilting entrance number for the Prince, casting his eyes around the village girls for a prospective bride ("J'aime l'oiseau"), and a third-act waltz ("Voyons d'abord") for the same character, whilst the Opéra-Comique's Ismaël was given the Chanson de la brune et de la blonde on which to expend his rich basso voice.

In spite of its top-drawer cast, Victor Koning's Paris production of *La Jolie Persane* was not a genuine success, and although the producer tried hard to get a run out of it, he was obliged to withdraw it on 4 January, after a little over two months of performances. This less-than-a-half success, however, did not stop other venues from taking up Lecocq's latest show. Vienna saw Hermine Meyerhoff as *Die hübsche Perserin* (ad F Zell, Richard Genée) alongside Felix Schweighofer (Moka), Carl Adolf Friese (Salamalek), Alexander Girardi (Brududur) and Frln König (Schrias-Kuli-Khan) 23 times; Germany saw a different German version at Aachen, then at Hamburg (17 April 1881) and ultimately in Berlin; Budapest got *A szép perzsalány* (ad Lajos Evva), with Aranka Hegyi starred as its heroine, 11 times; and San Francisco got the first English version in 1880 under the title *The Pretty Persian.* However, the piece finally did find genuine success when it was done over and into English by Sydney Rosenfeld, under the title *The Oolah,* as a Broadway vehicle for comedian Francis Wilson.

The change in title clearly showed the change in emphasis, away from the music and towards the sort of low comedy both Rosenfeld and Wilson did best with, but it was a shift that also ensured the show a run. Wilson (Hoolah Goolah), Marie Jansen (Tourouloupi), Hubert Wilke (Prince) and Harry MacDonough (Cadi) headed the cast of the show past its 100th Broadway night on 19 August, and *The Oolah* ran on merrily until October (156 performances) before going into the American regions . . . where J W Norcross was still touring *The Pretty Persian.* Often-battered and interpolated-into versions of the latter got occasional showings in American summer seasons in the 1890s, but *The Pretty Persian* too could still be sighted on the road in 1895, as played by the Andrew Opera Company.

Austria: Theater an der Wien *Die hübsche Perserin* 16 January 1880; Hungary: Népszínház *A szép perzsalány* 10 September 1880; Germany: Aachen *Die schöne Perserin* 29 May 1880, Carl-Schultze Theater, Hamburg 17 April 1881, Belle-Alliance-Theater, Berlin 3 January 1887; USA: Tivoli Opera House, San Francisco *The Pretty Persian* 25 November 1880, Broadway Theater, New York *The Oolah* 13 May 1889

JOLSON, Al [YOELSON, Asa] (b Srednike, Lithuania, 26 March 1886; d San Francisco, 23 October 1950). Famous blackface Mammy-singer of the stage and screen, whose run of successful theatrical vehicles can only barely be regarded as book musicals.

Jolson ran away from home to go into show business, and he made his first appearances in variety, in circus and, at the age of 13, in the play *The Children of the Ghetto.* He eventually made himself a career in minstrel shows and in vaudeville, and made his first Broadway appearance in a musical show when the Shuberts cast him in the blackface role of Erastus Sparkler, alongside some of the more glamorous ladies of the musical and revue stage, in the revusical *La Belle Paree* at the Winter Garden. His extravagantly emotional delivery of sentimental, patriotic and exuberant songs quickly made him popular, and he rose through a series of revusical musical plays, beginning with an adaptation of the Viennese hit *Vera Violetta* (''Rum Tum Tiddle''), and then continuing, in the character of the black ''boy,'' Gus, through *The Whirl of Society, The Honeymoon Express* (''Who Paid the Rent for Mrs Rip van Winkle''), *Dancing Around, Robinson Crusoe Jr* (''Yackey Hula Hickey Dula,'' ''Down Where the Swanee River Flows,'' ''Where the Black-Eyed Susans Grow'') and *Sinbad* (''Rock-a-Bye Your Baby with a Dixie Melody,'' ''My Mammy,'' ''Chloe,'' ''You Ain't Heard Nothin' Yet'') to major stardom in the American theatre.

Eventually, Jolson's shows developed into a two-part affair—a sketchy little musical comedy in the first act, and a second act in which the audience got little more than Jolson, singing his songs with blithe disregard for any dramatic coherence which the first half might have pretended, and with a consummate ability to hold an audience in the palm of his hand. On his way through a decade and more of celebrity, Jolson made enduring hits of some of the handful of songs which he interpolated into the scores of his various shows, some of which numbers bore his name as co-author much on the same principle as that adopted by the 19th-century music-hall stars, who considered that ''creating'' a song earned them a co-authorial credit, not to mention a share in the royalties.

Jolson abandoned the character of Gus to play the title role in *Bombo* (''April Showers,'' ''Toot Toot Tootsie,'' ''California, Here I Come'') at the Jolson Theater, but he returned to his old all-purpose character once more in 1925 in *Big Boy.* His illness cut short *Big Boy*'s run, but the show went on the road and returned to Broadway when the star had recovered. After 15 years at the top, however, Jolson's position in public favor had now become slightly wobbly, but he returned vigorously to the forefront with the coming of the sound film, starring in the famous *The Jazz Singer* and a series of similar films in the next few years (*The Singing Fool, Sonny Boy, Mammy, Big Boy*).

In 1931 he returned to Broadway to appear, this time without the famous blackface, in a version of the Austrian hit cabaret-musical *Die Wunder-Bar* (*Wonder Bar*). The production was not a success, and Jolson turned back to films to continue through another decade of movies (*Wonder Bar, Go into Your Dance, The Singing Kid, Rose of Washington Square, Swanee River,* etc) with mostly decreasing results. In 1940 he made one last return to the stage, this time in a regular musical play, *Hold on to Your Hats,* with an end-to-end construction and no second-half Jolson concert. He took the part of a radio

Plate 193. **Al Jolson** *(right) in* Robinson Crusoe Jr.

cowboy character who is set to performing real-life heroics, but he found the limitations of a straight script and the fact that he was not the solo star of the show more than he could take for too long, and *Hold on to Your Hats* was scuppered after five months on Broadway.

Jolson had a third period in the limelight when Hollywood made a highly successful biopic of his life as *The Jolson Story* in 1946. To Jolson's disappointment, Larry Parks appeared as him, but it was his singing voice which was heard both in that film and in a sequel, *Jolson Sings Again* (1949).

Although he had no monopoly on the genre, even in his own latter-day period, Jolson became accepted throughout the world as the archetype of the blackface singer, much in the same way that Marie Lloyd came facilely to represent virtually the whole of the English music-hall tradition to later generations, and he was ''imitated'' many times in later revues and musical shows. Several attempts were made in the 1970s to mount a stage biomusical based on Jolson's life, using much of the star's old material. Neither *Al Jolson Tonight!* (Kansas City, 1978) nor *Joley* (Northstage Theater, Glen Cove 2 March 1979), with Larry Kert starred as Jolson, found its intended way to Broadway. However, the West End finally got the Jolson quasi biomusical that Broadway had shunned when, in 1995 (22 October), a compilation called *Jolson* was mounted at the Victoria Palace, the theatre that had been for so many successful years London's Mecca of blackface as the home of *The Black and White Minstrels.* Brian Conley impersonated the Mammy-singer, but *Jolson* didn't rival its famously long-lived predecessor. It nevertheless had a good run and got itself onto the American tour circuits, where Mike Burstyn impersonated Jolson.

Jolson was married to stage and film ingenue Ruby Keeler.

Biographies: Jolson, H, Emley, A: *Mistah Jolson* (House-Warren, New York, 1951), Seiben, P: *The Immortal Jolson* (Fell, New

York, 1962), Anderton, B: *Sonny Boy* (1975), Freedland, M: *Jolson* (fictionalized biography) (Stein & Day, New York, 1972), Oberfirst, R: *Al Jolson* (A S Barnes, New York, 1980), Goldman, H: *Jolson: The Legend Comes to Life* (OUP, New York, 1988), etc

JONAS, Émile (b Paris, 5 March 1827; d Saint-Germain-en-Laye, 22 May 1905). Composer for the early French opéra-bouffe stage.

A teacher at the Paris Conservatoire for some 20 years, musical director at Paris's Portuguese synagogue and, subsequently, bandmaster of the Garde Nationale, Jonas was an early contributor to the programs mounted by Offenbach at the Théâtre des Bouffes-Parisiens, providing the scores for a number of one-act opérettes, of which *Les Petits Prodiges* (add mus Offenbach), played by the Bouffes company both at home and on its European tours, was the most generally popular. His little *Les Deux Arlequins* (100th Parisian night 1 July 1866) was also exported, and had the distinction of being played as part of the opening program at London's Gaiety Theatre (ad Gilbert a' Beckett 21 December 1868), whilst *Avant la noce* was played in London as *Terrible Hymen* (ad Gilbert a' Becket, Covent Garden 26 December 1866) and in America in the repertoire of Mrs Pyne Galton's little touring operetta troupe (Chestnut Street Theater, Philadelphia 17 January 1870).

Jonas had his greatest success with his first full-scale opéra-bouffe, the extravagantly comical *Le Canard à trois becs,* played throughout the world after its first fine Parisian season, and he confirmed that success with an opéra-bouffe score written for John Hollingshead and London's Gaiety Theatre as *Cinderella the Younger.* Under the title of *Javotte,* that piece—still arguably the best version of the Cinderella tale written for the light-musical stage—was also seen all round Europe. But if *Javotte* made its way back to Paris, as part of its international exposure, Jonas's next two pieces did not. *Die Japanesin* and *Goldchignon,* although originally written to French texts, were both premiered in translation in Austria and, although the second-named went on to productions in Brussels (Fantaisies-Parisiennes, Brussels 17 October 1874), where Pauline Luigini and Alfred Jolly starred, and in Budapest (*Az arany chignon* Budai Színkör 6 June 1874) following its introduction at the Vienna Strampfertheater, Jonas could not find either of them a place in his hometown. The two amongst his pieces which were mounted there, *La Bonne Aventure* and *Le Premier Baiser,* were both unsuccessful, and it was *Le Canard à trois becs,* his two little pieces, and *Javotte* which remained his principal references as a theatre composer.

1855 **Le Duel de Benjamin** (Eugène Mestépès) 1 act Théâtre des Bouffes-Parisens October

1856 **La Parade** (Jules Brésil) 1 act Théâtre des Bouffes-Parisiens 2 August

1857 **Le Roi boit** (Mestépès, Adolphe Jaime) 1 act Théâtre des Bouffes-Parisiens 9 April

1857 **La Momie de Roscoco** (w E Ortolan/Émile de Najac) 1 act Théâtre des Bouffes-Parisiens 27 July

1857 **Les Petits Prodiges** (Jaime, Étienne Tréfeu) Théâtre des Bouffes-Parisiens 19 November

1863 **Job et son chien** (Mestépès) 1 act Théâtre des Bouffes-Parisiens 6 February

1864 **Le Manoir des Larenardière** (Mestépès) 1 act Théâtre des Bouffes-Parisiens 29 September

1865 **Avant la noce** (Mestépès, Paul Boisselot) 1 act Théâtre des Bouffes-Parisiens 24 March

1865 **Le Roi Midas** (Charles Nuitter) privately

1865 **Les Deux Arlequins** (Mestépès) 1 act Fantaisies-Parisiennes 29 December

1867 **Marlbrough s'en va-t-en guerre** (w Georges Bizet, Isidore Legouix, Léo Delibes/William Busnach, Paul Siraudin) Théâtre de l'Athénée 15 December

1869 **Le Canard à trois becs** (Jules Moinaux) Théâtre des Folies-Dramatiques 6 February

1869 **Désiré, Sire de Champigny** (Désiré) 1 act Théâtre des Bouffes-Parisiens 11 April

1871 **Cinderella the Younger** (*Javotte*) (Alfred Thompson) Gaiety Theatre, London 23 September

1873 **[Der] Goldchignon** (*Chignon d'or*) (Eugène Grangé, Tréfeu) Strampfertheater, Vienna 20 May

1874 **Die Japanesin** (Grangé, Victor Bernard ad Richard Genée, F Zell) Theater an der Wien, Vienna 24 January

1882 **La Bonne Aventure** (Henri Bocage, de Najac) Théâtre de la Renaissance 3 November

1883 **Le Premier Baiser** (de Najac, Raoul Toché) Théâtre des Nouveautés 21 March

1887 **La Chatte blanche** (Cogniard brothers ad Émile Blavet, Jules Prével) Théâtre du Châtelet 2 April

JONES, [James] Sidney (b Islington, London, 17 June 1861; d London, 29 January 1946). The most internationally successful composer of the Victorian British romantic musical theatre.

Sidney Jones was the son of the bandmaster and conductor, also called [James] Sidney Jones (b Ispwich, c1838; d Plumstead, 19 June 1914), who was for many years a prominent figure in the musical life of the city of Leeds, where he held not only the position of musical director at the Grand Theatre but also presided over the city band. The younger Sidney began his musical life playing clarinet under his father's baton, but he soon found his own feet and left Leeds, while still in his early twenties, to go on the road as musical director with a company playing the popular American ''musical comedy oddity'' *Fun on the Bristol.* He subsequently worked in a similar capacity with Alfred Hemming's comedy burlesque company, conducting their burlesque of *The Flying Dutchman,* and with the Vokes family, touring their enduring farcical entertainment *In Camp,* and it was for this low comic tale of amateur theatricals in a military camp that Jones composed his first theatre music, in the shape of fresh incidental music and songs to be added to what was virtually the Vokes's "act."

In 1886 the young Jones's talents as a musical director came under the ever discerning eye of actress-producer Kate Santley, who hired him as musical director for the tour of her musical *Vetah.* His next employer was the newly rich Henry Leslie, for whom he worked for nearly four years as conductor of the number one touring companies of the phenomenally successful *Dorothy* (starring Lucy Carr-Shaw, sister to George Bernard), *Doris* and *The Red Hussar.* He then took musical control of a tour of the Gaiety Theatre success *Little Jack Sheppard* under the management of comedian J J Dallas, and this last engagement resulted in his coming to the notice of George Edwardes, who hired him as musical director for the Gaiety Theatre's prestigious 1891 tour of America and Australia, conducting a company which included Nellie Farren and Fred Leslie, and playing the burlesque *Ruy Blas and the Blasé Roué.* When the company produced *Cinder-Ellen Up Too Late* in Australia, Jones contributed a dance number to Meyer Lutz's score.

On his return to London, Jones remained in Edwardes's employment, and took up the baton for the first time in the West End as conductor of the new musical comedy *In Town* at the Prince of Wales Theatre. He was obliged to give up this position when the show transferred to the Gaiety Theatre, and resident musical director, Meyer Lutz, took over command of the orchestra but, now established as one of the principal conductors of the West End theatre, he was soon engaged for another important and successful new musical comedy, *Morocco Bound,* produced under the management of Fred Harris at the Shaftesbury Theatre.

In the meanwhile, Jones had also begun to establish himself as a composer. He composed original music for the pantomime *Aladdin II* at Leeds (1889), an operetta, *Our Family Legend,* written with Reginald Stockton, was staged at the Brighton Aquarium, and he also supplied some individual numbers for interpolation into London and touring scores. One of these, "Linger Longer, Loo," was taken up by Edwardes and subsequently became a hit at the Gaiety in the burlesque *Don Juan* (1893), but by that time Jones had already made his mark in a more substantial manner. The society journalist Jimmy Davis ("Owen Hall") had, so it is related, spoken disparagingly to Edwardes of the qualities of *In Town,* and Edwardes had challenged him to come up with a better script. When Hall produced the book of *A Gaiety Girl* it was given to Jones to set to music and the result was a show which, even more than *In Town* and *Morocco Bound,* set the trend for a new era of light musical theatre. It was music which had a popular ring, no doubt gleaned from the composer's early years with the touring variety combinations, allied to something of the substance of the classic light-theatre music of Sullivan and, more particularly, of Cellier, which he had so long conducted for Leslie.

Whilst continuing to work as a conductor, both for his own works and for such pieces as the hit London production of Ivan Caryll's *The Gay Parisienne,* and while continuing to provide additional pieces of music both for touring musicals such as *Giddy Miss Carmen* and his old employer J J Dallas's *One of the Girls,* and for town shows (*Lost, Strayed or Stolen,* etc), Jones settled down to a steady career as what eventually became house composer to George Edwardes's new Daly's Theatre. When *A Gaiety Girl* finished its splendid run, at Daly's, Jones again combined with Hall and lyricist Harry Greenbank on a successor, *An Artist's Model,* and this, in turn, was followed by the three most substantial light musical pieces of the era: *The Geisha, A Greek Slave* and *San Toy.*

With Edwardes's famous Daly's star team to write for, Jones turned out ever more masterly scores, including a fine supply of individual hit songs ("The Amorous Goldfish," "Chin, Chin, Chinaman," etc). His soprano solos, such as "A Geisha's Life" and the waltz song "Love, Love" from *The Geisha* or "The Golden Isle" from *A Greek Slave* and baritone ballads such as "The One in the World" (*San Toy*) and "The Girl of My Heart" (*Greek Slave*), were outstanding examples of late-19th-century romantic show music, set in shows which could still dip near to the music hall in some of their point numbers, such as the insistently anthropomorphic fables of "The Interfering Parrot" or "A Frog He Lived in a Pond," and rise to some magnificently tuneful concerted finales, such as that written by Jones for the ending of the first act of *A Greek Slave,* a piece of ensemble music which bordered on the light operatic without ever becoming too heavy for the kind of musical play which housed it.

Both *The Geisha* and *San Toy* became international hits, being played over several decades not only in Britain and the colonies but all round the world. Both were played in Germany, in Hungary and in Austria, where *The Geisha* became the most successful English-language musical of all time, being played regularly in metropolitan and provincial houses for more than half a century and taking a firm place in the regular repertoire, as it did also, in a lesser way, in Italy. If *A Greek Slave* took a definite third place to these two works, this was in no way due to any failings in its musical score, which held some of Jones's most attractive work.

After his series of successes at Daly's, Jones tried his hand at a comedy opera, *My Lady Molly,* an old-fashioned costume musical with strong affiliations with *Dorothy.* Given that the vogue for such pieces had long been drowned in the tide of success created by Jones's own musicals, on the one hand, and the lighter fare purveyed at the Gaiety Theatre on the other, the show was a fine success, but when Jones and Hall were hired by Tom Davis, grown rich on the triumph of *Florodora,* to write him a piece for his Lyric Theatre, the resultant *The Medal and the Maid,* again rather more by Hall's fault than Jones's, was a failure—the first in the composer's and the author's careers. A return to oriental topics in the pretty *See See* did rather better, but Jones had to wait for a further sizeable success until 1908, when he combined with the young Frederick Lonsdale in another trend-setting show, the archetypal modern Ruritanian musical *King of Cadonia,* mounted in the West End with singular success under the management of Frank Curzon. Its successor, *A Persian Princess,* failed, but when Jones changed direction yet again he once more found at least a measure of success, back with Edwardes, this time at the more lighthearted Gaiety Theatre, with *The Girl from Utah.*

It was now 1913, and musical tastes were taking a very heavy turn away from Victorian ballads and point songs, from romantic lyric music and concerted finales and ensembles, towards the syncopated dance-based rhythms coming from America. Jones was not at home in this musical atmosphere. He turned one last time back to Daly's Theatre to supply the score for the post-Edwardes production of the thoroughly Ruritanian *The Happy Day,* with José Collins and Bertram Wallis starring where Marie Tempest and Hayden Coffin had been, but although this last show fared well enough it was no *Geisha,* and it had nothing like the success of his most famous piece. At the age of 55 Jones withdrew from the world of the musical theatre and, for the last 30 years of his life, he wrote no more.

Rarely seen latterly in the musical-theatre world, he emerged in 1931 to conduct the overture on the opening night of the West End revival of *The Geisha.*

1892 **Our Family Legend** (Reginald Stockton) 1 act Brighton Aquarium 8 October

1893 **A Gaiety Girl** (Harry Greenbank/Owen Hall) Prince of Wales Theatre 14 October

1895 **An Artist's Model** (H Greenbank/Hall) Daly's Theatre 2 February

1896 **The Geisha** (H Greenbank/Hall) Daly's Theatre 25 April

1898 **A Greek Slave** (H Greenbank, Adrian Ross/Hall) Daly's Theatre 8 June

1899 **San Toy** (H Greenbank, Ross/Edward Morton) Daly's Theatre 21 October

1902 **My Lady Molly** (Charles H Taylor, Percy Greenbank/George H Jessop) Theatre Royal, Brighton 11 August; Terry's Theatre, London 14 March 1903

1903 **The Medal and the Maid** (Taylor/Hall) Lyric Theatre 25 April

1906 **See See** (Ross, P Greenbank/Charles H E Brookfield) Prince of Wales Theatre 20 June

1908 **King of Cadonia** (Ross/Frederick Lonsdale) Prince of Wales Theatre 3 September

1909 **A Persian Princess** (P Greenbank/Leedham Bantock, P J Barrow) Queen's Theatre 27 April

1913 **The Girl from Utah** (w Paul Rubens/Ross, P Greenbank, Rubens/James Tanner) Adelphi Theatre 18 October

1916 **The Happy Day** (w Rubens/Ross, Rubens/Seymour Hicks) Daly's Theatre 13 May

A brother, **[John] Guy [Sidney] JONES** (b Dublin, 5 November 1874; d Surbiton, 8 February 1959), also pursued a career as a musical director (*The Lady Slavey, The French Maid, Bilberry of Tilbury, The Medal and the Maid, The Blue Moon, The Grass Widows*) and as a composer, his one substantial score being that for Charles Frohman's production of the successful Seymour Hicks musical *The Gay Gordons* (1907). A 1910 musical, *The Heiress* (Theatre Royal, Birmingham, lib: Follett Thorpe, Harold Weston 13 June) was played by amateurs.

1898 **Bilberry of Tilbury** (George D Day, Silvanus Dauncey) Criterion Theatre 8 August

1899 **The American Heiress** (w Herbert Simpson, et al/Day, Arthur Branscombe) Theatre Royal, Birmingham 3 April

1899 **A Test Match** (Frederick Bowyer, Gerald Fitzgibbon) 1 act Oxford Music Hall 28 July

1907 **The Gay Gordons** (Seymour Hicks/Arthur Wimperis) Aldwych Theatre 11 September

1911 **Belle of the Skies** (Graham Squiers) 1 act Theatre Royal, Birmingham 22 May

1912 **The Democrats** (St John Hamund, Squiers) 1 act Theatre Royal, Birmingham 13 May

1915 **Menari, the Malay Dancing Girl** (Charles Ward-Jackson) 1 act Golders Green Empire 15 March

JONES, Tom (b Littlefield, Tex, 17 February 1928).

Jones teamed up with songwriting partner Harvey Schmidt during their university days and the pair made their earliest stage ventures in college shows. They placed songs in such revues as Julius Monk's *Demi-Dozen* and *Pieces of Eight,* and *Shoestring '57* before their first book musical *The Fantasticks* ("Try to Remember") was brought to the professional stage. The immense success of this little piece won Schmidt and Jones the opportunity to work on a very much larger show, the adaptation of the play *The Rainmaker* into the musical *110 in the Shade* but, although the piece had a certain success, they intelligently returned to what they recognized they did best and produced another intimate piece, the two-handed musical adaptation of Jan de Hartog's *The Fourposter* as *I Do! I Do!* This time, however, the piece was not staged like an intimate musical. It was mounted not in a tiny house like that which housed *The Fantasticks,* but on a regular Broadway-sized plateau, but the result was, just the same, another long-running hit.

Thereafter, however, success deserted the pair and, as *The Fantasticks* continued its run into the record books, their several attempts at a biomusical on the French writer and music-hall artist, *Colette;* a small-scale allegoric piece, with multiple echoes of *The Fantasticks* and of its 1960s era, entitled *Celebration* (110 performances); and a classical burlesque, *Philemon,* failed to confirm their popularity, as established by their first three shows. Like the largest version of *Colette,* mounted in 1982 with Diana Rigg starred as the novelist, a musical version of the Thornton Wilder play *Our Town,* produced under the title *Grover's Corners,* did not make it to Broadway.

Schmidt and Jones were responsible for establishing Portfolio Theater, a small-scale experimental musical theatre for workshopping new pieces.

1960 **The Fantasticks** (Harvey Schmidt) Sullivan Street Playhouse 3 May

1960 **Anatol** City Hall Theater, Hamilton, Bermuda

1963 **110 in the Shade** (Schmidt/w N Richard Nash) Broadhurst Theater 24 October

1966 **I Do! I Do!** (Schmidt) 46th Street Theater 5 December

1969 **Celebration** (Schmidt) Ambassador Theater 22 January

1970 **Colette** (Schmidt/w Elinor Jones) Ellen Stewart Theater 6 May

1975 **The Bone Room** (Schmidt) Portfolio Studio 28 February

1975 **Philemon** (Schmidt) Portfolio Studio 8 April

1982 **Colette** revised version 5th Avenue Theater, Seattle 9 February

1983 **Colette Collage** revised version of *Colette* York Players 31 March

1987 **Grover's Corners** (Schmidt) Marriott Lincolnshire Theater, Chicago 29 July

1996 **Mirette** (Schmidt/Elizabeth Diggs) Goodspeed Opera House, Chester 1 August

JOSEFFY, Josef [ICHHÄUSER, Josef] (later JOSEPHI) (b Kracow, 15 July 1852; d Berlin, 8 January 1920). Longtime leading man of the Viennese stage who created many notable Operette roles.

Joseffy came to Vienna from his hometown in 1873 to work in a bank, but it was not long before he abandoned money to begin a career as an actor. When he was thrown on, without rehearsal, in a provincial theatre to play Ange Pitou in *La Fille de Madame Angot,* he scored a considerable success and he thereafter began to orientate himself towards musical theatre. In 1878 he was engaged by Strampfer for the Ringtheater, but he soon moved on, first to the Carltheater (Evangelista in *Donna Juanita,* Duc des Ifs in *Olivette,* Marquis des Millefleurs in *Rosina*), and then to the Theater an der Wien where, from 1882 he began a long series of important roles in Operetten, including both dashing tenor/baritone heroes and some more comical characters.

Amongst the roles he created were leading parts in Zeller's *Die Carbonari* (1880, Bruto), Suppé's *Der Gascogner* (1881, James, Duke of Monmouth), *Herzblättchen* (1882), *Der Bettelstudent* (1882, as Jan Janicki to the Symon of Girardi), *Die Afrikareise* (1883, Antarsid), *Gasparone* (1884, Graf Erminio) and *Der Feldprediger* (1884, Hellwig), and he also appeared as Lotteringhi (*Boccaccio*) and later as Gaston Dufaure in *Donna Juanita,* whilst his original role was taken by the young Girardi. He created a number of roles in Johann Strauss Operetten, appearing in the premieres of *Der Zigeunerbaron* (Homonay, introducing the celebrated Recruiting Song, though he would later play both Zsupán and Barinkay), *Simplicius* (Der Einsiedler), *Fürstin Ninetta* (Baron Mörsburg), *Jabuka* (Bambora), *Waldmeister* (Tymoleon) and *Die Göttin der Vernunft* (Furiaux), as well as playing variously Eisenstein or Falke in *Die Fledermaus,* Sebastiani in *Der lustige Krieg,* Hesse in *Carneval in Rom* and the Duke of Urbino in the first Vienna performances of *Eine Nacht in Venedig.*

Other important creations included the role of the poet, Carl Bellman, in *Bellman* (1887), further Millöcker roles as Godibert in *Die Jungfrau von Belleville,* Sir Lothar in *Das Sonntagskind* (1892), Rodomonte in *Der Probekuss* and Jussupov in *Nordlicht,* and the leading role of Paul Aubier in Heuberger's *Der Opernball* (1898). He also appeared in the French repertoire as the Marquis in *Les Cloches de Corneville,* in the title role of Planquette's *Rip van Winkle* (*Rip-Rip,* 1885), as Matthieu in *Die Zaubergeige,* as Fortunio, as Champlâtreux in *Mam'zelle Nitouche* (1890), as Lorémois in *La Poupée* (*Die Puppe*) and as Coquenard in Vienna's version of *Véronique* (*Brigitte*), as well as in the British musicals *Weather or No* with Annie Dirkens, *A Runaway Girl* (Tamarinde Dubois) and *A Greek Slave* (Marcus Pomponius). He also played in revivals of such pieces as *Nanon* (d'Aubigné), *Drei Paar Schuhe* (Flink), *Der arme Jonathan* (Jonathan), *Der Vogelhändler* (Adam), *Die sieben Schwaben* (Theophrastus) and *Leichte Kavallerie* (János).

Alongside these more successful or noteworthy pieces, Joseffy also took part in the theatre's premieres of the less enduring *Der kleine Prinz* (Paolo), *Der schöne Nikolaus* (Pastorel), *Zwillinge* (Blondeau), *Gillette de*

Narbonne (Robert de Lignolles), *Der Hofnarr* (Graf Rivarol), Brandl's *Der liebe Augustin* (von Hocher), *Madame Bonbon* (Hannibal), *Krawelleria musicana* (Assio), Weinberger's *Pagenstreiche* (von Himmel), Geiringer's *Die indische Witwe* (Dschihan), Kremser's *Der Schlosserkönig* (Luiz von Robello), the Viennese version of *Miss Helyett* (Paul Landrin), *Fanchons Leyer* (Chevalier de St Florent), *Der Millionenonkel* (Wunibald), *Der Schwiegerpapa* (Hassan), *Husarenblut* (Michael Barna), Dellinger's *Die Chansonette* (Marchese Bonelli), *Die Karlsschülerin* (Major von Seeger), *Die Blumen-Mary* (Géza Budai), *Der goldene Kamerad* (Fred Hamlin), *General Gogo* (Florian Ducôt), *Mister Menelaus* (Johnny Tackleton), *Der Wunderknabe* (Patricio Gordoni), *Der Löwenjäger* (Casimir Brisson), *Die Schwalben* (Sykora), *Die Küchen-Komtesse* (Franz von Wuck), *Der Dreibund* (Kurt Koller), *Der Blondin von Namur* (Leroche), *Fräulein Hexe* (Graf Stelzenberg), *Katze und Maus* (Baron Montrichard), *Ihre Excellenz* (Prince Santiago de Merimac), *Fräulein Präsident* (Don Abricolaves), *Die Strohwitwe* (Snopper), *Der Sechs-Uhr Zug* (Camille Colineau), *Die Stiefmama* (Bodin Bridet) and a continuing list of others.

One of the mainstays of the Theater an der Wien company through its golden age, progressing from juvenile roles to principal comedy parts in direct competition with Girardi (some of whose roles he subsequently played), he ultimately left Vienna in 1900 and moved to Berlin, where he appeared at the Friedrich-Wilhelmstädtisches Theater and at the Metropoltheater, most especially in revue, with great success. In 1909 he was again seen on the Viennese stage when he played at the Johann Strauss-Theater in *Der Fürst von Düsterstein* and as Eisenstein, and in 1911 when he starred as Simplicitas in Vienna's version of *The Arcadians,* as Fierabras in Straus's *Venus im Grünen,* and in the two-handed Singspiel *Verliebte Plakate.* As late as 1917 he was seen at the Bürgertheater as Ollendorf, and in the new pieces *Brüderlein und Schwesterlein* (August Better) and *Bruder Leichtsinn* (Karl Pampinger), and in 1919 created a final major role as Vater Benedikt in Künneke's *Das Dorf ohne Glocke* at Berlin's Friedrich-Wilhelmstädtisches Theater.

JOSEPH AND THE AMAZING TECHNICOLOR DREAMCOAT Musical in 1 act with lyrics by Tim Rice. Music by Andrew Lloyd Webber. Haymarket Ice Rink, Edinburgh, 21 August 1972; Young Vic Theatre, London, 16 October 1972.

The first produced stage piece by Tim Rice and Andrew Lloyd Webber, *Joseph and the Amazing Technicolor Dreamcoat* was originally written as a 15-minute staged cantata, to be performed by the pupils of Colet Court School (1 March 1968). It was given a second performance at Westminster's Central Hall (12 May 1968) and, gathering momentum and additional pieces of music each time, on several other occasions, profiting from the enthusiasm of music critic Derek Jewell (father of a Colet's Court pupil), music publishers Novello and recording man Norrie Paramor. By the time the piece made it onto its first record, it had become 35 minutes in length.

After the success of *Jesus Christ Superstar, Joseph* was given its first professional performance by the Young Vic company at the Edinburgh Festival of 1972, with Gary Bond featured as Joseph. That production was transferred to London's Young Vic (14 performances) and, under the management of *Superstar* producer Robert Stigwood, to the Roundhouse (43 performances). Early the next year Stigwood and Michael White remounted the production at the Albery Theatre, with *Joseph* sharing the bill with another Rice/Lloyd Webber one-acter, *Jacob's Journey,* but a run of 243 performances proved disappointingly brief.

However, in spite of this semi-failure, *Joseph* continued to grow. Now a full, if short, evening's entertainment, it was played in provincial and overseas English-speaking theatres with great success, and a West End Christmas season in 1978 with Paul Jones as Joseph (Westminster Theatre 27 November) did well enough for a repeat season to be mounted by the same management the following year, followed in 1980 by a colorful Bill Kenwright production, starring former pop star Jess Conrad, which emphasized the family entertainment aspect of the show. This production became a provincial phenomenon, setting up a record as the longest-lived touring show of the postwar era and returning regularly to London for holiday seasons. By this time the text and music of the piece had become reasonably settled, and the originally all-male casting had been eased open not only to include the Potiphar's Wife of the early expansion, but (to less than perfect effect) to give the large role of the narrator, originally written for a man, to a female voice.

The story of Joseph and his brothers is acted out by a group of performers featuring a Joseph, a Pharoah, a Narrator and the team of brothers, with a children's choir supplying a backing without normally physically taking part in the action. The sung-through tale is told in a lively, modern fashion, with Joseph sharing with the Narrator the bulk of the music, but only occasionally bursting into what might be a full-scale song (''Close Every Door to Me''). Pharoah introduces himself as a pseudo–Elvis Presley, and the additions of the years included several other pieces of musical parody: a burlesque Western carol, ''There's One More Angel in Heaven,'' a parody of the French chanson (''Those Canaan Days'') and calypso for the brothers (Benjamin calypso).

Joseph had been staged regularly in American school productions from 1969 (Cathedral College, Douglaston, Long Island 3 October) onwards, and had been given its first professional productions at the Brooklyn Academy of Music in 1976 and 1977 with David James Carroll in the role of Joseph. However, in 1981, following a successful production in Baltimore, the show was given at off-Broadway's Entermedia Theater under the management of Zev Bufman and Susan Rose and, after 77 performances, transferred uptown to Broadway's Royale Theater. There it played for a fine run of 747 performances, with original Joseph, Bill Hutton, being succeeded by several other performers, including the pop world's Andy Gibb and David Cassidy, as the show, more than a decade on from its original production, established itself as a favorite in America.

Oddly, given the enthusiasm the show aroused in Britain and America, it simply did not go in Australia. A first production, at Sydney's York Theatre in 1975 with Mark Holden as Joseph, failed, and a later attempt to stage a version of the all-conquering Kenwright production also went under in a barrage of financial question marks.

However, *Joseph* proved popular virtually everywhere else it went, appearing around the world translated into a number of languages, but ever most popular in the original English.

In 1991, after the publishing rights to the show had been recuperated from Novello by Lloyd Webber's Really Useful Company, London saw a new production of *Joseph,* mounted with great splendor in the large auditorium of the London Palladium (12 June 1991). Australian teeny-idol Jason Donovan (later kiddie TV-host Philip Schofield) starred as Joseph, the children were brought out of their choir bleachers to join in the action for the first time, and the now enormous and spectacular show at last proved to be the West End hit that it had not been, in its more reduced shape, the first time around. Donovan's version of ''Any Dream Will Do'' made it to the top of the British hit-parades 20 years after its first hearing. This version of the show was also mounted on the American touring circuits (25 February 1993) and later brought to Broadway, with Michael Damian featured as Joseph (10 November 1993) for a less than satisfying run of 231 performances. It was also produced in Australia, but Australia once again proved indifferent. In 1996 a first German production (ad Heinz Rudolf Kunze), based on the new large format *Joseph,* was mounted at Essen with Andreas Bieber as its hero.

A video version, with Donny Osmond as Joseph, and Richard Attenborough and Joan Collins featured as the Potiphars was produced in 1999.

Joseph of the many-colored coat had previously been portrayed on the musical stage in the 1897 French opérette *Madame Putiphar* (Edmond Diet/Léon Xanrof, Ernest Depré). Baron fils played Joseph, Vauthier was Pharoah and Matrat and Mily-Meyer were the Putiphars in a piece which was considered so ''audacious'' that the British press refused to print the plot. It seems, in any case, to have concentrated wholly on the seductive bit of Joseph's story rather than the mystical bits. The Potiphar family were also seen on the Belgian stage in 1857 (19 August, Château des Fluers, Brussels) in Pellaert's *Monsieur et Madame Putiphar* and the tale of Joseph was parodied in highly successful opéra-bouffe *Joséphine vendue par ses soeurs.*

USA: Brooklyn Academy of Music 22 December 1976, Entermedia Theater 18 November 1981, Royale Theater 27 January 1982; Australia: York Theatre, Sydney 26 November 1975; Hungary: Madach Színház *Jéozsef és a sziness, szélesvéasznú Ealomkasát* January 1991; Germany: Colosseum, Essen 13 December 1996

Recordings: original cast (RSO), London cast (MCA), Irish cast (RAM), South African cast (EMI), Israeli cast (Hed-Arzi), Mexican cast (Melody), Broadway cast (Chrysalis), Austrian cast (Ha-Ha), London revival cast (Polygram), Canadian cast (Kerygma), Hungarian cast (Média), Broadway revival cast (Polydor), Swedish cast 1995 (Four Leaf Clover), German cast (Colosseum Essen), German cast 1997 (Polydor), etc

Video: 1999

JOSÉPHINE VENDUE PAR SES SOEURS Opéra-bouffe in 3 acts by Paul Ferrier and Fabrice Carré. Music by Victor Roger. Théâtre des Bouffes-Parisiens, Paris, 20 March 1886.

Joseph and the Amazing Technicolor Dreamcoat was not the first musical to utilize the biblical tale of Joseph for its libretto, but the 1886 *Joséphine vendue par ses soeurs* treated the tale rather differently. Ferrier and Carré called their piece an opéra-bouffe, and there was little doubt that it treated Joseph's story in a burlesque fashion, even if the result was a finished and funny French farce with little of the burlesque extravagance of earlier years about it. To start with, as the title made plain, *Joséphine* had its sexes reversed.

The widowed concierge Madame Jacob (Mme Macé-Montrouge) has 12 daughters but, whilst the others have to tighten their belts and go out to work, Joséphine (Jeanne Thibault) is the spoiled darling who wants for nothing. For Joséphine is at the Conservatoire and she is training to be a musical-theatre star. The exasperated sisters plot together and they manage things so that Joséphine is finally ''sold'' to the love-struck Egyptian Alfred Pharaon Pasha (Édouard Maugé), with what she thinks is a contract to star at the Cairo opera. However, when Joséphine gets to Egypt she finds that it is the Pasha's harem rather than his theatre that is in store for her. Madame Jacob and her daughters and Joséphine's beloved baritone, Montosol (Piccaluga) are, however, hot on the Egyptian trail, and the wily concierge soon takes control. She is determined that Joséphine will indissolubly wed the fabulously wealthy Pasha before bedtime, and that Alfred shall spend his fortune on getting her dozen daughters good (rich) husbands. But Alfred, dragged off to Paris by Madame and her girls, ends up being sacked from his regal post for neglecting his offices for the sake of his amours. When he finally gives up his amorous pursuit, his bank balance battered and his masculinity thoroughly tried, Joséphine is left virginally to wed her persevering baritone, while Madame Jacob settles down, without a single daughter, in the nice new concièrgerie he has lavished on her. The daughters have all, as she planned, been nicely married off, thanks to the dowries supplied by Alfred. The principal soubret parts of the show were Joséphine's youngest sister, Benjamine (Mily-Meyer), and Alfred's traditionalist, anti-French nephew, Putiphar Bey (Charles Lamy), whom she ultimately subdues.

The humor of the text permeated the whole of the show's score. Even the nominal lovers of the play, Joséphine and Montosol, gave forth with humorous numbers, albeit in a lyrical mode. Joséphine justified her choice of a baritone in the first act Couplets du conservatoire, pleaded with Alfred to let her return to Paris (''the conservatoire, the rain, and the omnibus accidents'') in a rondeau-valse, launched into extravagant operatic duo with Montosol in a first-act rehearsal and again in the second act (''Je lui disais encore''), on both occasions to splendidly funny effect, and repulsed poor Alfred in a third-act ronde. Montosol gave forth with operatic fervor, beginning with a romance in the first act (''Je ne vois que vous seule'') and topping his second-act solo with what he vowed would be his last high A flat in what he vowed would be his last serenade, before launching into the big duo of the evening. The soubrette role of Benjamine also had a large share in the music, with a number in each of the first two acts, a duo with Putiphar in the third, and, above all, the famous section of the first act's quartet in which she downed the operaticizing of her sister and Montosol with a brisk little bit of sexy nonsense illustrating her own rather lighter taste in music: ''Ugène, Ugèn' tu me fais languir, où y a d'hygiène y a plus de plaisir.'' Alfred, Putiphar and, briefly, Madame Jacob, all took a share in the music, which included several ensembles and concerted finales alongside its principal numbers.

Joséphine was a great success on its production in Paris, with Mily-Meyer, in particular, winning a triumphant reception as the perky and highly-featured little baby of the family. It played through till the summer break, and took up its place again as soon as the house reopened, passing its 100th performance on 20 September and its 200th on 22 December before being replaced

Plate 194. **Joséphine vendue par ses soeurs.** *Ilka Pálmay as Benjamine in Hungary's version.*

by Lecocq's newest piece in the first week of January, when it shifted across to the Menus-Plaisirs. The show became a regular part of the French repertoire and it was brought back at the Bouffes following the flop of *Sosie* later in 1887 with Mlle Desgrenais, Gourdon and Mlle Toudouze, and again with Mily-Meyer repeating her famous performance as Benjamine, in 1889 and 1890. It returned yet again at the Eldorado in 1896, at the Bouffes-Parisiens again in 1900 with Anna Tariol-Baugé and Jean Périer teamed with Mily-Meyer, at the Château d'Eau in 1903, and one more time at the Bouffes in 1906.

The first foreign productions followed quickly behind the remarkable Parisian success, and before the end of 1886 *Joséphine* had been seen in New York, Budapest, London and Vienna. Brussels welcomed it in 1887 (Galéries Saint-Hubert 14 September). However, for some strange reason, it caused nothing like the merry stir it had done at home. America's *Josephine Sold by Her Sisters* (ad William von Sachs) featured De Wolf Hopper (Alfred), Emily Soldene (Madame Jacob), Herndon Morsell

(Putiphar) and Mathilde Cottrelly (Benjamine), with Louise Parker (Josephine) and the novice Eugene Oudin (Montosol) as the operettic lovers. Colonel McCaull's production was well received and played through the six weeks' slot allotted to it in his season at Wallack's, but when it hit the McCaull tour trail it proved not to be a major hit. In Budapest (ad Viktor Rákosi) Ilka Pálmay (Benjamine), Aranka Hegyi (Josephine), Zsófi Csatay (Mme Jacob), Pál Vidor, József Németh and Vidor Kassai headed a top-flight Népszínház cast for just a dozen performances, whilst in London a Charles Marsham Rae adaptation/production called *Our Diva,* which featured Frank Celli (Montosol), Frank Wyatt (Alfred), Madame Amadi (Madame Jacob), Effie Clements (Caroline, ie, Josephine) and Minnie Marshall (Fifine, ie, Benjamine), and which chastely removed the biblical parallels, lasted only from the end of October till mid-December (48 performances). It did better, however, than the disappointing production (ad Heinrich Osten) mounted by Carl Tatartzy at the Vienna Carltheater. Wilhelm Knaack (Alfred), Adolf Brackl (Montosol) and Sophie Link (Josephine) were featured in a version which interpolated some pieces of music by Louis Lackenbacher, had the director's wife in the plum role of Madame Jacob, and folded in a fortnight. But France loved it.

USA: Wallack's Theater *Josephine Sold by Her Sisters* 30 August 1886; Hungary: Népszínház *Jozefa Egyptomban* 9 October 1886; UK: Opera Comique *Our Diva* 28 October 1886, Austria: Carltheater *Josephine und ihre Schwestern* 25 December 1886

LE JOUR ET LA NUIT Opéra-bouffe in 3 acts by Albert Vanloo and Eugène Leterrier. Music by Charles Lecocq. Théâtre des Nouveautés, Paris, 5 November 1881.

When Lecocq and producer Koning broke up their long and profitable association after the failure of *Janot,* the composer moved on to the Théâtre des Nouveautés and promptly turned out two of the best works of the later part of his career in *Le Jour et la nuit* and *Le Coeur et la main* for manager Brasseur. The first of these two works started out with the advantage of a fine, farcical libretto from the top team of Leterrier and Vanloo.

Manola (Marguerite Ugalde) is the intended of Miguel (Montaubry), steward to Don Brasiero de Tra os Montes (Berthelier), the Governor of a Portuguese province. She is also, however, lusted after by the ubiquitously lustful Portuguese prime minister, Prince Picrates de Calabazas (Jules Brasseur). Brasiero has just been proxy wed to a new wife, Béatrix (Juliette Darcourt), selected by his trusted and aristocratic cousin Degomez (Scipion), but since a little war has happened on his frontier, he is away from home when she is due to arrive. Before she does, however, Manola turns up, fleeing from the fingers of Calabazas, and Miguel's defense against the slavering prime minister is to pretend that it is Manola who is, untouchably, the new wife of the governor. Good friend Béatrix helps keep up the charade, so whilst Manola plays wife to the duly returned nobleman by day, it is Béatrix, with the lights out, who enjoys the nighttime part of marriage. The trick almost works, but unfortunately the unquenched Calabazas switches his amorous intentions on to Béatrix, and the deceptions and avoidances only multiply until the truth comes out. But the vengeance of the furious prime minister is stifled by his sacking—he has been off chasing skirt too long and the King has decided to get a new prime minister.

Lecocq's score was in his most attractive vein, popularly topped by Calabazas's lively if unlikely insistence that "Les Portugais sont toujours gais." Manola's role was a particularly well-served one, featuring a first-act air ("Eh bien! oui, je suis la baronne") in which she challenged her would-be seducer with her false rank, a series of numbers in which she frantically attempted to recall a tune sung to Brasiero by his nighttime wife, the seductive "J'ai vu le jour dans un pays" and Chanson Indienne, with which, after the turn of the plot, she attempts to distract Calabazas from Béatrix, and her last act waltz duo with Miguel, "Nous sommes deux amoureux." Miguel's romantic moments included a charming romance, "Laissez-moi rallumer, ma belle," and his despairing ones a duet with Manola in the opening act deciding that the only way out of the situation is a quick double suicide ("Tuons-nous"). The two comedians both had fine moments, Calabazas regretting his unstoppable lascivious tendencies ("Les femmes! ne m'en parlez pas!") and walloping out his Portuguese number, and Brasiero proffering his act-now philosophy ("Mon cher ami, sache bien qu'ici-bas") or rapturizing over his new bride (Ballade de la lune) in a first-act finale of particular quality and appeal.

Le Jour et la nuit was a major hit for Brasseur's theatre. Its first run totaled 197 performances, and it was brought back in 1883 (20 September) for a further 34 performances. It was later seen at the Athénée-Comique in 1897 (27 April) with Jeanne Petit (Manola), Édouard Maugé (Calabazas), Dekernel (Brasiero) and Albert Piccaluga (Miguel), at the Château d'Eau in 1911 (3 November) and in 1923 at the Gaîté. In the meanwhile, it had spread itself around the world, though not always with the kind of success it had found at home.

In Hungary (ad Lajos Evva, Béla J Fái) *Nap és hold* was a major hit, with Ilka Pálmay (Manola), Aranka Hegyi (Béatrix), Vidor Kassai (Calabazas), Elek Solymossy (Brasiero) and János Kápolnai (Miguel) heading the cast through an initial season of 69 performances, followed by revivals in 1899 (9 September) and 1906 (28 December). In America the piece did not get a regular Broadway run, as both the English and French-language productions were played only in repertoire companies. An English *Manola* with Catherine Lewis (Manola), Marie Jansen (Beatrice), John Howson (Calabazas), Fred Leslie (Brasiero) and Charles J Campbell (Miguel) was quickly followed (1 May 1882) by Maurice Grau's French company with Paola Marié (Manola), Mlle Grégoire (Béatrix), Mezières (Calabazas), Nigri (Miguel) and Duplan (Brasiero), and both proved to be well-enough liked for the piece to get showings around the country.

London's English version (ad H B Farnie) opened just a few days after New York's, with a cast that did not match the starry teams chosen for the piece elsewhere. Rosa Leo, Irene Verona, Henry Ashley, Eugène Desmonts and W J Hill featured in Alexander Henderson's production (which allowed the interpolation of a number by Leopold Wenzel) and ran for just a respectable three months at the Strand Theatre. Its relative failure can probably be put down to the bowdlerizing practiced on a libretto judged too sexual for English-hearing ears, as much as to its undercasting. It is hard to believe that the same kind of sanitization went on in Vienna, but the result there was even poorer. Franz Steiner's production of an uncredited German version at the Theater an der Wien, with Carl Adolf Friese (Calabazas), Alexander Girardi (Brasiero), Rosa Streitmann (Béatrix), Karoline Finaly (Manola) and Hubert Wilke (Miguel), was played only six times.

Hungary: Népszínház *Nap és hold* 7 January 1882; USA: Fifth Avenue Theater *Manola, or Blonde and Brunette* 6 February 1882; UK: Strand Theatre *Manola* 11 February 1882; Austria: Theater an der Wien *Tag und Nacht* 13 March 1882; Australia: Opera House, Melbourne *Manola* 13 September 1882

Recording: complete (Gaîté-Lyrique)

JUBILEE Musical comedy in 2 acts by Moss Hart. Music and lyrics by Cole Porter. Imperial Theater, New York, 12 October 1935.

Apparently suggested by the silver jubilee of King George V of Britain (but bearing a worrying resemblance to, in particular, Willie Gill's flop *A Royal Tramp* of nearly half a century earlier), Moss Hart's libretto for *Jubilee* took up the once favorite, very old comic opera theme of disguised princes and princesses out for adventure in the real world. On this occasion, the whole royal family goes gallivanting at once, because some minor royal has got greedy and decided to have a little revolution, putting them out of a job. Leaving the now unburdened King Henry (Melville Cooper) at home to play the parlor games which are his chief delight, the Queen (Mary Boland), Princess Diana (Margaret Adams) and Prince James (Charles Walter) leave behind the luxuries and responsibilities of royalty and dash off in search of a bit of unspied-upon romance. The Queen does well enough in batting her eyelashes at movie star Charles Rausmiller (Mark Plant), the Princess becomes briefly involved with the writer Eric Dare (Derek Williams), whilst the Prince sings and dances the night away with the dancer Karen O'Kane (June Knight) before the revolution fizzles out and they all have to go back home to work. The show's innish-joke was that Rausmiller was a Johnny Weismuller copy, Dare modeled on Noël Coward, another character on Elsa Maxwell, and one was supposed to think, for example, of Queen Mary having a flirt with Tarzan.

The score to *Jubilee* produced one of Porter's best-loved songs, when June Knight led off a dance number with her prince telling what happens when they "Begin the Beguine." The same pair also had the show's other most successful song, the enduring "Just One of Those Things," as well as the description of "A Picture of You without Me," whilst the Princess demanded of herself "Why Shouldn't I?" at the first whisperings of romance, and her writer sang in the Cowardesque Samolan fashion of "The Kling-Kling Bird on the Divi-Divi Tree."

The songs which became standards and the Queen-meets-Tarzan joke did not prove sufficient to keep *Jubilee* afloat for very long. Sam H Harris and Max Gordon's production played just 169 performances on Broadway, but *Jubilee* nevertheless rendered up more reusable musical parts than many shows which lasted twice or thrice as long.

Jubilee, with its jokes now stale and/or dead, has however been revived in San Francisco in the 1990s.

Recording: composer (Columbia)

JUDIC, Anna [DAMIEN, Anne Marie Louise] (b Semur-en-Auxois, 18 July 1849; d Golfe-Juan, 15 April 1911). Saucy, skillful megastar of the Parisian opérette and vaudeville stage.

The young Mlle Damiens, niece of manager Lemoine Montigny of the Théâtre du Gymnase, and daughter of that theatre's box-office lady, did her first work as a chanteuse at the Eldorado café-concert and, whilst there, she married (25 April 1867) the regisseur Émile Israël, known as Judic, whose name she used thereafter for her stage appearances. She made the first of those appearances at the Gymnase (2 June 1867) in *Les Erreurs d'un bel ange.* After several undistinguished ingenue parts, however, she returned to the cafés-concerts ("Ne me chatouillez pas," "La Première Feuille," "Les Baisers," etc) appearing not only at the Eldorado in song and in opérette (*Paola et Pietro,* 1868, etc), but at the Marseilles Alcazar and at the Folies-Bergère where, in 1871, she scored a considerable hit in Grisart's little opérette *Memnon.* In 1870 (11 September) she also visited Belgium. She returned to the theatre in 1872 when she was hired for the company at the Théâtre de la Gaîté, and there she

Plate 195. **Anna Judic.** *Paris's musical-comedy megastar of the 1880s.*

created her first important opéra-bouffe role as the Princess Cunégonde in Offenbach's *Le Roi Carotte.*

Mlle Judic was subsequently snapped up by the Théâtre des Bouffes-Parisiens, and she made a sensation in her very first role there, as the innocently scabrous heroine of Vasseur's hit musical, *La Timbale d'argent.* Her reputation thus made, she created, over the next three years, a series of lead roles at the Bouffes in often less than successful shows, including the title role of the café-chanteuse in Offenbach's little *Bagatelle,* Vasseur's *La Petite Reine,* Fanfare in Léon Roques's *La Rosière d'ici, La Branche cassée,* as the actress Nina (with disguises as an Auvergnat peasant, a music mistress and a pifferaro) in the quick flop *Les Parisiennes* (1874), as the titular Marietta in Offenbach's successful *Madame l'Archiduc,* and, stained black, as his *La Créole,* Dora. During the summer closures she was seen in St Petersburg, in London, and at Brussels's Galeries Saint-Hubert.

In 1876 she quit the Bouffes and moved on to the Théâtre des Variétés and the management of Eugène Bertrand. There, she confirmed herself as one of Paris's top musical-comedy players as she appeared in a mixture of classic opérettes (Hélène, Périchole, etc) and new pieces (Prascovia in *Le Docteur Ox* 1877, Thérèse Valpinçon in *Les Charbonniers* 1877, *Chanteuse par amour* 1877, etc), before causing a second sensation—six years after the first—in the starring role of the vaudeville *Niniche,* in which she shocked public opinion deliciously by appearing on stage in a bathing suit.

The successors of *Niniche,* constructed specially in the same play-with-songs manner and each made to feature its star in a vast, bravura role, hoisted Judic to her highest popularity. *La Femme à papa* (1879), *La Roussotte* (1881), *Lili* (1882) and *Mam'zelle Nitouche* (1883) were each a long-running triumph for her, and each supplied her with at least one all-pervading hit song, in five solid years at the very top of her profession. In 1883 she visited London's Gaiety Theatre, Vienna—where in five hectic days she introduced the Theater an der Wien to *Niniche, La Femme à papa, Lili* and supporting programs including *Les Charbonniers* and *La Princesse*—and Budapest (23 November) but, on her return, her series of successes came to an end with the rather less than triumphant production of the latest made-to-measure piece, *La Cosaque* (1884).

With the fashion having turned away from the now rather too similar run of vaudeville-opérettes, Judic left the Variétés to try her hand as an actress (*Elle et Lui* 1885 at the Palais-Royal, with a couple of interpolated songs), but after a couple of flops she returned once more to the musical stage, to star in revivals of her earlier hits, the co-author of which, Albert Millaud, she had in the meanwhile married. She toured through Scandinavia in 1884, and then in 1885 she traveled to America for Maurice Grau. There she played her staple roles (*La Femme à papa, Mam'zelle Nitouche, Niniche, Lili, La Cosaque*) and also appeared in pieces such as *La Mascotte, Le Grand Casimir, La Périchole, La Grande-Duchesse, La Jolie Parfumeuse, La Vie parisienne* and the comedy *Divorçons,* all round the country and in a season at New York's Star, Wallack's and Casino Theaters with considerable success. She had to be a success, as Judic—the biggest French musical star to visit America in years—had apparently extorted quite a deal from her manager: a reported guarantee of the equivalent of $42,000 for the eight months (25 percent payable to her Paris bank in advance), travel and hotels paid, and her own personal train for touring. She also followed the golden trail previously taken by Aimée and Paola Marié to Mexico and Cuba (1886).

Back in France the now rather portly actress subsisted over the years that followed largely on further reprises of her Variétés hits and on revivals of such pieces as *La*

Belle Hélène and *La Grande-Duchesse* (paired in both with the even more aging original star of those pieces, José Dupuis), *Madame l'Archiduc* (1889) *Madame Favart* (1889) and notably, opposite Jeanne Granier, who had succeeded to her prima donna assoluta's crown in Parisian eyes, as Lange in *La Fille de Madame Angot.* Her essays at new pieces, such as *La Noce à Nini* (1887, Virginie Bridoux) and *La Japonaise* (1888, Christine Vatencourt) were unfruitful.

She visited Vienna and Budapest again in 1889 with the Variétés company and Dupuis, playing *Niniche, Lili, La Femme à papa, Les Charbonniers* and *Mam'zelle Nitouche,* then again the following year, in 1891 and in 1892, with *La Roussotte* and the little *Joséphine* added to her repertoire. She visited Budapest's Népszínház to play *Nitouche* in 1892 and repeated her famous roles in Paris in 1894, but she latterly made her Paris appearances largely on the straight stage, although she continued to perform her famous songs out of their theatrical context. After five years of "retirement" she returned to the Paris stage in 1901, playing *Niniche* at the Variétés once again, and in 1903 she was seen in the revue *Paris aux Variétés* ("time has dealt gently with this gifted artiste") playing alongside Ève Lavallière, Max Dearly, Jeanne Saulier and Alice Bonheur of the new generation . . . but with Baron and Brasseur still there as well. She subsequently took a turn at management, taking over the Palais-Royal in 1906, but without notable success.

Judic's granddaughter, Simone Judic, originally a shopgirl in her family's hairdressing business, also took to the stage (at first as Simone Réva) performing her grandmother's numbers, but later in revue at the Cigale and the Folies-Bergère and then as a leading lady in 1920s musical comedy (Fourdrain's *Cadet-Roussel, Mariage princier, Marché d'amour, Rapatipatoum, La Princesse Carnaval, La Belle du Far-West, La Sirène, La Ceinture de Vénus, You-You, Dolly, Pouick, Prends-moi, Les Rendezvous clandestins,* etc).

JUMBO Musical comedy in 2 acts by Ben Hecht and Charles MacArthur. Lyrics by Lorenz Hart. Music by Richard Rodgers. Hippodrome, New York, 16 November 1935.

Jumbo was conceived by producer Billy Rose as a gigantic circus-spectacular-cum-musical, to be built around the greatest circus acts in the world which he, characteristically, had little doubt he could secure. What he did secure, in order of importance, was the vast old New York Hippodrome—the home of so many spectacular Charles Dillingham shows in the early years of the century—George Abbott, who had never staged a musical, as book director (John Murray Anderson was already hired with a "production staged by" credit), Rodgers and Hart for the songs, and Hecht and MacArthur, the authors of *The Front Page* and *Twentieth Century,* as neophyte librettists.

Having acquired the Hippodrome, Rose proceeded to tear its interior to pieces to make the place resemble a circus tent and, in place of the most famous acts in the world (which were, not wholly surprisingly, not available at short notice), he hired a mass of jugglers, trapeze artists, clowns, riders and a female elephant to play Jumbo, all of who rehearsed their way in and around the musical-comedy portion of the show for rather longer than was usual. Rose, who was flinging money around wildly on some aspects of the production, made a saving when he somehow persuaded Actors' Equity to agree that the show was not a musical but a circus and that, therefore, he had no reason to pay rehearsal wages to his cast. In spite of this economy, the production budget rose to the then enormous amount of $340,000.

Hecht and MacArthur's libretto was a run-of-the-mill affair about two rival circus owners (W J McCarthy, Arthur Sinclair), one of whom has a son (Donald Novis), the other a daughter (Gloria Grafton), and both of whom have a predictable ending. Top-billed comedian Jimmy Durante was cast as Claudius B Bowers, a circus press agent. Rather better were the songs. McCarthy and Miss Grafton had the best, the waltzing "The Most Beautiful Girl in the World," but the heroine's "Little Girl Blue" and her duo with her boy, "My Romance," also found popularity, alongside the ensemble "The Circus Is on Parade." Durante's contribution was "Laugh." One song did not make it to opening night, and Rodgers and Hart put aside "There's a Small Hotel" for later (but not much later) use.

Jumbo's spectacle and songs earned it a fine reception, but Rose's limits as a producer soon showed up. He had done his sums ridiculously poorly and, even playing to good houses, the show could not make ends meet. It had to be closed after 233 performances, and there was little chance that it could ever be staged again. In fact, it was, but on the screen: 27 years later MGM made a movie version which they christened *Billy Rose's Jumbo.* They threw out the bulk of the Hecht/MacArthur book and Sidney Sheldon developed a new story on not dissimilar lines, featuring Durante as the circus owner and Doris Day as his daughter who falls in love with the son (Stephen Boyd) of the rival proprietor (Dean Jagger), who has come in disguise to try to steal Jumbo from them (steal an elephant?). Martha Raye was Durante's love interest, as a circus lady called Madame Lulu. The half-dozen principal numbers of the Jumbo scored were topped up with "This Can't Be Love" (*On Your Toes*) and "Why Can't I?" (*Spring Is Here*) and a number by associate producer Roger Edens, and film gave production values to the piece which even the New York Hippodrome couldn't hold.

Jumbo actually made his way onto the musical stage many years before Mr Rose. In 1882 Tony Pastor mounted a burlesque *Jumbo, the Trick Elephant* at the 14th Street Theater hot on the heels of Barnum's importation of the beast in question.

Film: MGM 1962

Recordings: film soundtrack (CBS), selection (RCA)

JUNE [TRIPP, June Howard] (b Blackpool, 11 June 1901; d New York, 14 January 1985). British dancing ingenue of the 1920s.

Daughter of actor Howard Tripp EDGAR (né Walter Howard TRIPP), and trained as a balletic dancer, June appeared at the Palace Theatre as an 11-year-old support to Pavlova, then later at the Folies-Bergère, and in revue in London (*Watch Your Step, Buzz Buzz*). She had her first featured role in a musical playing the part which ended up being called Aspasia in C B Cochran's unrecognizable version of the Parisian hit *Phi-Phi* (1922), and followed up in the title role of the London production of George M Cohan's *Little Nellie Kelly* under the same management. She played juvenile leads opposite Jack Buchanan in *Toni* (1924, Princess Stephanie) and *Boodle* (1925, Daphne Drew), and—although she was at one stage announced to lead the cast of Broadway's *Riquette*—in two imported musicals in London, the highly successful *Mercenary Mary* (1925, June Somers) and the very quick flop *Happy-Go-Lucky* (1926, June Willard).

Thereafter she played principally in revue, although she visited America to play the title role of the unsuccessful *Polly* (1929) and, having spent a rather unsatisfactory if intermittently high-living period of time out as Lady Inverclyde, returned to the stage to replace the insufficient Lili Damita opposite George Robey in *Here's How!* (1934). Later engagements in revue and occasional film in America were discreet.

Autobiographies: *The Whole Story* (1932), *The Glass Ladder* (Heinemann, London, 1960)

DIE JUNGFRAU VON BELLEVILLE Operette in 3 acts by F Zell and Richard Genée based on *La Pucelle de Belleville* by Paul de Kock and its stage version, *Agnès de Belleville,* by de Kock and the Cogniard brothers. Music by Carl Millöcker. Theater an der Wien, Vienna, 29 October 1881.

Although never as popular or as successful as Millöcker's most famous works, *Die Jungfrau von Belleville* nevertheless attracted plenty of producers in the 1880s, and was seen throughout the world in a variety of languages. The text was based on the vaudeville *Agnès de Belleville* (Folies-Dramatiques, 1835), itself a stage version of the novel of the same title, which told the tale of a rather *Mam'zelle Nitouche*–like creature called Virginie Troupeau (Rosa Streitmann), daughter of a rich manufacturer (Felix Schweighofer) and tyrannically guarded by her aunt, the dragonistic Mlle Javotte Bergamotte (Therese Schäfer). Virginie, whose virtue is the pride of all Belleville, is anxious to marry anyone at all to escape life with her aunt, and has been practicing love-making with goofy neighbor Doudoux (Schütz) in preparation. Her father proposes the aging rake Count Archibald de Châteaurien (Grevé), his friend Vaudoré (Ausim) proposes his son, and Virginie gets her pitter-pats from a visiting Sergeant Godibert (Alexander Girardi). When she is nearly caught out in her ''practicing,'' her poor cousin Adrienne (Frln Scholz) takes the blame, but finally all is sorted out: Adrienne gets the painter Émile Montreux (Steiner) she adores, and Virginie settles for the Count who will be, at least, a complaisant husband. The piece was set with some typically attractive Millöcker music, with a first-act march proving particularly popular among the more lyrical numbers which illustrated the second-act love affairs.

The Theater an der Wien's production was played 35 times during its first 12 months in the repertoire, and it ultimately passed the 50 mark as the show went on to be mounted successively in Dresden, Hamburg, Berlin and at New York's Thalia Theater. Max Lube, Emmy Meffert, Habrich, Bertha Schulz, Junker, Elsbach, Rank and Schütz featured for a handful of performances in America's German-language production, and although George Lederer's subsequent English version (ad Richard Stahl)—mounted at the Star Theatre with Alice Harrison replacing the originally slated Marie Aimée in the central role of a gag-filled, ill-translated piece was—swiftly (14 performances) booted out to Philadelphia; there it was a decided success and outran its intended slot decisively. It was subsequently sent on the road by Lederer and Robert Grau, with Madeleine Lucette starred. *Die Jungfrau von Belleville* later turned up again in Chicago and once more, in 1891, at New York's German-language Terrace Garten.

Paris briefly saw a French version (ad Alexandre Beaumont, Charles Nuitter), with Mily-Meyer as Virginie, more than six years after the show's premiere, and later the same year Budapest got an Hungarian version (ad Andor Kozma). Neither won any particular favor. But *Die Jungfrau von Belleville* carried on. It was seen at the Johann Strauss-Theater in 1910, and it continued longer than expected to hold a revivable place in the Millöcker repertoire which was not really in line with its lack of real theatrical success.

La Pucelle de Belleville was used as the basis for another Operette, *Die Jungfrau von Paris,* written by Günther Schwenn, composed by Friedrich Schröder and produced at the Vienna Raimundtheater in 1969.

Germany: Residenztheater, Dresden 25 June 1882, Friedrich-Wilhelmstädtisches Theater, Berlin 29 September 1882; USA: Thalia Theater 6 May 1886, Star Theatre *The Maid of Belleville* 24 June 1886; France: Théâtre des Folies-Dramatiques *La Demoiselle de Belleville* 29 February 1888; Hungary: Népszínház *A bellevillei szüz* 3 November 1888

DER JUXBARON Operette in 3 acts by Alexander Pordes-Milo and Hermann Haller. Lyrics by Willi Wolff. Music by Walter Kollo. Carl-Schultze Theater, Hamburg, 14 November 1913.

The ''joke-baron'' of Pordes-Milo's title is the vagabond Blaukehlchen. When Hans von Grabow and his new little wife Hilda go off to enjoy their honeymoon they are threatened with the extremely unwanted company of Hilda's parents and her sister, Sophie, so they pretend that the only other available room in the house is taken up by their friend Alexander Christlieb, Baron von Kimmel. When the family turn up anyhow, and Alexander has not arrived, they have quickly to find a deputy. Blaukehlchen agrees to play the part. He plays it with extravagant gusto, drags the in-laws off to a vagabond's ball, gets engaged to Sophie and then, when the real Baron arrives and all is revealed, shrugs happily off on the road once more.

Kollo's jolly score ranged through such made-for-dancing pieces as ''Bubi, mein lieber süsser Bubi,'' ''Wozu hast du denn die Beene, kleine Maus,'' ''Kleine Mädchen müssen schlafen geh'n'' and ''Wenn ein Mädel einen Herrn hat,'' with soubrette Sophie and the phony baron winning the best of the song and dance moments.

A fine success in Hamburg, *Der Juxbaron* was seen in Berlin first at the Berliner Theater and, later, for a two-month revival at the other bastion of Kollo's fame, the Theater am Nollendorfplatz (25 December 1918), at that stage run by co-librettist Haller. It was produced in Vienna during the war, in a ''localized'' version, by Oskar Fronz and his Bürgertheater company, with Ludwig Herold and Emmy Petko as the newlyweds, Arthur Guttmann as the false baron, now called Stieglitz, and Alexander Hernfeld and Victoria Pohl-Meiser as the interfering in-laws. It played for a month at that house, then moved to the Colosseum when the Berliner Theater ensemble arrived for a season (50th 4 April 1915), returning to play its last performances at the Bürgertheater in May. Although Comstock and Gest promised the show for 1915 as *Baron de Gink* and the Shuberts announced the forthcoming production of *The Fake Baron* (w F Ray Comstock) later in the 1915-16 season, it did not apparently see the light of English-langauge day and America's only viewing of the show seems to have been at New York's German-language Irving Place Theater in 1918, with Christian Rub starring as the vagabond, supported by Lotte Engel, Hanns Unterkirchner, Flora Arndt and Bruno Schlegel.

Hungary: Royal Orfeum *Link báró* 11 February 1915; Austria: Wiener Bürgertheater 23 February 1915; USA: Irving Place Theater 1 February 1918

K

KACSOH, Pongrác (b Budapest, 15 December 1873; d Budapest, 18 December 1923). Composer of Hungary's most popular and enduring folk operett.

Brought up in Kolozsvár, the young Kacsoh spread his studies between mathematics and science on the one hand, and a musical education at the local conservatoire on the other. He later became a secondary-school teacher, teaching mathematics and science in Budapest, and, whilst pursuing a continuing scientific career, he also furthered his musical studies and ultimately became a music critic, editor of the musical paper *Zenevilág* (1905–7), and both a writer and a composer.

His first contribution to the theatre was in the form of a set of songs for the musical play *Csipkerózsika,* but in 1904 he composed the score for the light opera *János vitéz,* the Hungarian folktale of John the Hero as told in the dramatic poem by Sándor Petőfi and adapted to the stage by Károly Bakonyi, and with that piece he won an outstanding musical theatre success. The half-fairy-tale of the shepherd boy János who is chased from his home and his beloved Iluska by her murderous stepmother, and who, after becoming a military hero, throws up glory and sets out to the afterworld to find his lost love, was illustrated with a richly constructed, movingly wistful score of folk-based music which complemented its subject perfectly. *János vitéz,* regularly played throughout Hungary ever since its first production, has become virtually the country's national operett.

Kacsoh's two other principal works, in a small output, were *Rákóczi,* another Hungarian piece authored by Bakonyi, based on the tale of Ferenc Rákóczi, the 18th-century monarch who spread his Protestant power over Hungary and Transylvania, but who was subsequently defeated and exiled by the Austrians (a subject simultaneously used for an operatic trilogy by Zichy at the Magyar Királyi Operaház); and an operettic adaptation of Israel Zangwill's 1904 London play, *Merely Mary Ann.* He also supplied part of the music for the Árpád Pásztor Singspiel *A harang* which became better known in a subsequent musical setting, by Eduard Künneke, as *Das Dorf ohne Glocke.* All of these pieces were produced at the Király Színház, where *János vitéz* had established Kacsoh's reputation, and each found some success, but thereafter he limited his stage compositions to such assignments as the incidental music for Ferenc Molnár's plays *Liliom* (1909) and *Fehér felhő* (1916).

His final work, *Dorottya,* a comic opera based on a classic Hungarian poem, was produced posthumously. An 18th-century tale of a spinster who herself finds love whilst trying to settle the amorous affairs of her younger sister, it was well regarded although its music was judged more ambitious and less individual than that of *János vitéz.*

Kacsoh also wrote several historical works on music.

1904 **Csipkerózsika** no production traced

1904 **János vitéz** (Jenő Heltai/Károly Bakonyi) Király Színház 18 November

1906 **Rákóczi** (Sándor Endrődi, Árpád Pásztor/Bakonyi) Király Színház 20 November

1907 **A harang** (w Ákos Buttykay/Pásztor) Király Színház 1 February

1908 **Mary Ann** (Andor Gábor/Sándor Hajó) Király Színház 5 December

1929 **Dorottya** Szeged 9 January

KAHN, Gus (b Koblenz, 6 November 1886; d Beverly Hills, Calif, 8 October 1941). Lyricist for popular songs and films and for a small but song-productive group of stage shows.

Brought up in Chicago, and at first employed in the hotel supplies trade, Kahn had his first song published at the age of 21. Thereafter he became a prolific popular-music lyric writer and supplied the songwords for four Broadway shows, of which the comical Eddie Cantor vehicle *Whoopee* (1928, "Makin' Whoopee," "I'm Bringing a Red, Red Rose," "Love Me or Leave Me"), written in collaboration with his most frequent songwriting partner, Walter Donaldson, was the most successful example.

The first Broadway show for which he took a major credit was an adaptation of the German light opera *Früh-*

ling im Herbst (1920), played by *Naughty Marietta* star Orville Harrold and his daughter Patti with only limited success in the 1925–26 season, the second the lively musical farce *Kitty's Kisses,* in which his words were paired with Con Conrad's music to rather better effect and a much more enduring life, and the last, before Kahn's abandonment of Broadway in favor of Hollywood, a collaboration with George and Ira Gershwin, amongst others, on the indifferent Ziegfeld spectacular *Show Girl,* the hit of which, ''Liza'' (''All the Clouds'll Roll Away'') fell not to Kahn but to the Gershwins.

Although Kahn had but few full-scale Broadway credits, many of his songs were individually interpolated in musical comedies and revues of the 1910s and 1920s, the more memorable including ''Toot, Toot, Tootsie'' (w Dan Russo, Ernie Erdman) for Al Jolson in *Bombo,* ''I'll Say She Does,'' '''N' Everything'' and ''You Ain't Heard Nothin' Yet'' (w Jolson, B G De Sylva) for the same star in *Sinbad, Whoopee*'s ''Love Me or Leave Me'' (w Walter Donaldson) recycled into *Simple Simon,* ''Pretty Baby'' (w Egbert van Alstyne, Tony Jackson) in *The Passing Show of 1916, A World of Pleasure* and London's *Houp-La* and ''Carolina in the Morning'' (w Donaldson) in *The Passing Show of 1922.* A good number of his *Kitty's Kisses* songs were interpolated into the show that London preferred to call *The Girl Friend* (although it contained much more of *Kitty's Kisses*), and his ''I Wonder Where My Baby Is Tonight'' was used in the British revue *The Co-Optimists.* ''Ain't We Got Fun'' (w Raymond Egan, Richard Whiting) and ''It Had to Be You'' (w Isham Jones) turned up, many years later, in pasticcio London shows—*A Day in Hollywood, A Night in the Ukraine* and *Ziegfeld* respectively.

Kahn also introduced songs into many film scores of the period, including the screen versions of the stage musicals *The Chocolate Soldier* (''While My Lady Sleeps''), *The Merry Widow* (''Tonight Will Teach Me to Forget''), and *Rose-Marie* (''Just for You,'' ''Pardon Me, Madame''), as well as providing several fresh numbers for the cinematic *Whoopee* (''My Baby Just Cares for Me'').

Of Kahn's other songs, many of which have been used repeatedly in revues, theatrical compilation shows and musical films, the most successful included ''Yes Sir, That's My Baby,'' ''That Certain Party,'' ''There Ain't No Maybe in My Baby's Eyes,'' ''My Blackbirds Are Bluebirds Now,'' ''Beside a Babbling Brook'' (all w Donaldson), ''Some Sunday Morning'' (w Egan, Whiting), ''The Shores of Minnetonka'' (w Percy Wenrich), ''The One I Love Belongs to Somebody Else,'' ''I'll See You in my Dreams'' (w Isham Jones) and ''Chloe'' (w Neil Moret).

During the 1930s in Hollywood, Kahn supplied the words for many songs for artists such as Grace Moore, Eddie Cantor, Dick Powell and Jeanette MacDonald, in films including *Flying Down to Rio* (''Flying Down to Rio,'' ''Carioca'' w Youmans, Edward Eliscu), *One Night of Love* (w Victor Schertzinger), *Kid Millions, The Girl from Missouri, On Wings of Song* and *Thanks a Million,* a list topped by Jeanette MacDonald's celebrated title song to *San Francisco* (w Walter Jurmann, Bronislav Kaper).

Kahn was impersonated by Danny Thomas in the 1951 musical biofilm *I'll See You in My Dreams.*

1925 **Holka Polka** (aka *Spring in Autumn, Nobody's Girl*) (*Frühling im Herbst*) English lyrics (Lyric Theater)

1926 **Kitty's Kisses** (Con Conrad/Philip Bartholomae, Otto Harbach) Playhouse Theater 6 May

1928 **Whoopee** (Walter Donaldson/William Anthony McGuire) New Amsterdam Theater 4 December

1929 **Show Girl** (George Gershwin/w Ira Gershwin/J P McEvoy ad McGuire) Ziegfeld Theater 2 July

DIE KAISERIN (aka *Fürstenliebe*) Operettenspiel in 2 acts by Julius Brammer and Alfred Grünwald based partly on the play *Maria Theresia* by Franz von Schönthan. Music by Leo Fall. Metropoltheater, Berlin, 16 October 1915.

Leo Fall's *Die Kaiserin* owed its production in Berlin to censorship. In the same manner that Rodgers and Hammerstein's projected musical about Queen Victoria was banned from the British stage, the Austrian authorities would not allow a piece which presented an ancestor of their then reigning monarch to appear as a singing and dancing character in the musical theatre. In fact, as it proved, the story was a fairly harmless one, and one which had no need to be tacked on to the character of the Empress Maria Theresia, but *Die Kaiserin* was given its first production at the Berlin Metropoltheater, with Fritzi Massary starring in its title role, instead of in Vienna.

Having defied her advisers and married the Prinz August Franz von Lothringen (Rolf Brunner), the young monarch discovers the difficulty of being both queen and wife to her husband. Her lively friend the Countess Adelgunde (Rosa Valetti) gives some worldly, womanly advice which helps matters to a happy end. The book was credited as being based on a work by Franz von Schönthan, but the backbone of the text was not so very different from that of the French hit *Le Prince consort* nor even of *Ein Walzertraum.*

The score to *Die Kaiserin* gave its prima donna every opportunity she could wish, from the twinkling, lightfooted ''Zwei Füsserl zum Tanzen'' to the soaring showpiece aria ''Du, mein Schönbrunn,'' in which the Empress serenades her magnificent Viennese palace and all that it represents, and a huge waltz duet with her Franz (''Mir hat heute Nacht''). The show is, however, composed in classic Operette proportions: the tenor Franz has his big moment in the lively ''Dir gehört mein Herz,'' and Adelgunde and her light-comic partner, Graf Pepi Cobenzl, have contrastingly tripping numbers to set off the more romantic and seriously sung pieces of the score.

Following its German premiere, the work, delicately remade as *Fürstenliebe,* was played at Vienna's Carltheater, under the description ''ein Operettenspiel aus dem fröhlichen Rokoko.'' Mizzi Zwerenz starred as ''the Princess'' and later as ''the Regent'' to the Franz von Baldrigen of Victor Norbert, in a piece which was described as taking place ''at the court of a principality of the rococo era.'' The nonroyal Countess Adelgunde (Gerda Walde) was allowed to remain the Countess Adelgunde. *Fürstenliebe* played for 119 performances at the Carltheater, a respectable but ultimately slightly disappointing run, particularly in the eyes of Fall, who considered his score one of the best that he had ever written, as well as his own personal favorite.

Die Kaiserin was repeated, in its original version, at the same house for three weeks in 1925, after the end of the Habsburg years, with manager's wife Dora Keplinger-Eibenschütz starring as Maria Theresia alongside Norbert, Mimi Vesely (Adelgunde) and Oscar Karlweis (Pepi), and again at the Bürgertheater in 1931 with Maria Horstwig, Walter Kochner and Mimi Shorp, and former prima donna Mizzi Günther as Gräfin Fuchs, but it never succeeded in establishing itself as part of the standard repertoire.

Austria: Carltheater (as *Fürstenliebe*) 1 February 1916, (as *Die Kaiserin*) 4 December 1925

Recordings: radio cast (RCA, Germany), selection (Centaur)

KÁLMÁN, Emmerich [KÁLMÁN, Imre] (b Siófok, Hungary, 24 October 1882; d Paris, 30 October 1953). One of the principal composers for the Hungaro-Viennese ''silver age'' of Operette.

Balked in his hopes of becoming a concert pianist by meagre finances and a hand injury, the young Kálmán subsequently led parallel studies at Budapest University's law faculty and in music theory and composition at the Budapest Zeneakadémia under János Koessler, through whose classes had passed such musicians as Bartók, Dohnányi and Kodály. His first musical compositions were largely in the form of orchestral and vocal concert works, written in the late romantic style. One of them, a song cycle, won him a civic award, the Franz-Josef Prize (1907), whilst another, the symphonic poem *Saturnalia,* was performed in concert at the Magyar Királyi Operaház (1904).

Between 1904 and 1908 Kálmán worked as a répétiteur at Budapest's Vígszínház and as a music critic for the *Pesti Napló,* and, following a dip into the popular-

Plate 196. **Emmerich Kálmán**

music world with some pseudonymous cabaret music, he made his first essay as a theatre composer with songs for Samuel Fényes's musical comedy *A pereszlényi juss* (1906) at the Magyar Színház. After contributing to another piece in a similar vein, he then ventured, at the age of 26, his first full-scale operett, *Tatárjárás,* to a libretto by the celebrated author of *János vitéz* and *Bob herceg,* Károly Bakonyi. Produced at the Vígszínház, *Tatárjárás* proved to be one of the most successful of all Hungarian operetts at a time when, with Kacsoh's *János vitéz* and *Rákóczi,* Huszka's *Gül Baba* and *Bob herceg* and Buttykay's *A bolygó görög* and *A csibészkirály* all having appeared in the few years before its production, the native musical theatre in Budapest was beginning to flourish merrily.

Unlike these earlier works, the success of which had been large but limited almost entirely to their country of origin, Kálmán's piece found a considerable audience not only in Hungary but beyond its frontiers. Eleven months after its Budapest premiere, *Tatárjárás* was produced in Austria under the title of *Ein Herbstmanöver* by Wilhelm Karczag, the Hungarian director of Vienna's Theater an der Wien, in an adaptation by Robert Bodanzky. *Ein Herbstmanöver* scored a major Viennese success, totting up a total of over 250 performances in its first run and setting the show off on an international career which took the young composer's work to London (*Autumn Manoeuvres*) and New York (*The Gay Hussars*) as well as to Moscow, Berlin and most other European theatre capitals.

Kálmán's second piece, another if rather differently styled military piece entitled *Az obsitos,* also produced at the Vígszínház, thoroughly confirmed his rising star. After its hometown success, it followed *Tatárjárás* to Vienna where, under the title *Der gute Kamerad,* it was played at the Bürgertheater. And this time the composer went with it. Kálmán left Hungary and settled in Vienna, where he became ''Emmerich'' instead of ''Imre'' and where he remained for the large part of the rest of his life.

Kálmán's first works for the Viennese theatre appeared towards the end of 1912. One, *Der kleine König* (*A kis király*), produced at the Theater an der Wien, still bore its Hungarian origins in the form of a libretto by Bakonyi and Ferenc Martos, which had been translated into German for its premiere. However, it was his other offering of this season, Kálmán's first genuinely Viennese piece, in spite of having a deeply Hungarian story and score, which gave the composer his next big success. *Der Zigeunerprimás,* with Alexander Girardi starring as the old gypsy violinist of the title (''Mein alter Stradivari''), was a Viennese hit which was soon exported with singular success around Europe as well as to Broadway where, under the title of *Sári,* it proved to be one of the most successful of all Kálmán's works on the New York stage.

In 1914 *Gold gab' ich für Eisen,* a new version of *Az obsitos,* was staged in Vienna, its libretto heavily revised to make it into a piece of morale-boosting wartime propaganda, and, perhaps surprisingly, it was picked up and played (admittedly in a thoroughly botched form) both in America (*Her Soldier Boy*) and in Britain (*Soldier Boy*). In addition to this remake, Kálmán brought three new pieces to the stage during the war. The first, *Zsuzsi kisasszony,* began its life in Hungary, but, in the wake of the success of *Sári,* it was quickly picked up for Broadway where it was staged, to genuine success, as *Miss Springtime.* In 1917 Kálmán reused some of the *Zsuzsi kisasszony* score in his successful Vienna musical *Die Faschingsfee.*

In the interim, however, Vienna had seen the production of the composer's most successful Operette to date—*Die Csárdásfürstin,* produced at the Johann Strauss-Theater in November 1915. With its textbook combination of lushly romantic and light comic elements in both script and score, spiced with the gutsy Hungarian flavor which permeated all the best of Kálmán's works and gave them just that spicy iota of a difference from their Viennese fellows, and with a star performance from Mizzi (*Die lustige Witwe*) Günther in its title role, *Die Csárdásfürstin* clocked up nearly six hundred performances in the two years of its original run and became one of the greatest European successes of its time. Although, initially, badly botched in America (*The Riviera Girl*) and meeting an odd indifference in Britain (*The Gipsy Princess*) the show has, nevertheless, remained a member of the basic Austrian Operette repertoire, and won recent revivals even outside Continental Europe.

After the war, Kálmán continued to turn out often outstanding, and outstandingly successful, new musicals. The not-terribly-Dutch *Das Hollandweibchen* was perhaps a mite more discreet than his biggest successes, but it nevertheless ran for 13 months and 362 performances at the Johann Strauss-Theater, went round the world, and was the subject of a notable production in London where the *Little Dutch Girl* of the title was impersonated by opera star Maggie Teyte. However, his next two works, *Die Bajadere* and *Gräfin Mariza,* represented some of the best—and perhaps the very best—of all the composer's musical-theatre output. *Die Bajadere* mixed a tale of romance between an Indian prince and an Operette star with a joyously comical one-wife/two-husbands ménage and a combination of lush Viennese melodies (''O Bajadere,'' etc) and lively up-to-date song-and-dance numbers, in a score which was probably the most outstanding, musically, of the composer's ''Viennese'' works. *Gräfin Mariza,* conversely the most thoroughly Hungarian of all the scores of Kálmán's peak years, rendered up some of his most memorable individual numbers, from the striking tenor ''Komm' Zigany!'' to the loopy ''Komm mit nach Varasdin,'' in a tempestuous Magyar love story lightened judiciously with a little fun.

Both pieces were splendid successes in Vienna, where *Die Bajadere* initially played a full year (353 performances) at the Carltheater and *Gräfin Mariza* even longer (374 performances) at the Theater an der Wien. Both also triumphed throughout Europe but, of the two, *Gräfin Mariza* had a much more significant career in the decades which followed. Neither, however, truly won its due outside Europe. America, still not having learned that botching the big European hits of Kálmán (or anyone else, for that matter) almost invariably led to failure, turned *Die Bajadere* into *The Yankee Princess,* and London quite simply passed. *Countess Maritza* suffered less defacing and, probably not uncoincidentally, was rewarded with a splendid 321 Broadway nights. It did not, however, turn out a genuine hit in London. In Europe, however, both pieces had their due firmly and first time round, and *Gräfin Mariza* settled solidly into the backbone repertoire.

Success struck for Kálmán yet again with the Viennese production of the scenically nifty and musically joyous *Die Zirkusprinzessin* (''Zwei Märchenaugen''), but the composer finally faced disappointment, after years of virtually unshadowed triumph, when he attempted an original musical for the Broadway which had been so prodigal with its reception of its versions of his earliest shows and, so recently, *Gräfin Mariza. Golden Dawn,* concocted with a handful of Hammersteins and various other folk was a ludicrous piece—a custom-made botched show—which nevertheless played for 184 performances at the new Hammerstein's Theater. It produced one number (the villain's baritone exhibition of ''The Whip'') which left memories with some audience members, and it was subsequently filmed. It was not, however, the kind of hit that Kálmán had produced so regularly at home. As Jacobi and Szirmai had also so sadly found, even the greatest Hungarian talent often did not flourish under Broadway conditions.

Kálmán next turned out a European Operette with an American tinge in the Yankee-meets-Ruritania tale of *Die Herzogin von Chicago.* Some critics found the show's mixture of traditional Kálmán style and modern dance-rhythms uncomfortable, but the show gave the composer another Viennese success. *Das Veilchen vom Montmartre,* a flimsy period piece of La Bohèmerie in the composer's least virile Viennese style, also had a fair two-part run at the Johann Strauss-Theater and the Theater an der Wien, as well as some subsequent overseas productions, but the composer had now given all his best and even his second-best work, and the shows he turned out in the later part of his career were the least impressive and enjoyable of his opus.

Kálmán composed the score for the 1931 Reinhold Schunzel and Emmerich Pressburger film *Ronny,* one last Operette for Vienna, *Der Teufelsreiter,* and one which was produced in Zürich, before quitting Europe in 1938 to take shelter from Hitler in the United States. There, the composer of *Gräfin Mariza* and *Sári* found himself in a theatrical atmosphere in which more of his projects were aborted than came to fruition, but he had one further score heard on Broadway when the 1945 musical *Marinka,* the umpteenth rehash of the Mayerling tale (but this time given a happy ending), was played for some five months at the Winter Garden Theater and subsequently exported to a brief showing in Australia.

Kálmán returned to Europe after the Second World War but his only subsequent stage work, another American-flavored piece called *Arizona Lady,* was not produced until after the composer's death in 1953.

A 1958 CCC-Farbfilm entitled *Der Csárdáskönig,* which insisted in its subtitle that it was ''Die Emmerich-Kálmán-Story,'' featured Gerhard Riedmann as the composer, alongside Camilla Spira (original star of *Im weissen Rössl*) as Frau Kálmán, Marina Orschel as Vera, and Rudolf Schock as a tenor János, and a rather better Hungarian-Russian biofilm, *Az elet muzsikaja* was brought out for the composer's centenary in 1982 with Péter Huszti playing Kálmán.

Kálmán's son, **Charles KÁLMÁN** (b Vienna, 17 November 1929), has also composed a number of Operetten including *Babes in the Wood* (USA, 1951), *Wir reisen um Welt* (aka *Der grosse Tenor*) to a text by his sister, Elisabeth (Wiesbaden, 1955), *Rendezvous mit dem Leben* (Würzburg, 1969), *Alfie* (Cologne, 1969, lib: Peter Goldbaum), *Antonia* (Vienna, 1970), *Frau Warrens Gewerbe* (Theater am Dom, Cologne 23 December 1974), *Iszteni komédia* (Budapest, 1984 lib: Ivan Szénes), *Quasimodo* (Schauspielbühne, Munich 16 November 1989, lib: Maria Caleita, Mariello Momm) and *Der blaue Engel* (w Peter Raben/Tankred Dorst, Theater des Westens, Berlin 28 May 1992).

1906 **A pereszlényi juss** (Samuel Fényes) Magyar Színház, Budapest 7 April

1907 **Bernát** (Jenő Heltai) Vígszínház, Budapest 1 June

1908 **Tatárjárás** (Károly Bakonyi, Andor Gábor) Vígszínház, Budapest 22 February

1910 **Az obsitos** (Bakonyi) Vígszínház, Budapest 16 March

1912 **Der Zigeunerprimás** (Fritz Grünbaum, Julius Wilhelm) Johann Strauss-Theater 11 October

1912 **The Blue House** (Austen Hurgon) 1 act London Hippodrome 28 October

1912 **Der kleine König** (Bakonyi, Ferenc Martos ad Robert Bodanzky) Theater an der Wien 27 November

1913 **Kivándorlók** (Gábor) Modern Színház, Budapest 28 September

1914 **Gold gab' ich für Eisen** revised version of *Az obsitos* / *Der gute Kamerad* (Theater an der Wien)

1915 **Zsuzsi kisasszony** (Martos, Miksa Bródy) Vígszínház, Budapest 27 February

1915 **Die Csárdásfürstin** (Leo Stein, Béla Jenbach) Johann Strauss-Theater 17 November

1917 **Die Faschingsfee** (A M Willner, Rudolf Österreicher) Johann Strauss-Theater 21 September

1920 **Das Hollandweibchen** (Stein, Jenbach) Johann Strauss-Theater 31 January

1921 **Die Bajadere** (Julius Brammer, Alfred Grünwald) Carltheater 23 December

1924 **Gräfin Mariza** (Brammer, Grünwald) Theater an der Wien 28 February

1926 **Die Zirkusprinzessin** (Brammer, Grünwald) Theater an der Wien 26 March

1927 **Golden Dawn** (w Herbert Stothart/Otto Harbach, Oscar Hammerstein) Hammerstein's Theater, New York, 30 November

1928 **Die Herzogin von Chicago** (Brammer, Grünwald) Theater an der Wien 5 April

1930 **Das Veilchen vom Montmartre** (Brammer, Grünwald) Johann Strauss-Theater 21 March

1932 **Der Teufelsreiter** (Rudolf Schanzer, Ernst Welisch) Theater an der Wien 10 March

1936 **Kaiserin Josephine** (Paul Knepler, Géza Herczeg) Stadttheater, Zürich 18 January

1945 **Marinka** (aka *Song of Vienna*) (Karl Farkas, George Marion jr) Winter Garden Theater, New York 18 July

1954 **Arizona Lady** (Grünwald, Gustav Beer) Stadttheater, Berne 14 February

Biographies: Österreicher, R: *Emmerich Kálmán: der Weg eines Komponisten* (Amalthea-Verlag, Vienna, 1954), Bistron, J: *Emmerich Kálmán* (Karczag, Leipzig, 1932), Kálmán, V: *Grüss' mir die süssen, die reizenden Frauen* (Hestia Verlag, Bayreuth, 1966)

KALMAR, [Al]Bert (b New York, 16 February 1884; d Los Angeles, 18 September 1947). Song, stage and film wordsmith whose teaming with Harry Ruby left some fine numbers.

Bert Kalmar began his theatre career as a child, performing firstly as a magician, then as a comedian in vaudeville (in a partnership with his future wife, Jessie Brown), and even on occasion in musical comedy (Frank D Weyman in *Li'l Mose,* 1908, etc). He later turned to songwriting, and had his earliest musical-theatre efforts heard on the Chicago stage before, in 1918, he joined songwriting forces with composer-author Harry Ruby. He made his first Broadway appearances as a lyricist with individual songs in revues such as *The Ziegfeld Follies of 1920* (''I'm a Vamp from East Broadway'' w Irving Berlin) *The Passing Show of 1921* (''My Sunny Tennessee'') and *The Greenwich Village Follies of 1922* (''Beautiful Girls''), and also contributed to Chicago's *Arabian Knights,* before the pair provided the score for George S Kaufman and Marc Connelly's *Helen of Troy, New York* (1923). It was one of those rare cases where the book of a musical won better notices than its songs.

Whilst regularly turning out material for the ubiquitous revues of the time over the next half-dozen years, Kalmar also supplied the songs or lyrics and/or libretti for 10 musicals, of which the lively ''fairytale in modern clothes'' *The Five o'Clock Girl* (1927, ''Thinking of You'') was the only one to attract attention in theatres beyond America. The Marx Brothers show *Animal Crackers* (1928, ''The Musketeers,'' ''Hooray for Captain Spalding'') was another popular success which, if its international potential was negated by its being so very much a custom-made vehicle, was made into a film by its inseparable stars, two years after its Broadway run.

The other Kalmar and Ruby shows, if less than memorable in the theatre, nevertheless produced both some good runs and some popular individual numbers. In spite of bad notices, *The Ramblers* (1926), a loose-limbed piece with a filmland setting, was helped to a 290-performance Broadway run and a long afterlife by the antics of comics Clarke and McCullough, and gave the songwriters a hit with ''All Alone Monday,'' whereas *Good Boy* (1928) lasted 253 performances and produced the song ''I Wanna Be Loved By You,'' famously squeaked out by the ''boop-a-doop'' girl, Helen Kane.

Kalmar and Ruby were, along with Guy Bolton, given a ''based on'' credit on the London Rodgers and Hart musical *Lido Lady,* after Ronald Jeans had worked over an unused libretto of theirs to create a new ''American'' musical to order for Cicely Courtneidge and Jack Hulbert. The piece had a 259-performance London run, toured merrily and was exported to Australia and to Paris's Théâtre Apollo, where it was staged ''à grand spectacle.''

Less fortunate Kalmar and Ruby ventures included three attempts to get an adaptation of Aaron Hoffman's *Nothing But Lies* into musical-comedy shape in 1924–25, a share in the adaptation of the ''rather serious'' German musical *Frühling im Herbst* (at various times called *Holka Polka, Spring in Autumn* and *Nobody's Girl*), and a disappointing collaboration with Jerome Kern on a piece called *Lucky,* which failed to live up to its title in 71 performances on Broadway. A genuine pairing with Rodgers and Hart on *She's My Baby* had all the star values of *Lido Lady* (Clifton Webb, Jack Whiting, Beatrice Lillie, Irene Dunne) but none of the same success.

During the 1930s Kalmar and Ruby spent a period in Hollywood, during which they provided the scores for further Marx Brothers films (*Duck Soup, Horsefeathers*), which included such songs as ''Show Me a Rose'' and ''Timbuctoo,'' for Eddie Cantor's *The Kid from Spain* and for *Three Little Words* (''Three Little Words''). Kalmar continued to write film songs up to his death in 1947, returning only once to Broadway for *High Kickers* (1941), a vehicle for George Jessel and Sophie Tucker.

Some of Kalmar's songs were used in the briefly displayed off-Broadway musical *The Cockeyed Tiger* (1977).

In the 1950 musical biofilm *Three Little Words,* Fred Astaire played Kalmar to the Ruby of Red Skelton.

1914 **One Girl in a Million** (Ted Snyder/w Edgar Leslie/ Addison Burkhard, Charles Collins) La Salle Theater, Chicago 6 September

1923 **Helen of Troy, New York** (Harry Ruby/George S Kaufman, Marc Connelly) Selwyn Theater 19 June

1924 **The Town Clown** (Ruby/Aaron Hoffman) Illinois Theater, Chicago 6 January

1924 **The Belle of Quakertown** revised *The Town Clown* Stamford, Conn July

1924 **No Other Girl** revised *The Belle of Quakertown* Theater 13 August

1925 **Holka Polka** (aka *Spring in Autumn, Nobody's Girl*) (*Frühling im Herbst*) English version w Ruby (Lyric Theater)

1926 **The Fly-by-Nights** (w Ruby/Guy Bolton) Werba's Theater, Brooklyn 30 August

1926 **The Ramblers** (ex *The Fly-by-Nights*) (Ruby/w Bolton) Lyric Theater 20 September

1926 **Lido Lady** (Richard Rodgers, Lorenz Hart/w Bolton, Ruby ad Ronald Jeans) Gaiety Theatre, London 1 December

1927 **Lucky** (Jerome Kern/w Harbach, Ruby) New Amsterdam Theater 22 March

1927 **The Five o'Clock Girl** (Ruby/Bolton, Fred Thompson) 44th Street Theater 10 October

1928 **She's My Baby** (Rodgers/Hart/w Bolton, Ruby) Globe Theater 3 January

1928 **Good Boy** (Herbert Stothart/w Ruby/Harbach, Oscar Hammerstein, Henry Meyers) Hammerstein's Theater 5 September

1928 **Animal Crackers** (Ruby/Kaufman, Morrie Ryskind) 44th Street Theater 23 October

1929 **Top Speed** (w Ruby/Bolton) 46th Street Theater 25 December

1941 **High Kickers** (w Ruby/w George Jessel) Broadhurst Theater 31 October

KANDER, John [Harold] (b Kansas City, Kans, 18 March 1927). Composer of several hit shows of the Broadway 1960s and 1970s.

Kander's earliest musical-theatre assignments were as pianist for the tryout of the futureless musical *The Amazing Adele* and for a tour of *An Evening with Beatrice Lillie,* and as musical director for the Barbizon Plaza revival of Noël Coward's *Conversation Piece.* He subsequently arranged the dance music for *Gypsy* and for the Broadway version of *Irma la Douce,* before he had his first theatre score as a composer heard in 1962 when Andrew Siff produced *A Family Affair* at the Billy Rose Theater. With a cast headed by Shelley Berman, Eileen Heckart and *West Side Story* star Larry Kert, the show ran for 65 performances.

Kander supplied incidental music for a production of *It's Never Too Late* at the Playhouse, and then moved into what would be the most successful phase of his career when he teamed up with lyricist Fred Ebb to write, at first, a number of successful songs (''My Colouring Book,'' etc) and then a series of stage musicals. After an indifferent beginning with the tale of *Flora the Red Menace,* the pair scored a major international hit with *Cabaret* (''Cabaret,'' ''Willkommen,'' etc), a success magnified hugely by its transformation into one of the most successful musical films of the postwar era (''Maybe This Time,'' ''Money''). After a switch into gentler tones for the not-unsuccessful *The Happy Time,* the team found further and sizeable international success with the virile tale of *Zorba* (''Happy Birthday'') and with the darkly comic, bitingly glittery vaudeville *Chicago* (''Razzle Dazzle,'' ''All That Jazz,'' ''All I Care About Is Love,'' ''Cell Block Tango,'' etc).

Having, in their earlier shows, demonstrated a considerable versatility, as well as a particularly sure touch with what might best be described as stand-up or out-front material, the pair, who had throughout their association also provided a considerable amount of special material and songs to cabaret, nightclub and television performers, now put themselves at the service of the oversized female star-name for a series of shows. If *The Act,* a show about a show manufactured for vocalist Liza Minnelli, the enormously successful star of their *Cabaret* film, had only a medium run, a musicalization of the screenplay *Woman of the Year,* with further film names, Lauren Bacall and later Raquel Welch and Debbie Reynolds featured, played rather longer in town and also found its way to Europe. A third piece, *The Rink,* which paired Miss Minnelli with Chita Rivera, had a fair Broadway run and proved popular in Germany, but, like its two predecessors, it did not have either the attractions or the wide success of the team's three major shows.

In the decade since *The Rink,* Kander and Ebb have been represented on Broadway by a reprise of *Cabaret,* a musical version of the film and play *Kiss of the Spiderwoman*—another piece allowing the introduction of performance material into the fabric of its story and, yet again, featuring a large and now more than slightly grotesque feminine star personality—and an unloved show centered on the marathon dance craze of the 1930s and entitled *Steel Pier,* which folded in 76 performances leaving remountings of the ever-popular *Chicago* and *Cabaret* to represent its songwriters on the Broadway stage at the dawn of the new century.

A five-handed compilation show of Kander and Ebb songs, *And the World Goes Round: The Songs of Kander and Ebb,* has been played with considerable success at off-Broadway's Westside Theater (18 March 1991) and in other venues around America.

1962 **A Family Affair** (James Goldman, William Goldman) Billy Rose Theater 27 January

1965 **Flora, the Red Menace** (Fred Ebb/George Abbott, Robert Russell) Alvin Theater 11 May

1966 **Cabaret** (Ebb/Joe Masteroff) Broadhurst Theater 20 November

1968 **The Happy Time** (Ebb/N Richard Nash) Broadway Theater 18 January

1968 **Zorba** (Ebb/Joseph Stein) Imperial Theater 17 November

1971 **70, Girls, 70** (Ebb/Joe Masteroff) Broadhurst Theater 15 April

1975 **Chicago** (Ebb/Ebb, Bob Fosse) 46th Street Theater 3 June

1977 **The Act** (aka *Shine It On*) (Ebb/George Furth) Majestic Theater 29 October

1981 **Woman of the Year** (Ebb/Peter Stone) Palace Theater 29 March

1984 **The Rink** (Ebb/Terrence McNally) Martin Beck Theater 9 February

1990 **Kiss of the Spiderwoman** (Ebb/McNally) Westchester 1 May; Shaftesbury Theatre, London 20 October 1992

1997 **Steel Pier** (Ebb/David Thompson) Richard Rodgers Theater 24 April

1999 **Over and Over** (Ebb/Stein) Signature Theater, Arlington, Va 9 January

KÁPOLNAI, János [KIRCHNER, János] (b 1842; d Budapest, 11 December 1907).

The handsome, curly-headed principal tenor of the Népszínház, Budapest, from its earliest days, Kápolnai introduced many of the principal roles of the French and Viennese classic repertoire to the Budapest theatre. He was seen during the 1870s and 1880s as Offenbach's Barbe-bleue, Ange Pitou, Pygmalion, Grénicheux, Fritellini, Lotteringhi, Jan Janicki to the Symon of Lujza Blaha, Lamberto (*Kapitány kisasszony,* ie, *Der Seekadett*), Miguel (*Nap és hold,* ie, *Le Jour et la nuit*), Frikkel (*Kisasszony feleségem,* ie, *La Marjolaine*), Ritenuto (ie, Alfred) in *Denevér* (*Die Fledermaus*), in *A furcsa háború* (*Der lustige Krieg*), *Háromcsőrű kacsa* (*Le Canard à trois becs*), *Kanári hercegnő* (*La Princesse des Canaries*) and many such other pieces. He played Sándor Barinkay in Hungary's first *Zigeunerbaron* at Kolozsvár and introduced the Hungarian version of Offenbach's Hoffman, as well as creating roles in some of the earliest Hungarian operetts (Bruno in Erkel's *Katalina Székely,* 1880, etc).

KARCZAG, Wilhelm [KRAMMER, Vilmos] (b Karcag, Hungary, 15 August 1859; d Baden bei Wien, 11 October 1923). Manager of the Theater an der Wien through some of its greatest hours.

The son of an Hungarian grain merchant, Karczag made his earliest steps in the theatre as a writer, placing his first one-act play, *Szent a béke,* with the theatre in his home town of Debrecen at the age of 18. He wrote a number of other stage pieces over the following 17 years, including several comedies, a five-act drama, and, most successfully, the three-act *Lemondás,* the majority of which were produced at Budapest's Nemzeti Színház. He also authored one operett, *A leánypapa,* with music by Isidor Dreysach, which was produced in 1881. In 1894 he moved from Budapest to Vienna and, over the following years, worked as a writer and a journalist whilst his wife, the highly popular soubrette Juliska Kopácsi-Karczag, reaped the family's theatrical honors as one of the city's favorite Operette performers.

The most successful part of Karczag's theatrical life began on 9 May 1901. The Theater an der Wien had been going through a low time since the decline of the kind of Viennese Operette which had been its staple diet under the management of the Steiners and Alexandrine von Schönerer. With Strauss, Suppé and Millöcker no longer supplying the theatre with their popular works, it had begun to lose its way, and its last manager, Karl Langkammer, had lasted only part of a season before throwing in his hand. The theatre was for the taking, and Karczag took it. He acquired a long lease and set himself to work to get the house playing the best of Operette to the best effect, as it had in its palmiest days.

The opposition in 1901 didn't seem too great. The Carltheater had found itself a hit with Reinhardt's *Das süsse Mädel* to compensate for the lesser runs of Millöcker's *Die Damenschneider* and Zamara's *Die Debutantin;* the Raimundtheater had been living on revivals of classic pieces before getting round to producing *Der Kellermeister*; and the adventurous Gabor Steiner had tried Kappeller's version of the French spectacle *Die verkehrte Welt* (*Le Royaume des femmes*) at Venedig in Wien, gone to Germany for Lincke's *Venus auf Erden* and to Britain for a score from Ivan Caryll for *Die Reise nach Cuba,* and produced Eysler's *Das Gastmahl des Lucullus* at Danzers Orpheum, but none had met with particular success. Most of the other houses were relying on repeats. But the best Karczag could manage, for the moment, was a revival of *The Geisha,* which, for all its several-years-old charms, was not about to challenge the sprightly *Das süsse Mädel.*

However, the new manager hung on, and 1902 got better. He landed one of the best new Operetten that had turned up in Vienna for several years with Ziehrer's *Der Fremdenführer* and, although no one was yet to know it, the best new composer as well. For if Steiner went to Berlin, Paris and London for his material and inspiration, Karczag went home to Hungary. Or rather, Hungary, as represented by the young Franz Lehár, came to him, and Karczag produced the young composer's first major Operette, *Wiener Frauen,* at the Theater an der Wien, with Girardi starring. The good luck, or good management, continued. The year 1903 brought the first major work and first hit of another young composer, Edmund Eysler's *Bruder Straubinger.* With Girardi again in the starring role, this delightful piece gave the theatre one of the biggest successes it had ever known. Then, after a curious flop with another debut work, Leo Fall's *Der Rebell,* in 1905, Karczag produced Lehár's *Die lustige Witwe.* The show made all its participants rich—and the most important the richest—and it soon propelled the Theater an der Wien right back to the top, as the leading musical theatre of Europe. Fall's *Die Dollarprinzessin* (1907), Lehár's *Der Mann mit den drei Frauen* and Oscar Straus's *Der tapfere Soldat* (1908), the Vienna debut of another Hungarian composer, Emmerich Kálmán, with the hugely successful *Ein Herbstmanöver* (1909), Lehár's *Der Graf von Luxemburg* (1909) and Fall's *Die schöne Risette* (1910) all helped—some less, some very much more—to continue the newly refound prosperity of the Theater an der Wien, and, in 1908, Karczag took the opportunity to spread himself, with the financial backing of Karl Wallner, into the management of the Raimundtheater, which had in recent years fallen into disastrous straits.

He brought to the failing theatre not only the Theater an der Wien repertoire but also its stars, notably the one-and-only Girardi, and he even produced several new Operetten there, including one of the biggest hits Vienna had ever seen. But, although he got the Raimundtheater back on its financial feet in 12 years of management, he found himself constantly obstructed by a faction on the theatre's board of directors (who were, of course, not paying the bills) who insisted that the theatre should play the traditional old Vienna repertoire it had been originally founded to house. And so, what the productions of the plays of Raimund and Nestroy, mounted to appease these ''businessmen,'' lost, the Operette productions the retrograde gentlemen of the board so artsily despised earned back, to keep their theatre alive.

At the Theater an der Wien, Karczag continued to produce the same fine fare as before: Lehár's *Die ideale Gattin* (1913) and *Endlich allein* (1914), Kálmán's war effort *Gold gab' ich für Eisen,* and, most particularly, Leo Fall's *Die Rose von Stambul* (1916), a wartime triumph which provided the producer with his biggest success since *Die lustige Witwe.* In fact 1916 was a spectacular year for him, for, across town at the Raimundtheater, in the same year, he produced the biggest hit that theatre had ever had or would ever have: the Schubert biomusical *Das Dreimäderlhaus.* And in the euphoria thus created, Karczag took on a third house, the Wiener Stadttheater.

The Theater an der Wien continued with *Wo die Lerche singt* (1918), *Die blaue Mazur* (1920), a superb success with Oscar Straus's splendid *Der letzte Walzer* (1921), Lehár's *Frasquita* (1922) and *Die gelbe Jacke* (1923); the Raimundtheater followed *Das Dreimäderlhaus* with its musequel *Hannerl,* Granichstaedten's *Das alte Lied,* Künneke's *Das Dorf ohne Glocke,* a Berlin Mendelssohn pasticcio *Dichterliebe,* Ascher's *Was Mädchen träumen* and Stolz's *Der Tanz ins Glück*; whilst the Stadttheater also joined in Karczag's Operette blitz.

After a few years of this triple burden, however, Karczag started to shed his enormous workload. More and more of the responsibility at the Theater an der Wien fell onto his son-in-law, the longtime principal tenor of the house, Hubert Marischka, and in 1921, after nearly 13 years of fighting to keep a solvent ship at the Raimundtheater, he turned in his management there. It was ironic that, now given their heads, the we-only-do-what-we-consider-upmarket-plays gentlemen of the Raimundtheater quickly got into difficulties. Only a few years later, they would call Hubert Marischka and Operette back to rescue them from bankruptcy once again. A scenario not unfamiliar in more recent days and more state-subsidized circumstances.

In fact, Karczag now had little time left to live but when he died in 1923 his record over two decades of musical-theatre production made him unchallengedly the most remarkable and internationally successful producer of his era.

KARNILOVA, Maria [DOVGOLENKO, Maria Karnilovitch] (b Hartford, Conn, 3 August 1920). Dancer and character actress on the Broadway stage.

In the early part of her career, Miss Karnilova appeared as a dancer at the Metropolitan Opera, with the Ballet Theater, and in a number of musicals and revues (*Stars in Your Eyes, Hollywood Pinafore, Call Me Mister, High Button Shoes, Miss Liberty, Out of This World, Two's Company, Kaleidoscope*) both on Broadway and elsewhere. Her first notable role came in the 1959 musical *Gypsy,* in which she created the part of the stripper Tessie Tura (''You Gotta Have a Gimmick'').

She moved into non-dancing, accented-acting roles in *Bravo Giovanni* (1962, Signora Pandolfi), and followed this up with a famous creation as the milkman's wife, Golde, starred opposite Zero Mostel in the original production of *Fiddler on the Roof* (1964). Four years later she had another fine role, as the sweetly heart-wringing cocotte Hortense (''Happy Birthday'') in *Zorba* (1968). She took the part of Mamita in a 1973 attempt to put the Loewe/Lerner film score *Gigi* on to the stage, in 1981 appeared briefly in the effort to *Bring Back Birdie,* and subsequently played opposite Herschel Bernardi in a revival of *Fiddler on the Roof.* In 1993 she was seen as the Queen in *Cinderella* with the New York City Opera.

She appeared as Daphne in the film version of *The Unsinkable Molly Brown.*

Miss Karnilova is married to actor George S Irving.

KARTOUSCH, L[o]uise (b Linz, 17 August 1886; d Vienna, 13 February 1964). The favorite soubrette of the heyday of 20th-century Viennese Operette.

After studying music in her hometown and in Vienna, the young Luise Kartousch worked at first in provincial theatres, moving from children's roles in Linz to adult ones in Graz where, from 1902, she played soubrette parts in Operette and the occasional opéra-comique and even, in repertoire, such small operatic roles as Mercedes in *Carmen* and a minor Walküre in *Die Walküre.*

Before long, however, she made her way back to Vienna and to the Theater an der Wien where, at the age of 21, she created first the role of Mary in Stritzko's short-lived *Tip-Top,* and then the juvenile soubrette, Daisy, in the highly successful first performances of *Die Dollarprinzessin,* joining with Karl Meister to introduce the jolly song and dance of ''Wir tanzen ringelreih'n'' to the

Plate 197. **Maria Karnilova** *as Golde in* Fiddler on the Roof.

Viennese public. Show by show thereafter, she established herself as the adored little favorite of the Theater an der Wien audiences: *Der Mann mit den drei Frauen* (Coralie), *Der schöne Gardist* (Franziska), *Der Frauenjäger* (Fioretta), as the pining cousin Masha in *Der tapfere Soldat* (1908), as the lively Juliette in *Der Graf von Luxemburg* (1909) and, in a personal triumph which outdid all her previous efforts, in travesty as the highly featured little army cadet Márosi in the extremely successful Viennese production of Emmerich Kálmán's *Ein Herbstmanöver* (1909). It was this role and this production which marked the real confirmation of Kartousch's position as one of the city's favorite musical stars.

In the years that followed she appeared as Honoria Leontieff in Kerker's *Schneeglöckchen* (1910), Orestes in a revival of *Die schöne Helena,* Pauline in *Pariser Leben* and Pedro in *Giroflé-Girofla,* and created such roles as Princess Margot in *Die schöne Risette,* Milli Gärtner in *Ihr Adjutant* (1911) and the piquant Pipsi Paquerette who lends the liveliness to Lehár's tale of *Eva* (1911). She played in *Der kleine König* (Zaza) and *Der blaue Held* (Lottenbusch) and, in 1913, got into boy's clothes again as Prince Max in *Prinzessin Gretl.* She created the roles of Carmen de Serrantis in *Die ideale Gattin* and Tilly in Lehár's *Endlich allein,* played Xaver in the patriotic wartime *Gold gab' ich für Eisen* and, again in pants, the boy Henri in a revival of *Der Opernball,* before returning to skirts as Hilma, the title lass of *Die schöne Schwedin* (1915). In 1916 she created the role of Lilly in Lehár's *Der Sterngucker* and found one of the best parts of her career as the harem girl Midili Hanum in the long-running *Der Rose von Stambul,* introducing ''Fridolin, ach wie dein Schnurrbart sticht,'' the Schnucki-Duett and ''Papachen, Papachen'' with her partner of almost always, Ernst Tautenhayn.

Continuing to mix girls' and boys' roles, Kartousch returned to Lehár for *Wo die Lerche singt* (Margit), played little Baron Boris in the ''official wife'' musical

Nimm mich mit! (1919) and the soubrette Louisl in *Dorfmusikanten,* and scored with a fine run of roles in the early 1920s: Gretl Aigner in *Die blaue Mazur,* Sophie Lavalle in *Die Frau im Hermelin* and, at the Carltheater, the sparky Marietta who only fancies her husbands when she is not married to them in *Die Bajadere* (''Schatzi, ich möchte einen Zobel von dir!,'' ''Der kleine Bar dort am Boulevard''). Back at the Theater an der Wien she created the role of Mi—the prototype of *Das Land des Lächelns'* Chinese princess—in *Die gelbe Jacke,* but, after a last appearance there in Granichstaedten's *Die Bacchusnacht,* she put an end to some 15 years' association with the Theater an der Wien and moved on, still the eternal soubrette, to perform in musical and also non-musical shows at most of Vienna's other principal theatres.

An appearance at the Raimundtheater in Schnitzler's play *Vermächtnis* led the critics delightedly to compare her to Hansi Niese, the great comic soubrette of the Vienna stage of earlier years. However, she did not take the non-singing route, and returned to Operette at the Bürgertheater in the title role of Robert Stolz's successful *Mädi* (1923), in *Agri* (1924, Violet), as Lehár's little cabaret girl in *Cloclo* (1924) and in the juvenile lead of Dorothy in *Revanche* (1924). A second period at the Raimundtheater had her starring in Jerome K Jerome's play *Lady Fanny and the Servant Problem,* pairing with Tautenhayn in the Operette *Ich hab' dich Lieb,* playing Nettl in *Das Schwalbennest* and Denise in *Mam'zelle Nitouche,* whilst on a visit to Ronacher she appeared in *Spiel um die Liebe* (Erzherzogin Immaculata) and in the title role of Straus's *Teresina.* In 1927 she appeared in the title role of *Dorine und der Zufall* at the Rolandbühne, at the Carltheater in *Eine einzige Nacht* and, in her oddest male role yet, in the part of the detective, Mister Quick, alongside Tautenhayn in the Revue-Operette *Die Lady vom Lido* at the Johann Strauss-Theater.

Still just a little over 40, Kartousch returned briefly to the Theater an der Wien in 1930 to take over from Hella Kürty the role of Mi in *Das Land des Lächelns* and she appeared there again, as a guest artist, in 1933 for Straus's *Zwei lachende Augen* (Grossfürstin Maria Helene), as Prinz Orlofsky, and in 1935 as Madame Sauterelle in *Die Dubarry.* In 1934 she played at the Scala Theater in *Ein Kuss—und sonst gar nichts* (Ein aufgeregte Frau), and in 1936 in *Warum lügst du, Chérie* (Erszy Körmendi). She later returned also to the Raimundtheater, playing there in both Operette and plays during the war years (Resi-Tante in *Der Fremdenführer,* etc), and appeared in several musical films (*Zauber der Bohème,* etc).

She was still to be seen on the Operette stage in her sixties (Kathi the Haushälterin in *Abschiedswalzer,* etc) after a long career in which the difficult years between

Plate 198. **Luise Kartousch.** *Vienna's favorite soubrette through the years of the Austrian stage's greatest supremacy.*

soubrette and character parts (she never became a komische Alte comedienne) had been covered without any real break in activity.

KASSAI, Vidor [KOSSITZSKY, Vidor] (b Gyála, 16 February 1840; d Vác, 29 July 1928).

Comedian and operettic buffo at Budapest's Népszínház for many years, Kassai introduced many celebrated opéra-bouffe and opéra-comique roles to Hungarian audiences from the 1860s onwards. He was Budapest's first Baron Grog in *La Grande-Duchesse,* the first Frank (Fujo) in the Hungarian *Die Fledermaus,* played Madame Madou in *Mesdames de la Halle* (aged 25), Sebastiani in *Der lustige Krieg,* von Bontrouche in *Le Canard à trois becs,* Calabazas (*Le Jour et la Nuit*), Laurent (*La Mascotte*), Lambertuccio (*Boccaccio*), Ménélaos, John Styx and Saint Hypothèse (*Lili*) and also created roles in a number of original Hungarian works, including Marx in Konti's *Királyfógas* (1886), Rettenetes in *A kis alamuszi* (1894) and Tamás Pöl in *A citerás* (1894). At the other end of the repertoire, he was also seen as the Fool in *King Lear.*

KATALIN Operett in 3 acts by Izor Béldi. Music by Jenő Fejer. Népszínház, Budapest, 4 October 1901.

Plate 199. *The cast of Broadway's* **Katinka** *assemble as events rise to their finale: Olga (Edith Decker), Boris (Count Lorrie Grimaldi), Katinka (May Naudain), Thaddeus Hopper (Franklin Ardell), Mrs Hopper (Adele Rowland), Ivan Dimitri (Samuel Ash), Arif Bey (Edward Durand) and Knopf (W J McCarthy).*

The earliest original Hungarian operett to be played for one hundred performances in Budapest—even though the hundred were spread over five years—*Katalin* was first produced at the Népszínház with Aranka Hegyi as Katalin and Klára Küry, József Németh and Imre Szirmai in the other principal roles of a reasonably conventional story of the first romance of a young royal. By the time the record-making 100th performance arrived, however, the first famous works of Huszka and Kacsoh had come to the stage and *Katalin* and its record run were soon eclipsed.

Küry took over the lead role alongside two other star ladies, Mizzi Günther (Katharina II) and Mizzi Zwerenz (Anita), when the piece was played in Vienna as *Der kleine Günstling* for a season of 17 performances in 1902.

Austria: Carltheater *Der kleine Günstling* 12 April 1902

KATINKA Musical play in 3 acts by Otto Hauerbach (Harbach). Music by Rudolf Friml. 44th Street Theater, New York, 23 December 1915.

Produced by Arthur Hammerstein in the wake of his Friml/Hauerbach (as the latter was then still spelling his name) successes with *The Firefly* and *High Jinks, Katinka* gave the team of producer, composer and librettist a third successive hit. Hauerbach's libretto was altogether more old-world-Operette than the previous two pieces he had written or adapted, with Viennese and Turkish harem settings, a hero and villain and chorus of dancers who were Russians, and a foolish American for its low comedy.

Katinka (May Naudain) wants to marry Ivan Dimitri (Samuel Ash), an attaché at the Russian embassy in Vienna, but it is the ambassador himself, Boris Strogoff (Lorrie Grimaldi), who is leading her unhappily to the altar as the piece begins. Rather than consummate the marriage, she climbs out of the window of her nuptial bower on her wedding night and is helpfully hidden away by comical Yankee Thaddeus Hopper (Franklin Ardell), much to the annoyance of his suspicious wife (Adele Rowland). However, after the process of hiding the fleeing bride has led the action through some harem high-jinks, a certain Olga Nashan (Edith Decker), bigamous Boris's already wife, turns up to claim her husband, and Katinka and her Ivan can be united.

The show's score, also laid out on traditional Operette lines, with full-scale finales to the first two acts, solos and ensembles and at least one dance speciality per act, included several numbers which became popular: Katinka's song of the pigeon "Rackety-Coo," Olga's Eastern number "Allah's Holiday," Ivan's maestoso solo "My Paradise" and his first act farewell duet with Katinka, "'Tis the End." The quota of comical numbers featured Mrs Hopper's declaration that "I Want to Marry a Male Quartet" (not because there are four of them, you understand, but because they are good at harmony) and her "Your Photo" in which she encourages her beloved to hurry home, because his glossy picture is nasty and chilly against her bosom.

Brought swiftly from its tryout at Morristown, New Jersey, to open at the 44th Street Theater on the same night that the decidedly different *Very Good Eddie* made its debut at the smaller Princess, *Katinka* was swiftly established as a solid success. It ran for 220 performances on Broadway before heading for the touring circuits and, eventually, to overseas productions. J C Williamson's wartime Australian production (first actually put on stage in Wellington, New Zealand), which starred the young Gladys Moncrieff (Katinka), Florence Young (Mrs Hopper) and Phil Smith (Hopper), was a genuine hit and the piece earned regular revivals in Australia as a vehicle for the idolized Miss Moncrieff up until 1944. But, in spite of the fine London success of *High Jinks,* it was not until 1923 that *Katinka* appeared in Britain, produced by Robert MacDonald (ad Bertram Davis) at the Shaftesbury Theatre, with Helen Gilliland and George Bishop as the lovers, Joe Coyne and Binnie Hale heading the fun, and Peter Gawthorne as the libidinous Russian. It lasted only a disappointing 108 performances, although it proved good for two seasons in the provinces.

Like Friml's other early hits, *Katinka* was not produced in Europe, but another piece under the same title was staged with some success by Louis Brigon at Paris's Théâtre de l'Empire (22 February 1933). This was, in effect, an adaptation of the Hungarian opérette *Őfelsége frakkja* (Budapest, 1931), with text by István Békeffy (ad André Barde, Pierre Varenne, Robert Delamare) and music by Lajos Lajtai. The Viennese diva Rita Georg, Adrien Lamy, Saint-Granier and Lyne Clevers starred in Brigon's production, a production which led to some French composers publicly stamping their feet and accusing managers of jiggery-pokery on the royalty front, or, worse, of unpatriotically preferring foreign-made foxtrots, tangos, waltzes and marches to their own efforts at foxtrots, tangos, waltzes and marches.

Two further *Katinka*s—the first and the last of the group—were produced, logically enough, in Hungary, where Zoltán Thury and Árpád Orban turned out an 1898 operett (Budai Színkör 21 August), and Nándor Bihary (text) and István Máthé (music) combined on a piece premiered at the Városi Színház in February 1938, its title role played by the young Sári Bárabás.

Australia: Her Majesty's Theatre, Melbourne 8 June 1918; UK: Shaftesbury Theatre 30 August 1923

KATJA, DIE TÄNZERIN Operette in 3 acts by Leopold Jacobson and Rudolf Österreicher. Music by Jean Gilbert. Johann Strauss-Theater, Vienna, 5 January 1923.

The Princess Katja Karina (Mizzi Günther) has been deposed from her Ruritanian throne and has ended up, like all the best deposed operettic monarchs, working as a dancer and singer in a Paris nightclub. One night, at a reception, she encounters the aristocratic and attractive Eusebius von Koruga (Karl Bachmann) and, before that evening and the Operette are over, the two have not only fallen in love but discovered that Eusebius is the very prince who deposed Katja. While their romancing was going on, the lighthearted part of the evening was looked after by the American ambassador Lallan Webster (Max Brod), his daughter Maud (Gisela Kolbe) and his private secretary, Leander Bill (Fritz Imhoff). It centered on the efforts of the last-named pair to get together in spite of Papa's objections.

Gilbert's score spread itself in less than classic proportions between the romantic moments and the soubret and comic ones: the bulk of the music was the property of the soprano and her tenor. Katja introduced herself to music ("Spiel' auf, Kamerad . . ."), and whilst Eusebius soliloquized "O du verflixte Politik! Du nimmst uns Menschen soviel Glück . . . ," her soprano tones could be heard outside serenading in "Heut' Nacht beim Mondenschein." She was soon inside and joining him in their first duet ("Sie dachten, da ist eine Tänzerin") and the stage was only left for the space of a duo to Maud and Leander ("Komm morgen zu mir") before the romantic principals were back with a long and strong finale. In the second act Maud got a little more of a look-in, with duets with both Eusebius and Leander, and although Katja and Eusebius with a duo, a trio, another big finale and even a solo (him) dominated again, it was that little soubret duo which invited "Komm, Liebchen, wander mit deinem Leander . . ." which proved the takeaway gem not only of the act but of the piece. As in so many Operetten, the third act was little more than a perfunctory wind-up, holding only a trio, a number for a supporting character and a couple of little pieces before the evening was played out on a replay of the jaunty "Leander" duo.

Produced by Erich Müller at the Johann Strauss-Theater, *Katja die Tänzerin* was played for 207 performances in its first run, and for several further nights in a break between productions some months later. Herbert Trau produced the piece at Berlin's Neues Operetten-Theater less than a month after the Vienna premiere with

Margit Suchy (Katja), Erik Wirl (Sacha), Jacob Wiedtke (Webster), Ilse Muth (Maud) and Harald Paulsen (Leander Bill) starred, and Budapest's Fővárosi Operettszínház was close behind, with a production in which Marinka (as she had now become in Zsolt Harsányi's version) was played by Sári Petráss, and which ran up its first one hundred performances in repertoire in just five months. In 1927 *Marinka, a táncosnő* was played at the Budai Színkör (9 September) and in 1938 it was revived at the Royal Színház (12 November).

In Britain, James White produced *Katja the Dancer* (ad Harry Graham, Frederick Lonsdale) in Manchester, under the cheekily appropriated ''George Edwardes presents'' banner, with soprano Lilian Davies and Gregory Stroud in the romantic roles, Gene Gerrard and Ivy Tresmand as soubrets, and René Mallory as a newly tacked-in ''heroine's friend'' character with two reallotted songs. When the Gaiety Theatre fell free through the failure of *Poppy,* he quickly moved the clearly successful show to London. It proved a rare hit for the now rather sad Gaiety, and Gerrard and Miss Tresmand saw their ''Leander'' become a major success. However, after a seven-month run, White elected to transfer the show to Daly's, provoking a vicious (and unsuccessful) strike against the continued employment of their Gaiety colleagues by the current Daly's choristers, who expected to go unchallenged from one show into the next at ''their'' theatre, and leaving the Gaiety once again to its woes. As no fewer than three touring companies took to the road, *Katja the Dancer* sailed on for another eight months at Daly's, closing only after a total of 501 West End performances, and joining *Lilac Time* and Gilbert's other most recent hit *The Lady of the Rose* as one of the three longest-running London musicals of the postwar period.

In Australia, with Marie Burke starring alongside Marjorie Hicklin (Maud) and R Barrett-Lennard (Leander), *Katja the Dancer* and ''Leander,'' as delivered by the last two named artists, once again made a hit. The show played a splendid 131 performances in Sydney, before setting off round the country and to New Zealand. In America, however, things went a little less well. The Shuberts, inevitably, botched the British version of *Katja* (who was no longer titularly a dancer) with ''additional scenes by Isobel Leighton,'' ''additional lyrics by Clifford Grey'' and ''additional music by Vernon Duke.'' The additional numbers (''Try a Little Kiss,'' ''Back to My Heart''), which actually had lyrics by London's Percy Greenbank and Arthur Wimperis, seemed to be leftovers from Duke's London botching of another Gilbert piece or three as *Yvonne.*

Having originally announced the show (interestingly if curiously given its vocal demands) as a vehicle for dancer Marilyn[n] Miller, the producers finally imported the British soprano Lilian Davies to repeat her role opposite the Prince Carl of Allen Prior in a version set in Monte Carlo. Denis Hoey was the villanous Ivo and soubrette Doris Patston (Patricia) and Jack Sheehan headed ''Leander.'' *Katja* was adjudged ''a worthy and respectable candidate for Shubert operatic honours, containing as many virtues and fewer faults than most of such enterprises'' and it ran for 112 Broadway performances without winning the larger popularity it had elsewhere.

Germany: Neues Operetten-Theater 2 February 1923; Hungary: Fővárosi Operettszínház *Marinka a táncosnő* 24 February 1923; UK: Gaiety Theatre *Katja the Dancer* 21 February 1925; Australia: Theatre Royal, Sydney 19 December 1925; USA: 44th Street Theater *Katja* 18 October 1926

KATSCHER, Robert (b Vienna, 20 May 1894; d Hollywood, Calif, 23 February 1942). Songwriter with a revusical bent who scored one sizeable international success.

Viennese-born Katscher composed music for revue and, in particular, for what became known as the Revue-Operette, during the late 1920s and early 1930s, scoring a particular and international success with the nightlife-with-numbers tale of the cabaretty goings-on in *Die Wunder-Bar* (''Elizabeth,'' ''Tell Me I'm Forgiven''). His other major musical-theatre productions had mixed fortunes. The Revue-Operette *Die Lady vom Lido* lasted only a month and a half on the Viennese stage in spite of a cast led by patented local stars Luise Kartousch (as a male detective) and Ernst Tautenhayn, and was bundled off the Johann Strauss-Theater stage to be replaced by a visit from a certain *Dreimal Hochzeit* (otherwise Abie's *Irish Rose*). Katscher and his collaborators did, however, find some later success with another up-to-date and picturesque piece, *Der Traum-Express,* a revusical show developed from an earlier work that Katscher and Herczeg had had staged in Budapest. Set on the Blue Train between Paris and Nice and with an American film man (Hubert Marischka) as hero, what was described as an ''unbeabsichte (unintentional) Operette'' ran 136 performances at the Theater an der Wien.

Katscher's other principal showing, however, came not only after his flight from Hitlerian Europe back towards the filmlands of America (which he had visited previously in the early 1930s) but largely after his death. He was responsible for the original musical setting of *Bei Kerzenlicht,* an internationally produced small-scale play written by Siegfried Geyer, with whom Katscher had previously combined on a comedy with songs produced disastrously in London as *The Gay Princess* and a little ''Märchen aus Wien'' *Essig und Öl* played in Budapest as *Ecet és olaj* (ad István Békeffy, János Vaszary Andrássy-uti Színház, Budapest 27 November). *Bei Kerzenlicht* (''Bei Kerzenlicht,'' ''Wenn's Mai wird,'' ''Ich bin nur eine Mizzi!,'' ''Wo bist du?,'' ''Es ist nicht leicht, Mondän zu sein,'' ''Mit Klavierbegleitung''), to all evidence first produced not in German, but in Hungarian in Budapest (*Gyertyafényél* Royal Színház 1 October 1937), later won productions in Vienna; in a heavily botched version in New York (*You Never Know* with Katscher still slightly credited but mostly with new material by Cole Porter); and, almost entirely rewritten, in London where the piece was ill-treated by Eric Maschwitz (text) and Sam Coslow (replacement music) and, as *Romance by Candlelight,* was a quick failure.

Katscher's second American episode was not a success. He found little work in Hollywood, where his only real reference turned out to be the fact that his song ''Madonna'' had found some currency in a version by Buddy De Sylva called ''Day Is Done,'' and he died soon after from a liver ailment, apparently a legacy of his maltreatment in a German concentration camp.

1924 **Das Mädel mit dem Storch** (Wolfgang Pollaczek) Kammerspiele 4 March

1924 **Was Frauen träumen** (Katscher, Karl Farkas) Kammerspiele 27 June

1924 **Küsse am Mitternacht** (Katscher, Farkas) Kammerspiele 30 October

1925 **Frauenträume am Mitternacht** (Katscher) Carltheater 29 April

1927 **Die Lady vom Lido** (Katscher, Otto Florian) Johann Strauss-Theater 17 August

1929 **Riviera Express** (Géza Herczeg) Fővárosi Operettszínház, Budapest 30 March

1930 **Die Wunder-Bar** (Herczeg, Farkas) Kammerspiele 17 February

1931 **The Gay Princess** (Siegfried Geyer ad A P Herbert, Harold Simpson) Kingsway Theater, London February

1931 **Der Traum-Express (Paris-Nizza)** revised *Riviera-Express* (Herczeg, Farkas, Fritz Grünbaum) Theater an der Wien 5 June

1932 **Essig und Öl** (w Geyer/Geyer, Paul Frank) Kammerspiele 2 September

1933 **Pech muss man haben** (Julius Berstl) Kammerspiele 24 February

1937 **Gyertyafényél** (*Bei Kerzenlicht*) (Geyer ad Farkas) Hungarian version by Armand Szántó, mihály Szécsen (Royal Színház)

Plate 200. **Robert Katscher** *supplied words and/or music to many revusical entertainments in central Europe between the wars.*

KATTNIGG, Rudolf (b Oberdorf, 9 April 1895; d Klagenfurt, Austria, 2 September 1955). Dusktime composer in the Viennese tradition.

Kattnigg began by studying law in Graz, but in the years after the war he turned his ambitions to the world of music and, after further studies in Vienna, he became first a répétiteur and then a theatrical conductor. He spent some years in this capacity in Innsbruck (1928–34) and then, after four years of fairly constant movement from one town and theatre to another, returned to Vienna and took up a teaching post at the Akademie für Musik.

During his years as a conductor in the provinces, Kattnigg had taken his first steps as a composer of Operette, and in 1937 his *Kaiserin Katharina* won a production at Berlin's Admiralspalast. However, his most successful piece was the lushly romantic Operette *Die Gräfin von Durazzo,* first produced in Leipzig but later, as *Balkanliebe,* played widely in Germany and Austria. In 1942 he composed a three-act fairy-tale piece as a Christmas entertainment for the Vienna Opera; in 1949 he supplied the score for an Operette, *Bel Ami,* based on the work by de Maupassant, in which Johannes Heesters, as the hero of the title, and Gretl Schörg starred at Vienna's Raimundtheater; and in 1953 he turned out an opera, *Donna Miranda.* A final piece for the musical stage, *Rendezvous um Mitternacht,* was produced posthumously at the Raimundtheater in 1956.

Kattnigg was conductor of the Wiener Symphoniker and Opernhaus orchestra from 1939 and also wrote orchestral and chamber music and several film scores, including the arrangement of Suppé's music for the 1953 biopic *Hab ich nur deine Liebe.*

1936 **Der Prinz von Thule** (Oskar Walleck, ''Erik Kahr'') Stadttheater, Basel 13 December

1937 **Kaiserin Katharina** (Hans Fritz Beckmann, Paul Beyer) Admiralspalast, Berlin 3 February

1937 **Die Gräfin von Durazzo** (aka *Balkanliebe*) (''Erik Kahr,'' Bruno Hardt-Warden) Neues Operetten-Theater, Leipzig 22 December

1938 **Mädels vom Rhein** (Gustav Quedtenfeldt) Staatstheater, Bremen

1939 **Die Mädel von St Goar** (Quedtenfeldt) Staatstheater, Bremen 4 February

1941 **Der Feldprediger** musical revision of Millöcker's Operette (Opernhaus, Nuremberg)

1942 **Hansi fliegt zum Negerkral** (Hera Kassmekat) Opernhaus 16 December

1949 **Bel Ami** (Fritz Eckhardt) Raimundtheater 18 January

1956 **Rendezvous um Mitternacht** (Otto Emmerich Groh) Raimundtheater 20 May

KAUFMAN, George S[imon] (b Pittsburgh, Pa, 14 November 1889; d New York, 2 June 1961). Comic playwright and stage director who had several hits, in both capacities, in the musical theatre.

Originally a newspaper writer in Washington and then in New York, at first as a humorist and later as a drama critic, Kaufman began to write for the theatre in his twenties and had his first important success with the play *Dulcy* (1922, w Marc Connelly). He and Connelly subsequently collaborated on other successful plays (*To the Ladies, Merton of the Movies*) before being commissioned to write what was for Kaufman a first musical play. The producer of the piece had as a predestined title a not-very-novel joke and wanted the piece called *Helen of Troy, New York* (there is a place called Troy in New York State). If the piece's book was rather funnier than the title—which in any case had already done service as far back as July 1908 for a musical at Palisades Amusement Park—it was still not enough to give what was basically a formula musical comedy more than a 191-performance run, a record which was pale beside those the pair had compiled with their three hit plays.

Kaufman joined Robert Benchley to supply sketches for Irving Berlin's *Music Box Revue* (1923) and ventured with Connelly on a second musical, *Be Yourself,* based on an unproduced play called *Miss Moonshine* which the two had written in the years before their first success. With the great British comedian G P Huntley starring as the satirized Joseph Peabody Prescott alongside veteran Georgia Caine and the dances of Queenie Smith and Jack Donahue, it was noticed as having ''a screamingly funny first act,'' but apparently little thereafter. Its story of a Tennessee feud was seen only 93 times on Broadway.

As the play hits continued through the mid-1920s (*Beggar on Horseback, The Butter and Egg Man, The Royal Family*), Kaufman also produced his first musical-comedy successes—the scripts for the Marx Brothers' vehicles *The Cocoanuts* and *Animal Crackers*—but in between these two he ventured an interesting failure. *Strike Up the Band* was a burlesque-satire which struck out at politicians, businessmen, warmongers-for-profit, other peripheral moneygrubbers and anyone else who had a whiff of ''have'' about him, to the accompaniment of a set of Gershwin songs. It didn't interest Long Branch, New Jersey, and was closed down on the road, but three years later, with some of its pricklier thorns removed, it won a showing on Broadway. It ran for precisely the same time as had *Helen of Troy, New York.*

In spite of this, the following year Kaufman, collaborator Morrie Ryskind, and the Gershwins tried another piece in a similar vein. *Of Thee I Sing,* a gently but highly comical burlesque of the American political system and people, gauged public and critical taste rather better than had *Strike Up the Band.* It was rewarded with a long Broadway run, a Pulitzer Prize, and respected places in American musical-theatre history and on the fringe of the standard repertoire.

Around the same time Kaufman turned out one of his most famous plays, *Once in a Lifetime* (w Moss Hart), and contributed further and with some success to revue (*The Little Show* 1929, *The Bandwagon* 1931), but in the musical theatre, thereafter, things went less well. The success of *Of Thee I Sing* was not repeated when, in 1933, he and Ryskind essayed a musequel, *Let 'em Eat Cake,* nor, after further play successes (*Merrily We Roll Along, Stage Door, You Can't Take It with You*), when he went to the well yet again, with another Presidential musical, *I'd Rather Be Right* (1937).

Kaufman made several further, if intermittent, musical-theatre ventures in the next 20 years, turning out a comical if perhaps rather too in-jokey rewrite of *HMS Pinafore* in a Hollywood setting, and a confused and confusing flop called *Park Avenue* (1946). He collaborated, with rather better results, on the musicalization of the cold war tale of Ninotchka as *Silk Stockings,* as well as contributing to such revues as *Sing Out the News* (1938, w Hart) and *Seven Lively Arts* (1944), whilst continuing, all the time, to make play hits with such pieces as *The Man Who Came to Dinner* and *The Solid Gold Cadillac.*

Parallel to his life as a playwright, Kaufman led a second career, virtually as successful, as a director, principally of plays, but also of some musicals. He staged *Of Thee I Sing, Let 'em Eat Cake, Hollywood Pinafore* and *Park Avenue* of his own works, and also Irving Berlin's 1932 *Face the Music* (w Hassard Short) and, with the most singular success, the original production of *Guys and Dolls* (1950).

Two of Kaufman's plays have been adapted to the American musical stage with rather less success than their originals: *The Man Who Came to Dinner* became *Sherry!* (Alvin Theater 27 March 1967, Laurence Rosenthal/James Lipton), whilst *Merrily We Roll Along* was musicalized under the same title by George Furth and Stephen Sondheim (Alvin Theater 16 November 1981). *You Can't Take It with You* was produced as a musical play in Budapest under the title *Így élni . . . Ő!* (Magyar Színház 26 June 1948, mus: Charles Bradley).

1923 **Helen of Troy, New York** (Harry Ruby/Bert Kalmar/w Marc Connelly) Selwyn Theater 19 June

1924 **Be Yourself** (Lewis Gensler, Milton Schwarzwald/w Ira Gershwin/w Connelly) Harris Theater 3 September

1925 **The Cocoanuts** (Irving Berlin) Lyric Theater 8 December

1927 **Strike Up the Band** (George Gershwin/I Gershwin) Broadway Theater, Longbranch, NJ 29 August; Shubert Theater, Philadelphia 5 September

1928 **Animal Crackers** (Kalmar, Ruby/w Morrie Ryskind) 44th Street Theater 23 October

1930 **Strike Up the Band** revised version w Ryskind Times Square Theater 14 January

1931 **Of Thee I Sing** (G Gershwin/I Gershwin/w Ryskind) Music Box Theater 26 December

1933 **Let 'em Eat Cake** (G Gershwin/I Gershwin/w Ryskind) Imperial Theater 21 October

1937 **I'd Rather Be Right** (Richard Rodgers/Lorenz Hart/w Moss Hart) Alvin Theater 2 November

1945 **Hollywood Pinafore** burlesque of *HMS Pinafore* Alvin Theater 31 May

1946 **Park Avenue** (Arthur Schwartz/I Gershwin/w Nunnally Johnson) Shubert Theater 4 November

1955 **Silk Stockings** (Cole Porter/w Leueen McGrath, Abe Burrows) Imperial Theater 24 February

Biographies: Goldstein, M: *George S Kaufman: His Life, His Theatre* (OUP, New York, 1979), Teichmann, H: *George S Kaufman: An Intimate Portrait* (Angus & Robertson, London, 1973), Meredith, S: *George S Kaufman and His Friends* (Doubleday, New York, 1974)

KAYE, Danny [KOMINSKY, David Daniel] (b Brooklyn, NY, 18 January 1911; d Los Angeles, 3 March 1987). Lightning-lipped comedian who starred in a handful of musicals.

Previously part of a vaudeville act, The Three Terpsichoreans, the quick-fire comic first appeared on Broadway in *The Straw Hat Revue* (1939), but made his musical-theatre name as the effeminate Russell Paxton in *Lady in the Dark,* in which he performed memorably the frenetic catalogue of composers' names entitled ''Tschaikowsky.'' He subsequently starred in the Dorothy and Herbert Fields/Cole Porter musical *Let's Face It* (1941, Jerry Walker) performing a similar piece of material (the interpolated ''Melody in Four F,'' later included in the film *Up in Arms*), before moving on to a starring film career. Kaye returned to the stage in 1970 to star in the Rodgers and Charnin musical *Two by Two,* appearing as a 600-year-old Noah faced with worldly problems and an ark. Much in the way of the old-time musical comedians, he turned the show into a festival of individual gags (aided for a while, following an accident, by a wheelchair and a plaster cast) for the year of its run.

Kaye's musical film credits included the title role of Frank Loesser's *Hans Christian Andersen,* a score later turned several times into a stage musical.

Biographies: Singer, K: *The Danny Kaye Saga* (Hale, London, 1957), Richards, D: *The Life Story of Danny Kaye* (Convoy, London, 1949), Freedland, M: *The Secret Life of Danny Kaye* (St Martin's Press, W H Allen, 1985)

KEARNS, Allen [B] (b Brockville, Ontario, 1893; d Albany, NY, 20 April 1956). A juvenile and leading man on both sides of the Atlantic in the 1910s and 1920s.

The Canadian actor and singer worked as a child in Gus Edwards's juvenile troupe, and first appeared on Broadway as a teenager, in the chorus of the Marie Dressler vehicle *Tillie's Nightmare* (1910), and in very minor parts in Jerome Kern's *The Red Petticoat* (1912, Slim) and the sweetly slightweight *Miss Daisy* (1914, Frederic). After a naval stint as a second-class cook during the war, he returned with a supporting role in uniform (Private Barker) in the short-lived *Come Along* and then replaced Ward de Wolf as the young man forced to pretend to be a boy in the musical version of *The Magistrate,* here retitled *Good Morning, Judge* (1919).

He followed up in *Tickle Me* (1920, Jack Barton), *Tangerine* (1921, t/o Lee Loring), in the unfortunate Jimmy Powers show *The Little Kangaroo* (1922, Billy Irving), *Lady Butterfly* (1923, Billy Browning), and in the second lead of *Little Jessie James* (1923, Tommy Tinker) before having his first singing/light-comedy leading role in *Mercenary Mary* (1925, Jerry). He took the last, confirming step to leading-manhood playing Steve Burton, the rich man who falls for the dancing heroine (Queenie Smith) and who sings ''That Certain Feeling'' in Gershwin's *Tip-Toes.* He played this piece in America and, opposite Dorothy Dickson, in Britain, took another jeune premier role, in Ziegfeld's production of *Betsy,* on Broadway and then returned to London for two more similar parts, in the short-lived import from Chicago *Castles in the Air* (Monty Blair) and in the slightly more successful local musical, *Up with the Lark* (Freddy van Bozer).

Broadway gave Kearns some better quality stuff than these with the leading juvenile/romantic roles in *Funny Face* (1927, Peter Thurston, introducing ''He Loves and She Loves'' and '''S Wonderful''), *Here's Howe* (1928, Billy Howe), *Hello Daddy* (1928, Lawrence Tucker) and, still well short of his fortieth birthday, in *Girl Crazy* (1930, Danny Churchill, singing ''Embraceable You'' to and with Ginger Rogers). For some reason, this, one of his better roles, was his last on Broadway. He appeared once more in London, as the hero of the not-very-successful *Love Laughs—!* (1935, Tony Thornton), but in later years confined himself largely to television appearances.

KEEL, Howard [LEEK, Harold Clifford] (b Gillespie, Ill, 13 April 1919). Handsome musical leading man largely lost to films and television.

The richly baritonic Keel succeeded to the roles of Billy Bigelow (*Carousel*) and Curly (*Oklahoma!*) on Broadway and (still billed as ''Harold Keel'') introduced the latter role to London audiences in 1947. Thereafter he was seen exclusively in film musicals for almost a decade, appearing notably in the screen versions of *Annie Get Your Gun* (1950, Frank Butler), *Show Boat* (1951, Gaylord Ravenal), *Kiss Me, Kate* (1953, Fred), *Rose Marie* (1954, Jim Kenyon) and *Kismet* (1955, Hajj). His combination of heroic singing, impressive physique and willingness for a comic touch helped to steam his image onto these roles forever for much of the cinema-going world. He also played the leading male roles of the screen's *Calamity Jane* (1953) and *Seven Brides for Seven Brothers* (1954), both pieces later to be remade as stage musicals.

On the stage, he did not find the same kind of opportunities. He appeared in a further production of *Carousel* (1957), as the raffish and vengeful hero of Harold Arlen's *Saratoga* (1959, Clint Maroon), succeeded Richard Kiley as the leading man of *No Strings* (1963), and performed regionally in such pieces as *Kiss Me, Kate, South Pacific, Camelot, Show Boat, On a Clear Day You Can See Forever, I Do! I Do!,* and *Man of La Mancha,* creating his last stage role as the star of an unsuccessful musical based on Henry James's *The Ambassadors* (*Ambassador* London 1971, New York 1972).

His subsequent television success as the older love interest of the serial *Dallas* brought him a second period of fame which included concert tours as a vocalist, but no further musical-theatre roles either on Broadway or in London.

KEELER, Ruby [KEELER, Ethel Hilda] (b Halifax, Nova Scotia, 25 August 1909; d Rancho Mirage, Calif, 28 February 1993). Dancing ingenue of the musical screen.

After some small beginnings as a dancer in Broadway musicals, starting with *The Rise of Rosie O'Reilly* (1923) at the age of 14, then in increasingly important roles in *Bye, Bye Bonnie* (1927, Ruby), *Lucky* (1927, Mazie), *The Sidewalks of New York* (1927, Mamie) and *Show Girl* (1929, Dixie Dugan), in which she featured the show's most successful song, ''Liza (all the clouds'll roll away),'' the small and young-looking Miss Keeler came to international fame as the show-must-go-on heroine of the film *42nd Street* (1933). Her career in the 1930s was made in similar Warner Brothers films (*Gold Diggers of 1933, Dames, Go Into Your Dance*) in which her frenetic tap-dancing and angelic features combined to make her the ideal girl of a hundred thousand households next door. She made a return to the musical stage in later life star-billed in Harry Rigby's revival of *No, No, Nanette,* performing a dancer's ''I Want to Be Happy'' and ''Take a Little One Step'' in the role of Sue.

Miss Keeler was married for a period to performer Al Jolson.

KELLY, Edwin J (b Dublin, Ireland, 1831; d Adelaide, Australia, 1 January 1899).

The American minstrel team of Edwin Kelly and Francis Leon had a considerable success in America during the 1860s and 1870s, performing high-class minstrel programs of which the most effective highlight was a spectacularly produced burlesque of a currently popular show, normally featuring the square and sober-looking Kelly, the interlocutor and business manager of the troupe, in the leading male roles and starring largely the blondly softer and shorter Leon, with his skilled dancing and amazing soprano voice, as prima donna. Their most successful burlesques included homemade or made-over versions of *Cinder-Leon,* (''The best thing of its kind offered in this city for a long time'') *The Black Crook, The Grand Dutch-S, La Belle LN, Barber-Blu, Orphée, Frow-Frow, Kill Trovatore* and *Gin-nevieve de Graw,* and in 1870 they presented their version of Hervé's opéra-bouffe *Le Petit Faust* (with Kelly as Faust and Leon as Marguerite) even before a conventional production of the show had reached America. When they produced *Les Brigands* in San Francisco in 1873, the burlesque was so sizeable that the usual first part of the program had to be omitted. In the early 1870s they added such opérettes as Offenbach's *Lischen et Fritzchen, Ba-ta-clan, Monsieur Choufleuri, La Chatte métamorphosée en femme* and *La Rose de Saint-Flour,* Suppé's *Die schöne Galathee* and Legouix's *The Crimson Scarf* (*La Tartane*) to their repertoire, but still played these in their usual, genuinely burlesque manner with Leon as the (gradually more lightly blackfaced) feminine star. In this way, they introduced a number of important French opéra-bouffe pieces to the American theatre.

In spite of several attempts, various alliances, a decidedly superior level of performance, and a genuine popularity, the pair did not manage to establish themselves permanently in New York where competition was high (Kelly was acquitted after shooting and killing—in self-defense, and/or defense of Leon, so it was agreed—the brother of a rival manager in 1867, and on another occasion their theatre was burned down) and the summer weather prohibitive, and they spent part of their year, and on one occasion an entire year, on the road. They also tried performing white-face, in drama and farce, gathered and disbanded companies regularly for minstrel seasons, and once or twice even took engagements under other banners, but they were never so successful as when presenting their burlesques of opera and opéra-bouffe in New York and the other main centers. In 1869 the two stars visited Britain and gave a season at the Strand Theatre.

In 1878 Hayman and Hiscocks took the pair and their team to the south Pacific where, after introducing their programs—including such pieces as *M Choufleuri, Belles of the Kitchen, Galatea, La Rose de Saint-Flour,* their own musical comedy *His Grace, the Duke* and a burlesque of *Norma,* a number of these new to Australia—in Sydney, Melbourne, the Australian provinces and New Zealand with great success, they won a triumph and a certain notoriety when they produced early, pirated versions of *HMS Pinafore* and later *The Sorcerer,* played in the burlesque manner. When J C Williamson came on the scene with the legal rights to the pieces, Kelly negotiated to sublet those rights for certain areas, but shortly afterwards the Kelly and Leon team split up.

Leon returned, at first, to America whilst Kelly remained in Australia and, after not very successful attempts at launching further minstrel entertainments, he mounted a comic opera company playing straight versions of *Fatinitza* (Kantschukoff), *Giroflé-Girofla* (Mourzouk), *La Fille de Madame Angot* (Larivaudière) and *Les Cloches de Corneville* (Gaspard) in which he took the chief comic roles. He soon renounced management, however, joining up instead with Williamson, Garner and Musgrove's powerful comic-opera company with whom he played the Major General and later the Pirate King (*Pirates of Penzance*), Major Murgatroyd and later Grosvenor (*Patience*), Monthabor (*La Fille du tambour-major*), Gaspard (*Les Cloches de Corneville*), Merimac (*Olivette*), Rocco (*La Mascotte*), Mincing Lane (*Billee Taylor*) and other leading character/comic roles in opéra-bouffe and -comique for a number of years.

He continued a flourishing comic-opera career in Australia through the 1880s, starring with Majeroni and Wilson's company as the Black Rover in Luscombe Searelle's local comic opera *Isidora* and as Pomposo in his *Estrella,* and being seen as Brother Pelican in *Falka,* as Sir Lothbury Jones in *The Merry Duchess,* Don José in *Manteaux Noirs,* Lotteringhi in *Boccaccio,* Nick Vedder in *Rip van Winkle,* King Portico in Gilbert and Clay's *Princess Toto,* Pietro in *Les Brigands,* the old Prisoner in *La Périchole,* Larivaudière in *La Fille de Madame Angot,* Montefiore in *Maritana,* the Beadle *in Nell*

Plate 201. **Edwin Kelly** *as Rocco in J C Williamson's production of* La Mascotte.

Gwynne, Mourzouk in *Giroflé-Girofla,* Hannibal Grosgrain in *Babiole,* the Chevalier de Brabazon in *Erminie,* the Mikado, Nicholas in *Marjorie,* Bumpus in *Charity Begins at Home* as well as in pantomime (King Brokendown-o in *Cinderella,* Fitzwarren in *Dick Whittington*), before gradually turning more and more to non-musical shows and roles.

In the 1890s, whilst still appearing occasionally on the musical stage (Baron Badde in *Randolph the Reckless* with Coppin, Trenchard in *Little Jack Sheppard*), he became a regular and well-rated elderly character player in the Australian theatre, appearing with J C Williamson, George Darrell, Bland Holt, Arthur Garner, Mrs Brown Potter and Kyrle Bellew and other major companies, and he died, still in harness, whilst on tour in Adelaide from, so reported his death certificate, "failure of the heart's action."

Kelly's eldest son, who worked under the name of **Edwin LESTER** [Edwin Lester KELLY] (b New York, 1851; d Melbourne, Australia, 28 April 1936), was a member of the Kelly and Leon troupe in America and went with his father to Australia, where he appeared with the minstrels (Babylas in *Choufleuri,* Ganymede in *Galatea,* Smith in *La Rose de St-Flour,* etc), in the short-lived opera company (Julian in *Fatinitza,* etc) and later in both musical (*Isidora,* etc) and non-musical shows for other managements. He remained in Australia with his father and stepmother and in later life became a popular and praised character actor in the Australian theatre.

The vast turnover of sketches, playlets and burlesques produced by Kelly and Leon were rarely if ever credited, although it seemed to be understood that the two performers were themselves usually the authors and musical arrangers for their long run of merry musical pieces. If Leon was often mentioned when his own starring vehicles were concerned, Kelly seems to have been, notably, the author of *His Grace the Duke,* a musical comedy featuring Leon as a husband-hunting dame and Kelly as a theatrical manager, Theophilus Nubbs, whom she mistakes for a Duke, which was announced as having been played for over one thousand performances in America and Australia.

The following list of credits includes those works allegedly by Kelly and/or Leon.

1862 **La Vivandière** (pasticcio) 1 act Barnum's Museum 21 July

1862 **The Prima Donna from the Country** (pasticcio) sketch Barnum's Museum 28 July

1866 **The Two Doves** Kelly and Leon's Opera House 1 October

1866 **The Doctor of All-can-tear-her** Kelly and Leon's Opera House 8 October

1866 **My-deah Restore Her** Kelly and Leon's Opera House 15 October

1866 **Matrimony** Kelly and Leon's Opera House 3 December

1866 **The Black Statue** Kelly and Leon's Opera House 3 December

1867 **$7,000** Kelly and Leon's Opera House 7 January

1867 **Cinder-Leon** Kelly and Leon's Opera House 14 January

1867 **The Two Prima Donnas** Kelly and Leon's Opera House

1867 **Black Crook** burlesque Kelly and Leon's Opera House

1867 **Norma** burlesque (aka *Norma on the Half Shell*) Kelly and Leon's Opera House 24 March

1867 **Ernani** burlesque Kelly and Leon's Opera House

1867 **Kill Trovatore** Kelly and Leon's Opera House 26 August

1867 **Faust** burlesque Kelly and Leon's Opera House 4 November

1868 **The Grand Dutch-S** Kelly and Leon's Opera House 3 February

1868 **La Belle LN** Kelly and Leon's Opera House 8 June

1868 **Barber-Blu** Brooklyn 24 August, Kelly and Leon's Theater 31 August

1868 **Orphée aux enfers** Kelly and Leon's Opera House 2 November

1868 **Tame Cats** Kelly and Leon's Opera House 30 November

1869 **Gin-nevieve de Graw** Kelly and Leon's Opera House 2 January

1870 **Le Petit Faust** revised version of Robert Reece's English version (Kelly and Leon's Opera House)

1870 **Frow-Frow** Kelly and Leon's Opera House 18 April

1870 **Lischen et Fritzchen** revised English version (Kelly and Leon's Opera House)

1870 **Galatea, or The Black Sculptor** (*Die schöne Galathee*) revised English version (Kelly and Leon's Opera House)

1870 **Ching Chow Hi** (*Ba-ta-clan*) revised version of William Brough's English version (Kelly and Leon's Opera House)

1870 **The Babies of the Period** Kelly and Leon's Opera House 12 September

1870 **La Rose de Saint Flour** revised English version (Kelly and Leon's Opera House)

1871 **The Babes in the Wood** Hooley's Theatre, Brooklyn 1 January

1873 **The Crimson Scarf, or The Council of Ten** (*La Tartane*) revised English version (Opera House, Brooklyn)

1873 **Mons Choufleuri at Home** (*Monsieur Choufleuri restera chez lui le..*) new version (11th Street Opera House, Philadelphia)

1873 **The Haunted Mill** (Offenbach ad) adaptation (Alhambra, San Francisco)

1873 **The Brigands** burlesque (Alhambra, San Francisco)

1876 **His Grace, the Duke** (''music by Verdi'') Kelly and Leon's Opera House 1 May

1876 **Norma, or Titiens in a Minstrel Band** Kelly and Leon's Opera House 12 June

1876 **The Two Off'Uns** Kelly and Leon's Opera House 12 June

1876 **The Island of Bachelors** (*Les Cent Vierges*) version of Robert Reece's English version (Kelly & Leon's Opera House)

1876 **Sir Dan o'Pallas, or The Chief of the Assyrian Jim-Jams** Kelly and Leon's Opera House 2 September

1877 **The Police Force** (pasticcio) Kelly and Leon's Opera House 15 January

1877 **The Enchanted Cat** (*La Chatte métamorphosée en femme*) revised version of uncredited English adaptation (Kelly and Leon's Opera House)

1879 **Sir Joseph at Sea** (pasticcio) Kelly & Leon's Opera House, Sydney

1879 **Pin-a-4** (pasticcio) Kelly & Leon's Opera House, Sydney

KELLY, Gene [KELLY, Eugene Curran] (b Pittsburgh, Pa, 23 August 1912; d North Hollywood, Los Angeles, 2 February 1996). Screen dance star with a handful of theatre credits.

Kelly made his first appearance on the Broadway stage as a dancer in *Leave It to Me!* (1938), played in revue, and directed the shows at the Diamond Horseshoe before he was cast in the title role of the original production of *Pal Joey* (1940, ''I Could Write a Book''). The following year he choreographed the musical *Best Foot Forward,* but from 1942 his career was made in films where he became the epitome of the Hollywood song-and-dance man. He took starring roles in a long series of movies which included celluloid versions of *Dubarry Was a Lady, Anchors Aweigh, The Three Musketeers, On the Town* (also co-director) and *Brigadoon,* as well as the made-for-film musicals *The Pirate, An American in Paris, Singin' in the Rain, Les Girls* and many others.

He later returned to the musical theatre intermittently as a director (*Flower Drum Song, Clown Around*) and, regionally, as a performer (*Take Me Along,* 1974, etc), and in 1969 he directed the film version of *Hello, Dolly!*

Biography: Hirschhorn, C: *Gene Kelly* (W H Allen, London, 1974)

KENNEY, Charles Lamb (b Bellevue, France, 29 April 1821; d London, 25 August 1881).

The son of the prolific and successful playwright and librettist James Kenney, and the godson of Charles Lamb (thus the name, which F C Burnand insisted ''did a great deal for him''), Kenney was hired as a playreader for the Covent Garden Theatre at the age of 16 (''at £3 per week''), and worked as a journalist from the age of 19, but still found time to become secretarially involved in all sorts of other projects, notably with Joseph Paxton on organizing the transport services during the Crimean War and with de Lesseps on launching the scheme for the Suez Canal. Kenney moved comfortably in high London literary circles, and he worked latterly as a dramatic author and a critic (*Times*), writing a number of successful pieces for the West End stage, including the play *The Spitalfields Weaver* and the English versions of the operas *The Mock Doctor* (Gounod's *Le Medecin malgré lui*) and *L'Africaine* for the Theatre Royal, Covent Garden.

This theatre was also the venue for the landmark British production of Offenbach's *La Grande-Duchesse de Gérolstein* for which Kenney supplied the English version, a version which became the standard English text of this most popular of pieces and which brought his estate returns many years after his death. It also brought him, living, a series of further commissions for opéra-bouffe adaptations. ''Epigrammatically brilliant and invariably, because constitutionally, lazy,'' Kenney nevertheless published a number of works on a variety of subjects, which included the Suez Canal apologue *The Gates of the East,* a *Life and Letters of Balzac,* a biography of the composer Balfe and another of Dion Boucicault (*The Life and Career of Dion Boucicault* (New York, 1883 w Boucicault).

His son, **Charles H[orace] KENNEY** (b c1857; d London, 18 September 1909), had a successful career as a performer (originally under the name ''Horace Gay''), appearing in the burlesque *Touch and Go* (1886, Nurse); as Flint in Lydia Thompson's London production of *The Sultan of Mocha* (1888); with the same lady's company in America (Icarius in *Penelope,* etc, 1888); as the Mayor in *Rhoda* and as Biscotin in *Madame Favart* at the Avenue Theatre; as a dame in pantomime and burlesque; and on tour in America in the extravaganza *Spider and Fly* and in Britain in *Newmarket* (Jemmy Smart), *The American Heiress* (Fritz) and other musical and non-musical pieces. He also co-directed and played in Marie Lloyd's one attempt at a musical, *The ABC* (1898), in the provinces.

- 1859 **The Swan and Edgar, or The Fairy Lake** (w Sutherland Edwards) St James's Theatre 16 November
- 1867 **Wanted, Husbands for Six** (*Six demoiselles à marier*) English version mus arr J H Tully (Theatre Royal, Drury Lane)
- 1867 **La Grande-Duchesse** English version (Theatre Royal, Covent Garden)
- 1869 **Barbe-bleue** English version (Standard Theatre)
- 1870 **La Princesse de Trébizonde** English version (Gaiety Theatre)
- 1871 **La Belle Hélène** English version (Gaiety Theatre)
- 1873 **The Wonderful Duck** (*Le Canard à trois becs*) English version (Opera Comique)
- 1875 **La Jolie Parfumeuse** English version (Birmingham)

KENNY, Sean [Noël] (b Portroe, Ireland, 23 December 1929; d London, 11 June 1973).

Architect turned theatrical designer, Kenny made his name with the sets for Peter Coe's London production of *Lock Up Your Daughters*—a series of non-representational, skeletal constructions which served as a multiplicity of settings—and, most particularly, for Coe's subsequent *Oliver!* His collection of moving rostra and stairs, which came swiftly together in different groupings to make up the many settings of Bart and Dickens's tale, helped materially in keeping the impetus of the show's story going, and *Oliver!*'s scenery, reused over and over in revival, was long quoted as an outstanding piece of theatre mechanics and design.

In the 1960s he then designed, amongst others, the productions of *Stop the World—I Want to Get Off* (London and New York), the hugely scenic *Blitz!, The Roar of the Greasepaint . . . the Smell of the Crowd* (New York), *Pickwick* (London and New York), *Maggie May* and *The Four Musketeers,* by which time the qualities which had made his early work so interesting had, through repetition and imitation, themselves become clichés.

Kenny also worked on a number of theatre buildings, conceiving and designing his ''theatre of the future,'' the New London Theatre, from the ground up, on the site of the old Winter Garden Theatre. The theatre of the future seemed, for a long time, as if it had no future. Its many movable stage and auditorium parts lay idle for years before Cameron Mackintosh, already reponsible for successfully redisplaying Kenny's *Oliver!* sets to a new generation, put *Cats* into the New London. *Cats* not only utilized a number of Kenny's stage machines and concepts for the first time, it also virtually saved the theatre from dwindling away into non-use.

KENT, William [Thomas] (b St Paul, Minn, 29 April 1886; d New York, 4 October 1945). Agile, spindle-shanked comedian who had more than a decade of starring roles on the musical stage.

Kent began his career working in music hall (Looey from Louisville in *The Athletic Girl,* 1905, etc) and after a number of youthful years in regional and touring productions (*Miss Hook of Holland, Have a Heart, Look Who's Here,* t/o in *A Modern Eve,* etc), he had his first Broadway role as the campy Hyperion Buncombe in Jerome Kern's *Toot-Toot!* (1918). There then followed a succession of larger comic parts in Broadway musicals: as the show-stealing, henpecked Uncle Toby alongside Nora Bayes in *Ladies First* (1919), the best man in a spot, Sam Benton in *Somebody's Sweetheart* (1919, until he walked out) and the comical hero, Dick Crawford, in *Pitter Patter* (1920), but he came to grief with the "ultimate in intimate musicals" when Victor Herbert's *Oui, Madame,* which featured him as a janitor singing about being "Sincopated," folded out of town.

Kent took a rather plot-incidental role as Steve Simmons in the long-running *Good Morning, Dearie,* performing "Sing Song Girl" and "Melican Papa" and getting to imitate a Chinese waiter, and he played Hozier in support of Charles Ruggles's *Battling Butler* in the musical comedy of that title, before landing his most memorable role as the anything but Hard-Boiled Herman of Friml's *Rose Marie* (1924, "Hard-Boiled Herman," "Why Shouldn't We?"). He made a dumb decision when he elected to come out of *Rose Marie* to take the principal comedy role in an Americanization of Lehár's *Frasquita* alongside opera star Geraldine Farrar, for it folded after one night out of town. But Kent was still riding high: in 1926 he took Walter Catlett's role of Watty Watkins alongside the Astaires in the London version of *Lady, Be Good!,* and in 1927 he shared the stage with the same pair as he created the part of the comical crook Duggsie Gibbs, in a double act with Victor Moore, in *Funny Face.*

He appeared as the phony mountain climber Billings in a rip-off of *Going Up* called *Ups-a-Daisy* (1928), visited Australia to star in the revue *Clowns in Clover,* and then, on his return, landed another fine role as Ethel Merman's father in *Girl Crazy* (1930). His later Broadway shows and parts were less happy (*A Little Racketeer, Music Hath Charms, Revenge with Music*) although he toured and/or played regionally in such proven pieces as *Show Boat* (Cap'n Andy), *Blossom Time* (Tscholl), *The Merry Widow* (Nisch), *Balalaika* (Nicki) and *Anything Goes* (Moonface) in the latter years of his career, being seen as Nisch, in his last appearance, in the year before his death.

KERKER, Gustav[e] [Adolph] (b Westphalia, Germany, 28 February 1857; d New York, 29 June 1923). Prolific illustrator and botcher of Broadway shows who popped out one worldwide novelty hit show among reams of the merrily utilitarian.

A descendant of a family of German musicians, Kerker was taken to America at the age of 10 and settled with his family in Louisville, where he began his career in the theatre as an orchestral 'cellist. He subsequently became a theatrical conductor and at the same time began composing with an eye to the stage. A regional touring production of his first operetta, *Cadets,* a piece written in conjunction with Texan journalist Morris H Warner (d Galveston, Tex, 17 November 1891) and mounted (after a couple of false starts) in repertoire by a Grau touring company whose main offering was *Fatinitza,* won the 22-year-old composer the notice of and a position with E E Rice, as musical director of his touring opéra-bouffe company. In the years that followed he also waved his baton in front of companies run by H B Mahn (*Donna Juanita,* 1882), Miles and Barton and Charles E Ford, and for a selection of the touring and summer comic-opera companies which proliferated at the time around America. He also arranged the score (w John J Braham) for Willie Gill's latest remake of the burlesque *Oxygen* (1885) for Lydia Thompson.

Kerker's first full-time engagement in New York, again under Rice, was as conductor at the Bijou Theater, and it was at that house that he had his first music presented on the Broadway stage. It took the form of some considerable interpolations in a successful adaptation of Lecocq's *Fleur de thé,* there played under the title *The Pearl of Pekin.* He continued to double as a composer and a conductor and, when he was subsequently engaged as musical director at the Casino Theater (1888), his own music straight away began to find its way, in varying amounts, into the scores of most of the imported opérettes presented there. In 1890 he wrote his first full score to a libretto by Charles Alfred Byrne, the adaptor of *Fleur de thé,* and the resulting piece, a rip-off of Offenbach's *Les Bavards* entitled *Castles in the Air,* was produced by the De Wolf Hopper Comic Opera Company with a fine cast including Della Fox, Thomas Q Seabrooke, Marion Manola and the future Mrs Kerker, Rose Leighton, for a respectable three-months-plus Broadway run.

The young composer's name appeared nebulously on the bills of a Casino piece called *The Brazilian* which was supposed to be the work of the then red-hot Francis Chassaigne (Kerker later called himself the "composer" of this piece), but it was several seasons before his next own Broadway musical, *Prince Kam,* a revised version of an extravaganza played for a fine season in Boston as *Venus* the previous year, was produced at the Casino in 1894. It proved to have rather less appeal for New York. Another similar effort, called *Kismet,* with a libretto as deeply indebted to Offenbach's *L'Île de Tulipatan* as *Castles in the Air* had been to *Les Bavards,* lasted but three weeks on the Broadway stage. A second sizeable piece of botching for the Casino, a revamped version of *The Lady Slavey,* did rather better. Producer George Lederer had had this long-running English variety musical comedy rewritten to such an extent that little remained of the original show except its joyously comical Cinderella story line and characters, and Kerker was responsible for the songs which replaced almost all of the original British score. If the new version did not in any way approach the original *Lady Slavey*'s vast success in Britain, it nevertheless did well enough, without the musical score gaining any particular kudos.

Kerker and his fellow "adapter," Hugh McLellan, followed up their remade *The Lady Slavey* with a series of original musicals for the Casino, beginning with the revusical *In Gay New York* (1896) and continuing with the musical comedy *An American Beauty,* featuring Lillian Russell in its title role, the revue *The Whirl of the Town* (1897) and a jolly ragbag of a variety musical, built on *Lady Slavey* lines and called *The Belle of New York. The Belle of New York* ("The Belle of New York," "Teach Me How to Kiss," "They All Follow Me") lasted only 56 performances at the Casino, but it pleased Boston much better and, when the Australian impresario George Musgrove took the gamble of transporting the show and its company to the Shaftesbury Theatre, London, the piece became a novelty hit of huge proportions, leading to years of productions throughout Europe and around the world where *The Belle of New York* became accepted as the epitome of the American musical comedy.

Gaston Serpette's French vaudeville *La Demoiselle du téléphone* was subsequently given the same treatment as had been meted out to *The Lady Slavey* and Kerker supplied the Casino with one last revue, *Yankee Doodle Dandy* (1898), before, on the strength of the reputation won for him overseas by *The Belle of New York,* moving out to work with other managements and theatres. Amongst a series of mostly serviceable but scarcely memorable musicals, over the following years, he collaborated with Ludwig Englander and Reginald De Koven on the score for the successful extravaganza *The Man in the Moon* and composed a new show for his *Belle of New York* star, Edna May, *The Girl from Up There* (1900). Although this piece came nowhere near the earlier one in the extent of its success, it nevertheless had fair runs in both New York and London and was played in Vienna (*Die Eisjungfrau*), where *The Belle* had had the same kind of novelty effect as in London, in a revised version, with Kerker's score revamped by Josef Hellmesberger in much the same way Kerker had botched so many Continental scores for the American stage.

Two further musicals, *The Tourists* (124 performances) and *The White Hen,* fared respectably in America and a third, *Schneeglöckchen,* premiered at Vienna's Theater an der Wien (which had previously hosted *Die Schöne von New-York*), during Kerker's short-lived attempt to establish himself as a composer in Europe, was later played on Broadway as *Two Little Brides* (Providence, RI 14 March 1912, Casino Theater 28 April 1912) and also won a brief London showing in the same year as *The Grass Widows.* London also saw one of Kerker's less likely works, the little burlesque *Burning to Sing,* originally written for a benefit performance in New York, and subsequently mounted by J C Williamson in Australia and by George Edwardes, as part of a bill at the London Empire, as *Very Grand Opera* (1906).

It was a further European work, however, which brought him his biggest success since *The Belle of New York. Der oberen Zehntausend* attempted, as Adolf Philipp had done to not negligible success a decade earlier, to take New York to Berlin. Imported stars Madge Lessing and Fred Wright (playing a 16-year-old boy) starred with Guido Thielscher and a local company in a piece which was angled heavily towards the most up-to-date in American dance rhythms and dance numbers and the result was not only a novelty but a decided success. *Der oberen Zehntausend* proved a great draw and had a splendid run, right into the Berlin summer months.

In his later years, Kerker still worked as a musical-theatre conductor (*The Seventh Chord* Chicago, 1913, etc), and his last Broadway songs were heard in the revue *Some Party* the year before his death.

Kerker was often dismissed by commentators as a hack, and there is no doubt that he did his own cause little good by placing his melodies alongside those of the Continental masters of the period in his days of botching imported shows at the Casino Theater. However, unlike some interpolating songwriters, whose frankly simplistic music-hally songs, with their endlessly repeated phrases and refrains, could be relied on to catch only an undemanding ear, Kerker did in fact more or less aspire to writing in the same kind of strains as the composers he was "supplementing." As a result, he neither had "hit" songs nor, lacking the class of an Offenbach or a Lecocq, did he win any critical acclaim. His one hit, with *The*

Belle of New York, may indeed have been due largely to the novelty of the show's style for overseas audiences, but its score alone contains sufficient in the way of lively, attractive music to show that Kerker at his uncomplicated best was indeed capable of writing both charming and catchy music.

Kerker was the first legal husband of the English comic-opera contralto **Rose LEIGHTON** [Rosina KEENE] (b Shepherd's Bush, London, 1850), who had a prominent Broadway career in the last decades of the 19th century. She appeared in London under her given name, replacing Catherine Lewis as Friquette in *Les Prés Saint-Gervais* (1875) and playing Pedro in *Giroflé-Girofla* (1875), before coming to America with Julia Mathews's company in 1875 playing Fleurette in *Barbe-bleue* and as Pedro in *Giroflé-Girofla.* Following the company's collapse she remained in America and appeared as Broadway's first Plaintiff in *Trial by Jury* opposite G H MacDermott. She subsequently worked in the legshow at the Parisian Varieties (as ''Rosie Keene''), playing Clairette in *La Fille de Madame Angot* (1876), with Lydia Thompson, with Samuel Colville's company in *The Babes in the Wood* (1877, Queen of Tragedy), etc, for Edward Rice in *Evangeline* (1878, Eulalie) and *HMS Pinafore* (Hebe), with Colville again in *The Magic Slipper* (1879, Elfina), *Oxygen* (Suzel) and *Ill-Treated Travatore* (Inez), and with C D Hess's company (1882, Lazarillo in Maritana, etc), S W Fort's Academy Opera Co and, later, in a long series of comic-opera character roles at New York's principal musical houses and with John McCaull's companies on the road: as the Prince and later Sophistica in *Prince Methusalem,* Mrs Partlett in *The Sorcerer,* Donna Olympia in *Donna Juanita,* Germaine in *Les Cloches de Corneville,* Gypsy Queen in *The Bohemian Girl,* Lady Allcash in *Fra Diavolo,* Palmatica in *The Beggar Student,* Lady Saphir in *Patience,* Thomas Darrell in *Little Jack Sheppard,* Mrs Privett in *Dorothy,* Catarina in *The Queen's Mate,* Buccametta in *A Trip to Africa,* Inez in *The Gondoliers,* Angélique in her husband's *Castles in the Air* and Ramadamus in his *Kismet,* and Aurore in *Giroflé-Girofla.* She appeared as well in a number of less successful pieces, ranging from *Dovetta* and Sousa's *Desiree* (1884, Laurie) to the Baltimore comic opera *Jack Sheppard* (1885, Edgeworth Bess) and *The Birth of Venus* (1895) and was also later in farce comedy (Mrs Ungerblotz in *U & I,* 1891, etc).

Miss Leighton's first ''husband'' (an existing wife made an actual marriage impractical) was **William FORRESTER** (b London, c1848; d Baltimore, 7 February 1885) who, after switching from straight theater to comic opera as the Duke in the Standard Theatre's *The Island of Bachelors* (1875), came with her to America in 1875 (Saphir in *Barbe-bleue,* Prince Paul in *La Grande-Duchesse,* Marasquin in *Giroflé-Girofla,* Broadway's first Defendant in *Trial by Jury,* Ange Pitou in *La Fille de Madame Angot,* etc). He later appeared with Lydia Thompson in 1877 (Niklausse in *Oxygen,* Wai-Ho in *Robinson Crusoe*) and was seen on Broadway in 1878 in *Evangeline* (Le Blanc), in 1879 as Sir Joseph Porter in *HMS Pinafore,* in 1880 in skirts in *Ill-Treated Trovatore* (Madame Catalina Grimalkina), with the Colville company and in Gill's Our Goblins (1881, Octavius Longfellow Warbler). He later became stage director for the Boston Ideal Company.

1879 **The Cadets** (Morris H Warner) MacCauley's Theater, Louisville 17 September

1884 **Those Bells** burlesque (w E N Catlin/Sydney Rosenfeld) 1 act Park Theater, Boston 14 January

1890 **Castles in the Air** (Charles Alfred Byrne) Broadway Theater 5 May

1892 **A Society Fad** (comp & arr w Alexander Haig/John G Wilson) Bijou Theater 5 December

1893 **Venus** (Byrne, Louis Harrison) Park Theater, Boston, 11 September

1894 **Prince Kam, or A Trip to Venus** revised *Venus* Casino Theater 29 January

1894 **Kismet** (Richard F Carroll) Boston July; Herald Square Theater, New York 12 September 1895

1895 **The Flying Dutchman** (w Frank Howson, Anton Reiff/ Charles Harbury) Columbia Theater, Boston 25 March

1896 **The Lady Slavey** (George Dance ad C M S McLellan) American version w new songs Casino Theater 3 February

1896 **In Gay New York** (McLellan) Casino Theater 25 May

1896 **An American Beauty** (McLellan) Casino Theater 28 December

1897 **The Whirl of the Town** (McLellan) Casino Theater 25 May

1897 **The Belle of New York** (McLellan) Casino Theater 28 September

1897 **The Telephone Girl** (*La Demoiselle du téléphone*) (McLellan) American version w new songs Casino Theater 27 December

1898 **Yankee Doodle Dandy** (McLellan) Casino Theater 25 July

1899 **The Man in the Moon** (w Ludwig Englander, Reginald De Koven/Stanislaus Stange, Harrison) New York Theater 24 April

1901 **The Girl from Up There** (McLellan) Herald Square Theater 7 January

1902 **The Billionaire** (Harry B Smith) Daly's Theater 29 December

1903 **The Blonde in Black** (aka *The Sambo Girl*) (H B Smith) Knickerbocker Theater 8 June

1903 **Winsome Winnie** (Frederick Ranken) Casino Theater 1 December

1904 **Burning to Sing, or Singing to Burn** (aka *Very Grand Opera*) (R H Burnside) 1 act Lyric Theater 10 May (Lambs' Club Gambol)

1904 **Die Eisjungfrau** revised version of *The Girl from Up There* (ad Carl Lindau, Julius Wilhelm) Venedig in Wien, Vienna 3 June

1904 **The Sambo Girl** revised *The Blonde in Black* Nesbitt Theater, Wilkes-Barre, Pa 5 September

1905 **Der oberen Zehntausend** (Julius Freund) Metropoltheater, Berlin 24 April

1905 **In Lebensgefahr** (Freund) Walhalla-Theater, Berlin 1 November

1906 **The Social Whirl** (Joseph W Herbert, Charles V Doty) Casino Theater 7 April

1906 **The Tourists** (Burnside) Lyric Theatre, Philadelphia 21 May; Daly's Theater 25 August

1906 **The Great Decide** (Glen MacDonough) 2 scenes Herald Square Theater 15 November

1907 **The White Hen** (ex- *The Girl from Vienna*) (Paul West/ Roderic C Penfold) Hyperion Theater, New Haven (as *The Girl from Vienna*) 9 February; Casino Theater 16 February

1907 **Fascinating Flora** (Burnside, Herbert) Casino Theater 20 May

1907 **The Lady from Lane's** (George Broadhurst) Lyric Theater 19 August

1910 **Schneeglöckchen** (A M Willner, Wilhelm) Theater an der Wien, Vienna 14 October

KERN, Jerome D[avid] (b New York, 27 January 1885; d New York, 11 November 1945).

A major figure in the American musical theatre for more than two decades, Jerome Kern composed, during a long career, music and songs for a wide variety of musical plays, ranging from additional material for the musical comedies of the heyday of the London Edwardian stage, through sets of numbers for the comedy musicals of the American wartime years, to full-scale scores for more musically ambitious projects such as *Show Boat* and *Sweet Adeline* and, in the 1930s, a kind of mid-Atlantic brand of operetta.

Kern became an adept pianist at an early age, was composing songs for school and amateur shows in his early teens, and had his first piece of music published at the age of 17, whilst he was working in the accounts section of the music publishers Edward Marks. He soon moved on to work for another publisher, Max Dreyfus, in a more congenial position as a staff writer (later becoming a junior partner in Dreyfus's T B Harms when an inheritance allowed him to buy a share in the firm), and in that capacity he had his first opportunity to write songs which could, in the rather haphazard manner of the time, be interpolated by the plugging publisher in Broadway musical comedies.

The first of these shows were three British imports, two of which, *An English Daisy* and *Mr Wix of Wickham,* had never made it to London's West End. Nevertheless, in the scrabble amongst American producers for the right to produce the popular and fashionable British-made entertainments that were the backbone of Broadway entertainment at the turn of the century, they won themselves a showing in New York. The third was the post-Broadway tour of the London and New York success *The Silver Slipper.* Kern had two songs heard in *An English Daisy,* but by the time *Mr Wix* arrived in town no less than a dozen of his numbers had been crammed in to the score, virtually ousting the show's original songs. Neither show proved popular.

Kern then began an association with producer Charles Frohman, which resulted in his placing numbers in Frohman shows both on Broadway (*The Catch of the Season, The Babes and the Baron*) and in London (*The Beauty of Bath*), whither Kern moved temporarily in 1905. It was clearly not an exclusive engagement, as Kern was soon supplying songs to London's William Greet (*The Talk of the Town*) and George Edwardes (*The Spring Chicken, The Little Cherub*), and the composer's first song hit "How'd You Like to Spoon with Me?" was first heard in the Shuberts' Broadway production of the imported *The Earl and the Girl.* In the years that followed, Kern continued to provide a flood of additional material for the Broadway and, occasionally, the London stage, contributing sometimes just one song, at others a significant part of the show's song schedule. Many of these shows were American versions of the fairly elastically constructed contemporary British musical comedies—*The Rich Mr Hoggenheimer, The Little Cherub, My Lady's Maid, The White Chrysanthemum, The Orchid, The Dairymaids, Kitty Grey, King of Cadonia, The Girls of Gottenberg, Our Miss Gibbs*—whilst others were fresh-made American material (Kerker's *Fascinating Flora,* the revue *The Gay White Way, Fluffy Ruffles,* Julian Edwards's *The Girl and the Wizard, The Hen Pecks, The Echo* and a shortlived Shubert production called *The Golden Widow*). In the wake of *The Merry Widow,* some were also from the newly super-popular Austrian theatre (*A Waltz Dream, The Dollar Princess, The Gay Hussars*). By and large, these more consistently constructed and composed shows took interpolations much less happily. But several of the botched-in numbers nevertheless proved popular. In London, George Edwardes's unsuccessful production of *A Waltz Dream, The Dollar Princess* and the Frohman costume piece *The Dashing Little Duke* all took in a ration of Kern songs.

In 1906 Seymour Hicks announced that he would write his next musical, *The Lady of Bath,* with Kern as his composing partner, but the composer ultimately contributed only a little music to Herbert Haines's score for what became *The Beauty of Bath.* Then in 1908 George Grossmith announced the forthcoming production of a musical comedy, *The President's Daughter,* to be written by his *Girls of Gottenberg* associate L E Berman and composed by Kern, but this project never saw stagelight.

It was to be three further years before, after nearly a decade of successful if rarely enduring songwriting, Kern finally got billing for the first time as the principal composer of a show when he contributed to the revusical piece *La Belle Paree* not in London but in New York. Amongst the cast of *La Belle Paree* were included ex-Edwardes employees Jeannie Aylwin and Kitty Gordon, the newly arrived Hungarian starlet Mizzi Hajós (aka Mitzi) and the young Al Jolson, and, played as an item on a Winter Garden program, the piece had a respectable run. Although Kern would continue for many years to be one of Broadway's busiest interpolaters and, most notably, one of the more active botchers of the Continental Operetten which were then crowding onto American stages (Fall's *The Siren,* Berény's *The Girl from Montmartre,* Ziehrer's *The Kiss Waltz,* Heuberger's *The Opera Ball,* Jean Gilbert's *A Polish Wedding,* Eysler's *The Woman Haters,* Fall's *The Doll Girl* and *Lieber Augustin,* Victor Jacobi's *The Marriage Market*), he was at last on the road to becoming a successful show composer in his own right.

The success did not come immediately. The Shubert production of *The Red Petticoat,* an adaptation of a Rida Johnson Young play, failed in 61 Broadway performances, and a version of the French comedy *Une nuit de noces,* previously a hit play as *Oh, I Say!,* lasted just 68. It did, however, confirm the trend, already seen in Ivan Caryll's French-comedy-based shows (*The Pink Lady, Oh! Oh! Delphine,* etc) and in George Grossmith's earlier adaptations of Paris's *Le Coquin de printemps* (*The Spring Chicken*) and *L'Amorçage* (*Peggy*), towards a very satisfying kind of musical comedy—a type of piece on the lines of the French vaudeville in which a coherent and, in these cases, proven farcical tale provided the solid theatrical-comical basis for a set of lively and up-to-date songs and ensembles in a show which had no extravagant production, no large ''beauty'' chorus and/or glued-in ''pop'' songs to cover weaknesses in plot, character or score. It was a kind of show to which the composer would return regularly over the following years.

At the same time, however, Kern was himself still supplying such ''pop'' songs, although often of a more soigné character than those by some of his contemporaries—whether for use in Viennese Operetten (*The Laughing Husband, The Queen of the Movies, A Modern Eve*), homemade star vehicles (*When Claudia Smiles, When Dreams Come True*) or in the now-dwindling selection of imports from Britain (*The Sunshine Girl, The Girl from Utah*). It was one of these last, however, which gave him his most serious song hit since ''How'd You Like to Spoon with Me?'' when Julia Sanderson and Donald Brian introduced ''They Didn't Believe Me'' in Sidney Jones and Paul Rubens's score for *The Girl from Utah.* There were fine songs, too, in Kern's own next show, *Ninety in the Shade,* a ramshackle creation tailored for aging stars Richard Carle and Marie Cahill that quickly went under, and the composer rescued the best of the slightly used numbers for later reuse. Reuse, in the meanwhile was already going on in London, where Frohman took up some Kern material to bolster Herman Darewski's score for J M Barrie's curious, revusical *Rosy Rapture.*

Kern's next Broadway assignment started out as another fairly routine botching job, but it ended up as something rather better. Hired to do over the music of *Mr Popple of Ippleton,* Paul Rubens's charming London comedy with songs, for the new, tiny and financially limited Princess Theater, he ended up composing an entire set of songs (with the inevitable interpolations) to a revised Guy Bolton libretto effectively to make up a nearly new and necessarily ''intimate'' musical on the lines of *Oh, I Say!* and its predecessors. The piece was no longer *Mr Popple,* and in some ways it was less good than *Mr Popple,* but *Nobody Home* (as it was now called) proved an attractive, enjoyable, small-scale piece, and it caught on so happily that its producers, F Ray Comstock and Bessie Marbury, soon moved it to a larger house to cash in. Naturally, they also followed up *Nobody Home* with more of the same, and Kern was next hired to provide the songs for a musical adaptation of a successful farce, *Over Night.*

Whilst Kern busily manufactured short scores for two star-vehicles—Julian Eltinge's *Cousin Lucy* and Elsie Janis and Irene Bordoni's *Miss Information*—*Over Night* was turned into *Very Good Eddie* (''Babes in the Wood''), and Kern and his producers found themselves with a second, and more considerable, success on their hands, one which, once again, ultimately moved into a lucrative house. However, there was no sign as yet of making these ''intimate'' musical shows larger. They retained their musical-farce-in-two-sets layout and their limited production values and they continued to be popular and fashionable in their little home and after it. However, Bolton and Kern were not involved with the next of Comstock's productions: they turned down his plan to musicalize Charles Hoyt's *A Milk White Flag,* and Kern instead supplied half a score to his old friend George Grossmith for his musical of the hugely successful French farce *Theodore & Co* (503 performances) at London's Gaiety Theatre, some interpolations for Klaw and Erlanger's version of Kálmán's Budapest show *Zsuzsi kisasszony* (*Miss Springtime*) and the scores for two new works which opened almost simultaneously on Broadway.

One of this pair was the first piece to come from what was to be a not very prolific but fondly remembered three-sided partnership: Kern/P G Wodehouse/Bolton. However, Henry Savage's production of their *Have a Heart*—written for the Princess Theater but given to Savage after a lawsuit—had only a disappointing two-month run on Broadway, and the fashionably dance-filled Shubert production of *Love o' Mike* did much better. Neither, however, topped *Very Good Eddie,* and the new trio had to wait for a return to the Princess Theater for a return to that kind of success. Back in the cradle of the small-scale musical they together provided Comstock with the two best pieces written for his little house: *Oh, Boy!* (1917, "Till the Clouds Roll By"), and *Leave It to Jane* (1917, "The Siren's Song," "The Crickets are Calling") which arrived before *Oh, Boy!* had done its run and ended up, probably to its disadvantage, being played at the Longacre Theater instead of at the little house whose kind of entertainment it characterized. When *Oh, Boy!* was done, the team were ready with another made-to-the-same-measure piece to take its place in *Oh, Lady! Lady!!,* and then, to all intents and purposes, the little series which had looked so promising halted. Kern split from the team, other folk took over the making of the town's most successful intimate musicals, and after two more productions Comstock gave up intimate musicals to continue with pieces like the vastly spectacular *Mecca* (1920).

Kern, who had, in the meanwhile, contributed to the unhappy Dillingham revue *Miss 1917,* moved on through several unexceptional works—*Toot-Toot!* and a Mitzi-vehicle called *Head Over Heels* for Savage; *Rock-a-Bye Baby,* a version of the successful if rather distasteful Margaret Mayo play *Baby Mine* for the Selwyns; and *She's a Good Fellow* for Dillingham—before suffering the indignity, for the first time in his long and full career, of having a show fold on the road. It was a reunion with Bolton and Comstock, an adaptation of the hugely successful farce *Brewster's Millions* apparently intended to carry on the Princess Theater line of small-sized, play-based shows, and it ground to a halt after three weeks on the road.

Kern bounced back quickly. His delightful score to Anne Caldwell's adaptation of Alexandre Bisson's *Le Controlleur des Wagons-lits* as *The Night Boat* ("Whose Baby Are You?," "Good Night Boat," "Left All Alone Again Blues") helped materially towards the show's 313-performance Broadway run, before, following another brief interlude writing for revue with the indifferent *Hitchy Koo of 1920,* he moved to an ever bigger success with the winsome tale of *Sally* (1920). Ziegfeld's favorite star Marilyn[n] Miller sang of being "A Wild Rose" and duetted that one should "Look for the Silver Lining" to enormous effect, and *Sally* gave Kern his most substantial international hit up to that time.

It was a level of attainment which could not come every year, and in fact it was seven years before an equivalent triumph again came his way. Those years, nevertheless, brought forth some highly agreeable results and some happy songs. He composed the scores for two London musicals for George Grossmith of which *The Cabaret Girl* proved the better, and he took part in no less than five further collaborations with Ms Caldwell. Of these, *Good Morning, Dearie* ran for 347 performances and ended Kern up in court, charged (at the eventual cost of $250) with plagiarizing the hit song "Dardanella" for his "Ka-lu-a"; *The Bunch and Judy,* in spite of the Astaires, folded in 63 nights; *The City Chap* did no better; and two pieces for Fred Stone, *Stepping Stones* and *Criss-Cross,* if less distinguished than the comedian's best and earlier shows, nevertheless served his purposes. A final, disappointing attempt to team once more with Bolton and Wodehouse in *Sitting Pretty* (95 performances), *Lucky* (71 performances) and *Dear Sir* (14 performances) resulted in three straightforward failures. Amongst this mixed bag, however, the most sizeable success amongst Kern's new shows of this period was Dillingham's production of *Sunny* (1925), another Marilyn[n] Miller vehicle, which topped 500 Broadway performances, brought "Who?," "Sunny" and "Two Little Bluebirds" to the standards list, and which followed *Sally* on to the international circuits without having quite the same qualities or the same success.

Kern had for many years threatened to go "serious," to abandon foxtrots and one-steps for more dramatically and lyrically substantial forms. When he did, it proved to be in combination with a splendid text by the librettist of the textually indifferent *Sunny,* Oscar Hammerstein II, and the most extravagantly fearless of producers, Florenz Ziegfeld. The result was *Show Boat*—one of the most artistically complete and impressive, and also the most popularly enduring Broadway musical shows of its era. In *Show Boat* ("Ol' Man River," "Can't Help Lovin' Dat Man o' Mine," "Bill," "Make Believe," etc), Kern turned out a score which was in a different mode to the light-footed dance-and-songs of *Sally* or *Sunny* and proved, once for all time, that this songwriter had more than one color of ink in his pen.

After *Show Boat* he never again turned back to his old, breezy style of song-and-dancewriting for the musical theatre. A rather limp Scottish operetta, *Blue Eyes,* written for London before *Show Boat*'s opening, had a fair life without leaving Britain, but for New York henceforth Kern supplied more consciously substantial fodder. *Sweet Adeline,* a rather downbeat vehicle for *Show Boat* star Helen Morgan, produced the plangent "Why Was I Born?" but fell victim to the stock market crash. However, two considered attempts to write operetta in the Continental manner did better. The Bruxelloise love story of *The Cat and the Fiddle* ("She Didn't Say 'Yes,'" "The

Night Was Made for Love'') was rather happier libretto material than the saccharine operettic tale of *Music in the Air* (''I've Told Ev'ry Little Star''), but both produced some memorable music, had fine runs, foreign productions and considerable lives thereafter. Kern struck libretto problems again in the uninteresting frock-shop tale of *Roberta* (in the après–*Pink Lady* period, libretti mattered more than before), but the piece's score simply rustled with good things (''Yesterdays,'' ''Smoke Gets in your Eyes,'' ''I'll Be Hard to Handle,'' ''You're Devastating'') from a man who, 30 years into his career, seemed to be enjoying himself exploring a new register of musical theatre. *Roberta*'s future, after a disappointing 259 Broadway performances, turned out to be in films rather than in further stage productions.

The same went for Kern. Whilst London's *Three Sisters* (1934, ''I Won't Dance''), the St Louis Municipal Opera's *Gentlemen Unafraid* (1938) and Broadway's *Very Warm for May* (1939, ''All the Things You Are'') failed in the theatre, Kern was having a simultaneous success (mostly) with film versions of *Roberta* (1933) and *Show Boat* (1936) and the scores for such original films as *Swing Time* (1936), *High, Wide and Handsome* (1937) and *Joy of Living* (1938). This celluloid success continued (mostly) with *One Night in the Tropics* (1940), *You Were Never Lovelier* (1942), *Cover Girl* (1944), *Can't Help Singing* (1944) and his final, posthumously released film, *Centennial Summer* (1946). At the time of his death, he was preparing to embark on one more Broadway score, a score to a Herbert and Dorothy Fields libretto about the sharpshooting Annie Oakley.

Only one Jerome Kern work, *Show Boat,* has remained actively in the standard repertoire—a repertoire which has always preferred the musically more substantial, operetta kind of musical to the lighthearted comedy-with-songs style of piece to which Kern devoted most of his career. On the other hand, the most popular of his individual show songs have held a continuing and prominent place in the recital and recording repertoire. In recent decades, however, his work—again, most often the songs separated from their shows rather than whole shows—has been given detailed and appreciative attention by theatre writers and by performers, and his songs have been used as the material for several of the rash of compilation shows which have been seen on musical stages. This attention has come mainly in America where Kern has become perceived as ''the recognized father of the modern [American] musical theatre'' and ''the father of the American popular theater song.'' In an era when the kind of songwriting which he practiced, most particularly in the first 20 years of the century, has virtually ceased, a large number of his previously forgotten show numbers, which had been hidden behind those that became standards, have been brought out, and performed and recorded with an energy devoted to few other composers.

If tags such as those quoted, and the others which have been glibly attached to his works—notably *Show Boat* and the song ''They Didn't Believe Me''—have a simplistic and, therefore, debatable ring to them, they cannot mask the fact that Kern supplied the musical theatre, principally in America but also in Britain, with some of the happiest show songs of the 1910s and 1920s, helped produce one of the great romantic stage musicals of the time with his score to *Show Boat,* and continued, virtually to the end of his life to give of his very best material in a way that so many other writers, after a handful of successes, have failed to do. To call him the ''father of the modern [American] musical'' is to do poor service both to those who preceded and those who were contemporary with him, but if a sole paternity had to be established, Kern would certainly have to be queueing for a blood test.

1911 **La Belle Paree** (Edward Madden, et al/Edgar Smith) Winter Garden Theater 20 March

1912 **The Red Petticoat** (ex- *Look Who's Here*) (Paul West/Rida Johnson Young) Daly's Theater 13 November

1913 **Oh, I Say!** (aka *Their Wedding Night*) (Harry B Smith/Sydney Blow, Douglas Hoare) Casino Theater 30 October

1915 **Ninety in the Shade** (H B Smith/Guy Bolton) Knickerbocker Theater 25 January

1915 **Rosy Rapture, the Pride of the Beauty Chorus** (w Herman Darewski, John Crook/''F W Mark'' (E V Lucas)/J M Barrie) Duke of York's Theatre, London 22 March

1915 **Nobody Home** (Paul Rubens ad Bolton) Princess Theater 20 April

1915 **Cousin Lucy** (Schuyler Greene/Charles Klein) Cohan Theater 29 August

1915 **Miss Information** (Paul Dickey, Charles W Goddard) Cohan Theater 5 October

1915 **Very Good Eddie** (Greene/Philip Bartholomae, Bolton) Princess Theater 23 December

1916 **Theodore & Co** (w Ivor Novello/Adrian Ross, Clifford Grey/H M Harwood, George Grossmith) Gaiety Theatre, London 19 September

1916 **Girls Will Be Girls** (H B Smith/T Sidney) Lyric Theater, Philadelphia 20 November

1917 **Have a Heart** (P G Wodehouse/Bolton) Liberty Theater 11 January

1917 **Love o' Mike** revised *Girls Will Be Girls* Shubert Theater 15 January

1917 **Oh, Boy!** (Wodehouse/Bolton) Princess Theater 20 February

1917 **Houp-La** (Edgar A Woolf) Parsons' Theater, Hartford, Conn 25 June

1917 **Leave It to Jane** (Wodehouse/Bolton) Longacre Theater 28 August

1918 **Oh, Lady! Lady!!** (Wodehouse/Bolton) Princess Theater 1 February

1918 **Toot-Toot!** (Woolf, Berton Braley) Cohan Theater 11 March

1918 **Rock-a-Bye Baby** (Herbert Reynolds/Woolf, Margaret Mayo) Astor Theater 22 May

1918 **Head Over Heels** (Woolf) George M Cohan Theater 29 August

1919 **She's a Good Fellow** (ex- *A New Girl*) (Anne Caldwell) Globe Theater 5 May

1919 **Zip Goes a Million** (B G De Sylva/Bolton) Worcester Theater, Worcester, Mass 8 December

1920 **The Night Boat** (Caldwell) Liberty Theater 2 February

1920 **Sally** (Clifford Grey/Bolton) New Amsterdam Theater 21 December

1921 **Good Morning, Dearie** (Caldwell) Globe Theater 1 November

1922 **The Cabaret Girl** (Wodehouse/George Grossmith) Winter Garden Theatre, London 19 September

1922 **The Bunch and Judy** (Caldwell, Hugh Ford) Globe Theater 28 November

1923 **The Beauty Prize** (Wodehouse/Grossmith) Winter Garden Theatre, London 5 September

1923 **Stepping Stones** (Caldwell, R H Burnside) Globe Theater 6 November

1924 **Sitting Pretty** (Wodehouse/Bolton) Fulton Theater 8 April

1924 **Dear Sir** (Howard Dietz/Edgar Selwyn) Times Square Theater 23 September

1925 **Sunny** (Hammerstein, Otto Harbach) New Amsterdam Theater 22 September

1925 **The City Chap** (Caldwell/James Montgomery) Liberty Theater 26 October

1926 **Criss Cross** (Caldwell, Harbach) Globe Theater 12 October

1927 **Lucky** (Harbach, Bert Kalmar) New Amsterdam Theater 22 March

1927 **Show Boat** (Oscar Hammerstein) Ziegfeld Theater 27 December

1928 **Blue Eyes** (Graham John/Bolton) Piccadilly Theatre, London 27 April

1929 **Sweet Adeline** (Hammerstein) Hammerstein's Theater 3 September

1931 **The Cat and the Fiddle** (Harbach) Globe Theater 15 October

1932 **Music in the Air** (Hammerstein) Alvin Theater 8 November

1933 **Roberta** (Harbach) New Amsterdam Theater 18 November

1934 **Three Sisters** (Hammerstein) Theatre Royal, Drury Lane, London 9 April

1938 **Gentlemen Unafraid** (Hammerstein, Harbach) Municipal Opera, St Louis 3 June

1939 **Very Warm for May** (Hammerstein) Alvin Theater 17 November

Biographies: Bordman, G: *Jerome Kern* (OUP, New York, 1980), Lamb, A: *Jerome Kern in Edwardian England* (ISAM, City University of New York, 1985); Literature: Suskin, S: *Berlin, Kern, Rodgers, Hart, and Hammerstein: A Complete Song Catalogue* (McFarland, Jefferson, NC, 1990)

KÉROUL, Henri [QUEYROUL, Henry Alexis Antoine Simon] (b Corte, Corsica, 9 February 1854; d Paris, 14 April 1921).

The successful author of many Parisian songs, libretti and plays, Kéroul confined his musical-theatre work largely to the early part of his career, during which he collaborated with a half-dozen different composers on as many works, and turned out amongst them two pretty sizeable hits. *L'Oncle Célestin,* a lively vaudeville with a score by Audran, had a great Parisian success through 150 performances in its first season and subsequently went round the world, whilst *Cousin-Cousine,* a collaboration with composer Gaston Serpette and, like the earlier success, with co-librettist Maurice Ordonneau, also had an international career following a 90-performance Paris run. His *L'Élève de Conservatoire,* a vehicle for star soubrette Mily-Meyer, once again had an agreeable career but, at the other end of the scale, his earliest musical effort *Le Sosie* was an 18-night flop, a rather tasteless piece called *Les Colles des femmes* folded in 36 performances at the Menus-Plaisirs and a disappointing collaboration with Varney on *La Belle Épicière* also failed. After one further attempt, Kéroul abandoned the musical theatre for more than 20 years, during which period he turned out a number of highly successful plays, notably in a long collaboration with Albert Barré.

Several of these plays proved the meat for other men's musicals. Kéroul and Barré's 1904 Paris hit *Une nuit de noces* became the British play *Oh, I Say!* (ad Sidney Blow, Douglas Hoare), which was made up into a musical under the same name (Casino Theater, 1913, music by Jerome Kern, aka *Their Wedding Night*) in America, as *Telling the Tale* (Ambassadors Theatre, 1918, music by Philip Braham) in Britain, and as *La Supermoglie* (music by G F Checcacci, Teatro Fossati, Milan 13 January 1920) in Italy. The pair's *Le Portrait de ma tante* became *Léni néni* in the hands of Hungarian adapter Jenő Heltai and composer Zsigmond Vincze (Magyar Színház 2 May 1914), whilst Paul Lincke's Berlin musical *Ihr Sechs-Uhr Onkel* (w Alfred Schönfeld/Jean Kren, Thalia Theater 15 August 1907) also allowed that it was based on an unidentified Kéroul and Barré work.

Apart from concocting a festive season féerie for the Châtelet in 1907, the Kéroul and Barré combination collaborated on just one musical piece during their partnership, the libretto for *Les Maris de Ginette,* an unpretentious piece which, with a score by Félix Fourdrain and Mariette Sully starring, played successfully at the Théâtre Apollo in 1916–17.

Kéroul subsequently had some success as an author of early silent film scenarios.

1879 **La Sarbacane** (Châtau) 1 act Scala 30 August

Plate 202. **Henri Kéroul** *and Albert Barré's* Une nuit de noces *made up into the musical* Telling the Tale *in London. Marie Blanche starred as Sidonie de Matisse and her gentlemen included Arthur Margetson, Bruce Winston, C Denier Warren, Douglas Blore and Gerald Kirby.*

1887 **Le Sosie** (Raoul Pugno/w Albin Valabrègue) Théâtre des Bouffes-Parisiens 8 October

1891 **L'Oncle Célestin** (Edmond Audran/w Maurice Ordonneau) Théâtre des Menus-Plaisirs 24 March

1893 **Les Colles des femmes** (Louis Ganne/w Adolphe Jaime) Théâtre des Menus-Plaisirs 29 September

1893 **Cousin-Cousine** (Gaston Serpette/w Ordonneau) Théâtre des Folies-Dramatiques 23 December

1894 **L'Élève de Conservatoire** (Léopold de Wenzel/w Paul Burani) Théâtre des Menus-Plaisirs 29 November

1895 **La Belle Épicière** (Louis Varney/w Pierre Decourcelle) Théâtre des Bouffes-Parisiens 16 November

1896 **La Noce de Grivolet** (Marius Carman/w Charles Raymond) Théâtre Déjazet 24 October

1907 **La Princesse Sans-Gêne** (Marius Baggers/w Albert Barré) Théâtre du Châtelet 16 November

1916 **Les Maris de Ginette** (Félix Fourdrain/w Barré) Théâtre Apollo 18 November

KERT, Larry [KERT, Frederick Lawrence] (b Los Angeles, 5 December 1930; d New York, 5 June 1991).

After early experience as a child actor, stuntman and stand-in in films (he doubled for Roddy McDowell in *Lassie Come Home*), in variety, in revue and in stock companies, Kert made his first Broadway appearances in the revues *Tickets Please* (1950) and *John Murray Anderson's Almanac* (1953). After the *Ziegfeld Follies of 1956* closed pre-Broadway, he took over a supporting part in *Mr Wonderful* (1956) before winning his one memorable Broadway creation as Tony, the West Side Romeo of *West Side Story* (''Maria,'' ''Something's Coming,'' ''Tonight''). He subsequently appeared regionally in Menotti's *The Medium* and *The Telephone,* in *The Merry Widow* and in his *West Side Story* role, and after John Kander's maiden musical, *A Family Affair* (1962, Gerry Seigel), had closed its brief run, he replaced

Elliot Gould as the young ''hero'' of *I Can Get It for You Wholesale* (1962).

Kert suffered a second out-of-town closure in *Holly Golightly* (1966), the musical version of *Breakfast at Tiffany's,* and a quick Broadway flop in *La Strada* (1969, Mario), in between which he spent a period playing the role of Cliff in Broadway's *Cabaret.* He similarly took over, this time very soon after the show's opening, in the central part of Robert in *Company* (1970), a role which he subsequently played in London's production of the show (1972). He appeared on tour in *Gentlemen of Verona* (Proteus), in *Music! Music!, Sugar, Irma la Douce* and *La Cage aux Folles* (Georges), succeeded David Kernan in the cast of the compilation show *Side by Side by Sondheim* and played the role of Al Jolson in a series of attempts to put together a biomusical about *Joley* (1979 aka *Al Jolson Tonight,* 1978) which stopped short of Broadway. In 1980 he appeared at off-Broadway's Theater de Lys in the short-lived *Changes,* and in 1986, for the last time on Broadway, in another failure, *Rags.* He was again seen in the off-Broadway piece *The Rise of David Levinsky* before his final illness.

DIE KEUSCHE BARBARA Operette in 3 acts by Rudolf Bernauer and Leopold Jacobson. Music by Oskar Nedbal. Theater Weinberge, Prague, 14 September 1910.

Nedbal's first Operette was a piece set in England in the ''Gainsborough period,'' and the virtuous Barbara was little Miss Knox, daughter of the landlord of the alehouse ''Zur keuschen Barbara'' who is—like W S Gilbert's Phyllis—sighed over by the whole House of Lords. Most unoperettically, she weds her preferred Lord Halifax by the end of Act I, but for all the wrong reasons. Halifax is the promoter of a law by which a gentleman who compromises a lady must wed her, and he is accidentally caught in his own clauses. It takes two more acts for the marriage to turn from forced to full-blooded, thanks to the interference of Halifax's tenant, the House of Commonser Pittifox, who suspects the Lord of writing suggestive letters to his wife, Mabel. Pittifox's young niece, Kitty, and her sailorboy Jony [*sic*] Burns get mixed up in the resulting moral and amorous misunderstandings, all of which are happily cleared up for the final curtain.

Halifax rendered a waltz on morals (''Mein Grossvater in seiner Jugend'') and a march song with a sextet of supporting Lords (''Weib den braven Mann verlässt''), Barbara a not-very-English mazurka (''Ich zugle meine Leidenschaft'') and the comic pair duetted to the strains of the waltz, the minuet, the cancan, the cakewalk and the maxixe.

First produced in Prague, *Die keusche Barbara* was quickly picked up by Wilhelm Karczag for the Raimundtheater where, with Betty Fischer, Otto Storm, Ernst Tautenhayn and Franz Glawatsch starring and the composer conducting, it was played for 33 performances. After the success of Nedbal's later *Polenblut,* it was also produced in Hungary (ad Zsolt Harsányi) but, if its runs were generally limited, its several productions in central Europe nevertheless marked Nedbal out as a promising writer.

Germany: ?1911; Austria: Raimundtheater 7 October 1911; Hungary: Budai Színkör *Az Erénycsősz* 22 April 1921

DIE KEUSCHE SUSANNE Operette in 3 acts by Georg Okonkowski adapted from the farce *Fils à papa* by Antony Mars and Maurice Desvallières. Lyrics by Alfred Schönfeld. Music by Jean Gilbert. Wilhelm-Theater, Magdeburg, 26 February 1910; Neues Operetten-Theater, Berlin, 6 August 1911.

One of the outstanding and outstandingly successful shows of its era, *Die keusche Susanne* was a germanicized version of a Parisian Palais-Royal vaudeville set with a score of sparkling dance-and-song music by German composer Jean Gilbert. Very serious commentators and writers of German program copy purport to see in its text a ''satire of middle-class values in France'' (and, by transfer, Germany or anywhere else), but this musicalized version of *Fils à papa* is, of course, nothing but a rattling good sex comedy which its composer fitted out with delightful melodies well adapted to the more popular and enduring dance rhythms of the day.

Apparently model papa des Aubrais strictly refuses to allow his daughter Jacqueline to wed the womanizing René Boislurette, yet he himself—unbeknown to all—has the habit of sneaking off for jolly, disguised evenings in the company of various ladies at the Moulin-Rouge. Unfortunately, on the particular occasion involved in this play, he there encounters not only Jacqueline, out on the town with René, but also his son Hubert in the company of the advertisedly ''virtuous'' Susanne Pomarel, the wife of a provincial friend. A panoply of disguises and hidden identities entwine their way through an action which hots up dangerously when Monsieur Pomarel, egged on by the jealous moral crusader Charencey, brings in the police, only to discover that des Aubrais's partner of that evening is . . . Madame Charencey. The next morning mutual interest ensures that everything is ''forgotten,'' René and Jacqueline are allowed to become engaged, Pomarel is reassured of his wife's modesty, and Madame des Aubrais—who never got out of the house—remains sweetly unaware of the fact that her children clearly, if secretly, take after their father.

The 14-piece score was a lively affair, topped by the waltz ''Wenn die Füsschen sie heben und schweben'' for Jacqueline and René and by a march duo for Aubrais and Hubert, ''Wenn der Vater mit dem Sohne auf den Bummel geht,'' both of which duly became extremely popular outside the show as well as in it.

Die keusche Susanne was a great success on its initial showing at Magdeburg, and it quickly took its first steps onwards in what was to be a long and high-profile international career. The earliest foreign production—mounted before the show had even made its way to Berlin's Neues Operetten Theater—was Sigmund Eibenschütz's Austrian one, at the Carltheater, which starred Mizzi Zwerenz as Susanne with Karl Blasel as her husband, Richard Waldemar as the naughty des Aubrais, handsome Josef König and Olga Barco-Frank as his children and Willi Strehl as the tenor lieutenant. After a first run of 128 performances, straddling the summer break, the show was held in the repertoire for the next two seasons. During this time Budapest welcomed Juci Lábass as *Az artátlan Zsuzsi.*

The musical's most ringing success of this period, however, came in Britain. Produced by Philip Michael Faraday, the happy London co-producer of *The Chocolate Soldier,* in a version by Frederick Fenn and Arthur Wimperis, it swapped its slightly sexy title for the less apt *The Girl in the Taxi,* the title used for the American production of the source play. The reference was to Madame Charencey (now called Charcot) whom the Baron Dauvray [*sic*] encounters when they share a taxi to the Restaurant ''Jeunesse Dorée'' (no longer the Moulin-Rouge), but the change in name was really an attempt to capitalize on the major London success of the recent *The Girl in the Train,* a more apt title for Fall's *Die geschiedene Frau,* with another ''girl-y'' title. Yvonne Arnaud (Suzanne), ex-D'Oyly Carte comic C Herbert Workman (Pomarel), Arthur Playfair (Dauvray), Amy Augarde (Mme Dauvray) and Alec Fraser (René) were the name artists in a production which kept pretty close to the original and which scored an immense success with its fun, its songs—notably ''Waltzing'' (''Wenn die Füsschen'')—and its tangos and one-steps, and which played for 385 performances in a year at London's Lyric Theatre.

The Girl in the Taxi was sent out in triplicate on the road, and returned quickly to London (1 November 1913) following the failure of Straus's *Love and Laughter* for another six weeks at the Lyric Theatre, and again in 1915—in spite of the virtual ban on all German shows—for another splendid run of 155 performances at the Garrick (23 January), the New and the Criterion. This series of repeats brought its record to a total of nearly six hundred metropolitan performances in two and a half years, a figure which ranked it alongside *The Chocolate Soldier* as the most successful imported show of the decade. When Australia took in the same version of *The Girl in the Taxi* two years later it found a similar welcome. A cast headed by Maggie Jarvis (Suzanne), Dorothy Brunton (Jacqueline), Millie Engler (Delphine), W H Rawlins (Dauvray) and Workman in his London role totted up 60 consecutive Sydney performances—one of the best musical-comedy records of the time—before the show went on to Melbourne (Her Majesty's Theatre 24 October 1914) and to a number of return visits to both cities and others further afield over the following years.

America first saw *Die keusche Susanne* in the original German, and when it was produced at New York's Irving Place Theater in 1911, with Adolf Kühns and Emma Malkowska featured, it gathered rave notices. The following year A H Woods produced his rather-different-from-the-English version of the show (ad Harry and Robert B Smith) which he entitled *Modest Suzanne* (the *Girl in the Taxi* title having, of course, been preempted on Broadway). Sallie Fisher starred as Suzanne and a couple of Jean Schwartz numbers, ''The Tangolango Tap'' and ''I Would Like to See the Peaches,'' were tacked into the score. What remained of the show's original Palais-Royal gaiety was found ''vulgar'' and ''debauched''—though the music was spared such critical quiverings—and it still flopped in 24 Broadway performances.

France, on the other hand, took a predictably distinct and unprudish liking to *La Chaste Suzanne,* a liking which ultimately outstripped even London's enthusiasm. The show was first mounted at Lyon, in a version by the authors of the original play, under the management and direction of Montcharmont, the producer and agent who had his French finger firmly on central Europe's output. Montcharmont then sold it briskly to Alphonse Franck, Paris's *Veuve joyeuse* producer, for his Théâtre Apollo. With little-known American actress Bella Atkins (Suzanne) featured alongside Tréville (des Aubrais), *Veuve joyeuse* star Henri Defreyn (Hubert) and the future Opéra-Comique tenor Edmond Tirmont (René), and with Josef Szulc at the baton, the show had a stunning premiere with ''almost the entire score played twice, given the encores demanded for the songs and, above all, the dances,'' and a popular success which led to its being played 108 consecutive times as a first run. Thereafter it toured limitlessly, reappeared in Paris in 1913 (Théâtre Cluny), 1921 (Théâtre de l'Eden under the management of Léon Volterra, with Max Dearly starred), and at the Théâtre de la Gaîté-Lyrique in 1935, in 1945 and again in 1960 with manageress Germaine Roger starring as Suzanne. In the 30 years since, *La Chaste Suzanne* has remained an active item in the French repertoire—almost the only German musical comedy so to do—just as it has in the Spanish (*La casta Susanna*).

The success of *Die keusche Susanne* on the international stage was almost equaled by its cinematic success. A German film was issued in 1926 with Lillian Harvey and Willy Fritsch starred, and in 1937 André Berthommier made parallel French and English versions—the former starring Meg Lemonnier, Henri Garat and Raimu, the latter teaming Garat with the blonde bit of shrapnel that was Frances Day and with Lawrence Grossmith. Another, Spanish-language version was made in the Argentine, where Gilbert spent his last days, and further films appeared in France in 1950 (*La P'tite Femme du Moulin-Rouge*) and in 1951 (*La Chaste Suzanne,* with the voice of Mathé Altéry) and in Mexico.

Gilbert's son, Robert Gilbert, rewrote *Die keusche Susanne* in 1953 rather in the same way that Kollo junior had done with his father's most profitable pieces. He plucked the hit songs from Jean Gilbert's other shows—"Puppchen du bist mein Augenstern" from *Puppchen* became a duo for the Baron Conrad von Felsneck and Rosa Hintzmeier (as Aubrais and Mme Charency had become in a curious shift of national setting) and "Das haben die Mädchen so gerne" from *Autoliebchen* was a duo for René (who actually kept his first name) and Pauline (ex- Jacqueline)—squeezing out some of the original material in the process, and this altogether rather over-egged Neubearbeitung was republished as a fresh copyright. Which was, of course, the point of the exercise. No one preferred the new *keusche Susanne* to the old one.

Austria: Carltheater 18 March 1911; USA: Irving Place Theater (Ger) 12 April 1911, Liberty Theater *Modest Susanne* 1 January 1912; Hungary: Budai Színkör *Az artátlan Zsuzsi* 11 May 1912, Király Színház (Ger) May 1913; UK: Lyric Theatre *The Girl in the Taxi* 5 September 1912; France: Théâtre des Célestins, Lyon *La Chaste Susanne* 7 February 1913, Théâtre Apollo, Paris 29 March 1913; Australia: Her Majesty's Theatre, Sydney *The Girl in the Taxi* 8 August 1914

Films: Eichberg & Sturm 1926, André Berthommier 1937 (Fr), *The Girl in the Taxi* 1937 (Eng), *La Casta Susanna* (1944), (Fr) *La P'tite Femme du Moulin Rouge* 1950, *La Chaste Susanne* 1951, *El casto Susanna* 1952, etc

KEYS, Nelson [Waite] (b London, 7 August 1886; d London, 26 April 1939).

Principally known for his performances in revue, the diminutive and sometimes rather disagreeable comedian created several musical-comedy roles in the early part of his career. Amongst these were the small role of Bobby, the jockey, in *The Arcadians* in which he introduced the song "Back Your Fancy," originally intended for another artist; the comic little Lieutenant Makei, opposite Cicely Courtneidge, in The Mousmé; and the non-singing Ensign Pips in *Princess Caprice*—all three pieces produced under the Courtneidge management—as well as Lieutenant Skrydloff in Oscar Straus's unfortunate London musical *Love and Laughter.* He also took over as the out-on-the-town youngster Hubert des Aubrais in Phillip Michael Faraday's production of *The Girl in the Taxi.*

Keys's diminutive stature later made him a natural for the role of Eddie Kettle in the botched and brief London version of *Very Good Eddie* (1918), but thereafter he stuck to revue, and less prominently film, only returning to the West End musical stage for a period to play, in succession to Billy Merson, the part of Hard-Boiled Herman in the Drury Lane production of *Rose Marie* (1926).

Biography: Carstairs, J P: *Bunch* (Hurst & Blackett, London, 1941)

KID BOOTS Musical comedy of "Palm Beach and Golf" in 2 acts by William Anthony McGuire and Otto Harbach. Lyrics by Joseph McCarthy. Music by Harry Tierney. Earl Carroll Theater, New York, 31 December 1923.

Eddie Cantor starred in Florenz Ziegfeld's first musical comedy production since *Sally* in what was a patent attempt to repeat the formula of that show: the successful teaming of one star comedian and one blonde, dancing ingenue. The billing values, between the two shows, were about equal for if Cantor was a priori a bigger draw than Leon Errol, pretty little Mary Eaton, the principal dancer of the last *Ziegfeld Follies,* did not have the pull of a Marilyn[n] Miller. She got the same sized billing as Ziegfeld and Cantor, but they (and Ziegfeld first) were above the title, whilst she was blessed with a "with" prefix and followed underneath the title.

Cantor was featured as "Kid" Boots, a down-South golf-club caddy-chief who is into bootlegging and fixing golf balls (for a small sum) to help the undertalented defeat the over-practiced at this newly mass-popular sport. Unfortunately, his pal Tom Sterling (Harry Fender), the most accomplished golfer in the whole place, accidentally gets hold of one of Kid's doctored balls and uses it in his big match against the Champion of Hudson River Golf Club (Robert Barrat). Mary Eaton played Polly Pendleton, Tom's love interest and the daughter of sporting-goods manufacturer Herbert Pendleton (Paul Everton), whose business rivalry with fellow club member Peter Pillsbury (Robert Cummings) was another, parallel portion of the plot. Marie Callahan played Kid's girlfriend Jane Martin ("in charge of ladies' lockers"), Ethelind Terry was a glamorous soprano Carmen Mendoza, whilst Jobyna Howland played a lady doctor, Dr Josephine Fitch, whose main part in the proceedings was a pair of comical routines with the star: one in the club gymnasium, featuring some electrical treatment, and the other a golf lesson. There were also three principal dancers, not including Miss Eaton, and George Olsen and his orchestra to supply both the accompaniment and their own spot ("The Cocoanut Ball").

Harry Tierney and Joseph McCarthy, still floundering somewhat in trying to repeat the success and attractions of the score of *Irene,* didn't do much better for *Kid Boots* than they had for the short-lived *Up She Goes* and *Glory* the previous year. The juveniles duetted "If Your

Heart's in the Game,'' whilst Cantor advised ''Keep Your Eye on the Ball,'' delivered a ''Rain Song'' and topped up the not terribly impressive basic score with a winning interpolation in ''Dinah'' (Joe Young, Harry Akst, Sam Lewis). ''Dinah (is there anyone finah . . .)'' gave *Kid Boots* a genuine hit which would go on to be liberally recorded and performed outside the show, used in two films, and become the theme song of popular vocalist Dinah Shore.

Ziegfeld's production was mounted in picturesque style, with its lavish sets depicting scenes of the Floridean golf club's putting green, clubhouse, trophy room (''the tarpon in this scene caught at Palm Beach by Miss Billie Burke-Ziegfeld'') and the final Cocoanut Ball, but Cantor remained the main attraction. He clowned his way through the action in what was thought his ''best performance to date'' without the aid of his usual blackface makeup, until he arrived at the moment where he was due to do what was little more than his ''act.'' A timely explosion then sufficed to get him into smut-soiled blackface. Largely thanks to its star, *Kid Boots* proved to have sufficient mainly comical attractions to last through a whole season and it eventually ran up a total of 482 Broadway performances before going on the road.

An English production, sponsored by Grossmith and Malone as the latest in their series of American musical shows at the Winter Garden Theatre, starred their enormously popular regular comedian, Leslie Henson, in Cantor's role. The score was again topped up, this time by Vivian Ellis, but *Kid Boots* proved to have few of the attractions of the Winter Garden's recent imports or virtual imports: Kern's *Sally, The Cabaret Girl* and *The Beauty Prize,* Gershwin's *Primrose* or even *Tell Me More!* It dwindled away in 163 performances, effectively putting Grossmith out of the producing business.

In Australia, George Gee took the show's title role alongside Josie Melville (Polly), George Vollaire (Tom), Fiole Allen (Jane) and Jean Newcombe (Dr Fitch) through 11 weeks in Sydney and two months in Melbourne (Her Majesty's Theatre 25 June 1925).

In 1926 Cantor ventured into films for the first time to put *Kid Boots* on celluloid. Clara Bow (now called Clara), Billie Dove (Eleanor), and Lawrence Gray as Tom supported.

Australia: Her Majesty's Theatre, Sydney 4 April 1925; UK: Winter Garden Theatre 2 February 1926

Film: Paramount 1926

KIDD, Michael [GREENWALD, Milton] (b New York, 12 August 1919). Choreographer in Broadway's peak postwar years.

Kidd danced with Ballet Caravan, the Eugene Loring Dancers and, between 1942 and 1947 as a member of the Ballet Theatre, with whom he created a principal role in *Fancy Free,* latterly taking some choreographic assignments in addition to performing. He made his Broadway debut as a choreographer with *Finian's Rainbow* (1947), and continued with the short-lived college musical *Hold It!* (1948), *Love Life* (1948), and *Arms and the Girl* (1950) before creating the dances for the original production of *Guys and Dolls* (1950) and for *Can-Can* (1953) with its Montmartre dances and its spectacular Garden of Eden ballet sequence.

For the successful production of *L'il Abner* (1956) he turned both producer and director, and he doubled again as director and choreographer on his three subsequent shows: the comical western *Destry Rides Again,* the Lucille Ball vehicle *Wildcat* and the less successful *Subways Are for Sleeping.* Latterly, however, he failed to find the success of the best of his earlier pieces and although *Here's Love* had both charm and a year's run, *Ben Franklin in Paris* (director and co-producer), *Skyscraper, Holly Golightly, The Rothschilds, Cyrano* and the 1974 revival of *Good News* were less than hits. In 1993 he directed the musical version of *The Goodbye Girl* on Broadway.

His Broadway record and its five accompanying Tony Awards (*Finian's Rainbow, Guys and Dolls, Can-Can, Li'l Abner, Destry Rides Again*) were equaled only by his success in the cinema where he choreographed the screen versions of *Where's Charley?* and *The Band Wagon,* the memorably masculine routines of *Seven Brides for Seven Brothers, Guys and Dolls* and *Hello, Dolly!*

Kidd was seen as an actor—playing the role of a choreographer—in the film *Smile.*

KIEFERT, Carl Johann (b Cologne, 10 May 1855; d Eastergate, Bognor Regis, 26 November 1937). The man who made the sound of the British theatre orchestra of the Victorian and Edwardian musical comedy.

Son of a military bandmaster and originally a 'cellist, the German-born Kiefert visited London in 1880 as a member of the Saxe-Meiningen court orchestra for a series of performances at the Theatre Royal, Drury Lane. He remained in Britain thereafter, working with Richter's orchestra, as an arranger and from 1892 as conductor at the Prince of Wales Theatre, and became an important if low-profile contributor to the success of the British musical comedy during the 1890s and 1900s. Osmond Carr, then Lionel Monckton, and subsequently almost all of the principal musical-comedy composers of the time confided their theatre scores to him for orchestration and, as a result, he set the tone and style for the sound of theatre music of the era. Such was his popularity that eventually all the theatre orchestras of London began to sound the same, because their music had been arranged and orchestrated either by Kiefert himself or else by others who copied his effective, classic if, perhaps, unadventurous style.

Carr also got Kiefert some of his first important erngagements as a conductor, and he led the orchestra for that composer's *Morocco Bound* (1893), *Go-Bang* (1894) and *His Excellency* (1894) before taking up the baton at Daly's Theatre for *An Artist's Model* (1895), at the Court Theatre for *All Abroad* (1896) and *The Belle of Cairo* (1896), and joining Tom Davis as the original conductor and orchestrator of *Florodora* (1899). Amongst a series of end-to-end assignments, he also led the orchestra for Stuart's *The School Girl* (1903), joined Charles Frohman as musical director for *The Catch of the Season* (1904), *Bluebell in Fairyland* (1905) and *The Beauty of Bath* (1906), and moved to the Gaiety to conduct a third Leslie Stuart musical, *Havana* (1908). After *A Persian Princess* (1909), he succeeded Ivan Caryll as conductor of *Our Miss Gibbs* (1909), and remained with George Edwardes to be the initial conductor/orchestrator of *The Quaker Girl* (1910), *The Dancing Mistress* (1911) and *The Girl from Utah* (1912). In 1915 he went to America to supervise and conduct the American production of *Sybil,* and in the 1920s his name was still appearing on Broadway bills as an arranger (*Honeydew, Suzette, The Chiffon Girl*).

Beyond his conducting and orchestrating activities, Kiefert was one of the most popular arrangers of published dance music over many years. He also ventured from time to time as a composer, initially with single songs for use in such touring musicals as *A Village Venus* (1895), *A Merry Madcap* (1896) and *The Dandy Detective* (1898), and then with two scores, also for the road, but which nevertheless found considerable success. *The Ballet Girl* (with additional numbers by Stuart) had two good tours and was produced in America by E E Rice, whilst *The Gay Grisette,* written with George Dance, toured Britain for many years and won a number of overseas productions.

1897 **The Ballet Girl** (James T Tanner/Adrian Ross) Grand Theatre, Wolverhampton 15 March

1898 **The Gay Grisette** (George Dance) Theatre Royal, Bradford 1 August

1901 **Hidenseek** (w others/Arthur Eliot, Edward Granville) Globe Theatre 10 December

1907 **The Zuyder Zee** (comp and arr/W H Risque) 1 act London Hippodrome 24 June

1907 **Honeyland** (F Neville Piggot) 1 act London Hippodrome 24 December

KIEPURA, Jan (b Sonowicz, Poland, 6 May 1902; d Rye, NY, 15 August 1966). Film and stage tenor, often in tandem with his wife.

Kiepura spent the early part of his career in opera in Poland, Austria, Italy and America before appearing in 1943 opposite his wife, Marta Eggerth, as Danilo in a revival of *The Merry Widow* at New York's Majestic Theater. He followed up on Broadway, again with his wife, in a romantic Chopin pastiche, *Polonaise* (1945, General Thaddeus Kosciusko), as Edwin to her Sylva in a souped-up *Princesse Csárdás* in Paris (Théâtre de Paris, 1950), as the Tauber-touched heroes of *Der Zarewitsch* (1954) and *Paganini* (1956) at Vienna's Raimundtheater, and repeated his Danilo to Eggerth's *Merry Widow* in London in 1955.

In spite of limited acting talents, Kiepura also played in films in Austria (*Zauber der Bohème*), Britain (*Farewell to Love, My Song for You, Be Mine Tonight*), America (*Give Us This Night*) and Italy (*Her Wonderful Lie*).

KILEY, Richard [Paul] (b Chicago, 31 March 1922; d Warwick, RI, 5 March 1999). One of the most impressive actor-vocalists of the postwar Broadway stage, only rarely served with winning roles.

After an early career in radio, in stock and in touring plays (Stanley Kowalski in the national tour of *A Streetcar Named Desire*), and an appearance on Broadway in Shaw's *Misalliance,* Kiley had his first musical role in the road-closing *A Month of Sundays* (1951, Joe Ross). He won his first musical success soon after when he was cast in the part of the Caliph in *Kismet* (1953), in which he created "And This Is My Beloved," "Stranger in Paradise" and "Night of My Nights."

After several years of non-musical assignments he returned to the musical stage in 1959 to play the role of hero Tom Baxter, paired with Gwen Verdon, in the music-hall mystery musical *Redhead* (Broadway and tour, Tony Award). He then appeared opposite Diahann Carroll as David Baxter, the hero of *No Strings* (1962), introducing "The Sweetest Sounds" with his co-star; took over from Craig Stevens as the straight man in Meredith Willson's Santa Claus musical *Here's Love* (1963); and played alongside Buddy Hackett as Sam the Shpieler in *I Had a Ball* (1964) before creating his second major musical role as Don Quixote in *Man of La Mancha* (Tony Award), singing "The Impossible Dream" and "Man of La Mancha" into the standards list.

He subsequently played the part of Julius Caesar in a musical version of Shaw's *Caesar and Cleopatra, Her First Roman* (1968), and repeated his *Man of La Mancha* role in a revival of the show in London (1969). Thereafter, however, Broadway gave him no further new musical roles. He played the aviator in the Lerner and Loewe musical film of *The Little Prince* (1975), appeared as Peter Stuyvesant in a season of *Knickerbocker Holiday* at Town Hall (1977), reprised his *Man of La Mancha* role at the Vivian Beaumont Theater in 1972 and again in a 1977 revival which toured the following year, and ap-

Plate 203. **The King and I.** *Hayley Mills and Tony Marinyo in the title roles of John Frost's Australian revival.*

peared in the Michel Legrand/Sheldon Harnick musical version of Dickens's *A Christmas Carol* (1981) outside New York, but played thereafter mostly in non-musical productions.

THE KING AND I Musical play in 2 acts by Oscar Hammerstein II based on Margaret Landon's novel *Anna and the King of Siam.* Music by Richard Rodgers. St James Theater, New York, 29 March 1951.

The historical tale of the British governess Mrs Anna Leonowens and her 19th-century adventures in the differently civilized land of Siam had been metamorphosed—in a suitably romanticized form—into a successful novel and into a Hollywood film (1946) in which Rex Harrison starred as the King of Siam, Irene Dunne as Mrs Leonowens and Linda Darnell as the erring royal wife, before Gertrude Lawrence approached Rodgers and Hammerstein, the reigning monarchs of the musical stage, with the suggestion that the tale be adapted into a musical play with the role of Mrs Leonowens tailored to suit her own talents. The show that resulted followed the lines of the film screenplay, although it eventually developed a lighter touch to its warmly sentimental plot, a touch which was perhaps not unconnected with its star's natural comedic style.

The no-nonsense, widowed Anna (Miss Lawrence) goes to Siam as governess to the royal household of a king (Yul Brynner) who is tentatively willing to adapt his and his country's ways to Western values. He allows himself to be tactfully guided in this ''progress'' by the governess, but the wild, proud ways of traditional kinghood inevitably assert themselves from time to time and it is the morally hidebound Anna who is unable to understand his values when he orders the execution of a Burmese emissary, Lun Tha (Larry Douglas), who has been planning to run away with one of the royal concubines (Doretta Morrow). The warm personal relationship between the willing but still royal King and the rather less flexible Anna seems damaged, but she returns to him as he lies on his deathbed and promises to remain at the side of his young son as the boy makes his first steps in what will, under the influence of Anna's teachings, be a new style of rule in Siam.

The score, laid out rather differently from that of the three earlier Rodgers and Hammerstein successes, *Oklahoma!, Carousel* and *South Pacific,* reflected the casting. Whereas the authors' heroines in the first two pieces had been light soprano ingenues or, in *South Pacific,* a soubrette, here they had as a leading lady a light-comedy actress with romantic possibilities and not much of a voice. They supplied her with vocally limited, charming songs: the chin-up "I Whistle a Happy Tune," the wistful "Hello, Young Lovers," the almost coy invitation to the King "Shall We Dance?" and, added on the road to town with the express intention of lightening the mood of the piece, a children-and-chorus number "Getting to Know You," fabricated from a cutout melody from *South Pacific.* The King's role, too, was vocally truncated for a Brynner who semi-talked his way through "A Puzzlement," and the lyrical values of the piece were sidewound into the supporting parts. The ill-fated romance between Tuptim and Lun Tha was illustrated by two thoroughly sentimental soprano/tenor duets ("We Kiss in a Shadow" and the pre-Broadway addition "I Have Dreamed") which, by their arioso nature and plot placing, held more of the musical-dramatic in them than the writers had previously used, and Lady Thiang (Dorothy Sarnoff), the King's devoted chief wife, hymned her understanding of her lord in the mezzo-soprano "Something Wonderful," perhaps the most beautifully worded of the series of big songs for big ladies' voices with which Rodgers and Hammerstein followed *Carousel*'s "You'll Never Walk Alone."

The dance element of the show, in line with its strongly book-based nature, was limited, but it nevertheless threw up one of the evening's highlights. Introduced in the 19th-century variety-musical manner as "an entertainment for the king," it took the form of a dance-play, "The Small House of Uncle Thomas," which related in Eastern terms the tale of *Uncle Tom's Cabin:* a meaningful story about a cruel despot whose slave runs away. Jerome Robbins's dance piece, assisted by a sincerely humorous narration, made its serious point whilst impressing both with its beauty and its fun. Robbins and director John van Druten also made a major effect with the simply staged presentation of the King's children ("The March of the Siamese Children") in a classic piece of winning kiddie display.

The King and I was an enormous Broadway success, giving Miss Lawrence her most outstanding musical-comedy role and launching Brynner (who had won the part at audition only after Rex Harrison and Alfred Drake had been sounded out) as a star. Sadly, Miss Lawrence was not to profit from her winning idea. Ill with cancer, she died during the show's run and, having already been temporarily substituted by Celeste Holm, was succeeded by Rodgers's lady friend, Constance Carpenter, as the show ran on to a 1,246 performance record in over three years. The rich-voiced Drake also took a brief turn at the role of the King, playing—and singing—it in rather a different style from Brynner.

Whilst *The King and I* ran on on Broadway, a London production was mounted at the Theatre Royal, Drury Lane, again under the management of the authors, with van Druten reproducing his Broadway direction, prematurely blocked in by a stage manager. Herbert Lom (King) and Valerie Hobson (Anna) starred, with Muriel Smith as a memorable Lady Thiang, and Drury Lane, which had already hosted extended runs of *Oklahoma!, Carousel* and *South Pacific,* continued to be the home away from home of the Rodgers and Hammerstein opus for a further 926 performances, bringing the pair's tenancy at London's famous house to nearly a decade. London's success was ultimately repeated in Australia, but only after that country's chief producing house, J C Williamson Ltd, had turned the show down, put off by the exhausting prospect of organizing multiple casts of children. Garnet Carroll took up the rights and staged the show—10 years after its Broadway premiere—and, with Jeff Warren and Sheila Bradley starring, scored a major hit through nearly seven months in Melbourne and, with Susan Swinford as Anna, four more in Sydney (Tivoli 17 July 1963).

In the meantime, thanks to a particularly successful 1956 film version which used almost the whole original score without interpolations, *The King and I* had already become an integral part of the international musical-show bank of memories and song standards. The filmed version saw Brynner repeat his stage role opposite an ideally cast Deborah Kerr (dubbed by Marni Nixon) and, if the lyric roles were less well served, the two stars gave memorable performances which helped to disseminate *The King and I* and its songs around the world. However, like other musicals of the period, it received only few and delayed productions in Europe. Germany, where the show has since gained some currency, was the first to venture its version, in 1966, whilst the Belgian Opéra Royal de Wallonie, whose management in recent decades followed a policy of presenting American musicals in the French language, initiated *Le Roi et moi* as late as 1985, with opérette diva Nicole Broissin starred as Anna. Like its source book and the original film, however, stage and screen versions of *The King and I* are banned in Thailand.

The King and I has maintained a high profile in the basic repertoire and on English-speaking stages in the decades since its production, and it has been given several major revivals. New York's City Center hosted reprises in 1960, 1963 and 1968, the Music Theater of Lincoln Center produced the piece in 1964 with opera star Risë Stevens as Anna, whilst in London a 1973 revival featured television detective Peter Wyngarde as a stirring King (260 performances). However, the show's most substantial revival of these years owed its existence to Brynner who, through a subsequent film and stage career, never shook off the image or the role of the King of Siam. In 1977 he returned to Broadway in a *King and I* which had undoubtedly reversed the show's original hierarchy of star values, with Brynner's King now both very much the centerpiece of the attention and also a much broader and barnstorming characterization. He trouped the show with enormous success through America, to London's Palladium (where the adept casting of Virginia McKenna as Anna went a long way towards reestablishing the old balance) and finally back to Broadway where he appeared for a second season (7 January 1985) shortly before his death.

One of the finest musical plays of its period, *The King and I* has, ironically, profited by being constructed with sympathetic roles at its heart for two star actors-who-sing-only-a-bit. Its indelible connection with the performance of Brynner, proved by no means to have hamstrung its continuing production prospects around the world, for *King and I* productions continued legion in the last years of the 20th century. In 1990 former ballet superstar Rudolf Nureyev toured America in the role of the King without making it to Broadway, and a 1991 British tour and Sadler's Wells season starred Japan's Koshiro Matsumoto and Susan Hampshire. In 1991–92 Australia also saw *The King and I* afresh when John Frost mounted a spectacular new production with Hayley Mills starred as Anna and Tony Marinyo as the King with such notable success that in 1996 this much praised production was restaged on Broadway where, with Donna Murphy and Lou Diamond Phillips starred (Neil Simon Theater 11 April), it proved still to have every bit as much public appeal as in it Brynner days. When Broadway had finished with it, it progressed to London's vast Dominion Theatre (3 May 2000) with Elaine Paige starred alongside Jason Scott Lee. From being a role written originally to feature a comedienne with a wisp of a voice, the part of Anna Leonowens had progressed, half a century on, to being the property of two of the musical-theatre's most outstanding vocalists.

In 1999 the show so memorably filmed nearly half a century earlier was refilmed. In line with the two-dimensional nature of the 1990s animated-screen-to-stage shows, this one went the other way. In a version which admitted only to being ''based on'' the musical, Anna and the King were made into cartoon characters. Christiane Noll and Martin Vidnovic were the cartoon voices.

In 1874 (20 November), the real-life Mrs Leonowens had presented herself at New York's YMCA, recounting her story ''in a quiet but firm voice'' to an audience who had paid 50 cents apiece to hear her. 125 years later, she had the stereophonic voice of Barbra Streisand and worldwide audiences coughing up millions of dollars, euros and yen to see her. That was some progress.

UK: Theatre Royal, Drury Lane 8 October 1953; Australia: Princess Theatre, Melbourne 22 December 1962; Germany: Theater am Gärtnerplatz, Munich *Der König und ich* 17 April 1966; Belgium: Opéra Royal de Wallonie, Verviers *Le Roi et moi* 22 March 1985

Film: Twentieth Century Fox 1956

Recordings: original cast (Decca), original London cast (Philips), German cast (Philips), New York revival 1964 (RCA), South African cast (RCA), Israeli cast (CBS), New York revival cast 1996 (Varese Sarabande), selections (MFP, Philips, RCA, Columbia, etc), Netherlands cast 1998 (CNR), film soundtrack (Capitol), cartoon soundtrack (Sony), etc

KING, Charles [J] (b New York, 31 October 1889; d London, 11 January 1944). Broadway leading man who introduced several durable songs.

Originally a player in minstrelsy and vaudeville, ''Charlie'' King was engaged in the chorus of *The Yankee Prince* and *The Mimic World* (1908, Artie), toured with *Marcelle* (1909, Bud Wilson, ''Mary's Little Lamb'') and *The Yankee Prince* (1910, ''imitating George M Cohan to perfection'' as Percy) and worked in a double act with Elizabeth Brice in vaudeville, before winning his first Broadway role alongside Elsie Janis in *The Slim Princess* (1911, Tod Norcross), singing ''Let Me Live and Die in Dixieland'' a song written with Miss Brice and used in their act. He appeared, again with Miss Brice, in the later stages of the run of Lew Fields' *The Hen Pecks* (1911) and as Wilder Daly in the Ziegfeld rehash of *A Trip to Chinatown* (*A Winsome Widow,* ''Be My Little Baby Bumble Bee'') and as Dick Cunningham in the Arthur Hammerstein/Shubert revival of *The Geisha,* before playing in and out of Broadway in revue (*The Passing Show of 1913, The Honeymoon Express*) and featuring in New York in two further revusical productions: Irving Berlin's *Watch Your Step* (1914, Algy Cuffs) and Ziegfeld's ill-fated *Miss 1917.*

In 1919 he took over as the boy Hughie in the musical version of Pinero's *The Magistrate, Good Morning Judge,* then toured in the leading role of *Buddies,* starred as Ned Spencer in the flop *It's Up to You* (1921) and won his best role to date when he created the part of Jerry Conroy, the Irish lad who defeats the rich chap in the contest for the hand and heart of George M Cohan's *Little Nellie Kelly* (''Nellie Kelly, I Love You'').

After a number of years working in vaudeville and revue, King returned to the musical stage to create the not-very-romantic lead role of Bilge Smith in Vincent Youmans's *Hit the Deck* (''Sometimes I'm Happy'') and the heroic Chick Evans who gets the girl in Rodgers and Hart's *Present Arms* (1928) before heading on to Hollywood, where he appeared in *The Broadway Melody* and a number of other early musical films. He returned to the stage to star as the bootlegger Al Spanish in *The New Yorkers* (1930) and, one last time, in a character role in *Sea Legs* (1937, Captain Nordstrom).

King was married to **Lila RHODES,** a cousin of George M Cohan, who played with the Cohan companies in *The Honeymooners* (1907, Gertie Gayland), *The Yankee Prince* (1908, chorus), *The Little Millionaire* (1911, Goldie Gray), *The Cohan Revue of 1916* (Major Barbara), etc.

KING, Dennis [PRATT, Dennis John] (b Coventry, England, 2 November 1897; d New York, 21 May 1971). British vocalist and actor who made himself a fine career in both capacities in America.

King first worked on the professional stage at Birmingham Repertory Theatre, aged 19, and he made his first musical theatre appearance touring in Robert Courtneidge's *Oh, Caesar!* (Dick Hamilton) in the same year. Three years later he played in London for the first time when he appeared in a supporting role in Messager's *Monsieur Beaucaire* (1919, Townbrake). When the company took the show to America his part was given to André Brouard, but King soon followed, taking up the role of Rakell in the show's tour, and from 1921 onwards he was based in America, performing not in the musical theatre but in plays. His first musical leading role came in 1924 when he was cast as Jim Kenyon in *Rose Marie* (''Rose Marie,'' ''The Indian Love Call''), and this performance established him as one of Broadway's most prized operetta stars. He subsequently used his combination of classic acting experience and a rich, firm baritone in creating further romantic musicals—as François Villon in the Broadway production of Friml's *The Vagabond King* (1925, ''Song of the Vagabonds,'' ''Only a Rose'' and on film), and in both America and Britain as D'Artagnan in the same composer's *The Three Musketeers.* In 1932 he appeared as Gaylord Ravenal opposite Norma Terris in a revival of *Show Boat,* and the following year he was the hero of the unfortunate London musical of C Stafford Dickens's Broadway play *Command Performance.*

King's musical appearances were spaced thereafter through a career in often ambitious straight theatre, but they included, in 1937, Richard Tauber's role of Goethe in Lehár's *Friederike,* Count Willi Palaffi who married Vera Zorina's angel in *I Married an Angel* (1938), the disreputable though Ducal hero of his own production of *She Had to Say ''Yes''* which folded on the road in 1940, the heroically singing hero of the 1951 revival of *Music in the Air* and, finally, an unfortunate musicalization of *Lost Horizon* under the title *Shangri La* (1956, Hugh Conway).

On film, as well as re-creating his *Vagabond King,* he appeared with Laurel and Hardy in a low comic version of *Fra Diavolo,* and on television he starred as Peter Stuyvesant in *Knickerbocker Holiday* (1950) and as the Astrologer in the 1958 CBS broadcast of Cole Porter's *Aladdin.*

His son, **John Michael KING,** also appeared on the Broadway musical stage, creating the role of Freddy Eynsford Hill in *My Fair Lady* (''On the Street Where You Live'').

KING, Walter Woolf *see* WOOLF, WALTER

KING DODO Musical comedy in 3 acts by Frank Pixley. Music by Gustave Luders. Studebaker Theater, Chicago, 27 May 1901; Daly's Theater, New York, 12 May 1902.

The first work of the Luders/Pixley combine, *King Dodo* failed to find a producer until the success of the pair's *The Burgomaster* suddenly made them and their show saleable. Henry Savage secured *King Dodo* and produced it in Chicago, where it duly had as big a success as its predecessor, then sent it off round the touring circuits on a long run which finally—nearly a year later—led it to an appearance in New York.

Set in the kind of crazy fantasyland, derived from extravaganza, that was the favorite setting of turn-of-the-century American musicals, the show told the story of King Dodo of Dodo Land, ''a ruler by divine right only'' (William Norris), who attempts to boost his courtship of lovely Queen Lili of Spoojus (Maude Lambert) by seeking out a fountain of youth which rejuvenates him by 30 years, only to find that the lady prefers to take an older, and therefore wiser, husband. He changes back in time for a happy ending. The court historian (Charles W Meyer) decreed in topical song that he'd ''Look in the Book and See,'' the court physician introduced himself as ''The Eminent Doctor Fizz,'' the King's ward Angela (Celeste Wynne) and her beloved ''Lad Who Leads,'' Piola (played in travesty by Lillian Green), supplied the pretty romantic music (''Two Hearts Made One''), and the soon-to-be-famous basso William Pruette as the Queen's Prime Minister declared himself a ''True, Barbaric Soldier'' in rich tones, but the score's two veritable hits came in Angela's jaunty, raggy ''Diana'' and in Dodo's ''The Tale of a Bumble-Bee,'' a comical piece with a throbbingly tongue-in-cheek refrain.

Broadway's version of *King Dodo* introduced the eccentric comedian Raymond Hitchcock as a grotesque, white-faced, spiky-haired Dodo, in a performance which set him off on a star career, and the show was pronounced "a genuine success," but when the summer break arrived, 64 performances later, the musical headed back to the touring circuits and there it remained for a good number of years. An Australian version (ad "J Francis," ie, J F Sheridan), well botched and reorganized into two acts, was later produced by John F Sheridan, featuring himself as Dodo and Maud Amber as Lili, as part of a 1905 repertoire season.

Australia: Criterion Theatre, Sydney 10 June 1905

KING KONG Jazz opera in 2 acts by Harry Bloom. Lyrics by Pat Williams. Music by Todd Matshikiza.

A South African musical, apparently based on a real character, but with his story conventionally romanticized, *King Kong* told the tale of a boxer (Nathan Mdlele) who gets jailed for a killing and thereafter goes on the skids, finally murdering the girl, Joyce (Miriam Makeba), whom he had in better days attracted away from gang leader Lucky (Joseph Mogotsi). Sentenced to prison, King Kong kills himself.

Highly successful on its original production in South Africa, *King Kong* was taken to Britain by Jack Hylton, and produced in a revised version with its two original lead men and Peggy Phango starred. Its enormous zest, and such novelties as the Gumboot Dance, won it favor and, although the management found that the extent of the performers' exuberant energies meant they couldn't sell the sweat-stained front stalls, it played for 201 West End performances.

UK: Prince's Theatre 23 February 1961

Recordings: original cast (Gallotone), London cast (Decca)

[THE] KING OF CADONIA Musical play in 2 acts by Frederick Lonsdale. Lyrics by Adrian Ross. Music by Sidney Jones. Prince of Wales Theatre, London, 3 September 1908.

Frederick Lonsdale had his first piece produced on the London stage, when, to replace an unexpected flop, Frank Curzon hurried on the musical *King of Cadonia* (initially announced as *Princess Marie*) for which the young playwright had written the libretto.

Nobody wants to be the King of Cadonia, because the population have a habit of getting rid of their kings in unpleasant fashion. The current young monarch, Alexis (Bertram Wallis), is watched over nervously by his official heir, the comical Duke of Alasia (Huntley Wright), whose daughter Marie (Isabel Jay) has been nominated as future Queen. To his horror, however, the young folk—who object to all the restrictions placed on them for their safety—both run away, meet, fall in love, and ultimately, because the incognito King has become meanwhile chummy with the populous, are able to return to take up the throne together unmolested.

Lonsdale's libretto was more imaginative and literate in its style than many musical-comedy books, and Sidney Jones's score was similarly classy, from its romantic baritone and soprano music for the handsome Wallis and former D'Oyly Carte prima donna, Miss Jay ("There's a King in the Land Today," "Castles in the Air"), to some happily comic numbers for Wright ("Do Not Hesitate to Shoot") and for Gracie Leigh ("Situations") as a Balkan wench called Militza.

Critical praise was warm, success considerable, and *King of Cadonia* won a fine 333-performance London run. It quickly sent out three British touring companies, and was briskly and successfully opened in Australia, before the year was out, with Herbert Clayton and Dorothy Court starring and Susie Vaughan featured as the Duchess of Alasia in a production which included an interpolated performance of the latest craze, the danse apache. The Shuberts took up the piece for New York and then proceeded to dismember it. They featured Robert Dempster (Alexis), Marguerite Clarke (Marie), William Norris (Alasia) and Clara Palmer (Militza) in a version which did over Lonsdale's superior text, and dropped great chunks of Jones's score which were replaced by a virtual actful of M E Rourke/Jerome Kern numbers which had precious little to do with Cadonia. They had no latitude for surprise when the resultant show folded expensively after 16 performances.

Australia: Her Majesty's Theatre, Melbourne 12 June 1909; USA: Daly's Theater 10 January 1910

THE KING'S DRAGOONS Comic opera in 3 acts by J Wilton Jones. Music by John Crook. Theatre Royal, Manchester, 1 November 1880.

Produced in the same year as *The Pirates of Penzance* and *Billee Taylor, The King's Dragoons* did not take their sophisticated burlesque tone, but instead looked back to the classic comic-opera style of earlier years in its tale of pretty 18th-century Alice (Gertrude Cave-Ashton) who vows to wed the man who will take the place of her rash young brother (Fred J Stimson) in the army. It is not the horrid Marquis (Richard Cummings) but his son, handsome Edgar (Henry Walsham), who—after some tricky ins and outs—wins the prize. John Crook's score, in a ballad-opera strain, served the piece well and, produced with a distinguished cast, *The King's Dragoons* scored well at Manchester, in several other Midlands productions, and in Australia and New Zealand where it was produced by Alfred T Dunning with

Knight Aston, Annette Ivanova and Thomas B Appleby starred. Boston got as far as announcing a production, but not apparently to staging it.

Australia: Opera House, Melbourne 18 November 1882

KING'S RHAPSODY Musical romance in 3 acts by Ivor Novello. Palace Theatre, London, 15 September 1949.

King's Rhapsody was the last of the highly successful series of large-scale romantic musicals with which Ivor Novello filled the Theatre Royal, Drury Lane before the war, and other houses around London and Britain thereafter. Novello himself starred (as he had in all but one of the series), as the newly acceded King Nikki of Murania, unwillingly called back from Paris and the arms of his actress mistress, Marta Karillos (Phyllis Dare), to rule his country and to wed an unknown bride of state, the Princess Cristiane (Vanessa Lee). Aware of his unwillingness, Cristiane, disguised as a peasant, gets herself seduced by the King before the wedding. But the rather unroyal Nikki is so irked by the way the women around him—in particular his mother, Queen Elena (Zena Dare)—take him for a kingly cypher, simply to be managed, that he refuses to conform and runs back to Marta. Whilst the ungracious king grows more and more unpopular in his country, Cristiane—soon the mother of his child—becomes adored by the people, and when Nikki tries to interfere in the government and is forced to flee Murania, she stays behind to bring up their child to be king.

The return to the Ruritania which Novello had so successfully mined with *Glamorous Night,* the first of his series, proved a great success. The libretto of *King's Rhapsody* was arguably the best of its kind that he had written (the same could scarcely be said for the title), and the score which he attached to it—for once, not pretending to be show songs within a show—turned out his now almost inevitable ration of, in particular, lovely soprano ballads. Vanessa Lee's crystal rendition of ''Someday My Heart Will Awake'' was the highlight of the show, and contralto Olive Gilbert as her duenna boomed out the lullaby ''Fly Home, Little Heart'' to great effect. The soprano had further lovely melodies in ''When the Violin Began to Play'' and ''If This Were Love,'' and Phyllis Dare sang of ''The Mayor of Perpignan'' whose situation—with his wife liked so much better than he by his people—is a lesson to the sullen King.

King's Rhapsody was as great a success in London as *The Dancing Years* and *Perchance to Dream* had been, and it seemed likely to become Novello's longest-running musical play, but its prospects were sadly damaged when, 18 months into the run, the author-star died. Another middle-aging star, Jack Buchanan, took over his role, but in spite of Buchanan's popularity, the show was not the same without Novello and it closed after a total of a little over two years at the Palace Theatre (839 performances). It had an extended touring life thereafter, both in its full-sized version and, later, in a scaled-down one, and was both filmed (w Errol Flynn as Nikki and Martita Hunt as Elena) and televised (1957 w Griffith Jones and Miss Lee) without being given a major production outside Britain. In 1988 a small-cast rewritten version (ad Michael Pertwee), which replaced much of the libretto's romanticism with humor and scattered the score with numbers from other Novello shows, was seen outside the West End.

Film: Everest (1955)

Recordings: original cast recordings (HMV, WRC), selection (Columbia), film selection (Parlophone)

Plate 204. **King of Cadonia.** *The King (Bertram Wallis) comes upon a gaggle of girls in the garden. And one of them is Isabel Jay.*

DIE KINO-KÖNIGIN Operette in 3 acts by Georg Okonkowski (and Julius Freund). Music by Jean Gilbert. Deutsches Operettentheater, Hamburg (as *Die elfte Muse*), 22 November 1912; Metropoltheater, Berlin, 8 March 1913.

The noble Victor von Gardennes (Karl Bachmann), who moonlights as a clandestine film actor, inadvertently compromises Annie (Helene Ballot), the daughter of Josias Clutterbuck (Guido Thielscher), President of the Temperance League, Vice-President of the Crusade Against Trashy Books, and an anti-cinema advocate, on the day of her wedding to Boppi Lopp (Victor Norbert) and he is thus, by the laws of Operette, obliged to marry her. The jealous movie star Delia Gill (Ida Russka) tricks old Clutterbuck into being seen with her in public and thus ruins his credibility as a moral crusader, but Victor has a change of heart and he turns things round by announcing that Josias is going to make a useful marriage between morals and movies—he will use film productions to bring poverty and injustice to general notice. And so Victor keeps his little bride, and the slightly slighted Delia has to make do with the arms of a less aristocratic actor.

Gilbert's work came hot on the heels of Walter Kollo's widely played *Filmzauber,* the first significant German piece to use the newly popular silent movies and their performers as subject matter. Originally called *Die elfte Muse* (''the eleventh muse'' . . . cabaret was supposed to be the 10th!) in its Hamburg production, the Operette was revised by Julius Freund and rechristened with the more commercial title *Die Kino-Königin* for Berlin where it joined *Polnische Wirtschaft, Autoliebchen, Puppchen* and *Die Reise um die Erde in 40 Tage* to establish Gilbert at the forefront of the German musical-comedy scene in just a few brief seasons.

Gilbert's score for *Die Kino-Königin* was filled with dancing melodies, and one—the march song ''In der Nacht (wenn die Liebe erwacht)''—became a major song hit. Amongst the remainder, the Kino-Walzer ''Man lacht, man lebt, man liebt!,'' the heroine's dance duet with her ''victim,'' ''Ach, Amalia!,'' and Victor's lighthearted ''Liebliche kleine Dingerchen'' topped the musical list, and all gave opportunities for a display of the dance element which was now so liberally emphasized in local musical shows.

Die Kino-Königin proved a great success far beyond Hamburg. Following its initial season in Berlin it went on to run up a long series of productions in the German provinces where it was subsequently rated second in popularity only to *Die keusche Susanne* in the long list of Gilbert's works and, whilst its record overseas was not quite as fine, given that it appeared in time of war, it nevertheless was played widely and well.

In Vienna Mizzi Freihardt (Delia), Paul Harden (Victor) and Oskar Sachs (Josias) played a season at the Établissement Ronacher before the show was moved up to the temporarily at-a-loss Carltheater (2 June 1914), where it soon passed its 100th performance (30 June). It had to be withdrawn when the theatre got a production of its own together, and it moved back to Ronacher, but such was its popularity that the following year, in an almost unprecedented move, Carltheater director Eibenschütz remounted the piece, again directed by Miksa Preger, with the theatre's own star Mizzi Zwerenz as Delia alongside Richard Waldemar's Josias. It ran right through the summer and closed after its 286th performance. The wartime playbills credited the music to ''Max Winterfeld'' but reminded patrons in brackets that he was the same person who once liked to pretend he was the French ''Jean Gilbert'' in the days when being French was all right. In 1924 *Die Kino-Königin* was again seen at the Carltheater, with Freihardt and Fritz Imhoff starred.

The first foreign-language version to hit the stage was a French one (ad A de Graef) mounted at the Brussels Scala in 1913 (23 December), but it did not progress to Paris. There was more success for Thomas Ryley's American production of *The Queen of the Movies* (ad Glen MacDonough, Edward Paulton), starring Valli Valli (Delia) and Frank Moulan (Josias) and featuring additional numbers by Leslie Stuart (''Whistle'') and Irving Berlin (''Follow the Crowd''), which ran a good 106 nights at the Globe Theater and popularized ''When the Moon Slyly Winks in the Night'' (''In der Nacht'') around America, whilst in Britain, Robert Courtneidge's staging of *The Cinema Star* (ad Jack Hulbert, Harry Graham) with Dorothy Ward playing the title role alongside Lauri de Frece, Harry Welchman, Cicely Courtneidge and Hulbert, seemed set for a long run, when it was hit by considerations of loyalty (Gilbert was, after all, reported actually to be fighting on the war's other side) and had to be closed after 109 performances. Courtneidge nevertheless managed to keep his show going on the road, where apparently such considerations of origin counted for less than in London, for four seasons.

Australia, similarly, had no foolish qualms about the sources of its entertainment, and *The Cinema Star* was mounted there in 1916 with Ethel Cadman (singing ''On the Beach at Waikiki''), Florence Young, Minnie Love (performing Louis Hirsch's ''My Radium Girl'' and ''The Broken Doll''), Reginald Roberts, Derek Hudson and Phil Smith declaring ''I Want to Go Back to Honolulu'' (Sonny Cunha/William Warren) as Clutterbuck at the head of its cast. A fine eight weeks in Melbourne and six as a Christmas entertainment in Sydney (Her Majesty's Theatre 23 December 1916) recompensed a show which did not, by this stage, seem to be very largely *Die Kino-Königin,* in its music at least.

There was a Berlin revival at the Metropoltheater in 1948 and a fresh German version of the piece, heavily rewritten by Gilbert's son Robert and Per Schwenzen, and with numbers from other Gilbert shows introduced, was produced at the Opernhaus, Nuremberg in 1961, thus creating a new copyright for the show. This version was played at the Metropoltheater in 1964.

It appears, by the way, that *Die elfte Muse* was far from being the first movieland musical. I have noticed the title *El cinematografo parlante* ''a zarzuela in one act by Diaz and Manuel Mauri'' recorded as having taken to the stage in Spain as early as 1901. Talkies, already!

USA: Globe Theater *The Queen of the Movies* 12 January 1914; Austria: Ronacher 1 April 1914; UK: Shaftesbury Theatre *The Cinema Star* 4 June 1914; Hungary: *A mozitündér* Népopera 31 October 1914; Australia: Her Majesty's Theatre, Melbourne *The Cinema Star* 7 October 1916

KIRÁLY, Ernő (b Kiskeszi, 26 April 1884; d New York, 2 September 1954). Fine-featured high baritone who starred in two decades of Hungarian operetts and musical comedies.

Király joined the Népszínház company as a chorus singer at the age of 18, and subsequently worked his way up to principal roles in provincial houses before returning in 1907 to Budapest and the Király Színház. There, with his elegant style and pleasing light baritone, he quickly became one of the favorite stars of Budapest's musical stage. In 1908 he succeeded Ákos Ráthonyi as Danilo in *A víg özvegy* (*Die lustige Witwe*) and played Papp in *Hollandi lány* (*Miss Hook of Holland*), and he subsequently appeared as Hungary's first Karel van Lysseweghe in *Elvált asszony* (1909, *Die geschiedene Frau*), as René in *Luxemburg grófja* (*Der Graf von Luxemburg*), as Edwin in *Csárdáskirálynő* (1916, *Die Csárdásfürstin*), as Sándor in the premiere of Lehár's *Pacsirta* (*Wo die Lerche singt,* 1918) and, later, as Tassilo in *Marica grófnő* (1925, *Gräfin Mariza*). He also created starring roles in some of the most important Hungarian operetts of the time: the title role of Rényi's *A kis gróf* (1911), the cowboy Tom Migles in *Leányvásár* (1911), the Grand Duke to Sári Fedák's *Szibill* (1914), Iván Baracs in *Mágnás Miska* (1916), the title role of Szirmai's *Gróf Rinaldo* (1918) and the Count Dániel Cziráky, opposite Emmi Kosáry's Xenia, in Buttykay's *Az ezüst sirály* (1920). In 1921 he directed the successful Budapest production of Stolz's *Die Tanzgräfin* (*A kis grizett*) at the Vígszínház.

His other roles included the Marquis in *Kornevillei harangok* (*Les Cloches de Corneville*), Tom in *Aranyhattyú,* Mihajlovics in *Bíborruhás asszony* (*Das Weib im Purpur*), Bagó in *János vitéz,* László Tassy in *Párizsi divat* and György Honti in *Mesék az írógépról.*

Király visited the Vienna Carltheater in 1913 (Bagó, Prinz Georg in *Limonádé ezredes,* Octave in *Eva*), played *Az ezüst sirály* in Vienna as *Liebesrausch* and appeared in both Austria and Germany in 1922 with Hungarian companies. He was later also seen in New York, where he eventually settled in 1935, and opened an Hungarian restaurant.

KIRK, Lisa [KIRK, Elise Marie] (b Brownsville, Pa, 25 February 1926; d New York, 11 November 1990).

Best known as a nightclub and recording vocalist, tough-voiced Lisa Kirk created the roles of Emily in *Allegro* (1947, ''The Gentleman is a Dope''), the delectable Lois Lane in *Kiss Me, Kate* (1948, introducing ''Always True to You in My Fashion'' and ''Why Can't You Behave?'') and, 26 years on, that of Lottie Ames in *Mack and Mabel,* inviting the world to ''Tap Your Troubles Away.'' She also appeared on Broadway in *Here's Love* (1964), replacing Janis Paige in the feminine lead, closed out of town with *Home Again, Home Again* (1979) and loaned her voice to Rosalind Russell to dub parts of her role as Rose in the film version of *Gypsy* (1963).

KIRKWOOD, Pat[ricia] (b Salford, 24 February 1921). British soubrette of the 1940s and 1950s.

After teenage successes in pantomime and revue, Miss Kirkwood played principal soubrette roles opposite Stanley Lupino in *Lady Behave* (1941) and in London's edition of *Let's Face It* (1942). In a subsequent career similarly dominated by revue and pantomime, she had a nervous breakdown over her role in America's *Sweet Bye and Bye* and went home, leaving the later performances to Dolores Gray, and later took leading parts in the short-lived *Roundabout* (1949), as the cabaret vocalist Pinkie Leroy in Noël Coward's *Ace of Clubs* (1950, ''Chase Me Charlie''), as Ruth in the London edition of *Wonderful Town* (1955) and as Chrysanthemum Brown, the dashingly persecuted heroine of *Chrysanthemum* (1958, ''Love Is a Game''). Intermittent provincial musical appearances in later years included Mrs Squeezum in *Lock Up Your Daughters* and Vera Simpson in *Pal Joey,* and after a long break, in the 1990s in a pair of compilation shows.

She was for a time married to **Hubert [R H] GREGG** (b 19 July 1914), actor, director, sometime lyricist and broadcaster, who appeared with her in *Chrysanthemum* and *Lock Up Your Daughters.*

Autobiography: *The Time of My Life* (Robert Hale, London, 1999)

A KIS GRÓF Operett in 3 acts by Ferenc Martos. Music by Áladár Rényi. Király Színház, Budapest, 9 September 1911.

Produced in 1911, in a period when the blossoming Hungarian operett tradition was turning out some of the most interesting works in Europe, *A kis gróf,* composed to a libretto by top text-writer Ferenc Martos, was premiered on the 23rd (or, according to some sources, 26th) birthday of the hitherto untried Áladár Rényi.

The tale was a very simple one, finding its virtue in Martos's telling. The little count of the story was Count Laci d'Ennery (Ernő Király), son of the Count Guidó Agárdy (Imre Szirmai), whose father has decided that he shall wed the decidedly attractive and rich American widow Dorothy Howard (Anna Lonzay). Unfortunately, Laci is a very inexperienced young man so, prior to marriage with a woman who has already experienced all an American millionaire has to offer, he sets out to get some practice with a lady of the stage. Rózsi (Sári Fedák) is the chosen one. Of course the practice soon turns serious. Papa intervenes determinedly, Rózsi tries some self-sacrificing pretences, but by the end of the evening young love has its way, especially as Dorothy, who prefers older men, has both given the ''little count's'' romance a helping hand, and turned her attractions most successfully onto her intended's father.

The score was in the traditional mode, featuring Hungarian-flavored waltzes and marches—as in Rózsi's ''Kettesben csókok közt . . .'' and her Katonasári induló respectively—whilst Dorothy tra-la-laed out the refrain to a tale of ''Daphnis és Chloé'' in soubrette style and the fun was looked after by star comic Márton Rátkai (Roth) with such pieces such as the ''Csetneki Roth'' couplets.

A kis gróf ran straight through to its 50th performance at the Király Színház on 28 October and, in spite of the fact that it was succeeded in November by an even bigger success in the shape of Jacobi's *Leányvásár,* it maintained its popularity, was played at the Budai Színkör (25 May 1912), and reached its 250th Budapest performance in November 1913. In the meanwhile it had begun to be seen elsewhere. Vienna's Carltheater production (ad Julius Wilhelm), which reallotted the characters' names and rechristened the work *Susi,* starred Mizzi Zwerenz as Susi alongside Hubert Marischka (Stefan), Dora Keplinger (Aglaia), Blasel (Dr Häring) and Richard Waldemar (Szigetváry) and opened for the 1912 Christmas season. It proved a distinct hit, running right through the winter and spring—with a slight break for the visit of the Budapest Király Színház company, during which it emigrated to Ronachers ''Établissement Parisien''—till the summer recess (143 performances). It returned again both to open the new season and as an occasional matinée during the 1913–14 hit run of Nedbal's *Polenblut.* It was brought out again in 1917 for further performances.

Susi was produced in Stockholm (1 April 1913) and in Leipzig, later the same year, and Lew Fields staged a version on Broadway, with José Collins (now Suzi), Connie Ediss (Lina Blazer), Robert Evett (Stefan), Lew Hearn (Herr Horn) and Melville Stewart (Count Emmerich) starred, which, in spite of being greeted as ''far above the average musical comedy'' was bumped from the Casino to the Shubert Theater and then out of town after just 55 performances. In true Broadway style, it was a version (ad Otto Harbach) which had been regularly botched, but Fields had showed a little more taste than some of his fellow producers by taking his ''additional songs'' from the best Continental sources. The interpolations, whose melodies at least melded stylistically with the original score, included a Lehár melody relyricked as ''The Best Toast of All'' and a piece of Lincke performed under the gulpful title ''Teenie, Eenie, Weenie.''

Austria: Carltheater *Susi* 20 December 1912; Germany: Leipzig *Susi* May 1913; USA: Casino Theater *Suzi* 3 November 1914

KISMET Musical Arabian Night in 2 acts by Charles Lederer and Luther Davis based on Edward Knoblock's play of the same title. Music, adapted from the works of Alexander Borodin, and lyrics by George Forrest and Robert Wright. Ziegfeld Theater, New York, 3 December 1953.

Like their first great success, *Song of Norway,* Wright and Forrest's musical *Kismet* was written for and produced by Edwin Lester's Los Angeles and San Francisco Light Opera Company, opening its initial West Coast run at the San Francisco Philharmonic Auditorium on 17 August 1953 before going on to establish itself as one of the outstanding Broadway operettas of the postwar period at the top of a long international career.

The libretto for the show was based on Eddie Knoblock's successful London *Kismet* of 1911, a colorful oriental play (itself a derivate of *The Caliph of Baghdad* operaticized by Boïeldieu in 1800) in which Oscar Asche had made a sensation as the expansively comic-dramatic rogue beggar Hajj, before it went on to play Broadway, with Otis Skinner starred, to Paris, where Luicien Guitry was Hajj, and then all round the world in a multitude of languages. By and large, the original tale was well adhered to in the libretto for the musical.

The opportunistic street poet Hajj (Alfred Drake), with the help of a fine set of coincidences, works his way into the confidence of the power-crazy Wazir of Baghdad (Henry Calvin), who is plotting, for his own benefit, to wed the young Caliph (Richard Kiley) to several wealthy foreign princesses. But the Caliph has fallen in love with, and then lost track of, pretty Marsinah (Doretta Morrow), Hajj's daughter, and the rhymester does not realize that in aiding the Wazir he is risking losing a royal son-in-law. After some dramatic ups and downs, and a visit to the harem of the Wazir, the lovers are united, the villain is suppressed, and Hajj goes off to purge the punishment for his sins in exile . . . in the company of the Wazir's lush widow, Lalume (Joan Diener).

The score which Wright and Forrest evolved for this story included several pieces which would become musical-theatre standards. Hajj's vibrantly baritonic parable of ''The Olive Tree,'' the beautiful quartet ''And This Is My Beloved,'' Marsinah's realization that she can afford ''Baubles, Bangles and Beads,'' and the love duet ''A Stranger in Paradise'' (derived from the famous Polovtsian Dances) were set alongside the supremely comical

Plate 205. **Kismet**

mezzo-soprano recital of the debaucheries of Baghdad, ''Not Since Nineveh'' (ex- another portion of the Polovtsian Dances), and the Wazir's gloating ''Was I Wazir'' in a score full of hit songs which brought Borodin's melodies to a wider audience than they might ever have expected.

The $400,000 production of *Kismet* moved from the West Coast to the east in December, under the comanagement of Charles Lederer and Lester, and arrived in New York in the middle of a newspaper strike. The strike and its resultant lack of reviews certainly seemed to do no harm: word soon got round that *Kismet* was an exceedingly good thing and, come the time of year for prize-giving, the prize-givers nodded their assent. *Kismet* garnered Tony Awards as best musical, libretto and score, as well as for Drake's Hajj, as it settled in for 583 performances at Broadway's Ziegfeld Theater before beginning its touring life. Earl MacVeigh and William Johnson were the earliest road Hajjs.

Drake and Misses Morrow and Diener repeated their original characters in Jack Hylton's 1955 London production which stretched to an even longer 648 performances, and Garnet Carroll's Australian mounting, with Hayes Gordon (Hajj), Madge Stephens (Marsinah) and Morgan St John (Lalume) in the leading roles scored such a hit in its nine months in Melbourne and subsequent Sydney season (20 August 1956) as to launch its producer on an important career in the Australian musical theatre.

A film version was issued in the same year, featuring Howard Keel in one of his outstanding film appearances as Hajj supported by Ann Blyth (Marsinah), Vic Damone as a croony Caliph and Dolores Gray as a voluptuous if vocally truncated Lalume. It included much of the stage score (the Wazir's song being a notable casualty), the famous dances designed by Jack Cole, and added one fresh number (''Bored'').

Kismet swiftly settled itself firmly into the standard English-language repertoire. It was played and recorded regularly, televised (1967 w José Ferrer) and given major revivals in America both in 1962, with Drake teamed with Calvin, Anne Jeffreys, Lee Venora and Richard Banks, and again in 1965 (Lincoln Center w Drake and Anne Jeffreys) and back at the Civic Light Opera in 1976 with John Reardon starred. This last production, with Reardon repeating his forever-memorable Hajj, was exported to London's Shaftesbury Theatre in a scenically cutdown version the following year. Around the same time, *Kismet* was first heard in German (ad Janne Furch) in Koblenz, and also suffered a racial and musical reorganization (which admitted that it was ''based on'' *Kismet*) to be produced on Broadway as *Timbuktu!* (Mark Hellinger Theater 1 March 1978). Ira Hawkins played Hadji, Melba Moore was Mars, Gilbert Price the Mansa of Mali, and Eartha Kitt's Sahleem La-lume provided the marquee value through 243 performances.

An earlier musical *Kismet* subtitled *or Two Tangled Turks,* written by Richard Carroll jr and composed by Gustave Kerker, was seen on Broadway in 1895. This *Kismet,* although suitably Eastern, had nothing to do with ''fate.'' It was the name of the heroine (Lizzie MacNichol) who was disguised as a male child, in good operettic fashion, in order to succeed to a throne. It lasted but three Broadway weeks before hurrying back to the country.

UK: Stoll Theatre 20 April 1955; Australia: Princess Theatre, Melbourne 10 November 1955; Germany: Theater der Stadt, Koblenz 22 January 1977

Film: MGM 1955

Recordings: original cast (Columbia, USA), 1965 revival cast (RCA, USA), film soundtrack (MGM, USA), complete (TER), selections (London, Sony, Capitol), etc

KISSING TIME

The only example in the musical theatre of a composer writing two almost contemporaneous shows with different scores but with the same title. And, just to make things even more difficult, both shows were actually played under other titles before they were called *Kissing Time.*

The first *Kissing Time* was a musical comedy in 2 acts by Guy Bolton and P G Wodehouse based (uncredited) on the wartime farce *Madame et son filleul* by Maurice Hennequin and Pierre Veber (Palais-Royal 12 September 1916). Additional lyrics by Clifford Grey. Music by Ivan Caryll. However, by the time it became *Kissing Time,* in postwar London, it had already run its Broadway life under Klaw and Erlanger's management and the wartime title of *The Girl Behind the Gun* (New Amsterdam Theater, New York 16 September 1918).

The actress Georgette Bréval (Ada Meade) has patriotically ''adopted'' a serving soldier, Brichoux (John E Young). However, Lambrissac (Donald Brian), a fellow soldier and an aspiring dramatist, decides to substitute himself for Brichoux and pay a visit to the actress in the hope of making a connection or two that will help get his play produced. Amorous complications follow, with Georgette's uncle, the Colonel Servan (Frank Doane), assuming that Lambrissac is Georgette's husband until the real Brichoux, the real husband (John E Hazzard) and Madame Lucienne Lambrissac (Wilda Bennett) all arrive on the scene to complicate matters further.

Lucienne drew the plum of the score, the wartimely yearning ''Some Day the Waiting Will End,'' duetted ''There's a Light in Your Eyes'' with her husband at the show's end and gave the title song, ''The Girl Behind the Gun.'' Bréval had a comical ''Women Haven't Any Mercy on a Man'' and Georgette headed a piece about ''[Godsons and] Godmothers'' alongside a pleasing ration of ensembles (''I Like It,'' ''How Warm It is Today,'' ''Back to the Dear Old Trenches'').

The show ran a fine 160 performances in New York, during which time it was seen by London's George Grossmith, over in America and freshly free from the cares of war. He realized there was a good part for himself in the show, and snapped up *The Girl Behind the Gun* for a London production. He cast it royally, with himself (Max, ie, Lambrissac) and Leslie Henson (Bibi, ie, Brichoux) playing the two comic roles, Yvonne Arnaud (Georgette) and Phyllis Dare (Lucienne) as principal ladies, and such rising names as Tom Walls (Colonel Bollinger) and Isobel Jeans (Lady Mercia) and a young seaside comic called Stanley Holloway (Captain Wentworth) in his first West End appearance in supporting roles.

Kissing Time (as it was now rechristened) opened Grossmith and Laurillard's brand new theatre, the Winter Garden, risen on the site of the famous old ''Mogul'' music hall. It rose a little slowly, which meant that *Kissing Time* got five months of rehearsals, but when it did open, on 20 May 1919, it proved just the kind of show London wanted for its continuing victory celebrations.

The brisk comic tale was attached to a score of of-the-moment songs including 11 of the original 17, now topped up by some new ones. Miss Dare sang ''Some Day'' and the new ''Thousands of Years Ago,'' Henson gave a lighthearted ''My Motors'' (replacing Brichoux's ''True to Me'') and filched ''Women Haven't Any Mercy on a Man,'' Grossmith detailed his ''Desertions'' in another new piece, and spent his light comic-romantic moments with Miss Dare in ''There's a Light in Your Eyes'' and another fresh number, ''Joan and Peter.'' The whole was topped off by a French song for the French Mlle Arnaud (''Oh, ma chérie'') written by the Winter Garden's French md, Willie Redstone. It all proved just the ticket, and it remained the ticket for no less than 430 performances in London's West End as a preface to a long career in the provinces and the colonies.

Australia, in particular, took a strong shine to *Kissing Time.* It saw its first performance (Theatre Royal, Melbourne 31 January 1920) only eight months after the London premiere, with Maud Fane (Lucienne), Gladys Moncrieff (Georgette), Leslie Holland (Max), Arthur Stigant (Bollinger) and Theodore Leonard (Bibi) playing in the lead roles through no less than four months in two theatres in Melbourne, before going on to Sydney (Her Majesty's Theatre 29 May 1920) for nearly three months

Plate 206. **Kissing Time.** *Leslie Henson, Tom Walls, George Grossmith and Yvonne Arnaud line up a cue for a song-and-dance of mistaken identities.*

more. It was brought back several times thereafter, notably in 1924 with Madge Elliott and Alfred Frith and again as late as 1941, for another wartime showing, and it proved itself there one of the favorite musical comedies of its era.

Soon after the Australian opening of *Kissing Time* Mark I, *Kissing Time* Mark II began its career. This one was described as ''a musical comedy in 2 acts by George V Hobart based on the libretto *Mimi* by Adolf Philipp and Edward A Paulton, with music by Ivan Caryll,'' and was produced at the Lyric Theatre, New York, on 11 October 1920. Before it was produced in New York, however, it had actually been produced as *Mimi,* without Caryll's music, but with a score by the multi-talented Philipp and by Frank E Tours, patently trying to repeat the formula of Philipp's earlier hit show *Alma, Where Do You Live?* Having started out on its tryout tour at the Shubert Belasco in Washington on 14 March 1920, *Mimi* soon vanished from the road schedules. But seven months later *Kissing Time* surfaced on Broadway equipped with no Tours or Philipp songs but a whole score of Caryll ones, a libretto credited to Hobart based on Philipp and Paulton's alleged ''translation from the French'' and lyrics by a journalist and striving poet called Philander Chase Johnson (an ex-drama critic of the *Washington Star* who made much noise around dramatic circles, but no other mark on the musical stage), together with Clifford Grey and Irving Caesar. Broadway, of course, hadn't had a *Kissing Time,* because *Kissing Time* Mark I had still been *The Girl Behind the Gun* when it had played New York, and since it had played New York, there was no likelihood of it doing so again with its new title. The title was up for grabs, and Caryll, at least, clearly though it was worth saving.

The story that had, similarly, been thought worth saving (from *Mimi*) was barely an original one, and soubrette Mimi (Dorothy Maynard) of the Maison Mimi wasn't quite the central figure in it. That was ''the other Mimi,'' otherwise Clarice (Edith Taliaferro), a little lass from Dijon, who poses as the wife of an unmarried man so that he can get a married man's raise from his boss. William Norris (Polydore Cliquot, Mimi's admirer) was chief comic, Frank Doane (Armand Moulanger, another Mimi admirer) number two comic, Paul Frawley (Robert Perronet, admired by Mimi) the juvenile man, and Carl Hyson and Evelyn Cavanaugh a ubiquitous pair of speciality dancers. Caryll's songs included three duos for Miss Taliaferro and Frawley—an invitation to ''Bill and

Coo,'' the tale of ''Love's Telephone'' (an instrument already investigated in Caryll's *The Little Cherub*) and their assertion of being ''Absolutely Certain''—whilst the real Mimi sang of being ''Mimi,'' headed the ''Mimi Jazz'' and joined the juveniles and Cliquot in ''So Long as the World Goes Round.'' Frawley had a solo title song (which London's *Kissing Time* hadn't had), whilst Norris described himself as ''An Absolute Son of a Juan'' and the dancers encouraged ''Keep a Foxtrot for Me.''

The plot of *Kissing Time* actually won critical praise, simply for being a plot in an age where a musical didn't always have one, Caryll's ''pleasant, singable and danceable melodies'' didn't demerit, and one critic also found to his surprise that ''the ladies of the chorus manage to look more like intelligent human beings than is usually the case.'' All these elements put together, however, earned *Kissing Time* but nine weeks on Broadway, and this time there was no export.

KISS ME, KATE Musical comedy in 2 acts by Sam and Bella Spewack. Music and lyrics by Cole Porter. New Century Theater, New York, 30 December 1948.

Following the successful quintet of colorful, light song-and-dance shows which he had written with Herbert Fields in the late 1930s and the early 1940s, Cole Porter switched here to a rather more substantial kind of show and, in collaboration with the authors of his earlier *Leave It to Me,* turned out the musical which was to be his most successful and most enduring of all in *Kiss Me, Kate.*

Fred Graham (Alfred Drake) and Lilli Vanessi (Patricia Morison) were once man and wife, but they are now divorced. However, they are stage stars and the forces of show business and the pursuit of profit mean that they still work together. At the moment they are starring in a production of a musical based on *The Taming of the Shrew,* directed by Fred, which is being got into shape at Ford's Theater in Baltimore. Fred has, for not entirely blameless reasons, cast a perky cabaret performer called Lois Lane (Lisa Kirk) in the role of Bianca, and the other half of her double-act, Bill Calhoun (Harold Lang), has been found a role as Lucentio. Lilli—who is being intensely courted by a wealthy politician—finds she still gets miffed watching Fred's attentions to Lois, but it is Bill who really upsets the applecart. Heavily done down in a rough game of cards, he has signed the IOU as ''Fred Graham,'' and on opening night a pair of gangsters (Harry Clark, Jack Diamond) turn up to collect their boss's winnings from Fred. The evening is a tough one for Fred, for he has more than just gangsters on his plate: he has an ex-wife. Lilli is in a rage, for a replica of her wedding bouquet, sent from Fred, has been delivered to her, and, having let down her guard and admitted that she still loves her ex-husband, she has discovered that the flowers are addressed to Lois. She glowers through the first act, until Fred takes advantage of the play's script to administer his temperamental co-star a good spanking. Lilli refuses to continue the show, but Fred reminds the gangsters that they won't get their money if the box office take has to be returned, so the leading lady is frog-marched through the last act by two nutty gangsters, right up to the inevitable all-round happy ending.

Cole Porter's brimming-over scoreful of songs illustrated both the Fred-and-Lilli and Bill-and-Lois tales and also the show-within-the-show, allowing the songwriter to spread himself over a much wider variety of numbers than was usual in his theatre scores. And the celebrity telephone book never even got opened. In the first group, Fred and Lilli reminisced about their early touring days in a burlesque of Viennese Operette, ''Wunderbar'' (''gazing down on the Jungfrau . . .'' is, of course, a physical impossibility), and Lilli gave out one of Porter's warmest romantic numbers, admitting that she is ''So in Love'' with her ex-husband, whilst Lois bemoaned Bill's irresponsibility in ''Why Can't You Behave?'' and excused her own in the revusical ''Always True to You in My Fashion.''

The Taming of the Shrew had Petruchio/Fred thinking over his old conquests in ''Where Is the Life That Late I Led'' whilst admitting ''I've Come to Wive It Wealthily in Padua'' and rudely wooing Kate/Lilli in ''Were Thine That Special Face,'' Lilli spitting out ''I Hate Men'' with virulent overtones whilst Bianca/Lois played with her suitors in ''Tom, Dick or Harry,'' alongside a choral introduction ''We Open in Venice'' and, a rare thing in a Porter score, a winning concerted finale, ''Kiss Me, Kate.'' On top of all this, there was still space for a front-cloth kind of Gallagher-and-Shean number for the gangsters, advising in more typical, cataloguing, Porter tones that you should ''Brush Up Your Shakespeare'' to make a wow with the ladies, a lazy dance number performed by the stage-door keeper as an opener to the second act (''Too Darn Hot'') and an opening, hymning the out-of-town tryout in ''Another Op'nin', Another Show.''

Saint Subber and designer Lemuel Ayres's production of *Kiss Me, Kate* was a full-scale Broadway hit. It picked up, in the days before the proliferation of award categories, the initial Tony Award for best musical as well as the citations for best book and best score, and went on to a run of 1,077 performances. Keith Andes and Anne Jeffreys headed out the first touring company, before moving into town to replace the original stars, whilst the same company's Julie Wilson (Lois) also left what was to eventually be an almost two-year tour to go to London, where the first overseas *Kiss Me, Kate* was mounted, under the management of Jack Hylton, early in

Plate 207. **Kiss Me, Kate.** *Lilli Vanessi (Elisabeth Kales) ignores the chorused advice to kiss her ex-husband, Fred Graham (Peter Minich), in spite of the plot of their play, at the Vienna Volksoper, 1989.*

1951. There Miss Morison repeated her original role alongside Bill Johnson's Fred, Danny Green paired with Sidney (later to be film-famous as just Sid) James as the gangsters, and the show repeated its Broadway success, running for just short of 12 months (400 performances) as Helena Bliss (Lilli) and Valerie Tandy (Lois) took over from the original stars.

The following year, Australia welcomed its production of *Kiss Me, Kate* with Hayes Gordon (Fred), Joy Turpin (Lilli), Maggie Fitzgibbon (Lois) and Alec Kellaway and Morgan Davis (gangsters) featured, for five months in Melbourne and then four more in Sydney (Theatre Royal 2 August 1952), before Hollywood issued its 1953 celluloid version with Howard Keel (Fred), Kathryn Grayson (Lilli), Ann Miller (Bianca) and Tommy Rall (Bill) starred. In 1955 the show made something of a breakthrough when it was produced at Frankfurt (ad Günter Neumann), the first postwar American musical to have made its way to the Continental stage. From Frankfurt, the show slowly but surely worked its way through Europe, becoming, in the process, not only a groundbreaker, but also the most popular and enduring of all the transatlantic musical shows of the 1950s and 1960s which then began, tentatively at first, to follow in its wake. In 1963 *Csókolj meg Katám* became the first American musical to be played at Budapest's main musical house, the Fővárosi Operettszínház (ad Tamás Ungvári, György Dénes), opening the way for Britain's *Expresso Bongo* and France's *Irma la Douce* the following year, and for *My Fair Lady* two seasons later. That season saw a Budapest revival of *Kiss Me, Kate,* which also made its first appearance in Berlin in the same year.

In 1973 a version directed, designed and ''revised by'' Helmut Käutner was mounted at the Theater an der Wien, Vienna (which had begun its Broadway period with a visit from *My Fair Lady* in 1963) with Harald

Serafin (Fred), Naëmi Priegel (Lilli), Olivia Molina (Chiquita!?) and Joachim Kemmer (Bill) featured, and a vast amount of extraneous dancing tacked in for the theatre's resident corps de ballet (78 performances). Nearly a decade later (5 March 1982) the show was taken into the repertoire at the Volksoper, with Peter Minich (Fred), Dagmar Koller (Lilli) and Melanie Holliday (Bianca) featured in roles which they were still playing a further decade on, as *Kiss Me, Kate* confirmed itself as one of the pillars of American musical-theatre repertoire in Austria, in the same way that it had in Germany and in Hungary. The Volksoper mounted a new production in 1995 (30 October) with Mario Adorf and Julia Stemberger featured, and Budapest saw the show again at the Ódry Színpad in 1996 (8 March) with Attila Baráth and Barbara Dorogi.

Kiss Me, Kate held its place firmly in the repertoire in English-language countries as well, but for a long time in the regional theatre rather than in the main centers. Although it was seen at New York's City Center, and on American television (1970, with Robert Goulet and Carol Lawrence), there was, in spite of the enormous push for Porter productions in fin de siècle decades, no Broadway revival of this most complete (and, thus, least fiddleable-with) of his shows until half a century after the original one. London, on the other hand, saw the show twice, but each time in most unlikely circumstances and in the subsidized rather than the commercial theatre. In 1970 the English National Opera produced a semi-operatic version (London Coliseum 24 December) with its members Émile Belcourt (Fred) and Ann Howard (Lilli) supported by musical-comedy players Judith Bruce (Lois) and Teddy Green (Bill), and some 17 years later the Royal Shakespeare Company followed suit (Old Vic 19 May 1987) with a production which barely used their company at all—just their name and their subsidy. Paul Jones (Fred), Nichola McAuliffe (Lilli) and Fiona Hendley (Lois) featured in a revival which followed its Old Vic season with a run at the Savoy Theatre (18 January 1988). The Broadway revival came to the Martin Beck Theater in 1999 (18 November) with Brian Stokes and Marin Mazzie starred and met with a largely favorable reception.

In 1992 a French-language version (ad Alain Marcel) made its first appearance in Geneva with Bernard Alane (Fred), Marie Zamora (Lilli), Fabienne Guyon (Lois) and Jacques Verzier (Bill) featured. It was subsequently shown in Paris at the Théâtre Mogador the following year.

UK: London Coliseum 8 March 1951; Australia: His Majesty's Theatre, Melbourne 2 February 1952; Germany: Städtische Bühnen, Frankfurt 19 February 1955, Metropoltheater, Berlin 9 April, 1965; Hungary: Fővárosi Operettszínház *Csókolj meg Katám* 15 November 1963; Austria: Theater an der Wien 6 February 1973, Volksoper 5 March 1982: France: Théâtre Mogador 26 January 1993.

Film: MGM 1953

Recordings: original cast (Columbia), London cast on *Cole Porter in London* (WRC), London cast 1987 (First Night), Dutch cast (Philips, CNR), complete (EMI), film soundtrack (MGM, CBS), selection (Reprise, etc), selection in German (Ariola), etc

KISS OF THE SPIDERWOMAN Musical in 2 acts by Terrence McNally based on the novel by Manuel Puig. Lyrics by Fred Ebb. Music by John Kander. Bluma Appel Theater, Toronto, Canada, 14 June 1992; Shaftesbury Theatre, London, 20 October 1992.

Manuel Puig's novel, *Kiss of the Spiderwoman* was successfully transformed into both a play and a film (1985, with William Hurt and Raul Julia) before becoming a musical in the hands of the creators of *Chicago, Zorba* and *Cabaret.* First played in May 1990 as a work in progress by a New Musicals program at SUNY Purchase, the show was subsequently produced by the Canadian organization Livent in Toronto and, avoiding Broadway and its then critic, opted instead for a London launch.

Molina (Brent Carver), a flamboyant homosexual and Valentin (Anthony Crivello), a political prisoner, share a cell in a South American jail. Molina escapes from the awful reality surrounding him by fantasizing about the glamorous film star Aurora (Chita Rivera), famous for her role as ''the Spiderwoman,'' Valentin—who is being tortured by the prison authorities so that he will betray his collaborators—gets through by thinking of his girlfriend, Marta (Kirsti Carnahan). When Molina is allowed out of jail to visit his sick mother (Merle Louise), Valentin persuades him—by a calculated seduction—to make a telephone call. But Molina is followed, his collusion discovered and, when he refuses to reveal what he knows, he is shot by the prison warder. As he dies, he sees himself in the arms of Aurora the Spiderwoman, poisoned by her kiss.

Aurora's set song and dance pieces (''Her Name is Aurora,'' ''Where You Are,'' ''I Do Miracles,'' ''Gimme Love,'' the seductive ''Kiss of the Spiderwoman''), which made up the backbone of the score, were pieces with a period filmland flavor to their words and music, but in spite of their pastichey nature they appealed more than the men's pieces—a camp window-dressing number, and a wannabe-a-woman piece for Molina, a rampaging autobiographical piece for Valentin (''The Day After That'')—which seemed rather too shallow and lightweight to point a dramatic contrast. A simple, gentle piece for Molina's mother and Marta, ''Dear One'' proved the most attractive number.

The story was a natural for the musical stage, the well-tried traditions of the ''dream'' or fantasy musical being solidly encased in a version of a proven play which provided a fashionable shell of fin de siècle sex, politics and drama with the obligatory unhappy ending. If the result was less satisfying than the same songwriters' sex-law-and-drama *Chicago,* that was undoubtedly because—in line with the style of the modern musical—humor was rather less in evidence. There was also another point. A London journalist's review summed up what had, over the decades, become an important part of the appeal of Ebb and Kander's material: "What was a love story about two individuals becomes a generalised monument to gay taste, with [. . .] Rivera taking the place as icon once occupied by Judy Garland." There are, of course, plenty of "gay" folk to whom Ms Garland, Spiderwomen and all they represent are utter gushing anathema, and those same utter anathemists were among those who found it a shame that one of the few modern musicals (amongst an endless number of modern plays, not a few of them by librettist McNally) to represent a gay character on the stage as anything but the clichéd effeminate "interior decorator" of once upon a time, had to choose that character's turn-of-the-century equivalent, the "grande-dame queen," complete with his grande dame. There were many others whose tastes simply didn't run to this kind of entertainment.

However, folk with so-called gay taste held up the show for 390 performances in London, after which it made the move to Broadway. There, with the same three performers featured, it took the year's Tony Award for best musical and played for 906 performances without, however, recouping its investment. It also traveled on to South America (Teatro Lola Membrives, Buenos Aires 2 May 1995) and to central Europe, where "gay taste" in the musical theatre thrives most spectacularly in the turn-of-the-century years, and a German-language version (ad Michael Kunze) was mounted at the Vienna Raimundtheater with Günter Mokesch (Molina), Thorsten Tinney (Valentin), Yamil Borges (Aurora) and former Volksoper star Sigrid Martikke (mother) featured.

USA: Broadhurst Theater 3 May 1993; Austria: Raimundtheater *Kuss der Spinnenfrau* 28 November 1993

Recordings: original cast (First Night), Broadway casts (BMG, Mercury), Viennese cast (Ariola Reverso), Argentine cast *El Beso de la Mujer Arana* (BMG)

KITTY GREY Musical comedy in 3 acts adapted by J Smyth Piggott from *Les Fêtards* by Antony Mars and Maurice Hennequin. Music by Lionel Monckton, Howard Talbot, Augustus T Barratt and Victor Roger. Bristol, 27 August 1900; Apollo Theatre, London, 7 September 1901.

George Edwardes first produced his British version of the dazzling French musical comedy *Les Fêtards* (ad J Smyth Piggott) as a non-musical play (*Kitty Grey* Vaudeville Theatre 25 April 1900). However, he changed his mind in mid-run and, closing the production after 107 West End performances, he had the play briskly remusicalized so that, less than three weeks after the London closure, he was able to open a new, musical version of *Kitty Grey* in Bristol with several of the same players still holding their London roles.

In a very strong Edwardes cast, Ethel Sydney played the Quakerish Baronne de Trègue and Maurice Farkoa (whose Smyrnese accent was responsible for this character being remade French instead of English as in the play version) her philandering husband, with Evie Greene as Kitty, the actress who teaches the lady about sex and how to use it to control an errant mate. Plump and funny Lillie Belmore took the plum character role of the wardrobe lady which had been created by Marie Desclauzas, Harry Monkhouse was the sex-seeking King of Illyria and G P Huntley the goofy and scene-stealing Lord Plantagenet. If the strong text of the original play was well adhered to, the musical part was a bit of a patchwork, a little of Roger's Parisian music being retained, and other songs being supplied by Edwardes's loyal Lionel Monckton, conductor Howard Talbot and others mostly less eminent. Monckton came out with the most successful song, a piece for expansive Mrs Bright, describing how she was once, in her slimmer days, "Little Zo-Zo" of the circus.

The new *Kitty Grey* proved such a success on the road that Edwardes decided to bring it back to town. Evie Greene, in spite of the fact that a special role had been written for her in Edwardes's upcoming *Three Little Maids,* stayed on and was paired with suitably American Edna May (the Baronne de Trègue was an American in the original script) for whom extra songs were supplied to make her part the co-lead, with Huntley repeating his road success alongside Farkoa, Charles Angelo (King) and Gladys Homfrey (Mrs Bright). In spite of the fact that it was Mars and Hennequin's delicious play and characters that were the heart of *Kitty Grey,* the version with music outran the play comprehensively: 220 London performances, umpteen tours (as soon as Farkoa was gone his role reverted to being "Sir John Binfield"), and productions throughout the colonies over many years.

For the first of these, in Australia, George Edwardes sent out almost an entire principal cast from Britain. The "Gaiety Company" carried *The Girl from Kays* and *Three Little Maids* as well as *Kitty Grey,* and the cross-casting was done in function of *Three Little Maids,* but Huntley and Farkoa were both there in their original roles, alongside two of the three little maids, Madge Crichton (Kitty) and Delia Mason (Baronne), J Edward Fraser as the King and Clara Clifton as Mrs Bright. The show was not given for a run, but played for limited seasons in repertoire with its two fellows.

America had already had its own version of *Les Fêtards* (*The Rounders*) some time previously but, a number of years later when Charles Frohman needed a Broadway vehicle for Huntley and Julia Sanderson, he produced the comedian's old hit for 50 New York performances at the New Amsterdam Theater. For that occasion the London "balance" between the lady stars was abolished: Miss Sanderson sang five songs and a duet (including Jerome Kern's "If a Girl Wants You" and "Just Good Friends"), Valli Valli (Lady Binfield) had half a duet and "Little Zo-Zo" had been suppressed. Only Angelo, now living in America and repeating his London role, got much of a sing otherwise.

An atypical musical in turn-of-the-century Britain, the very libretto-orientated *Kitty Grey* was an important forerunner to the farcical musical comedies of the post-war years. Unlike them, it did not make a feature of modern dance fashions, and its music was the music of the standard Victorian musical comedy rather than of the dance floor, but its long and wide popularity showed that there was a market for reasonably sophisticated musical plays on the lines of the French vaudeville, as opposed to extravaganza, to spectacle or to the styles practiced by Edwardes at either the Gaiety or Daly. Yet, in spite of the fact that several successful pieces based more or less on good French plays followed it (*The Girl from Kays, Madame Sherry, The Spring Chicken, Peggy*), it was a style of piece that was oddly slow finding its feet in the English-speaking world.

Australia: Princess Theatre, Melbourne 25 June 1904; USA: New Amsterdam Theater 25 January 1909

KITTY'S KISSES Musical comedy in 2 acts by Philip Bartholomae and Otto Harbach adapted from Bartholomae's play *Little Miss Brown.* Lyrics by Gus Kahn. Music by Con Conrad. Playhouse Theater, New York, 6 May 1926.

A musical version of Bartholomae's 14-year-old play *Little Miss Brown,* the less accurately but more catchily titled *Kitty's Kisses* told the tale of little Kitty Brown (Dorothy Dilley) who, through a little bit of almost French misunderstanding, unintentionally spends a night asleep in a hotel room which is also (if chastely and elsewhere) occupied by Robert Dennison (Mark Smith), a perilously married man. However, the divorce lawyer summoned the next morning by Mrs Dennison (Frances Burke) to deal with the situation turns out to be a young man called Robert Mason (John Boles) who had fallen for Kitty during her eventful trip to the hotel the previous day, and, when all the farcical doings are sung, danced and done, he is able to sort things out to everybody's satisfaction. William Wayne and Ruth Warren as a couple of hotel employees supplied the traditional soubretteries.

Kitty's Kisses was a piece well in the 1920s fashion for frantic and funny farce with loads of lively dances which were not obliged to take too much notice of the locations or the story: "a rough and tumble of dancing men and women, individually and in chorus, at the pace that exhilarates while it kills[;] . . . as soon as the first curtain goes up the chorus begins ecstatically dancing between the railroad tracks and, from then on, it glides, pops, swoons, careens and charlestons through hotel corridors, lobbies, bedrooms and gardens indiscriminately." The show also sported some light and bright summer fashions and some jolly songs, including a deliciously bright title number put over by Kitty and Robert who also joined to romantically sigh over "Whenever I Dream," the hero's admission that "I'm in Love," Kitty's tale of "Two Fellows and a Girl," her duo with Dennison ("Early in the Morning") and her insistence in the face of the rest of the Dennison family that "I Don't Want Him." The soubrets bounced out a "Thinking of You" and the second act danced to its feet "Steppin' on the Blues." It was all lively, well-constructed, harmlessly tuneful fun and, as a result, spent a fine 22 weeks on Broadway.

A sizeable portion of the show also made its way to London. Producer Jack Waller, on a shopping trip to New York, purchased both *Kitty's Kisses* and another of the season's successes, *The Girl Friend,* with a score by Rodgers and Hart. In one of history's better bits of botching, he then took the solid comical libretto of *Kitty's Kisses* plus "Steppin' on the Blues," "I'm in Love" and a number of other pieces of Con Conrad's score, welded them to some of the score of *The Girl Friend,* added a couple of Rodgers and Hart songs from *The Garrick Gaieties* ("Mountain Greenery," "What's the Use of Talking?"), filled up the gaps with some local numbers by Vivian Ellis, had the whole lot shaken and stirred by musical comedy men-of-all-work Bert Lee and R P Weston and presented the show—which was altogether more *Kitty's Kisses* than it was *The Girl Friend*—at the Palace Theatre under the title of the latter. The hybrid show, with Roy Royston, Louise Browne and Clifford Mollison starred, proved delightful. It ran for a year (421 performances) in London, toured, was successfully produced in Australia with Annie Croft starred as Kitty, adapted into Hungarian and staged in Budapest, and went on to be given periodic revivals throughout Britain for many decades thereafter . . . all in and under the name of *The Girl Friend.*

The most recent production of a version of this version, at Colchester's Mercury Theatre in 1987, used five *Kitty's Kisses* numbers alongside just two and a half by Rodgers and Hart who nevertheless had their names billed large above the title for a piece which, even more than Britain's original production, was much more

Kitty's Kisses than *The Girl Friend.* And altogether the better for it.

Recording: Colchester cast (as *The Girl Friend*) (TER)

KLAW, Marcus [KLAU, Markus] (b Paducah, Ky, 29 May 1858; d Bracken Fell, Hassocks, 14 June 1936). Powerful Broadway producer of the early 20th century.

Lawyer Klaw had his first connection with the theatre when he dealt with a suit against theatrical pirates for Gus Frohman. He soon made serious inroads into the show-business world, however, when, after first having tried his hand at touring management (as early as 1881 he was general manager of Madison Square Gardens tours), he moved to New York and joined with Abe Erlanger to take over an important theatrical agency (1888). Their influence and power soon spread, and the partners were the moving force in the establishment of the Theatrical Syndicate, a body which sought to bring order to the touring booking systems of the time and which was regarded (by those who were not part of it) as an attempt to monopolize the management of the American theatre.

During the years in which they had an effective control of a large section of the New York and regional theatres, Klaw and Erlanger produced many musical shows as product for their houses. These included the Rogers Brothers series, dialect low-comedy shows intentionally set up to challenge the productions of the unsubdued Weber and Fields on their own ground, *A Little of Everything* (1904), *In Newport* (1904), Sousa's *The Bride Elect* (1898) and *The Free Lance* (1906), *The Pearl and the Pumpkin* (1905), *Fritz in Tammany Hall* (1905), the McIntyre and Heath musical *The Ham Tree* (1905), George M Cohan's *Forty-Five Minutes from Broadway* (1906), the Luders/Pixley *The Grand Mogul* (1906), the Lulu Glaser vehicle *Lola from Berlin* (1907), Victor Herbert's cartoon musical *Little Nemo* (1908), *In Hayti* (1909), *The Silver Star* (1909) with Adeline Genée as star, *The Bachelor Belles* (1910), *The Merry Martyr* (1913) such imports as the Drury Lane pantos *Mother Goose* (1903), *Humpty Dumpty* (1904) and *The White Cat* (1905), *Véronique* (1905), *The Spring Chicken* (1906), *La Mascotte* (1909), *The Count of Luxembourg* (1912), *Eva* (1912), Kálmán's *Miss Springtime* (*Zsuzsi kisasszony*) (1916) and *The Riviera Girl* (*Die Csárdásfürstin*) and the semi-imported *The Man from Cook's,* and the series of Ivan Caryll musicals beginning with the vastly successful *The Pink Lady* (1911) and *Oh! Oh! Delphine* (1912), the first of which they also presented in Britain, and going on to *The Little Café* (1913) and *Papa's Darling* (1914).

The thin-faced, droopy-moustachioed Klaw appeared as the gentlemanly and receptive half of the feared and disliked (by their rivals) partnership with the pugnacious, pudgy and bald Erlanger. However, there can be little doubt, for all that he liked to have it believed otherwise, that the former lawyer had as much to do as his more openly dislikeable—and equally efficacious—partner with the hard-edged hard-business policies and actions (in a business which has always had room for the enthusiastic not-very-businessman) that earned Klaw and Erlanger their hated position.

In 1919 the partnership broke up, and Klaw, who built the Klaw Theater in the following year, continued to produce on his own for several more years. His first, and sole musical, venture, *Dere Mabel* (1920), a piece written by the daughter of a Bostonian businessman and produced in her hometown, folded there. In 1927 he sold up and, two years later, moved to Britain where he lived in retirement for his last 10 years.

KLEIN, [Philip] Charles (b London, 7 January 1867; d at sea, 7 May 1915). Playwright and librettist to the turn-of-the-century Broadway stage.

The third-born son of a Russian language teacher, Hermann Klein, who had settled in Britain in the 1850s, Charles Klein worked as an actor from the time of moving to America at the age of just 16. He had his first play as an author, a locomotive melodrama with interpolated specialities and songs called *A Mile a Minute* which he wrote to order around some spare props and posters, produced in in 1891. He ventured into the musical theatre at first by way of the pasticcio farce-comedy (*A Happy Little Home* for George W Monroe, etc), sometimes apparently without allowing his name on the program, and of adaptation, turning out one of the many versions of *Niniche* which found their way to the world's stages following the vaudeville's original Paris production. *The Merry Countess* starred Marie Jansen and Dan Daly in its leading roles for 10 Broadway performances.

He found significant success with his first original libretto, the text for John Philip Sousa's enduring comic opera *El Capitan,* and thereafter wrote several highly successful plays (*Heartsease, The Music Master, The Lion and the Mouse*), whilst returning regularly to the genuine musical stage. *The Charlatan,* a second collaboration with Sousa, proved an excellent vehicle for De Wolf Hopper and his company, and *Mr Pickwick,* with a score by Klein's brother Manuel, gave the comedian a fine Dickens role in a musical which was well liked on the road if not noticed in New York. Of his other very varying musical shows *A Royal Rogue* was mounted for the "Jefferson de Angelis Musical Comedy Company," *The Red Feather* was a Ziegfeld romantico-swashbucker of a piece starring the specifically soprano Grace van Studdiford, whilst *Cousin Lucy* was written to feature female impersonator Julian Eltinge.

Klein was traveling to Europe with Charles Frohman, for whom he had originally worked as play-reader and to whom he had later become house adaptor, when the *Lusitania* was sunk and both men were drowned.

Klein's play *Maggie Pepper* (1913), which had originally housed a notable performance by Rose Stahl as the lady of the title, was subsequently turned into a musical comedy vehicle for Charlotte Greenwood as *Letty Pepper* (1922).

1891 **A Mile a Minute** (pasticcio) People's Theater 9 February

1895 **The Merry Countess** (*Niniche*) American version w Thomas Frost (Garrick Theater)

1895 **A Happy Little Home** (various) 14th Street Theater 25 November

1896 **El Capitan** (John Philip Sousa/Frost, Sousa) Broadway Theater 20 April

1898 **The Charlatan** (aka *The Mystical Miss*) (Sousa) Knickerbocker Theater 5 September

1900 **A Royal Rogue** (W T Francis/Grant Stewart) Ford's Theater, Baltimore 24 September; Broadway Theater, New York 24 December

1902 **Mr Pickwick** (Manuel Klein) Academy of Music, Montreal 7 September; Herald Square Theater 19 January 1903

1903 **The Red Feather** (Reginald De Koven/Charles Emerson Cook) Lyric Theater 9 November

1915 **Cousin Lucy** (Jerome Kern, et al) George M Cohan Theater 29 August

KLEIN, Manuel [Joachim] (b London, 6 December 1876; d Yonkers, NY, 1 June 1919).

Manuel Klein followed his elder brother, Charles, to America at 20 years' distance and worked there as a theatre conductor, notably for 10 years at the New York Hippodrome (1905–15), and as a composer of musical scores and occasionally also of lyrics. Most of these scores were incidental music of one kind or another composed to accompany the vast spectacles staged at the Hippodrome, but his credits also included two children's musicals and a Dickensian vehicle for De Wolf Hopper. He was sacked by the Shuberts in 1915 for ''insubordination,'' and subsequently returned to Britain where he acted as musical director for Grossmith and Laurillard's Gaiety Theatre production of *Tonight's the Night.* He suffered a traumatism when the theatre came under fire from a German zeppelin and was forced to give up work, returning to America where he died a few years later, having never recovered from the shock. The Klein family subsequently sued the German government for encompassing the deaths of the two brothers.

In 1921 some of the songs he had written for the out-of-town flop *High and Dri* were posthumously used to make up the score of the musical *It's Up to You* at the Casino Theater. His of-the-moment song successes included ''Moon Dear'' and ''Red Sky,'' whilst his ''Lucia'' made its way back to Britain to be interpolated in the score of Seymour Hicks's *The Gay Gordons.*

1903 **Mr Pickwick** (Charles Klein) Academy of Music, Montreal 7 September; Herald Square Theater 19 January

1905 **A Yankee Circus on Mars** (w Jean Schwartz/Harry Williams/George Hobart) New York Hippodrome 12 April

1905 **Tomorrowland** (John Kendrick Bangs) New York Hippodrome in *A Yankee Circus on Mars*

1905 **A Society Circus** (w Gustave Luders/Sydney Rosenfeld) New York Hippodrome 13 December

1906 **The Man from Now** (Vincent Bryan/Bangs) Tremont Theater, Boston 28 May; New Amsterdam Theater 3 September

1906 **Neptune's Daughter** (w Edward P Temple) 1 act New York Hippodrome 28 November

1907 **The Top of the World** (Anne Caldwell/James O'Dea/Mark E Swan) Majestic Theater 19 October

1907 **The Auto Race** (w Temple) New York Hippodrome 25 November

1908 **Sporting Days** (R H Burnside) New York Hippodrome 5 September

1908 **The Battle in the Skies** (Burnside) in *Sporting Days*

1908 **The Pied Piper** (ex- *What Happened Then*) (Burnside, Austen Strong) His Majesty's Theater, Montreal 14 September; Majestic Theater 3 December

1909 **A Trip to Japan** (Burnside) New York Hippodrome 4 September

1910 **The International Cup** (Burnside) New York Hippodrome 3 September

1911 **Bow Sing** (Carroll Fleming) 1 act Winter Garden 20 March

1911 **Around the World** (Fleming) New York Hippodrome 2 September

1911 **Undine** (M Klein) 1 act Winter Garden 20 November

1912 **Under Many Flags** (Fleming, Arthur Voegtlin) New York Hippodrome 31 August

1913 **America** (Voegtlin, John P Wilson) New York Hippodrome 30 August

1913 **Hop o' My Thumb** (George Sims, et al, ad Sydney Rosenfeld) Manhattan Opera House 26 November

1914 **The Wars of the World** (Voegtlin) New York Hippodrome 5 September

1919 **High and Dri** (Augustus McHugh, Edward Paulton, A Douglas Leavitt)

1921 **It's Up to You** (revised *High and Dri*) Casino Theater 24 March

A third of the six Klein brothers, **Alfred [Asher] KLEIN** (b Norwich, 12 May 1861; d Amityville, NJ, 21 February 1904), also worked in the theatre, musical and comic, as a performer from his earliest age, playing Sir Joseph in a juvenile *Pinafore* company in 1879, appearing as Buttons in *The Rajah,* and rising to the Girardi role of Miradello in *A Trip to Africa* in German and English. He spent a considerable amount of his career with John McCaull (Vulcanio in *Prinz Methusalem,* Pelican in *Falka,* Benozzo in *Gasparone,* Duke of Parma in *Jacquette,* Mefflin in *The Black Hussar,* Assinelli in *Amorita,* Simon in *Erminie,* in *Jacquette*) and in particular with De Wolf Hopper's companies (Repetitio in *Castles in the Air,* Lord Lawntennis in *Dr Syntax,* Pozzo in *El Capitan,* Don Jose in *Panjandrum,* Jellikoff in *The Charlatan,* Pepat in *Wang*), where his tiny, rotund figure and permanently worried expression (''the living incarnation of 'oh, dear me''') made him a fine foil to the extremely tall star.

A fourth brother, **Herman KLEIN** (b Norwich, 23 July 1856; d 10 March 1934), was a music critic and teacher of voice. He authored several books including *Thirty Years of Musical Life in London* (William Heinemann, London, 1903), *Unmusical New York* and four volumes of *Musical Notes,* and made English versions of several operas, including *Carmen.*

KNAACK, Wilhelm (b Rostock, Germany, 1823; d Vienna, 29 October 1894). Top-rank comic of the mid-19th century Vienna stage.

On the stage from his early twenties, Knaack played in Stralsund, Greifswald, Güstrow, Lübeck and, from 1852, at the Friedrich-Wilhelmstädtisches Theater in Berlin before he moved in 1857 to Vienna and was engaged at the Carltheater. He remained there for virtually the whole of the rest of his life, apart from one brief period with Treumann at the Theater am Franz-Josefs-Kai and another which he spent playing in German-language theatre in America, and in harness with Karl Blasel and Josef Matras he made up the trio of great and enormously popular Viennese comedians of the time.

Knaack introduced the German versions of a plethora of opéra-bouffe roles including Offenbach's Crécy-Crécy (*Toto*), Boboli (*Die schöne Weiber von Georgien*), Baron Gondremarck (*Pariser Leben*), Sparadrap (*Die Prinzessin von Trapezunt*), John Styx (*Orpheus in der Unterwelt*), *Trompeter und Näherin,* Romboïdal (*L'Île de Tulipatan*), Tschin-Tschin (*Tschin-Tschin*), Der kleine Arthur (*Die schöne Magellone*), Baptist (*Die Seufzerbrücke*), Christobal (*Die Schwätzerin von Saragossa*), Frau Hetschepetsch (*Die Damen von Stand*), Jean Brösel (ie, Petermann, *Salon Pitzelberger*), Ignazio (*Tromb-al-ca-zar*), Plumotzeau (*Apotheker und Friseur*), Bellecoeur (*Kakadu*), Arsenico (*Coscoletto*), Marquis von Fontrose (*Die Schäfer*), Balabreloque (*Schneeball*), Chrisostome (*Schönröschen*) and von Tricasse (*Doktor Ox*). He also succeeded Nestroy in the role of Pan in *Daphnis und Chloë,* and appeared in such other Viennezed French works as Alcidor von Rosenville (*Die Reise nach China*), Wetterhahn (*Confusius IX*), Larivaudière (*Angot*), Grison (*Die schöne Bourbonnaise*), Casteldémoli (*Graziella*), Graf Cornisti (*Niniche*), Prinz Charles (*Der grosse Casimir*) and Bodin-Bridet (*Papas Frau*).

Knaack also played in some of the earliest original Viennese works of the era, appearing as Hieronymus Geier in *Flotte Bursche* and Svermazet in *Mannschaft am Bord,* as Ritter Hannibal vom Bisamberg (*Das Donauweibchen*), Nicodemus Violette (*Isabella*), Breselmaier (*In der Sackgasse*) and Lord Blessington (*Fitzliputzli*), and he created, amongst others, the more important roles of Graf Kantschukoff in *Fatinitza* (1876), Herzog von Ricerac in *Prinz Methusalem* (1877), Mephisto in *Der Teufel auf Erden,* Bob Chester in *Die Mormonen* (1879), Muzinard in *Der Kukuk* and Barnacle in *Nisida* (1880).

After his trip to America, where he appeared at the Thalia Theater with the Gallmeyer-Tewele combination, in their challenge to Geistinger and her company, in his roles in *Niniche, Die Prinzessin von Trapezunt* and a series of comedies, he returned to the Carltheater in 1886 to carry on with a series of new shows and roles: Iwan der Schrecklich (*Der Vagabund*), Alfred Pharoa Pascha (*Josefine und ihre Schwestern*), Van der Putt-Putt (*Rikiki*), Eustachio fa Presto (*Die Dreizehn*), Lord Middleditch (*Der Glücksritter*), Prince Prostamento (*Der Sänger von Palermo*), Wilfred Shadbolt (*Capitän Wilson*), Campistrel (*Colombine*), Bluff (ie, Dufois) (*Erminie*), Schnerb (*Die Uhlanen*), Pierre Josua Favart (*Die Kätzchen*), Pichard (*Das Fräulein vom Telephone*), Verduron (*Susette, oder Zweihundert millionen*) and Van der Beerenboom (*Lachende Erben*). Even when turned 70, he was still to be seen in his old roles of Gondremarck, Kantschukoff and Sparadrap, as well as in the occasional new part such as Borgos in *Edelweiss* or the American David Osteborn in the French spectacular *Das Goldland.* Shortly before his death, he played Spettigue to the Fancourt Babberly of the equally veteran Blasel in the play *Charley's Aunt.*

KNEPLER, Paul [KNÖPLER, Paul] (b Vienna, 29 October 1879; d Vienna, 17 December 1967). Viennese composer turned librettist.

Like Genée and Hopp before him and others since, Paul Knepler set out to be a composer for the musical theatre and yet had his most considerable success as a librettist and lyricist. Nevertheless, he did well enough with his first produced work as a composer-author, a romanticized biomusical of the favorite Viennese 19th-century soubrette Josefine (''Pepi'') Gallmeyer. Produced at the Wiener Bürgertheater with Rosy Werginz (Gallmeyer) and Fritz Schrödter (Josef Matras) starring, and with such old-time favorites as Anna Grobecker (Paula Bäck), Karl Treumann (August Nietl) and Offenbach himself (Heinrich Pirk) represented on the stage, it ran for 139 performances.

In 1924 Knepler teamed with librettist Ignaz Michael Welleminsky on a second Operette *Wenn der Hollunder blüht,* which was produced in Berlin, and at the same time he sent a libretto he had written based on the putative love life of another historical character, the violinist Paganini, to Lehár. Lehár accepted it with some delight and put Knepler to work on his text with the proven Béla Jenbach. The success of the resultant Operette established its author as a librettist, and thereafter, often in collaboration with Welleminsky, he turned out books for many of the best composers of the time, including Leo Ascher, Eduard Künneke, Oscar Straus and Emmerich Kálmán. However, although he had a certain success with yet another text set in theatreland, the tale of the actor Devrient and his Spanish dancer as told in Künneke's *Die lockende Flamme* (87 performances), and again with his adaptation to the stage of the film script *Zwei Herzen im Dreivierteltakt* (yet another show about a show), of his original texts it was his only other collaboration with Lehár, on the grimly passionate libretto for the composer's last work, *Giuditta* (1934), and above all the three-generations tale of *Drei Walzer* (1935) which won him, at length if at not at the time of production, any kind of lasting laurels.

Knepler also translated the zarzuela *El barberillo de Lavapiès* (w Fred Salo Tysh) as *Lamparilla* for the German-language stage, and worked on adaptations of several classic Operetten. He had notable success with his rewrite of Millöcker's *Gasparone* (which introduced the famous ''Dunkelrote Rosen'') and also of the fresh book for Theo Mackeben's musical remake of Millöcker's *Gräfin Dubarry* as *Die Dubarry.* Both versions, conforming more readily to operettic styles of the years between the wars than their originals, found themselves a place in the repertoire they would not otherwise have recovered.

1921 **Josefine Gallmeyer** (Knepler) Wiener Bürgertheater 22 March

1924 **Wenn der Hollunder blüht** (Knepler/w Ignaz M Welleminsky) Bundestheater (Metropoltheater), Berlin 1 July

1925 **Paganini** (Franz Lehár/w Béla Jenbach) Johann Strauss-Theater 30 October

1927 **Die Glocken von Paris** (Richard Fall/w Welleminsky) Carltheater 14 October

1931 **Bei der Wirtin Rosenrot** (Leo Ascher/w Fritz Löhner-Beda) Theater des Westens, Berlin 14 March

1931 **Die Dubarry** (Carl Millöcker arr Theo Mackeben/w Welleminsky) Admiralspalast, Berlin 14 August

1931 **Die Toni aus Wien** (Ernst Steffan/Willner, Rubricius ad w Steffan)

1932 **Tanz durchs Leben** (R Düringer/w Welleminsky) Stadttheater, Danzig 13 November

1933 **Gasparone** revised version w Steffan (Volksoper)

1933 **Zwei Herzen im Dreivierteltakt** (*Der verlorene Walzer*) (Robert Stolz/Robert Gilbert/w Welleminsky) Stadttheater, Zürich 30 September; revised version Centraltheater, Dresden 26 December

1933 **Die lockende Flamme** (Eduard Künneke/w Welleminsky) Theater des Westens 25 December

1934 **Giuditta** (Lehár/w Löhner-Beda) Staatsoper, Vienna 20 January

1935 **Drei Walzer** (Johann Strauss I arr, Johann Strauss II arr, Oscar Straus/w Armin Robinson) Stadttheater, Zürich 5 October

1936 **Kaiserin Josephine** (Emmerich Kálmán/w Géza Herczeg) Stadttheater, Zürich 18 January

1948 **Die Musik kommt** (Oscar Straus/w Robinson) Stadttheater, Zürich 6 November

1950 **Ihr erster Walzer** revised *Die Musik kommt* ad Robert Gilbert Bayerische Stadttheater, Munich 31 March

1963 **Rhapsodie der Liebe** (Nico Dostal/w Peter Herz) Städtische Bühnen, Nürnberg-Fürth 9 November

Other work credited: *Tanz um Daisy* (Victor Reinshagen/André Perrot ad)

KNICKERBOCKER HOLIDAY Musical comedy in 2 acts by Maxwell Anderson based on Washington Irving's *Father Knickerbocker's History of New York.* Music by Kurt Weill. Barrymore Theater, New York, 19 October 1938.

A costume musical which utilized the low-comedy ''Dutch'' accent, so popular on the musical stage 30 to 50 years earlier, in a tale of old New York, *Knickerbocker Holiday* told the story of knifegrinder Brom Broeck (Richard Kollmar) who has to fight against both a peremptory town council and the Governor, Pieter Stuyvesant (Walter Huston), in order to get the girl he wants (Tina, played by Jeanne Madden). In fact, he succeeds not by his own exertions but only when author Washington Irving (Ray Middleton) century-hops and deters Stuyvesant from hanging the insubordinate fellow by threatening him with the thumbs-down verdict of posterity.

Anderson's libretto and dialogue included some tetchily social, political and even jingoistic moments in the unrolling of its standard comic-opera story, whilst taking time off for such personal jibes as calling one buffoonish councillor Roosevelt and another Vanderbilt. Weill's score, on the other hand, was sometimes adventurous in its form but scored best when following the traditional song patterns that produced Stuyvesant's ''September Song,'' crackled out by Huston in a rueful look at approaching age. ''September Song,'' which found its way into the score only when Huston requested a number that would give his rather one-dimensional character some personality, has remained the most popular single number composed by Kurt Weill for a Broadway show.

The show was dubbed ''unwieldy . . . the light fantastic vein of musical comedy does not become [Anderson's] serious mind—or vice versa'' and, in spite of a memorable performance by top-billed Huston, who negated some of Anderson's intent by making the Governor a warmly likeable character as he danced along peg-legged at the head of a line of little Dutch girls, the Playwrights' Company production of the rather ill-assorted *Knickerbocker Holiday* lasted only 168 performances on Broadway.

It was subsequently filmed, with Charles Coburn starred as Stuyvesant, Constance Dowling as Tina and Nelson Eddy as Broeck, in a version which used but four numbers from the original score, topped up with contributions from Werner Richard Heymann, Jule Styne, Sammy Cahn, Theodore Paxton and with both Forman Brown and Eddy himself having a go at lyricking Weill's music. In 1950 (17 November) it was televised with Dennis King, Doretta Morrow and John Raitt featured, and its writers' reputations and political standpoint have helped ensure it regular regional and occasional performances since. An attempt at a major Broadway-bound revival, mounted at the San Francisco Light Opera in 1971 with Burt Lancaster starred as Stuyvesant and Anita Gillette and David Holliday in support did not make it to the East Coast.

Germany: Städtische Bühnen, Essen 25 November 1948.

Film: United Artists 1944

Recordings: original cast compilation (AEI), film soundtrack (Joey)

A KNIGHT FOR A DAY Musical comedy in 2 acts by Robert B Smith. Music by Raymond Hubbell. Wallack's Theater, New York, 16 December 1907.

Musical-comedy star Sallie Fisher's Chicago successes earned her a fairly transparent title role in *Mam'selle Sallie,* a musical manufactured by Robert B Smith (and originally intended to be called *The Other Locket*) with songs by Raymond Hubbell, which was duly trouped from Poli's Theater, Waterbury, Conn (15 October 1906) around the country and eventually, and almost incidentally, towards New York. Miss Fisher played a Mittel-European washerwoman disguised as a brigand who is trying to get back the missing proofs of her pals' noble birth, to the accompaniment of a set of lively songs which had little of the Continental about them, and of a good deal of low comedy from British ''slavey'' star Katie Barry and John Slavin.

A brief touring visit to the combination house grandly known as the Grand Opera House (26 November 1906) and 16 performances at the New York Theater saw the show out of town and back on the road, but producer John C Fisher did not give up. *Mam'selle Sallie* was given a wash and brush-up and turned up again the following season under the title *A Knight for a Day.* The plot was much as before, Miss Fisher (now playing a Muriel from Evanston rather than a European Sallie, but still doing the Corsican bandits bit) and Slavin still starred, May Vokes replaced Miss Barry, and the score had simply been jollied up with more of the same (notably a couple of Clare Kummer ditties for the star), but this time Broadway liked it well enough to keep it running for 176 performances. Equipped with this statistical record—a much longer run than many of the most memorable shows of its time—it headed out onto the roads again with the cachet of Broadway success attached. One road even led as far as Australia where W S Percy, Bert Gilbert, Herbert Clayton, Toby Claude and Grace Edinsell featured in a brief production under the banner of the J C Williamson comic-opera company.

Australia: Her Majesty's Theatre, Sydney 9 July 1910

KNOBLOCK, Edward [KNOBLAUCH, Edward] (b New York, 7 April 1874; d London, 19 July 1945). Writer for all fields who had some success in the musical theatre.

Eddie Knoblock began his working life as an actor in the British theatre, but he soon switched to playwriting and had a pair of memorable successes on the London stage with *Kismet* (1911) and *Milestones* (1912). He wrote several short musical pieces for the variety theatre, including a musical sketch on the *Kismet* character of *Hajj* for Oscar Asche and Lily Brayton, before, in 1919, he combined with the *Maid of the Mountains* composer Harold Fraser-Simson and lyricist Harry Graham to provide a new vehicle for their show's star, José Collins. The resultant *Our Peg,* based exceedingly loosely on the loves of the historical Irish actress Peg Woffington, was tried out successfully in Manchester, but the long runs of its predecessors in London shut it out from Daly's Theatre and, although it toured extensively, without Miss Collins, the piece never played town.

The East End musical *Cherry* which Knoblock wrote for C B Cochran the following year had only a limited run, and he had thereafter but an intermittent connection with the musical theatre. In 1931, in collaboration with J B Priestley, he authored a stage version of *The Good Companions* with songs by Richard Addinsell and in 1944 he did a hatchet-job of an adaptation on *Merrie England* for a highly successful revival of Edward German's musical.

The author of several screenplays, he wrote the well-devised film version of *Chu Chin Chow* (w L du Garde Peach, Sidney Gilliatt), a piece which had been written very much along the lines of his *Kismet* by original *Kismet* star, Oscar Asche. *Kismet* was, in its turn, most successfully adapted into a musical comedy by Charles Lederer and Luther Davis, with a score compiled by George Wright and Robert Forrest from the melodies of Borodin, putting Knoblock posthumously into the repertoire of classic musical theatre.

1914 **England Expects** (Edward Jones/w Seymour Hicks) 1 act London Opera House 17 September

Plate 208. **Walter Kollo's** Die tolle Komtess.

1915 **Hajj** (Christopher Wilson) 1 act Palace Theatre 22 February

1919 **Our Peg** (Harold Fraser-Simson/Harry Graham) Prince's Theatre, Manchester 24 December

1920 **Cherry** (Melville Gideon) Apollo Theatre 22 July

Autobiography: *Round the Room* (Chapman & Hall, London, 1939)

KOLLO, Walter [KOLLODZIEYSKI, Elimar Walter] (b Neidenburg, Germany, 28 January 1878; d Berlin, 30 September 1940). One of German's leading composers of musical comedy in the early decades of the 20th century.

Intended by his father to follow him in the shopkeeping trade, Kollo worked effectively enough on his mother to be allowed at the age of 16 to go, instead, to study at the conservatoire at Sondershausen. Although his first bent was towards church music, he ended up working in a more popular area, writing songs and cabaret music, before moving on to become a répétiteur and then a conductor at the Luisen-Theater in Königsberg. It was in that town that his name appeared for the first time on a theatre-bill as a composer, when the local Tivoli produced a little burlesque called *Die versunkene Glocke* with "music by W Kollodzieyski." Thereafter his pieces were signed more succinctly.

He subsequently moved on to the very active Bellevue Theater at Stettin and then to Berlin, where he worked as a cabaret pianist as he began placing his songs in cabaret and revue. In 1907 he and his songwriting partner, Hermann Frey, saw their first metropolitan Operette *Ali Ben Mocca* produced at the Apollotheater. Kollo had further songs and small theatrical pieces played when Frey briefly and disastrously opened his own little cabaret theatre, but if the experience ruined his friend, it gave the composer sufficient exposure for him to be asked to set a little playlet written by the well-placed authors Rudolf Schanzer and August Neidhart. *Sein Herzensjunge* was well enough received at Elberfeld and in Vienna to ease Kollo further into the musical-theatre establishment, and within little more than a year his first significant successes had begun.

After resetting the saucy American success *Alma, wo wohnst du?* for the German stage, he moved on to join the co-founder of the newly activated Berliner Theater, Rudolf Bernauer, and his libretto-writing collaborator, Schanzer, on their highly successful New Year's Eve Posse *Grosse Rosinen* and the trio subsequently stayed together to manufacture what would become a series of musical comedies. The first of these, *Filmzauber,* which capitalized on the new craze for moving pictures, was a grand Berlin success, and it was subsequently exported throughout the world (*The Girl on the Film, A mozikirály,* etc), giving the composer his first general international exposure and thereafter Kollo remained as resident composer at the Berliner Theater for seven years. There he provided the scores (often in collaboration with the musical director Willi Bredschneider) for a further seven more-or-less annual musical comedies and Operetten which began with the most widely played, *Wie einst im Mai* (1913), then continued, end-to-end, through the war years, with *Extrablätter,* the "Scherzspiel mit Gesang" *Wenn zwei Hochzeit machen* ("Alle Englien lachen, wenn zwei Hochzeit machen," "Hindenburg-Marsch," "Ein Jüngling kann nicht gut allein," "Puppe, sei nicht so neutral!," "Du süsses Gulaschmägdelein") and *Auf Flügeln des Gesanges,* and peaked with the longest-running, the Operette *Die tolle Komtess* (more than 350 performances in 1917–18, revival 1919, "Dein auf ewig," "Edelweiss-Marsch," "Junges Herz lass die Liebe ein"), *Blitzblaues Blut* (nearly 300 performances, "Immer hinterdrein," "Jeder Mann hat einen dunkeln Punkt," "Liebe auf den ersten Blick," "Mädchen, Ihr seid wie das Mailicht") and seven months of *Sterne, die wieder leuchten.*

During this prewar and wartime period, however, the composer spread himself and his music far beyond the Berliner Theater. A commission from Hamburg produced *Der Liebesonkel* which duly made its way to Berlin and ultimately to New York's Irving Place Theater under the title *Die tolle Dolly* (1918), and a second Hamburg piece, the comical *Der Juxbaron,* followed it with even wider success. Then, with the triumph of *Wie einst im Mai* at its height, Kollo began simultaneously supplying Hermann Haller with what was to become a second wartime series of not quite end-to-end Operetten for his Theater am Nollendorfplatz. The patriotic four-act ''Vaterländisches Volksstück'' *Immer feste druff!* (''Das Vergeissmichnicht,'' ''Die Augen einer schönen Frau,'' ''Unser Kaiser,'' ''Der Soldate,'' ''Marine und Zeppeline,'' ''Auf der Banke an der Panke,'' ''Wenn man ein Mädchen küsst'') set things rolling with a run of nearly two years and more than 650 performances, and after Nelson's *Blaue Jungens* (with lyrics by Kollo's old friend, Frey) had run through six months, Kollo followed up with *Die Gulaschkanone* and a second long-running hit, a version of J M Barrie's *Quality Street,* with its wartime message couched in music. As *Drei alte Schachteln* (''Ach Jott, was sind die Männer dumm,'' ''Drei alte Schachteln geh'n zum Ball,'' ''Ein Märchenglück, ein Sommertraum,'' ''Was nützt denn dem Mädchen die Liebe'') it ran for over 450 performances, went on to Vienna, and even eventually ended up (briefly) on Broadway. And amongst all this activity, on two fronts, Kollo still found time to supply a further hit, *Der selige Balduin* (''Rechts im Arm ein süsses Mädel,'' ''Mausi, wenn's dunkel ist,'' ''Dolores,'' ''Ja, wen der Storch im Mai gebracht''), to Max Monti's Operetten-Theater.

The hugely successful composer now began to diversify his interests. Whilst still composing such pieces as the distinctly popular *Fräulein Puck,* produced in Munich for 150 performances before moving on to Berlin, he founded his own publishing house and then took on first the management of the Bellevue-Theater in Stettin (1919–22), then that of Berlin's Theater in der Kommandantenstrasse, where he revived Bromme's *Die Dame in Frack* and produced his own *Der verjungte Adolar,* and finally the Neues-Operetten-Theater am Schiffbauerdamm where he staged his *Die Königin der Nacht* and *Lady Chic.* He had, however, ill chosen his moment to venture into business. By 1922 his ventures had been flattened by the postwar inflation of the mark. However, he continued to cling to a managerial chair just a little longer with the tiny Kabarett Pot-Pourri until that, too, finally went under.

If his career as a businessman was more or less done, Kollo, however, continued to compose. He returned to Haller to write the music for the vastly popular and glitzy revues which the manager staged at the Admiralspalast between 1923 and 1927 (*Drunter und Drüber, Noch und Noch, Achtung, Welle 505!, An und Aus, Wann und Wo, Schön und Schick*), scoring one of his greatest song hits with ''Solang noch Untern Linden'' in the 1923 *Drunter und Drüber,* and he continued to turn out a regular supply of Operetten, both for Haller and for other managers. In 1923 his 19-year-old son Willi made his theatrical debut as a lyricist on Hugo Hirsch's *Der Fürst von Pappenheim* (''Eine Frau wie ich ist ne Sache für sich'') and he then joined in tandem with his father on *Marietta* (''Was eine Frau im Frühling traümt'') and on *Die Frau ohne Kuss* (''Das ist der Frühling von Berlin'') which followed its Berlin production with 80 performances at Vienna's Rolandbühne in 1927.

However, although Berlin welcomed several of Kollo's pieces over the next 15 years, and a handful ventured as far as Vienna, and although he continued to turn out a regular supply of popular Berliner songs, he was never again to taste the kind of theatrical success he had had during the whirlwind war years. Only *Marietta* (''Warte, warte nur ein Weilchen'') and the 1927 Operette *Drei arme kleine Mädels,* a piece written in blatant imitation of *Wie einst im Mai* which reached Vienna, Budapest and America as the Shuberts' *Three Little Girls* (1930, ad Marie Armstrong Hecht, Gertrude Purcell), came anywhere near drawing the attention Kollo had attracted in the half-dozen years he had spent challenging Jean Gilbert at the forefront of the German Operette, during its most effective period.

In fact, even during that time, Kollo never found the grand overseas success that his contemporary did. In Britain, he was represented only by a revamped version of *Filmzauber,* played as *The Girl on the Film* (add mus Szirmai), and although a number of his pieces were staged in America, he came out of the action very poorly. *Wie einst im Mai* became a huge hit as *Maytime,* but Kollo's entire score had been replaced by Sigmund Romberg. *Alma, wo wohnst du?* had won success with a score by librettist Adolf Philipp (masquerading as ''Jean Briquet''), before Kollo remusicked it for Germany; *Sterne, die wieder leuchten* underwent a major botching before flopping as Springtime of Youth; *Drei alte Schachteln* lived for even less time as *Phoebe of Quality Street;* and only *Three Little Girls* (103 performances) and *The Girl on the Film* of the American versions of his plays, plus the German-language presentation of *Der Juxbaron,* gave him any kind of worthwhile New York representation. The nearest he came to a hit song on Broadway was when one of his songs was hijacked into Eysler's *Die Frauenfresser* as ''Come on Over Here.''

In Hungary, Kollo was represented by *Pintyőke* (*Alma*), *A mozikirály* (*Filmzauber*), *A családfő* (*Der selige Balduin*), *Három a venlány* (*Drei alte Schachteln*), *Egyszer volt* (*Wie einst im Mai*), *Éj Királynő* (*Die Königin der Nacht*), *Link báró* (*Der Juxbaron*), *Katicabogár* (whatever that was) and *A kis szelburdi* (*Die tolle Komtess*), whilst France got a brief glimpse of *Pour plaire aux femmes* (*Frauen haben das gerne*) in the late 1930s.

1897 **Die versunkene Glocke** (Paul Kasten) Tivoli, Königsberg 27 July

1907 **Ali Ben Mocca** (Hermann Frey, F W Hardt, Louis Hermann) Apollotheater 2 March

1909 **Meyer mit 'n Hängeboden** (Paul Bendix) 1 act Buggenhagen 1 October

1909 **Der süsse Leutnant** (Henry Bender/Robert Breitenbach, Leopold Ely) 1 act Passage-Theater 2 October

1909 **Sherlock Holmes in Treuenbrietzen** 1act Buggenhagen

1911 **Sein Herzensjunge** (Rudolf Schanzer, August Neidhart) Thalia-Theater, Elberfeld 1 April

1911 **Der Brettlkönig** Liebichs Établissement, Breslau 18 September

1911 **Alma, wo wohnst du?** (Adolf Philipp) Luisen-Theater 17 October

1911 **Grosse Rosinen** (w Willi Bredschneider, Bogumil Zepler, Léon Jessel/Schanzer, Rudolf Bernauer) Berliner Theater 31 December

1912 **Ein aufgelegtes Geschäft** (Frey, Hardt) Komische Oper 7 April

1912 **Der Liebesonkel** (aka *Die tolle Dolly*) (w Walter Schütt/Frey, Alexander Pordes-Milo) Neues Theater, Hamburg 3 August; Walhalla-Theater, Berlin 13 August 1913

1912 **Filmzauber** (Schanzer, Bernauer) Berliner Theater 19 October

1912 **So wird's gemacht** revised *Ein aufgelegtes Geschäft* Neues Theater, Hamburg December

1912 **Juhu, es ist erreicht** (Hardt) Rose-Theater

1913 **Wie einst im Mai** (w Willi Bredschneider/Bernauer, Schanzer) Berliner Theater 4 October

1913 **Der Juxbaron** (Willy Wolff/Pordes-Milo, Hermann Haller) Carl-Schultze Theater, Hamburg 14 November

1913 **Komtess Hopsassa** (Pordes-Milo)

1914 **Immer feste druff!** (aka *Gloria Viktoria*) (Haller, Wolff) Theater am Nollendorfplatz 1 October

1914 **Extrablätter** (w Bredschneider/Schanzer, Heinz Gordon) Berliner Theater 24 October

1914 **Rund um die Spree** (Frey) Walhalla-Theater

1915 **Wenn zwei Hochzeit machen** (w Bredschneider/Bernauer, Schanzer) Berliner Theater 23 October

1916 **Der selige Balduin** (Erich Urban, Wolff) Montis Operetten-Theater 31 March

1916 **Auf Flügeln des Gesanges** (w Bredschneider/Bernauer, Schanzer) Berliner Theater 9 September

1917 **Die tolle Komtess** (Bernauer, Schanzer) Berliner Theater 21 February

1917 **Die Gulaschkanone** (Haller, Wolff) Theater am Nollendorfplatz 23 February

1917 **Drei alte Schachteln** (Rideamus/Haller) Theater am Nollendorfplatz 6 October

1918 **Blitzblaues Blut** (Bernauer, Schanzer) Berliner Theater 9 February

1918 **Sterne, die wieder leuchten** (Bernauer, Schanzer) Berliner Theater 6 November

1919 **Fräulein Puck** (Franz Arnold, Ernst Bach) Volkstheater, Munich 25 June

1920 **Der verjüngte Adolar** (Kurt Kraatz, Richard Kessler, Frey) Theater in der Kommandantenstrasse 4 October

1921 **Die Königin der Nacht** (Arnold, Bach) Neues Operetten-Theater 2 September

1922 **Lady Chic** (Kraatz, Kessler, Willy Steinberg) Neues Operetten-Theater 11 March

1922 **Madame empfängt** (Frey, Heye) 1 act Kaberett Potpourri

1923 **Marietta** (Willi Kollo/Robert Bodanzky, Bruno Hardt-Warden) Metropoltheater 22 December

1924 **Die tanzende Prinzessin** (Willi Kollo/Kessler) Komische Oper 15 April

1924 **Die Frau ohne Kuss** (Willi Kollo/Kessler) Schillertheater 5 July

1924 **Die vertagte Nacht** (Robert Gilbert/Arnold, Bach) Stadttheater, Mainz 11 November

1924 **Die vertauschte Frau** (Willi Kollo/Arnold, Bach) Neues Operettenhaus 22 December

1925 **Olly Polly** (Willi Kollo/Arnold, Bach) Theater am Zoo 3 September

1926 **Nur Du** (Hardt-Warden, Willi Kollo) Berliner Theater 23 December

1927 **Drei arme kleine Mädels** (Willi Kollo/Bruno Hardt-Warden, Feiner) Theater am Nollendorfplatz 2 April

1927 **Gaby und die Drei** (Kurt Robitschek, Paul Morgan) 1 act Johann Strauss-Theater, Vienna 26 May

1928 **Die grosse Kaiserin** (Robitschek, Morgan) 1 act Kabarett der Komiker 1 April

1928 **Kitty macht Karriere** Kabarett (Willi Kollo/Robitschek, Morgan) Kabarett der Komiker 1 September

1928 **Arme Ritter** (Günther Bibo, Kurt Schwabach/Arnold, Bach) Volkstheater, Munich 22 September

1928 **Jettchen Gebert** (Wolff, Martin Zickel) Theater am Nollendorfplatz 22 December

1928 **Der Liebeschauffeur** (Kurt Schwabach, Kessler)

1928 **Losgelassen** (Max Reinhardt)

1930 **Der doppelte Bräutigam** (Haller, Wolff) Theater am Schiffbauerdamm 7 March

1930 **Majestät lässt bitten** (Rideamus) Komische Oper 5 April

1931 **Frauen haben das gerne** (Arnold, Bach) Komische Oper 4 June

1933 **Die Männer sind mal so** (Halton, Rideamus) Schillertheater 4 January

1933 **Lieber reich—aber glücklich** (Willi Kollo/Arnold, Bach) Komödienhaus 3 November

1934 **Derfflinger** (Karl Bretschneider, Frey) Metropoltheater 17 February

1935 **Heirat nicht ausgeschlossen** (Kessler) Komische Oper 4 January

1935 **Ein Kaiser ist verliebt** (Theo Halton) Deutsches Nationaltheater, Osnabruck 22 August

1935 **Berlin wie es weint—Berlin wie es lacht** (*Die alten und die Jungen*) (Hans Brennecke) ''Plaza''-Theater der 3000 10 October

1936 **Die wilde Auguste** (Halton) Volksoper, Hamburg 18 February

1936 **Mädel Ahoi!** (Halton) Deutsches Nationaltheater, Osnabrück 17 April

1936 **Tausend Worte Liebe** (Hardt-Warden, Ritter) Theater im Europahaus 25 December

1938 **Das Schiff der schönen Frauen** Apollotheater, Cologne 25 December

1942 **Ich bin in meine Frau verliebt** (w Willi Kollo) revised *Olly Polly* Raimundtheater December

His son, **Willi KOLLO** (b Königsberg, 28 April 1904; d Berlin, 4 February 1988), worked widely in cabaret (Weisse Maus, Korso am Kurfüstrstendamm, Kabarett der Komiker, Hamburg Bonbonnière), and wrote several plays, musical and otherwise (*Meine Freundin Barbara, Frau Jenny Triebel, Eine Frau die ich kannte,* etc), as well as revue material (*Von A-Z, Der Zug nach dem Westen, Wieder Metropol, Du und ich, Gruss und Kuss, Scala-Revue,* etc), screenplays, songs and theatre lyrics. He also adapted his father's *Wie einst im Mai* for a second copyright life by adding other pieces of both his own (''Es geht doch nischt über Berlin'') and of Walter's music to the score and removing Bredschneider's contribution. He also composed music for both the stage and the screen (Die blonde Nachtigall, Wir tanzen um die Welt, Dolly macht Karriere, etc). His son, **René KOLLO** (b Berlin, 20 November 1937), became celebrated as a Heldentenor and also composed a number of songs. He appeared on the Operette stage in 1966 at the Braunschweig Oper as Fritz Jüterbog in a revival of *Wie einst in Mai* and again in 1992 at Munich and Berlin's Metropoltheater.

In 1958 Willi Kollo produced and directed a film, *Soland noch Untern Linden,* in which René Kollo portrayed Walter Kollo.

1923 **Der Fürst von Pappenheim** (Hugo Hirsch/w Alfred Berg/ Ernst Bach, Franz Arnold) Deutsches Künstlertheater 16 February

1923 **Die rote Katze** (Karóly Hajós/Eugen Burg, Louis Taufstein) Thalia Theater 27 April

1923 **Marietta** (Walter Kollo/Robert Bodanzky, Bruno Hardt-Warden) Metropoltheater 22 December

1924 **Die tanzende Prinzessin** (Walter Kollo/Kessler) Komische Oper 15 April

1924 **Die Frau ohne Kuss** (Walter Kollo/Kessler) Schillertheater 5 July

1924 **Die vertauschte Frau** (Walter Kollo/Arnold, Bach) Neues Operettenhaus 22 December

1925 **Olly Polly** (Walter Kollo/Arnold, Bach) Theater am Zoo 3 September

1926 **Nur Du** (Walter Kollo/w Hardt-Warden) Berliner Theater 23 December

1927 **Drei arme kleine Mädels** (Walter Kollo/Bruno Hardt-Warden, Feiner) Theater am Nollendorfplatz 2 April

1928 **Fräulein Mama** (Hugo Hirsch/Richard Kessler) Deutsches Schauspielhaus, Hamburg 1 July

1928 **Kitty macht Karriere** Kabarett (Walter Kollo/Kurt Robitschek, Paul Morgan) Kabarett der Komiker 1 September

1933 **Lieber reich—aber glücklich** (Walter Kollo/Arnold, Bach) Komödienhaus 3 November

1935 **Schminke** Komödienhaus 26 September

1938 **Besuch am Abend** (w Engelbrecht) Theater am Schiffbauerdamm 23 September

1940 **Es könnte dein Glück sein** 1 act Kabarett der Komiker 30 August

1942 **Ich bin in meine Frau verliebt** (w Willi Kollo) revised *Olly Polly* Raimundtheater December

1943 **Wie einst im Mai** revised version w Walter Lieck (Theater des Volkes)

1946 **Dornröschen** Kabarett Bonbonnière, Hamburg September

1949 **Die hellgelben Handschuhe** Komödie, Lübeck 12 July

1949 **Geschichte vom armen Hamburger Mädchen** Theater in Eppendorf, Hamburg 3 December

1958 **Die kleine Parfumerie**

1970 **Wer hat Angst von dem starken Mann** Kleines Theater 1 April

KOMJÁTI, Károly (b Budapest, 8 May 1896; d Budapest, 3 July 1953). Hungarian composer for his local and for Viennese stages.

Komjáti studied at the Budapest Zeneakadémia and went on from there to a fine career in the musical theatre. He began as a répétiteur, chorusmaster and theatrical conductor at Kolozsvár, Bremen and, ultimately, Budapest's Magyar Színház, and was but 22 when his first operett, *A kóristalány,* written to a text by top librettist Jenő Faragó, was staged at the Városi Színház. It was later played also at Vienna's Bundestheater (*Die Lily vom Chor* ad Felix Dörmann). It was, however, his second piece, produced just a few months after the first, that made his name. *Pillangó főhadnagy* (''Lieutenant Butterfly''), a military operett in the vein of the recent Kálmán hit *Tatárjárás,* composed to a text by another expert librettist, Ferenc Martos, and with lyrics by the equally respected Imre Harmath, was produced at Budapest's principal musical house, the Király Színház, where the last new native work mounted had been Szirmai's highly successful *Mágnás Miska,* and where the premieres since had been of no lesser works than *Liebeswalzer, Die Csárdásfürstin, Die Rose von Stambul* and Lehár's *Wo die Lerche singt.* The young composer's show was a wild success, reached its 200th Budapest performance within two years and was given a major revival in 1926 (Király Színház 22 May) whilst further productions proliferated round the country.

He followed up with several other well-regarded and successful pieces, of which *A harapós férj* (''the snapping husband'') was twice revived in various forms following its original production at the Fővárosi

Operettszínház; *Fizessen nagysád,* a tale of the French Riviera, clocked up a fine 44 performances at the Vígszinház; and the 1932 *Éjféli tangó,* his most popular piece since his first great hit, traveled on from its original Király Színház production through Hungary, Germany (*Tango um Mitternacht* Neues Operetten-Theater, Leipzig 25 August 1932), Holland (*Tango der Liebe* Scala Theater, The Hague 1933 with Beppi de Vries and Johannes Heesters) and Austria (Volksoper 8 April 1933). Vienna, in fact, saw two Komjáti Operetten in 1933, for in that year Hubert Marischka also produced *Ein Liebestraum* at the Theater an der Wien (27 October 1933) with Hungarian soprano Marta Eggerth and Wilhelm Klitsch starred through a season of 49 performances.

The Király Színház produced one further Komjáti piece, *A szegény ördög* (''the poor devil''), a piece based on Machiavelli, in 1934; the Városi Színház presented his *Bécsi tavasz* (''spring in Vienna'') with Hanna Honthy and Árpád Latabár the following year; and the Fővárosi Operettszínház produced both his *Antoinette,* with Gitta Alpár starring in the role of Marie Antoinette (as perceived in Max Bertuch's novel), and his final work, *Csicsónénak három lánya,* with Hanna Honthy starred—but in spite of fulfilling more than 20 highly satisfying years of a writing career, Komjáti's single most successful piece remained the work he had written at 22 years of age.

1918 **A kóristalány** (Jenő Faragó) Városi Színház 18 January

1918 **Pillangó főhadnagy** (Imre Harmath/Ferenc Martos) Király Színház 7 June

1922 **Három a tánc** (István Szomaházy, Faragó) Király Színház 20 May

1931 **A harapós férj** (Tamás Emőd, Rezső Török) Fővárosi Operettszínház 22 March

1931 **Phryné a fótargyaláson** (Endre Nagy, Viktor Lányi) 1 act Vígszínház 31 December

1932 **Fizessen nagysád** (Emőd, Török) Vígszínház 23 January

1932 **Éjféli tangó** (István Békeffy, László Vadnai) Király Színház 27 February

1933 **Ein Liebestraum** (Martos, László Szilágyi ad Heinz Reichert) Theater an der Wien 27 October

1934 **Szeressen kedves!** (Ernő Andai) Fővárosi Operettszínház 1 April

1934 **A cirkusz csillaga** (w Mihály Eisemann/Békeffy/László Bús Fekete) Vígszínház 22 June

1934 **A szegény ördög** (Emőd, Török) Király Színház 29 September

1935 **Grand Café** (Török, Andor Kellér) Fővárosi Operettszínház 21 March

1935 **Bécsi tavasz** (Harmath/Török, Adorján Stella) Városi Színház 15 November

1937 **Antoinette** (Harmath/Armand Szántó, Mihály Szécsén) Müvész Színház 23 December

1945 **Vannak még férfiak** Márkuspark Színház 3 July

1946 **Csicsónénak három lánya** (Dezső Kellér, Békeffy) Fővárosi Operettszínház 5 October

1949 **Ipafai lakodalom** revised version of *A harapós férj* Fővárosi Operettszínház 25 May

KÖNIG, Josef (b 1877; d Vienna, 26 February 1938). Viennese song-and-dance man who created several important roles in a busy career in the 1910s and 1920s.

Unless he was the Herr König who played the young Fredy in *Ein tolles Mädel* at Danzers Orpheum in 1907, it would seem that Josef König began the visible part of his career at the Carltheater where he played six years of soubret and light-comic roles from 1908 onwards. Amongst the best of these were the character role of the naughty sleeping-car attendant Scrop in *Die geschiedene Frau* (1908), the desperate-to-gallivant young Hubert in *Die keusche Susanne* (1910) and the hero's best friend, Bronio von Popiel, in *Polenblut.* During this period he also created and/or played roles in *Der schwarze Tenor* (1908, Mister Tom), *Johann der Zweite* (1908, Bobby), *Der Glücksnarr* (1908, Prince Alberich), *Das Puppenmädel* (1910, Romuald Talmi), *Majestät Mimi* (1911, Fürst von Lepanto), *Alt-Wien* (1911, Franz Stelzer), *Der liebe Augustin* (1912, Nicola), *Susi* (1912, Horn), *Fürst Casimir* (1913), *Der erste Kuss* (1914, Dr Rottermann) as well as Pietro in *Boccaccio* and other mostly light-comedy and youthful parts in the revived repertoire.

In 1915 he moved to the Johann Strauss-Theater where he took over the part of Vincenz in *Rund um die Liebe,* played Schmink in *Er und sein Schwester* and then created his most enduring role as Gróf Boni Káncsiánu in *Die Csárdásfürstin,* serenading ''Die Mädis vom chantant.'' From 1917 he teamed with Mizzi Zwerenz at the Apollotheater, playing in *Der Aushilfsgatte* (1917), *Walzerliebe* (1918), as Rosenstock in *Rosenstock und Edelweiss,* in Jean Gilbert's *Die Fahrt ins Glück* (1918, Kurt von Bodegg), in *Der Favorit* (1919, Peter Heller) and *Die Dame vom Zirkus* (1919). He played alongside Sári Fedák in *Der Pusztakavalier* (1920) at the same house, and was seen in *Fräulein Puck* (1920), *Die Tangoprinzessin* (1921, Don Gil de Tenorio), *Indische Nächte* (1921), *Der Geiger von Lugano* (1921), *Apachen* (1921, Redingote) and *Die Strassensängerin* (1922, Martin Schurf) before abandoning the Apollo and moving on to more profitable houses.

In the 1920s he appeared in most of Vienna's principal musical theatres—at the Carltheater in *Faschingshochzeit* (1921, Gustl Engel) and *Das Milliardensouper* (1925, Jimmy Twinkle); at the Wiener Stadttheater in *Die Siegerin* (1922, Wassili Bronin), *Offenbach* (Basco) and *Libellentanz* (Bouquet); at the Theater an der Wien in *Bacchusnacht* (1923, Metellus) and *Die gelbe Jacke* (1923, Claudius) and, in succession to Max Hansen, as

Zsupán in *Gräfin Mariza* (1924); at the Johann Strauss-Theater in *Ein Märchen aus Florenz* (1923, Don Carlos y Riminez), *Bajazzos Abenteuer* (1923, Cyprian Gunkel), *Marietta* (1924, Nicolo Tromboni), and *Des Königs Nachbarin* (1924, Major von Fehlow); at the Bürgertheater in *Das Land der Liebe* (1926, Martin); then in *Ich hab' mein Herz in Heidelberg verloren* (1927, Hieronymus Strudelmayer) at the Volksoper; in *Eine einzige Nacht* (1927, Fürst Severin) and *Prinzessin Ti-Ti-Pa* (1927, Árpád Basarhely), both back at the Carltheater; and in Straus's *Hochzeit in Hollywood* (1928, Ein Filmregisseur)—taking increasingly more senior and, finally, less important roles.

DIE KÖNIGIN Operette in 3 acts by Ernst Marischka and Bruno Granichstaedten. Music by Oscar Straus. Deutsches Künstlertheater, Berlin, 5 November 1926.

After *Riquette* and *Teresina* in 1925, *Die Königin* was the last in the series of 1920s Operetten composed by Oscar Straus and produced by Heinz Saltenburg at Berlin's Deutsches Künstlertheater as a vehicle for Berlin's queen of Operette, Fritzi Massary. *Die Königin* featured the star as ex-Königin Helena, who comes together in a ''fashionables Berghotel in der Schweiz'' with the President who has replaced her at the head of her country. She is a soprano, he a tenor, and it is quite clear that by the end of the evening they will, in the best operettic fashion, get together. Hopefully, Präsident Nikola Tonitscheff has fallen sufficiently in love not to regret the fact that his shortsighted republican actions have deprived him of a royal crown. There were plenty of other guests at the hotel—Willibald Netzerle and his pals, Harry and Fred, Miss Mabel Rostaslowitsch, her papa Vlasta and her pals, Mary and Gerda, and a group of military gents—all of whom joined the hotel's staff members in supplying the comic and soubret material which offset the romantic plot.

Saltenburg gave only three months of performances of *Die Königin* before removing the piece to produce Lehár's *Der Zarewitsch,* but when *Die Königin* was produced the following year in Vienna it got a much better run. Vienna's production was mounted at the Theater an der Wien, under the management of Hubert Marischka, with Betty Fischer as Königin Helena, Marischka as Tonitscheff, Fritz Steiner as Willibald, Richard Waldemar as Vlasta Rostaslowitsch and Lizzi Holzschuh as Mabel. Marischka himself directed, and the dances were arranged by Franz Bauer of the Staatsoper and George Shurley from London's Palace Theatre. The piece proved a definite success, running for 177 straight performances as understudy Ernst Nadherny, Raoul Aslan and then no less a star than Louis Treumann succeeded the manager-director-star, Maria Schwarz and Anny Coty relieved Frln Fischer, and Elsie Altman stepped into the soubrette role. After a revival of *Der Orlow, Die Königin* returned, and passed its 200th performance on 11 August.

Austria: Theater an der Wien 4 February 1927

KONING, Victor [KÖNIG, Victor] (b Belleville, 4 April 1842; Paris, 1 October 1894). Wheeler-dealer turned top Parisian producer of the 1880s.

Koning began work at the age of 15 as a Parisian journalist and was soon purveying his own particular brand of witticisms and theatrical gossip in *Le Figaro.* He quickly made his name by making his columns the nastiest and most viciously personal in town, and wielded his journalistic influence in such a way as to compel all but the bravest members of the theatrical establishment to ''collaborate'' with him, whether journalistically or in the furtherance of his own ambitions in the theatre, at the risk of being cleverly assassinated in print.

One of Koning's ambitions was to run his own theatre and, in 1869, he rashly took over the management of the large Théâtre de la Gaîté. The experience was a short and costly one—the power he wielded over the profession could not be wielded over the public—but Koning hung on in the theatrical world after his failure at the Gaîté and tried instead to make himself a place in—and an income from—the theatre by turning himself into an ''author.'' He achieved his ambition—like many another powerful ''co-author'' of the time—without writing a word, most particularly, in a curious collaboration with Paul Siraudin and the celebrated vaudevillist Clairville. The curiosity of this ''collaboration'' came from the fact that Siraudin—a lazy but bright writer—provided the ideas, the indefatigable Clairville wrote the pieces on the bones provided, and Koning, thanks to his influence in the theatre world, sold the resultant show. He placed several of the team's revues at the Théâtre des Variétés and a couple of comic féeries, *La Cocotte aux oeufs d'or* and *La Reine Carotte,* at the Théâtre des Menus-Plaisirs, but his biggest success came when he got his collaborators together with the composer Lecocq and theatre manager Eugène Humbert in Brussels. The result was the *La Fille de Madame Angot* (1872). Koning took up the provincial and touring rights to the show himself, and when *La Fille de Madame Angot* proved to be the most successful musical stage piece of its time he was thoroughly launched on a managerial career.

In 1875 he took over the management of the Théâtre de la Renaissance in Paris and there, for a number of years, he presided over what quickly became one of the most thriving centers of musical theatre in Paris, proving himself an extraordinarily talented, if thoroughly loathed, producer. Reading between the contemporary lines, however, it seems that at least a part of the loathing was caused by the tight-ship, letter-of-the-contract, nothing-for-nothing style of management he practiced in a Parisian theatre all too used to less worldly and more easy-going employers.

At the Renaissance Koning produced a long series of internationally successful Lecocq opérettes, beginning with *La Petite Mariée* (1875) and continuing over the next five years with *Kosiki, La Marjolaine, Le Petit Duc, La Camargo, La Petite Mademoiselle, La Jolie Persane* and, finally, *Janot,* the series being interspersed with the occasional new work from other composers such as Humbert's latest Brussels production, Vogel's *La Filleule du Roi,* the adaptation of Johann Strauss's *Die Fledermaus* as *La Tzigane,* Planquette's *Les Voltigeurs de la 32ème* and Offenbach's posthumous *Belle Lurette.*

Le Petit Duc, with Jeanne Granier starring in the title role, gave him his most outsized success since *La Fille de Madame Angot,* and the combination Koning/Lecocq/Granier was for several years the most potent musical-theatre force in town. After a while, however, the formula of their shows became rather too predictable and, following the comparatively only good-to-fair showings of *La Petite Mademoiselle* and *La Jolie Persane* (Starring Mme Koning instead of Granier), the unequivocal failure of *Janot* in 1881 resulted in a breach between the manager and the composer.

Lecocq moved on to the Théâtre des Nouveautés to produce some of his best works for Jules Brasseur (*Le Jour et la nuit, Le Coeur et la main*) and, after staging a handful of revivals (*Le Canard à trois becs, L'Oeil crevé,* etc), Koning, in timely fashion, gave up his lease on the Théâtre de la Renaissance, having lost in the last days a deal of the fortune he had made with his string of early Lecocq hits. He moved his center of activity to the Théâtre du Gymnase, where Montigny had just given up his lease, and away from musical productions. After some initial success and, from 1889 on, a subsequent and swift failure, he once more moved on, this time to build a theatre of his own, the Comédie-Parisienne (later the Théâtre de l'Athénée). The venture took the last of his fortune and he died in 1894, in want and insane, aged 52. One of his obituaries read ''no man in our theatrical world had so many enemies, nor was so thoroughly detested.''

KONTI, József (b Warsaw, 24 October 1852; d Budapest, 23 October 1905). The composer of the earliest group of successful Hungarian operetts.

Konti studied music from the age of 12, first at the Warsaw conservatoire and later in Vienna, and he began his working life in the theatre as an assistant conductor at the Theater in der Leopoldstadt and as a conductor at Salzburg. He subsequently held theatre posts as chef d'orchestre in Debrecen (1876) and then in Kolozsvár (1878) before settling in Budapest where he became, at first, conductor at the Várszínház.

In 1884 his first significant stage work as a composer was produced. *Az Eleven ördög* (''the living devil'') was a comic-opera treatment of Bayard and Dumanoir's long-popular play *Le Vicomte de Letorrières,* a piece already musicalized by several other writers, written to a libretto by Antal Deréki and produced initially at Ödenburg. The piece was subsequently brought to Budapest's Budai Színkör where it scored a fine success and the following year both the show and its composer were taken up by the city's most important musical house, the Népszínház. There had been, intermittently, good and successful Hungarian musical plays and operetts before, but *Az Eleven ördög* was a landmark both in its quality and in the success it won, and its Népszínház production with the darling of the Hungarian stage, Lujza Blaha, starring in travesty as the Vicomte was—even though a French-style work written by a Polish composer trained in Vienna—an important step in the development of native musical theatre in Hungary.

In the 18 years that Konti remained as chief conductor at the Népszínház, he turned out, between regular revivals of his first work (1897, 1900, etc), five further major operetts and the incidental music for innumerable plays, establishing himself as the first major composer of the Hungarian musical theatre. Of his principal pieces, *Királyfogás* (''the king's capture''), first mounted with Pál Vidor as Count Radziwill and Blaha as Fjóra in the starring roles, was played 50 times over five years in the Budapest repertoire whilst winning productions throughout the country and even a single showing by a local Hungarian company at New York's Terrace Garden (2 April 1899), whilst *A suhanc,* for which he returned to the works of Bayard with an adaptation of the French playwright's *Le Gamin de Paris* (w Émile Vanderburch), was another considerable success. Blaha starred again, this time in trousers as the ''gamin'' of the title. Its hometown reception—a first run of 94 performances—was sufficient, this time, to win Konti's piece more considerable notice abroad, and *A suhanc* was produced at Berlin's Theater Unter den Linden (*Der Taugenichts* ad Genée 9 June 1893), before being given a major Budapest revival in 1904 (Népszínház 23 April).

A kópé (''the crafty one''), an adaptation of August Kotzebue's *Pagenstreiche,* did less well (9 performances), apparently hampered by an unadventurous book which had done even worse a few years previously when adapted by Hugo Wittmann for a Carl Weinberger Operette at Vienna's Theater an der Wien, but Konti had further success with *A citerás* (''the zither-player''), which featured the Népszínház's new star Klára Küry through a first run of 33 nights, and *Talmi hercegnő* (''the counterfeit countess'') which brought the theatre's two old-guard stars, Blaha and Aranka Hegyi, together again to give the composer a final Népszínház run of 29 performances.

In 1903 Konti moved as musical director to the newly opened Király Színház. There his final operett *A fecskék,* a musical version of Dumas's *Les Demoiselles de Saint-Cyr,* was produced as one of the three new Hungarian operetts introduced in an eclectic first year's production which included the British musical *The Toreador,* the American *Robin Hood* and Germany's *Lysistrata* alongside Austrian and French musical pieces, *Il barbiere di Siviglia,* an Hungarian version of Shaw's *Arms and the Man* and a visit from Sarah Bernhardt. Konti's new position was, however, of short duration: he died in 1905 at the age of 53.

Amongst the long list of plays for which Konti supplied varying degrees of music were *Szeget szeggel* (1883, Aurél Follinusz), *Szikra Panna* (1885, Mihály Kiss) *A cigányprinc* (1885, József Szigeti), *A tunikás leányok* (1886, Károly Gerő), *A dezentor* (1886, Viktor Rákosi), *Rokolyás biró* (1887, Szigeti), *Az ezres bankó* (1887, Dezső Margitay), *A kupéban* (1888, Ede Kabos), *Kisvárosi hirességek* (1888, Hippolyte Raymond, Maxime Boucheron ad), *Haluska Benedek* (1889, Lajos Bartók), *A szép Darinka* (1892, Ilka Klárné Angyal), *Holtomiglan* (1896, György Ruttkay, Miska Rothauser), *Nászuton* (1896, Ferenc Herczeg) and the highly successful *A gyimesi vadvirág* (1897, István Géczsy).

1878 **A vadászok** 1 act Nagyvárad 29 August

1883 **Ein Wachsfigurenkabinett** (K Bayer) 1 act Fürsttheater, Vienna 15 May

1884 **Az Eleven ördög** (Antal Deréki) Budai Színkör 8 August

1886 **Királyfogás** (Gergely Csiky) Népszínház 29 October

1888 **A suhanc** (Ignác Nagy) Népszínház 12 January

1890 **A kópé** (August Kotzebue ad) Népszínház 7 February

1894 **A citerás** (Károly Murai ad Csiky) Népszínház 23 February

1898 **Talmi hercegnő** (Emil Makai, Albert Kövessy) Népszínház 4 February

1904 **A fecskék** (Árpád Pásztor) Király Színház 20 January

KOPÁCSI-KARCZAG, Juliska [née KOPÁCSI] (b Komárom, 13 February 1868; d Budapest, 20 February 1957).

A joyously fresh-faced soubrette, Julie Kopácsi was engaged at Budapest's Népszínház between 1890 and 1894, beginning there in *Der arme Jonathan* and *Die schöne Helena* and creating leading roles in Miklós Forrai's *A libapásztor,* and, in her last appearance there, as Sarah, opposite the Vicomte Renard of Aranka Hegyi, in Bokor's successful *A kis alamuszi* (1894). During this time, she married the rising Wilhelm Karczag and, after the couple's move to Vienna in 1894, she was employed at the Carltheater (1894–95), creating leading roles in Jakobowski's *Die Brillantenkönigin* (Betta), *Die Königin von Gamara* (Polly), *Lady Charlatan* (Emma Lion), *Coeur d'Ange* (Gräfin Ilona), *Olympia die Muskelvenus* (ie, Varney's *Les Forains,* Olympia), *Die Lachtaube* (Tatjana), Suppé's *Das Modell* (Coletta) and *Die Prima Ballerina* (Rosita Tremelli) and appearing as Helena and Adele in the house repertoire. In 1896–97 she appeared at the Theater an der Wien, creating Jeanette Millefleur in Weinberger's *Der Schmetterling,* Marina in Millöcker's *Nordlicht* and Ernestine in *Die Göttin der Vernunft* and again playing Helena.

In 1898 she visited America where she repeated her Adele and starred in *Die Lachtaube* at the Irving Place Theater, and in 1899 she appeared once more at the Carltheater in the title role of Ludwig Englander's *Der kleine Korporal.* In 1901 she starred in her old part, at the Theater in der Josefstadt, in the remade version of *Die Prima Ballerina* (*Auch so eine!*) and at Berlin's Theater des Westens in *Das Modell.* She took some of the leading roles at the Theater an der Wien in the first days of her husband's management there (King in *Das Spitzentuch der Königin,* Adele, Eurydice) and was seen on the Vienna stage as late as 1909, still appearing in such decidedly juvenile roles as Denise in *Mam'zelle Nitouche.*

During her starring years as a soubrette, although she made a particular and repeated success as Offenbach's *La Belle Hélène,* first and foremost a personality role, Kopácsi-Karczag was also able to encompass the vocal difficulties of a role like *Die Fledermaus*'s Adele. This duality was also evident in her appearances in opéra-comique, where she was seen, amongst other roles, as Bizet's Carmen.

KORNGOLD, Erich Wolfgang (b Brünn, 29 May 1897; d Hollywood, 29 November 1957). Operettic arranger whose main career was in film music.

Korngold had a promising beginning to a career as an operatic composer when his operas *Der Ring des Polykrates* and *Violanta* were produced at the Vienna Hofoper in 1916 when the composer was still under 20, and he confirmed that promise with *Die tote Stadt,* his best known work, in 1920. However, after *Das Wunder der Heliane* (1927) he produced just one more opera, *Kathrin* (Stockholm, 1939), devoting his attentions rather to a career in the light musical theatre and film.

Korngold, in fact, wrote no original score for the Operette stage, but limited himself to remaking the already-famous works of other composers. He rearranged such classics as *Eine Nacht in Venedig, Die schöne Helena*—a major reworking with a quantity of Offenbach music culled from other shows inserted into the score—and *Die Fledermaus*—a remake which did similarly inartistic things to Strauss's work—as spectaculars for Max Reinhardt and subsequently stages further afield, and his continuing name value was emphasized by the vast above-the-title billing given him by the Theater an der Wien when he conducted his reconstitution of the Leo Fall (billed small) Operette *Rosen aus Florida* which had been left uncompleted at the celebrated composer's death. Korngold's intimate association with a lady member of the Fall family assured him a free hand with the contents of the late great man's trunk of unused music, and unkind tongues were heard to say thereafter that some Korngold melodies of the years that followed had a remarkable flavor of Fall to them. He was also responsible for the musical manufacture of both the Strauss pasticcio *Das Lied der Liebe* played in Berlin by Richard Tauber, and of the widely successful *Walzer aus Wien,* a biomusical illustrated by a score compiled from the music of the Strausses, father and son, done for the Wiener Stadttheater in 1930 and subsequently played around in the world in various further reworked versions.

In 1934 he moved to Hollywood where he became a favorite composer of scores for more than a decade of pictures including *Captain Blood, Anthony Adverse, A Midsummer Night's Dream, The Adventures of Robin Hood, Elizabeth and Essex, The Sea Wolf, King's Row, The Constant Nymph, Of Human Bondage* and *Escape Me Never,* winning two Academy Awards in the process.

In 1951 he provided incidental music and songs for the musical radio play *Die stumme Serenade,* subsequently produced on the stage at Dortmund.

1923 **Eine Nacht in Venedig** revised version w Ernst Marischka (Theater an der Wien)

1927 **Cagliostro in Wien** revised version w Ludwig Herzer (Wiener Bürgertheater)

1929 **Rosen aus Florida** (Leo Fall arr/A M Willner, Heinz Reichert) Theater an der Wien 22 February

1929 **Die Fledermaus** revised version (Deutsches Theater, Berlin)

1929 **Eine Nacht in Venedig** second revised version (Hofoper, Vienna)

1930 **Walzer aus Wien** (Johann Strauss arr w Julius Bittner/Willner, Reichert, Ernst Marischka) Wiener Stadttheater 30 October

1931 **Die schöne Helena** revised version (Theater am Kurfürstendamm, Berlin)

1931 **Das Lied der Liebe** (Johann Strauss arr/Ludwig Herzer) Metropoltheater, Berlin 23 December

1933 **Die geschiedene Frau** (*Abenteuer im Schlafcoupé*) revised version w Max Colpet (Theater am Nollendorfplatz, Berlin)

1954 **Die stumme Serenade** (Bert Reisfeld, William Okie/Victor Clement ad Raoul Auernheimer) Städtische Bühnen, Dortmund 10 November

Biographies: Korngold, L: *Erich Wolfgang Korngold* (Vienna, 1967), Carroll, B G: *The Last Prodigy* (Amadeus, 1997)

KOSÁRY, Emmi (b Kisszeben, 31 May 1889; d Budapest, 22 October 1964). Hungarian prima donna who created important roles in two Lehár Operetten and also in many homemade ones.

After early experience in the chorus at the Király Színház, Kosáry at first made a career in opera in Berlin and Budapest and appeared, aged 23, as the heroine of the *Hamupipőke* (Cinderella) written by her husband, composer Ákos Buttykay, at the Budapest Opera. She scored a great success when she turned to the musical theatre and appeared as Budapest's Sylva Varescu in *Die Csárdásfürstin* at the Király Színház (1916), and she followed this up by creating the role of Juliska in Lehár's *Pacsirta* (*Wo die Lerche singt*), and the prima donna part of Szirmai's *Gróf Rinaldo* (1918). She also played Germaine to the Serpolette of Juci Lábass (1919) and Médi in *Három a kislány* (*Das Dreimäderlhaus*) as well as introducing the star role of Xénia, opposite her *Csárdáskirálynő* and *Pacsirta* partner, Ernő Király, in Buttykay's highly successful *Az ezüst sirály* (1920, ''the silver seagull''). The pair repeated their performances when the show was staged shortly after in Vienna, under the title *Liebesrauch,* running for two hundred performances at the Carltheater.

She starred in Budapest in Stolz's *A kis grizett* (*Die Tanzgräfin,* Városi Színház, 1921), created the title role in her husband's *Olivia hercegnő* (Fővárosi Operettszínház, 1922) and also visited America to repeat her *Ezüst sirály* role (1923) and to appear as Catherine the Great in the tryout of the Tschaikowsky pasticcio *Die Siegerin.* In 1924 she succeeded to the role of *Gräfin Mariza* at the Theater an der Wien and she remained in Vienna to create her first major role there, starring opposite Carl Clewing as Maria Anna Elisa in Lehár's *Paganini* at the Johann Strauss-Theater (1925). She went on to appear at the same house in the Viennese version of Szirmai's *Alexandra* (1926) and at the Carltheater for the 160 performances as the top-billed star of Stolz's Black-Bottomful *Eine einzige Nacht* (1927, Ora Kolorewna) alongside Luise Kartousch, Josef König and Ernst Tautenhayn.

She then returned to Hungary where she appeared at the Városi Színház in *A bíborruhás asszony* (*Das Weib im Purpur*), and took on another major Lehár role in Vienna in 1928 when she appeared as Sonja to *Der Zarewitsch* of Hans-Heinz Bollmann at the Johann Strauss-Theater. She subsequently appeared in Germany, America (a Philadelphia tryout of *Arms and the Maid,* ie, *Hotel Stadt Lemberg*) and in Budapest, in pieces such as *Die Csárdásfürstin, Das Land des Lächelns,* as the original Ottilie in Hungary's version of *Im weissen Rössl,* and in homemade pieces including Lajtai's *Őfelsége frakkja* (1931), *Amikor a kislányból nagylány lesz* (1932) and *A kék lámpás* (Király Színház, 1933, Nagyhercegnő) with Hanna Honthy, and *Marion* (1940), and appeared as Katinka in Tamás Hegedüs's *Kata, Kitty, Katinka* at the Operettszínház in 1942 in the latter part of a fine career.

KOSIKI Opéra-comique in 3 acts by William Busnach and Armand Liorat. Music by Charles Lecocq. Théâtre de la Renaissance, Paris, 18 October 1876.

Zulma Bouffar, back in stage-trousers yet again, starred in Lecocq's opéra-comique as Kosiki, ''the son of the sun'' and the boyish inheritor of the throne of the eastern principality of Yeddo. The new monarch finds both politics and married life tricky. He cannot bear to be surrounded by counsellors like the pompous Xicoco (Berthelier) and he causes a scandal by appointing a little juggler called Fitzo (Félix Puget) to be his closest minister. Similarly, duly wed to Xicoco's pretty daughter, Nousima (Marie Harlem), much to the despair of her kissing cousin, Sagami (Urbain), he finds that he can get up no interest in things marital. The reason is, of course, is that the ''he'' is a girl and the real sovereign is apparently Namitou (Vauthier), a state prisoner who is prison-employed decorating hats and who now proposes to wed Kosiki as he ascends the throne. She refuses him, and goes off to be a fairground performer with Fitzo who, by the end of the third act, is predictably found to be the real heir of Yeddo.

Both the soprano role of Kosiki and the tenor part of Fitzo—a role which required Puget to juggle, balance and do a knife-throwing act with Mlle Bouffar as his target—were equipped with vocally demanding numbers and ensembles in Lecocq's best style, ranging from her discovery of the ''drôle d'effet'' of his presence, and his romance with its final high C, to their balancing solo and knife-throwers' duet, whilst Namitou's baritone tale of the baby-swapping (''Jadis certaine altesse'')—a sort of Franco-Japanese equivalent to W S Gilbert's ''I Stole the Prince'' in *The Gondoliers*—and his over-drinking song, ''Dans la forteresse où naguère,'' headed the comic moments.

Kosiki scored a fine Paris success, without equaling the popularity of the very top group of Lecocq favorites. It ran to the end of 1876 at the Théâtre de la Renaissance and was revived the following year when, during the illness of the theatre's star, Jeanne Granier, Koning remounted *Kosiki* with Mlle Bouffar. He saw it pass its 100th performance on 11 September, before being replaced a week or so later by another Lecocq revival. In the meanwhile the show had already been seen with some considerable success in Budapest, with Lujza Blaha starring, and it was subsequently played in Germany and in Vienna (ad Carl Treumann) where Lori Stubel (Kosiki), Karl Drucker (Fitzo) and Kuhle (Namitou) headed the not very starry cast for Strampfer's production at the Carltheater. None of this, however, proved sufficient to establish *Kosiki* in the revivable repertoire. English-language theatres seem to have passed the tale of the androgynous ''son of the sun'' by.

Hungary: Népszínház 27 April 1877; Germany: Centraltheater, Hamburg *Mikado Kosiki* 11 July 1880, Krolls Theater, Berlin 16 October 1880; Austria: Carltheater 28 November 1882

KOSTA, Tessa (b Chicago, 10 December 1893; d New York, 23 August 1981).

Recognized as having one of the loveliest soprano voices on the American musical stage in the years after the First World War, the beautiful, dark-haired Miss Kosta starred on Broadway in a number of famous Continental and British musicals which did not equal their original success in their American versions, and in a number of original musicals of which only the picturesque *Song of the Flame* gave her the kind of opportunities on which she could capitalize.

She played early on in the road company of *The Pink Lady,* featured as a ''lady revolutionist'' alongside Alice Dovey and Maclyn Arbuckle in the unfortunate *The Merry Martyr* (1913), and made her first appearances on Broadway in *The Beauty Shop* (1914, Anna Budd) and as a takeover in Irving Berlin's *Stop! Look! Listen!* (1916). Her first leading roles came in 1917 when she was cast first as Peggy in Andreas Dippel's touring *The Love Mill* and then as Marjanah in the American production of *Chu Chin Chow* (1917). She subsequently played heroines in George M Cohan's burlesque operetta *The Royal Vagabond* (1919, Anitza Chefchek), the highly rated *Lassie* (1920, Kitty McKaye) and *Princess Virtue* (1921, Lane Demarest) before taking on the very vocal starring roles of Nadina in a revival of *The Chocolate Soldier,* Kondja Gül in Leo Fall's *The Rose of Stamboul* and Caroline Lee in *Caroline* (*Der Vetter aus Dingsda*). She later appeared in the title role of the Carlo and Sanders musical play *Princess April,* as Princess Ida in a revival of Gilbert and Sullivan's comic opera (1925) and as the romantic Russian heroine of Gershwin's *Song of the Flame* (1925, Aniuta), and starred in Alice Nielsen's double role in *The Fortune Teller* in the Shubert's operetta season of 1929, before disappearing from Broadway playbills.

KOVAL, [René] [KOVALSKY, René] (b Paris, 26 May 1885; d Paris, 17 August 1936). Tall, slim and dapper character man of the French musical comedy stage.

Koval, who appeared as the essence of Parisian-ness in the London revue *Kill That Fly* as early as 1912, later created more than a decade of comic Americans, Englishmen and, much less frequently, Frenchmen in Paris musicals of the 1920s and 1930s. He made an early mark with his last-act portrayal of the composer Olivier Métra in the original production of *Ciboulette* (1923), appeared alongside that show's star, Edmée Favart, in the 1924 revival of *Madame l'Archiduc* and went on to create such featured comedy roles as the American ex-husband of the heroine of *Pas sur la bouche* (1925, Eric Thompson, ''Pas sur la bouche'') who will never allow himself to be kissed on the lips, the tipsy American millionaire with a young wife to lose in *Passionnément* (1926, William Stevenson, ''Le Régime sec'') and a third American in Christiné's *J'aime* (1926, Harry Stone). He was the English Reverend Good-Bye, father to the heroine of *Flossie* (1929), singing of ''Paris,'' another Englishman as Bob, the bemused host of *Un soir de réveillon* (1932), and even one Spaniard, Pedro Hernandez, the plantation owner, performing the celebrated Duo des palétuviers with Pauline Carton, in *Toi c'est moi* (1934).

Koval played an American in a genuine American piece when *Mercenary Mary* came to Paris, taking the top-billed role of the money-seeking Charley, and he also appeared in *J'adore ça* (1925, André de Saint-Assise), *Le Madelon de la Victoire* (1925), *Elle ou moi* (1925, Siegfried), *La Marraine de l'Escouade* (1927), *Déshabillez-vous* (1928, ''Breton, Bretonne''), Honegger's *Les Aventures du Roi Pausole* (1930, Taxis), *Arsène Lupin Banquier* (1930, the tricksy banker, Lord Turner with his ''Marche de Lupin''), *La Pouponnière* (1932), *Azor* (1932), Guitry's *O mon bel inconnu* (1933, Hilarion Lallumette), *Pour ton bonheur* (1935), *Trente et quarante* (1935) and *Simone est comme ça* (1936), and was last seen in a revival of *Flossie* shortly before his death.

KRAATZ, Kurt (b Berlin, 2 September 1856; d Wiesbaden, 30 April 1925).

A playwright, whose considerable output was largely in the non-musical theatre, Kraatz nevertheless also authored a number of successful musical comedies.

His earliest significant venture in the musical-comedy field seems to have been the musical adaptation of his own Schwank *Eine lustige Doppel-Ehe,* a play originally mounted in Cologne in 1904 and later turned into a musical for Berlin's Thalia-Theater. This was swiftly followed by the highly successful *Eine tolles Mädel*—which went on from its initial production in Wiesbaden to be seen in Berlin, in Vienna (Danzers Orpheum 8 November 1907) and in America (*Mlle Mischief*)—and then by his biggest hit of all, the Posse *Polnische Wirtschaft,* which moved from Cottbus to Berlin's Thalia-Theater, scored a huge success there, launched its author and composer Jean Gilbert to the top of their professions, and went on to be played internationally.

Kraatz subsequently teamed with the Thalia's Kren and Schönfeld, and also with Gilbert, on several other shows which were housed for good runs at the theatre where *Polnische Wirtschaft* had scored its great Berlin triumph, and also paired with Hermann Haller to produce the text for *Blaue Jungens,* played for a run of six months at the Theater am Nollendorfplatz.

His play *Mädel als Rekrut* (w Heinrich Stobitzer), produced in America as *The Girl in the Barracks,* was made into a virtual musical when it was decorated with six songs and several dances during its American touring life (New Rochelle, NY 7 September 1907).

1896 **Olympische Spiele** (Max Schmidt/w Max Neal) Cologne 11 November; Thalia-Theater 8 March 1907

1903 **Der Hochtourist** (Schmidt/w Neal) Thalia-Theater September

1904 **Götterweiber** (Julius Einödshofer/w Wilhelm Jacoby) Belle-Alliance Theater 4 February

1906 **Eine lustige Doppel-Ehe** (Paul Lincke/Alfred Schönfeld) Thalia-Theater 27 November

1907 **Eine tolles Mädel** (Carl Michael Ziehrer/Wilhelm Sterk/w Heinrich Stobitzer) Walhalla-Theater, Wiesbaden 24 August; Danzers Orpheum, Vienna 8 November

1909 **Polnische Wirtschaft** (Jean Gilbert/ w Georg Okonkowski) Stadttheater, Cottbus 26 December; revised version ad Kren, ly Schönfeld, Thalia-Theater 6 August 1910

1912 **Puppchen** (Gilbert/Schönfeld/w Kren) Thalia-Theater 19 December

1913 **Die Millionenbraut** (Johannes Döbber/Schönfeld/w Jean Kren) Wilhelm-Theater, Magdeburg 17 February

1913 **Die Tangoprinzessin** (Gilbert/Schönfeld/w Kren) Thalia-Theater 4 October

1915 **Des Kaisers Rock** (Döbber/w Kren) Residenz-Theater 19 February

1916 **Loge nr 7** (Victor Holländer/w Theo Halton) Residenztheater 28 January

1916 **Blondinchen** (Gilbert/Schönfeld/w Kren) Thalia-Theater 4 March

1916 **Blaue Jungens** (Rudolf Nelson/Hermann Frey/w Hermann Haller) Theater am Nollendorfplatz 25 August

1918 **Inkognito** (Nelson/w Richard Kessler) Berlin Kammerspiele 4 June

1919 **Die Kabarett-Diva** (Rudolf Kaiser/w Kessler) Schauspielhaus, Potsdam 30 April

1920 **Die Löwenbraut** (Otto Gaze/w Halton) Albert-Schumann-Theater, Frankfurt am Main 12 February

1920 **Der verjüngte Adolar** (Walter Kollo/w Kessler, Frey) Theater in der Kommandantenstrasse 4 October

1921 **Der Alpenrosenkavalier** (Karl Grandauer/w Neal) Orpheum, Darmstadt 7 August

1922 **Lady Chic** (Kollo/w Kessler, Willy Steinberg) Neues Operetten-Theater 11 March

1928 **Zu Befehl—schöne Frau** (Ottberg/w Kessler) Neues Theater am Zoo 23 March

Other title attributed: *Lolas Rache* (Josef Snaga/w Halton)

[KRASZNAY]-KRAUSZ, Michael [KRASZNAI-KRAUSZ, Mihály] (b Pancsova, 11 April 1897; d during the Second World War). Composer for European stages between the wars.

Krausz studied at the Budapest Zeneakadémia, and in his twenties wrote several pieces for the operatic stage (*Marika,* 1919, *Táncosnő*) before moving to Vienna and to Berlin and devoting himself to the musical theatre. His first Viennese Operette, *Bajazzos Abenteuer,* produced at the Johann Strauss-Theater, was in a very different idiom from his early efforts, featuring such items as the shimmy and the ''Aequetor-Java'' in a score which wed traditional musical styles with popular and foreign dance rhythms. It played for only two months, but a second piece for the same house, *Pusztaliebchen,* outran it comprehensively with a fine run of 110 nights. *Glück in der Liebe,* with Gisela Werbezirk starred, had a good run of 103 performances, also at the Johann Strauss-Theater, and was later seen at Berlin's Metropoltheater, whilst *Eine Frau von Format,* successfully introduced along with its hit song ''Wir wollen tun, als ob wir Freunde wären'' in Berlin in 1927 (56 performances), was later played in Vienna (21 April 1935, 27 performances), and in Budapest, as *A fenséges asszony* (ad Andor Szenes, Király Színház 8 May 1935).

The latter part of Krausz's career in the theatre was less fulfilling than the first decade. His *Yvette und ihre Freunde* managed only a little over a month at the Bürgertheater, and his most successful subsequent pieces, a musical adaptation of the Hungarian *Sárga liliom*—first produced in Budapest, then in Teplitz-Schönau (12 May) and later an 81-performance semi-success at the Theater an der Wien—and the musical crime-story *Dixie* (42 performances) were also less long-lived. Another musical comedy, *Eső utan köpönyeg,* otherwise *Verzeih', das ich dich lieb',* which played an initial 56 performances at Vienna's Johann Strauss-Theater (1 March 1937) was, however, well enough liked to be revived in 1946. His last work, *Marion,* produced in Budapest nearly 20 years after his first, was mounted with the end-of-career Emmi Kosáry in its title role.

Krausz supplied two additional songs for the Berlin production of *The Student Prince* (1932), adapted Fall's *Der süsse Kavalier* (Fall ad Krasznay-Krausz/ad) with librettist Welisch under the title *Der junge Herr René* (1935) and also wrote for the musical screen (*Die Lindwirtin vom Rhein* for Käthe Dorsch, etc).

1923 **Pusztaliebchen** (Wilhelm Sterk) Johann Strauss-Theater 19 December

1923 **Bajazzos Abenteuer** (Ludwig Stark, Adolf Eisler) Johann Strauss-Theater 22 December

1927 **Glück in der Liebe** (Julius Horst, Peter Herz) Johann Strauss-Theater 25 February

1927 **Eine Frau von Format** (Rudolf Schanzer, Ernst Welisch) Theater des Westens, Berlin, 21 September

1927 **Yvette und ihre Freunde** (Sterk, Rudolf Österreicher) Bürgertheater 18 November

Plate 209. **Krausz's** *first Viennese Operette.*

1929 **Die Frau in Gold** (Leopold Jacobson, Bruno Hardt-Warden) Neues Operettenhaus, Leipzig 28 February

1930 **Das Herrgottslied** (Hardt-Warden) Neues Wiener Schauspielhaus 21 November

1933 **Die Lindenwirtin** (Schanzer, Welisch) Metropoltheater, Berlin 30 March

1933 **A papucs** (Paul Armont, Marcel Gerbidon ad Sándor Lestyán) Pesti Színház 18 November

1934 **Sárga liliom** (*Die gelbe Lili*) (Lajos Biró ad Géza Herczeg, István Zágon) Fővárosi Operettszínház, Budapest 5 January

1936 **Eső után köpönyeg** (Mihály Szécsén/István Békeffy) Andrássy uti Színház, Budapest 6 November

1938 **Dixie** (Farkas, Mathilde Schürz) Theater an der Wien 8 February

1940 **Marion** (Maurice Dekobra ad Attila Orbók) Városi Színház, Budapest 23 March

KREISLER, Fritz (b Vienna, 2 February 1885; d New York, 29 January 1962).

Fritz Kreisler studied under Hellmesberger in Vienna and Delibes in Paris, and made a famous career as a virtuoso violinist, using melodies composed and arranged by himself as a popular part of his concert repertoire. He put some of these melodies to use in two musical plays, an updated version of Dumas's *Un Mariage sous Louis XV* called *Apple Blossoms* (w Victor Jacobi), produced by Charles Dillingham at Broadway's Globe Theater in 1919 during Kreisler's wartime and post-wartime decade in America, and the 1932 *Sissy,* a costume Operette staged at Vienna's Theater an der Wien after the violinist's return to Europe, and later expanded and reorganized for a spectacular production in France as *Sissi, future impératrice.* His music was also put to use in *Broadway's Rhapsody* (John Latouche, Russell Bennett/Leonard Levinson, Arnold Sundgaard, Century Theater 22 November 1944) in arrangements by Bennett, and was heard off-Broadway as recently as 1996 when a ''Love's Sorrow'' was sung in the musical *Cowgirls* (Minetta Lane Theater 1 April).

1919 **Apple Blossoms** (w Victor Jacobi/William le Baron) Globe Theater, New York 7 October

1932 **Sissy** (Ernst Marischka, Hubert Marischka) Theater an der Wien, Vienna 23 December

KRELING brothers

Joseph Kreling (b Germany, c1855; d San Francisco, 26 June 1887).

William Kreling (b Germany, c1850; d San Francisco, 15 December 1893).

The brothers Kreling were the instigators of America's most novel, enterprising and long-surviving musical theatre of the nineteenth century, the Tivoli Opera House in San Francisco. The original ''Tivoli Gardens,'' on the corner of San Francisco's Sutter and Stockton, was instituted by German New Yorker Joe Kreling in October 1875, and it was operated on the lines of a pleasure garden, a setup something like a café-concert on the French lines, or those entertainments formerly given in the pleasure gardens and early music halls of London. ''A ladies' orchestra and good beer,'' a contemporary described it. The Tivoli Gardens proved so successful that, in 1879, Kreling—by now assisted by his brother, John, and various other family members—expanded his operation. He leased a piece of land at 28-32 Eddy Street, and there he constructed a larger hall, a three-story clapboard building with a galleried concert-hall capable of seating one thousand people. John ran the upstairs bar, a couple of other Krelings were in charge of the downstairs bar, and Joe himself took charge of the increasingly important entertainment element. The entertainment, in fact, was now sufficiently important in the scheme of things that the place was no longer known as the ''Tivoli Gardens,'' but more theatrically as the ''Tivoli Opera House'' (12 April 1879). And with good reason too, for, in their handsome new premises, from 3 July of 1879, Joe Kreling began mounting full-scale productions of the latest musical-theatre novelties of the day, with a more or less resident cast, playing each piece seven nights a week for two, three or sometimes even four week spots before switching the bill to something fresh. He acted as manager, director and adaptor (when required, and sometimes when not). The program at the ''Tivoli Opera House'' in its first months, between December 1879 and May 1880 included productions of the then fairly new *HMS Pinafore* and *Trial by Jury,* followed by the burlesque *The Wreck of the Pinafore, The Doctor of Alcantara, The Sorcerer, La Fille de Madame Angot, Giroflé-Girofla, The Little Duke, La Grande-Duchesse, Fatinitza* and Offenbach's *Bluebeard.*

Joe Kreling—whose crazy schedule had included the running of a furniture factory and salesroom alongside his Tivoli activities—died in 1887, aged only 32, during the rehearsals of the Tivoli's biggest original show to date, and the entertainment side of the operation—with the house now enlarged now to a 2,000-seater—was then taken over by brother William. Brother John still supervised the beer.

The Tivoli long retained its special ''beer garden'' nature, with tables and chairs instead of rows of seats, and smoking allowed along with, of course, drinking. It always retained its low prices, prices which included 10¢ worth of wet money—a coupon for beer ''or other refreshment'' being provided with the entertainment ticket—and, through and in spite of several attempts to set up rival companies in a similar style in San Francisco, it maintained its popularity for many years.

The repertoire at the Tivoli quickly got more ambitious, and the popular comic operas that had been its original diet were varied not only with grand operas (Tetrazzini made her first American appearance at the Tivoli), but also with a regular diet of ''firsts''—first American productions of Continental Operetten and opérettes which the East Coast sometimes never saw, and original comic operas from American hands—something which in the 1880s and 1890s was a far from common occurrence.

The Tivoli's casts were often second-best, but performers such as comic Ferris Hartman and soprano Tellula Evans became local favorites, and their was a regular stream of slightly-past-their-best ''names,'' including the top basso William H Hamilton, patent megastar Emily Soldene and international comic opera soprano Camille D'Arville, who took up one or more of the Tivoli's three-month contracts.

Their productions, too, though well-staged were not always faithful. Many a local journalist had his susceptibilities assuaged by the inclusion of one of his lyrics, set by the Tivoli's musical director, into the show of the week, and Dick Deadeye was liable to come out in the middle of *HMS Pinafore* with ''Rocked in the Cradle of the Deep.''

Amongst the Krelings' ''firsts,'' during Joe and William's years, were included English-language productions of Suppé's *Light Cavalry* (23 August 1880), Lecocq's *La Jolie Persane* (*The Pretty Persian* 25 November 1880), Planquette's *Les Voltigeurs* (16 June 1882), Varney's *Coquelicot* (7 August 1882) and Offenbach's *The Tales of Hoffmann* (25 September 1882); a pretty correct version of Audran's *Gillette de Narbonne* (7 July 1884); a Christmas entertainment called *Prince North Pole* (25 December 1884), said to be "from the German" of Richard Genée and musicked by a certain Görner; an Oscar Weil adaptation of Offenbach's *Les Braconniers* as *The Pretty Poacher* (19 May 1885); Offenbach's *Les Georgiennes* (August 1885); a musicalized version of *Der Bibliothekar* as *The Medium* (April 1886) done by a "celebrated Australian comedian" called F M Page, who took the leading role in what turned out a frightful flop; one of Serpette's pieces "for the first time in America" under the title *The May Queen* (17 March 1887); an unidentifiable comic opera called *Benvenita* "adapted from the French by Colonel J E Milliken" (1888); the first American viewings of André Messager's *The Nightingale* (*La Fauvette du Temple* 11 February 1889) and Suppé's *The Gascon* (*Der Gascogner* 24 March 1890); Lecocq's *La Marjolaine* in English, for what seems to have been the first time in America; and the maiden American stagings of *The Privateer* (in other words Planquette's *Surcouf* 22 September 1890), *Madame Cartouche* (23 November 1891) and *The Red Bird* (ie, Lecocq's *L'Oiseau bleu* 20 October 1892). They also mounted the "world premiere" of the New Zealand musical *The Fakir of Travancore* (6 June 1881) while its composer, Luscombe Searelle, briefly held the baton at the Tivoli, and other little-seen pieces such as Searelle's *Estrella,* Bucalossi's *Manteaux Noirs,* Teddy Solomon's *Virginia,* Lecocq's *Le Grand Casimir* (as *The Circus Queen*) or Dellinger's *Captain Fracasse* and *Lorraine* also got showings at the Tivoli.

In 1886 (27 September) the Tivoli mounted a "new musical comedy" by Joe Kreling, *Business Is Business*—apparently adapted from a German comedy called, of course, *Geschäft ist Geschäft.* It included an interrupted wedding, a photograph gallery, a dangerous drugstore and an entrapped Russian convict, a French actress, a Polish Jewish watch-vendor, a detective, etc, and seems to have had a pasticcio score arranged by md William Furst. They had a considerable success with an original home-made comic opera called *Said Pasha* (18 June 1888) (re)written by Scott Marble and with music by the theatre's conductor, Richard Stahl, which broke the house records before going east (Grand Opera House, Philadelphia 14 January 1889) and round America. They subsequently produced a locally made musical version of Rider Haggard's *She* (4 July 1887), with music by Furst, which also went east after its Tivoli showing; *Yetiva* (25 February 1889), a new American comic opera by "the Hon George Morgan, late a member of the Pennsylvania legislature, with music by Ion Arnold" and set in Albuquerque (later produced in the east as *A Trip to the Rockies*); *The First Lieutenant* by H Clark Wise and N Clifford Page (a pair of locals, aged 21 and 22, 6 May 1889); *Theodora* (Furst's musical version of Sardou's play, 26 September 1889); a not-so-successful extravaganza, *Furiosa, or The Daughter of Hades,* written by former Tivoli lead vocalist Fritz La Fontaine and Theodore Vogts (13 January 1890); a *Pied Piper* derivative composed by New York's German-Theater impresario and conductor Adolf Neuendorff as *Der Rattenfänger von Hameln* played in English as *The Rat-Charmer* (1 June 1891); an extravagant and unattracting *Nenajo* (J A Zander/ Constance P Fiske 22 June 1891); *Aquilo* (Adolf Bauer/R C White, 3 August 1891); *The Island of Zanobar, or The Princess of Benedicta* (21 December 1891); a *Bluff King Hal* (H J Stewart/O'Connell, 21 March 1892); and a *Beauty and the Beast* (Adolf Bauer/J P Wilson, 7 August 1892). They also took in (9 March 1893) the production of the local comic opera *His Majesty* (H J Stewart/Peter Robertson), originally staged at the Grand Opera House.

After William's death his widow, Ernestine (née Krause) continued the house's policy and amongst her new productions were included a *Dick Turpin* (Bowness Biggs, H Grattan Donnelly, 9 July 1894), a festive season burlesque *Lallah Rookh* (Joseph Hirschback, James Wilson, 24 December 1894), *The Gentle Savage* (Estelle Clayton/A C Wheeler, February 1896), a Ferris Hartman version of *Babes in the Wood* with a score of "up-to-date-songs" (13 October 1896), *Mother Goose, or The Strange Adventures of Jack and Jill* (comp & arr Max Hirschfeld/Edwin Stevens, 18 December 1897) and an imaginative piece called *The Poster* (Chester S Packard/L G Carpenter, C Wilson, 23 May 1898).

The clapboard Opera House was condemned under fire regulations in 1903, and the Tivoli operation (by then run by "Doc" Leahy, the new husband of the widow of Kreling, and a shadow of its former self) shifted to the old Olympia. The policy was now rather less exciting, though a *Miss Timidity* which was nothing more nor less than a remusicked, reorganized version of Audran's *Miss Helyett* done by an aspiring young local was premiered on 2 April 1906. His presumption was rewarded, for *Miss Timidity* was on the bill when the newest home of the Tivoli was destroyed in the earthquake. A fourth Tivoli—the New Tivoli—later emerged, only to go under in 1913 (12 March) to that entertainment tidal wave known as the cinema. But in San Francisco, where theatres and managements in those days collapsed yearly or even monthly, to have survived for nearly half a century—and more or less throughout under the same family management—made the Tivoli a truly remarkable institution.

KREN, Jean (b Berlin, 31 March 1862; d Berlin, 11 September 1922). Manager and author who turned out a series of Berlin's most successful-ever shows.

Kren began his theatrical career as an actor, but successes with his earliest attempts at a musical play, *Im siebenten Himmel* and *Leute von heute,* each played first in Berlin and later as far afield as the German Amberg Theater in New York (1892), set him off on a career as a playwright instead. He collaborated with the Centraltheater's resident dramaturg, Alfred Schönfeld, and musical director/composer Julius Einödshofer on several further musical Possen and Schwänke, but when the theatre's management preferred to turn to Julius Freund and Wilhelm Mannstädt for more and more of their shows, Kren and Schönfeld decided to move on. Their first stop was at the Adolf-Ernst-Theater, where they turned out first a German version of Audran's opérette *Madame Suzette* for Ernst, and then a series of pieces including the successful Posse *Im Himmelshof* for his successor. Then, at the turn of the century, Kren and Schönfeld began the next phase of their theatre life by taking over the direction of the theatre themselves. They rebuilt it into a 1,200-seat house and called it the Thalia-Theater.

The Thalia-Theater became the home of a long series of successful Kren/Schönfeld Possen and Schwänke, usually with libretti written or adapted by Kren and with lyrics by his partner. The musical part, whether it were arranged, additional or new was supplied, successively, by Einödshofer, Max Schmidt, Paul Lincke and Viktor Holländer, before the partners hired the young Jean Gilbert, fresh from his first success with *Polnische Wirtschaft* at Cottbus, as their resident composer. Together Kren, Schönfeld and Gilbert wrote, and the managers produced, such successful musical comedies as *Autoliebchen* and *Puppchen,* and the Thalia-Theater prospered on a continuous run of their works. Their pieces were produced, in principle, twice yearly, although some, like *Blondinchen,* ran beyond their allotted six months and others, such as the later *Zur wilden Hummel* and *Die närrische Liebe,* managed only three.

Kren and Schönfeld also produced pieces by other writers, but although many of these proved at least adequate propositions, no major successes arose from their productions of such musical comedies as *Jungfer Sonnenschein,* Goetze's very short-lived *Amor am Reisen, Der dumme Franzl, Botschafterin Leni* or *Schäm dich, Lotte,* although Gellért's very respectable *Unter den blühenden Linden* and Walter Bromme's *Mascottchen* both had good runs, and Goetze's *Ihre Hoheit die Tänzerin,* brought in from Hanover, began a fine run at the Thalia before being transferred to the Friedrich-Wilhelmstädtisches Theater.

Business was good enough at the Thalia that when Max Monti, one of their most serious rivals in the Berlin musical theatre, went into retirement, Kren (Schönfeld had died in 1916) was able to take over his Montis Operettentheater which he ran thereafter as the Neues Operettenhaus, playing, again, a mixture of his own and other people's musicals. His own most notable contribution to the Spielplan of the new house was his first production there, Leo Ascher's hugely successful wartime musical comedy *Der Soldat der Marie,* which ultimately proved to be one of Kren's greatest successes as both an author and as a producer. A collaboration with Robert Winterberg on *Die Dame vom Zirkus* brought another six months' success, and it was Winterberg who was Kren's partner on his last profitable work, *Die Herrn von und zu,* produced at the Thalia-Theater in January 1922 and still running there until just a few days before its author-producer's death in September.

In 30 years as a prolific writer, Kren had many successes in the Berlin theatre, but few followed *Im Himmelshof* (adapted by George V Hobart as *Hodge, Podge and Co* for the American stage) and *Autoliebchen* to productions outside central Europe. As a producer, whilst giving obvious attention to his own work, he nevertheless used and promoted local talent—Gilbert being the most successful example—and new local shows, and almost never hosted imported and/or translated pieces in his theatres.

- 1891 **Im siebenten Himmel** (Johannes Döbber) Thomastheater 31 July
- 1891 **Leute von heute** (Gustav Steffens) Centraltheater
- 1892 **Das grosse Los** (Döbber/w Alfred Schönfeld) Tivoli Theater, Bremen 6 August
- 1893 **Berliner Vollblut** (Julius Einödshofer/w Schönfeld) Centraltheater 31 August
- 1894 **Ein gesunder Junge** (Einödshofer/w Schönfeld) Centraltheater 6 March
- 1894 **Der neue Kurs** (Einödshofer/w Leopold Ely) Centraltheater
- 1894 **Die ewige Braut** (Steffens, Roth/w Mannstädt) 1 act Adolf-Ernst Theater 4 November
- 1894 **Ein fideles Corps** (*A Gaiety Girl*) German version w Eduard Jacobson (Adolf-Ernst-Theater)
- 1895 **Madame Suzette** German version w E Jacobson (Adolf-Ernst Theater)
- 1896 **Mamsell Vielliebchen** (revised *Im siebenten Himmel*) (arr Steffens) Belle-Alliance-Theater 8 October
- 1897 **Ein fideler Abend** (Einödshofer/w Wilhelm Mannstädt) Centraltheater 7 February
- 1897 **Heirath auf Probe** (*Próbaházasság*) (Leopold Kühn/Károly Gerő ad Bernhard Buchbinder, Ferenc Rajna) Berlin version w lyrics by G Görss Thalia-Theater 10 April
- 1899 **Der Platzmajor** (Gustav Wanda/w Schönfeld) Thalia-Theater 30 September
- 1899 **Im Himmelshof** (Max Schmidt/Schönfeld) Thalia-Theater 23 December
- 1900 **Der Liebesschlüssel** (Schmidt/Schönfeld) Thalia-Theater 8 September

1900 **Der Amor von heute** (Wanda/w Schönfeld) Thalia-Theater 30 November

1901 **Der Cadetten-Vater** (Schmidt, Conradi/Schönfeld) Thalia-Theater 9 March

1901 **Ein tolles Geschaft** (Einödshofer/Schönfeld) Thalia-Theater 7 September

1901 **Die Badepuppe** (Einödshofer/Schönfeld) Thalia-Theater 26 November

1902 **Seine kleine** (Einödshofer/Schönfeld/w Ely) Thalia-Theater 18 January

1902 **Die bösen Mädchen** (Einödshofer/Schönfeld/w Ely) Thalia-Theater 23 December

1903 **Der Posaunenengel** (Einödshofer, Schmidt/Schönfeld) Thalia-Theater 24 March

1903 **Der reicheste Berliner** (Einödshofer, Schmidt/Schönfeld) Belle-Alliance-Theater 23 December

1904 **Freut euch des Lebens** (Einödshofer/Schönfeld/Wilhelm Jacoby, Robert Stein ad) Belle-Alliance-Theater 14 April

1904 **Kam'rad Lehmann** (Einödshofer, Julius Stern/Schönfeld/F Zell ad w Ely) Belle-Alliance-Theater 7 May

1904 **Der Weiberkönig** (Einödshofer/w Schönfeld, Ely) Thalia-Theater 15 September

1904 **'s Zuckersgoscherl** (J Wolffsgruber/Schönfeld) Carltheater, Vienna 15 October

1904 **Der grosse Stern** (Einödshofer/Schönfeld) Thalia-Theater 23 December

1905 **Der beste Tip** (Schmidt) Belle-Alliance-Theater 9 February

1905 **Noch einmal so leben** (Schmidt/Schönfeld) Belle-Alliance-Theater 1 April

1905 **Madame Tip-Top** (Karl Woytschach/Arthur Lippschitz, Fritz Friedmann-Friedrich ad) Belle-Alliance-Theater 31 May

1905 **Bis früh um Fünfe** (Lincke/w Lippschitz) Thalia-Theater 26 August

1906 **Hochparterre-Links** (Lincke/Schönfeld/w Arthur Lippschitz) Thalia-Theater 7 April

1906 **Wenn die Bombe platzt** (Lincke/Schönfeld/w Lippschitz) Thalia-Theater 25 August

1907 **Wo die Liebe hinfällt** (Schmidt/Schönfeld/w Lippschitz) Thalia-Theater 20 April

1907 **Ihr sechs-Uhr Onkel** (Lincke/Schönfeld/Henri Kéroul, Albert Barré ad) Thalia-Theater 25 August

1908 **Immer obenauf** (Lincke/Schönfeld/Buchbinder ad) Thalia-Theater 22 January

1908 **Doktor Klapperstorch** (Schmidt/Schönfeld/w Georg Okonkowski) Thalia-Theater 28 March

1908 **Das Mitternachtsmädchen** (Viktor Holländer/Schönfeld/w Lippschitz) Thalia-Theater 14 August

1909 **Meister Tutti** (Holländer/w Schönfeld) Thalia-Theater 15 January

1909 **Wo wohnt sie denn?** (Holländer/Schönfeld/w Okonkowski) Thalia-Theater 12 February

1909 **Prinz Bussi** (Holländer/Schönfeld) Thalia-Theater 13 August

1909 **Die ewige Lampe** (Max Schmidt/Schönfeld) Thalia-Theater 30 October

1909 **Die süsse Cora** (Holländer/w Lippschitz) Thalia-Theater 11 December

1910 **Die lieben Ottos** (Jean Gilbert/Schönfeld) Thalia-Theater 30 April

1912 **Autoliebchen** (Gilbert/Schönfeld) Thalia-Theater 16 March

1912 **Puppchen** (Gilbert/Schönfeld/w Kurt Kraatz) Thalia-Theater 19 December

1913 **Die Millionenbraut** (Döbber/Schönfeld/w Kraatz) Wilhelm-Theater, Magdeburg 17 February

1913 **Die Tangoprinzessin** (Gilbert/w Kraatz) Thalia-Theater 4 October

1914 **Wenn der Frühling kommt!** (Gilbert/Schönfeld/w Georg Okonkowski) Thalia-Theater 28 March

1914 **Kam'rad Männe** (Gilbert/Schönfeld/w Okonkowski) Thalia-Theater 3 August

1915 **Des Kaisers Rock** (Döbber/w Kraatz) Residenztheater 19 February

1915 **Drei Paar Schuhe** (Gilbert/Schönfeld) Thalia-Theater 10 September

1916 **Blondinchen** (Gilbert/Schönfeld/w Kraatz) Thalia-Theater 4 March

1916 **Der Soldat der Marie** (Leo Ascher/Schönfeld/w Buchbinder) Neues Operettenhaus 2 September

1916 **Das Vagabundenmädel** (Gilbert/Schönfeld/w Buchbinder) Thalia-Theater 2 December

1917 **Egon und seine Frauen** (Ascher/w Buchbinder) Thalia-Theater 25 August

1918 **Graf Habenichts** (Robert Winterberg/w Buchbinder) Wallner-Theater 4 September

1919 **Zur wilden Hummel** (Gilbert/w Eduard Ritter) Thalia-Theater 19 March

1919 **Die Dame vom Zirkus** (Winterberg/w Buchbinder) Neues Operettenhaus 31 May

1919 **Die närrische Liebe** (Leon Jessel) Thalia-Theater 28 November

1920 **Prinzessin Friedl** (Ascher/w Buchbinder) Neues Operettenhaus 14 May

1922 **Die Herrn von und zu** (Winterberg/w Richard Bars) Thalia-Theater 3 January

KRENN, Leopold (b Vienna, 6 December 1851; d Vienna, 2 October 1930).

Krenn led a career as an official in the Austrian railways whilst simultaneously contributing a 30-year run of texts to the Viennese stage. The large part of these were for the musical theatre, initially in the form of Possen, and were written in collaboration first with Karl Wolff and then, most productively of all, with Carl Lindau.

Krenn and Lindau had singular successes with their musical comedies *Ein armes Mädel* and *Heisses Blut* in the 1890s before moving on, at the turn of the century, to work with Gabor Steiner, adapting foreign musical plays and revues for his theatres and writing the texts for a number of the new Operetten which he produced. *Die Landstreicher,* musically set by Carl Michael Ziehrer, turned out to be the most popular. The pair also supplied the libretti and lyrics to Ziehrer's other most enduring work, *Der Fremdenführer,* produced at the Theater an der Wien, and for Hellmesberger's one big hit, *Das Veilchenmädel,* mounted at the Carltheater two years later.

The Krenn-Lindau collaboration ended in 1911, and Krenn—either on his own or with other, occasional collaborators—subsequently provided several more texts to Steiner and to the Raimundtheater, before, in his sixties, virtually retiring. His name returned on a playbill, however, in 1926, half a century after its first appearance, along with that of Lindau, when the pair were credited as authors of the source material for the revusical *Donauweibchen* at the Bürgertheater.

1876 **Ein falsches Spiel** (Franz Roth/w Karl Wolff) Theater in der Josefstadt 25 November

1877 **Schwere Zeit, leichte Leut** (Roth/w Wolff) Theater in der Josefstadt 10 February

1877 **Ein Mann für alles** (Roth/w Wolff) Theater in der Josefstadt 7 July

1878 **Schwester Lori** (Henrik Delin/w Wolff) Theater in der Josefstadt 13 April

1878 **Die Vorstadtprinzessin** (Roth/w Wolff) Fürsttheater 22 June

1878 **Helden von heute** (Adolf Müller/w Wolff) Ringtheater 7 December

1879 **Die Jockeys** (Roth/w Wolff) 1 act Ronacher 23 August

1880 **Lorely** (von Weinzierl/w Wolff) 1 act Ronacher 11 May

1880 **Die Liebe war daran schuld** (Max von Weinzierl/w Wolff) 1 act Ronacher 20 May

1881 **Wiener Kinder** (Carl Michael Ziehrer/w Wolff) Carltheater 19 February

1883 **Auf goldenem Boden** (Louis Roth/w Wolff) Theater in der Josefstadt 19 January

1883 **Ein schieches Ding** (Paul Mestrozzi/w Wolff) Theater in der Josefstadt 7 December

1885 **Ein alter Junggeselle** (Mestrozzi) Theater in der Josefstadt 3 November

1886 **Husar und Grenadier** (Mestrozzi/w Engel) Fürsttheater 28 August

1890 **Die Frau Sopherl von Naschmarkt** (C W Löw/w Vincenz Chiavacci) Theater in der Josefstadt 25 January

1892 **Einer von der Burgmusik** (Karl Kleiber/w Chiavacci) Theater in der Josefstadt 14 January

1892 **Heisses Blut** (Heinrich Schenk/w Carl Lindau) Theater an der Wien 17 April

1893 **Der letzte Kreuzer** (Kleiber/w Chiavacci) Theater in der Josefstadt 28 January

1893 **Ein armes Mädel** (Leopold Kuhn/w Lindau) Theater an der Wien 6 May

1893 **Die Wiener in Amerika** (Fritz Lehner/w Chiavacci) Theater in der Josefstadt 21 October

1895 **Der Nazi** (L Kuhn/w Lindau) Theater an der Wien 3 October

1896 **Im siebenten Himmel** (Ferdinand Pagin/w Lindau) Theater an der Wien 29 April

1897 **Die fesche Pepi** (Wilhelm Argauer/w Lindau) Theater an der Wien 23 January

1897 **Der Herr Pomeisl** (von Weinzierl/w Lindau) Raimundtheater 23 October

1898 **Moderne Weiber** (L Kuhn/ad w Lindau) Carltheater 10 April

1898 **Der schöne Rigo** (Ziehrer/w Lindau) Venedig in Wien 24 May

1899 **Ein durchgegangenes Mädel** (*A Runaway Girl*) German version w Lindau (Theater an der Wien)

1899 **Die Landstreicher** (Ziehrer/w Lindau) Venedig in Wien 29 July

1900 **Die Schöne von New-York** (*The Belle of New York*) German version w Lindau (Venedig in Wien)

1901 **Die verkehrte Welt** (*Le Royaume des femmes*) (Karl Kappeller/ad w Lindau) Danzers Orpheum 22 February

1901 **Die drei Wünsche** (Ziehrer/w Lindau) Carltheater 9 March

1901 **Die Reise nach Cuba** (Ivan Caryll/w Lindau) Venedig in Wien 3 August

1902 **(Ei)ne feine Nummer** Austrian version w Lindau (Venedig in Wien)

1902 **Der Fremdenführer** (Ziehrer/w Lindau) Theater an der Wien 11 October

1902 **Das Cirkusmädel** (*The Circus Girl*) German version w Lindau (Danzers Orpheum)

1902 **Der Laufbursche** (*The Messenger Boy*) German version w Lindau (Danzers Orpheum)

1903 **An der schönen blauen Donau** (pasticcio) Danzers Orpheum 4 November

1904 **Das Veilchenmädel** (Josef Hellmesberger/w Lindau) Carltheater 27 February

1904 **Jung Heidelberg** (Millöcker arr Reiterer/w Lindau) Venedig in Wien 9 July

1904 **Ein nasses Abenteuer** (F Roth/w Lindau) Deutsches Volkstheater 27 August

1905 **Die Ringstrassenprinzessin** (*Messalinette*) German version w Lindau (Danzers Orpheum)

1905 **Fesche Geister** (Ziehrer/w Lindau) Venedig in Wien 7 July

1905 **Der Nabob** (Felix Albini) Carltheater 23 September

1906 **Eine vom "Moulin-Rouge"** (Hellmesberger) 1 act Danzers Orpheum 21 December

1907 **Es gibt nur a Kaiserstadt** (Leo Ascher) 1 act Danzers Orpheum 27 September

1909 **Die arme Lori** (Ascher) Raimundtheater 12 March

1909 **Miss Gibbs** (*Our Miss Gibbs*) German version w Lindau, Max Baer (Ronacher)

1910 **Hupf mein Mäderl!** (Viktor Holländer/w Lindau) Ronacher 13 August

1910 **Der Dumme hat's Glück** (Béla von Ujj/w Lindau) Raimundtheater 10 September

1910 **Chantecler** (von Ujj/w Lindau) 1 act Ronacher 25 October

1911 **In fünfzig Jahren** (pasticcio arr Ziehrer/w Lindau) 1 act Ronacher 7 January

1911 **Der Veilchenkavalier** (Hellmesberger) Ronacher 16 April

1911 **Die schöne Helena von heute** (Offenbach arr Ludwig Gothov-Grüneke/w Gábor Steiner) Ronacher 1 September

1912 **Der Teufelswalzer** (Hans May/Ernst Ress) Ronacher February

1913 **Die tolle Therese** (Strauss père arr Otto Romisch/w Julius von Ludassy) Raimundtheater 21 November

1926 **Donauweibchen** (Egon Neumann/w Lindau ad Karl Farkas) Wiener Bürgertheater 22 May

KREOLENBLUT Operette in 3 acts by Ignaz Schnitzer and Emmerich von Gatti. Music by Heinrich Berté. Neues Operetten-Theater, Hamburg, 25 December 1910.

The plot of *Kreolenblut* centered on the President of one of those comic-operatic exotic isles so popular on turn-of-the-century stages. This head of state, however, unlike most of his fellows, is actually encouraging revolution. He is keen to be deposed so that he can go off to the kind of luxurious exile in France which was (and still is) the lot of the deposed.

First produced in Hamburg, *Kreolenblut* had a rather curious afterlife. Although it was apparently played neither in Berlin nor in Vienna, it was given in an Hungarian version (ad Zsolt Harsányi) in Budapest, in a French version (ad Maurice Ordonneau, Bénédict) in Lille, and even produced in America, by John Cort, in a version written by the unlikely combination of London comedian John L Shine and wheeler-dealer-adapter Sydney Rosenfeld. The ''French prima donna'' Chapine (real name Helen Benedeck) and Forrest Huff took the leading roles, speciality interpolations enlivened the evening and it was gone after 24 performances. Its post-Broadway tour fell apart in Chicago. The other two adaptations proved equally unsuccessful.

Hungary: Budai Színkör *Kreolvér* 7 July 1911; USA: Daly's Theater *The Rose of Panama* (*Jacinta*) 2 January 1912; France: Lille *Coeur de créole* 1913

KRETZMER, Herbert (b Kronstadt, South Africa, 5 October 1925).

For many years the dramatic critic of London's *Daily Express,* Kretzmer authored and/or lyricked several adaptations for the musical stage, beginning with a version of *The Admirable Crichton* in which Tweeny became the principal character, continuing with a burlesque-style *The Four Musketeers* which featured Harry Secombe above the title, and, most successfully, the final English version of the French musical play *Les Misérables.*

He has also written the lyrics for a number of songs, most notably Charles Aznavour's ''She,'' Peter Sellers's ''Goodness Gracious Me'' and ''Yesterday When I Was Young.''

1964 **Our Man Crichton** (David Lee) Shaftesbury Theatre 22 December

1967 **The Four Musketeers** (Laurie Johnson/Michael Pertwee) Theatre Royal, Drury Lane 5 December

1985 **Les Misérables** English version (Barbican Theatre)

1996 **Martin Guerre** revised version w Alain Boublil (Prince Edward Theatre)

KREUDER, Peter [Paul] (b Aachen, 18 August 1905; d Salzburg, 28 June 1981). Composer of several of the more popular musical comedies of the German and Austrian stages of the postwar period.

Son of an opera singer, Kreuder had a musical education from a young age and performed as a juvenile pianist. He studied music in Munich and Hamburg, was musical director to Max Reinhardt in Berlin at 23, and composed during these years both for cabaret and for the theatre. His earliest stage works were an Operette *Bis hierher und nicht weiter* and a new musical version of the British farce *Tons of Money,* played under the title *Geld wie Heu* at Berlin's Neues Theater am Zoo. From 1929, with plenty of songwriting success already under his belt, he began composing music for film, and in the years that followed, although he turned out a certain amount of incidental theatre music, he wrote but few pieces for the musical stage.

In 1930 he moved to Munich, where he spent several years as musical director at the Schauspielhaus, and then, with the coming of National Socialism, shifted successively to America and to the Argentine, where he worked as a radio conductor, whilst continuing to supply music to the German screen (*Es lebe die Liebe, Es fing so harmlos an, Frech und verliebt,* etc). He returned to Munich in 1951, and it was in this later part of his career that he composed the scores of his best known stage works. Vienna's Raimundtheater staged *Madame Scandaleuse* with Zarah Leander in the title role, followed (in spite of their having produced a Kattnigg Operette on the same subject a decade earlier) by his musical version of Guy de Maupassant's *Bel Ami,* a piece which then went on to be seen in Germany (Dresden Staatsoperette, 1961). The Raimundtheater also produced his version of *Lady Windermere's Fan,* under the title *Die Lady aus Paris,* with Leander in the role of Mrs Erlynne. This piece of musical Oscar Wilde subsequently played at Berlin's Theater des Westens (19 March 1965, 50 performances). He had a further success with his final work for the adult musical stage, *Wedding Mary,* first mounted in Schleswig-Holstein. His last piece, *Silla, Pupsi und Kulline,* was a piece for children.

1925 **Bis hierher und nicht weiter** (w Walter Basny/Gustav Quedtenfeldt) Cherubintheater, Munich 30 July

1930 **Geld wie Heu** (Leo Walther Stein/Anton Exl) Neues Theater am Zoo, Berlin 11 November

1938 **Liebe, Trommeln und Fanfaren** (Arthur Wagner) Bayerische Staatsoper, Munich 30 July

1939 **Frackkomoedie** (Fritz Schwiefort) Deutsches Volkstheater 13 May

1940 **Franzi** (Ernst Marischka) Leipzig 12 September

1941 **Lips** (*Der Zerissene*) (Hans Martin Kremer) Stockholm 15 September

1957 **Unsere Träume** (Johannes Majo) Städtische Bühnen, Nuremberg-Fürth 29 June

1958 **Madame Scandaleuse** (Ernst Nebhut) Raimundtheater, Vienna 3 September

1960 **Bel Ami** (Therese Angeloff/Angeloff, Franz Gribitz) Raimundtheater, Vienna 27 May

1964 **Die Lady aus Paris** (Karl Farkas) Raimundtheater, Vienna 22 October

1976 **Wedding Mary** (Schwenn/Erika Lanz) Landestheater, Schleswig-Holstein 25 December

1977 **Silla, Pupsi und Kulline** (Rosita Magnus)

Autobiographies: w Sailer, A: *Schön war die Zeit* (Munich, 1955), *Nur Püppen haben keine Tränen* (Percha, 1971)

KRIEGER, Henry (b New York, 9 February 1945). The composer of two long-running Broadway musicals of the early 1980s.

Krieger initially worked off- and off-off-Broadway before first having his music played on Broadway as interlude music to the hit comedy *Same Time Next Year.* He had a major hit in America with his first full-scale book musical, the pop-music saga of *Dreamgirls* (''And I'm Telling You I'm Not Going,'' ''One Night Only'') which played for 1,522 performances in its first run in New York, and he followed up that success two seasons later with the songs for a second successful gotta-make-it-good-in-showbiz musical, the rather less high-powered tale of *The Tap Dance Kid* (669 performances).

He subsequently provided music for children's theatre (a rewrite of the French musical *Le Cochon qui voulait maigrir*) and television (the songs for CBS's *Captain Kangaroo*), collaborated with his *Dreamgirls* partner, Tom Eyen, on one further musical, and supplied several numbers to Radio City's Christmas spectacular before being again sighted on Broadway with his score for the 1997 musical *Side Show.* This interesting piece about Siamese twins pleased connoisseurs, but both public and prizegivers opted for the season's more obvious pocket-pleasers and it lasted only 90 performances.

1975 **(Tom Eyen's) Dirtiest Musical** (Tom Eyen) Truck and Warehouse Theater

1981 **Dreamgirls** (Eyen) Imperial Theater 20 December

1983 **The Tap Dance Kid** (Robert Lorick/Charles Blackwell) Broadhurst Theater 21 December

1988 **Dangerous Music** (Eyen) Burt Reynolds Theater, Jupiter, Fla 18 October

1988 **Fat Pig** (*Le Cochon qui voulait maigrir*) ad Mark Bramble, Jenny Hawkesworth with new score Haymarket Theatre, Leicester 20 November

1997 **Side Show** (Bill Russell) Richard Rodgers Theater 16 October

KRÖGER, Uwe (b Hamm, 4 December 1964). Central Europe's most prominent musical leading man of the turn-of-the-century years.

Dark-blonde, tenor-voiced and handsome, Kröger made his earliest appearances in the musical theatre in *Godspell* (1986, Hamm), the German edition of *Le Cochon qui voulait maigrir* (1987, Quak-Quak) and *The Rocky Horror Show* (1988, Eddie) before joining the cast of the German edition of *Starlight Express* (1988, Flattop, t/o Rusty). During the Raimundtheater run of *Les Misérables* (1989) he was seen as both Marius and as Enjolras, a role which he went on to repeat in the Amsterdam production of the same show (1991). He appeared as Jesus in two productions of *Jesus Christ Superstar* (1990, 1992), as Ziggy in the original German production of *Starmania* (1991) and as Frank'n'furter in a Vienna revival of *The Rocky Horror Show* (1993), and in 1992 took the last step to stardom creating the leading role of Death in the hit Viennese musical *Elisabeth.*

He subsequently appeared in the leading roles of a series of Austrian and German productions of major foreign musicals—as Chris in *Miss Saigon* (1994), Joe Gillis in *Sunset Boulevard* (1995), the Beast in *Beauty and the Beast* (1997)—and made a notable hit as the MC in a Viennese revival of *Cabaret* (1998), before creating a second important role, as the Archbishop Colloredo in the Theater an der Wien's *Mozart!* (1999). In 2000 he was seen in London, playing the title role in the musical *Napoléon.*

He has appeared widely in concert (*[Still] In Love with the Musical,* etc), on television, recorded several solo albums and provided the voice for the German version of Jack in the Disney film *Newsies.*

KULINYI, Ernő (b Szeged, 18 June 1893; d Bruck, 2 February 1945). Successful Hungarian lyricist and adaptor.

A journalist from his late teens, Kulinyi became, in his twenties, a prolific adaptor of foreign musicals of all kinds for the Hungarian stage. He also provided lyrics, and less frequently, libretti for a number of native musical plays, amongst which his adaptation of Gyula Pekár's comedy *Kölcsönkért kastély* as the libretto to Vincze's *A hamburgi menyasszony* had a fine run of over one hundred nights at the Városi Színház in 1922 and Károly Czobor's *Szépasszony kocsisa* also scored over one hundred performances at the Lujza Blaha Színház the following year. As a lyricist, too, he scored a number of hits, providing the songwords to popular songwriter Béla Zerkovitz's *Árvácska,* which ran up its century as it moved from the Budai Színkör to the Király Színház in 1924, and for Zerkovitz's score to Bús-Fekete's adaptation of his own play as *A nóta vége,* a one-hundred-night success at the Budai Színkör before going on to top three hundred nights in an outstanding run at the Városi Színház.

Kulinyi died in a concentration camp in 1945.

1918 **Pintyőke** (*Alma, wo wohnst du?*) Hungarian version (Margitszigeti Színház)

1920 **A cigánygrófné** (Zsigmond Vincze/Ferenc Martos) Király Színház 13 March

1920 **Yu-shi** (*Yushi tanzt*) Hungarian version (Eskü-téri Színház)

1921 **A tündérek cselédje** (*Irene*) Hungarian version (Lujza Blaha Színház)

1921 **A reichstadti herceg** (*Der Graf von Reichstadt*) Hungarian lyrics (Városi Színház)

1921 **A hollandi menyecske** (*Das Hollandweibchen*) Hungarian version (Király Színház)

1922 **A hamburgi menyasszony** (Vincze) Városi Színház 31 January

1922 **Babavásár** (Mihály Nádor/Andor Kardos) Király Színház 16 February

1922 **Vigyen el az ördög** (*Hol' mich der Teufel*) Hungarian version w Imre Liptai (Lujza Blaha Színház)

1922 **Az éj királynője** (*Die Königin der Nacht*) Hungarian version w Liptai (Renaissance Színház)

1922 **Detektivkisasszony** (*Das Detektivmädel*) Hungarian version (Fővárosi Nyári Színház)

1922 **A bajadér** (*Die Bajadere*) Hungarian version (Király Színház)

1923 **Cowboy** (Alfréd Márkus) 1 act Várszínház 26 January

1923 **A gárdista** (Vincze) Városi Színház 15 February

1923 **A sárga kabát** (*Die gelbe Jacke*) Hungarian version (Király Színház)

1923 **Tangókirálynő** (*Die Tango-Prinzessin*) Hungarian version (Budai Színkör)

1923 **Szépasszony kocsisa** (Károly Czobor/Ferenc Rajna) Lujza Blaha Színház 19 May

1923 **Mintha álom volna** (Izsó Barna/w Mihály Erdélyi) Budai Színkör 1 September

1924 **A balga szűz** (*Die torichte Jungfrau*) Hungarian version (Lujza Blaha Színház)

1924 **A nóta vége** (Zerkovitz/Bús Fekete) Budai Színkör 24 June

1924 **Árvácska** (Béla Zerkovitz/László Bús Fekete) Budai Színkör 1 July; Király Színház 13 September

1924 **Egy éj Velencében** (*Eine Nacht in Venedig,* revised version) Hungarian version (Városi Színház)

1924 **Krizantém** (Nádor/Gustav Beer, Hans Kottow ad) Városi Színház 19 December

1925 **Anna-bál** (Robert Volkmann ad Vincze/Ferenc Martos) Király Színház 30 September

1925 **A nagy nő** (*Geliebte seiner Hoheit*) Hungarian version (Városi Színház)

1926 **Csuda Mihály szerencséje** (Zerkovitz/Bús Fekete) Magyar Színház 22 May

1926 **Paganini** Hungarian version (Városi Színház)

1926 **A cirkuszhercegnő** (*Die Zirkusprinzessin*) Hungarian version (Király Színház)

1926 **Asszonykám** (Béla Nagypál/Dezső Uray) Városi Színház 18 December

1927 **Kiss és Kis** (Vincze/Bús Fekete) Városi Színház 22 January

1927 **A bíborruhás asszony** (*Das Weib im Purpur*) Hungarian version (Városi Színház)

1927 **A cigánykirály** (Nagypál/Uray) Városi Színház 30 December

1928 **Bocánat felség** (Laura Lengyel Dánielné) Andrássy-uti Színház 9 January

1928 **A cárevics** (*Der Zarewitsch*) Hungarian version (Városi Színház)

1928 **A csikágói hercegnő** (*Die Herzogin von Chicago*) Hungarian version w Adorján Stella (Király Színház)

1929 **A palatinus rózsái** (Nagypál/Uray) Városi Színház 1 February

1929 **Naplopó** (Géza Marton/Imre Liptai, Gábor Drégely) Pécs 27 April

1929 **Aranyszőrű bárány** (Vincze/Ferenc Móra) Szeged 15 November

1932 **Vőlegényem a gazember** (Sándor Szlatinay/w Imre Füredi/Uray) Városi Színház 3 March

1933 **Kék Duna** (Johann Strauss ad Nagypál/Gyula Halász, Károly Kristóf) Király Színház 23 December

1935 **Tarantella** (Suppé arr Béla Nagypál/Kristóf Károly, Halász) Városi Színház 23 January

1936 **Urilány szobát keres** (Pál Zsigmondi/Jenő Rejtő) Kamara Színház 23 December

KUMMER, Clare [née BEECHER, Clare Rodman] (b Brooklyn, NY, 9 January ?1888; d Carmel, Calif, 22 April 1958).

A cousin of actor William Gillette and a relation of Henry Ward Beecher and of Harriet Beecher Stowe, Miss Beecher married playwright Frederick Arnold Kummer and, although they subsequently divorced, she kept his name, under which she had made her first success as a songwriter. That first success came with the song "Dearie," originally written as a valentine card greeting, which was later interpolated along with her "On the Rialto" into Broadway's version of the British musical *Sergeant Brue* (1905). Mrs Kummer had several other song successes in the first decade of the 20th century, both as a composer and a lyricist, and she had songs displayed in a number of musical plays including *The Girl from Kays* (1903, "Egypt," "Sufficiency"), Marie Cahill's tours ("June," "I'm Goin' to Change My Man"), *Vivian's*

Papas (1904, ''Take Your Name Off Ma Door''), *The Rollicking Girl* (1905, ''Miranda''), *Smiling Island* (1905, ''Dingle Dongle Dell''), *A Knight for a Day* (1906, Miss Fisher doing ''My Very Own'' again, then ''Garden of Dreams''), her own *Noah's Ark* (1907, ''Wilderness,'' ''My Very Own'' for Sallie Fisher), *Lonesome Town* (1908, ''Diana''), *The Girl in the Train* (1910) and even in Edward German's comic opera *Tom Jones* (''The Road to Yesterday'') in New York, as well as in the occasional London show (''Egypt'' in *A Chinese Honeymoon*).

She ventured in the Broadway theatre with her adaptation of the text of Heuberger's *Der Opernball,* but she had her greatest stage success as a straight playwright, with the comedy *Good Gracious Annabelle,* into which Lola Fisher nevertheless inserted the authoress's song, ''Other Eyes,'' and she soon found herself acclaimed as one of the most promising and skillful modern playwrights of the American theatre. Although she adapted several other Continental musicals for the Broadway stage, turned out further interpolatable songs (''Jolly Good Fellow,'' ''Lonely in Town,'' ''Wonderful Days'' in *Ninety in the Shade,* etc), and authored what she called a ''play with songs'' titled *Amourette* in 1933, her sole venture as a musical-comedy librettist in over 30 years of theatrical activity was with an adaptation of her own hit play, set to a Sigmund Romberg score, as *Annie Dear.*

1909 **Noah's Ark** Academy of Music, Baltimore 22 April

1912 **The Opera Ball** (*Der Opernball*) English version w Sydney Rosenfeld (Liberty Theater)

1921 **The Choir Rehearsal** 1 act Punch and Judy Theater 28 February

1921 **Chinese Love** 1 act Punch and Judy Theatre 28 February

1923 **One Kiss** (*Ta bouche*) American version (Fulton Theater)

1924 **Annie Dear** (Sigmund Romberg) Times Square Theater 4 November

1924 **Madame Pompadour** American version (Martin Beck Theater)

1933 **Amourette** (Kummer) Henry Miller Theater 27 September

1937 **Three Waltzes** (*Drei Walzer*) American version w Rowland Leigh (Majestic Theater)

KÜNNEKE, Eduard (b Emmerich-am-Rhein, 27 January 1885; d Berlin, 27 October 1953). The most appreciable German composer for the mid-20th-century musical stage.

Born at Emmerich, near the German border with the Netherlands, Künneke studied music in Berlin and became first, at the age of 22, chorus-master at Victor Palfi's Neues Operetten-Theater and later a conductor at the Deutsches Theater. During this period, he won his first professional stage production as a composer with a comic opera, *Robins Ende,* which featured King Charles II of England as its central character. A second piece, *Coeur-As,* labeled as an opera, was produced several years later at the Dresden Hofoper (November 1913), before Künneke joined the wartime army as a horn player in an infantry regiment.

In 1916 he put aside the horn and was engaged as a conductor at Berlin's Friedrich-Wilhelmstädtisches Theater. There he acted as a musical director for the extremely long run of the Schubert pasticcio *Das Dreimäderlhaus* and, thus inspired, decided himself to compose a piece which, like the Viennese work, called itself a Singspiel. He took as his libretto a 12-year-old Hungarian piece by Árpád Pásztor, already set with no little success by Pongrác Kacsoh and Ákos Buttykay for Lujza Blaha and Budapest's Király Színház as *A harang* (''the bell''), and made it into *Das Dorf ohne Glocke.* The piece was produced at the Friedrich-Wilhelmstädtisches Theater following the more than a thousand performances of *Das Dreimäderlhaus* and the rather shorter run of its sequel, *Hannerl.* Although it did not achieve anything like that kind of a run, it was sufficiently well liked not only to win itself a Vienna production (Volksoper, 2 December 1925) but also to arouse the interest of Hermann Haller, the new manager of the Theater am Nollendorfplatz.

Haller commissioned Künneke to set an umpteenth version of Bayard's celebrated play *Le Vicomte de Letorrières,* written by himself and the nimble lyricist ''Rideamus,'' and the resultant Operette, produced at Haller's theatre under the title *Der Vielgeliebte,* was a six-month success. Whilst Bromme's *Eine Nacht im Paradies* followed *Der Vielgeliebte* on to the Nollendorfplatz stage, Haller, Rideamus and Künneke concocted a second Operette, *Wenn Liebe erwacht*—this time an original piece—and they were gratified with another six-month run (218 performances). When *Wenn Liebe erwacht* had left Berlin to move on to other productions, as well as several other countries and other versions, the team were ready with a third piece. It was this third little Operette—a piece which shunned both the classic glamor of *Le Vicomte de Letorrières* and the colorful romanticism of *Wenn Liebe erwacht,* and returned to something like the winning simplicity of *Das Dorf ohne Glocke*—which was to turn out to be the highlight of their collaborating years. *Der Vetter aus Dingsda,* with its intimate family story, its cast of nine, and its delightfully dreamy and comical score, was a major hit. It duly ran out its allotted six-month spot in the theatre's calendar but, when its successor, *Die Ehe im Kreise,* took over, it continued its life with much more vigor than its predecessors, heading to productions in the provinces, through Europe and to almost every major country where musical theatre was played.

Die Ehe im Kreise duly ran out its six months without winning a comparable afterlife, but its successor *Ver-*

liebte Leute did less well (138 performances) and it marked the end of the Künneke series at the Theater am Nollendorfplatz. Haller decided instead to produce the French hit *Ta bouche* and, soon after, he was obliged to give up his theatre. Künneke moved on to supply one piece to the rival Metropoltheater before, in 1924, setting off to pick up some of the gold lying in the streets of America.

In New York he worked for the Shuberts on the adaptation of an Hungarian pasticcio *Offenbach,* a biomusical with which they hoped to imitate the success of *Das Dreimäderlhaus / Lilac Time,* and he composed a part of the original score for a musical version of Arthur Richman's play *Not So Long Ago,* produced as *Mayflowers* with Ivy Sawyer and Joseph Santley starred. Neither piece was a success, and Künneke's subsequent commission to write a piece for London resulted in an even worse failure when *Riki-Tiki* folded after only 18 performances.

Back in Germany, he did rather better with *Die hellblauen Schwestern,* and he returned to something like his old level of success with *Lady Hamilton,* a piece dealing with an operetticized version of the lady in question's relationship with Lord Nelson. First produced at Breslau, *Lady Hamilton* eventually made it to London where, either through respect or because the story was too patently unhistorical for British consumption, the leading characters had their names changed and the title became *Song of the Sea.*

Künneke had a number of Operetten produced in the following years at Breslau, Altenberg and Prague, and an opera, *Nadja* (1931), was played at Kassel, but it was five years since his last metropolitan production when his music was once again heard in the Berlin theatre. Once again, it was under the management of his old collaborator Haller, who was now at the head of the Admiralspalast and who had become celebrated over recent years as the most prominent purveyor of glitzy revue to Berlin striving-towards-high-society. The piece Haller mounted was *Liselott,* a revision of one of Künneke's out-of-town pieces, with Käthe Dorsch starring as a royal Austrian lady who saves her home country from war by being nice to her bellicose brother-in-law, the King of France. *Liselott* did well enough, but it was Künneke's next piece which gave him his biggest hit since *Der Vetter aus Dingsda.*

Glückliche Reise was altogether different in tone from his first big hit. It was a bright, modern musical comedy with bright up-to-date music, light years away from the charmingly stylish and atmospheric *Vetter,* but it proved, in that day and age, almost equally as popular. *Glückliche Reise* began its career at the Theater am Schiffbauerdamm and has been "journeying happily" around European theatres ever since.

Künneke continued to turn out regular new works for another decade without finding a third major success, but he nevertheless produced several works, widely varying in style and tone, which evoked more than passing interest during years when the flight of Jewish writers from Nazi Germany left him at the head of a now miniscule group of able Operette composers. The comfortably old-world Singspiel *Die lockende Flamme,* with its theatrical tale of the actor Devrient and the poet Hoffmann and their unrequited rivalry for the love of a Spanish dancer; one of most vocally challenging of all costume Operettes, *Die grosse Sünderin,* produced at the Berlin Staatsoper Unter den Linden with Helge Roswaenge and Tiana Lemnitz; the spectacular *Hochzeit in Samarkand,* Künneke's last Berlin work; and the more modern-sounding movieland musical comedy *Traumland* all had their moment.

Apart from the thoroughly international career of *Der Vetter aus Dingsda,* Künneke's works were seen largely only in Germany. Alongside his unfortunate American and British commissions, *Wenn Liebe erwacht* was played in Vienna and, for a brief 35 performances, as *Love's Awakening* in London, where *Lady Hamilton / Song of the Sea* had a rather longer life. His two principal works, however, have remained in the German-language repertoire up to the present day, whilst the best of his other works still win occasional attention.

Künneke also wrote scores for the screen, and a certain amount of instrumental and piano music.

1909 **Robins Ende** Hoftheater, Mannheim Hoftheater 5 May 1909; Komische Oper 23 March 1910

1919 **Das Dorf ohne Glocke** (Árpád Pásztor) Friedrich-Wilhelmstädtisches Theater 5 April

1919 **Der Vielgeliebte** (Herman Haller, "Rideamus") Theater am Nollendorfplatz 17 October

1920 **Die Schöne von Baden-Baden** (Hermann Beutten arr/ August Neidhart) Kurhaustheater, Baden-Baden 12 June

1920 **Wenn Liebe erwacht** (Haller, Rideamus) Theater am Nollendorfplatz 3 September

1921 **Der Vetter aus Dingsda** (Haller, Rideamus) Theater am Nollendorfplatz 15 April

1921 **Die Ehe im Kreise** (Haller, Rideamus) Theater am Nollendorfplatz 2 November

1922 **Verliebte Leute** (Haller, Rideamus) Theater am Nollendorfplatz 15 April

1923 **Casino-Girls** (Georg Okonkowski) Metropoltheater 15 September

1925 **The Love Song** (Offenbach) musical revision, American version w Offenbach arr, Century Theater, New York 13 January

1925 **Die hellblauen Schwestern** (Albrecht Salfeld, Franz Richthoff) Theater am Nollendorfplatz 22 August

1925 **Mayflowers** (Clifford Grey) Forrest Theater, New York 24 November

1926 **Riki-Tiki** (Leslie Stiles) Gaiety Theatre, London 16 April

1926 **Lady Hamilton** (Richard Bars, Leopold Jacobson) Schauspielhaus, Breslau 25 September

1927 **Die blonde Liselott** (Richard Kessler) Landestheater, Altenburg 25 December

1928 **Die singende Venus** (Gustav Beer, Fritz Lunzer) Schauspielhaus, Breslau 9 June

1930 **Der Tenor der Herzogin** (Kessler) Deutsches Theater, Prague 8 February

1932 **Lieselott** revised *Die blonde Liselott* (Kessler, Carl Stobitzer) Admiralspalast 17 February

1932 **Glückliche Reise** (Max Bertuch, Kurt Schwabach) Theater am Kurfürstendamm 23 November

1933 **Die Fahrt in die Jugend** (Bela Jenbach, Ludwig Hirschfeld) Stadttheater, Zürich 26 March

1933 **Klein Dorrit** (Franz von Schönthan, Kessler) Stadttheater, Stettin 28 October

1933 **Die lockende Flamme** (Paul Knepler, Ignaz Welleminsky) Theater des Westens 25 December

1934 **Liebe ohne Grenzen** (Bertuch, Schwabach) Neue Wiener Stadttheater 29 March

1935 **Herz über Bord** (Eduard van der Becke) Opernhaus, Zürich 30 March

1935 **Die grosse Sünderin** (Katharina Stoll, Hermann Rommer) Staatsoper Unter den Linden 31 December

1937 **Zauberin Lola** (Alfred Brieger, Sigmund Graff) Stadttheater, Dortmund 24 April

1938 **Hochzeit in Samarkand** (Kessler) Theater des Volkes, Berlin 14 February

1938 **Der grosse Name** (Ferdinand Julius, Ursula Renate Hirt) Städtische Bühnen, Düsseldorf 14 May

1941 **Die Wunderbare** (Kurt Aadalbert, Just Scheu) Stadttheater, Fürth 25 January

1941 **Traumland** (Eduard Rhein) Theater des Volkes, Dresden 15 November

1949 **Hochzeit mit Erika** (Willi Webel) Opernhaus, Düsseldorf 31 August

Biographies: Schneidereit, O: *Eduard Künneke der Komponist aus Dingsda* (Henschelverlag, Berlin, 1978), Karl, V: *Eduard Künneke: Komponistenporträt und Werkverzeichnis* (Ries & Erler, Berlin, 1995)

KÜNSTLERBLUT Operette in 2 acts by Leo Stein and Carl Lindau. Music by Edmund Eysler. Carltheater, Vienna, 20 October 1906.

Künstlerblut was written by Stein and Lindau as a vehicle in which Vienna's most important musical star, Alexander Girardi, might follow up his great Carltheater success in their *Schützenliesel* (1905). Whilst the star took a turn to the Theater in der Josefstadt to appear in the Posse *Der Schusterbub* with Hansi Niese, and whilst the Carltheater found only Oscar Straus's *Hugdietrichs Brautfahrt* of their five new shows capable of standing up more than a few performances, the authors dreamed up and wrote down a piece which cast Girardi as an aging comedy actor/manager called Franz Torelli—a role modeled on the famous Raimund himself. They also took a slightly daring turn: this time, at the end of the evening, the star did not come to a happy ending with the show's female star Mizzi Zwerenz, who was cast in their play as Nelli Leissner, the beloved soubrette of Torelli's company. It was the tenor, Max Rohr, in the role of the star-struck Alfred Blank, who got the girl who had originally set out to disillusion him, but finally fell in love with him. The curtain fell on Torelli looking sadly in the mirror at his greying hair as the younger man won Nelli from him.

Shooting bullets apparently forged by his wife, who was altogether indignant at the idea of her megastar husband appearing grey-haired and defeated, the 55-year-old Girardi announced that he was not old enough to play such a part, and turned the show down. However, the authors persuaded their star of the benefits of sympathetic, tragic scenes and a heart-tugging ending, and he ultimately agreed to go ahead. Composer Eysler played his part once more by supplying the role with a dainty Schmetterlingslied which which Girardi could follow up his famous hit with the Mutter-Lied in *Schützenliesel,* and *Künstlerblut* turned out to be every bit as big a success as its predecessor. Girardi's impersonation of Torelli was acclaimed as one of his best ever performances, and he played *Künstlerblut* for 101 successive nights in its first run. Unlike so many of his other highly successful shows, this one was also a piece to which the star would return. He played Torelli again in 1910 in a Girardi season at the Raimundtheater (30 April), and again in 1915, back at the Carltheater, as it became more and more what even his wife could not deny was a "suitable" role for him.

The score of *Künstlerblut* proved a fine adjunct to its solid story. If the Schmetterlingslied was the evening's biggest hit, Mizzi Zwerenz's march-tempo Gassenbubenlied ("Ein jeder, der mich näher kennt") ran it a close second, and the tenor was given a fine waltz, "Wie scheint das Leben mir so wonnig." The bulk of the music, however, fell to the show's star, and it ranged with Eyslerian tunefulness from the score's biggest and most oft-repeated waltz theme, "So vergehen der Tage gar viel," via another waltz ("Einst und jetzt"), to Torelli's big Rauschszene, leading into the first-act finale, and the Schmetterlingslied.

Whilst *Künstlerblut* established itself through the years as a thorough Viennese hit, it also won itself a good showing elsewhere. Germany (where Girardi himself played it at the Thalia-Theater in 1908), Hungary (ad Adolf Mérei) and Italy (*Sangue d'artista*) all produced versions, whilst America's Henry Savage picked up not only *Künstlerblut* but also Eysler's less successful *Johann der Zweite* and *Das Glücksschweinchen* which he dismembered for additional numbers to make up what he considered a more Broadway-sized score for his show. Even then he called on Augustus Barratt for additional bits. Oliver Herford's adaptation, awkwardly christened *The Love Cure,* was produced with great fanfare, with Charles J Ross (Torelli) and Craig Campbell (Alfred) starred alongside Elgie Bowen—although Annie Dirkens had been announced—as Nelly and the action of the piece shifted to New York. The ''haunting and bewitching melodies'' won praise, but *The Love Cure* stretched to only 70 Broadway performances before it went on the road with Theater an der Wien ingenue Lina Abarbanell taking over the role of Nelly.

Germany: Centraltheater 22 December 1906; Hungary: Fővárosi Nyári Színház *Szinésvér* 30 July 1909; USA: New Amsterdam Theater *The Love Cure* 1 September 1909

KUNZE, Michael [Rolf] (b Prague, 9 November 1943).

Initially destined for the law, Michael Kunze found early and international success in the 1970s as a songwriter (''Fly, Robin, Fly,'' ''Mr Music,'' ''One-Two-Three-Four Fire,'' ''Lady Bump,'' ''Get up and Boogie,'' etc) and record producer (Silver Convention, Grammy Award, etc).

He made his first appearance in the musical theatre with the adaptations of *I Love My Wife* for the German stage and of Tim Rice's *Evita* (1981) for its Viennese production, and subsequently, through the 1980s and 1990s, adapted many of the most successful shows of the English-singing stage for their German-language mountings.

His first original musical *Hexen Hexen,* drawn from the author's legal studies of the 16th century Munich witch trials, was produced in the open-air theatre at Heilbronn in 1990, and the second, a piece written around the history of the already much-musicalized Empress Elisabeth of Austria, at the Theater an der Wien in 1992. This *Elisabeth* turned out to be not only the most successful version of the ''Sissy'' story, but the most successful European musical of the postwar era, running through several seasons at the Theater an der Wien, and totaling 1,278 Viennese performances, whilst going on to productions in Japan, Hungary, Germany, Holland and Scandinavia.

Elisabeth was followed up by another hit with *Dance of the Vampires,* a burlesque of the vampire legend based on the 1960s Roman Polanski film *The Fearless Vampire Killers* and directed by Polanski at the Raimundtheater, and by *Mozart!,* a musical which treated of the composer's attempts to live an adult life, whilst dogged by the ever-present image of the ''wonderful child,'' which was produced at the Theater an der Wien in 1999. Both scored notable successes in their original productions and at the time of writing seem likely to move on to worldwide careers.

Kunze has also authored television scripts and a number of books on legal, social and political topics.

1980 **I Love My Wife** German version (Theater Oberhausen)
1981 **Evita** German version (Theater an der Wien)
1983 **Cats** German version (Theater an der Wien)
1985 **Le Cochon** (*Le Cochon qui voulait maigrir*) German version (Burgtheater)
1985 **Song and Dance** German version (Deutsches Theater, Munich)
1986 **A Chorus Line** German version (Raimundtheater)
1986 **Little Shop of Horrors** German version (Szene Wien)
1987 **Wodka-Cola** (*Leave It to Me*) German version w Dietrich Hilsdorf, Michael Quast, Dieter Glawaschnig (Staatstheater, Stuttgart)
1988 **The Phantom of the Opéra** German version (Theater an der Wien)
1988 **Avos!** German version (Stadttheater, Grosses Haus, Freiburg)
1989 **Czechow** German version (Theaterfestival Konstanz)
1990 **Into the Woods** German version (Stadttheater, Heilbronn)
1991 **Hexen Hexen** (Sylvester Levay) Deutschhof, Heilbronn 15 June
1991 **Follies** German version (Theater des Westens, Berlin)
1992 **Elisabeth** (Levay) Theater an der Wien 3 September
1992 **Dorian Gray** German version (Stadttheater, Heilbronn)
1993 **Assassins** German version (Stadttheater, Heilbronn)
1993 **Kiss of the Spiderwoman** German version (Raimundtheater)
1995 **City of Angels** German version (Stadttheater, Heilbronn)
1995 **Sunset Boulevard** German version (Rhein-Main-Theater, Niedernhausen)
1996 **Aspects of Love** German version (Staatsoperette, Dresden)
1997 **Dance of the Vampires** (Jim Steinman) Raimundtheater 4 October
1999 **The Hunchback of Notre Dame** (Alan Menken/Stephen Schwartz/James Lapine ad) Theater des Westens 5 June
1999 **Mozart!** (Levay) Theater an der Wien 2 October

KÜRY, Klára [aka HAJNAL, Klárika] (b Jászkisér, 27 March 1870; d Budapest, 27 April 1935). Hungary's favorite musical soubrette of the turn of the century.

Plumply pretty Klára Küry made her earliest stage appearance at the Nemzeti Színház in Kolozsvár, under the name Klárika Hajnal, playing Louise in *Les Mousquetaires au couvent,* and there earned herself the attention of Lajos Evva, manager of the Budapest Népszínház. As a result, in October 1892 she made her debut at the capital's most important musical house in the star role of Denise de Flavigny in *Mam'zelle Nitouche.* She followed up a week later in the title role of Varney's *La Fille de Fanchon la vielleuse* and, less than another week later, created the role of Roxelán, the heroine of one of the most important Hungarian operetts of the time, György Verő's *A szultán,* hoisting herself at 22 to an immediate popularity and a place alongside the most important stars of the Hungarian musical theatre.

Over the following years she appeared at the Népszínház in leading roles in both plays and musicals in a repertoire which introduced Konti's newest work *A citerás* (1894, Rozetta), the Hungarian versions of Roger's *Clari-Clara,* Serpette's *Le Dot de Brigitte,* Banès's *Toto,* Wenzel's *Le Dragon de la Reine,* Varney's *La Falote,* and another successful Hungarian operett, Szabados's *Rika.* She also succeeded to some of the star roles in the standard repertoire such as La Belle Hélène, Serpolette, Eurydice and Hervé's Lili, whilst continuing to add to her credits new ones French (Alésia in *La Poupée,* the title role of Audran's *La Toledad, Les Fêtards*), British (Molly in *The Geisha, San Toy,* Iris in *A Greek Slave,* Winifred Grey in *A Runaway Girl, A Chinese Honeymoon, The Silver Slipper*) and homemade (Pásztor's *Kadétkisasszony,* Barna's *Casanova,* Hüvos's *Katinka grófnő*), the most important of which was the role of the tzarina's page, Germain Duplessis, in Izor Béldi's highly successful *Katalin* (1901). It was this piece which gave Küry her first Vienna exposure, when she visited the Carltheater to star as Katalin in the retitled *Der kleine Günstling* in 1902, nearly a decade after her visit to Berlin's Theater Unter den Linden to play the title role in Konti's *A suhanc* (1893, *Der Taugenichts).*

Just as Küry had moved in a decade earlier to challenge Ilka Pálmay and Aranka Hegyi for their musical-comedy throne, she herself, in her mid-thirties, now saw the arrival of a new challenger in the young Sári Fedák. Intrigue rustled at the Népszínház and, in 1904, Küry left. It was, to all intents and purposes, the end of her reign as Budapest's princess of musical comedy. She visited Vienna again in 1906 to star opposite Mizzi Zwerenz as Ilka Etvös in a short-lived musical version of the famous play *Krieg im Frieden,* and was seen again on the Budapest stage in local versions of *Die Förster-Christl* (1906, Városligeti Nyári Színház), in the role created by Hansi Niese, and in *The Sho-Gun, Die lustige Witwe, Die keusche Susanne* and *Die Musikantenmädel,* but without regaining the popularity she had known in her twenties.

L

LÁBASS, Juci (b Zilah, 22 July 1896; d Budapest, 25 August 1932). Popular Hungarian soubrette whose career as a musical star was cut short by a premature death.

Juci Lábass left stage school to make her debut at the Király Színház, at the age of 17, in Jean Gilbert's *Buksi* (*Puppchen,* 1913, Lori), and subsequently became a favorite operett soubrette and leading lady in Budapest, appearing in local productions of such pieces as *Die geschiedene Frau* (revival, Gonda van der Loo), *Die keusche Susanne* (1913, Susanne), *Rund um die Liebe* (1915, Stella), *Die Rose von Stambul* (1916, Midili), *Bacchusnacht* (1924, Chloris), *Gräfin Mariza* (1924, Mariza), *Der Orlow* (1925, Nadja), *Die Zirkusprinzessin* (1926, Fedora) and *Die Blume von Hawaii* (1932, Princess Lilia), and in such classic roles as Eurydice, Serpolette, Lisbeth (*Rip*) and Boccaccio.

She also created the principal soubrette roles in several notable Hungarian operetts including the lead role of *Nemtudomka,* the part of Sarah, paired with the Poire of Márton Rátkai, in *Szibill* (though in her later, post-soubrette days she would play the title role), Rolla in *Mágnás Miska* (1916) and Katinka in *Pillangó főhadnagy* (1918). She also appeared in the soubrette role of Szirmai's *Gróf Rinaldo,* as Hortense Schneider in the Hungarian biomusical *Offenbach* (1920), and starred in such other homemade pieces as *Chopin* (1926, Aurora), *A királynő rózsája* (1926, Suzy), *Aranyhattyú* (1927, Elinor), *Eltörött a hegedüm* (1928, Rózsika), *Cigánygrófné* (Panni), *Pesti család* (1929, Margit), *Alvinci huszárok* (1930), *Fehér orchideák* (1931, Elena), *Hajnali csók* (1931) and *Éjféli tangó* (1932) and made a Vienna appearance in the star role of *Die Herzogin von Chicago* (1929, t/o Mary) before her death at the age of 36.

LABICHE, Eugène [Marie] (b Paris, 6 May 1815; d Paris, 22 January 1888).

Like George Bernard Shaw, the apparently tone-deaf French vaudevillist and co-author of *Un chapeau de paille d'Italie* (1851, w Marc-Michel) and *La Station Champbaudet* avowed a certain lofty distaste for the musical theatre. However, unlike the Irish author, he was tempted from time to time, by the monetary gains possible, to dip into the despised area. He wrote his libretti largely for composers at the opéra-comique end of the musical-theatre scale—Delibes, Massé, Poïse—and, most significantly, for François Bazin. Bazin's comical musical play *Le Voyage en Chine,* composed to a brightly humorous Labiche and Delacour text, became an enormous international success and served as the model for a number of pieces in the budding English-language musical-comedy tradition. An attempt to pair Labiche with Offenbach failed when the playwright (purposely?) wrote his libretto for the intended opérette, *Les Trente Millions de Gladiateur* (w Philippe Gille), at such length that there was no space for musical numbers, and the show in question was finally presented as a straight play.

Apart from *Le Voyage en Chine,* the nearest Labiche came to authoring a regular musical was with a vaudeville, *Le Roi dort,* for the Théâtre des Variétés. It was presented with sufficient of the accessories of a féerie, and with a substantial enough musical score by the theatre's former musical director, Marius Boullard, for the latter to assert that it was a genuine opérette. It was in any case a genuine flop, withdrawn after just a few nights. Labiche also co-authored the féerie-vaudeville *Les Secrets du Diable* (w Clairville, Jules Cordier) for the Théâtre du Vaudeville (23 February 1850), had his 1868 *Le Roi d'Amatibou* (w Edmond Cottinet) at the Palais-Royal illustrated musically by Hervé, and also wrote a handful of short vaudevillesque texts, subsequently produced as one-act opérettes.

Needless to say, in the manner of the time, many of Labiche's original vaudevilles were illustrated with a handful of pasticcio couplets, but in his later days he tried, where he could, to avoid any musical portions in his plays. Again like Shaw, but in Labiche's case largely posthumously, his works later became the meat for musical-comedy authors, but unlike Shaw he had no *Der tapfere Soldat* or *My Fair Lady* emerge as a result. Labiche musicals have not precisely flourished.

Un chapeau de paille d'Italie was originally produced as a vaudeville with songs attached, the pasticcio score of more than 20 items including music from Auber's *Le Serment* and Hérold's *Zampa,* from other vaudevilles of the 1830s and 1840s, and even items from shows of the previous season. This score has not endured, but *Un chapeau de paille d'Italie* has been the most frequently adapted of Labiche's works, remade notably in a version by W S Gilbert who, with George Grossmith as composer, musicalized his own London version of the play, *The Wedding March* (itself played, like the original, with interpolated songs), as *Haste to the Wedding* (Criterion Theatre 27 July 1892). In Italy, Giovanni Maria Sala, Mario Borciani and Lores produced a *Capello di paglia di Firenze* at Verona's Teatro Ristori, and Nino Rota later provided the music for a light-operatic version under the same title, whilst in France Guy Lafarge and André Grassi turned out a musical *Un chapeau de paille d'Italie* at the Opéra de Strasbourg in 1966 (22 October). Hungary got a *Florentin kalap* in an adaptation by István Békeffy, music by Tibor Polgár, at Budapest's Fővárosi Operettszínház (19 April 1946), a second in 1979 at the same theatre (ly: Iván Szenes, mus: Szabolcs Fényes, 30 March), and a third—*Olasz szalmakalap*—with a book credited to Adorján Stella and music by Szabolcs Várady, which was played at the Vigszínház in 1997 (23 March). The piece has also appeared in two American versions, a disastrous off-Broadway piece called *That Hat* (1964, Cy Young) which ran one performance, and a rather more successful one by Alfred Uhry and Robert Waldman with an even nippier title, *Chapeau* (John Houseman Theater, Saratoga 24 July 1977). *Un chapeau de paille d'Italie* was also the source for Genée's comic opera *Rosina* (Carltheater 25 December 1881), for the German pasticcio *Hochzeit mit Hindernissen* (Offenbach arr K Martens) produced in 1930 at the Leipzig Altes Theater (16 February) and for a Burleske mit Musik, *Der Florentiner Hut* (Werner Kruse/H Budjuhn, Hans Weigel), mounted at Brauschweig's Staatstheater in 1965 (31 January).

The next most lets-make-a-musical-ly popular Labiche piece, *La Cagnotte,* became the Posse mit Gesang *Vergnügungszügfer* (Karl Stix/C F Stenzl, Carltheater) in Austria in 1870, *Die Sparbüchse* (Ludwig Kusche/ Charles Regnier Saarbrücken Stadttheater 31 December) in Germany in 1953 and, in France, *La Cagnotte* (Jack Ledru/Guy Lafarge), produced at Lille in 1983. It was also plundered, without credit but with some success, for a bristling British musical comedy entitled *Eldorado,* written by H B Farnie for the Strand Theatre in 1874 (19 February) and with similarly little credit and no success for a shabby British musical called *Instant Marriage. Le Voyage de M Perrichon* was made into an Italian musical *Il viaggio di Perrichon* with music by the Contessa Cento della Morea and into an American off-off-Broadway one, *Bon Voyage,* with a pasticcio Offenbach score (York Players ad V B Lawrence/Edward Mabley 18 November 1978), and Guy Lafarge adapted a third Labiche piece as a musical when he combined with Grassi on a version of *Les Noces de Bouchencoeur,* produced at the Théâtre de Besançon in 1966. In the 1990s Labiche was still turning up with songs attached: Budapest's Új Színház mounted an András Forgách version of *L'affaire de la rue Lourcine* in 1995 (1 October), under the title *Gyilkosság villásreggelivel.*

The 1874 Lecocq (et al) pasticcio put together by H B Farnie as *The Black Prince* for the London stage and said to be based on a combination of three separate French plays, credited Labiche and Delacour as its source and clearly owed part, at least, of its plot to *Le Voyage en Chine,* whilst another piece, the little *A Professional Beauty* played by Letty Lind in London, was apparently taken from his *Un mari qui lance sa femme* (Théâtre du Gymnase 23 April 1864). America got its first original Labiche musical when Australia's John Howson adapted *La Poudre aux yeux* (w Martin) as *Putting On Style* (mus: Frank Howson, Fred J Eustis and pasticcio) for production at the Opera House, Paterson, NJ, in 1885 (10 September), and a second when Newton Calspell put together a song-studded version of *Si jamais je te pince* (w Michel, mus: Arthur Selden, et al) premiered by Aimée at San Francisco's Bush Theater in 1886 (24 December).

Other Labiche derivatives were only nebulously credited. *Die Doppelhochzeit* (Hellmesberger/Léon, von Waldberg), produced at Vienna's Theater in der Josefstadt in 1895 (21 September), was given as ''based on Labiche'' without its source being made specific, and the same went for *Auf der Rax* (w Martin), played at the Theater an der Wien in a version by Theodore Taube with music by the younger Adolf Müller; *Die Familie Pfifferling* (Ringtheater 3 December 1881, mus: A Grüber); for Hungary's successful *Az első és a második* (Béla Szabados/Jenő Rákosi, Népszínház 8 April 1891); and the one-act vaudeville *Sein Bébé* (ad H Paul), to which Hugo Felix composed a score (15 January 1898). Few, however, had a success of the kind that would indicate that Labiche's often very full evenings of comedy were, or are, ideal sources for musical plays.

1859 **L'Omelette à la Follembuche** (Léo Delibes/w Marc-Michel) 1 act Théâtre des Bouffes-Parisiens 8 June

1865 **Le Voyage en Chine** (François Bazin/w Alfred Delacour) Opéra-Comique 9 December

1867 **Le Fils du brigadier** (Victor Massé/w Delacour) Opéra-Comique 25 February

1868 **En manches de chemise** (A Villebichot/w Auguste Lefranc, Eugène Nyon) Alcazar 2 April

1868 **Le Roi d'Amatibou** (Hervé/w Edmond Cottinet) Palais-Royal 27 November

1868 **Le Corricolo** (Ferdinand Poïse/w Delacour) Opéra-Comique 27 November

1876 **Le Roi dort** (Marius Boullard/w Delacour) Théâtre des Variétés 30 March

1879 **Embrassons-nous Folleville** (Avelino Valenti/w Lefranc) Opéra-Comique 6 June

DER LACHENDE EHEMANN Operette in 3 acts by Julius Brammer and Alfred Grünwald. Music by Edmund Eysler. Wiener Bürgertheater, Vienna, 19 March 1913.

In a period when the Viennese musical theatre was casting its first glances towards the more sombrely romantic, less frivolous dramatic and musical styles which would become even more marked a trend after the First World War, Edmund Eysler and his collaborators remained cheerfully and successfully attached to the comic, lighthearted and brightly tuneful mode which had characterized the past decade of Viennese triumphs. After their successes at the Bürgertheater with *Der unsterbliche Lump* and *Der Frauenfresser* they produced there, in *Der lachende Ehemann,* a piece with the practiced air of a traditional Parisian comedy in its libretto and everything that the name of Eysler meant in indubitably Viennese, dancing, melodious music as a score.

Novelist Hella Bruckner (Betty Myra) loves her husband Ottokar (Fritz Werner) dearly, but he seems to take her for granted and is interested only in his business—the manufacture of artificial butter. So, seeking someone with whom she can share her interest in modern music, art and literature, Hella strikes up a friendship with the amorous Graf Selztal (Ludwig Herold). Ottokar's maiden cousin, Dr Lucinde von Sperrholz (Viktoria Pohl-Meiser), warns the husband that for the good of his marriage he should get out and acquire himself some quick culture, and the buttermaker announces that he will go to Italy for that very purpose. In fact, he simply slips away to his hunting lodge. Unfortunately, it is there that, in his putative absence, Hella decides to have an arty party. Events wind up to a pitch where Ottokar, urged on by his two-faced friend Pipelhuber (Leopold Strassmayer), who has himself designs on the faithful wife, is about to sue for a divorce, but when he becomes aware that the figure of fun in Hella's latest novel, ''Der lachende Ehemann,'' is not the husband but the lover, he realizes how Hella truly loves him. Pipelhuber, by way of retribution, is snared by the acidulous Lucinde.

The score of the piece ranged through the gamut of dance rhythms from a polka-duet in Act I, via mazurka, gavotte and a snatch of Ländler, to the most successful piece of the evening, Ottokar's temptingly lazy second-act waltz ''Fein, fein schmeckt uns der Wein,'' to a particularly successful march ''Wohl dem, der meine Lehr benützt'' and a parody of Italian gondola music in Lucinde and Ottokar's first-act duet ''Am Molo dort beim Canaletto.''

Der lachende Ehemann followed happily in the footsteps of the previous Eysler/Bürgertheater successes. It was played for 201 performances in its first run, then returned for a further series the following year, with Vincenz Bauer starring. It received a third run in 1915 at the Raimundtheater with Franz Glawatsch and Rosa Mittermardi in the leading roles, and at the same time it set off on an international career. Hungary was quickest off the mark, with a localized production (ad Adolf Mérei) at the Népopera which featured Imre Szirmai as Ottokár Bárdos and Nelly Hudacsek as Etelka (ex- Hella) alongside Ferenc Pázmán as gróf Szapolczay (ex- Selztal), Lili Berky as Charlotte (ex- Lucinde), Lajos Ujváry as Kakuk Istók (Pipelhuber) and Sándor Horti as Dr Rosenroth. The show, however, found its perhaps biggest success in Germany where, after its initial production at Max Monti's Operettentheater, with Julius Spielmann playing Ottokar alongside Frln Kriwitz (Hella) and Kutzner (Selztal), it won both a three-month return season at the Neues Operetten-Theater (17 February 1921) and productions all round the country, making it one of the most popular and widely played of all Eysler's long list of Operetten in German theatres.

Its English-language productions proved less fortunate. Philip Michael Faraday's London mounting (ad Arthur Wimperis) starred Courtice Pounds (Ottokar), Daisie Irving (Hella) and Georges Carvey (Selztal), with James Blakeley in the stand-out comic role of the lawyer who effects the reconciliation not only of the leading pair but also of three other pairs in the final act. It started indifferently, and Faraday took it off after 78 performances, revised it, and restaged it at his own Lyric Theatre, where his production of Straus's *Love and Laughter* had foundered, under the more provocative title of *The Girl Who Didn't* (18 December). The second try lasted no longer than the first before the show was taken out of the West End and put onto the road.

In America, where *The Laughing Husband* was produced under the management of Charles Frohman, a different script, adapted by Harry B Smith, was used and Eysler's score was botched with local additions, four of which came from the pen of Jerome Kern. One of these, ''You're Here and I'm Here,'' survived to be shifted into another show when Courtice Pounds (Ottokar, rushed in to replace an insufficient Julius Steger at the last minute), Betty Callish (Hella), Fred Walton (Andreas Pipelhuber), Gustave Werner (Selztal), William Norris (Mr Rosenrot), the lovely Frances Demarest and Venita Fitzhugh left Broadway after 48 performances.

A French language version (ad de Caigny) was given at the Brussels Alhambra in 1914 (15 February).

Germany: Montis Operettentheater 14 May 1913; Hungary: Népopera *A nevető férj* 26 September 1913; UK: New Theatre *The*

Laughing Husband / The Girl Who Didn't 2 October 1913; USA: Knickerbocker Theater *The Laughing Husband* 2 February 1914

Film: Rudolf Walther-Fein 1926

LACOME, Paul [LACOME D'ESTALENX, Paul Jean-Jacques] (b Houga (Gers), 4 March 1838; d Houga, 12 December 1920). 19th-century Parisian composer who scored two attractive successes in the musical theatre.

The son of a wealthy Gascon family, Lacome studied music at Aire-sur-l'Ardour in his native Gers and, at the age of 22, won a composing competition, promoted by a magazine, with his one-act opérette *Le Dernier des paladins.* This success encouraged him to move to Paris to pursue a career in music.

Over the next decade he composed songs and orchestral and chamber music as well as contributing articles and criticism to various journals, but it was not until 1870 that his first stage work, the one-act *Épicier par amour,* was staged at the Folies-Marigny. He collaborated on a pair of further short works, produced at the Café Tertulia, with librettist Georges Mancel, before the two men turned out their first full-length piece, the opéra-bouffe *La Dot mal placée* (1873). It was produced at the Théâtre de l'Athénée, where it proved sufficiently successful for Louis Cantin to give Lacome the opportunity to compose a small part of the score for a Clairville/Delacour libretto for which he was having difficulty in finding suitable music. It had been effectively turned down by Offenbach, whose hesitance, apparently, was not unconnected with the fact that *Jeanne, Jeannette et Jeanneton,* as its title suggests, had not one but three prima donnas. Seven other attempts to find a composer for what had become a virtual Cantin audition piece had also failed.

Lacome took the libretto, and swiftly wrote two whole acts. When he presented his music to Cantin, the director happily agreed that he should complete the score alone. *Jeanne, Jeannette et Jeanneton* (1876), presented at the Folies-Dramatiques with Mme Prelly, Berthe Stuart and the novice Marie Gélabert as its three heroines, was a great success, and was subsequently played in London, New York, Vienna and a long list of other centers as well as coming round again in a series of revivals.

Over the next two decades Lacome produced a well-spaced series of elegantly tuneful and well-orchestrated scores for all types of musical plays, which were shared amongst practically all of the major Parisian musical theatres. However, only with the spicy tale of *Madame Boniface* did he ever again approach the sizeable success of *Jeanne, Jeannette et Jeanneton.* His one-act *La Nuit de Saint-Jean* was played at the Opéra-Comique (1882, 1889), whilst *Ma mie Rosette* (1890), a Paris failure, found some friends, particularly in Australia, in a rewritten London version with much of the score replaced by Ivan Caryll and, like the attractive *Madame Boniface* (1883)—which was seen for two performances at the Theater an der Wien in 1891 as *Madame Bonbon* (ad Heinrich Thalboth, Richard Genée) and in America following its Paris success—it won itself revivals in France.

Le Beau Nicolas was given two performances in Vienna as *Der schöne Nikolaus* but, when a version of *La Gardeuse d'oies* was produced in America, a hackwork score replaced the original music. *Les Quatre Filles Aymon,* Lacome's final work at the age of 60, achieved a respectable run and a production at Budapest's Magyar Színház (*Négy menyasszony* ad Ferenc Rajna 16 March 1901) but, although the composer continually found some partisans for his music amongst the cognoscenti, none of his later works survived long beyond their usually brief first runs.

Lacome's other stage works included a ballet, *Le Rêve d'Élias* (1898), and incidental music to Pesquidoux's dramatic poem *Salomé* (1898), and his non-theatrical work a large number of songs and instrumental pieces and several books on musical subjects.

1870 **Épicier par amour** (Georges Mancel) 1 act Théâtre des Folies-Marigny 16 July

1872 **En Espagne** (Mancel) 1 act Café Tertulia 10 May

1872 **J'veux mon peignoir** (Mancel) 1 act Café Tertulia 11 May

1873 **La Dot mal placée** (Mancel) Théâtre de l'Athénée 9 March

1873 **Le Mouton enragé** (Jules Noriac, Adolphe Jaime) 1 act Théâtre des Bouffes-Parisiens 27 May

1875 **Amphytrion** (Charles Nuitter, Alexandre Beaumont) 1 act Théâtre Taitbout 5 April

1876 **Jeanne, Jeannette et Jeanneton** (Clairville, Alfred Delacour) Théâtre des Folies-Dramatiques 27 October

1877 **La Chaste Suzanne** (w Jules Bariller/Paul Ferrier) Palais-Royal 4 July

1879 **Pâques fleuries** (Clairville, Delacour) Théâtre des Folies-Dramatiques 21 October

1880 **Le Beau Nicolas** (Eugène Leterrier, Albert Vanloo) Théâtre des Folies-Dramatiques 8 October

1882 **La Nuit de Saint-Jean** (Erckmann-Chatrian ad Delacour, J de Lau-Lusignan) 1 act Opéra-Comique 13 November

1883 **Madame Boniface** (Ernest Depré, Charles Clairville) Théâtre des Bouffes-Parisiens 20 October

1885 **Myrtille** (Émile Erckmann, Chatrian, ''Maurice Drack'' [ie, A Poitevin]) Théâtre de la Gaîté 27 March

1887 **Les Saturnales** (Albin Valabrègue) Théâtre des Nouveautés 26 September

1888 **La Gardeuse d'oies** (Leterrier, Vanloo) Théâtre de la Renaissance 26 October

1890 **Ma mie Rosette** (Jules Prével, Armand Liorat) Théâtre des Folies-Dramatiques 4 February

1890 **La Fille de l'air** (Cogniard brothers ad Liorat, Hippolyte Raymond) Théâtre des Folies-Dramatiques 20 June

LEFT: Plate C-20. Havana. *Evie Greene and her cigarette.* **BELOW: Plate C-21. HMS Pinafore.** *The original "big, big D!"*

LEFT: Plate C-22. Im weissen Rössl. *The show started huge but showed its quality by shrinking to great effect. Meret Becker and Ursli Pfister meet behind the cowshed in the Berlin Bar Jeder Vernunft's tiny production.* **BELOW: Plate C-23. In Dahomey/A Night Out.** *Two dancing musicals.*

Left: Plate C-24. Iolanthe. *The Fairy Queen (Jill Pert) would like to do all sorts of things with gossamer and buttercups not to mention a bit of gamboling, but noblesse obliges for two whole acts before a particularly handsome guardsman turns up.* **Below: Plate C-25. Jesus Christ Superstar.** *John Nineteen Forty-One.*

LEFT: Plate C-26. Là-Haut. *Maurice Chevalier does the one-step.* **BELOW: Plate C-27. Bonnie Langford.** *From child star to Charity.*

ABOVE: Plate C-28. Gracie Leigh. *Two costume sketches for comical Gracie in* My Mimosa Maid. **RIGHT: Plate C-29. Little Miss Nobody.** *The poster-maker was a bit premature. Top-billed Florence Perry dropped out of the cast, Kate Cutler was upped to the title role, and Gracie Leigh was brought in to play Trixie and thus start a memorable career.*

Plate C-30. Julia McKenzie *as Lily Garland to the Oscar Jaffee of Keith Michell in London's memorable reproduction of* On the Twentieth Century.

CLOCKWISE: Plate C-31. La Mascotte. *Kissing? That's not what the plot says.* **Plate C-32. The Messenger Boy.** *I don't think the Opera House, Harrogate, ran to a camel.* **C-33. The Mikado.** *D'Oyly Carte's earliest touring poster.*

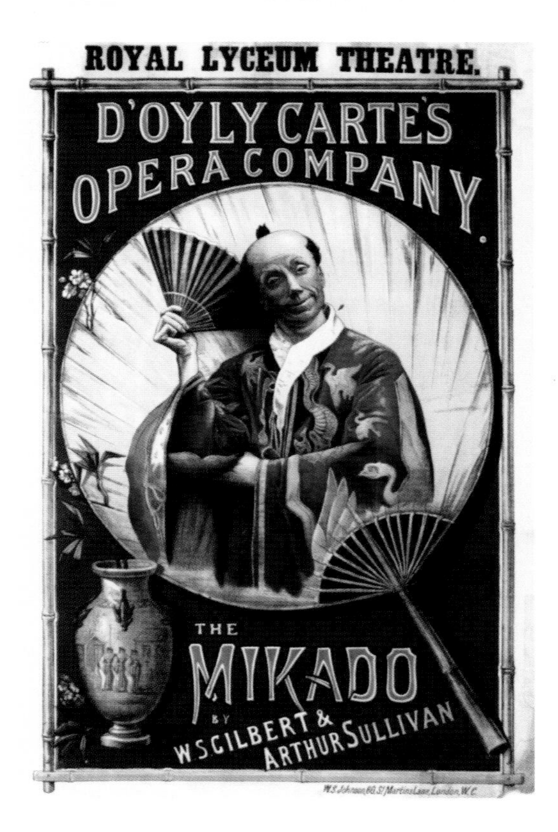

Plate C-34. The Nautch Girl. *Percy Anderson's designs for the Savoy Theatre's Jessie Bond, Leonore Snyder, Courtice Pounds, Rutland Barrington and a mosquito dancer.*

1891 **Mademoiselle Asmodée** (w Victor Roger/Ferrier, C Clairville) Théâtre de la Renaissance 23 November

1893 **Le Cadeau de noces** (Liorat, Fernand Hue, Stop [ie, Morel-Retz]) Théâtre des Bouffes-Parisiens 20 January

1895 **La Bain de Monsieur** (Octave Pradels, Mancel) 1 act Eldorado 12 September

1896 **La Fiancée en loterie** (w André Messager/Camille de Roddaz, Alfred Douane) Théâtre des Folies-Dramatiques 13 February

1898 **Le Maréchal Chaudron** (Henri Chivot, Georges Rolle, ''Jean Gascogne'' [ie, E Ratoin]) Théâtre de la Gaîté 27 April

1898 **Les Quatre Filles Aymon** (w Roger/Liorat, Albert Fonteny) Théâtre des Folies-Dramatiques 20 September

LA-DI-DA-DI-DA Farcical musical in 2 acts based partly on the musical *That's a Pretty Thing* by Stanley Lupino. Additional dialogue by Barry Lupino and Arty Ash. Music by Noel Gay. Victoria Palace, London, 30 March 1943.

To follow the successes of *Me and My Girl* and *Twenty to One* at the Victoria Palace, Lupino Lane produced a fresh vehicle for himself which, without ever reaching the level of the two earlier shows, carried on his run of good fortune. *La-di-da-di-da* was a new version of the 1933 musical *Paste,* a piece written by his cousin Stanley Lupino around a multiplicity of stolen or pawned jewels. Retitled *That's a Pretty Thing,* it had been played for 103 performances at Daly's Theatre (22 November 1933) with a comic cast headed by Bobbie Comber, Sara Allgood, George Gee and Jerry Verno.

Reorganized by another member of the family, Barry Lupino, and with ''additional dialogue by'' jokes specialist Arty Ash, the show was again retitled, this time as *La-di-da-di-da.* The excuse for this apparently meaningless title was that it was the name of the original show's most successful number, a comical piece recommending deep breathing for what ails you. The new version re-routed the jeweled action into a nightclub (nightclubs being currently in fashion, and helpfully allowing the introduction of a cabaretful of speciality acts) and to Scotland for a picturesque finale to the accompaniment of some old and some new Noel Gay songs. It ran for 318 performances largely on the popularity of its star and his team, a team which included brother Wallace Lupino and wife Violet Blythe.

LADY, BE GOOD! Musical play in 2 acts by Guy Bolton and Fred Thompson. Lyrics by Ira Gershwin. Music by George Gershwin. Liberty Theater, New York, 1 December 1924.

One of the most successful of the American dance-and-comedy musicals of the 1920s, *Lady, Be Good!* gave its composer, George Gershwin, paired here for the first time on a Broadway score with brother Ira as lyricist, his first notable musical comedy success, and confirmed the newly established stardom of Fred Astaire and his sister Adele.

Guy Bolton and Fred Thompson's book cast the duo as brother and sister, Dick and Susie Trevor, an impecunious pair thrown out of their lodgings by the machinations of beastly, rich Josephine Vanderwater (Jayne Auburn), who thinks that this is the way to throw discomforted Dick into her money-padded embrace. But Dick is in love with gentle Shirley (Kathlene Martyn). As for Susie, she takes a fancy to a tattered passerby called Jack Robinson (Alan Edwards). Most of the evening's action is precipitated by the comical lawyer, Watty Watkins (Walter Catlett), who, for reasons connected with guilt and a very big Mexican with a knife, gets Susie to impersonate an imprisoned Mexican lady who is anxious to collect the fortune of her rich and ''accidentally'' deceased American husband. Of course, the husband in question is Jack, who escaped his ''accident'' and who is only a temporarily disinherited millionaire, so by the final curtain everyone is as rich and happy as they have been since the invention of musical-comedy final curtains.

The liveliest of the songs which punctuated the comedy included the jaunty title song vamped out by Catlett, the stars' duet ''Hang on to Me,'' Fred Astaire's delightfully exasperated ''The Half of It Dearie, Blues,'' and, above all, the incidental ''Fascinating Rhythm'' performed by stand-up performer Cliff Edwards (aka Ukelele Ike) who had no place or character in the action, but who appeared to sing two or three numbers during the course of the evening (''Little Jazz Bird,'' and at one stage his own ''Insufficient Sweetie'') with considerable success. The loveliest piece, in a show where lovely songs were not really required, was Susie and Jack's winning ''So Am I,'' but another soulful piece, cut on the road, eventually proved more memorable: ''The Man I Love.''

In a season that included such hits as *Rose Marie* and *The Student Prince,* the stars and the songs of *Lady, Be Good!* nevertheless outpointed such other light-footed musical comedies as the much-boosted *Louie the 14th,* the futureful *Mercenary Mary,* and the Duncan Sisters' virtually two-handed version of *Uncle Tom's Cabin* (*Topsy and Eva*). The show had a 41-week, 330-performance run on Broadway before producers Alex Aarons and Vinton Freedley arranged with Alfred Butt to take it to London, where the Astaires had been so well received in *Stop Flirting.* A few minor changes were made for the production at the Empire Theatre, with the stars garnering an extra duet, ''I'd Rather Charleston''

Plate 210. **Lady, Be Good!** *What exactly is he saying . . . ?*

(ly: Desmond Carter). William Kent took on Catlett's role and Buddy Lee was the incidental Jeff, taking the place previously occupied by Ukelele Ike. The piece and its stars won London's approval as much as they had New York's, and the production ran for 326 performances. Whilst the Empire Theatre then shuttered its dressing rooms and took in movies, *Lady, Be Good!* went out for a season's touring around Britain.

An Australian production, mounted by Hugh J Ward, featured the favorite team of soubrette Elsie Prince and comedian Jimmy Godden (Watty) and introduced a ukelele player called Jack Smith to take the moments originally belonging to Ike. However, the show did not take off as well as it had with its original stars. It managed only a fair-to-medium seven weeks in Melbourne, and later played Sydney under the auspices of Sir Benjamin and John Fuller (St James Theatre 30 July 1927). It was given a brief revival at Melbourne's Apollo Theatre in 1936.

Lady, Be Good! has remained in the regional repertoire of English-speaking countries over the years as a favorite example of a 1920s musical comedy, but it has been played almost invariably in heavily souped-up versions. Both of the major productions of recent years—an unfortunate London revival (Saville Theatre 25 July 1968) starring Lionel Blair and Aimi MacDonald, and a Goodspeed Opera House version (3 June 1974)—have filled up the piece's song list with additional Gershwin numbers culled from other shows, revues and films (five in the case of the first, four for the second). What passed for a film version, inevitably, did the same, using Kern's ''The Last Time I Saw Paris'' and the Arthur Freed/Roger Edens ''You'll Never Know'' alongside bits of Gershwin's score, as Eleanor Powell and Robert Young played out what was, in any case, a different story under the show's title.

Lady, Be Good! put in its most recent metropolitan appearances at London's Open Air Theatre in 1992 (28

July) with Bernard Cribbins, Joanna Riding and Simon Green at the head of its cast and at Berlin's Neuköllner Oper (ad Peter Lund) in 1997 with Karen Probst and Tilmann von Blomberg featured.

UK: Empire Theatre 14 April 1926; Australia: Princess Theatre, Melbourne 18 September 1926; Germany: Städtische Bühnen, Dortmund 19 September 1976, Neuköllner Oper, Berlin 19 June 1997

Film: MGM 1941

Recordings: London cast (WRC, part record), archive collection (Smithsonian/Columbia), studio cast (Elektra-Nonsuch)

LADY BEHAVE Musical comedy in 2 acts by Stanley Lupino. Additional dialogue by Arty Ash. Lyrics by Frank Eyton. Music by Edward Horan. His Majesty's Theatre, London, 24 July 1941.

Jack Hylton's wartime production *Lady Behave* chose the currently popular Ruritania of Hollywood for its setting, in which were followed the twin stories of a film star (Bernard Clifton) in love with a humble stand-in (Sally Gray), and of a comic stunt man (Stanley Lupino) rivaled for the love of his soubrette (Pat Kirkwood) by a gangster (Arthur Gomez). The love affairs were topped by some further comedy gleaned from the antics of a scriptwriter (Hartley Power) who is forced into feminine clothes for a mock wedding in one of the oldest turns in the history of musical theatre.

Stanley Lupino's libretto was a hotchpotch of used themes, and not in the same class as his Gaiety musical comedies of the 1930s, but *Lady Behave* was bright and escapist entertainment which gave the opportunity for some light if insignificant songs (of which Lupino's own ''I'm a Nil'' proved the most popular) and rather less dancing than had been the habit in his Laddie Cliff series of shows. It wisely played a twice-daily schedule, at 2 PM and 5:15 PM, for an audience which had no wish to be out on the nighttime streets of wartime London and, as the only new musical in town alongside reprises of *Me and My Girl* and *Chu Chin Chow,* it succeeded in holding up for nine months (401 performances). During the run Lupino fell ill and was temporarily replaced by Bobby Howes, who then headed a touring company into the provinces when the star/librettist returned, but Lupino was still ill and he died shortly after the show closed, as *Lady Behave* continued its second tour around the provinces.

A Lupino sequel to *Lady Behave, The Love Racket,* which used what were allegedly, at least, the same set of characters for a second Hollywood adventure, was posthumously produced at the Victoria Palace (21 October 1943). With Arthur Askey starring, it proved even more successful than the first piece, playing through good runs both in Britain and, under the management of David N Martin, in Australia (Tivoli, Melbourne 23 December 1949).

LADY IN THE DARK Musical play in 2 acts by Moss Hart. Lyrics by Ira Gershwin. Music by Kurt Weill. Alvin Theater, New York, 23 January 1941.

The piece which ultimately became *Lady in the Dark* was conceived by author Moss Hart as a play for Katharine Cornell, but during the course of its writing he became convinced that the fantastical dream sequences he envisaged as a part of the psychoanalysis of his heroine would be better played with music, and he approached Ira Gershwin and Kurt Weill to turn the play into a musical for Gertrude Lawrence.

Miss Lawrence played Liza Elliott, a smart and successful New York magazine editor who, in spite of her healthy material and business position and an apparently uncomplicated love life with the rich if married Kendall Nesbitt (Bert Lytell), finds herself sufficiently ill at ease to consult a psychiatrist (Donald Randolph). It is finally resolved that Liza has a hang-up left over from a childhood in which her father overstressed the beauty of her mother, and this hang-up has led her to push herself to excel in life to make up for what she sees as an inability to compete as an attractive woman. Once she understands the whys of her uneasiness and dissatisfaction, she can finally give up the safe, unavailable Kendall, refuse the men who need her rather than want her, and start afresh on a less aggressive and defensive business and love life.

The musical portion of *Lady in the Dark* was, as Hart planned, virtually restricted to four dream sequences, three long and one brief, sequences which were the main substance and raison d'être of the show. The first (''O Fabulous One in Your Ivory Tower''/''The World's Inamorata''/''Only One Life to Live''/''Girl of the Moment''/''It Looks Like Liza'') presented Liza as a matchless beauty, until blown apart by a portrait of the stern, besuited woman of business; the second (''Mapleton High Chorale''/''This Is New''/''The Princess of Pure Delight''/''This Woman at the Altar'') visited schooldays, saw her involved with film star Randy Curtis (Victor Mature) and then threatened with a marriage which she knows she does not want; and the third (''The Greatest Show on Earth''/''He Gave Her the Best Years of His Life''/''Tschaikowsky''/''Jenny'') mixed a circus, featuring office photographer Russell Paxton (Danny Kaye) as ringmaster, with a court scene in which her employee Charley Johnson (Macdonald Carey) pounded out accusations. It was this third (originally written as a minstrel show, with the principal number being a piece about the signs of the zodiac) that introduced two of the show's three set songs. Kaye caused a sensation with a madly pattering nonsense song of composers' names (''Tschaikowsky''), and Miss Lawrence followed with the saga of ''Jenny'' the girl who would make up her mind, and, by a purposefully pianissimo (and bumpingly sexual) performance, topped Kaye's number. The third and most popular number in the score came in the final dream. ''My Ship'' was the melody which represented Liza's fears and which reappeared at her moments of crisis. It was also the one number of the score in which Weill's music was able to come to the fore over Gershwin's character- and plot-important words.

Hassard Short's production of *Lady in the Dark* was a fine Broadway success. If the work was seemingly somewhat daunting in its subject matter—although dream sequences were as old as the musical theatre and mental processes had been explored as recently as Herbert Fields's *Peggy-Ann*—it was produced with considerable glamor both in its dream portions and in the part of the play set in Liza's fashion magazine's offices, and it had three strong songs and as many outstanding players. Miss Lawrence, in spite of a psychoanalysable tendency to play the clown and upstage her fellow players, gave one of her finest performances as Liza, whilst Kaye's explosion of patter in ''Tschaikowsky'' was his first step to stardom. Victor Mature, here cast as a piece of soft beefcake, was on the same track. The show ran through 467 Broadway performances, with a two months-plus summer break during which the leading men were replaced.

The cost of the production and wartime conditions were surely at least partly responsible for the failure of *Lady in the Dark* to win a first-class production outside America, and any possibility of this being remedied in the postwar years was wiped out by the release of Paramount's 1944 film in which Ginger Rogers starred as Liza Elliott in a version ''based on'' the Broadway show. The dream sequences were filleted and supplemented with Victor Schertzinger's ''Dream Lover'' and the Johnny Burke/Jimmy van Heusen ''Suddenly It's Spring.'' These alterations were, however, made good for a 1954 television production in which Ann Sothern was featured.

A German version of the piece was finally produced in Kassel in 1951 under the give-away title of *Das verlorene Lied* (''the lost song,'' ad Maria Teichs, R A Stemmle) with Vera Salvotti-Stoern as Liza, and, in Britain too, when *Lady in the Dark* was finally played there, 40 years after its initial production, it was in a provincial theatre, without a chorus, with an orchestra of nine, and with a cast of mostly expatriate Americans (Kenneth Nelson, Don Fellowes, Edward Wiley) supporting the specially imported Celeste Holm. Shorn of its production values, and with Hart's once ever-so-slightly daring psychoanalytic details seeming banal and almost jokey in an age where the stereotypical New Yorker is known to see a psychiatrist more often than he sees the sky, it proved singularly less workable than it had in the 1940. However, the well-fostered fin de siècle fashion for the works of Weill saw the piece brought to London in 1997. Not in a commercial production, but in the public-money-padded security of Britain's Royal National Theatre. Maria Friedman played Liza for the occasion and the lack of workability noted at Nottingham was confirmed.

The idea of using psychoanalysis as an up-to-date version of the ''dream'' musical was taken to its illogical conclusion in an Anglo-Viennese musical *Freudiana* (Eric Woolfson, Theater an der Wien 19 December 1990).

Germany: Staatstheater, Kassel *Das verlorene Lied* 24 May 1951; UK: Playhouse, Nottingham 9 December 1981; Royal National Theatre, London 15 March

Film: Paramount 1944

Recordings: original cast (RCA, Columbia, AEI), TV cast (RCA), London cast (TER), film soundtrack (Curtain Calls), selections (Columbia, Decca), etc

Literature: McClung, B: *American Dreams: Analyzing Moss Hart, Ira Gershwin and Kurt Weill's ''Lady in the Dark''* (UMI, Ann Arbor, Mich, 1997)

LADY LUCK Musical play in 2 acts by Firth Shephard, based on the libretto *His Little Widows* by William Cary Duncan and Rida Johnson Young. Additional scenes by Greatrex Newman. Lyrics by Desmond Carter. Music by H B Hedley and Jack Strachey. Carlton Theatre, London, 27 April 1927.

Producer Laddie Cliff followed up his semi-successful debut show *Dear Little Billie* with another musical written by the same team. Firth Shephard, who had done the anglicization of Duncan and Young's *His Little Widows* for the London stage, borrowed the plot from the American musical and used it as the backbone for a vehicle for Cliff, a second dancing light-comedian in Cyril Ritchard, and an out-and-out comic star in Leslie Henson as three American stockbrokers who invest in the ''Lady Luck'' mine. After jagged fortunes, it renders pay dirt at the final curtain. There was a theatrical subplot line which involved little Jane the milliner's assistant (Phyllis Monkman) becoming a sudden leading lady, and another—the *Little Widows* one—in which Henson inherited a fortune from a Mormon uncle on the condition that he weds all his wives.

Each element was a well-used one, but the appeal of *Lady Luck* was in the telling rather than the tale or, more accurately in the star comedy performances and in the dancing which was one of the show's main attractions. Cliff did a gracefully eccentric turn to a number called ''Syncopated City,'' Ritchard performed a smooth routine to ''Happy'' and paired with his long-legged Australian partner Madge Elliott in ''I've Learned a Lot,'' Phyllis Monkman sang and danced ''Blue Pipes of Pan'' and the John Tiller Girls did their bit in unison. The suitably dance-rhythmed ''tinkling tunes'' of Hedley and Strachey were supplemented, in the fashion of the time, by two American songs: ''Sing'' and ''If I Were You'' culled from Rodgers and Hart's Broadway flop *Betsy.*

Lady Luck opened the new and short-lived (as a live theatre) Carlton Theatre in London's Haymarket, and Cliff and Shephard proved to have gauged the public taste well. Alongside the town's other, and more romantic, musical hits, *The Desert Song* and *The Vagabond King,* their show ran for 324 performances and established Cliff and his team for a series of popular musicals in the same dance-and-laughter vein over the following years. Two *Lady Luck* companies went into the country whilst the London run continued, followed soon by a third, and the show held its place on the touring lists through into 1929 before being superseded by other British and American musicals in the same style.

LADY MADCAP Musical comedy in 2 acts by Paul Rubens and N Newnham Davis. Lyrics by Paul Rubens and Percy Greenbank. Music by Paul Rubens. Prince of Wales Theatre, London, 17 December 1904.

Following on behind the success of the winsome *Three Little Maids,* George Edwardes commissioned another musical comedy from author-composer Paul Rubens. *Lady Madcap* had a tiresome little heroine (Adrienne Augarde) of the madcap variety beloved by Victorian and Edwardian playgoers, who fools her father into hurrying away from the country on fake business so that she can entertain a whole lot of soldiers and trick a French Count (Maurice Farkoa) and a couple of burglars pretending to be millionaires (Aubrey Fitzgerald, Fred Emney) into mistakenly flirting with her disguised maid, Gwenny (Delia Mason) instead of her clever little self. She her clever little self goes for one plain ordinary Trooper Smith (G P Huntley), who is, of course, a millionaire in disguise. The libretto was even weaker than that for *Three Little Maids* had been, and it was supported by a score which was occasionally pretty, often inane, and at its most popular when pinkly suggestive, as in Maurice Farkoa's serenade ''I Like You in Velvet'' with its clear indication that he would prefer the lady without her velvet, or indeed anything else, on. Farkoa ''wore a pale mauve suit and a diamond ring and was voted fascinating'' and, although now plumpish and 40, was as much of an attraction as the charmingly comical Huntley and the pretty girls of the cast.

In spite of its weaknesses (which were obviously not considered such), *Lady Madcap* found itself an audience as Edwardes poured into the cast some of his most attractive artists as periodic replacements (Madge Crichton, Zena Dare, Marie Studholme, Lily Elsie, Gabrielle Ray, Maud Hobson, Mabel Russell, Blanche Massey). Nine months in, he revamped the show thoroughly and advertised ''a new edition'' which included several new numbers, amongst them Blanche Ring's pair of American hit songs, ''Sammy'' and ''Bedelia,'' performed by Farkoa in French. *Lady Madcap* maintained its popularity for nearly a year (354 performances) before going on the road in two companies (soon reduced to one) for one season's touring, and beginning overseas productions. The Shuberts produced the show on Broadway in an Americanized version (ad Edward Paulton, R H Burnside, Percy Greenbank) as *My Lady's Maid* with several of the London cast (Madge Crichton, Delia Mason, George Carroll) repeating their roles and Joe Coyne as the disguised hero. It was scolded by the critics and lasted only 44 performances. Australia's version, the following year, featured Daisy Wallace and Myles Clifton and found only a very little more popularity.

USA: Casino Theater *My Lady's Maid* 20 September 1906; Australia: Princess Theatre, Melbourne 3 August 1907

LADY MARY Musical play in 3 acts by Frederick Lonsdale and J Hastings Turner. Lyrics by Harry Graham. Music by Albert Szirmai. Additional numbers by Phil Charig, Richard Myers and Jerome Kern. Daly's Theatre, London, 23 February 1928.

Producers Lee Ephraim (*The Desert Song, Sunny*) and Jack Buchanan lined up an impressive writing team for *Lady Mary,* with Hungary's Albert Szirmai, who had recently been represented in London by *Princess Charming* (*Alexandra*) and by *The Bamboula,* his first made-for-Britain piece, as theoretically principal composer. If the libretto was rather conventional in its plotting (heir-to-earldom wins pretty lady from rotter), the show's action was peopled with enjoyable characters—notably the kindly self-made millionaire Hatpin Pinge (George Grossmith), who proposes to the heroine's sister (Dorothy Field) 68 times before being accepted, and his sidekick Waghorn (Herbert Mundin), who has to fight a fearsome butler (Thomas Weguelin) to win Lady Mary's maid (Vera Bryer). The incipient Earl was played by Paul Kavanagh and Lady Mary by star soprano Helen Gilliland. Some originality was obtained by setting the first act in Australia, but the effect was apparently rather spoiled by a chorus of jackaroos ''who,'' the *Observer* critic noted, ''left me with the impression that if a little woolly lamb said 'Baa' to them, they would fall into a deep swoon.''

The jigsaw score for the piece was very curiously credited. Some of the songs were labeled as the joint work of Szirmai and of Richard Myers, an American show-songwriter who must still just about hold the highest strike-out average of pre-Broadway closures, others of Szirmai and a second and slightly more successful transatlantic composer, Phil Charig. Who did what and to whom must remain a mystery. The most winning song of the evening, Mary's pretty farewell to Australia, ''Calling Me Home,'' was credited to Szirmai and Myers. Unlike ''Calling Me Home,'' a number of the tunes—in spite of the Australian and British settings of the piece—strove towards being or, with the help of a half-dozen further American contributors, really were American and up-to-date, but no one semed to worry too much about such incongruities, and numbers such as Kalmar and Ruby's ''You Can't Have My Sugar for Tea'' duly found a place in the entertainment. Szirmai and Charig supplied a jaunty duet, ''I've Got a Feeling for Somebody,'' for Mundin and Miss Bryer, and the soubrette had another catchy, bouncy number, ''What About Me?'' (Szirmai unaided), both of which were rather more fun than the other songs given to Grossmith (''You Came Along,'' Charig's ''Why Should I Feel Lonely'') and to Miss Gilliland (Charig's ''I'll Go Where You Go,'' Jerome Kern's ''If You're a Friend of Mine'' recycled from *Stepping Stones* where it had been ''In Love with Love'').

The libretto of the show was very well reviewed and, although there were general reservations about the potpourri score, *Lady Mary,* with Grossmith and Mundin as draws, began well, even breaking Daly's Theatre's house record in an early performance. However, something failed to click, and the show resolutely refused to become a hit. It was closed after 181 striving performances and sent on the road in two companies, but there too it simply failed to take and it ultimately closed in indifference.

THE LADY OF THE SLIPPER, or A Modern Cinderella Musical comedy in 3 acts by Anne Caldwell and Lawrence McCarthy. Lyrics by James O'Dea. Music by Victor Herbert. Globe Theater, New York, 28 October 1912.

Charles Dillingham's spectacular fairy story show top-billed comedians Montgomery and Stone as a couple of jolly fellows from a cornfield called Punks and Spooks who more or less help their modern Cinderella (Elsie Janis) to get, first, to the ball and then into her prince's arms, in much the same way that the same two comedians had helped Dorothy and her dog get to the Emerald City nearly a decade previously. With three stars who had little in the way of singing ability, Herbert channeled his most attractive writing into the dance numbers (Witches' Ballet, Harlequinade) and descriptive music. Stone was left to take out his energies on a burlesque routine, the Punch Bowl Glide, whilst Miss Janis encompassed an A sharp below the stave to an E on its top edge in her ''Princess of Far Away,'' duetted with Mouser, her cat (David Abrahams), in ''Meow! Meow! Meow!'' and droned away on Cs and Ds whilst her more vocally equipped Prince Maximilan (Douglas Stevenson) scampered up, in compensation, to a baritone G in ''A Little Girl at Home.'' In spite of this Cinderella having cornfield-bred help, there was still a fairy godmother (Vivian Rushmore) in the story, not to mention a couple of creatures called, in a fashion which sounded more *Rocky Horror Show* than 1912, Dollbabia (Lillian Lee) and Freakette (Queenie Vassar), whose performances were for the delectation of the rather older children in the audience.

The Lady of the Slipper was Dillingham's third successive production with Montgomery and Stone, following *The Red Mill* and *The Old Town,* and their third success together. It ran for 232 performances on Broadway, saved the producer from severe difficulties brought about by losses recently incurred on less popular shows, and served the comic partners and their promoter splendidly for good runs in Chicago and Boston and for two seasons of touring throughout America, until they traded it in for a newer model, based this time on *Aladdin.*

THE LADY SLAVEY Musical go-as-you-please in 2 acts by George Dance. Music by John Crook, et al. Theatre Royal, Northampton, 4 September 1893; Avenue Theatre, London, 20 October 1894.

One of the earliest pieces in the new modern-dress ''musical comedy'' style of the 1890s, and also one of the most phenomenally successful. H Cecil Beryl's production of *The Lady Slavey* immediately postdated George Edwardes's mounting of *In Town* and Frank Harris's hit *Morocco Bound* and it leaned in the same direction as these two pieces by unashamedly including a large variety content in its second act.

The first act set up the show's plot in which youngest daughter Phyllis (Kitty Loftus) dons a maid's cap and apron to give ''tone'' to her under-funded family home when the tinned-tomato millionaire Vincent Evelyn (J C Piddock) comes around in search of a wife. The kindly bailiff Roberts (Witty Watty Walton) agrees to pose as butler, in the hope of getting his money if the can-man is hooked. Of course, Evelyn chooses for his final-curtain mate neither one of Phyllis's sisters (Amy Thornton, Florence Wilson) nor the determinedly pursuing music-hall star Flo Honeydew (producer's wife Edith Rosenthal), but Phyllis. Evelyn calculatedly lets it slip out that it is Roberts who is the real millionaire, in disguise, and as the ladies—all but Phyllis, of course—set their sights on the comical bailiff, things begin to go sufficiently unsmoothly to allow the show to run into a second act in which an ''entertainment,'' in which each of the performers has a number or a spot, is staged for the benefit of the houseguests before the happy ending is tied up.

George Dance's book was accurately aimed at the tastes and predilections of *The Lady Slavey*'s provincial audiences, and John Crook's score, a compound of lively pieces from which the concerted music and a comic number for Roberts called ''The Big Boss Dude'' stood out, was perforated with a series of interpolated numbers including such popular songs as ''Daisy Bell,'' ''After the Ball,'' ''Wotcher'' and ''The Seventh Royal Fusiliers,'' an original piece by Miss Rosenthal called ''Paddy Murphy Had a Pig,'' and a song Dance had written with Charles Graham two years earlier called ''In Friendship's Name.'' The mixture proved a vast success in its first 14-week tour, in a simultaneous number-two tour run by William Greet, and also in a quickly launched number-three company under Charles K Chute. All three tours were resumed after the Christmas pantomime season had passed and Greet's tour eventually ran virtually nonstop for 11 years, Chute's for 4 and Beryl's for no less than 15.

The Lady Slavey that totted up such amazing totals was, however, a rather different piece from the original, for in October 1894, after having long hesitated to bring such an unsophisticated show before Londoners, Beryl produced his musical at the Avenue Theatre with American performers May Yohé (Phyllis) and Jenny McNulty (Flo) starred alongside Charles Danby (Roberts) and Henry Beaumont (Evelyn). The libretto was little changed, although one new comedy character was introduced, but the score was largely remodeled and the ''borrowed'' popular songs replaced by some new material written by Crook and by some modern interpolations. Miss Yohé sang ''What's a Poor Girl to Do?'' (Joseph and Mary Watson), ''Tis Hard to Love and Say Farewell'' (Frank Isitt), and a plantation song ''The Land of Dreams'' (Albert Cammeyer/Herbert Walther), but she had her biggest success in duet with Danby in Crook's topical ''It's a Very Wise Child that Knows.'' Danby, however, topped the lot with his ''Big Boss Dude.'' The hero retained ''In Friendship's Name'' and scored with ''Wanted a Wife for a Millionaire'' in the first-act finale whilst Adelaide Astor, as one of the sisters, danced and sang a little number called ''Dorothy Flop'' written by her more famous sister Letty Lind.

Handicapped by Miss Yohé, who not only gave a disappointing performance but also hit the headlines in a less than happy manner when her husband Sir Francis Hope (owner of the infamous Hope diamond) was declared bankrupt and she thereafter declared herself off sick, the show ran for only 96 London performances. But *The Lady Slavey* left Miss Yohé and her diamond to their inexorable downward path and hurried back to its home on the road, there to continue its upward and onward perambulations in its new and musically improved version.

The Lady Slavey went round the English-speaking world, being played alongside the blossoming musicals of the Gaiety Theatre repertoire on the African, Pacific and Oriental circuits (where it was many years a feature of the repertoire of the children's company, Pollard's Lilliputians) and in 1896 George Lederer and Thomas Canary presented what passed for a version of the show (ad variously attributed) on Broadway. Little remained of Dance's dialogue and—according to the billing—nothing of Crook's score, which had been replaced by some Gustave Kerker pieces. However, London's ''Whoop-de-dooden-do'' and ''The Harmless Little Girlie with the Downcast Eye'' still appeared on the programs. Virginia Earle (Phyllis), Dan Daly (Roberts) and Marie Dressler (Flo) were featured in a satisfactory run of 128 performances, which was followed by a second season (72 performances) two years of solid touring later.

John F Sheridan introduced *The Lady Slavey* in Australia some years later, starring himself as Roberts and Celia Mavis as Phyllis in a version which had, he assured his audiences, been ''increased in size,'' and he played it there through several seasons in repertoire. Nowhere, however, did the show harvest the same rewards as in Britain, where the London version of *The Lady Slavey* just went on and on. Even after the end of its two marathon tours, it continued to be played in Britain's provincial houses right through into the 1920s.

USA: Casino Theater 3 February 1896; Australia: Criterion Theatre, Sydney 2 August 1902

LÀ-HAUT Opérétte-bouffe in 3 acts by Yves Mirande and Gustave Quinson. Lyrics by Albert Willemetz. Music by Maurice Yvain. Théâtre des Bouffes-Parisiens, Paris, 31 March 1923.

The musical comedy *Là-haut,* written and produced to be music-hall star Maurice Chevalier's follow-up to the highly successful *Dédé* as a legitimate stage vehicle, was a piece well and truly in the insouciant, sexy and dance-filled style that was the rage of the Parisian années folles. Yves Mirande (in a nominal collaboration with producer Quinson) supplied a suavely comical role for the star and Maurice Yvain, riding high after the triumph of *Ta bouche* at the Théâtre Daunou, and the ubiquitous Albert Willemetz provided a set of songs in a suitably insinuating music-hall mode.

The late Evariste Chanterelle (Chevalier) arrives in Heaven and there learns that his widowed wife Emma (Mary Malbos) is already being amorously pursued by her horrid little cousin, Martel (Louis Blanche). He begs St Peter (Gabin père) to let him have 24 hours extra on earth to put the pest in his place. He is allowed to go, accompanied by a guardian angel called Frisotin (another major music-hall star, Dranem), but when his time—

mostly spent romancing his widow—is up, he brings the pregnant Emma back with him. Horrified at the thought of a celestial birth, St Peter throws the pair out of Heaven. Then Evariste wakes up.

Yvain's score was a bundle of catchy, comical songs made to the measure of his two stars, who shared the bulk of the musical content of the show between them. Chevalier was well served with a fox-trotting paean to Paris (''C'est Paris'') which compared it favorably with Paradise, a very funny and catchy plea for sexual tolerance, ''Si vous n'aimez pas ça,'' which encouraged ''just because you don't like 'ça,' don't put other folk off'' (the identity of ''ça'' varied from verse to verse), the lively title song and the incidental ''Ose Anna,'' whilst Dranem sighed over the naughty things a guardian angel has to watch his client get up to without being able to partake himself, giggled over some ghastly puns in ''L'Hilarité céleste,'' took literally the phrase ''C'est la vie,'' ran through some literary burlesques in the clipping ''Aime-moi, Emma,'' and cheeked St Peter in ''J'm'en balance'' as well as indulging in a pantomime scene of heavenly drunkenness. In the smaller feminine part of the show, Mlle Malbos lined up the advantages and disadvantages of widowhood and explained ''Parce que,'' whilst Simone Montalet, as an amorous angelette, swooned over Chevalier in the Duo de la tentation.

Là-haut was a splendid success, and Chevalier's triumph in *Dédé* seemed confirmed, but the star was not happy. Dranem, in what was theoretically the second role of the angel, had made a stunning major musical-theatre debut and Chevalier, quickly noticing that his partner was gathering the largest applause of the night for his characterful and often liberty-taking performance, stamped his foot. Since there could be no question of reducing Dranem's role or crushing his hugely popular extravagances, it did no good. So Chevalier walked out of the show and out of a career in the musical theatre, whilst Dranem went on to become one of the all-time great comic stars of the French musical stage.

The show did not suffer noticeably from its star's departure, and Boucot and Harry Arbell both replaced him happily, first opposite Dranem and then alongside his replacement, the comedian Serjius, as the show played out the year at the Bouffes-Parisiens. The initial run was followed by a quick revival at the Folies-Dramatiques (14 April 1924), before *Là-haut* began a long and enduring career in the French provinces. Ultimately, the show even returned to Paris when a major revival mounted at Lyons in 1996 was picked up and brought to the Théâtre des Variétés two years later (10 July 1998) with Jean-Paul Lucet and Patrick Haudecer in the leading roles.

Recordings: complete (Decca), original cast selection on *L'Opérette française par ses créateurs* (EPM)

LAHR, Bert [LAHRHEIM, Irving] (b New York, 13 August 1895; d New York, 4 December 1967).

A clownish, flappy-faced comic, who started his performing life in vaudeville and burlesque, Lahr made his first appearances in the musical theatre as a wobbly boxer in *Hold Everything!* (1928, Gink Schiner), as an incompetent air mechanic in *Flying High* (1930, Rusty Krause) and in the less effective *Hot-Cha!* (1932, Alky Schmidt) before extending his Broadway fame in revue. He had his best Broadway musical part as the little chappie who dreams he is Louis XV in Cole Porter's *Dubarry Was a Lady* (1939), joining with Ethel Merman to celebrate ''Friendship,'' and his last, after a quarter of a century in mostly non-musical shows (*Waiting for Godot, Hotel Paradiso, The Winter's Tale,* etc) and the occasional revue, was the title role of *Foxy,* a musical-comedy version of Ben Jonson's *Volpone,* in 1964.

Lahr was seen on television in *Let's Face It* and *The Fantasticks,* but his most famous screen musical portrayal remains his Cowardly Lion in the cinematic version of *The Wizard of Oz* (''If I Were King of the Forest'').

Biography: Lahr, J: *Notes on a Cowardly Lion* (Knopf, New York, 1969)

LAJTAI, Lajos (b Budapest, 13 April 1900; d Budapest, 12 January 1966).

Lajtai studied in Budapest and Vienna and, after a period in the army, made his first efforts as a theatre composer with music for the revues *Das nackte Ballet* and *Der Liebestrompeter,* produced at the Vienna Trocadero. The bulk of his work thereafter was mounted in Budapest, where his first book musicals, including an adaptation of Paul Gavault and Robert Charvay's 1904 Paris success *Mademoiselle Josette, ma femme* (*Az ártatlan özvegy*), were staged in the early 1920s. He wrote liberally for all kinds of stages throughout that decade, supplying songs for children's shows, and scores or part-scores for several spectacular operett-revues or revue-operetts or even unqualified revues such as *A meztelen Pest* (Budapesti Színház, 1925) and the Fővárosi Operettszínház's *Nézze meg az ember* (1926), as well as for regular musical plays.

Lajtai's 1927 musical comedy *Mesék az írógépről* ran up more than 50 performances at the Városi Színház, but his first international success came with the 1928 *A régi nyár* (''once upon a time in summer''), a Budapest triumph with a first run of over one hundred performances, and subsequently seen under the title *Sommer von Einst* (ad Hans Hellmut Zerlett, Swariowsky) at Nuremberg (9 November 1929) and at Stuttgart (12 May 1931). Thereafter, a fine series of successful musicals followed, several of which won subsequent productions beyond Hungary. *Sisters,* created by Rózsi Bársony and

Ilona Titkos as two little girls from Pest who become a sister act at the Moulin-Rouge before going home to happiness, was played for two months in German (ad Béla Jenbach) at Vienna's Johann Strauss-Theater (22 October 1930) with Irén Biller and Grete Hornik starred; the musical comedy *Az okos mama,* revived several times in Budapest after its original successful run with Sári Fedák as the ''clever mama'' of the title, appeared as *Die kluge Mama* (ad Jenbach) at the Vienna Volksoper in 1931 (6 April); and the costume piece *Őfelsége frakkja* (''His Majesty's overcoat''), a three hundred–performance hit with Emmi Kosáry, Márton Rátkai and István Gyergyai in Budapest, became *Katinka* (ad André Barde) on the Paris stage. At home, there were further successes with the revusical *A régi orfeum* (old time music hall) and a piece about the Rothschilds, starring Vilma Medgyasszay as a musical Mama Rothschild, watching her youngest son, Jacob, through an entanglement with a Parisian singer (Hanna Honthy) before coming back to his hometown Betty.

Lajtai's output, and virtually his career in the theatre, came to an end at the age of 35. With the rise of Nazism, he left Hungary and, after a detour via Paris, where he capitalized on his success with *Katinka* by supplying some further music to the Théâtre des Nouveautés, settled in Sweden. Although he returned regularly to his homeland after the end of the War, his only ''new'' stage show produced thereafter was *Három tavasz* (''three springtimes''), a piece which reused favorite songs from his previous shows as its score. His works have survived less strongly in the repertoire than those of such as Eisemann, but the 1990s has seen productions of both *Â régi nyár* (Székesfehérvár 2 July 1993, Tatabánya 14 June 1996, Szeged 21 March 1997, Győr 21 October 1997) and *Párizsi divat* (József Attila Színház 13 April 1996).

1923 **Az asszonyok bolondja** (István Bródy) Budai Színkör 9 May

1925 **Az ártatlan özvegy** (Paul Gavault, Robert Charvay ad Harmath) Városi Színház 25 December

1926 **Az alvó feleség** (Mátyás Feld, Imre Harmath) Budapesti Színház 13 July

1927 **Mesék az írógepről** (István Békeffy, István Szomaházy) Városi Színház 8 October

1927 **Mackó urfi kalandjai** (Gyula Komor) Fővárosi Operettszínház 19 November

1928 **A Jégkirály kincse** (Arthur Lakner) Fővárosi Operettszínház 6 January

1928 **Postás bácsi szerencséje** (Károly Breitner) Fővárosi Operettszínház 4 March

1928 **A régi nyár** (I Békeffy) Budai Színkör 15 June

1928 **Dörmögő Dömötör** (Károly Beretvás) Fővárosi Operettszínház 17 November

1928 **Párizsi divat** (I Békeffy) Városi Színház 22 December

1929 **Sisters** (I Békeffy, László Vadnai) Belvárosi Színház 2 March; Király Színház 10 January 1930

1930 **Lila test, sárga sapka** (I Békeffy, László Békeffy) Nyári Operettszínház 7 June

1930 **Az okos mama** (I Békeffy, Béla Szenes) Király Színház 26 November

1931 **Őfelsége frakkja** (I Békeffy) Király Színház 19 September

1932 **A régi orfeum** (I Békeffy, Jenő Faragó) Fővárosi Operettszínház 12 March

1932 **Amikor a kislányból nagy lány lesz** (I Békeffy) Budai Színkör 10 June

1932 **A fekete lány** Labriola Színház (Városi Színház) 16 October

1932 **A Rotschildok** (I Békeffy, Ferenc Martos/Martos) Fővárosi Operettszínház 25 November

1933 **Az a huncut postás bácsi** (Beretvas) Fővárosi Operettszínhaz 1 January

1933 **Katinka** (revised French *Őfelsége frakkja,* ad André Barde) Théâtre de l'Empire, Paris 22 February

1933 **Tánc a boldogságért** (Andor Szénes/Adorján Bonyi) Budai Színkör 14 June

1933 **Sült galamb** (László Szilágyi) Király Színház 7 October

1934 **Nápolyi kaland** (I Békeffy, Vadnai) Fővárosi Operettszínház 10 November

1935 **Tonton** (Barde) Théâtre des Nouveautés, Paris 19 March

1936 **La Poule** (w Henri Christiné/Henri Duvernois/ad Barde) Théâtre des Nouveautés, Paris 9 January

1958 **Három tavasz** (Dezső Kellér) Fővárosi Operettszínház 19 December

LALOR, Frank [T] (b Washington, DC, 20 August 1869; d New York, 15 October 1932).

Comedian Lalor made his first stage appearances as a child in variety and played for a number of years as half of the double act ''Dunn and Lalor'' before beginning a long and ultimately prominent career in musical comedy in the Wolford Comedians' collapsible farce comedy *Our Strategists* (1891, Terence O'Flam). He was first seen on Broadway in the Rays' farce comedy *A Hot Old Time* (1897, Jack Treadwell), and more prominently in *The Show Girl* (1902, Dionysius Fly), as Bliffkins in *An English Daisy* (1904), and as Shamus O'Scoot in *Mr Wix of Wickham* (1904). He appeared in Boston and on the road in E E Rice's remake of *Mr Wix* as *The Merry Shop Girls* (1905), played in vaudeville houses in *The Athletic Girl* (1905, Captain O'Shiver), took the role of Bunny Hare in Chicago's *The Filibuster* (1905) and again on Broadway when it was renamed *The Press Agent* (1905), and went on the road in *Comin' Thru the Rye* (1906, Nott), and Karl Hoschna's early *Prince Humbug.* In his forties, he played in such pieces as *The Candy Shop* (1909, Saul Wright) and the *The Bachelor Belles* (1910, Tom Jones) before making a big success as the comical-satirical ''Donny'' Dondidier, in Ivan Caryll's hit musical *The Pink Lady* (1911, ''I Like It!,'' ''Donny Didn't, Donny Did''), a part which he repeated on the London stage (1912).

A series of good comic roles followed this success, as Lalor appeared in the short-lived but admired-by-some *Iole* (1913, Clarence Guildford), as the philandering professor of Caryll's *Papa's Darling* (1914, Achille Petipas), in the revusical Gaby Delys vehicle *Stop! Look! Listen!* (1915, Gideon Gay) and as the chief comic of Marc Connelly's Broadway debut show, *The Amber Express* (1916, Percival Hopkins). He featured alongside Fred Stone and Charlotte Greenwood in the Mormon musical *His Little Widows* (1917, Abijah Smith), and starred in the Chicago musical *Good Night Paul* (aka *Oh! So Happy,* 1917, Frank Hudson), but he had to return to London to find himself another real winner. In 1918 he appeared as Prosper Woodhouse (''All Line Up in a Queue'') in the long-running West End hit *The Lilac Domino,* and he remained in London to take part in the quick-flop import *Nobody's Boy* (1919, Colonel Bunting).

Lalor's last shows brought no such hits, whether in America—*The Cameo Girl* (1921, Jones), four performances of *Suzette* (1921, Tony), the botched *Phi-Phi* (Phi-Phi), *Luckee Girl* (1928, Pontavès), a brief appearance in Busby Berkeley's *The Street Singer,* Friar Tuck in a 1932 revival of *Robin Hood*—or in London, where he played, subordinate to W H Berry, as Oliver J Oosenberry in Szirmai's *The Bamboula,* and when time came to tally up it was seen that the memorable shows of his career finally totaled few, even though the leading roles had been many.

LAMY, Charles [CASTARÈDE, Charles Désiré] (b Lyon, 28 August 1857; d Orléans, 15 June 1940).

The son of Adrien Castarède, the director of Lyon's celebrated Théâtre des Célestins, and the foremost of a family of light-tenor vocalists of charm (his brother Maurice and his son Adrien followed the same path), Charles Lamy had a 40-year career in the musical theatre, at first as a sweet-voiced tenor juvenile, and later as a full-blooded comedy player of some finesse. After beginning his career in the theatre as an orchestral violinist at the Théâtre de Saint-Étienne, he made his first stage appearances at the same house, but he began his lyric career in earnest, after some studies at his local conservatoire, playing opérette in Marseille (1876–77), touring in Italy (1877–78) and playing at the Galeries Saint-Hubert in Brussels (1879) before he was engaged at the Paris Théâtre des Bouffes-Parisiens in 1880.

His first role at the Bouffes was probably his most memorable of all for, in December 1880, he created the high tenorino-cum-comedy part of the Prince Fritellini in Audran's *La Mascotte* (''Le Je ne sais quoi poétique''), but there were plenty of other fine parts to follow. Prince Olivier in Audran's next work, *Gillette de Narbonne* (1882), and the goofy Egyptian Putiphar Bey in Victor Roger's comical *Joséphine vendue par ses soeurs* (1886) were amongst his other most important creations in the first part of a career which also included roles in such further new works as *Coquelicot* (1882, Pérez), Lacome's successful *Madame Boniface* (1883, Fridolin), *La Dormeuse éveillée* (1883, Saturnin), Serpette's *La Gamine de Paris* (1887, Hercule), Lecocq's *Les Grenadiers de Mont-Cornette* (1887, Canut), Pugno's *Sosie* (1887, Neradi/Ravaja), the vaudeville *Le Microbe* (1887, Petrewski), Audran's *Miette* (1888) and *La Gardeuse d'oies* (1888), Pugno's *Le Valet de Coeur* (1888), the military spectacle *Mam'selle Piou-Piou* (1889, Camille), Roger's *Le Fétiche* (1890, Valentin des Hauts-Crénaux), Varney's *La Fille de Fanchon la vielleuse* (1891, Jules), *La Famille Vénus* (1891) and Paul Vidal's *Eros* (1892, Fortuny). He also performed the tenor roles—Gontran in *Les Mousquetaires au couvent,* etc—in the theatre's repertoire of revivable shows.

The vocal demands grew progressively less and the comic ones more prominent as he moved on through such pieces as Pessard's *Mam'zelle Carabin* (1893, Monsieur Chose), Messager's *Madame Chrysanthème* (1893, Kangourou), Varney's *Les Forains* (1894, lion-tamer Jules César), Banès's *Le Bonhomme de neige* (1894, Fricotin), Diet's *Fleur de vertu* (1894, Casimir), *L'Élève de Conservatoire* (1894, Gedéon), *La Saint-Valentin* (1895, Bertiquet), *La Belle Épicière* (1895, Pomponneau), the winning vaudeville *La Dot de Brigitte* (1895, Mulot), Audran's successful *L'Enlèvement de la Toledad* (1895, Gaston Lombard) and the part of the secret agent in *Monsieur Lohengrin* (1896, Boussard) to what was undoubtedly the best new role of this later period of his career as the joyously silly-âne Duc Jehan de Beaugency of *Les Fêtards* (1897).

In 1897 Lamy became a member of the company at the Palais-Royal, where *Les Fêtards* was included amongst the occasional musical productions in a program of mainly comedies, but he still made intermittent forays on to other musical stages, creating memorably the part of a low-comical Paris in Claude Terrasse's *Paris, ou le bon juge* (1906, revived 1922), and latterly onto the cinema stage. He played in Terrasse's *Le Coq d'Inde* (1908), appeared in revue and, in 1920, took the role of Ischabod in the production of *Rip!* which opened the new Théâtre Mogador and in which his son, Adrien, played the small part of Pickly. He died alongside that same son, and their wives, in the German bombardement of Orléans in 1940 at the age of 83.

Adrien LAMY [Adrien Maurice Édouard CASTARÈDE] (b Paris, 17 May 1896; d Orléans, 2 July 1940), a clean-necked, boyish, light vocalist, dancer and actor, had a lively career in the Paris musical theatre of the 1920s, playing juvenile lead in the French version of *The Pink Lady,* replacing Urban in the title role of *Dédé,* and appearing in prominent juvenile parts in a full list of other popular Jazz Age musicals including the Théâtre Marigny's *Je t'veux* (1923, Vignac, ''C'est fou la place que ça tient,'' ''Si c'était pour en arriver là'' and the shimmy orientale ''Là-bas''), Szulc's *Le Petit Choc* (1923, Alfred de Marigny, ''L'Ouverture de la pêche,'' ''Il faut savoir prendre les femmes''), and Moretti's *En chemyse* (1924) and *Trois jeunes filles . . . nues!* (1925). In 1926 he was the first French Tom in *No, No, Nanette,* introducing Paris to ''Thé pour deux'' and ''J'ai confessé à la brise'' in partnership with Loulou Hégoburu, with whom he teamed again in Paris's *Tip-Toes* (Steve Burton), performing ''La Femme que j'aimais'' (a reverse-sex ''The Man I Love'') and ''Un sentiment'' (''That Certain Feeling''). He played the put-upon young hero Étienne Fanoche in *Zou!* (1930), appeared in Moretti's *Rosy* (1930) and was Orphée to the Eurydice of Marise Beaujon in the Mogador's starry 1931 revival of *Orphée aux enfers.* In the subsequent 1930s he appeared in the Parisian-Hungarian *Katinka* (1933, ''En écoutant les petits oiseaux'' w Lyne Clevers), as Frontignac in the Josephine Baker *La Créole* (1934) and in such productions as *Les Soeurs Hortensia* (1934, film version 1936), *Un p'tit bout de femme* (1936) and *Les Jolies Viennoises* (1938).

Maurice LAMY [Maurice CASTARDÈDE] (b Lyon, ?1863; d April 1930) created two major musical comedy roles—the bedazzled shopboy Aristide in Messager's *Les P'tites Michu* and the comical Loustot of the same composer's *Véronique*—in a career which ran closely alongside that of his brother, Charles. He also appeared in the premieres of such pieces as *Les Pommes d'or* (1883), Lecocq's *La Belle au bois dormant* (1889, Le Taupier), the French version of *Donna Juanita* (1891), *Le Cocarde Tricolore* (1892, M Bosthonn), *Cliquette* (1893, Nicolas), Serpette's *Cousin-Cousine* (1893) and *Shakespeare!* (1899, Jack), *Sa Majesté l'amour* (1897, Tricala), *La Petite Tache* (1898, La Bûche), Pessard's *La Dame de trèfle* (1898, Roger), *La Fille de Paillasse* (1894, Joséphin), *La Demoiselle aux caméllias* (1899, Octave) and *La Fille de la mère Michel* (1903, Quatrebard). He also played des Toupettes in the 1897 revival of *Les Douze Femmes des Japhet.* He later appeared in supporting roles in several of Louis Ganne's works including *Hans, le joueur de flûte* (Petronius) and *Rhodope* at Monte-Carlo, where he was, from 1913 director of the Casino, in *Cocorico* (Margrave Jean-François) and in Banès's *Léda* (1909, Ménélas) and, in his sixties, took a four-line role as Le Directeur du Casino in Hahn's *Le Temps d'aimer* (1926).

Plate 211. *East fails to meet West for longer than two acts. Gunter Neubert as Sou Chong and Gail Steiner as Lisa in a Nuremberg Städtische Bühnen production of* **Das Land des Lächelns.**

DAS LAND DES LÄCHELNS Romantic Operette in 3 acts by Ludwig Herzer and Fritz Löhner-Beda based on the libretto *Die gelbe Jacke* by Victor Léon. Music by Franz Lehár. Metropoltheater, Berlin, 10 October 1929.

Die gelbe Jacke, written from a libretto by Léon—the partner of Lehár's earliest success, *Der Rastelbinder* (1902), and of his greatest triumph, *Die lustige Witwe* (1905)—and produced by Karczag at the Theater an der Wien in 1923 (9 February), was another version of the East-has-difficulty-meeting-West theme so popular in such turn-of-the-century works as *The Geisha.* Hubert Marischka appeared as the Chinese Prince Sou Chong Chwang whose marriage to the Viennese Lea von Limburger (Betty Fischer) threatens to founder when she cannot cope with oriental customs. Luise Kartousch as his sister, Mi, was paired with Josef König (Claudius von Wimpach) in a parallel soubret story.

Die gelbe Jacke won some appreciative comments for its attractive mixture of Chinese and Viennese tones (one critic apparently nicknamed it *Monsieur Butterfly*) and it proved a tidy, unspectacular success, running for three months and 98 performances at the Theater an der Wien. Just before its closure there, it was produced at Budapest's Király Színház (*A sárga kabát* 5 May 1923) with Tivadar Uray, Erszi Péchy, Árpád Latabár, Márton Rátkai and Hanna Honthy starred. It was not a success, however, to compare with the previous year's *Frasquita* or with the Theater an der Wien's other recent Operetten, *Der letzte Walzer, Die Frau im Hermelin* or Lehár's own *Die blaue Mazur* and *Wo die Lerche singt,* and it was positively overshadowed in the two following seasons by the huge successes of *Gräfin Mariza* and *Der Orlow,* all of which may help to explain why the myth has developed that *Die gelbe Jacke* was a thorough failure. It wasn't. It just wasn't a big hit.

When Lehár moved soon after into his tenor-dominated Tauber era of writing, *Die gelbe Jacke* was given a second chance. Tauber's greatest successes of the 1920s had been in Berlin, and the Rotter brothers of the Berlin Metropoltheater, who had hosted the tenor's successes in *Paganini* and *Friederike,* asked the composer for another Tauber vehicle. Never loath to reuse the scores of his less enduring shows, Lehár had already produced a second version of *Wiener Frauen* and third versions of *Der Göttergatte* and *Der Sterngucker,* and now, to follow his successes with the lushly sentimental *Paganini, Der Zarewitsch* and *Friederike,* he decided on a romantic tenor remake of the tale of either *Endlich allein*'s mountaineering prince or of *Die gelbe Jacke*'s Chinese one. It was the Chinaman who ultimately got the nod, but instead of returning the original libretto to Léon to be Tauberized, Lehár instead handed the seven-year-old work to Ludwig Herzer and Fritz Löhner, the librettists of *Friederike,* for a rewrite. He himself revamped part of his score, principally to turn the role of the Prince into the kind of all-singing, all-emoting Tauber-Rolle which the success of the singer's previous Operetten had made a sine qua non.

The most obvious alteration to the *Die gelbe Jacke* book was the exchange of Léon's original reconciliatory ending for the now obligatory and fashionably unhappy one, in line with the bruised-to-brokenhearted final curtains featured in the three last Operetten. The most obvious change in the score was a large new number for the star, written in the ringing style of *Paganini*'s "Gern hab' ich die Frau'n geküsst" or *Friederike*'s "O Mädchen, mein Mädchen." "Dein ist mein ganzes Herz" was to turn out to be the most successful of all Lehár's throbbingly romantic songs for Tauber.

In *Das Land des Lächelns* (the title was already an improvement), the impassive Prince Sou Chong (Tauber) weds Viennese Lisa (Vera Schwarz) and takes her back to his homeland. There she discovers that the Prince is expected by custom to take Chinese brides as well. He is unable to defy the traditions of his country and she, in spite of her love for him, cannot bend to them. Aided by Sou Chong's sister, Mi (Hella Kürty), a trapped little soubrette who longs for a taste of the freedom that she sees Western women have, and by her Viennese friend Graf Gustl von Pottenstein (Willi Stettner), she plans an escape. When the Prince catches the fleeing foreigners he realizes that it is better to let Lisa go. Brokenhearted but impassive, he remains to rule his country.

Although the applause-tugger of Tauber's role was the new song, the part of Sou Chong contained some less obvious but more beautiful pieces, notably his two first-act songs, the philosophical "Immer nur lächeln" and the gentle love song "Von Apfelblüten einen Kranz," as well as some ringingly dramatic moments in the long and two-handed second-act finale which the tenor shares with the soprano. The prima donna, too, had many fine moments, ranging from her lighthearted first-act entry song and the tiptoeing duet "Bei einem Tee à deux" to the romantic duet "Wer hat die Liebe," but it was the powerful light-operatic "Ich möcht wieder einmal die Heimat seh'n," in which Lisa pours out her longing for her homeland in tones which have nothing to do with the usual Do-you-remember-Vienna type of song, which was her great moment and is, in spite of all the tenorizing propaganda to the contrary, arguably the musical highlight of the score. The soubrette role of Mi was equally well parted, the little princess's shy longing for Western freedom, expressed trippingly in the song "Im Salon zur blau'n Pagoda," and her gently comical duos with Gustl ("Meine Liebe, deine Liebe," "Zig, zig, zig") contrasting breath-catchingly with the powerful emotions and big singing of the other two principals.

The Berlin premiere of *Das Land des Lächelns* was an outstanding success, the hit song quickly became a mega-favorite, and productions of the show flourished throughout Germany in the years that followed, with Tauber guesting as the star in several of the main centers. Hungary, as usual, was first off the mark with a foreign production, opening *A mosoly országa* at Budapest Operaház with Ferenc Székeleyhidy (Szu Csong), Margit Nagy (Liza), Júlia Orosz (Mi) and Lajos Laurisin (Feri Hatfaludy), just a few days before the Theater an der Wien premiered their Viennese production, with Tauber again starring opposite Vera Schwarz and Hella Kürty again as Mi. The two original stars did not stay long with this production, and Margit Suchy and Otto Maran soon succeeded to their roles, whilst Luise Kartousch, the original Mi of *Die gelbe Jacke,* took up the new version of her old part during the 101 performances that Vienna's version played. The production was reprised for a fortnight the following year, but, in spite of this limited first Viennese run, *Das Land des Lächelns* established itself as a repertoire favorite in Austria just as it did in Hungary.

Paris was once again beaten to the nod by the Belgians who produced the first *Le Pays du sourire* (ad André Mauprey, Jean Marietti) at Ghent (Théâtre Royale 1 April 1932) with Louis Izar and Germaine Roumans in the leading roles, but the French production, mounted six months later, with Willy Theunis and Georgette Simon starred, was a prodigious success, securing *Le Pays du sourire* a prominent place in the permanent repertoire of the French musical theatre where it has remained, through regular revivals, ever since.

In spite of its success in Europe, however, the Operette did not catch on in Britain or in America. Tauber himself introduced his show to London's Theatre Royal, Drury Lane, with Renée Bullard as his Lisa and Hella Kürty again as Mi, but *The Land of Smiles* (ad Harry Graham) failed to appeal. It was not simply Tauber's well-publicized absences from the cast that deterred British audiences of the dawning 1930s from patronizing the show, it was rather that their pleasure was found in the then-popular dance-and-laughter musicals and their taste at the time did not run to a Very Big Romantic Operette. The show closed after 71 underfilled performances. Tauber repeated his Sou Chong in London in 1932 (Dominion Theatre 31 May) and again 10 years later (Lyric Theatre 18 June 1942), each time paired with Josie Fearon and Miss Kürty, but the show never won a London run. In 1959 it was produced by the Sadlers Wells Opera Company (w Charles Craig, Elizabeth Fretwell, June Bronhill, ad Christopher Hassall) but it did not remain in their repertoire.

In America, Graham's version was further adapted (ad Harry B Smith, Edgar Smith, Harry Clarke) and the resultant piece produced as *Prince Chu Chang* with Clifford Newdahl and Gladys Baxter starring in a hideously bowdlerized tale in which the Prince and Lisa did not actually get married in Act I at all, and she ended up finding consolation in the arms of Gustl. It folded on the road. It was only after a St Louis Muny production and a second prematurely folding stab at a Broadway version (26 December 1932, w Charles Hackett, Nancy McCord) that the Shuberts finally got yet another adaptation (ad Ira Cobb, Karl Farkas, Felix Günther) of the show to Broadway in 1946 under the title *Yours Is My Heart.* Sixteen years on, Tauber again starred, alongside Stella Andreva and Lillian Held (equipped with a Paul Durant interpolation explaining for reasons unexplained that ''Paris Sings Again''), but yet again an English-language version of *Das Land des Lächelns* failed.

Tauber put his *Das Land des Lächelns* on film soon after the show had been produced, and in 1952 another version (scr: Axel Eggebrecht, Hubert Marischka), with the music adapted by Alois Melichar, was produced with Jan Kiepura and Marta Eggerth starring. Prince Sou became a singer (!) who falls in love with his Lissy over a duet and the pair produce a little Chrysanthemum on their way to their unhappy ending. Ludwig Schmitz featured as Chief Eunuch Kato. A third film, with René Kollo and Birgit Pitsch-Sarata featured, was issued in 1973.

Das Land des Lächelns remains a prominent fixture in the repertoire in Germany and in Austria, where it was played at the Staatsoper in 1938 (again with Tauber) and from 1985 at the Volksoper, where Siegfried Jerusalem and Nicolai Gedda have both appeared at various times as Sou Chong. The newest production, in 1996 (28 September), featured Johan Botha and Silvana Dussmann. It also holds a continuing place both in France and in Hungary (ad Zsolt Harsányi), where it was remounted a recently as 1998 at the Budapesti Operett Színház (26 June). However, in spite of regular exposure through recordings and broadcasting, and the wide popularity of its tenor bonbon, *The Land of Smiles* remains generally unplayed in English-language countries.

Hungary: Magyar Királyi Operaház *A mosoly országa* 20 September 1930; Austria: Theater an der Wien 26 September 1930; UK: Theatre Royal, Drury Lane *The Land of Smiles* 8 May 1931; France: Théâtre de la Gaîté-Lyrique *Le Pays du sourire* 15 November 1932; USA: Shubert Theater *Yours Is My Heart* 5 September 1946

Films: Max Reichmann 1931, Berolina/Union Films 1952, Arthur Maria Rabelnalt 1973

Recordings: complete (Columbia, EMI, Eurodisc), complete in French (EMI, De Plein Vent), selections (Philips, Polydor, EMI, Preiser, Telefunken etc), selection in Hungarian (Qualiton), selection in English (HMV, Telarc), selections in French (Decca, Philips), selection in Italian (Fonit-Cetra), selection in Czech (Supraphon)

LANDESBERG, Alexander (b Grosswardein, 15 July 1848; d Vienna, 14 June 1916).

At first a journalist in Budapest and then in Vienna, Landesberg was also for some 20 years a librettist and lyricist mostly for the Viennese stage. He had his one great success with the text for Heinrich Reinhardt's Operette *Das süsse Mädel,* a long-running Carltheater hit in 1901 prior to productions around the world, but never approached the record established by *Das süsse Mädel* with his other works. Amongst these, several collaborations with Eugen von Taund brought forth two reasonably successful pieces in *Der Wunderknabe* (later seen in Britain as *The Little Genius*) and *Die Lachtaube,* which was exported to Berlin (Theater Unter den Linden 10 August 1895) after its 51-performance Viennese run, whilst a version of the French comedy *Nelly Rosier,* entitled *Fräulein Präsident* and composed by Alfred Müller-Norden, went on from its 25 nights in Vienna to be seen in Budapest as *Elnők kisasszony* (ad Károly Stoll, Fővárosi Nyári Színház 20 July 1900).

He had a number of works produced at the Theater an der Wien where his *Die Blumen-Mary* played 40 nights, *Der Lebemann* was seen 31 times, Reinhardt's *Der Generalkonsul* with Girardi in its starring role reached its 78th night before going on to Budapest as *A főkonsul, Das Garnisonsmädel* (*Huszárvér* in Hungary) played 53 performances consecutively, and *Der schöne Gardist* lasted just a month prior to its Hungarian production (*Szép gárdista*). *Clo-Clo,* with Fritzi Massary in the title role, also played a month at Danzers Orpheum, whilst a further Reinhardt work, *Der liebe Schatz,* played 45 nights at the Carltheater, the best run of three latter-day Landesberg Operetten produced there.

1886 **Fioretta** (Max von Weinzierl, Alfred Strasser) Deutsches Theater, Prague 3 April

1889 **Das Familie Wasserkopf** (Julius Stern/w D Schild) Carltheater 24 March

1889 **Page Fritz** (von Weinzierl, Strasser/w Richard Genée) Deutsches Theater, Prague 24 November; Friedrich-Wilhelmstädtisches Theater, Berlin July 1891

1889 **Das Paradies** (Adolphe Ferron/w Leo Sendach) Brünn 21 May

1893 **Münchener Kind'l** (Carl Weinberger/w Leo Stein) Theater Unter den Linden, Berlin 7 November

1895 **Die Lachtaube** (Eugen von Taund/w Stein as "Otto Rehberg") Carltheater 14 April

1896 **Im Pavilion** (Karl Kappeller/Blum, Toché ad w Ludwig Fischl) Theater in der Josefstadt 6 March

1896 **Der Wunderknabe** (von Taund/w Stein) Theater an der Wien 28 March

1897 **Das rothe Parapluie** (*Le Voyage de Corbillon*) German version w Fischl w music by Kappeller Theater in der Josefstadt 27 February

1897 **Der Prokurist** (von Weinzierl/w Leo Gerhard) Raimundtheater 25 September

1897 **Die Blumen-Mary** (Carl Weinberger/w Stein) Theater an der Wien 11 November

1898 **Der Dreibund** (von Taund/w Stein) Theater an der Wien 28 April

1899 **Fräulein Präsident** (Alfred Müller-Norden/w Fischl) Theater an der Wien 6 May

1901 **Die Primadonna** (Müller-Norden/ad w Fischl) Carltheater 31 January

1901 **Das süsse Mädel** (Heinrich Reinhardt/w Stein) Carltheater 25 October

1902 **Der liebe Schatz** (Reinhardt/w Stein) Carltheater 30 October

1902 **Clo-Clo** (Ferdinand Pagin/w Stein) Danzers Orpheum 23 December

1903 **Der Lebemann** (Alfred Grünfeld/Josef Stolba ad w Fischl) Theater an der Wien 16 January

1904 **Der Generalkonsul** (Reinhardt/w Stein) Theater an der Wien 29 January

1904 **Das Garnisonsmädel** (Raoul Mader/w Stein) Theater an der Wien 29 October

1907 **Der selige Vincenz** (Mader/w Stein) Carltheater 31 January

1907 **Der schöne Gardist** (Heinrich Berté/w E Limé, A M Willner) Neues Operetten-Theater, Breslau 12 October; Theater an der Wien 4 April 1908

1908 **Der Glücksnarr** (Berté/E Limé ad w Willner) Carltheater 7 November

THE LAND OF NOD Musical comedy in 2 acts by Frank R Adams and Will Hough. Music by Joe Howard. Additional material by George V Hobart and Victor Herbert. Opera House, Chicago, 17 June 1905; New York Theater, New York, 1 April 1907.

A children's extravaganza on the accepted large-scenery model of the period, *The Land of Nod* was first produced by the Majestic Extravaganza Company in Chicago, where authors Hough, Adams and Howard had already combined to produce a long line of highly successful shows. It was named after a song from their earlier hit, *His Highness, the Bey.* Too big a piece for the little La Salle Theater, it was shifted instead to the Chicago Opera House where Mabel Barrison, the original babe heroine of *Babes in Toyland,* and wife to composer Howard, appeared as little Bonnie who goes to sleep and dreams herself into a series of lavishly staged adventures in the land of Nod—much in the same way that little Dorothy had got herself into her adventures in Oz a few seasons earlier, and that Miss Barrison and her fellow babe had more recently traveled through Toyland. May de Sousa (Jack of Hearts) was the jeune premier of the evening, Juliet Wood was soubrette Rory Bory Alice and the main credit for the evening's visuals went to designer Ansel Cook.

Two years after its first Chicago production, *The Land of Nod* was taken up by the Will J Block Company and, suitably revamped by George Hobart (add songs Josh Hart), it was produced in New York. The baddie of the piece, the Sandman, out to steal the hearts from the pack of cards, was played by William Burress, the goodies were Miss Barrison as little Bonnie and Helen Bertram as her beloved Jack of Hearts, and the outcome, of course, was a picturesque and happy ending. Composer Howard appeared as the Moon, originally played in Chicago by Miss Barrison's *Babes in Toyland* partner, William Norris. To add a little more adult interest to the show, the producers squeezed a scena which Hobart and Victor Herbert had written for performance at the Lamb's Club into the loose fabric of the show. *The Song Birds* was a topical operatic burlesque which made fun of the current rivalry between operatic producers Oscar Hammerstein of the Manhattan Opera House and Hans Conried of the Metropolitan.

Like most Chicago products, *The Land of Nod* did not find itself a run on Broadway, but this time it was not public indifference which did the show down. *The Land of Nod* was closed after 17 performances when a fire struck the New York Theater. The show, however, did not go wholly under. A decade on from its first staging,

Australia's William Anderson put out a version in Melbourne. Although the American authors still got billing, and much of their work was still on view, the Australian *Land of Nod* was played at the pantomime season and additions and alterations accrued accordingly. Anna McNab was Bonnie, Tom Cannan the Sandman, Maudie Chetwynd made a hit as Rory Bory Alice, Tom Armstrong was the Man in the Moon, and such established hits of the period as ''You Made Me Love You,'' ''M.I.S.S.I.S.S.I.P.P.I.'' and ''Same Old Moon'' were performed alongside ''Australia Calls'' and ''Mine's Australia'' through a fine 70 Christmas-season performances, followed by a six-week season at Sydney's Palace Theatre (28 February 1914).

The title *The Land of Nod* was used in Britain for an 1897 musical written by and as a vehicle for popular singer Albert Chevalier. The score was provided by his accompanist Alfred H West. After touring for 29 weeks, it was brought to the West End's Royalty Theatre (24 September 1898) where it collapsed in six performances at a loss of £2,500.

Australia: King's Theatre, Melbourne 20 December 1913

DIE LANDSTREICHER Operette in 2 acts and a Vorspiel by Leopold Krenn and Carl Lindau. Music by Carl Michael Ziehrer. Venedig in Wien, Vienna, 29 July 1899.

When the tramps August (Anton Matscheg) and Bertha (Frln Augustin) Fliederbusch are arrested on suspicion of theft, they escape from the police station disguised in the overcoats of Count Adolar Gilka (Karl Tuschl) and the dancer, Mimi (Frln Dorn), who have come there to report a jewel robbery. In fact, Mimi's jewels have been found by August and Bertha and they would be more than happy, if they were permitted, to return them and win the 5,000-mark reward offered. But the problem is that the canny Count had intended that Mimi should have only paste copies. However, before he can stop it, August has given the dancer the real jewels and Gilka has to hire him to steal them back again. In the midst of a masked ball, the clever pair effect the exchange only to find, in the end, that the second set of jewels is as phony as the first!

Ziehrer's score to Krenn and Lindau's crook musical was one of his most successful. The first-act closer, the waltzing tenor solo ''Sei gepriesen du lauschige Nacht,'' sung by Roland (Sigmund Steiner), the official responsible for the escape of the two Landstreicher but also the piece's love interest, as a ''number'' in the incidental celebration around a rustic golden wedding, proved the success of the evening and became a half-million seller. A march-duet for two extravagant soldiers (Anna Bachler, Ludmilla Gaston) ''Das Leutnant Rudi Muggenhain und Fähnrich Mucki Rodenstein . . . ,'' describing ''Der Zauber der Montur''—the magic of a uniform—in attracting girls, turned out to be the other take-away hit of the evening whilst a cancan duet for the Count and Mimi (''Wie war entzückt ich neulich''), another march (''Ich komme von Marokko'') performed by the tramps and the count, all disguised in the same Arab outfit for their tricks at the ball, a Spanisches Lied for Mimi, Roland's love song ''Mein herzliche Bua'' and a comical trio for Mimi and the two officers (''Der Soldat muss stets marschieren'') all contributed tunefully to the success of the piece.

Die Landstreicher was first produced on the stage of the Englisher Garten ''Venedig in Wien,'' Gabor Steiner's outdoor summer theatre in the Prater which operated during the main theatres' closed season, and it was mounted by its producer with considerable spectacle, including a ballet of two hundred which performed ''grosse militärische Evolutionen'' staged by choreographer Louis Gundlach in the styles of 10 countries (topped by Austria) in the second act. It turned out to be the most successful among a number of durable pieces which librettists Carl Lindau and Leopold Krenn, who were by way of being house writers to Steiner's enterprise, turned out during the manager's years of activities in Vienna. Following its summer season in 1899 it was repeated in the Prater in 1900 and was played the next year at Steiner's winter house, Danzers Orpheum (8 February 1901), before being given for nine performances at the Theater an der Wien (26 March 1902). It was later played at the Raimundtheater (w Franz Glawatsch, Gerda Walde) in 1909, in 1920 at the Bürgertheater (12 October, w Josef Viktora, Rosa Koppler, Emmy Stein, Richard Waldemar) and as recently as 1980 at the Raimundtheater.

In Germany, following productions at the Friedrich-Wilhelmstädtisches Theater and the Luisen-Theater (2 May 1902), *Die Landstreicher* became far and away the most popular of Ziehrer's works, and it has been produced regularly throughout the country through the century since its creation, most recently in a rearranged version (ad Hans Fretzer, Herbert Mogg Staatsoperette, Dresden 8 March 1985), whilst in Hungary (ad Aurél Föld, Adolf Mérei), after beginning its career at the Városligeti Színkör, it moved on to the Magyar Színház and then to other theatres with equal popularity.

In America, the story of *Die Landstreicher* was retained as the libretto for the musical comedy *The Strollers* (ad H B Smith, Knickerbocker Theater 24 June 1901), a George Lederer vehicle put together for comedian Francis Wilson, but in a fashion of the time which undoubtedly had something to do with finances, Ziehrer's score was replaced by a new one by Ludwig Englander. Wilson sang an English coon song (''Little Daffy Pipedreams'') burlesquing Leslie Stuart's ''Little Dolly Daydream''

Plate 212. **Die Landstreicher.** *August (Heinz Zimmer) and Bertha (Helga Schulze Margarf) Fliederbusch make their hurried escape from the police (Mario Dehne) in the Dresden Staatsoperette's production.*

and annexed a larger part of the now shorter score (''Song of the Strollers,'' ''When the Orchestra Plays''). Roland (Harry Fairleigh), who had descended to being a bass, had to be content with a waltz ''Song of Loretta'' which did not compensate for his lost hit. Irene Bentley gave ''A Lesson in Flirtation'' as Bertha, Marie George was the dancer and one Edwin Foy had a supporting role as a comedy jailor (developed from Franz Glawatsch's part of Kampel in the original script). A piece called ''The Kaiser's Bold Hussars'' supplied a more Ziehrer-ish and Continental flavor, elsewhere submerged, which recalled the show's origins. *The Strollers* had a reasonable Broadway run of 70 nights without ever looking like equaling the success of *Die Landstreicher* before Wilson, and later Marguerite Sylva and George C Boniface jr, took it to the rest of the country.

A film version was made in Germany in 1937 with Paul Hörbiger, Lucie Englisch and Erika Drusovich featured.

Hungary: Városligeti Színkör *A svihákok* 19 July 1901; Germany: Friedrich-Wilhelmstädtisches Theater 21 September 1901

Film: Carl Lamac 1937

LANE, Burton [LEVY, Burton] (b New York, 2 February 1912; d New York, 5 January 1997). Film songwriter whose handful of ventures on to the stage produced a bundle of popular numbers.

Lane joined the Remick music-publishing company as a staff pianist and writer at an early age, and he published his first songs at the age of 19. In the early 1930s he provided material for several revues (*Three's a Crowd, Earl Carroll's Vanities of 1931, The Third Little Show, Americana*), a couple of musicals—the flop *Singin' the Blues,* and the Shubert remake of the British show *Dear Love* as the revusical *Artists and Models* (w Sam Lerner)—and to films, scoring an early success with ''Everything I Have Is Yours'' (ly: Harold Adamson) in *Dancing Lady* (1933). For more than 20 years supplied music and songs to such Hollywood screenplays as *Swing High, Swing Low* (title song for Dorothy Lamour, w Ralph Freed), *Some Like It Hot* (1939, ''The Lady's in Love with You,'' w Frank Loesser), *Babes on Broadway* (1941, ''How About You?,'' w Freed), *Wedding Bells* (US: *Royal Wedding* 1951, ''Too Late Now,'' ''How Could You Believe Me When I Said I Loved You When You Know I've Been a Liar All My Life,'' w Alan Jay Lerner for Fred Astaire and Jane Powell), *College Swing,* and *Dancing on a Dime* (''I Hear Music,'' w Loesser) as well as contibuting occasional numbers to filmed musicals (''Madam, I Love Your Crêpe Suzette'' w Ralph Freed, Lew Brown in *Dubarry Was a Lady*; ''Salomé'').

Lane's first major stage venture was *Hold on to Your Hats,* a vehicle for the aging Al Jolson who was returning to Broadway after a 10-year absence. His score (''There's a Great Day Coming,'' ''Don't Let It Get You Down,'' ''Walkin' Along Mindin' My Business'') was, however, peppered with Jolson standards as desperation set in and the show ran only for 158 fairly unsatisfactory performances. The composer had a slightly happier time with Olsen and Johnson's revue *Laffing Room Only* (''Feudin' and Fightin'''), and then won a considerable Broadway success with his next book musical, *Finian's Rainbow.* Although the show subsequently failed in productions outside America, it won a long initial run in New York and considerable popularity at home and its score produced a solid phalanx of Lane's most popular songs (''How Are Things in Glocca Morra?,'' ''Old Devil Moon,'' ''Look to the Rainbow,'' ''When I'm Not Near the Girl I Love,'' ''If This Isn't Love'').

It was nearly two decades before Broadway heard another Lane musical comedy score. *On a Clear Day You Can See Forever* had a respectable if unprofitable New York run and, like *Finian's Rainbow,* was made into a film, but it won out mainly by the enduring nature of its principal songs (''Come Back to Me,'' ''On a Clear Day You Can See Forever''). Lane returned only once more to Broadway, as the composer of *Carmelina* (1979), a musical version of the screenplay *Buona Sera Mrs Campbell.* It had a very short run, but it also threw up several attractive songs (''Someone in April,'' ''One More Walk Around the Garden'') which, nevertheless, did not outlive their show or travel as the best numbers from his two principal stage shows had done.

1940 **Hold on to Your Hats** (E Y Harburg/Guy Bolton, Matt Brooks, Eddie Davis) Shubert Theater 11 September

1947 **Finian's Rainbow** (Harburg/Fred Saidy) 46th Street Theater 10 January

1965 **On a Clear Day You Can See Forever** (Alan Jay Lerner) Mark Hellinger Theater 17 October

1979 **Carmelina** (Lerner/Joseph Stein) St James Theater 8 April

LANE, Lupino [LUPINO, Henry William George] (b Hackney, London, 16 June 1892; d London, 10 November 1959).

Born into a famous family of dancers and acrobats, ''Harry'' Lane was trained in the family business from early childhood and appeared on the stage from the age of 11 in music hall and variety, performing at first under the name of ''Master Harry'' or ''Nipper'' Lane. In 1907 he was featured at the Hippodrome in a song and dance (''he brings down the house'') in the musical scena *Zuyder Zee* (Peterkin). He came to the theatre by way of revue at the beginning of the dancing-craze years, appearing in *Watch Your Step, Follow the Crowd, We're All in It* and *Extra Special,* before tasting first the straight stage and then the musical. He was first seen in a book musical under the management of C B Cochran, when he played the role of Coucourli alongside Alice Delysia in the London version of *Afgar* (1919), and he journeyed to America with the French star to repeat his part briefly on Broadway the following year.

After several further years in revue on both sides of the Atlantic (*League of Notions, Brighter London, Ziegfeld Follies of 1924*), he returned to the musical stage as an acrobatic and unconventional Ko-Ko in a New York revival of *The Mikado* and in Willie Edouin's famously extravagant role of George Medway in a British musical version of the farce *Turned Up* (1926). He subsequently took leading comic parts in London's version of *Der Orlow* (*Hearts and Diamonds,* Jefferson), in the Dominion Theatre's spectacular operetta *Silver Wings* (1930, Jerry Wimpole), in the London version of Broadway's *Smiles,* played under the title *The One Girl* (1932, Freddy Stone), and in the London Coliseum Schumann pasticcio *The Golden Toy* (1934, the Barber) before going into management himself to present a racing farce with songs called *Twenty to One.*

Lane starred in *Twenty to One* as a cheeky little bowler-hatted chappie called Bill Snibson and he scored a fine success, first on the road and then—with the show slimmed and recast—at London's Victoria Palace where the show, mounted as a Christmas attraction, ultimately ran for six months. Lane then took his musical on the road, and when it was done he started back towards the West End with a soi-disant ''sequel'' (actually, the only continuing feature was the name of Lane's character) called *Me and My Girl.* A major wartime hit, in which its star introduced ''The Lambeth Walk'' and the title song, *Me and My Girl* provided Lane with a considerable fortune and with a vehicle to which he would return time and again in the remainder of his career. For the next 10 years he and his company (including a good number of his family) occupied the Victoria Palace through a revival of *Twenty to One, La-di-da-di-da, Meet Me Victoria* and *Sweetheart Mine* in which, after being called ''Bill'' in all the other shows Lane finally became ''Harry.''

The line of shows ended in 1947, and Lane's fortunes turned expensively sour when he bought the old, war-damaged Gaiety Theatre for the huge sum of £200,000, with a dream of restoring it to its Edwardesian splendor. The Gaiety drank up his money greedily, but it never reopened and was ultimately put down by the London city council. Lane rarely appeared on the stage thereafter. He was seen in pantomime and the odd play and occasionally as Bill Snibson in revivals of *Me and My Girl* before he died, whilst still in his sixties.

Parallel to his stage career, Lane ran another in films. Having made early silents as a young man, he subsequently appeared in such British stage musicals-turned-movies as *The Lady of the Rose, The Yellow Mask* (Sam Slipper) and *The Lambeth Walk* (ie, *Me and My Girl,* Bill Snibson), and he also visited Hollywood, where he was seen in a number of non-musical films and, with Maurice Chevalier and Jeanette MacDonald, in *The Love Parade.* In Britain he directed several early sound movie musicals, including *Love Lies* and *The Maid of the Mountains* and the non-musical version of the stage musical *The Love Race.*

Lane's wife, **Violet BLYTHE** (née BLYTH), at first a buxom showgirl in Robert Courtneidge's shows (*The Pearl Girl, The Cinema Star*) and later a supporting principal at the Adelphi (*High Jinks, Who's Hooper?*), appeared with her husband in *Afgar* in America (Musauda) and in small, usually imposing and/or aristocratic roles in the series of shows at the Victoria Palace. His brother, **Wallace [Arthur] LUPINO** (b Newington, Edinburgh 23 January 1897; d Middlesex, 11 October 1961), who played for many years in pantomime, concert party and musical comedy, created the role of Parchester (''The Family Solicitor'') in *Me and my Girl* (1937) and took supporting roles in the other Lupino Lane musicals at the Victoria Palace. Lupino Lane's son **Lauri Lupino LANE** [Lauri Henry LUPINO] (b St Giles, London, 26 July 1921; d Fulham, London, 4 June 1986), also a performer, began as a child at the Victoria Palace and appeared in his father's role in later revivals of *Me and My Girl.*

1944 **Meet Me Victoria** (Noel Gay/Frank Eyton/w Lauri Wylie) Victoria Palace 8 April

1946 **Sweetheart Mine** (Gay/Eyton/Albert Chevalier, Arthur Shirley ad w Eyton) Victoria Palace 1 August

Biography: Dillon White, J: *Born to Star* (Heinemann, London, 1957)

LANG, Harold [Richard] (b Daly City, Calif, 21 December 1923; d Cairo, Egypt, 16 November 1975). Dancing actor who created one important role and re-created another to great effect.

Lang worked as a dancer with the Ballets Russes de Monte-Carlo and the American Ballet Theater before his first appearances in Broadway musicals in *Mr Strauss Goes to Boston* (1945) and *Look Ma, I'm Dancin'* (1946). In 1948 he had his one major new role when he created the part of the trouble-making dancer Bill Calhoun in *Kiss Me, Kate* and he then teamed with Helen Gallagher as the number-two pair (with dances) in the less successful *Make a Wish* (1951), before taking the title role in the revival of *Pal Joey* (1952), which established this show as a fashionably unfrilly item in the standard repertoire. He appeared subsequently in *Shangri-La* (1956), as Gabey in a 1959 revival of *On the Town,* and as garment salesman Teddy Asch in *I Can Get It for You Wholesale* (1962).

LANGFORD, Bonnie [LANGFORD, Bonita] (b London, 22 July 1964). Child star become musical-comedy leading lady.

Bonnie Langford made her first appearance on the musical stage creating the role of the child, Bonnie, in the musical version of *Gone with the Wind* (1972) at the Theatre Royal, Drury Lane. She subsequently appeared as a very noticeable Baby June in London's edition of *Gypsy* and went on to play the same role in South Africa, on Broadway, and around America. After a number of years working largely in television (notably, in a memorable portrayal of the appalling Violet Elizabeth Bott in the *Just William* series) and attending school, she returned to the musical stage to create the cat-burgling Rumpleteazer (''Mungojerry and Rumpleteazer'') in *Cats* (1981), to play Kate in the Drury Lane revival of *The Pirates of Penzance* (1982), to feature in the title role of London's version of the musical-comedy *Peter Pan* (1985) and to succeed to the role of Sally Smith in *Me and My Girl* (1988).

She was also seen around Britain as *Peter Pan,* as Mabel in three tours of *The Pirates of Penzance* (1985, 1989, 1993, and a season at the London Palladium in 1990), in the title role of the revived *Charlie Girl* (1987), as Peggy Sawyer in *42nd Street* (1991) and in *Oklahoma!* (1994, Ado Annie) before returning to the West End in 1997 as an actor-manager, playing Charity in a revival of *Sweet Charity.*

In a career which has included every kind of entertainment from variety and pantomime to drama, radio and television hosting and a one-woman show, she also appeared in child roles in the musical films *Wombling Free* (1977) and *Bugsy Malone* (1976, Lena Marelli), and in the televised version of Coward's *Family Album* (1991, Emily).

LANNER, Josef (b Vienna, 12 April 1801; d Oberdöbling, 14 April 1843).

The great Viennese dance-music composer of his time, Lanner wrote only occasionally for the theatre—a pantomime, a ballet and a fairy-tale piece for the Theater in der Josefstadt, a divertissement for the Kärntnertör-Theater—but his melodies, arranged by Emil Stern, were used as the basis for the score for the successful Operette *Alt-Wien* (Carltheater 23 December 1911) written to a libretto by Gustav von Kadelburg and Julius Wilhelm. He was also made the subject of a biomusical (labeled a Genrebild), *Josef Lanner,* produced at the Theater in der Josefstadt in 1880 (musical arrangements: Ludwig Gothov-Grüneke and Philipp Fahrbach; text: Franz von Radler, 30 September) which was later reprised at the Carltheater (1887, with Carl Adolf Friese as Lanner), the Theater in der Leopoldstadt (1888), at the Rudolsheim Colosseumtheater (1894) and at the Volksoper (1900). He was also portrayed on the Carltheater stage in 1894 by Siegmund Natzler in the Festspiel *Sein erster Walzer* celebrating Johann Strauss's 50 years in the theatre.

His daughter **Kathi** [later Katti] **LANNER** (b Vienna, 14 September 1829; d Clapham, London, 15 November 1908) was a highly successful dancer who appeared as a soloist in Austria (''of the Royal Imperial Opera, Vienna''), Germany (*Sitala das Gauklermädchen, Uriella, der Dämon der Nacht,* etc), Hungary and other European countries as well as in New York, where she first appeared with her Viennoise Ballet Troupe in the summer of 1870 in *Giselle,* and her own *Hirka* and *Sitala the Juggler-maiden.* In 1872 she was star dancer at Niblo's Garden (*Leo and Lotos, Azraël,* etc) and choreographed *A Midsummer Night's Dream* with G L Fox and a version of *The Black Crook.* She ultimately settled in London, where she had first performed her *Giselle* in 1870, and became celebrated as a ballet mistress (Her Majesty's, Drury Lane) and choreographer (*Cinder-Ellen Up Too Late* w Willie Warde, the original productions of *Dorothy* and of Planquette's *Nell Gwynne, Toledo, Madame Cartouche, The Naiad Queen* 1883, etc) and teacher (Directress of the National Training School for Dancing, etc). She was in charge of the ballets at the Empire Theatre from its opening until 1905, and some of her choreography for that house was reproduced in parallel Paris establishments (*Brighton* Olympia, 1898, etc).

The American adapters of *Walzer aus Wien* introduced Kathi [*sic*] Lanner into their version of the show as a character.

Biography: Krenn, H: *Lenz-Blüthen: Josef Lanner, sein Werk, sein Leben* (Böhlau Verlag, Vienna, Köln, Weimar, 1994)

LANSBURY, Angela [Brigid] (b London, 16 October 1925).

Miss Lansbury moved from Britain to America during the Second World War and there began an eminently successful career in films (*Gaslight, National Velvet* as Elizabeth Taylor's sister, *The Picture of Dorian Gray, The Harvey Girls, Till the Clouds Roll By, The Court Jester, The Long Hot Summer, The Dark at the Top of the Stairs, The Manchurian Candidate,* etc). In 1964 she made her first musical-stage appearance as the voracious Cora Hoover Hooper in the short-lived *Anyone Can Whistle,* but she found singular success and a Tony Award shortly afterwards when she introduced the title role of the musicalization of *Auntie Mame* (*Mame,* 1966 ''If He Walked into My Life,'' ''Bosom Buddies'').

She subsequently starred as the Madwoman of Chaillot in Jerry Herman's musical version of Giradoux's play entitled *Dear World* (1969) and closed out of town in *Prettybelle* (1971) before scoring a fresh personal success in the role of Rose, created on Broadway by Ethel Merman, in a revival of *Gypsy,* first on the West End stage and then on Broadway where the performance earned her a second Tony Award. In 1977 she took over the role of Anna, opposite Yul Brynner, in a revival of *The King and I* and in 1979 created the part of Mrs Lovett in Stephen Sondheim's musical melodrama *Sweeney Todd,* hawking ''The Worst Pies in London'' which end up containing ''A Little Priest'' before her blood-bespattered end in her own furnace.

In between her stage appearances, she continued a film career (*Bedknobs and Broomsticks,* etc) and since 1984 she has appeared constantly on the world's television screens as small-town supersleuth Jessica Fletcher, America's answer to Miss Marple, in the enormously successful *Murder She Wrote.* She appeared in the television musical piece *Mrs Santa Claus* in 1996 and in 1998 provided the voice of the Empress Marie in the cartoon musical version of *Anastasia.*

Biographies: Edelman, R & Kupferberg, A E: *Angela Lansbury* (Birch Lane, New York, 1976 and 1996), Gottfried, M: *Balancing Act* (Little, Brown, Boston, 1998)

LAPINE, James (b Mansfield, Ohio, 10 January 1949). Director with book input for a handful of often unusual musicals of the last part of the 20th century.

At first active off-Broadway, where his play *Twelve Dreams* was mounted in 1978 (rev 1981 and 1995) and at Playwrights' Horizons where he directed his play *Table Settings* (1979, 264 performances) and the musical *March of the Falsettos* (1980), Lapine subsequently directed several pieces at the New York Shakespeare Festival before making his mark on musical Broadway when *Sunday in the Park with George,* which had been developed at Playwrights Horizons, was produced at Booth's Theater in 1984. Lapine was credited for the largely sung show's book and direction.

He subsequently combined further with the piece's writer Stephen Sondheim on a revamped version of the composer's *Merrily We Roll Along* at the La Jolla Playhouse, California, and as librettist-director on both the fairy-tale burlesque *Into the Woods* (Tony Award, book) and the darkly powerful *Passion* (Tony Award, book).

He teamed again with *March of the Falsetto* writer William Finn on that piece's musequel *Falsettoland* (dir,

Plate 213. **Angela Lansbury** *as Patrick Dennis's* Auntie Mame.

co-lib), on the fusion of the two shows into the Broadway *Falsettos* (dir, co-lib) and on the briefly seen *A New Brain* (dir, co-lib), before joining the growing stable of musical-theatre names harnessed in the last years of the century by the Disney organization, on the adaptation of their Victor Hugo cartoon, *The Hunchback of Notre Dame,* to the musical stage (1999, also director).

1984 **Sunday in the Park with George** (Stephen Sondheim) Booth's Theater 2 May

1987 **Into the Woods** (Sondheim) Martin Beck Theater 5 November

1992 **Falsettos** revised *March of the Falsettos* and *Falsettoland* (w William Finn) John Golden Theater 29 April

1994 **Passion** (Sondheim) Plymouth Theater 9 May

1998 **A New Brain** (Finn/w Finn) Lincoln Center Theater 18 June

1999 **The Hunchback of Notre Dame** (Alan Menken/Stephen Schwartz/ad Michael Kunze) Theater des Westens, Berlin 5 June

LATABÁR

The founding father of five generations of Latabárs in the Hungarian theatre was **Endre LATABÁR** (b Kiskunhalas, 16 November 1811; d Miskolc, 10 July 1873), who, in a career which involved performing, directing and writing, was the translator of some of the earliest opéras-bouffes and operettes to be played in Hungary. His adaptation credits include *Nőnövelde* (*Das Pensionat*), *Szép Dunois lovag* (*Le Beau Dunois*), *Az átváltozott macska* (*La Chatte métamorphosée en femme* w Kálmán Szerdahelyi), *Párizsi élet* (*La Vie parisienne*), *Szép Galathea* (*Die schöne Galathee*), *Tiz leány, egy férj* (*Zehn Mädchen und kein Mann*), *Szép Helena* (*La Belle Hélène*), *Orfeusz az alvilágban* (*Orphée aux enfers*), *Utazás Kinába* (*Le Voyage en Chine*) and *Genoveva* (*Geneviève de Brabant*).

Endre's son Kálmán Latabár (1855–1924) worked only in the non-musical theatre, but his son **Árpád LATABÁR** (b Miskolc, 19 September 1878; d Budapest,

22 August 1951) had a long career as a performer on the musical stage. He played in *Das verwunschene Schloss* at the age of 18, and joined the company at the Budapest Király Színház in his early thirties, making his first appearance there in the local version of *The Balkan Princess* and going on to appear in a long line of important character roles in both Hungarian and foreign musicals. These ranged from the classic Viennese repertoire—*Die Rose von Stambul* (Müller), *Die Csárdásfürstin* (Feri), *Die Zirkusprinzessin* (Sergius Wladimir), *Eva, Der Zigeunerprimás, Die Bajadere*—to the American imports of the 1920s—*Rose-Marie* (Mountie Malone), *Mersz-e Mary?* (Harry) or the curious *Amerikai lányok*—up-to-date imports like Katscher's *Wunder-Bar* or Ábrahám's *Die Blume von Hawaii,* and a whole range of Hungarian pieces, including such pieces as *Leányvásár* (gróf Rottenberg), *Szibill* (The Governor), *Pillangó főhadnagy* (Morvay), *Alexandra* (gróf Szuvarov), *Éva grofnő* (Guido Bonyhady), *Aranyhattyú* (Dicky), *Mágnás Miska* (Korláth gróf), *Eltörött a hegedűm* (Lojzi), *Sisters* (Müller), *Alvinci huszárok, Lámpaláz, Hajnali csók, Sültgalamb, Kék Duna, Ördöglovas, Csak azért, Bécsi tavasz, Josephine császárnő, Gólyaszanatórium, Éva a paradicsomban, Ki gyereke vagyok én?* and *Becskereki menyecske,* a series which carried on through into his sixties.

The two long-faced sons of this tall moon-faced comedian, **Kálmán LATABÁR** (b Kecskemét, 24 November 1902; d Budapest 11 January 1970) and **Árpád LATABÁR** (b Satoraljaújhely, 22 November 1903; d Budapest, 1 December 1961) both became popular musical-theatre comedians. Árpád, after an early career which took him from Hungary (*Szeretlek, Lámpaláz,* etc) to Africa, the Netherlands and Italy, returned to Budapest and, through the 1930s and 1940s, took over some of his father's roles, such as Rottenberg and Feri bácsi, Zsupán in *Der Zigeunerbaron,* Château-Gibus in *Mam'zelle Nitouche* and the head waiter in *Ball im Savoy,* and played in and created a long list of new roles in Hungarian works (*Száz piros rózsa, Kata, Kitty, Katinka, Bástyasétány 77,* etc). From 1954 he was a member of the company at the Fővárosi Operettszínház.

Kálmán stayed closer to home, although he created the role of Graf Sacha Karlowitz in *Schön ist die Welt* at the Theater an der Wien (1931) and paired with his brother in Vienna's *Lady vom Lido* (1927, Dr Hitschi-Harschi/Buster Keaton), and he made a memorable career on stage and screen as a gangling, monocled and light-footed comic actor. His roles, over the years, included Offenbach's Menelaus, General Boum, Fritz in *Leányvásár,* Zsupán in *Gräfin Mariza,* Basil in *Der Graf von Luxemburg* as well as a long line of both other imports (Christiné's *Szeretlek,* Jim in *Mr Cinders,* Yvain's *Cserebere* and several of the Russian musicals played in Budapest under communism), and more than 30 years of native pieces from the classically styled to the pseudo-American shows of the 1930s (*Weekend, Manolita, Amit a lányok akarnak, Bolondóra, Szegény Ördög, Én és kisöcém, Történnek még csódak, Szépsegkirálynő, Budapest-Wien, A nagyhercegnő és a pincér, Eső után köpönyeg,* Benatzky's *Egy lány, aki mindenkié, Romantikus asszony, Antoinette, Kávé habbál, Egy bolond százat csinál, Pusztai szerenád, Pozsonyi lakodalom, Handa Banda, Sárgarígofészek, Bécsi györs, Fiatlalság-bolondság, Ilyenek a férfiak, Fityfiritty, Múzsák muzsikája, Maya, Maria főhadnagy, Csicsónénak három lánya, vagy?, VIII osztály, Ipafai lakodalom, Bécsi diákok, Szelistyei asszonyok, Kard és szerelem*), in some of which he appeared alongside his brother. In *Csak azért* (1934), *Zimberi, Zombori szépasszony* (1938) and *Fekete Liliom* (1946) the three Latabárs all appeared together in the same show.

Kálmán Latabár also directed a number of new musical shows, and continued to appear at the Operettszínház into the 1960s, appearing as Pietro in a *Boccaccio* rewritten to provide roles for him and for Hanna Honthy as his wife (1961), as Don Moskitos in a version of Offenbach's *Les Brigands,* as Frosch, Negus (*Die lustige Witwe*) and—now alongside his son, the third Kálmán Latabár—as Saint-Hypothèse in *Lili* in the last years of a career in which he was, alongside Honthy, the most popular representative of the glorious bygone years of the musical theatre.

He also appeared in the comic roles of 38 Hungarian films between 1937 and 1962.

Biography: *A Latabárok: egy szinészdinasztia a magyar Színháztörténetben* (NPI, Budapest, 1983)

LATOUCHE, John [Treville] (b Richmond, Va, 13 November 1917; d Calais, Vt, 7 August 1956). American lyricist whose best work won special praise for its literacy and ingenuity.

Early examples of Latouche's lyrics were heard in revue in 1939 when he contributed a song to *Pins and Needles* and several to *From Vienna* and *Sing for Your Supper* (''Ballad for Americans'' w Earl Robinson) before he made a notable first appearance in the musical theatre with the lyrics to Vernon Duke's music for the negro fantasy *Cabin in the Sky* (1940). Even though the words for the most durable song of the score ''Taking a Chance on Love'' came from the pen of Ted Fetter, Latouche was responsible for the lyrics to the show's title song and ''Honey in the Honeycomb.'' Further success, however, did not come quickly. Additional collaborations with Duke on a musical version of *Three Men on a Horse* (*Banjo Eyes*) for Eddie Cantor and on *The Lady Comes Across* were less productive, and a turn into pastiche operetta with pieces based on the music of Kreisler and Chopin did no better, whilst a rewrite of *The Beggar's Opera* in collaboration with Duke Ellington (*Beggar's Holiday*) found only a limited circle of admirers.

It is the 1954 musical *The Golden Apple* (mus: Jerome Moross), a piece that has remained a strong favorite with musical-theatre intellectuals since its first production, on which Latouche's continuing reputation almost wholly rests. A written-through piece using classical mythology, in time-honored style, to poke fun at modern society and institutions, it had only a limited stage life, but it yielded up some particularly attractive pieces of writing and composing (''Windflowers,'' ''Lazy Afternoon,'' ''It's the Going Home Together,'' ''The Judgement of Paris,'' etc), many of which were pieces not safely extractable from the fabric of the show. Disappointingly, *The Golden Apple* was to be almost without tomorrow. A spectacular Hollywood burlesque, *The Vamp* (1955), encouraged camp rather than wit, and Vernon Duke's *The Littlest Revue* (1956) went the way of most of Duke's later works. By the time the first genuine success with which Latouche had been involved since *Cabin in the Sky* was produced, he was dead, having suffered a heart attack at the age of 38. His posthumous lyrical contribution to Leonard Bernstein's *Candide* was, in fact, his only work to ensure him a lasting place in the repertoire.

Latouche's other credits ranged from special material for New York nightclub perfomer Spivy to the texts for Douglas Moore's opera *The Ballad of Baby Doe* (Colorado, 1956), and for three dance plays called *Ballet Ballads,* containing songs, composed by Moross (Music Box Theater, 1948).

1940 **Cabin in the Sky** (Vernon Duke/Lynn Root) Martin Beck Theater 25 October

1941 **Banjo Eyes** (Duke/w Harold Adamson/Joe Quillan, Izzy Ellinson) Hollywood Theater 25 December

1942 **The Lady Comes Across** (Duke/Fred Thompson, Dawn Powell) 44th Street Theater 9 January

1944 **Rhapsody** (Kreisler arr Robert Russell Bennett/w Bennett, Leonard Levinson, Arnold Sundgaard) Century Theater 22 November

1945 **Polonaise** (Chopin arr Bronislaw Kaper/Gottfried Reinhardt, Anthony Veiller) Alvin Theater 6 October

1946 **Beggar's Holiday** (Duke Ellington) Broadway Theater 26 December

1954 **The Golden Apple** (Jerome Moross) Alvin Theater 20 April

1955 **The Vamp** (James Mundy/w Sam Locke) Winter Garden Theater 10 November

1956 **Candide** (Leonard Bernstein/w Richard Wilbur, Dorothy Parker/Lillian Hellman) Martin Beck Theater 1 December

LATTÈS, Marcel (b 1886; d 1943).

A much-liked young musician who moved around to good effect in Parisian society, Lattès wrote several short scores for both opérettes and opéras-comiques before making his full-length debut with *La Jeunesse dorée,* a piece set in the 1830 Paris of the ''dandys'' and starring Henri Defreyn and Brigitte Régent as an English lord and a dancer entangled in a rather curious, pedophilic plot. In the midst of the fashion—particularly at the Théâtre Apollo, where it was staged—for Viennese Operette, *La Jeunesse dorée* won some compliments for its distinctly French music. It won none for its book, however, and after 17 performances the Apollo hastened back to *La Veuve joyeuse* and *Le Comte de Luxembourg.*

Lattès's second piece was produced not in France, but in London, where C B Cochran mounted an English version of his musical comedy *Maggie* at the Oxford Theatre in succession to the wartime hit *The Better 'Ole.* Handicapped by an ''inventive'' chief comic and the switch in the kind of fare at the Oxford, *Maggie* lasted only 108 performances, but it was exported with some success to Australia (Tivoli, Melbourne 30 October 1920) and was later given a kinder production at Paris's Théâtre de la Gaîté-Lyrique where, with Yane Exiane starring as *Nelly* (ad Jacques Bousquet, Henri Falk), it played for a reasonable run.

In a career which embraced both the stage and the cinema as well as the composition of occasional and salon music, Lattès later turned out several further musical plays which found some success. Mlle Régent was again the star of *Monsieur l'Amour* at the Mogador, *Le Diable à Paris* featured Dranem as the ''diable'' at the head of a starry cast including Edmée Favart, Raimu and Jeanne Cheirel, *Arsène Lupin, banquier* featured René Koval as the famous criminal aborting a fabulous plan for the sake of the pretty smile of his victim's niece, and *Xantho chez les courtisanes,* adapted from Jean Richepin's successful play, starred Gabrielle Ristori as an ancient Greek femme honnête learning about love from a team of courtesans headed by Arletty.

Each of Lattès's works was praised for its musicality and its melodic distinction, and he was considered a fine and ever-promising composer, but, in spite of some success, he did not manage to turn out a *Ciboulette* or a *Véronique* for the Parisian 1930s (which didn't really want one, anyhow), his export rate was low to nonexistent, and he spent the large part of the 1930s composing for the cinema screen (*Un fil à la patte, Primerose, Du haut en bas,* etc).

1908 **Fraisidis** (Jacques Redelsperger) 1 act Comédie-Royale 16 November

1912 **La Cour mauresque** (Fernand Nozière) privately, Maisons-Lafitte 21 June

1913 **Il était une bergère** (André Rivoire) 1 act Opéra-Comique 16 April

1913 **Pas davantage** (Nozière) 1 act Théâtre Michel 25 April

1913 **La Jeunesse dorée** (aka *Les Dandys*) (Henri Verne, Gabriel Faure) Théâtre Apollo 29 May

1919 **Maggie** (Adrian Ross/Fred Thompson, H F Maltby, Étienne Rey, Jacques Bousquet) Oxford Theatre, London 22 October

1921 **Nelly** (ad Bousquet, Henri Falk) revised French version of *Maggie* (Théâtre de la Gaîté-Lyrique)

1922 **Monsieur l'Amour** (Falk, René Peter) Théâtre Mogador 18 February

1927 **Le Diable à Paris** (Albert Willemetz, Robert de Flers, Francis de Croisset) Théâtre Marigny 27 November

1930 **Arsène Lupin, banquier** (Yves Mirande) Théâtre des Bouffes-Parisiens 7 May

1932 **Xantho chez les courtisanes** (Jacques Richepin) Théâtre des Nouveautés 16 March

1935 **Pour ton bonheur** (Léopold Marchand, Albert Willemetz) Théâtre des Bouffes-Parisiens 20 September

LAURENT DE RILLÉ [LAURENT, François Anatole] (b Orléans, 30 November 1824; d Paris, 26 August 1915).

Inspector of vocal music for the Parisian school area, Laurent de Rillé was also the composer of a regular flow of songs, choral pieces and short opérettes, the majority of which last were written for and produced at Hervé's Folies-Nouvelles in the late 1850s. He had a more substantial success, however, on the few occasions that he stretched to full-length works, notably with the setting of Leterrier and Vanloo's *Le Petit Poucet* (subsequently played in Austria and Germany as *Der Däumling*), and with the little rustic tale of *Babiole* which, following its Parisian production, was played in Britain, Australia and, with its original star, Paola Marié, in America. His *Le Liqueur d'or,* however, was shut down by the law, when the actors were caught popping back in the rude bits that the censor had cut out. Of his shorter pieces, it was *Les Pattes-blanches,* a little two-handed tale of a couple of white folk adrift in a black country, introduced by Potel and Édouard Georges at the Bouffes-Parisiens in 1873, which proved his most popular.

An anecdote says that it was he who first set what ultimately became Offenbach's *Apothicaire et perruquier.* Offenbach the manager lost the score he had commissioned, so he put on his other hat and composed a new one himself. Maybe.

1855 **Le Sire de Framboisy** 1 act Folies-Nouvelles 2 February

1857 **Aimé pour lui-même** (Machiat de la Chesneraye) 1 act Folies-Nouvelles 3 February

1857 **Bel-Boul, ou une métempsychose** (Chesneraye) 1 act Folies-Nouvelles 14 March

1857 **Achille à Skyros** (Ernest Alby, Delmare [ie, Commerson]) 1 act Folies-Nouvelles September

1857 **La Demoiselle de la Hoche-Trombelon** (Jules Moinaux) 1 act Folies-Nouvelles 20 October

1858 **Trilby** (Chesneraye) 1 act Folies-Nouvelles 1 January

1858 **Frasquita** (Alfred Tranchant) 1 act Théâtre des Bouffes-Parisiens 3 March

1858 **Le Moulin de Catherine** (Alby) 1 act Folies-Nouvelles 1 September

1859 **Le Sultan de Mysapouf** 1 act Folies-Nouvelles 12 February

1859 **Le Jugement de Paris** (Alby, Commerson) 1 act Folies-Nouvelles 11 February

1859 **Elle a des bottes** (G Albert, Eugène Audray-Deshortier) 1 act Folies-Nouvelles 30 March

1859 **Au fond du verre** (Ernest Dubreuil) 1 act Baden-Baden, Théâtre Déjazet March 1861

1868 **Le Petit Poucet** (Eugène Leterrier, Albert Vanloo) Théâtre de l'Athénée 8 October

1873 **Les Pattes-blanches** (Marc Constantin, Léon Coron)1 act Théâtre des Bouffes-Parisiens 21 May

1873 **La Liqueur d'or** (William Busnach, Armand Liorat) Théâtre des Menus-Plaisirs 11 December

1878 **Babiole** (Clairville, Octave Gastineau) Théâtre des Bouffes-Parisiens 16 January

1880 **La Princesse Marmotte** (Clairville, Busnach, Gastineau) Nouvelles Galeries Saint-Hubert, Brussels 24 January

1882 **Frasquita** (Lucien Solvay, Georges de Boesch) 1 act Galeries Saint-Hubert, Brussels October

1891 **La Leçon de chant** (Eugène Adénis) 1 act Théâtre de la Galerie Vivienne 21 June

LAURENTS, Arthur (b New York, 14 July 1918).

The author of several plays and screenplays in the 1940s and early 1950s, Laurents scored his most considerable early successes with the stage play *The Time of the Cuckoo* (1952, subsequently filmed as *Summer Madness*), the Alfred Hitchcock film *Rope* (1948) and the Twentieth Century Fox movie version of *Anastasia* (1956), which netted an Academy Award for Ingrid Bergman.

His first venture into the musical theatre was as librettist for *West Side Story* (1957), a venture which hoisted him immediately to the top of another section of his professions, and he confirmed this success when he collaborated with lyricist Stephen Sondheim a second time in the writing of *Gypsy,* a musical based on the tale of iconized stripper Gypsy Rose Lee and her stage mother. A third collaboration between the two, this time with Sondheim acting as composer as well as lyricist, resulted in a curious, grotesque parable called *Anyone Can Whistle* which was a quick failure (9 performances).

In 1965 Laurents adapted his *The Time of the Cuckoo* as a musical, with Richard Rodgers and Sondheim supplying the score but, in spite of top-class work from all the writers involved, *Do I Hear a Waltz?* hit concept problems on the road and ended up not being a success. Given the markedly superior quality of Laurents's earlier works, the libretto for *Hallelujah, Baby!* (1967) was a disappointment. A piece which mixed a conventional tale of making good in showbiz with some simplistic racial and civil rights elements and a dose of 1960s-isms, it followed all-purpose Georgina—an eternal 25—through four decades of situations on her way to the present day. Its 293 Broadway performances, nevertheless, outdid the 220 of the more sophisticated *Do I Hear a Waltz?*

In 1962, whilst still working on all three fronts as a dramatist, Laurents began a parallel career as a director for the musical theatre with the production of *I Can Get It for You Wholesale* and he subsequently directed *Anyone Can Whistle* (1964), the London (1973) and Broadway (1974) revivals of *Gypsy* and *La Cage aux Folles* (1983).

Laurents proved himself, with his eminently theatrical and intelligent libretti for *West Side Story, Gypsy* and *Do I Hear a Waltz?,* to be one of the most effective librettists of his era but, in the quarter of a century since *Hallelujah, Baby!,* his only further authorial contributions to the musical theatre were *The Madwoman of Central Park,* a one-woman entertainment written with and for Phyllis Newman (22 Steps Theater 13 June 1979) and the text for the disappointing and short-lived *Thin Man* musical *Nick and Nora* (1991, also director).

1957 **West Side Story** (Leonard Bernstein/Stephen Sondheim) Winter Garden Theater 26 September

1959 **Gypsy** (Jule Styne/Sondheim) Broadway Theater 21 May

1964 **Anyone Can Whistle** (Sondheim) Majestic Theater 4 April

1965 **Do I Hear a Waltz?** (Richard Rodgers/Sondheim) 46th Street Theater 18 March

1967 **Hallelujah, Baby!** (Styne/Comden, Green) Martin Beck Theater 26 April

1991 **Nick and Nora** (Charles Strouse/Richard Maltby jr) Marquis Theater 8 December

Autobiography: *Original Story By* (Knopf, New York, 2000)

LAURILLARD, Edward (b Rotterdam, 20 April 1870; d New York, 7 May 1936). Cinema owner turned musical producer who scored several London hits in partnership with George Grossmith and who launched two West End theatres.

From his early twenties, Dutchman Laurillard worked as a company manager with theatrical managements in Britain: under Fred Harris and C J Abud on their West End production of *King Kodak* and then on the tour circuits, at first for William Greet and later for Hardie, von Leer and Gordyn. He moved into production on his own account in 1897 with the play *Oh! Susannah* and made his first venture into the musical theatre with George Grossmith's musical *The Lovebirds,* which he produced unsuccessfully at the Savoy Theatre in 1904.

Laurillard subsequently moved sideways, into the cinema world, and there he expanded his interests until he controled some two dozen film theatres. Thus enriched, he turned back to the theatre and formed a partnership with Grossmith for producing plays and musical comedies. For some six years, from 1914 on, the two men mounted many successful pieces, beginning with the wartime comedy *Potash and Perlmutter* and continuing with the musicals *Tonight's the Night, Theodore & Co,* the London production of Victor Herbert's *The Only Girl, Mr Manhattan, Yes, Uncle!,* a version of Broadway's *Oh, Boy!* played in London under the title *Oh, Joy!,* and *Baby Bunting.* Their partnership culminated in the building of the Winter Garden Theatre and its opening with the successful importation of Ivan Caryll's Broadway musical *The Girl Behind the Gun,* remade for London under the title *Kissing Time.*

The partners produced Friml's *The Little Whopper* for a short run and Cuvillier's *The Naughty Princess* (*La Reine s'amuse*) for a longer one, and in 1920 mounted a second highly successful Winter Garden show, an original musical version of the famous farce *L'Hôtel du Libre-Échange* played as *A Night Out.* Around this time they were reported to have purchased the Gaiety and the Adelphi Theatres and to have made plans for the production at the latter for Lincke's *Gri-gri,* but they were outmaneuvered in their efforts to pick up the pieces of George Edwardes's empire, and Grossmith and Laurillard made only one further venture together, a disastrous attempt to bring burlesque back to the Gaiety Theatre with *Faust on Toast,* before the partnership was dissolved.

Whilst Grossmith continued to run the Winter Garden in tandem with Pat Malone, Laurillard took on the Apollo Theatre, and essayed a number of other producing ventures including a disastrous English version of Künneke's Berlin hit *Love's Awakening* (*Wenn Liebe erwacht*), a happier one of his *The Cousin from Nowhere* (*Der Vetter aus Dingsda*) and the revusical *The Smith Family* (w Alfred Butt), before attempting to export *A Night Out* to America. It closed expensively out of town. In 1928 he opened a second new London theatre, the Piccadilly, where he arranged with Lee Ephraim for the production of what would be his final musical show, the Jerome Kern costume operetta *Blue Eyes.* He maintained an active interest in the theatre up to his death, but in his later years, although he was to be seen ''shopping'' around Broadway from time to time, he did not bring any further productions to the stage.

Laurillard's second wife was musical comedy actress **Adrah FAIR** [Audrey BRUNNER] (b Paducah, Ky, 18 January 1897) who appeared in *Tonight's the Night* in New York and London (1914–15, Yvette la Plage), in *Theodore and Co* (1916, Cleo, the Tiptoe Queen) and in *Arlette* (1917, Cherry).

LAVALLIÈRE, Ève [FENOGLIO, Eugénie Pascaline] (b Toulon, 1 April 1866; d Thuillières, Vosges, 10 July 1929). A gentlemen's delight of the turn-of-the-century years on the Paris musical stage who quit the stage for a convent after a career of three decades.

Orphaned at the age of 18 by the murder of her mother and the suicide of her father, the pretty, diminutive Mlle Fenoglio was taken on as a member of a touring theatre troupe where she found experience, a fairly rich protector and her new name. She kept the name when she headed for Paris and won herself a job in revue at the Théâtre des Variétés. Soon after she replaced the fairly rich protector with a very influential one—Fernand Samuel, the new manager and director of the theatre. Samuel turned Svengali, and the following year Mlle Lavallière scored her first stage success as Oreste in a revival of *La Belle Hélène.* She appeared regularly at the Variétés from then on, in revue, as the Baronne in *La Vie parisienne* and in a series of the travesty boy roles for which her small stature and attractive figure fitted her: Adolphe de Valladolid (*Les Brigands*), Siebel (*Le Petit Faust*), Cupidon (*Orphée aux enfers*), Ernest (*L'Oeil crevé*), Orèste, and Prince Orlofsky in the first French production of *La Chauve-Souris.*

The birth of her daughter and a serious accident interrupted her career in the late 1890s, but she came back to create roles in the spicy Variétés spectaculars *Le Carnet du Diable* (1895, Jacqueline) and *Le Carillon* (1896, Prince Colibri), in *Madam Satan* (1893, Olympe), *Le Pompier de service* (1897, Mimile), *Les Petites Barnett* (1898, Lucie), *Mademoiselle George* (1900, Josette) and a number of other pieces. She had important parts in the original productions of the two most popular works of Claude Terrasse—*Le Sire de Vergy* (1903, where, in the role of Mitzy, she caused a sensation with her belly dance and a dromedary dance) and *Monsieur de la Palisse* (1904, Inésita)—appeared as Mimi in Henri Hirschmann's *La Petite Bohème* (1905), as La Collégienne in *L'Age d'or* (1905), and also took part in a series of plays, whilst at the same time playing a regular round of revivals (Hermia in *Barbe-bleue,* a thoroughly miscast *Miss Helyett,* etc).

In 1917 she starred in Émile Lassailly's *Carminetta* and then, still apparently in fine form at over 50, and after nearly 30 years as a member of the Variétés company, she suddenly (or opportunely, depending which version you believe) got religion. She retired from the stage and spent the remainder of her life first as a missionary in Tunisia and then in a closed Franciscan convent.

Biography: Engelbert, O: *La Vie et conversion d'Ève Lavallière* (Librairie Plon, Paris, 1936), etc

LAVERNE, Pattie [MARDON, Martha Maria] (b London, 10 December 1844; d London, 24 April 1916).

Plate 214. **Pattie Laverne.** *Pattie wasn't too conventionally pretty, but she could set an opéra-bouffe audience alight with a glance and a trill.*

A plain-faced but marvelously vivacious and popular leading lady of the British opéra-bouffe and burlesque stage, soprano Pattie Laverne was seen in prominent roles in a decade of productions which ranged from the works of Offenbach and Hervé, through British extravaganza and burlesque and the earliest English light operas, to the first Viennese pieces to be staged in English-speaking houses.

''Pattie'' made her debut as a singer in concert under a Frenchified version of her married name (Mrs James Hadley Laver) at the Store Street Concert Rooms in 1870, and appeared in various concerts, and as an assistant in Mrs Howard Paul's Entertainment, before allegedly making her stage debut when she was shoved on to deputize briefly for an ailing Julia Mathews during a tour of *La Grande-Duchesse.* She made a more regular stage debut back in London when she was cast as ''Louise'' (ex-Baronne Gondremarck) in the unsuccessful *La Vie Parisienne in London* (1872), but she caught attention well and truly soon after in a succession of roles at the Opera Comique where she was co-starred first with Miss Mathews, then with Rose Bell in *L'Oeil crevé* (1872, Dindonette), Offenbach's *The Bohemians* (1873, *Le Roman comique,* Guillerette), *The Wonderful Duck* (1873, Ulrica) and in the title roles of *Kissi-Kissi* (1873, *L'Île de Tulipatan*) and the burlesque *Tom Tug* (1873).

She subsequently played Clairette to the Lange of Emily Soldene at the Opera Comique and of Blanche Tersi in Liston's touring *La Fille de Madame Angot* Company, apeared as Margotte in *The Broken Branch* (1874), Ixion in the Opera Comique revival *Ixion (Re-wheeled)* (1874) and Cunégonde in the Hervé piece *Dagobert (*1875) in town and the *Grande-Duchesse* (1875) in Manchester. She also created the role of Nell Gwynne in Cellier's musical of that name at Manchester (1876) and that of Trainette in Mrs Liston's production of Bucalossi's *Pom* (1876) before going on to tour with D'Oyly Carte and Richard South's opéra-bouffe companies, and to play in the extravaganza *Wildfire* (1877, Baroness Hey Derry Down) at the Alhambra, where she later took over the title role of *Fatinitza.* In 1878 she appeared in the title role of the British production of de Rillé's *Babiole* (1879), but she made the greatest success of the latter years of her career when she was recruited by Australia's George Musgrove as the leading lady of his first comic-opera company. She starred as Stella in Musgrove's landmark Australian production of *La Fille du tambour-major* (1880), and then, through 1881, in the title roles of his mountings of *Madame Favart* and *Olivette* and as Serpolette in *Les Cloches de Corneville* before quitting Australia, where she had become an enormous favorite, and heading home. She stopped off in San Francisco where she played *Madame Favart* to great acclaim, but that seems to have been her last appearance on the stage. When she got home to Mocca's Cottages, Camden Town she quite simply quit performing and—still not yet 40—went instead into a quiet and long suburban retirement.

LAW, [William] Arthur [aka West CROMER] (b Northrepps, 22 March 1844; d Parkstone, Dorset, 2 April 1913).

The son of a country clergyman, Law took up a commission in the Royal Scots Fusiliers at the age of 20 and he served with the regiment for eight years, in Britain and Burma, before resigning his commission in 1872 to become an actor. After touring for two years in stock with Joseph Eldred, he joined the German Reed company at London's St George's Hall and, during and after a period of more than two years acting with the company, he wrote the libretti of many of the short operettas which made up the Reeds' entertainments.

He later also wrote several successful plays for the regular theatre, including *The Mystery of a Hansom Cab* (1888) and *The New Boy* (1894), and four full-length musical plays, amongst which were Kate Santley's touring vehicle *Chirruper's Fortune*—a piece resembling an extended version of the polite and traditional little stories which had made up his German Reed opus—which was later toured in America by Kate Castleton as *A Paper Doll,* and *The Magic Opal,* a comic opera in the old brigands-and-witches style set to music by Albéniz. His play *The New Boy* gave him one additional and, probably, unwitting musical-theatre credit. It apparently underwent some musical decoration on its voyage from London's Court Theatre to Australia (Palace Theatre, Sydney 22 December 1906) where Harry Macdona billed it (and played it) as a farcical musical comedy.

Married to Fanny Holland, the soprano of the German Reed company, Law also toured for a period with his wife in a drawing-room entertainment (*Wanted, a Ladies' Companion, Victoria Villa*).

1877 **A Night Surprise** (Thomas German Reed) 1 act St George's Hall 12 February

1877 **A Happy Bungalow** (Charles King Hall) 1 act St George's Hall 11 June

1878 **An Artful Automaton** (Hall) 1 act St George's Hall 10 July

1879 **$100 Reward** (R Corney Grain) 1 act St George's Hall 27 May

1880 **Castle Botherem** (Hamilton Clarke) 1 act St George's Hall 16 February

1880 **A Flying Visit** (Grain) 1 act St George's Hall 31 May

1880 **A Merry Christmas** (Hall) 1 act St George's Hall 26 December

1881 **All at Sea** (Grain) 1 act St George's Hall 28 February

1881 **Uncle Samuel** (George Grossmith) 1 act Opera Comique 3 May

1881 **A Bright Idea** (Arthur Cecil) 1 act St George's Hall 30 May

1881 **Cherry Tree Farm** (Clarke) 1 act St George's Hall 30 May

1882 **The Head of the Poll** (Eaton Fanning) 1 act St George's Hall 28 February

1882 **Nobody's Fault** (Clarke) St George's Hall 5 June

1882 **Mr Guffin's Elopement** (Grossmith) 1 act Alexandra Theatre, Liverpool 29 September; Toole's Theatre 7 October

1882 **A Strange Host** (Hall) 1 act St George's Hall 13 December

1883 **A Treasure Trove** (Alfred J Caldicott) 1 act St George's Hall 6 June

1883 **A Moss Rose Rent** (Caldicott) 1 act St George's Hall 17 December

1884 **A Double Event** (Grain/w Alfred Reed) 1 act St George's Hall 18 February

1884 **A Terrible Fright** (Grain) 1 act St George's Hall 18 June

1884 **A Peculiar Case** (Grossmith) 1 act St George's Hall 8 December

1885 **The Great Taykin** (Grossmith) 1 act Toole's Theatre 30 April

1885 **Chirruper's Fortune** (Florian Pascal, Georges Jacobi, Grossmith, Caldicott, et al) Theatre Royal, Portsmouth 31 August

1888 **A Paper Doll** (revised *Chirruper's Fortune*) Wieting Opera House, Syracuse, NY 24 September

1889 **John Smith** (Caldicott) 1 act Prince of Wales Theatre 28 January

1890 **All Abroad** (Caldicott) 1 act Prince of Wales Theatre 21 February

1893 **The Magic Opal** (aka *The Magic Ring*) (Isaac Albéniz) Lyric Theatre 19 January

1898 **The Showman's Sweetheart** (George Byng/w Guy Eden) Queen's Theatre, Crouch End 29 August

1900 **Punch and Judy** revised *The Showman's Sweetheart* (Byng, Arthur Meredyth) Theatre Royal, Croydon 25 June

LAWRENCE, Gertrude [KLASEN, Gertrude Alice Dagmar Lawrence] (b London, 4 July 1898; d New York, 6 September 1952). British revue performer and actress who introduced several major roles in Broadway musical plays.

Gertrude Lawrence began her life on the stage as a child in pantomime and variety, and had her earliest musical-theatre experience dancing in the Liverpool Repertory Company's fantasy *Fifinella.* She toured minor dates in the provincial musical comedies *Miss Lamb of Canterbury* and *Miss Plaster of Paris,* more worldly ones as Blanche-Marie in *Les P'tites Michu* and made her first London appearance at the age of 18 as understudy to the ill-fated Billie Carleton in the revue *Some.* For several years thereafter, she played in revue—*Cheep, Tabs, Buzz-Buzz, A to Z*—and in the newly fashionable cabaret *The Midnight Frolics,* establishing herself on the way as a singing comedienne of charm.

Miss Lawrence had her first major musical-comedy role as Denise in the London version of *Dédé* (1922) before returning to revue for a second series of engagements, now at the top of the bill: *Rats, London Calling* (creating ''Limehouse Blues''), *Charlot's Revue of 1924* on Broadway, *Charlot's Revue* (London) and *Charlot's Revue of 1926* (New York). Later in 1926, she created the comical (and suitably English—the show was originally called *Cheerio!,* for her benefit!) Lady Kay in the American musical remake of Paris's *La Présidente* as *Oh, Kay!,* introducing George Gershwin's ''Someone to Watch Over Me'' and ''Do, Do, Do'' and scoring a singular success. She repeated that role and that success the following year in London.

In 1928, after playing her first adult part in a nonmusical show as Jane Crosby in *Icebound,* she returned to New York to star in Gershwin's less-successful *Treasure Girl* (1928, Ann Wainwright) and the *International Revue* (1930). From that time on, with her revue days now behind her, she appeared largely in plays (of which *Private Lives* with Noël Coward remains the best remembered), returning only episodically to the musical stage, first in 1933 to create the starring role of Cole Porter's short-lived *Nymph Errant* (''The Physician''), then to pair again with Noël Coward in the series of short and intermittently musical playlets of *Tonight at 8.30* (London, New York and revival) and in 1941 as Moss Hart's psychoanalyzable heroine in *Lady in the Dark* (''My Ship,'' ''Jenny'').

In 1951 Miss Lawrence created her last and best remembered musical role as Anna Leonowens, the ''I'' of *The King and I,* performing the Rodgers and Hammerstein songs written especially to suit her sweet but slightly frayed and short-ranged voice—''I Whistle a Happy Tune,'' ''Hello, Young Lovers,'' ''Getting to Know You'' and ''Shall We Dance'' (w Yul Brynner). She was forced out of the show by illness and died from cancer whilst the piece which she had dreamed up continued its run.

An approximative Hollywood film about her life was produced in 1968 as *Star!,* with Julie Andrews playing Miss Lawrence and Daniel Massey her Noël Coward.

A stage musical about *Noël and Gertie* written by Sheridan Morley was produced at the May Fair Theatre in 1980 with Gary Bond and Mark Wynter, acting and singing (respectively) Noël Coward and Maria Aitken and Liz Robertson doing the same for Miss Lawrence. Later adapted as a two-hander, *Noël and Gertie* was seen as played by Lewis Fiander and Patricia Hodge at the Donmar Warehouse (1985) and was performed thereafter regularly in small houses around the world. In 1989 it played a season at the West End's Comedy Theatre and in 1999 it was seen for a season at off-Broadway's Lucille Lortel Theater under the title *If Love Were All.* Twiggy was the Gertie on this occasion.

Autobiography: *A Star Danced* (Doubleday, Doran, New York & W H Allen, London, 1945); Biographies: Aldridge, R: *Gertrude Lawrence as Mrs A* (Greystone, New York, 1954), Morley, S: *A Bright Particular Star* (Weidenfeld & Nicolson, London, 1981)

Recording: *Noël and Gertie* (TER)

LAWRENCE, Jerome (b Cleveland, 14 July 1915).

In collaboration with **Robert E[dwin] LEE** (b Elyria, Ohio, 15 October 1918; d Los Angeles, 8 July 1994), Lawrence wrote two highly successful plays: the dramatization of the tale of the bible-belt Bertram Scopes ''Monkey Trials'' as *Inherit the Wind,* and that of Patrick Dennis's comic novella about his extravagant *Auntie Mame.* This latter piece provided the pair with the basis for their most successful musical play, *Mame.*

Before their play successes, Lawrence and Lee had already ventured into the musical theatre when they pro-

Plate 215. **Evelyn Laye.** *London's loveliest ingenue of the years between the wars.*

vided the libretto to the songs of Hugh Martin for *Look Ma, I'm Dancin'!,* a vehicle for comedienne Nancy Walker as a rich lady who drags a ballet company into modern dance which had run through 188 performances on Broadway. They subsequently adapted James Hilton's famous *Lost Horizon* into a short-lived musical called *Shangri-La,* and Giraudoux's *The Madwoman of Chaillot* as a second vehicle for *Mame* star Angela Lansbury. Produced under the title *Dear World,* it ran for a disappointing 132 performances.

1948 **Look Ma, I'm Dancin'!** (Hugh Martin/w Lee) Adelphi Theater 29 January

1956 **Shangri-La** (Harry Warren/w Lee, James Hilton) Winter Garden Theater 13 June

1966 **Mame** (Jerry Herman/w Lee) Winter Garden Theater 24 May

1969 **Dear World** (Herman/w Lee) Mark Hellinger Theater 6 February

LAYE, Evelyn [LAY, Elsie Evelyn] (b London, 10 July 1900; d London, 17 February 1996). Beautiful British ingenue whose additional gift of a sweet and strong soprano voice made her the West End's outstanding musical leading lady between the wars.

Miss Laye made her first stage appearance at the age of 15, and played in her first book musical a year later when she went on tour with her father, Gilbert Laye, in Robert Courtneidge's production of *Oh, Caesar!* (1916, Myrrha). She appeared on the West End stage for the first time as a 17-year-old when she took over a supporting role in *The Beauty Spot* at the Gaiety Theatre (1918, Leonie Bramble), and she remained there to take her first leading ingenue role in the London production of *Going Up* (1918, Madeline Manners). With only the occasional break for a play or revue, she then continued over the following years to sweep many of the best of the West End's ingenue roles before her, beginning with Dollis Pym in *The Kiss Call,* Bessie Brent in *The Shop Girl* revival, Mary in Louis Hirsch's *Mary,* and Helen in C B Cochran's botched *Phi-Phi.* She moved up to a different calibre of music when she went to Daly's Theatre in 1923 to star in Jimmy White's revivals of *The Merry Widow* and *The Dollar Princess* and she scored one of her greatest successes at that house when she took on the made-for-Massary title role of Fall's *Madame Pompadour* (1923–24). White's subsequent production of Straus's *Die Perlen der Kleopatra* (1925, Cleopatra), in which she appeared in another Massary title role, was, however, not a success.

The star mixed musical weights merrily as she starred in the title roles of two light musical comedies, *Betty in Mayfair* (1925, Betty) and *Merely Molly* (1926, Molly), took over as leading lady in Szirmai's *Princess Charming* (1927, *Alexandra,* t/o Princess Elaine), appeared in the lead soprano part in *Lilac Time* for two London seasons and then starred in the opening attraction at the Piccadilly Theatre, Jerome Kern's *Blue Eyes* (1928, George Ann Bellamy), as the girl who saved Scotland, before moving to Drury Lane to take up the star role in London's production of *The New Moon* (1929, Marianne Beaunoir).

Having refused the part of Sarah Millick in the original production of Noël Coward's *Bitter-Sweet* in London because of a quarrel with the author, whom she suspected of being at best on the other woman's side in the recent luring-away of her husband, she later agreed (things having been explained away) to play it on Broadway. Following an enormous personal success, she then returned to play the same part in the last part of the run in London. She was subsequently seen as Helen of Troy in an all-star C B Cochran rehash of Max Reinhardt's rehash of Offenbach's *La Belle Hélène* (1932) and then, in contrast, appeared with Flanagan and Allen in the variety musical comedy *Give Me a Ring* (1933, Peggy). In 1937 she starred opposite Richard Tauber in the very vocal role of the Princess Anna Elisa in the London production of Lehár's *Paganini* and she then moved to Broadway to appear in the very differently toned Dietz and Schwartz musical comedy *Between the Devil* (1937, Natalie).

Now in her forties, Miss Laye made her final London appearances as juvenile lady on the musical stage in Edna May's famous role of Violet Grey in a revival of *The Belle of New York,* in Sigmund Romberg's short-lived *Sunny River* (1943, Marie Sauvinet) and, as a bonne-bouche, in a performance fit to challenge Yvonne Printemps, in the role the French star had made her own in an English adaptation of *Three Waltzes* (1945, Katherine). After this she appeared in plays, in pantomime where she was a much-prized principal boy, and in revue, but she finally did return, no longer an ingenue but a dashing leading lady, to star with Anton Walbrook in the successful musical *Wedding in Paris* (1954, Marcelle Thibault, "In the Pink"). Noël Coward subsequently suggested adding songs to his play *La Marquise* as a vehicle for Miss Laye, but ultimately she toured the play without singing.

In her sixties, she played Annie Besant in the short-lived *Strike a Light* and then, having temporarily replaced the spelling Anna Neagle in the role of Lady Hadwell in Harold Fielding's production of *Charlie Girl,* had a star role built for her in the next Fielding show, *Phil the Fluter* (1969, Mrs Fitzmaurice). The show ran but briefly, but Miss Laye's "They Don't Make Them Like That Any More" went down as an anthology piece. She later appeared in the British provinces as Madame Armfeldt in a tour of *A Little Night Music* in the final episode of one of the most remarkably long and successful careers in the British musical theatre.

Autobiography: *Boo, to My Friends* (Hurst & Blackett, London, 1958)

LAYTON, Joe [LICHTMAN, Joseph] (b New York, 3 May 1931; d Key West, Fla, 5 May 1994). Choreographer-turned-director who won international success with his dances for *The Sound of Music* and his direction of the circus musical *Barnum.*

After an early career as a dancer in Broadway shows (*Oklahoma!, High Button Shoes, Gentlemen Prefer Blondes, Miss Liberty, Wonderful Town*), Layton joined the US Army where he was given his first opportunities to direct and choreograph musical productions. One of his earliest efforts in his post-forces period was the burlesque *The Princess and the Pea* (1958), and his New York choreography career began with the 1959 revival of *On the Town* and the off-Broadway development of *The Princess and the Pea* into *Once Upon a Mattress* (also London). He subsequently created the dances for the original production of *The Sound of Music* (1959 and London 1961), for *Greenwillow* (1960), *Tenderloin* (1960) and Noël Coward's *Sail Away* (1961 and London 1962).

Layton's first Broadway directing assigment was on Richard Rodgers's *No Strings* (1962) and, although the show itself had a limited success, his contribution won him half of the year's Tony Award for choreography. He subsequently directed another *On the Town* revival (London, 1963), Coward's *The Girl Who Came to Supper, Drat! The Cat!, Sherry!* and the George Cohan biomusical *George M!* (which brought his total to four exclamation points in three shows and won him a second choreographer's Tony Award), as well as *Dear World* (1969) and another Richard Rodgers piece, *Two by Two* (1970). He visited Japan in 1970 to stage the musical *Scarlett,* based on *Gone with the Wind,* and in 1973 he directed an English-language *Gone with the Wind* musical at London's Theatre Royal, Drury Lane.

Following a period devoted largely to revue, television, and nightclub work, Layton returned to Broadway to direct the musical *Platinum* (1978) before creating his greatest success with the all-circus staging of *Barnum* (1980), a staging subsequently repeated in various versions in the show's many productions all around the world. In 1988 he directed and choreographed the London extravaganza *Ziegfeld.* Already unwell, he could no longer put on the stage the things he imagined and described, and the result was an under-prepared fiasco.

LEANDER, Zarah [HEDBERG, Zarah Stina] (b Lake Vaner, Karlskrona, Sweden, 15 March 1907; d Stockholm, 23 June 1981).

Daughter of a provincial Swedish pastor, Zarah Leander, equipped with a limited and extremely low singing voice of a highly individual character, seemed scarcely set to take her stage talents into the musical field. However, after beginnings in revue she made a success as Lehár's "glada anken" (merry widow) in a Stockholm production which tactfully lowered the entire role into her range, and it was thereafter as a singing actress that she established herself in Sweden.

She made her Vienna debut as the star of Benatzky's successful musical comedy *Axel an der Himmelstür* (1936) at the Theater an der Wien and, as a result of the film version that followed, began a prominent career in musical films, to the accompaniment of a series of successful songs. After the Second World War, she returned to the screen and later to the stage, starring in Vienna in Peter Kreuder's *Madame Scandaleuse* (1958) and as Mrs Erlynne in his musical version of *Lady Windermere's Fan, Lady aus Paris* (1964). Her final Vienna appearance was as Madame Armfeldt in *A Little Night Music,* produced at the Theater an der Wien in 1975, nearly 40 years after her first starring role there in *Axel an der Himmelstür,* and her final stage appearance was in the same role in a Swedish production.

In 1992 (3 July) the singer was the subject of a "one-person musical" staged at Greifswald's Stadttheater as

Zarah 47-Das tote Lied. The musical part of the evening was a selection of Leander's best-known screen songs.

Autobiography: *Es war so wunderbar* (Ullstein, Frankfurt, Berlin, 1983)

LEÁNYVÁSÁR Operette in 3 acts by Miksa Bródy and Ferenc Martos. Music by Viktor Jacobi. Király Színház, Budapest, 14 November 1911.

Viktor Jacobi, although still only 28 years of age, was already well established as one of Budapest's most appreciable composers of operett, with half a dozen shows including the successful *Tüskerózsa* and *Van, de nincs* to his credit, by the time he wrote *Leányvásár,* the piece which would open up the international theatre scene to him. This expansion was not unpremeditated, for, in the climate of that time, when central European Operette was the rage of London and New York, many Viennese and Hungarian composers were writing their works more with a view to export than for the home market. Jacobi's librettists purposely set out their book to *Leányvásár* on "English" principles and persuaded the composer to do the same with his score.

The story of the show was a sort of not-very-wild-West version of the much-used tale which, up till now, had had its apotheosis in von Flotow's *Martha.* Lucy Harrison (Sári Petráss), the daughter of a millionaire San Francisco congressman (Endre Boross), is destined unenthusiastically to become the wife of Fritz (Márton Rátkai), the son of Count Rottenberg (Árpád Latabár sr). One day, she goes off for a bit of fun to the marriage market at "a village near San Francisco" and there she gets herself paired off with a handsome vagabond called Tom Migles (Ernő Király). Migles turns out to be Tom Fleetwood, the son of a once wealthy San Franciscan gentleman who was ruined by playing the money market opposite Lucy's father. Lucy thinks that he has entrapped her into what is apparently a binding marriage as a form of revenge and she angrily and unhappily agrees to follow her father's wishes and wed Fritz. However, by the time the last scenes are reached it turns out that the little nobleman has already tied himself to Lucy's maid, Bessy (Sári Fedák), so the way is left clear for a pretty reconciliation and a happy if conventional ending.

Jacobi's score may have been lined up in an "English" shape, with its two central singing lovers, its supporting pair of soubrets and its accent on comedy, but its flavor was unmitigatedly Hungarian with, advisedly, a rather more prominent ration of Viennese waltzes than was hitherto usual out east. It was also easily his best score to date, a mixture of light romantic and dancing comic melodies which produced a whole line of successful single numbers as well as some memorable ensembles. The best of the romantic music was in the prima donna's role—a swooping, rhythmic entrance waltz (Lucy belépője) and a lovely third-act solo "Tele van a szívem" as well as a series of duets with the tenor Tom, of which the waltzes of the first-act finale ("De nagyot iramodtam") and the second act ("Mondjad igazán") stood out—but it was the light comic music of the show which supplied the real hits. Fedák and Rátkai scored in the first act with the tripping song-and-dance "Kettecskén," again with the jaunty waltz duo "No, de méltóságos úr," and topped the set with the bristling "Dzsilolo," accompanied by a lively dance routine choreographed by the theatre's ballet master Izsó Geiger which became famous in itself. Fedák hit the heights again with a marching sailor song (Tengerész-dal) in a role of proportions altogether out of line with her part in the plot, but altogether in line with her star status.

Leányvásár was one of the greatest successes that the Király Színház had known in its six years as Budapest's principal theatre for both imported and original Operette. It topped both all of Jacobi's own previous works and such pieces as Rényi's *A kis gróf,* produced with great success earlier the same year, and outdid all but the very particular *János vitéz* of the works of earlier composers. It established itself firmly as a part of the basic Hungarian repertoire and promptly began the march around the world which had been hopefully planned for it. That march started disappointingly, for Victor Palfi's Berlin production at the Neues Operetten-Theater (ad Fritz Moss) was only a very relative success—being distinctly outpointed by Fall's *Der liebe Augustin* at the Theater des Westens—and *Das Mädchenmarkt* did not ever really establish itself in Germany. Perhaps as a result, although the Király Színház company introduced their show to Vienna in a season at the Carltheater in 1913, it was 1915 before Vienna saw the German version, and then it was produced not at one of the major houses but at Ronacher with Susanne Bachrich (Lucy), Mizzi Freihardt (Bessy), Karl Pfann (Tom), Carlo Böhm (Fritz) and Oskar Sachs (Rottenberg) featured.

If the German-language version failed to live up to the original success, however, the targeted British one did not. In London, George Edwardes mounted *The Marriage Market* at Daly's Theatre, following the line of Viennese successes there which descended from *The Merry Widow* through *The Dollar Princess* and *The Count of Luxembourg* to *Gipsy Love.* But, in spite of the authors' efforts to be English, the show which he staged had undergone some significant alterations. Gladys Unger's libretto beefed up the amount of comedy by making the first soubrette role a new "heroine's best friend" called Kitty for top-billed Gertie Millar, to whom "Dzsilolo" was allotted as one of four solos—a total which later included a tacked-in piece called "Silly Billy," written by

Paul Rubens. Kitty went with Mariposa (as the heroine was now called) to the fair and won a Lord Hurlingham (comedian G P Huntley) as a prize. Bessy the maid did not quite disappear, although Emma (Avice Kelham) was now largely there to be paired off with the show's other star comic, Bill Berry, who appeared in a wholly new role as Huntley's valet, Blinker, and appropriated "No, de méltóságos úr" made over as a song called "A1." He also had his part expanded by Rubens with a number called "I Don't Believe in Fairies Now" and later with a Lionel Monckton piece called "Joy Bells."

With all this comedy and these comedy solos padding out the piece, Mariposa (Sári Petráss, repeating her original role) and Jack (Robert Michaelis) were limited to duets—although they did have four of them. Lucy belépője was no longer a belépője (entrance) but appeared in the second-act finale, whilst "Kettecskén" became a quartet. Vocalist Harry Dearth as an incidental seaman rendered a baritone song which was also eventually replaced by one by Rubens during alterations intended to freshen the show six months into its run. The piece as made over proved strongly to London tastes—more so than either of the Viennese works which had preceded it at Daly's—and, in a 14-month run, Edwardes won 423 London performances from Jacobi's slightly souped-about operett before sending it on the road.

In America, Charles Frohman had no such good fortune with an even more botched version which was based on the London one, but which wandered much further away from the original. "Kettecskén" ("Hand-in-Hand"), "Ha lennék" ("The One I Love") and the Sailor Song were still there, but the Rubens and Monckton interpolations had also been retained at the expense of much of the rest of Jacobi's score which was replaced by songs by Jerome Kern (three), Edwin Burch (two), Pedro de Zulueta (one) and leading man Donald Brian (one). Venita Fitzhugh was the heroine, and Moya Mannering and Percival Knight headed the comedy for a 10-week Broadway run.

J C Williamson Ltd returned to what was largely the London version when *The Marriage Market* was produced in Australia with Ethel Cadman (Mariposa), Thelma Raye (Kitty), Derek Hudson (Jack), Leslie Holland (Hurlingham) and Phil Smith (Blinker) featured for seasons in Melbourne and Sydney (Her Majesty's Theatre 3 July 1915), but it was Lionel Monckton's English "Joy Bells" and Smith's Jerome and Schwartz ragtime song "You Can't Get Away from It" which caught on best from the now internationally composite score, rather than the markedly rhythmic remaining Hungarian numbers.

Leányvásár took its time to reach France, where Jacobi never succeeded in gaining the foothold that he had in Britain, but it was ultimately produced by Charles Montcharmont at his Lyon theatre, in a version by Charles Quinel and Pierre d'Aumier, a dozen years after its Hungarian debut. The French version, although crediting only the original librettists, was, however, based on the English text and Lilian Backson (Cécile Dessaud) and Jack Grims (Géo Bury) romanced, Ketty (Gabrielle Ristori) and Comte Montegrisky (Armand Franck) soubretted and comedian Morton played the valet Brichton opposite Denise Cam as the English maid Phoebe. The score, whilst ignoring the English incrustations, again underwent some alterations, but Ketty retained "Psilolo" and Brichton and Phoebe got back most of their pilfered duets. *Le Beau Voyage* did not, however, make it to Paris where, by this time, the one-step and the fox-trot were reigning instead of the waltz and Hungarian novelties were not à la mode.

Leányvásár has held a place in the Hungarian repertoire, being given a major revival at the Fővárosi Operettszínház (12 November 1993) with Mónika Sáfár (Lucy), Sándor Sasvári (Migles) and Marika Oszvald (Bessy) and it has been seen as recently as 1995 in its German version (Luxembourg 29 March).

Germany: Neues Operetten-Theater *Das Mädchenmarkt* 7 April 1912; Austria: Carltheater (Hun) 7 May 1913, Ronacher *Das Mädchenmarkt* 1 March 1915; UK: Daly's Theatre *The Marriage Market* 17 May 1913; USA: Knickerbocker Theater *The Marriage Market* 22 September 1913; Australia: Her Majesty's Theatre, Melbourne *The Marriage Market* 20 May 1915; France: Théâtre des Célestins, Lyon *Le Beau Voyage* 15 March 1923

Recording: selection (Qualiton)

LEAVE IT TO JANE Musical comedy in 2 acts by Guy Bolton and P G Wodehouse based on George Ade's play *The College Widow.* Music by Jerome Kern. Longacre Theater, New York, 28 August 1917.

F Ray Comstock and Morris Gest planned to follow the successful production of *Oh, Boy!,* at the little Princess Theater, with another Bolton/Wodehouse/Kern collaboration and, to that end, they purchased the rights to musicalize George Ade's highly successful comedy *The College Widow,* an ingenuous piece of school-days romance with footballing frills which had run up a fine 278-performance sequence for producer Henry Savage at the Garden Theater in 1904–5. The plot of the original play was retained as the central story of the more jovially titled musical *Leave It to Jane,* which told of how Jane Witherspoon (Edith Hallor), daughter of the President of Atwater College, uses her charms to make footballing star Billy Bingham (Robert Pitkin) abandon his own father's alma mater and secretly attend Atwater to be near his girl. Billy wins the big match for Atwater and then discovers the treachery, but the repentant Jane comes good for a happy ending. There were plenty of comic incidentals surrounding this tale, with Oscar Shaw (Stub Talmadge) and Ann Orr (Bessie Tanner) playing a football-mad pair of students; Georgia O'Ramey sweeping up the low comedy as a landlady's daughter determined to get romantic and/or financial satisfaction from an ex-boarder, the weedy Harold Hicks (Olin Howland), who has since grown too big for his boots and for her; and Will C Crimans as Billy's rampaging papa, dashed off by the students on a happily youthful spree so that he will not notice that his son is playing on the wrong side in the big match.

Kern supplied a suitably feather-light, youthful set of songs, some of which were leftovers from earlier works, to match the libretto. The title trio, performed by Misses Orr and Haller and Pitkin, was a rewritten version of *Ninety in the Shade*'s ''Whistling Dan,'' ''When the Orchestra Is Playing Your Favorite Waltz''/''There It Is Again'' was an *Oh, Boy!* cut-out, whilst the delightful ensemble ''I'm Going to Find a Girl'' reused a melody Kern had written for a silent film score. The favorite numbers, however, were custom-made: the revusical ''Cleopatterer,'' performed by Miss O'Ramey, the incidental comedy trio ''Sir Galahad'' (Shaw, Ramey, Howland), a pretty duo ''The Crickets Are Calling'' for Pitkin and Miss Hallor and, most notably, the languid Siren's Song performed with intent by the girls of Atwater. These were supplemented by some jolly, lively pieces, principally for Shaw and Miss Orr (''Just You Watch My Step,'' ''The Sun Shines Brighter'') which ensured that the ingenuous collegiate spirits of the show never slackened.

Leave It to Jane started out of town happily, was given a smart wash-and-brush-up on the way to town (including the wiping of four numbers, only two of which were replaced), and, given that *Oh, Boy!* was still happily running at the Princess Theater, opened on Broadway at the much larger Longacre instead. It did well enough, holding its place there for 167 performances before moving on to the touring circuits in no less than three separate companies, but it did not establish itself in the same way that the rather less ingenuous *Oh, Boy!* had done, and its post-Broadway career was, with one exception, confined to America.

That exception was Australia. J C Williamson Ltd took up *Leave It to Jane* and presented Genevieve Davis/Margery Hicklin (Jane), Maude Fane (Bessie), Winnie Collins (Flora), Leyland Hodgson (Stub) and Athol Tier (Bub) for a fine 11 weeks in Sydney, 6 in Melbourne (Theatre Royal 5 June 1926) and a subsequent trip to New Zealand.

In 1959 Joseph Beruh and Peter Katz produced a revival of *Leave It to Jane* at off-Broadway's Sheridan Square Theater (25 May 1959). A few alterations were made to the score, including the reinstating, for the benefit of top-billed Dorothy Greener as Flora, of ''Poor Prune,'' a number cut on the road, and the dropping of a couple of other songs, but by and large the revival reproduced the show much as it had been originally played on Broadway, if on a smaller scale. Kathleen Murray (Jane), Vince O'Brien (Billy), Angelo Mango (Stub) and George Segal (Ollie) were amongst the cast of the show which found an appreciative audience for a splendid 928 performances amongst those who appreciated a little nostalgic relaxation from the bigger and slicker products of contemporary Broadway. In 1985 a Goodspeed Opera House revival (2 October) with Rebecca Luker (Jane), Faith Prince (Flora), David Staller (Billy) and Michael O'Steen (Stub) was sent on tour with Broadway as a goal, but it petered out before reaching New York.

Australia: Her Majesty's Theatre, Sydney 24 October 1925

Recording: 1959 revival cast recording (Strand)

LEAVE IT TO ME! Musical comedy in 2 acts by Bella and Sam Spewack based on their play *Clear All Wires.* Music and lyrics by Cole Porter. Imperial Theater, New York, 9 November 1938.

Mrs Alonzo P Goodhue (Sophie Tucker) had ambitions for her husband (Victor Moore), so she dug into her deep bank accounts and backed Mr Roosevelt for President. As a result, with Roosevelt safely in the White House, Alonzo has been nominated as US Ambassador to Russia. But he doesn't want to be Ambassador to Russia, and once he gets there he tries everything in his power to get himself sacked. He has some help from a young newspaperman called Buckley Joyce Thomas (William Gaxton), an employee of tycoon J H Brody who had thought himself a shoo-in for the ambassadorial job, and who has sent his minion to Moscow under orders to try to get Goodhue disgraced. But no matter how badly Alonzo the ambassador behaves, things always seem perversely to turn out in his favor. It is only when he has ruefully given up, settled in, and is concocting a Goodhue plan for world peace that the State Department takes fright, and it is deemed advisable to get rid of him. Next thing Mrs Goodhue will have him standing for president. The feminine interest in this mostly masculine plot was provided by giving Mrs Goodhue a troupe of dancing girls to export ''culture'' to Russia, by giving Thomas a girl called Colette (Tamara) and by introducing a nymphet of Thomas's acquaintance (and Brody's) called Dolly Winslow (Mary Martin) with a song.

That song came out at the top of a not-really-top-notch score which nevertheless rendered up a couple of Porter durables. Miss Martin's singing of ''My Heart Belongs to Daddy,'' whilst delicately removing her furs, and all oblivious to the Siberian cold, established both the number and the artist as hits. Elsewhere, Tamara insisted "Get Out of Town" and Miss Tucker disserted on the fact that "Most Gentlemen Don't Like Love" with (probably because the number was a cutout rescued from an earlier show) rather less relevance to what was going on than her punning declaration in the first act that she was "taking the Steps to Russia" and "making Communism thwing." Moore simply cried "I Want to Go Home" and, in a typical Porter catalogue of fun, listed some reasons why. The finale of the first act hailed "Comrade Alonzo" and had Joseph Stalin (Walter Armin) doing a little dance to a jazzed-up version of the Internationale.

Although the authors actually had the experience of having been journalists in Russia, *Leave It to Me!* was just another colorful Ruritanian song and dance show pretending to be "biting satire," and just another on the recent heap of (mostly better) musical comedies which had decided that Presidents and politics—preferably ridiculed—were smart material for the musical stage. However, with the best of Porter's songs and its fine cast, headed by the inimitable *Of Thee I Sing* and *Anything Goes* pairing of Moore and Gaxton, as advantages, Vinton Freedley's production stayed 291 performances on Broadway before going on the road. By this stage, however, events had moved on in Europe and Stalin's rapprochement with the Nazis had not only rather messed up one bit of the plot, it had changed a few of even the most enthusiastically liberal Americans' thoughts on the OK-ness of the Russian leader. It was judged wiser to expunge the dancing dictator from the show.

Britain and Australia did not take up *Leave It to Me!*, and the piece was laid to rest, leaving its favorite songs to carry on alone. However, it finally did find its way further afield in 1987 when, on the crest of the revived fashion for Porter's work, a German production, which swapped the show's original catchphrase title for the more apt and amusing *Wodka Cola* (ad Michael Kunze, Dietrich Hilsdorf, Michael Quast, Dieter Glawaschnig), was put together at Stuttgart. *Wodka Cola* used the plot and much of the score of *Leave It to Me!* but, in the musical jigsaw manner of modern Porter productions, interpolated numbers from *Seven Lively Arts, Out of This World* and *Anything Goes.* In a reverse of this process, four numbers from *Leave It to Me!* were inserted into a Porter pasticcio score for an (extremely) unfortunate London musical based on the film *High Society.*

The title *Leave It to Me!* had been used previously for the 1925 out-of-town tryout of a musical comedy which ultimately came to Broadway in a revised version as *Sweetheart Time* (19 January 1926).

Germany: Staatstheater, Stuttgart *Wodka Cola* 9 December 1987

Recordings: original cast recordings (Decca, Smithsonian), *Wodka Cola* (Boyer)

LECOCQ, [Alexandre] Charles (b Paris, 3 June 1832; d Paris, 24 October 1918). The most potent musician in the development of the French opérette tradition in the 1870s, and for a decade the musical theatre's most successful composer.

A sickly child, Charles Lecocq has long been said to have suffered from an illness which left him with a permanent limp and the need to use crutches. It appears, however, that in truth his handicap was the result of his having been dropped, by his sister, whilst a baby. During his youngest years the physically limited boy developed the interest in music which led him to prefer a musical education to a general college one, and at the age of 16 he entered the Paris Conservatoire. The need to earn a living ultimately obliged him to give up his studies and devote himself to teaching and to work as an occasional pianist, but at the same time he made his first steps as a composer with a series of piano pieces. He was able to find a publisher for some of these, however, only when he pretended that they were the work of a fashionably German composer.

The struggling young man first came to general notice as a composer at the age of 24 when his setting of a Léon Battu/Ludovic Halévy text called *Le Docteur Miracle* tied for first place with that by his Conservatoire contemporary, Georges Bizet, in a contest organized by Offenbach for the Théâtre des Bouffes-Parisiens. The winning pieces were produced at the Bouffes, and Lecocq's stage career was launched. That launching was, however, to prove to be a very slow one. Although he continued to write regularly for the theatre and, during the next 15 years, succeeded in placing as many pieces—principally one-act opérettes but also several longer pieces—on the Paris stage, Lecocq did not manage to force his way through to a position in the first rank of opérette composers.

The most substantial and successful of these early pieces was the three-act oriental opéra-comique *Fleur de thé* (1868), mounted at the Théâtre de l'Athénée under the management of the eccentric William Busnach, the same producer who had given Lecocq—whom he had engaged on the music staff at his short-lived theatre—his first opportunity with a larger piece a couple of seasons earlier. The two-act *L'Amour et son carquois* had been a semi-success which had been sufficient to win him a libretto from the rising Chivot and Duru, recently the librettists of Hervé's *Les Chevaliers de la table ronde.* The swingeingly saucy *Fleur de thé* was given a good Parisian run in its unfashionable little house and, at the height of the fashion for French opéra-bouffe, it went on to be played in most of the main theatrical centers of the world. Lecocq's name and reputation had begun to get around, but in a theatrical world where star composers were made within years of coming out of short pants and the Conservatoire, he was already heading for his 40th birthday.

Thereafter, however, his works began to win more attention. Three short pieces produced at the Théâtre des Bouffes-Parisiens—*Gandolfo, Le Rajah de Mysore* and *Le Testament de M Crac*—were given productions throughout Europe and occasionally beyond, and the two-act *Le Beau Dunois* went on from its Paris production to be played both in Vienna and in Budapest, where it was the first of Lecocq's works to be produced. However, Lecocq still had to struggle for commissions and productions, and the closest he got to a new production in Paris was the announcement that he was to write a new opéra-bouffe, entitled *Gésier XIV,* with Jules Moinaux for the Folies-Dramatiques. Apparently because of legal complications, *Gésier XIV* was never produced, and it was not until the Franco-Prussian War encouraged Lecocq temporarily to quit Paris that he found the opportunity that would set him on the road to real international success.

His next collaboration with Chivot and Duru, and this time with the famous vaudevilliste Clairville as well, was *Les Cent Vierges,* an extravagantly comical piece of musical-farce writing which was accepted for production by the enthusiastic Eugène Humbert at Brussels's Théâtre des Fantaisies-Parisiennes. Splendidly mounted, *Les Cent Vierges* was a grand success in Belgium, and within two months of its first Brussels performance it was transferred to the Paris stage before being exported worldwide (*To The Green Isles Direct, The Island of Bachelors, Hundert Jungfrauen, Száz szüz,* etc). A second piece for Humbert, *La Fille de Madame Angot* (1872), was even more successful. A combination of a splendidly shapely libretto and a score which offered one sveltely melodious song and ensemble after another, it went swiftly to Paris and then around the world several times. On the way, it proved itself internationally as the most consequent work of the period, and it firmly and finally established Lecocq and his light comic-opera style of writing at the forefront of the French and international musical theatre scene, in place of the outrageous frivolities of the prewar opéras-bouffes of Offenbach and Hervé.

The success of *La Fille de Madame Angot* and *Les Cent Vierges* sent theatre directors off in the same kind of spin searching for more Lecocq works that they had earlier displayed in chasing Offenbach pieces. They dug back and, in London for example, where the new rage burned brightest, his *Le Carnaval d'un merle blanc* was produced in a botched version as *Loo, or The Party Who Took Miss,* whilst such short pieces as *Les Ondines au champagne* (Folly, 1877), *Le Rajah de Mysore* (Gaiety, 1878) and *Gandolfo* (Drury Lane, 1878) were given belated first showings. Less scrupulous directors fabricated their own Lecocq opérettes from music pilfered from his old works.

The composer's next piece, *Giroflé-Girofla,* was also produced in Belgium. A delicious comic opera, much more in the old-fashioned, low-comic vein of *Les Cent Vierges* than in the dramatic and historic/political mode of *La Fille de Madame Angot* with its true-to-life characters, it proved a third consecutive international hit for Lecocq. With the Parisian theatres crying out for the services of the composer of *La Fille de Madame Angot* and *Giroflé-Girofla,* Lecocq—after an aborted start on a fourth show, *Le Grand Frédéric* (w Prével, Saint-Albin) for Humbert—now returned to France. There, his first new works had a mixed reception. A distinctly more polite and rather old-fashioned comic opera, *Les Prés Saint-Gervais* (1874), written to a text by Sardou and Philippe Gille and produced at the Théâtre des Variétés, had neither the comic flavor nor the drama of his more popular pieces, but, after a disappointing Paris run, it nevertheless followed its predecessors on to the international circuit (*Prinz Conti, Conti herceg,* etc). A bandit piece, *Le Pompon* (1875), was firmly rejected by the Paris public, but it too won some exposure away from home (*Tivolini*) and scored a long-lasting success in Hungary where, as *A kis doktor,* it was given a respectable first run at the Király Színház and remained more than 15 years in the general repertoire.

Following these two less-than-wholly-successful pieces, Lecocq teamed up again with his *La Fille de Madame Angot* collaborator, wheeler-dealer Victor Koning, who was now spending his vast royalties on being the director of the Théâtre de la Renaissance. Over the next six years Lecocq composed, Koning presented, and the reigning queen of Parisian opérette, Jeanne Granier, (mostly) starred in eight new opéras-comiques, beginning with *La Petite Mariée* (1875), peaking with *Le Petit Duc* (1878) and including such other internationally played pieces as *La Petite Mademoiselle, La Marjolaine, La Jolie Persane* and *La Camargo.* These Théâtre de la Renaissance shows, written to texts by a variety of librettists and lyricists, were a remarkably consistent body of works musically and they confirmed Lecocq's position, through the 1870s, at the head of his profession. However, the dismal failure of *Janot* (1881), written after a period of illness and unhappiness, led to a split between the composer and his producer, and it was bruited about that Lecocq, accused now of turning out works which were all too much musically alike, might be on the downward slope. A change of venue, of producer and of cast, however, proved to be salutary and Lecocq, who had already had some lively success at other houses with his music for the vaudevilles *Le Grand Casimir* and *La Roussotte* (w Hervé, Marius Boullard) at the Variétés, and his accompaniment to the grandiose spectacle of *L'Arbre de Noël* at the Porte-Saint-Martin, moved back into top gear with his next two pieces, *Le Jour et la nuit* (1881) and *Le Coeur et la main* (1882), both produced by Brasseur at the Théâtre des Nouveautés. Both, equipped with the kind of dashingly farcical libretti which suited him so well, were splendid successes which, like his earlier triumphs, were swiftly played throughout the world. Chivot and Duru's *La Princesse des Canaries* (1883), which followed quickly on the heels of this pair of hits, had a more limited home success, but it, too, exported well, and the same authors' *L'Oiseau bleu* also found some takers at home and abroad (San Francisco as *The Red Bird,* Amsterdam as *Der Wondervogel*) without ever looking like challenging the composer's most popular works.

Thereafter Lecocq, ''very rich, in love with his art, cats and old books,'' genuinely did become somewhat bogged down in his own style and, deprived by the depredations of time of the support of his (and everyone else's) favorite authorial teams of Leterrier/Vanloo, Chivot/Duru and Meilhac/Halévy, the shows and scores he produced became less and less successful. *Plutus,* his first work premiered at the Opéra-Comique, was a failure, *Les Grenadiers de Mont-Cornette* disappeared in 18 performances at the Bouffes-Parisiens, and *L'Égyptienne* (1890) did even worse. Only one work, *Ninette* (1896), his version of the Cyrano de Bergerac story, had any kind of a run, but even it did not begin to approach the composer's great works of the 1870s and 1880s.

A master of the charming and even the beautiful in light theatre music—this last quality best witnessed by the melodies written for the hero and heroine of *Le Petit Duc*—Lecocq could also turn his hand to lustier strains, such as those of the celebrated Quarrelling Duet and ''Marchande de marée'' in *La Fille de Madame Angot,* and to swirling dance music as epitomized in the waltzing finale to the second act of the same piece. His work did not in any way lack comical strains, but his musical turn of phrase in comic situations was always more genteel than the cheerfully vulgar and belly-laugh burlesque effects of such musicians as Hervé. It is perhaps this lack of very obvious coloring that has led to his works being disproportionately neglected in modern times where only *La Fille de Madame Angot* and, to a lesser extent, *Le Petit Duc* remain in the repertoire in France.

Unlike Offenbach, Lecocq seems to have suffered but a little from the pastiche-makers down the years. He caused a great storm in the press when H B Farnie put together a ''new Lecocq opéra-bouffe'' called *The Black Prince* for London, which may have been why another and much less talented British cobbler together of semi-borrowed pieces ducked his head a little. ''Austin Fryers'' produced two musical plays, *The Japanese Girl* (1897) and the one-act *Eulalie* (1890), played by the Arthur Rouseby company (1895) on a triple bill with *Cavalleria rusticana* and *Die schöne Galathee,* each of which boasted a musical score by one ''Charles Lacock.'' The ''coq'' had become anglicized and changed its gender, but I think there is little doubt as to the source of Fryers' scores. A piece called *Una* (Dublin 5 April 1875), written by Harry Paulton for a short touring life, also sported a Lecocq pasticcio score.

1857 **Le Docteur Miracle** (Léon Battu, Ludovic Halévy) one act Théâtre des Bouffes-Parisiens 8 April

1859 **Huis-clos** (Adolphe Guénée, Adolphe Marquet) 1 act Folies-Nouvelles 28 January

1864 **Le Baiser à la porte** (Jules de la Guette) 1 act Folies-Nouvelles 26 March

1864 **Liline et Valentine** (de la Guette) 1 act Théâtre des Champs-Élysées 25 May

1865 **Les Ondines au champagne** (Hippolyte Lefèbvre, Jules Pelissié [ie, Victorien Sardou], Merle) 1 act Folies-Marigny 5 September

1866 **Le Myosotis** (''Cham,'' William Busnach) 1 act Palais-Royal 2 May

1867 **Le Cabaret de Ramponneau** (Lesire) 1 act Folies-Marigny 11 October

1868 **L'Amour et son carquois** (Marquet, Delbès [ie, Busnach]) Théâtre de l'Athénée 30 January

1868 **Fleur de thé** (Henri Chivot, Alfred Duru) Théâtre de l'Athénée 11 April

1868 **Les Jumeaux de Bergame** (Busnach) 1 act Théâtre de l'Athénée 20 November

1868 **Le Carnaval d'un merle blanc** (Chivot, Duru) Palais-Royal 30 December

1869 **Gandolfo** (Chivot, Duru) 1 act Théâtre des Bouffes-Parisiens 16 January

1869 **Deux portières pour un cordon** (w Hervé/Isidore Legouix, et al/''Lucian'' [ie, Lefebvre, L Dubuis]) 1 act Palais-Royal 15 March

1869 **Le Rajah de Mysore** (Chivot, Duru) 1 act Théâtre des Bouffes-Parisiens 21 September

1870 **Le Beau Dunois** (Chivot, Duru) Théâtre des Variétés 13 April

1871 **Le Testament de M Crac** (Jules Moinaux) 1 act Théâtre des Bouffes-Parisiens 23 October

1871 **Le Barbier de Trouville** (Adolphe Jaime, [Jules Noriac]) 1 act Théâtre des Bouffes-Parisiens 19 November

1871 **Sauvons la caisse** (de la Guette) 1 act Café Tertulia 22 December

1872 **Les Cent Vierges** (Chivot, Duru, Clairville) Fantaisies-Parisiennes, Brussels 16 March

1872 **La Fille de Madame Angot** (Clairville, Victor Koning, Paul Siraudin) Fantaisies-Parisiennes, Brussels 4 December

1874 **Giroflé-Girofla** (Eugène Leterrier, Albert Vanloo) Fantaisies-Parisiennes, Brussels 21 March

1874 **Les Prés Saint-Gervais** (Victorien Sardou, Philippe Gille) Théâtre des Variétés 14 November

1875 **Le Pompon** (Chivot, Duru) Théâtre des Folies-Dramatiques 10 November

1875 **La Petite Mariée** (Leterrier, Vanloo) Théâtre de la Renaissance 21 December

1876 **Kosiki** (Busnach, Armand Liorat) Théâtre de la Renaissance 18 October

1877 **La Marjolaine** (Leterrier, Vanloo) Théâtre de la Renaissance 3 February

1878 **Le Petit Duc** (Henri Meilhac, Halévy) Théâtre de la Renaissance 25 January

1878 **La Camargo** (Leterrier, Vanloo) Théâtre de la Renaissance 20 November

1879 **Le Grand Casimir** (Jules Prével, Albert de St-Albin) Théâtre des Variétés 11 January

1879 **La Petite Mademoiselle** (Meilhac, Halévy) Théâtre de la Renaissance 12 April

1879 **La Jolie Persane** (Leterrier, Vanloo) Théâtre de la Renaissance 28 October

1880 **L'Arbre de Noël** (Leterrier, Vanloo, Arnold Mortier) Théâtre de la Porte-Saint-Martin 6 October

1881 **Janot** (Meilhac, Halévy) Théâtre de la Renaissance 22 January

1881 **La Roussotte** (w Marius Boullard, Hervé/Meilhac, Halévy, Albert Millaud) Théâtre des Variétés 28 January

1881 **Le Jour et la nuit** (Leterrier, Vanloo) Théâtre des Nouveautés 5 November

1882 **Le Coeur et la main** (Charles Nuitter, Alexandre Beaumont) Théâtre des Nouveautés 19 October

1883 **La Princesse des Canaries** (Chivot, Duru) Théâtre des Folies-Dramatiques 9 February

1884 **L'Oiseau bleu** (Chivot, Duru) Théâtre des Nouveautés 16 January

1885 **La Vie mondaine** (Paul Ferrier, Émile de Najac) Théâtre des Nouveautés 13 February

1886 **Plutus** (Millaud, Gaston Jollivet) Opéra-Comique 31 March

1887 **Les Grenadiers de Mont-Cornette** (Daunis, Delorme, Édouard Philippe) Théâtre des Bouffes-Parisiens 4 January

1887 **Ali Baba** (Vanloo, Busnach) Théâtre de l'Alhambra, Brussels 11 November; revised version Théâtre de l'Eden, Paris 28 November 1889

1888 **La Volière** (Nuitter, Beaumont) Théâtre des Nouveautés 11 February

1890 **L'Égyptienne** (Chivot, Nuitter, Beaumont) Théâtre des Folies-Dramatiques 8 November

1894 **Nos bons chasseurs** (Paul Bilhaud, Michel Carré) 1 act Nouveau-Théâtre 10 April

1896 **Ninette** (Charles Clairville, Eugène Hubert, Christian de Trogoff) Théâtre des Bouffes-Parisiens 28 February

1898 **Ruse d'amour** (Stéphane Bordèse) 1 act Casino, Boulogne-sur-Mer 26 June

1900 **La Belle au bois dormant** (Vanloo, Georges Duval) Théâtre des Bouffes-Parisiens 19 February

1903 **Yetta** (Fernand Beissier) Galeries Saint-Hubert, Brussels 7 March

1904 **Rose mousse** (André Alexandre, Peter Carin) 1 act Théâtre des Capucines 28 January

1905 **La Salutiste** (Beissier) 1 act Théâtre des Capucines 14 January

1905 **Les Poupées de M Dupont** (Paul Gavault) 1 act Théâtre des Variétés 26 May

1910 **La Trahison de Pan** (Bordèse) 1 act Théâtre du Cercle, Aix-les-Bains 13 September

Biographies: Schneider, L: *Les Maîtres de l'opérette francaise: Hervé, Charles Lecocq* (Librarie Académique Perrin et Cie, Paris, 1924), *Une heure de musique avec Charles Lecocq* (Editions Cosmopolites, Paris, 1930)

LEDERER, George W (b Wilkes-Barre, Pa, 1861; d Jackson Heights, NY, 8 October 1938). Turn-of-the-century Broadway producer, ''twice worth about a million,'' who had his best moments at the head of the Casino Theater, but also lot of bad ones.

Professedly ''a descendant of Baron Lederer, the first Austrian Ambassador to America,'' George Lederer had his first connection with the stage as a boy soprano. Having subsequently dipped into acting, playwriting and journalism, he made his maiden venture as a theatrical producer at the age of 22, in partnership with the barely reliable Sydney Rosenfeld on a Philadelphia piece called *Florinel* (1883). During the mid-1880s he worked in variety and burlesque, notably managing Alice Harrison's company in the successful variety musical *Hot Water* (1885), ventured into comic opera for the first time with the production of *The Maid of Belleville* (1886) and went out with one of the seamier legshow outfits of the time—M Ben Leavitt and Abe Leavitt and their Rentz-Santley company (1887)—before going on to look after something called ''Bartholomew, an Equine Paradox'' (1888), to spend a spell with Randall's Theatrical Bureau (1889), to manage ''Professor Herrmann's American Amusement Enterprises'' and Herrmann's Transatlantiques (1890) and at the dawn of the '90s to tour ''George W Lederer's Players'' with the farce comedy *U & I* (1891) with notable success. However, he became more thoroughly respectable when, in September 1893, he and **Thomas CANARY** (b New York, 1836; d Raritan Landing, NJ, 12 February 1899) took over the management of Broadway's Casino Theater following the squeezing out of its financially frowsy founder, Rudolf Aronson, from its directorial chair. Lederer and his partner produced a series of musical shows at the Casino, beginning with the local musicals *The Princess Nicotine, Prince Kam* and *The Little Trooper,* and including the early American revue, *The Passing Show,* before Canary withdrew and Lederer took over as sole manager. He soon allied himself with George B McLellan, brother of the librettist C M S McLellan, but by the end of 1899 that partnership too was dissolved. In spite of many precarious moments thereafter, Lederer managed to keep control of the theatre, both as a letting proposition and also as a producing management, until 1904 when reality, theatre-owners the Sire Brothers, and New York's bank managers finally caught up with him.

Amongst the long list of new musicals, revues and imports which Lederer produced (either alone or in partnership) and/or directed at the Casino during his decade in charge were the homemade *In Gay New York, The Whirl of the Town, An American Beauty, The Belle of Bohemia, The Casino Girl,* Alice Neilsen's production of Victor Herbert's *The Singing Girl,* and, ultimately the most successful of his own productions there, *The Belle of New York*—as well as American versions of the British hit *The Lady Slavey* (on which he grabbed an intermittent author's credit), the French *La Demoiselle du téléphone* (*The Telephone Girl*), *La Falote* and *Les Fêtards* (*The Rounders*), and the Austrian *Heisses Blut* (*A Dangerous Maid*).

Lederer also expanded outwards, and he mounted pieces at Broadway theatres other than the Casino—*The Strollers* (*Die Landstreicher*), *The Blonde in Black* (1903) and *The Wild Rose* at the Knickerbocker Theater, *The Man in the Moon* at the New York Theater, *The Jewel of Asia* (1903) at the Criterion, *The Jersey Lily* (1903) at the Victoria Theater and *Sally in Our Alley* (1902) at the Broadway Theater, and a burlesque double-bill *George Lederer's Midsummer Night's Fancies* (1903) at the Crystal Gardens—as well as taking an interest in the London productions of his pieces, notably the hugely successful version of *The Belle of New York* organized in London by George Musgrove and a London season of *An American Beauty* (1900), and even touring the Casino Theater company to the Continent.

After his eviction from the Casino, Lederer took the semi-black musical *The Southerners* (1904) on the road (also director) and, after getting his breath and presumably at least part of his purse back after the awkward end of his Casino adventure, this unprofitable exercise, and a vast $170,000 bankruptcy, he once again went back into producing. He toured such pieces as *The Smiling Island* (1904), the staunch *Coming Through the Rye* (1905, w Elias and Konig) and the ''musical drama'' hotchpotch spectacle *The Girl Rangers* (1907) and then, partnered with the young H H Frazee, he produced and directed the highly successful *Madame Sherry* (1910 w A H Woods) and found himself temporarily back on the map. This kind of success did not, however, come again. In the 1910s he (co-)produced and/or directed W T Francis and Jeff de Angelis's unfortunate *The Ladies' Lion* (1911), Richard Carle's *Jumping Jupiter* (1910, co-producer w Frazee only), Junie McCree's *The Happiest Night of His Life* (1911 w Frazee) and *Mama's Baby Boy* (1912), the hopelessly pretentious *The Seventh Chord* (1913), *The Charity Girl* (1912) and the nine-performance megaflop *Madame Moselle* (1914), but spent more time in employed positions, managing Chicago's Colonial Theater, working for Klaw and Erlanger on the west coast and/or traveling as an advance rep in vaudeville. He was even very briefly managing director of the Reliance Film Company (1913) prior to one of his loud and periodic bankruptcies (January 1914), and surfaced in filmland again in 1915 producing *The Siren's Song* and other moving pictureplays. But Lederer returned ever to the theatre mounting *Angel Face* in 1919 and his last Broadway production, Victor Herbert's *The Girl in the Spotlight,* in 1920. Several subsequent musical comedies, such as the slightly Hungarian *Peaches* (1923) and *The Pajama Lady* (1930), designed for New York, foundered on their way in.

In his last years Lederer became general manager for producer Sam Harris.

Lederer was at one stage married to Reine Davies, a vaudeville vocalist and sister to the more famous Marion. His son, **Charles LEDERER** (b New York, 31 December 1910; d Los Angeles, 5 March 1976), a screen and stage author, was co-adaptor of Edward Knoblock's play *Kismet* as the libretto for the successful musical of the same name which he presented on Broadway in 1953 and worked on the movie versions of *Red, Hot and Blue!, Gentlemen Prefer Blondes* and *Can-Can,* whilst an elder son, **George W Lederer jr** (b 1891; d New York, 17 December 1924) worked as a New York theatre agent until an early death. Lederer's nephew, **Norman J Norman** (b Philadelphia, 12 November 1870; d London, 10 October 1941), who went to Britain as the company manager of the *Belle of New York* company, remained there and became European manager for the Shuberts and an occasional producer or general manager. He was also associated with the construction of the Apollo Theatre, and the opening of the Waldorf Theatre. His wife was the successful soubrette, **Marie GEORGE** (b New York, 25 June 1874; d Hammersmith, 14 July 1955), who appeared on Broadway in *The Lady Slavey* (1897), *The Belle of New York* (1897, Kissie Fitzgarter), *In Gay Paree* (Denise), *Yankee Doodle Dandy* (1898, Angela Swansdowne), *A Dangerous Maid* (1899, Lena), *The Rounders* (1899, Stella Giltedge), in several London musicals, notably the imported *An American Beauty* (1900, Rose Budd), *The Casino Girl* and *The Belle of Bohemia* (1900, Katie), *The White Chrysanthemum* (1905, Cornelia Vanderdecken), *Lady Tatters* (1907, Poll Merrie), *Baron Trenck* (1911, Mariza) and her own production of *The Boy Scout* (1912, Paul) as well as in many pantomimes. She was later seen as Mrs Pineapple in a revival of *A Chinese Honeymoon* (1915) and as Miss Trask in *Just a Kiss* (1926).

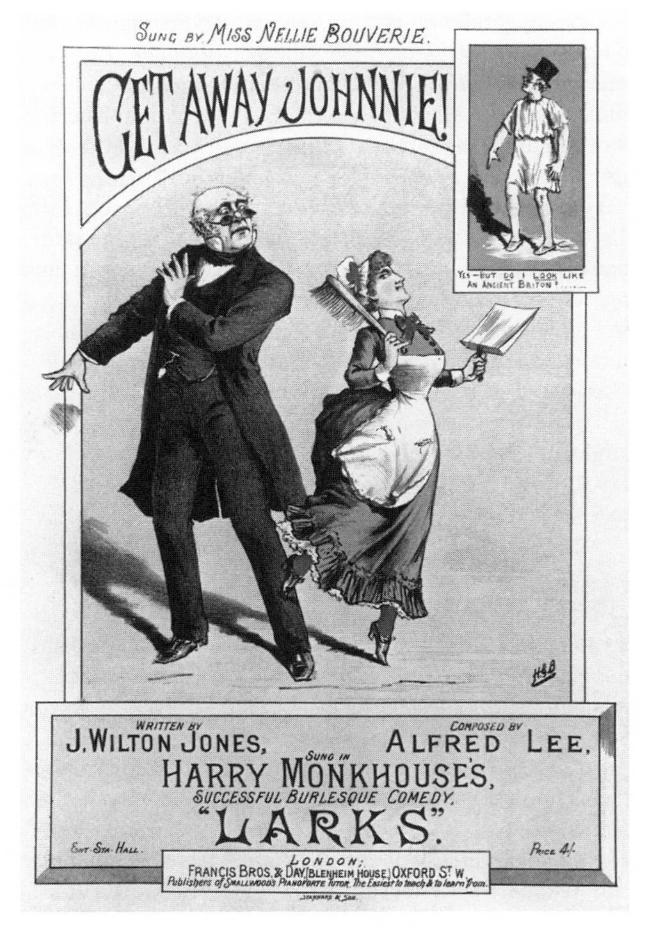

Plate 216. **Alfred Lee** *turned out a lifetime of lively songs for the musical comedy and music-hall stage.*

LEE, Alfred [Augustus] (b ?Bishopwearmouth, ?1839; d Walworth, 14 April 1906).

At first a piano tuner for Messrs Peachey, later a music-hall piano player, the purveyor of his own 1860s touring Entertainment, an arranger for the publishing house of Charles Sheard, a sometime musical director both for burlesque and touring musical comedy (*Larks, Pat,* etc) and also at London's Duke's and Astley's Theatres, Lee had some singular successes as a popular songwriter. Among a long list of music-hall songs such as "The Girl at the Telegraph," "The Jolly West End," "We Cards in the Guards," "Burgundy Ben," "Nobody's Child," "Walking in the Zoo," "Not for Joseph" or "The Late Lamented Jones" it was "Champagne Charlie" and "The Man on the Flying Trapeze" (w George Leybourne) which proved the most enduring. As a theatre composer, he arranged the music for a number of burlesques and pantomimes, and also composed several original scores and part-scores, including an operetta for the concert party run by Alfred Vance (*Swells and Shells*), a burlesque for another music-hall star in Arthur Lloyd (*Bluff King Harry*), a fresh set of songs for an expanded version of Burnand's record-breaking burlesque *Black-Eyed Susan,* mounted by William Holland (who had produced his *Roi Carotte* burlesque *Carrot and Pa-snip* a dozen years earlier) at the Alhambra in 1884, and additional numbers for two decades of shows (*Rustic Roses* 1872, *Spectresheim* 1874, *Pat* 1886, etc). His music-hall hits also found their way into the scores of many a burlesque, pantomime and touring show, and the melody of "Champagne Charlie" became one of the show-song hits of its era when adapted as "Captain Crosstree is my name" in the original edition of Burnand's *Black-Eyed Susan.*

1870 **Pom Pom** (Adolphus C Shelley) 1 act

1870 **Shells and Swells** (Hugh Willoughby Sweeney) 1 act Drill Hall, Bristol 4 April

1870 **The Beggar's Uproar** (Hubert Jay Morice) Surrey Theatre 7 May

1872 **Carrot and Pa-snip** (Frank W Green) North Woolwich Gardens 11 May

1875 **Crusoe the Second** (Green) Surrey Theatre 3 March

1877 **The Lying Dutchman** (Frederick Hay, Arthur Clements) Strand Theatre 21 December

1878 **Bluff King Harry, or The Scrapes of a Royal Rake** (w Arthur Lloyd/Green) Theatre Royal, Barrow in Furness 2 September

1884 **Black-Eyed Susan** (F C Burnand) Alhambra Theatre 2 August

1886 **Larks** (w John Crook, Oscar Barrett, et al/J Wilton Jones) Winter Garden, Southport 22 February

1891 **Pat** (John Crook, Edward Solomon, Fred Eplett/Mark Ambient, Frederic Wood/Harry Monkhouse, George Roberts) Royal Artillery Theatre, Woolwich 16 November; revised version w add mus Edward Jakobowski Aquarium, Yarmouth 1 August 1892

LEE, Bert [LEE, Albert George] (b Ravensthorpe, 11 June 1880; d Llandudno, 23 January 1946). Songwriter and musical-comedy man-of-all-parts in the British years between the wars.

Yorkshire-born Bert Lee played the organ from a young age, and cemented his connection with music when he took his first employment as a piano tuner in Manchester at the age of 15. He subsequently joined a concert party as a pianist and, when he was 19, began to try his hand composing songs. In 1910 he had a major hit with "Joshua" (ly: George Arthurs), and he made an early appearance in the West End musical theatre when his song "I Feel So Lonely" was interpolated into the musical *The Islander.* He supplied some additional songs for the inveterately touring *The Lady Slavey* (1913) and hit the bull's-eye again in the same year with the song "Hello! Hello! Who's Your Lady Friend?" (w Worton

David, Harry Fragson) before, in 1915, under the guidance of music publishers Francis, Day and Hunter, he came together with fellow songwriter R P Weston. The two then began a partnership which was to produce a 20-year run of hit songs, a considerable list of stage musicals and revues (both as joint-composers and text writers), as well as screenplays and musical scores for a number of films.

Weston and Lee began in the musical theatre supplying interpolations for *A Night Out* (1920) and the score for Herbert Clayton's touring revue *Sunshine and Laughter* (1923) before contributing the lyrics for Clayton's next venture, a touring musical version of the play *Tilly of Bloomsbury* produced in collaboration with Joe Waller. *Tilly* was played for one week at the Alhambra, giving the pair a first real West End credit. They supplied "additional material" for C B Cochran's *Turned Up* and then, with their producer pals Clayton and Waller suddenly having become big news thanks to their canny purchase of *No, No, Nanette,* they were pitchforked into the West End as adaptors of the mélange of American musicals which their mentors staged under the title *The Girl Friend.* In the following decade, Lee—and Weston up till his death—worked steadily for Clayton and/or Waller. In fact, Lee's final full West End show, in 1938, was, like his first, under Waller's management.

In between, he had contributed libretti and lyrics to a whole rang of Waller's shows—including the producer-composer's own *Virginia* ("Roll Away Clouds"), his Bobby Howes comedy musicals *Tell Her the Truth* ("Horrortorio," "Sing, Brothers") and *He Wanted Adventure* ("Smile and Be Bright"), the Howes/Binnie Hale hit *Yes, Madam?* ("Sitting Beside o' You," "Dreaming a Dream," "Czechoslovakian Love") and *Please, Teacher* ("Song of the Cello") and its successors at the Hippodrome—as well as to the Flanagan and Allen show *Give Me a Ring* and many other successful interwar comedy musicals. He also collaborated on the screenplays for the movie versions of the stage musicals *Hold My Hand* and *Yes, Madam?*

The extensive list of Lee's song hits encompasses "Any Complaints? No!," "In a Land Fit for Heroes," "Goodbyee," "Paddy McGinty's Goat," "What I Want Is a Proper Cup of Coffee," "My Word, You Do Look Queer," Stanley Holloway's comical "With Her Head Tucked Underneath Her Arm" and "Brahn Boots," "Stop and Shop at the Co-Op" as performed by Gracie Fields, "Shall I Have It Bobbed or Shingled?," the melodrama classic "And the Great Big Saw Came Nearer," Violet Loraine's "The Gipsy Warned Me" and "Fancy You Fancying Me," and his contribution to the revue stage included doctoring, adding to or just plain writing for *Who's Who, Looking Around* with Jack Norworth, *Cheep* with Harry Grattan, *US* with Hastings Turner, *Back Again, Brighter London, Carte Blanche, Pot Luck* and, after Weston's death, George Black's *London Rhapsody.*

A compilation show written by Roy Hudd based on the life and songs of Weston and Lee was produced at the Haymarket Theatre, Leicester, under the title *Just Another Verse and Chorus.*

1913 **The Soldier and the Girl** (w Worth David) sketch Chiswick Empire 21 April

1913 **After the Production** sketch Empress Theatre, Brixton 28 April

1924 **Tilly** (Haydn Wood, Jack Waller/w R P Weston/Herbert Clayton, Con West) Empire Theatre, Leeds 21 July; Alhambra 3 November

1924 **Mr Tickle MP** (w Weston) Grand Theatre, Blackpool 29 September

1926 **King Rags** (Harris Weston/w Weston) Empire Theatre, Leeds 23 August

1927 **The Girl Friend** English adaptation of the libretto of *Kitty's Kisses* w Weston (Palace Theatre)

1928 **Billy Blue** (w Joseph A Tunbridge, Fred Elkin, Weston/Harold Dayne) Empire Theatre, Newcastle 6 August

1928 **Virginia** (Waller, Tunbridge/w Furber, Weston/Clayton, Waller) Palace Theatre 24 October

1928 **Lucky Girl** (Phil Charig/w Douglas Furber, Weston) Shaftesbury Theatre 14 November

1929 **Merry, Merry** English adaptation and new lyrics w Weston (Carlton Theatre)

1929 **Hold Everything!** English adaptation w Weston (Palace Theatre)

1929 **Here Comes the Bride** (Arthur Schwartz/Desmond Carter, Howard Dietz/w Weston) Opera House, Blackpool 7 October; Piccadilly Theatre, London 20 February 1930

1930 **Sons o' Guns** English lyrics w Weston (London Hippodrome)

1930 **Little Tommy Tucker** (Vivian Ellis/w Carter, Caswell Garth, Weston) Daly's Theatre 19 November

1932 **Tell Her the Truth** (Waller, Tunbridge/w Weston) Saville Theatre 14 June

1933 **He Wanted Adventure** (Waller, Tunbridge/w Clifford Grey, Weston/w Weston) Saville Theatre 28 March

1933 **Give Me a Ring** (Martin Broones/Graham John/w Guy Bolton, Weston) London Hippodrome 22 June

1934 **Yes, Madam?** (Waller, Tunbridge/w K Browne/w Weston) London Hippodrome 27 September

1935 **Please, Teacher!** (Waller, Tunbridge/w Browne, Weston) London Hippodrome 2 October

1936 **Certainly, Sir!** (Waller, Tunbridge/w Weston) London Hippodrome 17 September

1937 **Big Business** (Waller, Tunbridge/w Carter/w Carter, Browne) London Hippodrome 18 February

1937 **Oh! You Letty** (Paul Sharon/Grey/w Geoffrey Kerr) Palace Theatre 8 December

1938 **The Fleet's Lit Up** (Vivian Ellis/w Thompson, Bolton) London Hippodrome 17 August

1938 **Bobby Get Your Gun** (Waller, Tunbridge/w Grey, Carter, Bolton, Thompson) Adelphi Theatre 7 October

1940 **Present Arms** (Noel Gay/Thompson) ''additional dialogue'' Prince of Wales Theatre 13 May

LEE, Gypsy Rose [HOVICK, Rose Louise] (b Seattle, 9 January 1914; d Los Angeles, 26 April 1970).

Labeled and classified in showbusiness history as the archetypal stripper, Miss Lee was once a player in vaudeville, and was subsequently seen in a handful of 1930s Broadway shows (*Hot-Cha!, Melody, Ziegfeld Follies*). In the early 1940s she suceeded Ethel Merman in the star role of *Dubarry Was a Lady,* and appeared alongside Bobby Clark as the principal attraction of the burlesque revue *Star and Garter* (1942).

Her memoirs, *Gypsy,* became the basis of the Styne/ Sondheim/Laurents musical of the same title which, ultimately, was more about the ambitions and staunchly stentorian heartaches of the star's mother, and in which ''Louise'' was played by Sandra Church (stage) and Natalie Wood (film).

Miss Lee's sister, **June HAVOC** (b 8 November 1916), the ''Baby June'' of the musical *Gypsy,* had a longer but equally intermittent career in the musical side of the theatre. She played in musicals at the St Louis Muny at the age of 19, appeared on Broadway in *Forbidden Melody* (1936, Rozsa), *Pal Joey* (1940, Gladys), *Mexican Hayride* (1944, Montana) and *Sadie Thompson* (1944, Sadie) and as late as 1982 starred as Mrs Lovett in *Sweeney Todd* on tour. She also authored a musical, *Oh Glorious Tintinnabulation* (Actors Studio 23 May 1974).

Miss Lee was married to film director Otto Preminger.

Literature: Preminger, E L: *Gypsy and Me* (Little, Brown, Boston, 1984)

Autobiography: *Gypsy* (Harper, New York, 1957)

LEE, Robert E[dwin] *see* LAWRENCE, JEROME

LEE, Sammy [LEVY, Samuel] (b New York, 25 May 1890; d Woodland Hills, Calif, 30 March 1968).

After appearing in his twenties as a dancer in *The Firefly* (1912, Pietro, ''special dances by'') and *The Belle of Bond Street* (1914, t/o Jack Richley), Lee made a career as a choreographer, providing the dances for more than two dozen musical comedies and revues during a decade of Broadway work. Amongst the most important shows on which he worked were the Astaires' *Lady, Be Good!* (1924), the subsequent Gershwin shows *Tell Me More!, Tip-Toes* (with its ex-ballet-dancer heroine, Queenie Smith) and *Oh, Kay!, No, No, Nanette,* the Marx Brothers vehicle *The Cocoanuts,* the spectacular *Rio Rita* with its call for everyone to do ''The Kinkajou,'' the original production of *Show Boat* and the 1927 edition of the *Ziegfeld Follies.* Lee subsequently went to Hollywood, where his work from the early 1930s was in films.

LEE, Vanessa [MOULE, Winifred Ruby] (b London, 18 June 1919; d London, 15 March 1992).

Miss Lee made her first appearance on stage at the age of 13, and on the London musical stage when she was 16 playing a schoolgirl in Anne Croft's twice-a-day *Tulip Time* (as Ruby Moule). She toured in the leading soprano parts of *Chu Chin Chow* and *The Belle of New York* and then returned to London to take over a small part in Richard Tauber's *Old Chelsea* (1942, t/o Countess of Stafford). In 1947 she understudied Jessica James as Maria Ziegler in *The Dancing Years* and she was subsequently given the principal soprano role in the post-London run of *Perchance to Dream,* playing opposite Ivor Novello in his tours of South Africa and Britain. When Novello's last show, *King's Rhapsody,* was produced, she again played opposite the author, creating the role of the Princess Cristiane and the song ''Some Day My Heart Will Awake.'' She appeared as Lady Windermere in *After the Ball,* Noël Coward's musical version of *Lady Windermere's Fan,* toured as *The Merry Widow* and played Maria in *The Sound of Music* in Australia, but thereafter limited her stage appearances to the straight stage for a number of years before retiring.

Miss Lee was the wife of actor **Peter GRAVES** [Lord] (b London, 21 October 1911; d Calais, 6 June 1994) who appeared in several of Novello's musicals, sometimes understudying and playing for the star and, in *Arc de Triomphe* (1943), creating the lead role of Pierre Bachelet built on Novello lines. He played in the original productions of Novello's *Glamorous Night* (Nico), *Careless Rapture* (Jimmy Torrence), *The Crest of the Wave* (Lord William Gantry) and *The Dancing Years* (Franzel). Graves was Lord Windermere to his wife's Lady in *After the Ball,* appeared as Orlofsky in *Gay Rosalinda,* starred as Valentine Brown in the musical of *Quality Street, Dear Miss Phoebe,* and in 1952 played Danilo to the Widow of Margaret Mitchell. He later appeared in the stage-musical version of *The Water Gipsies* and a provincial rerun of *Old Chelsea.* In a long parallel career in British films he was seen in the screen versions of *Waltz Time* (1945) and *Derby Day* (1952).

LEFTWICH, Alexander [Thornton] (b Baltimore, 24 December 1884; d Hollywood, 13 January 1947).

A former actor and production assistant, Sandy Leftwich worked behind the scenes first in variety and then in the theatre, for Daniel Frohman and later for the Shuberts. In a bright Broadway career as a director, the heart of which lasted only the half-dozen years before filmland started claiming the talents of the musical theatre, Leftwich staged a heavy schedule of revues and musicals from which his first book show, Al Jolson's *Big Boy* (1925), and the later *Hit the Deck* (1927) and *A Connecticut Yankee* (1927), both for Lew Fields, *Strike Up the Band* (1930) and Aarons and Freedley's *Girl Crazy* (1930) emerged as the most interesting and/or successful.

LEGOUIX, Isidore [Édouard] (b Paris, 18 April 1834; d Boulogne, 15 September 1916).

A Conservatoire-trained musician and composer, Isidore Legouix was an early purveyor of one-act entertainments to the Paris theatre. He had a wider success with the little piece *La Tartane,* played in Britain (Alhambra, 1871, Haymarket Theatre 3 January 1874), Australia and in America (Brooklyn Opera House 31 March 1873) in H B Farnie's version as *The Crimson Scarf* and Farnie was also responsible for *Deux portières pour un cordon,* another one-act piece to which Legouix contributed, getting a wider showing under the title *Retained on Both Sides. Un Othello* was played in Vienna as *Der Rächer* in 1872 (Strampfertheater 5 January).

1863 **Un Othello** (Charles Nuitter, Alexandre Beaumont) 1 act Théâtre des Champs-Élysées 20 June

1864 **Le Lion de Saint-Marc** (Nuitter, Beaumont) 1 act Théâtre Saint-Germain 24 November

1866 **Ma fille** (Alexis Bouvier) 1 act Délassements-Comiques 20 March

1867 **Marlborough s'en va-t-en guerre** (w Georges Bizet, Léo Delibes, Émile Jonas/William Busnach, Paul Siraudin) Théâtre de l'Athénée 15 December

1868 **Le Vengeur** (Nuitter, Beaumont) 1 act Théâtre de l'Athénée 20 November

1869 **Deux portières pour un cordon** (w Charles Lecocq, Hervé, et al/''Lucian'' [ie, Hippolyte Lefèbvre, L Dubuis]) 1 act Palais-Royal 15 March

1869 **L'Ours et l'amateur de jardins** (Busnach, Adolphe Marquet) 1 act Théâtre des Bouffes-Parisiens 1 September

1871 **La Tartane** done as *The Crimson Scarf* (ad H B Farnie) 1 act Alhambra, London 24 April

1874 **Les Dernières Grisettes** (Nuitter, Beaumont) Fantaisies-Parisiennes, Brussels 12 December

1876 **Le Mariage d'une étoile** (Eugène Grangé, Victor Bernard) 1 act Théâtre des Bouffes-Parisiens 1 April

1877 **Madame Clara, sonnambule** (Albert Vanloo, Eugène Leterrier) 1 act Palais-Royal 15 March

Other title attributed: *Le Clef d'argent*

LEHÁR, Franz [LEHÁR, Ferencz] (b Komárom, Hungary, 30 April 1870; d Bad Ischl, Austria, 24 October 1948). The celebrated composer of *Die lustige Witwe,* who switched with almost equivalent success to writing romantic Operette in the years between the wars, and whose works remain an important part of the backbone of the 20th-century Viennese repertoire.

The son of an orchestral horn-player and bandmaster, Franz Lehár studied music, and principally the violin, at Sternberg and, from the age of 12, at the Prague Conservatorium. He worked first as a teenaged violinist in the theatre orchestra of Barmen-Elberfeld then, at 19, joined a regimental band, subsequently becoming a military bandmaster in Losoncz. During this period he first tried his hand at composing opera (*Der Kürassier, Kukuska*) without success, although the latter work, written to a text by Felix Falzari, was produced at Leipzig and Königsberg in 1896 and at Budapest's Magyar Királyi Operaház in 1899, and was subsequently revised (ad M Kalbeck) and re-presented as a ''dálmű'' under the title *Tatjana.*

Lehár held several army posts before finally quitting the military to take up a position as a theatre conductor at Trieste and there, putting aside his ambitions as an operatic composer, he made his first attempts at writing for the lighter musical theatre. After several false starts *(Arabella die Kubanerin, Fräulein Leutnant, Das Club-Baby*) one of his works was accepted by his fellow Hungarian, Wilhelm Karczag, the recent lessee of Vienna's Theater an der Wien, and it was under Karczag's management that *Wiener Frauen* was produced at the Theater an der Wien in 1902, with the composer waving the baton for the occasion.

Fashionably admitting to be ''partly based on French material,'' *Wiener Frauen* featured Alexander Girardi, Oscar Sachs, soubrette Lina Abarbanell, tenor Karl Meister, and grande dame Sarolta von Rettich-Birk in its principal parts, with Julius Brammer, who would later serve Lehár as a librettist listed amongst the ''wedding guests'' in a frothy evening's entertainment. It was given a reasonable reception, played out precisely 50 performances (a favorite contractual number) and was then removed, returning the following year for another 10 performances into which were interpolated an act by Mlle Célia Galley ''of the Nouveautés, Paris'' doing her imitations of Sarah Bernhardt, Réjane, Yvette Guilbert, la Belle Otéro and other such ''Wiener Frauen.'' It played its 75th and last performance at the Theater an der Wien on 14 September 1905. The piece was also mounted at Budapest's Budai Színkör in a version which made the Frauen into local ones—*Pesti nők* and later *Pesti asszonyok.*

In the meanwhile, however, Lehár's reputation had been well and truly made. Just a month after the production of *Wiener Frauen,* Andreas Aman produced the composer's second Operette, the folksy tale of *Der Rastelbinder,* at the opposition Carltheater, with the young comic actor and singer Louis Treumann starring as the onion-seller Wolf Bär Pfefferkorn. The piece was an immediate and major hit. Whilst other Operetten came and went from the Carltheater stage and repertoire in the months that followed, *Der Rastelbinder* continued to be heavily featured in the theatre's Spielplan. By the end of the following year it had been played 189 times, it passed its 300th performance in late 1908 and continued for decades as a popular part of the Viennese repertoire whilst concurrently winning a very long list of productions throughout Europe. Franz Lehár had his first major hit in the musical theatre.

He followed up with further shows for both of Vienna's principal stages. *Der Göttergatte,* a comical retelling of the mythological Amphytrion tale, gave him a semi-success, being played for a decade (latterly in a revised version) in the repertoire of the Carltheater, but *Die Juxheirat* was a 39-performance failure at the Theater an der Wien in spite of the presence of Girardi at the head of its bill. It was no better liked back home in Hungary (*Mókaházasság,* Magyar Színház 7 September 1906) even though it managed to knock up its half-century at Berlin's Centraltheater (28 January 1905). This serious flop temporarily damped the composer's élan. Karczag, however (apparently, so it is said, with some persuasion from a friendly employee), stuck by the musician whose only real hit to date had been at the opposition theatre, and when a composer was needed for Léon and Stein's libretto to *Die lustige Witwe* it was to Lehár that the assignment was eventually given.

Lehár's *Die lustige Witwe* was not just the musical-theatre sensation of its time, both in Vienna and beyond (*The Merry Widow, La Veuve joyeuse, A víg özvegy,* etc). It was also the show which gave the all-important outward-moving impetus to the 20th-century Viennese and Hungarian school of Operette which, as a consequence, was to dominate the world's stages for the following decade and hold a fine place on them for even longer. And as the composer of *Die lustige Witwe,* Lehár would remain the standard-bearer of that school through the days of its greatest popularity.

Further hits did not follow immediately. There was a remake of *Wiener Frauen,* the first of many occasions on which Lehár would work on revisions of his moderately successful or unsuccessful shows; there was a children's piece, *Peter und Paul reisen ins Schlaraffenland,* played for a dozen matinées at the Theater an der Wien in 1906 and again for the two following Christmases, and the first and most successful of a handful of one-acters written for the same theatre's studio theatre, Hölle, called *Mitislaw der moderne,* an opérette-bouffe which had fun with the grisettes of *Die lustige Witwe* and a Danilo clone called Mitislaw. But no new *lustige Witwe.*

It was two years after the production of his hit show before Lehár presented his next major work, *Der Mann mit den drei Frauen,* again written with *Juxheirat* librettist Julius Bauer, and again mounted at the Theater an der Wien. Rudolf Christians starred as the man of the title and Mizzi Günther as the wife whom he finally keeps, but this piece of modern-day musical-beds musical comedy had few of the attractions of its famous predecessor and was played out in a two-part Vienna run of 90 performances. Nevertheless, as the next work by the internationally worshipped composer of *Die lustige Witwe, Der Mann mit den drei Frauen* won its ration of foreign productions.

Success returned more surely when Lehár returned to the land of princes and princesses and counts and countesses to turn out the scores for *Das Fürstenkind,* which featured *Die lustige Witwe* stars Treumann and Mizzi Günther through a first run of two hundred performances at the Johann Strauss-Theater and *Der Graf von Luxemburg,* a recomposed version of a libretto first (and not successfully) set by Johann Strauss, which clocked up 179 Vienna performances with Lehár's melodies attached to it before going on to a fine national and international career.

Some rather more sombre and dramatic coloring crept into much of Lehár's score for the often turbulent love story of *Zigeunerliebe* which, when it was produced in early 1910 at the Carltheater, for a period gave the composer the monopoly of Vienna's three major musical theatres: the Carltheater, the Johann Strauss-Theater (*Das Fürstenkind*) and the Theater an der Wien (*Der Graf von Luxemburg*). *Zigeunerliebe*'s score gave a foretaste of the more sentimental and romantic style of show that Lehár would give to the postwar musical theatre, but the tones with which the composer imbued the music of this early ''romantische Operette'' were the freshest and most exciting of all that he would accomplish in a field in which he would later linger a little more self-indulgently. Mizzi Zwerenz top-billed, and *Zigeunerliebe* did even better than the composer's other two Operetten in 1910 Vienna, ending its first run after 232 performances before going on to productions around the world.

The Theater an der Wien followed up with Treumann and Günther in *Eva,* a less colorful piece which nevertheless confirmed the previous run of success with a fine 226 performances, and, after a short interlude in which Lehár composed music for two little pieces for the Hölle studio theatre and an incidental minuet for Árpád Pasztor's Budapest play *A lányom,* the composer followed up with *Die ideale Gattin* (a rewrite of *Der Göttergatte*), which had only an indifferent run (111 performances), and the decidedly individual ''mountain musical'' *Endlich allein* in which Mizzi Günther and Hubert Marischka spent time up a Swiss alp working out their love story for the same number of first-run performances. If Vienna did not decide statistically between the two, the rest of the world did, and the more enjoyable *Endlich al-*

lein had easily the better career of the pair until it was put down by becoming Lehár's latest candidate for a remake. The Theater in der Josefstadt's production of *Der Sterngucker* (1916) proved Lehár's least welcomed piece since the days of *Die Juxheirat* (79 performances), and even when it was rewritten and restaged later the same year at the Theater an der Wien, it had no more success. The music duly went into the drawer of "scores to be recycled" and, like the preceding two pieces, it was, frequently.

Following this run of less than triumphant productions on the Viennese stage, Lehár saw his next premieere take place in his native Hungary. *A pacsirta* ("the lark"), a piece composed to a libretto by Ferenc Martos, was produced at Budapest's Király Színház and the slim Hungarian tale ran for a season there, with Emmi Kosáry, Ilona Dömötör and Ernő Király starring, before being produced in Vienna the following month. At the Theater an der Wien the retitled *Wo die Lerche singt* took off solidly and it ran with all the vigor typical of a well-liked and escapist wartime show, to such effect that it piled up the longest initial season of any Lehár musical since *Die lustige Witwe* (379 performances). When the fighting died, however, the piece did not prove to be as attractive as many of his others and it did not have a significant international career.

After the First World War, however, the kind of success Lehár had achieved with *Wo die Lerche singt* continued. The up-to-date musical comedy *Die blaue Mazur* (1920) kept the Theater an der Wien occupied for 11 months, Carlo Lombardo's revusical-spectacular remake of *Der Sterngucker* as *La danza delle libellule* did well enough in Italy finally to put Lehár's score, with its hit number "Gigolette," into international orbit at the third time of asking, and the Spanish story of *Frasquita* allowed Betty Fischer to vamp her way through the composer's not very serious attempt at Iberian-flavored music opposite Hubert Marischka and take over Richard Tauber for some six months at a Theater an der Wien where the repertoire (*Eva, Die lustige Witwe, Zigeunerliebe, Die blaue Mazur, Der Graf von Luxemburg, Wo die Lerche singt, Der Rastelbinder*) in late 1922 seemed to be entirely made up of Lehár works, old, very old and new.

A Chinese Operette, *Die gelbe Jacke,* played 104 performances at the Theater an der Wien, and another musical-comedy piece, apparently aimed at the international market and featuring Theater an der Wien star Luise Kartousch as the eponymous Parisian revue star of *Cloclo* (1924), was played at the Bürgertheater for two and a half months before reaching its hundredth performance at the Johann Strauss-Theater later in the year and duly going out for export.

It was now, however, that the receipt of an unsolicited manuscript sent Lehár out on a track leading far from the French farcicalities of *Cloclo* and into an area of which intimations had been heard more than a decade earlier, in *Zigeunerliebe.* Paul Knepler's libretto for *Paganini* was a piece written squarely in the romantic mode, and Lehár set it with a lushly romantic score in which the leading tenor role, created by actor-turned-opera-star Carl Clewing, was paramount. The show had a five-month run in Vienna, but it did better in Berlin where Richard Tauber appeared as Paganini and made "Gern hab' ich die Frau'n geküsst" his own. That song ("Girls Were Made to Love and Kiss") went around the world and it ultimately became more widely popular than the Operette, the success of which remained limited to Germany and France.

Paganini's Berlin season, however, had made a notable effect and, from this time on, Lehár's new works were mounted almost exclusively in Germany. They also stuck textually close to the kind of romantic Operette outline which Knepler and *Paganini* had used and which was very quickly to become a sine qua non and, eventually, a cliché of the Operettic stage. Boy (tenor and Tauber, for preference) loves girl, wins girl and ultimately has to renounce girl for reasons of state, career or some other shade of incompatibility at the final curtain. The unhappy ending was obligatory, and only once in the following years, in a remake of the old *Endlich allein,* did Lehár and his librettists allow an "old-fashioned" happy ending as a climax to one of their works. The result of all this textual unhappiness was to set the composer loose on a lot of often sad and dramatic sentiments, and it was romantic music often deeply dyed with misery which made up much of the scores of Lehár's later Operetten. Much of it, also, was tenor music, for Lehár's on- and off-stage friendship with Tauber meant that the starring roles in these Operetten were custom-made for the popular singer. Much of it, again, was splendid music and Lehár's talent shone as brightly in the best of his postwar scores as in his prewar ones, but the color of the shine was a different one.

The first, and deepest dyed, of the series that followed *Paganini* was a version of Gabryela Zapolska's romantic novella about a Russian princeling *Der Zarewitsch* who, having been slow to find his sexuality and romance, has to give it up in *Alt-Heidelberg* fashion, when the time comes to take up his crown (1927). The second, which put the poet Goethe into the same kind of sorry love affair already inflicted on poor Paganini and the semi-historical Russian, allowed his sweet *Friederike* (1928) to do the renouncing whilst he secured the vocal bonbon of the show "O Mädchen, mein Mädchen." Once again, the bonbon traveled better than the show, but both Operetten were thoroughly appreciated in their original productions (though much less in export) and have remained popular in central Europe for more than half a century.

The most successful of the Lehár romantic musicals, however, was none of these new pieces but another remake. *Das Land des Lächelns* (1929) was a Tauberized version of *Die gelbe Jacke* with the happy ending of the original changed to an unhappy one to fit the fashionable formula, and a new tenor number, "Dein ist mein ganzes Herz," prominent in the star role. A major hit in several languages in Europe and one of the bastions of the European Operette repertoire to this day, it did not, however, make itself a career beyond. "Dein ist mein ganzes Herz," under the titles "You Are My Heart's Delight" (UK) and "Yours Is My Heart Alone" (USA), like Lehár's previous tenor solos, did very much better with English-speaking audiences than the show that hosted it. The successor to *Das Land des Lächelns* was another remake, this time of *Endlich allein.* Once again, however, although *Schön ist die Welt* proved to be a long-running hit at home, it turned out to be of little interest outside Europe.

This line of deeply sentimental and musically lush costume pieces, each with its modish downbeat ending and far, even in their lighter moments, from displaying the sparkling frivolity of Lehár's earlier works, culminated in the composer's biggest-sing Operette of all, the tempestuous "musikalische Komödie" *Giuditta,* produced at the Vienna Staatsoper with Tauber starring opposite cruiserweight soprano Jarmila Novotna. *Giuditta* had a limited life in its unlikely home (42 performances), although, like its predecessors, it left a legacy of several beautiful songs—soprano ones, this time—to the light-opera repertoire.

Giuditta was Lehár's last original work. The striving towards an operatic Operette already evidenced in his rearrangement of *Frasquita* for Paris's Opéra-Comique, and in his angling of the score of *Giuditta* towards operatic voices, was continued in a rewrite of *Zigeunerliebe* as an opera for the Budapest Operaház, but otherwise he limited himself, in the years running up to the Second World War, to a handful of film scores (*Grossfürstin Alexandra, Die ganze Welt dreht sich um Liebe, Eine Nacht in Wien, Die Gefährten des Odysseus*) and to efforts to reassemble the publishing of his work under the banner of his own firm, Glocken Verlag.

Lehár's non-Operettic stage music included a share in the score for the wartime Volksstück (w Eysler) *Komm, deutscher Bruder,* accompanying waltz music for the 1916 György Ruttkay play *Keringő* (*Walzer* Magyár Színház 23 September 1916) and "musikalische Illustrationen" to Heinrich Ilgenstein's Schwank *Der Walzer von heute Nacht* (Kleines Theater, Berlin 17 January 1930).

Lehár's body of work, one of the most important in the 20th-century European Operette at the period of its greatness, falls clearly into two halves. The earlier contains his most attractive work, the later, deliberately more pretentious, his most impressive. But, although the individual songs from his romantic Operetten still have international success and the best of the shows which housed them still win regular performances in Europe, it is the gaily glittering *Die lustige Witwe* which, with Strauss's *Die Fledermaus,* remains the worldwide epitome of Viennese Operette and Lehár's enduring monument.

1902 **Wiener Frauen** (aka *Der Klavierstimmer*) (Ottokar Tann-Bergler, Emil Norini) Theater an der Wien 21 November

1902 **Der Rastelbinder** (Victor Léon) Carltheater 20 December

1904 **Der Göttergatte** (Léon, Leo Stein) Carltheater 20 January

1904 **Die Juxheirat** (Julius Bauer) Theater an der Wien 22 December

1905 **Die lustige Witwe** (Léon, Stein) Theater an der Wien 30 December

1906 **Der Schlüssel zum Paradies** (revised *Wiener Frauen*) Stadttheater, Leipzig October

1906 **Peter und Paul reisen ins Schlaraffenland** (Fritz Grünbaum, Robert Bodanzky) Theater an der Wien 1 December

1907 **Mitislaw der moderne** (Grünbaum, Bodanzky) 1 act Hölle 5 January

1907 **Tatiana** (revised *Kukuska* Felix Falzari ad M Kalbeck) Magyar Király Operaház 28 April

1908 **Der Mann mit den drei Frauen** (Bauer) Theater an der Wien 21 January

1909 **Das Fürstenkind** (Léon) Johann Strauss-Theater 7 October

1909 **Der Graf von Luxemburg** (aka *Der Graf von Luxenburg*) (A M Willner, Bodanzky) Theater an der Wien 12 November

1910 **Zigeunerliebe** (Willner, Bodanzky) Carltheater 8 January

1911 **Die Spieluhr** (T Zasche) 1 act Hölle 7 January

1911 **Eva (das Fabriksmädel)** (Willner, Bodanzky) Theater an der Wien 24 November

1912 **Rosenstock und Edelweiss** (Bauer) 1 act Hölle 1 December

1913 **Die ideale Gattin** (revised *Der Göttergatte*) Theater an der Wien 11 October

1914 **Endlich allein** (Willner, Bodanzky) Theater an der Wien 30 January

1914 **Komm, deutscher Bruder** (w Edmund Eysler/Carl Lindau, August Neidhart) Raimundtheater 4 October

1916 **Der Sterngucker** (Fritz Löhner-Beda, Willner) Theater in der Josefstadt 14 January (revised version Theater an der Wien 26 September)

1918 **A pacsirta** (*Wo die Lerche singt*) (Ferenc Martos) Király Színház, Budapest 1 February

1920 **Die blaue Mazur** (Stein, Béla Jenbach) Theater an der Wien 28 May

1921 **Die Tangokönigin** (revised *Der Göttergatte*) Apollotheater 9 September

1922 **Frühling** (Rudolf Eger) 1 act Hölle 20 January

1922 **Frasquita** (Willner, Heinz Reichert) Theater an der Wien 12 May

1922 **Libellentanz** (aka *Die drei Grazien*) (revised *Der Sterngucker,* as *La danza delle libellule*) (ad Carlo Lombardo) Teatro Lirico, Milan 27 September

1923 **Die gelbe Jacke** (Léon) Theater an der Wien 9 February

1924 **Cloclo** (Jenbach) Bürgertheater 8 March

1925 **Paganini** (Paul Knepler, Jenbach) Johann Strauss-Theater 30 October

1926 **Gigolette** (revised *La danza delle libellule*) (ad Lombardo, Gioacchino Forzano) Teatro Lirico, Milan 30 October

1927 **Der Zarewitsch** (Jenbach, Reichert) Deutsches Künstlertheater, Berlin 21 February

1928 **Das Frühlingsmädel** (pasticcio/Rudolf Eger) Theater am Zoo, Berlin 29 May

1928 **Friederike** (Ludwig Herzer, Löhner-Beda) Metropoltheater, Berlin 4 October

1929 **Das Land des Lächelns** (revised *Die gelbe Jacke*) (Herzer, Löhner-Beda) Metropoltheater, Berlin 10 October

1930 **Schön ist die Welt** (revised *Endlich allein*) Metropoltheater, Berlin 3 December

1932 **Der Fürst der Berge** (revised *Das Fürstenkind*) Theater am Nollendorfplatz, Berlin 23 September

1934 **Giuditta** (Knepler, Löhner-Beda) Staatsoper, Vienna 20 January

Biographies: Decsey, E: *Franz Lehár* (Drei Masken Verlag, Berlin, 1924), Czech, S: *Franz Lehár: Sein Weg und sein Werk* (Franz Perneder, Berlin, 1942) and as *Schön ist die Welt: Franz Lehárs Leben und Werk* (Berlin, 1957), Peteani, M von: *Franz Lehéar, seine Musik, sein Leben* (Glocken Verlag, Vienna, 1950), Grün, B: *Gold and Silver: The Life and Times of Franz Lehár* (David McKay, New York, 1970), Schneidereit, O: *Franz Lehár: Eine Biographie in Zitaten* (Pinguin-Verlag, Innsbruck, 1984), Frey, S: *Franz Lehár oder Das schlechte Gewissen der leichten Musik* (Niemeyer, 1995), Haffner, H, Haffner, I: *Immer nur lächeln: Das Franz Lehár-Buch* (Heyne, Munich, 1998), Frey, S: *Was sagt ihr zu diesem Erfolg: Franz Lehár und die Unterhaltungsmusik im 20. Jahrhundert* (Insel, Frankfurt, 1999), etc

LEHMANN, Liza [LEHMANN, Elizabeth Nina Mary Frederika] (b London, 11 July 1862; d Pinner, Middlesex, 19 September 1918).

The daughter of the Hamburg-born painter Rudolf Lehmann, Liza Lehmann was brought up in a home where the famous and fashionable of London were often to be found. Thoroughly educated in all the arts, she was at first a concert singer, and then a composer, becoming well known for her parlor music and, in particular, for the song cycles "In a Persian Garden" (1896) and "The Daisy Chain" and an "In Memoriam" based on Tennyson's poem. In 1904 she was commissioned by Frank Curzon, who had just had record-breaking success with the musical comedy *A Chinese Honeymoon,* to provide the score for another piece in a similar vein. Teamed with top librettist Owen Hall and lyricist James Hickory Wood, Miss Lehmann turned out a fine set of popular-styled songs for the musical comedy *Sergeant Brue* without writing anything that was likely to wear out the barrel organs of the town.

Sergeant Brue had a good London run and a Broadway production (1905) but, irritated at the way Curzon had interpolated other composers' music into her score despite her announced willingness to supply any extra music, Miss Lehmann wrote no more for the musical-comedy stage. She did, however, provide an elegant score to a text by Laurence Housman for a comic-opera version of *The Vicar of Wakefield* (1906). This time it was the librettist who flounced angrily out when his over-long book was cut to make room for the vast amount of music his composer had supplied. *The Vicar of Wakefield* was produced in the West End by vocalist David Bispham with some success, but once again the composer ventured no further. After one musical comedy and one comic opera she moved on to compose the score for one opera, *Everyman,* which was produced by the Beecham Opera Company in 1916. She also composed a score of incidental music for a stage version of Oscar Wilde's *The Happy Prince* (1909).

1904 **Sergeant Brue** (Owen Hall, James Hickory Wood) Strand Theatre 14 June

1906 **The Vicar of Wakefield** (Laurence Housman) Prince of Wales Theatre 12 December

Autobiography: *The Life of Liza Lehmann by Herself* (T Fisher Unwin, London, 1919)

LEHMANN, Maurice (b Paris, 14 May 1895; d Paris, 17 May 1974). Paris's champion of the opérette à grand spectacle through several decades, particularly at the helm of the vast Théâtre du Châtelet.

Originally an accountant in an automobile emporium, then an actor (at first as "Dormel") at the Comédie-Française and at the Théâtre de la Porte-Saint-Martin, Lehmann became the director of the Nouvel-Ambigu and of the Porte-Saint-Martin in the early 1920s. In 1928 he was taken on as the partner of Alexandre Fontanes at the head of the Théâtre du Châtelet and, soon after, was left at the sole head of the management of that great auditorium. He was to run it for most of the next 40 years and, during his tenancy, bring to Paris a long series of musical productions with a heavy accent on spectacular staging.

The series began in 1929 with the production of the French version of *Show Boat* (*Mississippi*) and continued through its first decade with *Robert le Pirate* (*The New Moon*), Joseph Szulc's North African extravaganza *Sidonie Panache,* the long run of *Nina Rosa* and an original work commissioned from that show's composer, Sigmund Romberg, for the Châtelet stage and entitled *Rose de France.* These were followed by the picturesque *Au temps des merveilleuses,* Yvain's *Au soleil du Mexique, Yana,* Romberg's *Le Chant du tzigane* (*Forbidden Melody*) and the comical and (of course) scenery-filled chase after the contents of *Le Coffre-fort vivant,* mixed with occasional productions of such Châtelet traditionals as the long-loved everything-that-moves mounting of the stage version of Verne's *Le Tour du monde en 80 jours.*

The war years were filled, as war years so often are, with revivals as well as two new shows, *Valses de France* and *Le Beau Voyage d'un enfant à Paris;* the years following the war brought the filmland *Les Chasseurs d'images, La Maréchale Sans-Gêne* and *Annie du Far-West* (*Annie Get Your Gun*) as well as revivals of, in particular, the frequently recalled *L'Auberge du Cheval Blanc* and *Valses de Vienne,* before in 1950 Lehmann called in composer Francis Lopez, the newly popular writer of *La Belle de Cadix,* to supply him with his next piece. Lopez became, for a period, chief supplier of music to the Châtelet, following the romantic Hispanneries of *Pour Don Carlos* with the 905-performance run of Luis Mariano's newest star-vehicle *Le Chanteur de Mexico,* musical adventure in oil-rich Turkestan in *La Toison d'or* and a saga of smuggling skulduggery in song amid the islands of the *Méditerranée* with Corsican star Tino Rossi at its head. In the late 1950s, Lehmann mounted *Maria Flora,* the Lehár pasticcio *Rose de Noël* and Lopez's *Le Secret de Marco Polo,* and in the 1960s a French version of *Some Like It Hot* (*La Polka des Lampions*), *Eugène le Mystérieux* and Charles Aznavour's *Monsieur Carnaval* amongst continuing reprises of the most popular older pieces. *Monsieur Carnaval* was Lehmann's last production at the Châtelet from which he retired in 1966.

From 1933 Lehmann turned the Porte-Saint-Martin over to musical shows as well, staging opera, opéra-comique and opérette and including amongst his productions both grandiose revivals of the classic repertoire, modern imports (*La Dubarry, Valses de Vienne, Violette de Montmartre*), such occasional new pieces as Pierné's *Fragonard* and, with more success than any of these, the musical comedy *Ignace* with Fernandel starred, until he handed over the management in 1938. At this stage he took over the Théâtre Mogador where, alongside his Châtelet shows, he produced further large-scale musical shows—the British *Balalaika,* the ex-Austrian *Billy et son équipe* and a revival of the eternal *Rose Marie*—before the wartime closures intervened.

After the war he was engaged in the reopening of the Paris Opéra and the Opéra-Comique, and he later returned to this arena between 1952 and 1955, but his principal fame in the Paris theatre was won in his long tenancy of the Châtelet and his championing there of the opérette à grand spectacle.

1948 **La Maréchale Sans-Gêne** (Pierre Petit/Albert Willemetz/ Victorien Sardou, Émil Moreau ad) Théâtre du Châtelet 17 February

Autobiography: *Trompe l'oeil* (Editions de la pensée moderne, Paris, 1971)

LEICHTE KAVALLERIE Comic Operette in 2 acts by Karl Costa. Music by Franz von Suppé. Carltheater, Vienna, 21 March 1866.

Following the success of his short pieces *Das Pensionat, Zehn Mädchen und kein Mann, Flotte Bursche* and *Die schöne Galathee,* Suppé ventured for the first time into a two-act Operette format, in collaboration with the prolific and successful playwright Karl Costa, on *Leichte Kavallerie.*

The orphan Vilma (Frln Mayer) has grown up so pretty that the wives of the Burgermeister Bums (Grois) and city official Pankraz (Josef Matras) cannot bear to have her around, even though the girl has eyes only for her own Hermann (Telek). When the lascivious Burgermeister refuses to allow her to wed Hermann, the boy enlists the help of two Hungarian cavalry officers, János (Carl Treumann) and Carol (Frln Völl), to stage a series of rendezvous which will allow the jealous wives (Fr Walter, Fr Bachmann) to catch their husbands misbehaving. János plays his part in the charade, but, as he does, he cannot help thinking of his old, lost love and the song they sang together. Then he hears that song. It is Vilma singing—the orphan is an orphan no longer, she has found her father and he is only too happy for her to wed Hermann. Then the trumpets sound and, their duty done, the Light Cavalry leave town.

Of Suppé's score to this, one of the most successful of his earliest Operetten, only the celebrated overture is heard today, but the rest of the score, put together with the aid of some popular Hungarian military melodies, produced a number of attractive and/or humorous pieces of which a number mocking jumped-up local officials (''Wie gescheit, wie gescheit, wir von der G'meind'') proved the favorite.

After its first season at the Carltheater, *Leichte Kavallerie* was regularly reproduced in Vienna, appearing at the Hietzing ''Zur neuen Welt'' (20 July 1870), returning to the Carltheater in 1872 (11 performances), 1873 (11 performances), 1874 (1 performance), 1875 (4 performances) and in 1876 (5 performances) with Blasel (Bums) and Karoline Finaly (Vilma). Later it played at the Theater an der Wien, first from 17 January 1888, then in 1898 in a double bill with *La Chanson de Fortunio* in which Joseffy played János and Streitmann was Hermann, and as late as 1914 (paired with *Flotte Bursche*), as well as appearing on a bill at Ronacher (9 August 1896), and again at the Carltheater in 1905 with Blasel still playing Bums.

The show was first seen in Hungary in 1867, being performed at the Budai Színkör one night in the original German and the next, as *Magyar huszárok,* in Hungarian, by István Bényei's company. It was subsequently played there also under the title *Könnyű lovasság,* and duly appeared in Germany and in the German theatres in America. An English version (ad Harry Gates), which was noted as being ''revised and adapted'' was given at the San Francisco Tivoli in 1880 with Hattie Moore as its Vilma. However, apart from that eternal overture, it did not evoke sufficient interest anywhere else outside central Europe to win productions in an era of musical theatre which was very largely devoted to the many and very available works of Offenbach. A French-language version was made by Gustave Lagye but, although it may have been performed in Belgium, there is no record of a first-class professional staging of *Cavalerie légère* in France.

Germany: ?1866; Hungary: Budai Színkör (Ger) 10 May 1867, *Magyar huszárok* 11 May 1867; USA: Stadttheater 1 October 1869, Tivoli Opera House, San Francisco *Light Cavalry* 23 August 1880

LEIGH, Carolyn [ROSENTHAL, Carolyn Paula] (b New York, 21 August 1926; d New York, 19 November 1981).

At first a writer of radio link material and advertising copy, Carolyn Leigh won her first contract to compose song lyrics in 1951 and subsequently produced a number of successful songs including ''Young at Heart'' (w Johnny Richards) sung in the 1954 Frank Sinatra film of the same title, ''The Day the Circus Left Town'' (w E D Thomas), ''Witchcraft'' (w Cy Coleman) and ''You Fascinate Me So'' (w Coleman). She made her first input to the musical theatre when, on the initiative of Mary Martin, she was invited to supply the lyrics to Moose Charlap's songs for the 1954 Broadway version of *Peter Pan* (''I'm Flying,'' ''I Won't Grow Up'').

She contributed to the revues *Shoestring '57* (w Phillip Springer), *Take Five* (1957, w Springer), *The Ziegfeld Follies of 1957* (w Springer) and *Demi-Dozen* (1958 w Coleman) and later to the unhappy attempt to write a new *Hellzapoppin* (1976 w Coleman, Jule Styne), but her principal successes on the musical stage came with two collaborations with Coleman, the Lucille Ball vehicle *Wildcat,* in which the star introduced ''Hey, Look Me Over,'' and the Neil Simon burlesque *Little Me* from which ''Real, Live Girl,'' ''I've Got Your Number'' and ''The Other Side of the Tracks'' added to her palette of song hits. Her fourth and final Broadway musical was *How Now, Dow Jones,* written with composer Elmer Bernstein, who had supplied additional music to *Peter Pan.*

In 1955 Miss Leigh supplied the lyrics for a NBC television musical version of the children's tale *Heidi* (C Warnick, M Pahl, Irwin Kostal/Beil Simon, William Friedberg 1 October).

1954 **Peter Pan** (Moose Charlap, Jule Styne/w Adolph Green, Betty Comden) Winter Garden Theater 20 October

1960 **Wildcat** (Cy Coleman/N Richard Nash) Alvin Theater 16 December

1962 **Little Me** (Coleman/Neil Simon) Lunt-Fontanne Theater 17 November

1967 **How Now, Dow Jones** (Elmer Bernstein/Max Shulman) Lunt-Fontanne Theater 7 December

LEIGH, Gracie [ELLIS, Edith] (b Chelsea, ?1875; d Box, Glos, 24 June 1950). Musical comedienne who had nearly 30 years of stage stardom in Britain.

Daughter of artist Edwin Ellis and his actress wife, pert little Gracie Leigh went on the stage at a young age and was to be seen touring in the title role of *Little Red Riding Hood* for Rothbury Evans as early as 1890. She came to notice in no uncertain way in her very first London role, playing the music hall's common little Trixie Triplet in the musical *Little Miss Nobody* (1898). Brought in to take up the principal soubrette part during a cast reshuffle in rehearsals, she went on to make a notable personal success. She was subsequently hired by George Edwardes and sent on tour as soubrette in *A Greek Slave* (1899, Iris) but when Ada Reeve walked out of the show's chief feminine comic role of Dudley in *San Toy* (1899), also in rehearsals, Leigh was again called in as an emergency, and once again she went on to score a personal hit. She was thereafter kept several years on the payroll by Edwardes for whom she played important female comedy roles in *A Country Girl* (1902, t/o Madame Sophie) and *The Cingalee* (1904, Peggy Sabine) at Daly's, becoming in the course of these years one of the town's most popular musical comediennes. In between time she also played in Edwardes's unfortunate *The Merry-Go-Round,* in several comedies and short musical pieces, and also took over from Marie Dainton for a period as Mrs Pineapple in the long-running *A Chinese Honeymoon.*

She appeared in the short-lived London production of *The Gay Lord Vergy* (1905, *Le Sire de Vergy*) in the role of the belly-dancing Mitzy created in Paris by Ève Lavallière, dropped out of the small-scale *The White Chrysanthemum,* and was seen in a typical low-comedy role in the popular *The Dairymaids* (1906, Eliza) before she was contracted by Frank Curzon for the Prince of Wales Theatre. There she scored her biggest success of all when she created the comedy-soubrette role of Mina in *Miss Hook of Holland* (1907, ''A Pink Petty from Peter,'' ''The Flying Dutchman''). Similar clowning, song-and-dance roles followed in *My Mimosa Maid* (1908, Popotte), *King of Cadonia* (1908, Militza) and

Dear Little Denmark (1909, Ophelia), before she left the Prince of Wales and returned to the Edwardes stable to create the lead comedy parts of *The Quaker Girl* (1912, Phoebe), the English version of Kálmán's *Autumn Manoeuvres* (1912, Lady Larkin), *The Dancing Mistress* (1912, Jeannie McTavish) and *The Girl from Utah* (1913, Clancy). In 1913 she visited America to star alongside Hazel Dawn in Ivan Caryll's *The Little Café* (Katziolinka).

During the First World War Miss Leigh appeared in a revival of *Miss Hook of Holland* and in the revue *Airs and Graces,* but thereafter abandoned the stage for several years. She returned in 1921 to take the comedy role of Wei Wa Shei in *Cairo,* Oscar Asche's successor to *Chu Chin Chow,* and appeared in the quick flop *Almond Eye* (1923) and in several plays before scoring the best and last success of the second part of her career as the maid, Pauline, in the London production of *No, No, Nanette* (1925).

Her husband, **Lionel MACKINDER** (b Faversham, Kent, 17 June 1868; d Le Touret, France, 9 January 1915), after an early actor-manager experience with the touring ''nautical burlesque drama'' *The Water Babes* (1894) worked for a number of years—and very largely for Edwardes—as a musical-comedy juvenile man, appearing in *The Shop Girl* (1895, t/o Charles Appleby, Miggles), *The Circus Girl* (1896, Hon Reginald Gower), *Little Miss Nobody* (1898, Gussie Stilton), *The Merry-Go-Round* (1899, Charlie Dalrymple), *San Toy* (1899, Lt Harvey Tucker), *The Messenger Boy* (1900, Clive Radnor), *The Toreador* (1901, Augustus Traill), *The Orchid* (1903, Dr Ronald Fausset), *The Spring Chicken* (1906, Boniface), *The Girls of Gottenberg* (1907, t/o Prince Otto), *Bonita* (1911, Frederico), etc. He was killed in action with the Royal Berkshire Regiment during World War I.

LEIGH, H[enry] S[ambrook] (b London, 29 March 1837; d London, 16 June 1883).

Sometime journalist, adaptor, stagewriter and lyricist, and a cousin of Charles J Mathews, the bohemian bachelor Leigh was known as a man of culture and wit and a very devil at whist in the purlieus of London's Savage Club. His speciality was the writing of satirical verses and of songs, set to simple melodies, which he played and sang himself and, occasionally, inserted into a topical burlesque (*Robin Hood* Victoria Theatre, 1871, etc). With the coming of opéra-bouffe, he turned his talents firmly to the theatre, and he was responsible for the English-language stage versions of a number of popular large-scale opéras-bouffes and Operetten of the 1870s and 1880s. He also supplied verses to the Moore and Burgess Minstrels (''Le choeur des cuisiniers'' from *Les Cent Vierges,* 1874, etc), published several collections of lyrics (*Gillot and Goosequill, Carols of Cockayne*—including the famous ''Uncle John,'' *A Town Garland, Strains from the Strand*) and authored both an operatic version of *Cinderella* (music: John Farmer, Harrow, 1883) and an English version of Paladilhe's *Suzanne* (Theatre Royal, Portsmouth, 1884) before his death at the age of 46.

1871 **Falsacappa** (*Les Brigands*) English version (Globe Theatre)
1872 **Le Roi Carotte** English version (Alhambra Theatre)
1872 **Le Pont des soupirs** English version (St James's Theatre)
1875 **La Chatte blanche** English version (Queen's Theatre)
1876 **Le Voyage dans la lune** English version (Alhambra Theatre)
1878 **Fatinitza** English version (Alhambra Theatre)
1879 **La Petite Mademoiselle** English version w Robert Reece (Alhambra Theatre)
1879 **Le Grand Casimir** English version (Gaiety Theatre)
1883 **Lurette** (*Belle Lurette*) English lyrics (Avenue Theatre)
1883 **Prince Methusalem** (*Prinz Methusalem*) English version (Folies Dramatiques)

LEIGH, Mitch [MICHNIK, Irwin] (b Brooklyn, NY, 30 January 1928). The composer of one major Broadway hit who never came near repeating that success.

Leigh studied music at Yale and began a career in 1954 as a composer of television and radio commercial music. He subsequently founded the commercial production house Music Makers. He wrote incidental music for several plays in the early 1960s (*Too True to Be Good, Never Live Over a Pretzel Factory*) and put music to a version of Sean O'Casey's *Purple Dust,* before breaking through as a Broadway composer with his score for *Man of La Mancha* (1965, ''The Impossible Dream,'' ''Man of La Mancha,'' Tony Award). Whilst *Man of La Mancha* continued to travel around the world's stages, Leigh's subsequent efforts at stage musicals foundered, with two shows closing on the road and two others closing after one and eight performances on Broadway, respectively.

A 1979 musical *Sarava,* based on *Doña Flor and Her Two Husbands,* which never officially opened on Broadway, nevertheless lasted several months there, whilst a Mike Todd biomusical produced in Philadelphia in 1988 and seen subsequently on Broadway as *Ain't Broadway Grand* also got into double figures.

Leigh subsequently operated more successfully as a producer when his Mitch Leigh Company mounted the highly successful Yul Brynner revival of *The King and I* of the 1980s, but the company later failed in an effort to bring his *Chu Chem* from a revival at the Jewish Repertory Theater to Broadway (w William D Rollnick, 44 performances).

1965 **Purple Dust** (Sean O'Casey ad) Goodspeed Opera House, East Haddam August

1965 **Man of La Mancha** (Joe Darion) Goodspeed Opera House, East Haddam 28 June; ANTA Washington Square Theater, New York 22 November

1966 **Chu Chem** (Jim Haines, Jack Wohl/Ted Allan) New Locust Street Theater, Philadelphia 15 November; Ritz Theater, New York 17 March 1989

1970 **Cry for Us All** (William Alfred, Phyllis Robinson/Alfred, Albert Marre) Broadhurst Theater 8 April

1972 **Halloween** (Sidney Michaels) Bucks County Playhouse 20 September

1976 **Home Sweet Homer** (aka *Odyssey*) (Forman Brown, Charles Burr/Roland Kibbee, Marre) Palace Theater 4 January

1979 **Sarava** (N Richard Nash) Mark Hellinger Theater 13 February

1980 **An April Song** (Sammy Cahn/Marre) John Drew Theater 25 August

1988 **Ain't Broadway Grand** (ex- *Mike*) (Lee Adams/Thomas Meehan) Walnut Street Theater, Philadelphia 26 March; Lunt-Fontanne Theater, New York 18 April 1993

LELY, Durward [LYALL, James Durward] (b Arbroath [Forfar], 2 September 1852; d Hillhead, Glasgow, 29 February 1944).

Born in Arbroath, brought up in Blairgowrie, the young Durward Lyall was trained for the law. However, having discovered a tenor voice, he began singing in concert and, with the support of a local Maecenas, was sent to Italy for five years of study. He made his stage debut singing Manrico at Rimini, and on returning home won leading roles with the Italian opera companies. ''Signor Leli'' was Britian's first English-language Don José to the Carmen of Selina Dolaro, and he subsequently toured Britain playing the same role with Emily Soldene. It was Soldene who edged him into the musical theatre when she cast him in her repertoire as Don Florio in *The Naval Cadets.* In 1880 he was hired by D'Oyly Carte to succeed to the role of Frederic in *The Pirates of Penzance,* and he remained with Carte's company for the next six years and five shows, creating the roles of the Duke of Dunstable in *Patience* (1881), Lord Tolloller in *Iolanthe* (1882), Cyril in *Princess Ida* (1884), Nanki-Poo in *The Mikado* (1885, ''A Wandering Minstrel, I''), and Richard Dauntless in *Ruddigore* (1887) and playing Alexis in the first revival of *The Sorcerer* (1884).

Thereafter he mixed concert tours, often alongside Adelina Patti, and operatic roles (creating Glaucus in *Nydia,* King James in *Holyrood* 1896) with intermittent appearances on the musical stage, playing in *Carina* (1888, Don Felix de Tornado), *La Girouette* (1889, Hildbert), *The Golden Web* (1893, t/o Geoffrey Norreys) and making a speciality of playing Osbaldistone in the eternally popular musical drama *Rob Roy.* In his later years he toured as a Scots entertainer.

Plate 217. *Scotsman* **Durward Lely** *created many a tenor role for Sullivan and Gilbert, but he was also the world's first English-singing Don José (Carmen).*

LENO, Dan [GALVIN, George Wild] (aka Dan Patrick) (b London, 20 December 1860; d London, 31 October 1904).

The famous music-hall clog dancer, acrobat and comic singer began by parodying the musical theatre (his perversion of Cellier's ''Queen of My Heart'' as ''Queen of the Tarts'' was withdrawn after a complaint from the composer) and ended up playing in it. His first venture as a musical-comedy actor was at the Crystal Palace where he appeared in Horace Lennard's burlesque *Too Lovely Black-Eyed Susan* (1888) and the following year he appeared at a matinée performance as Pitcher to the Tosser of Rutland Barrington, vying for the affections of Kate Everleigh's *Penelope* (1889) in Edward Solomon's musical version of the popular farce *The Area Belle.* His regular start as a musical-theatre player came when provincial producer Milton Bode signed him for a musical comedy at a vast salary of $125 a week and commissioned Basil Hood and Walter Slaughter to write *Orlando Dando* (1898), featuring the little comic in a suitably protean role.

Although he played *Orlando Dando* for only a short season, owing to more lucrative commitments, he returned the following year for a longer tour of another piece commissioned by Bode, playing Aubrey Honeybun in *In Gay Piccadilly* (Clarence Corri/George Sims), and a third time in 1902 with a piece by Herbert Darnley, who had previously written music-hall songs for him, as the benighted little hero of *Mr Wix of Wickham.* None of the three pieces ventured near the West End, and Leno (perhaps warned by the less-than-successful venture of fellow music-hall star Little Tich in a London musical) never appeared in a regular London production other than his highly successful pantomimes at the Theatre Royal, Drury Lane.

Biographies: Wood, J Hickory; *Dan Leno* (Methuen, London, 1905), Brandreth, G: *The Funniest Man on Earth* (Hamilton, London, 1977)

LENYA, Lotte [BLAMAUER, Karoline Wilhelmina] (b Vienna, 18 October 1898; d New York, 27 November 1981).

During her early career as an actress in Berlin, Miss Lenya appeared in the several pieces composed by her husband, Kurt Weill: the *Mahagonny Singspiel, Die Dreigroschenoper,* first as Jenny (''Seeräuber-Jenny,'' ''Barbara-Lied'') and subsequently as Lucy, and the full-scale *Aufstieg und Fall der Stadt Mahagonny* (1931, Jenny).

She left Germany together with her husband in 1932, and made her way to Paris (Anna I in *Die sieben Todesünden,* 1933), London, and finally New York, where the couple settled in 1937. There she appeared in several plays and in Weill's *The Firebrand of Florence* (1945, Duchess) and found an enthusiastic following with her performance as Jenny in the 1954 revival of *The Threepenny Opera* which brought the piece tardily to the notice of the English-language world. In a subsequent career which was angled very largely towards the works of Weill and of his sometime collaborator, Bertolt Brecht, she created a single Broadway musical role as the Berlin landlady, Fräulein Schneider, in *Cabaret* (1966).

Lenya appeared in the 1930 film version of *Die Dreigroschenoper,* but made her most memorable screen appearance in a non-singing role as the archvillainess Elsa Krebs (equipped with a dagger in her toes) in the James Bond film *From Russia with Love* (1964).

Biographies: Spoto, D: *Lenya: A Life* (Little, Brown, Boston, 1989), Farneth, D: *Lenya, the Legend* (Overlook Press, Woodstock, NY, 1998)

LEON, Francis (''The Only Leon'') [GLASSEY, Patrick Francis] (b New York, 21 November 1844). Minstrel performer who was the finest travesty player of his era—and perhaps of any era—and who introduced a number of important burlesque musicals both to America and to Australia.

Leon made his first appearance as a boy soprano at New York's St Stephen's Church and his first stage appearance singing at Buckley's Music Hall. He joined up with Christy and Wood's Minstrels at the age of 14 and thereafter worked the minstrel circuits, billed as ''the Ethiopian Cubas'' and ''the wonderful danseuse and soprano singer,'' for a number of years before, in 1864, going into partnership with Edwin Kelly to form the company known as Kelly and Leon's Minstrels. The company did well and Leon quickly made himself a reputation as the outstanding minstrel ''prima donna'' of his day, starring as leading lady in the lavishly produced burlesques (advertised as ''Africanised opéra-bouffe'') which formed the heart of Kelly and Leon's minstrel programs. Amongst the burlesques in which he appeared were *Mydeah Restore Her* (parodying Ristori's Medea), *Lucrezia Borgia, The Great Black Crook Burlesque,* as Leon Hurra in *Kill Trovatore,* Mag-you're-right in *Faust,* in the title roles of the opéra-bouffe burlesques *La Belle LN* and *The Grand Dutch-S,* as *Frow-Frow* (taking off Agnes Ethel's performance as Frou-Frou), *Barber-blu* (burlesquing Mlle Irma) and *Gin-neviève de Graw* (mimicking Rose Bell, the current star of the real *Geneviève de Brabant*). He also played Marguerite in Hervé's *Le Petit Faust* and the feminine leads of such Offenbach pieces as *Lischen et Fritzchen, Ba-ta-clan, La Rose de Saint-Flour* and as the vocally perilous Ernestine of *Monsieur Choufleuri at Home, or Prima Donna for a Night.* He played Limonia in Suppé's *Zehn Mädchen und kein Mann* and Galatea in his *Die schöne Galathee,* top-featured in Legouix's *The Crimson Scarf,* burlesqued Jenny Lind in the celebrated parody of the operatic star called *Leatherlungs,* and appeared as a man-hunting widow (and without his usual blackface) in Kelly's musical comedy *His Grace the Duke* and as three different girls and one boy in the made-to-measure tale of *The Pretty Detective.* In 1870, when he included the burlesque *The Kneelson Concert* in his repertoire, complete with *Hamlet* mad scene, opera diva Christine Nilsson went to see Leon's version of ''herself'' and came away delighted.

After more than a decade as favorites in New York and throughout America, Kelly and Leon were taken to New Zealand and Australia in 1878 by Hiscocks and Hayman. There they found less competition and a marked success, particularly when they produced an early and unofficial version of *HMS Pinafore* with Leon featured as Little Buttercup. When J C Williamson, the official rights-holder of the work, stopped these performances, they announced a sequel, *Sir Joseph at Sea,* and produced a burlesque *Pin-a-4* (the difference in attitude was marked by the fact that Leon now played Josephine). They also presented such pieces as *The Sorcerer* (Aline), *Trial by Jury* (Plaintiff), *Rose Michon, or The Little Bride* (ie, *La Jolie Parfumeuse,* Rose Michon), the Vokes's famous *Belles of the Kitchen* and a burlesque *Norma on a Half Shell* (Norma) and the ''prima donna'' drew the comment ''Mr Leon's female impersonations are certainly exceedingly clever, and although he has no great vocal power, except in the upper range of a falsetto voice, he has extraordinary execution and in his imitation of di Murska took some florid runs in a remarkable manner. He is an excellent light comedian, and plays the female parts without the slightest vulgarity, which has been the bane of most female impersonators.'' In other words, instead of burlesquing womanhood in the manner of the music halls, Leon was quite simply playing a woman.

In 1880 Kelly and Leon split up. The ''divine and only'' Leon continued briefly to lead a minstrel company under the Kelly and Leon banner but he soon returned to America where he joined Haverley's Mastodon Minstrels at a reputed salary of $200 a week. However, after some months he quit Haverley ''with acrimony,'' taking with him his versions of *Lischen et Fritzchen* (*The Alsatians*), *Monsieur Choufleuri (Her Majesty's Opera, or Patti's visit to Vanderbilt),* his latest hit burlesque *Langtry, or Ben Butler and the Jersey Lily* (''her gown was a stifled sigh trimmed with superfluous regrets '') and his latest wardrobe of gowns from Worth of Paris. He also took Haverley's ''leading man,'' Frank Cushman. The pair moved first to the San Francisco Minstrels (1883, *X-Seltzer,* etc) and thence to several other minstrel groups and to Edward E Kidder's *On the Stage* (1886, Pomona Potter Pommery, etc) combination, but, after having ''made a round of the earth,'' Leon and Cushman returned to Australia (1886) with their own minstrel company. Their features included the burlesques *Ill-fed Dora* and *A Tough Gal-a-tea,* the musical extravaganza *Vassar Girls* and a production of *Uncle Tom's Cabin* mounted to allow Leon to play the popular role of Topsy to the Tom of Cushman. A local journal noted ''his make-up was perfect and his voice as good as ever'' but the difference in the style of the company was seen in their repertoire: instead of playing Suppé's Galatea, Leon now appeared alongside Cushman's Hogmalion in a broad, traditional burlesque.

After touring through New Zealand, Leon returned at the end of the year to America. There he had a continuing career in minstrelsy (as ''The Only Leon''), at first with Cushman under their own banner then with other groups; in vaudeville; and, occasionally—though still in feminine garb—in the musical theatre. He successfully repeated his performance as a stage-struck society girl, Pomona Potter Pommery, in *On the Stage* through 1888, but an 1890 attempt to revive Kelly and Leon's Minstrels (without Kelly) in Chicago went astray when the money men started playing tricks with their headliner-cum-manager. Thus, whilst his old partner worked out the end of his career as a busy character actor in Australia, Leon donned his skirts again to feature as the Baroness to Joseph Herbert's Baron in the Chicago extravaganza *Babes in the Wood* (1890), to play Mrs McBrannigan Mack in *A High Roller* (1891) with Barney Fagan and to tour in Will Mestayer and in Theresa Vaughn's variety musical *Grab Bag* before retiring from the theatre. He retired so completely that, although I know he was still alive in 1900, I do not know when and where he took his last curtsey before the Almighty.

Leon was the author or adaptor, either in parnership with Kelly or sometimes alone, of a number of the burlesque operatic sketches which he performed.

LÉON, Victor [HIRSCHFELD, Viktor] (b Vienna, 4 January 1858; d Vienna, 3 February 1940).

Vienna-born journalist Viktor Hirschfeld adopted a French name for his career in the theatre, whilst his brother, Leopold, opted for a definitely German one as Leo Feld. Léon's choice turned out to be a significant one, for, during a career as an Operettic librettist which took him to the top level of his profession at the time when Austrian Operette was the most popular kind of musical theatre throughout the world, his first and his greatest successes were based on works borrowed from the French comic theatre.

Léon's earliest stage works, written while he was in his twenties, were in the usual beginner's mold: one-act pieces for Vienna houses and full-sized texts for regional theatres, in his case the important Carl-Schultze Theater in Hamburg, which produced Rudolf Raimann's setting of Léon's first substantial work—already based on a French original, Dumas's *Les Trois Mousquetaires*—and the Deutsches Theater in Pest which hosted Emil Rosé's *Tizianello.*

The first major work from Léon's pen to be presented in Vienna was Alfred Zamara's *Der Doppelgänger,* which was brought from its Munich production to Berlin and then to the Theater an der Wien (1 October 1887) prior to a mass of further showings throughout Germany, and later the same year his musical-comedy adaptation of Grimmelhausen's *Simplicius Simplicissimus,* set by Johann Strauss as *Simplicius,* was produced at the same theatre. Both were, however, Vienna failures, *Der Doppelgänger* playing for just two weeks and the collaboration with Strauss, which had seemed like an engraved-not-printed passport to success, a disastrous 31 performances.

Another such opportunity did not come quickly. During the 1890s Léon tried his hand at opera—supplying texts to Josef Beer (*Friedl mit der leeren Tasche, Der Strike der Schmiede*), Ignaz Brüll (*Gringoire,* 1893, *Schach dem König, Der Husar*) and Julius Stern (*Narciss Rameau*)—adapted several foreign musical texts for the Carltheater, wrote Possen and Volksstücke, and spent a period as dramaturg at the Theater in der Josefstadt where his Operettic contribution was limited to adapting French musicals for the Vienna stage and organizing the composition of an early biomusical on the father of his erstwhile collaborator, Johann Strauss.

He was represented on the Vienna stage of the later 1890s, however, by several original Operetten of which two found some small measure of success: Dellinger's *Die Chansonette,* imported from Dresden, lasted only a fair 37 performances at the Theater an der Wien but went on to be seen in Munich and Berlin, whilst Suppé's *Das Modell* was played intermittently in the Carltheater repertoire for some three years. Another collaboration with Suppé and Ludwig Held, *Die Pariserin,* fell flat in 11 performances.

Léon's next contribution to the Carltheater was not an original text, but an adaptation: a version of Bayard and Scribe's *La Frontière de Savoie.* As *Der Cognac-König,* it fell flatter than ever in just 10 performances in Vienna and in a production at Berlin's Theater Unter den Linden, but Léon continued to delve into the French theatrical libraries as Zell and Genée had so successfully done before him, and at his next essay he came up trumps. After 20 not very impressive years in the business, he finally got his hit. The breakthrough came with an adaptation of the famous farce *Les Dominos roses,* written with his co-author of a decade, the Baron von Waldberg, and set to music by the unproven Richard Heuberger, with whom Léon had worked a couple of years previously on a ballet-pantomime *Struwwelpeter* (6 January 1897) for Dresden. Produced at the Theater an der Wien, *Der Opernball* was a singular success, and Léon went on to dip further into the French opus and turn out texts based on Scribe's *La Bataille des femmes* (set by the youngest Johann Strauss as *Katze und Maus*), on Alfred Hennequin and Albert Millaud's *Niniche* (*Ihre Excellenz*), and on Meilhac's *Décoré* (*Der Sechsuhrzug*). None, however, found anything like the same success as *Der Opernball.* He also dipped, with rather more success, back into the Strauss family's works and produced a French-style Viennese text to a Johann jr pasticcio score for the Carltheater under the title *Wiener Blut* and another, illustrated by a pasticcio of the same Strauss's *Simplicius* and *Blindekuh* music, which played for a fair season at Venedig in Wien as *Gräfin Pepi.*

However, there were other successes for him in those turn of the century years, and the first and most important of these was a first collaboration with the young Franz Lehár on the composer's earliest success, *Der Rastelbinder.* He combined again with Lehár on a willfully Offenbachian classical burlesque, *Der Göttergatte,* and with another young composer on the way up, Leo Ascher, on the Theater an der Wien's *Vergeltsgott* (42 performances), but he returned to French sources for his next success. Whilst Heuberger, whom Léon had apparently wanted to set his adaptation of Meilhac's *L'Attaché d'ambassade* for the Theater an der Wien, instead composed his Volksoper *Barfüssele* for Dresden, it was Lehár who turned Léon and Leo Stein's version of Meilhac's piece into *Die lustige Witwe,* a success which eclipsed not only *Der Opernball* but every other Operette of the past decades.

The years which followed *Die lustige Witwe* housed Léon's other greatest and most enduring successes—the German *Der fidele Bauer* and the French-borrowed *Die geschiedene Frau* with Leo Fall and *Das Fürstenkind* with Lehár—but thereafter major success again avoided him. In the 1910s and up to his last venture in 1925, his output continued at the same staunch level as before, but not one outstanding hit emerged from amongst the two dozen titles, large and small, to which his name was affixed. Two works written with Péter Stojanovits had good runs at the Carltheater (*Liebchen am Dach* 183 performances, *Der Herzog von Reichstadt* 111 performances), but collaborations with Straus brought nothing more durable than *Liebeszauber* (77 performances), those with Fall produced at best 55 nights of *Der Nachtschnellzug,* with Granichstaedten 60 of *Glück bei Frauen* and with Nedbal 52 of *Donna Gloria.* The only other one of his pieces to clear the one hundred performance mark was his sole further work with Lehár, *Die gelbe Jacke* (104 performances).

It was five years after Léon's last contribution to the Viennese stage when Fritz Löhner-Beda and Ludwig Herzer remade this last-named libretto into the rather more successful *Das Land des Lächelns.* If Léon had really not, as the tale goes, wanted Lehár as his partner on *Der Rastelbinder* and/or *Die lustige Witwe,* the composer was now, in some small way, revenged. He returned to Léon, however, two years later for a revision of the librettist's text to *Das Fürstenkind,* staged in Berlin as *Der Fürst der Berge.* It was no *Land des Lächelns* and it was Léon's last stage credit.

From 1908, in parallel to his work as a librettist, Léon acted as director for many of his Operetten. He mounted the original Vienna productions of *Der fidele Bauer* (1908), *Gold gab ich für Eisen* (1914) and *Die gelbe Jacke* (1923) at the Theater an der Wien; the premieres of *Das Fürstenkind* (1909), *Das erste Weib* (1910) and *Der Nachtschnellzug* (1913) at the Johann Strauss-Theater; *Der gute Kamerad* (1911) and *Liebeszauber* (1916) at the Bürgertheater; and *Die geschiedene Frau* (1908), *Liebchen am Dach* (1917), *Der Herzog von Reichstadt* (1921), *Glück bei Frauen* (1923) and *Donna Gloria* (1925) at the Carltheater. He also directed his *Der Millionendieb* with Mizzi Günther and Louis Treumann at Ronacher.

Léon was also the author of a number of non-musical plays including *Gebildete Menschen, Die Rheintochter* (w Waldberg), *Ein dunkler Ehrenmann, Man sagt* (w Waldberg), *Toeff-Toeff* (w Alexander Engel) and *Der grosse Name* (w Leo Feld, music by Robert Stolz), in which the central character was a crazy Operette composer. Popular opinion had it, and no one contradicted the idea, that the composer the brothers were having a go at was . . . Franz Lehár. He also texted further operas, among them a folk opera, *Barfüssele,* with music by Heuberger, first produced at the Dresden Königliches Operntheater (11 March 1905) and later at the Vienna Volksoper (22 December 1915), a version of Erckmann-Chatrian's famous play as *Der Polnische Jude* (1902, music by Karl Weis w Richard Batka) and *Die Schönen von Fogaras* (1907, Alfred Grunfeld). *Toeff-Toeff* was later musicalized by Zsolt Harsányi and composer Adorján Ötvös under the title *Özvegy kisasszony* (Budai Színkör 1 September 1916).

In spite of the fact that very many of his pieces had short lives, Léon left a solid handful of often first-rate pieces which remain in the European repertoire nearly a century after their first productions: *Der Opernball, Wiener Blut, Der Rastelbinder, Der fidele Bauer, Die geschiedene Frau,* and *Das Land des Lächelns,* for which he must be allowed at least a slice of the credit. However, it is as the librettist of *Die lustige Witwe* that he principally remains amongst the star names of the Viennese Operette tradition.

Léon's brother, Leo HIRSCHFELD (b Augsburg, 14 February 1869; d Florence, 9 September 1924), who wrote for the theatre under the name of **Leo FELD,** was Léon's partner on the successful *Der grosse Name* and also supplied libretti for the comic operas *Kleider machen Leute* (Zemlinsky/w Keller, Volksoper 2 December 1910) and *Die Stunde* (Lafite, Volksoper 25 October 1932).

1880 **Beim Schützenfest in Wien** (Max von Weinzierl) 1 act Ronacher 17 July

1881 **D'Artagnan [und die drei Musketiere]** (Rudolf Raimann) Carl-Schultze Theater, Hamburg 18 September

1883 **Tizianello** (Emil Rosé) Deutsches Theater, Pest 29 March

1883 **O diese Gotter!** (Karl Stix) 1 act Ronacher 8 August

1884 **Die Königin von Arragon** (Alfred Zamara) 1 act Ronacher 1 May

1886 **Der Doppelgänger** (Zamara) Theater am Gärtnerplatz, Munich 16 September; Friedrich-Wilhelmstädtisches Theater 9 March 1887

1887 **Simplicius** (Johann Strauss) Theater an der Wien 17 December

1888 **Der Savoyarde** (Ottokar Feith/w Franz Josef Brackl) Theater am Gärtnerplatz, Munich 19 June

1889 **Der Herr Abbé** (Zamara/w Brackl) Theater am Gärtnerplatz, Munich 10 August

1889 **Capitän Wilson** (*The Yeomen of the Guard*) German version w Carl Lindau (Carltheater)

1890 **Erminy** (*Erminie*) German version w Heinrich von Waldberg (Carltheater)

1890 **Der bleiche Gast** (Josef Hellmesberger, Zamara/w von Waldberg) Carl-Schultze Theater, Hamburg 6 September

1892 **Der Bajazzo** (Alfons Czibulka/w von Waldberg) Theater an der Wien 7 December

1894 **Tata-Toto** (*Toto*) German version w F Zell (Theater in der Josefstadt)

1894 **Die Chansonette** (Rudolf Dellinger/w von Waldberg) Residenztheater, Dresden 16 September; Theater Unter den Linden, Berlin 22 August 1895

1894 **Johann Strauss** (Strauss arr Klimsch) 1 act Theater in der Josefstadt 12 October

1895 **Die eiserne Jungfrau** (*Le Brillant Achille*) German version w add mus by Karl Kappeller (Theater in der Josefstadt)

1895 **Die Doppelhochzeit** (Hellmesberger/w von Waldberg) Theater in der Josefstadt 21 September

1895 **Das Modell** (Franz von Suppé/w Ludwig Held) Carltheater 4 October

1896 **Toledad** (*L'Enlèvement de la Toledad*) German version w Waldberg (Theater in der Josefstadt)

1897 **Der Cognac-König** (Franz Wagner/w Held) Carltheater 20 February

1898 **Der Opernball** (Richard Heuberger/w von Waldberg) Theater an der Wien 5 January

1898 **Die Pariserin** (von Suppé/w Held) Carltheater 26 January

1898 **Katze und Maus** (Johann Strauss III/w Ferdinand Gross) Theater an der Wien 23 December

1899 **Ihre Excellenz** (*Die kleine Excellenz*) (Heuberger/w von Waldberg) Centraltheater, Berlin 17 January

1899 **Wiener Blut** (Strauss arr Müller/w Leo Stein) Carltheater 26 October

1899 **Die Strohwitwe** (Albert Kauders/w von Waldberg) Theater an der Wien 4 November

1899 **Tohu-Bohu** (*L'Auberge du Tohu-bohu*) German version (Theater in der Josefstadt)

1900 **Frau Lieutnant** (*La Dot de Brigitte*) German version w von Waldberg (Theater in der Josefstadt)

1900 **Der Sechsuhrzug** (Heuberger) Centraltheater, Berlin 17 January

1901 **Die verwünschene Prinzessin** (Eduard Gärtner) Carltheater 4 January

1901 **Das Medaillon** (Walter Mortier) 1 act Friedrich-Wilhelmstädtisches Theater, Berlin 31 March

1902 **Tarok** (Raimann) Raimundtheater 8 February

1902 **Das gewisse Etwas** (Weinberger/w Stein) Carltheater 15 March

1902 **Gräfin Pepi** (Strauss arr Ernst Reiterer) Venedig in Wien 5 July

1902 **Der Rastelbinder** (Franz Lehár) Carltheater 20 December

1903 **Der Herr Professor** (Béla von Ujj) Theater an der Wien 4 December

1904 **Der Göttergatte** (Lehár/w Leo Stein) Carltheater 20 January

1905 **Kaisermanöver** (von Ujj) Carltheater 4 March

1905 **Vergeltsgott** (aka *Der Bettlerklub*) (Leo Ascher) Theater an der Wien 14 October

1905 **Die lustige Witwe** (Lehár/w Stein) Theater an der Wien 30 December

1907 **Der fidele Bauer** (Leo Fall) Hoftheater, Mannheim 27 July

1907 **Der Frauenmörder** (Oscar Straus) 1 act Danzers Orpheum 8 November

1908 **Die geschiedene Frau** (Fall) Carltheater 23 December

1909 **Little Mary** (Straus/ad Auguste Germain, Robert Trébor) 1 act Comédie-Royale, Paris 8 January

1909 **Das Fürstenkind** (Lehár) Johann Strauss-Theater 7 October

1909 **Didi** (Straus) Carltheater 23 October

1910 **Das erste Weib** (Bruno Hartl) Johann Strauss-Theater 22 October

1910 **Die Post im Walde** (Oehl) 1 act Colosseum October

1911 **Der andere Herr war nicht so** (aka *Die anderen Herren sind nicht so*) (Straus) 1 act Hölle 1 February

1911 **Der gute Kamerad** (*Az obsitos*) German version (Wiener Bürgertheater)

1911 **Die eiserne Jungfrau** (Robert Stolz) Raimundtheater 11 November

1913 **Die Studentengräfin** (Fall) Theater am Nollendorfplatz, Berlin 18 January

1913 **Der Nachtschnellzug** (Fall/w Stein) Johann Strauss-Theater 20 December

1914 **Gold gab ich für Eisen** revised German version of *Az Obsitos* (Theater an der Wien)

1915 **Das Lumperl** (revised *Die eiserne Jungfrau*) Operntheater, Graz 4 April

1915 **Man steigt nach!** (Straus/w Heinz Reichert) Carltheater 2 May

1915 **Otto oder Otto** (Hans Tegern) 1 act Apollotheater 7 September

1916 **Im Apollo** (Tegern) Apollotheater 1 act 2 January

1916 **Liebeszauber** (Straus) Wiener Bürgertheater 28 January

1916 **Die Wachsfigur** (Oskar Stalla) 1 act Apollotheater 1 April

1917 **Wiener Kinder** (Johann Schrammel arr Stalla/w Léon) Johann Strauss-Theater 16 May

1917 **Liebchen am Dach** (Péter Stojanovits) Carltheater 19 May

1917 **Der weisse Adler** (Chopin arr Raoul Mader/w Hugo H Regel) Volksoper 22 December

1918 **Der Millionendieb** (Friedrich Mayer) 3 scenes Ronacher 30 September

1920 **Die Pawlatsch'n** (Robert Mahler) Raimundtheater 19 May

1920 **Wiener Volkssänger** (Mahler) Raimundtheater 21 May

1920 **Hol' mich der Teufel** (Leopold Reichwein/w Reichert) Wiener Bürgertheater 29 October

1921 **Der Herzog von Reichstadt** (Stojanovits/w Reichert) Carltheater 11 February

1923 **Die gelbe Jacke** (Lehár) Theater an der Wien 9 February

1923 **Glück bei Frauen** (Bruno Granichstaedten/w Reichert) Carltheater 4 December

1925 **Donna Gloria** (Oskar Nedbal/w Reichert) Carltheater 30 December

1930 **Das Land des Lächelns** revised *Die gelbe Jacke* by Fritz Löhner-Beda, Ludwig Herzer, Theater an der Wien 26 September

1932 **Der Fürst der Berge** revised *Das Fürstenkind* Theater am Nollendorfplatz, Berlin 23 September

LEONCAVALLO, Ruggiero (b Naples, 8 March 1858; d Montecatini, 9 August 1919).

The composer of *I Pagliacci* dipped on a number of occasions into the light musical theatre, reasoning if that Lehár, whom he judged his musical inferior, could make such a killing there, there was a lucrative place for him too. It turned out that there wasn't, although Leoncavallo made regular attempts, ranging from an early *Songe d'une nuit d'été* which was not played publicly, to a charming *Reginetta delle rose,* first produced in Rome in 1912, which was said to have been inspired by Gaby Deslys's escapade with the King of Portugal. It was afterwards played also in Paris as *La Petite Reine des roses* (Théâtre Apollo 10 May 1913, ad Claude Berton, Charles Maral), but Andreas Dippel's proposed American version (ad H B Smith, R B Smith), which announced that it would take in "syncopated and special numbers by L Wolfe Gilbert and Malvin Franklin" to dizzy up Leoncavallo's score, fortunately seems never to have hit the stage. He later made a disastrous attempt to break into London with a telephone-girl musical comedy glitzily misstaged by revue specialist Albert de Courville (who also mounted the composer's short opera *I Zingari* on a variety bill) and turned out a series of musical stage pieces in his later years, following the failure of his operatic ventures to produce another *I Pagliacci.*

1910 **Malbruck** (Angelo Nessi) Teatro Nazionale 19 January

1912 **La reginetta delle rose** (Gioacchino Forzano) Teatro Costanzi 24 June

1913 **Are You There?** (Edgar Wallace/Albert de Courville) Prince of Wales Theatre, London 1 November

1915 **La candidata** (Forzano) Teatro Nazionale 6 February

1916 **Prestami tua moglie** (Edmondo Corradi) Casino, Montecatini 2 September

1919 **A chi la giarrettiera?** (Corradi) Teatro Adriano 16 October

1923 **Il primo bacio** (Luigi Bonelli) 1 act Kursaal, Montecatini

1925 **Émile Collet** (Polieri, Bonelli) Politeama, Naples July

1925 **La maschera nuda** (ad Salvatore Allegra)

LÉONCE [NICOLE, Édouard Théodore] (b Paris, 12 January 1820; d Le Raincy, 19 February 1900). Slim, bespectacled (off-stage) low comedian with a musical education whose particularity it was that in spite of playing and singing in what one critic called his "voix de flûte," with much ad-libbing and physical foolery, he managed always to keep in tune.

Engaged at the Bouffes-Parisiens in the 1850s, Léonce there created a number of roles, male and character-female, in opéras-bouffes both large and small, including Offenbach's *Un postillon en gage* (1856, Hélène de Saint-Bourdon), *Tromb-al-ca-zar* (1856, Vert-Panné), *Dragonette* (1857, Madame Schaubraque), *Croquefer* (1857, Boutefeu), *Les Deux Pêcheurs* (1857), *Vent du soir* (1857, Le Lapin Courageux), *Mesdames de la Halle* (1858, Madame Poiretapée), *Orphée aux enfers* in which he introduced the part of Pluton/Aristée (1858), as originally played for its comedy rather than any tenorial values, and *Geneviève de Brabant* in which he created the central part of Sifroid (1859). He introduced two more of his gallery of grotesque ladies as the Baronne de Follembuche in Delibes's *L'Omelette à la Follembuche* (1859) and Madame Potichon in his *Deux vieilles gardes* (1856) and yet another as the gushing guest, Madame Balandard, in *Monsieur Choufleuri* (1861); took further Offenbach roles in *Le Roman comique* (1861, La Rancune), as Patrocle, the younger Dunanan, in *Le Voyage de MM Dunanan père et fils* (1862), Boboli in *Les Géorgiennes* (1864) and the Marquis de Fonrose in *Les Bergers* (1865); appeared in Hervé's first full-length opéra-bouffe *Les Chevaliers de la table ronde* (1866), as Pan in a revival of *Daphnis et Chloë* (1866) and, alongside Beauce, Desmont and Mlle Petit in his own little musical pochade, *Une femme qui a perdu ses clefs* (1866), before leaving the Bouffes-Parisiens after a solid decade of work and moving to William Busnach's newly launched Théâtre de l'Athénée. If much of the material he found there was of a lesser quality than at the Bouffes (Archiduc in *Marlbrouk s'en va-t-en guerre* 1867, *Les Horreurs de la guerre* 1868, Legouix's *Le Vengeur* 1868, *Le Petit poucet* 1868, "in which M Léonce enters on a velocipide"), the engagement did allow him to appear in two of the earliest full-scale works by the young Lecocq, *L'Amour et son carquois,* and as the mandarin Ka-o-lin in *Fleur de thé* (1868) before the Athénée fizzled out of his life.

He played his original role in a revival of *Fleur de thé* at the Théâtre des Variétés the following year, as well as appearing there as Volteface in Delibes's *La Cour du Roi Pétaud* and, in perhaps his greatest creation in a full-sized musical play, as Antonio, the harmless-seeming caissier with a womanful past in *Les Brigands* (1869), and thereafter, he made his artistic home at the Variétés. Over the next two decades he created a long list of roles in, at first, opéra-bouffe, then opéra-comique, and in latter days in the vaudeville-opérettes which became the rage of the early 1880s. Amongst the parts he introduced and played were included Caprican in *Le Beau Dunois* (1870), Buckingham in *Le Trône d'Écosse* (1871), Oscar in the Variétés revival of *Barbe-bleue* (1872), Briddidick in the Paris premiere of *Les Cent Vierges* (1872), Zizibar in *La Veuve du Malabar* (1873), Bibès in *Les Braconniers* (1873), Don Pedro in the expanded *La Périchole* (1874), Délicat in *La Boulangère a des écus* (1875), Melinard in *Le Manoir du Pictordu* (1875), Ygène in *Le Docteur Ox* (1877), Tardivel in *Les Charbonniers* (1877), Sotherman, the lascivious clown in *Le Grand Casimir* (1880), Savarin in *La Roussotte* (1881), Bonpain in *Lili* (1882), the soldier Loriot with his stand-up comedy routine in *Mam'zelle Nitouche* (1883) and Le consul d'Illyrie in *La Cosaque* (1884). He also gave repeats of his Pluton and Caissier, of Ménélas in *La Belle Hélène,* Alfred in *La Vie parisienne,* and a vast number of comedy roles in the plays which made up an important part of the Variétés repertoire.

In 1889 he was seen at the Théâtre de la Renaissance in the opéra-bouffe *La Tour de Babel* as Ephel, the builder of the Tower of Babel, in the last musical creation of a career of 45 years on the stage.

1866 **Une femme qui a perdu ses clefs** (Frédéric Barbier/w Bar) 1 act Théâtre des Bouffes-Parisiens 21 October

LERNER, Alan Jay (b New York, 31 August 1918; d New York, 14 June 1986). Librettist/lyricist to some of the happiest musicals of Broadway's postwar heyday.

Born into a well-off garment chain-store family and educated in Britain and at Harvard, Lerner first worked on college shows and, after graduation, as a radio writer. In 1942 he came together for the first time with composer Frederick Loewe when the two worked on remaking a show called *Patricia,* a musicalized version of the successful play *The Patsy* done by George Grandee, J Keirn Brennan and Barry Connors, in which Dorothy Stone had played the previous season in San Francisco. Lerner was hired on this occasion to redo the libretto, with Earle Crooker (Loewe's partner on an earlier show) working on the lyrics of what was now called *The Life of the Party. The Life of the Party* got no nearer to Broadway than *Patricia* had done.

The following year Lerner and Loewe repeated their collaboration on *What's Up?,* a curious piece redolent of turn-of-the-century comic opera which did make it to Broadway but closed after eight weeks. A third effort together, *The Day Before Spring,* marked further progress: it had a life of 164 performances at Broadway's National Theater, and produced some fine (and some recyclable) songs in the midst of an uninteresting libretto which was weighted down with a barrage of ballets that were more *Oklahoma!* than *Oklahoma!*

The curve of fortune continued to ascend and, when Lerner abandoned the little love lives of everyday people and reached into the world of romantic fantasy for his libretto for *Brigadoon,* a piece consciously constructed and written in the revived Broadway operetta style made fashionable by the success of *Oklahoma!,* the partners found a major success. The simple, charming tale of *Brigadoon* was illustrated with some particularly winning and suitable songs, both sentimental and comical (''Come to Me, Bend to Me,'' ''Almost Like Being in Love,'' ''The Heather on the Hill,'' ''There But for You Go I,'' ''The Love of My Life,'' etc), and these quickly found their way to as much popularity out of the show as in it.

In his next piece, *Love Life,* Lerner returned to more prosaic folk and their more prosaic relationships, but approached them in a less-than-straightforward way. His text followed its couple through 150 years of a slowly developing married life to a score by Kurt Weill which did not turn out any individual pieces to equal the popularity of those from *Brigadoon.* The show had a fair, if insufficient, run of 252 performances. A return to Loewe for the vigorously romantic go-West-young-woman *Paint Your Wagon* provided more songs that lingered (''They Call the Wind Maria,'' ''Wanderin' Star,'' ''I Still See Elisa,'' ''I Talk to the Trees'') and a slightly longer, if still insufficient, run, at a time when the competition included such shows as *Guys and Dolls* and *The King and I,* but their 1956 work, *My Fair Lady,* both outshone and outran all and any competition. Lerner's adaptation of George Bernard Shaw's *Pygmalion,* and the score which he and Loewe devised to illustrate it, came together to produce a show which was as much the key show of its time as *Die lustige Witwe* had been half a century earlier in Vienna or *Orphée aux enfers* a century earlier in Paris. It was not that it was influential, or at the beginning of anything, it was simply a show which would spread itself, on stage and disc, to corners of the earth where few other Broadway musicals of the era had been, there to become accepted as the flag-bearer of this most successful age of the American musical stage.

To follow such a work and such a success was difficult, not to say impossible, but Lerner found fruitful material for adaptation in T H White's whimsical Arthurian tale *The Once and Future King,* and the result was another highly successful show. The stage musical which the authors called *Camelot* was ultimately more sentimental than whimsical (not to mention decoratively spectacular), but it was full, once again, of tasty songs, both romantic and brightly and unforcedly comic (''I Loved You Once in Silence,'' ''How to Handle a Woman,'' ''If Ever I Would Leave You,'' ''The Simple Joys of Maidenhood,'' ''Take Me to the Fair'') and it proved a resounding and enduring international triumph.

With Loewe's subsequent retreat into real or imagined delicate health, Lerner was forced to look for other collaborators, but in spite of his tying up with several writers of reputation the kind of success he had enjoyed with his first partner did not repeat itself. The first of his ''outside'' collaborations, a musical about ESP, *On a Clear Day You Can See Forever,* written with composer Burton Lane, did the best. It lasted for 280 performances on Broadway, provided the basis for a film, won subsequent regional productions, and launched both its title song and ''Come Back to Me'' as singles. It did not, however, become an international property any more than did a biomusical on couturiere Coco Chanel (*Coco*) mounted with Katharine Hepburn as an unlikely Chanel through 332 Broadway performances.

An attempt to make a musical out of Nabokov's much-discussed teeny-porn novella *Lolita* curled up out of town, and another nymphet musical—a stage version of Lerner and Loewe's enormously successful musical film of Colette's *Gigi*—failed to get off the ground in spite of several tries. *1600 Pennsylvania Avenue,* the umpteenth (but, alas, not the last) presidential musical, with an extended time span and a score by Leonard Bernstein, lasted a week before going nowhere except into the scrapbooks of those who adore one-week flops by superior writers; a pretty but impotent musical version of the screenplay *Buona Sera Mrs Campbell,* produced as *Carmelina,* lasted little longer; and a final essay, an awkwardly updated version of the hit play *Idiot's Delight* as *Dance a Little Closer,* was a one-performance flop.

Always a very much better lyricist than a librettist, Lerner nevertheless wrote the texts for all his musicals. Given the success of his spot-on musical comedy slimming of Shaw's *Pygmalion,* there was no reason why he should not have. But many of his texts were inclined to wander and none, not even those for *Camelot* (subsequently severely altered in revival) or *Brigadoon,* reached the same level. His show songs, however, included a bookful of the most memorable of the 1950s and 1960s produce of Broadway's musical stage.

Five of Lerner's musicals reached the screen—*Brigadoon, My Fair Lady, Camelot, On a Clear Day You Can See Forever* and *Paint Your Wagon*—and he had further success on film, most notably with *Gigi* (subsequently turned into a stage piece) and with *An American in Paris* (1951, Academy Award). He also wrote an autobiography and a book of musical-theatre history, both of which unfortunately showed evidence of a faulty memory and/or careless copyediting. His collected lyrics (ed Benny Green) were published in 1987 under the title *A Hymn to Him: The Lyrics of Alan Jay Lerner.*

1942 **The Life of the Party** (revised *Patricia*)(Frederick Loewe, et al/Earle Crooker, et al) Wilson Theater, Detroit 8 October

1943 **What's Up?** (Loewe/w Arthur Pierson) National Theater 11 November

1945 **The Day Before Spring** (Loewe) National Theater 22 November

1947 **Brigadoon** (Loewe) Ziegfeld Theater 13 March

1948 **Love Life** (Kurt Weill) 46th Street Theater 7 October

1951 **Paint your Wagon** (Loewe) Shubert Theater 12 November

1956 **My Fair Lady** (Loewe) Mark Hellinger Theater 15 March

1960 **Camelot** (Loewe) Majestic Theater 3 December

1965 **On a Clear Day You Can See Forever** (Burton Lane) Mark Hellinger Theater 17 October

1969 **Coco** (André Previn) Mark Hellinger Theater 18 December

1971 **Lolita, My Love** (John Barry) Shubert Theater, Philadelphia 16 February

1973 **Gigi** (Loewe) Uris Theater 13 November

1976 **1600 Pennsylvania Avenue** (Leonard Bernstein) Mark Hellinger Theater 4 May

1979 **Carmelina** (Lane/w Joseph Stein) St James Theater 8 April

1983 **Dance a Little Closer** (Charles Strouse) Minskoff Theater 11 May

Autobiography: *On the Street Where I Live* (Hodder and Stoughton, London, 1978); Biographies: Lees, G: *Inventing Champagne* (St Martin's Press, New York, 1990), Shapiro, D: *We Danced All Night* (Morrow, New York, 1990)

Plate 218. **Fred Leslie** *as Rip van Winkle.*

LESLIE, Fred [HOBSON, Frederick George] (b Woolwich, London, 1 April 1855; d London, 7 December 1892).

The most popular British musical comedian of his era, Leslie—in tandem with "boy" specialist Nellie Farren—fronted a series of musical burlesques at George Edwardes's Gaiety Theatre between 1885 and 1892 which were the centerpiece of the popular musical theatre of their time.

Leslie began acting as an amateur before being hired by Kate Santley (at the age of 22) to play old Colonel Hardy in the play *Paul Pry.* Miss Santley's main production diet, however, was musicals, and a month later Leslie made his first London appearance as a musical-comedian as an almost as aged Agamemnon in *La Belle Hélène,* following this debut with parts in *La Jolie Parfumeuse* (Poirot), the burlesque *Over-Proof* (Duc d'Aubeterre), *La Marjolaine* (Burgomaster) and *Tita in Thibet* (Po-Hi) with Santley, and *Les Dragons de Villars* (Thibaut), *La Périchole* (Panatellas) and the burlesque *Another Drink* (Folly Slantier) alongside Selina Dolaro. He joined the company at the Alhambra Theatre to play a leading role in *La Petite Mademoiselle* (Manicamp), toured as Hector in *Madame Favart* (with the young Beerbohm Tree as Pontsablé), and then returned to the Alhambra to appear in a group of widely differing roles in French musicals—as the heroine's father in *La Fille du tambour-major* (aged all of 24), Faust in *Mefistofele II* (ie, *Le Petit Faust,* 1880), the comic little Briolet in *Jeanne, Jeannette et Jeanneton* and Prince Toko in Auber's opéra-comique *The Bronze Horse.*

In 1881 Leslie was engaged to appear in America and visited Broadway for the first time to play for Comley and Barton in *Madame Favart* (now as Favart), *Manola* (Brasiero) and *Olivette* (Duc des Ifs). He returned to London to leading comic roles in *Madame Favart* (a third different role, the aged comedy of Pontsablé this time) and Bucalossi's highly successful *Manteaux Noirs.* By this time he had become admired as a quite exceptional musico-comic actor, and H B Farnie and Planquette, the composer of the record-breaking *Les Cloches de Corneville,* came together, under the aegis of producer Alexander Henderson, to write a vehicle for him in which—profiting from his ability to play both young and old—he could star as a musical Rip van Winkle. Leslie's performance in this role placed him firmly at the head of his profession, but contractual quarrels led him eventually to quit the part and to return to America. There he starred in John McCaull's comic opera company in such pieces as *The Queen's Lace Handkerchief* (Villalobos), *The Beggar Student* (Ollendorf), *The Merry War* (Balthazar) and *Madame Favart* (Favart), returning home to repeat his Ollendorf at the London Alhambra, appear again as Rip van Winkle and to play at the Comedy Theatre in *The Grand Mogol* (Ayala) and *Barbe-bleue* (Popolani).

Leslie was appearing in a feeble, fantastical piece called *Fay o' Fire* for a novice management when he was approached with a proposition to star opposite Gaiety Theatre favorite Nellie Farren in a burlesque on the Jack Sheppard tale. Fortunately for his future, *Fay o' Fire* folded quickly and Leslie went to the Gaiety where his performance as Jonathan Wild in *Little Jack Sheppard* gave him the last fillip to megastardom. Thereafter, under the newly instituted management of George Edwardes, he starred with Nellie Farren in the Gaiety's series of "new burlesques": as Noirtier to the Dantès of Miss Farren in *Monte Cristo Jr,* as the Monster to Nellie's Frankenstein in *Frankenstein* (the least successful of the series), as Don Caesar de Bazan to his partner's Ruy in *Ruy Blas and the Blasé Roué* and, finally, as "the servant" who turns out to be the comedy value in *Cinder-Ellen Up Too Late,* but this time not opposite Nellie, who was now incapacitated with rheumatism. The pair toured their successes through Britain and took them to America and to Australia, where they also appeared in *Miss Esmeralda,* one of the similar pieces with which Edwardes filled the Gaiety stage during his stars' hugely popular and lucrative touring absences. The partnership with Nellie Farren, hopefully only suspended for *Cinder-Ellen,* was, however, never to be resumed. Whilst Leslie was planning his next piece—a burlesque of *Don Juan*—he was taken ill and, at the age of 37, died of typhus.

In the era of the creative comic actor, Leslie supplied much of the material with which his parts in the early Gaiety burlesques were made. As a result, he decided to turn author officially, and, under the fairly transparent pseudonym of "A C Torr" co-wrote the libretti for his last three shows, as well as one on commission from fellow comedian Arthur Roberts (*Guy Fawkes Esq,* 1890).

Leslie's elder son, **Fred LESLIE** [William Herbert Leslie HOBSON], had a good career in musical comedy as a light-comedy supporting gentleman. He began in a small role in George Grossmith's *The Lovebirds* (1904, Maharajah of Mohook), toured America in *The School Girl* and took over in *Lady Madcap* (1905, t/o Stony Stratford) in the West End before spending some time on tour with George Edwardes's and Seymour Hicks's companies. He played in a revival of *The Dairymaids* (1908, Frank), covered Joe Coyne as Danilo in *The Merry Widow,* and had his first good West End role as Nicola in Robert Courtneidge's *Princess Caprice* (*Der liebe Augustin*), a part he repeated in New York (1913). After *Dancing Around* (USA, 1914, Lord Graham) and *The Miller's Daughters* (London, 1916, t/o Jack Charlton) he joined the company of *Theodore & Co* (1917, Rt Hon George Wye) at the Gaiety Theatre, thus beginning an association with producers Grossmith and Laurillard which gave him good number-two light-comedy roles in the hit musicals *Yes Uncle!* (1917, George Bellamy Stark), *Kissing Time* (1919, t/o Max Touquet) and *A Night Out* (1920, Maurice Paillard). He appeared in 1922 with Jack Buchanan in *Battling Butler* (Hugh Bryant), in 1923 in *Toni* (Von Koompf), and in 1924 visited Broadway one last time with Charlot's revue company.

1887 **Miss Esmeralda** (Meyer Lutz/w Horace Mills) Gaiety Theatre 8 October

1889 **Ruy Blas and the Blasé Roué** (Lutz as "A C Torr" w Herbert F Clark) Gaiety Theatre 21 September

1890 **Guy Fawkes Esq** (George W Byng/"Doss Chidderdoss"/w Clark) Theatre Royal, Nottingham 7 April

1891 **Cinder-Ellen Up Too Late** (Lutz, et al/w W T Vincent) Princess Theatre, Melbourne 22 August

Biography: Vincent, W T: *Recollections of Fred Leslie* (2 vols) (Kegan, Paul, Trench, Trübner & Co, London, 1894)

Another Fred Leslie [Frederick William Daniel STONEHAM] (b Carlton, Melbourne, 14 February 1882; d Geelong, 1969), an Australian dancer, light-comedy actor and choreographer, worked on the revue and musical comedy stage in both Australia—where he co-starred with John Ford in 1908 in the local production of *The Red Mill*—and (as **Fred A LESLIE**) in Britain. His West End choreographic credits included *Cash on Delivery* (1917), *Oh, Julie!* (1920, also pd w Ninette de Valois), *The Beauty Prize* (1923), *The Street Singer* (1924), *Love's Prisoner* (1925), *Sylvia* (1927), *Mr Cinders* (1929 w Charles Brooks, et al), *Tell Her the Truth* (1932), *Prudence* (1932), *He Wanted Adenture* (1933), *That's a Pretty Thing* (1933, also dir), *Jack of Diamonds* (1934), *Lucky Break* (1934 w Buddy Bradley), *Twenty to One* (1935), *Me and my Girl* (1937, including "The Lambeth Walk"), *Runaway Love* (1939), *Susie* (1942) and *La-di-da-de-da* (1943 w Bradley, John Regan).

His grandfather, father and uncle had each worked as wind and brass players in the orchestra with Australia's Simonsen comic opera company in the 1870s under their given names.

LESLIE, Henry J[ohn] (b Stepney, London, 16 January 1854; d London, 14 June 1900). Briefly but dramatically successful London producer and the builder of the West End's Lyric Theatre.

Originally an accountant with a musical and theatrical bent, Leslie worked in accounts at the Gaiety Theatre whilst occasionally inserting an original song into such of the theatre's shows as *Little Jack Sheppard* and *Monte Cristo Jr,* until the time when George Edwardes produced Alfred Cellier's comic opera *Dorothy.* After *Dorothy* had run an adequate fill-in season at the Gaiety, Edwardes transferred it to the Prince of Wales Theatre when his main company returned for the newest burlesque production. Soon he lost interest in the show and would have closed it had not Leslie offered to buy the production from him. For £500 the accountant became a producer and by recasting the old-style comic opera with some more vivacious performers, most notably the young Marie Tempest in the title role, he turned it into the longest-running London show of the century and made himself a fortune.

Leslie built Shaftesbury Avenue's Lyric Theatre on the proceeds of *Dorothy,* and there he produced Cellier's next piece, *Doris,* with sufficient if not equivalent returns whilst sending out long and large tours of both pieces. After the success of *Dorothy,* Leslie had put a lien on Cellier's future works and he took Lydia Thompson to court when she produced the 1874 *Sultan of Mocha.* He lost when *The Sultan of Mocha,* although heavily revised, was adjudged an "old" work. Leslie then abandoned Cellier, and turned for his next production to Edward Solomon, whose *The Red Hussar* he staged in 1889. Miss Tempest, with whom (though both were married) he had been carrying on a rather indiscreet affair which brought him again to court—this time as a co-respondent with £5,000 in damages to pay to the wounded husband—again starred, and with an undoubted success. However the ex-accountant's finances became more and more parlous as he became more and more ambitious.

A hugely spectacular pantomime, *Cinderella,* which he set up at Christmas 1889 at Her Majesty's Theatre in a hopeless attempt to outdo the traditional Drury Lane one, lost him his fortune and his theatre, an attempt to take the pantomime *The Babes in the Wood* (w J C Duff) to Broadway lasted but 48 Niblo's nights and his *Cinderella* got but 40 nights at the Academy of Music and, in spite of Miss Tempest's success in *The Red Hussar* in America, he went further under when a surfeit of top notes forced her voicelessly to cancel the tour. She returned to Britain, whilst he, having gone suddenly blind, remained in America. He later regained his sight, but his health was gone and his career in the theatre was over.

1887 **Jubilation** (w Ivan Caryll/"Richard Henry") 1 act Prince of Wales Theatre 14 May

1888 **Warranted Burglar Proof** (w Caryll/B C Stephenson)1 act Prince of Wales Theatre 31 March

LESTER, Alfred [LESLIE, Alfred Edwin] (b Nottingham, 25 October 1870; d Madrid, Spain, 6 May 1925). Little British musical comedian who followed in the tradition set by Teddy Payne at the Gaiety.

Born into a theatrical family, Lester worked on the stage from his earliest years, and spent the first part of his career touring the provinces in comedy and drama. In 1904 he appeared in London in the musical comedy *The Officer's Mess* (of which he was also the director) and scored a particular success with a comic scene-shifting act which he had invented for the halls, and now interpolated into the show. When *The Officer's Mess* closed he was hired to repeat his act (now entitled *The Scene Shifter's Lament*) at the Palace Music Hall.

Lester successfully followed this variety stage performance with others round the country (*The Labour MP,* etc) before he was drawn back into musical comedy by George Edwardes, who hired him to appear in the Gaiety show *The New Aladdin* (1906, The Lost Constable). Although this musical turned out to be one of the Gaiety's least popular, Lester scored a personal hit as a bewildered London bobby magicked into an ideal London. He returned to the Gaiety to take the principal comic role in *Havana* (1908, Nix) and then found a huge success when he created the part of the lugubrious jockey, Doody, in *The Arcadians* (1909), introducing the ludicrous song "My Motter." Kerker's *The Grass Widows* (1912) was a failure, but *The Pearl Girl* (1913, Byles), which cast him as a lovelorn shopboy, served him better and he had the second outstanding role of his career when he appeared as one of the Bing Boys, teamed with George Robey, in the triumphant Franco-English revue *The Bing Boys Are Here* at the Alhambra.

Lester subsequently played in the unsuccessful *Shanghai* and *The Eclipse* (1919, George), and he made his last appearance in a musical comedy in Teddy Payne's role of Miggles, another little shop boy, in the year-long revival of *The Shop Girl,* before spending his final years playing in revue. He withdrew, ill, from the cast of *The Punch Bowl* and went to Spain in search of health, dying there at the age of 54.

LESTER, Edwin (b Providence, RI, 30 March 1895; d Beverly Hills, Calif, 13 December 1990). American producer responsible for much of the best action on that country's western seaboard through several decades.

A child singer and pianist, a sometime conductor and mounter of the prologues at Grauman's Chinese Theater, sales manager with a Los Angeles music company, then a talent agent, Lester began producing for the benefit of his clients. He founded the San Francisco Light Opera Association (w Homer Curran) in 1937 and the Los Angeles Light Opera Association the following year. Amongst the productions of their first years, which from the beginning attained a high level of staging and casting (if not always of textual fidelity), were included *Blossom Time* with John Charles Thomas, a heavily reorganized *Gipsy Baron, A Waltz Dream,* Allan Jones in *The Desert Song, HMS Pinafore,* Jarmila Novotna as *The Merry Widow, The Red Mill,* Thomas and Irra Petina in *The Chocolate Soldier, Bitter-Sweet* with Muriel Angelus, *Music in the Air,* an "adapted" version of *Die Fledermaus* as *The Rose Masque* and a Strauss pasticcio called *The Waltz King.*

Lester had a major success and a Broadway transfer with another original pasticcio, *Song of Norway,* and thereafter he hosted and commissioned a number of other pasticcio and arranged pieces including, most successfully, Wright and Forrest's *Kismet* (1953) and, after several attempts, a new version of *Walzer aus Wien* produced as

The Great Waltz. Other productions included a Tchaikovsky pasticcio *Song without Words* (aka *Music in My Heart*) with Margit Bokor starred, yet another made-over *Fledermaus* based on the Reinhardted-and-Korngoldized version and called *Rosalinda,* Wright and Forrest's Victor Herbert remake *Gypsy Lady* (1946) and their Saint-Saëns pasticcio *Dumas and Son.* He also mounted some new musicals, ranging from stage versions of *Gigi* (1973) and Robert Stolz's musical film *Two Hearts in Waltz Time* to a musical *Peter Pan* (1954), Wright and Forrest's *Magdalena* (1948) and *At the Grand* and Vernon Duke's *Zenda.*

Separately, and later in tandem, the two companies flourished, although over the years the production schedule was forced down by rising costs and the season was ultimately obliged to include brought-in productions. Lester retired in 1976.

LET 'EM EAT CAKE Musical comedy in 2 acts by George S Kaufman and Morrie Ryskind. Lyrics by Ira Gershwin. Music by George Gershwin. Imperial Theater, New York, 21 October 1933.

Conceived as a sequel to the successful *Of Thee I Sing, Let 'em Eat Cake* followed the fortunes of President John P Wintergreen (William Gaxton), his winsome wife Mary (Lois Moran) and his ever-forgotten vice president, Throttlebottom (Victor Moore)—partially recognizable in their new antics as the joyous folk of the former show—following their ejection from office after one term. In a plot redolent of 19th-century comic opera, they open a clothing store, espouse revolution in order to sell their blue shirts as the uniform of rebellion, end up back in power after toppling the legitimate president, and get court-martialed out of power and in the direction of the gibbet following a baseball match between the League of Nations and the Supreme Court (prize: double or nothing on the war debts). Mary's manipulation of feminine America saves their necks, and the ex-presidential pair end up going back into the garment trade whilst Throttlebottom becomes president.

Lightning did not strike twice. The happy, witty burlesque tone which had made the first piece a success was missing second time round: the Gilbertian sparkle was replaced by a grey zaniness. From the score, only the extractable ''Mine'' (which was indeed extracted and used in a later version of *Of Thee I Sing*) won notice. *Let 'em Eat Cake* ran for 90 performances, and its closing marked the end of George Gershwin's contribution to the light musical theatre.

Recording: 1987 concert (CBS)

LETERRIER, [Stéphane] Eugène (b Paris, 15 May 1842; d Maisons-Lafitte, 22 December 1884). One of the most successful librettists for the Parisian opéra-comique in the years of its greatest prominence.

The young Leterrier, a clerk at the Paris Hôtel de Ville, began his theatrical career as he would finish it, in partnership with the even younger Albert Vanloo, who was at that time a not entirely enthusiastic law student. Their first work together, a version of the ''Tom Thumb'' story set to music by Laurent de Rillé, was given a production by William Busnach—the manager who had recently given his first major opportunity to the young composer Charles Lecocq—at his short-lived Théâtre de l'Athénée. However, it was five years of occasional one-acters, burlesques and flops before the pair found their first really productive opportunity in the musical theatre—one which came courtesy of the same Lecocq, now the celebrated composer of *La Fille de Madame Angot.* Leterrier and Vanloo, his friends from the days when he had been accompanist at the Athénée, were given the opportunity to supply the text for the new Lecocq work which producer Humbert anxiously awaited to follow his explosive hit, and they did not let him down. Their hilariously foolish text for *Giroflé-Girofla,* with its double-headed prima-donna role, added greatly to the success of the show which confirmed the tonitruant arrival of Lecocq at the musical-theatre forefront. It also marked the arrival of his new librettists.

Over the next decade, Leterrier and Vanloo—always working together—provided Lecocq with five further opéra-comique texts in the best and most intricately saucy farcical style of the time. Virtually all were successful, all were internationally played, with *Le Jour et la nuit, La Marjolaine* and *La Petite Mariée* each, in different areas, the most popular, and *La Jolie Persane* and *La Camargo* only a little in retreat. A sixth joint piece, in a different vein, was *L'Arbre de Noël* (w Arnold Mortier), a spectacular Christmas féerie in no fewer than 30 scenes, which was produced with considerable success at the Porte-Saint-Martin in 1880 and thereafter throughout Europe.

At the same time that they were turning out their Lecocq hits, the team also supplied texts to several of the other greats of the Paris musical stage, beginning, in the year following the production of *Giroflé-Girofla,* with Offenbach himself. Their *Le Voyage dans la lune* (w Mortier) proved a splendidly spectacular and durable piece of writing, but they worked on only one other occasion with Offenbach, and that was on a one-act piece which took many years to find its way to the stage. They also supplied the young Chabrier with the libretto for his *L'Étoile*—a libretto which subsequently went a good deal further than its score, being adapted to the uses of the American (*The Merry Monarch*), Hungarian (*Uff király*) and British (*The Lucky Star*) stages, without the benefit of Chabrier's music. Later, the same American writer who had helped himself to *L'Étoile,* Cheever Goodwin, would also borrow the libretto of their *La Gardeuse d'oies* for his William Furst musical *A Normandy Wedding* (aka *Papa Gougou*).

Lacome's *Le Beau Nicolas,* Lajarte's *Le Roi de carreau* and Messager's *La Béarnaise* all had respectable runs and traveled to productions overseas, but it was Leterrier and Vanloo's collaboration with Francis Chassaigne, *Le Droit d'aînesse,* which provided their biggest success of all outside France. Adapted by Henry Farnie as *Falka, Le Droit d'aînesse* was carried triumphantly across English-speaking stages from one side of the globe to the other, outdoing even *Giroflé-Girofla* in popularity and becoming easily the most often played of the partners' works in those areas.

Leterrier died at the age of 42 but, in an effective career of little more than 10 years, he had made a significant contribution to the musical theatre of his time with a dozen notably well-made and internationally played works, a number of which still receive intermittent productions more than a century later.

1868 **Le Petit Poucet** (Laurent de Rillé/w Albert Vanloo) Théâtre de l'Athénée 8 October

1869 **Madeleine** (Henri Potier/w Vanloo) 1 act Théâtre des Bouffes-Parisiens 10 January

1869 **La Nuit du 15 Octobre** (Georges Jacobi/w Vanloo) 1 act Théâtre des Bouffes-Parisiens 25 October

1871 **Nabucho** (A Villebichot/w Vanloo) Folies-Nouvelles 13 September

1874 **Giroflé-Girofla** (Charles Lecocq/w Vanloo) Fantaisies-Parisiennes, Brussels 21 March; Théâtre de la Renaissance 11 November

1875 **Le Voyage dans la lune** (Jacques Offenbach/w Vanloo, Arnold Mortier) Théâtre de la Gaîté 26 October

1875 **La Petite Mariée** (Lecocq/w Vanloo) Théâtre de la Renaissance 21 December

1877 **La Marjolaine** (Lecocq/w Vanloo) Théâtre de la Renaissance 3 February

1877 **Madame Clara, sonnambule** (Isidore Legouix/w Vanloo) 1 act Palais-Royal 15 March

1877 **L'Étoile** (Emmanuel Chabrier/w Vanloo) Théâtre des Bouffes-Parisiens 28 November

1878 **La Camargo** (Lecocq/w Vanloo) Théâtre de la Renaissance 20 November

1879 **Une education manquée** (Chabrier) 1 act Cercle Internationale de la Presse 1 May

1879 **La Jolie Persane** (Lecocq/w Vanloo) Théâtre de la Renaissance 28 October

1880 **L'Arbre de Noël** (Lecocq/w Vanloo, Mortier) Théâtre de la Porte-Saint-Martin 6 October

1880 **Le Beau Nicolas** (Paul Lacome/w Vanloo) Théâtre des Folies-Dramatiques 8 October

1881 **Der Weihnachtsbaum** German version of *L'Arbre de Noël* w music by Louis Roth (Theater an der Wien, Vienna)

1881 **Mademoiselle Moucheron** (Offenbach/w Vanloo) 1 act Théâtre de la Renaissance 10 May

1881 **Le Jour et la nuit** (Lecocq/w Vanloo) Théâtre des Nouveautés 5 November

1883 **Juanita** (*Donna Juanita*) French version w Vanloo (Galeries Saint-Hubert, Brussels)

1883 **Le Droit d'aînesse** (Francis Chassaigne/w Vanloo) Théâtre des Nouveautés 27 January

1883 **Le Roi de carreau** (Théodore de Lajarte/w Vanloo) Théâtre des Nouveautés 26 October

1885 **Le Petit Poucet** (André Messager, et al/w Vanloo, Mortier) Théâtre de la Gaîté 28 October

1885 **La Béarnaise** (André Messager/w Vanloo) Théâtre des Bouffes-Parisiens 12 December

1887 **La Gamine de Paris** (Gaston Serpette/w Vanloo) Théâtre des Bouffes-Parisiens 30 March

1888 **La Gardeuse d'oies** (Lacome/w Vanloo) Théâtre de la Renaissance 26 October

LET'S FACE IT Musical comedy in 2 acts by Herbert and Dorothy Fields based on the play *Cradle Snatchers* by Russell Medcraft and Norma Mitchell. Music and lyrics by Cole Porter. Imperial Theater, New York, 29 October 1941.

The Fields, brother and sister, working here together for the first time, adapted the play *Cradle Snatchers* to wartime musical comedy conditions by a little switching of characters. In the original play, the three ladies of the piece go and get themselves a gigolo apiece when they think their husbands are cheating on them. In the musical version, the ladies (Vivian Vance, Eve Arden, Edith Meiser) pick themselves up three soldiers (Danny Kaye, Benny Baker, Jack Williams) who are already equipped with sweethearts (Mary Jane Walsh, Sunny O'Dea, Nanette Fabray), who are, in fact, being romanced by the husbands. All the combinations came to a peak in some farcical scenes which finally restored the status quo.

Cole Porter's score was built on a veritable parade of for-the-moment lyrics: Mary Jane Walsh hymned ''Jerry, My Soldier Boy'' and the title song had the army facing it ''for Uncle Sam'' but, war or no war, the composer returned to his favorite style in ''Let's Not Talk About Love,'' a duo for Kaye and Miss Arden decorated with a bevy of topical and social names; a second name-dropper describing how celebrities go ''Farming''; a catalogue song on ''You're the Top'' lines called ''You Irritate Me So,'' which was shared by Williams and Miss Fabray; and a trio for the three girls advising each other always to have an ''Ace in the Hole.'' The lyric of this last had to be altered when one of its plugged personalities, Carole Lombard, was killed during the show's Broadway run. However, the most winning lyric was one of the few that refreshingly mentioned scarcely a star or brand name: a weary trio for the three wives explaining why ''A Lady Needs a Rest.''

Danny Kaye came to the cast of *Let's Face It* direct from his big success in *Lady in the Dark,* and he was allowed to develop his role into a festival of personal comedy amongst the more general comedy of the rest of the show. He also interpolated a pair of songs written with his wife, Sylvia Fine: a travestied Fairytale, and a gobbledegook scena to music called ''Melody in 4F'' in which he followed through the stages of the induction of an army recruit, and which proved to be amongst the comic highlights of the evening.

Let's Face It was greeted as ''brisk and bright and continuously enjoyable . . . swift and dry-humored comedy, a good thing in the vein of high pressure fooling.'' With appreciable help from Kaye and his comicalities during the first part of its run (he was later succeeded by José Ferrer) and, no doubt, also from the usual wartime long-run phenomenon, Vinton Freedley's lively production racked up a splendid 547 performances on Broadway. London gave the show an equally warm welcome, and Jack Waller and Tom Arnold's production, with Bobby Howes appearing in Kaye's role alongside Joyce Barbour, Noele Gordon and Babette O'Deal (wives), Pat Kirkwood, Pat Leonard and Zoe Gail (girls) and Jack Stanford and Leigh Stafford (soldiers), ran for 348 performances in the West End.

The score underwent alterations on Broadway when Kaye left the cast, and a number borrowed from *Dubarry Was a Lady* was inserted to replace his double-talk material for the benefit of Ferrer. It was this un-Kayed version which was subsequently played both in Britain and in Australia where Yvonne Banvard/Marjorie Gordon, Marie La Varre and Lily Moore featured as the three ladies and Don Nicol (who kept the Fairytale), Ron Beck and Fred Murray were the three fellows for a two and a half months' season at Sydney's Theatre Royal and another the following year at Melbourne's Her Majesty's (20 November 1943), during a wartime period which saw few other new productions relieving the flow of revivals in the area.

A 1954 television version with a cast including Bert Lahr, Gene Nelson and Vivian Blaine snaffled two additional elsewhere-Porter songs (''It's De-Lovely'' and ''I've Got You under My Skin''), whilst a film adaptation which starred Bob Hope alongside Betty Hutton and Miss Arden went the opposite way and shrank the song content, retaining only the title song and ''Let's Not Talk About Love'' alongside some studio-baked songs.

Australia: Theatre Royal, Sydney 12 September 1942; UK: London Hippodrome 19 November 1942

Film: 1943

Recording: archival reconstruction (CBS/Smithsonian Institution)

DIE LETZTEN MOHIKANER Komische Operette in 3 acts by F Zell. Music by Richard Genée. Theater am Gärtnerplatz, Munich, 10 September 1878; Friedrich-Wilhelmstädtisches Theater, Berlin, 8 May 1879.

Zell and Genée's Operette had nothing to do with J Fenimore Cooper's tale of American frontier life, but was set in Germany, with much of its action located around a rowing club, and had for its chief characters a rowing photographer, a plumber and the plumber's girlfriend. Liberally played in central Europe after its premiere in Munich (Leipzig, Vienna, Brünn, Berlin, Nuremberg, Prague, etc) it lasted only 12 performances when it was mounted at Vienna's Theater an der Wien in spite of the presence of Albin Swoboda, Alexander Girardi and Hermine Meyerhoff in its principal roles. It continued to win productions in Germany, however, and was mounted as a burlesque spectacular at Hamburg's Centraltheater in the 1885–86 season. In 1881 an English-language version was announced by the Emilie Melville Opera Company in San Francisco, but I can find no record of its having ever been played.

Austria: Theater an der Wien 4 January 1879

DER LETZTE WALZER Operette in 3 acts by Julius Brammer and Alfred Grünwald. Music by Oscar Straus. Berliner Theater, Berlin, 12 February 1920.

By 1920 more than a decade had passed since Oscar Straus's two big international hits with *Ein Walzertraum* and *Der tapfere Soldat* and, although he had subsequently composed Operetten and musical plays for the Austrian, German, British, French and Hungarian stages, including such not-inconsiderable pieces as the long-running *Rund um die Liebe, Die schöne Unbekannte, Die kleine Freundin, Eine Ballnacht, Liebeszauber* and *Dorfmusikanten,* none of these had achieved the same wide-ranging popularity that his two early hits had.

After the First World War Straus settled in Berlin, and his first work for the Berlin theatre was *Der letzte Walzer,* written to a libretto by Julius Brammer and Alfred Grünwald. Their plot centered on Vera Lisaweta (Fritzi Massary), eldest daughter of the widowed Countess Opalinski, who has rejected the pressing advances of the powerful Prince Paul and ultimately had to be rescued from his importunities by an unknown young man. Paul, however, has had his revenge. He has had the interfering Count Dmitri Sarrasow (Otto Storm) condemned to death and has commanded the elderly General Krasinski to wed the so-very-particular Vera Lisaweta. Dmitri, under arrest in Krasinski's castle, is allowed a reasonable freedom on his honor and, on the night before his transfer to the death cell, he encounters the woman who is now the General's fiancée at a ball. Together they dance what will be his last waltz. Vera arranges an escape for the man she loves, but Dmitri refuses to break his word. Paul, however, does not mean to kill the Count, he means merely to humiliate both him and Vera, and so the vehicles taking the prisoner to Warsaw and the bride to her wedding are rerouted to the Prince's palace. There, however, Vera gains the upper hand. She points out to the Prince that Dimitri is emerging in the eyes of the world as the hero of the affair and he as a petulant loser, a situation which can be turned around if he now orders Vera and Dmitri to be wed. The light comedy of the piece was ensured through the first two acts by Vera's sisters, notably the youngest, Babuschka, and by their en masse suitor Baron Ippolith, all of whom were then tactfully faded out of the picture to allow the final triangle to be worked out without interruption.

Straus's score for *Der letzte Walzer* was one of his most sweepingly romantic and melodious and, if it did not bring forth such obvious bonbons as *Ein Walzertraum*'s famous duet or *Der tapfere Soldat*'s "My Hero" waltz, it was nevertheless filled with richly written music in the very best and most beautiful contemporary Viennese vein. The best role and the bulk of the romantic music fell to the prima donna: her mirror song "Tanze, Vera Lisaweta" as she persuades herself that she can convince Dmitri to flee, the waltzing "Rosen die wir nicht erreichten," the csárdás of the second-act finale, the contrastingly taunting "O du pikantes, süsses o-la-la" of her third-act encounter with the Prince, and her rousing waltz duets with the tenor ("Das ist der letzte Walzer," "Hörst du die liebliche zwingende singende werbende Walzermusik"). The tenor role had its best moments in duet, and in Dmitri's carefree farewell to life, "Bei Lied und Wein," but the other highlights of the show's score came in the light numbers: Ippolith's appreciation of Babuschka's dimples ("Du hast zwei Grübchen") and his polka-ed dilemma, before the appearance of the youngest, over which delicious sister to choose (Der Polkakavalier: "O kommt, o kommt und tanz mit mir").

Der letzte Walzer scored a major success through 280 performances in Berlin, sealing a collaboration between Straus and Fritzi Massary which would last, to their great mutual advantage, through five further shows, and it soon found its way to the stages of the world in a way that only his two most popular pieces had previously done. Hungary, as almost always, was first off the mark with *Búcsúkeringő* (ad Zsolt Harsányi), followed by America and the Shuberts whose Broadway production of *The Last Waltz* (ad Edward Delaney Dunn, Harold Atteridge) starred Eleanor Painter and Walter Woolf, two of the most considerable musical-theatre vocalists of the time, as Vera and her Count. In a fashion which had not yet, sadly, seen its day, they also botched Straus's score with interpolations by house writer Al Goodman and by Rudolf Nelson and Ralph Benatzky. *The Last Waltz* was, nevertheless, a distinct success and played for 199 performances at the huge Century Theater.

Having taken its time to reach Vienna, *Der letzte Walzer* was no less of a hit when it finally appeared there, in the wake of Gilbert's not dissimilar *Die Frau im Hermelin,* with Betty Fischer (Vera), Hubert Marischka (Dimitry), Lilly Welly (Babuschka), Kurt Ehrle (Paul) and Walter Huber (Ippolith) starring at the Theater an der Wien for a first run of 221 performances and a 34-performance reprise. In Britain, the piece was picked up by Robert Evett as the first independent vehicle for *Sybil* star José Collins following her departure from Daly's Theatre. Played at the Gaiety in a version by Evett and Reginald Arkell, with vocalist Kingsley Lark as Dmitri and Miss Collins's handsome Daly's Theatre co-star Bertram Wallis as Prince Paul, *The Last Waltz* set the new management off to a fine start with a 280-performance run which, if less than that achieved by *Sybil,* was to be the best that any of their ventures would achieve.

Oddly, it took six years for the show to reach France, the French version (ad Jean Marietti, Léon Uhl) being given first at Geneva, where Odette Sardo created the French Vera Lisaveta opposite Pagnoulle and Monval. When it did arrive in Paris, it was at Louis Masson's well-meaning repertoire theatre, the Trianon-Lyrique, where Germaine Revel, René Rudeau and Monval headed the cast. However *La Dernière Valse* received a more substantial Parisian showing a decade later when it was played at the Gaîté-Lyrique (21 May 1936), with Suzanne Laplace, Raymond Chanel and André Balbon at the head of its cast.

In spite of its obvious attractions and its strong initial runs *Der letzte Walzer* subsequently rather slipped from the standard repertoire, but it was filmed in Germany on two occasions, the first in 1934 with Camille Horn and Ivan Petrovitch starred, and the second in 1953. This second version (ad Curt Braun, music arr Bruno Uher) kept a little (but not much) closer to the original story than the bulk of European Operette films, as Eva Bartok pleaded with O E Hasse for the life of Curd Jurgens. Robert Gilbert and Fritz Rotter wrote fresh text for new numbers interpolated into what remained of the score and maturing Operette star Christl Mardayn appeared as the heroine's mother. In 1936 a British film version, starring Harry Welchman and Jarmila Novotna, and a simultaneous French version which paired Novotna with Jean Martinelli were made.

Hungary: Városi Színház *Búcsúkeringő* 29 December 1920; USA: Century Theater *The Last Waltz* 10 May 1921; Austria: Theater an der Wien 27 October 1921; UK: Gaiety Theatre *The Last Waltz* 7 December 1922; France: Trianon-Lyrique *La Dernière Valse* 5 May 1926

Films: Georg Jacoby 1934, *The Last Waltz* 1936, *La Dernière Valse* 1936, International Films 1953

Recording: selection (Period)

LEVEY, Ethel [FOWLER, Grace Ethelia] (b San Francisco, 22 November 1880; d New York, 27 February 1955).

Ethel Levey made her first professional stage appearance at the age of 17, singing a coon song in a West Coast production of the musical farce-comedy *A Milk White Flag.* She soon moved east, and she appeared in New York in music hall and burlesque at Koster and Bial's and Weber and Fields's music halls before joining Josh Hart's Speciality Company (1899) and Hyde and Behman's company. This last shift was made in order to stay at the side of the man who shortly after (10 July 1899) became her husband, George M Cohan. She appeared with Cohan, between 1901 and 1907, in the run of musical comedies which he wrote, composed and starred in: *The Governor's Son* (1901, Emerald Green, later Mrs Dickey Dickson), *Running for Office* (1903, Gertie Gayland), *Little Johnny Jones* (1904, as the persecuted heroine, Goldie Gates) and *George Washington Jr* (1906, Dolly Johnson). During this period she also took over the title role of Sidney Jones's much more musically substantial comedy opera, *My Lady Molly,* on the road.

After divorcing Cohan, Miss Levey appeared on Broadway in the musical *Nearly a Hero* (1908, Angeline de Vere) and appeared with Laddie Cliff in the revusical *Gaby* (1911, Gaby), but she worked largely in music hall and revue, both in America and in Europe, performing Blanche Ring's successful ''Rings on My Fingers'' and ''Prairie Mary'' at Vienna's Apollotheater and scoring a big success in London in 1912 when she starred in the early revue *Hullo, Ragtime!,* dancing Jack Mason's choreography to the ''Bacchanale Rag'' with Checkers von Hampton. She subsequently spent a number of years in Britain where she devoted most of her time to revue but also appeared in the title role of Ernest C Rolls's musical comedy production *Oh! Julie* (1920, Julie), winning a personal success in the show's fair-to-medium run. She was seen in New York in 1922 as the Mabel of *Go Easy, Mabel* and three years later, back in London, as Totoche in *The Blue Kitten,* but her musical stage performances thereafter were few and, as far as Broadway was concerned, limited to character roles in Romberg's *Sunny River* and Kálmán's *Marinka* when she was in her sixties.

LEVIN, Herman (b Philadelphia, 1 December 1907; d New York, 27 December 1990).

A lawyer in New York, Levin entered theatrical production as co-producer of the revue *Call Me Mister* in 1946. His first musical play venture was a combination with Paul Feigay and Oliver Smith on *Bonanza Bound!* (1947), which closed on the road. His first Broadway musical was *Gentlemen Prefer Blondes* (1949) and he more than confirmed this promising start with his second, the triumphant *My Fair Lady* (1956), which he sponsored both in America and Britain.

Thereafter, however, the winning touch deserted him. Noël Coward's *The Girl Who Came to Supper* (1963), although patently geared to the *My Fair Lady* formula, failed to repeat that show's results, *Lovely Ladies, Kind Gentlemen,* a musical version of *The Teahouse of the August Moon,* was a quick flop in 1970, and *Tricks,* a musical-comedy adaptation of Molière, an even quicker one three years later.

LEWENSTEIN, [Silvion] Oscar (b London, 18 January 1917; d Hove, 23 February 1997).

The manager of several British theatres (Unity Glasgow, Embassy, Royal Court), Lewenstein produced or co-produced a number of plays, often with a bias towards the experimental and/or the left-wing, in the 1950s and the 1960s. His first musical-theatre venture was a revival of *The Threepenny Opera* (1956), but having commissioned a first original musical, the adventurous *Valmouth,* from Sandy Wilson as a vehicle for American star Bertice Reading, he did not ultimately produce it. Two years later, however, he did mount an equally impressive original musical in *Expresso Bongo* (David Heneker, Julian More, Monty Norman/Wolf Mankowitz) and, following its success, sponsored the same authors' next piece, *Make Me an Offer* (1959), a musical play which was, like its predecessor, one of the best British musicals of its time. *The Lily White Boys* at the Royal Court and the British production of Broadway's *Fiorello!* were both unsuccessful and thereafter Lewenstein stuck principally to producing straight plays, making just one last but unmemorable musical venture with the short-lived London version of the off-Broadway import *Your Own Thing* (1969).

Autobiography: *Kicking Against the Pricks* (Nick Hern Books, London 1994)

LEWIS, Ada (b New York, 17 March 1872; d Hollis, NY, 24 September 1925). One of the most effective character actresses of the Broadway musical theatre in the 1910s and 1920s.

Ada Lewis made her stage debut walking on at $3 a week in *Siberia* at the Alcazar, San Francisco in 1887. She passed much of her juvenile days in the stock company at the Alcazar, before catching the eye of Ned Harrigan during the star's guest appearance there in 1889. Harrigan wrote the teenaged girl into his *Reilly and the Four Hundred* (1890) and she scored a fine personal success in the role of the ''tough girl'' Kittie Lynch. She appeared in another similar role in Harrigan's *The Last of the Hogans* (1891, Mary Ann Brennan), and thereafter made herself a reputation and a pigeonhole as a strong lady in a string of farce comedies and variety musicals—*Squatter Sovereignty* (1892 revival, Louisa Kringle), *The Mulligan Guards Ball* (1892 revival, Kitty Lochmuller), *The Midnight Express* (1892), as Ellen McFuss in the revived *Cordelia's Aspirations* (1893), Margie McIntyre in *A Country Sport* (1893), Felicity Jones in *The Widow Jones* (1895), Mme Nocodi in *Courted into Court* (1896, making a hit with the song "Ooompah"), Mamie Muggins in the vaudeville extravaganza *Cook's Tour* (1898) at Koster and Bial's, Clementine Clapper in *A Reign of Error* and the burlesque *Mdlle Ka-za-za* (1899), Lotta Hintz in *The Rogers Brothers on Wall Street* (1899), La Dollie in *The Widow's Husband* (1900) back at the San Francisco Alcazar, Letitia Campbell in Peter F Dailey's *Champagne Charlie* (1901), Kate in *The Supper Club* (1901) and Lil McGrain in *Fritz in Tammany Hall* (1905). She also starred in Philadelphia's *The Wanderer* (1905, Angeline Jones), which didn't go on, as hoped, to bigger things. She subsequently moved "up" to the Casino Theater where she took further roles in the same line in *The Social Whirl* (1906, Kitty La Verne), *Fascinating Flora* (1907, Winnie Wiggins) and *Nearly a Hero* (1908, Gwendolyn Doolittle).

In the following years, as she matured from "tough girl" into a comical character actress, she played in such pieces as Boston's *The Yanklee Mandarin* (1909, "Gypsy of Poughkeepsie"), *Old Dutch* (1909, Alma Villianyi), *The Summer Widowers* (1910, Mrs Guinevere McGuirk), the Folies-Bergère double-bill (1911) of *Gaby* (The Royal Governess) and *Hell* (impersonating Maude Adams, and playing Mrs Devil) and the Weber and Fields burlesque *Bunty Bulls and Strings* (1912, Susie Slimson, a female villain). She supported Al Jolson in *The Honeymoon Express* (1913, Mme de Bressie), appeared briefly in the substandard *The Dancing Duchess* (1914, Tilly, the housemaid), took over in Chicago's *One Girl in a Million* (1914) and then, at the age of 40 (perhaps), landed her best role for some time as Madame Matroppo, the extravagantly forgetful singing teacher of *Very Good Eddie.*

Her next musical appearance was in the long-running *Listen, Lester* (1920, Tillie Mumm), after which she appeared in two further Jerome Kern musicals: as the gorgonic mother-in-law of *The Night Boat* (1920, Mrs Maxim) and the comical couturiere of *Good Morning, Dearie.* In 1924 she starred alongside John E Hazzard as Madame Doremi, the American version of Jeanne Cheirel's celebrated role of the "Comtesse" in *Ta bouche* (*One Kiss*) and she was signed to appear in a further Kern piece, *Sunny,* when, at a time and age when she might have been expected to have continued into a career as a major star older comedy/character lady, she collapsed with a nervous breakdown and died.

LEWIS, Bertha [Amy] (b Forest Gate, 12 May 1887; d Cambridge, 8 May 1931).

At first a supporting member and then, for many years, the principal contralto of the D'Oyly Carte Opera Company, the imposing, squarely built Bertha Lewis became identified with the heavy ladies of the Gilbert and Sullivan repertoire to a generation of British theatregoers and early record buyers. She was killed in a car crash, aged 43, while touring with the company.

LEWIS, Catherine (b Swansea, 6 May ?1853; d Hove, 15 February 1942). Leading lady of the international musical stage who later transformed herself into a classic character actress.

The daughter of artist Richard Jeffries Lewis RA, the young Catherine made her first appearance on the stage in comedy at the Lyceum at the age of something like 19. She moved on from there to play with Carl Rosa's newly established opera company (1873, Cherubino then Susanna to the Countess of Rose Hersee, Leila in *Satanella,* Donna Carmen in *The Rose of Castile* and Isabella in the first British performance of *The Doctor of Alcantara*), and made her first notable appearance on the London stage soon after when she took over from Selina Dolaro as Clairette in *La Fille de Madame Angot* at the Philharmonic Theatre. At Christmas 1874 she appeared at Covent Garden in the pantomime and the operetta *La Vivandière,* and the following year she took the feminine lead in the London production of Lecocq's *Les Prés Saint-Gervais,* playing Friquette to the Prince Conti of Pauline Rita, and appeared at Manchester as Dolly in the first revival of *The Sultan of Mocha.* In 1875–76 she toured Britain in the big double title role of Mrs Liston's production of *Giroflé-Girofla.*

In 1877 she visited Australia, starring in *Giroflé-Girofla, La Petite Mariée, La Fille de Madame Angot* and *Madame l'Archiduc,* but she could not equal the popularity there of the more incisively vivacious American star, Emilie Melville, and she soon moved on to San Francisco. There she starred at Baldwin's Theater with Fred Lyster's troupe as Clairette and *Giroflé-Girofla* (1878) and at Emerson's Opera House in a wide variety of musical pieces including the burlesque *Kenilworth* (Amy Robsart), *Fra Diavolo, Les Cloches de Corneville* (Serpolette), *Giroflé-Girofla* and *Zampa.* She also appeared in the spectacular *Zapha* at San Francisco's Grand Opera House before, in November 1878, she made her first appearance in New York, with Tracy Titus's operetta company. With the arrival of the *HMS Pinafore* craze, she took up the role of Josephine with Alexander Henderson's company, then moved on to join Augustin Daly's well-considered repertoire company, appearing in both plays and musicals and taking, amongst others, the lead role of versions of *Niniche* (*Newport,* Hon Mrs Peter Porter) and *L'École des femmes* (*Wives,* Agnes). It was in her next engagement, however, that she hit her peak as a star, playing Fanchette Michel in *The Royal Middy* (1880), a role for which she received a reported salary of $75 a week. She earned that salary, however, as this version of Genée's *Der Seekadett* was a major hit and she its most appreciated asset. When Daly's production of the show was subsequently set to tour, American managers refused to take it in without its star and Daly, who had sacked his star shortly before, during one of their spats, was obliged to hire the ''brilliant, dashing actress'' back—at $150 per week.

She scored another major Broadway hit when she starred as Audran's *Olivette* with the Comley-Barton troupe, winning enormous popularity with ''her kittenish ways and her catchy way of singing,'' appeared in Boston as Merope Mallow in Rice & Goodwin's production of *Cinderella at School* (1881) and as Bettina in *La Mascotte,* and went on to score heavily in the title roles of *Madame Favart* (1881) and *Manola* (*Le Jour et la nuit,* 1882). She subsequently toured as Mignapour in *Le Grand Mogol* (1882), played Régina in *The Princess of Trébizonde* and featured as the first American-language *Prince Methusalem* (1883) before disappearing from the Broadway stage into a long series of comic-opera summer seasons and tours, latterly with noticeably lessening vocal powers. In 1884 she and her touring company played the first English-language *Madame Boniface* in America before collapsing, in 1885 she put out her own company with the musical comedy *Gladys* which stayed strictly away from New York, and in the years that followed things didn't get much better. In 1895 she was seen scraping the bottom of the Broadway barrel as Ophelia in a burlesque of *Hamlet II* at the Herald Square Theater.

Catherine Lewis nevertheless returned to metropolitan prominence 15 years on, playing both in classic plays—she was Daly's Maria in *Twelfth Night*—and also in character roles in such musical productions as *La Poupée* (1898, Madame Hilarius), *The Circus Girl* (1898, Mme Drivelli), A *Runaway Girl* (1898, Lady Coodle), *The Cadet Girl* (1900, Madame Majeste), Aimé Lachaume's *The Prima Donna* (1901, Mrs Chumpley), and in her last Broadway appearance, *Sally in Our Alley* (1902, Calanthe Marigold) before going into a long retirement.

In 1905 she mounted the Lenten Mystery Plays at Carnegie Hall with her daughters Constance Arfwedson and Catherine Robertson in the cast, and as late as 1921 ''Miss Catherine Lewis's Educational Theatre Company'' was to be seen at London's Bedford Hall giving a series of biblical plays, under the management of daughter Constance.

Her sister, **Mary [Jeffreys] LEWIS,** had a fine career as a star actress on the Broadway and West Coast stages under the name Jeffreys Lewis, and made appearances in a non-singing capacity in the slightly musical-comedy *Easy Dawson* (1905, Mrs Churchill-Churchill-Brenton) and in the Chicago musical *The Girl and the Drummer* (1910, Mrs Goodly). A second sister, **Constance [Florence] Lewis** (b Swansea, 24 December 1858), also appeared on the musical stage in Britain and in America.

LIBELLENTANZ Revue-Operette in 3 acts by Carlo Lombardo, a revised version of *Der Sterngucker* by Fritz Löhner-Beda and A M Willner. Music by Franz Lehár. Produced as *La danza delle libellule,* Teatro Lirico, Milan, 27 September 1922.

Franz Lehár's *Der Sterngucker,* produced at Vienna's Theater in der Josefstadt in 1916 (14 January), had a libretto in which an unworldly young astronomer gets involved simultaneously with three of his sister's girlfriends and has to be brought severely down to earth. Seventy-nine performances at the Theater in der Josefstadt were followed by a second attempt, with a ''Neubearbeitung,'' which played for a further 60 nights from September of the same year, with all the forces of the Theater an der Wien behind it (Hubert Marischka, Betty Fischer, Luise Kartousch, Ernst Tautenhayn), but, although the piece was substantially played in Germany (Montis Operettentheater) and won productions in Budapest (*A csillagok bolondja* Népopera 10 October 1916) and in America (*The Star Gazer* Plymouth Theater 26 November 1917, 8 performances), it was not anywhere considered a success.

When subsequently approached for a score by Carlo Lombardo, Lehár, who was never chary of reusing ''wasted'' music, exhumed the *Der Sterngucker* score and handed it over to the enterprising Italian manager and writer. Lombardo put together a wholly new libretto in which the disguised Charles, Duke of Nancy, finds himself a young widow for a Duchess during the course of some amateur theatricals, and he produced the resulting piece, under the description of a ''revue-operetta'' and the title *La danza delle libellule,* in Milan. *La danza delle libellule* proved noticeably more successful than *Der Sterngucker,* and following its Italian production it was duly reexported to Vienna where it was mounted by Herbert Trau at the Neues Wiener Stadttheater as *Libellentanz* with Otto Storm starring as the Herzog von Nancy, Lia Lüdersdorff as his Hélène Cliquot, and Josef König, Lisa Rado and manager's wife Olga Bartos in the other principal roles.

The show, as it now stood, consisted of a very light and slight story—which depended as much on the flirtations of the ex-chorus-girl wives of local gentlemen who join in the theatricals as on its main threadlet—decorated with many dances of which a Snowball Ballet was the feature, not to mention a parade of ladies' underwear, a classical burlesque, harp and violin solos, an extensive wardrobe and a very full score of no fewer than 25 musical numbers. From that score, which Lombardo (who was a composer and musical director as well as a librettist, adaptor, producer and performer) had remodeled to appeal to the international dance-music tastes of the time, there emerged one genuine international hit, the fox-trot "Gigolette," sung by the two principals, as well as several other appreciated numbers amongst which were the song-and-dance duo "Bambolina" (Storm and Frau Trau), a waltz song for Frln Rado, a quartet in the form of a java-gavotte and a Butterfly Duet in which König threatened to net Frau Trau.

If Germany and America, who had both previously hosted *Der Sterngucker,* refrained from taking up *Libellentanz,* Hungary had no such qualms. Budapest was both the first and the most successful to stage its version, but nevertheless balked at Lombardo's title. The show, staged as *A három grácia* ("the three graces," ad Zsolt Harsányi), scored a major triumph at the Fővárosi Operettszínház with Irén Biller starring, and it was played more than two hundred times there during 1923–24. Elsewhere, those countries which had passed on the original show moved in to try the revised one. In Paris, Mme Rasimi produced Roger Ferréol and Max Eddy's French version of the show at the Ba-ta-clan (the busy productrice being herself responsible for what she billed as "300 costumes"), with Maria Kousnezoff and Jacques Vitry in the lead roles and Marthe Ferrare, Marie Dubas and Félix Oudart in rich support, and it again won a comfortable success. If the French retained Lombardo's title—in spite of the fact that the word "libellule" (dragonfly) had suffered something of the same denaturization there as the English "gay"—England followed the Hungarians, calling its version of the piece *The Three Graces.* Produced by Joe Sacks in a version by the young playwright Ben Travers, with the well-known vocalists Thorpe Bates and Winifred Barnes starring, it suffered the fate of most of Lehár's middle and later works in Britain and managed only a mediocre run of two and a half months (121 performances) in a season in which Gilbert's *Lady of the Rose,* Kern's *Sally* and a variegated selection of revues dominated the London scene. It was sufficient time, however, for "Gigolette" to become a London dance-band hit.

The name value of this hit song was sufficient, and sufficiently international, for the piece to be later reproduced (in a further revised version, with the addition of numbers from other Lehár works) in Milan under the title *Gigolette* (Teatro Lirico 30 December 1926), but the new version did not succeed in superseding the previous one.

Austria: Neues Wiener Stadttheater *Libellentanz* 1 April 1923; Hungary: Fővárosi Operettszínház *A három grácia* 6 June 1923; France: Théâtre Ba-ta-clan *La Danse des libellules* 14 March 1924; UK: Empire Theatre *The Three Graces* 26 January 1924

Recordings: selections in Italian (COS, Fonit Cetra, Oxford, Vesuvius)

Video: Ricordi 1990

LIDO LADY Musical comedy in 3 acts by Ronald Jeans based on a libretto by Guy Bolton, Bert Kalmar and Harry Ruby. Lyrics by Lorenz Hart. Music by Richard Rodgers. Gaiety Theatre, London, 1 December 1926.

In the post-*Nanette* period, when simply anything American that sang and danced was all the rage in the London theatre, *Lido Lady* was commissioned by London producers Jack Hulbert and Paul Murray from the American songwriting team of Rodgers and Hart, hard on the heels of the duo's first Broadway successes with *The Garrick Gaieties, Dearest Enemy* and *The Girl Friend,* and before any of their shows had as yet been presented to the London public. Here, the pair had their first experience of being presented with a ready-made book to illustrate (their earlier musicals had been evolved in collaboration with Herbert Fields) and a star team already in place (Hulbert, his wife Cicely Courtneidge and Phyllis Dare). The jolly, nonsensical book, which opened on the Lido at Venice, featured Miss Dare as Fay Blake, daughter of sporting-goods magnate, and revolved around a stolen formula for a tennis ball. It spent most of its time looking at the various set-up efforts staged by the boys of the piece to impress their chosen girls with their particular sporting prowesses, and it took time off from things sporting to enjoy the attempts of a budding starlet called Peggy Bassett (Miss Courtneidge) to find herself publicity.

Rodgers was less than happy with the situation (and also with the lack of fuss made over him by his employers), and this disenchantment came out in his work. The best number in *Lido Lady* was not composed for the show, it was none other than "Here in My Arms," lifted from *Dearest Enemy* and here performed by Hulbert and Miss Dare. Miss Courtneidge duetted with Harold French (as Spencer Weldon) about "A Tiny Flat Near Soho Square" and with Hulbert (playing her brother, Harry) in "Try Again Tomorrow," whilst Miss Dare got the best of the new numbers, the "Atlantic Blues," as well as a De Sylva, Brown and Henderson interpolation "It All Depends on You," taken from Broadway's *Big Boy.* It shared the evening's honors with the other second-hand song as the best liked numbers in the show.

Lido Lady was carefully produced out of town (Alhambra, Bradford 4 October) and run in thoroughly in the provinces before moving into town where its brisk fun and star team won it a seven-and-a-half-month (261 performances) stay. It subsequently went on the road in 1928 with George Clarke and Ella Retford featured, was trotted out again in 1929, and was mounted by the Fuller organization in Australia with Elsie Prince (Peggy), Billy Leonard (Harry), Jimmy Godden (Bill), Yvette Armina as Fay, singing the ''Atlantic Blues,'' and director Charlton Morton as Spenser. A good Sydney run was followed by six weeks at Melbourne's Princess Theatre (10 May) where the show had the misfortune to follow in behind one of the biggest Australian hits of the era, *Rio Rita.*

Lido Lady also appeared briefly on the Paris stage (ad Charles Tutelier, Georges Gilbert, with additional songs by musical director Max Alexis) under the management of Edgard H Tietjens and advertised as a ''comédie musicale à grand spectacle.'' Violet Warland (succeeded by Mireille) sang the ''Atlantic Blues'' and ''Tout ça dépend sur vous'' with Lucien Mussière, who shared ''Reviens un autre jour'' with Yvonne Louis. ''Here in My Arms'' became ''Rien n'est plus doux'' in the show, but was given under its American title as the theme of the intermission music, arranged by M Alexis to feature trumpet and piano solos. The 16 Dolly Dorne's Girls and the 8 Apollo's Boys supported, and the second act featured ''La Parade de la Reine de Saba'' as an entertainment at the Fête du Sporting Club. *Lido Lady* was not, however, transported back to America, where its best pieces had already been used, and the unused parts were, on the evidence, not reckoned by their writers (or anyone else) to be recyclable on home ground.

Vienna did not take up London's *Lido Lady,* but soon after its closure in the West End the Johann Strauss-Theater came up with a Revue-Operette in seven scenes by Otto Florian and Robert Katscher, directed by Leo Strassberg and starring Luise Kartousch as Mister Quick the Detective in the tale of *Die Lady vom Lido* (12 August 1927). It didn't actually get to the Lido until scene seven, having spent its time in such revusical places as the Highschool for Charlestonning, A Revuetheater in Rehearsal and Amongst Cannibals. All of which sounded more fun than the Lido. Or Soho Square.

Italy was not far behind Britain and Austria when it came to Lido-ing, and Rome's Teatro Nazionale hosted a musical christened *Lady Lido* (Virgilio Ranzato/D Marchi) in 1929 (31 July).

Australia: St James Theatre, Sydney 23 February 1929; France: Théâtre Apollo

DER LIEBE AUGUSTIN Operette in 3 acts by Rudolf Bernauer and Ernst Welisch, a revised version of their *Der Rebell.* Music by Leo Fall. Neues Theater, Berlin, 3 February 1912.

Leo Fall's first venture as a composer of Operette was *Der Rebell,* a piece written to a libretto by Bernauer and Welisch and produced in no less a venue than the Theater an der Wien (29 November 1905) with a cast headed by Louis Treumann, Karl Streitmann, Dora Keplinger, Gerda Walde and Franz Glawatsch. It was an utter failure, playing for just five performances before being withdrawn, leaving manager Karczag hurriedly to rehearse and replace it with a piece by another promising and slightly more experienced composer, Franz Lehár. The failure of *Der Rebell* was forgotten in the success of *Die lustige Witwe.*

Half a dozen years later, Fall, now the internationally idolized composer of *Der fidele Bauer, Die Dollarprinzessin* and *Die geschiedene Frau,* and pressed from all sides and all parts of the world for new shows and new compositions, exhumed his score for *Der Rebell* and reworked it, with the original librettists, under the title *Der liebe Augustin,* with its catchy reminiscence of the popular song. The beloved Augustin, in this story, was the piano teacher of Princess Helene (Fritzi Massary), daughter of the desperately impecunious Bogumil of Thessaly who is intent that his child wed the rich Prince Nicola of Mikolics to save the family furniture from the hands of the bailiffs. Helene attempts to dissuade her bridegroom with a display of temper tantrums, but he is set on getting his hands on the Thessalian throne, even if he is obliged to wed a shrewish wife to get it, and he already has his eye on Helene's maid Anna as a candidate for the post of consoling royal mistress. Fortunately, it turns out that batty Bogumil and Anna's father Jasomirgott got their babies mixed up, 20-something years back, whilst fleeing from an old revolution, so Nicola gets both the crown and Princess Anna, whilst Helene goes off happily to picturesque poverty with her piano teacher.

Fall's score was made up from a series of such winning melodies that it was almost impossible to believe that they had escaped popularity six years earlier. The big hit of the show was the duet for Helene and Augustin, blissfully dreaming of a paradise for two in the waltz ''Und der Himmel hängt voller Geigen,'' but there were many more. The same pair shared a jaunty duo in a soundless piano lesson after the bailiffs have taken the piano (''Es war einmal ein Musikus'') and took the first steps to special friendship in the lilting ''Sei mein Kamarad,'' whilst Anna joined Jasomirgott and Augustin in the leaping ''Anna, was ist denn mit dir?'' and there were splendid numbers for Augustin (''Lass' dir Zeit''/''Was es Schönes gibt'') and Helene (''Wenn die Sonne schlafen geht'') as well as bouncy, tuneful comic material for the comedy men (''Heut' Nacht, nach acht,'' ''Wo steht denn das Geschrieben'').

Der liebe Augustin was a singular hit for the Neues Theater and—as its total of performances rose at a rate which would, within a decade, put it in the all-time top 20 of musical shows in Germany (Otto Keller's calculations, made up to the early 1920s, placed it 16th with 3,660 performances)—the foreign-language productions began.

The first of these was in Budapest, where Adolf Mérei's Hungarian version was mounted at the Népopera, prior to the city seeing the piece in German during a guest appearance by the Carltheater company at the Király Színház the following year. The second was in London, where Robert Courtneidge produced a version entitled *Princess Caprice* (ad Alexander M Thompson, A Scott Craven, Harry Beswick, Percy Greenbank) with Harry Welchman and Clara Evelyn starring in the romantic roles alongside top comedians Courtice Pounds (Jasomirgott) and George Graves (Bogumil) and Marie Blanche as Anna. Producer's daughter Cicely appeared in an added role as Nicola's sister, Clementine, which involved some reallocating of the score. The show was a fine London success through 265 performances before taking to the road for a provincial career which was somewhat handicapped by the First World War and the subsequent campaign mounted against shows by German and Austrian composers. In the meantime, however, *Der liebe Augustin* had reached Vienna where, with Mizzi Zwerenz and Hubert Marischka starred alongside Richard Waldemar (Bogumil), Josef König (Nicola), Karl Schöpfer (Jasomirgott) and Magda Szécsy (Anna), Sigmund Eibenschütz's production won a fine reception through 66 first-run performances. In Berlin it played 48.

What was allegedly another and original English version (ad Edgar Smith, but including the added character of Clementine and, inevitably, musically botched) was produced in America by the Shuberts. George Macfarlane and May de Sousa played the lovers and De Wolf Hopper headed the comedy whilst Fred Leslie repeated his London role as Nicola. Yet again, a botched Continental hit failed on Broadway, and *Lieber Augustin* was sent on the road after just five weeks, retitled for the occasion *Miss Caprice.* This production did, however, last longer than an Australian one of the British *Princess Caprice* version which was mounted in Melbourne with Elsie Spain (Helen), Derek Hudson (Augustin), John Ralston (Jasomir), Dorothy Brunton (Clementine), Jack Cannot (Digomir), Phil Smith (Nicola) and Olive Goodwin (Anna) featured. It played only six nights as a tryout, and J C Williamson Ltd decided not to persevere with it.

Der liebe Augustin became part of the standard repertoire and was played for many years in central Europe, losing its place only when Fall, in his time perhaps the most saleable of all composers, faded as a money-making name.

Other Operetten with the same title were produced in Vienna at the Theater an der Wien (15 January 1887, Brandl/Klein) and at the Volksoper (11 June 1917, Julius Bittner), and in Germany at Brandenburg in 1906 (H Chemin-Petit/Hans Gaus, Sommertheater 2 September) and Berlin's Theater des Volkes in 1942 (Josef Rixner/ Rudolf Köller, Bruno Hardt-Warden 18 December).

Hungary: Népopera *Kedves Augusztin* 9 March 1912; UK: Shaftesbury Theatre *Princess Caprice* 11 May 1912; Austria: Carltheater 12 October 1912; USA: copyright performance 28 March 1913, Casino Theater *Lieber Augustin* (aka *Miss Caprice*) 3 September 1913; Germany: Theater des Westens 3 April 1913; Australia: Her Majesty's Theatre, Melbourne *Princess Caprice* 17 October 1914

Recordings: selection (EMI-Electrola, Eurodisc)

LIEBE IM SCHNEE Singspiel in 2 acts and a Nachspiel by Ralph Benatzky and Willy Prager. Music by Ralph Benatzky. Ronacher, Vienna, 2 December 1916.

When the time comes for Princess Gertrud (Mizzi Günther) to choose a husband, she is still going through the crush phase of being passionately in love with the opera singer Hendryk van Rhyn (Karl Pfann). A taste for the theatre evidently runs in the royal family, for her father, the Landesfürst Dagobert of Landskron (Arthur Guttmann), is currently linked with the dancer Ellen Kramer (Margit Suchy). Both couples have spent some idyllic times in the snowy market town of Sassen, in the inn run by another of the Landesfürst's old flames (Alma Sorel). However, the Herzog Kilian Dietrich von Parthey (Adolf Klein) is determined to win the Princess and when, during the court theatricals which precede the naming of her official fiancé, she goes so far as defiantly to kiss her leading man—Hendryk—on the lips, it is he who steps cleverly in to save the situation. After their marriage, he tactfully arranges for Hendryk to be offered a job he can't refuse in another city and, when he accompanies the Princess to the singer's farewell performance, she is able uncomplicatedly to say goodbye to her old love, secure in the presence of the new.

Waltz songs predominated in Bentazky's score: the title song, the lilting "Was jede Köchin summt!," the Princess's declaration "Ich will frei sein!" and "Du, mein Geliebter" all moved the romance along in 3/4 time, contrasted with square-time songs of which the most popular were "Im Januar, im Februar" and the march rhythms of the presentation of the Princess's suitors ("Wir vier Thronprätendenten").

Liebe im Schnee secured a very good reception in both Austria, where it was produced at Ronacher under Oscar Straus's management (dir: Miksa Préger, md: Oskar Jascha, 100th performance 26 February 1917), and in Germany, as well as in an Hungarian version (ad Zsolt Harsányi) which was played in Budapest with Erzsi Péchy, Ferenc Galetta and Áládar Sarkadi starred. In each center it was recognized as being musically one of Benatzky's best works.

An American version (ad Rowland Leigh), produced by the Shuberts many years later, after the Broadway success of Benatzky's *Im weissen Rössl,* folded on the road.

Germany: Komische Oper, August 1920; Hungary: Városi Színház *Hóvirág* 9 March 1918; USA: Bushnell Memorial Theater, Hartford *Love in the Snow* 15 March 1946

LIEBESWALZER Operette in 3 acts by Robert Bodanzky and Fritz Grünbaum. Music by Carl Michael Ziehrer. Raimundtheater, Vienna, 24 October 1908.

A jealous Austrian Count, Graf Artur Wildenburg (Ludwig von der Bruch), his jealous wife, Jenny (Gisela Noris), and her glittering man-trap of a cousin, the Baroness Yella von Bernau (Flora Siding), a wealthy tradesman called Leopold Führinger (Franz Glawatsch) and his wife Kathi (Louise Lichten) and daughter Antschi (Rose Karin-Krachler), a seductive Italian violin virtuoso, Guido Spini (Franz Gross), and a non-existent ballerina called Lisa Lizza (to rhyme conveniently with the city of Nizza), all caught up in the lightly amorous complications provoked by the Italian's apparent duplicity during a stay on the French Riviera, made up the action of *Liebeswalzer.* Ziehrer's score featured the popular Viennese strains for which he was best known in a Fiakerduett for father and daughter on ''Das Wien der alten Zeit,'' the tradesman's solo ''Wie ich einmal noch jünger war,'' his family trio ''Wenn man Geld hat'' and a spanking entrance number for Yella, ''Mädel guck, Mädel schau,'' alongside a polka trio and a piece in praise of the usefulness of the newfangled motor car, a vehicle which played a vitally deus-ex-mechnical part in the complexities of the plot.

Produced by Wilhelm Karczag and Karl Wallner in repertoire at the Raimundtheater, *Liebeswalzer* reached its 50th performance there by the end of the year, its 100th on 28 October 1909, and ultimately its 150th almost five years after its first performance (29 September 1913). It was played in Paris as part of a 1911 repertoire season by the Viennese company, was well received in Germany where, following its initial production with Conrad Dreher in the role created by Glawatsch, it proved the most popular of Ziehrer's works behind the untouchable *Die Landstreicher,* whilst an American production (ad Edgar Smith, Matthew Woodward) was put on in two stages under the management of the Shuberts. *The Love Waltz* started out at New Haven in May, with Eva Davenport, Van Rensslaer Wheeler, Charles Bigelow and Elsa Ryan top-billed. The producers were dissatisfied with the reaction to their piece, ordered a face-lift, and by the time the swiftly retitled *The Kiss Waltz* arrived in town via the Shubert, Boston, et al, four months later it had a remade libretto and a score botched with five Jerome Kern and two Louis Hirsch numbers, alongside what remained of Ziehrer's music. With Flora Zabelle (Nella, ex- Yella), Adele Rowland, Robert Warwick and William Pruette starred, it ran for 88 performances before leaving town with the shapely Valeska Suratt now at the head of its bills to score a fine success on the tour circuits.

Germany: Apollotheater 4 February 1910; USA: Hyperion Theater, New Haven *The Love Waltz* 18 May 1911, Casino Theater *The Kiss Waltz* 18 September 1911; France: Théâtre du Vaudeville (Ger) 1911

Recording: selection (Amadeo)

LI'L ABNER Musical comedy in 2 acts by Norman Panama and Melvin Frank based on the cartoon characters of Al Capp. Lyrics by Johnny Mercer. Music by Gene de Paul. St James Theater, New York, 15 November 1956.

Li'l Abner was a musical comedy built around the well-known cartoon characters who had peopled the extravagantly crazy cornseed town of Dogpatch, USA, in the *New York Daily Mirror*'s strip of the same name for more than 30 years: the bulgingly healthy and strappingly naive Abner; the burstingly promising Daisy Mae, only just held in by her tiny, tattered dress; pipe-sucking, fly-attracting Mammy Yokum; and all those that get in their way. After several other better-known names, including Alan Jay Lerner, had dithered with the project, it was film men Norman Panama and Melvin Frank who ultimately put together a libretto which tri-centered on a love story, a patriotic-political story and a sex-and-secret-formula story. On the one hand, there were the endless efforts of Daisy Mae (Edith Adams) to get herself L'il Abner (Peter Palmer) as a mate, aided by that awesomely terrifying institution known as Sadie Hawkins Day, on which Dogpatch ladies go out and physically catch themselves a husband. On the second hand, there was the threat to the very existence of Dogpatch, nominated because of its utter uselessness as an atom-bomb test site, and, on the third hand, there were the attempts of the horrid General Bullmoose (Howard St John) to steal the recipe for Mammy's (Charlotte Rae) Yokumberry tonic, the elixir which turns the feeblest of men into specimens like Abner. After a disastrous Sadie Hawkins race in which Abner is cornered by Bullmoose's protégée, Appassionata von Climax (Tina Louise), and Daisy Mae is set to wed the aptly named Earthquake McGoon (Bern Hoffman), and after the bomb-carrying planes have circled Dogpatch with their cargo of doom, everything comes right, *Pirates of Penzance*-fashion, thanks to the magic of the name of Abraham Lincoln.

The filmland writing team was completed by director-choreographer Michael Kidd, who joined the authors both on the development of the project and as its producer, and his *Seven Brides for Seven Brothers* colleagues, songwriters Johnny Mercer and Gene de Paul, who were brought in to compose the songs. *Li'l Abner's* score turned out a genuine hit in the lively tale of the town's founding father ''Jubilation T Cornpone'' as sung by Stubby Kaye in the role of Dogpatch's Marryin' Sam and, if it proved a little difficult to endow the comic-strip folk with ballady sentiments (''Namely You''), they were more than happy with a series of wordful, topical songs (''The Country's in the Very Best of Hands,'' ''Progress is the Root of All Evil'') and another number for Kaye celebrating the happy ending of the show with the ''Matrimonial Stomp.'' A non-musical highlight of the evening was the hero's entrance, accompanied by a flock of real, live geese.

Li'l Abner had a fine Broadway success and a 693-performance run but, perhaps because of its extremely broad outback Americanness, it failed to attract export propositions. It did, however, make its way back to Hollywood where, under the direction of the authors, ex-college footballer Palmer repeated his impersonation of the beefcake Abner alongside Kaye and Leslie Parrish (Daisy Mae) on film.

The characters of Dogpatch were later set to music for television both by ABC (26 April 1971) and, in a version which planted them in the there and then, by NBC (9 November 1978).

Film: Paramount 1959

Recordings: original cast (Columbia), film soundtrack (Columbia)

LILAC TIME *see* DAS DREIMÄDERLHAUS

DER LILA DOMINO Operette in 3 acts by Emmerich von Gatti and Béla Jenbach. Music by Charles Cuvillier. Stadttheater, Leipzig, 3 February 1912.

An Operette by a French composer, produced in Germany, which made him for several years the most sought-after musician in Britain, *Der lila Domino* (or, more correctly, *The Lilac Domino*) was a curious theatrical phenomenon—a musical which wandered the world without notable success until it was six years old, and then became a major hit.

Before this explosion of interest in his music, Cuvillier had had an agreeably successful Parisian career, mostly in smaller theatres, with such pieces as the winningly witty *Son p'tit frère*. Like many other French composers, he had also found some popularity in neighboring Belgium, but history does not relate how he came suddenly to be involved in writing a score to a German-language libretto for Leipzig. It was an unexceptional, conventional libretto, more than a little redolent of the successful American comedy *Captain Jinks of the Horse Marines,* whose heroine, Georgine, gets into a lilac domino at a ball, gets kissed by a disguised Count Anatol de Saint-Vallé, and then has the stars in her eyes doused when she finds he has taken a wager to find a rich wife. By the final curtain she predictably gets her man who had, of course, regretted the bet from the moment of the kiss.

The Leipzig production was well enough received for *Der lila Domino* to be produced later the same year in Budapest, but it created little interest in Europe and neither Berlin nor Vienna nor Paris took it up. Its next major premiere was in America where it appeared, two years after its debut, in a version adapted by Harry and Robert Smith, under the management of Andreas Dippel. Eleanor Painter (Georgine) was the girl in purple (thanks to Emmy Wehlen being struck down by what was announced as appendicitis), John E Hazzard (Prosper) played the comedy, Wilfred Douthitt (André), René Dettling (Léonie), Jeanne Maubourg (Baroness de Villiers) and Robert O'Connor (Casimir) supported, the evening was enlivened by some colored motion pictures depicting the carnival at Nice, and the show ran for a fair-to-pretty-all-right 110 performances on Broadway before going to the country, with Yvonne Darle as Georgine, through into 1916.

In spite of the show's only reasonable, rather than exceptional, record to date, the British rights to *Der lila Domino* were taken up by a maverick little Russian-South African producer called Joe Sacks, who had recently ventured onto the London stage with a nearly successful revue called *Three Cheers* (1916). He had the American lyrics given a facelift by journalist S J Adair Fitzgerald, popped in a few additional songs by musical director Howard Carr and lyricist Donovan Parsons, and produced his show at the Empire Theatre with what was, for wartime, some splendor. A fine soprano in Clara Butterworth was cast as Georgine, but the cast did not in any way glitter with known names. Out of the blue, *The Lilac Domino*—the only ''German'' show left in town (and obviously, because of Cuvillier not regarded as such)—became not just a success but a vast success, almost on the scale of the town's two monster war-aided hits *The Maid of the Mountains* and *Chu Chin Chow.* The show's title song, as performed by Miss Butterworth, Vincent Sullivan and R Stuart Pigott, became one of the hits of the day, and Cuvillier's ''What's Done You Never Can Undo'' (Miss Butterworth, Jamieson Dodds) and Carr's ''For Your Love I Am Waiting'' (Josephine Earle) and ''All Line Up in a Queue'' (American comedian Frank Lalor as Prosper) all became popular. When Miss Earle's lyrical ''True Love Will Find a Way'' was replaced by the saucier ''We Girls Don't Like Them Shy,'' another song success was added to the total.

Before the end of the year Sacks had two companies touring his hit show in the provinces and Cuvillier had put in an appearance in London to take part in concerts for André Charlot and to talk to managements about new shows. And while all this was going on, the London *The Lilac Domino* ran on until it reached a total of 19 months and 747 performances. Four weeks after its West End closure it was already back in town again for further performances, this time at the Palace Theatre (23 October). It was also exported, on the crest of its London success, to Australia, where West End hero Jamieson Dodds was paired with a young local soprano, René Maxwell, at the head of a cast featuring Marie La Varre, Ivy Shilling, A H Majilton, George Gee, Hugh Steyne, John Delacey and William Valentine. Once again the show was a major hit, running for 155 performances in three different theatres in Sydney, prior to playing in Melbourne (Theatre Royal 16 July 1921) and in New Zealand, where Miss Maxwell was paired with the robust ex-Savoyard Claude Flemming. It was revived on the Australasian stage on several occasions thereafter.

The Lilac Domino remained on the British touring circuits for many years, established itself as an operatic society favorite, and returned during the Second World War for a West End revival (ad Herbert Sargent, His Majesty's Theatre 5 April 1944) under the management of Jack Hylton. With his lady friend, Pat Taylor, starring as Georgine it once again proved popular and played for 224 performances in a run bisected by bombing. In between its two profitable wartimes, however, the piece's popularity had been thoroughly retained, even to the extent, in 1937, of its being made into a film. June Knight starred in the cinematic version alongside dashing Richard Dolman, Michael Bartlett and comedians Athene Seyler, Cuddles Szakall and Fred Emney.

Whether *The Lilac Domino* would have become the success it did without the aid of wartime circumstances to establish it as a favorite cannot be guessed. It is certainly not Cuvillier's best score, and it is attached to a much less imaginative libretto and lyrics than some of his Parisian works, but it nevertheless won the composer the international popularity which his other works were denied and became a durable English repertoire staple for many years.

Hungary: Népopera *A lila dominó* 5 November 1912; USA: 44th Street Theater *The Lilac Domino* 28 October 1914; UK: Empire Theatre 21 February 1918; Australia: Tivoli, Sydney *The Lilac Domino* 18 December 1920

Film: Grafton-Capitol-Cecil (Eng) 1937

Recording: selection in English (HMV 45EP)

LILI Comédie-opérette in 3 acts by Albert Millaud, Alfred Hennequin [and Ernest Blum]. Music by Hervé. Théâtre des Variétés, Paris, 10 January 1882.

One of the hugely successful series of Parisian vaudeville-opérettes produced in the late 1870s and early 1880s under the management of Eugène Bertrand, with Anna Judic, at the peak of her popularity, in the starring role, *Lili* followed *Niniche, La Femme à papa* and *La Roussotte* on to the stage of the Théâtre des Variétés and proved as successful as the best of them. Madame Judic appeared as the *Lili* of the title, in a role which permitted her to run the now-expected gamut: as a young woman in 1842, a middle-aging married lady in 1850 and an aged grandmother of the 1880s.

Amélie Bouzincourt, known as Lili, a strictly-brought-up young lady of the provincial noblesse, is tactless enough to fall in love with Antonin Plinchard (José Dupuis), a poor soldier who had come to her home to court the kitchen maid. They have their moment of passion, but then go their separate ways. Eight years on, when they meet again, Lili is the Baronne de Lagrange-Batelier and Plinchard has risen to the rank of lieutenant. Their moment of passion is still visible, in the person of Lili's daughter, Antonie (also Judic), but it is now too late to upset the lives into which they have settled. Years later, General Plinchard and the Baronne meet once more, when it is now safe to reminisce over what happened, and what might have happened but did not. The stalwarts of the Variétés company—Baron (Vicomte St Hypothèse), Léonce (Professor Bompain) and Lassouche—had fine supporting comic roles whilst Rosine Maurel appeared in the next-best feminine role as Madame Bouzincourt.

The score, largely devoted to its female star, more than fulfilled its purposes. Hervé came up once again with the kind of hit song which Judic had made a feature of these shows, and his Chanson provençale (''Du Pont du Garde à la Durance''), ''a mixture of provençal accent and Parisian wit,'' was the musical moment of the evening. The Duo de la reconnaisance between Lili and Plinchard proved enormously popular as well, and the star also turned out a rondeau (''Celui que j'aime est un pioupiou'') and a saucy song about ''Le plus beau jour de ma vie'' (it begins as her wedding day, and in the last verse it's the day her husband decides on separate bedrooms), and there were some wistfully touching musical moments in the final act as the two lovers relived their early escapade.

Lili's success ran to 233 performances at the Variétés before it gave way to its successor, Hervé's latter-day masterpiece and another triumph for Judic, *Mam'zelle Nitouche*. The star, however, kept her splendid vehicle warm, and, in the years that followed, she reappeared in *Lili* on several occasions on the Paris stage. The first was a brief 1884 reprise following the indifferent run of *La Cosaque,* the second in 1885 when the actress, now engaged at the Palais-Royal, returned to the Variétés for a few performances of each of her fondly remembered roles, the last in 1894 when, fatter and fortyish, she made one last appearance as Amélie-Lili. In the meanwhile, however, Judic had gone around the world, appearing in London, Vienna and Budapest in 1883 and in America in 1885, with *Lili* always a part of her baggage.

Whether it was Judic's performance that dissuaded many folk from trying to produce *Lili* with another star or whether the piece simply had limited appeal for foreign producers, the show was little taken up outside France—with one very notable exception, in Hungary. A version by Lajos Evva and Béla J Fái was produced at the Budapest Népszínház 10 months after the Paris premiere with that theatre's star vocalist Aranka Hegyi taking the Judic role opposite Miklós Tihanyi (Plinchard). Hegyi and *Lili* scored a triumph every bit as grand as Judic and *Lili* had done in Paris. The piece was revived in 1883 (13 December) and in 1894 (5 October) with Hegyi's successor Klára Küry at the Népszínház (100th performance 9 December 1898, 150th 2 February 1907), at the Népopera in 1915 and at the normally non-musical Nemzeti Színház with Gizi Bajor in 1926, and it became an oft-revived part of the Hungarian standard repertoire, reappearing as recently as 1967 at the Fővárosi Operettszínház (new ad Ernő Andai) with Zsuzsa Lehoczky starred, many years after its last sighting in France.

Vienna, which had first seen the piece in German (ad F Zell) with Frln Jona starred alongside Felix Schweighofer (Hypothèse), Alexander Girardi (Plinchard) and Carl Adolf Friese (Bompan), in advance of Judic's visit, also welcomed several reprises. The undaunted Marie Geistinger played the role before Viennese audiences just months after Judic had departed (and beat her to the punch in New York) and the city was also given Klára Küry's Hungarian version during her 1902 Vienna season with *Der kleine Günstling*. There was a Vienna revival of the German adaptation at the Theater in der Josefstadt as late as 1909. In Germany itself, the show took some time to make it to the capital, and when it did it was noticeable that the music was credited to Hervé and Julius Stern. Schweighofer took his old role alongside the Lili of Vienna's Leopoldine Augustin. Berlin got a reprise in 1905 (Berliner Theater 10 June, ad Schönau) with Annie Dirkens and Leopold Deutsch in the star roles.

Austria: Theater an der Wien 21 October 1882, Theater an der Wien 18 November 1883 (Fr); Hungary: Népszínház 17 November 1882; Germany: Teplitz 13 July 1884, Wallner-Theater, Berlin 25 December 1890; UK: Gaiety Theatre (Fr) 4 June 1883; USA: Thalia Theater (Ger) 19 November 1883; Wallack's Theater (Fr) 5 October 1885

LILI BÁRÓNŐ Operett in 3 acts by Ferenc Martos. Music by Jenő Huszka. Városi Színház, Budapest, 7 March 1919.

One of the classics of the Hungarian musical comedy repertoire, *Lili bárónő* has remained a favorite on the stages of the country of its origin ever since its production just after the end of the First World War, even though it has rarely been staged outside Hungary. Although it had been some years since Huszka's biggest successes with *Bob herceg* (1902), *Aranyvirág* (1903) and *Gül Baba* (1905), the postwar musical tale of the Baroness Lili found him back on the top, with a fourth enduring piece to add to his already impressive list.

Ferenc Martos's libretto was made up of elements familiar to Victorian followers of musical theatre. The penniless Count Illésházy (Ferenc Galetta) dons the clothes of his valet and, in this disguise, woos young Lili (Erzsi Péchy), daughter of the Baron Malomszegi (Rezső Sik). But the jealous actress Clarisse (Manci Vigh) exposes the Count's identity and persuades Lili that he was making light with her. The little baroness returns chastened to her official fiancé, Frédi (Áládar Sarkadi). But one day on the racecourse her horse Tündér is left without a jockey and the Count appears to ride his way to victory and into Lili's arms. Clarisse, of course, gets Frédi.

The favorite pieces of the score included a Cigarette-Waltz duo for the hero and the soubrette and the heroine's "Egy férfi képe," as well as Clarisse's saucy "Gyere, csókolj meg," the lovers' duos "Tündérkirálynő légy a párom" and "Szellő szárnyán," the lighthearted "Drágám engem sohase féltsen" for Clarisse and Frédi, and a choral Jockeys March in the final act.

Repeatedly played since its initial production, and several times recorded, *Lili bárónő* was most recently heard in Budapest in 1989 (14 September) played in a cut version as part of a Huszka double bill, with *Gül Baba*, at the Fővárosi Operettszínház, and it has since been played both at Eger in 1992, and at Kecskemét in 1994.

Recording: selection (Qualiton)

LILLIE, Beatrice [Gladys] (b Toronto, 29 May 1894; d Henley-on-Thames, 20 January 1989).

An outstanding revue comedienne with a special vogue, "Bea" Lillie appeared rarely in the musical theatre. On the first (and best) occasion, which was also one of only two on the London stage, she took the leading comedy part of Jackie in the UK version of the Broadway musical *Oh, Boy!* (played as *Oh, Joy!*, 1919). In 1921, again in London, she played a multiple comedy role in the short-lived revusical *Now and Then*. Five years later, following her Broadway success in the Charlot revues, she was seen there as the comical "other woman" in Vincent Youmans's musical version of the Paris hit *La Présidente, Oh, Please!*, and then as a masquerading maid (in one of the most over-used plots in the business) in the Rodgers and Hart *She's My Baby*. Neither of this pair was successful. She made one last musical-comedy appearance, 35 years later, in the role of the batty medium

Madame Arcati in a musical version of Noël Coward's *Blithe Spirit* (*High Spirits*), giving more to the show than it gave to her, but without being able to make it into a worthwhile exercise.

Autobiography: *Every Other Inch a Lady* (Doubleday, New York, 1972); Biography: Laffey, B: *Beatrice Lillie: The Funniest Woman in the World* (Wynwood Press, New York, 1989)

THE LILY OF KILLARNEY Opera in 3 acts by John Oxenford and Dion Boucicault based on Boucicault's play *The Colleen Bawn,* itself an adapation of Gerald Griffin's story *The Collegians.* Music by Julius Benedict. Theatre Royal, Covent Garden, 8 February 1862.

Benedict's *The Lily of Killarney* was the third of the three basic romantic ''operas'' which, with the rather more popular *The Bohemian Girl* and *Maritana,* made up the basis of the repertoire of many English-language opera companies of the mid-19th century. Although called an opera—for its dramatic tale, even though it had a happy ending, forbade it at that stage any other kind of description—*The Lily of Killarney* was, musically at least, already a large step towards the romantic comic-operas of later years and its most outstanding songs, the male duo ''The Moon Has Raised His Lamp Above,'' Hardress Cregan's beautiful tenor serenade to ''Eily Mavourneen'' and the heroine's ''I'm Alone,'' for decades parlor favorites, were the forerunners of many a sentimental song in 19th-century musical-theatre writing in Britain and America.

Following its extremely successful original production, under the operatic management of William Harrison and Louisa Pyne, with Harrison as Myles na Coppaleen, Pyne as Eily O'Connor—the Colleen Bawn of Boucicault's play—Henry Haigh as Hardress Cregan and Charles Santley as Danny Mann, it was widely and frequently played on English-language stages of both hemispheres for several decades. In America it was first produced by Caroline Richings troupe with Miss Richings (Eily), William Castle (Cregan), S C Campbell (Danny) and Pierre Bernard (Myles) and it was played on Broadway as late as 1895 (20 May) in a production at the Grand Opera House with William T Carleton (Danny), Helen Bertram (Eily) and Payne Clarke (Myles) featured. It was also given in a German adaptation (ad F von Dingelstedt) throughout Germany. In the 20th century performances have become progressively less frequent as the fashion has militated against Victorian English works.

A film issued as *The Lily of Killarney* by A, P & B in 1934, with John Garrick, Gina Malo, Sara Allgood and Stanley Holloway amongst its cast, used some of Boucicault's plot and characters, but turned to old Irish melodies for its musical part rather than to Benedict's score.

Australia: Apollo Music Hall, Melbourne 2 August 1862; Germany: Brunswick *Die Rose von Erin* 28 January 1863, Berlin 9 February 1864; USA: National Theater, Washington, DC 2 October 1867, Academy of Music, New York 1 January 1868

Recordings: complete (Rare Recorded Editions), selection (part-record) (HMV)

LINCKE, [Carl Emil] Paul (b Berlin, 7 November 1866; d Clausthal-Zellerfeld, Germany, 3 September 1946). German revue and Operette composer who, in spite of the fact that he did not produce an international success, nor even one major full-length Operette, has become tagged as the landmark writer of the German musical theatre.

Musically trained in Wittenberg, Lincke worked his way through some menial musical jobs to a post, at the age of 18, as bassoonist in the orchestra of Berlin's Centraltheater, and then at the newly renamed Ostend-Theater (ex- Nationaltheater). He soon got opportunities to conduct, and in that capacity he moved from pleasure garden to second-class theatre, to touring company until, as a 26-year-old, he was engaged at the Apollotheater (Apollo-Variété-Theatre), a Berlin house formerly specializing in large musical and dance spectaculars but now become a less over-ambitious variety house. There he conducted the orchestra and supplied such music as was necessary to the running of its programs, sometimes less, sometimes, as for Senefeld's Posse *Die Spreeamazone,* which made up part of one Apollo program, a little more. At the same time, he also purveyed music to other Berlin houses, and an Eduard Jacobson ''ballet-phantasie,'' *Unter den Linden,* with music by Lincke, was mounted at the theatre of that name (14 November 1896).

It was, however, back at his old haunt, the Ostend-Theater, that he first found genuine success as a composer. Carl Weiss produced the Posse *Der deutsche Michel,* a little tale of adventures in foreign parts which dropped the Berlin Bombach family and their army-officer son, Michel (Weiss), into darkest Africa. The show, equipped with a scoreful of songs and incidental music by Lincke, had a splendid run, topping the one hundred performance mark which in those days signaled a genuine hit. However, this success was as nothing beside that which he made when he tried his hand at genuine (if small) Operette. The director of the Apollotheater decided to insert one-act Operette spectaculars into his variety programs, and Lincke was given the job of writing the scores. One of these, the picturesque, topical *Venus auf Erden* (1897), with its splendid, saucy staging and bright music, turned out a major Berlin hit.

Lincke abandoned the Apollotheater for the siren calls of France and the French equivalent of the Apollo, the Folies-Bergère, but two seasons in Paris brought him little joy, and in 1899 he returned home and to the Apollotheater where another and even more successful little

Grosse Ausstattungs-Operette from his pen, *Frau Luna,* was produced soon after. The fantastical *Frau Luna* was followed by another fine success in *Im Reiche des Indra* (''Nimm mich mit in dein Kämmerlein''), by the rather less-liked *Fräulein Loreley,* and then by another eventual winner in *Lysistrata* (Glühwürmchen-Idyll), and the Siamese-flavored *Nakiris Hochzeit,* all composed to Apollo-style libretti (ie, lots of scenery, topicals and girls) by his *Venus auf Erden* collaborator, Heinrich Bolten-Bäckers. This run of little pieces carried on through four Apollotheater seasons and Lincke, after a tour of Germany, Austria and the Netherlands with his repertoire, saw the most popular of them win further productions outside Germany, in a fashion that few German composers to that date had succeeded in achieving.

Increasingly rich, randy and lazy (he was fined by the courts and had his publishing contract with Salabert canceled when he passed off a pilfered American song as his own original work), Lincke devoted himself but episodically to his music, and these miniature successes were not followed by the full-length work that might have been expected. He returned to the Apollotheater in 1904 as conductor for the Operetten which now made up an increasedly important part of its program, and scored a fresh success with his scoreful of popular songs for the revusical *Berliner Luft* (1904, ''Das ist die Berliner Luft''). He provided some long-running revue and Posse scores both for Kren and Schönfeld at the Thalia-Theater and for the Metropoltheater (*Donnerwetter, tadellos!, Hallo! die grosse Revue*), where he subsequently became musical director for a period; he turned out some shorter pieces for the Apollotheater and for Vienna's Danzers Orpheum; set music to comic scenes for variety; and composed individual songs with and for various star performers, but still produced no genuine Operette. And when he was announced to compose the score for Florenz Ziegfeld's *Follies of 1910* he failed to come up with the goods.

Lincke's full-sized musical stage plays did finally come, but not until he had composed his last theatre pieces for Berlin. He was 44 years old when his musicalization of a Parisian farce was brought out at Cologne under the title *Gri-gri.* It was successful enough to win further productions, both in Germany and beyond, a little more successful than his second piece, *Casanova,* staged two years later at Chemnitz, and altogether more so than the third and a handful of further wartime pieces. Then Lincke, apparently at odds with the new, foreign dance rhythms invading the Continental stages, stopped writing.

He worked still occasionally as a conductor and at his publishing house, Apollo Verlag, and, as one of the very few successful German or Austrian composers with no apparent Jewish connection, found himself and his little turn-of-the-century Operetten prized and popular under the Nazi regime. But though he received honors from that regime and saw his old shows boosted into fresh productions, he lost everything in the final stages of the war and died soon after.

The high spot of Lincke's curiously unambitious career as a composer of musical theatre lies in the three seasons he spent at the Apollotheater after his return from Paris. The most successful of his little pieces there, *Frau Luna,* altered, expanded and decorated to make it up into a full evening's entertainment, has survived into the modern German repertoire, and *Lysistrata,* on the back of its internationally popular glowworm number, has followed on a lesser scale. Of *Gri-gri* and its fellows little is heard. But, in spite of the paucity of his product, Lincke remains pinned into position as the rather infertile follower of the almost as infertile Dellinger at the beginning of what would be—with the arrival of such writers as Gilbert and Kollo—Germany's busiest handful of years as a producer of original and internationally appreciated musical theatre.

1896 **Die Spreeamazone** (A Senefeld) Apollotheater, Berlin 16 May

1896 **Der deutsche Michel** (Rudolf Kneisel) Ostendtheater 4 September

1897 **Eine lustige Spreewaldsfahrt** (Alfred Schmasov) 1 act Apollotheater

1897 **Ein Abenteuer in Harem** (Wilhelm Mannstädt) 1 act Apollotheater

1897 **Venus auf Erden** (Heinrich Bolten-Bäckers) 1 act Apollotheater 6 June

1899 **Frau Luna** (Bolten-Bäckers) 1 act Apollotheater 1 May

1899 **Im Reiche des Indra** (Bolten-Bäckers, Leopold Ely) Apollotheater 18 December

1900 **Fräulein Loreley** (Bolten-Bäckers) 1 act Apollotheater 15 October

1902 **Lysistrata** (Bolten-Bäckers) Apollotheater 1 April

1902 **Nakiris Hochzeit** (Bolten-Bäckers) Apollotheater 6 November

1903 **Am Hochzeitsabend** (Bolten-Bäckers) 1 act Danzers Orpheum, Vienna 31 March

1904 **Berliner Luft** (Benno Jacobson) Apollotheater 28 September

1905 **Ausser Rand und Band** (Carl Lindau, F Antony) 1 act Danzers Orpheum, Vienna 4 November

1905 **Bis früh um Fünfe** (Alfred Schönfeld/Jean Kren, Arthur Lippschitz) Thalia-Theater 26 August

1905 **Prinzess[in] Rosine** (Bolten-Bäckers, Friedendorf) Apollotheater 18 November

1906 **Hochparterre-Links** (Schönfeld/Kren, Arthur Lippschitz) Thalia-Theater 7 April

1906 **Das blaue Bild** (Bolten-Bäckers) Apollotheater 18 May

1906 **Wenn die Bombe platzt** (Schönfeld/Kren, Lippschitz) Thalia-Theater 25 August

1906 **Eine lustige Doppel-Ehe** (Schönfeld/Kurt Kraatz) Thalia-Theater 27 November

1907 **Der Triumph des Weibes** ad mus for localized version by Benno Jacobson Apollotheater 24 March

1907 **Ihr sechs-Uhr-Onkel** (Schönfeld/Kren) Thalia-Theater 25 August

1908 **Immer oben auf** (Schönfeld/Kren, Bernhard Buchbinder) Thalia-Theater 22 January

1910 **Nu hat's geschnappt** (Oskar Sachs) 1 act Sans Souci 2 September

1911 **Gri-gri** (Bolten-Bäckers) Metropoltheater, Cologne 25 March; Berliner Theater 1912

1913 **Casanova** (Jacques Glück, Willi Steinberg) Altes Theater, Chemnitz 5 November

1915 **Fräulein Kadett** (Steinberg/Julius Winckelmann) Olimpia-Theater, Dortmund 25 December; Theater am Zoo, Berlin

1917 **Pst-Pst** (Steinberg/Leonhard Haskel) Neues Theater, Hamburg 12 January

1917 **Stahl und Gold** (Leo Leipziger) 1 act Stadttheater, Memel 29 September

1940 **Ein Liebestraum** (Alexander Erler, Max Neumann) Theater an der Reeperbahn, Hamburg 15 October

Biographies: Nick, E: *Paul Lincke* (Musikverlag Hans Sikorski, Hamburg, 1953), Schneidereit, O: *Paul Lincke und die Entstehung der Berliner Operette* (Henschelverlag, Berlin, 1974)

LIND, Letty [RUDGE, Letitia Elizabeth] (b Birmingham, 21 December 1861; d Slough, 27 August 1923).

The most successful of the five stageworthy Rudge sisters, Letty Lind was London's favorite musical-comedy soubrette at the peak of the George Edwardes era at Daly's Theatre.

On the stage from childhood as a juvenile actress (as ''Letty Rudge,'' Eva in *Uncle Tom's Cabin,* 1867, etc), then from age nine as a dancer (''Mdlle Letitia'') at Birmingham's Crystal Palace Music Hall, Letty (still as ''L Rudge'') appeared at Drury Lane as early as 1874 in the annual pantomime. In 1875 she played Columbine in *Puss in Boots* at Birmingham.

She spent a number of youthful years playing in the provinces, first with Howard Paul's entertainment, then in Minnie Palmer's famous role of Tina in *My Sweetheart,* and in several plays. She was seen at London Princess's Theatre alongside Paul in his playlet *Locked Out* (1879), but got sidelined for a while when the result of their propinquity turned out to be a little illegitimate Henry Paul Howard Rudge. She was again seen in London in the tiny role of Phebe in the 1883 revival of Offenbach's *Le Voyage dans la lune,* with Charles Duval's Entertainment at St James's Hall (1885), on tour as Dora in *Fun on the Bristol* (1885), in the comedy *Tact,* the burletta *A Fashionable Beauty* (1885, Madge Primrose) and in the secondary role of Clorinda in a revival of *Manteaux Noirs* (1885) at the Avenue Theatre, but her career took off when she was taken a shine to by author and journalist Henry Pottinger Stephens who plugged her extravagantly in his newspaper column and urged George Edwardes to take her on at the Gaiety.

She duly made her Gaiety debut succeeding Lottie Collins in the role of Mariette in the burlesque *Monte Cristo Jr* (1886), and she had her first new role, with a featured dance, as the gypsy Fleur-de-Lis in the next house burlesque, *Miss Esmeralda* (1887). She played Lizzina in *Frankenstein* (1887), visited America and Australia with her first two, previously mentioned Gaity shows and returned, now an accepted part of the number-one team, to contribute a polka and a valse chantante to the next Gaiety piece, *Ruy Blas and the Blasé Roué,* and a hornpipe and a spot with farmyard imitations to *Carmen Up-to-Data* (Mercedes). Her first leading part came when, following the illness of Nellie Farren, she ultimately took over in the title role of *Cinder-Ellen Up Too Late* (1892).

When burlesque gave way to musical comedy, Letty Lind appeared in one of the earliest such shows, *Morocco Bound* (1893, Maude Sportington), performing the famous skirt dance which her erstwhile understudy, Loie Fuller, was later to glossy-up and win history's credit for, and then had her first full-blown top-of-the-bill role as the ballerina heroine of the next work by the *Morocco Bound* team, *Go-Bang* (''Di, Di, Di,'' ''The Chinee Dolly''). After she had successfully taken over the central role of *A Gaiety Girl* (Alma Somerset, following Maud Hobson and Marie Studholme) for the last part of the show's run, George Edwardes slated her as the juvenile leading lady of his Daly's Theatre production *A Naughty Girl.* However, the late hiring of Marie Tempest meant she had to share the top spot, and give up the title. *An Artist's Model* (1895, Daisy Vane, delivering ''The Gay Tomtit'' and ''Daisy With the Dimple'' with ''a certain cynically humorous sentiment'' in her ''croakily fascinating voice''), however, proved a triumph for both women and established the Daly's star team, Tempest/Lind/Hayden Coffin, who, with comic Huntley Wright, were to be the backbone of the theatre's famous series of musicals during the late 1890s.

After scoring huge successes in the soubrette role of Molly Seamore in *The Geisha* (1896, ''The Interfering Parrot,'' ''The Toy Monkey''), and as Iris in *A Greek Slave* (1898, ''A Frog He Lived in a Pond'') Miss Lind broke up the team by leaving Daly's. After an ill-starred appearance in the unfortunate *The Gay Pretenders* (1900, Clotilde) she came back to Edwardes's management for an incidental role in *The Girl from Kays,* after which, aged just a little more than 40, she slipped from the forefront of the theatrical scene. She seems to have slipped,

Plate 219. **Letty Lind** *with the skirt she made famous.*

however, in useful company, for when Letty died at 61—eternally, in spite of all the gossip columns' rumors through the years, unmarried, though the mother of two sons—her will was executed by two peers of the realm.

Letty's next sister down, **Millie HYLTON** [Sarah Frances Louise RUDGE] (b Birmingham, 8 February 1870; d Steyning, 1 September 1920), also had a fine singing, dancing career, most notably as a male impersonator in music halls on both sides of the Atlantic (Tony Pastor's company 1888, 1889, etc). She made her first musical-theatre appearance at Liverpool's Alexandra at 16, her first London appearance when she took over as ''a Captain of Hussars'' in *Monte Cristo Jr* (1887) at the Gaiety and she went on from there to play principal roles in pantomime, returning intermittently to the musical theatre where she created the title role in the Gaiety burlesque *Don Juan* (1893), took over and toured as Lord Clanside in *In Town* (1893), replaced May Yohé in the title role of *Dandy Dick Whittington* (1895), and toured as Ada Smith in *The Shop Girl* (1895), as Mme Drivelli in *The Circus Girl* (1897) and as Mrs Bang in *The Messenger Boy* (1901). She was latterly seen in several music-hall musicals including Walter Slaughter's *S'Nero* (1906), in which she featured as Poppaea to the Nero of M R Morand, and on the tour circuits as La Boléro in *Mr Popple* (1906). In 1910 she played the halls with a ''dramatic song-scena'' called *The Dawn of a Tomorrow* and in 1912 went on the road in Connie Ediss's role in *Peggy*. Milllie Hylton was married to actor Harry E Clulow Sim who appeared in the provinces in such roles as Bertie Boyd in *The Shop Girl* (1895).

Adelaide ASTOR [Elizabeth Gertrude RUDGE] (b Birmingham, 15 December 1873; d London, 24 May 1951) also appeared on the London musical stage as a dancer and in smaller and lighter soubrette roles in such pieces as *Carmen Up-to-Data* (1891, t/o Zorah), *Cinder-Ellen Up Too Late* (1891, Templina, t/o Linconzina), *In Town* (1892, pas de quatre), *The Lady Slavey* (1894, Maud), *Go-Bang* (Sarah Ann, and u/s Letty as Di), *The Shop Girl* (UK, 1895, t/o Maud Plantaganet and USA), her husband's production of *The Gay Pretenders* (1900, Mary Lady Jolliffe), *The Gay Cadets* (1901, Nora) and *Morocco Bound* (1901 rev, Maude Sportington). She became the wife of the high-profile performer-manager George Grossmith jr.

Lydia FLOPP [Lydia Agnes RUDGE] (b Birmingham, 11 February 1877) appeared alongside her sisters in *Go-Bang* (1894, t/o Flo Wedderburn) and *An Artist's Model* (1895, Lucille, u/s Daisy Vane), created the role of the little midshipman Tommy Stanley in *The Geisha* (1896) and also appeared in *The Gay Cadets* (1901, Dora to Adelaide's Nora), in the leading role of the tour of *The Silver Slipper* (1901, Stella), *Three Little Maids* (1902, t/o Hilda), *The Girl from Kays* (1902, t/o Jane), *Mr Popple of Ippleton* (1905, t/o Louise) in the West End and as Sophia in *The Catch of the Season* and other supporting roles in Australia in a full and far-flung career of musical-comedy credits.

Fanny DANGO [Fanny RUDGE] (b Birmingham, 20 October 1878; d Mount Waverley, Victoria, Australia, 15 July 1972), the youngest sister, had the lengthiest career and the longest life. For a long time a dancer, understudy, taker-over and touring player in such British shows as *The Geisha* (replacing Lydia as Tommy Stanley), *A Runaway Girl, Little Miss Nobody* (1898, t/o Tiny Triplet), *Florodora* (1899, Juanita), *The Silver Slipper* (1901, Millicent, u/s Brenda Shallamar), *The Gay Cadets* (1901), *Three Little Maids* (1902, t/o Miss Price), *The Girl from Kays, The Medal and the Maid* (1903, Antoinette), *The Lovebirds* (1904, t/o Lillie de Jones), and *The Spring Chicken* (1905, Yvette), she came into her own in leading roles when she visited Australia and New Zealand. She appeared there, during a three-year stay, as Angela in *The Catch of the Season,* Peggy in *The Dairymaids,* Anita in *Havana,* Illyrine in *Les Merveilleuses,* Mitzi in *The Girls of Gottenberg,* Tina in *The Red Mill,* in *The Prince of Pilsen,* as Franzi in *A Waltz Dream* and in the title role of *The Merry Widow.* On her return to London in 1910, she married a well-off Australian and, after a festive season appearance in *Gulliver's Travels* at the Avenue (1910, Glumdalclitch), withdrew from the stage. She survived to the age of 91, dying almost half a century after her most famous sister.

The Rudge family's involvement in the musical theatre continued for one more generation when Millie's daughter **Millie [Helen R] Sim** (b 7 February 1895) appeared in *Riquette* (1925, Liane) and *Bitter-Sweet* (1929, Lotte) as part of her career as an actress. The Grossmith daughters **Ena [Sylvia V] Grossmith** (b London, 14 August 1896; d London, 20 March 1944) and Rosa Grossmith also followed musical-theatre careers.

LINDAU, Carl [GEMPERLE, Karl] (b Vienna, 26 November 1853; d Vienna, 15 January 1934). Prolific comic actor turned equally prolific librettist of the Viennese musical theatre.

Lindau went on the stage at the age of 17, playing the classic repertoire at Graz, and subsequently worked in Budapest, Frankfurt, Dresden, at Graz again and then at Olmütz before making his first Viennese appearances at the Theater an der Wien in supporting comic roles such as Degomez in *Tag und Nacht* and Josse in *Doctor Ox.* He joined Josefine Gallmeyer's American tour company in 1882 in a comedy team with Tewele and Knaack, playing in a range of shows from *Hamlet* (gravedigger) through Possen (*Die Näherin, Der Goldonkel*) to such opérettes and Operetten as *La Mascotte, Giroflé-Girofla, Les Cloches de Corneville, Der lustige Krieg, Gräfin Dubarry* and *La Princesse de Trébizonde,* and on his return he became a solid member of the Theater an der Wien company.

Over the next 15 years, with only one short break, he there created and played good supporting comic roles in a long list of plays and Operetten including *Rip-Rip* (1883, Nick Vedder), *Eine Nacht in Venedig* (1883, Barbaruccio), *Der Marquis von Rivoli* (1884, Baptiste), *Der Feldprediger* (1884, D'Alencourt), *Pfingsten in Florenz* (1884, Lorenzi), *La Princesse de Trébizonde* (1885, Trémolini), *Zwillinge* (1885, Avrillon), *Gillette de Narbonne* (1885, Barigoul), *Der Viceadmiral* (1886, Deodato), *Der Hofnarr* (1886, Der Kanzler), *Der liebe Augustin* (1887, Längler), *Bellman* (1887, Claasen Steen), *Die sieben Schwaben* (1887, Allgauer), *The Mikado* (1888, Mikado), *Pagenstreiche* (1888, Pomposo), *Der Schlosserkönig* (1889, Herzog von Uak), *Capitän Fracassa* (1889, Ali), *Das Orakel* (1889, Glaukos), *Der arme Jonathan* (1890, Graf Nowalsky), *Mam'zelle Nitouche* (1890, Loriot), *Der Vogelhändler* (1891, Süffle, one of the two crazy professors), *Madame Bonbon* (1891, Fridolin), *Die Kosakin* (1891, Fürst Cyrill Macshinstoff), *Miss Helyett* (1891, Bacarel), *Das Sonntagskind* (1892, Sheriff Plunkett), *Fanchons Leyer* (1892, August), *Der Millionenonkel* (1892, Jovan Zingaliri) and *Der Bajazzo* (1892, Monstroso). He played Melchior in his own new version of *Simplicius* and Lord Plato in Strauss's new *Fürstin Ninetta* (1893), created the role of mine-manager Zwack in *Der Obersteiger* (1894) and continued on in *Husarenblut* (1894, Pinter), *Jabuka* (1894, Sava), *Kneisel & Co* (1894, Eustachius Altgrübel), Millöcker's *Der Probekuss* (1894, Graf Pizzi), *Die Chansonette* (1895, Tromboni), *Der goldene Kamerad* (1895, Juba Bill), *Waldmeister* (1895, Sebastian), *General Gogo* (1896, Armand Charmant), *Mister Menelaus* (1896, Flips), *Der Wunderknabe* (1896, Graf Calmore), *Der Löwenjäger* (1896, Tonpin), *Der Schmetterling* (1896, Theodor de Saint Marco), *Die Schwalben* (1897, Satrapschil), *Der Blondin von Namur* (1898, General Fano), *Ihre Excellenz* (1899, Desablettes) and as Baron Bonifaz Nickel in *Ein durchgeganges Mädel* (*A Runaway Girl*), Calineau in *Fräulein Präsident* and Lord Fiddlepuds in *Der Gross-mogul* (1900), as well as repeating such classic parts as Agamemnon, Frank, Scalza, Bliemchen, Sindulfo and Stanglmeier, or later Nachtfalter, in *Drei Paar Schuhe.*

Lindau began a concurrent career as a playwright, librettist and lyricist in 1885, writing short plays, then translating French pieces, and writing first songwords and then text and lyrics for Possen, including several with good roles for his colleague Girardi. It was in this area that he found his first big successes as an author with *Ein armes Mädel* and, in particular, *Heisses Blut,* a genuine star vehicle with a role à tiroirs par excellence for its leading lady, which was later played throughout central Europe and in an American adaptation as *A Dangerous Maid. Der Nazi, In siebenten Himmel* (1896) for Girardi and *Die fesche Pepi* (1897) were amongst the other successful musical-comedy pieces which he turned out in the 1890s.

Lindau's first Operettic libretto, written at a time when one of his most successful roles was that of Gilbert's *Mikado,* was for a version of *Der Schelm von Bergen* (1888). A libretto by Ignaz Schnitzer, also based on Heine's poem, had been originally accepted and partly set by Strauss, but it was ultimately rejected by him on the excuse that it was too like *The Mikado.* Lindau's version—originally announced for setting by the aging Brandl—was ultimately set by the less famous Oelschlegl without success (17 performances). However, Lindau later worked with Strauss when he co-authored a revision of the libretto of his *Simplicius* (1894).

Writing mostly in collaboration with either Krenn or "F Antony," Lindau translated and adapted many of the most popular British and American musical-comedy imports of the turn of the century—in particular for Gabor Steiner's theatres, the open-air stage of Venedig in Wien and the "winter" house Danzers Orpheum—as well as the occasional Hungarian operett, or a Berlin show that needed to be "localized" with Viennese references for presentation in the Austrian theatre.

Of the original Operetten on which he collaborated, as part of this busy writing schedule, the most successful were two pieces composed by Carl Michael Ziehrer, *Die Landstreicher* (1899) and *Der Fremdenführer* (1902), and three with music by Edmund Eysler, Girardi's vehicles *Die Schützenliesel* (1905) and *Künstlerblut* (1906) and *Der Frauenfresser* (1911). A pastiche of Josef Strauss music attached to a version of Jaime and Duval's French farce *Coquin de Printemps* won considerable success for Steiner as *Frühlingsluft* (1903), prompting several other such pasticcii including the adding of a fresh libretto to Johann Strauss's *Indigo* score under the title *Tausend un eine Nacht* (1906). Berény's much-traveled *Lord Piccolo* (1910) was another fine success, and a set of collaborations with Josef Hellmesberger brought forth that composer's longest-running work *Das Veilchenmädel* (1904), which Lindau not only wrote but directed in its first Vienna presentation. He also directed *Die drei Wünsche* (1901) and *Der Schnurrbart* (1905) at the Carltheater and the Hungarian hit *Der Sultan* (1909) at the Johann Strauss-Theater.

Lindau also worked on libretti for several foreign composers—Ivan Caryll, Paul Lincke, Viktor Holländer, Ludwig Englander—all of whom had original pieces produced in Vienna, and, in later days, with his performing well behind him, he also contributed texts to the Berlin stage.

1885 **Die beiden Wenzel** (Paul Mestrozzi/w Wilhelm Mannstädt) Theater in der Josefstadt 26 September

1885 **Eine gute Partie** (Franz Wagner) Theater in der Josefstadt 12 December

1886 **Der Aprilnarr** (Karl Kleiber/w F Antony) Theater in der Josefstadt 13 April

1886 **Humbug der Geist des Schwindels** (Kleiber/w Mannstädt) Theater in der Josefstadt 11 September

1886 **Der Stabstrompeter** Viennese version w Antony w music by Hanns Krenn, Theater in der Josefstadt

1887 **Wien bleibt Wien** Viennese version w Antony w music by H Krenn, Theater in der Josefstadt 1 October

1887 **Peter Zapfel** Viennese version w Antony w music by Kleiber, Theater in der Josefstadt 17 December

1888 **Der Grasteufel** (Kleiber/w Mannstädt) Theater in der Josefstadt 3 April

1888 **Der Schelm von Bergen** (Alfred Oelschlegl/w Karl Löwe) Theater an der Wien 29 September

1888 **Ein Hundert Jahre** (Kleiber/w Franz von Radler) Theater in der Josefstadt 24 October

1889 **Capitän Wilson** (*The Yeomen of the Guard*) German version w Victor Léon (Carltheater)

1889 **Wiener Luft** (Carl Michael Ziehrer/ad w Heinrich Thalboth) Theater an der Wien 10 May

1889 **Der Wildfang** (*Mademoiselle Moucheron*) German version (Carltheater)

1890 **Das Paradies** (H Krenn/w Leon Treptow) Carltheater 11 January

1892 **Heisses Blut** (Heinrich Schenk/w Leopold Krenn) Theater an der Wien 17 April

1892 **Unser Volk unter Waffen** (Kleiber/w Antony, Thalboth) Theater in der Josefstadt 17 September

1893 **Ein armes Mädel** (Leopold Kuhn/w Krenn) Theater an der Wien 6 May

1894 **Simplicius** revised version Theater an der Wien 19 September

1895 **Wiener Touristen** (Karl Kappeller/w Antony) Theater in der Josefstadt 2 March

1895 **Der Nazi** (Kuhn/w Krenn) Theater an der Wien 3 October

1896 **In siebenten Himmel** (Ferdinand Pagin/w Krenn) Theater an der Wien 29 April

1897 **Die Ladenmamsell** (*The Shop Girl*) German version (Theater in der Josefstadt)

1897 **Die fesche Pepi** (Wilhelm Argauer/w Krenn) Theater an der Wien 23 January

1897 **Der Herr Pomeisl** (Max von Weinzierl/w Krenn) Raimundtheater 23 October

1898 **Moderne Weiber** (Kuhn, Johann Brandl/w Krenn) Carltheater 10 April

1898 **Der schöne Rigo** (Ziehrer/w Krenn) Venedig in Wien 24 May

1899 **Ein durchgegangenes Mädel** (*A Runaway Girl*) German version w Krenn (Theater an der Wien)

1899 **Die Landstreicher** (Ziehrer/w Krenn) Venedig in Wien 29 July

1899 **Der kleine Corporal** (*The Little Trooper*) German version w Golz brothers (Carltheater)

1900 **Die Schöne von New-York** (*The Belle of New York*) German version w Krenn (Venedig in Wien)

1901 **Die verkehrte Welt** (*Le Royaume des femmes*) (Kappeller/ad w Krenn) Danzers Orpheum 22 February

1901 **Die drei Wünsche** (Ziehrer/w Krenn) Carltheater 9 March

1901 **Die Reise nach Cuba** (Ivan Caryll/w Krenn) Venedig in Wien 3 August

1901 **Das Brautpaar vor Gericht** (*Trial by Jury*) German version (Danzers Orpheum)

1901 **Das Frauenduell** (Edmund Eysler/w Louis Gundlach) 1 act Danzers Orpheum 23 November

1901 **Das Gastmahl des Lucullus** (Eysler/w A Paulus) 1 act Danzers Orpheum 23 November

1902 **Eine feine Nummer** Austrian version w Krenn (Venedig in Wien)

1902 **Der kleine Günstling** (*Katalin*) German version (Carltheater)

1902 **Der Laufbursche** (*The Messenger Boy*) German version w Krenn (Danzers Orpheum)

1902 **Der Fremdenführer** (Ziehrer/w Krenn) Theater an der Wien 11 October

1902 **Das Cirkusmädel** (*The Circus Girl*) German version w Krenn (Danzers Orpheum)

1903 **Frühlingsluft** (Josef Strauss arr Ernst Reiterer/w Julius Wilhelm) Venedig in Wien 9 May

1904 **Das Veilchenmädel** (Josef Hellmesberger/w Krenn) Carltheater 27 February

1904 **Die Eisjungfrau** (*The Girl from Up There*) German version w Wilhelm, M Band and add mus by Hellmesberger (Venedig in Wien)

1904 **Jung Heidelberg** (Millöcker arr Reiterer/w Krenn) Venedig in Wien 9 July

1904 **Ein nasses Abenteuer** (Roth/w Krenn) Deutsches Volkstheater 27 August

1904 **'s Zuckergoscherl** (J Wolffsgruber/w Alfred Schönfeld, August Neidhart) Carltheater 15 October

1904 **Wien bei Nacht** (Hellmesberger/w Wilhelm) 1 act Danzers Orpheum 28 October

1905 **Der Schnurrbart** (*A bajusz*) German version w Leo Stein (Carltheater)

1905 **Die Ringstrassenprinzessin** (*Messalinette*) German lyrics (Danzers Orpheum)

1905 **Fesche Geister** (Ziehrer/w Krenn) Venedig in Wien 7 July

1905 **Frauenherz** (Josef Strauss ad Reiterer) Danzers Orpheum 29 September

1905 **Die Schützenliesel** (Eysler/w Stein) Carltheater 7 October

1905 **Ausser Rand und Band** (Paul Lincke/w Antony) 1 act Danzers Orpheum 4 November

1905 **Auf's in Orpheum** Viennese version (Danzers Orpheum)

1906 **Die drei Engel** (Hellmesberger/w Antony) Venedig in Wien 4 May

1906 **Künstlerblut** (Eysler/w Leo Stein) Carltheater 20 October

1906 **Tausend und Eine Nacht** (Johann Strauss arr Reiterer/w Stein) Venedig in Wien 15 June

1906 **Das Scheckbuch des Teufels** (*Le Carnet du Diable*) German version w Antony and add mus Max R Steiner (Danzers Orpheum)

1906 **Uber'm grossen Teich** (*Across the Big Pond*) Viennese version w Antony w music by Franz Ziegler (Theater an der Wien)

1907 **Der lustiger Witwer** Austrian version w Antony (Danzers Orpheum)

1907 **Monte Carlo** (Ludwig Roman Ehmel/w Antony) Neues Operetten-Theater, Leipzig 7 April

1907 **Die kleine Prinzessin** (Béla von Ujj/w Antony) Venedig in Wien 5 May

1907 **Eine Sensation** (von Ujj/w Antony) 3 scenes Danzers Orpheum 20 December

1907 **Miss Hook von Holland** (*Miss Hook of Holland*) German version (Venedig in Wien)

1907 **Weiberlaunen** (*Leányka*) German version w Leo Stein (Frankfurt-am-Main)

1908 **Das Glücksschweinchen** (Eysler/w Stein) Venedig in Wien 26 June

1908 **Johann der zweite** (Eysler/w Stein) Carltheater 3 October

1909 **Der Ehemännerzug** (Kappeller/w Alexander Engel) Stadttheater, Nuremberg 14 November

1909 **Der Sultan** (*A szultán*) German version (Johann Strauss-Theater)

1909 **Tanzhusaren** (*A táncos huszárok*) German version (Venedig in Wien)

1909 **Drei Stunden Leben** (von Ujj/w Antony) 1 act Apollotheater 1 November

1909 **Miss Gibbs** (*Our Miss Gibbs*) German version w Krenn, Max Baer, Ronacher 12 November

1910 **Hupf mein Mäderl!** (Viktor Holländer/w Krenn) Ronacher 13 August

1910 **Lord Piccolo** (Henrik Berény/w Rudolf Schanzer) Johann Strauss-Theater 1 September

1910 **Die verhexte Wien(erstadt)** (*The New Aladdin*) German version w Antony (Ronacher)

1910 **Der Dumme hat's Glück** (von Ujj/w Krenn) Raimundtheater 10 September

1910 **Chantecler** (von Ujj/w Krenn) Ronacher 25 October

1911 **In fünfzig Jahren** (arr Ziehrer/w Krenn) Wiener Stadttheater 7 January

1911 **Die romantische Frau** (Carl Weinberger/w Béla Jenbach) Johann Strauss-Theater 17 March

1911 **Vielliebchen** (Ludwig Engländer/w Rudolf Osterreicher) Venedig in Wien 5 May

1911 **Das geborgte Schloss** (Hermann Dostal/w György Verő) Stadttheater, Leipzig 15 May

1911 **Der Frauenfresser** (Eysler/w Stein) Wiener Bürgertheater 23 December

1912 **Autoliebchen** Viennese adaptation (Apollotheater)

1912 **Freddy und Teddy** (Digby la Touche/H L Melbourne ad w Neidhart) Theater am Nollendorfplatz, Berlin 23 December

1913 **Mein Mäderl** (Berény/w Eugen Burg, Schanzer) Raimundtheater 21 January

1913 **Die verbotene Stadt** (Bruno Granichstaedten/w Granichstaedten) Montis Operetten-Theater, Berlin 23 December

1914 **Teresita** (Émile Waldteufel arr von Ujj) Venedig in Wien 27 June

1914 **Komm, deutscher Bruder** (Eysler, Franz Lehár/w Neidhart) Raimundtheater 4 October

1914 **Frühling am Rhein** (Eysler/w Fritz Löhner-Beda, Oskar Fronz) Wiener Bürgertheater 10 October

1915 **Der Weltenbummler** (Richard Fall/w Löhner-Beda) Montis Operetten-Theater, Berlin 18 November

1915 **Die ledige Frau** (Karl Eibenschütz/w Neidhart) Landestheater, Linz 3 December

1917 **Liebessport** (Eibenschütz/w Neidhart) Theater am Gärtnerplatz, Munich 26 May

1921 **Der keusche Heinrich** (Hans Duval-Diamant/w Löhner-Beda) Lustspieltheater 29 March

1926 **Donauweibchen** (Egon Neumann/w Krenn ad Karl Farkas) Wiener Bürgertheater 22 May

LINDSAY, Howard [NELKE, Herman] (b Waterford, NY, 29 March 1889; d New York, 11 February 1968). Broadway director and producer and the author, at 25 years' distance, of two of the most enduring musical plays of their times.

At first an actor and stage manager, Lindsay directed several productions for Margaret Anglin's company and made his Broadway debut as a director (he also played a part) at the helm of George S Kaufman and Marc Connelly's highly successful *Dulcy* in 1921. The following year he directed the revue *The 49ers,* in which he made what would be his only Broadway appearance as a performer in a musical piece. Other directing assignments followed, including the 1932 Fred Astaire musical *Gay Divorce.*

Lindsay's initial stage play, *Tommy* (w Bertrand Robinson), was produced in 1927, and his first significant success as an author came six years later with Dwight Deere Wiman and Tom Weatherly's production of his play *She Loves Me Not* (1933), a piece which took in two Arthur Schwartz/Edward Heyman songs. He directed each piece, but did not perform.

Hired to direct the Cole Porter musical *Anything Goes* the following year, Lindsay became emergency librettist when events prompted a major rewrite. He teamed on this job with Russel Crouse and, following the enormous success of *Anything Goes,* the two worked together as a play- and musical-writing partnership for a 25-year stretch which was highlighted by some exceptionally big successes. Amongst their plays the Pulitzer Prize–winning *State of the Union* (1945) and the extremely long-running *Life with Father* (1939) were the most memorable, whilst the Irving Berlin musical which had Ethel Merman demanding that one *Call Me Madam* and Rodgers and Hammerstein's Mary Martin vehicle *The Sound of Music* gave them two major musical-theatre hits.

Lindsay also authored film scripts (*The Great Victor Herbert,* etc), continued occasionally to direct—staging both *Red, Hot and Blue!* and *Hooray for What!* of his own musical shows—and later produced several Broadway plays (w Crouse), notably the long-running *Arsenic and Old Lace.*

Lindsay and Crouse's 1942 play *Strip for Action* was turned into a musical of the same title (Jimmy McHugh/Harold Adamson/Paul Streger, Eli Blaser) which folded out of town in 1956.

1934 **Anything Goes** (Cole Porter/w Russel Crouse, Guy Bolton, P G Wodehouse) Alvin Theater 21 November

1936 **Red, Hot and Blue!** (Porter/w Crouse) Alvin Theater 29 October

1937 **Hooray for What!** (Harold Arlen/E Y Harburg/w Crouse) Winter Garden Theater 1 December

1950 **Call Me Madam** (Irving Berlin/w Crouse) Imperial Theater 12 October

1956 **Happy Hunting** (Matt Dubey, Harold Karr/w Crouse) Majestic Theater 6 December

1959 **The Sound of Music** (Richard Rodgers/Oscar Hammerstein/w Crouse) Lunt-Fontanne Theater 16 November

1962 **Mr President** (Berlin/w Crouse) St James Theater 20 October

Biography: Skinner, C O: *Life with Lindsay and Crouse* (Houghton Mifflin, Boston, 1976)

LINGARD, W[illiam] H[orace] [NEEDHAM, William Horace Thomas] (b London, 20 June 1837; d London, 12 January 1927). Buccaneering musical comedian who purveyed musical theatre to all corners of the English-speaking world for more than half a century.

At first a comic actor (J K Chute's company, etc), Horace Lingard made his first successes in Britain as a music-hall performer, singing about what happens "On the Beach at Brighton on a Summer's Day," "The Model Police," "The Life of William Shakespeare," and "Artful Dodger's Return" in an act built around a series of impersonations and comic songs. In 1866 he visited America and there caused a sensation with his songs, notably the number "Captain Jinks of the Horse Marines," and with what was claimed to be the first quick-change act ever seen in the country. He became hailed as "the best comic singer ever introduced to New York audiences." He played at New York's Theatre Comique in farce and burlesque and, supported by his second wife, music-hall serio-comic **Alice [Anne] DUNNING** (b London, 29 July 1845; d London, 25 June 1897) and her sister, Mrs Harriet Dalziel, who worked under the name of Dickie Lingard, he took over the management of the house (27 June 1868) for a short period, playing sketches and burlesque (*Pluto,* etc) until it was burned down, and the company moved out to Brooklyn, then to Boston (1869) where Lingard took over the local Theatre Comique (later Adelphi Theater).

The Lingards toured for a number of years in and out of New York with programs which included plays, burlesques and, later, short operettas featured alongside Horace's own stand-up performance. A tale is told of family rivalry in which Alice and Horace, each considering themselves the main attraction, came to hard words. To prove his point, Horace withdrew from the bill, leaving Alice to head it alone. When the receipts went down and his wager was apparently won, he came back.

Lingard shared his programs both with Susie Galton and Thomas and Blanche Whiffen (née Galton) and their family group, the earliest purveyors of Offenbach in English to American audiences, and with the Howard Pauls, and he traveled his company—playing everything from drama to burlesque—as far afield as the southern Pacific, appearing in Australia in 1875 billed as "the world-renowned comedian" in *Our Boys, David Garrick, Married in Haste,* the melodrama *Dead to the World* and a comic opera called *I Ladroni,* allegedly of his own making. However, *I Ladroni* (Theatre Royal, Sydney 19 February 1876), which he had first mounted in St Louis several years earlier, and which was allegedly musically compiled by Giuseppe Operti, bore a remarkably close resemblance both textually and musically to Burnand and Sullivan's early opéra-bouffe *The Contrabandista.*

In February 1879, hot on the heels of the first startling Broadway performances of *HMS Pinafore,* Lingard starred as John Wellington Wells in New York's first *The Sorcerer* and later the same year the Lingards sailed off again to New Zealand and Australia, playing *HMS Pinafore* (he as Joseph Porter, she as Josephine) and *The Sorcerer.* He was pursued legally, in a stranger-than-fiction saga of court appearances, featuring flights and at least one probably faked bankruptcy, by J C Williamson (who had played at the Theatre Comique under Lingard's management), who had bought the Australasian rights to Gilbert and Sullivan's show. Balked by the courts, Lingard eventually had to give up, but he continued to play in his repertoire his own "sequel," *The Wreck of the Pinafore,* which ultimately found its way very briefly to the London stage. He also performed a number of French works (notably as Frimousse to Alice's *Le Petit Duc*), as well as *Our Boys, Old Bachelors,* Gilbert's *The Happy Land,* H B Farnie's *Pluto* and the inevitable *I Ladroni.*

After touring the rest of the Pacific circuit—Japan, China, Hong Kong—the Lingards finally returned to

Plate 220. **Horace Lingard** *and his wife Alice Dunning played all kinds of theatre—comic, dramatic and musical—from one side of the world to the other.*

Britain where Horace mounted a special Gaiety Theatre matinée to promote his wife as a star, but metropolitan success did not come their way and it was ultimately in the British provinces that Lingard found himself a very comfortable niche. In collaboration with 'cellist-actor-producer Auguste van Biene, he produced and subsequently toured endlessly with English versions of such reputable French pieces as *Le Droit d'aînesse* (*Falka,* Tancred), *Les Voltigeurs de la 32ème* (*The Old Guard,* Polydore Poupart) and *La Princesse des Canaries* (*Pepita,* Inigo). In a rare venture into the West End he tried *Pepita* at Toole's Theatre in 1888 and was gratified with a run of 102 performances before going back on the road. He also played one London week of Messager's *La Fauvette du Temple* (1891) and produced a revival of Offenbach's *Les Brigands.* For this revival he used a youthful translation by W S Gilbert, published by Boosey and Hawkes, and once again found himself in court, on the receiving end of a writ from the author who had no wish to see his juvenilia thus displayed (nor, perhaps, for its influence on *The Pirates of Penzance* and *The Mountebanks* in particular to be noticed). For once, this time, Lingard was on the right end of the law.

Lingard also co-wrote (or at least put his co-name to) and produced a burlesque of his touring success *Falka* under the title *Brother Pelican* (1894) and mounted a new and short-lived show called *The Chorus Girl* (Caractacus Tire) as part of his repertoire in 1897. In 1899, now a widower, he was still to be found on the road, starring in the chief comic part of a musical called *An American Heiress* (Stuart McNab). He trouped his shows endlessly and, in his eighties, allowed himself to drop from star comic roles to smaller parts, whilst also taking time off to direct amateur productions of the works which he had performed in his younger days. He died in his ninetieth year.

The two daughters of Horace and Alice Lingard both married music. Lulu became Lulu Wicks, and Nellie—a leading lady in Australian musical theatre (*La Cigale, La Mascotte*) as Mowbray Lingard—having disposed of a certain Frank M Burbank (''of the Boston Theater''), became the wife of Arthur Godfrey, composer of the successful *Little Miss Nobody* (1898) and nephew to the more famous bandsman and arranger Dan Godfrey.

Lingard's first wife was actress and music-hall performer Minnie Foster. She worked as ''Mrs W H Lingard,'' and carried on doing so even after her husband ran away to bigamize with Alice Dunning. The pair were finally legally divorced in 1878, and Lingard then married Alice a second time to make it all legitimate.

1872 **I Ladroni** (Giuseppe Operti) 1 act De Bar's Opera House, St Louis 30 December

Plate 221. **Linie I.** *The company down in the underground.*

1880 **The Wreck of the Pinafore** (Luscombe Searelle) Princess's Theatre, Dunedin, New Zealand 29 November

1894 **Brother Pelican** (Operti, Ernest Allen, William C Levey/w Alfred Rae) Theatre Royal, Belfast 8 February

LINIE I Musikalische Revue (Stück) in 2 acts by Volker Ludwig. Music by Birger Heymann and the rock band No Ticket. Grips Theater, Berlin, 30 April 1986.

A loosely constructed musical journey which its author not unadvisedly christened ''revue,'' *Linie I* was first produced at Berlin's Grips Theater, a house specializing in young people's entertainment. The show followed its central character, a nameless girl (Jannette Rauch) come to the big city from West Germany to track down the rock singer who she thinks has made her pregnant, on a two-act back-and-forth trip along West-Berlin's underground ''Number One Line.'' On the way, the unsophisticated young woman runs into a series of fashionable 1980s types—the prostitutes, the drug dealer and his hangers-on (Thomas Ahrens, Dieter Landuris), the crazy lady (Else Nabu), the street musicians, the pimpled adolescent (Ilona Schulz), the suicide, the long-haired environment-freak (Landuris) and the singles-bar drifters, as well as some (obligatorily unsympathetically portrayed) middle-class adults—amid a series of youthfully preoccupied songs with a *Hair* flavor. There is, before the final curtain, a button on the show's tale: when the young woman's ''rock star'' finally is tracked down, he turns out to be a boring old-fashioned Schlager singer, so she dumps him for a with-it fellow in an overcoat (Folkert Milster) who's been dogging her paces since early in Act I.

The songs which illustrated our heroine's train trip through 1980s Berlin were simple, poppy items, with a strongly featured drummer, often as much spoken as sung: the tube-train number (''Du sitzt mir gegenüber'') of the folk who see each other every day without knowing each other at all, the jaunty exhortation ''Fahr mal wieder

U-Bahn,'' the pattering pick-up attempt of ''Der Anmacher'' or a quartet of ''Wilmersdorfer Witwen,'' fur-coated middle-class ladies (played by men) pounding out their longing for the good old days of National Socialism in beer-barrel tones. The show had its most effective musical moments, however, when its drum machine was switched off and its heart switched on, as in the moving song of an elderly man (Dietrich Lehmann) assuring the girl that, no matter what, it is wonderful just to be alive (''Herrlich zu leben'') or in the pimpled Maria's lament, ''Du bist schön auch wenn du weinst.''

Linie I was a great success in its little theatre and—aided by its small semi-singing cast and band and minimal production requirements—it soon moved on to be played throughout Germany, proving itself more popular in theatres all round the country than any other locally bred musical show in decades. In the 15 years since its creation it has been played in over one hundred German-speaking houses, whilst remaining a feature of the Grips repertoire to such effect that by February 2000 it had been played 943 times in the house of its birth. Its pre-reunification setting and tone, and the picture of a Berlin full of West German dropouts and draft dodgers that it presents, provoke an extraordinary kind of nostalgia in much the same way that pieces such as *Hair* can still do, a nostalgia which those who were not part of that world and of that time can find just as amusing today as a ''with-it'' Berliner of 1986 evidently found the ''Wilmersdorfer Witwen.''

The Grips company have also performed their piece in festivals around the world.

In 1988 a film version was produced by Reinhard Hauff with Landuris, Damitz, Lehmann, Ahrens, Christiane Reiff, Petra Zieser and Ilona Schulz of the original cast again featured and Inga Victoria Groetschel as the girl.

UK: 8 October 1986; Austria: Wiener Festwoche 27 May 1987; France: Paris 3 June 1987; USA: State University of New York 20 July 1988; Australia: Brisbane 23 August 1988

Film: Reinhard Hauff 1988

Recording: original cast (Polydor)

LINK, Antonie (b Budapest, 5 February 1853; d Vienna, June 1931). Star of some of the earliest Viennese Operetten who crammed a vast amount into a career which ended in her mid-twenties.

Having at first played children's roles at the Bürgertheater and then sung in the chorus at the Vienna Hofoper, the statuesque and poised teenage mezzo-soprano became a member of the company at the Carltheater where, at the age of 23 (or 19, if some reports of her birth date are to be believed), she created the title role in *Fatinitza* (1876) and, subsequently, those of Johann Strauss's *Prinz Methusalem* (1877) and, her greatest role, Suppé's *Boccaccio* (1879).

Link also originated and/or played roles in such early Viennese Operetten as Suppé's short-lived *Die Frau Meisterin* (Pierre), Conradin's *Flodoardo Wuprahall* (Donna Fiamina) and Zaytz's favorite *Mannschaft an Bord* (Grobecker's role of Max); appeared again in travesty as Frinke in *Flotte Bursche,* Pygmalion in *Die schöne Galathee,* as the midshipman Henrik in *Les Cent Vierges* (1873, with a song specially added for her in what was officially her debut), Pedro in *Giroflé-Girofla* and the heroine's bridegroom Bavolet in *Schönröschen* (*La Jolie Parfumeuse*); and in skirts as Manon in *Die schöne Bourbonnaise,* as the slavegirl Nakahira in the spectacular *Reise um die Erde in 80 Tagen* and opposite manager Franz Jauner as Constanze Mozart in a Singspiel called *Wolfgang und Constanze.*

She was also Vienna's first and blessedly young Madame Lange in *La Fille de Madame Angot* (1873), the first German-language *Petit Duc* in Lecocq's opérette, the first Boulangère of Offenbach's *Margot die reiche Bäckerin* (1877) and the Rose Friquet of the Viennese *Les Dragons de Villars.* She visited the Theater an der Wien to star in Offenbach's *Der Jahrmarkt von St Laurent* (1877, Bamboche) and Pest to play at the German-language theatre in *Die Prinzessin von Trapezunt* (1875), and she also appeared in such lighter operatic roles as Cherubino and Ännchen in *Der Freischütz.* At the age of 26 (surely not 22?), after playing just four long-remembered weeks in her final role as Boccaccio, she married and retired from the stage.

Antonie Link was introduced as a character in Willy Först's film *Operette* where she was impersonated by Trude Marlen.

Her sister **Sophie LINK** (b Budapest, 1860; d New York, 1 October 1900) played some Operettic roles in Hamburg and Vienna in the 1880s, appearing as Princess Blanche de Coligny in *Capitän Fracassa* at the Theater an der Wien, and as Josephine in the local version of *Joséphine vendue par ses soeurs* at the Carltheater before moving on to an operatic career. Her brother, comedian **Adolf LINK** (b Pest, 15 September 1851; d New York, 24 September 1933), was a former child actor who played in Olmütz, Budapest and Hamburg and was for a while a small-part player at the Theater an der Wien (Nux in *Königin Indigo,* Tabellion in *Les Cloches de Corneville,* Curtius in *Der Jahrmarkt von St Laurent,* Lamotte in *Das verwunschene Schloss,* Baldrian in *Der letzte Mohikaner,* Biscontin in *Madame Favart*) and Ronachers Operetten-Theater (Simplicius in *Der Graf von Gleichen,* Stutzerl in *Kapitän Ahlstrom,* Zwickel in *Die weiblichen Jäger,* etc). He later spent a number of years at the theatre in Meiningen and introduced and performed larger roles in

German-language Operette in America (Sebastiani in *Der lustige Krieg,* Sir Andrew in *Donna Juanita,* Fritellini in *La Mascotte,* Wenzel in *Der Chevalier von San Marco,* Prutschesko in *Apajune,* Anatol in *Hundert Jungfrauen, Capitän Nicol* w Geistinger, Taboreau in *Trompette, Der Vagabund,* etc). He moved definitively to America in 1911 playing at first at the Irving Place Theater and later in the English-speaking theatre. In 1923 he appeared in *Peaches* (Baron von Blowitz) in Philadelphia, and as late as 1931—at the age of 80—he was seen on Broadway playing Toni in a revival of *The Student Prince.*

LINNIT & DUNFEE LTD

Originally a London talent agency headed by Jack Dunfee and S E Linnit, a former general manager to Edgar Wallace, the firm began producing plays in 1936 with regular success. They made their first venture into the musical field with the small-scale *Cage Me a Peacock* (1948) but, in spite of mounting a couple of revue productions, did not again produce a musical until they picked up Julian Slade's *Salad Days* from the Bristol Repertory Company and brought it to the Vaudeville Theatre for what was to be the longest run of any musical piece up to that date.

Thereafter they produced Slade's further works (*Free as Air, Follow That Girl, Hooray for Daisy, Vanity Fair*) as well as the *Little Women* musical, *A Girl Called Jo,* written by the authors of their successful revue *Intimacy at 8.30.* Two Broadway imports, *Candide* and *High Spirits* (1964) were failures, and after the flop of another repertory theatre show, *The Matchgirls* (1966), the firm returned exclusively to producing plays.

LIONEL AND CLARISSA Comic opera by Issac Bickerstaff. Music by Charles Dibdin. Theatre Royal, Covent Garden, 28 February 1768.

One of the most enduring comic operas of its time, *Lionel and Clarissa* brought together a regular set of comic-opera characters in a lively, if regular comic opera-plot. Clarissa (Miss Macklin) is the daughter of Sir John Flowerdale (Mr Gibson), Lionel (George Mattocks) is the orphaned son of a friend brought up in Sir John's care. Before they can be happily paired off, Clarissa has to escape from a more advantageous match with the unwanted Lord Jessamy (Mr Dyer). The son of the boisterously old-English, wench-snatching Colonel Oldboy (Ned Shuter) and his affected, underwed Lady Mary, Jessamy has been raised by Lady Mary's brother as a powdered and painted exquisite of whom even his own father is in horror. British salt-of-the-earth outdoes Frenchified pansy at every turn, and of course gets the girl. A subplot dealt with Oldboy's encouragement of the jaunty Frank Harman (Mr Mahoon) to elope with his girl, unaware that the girl in question is his own daughter, Diana (Mrs Baker).

Bickerstaff's merrily bristling script, which gave more than three-quarters of its scenes to the comical folk and only occasional moments to the amorous mopings of the two title characters, was illustrated with 24 musical numbers, mostly solos, and mostly original music from the pen of Dibdin (''for which I received at different times £48, giving up the copyright'').

An indifferent success on its ill-prepared first production under Colman at Covent Garden, when it was played but 11 times, the show was seen at the Theatre Royal, Drury Lane, two seasons later, under the new title of *The School for Fathers* (8 February 1770) to better advantage. But if its initial London career was scarcely brilliant, the piece—in each of its versions—went the rounds of the world's English-speaking stages with great success and it was revived at Drury Lane in 1807 (12 December) and at several other houses in the early 1800s. A version of *Lionel and Clarissa* (mus arr Alfred Reynolds) was given a modern revival at the Lyric Theatre, Hammersmith (28 October 1925, 171 performances), during the management of Nigel Playfair, as one of his ballad-opera attempts to follow up the theatre's major success with a reorganized version of *The Beggar's Opera.*

USA: Southwark Theater, Philadelphia *A School for Fathers* 14 December 1772, New York 21 February 1794

THE LION KING Musical in 2 acts by Roger Allers and Irene Mecchi adapted from the screenplay by Irene Mecchi, Jonathan Roberts and Linda Woolverton. Music and lyrics by Elton John and Tim Rice. Additional music and lyrics by Lebo M, Mark Mancina, Jay Rifkin, Julie Taymor and Hans Zimmer. Produced at the New Amsterdam Theater, New York, 13 November 1997.

The second of Walt Disney's animated features to be remade for the spectacular musical stage, *The Lion King* was not, as the majority of the other Disney features of the 1990s were, based on a familiar fairy tale or work of fiction. Its story, if a traditional and straightforward example of its fabular kind, was indeed an original one, something which in the last years of the century had become increasingly rare in musical-theatre books.

When the tale begins, the Lion King is the regal Mufasa (Samel E Wright). But the crown of the King of the Pridelands, destined for Mufasa's well-loved and loving son, Simba (Scott Irby-Rannier/Jason Raize) is coveted by the monarch's envious brother, Scar (John Vickery). Scar engineers Mufasa's death in a wildebeest stampede, and leads the lion cub to believe that it was because of him that his father died. Brokenhearted and tormented, Simba runs away from Pride Rock, leaving Scar to take upon himself the crown of the Lion King. In his exile, Simba falls in with the show's low comedians, a warthog called Pumbaa (Tom Alan Robbins) and a meerkat, Timon (Max Casella), and in their company he grows into a fine young lion. Meanwhile, back home, Scar proves a Bad King. To win his place, he had made an alliance with the lions' traditional enemy, the hyenas (Tracey Nicole Chapman, Stanley Wayne Mathis, Kevin Cahoon), and under his and their rule and influence the Pridelands falls low. But, in the last reel, Simba returns to claim his own, and Scar meets the sticky end he has deserved. A love interest was provided for Simba in the form of the young lioness, Nala (Heather Headley).

The score of the stage show was made up of the five jaunty Elton John/Tim Rice numbers which had made up the score of the original, juvenile-orientated film (''Can You Feel the Love Tonight,'' ''The Circle of Life,'' etc), topped up by three new comic pieces in a similar vein by the same writers, by the addition of a version of the sixties pop song ''The Lion Sleeps Tonight,'' and by a significant amount of African-flavored music, chants, songs and orchestrations by other writers.

The remake of *The Lion King* for the stage proved a triumph. If the previous Disney transfer, *Beauty and the Beast,* had gained no extra dimension or attractions in its transfer from the animated screen to the animated stage, this piece certainly did. The seams that were let out of the original 75-minute story allowed the cartoon characters to win in warmth and humanity, and the additional African-style music lifted the score from being just another set of jolly movieland songs to being something both richer and more individual in both texture and sound—but the great triumph of the exercise came in the entire reconception of the original tale for its stage production. *The Lion King* stage version was re-created by director-choreographer-designer Julie Taymor with an imaginative flair that resulted in a physical production of a dazzling originality the like of which had not been seen in the musical theatre in living memory. The piece was played in vibrantly colored scenery and costumes with an air of Braque or Matisse to them which echoed with a feeling both primitive and modern, and the animals of the story and of the African savanna were re-created by combining puppets and masks with human performers to the most amazing effect. The result was both a triumphant piece of spectacular theatre in a genre where ''spectacle'' had, through years of repetitive excesses, been becoming a dirty word and a major hit. *The Lion King* won itself and its creatress-in-chief stunning reviews, walk-away Tony Awards, and all-round acclaim, and the piece duly settled into its ''new'' Broadway theatre for what will evidently be a very, very long run.

The Lion King opened in London two years on from its Broadway bow, after a long and dangerous blast of pre-production rave. The cast at the Lyceum Theatre was headed by Rob Edwards (Scar), Cornell John (Mufusa), Roger Wrght (Simba), Martyn Ellis (Puumba) and Simon Gregor (Timor). Overcoming all the hype, and outriding all the expectations, London, like New York, welcomed the piece with acclamation as *The Lion King* set out on what seem likely to be considerable travels.

An earlier *The Lion King* produced at London's Victoria Theatre in 1851, dealt not with the king of the jungle but with King Richard of the lionheart. It was subsequently given a sequel called *The Lion Queen* (1852). Watch this space.

UK: Lyceum Theatre 19 October 1999

Recordings: cartoon soundtrack (Disney), original cast (Disney)

Literature: Taymor, J: *The Lion King: Pride Rock on Broadway* (Hyperion, New York, 1997)

LIORAT, Armand [DÉGAS, Georges] (b Sceaux, 10 January 1837; d Paris, 7 August 1898).

For more than 30 years both a civic accountant and a librettist and lyricist for the Parisian stage, Liorat had a fair share of success in his ''other'' job, notably in his collaborations with the composer Varney, with whom he worked on the opérettes *L'Amour mouillé, La Falote, Les Petites Brebis* and *La Fille de Fanchon la vielleuse,* all of which were also played through Europe and, occasionally, further afield after their Parisian successes. Others of his works which traveled beyond their original productions included Lecocq's *Kosiki,* Grisart's *Les Poupées de l'Infante* (played in Hungary as *A kisasszony babui* and in Boston as *Puppets*), *Le Petit Bois* (*A farkas meg a bárány* in Budapest), Lacome's *Ma mie Rosette,* which was seen on the London stage and became a long-term favorite in Australia, and, most successfully of all, Francis Chassaigne's Hungarian tale of *Les Noces improvisées* which, reworked as *Nadgy,* found particular success in America. His *La Rosière d'ici,* however, was found too risqué even for the Paris stage. It was banned by the censor, expurgated and, not unexpectedly, flopped.

Outside the opérettic field, Liorat collaborated with Pierre Decourcelle on the libretto for d'Erlanger's 1897 opera *Inès Mendo,* contributed to the drama *La Belle aux cheveux d'or* (1882), lyricked a series of popular songs and joined Clairville in writing revue for the Théâtre de l'Athénée (*De bric et de broc, Boum! Voilà!,* 1876).

His last work, *Les Quatre Filles Aymon* was produced posthumously, the author having died the day before he was due to read it to the Folies-Dramatiques company.

1869 **Un mariage au gros sel** (Frédéric Barbier) 1 act Eldorado 10 July

1870 **Un souper chez Mlle Contat** (Barbier) 1 act Eldorado 5 February

1871 **Une entrevue** (Charles Lecorbeiller) 1 act Eldorado 1 October

- 1871 **Un drame à Nogent** (Paul Wachs) 1 act Alcazar 9 October
- 1872 **Les Brioches du Doge** (F Demarquette/w William Busnach) 1 act Folies-Bergère 16 March
- 1872 **Le Valet de chambre de Madame** (Olivier Métra) 1 act Folies-Bergère November
- 1872 **La Belle Kalitcha** (Wachs) 1 act Folies-Bergère December
- 1873 **La Belle Indienne** (Wachs) 1 act Alcazar
- 1873 **La Rosière d'ici** (Léon Roques) Théâtre des Bouffes-Parisiens 27 March
- 1873 **Mariée depuis midi** (Georges Jacobi/w Busnach) 1 act Marseille 20 August; Théâtre des Bouffes-Parisiens 6 March 1874
- 1873 **La Leçon d'amour** (Wachs) 1 act Théâtre des Bouffes-Parisiens 14 September
- 1873 **La Liqueur d'or** (Laurent de Rillé/w Busnach) Théâtre des Menus-Plaisirs 11 December
- 1874 **Une pleine eau à Chatou** (Wachs) 1 act Folies-Bergère 21 November
- 1876 **Kosiki** (Lecocq/w Busnach) Théâtre de la Renaissance 18 October
- 1878 **Le Pont d'Avignon** (Charles Grisart) Théâtre des Bouffes-Parisiens 3 September
- 1879 **Le Petit Abbé** (Grisart/w Henri Bocage) 1 act Théâtre du Vaudeville 9 October
- 1881 **Les Poupées de l'Infante** (Grisart/w Bocage) Théâtre des Folies-Dramatiques 9 April
- 1883 **Le Pot au lait** (Wachs/w Busnach) 1 act Palais-Royal 1 May
- 1886 **Les Noces improvisées** (Francis Chassaigne/w Albert Fonteny) Théâtre des Bouffes-Parisiens 13 February
- 1887 **L'Amour mouillé** (Louis Varney/w Jules Prével) Théâtre des Nouveautés 25 January
- 1888 **Le Bossu** (Grisart/w Bocage) Théâtre de la Gaîté 19 March
- 1889 **La Vénus d'Arles** (Varney/w Paul Ferrier) Théâtre des Nouveautés 30 January
- 1890 **Ma mie Rosette** (Paul Lacome/w Prével) Théâtre des Folies-Dramatiques 4 February
- 1890 **La Fille de l'air** (Lacome/Cogniard brothers ad w Hippolyte Raymond) Théâtre des Folies-Dramatiques 20 June
- 1891 **La Fille de Fanchon la vielleuse** (Varney/Busnach, Fonteny) Théâtre des Folies-Dramatiques 3 November
- 1893 **Le Cadeau de noces** (Lacome/w Fernand Hue, Stop [ie, L Morel-Retz]) Théâtre des Bouffes-Parisiens 20 January
- 1893 **Le Petit Bois** (Grisart) 1 act Théâtre des Bouffes-Parisiens 7 March
- 1894 **La Fille de Paillasse** (Varney/w Louis Leloir) Théâtre des Folies-Dramatiques 20 April
- 1895 **Les Petites Brebis** (Varney) Théâtre Cluny 5 June
- 1896 **La Falote** (Varney/w Maurice Ordonneau) Théâtre des Folies-Dramatiques 17 April
- 1896 **Le Lézard** (Frédéric Toulmouche) 1 act Scala 29 August
- 1898 **Les Quatre Filles Aymon** (Lacome, Victor Roger/w Fonteny) Théâtre des Folies-Dramatiques 20 September

THE LISBON STORY Play with music in 2 acts by Harold Purcell. Music by Harry Parr Davies. London Hippodrome, 17 June 1943.

George Black's wartime production of *The Lisbon Story* was a curious concoction of drama, sentiment and patriotism on the one hand and song and dance on the other—rather like a hybrid of an Ivor Novello romantic musical and a purposeful film melodrama. Harold Purcell's book was filmic in style, following episodically the career of Parisian prima donna Gabrielle Girard (Patricia Burke), who agrees to the insistent offers of Nazi cultural boss von Schriner (Albert Lieven) to return to the Paris stage only so that she can help a French scientist to escape with a vital wartime secret. On opening night, Gabrielle takes the place of the man's daughter in the show's ballet, a depiction of the rape of Innocence by Evil, whilst the pair escape, but when she steps forward to underline the ballet's message in words von Schriner shoots her. As she dies, the Allied bombs pound onto Paris and the cast joins in the Marseillaise.

Harry Parr Davies (in spite of being currently in the Life Guards) supplied a score in which, in good Novello style, the numbers were given to the prima donna and to some incidental vocalists, but not to the hero or the villain. Miss Burke had a successful waltz, ''Someday We Shall Meet Again,'' with an infallible wartime lyric, a fruit-seller sang the tenor ''We Must Never Say Goodbye'' and a café singer rendered ''Music at Midnight.'' However, *The Lisbon Story*'s most successful song was a late addition. Purcell's quick-cuts film-style writing made for some awkward scene changes, and it was decided that one was serious enough to require the front cloth to be dropped and the wait to be covered by a song. The Vincent Tildesley Mastersingers, who acted as backing vocalists, were given a whistling song called ''Pedro the Fisherman'' which they harmonized effectively to cover the bumps and bashes of the scene change. ''Pedro'' became one of the most popular songs of the war years. The show was also heavily equipped with dance, and the Polish dance stars Alicia Halama and Czeslaw Konarski were featured both in the ballet-within-the-opérette and in a long set-piece Portuguese festival routine in which Wendy Toye deftly mixed balletic and music-theatre dance to produce one of the highlights of the show.

The Lisbon Story evoked some startled responses (''The Heroine Is Shot At the End . . . at the Hippodrome of all places!''). It was clearly not what a musical show should be. It was serious. There was hardly any comedy. And The Heroine Got Shot at the End. But the public didn't mind. Quite the contrary. *The Lisbon Story* ran through 492 performances before it was chased from town by some indignant German bombs. Three months later it returned, with Viennese soprano Maria Elsner and Karel Stepanek replacing the stars and Raymond Newell singing ''Pedro'' as a baritone solo, but it failed to take off a second time and ended its run after 54 further per-

Plate 222. *The Vincent Tildesley Mastersingers sing the front-cloth hit of* **The Lisbon Story,** *''Pedro, the Fisherman.''*

formances. It went promptly on the road with Jessica James starring and in 1946 it was filmed.

British National determined to make *The Lisbon Story* an all-star affair and, although they failed after much trying to persuade the busy Sadler's Wells Ballet to take part, they ended up with a fair plateau of ''names'' including vocalists Richard Tauber, Harry Welchman and Lorely Dyer and violinist Stéphane Grappelly featured alongside Miss Burke, the Polish dance stars and Walter Rilla as the villain.

Film: British National 1946

LISCHEN ET FRITZCHEN Saynète (conversation alsacienne) in 1 act by Paul Boisselot (and Charles Nuitter, uncredited?). Music by Jacques Offenbach. Théâtre du Kursaal, Bad Ems, 21 July 1863.

Lischen et Fritzchen was a two-handed ''conversation'' for a pair of young folk who have the same Alsatian accent. Fritzchen (Jean-Paul) has been sacked because his ''improper'' French has led him to mistake the word ''pierre'' for ''bière'' and commit an embarrassing error in front of his master's sweetheart. Lischen (Zulma Bouffar) is having a problem making ends meet selling brooms (probably because she pronounces ''balais'' as ''palais''), and is thinking of giving up and going home. The two meet on the road, and are rather taken with each other, only to discover that they have the same surname . . . they are brother and sister! But the disappointed Fritzchen can read (which Lischen cannot), and he reads a letter which the girl has kept on her. It is from her mother, admitting that her so-called daughter is really the child of her unfortunate sister. And so Lischen and Fritzchen can head off towards Alsace and a happy un-brotherly-and-sisterly ending, arm in arm.

The musical part of the little piece consists of five portions: entry songs for Fritzchen (''Me chasser'') and Lischen (''P'tits balais''), the girl's tale of the Rat de Ville and the Rat de Campagne, a duo finale, and, most effectively, the delightful duo in which the two discover their similar origins (''Je suis alsacien, je suis alsacienne'').

First produced at Ems, where Offenbach spent many a holiday and where, from 1862, a number of his short pieces were given their first performance, the little saynète was a great success and it was taken into the repertoire of Offenbach's Théâtre des Bouffes-Parisiennes the following season with Désiré and Mlle Bouffar playing the two heavily accented sweethearts. Within months it was seen in Vienna (ad Poly Henrion) and in Berlin, and soon after in Budapest, but it was several years more before, with the slowly growing vogue for Offenbach's works in England and America, the piece was given its first performances in English-speaking countries.

America was given *Lischen et Fritzchen* first in French, played by Lucille Tostée and Dardignac in H L Bateman's repertoire (Academy of Music), and by Mlle Irma with James Fisk's company, whilst Kelly and Leon's minstrels performed Leon's English adaptation (15 March 1870, with him as Lischen) and the little English company of the Galton sisters and Thomas Whiffen purveyed a more normally cast vernacular version. In 1871 the visiting Charles Wyndham company from London included the little piece in its repertoire, as played by W H Woodfield and Annie Goodall. Kelly and Leon later played their unisex *Lischen and Fritzchen* in Australia, half a dozen years after it had been seen there for the first time, played at Sydney's Royal Victoria Theatre for a handful of nights by Annette Hirst and her husband, David Miranda ''from the Theatre Royal, Covent Garden'' (he'd sung there once in a six-night flop). Leon kept the piece in his repertoire (as *The Alsatians*) through the 1880s.

In London, one English version, *A Happy Result,* was given at the Gallery of Illustration in 1865, 1868 and again in 1869, a second, also in 1869 (ad Wellington Guernsey, 9 August) at the newly opened Gaiety Theatre, and a third at Covent Garden (27 December 1869), performed by Julia Mathews and Wilford Morgan as a forepiece to the Christmas pantomime, prior to intermittent performances around Britain over the following years.

Lischen et Fritzchen and its various national variants proved long popular as a part of multiple bills or as a benefit item, and the little piece still wins occasional performances today.

France: Théâtre des Bouffes-Parisiens 5 January 1864; Austria: Carltheater *Französiche Schwaben* 16 April 1864; Germany: Friedrich-Wilhelmstädtisches Theater 23 June 1864; UK: Gallery of Illustration *A Happy Result, or an Alsatian Dialogue* 3 November 1865, St James's Theatre (Fr) 2 June 1868; Hungary: Budai Színkör *Liesl und Fritzl, oder Die Französichen Schwaben* 21 June 1866; USA: Academy of Music (Fr) 25 June 1868, Williamsburgh (Eng) 8 October 1868; Australia: Royal Victoria Theatre, Sydney 9 March 1872

Recording: complete (Bourg)

LISTEN LESTER Musical comedy in 2 acts by Harry L Cort and George E Stoddard. Music by Harold Orlob. Knickerbocker Theater, New York, 23 December 1918.

The comedian of the title (Hansford Wilson) and his pal (Fred Heider) gallivant lightheartedly around ''the Ritz Hotel, Palm Beach'' attempting to get back some incriminating letters from Miss Arbutus Quilty (Gertrude Vanderbilt), warningly described on the theatre program as ''a live one.'' The juvenile songs and dances in Orlob's ultra-light score (''Waiting,'' ''For You—Just You'' and the fox-trot ''Two Is Company'') featured the young Clifton Webb and Ada Mae Weeks, The Four Entertainers provided the harmony and Eddie Garr and Heider got the jolliest song of the evening in ''Who Was the Last Girl You Called By Her First Name?''

John Cort's cast played 272 performances of the featherweight comedy and frequent dance routines of *Listen Lester* at the Knickerbocker Theater in the 1918–19 season, and the surprise-success show toured in three companies in the following one, encouraging the Corts to continue with a series of similar musical comedies (one, *Jim Jam Jems,* was temporarily called *Hello, Lester!* to emphasize a non-existent connection), none of which found anything like an equivalent success.

Listen Lester's announced C B Cochran production in London did not come off, but the show was given a mounting in Australia, under the J C Williamson Ltd banner, with a cast headed by Charles Norman, Renie Riano, Sydney Burchall and Jack and Sylvia Kellaway. The Sydney press sniffed that although it was ''not entirely dreary'' and had ''some pleasant dancing'' it also had ''hardly any plot . . . and is a traditional melange of 'wisecracks,' brightly dressed chorus girls, miscellaneous dancing and a pair of lovers.'' Williamson did not bother to take it on to Melbourne.

Australia: Criterion Theatre, Sydney 10 February 1934

LISTEN TO THE WIND Musical play in 2 acts taken from the book by Angela Ainley Jeans. Music by Vivian Ellis. Oxford Playhouse, 15 December 1954; Arts Theatre, London, 16 December 1955.

A superior children's musical, in the best British tradition, *Listen to the Wind* was based on a pretty nursery tale which had a nasty butler conniving with gypsies to whisk three children away from their happy home. The children get help from the winds and they escape the baddies through a series of adventures with a moonbeam, sunshine, a thundercloud and a sea witch called Miranda before returning home in time for tea. Ellis decorated the tale with a suitable score which included ''The Bread and Butter Song,'' ''Listen to the Wind,'' ''Whistle Down the Chimney'' and the traditional Suffolk ''Timothy's Under the Table.''

The Oxford production included several to-be-well-known names in its credits: director Peter Hall, designer Disley Jones, musical director Raymond Leppard, and amongst the cast Ronald (later to be Ronnie) Barker, Julia Smith (godmother to TV's *East Enders*), Derek Francis, Vivienne Martin and Sylvia Coleridge. The following year Hall, appointed director of the Arts Theatre, brought *Listen to the Wind* to London for a season. This time the cast included Clive Revill as the butler, Roderick Cook (Gale Bird), Miriam Karlin (Miranda) and Barker. The changing taste in children's entertainment meant that *Listen to the Wind*'s life was not as long as it might have been and the show was for many year best known by record collectors—its 45 EP recording being the rarest commercially issued British show disc in existence. However, in 1997 Dan Crawford, the British musical theatre's most enthusiastically active reviver of ought-not-to-be-forgotten shows, gave *Listen to the Wind* a seasonal revival (10 December, with 3 new songs) at his King's Head Theatre Club. Television actress Paula Wilcox featured as the Sea Witch, and the show won fond adherents among a new generation of theatregoers.

Recordings: studio cast selection (EP) (World Records), King's Head revival (TER)

LITOLFF, Henry Charles (b London, 6 February 1818; d Bois-Colombes, 6 August 1891).

Best known as a pianist and a conductor, Litolff also composed overtures for the dramatic theatre and wrote several pieces for the operatic and opérette stage. If his first attempt at a Parisian opérette, *La Boîte à Pandore,* was a failure, his second, a musical-comedy version of the medieval tale of *Heloïse et Abélard,* found a much happier outcome (both for Abélard and for the composer), playing a good first run, being subsequently revived and also performed outside France. Another potentially "hot" subject, that of *Mazeppa,* for which the composer was announced in the same season did not materialize: when the show came out (7 September 1872) it had a score by Pourny.

Litolff subsequently composed the music for the féerie *La Belle au bois dormant* at the Châtelet, which had previously mounted his "symphonie dramatique" *Les Guelfes* (18 February 1872), and attempted several other lighter musical stage pieces, one of which, *L'Escadron volant de la reine,* was played at the Opéra-Comique, without equivalent success.

He later composed the score for the opera *Les Templiers,* produced in Brussels in 1886 (Théâtre de la Monnaie 25 January, lib: Jules Adénis, Armand Silvestre, Lionel Bonnemère), and music for other lyric-dramatic pieces.

1866 **Le Chevalier Nahal** (Édouard Plouvier) 1 act Baden-Baden 10 August

1871 **La Boîte à Pandore** (Théodore Barrière) Théâtre de Folies-Dramatiques 17 October

1872 **Heloïse et Abélard** (Clairville, William Busnach) Théâtre des Folies-Dramatiques 19 October

1874 **La Belle au bois dormant** (Busnach, Clairville) Théâtre du Châtelet 4 April

1874 **La Fiancée du roi de Garbe** (Adolphe d'Ennery, Henri Chabrillat) Théâtre des Folies-Dramatiques 29 October

Plate 223. **Listen Lester**

1876 **La Mandragore** (Jules Brésil) Fantaisies-Parisiennes, Brussels 29 January

1888 **L'Escadron volant de la reine** (d'Ennery, Brésil) Opéra-Comique 14 December

THE LITTLE CAFÉ Musical comedy in 3 acts by C M S McLellan based on Tristan Bernard's play *Le Petit Café.* Music by Ivan Caryll. New Amsterdam Theater, New York, 10 November 1913.

Tristan Bernard's delightful comic play had a memorable Parisian success when it was first produced at the Palais-Royal (12 October 1911) with the comedian Le Gallo in its starring role and, in the era where French-language comedies were considered the most effective starting point for English-language libretti, it was a natural choice for musicalization. Composer Ivan Caryll, who had long shared his time between England and France before settling in America, had become something of a specialist in this area. He had had notable successes with adaptations of *Madame Sans-Gêne* (*The Duchess of Dantzic*), *Coquin de printemps* (*The Spring Chicken*), *Le Prince Consort* (*S.A.R.*), *Le Satyre* (*The Pink Lady*) and *La Grimpette* (*Oh! Oh! Delphine*), and he was quick to snap up this latest piece for the same purposes. *The Little Café,* produced, like the last two named musicals, by Broadway's Klaw and Erlanger, gave him yet another hit.

Plate 224. **The Little Café.** *Even when the book-based musical hit Broadway, there still had to be a line of leggy lassies to troop across the stage between the bits of plot.*

The story centered on the little waiter Albert Loriflan (John E Young), who inherits a whole heap of money but is unable to hand in his notice because of a very strict contract with his employer (Harold Vizard). And so, whilst he demurely serves customers in the ''petit café'' by day, Albert leads a lively and extravagant life at night, getting into the clutches of not one but two colorful women and also of the crooked Bigredon (Tom Graves) before ending up safely in the arms of his boss's daughter, Yvonne (Alma Francis). The ''other women'' were played by Hazel Dawn, repeating her famous demi-mondaine portrayal of *The Pink Lady,* as Gaby Gaufrette, Queen of the Night Restaurants, and English low comedienne Gracie Leigh as Katziolinka, an Hungarian singer.

Young had the jolly songs (''You Little Café, Good Day,'' ''They Found Me'' and the well-plugged ''Serve the Caviar'' which returned as the piece's finale), Miss Francis the pretty ones (''I Wonder Whom I'll Marry,'' ''This Gay Paree''), and Miss Leigh the extravagantly comical as she chased after the little hero declaring ''I'm a Hunting Jaguar'' or recommended Hungarian dancing instead of the clinch-and-crawl variety in ''You Call That Dancing?'' The show's big number, however, was saved for Miss Dawn. She had scored a major hit with *The Pink Lady*'s famous waltz song, and here Caryll provided her with another, as near as was possible in style to the last one. Lightning did not strike again, and although ''Just Because It's You'' was a charming piece it did not make the effect of the earlier number, perhaps by virtue of that very noticeable similarity.

The Little Café ran for 148 performances on Broadway before taking to the road but, unlike *The Pink Lady* and *Oh! Oh! Delphine,* it was not produced in London or in Continental Europe. The original play, however, subsequently served as a libretto for further musical comedies both in Austria and in France. Ralph Benatzky's *Das kleine Café* was introduced under the management of Rolf Jahn at Vienna's Deutsches Volkstheater in 1934 with Max Hansen playing the waiter Franz, whilst librettist Jean Valmy turned out a French piece produced as *Le Petit Café* at the Grand Theatre, Mulhouse (mus: Guy Lafarge, Jack Ledru, 14 December 1980).

Le Petit Café also served as the basis for the musical film *The Playboy of Paris* (1930) in which Maurice Chevalier took the starring role.

THE LITTLE CHERUB Musical play in 3 acts by Owen Hall. Lyrics by Adrian Ross. Additional lyrics by

George Grossmith jr and W H Risque. Music by Ivan Caryll. Additional music by Frank E Tours and Paul Rubens. Prince of Wales Theatre, London, 13 January 1906.

The Little Cherub was one of the very few pieces which issued from the pen of librettist Hall that was less than wholly successful, and also the only one which reckoned itself to be based on someone else's work. The supposed source was Henri Meilhac's play *Décoré* (earlier the basis of the 1900 Viennese musical *Der Sechs-Uhr-Zug*) but, in fact, only one insignificant subplot resembled the French play in a story which had a straight-laced earl (Fred Kaye) blackmailed by his daughters (Zena Dare, Gabrielle Ray, Lily Elsie, Grace Pindar) into letting them be coached in their amateur dramatics by a real actress (Evie Greene) who ultimately hooks their Papa. Maurice Farkoa featured as a lecherous Rajah, Lennox Pawle was the asinine Algy who, in the *Décoré* piece of plot, saves a drowning man who isn't, and the to-be-star comedian W H Berry made his first professional musical-theatre appearance as a valet.

Ivan Caryll's attractive music was often weighed down by some tiresome and repetitively suggestive lyrics as Miss Greene scored the evening's hit singing coyly of having had ''Experience,'' Farkoa praised the ''Supper Girl,'' as opposed to the less easy girls who only accept invitations at lunchtime, and Gabs Ray aimed for yet another rich husband on ''Cupid's Rifle Range.'' Berry got some topical comedy in ''I Wasn't Engaged for That'' and the servant characters amusingly described ''Couples'' on a dance floor.

The Little Cherub started dubiously. It opened on election night when the cast was salutorily booed for trying to bring politics into their ad-libs, and thereafter it refused to become the usual kind of George Edwardes success. The producer tried some cosmetics, then acted more strongly by putting star comic Willie Edouin into the role of the Earl and replacing the less-than-manly matinée idol Farkoa with staunch Louis Bradfield. Still it didn't go. So, after 114 performances Edwardes took the show off, commissioned a major rewrite and ordered a half-dozen new songs from specialist interpolators Frank Tours and Jerome Kern. A week after closing, the show reopened with the title *The Girl on the Stage*. Four weeks later it closed definitively.

In spite of this indifferent showing, Charles Frohman took *The Little Cherub* to Broadway. He put Hattie Williams and British comic Jimmy Blakeley in the leads, went mostly back to the original book, flung in a handful more new songs by Kern and Jean Schwartz, and produced the piece for a limited Broadway run prior to touring. But this time *The Little Cherub* refused to be limited. The performance led to newspaper musings on ''the obvious superiority of such British compositions'' to local ones—''several of Mr Caryll's songs were capital, being imbued with a delightful originality; Mr Caryll deserves to be complimented on having achieved the difficult task of not 'unconsciously remembering'''—and the show remained at the Criterion Theater for a profitable five months and 169 performances. It then took to the road on a tour which was eventually directed back to Broadway for a three-week return engagement, and carried on to a fine life on the American touring circuits, long after its parallel existence had ended in Britain. Thus, *The Little Cherub* became one of the very few British musicals in history to have done better on and beyond Broadway than in its country of origin.

USA: Criterion Theater 6 August 1906

LITTLE CHRISTOPHER COLUMBUS Burlesque opera in 2 acts by George R Sims and Cecil Raleigh. Music by Ivan Caryll. Lyric Theatre, London, 10 October 1893.

One of the latter-day London burlesques, produced on the cusp of burlesque's eclipse by ''musical comedy,'' *Little Christopher Columbus* had, typically, very little to do with its alleged subject or hero. The best that could be said was that its Little Christopher did make a voyage from Europe to America—albeit a thoroughly discovered America, and with him disguised as a girl. Sims and Raleigh's Christopher (May Yohé) was a naughty cabin boy in love with Genevieve (Maud Holland), the daughter of Chicago meat king Silas Block (John Furneaux Cook). Pursued, for a complexity of reasons, by a Spanish policeman (George Tate) and by an Irish detective called O'Hoolegan (E J Lonnen), he escapes from Europe across the waters by swapping clothes with the dancer Pepita (Eva Moore), who has been engaged to perform at the World's Fair (cue for the interpolation of such variety acts as were required). The convolutions of the book existed merely to house the songs and dances and a goodly dose of comical scenes, and the show depended for its success on these elements, and not on its story line. The songs and dances proved, fortunately, much better than the scenes. Ivan Caryll, writing his first full score for the London theatre after doing some hefty but successful botching on *La Cigale* and *Ma mie Rosette,* provided two lively comedy songs for Gaiety burlesque star Lonnen (''The Indiarubber Shoe,'' ''Rumpty Tumpty'') and a plantation song ''Oh, Honey, My Honey'' and siesta song (''Lazily, Drowsily'') for his co-star, Miss Yohé. The last three numbers all became major song successes, in spite of the fact that the lady's solos had all to be written within the 10-or-less tones that comprised her vocal range.

Little Christopher Columbus started indifferently, in spite of the quick popularity of its best numbers, and the blame was firmly laid on the libretto. Lonnen's role was a patchwork of his earlier successes and both story and dialogue were banal. George Edwardes set his team to work to straighten things out, but when the show was taken off after 74 performances ''or renovations'' that wording seemingly covered—as it has so many show-business times before and since—a tactful closure. However *Little Christopher Columbus* reopened shortly after and from then it never looked back. It had, admittedly, been much improved since opening, and the biggest single improvement was the addition of American dame-comedian John Sheridan (the creator of Widow O'Brien in *Fun on the Bristol*) to the cast as the Second Mrs Block. This role, originally intended as a parody of the current play hit *The Second Mrs Tanqueray,* but ultimately a two-line part played by Adelaide Newton, was worked up into a low-comic tour de force by and for Sheridan who became the show's star in all but pecking order (May Yohé and her lordly boyfriend had ''bought'' her role and status with a large investment in the production, so she was top-billed come what may). Sheridan helped *Little Christopher Columbus* to a run of 421 performances in 14 months before it took to the road.

The following year Edward Rice produced the show in America with Helen Bertram (succeeded by Bessie Bonehill) in the title role, London's George Walton in Lonnen's part, Harry McDonough as Mrs Block and eight songs by Gustave Kerker added to the score. The entertainment also included a ''sensational fantastic danseuse,'' a Royal Marionette Dance, an eccentric step dance, duet items by the Twin Sisters Abbott, a representation as ''The Puritan Maiden'' by Miss Clara Lane, a tramp act, a topical song act, tableaux vivants by the Kilyani Troupe and a slide show between the acts showing ''novel and beautiful illustrations . . . of the World's Columbian Exposition.'' This now vastly over-stuffed variety musical proved a jolly evening's entertainment and ran for 264 performances at the Garden and later Palmer's Theater.

The show was subsequently and regularly played in Australia as part of Sheridan's repertoire during his later career in that country. It was, however, played in a version which he advertised as ''funnier than a pantomime,'' which warned on its bills that the score was ''arranged by George Gardener,'' and which seemed as if it might have come quite a long way (in more ways than one) since its days at the Lyric Theatre.

Little Christopher Columbus, not unsurprisingly, did not find his way to the Paris stage, but his two hit songs did. ''Lazily, Drowsily'' turned up in a revue at the Variétés, whilst ''O Honey, My Honey'' was reused as part of Caryll's contribution to *La Marraine de Charley*—the French version of *Charley's Aunt*—which was decorated with several songs of his making.

Christopher Columbus had already been present on the stage for several decades, as the hero of a run of Italian operas, and more recently of a Spanish one (*Cristóbal Colón* by Francisco Vidal y Careta, 1892), and he had served since as the star of a handful of musical-theatre pieces in both Britain and America. In London, after being first seen at Covent Garden in Thomas Morton's 1792 Christmastide ''historical play'' *Christopher Columbus, or The World Discovered* and then, grotesquely, in Tom Taylor's 1853 pantomime *Harlequin Columbus, or the Old World and the New* at the Olympic, he had been the star of a burlesque *Columbus, or The Original Pitch in a Merry Key* (Alfred Thompson, Gaiety Theatre 17 May 1869) where he was played by Nellie Farren in breeches. In New York he had previously appeared in John Brougham's burlesque *Columbus Reconstructed* (Winter Garden 9 July 1866), as portrayed by the British actor-author himself alongside Emilie Melville as the Goddess of America, and as played by Edmund Shaftesbury—to the Isabella of Pauline Markham—in the 1890 extravaganza *Christopher Columbus, or The Discovery of America* (Windsor Theater 18 August). The same year Willie Gill and Robert Fraser's *Hendrik Hudson, or The Discovery of Columbus* gave the star role to Fay Templeton as Hudson—Eva Randolph being another be-tighted Columbus, and one more Columbus appeared in 1893 in the person of the tenorious Sgr Perugini (real name, John Chatterton) featured in a R A Barnet/Pfluger piece called *1492,* mounted by E E Rice's Surprise Party. A further Rice piece, *The World's Fair,* written around the theory that Columbus lies buried not in Spain but in Wayback, USA, had comedian Joseph W Herbert as Christopher, as well as as Pygmalion, Don Jose and several other characters. A *Columbus il Filibustero* burlesque was produced in San Francisco in 1865 with Charles Wheatleigh in the title role and Annie Yeamans in breeches, the Fields minstrels did a *The Darktown Circus, or America Discovering Columbus* (1892), Frank Dumont turned out an *America, or The Discovery of Columbus* (1892) for the Rentz-Santley burleycue troupe, and the most famous burlesquer of them all, Lydia Thompson, was also seen as Christopher when, in her last tour of America, she played a *Columbus* written to her measure by George Dance and Archibald Gordon (Grand Opera House, Los Angeles 11 January 1889). However, it seems that Philadelphia may have been the first American city to get a singing-dancing Columbus when, in 1847, a certain South American Sgr Noronha (''sometime violinist to the Emperor of Brazil'') and his wife produced their version of the tale of America's ''discoverer'' on the Pennsylvanian stage.

Vienna saw Columbus on its stage in the spectacular *Die Entdeckung Amerikas* (Emil Korolanyi/Karl Alexander Raida) at the Jantschtheater in 1904 (23 December),

Cassel took pity on *Armer Columbus* in a 1928 opéra-bouffe (Artur Zeininger/Erwin Dressel) whilst Darius Milhaud put out a serious *Christophe Colombe* in the same year and Werner Egk devoted a whole three-part opera (1933 radio, 1942 stage) to *Columbus.* More recently, a winning *Christopher Columbus,* a pastiche Offenbach opéra-bouffe (ad Don White), was staged in Britain, and the Columbus demi-millennium provoked a gaggle of theatrical pieces using the mariner as a subject (or an excuse), ranging from the Metropolitan Opera's *The Voyage* (Philip Glass/David Henry Hwang 12 October) to a *Christopher Columbus, or Business as Usual,* ''a musical about multiculturalism and American history as seen through the eyes of a fourth grader'' performed in a Brooklyn park. It would have been fun to see George Sims find a rhyme for ''multiculturalism.'' In 1999 the most recent musical *Columbus* (Dietrich Stern/Matthias Lösch/Monika Dobrowianska, Walter Weyers) was given its premiere at Memmingen (4 November).

Amongst all these musical Columbuses was a little one featured in the film *Where Do We Go from Here?* (Kurt Weill/Ira Gershwin, 1945).

USA: Garden Theater aka *Little Christopher* 15 October 1894; Australia: Lyceum Theatre, Sydney 4 November 1899

LITTLE JACK SHEPPARD Burlesque operatic melodrama in 3 acts by Henry Pottinger Stephens and William Yardley. Music by Meyer Lutz. Additional music by Florian Pascal, Arthur Cecil, Hamilton Clarke, Henry J Leslie, Alfred Cellier and R Corney Grain. Gaiety Theatre, London, 26 December 1885.

Little Jack Sheppard was the first full-length burlesque produced at the Gaiety Theatre, and the first of the famous series of so-called Gaiety new burlesques which went round the world in what was the last long-term period of success for the burlesque genre in the English-language theatre. Earlier in 1885 John Hollingshead, ill, overworked and near the effective end of his career, had accepted and staged a burlesque by his friends Bill Yardley and ''Pot'' Stephens called *The Vicar of Wide-awake-field* which used an original score by music-publisher-cum-composer ''Florian Pascal'' rather than the usual paste-up of popular melodies. Thanks largely to Arthur Roberts's and Laura Linden's imitations of Irving and Ellen Terry in the central roles, it did fairly well, and Hollingshead planned a second piece—full-length this time—to follow it. By the time *Little Jack Sheppard* went on, however, his successor George Edwardes, who would lead the ''new burlesque'' to its triumphs, had in effect taken over the running of the theatre.

Little Jack Sheppard burlesqued Harrison Ainsworth's novel and the old tale of the thief Sheppard, who was here made into a loveable scamp as a role for the Gaiety's favorite burlesque ''boy,'' Nellie Farren. The well-known comic actor David James played Blueskin, and the thief-taker, Jonathan Wild, was made into a large comedy role for the popular singing comedian Fred Leslie, a newcomer to the Gaiety. In later years, Hollingshead and Edwardes both claimed to have brought Leslie to the Gaiety where he created with Miss Farren the most famous musico-theatrical partnership of the century. The fact that the artist was rehearsing and playing in another (flop) show till three weeks before *Jack Sheppard*'s opening seems to give credence to Edwardes, but it is perfectly possible that Hollingshead had approached him earlier and found him unavailable.

The libretto of the new show was rhyming, metred and often punning, in line with the old burlesque tradition. However, sometimes it moved into a style more akin to legitimate comedy and its lyrics made no concession to burlesque style but remained staunchly popular songs. These lyrics also had original music for, in spite of the reservations of the press over the original music in *The Vicar of Wide-awake-field,* Edwardes stuck to the no-pasticcio principle of the earlier show and musical director Meyer Lutz composed (mostly) and collected from several colleagues a score of almost entirely new music. If the most successful number of the night turned out to be an arrangement of ''Botany Bay'' made by Lutz for David James (one of only two non-original numbers out of 24) there were nevertheless bright moments for Leslie declaring ''I'm Jonathan Oscar Wild'' and for Nellie Farren insisting irresistibly ''Jack Keeps 'em All Alive-o.''

The Fred-and-Nellie team, a splendid physical production of which the highlight was the escape of Jack and Blueskin from Newbury jail and the chase across the London rooftops that followed, and a whole evening's feast of songs and dances secured the success of *Little Jack Sheppard,* the future of the ''new burlesque,'' of Edwardes and of the Gaiety Theatre. The piece ran for 155 performances and, when it was removed to allow the pre-booked summer season of French plays to come in, Edwardes sent it on the road with Fred and Nellie starring, giving the provinces a rare glimpse of such London stars.

Whilst Fred and Nellie toured, Colonel R E J (''Bob'') Miles and his partner Barton Keys mounted a Broadway version of *Little Jack Sheppard* with Nat Goodwin (Wild) and Loie Fuller (Jack) in the starring roles, and author Yardley directing (''with Mr Goodwin'')—a production which like its London equivalent would pass its 100th performance—and the newly fledged Brough and Boucicault company produced the piece in Australia with Brough himself starring opposite Fanny Robina and E W Royce, from the Gaiety, as Blueskin. Once again the result was a major success, leading Brough to repeat the piece the following year and again in 1888 before subletting it to other managers. In 1892 an Australian revival featured Billie Barlow and George Walton, with Royce repeating his Blueskin and another famous veteran, Edwin Kelly, as Trenchard.

Even when the later and rather better-made new burlesques came on the scene, *Little Jack Sheppard* continued to be fondly played throughout the English-speaking world and in 1894, when the new burlesque had become very old hat, Edwardes, needing a stopgap in his program at the Gaiety, even revived the old piece in the West End (18 August). Seymour Hicks was Wild and the music-hall artiste Jessie Preston played Jack, but memories of the adored Fred and Nellie partnership were too fresh in the public's minds and 42 performances were all that the revival achieved. The piece was still to be seen in the 1890s not only in Britain, but also on the American road.

A singing Jack Sheppard returned briefly to London, many years later, portrayed by Nicky Henson in the musical *Stand and Deliver* (Monty Norman/Wolf Mankowitz, Roundhouse 24 October 1972, 14 performances).

The tale of Jack Sheppard (suddenly, but temporarily, banned in 1859 as a stage subject in Britain by a brainstormed Lord Chamberlain) had been previously burlesqued with much success in H B Farnie's 1870 [*Little Jack Sheppard, or*] *The Idle 'Prentice* produced at London's Strand Theatre (10 September) and by Lina Edwin on Broadway (29 November 1870). An American burlesque *Little John Sheppard and Joseph Blueskin* by John F Poole was played at Tony Pastor's Opera House in 1870 and again in 1874, with Edith Blande as Jack, and a more substantial musical *Jack Sheppard* (Adam Itzel/Albert Kimberley Fulton) was seen on the stage of Baltimore's Academy of Music in 1885 (23 November) with English tenor George S Appleby starred as Thames Darrell to Jeannie Winston's Jack and the Wild of Joseph Fay. Another Pastor-Poole burlesque boasting (and delivering) *Forty Female Jack Sheppards* (22 April 1867) proved to be merely a version of *The Forty Thieves.* The most celebrated version of the tale to have been seen on the British stage, however, remains the Adelphi Theatre production of 1839 (28 October) in which Mrs Keeley appeared as Jack, Paul Bedford Blueskin, and Lyon the thieftaker.

USA: Bijou Theater 13 September 1886; Australia: Opera House, Melbourne 19 October 1886

LITTLE JESSIE JAMES Musical comedy in 2 acts by Harlan Thompson. Music by Harry Archer. Longacre Theater, New York, 15 August 1923.

A bedroom-and-livingroom farce of the most cheerful and blissfully busy kind, *Little Jessie James* was set in a New York apartment (one set throughout) which welcomed rendezvous of both licit and apparently illicit kinds, as well as a series of business dealings, all of which got mixed up with one another amidst the welter of comic scenes, songs and dances given by the small principal cast and eight-girl chorus. The highlight of the comic action was a scene with a retractable bed into which members of the cast disappeared in a frantic and farcical scene of semi-sexual shenanigans. The Jessie of the title was not a sharpshooting misprint, but the noisiest lady of the piece, one Miss Jessie Jamieson (Nan Halperin) who, it is said, always gets her man. Jay Velie, Ann Sands, Allen Kearns and Miriam Hopkins were amongst the cast, and the accompaniment to Harry Archer's score was provided by Paul Whiteman's band, The James Boys. That score produced Broadway's surprise hit song of the season, "I Love You," sung by Velie and Miss Sands, a hit which helped to ensure the economy-sized *Little Jessie James* a magnificent run of 393 performances without, however, encouraging other producers to forsake large casts and spectacular productions in the search for similar results.

The show subsequently had a very much wider showing than was usual for American musical comedies of the period. The year after its production it turned up in Germany, where the adapters took the show's original title at face value and rechristened their version variously *Das Wildwestgirl* or *Wildwestmädel,* and it also got a showing in Hungary where Jenő Faragó also dropped the title, whose joke clearly didn't work too well outside America, and simply christened his version by the title of the hit song, *I Love You.* Australia was alone in keeping the original title when the Fuller-Ward management mounted the show with local star Dot Brunton as Jessie, supported by Mary Gannon, Elsie Parkes, Leslie Pearce, Harry Angers, the Boys Symphonic jazz orchestra and, in standard Australian style, with a couple of non-Archer songs edged into the score. It played a good 10 weeks in Melbourne and seven in Sydney (Grand Opera House 27 July 1925).

A decade later, the show finally even turned up in Britain. In 1929 Clayton and Waller had some success with their version of another Archer/Thompson show *Merry, Merry* and a few years later Leslie Henson and Firth Shephard followed where the producers of the moment had led and picked up the earlier *Little Jessie James* as a vehicle for Henson. The libretto was anglicized by Douglas Furber under the title *Lucky Break*—although its original outlines and, of course, the retractable bed remained—and the song schedule was reorganized by Archer with some of the *Jessie James* songs (more or less relyricked by Furber), complemented by other Archer songs written with Walter O'Keefe ("A Kick in the Pants"), Will B Johnstone ("You Can't Take It") and Wolsely Charles ("Hush, Hush"). Strangely, "I Love

You,'' which had already become popular in Britain 10 years earlier, as recorded by Whiteman and by Jackie Gleason, and which had also been heard in the film *The Sun Also Rises,* was amongst those numbers dropped. Henson, Heather Thatcher, Adele Dixon, Richard Hearne, David Hutcheson, Sydney Fairbrother and nine athletic chorus girls who danced out of a bookcase as ''Bookworms'' kept the fun and the show alive for 198 London performances.

In 1942 an attempt was made to revive *Little Jessie James* in America. It was rewritten by Thompson and Gladys Shelley into a wartime setting, equipped with what seem to have been new Archer songs (''I Just Want to Make Friends,'' ''Teach Me to Dance,'' ''Who's to Blame,'' ''Rainy Afternoon,'' ''Gotta Have a Man Around the House'') to such an extent that, apparently, little more than the famous scene with the bed remained. Produced as *Heels Together* at Scarsdale, New York (15 September) it folded before making it to the metropolis. In 1953 Archer himself masterminded another attempt to revive the piece, with the old book, the new songs and the old title, but it too folded after three weeks on the road.

Hungary: Lujza Blaha Színház *I Love You* 31 August 1924; Germany: Stadttheater, Düsseldorf *Das Wildwestgirl* 16 December 1928; Australia: New Princess Theatre, Melbourne 11 April 1925; UK: Strand Theatre *Lucky Break* 2 October 1934

Plate 225. **Little Johnny Jones.** *George M Cohan in the title role of his musical.*

LITTLE JOHNNY JONES (The American Jockey) Musical play in 3 acts by George M Cohan. Parsons' Theater, Hartford, Conn, 10 October 1904; Liberty Theater, New York, 7 November 1904.

It was only three years since the young and multi-talented George M Cohan had first turned his hand to creating and playing full-length musical comedies rather than the comic song-and-dance sketches contained in the Cohan family's vaudeville act, and *Little Johnny Jones* was already his third such piece. Now more widely ambitious, however, he moved for this occasion into an alliance with producer Sam H Harris (''manager Charles C Stumm''), and stepped his sights up a notch to write, direct and perform *Little Johnny Jones* with, this time, instead of the billing ''the Four Cohans in . . . ,'' the simple statement ''George M Cohan in . . .'' The others were still there, but George was the solo star. ''He is not only the central star, but every line and every song including the music is of his own composition'' gasped the critic at Hartford, Conn. The gasp was understandable, at a time when American musical-comedy scores were mostly made up of a patchwork of publisher-pushed numbers rather than songs made specially to suit their show. Cohan's ambition showed up in another way, too: *Little Johnny Jones* made its way swiftly to Pennsylvania and then, rather than to one of the less up-market New York houses which had housed his first two pieces, to Broadway's new Liberty Theater.

The new show and Cohan's character in it were suggested by the exploits of the American jockey Tod Sloane who had ridden in the English Derby the previous year. Cohan appeared as jockey Johnny Jones, over in England to ride the colt ''Yankee-Doodle'' in the blue riband of the turf. He doesn't have an easy time. He loses the race, beastly Anthony Anstey (played by Cohan's father, Jerry J Cohan) revengefully gets the boy warned off the turf for allegedly pulling his horse, and rich, crusading Mrs Kenworthy (mother Helen F Cohan) arranges for her niece Goldie Gates (wife Ethel Levey), whom Johnny loves, to wed a titled Englishman. It takes two further acts of action and music, including some kidnapping highjinks in San Francisco's Chinatown, for Johnny to clear his name, defeat Anstey and rescue and win the kidnapped Goldie in a series of events which didn't seem too far away from the more melodramatic moments of *Fritz, Our Cousin German* and other such old-time favorites.

Little Johnny Jones, however, had a different, rather insouciant flavour to it which contrasted wholly with *Fritz* and its ilk, just as the red-white-and-true-blue Cohan himself contrasted utterly with the quaint, accented Emmet and his kind. This *Boy's Own* tale was a thoroughly American one. It was also easily Cohan's best show and role to date and, through the many that followed, it remained one of his finest. The part of the bright and bouncy little jockey, idolized by the girls yet true to his Goldie, ill-done-by but determined, and ultimately all-American heroic, gave him every opportunity he needed, and the songs with which he furnished the character proved to be amongst his most popular. "The Yankee Doodle Boy," "Life's a Funny Proposition After All" and "Give My Regards to Broadway" gave the author-star three hits in one production. Miss Levey had a fine role as Goldie, disguised variously as her own British fiancé and as a French girl and all but tied to the railway tracks in the last act, and several songs ("Goodbye Flo," "Mademoiselle Fanchette"); the rising juvenile man Donald Brian complemented Cohan's plug for Broadway by singing in praise of "Good Old California"; and Truly Shattuck played a busybody newspaper lady and sang apropos of nothing at all about "Nesting in a New York Tree," whilst the plot was intermittently helped along by Tom Lewis as a detective disguised, variously, as a fop, a lady and a San Francisco "Chink." The show's lively selection of songs was complemented by several choruses and by a (distinctly un-American) double sextet on *Florodora* lines for six London cabdrivers and six little American girls ("'Op in Me 'Ansom").

Cohan's expertise also extended to the staging of the piece, and his second-act closing became famous. Johnny, left in Britain to clear his name, stands on the pier whilst the ship on which he should have sailed heads for America across the back of the stage. Then, from the ship, a rocket goes up—a message from his detective ally that he has found the evidence they need of Anstey's villainy—and on this cue Cohan leapt joyfully into action with a vigorous one-man reprise of "Give My Regards to Broadway" in a finale which brought down the house. But although there was plenty of song and dance for the audience's entertainment, the admittedly melodramatic and episodic story was never out of sight for long, and all of the play's characters had a part and a purpose in that story. *Little Johnny Jones* did not tail away into a virtual variety show of acts and interpolated numbers like so many so-called musical comedies of the time. It also had, amongst the conventionalities of its disguises and horrid foreigners, some little originalities: rare was the musical-comedy hero who rode in the Derby and lost!

Little Johnny Jones was not destined for a long Broadway run. After just 52 performances Cohan uprooted his show from the Liberty Theater and took it on the road, where the principal and most lucrative of his activities had always been, but he returned the show to New York the following May (New York Theater 8 May, 128 performances), again in November (New York Theater 13 November) and yet again in 1906, so that ultimately Broadway saw some two hundred performances of *Little Johnny Jones.*

Very few of Cohan's works were ever produced abroad, and the career of *Little Johnny Jones,* with its starry-and-stripey chauvinism, was limited to America. It was given a major revival in 1980 (ad Alfred Uhry, 25 June) when it was produced at the Goodspeed Opera House with Tom Hulce in the role Cohan had written for himself. It was subsequently toured and brought to Broadway almost two years later (Alvin Theater 21 March 1982) with the popular vocalist Donny Osmond starring, where it played for one performance.

A 1923 film entitled *Little Johnny Jones* based itself on the character Cohan had invented rather than on the show. Johnny Hines played the jockey alongside Wyndham Standing as the Earl of Bloomsbury.

Another, one-act and British piece called *Little Johnnie Jones* written by Harry Vernon with songs by Frank E Tours and Preston Wayne was produced on a music-hall bill at the Tottenham Palace, London, 9 May 1910.

LITTLE MARY SUNSHINE New musical about an old operetta in 2 acts by Rick Besoyan. Orpheum Theater, New York, 18 November 1959.

A little burlesque of bits plucked here and there from the Broadway musical theatre of the first 30 or 40 years of the century, *Little Mary Sunshine* was set amongst the same Rocky Mountains that had hosted *Rose Marie* where Forest Rangers who have wandered in from *Naughty Marietta* serenade the owner of the local pub (Eileen Brennan) before breakfast. Mary is a foundling, like *Sally,* and she sings *Sally*-ish songs with such titles as "Look for a Sky of Blue." Captain "Big Jim" Warington (William Graham), the head of the Rangers, is a baritone and he expresses himself baritonically in terms such as "You're the Fairest Flower" to little Mary. Big Jim has a subordinate called Billy Jester (John McMartin) and Mary has a maid called Nancy Twinkle (Elmarie Wendel) to supply the soubret work, and the Viennese influence arrives with a vocalist called Mme Ernestine Liebich (Elizabeth Parrish), who describes "Izzenschnooken on the Lovely Essenzook See" as if she had recently been to see *Music in the Air* (but certainly never a real Viennese show) and demands of a passing General (Mario Siletti) "Do You Ever Dream of Vienna?" in predictable Amerikanerstrüdel style. Some of the score's more direct parodies included a "Colorado Love Call" echoing *Rose*

Marie, a ''Naughty, Naughty Nancy'' which recalled *Naughty Marietta* and, popping back for a bit to the 19th century, a *Florodora* double-sextet called ''Tell a Handsome Stranger.'' As for the plot well, the piece's nasty Indian is reformed, its nice Indian is given a great chunk of Colorado, and all ends happily.

The show first saw the light of stage in a much shorter form during the mid-1950s, and it was subsequently extended to its full two-act form and produced by Howard Barker, Cynthia Baer and Robert Chambers at off-Broadway's Orpheum Theater. Staged by its author, a former light-opera vocalist, in an imitation of the precious style of some of the worse and more stilted operatic and operettic productions of not only earlier years but of the present day, it proved highly popular, remaining at the Orpheum for three years and 1,143 performances. It was subsequently produced in Britain with Patricia Routledge (Mary), Terence Cooper (Jim), Bernard Cribbins (Billy), Joyce Blair (Nancy) and Gita Denise (Ernestine), but its parodies appeared more amateurish than endearing to English audiences and it became another on the long list of successful off-Broadway musicals to founder in the West End (44 performances). An Australian production under the management of the Elizabethan Theatre Trust and Garnet Carroll, featuring Geraldene Morrow and Myron Natwick, also flopped in just a month's run in Sydney.

UK: Comedy Theatre 17 May 1962; Australia: Palace Theatre, Sydney 10 February 1962

Recordings: original cast (Capitol), London cast (Pye/DRG)

LITTLE ME Musical comedy in 2 acts by Neil Simon based on the novel of the same name by Patrick Dennis. Lyrics by Carolyn Leigh. Music by Cy Coleman. Lunt-Fontanne Theater, New York, 17 November 1962.

Patrick Dennis's brilliantly funny and best-selling burlesque of the star autobiography genre, *Little Me,* was translated to the stage by Neil Simon, who had not long since had his first Broadway triumph with the comedy *Come Blow Your Horn.* Cy Coleman and Carolyn Leigh, whose first Broadway musical *Wildcat,* two years earlier, had produced some success and a hit song, provided the score. It proved to be an outstanding combination, with Coleman matching the extravagantly witty burlesque humor of the text with music that was equally as humorous, and displaying for the first time his unequaled ability amongst modern composers as a writer of genuine and sophisticated burlesque, as opposed to the soupy imitation-cum-parodies of earlier styles involved in such pieces as the then recent off-Broadway success, *Little Mary Sunshine.*

Little Me is Belle Poitrine (Nancy Andrews), née Schlumpfert on the very wrongest side of the tracks. The aging Belle is dictating her autobiography, the story of her young self (Virginia Martin) and her attempt to acquire the wealth, culture and social position which the devastatingly rich, cultured and social mother (Nancy Cushman) of Noble Eggleston (Sid Caesar) had told her were indispensable for anyone with ambitions to be her son's wife. Armed with nothing more than the best and biggest pair of bazooms in Illinois, Belle went via slum landlord Mr Pinchley (money) and a spell in vaudeville (culture), to marriage first with a gormless GI called Fred Poitrine, thus acquiring her mammarily predestined name, and then with French singing star Val du Val, whose demise in the sinking of the *Gigantic* brought her more money. Thus equipped, she entered films (more . . . er . . . culture), won a Golden Turkey for her biblical spectacular *Moses Takes a Wife* (even more culture), and had oil discovered on her back lot (more money than you can count), before going off to Europe to find social position. In Monte Carlo she chummed up with a penniless Prince, helped him with his national debt and in return was given a Rosenzweigan title (definitely social position). All three aims accomplished after so many years, she returned to America and Noble. At last they could be wed! But the celebratory champagne turned teetotal Noble into a raving alcoholic and in no time the man whose life had been a double dose of success from his cradle was a bum. So Belle gave up and married George Musgrove (Swen Swenson) who'd been pursuing her bazooms since the beginning of Act I and settled down to write her autobiography. But wait! All is not yet over. It may have taken time, but there is a walk-in sunset waiting for our heroine at the final curtain.

The score included three take-away songs: Belle's determined carol to escaping from ''The Other Side of the Tracks,'' George Musgrove's song-and-dance seduction ''I've Got Your Number'' which, on the stage, featured a memorably slick Bob Fosse solo routine for the handsome, gangstery Swenson, and Fred Poitrine's myopic meeting with ''A Real Live Girl'' (''pardon me, Miss, but I've never been kissed by . . .''), later reprised longingly by the entire American army. Amongst the rest, the most plot-worthy was the tune ''I Love You'' which rang out every time Belle and Noble touched each other. Initially introduced at their first meeting in Drifter's Row with Noble covered in the slops slung from Belle's rubbish-pail, it returns throughout, rising to operettic proportions as the pair duet magnificently on the rapidly subsiding deck of the doomed ship *Gigantic.* Belle's insistence that old Pinchley is a real nice person ''Deep Down Inside,'' her vaudeville turn ''Dimples'' and her film-starry ''Poor Little Hollywood Star,'' Val du Val's cabaret song ''Boom-Boom'' and a title song shared by the old and young Belles also contributed to the fun, whilst a crisply mannered dance to ''The Rich Kids Rag'' turned up another memorable dance moment.

If the role of Belle cornered most of the score and much of the comedy, the largest share of the latter went to Sid Caesar who, in Simon's text, appeared as each and every one of the men in Belle's life with the exception of the ultimately unlucky George Musgrove. Caesar's top billing was justified by a virtuoso role which allowed him to impersonate the aged Pinchley, the Frenchman, the gormless Fred and the Rosenzweigian Prince in a gala of comic acting.

Even with the very popular Caesar at its masthead, *Little Me* did not have the success it might have had on Broadway. A fair rather than a fine run of 257 performances prefaced a London production sponsored by Bernard Delfont, Arthur Lewis and Tom Arnold in which Bruce Forsyth and Eileen Gourlay starred. This did better, with a run of 10 months (334 performances), but it was clear that upmarket burlesque of this kind, whilst it had very strong partisans amongst its partisans (''the most witty and richly entertaining comedy musical to come to us from America since *Pal Joey*'') did not have battalions of them.

In 1982 a clutch of seven individuals and corporations produced a Broadway revival of a lightly revised *Little Me* (Eugene O'Neill Theater 21 January 1982). Several numbers were removed (''Dimples,'' the vaudeville duet ''Be a Performer'' and ''Poor Little Hollywood Star'') whilst a new opening song for Belle (''Don't Ask a Lady'') replaced the original one. More surprisingly, the Sid Caesar role was cut in two for Victor Garber and James Coco. The revival folded after 36 performances, but Bernard Delfont's office remounted the show at London's Prince of Wales Theatre (30 May 1984) with television comedy star Russ Abbott playing the reconstituted multiple role and Sheila White as a Belle who had got her ''Dimples'' back. Once again, London welcomed the show more warmly than Broadway, through a run of 423 performances.

New York was given one more chance in 1998 (Roundabout/Stage Right 12 November) to appreciate *Little Me* in a version again revised by Simon which went the opposite way to the last. Faith Prince got to double both the old and the young Belle, and Martin Short added one extra role, that of a Buchsbaum brother (who presumably wasn't a man in Belle's life, but who's counting), to the original list. It totted up one hundred performances.

UK: Cambridge Theatre 18 November 1964

Recordings: original cast (RCA), London cast (Pye), revival cast 1998 (Varese Sarabande)

THE LITTLE MILLIONAIRE Musical comedy in 3 acts by George M Cohan. George M Cohan Theater, New York, 25 September 1911.

Although not one of Cohan's most memorable shows, *The Little Millionaire,* with its author at its head ''a human dynamo of nervous energy,'' found itself a willing Broadway public for 192 performances and a nationwide one for even longer. The entertainment served up much the same red-white-and-not-the-slightest-bit-blue mixture that Cohan had been serving up for the past decade to a fond public which knew precisely what to expect from him. There was a simplistic story of a father (Jerry Cohan) and son (George Cohan) out to get themselves wed in order to inherit, to which was addded a bunch of the author's usual lively and straightforward type of songs and some colorful production numbers. George ended up getting Goldie Grey (Lila Rhodes) and his father Mrs Prescott (Nellie Cohan), although neither got any Cohan song hits from amongst ''The Musical Moon,'' ''Oh! You Wonderful Girl,'' ''Any Place the Old Flag Flies,'' ''Barnum Had the Right Idea,'' ''New Yorkers,'' ''We Do the Dirty Work,'' ''The Little Millionaire'' and ''Come with Me to the Bungalow'' (Cohan's Bungalow Song) to line up alongside those from the best of the previous shows. The busy Cohan and his partner, Sam H Harris, did however get a tidy profit out of *The Little Millionaire* during a season in which they had a mass of productions—mostly non-musical—on the road, confirming, if it needed confirming, the continuing popularity of both the star and his exuberantly, even agressively, American style of show.

LITTLE MISS NOBODY Musical comedy in 2 acts by H Graham. Music by Arthur E Godfrey. Additional music by Landon Ronald. Added songs by Paul and Walter Rubens. Lyric Theatre, London, 14 September 1898.

In a London musical theatre dominated by George Edwardes and a handful of other producers, unexpected musical-comedy hits from untried producers were few and far between. *Little Miss Nobody* was one. Written by the playwright H Graham, author of the comedy *The County Councillor,* with music by ballad composer Arthur Godfrey, the piece was played for one tryout performance at Cheltenham's Opera House (5 March 1898) under the management of actor and would-be producer Yorke Stephens. There it was seen and taken up by Tom B Davis, a former solicitor and theatre-manager, who had the show titivated with some songs from Paul Rubens and his brother Walter, sold the American rights to Charles Frohman, and then produced it himself at London's Lyric Theatre.

Kate Cutler starred as Elsie Crockett, the little governess of the title, who wins noble Guy Cheviot (Yorke Stephens), Fred Eastman was the moneylender Potter, and Gracie Leigh, Lydia West and Dora Dent played three music-hall artists, all of whom end up in a Scots castle mistaken for aristocrats. The grand old comedian Lionel Brough played the heroine's father and the Gaiety's dragon Maria Davis was Guy's lofty aunt. The score was an unexceptional one, with some jolly, ephemeral numbers being topped by one deprecating the ghastly "Gay Excursionist" as described by Miss Leigh. A later addition, however, proved the most popular: "Trixie of Upper Tooting," an early Paul Rubens hit described an unpleasant little lady to a jaunty tune. Sung in the show by Lionel Mackinder and later George Grossmith, it became a music-hall success in the hands of Ada Reeve who later claimed to have written the tasteless lyric which the sheet music attributed to Rubens.

Frohman's production actually opened first, in Philadelphia, with ex-D'Oyly Carte chorister Ethel Jackson in the title role and comic William Norris top-billed. The undercast mounting was shuddered at as being "heavy English" (by a critic who apparently preferred "light American") and proved a disaster, and two weeks at the Broad Street Theater and a quick visit to Baltimore, et al, finished its American life. It also finished the life of its co-producer, journalist and playwright Nat C Childs, who committed suicide soon after.

On Shaftesbury Avenue, however, *Little Miss Nobody* became a quick and comfortable success, running for more than six months and two hundred performances during which Davis's cast went decidedly upmarket with the addition of such performers as comedian John Le Hay and operatic singer John Coates, for whom the role of Guy was made into a considerable singing one. Equally, the neophyte producer did not shrink from enlivening his "bill" with such plot-irrelevant items as Loie Fuller doing what one paper described as "posing in coloured lights."

Before the show closed in London, Edward Compton's Company had taken it on the road with Hettie Dene, Sidney Barraclough and young Adrienne Augarde in the tiny role of Maggie, and this was soon followed by a second company which played two seasons on the road. In 1903 George Walton produced the show in South Africa and in 1904 a revised version again played the British provinces. And as late as 1923 someone still fondly remembered *Little Miss Nobody,* for in that year its story was used as the subject for a silent film!

The authors of *Little Miss Nobody* never confirmed their success, but other *Little Miss Nobody* beginners did: Davis went on to produce *Florodora* the next year, Gracie Leigh (who had won her London debut only by the late drop-out of soprano Florence Perry from the cast) went on to become a major musical-comedy star, and Ethel Jackson became Broadway's "merry widow."

USA: Broad Street Theater, Philadephia 5 September 1898

Film: Carlton Productions/Wilfred Noy 1923 (silent)

LITTLE NELLIE KELLY Song and dance show in 2 acts by George M Cohan. Liberty Theater, New York, 13 November 1922.

The only one of George M Cohan's long list of mostly successful American musical comedies to be internationally played, *Little Nellie Kelly* was a sentimental bog-American-Irish tale with considerable family resemblances to the *Irene*/ *Sally* school of Cinderella musicals, and with perhaps rather less to the vigorous pieces Cohan had written for himself 15 and 20 years earlier.

Little Nellie Kelly (Elizabeth Hines) is an American-Irish shopgirl who is courted by the wealthy Jack Lloyd (Barrett Greenwood) but who prefers to give her hand and heart to the rough and ready, but Irish, Jerry Conroy (Charles King), in spite of the fact that he sings dubious things like "You Remind Me of My Mother" to her. The subplot involved Jerry in accusations of stealing some jewels from Jack's aunt, Mrs Langford (Georgia Caine). If this was all conventional-sounding stuff, it had to be noted that Sally, Irene and even Mary, the musical-comedy megaheroines of the era, all found their love with wealthy heroes, and giving up a life of musical-comedy luxury for a lad, even if he were Irish, was probably either old-fashioned or just plain dumb. For the moment it was also, at least, different. The show's songs included such titles as "Dancing My Worries Away," "The Name of Kelly," "The Hinky Dee," "Until My Luck Comes Rolling Along" and "All My Boys," but far and away the most successful piece of the evening was Jerry's love song "Nellie Kelly, I Love You," a number which turned out to be Cohan's biggest song success in years.

Little Nellie Kelly ran for 274 performances at Broadway's Liberty Theater before heading not only out onto the American road, as was normal and expected with a Cohan show, but overseas, which was not. C B Cochran took up the London rights and produced the show at the Oxford Theatre, where he had recently had a considerable hit with *The Better 'Ole.* Ralph Whitehead outdid Roy Royston for the hand of June in a cast that also included Anita Elson, Maidie Hope and Sonnie Hale. It had taken 20 years for a Cohan show to get to play London, but, now, the one that did proved to be thoroughly to London's taste. With a score of 265 West End performances *Little Nellie Kelly* did nearly as well in Britain as on Broadway.

In 1923 Hugh J Ward produced the show in Australia as a successor to his highly successful mountings of Broadway's *The O'Brien Girl* and *Tangerine* and, if it did not quite equal the splendid record put up by the former of those shows, Mamie Watson and Leyland Hodgson were nevertheless seen in Australia's version of *Little Nellie Kelly* for a fine four months in Melbourne and two and a half in Sydney (Grand Opera House 9 August 1924).

In 1940 a film was made by MGM under the title *Little Nellie Kelly* with Judy Garland starred as Nellie. Jack McGowan's screenplay kept virtually nothing of Cohan's story, and Roger Edens's songs made space only for "Nellie Kelly I Love You" after the originally scheduled "You Remind Me of My Mother" ended up on the cutting-room floor. The score did, however, include one song that would be considerably bigger even than Cohan's not inconsiderable hit—"Singin' in the Rain."

UK: Oxford Theatre 2 July 1923; Australia: New Princess Theatre, Melbourne 22 December 1923

LITTLE NEMO Musical play in 3 acts by Harry B Smith. Music by Victor Herbert. New Amsterdam Theater, New York, 20 October 1906.

Little Nemo was one of the spectacular, variety-filled children's musical shows that prospered as family entertainment on Broadway in the early part of the 20th century much as pantomime prospered in Britain, and of which such pieces as *The Wizard of Oz* and *Babes in Toyland* were enduring examples. Harry Smith developed this one for Klaw and Erlanger from Winsor McKay's *New York Herald* comic strip of the same name.

In Smith's story, Little Nemo (Master Gabriel, not actually a child actor but a midget) goes off to Slumberland to find the elixir of youth. On his travels he encounters the nice King of the land, Morpheus (W W Black), but also the villainous Dr Pill (Joseph Cawthorn), and a great deal of scenery (Young brothers and Boss, Ernest Albert and John Young) and dancing. The scenic plot led Little Nemo through Slumberland, the Land of Saint Valentine, a Weather Factory in Cloudland, the shipwreck of the Ship of Dreams, the Island of the Table d'hôte, a Dream of the Fourth of July and a battleship where the entire company paraded in naval whites. One writer voted that it was rather "like *Peter Pan* . . . with the accompaniment of stirring and tuneful music, capital songs, glittering pageants, graceful ballets and clever fooling by those inimitable comedians Joseph Cawthorn, Billie B Van and Harry Kelly." Victor Herbert's score did not produce any lasting pieces to equal his *Babes in Toyland* bonbons, but such numbers as "Won't You Be My Sweetheart?" for Nemo and the Little Princess (Aimée Erlich), "If I Could Teach My Teddy Bear to Dance" as sung by the Candy Kid (Florence Tempest) and "The Happy Land of Once Upon a Time" served their purpose in the show alongside orchestral music accompanying a Valentine sequence, a Will o' the Wisp routine, a Cannibal scene, a review of athletes, a barbecue, and a comical zouave march featuring Van and Kelly.

Richard Rodgers and Vincent Youmans apparently both remembered seeing *Little Nemo* as one of the earliest theatrical parts of their childhood, but it does not seem to have left any influence on their writing. However, an ad-lib by Joseph Cawthorn in a catalogue of imaginary animals with which he enlivened his part apparently introduced the "whiffenpoof" into the American language, and the Yale University society which took up the creature as their name, and the title of their famous club song, lasted rather longer than anything else from *Little Nemo's* 111 Broadway performances. These performances were followed by two seasons of touring, touring which was limited in scope by the amount of scenery that Herbert Gresham's production required to be carried. ("[I]t can travel only on private trains, as it requires ten cars to carry the scenery and the company. The production is so big that week stands will have to made out of cities in which a company usually remains only two or three nights.") A revised edition was put on the road by Klaw and Erlanger in 1910.

In 1992 *Little Nemo (Adventures in Slumberland)* made his way to the cinema screen, but film producers Hemdale did not avail themselves of Herbert's music as an accompaniment.

A LITTLE NIGHT MUSIC Musical comedy in 2 acts by Hugh Wheeler suggested by the screenplay *Smiles of a Summer Night* by Ingmar Bergman. Music and lyrics by Stephen Sondheim. Shubert Theater, New York, 25 February 1973.

Following on behind his two revusical American pieces of the early 1970s, *Company* and *Follies,* Stephen Sondheim expanded his talents as both lyricist and composer into a rather different sphere with the score to Hugh Wheeler's stage adaptation of the screenplay of the atmospheric 1955 Swedish film *Smiles of a Summer Night.*

Fredrik Egerman (Len Cariou) is a middle-aged lawyer whose second wife is the young and still decidedly immature Anne (Victoria Mallory). It is an immaturity which means that Anne, in spite of months of marriage, is still a virgin, and she is showing no signs of becoming anything else. Whilst Fredrik holds back with decreasing patience from leaping amorously upon his wife, the theatre company in which Desirée Armfeldt (Glynis Johns) is playing comes to town. Desirée, who troupes the cities of Sweden whilst her young, illegitimate daughter, Fredrika (Judy Kahan), remains in the care of her grandmother, Madame Armfeldt (Hermione Gingold), is now in the throes of an affair with a bristling hussar, Carl Magnus Malcolm (Lawrence Guittard), a sexual despot with a total belief in the rights of man (as opposed to those of woman). The Count's predecessor, however, as witnessed in the name of Desirée's child, was the between-wives Fredrik. When Desirée hears of her ex-lover's predicament she offers, first, practical consolation, and then a different kind of invitation. And, thus, it happens that all the protagonists of this amorous sex-tangle turn up one weekend at the palatial home of Madame Armfeldt: Fredrik, Anne, Carl Magnus, his miserably maltreated wife Charlotte (Patricia Elliott), Desirée, and Fredrik's burstingly teenaged son, Henrik. As the young (Fredrika), the old (Mme Armfeldt) and the amused, uncomplicated servants (Petra, Frid) look on, the waltz of changing partners begins. Hearts and other parts are bared, realizations blossom, practicalities emerge in a series of events and encounters often more farcical than romantic, before Anne runs off with Henrik, Charlotte drags Carl Magnus at least temporarily back, and Fredrik and Desirée relax, with a little bit of Petra's practicality, into a comfortable, middle-aged partnership which is so much more suitable than their respective chases after exhaustingly active youth.

The wry, sophisticated comicalities of the show's script were dazzlingly echoed in a waltzing score which was musically far in advance of its predecessors. It skated excitingly through the full range of male and female voices, blending into some of the most fascinating ensembles heard on Broadway in decades, yet always in allegiance with its witty and elegant words, and at the same time both melodic and interesting. There were solos which touched on the style of Sondheim's earlier works—Petra (D Jamin Bartlett) explaining that she will naturally marry ''The Miller's Son'' one day, but seeing that as no bar to a healthy sex life in the meanwhile, and Madame Armfeld mooning over the debased status of ''Liaisons'' since the days when she was the plaything of royalty—but others took on a less set-piece tone. Fredrik debates patteringly whether to make his move on his wife ''Now,'' whilst she promises in soaring soprano tones that ''Soon'' she won't shy away, and pubescent Henrik, curdled with impatience at always being always told to wait till ''Later,'' supplies what becomes a frantic tenor and cello obbligato when the three solos interlace in a trio of musical frustrations. The rest of the ensemble music included a piece expressing everyone's feelings over the prospect of ''A Weekend in the Country''—the reasons for not going are manifold, but no one would dream of missing out—and two illustrative pieces for the quintet of vocalists which served the essentially intimate piece as a chorus (''Night Waltz,'' ''The Sun Won't Set''), whilst Fredrik enthused unenthusiastically to Desirée that ''You Must Meet My Wife,'' turned over comical maybes in his mind in parallel to Carl Magnus's different ones in ''It Would Have Been Wonderful,'' and Anne and Charlotte ran down marriage in ''Every Day a Little Death'' in some of the evening's musical duologues.

The piece of the show's score which became a popular success, however, was none of these. It was a rueful, gentle, rather obscurely lyricked piece delivered by Desirée, in the midst of all the hurly-burly of the house party, as she sits and wonders if she hasn't rather made a mess of things. Before *A Little Night Music* had finished making use of it, ''Send in the Clowns'' made its way into the repertoire of Frank Sinatra, on to the radios and gramophones of the world, and via cabaret and concert to the list of Broadway standards, where it stands alongside ''Don't Cry for Me, Argentina'' as one of the unlikeliest out-of-context show hits of the era.

A Little Night Music took the season's Tony Awards for best musical, book and score (Sondheim's third consecutive win in this category), and for Miss Johns's performance, and went on to play for 601 performances on Broadway. It was only nine months into its run when an Australian production appeared, under the management of J C Williamson Ltd, with Tania Elg (Desirée), Bruce Barry (Fredrik), Tim Page (Henrik) and comedienne Anna Russell (Mme Armfeldt) starred in what proved to be one of the country's most outstanding musical productions in years. However, like its American counterpart (still in the red at the end of its run), it found that cash returns and artistic merits did not necessarily go together. It played but four months in Sydney and as many weeks in Melbourne (Her Majesty's Theatre 10 July 1974). These considerations prompted London to pull the plug on its already cast and prepared production, but the show did ultimately make it to London, in 1975, with Jean Simmons, who had been touring America in the role of Desirée, starring alongside Miss Gingold, repeating her original role, Joss Ackland (Fredrik), Terry Mitchell (Henrik) and Veronica Page (Anne) in a reproduction of the Broadway version. Once again the production created great enthusiasms, and once again it struggled to make ends meet through 406 performances.

An Austrian version, which again reproduced the ingenious and much-praised Broadway scenery and production, went back to the film title, *Das Lächeln einer Sommernacht.* Susanne Almassy starred as Desirée, performing ''Wo sind die Clowns,'' Gideon Singer played Fredrik, Zarah Leander supplied the marquee value in the role of Madame Armfeldt, and the young Dagmar Koller appeared as Petra through 65 performances. A film version, which featured several of the original cast, Elizabeth Taylor as Desirée and a lot of dubbing, went through all kinds of problems and finally sneaked out late, lavishly cut and low-profile.

Following its initial major productions, *A Little Night Music* went through a long and widespread series of stagings in regional theatres all around the world, becoming in the process a standard item in the international repertoire. In 1989 it was given a return season in London under the management of H M Tennent Ltd, in a production transferred from the Chichester Festival (Piccadilly Theatre 10 October, 152 performances) with Dorothy Tutin (Desirée), Eric Flynn (Fredrik) and Lila Kedrova (Mme Armfeldt), in 1990 (3 August) the New York City Opera mounted a production, with Sally Ann Howes featured as Desirée, which they reprised on several occasions, and in 1995 (Olivier Theatre 26 September) Britain's National Theatre mounted a production with Judi Dench playing Desirée alongside Laurence Guittard, now as Fredrik, and the inevitable once-cut now-replaced "additional number" (for Charlotte). The Melbourne Theatre Company brought the piece back for a fresh run (Playhouse 1 February 1997) in Australia's main centers as well, with Helen Morse (Desirée), Ruth Cracknell (Mme Armfeldt), John O'May (Fredrik) and Lisa McCune (Anne) featured, and for a Sydney season (1 September 1998), as the 25-year-old *A Little Night Music* settled comfortably into its rightful place as a musical-theatre classic of the first order.

Australia: Her Majesty's Theatre, Sydney 30 November 1973; Austria: Theater an der Wien *Das Lächeln einer Sommernacht* 14 February 1975; UK: Adelphi Theatre 15 April 1975; Hungary: Madách Színház *Egy nyári éj mosolya* 20 March 1997

Film: New World/Sascha-Wien Films 1978

Recordings: original cast (Columbia), London cast (RCA), film soundtrack (Columbia), selection in German (Preiser, Austria), studio cast (TER), London revival 1995 (Tring)

LITTLER, Emile (Sir) [né RAINES, Norman] (b Ramsgate, 9 September 1903; d Ditchling, 23 January 1985). British producer of London and provincial shows through more than three decades.

The son of suburban theatre managers, Frank LITTLER [né RAINES] and Agnes [Mary] LITTLER, Littler had his first theatrical job as assistant manager at the Ambassador's Theatre in Southend-on-Sea. He subsequently fulfilled a series of company management and stage management positions on both sides of the Atlantic before in 1931 taking over the running of the Birmingham Repertory Theatre. In the mid-1930s he began a commercial producing career, touring both plays and musical comedies. The musicals were mostly revivals of proven favorites, but occasionally, as with the South Seas musical *Aloma and Nutane* (1938) starring Carl Brisson and Gabrielle Brune, they were billed fatally as "prior to London presentation" and didn't make it.

It was in the early 1940s that Littler made his first London ventures with wartime revivals of *The Maid of the Mountains* with Sylvia Cecil, *The Belle of New York* with Evelyn Laye and a successful, rewritten version of *The Quaker Girl* featuring Celia Lipton. He had less luck with his first London production of an original musical, when a version of the famous farce *When Knights Were Bold,* in which he himself had had a hand in the adaptation and the direction, was a 10-performance flop. Sigmund Romberg's *Sunny River* with which he followed it at the Piccadilly Theatre lasted only two months, but he had better fortune when he took a small interest in Lee Ephraim and Tom Arnold's presentation of the Cicely Courtneidge/Jack Hulbert musical *Something in the Air* (1943) and then joined them more fully in the London version of Cole Porter's *Panama Hattie.*

His breakthrough in the London theatre came with the considerable success of two further imports, *Song of Norway* (1945) and *Annie Get Your Gun* (1947), although others, such as the revived *The Red Mill* (1947), failed to make the grade. Littler made several further attempts with original musicals, and scored successes with a pretty musicalization of *Quality Street* (*Dear Miss Phoebe* 1950), a comical one of the famous farce *Hurra! eine Junge!* (*Blue for a Boy,* 1950) with Fred Emney, with the George Formby *Brewster's Millions* show *Zip Goes a Million* (1951), and with the *Daddy Long-Legs* with music entitled *Love from Judy* (1952). Others, such as the Robert Stolz spectacular *Rainbow Square* (1951), *Happy Holiday* (based on *The Ghost Train*) and *Romance by Candlelight* (from *Bei Kerzenlicht*) were unmitigated flops.

Littler took a 10-year tuck in his musical presentation schedule, returning to the West End in 1967 with three months of a Broadway import, *110 in the Shade.* A revival of *The Student Prince* with popular touring tenor John Hanson had a good run, but an attempt to bring back Littler's own idea of a sure-fire success with a version of *The Maid of the Mountains,* revamped in the same way that he had treated *The Quaker Girl* and *Miss Hook of Holland* 30 years earlier, was a costly disaster.

A major presence on the touring circuits throughout the 1940s and 1950s, Littler was also extensively and lucratively involved for many years with the presentation of Christmas pantomimes throughout Britain and owned both the Palace and Cambridge Theatres in London's West End. He was knighted in 1974.

His brother **Prince LITTLER** [Frank RAINES] (b Hackney, 25 July 1901; d Henfield, 17 September 1973), originally a producer of mainly touring shows and pantomimes, and sometime chairman of Moss Empires Ltd, was for many years the most influential theatre owner in Britain, whilst his sister **Blanche LITTLER** [Blanche RAINES] (b Ramsgate, 26 December 1899; d Brighton, 7 June 1981) partnered Prince in early productions and subsequently became even more theatrically prominent as Lady Robey (ie, Lady Wade), the wife of comedian George Robey (né Wade).

1943 **The Knight Was Bold** (ex- *Kiss the Girls*) (Harry Parr Davies/Barbara Gordon, Basil Thomas/w Thomas Browne) Piccadilly Theatre 1 July

LITTLE SHOP OF HORRORS Musical in 2 acts by Howard Ashman based on the film by Charles Griffith. Music by Alan Menken. WPA Theater, New York, 6 May 1982; Orpheum Theater, 27 July 1982.

The most internationally successful wholly off-Broadway musical since *The Fantasticks, Little Shop of Horrors* began its career at the little WPA Theater, where author Ashman was co-director, before moving up to off-Broadway's premiere house, the Orpheum, with the massed might of Cameron Mackintosh, the Geffen Organization and the Shubert Organization behind it, for the bulk of what was eventually a 2,209-performance run in more than five years.

The musical was a burlesque of the period horror-movie genre in general, and of the 1960 film *Little Shop of Horrors,* made by Roger (*Not of This Earth, Teenage Caveman, A Bucket of Blood*) Corman, in particular. It was written in a tightly controlled and tautly funny combination of dialogue and lyrics which lovingly and knowledgeably parodied its original whilst still making the show funny to those who had never seen a horror movie. The doom-laden newsreadery tones of the voice-over narrator, a period trio of girl singers just too girl-group to be true, and a set of impossibly wide-eyed characters featuring shopboy hero Seymour (Rick Moranis) and his beloved workmate, the vacuous blonded Audrey (Ellen Greene), her sadistic leather-clad dentist boyfriend, Orin (Franc Luz), and a man-eating plant (Ron Taylor/Martin P Robinson) which grew and grew and grew, all went to make up the flavor of the most winning small musical in ages.

Seymour and Audrey work for florist Mr Mushnik (Hy Anzell) on Skid Row, where Seymour nurses this strange and interesting plant which he has called Audrey II after his adored one. The plant proves a major attraction and clients start to pour in to the once neglected shop, but there is one problem: the plant doesn't drink water, it drinks blood. And when Seymour's fingers are whitened with pinpricks, it even talks! It says ''Feed Me!'' The beastly Orin snuffs it whilst getting his kicks on laughing gas, and Seymour feeds him to the hungry plant, then Mr Mushnik gets on the trail, and he becomes the next victim. Seymour is becoming famous, but he's also losing control. Audrey is the next to fall, and finally Seymour realizes what is happening: this is not horticulture, it is a plan for Global Domination by Creatures From Outer Space. He attacks his plant, and is gobbled up in his turn, as Audrey II prepares to take over the world.

The musical part of the show was launched with the three girls boopsing out their harmonized history of ''Little Shop of Horrors,'' and went on to a row of endearingly funny pieces. Seymour encouraged the baby plant to ''Grow for Me,'' Audrey mooned over the fate of those who live ''Downtown,'' longed for sweet suburbia in ''Somewhere That's Green'' and rose rhapsodically with Seymour to the heights of ''Suddenly Seymour,'' and the dentist laughed himself to death in song (''Now''/''It's Just the Gas''), but the musical highlight of the night came when Audrey II burst forth with a big, black, husky voice demanding ''Feed Me!'' and gloating over making Audrey its ''Suppertime.''

Plate 226. **Little Shop of Horrors.** *Seymour (Brad Moranz) and Audrey (Faith Prince) in the jaws of Audrey II.*

Mackintosh took *Little Shop of Horrors* to London and was faced with the eternal dilemma of what to do with an off-Broadway show in a city with no equivalent area. He opted for the West End's little Comedy Theatre, made it littler by closing the dress circle, but still could not quite reproduce the special atmosphere engendered by off-Broadway. Miss Greene repeated her original role alongside Barry James (Seymour), Harry Towb (Mushnik) and Anthony B Asbury/Michael Leslie (Audrey II) and although the show struggled, it nevertheless managed to put up a better performance than previous off-Broadway shows had done in London, playing 813 West End performances before recouping some extra cash when the complex Audrey II puppet proved a rental prospect in view of the rush of regional houses anxious to mount the nine-handed, one-set musical.

An Australian production, mounted at Sydney's unsuitably handsome, modern Theatre Royal and at Melbourne's Comedy Theatre (26 February 1985), performed disappointingly, before the show moved into its foreign-language showings. Hungary was, as so often, at the head of the field with a version adapted by Mária Révész and produced at the Városmajori Parkszínpad, and the following season France's Claude Martinez and Paul Ledermann gave *La Petite Boutique des horreurs* (ad Alain Marcel) a fine production with Vincent Vittoz (Seymour), Fabienne Guyon (Audrey) and Jacques Martial/Charles Philippe Klanit (Audrey II) in the starring roles for a four-month Paris season. In Germany *Der kleine Horrorladen* (ad Michael Kunze) was played in Gelsenkirchen and in Austria Vienna's Szene Wien also mounted a German-language version. Japan, Scandinavia, South Africa, Israel, Iceland and other countries all saw productions, as the show moved into provincial and small-city houses around the world, and there often found an atmosphere more favorable to its success than in oversized or over-sophisticated metropolitan theatres.

In 1986 a film version was put out by the Geffen Company. Rick Moranis (Seymour) and Miss Greene featured in a glossy A-minus movie version of the parody of the musical based on a Z-movie, which topped up the main portions of the original score with several fresh musical pieces including a rip-roaring ''Mean Green Mother from Outer Space'' for the plant.

UK: Comedy Theatre 12 October 1983; Australia: Theatre Royal, Sydney 8 November 1984; Hungary: Városmajori Parkszínpad *Rémségek kicsiny boltja* 15 August 1985; France: Théâtre Déjazet *La Petite Boutique des horreurs* 19 June 1986; Austria: Szene Wien *Der kleine Horrorladen* 7 May 1986; Germany: Musiktheater im Revier, Gelsenkirchen *Der kleine Horrorladen* 31 March 1989, Berliner Kammerspiele 4 April 1989

Film: Geffen Co 1986

Recordings: original cast (Geffen), French cast (Martinez Lederman), Icelandic cast (Steinar), Spanish cast (*La botica dels horrors*) (Musica per a Anna), German cast (Polydor), film soundtrack (Geffen)

LLEÓ [I Balbastre], Vicente (b Valencia, 19 November 1870; d Madrid, 28 February 1922).

Composer, conductor and producer of zarzuelas, Vicente Lleó turned out a long list of scores for the Spanish stage over a period of more than 20 years, beginning with *Las de farandul* (lib: Lopez Marin, Teatro Maravillas 19 August 1898) and following up with a veritable rush of pieces over the next months, composed both in collaboration and alone: *Los cenceros* (Ramirez, Teatro Romea 11 February 1899), *Variétés* (w Zavala/Montesinos, Luis Pascual Frutos, Nuevo Teatro April 1899), *Extraje de boda* (w A Rubio/Miguel Palacios, Guillermo Perrin, 7 April 1899), *Los gladiatores* (w Chalons/Pazos, Gijon, Teatro Zarzuela 5 June 1899), *El estado di sitio* (w Calleja/Soriano, Falcado, Teatro Maravillas 20 June 1899), *Cambios naturales* (w Rubio/Ventura de la Vega, Teatro Maravillas 19 August 1899), *Venus Salón* (w Calleja/Limendoux, Lopez Marin, Teatro Romea 14 December 1899) and *La tiple mimada* (Enrique Prieto, Teatro Martin 17 October 1899).

He subsequently worked on a long list of pieces with Rafael Gomez Calleja, amongst which were included *La maestra* (1901 w Barrera), *Jilguero chico* (1901), *El dios Apolo* (1901), *Gubasta nacional* (1902), *Arlequin rey* (1903), *El mozo crúo* (1903), *Copito de nieve* (1903), *Gloria pura* (1904), *Quo vadis, montero* (1905), *La Golfa del Manzanares* (1908), *El rey del valor* (1914), *El premio de honor, El famoso Colirón, Los hijos del mar, Los presupuestos de Villapierde* and *Venus Kursaal,* but his most important success came well into his career with a piece composed alone, the 1909 zarzuela *La corte de faraón* (lib: Miguel Palacios, Guillermo Perrin).

Lleó's long list of further credits includes the following titles: *La pierras preciosas* (1905), *La taza de thé* (1906), *La guedeja rubia* (1905), *La loba* (1907), *Tupinamba* (1907), *Episodios nacionales* (1908 w Amadeo Vives), *Mayo florido* (1908), *La vuelta del presidio* (1908), *La république del amor* (1908), *La balsa de aceite* (1908), *Si las mujeres mantasa* (1908, w Luis Foglietti), *Las molineras* (1908), *Ninfas y satiros* (1909), *La moral en peligro* (1909), *La partina della porra* (1911), *Livio* (1911), *El barrio latino* (1912), *La Tirrena* (1913), *La Pandereta* (1915 w Jimenéz), *Siera Morena* (1915), *To esta pagas* (1920), *La alegre trompetaria, La carne flaca, Apaga y vamonos, Ave Cesár, El metodo Gorriz, El crimen pasional, El ilustre Recóchez, El maestro Campanone* and *El principe sin miedo.*

LLOYD WEBBER, Andrew (Lord) (b London, 22 March 1948).

The most successful musical-theatre composer of the fin de 20th siècle years.

The son of William Lloyd Webber, musician, composer and principal of the London College of Music, Andrew Lloyd Webber began writing songs in his teens, soon in collaboration with an ephemeral law student, Tim Rice. In the wake of the success of the children-heavy musical *Oliver!,* the two attempted a stage musical based on the life of children's-homes founder Doctor Barnardo (a subject which would come to the London stage years later in other hands and disastrously), but their first produced piece was one of more modest proportions, brought out under modest circumstances. *Joseph and the Amazing Technicolor Dreamcoat* was a 15-minute staged cantata, written for and first played by a boys' school choir. It did, however, lay the bases for the style which its writers would follow thereafter with outstanding success: lively, colloquial lyrics illustrated by music which blended popular modern tones with more classic elements, and which found much of its humor in burlesque.

Joseph was subsequently expanded, little by little, into a full-length show, but it was a second biblically based piece, produced before an evening-long *Joseph* had been developed, that made its composer's reputation. *Jesus Christ Superstar,* the story of the last days of the life of Christ as seen through the eyes of Judas Iscariot, was conceived as a stage musical, first heard as a two-record, pre-original-cast recording, and ultimately premiered at Broadway's Mark Hellinger Theater in 1971. Advisedly described as a ''rock opera,'' it took the modern-toned, written-through cantata style used in *Joseph* a step further, produced its composer's first hit songs (''Jesus Christ Superstar,'' ''I Don't Know How to Love Him''), scored an important success, became London's longest-running musical of all time and was played thereafter throughout the world, in productions varying from the extravagantly trendy to the wholly devotional.

After a sidewind into a conventional musical comedy with the period-piece set of songs for the short-lived *Jeeves,* Lloyd Webber returned to Rice and to the particular style they were developing with a musical show set this time not in the religious, but in the political arena. Maintaining the sung-through idiom, which was fast becoming accepted by other young writers as the modern style, and which they here further developed to fit a more substantial and modern dramatic subject, they told, to a musical score richer than before, the tale of Argentinian politician's wife Eva Peron, otherwise known as *Evita* (''Don't Cry for Me, Argentina,'' ''O What a Circus,'' ''Another Suitcase in Another Hall''). The worldwide triumph of *Jesus Christ Superstar* was more than confirmed as *Evita* triumphed over the foreseeable politically dying-to-be-correct howls about its subject matter and joined its predecessor at the head of the list of the most internationally successful musicals of the 1970s.

Leaving, for the moment, historical and dramatic subjects and his collaboration with Rice, Lloyd Webber took a turn into a lighter vein with his musical setting of the *Old Possum* poems of T S Eliot, brought to the theatre in 1981 as the song-and-dance spectacular *Cats* (''Memory''). *Cats* was a piece far from the 20th-century traditions of the book musical in its layout and its staging, but it would become the theatrical sensation of its era, outrunning even its record-breaking predecessors on the London and New York stages and breeding productions throughout the world.

The composer essayed further into the area of the theatre spectacular and further away from the musical-dramatic style of *Jesus Christ Superstar* and *Evita* with the pop-orientated wheelie extravaganza *Starlight Express* (1984) and had another success with the equally unusual staged pairing of his solo song-cycle ''Tell Me on a Sunday'' and a choreographed version of his 'cello variations on a theme by *Paganini* under the title *Song and Dance* (1982), before taking a turn into yet another field with the romantic musical melodrama *The Phantom of the Opéra* (1986). More musically substantial than his most recent works, Lloyd Webber's score for *The Phantom of the Opéra* paired opera pastiche and lush love songs with some highly developed ensembles and produced no fewer than three hit-parade songs (''Music of the Night,'' ''All I Ask of You,'' ''The Phantom of the Opéra'') before following its composer's earlier works to outsized international success.

Plate 227. **Andrew Lloyd Webber**

In spite of the popularity of this romantic costume piece, Lloyd Webber followed the lavishly staged *The Phantom of the Opéra* with a musical play which was of a wholly different genre, the comparatively intimate and sophisticated *Aspects of Love,* a piece based on a successful 1940s British novel dealing largely with the fairly unspectacular affairs of the heart of one family over some 20 years. Once again, Lloyd Webber's written-through score rendered up hit parade songs (''Love Changes Everything,'' ''Anything But Lonely'') as the musical settled in for a run which gave its composer the unusual distinction of having five shows running concurrently in the London of the early 1990s (*Cats, Starlight Express, The Phantom of the Opéra, Aspects of Love, Joseph and the Amazing Technicolor Dreamcoat* revival), and three simultaneously on Broadway (*Cats, The Phantom of the Opéra, Aspects of Love*), a record not even Ivan Caryll and the other most outstanding (and much more prolific) musical-theatre composers of the past had achieved.

The 1990s, however, did not bring further successes of the outsize proportions the composer had led the public to take almost as foreseeable. Whilst major revivals of a now hugely spectacularized *Joseph* and of *Jesus Christ Superstar* and a remake of *Jevees* as a small-scale *By Jeeves* in turn joined the still-running *Cats* and *Phantom of the Opéra* to keep up Lloyd Webber's remarkable full-handed presence in the West End and around the world, two new shows fared a little less extravagantly well in public favor. An attempt to turn the claustrophobic film-tale of *Sunset Boulevard* into a large-stage musical produced more splendid musical numbers (''With One Look,'' ''It's as if we Never Said Goodbye'') but failed to convince wholly as a theatre piece, whilst another musicalized film script, a musical based on the Hayley Mills film *Whistle Down the Wind* reproduced in London after a false start in America, produced some exciting and even moving theatrical moments and several chartable songs (''Tire Tracks and Broken Hearts,'' ''Whistle Down the Wind,'' and the Boyzone number one hit ''No Matter What'') but established itself as only a sure value rather than a top-notch theatre hit.

At the time of writing Lloyd Webber's first musical of the 2000s is in preparation. Leaving behind the cinema screenplays and returning to every(English)man's most precious preoccupations for his subject, *The Beautiful Game* is centered on the game of association football.

In between the successes of *Cats* and *Starlight Express,* and at the termination of the management contract under which he had worked from his earliest days, Lloyd Webber founded the Really Useful Company as a production and exploitation company for his works. The company (which subsequently became for a period the Really Useful Group and a public company) has co-produced or produced each of his subsequent musicals, and has also produced both plays (*Daisy Pulls It Off, Lend Me a Tenor*) and, less successfully, musicals (*The Hired Man, Café Puccini*) by other writers. Embryonic versions of Lloyd Webber's own pieces have been tried out at his private Sydmonton Festival, and there too the works of other writers have been tested, including two (*Masquerade, Café Puccini*) that were subsequently played in London. Another stage piece, a collaboration with Rice on an occasional one-act operetta called *Cricket,* was also staged privately, and in 1985 he composed a requiem mass, performed first at New York's St Thomas's Church, later in London, and ultimately staged as a ballet. His other work includes two film scores (*Gumshoe, The Odessa File*).

In 2000, the Really Useful Group became co-owners of the former Stoll Moss group of West End theatres, a package including the Theatre Royal, Drury Lane, Her Majesty's Theatre and the London Palladium, making it the largest and most important theatrical landlord in London.

The most important and innovative—not to say phenomenally successful—theatre composer of his era, Lloyd Webber has, in his 11 full-length theatre shows to date, displayed a considerable musical range within his preferred idiom, whilst always remaining not only accessible, but popular to the extent of placing regular numbers from his musicals in the pop charts, an area in which the musical-theatre music of the past 40 years has appeared less and less frequently.

1971 **Jesus Christ Superstar** (Tim Rice) Mark Hellinger Theater, New York 12 October

1972 **Joseph and the Amazing Technicolor Dreamcoat** (Rice) Haymarket Ice Rink, Edinburgh 21 August; Young Vic Theatre, London 16 October

1973 **Jacob's Journey** (Rice) 1 act Albery Theatre 17 February

1975 **Jeeves** (Alan Ayckbourn) Her Majesty's Theatre 22 April

1978 **Evita** (Rice) Prince Edward Theatre 21 June

1980 **Tell Me on a Sunday** (Don Black) 1 act Royalty Theatre January

1981 **Cats** (T S Eliot ad) New London Theatre 11 May

1982 **Song and Dance** (Black) Palace Theatre 26 March

1984 **Starlight Express** (Richard Stilgoe) Apollo Victoria Theatre 19 March

1986 **The Phantom of the Opéra** (Charles Hart/w Stilgoe) Her Majesty's Theatre 9 October

1989 **Aspects of Love** (Hart, Black) Prince of Wales Theatre 17 April

1993 **Sunset Boulevard** (Black/Christopher Hampton) Adelphi Theatre 12 July

1996 **By Jeeves** revised *Jeeves* Stephen Joseph Theatre, Scarborough 24 April; Duke of York's Theatre, London 2 July 1996

1996 **Whistle Down the Wind** (Jim Steinman/Patricia Knop) National Theater, Washington, DC 12 December; revised version Aldwych Theatre, London 1 July 1998

2000 **The Beautiful Game** (Ben Elton) Cambridge Theatre 26 September

Literature: Richmond, K: *The Musicals of Andrew Lloyd Webber* (Virgin, London, 1995), Mühe, H: *Die Musik von Andrew Lloyd Webber* (Kovacs, Hamburg 1995), Coveney, M: *Cats on a Chandelier* (Hutchinson, London, 1999)

Biographies: Mantle, J: *Fanfare—The Unauthorised Biography of Andrew Lloyd Webber* (Michael Joseph, London, 1989), Walsh M: *Andrew Lloyd Webber* (Viking, London, 1989)

LOCK UP YOUR DAUGHTERS Musical play in 2 acts by Bernard Miles adapted from *Rape upon Rape* by Henry Fielding. Lyrics by Lionel Bart. Music by Laurie Johnson. Mermaid Theatre, London, 28 May 1959.

Bernard Miles, the brainfather and manager of the Mermaid Theatre in London's Puddle Dock, opened his newly built house in 1959 with a musical for which he himself had written the libretto. *Lock Up Your Daughters* was a lusty adaptation of Henry Fielding's 1730 tale *Rape upon Rape,* to which, after several writers had turned down the opportunity, the musical part was supplied by film composer Laurie Johnson and the 28-year-old Lionel Bart, the lyricist of the recent *Fings Ain't Wot They Used t' Be.*

The rape of the story's title did not actually happen. 18th-century Hilaret (Stephanie Voss) has snuck out to meet her lover, Captain Constant (Terence Cooper), but become embroiled in the dangers of the city. One of these is Ramble (Frederick Jaeger), and when Hilaret deters his advances by squealing ''Rape!'' both of them are dragged before Justice Squeezum (Richard Wordsworth). Squeezum is himself an even greater danger than the lowest streets of London, and while he is dribbling all over Hilaret, his wife (Hy Hazell) makes merry with Ramble. However Hilaret is not all winsomeness, and she arranges a booby-trapped rendezvous with the lascivious judge who, by the final curtain, ends up in his own jail. The songs ranged from a lusty title number, through two comical pieces for Mrs Squeezum (one demanding ''When Does the Ravishing Begin?'' and the other vengefully threatening her prison-bound husband ''I'll Be There''), the gentle wonderings of the wine-sodden Sotmore (Keith Marsh) over Hilaret's smartness (''If I'd Known You''), and the heroine's ingenuously comical seduction of the boggling Judge, describing her deflowering on ''A Sunny Sunday Morning'' as she removes her clothes.

Staged by the Mermaid's 29-year-old artistic director, Peter Coe, on a multiple-purpose setting constructed on scaffolding by the architect Sean Kenny, *Lock Up Your Daughters* was a singular success. Intended only for a six-week season at what was planned to be a house with a regular turnover of productions, it ran and ran, paying off the entire building cost of the theatre and setting the venture off on a very firm foot. But the house's trustees required productions, not success and profit, and they urged that the show be closed. Finally, after six months and 330 performances, it was taken off. The round of international productions began soon after in South Africa, but an American version, Broadway-bound under the management of Douglas Crawford, and with Harry Locke, Nancy Dussault and John Michael King teamed with Miss Hazell, folded on the road amidst little cries of horror at the show's indecent content. Australia proved less tender-eared and welcomed *Lock Up Your Daughters* the following year with Wordsworth in his original role and Miss Hazell in the part she had made all her own for an eight-week limited season in Melbourne and then in Sydney (Palace Theatre 8 June 1961).

In 1962 the Mermaid revived its most successful piece with Bernard Miles and Sally Smith featured, and after 111 more performances there it was shifted into the West End's Her Majesty's Theatre. Wordsworth and Miss Voss took up their original roles again, and the piece played 15 further months and 553 performances. *Lock Up Your Daughters* was regularly mounted in English theatres thereafter. It played a 10th anniversary season at the Mermaid (31 March 1969) and it was to have been included in the first season of the newly rebuilt Mermaid in 1981. This production was canceled when the ill-conceived, -cast and -staged new piece which this time opened the theatre proved such a failure that the rest had to be abandoned and Miles ultimately lost his theatre.

Sydney's Q Theatre mounted a revival in 1977, and in 1982 Goodspeed Opera House made another attempt to interest America in the show (30 March), but the production, with Carleton Carpenter and Dena Olstad in its leading roles, played its two-and-a-half-month regional season and ended.

Coe, whose directing assignment on *Lock Up Your Daughters* was his first musical in what was to be a distinguished career, later made a film under the same title which, in fact, used Johnson's score only as incidental music.

The success of *Lock Up Your Daughters* provoked a rash of attempts at Restoration musicals, none of which approached the success of the first. It also tempted the Mermaid into a number of other musicals, most of which—and particularly the last—were not on the same professional level, so that the musical theatre, which had been the original source of the Mermaid's financial and popular strength, ultimately proved its downfall. But what might have happened had *Lock Up Your Daughters* not been forced off the Mermaid stage first time round . . . ?

USA: Shubert Theater, New Haven 27 April 1960; Australia: Princess Theatre, Melbourne 12 April 1961

Recording: original cast (Decca)

LOESSER, Frank [Henry] (b New York, 29 June 1910; d New York, 26 July 1969). Songwriter turned show-writer who, in spite of a very short theatrical output, turned out three of the most outstanding musical comedies of the postwar era.

Plate 228. **Frank Loesser**

The son of a piano teacher, Loesser evinced an early interest in popular music and songwriting, but he found little success in his early attempts to write songwords. When he finally broke into the world of popular music as a house lyricist for the publishing firm of Leo Feist, it was only to find himself dismissed after one year as inadequate, but it was, nevertheless, Feist who published his first printed song, ''In Love with the Memory of You'' (mus: William Howard Schuman) in 1931. In spite of working with such established names as Hoagy Carmichael and Joseph Meyer, Loesser found that success still slouched at coming, and the only one of his numbers to catch the ear, as he worked as a nightclub pianist to make ends meet in the early 1930s, was ''I Wish That I Were Twins'' (w Joseph Meyer, Eddie de Lange).

In 1935 Loesser contributed lyrics to the quasi-amateur *The Illustrators' Revue* and as a result won the interest of Hollywood. He moved out West in 1936 and subsequently, at first for Universal and then for Paramount, RKO and MGM, provided seven years' worth of lyrics for cinema songs. Here he at last built, albeit slowly, a genuine success and the series of popular songs on which he collaborated included several which were to become standards: ''Moon of Manakoora'' (1937, Alfred Newman, *The Hurricane*), ''Says My Heart'' (1938, Burton Lane, *The Cocoanut Grove*), ''Two Sleepy People'' (1938, Hoagy Carmichael, *Thanks for the Memory*), ''The Lady's in Love with You'' (1939, Lane, *Some Like It Hot*), ''The Boys in the Back Room'' (1939, Frederick Hollander, *Destry Rides Again*), ''Say It'' (1940, Jimmy McHugh, *Buck Benny Rides Again*), ''Dolores'' (1941, Louis Alter, *The Gay City*), ''I'll Never Let a Day Pass By'' and ''Kiss the Boys Goodbye'' (1941, Victor Schertzinger, *Kiss the Boys Goodbye*), ''Katy Did, Katy Didn't'' (1941, Carmichael, *Hoppity Goes to Town*), ''I Don't Want to Walk without You'' (1942, Jule Styne, *Sweater Girl*), ''Jingle, Jangle, Jingle'' (1942, Joseph Lilley, *The Forest Rangers*), ''Touch of Texas,'' ''Can't Get Out of This Mood'' and ''I Get the Neck of the Chicken'' (1942, McHugh, *Seven Days Leave*), ''Let's Get Lost'' and ''Murder, He Says'' (1943, McHugh, *Happy Go Lucky*), ''They're Either Too Young or Too Old,'' ''How Sweet You Are,'' ''The Dreamer'' and ''I'm Riding for a Fall'' (1943, Arthur Schwartz, *Thank Your Lucky Stars*), ''Hello, Mom'' (Arthur Jones, Eddie Dunstedter).

It was in 1942 that Loesser first made his mark as a composer. He was in the habit of composing his lyrics to dummy tunes, and when ''Praise the Lord and Pass the Ammunition'' was not only accepted for publication with its ''dummy'' melody unreplaced, but also became a major hit, he continued to write songs alone. Amongst those which he turned out and which were used by Hollywood over the following years were ''Spring Will Be a Little Late This Year'' (1944, *Christmas Holiday*), ''I Wish I Didn't Love You So,'' ''Poppa Don't Preach to Me,'' ''The Sewing Machine'' (1947, *The Perils of Pauline*), ''Tallahassee'' (1947, *Variety Girl*), ''Bloop Bleep,'' ''On a Slow Boat to China,'' ''Baby, It's Cold Outside'' (1949, *Neptune's Daughter,* Academy Award) and ''Now That I Need You'' (1949, Betty Hutton in *Red, Hot and Blue!*).

In 1948 Loesser came to the Broadway stage for the first time with a musicalized version of the famous farce *Charley's Aunt.* The lyrics and music for *Where's Charley?,* written to fit the elderly and extremely English play, included one which was popular at the time (''My Darling, My Darling'') and another which lasted a little better (''Once in Love with Amy''), but Loesser's score was only a supporting item to the joyous antics of Ray Bolger who led *Where's Charley?* to a long-running Broadway success. However, a second essay at the musical stage, one with a thoroughly American and New York subject, produced something very different. The bookful of colorful and characterful songs which Loesser provided for the adaptation of Damon Runyon's stories as the musical *Guys and Dolls* (1950) remains to this day one of the most outstanding of American musical-theatre scores (Adelaide's Lament, ''Sue Me,'' ''Marry the Man

Today,'' ''Take Back Your Mink,'' ''My Time of Night,'' ''I've Never Been in Love Before,'' ''A Bushel and a Peck,'' ''Sit Down, You're Rockin' the Boat,'' ''If I Were a Bell''). The show ran for twelve hundred Broadway performances prior to winning itself an international career on English-language stages and a place amongst the classics of the musical theatre.

After a highly successful Hollywood venture with the score for the Danny Kaye film of *Hans Christian Andersen* (''The King's New Clothes,'' ''Thumbelina,'' ''Wonderful Copenhagen''), Loesser returned to Broadway with another outstanding musical play. *The Most Happy Fella* (1956), for which he provided both text and score, was once again a show that breathed ''America'' from every pore. But it took a different turn from its toughly endearing predecessor, seamlessly mixing operatic vocalizing with broad Broadway show songs in a show score of considerable scope and substance, as the accompaniment to a gentle, intimate love story. ''Standing on the Corner,'' ''Big D,'' ''Ooh, My Feet'' and ''Joey, Joey, Joey'' were amongst the popular singles that emerged as *The Most Happy Fella* became a Broadway hit and a perennial favorite.

In the 1960 *Greenwillow* Loesser attempted to step too far away from the genre which had proven itself as his forte and, in the area of near fantasy, met failure for the first time, but his final Broadway musical, the brisk, modern *How to Succeed in Business without Really Trying,* brought him back to the forthright American folk who suited him best, whilst allowing him to expose more fully the satirical facet of his style in its story of one ingenuous-seeming young man's drive to the very top of the business tree (''Brotherhood of Man,'' ''A Secretary Is Not a Toy,'' ''Happy to Keep His Dinner Warm,'' ''Been a Long Day,'' ''I Believe in You''). *How to Succeed in Business without Really Trying* gave Loesser his longest Broadway run (1,417 performances), his widest international coverage (it made it to a French production, for example, which few Broadway shows ever managed) and a Pulitzer Prize.

A final musical, *Pleasures and Palaces,* which went—in company with its sources, Sam and Bella Spewack's *Once There Was a Russian*—back to the days of Catherine the Great, closed out of town, but Loesser's total of musical-theatre successes was increased posthumously when his score for the 1952 film *Hans Christian Andersen* became the basis for a London stage musical, *Hans Andersen* in 1974. His works were also the bases for a compilation show *Perfectly Frank* played at Broadway's Helen Hayes Theater in 1980 (ad Kenny Solms, 30 November, 16 performances), and 1985 saw the mounting of *Señor Discretion Himself,* a piece written to a text by Budd Schulberg, in a showcase at New York's Musical Theater Works.

The most versatile and inventive musical-comedy writer of his time, Loesser displayed a warmth and wit in creating the songs of the almost inevitably likeable, and always comprehensible American characters who people, in particular, his three great musical shows, each of which remains a classic and a solid part of the basic musical-theatre repertoire.

Loesser's first wife, Lynn, was co-producer of *The Most Happy Fella* (w Kermit Bloomgarden) and of several other shows (*The Carefree Heart, The Love Doctor, High Fidelity,* etc) but is remembered principally for having inspired the irritated soubriquet ''the evil of two Loessers.'' His second wife was soubrette **Jo SULLIVAN** [SULLIVAN, Elizabeth Josephine] (b Mound City, Ill, 28 August 1928), a bitingly pert little ingenue with a strong soprano voice who made her most notable musical-theatre appearances in off-Broadway's *Threepenny Opera* (Polly Peachum) and as ''Rosabella,'' the waitress heroine of *The Most Happy Fella* (''My Heart Is So Full of You''). Rosabella, however, surprisingly turned out to be her only Broadway role. She played at the City Center as Julie in *Carousel,* Eileen in *Wonderful Town* and Magnolia in *Show Boat* and regionally as Dorothy in *The Wizard of Oz,* Sharon (*Finian's Rainbow*), Kathie (*Student Prince*) and Kitty (*Charley's Aunt*) and appeared in the musical version of *Of Mice and Men* at the Provincetown Playhouse (1958). In later years she administered the musical legacy of her late husband and appeared in a show—*Perfectly Frank*—compiled from his works.

Loesser's daughter, **Emily LOESSER,** has also appeared on the Broadway musical stage.

1948 **Where's Charley?** (George Abbott) St James Theater 11 October

1950 **Guys and Dolls** (Abe Burrows, Jo Swerling) 46th Street Theater 24 November

1956 **The Most Happy Fella** Imperial Theater 3 May

1960 **Greenwillow** (w Lesser Samuels) Alvin Theater 8 March

1961 **How to Succeed in Business without Really Trying** (Burrows, Jack Weinstock, Willie Gilbert) 46th Street Theater 14 October

1965 **Pleasures and Palaces** (w Sam Spewack) Fisher Theater, Detroit 11 March

1974 **Hans Andersen** (Beverley Cross, Tommy Steele) London Palladium 17 December

1985 **Señor Discretion Himself** (Budd Schulberg) Musical Theatre Works 20 November

Biography: Loesser, S: *A Most Remarkable Fella: Frank Loesser and the Guys and Dolls in His Life* (Donald I Fine, New York, 1993)

LOEWE, Frederick [LÖWE, Fritz] (b Berlin, 10 June 1901; d Palm Springs, Calif, 14 February 1988). Composer who combined with Alan Jay Lerner on the scores for several enduring hits, topped by *My Fair Lady,* during the peak years on postwar Broadway.

Frederick Loewe was born in Berlin, the son of **Edmund LÖWE** (b Berlin, 3 March 1880; d Los Angeles, 21 April 1971), a popular Operette light comedian who appeared on the musical stage in Berlin and Vienna (Theater an der Wien as Célestin to Lina Arbarbanell's *Nitouche,* Alphonse in *Die Dame aus Trouville,* original Niki in *Der Fremdenführer,* etc), and in New York (1903, Florian in *Das süsse Mädel, Die Puppe* and *Die Geisha* with Ferenczy's Centraltheater Company, 1905–6 as Hildebrandt in *Frühlingsluft* and in *Mam'zelle Nitouche* with Abarbanell, etc).

''Fritz'' studied music, and, in particular, piano as a youth, but when he moved with his father to America at the age of 20, he found himself unable to make the kind of performing career he had hoped for. He also tried his hand at composing, but it was a decade more before he found any signs of hope in a career in the musical theatre. He managed to place occasional individual numbers, but his first produced shows, written in collaboration with Earle Crooker, did not set him off to a flourishing start. Richard Berger's production of *Salute to Spring,* with Guy Robertson starring, did not make it out of St Louis, whilst a piece called *Great Lady*—again with name value on the marquee in the persons of Irene Bordoni, Helen Ford and Norma Terris, and with an exhaustingly time-warping libretto—lasted just 20 performances on Broadway. He worked with Crooker again on a revised version of a musical entitled *Patricia* (itself a musicalized version of the successful play *The Patsy*) in which Dorothy Stone had played a reasonably successful season on the West Coast in 1941. The doctor on the textual side was a young man named Alan Jay Lerner. *The Life of the Party,* again with Dorothy Stone starred, played a second season but kept away from Broadway.

After their work together on this project, Loewe and Lerner collaborated on two further pieces, *What's Up?* (63 performances) and, improving their hit-rate all the time, *The Day Before Spring* (165 performances), before they finally won success, in the wake of *Oklahoma!,* with a delightfully unpretentious piece of romantic Scottish fantasy. *Brigadoon* enchanted both Broadway and London as it set the partners on the road to even bigger triumphs. Loewe successfully submerged any signs of Vienna in such winning numbers as ''Come to Me, Bend to Me,'' ''It's Almost Like Being in Love'' and ''I'll Go Home with Bonnie Jean,'' just as he turned thoroughly and believably Western for the dashing songs of the pair's next musical *Paint Your Wagon* (''Wand'rin' Star,'' ''They Call the Wind Maria,'' ''I Talk to the Trees,'' ''I Still See Elisa''). *Paint Your Wagon* did a little less well than *Brigadoon,* but the partnership's most memorable triumph came with their next and fifth Broadway show together, the musical adaptation of G B Shaw's *Pygmalion* as *My Fair Lady.*

My Fair Lady's record-breaking Broadway run, its worldwide productions, penetrating even countries where the American musical was otherwise little known, made it the most popular and played show of its era. Once again, Loewe successfully adapted his musical style to a foreign setting and, after being Scots and wildish-Western, came up with some colorable if smooth-edged English music-hall numbers (''A Little Bit o' Luck,'' ''Get Me to the Church on Time'') as well as a Spanish-flavored trio and a serenade (''On the Street Where You Live'')—which was related to European serenades only in being sung under a window—and sent his heroine off into pre-ball raptures to the memorable strains of ''I Could Have Danced All Night'' not in a normally inevitable waltz time, but in 4/4.

Success came for a fourth consecutive time with the human and humorous retelling of the tale of Arthur, Lancelot and Guenevere in *Camelot* (1960, ''If Ever I Would Leave You,'' ''I Loved You Once in Silence,'' ''How to Handle a Woman''), before Loewe, convinced that he was unwell, retired from the theatrical scene. He emerged briefly in 1973 to supply additional material for an unfortunate first stage version of the partnership's 1958 film hit, *Gigi,* and combined again with Lerner on the film score *The Little Prince* (1975), but otherwise he remained quiet. As is so often the case, he survived another 15 years, seeing his incessantly active partner pass away first before he himself died at the fine age of 84.

Loewe's basically romantic music, staunchly rooted in the values (if not necessarily the styles) of the prewar European operetta, had, like that of the latter-day Richard Rodgers, a substance which had often been absent in a musical theatre where the large proportion of show scores had, for many years, been the works of songwriters and modern-dance composers. Fresh, characterful and singable, and tidily in keeping with its subject, it helped give the Lerner/Loewe collaborations a fine cohesiveness, whilst still producing a large percentage of show standards.

1937 **Salute to Spring** (Earle Crooker) Forest Park, St Louis 12 July

1938 **Great Lady** (Crooker/Crooker, L Brentano) Majestic Theater 1 December

1942 **The Life of the Party** revised *Patricia* (w George Grandee/Earle Crooker, J Keirn Brennan/Barry Connors, Alan Jay Lerner) Wilson Theater, Detroit 8 October

1943 **What's Up?** (Lerner, Arthur Pierson) National Theater 11 November

1945 **The Day Before Spring** (Lerner) National Theater 22 November

1947 **Brigadoon** (Lerner) Ziegfeld Theater 13 March

1951 **Paint Your Wagon** (Lerner) Shubert Theater 12 November

1956 **My Fair Lady** (Lerner) Mark Hellinger Theater 15 March

1960 **Camelot** (Lerner) Majestic Theater 3 December

1973 **Gigi** (Lerner) Uris Theater 13 November

Biography: Lees, G: *Inventing Champagne: The Worlds of Lerner and Loewe* (St Martin's Press, New York, 1990)

LOFTUS, Kitty [NEWMAN, Katharine] (b Whitecliffe, Gloucs, 16 June 1867; d London, 17 March 1927). Star soubrette of the British stage of the 1890s and 1900s.

One of the several singing, dancing daughters of touring actor George F Newman and his actress wife Mary, tiny, blonde Kitty Loftus began a stage career as a child in plays and in pantomime before going touring with the Milton-Rays. She later appeared in a series of new burlesque roles (Psyche in *Venus* 1890, Jack in *Little Jack Sheppard,* Siebel in *Faust Up-to-Date,* Cinderellen in *Cinder-Ellen Up Too Late* 1893) and in 1893 created the title role in the most successful of the early variety musical-comedies, *The Lady Slavey* (Phyllis), on the road. She made her first major London appearance starring as Emma, the housemaid, opposite the *Gentleman Joe* of Arthur Roberts (1895) and paired with the unreliable comic again in *Biarritz* (1896, Janet) and *The White Silk Dress* (1896, Mrs Bailey). She also starred in the allegedly Armenian musical *The Yashmak* (1897, Dora Selwyn), succeeded Kate Cutler to the title role of *The French Maid* (1898, Suzette), played in the unlucky *Her Royal Highness* (1898, Princess Petula) and crossed the ocean to play in New York in *In Gay Paree* (1899, Denise).

She went into court to challenge her old partner Roberts when he dropped her as co-star for his West End season of *HMS Irresponsible* (1900, Victoria Chaffers) after the pre-London tour in favor of Miss Cutler. In the incomprehensible way of theatrical lawsuits, she somehow managed to lose, and so instead went off to play in Shakespeare with Benson, a revival of *Morocco Bound* (1901, Maude Sportington) and on the road in the title role of the musical comedy *Bébé* (1901). In 1902 she brought her own touring musical, *Naughty Nancy* (Nancy, producer), written by Lord Tiverton, to the then-hallowed walls of the Savoy and scored a surprisingly good run with what was essentially a variety musical in the home of comic opera. In 1904 she appeared at Terry's Theatre under her own management in the burlesque *The Duchess of Sillie-crankie* (Duchess, producer) before going on to see out the last part of her career in variety, in the colonies (South Africa 1906 w George Robey) and the provinces.

Her sisters **Rosie LOFTUS-LEYTON** [Rose NEWMAN] (b Tyldesley, Lancs, 17 January 1877; d Eastbourne, 17 March 1902) (*Bonnie Boy Blue, A Trip to Chinatown, Dandy Dan, My Sweetheart, The Lady Slavey*), **Mabel Luxmore** (b 30 April) and **Olive Loftus-Leyton** (b 15 February) were all occupied in the mostly musical theatre.

LOGAN, Joshua [Lockwood] (b Texarkana, Tex, 5 October 1908; d New York, 12 July 1988). Broadway director of several major hits of the postwar era.

First an actor, then a director of plays and films, Logan made his bow as a director of Broadway musicals in 1938 with the Rodgers and Hart *I Married an Angel* and the Maxwell Anderson/Kurt Weill *Knickerbocker Holiday. Stars in Your Eyes* (1939), with Ethel Merman and Jimmy Durante, and Rodgers and Hart's *Higher and Higher* (1940), in which Logan also took a hand in the libretto, did less well than his first essay, but success reared its head again in 1942 when he staged Rodgers and Hart's classical burlesque *By Jupiter.*

Logan subsequently directed Irving Berlin's wartime revue *This Is the Army* and, in consequence, was employed for the same task on Berlin's book musical *Annie Get Your Gun.* Following the huge and worldwide success of that musical, he joined Rodgers and Hammerstein as co-producer, co-librettist and director of *South Pacific* with equally memorable results. He filled the same multiple role on two further Broadway successes: the easy-going summer-camp piece *Wish You Were Here* (1952) and the three-into-one musicalization of Pagnol's Marseille tales as *Fanny* (1954), but thereafter he returned for a long time solely to directing. However, the college musical *All American* (1962) and Berlin's *Mr President* (1962) measured their runs in months, *Hot September* (1965) didn't measure its at all, and a final Broadway engagement, *Look to the Lilies* (1970), counted its life in days. A last attempt at producing/writing/directing with a musical version *of The Corn Is Green,* produced under the title *Miss Moffat,* folded out of town.

Logan had considerable success with several non-musical ventures both as an author (*Mr Roberts*) and a director (*The World of Suzie Wong*). He also directed the screen versions of *South Pacific* with its technicolor Pacific skies, *Camelot* and *Paint Your Wagon,* as well as the filmed *Fanny* without its music.

1940 **Higher and Higher** (Richard Rodgers/Lorenz Hart/w Gladys Hurlbut) Shubert Theater 4 April

1949 **South Pacific** (Rodgers/Oscar Hammerstein/w Hammerstein) Majestic Theater 7 April

1952 **Wish You Were Here** (Harold Rome) Imperial Theater 25 June

1954 **Fanny** (Rome/w S N Behrman) Majestic Theater 4 November

1974 **Miss Moffat** (Albert Hague/Emlyn Williams/w Williams) Shubert Theater, Philadelphia 7 October

Autobiographies: *Josh* (Delacorte, New York, 1976), *Movie Stars, Real People and Me* (Delacorte, New York, 1978)

LÖHNER, Fritz [aka BEDA or LÖHNER-BEDA, Fritz] (b Wildenschwert, 24 June 1883; d Auschwitz, 4 December 1942).

Dr Löhner (he was a doctor of law) made a career as a musical theatre librettist, a writer of revue, and, under the pseudonym of ''Beda,'' the lyricist of a large number of popular songs of the 1910s and 1920s, both original German pieces—many in the American style—with titles ranging from ''Tutenkhamen Shimmy'' to the ''Komm, meine kleine Colombine'' fox-trot, and German versions of foreign numbers (amongst which a German translation of ''Yes, We Have No Bananas'' as ''Ausgerechnet Bananen'').

His first major stage work, Edmund Eysler's *Frühling am Rhein,* staged at the Bürgertheater with Louis Treumann starring through 62 performances was produced (as by ''Fritz Beda'') during the Great War, but it was well into the 1920s before Löhner found real theatrical success with his libretto for the Operette written around Fred Raymond's hit song *Ich hab' mein Herz in Heidelberg verloren* and the fictionalized romance about the poet Goethe set by Lehár as *Friederike.* Thereafter, he was allotted the task of revising earlier Lehár works—Tauberizing *Die gelbe Jacke* into *Das Land des Lächelns* and *Endlich allein* into *Schön ist die Welt*—and he also collaborated with Paul Knepler on the heavily dramatic libretto for Lehár's last work, *Giuditta.*

Löhner found a second fruitful collaboration with the Hungarian composer Pal Ábrahám, whose two most successful works he adapted from their original Hungarian into German (*Viktoria und ihr Husar, Die Blume von Hawaii*) before writing the text for the composer's third and last major hit, *Ball im Savoy,* and he later worked successfully with other Hungarian composers, Eisemann and Brodzsky, and with the Czechoslovakian Jára Beneš. Imprisoned in Auschwitz in late 1939, he died there three years later.

1910 **Die keusche Susanne** (Leo Ascher) 1 act Kabarett Fledermaus 1 February

1910 **Die fromme Silvanus** (Ascher) 1 act Kabarett Fledermaus 3 November

1911 **Rampsenit** (Ascher) 1 act Kabarett Fledermaus 1 January

1911 **Eine fidele Nacht** (Ascher) 1 act Colosseum 11 September

1913 **Die goldene Hanna** (Ascher) 1 act Apollotheater 4 January

1913 **Das Gartnerhäuschen** (Béla Lazsky) 1 act Künstlerspiele 1 December

1914 **Frühling am Rhein** (Edmund Eysler/w Carl Lindau, Oscar Fronz) Wiener Bürgertheater 10 October

1915 **Der Weltenbummler** (Richard Fall/w Lindau) Montis Operettentheater, Berlin 18 November

1916 **Der Sterngucker** (Franz Lehár) Theater in der Josefstadt 14 January

1917 **Die Dame von Welt** (R Fall/w Hans Kottow) Apollotheater 31 January

1917 **Die Anne-Marie** (Franz Schubert arr Max Egger) 1 act Ronacher 1 November

1918 **Muschi** (Robert Stolz) 1 act Gartenbau 1 January

1918 **Das Zuckergoscherl** (R Wagner, Arthur Guttmann) 1 act Hölle 31 August

1921 **Kirikiri** (Stolz/w Otto Hein) Rolandbühne 1 January

1921 **Der Herr der Welt** (Károly Hajós/w Carl Bretschneider, Franz Wolf) Komische Oper 4 October

1922 **Der schwarze Pierrot** (Hajós) Theater am Nollendorfplatz, Berlin 19 May

1923 **Die Brasilierin** (Oskar Jascha/w Max Neal) Carltheater 12 January

1923 **Der keusche Heinrich** (Hans Duval-Diamant/w Lindau) Jantschtheater 29 March

1924 **Revanche** (Jascha/Fritz Lunzer) Wiener Bürgertheater 8 November

1925 **Die Bojarenbraut** (Willy Engel-Berger/w Kottow) Carltheater 22 September

1927 **Ich hab' mein Herz in Heidelberg verloren** (Fred Raymond/Ernst Neubach/w Bruno Hardt-Warden) Volksoper 29 April

1928 **Friederike** (Lehár/w Ludwig Herzer) Metropoltheater, Berlin 4 October

1929 **Das Land des Lächelns** (Lehár/Léon ad w Herzer) Metropol theater, Berlin 10 October

1930 **Frühling in Wienerwald** (Ascher/w Lunzer) Neues Wiener Stadttheater 17 April

1930 **Viktoria und ihr Husar** (*Viktória*) German version w Alfred Grünwald (Stadttheater, Leipzig)

1931 **Bei der Wirtin Rosenrot** (Ascher/w Paul Knepler) Theater des Westens, Berlin 14 March

1931 **Schön ist die Welt** revised *Endlich allein* w Herzer, Theater an der Wien 21 December

1931 **Die Blume von Hawaii** German version w Grünwald (Neues Theater, Leipzig)

1932 **Ball im Savoy** (Pál Ábrahám/w Grünwald) Grosses Schauspielhaus, Berlin 23 December

1933 **Rosen im Schnee** (Karl Löwe arr Jascha/w Hardt-Warden) Volksoper 20 January

1933 **Katz im Sack** (*Zsákbamacska*) German lyrics (Die Komodie)

1934 **Giuditta** (Lehár/w Paul Knepler) Staatsoper 20 January

1934 **Märchen im Grand-Hotel** (Ábrahám/w Grünwald) Theater an der Wien 29 March

1934 **Der Sterne der Manege** (*Vadvirág*) German version w Hugo Wiener

1934 **Der Prinz von Schiras** (Josef Beer/w Herzer) Theater an der Wien 20 November

1934 **Die verliebte Königin** (*A szerelmes királynő*) German version w Grünwald (Scala-Theater)

1935 **Dschainah, das Mädchen aus dem Tanzhaus** (Ábrahám/w Grünwald) Theater an der Wien 20 December

1935 **Der gütige Antonius** (Jára Beneš/w Wiener) Volksoper 23 December

1936 **Auf der grünen Wiese** (*Na t louce zelen*) (Beneš/V Tolarsky ad w Wiener) Volksoper 9 October

1937 **Polnische Hochzeit** (J Beer/w Grünwald) Stadttheater, Zürich 3 April

1938 **Grüss und Kuss aus der Wachau** (Beneš/w Wiener, Fritz Eckhardt/Wiener, Kurt Breuer) Volksoper 17 February

Biography: Schwarberg, G: *Dein ist mein ganzes Herz: Die Geschichte von Fritz Löhner-Beda, der die schönsten Lieder der Welt schrieb und warum Hitler ihn ermodern liess* (Steidl Verlag, Göttingen, 2000)

LOLA MONTEZ Musical in 2 acts by Alan Burke. Lyrics by Peter Benjamin. Music by Peter Stannard. Union Theatre, Melbourne, 19 February 1958. Revised version Her Majesty's Theatre, Brisbane, 1 October 1958.

One of the periodic attempts in Australia to produce a musical with international possibilities, *Lola Montez* was sponsored by the financially pressed Elizabethan Theatre Trust, a straight theatre organization which hoped to cash in with a run on the lines of those achieved by the profitable imported musicals of the time. It was written by one of their former producers, with songs by two young men whose principal experience had been in university revue. An early, small-scale version of the show was tried out, under the Trust's aegis, at the Union Repertory Company in Melbourne, with operatic vocalist Justine Rettick as Lola, and seven months later an enlarged and revised version, with one number cut and two fresh ones inserted, was produced at Brisbane, with English dancer Mary Preston as the heroine, before being brought to the Trust's Sydney Theatre. The much-publicized show (using the byline ''a gay, virile Australian musical'') proved to be agreeable but undistinguished by anything except being ''local'' and it folded with severe losses.

Ms Montes [*sic*] had an earlier showing as the heroine of an Amadeo Vives/Yrayroz zarzuela produced at Madrid's Teatro de la Zarzuela in 1902 (11 June), ''an episode of her life'' made up the subject of Leo Fall's 1913 *Die Studentengräfin,* and she became *Zauberin Lola* in Eduard Künneke's 1937 Operette.

Recording: original cast (Columbia)

LOMBARDO, Carlo [aka BARD, Leon, etc] (b Naples, 28 November 1869; d Milan, 19 December 1959). Italian musical man-of-all-parts who contributed to much of the best of his country's musical theatre for many years.

Lombardo began in the musical world as a writer of songs, and apparently made his first attempts at stage musical pieces in his early twenties. He became musical director of a touring operetta company, a job which he subsequently traded in for that of chief comedian in the same group before founding his own company, with himself as leading player and his brother Costantino taking over the post of musical director. For that company, he turned out Italian versions of a number of foreign musical shows. The fidelity of those versions can only be guessed at, but given Lombardo's later depredations on other folk's works, it is unlikely that the originals survived in a very recognizable state. His company toured in Italy and in Northern Africa, where he trouped in 1907 with a repertoire consisting of versions of such pieces as *The Geisha, The Toreador* and *The Orchid.*

Lombardo had a singular success when (under the pseudonym of ''Leon Bard'') he reorganized Bruno Granichstaedten's *Majestät Mimi* into a piece which he called *La Duchessa del Bal Tabarin,* and another when he mixed some of the score of Josef Szulc's hit musical comedy *Flup..!* with pieces borrowed from Cuvillier's *Der lila Domino,* and from Offenbach, Lehár and Vicente Lleó with a libretto set in a Paris nightclub, under the title *Madama di Tebe.* Other composers who came under his pasticcio-making hand included Vienna's Leo Ascher (*La Regina della fonografo*) and Budapest's Béla Zerkovitz (*La bambola della prateria*), but his cheeky request to Lehár for a new operetta won him instead the opportunity to rework an old one. The revue-operetta which he fabricated around the composer's *Der Sterngucker* score under the title *La danza delle libellule* proved sufficiently popular for the show later to be retranslated into German and played in Vienna and elsewhere mostly with more success than *Der Sterngucker* had had.

Lombardo worked both as a musician and a text-writer, or sometimes as both, but his most successful operettas were those in which he had a proven composer as a partner. A collaboration with composer Mario Costa produced two of the most effective of Italian native operettas, *Scugnizza* and the pasticcio *Il re di Chez Maxim,* and another with Virgilio Ranzato produced two further Italian standards, *Il paese dei campanelli* and *Cin-ci-là.* The best of his later works, *La casa inamorata,* a collaboration with Renato Simoni, was another piece that became part of the Italian repertoire.

In the fashion of the time (or slightly earlier) Lombardo turned out a number of libretti based on French comedy texts. Amongst the famous plays which he borrowed were Feydeau's *La Dame de chez Maxim* (*La dama di Montmartra*), Moreau and Sardou's *Madame Sans-Gêne* (*Cri-cri*), de Flers and de Caillavet's *Primerose* (*Primarosa*) and, in the making of yet another pasticcio, this time of the music of Robert Stolz, a version of Hennequin and Veber's *La Présidente* (*La Presidentessa*).

His brother, **Costantino Lombardo,** also composed several operettas, including a musical version of Mélesville's *Sullivan* (1914), and works on such popular subjects as *Vita d'artista* (1916), *La Pompadour* (1918), *La Sirena delle Folies-Bergère* (1920) and *Diana al bagno* (1924).

1891 **Un viaggio di piacere** (E Favi) Teatro Gerbino, Turin 30 January

1892 **I coscritti** (L Manna) Teatro Alfieri, Turin 10 May

1892 **Il borgomastro** (w Achille Grafigna/G Maresca) Teatro Quirino, Rome 26 October

1896 **La milizia territoriale** (Maresca) Teatro Balbo, Turin ?April

1910 **Amor de principi** (*Pufferl*) Italian version (Teatro Fossati, Milan)

1914 **La signorina del cinematografo** (*Der Schmetterling*) Italian version

1916 **La signora mia moglie** (Felice Checcacci) Teatro Miramar, Naples 2 September

1916 **Il marito decorativo** (Adolfo Bossi/ad)

1917 **La regina della fonografo** (Leo Ascher ad/w ''Gil Blas'') Teatro Fossati, Milan 3 February

1917 **La Duchessa del Bal Tabarin** (*Majestät Mimi*) revised Italian version

1917 **Linotte** (Ernest Coop) Teatro Quirino, Rome 3 July

1918 **Il figlio in accomandita** (Carlo Nicolò) Teatro del Casino, Montecatini September

1918 **Cloclo** (Emilio Gragnani) Politeama Nazionale, Faenza 7 November

1918 **Madama di Tebe** pasticcio based on the score of *Flup..!* et al (Teatro Fossati, Milan)

1919 **Il re di chez Maxim** (Mario Costa arr/Arturo Franci) Teatro Fossati, Milan 10 May

1919 **Si** (*La Dame des Folies-Bergère*) (Pietro Mascagni/Franci) Teatro Quirino, Rome 13 December

1920 **Changez la dame** (Coop/Georges Berr ad) Politeama Chiarella 14 February

1922 **La danza delle libellule** revised Italian version of *Der Sterngucker* (Teatro Lirico, Milan)

1922 **Il paese dei campanelli** (Virgilio Ranzato) Teatro Lirico, Milan 23 November

1922 **Scugnizza** (Costa) Teatro Alfieri, Turin 16 December

1923 **La bambola della prateria** (Béla Zerkovitz ad) Teatro Fossati, Milan 12 May

1923 **La Presidentessa** (Robert Stolz arr)

1924 **Luna Park** (Ranzato) Teatro Lirico, Milan 26 November

1925 **La dama di Montmartre** (Ermete Liberati/Feydeau ad)

1925 **La Fornarina** (pasticcio ad/Giuseppe Adami)

1925 **Cin-ci-là** (Ranzato) Teatro dal Verme, Milan 18 December

1926 **Primarosa** (Guiseppe Pietri/w Renato Simoni) Teatro Lirico, Milan 29 October

1926 **Gigolette** revised *La Danza delle libellule* w Gioacchino Forzano Teatro lirico, Milan 30 December

1927 **La città rosa** (w Ranzato/Carlo Ravasio) Teatro Lirico, Milan 13 April

1927 **Miss Italia** (Alfredo Cuscina/w A Zorzi ad)

1928 **Cri-cri** (Ranzato) Teatro dal Verme, Milan 28 March

1928 **Il trillo del diavolo** (Cuscina/w A Lanocita) Teatro Lirico, Milan 2 May

1928 I **Merletti di Burano** (w Ranzato/w Ravasio) Teatro Lirico, Milan 22 December

1929 **Zig-Zag** (Ivan Darclée) Teatro dal Verme, Milan 2 February

1929 **L'isola verde** (Pietri/w Luigi Bonelli) Teatro Lirico, Milan 16 October

1929 **La casa inamorata** (Renato Simoni) Teatro Lirico, Milan 15 November

1930 **Mille e un bacio** (Vittorio Mascheroni/w Lanocita) Teatro dal Verme, Milan 1 February

1930 **La Duchessa di Hollywood** (Ranzato) Teatro dal Verme, Milan 31 October

1931 **Le tre lune** (Lombardo) Teatro Verdi, Florence 5 February

1932 **Prigioni di lusso** (Ranzato/w Ravasio) Odeon, Milan 26 March

1932 **L'appuntamento nel sogno** (Simoni) Odeon, Milan 22 October

1932 **Parigi che dorme** (Lombardo) Teatro Argentina, Rome 16 December

1937 **I mulini di Pit-Lil** (w Colombini) Teatro Lirico, Milan 2 February

Other titles attributed: *Crema di chic, Il Viaggio di Perrichon, Tre studenti e una cocotte, Diavolo e jazz,* Italian versions of *Coquelicot, Fanfan la Tulipe, Der Fremdenführer* (*Cavaliere della luna*), etc

LONNEN, E[dwin] J[esse] (b Myton, Hull, 12 August 1861; d Ipsden, Warwickshire, 31 October 1901). Star comedian of the Gaiety new burlesques.

The son of minor circuits actor-director-manager William CHAMPION [William Rooles LONNEN] (b Portsmouth, c1832; d London, 30 July 1890), Lonnen played in stock companies in his teens, and subsequently took bit parts with the barnstorming Barry Sullivan in Shakespeare and on the road with The Miltons (1881) and with Edward Terry in comedy and burlesque (1884, *Robbing Roy,* etc). He had early musical-theatre experiences as Tarradiddle in a butchered version of *La Vie parisienne* (1884) and in the comic opera *The Bachelors* (1885, Sam Sleepy) at Manchester, but his first successful London venture was in burlesque at the Avenue Theatre, where he appeared under the management of Alexander Henderson in the supporting role of Tony Foster in *Kenilworth* (1885), with a cast including Arthur Roberts, J J Dallas, Violet Cameron and the Broughton sisters. He played Skraggestein in the same company's *Lurline* (1886), appeared in Henderson's production of *Falka* (1886, Tancred), then moved to the new Prince of Wales Theatre for Messager's *La Béarnaise* (1886, Girafo) after which—with the transferred *Dorothy* taking over the Prince of Wales—he was loaned to George Edwardes as a supporting comedian to Fred Leslie for the Gaiety's new burlesque productions.

Lonnen's first appearance at the Gaiety was as the policeman, de Villefort, in *Monte Cristo Jr* (1886). He made a great success singing Robert Martin's Irish song "Ballyhooley" and when Leslie and Nellie Farren took *Monte Cristo Jr* on tour, he remained behind to head the Gaiety's alternative company as Claude Frollo, "a monk and a villain of deepest dye," in *Miss Esmeralda* (1897). The French monk also had an Irish song, and "Killaloe" proved even more popular than its predecessor as Lonnen quickly established himself as one of the hottest comedy stars in town. He appeared as Visconti in *Frankenstein* (1887) and then as Mephistopheles in *Faust Up-to-Date* (1888, "Enniscorthy," "McCarthy's Widow," "Donegal," "I Shall 'ave 'em") and, after Fred and Nellie had had their turn with *Ruy Blas and the Blasé Roué,* he returned from the road to create Don José to Florence St John's Carmen in *Carmen Up-to-Data* (1890). This time he sang of "The Jolly Boys' Club" and, instead of the usual Irish song, a nigger minstrel number, "borrowed" from the repertoire of the Christy Minstrels. "Hush, the Bogie" turned out to be the greatest of his many great hit songs.

Lonnen took over John Shine's role of Charles VII in *Joan of Arc* when that show transferred to the Gaiety and caused a sensation with the rather-too-topical "Jack the Dandy, Oh, "but when in *Cinder-Ellen Up Too Late* (1891) the two Gaiety burlesque teams joined up again, Lonnen had to take second place in the comic cast, playing Prince Belgravia to Fred Leslie's Servant (ie, Buttons), and introducing Lionel Monckton's first Gaiety song, "What Will You Have to Drink?" and the Irish "Teaching McFaddyen to Dance." At the end of *Cinder-Ellen* he headed the latest and last of the great Gaiety tours to Australia (1892) playing Frollo, Arthur de Richemont (*Joan of Arc*), Don José and Mephistopheles with a company including Marion Hood, Robert Courtneidge and Addie Conyers.

When he returned, it was to find that the new burlesque, of which he had been one of the brightest stars, was almost a thing of the past. However, he had one last grand burlesque role to come—this one at the Lyric, and not at the Gaiety where he had passed his seven years of stardom—as the detective O'Hoolegan in *Little Christopher Columbus,* equipped with a mass of disguises and Ivan Caryll's "The Indiarubber Shoe," "I Pay No Attention to That" and the popular "Rumpty Tumty."

Lonnen never took to musical comedy as he had to burlesque. He went to South Africa with Alice Lethbridge under the management of Luscombe Searelle and ended up getting imprisoned by the Boers in Pretoria; he succeeded Shine as William White in London's version of *The New Barmaid* (1896); he played large roles in the adaptation of Eugen von Taund's *Der Wunderknabe* as *The Little Genius* (1896, Chevalier Tween) and the flop musicals *Man About Town* (1897, Frank Ennesleigh) and *The Maid of Athens* (1897, The O'Grady); he played Cabestan in Willie Edouin's production of *Toto and Tata* (1897) at Leeds; and guested as a Huntsman in *Dorothy* for Furneaux Cook's starry benefit, before renouncing musical comedy for the music halls and an essay at a play. He returned, at the last, to the Gaiety when Edwardes cast him in a supporting role in *The Messenger Boy,* but at the end of the show's run he was taken ill and he died a few months later at the age of just 40.

Lonnen's three brothers also partook of theatrical careers. **Walter [Champion] LONNEN** (b Bishop Auckland c1867; d London, 2 December 1903) was a supporting comedian in musicals, **Lonnen MEADOWS** (b Hull) was a comedian and pantomime player, and **Victor CHAMPION** (b Liverpool, c1864) was a conductor, mostly on the touring circuits and in suburban theatres but also, occasionally, at the Gaiety, other London houses, and latterly in Australia. Edwin's elder daughter **Jessie LONNEN** [Beatrice Helen LONNEN] (b Bristol, 6 February 1886) also went on the stage and appeared in a number of musical comedies, both in Britain (*Bluebell in Fairyland,* First Flower in *The Cherry Girl, The Beauty of Bath,* the juvenile lead of *Butterflies, Our Miss Gibbs, The Quaker Girl,* Zoraida in *A Persian Princess* 1909, Avis von Senzburg in *The King's Bride* 1911, tours of *A Country Girl, Tina, The Maid of the Mountains, A Southern Maid, Petticoat Fair, Our Peg,* etc) and in Australia (Phoebe in *The Quaker Girl,* Delia Dale in *The Sunshine Girl* 1912–13). A second daughter **Nellie LONNEN** [Ellen Farren LONNEN] (b London, 25 September 1887) also made a career in the musical theatre appearing with her sister in *Bluebell in Fairyland* and as A Sunbeam in *The Cherry Girl,* for George Edwardes in *The Spring Chicken* and *The New Aladdin,* in *The Gay Gordons* (1907, Lady Millicent) and *The Dashing Little Duke.*

LONSDALE, Frederick [LEONARD, Lionel Frederick] (b St Helier, Jersey, 5 February 1881; d London, 4 April 1954).

Variously a private soldier, an employee of the London and South Western Railway and a winning layabout, the young Lonsdale struggled for a number of years to make a career as a playwright until his wife, who had taken a job as a chorus girl for William Greet to make ends meet, got his work read by her employer. Greet sent it to fellow producer Frank Curzon, who not only put the young man on a retainer but eventually produced his first work: the musical play *King of Cadonia,* which he had set to music by none other than the composer of *The Geisha,* Sidney Jones, and the doyen of lyricists, Adrian Ross. It was, however, Lonsdale's very much more substantial than usual dialogue for the show's Ruritanian comic opera plot which both won *King of Cadonia* fine notices and helped the musical to a long career. After a couple of indifferent runs with straight plays, he turned out a second successful musical for Curzon. *The Balkan Princess* was basically little more than *King of Cadonia* with the sexes reversed, but it, too, had a good London run and a remarkably long and wide provincial and export life.

After a hiatus of some five years, during which Curzon turned down his author's newest text, Lonsdale reappeared on the London musical stage under the patronage of George Edwardes with the libretto for another successful musical, *Betty,* produced at Daly's Theatre. Following Edwardes's death he submitted the text Curzon had rejected to Daly's Theatre manager Bobby Evett, who staged it as *The Maid of the Mountains,* and the show went on to become one of the phenomena of the wartime London theatre, compiling one of the longest runs in the history of the musical theatre and establishing itself as a classic of the British musical stage.

As Lonsdale moved on towards a career which would establish him as one of London's favorite writers of classy comedy, he did not abandon the musical stage. He adapted Booth Tarkington's *Monsieur Beaucaire* as a highly successful light opera for André Messager, and he supplied the English texts for the enormously popular British productions of Jean Gilbert's *Die Frau im Hermelin* (*The Lady of the Rose*) and *Katja, die Tänzerin* and for Leo Fall's *Madame Pompadour,* but he wrote only two more original libretti. His Parisian tale of *The Street Singer,* commissioned by and devised for Phyllis Dare and with additional numbers supplied by his Jersey compatriot Ivy St Helier, told another conventional operetta tale in a manner that ensured it a more than conventional success, but his final piece, *Lady Mary,* 20 years after his splendid beginning with *King of Cadonia,* turned out to be the one musical venture from his pen which was rather less than a hit. From this time on Lonsdale wrote only plays but, after two decades of success, it seemed evident by the early 1930s that his era was past.

Remembered today principally for the four or five comedy hits of his career (*On Approval, The Last of Mrs Cheney,* etc), Lonsdale, nevertheless, had considerably more, and more lucrative, successes in the musical theatre. He wrote the text for one of the greatest hits of the London musical stage in *The Maid of the Mountains,* and, if his other musicals are no longer played in Britain, *Monsieur Beaucaire* has remained in the repertoire in France for the 70 years since its original production.

Lonsdale's daughter, Frances Donaldson, became an author of, amongst other books, her father's biography, whilst his illegitimate daughter Angela became the mother of Britain's theatrical Fox family: actors Edward and James and producer Robert (*Chess,* etc).

1908 **King of Cadonia** (Sidney Jones/Adrian Ross) Prince of Wales Theatre 3 September

1910 **The Balkan Princess** (Paul Rubens/Arthur Wimperis/w Frank Curzon) Prince of Wales Theatre 19 February

1915 **Betty** (Rubens/w Gladys Unger) Daly's Theatre 24 April

1916 **High Jinks** English adaptation (Adelphi Theatre)

1917 **The Maid of the Mountains** (Harold Fraser-Simson/Harry Graham) Daly's Theatre 10 February

1919 **Monsieur Beaucaire** (André Messager/Ross) Prince's Theatre 19 April

1922 **The Lady of the Rose** (*Die Frau im Hermelin*) English version (Daly's Theatre)

1923 **Madame Pompadour** English version (Daly's Theatre)

1924 **The Street Singer** (Fraser-Simson/Percy Greenbank) Lyric Theatre 27 June

1925 **Katja the Dancer** (*Katja, die Tänzerin*) English version w Harry Graham (Gaiety Theatre)

1928 **Lady Mary** (Albert Szirmai, Phil Charig/w John Hastings-Turner) Daly's Theatre 23 February

Biography: Donaldson, F: *Freddy Lonsdale* (Heinemann, London, 1957)

LOPEZ, Francis [LOPEZ, Francisco] (b Montbéliard, 15 June 1916; d Paris, 5 January 1995). The brightest musical star of the postwar years in France, whose output frittered away into embarrassing imitations of himself after he had produced some of the happiest Parisian scores of the 1950s.

Trained as a dentist, Lopez had his first musical successes as a part-time songwriter before turning to the theatre for the first time in 1945. His initial opérette, *La Belle de Cadix,* a colorful, vivacious piece hastily written to play six weeks at the small Casino-Montparnasse, ran for two years and provided the French musical theatre with the same kind of new acceleration that *Oklahoma!* had recently provided in America. Lopez and his librettist/lyricist Raymond Vincy followed up with a series of like pieces for larger Parisian stages over the next decade, pieces which, like *Oklahoma!,* returned to the classic romantic operettic proportions in a deft textual and musical mixture of the sentimental and the comic set in the most colorful of venues (*Andalousie, Pour Don Carlos, Le Chanteur de Mexico, À la Jamaïque, La Toison d'or, Méditerranée*). Unlike their American counterparts, however, the pair also worked simultaneously on a number of more intimate comedy musicals such as *Quatre Jours à Paris* and *La Route fleurie* which were mounted at smaller venues with success equal to that won by their bigger shows, thus allowing Vincy and Lopez to dominate the postwar musical theatre large and small.

After Vincy's death, Lopez continued writing ostensibly the same kind of pieces, to mostly much less able texts, supplying a series of often long-running if very obvious opérettes à grand spectacle to the large stage of Paris's Théâtre du Châtelet and only occasionally, as in *Viva Napoli* (1970), finding again the hearty freshness of his earlier work. Familiar strains set to what became thin and painfully predictable libretti and feeble orchestrations became the order of the day in the 1980s as Lopez became his own producer at, successively, the Théâtre de la Renaissance, the Élysée Montmartre and the Eldorado, producing scrappily written and staged shows in which his then wife, Anya, and son, Rodrigo, often took a hand. Madame Lopez and her son were credited with the score for *La Perle des Antilles* (nevertheless billed as ''opérette de Francis Lopez''; Théâtre de la Renaissance 17 February 1979), and the younger Lopez also composed the music for his father's production of *Aventure à Tahiti* (1988).

Whilst Lopez's more recent shows, and intermittent revivals of his earlier ones, played to their particular audience at his Parisian base, contributing no little to the falling reputation and image of ''opérette'' amongst the French younger generation, the provincial theatres of France continued to welcome productions of his earlier works, and even at the turn of the 21st century no season passes in the French theatre without numerous revivals of his best (and, occasionally, also his less good) musicals being seen in all corners of the hexagon.

Unsophisticated though it may often be, the rhythmic, sentimental and immensely singable music of his earliest opérettes is in the happiest tradition of popular light musical-theatre, and his best scores remain as admirable as the last are inane. When these are attached to the best of Vincy's texts (*Quatre Jours à Paris, Andalousie*) they make up into delightful theatre pieces.

Several of Lopez's early opérettes were made into films (*La Belle de Cadix, Andalousie, Quatre Jours à Paris, Le Chanteur de Mexico, À la Jamaïque*), and the composer also supplied songs and scores for a good number of musical films of the 1940s and 1950s, including *Je n'aime que toi, L'Aventurier de Séville, Sérénade au Texas* and the musical film remake of *Violettes impériales,* composed for the theatre by Vincent Scotto.

A 1987 autobiography concentrated more on the composer's career as a lady-killer than on his work for the theatre.

1945 **La Belle de Cadix** (Maurice Vandair/Raymond Vincy, Marc-Cab) Casino Montparnasse 24 December

1947 **Andalousie** (Vincy, Albert Willemetz) Théâtre de la Gaîté-Lyrique 25 October

1948 **Quatre Jours à Paris** (Vincy) Théâtre Bobino 28 February

1949 **Monsieur Bourgogne** (Vincy, Jean-Jacques Vital) Théâtre Bobino 12 March

1950 **Pour Don Carlos** (Vincy, André Mouëzy-Éon) Théâtre du Châtelet 17 December

1951 **Le Chanteur de Mexico** (Henri Wernert/Vincy, Félix Gandéra) Théâtre du Châtelet 15 December

1952 **La Route fleurie** (Vincy) Théâtre de l'ABC 19 December

1953 **Soleil de Paris** (Vincy) Théâtre Bobino 7 March

1954 **À la Jamaïque** (Vincy) Théâtre de la Porte-Saint-Martin 24 January

1954 **La Toison d'or** (Vincy) Théâtre du Châtelet 18 December

1955 **Méditerranée** (Vincy) Théâtre du Châtelet 17 December

1956 **El Aguila de fuego** (Arturo Rigel, Francisco Ramos de Castro) Teatro Maravillas, Madrid 19 January

1957 **Tête de linotte** (Vincy) Théâtre de l'ABC 14 December

1957 **Maria-Flora** (w Henri Betti/Vincy) Théâtre du Châtelet 18 December

1957 **La Cancion del amor mio** (M Brocey, A Quintero, Arozamena) Madrid December

1958 **S E la Embajadora** (Rigel, Jesus M de Arozamena) Teatro Alcázar, Madrid 21 November

1959 **Le Secret de Marco Polo** (Vincy) Théâtre du Châtelet 12 December

1960 **Dix millions cash!** revised *Monsieur Bourgogne* Théâtre de la Porte-Saint-Martin 10 December

1961 **Visa pour l'amour** (Vincy) Théâtre de la Gaîté-Lyrique 22 December

1963 **Cristobal le Magnifique** (Vincy) Théâtre de l'Européen 21 December

1963 **Le Temps des guitares** (Vincy, Marc-Cab) Théâtre de l'ABC 28 October

1967 **Le Prince de Madrid** (Jacques Plante/Vincy) Théâtre du Châtelet 4 March

1969 **La Caravelle d'or** (Plante/Jean Valmy) Théâtre du Châtelet 19 December

1970 **Viva Napoli** (Daniel Ringold/René Jolivet) Lille 20 December; Théâtre Mogador 4 September

1971 **Restons françaises** (w Anja Lopez/R Barbe) Théâtre des Capucines 24 December

1972 **Gipsy** (Ringold/Claude Dufresne) Théâtre du Châtelet 18 December

1974 **Les Trois Mousquetaires** (w Anja Lopez/Ringold/Jolivet) Théâtre du Châtelet 23 February

1975 **Fiesta** (Dufresne) Théâtre Mogador 23 February

1976 **Volga** (Plante, Ringold/Dufresne) Théâtre du Châtelet 26 November

1980 **Viva Mexico** revised *Fiesta* (Plante, Ringold/Dufresne) Théâtre de la Renaissance 22 February

1981 **Aventure à Monte-Carlo** (Ringold/Dufresne) Théâtre de la Renaissance 14 March

1981 **Soleil d'Espagne** (Ringold/Dufresne) Théâtre de la Renaissance 3 October

1981 **La Fête en Camargue** (Ringold/Dufresne) Théâtre de Saint-Etienne 3 December

1982 **Le Vagabond tzigane** (Ringold/Dufresne, Fernand Cayol) Théâtre de la Renaissance 2 October

1982 **Vacances au soleil** (Ringold/Dufresne, Cayol) Théâtre de Besançon 4 December

1983 **L'Amour à Tahiti** (Ringold/Dufresne) Théâtre de l'Élysée-Montmartre 1 October

1984 **Les Mille et une nuits** (Ringold/Dufresne) Théâtre de l'Élysée-Montmartre 6 October

1985 **Carnaval aux Caraïbes** (w Rodrigo Lopez/Ringold/Dufresne) Théâtre de l'Élysée-Montmartre 27 September

1986 **Le Roi du Pacifique** (Ringold/Dufresne) Théâtre de l'Élysée-Montmartre 24 September

1987 **Fandango** (Ringold/Dufresne) Théâtre de l'Élysée-Montmartre 16 January

1988 **Rêve de Vienne** (Ringold/Dufresne) Théâtre de l'Eldorado 30 September

1989 **La Marseillaise** (Ringold/Dufresne) Théâtre de l'Eldorado 7 July

1989 **La Belle Otéro** (Ringold/Dufresne) Théâtre de l'Eldorado 30 September

1990 **Portorico** (Ringold/Dufresne) Théâtre de l'Eldorado 30 September

1991 **Sissi** (w R Lopez/Ringold/Dufresne, Nadine de Rotschild) Théâtre de l'Eldorado 8 September

1992 **Mariane mes amours** revised *La Marseillaise* Théâtre de l'Eldorado 26 September

1993 **Les Belles et le gitan** (w R Lopez/Ringold/Dufresne) Théâtre de l'Eldorado 9 October

Autobiography: *Flamenco: La gloire et les larmes* (Presses de la Cité, Paris, 1987)

LORD PICCOLO Operette in 3 acts by Carl Lindau and Rudolf Schanzer. Music by Henri Berény. Johann Strauss-Theater, Vienna, 1 September 1910.

Berény's most successful Operette, produced by Leopold Müller at the Johann Strauss-Theater, starred Lisa Weise as Daisy, the barmaid from the Parisian Tabarin dance hall who pretends to be the little lost heir to the Scottish earldom of Goberdeen long enough to allow her foster brother, Jim (Carlo Böhm), to win his rightful place. Louis Treumann shared the top billing as the comical detective, Arsène Dupont, set on the trail of the missing heir by Lord Goberdeen (Oscar Sachs) and Eduard Rose was Gaston, Marquis de Champ d'Azur, who is Daisy's ultimate reward.

Berény's score, composed in classic proportions with numbers for Daisy (mostly), Gaston, Dupont and Lord Goberdeen featured alongside a ration of duets, a trio, a quartet and a full-scale first-act finale, was topped by a waltz duo for Gaston and Daisy in the first act.

Lord Piccolo played to its 50th performance on its first run, was brought back for some matinée showings the following year, and was later produced, without arousing too much enthusiasm, both in Germany and in Hungary. In America, however, it had a genuine success. Adapted in two acts by Edward Paulton and A E Thomas, the piece was presented by Henry Savage under the title *Little Boy Blue,* with lyrics by Grant Stuart and a number of other folk, and with some additional numbers with a Scots flavor written and composed by Scotland-born (but not bred) Paulton and by musical director Arthur Weld, one of whose two pieces was a medley of popular Scots tunes. A little-known actress, Gertrude Bryan, starred as Daisy and won herself praise as ''the musical comedy find of the season,'' alongside Otis Harlan (detective), John Dunsmure (Earl) and Charles Meakings (Gaston) as the production ran with singular vigor through a very appreciable 174 performances on Broadway before going on to a further fine life through several seasons on the road.

Germany: Gross-Berlin Operetten-Theater 1 March 1911; Hungary: Temesvár 18 April 1911, Budai Színkör 28 September 1911; USA: Lyric Theater *Little Boy Blue* 27 November 1911

LOSEBY, Constance (b Nottingham, 11 September 1842; d Milford, Surrey, 13 October 1906). Star soprano of the British opéra-bouffe stage who introduced many important roles to the 19th-century London stage.

In the mid-1850s the young barely teenaged Connie Loseby joined her mother, Elizabeth, née Foster (''Madame Losebini'')—''a celebrated vocalist of high musical standing'' and established as a class act in the music halls for some years—in a duet-singing double act (''Constance and Losebini'') in which the daughter quickly became the anchor and the main attraction. They played in music halls throughout the country, and paired regularly in pantomimes (Beauty in *King Pumpkin* at the Surrey 1864, Freddy in *Pat a Cake Baker's Man* at the Standard 1865), where Connie with her ''fine commanding figure and powerful contralto voice'' was on occasion seen as principal boy to her mother's principal girl (*Ding Dong Bell* at the City of London 1866, *Robin Hood* at the East London 1867, etc).

Constance and Losebini were seen at all the top London music halls during the mid-1860s, including the Alhambra. There they came under the house-management of John Hollingshead and when, in 1868, Hollingshead opened the new Gaiety Theatre, he engaged the now 26-year-old Miss Loseby as one of his original company. She appeared there, in her legit theatre debut, on the theatre's opening night playing opposite Charles Lyall as Columbine in Jonas's *The Two Harlequins* and as Raimbault in Gilbert's *Robert the Devil* burlesque. She remained at the Gaiety for some seven years, appearing in burlesque and extravaganza (Don Diego in *Columbus,* Linda in *Linda of Chamouni,* Ellen Tyler in *Wat Tyler MP,* Morgiana in *Ali Baba à la Mode* and again in *The Forty Thieves,* Lionel in *Martha,* Tresham in *Guy Fawkes,* Flora Sorbetto in the remake of *MM Dunanan* as *The Great Metropolis,* Donna Anna in *Don Giovanni in Venice,* Winifred Duxford in *Snae Fell*), in comedy (*London Assurance,* Young Lady Lambert in *The Hypo-*

crite, Oberon in *A Midsummer Night's Dream,* Mrs Ford in *The Merry Wives of Windsor*), ballad opera (Polly Peachum in *The Beggar's Opera*), English opera (Countess in *Letty the Basketmaker*) and in opéra-bouffe of all kinds. She appeared as Prince Raphaël in London's first *The Princess of Trébizonde,* as Princess Hermia in *Barbe-bleue,* Caesarine in *Malala* (ad fr *Fleur de thé*), Gabrielle in *The Island of Bachelors* (*Les Cent Vierges*), Clairette in *La Fille de Madame Angot,* Paris in *La Belle Hélène,* Gigolette in *Tromb-al-ca-zar,* Rigobert in *The Magic Fife,* Lischen in *Lischen and Fritzchen,* as Galatea to the Ganymede of Nellie Farren in the Gaiety's version of *Die schöne Galathee,* as Emily Flutterby in the remake of Gastinel's *L'Opéra aux fenêtres* as *An Eligible Villa* and also in several of the earliest British musicals presented there: as Princess Veloutine to the Aladdin of Farren in *Aladdin II,* as the ''ugly'' sister Bellezza in *Cinderella the Younger,* and as Nicemis in Gilbert and Sullivan's *Thespis.*

During this period she also toured at the head of the Gaiety's musical company, and played regular ''outside'' summer engagements, including a brief return to the halls, and a season of musical classics (*Guy Mannering, The Waterman, Rob Roy, The Beggar's Opera*) at Brighton opposite the famous tenor Sims Reeves.

In 1876 she went to Manchester to play the heroine of Cellier's *The Sultan of Mocha* and subsequently toured with his *Geneviève de Brabant* company before joining in 1878 the company playing London's most spectacular productions of opéra-bouffe at the Alhambra. With just a few forays out, she remained at the Alhambra for five years starring as Geneviève in *Geneviève de Brabant,* Florine in *La Poule aux oeufs d'or,* Angelo in *Venice* (1879, *Le Pont des soupirs*), Prince Raphaël, Countess Cameroni in *La Petite Mademoiselle,* Rothomago in *Rothomago,* Stella in *La Fille du tambour-major,* Marguerite in *Mefistofele II* (*Le Petit Faust*), Jeanneton in *Jeanne, Jeannette et Jeanneton,* Black Crook in the Alhambra's version of the *Biche au Bois / Black Crook* tale, Mistigris in *Babil and Bijou,* and Violetta in Strauss's *The Merry War,* returning after the fire which destroyed the theatre during the last-named show to star again as Sirene in *The Golden Ring.* Her outside engagements during this period included the leading roles in two new British pieces, the comic opera *The Lancashire Witches* (1882, Alizon) and Luscombe Searelle's *Estrella,* in which she took the title role (1883). She toured in 1884 as Nell Gwynne, but withdrew from the cast to attend to her mother in her last illness. She returned to the stage to join Violet Cameron's scandal-sabotaged trip to America with *The Commodore* in 1886, but then, still only in her early forties (and admitting to half-a-dozen years less), and after a remarkable career of some 15 years as one of the West End's leading musical artists, Connie Loseby retired from the stage.

Plate 229. **Constance Loseby.** *Connie brought her grand soprano voice from the halls to become the Gaiety Theatre's first leading lady.*

Connie was married to **Johnnie CAULFIELD** (b London, c1837; d Brixton 25 April 1880), the son of the celebrated comic-singing-actor, songwriter and music-hall chairman John [Henry] CAULFIELD (b ?April 1809; d London, 24 April 1865), stepson to his equally celebrated wife Louisa [née Louisa Rachel MATTLEY, ka **''Mrs Caulfield''**] (b ?1823; d Lambeth 15 September 1870), of the Haymarket Theatre and many a music hall and warmly if inaccurately christened by commentators ''the first of the serio-comics,'' and half brother to the infamous opéra-bouffe actress known as **Lennox GREY** [Louisa CAULFIELD] (b Covent Garden, 26 March 1845). A music-hall musician from his childhood, Johnnie went on to become assistant musical director at the Gaiety Theatre, a post he held till ill health forced him to retirement. He then took on the White Horse pub in Brixton, and after his death Connie carried on where he had left off. In 1896 she was the licensee of the Greyhound in Bushey Park, and at her death was at the helm of the Red Lion in Milford.

LOST IN THE STARS Musical tragedy in 2 acts by Maxwell Anderson and Alan Paton based on Paton's novel *Cry, the Beloved Country.* Music by Kurt Weill. Music Box Theater, New York, 30 October 1949.

An ''operaticized'' version of the highly successful South African novel *Cry, the Beloved Country, Lost in the Stars* told the tale of Absalom (Julian Mayfield), the son of a black minister (Todd Duncan), who murders the son of one of his father's white neighbors during an attempted robbery and is sentenced to hang. In this racially orientated tale, however, the accent is not on the ''murder'' and the ''robbery,'' but on the ''black'' and the ''white,'' as the father of the killer and the suddenly liberalized father (Leslie Banks) of the victim come together, at the end of the evening, in some kind of an unsteadily improved understanding.

The bulk of Kurt Weill's musical score fell to the role of the churchman (''Lost in the Stars,'' ''Thousands of Miles,'' etc), whilst the feminine part of the musical entertainment rested largely with Absalom's mistress, Irina (Inez Matthews), and a prominent place was reserved for a chorus which narrated and commented on the action. In spite of the respected names attached to it, the Playwrights' Company production of this ''musical tragedy'' had only a respectable but ultimately insufficient run of 281 performances on Broadway.

A 1972 revival (Imperial Theater 18 April) ran 39 performances, and a filmed version was made in 1974 with that production's lead man, Brock Peters, repeating his role. *Lost in the Stars* is played regularly in America, mostly in non-professional situations where its theme of the former South African apartheid politic and/or racial disharmony in general are fashionable, and also occasionally under similarly predisposed professional circumstances. A revised version produced at Chicago's Goodman Theater in 1993 (28 June), ''newly adapted from Alan Paton by Frank Galati,'' disposed of Anderson's libretto whilst keeping his lyrics. In 1998 (29 August) the show was seen in South Africa in a charity performance at the Roodepoort City Opera.

Germany: Opernhaus, Nuremberg *Der weite Weg* 7 May 1961; Austria: Staatsoper *Der weite Weg* 1962

Film: AFT 1974

Recordings: original cast (Decca, MCA), studio cast (Music Masters), selections (World Records, Decca)

LOST, STOLEN OR STRAYED (aka *Lost, Strayed or Stolen*) Musical farce in 3 acts by J Cheever Goodwin based on the play *Le Baptême du petit Oscar* by Eugène Grangé and Victor Bernard. Music by Woolson Morse. McVicker's Theater, Chicago, 15 June 1896; Fifth Avenue Theater, New York, 21 September 1896.

One of the earliest examples on the American musical stage of a genuine ''musical comedy,'' in the mold of the French vaudeville, fabricated from a translation of an original and successful (French) play, and a set of custom-written songs. Produced by the American Theatrical Syndicate, as their maiden production, at Chicago's McVickers Theater, with the English musical comedian Fred Wright jr starred, the piece was hailed as ''something new'' and the Chicago press decided patriotically that though it was ''built on the general plan of English pieces like *The Gaiety Girl* and *An Artist's Model*'' it was ''decided novelty, and an improvement on the British article.'' The show proved a firm success in its three-week season in Chicago, and was taken east at the start of the new season. Since Wright (Bidart) was continuing his international traveling, and leading lady Jennie Goldthwaite (Rose d'Été) opted for marriage instead of Broadway, it reached New York in a slightly recast form.

On the day of his christening, the baby of Monsieur Bidart goes astray. The nursemaid went and gave him to a soldier in the Luxemburg Gardens to hold, and now that soldier cannot be found. So Bidart (Louis Harrison) and the baby's three godfathers, the portly but exuberant Chachignon (Mike A Kennedy), string-bean, misanthropic Courte Botte de Roquencourt (Joseph W Herbert) and the bright little notary Galampois (Claude Brooke), set out to find baby Oscar. They gallop through the barracks and through the boudoir of Mlle Rose d'Été (Georgia Caine), having to assume ridiculous disguises when found where they shouldn't be and braving the poisonous handshake of the lady's irate Cuban guardian (Henry Bergman) on the way, before baby is found.

Morse and Goodwin illustrated the French antics with a score of lively songs, from which Rose and Gaston's ''When Two Hearts Love'' proved the favorite, and the show, with a cast completed by Irene Verona (Françoise), Rose Beaudet (Catherine), Cyril Scott (Gaston de Champignol, Rose's gentleman friend), Emma Janvier (Louise) and Fannie Bulkeley (Honorine Girardin, the baby's godmother) went on to a respectable stay of 69 nights through some two and a half months at Broadway's Fifth Avenue Theater before moving on both to success around America (''the biggest musical hit in Boston this season'') and, a rare thing for an American musical at the time, to Britain.

Exported to a London at the peak of the British musical-theatre boom, *Lost, Strayed or Stolen* was mounted with South African comedian Frank Wheeler as Bidart alongside Decima Moore (Rose), Ethel Sydney (Honorine) and J H Barnes, Arthur Appleby and Herman de

Lange as the three godfathers. It was well noticed as a jolly entertainment, and Johnnie D'Auban's eccentric dance routines won rave notices, but it failed to attract. The producers took no half-measures. They hired Louie Freear, the comic star of *The Gay Parisienne,* and wrote in a role for her, they changed other cast members and the show's title (*A Day in Paris*), souped up the second act, and what little remained of the original score ("When Two Hearts Love," "Two Heads Are Better Than One," "Jean and Jacques," etc) was complemented by a barrage of local numbers: Arthur Godfrey's "Why Did the Little Fly Fly?" and "Summer Tide," Leslie Stuart's "The Goblin and the Fay," Herbert Darnley's "Blowed if Father Ain't Commenced to Work" for Louie Freear, "She Just Walks On" (Mills/Scott), "An Extra Little Bit Thrown In" (Sidney Jones/Bowyer), "It's Painfully True" (Roby/Cross). It was all to little avail, and the show was shunted out to Islington after 10 weeks.

A Berlin musical farce, *Berliner Fahrten* written by Freund and Mannstädt and produced at the Centraltheater in 1897 bore a remarkable resemblance in its plot to Grangé and Bernard's piece, but admitted of no influence.

UK: Duke of York's Theatre (aka *A Day in Paris*) 27 April 1897

LOUDON, Dorothy (b Boston, 17 September 1933). Versatile actress who came into her own in the musical theatre in character roles.

After early work in stock and revue, Miss Loudon made her first Broadway appearance in the short-lived Izzy and Moe musical *Nowhere to Go But Up* (1962). In a career mixing straight and musical-theatre appearances, she toured as the *Unsinkable Molly Brown* and Reno Sweeney, in *The Apple Tree* and *High Spirits,* appeared on Broadway in *The Fig Leaves Are Falling* (1968, Lillian Stone) and stopped short in *Lolita My Love* (1971, Charlotte Haze), before memorably creating the role of the kiddie-loathing Miss Hannigan in a very different kind of nymphet musical, *Annie* ("Little Girls," "Easy Street"), in its metropolitan production.

She subsequently succeeded to the role of Mrs Lovett in Broadway's *Sweeney Todd,* starred opposite Vincent Gardenia as Bea Asher in *Ballroom* (1978), repeated her Annie role in the "Miss Hannigan Fights Back" version of the musequel *Annie* 2, was seen on the road as Parthy Ann in *Show Boat* (1997) and created the role of Lulu Shriner in *Over and Over* (1999).

LOUISIANA PURCHASE Musical comedy in 2 acts by Morrie Ryskind based on a story by B G De Sylva. Music and lyrics by Irving Berlin. Imperial Theater, New York, 28 May 1940.

One of the later examples of the group of mostly 1930s musical comedies which liked to pretend they were politically satirical (rather than just funny and sexy), *Louisiana Purchase* followed hopelessly clean Senator Oliver P Loganberry (Victor Moore) down to New Orleans where he has been ordered to carry out an investigation into the indubitably dubious activities of the Louisiana Purchase Company. The company's lawyer Jim Taylor (William Gaxton) sets out to divert and compromise Loganberry, bringing in such big guns as the alluring Marina van Linden (Vera Zorina) and Madame Bordelaise (Irene Bordoni) to knock him off his high moral standards. After some musical-comedy ups and downs, and a lot of winning comedy from Moore—cast yet again as a buffonish politician, following his double helping of Throttlebottoms in *Of Thee I Sing* and *Let 'em Eat Cake* and his unable-to-do-wrong ambassador in *Leave It to Me!*—the loveable senator ends up wedding la Bordelaise, whilst Taylor gets Marina, in good, tidy Gilbert and Sullivan style.

Irving Berlin's score of a dozen numbers accompanied the story brightly, with Miss Bordoni's assertion that "It's a Lovely Day Tomorrow" (always a winner of a title for wartime, even other people's wartime) coming out as the most popular single number, alongside her suggestive "Latins Know How," a happy title song, an opening called "Sex Marches On" and some less louche lyrics such as "You're Lonely and I'm Lonely," "Outside of That, I Love You," "What Chance Have I (with love)?" and "Dance with Me (tonight at the Mardi Gras)."

A winning combination of grand comedy, songs, production values and a fine cast, Buddy De Sylva's production of *Louisiana Purchase* settled down as the principal hit of 1940 (which nevertheless included *Panama Hattie, Pal Joey* and *Cabin in the Sky*), running through 444 performances on Broadway, and bundling directly into the movie studios where Mlles Bordoni and Zorina again vamped Moore who was pitted this time against Bob Hope in the role of Taylor. Only three of the show's songs ("It's a Lovely Day Tomorrow," "You're Lonely" and the title song) survived into a film which, since only one other number was added, was rather shorter on music than the original piece.

Moore, Gaxton and Miss Bordoni took up their roles again for a tightened-up TV version in 1951, and in 1996 the piece was disinterred for a concert performance at Carnegie Hall, with George S Irving (Loganberry), Taina Elg (Bordelaise), Michael McGrath (Jim) and Judy Blazer (Marina) featured, but *Louisiana Purchase* did not travel beyond America and ultimately none of its songs made its way into the Irving Berlin book of standards.

The Louisiana Purchase was made the subject of an extravaganza produced at the St Louis World's Fair of

1904. A vast spectacle written by Hiram Wencislaus Hayes, musically illustrated by William John Hall and Anton Heidl (with a couple of interpolations by A Baldwin Sloane) and mounted by Max Freeman at the Delmar Gardens (29 May), it had Miss Dixie (Frances Merton) singing about being ''The American Girl'' and Davy Crockett (William G Stuart) serenading ''My Sweet Dakotah Girl'' amid lashings of scenery and a chorus of 170. Not to be left out, the spectacle-specializing Kiralfy Family mounted their *Louisiana Purchase* simultaneously at the Odeon with Bolossy Kiralfy's inevitable Pony Ballet, a radium dance and other such historical accessories featured, but without much success.

Film: Paramount 1941

Recording: New York concert recording 1996 (DRG), compilation from original production (JJA)

LOUIS XIV Opérette in 3 acts by Serge Veber. Music by Georges van Parys and Philippe Parès. Théâtre de la Scala, Paris, ?October 1929.

Serge Veber's musical-comedy vehicle for the celebrated singing comedian Dranem cast him as a grocer in prey to a celluloid passion for film star Diamond Black (Lily Zévaco). When a film director spots in him the sosie of King Louis and stars him opposite his dream girl in a *Louis XIV* film, the grocer takes all his friends to filmland with him and Versailles becomes an on-screen havoc. In his royal garb, little Louis briefly succeeds in winning Miss Black before going back to grocering, and, since his battle-ax wife (Martine Lestac/Pauline Carton) has gone off with a svelte screen star (Jacques Vitry/Pierre Dorly), he takes the faithful little shopgirl Odette (Suzette O'Nil) with him. Urban and Morton added to the comedy as two of Odette's other soupirants.

Veber's script earned him accusations of plagiarism from André Vivolette, the French adaptor of *Merton of the Movies,* but the local piece got to the stage first and suffered not a whit from such aspersions. Henri Darcet's production at the Scala boasted ''la fleur des comiques'' in its advertising and indeed the comedy of Veber's libretto and the cast of top comedy players did much towards the success of *Louis XIV.* It had a fine first run (at the end of which Urban married Lily Zévaco), and it was reprised at the Théâtre de l'Étoile in 1945, under the title *On cherche un roi,* with Champi cast in Dranem's role and Urban repeating the part he had created 16 years earlier.

A Florenz Ziegfeld Broadway show (Sigmund Romberg/Arthur Wimperis, Ziegfeld-Cosmopolitan Theater 2 March 1925) went in for phonetics, calling itself *Louie the 14th.* Like the French piece, it wasn't about the King of France at all, but was a version of the German play, *Ludwig XIV* (Theater des Westens 15 March 1918, 41 performances), by Julius Wilhelm and Paul Frank about an army chow-puncher who gets invited to a posh dinner to prevent there being an unlucky 13 guests at the table. Comedian Leon Errol performed his regular routines, whilst getting to imitate the cook, a mountain guide and a nobleman, alongside leading lady Doris Patston, without the show—which Ziegfeld had boomed fatally as ''the greatest musical comedy ever''—ever taking off. It played 79 performances on Broadway, and closed its subsequent tour in Chicago after the star had had time off with an injured leg.

LOVE FROM JUDY Musical comedy in 2 acts by Eric Maschwitz adapted from the play *Daddy Long-Legs* by Jean Webster. Lyrics by Hugh Martin and Timothy Gray. Music by Hugh Martin. Saville Theatre, London, 25 September 1952.

Love from Judy was an attempt to create an American musical in Britain in which producer Émile Littler teamed local librettist Eric Maschwitz with American stage and film composer Hugh Martin (*Meet Me in St Louis, Best Foot Forward,* etc) and the 1914 Broadway play *Daddy Long-Legs,* a 264-performance success at New York's Gaiety Theater (28 September) and a triumph at London's Duke of York's Theatre two years later (514 performances).

The sentimental story of an orphanage girl, Judy Abbott (Jeannie Carson), and her mysterious benefactor, Jervis Pendelton, whom she calls Daddy Long-Legs (Bill O'Connor), was a natural for adaptation into an equally sentimental musical. Maschwitz kept the well-known plot, in which Pendleton—who is not, as the girl supposes, an old man—eventually wins Judy's love as well as her gratitude, placed the action in more picturesque surroundings to supply some spectacle, and added 17 mostly incidental numbers including an old-fashioned concert scene and a for-the-times-obligatory dream-ballet on Agnes de Mille lines.

There was an orphans' chorus, a Mardi Gras number, a deep-South blackface ''Go and Get Your Old Banjo,'' a black maid (Adelaide Hall) to sing of ''A Touch of Voodoo,'' a smooth title song for the hero, a perky blonde soubrette (June Whitfield) to squawk out the most enjoyable piece of the evening with the denial that she was ''Dum-dum-dum,'' and a series of other pieces which all sounded like a purée of Broadway and Hollywood as illustration to a piece which, if unoriginal, proved, at least, likeable. The orphans, the sentiment, the liveliness and a winning performance from Miss Carson helped the made-to-formula *Love from Judy* to a 594-performance run in London, followed by four years of touring.

Recording: original cast recordings on *Three by Hugh Martin* (JJA Records/Encore)

LOVE IN A VILLAGE Comic opera in 3 acts by Isaac Bickerstaff based on *The Village Opera* by C Johnson. Music composed, selected and arranged by Thomas Arne and Edward Toms. Theatre Royal, Covent Garden, London, 8 December 1762.

One of Bickerstaff's most popular comic operas, *Love in a Village* was based, like so many contemporaneous pieces, on a plot designed to get young aristocrats paired off as their hearts rather than their parents desire. Rossetta (Charlotte Brent) runs away and disguises herself as chambermaid to her friend, Lucinda Woodcock (Miss Hallam), rather than marry unseen the son of Sir William Meadows (Mr Collins), who himself runs away rather than obey his father's orders to wed Rossetta. Young Meadows (George Mattocks) ends up disguised as a gardener at the Woodcock's house, and predictably falls for the disguised Rossetta. In the meanwhile Lucinda is planning to elope with her beloved Jack Eustace (Mr Dyer), who is posing as a music master in the house, under the noses of Justice Woodcock and his tight-lipped maiden sister Deborah (Mrs Walker). Deborah catches them out, but Jack's credentials and Deborah's opposition combine to make the Justice permit the match. The supporting characters included a jolly country squire, Hawthorn (John Beard), and a pair of comical servants, Hodge (Mr Dunstall) and Madge (Miss Davies).

The accompanying musical part included some 30 to 43 numbers (added to, latterly, by a whole series of ad-lib interpolations), including ''The Miller of Dee'' as performed by Hawthorn as his entrance piece, and seven original tunes composed specifically for the piece by Arne (five) and Samuel Howard (two). It has been argued by some folk who like labels pinned on things that this original contribution, and the more substantial than usual nature of the score, disqualifies the piece from being considered a ballad opera and makes it ''the first English comic opera.''

Love in a Village was played 37 times in its first season in the repertoire at Covent Garden, was a major success, and was repeated on English-language stages for many decades thereafter. In 1853 it was played at the Strand Theatre with Rebecca Isaacs as Rossetta and the young Isabelle Featherstone as Madge.

During the brief fashion for 18th-century musical shows in London during the 1920s, *Love in the Village* was given a revival at the Everyman Theatre (21 December 1923, mus arr Julian Herbage), and another at the Lyric, Hammersmith (19 April 1928, 124 performances) in a version with a score rearranged by Alfred Reynolds. Rose Hignell (Rossetta), Sybil Crawley (Lucinda), Frederick Ranalow (Hawthorn), Una O'Connor (Deborah) and Nigel Playfair (Meadows) featured, with veteran Savoyard H Scott Russell in a small role.

USA: Southwark Theater, Philadelphia January 1767, New York 11 January 1768; Australia: Theatre Royal, Sydney 22 February 1836

LOVE LIES Musical play in 2 acts by Stanley Lupino and Arthur Rigby. Lyrics by Desmond Carter. Music by ''Hal Brody.'' Gaiety Theatre, London, 20 March 1929.

Following his success with *Lady Luck* and a larger one with *So This Is Love,* producer-performer Laddie Cliff continued with a third piece in the same dance-and-laughter mode, written and played by the same team that had been involved in the previous show. Lupino and Rigby's silhouette-slight book involved the usual wealthy uncles and scallywag nephews who have got entangled with girls without asking the permission of those relations from whom they have expectations. The functions of each artist were maintained, Lupino going in for the low comedy and a whole lot of disguises, Cliff taking the tricky dancing and little-fellow comedy, and Cyril Ritchard and Madge Elliott being the romance and the graceful dancing. The songs, mostly by the team of British songwriters who were still pretending to be a fashionably American ''Hal Brody,'' were a bundle of the lightly dancing kind from which ''You've Made a Difference to Me'' as delivered by Ritchard and Miss Elliott emerged as the best. As so often, however, it was the interpolations which proved the most popular: Billy Mayerl's ''A House on a Hill Top,'' Leslie Sarony's nonsensical ''I Lift Up My Finger (and say tweet-tweet)'' as performed by Lupino, and De Sylva, Brown and Henderson's ''I'm on the Crest of a Wave'' borrowed from one of *George White's Scandals.*

Cliff took *Love Lies* to the famous Gaiety Theatre, which had fallen onto sadly hard times, and the show gave that house its biggest success since *Going Up* a decade earlier. It won delighted notices, which compared it and its performers favorably with the recent *Funny Face,* a production which had featured no less artists than the Astaires and Leslie Henson, and it settled in for a run of 347 performances. Before the London run was done, there were two companies on the road taking *Love Lies* to the provinces, a total which rose to three when the London company took to touring at the end of its run, and the show was still to be seen on the provincial lists in 1931, by which time Cliff and his team had compounded their success with more shows of the same type.

An Australian production under the management of Richard White and Eric Edgley featured Dan Agar, Bobby Gordon, Rita McLean, Clem Dawe and Compton Coutts, for four-week seasons in Melbourne and Sydney (Theatre Royal 24 May 1930).

A 1931 BIP film version scripted by and starring Lupino, and directed by Lupino Lane, omitted the music.

Australia: King's Theatre, Melbourne 5 April 1930

LOVE LIFE Vaudeville in 2 acts by Alan Jay Lerner. Music by Kurt Weill. 46th Street Theater, New York, 7 October 1948.

Like Rodgers and Hammerstein's *Allegro* of the previous season, Alan Jay Lerner and Kurt Weill's *Love Life* sported a libretto which looked at its two principal characters, from a standpoint apart, more as the victims of their environment than as real people of action. The story of the love life of Sam (Ray Middleton) and Susan (Nanette Fabray) Cooper was told in a revusical fashion, in a series of scenes which (after a prologue set in the present) took them through various periods of time from 1791 through 1821, 1857, 1890 and the 1920s, back to the present. Like the couple of *Allegro* they progress from a promising start to infidelity, and it is all the fault of the American way of life and its economic pressures which Lerner apparently considered—for the purposes of this piece, at least—to have been less in 1791 than in 1948.

The songs of *Love Life* included some which were set in the action, notably the winning first-scene duo for the two principals, ''Here I'll Stay,'' and others which were presented between the scenes, repeating in song what was played in the action in the style of traditional Jewish theatre (''Economics,'' ''Progress''). The second act, wholly set in present time, and including a dance sequence featuring Punch and Judy in the throes of divorce and a long scena played as a stylized minstrel show, ultimately gave forth some hope for the future of marriage in this hard, modern world. As long as you go into it with your eyes and wallet open. The other principal dance sequence of the entertainment was the first-act ''Green-Up Time,'' and the score also included a number entitled ''I Remember It Well'' whose lyric was later made over for Maurice Chevalier and Hermione Gingold for reuse in the film *Gigi.*

In spite of being equipped with two fine star performances in its not very coherent leading roles, with Michael Kidd's lively choreography and with much in the way of colorful spectacle to assist its unconventionally shaped tale and score, *Love Life* failed to become a success. It ran 252 Broadway performances without either breaking even or establishing itself in the exportable or revivable repertoire. It was given a 1990 staging at the American Music Theater Festival of Philadelphia (10 June) with Richard Muenz and Debbie Shapiro featured in a tinkered-with version, and subsequently given its first British showing in the unlikely hands of one of the country's top opera organizations, Opera North, with Alan Oke and Margaret Preece as Sam and Susan.

UK: Grand Theatre, Leeds 25 January 1996

Recording: selection on *Lyrics by Lerner* (Walden/DRG)

LOVE OFF THE SHELF Musical in 2 acts by Roger Hall. Lyrics by A K Grant. Music by Philip Norman. Fortune Theatre, Dunedin, New Zealand, 29 August 1986.

A revusical eight-hander written by New Zealand's most popular playwright, Roger Hall, who had had a London stage success with his play *Middle-Age Spread* shortly before, *Love off the Shelf* took the romantic novel as its subject and source of fun. John (Barry Dorking) is a serious but unpublished writer who has spent ages working on a book about a minor poet. Mary (Helen McGowan) is his serious research assistant. On the side, each begins to write romantic fiction, and the action of the show sees the characters of their pink novellas come off the page to tangle with their authors and with each other in a series of comic scenes and songs which culminates in a suitably romantic ending. The score was in an ultralight, revusical vein, producing comical moments as two wide-eyed and be-skied characters met on ''The Virgin Slopes of Love,'' as that novelist's sine qua non the ''Deus ex Machina'' put in an appearance, or as a bemused stock character bewailed ''You'd Think It Was Fine to Be Virile.''

A successful New Zealand production was followed by a six-month tour and then by a production in Southampton, England. Marilyn Cutts and Barry James led the company in a more revue-like version of the show which cut some of the structure from the libretto whilst maintaining most of the score unchanged. Well received, it was mooted for a London showing which failed to get off the drawing board in a period when West End audiences and producers were still concentrating on the large-scale musical spectaculars and pastiche shows that had been their diet for some years. Instead, it won a fresh production under the aegis of Alan Ayckbourn at his Scarborough theatre (15 October 1993). In 1998 the show was given an Australian premiere in a month's run at Canberra's Universal Theatre with Grant Dodwell, Elaine Smith, Nick Carrafa and Anna McCrossin featured, and a further British production at Harrogate (17 September) and Southampton (29 October) with Simon Robson and Amanda Waring in the central roles.

Love off the Shelf remains the first New Zealand–bred musical to have been played in Great Britain since *The Wreck of the Pinafore* over a century earlier.

Hall, Grant and Norman also produced the successful musical based on the favorite New Zealand comic strip *Footrot Flats* (Court Theatre, October 1983), and Hall and Norman have collaborated on two other small-house pieces, *Making It Big* (Fortune Theatre, November 1991) and *Dirty Weekends,* ''a gardening musical in four seasons'' (Fortune Theatre, October 1997).

UK: Nuffield Theatre, Southampton 17 December 1987; Australia: Universal Theatre, Canberra 3 June 1998

Recording: original cast (Kiwi Pacific Records)

Autobiography: [Hall] *Bums on Seats* (Viking, Auckland, 1998)

LOVE O' MIKE Musical comedy in 2 acts by "Thomas Sydney" (Sydney Smith and Augustus Thomas). Lyrics by Harry B Smith. Music by Jerome Kern. Shubert Theater, New York, 15 January 1917.

The show which eventually became *Love o' Mike* was first produced at the Lyric Theater, Philadelphia (20 November 1916), under the title *Girls Will Be Girls,* as a joint production by the Shuberts and Elisabeth Marbury but, after an unsuccessful start, it was taken off after two weeks of performances and given a thorough overhaul. In just two further weeks major revisions were made to the text and the score (four songs were jettisoned and replaced by five others, in spite of the fact that composer Kern was working concurrently on another show), several of the lead roles were recast and the show reopened at New Haven (25 December 1916) under the new title of *Love o' Mike.* Three weeks later it was on Broadway.

English actor Lawrence Grossmith (brother to the more famous George) was the Mike of the title, an English soldier and Lord whose dashing presence cuts out all the other fellows at the house party run by Mrs Marvin (Alison McBain). Whilst the girls cluster, the boys try to discredit Mike, but the comical butler (George Hassell) spoils their plans and Mike comes out as heroic as ever at the end of the evening, with his choice of the girls (Vivian Wessell) to boot. The pick of the songs turned out to be one of the additions, "It Wasn't My Fault" (ly: M E Rourke), which Kern had lifted from the score of his 1915 flop *Ninety in the Shade* to be performed here by Grossmith and Miss Wessell. Grossmith's limited voice was not taxed much further, and the bulk of the songs went to the boys and girls of the house party amongst whom were to be found the young Peggy Wood singing of "A Lonesome Little Tune" and Clifton Webb and Gloria Goodwin duetting "It's in the Book." Miss Wessel retained two of the best of the original songs, "I Wonder Why" and "The Baby Vampire."

The two weeks of hard work proved to have been worth their while, and the bright and extremely lightweight piece of entertainment ran for 192 Broadway performances at the Shubert, Maxine Elliott and Casino Theaters. On the road, however, it was less successful and did not confirm its happy New York run.

THE LOVE RACE Musical play in 2 acts by Stanley Lupino. Lyrics by Desmond Carter. Music by Jack Clarke. Additional numbers by H B Hedley and Harry Acres. Gaiety Theatre, London, 25 June 1930.

After the success of *Love Lies,* Laddie Cliff attempted to repeat the formula which George Edwardes had successfully used at the Gaiety Theatre in the 1880s by

Plate 230. **Love off the Shelf.** *Novelist Mary (Helen McGowan) gazes in delight at the creature (Debbie Cairns) who has stepped out of her pages.*

sending his star team on the road, with the original show to play and a new one to prepare, whilst holding the theatre open with a second team and another musical show. The second team and *Darling, I Love You* did not come up to hopes and expectations, and *The Love Race* promptly brought the A-team back to town.

Disapproving elders and youthful love were again the theme of the piece, with Cyril Ritchard as a film star and Madge Elliott playing the daughter of a socialist MP who disapproves of film stars, whilst Stanley Lupino was the son of a car magnate in love with Fay Martin as the daughter of a rival manufacturer. Laddie Cliff was her brother, Fred Conyngham and Esmé Tosh were a supporting song-and-dance pair, Drusilla Wills provided low comedy, Connie Emerald (Mrs Stanley Lupino) the soubrette comedy, and Violet Farebrother, Arthur Wotton and Arthur Rigby jr played the heavy parents.

The team was equipped with plenty of comedy, light and low, and nine mostly dance-orientated numbers of which the three star men singing and dancing "You Can't Keep a Good Man Down" and Laddie Cliff's "Spring Is in the Air" proved the best. Lupino's would-be hit-clone "I Stamp My Foot" did not come up to *Love Lies*'s "I Lift Up My Finger." The stars scored a repeat success, to which had to be added a success for costumier Irene Segalla who had, in the age of naked kneecaps, put her ladies back into long dresses, a decision perhaps not unconnected with the improving billing of the elegant and longiline Miss Elliott. *The Love Race* ran 237 performances, rather short of the producers' most hopeful expectations, but it lasted for two provincial seasons and confirmed Cliff and Lupino in their successful ways.

J C Williamson Ltd later mounted a production in Australia with Gus Bluett, Leo Frankyln, Alfred Frith, Elsie Prince and Josie Melville featured in a starry cast, but the piece proved to have no future beyond its Sydney season.

A 1931 film starring Lupino followed the pattern set with *Love Lies* and omitted the music.

Australia: Her Majesty's Theatre, Sydney 16 May 1931

THE LOVE RACKET Musical play in 2 acts by Stanley Lupino. Additional dialogue by Arty Ash. Lyrics by Frank Eyton, Barbara Gordon and Basil Thomas, and Leslie Gibbs. Music by Noel Gay. Additional numbers by Hubert Gregg and Freddie Bretherton. Victoria Palace, London, 21 October 1943.

Allegedly a successor to *Lady Behave,* in the same dubious style that *Me and My Girl* had been billed a sequel to *20 to 1, The Love Racket* repeated the names of some of the earlier piece's characters but without even the connection of having them played by the same artist. Author and *Lady Behave* star Stanley Lupino was, in fact, dead by the time Jack Hylton and Lupino Lane staged his last stage work, and his role was taken by Arthur Askey who starred alongside Roy Royston, Harry Milton, Valerie Tandy, Carole Raye and Peggy Carlisle as the six filmland folk of the earlier show, this time mixed up in problems over the making of a film which is apparently a cert to be the blockbuster of its era. The accompanying songs included ''Happy Days'' (Harry Milton, Carol Raye) and ''Reaching for the Moon'' (Carol Raye) amongst a pleasant dance-and-laughter set.

The Love Racket proved a viable vehicle, and Askey confirmed himself as the legitimate successor to Lupino Lane at the theatre where Lane had triumphed in *Me and My Girl,* but the show's run was interrupted by Lane's decision to return to ''his'' theatre himself in *Meet Me Victoria,* which necessitated the removal of the still-profitable *Love Racket* to the Prince's Theatre. It was interrupted again by enemy bombing which, after eight and a half months and 324 performances, forced the show out of town. It was taken on an ENSA round of service entertainment, and then on a regular provincial tour, returning to London five months later for a Christmas season at the Adelphi Theatre (23 December 1944, 36 performances). Askey then took the show back on the ENSA trail, and around the provinces again, before, after more than two years in his role, handing it over to Ernie Lotinga. However, in 1949 he took up the part one more time for an Australian production which confirmed both his own popularity and that of his show.

Australia: Tivoli, Melbourne 23 December 1949

LOVE'S LOTTERY Comic opera in 2 acts by Stanislaus Stange. Music by Julian Edwards. Broadway Theater, New York, 3 October 1904.

History does not relate how producer F C Whitney persuaded 43-year-old Metropolitan Opera star Mme Ernestine Schumann-Heink away from her operatic and concert pursuits to appear on the musical stage. One can only suppose that the lure was either money, or the unusual opportunity for the contralto to play the heroine. The vehicle which Whitney provided was a comic opera which cast Mme Schumann-Heink as a German laundress called Lina (which took care of the hefty accent if not the lady's ingenuous acting style) and paired her with English baritone Wallace Brownlow, the original Luis of *The Gondoliers,* in a story of true love in the England of the Napoléonic wars.

Julian Edwards's score was by no means overwhelmingly written for his star, nor, curiously, did it seek to capitalize on her gifts. She had four songs, two in each act, but if ''She Is the Right Girl for Your Money'' gave her a little cadenza, and the closing ''Sweet Thoughts of Home'' allowed a few cello-like low A-flats, ''Kind Fortune Smiles Today'' and ''A Spanish Grandee'' were pretty standard stuff with vocal lines which never ventured above the stave and rarely more than a tone or two below. Brownlow had a solo in each half and a duo and a trio with the star, Louise Gunning and George L Tallman were the number-two couple and John Slavin as Barney O'Toole provided the comedy (''The Blarney of Killarney''). *Love's Lottery* was produced at Detroit in September, and took in a set season of 50 performances on Broadway, but the tour came to grief in Cleveland when the recently remarried star (husband Schumann had died whilst the show was playing an early date in Boston), involved in all sorts of grief with the German government and her sons in the German army, went and lost her voice.

DES LÖWEN ERWACHEN Operette (comic opera) in 1 act by Julius Rosen. Music by Johann Brandl. Carltheater, Vienna, 26 April 1872.

A four-handed, one-act Operette on the Offenbach model, Rosen and Brandl's piece centered on the young 18th-century Gaston (Hermine Meyerhoff), the second son of the local lord, who has been brought up, without expectations, by the local teacher Placide (Karl Blasel).

To keep his ward, Paquerette (Frl Guilleaume), safe from the pubescent boy, Placide locks her up in the mill, but when news comes that the Herzog's eldest son has died and that Gaston is now his heir, Placide decides that a boy with that kind of expectations needs a different kind of education. Part of that education involves letting Paquerette out of the mill. By the time Placide discovers that the news was incorrect and bundles the girl back inside, it is too late—the lion of the title has awakened. But fortunately the Herzog has given Gaston a commission, so he marches away leaving the girl safe with her rural lover (Herr Küstner).

The most enduring of the many pieces (few of which, however, were legitimate Operetten) written by Carltheater musical director Brandl, and one of the best of the early attempts at short "French" Operetten by Viennese composers, *Des Löwen Erwachen* was played 18 times during 1872, and became a firm favorite in Vienna thereafter. It was reprised regularly at the Carltheater, and played at the Strampfertheater (25 December 1872), the Theater an der Wien (31 March 1886), the Hofoper (22 October 1893) and at Venedig in Wien (31 August 1900), as well as throughout Germany.

Germany: ?1873

LOWENFELD, Henry [Hans] (b Poland; d Paris, 20 November 1931).

A wealthy businessman, owner of the Kops Ale (temperance) brewery, of a stockbroking firm and, if word told true, of a fair chunk of the Isle of Wight as well, Lowenfeld moved into the musical theatre in 1893 when he picked up Albéniz's failing comic opera, *The Magic Opal,* had it rewritten, leased the Prince of Wales Theatre and reproduced it there. Its refailure apparently daunted him not, and he continued to run musicals at the Prince of Wales, scoring notable successes with Arthur Roberts in *Gentleman Joe* (1895) and, above all, with the French musical *La Poupée* (1897), a long-running hit which he had picked up from Paris after most of London's managers had rejected it. He met with failure, however, when he put his trust in French composer Justin Clérice, first with the previously unproduced *The Royal Star* and then in an English version of the composer's Portuguese success *O Moliero d'Alcala,* presented as *The Coquette* (1899). Infuriated by a section of the first-night gallery audience which drowned a perfectly adequate musical with their whistling and shouting, he went on stage and harangued the self-appointed arbiters of his show. Soon after, although *The Coquette* showed every sign of running, he removed it, sold his lease, and got himself and his money out of a business which did not behave like a business, but where profit and loss could be decided by a handful of irresponsible (or paid) whistlers.

LUDERS, Gustav [Carl] (b Bremen, 13 December 1865; d New York, 24 January 1913). One of the best and most successful composers for the comic opera stage at the turn of the American century.

Having spent his youth and study years in Germany, where he worked latterly as a band musician, Luders moved to America in 1888 and settled in Milwaukee. There he worked first as a theatre and pleasure-garden musician, later as a conductor, and he had his first taste of musical theatre putting together the score for a piece called *A Night in Egypt* played at the new People's Theatre, where he was engaged as musical director for a summer season of burlesque. The show lasted two weeks, management policy four, but after the dropping of the theatre part of the program Luders stayed on to provide the house with new music for its orchestra through the rest of the summer.

He subsequently became a staff arranger for the music-publishing company of Witmark, and it was under Witmark's banner that he found his first slice of wider success when his transcription of Barney Fagan's song "My Gal is a Highborn Lady" became a hit. The music publisher and songwriter Charles Harris encouraged him to move to the more musically active Chicago, where there was currently a shortage of trained musicians in the publishing trade, and there, whilst playing in the orchestra at the Schiller Theater, Luders began his career as a theatre composer by composing the scene music for the theatre's production of *The Witch,* putting together a score for Joel Marks's quick-flop touring production of the "farcical burletta" *A Trip to Turkey* (1892), and then by writing a stopgap score for Harry B Smith's *Little Robinson Crusoe* (1895). "Professor Luders" subsequently acted as musical director to the Schiller Theater stock-and-variety house, and as conductor of the grandly named Philharmonic Orchestra at another local vaudeville house, the Gaiety. There he put together the music for the burlesque *Little Miss Chicago,* led the "Philharmonic" in afternoon pops, provided music for the stock company, and teamed with J A Fraser on an (apparently unproduced) musical version of a French drama under the title *The Merry Robbers.* Around this time, he also placed the odd number in such traveling musicals as *By the Sad Sea Waves* ("In Dear Old London") and *The Rogers Brothers in Wall Street* ("You Told Me You Had Money in the Bank"), with which he went on the road as conductor. Also around the same time, he paired up with Frank Pixley, a Chicago journalist and budding playwright, to write more ambitious stage pieces. Luders and Pixley were unable to find a producer for their first musical comedy *King Dodo* (though in the summer of '98 Luders announced to the Chicago press that he was going to New York for its production), but a second effort, *The Burgo-*

master, was taken up by the local Dearborn Theater. It turned out to be a major Chicago success. *The Burgomaster* had but a brief subsequent Broadway run (33 performances) with Raymond Hitchcock and Zelma Rawlston featured, but it proved highly popular through several years of touring for manager William Cullen and the previously unwanted *King Dodo* was now snapped up by Henry Savage. It duly followed a similar path from Chicago to New York (64 performances) and to a long life on the lucrative road.

The third Luders/Pixley work, *The Prince of Pilsen,* turned out to be their best and their most successful. This time even Broadway took notice of the happily American-Continental comic opera with its fine ''Stein Song'' and its pretty ''The Message of the Violet,'' and the piece, certainly one of the best of all early American comic operas, not only lived out many years on the road but returned for repeated revivals and even traveled to London and to Paris with some success after its initial 143 nights in New York.

This run of success finally prompted a call eastwards for Luders, and a commission to provide the score for Florenz Ziegfeld's production of *Mam'selle Napoléon,* a Jean Richepin piece he was having adapted as a vehicle for Anna Held. In 1905 the composer had a second Broadway job, writing part of the score for the Hippodrome spectacular *A Society Circus,* but, in between, he turned out two further pieces in his own Chicago vein. George Ade's *The Sho-Gun,* after splendid seasons in Chicago and New York (125 performances) and a long tour, proved to be another export when, by some chain of events, it was staged with notable success at the Király Színház in Budapest, and the pretty fantasy *Woodland* (83 Broadway performances), written again with Pixley, also had a good life on the home circuits.

The last three of the Pixley/Luders team's shows were, however, disappointing. Klaw and Erlanger's production of the old-fashioned *The Grand Mogul* (40 performances), *Marcelle* (68 performances) and *The Gypsy* (12 performances), all built on the same format of easy comedy and well-written, tuneful songs were simply a little less fresh than their first attempts, and they duly did increasingly less well. Luders's simultaneous collaborations with Ade on the college musical *The Fair Co-Ed* (136 performances)—a follow-up to the librettist's *The College Widow* starring Elsie Janis—and on a Montgomery and Stone vehicle for Charles Dillingham, *The Old Town* (171 performances), each helped not a little by the popularity of its respective stars, had much longer Broadway lives.

With Pixley having gone into retirement after the flop of *The Gypsy,* Luders paired for his next Broadway show with the young Avery Hopwood, but Henry Savage's production of their *Somewhere Else* proved to be the composer's quickest-ever failure. Four days after the premiere Luders died, reportedly of a broken heart. His estate amounted to just $160.

A composer of well-written, unpretentiously attractive music with a delightfully catchy lilt—ranging from bubble-light waltzes with a tinge of the Old World right through the gamut of song styles to coon songs and politely ragtimey numbers which were wholly of the New World—as well as of thoroughly musical ensembles in the best comic-opera tradition, Luders was one of the most effective composers in the American musical theatre of his time. His best shows rank musically alongside those of Herbert and Caryll as the choice produce of the Broadway stage in the first decade and a bit of the century.

1890 **A Night in Egypt** People's Theater, Milwaukee 14 June

1892 **A Trip to Turkey** (J W Kelly) Carlisle, Pa 1 December

1895 **Little Robinson Crusoe** (w W H Batchelor/Harry B Smith) Schiller Theater, Chicago 15 June

1897 **Little Miss Chicago** Gaiety Theater, Chicago 23 February

1900 **The Burgomaster** (Frank Pixley) Dearborn Theater, Chicago 17 June; Manhattan Theater 31 December

1901 **King Dodo** (Pixley) Studebaker Theater, Chicago 27 May; Daly's Theater 12 May 1902

1902 **The Prince of Pilsen** (Pixley) Tremont Theater, Boston 12 May; Broadway Theater 17 March 1903

1903 **Mam'selle Napoléon** (Joseph W Herbert) Knickerbocker Theater 8 December

1904 **The Sho-Gun** (George Ade) Studebaker Theater, Chicago 4 April; Wallack's Theater 10 October

1904 **Woodland** (Pixley) Tremont Theater, Boston 25 April; New York Theater 21 November

1905 **A Society Circus** (w Manuel Klein/Sydney Rosenfeld) New York Hippodrome 13 December

1906 **The Grand Mogul** (Pixley) Colonial Theater, Chicago 7 December; New Amsterdam Theater 25 March 1907

1908 **Marcelle** (ex- *The Baron of Berghof*) (Pixley) Casino Theater 1 October

1908 **The Fair Co-Ed** (Ade) Studebaker Theater, Boston 23 November; Knickerbocker Theater 1 February 1909

1910 **The Old Town** (Ade) Studebaker Theater, Chicago 23 September; Globe Theater 10 January

1911 **Ladies' Day** (Vernon Cassard) Ladbroke Hall, London 4 October (copyright performance); Lyric Theater, Philadelphia 13 January 1913

1912 **The Gypsy** (Pixley) Park Theater 14 November

1913 **Somewhere Else** (Avery Hopwood) Broadway Theater 20 January

LUIGINI, Pauline [LUIGGINI, Pauline Marie] (b Toulouse, 27 January 1854).

The daughter of composer François [Maximilien Caiëtan] Luigini, 30 years orchestral leader at Toulouse,

Pauline Luigini was a leading member of the company at the Brussels Fantaisies-Parisiennes under the management of Eugène Humbert in the early 1870s. As such, she became the creator of the role of Clairette Angot in *La Fille de Madame Angot* (1872), the title role of *Giroflé-Girofla,* Marion in Vogel's *La Filleule du roi* (1875) and the leading role of the French version of Jonas's *Chignon d'or.* Having seen the first two roles recast for Paris whilst she played on with the Brussels company, she was finally given the third on its production in France, only to have the show prove very much less liked than its two brilliant predecessors.

Mlle Luigini subsequently appeared in the Parisian premiere of Offenbach's *La Boîte au lait* (1876, Paméla); starred opposite Louise Théo as Fortunato in *Madame l'Archiduc* (1876) and as Bavolet in a revival of *La Jolie Parfumeuse* (1877); featured in the opéras-comiques *Capitaine Fracasse* at the Théâtre Lyrique and *Scheinn Baba* (1879) at Nice; and, back at Brussels, was cast as Lydia in *Fatinitza* (1881)—but she had her best metropolitan chances when her manager husband, Taillefer, took over the Théâtre Cluny in 1881–82 and featured her as Bibletto in *Les Braconniers,* Stella in *La Fille du tambour-major,* and in the title role of Michiels's new but unsuccessful opérette *Mimi Pinson* (1882). Taillefer also mounted her father's opérette *Faublas* (1881), in which she appeared for its life of three nights. ''She is too provincial to please Parisians,'' remarked one critic, noting her ''superabundant energy and action'' and also the fact that ''her voice has gone off greatly since last summer.''

In fact, Mlle Luigini's greatest moments had come in Brussels and in London where, whilst Paola Marié and Jeanne Granier gleaned the real fame from the parts of Clairette and Giroflé-Girofla in Paris, she had traveled to play her famous roles with the Brussels company.

LUISA FERNANDA Zarzuela in 3 acts by Federico Romero and Guillermo Fernández Shaw. Music by Federico Moreno Torroba. Teatro Calderón, Madrid, 26 March 1932.

Although belonging to a later period than most of the best and longest-lived Spanish works, *Luisa Fernanda,* written in the early 1930s, remains one of the most popular full-length pieces in the zarzuela repertoire.

Like that other staple of the zarzuela repertoire, *El barberillo de Lavapiés, Luisa Fernanda* mixed pictures of everyday Spanish life, particularly in Madrid, with a tale of royalty-versus-republican politics and plotting. Luisa Fernanda (Selica Perez Carpío) is a Madrid lass, whose soldier lover, Javier (Faustino Arregui), has risen above her, to the rank of Colonel. Whilst he mixes in royal circles, she is assiduously courted by the wealthy country landowner Vidal Hernando (Emilio Sagi-Barba), but she longs still for Javier. When a group of republicans stage an armed uprising, the apolitical Vidal fights with them solely to have the chance to challenge Javier in the field and he bests and imprisons his rival. The royal troops are finally victorious, but when Luisa sees Javier depart with the Queen's lady-in-waiting, the Duquesa Carolina (Laura Nieto), she at last agrees to marry the brave Vidal. However, following the Queen's deposition and Carolina's flight into exile and in the midst of Luisa's marriage preparations, Javier turns up in Extremadura. Before long Vidal realizes that he must lose the woman he loves to the soldier.

The shape of the piece was interesting in that, like others of the zarzuela grande genre and unlike most traditional Operette libretti, it had no space for low comedy, and, although there were fine featured roles for regular soubrettes (innkeeper Mariana, dressmaker Rosita), its male roles were less predictable. Of its two leading men it was the less worthy Javier, rather than the brave and gentlemanly Vidal (who in a French or Viennese script would have been an aging buffoon), who was capable of inspiring the love of the heroine.

The score included numbers in the popular dance rhythms—a habanera for an organ-grinder (''Marchaba á ser soldado''), a mazurka chorus (''A San Antonio'')—alongside the main body of romantic and lyric numbers, the best and most of which fell to the men of the cast. Javier sang of his rise to high position in a romanza (''De este apacible rincón de Madrid''), responded to Carolina's come-hither (''Caballero del alto plumo'') and forced a quarrel on Vidal and Luisa (''¡Cuanto tiempo sin verte, Luisa Fernanda!'') before getting to his final duet (''Cállate corazón''), whilst Vidal poured out his love to Luisa (''En mi terra estrameña''), spurned the flirtations of Carolina (''Para comprar á un hombre''), went into battle for his love (''Por el amor da una mujer'') and rejoiced in heartfelt fashion over his marriage (''En una dehesa de la Extramadura'') before being left, at the finish, to nothing but despair (''Si por el rido'').

Recordings: complete (Auvidis Valois, Columbia, Alhambra, Montilla, Hispavox, EMI, etc)

LULU Operette in 3 acts by Serge Veber. Music by George van Parys and Philippe Parès. Théâtre Daunou, Paris, 14 September 1927.

The first Parisian show of the young van Parys/Parès team of songwriters, mounted just a few months after their *La Petite Dame du train bleu* had seen stagelight in Brussels, *Lulu* was written to an up-to-date comedy script by another young writer, Serge Veber, who had already tasted Parisian success—in collaboration with his father, the celebrated author of comedies Pierre Veber—with *Quand with est trois.*

Bernard (Pizella) and Yette (Davia) have been wed, he swearing to her all along that he has led a blameless youth, so when the little actress Lulu (Christiane Dor) bounces out of his past and into their home, Yette goes home to daddy (Paul Asselin). Then Bernard's rich Aunt Chloë (Marcelle Yvren) turns up with her son Jeff (Fernand Graavey) and a dowry and, presuming that Lulu is Bernard's new wife, destines Yette for Jeff. In the third act, everyone goes off to Venice where things get worse before they finally get better and the inevitable tidy pairing-off (equipped with happy financial arrangements) brings down the curtain.

The young composers' score included a fox-trot title song for Pizella, who also pleaded liltingly ''Fais ça pour moi,'' whilst Mlle Davia went on pinkly about ''Un petit quelquechose,'' and Mlle Dor explained (''J'ai une nature'') that whilst other performers had talent and could play Iphigenia or Mademoiselle Beulemans she got by very nicely on ''une nature, une bonne figure.''

Lulu was produced by Jane Renouardt on the stage of the little Théâtre Daunou and it scored an instant success. It held its place on the Paris stage for the best part of a year, being joined after just a few weeks by a quick transfer of *La Petite Dame du train bleu* and, when it was time for a change, it was replaced by the young team's next work, *L'Eau à la bouche.* The show went merrily into the provinces, and even traveled as far as Budapest where it was brought into the adventurous and eclectic Fővárosi Operettszínház (ad Adorján Stella, Zsolt Harsányi), following in behind a no less adventurous production: *Abris Rózsája*—otherwise *Abie's Irish Rose.*

Another musical of the same name written by Alain Monjardin and composed by Victor Alix was produced at Caen in 1922 (29 December), an Hungarian *Lulu* with a Szabolcs Fényes score was produced at Budapest's József Attila Színház in 1967 (20 May) and an American one, based on the plays of Wedekind, was played in New York in 1977. The title had also been previously used for what later became *The Girl in the Private Room* (Gitz Rice/Edward Clark, New Haven 20 September 1920) and ultimately the Broadway success *The Blushing Bride.*

Hungary: Fővárosi Operettszínház 14 September 1928

LUNA [y Carne], Pablo (b Alhama de Aragón, 21 May 1879; d Madrid, 28 January 1942).

Pablo Luna worked as a violinist at the Teatro Apolo, and later as a conductor at the Teatro de la Zarzuela, whilst leading a career as a composer for the theatre which would make him one of the main and most successful practitioners of the genéro grande—the full-length zarzuela as opposed to the shorter and more widely popular genéro chico or short musical play.

He began his career with several provincial and shorter pieces—*La escalera de los duendes* (Bilbao, 1904), *Musetta* (1908), *La reina de los mercados* (1909), *El club de las solteras* (1909, w Luis Foglietti), *Huelga de criados* (1910, w Foglietti)—one of which, the 1910 *Molinos de viento* (lib: Luis Pascual Frutos), produced at first in Seville (2 December) and then the following year in Madrid, gave him his first popular success.

Amongst his longer works, the 1918 *El niño judío* (lib: Enrique García Alvárez, Antonio Paso y Cano, Teatro Apolo, Madrid 5 February) proved to be his most successful single piece, but it was his 1916 *El asombro de Damasco* which became the only full-length zarzuela to be adapted for a commercial run on the British stage. It was produced by William J Wilson at the Oxford Theatre under the title *The First Kiss* (ad Boyle Lawrence) with a cast including Desirée Ellinger and Courtice Pounds (10 November 1924) for a run of 43 performances.

His other major works included *Los cadetes de la reina* (1913), *Benamor* (1923), *La pícara molinera* (1928), *La chula de Pontevedra* (1928 w Enrique Brú) and, in later years, *Cock-tail, o un copla hecha mujer* (1939) and *Las calatravas* (1941) from a long list of works amongst which are numbered *Sangre y arena* (1911), *Canto de primavera* (1912), *La alegria de amor* (1913), *El rey del mundo* (1914), *El potro salvaje* (1914, w Joaquín Quinito Valverde), *La corte de Risalia* (1914), *Amores de aldea* (1915), *Ni rey, ni roque* (1915), *El boton de nácar* (1916), *El sapo enamorado* (1916), *Trina la clavellina* (1918), *Los Calabreses* (1918), *Munecos de trapo* (1919), *La mecanógrafa* (1919), *Pancho Virondo* (1919), *Llévame al' metro mamá* (1919), *El suspiro de moro* (1919), *La Venus de las pieles* (1920), *Su Alteza se casa* (1921), *El sinverguenza en palacio* (1921 w Amadeo Vives), *La moza de campanillas* (1923), *Turquía* (1924), *Sangre de reyes* (1925), *La pastorela* (1926), *La Manola del Portillo* (1928), *Encantanda o flor de cerezo* (1939), *El rey flojo* and *La conquista de la gloria.*

Luna also wrote for the musical screen.

Biography: Sagardía, A: *Pablo Luna* (Espasa-Calpe, Madrid, 1978)

LUNZER, Fritz (b Prague, 19 October 1877; d Vienna, 16 March 1940).

The author of more than 30 years of libretti—many of which were short pieces—for the Viennese stage, Lunzer had a single international success with his libretto to *Die Siegerin,* a tale of Catherine the Great set with a pasticcio score of Tchaikovsky music. Of his other pieces, another pasticcio, a Johann Strauss show called *Faschingshochzeit,* ran over one hundred nights at the Carltheater in 1921, a remake of his early Ziehrer Operette *Manöverkind* as *Husarenblut* was played 51 nights at the Raimundtheater, Robert Stolz's *Prinzessin Ti-Ti-Pa* played 53 Viennese performances and *Revanche* lasted two and a half months at the Bürgertheater.

1901 **Die Luftzauberin** (Julius Eibenschütz/Richard Manz ad w Eduard Lunzer) Jantschtheater 27 November

1904 **Der jüngste Tag** (Georg Klammer/w E Lunzer) Jantschtheater 14 October

1908 **Ein Wiener Märchen** (Julius Heller) Wiener Colosseum 7 October

1911 **Die schöne Estrella** (Tomás Lopez Torregrosa/w Friedmann) 1 act Ronacher

1911 **Im Schilderhaus** (Donell/w Friedmann) 1 act Ronacher 22 February

1911 **Die Arkadier** (*The Arcadians*) German version w Oskar Friedmann (Ronacher)

1912 **Adam und Eva** (A M Schweiger) 1 act Ronacher 1 March

1912 **Die Frau im Negligée** (*Die Frau im Hemd*) (Karl W Zeller/w Alfred Spitzer) Ronacher 1 March

1912 **Manöverkind** (Carl Michael Ziehrer/w Friedmann) Venedig in Wien 22 June

1912 **Fräulein Bijou** (Richard Grünfeld/w Ludwig Rottmann) 1 act Wiener Colosseum 1 October

1912 **Kittys Ehemänner** (Ludwig Engländer/w Emil Kolberg) 1 act Hölle 1 November

1913 **Der dreifache Gatte** (Oskar Porges/w Friedmann) 1 act Intimes Theater 5 April

1913 **Die Ballkönigin** (*The Catch of the Season*) German version w Karl Tuschl (Theater an der Wien)

1913 **Das Liebesnest** (Nicolas Hédas) Strasbourg

1913 **Das grosse Abenteuer** (Hans May/w C Clermont)

1913 **Wie Frauen lieben** (Karl List/w Ludwig Johannes) Venedig in Wien 1 May

1913 **Husarengeneral** (revised *Manöverkind*) (Ziehrer/w Friedmann) Raimundtheater 3 October

1914 **Eine verschenkte Nacht** (Béla Laszky/w Gustav Beer) 1 act Deutsches Künstlertheater 1 February

1917 **Die Bauernprinzessin** (Robert Stolz/w Anton Aldermann) Volkstheater, Munich 3 March

1918 **Leute von heute** (Edmund Eysler, Stolz, Arthur M Werau/w Arthur Rebner) Bundestheater 22 June

1919 **Daniel in der Löwenhöhle** (Hans May) 1 act Kleinkunstbühne, Munich 1 December

1920 **Liebe auf den ersten Blick** (Robert Rakowianu/w Friedmann) Bundestheater 19 May

1920 **Ein alter Steiger** (Oskar Dub) 1 act Rolandbühne 1 June

1920 **Heimkegekehrt** (Károly Újvári) 1 October

1921 **Der Theatergraf** (Walter Bransen) Landestheater, Gotha 24 April

1921 **Faschingshochzeit** (Johann Strauss arr Josef Klein/w Friedmann) Carltheater 25 May

1922 **Die Siegerin** (Tchaikovsky arr Klein/w Jenbach, Friedmann) Neues Wiener Stadttheater 7 November

1923 **Der Hampelmann** (Stolz/w Beer) Komödienhaus 9 November

1924 **Die Afrikareise** new libretto (Bürgertheater)

1924 **Revanche** (Oskar Jascha/w Löhner-Beda) Bürgertheater 8 November

1928 **Prinzessin Ti-Ti-Pa** (Stolz/w Beer) Carltheater 15 May

1928 **Die singende Venus** (Eduard Künneke/w Beer) Schauspielhaus, Breslau 9 June

1930 **Das Strumpfband der Pompadour** (Eysler/w Emil von Meissner) Stadttheater, Augsburg 16 March

1930 **Frühling im Wienerwald** (Ascher/w Löhner-Beda) Stadttheater 17 April

1930 **Durchlaucht Mizzi** (Eysler/w Beer) Neues Wiener Schauspielhaus 23 December

1935 **Valentino, der Liebling vom Broadway** (Ludo Philipp/Kurt Breuer) Volksoper 10 February

LUPINO, Stanley [HOOK, Stanley] (b London, 15 May 1894; d London, 10 June 1942). Startled-looking little star comedian and author of two decades of British musicals.

The son of dancer **George LUPINO** [George Emanuel Samuel Lupino HOOK] and a member of a famous family of dancers and acrobats, Lupino worked as a child in an acrobatic act and in pantomime, and, as a young man, in revue, variety (his first musical-comedy appearance being in the one-act *Go to Jericho* in a variety house) and at the Theatre Royal, Drury Lane, in animal roles in pantomime. He had his first good musical-comedy role in 1917 at the age of 24 supplying the supporting comedy in the Gaby Deslys vehicle *Suzette* (Tibbs) and he made a notable success later the same year in the principal comic part of *Arlette* (Rono), in which he made the hit of the evening with his performance of Ivor Novello's song "On the Staff."

Established as a leading comic, he mixed musicals and revues over the years that followed, appearing at the Gaiety in *The Kiss Call* (1919, Dr Pym), in *Oh! Julie* (1920, t/o Mumps), *His Girl* (1922, James Hicks) and Cochran's remade *Phi-Phi* (1923, Mercury), before making his American debut alongside Vivienne Segal (pre-Broadway) and later Mitzi in the local version of Oscar Straus's (*Naughty*) *Riquette* (1925/26, Théophile Michu). He remained in America to play in the Jenny Lind biomusical *The Nightingale* (1927, Mr Carp). During this period he won his first West End credit as a writer when he supplied some material to C B Cochran's many-handed musical version of the famous comedy *Turned Up*.

Back in Britain, he was seen in the farcical *Up with the Lark* on the road before he teamed up with rising producer Laddie Cliff as co-librettist and co-star of the new-style dance-and-laughter musical *So This Is Love* (1928, Potiphar Griggs). The piece was a substantial success, and many of the team it created continued together over the following years, playing in a number of further shows in the same vein, written and directed by Lupino, produced by Cliff and starring the pair as chief comedians (Jerry Walker in *Love Lies,* Reggie Powley in *The Love Race,* Percy Brace in *Sporting Love,* Tommy Teacher in *Over She Goes,* Bertie Barnes in *Crazy Days*) with decided success.

Lupino also rewrote the already rewritten libretto of the American musical *So Long, Letty!* for Cliff, in an unsuccessful attempt to get it into shape for town; wrote, directed and starred in *Hold My Hand* (1931, Eddy Marston); wrote and then rewrote *Paste / That's a Pretty Thing,* which was ultimately played at Daly's Theatre without him in the cast and without equivalent success, and was credited with the ''book'' to the wartime revue *Funny Side Up* (1940) produced at His Majesty's Theatre with a score made up of a mass of songs mostly culled from the backlists of American publishers.

After his winning partnership with Cliff and their series of shows together was ended by the little producer-dancer's premature death, Lupino went on to star at the Hippodrome in *The Fleet's Lit Up* (1938, Horatio Roper) and took the leading comic role in his own Hollywood saga, *Lady Behave* (1941, Tony Meyrick, also director). But he himself was taken ill during the run of this last show, and died at the age of 48. He was represented posthumously as an author in two further shows, a remake of *That's a Pretty Thing* called *La-di-da-di-da* and *The Love Racket,* both successfully produced by his cousin, Lupino Lane, in 1943.

Lupino worked widely in early British musical films, both as an author and an actor, writing the screenplay with Arthur Rigby and Frank Miller for the cinema version of *Love Lies* and starring in that piece as well as in the screen versions of *The Love Race, Hold My Hand* and *Over She Goes.*

Lupino's wife **Connie EMERALD** [née O'SHEA] (b ?1889; d December 1959) appeared in supporting roles in several musicals in the provinces (*The Belle of New York, Our Miss Gibbs,* Kathie in *The King's Bride,* Bon Bon in *The Algerian Girl*), in Australia (*The Swiss Express*), in London (*The Prince of Pilsen, Nobody's Boy,* and alongside her husband in the majority of his 1920s and 1930s shows) and in New York (*Naughty Riquette*).

His brother **Barry LUPINO** [George Barry HOOK] (b London, 7 January 1884; d Brighton, 26 September 1962) worked as a musical comedian in Australia (Eddie Kettle in *Very Good Eddie, The White Chrysanthemum* 1917), America (Howell Lowder in *Robinson Crusoe Jr* 1916, Reginald Pargeter in *The Love Call,* Hercule in *The Red Robe,* Gonzorgo in *Babes in Toyland*) and in Britain where he was seen in the provincial extravaganza *Admiral Jack* as early as 1902 (Lord Mylkensop), played at the Gaiety in *The Love Race* (1931, Reggie Powley) and *The Millionaire Kid* (1931, Charlie Bang), and toured in later years in good roles in the family musicals (both Stanley's and Lupino Lane's), returning to London to feature as Sir John in the 1941 revival of *Me and My Girl* and to play in *Sweetheart Mine* (1946, Mr Sam) at the Victoria Palace. He was also for many years a great favorite as a pantomime dame. Barry Lupino co-authored the libretti for the touring musical *Happy Birthday* and the London show *Runaway Love* and also provided additional material to *La-di-da-di-da.* Stanley Lupino was the father of **Ida LUPINO** (b London, 4 February 1918; d Hollywood, Calif, 3 August 1995), who made her fame in the cinema. She was seen as Hope Harcourt in the 1936 film of *Anything Goes.*

- 1926 **Turned Up** (Joseph Tunbridge/w others/Arthur Rigby) New Oxford Theatre 11 January
- 1928 **So This Is Love** (''Hal Brody''/Desmond Carter/w Arthur Rigby) Winter Garden Theatre 25 April
- 1928 **Oh, Letty!** (ex- *So Long, Letty!,* later *Change Over*) (Billy Mayerl/Frank Eyton/w Austin Melford) revised English version (Sheffield)
- 1929 **Love Lies** (''Hal Brody''/Carter/w Rigby) Gaiety Theatre 20 March
- 1930 **The Love Race** (Jack Clarke/Carter) Gaiety Theatre 25 June
- 1931 **Hold My Hand** (Noel Gay/Carter) Gaiety Theatre 23 December
- 1933 **That's a Pretty Thing** (ex- *Paste*) (Gay/Carter) Daly's Theatre 22 November
- 1934 **Sporting Love** (Mayerl/Carter, Eyton/w Rigby, Arthur Ash) Gaiety Theatre 31 March
- 1936 **Over She Goes** (Mayerl/Carter, Eyton) Saville Theatre 23 September
- 1937 **Crazy Days** (Mayerl/Carter, Eyton) Shaftesbury Theatre 14 September
- 1941 **Lady Behave** (Edward Horan/Eyton) His Majesty's Theatre 24 July
- 1943 **La-di-da-di-da** revised *That's a Pretty Thing* Victoria Palace 30 March
- 1943 **The Love Racket** (Gay/Eyton, et al) Victoria Palace 21 October

Autobiography: *From the Stocks to the Stars* (Hutchinson, London, 1934)

LuPONE, Patti (b Northport, NY, 21 April 1949). Staunch-voiced leading lady of the 1980s and 1990s.

In an early career shared between the musical and non-musical theatre, Patti LuPone was seen musically on Broadway for a fortnight with John Houseman's Actors Company in the Alfred Uhry musical *The Robber Bridegroom* (1975), in the Stephen Schwartz/Joseph Stein adaptation of Pagnol's *La Femme du boulanger* as *The Bakers Wife* (1976, ''Meadowlark'') which ran out of steam pre-Broadway, and in *Working* (1978), before in 1979 being cast as Broadway's original *Evita* (Tony

Plate 231. **Patti LuPone** *as Eva Peron shares a podium with Bob Gunton (Peron) in Broadway's* Evita.

Award). She subsequently appeared in *The Beggar's Opera* (1982), as Nancy in the brief 1984 revival of *Oliver!,* and in 1985 she was seen in London playing in the empty-houses season of *The Cradle Will Rock,* an engagement which, however, led to her introducing the part of Fantine in the English adaptation of *Les Misérables* (1985, ''I Dreamed a Dream''). She found a further success playing Reno Sweeney in the Lincoln Center revision of *Anything Goes* (1987) before returning to playing largely in film and television. In 1993 she created her first original musical-theatre role since *The Robber Bridegroom* as Norma Desmond in *Sunset Boulevard* (1993, ''With One Look'') in London, but in one of the Really Useful Company's then regular star-casting crises, she was replaced for the show's Broadway production. She subsequently appeared as Vera Simpson in a concert presentation of *Pal Joey* (1995), and appeared during the 1995–96 season for 46 performances in the solo (with quartet) show *Patti LuPone on Broadway* before taking over the role of Maria Callas in the play *Master Class* (1996). She has subsequently given another solo performance entitled *Matters of the Heart.*

DER LUSTIGE KRIEG Operette in 3 acts by F Zell and Richard Genée based on the libretto to *Les Dames capitaines* by Mélesville. Music by Johann Strauss. Theater an der Wien, Vienna, 25 November 1881.

The eighth in Strauss's list of Operetten, *Der lustige Krieg* followed behind the disastrous *Blindekuh* and the rather more successful *Das Spitzentuch der Königin,* and it reunited the composer with the Theater an der Wien's most successful librettists, Zell and Genée (the veritable author of his *Die Fledermaus* book), with whom he had previously combined on the indifferent *Cagliostro in Wien.*

There is war between Massa-Carrara and Genoa, over the fact that these countries' rulers are each claiming a binding contract with a certain ballet star, but it is a war

Plate 232. **Der lustige Krieg** *made its way to Belgium but steered clear of Paris—possibly because Messrs Mélesville and Reber hadn't been consulted over the ''borrowing'' of their text.*

where no one has yet come to blows, even though battle lines are drawn. Violetta (Karoline Finaly), niece of the Princess Artemisia (Therese Schäfer) who heads the all-female army of Massa-Carrara, is to be married to the Duke of Limburg, in exchange for reinforcements, but her voyage to the wedding ceremony is betrayed to the Genoese by the chattery Marchese Sebastiani (Alexander Girardi). The Genoese commander Umberto Spinola (Ferdinand Schütz) intercepts both Violetta and the proxy husband sent by Limburg and, having fallen in love with the lady at first sight, he himself takes the deputy bridegroom's place in a hasty wedding. Spinola forces a little Dutch tulip-grower, Balthasar Groot (Felix Schweighofer), who has unknowingly wandered into the war lines, to pretend to be the Duke and he then follows Violetta and her ''husband'' to Massa-Carrara. But there, Sebastiani recognizes him and uncovers Groot's impersonation, at which it becomes apparent that Violetta has married . . . a Genoese! Since she is by now thoroughly in love with him, she has no objection to the fact, and since there seems similarly no longer to be a need for battle lines, the merry war is declared over.

The splendidly silly book—easily the best of those with which Strauss was supplied in his post–*Die Fledermaus* period—was based on that used for Henri Reber's 1857 French opéra-comique *Les Dames capitaines,* and it spurred the composer to one of his most attractive and versatile scores. The musical numbers ranged from the glittering coloratura of Violetta's polka ''Für diese Kriegezugs Wohl und Wehe'' to the bristling march strains of her ''Es war ein lustig' Abenteuer''; to the warmly beautiful song for the Dutchman's little wife (Rosa Streitmann), who has lost her husband and his cargo of precious tulip-bulbs somewhere amongst the war (''Durch Wald und Feld''); their third-act duet, woefully and sweetly wondering when they will ever get out of this mess and back to their little Dutch family (''Zwei Monat sind es schon''); and the first-act waltz quintet, ''Kommen und gehen.''

However, *Der lustige Krieg* had not only a delicious score, it had a hit number, one which (like so many of its fellows before and after) was not originally in the show. Alexander Girardi, one of the Theater an der Wien's principal comedians, here cast as Sebastiani, threatened to strike unless he was given a solo. Strauss wearily complied, Franz Wagner supplied the extra songwords which Genée was too busy to come up with, and Girardi squeezed ''Nur für Natur'' into the show's second act. The waltz turned out to be not only the hit of the show, but the biggest theatre song-hit in years. It played a significant part in initially helping *Der lustige Krieg* to success, and his light, comic tenor performance of it made Girardi—who had been around for a few years in increasingly worthwhile roles—into a major star overnight.

Der lustige Krieg held the stage at the Theater an der Wien through the Christmas and New Year period before being removed to allow some guest performances to be played, but it returned later in the year to notch up its 100th performance at the beginning of September. By this time, however, it had run half way round the world. An extremely fine success in Germany—it got no fewer than two hundred performances in just nine months at the Friedrich-Wilhelmstädtisches Theater—was quickly followed by an excellent reception in Budapest (ad Lajos Evva, Béla J Fái) where a topline Népszínház cast was headed by Aranka Hegyi, Mariska Komaromi, Zsöfi Csatay, János Kápolnai and Elek Solymossy and featured Vidor Kassai as the now all-important Sebastiani.

Six weeks later New York saw the piece (already announced as ''a success in 27 German cities'') in the original German as played by Jenny Stubel (Violetta), Marie Seebold (Else), Adolf Link (Sebastiani) Gustav Adolfi

(Groot) and Alexander Klein (Umberto), and three months after that *The Merry War* was seen on Broadway in English (ad L C Elson) in the repertoire of J W Norcross's Opera Company. This production ended up transferring to the Metropolitan Alcazar where the company happily jettisoned the rest of its repertory for the season and simply played one and the same show for a remarkable seven consecutive weeks. W T Carleton, Dora Wiley, Belle Cole, Louise Paullin, Richard Golden and Adolfi (this time in English) headed this cast which brought the piece back for two further weeks later in the same season, before Carleton took the show touring far and wide under his own banner. New York was, however, far from finished with its favorite Strauss Operette, for in September 1882 *Der lustige Krieg* was remounted at the Thalia Theater, in October it was burlesqued by Irene Worrell and Lina Aberle at Aberle's Theater, and at the beginning of 1884 the Casino Theater staged a major revival with Lilly Post starred as Violetta, which added two further months to *The Merry War*'s Broadway tally. Between 1885 and 1889 it was again played each season in repertoire in the German theatres, and Carleton and his company toured the English version throughout the country for several seasons. *The Merry War* was undoubtedly the most successful of all Strauss's works on the American stage in the century of its creation.

Prague, Naples, Strasbourg and Stockholm had all hosted the show before London put out its version (ad Robert Reece) on the vast stage of the Alhambra, which had already hosted Strauss's *Die Fledermaus* and *King Indigo* without exceptional results. Constance Loseby (Violetta), Henry Walsham (Spinola), Vienna's Lori Stubel (Else) and Albert Lefevre headed the cast. Unfortunately, Miss Stubel miscalculated London's tastes and, when she pulled up her partner's stocking-tops in what London first-nighters found a rather vulgar fashion, she drew the wrath of the audience on her. She promptly thumbed her nose back at them. Things Viennese did not impress some of the more hidebound London music critics either. One sniffed ''dance music such as [Strauss] writes is very attractive in the ballroom, but it is apt to weary the hearer when polka and waltz melodies are given throughout the entire opera.'' However *The Merry War* (with Frln Stubel quickly replaced by Kate Sullivan) had settled in nicely when, five weeks into the run, the Alhambra was burnt down. It was 56 years before the piece got another London showing (New St Pancras Theatre 2 January 1939), and Strauss's most melodious show never recovered from the overheated start which prevented it establishing itself in England.

La Guerre joyeuse (ad Alfred and Maurice Hennequin) was produced in Brussels (Alcazar Royale, Brussels 21 November 1885) with Claire Cordier as Violetta and Monsieur Minne singing ''Pour la nature'' in a score which had been ''adapté par Maurice Kufferath,'' but it did not make its way to Paris. This may very well have been because Strauss was not keen, after the fuss that had been made over his librettist's unauthorized borrowing of *Le Réveillon* as the source for *Die Fledermaus,* similarly to tangle with the representatives of the original French author of the ''borrowed'' *Les Dames capitaines.*

In Vienna, *Der lustige Krieg* was played in repertoire through 1882 and 1883, and in 1885 the Theater an der Wien mounted a new production with Girardi teamed with Marie-Theresia Massa and Josef Joseffy. It was revived at the Carltheater in 1898 with Ottilie Collin and Natzler and at the Johann Strauss-Theater in 1911–12 with Grete Holm as Violetta, and it had a continuing success through the 19th and early 20th centuries, holding an indubitable third place behind *Die Fledermaus* and *Der Zigeunerbaron* as the most popular of Strauss's works in central Europe. Only with the coming of increasingly sentimental and romantic tastes (as opposed to the continuous comedy this work displays) in the later 20th century did it give way to the revamped, scenery-worthy *Eine Nacht in Venedig* and to the pasticcio *Wiener Blut,* which are now played and recorded in preference to it.

A hacked-about version of the show rewritten by Wilhelm Sterk, with the music rearranged by Felix Günther, in which Balthasar (Richard Waldemar) became a strolling player, Else disappeared and Violetta (Anni Ahlers) acquired a sister called Nina (Marianne Küpfer) alongside Hans Heinz Bollmann's Umberto and Ernst Tautenhayn's Cipriani, was produced at the Johann Strauss-Theater on 23 December 1929 by Erich Müller, and subsequently in Hungary (*Asszonyháború* Városi Színház 13 November 1931), and another partially rewritten version was produced at Augsburg in 1957 (Städtische Bühne 23 August ad Eugen Mühl) under the title *Fürstin Violetta.*

Germany: Friedrich-Wilhelmstädtisches Theater 19 January 1882; Hungary: Népszínház *A furcsa háboru* 31 January 1882; USA: Thalia Theater 15 March 1882, Germania Theater *The Merry War* 27 June 1882; UK: Alhambra Theatre *The Merry War* 16 October 1882

Recordings: complete (Austrian radio cast 1999) (ORF), selections (Philips, etc)

DIE LUSTIGEN NIBELUNGEN Burlesque Operette in 3 acts by Rideamus. Music by Oscar Straus. Carltheater, Vienna, 12 November 1904.

Oscar Straus's first produced Operette—written in collaboration with the cabaret satirist ''Rideamus'' (Fritz Oliven), with whom he had previously concocted a series of songs polyglottishly described as ''lustige Chansons''—was a burlesque of the legend which had been the basis for Richard Wagner's Ring Cycle or, more properly, of the material used for one plot strand of the last two operas: the marriage of Günther and Brünnhilde and the fate of Siegfried.

In Rideamus's version, flabby Günther (Friedrich Becker) is obliged to go into single combat with Brünnhilde (Hermine Herma) to win her as his bride. He is all for catching the first train out of town, but Herr Siegfried von Niederland (Willi Bauer) comes to his aid and, invisible under his magic nightcap, complies with the rules set down by referee Hagen (Karl Blasel) and floors Brünnhilde, both shoulders to the ground, all for the sake of Günther's pretty sister Kriemhild (Helene Merviola). At the beginning of Act II the two couples are supposed to be getting wed, but there are plenty more troubles in store. Hagen tries to get Kriemhild to woo from Siegfried the secret of his dragon's blood baths and Günther gets into a squabble with Brünnhilde over domestic matters and calls again for Siegfried's help as his invisible arm. But this time Hagen spots the marks left on the ground by the invisible man's gown and he fells his opponent with a nifty blow. Battered Siegfried goes off to have a restorative dragon's blood bath and while he is away Günther confesses, Brünnhilde takes umbrage, Kriemhild gets a better offer, and they all decide to get rid of Siegfried. However, a friendly canary brings the Hero all this latest news and, fore-warned and -armed, he is finally able to win everyone around and Brünnhilde to bride.

Straus replaced Wagner's tonitruant score with one in very different and almost Sullivan-esque rhythms, one from which a ''Rheingold'' waltz-song (''Einst hatte ich geld und Got''), a Lindenblatt-duet (''Das ist die Stelle mit dem Lindenblatt''), and a round-dance (''Nun so lasst uns denn Siegfried ermordern'') stood next to some more spoofingly splendid music, which was paired with ridiculous words in the best traditions of burlesque. Siegfried emerged the best with two such numbers ''Ich bracht's auf dem Gymnasium'' and ''Ich hab ein Bad genommen,'' alongside a catching march, which opened the second act burlesquing the recent declarations of the Kaiser Wilhelm with its ''Das ist der Furor teutonicus.''

Announced for Berlin's Buntes-Theater as early as 1902, *Die lustigen Nibelungen* finally made it to the stage only in 1904, and in Vienna. It won only a fair reception on its production at the Carltheater for, in spite of its gleefully foolish fun and its attractive, well-made music, its genuine opéra-bouffe score (a prizeworthy rarity in the Germanic theatre), with its mixture of the witty and the beautiful and the cancanning, contained none of the heavily rhythmed, take-away songs that the public expected from the composer of so many Überbrettl songs and Volkslieder. And burlesque was scarcely in its heyday. Andreas Aman's production was withdrawn after a first run of 26 performances, although it was given occasional repertoire performances over the next three years. It was better received in Berlin, where, in spite of some grumblings about the decency of taking the mickey out of the revered Volsung saga (grumbling which rather recalled the howls over *Orphée aux enfers* and its burlesque of the ancient world), it set up a good run at the Theater des Westens (134 performances). It was also subsequently produced in Hungary (ad Adolf Mérei), and kept a small place in the repertoire for a number of years, establishing Straus on the springboard from which he would shortly leap to fame with *Ein Walzertraum.* Straus himself revived the show at the Établissment Ronacher in 1916 with Mizzi Freihardt featured as Brünnhilde, it was played at Helsenkirchen's Musiktheater im Revier in 1977 (28 February) and as recently as 1987 it was seen again in Vienna in a production at the Wiener Kammeroper.

An earlier Nibelungenlied burlesque, *La Petite Valkyrie,* was brought out at Brussels's Alcazar in 1887, and a more recent one, with the action of the saga transferred to Texas, was produced at Seattle Opera in 1991 under the title *Das Barbecü* (Scott Warrender/Jim Luigs) and subsequently at the Goodspeed Opera House (Norma Terris Theater 1993) and at off-Broadway's Minetta Lane Theater (10 November 1994). Clairville's Parisian opérette *La Dame de trèfle* (Bouffes-Parisiens 13 May 1898, mus: Pessard) was written around the story of a provincial civic worthy who writes and produces an improved version of *Die Walküre.*

Hungary: Király Színház *Víg Nibelungok* 30 August 1907; Germany: Theater des Westens 4 March 1911

Recording: complete (Capriccio/WDR)

DIE LUSTIGE WITWE Operette in 3 acts by Victor Léon and Leo Stein, based on *L'Attaché d'ambassade* by Henri Meilhac. Music by Franz Lehár. Theater an der Wien, Vienna, 30 December 1905.

Henri Meilhac's play *L'Attaché d'ambassade,* produced at Paris's Théâtre du Vaudeville in 1861, was not a success. It was played for just 15 performances in the French capital. Yet, in the way of the time, this failure did not affect its export prospects and the piece found its way to the Vienna stage the following year. There, played at the Carltheater in an adaptation by ''Alexander Bergen'' as *Der Gesandschafts-Attaché,* it became not only a success but a piece which was popular enough to win regular revivals over a number of years.

The first years of the 20th century in the Viennese musical theatre were not rich in successes. The staple composers of earlier years—Suppé, Strauss, Millöcker—were gone, and the last real new successes which the Theater an der Wien had hosted had been Richard Heuber-

Plate 233. **Die lustige Witwe.** *The Pontevedrian ambassador and his staff of noble gentlemen have money problems . . . and, some of them, woman problems too (Vienna Volksoper, 1987).*

ger's *Der Opernball*—a musical version of the French comedy *Les Dominos roses*—and the young Edmund Eysler's *Bruder Straubinger.* It was logical, then, that librettist Victor Léon, the co-author of *Der Opernball,* should present Theater an der Wien director Karczag with another French-flavored libretto for Heuberger to set—a musical version of *Der Gesandschafts-Attaché.* One version of the story goes that Heuberger actually set Léon and Leo Stein's piece, but that Karczag did not like the score he provided and took back the libretto. On the encouragement of theatre secretary Emil Steininger, he then proposed to offer it to Lehár, whose debut piece, *Wiener Frauen,* had been played at the Theater an der Wien three years earlier. Léon, however, objected. Although he had had a major success with Lehár on *Der Rastelbinder* at the rival Carltheater, he and Stein had subsequently worked with the composer on the barely successful *Der Göttergatte* in which the composer had clearly failed to catch the Offenbachian opéra-bouffe flavor the librettists intended their piece to have. But, in the end, he agreed that Lehár should be given the opportunity to set a portion of the piece, as a kind of an audition. When the composer played Léon the melody which he had set to the Hanna/Danilo duet ''Dummer, dummer Reitersmann,'' the librettist allowed himself to be convinced.

Karczag, however, showed little enthusiasm for the show. During 1905 little had gone right for him. Star comic Girardi had gone off after the production of *Pufferl* taking the most promising composer of the time, Edmund Eysler, with him, and if some performances of the second-hand Strauss pastiche *Wiener Blut* had filled a gap, neither a German version of Huszka's *Bob herceg* (10 performances) nor Léon's collaboration with another young composer, Leo Ascher, on *Vergeltsgott* (69 performances) had proved a hit. Another essay with an untried composer, Leo Fall's *Der Rebell,* had been a total disaster, folding after just five performances. There was little incentive for Karczag to invest heavily in another new piece in which he had little confidence, and so, when *Die lustige Witwe* was hurriedly produced to fill the gap left by the flop of *Der Rebell* (in preference, according to Harry B Smith's memoirs, to De Koven's *Robin Hood,* which was also on Karczag's waiting list), it was done so on the proverbial shoestring with recycled scenery and costumes. Four weeks after the closure of Fall's Operette, *Die lustige Witwe* opened.

Léon and Stein's piece, which was shyly announced only as being ''teilweise nach einer fremden Grundidee'' (''partly based on a foreign idea''), was set in contemporary Paris at the Embassy of the Balkan state of Pontevedro rather than in the Germanic Birkenfeld of the original play or in Léon's originally posited, but too real, Montenegro. Baron Mirko Zeta (Siegmund Natzler) is desperate to find a Pontevedran husband for the ''merry widow,'' the young and hugely wealthy Hanna Glawari (Mizzi Günther) who is currently being chased by half of male Paris. He and the fatherland cannot afford to let Hanna's millions go into a foreign exchequer. He selects for this delicate patriotic task the womanizing, boozing but indubitably charming attaché Count Danilo Danilowitsch (Louis Treumann). Unfortunately Danilo and Hanna are rather more than old friends from the days before Hanna's wealthy marriage and Danilo has sworn that he will never again say ''I love you'' to the woman he regards as venal. It soon becomes clear, however, what his feelings really are, for when Hanna steps in to save the Ambassador's wife, Valencienne (Annie Wünsch), from an embarrassing if innocent exposure in a tete-à-tete with the sexy young Camille de Rosillon (Karl Meister), the furious Danilo sweeps off to Maxim's to find consolation with the girls of that friendly establishment. Hanna sets up part of her mansion as an imitation of Maxim's and, there, the amazed Danilo comes to discover that the merry widow loses her money should she remarry. His pride assuaged, he now proposes, only to find—as all ends happily—that the money goes to the new husband.

Lehár's score gave his four principals plenty of opportunities, both the leading pair who, in good Gaiety Theatre tradition, were light-comedy actor/singers, and their straighter-singing secondary counterparts. Hanna made her first entrance to a cascading number (''Bitte meine Herr'n'') which immediately established her as lustige, performed the mythological tale of the ''Vilja'' as a party-piece, and shared the ''Dummer Reitersmann'' duo and the evening's big waltz tune, ''Lippen schweigen,'' with Danilo, whilst he, apart from the duets, saluted the high life in ''Da geh' ich zu Maxim'' and the ''Ballsirenen'' waltz. Valencienne and Camille shared three soprano/tenor set piece duets (''Zauber der Hauslichkeit,'' ''Ich bin eine anständige Frau'' and the Pavilion duo with Camille's fine-spun solo ''Wie eine Rosenknospe'') in more vocal manner. The lower-comedy area, headed by Zeta and his colleagues Cascada (Carlo Böhm) and Saint-Brioche (Leo von Keller), came to the fore in a swinging march octet (''Ja, das Studium der Weiber ist schwer''), whilst Valencienne led the grisettes of Maxim's in a lively song-and-dance routine (''Ja, wir sind es die Grisetten''), choreographed by Professor van Hamme, alongside some particularly fine finales. Almost every portion of the *Die lustige Witwe* score became familar and popular in the years which followed but it was, perhaps, the big waltz duet and the march octet which stood out from the crowd at first.

The success of *Die lustige Witwe* was never in doubt. The show ran through the spring at the Theater an der Wien, totaling 119 performances by the time, at the end of April, that the traditional summer closure began. *Die lustige Witwe* did not, however, close but transferred first to the Raimundtheater and then to the Volksoper to continue its run with some 69 guest performances. The two stars held their places, but amongst the minor characters now appeared both Julius Brammer (Cascada, after having originally been Pritschitsch) and Robert Bodanzky (Pritschitsch), before long to be much better known as librettists. When the Theater an der Wien reopened in September, *Die lustige Witwe* resumed and on 11 January 1907 it passed its 300th, and on 24 April 1907 its 400th performance. Lehár composed a new overture (''Eine Vision'') for the latter occasion, and conducted an expanded orchestra of a hundred players in celebration.

In the meanwhile, the foreign productions had begun. Max Monti opened *Die lustige Witwe* at Hamburg's Neues Operetten-Theater, with Marie Ottmann and Gustave Matzner starred and Poldi Deutsch as the Ambassador for ''Pontenegro,'' little more than two months after seeing it at the Vienna premiere and, soon after, the Hamburg company, which had played some 250 performances on its home ground within seven months, introduced the show to Berlin. Their success was, again, indubitable, and the show was promptly taken up for a local production at the Theater des Westens (1 March 1907). It remained there for 262 performances.

Budapest followed with, as usual, the first foreign-language version, an Adolf Mérei adaptation produced at the Magyar Színház with Olga Turchányi (later Klára Küry, Ilona Szoyer) and Ákos Ráthonyi starred. It passed its 200th performance at the end of May before the show was taken up by the Király Színház, where Ráthonyi was paired with Sári Fedák, and then at the Budai Színkör. *Die lustige Witwe* was translated into Czech, Norwegian, Russian, Swedish, Croatian and Italian (Milan 27 June 1907) before it received its first English performance, at

London's Daly's Theatre, in a version credited variously to Edward Morton (best known as the author of *San Toy*) or to Basil Hood, and lyricist Adrian Ross.

The book underwent some alterations for the London presentation of the show initially announced as *The Jolly Widow*. Some tended to the clichéd—Danilo became a Prince, for example—others removed things which would have seemed odd to English ears. In the British version the final scene takes place in the real Maxim's rather than a reproduction at the widow's home (yet years later the libretto for London's *Primrose* pinched precisely Léon and Stein's plot line). Lehár himself was on hand to help with the adaptation and, at Edwardes's request, he provided two additional songs, one to feature Mabel Russell as a third-act grisette (''Butterflies'') and the second to give Bill Berry, cast in the small role of Nisch, a number declaring that although ''I was born, by cruel fate, in a little Balkan state . . .'' he had now become ''Quite Parisian.'' There were other alterations, too. The ''Zauber der Hauslichkeit'' duet was turned into a solo for Robert Evett as Camille, and the role of Valencienne (here called Natalie) was reduced further by giving the Grisetten-Lied of the last act to Gertrude Lister as another grisette.

Edwardes followed the light-comedy lead casting of the Viennese production by choosing American Joe Coyne, who had played light-comedy roles for Edwardes in America before making his British debut earlier in the year as the comic hero of *Nelly Neil,* to be his Danilo. Lily Elsie, who had been moving up through smaller roles in Edwardes productions, was cast as a younger, prettier, and slimmer widow (now called Sonia) than previously, and accredited comic George Graves was given leave to play up the role of Zeta (now called Popoff), which he did largely by sticking in a self-written chat about a fowl called Hetty and her propensity for producing bent eggs. The fine singing was left to Evett and another American, soprano Elizabeth Firth (Natalie). The English Widow proved as popular as her Continental counterpart, running solidly for two years and two months, a total of 778 performances, before beginning the round of tours, and it launched in Britain, as it would elsewhere, a mad rage for Viennese shows which would last until the war. Its songs and a bit of millinery merchandising called the ''Merry Widow Hat'' became the hits of the day.

Henry Savage's New York production continued the series of *Merry Widow* triumphs. Savage used the London adaptation, now uncredited and with ''Quite Parisian'' omitted, and cast the bright and friendly looking actor-dancer-singer Donald Brian as Danilo with Ethel Jackson, a former D'Oyly Carte chorine whose Broadway credits over half-a-dozen years were good if scarcely starry, as Sonia. The waltz, the hat, the stars and the strains of Vienna all came together once more in an enormous hit which produced 419 Broadway performances and, as in London, set up the fashion for all that's Viennese.

Theatrical mythology has every country unwillingly taking on *Die lustige Witwe* without any expectation of success. Given its untarnished record of triumph, this seems unlikely. Yet Paris did not welcome *La Veuve joyeuse* until more than four years after the Vienna production—by which time it had been seen in Cairo, in Shanghai, in Melbourne and in Johannesburg—and it was not one of the major Parisian musical producers but Alphonse Franck at the Théâtre Apollo who finally ventured. Franck gave the text to the most popular upmarket comedy writers of the day, Gaston de Caillavet and Robert de Flers, for adaptation and they, like the British, made their amendments to the original. The widow, now called Missia, became an American brought up in Marsovie (ex- Pontevedro, Pontenegro, Montenegro). Whether this was because Franck cast British soprano Constance Drever (a London takeover) in the role, or whether Miss Drever was cast because of the change of nationality (American, after all, at this period, always meant rich), is not known, but to this day the French script of *La Veuve joyeuse* bears the instruction that Missia is to be played with an English [*sic*] accent, touched with a little Slav. The French Danilo is a Prince gone broke through gambling. In line with London, the Ambassador remained Popoff and the last act went to Maxim's, although the extra numbers disappeared along with Graves's excrescences and Hetty the Hen. The truly dashing light baritone Henry Defreyn was cast opposite Miss Drever, Charles Casella (Camille de Coutançon) and Thérèse Cernay (Nadia) had the duets, and Félix Galipaux was Popoff. Franck's production was an enormous success, played 186 times consecutively for its first run, and was regularly reprised at the Apollo in the years that followed, with Defreyn repeating his role endlessly opposite Alice O'Brien and other Anglophone (and later not so very Anglophone) ladies.

Australia followed the personality-plus-singing style in casting its *Merry Widow* when local soubrette Carrie Moore, who had had considerable success on the London stage, introduced the role of the widow to audiences in Melbourne and later the rest of the country. The piece had a fine success, and it was regularly played in Australia thereafter, with the change in values from personality performance to singing ability being particularly noticeable as local divas such as Gladys Moncrieff and, later, Joan Sutherland succeeded to the role of Hanna/Sonia.

The success of *Die lustige Witwe* prompted many burlesques throughout the world. In Germany, Julius Freund authored a pasticcio, *Der lustiger Witwer,* with music by Max R Steiner and others attached, which later played Danzers Orpheum in Vienna (ad Lindau, Antony 9 February 1907); the Folies-Caprice presented a one-act *Die lästige Witwe* (20 August 1908); and a ''sequel'' depicting *Die lustige Witwe in zweite Ehe* (''the merry widow's second marriage''), written by Max Hanisch and composed by Karl von Wegern, was played both in Vienna (Apollotheater 1907), where Annie Danninger and Eugen Borg burlesqued Günther and Treumann's creations, and in America (Deutsches Theater, Philadelphia 10 May 1909, and as *The Merry Widow Remarried* at Cincinatti, July 1909). In Vienna, Lehár himself had fun with a little bit of his show, turning out a one-acter for the Theater an der Wien's studio theatre, Hölle, called *Mitislaw der moderne,* which allowed Louis Treumann to parody his own performance as Danilo.

Hungary saw *A vígadó özvegy* (Albert Heidelberg/Károly Ujváry, Emil Tábori, Budai Színkör 25 July 1907); France a dozen or so parodic pieces including *La Veuve soyeuse* (Eugène Joullot, Henry de Farcy, 5 March 1909) at the Parisiana, *Moins veuve que joyeuse, Ni veuve, ni joyeuse* and *La petite veuve joyeuse* (Café Belleville 22 March 1913); whilst in New York Joe Weber produced a highly successful *Merry Widow Burlesque,* which allowed Lulu Glaser and Blanche Ring as ''Fonia'' an unlikely crack at the widow's role. The American musical *His Honor the Mayor* threatened in song ''I Wish I Could Find the Man Who Wrote the Merry Widow Waltz'' and went on to say what the singer would do to him. In London, George Edwardes sued Henri Pélissier's *Follies* not for burlesquing the *Merry Widow* but for playing its music whilst he was still running the show. That problem, of course, raised its head elsewhere and a curious lawsuit arose in New York when Savage attacked one variety house for playing *The Merry Widow* without permission. The producers claimed that their production was not *The Merry Widow,* it was an adaptation of *L'Attaché d'ambassade* with music taken from Planquette's *Le Paradis de Mahomet* and other sources which just happened to sound like Lehár's score.

Inevitably, *Die lustige Witwe* made its way on to film. The first films, including a Hollywood one with Mae Murray and John Gilbert, were silent; later versions proved not terribly faithful, whether emanating from America (MGM's 1934 version with Chevalier and Jeanette MacDonald and a 1952 repeat with Lana Turner and Fernando Lamas) or from Austria (1962 with Karin Hübner and Peter Alexander). A projected 1980s British film which, like the last-mentioned, used the Operette as part of another story, vanished off the schedules without being made. Two pieces put out by Vitagraph in 1910 as *Courting the Merry Widow* and *The Merry Widow Takes Another Husband* were fakers that used the famous title to try to interest customers in what was no more that a one-lady, two-men short.

Major revivals have appeared regularly in all the main musical-theatre centers in the 90-plus years since the widow's first stage appearances as *Die lustige Witwe* established the piece as the outstanding representatative of Vienna's Silver Age on the international stage. London saw Carl Brisson three times as Danilo, paired with Evelyn Laye, Nancie Lovat and Helen Gilliland, but if the last of these signaled a switch to a more legit singing widow, a reprise starring Madge Elliott and Cyril Ritchard put the ball squarely back in the light-comedy area. The last commercial London production of the piece was in 1969 with Lisbeth Webb. In New York, where revivals had passed in 1921, 1929 and 1931, musical film stars Marta Eggerth and Jan Kiepura played the piece in 1943 before going on to repeat their performances around the world. In both countries the piece then passed into the opera houses, with June Bronhill initiating the Sadler's Wells Opera production with Christopher Hassall's new translation, and the New York City Opera and Beverley Sills putting the new very vocal slant on the piece in America. Since then the role of the widow has become meat for such operatic divas as Roberta Peters, Joan Sutherland, Lisa della Casa and Anna Moffo—a long way from the pretty-voiced personality performances of such as Mizzi Günther and Lily Elsie.

In Vienna the piece remains regularly in the repertoire of the Volksoper, which admits it finds it difficult to cast a Hanna with the personality the role has traditionally maintained in Austria but also with the now more solid vocal equipment modern tastes require, but the show stood up for a commercial run as recently as 1967 when the Theater an der Wien hosted a season of 309 performances with the aging but ineffably dapper Johannes Heesters, repeating the Danilo on which Lehár had earlier posed ''best ever'' laurels, playing opposite Ilona Szamos. In Germany, on the other hand, the piece, which has elsewhere suffered surprisingly little from the depredations of directors out to make themselves noticed by setting it in Greenland or the 14th century, has had some rather extreme treatments. An extravagantly reorganized and reorchestrated version (ad Rudolph Schanzer, Ernst Welisch), with Fritzi Massary and Max Hansen, was staged by Erik Charell at the Grosses Schauspielhaus in 1929, and in 1979 the Deutsches Oper hosted a version in which Wagnerian soprano Gwyneth Jones (who is not, in fact, the only Brünnhilde to have also played the widow in Germany) appeared as Hanna.

In Paris, with no operatic venue into which to retreat, *La Veuve joyeuse* has remained resolutely opérettique through regular revivals, the most recent of which was at the Châtelet in 1982. After Mary Lewis (1925) and

Corinne Harris (1934), the French productions stopped importing their Missias and Jeanne Aubert starred with Opéra-Comique baritone Jacques Jansen in 1942, followed by singing actress Marina Hotine (1951), Jenny Marlaine (1957) and the Opéra-Comique's Géori Boué (1962) before a multi-cast effort in 1982.

Budapest, too, has welcomed regular revivals of Merei's adaptation, most recently at the Fővárosi Operettszínház in 1995 (24 March).

The score of *Die lustige Witwe* has been used as the basis for two ballets, one by Maurice Béjart (1963) and the second, with the score arranged by John Lanchbery, produced by the Australian Ballet. This latter arrangement, which included choral pit vocals, was played in New York and at the London Palladium with Marilyn Jones/Margot Fonteyn dancing the role of the widow.

Germany: Neues Operetten-Theater, Hamburg 3 March 1906, Berliner Theater, Berlin 1 May 1906; Hungary: Magyar Színház *Víg özvegy* 27 November 1906; UK: Daly's Theatre *The Merry Widow* 8 June 1907; USA: New Amsterdam Theater *The Merry Widow* 21 October 1907; Australia: Her Majesty's Theatre, Melbourne 16 May 1908; France: Théâtre Apollo *La Veuve joyeuse* 28 April 1909

Films: MGM 1925 (silent), MGM (Eng) 1934, MGM (Eng) 1952, Sacha Films/Herbert Gruber (Ger) 1962

Recordings: 2-record ''complete'' (EMI and many others), selection in English (CSD and many others), selection in French (EMI-Pathé and many others), 2-record ''complete'' in Italian, 2-record ''complete'' in Russian (Melodiya), selection in Swedish (London), selection in Hungarian (Hazam, Qualiton), selection in Romanian (Electrecord), selection in Spanish (Montilla), etc

LUTE SONG Musical play (love story with music) in 2 acts by Sidney Howard and Will Irwin based on the play *Pi-Pa-Ki.* Lyrics by Bernard Hanighen. Music by Raymond Scott. Plymouth Theater, New York, 6 February 1946.

The musical *Lute Song* was based on a classic 14th-century Chinese play, adapted into English by Sidney Howard, the author of such outstanding successes as *They Knew What They Wanted* (subsequently musicalized as *The Most Happy Fella*), *The Silver Cord, The Late Christopher Bean* and *Alien Corn,* in collaboration with Will Irwin. The piece failed to find a production as a play, but producer Michael Meyerberg had it set as a ''love story with music'' and it was finally produced, seven years after Howard's death, with Mary Martin as the Chinese wife Tschao-Ou-Niang whose husband Tsai-Yong (Yul Brynner) becomes too successful at court and who finds himself commanded to wed a royal Princess, Nieou-chi. Ultimately, the Princess realizes that her husband loves his first wife and relinquishes him.

The score included as much in the way of incidental and dance music as of vocal numbers, the most successful of the latter being Miss Martin's opening song ''Mountain High, Valley Low.'' In spite of a production which was praised for its beauty, *Lute Song* proved too far from the Broadway mainstream to attract the audiences needed, and it folded after 142 performances. It was, however, taken up by the once-proud London manager Albert de Courville, of *Hullo Ragtime!* and variety fame, and staged by him at the Winter Garden—a rather larger venue than Broadway's Plymouth Theater—with Brynner starred alongside Dolly Haas and Iris Russell. It failed in 24 performances.

Lute Song was seen once more when it was revived at New York's City Center in 1959.

UK: Winter Garden Theatre 11 October 1948

Recordings: selection (Decca, Ace of Hearts)

LUTZ, W[ilhelm] Meyer (b Münnerstadt, Kissingen, (16 or) 19 May 1829 (or 1828); d London, 31 January 1903). London conductor and composer of a half-century of all kinds of music and musical theatre.

Meyer Lutz was born in Germany, a younger brother of the Baron von Lutz, Prime Minister of Bavaria, whose principal claim to be remembered is that he was the ''villain'' who committed the ''mad'' King Ludwig of Bavaria. The younger Lutz studied music with his organist father, then at Würzburg under Eisenhöfer, made his first public appearance at eight, and visited Britain for the first time in 1846 to play piano in a series of concerts in Birmingham. He returned for a second visit in 1848 and this time he remained. He became, briefly, organist at St Chad's Church in Birmingham and at St Ann's, Leeds, before taking up a similar post at St George's Catholic Cathedral in Southwark, London, which he would maintain for over forty years. He paired this last engagement, initially, with a position as conductor at Surrey Theatre (1850–55). There he conducted the Romer family's productions of operas (the premiere of Balfe's *The Devil's in It, Ernani, Robert le Diable, La Juive, Lucia di Lammermoor,* etc) and composed, arranged and conducted the music for the house's dramatic productions. There, too, his own first composed works, including a light-operatic version of *Faust and Marguerite,* were played. During this same period he performed as a piano soloist and conductor in concert, notably as musical director of the Exeter Hall Wednesday concerts, and founded and ran musical ''Metropolitan Evening Classes for Young Men.''

During the later 1850s and the 1860s he toured as conductor of a series of English opera companies—Alfred St Albyn and Mlle Nau's Opera Company (1855), the Grand National Opera Company (1861, Eliot Galer, Jenny Bauer, Eugene Corri, Fanny Reeves, etc), the London Grand Opera Company (1862, Sims Reeves, Elliot

Galer, Rebecca Isaacs, Oliver Summers, etc), Henri Corri's English Opera Company (1864, *Faust, Maritana, No Song, No Supper, The Bohemian Girl, The Waterman, Lurline, The Rose of Castile,* etc), Galer and Fanny Reeves's Royal English Opera Company (1866, *La Sonnambula, Il Trovatore, Satanella, Faust, The Bohemian Girl,* Burnand's *Dido,* etc), Florence Lancia's Grand English Opera Company (1868)—and also with various concert combinations which included such artists as Mario and Mme Sainton Dolby. He appeared in London on a number of occasions, including several seasons with Galer and his wife in burlesque and operetta at the Royalty Theatre in the mid-1860s.

At the same time, he turned out a steady stream of music ranging from a mass for Southwark Cathedral to a number of short operettas—notably for Galer and Miss Reeves who had mounted and starred in his *Zaida* as early as 1859 (''Herr Lutz has been known for some years as a graceful composer in the school of Auber'')—and cantatas including *Herne the Hunter* (Crystal Palace 19 December 1862), *The Legend of the Lys* (lib: Robert Reece, Covent Garden 6 October 1873) and a 1863 Christmas cantata *King Christmas,* which was was performed at the Oxford Music Hall under Charles Morton with a cast including the young Emily Soldene. He also composed a scena *Xenia, the Sclavonian Maiden* for soprano Christine Nilsson, a selection of parlor songs, and, when the craze for Minstrelsy struck, he was for a time the principal purveyor of songs, scenas and burlesque music to the Christy Minstrels and their Moore and Burgess successors.

His peripatetic life was stilled in February 1869 when John Hollingshead engaged him to replace the Belgian musician Aloys Kettenus as musical director of the two-month-old Gaiety Theatre. There, in his first year, he composed and arranged the pasticcio scores for such burlesques as *Columbus* (1869, and including three original numbers by Lutz), *Linda di Chamouni* (1869) and *Wat Tyler MP* (1869) and the operetta *The Happy Village* (1869), and composed incidental music for several plays including the popular *Uncle Dick's Darling.* In the years following, he continued to turn out a liberal supply of mostly pasticcio-burlesque scores, whilst also conducting the opéras-bouffes—including the Gaiety's original works *Aladdin II, Cinderella the Younger* and *Thespis*—on the program of the theatre which was rapidly becoming recognized as central London's top musical house. During the Gaiety's summer closure, he would conduct at seaside resorts, in later years on a regular basis at Scarborough, one of most charming and upmarket of such English holiday venues.

A conductor, répétiteur and musical amanuensis by day and evening, Lutz continued as a composer by night, working not only on the house pasticcio scores (*Little Don Caesar de Bazan, Ariel, The Bohemian G'yurl, Camaralzaman, Gulliver, The Forty Thieves, Little Doctor Faust, Robbing Roy, Little Robin Hood, Mazeppa,* etc, etc), to which he supplied original melodies if and when necessary, but on some original, if distinctly old-fashioned little operettas and light operas, several of which were played on matinée or benefit programs at the Gaiety. His most successful compositions, at this stage, were two little pieces—*On Condition* and *Posterity*—played by Lila Clay's all-women concert party, and a song, ''Eyes of English Blue,'' performed by Alice Atherton in the touring scenas *The Japs* (1885) and *Blackberries* and interpolated into most of her other shows as well.

After 35 years in the business and 15 at the Gaiety, it seemed unlikely that the aging musician would suddenly become a hot property, but when pasticcio scores began to give way to original music at the Gaiety, under the management of George Edwardes, Lutz provided at first a portion (*Little Jack Sheppard,* 13 of 24 numbers) of the scores required and, very soon, virtually all the music for the hugely popular run of shows starring Nellie Farren and Fred Leslie and their contemporaries. He had a major hit with the barn-dance music for the pas de quatre in *Faust Up-to-Date,* but he also supplied the basic scores (into which interpolations were regularly made) for the whole series of new burlesques from *Monte Cristo Jr* and *Miss Esmeralda* through to the last, *Don Juan.*

At the same time, Lutz continued his conducting duties (notably as the original conductor of *Dorothy*) and also turned out a regular mass of contributions to mostly touring shows, including Willie Edouin's *Blackberries* and Harry Monkhouse's *Larks,* an activity which he pursued further when the burlesque fashion faded and newer composers stepped in to provide scores for the ''musical comedy'' productions at the Gaiety. *Cupid & Co, Giddy Miss Carmen* (1894), *Baron Golosh, One of the Girls* (1896), *The Merry-Go-Round* (1899), *Hidenseek* (1901) and *The Girl from Kays* (1902) were amongst the shows to which he supplied more or fewer individual numbers.

Lutz conducted the early musical comedy *In Town* at the Gaiety before finally quitting his post there, although he continued to conduct some ill-advised ventures such as *Baron Golosh* (*L'Oncle Célestin*), Nellie Farren's attempt at management with his *A Model Trilby* and, at the age of 72, the desperate *Hidenseek,* as well as spending a period working under Edward Terry at the Strand Theatre.

A well-trained and versatile musician, and a prolific composer, who held an important place in the light musical theatre through the whole of the opéra-bouffe and burlesque eras and into that of Edwardesian musical comedy, Lutz leaned naturally to a somewhat polite and academic style in his writing, but he won his greatest successes with comic songs and lively dances of which the famous *Faust Up-to-Date* dance was the most enduring.

1852 **The Charmed Harp** (John Courtney) 1 act Surrey Theatre 30 August

1855 **Mephistopheles, or Faust and Marguerite** (Henri Drayton) Surrey Theatre 26 May

1859 **Zaida, or The Pearl of Granada** (Oliver Summers) Liverpool Amphitheatre 14 February

1861 **Blonde or Brunette, or The Belle of Ballengarry** (John Pratt Wooler) 1 act Cork, April; Royalty Theatre 19 May 1862

1863 **Cousin Kate** (Eliot Galer) 1 act Polytechnic Hall 14 December; St James's Theatre 16 May 1864

1865 **Felix, or The Festival of the Roses** (John Oxenford) 1 act Royalty Theatre 23 October

1872 **The Miller of Millberg** 1 act Gaiety Theatre 13 April

1881 **All in the Downs** (Douglas Jerrold ad) Gaiety Theatre 5 November

1882 **Oh! Those Girls** (*Zehn Mädchen und kein Mann*) comp and arr score for English version by Robert Soutar, Gaiety Theatre

1882 **On Condition** (Robert Reece) 1 act Opera Comique 9 October

1882 **The Knight of the Garter** (J Sheddon Wilson) 1 act Gaiety Theatre 7 December

1883 **The Laundry Belle** (Wilson) 1 act Gaiety Theatre 5 December

1884 **Posterity** (Augustus M Moore) 1 act Theatre Royal, Newcastle 10 March

1884 **High Life Below Stairs** played with songs Gaiety Theatre 28 July

1885 **Won by a Trick** (Wilson) 1 act Gaiety Theatre 15 April

1885 **Little Jack Sheppard** (w Florian Pascal, et al/William Yardley, H Pottinger Stephens) Gaiety Theatre 26 December

1886 **Carl** (Wilson) 1 act Gaiety Theatre 3 May

1886 **Monte Cristo Jr** (w Ivan Caryll, et al/''Richard Henry'') Gaiety Theatre 23 December

1887 **Miss Esmeralda** (w Robert Martin, et al/''A C Torr'' [ie, Fred Leslie], Horace Mills) Gaiety Theatre 8 October

1887 **Frankenstein** (w Martin, et al/''Richard Henry'') Gaiety Theatre 24 December

1888 **Faust Up-to-Date** (G R Sims, Henry Pettitt) Gaiety Theatre 30 October

1889 **Ruy Blas and the Blasé Roué** (''A C Torr,'' Herbert F Clark) Gaiety Theatre 21 September

1890 **Carmen Up-to-Data** (Sims, Pettitt) Gaiety Theatre 4 October

1891 **Cinder-Ellen Up Too Late** (''A C Torr,'' W T Vincent) Princess Theatre, Melbourne 22 August; Gaiety Theatre, London 24 December

1893 **Frasquita** (W Godfrey) 1 act Gaiety Theatre 29 May

1893 **Don Juan** (Adrian Ross/James T Tanner) Gaiety Theatre 28 October

1895 **A Model Trilby, or A Day or Two After Du Maurier** (C H E Brookfield, Yardley) 1 act Opera Comique 16 November

1896 **One of the Girls** (w John Crook, Sidney Jones/Herbert Darnley, J J Dallas) Grand Theatre, Birmingham 9 March

1899 **The Merry-Go-Round** (w others/Aubrey Hopwood/Seymour Hicks) Coronet Theatre 24 April

UN LYCÉE DE JEUNES FILLES Vaudeville-opérette in 3 acts by Alexandre Bisson. Music by Louis Gregh. Théâtre Cluny, Paris, 28 December 1881.

A lively piece from the pen of top comedy-writer Bisson which dealt with a decidedly eccentric young ladies' establishment, set up by an ancient actor and his one-time-Juliet sister, both of whom let their old profession flow over into their new one, with the result that in English lessons the headmaster impersonates an Englishman, in German a frightful ''meinherr,'' and so forth. The pursuit of Valentine, the headmaster's daughter, by the sweetly klutzy usher Simplice and the womanizing Raoul Vol de Vent provided much of the comic action of the piece. With established funny men Guy (Simplice) and Mesmaecker (headmaster Cavénécadas) in its lead roles, with Blanche Ghinassi (Suzette) and Marguerite Luther (Valentine) supplying the feminine moments, to the accompaniment of some self-effacing numbers from Louis Gregh, *Un Lycée de jeunes filles* proved to be good for a run of more than 50 nights under Taillefer's management at the Théâtre Cluny on its first showing. It was also good for a series of repeats thereafter. Paris saw the piece again when Fernand Samuel mounted it at the Théâtre de la Renaissance in 1890, with Guy repeating his original lead comic role (3 May) and the 140 performances racked up by this reprise were sufficient encouragement for the director to repeat *Un Lycée de jeunes filles* when he took over at the Théâtre des Variétés (24 May 1892). Baron featured in this third production, alongside the young Ève Lavallière. This time it was a flop, but when the Folies-Dramatiques took the show up in 1895 (63 performances), followed by the Théâtre Déjazet in 1897 and, finally, the Gaîté-Lyrique in 1904 (1 July), with Berthe Legrand featured alongside Guyon fils, Regnard and Bardès, it was evident that the Variétés season had been the odd man out.

France was not the only country to welcome Bisson's tale of mildly immodest mix-ups in a girls' school. The Brussels Théâtre des Nouveautés hosted a popular production in January 1882, with Mme Raimbault as sister Polymnie, Zinquet as Simplice and Gregh conducting his own score, and the Renaissance revival inspired within months an Hungarian mounting for a good 24 nights at the Népszínház (ad Lajos Evva, Viktor Rákosi as ''theatre school''), followed by performances at the Budai Színkör (1 June 1892) and elsewhere, and Berlin saw a version adapted by Richard Genée who also supplied some fresh music to supplement Gregh's score.

Hungary: Népszínház *Színitanoda* 7 November 1890; Germany: Thomas Theater *Mädchenschule* 25 September 1891

LYNNE, Gillian [PYRKE, Jillian Barbara] (b Bromley, 20 February 1926). Performer turned choreographer whose dances for *Cats* and other musicals of recent years have made her Britain's most internationally successful dance arranger since the days of E W Royce.

Miss Lynne made her earliest theatre appearances in ballet, dancing for seven years with the Sadler's Wells company (Lilac Fairy, Queen of the Wilis, Black Queen in *Checkmate, Adam Zero,* etc) before moving into variety at the London Palladium and into jazz dance with her own group, Collages. She made her first major musical appearance in the West End in 1953 when she played the part of Claudine in the London production of *Can-Can,* and was subsequently seen as Wanda in a revival of *Rose Marie* and in several revues.

She began her career as a choreographer in 1962 with the Western Theatre Ballet and choreographed several revues and films before taking on her first musical shows, *The Roar of the Greasepaint . . . the Smell of the Crowd* (England 1964, USA 1965) and *Pickwick* (USA 1965, TV 1970). She directed and choreographed *The Matchgirls* at the Leatherhead Repertory Theatre (1965) and on its West End transfer and subsequently fulfilled the same double function for a 1969 production of Offenbach's *Bluebeard* at Sadler's Wells, the unlucky musical version of *Love on the Dole* (Nottingham, 1970) and a wild-Westernized *She Stoops to Conquer* written by Caryl Brahms and Ned Sherrin (Liberty Ranch, 1972). She also choreographed Broadway's *How Now Dow Jones* (1968) and London's *Phil the Fluter* (1969), *Ambassador* (1971), *The Card* (1973), *Hans Andersen* (1974), *My Fair Lady* revival (1979) and *Songbook* (1979).

In the late 1970s Miss Lynne had a personal success with her musical staging of two Royal Shakespeare Company productions, *A Comedy of Errors* and *Once in a Lifetime,* and she teamed again with RSC director Trevor Nunn to create the original production of the dance-based Andrew Lloyd Webber musical *Cats.* She subsequently directed and choreographed productions of *Cats* in many parts of the world, teamed with Hal Prince on *The Phantom of the Opéra* and with Nunn again on *Aspects of Love,* and directed and choreographed the compilation show *Tomfoolery* (1980), a London revival of *Cabaret* (1986), the musicalized Shaw piece *Valentine's Day* (1992) and a *Gigi* revival (1999) at the Vienna Volksoper.

Miss Lynne choreographed the film versions of *Half a Sixpence* (1966), *Man of La Mancha* (1972) and *Yentl* (1982). In 1985 she created a ballet, *Café Soir,* to the music of *A Little Night Music* for the Houston Ballet and in 1990 the BBC-TV's *The Look of Love* (dir and ch) based on the songs of Burt Bacharach and Hal David.

LYSISTRATA Spectacular Operette with ballet in 2 acts by Heinrich Bolten-Bäckers. Music by Paul Lincke. Apollotheater, Berlin, 1 April 1902.

One of the successors to Lincke and Bolten-Bäckers's enormously successful spectacle-fantasy *Frau Luna* as part of the variety program at Berlin's Apollotheater was a comic-burlesque treatment of Aristophanes' celebrated war-or-sex tale. Bolten's Lysistrata inflicted her ''Bettstreik'' on her husband, Athenian generalissimo Themistokles, and encouraged her nieces Cypris and Bachis and the Apollotheater's glamor chorus to do the same to their husbands, to the accompaniment of a lively set of songs, dances, marches and ensembles. *Lysistrata* proved to have less attraction for the Apollotheater's audiences than *Frau Luna* or *Im Reiche des Indra,* but from amongst several agreeable pieces its score brought forth the number which was to become the most internationally successful single item in Lincke's opus. The Glühwürmchen-Idyll, a delicious, twinkling ensemble used as an intermezzo in the show, became a worldwide hit, traveling to all kinds of countries where *Lysistrata* itself did not go. On Broadway it was inserted into the production of *The Girl Behind the Counter,* sung as a solo by May Naudain.

In 1903 Adolf Klein's Apollotheater production, with Lucie Medlon in the title role, was taken to Vienna's Danzers Orpheum by Gabor Steiner. There it shared the bill with a Lincke/Bolten-Bäckers one-acter, *Am Hochzeitsabend,* and a variety program, and was played in repertoire with the Apollo's other pieces, *Frau Luna* and *Im Reiche des Indra,* for a season. The ''electric'' ballet *Leuchtende Brillanten,* ''by H Harndin from the Folies Bergères [*sic*] in Paris and the Alhambra-Theater in London,'' was interpolated into each of the three Operetten.

P-L Flers's French version was played at the Moulin-Rouge, in the wake of the Parisian success of Steiner's earlier success, *The Belle of New York,* with the beautiful, aggressively corseted soprano Germaine Gallois starred in the title role and Angèle Gril and Sulbac featured. Flers added additional scenes and tableaux-vivants to the libretto and also interpolated extraneous songs, turning the piece into a full evening's entertainment which showed off the scenic and feminine specialities of the Moulin-Rouge at their lushest. With typical theatrical mensongerie, the show was advertised as having been played nearly ten thousand times in America and Britain: it had actually been seen in neither. It had, however, reached Hungary (ad Ferenc Molnár, Jenő Faragó), where it was played at the Király Színház in 1903.

In spite of an indifferent start, *Lysistrata* survived. It was revived at Budapest's Scala Színház as *Lysistrata* with Hanna Honthy in the title role (14 August 1920), and it remains on the fringe of the German-language repertoire in one of those reorganized versions which, like Flers's effort, brings it up to the length of a full evening's entertainment. One such version was produced at the Neuköllner Oper in Berlin in 2001. However, the "Glow-Worm" is still heard more than the Operette.

Lysistrata has been seen on the musical stage on a number of other occasions since she was given Schubert music in 1861 in the little *Der Verschworenen, oder Der häusliche Krieg* (lib: I F Castelli, Frankfurt 29 August). Aristophanes' sex-based tale was a natural prey for musical-makers of the naughty-words-are-thrilling era. Myers and Cass turned out a *Liz* for Canterbury's Marlowe Theatre (17 August 1968), a Frank Vinciguerra/Danny Liebstein rock musical *Lysistrata* was played at Hunter College Theater Workshop in the same year, and another American musical of the same title was produced in New York in 1972 (Brooks Atkinson Theatre 13 November Peter Link/Michael Cacoyannis). A 1963 Romanian operetta by Nicouzor Constantinescu and George Voinescu, music by Gherase Dendrino, and a 1971 Czechoslovakian piece (*Der schönste Krieg*) by Hana Čináková, Vladimir Renčin and composer Jiři Bedná went to the same source, whilst a British piece mixed the tale with a cowboy setting and called itself *Wild, Wild Women* as it made its way from Richmond to Windsor to London's Astoria (ex-movie) Theatre. A piece called *Lysistrata 2001* appeared in Munich in 1986 (Musiktheater 21 December), and off-Broadway's Samuel Beckett Theater got a *Lyz!* (with exclamation point) in 1998. So far none has come up to Bolten-Bäckers and Lincke's effort nor produced anything to rival his Glühwürmchen-Idyll.

Austria: Danzers Orpheum 31 March 1903; Hungary: Király Színház *Mákrancos Hölgyek* 16 December 1903; France: Théâtre du Moulin-Rouge 15 April 1904

Recording: selection (EMI)

LYTTON, Henry A[rthur] (Sir) [aka Henry HENRI] [JONES, Henry Arthur] (b London, 3 January 1865; d London, 15 August 1936). Light-comedy baritone and longtime chief comedian of the D'Oyly Carte company.

Lytton made his earliest stage appearances (as H A Henri, pretending to be his wife's brother) as a chorister for Violet Melnotte in *Erminie* and Ivan Caryll's first musical *The Lily of Léoville,* on Broadway with Violet Cameron's company (*The Commodore,* Wayland Smith in *Kenilworth*) and on the road with one of D'Oyly Carte's companies. He played briefly for George Grossmith in *Ruddigore* and George Temple in Broadway's *Gondoliers* and, after some eight years playing Gilbert and Sullivan in the provinces, was brought into the Savoy Theatre company to replace the failing Grossmith in the lead role of Carte's production of *His Majesty* (1897). Thereafter he remained at the Savoy to appear in D'Oyly Carte's main company in the Gilbert and Sullivan repertoire (Shadbolt, Dr Daly, Strephon, Mikado, etc), as Prince Paul in the Savoy's revival of *The Grand Duchess,* and to create important roles in *The Lucky Star* (1899, Baron Tabasco), *The Rose of Persia* (1899, Sultan Mahmoud), *The Emerald Isle* (1901, Pat Murphy), *Merrie England* (1902, Earl of Essex, "The Yeomen of England") and *A Princess of Kensington* (1903, Jelf).

When William Greet took the Savoy company into musical comedy, Lytton starred as juvenile lead in *The Earl and the Girl* (Dick Wargrave, "My Cosy Corner Girl") and continued in similar roles in *The Talk of the Town* (Reggie Drummond), *The White Chrysanthemum* (Reginald Armitage), as a takeover for the younger George Grossmith in the Gaiety's *The Spring Chicken* (Boniface) and in *The Little Michus.* In 1906 he went on the halls in a two-handed musical comedy *United Service* with Connie Ediss. He was subsequently cast as a Seymour Hicks clone in *My Darling* (1907) and played the Pavilion in the musical sketch *An Amateur Raffles* (1908, Hon Percy Gower) in his last musical-comedy performances before rejoining the D'Oyly Carte company in 1908 (Mikado, Dick Deadeye, Strephon, Pirate King, etc). He remained with the company for the rest of his long career, graduating from the Richard Temple roles to the George Grossmith ones, and making himself an enduring name as the comic star of the Gilbert and Sullivan repertoire over a quarter of a century. He retired in 1934.

Lytton's wife, **Louie Henri** (b ?1862; d 2 May 1947), who began a career as a chorus singer before her husband (*The Merry Duchess,* etc), played alongside him thereafter both with Miss Melnotte and then with Carte, first as a chorister and later as a soubrette during their eight years of touring. She appeared as Tessa in the 1891 revival of *The Gondoliers* before retiring to family life.

Their son **Henry Lytton jr** [Lord Alva JONES] (b London 1904; d London, 16 September 1965) played in musical comedy (*The Beauty Spot,* Toby Kerwyn in *Archie, The Girl Friend, Here Comes the Bride,* etc) and revue and was at one stage the husband of revue star Jessie Matthews.

Autobiographies: *Secrets of a Savoyard* (Jarrolds, London, 1922), *A Wandering Minstrel* (Jarrolds, London, 1933)

M

MacCUNN, Hamish (b Greenock, Scotland, 22 March 1868; d London, 2 August 1916).

A composer of orchestral music and of two operas (*Jeanie Deans, Diarmid*), MacCunn began his composing and conducting careers (Carl Rosa Opera, Moody-Manners Opera) in classical music before, in 1902, moving to the Savoy Theatre where, as principal conductor, he musically directed the original productions of *Merrie England* and *A Princess of Kensington.* When manager William Greet moved on from the Savoy and comic opera to the Lyric Theatre and musical comedy, MacCunn went with him as the conductor for *The Earl and the Girl* and *Little Hans Andersen.* He subsequently conducted *The Blue Moon* (1905), *The Talk of the Town* (1905), Liza Lehmann's light opera *The Vicar of Wakefield* (1906), *Tom Jones* (1907) and German's last musical, *Fallen Fairies* (1909). He then joined the Beecham Opera Company with whom he was the musical director for Beecham's 1910 revival of C V Stanford's *Shamus O'Brien.*

MacCunn supplied occasional songs for interpolation into a number of West End shows and in 1905 he wrote the score for the musical comedy *The Golden Girl,* toured by H Cecil Beryl.

MacCunn's brother, **Andrew MacCunn,** at first a deputy conductor with the Moody-Manners Opera Company, later also worked as a musical director in the musical theatre. He toured for George Edwardes in South Africa, but made the large part of his career in Australia where he became established as the senior theatre conductor of his time.

1905 **The Golden Girl** (Basil Hood) Prince of Wales Theatre, Birmingham 5 August

1912 **The Sailor and the Nursemaid** (Charles Childerstone) 1 act Aldwych Theatre 27 June

MacDERMOT, Galt (b Montreal, 18 December 1928). The composer of the songs for *Hair.*

MacDermot's achievement at the age of almost 40 was sufficiently limited for him to describe himself in the program of his first musical, amongst the lists of credits of his companions, solely and briefly as ''piano player, organist, choir director, African and love-rock musicologist.'' In fact, he had made some inroads into the popular-music world, and had had some success with a 1961 song, ''African Waltz,'' but that was small beans compared to the success which that first musical would bring him. *Hair* turned out to be an enduring international hit, and its favorite song, ''Aquarius,'' became and has remained ever since the anthem of the 1960s people of every decade.

In spite of its huge success, *Hair* won no awards (the 1968 Best Musical Tony went to *Hallelujah, Baby!*), and it almost seemed like a slightly shamefaced acknowledgment of that fact that, in 1972, MacDermot's modern musical-comedy version of Shakespeare's *Two Gentlemen of Verona,* brought to Broadway, like *Hair,* from the New York Shakespeare Festival's Public Theatre, did take the principal award. *Two Gentlemen of Verona* proved quite successful—although not anywhere as successful as *Hair*—finding a good run on Broadway and a number of productions overseas.

Thereafter, however, MacDermot failed to find again the success that the 1960s and its trends, attitudes and tastes had brought him. *Dude,* mounted by *Hair* director O'Horgan (another whose triumphs lasted only those few years of the late 1960s and early 1970s), was a quick failure; an Andrew Lloyd Webber–style sung-through *Via Galactica* which was mounted by Peter Hall at the new Uris Theater was gone in a week; and a version of Tirso de Molina's *El Burlador de Sevilla,* originally commissioned by Britain's Royal Shakespeare Company, was eventually seen only in Trinidad.

MacDermot returned to the musical theatre in the 1980s with another score for Joseph Papp and the Public Theatre, but *The Human Comedy* followed its 79 performances at the Shakespeare Festival with just 13 at Broadway's Royale.

MacDermot has also written ballet and church music and composed an operatic *Troilus and Cressida* (1969), as well as incidental music for the Public Theatre's productions of *Hamlet* and *Twelfth Night* and Derek Walcott's *The Odyssey* (1994), and 30 years on from his big success, his name appeared once more among the credits for the revue *Time and the Wind* (w Norman Matlock) produced at the John Houseman Theater (9 August 1995).

1967 **Hair** (Gerome Ragni, James Rado) Anspacher Theater 17 October; Biltmore Theater 29 April 1968

1970 **Isabel's a Jezebel** (William Dumaresq) Duchess Theatre, London 15 December

1971 **Two Gentlemen of Verona** (John Guare, Mel Shapiro) St James Theater 1 December

1972 **Dude** (*The Highway Life*) (Ragni) Broadway Theater 9 October

1972 **Via Galactica** (Christopher Gore, Judith Ross) Uris Theater 28 November

1973 **The Karl Marx Play** (Rochelle Owens) American Place Theater 16 March

1973 **Aunt Harriet** (MacDermot) Theater for the New City 21 November

1974 **The Charlatan** (Derek Walcott) Mark Taper Forum, Los Angeles 23 May

1974 **The Joker of Seville** (Walcott) Little Carib Theater, Trinidad November

1983 **The Human Comedy** (Dumaresq) Public Theater 28 December; Royale Theater 5 April 1984

1985 **The Special** Jewish Repertory Theater 19 October

1991 **Steel** (Walcott) American Repertory Theater, Cambridge, Mass 14 April

MacDONALD, Christie (b Pictou, Nova Scotia, 28 February 1875; d Westport, Conn, 25 July 1962). Attractive, sweet-voiced leading lady on the turn-of-the-century Broadway stage.

Born in Nova Scotia and educated in Boston, the palely pretty young Christie MacDonald made her first stage appearance as a chorus singer in *Erminie* and *Puritania* with Pauline Hall. She subsequently played bits with Francis Wilson's company in such comic operas as *The Lion Tamer* (*Le Grand Casimir*), *The Merry Monarch* (*L'Étoile*) and *Erminie* again (Marie) before being promoted to a slightly larger role in *The Devil's Deputy* (*Babolin,* 1894, Bob). She appeared in the Boston musicals *The Sphinx* (1895, Shafra) and *The Walking Delegate* (1897, Woo Me), and featured alongside Wilson again both as Dolly Grigg in the Broadway version of Sullivan's *The Chieftain* (1895) and in *Half a King* (1896, *Le Roi de carreau,* Lucinde), and had her best new role to date as the Princess Minutezza in Klaw and Erlanger's production of Sousa's *The Bride Elect* (1898).

Thereafter a string of leading ingenue roles followed, both in American musical comedies and extravaganzas—*The Man in the Moon* (1899, Diana), *In Gay Paree* (1899, Louisette), *The Princess Chic* (1900, Chic), *The Cadet Girl* (1900, Marguerite), alongside Peter Dailey in his *Hodge, Podge & Co* (1900, Priscilla Hodge) and *Champagne Charlie* (1901, Dorothy Williams), *The Sho-Gun* (1904, Princess Hunni-Bun), *Mexicana* (1906, Tita), *The Prince of Bohemia* (1910, Angela Tritton)—and in imports such as *The Cadet Girl* (1900, *Les Demoiselles de Saint-Cyriens,* Antoinette), the Gaiety Theatre musical *The Toreador* (1902, Nancy Staunton), *An English Daisy* (1904, Daisy), and *The Belle of Mayfair* (1906, playing the Juliet role created in London by Edna May). She found particular success in the title role of *Miss Hook of Holland* (1907), as Pitti-Sing in the all-star *Mikado* revival of 1910 and as the star of the long-running American production of Reinhardt's *The Spring Maid* (1910, *Die Sprudelfee,* Princess Bozena). In 1913 she created the ingenue lead—yet another disguised princess—in Victor Herbert's *Sweethearts* (Sylvia) before, no longer an ingenue at almost 40, disappearing from the forefront of the musical stage.

She returned in 1920 to play the star character role of Lady Holyrood, created by Ada Reeve, in a revival of *Florodora,* before putting an end to her career.

MacDONALD, Jeanette [Anna] (b Philadelphia, 18 June 1901; d Houston, Tex, 14 January 1965). Hollywood's most successful soprano star of celluloid operetta.

After beginning her singing career as a teenager in the chorus of a New York revue, Miss MacDonald appeared in Jerome Kern's *The Night Boat* (1920), acted as understudy to the title role of *Irene* in Chicago and played a chorus part at the Casino Theater in *Tangerine* (1921). She won improving roles alongside Mitzi in *The Magic Ring* (1923, Iris Bellamy), and (sporting two ''n''s in her name in the playbill) as Sylvia Metcalf, the second female part to Queenie Smith, in *Tip-Toes* (1925), accompanying another fine voice, Robert Halliday, in the strains of ''Nice Baby.'' She had a leading role, alongside touring stars Cecil Lean and Cleo Mayfield, in a musical version of *Brewster's Millions* called *Bubbling Over* (1926) which stumbled out of town, and she moved on instead to the title role (which was not quite as good as it sounded) of another fine farce, *Nothing But the Truth,* set to music as *Yes, Yes, Yvette* (1927). This one made Broadway, but she stopped short of New York once again in *The Studio Girl,* a flop version of the *Trilby* tale musicalized by the perennially flopping Will Ortmann, in which she had been cast as the mutable heroine.

Miss MacDonald continued in ingenue roles through a further trio of undistinguished shows in 12 months—*Sunny Days* (1928, Ginette Bertin), *Angela* (aka *The Right Girl,* 1928, Princess Angela) and *Boom Boom* (1929, Jean)—before moving on to a film career which

Plate 234. **Christie MacDonald.** *This little lady from* Sweethearts *may look like a Netherlandish washergirl, but she is . . . of course . . . really and truly a Princess.*

Plate 235. **Jeanette MacDonald**

made her one of the most famous leading ladies of the heyday of the musical screen. She starred through more than a decade in (not always recognizable) film versions of *The Vagabond King* (1930), *The Cat and the Fiddle* (1934), *The Merry Widow* (1934), *Naughty Marietta* (1935), *Rose-Marie* (1936), *The Firefly* (1937), *Maytime* (1937), *Sweethearts* (1938), *Bitter-Sweet* (1940) and *I Married an Angel* (1942), as well as in such made-for-the-screen musical movies as *The Love Parade, One Hour with You, Love Me Tonight* and *San Francisco.* She later appeared on the stage in concert, but returned only intermittently to the musical theatre (*Bitter-Sweet* 1954, *The King and I* 1956) where, *Tip-Toes* apart, she had drawn a fairly feeble lot of shows in her ingenue days.

Biography: Turk, E B: *Hollywood Diva* (University of of California Press, Berkeley, 1988)

MacDONOUGH, Glen (b Brooklyn, NY, 12 November 1870; d Stamford, Conn, 30 March 1924). Eclectic musical-theatre writer whose works ranged from touring comedy to fantasy to Viennese adaptations.

MacDonough began his theatre career as an actor, and he subsequently wrote several farces before making his first essays into the musical theatre with Marie Jansen's not very successful touring vehicle *Miss Dynamite* and in a collaboration with Victor Herbert on a piece called *The Gold Bug* (1896). In spite of the last-minute interpolation of two lively and appreciated young performers called Bert Williams and George Walker into its cast, *The Gold Bug* expired after one week. MacDonough supplied farcical vehicles for Sam Bernard (*The Marquis of Michigan*) and May Irwin (the play with songs *Kate Kip, Buyer,* the musical comedy *The Belle of Bridgeport*), concocted a low-comical American-in-Paris text to star Dan Daly as one of *The New Yorkers* and adapted the Strauss pasticcio *Wiener Blut* for Rudolf Aronson, but he found his first major success only when he came back together with Herbert, seven years after their disastrous first collaboration, to write the spectacular children-of-all-ages extravaganza *Babes in Toyland.*

The association was pursued in a successful piece of Ruritanian musical comedy, *It Happened in Nordland,* in a pretty fantasy called *Wonderland* (based on the Brothers Grimm tale *The Dancing Princesses*), which did not, in spite of a respectable run, win the same audience that had clustered around *Babes in Toyland,* and an oriental comic opera called *Algeria.* Herbert's delightful score for this last piece was too good to jettison, so when the piece failed to come up to expectations MacDonough partly rewrote the libretto and it was given a second chance the following season as *The Rose of Algeria.* But it still failed to take off.

The end of MacDonough's collaboration with Herbert overlapped with the beginning of his contribution to a mostly successful series of ''summer musicals.'' These were frivolous, light pieces of only fairly coherent comedy, illustrated by B-grade but pluggable songs in the mode of the moment (at first by Raymond Hubbell, later by Baldwin Sloane), pretty girls, specialities and scenic effects, and intended not only for the businessman who was tired and hot, but also for his equally exhausted wife and family. After the success of the first, *The Midnight Sons,* producer Lew Fields played the series summer and winter at the Broadway Theater until the vein ran out some three years later.

MacDonough subsequently adapted several of the freshly fashionable Viennese musical shows into American-style shows for Klaw and Erlanger with some success, remade Leo Birinski's *Narrentanz* as the libretto for a piece called *The Merry Martyr* without any, and had his last brush with something like a winner when he contributed the text to Raymond Hubbell's *The Kiss Burglar* in 1918. His last work for the musical theatre included four songs (w Hubbell) for the 1916 *Come to Bohemia,* material for the revues *Fads and Fancies, As You Were* (American adaptation), *Hitchy Koo of 1920* (book and lyrics to the music of Jerome Kern) and *Snapshots of 1921,* and five projects that all stopped short of Broadway: De Koven's last comic opera, May Irwin's last star vehicle, a musical version of the comedy *It Pays to Advertise,* a botch job on the Paris hit *Phi-Phi* and an unsuccessful musical-comedy vehicle for the usually successful female impersonator Julian Eltinge, produced by Jacques Pierre as *The Elusive Lady.*

1894 **The Brownies** revised libretto

1894 **Miss Dynamite** (various) Bijou Theater 5 November

1896 **The Gold Bug** (Victor Herbert) Casino Theater 21 September

1897 **The Marquis of Michigan** (A Baldwin Sloane/w Edward W Townsend) Collingwood Opera House, Poughkeepsie 26 August; Bijou Theater 21 September 1898

1898 **Kate Kip, Buyer** (various) Grand Opera House, Kansas City 13 May; Bijou Theater 31 October

1899 **Chris and the Wonderful Lamp** (John Philip Sousa) Hyperion Theater, New Haven 23 October; Victoria Theater 1 January 1900

1899 **Sister Mary** (various) Bijou Theater 27 October

1900 **The Belle of Bridgeport** (various) Bijou Theater 29 October

1901 **Vienna Life** (*Wiener Blut*) American version (Broadway Theater)

1901 **The New Yorkers** (Ludwig Englander/George V Hobart) Herald Square Theater 7 October

1903 **Babes in Toyland** (Herbert) Majestic Theater 13 October

1904 **It Happened in Nordland** (Herbert) Lew Fields Theater 5 December

1905 **Alice and the Eight Dancing Princesses** (Herbert) Star Theater, Buffalo 14 September; Grand Opera House, Chicago 18 September

1905 **Wonderland** (revised *Alice and the Eight Princesses*) (Herbert) Majestic Theater 24 October

1906 **The Great Decide** (Gustave Kerker) 2 scenes Herald Square Theater 15 November

1907 **Too Near Home** (Herbert) Walnut Street Theater, Philadelphia 7 January

1908 **Algeria** (Herbert) Broadway Theater 31 August

1909 **The Midnight Sons** (Raymond Hubbell) Broadway Theater 22 May

1909 **The Rose of Algeria** revised *Algeria* Herald Square Theater 20 September

1909 **The Girl from the States** (later *The Golden Widow*) (Hubbell, A Baldwin Sloane) Adelphi Theater, Philadelphia 11 October

1910 **The Jolly Bachelors** (Hubbell) Broadway Theater 6 January

1910 **The Summer Widowers** (Sloane) Broadway Theater 4 June

1911 **The Hen Pecks** (Sloane/E Ray Goetz) Broadway Theater 4 February

1911 **The Never Homes** (Sloane/Goetz) Broadway Theater 5 October

1912 **The Count of Luxembourg** (*Der Graf von Luxemburg*) American version (New Amsterdam Theater)

1912 **Eva** American version (New Amsterdam Theater)

1913 **The Merry Martyr** (Hugo Riesenfeld) Colonial Theater, Boston 8 September

1914 **The Queen of the Movies** (*Die Kino-Königin*) American version w Edward A Paulton (Globe Theater)

1916 **Come to Bohemia** (Kenneth M Murchison/w George S Chappell/Chappell) Maxine Elliott Theatre 27 April

1918 **The Kiss Burglar** (Hubbell) George M Cohan Theater 9 May

1919 **Yesterday** (Reginald De Koven) Playhouse, Wilmington, Del 10 March

1919 **Raising the Aunty** (aka *The Water's Fine*) (Ted Snyder/Joe Sam Lewis, Joe Young/w Aaron Hoffman) Poughkeepsie, NY 19 March

1919 **Among the Girls** (Hubbell/w Henry Blossom/Blossom, Roi Cooper Megrue) Park Square Theater, Boston 19 May

1921 **Phi-Phi** American version w Harry Wagstaffe Gribble, Goetz (Globe Theater, Atlantic City)

1922 **The Elusive Lady** (Hubbell) Ford's Theater, Baltimore 2 October

MACÉ-MONTROUGE, Marguerite [Élise] [née MACÉ] (b ?1836; d Paris, ?28 November 1898).

Marguerite Macé began her career as an actress at the Gymnase (1850) and during the 1850s worked at the Délassements-Comique and, from 1855, at the Bouffes-Parisiens, where she made up part of Offenbach's original little company. At one stage she was the only female member. She remained with the composer to create roles in a number of his early works, including *Une nuit blanche* (Fanchette), *La Chatte métamorphosée en femme* (Marianne) and, most notably, the part of L'Opinion Publique in *Orphée aux enfers,* and she also created roles in such little opérettes as Jonas's *Le Duel de Benjamin* (1855), the prize opérette *Le Docteur Miracle* (1857, Véronique), *Les Ondines au Champagne* (1865, Coquilette), *Le Cabaret de Ramponneau* (1867, Bellhumeur) and *Sauvons la caisse* (1871). She was described by a contemporary as "une chanteuse d'opérette exquise de legèrté, blonde, spirituelle, enragée, vapoureuse, fibe, tendre, ironique."

Madame Macé-Montrouge had a long career as an actress and a vocalist, successfully transferring to character parts in later years and creating two important senior musical-comedy roles, the conniving Madame Jacob in *Joséphine vendue par ses soeurs* (1886) and La Señora, the vigorous duenna of *Miss Helyett* (1890). She also appeared as La Baronne in *Le Droit du seigneur* (1878), in *Les Cent Vierges* (1885, Eglantine), *Mamselle Crénom*

(1888, Mlle Chipoix), Pugno's *Le Valet de coeur* (1888), in the title role of *Oscarine* (1888), in *Mariage avant la lettre* (1888, Archiduchesse), *Le Royaume des femmes* (1889, Jérémia), *Le Mari de la reine* (1889, Madame Patouillard), *La Vocation de Marius* (1890, Mme Charles) and a number of other musical shows, at first at the Bouffes, then from 1890 at the Nouveautés, amongst an always busy program of the plays which became her principal occupation. She made her last stage appearance in 1897.

Her husband, **MONTROUGE** [Louis HESNARD] (b 1825), who came to fame as a comic actor in the musical theatre, had begun his working life as an architect. After being involved in the restoration of the Théâtre des Batignolles in 1855 he became its associate director, and he moved on from there to manage Offenbach's original little Bouffes-Parisiens, by then known as the Folies-Marigny (1863–68), and later, after a three-year stint in Cairo, the Théâtre de l'Athénée Comique (1876 until its destruction in 1883, "retiring with a comfortable fortune"), the new Bouffes-Parisiens and the Châtelet. He simultaneously had a long career as a performer, making a particular mark as a compère in revue ("le roi des compères et des féticheurs") and creating many musical-theatre roles, from early days in *Le Testament de M Crac* (1871, Capoulade) and alongside his wife in *Le Cabaret de Ramponneau* (Ramponneau) and *Les Ondines au Champagne* (Vent-Contraire), to good character roles in *Le Droit du seigneur* (1878, the Baron), *François les bas-bleus* (1883, Marquis de Pontcornet), *Le Naufrage de M Godet* (1885, Godet), *Surcouf* (1887, Kerbiniou), *Le Valet de coeur* (1888), *Oscarine* (1888, Pavillon), *Mam-selle Crénom* (1888, Vincent), *Le Mari de la reine* (1889, Patouillard), *Miss Helyett* (1890, Smithson), etc.

MacGREGOR, Edgar J (b Rochester, NY, 1879; d New York, 3 April 1957).

For 30 years one of the busiest stage directors in the American musical theatre, McGregor began his career working in the straight theatre before directing his earliest Broadway musicals. *The Kiss Burglar* (1918) gave him a promising start, and Abe Erlanger's productions of Ivan Caryll's *The Girl Behind the Gun* and Victor Herbert's *The Velvet Lady,* May Irwin's *Raising the Aunty* and the 1919 edition of *George White's Scandals* helped to establish his reputation.

In 1920 MacGregor joined William Moore Patch to produce Hugo Felix's *The Sweetheart Shop* (dir: Herbert Gresham), a fine success in Chicago and a respectable one in New York, before he returned to directing with John Cort's *Jim Jam Jems* and Sigmund Romberg's essay as a producer with *The Love Birds.* In 1922 he directed a piece called *Love and Kisses,* the first production of the young Laurence Schwab, and after the show had been turned into *The Gingham Girl* and, at the same time, into a success, McGregor directed eight further shows for Schwab and his sometime partner Frank Mandel, in a collaboration that produced his most memorable triumphs—*The Desert Song* (1926), *Good News* (1927) and *The New Moon* (1928)—as well as *Sweet Little Devil* (1924), *Captain Jinks* (1925), *Queen High* (1926) and *Follow Thru* (1929). Amongst a contrasting selection of less successful pieces, ranging from the Sissle and Blake show *Elsie* (1923), Gershwin's grim *Our Nell* (1922), *Adrienne* (1923, the show which didn't turn up at the theatre for its out-of-town first night) and the Tchaikovsky pasticcio *Natja* (1925) to the splashy vanity production *Fioretta* (1929), he also staged a couple of hits for other producers: Eddie Dowling's ingenuous *Honeymoon Lane* (1926) and Aarons and Freedley's production of *Funny Face* (1927) with Fred and Adele Astaire in its star roles.

In the early 1930s MacGregor directed several Earl Carroll revues and Ziegfeld's *Hot-Cha!,* but after one last show, *Take a Chance,* for Schwab, he abandoned Broadway in favor of filmland. He returned only in 1939 to direct Cole Porter's *Dubarry Was a Lady,* and followed it up with three further fine successes in two seasons: Berlin's *Louisiana Purchase,* and Porter's next two pieces, *Panama Hattie* and *Let's Face It,* before fizzling away into a few failures *(My Dear Public, Nellie Bly, Louisiana Lady)* in his last Broadway assignments.

MacGregor has sometimes been listed as co-librettist of some of his shows, but these credits did not appear at the time of the productions, and it seems that his only effective input was directorial. He was also credited with a co-writer's share (w Otto Harbach) in the unproduced (screen)play which was transformed into the British musical *Here Comes the Bride.*

MACK AND MABEL Musical romance (musical love story) in 2 acts by Michael Stewart. Music and lyrics by Jerry Herman. Majestic Theater, New York, 6 October 1974.

A primary-colored almost-burlesque of the early days of the movies in America, through which runs the story of silent filmmaker Mack Sennett (Robert Preston) and Mabel Normand (Bernadette Peters), the girl he takes from the deli, makes into a film heroine, seduces, then loses (after she's invented custard-pie-throwing) to a more-reel filmmaker. This gap in his schedule makes Sennett invent his Bathing Beauties in time for a first-act closer. Boy and girl get together again five years later, but when he invents the Keystone Kops she leaves and goes off with her filmmaker. Her ambition to be more than a speechless comic, and his determination that the kind of slapstick films he makes are the only kind he can and will make, mean that no happy ending is available.

The songs of *Mack and Mabel*—very largely devoted to the two stars—fell into three categories: the movie numbers, bright and usually comical; the production numbers; and the romantic ballads. Mack set the evening going, singing (before moving into the flashback that was the main part of the piece) of how ''Movies Were Movies'' when he ran the show. He insisted that, in face of the fashion for spectaculars, weepies and dramas, his only credo was ''I Wanna Make the World Laugh''; he brought on the Bathers to ''Hundreds of Girls'' and declared ''My Heart Leaps Up'' every time a Keystone Kop falls down. Lisa Kirk, in the supporting role of Lottie Ames, also contributed to the showbizzy section with her description of the ''Big Time'' and a parodic encouragement to ''Tap Your Troubles Away.'' On the romantic side, Mack proposed sex with no attachments in ''I Won't Send Roses,'' whilst Mabel, who had set her evening off marveling at herself on film in ''Look What Happened to Mabel,'' spat out her preference for being ''Wherever He Ain't'' and torched her way through the disbelief that ''Time Heals Everything.'' She also benefited from a ''Hello, Dolly!'' style of entrance number as she was welcomed back to Mack's studio by the massed cast, hailing the effect that is made ''When Mabel Comes in the Room.''

Directed and choreographed, like *Hello, Dolly!,* by Gower Champion, the piece, with its uneasy mix of the two-dimensional and real feelings, proved not to have the same appeal for Broadway audiences as its blockbusting predecessor, and it closed after 65 performances. However, several years later, a magistral piece of plugging gave *Mack and Mabel* a strange sort of second life. The original-cast recording of the show was outrageously pushed by one British disc jockey on one British radio station and, little by little, the songs gained currency, and the score a cult status amongst a particular group of English musical-theatre devotees. A British provincial production of a rewritten-ish version with an alternative happy (?) ending tacked on was staged; West End producers went to look, shook their heads, and librettist Stewart set to re-rewriting the text which was being blamed for insufficiently supporting the now-familiar songs. Several times during the 1980s an announcement of a London production was whispered or even pronounced, but the nearest *Mack and Mabel* got to the London stage was a concert performance of the score, and at Stewart's death in 1987 he had got no closer to making an attractive libretto out of the tale of the basically distasteful man and the rather silly girl who make up the title and take up most of the text of the show.

However, *Mack and Mabel* did finally get its London showing in 1995 when a consortium of American and British producers mounted the re-re-(re?)written version at Leicester's Haymarket Theatre and the Picadilly Theatre. Howard McGillin and Caroline O'Connor featured in the title roles of an uncomfortably tuppence-colored production of an obviously patched-about show (ad Francine Pascal) which lasted from 7 November 1995 to 29 June 1996 on the stage of the Piccadilly Theatre and simply and finally confirmed *Mack and Mabel* as a set of now much-loved songs rather than as a viable piece of musical theatre.

Plate 236. **Cameron Mackintosh**

In spite of this, however, in 1998 a German version (ad Frank Thannhäuser) was produced at Karlsruhe with Miroslaw Nemec and Jolanta Teresa Kuznik in the title roles. It proved a financial disaster.

UK: Nottingham Playhouse 16 September 1981, Picadilly Theatre 24 October 1995; Germany: Badische Staatstheater, Karlsruhe 26 September 1998

Recordings: original cast (ABC/MCA), London concert 1988 (First Night), London cast (EMI), German (Karlsruhe) recording live (Bella Musica)

MACKINTOSH, Cameron [Anthony] (Sir) (b London, 17 October 1946). The dominant producer of the international musical theatre of the 1980s and 1990s.

Cameron Mackintosh began his life in the theatre working as a teenaged stagehand on *Camelot* at the Theatre Royal, Drury Lane, and as an ASM on the touring production of *Oliver!* He moved into production with a season of plays (w Robin Alexander, Hubert Woodward) at Henley's Kenton Theatre, and touched London for the first time with a version of *Little Women* mounted by ''Bloomsbury Plays'' at the Jeannetta Cochrane Theatre at Christmas 1967. Although the same year saw the 20-year-old neoproducer paragraphed in the press as preparing an Ireland Cutter/Tommie Connor musicalization of *A Portrait of Dorian Grey,* it was to be almost two years—spent whetting his teeth on the produce of such writers as Agatha Christie in the provinces—before Mackintosh got his first real West End production of a musical to the stage. It was a revival of a version of *Anything Goes,* mounted in collaboration with Laurier Lister at the Yvonne Arnaud Theatre, Guildford, and its stay at London's Saville Theatre was a brief one.

New and original musicals, however, were soon to follow. In partnership with Veronica Flint-Shipman, he brought a musical version of Pinero's *Trelawny of the Wells* (*Trelawny*) from the Theatre Royal, Bristol, to London for 177 performances in 1972; with Jimmy Wax he mounted a version of Arnold Bennett's *The Card* (1973) at Bristol and in London (130 performances); and with Mrs Flint-Shipman again, in the wake of *Jesus Christ Superstar,* he launched one of the biblical musicals which were briefly the rage—a *Rock Nativity* (1974, revised 1975 as *A New Tomorrow*) written by *Card* songwriters Tony Hatch and Jackie Trent. He also staged London seasons of two children's entertainments—Julian Slade's *Winnie the Pooh* and David Wood's *The Owl and the Pussycat Went to See*—whilst keeping up a busy schedule of touring activities.

After this burst of productivity, however, Mackintosh retrenched for a number of years into less adventurous, but slightly more profitable areas, and for the remainder of the 1970s he mounted no new musical play. He invested the touring circuits with a seemingly ceaseless touring version of *Godspell,* which returned on several occasions to London, and joined Michael White on a touring *The Rocky Horror Show.* He presented several seasonal editions of the popular children's musical *The Gingerbread Man,* brought the successful compilation show *Side by Side by Sondheim* (1976) to the Mermaid Theatre and then to the West End, and also produced fine revivals of several major classics: an *Oliver!* that remained 1,139 performances at the Albery Theatre and Arts Council–backed versions of *My Fair Lady* and *Oklahoma!,* which both found their way to London for good seasons from the touring circuits for which they had been originally designed.

In 1980 Mackintosh put together and mounted another compilation show, this one made up from the works of humorist Tom Lehrer (*Tomfoolery*), but it was the following year that he made his major breakthrough to success when, following the disappearance from the London theatre scene of Robert Stigwood, the producer of *Jesus Christ Superstar* and *Evita,* he began an alliance with composer Andrew Lloyd Webber. The partnership was initiated by the production of *Cats.* The vast success of this piece, which spread long and large throughout the world with results unparalleled in musical-theatre history, was compounded not only by two further pieces produced in collaboration with Lloyd Webber's Really Useful Company—the two-headed entertainment *Song and Dance,* and a second international blockbuster in the romantic operetta *The Phantom of the Opéra* (1986)—but by an involvement in the off-Broadway hit *Little Shop of Horrors* and, even more significantly, the production of the third of the three grandiose ''Cameron Mackintosh presents'' musical plays which were to dominate the late 1980s and early 1990s on the world's stages: the English adaptation of the French musical *Les Misérables* (1985).

Whilst Mackintosh rose to the top of the international producing heap, bestriding not only the Atlantic but a few other of the world's oceans as well, as carefully managed reproductions of his three big, spectacular musicals went from one corner of the globe to another, there were occasional less-profitable productions going on in their shadow. The 1983 *Blondel* was a failure, repeats of *Oliver!* in London and New York did not have the same success as his previous revival of the show (or of a later one at the London Palladium), an awkwardly choreographed-up revival of *The Boy Friend* convinced no more, and a late West End version of the Broadway musical *Follies* had a respectable London life without ringing any bells.

In 1989 he produced a fourth new large-scale musical, a modernized *Madam Butterfly* written by the authors of *Les Misérables* and christened *Miss Saigon.* This piece took the stereophonic-sound-and-scenery kind of sub-operatic spectacular that the musical theatre was then becoming, to (or perhaps beyond) bursting point but, as it set off—rather less surefootedly than its three famous forebears—to the areas beyond the West End which those forebears had established as almost an international circuit, *Miss Saigon* was worked up into what seemed to be (and what the producer filled newspaper space to assure the world in general and Sir Andrew Lloyd Webber—with whom, since *The Phantom of the Opéra,* he no longer saw eye-to-eye—in particular), a commercial success.

When his star writers chose the old French tale of *Martin Guerre* as the subject for their next stage musical, however, their producer was set a major task. In spite of a loyal struggle to make a success of a richly musical but physically unspectacular piece, including major post-opening rewrites on a scale unremembered in the West

End, the show failed to take. However, with a rare determination, Mackintosh mounted a fresh version of the show in the British provinces. This version was taken to America, but stalled in Los Angeles on its way to Broadway.

Mackintosh's most recent major musical production—a Drury Lane-sized adaptation of John Updike's *The Witches of Eastwick* (2000)—abandoned the more dramatically pretentious subjects and styles favored by megamusical-writers in the last decades of the 20th century, in a return to the more merrily spectacular values of yesteryear. If the producer has successfully sussed the growing trend for more fun in the musical theatre at the dawn of the 21st century, *The Witches of Eastwick* may well be around for the next edition of this *Encyclopedia.*

Although Cameron Mackintosh's public profile has, thanks to the vast success of the internationally visible and triumphant *Cats, Les Misérables* and *The Phantom of the Opéra,* become one of a producer of large-scale, spectacular shows, he has nevertheless also produced, in parallel, a considerable number of smaller, more intimately scaled pieces of entertainment including, in the 1980s, the internationally popular *Little Shop of Horrors,* a highly successful children's show made up from the music of the singing group Abba (*Abbacadabra,* 1983), and a charming but unloved Puccini pasticcio *Café Puccini.* In the 1990s, similarly, as the London productions of the three big hits and *Miss Saigon* all ran on in their original West End productions and in a multitude of other venues abroad, most of his new shows—give or take *Martin Guerre*—came in less voluminous packages. There were several compilation shows (the long-running *Five Guys Named Mo, Putting It Together*) and also some smaller-sized original pieces (*Just So,* the jokey *Moby Dick, or A Whale of a Tale,* the interesting but directorially schizophrenic *The Fix*), as well as a revival of the 1973 *The Card.* Unfortunately, none of the original pieces succeeded in making themselves a place in the sun alongside the three monoliths of the musical theatre.

Mackintosh has been active in other theatrical areas in the 1980s and 1990s. He founded the Chair of Contemporary Theatre at Oxford University, and his Mackintosh Foundation has sponsored musical-theatre productions both large—revivals of fashionable but usually uncommercial American musicals at Britain's National Theatre (including West End transfers with *Carousel* and a notably fine *Oklahoma!*)—and small, including provincial tryouts of new material at Oxford's Old Fire Station Theatre and Newbury's Watermill Theatre.

Through his company Delfont-Mackintosh Theatres he is the owner of the Prince Edward and the Prince of Wales Theatres.

Literature: Morley, S, Leon, R: *Hey, Mr Producer!* (Weidenfeld & Nicolson, London, 1998)

MACRAE, Arthur [SCHRÖPFER, William Arthur] (b Edmonton, 17 March 1908; d Brighton, 25 February 1962).

An actor from an early age, Macrae appeared largely in plays but also in the musical *Song of the Drum* at the Theatre Royal, Drury Lane (1931, ''Babe''). His first play was produced when he was 24, and he subsequently contributed to a number of revues (Charlot's *Char-a-Bang!, Shall We Reverse, The Town Talks*) before collaborating on the texts for the long-running series of Cicely Courtneidge musical-comedy vehicles which spanned the Second World War in Britain. He also supplied ''additional dialogue'' for James Hadley Chase's nightclub mystery-musical *Get a Load of This* (1941).

1938 **Under Your Hat** (Vivian Ellis/w Jack Hulbert, Archie Menzies) Palace Theatre 24 November

1942 **Full Swing** (George Posford, Harry Parr Davies/w Hulbert, Menzies) Palace Theater 16 April

1943 **Something in the Air** (Manning Sherwin/Harold Purcell, Max Kester/w Hulbert, Menzies) Palace Theatre 23 September

1945 **Under the Counter** (Sherwin/Purcell) Phoenix Theatre 22 November

MADAME Comédie-opérette in 3 acts by Albert Willemetz. Music by Henri Christiné. Théâtre Daunou, Paris, 14 December 1923.

When Gustave Quinson chose to stage Maurice Yvain's *Là-haut* at the Bouffes-Parisiens, the way was left free for Jane Renouardt of the Théâtre Daunou to mount the latest work by Henri Christiné, the darling of the modern musical theatre and formerly monopolized by her very good friend Quinson. She produced *Madame* with considerable success, and it followed a good Parisian run—including a quick revival at Quinson's Théâtre des Bouffes-Parisiens (28 April 1924)—with an equally good provincial life.

The Madame-to-be of the play's title is little Mlle Delicia (Andrée Alvar), who, with the encouragement of her friend Chicorée (Davia), tests her hold over her fiancé, Paul Fêtard (André Luguet), but goes too far and loses him. Chicorée, trying to atone for her unfortunate interference, gets them together in the same hotel, along with Delicia's father Romulus (Gabin père), his petite amie Blanche Farine (Christiane Dor), Paul's best friend Clichy de Lapinière (Louis Boucot) and Aunt Hortense (Jeanne Cheirel) and, after much in the way of farcical doings, everyone is safely and suitably paired off for the final curtain.

Christiné's score, abetted by some tasty Willemetz lyrics, had its most successful moment in Chicorée's rhythmic recipe for a plain girl's self-improvement, ''Ell' n'est pas si mal que ça,'' but there were plenty of other numbers of charm and wit, including Paul's description of how his eye first lit on Delicia because her father was such good fun (''Quand une fille possède un papa''); Delicia's waltz celebrating marriage, ''Être Madame''; Hortense's peremptory ''On l' dit . . . sapristi!'' and the ensemble ''L'annexe,'' in which Romulus at first protests against his offhand, out-of-the-way accommodation, until he realizes that, lodged in the hotel's annex, he can entertain Mlle Farine without being overseen.

MADAME BONIFACE Opéra-comique in 3 acts by Ernest Depré and Charles Clairville. Music by Paul Lacome. Théâtre des Bouffes-Parisiens, Paris, 20 October 1883.

Madame Boniface (Louise Théo), the wife of a little confectioner (Édouard Maugé), is altogether too pretty for her husband's peace of mind but, when he tries to send her away to the safety of Orléans, the rakish Comte Annibal de Tournedor (Piccaluga) takes the place of the coachman and whisks her off instead to his debauched home. Boniface goes after him and, unsuccessful in recapturing his wife, he then hurries to court to complain. Clever little Madame Boniface succeeds in keeping her virtue intact, but Tournedor's escapade costs him dear: whilst he has been trying to seduce the pretty confiseuse his own fiancée has gone off with his best friend, Fridolin (Charles Lamy). Désiré (Jacquot) and Mlle Levasseur (Isabelle) headed the support cast.

Apart from the lead role, which was well equipped with a Chanson Auvergnat in the final act and with a catchy ''Il faut s' taire,'' Lacome's score most favored the baritone part of the Count (the romance ''Comme la fleur,'' ''Moi, si j'étais époux''), with best friend Fridolin supplying the tenor notes.

Tailor-made for the piquant, vocally limited Théo, who was freshly back from one of her American tours, *Madame Boniface,* was modeled verly closely on the lines of her early success, *La Jolie Parfumeuse.* Produced by Louis Cantin—much in need of a successor to *La Mascotte* at the Bouffes-Parisiens—it won an agreeable success through 76 performances before Théo disappeared off to Nice for a ''previous engagement,'' then was brought back the next season for a further 23 performances (29 April 1884). When the star went back to America she took her show with her and it was played by Maurice Grau's troupe with Mezières (Boniface) and Francis Gaillard (Tournedor) appearing alongside Mlle Théo at Wallack's Theater in 1884 and at the Star in 1885. In Paris, *Madame Boniface* was revived in 1916 (Théâtre Apollo 29 March) with Jenny Syril starred, and it was played again in 1919 and in 1924 at the Trianon-Lyrique.

The first English-language production (ad J F Milliken) was mounted in America just a week after Théo had introduced the piece to Broadway audiences when Catherine Lewis's touring company introduced its manageress as Friquette in New Jersey. However, the company collapsed after just one week's touring. The following year the piece was featured at Boston's Oakland Gardens (15 August) with Madeleine Lucette starred, but although she then took her show on the road Miss Lucette's company did not look like bringing the English *Madame Boniface* to Broadway any more than its unfortunate predecessor had done. In 1886 Milliken himself mounted the show in Chicago (Criterion Theater, September) in summer season.

An 1891 production by Alexandrine von Schönerer at Vienna's Theater an der Wien (ad Heinrich Thalboth, Richard Genée) starred Therese Biedermann as the cutely named Friquette Bonbon, alongside Siegmund Natzler (Bonbon), Josef Joseffy (Tournedor) and Carl Lindau (Fridolin), but the piece proved not at all to Viennese tastes and was played only three times. It was, nevertheless, given an Hungarian showing (ad Károly Murai) under the title of *A kis cukrászné* (''the little confectioner'') in 1897.

USA: Wallack's Theater (Fr) 8 September 1884, Orange, NJ (Eng) 15 September 1884; Austria: Theater an der Wien *Madame Bonbon* 15 May 1891; Hungary: Kisfaludy Színház *A kis cukrászné* 31 August 1897

MADAME CARTOUCHE Opérette in 3 acts by Pierre Decourcelle and William Busnach. Music by Léon Vasseur. Théâtre des Folies-Dramatiques, Paris, 19 October 1886.

The actress Sylvine (Mme Grisier Montbazon) is carried off by Labretèche (Vauthier), lieutenant of the brigand Cartouche, to a fate not quite as bad as death, but when she has been compulsorily installed as a brigandesse she gets her revenge on her captor by tricking him out of both the booty he has stolen from the wealthy Grippardin (Riga), and the conquest of pretty Olympe (Jeanne Becker), wife of the barkeeper Grégoire (Gobin), whom he was sure of winning into his bed. The heart of the opérette's action had the heroine masquerading as the Mexican Carmen de las Pampas, the betrothed bride of Grippardin, complete with Mexican entourage and a bolero sextet, in order to effect her anti-robbery. Vasseur's score paired the heroine musically with her baritone captor, and with Guy in the role of the violinist whom she loves, whilst the comic numbers fell principally to the almost-cuckolded Grégoire.

A disappointment at the Folies-Dramatiques, where it held the stage for just a month, *Madame Cartouche* was nevertheless staged both in Britain (ad Sutherland Edwards), where light-opera soprano Giulia Warwick, the original Constance of *The Sorcerer* something more than a decade earlier, took it on the road in 1891 for eight weeks, and in America at the ever adventurous Tivoli in San Francisco. Harry Gates's adaptation featured Tillie Salinger (Sylvine), Phil Branson (Labretèche) and Gracie Plaisted (Olympe) for the Tivoli's usual short season.

UK: Royal Opera House, Leicester 21 September 1891; USA: Tivoli Opera House, San Francisco 23 November 1891

MADAME CHRYSANTHÈME Comédie-lyrique in 4 acts, a prologue and an epilogue, by Georges Hartmann and André Alexandre, based on a work by Pierre Loti. Music by André Messager. Théâtre de la Renaissance (Théâtre-Lyrique), Paris, 30 January 1893.

Written during a period when Messager, with the successes of *La Fauvette du Temple* and the opéra-comique *La Basoche* now a couple of years behind him, turned out half-a-dozen scores in as many years in quest of a financial success, *Madame Chrysanthème* was a quick Paris failure (10 performances) when produced by Léonce Détroyat at his Théâtre Lyrique. However, in its short life it won many partisans for its elegant and extended opéra-comique score and its pretty story—which prefigured in (very) many ways that of John Luther Long and David Belasco's *Madam Butterfly* and Luigi Ilica's *Madama Butterfly.*

During his service in the East, the Breton naval officer Pierre (Delaquerrière) ''weds'' the oriental singing girl Chrysanthème (Jane Guy) through the offices of the marriage broker Kangourou (Charles Lamy) and then finds himself falling in love with her. His jealousy is aroused and the idyll spoiled when she takes a sick colleague's place and sings in public once more, and again when he fancies an attachment between the girl and his best friend and fellow officer, Yves (Jacquin). But it is Chrysanthème whose love is the more real, and whose heart is almost broken when her ''husband'' finally sails away with his ship leaving his loving ''wife'' behind him. Mlle Caisso (Madame Prune) and Declercq (Monsieur Sucre) helped the comedy along as Chrysanthème's temporary ''parents'' and Nettie Lynds had the soubrette role as Oyouli, Prune's young daughter.

The success of *Madama Butterfly* (1904) precluded a revival of the earlier work, which had been mooted at around that time for the Opéra-Comique, but the piece has continued to be prized by musicians and is still occasionally played, most recently at Rochefort in 1990.

MADAME FAVART Opéra-comique in 3 acts by Henri Chivot and Alfred Duru. Music by Jacques Offenbach. Théâtre des Folies-Dramatiques, Paris, 28 December 1878.

Madame Favart was produced in 1878, at a time when Offenbach's nearest real success, *Le Voyage dans la lune,* was three years in the past, and his recent shows had been failures (*La Boîte au lait, Maître Péronilla*) or, at best, half-successes (*Le Docteur Ox,* 42 performances, *La Foire Saint-Laurent,* 48 performances). The new show set the composer's reckoning right with a vengeance.

He was much aided in this return to form by the libretto served to him by Chivot and Duru, with whom, in spite of their eminence on the opérette stage, he had worked only once previously, almost a decade back, on *L'Île de Tulipatan.* Their book to *Madame Favart* tacked the name of famous actress Justine Favart—already the nominal subject of a comédie-vaudeville at the Palais-Royal half a century earlier (Masson, Boniface 24 December 1836)—on to a thoroughly comic-opera adventure, in much the same way English writers were inclined to do with such semi-historical actress figures as Nell Gwynne or Peg Woffington. The action was intricately filled with disguises and situations in the best French mode, and at the same time it developed the character of Justine into a first-rate rôle à tiroirs for the show's leading lady, who was given the opportunity of appearing in turn as a serving wench, an elderly lady and an elegant actress during the course of the night.

Justine Favart (Juliette Simon-Girard) has adeptly avoided the carnal desires of the powerful Maréchal de Saxe and, as a result, both she and her celebrated actor husband, Charles Favart (Lepers), are on the run from his vengeance. At first they hide in an inn, he in the basement, she disguised as a maidservant, and then—after Justine has posed as the wife of young Hector de Boispréau (Simon-Max) effectively enough to win him a police appointment from the lecherous Marquis de Pontsablé (Édouard Maugé)—they masquerade as Hector's servants. When Pontsablé visits Hector, Justine is obliged to become ''wife'' again—whilst the real wife, Suzanne (Marie Gélabert), temporarily becomes the maid—and then to impersonate a dowager who has threatened to expose her. The ''discovered'' Suzanne and Favart are dragged triumphantly off by Pontsablé to Fontenoy to appear before the mighty Saxe, followed by Justine and Hector, who are now disguised as Tyrolean peddlers, and things wind up to a pretty height before the vengeance of Saxe and of Pontsablé is defused by none other than the king himself.

Offenbach's score—opéra-comique music to its last semiquaver, and without a touch of joshing opéra-bouffe from end to end—accompanied this ever-active tale delightfully, with Madame Favart scoring the hit of the evening with her fake-rustic sauce in ''Ma mère aux vignes m'envoyit,'' playing the little wandering minstrelette in ''Je suis la petite vielleuse,'' the elderly grande dame in ''Je passe sur mon enfance,'' and the Tyrolean peasant in ''Mon grand frèr' vend des mouchoirs,'' and finally relating the whole of her complex tale to the king in ''J'entrai sous la royale tente.'' The baritone role of Favart was also well equipped with amusing songs, notably his ''Quand du four on le retire'' recalling his father's life as a pastry cook, whilst Hector (tenor) and Suzanne (soprano) provided the ingénu duets and solos, and the buffo part of the musical entertainment was assured by Pontsablé and by Suzanne's father, Cotignac (Luco).

Juliette Simon-Girard, the heroine of *Les Cloches de Corneville,* had her second role of a lifetime as Madame Favart, and the show was a splendid success, running for more than two hundred performances (interleaved with performances of the theatre's other main pieces) in its first year at the Bouffes-Parisiens and keeping away the following year solely because of the subsequent hit of Offenbach's next piece, *La Fille du tambour-major.* It was soon back, and in 1883 Marie Grisier-Montbazon (34 performances) succeeded to the role created by Mme Simon-Girard alongside Maugé and the Favart of Piccaluga. In 1889 Anna Judic took a turn as Madame Favart (Menus-Plaisirs, December).

Meanwhile, the show had set out swiftly on its international travels. Vienna's version (ad Julius Hopp), produced under Maximilian Steiner's direction, was on the stage six weeks after the Paris premiere. Marie Geistinger was his Madame Favart, with Girardi as her husband, Steiner and Hermine Meyerhoff as the young couple and Felix Schweighofer as Pontsablé. But even a cast of such voltage left Vienna unmoved: *Madame Favart* played only 23 times.

On the other hand, when Alexander Henderson produced the first English version (ad H B Farnie) at the Strand Theatre with the virtually unknown Florence St John starring alongside Claude Marius (Favart), Walter Fisher (Hector), Henry Ashley (Pontsablé) and Violet Cameron (Suzanne), he and his star both scored a sensational success. *Madame Favart* proved itself the genuine successor to London's record-breaking *Les Cloches de Corneville,* running alongside that piece and *HMS Pinafore* until it reached 502 performances, a total excelled in London's theatre history to that time only by its two direct competitors. Camille Dubois relieved the now starry Miss St John late in the run, but the new London ''queen of comic opera'' returned to the West End with her show again in 1882, in 1887 and one last time in 1893 (Criterion Theatre 9 November).

In America, Marie Aimée and Paola Marié both played *Madame Favart* in the original French, Marie Geistinger gave New Yorkers her German version and Emilie Melville played a vernacular Justine Favart to San Franciscans before the Comley-Barton Company brought the English *Madame Favart* to Broadway. The English pair Catherine Lewis and Fred Leslie starred as the Favarts with Australia's John Howson as Pontsablé, local star Marie Jansen as Suzanne and Alfred Cellier conducting, but New York sided with Vienna rather than with Paris and London, and the company was obliged to revert to Audran's *Olivette,* which Broadway had already certified as a hit, after only a short season. Only the French-speaking part of the New York population continued to welcome *Madame Favart* as it was repeated by Aimée and Paola Marié on their regular returns to town. The English-language version was played again the following year (Fifth Avenue Theater 23 January 1882) when the Comley-Barton troupe passed through town and it was also later played in Australia, where Pattie Laverne starred alongside Fred Mervin, Alfred Brennir and Nellie Stewart in George Musgrove's production in Sydney and Melbourne (Opera House 29 October 1881). It, too, shared a repertoire with *Olivette* and with the hit Australian production of *La Fille du tambour-major.* Stockholm, Leipzig, Berlin, Brussels and Naples all presented *Madame Favart* whilst it still held the stage in Paris, and in Hungary (ad Lajos Evva, Béla J Fái) it was given a fine 34 performances at the Népszínház with Lujza Blaha starred.

In spite of its great Parisian and British success, however, and in spite of the outstanding opportunities it offers to its star, *Madame Favart* has not become a genuine fixture in the 20th-century Offenbach repertoire. It has been given revivals in Paris (1911, 1913, 1934) and in Germany, where a revised version was produced in 1955 (Operetten-Theater, Leipzig 15 October), but it still exists a little in the shadow of *La Fille du tambour-major* amongst the composer's late works.

Austria: Theater an der Wien 7 February 1879; UK: Strand Theatre 12 April 1879; USA: Park Theater (Fr) 12 May 1879, Bush Street Theater, San Francisco (Eng) 28 June 1880, Fifth Avenue Theater (Eng) 19 September 1881; Germany: Leipzig 1 June 1879, Friedrich-Wilhelmstädtisches Theater, Berlin 15 August 1879; Hungary: Népszínház *Favartné* 14 November 1879; Australia: Theatre Royal, Sydney 17 September 1881

Recordings: 2-record sets (Discoreale, Rare Recorded Editions)

MADAME L'ARCHIDUC Opéra-comique in 3 acts by Albert Millaud (and Ludovic Halévy, uncredited?). Music by Jacques Offenbach. Théâtre des Bouffes-Parisiens, Paris, 31 October 1874.

An agreeable Millaud/Offenbach piece, but one which had little in the way of outstanding features in book or score, *Madame l'Archiduc* had a very much better international career than a number of the composer's other equally good or better works, possibly due to the appeal the large central prima donna role had for lady stars.

Hotel workers Marietta (Anna Judic) and Giletti (Habay) have just been wed when the exiled Comte (Lucien Fugère) and Comtesse (Berthe Perret) arrive at the inn where they work. The aristocratic pair are plotting the downfall of the local Archiduc Ernest (Daubray), but their steward Riccardo (Desmonts) discovers that Ernest has got wind of their conspiracy and so the disguised Marietta and Giletti are bribed to go to the castle in the aristocrats' place. The effects of this swap are alarming. Ernest goes loopy over Marietta, and before she knows what is happening she is under siege from the amorous overlord. He even goes so far as to abdicate and promote her to Archiduc in a frantic attempt to win her favors, whilst simultaneously bundling Giletti out of the way with a posting as Ambassador to Naples. However, when his ardor is continually doused by the newly married Marietta, Ernest gets sulky and, like the Grande-Duchesse de Gérolstein, he ends up joining the conspiracy against the one he has, with sexual self-interest, promoted. However, the moment Ernest gets to the conspiracy table down at the inn, and sees the real Comtesse, he transfers his affections so that, once Marietta is deposed and he is restored, it is the Comte who is bundled off to Naples. Marietta and Giletti, who have bought the inn where they worked with the money gained in the exercise, close it for three months and go to bed for a honeymoon. Laurence Grivot played the important, but not plotworthy, role of Fortunato, the young captain of the guard who is the hereditary favorite of the Archiduc's favorite.

Most of the solo highlights of Offenbach's score were for the benefit of his leading lady. Judic scored with the catchy ''Pas ça!'' and her ridiculing of Fortunato's overslicked appearance, ''P'tit bonhomme,'' described her husband's honeymoon arrangements (Couplets de la voyage de noces), spied on the Comte and Comtesse's heavy petting (''Pardonnez-nous, monsieur, madame'') and joined Giletti in a Duo des rires, laughing at themselves in their fancy court clothes. Fortunato had a jolly entrance song (Chanson du petit capitaine), Ernest described himself as ''Original! Original'' with particular success, and the Comte and Comtesse, pretending to be English tourists, had a merry burlesque Duo anglais and joined in some foolish, comical plotting pieces with their fellow conspirators.

The first run of the show, in spite of its song hits and, in particular, of the presence of the enormously popular Mme Judic in the cast, was a just a little disappointing. After three and a half months Charles Comte's production ran out of audience. However, in spite of this, *Madame l'Archiduc* proved to have a remarkable amount of staying power and it was seen again on the same stage in 1876 and, much to the annoyance of the authors, who had arranged for a new production at the Variétés with Judic, Comte kept his hands legally on the piece by playing it again—lawsuit or none—in 1877 (18 May, 45 performances) with Louise Théo and later Mary Albert taking the part created by Judic and with the tiny Paola Marié (succeeded by the very tall Blanche Miroir) as Fortunato. Judic took up her role again in 1889 at the little Théâtre des Menus-Plaisirs, with Bartel (Ernest), Clara Lardinois (Fortunato) and Ernest Vois (Giletti) in support, whilst a 1901 revival at the Bouffes-Parisiens (20 December) starred Juliette Simon-Girard as Marietta and Evelyne Janney as Fortunato and another, in 1920 at the Théâtre Mogador, featured Edmée Favart. A further revival was mounted at the Théâtre des Variétés in 1924 (10 October), and the piece still wins the occasional performance a century and more after its premiere. In December 1997 it was played at Rennes.

Madame l'Archiduc was seen far and wide after its Paris debut. It was first performed in America in English (ad uncredited) by Emily Soldene's visiting company, adapted, cast, rehearsed and produced in double-quick time and presented at the Lyceum Theatre with the diva taking the title role alongside Lizzie Robson (Fortunato), Edward Marshall (Archduke) and E D Beverley (Giletti) for one week at the end of her Broadway season, and later played in its original language by most of the opéra-bouffe repertoire companies, notably those led by Coralie Geoffroy and by Louise Théo. Soldene eventually took the show back to base, and played an 1876 London season with Kate Santley (Fortunato) and W J Hill (Ernest) in support. This was, ultimately, a rather slimmed-down version of Offenbach's original as the audience revolted loudly on the first night when the afterpiece *Trial by Jury* was canceled at midnight. Thereafter, London audiences got all of *Trial by Jury* and rather less of *Madame l'Archiduc* for the two months of the run. Théo later gave London her French version of the show, and Kate Santley took a personalized version (in which she now played Marietta, not Fortunato) to the British provinces in competition with Soldene.

Soldene also traveled her production to New Zealand and to Australia, where the piece had been introduced by Catherine Lewis (Marietta), Henry Bracy (Giletti) and Miss E A Lambert (Fortunato) just a few months earlier. She scored a solid success there (Theatre Royal, Sydney 15 September 1877) with Rose Stella (Fortunato), Marshall and Charles J Campbell (Giletti) supporting. The piece was long retained in the Soldene repertoire and the buxom prima donna was responsible for taking *Madame l'Archiduc* around the largest part of the English-speaking world. The show was later repeated in Australia in a short season by Australian prima donna Lotty Montal and Annette Ivanova (Fortunato) in 1885.

In Vienna a version by Julius Hopp was mounted as *Madame ''Herzog''* at the Theater an der Wien with the theatre's co-manager Marie Geistinger starring alongside Karoline Tellheim (Fortunato), Carl Adolf Friese (Archduke) and Jani Szika (Giletti) and with the young Girardi playing a supporting conspirator, Scaevola. It played a splendid 51 performances and Geistinger then went on to repeat her performance in Berlin. A new and worked-over German version was later produced at the Stendal Landestheater in 1929 (ad Karl Kraus, 15 June). Prague, Naples, Stockholm and St Petersburg were amongst the other cities to host *Madame l'Archiduc* before Hungary's version (ad Lajos Evva, Béla J Fái) was seen at the Budai Színkör in 1877. The show was brought into the repertoire of the Népszínház in 1883 (23 April).

USA: Lyceum Theater 29 December 1874, Lyceum Theater (Fr) 6 September 1875; Austria: Theater an der Wien *Madame ''Herzog'' (Die Verschwörung zu Montefiasco)* 19 January 1875; Germany: Friedrich-Wilhelmstädtisches Theater *Madame ''Herzog''* 3 July 1875; UK: Opera Comique 13 January 1876; Australia: Opera House, Melbourne 26 May 1877; Hungary: Budai Színkör *A hercegasszony (A Montefiasconei összeesküves)* 12 June 1877

Recording: complete (Gaîté-Lyrique)

MADAME POMPADOUR Operette in 3 acts by Rudolf Schanzer and Ernst Welisch. Music by Leo Fall. Berliner Theater, Berlin, 9 September 1922.

The most successful of the postwar works of Leo Fall, and one of his most delightful, *Madame Pompadour* was written for the Berlin theatre and as a vehicle for its reigning queen of the musical stage, Fritzi Massary. Like those of many Operetten before and since, the amorous adventures of the plot had little to do with the historical Madame Pompadour, but were simply tacked on to the recognizable and title-worthy figures of France's Louis XV and his mistress.

René, Comte d'Éstrades, who has come up to Paris for a dirty weekend over carnival time, picks up a pretty girl in an inn. She turns out to be the Marquise de Pompadour (Massary), out on the town in disguise, and he consequently finds himself arrested and condemned to . . . her personal bodyguard. His drinking companion, Josef Calicot (Ralph Arthur Roberts), a would-be poet who had been singing rude songs about the royal mistress over his beer, is, in his turn, sentenced to write the amused Marquise a play. The jealous King Louis and his police chief get into a fiendish muddle trying to catch the Pompadour out with her unknown lover but, after a series of bedroom-farcical incidents, the lady neatly extracts herself from trouble. The comical Calicot, who had ludicrously been under suspicion, is paired off with her maid Belotte, and René, who turns out to be none other than the husband of the royal mistress's half sister, is packed off back to his wife, leaving the Marquise to her King—not to mention the remainder of her personal bodyguard.

The score followed one sparkling song with another. The tripping duet between Massary and Roberts, ''Josef, ach Josef,'' was a comical highlight, alongside Calicot's bouncing denunciation of ''Die Pom-, Pom-, Pompadour,'' whilst the leading lady made her entrance to the strains of ''Heut' könnt einer sein Glück bei mir machen,'' dazzled through her showy ''Madame Pompadour'' and encouraged René's invitation to ''Ein intimes Souper'' in her principal musical moments.

Bernauer and Meinhard's Berlin production of *Madame Pompadour* was a splendid success at the Berliner Theater and then at their Komödienhaus before Massary took the piece to Vienna's Carltheater. She starred there, alongside Ernst Tautenhayn (Calicot), Erik Wirl (René), Mimi Vesely (Belotte) and Ernst Rollé (King), for some 60 performances until Mimi Kott took over the star role and romanced first Willi Strehl and then Eric Deutsch-Haupt, with Ernst Arnold as Calicot, through to the end of the seven-month run. In Budapest (ad Zsolt Harsanyi), Sári Fedák played the Pompadour, whilst in New York, after producer Dillingham had sacked leading lady Hope Hampton on the road as ''incompetent and insubordinate,'' Wilda Bennett headed what was ultimately a disappointing production (ad Clare Kummer) which lasted only 80 performances on Broadway.

A much more successful English version of *Madame Pompadour* was the one made for the British stage by Frederick Lonsdale and Harry Graham. It, indeed, turned out to be the longest-running *Madame Pompadour* of all. Mounted at Daly's Theatre under Jimmy White's regime, with Evelyn Laye as the merry Marquise, Derek Oldham as René, the old Daly's favorite, Huntley Wright, as Calicot, and Bertram Wallis (King Louis) and Elsie Randolph (Belotte) in support, it was an enormous hit, running for 13 months and 469 performances. Australia, too, welcomed this version of the show, with the Dutch soprano Beppie de Vries as its Pompadour teamed with Frank Webster (René) and Arthur Stigant (Calicot).

It took some years before Paris saw *Madame Pompadour,* but the Operette finally won itself a French showing in the wake of an extravagantly produced ''Revue-Operette'' revival at Berlin's Grosses Schauspielhaus in 1926. In line with that house's reputation for botching, Massary had this time introduced the Arthur Guttmann/Julius Freund ''Im Liebesfalle,'' first heard in *Die Herren von Maxim,* adapted by Schanzer and Welisch as an additional solo. The French version (ad Albert Willemetz, Max Eddy, Jean Marietti, with the lady punctiliously rechristened Madame de Pompadour) was lavishly and successfully presented at the Théâtre Marigny by Léon Volterra. Raymonde Vécart, Robert Burnier and René Hérent starred, supported (in deference to the fashion for things American, even in period France) by ''les Merry

Plate 237. **Madame Pompadour.** *Silvia Holzmayer and the boys in the Vienna Volksoper's revival.*

Girls'' and ''les Smart Boys,'' as well as an orchestra of 40.

In more recent times, *Madame Pompadour* has been seen at the Vienna Volksoper which brought back a version of the show in 1976 and again in 1986, and at Budapest's Katona József Színház (16 October 1992), and it holds a place on the fringe of the revivable and revived repertoire where it is looked at by musicians with particular favor.

The Pompadour has been utilized a number of times as a character on the musical stage, even if she has proved a touch more discreet than such other members of her profession as Madame Dubarry. An operatic *Die Pompadour* by Emmanuel Mór was produced at Cologne in 1902, and an Italian operetta, *La Pompadour,* by Costantino Lombardo to a text by Antonio Lega, was produced at the Teatro Alfieri, Turin (25 September 1918).

A silent *Madame Pompadour* film, directed by Britain's Herbert Wilcox after the success of the musical in London, and with Lillian Gish in its title role, could be said to have been inspired by the stage show rather than being a version of it.

Austria: Carltheater 2 March 1923; Hungary: Fővárosi Operettszínház *Pompadour* 28 November 1923; UK: Daly's Theatre 20 December 1923; USA: Martin Beck Theater 11 November 1924; Australia: His Majesty's Theatre, Brisbane 21 May 1927, Her Majesty's Theatre, Sydney 4 June 1927; France: Théâtre Marigny 16 May 1930

Recording: selection (EMI Electrola)

MADAME SHERRY Operette in 3 acts by Benno Jacobson adapted from a libretto by Maurice Ordonneau [and Paul Burani]. Music by Hugo Felix. Centraltheater, Berlin, 1 November 1902.

Bachelor music teacher Anatole Mac Sherry has been supported for many years by his Canadian uncle, Epaminondas Mac Sherry, whom he has led to believe that he is an underfunded married man with two children. When the uncle inevitably and unexpectedly turns up, along with his pretty convent-bred niece Jane, Anatole has to produce an instant family. Housekeeper Catherine becomes the wife, the dancer Mistigrette with whom Anatole has been carrying on a flirtation is the daughter, and Leonard y Gomez, son of the president of Bolivia and one of Anatole's pupils, is the son. The pretence, complicated by the fact that Leonard's old flame, the tempestuous Pepita, is led to believe that Mistigrette is Madame Sherry junior—ie, Leonard's wife—is given a hard time during a hair-raising evening out at the ''Golden Key'' restaurant, but Uncle, who has finally to be told the truth, is mollified by the fact that Anatole and Jane have fallen in love and there will, at last, be a real Madame Sherry.

Felix's score was a pretty one, skipping merrily and effectively through the whole range of his performers' voices from top tenor and soprano to some basso rumblings from the men of the company. It was highlighted by the jaunty duet ''Youp-la! Catarina'' for Catherine and her (real) husband Aurillac and a comical dagger number for the stalking Pepita, but most particularly by its ensembles, including a charming vocal nocturne and a second-act finale in which a befuddled policeman, called in to sort out the brouhaha in the restaurant, is ''youp-la-ed'' off his feet by Catherine and waltzed through a laughing chorus by Jane.

A genuine hit as produced by Jose Ferenczy in Berlin, the show was brought quickly back for a second, summer season at Krolls Theater (June 1903) and was soon off on its way around the world. On the way it met a curious fate. Andreas Aman produced *Madame Sherry* at the Carltheater with Karl Blasel as the elder Mac Sherry, Louis Treumann as the younger, Karl Streitmann as the Bolivian, and Therese Biedermann (Catherine), the American divette Marie Halton (Jane), Else Stefans (Mistigrette) and Marie Gribl (Pepita) in the feminine roles, but in spite of its fine cast the show managed only a dozen performances. Its Berlin success was, however, sufficient reason for it to reach London (ad Charles E Hands, Adrian Ross) surrounded by vast pre-production ballyhoo. Florence St John (Catherine), Louis Bradfield (Andrew), Nigel Playfair (MacSherry) and Ruth Lincoln (Barbara, ex- Jane) headed George Edwardes's cast, the score was infiltrated by a couple of Paul Rubens ditties, and the agencies bought up thousands of pounds worth of tickets for the first six months of the run, only to find their fingers nastily burned when the show didn't run nearly that long. George Dance had the show revised, ''freeing it,'' as he insisted, ''of all blemish,'' added some songs by Ernest Bucalossi, and sent it on tour (Prince of Wales, Kennington 29 August 1904) with J Robert Hale as Mac Sherry, operatic Georgina Delmar as Catherine and the young Lily Elsie singing ''Under the Panama'' and ''The Ole Banjo'' in the role of Barbara in a piece which had come rather a long way from its original. It did only fairly.

Madame Sherry was also seen, in French, at Brussels's Galeries Saint-Hubert (14 April 1905), but did not make it to Paris or anywhere else in France.

Success for *Madame Sherry* beyond German shores was reserved only for America, but the *Madame Sherry* which was given to the American public by A H Woods, George Lederer and H H Frazee (Bloomington, Ill 3 April 1910; Colonial Theater, Chicago 11 April 1910; New Amsterdam Theater 30 August 1910) was a decidedly different one from that which had been played in Europe. Otto Harbach's libretto (billed as ''a three-act French vaudeville'' and initially announced as ''based on two French stories'') kept closely to Ordonneau's original plot but, with scenic and terpischorean considerations ever in view, it resituated the first act in a school of aesthetic dancing, and the other two . . . on board a yacht. Felix's score was quite simply replaced by an almost wholly new one written mostly by Karl Hoschna (with ''an Irish song by Elizabeth Murray and ensembles by Carl [*sic*] Felix''). It was a score with a different level of ambition. Felix's finales were replaced by act endings that were little more than tags; what ensembles there were, apart from the two lonely remaining bits of Felix material, were largely sung in unison; and the accent was on ''numbers'' and, very specifically, on dances.

Frances Demarest (as Lulu, ex- Mistigrette) and Carl Martens (Leonard) performed a burlesque aesthetic dance to ''Every Little Movement (has a meaning all its own),'' a melody which had been previously introduced in the opening chorus, and which was replugged both as a finale to the first act and in an intermezzo. It was this tune that became the most popular of the evening, in spite of a catchy waltz ''The Birth of Passion,'' which was given a similar treatment in the second act by the show's star, Lina Abarbanell (Yvonne, ex- Jane), and Jack Gardner (Edward, ex- Anatole). Comic Ralph Herz played Uncle Sherry, Elizabeth Murray was the youp-la-less Catherine, and English *Chinese Honeymoon* star and music-hall impressionist Marie Dainton was Pepita. By the time the show reached Broadway, the score also included the Albert von Tilzer/Junie McCree ''Put your Arms Around Me, Honey'' given as part of a pasted-in ''concert on the deck of the yacht *Yvonne.*'' The ''Irish Song'' that Miss Murray performed was Atteridge and Phil Schwartz's ''The Dublin Rag.'' Miss Abarbanell sang ''Ciri biri bin.''

Whatever purists might have thought, the producers had nevertheless judged their audiences aright in their remake of the show and Abarbanell, in particular, and *Madame Sherry* in general, were fine successes in Chicago, where the show ran for an amazing 20 weeks, on Broadway (231 performances) and thereafter on the road. In 1912 Woods, Frazee and Lederer had no less than five companies carrying *Madame Sherry* around America. As for "Every Little Movement," it completed the full circle. Stripped of Harbach's lyric, Hoschna's melody turned up back both in France—where Ordonneau had begun the whole thing—set to words by Lucien Boyer and purveyed to Parisians by Henri Leoni as "Je n' sais comment!," and again in Germany, where it was billed as the "Liebestanz aus Madame Sherry." Ah, but which *Madame Sherry*?

Berlin hosted a revival in 1919 (Theater des Westens 1 March, 51 performances) and in 1989 a revised version of the American version of the show (ad John Peters, Joe Goss, Shawn McEnaney), which introduced several of Felix's numbers as well as Hoschna's "Cuddle up a Little Closer" from *Three Twins* in preference to half-a-dozen pieces from the original (American) score, was played at the Goodspeed Opera House (28 June).

Austria: Carltheater 10 October 1903; UK: Apollo Theatre 23 December 1903; Hungary: Magyar Színház *Sherry* 9 January 1904

MADAME SUZETTE Opérette in 3 acts by Maurice Ordonneau and André Sylvane. Music by Edmond Audran. Théâtre des Bouffes-Parisiens, Paris, 29 March 1893.

Suzette Gabillot (Biana Duhamel), the daughter of a provincial hotelier (Édouard Maugé), needs to win time in her battle not to wed her father's candidate for her hand, for her beloved, an extremely moustachioed but penniless soldier (Dekernel), has to woo sufficient money from an old aunt to clear his hotel bill before they can announce his pretensions. When papa discovers that another, new pretender for Suzette's affections, William Robiquet (Piccaluga), is violently rich, he practically forces the young man into his daughter's bed, but William is a nice young man and he helps Suzette keep father quiet by pretending a liaison until her soldier returns, actually not from seeing any aunt at all but from breaking off another affair in Paris. Suzette then realizes that William is the better bargain of the two. A lightly pretty Audran score in his *Miss Helyett* vein, molded to suit *Miss Helyett*'s star, Mlle Duhamel, illustrated the story deftly, and the piece was played 79 times at the Bouffes before going on to be seen in a German version in Berlin (ad Eduard Jacobson, Jean Kren) with Frln Schlüter (Suzette) and Guido Thielscher (Gabillot) starred, and in an Hungarian one in Budapest (ad Ferenc Rajna).

Germany: Adolf Ernst Theater 23 March 1895; Hungary: Magyar Színház *Menyecske kisasszony* 8 January 1898

DAS MÄDEL VON MONTMARTRE Operette in 3 acts by Rudolf Schanzer adapted from *La Dame de chez Maxim* by Georges Feydeau. Music by Henrik Berény. Neues Theater, Berlin, 26 October 1911.

Feydeau's highly successful 1899 play *La Dame de chez Maxim,* with its showy comic roles for both leading man and lady—the latter memorably created by Armande Cassive in the play's premiere at Paris's Théâtre des Nouveautés (17 January 1899)—was natural fodder for the musical-farce stage. When model husband Dr Petypon is reluctantly dragged out for a night on the tiles by a friend, he ultimately rather overdoes things and wakes up squeamishly in the morning underneath the upturned sofa. There is an empty dress over the chair, and his bed is occupied by "the girl from Montmartre." Enter Madame Petypon, and the farcical complications and the crises of mistaken identity begin, galloping from Paris to a house party in the Touraine and ending only when, with his wife blissfully undeceived over the escapade which never really was one, Petypon succeeds in off-loading the embarrassing "la môme crevette."

Das Mädel von Montmartre had only an average run in Berlin and it did not travel to Vienna or to Budapest but, in the wake of the splendid Broadway success of Berény's previous Operette, *Lord Piccolo* (*Little Boy Blue*), not to mention the hit made in America by the production of the original, slightly musicalized, play a decade earlier (*The Girl from Maxim's* Criterion Theater 29 August 1899, starring Josephine Hall), it was snapped up for New York by that production's sponsor, Charles Frohman. Adapted by Harry B and Robert B Smith, peppered with a good half-dozen Jerome Kern songs (one of which suspiciously resembled a piece of Hugo Felix's original *Madame Sherry* score), plus two numbers pinched from *The Arcadians* and a Franz Wagner song relyricked by a Smith as "Something Like This" (thus leaving Berény represented by about 50 percent of the score), with Richard Carle (Petypon) and Hattie Williams (Praliné) in the two juicy star roles, and given an up-to-date touch by the use of a kinemacolor film section depicting the heroine's pursuit of the show's various characters in the last act, it had a modest 64 performances in town but served well enough—further peppered with non-Berény songs, and with a J M Barrie skit (*A Slice of Life*) pasted into its middle—when Carle took it out on the road.

La Dama di Montmartre (1925), an Italian musical by Carlo Lombardo and Ermete Liberati, and the Polish *Dama od Maxima* (1967) by Antoni Marianowicz and Ryszard Sielicki were also later based on the same Feydeau play, and New York's Weber and Fields musically burlesqued the original play in *The Girl from Martin's* (25 October 1899).

USA: Criterion Theater *The Girl from Montmartre* 5 August 1912

MADER, Raoul [MADER, Rezső] (b Pressburg, Hungary, 25 June 1856; d Budapest, 16 October 1940). Composer, conductor and administrator in the Austrian and Hungarian theatre.

The son of a schoolteacher, Mader showed an early preference for music and, after his first studies in his home town, he was sent to Vienna to attend the Conservatorium there. He won prizes in piano and composition, but was slow to make a career thereafter. His first musical theatre composition to be produced in Vienna was a Spieloper, *Die Flüchtlinge,* written with Bernard Buchbinder when he was already well into his thirties and staged at the Hofoper (19 February 1891), where Mader had been for nearly a decade a répétiteur. This was followed by a burlesque of *Cavalleria rusticana* (''mit verschiedene skandalösen Auftritten'') on the bill of which the musician was described, tongue-in-cheek, as the ''komponist der Mascagnischen Musik,'' and by two ballets, also for the Hofoper (*Die Sirenen-Insel* 1892, *Hochzeit in Frisirsalon* 4 October 1894), before his first Operette, *Engelsherz,* was presented at the Carltheater in 1895 with Julie Kopácsi-Karczag and Karl Blasel starred. It was played just 10 times.

In the same year Mader was engaged as a conductor at the Magyar Királyi Operaház in Budapest and he returned home to Hungary where his first new offerings to the theatre were further ballets (the highly successful *A piros cipő* [*The Red Shoes*] 1897, *She* 1898). He had some success with an operett, *Kadétkisasszony,* written with Árpád Pásztor and produced at the Népszínház (31 performances), and rather less with a second, written with the same partner, and played later the same year at the Magyar Színház (*Primadonnák*), before taking over as Director of the Operaház in November 1901. During his six-year tenure there, he had two more Operetten produced, both to libretti by Landesberg and Stein, and both in Vienna. The first of these, *Das Garnisonsmädel,* gave him his most considerable run to date with 55 performances at the Theater an der Wien and productions at Berlin's Theater des Westens (8 July 1905, 8 performances) and Budapest's Magyar Színház under the title *Huszárvér* (ad Adolf Mérei, György Ruttkay 2 December 1904). *Der selige Vinzenz,* produced at the Carltheater with Girardi and Mizzi Zwerenz as stars, played for one month.

Mader subsequently became director of the short-lived Népszínház-Vígopera (1907), and while there composed the musical score for his most enduring piece, Pásztor's musical version of Gergely Csiky's play *Nagymama,* in which the ageing Lujza Blaha scored one final triumph as the grandmother of the title. *Nagymama* went on to become Hungary's most popular vehicle for a senior female star. As Mader's career as a manager progressed from Budapest to Vienna's Volksoper (1916) and again to the Magyar Királyi Operaház (1922–25), his composing decreased, and his later works—another ballet, a puppet-play score for the Budapest opera house (*A bűvös bábú* 19 December 1924), and a Chopin pastiche for the Theater an der Wien—were few and far between.

1891 **Krawalleria musicana** (*Sizilianische Ehrenbauern*) (Alexander Weigl) 1 act Theater an der Wien 3 October

1895 **Engelsherz** (*Coeur d'ange*) (Hugo H Regel, Richard Genée) Carltheater 12 January

1900 **Kadétkisasszony** (Árpád Pásztor) Népszínház, Budapest 10 January

1900 **Primadonnák** (Pásztor) Magyar Színház, Budapest 29 December

1904 **Das Garnisonsmädel** (Alexander Landesberg, Leo Stein) Theater an der Wien 29 October

1907 **Der selige Vincenz** (Landesberg, Stein) Carltheater 31 January

1908 **A Nagymama** (Pásztor) Népszínház-Vígopera, Budapest 11 February

1917 **Die weisse Adler** (Chopin arr/Victor Léon, Regel) Volksoper 3 October

MÄDI Operette in 3 acts by Alfred Grünwald and Leo Stein. Music by Robert Stolz. Berliner Theater, Berlin, 1 April 1923.

The titular heroine of *Mädi,* the Countess Mädi von Birkenhof (Claire Waldoff), gets her straying Count Anatol Welsberg (Fritz Werner) to marry her by a ruse that is a slight twist on a much-used plot. She enlists the help of his best friend, Baron Aristid (''Stidi'') Stelzer (Hans Albers), who pretends that he wants to marry Mädi himself but, he explains, in order to inherit a fortune, he must only marry a divorcée. Will his good friend Anatol help him out by marrying his own ex-girlfriend for four weeks? It takes a honeymoon in a Wintersportshotel in the Swiss Alps (Act II) and a ride south on the Riviera-Express (Act III) before Mädi convinces the helpful but up-till-now chaste Anatol that the marriage should be left permanent. Stidi gets his reward for his helpfulness in the person of the soubrette, Clo Bernas (Hilde Wörner).

The 15 pieces of the show's score were shared out largely amongst the four principals, with Mädi and Anatol having the catch-number of the evening in their second-act ''what would you say if we were really husband and wife?'' duo, ''Mädi, mein süsses Mädi.'' Amongst the other musical pieces, Mädi sang of ''Was die kleinen Mädchen träumen'' and joined in the night's other top number, the two-step ''Halt dich fest, dass du die Balance nicht verlierst'' with Stidi and Clo, and in a Bummelntrio (''Wir fahren eine Strecke'') with the two men, whilst Anatol hymned ''Die süssen Mäderln'' and joined his wife with the Shimmy-invitation ''Nun komm doch, du kleine, du reizende Schampusfee.'' But it was pretty, incidental Clo—who delivered an introductory number (''Das ist ja Clo''), another in the last act (''Wenn du nur Einen kennst''), led a march to get the second act going (''Auf ja und nein'') and joined with Stidi in a pair of duets: the waltz ''Du brauchst nur treu zu sein'' and ''Du darfst alles, was du willst, mein Schatz''—who had what seemed the lioness's share in the evening's music.

Mädi had a fine run in Berlin, passing its 100th night (9 July) at the Berliner Theater and in October it was seen in Vienna, produced under the management of Siegfried Geyer and Oscar Fronz at the Bürgertheater. Louis Treumann and Luise Kartousch played the lovers, Hans Albers was again their comic helpmate, Magda Garden was the ubiquitous Clo, and *Mädi* ran a little short of three months. It was subsequently produced at Budapest's Király Színház (ad György Verő), not unreasonably retitled *Huncut a lány* (''the crafty girl'') with Hanna Honthy starred, but London preferred to stress the picturesque accoutrements of the staging rather than the plot and called its version (ad Reginald Arkell, Dion Titheradge) *The Blue Train.* Jack Hulbert and Paul Murray's production boasted a toboggan slide on the stage in the alpine act, additional numbers by Ivy St Helier (3), Howard Carr (2), and Jay Gorney and Dion Titheradge (a title song), and the return to the stage of the much loved heroine of *The Merry Widow,* Lily Elsie, as the the crafty Mädi, here rechristened Eileen. Arthur Margetson was the man she married and comedian Bobby Howes helped her do it. However, a London mad for such transatlantic novelties as *The Desert Song, The Vagabond King, Sunny* and the antics of Leslie Henson and Laddie Cliff in *Lady Luck* showed little interest in *The Blue Train* and, surprisingly, in Miss Elsie, and *The Blue Train* lasted only 116 performances.

A new version of *Mädi* with some additional numbers and revised lyrics by Robert Gilbert was produced in 1953 (Stadttheater, Zürich 9 April).

Austria: Wiener Bürgertheater 5 October 1923; Hungary: Király Színház *Huncut a lány* 19 April 1924; UK: Prince of Wales Theatre *The Blue Train* 10 May 1927

MAGGIE MAY Musical in 2 acts by Alun Owen. Music and lyrics by Lionel Bart. Adelphi Theatre, London, 22 September 1964.

Bart's successor to *Oliver!* and *Blitz!* had no exclamation mark and didn't need one. Having decided to construct a show around the old ballad character of Maggie May, Bart had a libretto written by the successful Liverpool playwright Alun Owen in which the docklands prostitute (Rachel Roberts) was really not central to the story. Her childhood sweetheart, docker Casey (Kenneth Haigh), dogged by having a famous union man for a father, is his own man. In spite of the jeers of his coworkers, to whom management is a born-not-bred enemy, he refuses to commit himself to unreasoning union action, but he ends up, in spite of himself, leading a wildcat strike and dying as he tries to ditch a cargo of guns intended for anti-riot police in South America.

In a strong if simplistic story (in which both bosses and union men were shown with plenty of warts), Owen created a set of colourful characters for whom Bart supplied an unusual collection of folky-sounding pieces and modern shanties which were far from making up a conventional musical-play score. The heroine's toughly pragmatic ''love'' song ''It's Yourself I Want,'' her duo with a fellow whore, ''I Told You So,'' and their mockery of the men's self-important preoccupation with union affairs in ''There's Only One Union'' stood alongside such ballady pieces as ''Dey Don't Do Dat T'day'' and ''Leave Her, Johnny, Leave Her'' and, it being Beatles time, a number for a Liverpudlian pop group, in a score which accompanied the play very effectively, rather than the other way around.

Bernard Delfont and Tom Arnold's production of *Maggie May* ran through 501 London performances, during which time the unreliable Miss Roberts was first deputized for by 21-year-old chorister Julia McKenzie, and then succeeded by Georgia Brown. However, in spite of being announced for Broadway by Delfont and David Merrick, it did not move on to further productions.

In 1992 a performance was given at the Royalty Theatre by the National Youth Theatre.

Recordings: original cast (Decca), original cast with additional songs (TER), selection (EP) (Capitol)

THE MAGIC OPAL Comic opera in 2 acts by Arthur Law. Music by Isaac Albéniz. Lyric Theatre, London, 19 January 1893. Revised version as *The Magic Ring,* Prince of Wales Theatre, 11 April 1893.

The music for *The Magic Opal* was composed by Albéniz whilst he was resident in Britain on a retainer from the wealthy banker and amateur author Francis Burdett Money-Coutts to set to music such libretti as the latter might write. In between Coutts's assignments, the composer wrote some additional music for interpolation into London's versions of *Le Coeur et la main* and *Der arme Jonathan* and also completed the full score for this comic opera, produced by Horace Sedger. Arthur Law's libretto followed a magic ring which makes the wearer irresistible. It affected a brigand chief (Wallace Brownlow) and his sister (May Yohé), an old hag (Susie Vaughan), the two juvenile leads (Aida Jenoure, John Child) and the heroine's father (Harry Monkhouse), all to the accompaniment of a fairly straightforward comic-opera score. *The Magic Opal* was well enough received and reviewed, but it aroused little interest and closed after 44 performances, leaving its touring company, which had gone out counting on London success, adrift.

However, brewery tycoon Henry Lowenfeld liked the show, leased the Prince of Wales Theatre, got rid of Miss Yohé (in spite of her already distinct personal following) and half the original cast and reproduced the show as *The Magic Ring* with Monkhouse, Miss Vaughan, Norman Salmond and the American soubrette Marie Halton featured. The critics liked it again, but again it lasted for just 37 performances. Later in the year it surfaced a third time, but this time in Madrid where, in Eusebio Sierra's translation, it was played as *La Sortija.*

The title *The Magic Ring* was once more the second choice name for a 1923 American musical comedy (Harold Levey/Zelda Sears, Liberty Theater 1 October) which had been originally produced by Henry Savage as *Minnie an' Me* (Stamford 2 April 1923), but it was first choice for a comic opera by Immanuel Liebich, tentatively produced in London in 1886 to a firm thumbs-down.

THE MAGIC SHOW Musical in 2 acts by Bob Randall. Music and lyrics by Stephen Schwartz. Cort Theater, New York, 28 May 1974.

A vehicle for the illusions of Doug Henning, *The Magic Show* cast the young magician as a young magician called Doug in a story line which had him saving a failing nightclub from extinction by his performances. One of the evening's highlights came when Doug sawed his girlfriend (Anita Morris) in half, and his jealous wife promptly ran off with one half—the bottom half, at that. The magic was spaced out by 11 bright songs for a supporting cast of nine (Henning did not sing) and band of seven. Partly thanks to these manageable proportions, Henning (temporarily spelled by Joe Abbaldo) and his show ran through 1,859 performances on Broadway. The star returned to Broadway in 1983 with another, less successful show, in which he appeared as *Merlin.*

An Australian production, mounted under the auspices of the Elizabethan Theatre Trust and Garnet Carroll, did not have Henning, was a two-month failure in Melbourne and did not brave Sydney.

Australia: Princess Theatre, Melbourne 2 August 1975
Recording: original cast (Bell)

MÁGNÁS MISKA Operett in 3 acts by Károly Bakonyi. Lyrics by Andor Gábor. Music by Albert Szirmai. Király Színház, Budapest, 12 February 1916.

Produced in Budapest during the most fecund period in Hungarian operett, Szirmai's wartime piece *Mágnás Miska* (''Miska the magnate'') stands alongside such pieces as Jacobi's *Leányvásár* and *Szibill* as one of the most successful products of its time and place.

During a sporty country-house weekend at the house of Count Kasimir Korláth (Kálmán Latabár), his daughter, Rolla (Juci Lábass), falls for the untitled Iván Baracs (Ernő Király) whose athletic prowesses have won him every event. Rolla's brother Gida (Ernő Szabolcs) and the other losers get it whispered about that she is simply leading the bourgeois fellow on, and in revenge Baracs introduces his groom, Miska (Márton Rátkai), to the dazzled aristocrats as the lofty Gróf Amadée, just returned from darkest Africa. But Rolla, who is wise to his trick, in turn disguises her kitchen maid, Marcsa (Sári Fedák), as Amadée's cousin, the Countess Lizzi. The antics of the two disguised ''aristocrats'' and the clearing of a path towards both their union and that of Rolla and Baracs comprise the action of the second and third acts.

Szirmai's score was a vigorously tuneful one, ranging from the fiendishly bouncing and folksy ''Hoppsza Sári'' and a rollicking march-time entry song for the heroine to some duets for the tenor and soprano which verged on the ''grand opérette'' style, yet which maintained a swinging sound which stopped them ever becoming too pretentious for their jolly little story. However, the heart of *Mágnás Miska* was in its comedy, and in the roles of Miska himself—a part in joyous line of descent from the *Erminie* style of masquerading rogue of 19th-century comic opera—and of soubrette Marcsa.

A great success in Budapest, *Mágnás Miska* passed its 150th performance at the Király Színház just eight months after its premiere, and was long regularly revived in Hungary, most recently at the Fővárosi Operettszínház in 1972 (27 October). The show was also briskly picked up for a German presentation (ad Robert Bodanzky) which ran through almost three months of performances at Berlin's Komische Oper, and this version was later played at Vienna's Apollotheater with Fedák repeating her original role (now called Rosi) alongside Josef König, Olga Bartos-Trau and Oskar Neruda. It apparently went no further west, but in Hungary it wins regular revivals, most recently at Zalaegerszeg (1992), Eger (1994), Győr (1995), Pécs (1996), Szeged and Nyíregyháza (1997) and at Budapest's Vigszínház (4 April 1996) with Erika Pápai as Rolla and Enikő Börcsök as Marcsa.

Germany: Komische Oper *Der Pusztakavalier* 16 November 1916; Austria: Apollotheater *Der Pusztakavalier* November 1920
Film: 1948

THE MAID OF THE MOUNTAINS Comic opera in 3 acts by Frederick Lonsdale. Lyrics by Harry Graham. Additional lyrics by ''Valentine'' and F Clifford Harris. Music by Harold Fraser-Simson. Additional music by James Tate and Merlin Morgan. Daly's Theatre, London, 10 February 1917.

One of the sensations of the London theatre during the First World War, *The Maid of the Mountains* arrived

Plate 238. **The Maid of the Mountains.** *Australia's Gladys Moncrieff made half a career out of playing "The Maid" round and round her homeland.*

at Daly's Theatre just in time to save George Edwardes's once-great theatre from financial disaster. Bobbie Evett, representing the Edwardes estate as manager of Daly's, accepted the libretto (originally rejected some years previously by Frank Curzon) from author Frederick Lonsdale and had it set by composer Harold Fraser-Simson. He then mounted the tale of swashbuckling banditry and low comedy with the darkly attractive prima donna José Collins playing the part of Teresa, "the maid of the mountains," whose love for her brigand chief, Baldasarre, is great enough for her to free him from his island prison knowing he will fly straight to the arms of her rival, the governor's daughter. *The Maid of the Mountains* followed the system which Lonsdale had set out in his first musical, *King of Cadonia,* by taking an old-fashioned comic-opera plot and characters and equipping them with rather better-made scenes and lines than was the custom, as well, in this case, as an unusual (at that stage) "unhappy" ending—which he was ultimately not permitted to keep. Miss Collins objected damply to the unconventional (for her) unhappy (for her) ending to the piece as originally written and forced her producer and her writer to invert it so that she and her leading man (Arthur Wontner) could sail off into the sunset together at the final curtain.

Fraser-Simson's score, topped by two lovely waltzes, "Farewell" and "Love Is My Life," for the prima donna, and some sprightly comic pieces ("I Understood," "Husbands and Wives") for the supporting comedy couple (Lauri de Frece, Mabel Sealby), illustrated Lonsdale's work splendidly. During the show's Manchester tryout, however, Evett decided the score needed further strengthening and he added three numbers written by Miss Collins's stepfather, songwriter James Tate, and one by musical director Merlin Morgan. Tate's songs included another hit for the star, "Love Will Find a Way," a solo for principal baritone Thorpe Bates (the role of Baldasarre was a non-singing one) declaring "A Bachelor Gay Am I," and a duet for the two of them, "A Paradise for Two." All three numbers subsequently became enormous favorites and ubiquitous concert items in English and colonial houses for half a century. Morgan's song didn't last out the run.

Oscar Asche, already the director (and author and star) of the West End's other great hit, *Chu Chin Chow,* staged the show which, arriving in town after its Manchester Christmas season, caused nothing short of a sensation at Daly's Theatre. It played there for 1,352 performances—a massive run for the time—and closed only when Miss Collins, who in spite of regular breaks was finding an endless run of Teresas nerve-racking, cried enough. She was so closely identified with the role that, although she had been ably deputized for by Dorothy Shale during various absences, there was no thought of replacing her, and Evett took the only way out—he produced a new show, *A Southern Maid,* as like as possible to the old one, with Miss Collins starring, whilst *The Maid of the Mountains* went on the road. It proved as big a hit in the provinces—without its star—as it had in London with her and, at one stage, no fewer than 12 different companies were on the road touring *The Maid of the Mountains* around Britain. José Collins reappeared as ''the maid' in 1921–22 as a farewell to Daly's, and the show returned to London in 1930 with Annie Croft and again, and most successfully, in 1942 with Sylvia Cecil starred, but a 1972 Émile Littler version, embarrassingly rewritten and with the score plumped up with some borrowed operetta pops (''Song of the Vagabonds,'' ''Pedro the Fisherman'') was a failure.

The Maid of the Mountains, similarly disfigured by unsuitable interpolations, also failed quickly (37 performances) when it was trekked down to America in a Canadian production with Sidonie Espero in its title role, but in Australia, where it was played as written, it proved, if anything, even more of a hit than in Britain. Soprano Gladys Moncrieff scored a huge personal success as Teresa and became as thoroughly identified with the role in Australia and New Zealand as Miss Collins had in Britain. Again and again she appeared on the Australian stage as ''the maid,'' always a reliable money-maker in a piece which producers J C Williamson Ltd re-mounted whenever another iffy venture had landed them in sharky waters (''Gladys, the ship is sinking . . .''). She made her final appearance in the role of the gypsyish brigand girl at the age of 59.

USA: Casino Theater 11 September 1918; Australia: Theatre Royal, Melbourne 21 January 1921

Recordings: original cast transfers (World Records), selection (World Records, Hyperion), revival cast 1972 (Columbia), etc

MAILLART, Aimé [MAILLART, Louis] (b Montpellier, 24 March 1817; d Moulins-sur-Allier, 26 May 1871).

Conservatoire-trained Aimé Maillart was the composer of a number of lyric theatre works including *Gastibelza, ou Le Fou de Tolède* (1847), *Le Moulin des tilleuls* (1849), *La Croix de Marie* (1852), *Les Pêcheurs de Catane* (1860) and *Lara* (1864), produced variously at the Opéra-Comique and at Adolphe Adam's Théâtre Lyrique. His most notable success came with the opéra-comique *Les Dragons de Villars,* composed to a book by Lockroy and Cormon which mixed a lighthearted soldiers-and-peasant-girls tale of (attempted) naughty doings in the ruins of a hermitage with a more serious story of a *Sound of Music*–style attempt by some persecuted folk (without children) to escape through the mountains to political safety. The piece was illustrated by a score which leaned tunefully towards the light musical theatre rather than the grand operatic. Produced by Léon Carvalho at the Théâtre Lyrique in 1856, *Les Dragons de Villars* was subsequently taken into the repertoire of the Opéra-Comique (1868) and became one of the handful of opéras-comiques of the early and middle part of the 19th century to survive into the repertoires of the touring French opéra-bouffe companies when the works of Offenbach, Lecocq and their fellow composers of the latter part of the century dominated the musical stages of the world to the exclusion of virtually all the musical works of the earlier sub-operatic stage.

MAJESTÄT MIMI Operette in 3 acts by Felix Dörmann and Roda Roda. Music by Bruno Granichstaedten. Carltheater, Vienna, 17 February 1911.

Granichstaedten's Operette presented Mizzi Zwerenz as a Parisian cabaret performer called Mimi who dances the cancan, insists that she is ''modern,'' has ''Temp'rament'' and sings in praise of ''Walzer und Wein''; and Willi Strehl as the cabaret-singer Prince of a mythical country called Bythinia, who is unhappily whisked away from his boyish bohemian life in Paris to Brussa (capital of Bythinia) to take up his royal duties—in precisely the same manner that Ivor Novello's Niki of Murania would be a few decades later. In spite of Granichstaedten's penchant for music with a modern and even transatlantic tinge, the two lovers spent most of the evening singing in 3/4 time and by the third-act finale they were even encouraging each other to ''Küss mich in dreivierteltakt'' as they waltzed into their happy ending. Josef König was the Fürst von Lepanto, the patter-singing representative of the Bythinia establishment; Otti Dietze (Princess Xénia) and Rudolf Kumpa (Ferry) supplied the soubret moments, again largely in waltz time (''Komm mit mir auf meine kleine Segelyacht . . . ,'' ''O, jui jui jui''); and veteran Karl Blasel had a virtual non-singing role.

Sigmund Eibenschütz's production of *Majestät Mimi* lasted but 27 performances at the Carltheater, and the piece was subsequently played without stirring too much interest in Hamburg. It did not, apparently, make it to Hungary where even the least of its composer's works was played and though Broadway whispered that Lillian Russell would do it if she didn't do *Der Opernball,* in the end she didn't do either. However, the show did find its way to Italy where, in the hands of Carlo Lombardo, a specialist in concocting semi-original shows out of other people's works, it was turned into a piece called *La Duchessa del Bal Tabarin*—its heroine was now no longer Mimi but Frou-Frou of the Bal Tabarin—with a considerable success. Granichstaedten's name was nowhere to be seen on the bill which described the piece as "an operetta by Leon Bard" (Lombardo's occasional nom de plume). After cleaning up in Italy, where it was reproduced many times in years to come, it moved on to repeat its Italian success in Spain (ad Enrique Gomez Carillo, José Juan Cadenas).

Germany: Deutsches Operetten-Theater, Hamburg 1 April 1911

Recordings: Italian recording *La Duchessa del Bal Tabarin* (Fonit-Cetra), Spanish recording *La Duquesa del Bal Tabarin* (Montilla)

MAKE ME AN OFFER Musical in 2 acts by Wolf Mankowitz taken from his novel of the same name. Lyrics and music by David Heneker and Monty Norman. Theatre Royal, Stratford East, 17 October 1959; New Theatre, London, 16 December 1959.

Developed from a novel (and subsequent film) that author Mankowitz had written around his own collector-mania for Wedgwood china, *Make Me an Offer* was the tale of market stallholder Charlie (Daniel Massey), who loves and knows the stuff he sells, but who is not much of a chat-happy businessman. When he takes part in an auction ring at a big sale, he gets enough cash to buy a beautiful vase. It's something he's dreamed all his life of owning, but he finds he has grown up enough to be able to sell it. He is a professional dealer, and he needs the cash both to support his wife (Diana Coupland) and babes and to develop his business. Temptation was represented not only by the vase, but by its pushy redheaded seller (Dilys Laye), whilst comedy was provided by the snappily professional, sell-you-anything Jewish market-vendors (Meier Tzelniker, Wally Patch) quarreling day in, day out until they finally unite in the face of a common prey as represented by a pair of American buyers (Victor Spinetti, Chuck Julian).

The show's songs and ensembles, often flowing over into and out of the text, were from two-thirds of the team responsible for *Expresso Bongo* and the English version of *Irma la Douce.* They were highlighted by Massey's musical epitomizing of life's problems in "Damn the Pram" and his longing for "A Lock-Up in the Portobello Road"; a first-act finale with Charlie on the phone to his wife and the redhead hovering dangerously near ("Make Me an Offer"); and a rhythmical set-piece auction scene. Like the writers' earlier work it was a show "for grown ups of all ages" which almost never tumbled into the stage Sohoisms of such recent pieces as *Fings Ain't Wot They Used t' Be* and *The Crooked Mile,* and its quality showed through as it won a transfer from the suburban Theatre Royal, Stratford East, to the West End's New Theatre where it remained for 267 performances before going on to be reprised in provincial theatres.

A German adaptation (ad Kurt Barthel) mounted in Rostock under the unlikely title "a breath of romance" elevated the previously unnamed "redhead" to being "Lady Rotkopf" in what otherwise seemed a faithful version.

Germany: Rostock *Ein Hauch von Romantik* 27 March 1966

Recording: original cast (HMV/AEI)

MALONE, J[oseph] A[rchibald] E[dward] (b Mhow, India, 1863; d London, 3 February 1929). George Edwardes's stage director through his greatest era of activity.

The son of a Royal Artillery riding master, "Pat" Malone was born while his father was stationed in India, and spent his youth in Manchester, Brighton, Dublin, Cheriton and other parental posting-towns. He began his theatrical life as a performer (one of his jobs was as a chorister in *Indiana,* 1887) before shifting to the stage-management and directing side of the business. He was engaged first for some half-dozen years at the Prince of Wales' Theatre in Liverpool, where he directed his first musical, William Duck's presentation of the comic opera *Herne's Oak,* in 1887, but from 1894 he worked under the wide-reaching management of the country's most important musical producer, George Edwardes, starting at a time when the manager of the Gaiety Theatre and Daly's Theatre was launching his double-headed series of musical plays towards the stages of the world.

Malone directed the initial production of *A Gaiety Girl* and in 1894 restaged *In Town, The Shop Girl* and *Gentleman Joe* for the Gaiety's world tour, with which he traveled as general manager. Following his return to Britain, he directed the majority of Edwardes's productions at the Gaiety Theatre (*The Circus Girl, A Runaway Girl, The Messenger Boy, The Toreador, The Girls of Gottenberg, The Sunshine Girl*), at Daly's (*The Geisha, A Greek Slave, San Toy, A Country Girl, The Cingalee, The Merry Widow*), in various other venues in London (*Kitty Grey, Three Little Maids, The Merry-Go-Round, The School Girl, Lady Madcap, The Little Cherub, A Waltz Dream, The Quaker Girl, The Dancing Mistress, The Girl from Utah*) and on Broadway (*The Geisha, In Town, The Circus Girl, The Girls of Gottenberg, The Dollar Princess, The Quaker Girl, The Sunshine Girl, The Girl from Utah*) over the following two decades.

After Edwardes's death, Malone continued as a director of his old boss's Musical Plays Ltd, running the Adelphi Theatre where he directed the successful *High Jinks* (1916), *Who's Hooper?* (1919) and *The Naughty*

Princess (*La Reine s'amuse*) for Alfred Butt. He also directed *The Beauty Spot* for Butt, with whom he was allied on the board of the Victoria Palace Theatre, at the Gaiety, Messager's *Monsieur Beaucaire* in London and New York and *The Maid of the Mountains* for Broadway, billed as "Captain J A E Malone" on a self-conscious program which also credited "additional music by Lieutenant Gitz Rice."

Alongside his directing activities, Malone was involved in various producing exercises. In 1904 he joined Robert Courtneidge and Arthur Hart on the management side of the first provincial production of *The Blue Moon,* and he deputized efficiently for the absent and ill Edwardes on *After the Girl* and *Adele* (1914) in the last days of the producer's Gaiety reign. However, he made his firmest effort in that area when, in 1920, he joined George Grossmith and Edward Laurillard in their production company and, on Laurillard's retirement from the partnership, teamed with Grossmith in the management of the Winter Garden, the Shaftesbury and His Majesty's Theatres and as the co-producer of the successful series of musicals staged at the Winter Garden (*Sally, The Cabaret Girl, The Beauty Prize, Tell Me More, Primrose, Kid Boots*) and also of such other London and provincial pieces as Jack Buchanan's *Toni* (1923).

Malone was for a period London representative of Australia's J C Williamson Ltd, for whom he was directing their London transfer of the musical *Mr Cinders* when he died in 1929.

He was married to the Cornish musical-comedy actress **Hilda MOODY** (b Redruth, 16 June 1876), younger sister of the operatic Fanny Moody of the Moody-Manners Opera Company who, after early performances with the D'Oyly Carte companies (Lisa in *The Grand Duke,* etc), appeared under Edwardes's management in leading roles in *A Greek Slave* (1898, Antonia), *A Gaiety Girl* revival (1899, Rose Brierly), *San Toy* (1899, Poppy Preston), *Three Little Maids* (1902, Hilda Branscombe) and *The Dollar Princess* (1908, Alice pre-London).

MALTBY, H[enry] F[rancis] (b Ceres, Cape Colony, 25 November 1880; d Hove, 25 October 1963).

For many years an actor and, in late life, a favorite screen character performer, big, bullet-headed Maltby wrote a number of successful postwar plays, beginning with the splendid *A Temporary Gentleman,* and innumerable film screenplays, as well as several West End musicals. The first of these, C B Cochran's production of *Maggie* with music by the French composer Marcel Lattès, proved only a semi-success (108 performances) in London before going on to productions in Australia and (as *Nelly*) in Paris, but the second, the musical comedy *For the Love of Mike*—originally written as a straight comedy, but rejected by Tom Walls for whom it had been intended—proved a musical-comedy hit for star Bobby Howes and producer Jack Waller (239 performances) and initiated a happy series of "plays with tunes" at the Saville Theatre in the early 1930s. *Jack o' Diamonds,* a comedy piece featuring Richard Dolman as a phony South African millionaire, won good notices for its text, but only a fair run (126 performances), while *Meet Me Victoria,* a Lupino Lane vehicle constructed on a Maltby story line continued the star's successful series at the Victoria Palace.

1906 **Fannikin** (w Kathleen Barry) 1 act Pier Pavilion, Hastings May

1919 **Maggie** (Marcel Lattes/w Fred Thompson) Oxford Theatre 22 October

1931 **For the Love of Mike** (Jack Waller, Joseph Tunbridge/Clifford Grey, Sonny Miller/w Grey) Saville Theatre 8 October

1935 **Jack o' Diamonds** (Noel Gay/w Grey) Gaiety Theatre 25 February

1942 **Susie** revised *Jack o' Diamonds* New Theatre, Oxford 13 June

1944 **Meet Me Victoria** (Gay/Frank Eyton/w Lupino Lane, Lauri Wylie) Victoria Palace 6 March

1948 **The Lilac Domino** (*Der lila Domino*) revised English libretto and lyrics

Autobiography: *Ring Up the Curtain* (Hutchinson & Co, London, 1950)

MAME Musical in 2 acts by Jerome Lawrence and Robert E Lee based on the novel *Auntie Mame* by Patrick Dennis and the play by Lawrence and Lee. Lyrics and music by Jerry Herman. Winter Garden Theater, New York, 24 May 1966.

The adventures of Patrick Dennis's extraordinary Auntie Mame, as she has ridden (doubtless bareback) from the printed page to the stage and the screen, have become as much part of American and international folklore as those of Rip van Winkle and the inhabitants of Uncle Tom's Cabin. Auntie Mame's first appearance on the stage—in the person of comedienne Rosalind Russell—was in a play version of her story, written by Lawrence and Lee and produced at the Broadhurst Theater (*Auntie Mame* 31 October 1956) for a triumphant run of 639 performances, and Miss Russell transferred her amiable antics to the screen in 1958 before, in 1966, *Mame* was given music by the newly celebrated composer of *Hello, Dolly!,* Jerry Herman.

Mame Dennis (Angela Lansbury) is a gourmand for all the latest fads and fancies, no matter how unsuitable they might seem for a nice middle-class American lady of middle years. If she thought at all, she could possibly be called a freethinker. When she is suddenly given charge of her young, orphaned nephew she fights off a hidebound trustee who wants him to have a strictly conventional upbringing, and drags the boy with her via martinis, kook religion and the sloughs of showbusiness up to young manhood. When he shows signs of marrying a horsey nincompoop, in spite of (or because of?) his off-the-elbow upbringing, Mame scuttles the liaison and Patrick (Jerry Lanning) ends up with a nice no-nonsense wife and, before the evening is over, a young son who, it seems, is going to give the aging Mame the chance to be a madcap surrogate mother all over again.

Herman's score obligatorily sported an equivalent to the title song of *Hello, Dolly!,* and, if the cakewalky serenade of the entire southlands of America, all dressed in hunting red, to the ''Mame'' who has just brought the fox back alive, didn't quite equal its predecessor in popularity, it very nearly disproved the old saw about lightning never striking twice. But if ''Mame'' was the most obviously big number in the lively score, there were other pieces in a different vein: Mame ruminating on whether she has done the best for her boy (''If He Walked into My Life''), Patrick's plain nanny, Agnes Gooch (Jane Connell), hilariously relating her finally achieved sky-dive from virginity (Gooch's Song), Patrick's comforting hymn to his aunt, ''You're My Best Girl,'' or Mame and best friend Vera Charles (Beatrice Arthur) declaring themselves ''Bosom Buddies'' with only the odd gallon of bitchery.

Mame won a fine Broadway success, staying at the Winter Garden Theater for 1,508 performances, and returned for a second showing in 1983 with Misses Lansbury and Connell repeating their original roles alongside Byron Nease (Patrick) and Anne Francine (Vera) (24 July, 41 performances). If it did not follow *Hello, Dolly!* on to the wide world's stages, it nevertheless had a highly satisfying run at London's Theatre Royal, Drury Lane, where Harold Fielding's production, with Ginger Rogers starred and Ann Beach (Gooch), Margaret Courtenay (Vera) and Tony Adams (Patrick) in support, played through 443 performances, closing only when Miss Rogers left the show. *Mame* was subsequently seen in South Africa with Joan Brickhill and in Australia with Gaylea Byrne starred as Mame alongside Geoff Hiscock (Patrick) and Sheila Bradley (Vera) for four months in Melbourne and, later, a rather shorter season in Sydney (Her Majesty's Theatre 8 February 1969). A Spanish-language version (ad Berta Maldonaldo, Jose Luis Ibañez), with Silvia Pinal featured as Mame was a very long-running success in Mexico, where the show survives to this day with a great vigor.

In 1974 the musical version of *Mame* was filmed, with Lucille Ball starred as Mame alongside Misses Arthur and Connell. Robert Preston featured as the wealthy bluegrass husband who falls off an alp on their honeymoon, leaving Mame a well-equipped widow, and was given an additional song for the occasion.

Australia: Her Majesty's Theatre, Melbourne 25 May 1968; UK: Theatre Royal, Drury Lane 20 February 1969; Germany: Nuremberg 1 October 1970

Film: Warner Brothers 1974

Recordings: original cast (Columbia), Mexican cast (Orfeon), film soundtrack (Warner Brothers)

MA MIE ROSETTE Opérette in 3 acts by Jules Prével and Armand Liorat. Music by Paul Lacome. Théâtre des Folies-Dramatiques, Paris, 4 February 1890.

Lacome's *Ma mie Rosette* was a pretty, if apparently run-of-the-mill, opérette based on a little adventure of ''lou nouste Henrique,'' France's favorite fictionally philandering monarch. It had only a limited run in France, yet it won itself an afterlife overseas and, ultimately, became a long-lived repertoire piece with the J C Williamson company in Australia.

Rosette (Juliette Nesville), the daughter of the rustic Moustajon (Bellucci), is all set to be happily wed to her Vincent (Gobin) when King Henri, with whom she had played as a child, passes by and sees what has become of his little playmate. To the annoyance of the official royal mistress, Corisandre (Mlle Vernon), the tasty little Rosette is lured up to the King's castle to deliver the milk and, before she knows where she is, she's decked out in jewels and silks and attending a court ball. Vincent is conveniently sent off to the wars. However, the determined Corisandre makes sure that Vincent is brought back on the scene and, although swords are drawn momentarily, the final act brings its happy, everyone-in-his-place, ending. The comedy was supplied by the royal valet who, disguised as a Duc, cocks an eye dangerously at Rosette's aunt, a dame in active search of a fourth husband.

The *Ma mie Rosette* which appeared in Britain was a little different from that seen in Paris. The piece had been done over into a two-act English version by George Dance, which turned the whole kingly episode ''harmlessly'' into nothing but Rosette's dream. It had also had its score adapted by Ivan Caryll, who added 8 or 9 new musical numbers of his own—including two finales—to the 13 or 17 remaining pieces of Lacome's score (the totals varied through the run). In a cast full of Savoy Theatre favorites, very young French soubrette Juliette Nesville came to Britain to repeat her Rosette alongside Eugene Oudin (Henry IV), Courtice Pounds (Vincent), Jessie Bond (Martha), Lawrance D'Orsay, Frank Wyatt, Cairns James, Scott Fishe and American soubrette Jennie McNulty (Corisandre). William Boosey and John Lart's production was well received (''a pretty, sentimental story slashed with streaks of genuine comedy'') and the show looked set for a fine run, but after an optimistic shift of theatre it suddenly faded and came off after just three months. During those months, however, it started a controversy in London's papers over the botching of French opérettes for the English stage. Teddy Solomon came out against, but Lacome and Serpette—apparently more interested in royalties than integrity—announced themselves in (English) print as pro! *Ma mie Rosette* got a British revival at Manchester in 1899 (Prince's Theatre 1 April) with Harrison Brockbank and Flora Macdonald featured.

The London version was the one which was played in Australia. Nellie Stewart was the first Australian Rosette, with Wallace Brownlow as Henri alongside Howard Vernon (Cognac), George Lauri (Bouillon), Florence Young (Corisandre) and Clara Thompson (Marthe), and the opérette established itself as a sufficient favorite to be revived periodically by the Williamson organization as late as 1925, when Gladys Moncrieff appeared as Rosette.

UK: Globe Theatre 17 November 1892; Australia: Princess Theatre, Melbourne 16 June 1894

MAMMA MIA! Musical in 2 acts by Catherine Johnson. Music and lyrics by Björn Ulvaeus and Benny Andersson. Some songs with Stig Anderson. Prince Edward Theatre, London, 6 April 1999.

An unpretentious and almost tongue-in-cheek show with a score compiled from the Euro-popular song hits of the outstandingly successful group Abba, *Mamma mia!* was a deftly woven together piece of pasticcio held together by a slight story of a middle-aged Abba-era mum, Donna Sheridan (Siobhán McCarthy), her romantic, about-to-be-wed daughter Sophie (Lisa Stokke) and the three men who might have been the girl's father (Nic Colicos, Hilton McRae, Paul Clarkson). ''*Shirley Valentine* meets *Carmelina*'' quoth one commentator.

The story, however, had no need to be anything but slight for it existed solely to give a setting to 27 Abba-songs (''Winner Takes All,'' ''Money, Money, Money,'' ''Dancing Queen,'' ''Chiquitita,'' ''Knowing Me, Knowing You,'' ''Take a Chance on Me,'' ''Thank You for the Music,'' ''Super Trouper,'' ''Does Your Mother Know?,'' Mamma mia!,'' etc) and the fun of the evening was derived from discovering just how, with minimal lyric changes, the familiar numbers had been squeezed into the evening's action. Just as in the old days of Victorian punning burlesque, the book's sneaky sashays into a quickly recognized piece of 20-year-old pop music brought forth squeals and groans from an audience just dying to squeal and groan, and when one number was finished the outstanding interest lay in waiting for and catching (preferably half a bar before your neighbor) the tag into the next one.

Brought out in London on the crest of the wave of semi- and demi-semi-musicals tacked-up around virtual concerts of middle-aged pop music (*Elvis, Buddy, Patsy Cline, The Boy from Oz, Smokey Joe's Cafe, Great Balls of Fire,* etc), but sparing its audiences a sugared-up retelling of the life history of the four members of the group—each of them, unlike the subjects of the other entertainments, thoroughly alive), *Mamma mia!* arrived at precisely its right time. After having for many a year reigned as Europe's best-selling group, Abba had become subsequently identified as what a non-fan, bred in decibel-days on such evanescent trends as punk and rap and hippity-hoppity, referred to bewilderingly as ''the uttermost height of naff.'' However, fueled by the half-loving, half-mocking use of the group's music in such popular movies as *Priscilla the Queen of the Desert* and *Muriel's Wedding,* an Abba revival had got severely under way in the 1990s, and it was noticeable that the daylong queues panting for tickets outside the Prince Edward Theatre in the weeks following the opening of the show were compiled not of Abba-age mums like Donna, but of young folk of her daughter's age. *Mamma mia!* quickly established as a serious hit, and entrenched itself cheerfully in Old Compton Street, in the sometime home of *Evita* and *Chess,* where it looks likely to stay for many years to come.

At the time of writing, a production of the piece in Canada has proved no less popular and successful, and Abba's offspring is Broadway-bound.

MAMOULIAN, Rouben (b Tiflis, Russia, 8 October 1897; d Los Angeles, 4 December 1987). Director of several highly successful Broadway musicals of the 1940s.

Having spent the early part of his career working in the straight theatre, in opera and comic opera, Mamoulian became in the mid-1920s stage director with the Theatre Guild, in which capacity he directed the original production of the play *Porgy* (1928). He moved on to a striking career as a director of films (*Applause, City Streets, Dr Jekyll and Mr Hyde,* the Jeanette MacDonald musical film *Love Me Tonight, The Gay Desperado,* Garbo's *Queen Christina,* etc) before returning to Broadway where he directed, amongst other pieces, the original production of George Gershwin's musical version of *Porgy, Porgy and Bess* (1935).

In 1943 Mamoulian was responsible for the staging of the Theatre Guild's venture into the musical theatre, Rodgers and Hammerstein's *Oklahoma!,* and following the enormous worldwide triumph of that piece, he directed, and occasionally co-wrote, a series of musicals, several of which were more than usually interesting if not always successful: a version of Somerset Maugham's *Rain* as *Sadie Thompson* (1944), another adaptation of a tragicomic classic, Ferenc Molnár's *Liliom,* as the highly successful *Carousel* (1945), Harold Arlen's dazzlingly musicked *St Louis Woman* (1946), the musical version of *Cry, the Beloved Country* written by Maxwell Anderson and composed by Kurt Weill as *Lost in the Stars* (1949) and the Theatre Guild's musical made out of their own play *The Pursuit of Happiness, Arms and the Girl* (1950). After the original productions of *Oklahoma!* and *Carousel,* he directed a number of further productions of each piece, notably in Britain and Germany.

His later film credits included the screen version of *Silk Stockings* (1957).

1944 **Sadie Thompson** (Vernon Duke/w Howard Dietz) Alvin Theater 16 November

1950 **Arms and the Girl** (Morton Gould/Dorothy Fields/w Herbert Fields, D Fields) 46th Street Theater 2 February

Biography: Milne, T: *Mamoulian* (Thames & Hudson, London, 1969)

MAM'ZELLE CARABIN Opérette in 3 acts by Fabrice Carré. Music by Émile Pessard. Théâtre des Bouffes-Parisiens, Paris, 3 November 1893.

A vaudevillesque piece of character and comic scene, *Mam'zelle Carabin* featured Juliette Simon-Girard as Olga, a would-be medical student who prides herself on having all the advantages of the two sexes, but who faints at the sight of a pricked finger. She nevertheless proves a fine psychologist as she helps her handsome but distractable fellow student and neighbor Ferdinand (Piccaluga) to study his books, renounce the tarty Nini (Mlle Boka) and, finally, to take her hand instead. In parallel to this plotlet ran the comic story of cousin Adolphe (Félix Huguenet), the eternal failed student, who exchanged lovers' tokens with his already mature mistress, Olga's aunt Caroline Quillette (Rosine Maurel), 16 years ago, and now wants to break it off. He can't, because the tokens were 100-franc pieces and he doesn't have that much money to give back. Charles Lamy played the idiotic Monsieur Chose, equipped with a dandy's lingo and a rare coin which Adolphe manages to swallow at the right moment to tie up the plot.

The comedy—which was substantial enough to have played without songs—was nevertheless illustrated by a well-regarded score of songs and ensembles, which did not hesitate to make comic references to such pieces of the operatic repertoire as *Manon* or *Samson et Dalila,* and which was devoted largely to the five principals. ''Carabin'' arrived in a whirl (''Je touche au terme du voyage''), was christened with her nickname (''Va pour Carabin''), explained to Adolphe the failings of man (''L'Être idéal, parfait en somme'') and, loosened up by an unaccustomed glass of wine, gave out in praise of love (''Pourquoi donc que toutes les femmes''), but she had her most amusing moment in a rondeau (''La belle amoureuse'') in which she described to the unbelieving Ferdinand the way in which Nini would pick herself up a man. As she sang, the cocotte, seen on the split stage meeting up with Monsieur Chose, was going through exactly the routine that was being described. In other musical moments, Mme Quillette drew her coin from her ample bosom (''Pendant seize ans'') only to find Adolphe unable to respond with his, and Nini tempted Ferdinand (''Faut pas m'la faire'') whilst Carabin pushed him to work (''Rien ne vaut le devoir austère''). A quartet for three students and a little Bichette in the first act (''Grand Salomon'') was also picked out for mention by the critics, who found Pessard's educated and well-orchestrated music decidedly to their taste.

Mam'zelle Carabin (the title meant ''Madame Sawbones'') scored a fine success in Paris, running for more than 150 nights at the Bouffes-Parisiens in its first series, returning for a second visit in October 1895 and, again, to the Théâtre de la Renaissance, in October 1900 with Rosalia Lambrecht in its title role for another 50 Parisian nights. It was also seen in Germany (ad Richard Genée, Richard Pohl), played in Munich under the title of *Mamselle Cerevis.*

Germany: Theater am Gärtnerplatz, Munich *Mamselle Cerevis* 6 October 1894

MAM'ZELLE NITOUCHE Comédie-vaudeville in 3 acts by Henri Meilhac and Albert Millaud [and Ernest Blum]. Music by Hervé. Théâtre des Variétés, Paris, 26 January 1883.

Of the series of enormously successful vaudevilles produced by Eugène Bertrand at the Théâtre des Variétés between *Niniche* and *La Cosaque,* with Anna Judic for their overwhelming female star, *Mam'zelle Nitouche* was, in the long run, the most enduringly successful of all.

Convent music-master Célestin (Baron) leads a double life. Outside teaching hours he composes opérettes, and one of his frothy little works is about to be presented at the local theatre. Unfortunately for him, his secret is discovered by his most innocent-looking but diabolically frisky pupil, Denise de Flavigny (Anna Judic). Without too much use of blackmail she manages to get first backstage, and finally on stage, at the theatre; she falls for a handsome soldier called Champlâtreux (Cooper), gets arrested climbing out of a window and is carried off to the barracks. She ends up, disguised as a soldier, on top of a table singing a jolly song before she is discovered, and she finally sneaks poor Célestin back into the convent in the early hours, blinking not an eyelash as she delivers

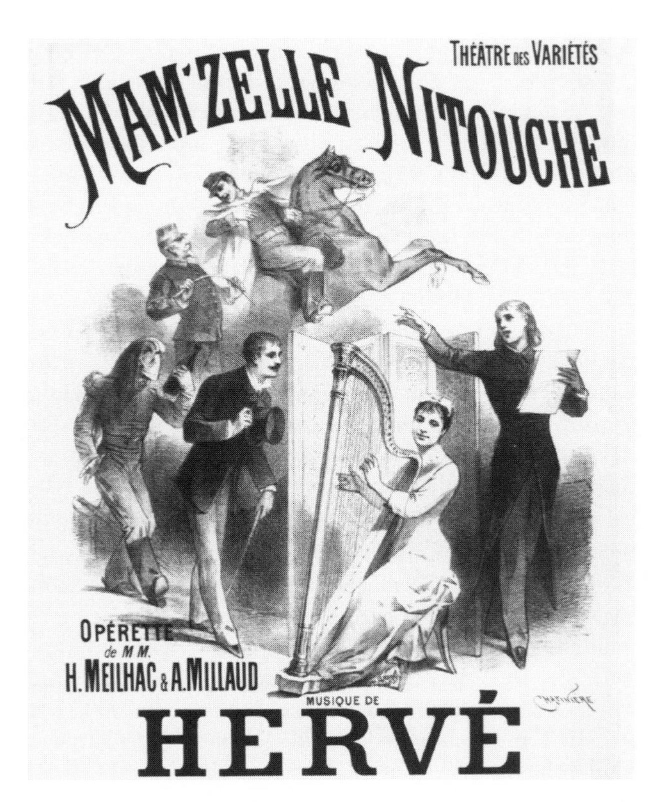

Plate 239. **Mam'zelle Nitouche.**

a plausible story for the benefit of the Mother Superior. She now announces she is going to become a nun rather than wed the unknown man her father has lined up for her, but then she discovers that that man is none other than her handsome soldier. But Mam'zelle Nitouche, little Miss Innocence, is perfectly able to do a volte face without anyone thinking anything but the very sweetest thoughts about her. Only her husband and her music master know the truth.

Hervé's light comic score provided Judic with her obligatory encorable chanson—this time the Légende de la grosse caisse, a thumpingly comical piece of tuneful foolery performed in her military disguise—and with a comical singing-lesson scene in which she and her music master sneak off into a duo from his opérette only to be recalled quickly to a ''Gloria'' when the Mother Superior heaves to. When the fire-breathing Major (Christian) with whom Nitouche has tangled both at the theatre and at the barracks turns up at the convent and accuses her of being one of his soldiers, she sweetly sings to him ''Que je n'ai rien de masculin.'' Her soldier had a musical moment romancing over ''Un mariage de raison,'' and there was a stand-up comedy scene and a number for a gormless soldier called Loriot (Léonce) at the opening of the third act (''Je suis de Saint-Étienne, Loire'') but, if there was comedy for everyone, the music was mainly for Judic in a piece which was a genuine musical comedy in the straightforward meaning of the two words.

Mam'zelle Nitouche was an instant hit. It played through the whole spring and returned immediately after the summer recess, with the star now equipped with a new Hervé song, ''La Cuirasse,'' to add to her already bulging role. It ran on to its 212th performance before Judic set off on her international travels, and the theatre hastened to mount a non-Judic piece that Bertrand didn't want to lose from his repertoire. When her next year's piece, *La Cosaque,* proved shorter-lived than hoped, *Mam'zelle Nitouche* was promptly brought back, but after 19 performances Judic's husband died, and the run had to be ended. In the years that followed, Judic played *Mam'zelle Nitouche* all around the world, but Paris was given the most opportunities to see her portrayal of the archetypical Miss Innocence, for she reprised the role there in 1885, in 1888 and again as late as 1894. Mathilde Auguez (1892), Jeanne Pierny (Folies-Dramatiques, 1897 w Jean Périer, Baron), Juliette Simon-Girard (1901), Angèle Gril (1913–14), Mary Malbos (1921, 1923), Andrée Alvar (1924), Germaine Roger (1945, 1960) and Madeleine Vernon (1954) have been amongst those who have followed, and if some of these ladies were, like Judic, just a decade or two too old to play a perky schoolgirl, such an accusation cannot be made about Paris's 1984 Nitouche, Fabienne Guyon, who starred opposite Jean-Marie Proslier at the Bouffes-Parisiens in the most recent Paris production.

Both in America and in Britain, the piece was first seen in English. The American actress Lotta, a specialist in little-girl roles though by then 37, latched on to *Nitouche* as a vehicle for herself and she starred as Denise in a Harry Jackson version which allowed her to appear for part of the evening as Kin Yai Me, a Japanese Princess, with Frank Wyatt (also co-producer) and Frederic Darrell supporting her in London, and alongside C H Bradshaw and Darrell in New York. London gave her seven weeks, but Broadway sent her on her way in three. Both cities later had a chance to see the genuine article when Judic played her repertoire at the Gaiety Theatre, London (a matter of weeks after Lotta had closed) and at Wallack's Theater in New York. Undismayed, Lydia Thompson gave her Denise at the Crystal Palace (7 October ad Harry Jackson) just weeks later. London saw the show again in English in 1893 when another American actress, May Yohé, gave her version of *Nitouche* at the Trafalgar Square Theatre (6 May) for some of the run of 104 performances (she was off more than she was on), and at the Court Theatre in 1896 (1 June) in a new and ''improved'' version boasting two extra numbers by Carl Kiefert and one by Ivan Caryll. Polyglot New York had a second, post-touring season of Lotta, as well as a piece called

Papa's Wife in which Anna Held used bits of both *Nitouche* and *La Femme à papa* to make up one show and, in 1906, a German version played at the Irving Place Theater with Lina Abarbanell and Edmund Loewe starred.

That German-language version had been very slow to get going. Although Vienna, Berlin, Hamburg and other centers had welcomed Judic's French seasons, it was apparently not until 1890, when the Hungarian star Ilka Pálmay came to the Theater an der Wien, that Richard Genée's German adaptation of the show was first mounted. Pálmay was paired with Girardi as a perfect Célestin, Josef Joseffy was Fernand, Carl Lindau played Loriot and Sebastian Stelzer the roaring major. Over the next 12 years the piece resurfaced every year for further performances in the repertoire. Therese Biedermann and Annie Dirkens took turns at the star role, Juliette Méaly visited from France with her version, and Lina Abarbanell and Edmund Loewe gave theirs before the piece was finally taken from the repertoire after 122 performances. In the meanwhile it had also been played at the Theater in der Josefstadt—in Czech (1893). In 1910 Girardi took up his role again, paired with Gerda Walde and then Julie Kopácsi-Karczag, at the Raimundtheater, whilst in 1914 Mimi Marlow and Fritz Werner played the piece at the Johann Strauss-Theater where it was repeated by Ernst Tautenhayn and Luise Kartousch in 1926 (18 February).

In Germany, too, the Genée version was popular, and, following its introduction, *Mam'zelle Nitouche* won regular revivals up until 1931 before the piece underwent several of the modern reorganizations dear to that country. One of these was played in 1954 at Berlin's Theater im Kurfürstendamm (ad Alexander Steinbrecher, Hans Weigel 25 February).

Pálmay, who introduced *Nitouche* to Vienna, also introduced her to Budapest, at the Népszínház (ad Lajos Evva, Viktor Rákosi) with Béla Pusztai (Célestin) and Imre Szirmai (Fernand) in the other lead roles. As elsewhere, the show was regularly seen thereafter, reaching its 100th performance in 1901, being revived at the Népopera in 1915 (28 February) and at the Városi Színház with Irén Biller in 1927 (6 January), at the Fővárosi Operettszínház in 1928 and again in a new adaptation in 1959, at the Magyar Színház in 1930 and at the Vígszínház in 1946, as it confirmed itself as a permanent part of the opérette repertoire. It was most recently seen at Budapest's Ódry Színpad in 1996 (18 October) with Zsolt Homonnay and Claudia Lugossy playing a later version by István Zágon.

Australia was particularly slow to pick up on *Mam'zelle Nitouche,* but the piece duly arrived there in 1894, mounted at the Sydney Lyceum with Nellie Stewart as Nitouche, George Lauri as Célestin and Wallace Brownlow as Champlâtreux. The role which had been good enough for Judic was apparently not, however, good enough for Miss Stewart: it seems that she ousted La Légende de la grosse caisse, wrote herself a Drum Song, had it set by musical director, Léon Caron, and a local journal staunchly reported that it was ''the biggest hit'' of the show. Miss Stewart gave her *Nitouche* in Sydney and in Melbourne (Princess Theatre 10 November 1894) without it becoming a lasting feature of the Australian repertoire.

Mam'zelle Nitouche remains a feature of the European repertoire to the present day although, like virtually all other such comedy-based pieces, it has faded from the spectacle-orientated English-language stage.

The show has also been twice filmed in France, initially in 1931 with Janie Marèse as Nitouche and Raimu in the role of Célestin, and on the second occasion with Pier Angeli in the title role and Fernandel starred as the music master. A German version of the first film, with Anny Ondra and Oskar Karlweis featured, was made simultaneously.

UK: Opera Comique 12 May 1884, Gaiety Theatre (Fr) 13 June 1884; USA: Daly's Theater (Eng) 15 September 1884, Wallack's Theater (Fr) 1 October 1885; Hungary: Népszínház *Nebantsvirág* 14 October 1887; Austria: Theater an der Wien 19 April 1890; Australia: Lyceum, Sydney 11 August 1894

Films: Paramount (Fr & Ger) 1931, 1953

Recordings: complete (Decca), selections (EMI, Decca)

MAM'ZELLE QUAT' SOUS Opérette in 4 acts by Antony Mars and Maurice Desvallières. Music by Robert Planquette. Théâtre de la Gaîté, Paris, 5 November 1897.

A period piece, set in the markets of Paris at the turn of the 19th century (1804), *Mam'zelle Quat' Sous* told of the fortunes and misfortunes of a little fishmonger, Michel Borniche (Paul Fugère), in a tale which had considerable airs of Alfred Duru's *Les Deux Noces de M Boisjoli.* Borniche is engaged to the market-girl Marion (Mlle Cocyte), but they have sworn not to wed until they have a 10,000-franc nest egg. Marion zealously puts aside every sou that they can earn—thus earning herself the nickname of ''Quat' sous''—but while she is doing so the local Don Juan, baker Anatole (Lucien Noël), is getting Borniche into trouble. Anatole chaffs Borniche over his faithful virginity, and the fishmonger gets his revenge by taking the baker's place at one of his spare blindish dates and making love to the pretty coal-merchant's niece Thérèsette Rascalou (Mariette Sully). Alas, he gets caught by the girl's uncle and condemned to marriage. The marriage is scheduled for the same day as his wedding with Marion (for she has saved up her sous at last) and, indeed, at adjoining restaurants. The double engagement inevitably comes to light, and the doubly dumped and downcast Borniche goes off to join the army. In the last act he comes back covered in glory, accompanied by the entire old guard, to reclaim his Marion. Thérèsette pairs off with Anatole, whilst pastrycook Isidore (Émile Soums) and little Denise (Mlle Deberio) make up the third pair.

Planquette's winning music included a jolly "Cris de Paris" for Fugère and a number in praise of "Les Fillettes de chez nous," whilst the military element of the tale once more gave the composer the opportunity to dip his pen into the martial strains which had found him fame with "La Sambre et Meuse" and which he had utilized repeatedly on the opérettic stage in such military pieces as *Les Voltigeurs de la 32ème, La Cantinière* and *Capitaine Thérèse.* The military scenes also supplied the opportunity for a display of marching, a parade of veterans and other such spectacular accoutrements, well suited to the large stage of the Théâtre de la Gaîté.

Mam'zelle Quat' Sous had a fine run at the Gaîté, and, although it proved not to be of the stuff revivals are made of, it nevertheless got itself seen throughout central Europe.

Budapest's Magyar Színház mounted its version (ad Emil Makai, Ferenc Rajna) the next year, and Munich got the first German version in 1901 before the show moved on to be seen in Austria. It was mounted at the Theater an der Wien (ad A M Willner, Robert Pohl) with Girardi starred in Fugère's role of Borniche and Betti Seidl (Thérèsette), Dora Keplinger (Marion) and Oskar Sachs (Rascalou) supporting, but the production had been hurried unwillingly on to meet contractual dates when the theatre held a big new hit with *Bruder Straubinger* in its repertoire and Planquette's piece was simply shoved in to play from 25 May till 5 June, leaving time for one last *Straubinger* before the season ended. It was played a handful more times in the autumn, but *Bruder Straubinger* dominated the bills, and after 17 performances *Die beiden Don Juans* was dropped.

An American version, announced by A H Woods under the title of *My Fiancée* in 1902 with Paula Edwardes slated to star, was canceled in rehearsals when the producer got what he said was ptomaine poising but sounds more like cold feet and/or his habitual financial problems.

Hungary: Magyar Színház *A garasos kisasszony* 12 November 1898; Germany: Theater am Gärtnerplatz, Munich *Die Sparmamsell* 10 October 1901, Theater des Westens 27 February 1903; Austria: Theater an der Wien *Die beiden Don Juans* 23 May 1903

MANDEL, Frank (b San Francisco, 31 May 1884; d Hollywood, Calif, 20 April 1958). Broadway producer and writer who was behind some of the most successful musicals of the 1920s American stage.

Mandel attended the University of California and Hastings Law School before going east and finding his first employment as a journalist whilst he endeavored to establish himself as a playwright. He made his first mark in the theatre when he collaborated with Helen Craft on an adaptation of Ludwig Fulda's play *Jugendfreude* under the title *Our Wives* (1912), and he made his debut in the musical theatre as the librettist for John Cort's Chicago production of *Miss Princess* (1912), a piece set to songs by the indefatigable and rarely successful Alexander and Will Johnstone.

Mandel followed up with several more plays, but, although Victor Herbert and Henry Blossom turned his *Our Wives* into *The Only Girl* in 1914 with some success, he did not venture back into the musical world for another seven years. When he did, he then simply deluged the musical stage with texts. After a good beginning with a slightly musical play called *My Lady Friends,* which put up a fine 228 performances at the Globe Theater with Clifton Crawford (who supplied his own song) in its star role, Broadway saw no fewer than four musicals to which Mandel had contributed within nine months. The first, *Look Who's Here,* written with Edward Paulton and composer Silvio Hein for Spiegels Productions, visited the metropolis only briefly prior to going on the road where its stars, Cecil Lean and Cleo Mayfield, had a faithful public, but the second and third, both produced by Arthur Hammerstein, teamed Mandel with a pair of writing partners in Otto Harbach and Oscar Hammerstein II who were of a different class to the hacking Paulton. *Tickle Me* (it was not an invitation, but the name of a ship) was a piece of filmland foolery evolved as a vehicle for vaudeville favorite Frank Tinney, which its star's antics helped hold up for 207 performances, whilst *Jimmie,* which leaned on the very old plot of putting a ringer in for a lost heiress, did rather less well (71 performances).

In between, however, Harbach and Mandel had found a genuine hit, one which would outdo even *My Lady Friends,* in a venture with producer George M Cohan. Their piece, which had started out on the road as *The House That Jack Built* even before *Tickle Me* had begun, cleaned up on the road, and by the time it came to town as *Mary,* their pretty if barely original little tale of a poor girl who weds a rich boy after two acts of minor difficulties was, no small thanks to the fact that the writers had allied themselves with a first-class composer in Louis Hirsch, already a sure-fire hit.

A second innocently Cinderellary show with the same team, *The O'Brien Girl,* also did well at home (164 performances) and in export; a vehicle for Nora Bayes as *Queen of Hearts* rather less (39 performances); but a piece called *Paradise Alley* which had had Mandel's name on the credits in Rhode Island, Boston and Philadelphia in 1922, no longer did so by the time the show reached Broadway in 1924. By that time, however, Mandel was pretty much in Paradise Alley himself, for he had well and truly hit pay dirt in the form of one of those outsized hits that come along in only a few folk's lifetimes. Harry Frazee, who had co-produced his play *My Lady Friends,* brought Mandel in to work on a musical version of that piece, and the resultant *No, No, Nanette* became the musical-comedy hit of its era.

Before *No, No, Nanette* reached Broadway, however, Mandel had teamed up with a new writing partner. Lawrence Schwab, looking for a collaborator to work with on his new show, asked publishers Harms for a suggestion. They put forward Mandel and the two writers got together for the first time on the smart-talking modern text for the George Gershwin musical *Sweet Little Devil.* After that show's 120-performance Broadway run, the pair formed a producing partnership which they launched in 1925 with a play, *The Firebrand,* and with their own musical version of Clyde Fitch's play *Captain Jinks of the Horse Marines. Captain Jinks* was a big hit in Philadelphia, but Lewis Gensler and Stephen Jones's score didn't throw up any popular songs and the 167 performances the show eventually played on Broadway did not quite come up to the great hopes that had been aroused on the road.

Mandel and Schwab were on the right tracks, however, and they hit the bull's-eye with their next production. The romantic musical play *Lady Fair* didn't cause the stir pre-Broadway that *Captain Jinks* had done, but when it reached town, now retitled *The Desert Song,* it proved another *Nanette*-sized hit for Mandel, this time as both author and producer. The team followed their biggest hit with the production of another memorable musical, *The New Moon,* in which Mandel had again some kind of hand in the writing (though quite what and how much is not sure), but the pair, now under full steam as producers, also mounted in this period several shows in which neither Mandel nor Schwab were involved authorially.

The first two were from the De Sylva, Brown and Henderson team, and both were hits: the favorite college musical of the day, *Good News,* and the golfing piece *Follow Thru.* The next was Rodgers and Hart's filmland piece *America's Sweetheart,* which did well enough, but the up-to-now apparently charmed partners hit their first dud when they mounted a small-scale Richard Whiting musical, written to a text by Schwab and Hammerstein and entitled *Free for All.* After the opening on Broadway Mandel and Schwab offered to sell out the show to the cast for the weekly break-even figure of $5,100, but the cast declined and *Free for All* closed at the end of the week. Returning to the area of romantic operetta, Mandel co-wrote and co-produced *Always Young* ("it looks like Schwab and Mandel have a worthy successor to *The New Moon*"), which became *East Wind* and flopped in 23 performances in New York.

Following this pair of failures Schwab and Mandel dissolved their association, and Mandel ventured only once more on to the Broadway musical stage, in 1935, when he adapted *The Happy Alienist,* a ludicrously old-fashioned romantic novel tricked out with a fashionable tinge of psychoanalysis, to Romberg's music as *May Wine.* The piece ran for a respectable 213 performances, but it was not in any way comparable with *The Desert Song* and *The New Moon.* Mandel subsequently spent some time in 1937–38 as a film director with Warner Brothers, but he finally withdrew from the arena of show business in 1942 and went into retirement.

1912 **Miss Princess** (Alexander Johnstone/Will B Johnstone) Garrick Theater, Chicago 11 November; Park Theater 23 December

1920 **Look Who's Here** (Silvio Hein/Edward Paulton) 44th Street Theater 2 March

1920 **Mary** (Louis Hirsch/w Harbach) National Theater, Washington, DC March; Knickerbocker Theater 18 October

1920 **Tickle Me** (Herbert Stothart/w Otto Harbach, Oscar Hammerstein II) Selwyn Theater 17 August

1920 **Jimmie** (Stothart/w Harbach, Hammerstein) Apollo Theater 17 November

1921 **The O'Brien Girl** (Hirsch/w Harbach) Liberty Theater 3 October

1922 **Paradise Alley** (Harry Archer/Howard Johnson/Carle Carlton, Hale Francisco) Providence, RI 18 September

1922 **Queen of Hearts** (Lewis E Gensler, Dudley Wilkinson/w Oscar Hammerstein II) Cohan Theater 10 October

1923 **No, No, Nanette** (Vincent Youmans/Harbach, Irving Caesar/w Harbach) Garrick Theater, Detroit 23 April; Globe Theatre, New York 16 September 1925

1924 **Sweet Little Devil** (George Gershwin/w Lawrence Schwab) Astor Theater 21 January

1925 **Captain Jinks** (Gensler, Stephen Jones/B G De Sylva/w Schwab) Martin Beck Theater 8 September

1926 **The Desert Song** (Sigmund Romberg/w Hammerstein, Harbach) Casino Theater 30 November

1927 **The New Moon** (Romberg/Hammerstein/w Hammerstein, Schwab) Chestnut Street Opera House, Philadelphia 22 December 1927; Imperial Theater, New York (revised version) 19 September 1928

1931 **East Wind** (Romberg/w Hammerstein) Manhattan Theater 27 October

1935 **May Wine** (Romberg/Hammerstein) St James Theater 5 December

MANHATTAN MARY Musical comedy in 2 acts by William K Wells and George White. Music and lyrics by B G De Sylva, Lew Brown and Ray Henderson. Apollo Theater, New York, 26 September 1927.

When the mum (Dorothy Walters) of Manhattan Mary loses all her money, the show's comic helps the girl to get a job in the *George White Scandals* and set things aright. If this was a fate just a little different from that of the vast number of other contemporary musical-comedy heroines, who almost invariably ended up as the star of the *Ziegfeld Follies,* this was because *Manhattan Mary* was produced by George White, on the very stage which housed the *Scandals.* Manhattan Mary was Ona Munson, the comic in question was Ed Wynn and George White's contribution to the production included appearing in the show as himself. This was not as unlikely as it might have been in the case of some producers, as White had been a top-class international tap-dancing performer before becoming a producer, and in the final act he showed that his talents were still intact. The McCarthy Sisters, who simply appeared, tacked in, as the McCarthy Sisters, also got into the musical action.

De Sylva, Brown and Henderson, whose *Good News* had opened with great success just three weeks earlier, supplied "My Bluebird's Home Again," "Just a Cozy Hide-Away," "Broadway," "Manhattan Mary," "I'd Like You to Love Me" and "It Won't Be Long Now" without turning out anything to challenge the other show's "Varsity Drag" or "The Best Things in Life Are Free," but it didn't really matter. The priorities of *Manhattan Mary* were evident in the billing it proposed to the public: George White (70 percent) presents Ed Wynn (200 percent) in *Manhattan Mary* (100 percent). There were also 100 George White Beauties, the George White Ballet, 24 Hudson Dusters, 17 scenes and curtains and costumes by Max Weldy from designs by Erté.

Wynn lisped his way endearingly through his role without too much apparent regard for what was going on around him, and did it for 264 revusical performances.

MANINA Operette in 3 acts by Alexander Lix. Lyrics by Hans Adler. Music by Nico Dostal. Admiralspalast, Berlin, 28 November 1942.

Produced by Heinz Hentschke in wartime Berlin, *Manina* profited from a good-old-days libretto treating of turn-of-the-century Ruritanian royal romance and from a lavish physical production to run for a full season at Berlin's Admiralspalast. Lix's book centered on the lives of King Jalomir of Catatea (who is never seen) and Hella von Lichtenau (Carla Spletter), who are condemned to be royally wed. He carries on with a cabaret singer (Elvira Erdmann) and she ends up in bed with the poet Mario Zantis (Julius Katona), who the next day writes a satirical poem about the king and gets himself arrested and banished. Hella eventually becomes Queen when Jalomir abdicates, but she has to abdicate herself before she can, at last, officially have her Mario. The Manina of the title was another who never appeared: she was the ideal heroine of Mario's epic work.

Dostal's rather oddly colored score aspired towards the big-sing Operette in the music for its principal lovers, notably in their ever-rising duet "Niemand weiss, warum auf einmal süss und heiss," although, in contrast, Mario explained "Ich such' in jeder Frau Manina" ("I look for Manina in every woman") to a tango rhythm, and the sounds of filmland crept in frequently. A pair of soubrets, Hella's cousin Carla (Herta Mayen) and good friend Ronni (Karl Heigl), and a duo of comical elders (former prima donna Cordy Millowitsch and Kurt Seifert) provided the lighter moments in a 1940s version of traditional style.

Manina was staged in Vienna after the War, with Steffi Schafel and Rudolf Reimer in the romantic roles and Fritz Imhoff as the comical Obersthofmarschall, through a run of five months, and it was subsequently seen in Norway, Switzerland and, in a French translation (ad René Rongé, Freddy Dedain, Marcel Désiron), in Belgium (Liège 7 December 1957).

Austria: Raimundtheater 8 September 1947

Recording: selection (part-set) (Eurodisc)

MANKOWITZ, [Cyril] Wolf (b Bethnal Green, London, 7 November 1924; d County Cork, 20 May 1998). Librettist to the best of the British theatre's attempts at a "Soho" musical in the 1950s.

The author of such East End of London novels as *Make Me an Offer* and *A Kid for Two Farthings,* Mankowitz had a first stage and film success with the play *The Bespoke Overcoat* (1953) and entered the musical theatre five years later when he expanded a newspaper novella he had written, a piece transparently based on the career of popular cockney singer Tommy Steele, into a musical play under the title *Expresso Bongo. Expresso Bongo* and its successor, *Make Me an Offer* (based on Mankowitz's earlier book), both produced by Oscar Lewenstein, led the field in the trend towards the Soho, low-life musicals of the London 1950s, but they had about them a quality and a gritty taste of unpretentious realism which those that tried to follow them—including a piece on which Mankowitz later joined Lewenstein as co-producer, *The Lily White Boys* (1960)—almost inevitably failed to repeat.

Belle, an attempt to adapt the tale of the murderer Crippen into a musical told in music-hall terms, did not catch on, and Mankowitz then abandoned the toughly realistic style of his earliest pieces to mold a jolly musical entertainment out of Dickens's *The Pickwick Papers* as a vehicle for tenor comedian Harry Secombe. *Pickwick* had a fine London career and something of an afterlife. Mankowitz moved further away from the adult world of his earliest works in the 1960s with his last contributions to the musical theatre, two pieces produced to diminishing success: an adaptation of the successful teeny-fumbling novel *Passion Flower Hotel,* followed by an advertisedly "bawdy" retelling of the Jack Sheppard tale, *Stand and Deliver.*

Elsewhere, he has written novels, works on the Yiddish cinema and on porcelain, and screenplays (*The Millionairess, The Long, the Short and the Tall, Casino Royale,* etc).

1958 **Expresso Bongo** (David Heneker, Monty Norman/ Heneker, Norman, Julian More/w More) Saville Theatre 23 April

1959 **Make Me an Offer** (Heneker, Norman) New Theatre 16 December

1961 **Belle, or The Ballad of Doctor Crippen** (Norman/ Beverley Cross ad) Strand Theatre 4 May

1963 **Pickwick** (Cyril Ornadel/Leslie Bricusse) Saville Theatre 4 July

1965 **Passion Flower Hotel** (John Barry/Trevor Peacock) Prince of Wales Theatre 24 August

1972 **Stand and Deliver** (Norman) Royal Lyceum, Edinburgh 20 September; Roundhouse 24 October

MANN, Terrence V (b Clearwater, Fla, 1 July 1951).

Prominent leading man of the fin de millennium Broadway stage.

Terrence Mann made his first Broadway appearance as the white-faced clown in the original cast of *Barnum* (1980), and subsequently succeeded to the role of the unicycle-riding Ringmaster. He went on to be the first American Rum Tum Tugger in *Cats* (1982) and the first American Javert in *Les Misérables* (1987), in between times featuring as Saul in the short-lived *Rags* (1986). He later succeeded to the central role of *Jerome Robbins' Broadway* and appeared off-Broadway in *Assassins* (1991, Leon Czolgosz) before creating the part of the Beast in the stage version of Disney's *Beauty and the Beast* (1994). He has since been seen on Broadway as Scrooge in the large festive-season *A Christmas Carol* (1995), another musical version of which he himself penned for the North Carolina Theater, Raleigh, and in *The Scarlet Pimpernel* (1997, Chauvelin).

He appeared as Larry in the filmed *A Chorus Line* and in the television musical *Mrs Santa Claus* (1996).

Mann is the husband of dancer Charlotte d'Amboise (*Song and Dance,* Roxie Hart in *Chicago,* etc).

1999 **Romeo and Juliet** (w Jerome Korman) Ordway Music Theater, St Paul, Minn 18 August

MANNEQUINS Féerie-opérette in 3 acts by Jacques Bousquet and Henri Falk. Music by Joseph Szulc. Théâtre des Capucines, Paris, 30 October 1925.

A happily sort-of-satirical small-scale piece, with a cast of 15, no chorus and accompanied just by composer Joseph Szulc at the piano, *Mannequins* was a shoestring hit at the little Théâtre des Capucines in 1925.

Shopboy Alfred (Louvigny) is more at home mooning over the pretty dummies in the shop's windows than in chatting up the real, live flowergirl Micheline (Edmée Favart). Then, one night, the mannequins all come to life. Alfred finds his attempts to win the glamorous Fleur de Pêcher (also Edmée Favart) impeded by the elegant Vicomte (Hiéronimus) and Marquis (Jean Périer) who are, each in turn, placed next to the lady mannequin as the chief window-dresser rearranges his display, and his hopes are finally ended by the arrival of a new dummy: the American millionaire. When Alfred wakes up, he realizes that Micheline is better value than a doll.

Christiane Dor as Rose, the Marquis's mannequin-maid turned poule de luxe, scored the song success of the evening with the saucy "Si ça n'est qu' ça" in a score which, although it was of the lightest kind was, nevertheless, not undemanding. A second-act finale with the whole cast running together up the stave in parallel semiquavers (admittedly to an ah-ah lyric but with no conductor!) was a more substantial piece of writing, for all its piano-only accompaniment, than much contemporary musical-comedy music.

The show was toured in France, produced at Budapest's Magyar Színház (ad Zsolt Harsányi, István Zágon), announced for London by C B Cochran, in an adaptation by Eddie Knoblock, and purchased by E Ray Goetz for America. It was apparently, however, not produced in either English-language case. In 1948 a German-language piece (ad H Adler) advertisedly taken from a work by Bousquet, Falk and Szulc turned up at Vienna's Theater in der Josefstadt under the title *Es schlägt 12, Herr Doktor* where it ran for a splendid 56 consecutive nights. Since the trio wrote nothing else together, and the stroke of midnight is definitely relevant, this would seem to have been a version of *Mannequins.*

Hungary: Magyar Színház *Párizsi kirakat* 9 April 1926; Austria: Theater in der Josefstadt *Es schlägt 12, Herr Doktor* 15 November 1948

DER MANN MIT DEN DREI FRAUEN Operette in 3 acts by Julius Bauer based on *Trois femmes pour un mari* by Ernest Grenet Dancourt. Music by Franz Lehár. Theater an der Wien, Vienna, 21 January 1908.

Lehár's first new full-scale Operette following the triumph of *Die lustige Witwe* moved far away from both the subject matter and the style of his big hit. Set, like the earlier piece, in the present time, and taken, like its predecessor, from a French play source (Théâtre Cluny 11 January 1884), it remained far from the ambassadorial circles of Paris in its modern-days tale of a Viennese rep for an international travel company. Hans Zipler (Rudolf Christians), in spite of having a happy home life with his wife (Mizzi Günther), acquires additional ladies in the branch-office cities of London (Mizzi Gribl) and Paris (Luise Kartousch). And it goes on from there. Generally reckoned a disappointment, the show lasted only 82 performances at the Theater an der Wien, and rendered up no reusable parts to a composer who very often recycled his ''lost'' music. It was still, however, picked up by overseas managements anxious for the latest Lehár show. In Budapest (ad Adolf Mérei) it was played a respectable 35 times. On Broadway (ad Paul Potter, Harold Atteridge, Agnes Bangs Morgan), where its score was dotted with a handful of interpolations including a ditty called ''Rosie'' composed by *Chu Chin Chow*'s composer Frederic Norton, the Shuberts' production starred Cecil Lean (Hans) with Alice Yorke (Lori), Cleo Mayfield (Alice), Charlotte Greenwood (Sidonie) and Dolly Castles (Olivia) as the ladies and lasted 52 performances.

The show did not quite manage the full circle back to its ''roots'' in Paris, but a French version was made by Maurice Ordonneau, and it saw the light of day at Brussels's Théâtre Molière under the title *Les Trois Amoureuses* in 1911 (15 December).

The American adaptation of Grenet-Dancourt's highly successful original play (ad J Milliken, *Three Wives for One Husband*) was put on the post-Broadway road (Opera House, New Haven 18 December 1884) with the subtitle *Nice and Warm* and songs added to the proceedings. J B Polk was the ''mari,'' Julia Polk, Genevieve Mann and Elsie Jerome the ''femmes.''

Germany: Neues Operettenhaus 18 March 1908; Hungary: Népszínház-Vígopera *Három feleség* 31 March 1908; USA: Weber and Fields Theater *The Man with Three Wives* 23 January 1913

MANNSCHAFT AN BORD Komische Oper in 1 act by J L Harisch. Music by Giovanni von Zaytz (''mit freier Benützung der Englisch bootman songs''). Carltheater, Vienna, 15 December 1863.

Zaytz was, along with C F Conradin, Johann Baptist Klerr and Franz von Suppé, amongst the first composers of the German-language stage to follow the Offenbach-inspired fashion for short Operetten, and his little *Mannschaft an Bord* (''crew on board'') followed and joined Suppé's *Das Pensionat, Zehn Mädchen und kein Mann* and *Flotte Bursche* and Conradin's *Flodoardo Wuprahall* as one of the early Viennese successes in the genre. The little semi-nautical tale was set in a French harbor where an English frigate has taken refuge. During the ship's stay, the old local cargo-man Piffard (Karl Treumann) helps one of the sailors, Max (Anna Grobecker), to win his steersman's ticket and, thus, the consent of the schoolmaster, Profond (Grois), for the boy to wed his daughter, Emma (Frln Fischer). Wilhelm Knaack featured as the dentist Svermazet and Fr Raab was Frau Bibiana Piffard alongside a half-dozen shapely-legged chorus ''sailors.'' The text was accompanied by a brightly catchy score, an effective part of which was made up of arrangements of English sea shanties (endearingly billed as ''Bootmansongs'').

After its original, successful production, *Mannschaft an Bord* remained some years in the Carltheater repertoire (50th performance, 16 February 1867), was picked up by the ''Zur neue Welt'' at Hietzing and other minor theatres, and returned to the Carltheater in 1873 (10 June) with Treumann (Piffard), Karl Blasel (Jean), Therese Schäfer (Bibiana) and Antonie Link (Max) in the cast to play 25 times over the next four seasons. It was played at Ronacher in 1883, at the Jantschtheater in 1902, at Budapest's Royal Orfeum in 1903 (*Legényseg a födelzeten*) and at the Johann Strauss-Theater in 1915, surviving, thus, more strongly than any but Suppé's most popular pieces as a representative of its period.

USA: Germania Theater 30 November 1873; Hungary: Budai Színkör (Ger) 27 April 1867, Budai Színkör *Matrózok a fedélzeten* (*Matrózok a kikotoban*) 17 May 1867

MANNSTÄDT, Wilhelm (b Bielefeld, 29 May 1837; d Steglitz, 13 September 1904).

A polytalented artist—painter, composer, poet, actor and theatrical conductor, notably at Berlin's Woltersdorff Theater—Mannstädt's most significant contribution to his country's culture was as an author for the musical-comedy stage. He actually made his debut in the musical theatre as a composer, supplying the songs for other folk's and then for his own pieces, but he soon found his niche as a librettist and over nearly 30 years' activity in the German theatre he wrote or co-wrote the texts of some 60 theatrical works of all kinds, the most and the best being a long series of Possen for the Berlin and Vienna stages. Amongst these, the Centraltheater Posse *Eine tolle Nacht*—the inspiration for George Edwardes's Gaiety musical *The Circus Girl*—was the most generally successful. Of the handful of Operetten to which he subscribed Czibulka's *Der Glücksritter,* played in Austria, Germany and in America (*The May Queen*), was the most widely seen.

1868 **Ein moderner Hexenmeister** (Fritz Mai) 1 act Theater in der Josefstadt, Vienna 6 September

1870 **Chor de mille fleurs** (Rudolf Hahn) 1 act Woltersdorff Theater

1875 **Luftschlösser** (Adolf Mohr/w A Weller) Woltersdorff Theater; Theater an der Wien, Vienna 11 July 1876 w music by Richard Genée

1875 **Eine resolute Frau** (Mohr/w Weller) Woltersdorff Theater

1876 **In harter Lehre** (Schramm, Michaelis/w Weller)

1877 **Die Tochter des Hollenfürsten** (w Henrik Delin/w Weller) Theater in der Josefstadt, Vienna 24 November

1878 **Schusserl, der Heiratsvermittler** (aka *Das Kind der Natur*) (w Delin/w Eduard Dorn) Theater in der Josefstadt, Vienna 2 March

1879 **Wildröschen** (Johann Brandl/w Weller) Carltheater, Vienna 4 July

1880 **Im Strudel** (Gustave Steffens/w Heinrich Sealsieb)

1881 **Unser Otto** (Steffens) Thalia-Theater

1882 **Eine neue Welt** (Steffens) Friedrich-Wilhelmstädtisches Theater

1882 **Der tolle Wenzel** (Steffens) Friedrich-Wilhelmstädtisches Theater

1883 **Die schöne Ungarin** (Steffens) Friedrich-Wilhelmstädtisches Theater

1883 **Ein Naturkind** (Karl Kleiber/w C B) Fürsttheater, Vienna 15 September

1884 **Die Millionenbraut von Sarajewo** (Kleiber/w Weller ad Bruno Zappert) Fürsttheater, Vienna 21 May

1885 **Die beiden Wenzel** (Paul Mestrozzi/w Carl Lindau) Theater in der Josefstadt, Vienna 26 September

1885 **Der Walzerkönig** (Brandl/w Karl Costa, Bruno Zappert) Carltheater, Vienna 9 October

1886 **Humbug, der Geist des Schwindels** (Kleiber/w Lindau) Theater in der Josefstadt, Vienna 11 September

1886 **Der Stabstrompeter** (Steffens/w Weller) Centraltheater; Theater in der Josefstadt, Vienna 2 October

1887 **Höhere Töchter** (Steffens/w R Schott) Centraltheater 3 September

1887 **Rikiki** (Josef Hellmesberger/w Genée) Carltheater, Vienna 28 September

1887 **Peter Zapfel** (Kleiber/ad Lindau, Antony) Theater in der Josefstadt, Vienna 17 December

1887 **Das Glücksritter** (Alfons Czibulka/w Genée, Zappert) Carltheater, Vienna 22 December

1887 **Der Spottvogel** (Steffens) Centraltheater

1887 **Der Waldteufel** (Steffens) Centraltheater

1887 **Die wilde Katze** (Steffens/w Weller) Centraltheater

1888 **Der Grasteufel** (Kleiber/w Lindau) Theater in der Josefstadt, Vienna 3 April

1891 **Der Tanzteufel** (Steffens/w Eduard Jacobson) Adolf-Ernst Theater 25 December

1892 **Berliner Pflaster** (Ludwig Gothov-Grüneke) Alexanderplatz Theater January

1892 **Modernes Babylon** (Steffens/G Görss/w E Jacobson) Adolf-Ernst Theater 25 December

1893 **Monsieur Hannibal** (Alfons Czibulka/w Karl Dreher) Theater im Gärtnerplatz, Munich 5 September

1893 **Goldlotte** (Steffens/w E Jacobson) Adolf-Ernst Theater 4 April 1894 **Die ewige Braut** (Steffens, Roth/w Kren) 1 act Adolf-Ernst Theater 4 November

1895 **Unsere Rentiers** (Einödshofer/w Julius Freund) Centraltheater 16 February

1895 **Eine tolle Nacht** (Einödshofer/w Freund) Centraltheater 4 September

1895 **Frau Lohengrin** (Steffens/Görss/w E Jacobson) Adolf-Ernst Theater 21 December

1896 **König Chilpérich** (*Chilpéric*) German version w E Jacobson (Carltheater)

1896 **Eine wilde Sache** (Einödshofer/w Julius Freund) Centraltheater 20 September

Plate 240. **Man of La Mancha.** *Joan Diener as Aldonza.*

1897 **Ein fideler Abend** (Einödshofer/w Freund) Centraltheater 7 February

1897 **Berliner Fahrten** (Einödshofer/w Freund) Centraltheater 4 September

1897 **Ein Abenteuer in Harem** (Paul Lincke) 1 act Apollotheater

1897 **Metella** (*Le Capitole*) German version (Alexanderplatz Theater)

1898 **Die Tugendfalle** (Einödshofer/w Freund) Centraltheater 22 January

1898 **Sterzl in Berlin** (Einödshofer/w Freund) Theater an der Wien, Vienna 2 April

1899 **Das Milkmädchen von Schöneberg** Belle-Alliance Theater 19 February

1902 **Der silberne Pantoffel** (*The Silver Slipper*) German version (Neues Königliches Opernhaus)

1906 **So sind sie alle** (w Weller) Luisen-Theater 21 December

MAN OF LA MANCHA Musical play by Dale Wasserman based on his television play *I, Don Quixote* and on Miguel de Cervantes y Saavedra's *Don Quixote.* Lyrics by Joe Darion. Music by Mitch Leigh. Goodspeed Opera House, Connecticut, 28 June 1965; ANTA Washington Square Theater, New York, 22 November 1965.

A version of the Don Quixote tale, developed from a television play by author Wasserman, *Man of La Man-*

cha was laid out in a manner often used by a director of a piece of dubious value to take the curse off his material. It was framed, or made into a play-within-a-play, thus putting the main story of the evening and its characters at one step's remove from any need to run too close to a convincing reality. The technique was one that could prove powerful when used on fine material, as Peter Brook's previous year's production of the *Marat/Sade* had proven, and in the case of *Man of La Mancha,* where the basic subject matter was anything but of dubious value, it worked most effectively once again. Wasserman's dramatically effective reduction of the Quixote story made up into a strongly projected play-within-a-play, equipped with a score which produced one hit song from amongst a set of vigorously written numbers and ensembles.

Cervantes (Richard Kiley) and his servant (Irving Jacobson) act out the story of the Knight of the woeful countenance as a sort of command performance before their fellow prisoners whilst waiting their turn to be called before the Inquisition. Cervantes impersonates the Don and the servant plays his servant Sancho Panza in their depiction of the adventures of the dream-a-day old Knight, living out his fine notions of the age of chivalry whilst struggling to keep clear of the clutches of the members of his greedily expectant family who are anxious to have him declared insane. Quixote and Sancho pass together by the famous encounter with the giant-cum-windmill, and arrive at an inn where Quixote pays homage to the vulgar wench Aldonza (Joan Diener) as his fair lady Dulcinea. His other-worldly idealism earns him only buffetings and robbings, and when Aldonza tries to follows his tenets of charity, chivalry and life led in keeping with a code of generosity, she too is made to suffer. But Quixote is undeterred, until he faces up to the great Enchanter. The Enchanter's weapon against Quixote is a mirror: the old man is forced to look at reality, at himself as he really is, and the great dream is chased away. The Enchanter is, of course, no Enchanter, but his rapacious son-in-law come to take him home. But the hope of a better world is never utterly extinguished. As Quixote lies dying, Sancho and Aldonza, the willing and the unwilling believers, come to him. With them at his side, the old man can go back into his dream for the last minutes of his life. Amongst the supporting cast, Ray Middleton (the original Frank Butler of *Annie Get Your Gun*) appeared as the Innkeeper and Robert Rounseville, the creator of Bernstein's *Candide,* was the family's hypocritical Padre.

Quixote's creed, The Quest, otherwise known as "The Impossible Dream," a crazily philosophizing piece with a strong flavor of 1960s idealism about it, was the song success of the show, but amongst the rest of the score a lusty title song for the Knight, some gently humorous pieces for Sancho ("I Like Him," "A Little Gossip"), Quixote's gentle dream of "Dulcinea" and a particularly accurate, nagging trio for the family, "I'm Only Thinking of Him," all contributed to the success of the show.

Albert Selden and Hal James's production of *Man of La Mancha* was a major hit. In a season which included *Sweet Charity* and *Mame* amongst its products, it virtually swept the board at the year's Tony Awards, taking prizes for best musical, score and libretto, for Albert Marre's direction and for Kiley's thrilling, rich-voiced performance in its title role, as it settled in at the ANTA Washington Square Theater for what would be one of the longest runs in Broadway history. By the time it closed, after 2,328 performances, *Man of La Mancha* had passed all but *Fiddler on the Roof, Hello, Dolly!* and *My Fair Lady* in Broadway longevity, and like those three exceptional pieces it had spread itself triumphantly to all corners of the globe.

The first American touring company, with Broadway takeover José Ferrer starring as Quixote, went out 10 months into the Broadway run, and the first foreign mounting appeared a year later, when an Australian production with Charles West and Sadler's Wells and Covent Garden soprano Suzanne Steele starred was mounted in Melbourne. Four months there were followed by four more in Sydney (Her Majesty's Theatre, February 1968), a tour through New Zealand, two repeat seasons at Melbourne's Comedy Theatre and one at Sydney's Theatre Royal (1 April 1971) as the piece established itself as a great favorite. In London, on the other hand, Donald Albery's reproduction of the Broadway staging failed wholly to catch on. Keith Michell (Quixote), Bernard Spear (Sancho) and Miss Diener headed a cast which included operetta favorites Oliver Gilbert and Alan Crofoot in its supporting ranks, but which could only keep the producer's theatre alight for 253 performances. Albery closed the show, but brought it back for a second attempt in June 1969 with Kiley crossing the Atlantic to repeat his original role. Again, it failed to take, and was shuttered in 118 performances. Michell, like Australia's West, however, went on to succeed to the role of Quixote in the continuing Broadway production.

France, which had not made a major hit of a Broadway musical since *Rose-Marie* and *No, No, Nanette,* gave *L'Homme de La Mancha* one of its more attentive hearings. Part of the reason for this, however, was its casting. The enormously popular Belgian vocalist Jacques Brel both adapted and starred in the Parisian production, with Jean-Claude Calon as Sancho and Miss Diener repeating in French the role she had already played in English in both America and Britain. *L'Homme de La Mancha* had sufficient success to be taken up in the French provinces and, in 1988, Paris saw a revival, brought in from Nantes, with Jean Piat as Quixote and Richard Taxy as Sancho (Théâtre Marigny 15 January).

If the show proved popular in French, it was even more so in its German-language version (ad Robert Gilbert). First produced by Vienna's Theater an der Wien (w Lawrence White, Paul Kijzer), with Josef Meinrad (Quixote), Fritz Muliar/Manfred Lichtenfeld (Sancho) and Blanche Aubry (Aldonza) in the leading roles, it played a fine 143 nights between its original season and a return visit in 1970, before going on to be seen in Hamburg—with Gideon Singer, also the star of the Israeli version and later a Broadway replacement, as Quixote, Peter W Staub (Sancho) and Dagmar Koller (Aldonza)—and then at Berlin's Theater am Kurfürstendamm. Thereafter it was seen throughout German-speaking areas where it is regularly played to the present day, being revived at the Volksoper in 1994 (28 May) with Karlheinz Hackl as Quixote. An Hungarian version (ad Tamás Blum) was taken into the repertoire of Budapest's Fővárosi Operettszínház in 1971, and although it did not find the same popularity there as the oft-repeated *Hegedüs a háztetön* (*Fiddler on the Roof*) or *My Fair Lady,* it nevertheless went on to further productions in Hungary, returning to Budapest's Nemzeti Színház in 1995 (6 October) with Sándor Szakácsi as Quixote, and again to the Ferencvárosi Nyári Játékok in 1998 (2 July).

A film version was produced by United Artists in 1972 with Peter O'Toole (singing dubbed by Simon Gilbert) cast as Don Quixote and James Coco as Sancho. Sophia Loren was a lushly beautiful Aldonza. The film version retained all but a couple of the show's songs but cut much of its other music.

On the stage somewhere at most times since it first appeared in the Connecticut countryside in 1964, with artists such as Howard Keel, Allan Jones and, for two New York reprises (1972, 1977), Kiley himself playing Quixote, *Man of La Mancha* ultimately returned to Broadway in a "25th anniversary" production (Marquis Theater 24 April 1992, 108 performances) which had originally been mounted on the American West Coast. Raul Julia and British pop vocalist Sheena Easton featured in the lead roles.

Australia: Comedy Theatre, Melbourne 30 September 1967; UK: Piccadilly Theatre 24 April 1968; France: Théâtre des Champs-Élysées *L'Homme de La Mancha* 1968; Austria: Theater an der Wien *Der Mann von La Mancha* 4 January 1968; Germany: Operettenhaus, Hamburg 1969, Theater am Kurfürstendamm 1969; Hungary: Fővárosi Operettszínház *La Mancha lovagja* 7 May 1971

Film: United Artists 1972

Recordings: original cast (Kapp/MCA), London cast (MCA), French casts (Barclay, Maison de la Culture de Loire Atlantique), Mexican cast (Decca), Austrian cast (Polydor), Hamburg cast (Polydor), Israeli cast (CBS), Spanish cast (EMI-Odeon), Belgian cast (Forlane), German/Essen cast 1994 (Drama), studio cast w Placido Domingo (Sony), film soundtrack (United Artists), selection (Columbia), etc

MANSELL, Richard [MAITLAND, Robert] (b Athlone, Ireland, c1847; d London, 28 February 1907).

A lively and popular Irishman whose theatrical ventures often ran short of money but rarely of skimpily clad girls, Mansell caused a sensation in the London theatre world when, at 23 years of age, he and his elder brother, **William Lauderdale MANSELL** [William Henry MAITLAND] (b Athlone, Ireland, ?1845; d London 28 July 1893), produced Hervé's *Chilpéric* at London's Lyceum in 1870. Staged under fledgling actor Mansell's own direction, in a version co-written by himself, Frederick Marshall and (mostly) Robert Reece and with the author/composer performing in the title role, this production largely helped set in motion the fashion in Britain for opéra-bouffe and for original music scores for burlesque and musical comedy in general.

Mansell subsequently produced Hervé's *Le Petit Faust,* with slightly less success, and leased the St James's Theatre in the 1872–73 season to produce the first British version of Offenbach's *Le Pont des soupirs.* His management there ended after four months when the money ran out, but he was responsible, with Henry Herman, for running up in two days a libretto for a scandalous version of what claimed to be Offenbach's *Vert-Vert,* played at the same theatre the following year. He tried again with another Hervé piece, *Dagobert,* at the Charing Cross Theatre the following year, but once again failed to repeat the success of *Chilpéric.*

He later returned to the stage as a touring and stock "star," playing in particular Irish roles of the Boucicault kind, and was for varying periods connected with the management of the Alexandra Theatre, Liverpool, and the Queen's, Manchester. He directed and produced melodrama for the provinces, produced a water pantomime on the Continent, and spent several years mounting English productions in Russia. He later sent out a version of *La Fille du tambour-major* updated to the Boer War (1900), and put in brief managerial appearances at the Brixton Theatre and Theatre Royal in Kilburn before settling to employment as house manager at various suburban London theatres, notably the Coronet Theatre, Notting Hill Gate, where he produced a 1903 revival of *Chilpéric* and reprises of those other classics of his heyday, *La Fille de Madame Angot* and *La Fille du tambour-major.* He died at the age of 57, as impecunious as ever.

William Maitland resumed his own name after his youthful venture into the theatre, and he also changed his calling—from the theatrical to that of a Hammersmith florist.

1870 **Chilpéric** English version w Robert Reece, Frederick Marshall (Lyceum Theatre)

1874 **Vert-Vert** English version w Henry Herman (St James's Theatre)

1875 **Dagobert** English version w Frank W Green (Charing Cross Theatre)

1881 **La Belle Normande** (*La Famille Trouillat*) English version w Alfred Maltby (Globe Theatre)

MANSFIELD, Richard (b Berlin, 24 May 1853; d New London, Conn, 30 August 1907). British musical comedian who turned himself into a classical actor on the other side of the water.

The son of the celebrated Russian vocalist Erminia Rudersdorff (b Ivanska, Crimea, ?1822; d Boston, 26 February 1882), but allegedly not of either of her husbands (''a certain professor of music took an almost parental interest in the child . . .''), the young Richard Mansfield was brought up largely in Boston, but made his first theatrical appearance in 1874, deputizing for Corney Grain as the Beadle in a revival of the operetta *Charity Begins at Home* in the German Reed entertainment at London's St George's Hall. He later joined the D'Oyly Carte touring companies and, as principal comedian of the A-company (Sir Joseph Porter, John Wellington Wells), played the role of Major General Stanley in the mocked-up, pre-production copyright performance of *The Pirates of Penzance* at Paignton. Whilst still desultorily studying law, he appeared in London in supporting roles in *La Boulangère* (1881, Coquebert), a revival of *Geneviève de Brabant* with Soldene (1881, Vanderprout), and in a Strand Theatre revival of *La Mascotte* (1882, Rocco) before going to America with Carte to play Harry Paulton's principal comedy part in *Manteaux Noirs* and Nick Vedder in *Rip van Winkle* on Broadway. He remained there, appearing in New York's first English-language *La Vie parisienne* (von Wienerschnitzel, ie, Gondremarck) and *Gasparone* (Nasoni), but thereafter, increasingly, in non-musical pieces.

He only occasionally used his limited singing voice thereafter, in such plays as *Prince Karl* and *The First Violin,* as he spread himself through all areas of the straight theatre until he eventually became regarded as one of America's foremost classical leading men. And the story of his early life became, thereafter, suitably fictionalized.

During his early days in Britain Mansfield was the author of a one-act musical play, *Ten Minutes for Refreshment,* and he later wrote another short opéra-bouffe under the title *Bouffes and Breezes* which or may not have achieved a production.

1882 **Ten Minutes for Refreshment** (James M Glover) 1 act Olympic Theatre 14 January

Biography: Winter, W: *The Life and Art of Richard Mansfield* (Moffat, Yard & Co, New York, 1910), etc

[LES] MANTEAUX NOIRS Comic opera in 3 acts by Walter Parke and Harry Paulton adapted from the libretto *Giralda, ou La Nouvelle Psyche* by Eugène Scribe. Music by Procida Bucalossi. Avenue Theatre, London, 3 June 1882.

Girola (Florence St John) has been needfully betrothed to the loutish miller Dromez (Charles Groves), but she sighs after the mysterious Luis (Henry Bracy), a gallant who one day rescued her from the hands of some ruffians. On the day of the wedding, the equally unenthusiastic Dromez secretly sells his bridegroom's place to a stranger (of course, its Luis), but on the wedding night, spent in the blackness of his mill, the lecherous King Philip (Claude Marius) comes sneaking around the pretty country girl. In the dark, the king, his chancellor (Fred Leslie) and Luis all get involved in the series of farcical who-shall-deflower-the-bride encounters which make up the comic heart of the play's action, before everything is straightened out in time for the final curtain.

Bucalossi's straightforward, old-fashioned comic opera score was highlighted by a comedy serenade for the philandering king and his chancellor, but the bulk of the music fell to the heroine, in ballad (''The Heart Sighs Ever to Be Free''), fandango (''Anita Is Sad''), rondo (''Six Months Ago'') or air (''I Never Could, Like Some Girls, Smile''). If not top-class stuff, it was sufficient to effectively complement Paulton and Parke's highly comical book, which, in the hands of such accomplished players as Marius, Leslie and the enormously popular young Miss St John, who had recently come to fame as London's Madame Favart, played hilariously enough to win the show 190 London performances, an 1885 revival, and many years of touring in the British provinces and colonies.

D'Oyly Carte snapped up the American rights to this challenger to his domination of the musical West End, and presented the piece in New York with a largely British cast headed by Selina Dolaro, W T Carleton, Richard Mansfield, J H Ryley and Arthur Wilkinson. It didn't take hugely, even when the two last-named actors decided to swap roles, and ended its Broadway run after 37 performances, but if New York didn't want it, the rest of the country did. In the wake of the 37 performances a rash of pirate productions, pasting Bucalossi's score to a variety of more-or-less adaptations of *Giralda* (and rip-offs of *Manteaux Noirs)* were played by touring, repertoire and summer season companies all round the country, under such titles as *Three Black Cloaks, Three Black Mantles* and *Girola, or the Miller's Bride,* for a decade and more.

A Vienna production (ad M Röttinger, Franz Wagner) which starred Jenny Stubel, Karl Drucker, Thaller, Rösike and Kühle played just eight times.

Giralda, originally set as an opéra-comique by Adolphe Adam (Opéra-Comique, Paris 20 July 1850), and popularized later as a straight play in Dion Boucicault's English adaptation (*Giralda / A Dark Night's Work*), was also used as the basis for the Hungarian operett *A kis molnárné* (Jenő Sztojanovits/Antal Radó, Népszínház 29 January 1892). Scribe's *Giralda* text was said itself to have been derived from Isaac Bickerstaff's well-known *The Maid of the Mill.*

USA: Standard Theater 26 September 1882; Austria: Carltheater *Drei Schwarzmäntel* 14 October 1882; Australia: Opera House, Sydney 11 July 1883

MARBURY, Elisabeth (b New York, 19 June 1856; d New York, 23 January 1933).

An important New York theatrical agent, ''Bessie'' Marbury is said to have been the first to negotiate a percentage of the box-office returns for her playwright clients—a claim that Dion Boucicault who, admittedly, is said to have done so on his own behalf, would doubtless have challenged.

Miss Marbury, ''equipped with an advisory board of Elsie de Wolfe (interior decoration), Robert Chanier (scenic effects), Peter Cooper Hewitt (electrical effects), Jerome Kern (light music), Melville Ellis (costumes) and Maurice (for dancing),'' was also involved in the turning of the intimate Princess Theater into a home for small musicals, and was associated with F Ray Comstock on the production of the first of the pieces staged there: *Nobody Home* (1915) and *Very Good Eddie* (1915). She was also the first producer to introduce Cole Porter to the professional musical stage when she (solo) mounted *See America First,* described as a comic opera, written by the young songwriter and his college chum, T Lawraston Riggs. She later mounted several other musicals including *Love o' Mike* (1917, w Lee Shubert), Philip Bartholomae's *Girl o' Mine* (Bijou 28 January 1918, 48 performances) and the small-scale *Say When* (1928 w Carl Reed), a musical version of the Amélie Rives/ Gilbert Emery play *Love in a Mist* put together by many hands, in a career in which she was first and foremost an artists' representative.

Autobiography: *My Crystal Ball* (Boni and Liveright, New York, 1923)

MARC-CAB [CABRIDENS, Marcel Eugène Henri] (b Nice, 11 December 1900; d Bandol, 18 October 1978).

French author, librettist and lyricist, Marc-Cab wrote at first largely for the revue stage, turning out pieces both in the Casino de Paris style and in the Marseillais genre. He made his first appearance as a musical-comedy librettist on the Paris stage with the texts for two opérettes by the conductor of the Marseillais pieces, Georges Sellers. After collaborating with Raymond Vincy on the libretto for the landmark musical *La Belle de Cadix,* he was connected with many further Parisian productions, ranging from such large, romantic opérettes à grand spectacle as *Les Amants de Venise* and the Tino Rossi vehicle *Naples au baiser de feu,* mounted by Henri Varna at the Théâtre Mogador, to small-scale comedy musicals, an area in which he was particularly successful with such shows as the extremely long-running *Mon p'tit pote, Coquin de printemps* and the Frères Jacques's musical *La Belle Arabelle.*

1933 **Pauline** (Vincent Scotto/w Gévaudan) Nice 6 January

1933 **Loulou et ses boys** (Michel Emer, Georges Sellers/w Paul Farges, Pierre Baylès) Théâtre Daunou 7 December

1935 **Nine** (Scotto/w Gévaudan, Danam) Eldorado, Nice 10 January

1940 **Ma belle marseillaise** (Sellers/w Audiffred, Charles Tutelier) Théâtre des Variétés 8 March (revised version 10 February 1978, Opéra de Toulon)

1945 **La Belle de Cadix** (Francis Lopez/Maurice Vandair/w Raymond Vincy) Casino Montparnasse 24 December

1949 **Symphonie Portugaise** (aka *Romance au Portugal*) (José Padilla/w Vincy) Théâtre de la Gaîté-Lyrique 9 October

1950 **Il faut marier maman!** (Guy Lafarge/w Lafarge/w Serge Veber) Théâtre de Paris 15 September

1952 **Schnock, ou L'École du bonheur** (Lafarge/w Jean Rigaux) Théâtre l'Européen

1953 **La Belle de mon coeur** (*The Belle of New York*) revised French version (Théâtre Mogador)

1953 **Les Amants de Venise** (Vincent Scotto/w Henri Varna, René Richard) Théâtre Mogador 5 December

1954 **Mon p'tit pote** (Jack Ledru/w Jean Valmy) Theatre l'Européen 29 September

1954 **Les Chansons de Bilitis** (Joseph Kosma/w Valmy) Théâtre des Capucines 30 January

1955 **Les Amours de Don Juan** (Juan Morata/w Varna, Richard) Théâtre Mogador 23 December

1956 **La Belle Arabelle** (Lafarge, Pierre Philippe/w Francis Blanche) Théâtre de la Porte-Saint-Martin 4 October

1957 **Naples au baiser de feu** (Renato Rascel/w Varna, Richard) Théâtre Mogador 7 December

1958 **Coquin de printemps** (Guy Magenta/Fernand Bonifay/w Valmy) Théâtre l'Européen 30 January

1958 **Le Moulin sans souci** (Georges van Parys, Philippe Parès/S Veber) Opéra, Strasbourg 24 December

1959 **Sissi, futur Impératrice** (*Sissi*) French lyrics (w Richard) (Théâtre Mogador)

1961 **À toi de jouer** (Ledru/w Valmy) Theatre l'Européen 24 November

1963 **Le Temps des guitares** (Francis Lopez/w Vincy) Théâtre de l'ABC October

1964 **Michel Strogoff** (Ledru/w Richard) Théâtre Mogador 5 December

1967 **SO6** (Jo Moutet/w Jacques Dambrois) Pacra/Théâtre du Marais 10 February

1967 **Vienne chante et danse** (Ledru, Strauss arr Ledru/w Varna, Richard) Théâtre Mogador 25 November

1971 **Hello, Dolly!** French version w Jacques Collard, André Hornez (Liège)

1972 **Le Pêcheur d'étoiles** (Alain Vanzo/w Francis Didelot, Marc Berthomieux) Théâtre Sebastapol, Lille 23 September; Opéra-Comique, Paris 28 September 1973

1973 **Quand fleurissent les violettes** (*Wenn die kleinen Veilchen blühen*) French version w Hornez (Liège)

1976 **Parade de printemps** (*Frühlingsparade*) French version w Hornez (Grand Théâtre, Bordeaux)

1977 **L'Oeuf à voiles** (Lafarge/Cami) Théâtre Graslin, Nantes 23 December

nd **Sang viennois** (*Wiener Blut*) new French version

MARCH OF THE FALSETTOS Music and lyrics by William Finn. Playwrights Horizons, New York, 1 April 1981, Chelsea Westside Arts Theatre, 13 October 1981.

March of the Falsettos was the second of what ultimately became a trio of short musicals dealing with a self-centered, neurotic Jewish New Yorker called Marvin (Michael Rupert) who has left the wife, Trina (Alison Fraser), whom he had acquired in Part One (*In Trousers,* Playwrights Horizons, February 1979) to make his home and love life with young Whizzer Brown (Stephen Bogardus). His psychiatrist, Mendel (Chip Zien, who had played Marvin in *In Trousers*), moves in with Trina. The fifth character of the show is Marvin and Trina's young son, Jason (James Kushner).

At first staged—like *In Trousers,* under the auspices of Playwrights Horizons—as *Four Jews in a Room Bitching* (the title of the opening song from the finished show), the piece was developed by Finn and director James Lapine through a workshop production before being staged off-Broadway as *March of the Falsettos.* It was received with mixed feelings, but from those who liked its unconventional story-in-sort-of-songs style and were interested in and/or identified with its drivingly egotistic small group of characters and their dissected sentiments, it won high and enthusiastic praise. Played off-Broadway for 268 performances, it was subsequently produced in Britain, at first at Manchester, but failed in 29 performances when brought to London with Barry James, Simon Green, Martin Smith and Paddy Navin in its cast.

The success of *March of the Falsettos* won a second chance for *In Trousers,* which had not progressed beyond its two dozen tryout performances in New York in 1979, but which was now brought back to off-Broadway's Promenade Theater. It did not confirm its sequel's success, closing after 16 performances.

Falsettoland (Lucille Lortel Theater 14 September 1990), the third Marvin musical, moving with the preoccupations of the times, dealt with what develops when Whizzer turns out to have AIDS. Following its off-Broadway run the piece was mounted in a number of regional houses, before a combination of pieces number two and three was put together by Graciela Daniele at Hartford Stage. The success of this mounting provoked a similar production, shortly afterwards, on Broadway, under the title *Falsettos* (John Golden Theater 29 April 1992). Rupert, Bogardus and Zien all repeated the roles which they had played a decade earlier, with Barbara Walsh as Trina, and director Lapine now had a co-librettist's credit. Barry and Fran Weissler's production picked up Tony Awards for music and lyrics (the "best musical" citation went to the even older paste-up *Crazy for You*) as *Falsettos* established itself through 14 months and 487 performances as one of the rare glimmers of musical-theatre light on a 1980s Broadway starved of well-written new works.

UK: Manchester Library Theatre 29 January 1987, Albery Theatre 24 March 1987; Germany: Delphi Theater, Hamburg 4 January 1996

Recordings: original cast (DRG), with *Falsettoland* (DRG)

LE MARIAGE AU TAMBOUR Opéra-comique in 3 acts by Paul Burani adapted from the play by Alexandre Dumas père, Adolphe de Leuven and Brunswick. Music by Léon Vasseur. Théâtre du Châtelet, Paris, 4 April 1885.

In order to help her brother, Vicomte Charles d'Obernay (Marcelin), escape from the republican lines to carry battle orders to the army of the princes, the dashing, lovely Louise (Mlle Perrouze) disguises herself as a peasant girl and, to keep up her masquerade, even goes through an in-the-field marriage with the attractive Sergeant Lambert (Vauthier). When order and the aristocracy are restored, and Charles is urging his sister to marry one of his comrades in arms, Lambert returns and proves to be the Marquis d'Argy.

Vasseur's musical score illustrated the military-spectacular part of the piece richly (the entire fourth tableau of the second act was devoted to the army setting out to war in a regimental parade headed by officers on horseback and ending with the ragtag of "volontaires, voltigeurs, tambours, clairons, cantinières"), whilst also supplying a varied selection of solos for Louise—in her various appearances as cavalier, peasant, vivandière and lady—and for her Lambert, and some perky pieces for the vivandière Gervaise (Mlle Dharville) and her comical suitors Fleur-des-Pois (Plet) and Spartacus (Romani).

Produced with plenty of spectacle at the Châtelet, the show proved to sit ill there. It was taken off after 11 performances, and shortly after was restaged less hugely at the Folies-Dramatiques (2 June 1885), with Félix Huguenet replacing Plet and Mlle Carlin as Gervaise. This time the result was altogether different and *Le Mariage au tambour* played happily through a good Paris run. It was subsequently translated into Hungarian (ad Béla J Fái, György Verő) for three performances at the Népszínház, and into German for a production at Berlin's Walhalla Theater.

Hungary: Népszínház *Esketés dobszóval* 1 May 1886; Germany: Walhalla Theater *Die Marketenderin* 26 February 1887

LE MARIAGE AUX LANTERNES Opérette in 1 act by Michel Carré and Léon Battu, a revised version of *Le Trésor à Mathurin* by Battu. Music by Jacques Offenbach. Théâtre des Bouffes-Parisiens, Paris, 10 October 1857.

One of the most successful and influential of Offenbach's long series of short opérettes, *Le Mariage aux lanternes* was developed by Michel Carré from a ''tableau villageois'' called *Le Trésor à Mathurin,* which Offenbach had composed to a text by Léon Battu at the very beginning of his career and which had been played at the little Salle Herz four years earlier (7 May 1853).

Pépito, Les Deux Aveugles, Le Violoneux, Ba-ta-clan, Tromb-al-ca-zar, La Rose de Saint-Flour, Le 66, La Bonne d'enfant[s] and *Croquefer* followed, all but the first staged under Offenbach's management at his Bouffes-Parisiens, before he introduced the made-over version of his little rustic opérette in which the farmer Guillot (Paul Geoffroy) and his cousin Denise (Mlle Mareschal) are brought together by a letter-writing uncle who sends them both to look for ''a treasure'' in the same place. The principal cast of the piece was completed by two gossiping-widow neighbors (Lise Tautin, Marie Dalmont) with an eye for the handsome and potentially wealthy farmer.

The score to *Le Mariage aux lanternes* had nothing of the burlesque extravagance of a *Ba-ta-clan,* but instead relied on the same kind of unpretentious melodic charm tasted with such widespread success in such pieces as *Le Violoneux* and *La Rose de Saint-Flour,* shot through with the comedy provided in the widows' pieces (''Mon cher mari quelquefois s'emportait,'' ''Ah! la fine, fine mouche''), and peaking in an Angelus Quartet in which Guillot digs on one side of the ''treasure'' tree, Denise dreams on the other, and the prospecting widows watch eagerly and vocally from behind the hedge.

A fine success on its first production in France, where it remains one of the best-loved of Offenbach's non-burlesque pieces, *Le Mariage aux lanternes* was the first of Offenbach's opérettes to be played in Vienna in the German language and its great success there helped set in motion the invasion of the Viennese stage by French opéra-bouffe and opérette. Adapted by actor Karl Treumann, with the music ''eingerichtet und instrumentiert'' by Carl Binder, it was presented under Johann Nestroy's management at the Carltheater with Treumann and Elise Zöllner as the treasures and Therese Braunecker-Schäfer and Anna Grobecker as the widows. It played for a splendid 14 straight nights (in a house where the bill was usually changed every couple of days) and then another dozen between some Possen and a Déjazet play season. Treumann re-produced the piece when he took on the Theater am Franz-Josefs-Kai (6 November 1860) with Anna Marek playing Denise alongside himself and his original widows, and it was later staged in spectacles coupés at several other houses, including Ronacher (12 June 1880), the Fürsttheater (26 April 1884) and the Theater an der Wien (18 February 1889). It was brought back again to the Carltheater in 1914 as part of an Offenbach season (1 June).

In Germany *Die Verlobung bei Laternenschein* proved easily the most popular of the large repertoire of Offenbach one-acters, whilst Hungary's version (ad Miklós Feléky), first seen in Kolozsvár, and then at Budapest's Nemzeti Színház with Kálmán Szerdahelyi, Vilma Bognár, Ida Huber and Ilka Markovics in its four roles, was again instrumental in setting off a local fashion for Offenbach in particular and French musical shows in general. *Eljegyzés lámpafényél* was widely and long played thereafter, notably in the repertoire at the Budapest Operaház (12 December 1890).

England had its first sight of the piece when the Bouffes-Parisiens company visited London in 1860, with Geoffroy playing his original role, and several English versions were subsequently produced. These included one played at the Royalty Theatre (ad Benjamin Barnett) with John [Wilford] Morgan as Guillot in 1862, a second—*The Treasure Found by Lanternlight*—toured in 1868 by Louisa Pyne's Comic Opera Company (which may have been the same as the *Treasure Trove* toured by Mrs Galton Pyne's operetta company to Halls and Mechanics' Institutes round the country and later played by Frank Crellin, Bessie Lovell, Susan Pyne and Harriet Everard at the St James's in 1869 [16 October]), and another at the Gaiety Theatre (11 October 1871) in which Frank Wood, Constance Loseby and Annie Tremaine were featured. The Galton family introduced their British version to America at Broadway's Wood's Museum in 1868, but by that time New York had already been able to see the piece both in German and in French. It was played first at the Stadttheater with Hübner and the ladies Siedenburg, Meaubert and Auguste Steglich-Fuchs, and on several later occasions in the next decade in the other German-language houses, as well as being played in French by Paul Juignet's Theatre Français company at Niblo's Saloon. A later English version entitled *Plighted by Moonlight* was produced by J Fred Zimmerman's company at the Metropolitan Alcazar (17 June 1882) with Fanny Wentworth, Adelaide Randall, Rosa Cooke and Sgr Montegriffo.

Austria: Carltheater *Die Verlobung bei Lanternsheine* 16 October 1858; Germany: Krolls Theater *Hochzeit bei Laternenschein* 17 June 1858; Hungary: Kolozsvár 28 December 1859, Nemetzi Színház *Eljegyzés lámpafényél* 21 November 1860, Budai Színkör (Ger) 1 May 1862; UK: Lyceum Theatre (Fr) 9 July 1860, Royalty Theatre *Marriage by Candlelight* 18 January 1862; USA: Stadttheater (Ger) 18 March 1860, Théâtre Français/ Niblo's Saloon (Fr) 6 February 1864, Wood's Museum *Married by Lanterns* 31 August 1868; Australia: Theatre Royal, Melbourne *Love by Lantern Light* 8 December 1877

UN MARI À LA PORTE Opéra-comique in 1 act by Alfred Delacour and Léon Morand. Music by Jacques Offenbach. Théâtre des Bouffes-Parisiens, Paris, 22 June 1859.

Un mari à la porte is a farcical little piece in which a husband called Henri Martel (Guyot) finds his newly wed wife, Suzanne (Coralie Geoffroy), has locked him out of their room. And there is a man in there with her. But Florestan (Paul Geoffroy), who has arrived over the roof and down the chimney, is only a silly fellow fleeing from a jealous husband and a bailiff, and his little flirtation is ultimately not with the wife, but with her pretty bridesmaid, Rosita (Lise Tautin). The show was a virtual three-hander, as the husband is heard but not seen until the final moments, when the door is at last opened. The features of the little score were a valse tyrolienne for Rosita (''J'entends, ma belle, la ritournelle''), some comical lamentations for Florestan who, it seems, is going to have to jump three floors to the ground to save the situation, a dilemma trio when the trellis he attempts to descend by breaks (''Juste ciel! Que vois-je?'') and, the big set piece of the show, a quartet with the husband outside joining in to provide the bottom line.

This comical opérette did well in France, where it was introduced at Offenbach's Bouffes-Parisiens, but it also won a particularly strong and widespread popularity in Austria and in Hungary. Karl Treumann followed up his successes with his versions of *Le Mariage aux lanternes, Pépito, Le Savetier et le financier, Le Violoneux* and *Le 66* by adapting *Un mari à la porte* for the Carltheater. With its adaptor playing the foolish Florian alongside Therese Braunecker-Schäfer and Helene Weinberger in a version which made great play of a lot of business with a painter's cradle and which seems to have been rather more joyously farcical than the French original, it gave him his biggest success since the first two—and still most popular—of his Offenbach rewrites. Treumann played *Der Ehemann vor der Thüre* both at the Carltheater and subsequently at his own Theater am Franz-Josefs-Kai, and it was later taken up at the Variététheater and at other houses specializing in spectacles coupés, appearing at Ronacher in 1880 and at the Theater an der Wien in 1884 (13 January) and again in 1894 with Karl Wallner, Ferdinand Pagin and Frlns Devall and Häckl featured for a series of 10 performances.

In Hungary, *Férj az ajto elött* (ad Kálmán Szerdahelyi) followed *Le Mariage aux lanternes* into the Nemzeti Színház. Thus, the second Hungarian-language Offenbach work in Budapest thoroughly confirmed the success of the first, and the piece was repeated regularly thereafter. Offenbach's company played *Un mari à la porte* there in French the same year, whilst István Benyey's team were seen in the Hungarian adaptation at the Budai Színkör (1867), where the show had been put on as early as 1860 in its German version, as the little piece made itself a firm place in the repertoire.

Although Europe enjoyed the piece (it was seen in Paris as recently as 1983, Théâtre Essaïon), it does not seem to have traveled significantly beyond there. America saw it in its German version, at the Stadttheater, several times with Minna von Berkel and Eugenie Schmitz featured, and later at the Germania (1873–74), but neither in America nor in Britain does it seem to have been staged in English in the century of its first appearance. That distinction seems to have fallen only to Australia where *The Wrong Side of the Door* was produced to considerable publicity as the first Offenbach opérette to play in the colony. The publicity was occasioned, however, more by the fact that local burlesque author William M Akhurst was announced as the ''author,'' and the show was spoken of as ''Mr Akhurst's long-promised operetta.'' H Humphreys (Pythias Callicado), E Reeve (Tapper), Kate Ryder (Mrs Tapper) and Milly Parker (Rosella Parrott) introduced the show for a brief season at Melbourne's Duke of Edinburgh's Theatre.

New York finally saw *The Husband Locked Out* produced by Mrs Dore Lyon at a matinée in 1910, and London got *A Husband on the Mat* in 1950 when Geoffrey Dunn's anglicization of the piece was played at the Fortune Theatre.

Austria: Carltheater *Der Ehemann vor der T(h)üre* 28 December 1859; Hungary: Budai Színkör *Der Ehemann vor der Tür* 16 June 1860, Nemzeti Színház *Férj az ajto elött* 12 March 1861; USA: Stadttheater *Der Ehemann vor der Tür* 1866, Berkeley Theatre *The Husband Locked Out* 11 November 1910; Australia: Duke of Edinburgh's Theatre, Melbourne *The Wrong Side of the Door* 7 November 1868; UK: Fortune Theatre *A Husband on the Mat* 21 February 1950

MARIANO, Luis [GONZALES, Luis Mariano Eusebio] (b Irun, Spain, 12 August 1914; d Paris, 14 July 1970). Svelte little singing idol of the French opérette à grand spectacle of the postwar stage and screen.

The son of a Spanish garagiste and taxi driver, brought up largely in Bordeaux, the young Mariano studied at the local Conservatoire whilst singing with a cabaret band. Jeanne Lagiscarde, a forceful lady who looked after the classical department at the local record shop, took him under her wing and finally sold up in order to take her ''discovery'' to Paris and make him a star. Three years of meagre pickings in the popular music world and several performances of *Don Pasquale* intervened before that stardom came when Mariano was cast in the leading role of the film star Carlos Médina in *La Belle de Cadix* (1945), the first opérette by the composer Francis Lopez. As a sometime art student, Mariano also designed the sets for the *Belle de Cadix*'s purse-pinched mounting on the little stage of the Casino-Montparnasse, but it was his singing rather than his painting which won the enthusiasm of all when the show opened. He created the famous, lilting title song ''La Belle de Cadix,'' the serenade to ''Maria Luisa'' and the longing ''Une nuit à Grenade'' and he made them and the show as well-known as they, in turn, made him.

Thereafter, the slim, dark little tenor swiftly became one of the most loved stars of the French entertainment world, leading a high-profile career in alternate stage and film productions, always in large made-to-measure roles full of ringing tenor songs in the popular vein, usually from the pen of the now-equally-famous Lopez. His films of the 1940s included *Histoire de chanter* (1946), *Cargaison clandestine* (1947), *Fandango* (1948), *Je n'aime que toi* (1949) and *Pas de weekend pour notre amour* (1949), whilst his stage successor to *La Belle de Cadix* was *Andalousie* (1947), a piece in similar vein to the former, and with an even brighter bag of tenor songs: ''Andalucia mia, ''Le Marchand d'alcarazas,'' ''Je veux t'aimer,'' ''La Fête à Seville,'' ''Olé torero'' and the ringing prayer ''Santa Maria.''

Le Chanteur de Mexico (1951, ''Mexico,'' ''Acapulco,'' Il est un coin de France,'' ''Maïtechu,'' ''Quand on voit Paris d'en haut,'' ''Rossignol de mes amours'') gave Mariano a third successive stage hit and, helped by the film versions of his stage opérettes and of *Violettes impériales,* perhaps his best film, it brought him to the peak of his career.

This record of unalloyed success had its first hiccup when Mariano essayed less suitable material with a weak musical called *Chevalier du ciel* (1954), which put him in uniform and gave him virtually the entire score to sing, and a botched film version of Lehár's *Der Zarewitsch* which found its star happier with the character than the music. He filmed several further Lopez stage pieces—*Le Chanteur de Mexico,* and two others in which he had not appeared on the stage, *Quatre jours à Paris* and *À la Jamaïque*—appeared in the film musical *Sérénade au Texas,* and played five more of Lopez's works in the theatre: *La cancion del amor mio* in Madrid (1958), the indifferent *Le Secret de Marco Polo* (1959), the lively *Visa pour l'amour* (1961) in which he paired with Annie Cordy to sing and dance the twist, and two further spectaculars, *Le Prince de Madrid* (1967) which cast him as Goya and, finally, *La Caravelle d'or* (1969). Although each had a good run and a long tour, none was of the same class as the early pieces and, latterly, Mariano too lost some of his éclat. He died during the run of *La Caravelle d'or* at the age of 56.

Plate 241. **Paola Marié.** *Star of Parisian and American opera-bouffe.*

Biographies: Montserrat, J: *Luis Mariano* (Pac, Paris, 1984), Chardans, J-L: *J'ai connu un prince* (Table Ronde, Paris, 1976), *Luis Mariano* (Ramsay, Paris, 1980), Château, R: *Luis Mariano* (1995)

MARIÉ, Paola (b Paris, 28 March 1851; d Nice, 22 September 1905). Opéra-bouffe star of the French and American stages.

Daughter of opera-singer Claude Félix Mécène MARIÉ DE L'ISLE [Jean-Baptiste MARIÉ], the tiny, dark and very lovely mezzo-soprano Paola Marié made her first appearance before the Paris public as a teenaged takeover in the role of Méphisto in *Le Petit Faust* (1869) and featured with notable success at the Bouffes-Parisiens in Potier's little *Madeleine* (1869), as a result of which she was hired for the company at the Brussels Galeries Saint-Hubert. She visited London with that company in 1871 (Inès in *Les Bavards,* Angélique to the Roland of Hervé in *Les Chevaliers de la table ronde,* etc). The following year she returned to Paris and joined the company at the Théâtre des Folies-Dramatiques, where she appeared as Méphisto (15 May), Marguerite in *Le Canard à trois becs* and as Bertrande in the original production of *Heloïse et Abélard* (1872), and she was seen in Britain for a second successive season when she played Galusinda in *Chilpéric,* Dindonette in *L'Oeil crevé* and *Le Canard à trois becs* with the Folies-Dramatiques company during their summer season at London's Globe Theatre.

She scored a considerable success when she appeared as the original Parisian Clairette in *La Fille de Madame Angot* in 1873, and she subsequently appeared on the Paris stage as Fiorella in the 1874 remake of Les Brigands; creating leading roles in Lecocq's *Les Prés Saint-Gervais* (1874, Friquette) and Offenbach's *La Boulangère a des écus* (1875, Toinon); playing Müler to the Molda of Judic in a revival of *La Timbale d'argent* (1876) and Fortunato to her *Madame L'Archiduc* (1876); stepping in as a very-last-minute replacement for the bereaved Mlle Luce in *Le Moulin du Vert-Galant* (1876, Jeanne); and featuring in *La Boîte au lait* (1876, Sosthène), the revived *La Princesse de Trébizonde* (1876, Raphaël) and also such little pieces as Legouix's *Le Mariage d'une étoile.* She guested at the profitable theatre at St Petersburg in 1876, and on her return to Paris starred in Vasseur's *La Sorrentine* (1877, Térésina), opposite Louise Théo as Fortunato in another revival of *Madame l'Archiduc,* created another major travesty role as Lazuli in *L'Étoile* (1877), and also starred in Laurent de Rillé's opérette villageoise *Babiole* (1878, Babiole), in Offenbach's short-lived *Maître Péronilla* (1878, Frimouskino) and in *La Marocaine* (1879, Fatime).

In 1879 Paola Marié went to America, making her first appearance there under the management of Maurice Grau in the role of Clairette (15 September), and over the next four years she toured the country playing a vast repertoire of opéras-bouffes, including *Giroflé-Girofla, Barbe-bleue, Les Brigands, La Périchole, La Vie parisienne, Le Petit Faust, La Grande-Duchesse, Le Petit Duc, Madame Favart, Les Cloches de Corneville* and *Olivette.* She introduced several new pieces to America, among them *La Petite Muette* (Mercédès), *La Camargo* (Camargo), *La Fille du tambour-major* (Stella), *Les Mousquetaires au couvent* (Louise, later Simonne), *Babiole* (Babiole) and *Le Jour et la nuit* (Manola) and she also starred in Sardou's play *Divorçons* and in the title roles of Bizet's *Carmen* and Ambroise Thomas's *Mignon,* both parts created in Paris by her sister.

Mlle Marié returned to the Paris stage in 1884, now tiny, dark and distinctly tubby, and with her 33-year-old voice beginning to curl up a little at the edges, and she made her reappearance at the Bouffes as Régine in the short-lived *Le Chevalier Mignon.* She went on to appear in Paris in a revival of *La Grande-Duchesse,* and came out of what looked already like retirement to appear at the Palais-Royal in the revue *Le Club des Pannés* in 1887, but soon put an end to a career which had taken her through a decidedly large number of countries in its span of nearly 20 years.

Two sisters of Paola Marié (she was number four, in line of age) were also singing stars. **Mlle IRMA** (aka Irma-Marié) [Marie Irma MARIÉ] (b Paris, 1 December 1841; d Paris, 9 January 1891), chosen by Offenbach to create his *L'Amour chanteur* (1864) and *Les Bergers* (1865, Daphne/Annette/La Rouge), was subsequently the prima donna at the short-lived Théâtre de l'Athénée where she created the role of Césarine in Lecocq's *Fleur de thé* and his *L'Amour et son carquois.* She made the most successful portion of her career in America where she was the first Broadway interpreter of Offenbach's Boulotte (*Barbe-bleue*) and of *La Périchole* and where she played in a repertoire of touring opéra-bouffe, before returning home to take her place, in 1877, amongst the supporting casts at the Opéra-Comique (Ambroise Thomas's *Psyché,* the Countess in Poïse's *La Surprise de l'amour,* etc) and eventually drifting into retirement.

Eldest sister **Galli-Marié** [Jeanne MARIÉ] (b Paris, November 1839; d Vence, 22 September 1905), made her career in a different and more purely vocal area. She was the creator of the title roles of Ambroise Thomas's *Mignon* and Bizet's *Carmen,* the first Friday in Offenbach's *Robinson Crusoe,* Fantasio in his *Fantasio* (1872) and for a long time a prima donna at the Opéra-Comique. She appeared alongside sister Irma, in 1869, in the little opérette *Madeleine* at the Bouffes-Parisiens, and again in Irma's Opéra-Comique debut in *La Surprise de l'amour* (1877, Colombine). She retired in 1885.

MARIETTE, ou Comment on écrit l'histoire Comédie musicale in 5 scenes by Sacha Guitry. Music by Oscar Straus. Théâtre Édouard VII, Paris, 1 October 1928.

Originally written by Sacha Guitry as a vehicle for Sarah Bernhardt, but ultimately rewritten for the benefit of his then wife, Yvonne Printemps, and himself, *Mariette* presented its star as a 100-year-old actress recalling her past to a journalist. Since her past is not quite what she would have liked it to have been, she improves on fact, and invents for herself a romance with Prince Louis Napoléon (Guitry). Her tale of that non-existent romance makes up the remainder of the show.

Mariette is seen as a girl of 20 in the 1848 of the first act, performing a boy's role in a provincial opérette (the audience saw the scene from behind the actors). The first contact with the Prince is made in a scene of pantomime, with the young woman initially refusing his advances, but ultimately accepting his invitation to ''supper.'' The piece then followed their subsequent affair before, in the overture to the fourth scene, it advanced musically through the years from the cancan and the waltz to the boston, the fox-trot, one-step, charleston and blues up to the present day.

The short score included musical pieces for several other artists (Jane Montange, Renée Sénac, Aquistapace), although not for the non-singing Guitry as the Prince, but it was the star who reaped the bulk of the music, ranging from a lovely Valse d'adieu (''Depuis trois ans passés'') to a coon song in the final act.

Mariette was a full-scale hit in Paris, with the duo who had previously triumphed in Guitry's *Mozart* triumphing all over again in a piece wholly different in style, and they subsequently played their piece in London, for a four-week season at His Majesty's Theatre, in the same way that they had done with the earlier show.

When *Mariette* was produced in Berlin, the Rotter brothers (who ran Berlin's musical theatre with a rubber hand in a rubber glove) decided that Guitry's sweet spider's-web of a book was not sufficiently obvious and throat-tugging, nor the score sufficiently conventional. They commissioned Alfred Grünwald to rewrite the text, adding a melodramatic scene of self-sacrifice for the heroine, and introduced a deal more vocal music for the leading man, turning the show from an elegant play with music into a full-blown, conventional Operette, which did not make anything like the same effect as the original had done. The new scene sat like a pustule on the face of the play as Käthe Dorsch and ex-opera baritone Michael Bohnen, supported by Ida Perry and Hermann Böttcher, played out a conventional Operettic season. A Vienna production of this Grünwald version starred Rita Georg and Hubert Marischka, Anny Coty and Fritz Imhoff through a total of 127 performances at the Theater an der Wien in 1929–30.

In America, an English-language version by Arthur Guiterman, with Helen Ford and Richard Hale featured, was produced under weekly stock conditions which were sufficiently uninspiring to damp its management's hopes that it might make its way to Broadway.

UK: His Majesty's Theatre (Fr) 3 June 1929; Germany: Metropoltheater *Marietta* 5 September 1929; Austria: Theater an der Wien *Marietta* 25 October 1929; USA: Stockbridge, Mass, *Marietta* 28 June 1937

Recording: items (HMV)

MARION, George F (b San Francisco, 16 July 1860; d Carmel, Calif, 30 November 1945). Actor turned musical-theatre director through three decades of Broadway productions.

At first a performer, Marion appeared on Broadway, alongside his brothers Sam and Dave, and in tandem with Morris Franks, with Dockstader's minstrels (''In the Soup'') and in several musical shows (Dr Dago Daggeri in *The Reign of Error,* Major Bombardos in *Papa's Wife,* Count Cassibianca in *The Little Duchess*), toured as a farce-comedy player (Hezekiah Muggins in *Mrs Partington* 1886, Jonah in *A Brass Monkey* 1889, Christopher Columbus jr in *A Texas Steer* 1890, Adam Scrowler in *Mr Macaroni* 1891, Willett Work and Berry U Decent in *Boys and Girls* 1891–92) and appeared in the Boston musicals *Westward Ho!* (1894, Colorado Sam) and *Prince Pro Tem* (1894, Justice). However, he found what was to be his niche, as a director, while still in his twenties, mounting the Afro-American Spectacular, Fantastical, Farcical and Musical Comedy *Down by the Suwanee Rover* (1896), Hoyt's *A Brass Monkey,* De Koven's *The Fencing Master, Papa's Wife* and *The Little Duchess* for Florenz Ziegfeld and Anna Held and *The Cadet Girl* (1900) for Adolphus H Chamberlyn. In the 1900s, for several years, he was house director for Henry Savage and, in that capacity, directed—along with a series of plays including *The County Chairman* and *The College Widow*—such successful early American musicals as *Peggy from Paris* (1903), *The Prince of Pilsen* (1904, USA, UK, France), *The Yankee Consul* (1904), *The Sho-Gun* (1904), *Woodland* (1904), *Easy Dawson* (1905), *The Man from Now* (1906), *The Student King* (1906) and *The Yankee Tourist* (1907), as well as Eysler's *The Love Cure* (*Künstlerblut,* 1909), Kálmán's *The Gay Hussars* (*Tatájárás,* 1909), and, mostly notably, Broadway's version of *The Merry Widow* (*Die lustige Witwe,* 1907). He also worked for Joe Weber (*Higgledy Piggledy,* 1904), the Shuberts (*Nearly a Hero,* 1908), Marie Cahill (*The Boys and Betty,* 1908) and Mort Singer (*The Girl Question, A Stubborn Cinderella*). He returned to the stage as an actor intermittently during these years, notably in Victor Herbert's *Algeria* (C Walsingham Wadhunter, 1908, also director).

In 1910 he directed the highly successful *The Spring Maid* for Werba and Luescher, and he followed up this second large Operette hit with a series of musicals of all kinds for A H Woods, John Cort, Savage and other managements, a list which included *Hell* and *Gaby* at the Folies-Bergère (1911), Julian Eltinge as *The Fascinating Widow* (1911), *Tantalizing Tommy* (1912), *The American Maid* (1913), *Her Little Highness* (1913), *The Debutante* (1914), *Pom-Pom* (1916), *Molly O* (1916), *The Amber Express* (1916), *Eileen* (1917, dances only), *The Love Mill* and *Head Over Heels* and American adaptations of the Continental *Gypsy Love* (1911), *Modest Suzanne* (1912), *The Rose Maid* (1912), *The Woman Haters* (1912), *The Purple Road* (1913 w Edward P Temple), *Sári* (1914), *The Maids of Athens* (1914) and *Suzi* (1914).

Although he was seen again as a performer in *The Grass Widow* (1917, Anton Pivert), his acting appearances from this time on were confined largely to plays (Christopherson in *Anna Christie,* 1921, etc) and films. As a director, however, he continued to be active in the musical theatre through the 1920s, staging musicals for the Shuberts and others up to his retirement (*The Right Girl, Tangerine, First Love, White Lilacs, Angela, Boom Boom*).

His son, **George MARION jr** (b Boston, 30 August 1897; d New York, 25 February 1968), wrote silent-movie scenarios, the subtitles for the early film of *Irene,* screenplays for such films as *The Gay Divorcee* and *Love Me Tonight* and later libretti, including the books for an unfortunate version of *Der Zigeunerbaron* for San Francisco (1938 w Ann Ronell), for *Too Many Girls* (1939), *Beat the Band* (w George Abbott), *Early to Bed* (1943), Kálmán's Mayerling musical, *Marinka* (1945), *Toplitzky of Notre Dame* (1946) and Guy Lombardo's *Arabian Nights* (Jones Beach, 1954).

Brother **Sam MARION** (d New York, 20 May 1906) played in the Hoyt farces and appeared on Broadway in *The Mandarin* (1896, Court Physician, also ch, with Dave), *The Good Mr Best* (1897, Hardis Lotte) and—with Joe Weber, for whom he became house choreographer and assistant director—in *Higgledy Piggledy* (1904, Pierre), *The College Widower* (The Town Policeman) and *Twiddle Twaddle* (1905, Capt Schmitt, Emperor Franz Josef). He also did the dances for *The Runaways* (1903), Nat Wills's *A Son of Rest* (1903), *The Sho-Gun* (1904), his brother's production of *Woodland* (1904), the Hippodrome extravaganza *A Yankee Circus on Mars* and George Broadhurst's *The Duke of Duluth* (1905).

1888 **O-Thel-O** (uncredited) sketch Dockstaders Minstrels 3 December

MARISCHKA, Ernst (b Vienna, 2 January 1893; d Chur, Switzerland, 12 May 1963).

The brother of the Theater an der Wien's Hubert Marischka, Ernst also spent his life in the world of Operette. He began as a librettist, scoring his most important successes at the family theatres with *Der Orlow* and the pasticcio *Walzer aus Wien* and in his collaboration with Hubert on *Sissy,* but subsequently became a busy and important figure in the film world, writing and/or directing many musical films (screenplays for *Das Abenteuer geht weiter, Die Fledermaus, Mein Herz ruft nach dir, Ich liebe alle Frauen, Frühjahrsparade, Zauber der Bohème, Konfetti, Rosen in Tirol* [ie, *Der Vogelhändler*], *Saison in Salzburg, Hochzeitsnacht im Paradies,* producer/director and screenplay for *Der Opernball, Das Dreimäderlhaus* with Rudolf Schock, etc). His screenplay for *Frühjahrparade* (*Spring Parade*) was subsequently adapted as a stage musical.

1911 **Der Minenkönig** (Robert Stolz/w Gustav Beer) 1 act Apollotheater 3 October

1914 **Das Narrenhaus** (Tivadar Pallós, Hans Albert Cesek/w Beer) 1 act Hölle 1 February

1916 **Das Kammerkatzerl** (w Max Blau) 1 act Rideamus Kabarett 1 April

1920 **Der König heiratet** (Edmund Eysler/w Beer) 1 act Künstlerbühne April

1923 **Die Bacchusnacht** (Bruno Granichstaedten) Theater an der Wien 18 May

1923 **Eine Nacht in Venedig** revised text (Theater an der Wien)

1924 **Puszipajtások** (Pallós/w Beer ad Zsolt Harsányi) 1 act Lujza Blaha Színház, Budapest 9 October

1925 **Der Orlow** (Granichstaedten) Theater an der Wien 3 April

1926 **Das Schwalbennest** (Granichstaedten) Raimundtheater 2 September

1926 **Die Königin** (Oscar Straus/w Granichstaedten) Deutsches Künstlertheater, Berlin 5 November

1927 **Alles auf Liebe** (Ralph Benatzky/w Karl Farkas) Stadttheater 30 September

1930 **Reklame** (Granichstaedten) Theater an der Wien 28 February

1930 **Walzer aus Wien** (Johann Strauss arr E W Korngold/w A M Willner, Heinz Reichert) Wiener Stadttheater 30 October

1932 **Sissy** (Fritz Kreisler/w Hubert Marischka) Theater an der Wien 23 December

1933 **Glück muss man haben** (Anton Profès/w Herman Feiner) Neues Wiener Stadttheater 10 March

1934 **Der singende Traum** (Richard Tauber/w Feiner) Theater an der Wien 31 August

1940 **Franzi** (Peter Kreuder) Leipzig 12 September

1949 **Frühling im Prater** (Stolz) Wiener Stadttheater 22 December

1964 **Frühjarsparade** (Stolz/w Hugo Wiener) Volksoper 25 March

MARISCHKA, Hubert (b Brünn, 27 August 1882; d Vienna, 4 December 1959). Longtime leading man and leading producer of the Viennese Operette theatre between the wars.

Marischka began his career as an actor and vocalist at St Pölten at the age of 21 and played at first in provincial theatres. During a successful engagement at Brünn, he was spotted by librettist Victor Léon and in 1908 he made his first appearances in Vienna, playing in a revival of Léon's Strauss pasticcio *Wiener Blut* and featuring alongside Karl Streitmann in *Die lustige Witwe* at the Raimundtheater. He also married Léon's daughter. From the Raimundtheater he moved to the Carltheater and leading-manhood, creating the roles of the temporarily divorced husband Karel van Lysseweghe in *Die geschiedene Frau* (1908), the cabaret-director Olivier in Oscar Straus's *Didi* (1909), the comical Kajetán in

Lehár's *Zigeunerliebe* (1910), and Tiborius in Fall's *Das Puppenmädel* (1910), as well as appearing as Hector to the Nanon of Mizzi Zwerenz in a revival of *Nanon* (1910). In 1912 he appeared in the title role of the Viennese premiere of *Der liebe Augustin* and as Stephan to the *Susi* of Zwerenz before switching his allegiance to the Theater an der Wien for what was to be a long and eventful stay.

Marischka began his life at the Theater an der Wien starring in *Die ideale Gattin* (1913, Pablo de Cavaletti), *Endlich allein* (1914, Baron Frank Hansen), and opposite Betty Fischer in Léon's newest, patriotic version of Kálmán's *Az obsitos, Gold gab ich für Eisen* (1914). He appeared as Dumésnil in a revival of *Der Opernball* and as Konrad in Granichstaedten's *Auf Befehl der Herzogin,* guested at the Apollotheater in Zerkowitz's *Das Finanzgenie* and a little scene called *Otto oder Otto,* and then returned to base to appear in *Der Sterngucker* (1916, Paul von Rainer). He also took a turn at playing Schubert in the Raimundtheater production of *Das Dreimäderlhaus,* but scored his greatest success to date when he introduced the archetypal romantic tenor role of Achmed Bey in the Theater an der Wien's long-running wartime hit *Die Rose von Stambul* (1916, "O Rose von Stambul," "Ihr stillen süssen Frauen").

Marischka went on to play the role of Sándor Zapolja in the Vienna version of *Wo die Lerche singt* (1918), created the title role of Friedl Pausinger in Straus's *Dorfmusikanten* (1919) and again visited the same management's Raimundtheater to star as Heinrich Heine in a biomusical made up of Mendelssohn music and called *Dichterliebe* (1920). He returned to the Theater an der Wien to create Count Julian Olinski in *Die blaue Mazur* (1920), to play the heroic Dimitri Sarrasow in *Der letzte Walzer* (1921), to introduce Armand Mirbeau (later to be taken by Richard Tauber) in *Frasquita* (1922) and Nero in Granichstaedten's *Die Bacchusnacht* (1923), and was also seen as Caramello in a revival of *Eine Nacht in Venedig.* Later in 1923 he starred as the prototype Prince Sou Chong (another role with which Tauber would later identify himself) in the first performances of *Die gelbe Jacke.*

During the period that had seen him rising to the top of the list of romantic leading men in the Viennese Operettic firmament, the widowed Marischka had married Lilian Karczag, the daughter of the director of the Theater an der Wien, and he had become progressively more and more involved in the running of the theatre. When Wilhelm Karczag died in 1923, his son-in-law (now billed as Marischka-Karczag) took over the management of the Theater an der Wien. He also soon took up the co-running of the Raimundtheater (1926), formerly under Karczag's control, where Rudolf Beer had yet again got himself into trouble producing possibly admirable but definitely unprofitable plays, and leavened that house's diet with some more popular Operette productions including the premieres of *Das Schwalbennest* and *Die Liebe geht um.*

Marischka began his managership of the Theater an der Wien by staging Oscar Straus's *Die Perlen der Kleopatra* (1923, with the playbills still giving Karczag as producer), and then found major success producing and starring opposite Betty Fischer as Count Tassilo ("Grüss mir die süssen, die reizenden Frauen," "Komm' Zigan!"), the impoverished nobleman in love with his employer, in Kálmán's *Gräfin Mariza* (1924). A first-rate hit which ran for a full year, *Gräfin Mariza* was followed up by the short-lived *Das Milliardensouper* (director) and a run of further splendid successes in *Der Orlow* (1925, dir: Alex Dorotschinsky), *Die Zirkusprinzessin* (1926, Mister X, introducing "Zwei Märchenaugen"), *Die Königin* (dir: Nikola Tonitscheff) and *Die gold'ne Meisterin* (1927, dir: Christian, "Du liebe gold'ne Meisterin").

In 1928 Marischka staged and starred in Kálmán's *Die Herzogin von Chicago* (1928, Sándor Boris), in 1929 did the same for Fall's posthumous *Rosen aus Florida* (Goliath Armstrong) and Straus's *Marietta* (Louis Napoléon), with Rita Georg as his partner, and in 1930 he directed Granichstaedten's *Reklame.* He was given the large-billed credit of "Künstlerische Oberleitung" (which he'd used on a few previous occasions) to the "Regie" of house director Otto Langer on the original Vienna production of *Das Land des Lächelns* (1930) in which Richard Tauber repeated his Berlin performance of Marischka's old role of Sou Chong.

In the earliest 1930s he appeared in revivals of *Wiener Blut* and *Die lustige Witwe* with leading lady Betty Fischer, as Leopold in *Im weissen Rössl* and in Girardi's role in *Bruder Straubinger* and directed and starred in the Theater an der Wien's productions of the disappointing *Der Bauerngeneral* (1931, Fedor Gregorowitsch Iritsch), his own *Sissy* (1932, Herzog Max to the Sissy of Paula Wessely), *Der Teufelsreiter* (1932, Rittmeister Graf Sándor) and *Zwei lachende Augen* (1933, Grossfürst Felician). In between these appearances, he left the star roles in such of his theatre's productions as Miksa Preger's staging of *Viktoria und ihr Husar* ("Künstlerische Gesamtleitung"), his own production of *Schön ist die Welt* (1931), Preger's mounting of *Die Blume von Hawaii, Das Veilchen vom Montmartre,* the Hungarian *Ein Liebestraum* (director), *Die Dame mit dem Regenbogen* (director) and Otto Preminger's visiting staging of *Märchen im Grand-Hotel* to such artists as Louis Treumann, Otto Maran, Hans Heinz Bollmann and Wilhelm Klitsch whilst he occasionally guested elsewhere. In 1930 he directed and created the role of the younger Johann Strauss in *Walzer aus Wien* at the Stadttheater, and in 1934 he played Erzherzog Salvator in the Hungarian children's musical *Kadettenliebe.*

In 1935 Marischka gave up the active management of the Theater an der Wien, which had fallen into severe difficulties in the depression, retaining only his lease on the property, and he thereafter devoted much of his time to writing screenplays and libretti, directing films and appearing in screen roles ranging from the heroic, such as his original part in *Gräfin Mariza* (1932), to the aging, such as Féri in Georg Jacoby's version of *Die Csárdásfürstin.* However, he continued to work and to appear in the theatre in such pieces as Jessel's *Der goldene Mühle* (Scala Theater, 1936), as author-director of *Die Straussbuben* (later staged in Hungary as *Tavaszi hangok*), as Ferdinand Lobmeyer to the Marie Geistinger of Elfie Meyerhofer in his own *Die Walzerkönigin,* in Schmidseder's *Abscheidswalzer* (Georg Ferdinand Waldmüller) and as director of Stolz's *Frühling im Prater.* In 1958, now a little stouter, but not a lot balder (a lot would not have been possible), he appeared at the Raimundtheater in his own Operette *Deutschmeisterkapelle.*

Marischka was the outstanding figure of his age in the Viennese theatre, both from a managerial point of view and as the archetypal leading man of the Austrian Operette for over 20 years. In spite of his place as the creator of the star roles and songs of some of the best Operetten of the Austrian stage canon, his reputation has been somewhat overshadowed outside Austria by the purely vocal talents of the better-publicized, -traveled and -recorded Richard Tauber, but it was Marischka who, whilst lacking the finer and more forceful vocal skills of a Tauber, a Bollmann or a Clewing, outshone and outlasted all his contemporaries as a complete performer: the darkly dashing romantic leading man (a tendency to baldness and squareness notwithstanding) with the winning tenor voice.

1932 **Sissy** (Fritz Kreisler/w Ernst Marischka) Theater an der Wien 23 December

1946 **Die Straussbuben** (Johann Strauss, Josef Strauss arr Oskar Stalla/w Rudolf Weys) Raimundtheater

1948 **Die Walzerkönigin** (Ludwig Schmidseder/w Aldo Pinelli) Wiener Bürgertheater 11 October

1949 **Abschiedswalzer** (Schmidseder/w Rudolf Österreicher) Bürgertheater 8 September

1954 **Der Feldernhügel** (Heinz Sandauer/Karl Farkas) Raimundtheater 24 March

1955 **Liebesbriefe** (Nico Dostal/w Österreicher) Raimundtheater 23 November

1958 **Deutschmeisterkapelle** (Carl Michael Ziehrer arr Max Schönherr/w Österreicher) Raimundtheater 31 May

Biography: Marischka, F: *Juhnke, Lehár und Papa* (Amalthea, Munich, 2000)

MARITANA Opera in 3 acts by Edward Fitzball based on the play *Don César de Bazan* by Adolphe d'Ennery and Philippe Dumanoir. Music by Vincent Wallace. Theatre Royal, Drury Lane, London, 15 November 1845.

Wallace's vastly popular romantic opera was one of the three great standards of the English-language opera repertoire in the middle years of the 19th century when troupes purveying such fare provided an important part of popular theatrical entertainment throughout Britain and the colonies. Based on a classic French play, which would later inspire a number of other musical theatre writers, including W S Gilbert on his *The Yeomen of the Guard, Maritana*'s Spanish tale of a blindfold wedding was illustrated by a score that included such hit numbers as ''Ah! Let Me Like a Soldier Fall'' and ''Scenes That Are Brightest,'' melodies which were the great musical-theatre hits of their day and which would later be used over and over again as fodder for burlesque and other pasticcio scores. Written in a spoken dialogue format with musical numbers, and boasting a happy ending, *Maritana* was, like its equally popular contemporary *The Bohemian Girl,* a legitimate ancestor of the English romantic operettas of later years.

The *Don César de Bazan* story in general, and *Maritana* in particular, came in for a considerable amount of burlesque treatment during the 19th-century reign of the burlesque over the popular musical stage, notably in F C Burnand's *Mary Turner, or The Wicious Willin and Wictorious Wirtue* (Holborn Theatre, 1867, mus arr: George Richardson) in which Fanny Josephs appeared as Mary (''Our Bol'eroine'') to the Don Caesar of Jenny Willmore, the Don Carlos of H J Montague, the Don José of Charlotte Saunders and the Queen Isabella of Mr Wilmott. An 1876 *Little Don Caesar de Bazan, or Maritana and the Merry Monarch* by H J Byron (Gaiety Theatre 26 August 1876) presented Kate Vaughan as Maritana, alongside Nellie Farren (Don Caesar), E W Royce (Don José) and Edward Terry as the King of Spain.

The principal plot line of the show, the case of the convenience marriage with a condemned man who then doesn't die after all, was reprised as late as 1927 in Broadway's *Half a Widow.* In this case, the husband was going not to the scaffold but into battle.

Austria: Theater an der Wien 8 January 1848; USA: Bowery Theater 4 May 1848; Germany: Hamburg 16 February 1849; Australia: Royal Victoria Theatre, Sydney 19 April 1849; Hungary: Budai Színkör (Ger) 20 June 1850

MARIUS, Monsieur [DUPLANY, Claude Marius] (b Paris, 18 February 1850; d at sea, 25 January 1896). ''Frenchman, play producer, actor, raconteur, and optimist'' (they might have added ''cricketer, sculptor, Bohemian and womanizer'') who made a fine career on the burlesque and opéra-comique stage in Britain.

''Mons'' Marius began his theatrical career at the age of 15, working as an extra, then a chorister at Paris's

Théâtre des Folies-Dramatiques while doing daytimes in a silk warehouse. He rose, through his teens, to small roles (Leucaste in *Chilpéric* 1868, Saxon in *Le Petit Faust* 1869) and understudies, and he was still only 19 when he was taken to Britain to play his first major role, as Landry to the Chilpéric of Hervé in the landmark London production of *Chilpéric* (1870).

Following the enormous British success of Hervé's opéra-bouffe (in which the young, prettily accented Frenchman won more than his share of applause) he remained on the left-hand side of the channel to play Siebel in London's *Le Petit Faust* before hurrying back to France to join the seventh batallion of the Chasseurs d'Afrique when war broke out.

Having done his bit against the Prussians at Champigny, he returned to England and there appeared at the Philharmonic Theatre, and round Britain, as Charles Martel (and later, deputising for Emily Soldene, in the normally travesty star role of Drogan) in *Geneviève de Brabant* (1872). In 1873 he was contracted to the Strand Theatre and there he won major star status in the long run of burlesques and musical comedies presented by the Swanborough family: *Nemesis* (1873, Roland de Roncevaux Ramponneau), *El Dorado* (1874, Patatras), *The Field of the Cloth of Gold* revival (1874), *Loo* (1874, Rimbombo), *Intimidad* (1875, Intimidad), *Flamingo* (1875, Hannibal Gobbler), *Antarctica* (1876, Amadis de Batignolles), *L'Africaine* revival (1876, Nelustan), a further *The Field of the Cloth of Gold* revival (1876), *Dan'l Traduced Tinker* (1876, burlesquing Forbes Robertson as Geoffrey Wynyard, the sailor hero of Gilbert's play), *The Maid and the Magpie* revival (1877, Fernando Vilabella), *Champagne* (1877, Chevalier de la Mayonnaise), *The Last of the Red Rover* (Red Rover), *Dora and Diplunacy* (1878, Orloff) and *The Baby* (1879, Rajar Real Jam). He also appeared in the Strand's occasional productions of original musicals, playing Prince Doro in Gilbert and Clay's *Princess Toto* (1876) and François Frenchipani in *The Lying Dutchman* (1876).

When Alexander Henderson brought in modern French comic opera to replace burlesque at the Strand, Marius was a natural for the leading roles. He was paired with Florence St John as Charles Favart in *Madame Favart* (1879), and with Violet Cameron as Merimac in *Olivette* (1880), before moving with Mrs St John (who was by now Mme Marius à la ville) to repeat his *Madame Favart* (1882) and play Don Philip of Aragon in *Manteaux Noirs* (1882), Malicorne in Offenbach's *Belle Lurette* (1883) and in revivals of *Olivette* and *Barbe-bleue* (Popolani), all at the Avenue Theatre under what was billed as his own management (one Edmund Burke was lessee, but Henderson was apparently behind his former star).

The Avenue speculation came to an end, and that with Mrs St John was regularized (7 January 1884) as Marius went on to appear as Prince Grégoire in *La Cosaque* with Kate Santley (1884), in the operetta *The Casting Vote* (1885), in *The Palace of Pearl* (1886, Mentor) at the Empire, where he was also momentarily manager, and for Violet Melnotte in *Mynheer Jan* (General Bombalo, 1887). He also patented, in 1888, "improvements concerning fireproof curtains." Around this time, the journalist Jimmy Davis took his pen to the actor in the pages of *The Bat*, sneering at him as an ex-waiter and suggesting he return to his old trade. Marius sued, proved he had never been a waiter, and was awarded £110 damages. Nevertheless, thereafter he increasingly devoted his attention to directing. His production of *Nadgy*, with Arthur Roberts and Marie Vanoni featured, was not wholly successful, but the olde English *Marjorie* (1889) did well and if an English version of *Madame Cartouche* (1891) stayed on the road, he won a fine run with the very delicately balanced sauciness of *Miss Decima* (1891).

In the 1890s Marius ventured further afield. He appeared with Mrs Bernard Beere in Britain, America and Australia (1892), succeeded to the role of Galeazzo Visconti in Broadway's *The Fencing Master* (1892), directed the production of E E Rice's successful Boston extravaganza *Venus* (1893) and appeared with the Louise Beaudet company in Philadelphia in the role of Metepec in *Jacinta* (1894). His last engagement, after several years of intermittent illness, was with George Edwardes's South African company. He died of consumption on board ship on the way back to Britain.

In 1885 his name appeared on the bills at Philadelphia's New Central Theatre as the author of a burlesque on *The Mikado* given by the Appleton and Randolph Novelty Burlesque Co.

Marius's first wife was the dancer **Laura [Ann] GERRISH** (b Islington, London, 1854), a featured member of the Philharmonic *Geneviève de Brabant* company.

LA MARJOLAINE Opérette in 3 acts by Alfred Vanloo and Eugène Leterrier. Music by Charles Lecocq. Théâtre de la Renaissance, Paris, 3 February 1877.

Modest Marjolaine (Jeanne Granier) has won the Brussels May Queen title for eight years running, and even though she is now married she wins it a for a ninth, for her husband, old Baron Palamède (Berthelier), has to admit that his bride is still a virgin. Annibal (Vauthier), gayest of a band of gay young blades, bets the resigned husband that he will change that and, though he fails in his naughty designs, he manages to give the appearance that he has succeeded. The baron pays up ruinously and Marjolaine is thrown out of the castle. By the time the truth comes out, she is past accepting her spouse's apologies, and she goes off instead with a little clockmaker, Frickel (Félix Puget), who is a tenor.

Granier was this time equipped with a role which had not the farcical possibilities of a *Giroflé-Girofla* or a *Petite Mariée,* but which nevertheless gave her plenty of opportunities to score points in dialogue as well as in song. Lecocq provided her with a pretty, coy first-act Rondo des Blés, a Duo des adieux and the Couplets des ''coucous'' with her little tenor, and another duo of ''no''s with the determined baritone, with whom she later shared a thought of what might have been, and finally a little tongue-in-cheek ''Complainte.'' Vauthier had his chance in his Couplets de Printemps and Berthelier had a few comic moments, but the best of the rest fell to Mlle Théo, as Aveline, the original girl who can't say no, who complained of a ''coeur trop sensible'' explaining ''c'est ma nature qui veut ça!,'' and joined in a bell song with Puget which came dangerously near, in lyrics at least, to that of the soon-to-be-concurrent *Les Cloches de Corneville* (''sonne, sonne, donc maudit carillon'').

If *La Marjolaine* was not adjudged quite up to its predecessors by the critics, it nevertheless pleased Victor Koning's Théâtre de la Renaissance public. It ran straight through the spring to packed houses (116 performances) and would have resumed after the summer recess had Granier not been taken ill. By the time she returned, other shows were under way, and it was not until 1880 that she reprised *La Marjolaine* at the Renaissance. But, in spite of this accident, the show was already on its way. Brussels staged the piece which was set in its own town square just a few weeks after the Paris opening, with Mlle Luce starred as Marjolaine; Bordeaux welcomed the Renaissance company headed by Mme Matz-Ferrare in the summer; and in the autumn the show began to appear further afield.

In September *Kisasszony feleségem* (ad Jenő Rákosi) opened at the Budapest Népszínház with no less a star than Lujza Blaha in the role of Marjolaine alongside János Kápolnai (Friquet), Elek Solymossy (Hannibal) and István Együd (Palamède) to great success and a series of 56 performances, the best for any opérette since the theatre's opening three years earlier, and outpointing both *La Fille de Madame Angot* and *Der Seekadett.* A firm hit, it was brought back in new productions in 1884 and in 1901. A few days later, London saw its version of *La Marjolaine* (ad Sutherland Edwards) starring Kate Santley alongside Fred Mervin, Lionel Brough and Walter H Fisher. London's critics, however, were not ready for a musical about virginity. They howled (''one of the most daring books in the long, dirty line of opéra-bouffe'') at the doubles entendres which had looked safe to the Lord Chamberlain on paper but which la belle Kate imbued with very different meanings—ignoring the fact that the audience were howling too, but with delight. Newspaper correspondence flowed, and when *The Era* announced that the piece had been changed (''nearly all the naughty speeches and wicked suggestions have disappeared''), the director, Maria Liston, hastened into print to deny ''the process of emasculation'' suggested. *La Marjolaine* ran for a fine four months, and returned the following autumn for a second season.

In America, Marie Aimée was quick to add *La Marjolaine* to her repertoire, and she kept it there as a popular item for a number of years. She also played it in Brussels on one of her trips back to Europe (1878). Louise Théo followed her American example from 1882, but apparently no one was game to try to produce the show on Broadway in English. Alice Oates, however, had no such qualms and she produced a version during her season in San Francisco in the fall of 1878, herself playing Marjolaine. A new version (ad Philip Hastings, Albert Raymond) was produced in San Francisco in 1891 (8 September).

In German, the famous doubles entendres either didn't entendre or else were not liked. A mounting at Vienna's Carltheater (ad not credited) with Frln Horty cast as Marjolaine alongside Karl Blasel (Palamède), Franz Eppich (Hannibal), Antonie Schläger (Frickel) and Rosa Streitmann (Aveline) played just 13 times. A Spanish version was mounted under the title *Amapola.*

Another musical entitled simply *Marjolaine* (Hugo Felix/Brian Hooker/Catherine Chisholm Cushing), produced in America (Broadway Theater 24 January 1922, 136 performances) and later played briefly in Britain, was a musical version of the Louis N Parker play *Pomander Walk* in which young love is thwarted by the fact that the lovers' parents had been involved in a jilt. But times had changed—this *Marjolaine* didn't have a double entendre in it anywhere.

USA: Booth's Theater (Fr) 1 October 1877, Bush Street Theater, San Francisco 18 November 1878; Hungary: Népszínház *Kisasszony feleségem* 14 September 1877; UK: Royalty Theatre 29 September 1877; Austria: Carltheater 18 October 1879

MARJORIE English comic opera in 3 acts by ''Lewis Clifton'' (Clifton Lyne) and Joseph J Dilley. Revised by Robert Buchanan. Music by Walter Slaughter. Prince of Wales Theatre, London, 18 January 1890.

Marjorie was the first and only English musical produced by the Carl Rosa Light Opera Company, a British company set up by the famous operatic manager in an attempt to pluck some of the pluckable cash from that lighter musical theatre which had eaten into his audiences. Written by an authorial partnership with little track record and a composer whose only notable achievement to date had been a children's musical version of *Alice in Wonderland,* it was a period light opera, in the style of *Dorothy,* with a feudal background, telling the tale of an amorous earl's attempts to win and wed the titular Marjorie by sending her lover, his serf, off to the wars. Tried out at a matinée during the very successful run of *Paul Jones,* the company's initial presentation, it was subsequently revised for production by the poet Robert Buchanan and made into a vehicle for contralto Agnes Huntington, who had won fame in *Paul Jones,* as the serf, Wilfred.

Miss Huntington walked out shortly after the opening, in newspaperworthy circumstances, but *Marjorie,* with its pretty old-English score, some vigorous low comedy from resident funny man Harry Monkhouse, ringing singing from the handsome baritone Hayden Coffin as the villain (''For Love of Thee''), and the hero's role restored to its original tenor, had a six-and-a-half-month run in London, toured successfully with Miss Emmott Herbert, ''the lady baritone,'' as hero, and was played in the repertoire of J C Williamson's Royal Comic Opera Company in Australia and in South Africa.

Another musical under the same title credited to Fred Thompson, Clifford Grey and Harold Atteridge (''additional dialogue''), with music by Romberg, Herbert Stothart, Philip Culkin and Stephen Jones, was produced at Broadway's Shubert Theater (11 August 1924). Elizabeth Hines in the title role vamped Roy Royston to charleston strains until he put her brother's play on the stage and married her 144 times.

Australia: Princess Theatre, Melbourne 20 December 1893

MARRE, Albert [MOSHINSKI, Albert] (b New York, 20 September 1925). Director whose several hits were big enough to make up for a welter of quick failures.

After posts in Cambridge, Massachusetts, and at the New York City Center as a director of drama, Marre made a successful start in the musical theatre when his first assignment, as director of the West Coast production of *Kismet,* gave him a major national and international success. He had less joy with the *Lost Horizon* musical, *Shangri La,* a camped-up Offenbach *Belle Hélène* retitled *La Belle,* and with two further shows by the *Kismet* team of Wright and Forrest, *At the Grand* and *The Love Doctor,* but he moored up against success once again with Jerry Herman's maiden musical, *Milk and Honey* (1961) and, most notably, with the original production of the Don Quixote musical *Man of La Mancha* (1965). His subsequent ventures with new musicals were wholly unfortunate. Four later shows by *La Mancha* composer Mitch Leigh (*Chu Chem, Cry for Us All, Halloween, Home Sweet Homer*) and a British extravaganza called *Winnie,* based on the life of Winston Churchill, all folded on the road or soon after.

Marre is married to performer **Joan DIENER** who appeared as Lalume in *Kismet,* as Aldonza in *Man of La Mancha* (USA, UK, France), as Helen in *La Belle,* in *At the Grand* (1958), *Cry for Us All* (1970), *Home Sweet Homer* (1976), etc.

1970 **Cry for Us All** (Mitch Leigh/William Alfred, Phyllis Robinson/w Alfred) Broadhurst Theater 8 April

1976 **Home Sweet Homer** (aka *Odyssey*) (Leigh/Forman Brown, Charles Burr/Roland Kibbee) Palace Theater 4 January

MARS, Antony (b Vence, 22 October 1861; d Paris, 17 February 1915). Expert author of vaudevilles and comedies whose works won substantial and far-flung success around Europe in the 1890s and 1900s, and on several occasions around the world.

Before making a success as a dramatist, Mars worked first in a solicitor's office and then as a clerk for the railways. His first significant hit in the theatre came with the play *Les Surprises du divorce* (1888, w Alexandre Bisson) and, as the play successes continued through the 1890s, he also began to write freely, both in collaborations and occasionally alone, for the musical theatre. He achieved a remarkable percentage of hits to productions, and his most enduring successes in the musical sphere came with two pieces with scores composed by Victor Roger: the vaudeville-opérette *Les Vingt-huit Jours de Clairette* with its merry tale of mistaken identities and a disguised lady loose in an army camp, and the superb *Les Fêtards,* with its comic/sentimental lesson on how to hold an errant husband. The libretto of *Les Fêtards* was later used as the basis for two further musicals, the highly successful *Kitty Grey* in England and *The Rounders* in America, as well as being played widely and long in Europe with Roger's original musical score attached, and on the West End stage as a straight play.

Three other Mars pieces originally set with scores by Roger for their French productions also traveled around Europe, sometimes with and sometimes without that music attached. *Le Voyage de Corbillon,* written by Mars alone, was adapted into German as *Das rothe Parapluie* (ad Alexander Landesberg, Ludwig Fischl) to be played at Vienna's Theater in der Josefstadt with a score by Karl Kappeller (26 February 1897), and also appeared in Hungary as *Az orleansi szüzek* (ad Sándor Peterdi, Városligeti Nyári Színkör 23 August 1906) with Roger's score intact. The vaudeville *Les Douze Femmes de Japhet,* written with Maurice Desvallières and played with some considerable success in France, Austria and Hungary, was also adapted into a German vaudeville, *Die zwölf Frauen des Japhet,* by Julius Freund and composer Viktor Holländer for the Berlin Metropoltheater. The later *La Poule blanche* (w Maurice Hennequin) turned up in Germany as *Das weisse Henne* (ad Bolten-Bäckers, Viktoria Theater 11 September 1898) and in Hungary as *Fehér csirke* (ad Emil Makai, Gyula Zempléni Népszínház 28 April

1899). Hungary also proved partial to one piece which France had cared less for: *Clary-Clara* had a fine run in Budapest as *Klári* (ad Ferenc Rajna, Viktor Rákosi Népszínház 14 April 1894, 31 performances) before its libretto was borrowed by László Szilágyi to be made over into the text for Béla Zerkovitz's extremely successful and enduring *Csókos asszony* (Városi Színház 27 February 1926). Hungary also welcomed Mars and Raymond's *Nicol-Nick,* under the title *Vegye el á lányomat* (ad Gyula Komor).

Another vaudeville, *La Demoiselle du téléphone,* this one originally set with a score by Gaston Serpette, provided Mars with a further worldwide success in a variety of musicalized forms, whilst the Serpette/Roger *La Dot de Brigitte* was played in Berlin and Vienna as *Frau Lieutenant,* and in Hungary as *Brigitta.*

The Robert Planquette vaudeville-opérette à grand spectacle *Mam'zelle Quat' Sous* and the Louis Varney opérette *Les Forains* also won both German- and Hungarian-language productions as *Die beiden Don Juans / A garasos kisasszony* and *Olympia, die Muskelvenus / Der Gaukler / Komediások* respectively. However, in spite of this outstanding strike rate in Europe, and in spite of the enormous popularity of versions of such of his plays as *Les Surprises du divorce, Le Truc de Séraphin* and *Fils à papa* in English-speaking countries, Mars's musical works—*Les Fêtards* and *La Demoiselle du téléphone* apart—were largely bypassed in Britain and America. *Les Surprises du divorce,* however, eventually turned up on the Broadway stage in musical form, played under the title *Honeydew* (Efrem Zimbalist/Joseph W Herbert Casino Theater 6 September 1920).

In later years, Mars devoted his attention largely to the non-musical theatre, but he collaborated with his earliest partner, Maurice Desvallières, on the French versions of two highly successful Operetten, *Die Dollarprinzessin* and *Die keusche Susanne,* the latter a musical version of his own play *Fils à papa* and, in the long run, his most international credit in the musical theatre.

His *Veuve Durosel* (w Bisson, Théâtre du Vaudeville 7 March 1888) was made into a musical in Czechoslovakia as *Mama vom Ballett* (Bernard Grün/Rudolf Stadler, Ernst Stadler Deutsches Theater studio 20 February 1926), whilst another, unidentified work was quoted as the source of the American entertainment *Exceeding the Speed-Limit* (Cohan's Grand Opera House, Chicago 23 December 1912), and producer A H Woods went into print to say that his Julian Eltinge musical *The Fascinating Widow* was developed from a Mars comedy.

A pretty little square, which once held Vence's one good second-hand bookshop, commemorates Mars in his hometown. But it spells his name wrongly on its bus stop.

1888 **Quand on conspire!** (P Devos) 1 act Salle Lancry 22 January

1890 **Les Douze Femmes de Japhet** (Victor Roger/w Maurice Desvallières) Théâtre de la Renaissance 16 December

1891 **La Demoiselle du téléphone** (Gaston Serpette/w Desvallières) Théâtre des Nouveautés 2 May

1891 **Le Mitron** (André Martinet/w Maxime Boucheron) Théâtre des Folies-Dramatiques 24 September

1892 **Les Vingt-huit Jours de Clairette** (Roger/w Hippolyte Raymond) Théâtre des Folies-Dramatiques 3 May

1892 **La Bonne de chez Duval** (Serpette/w Raymond) Théâtre des Nouveautés 6 October

1893 **Catherinette** (Roger/w Raymond) 1 act Lunéville 17 July

1893 **Pierre et Paul** (Roger/w Raymond) 1 act Lunéville 17 July

1894 **Les Forains** (Louis Varney/w Boucheron) Théâtre des Bouffes-Parisiens 9 February

1894 **Le Troisième Hussards** (Justin Clérice/w Maurice Hennequin) Théâtre de la Gaîté 14 March

1894 **Clary-Clara** (Roger/w Raymond) Théâtre des Folies-Dramatiques 20 March

1895 **Nicol-Nick** (Roger/w Raymond, Alfred Duru) Théâtre des Folies-Dramatiques 23 January

1895 **La Dot de Brigitte** (Serpette, Roger/w Paul Ferrier) Théâtre des Bouffes-Parisiens 6 May

1896 **Le Voyage de Corbillon** (Roger) Théâtre Cluny 30 January

1896 **Sa Majesté l'amour** (Roger/w M Hennequin) Eldorado 24 December

1897 **Les Fêtards** (Roger/w M Hennequin) Théâtre du Palais-Royal 28 October

1897 **Mam'zelle Quat' Sous** (Robert Planquette/w Desvallières) Théâtre de la Gaîté 5 November

1898 **La Geisha** (*The Geisha*) French version w Charles Clairville, Jacques Lemaire (Théâtre de l'Athénée)

1899 **La Poule blanche** (Roger/w M Hennequin) Théâtre Cluny 13 January

1910 **La Vie joyeuse** (Henri Hirschmann) Valence 17 November

1911 **La Princesse Dollar** (*Die Dollarprinzessin*) French version w Desvallières (Théâtre de la Scala)

1913 **La Chaste Suzanne** (*Die keusche Susanne*) French version w Desvallières (Théâtre des Célestins, Lyon)

MARSH, Howard [Warren] (b Bluffton, Ind, 18 August 1888; d Long Branch, NJ, 7 August 1969).

A good-looking leading man with a fine tenor voice, Marsh had his first good part on Broadway in 1917 as the leading man of Louis Hirsch's short-lived *The Grass Widow* (Comte Jacques de Cluny). He subsequently took over a supporting role in *Maytime* and toured in that piece alongside Grace van Studdiford, and appeared in the *Greenwich Village Follies* (1920) before his next important appearance on Broadway. This time he was in a hit, cast as Franz Schober, the tenor who gets the girl and Schubert's "Serenade" to sing in the American version of *Das Dreimäderlhaus* (*Blossom Time,* 1921). He followed this memorable performance with a second consecutive triumph when he created the star role of Sigmund Romberg's romantic operetta *The Student Prince* (Karl-Franz), a role equipped with another, almost as celebrated Serenade, and introducing the duets ''Deep in My Heart, Dear'' and ''Golden Days.'' Romberg's *Cherry Blossoms* (1927, Ned Hamilton) was a failure, but its closure at least made Marsh available to create the romantic lead of a third block-buster, as Gaylord Ravenal in *Show Boat,* joining Norma Terris in singing ''Make Believe,'' ''You Are Love'' and ''Why Do I Love You?'' for the first time on any stage. After this top-class trio of roles, however, there were no more successes and Marsh's final Broadway appearances came when he was paired again with Miss Terris in a swift flop called *The Well of Romance* (Poet) in 1930, little more than a decade after his first lead role, and in a season of revivals of Gilbert and Sullivan and other classic musicals (Nanki-Poo, Ralph Rackstraw, Marco, Frederic, Dunstable, Tolloller, Defendant, Robin Hood).

MARTIN, Ernest [MARKOWITZ, Ernest H] (b Pittsburgh, Pa, 28 August 1918; d Los Angeles, 7 May 1995).

Producer who, in collaboration with Cy Feuer, presented such Broadway musicals as *Where's Charley?, Guys and Dolls, Can-Can, The Boy Friend, How to Succeed in Business without Really Trying, Little Me, Skyscraper* and *Walking Happy* and the film version of *A Chorus Line.*

MARTIN GUERRE Musical in 2 acts by Alain Boublil and Claude-Michel Schönberg based on the French folk tale. Lyrics by Edward Hardy and Stephen Clark. Music by Claude-Michel Schönberg. Prince Edward Theatre, London, 10 July 1996.

The old is-he-or-isn't-he French tale of Martin Guerre, with the histories of ''Roger Tichborne'' and ''Anastasia'' one of the world's favorite histories of imposture, has—in spite of its inherently undramatic nature—been used down the years as the basis for a number of stage and screen dramas. One of these, E M Pearl's *Martin Guerre, or The Guilty Claim,* was brought out during the Tichborne affair (Theatre Royal, Woolwich 13 September 1873) with Charles Quayle playing both Martin Guerre and the impostor. A French film version, with Gérard Depardieu starred was brought out in 1982, and an American one, under the title *Sommersby* in 1993 with Richard Gere featured. Announced well in advance of its production as the next project of the writers of *Les Misérables* and *Miss Saigon,* the musical version of *Martin Guerre* found itself the most remarkable victim of the ''copycat'' syndrome. Musicals based on the same tale were brought out at Hartford, Conn (1993), Toronto (1994) and at Chicago's Goodman Theatre (*The House of Martin Guerre* 21 June 1996) whilst Cameron Mackintosh's production of Boublil and Schönberg's show was in preparation.

This version of the tale emphasized the influence over the lives of the individual of the Protestant/Catholic struggles in sixteenth-century France, rather than the mystery over the identity of ''Martin Guerre,'' which was never here posited as a mystery to the audience. Catholic landowner's nephew Martin Guerre (Matt Rawles) weds Bertrande de Rols (Juliette Caton), the daughter of a neighboring landowner in a move which will consolidate Catholic power and property in the village of Artigat. However, Martin is unready for marriage, the couple fail to produce an heir, and the despairing boy runs off to fight in the wars. Courted in his absence, with his uncle's and the village's approbation, by the ambitious but Catholic Guillaume (Jérôme Pradon), Bertrande finds comfort instead in the services held secretly by the Protestants of the area. And then, seven years on, Martin Guerre returns. Or so it seems to the villagers. But, in fact, the man who instals himself as Bertrande's husband and gets her with child is not Martin, but a friend and fellow soldier, Arnaud du Thil (Iain Glen). The two fall quickly in love, and—believing Guerre dead—decide to keep up the imposture. The jealous Guillaume, discovering the couple's Protestant sympathies, stirs up the villagers, and ''Martin'' is arrested for imposture. While the villagers clan against the revealed Protestants, Arnaud and Bertrande protest before the court that ''Martin'' is who he claims to be, and judgment seems likely to favor them when Martin Guerre turns up, alive. Arnaud is imprisoned, and when the understanding Martin helps them to escape, the furious Guillaume, who has led a revengeful riot through the village, tries to stab Martin. Arnaud takes the blow intended for his friend. Finally, Bertrande leaves a chastened Artigat, with the Protestants, and Martin Guerre stays on, alone, in the place destined for him as the leader of the village.

The music of the show saw Schönberg back in the form of *Les Misérables* with a score which peaked in a richly dramatic courtoom sequence, which ranged from the pathetic (''Me'') to the ringing (''Martin Guerre''), the romantic (''Someone'') and the ensemble (''The Impostors'') and featured such soaring pieces as the thrilling two-tenor duo ''Here Comes the Morning'' and a fine selection of choral music. A bit of the coarsly comic, as provided by the Thénardiers in the earlier show, was here given by the village commères discussing their late husbands in ''Sleeping on our Own.''

Martin Guerre had a troubled birth, fighting it way through rewrites, rearrangements and postponements to its opening night. On its production, it was met with diverse reactions by the press and public, but producer

Mackintosh and his production team continued to work on the show, and finally, after some three and a half months, the show was temporarily shut down for several days to allow a major restaging. On 11 November 1996 *Martin Guerre* reopened in a revised version with additional lyrics by Herbert Kretzmer and Alain Boublil. However, the piece's unshowy and deeply charactered nature was against its being boosted into a success as the visually spectacular and comic-strip charactered *Miss Saigon* had been, and in spite of all the efforts *Martin Guerre* was closed after some 16 further months and 700 nights.

Mackintosh did not, however, abandon *Martin Guerre.* With a tenacity he had already shown on other occasions with less than huge-hit shows, he had *Martin Guerre* largely rewritten, and this re-revised version, with both altered text and new songs, was produced at Leeds's West Yorkshire Playhouse (8 December 1998). Matthew Cammelle (Arnaud), Stephen Weller (Martin) and Joanna Riding (Bertrande) featured. The new version seemed to have focused inward from the larger picture in the original, concentrating more on the plight of the young people at its center, manipulated by men of religion and the envious to their own ends. Musically, if some of the outstanding moments of the original score—from the gentle ''Me'' to the stunning ''Here Comes the Morning'' but also the less attractive comic trio—had disappeared or been transmogrified, there were still some stirring pieces remaining for the leading lady or the chorus in a score largely devoted to the many tenor voices of the cast and as before climaxing in a rewritten court scene. The show's reception, this time, was much improved, and announcements of a series of overseas productions were made as the show set off to play the main British centers. An American production, which was first seen at Detroit, with Erin Dilly (Bertrande), Hugh Panaro (Martin) and Stephen Buntrock (Arnaud) featured, headed Broadwaywards at the end of 1999, but it did not get there. The show closed down, after a visit to Los Angeles, in February 2000.

USA: Tyrone Guthrie Theater, Minneapolis 17 September 1999

Recording: revised version (First Night)

Video: *Martin Guerre: A Musical Journey* (VCI)

MARTIN, Hugh (b Birmingham, Ala, 11 August 1914).

At first a chorister and member of the singing group The Martins in musical comedy (*Hooray for What!, The Streets of Paris, Louisiana Purchase, The Lady Comes Across,* pre-Broadway in *My Dear Public* and *Three After Three*), Martin joined with fellow singer **Ralph BLANE** (b Broken Arrow, Okla, 26 July 1914; d Broken Arrow, Okla, 13 November 1995) to compose the songs for the successful musical comedy *Best Foot Forward* (''Buckle Down, Winsocki'') and for a number of films, of which the most notable was *Meet Me in St Louis* (''Meet Me in St Louis,'' ''Trolley Song''). After the war, Martin returned to writing for the stage and supplied songs for *Look Ma, I'm Dancin'* (188 performances), *Make a Wish* (102 performances), Eric Maschwitz's neatly calculated attempt to write a British Broadway musical to the text of the play *Daddy Long-Legs* (*Love from Judy,* 594 performances), and a musicalization of Noël Coward's *Blithe Spirit* (375 performances, London 93 performances).

In 1989 an attempt to mount a Broadway stage-spectacular version of *Meet Me in St Louis*—previously played as a stage piece at the St Louis Municipal Opera in 1960—ran through an apparently forced 236 performances.

1941 **Best Foot Forward** (w Ralph Blane/John Cecil Holm) Ethel Barrymore Theater 1 October

1948 **Look Ma, I'm Dancin'!** (Jerome Lawrence, Robert E Lee) Adelphi Theater 29 January

1951 **Make a Wish** (Preston Sturges) Winter Garden Theater 18 April

1952 **Love from Judy** (Timothy Gray/Eric Maschwitz) Saville Theatre, London 25 September

1964 **High Spirits** (w Gray) Alvin Theater 7 April

1989 **Meet Me in St Louis** (w Blane/ad Hugh Wheeler) Gershwin Theater 2 November

MARTIN, Mary [Virginia] (b Weatherford, Tex, 1 December 1913; d Rancho Mirage, Calif, 3 November 1990). Broadway soubrette who became one of the American musical theatre's favorite leading ladies and who introduced two of Rodgers and Hammerstein's most memorable heroines.

Miss Martin first came to the fore at the age of 25 as the soubrette of *Leave It to Me!* in which, in the character of the popsie Dolly Winslow, she introduced Cole Porter's ''My Heart Belongs to Daddy.'' It was, however, some four years before she returned to Broadway, having closed out of town in the musicals *Nice Goin'* (1939, Billie Jackson) and *Dancing in the Streets* (1943, Mary Hastings) and spent some time in Hollywood, where her film assignments had included *The Great Victor Herbert* (1939) and *The Birth of the Blues* (1941). The character in which she returned was that of the brought-to-life statue of the goddess of love in *One Touch of Venus,* introducing Kurt Weill's ''Speak Low'' and ''I'm a Stranger Here Myself'' for a long and successful run. She subsequently appeared as the Chinese heroine of *Lute Song* (1946, ''Mountain High, Valley Low'') on Broadway and, miscast, as the prima donna heroine of Noël Coward's London musical *Pacific 1860* before going out to the rest of America as the star of the first touring company of *Annie Get Your Gun* (1947).

Miss Martin had her second great success when she created the role of Ensign Nellie Forbush, the button-bright little heroine of Rodgers and Hammerstein's *South Pacific* (1949, Tony Award), singing "(I'm in love with) A Wonderful Guy," "I'm Gonna Wash that Man Right outa my Hair" and "Honey Bun" to New York and London audiences. In 1954, now past the age of 40, she starred in a Broadway-style musical version of J M Barrie's *Peter Pan* which brought her a second Tony award and, thanks to a television recording, loving identification with this celebrated boyish role throughout America. However, her most memorable achievement came when she encouraged Rodgers and Hammerstein to write for her their musical version of the tale of Maria von Trapp and her singing family. As Maria in *The Sound of Music* ("My Favourite Things," "Do-re-mi," "The Sound of Music") Miss Martin scored yet another major triumph, took her third Tony Award, and launched a show which was to become—this time with a little help from someone else's film—one of the best-loved of all time.

If the star was less successful in the title role of the short-lived *Jennie* (1963), it was perhaps partly because she herself had ordered a disinfecting rewrite of the libretto and character, and her version of the title role of *Hello, Dolly!,* though well received on the touring circuits at home, proved not to be to the taste of Londoners. She turned up one final Broadway musical success, however, when in 1966 she starred opposite Robert Preston in the two-handed tale of marriage, *I Do! I Do!* ("My Cup Runneth Over," "Flaming Agnes").

I Do! I Do! turned out to be not only Miss Martin's last Broadway success, but her last Broadway musical. Although she appeared further on the stage over another 20 years, she did not move into senior roles in musicals, leaving her image, in line with her oft-reseen television film appearance as *Peter Pan,* as a youngish and spiritedly soubretty one.

Miss Martin was married to Richard Halliday, producer of *Jennie,* and was the mother of actor Larry Hagman, best known as the "JR" of television's *Dallas.*

Autobiography: *My Heart Belongs* (Morrow, New York, 1976)

Literature: Newman, S: *Mary Martin On Stage* (Westminster Press, Philadelphia, 1969), Rivadue, B: *Mary Martin, A Bio-bibliography* (Greenwood Press, New York, 1991)

MARTIN, Millicent [Mary Lillian] (b Romford, Essex, 8 June 1934). Top British soubrette of the 1950s who later returned to play character roles.

Originally a child performer (*Lute Song,* etc), Millicent Martin made her first adult London appearance at the age of 21 when she took over as Fay/Lolita in *The Boy Friend,* and her first on Broadway as Nancy in the same show. She made her mark soon after as the little cockney stripper, Maisie, in *Expresso Bongo* (1958) but another, rather similar, role in the less successful *The Crooked Mile* (1959, Cora) was followed only by the flops of *The Dancing Heiress* (1960), *State of Emergency* (1962) and a curiously adapted musical version of *The Admirable Crichton* (*Our Man Crichton*), reorganized to make her character of Tweenie extravagantly prominent. Thereafter she was seen principally on television, but she appeared at the Chichester Festival as Polly Peachum (*Beggar's Opera*) and had her best new musical-theatre part since *Expresso Bongo* as Ruth Earp opposite the Denry Machin of Jim Dale in *The Card* (1975) before finding a fine success with *Side by Side by Sondheim,* a compilation show of material from Stephen Sondheim's shows of which she was one of the original group of instigators.

After some years away from the musical theatre, Miss Martin succeeded, in the 1980s, to the roles of Dorothy Brock in Broadway's *42nd Street* and that of Phyllis in the London production of *Follies.* In 1998 she appeared in a concert tryout of a musical based on *Whatever Happened to Baby Jane?*

On film, she paired with Tony Tanner in a cinematic version of *Stop the World—I Want to Get Off.*

MARTIN, Robert [Jasper] (b Galway, Ireland, ?1841; d Ross, County Galway, 12 September 1905).

Bohemian Irish journalist, storyteller and songwriter, Unionist politician and Justice of the Peace, "Bob" Martin never had a musical-comedy score played in the London theatre, and would not, indeed, have been capable of writing one, but in the late 1880s his songs were amongst the greatest highlights of George Edwardes's Gaiety Theater new burlesques. Nellie Farren introduced "I'm a Jolly Little Chap all Round" and Edwin Lonnen made major hits of his "Ballyhooley" in *Monte Cristo Jr* (1886) and of his "Killaloe" in *Miss Esmeralda* (1887). "The Dispensary Doctor" written for the same artist in *Frankenstein* (1887) was, like the show, a little less successful, but "Enniscorthy" sung by Lonnen as Mephistopheles, and the topical duet "I Raise No Objection to That" in *Faust-Up-to-Date* (1888) were both serious hits.

Martin wrote lyrics for Teddy Solomon for two songs in *Ruy Blas and the Blasé Roué* (1889) and combined with Ernest Ford to produce an entire short musical called *Joan or the Brigands of Bluegoria* ("a story of the stock exchange") which was privately performed by himself and a group of fashionable friends including Sir George Power, David Bispham, Cosmo Gordon Lennox and Gabrielle Enthoven at the Opera Comique, but thereafter, although he continued to write individual songs ("Mullingar," "Mulrooney's Dog," "Thru Darkest Ire-

Plate 242. **Millicent Martin** *and the ladies' chorus in* The Crooked Mile.

land,'' ''On the Blatherumskite,'' etc) his name disappeared from London's playbills, emerging just once more, a decade later, on the program of Edwardes's revusical *The Merry-Go-Round.*

His one full set of songs was written for a burlesque called *Doctor Faust* produced in Dublin by military amateurs, and subsequently picked up by Maggie Morton for the Londonderry Theatre. It was also produced at the Chelsea Barracks in 1888, directed by Augustus Harris and with a new score by Edward Solomon.

1885 **Doctor Faust and Miss Marguerite, or The Young Duck with the Old Quack** (E A P Hobday) Queen's Theatre, Dublin 24 August; Londonderry 27 November

MARTINOT, Sadie [MARTINOT, Sarah Frances Marie] (b Jamaica, NY, 19 December 1861; d Ogdensburg, NY, 7 May 1923). Singing beauty who played in musical and non-musical theatre on both sides of the Atlantic.

At the age of 15 the lavishly glamorous Miss Martinot appeared as Cupid in a production of the burlesque *Ixion* at the Eagle Theater before going on the road with Adah Richmond's burlesque company (1877, *Chow Chow, Golden Butterfly, Three Musketeers* as ''Saidée Martinetti''). She played with E E Rice's company in Boston (Eulalie in *Evangeline,* Yenadizze and replacement Hiawatha in *Hiawatha* 1878, *Pippins* 1878) and, as a member of the company at the Boston Museum, played Hebe in that theatre's first American production of *HMS Pinafore.* She also played in the slightly musicalized Boston version of *Mein Leopold* (1878) and Pedro in the disastrously unprepared production of the ''original American opéra-bouffe extravaganza'' *Sancho Pedro* (Boston 16 June 1879). She subsequently toured with Fred Stinson as Gabriel in *Evangeline,* in *Babes in the Wood, Tit for Tat, Larks,* etc (1880), and then crossed to Britain where she played small roles in the Alhambra productions of *Mephistopheles II* (*Le Petit Faust,* 1880, Spirit of the Brocken) and *Jeanne, Jeannette et Jeanneton* (1881, Céline) and created her one important musical part, the ingenue Katrina in Planquette's *Rip van Winkle.*

Returning to America, she toured with the Grayson Opera Company (1881–82, Fiametta in *La Mascotte,* etc), appeared at the Boston Bijou in comic opera in the summer of 1883, and then announced to the press that she would never sing again. She concentrated largely on non-singing parts thereafter until the ''never'' got the better of her and she appeared at the Casino Theater for Aronson in the title role of Genée's *Nanon* (1885). She scored a major success. However, cast in the lead of the theatre's later production of *Nadgy,* she walked out of the show during rehearsals and appeared instead at the Amberg Theater playing Bettina in *La Mascotte* in German. After several successful years acting only in plays, she reappeared on the musical stage playing Suzette in *Le Voyage de Suzette* in 1893 and caused a sensation (more by her figure and revealing frock than anything else) as Lady Angela in a revival of *Patience* (1896). She later starred at the head of her own comedy and drama company for a number of years but appeared, between dramatic engagements, in the musical shows *The Gay Parisians* and *A Stranger in New York* (1897, Hattie) and later in character roles in such pieces as *Piff! Paff! Pouf!* (1905) on the road—before going into a retirement which ended, in the last seven years of her life, in an insane asylum.

In 1884 a ''Sadie Martinot'' chrysanthemum was introduced at a New York flower show. It was yellow.

MARTOS, Ferenc (b Arad, 10 January 1875; d Budapest, 24 November 1938). The most outstanding and successful librettist of the Hungarian musical theatre.

In a career of over 30 years which covered the most internationally flourishing era of the Hungarian musical theatre, Martos worked with virtually all the best local composers of his time, and he was responsible for the texts of a vast percentage of Hungary's most successful and enduring operetts.

Martos graduated as a Doctor of Law from Budapest university and took a post in the department of religious and public education of the public service. He began writing for the theatre in 1900 and his first produced piece, a verse comedy, *Balassa Bálint,* was staged in 1902 at the Nemzeti Színház. Later the same year he moved into the musical theatre for the first time when he provided the text for Jenő Huszka's highly successful operett *Bob herceg.* It was a libretto which involved British royalty in the same kind of preposterous doings that British librettists persisted in inflicting on central European kings and princesses, and the Prince Bob of the title was no less than the son of Queen Victoria. *Bob herceg* turned out to be the biggest native operett success up to its time, and thereafter, although Martos turned out a handful of successful plays and adaptations (including the Hungarian version of *His Official Wife*), the bulk of his career was spent as a librettist and lyricist for the musical theatre.

After further hits with Huszka (*Aranyvirág, Gül Baba*), he joined forces with the rising Viktor Jacobi. The pair had several home successes before they teamed on Jacobi's two most important shows, *Leányvásár* (*The Marriage Market*) with its Ruramerican-cowboy version of the *Martha* story, and the finely constructed combination of the romantic and comic that was *Szibill.* Both operetts would go round the world. Before they got there, however, *A kis gróf,* on which Martos had collaborated with the young Áladár Rényi, had already made it to Vienna and to Broadway under the title *Suzi.*

Martos wrote the texts for Kálmán's *A kis király* (*Der kleine König*) and *Zsuzsi kisasszony* (*Miss Springtime*), and for Lehár's *A pacsirta,* originally produced in Budapest but later more generally known under its German title of *Wo die Lerche singt,* and he paired with another young composer, Károly Komjáti, on what would be, as it had been with Rényi, the most important hit of the composer's career. The military operett *Pillangó főhadnagy* became another oft-revived staple in the Hungarian repertoire.

Martos then paired up with Albert Szirmai, for whom he provided the text for *Alexandra* (1925), one of his most internationally successful works, as well as for *Eva grófnő* (''a combination of *Enoch Arden* and *Madame Butterfly* with a happy ending'') and the successful *A Balerina.* By the time of his final works, some of which were staged in translation in Vienna (the Christmas show *Hanserl* [ex- *Jánoska*] and Komjáti's Singspiel *Ein Liebestraum*), the height of the European operett period had passed, and his remarkable total of hits was no further increased.

Martos's name appeared attached to a 1923 American musical called *Peaches* (Max R Steiner/Robert B Smith/ad Harry B Smith Garrick Theater, Philadelphia 22 January) but producer George Lederer was not specific about the source of his borrowing and the Swiss maid/heiress identity-swap of the show's tale certainly didn't belong to any of Martos's major plays.

- 1902 **Bob herceg** (Jenő Huszka/w Károly Bakonyi) Népszínház 20 December
- 1903 **Aranyvirág** (Huszka) Király Színház 6 November
- 1905 **A granadai vőlegény** (József Bahnert) Népszínház 11 February
- 1905 **Gül Baba** (Huszka) Király Színház 9 December
- 1905 **A legvitézebb huszár** (Viktor Jacobi) Magyar Színház 30 December
- 1907 **Tüskerózsa** (Jacobi) Király Színház 23 March
- 1907 **Tündérszerelem** (Huszka) Népszínház-Vígopera 20 December

1908 **Van, de nincs** (Jacobi) Király Színház 30 October

1909 **Jánoska** (Jacobi) Király Színház 7 May

1911 **A kis gróf** (Áladár Rényi) Király Színház 9 September

1911 **Leányvásár** (Jacobi/w Miksa Bródy) Király Színház 14 November

1913 **Szökik a nagysága** (w M Bródy) Budapesti Színház 22 March

1914 **A kis király** (Emmerich Kálmán/w Bakonyi) Népopera 17 January

1914 **Szibill** (Viktor Jacobi/w M Bródy) Király Színház 27 February

1915 **Zsuzsi kisasszony** (Kálmán/w M Bródy) Vígszínház 27 February

1918 **A pacsirta** (Franz Lehár) Király Színház 1 February

1918 **Pillangó főhadnagy** (Károly Komjáti/w Imre Harmath) Király Színház 7 June

1919 **Lili bárónő** (Huszka) Városi Színház 7 March

1919 **Kutyuskám** (Albert Szirmai) 1 act Andrássy-uti Színház 12 December

1920 **Cigánygrófné** (Zsigmond Vincze/Ernő Kulinyi) Király Színház 13 March

1925 **Anna-bál** (Robert Volkmann arr Vincze/Kulinyi) Király Színház 30 September

1925 **Alexandra** (Szirmai) Király Színház 25 November

1926 **Kitty és Kató** (Rényi) Király Színház 30 April

1926 **Hajtóvadászat** (Huszka) Városi Színház 22 October

1928 **Éva grófnő** (Szirmai) Király Színház 3 February

1929 **Katica** (Alfred Márkus) Városi Színház 7 December

1931 **A Balerina** (Szirmai) Király Színház 7 March

1933 **Ein Liebestraum** (Komjáti/w Szilágyi ad Heinz Reichert) Theater an der Wien 27 October

1935 **Szépségkirálynő** (József Paksy/w Andor Szenes) Király Színház 21 June

MARX BROTHERS

Harpo MARX [Arthur MARX] (b New York, 23 November 1888; d Hollywood, Calif, 28 September 1964); **Groucho MARX** [Julius Henry MARX] (b New York, 2 October 1890; d Los Angeles, 19 August 1977); **Chico MARX** [Leonard MARX] (b New York, 22 March 1891; d Hollywood, Calif, 11 October 1961); **Zeppo MARX** [Herbert MARX] (b New York, 25 February 1901; d Palm Springs, 29 November 1979).

The famous American comedy squad began their careers in vaudeville, touring in 1914 with their uncle Al Shean under their given names as ''Al Shean and the four Marx brothers,'' before appearing (reduced to four, by this stage, with the early loss of fifth brother, Milton-cum-Gummo), on the almost legitimate stage in three musical comedies. The first of these, *I'll Say She Is* (''a musical comedy revue''), written by Will B Johnstone in the form of an extended variety sketch (songs: Tom Johnstone), was built to allow the team to gallivant through the kind of extravagant comedy for which they became famous, and included an hypnosis section in which Groucho appeared as Napoléon, a courtroom ''drama'' and some spare moments for other specialities. It ran through 304 performances at the Casino Theater, encouraging the follow-up the next year with a vehicle written by an altogether classier team: George S Kaufman and Irving Berlin.

The equally zany and marginally more constructed *The Cocoanuts* was an even greater success than its predecessor (377 performances), and a third piece, *Animal Crackers,* again penned by Kaufman and by Morrie Ryskind (songs: Bert Kalmar and Harry Ruby)—presenting Groucho as the preposterous Captain Spalding, out to hunt down a stolen painting—also had a fine run (191 performances). The brothers then left Broadway to pursue the career which would give them international fame, in Hollywood. Amongst their screen ventures were included filmed versions of both *The Cocoanuts* and *Animal Crackers.*

Targets for often unimaginative impersonators for many years, the brothers finally won a clever and sympathetic treatment in the London revusical show *A Day in Hollywood, a Night in the Ukraine,* in which Sheila Steafel stole the evening as an appealingly mute Harpo in a one-act Marx-style perversion of *The Bear.* Perhaps just because it was successful, and success of course means money, this umpteenth imitation provoked a threat of legal action for plagiarism of the brothers' act. The team were also portrayed in the Broadway musical *Minnie's Boys* (Imperial Theater 26 March 1970), a *Gypsy*-ish tale of their ambitious stage mother, which avoided any such action by having a younger Marx on its writing team and paying Groucho Marx (Harpo and Chico were already departed) to be a ''production consultant.'' It folded after 80 performances.

Autobiographies: Marx, G: *Groucho and Me* (Bernard Geis, New York, 1959), Marx, H w Barber, R: *Harpo Speaks* (Gollancz, London, 1961), *The Groucho Letters* (Simon & Schuster, New York, 1967), w Anobile, R: *The Marx Brothers Scrapbook* (Norton, New York, 1973); Biographies: Crichton, K: *The Marx Brothers* (Doubleday, New York, 1950), Marx, A: *Son of Groucho* (David McKay, New York, 1972), Adamson, A: *Groucho, Harpo, Chico and Sometimes Zeppo* (Simon & Schuster, New York, 1973), etc

MARY Musical comedy in 2 acts by Otto Harbach and Frank Mandel. Music by Louis Hirsch. National Theater, Washington, DC, 31 March; Knickerbocker Theater, New York, 18 October 1920.

The most successful of composer Louis Hirsch's successors to *Going Up, Mary* was one of the best in the prettily naive ''Cinderella'' line of Broadway shows

Plate 243. **The Marx Brothers** *surrounded by their chorines in* The Cocoanuts.

which had been given such an impetus by *Irene* the previous season and which would be compounded a couple of weeks after *Mary*'s opening by *Sally.*

Mary's tiny story centered on Jack Keene (Jack McGowan), a go-getting young man who is so interested in trying to make a fortune out of building ''portable houses'' that he doesn't notice his mother's sighing little secretary, Mary (Janet Velie). Wealthy Madeleine (Florrie Millership) pursues Jack, and dashing Tommy (Alfred Gerrard) and womanizing Gaston (Charles Judels) pursue Madeleine, until the latter switches his attentions to Mary, but Jack finally gets around to recognizing true love round about the same time that his housing plot spouts oil. And so, whilst Gaston is gratefully grabbed by Mrs Keene (Georgia Caine), the happily-rich-and-wed ending that had been a foregone conclusion since Act I, minute one, duly arrives.

Originally entitled *The House That Jack Built* (even though he apparently didn't), George M Cohan's production was rechristened after its producer's famous old song (''it's a grand old name''), and the song itself was then eased into the show—which opened at Philadelphia in April. After four weeks it headed for Boston for the summer, then it repeated Philadelphia, then it returned to Boston, and all the time its favorite songs—the delightful hymn to ''The Love Nest,'' the lively ''We'll Have a Wonderful Party'' (strong shades of *Irene* here) and the jaunty ''Anything You Want to Do, Dear''—were becoming ingrained into the popular piano stool. By the time *Mary* eventually opened in New York, its score was well and truly whistled-in and two tours were on the road. Joe Sacks signed the piece for England within weeks of the Broadway opening, and the show looked set to be another *Irene.* But in the end *Mary* had a slightly disappointing metropolitan career.

Cohan's production played for a thoroughly respectable if not earth-shattering 219 performances at the Knickerbocker Theater, but Sacks's version with Evelyn Laye, Mabel Sealby (Madeleine), Ralph Lynn (Gaston), Alec Regan (Jack) and Bernard Granville (Tommy) lasted only 90 nights at London's not-so-big Queen's Theatre and soon after its closure the producer was declared bankrupt. Australia's production did not have such disastrous effects, and did rather better, all told. Maud Fane starred as Mary to the Jack of J Roland Hogue, alongside W S Percy (Gaston), Madge Elliott (Madeleine) and Ethel Morrison (Mrs Keene) through a tryout in Adelaide (30 September), a good 10-week run in two theatres in Melbourne, and 7 weeks in Sydney (Her Majesty's Theatre 7 July 1923) the following year with Phyllis Beadon as Mary.

If all this was a little less than might have been hoped, *Mary,* nevertheless, had a long and happy life which was lived out largely in the areas where she had first found popularity, wearing a much-loved trail around the American touring circuits for many seasons.

UK: Queen's Theatre 27 April 1921; Australia: Theatre Royal, Melbourne 7 October 1922

MASCHWITZ, [Albert] Eric [aka Holt MARVELL] (b Birmingham, 10 June 1901; d London, 27 October 1969). Librettist for several long-running London shows.

Cambridge-educated Maschwitz became first the editor of Britain's *Radio Times,* and subsequently director of variety programs at the BBC in the years prior to the war. His position gave him reasonably unhampered access to the airwaves, which he used (and not for the last time) pseudonymously to give an airing to his own unproduced romantic musical play *Goodnight Vienna* (mus: George Posford). *Goodnight Vienna* went on from its radio production to become a musical film with Jack Buchanan and Anna Neagle starred, whilst the pair turned out a second piece constructed on very similar plot lines, *The Gay Hussar,* for the British touring circuits. Three years later, in the wake of Ivor Novello's great success with *Glamorous Night,* Maschwitz exhumed *The Gay Hussar,* rewrote it in a similar style, hired as many of Novello's team as he could to stage it, and scored a singular success with what was now called *Balalaika* (''At the Balalaika'').

An attempt to follow up this winner with another large romantic musical failed twice (*Paprika, Magyar Melody*), as did a musical version of *Nymph Errant* (*Evangeline*), for which he supplied lyrics only, and a Chopin pasticcio biomusical ripped off from a recent Hungarian show. The indifferent performance of the Chopin piece deterred producer Jack Buchanan from continuing with his announced plans to mount Maschwitz's pasticcii of Tchaikovsky, Offenbach and Mendelssohn, but the author found much more success with a year's run of another romantic piece, *Carissima* (1948), made over from a Viennese musical by Armin Robinson and the expatriate composer Hans May, and, above all, with two further adaptations: a musical version of *Brewster's Millions* with popular singer George Formby starred (*Zip Goes a Million*), and a built-for-Britain Broadway musical called *Love from Judy,* with a book taken from the play *Daddy Long-Legs.* Both held the London stage for over five hundred performances. The vein, however, did not stay solid. Adaptations of Arnold Ridley's *The Ghost Train* (*Happy Holiday*) and of the musical version of Siegfried Geyer's widely successful play *Bei Kerzenlicht* (*Romance in Candlelight*) were both failures, and threatened musicals based on *Blood and Sand* and Neville Shute's *Beyond the Black Stump* never got to the stage.

Over the years since *Goodnight Vienna* had been taken from the screen to be played by amateur groups (and ultimately, outside London, by professionals), Maschwitz had, simultaneously, turned out a steady list of adaptations and pasticcio pieces intended for the lucrative amateur market. One of these, a biomusical on (of all people) Dvořák, called *Summer Song,* was professionally produced in 1956. An extremely adept follower, adaptor and imitator of and borrower from whatever musical-theatre styles and shows were in fashion, and equipped with the position and the connections to plug his works, Maschwitz made himself a good career in the musical theatre, from which he emerged with several enduring song credits (''These Foolish Things,'' ''A Nightingale Sang in Berkeley Square'') and a firm which purveys his product to operatic societies to this day.

1933 **The Gay Hussar** (George Posford) Manchester 2 October

1936 **Balalaika** (revised *The Gay Hussar*) Adelphi Theatre 22 December

1938 **Paprika** (Posford, Bernard Grün) His Majesty's Theater 15 September

1939 **Magyar Melody** (revised *Paprika*) His Majesty's Theatre 20 January

1942 **Waltz without End** (Frederic Chopin arr Grün) Cambridge Theatre 29 September

1946 **Evangeline** (Posford, Harry Jacobson/Romney Brent) Cambridge Theatre 14 March

1946 **Goodnight Vienna** (Posford/w Harold Purcell) Pavilion, Bournemouth 22 July

1948 **Carissima** (Hans May/Armin Robinson ad) Palace Theatre 10 March

1948 **Serenade** English version w Lauri Wylie (tour)

1949 **Belinda Fair** (Jack Strachey/w Gilbert Lennox) Saville Theatre 25 March

1951 **Zip Goes a Million** (Posford) Palace Theatre 20 October

1952 **Love from Judy** (Hugh Martin, Timothy Gray) Saville Theatre 25 September

1954 **Happy Holiday** (Posford) Palace Theatre 22 December

1955 **Romance in Candlelight** (*Bei Kerzenlicht*) English version with new songs by Sam Coslow, Piccadilly Theatre 15 September

1956 **Summer Song** (Anton Dvořák arr Grün) Prince's Theatre 16 February

MASCOTTCHEN Operette in 3 acts by Georg Okonkowski. Lyrics by Will Steinberg. Music by Walter Bromme. Thalia-Theater, Berlin, 15 January 1921.

Georg Okonkowski supplied a fine farcical libretto as the backbone of what would be the most successful of Walter Bromme's series of musical comedies for the Berlin stage. Its key rested in the fact that both the ladies of the piece—the young Countess von Castell-Steensdorf and the dancing girl Fräulein de Lorm—have the same name, Marion. They also have the same man, for the young Count Eric von Friisenborg who is now betrothed to the countess had previously been knocking about with the dancer. Worse, the fine house that Countess Marion's mama has purchased for the pair's honeymoon is none other than the former home of Marion the unaristocratic. The situation is obviously ripe for a bundle of mix-ups and misunderstandings, and when Marion the dancer's periodic sugar daddy, sea captain Krag von Westergaard, pulls into port with his nephew, Harald, a lad anxious to throw an eye (and probably something else) over uncle's bit of fluff, the trouble starts. Harald, of course, gets the wrong Marion. After a lot of shipboard and waterside comings and goings Eric goes back to the premarital Marion, Harald gets the upmarket one, and Krag (like all operettic over-30s) has to be content with his pipe and his grog.

Mascottchen ran past its 200th Berlin performance at the Thalia on 30 July before being taken off, and it was later seen in Vienna where Mimi Vesely and Klara Karry starred as the two Marions alongside Viktor Norbert (Eric), Paul Harden (Harald) and Oskar Sachs as the renamed Götz von Berlichingen through a season of 37 performances. The show was later revived at Berlin's Rosetheater.

Austria: Carltheater 26 September 1924

Plate 244. **La Mascotte.** *Maggie Moore as Bettina, the ''lucky charm'' in Australia's production of Audran's opérette.*

LA MASCOTTE Opéra-comique in 3 acts by Henri Chivot and Alfred Duru. Music by Edmond Audran. Théâtre des Bouffes-Parisiens, Paris, 29 December 1880.

Produced at Louis Cantin's Théâtre des Bouffes-Parisiens following the enormous success there of Varney's *Les Mousquetaires au couvent,* Audran's successor to his splendid debut with *Les Noces d'Olivette* was thus given two very difficult acts to follow. It triumphed unequivocally, giving the Bouffes-Parisiens another vast hit and going on to become and to remain one of the most popular French opérettes of all time.

The turkey-girl Bettina (Mlle Montbazon) is a ''mascot''—that is to say, she brings good luck to her household—and when she joins the working staff of the miserable farmer Rocco (Raucourt) his luck changes immediately. Bettina's boyfriend, Rocco's shepherd Pippo (Louis Morlet), isn't allowed too close, however, for a mascot ceases to be a mascot if she ceases to be a virgin. Alas, when her virtues are discovered by the interminably unlucky King Laurent (Paul Hittemans), poor Bettina is dragged off to court, much to the displeasure of the Princess Fiametta (Mlle Dinelli) who, obviously unaware of the rules of being a mascot, assumes the girl is her father's mistress. A whole barrage of complexities leads up to preparations for a double royal wedding, from which Pippo and Bettina escape just as Fiametta's rejected suitor, Fritellini (Charles Lamy), attacks the now instantly unlucky Laurent with his army. But luck has changed sides only for as long as it takes for Pippo and Bettina finally to get wedded and bedded. When all efforts to stop this disaster fail, both camps have to sit down and wait for nine months and hope the young mother will produce twins. One apiece. For it appears that mascotry is hereditary.

Chivot and Duru's joyously lubricious libretto built up to wilder and wilder comic scenes which, in the last act, bordered on the burlesques of earlier days, and the comedy was illustrated by a delicious Audran score. The hit number of the show was an ingenuous love duo for the shepherd and the turkey-girl with a ''glou-glou'' (her as the turkey) and ''bé-bé'' (he as a sheep) refrain, whilst Fritellini's melodic analysis of his own qualities (''Le je ne sais quoi poétique'') and his bamboozling of the naive

Pippo (''Ah, mon cher, que vous êtes naïf'') and Fiametta's appreciation of Pippo's muscles (''Ah! qu'il est beau!'') boasted the piece's loveliest melodies. The comic side was topped by Laurent's declaration of his main advantage as a husband for Bettina—his impotence (''J'en suis tout à fait incapable'').

La Mascotte was an overwhelming success at the Bouffes-Parisiens, playing for the entire season, and then for most of the next one as well. Cantin removed it in order to stage Louis Varney's *Coquelicot,* but when that piece failed to take he promptly brought back *La Mascotte* which proved far from having exhausted its public. It was nearly two years from its opening night when the show was finally taken off and replaced with the next Audran work, *Gillette de Narbonne. Gillette de Narbonne* was another fine success, but *La Mascotte* was naturally brought back in 1883 (11 April) with Piccaluga, Mme Gugot-Morlet (replacing a too pregnant original star) and Édouard Maugé for another 92 performances, and it resurfaced again in 1889 with Théo this time in the title role. Paris revivals were regular thereafter, including runs at the Menus-Plaisirs (1890, where on 14 July the show celebrated its 1,500th Parisian performance), the Gaîté (1897, 1901 w Germaine Gallois, 1915 w Angèle Gril), the Apollo (1913, 1914), the Mogador (1921, 1944) and the Porte-Saint-Martin (1933 w Edmée Favart, 1935, 1968) as *La Mascotte* confirmed itself as one of the surest pillars of the opérette repertoire.

The piece also traveled with considerable success. Although Vienna hosted an uncredited (and apparently insufficient) adaptation of *Der Glücksengel* with Josefine Gallmeyer given top billing in the role of Fiametta alongside Girardi (Pippo), Karoline Finaly (Bettina) and Carl Adolf Friese (Lorenzo) for only 23 performances, and Germany extended it only a slightly warmer reception, in Hungary, where Lujza Blaha took on the role of the turkey-girl with Pál Vidor as her Pippo, János Kápolnai (Fritellini) and Vidor Kassai as Laurent, *Az üdvöske* (ad Jenő Rákosi) was an undoubted winner and it followed its original production with many returns. Britain reacted similarly when, after an out-of-town tryout at Brighton (a most unusual thing at the time) Alexander Henderson brought *La Mascotte* (ad Robert Reece, H B Farnie) to the Comedy Theatre with Violet Cameron and the 22-year-old Savoyard baritone Francis Gaillard starred, Lionel Brough heading the comedy, and Lizzie St Quinten and Henry Bracy in the chief singing roles. After a first run of 199 performances it came back after just a month for a further season with Clara Merivale and Gaillard starred, whilst Kate Santley took her production and her Bettina to the provinces. In 1884 Florence St John paired with Gaillard in a rerun, in 1885 Violet Cameron repeated her original role, in 1888 the French prima donna Mary Albert gave a season in French and, finally, in 1893 the Gaiety Theatre staged a *La Mascotte* season with Miss St John (9 September), the sixth sighting of the show in London in a dozen years. Australia, in the meantime, had responded with equal delight to a J C Williamson production which featured his wife, Maggie Moore, as a truly lusty Bettina, alongside George Verdi (Pippo), W H Woodfield (Fritellini), Nellie Stewart (Fiametta), H M Harwood (Laurent) and Edwin Kelly (Rocco) in the first of what would be a long series of *La Mascotte* seasons.

The competition to get the first *La Mascotte* on to the American stage was all the hotter because of the vast success of the American version of *Les Noces d'Olivette,* but in the end it was the management of the ever to-the-fore Boston Museum who won the race. They mounted Theodore T Barker and J W Norcross's version of the show in April 1881 with Helen Carter, Seth Crane and Harry Brown in the principal roles. It was nearly a month after this before Broadway got its first glimpse of the new show at the Bijou Theater, the house which had so successfully staged the earlier piece. They brought in the touring Wilbur Opera Company's production, with Emma Howson (the original London Josephine of *HMS Pinafore*) and John Brand heading the cast, four days before the Boston company appeared at the Park Theater with their version. It was the Bijou which came out the better, for *La Mascotte,* an oversized hit in no time, ran there for an uninterrupted three months (108 performances,), the Gobble Duet became, as it had in Britain, one of the hits of the season, and the floodgates were opened for productions of the show around the country.

Over the next 12 months Selina Dolaro appeared as Bettina in a quick revival at the Bijou (60 performances); Geraldine Ulmar and H C Barnabee (Laurent) headed the Bostonians' production at Booth's; Paola Marié introduced the original French version, which was also played in repertoire by Louise Théo; Jenny Stubel and Alexander Klein gave *Der Glücksengel* at the Thalia-Theater in German; whilst the young Fay Templeton appeared in the title role of a remade-to-order production at the Windsor Theater. The flood slowed thereafter, but it did not stop for many years: Judic played Bettina during her 1885 tour, the Bijou revived the piece in 1887, a 1892 production at Palmer's Theater presented William Pruette as Pippo, Henry Dixey as Laurent and Camille D'Arville in the title role, and Raymond Hitchcock and his wife Flora Zabelle starred for a month in a 1909 Klaw and Erlanger production at the New Amsterdam Theater. The last sight of *La Mascotte* on Broadway was in 1926 (1 December) when Jenny Syril and Servatius starred in a revival at the Jolson Theater, by which time the show had proven itself one of the most standard standards of the American-French repertoire. Largely because Audran's name has not remained a fashionable one, it has not, however, followed Offenbach and Strauss's works into the modern opera houses.

A French film version was made in 1935 by Léon Mathot, with Germaine Roger as Bettina alongside Dranem, Lucien Baroux and Lestelly, but *La Mascotte* had undoubtedly its most curious film exposure in 1913 when it was presented as a three-reeler film starring Minnie Jarbeau "in three six-minute acts" with accompanying sound "by means of Edison's wonderful kinetophone." The experiment was apparently successful enough for the manufacturers to subsequently serve up the customers a version of *Les Noces d'Olivette* recorded in the same style.

Austria: Theater an der Wien *Der Glücksengel* 12 February 1881; Hungary: Népszínház *Az üdvöske* 10 April 1881; USA: Boston Museum 12 April 1881, Bijou Theater, New York 5 May 1881; UK: Comedy Theatre 15 October 1881; Germany: Friedrich-Wilhelmstädtisches Theater *Der Glücksengel* 25 October 1881; Australia: Theatre Royal, Sydney 25 October 1882

Film: Léon Mathot 1935

Recordings: complete (Clio, Decca), selection (EMI-Pathé), etc

MASKE IN BLAU Revue-Operette in 8 (later 6) scenes by Heinz Hentschke. Lyrics by Günther Schwenn. Music by Fred Raymond. Metropoltheater, Berlin, 27 September 1937.

A splendid success at Hentschke's Berlin Metropoltheater in 1937–38, the colorfully staged if textually feeble *Maske in Blau* followed the young artist Armando Cellini (Niko Stefanini) from San Remo to Argentina in pursuit of Evelyne (Carla Carlsen), the beautiful and rich plantation owner who is the subject of his painting. He takes along two pals and a noisy soubrette called Juliska (Clara Tabody) and together they foil the beastly Pedro who has caused the bust-up between the lovers in Scene Two. Then almost everyone (five into pairs doesn't go) pairs up for a multi-happy ending. Fred Raymond's score was mostly in a B-film vein, but it threw out two songs—both performed by the very prominent soubrette—which became highly popular: her insistence that she has "temperament" ("Ja, das Temp'rament") and that she is "Die Juliska aus Budapest." Most of the rest of the music fell to the two lovers, she singing of "Frühling in San Remo," he of "Maske in Blau" and both of them of being "Am Rio Negro," which didn't stop them being more than a little edged out of the limelight by the pushy Juliska. The fourth scene also introduced the Maxixe for South American flavoring.

The piece remained popular in Germany, returning to the Theater des Westens in 1966 (20 January, 122 performances) and in 1977 (18 March, 63 performances) and, in spite of its and Hentschke's Nazi connections, it was introduced to Vienna after the Second World War, playing first at the Sophiensaal (1946), then at the Titania Theater (1947 with Stefanini, Desa Valoni and Mimi Urban) and in 1964–65 at the Raimundtheater, with patented star Marika Rökk making Juliska even more prominent than before. In 1970 (6 November) the Operette was given an ice-rink production at Berlin's Deutschlandhalle (add mus Erwin Halletz), and it wins regional productions in Austria, and above all in Germany, up to the present day.

A 1942 film version featured Clara Tabody, Wolf-Albach Retty, Hans Moser and and seven sung numbers from the score, but a 1953 film had nothing to do with the show's plot, except that its leading lady (Frln Rökk) was called Juliska. She was a "revuestar" and never went near the Argentine. However, she was still "Die Juliska, die Juliska aus Buda-Budapest," still had "Temp'rament" and also sang with her painter (Paul Hubschmid) the principal soprano/tenor duet ("In dir hab ich mein Glück gefunden"). "Maske in Blau," "Schau einer schönen Frau" and "Frühling in Sam Remo" were all there too, in a film which had rather more of *Maske in Blau*'s score about it than its story.

Austria: Sophiensaal 15 June 1946

Films: Paul Martin/NFK 1942, Georg Jacoby/Röja Film 1953

Recordings: selections (Eurodisc, EMI, Telefunken, Philips), etc

MASSARY, Fritzi [MASSARIK, Friederike] (b Vienna, 21 March 1882; d Beverly Hills, Calif, 30 January 1969).

For 20 years the adored queen of the Berlin Operette stage, Massary at the peak of her powers won appreciative comments from the press of the whole world ("in a class by herself . . . the most finished operetta diva on the Continent") even though she did not venture beyond central Europe until she was past her best years.

She made her first appearances on stage as a child, then played in revue, toured to Russia in the chorus of an Operette company, worked in Linz, and in the 1900–1901 season became a member of the company at the Carl-Schultze Theater, Hamburg, where she played her first good roles as those most classic of soubrettes Christl (*Der Vogelhändler*) and Bronislawa (*Der Bettelstudent*). In 1901 she appeared at the Carltheater as Molly in *The Geisha* and in the summer joined Gabor Steiner's company, performing both at his summer theatre, Venedig in Wien, and at his winter Danzers Orpheum—as Kitty, the heroine's maid, in Ivan Caryll's *Die Reise nach Cuba* (billed as Frln Massari), as Cora Angélique in *Die Schöne von New York* (1901), La Favorita in the English musical *Das Cirkusmädel* (1902), Ninetta in *Eine feine Nummer* (1902), in the title role of Clotilde in Ferdinand Pagin's *Clo-Clo* (1902) and as "Sie" in Paul Lincke's little *Am Hochzeitsabend* (1903).

Massary went on from there to play in Cologne and in Prague, and in 1904 she stopped in Berlin. It was there that she was to make the bulk of the rest of her career. She joined the company at Richard Schultz's Metropoltheater, made her debut there in Viktor Holländer's *Die Herren von Maxims* (''Im Liebesfalle''), and performed thereafter in the revues which Lincke, Walter Kollo and Holländer composed for the house (*Auf's in Metropol,* etc). She revisited Vienna in 1908 to star in Eysler's *Das Glücksschweinchen* at her old haunt, Venedig in Wien, appeared as Helene in Leo Fall's *Der liebe Augustin* in its Berlin premiere, played in Vienna in Benatzky's vaudeville *Prinzchens Frühlingserwachen,* at the Theater Gross-Berlin am Zoo in Gilbert's *So bummeln wir!* and *Die Studentengräfin,* and at the Theater am Nollendorfplatz (1913) in *Die schöne Helena,* but she returned each time to the Metropoltheater.

The war years brought the déclic which lifted Massary from stardom to megastardom. Her performance in the title role of Leo Fall's *Die Kaiserin* (1915) won her stunning reviews and great popularity, and thereafter the Metropoltheater mounted a series of Operetten designed specifically for her. Some were pieces already played in Vienna, but as the years went on she created, or in some cases had created for her, some of the greatest of the period's works, as she became to Straus and to Fall what Hortense Schneider had been to Offenbach or the Savoy company to Gilbert and Sullivan. She starred successively in Betty Fischer's roles in *Die Csárdásfürstin* and *Die Rose von Stambul,* as Offenbach's *Grande-Duchesse,* in Kálmán's *Die Faschingsfee* and in the character created by Sári Fedák in *Szibill* (1919) before creating the star role of the richly vocal Vera Lisaweta in Straus's *Der letzte Walzer* (1920), Dolores Belamor in Leo Fall's *Die spanische Nachtigall* and the title role of his *Madame Pompadour* (1922).

Die Perlen der Cleopatra (1923) cast her as the queen of the Nile in Berlin and Vienna, and if *Geliebte seiner Hoheit* (1924), *Der Tanz um die Liebe* (1924), *Teresina* (1925) and *Die Königin* (1926) offered her fewer opportunities than a Vera Lisaweta or a Pompadour, she was able to return to the latter role in a splashy Erik Charell production at the Grosses Schauspielhaus in 1926. It was another Charell staging, however, a few years later, which resulted in her temporarily leaving the musical theatre. A badly disfigured, over-staged version of *Die lustige Witwe* drew the public's and critics' scorn, and the star suffered. She withdrew to the straight theatre, and remained there for two years, playing lead roles in plays in Germany and in Austria. She came back to the musical stage to star in the outstanding mother role of Oscar Straus's *Eine Frau, die weiss, was sie will* (1932), creating the song which would remain, more than any other, her trademark, ''Jede Frau hat irgendeine Sehnsucht.'' In 1933 she was obliged to quit Germany, and almost more than the flight of any or all the other Jewish makers of Operette, her departure signaled the end of an era in the German theatre.

The now-widowed Massary moved to London—where in 1938 she made her one appearance in the British musical theatre as the prima donna of Noël Coward's unfortunate *Operette*—and then to America. She ultimately retired to Beverly Hills, to the home of her son-in-law, where she died in 1969.

Massary was married to actor **Max PALLENBERG** (b Vienna, 18 December 1877; d Prague, 20 June 1934), another Austrian who made much of his career in Berlin. He was regarded by many as Germany's foremost comedian, but he also took a number of comic roles in Operette, with very limited vocal means but with considerable success.

Biography: Stern, C: *Die Sache, die man Liebe nennt. Das Leben der Fritzi Massary* (Rowohlt, Berlin, 1998)

MASSÉ, Victor [Félix Marie] (b Lorient, 7 March 1822; d Paris, 5 July 1884).

A winner of the celebrated Prix de Rome (1844), awarded to the outstanding composition student of the Paris Conservatoire, Massé did not ever fulfill the hopes this prize automatically placed in him for a career in serious music. He composed some attractive vocal pieces, one opera which was presented at the Paris Opéra, and nine works—full-length and short—which were produced at the Opéra-Comique. Two of the earliest of these, however, ensured that his musical survival would be distinctly more marked than many more ''successful'' winners of the Prix de Rome. The two-act comic opera *Galathée* (1852), dealing with the awakening of Pygmalion's statue, won considerable popularity (its libretto by Jules Barbier and Michel Carré later formed the basis for Poly Henrion's text for Suppé's *Die schöne Galathee*), whilst the little rustic opérette *Les Noces de Jeannette* (1853), written by the same authors, provoked a delightful score from the composer which has resulted in the piece being played throughout the world ever since, perched on the very cusp of the light-opera and opérette repertoires.

MASTEROFF, Joe (b Philadelphia, 11 December 1919).

Masteroff worked as an actor (he appeared in one Broadway play) and as an assistant director to Howard Lindsay whilst making his first attempts as a playwright, and he reached Broadway as an author in 1959 with the play *The Warm Peninsula* (86 performances). He moved into the musical theatre for the first time with his adaptation of the Hungarian play *Illatsertár* as the text for *She Loves Me,* but found his greatest success with a second adaptation, that of Christopher Isherwood's Berlin stories as the libretto for the internationally triumphant *Cabaret.* A third adaptation, of the classic British farce *Breath of Spring* as the confusingly titled *70, Girls, 70,* with songs by the composers of *Cabaret,* did not have the same success.

In 1996 a musical, *Paramour* (mus: Howard Marren), was given a staged concert reading at the National Music Theater Conference.

1963 **She Loves Me** (Jerry Bock/Sheldon Harnick) O'Neill Theater 23 April

1966 **Cabaret** (John Kander/Fred Ebb) Broadhurst Theater 20 November

1971 **70, Girls, 70** (Kander/Ebb) Broadhurst Theatre 15 April

1989 **Desire Under the Elms** (Edward Thomas) New York City Center 11 January

1992 **Six Wives** (Thomas) York Theater 4 October

MATHEWS, Julia [Ann Isabella] (b London, 14 December 1842; d St Louis, Mo, 18 May 1876). Top international prima donna of the English-language opéra-bouffe stage whose fame was extinguished by an early death.

Taken to Australia as a child, after a handful of juvenile appearances as a dancer and a pianist on the London stage (Surrey Theatre, Strand Theatre, Linwood Gallery), Julia Mathews made her first appearances on the southern stage (or whatever did duty for a stage) at Sydney's Royal Victoria Theatre (28 August 1854), Melbourne's Coppin's Olympic (30 July 1855) and in the goldfields, appearing in comedy, drama, comic opera and burlesque whilst still in her earliest teens. She subsequently made herself a considerable name as an actress and vocalist at the Princess Theatre in Melbourne (''the Queen of burlesque and song''). Amongst the musical shows in which she appeared were numbered *The Beggar's Opera* (Polly), *The Latest Edition of the Lady of Lyons, Midas, The Fair One with the Golden Locks* (Graceful), *Esmeralda* (Phoebus), *Bluebeard* (Alidor), *Prince Prettypet* (Prince), *Cinderella the Second* (Cinderella), *The Little Savage, Endymion* (Endymion), *Aladdin* (Aladdin), *The Daughter of the Regiment* (Marie), *The Queen of Beauty* (Queen), *The Miller and His Men* (Karl) and *Theseus and Ariadne* (Theseus) and, even in the theatre's production of dramas, a spot was usually found to break the action and allow Julia to sing a song or two.

She appeared at the Princess alongside a number of visiting stars, notably Joseph Jefferson, and she gained some additional notoriety when her name was linked with that of the ill-fated explorer R O'H Burke who apparently proposed marriage to her when she was 15 years old. Her parents, who kept a firm control over their lucrative daughter, sent him on his way. In 1863 the Mathewses crossed to the New Zealand goldfields, where Julia was engaged for the Dunedin Princess's Theatre, and there the young star took advantage of a moment's inattention by her parents to get herself wed to a shipping agent called William H Mumford. Two children later, Mumford had his wife back on the stage and he quickly proved as grasping a ''manager'' as father and mother had been.

Plate 245. **Julia Mathews** *came from the Australian goldfields to stun London as* La Grande-Duchesse de Gérolstein.

In 1866 the family returned to Melbourne, but after one quick rounds of the goldfields, they packed up and set out to return to Britain. Julia arrived in London in October 1867, and she established herself as one of the most celebrated stars of the opéra-bouffe stage when she introduced the title role in Offenbach's *La Grande-Duchesse de Gérolstein* to English audiences both in London (Theatre Royal, Covent Garden 17 November 1867) and in a substantial tour around the provinces. She returned to Covent Garden in 1869 in a double bill of *Lischen and Fritzchen* and the pantomime *The Yellow Dwarf.*

In 1870 the new singing star (having divested herself of Mr Mumford) made a first appearance at the Gaiety Theatre and the following year created the title role in Émile Jonas's *Cinderella the Younger* (1871) there. She also appeared with the Gaiety company as *La Belle Hélène,* as Boulotte in *Barbe-bleue,* as Gigolette in *Tromb-al-ca-zar,* in the title role of Balfe's *Letty the Basket-maker,* in *Lischen and Fritzchen* and in *No Song, No Supper*—whilst putting in regular provincial appearances in the kind of repertoire she had played in Australia (*The Daughter of the Regiment, The Bohemian Girl,* etc).

In 1872 she played Fleur de Noblesse in the London version of Hervé's *L'Oeil crevé,* and in 1873 she appeared as Mlle Lange to the Clairette of Selina Dolaro in the first English-language *La Fille de Madame Angot* at the Philharmonic, Islington. She followed up there in the dual title role of the English version of *Giroflé-Girofla* (1874) and, at Christmas of the same year, she created the part of Alice Fitzwarren in Offenbach's brand new *Whittington* at the London Alhambra. In 1875 she toured for Mrs Liston in *Giroflé-Girofla,* and then, after three ''farewell'' performances at the Gaiety, she set off to New York at the head of a company organized by Alexander Henderson and Samuel Colville. She played a season at Wallack's Theatre with *Giroflé-Girofla, La Grande-Duchesse, Les Prés Saint Gervais* and a mangled version of *Barbe-bleue,* before setting off on tour, but the company collapsed in its first date. Most of the company went home, but Julia stayed in America and, after struggling through some second-rate engagements, managed to set up a fresh tour. She started out in Indianapolis to glorious notices (''Her acting was modest and spirited, and her singing . . . thrillingly beautiful[;] . . . we have seen no-one worthy to be compared to her'') but six weeks later, in St Louis, she was off, ill. A few days later she was dead, at the age of just 33.

MATRAS, Josef (b Vienna, 1 March 1832; d Vienna, 30 September 1887). Star comic of the 19th-century Viennese stage.

Viennese-born Matras toured as a vocalist and chorister, appearing in the Austrian provinces and at Pest before coming back to play in his home town, first of all at Fürsts Singspielhalle in the Prater, and then, in 1862, at the Carltheater. There he became a popular and highly paid leading comedian, appearing in some of the foremost comedies of the Austrian classic and modern repertoire, in Possen and Volksstücke and, with the coming of the French opéra-bouffe, in this new brand of entertainment.

Amongst his operettic assignments in the 1860s and 1870s were included the Viennese versions of the French *Les Deux Aveugles* (Terzabeck, paired with Franz Eppich), *Les Géorgiennes* (Paterno), *L'Île de Tulipatan* (Cactus), *Le Château à Toto* (Massepain), *Les Cent Vierges* (Rumpelmeier), *La Princesse de Trébizonde* (Casimir), *La Boulangère a des écus* (Flammèche to the Delicat of Blasel), *Le Soldat magicien* (Robin), *Monsieur Choufleuri* (the travesty Madame Balandard, invented by Léonce), *Vert-Vert* (Binet), *Boule de Neige* (The Corporal), *Cannebas* (Augustin), *La Cour du Roi Pétaud* (Confusius IX), *La Permission de dix heures* (Lanternik), *La Belle Bourbonnaise* (Anselme), *Le Grand Casimir* (Little Wheel, the clown), *Les Prés Saint-Gervais* (Harpin), *La Marjolaine* (Peterschop) and *Le Petit Duc* (Frimousse). He also appeared in a number of the earliest native Viennese works, playing Fleck in *Flotte Bursche,* Midas in *Die schöne Galathee,* Bitterich in Julius Hopp's *In der Sackgasse,* Hans der Gerechte in *Die Jungfrau von Dragant,* the title role of *Flodorado Wuprahall* and Dr Tondolo in *Banditenstreiche.*

With the blossoming of the Austrian tradition, Matras found his finest musical roles, creating the parts of Izzet Pascha in *Fatinitza* (1876), Satanas in *Der Teufel auf Erden* (1877) and Fürst von Trocadero in *Prinz Methusalem* (1877), as well as playing in *Die Mormonen,* but his career came prematurely to an end in 1880 when his memory failed him, and he died a depressive in 1887 after spending the last five years of his life in a lunatic asylum declaring to all who would listen that he was being pursued by mysterious Russians.

Matras's daughter, actress Pepi Glöckner, was Vienna's first Mrs Peachum in *Die Dreigroschenoper.*

In the 1921 Wiener Bürgertheater Singspiel on *Josefine Gallmeyer,* Fritz Schrödter impersonated Matras in an operetticized retelling of the actor's love affair with his fellow star.

MATTHEWS, Jessie [Margaret] (b London, 11 March 1907; d London, 19 August 1981).

A petitely pretty and maniacally bright dancing soubrette, Jessie Matthews had a successful career as a star of London and occasionally New York revue in the 1920s and of British film musicals in the 1930s (*Evergreen, It's Love Again, The Good Companions, Waltzes from Vienna, Gangway,* etc). She also made isolated appearances in stage musicals, performing as a child in *Bluebell in Fairyland,* teamed with Harry Milton and Sonnie Hale as the ingenue of Stanley Lupino's musical comedy *Hold My Hand* (1931) and starring in the Marilyn[n] Miller role of Sally in a revised version of Kern's musical of the same name rechristened *Wild Rose* (1942). In 1939 she also starred with Sonnie Hale (then her husband), and his father as Sue Merrick in their own production of a piece called *I Can Take It* which died on the road, and in 1941 she disappeared from the cast of the Vernon Duke musical *The Lady Comes Across* between New Haven and New York, thus avoiding a three-night Broadway flop.

In her mid-sixties she appeared one final time on the London stage as Mrs Doasyouwouldbedoneby in a version of *The Water Babies* (1973).

Autobiography: *Over My Shoulder* (W H Allen, London, 1974)

MAY, Alice (b Yorkshire, c1847; d St Louis, Mo, 16 August 1887). The first prima donna of the Gilbert-Sullivan-Carte combine.

Alice May, ''a member of a remarkably musical family and a connection of Cipriani Potter,'' was born (under an unknown name, on an unknown date) in Yorkshire and studied singing initially with the area's most celebrated teacher, Mrs Wood (née Mary Ann Paton, and the creator of Rézia in *Oberon,* etc) of Wakefield. She later took lessons in London from George Benjamin Allen, made her earliest concert appearances under his accompaniment, and then ran away to Australia with him. There, although he had a family back home, she was known as ''Mrs Allen.''

''Mrs G B Allen'' made her first significant appearances as a singer in her adopted homeland, appearing first in concert (18 June 1870), then, under the banner of W S Lyster and Smith, in light opera (*The Daughter of the Regiment* 29 April 1871), and finally in prima donna roles in opéra-bouffe and comic opera with Lyster and Cagli's company (Zerlina in *Fra Diavolo,* Amina in *La Sonnambula,* the Grande-Duchesse, Boulotte, Agathe in *Freischütz,* Elvira in *The Rose of Castille,* Maritana, Arline, as Eurydice in Australia's first *Orphée aux enfers,* etc). She next played a season with her own ''Gallery of Illustration,'' a group set up at Sydney's Masonic Hall on the lines of London's German Reed establishment, playing *Cox and Box, The Rose of Auvergne* and *The Belle of Wooloomooloo,* before going on to star as Drogan in a seasonal version of *Geneviève de Brabant,* and as Balfe's *Satanella.* She had established herself as Australia's foremost light-opera star before the couple made their professional way first to New Zealand (May 1874), where they toured opéra-bouffe and light opera for over a year on a scale never before attempted in the colony and then, the following year, they traveled on through Calcutta, Bombay, Madras, Allahabad and so forth, back to Britain.

She made her first appearance on British soil on 11 December 1876, at the Liverpool Prince of Wales Theatre as the Grand Duchess; a fortnight later was featured in a special matinée at the Gaiety; and was soon on the road starring in *La Fille de Madame Angot, La Belle Hélène* and *La Grande-Duchesse* with Richard South's company. She soon left that company to make an attempt at opera, performing Marguerite in *Faust* and the title role in *Satanella* at Leicester, but she soon returned to lighter fare, establishing herself as one of the best opéra-bouffe sopranos of her time on the British stage, and making herself a place in history by creating the role of Aline in Gilbert and Sullivan's *The Sorcerer* (1877). Miss May left the *Sorcerer* company to appear for producer D'Oyly Carte as Drogan in a revival of *Geneviève de Brabant* (1878) and, whilst a more thorough Australian, Tasmanian-born Emma Howson, introduced the role that would have been hers in *HMS Pinafore,* she went on to appear in London's versions of Lecocq's *Le Petit Duc* (Duke), the revived *La Princesse de Trébizonde* (1879, Zanetta), *La Petite Mademoiselle* (1879, Madelon), *Les Mousquetaires au couvent* (1880, Simonne), *Jeanne, Jeannette et Jeanneton* (1881, Jeanne) and *The Bronze Horse* (1881, Sou-Sou) before—now distinctly plumper—going out in tandem with Emily Soldene to play opéra-bouffe, and half-a-handful of performances of Allen's comic opera *The Wicklow Rose* (1882) in the provinces. She later appeared with Joseph Eldred's company on the British road, and having now split with Allen, in 1883 she left Britain for America. She introduced herself to American audiences rather unwisely as Satanella with Barton's English Opera Company, but engagements followed swiftly, even if they were not perhaps quite the engagements she would have wished. Now, although only in her mid-thirties (?), she was already unwillingly abandoning heroines for character ladies. She toured with Charles Ford's comic-opera company (*Barbe-bleue, The Mikado, La Princesse de Trébizonde* and Symon in *The Beggar Student*), became regular heavy lady at St Louis's Uhrig's Cave summer season, joined John McCaull to play at the Casino Theater as Sophistica in *Prinz Methusalem* and on the road in *Falka* and with H B Mahn (Jelly in *Princess Toto,* Katisha, etc). Several of the companies with which she played were poor stuff and more than once she was stranded. She was playing at Uhrig's Cave in the summer of 1887 when she was suddenly taken ill. She died in St Louis City Hospital a few days later, and the company had to take up a collection to pay for her burial. Her death certificate revealed the reasons for her fall: ''cause of death: alcoholism.''

Miss May's undoubtedly always-de-facto husband, the conductor and composer **George B[enjamin] ALLEN** (b London, 21 April 1822; d Brisbane, 30 November 1897), had his moment of semi-fame as the original conductor of London's *The Sorcerer,* an engagement (like Alice's) apparently the result of a considerable financial investment towards the show's production budget. During his time in Australia he made himself a fine reputation as a conductor, directing Lyster and Cagli's productions of opéra-bouffe and opéra-comique in the early 1870s (*Barbe-bleue, Geneviève de Brabant, La Grande-Duchesse, Der Freischütz,* etc) and working reg-

Plate 246. **Edna May.** *Broadway's Belle of New York.*

ularly with Alice, notably on their big tour through New Zealand and the Orient. He also wrote several pieces for the musical stage, including the extravaganza *The Belle of Woolloomooloo* (1872) and two pieces played on the British stage, the one-act operettas *Castle Grim* (Royalty Theatre 2 September 1865, lib: Robert Reece), *A Wild Cherry* (Reigate 2 September 1867, lib: Reece) toured by Louisa Pyne's operetta company in 1867, and the full-length *The Wicklow Rose* (Prince's Theatre, Manchester 3 May 1882). After their split, he remarried and returned to Australia where, his larger ambitions disappointed, he spent his final days as a teacher in Queensland.

Miss May married, shortly before her death, the basso of the Uhrig's Cave company, Louis W Raymond, in a ceremony held in the lobby of Ford's Opera House at Baltimore.

MAY, Edna [PETTIE, Edna May] (b Syracuse, NY, 2 September 1878; d Lausanne, Switzerland, 2 January 1948). Palely pretty ingenue who made her name as The Belle of New York.

Having first played in juvenile Gilbert and Sullivan companies and in plays in her hometown, Edna May Pettie (still thus billed) made her first New York appearance at the age of 17 in a small part in the elder Oscar Hammerstein's comic opera *Santa Maria* (Clairette). After only a year on the professional stage she was hired by George Lederer to create the role of the Salvation Army lass Violet Gray in *The Belle of New York* (''They All Follow Me,'' ''The Purity Brigade''). She traveled to London with the show after its New York closure and there she made an enormous personal hit, establishing herself in this one performance as one of the most popular and sought-after stars of the London musical theatre.

Miss May appeared in London in another American musical comedy, *An American Beauty,* and in both America and Britain in the title role of *The Girl from Up There,* being largely responsible by her popular presence for the few months each piece held the stage. The earliest years of the new century were also largely spent in Britain where she starred opposite Evie Greene as the artless Baroness de Trègue in *Kitty Grey* (*Les Fêtards*), teamed with Hilda Moody and Madge Crichton as Paul Rubens's *Three Little Maids,* and created the title role of Leslie Stuart's *The School Girl* (1903).

After playing on Broadway with the American production of *The School Girl* (1904), Miss May remained there to play Alésia in a return season of *La Poupée* and the Cinderella role of Angela, written for Ellaline Terriss, in the imported *The Catch of the Season* (1905). She went to London once more to star in the latest Leslie Stuart show, *The Belle of Mayfair,* but walked out of the production when her star billing was threatened by the novelty attraction represented by ''the Gibson Girl'' Camille Clifford. As a replacement vehicle, Charles Frohman mounted *Nelly Neil,* a silly piece with a silly part calculatedly modeled on her *Belle of New York* role, but the show failed and Miss May left the theatre in favor of an advantageous marriage at the age of 29.

Memoir: (ed Danham, C): *The Casino Girl in London* (R E Fenno, New York, 1898)

MAY, Hans [MAYER, Johannes] (b Vienna, 11 May 1891; d Beaulieu, France, 1 January 1959). Viennese composer who had more theatrical success after emigrating to Britain.

May studied in Vienna and composed much accompanying music for silent films both in Germany and France as well as a list of small-scale Operetten in the 1910s and a handful of larger ones in the 1920s. He moved to Britain in the 1930s, an early part of the Jewish exodus which bled central Europe of most of its operettic talent, and continued there to make the largest part of his career in the cinema, composing film scores (*The Stars Look Down, Thunder Rock, The Wicked Lady, Brighton Rock, The Gypsy and the Gentleman*) and later conducting film music, whilst still supplying some music to the German stage (*Kolonne Immergrün,* Theater am Schiffbauerdamm 1932, etc) and screen.

His 1935 Operette *Die tanzende Stadt,* played in Vienna at the Theater an der Wien (26 performances), was produced at the Coliseum by André Charlot with Lea Seidl starred as Maria Theresia and without success, but two later pieces, an English adaptation of a piece originally written with Armin Robinson and here called *Carissima* and, particularly, the attractive *Wedding in Paris* (''Light Another Match,'' ''I Have Nothing to Declare,'' ''Wedding in Paris'') had fine runs, whilst a theatre version of his film *Waltz Time* had a reasonable touring career.

May had song successes with ''Ein Lied geht um die Welt'' (1933 ly: Ernst Neubach), introduced by Josef Schmidt in the film of the same name (and as ''My Song Goes Round the World'' in the English version) with Vera Lynn's ''Love of My Life,'' ''The Windsor Waltz'' and ''Throw Open Wide Your Window.''

1911 **Das süsse Gespenst** sketch Ronacher

1912 **Der Teufelswalzer** (Ernst Ress/Leopold Krenn) Ronacher ?February

1912 **Der Dreibund** (Alfred Spitzer) 1 act Hölle 1 March

1913 **Das grosse Abenteuer** (Fritz Lunzer, C Clermont)

1918 **Die schöne Blonde** (Hans Pflanzer) 1 act Hölle 1 October

1919 **Daniel in der Löwenhohle** (Lunzer) 1 act Kleinkünstbühne, Munich 1 December

1922 **Miss Blaubart** (Alexander Pordes-Milo, Ernst Neubach) Jantschtheater 22 December

1926 **Drei Mädel von Heute** (Dengraf, Max Steiner-Kaiser) Komödienhaus, Berlin 20 July

1932 **Traum einer Nacht** (Willy Wolff/Behr) Theater am Nollendorfplatz, Berlin 4 March

1935 **Die tanzende Stadt** (Karl Rossler, Arthur Rebner) Theater an der Wien 4 October

1935 **The Dancing City** revised *Die tanzende Stadt* by Harold Plumptre, David Yates Mason (London Coliseum)

1948 **Carissima** (Armin Robinson ad Eric Maschwitz) Palace Theatre, London 10 March

1949 **Waltz Time** (Conrad Carter, Harry C James/Alan Stranks) Winter Gardens, Morecambe 2 May

1954 **Wedding in Paris** (Sonny Miller/Vera Caspary) London Hippodrome 9 March

MAYA Operett in 3 acts by Imre Harmath. Music by Szabolcs Fényes. Fővárosi Operettszínház, Budapest, 10 December 1931.

The most successful of Fényes's operetts, *Maya* was first mounted in Budapest in 1931 with Hanna Honthy, the favorite soubrette of the Hungarian stage, playing the role of the Arabian dancer of the show's title.

The show's tale was begun in Paris. The meddling mama of Charley (Gábor Kertész) is determined to put an end to his love affair with unsuitable Madelaine (Olly Szokolay). She persuades friend Dixie (István Békássy) to help her in her plans, and Dixie consequently confides in Charley that he's been having an affair with his girl. Charley pulls a gun, shoots Dixie, and runs off to join the Foreign Legion. He doesn't much like the Foreign Legion, and he is helped to escape from Tangiers and back to Paris by Maya, a little dancer he once defended from a nasty soldier. Maya follows the man with whom she has fallen in love by forming an acrobatic trio with a couple of friends and getting a job in a Paris music hall. When Charley gets home, he quickly finds out that Dixie didn't fall down dead, just dead drunk, but whilst Charley's been gone he really has moved in with Madelaine. It takes Charley a whole further act, however, to realize that the little acrobat, who has meanwhile become a music-hall megastar in the metropolis, is the girl for him.

Maya went round Hungary, and proved a regular item in the repertoire at the Fővárosi Operettszínház where it was given new productions in 1945 (25 May), in 1957 (now billed as a ''revueoperett,'' 31 July) in a version from the Margitszigeti Színpad, and in 1967 in a production from the Parkszínpad (ad József Romhányi). It also went further afield—something fewer Hungarian operetts were doing by the 1930s—and was seen in a German-language version at Vienna's Theater an der Wien (ad Schanzer, Welisch) with Mary Lossef featured as Maya (30 performances).

Austria: Theater an der Wien 16 November 1935

MAYERL, Billy [MAYERL, Joseph William] (b London, 31 May 1902; d Amersham, 27 March 1959).

A longtime popular light-entertainment pianist and composer of piano music (''Marigold''), Mayerl at one time made up part of the famous concert-party team, the Co-Optimists, for whom he provided a considerable amount of performance material. He contributed music to a number of revues (*The Punch Bowl, The London Revue,* etc), appeared as a performer in others (*You'd Be Surprised, Shake Your Feet, White Birds*), and also had a career as a composer of the ultra-light kind of songs and dances popular in the interwar musical theatre.

Mayerl composed his first full show score, in collaboration with loyal lyricist Frank Eyton, for Laddie Cliff, recently risen to the top of London's producing tree, as replacement music for a local version of the American musical comedy *So Long, Letty!* In spite of several rewrites the show floundered out of town, but Cliff stuck with his songwriter, and after Mayerl had injected additional numbers into several London and touring shows during 1929–31 (*Love Lies, Darling, I Love You, Silver Wings, Meet My Sister*), Cliff hired him to compose the songs and/or act as musical director for several more of his musicals. *Sporting Love* and *Over She Goes* did splendidly, *The Millionaire Kid, Leave It to Love* and *Crazy Days* rather less well. Mayerl had his most substantial success in the musical theatre, however, when he supplied the score for the long-running Lupino Lane comedy with songs, *Twenty to One.*

In 1939 he turned producer-songwriter-musical director with the production of a not terribly successful piece called *Runaway Love.* He fulfilled this triple role again on *Happy Birthday* (w Barry O'Brien), but this one failed to make it to town and its failure effectively ended his musical-theatre career. His last musical-theatre contributions were unspectacular ones: to a touring musical comedy, *Kiki,* and a short-lived *Six Pairs of Shoes* at a minor London house.

Long eclipsed through the change in musical fashions, Mayerl's sometimes deceptively simple-sounding music began to again find aficionados amongst piano players in the 1990s.

1928 **So Long, Letty!** (later *Oh, Letty!*) (Frank Eyton/Austin Melford, then Stanley Lupino) Theatre Royal, Birmingham 22 October

1929 **Change Over** revised *Oh, Letty!* (S Lupino) Hippodrome, Portsmouth 8 April

1930 **Nippy** (Arthur Wimperis, Eyton/Melford) Prince Edward Theatre 30 October

1931 **The Millionaire Kid** (Eyton/Noel Scott) Gaiety Theatre 20 May

1934 **Sporting Love** (Desmond Carter, Eyton/Arthur Rigby, Arty Ash, Stanley Lupino) Gaiety Theatre 31 March

1935 **Twenty to One** (Eyton/L Arthur Rose) London Coliseum 12 November

1936 **Over She Goes** (Eyton, Carter/S Lupino) Saville Theatre 23 September

1937 **Crazy Days** (Eyton, Carter/S Lupino) Shaftesbury Theatre 14 September

1939 **Runaway Love** (Eyton/Barry Lupino) Saville Theatre 3 November

1940 **Happy Birthday** (Eyton/Eyton, B Lupino, Rigby) Opera House, Manchester 9 September

1942 **Kiki** (Eyton/Martin Henry) Grand Theatre, Leeds 30 March

1944 **Six Pairs of Shoes** (w Harry Roy, et al/Eyton, et al/Monica Disney Ullman) Playhouse 10 April

THE MAYOR OF TOKIO Farcical Japanese opera in 2 acts by Richard Carle. Music by William Frederick Peters. Studebaker Theater, Chicago, 12 June 1905; New York Theater, New York, 4 December 1905.

Richard Carle's author-actor-manager-director vehicle was a latter-day *Chinese Honeymoon* which starred him as Marcus Orlando Kidder, the actor-manager of Kidder's Komiques, let loose in a barrage of misunderstandings and romantic complications in Tokyo. Kow-Tow (Edmund Garvie/Fred Frear) introduced himself as "The Mayor of Tokyo," and his daughter Oloto (Hortense Mazurette) insisted that one "Pity My Pitiful Plight" before falling in love with the tenor of the Komique company (Edmund Stanley/Albert Wellerstedt), who sang "A Toast to the Moon." Her father ended up in cahoots with the wardrobe mistress (Emma Janvier). Soubrette Birdie Talcum (Minerva Courtney) and Rusty (William Mock) provided the light moments alongside Betsy Lincoln, an American heiress (May Boley/Adele Rowland), and Ivan Orfulitch, a Russian spy (Charles Meyers/Jo Smith Marba), all of whom still left room in score and scenes for Carle to sing of "Foolishness" and "I Like You" and earn his very-top-of-the-bill billing.

The Mayor of Tokio played only 50 Broadway performances, but it proved a rich touring vehicle for Carle, and as late as 1914 it even made it to Australia. There, however, produced by George Willoughby with George H Bogues, Gilbert H Emery, Carrick Major (Kidder) and Amy Murphy (Oloto) in the lead roles, it was voted "not as good as *The Tenderfoot,*" another Carle piece which had preceded it, and did not stay around long.

Australia: Adelphi Theatre, Sydney 2 May 1914

MAYTIME *see* WIE EINST IM MAI

McCARTHY, Joseph (b Somerville, Mass, 27 September 1885; d New York, 18 December 1943). Lyricist of the 1910s and 1920s who scored sizeable hits both in and out of the theatre.

Variously a vocalist, a music publisher in Boston, and a scion of Tin Pan Alley, McCarthy placed numbers in such stage pieces as May Irwin's *Getting a Polish* (1910 w Al Piantadosi) and *The Wall Street Girl* (1912), but made himself evident in the musical theatre for the first time in 1913 when Al Jolson used several of his songs, including the durable "You Made Me Love You" (w James Monaco) as part of his act in *Honeymoon Express.* He had further song successes with "Ireland Must Be Heaven (for my mother came from there)" (w Fred Fisher, Howard Johnson), "What Do You Want to Make Those Eyes at Me For?" (w Monaco, Johnson), which was interpolated both in Broadway's *Follow Me* and the London wartime musical *The Better 'Ole,* and "They Go Wild, Simply Wild Over Me" (w Fisher) before, in 1918, he collaborated with Harry Carroll on the score of a first Broadway musical, *Oh, Look!* Although short-lived at New York's little Vanderbilt Theater, this piece proved much more of a success on the road with the Dolly Sisters featured at the top of its bill, and it produced another McCarthy piece that was to become a standard, "I'm Always Chasing Rainbows" (mus: Chopin ad).

The following year he provided the whole of the lyrics for a second show produced at the Vanderbilt. This time his musical collaborator was Harry Tierney, another *Follow Me* contributor with whom he had also written two numbers for the Cohanized comic opera *The Royal Vagabond* earlier in the year, and the huge success of their *Irene* (''Alice Blue Gown'') cemented a partnership which was to last through five and a bit more musicals in the following decade. The comical *Kid Boots* and the spectacular, romantic *Rio Rita* (Rangers Song, ''Rio Rita'') were both played internationally but, in spite of some considerable success, they did not approach *Irene* in either charm or in longevity. The ''bit'' of the five and a bit was the Broadway production of the French opérette *Afgar* for which Tierney and McCarthy supplied a goodly number of interpolations.

McCarthy and Tierney also wrote for revue, contributing songs to the *Ziegfeld Follies* from 1919 on (''My Baby's Arms,'' ''They're So Hard to Keep When They're Beautiful,'' ''Take Oh Take Those Lips Away'') and being billed as principal writers for the 1924 edition (''Adoring You,'' ''All Pepped Up,'' ''The Old Town Band''). They also composed the songs for *The Broadway Whirl* (1921).

The 1973 revival of *Irene,* which gave the show a second and even more prosperous Broadway, London and Australian life, used a selection of McCarthy's early song hits written with composers other than Tierney as part of a score which featured only a part of *Irene*'s original music.

1918 **Oh, Look!** (Harry Carroll/James Montgomery ad) Vanderbilt Theater 7 March

1919 **Irene** (Harry Tierney/Montgomery) Vanderbilt Theater 18 November

1922 **Up She Goes** (Tierney/Frank Craven) Playhouse 6 November

1922 **Glory** (Tierney, Maurice de Packh/w James Dyrenforth/Montgomery) Vanderbilt Theater 25 December

1923 **Kid Boots** (Tierney/William A McGuire, Otto Harbach) Earl Carroll Theater 31 December

1927 **Rio Rita** (Tierney/Guy Bolton, Fred Thompson) Ziegfeld Theater 2 February

1928 **Cross My Heart** (Tierney/Daniel Kusell) Knickerbocker Theater 17 September

McCARTHY, Siobhán [Mary Ann] (b Dublin, 6 November 1957).

Plangent-voiced Irish singer and actress who created major parts in two important West End musicals.

Siobhán McCarthy came to London and to instant notice when, after a well-publicized ''nationwide search,'' she was cast to create the role of the schoolgirl Mistress (''Another Suitcase in Another Hall'') in the original production of *Evita* (1978). Later in the piece's long run she succeeded to the title role. She subsequently took over as Mary Magdalene in the last days of the long run of London's *Jesus Christ Superstar* and, after spending two years as a member of the singing group Wall Street Crash, returned to the musical theatre to play Frankie Frayne in the 1984 revival of *On Your Toes,* the title role in the Joan of Arc musical *Jeanne* (Birmingham, 1985) and the betrayed Russian wife, Svetlana, in the original production of *Chess* (1986, ''I Know Him So Well''). During the show's run she succeeded Elaine Paige in the leading role of Florence.

She played for periods both as Fantine in *Les Misérables* and as Mrs Johnstone in *Blood Brothers* in London, appeared in Ken Hill's *Zorro—the Musical* at the Theatre Royal, Stratford East and as Betty in a revival of *No Trams to Lime Street* at the Liverpool Playhouse and, after a detour to the non-musical theatre (*Dancing at Lughnasa*), returned to the Prince Edward Theatre for the third time to create a third major role as Donna Sheridan in the Abba musical *Mamma mia!* (1999).

McCAULL, John A (b Scotland, 1846; d Greensboro, NC, 12 November 1894). Broadway's most energetic producer of comic opera in the 1880s.

Colonel McCaull (apparently a genuine Colonel, from the Confederate ranks) was a Baltimore lawyer and sometime member of the Virginian state legislature whose first link with the theatre came in handling a number of stage lawsuits. In 1879, in partnership with Charles E Ford and James Barton Key, he became a theatrical manager, setting up first at the Fifth Avenue Theater where the partners hosted D'Oyly Carte's production of *The Pirates of Penzance* and, from March 1880, at the newly remodeled Bijou Theater which was opened with a spectacle coupé of English operettas (*Charity Begins at Home, Ages Ago, The Spectre Knight*). After six months, Ford dropped out and in the end McCaull continued alone, presenting Audran's *Olivette, La Mascotte* and *Le Grand Mogul* (*The Snake Charmer*), Gilbert and Sullivan's *The Sorcerer* and *Patience,* Solomon's *Billee Taylor* (as D'Oyly Carte's accredited American associate) and Lecocq's *Le Coeur et la main* (*Heart and Hand*), and scoring several notable successes. He hosted Willie Edouin's Sparks for a season at the Bijou with *Dreams* and also ventured briefly into comedy, but his career from this time on was virtually wholly in the musical theatre.

McCaull sponsored the Blanche Roosevelt Opera Company which folded after underprepared productions of Cellier's *The Sultan of Mocha* and *The Mask of Pandora* (1881), and he then set up the McCaull Opera Comique Company which became a much more significant and wide-ranging institution. For a while he joined forces with Rudolf Aronson, investing money in the Casino

Theater under an agreement to supply the house with operettic product. That agreement foundered when the two came to disagreement over Aronson's attempts to influence the staging of the shows, and McCaull moved his company on first to Wallack's (1884) and then to seasons in other theatres. In the years that followed he had at least one and sometimes three companies touring America with repertoires of usually two or three high-class, excellently cast comic operas, playing substantial seasons in the main centers, and notably in Philadelphia where he for a while took on his own theatre.

He numbered amongst his productions such imported pieces as *The Queen's Lace Handkerchief* (*Das Spitzentuch der Königin*), *The Sorcerer, La Princesse de Trébizonde, Der Bettelstudent, The Black Hussar* (*Der Feldprediger*), *Die Fledermaus, Falka, Jacquette* (*La Béarnaise*), *Bellman, Le Petit Duc,* Planquette's *Nell Gwynne, Indiana,* Dellinger's *Don Cesar, Lorraine* and *Capitän Fracasse, Joséphine vendue par ses soeurs, The Crowing Hen* (*Serment d'amour*), *Die sieben Schwaben, Prince Methusalem, Boccaccio,* the Viennese musical comedy *Die Näherin* (played as *Chatter*) and Suppé's *Die Jagd nach dem Glück* produced under the title *Clover,* and also produced two early American comic operas, *The Lady or the Tiger* and *The Begum* (1887), and the English-bred but American-premiered *Virginia [and Paul]* (1883).

McCaull became disabled after he slipped on the ice during a visit to Chicago and broke his right ankle (27 December 1887). He almost died right there in Chicago, thanks to the overdose of potassium bromide administered to him as a painkiller, but although he eventually recovered, after several years of struggle, his circumstances had become so reduced between times that a series of benefits was given for him by the profession—at the Metropolitan Opera House, in Chicago and in Philadelphia—raising $8,000 to help him through the last years of his life. In September 1890 Mathilde Cottrelly, his fairly silent partner of always, withdrew from the financial management of the McCaull Opera Company, and McCaull sold out to Harry Askin, a former employee, thus ending his connection with the company that bore his name. It didn't bear it for long, for Askin, who was supposed to pay Mrs McCaull $200 a week for use of the McCaull name, and assume all sorts of other responsibilities, mostly financial, as well, soon defaulted and the company slipped from existence. In May 1892 the warehouses full of scenery and costumes were sold off to an Atlanta syndicate for just $3,000. John McCaull survived but a little while the company which had made him a well-known name from one side of America to the other.

McGOWAN, John W (''Jack'') (b Muskegon, Mich, 12 January 1894; d New York, 28 May 1977). Juvenile lead man turned librettist for musical comedy.

McGowan had a first and distinctly prominent contact with the musical theatre as a performer, appearing on Broadway in a series of musical comedies in his twenties. He had lead juvenile roles in *Take It from Me* (1919, Tom Eggett), *Little Blue Devil* (1919, Philip Scarsdale) and *Mary* (1920, Jack Keene), took the principal comic role of Howard Rodney Smith in *The Rose of Stamboul* (1922) and appeared in *George White's Scandals,* in George M Cohan's *The Rise of Rosie O'Reilly* (1923) and, as takeover from Roy Royston, as Austin Bevans in *June Days* (1925).

He had a notable first success as a dramatist with the play *Mama Loves Papa* (1926) and later that same year he turned his play, with altogether less success, into a musical, under the title *Sweet Lady.* After a couple more plays (*Tenth Avenue, Excess Baggage,* with the odd song), he returned to the musical scene, this time more happily, as the co-librettist on De Sylva, Brown and Henderson's boxing musical, *Hold Everything!* A collaboration with Rodgers and Hart on a thorough rewrite of the musical which ended up being called *Heads Up!* was less satisfactory, but *Girl Crazy* (1930) with the Gershwins and a second venture with De Sylva, Brown and Henderson on another quickly written piece, *Flying High,* helped turn the 1929–30 season into a spectacularly lucrative one for their librettist.

The run did not continue, however. A rather curious ''melodrama with music'' called *Singin' the Blues* (1931), laced with black speciality acts, was a quick failure for producers Aarons and Freedley, as was *Pardon My English,* which McGowan directed for the same management. A final Broadway venture, *Say When,* with McGowan this time as co-producer as well as writer (w Ray Henderson), joined the revue *Strike Me Pink* (also director), on which the two men had worked together the previous season, in the debit column of his career.

McGowan then abandoned Broadway for Hollywood, where he subsequently worked as a screenwriter (*Sitting Pretty, Little Nellie Kelly, Babes in Arms, Lady, Be Good!, Panama Hattie, Broadway Melody of 1936, Broadway Melody of 1938, Born to Dance*) and as a director and performer.

1926 **Sweet Lady** (Delos Owen/Bud Green) Weiting Theater, Syracuse 2 December

1928 **Hold Everything!** (Ray Henderson/B G De Sylva, Lew Brown/w De Sylva) Broadhurst Theater 10 October

1929 **Heads Up!** (Richard Rodgers/Lorenz Hart/w Paul Gerard Smith) Alvin Theater 11 November

1930 **Flying High** (Henderson/De Sylva, Brown) Apollo Theater 3 March

1930 **Girl Crazy** (George Gershwin/Ira Gershwin/w Guy Bolton) Alvin Theater 14 October

1931 **Singin' the Blues** (Jimmy McHugh/Dorothy Fields) Liberty Theater 16 September

1934 **Say When** (Henderson/Ted Koehler) Imperial Theater 8 November

McGUIRE, William Anthony (b Chicago, 9 July 1885; d Beverly Hills, Calif, 16 September 1940). Broadway librettist and director who flourished in the 1920s, and floundered thereafter.

McGuire worked at first as a journalist on the *South Bend News* in Indiana, but he began to make his first efforts as a playwright in his teens and had a dozen plays under his belt, without notable success, before he tackled the musical theatre. In the early 1920s he wrote sketches for such revues as *Frivolities of 1920, The Ziegfeld Follies* (1924) and *No Foolin'* (1926), and worked on his first libretto, with Otto Harbach, for the successful Eddie Cantor vehicle *Kid Boots* (1923), whilst in the same period turning out the most successful of his straight plays, *Six-Cylinder Love* (1921) and *Twelve Miles Out* (1925).

McGuire directed the Broadway production of the Rodgers and Hart musical *Betsy* for Florenz Ziegfeld and, during 1928, doubled the functions of librettist and director on three shows, of which Friml's *The Three Musketeers* and Walter Donaldson's *Whoopee* both turned out to be sizeable hits. He had less success with the textual and directorial doctoring of Vincent Youmans's Broadway-bound *Great Day* (1929), with the starry and lavish Ziegfeld *Show Girl,* and with a Rip van Winkle vehicle for the fading Fred Stone and his daughter, *Ripples* (1930). Nor did he fare any better with his final effort, *Smiles,* for which Ziegfeld had again supplied all of what ought to have been the best in the way of music (Youmans), stars (Fred and Adele Astaire, Marilyn[n] Miller) and physical production.

Suffering by this stage from what had finally become a severe drink problem, McGuire was all but sacked from *Smiles.* After nine productions for Ziegfeld, he never worked for him again nor, indeed, for anyone else in the musical theatre.

1923 **Kid Boots** (Harry Tierney/Joseph McCarthy/w Otto Harbach) Earl Carroll Theater 31 December

1928 **Rosalie** (George Gershwin, Sigmund Romberg/Ira Gershwin, P G Wodehouse/w Guy Bolton) New Amsterdam Theater 10 January

1928 **The Three Musketeers** (Rudolf Friml/Wodehouse, Clifford Grey) Lyric Theater 13 March

1928 **Whoopee** (Walter Donaldson) New Amsterdam Theater 4 December

1929 **Show Girl** (G Gershwin/I Gershwin, Gus Kahn) Ziegfeld Theater 2 July

1930 **Ripples** (Oscar Levant, Albert Szirmai/Irving Caesar, Graham John) New Amsterdam Theater 11 February

1930 **Smiles** (UK: *The One Girl*) (Vincent Youmans/Grey, Harold Adamson/w others) Ziegfeld Theater 18 November

McKENZIE, Julia [Kathleen Nancy] (b Enfield, 17 February 1941). Actress and vocalist who won a triple-headed success, unparalleled in modern British show business, as an award-winning star of straight and musical theatre and television.

Originally trained as an operatic vocalist, Julia McKenzie made her earliest stage appearances on the road (*Rose Marie* tour, 1963) and in British regional theatres as well as appearing in the chorus and deputizing for Rachel Roberts in the lead role of *Maggie May* (1964) in London. She was subsequently seen in London in *Joey Joey* (1966), *Queenie* (1967), the showcase of the Worcester repertory theatre's musical production *A Present from the Corporation* (1967, Maggie Slater), *The Man with a Load of Mischief* and as a memorably simpering Gloria in *Mame* (1969). She took over the role of Marge in *Promises, Promises* (1970), appeared at the Old Vic in the York repertory theatre's production of *The Last Sweet Days of Isaac* (1971) and played the Ladybird in a Shaw Theatre production of *The Plotters of Cabbage Patch Garden* (1971) before, in 1972, she had her first contact with the works of Stephen Sondheim, a writer with whose works she was to have a special connection, when she took over the role of April in the London production of *Company* (1972).

Miss McKenzie subsequently appeared at Leatherhead in *I Do! I Do!* and at London's Mermaid Theatre in the musical compilation shows *Cowardy Custard* (1972) and *Cole* (1974), and she was one of the group which was instrumental in compiling and performing a similar show made up from the works of Sondheim, produced in London as *Side by Side by Sondheim* (1976). The notable success of this piece, which was largely reponsible for promoting a wider awareness of the author's work in Britain, was continued overseas, and the London team repeated their performances for an Equity-allowed period on Broadway. Miss McKenzie appeared there, by the will of that organization, as Julie N McKenzie.

After a period spent shunning the musical theatre in a purposeful attempt to establish herself as an actress in a country where, unlike others, ability as a vocalist is considered by the powers-who-cast to be a bar to acting ambitions (*Norman Conquests, Ten Times Table, Outside Edge,* etc), Miss McKenzie returned to the musical stage in London's production of *On the Twentieth Century,* giving the performance of an era in the demanding mixture of comedy and vocal versatility which make up the role of Lily Garland. Over the following years she was largely claimed by television (*Blott on the Landscape, Fresh Fields, French Fields,* etc), film (*Shirley Valentine,* etc) and the non-musical stage (*Woman in Mind,* etc), returning to the musical theatre only to play Adelaide in *Guys and Dolls* at the National Theatre (1982) and then two Sondheim works in the West End—as Sally in *Follies* (1987) and as the Witch in *Into the Woods* (1990)—and a third, *Sweeney Todd* (1993, Mrs Lovett), back at the National Theatre.

In recent years Miss McKenzie has varied her performing career with directing assignments, mounting the original production of the play *Stepping Out,* Britain's *Steel Magnolias* and musical pieces including *Just So,* a further Sondheim compilation *Putting it Together* (1992) and a musicalized *Stepping Out* (1997) from which she withdrew before it reached London failure.

McLELLAN, C[harles] M[orton] S[tewart] [aka MORTON, Hugh] (b Bath, Maine, 1865; d Esher, Surrey, 22 September 1916). Adept Broadway librettist who found success at the turn of the century with variety musicals and revues, and ended up adapting French comedies as the libretti for a landmark set of musical comedies in the 1910s.

A sometime journalist, and at one stage the editor of the New York journal *Town Topics,* McLellan made his first attempt at writing for the stage with the libretto to *Puritania,* an olde-American comic-opera vehicle for Pauline Hall as an English Earl out to save a 17th-century Salem girl accused of witchcraft. The piece did well enough, and McLellan followed up with a second piece for the star (*The Honeymooners*), but he chose to make his next ventures into musical theatre under the pseudonym ''Hugh Morton.'' After supplying some fresh lyrics for George Lederer's brutal remake of the British hit *The Lady Slavey* for the Casino Theater he worked on a number of further libretti and lyrics for Lederer and the Casino. *In Gay New York, The Whirl of the Town* and *Yankee Doodle Dandy* professed to be revues, *An American Beauty* and *The Belle of New York* were billed as musical comedies, but no matter what they called themselves, they were all basically lively ragbags of multi-colored entertainment, whose plots took more preposterous turnings than a politician and whose dialogue was eased aside to allow the introduction of songs, specialities and dance numbers on the one hand, and what were little more than stand-up turns from the chief comedians on the other.

The Belle of New York, however, turned out to be a phenomenon. Introduced into Britain, it proved a novelty attraction of huge drawing power, and subsequently became established throughout the world in the earliest years of the 20th century as the representative of ''American musical comedy'' to the outside world. McLellan failed to repeat this out-of-the-blue success with two further vehicles for *Belle of New York* star Edna May, *The Girl from Up There* (which had the heroine emerging from a block of ice at the North Pole) and a truly silly London piece called *Nelly Neil,* or with a musicalized version of his own farce *Glittering Gloria* (1904) which had been discreetly produced at London's Wyndham's Theatre the year before. His one success in the decade following *The Belle of New York* was, in fact, not in the musical field, but in one of a small handful of attempts at non-musical playwriting, with the drama *Leah Kleschna* (1904), which won productions throughout the world after its New York introduction by Minnie Maddern Fiske.

Musical-comedy success returned when McLellan allied himself again with Ivan Caryll, his partner on *Nelly Neil,* following the composer's removal to America. Caryll had a ready supply of first-rate French comedies optioned for musicalization, and it was McLellan whom he chose to do the English-language adaptations. *Mariage à la Carte,* at McLellan's old haunt, the Casino, was the first, but it was the next pair, *The Pink Lady* (from *Le Satyre*) and *Oh! Oh! Delphine* (from *La Grimpette*), two dazzling musical comedies which played an important part in establishing the more sophisticated book-based musical comedy on Broadway, which were both their librettist's biggest Broadway successes and the best of his writings. However, after one more successful collaboration with Caryll on a version of Tristan Bernard's *Le Petit Café,* McLellan reversed his partner's trail, and left America to go to live in Britain.

There, in the few years up till his death—and in spite of Klaw and Erlanger's 1915 announcement of one more McLellan-Caryll work, under the intriguing title *Here Comes Miss Tootsie*—he made little further contribution to the theatre, his final musical piece being a reversion to the now-fashionable revue form with *Round the Map* (mus: Herman Finck, ly: Hartley Carrick, Clifford Grey) produced at the Alhambra in 1915.

His brother, **George B[rinton] McLELLAN** (b Bath, Maine, 1867; d London, 1 February 1932) was for many years a theatrical manager. He ran the Fay Templeton Opera Company (w David Towers) in the early 1890s, teamed with George Lederer to produce several Casino Theater shows (*The Telephone Girl, Yankee Doodle Dandy,* etc), was for a period manager of that house, and subsequently moved to London where he was associated with the Shuberts in several productions and acted as their London and Continental representative. He later became the general manager for Sir Harold Wernher's London group of theatres, including the Adelphi, Shaftesbury, Gaiety, Apollo and His Majesty's Theatres. He was married successively to two particularly lovely Broadway musical stars in Pauline Hall and **Madge LESSING** (1866–1932, *Jack and the Beanstalk, A Dangerous Maid, The Rounders, Little Red Riding Hood, The Lady Slavey, The Monks of Malabar, The Belle of New York* revival,

Erminie revival, *Wang* revival, *Sergeant Brue, Noah's Ark, The Prince of Pilsen, The Prince of Pilsen* Paris, *Der oberen Zehntausend* Berlin, etc).

1892 **Puritania** (Edgar Stillman Kelly) Tremont Theater, Boston 6 June; Fifth Avenue Theater 19 September

1893 **The Honeymooners** (William W Furst) Columbia Theater, Boston 23 October

1896 **The Lady Slavey** American lyrics (Casino Theater)

1896 **In Gay New York** (Gustave Kerker) Casino Theater 25 May

1896 **An American Beauty** (Kerker) Casino Theater 28 December

1897 **The Whirl of the Town** (Kerker) Casino Theater 25 May

1897 **The Belle of New York** (Kerker) Casino Theater 28 September

1897 **The Telephone Girl** (*La Demoiselle du téléphone*) American libretto (Casino Theater)

1898 **Yankee Doodle Dandy** (Kerker) Casino Theater 25 July

1901 **The Girl from Up There** (Kerker) Herald Square Theater 7 January

1904 **Glittering Gloria** (Bernard Rolt) Daly's Theater 15 February

1907 **Nelly Neil** (Ivan Caryll) Aldwych Theatre, London 10 January

1911 **Marriage à la Carte** (Caryll) Casino Theater 2 January

1911 **The Pink Lady** (Caryll) New Amsterdam Theater 13 March

1912 **Oh! Oh! Delphine** (Caryll) Knickerbocker Theater 30 September

1913 **The Little Café** (Caryll) New Amsterdam Theater 10 November

McNALLY, John J[ames] (b Charlestown, Mass, 7 May 1854; d Brooklyn, NY, 25 March 1931). Librettist for farce comedy and variety musicals of the 19th and early 20th centuries.

Originally, if briefly, a Harvard law student, subsequently a journalist and drama critic in his native Charlestown and in Boston (drama critic of the *Times, Herald, Daily Star*), McNally began his career as a dramatist when he supplied the young E E Rice and his ''Surprise Party'' company with the loose-legged libretto for the early musical farce comedy *Revels* (1878). The piece, decorated with a set of songs gathered from hither and yon, served for many years of touring, and McNally (who went out with the company as Press Agent) followed it up with a run of like pieces—cheerful low comedies of the most unsophisticated kind, often in the German-accented style popular at the time, and effectively adaptable to a changing musical and variety-turn content.

McNally wrote several such pieces for the Dalys (revised *Vacation, Upside Down, Irish Heads and German Hearts*) and for May Irwin (the sketch *Army Tactics, Boys and Girls,* the highly successful *The Widow Jones* which put the seal on her stardom), and provided annual vehicles for the Rogers Brothers as part of Klaw and Erlanger's attempt to out-Weber-and-Fields Weber and Fields, beginning with the 1899 *A Reign of Error* and continuing to the last of the series in 1907. He also wrote the spectacular *Superba* (Harmanus Bleeker Hall, Albany 1 October 1890) for the Hanlon team of athletes, fabricated *Lola from Berlin* to feature Lulu Glaser in a Dutch comedy role, brought the *New York Herald*'s cartoon *Fluffy Ruffles* to the stage, and in 1909 put together *In Hayti* for the comedy team of McIntyre and Heath. He then took his distance from the theatre, after 30 years of supplying it with almost inevitably reviled libretti which had, simply, the merit of allowing their performers to show off whatever it was that they did best to an audience who had really only come to see them do that.

1878 **Revels, or Bon Ton George Jr** (pasticcio arr Henry Sator, various/w Dexter Smith) Grand Opera House, San Francisco 24 December; 14th Street Theater, New York 25 October 1880

1880 **Dreams, or Fun in a Photograph Gallery** (W A Rostetter, Woolson Morse, E E Rice, Harry Braham, et al/w Dexter Smith, Nat Childs, F T Robinson, et al/Willie Edouin, Childs) Park Theater, Boston 23 August; Bijou Theater, New York 30 August

1880 **The New Evangeline** revised version of *Evangeline* Haverly's 14th Street Theater

1887 **Vacation, or Harvard vs Yale** revised version of Thomas Daly and F G Maeder's piece

1887 **Upside Down** (comp & arr Charles Levenberg/w Daly) City Opera House, Dover, NH 27 August; Niblo's Garden 23 April 1888

1889 **Army Tactics** (various) sketch Howard's Athenaeum, Boston

1889 **Irish Heads and German Hearts** (various) Music Hall, Lowell, Mass 4 September

1890 **Grimes' Cellar Door** (various/w Thomas Addison) Proctor's Opera House, Wilmington 25 August

1890 **A Straight Tip** (various) Brockton, Mass 26 August; Bijou Theater 26 January 1891

1891 **Boys and Girls** (various) Park Theater 21 September

1892 **A Mad Bargain** (various/w Julian Mitchell) Bijou Theater 27 February

1893 **A Country Sport** (various) Bijou Theater 25 December

1895 **The Widow Jones** (various) Bijou Theater 16 September

1895 **The Night Clerk** (René Stretti, et al) Bijou Theater 11 November

1895 **Criss-Cross** (pasticcio) sketch Keith's Boston January 1896; Keith's Union Square 3 February 1896

1896 **A Good Thing** (various) Casino Theater 12 October

1896 **Courted into Court** (various) Bijou Theater 29 December

1897 **The Good Mr Best** (Henry J Sayres, Tom Le Mack, Frederick Dana, et al, arr Jesse Williams) Brockton, Mass 17 April; Garrick Theater, New York 30 August

1899 **A Reign of Error** (Maurice Levi) Victoria Theater 2 March

1899 **Mademoiselle Ka-za-za** (Levi) 1 act Victoria Theater 8 May

1899 **The Rogers Brothers in Wall Street** (Levi) Victoria Theater 18 September

1900 **The Rogers Brothers in Central Park** (Levi/J Cheever Goodwin) Victoria Theater 17 September

1900 **Star and Garter** (revised *Boys and Girls*) (various) New Haven, Conn 25 October; Victoria Theater 26 November

1901 **The Rogers Brothers in Washington** (Levi) Knickerbocker Theater 2 September

1901 **The Sleeping Beauty and the Beast** American version w Cheever Goodwin and Fred Solomon (Broadway Theater)

1902 **The Rogers Brothers at Harvard** (Levi/Goodwin, Edward Gardiner) Knickerbocker Theater 1 September

1903 **Mother Goose** American version w George V Hobart (New Amsterdam Theater)

1903 **The Rogers Brothers in London** (Max Hoffman, Melville Ellis/Hobart, Gardiner) Knickerbocker Theater 7 September

1904 **A Little of Everything** (J Rosamund Johnson, Bob Cole, George M Cohan, et al) Aerial Gardens 6 June

1904 **The Rogers Brothers in Paris** (Hoffman/Hobart) New Amsterdam Theater 5 September

1904 **Humpty Dumpty** American version (New Amsterdam Theater)

1904 **(Life) In Newport** (Bob Cole, James Weldon Johnson, J R Johnson) Liberty Theater 26 December

1905 **Lifting the Lid** (Jean Schwartz/William Jerome) Aerial Gardens 5 June

1905 **The Whole Damm Family** (various) 1 act Aerial Gardens 26 June

1905 **The Rogers Brothers in Ireland** (Hoffman/Hobart) Liberty Theater 4 September

1905 **Fritz in Tammany Hall** (Schwartz/Jerome) Herald Square Theater 16 October

1907 **The Rogers Brothers in Panama** (Max Hoffman) Broadway Theater 2 September

1907 **Lola from Berlin** (Schwartz/Jerome) Liberty Theater 16 September

1908 **Fluffy Ruffles** (W T Francis/Wallace Irwin) Criterion Theater 7 September

1909 **In Hayti** (Schwartz/Jerome) Circle Theater 30 August

Other titles credited: *Home Rule, A Sharp Tack, Turned Down* (burlesque), *Little Lord McElroy* (burlesque), *Rapid Delivery* (1892)

McNALLY, Terrence J (b St Petersburg, Fla, 3 November 1939).

Highly successful playwright and occasional librettist of the modern theatre.

Represented on and off Broadway from 1963 by a series of plays (*The Lady of the Camellias, Where Has Tommy Flowers Gone, The Ritz, Lips Together, Teeth Apart*), McNally made his first appearance in the musical theatre with the libretto to a musicalization of John Steinbeck's *East of Eden,* mounted under the title *Here's Where I Belong*. His name had disappeared from the bills by the time the show sank in one Broadway night, and it was 16 years before the by then established playwright ventured again into the musical theatre, this time with the libretto to the intimate Kander/Ebb musical *The Rink.*

As his often pleasingly politically and socially incorrect plays gained increasing success (*The Lisbon Traviata, Frankie and Johnny in the Clair de Lune, A Perfect Ganesh, Love! Valour! Compassion!, Master Class,* etc) he ventured again on to the musical stage with his adaptation of the play *Kiss of the Spiderwoman* (Tony Award), and a third time with the encapsulation of E W Doctorow's zany *Ragtime* (Tony Award) into a rather less zany and—for the author—surprisingly ''corrected'' piece of sentimental period-musical theatre. It nevertheless, in a period where humor and above all zaniness in the musical theatre had gone thoroughly out the window, found a certain degree of success. Better—much better—was however to come. At the time of writing, McNally's latest musical, an Americanized version of the British film *The Full Monty,* a first and welcome venture by the author into the (it seems) once again popular genre of the musical with merriment, has just opened on Broadway with every sign of being the newly minted hit the American musical theatre has lacked in recent years. Watch this space.

His play *Master Class* was built round a vocal class taken by former opera star Maria Callas.

In 1999 McNally contributed to the text for the opera *Central Park* produced by Glimmerglass Opera at Cooperstown, NY.

1968 **Here's Where I Belong** (Robert Waldmann/Alfred Uhry/ Alex Gordon credited) Billy Rose Theater 3 March

1984 **The Rink** (John Kander/Fred Ebb) Martin Beck Theater 9 February

1990 **Kiss of the Spiderwoman** (Kander/Ebb) Westchester 1 May; Shaftesbury Theatre, London 20 October 1992

1996 **Ragtime** (Stephen Flaherty/Lynne Ahrens) Ford Center, Toronto 8 December 1996; Ford Center, New York 18 January 1998

2000 **The Full Monty** (David Yazbec) Eugene O'Neill Theater 26 October

MÉALY, Juliette [JOSSERAND, Juliette] (b Toulouse).

Juliette Méaly ''with her abbreviated skirts, a wealth of rustling frills and a huge hat,'' not to mention a very fine soprano voice, led a full career in the European musical theatre, starring in many a Parisian role where a certain glamorous audacity was needed, yet proving herself a fine performer in a wide range of parts, from the classics to the music-hally, through a long career.

She made her earliest appearances at a very young age at the Eldorado in 1884, but she first came into fuller evidence as a young and appealing jeune première at the Théâtre des Menus-Plaisirs (Marcel in *La Fiancée des verts-poteaux,* 1887, etc) when she took over from Yvonne Stella in the central role of Audran's *L'Oncle Célestin* (1891). She followed up at the same house alongside Félix Huguenet in Roger's *Le Coq* (1891, Cécilia) and in the leading role of Audran's *Article de Paris* (1892, Jeanne) before moving on to appear in *La Vie parisienne* at the Variétés, and starring on the rather larger Gaîté stage as Michelette in *Le Talisman* (1893). She followed this distinct personal success by taking her new-found stardom to the rest of Europe, and later the same year she visited Budapest's Somossy Theatre, Bucharests's Théâtre Lyrique and the Vienna Carltheater playing Miss Helyett and Le Petit Duc. She then went on to London, where she appeared at Alhambra with Paul Fugère in a selection from *La Femme de Narcisse,* and was featured in a pasted-in ''green-room scene'' in *In Town* at the Gaiety Theatre (August), alongside American whistler Tom Browne and impersonator Cissie Loftus.

Back in Paris, she starred as Christiane in *Le Troisième Hussards* (1894) at the Gaîté, as the voluptuous Mimosa, nude scene and all, in the spectacular *Le Carnet du Diable* (1895, 1897, 1899) and as another near-the-knuckle demoiselle, Paquerette in *Le Carillon* (1896), both at the Variétés, where, under the direction of Fernand Samuel, she would make her ''home'' for most of the next two decades. In between her appearances in osée opérette à grand spectacle, she played in the Variétés revivals of the classics (Dindonette in *L'Oeil crevé,* Gabrielle in *La Vie parisienne,* Marguerite in *Le Petit Faust,* etc). In 1897 she created the role of the actress Fanny in *Le Pompier de service,* but the years which followed brought no new roles of value as Mlle Méaly appeared as Fragoletto to the Fiorella of Tariol-Baugé in *Les Brigands* and as Eurydice at the Variétés, and took another turn around central Europe, playing *Madame Méphisto*—Blondeau and Monreal's Parisian ''opérette-folie'' spectacle, which had her as a female demon taking vengeance on her underworld husband—*Mam'zelle Nitouche, Le Pompier de service* and *L'Auberge du Tohu-bohu* (Flora) at Budapest's Magyar Színház (16–20 April 1901), Berlin's Friedrich-Wilhelmstädtisches Theater (15 May 1901) and Theater des Westens (22 February 1901) and Vienna's Theater an der Wien and Carltheater.

She had her best fresh role for a decade when she starred as the Princess Bengaline in Planquette's posthumous *Le Paradis de Mahomet* (1906), and then stepped aside from the Variétés to appear at the Moulin-Rouge alongside Mistinguett in *La Revue de la femme* (1907) and the following year as the star of the opérette *Son Altesse l'amour,* this time in competiton with Gaby Deslys. She was seen regularly on the Paris stage for another decade, repeating her best roles (notably *La Vie parisienne*'s Gabrielle, but no longer those requiring a nude scene) and creating the occasional new role, as in *Les Merveilleuses* (1914) or, as late as 1921, in a return to the stage, in *La Galante Épreuve* at La Cigale.

Plate 247. **Juliette Méaly**—*with her clothes on.*

ME AND JULIET Musical in 2 acts by Oscar Hammerstein II. Music by Richard Rodgers. Majestic Theater, New York, 28 May 1953.

A regulation backstage musical which busied itself with the love affairs of a regulation operetta pair of pairings: one romantic—between a chorine (Isabel Bigley) and an ASM (Bill Hayes), which comes to a happy conclusion in spite of a lighting man (Mark Dawson) with the air of *Oklahoma!*'s Judd Fry—and one, between dancer Betty (Joan McCracken) and stage manager Mac (Ray Walston), which is comic. The authors of *Me and Juliet* (which was the title of the show within the show) considered that they had avoided the clichés of the backstage musical, using their theatre setting only as a colorful background to a pair of love affairs, but in throwing out the clichés (and it was not often evident that they had) they had also thrown out the color, and the tale and the action of *Me and Juliet* looked a little pale in the wake of such bristlingly bright theatrical shows as *Kiss Me, Kate.*

The score turned out one number, the lilting ''No Other Love,'' adapted from Rodgers's theme music for the film *Victory at Sea* and performed by the leading lovers, which became a Rodgers and Hammerstein standard (it was later shifted over into their *Cinderella* in London, when *Me and Juliet* failed to travel), as well as a pleasing ballad with the rather ungrammatical title ''Marriage Type Love'' for the leading man of the internal *Me and Juliet.* The characters and situations of the show did not allow its writers to stretch their ideas too far beyond the everyday in their numbers. But if the show was a touch unimaginative, it was also, as might have been expected, highly professional, and Rodgers and Hammerstein's names on the bill (they were producers as well as authors) gave it an extra impetus through 358 performances on Broadway.

Recording: original cast (RCA Victor)

ME AND MY GIRL Musical comedy in 2 acts by L Arthur Rose and Douglas Furber. Music by Noel Gay. Victoria Palace, London, 16 December 1937.

Following his success as the perky little hero of the musical comedy *Twenty to One,* Lupino Lane commissioned a second piece for himself which would allow him to repeat his characterization of cheeky cockney Bill Snibson. Arthur Rose, the author of the first piece, teamed with librettist-lyricist Douglas Furber to write a piece which was advertised as a sequel but which, in fact, apart from its general tone, had only Lane's character and his name in common with its predecessor. This time Lane was presented as the unwilling heir to an earldom, whisked from Lambeth and his girl, Sally (co-producer's wife Teddie St Denis), to suffer with due comicality being made into a ''fit and proper person'' for his new position by the dragonistic Duchess of Hareford (Doris Rogers). Betty Frankiss played the Lady Jacqueline, seductively angling for the new Earl, whilst veteran comedian George Graves made a sympathetic aristocratic ally for the little fellow in the role of Sir John Tremaine.

Noel Gay's handful of songs—whittled down to just seven on a run into town which, in a fashion most untypical in Britain, also saw the disappearance of the original duchess, Mignon O'Doherty, and director Gene Gerrard—illustrated the comedy with vigor. Brother Wallace Lupino sang and danced about the duties of ''The Family Solicitor,'' Miss Frankiss looked to ''Me'' and duetted comically with Lane that ''I Would if I Could,'' Sally kept a stiff upper lip and decided to ''Take It on the Chin'' and the servants of the house had ''A Domestic Discussion.'' However, it was Bill and Sally's title song and the jaunty dance number ''The Lambeth Walk'' (ch: Fred A Leslie) which proved the show's happiest numbers, and—with the original ''Lambeth Walk'' which had been touted round the music halls by Alec Hurley at the turn of the century quite forgotten—both went on to become perennial favorites.

Me and My Girl played a twice-nightly schedule at the Victoria Palace and, boosted by a clever introduction of ''The Lambeth Walk'' into the dance halls of the country, by broadcast and television versions and, ultimately, by wartime conditions which at first caused the show to take a short break, it settled in for a fine run. In the early stages of the war, as ''The Lambeth Walk'' went to the battlefields of Europe with the British troops, the production switched from evening performances to playing 1:45 and 4 PM matinées. Then, when ''We're Going to Hang Out the Washing on the Siegfried Line'' joined ''The Lambeth Walk'' at the top of the Tommies' marching songs, Lane interpolated that song into his show as well. By the time he had finished, the piece had racked up 1,646 performances on its 12-a-week schedule.

Me and My Girl became a perennial vehicle for Lane, who returned to London for a second season in 1941 (London Coliseum 25 June), a third, back at the Victoria Palace, in 1945 (6 August) and a fourth at the Winter Garden in 1949 (12 December) before his son Lauri took over to continue to troupe the piece around Britain and overseas.

In 1984, under the management of Richard Armitage, son of and publisher to the late Noel Gay, *Me and My Girl* was given a major revival in a revised version (ad Stephen Fry). The show's score was expanded to more conventional 1980s musical comedy proportions by the addition of a number of songs which the original writers had composed after the event to make their show more appealing to amateur musical companies, as well as several other Gay hits. Robert Lindsay in Lane's role (complete with some of the originator's well-known acrobatic comedy) was given ''Leaning on a Lampost,'' whilst his Sally (Emma Thompson) inherited the lovely ballad ''Once You Lose Your Heart'' from the amateur score. The new version of *Me and My Girl* proved, nearly half a century on, to be even more popular than the first. It settled down at London's Adelphi Theatre (4 February 1985) where, whilst running through a veritable parade

Plate 248. **Me and My Girl.** *Robert Lindsay (Bill Snibson) and Emma Thompson (Sally) introduced the revival that set Arthur Rose's comedy musical off for a worldwide series of productions—50 years after its first showing.*

of mostly television-comedy names at the top of its bill (Karl Howson, Gary Wilmot, Les Dennis) it remained for nearly eight years, taking the show's London total past 4,000 performances.

Exported to Broadway, the new *Me and My Girl* once again conquered by its charm and high spirits, won Lindsay acclaim for his performance, and remained for 1,420 performances before being crowded out of its theatre in a booking jam. In the meanwhile, the show progressed to all kinds of places that Lane would never have dreamed of. It was seen in an embarrassingly under-cast production in Australia (which hadn't, curiously, bothered about it first time round), in Mexico (as *Yo y mi chica*), in Hungary (ad Iván Bradányi) with Sándor Szakácsi, Judit Kocsis and György Bánffy featured at Budapest's József Attila Színház, and in a Japanese production mounted by the famed all-woman Takarazuka troupe, and, with the Second World War and "We're Going to Hang Out the Washing on the Siegfried Line" now expunged from the text, *Me and My Girl* (it retained its English title in Mary Miliane and Helmut Forche's adaptation) even ultimately appeared in Germany, having its first performance in Coburg with a cast headed by Roland Wagenführer (Bill), Carol Lentner (Sally) and Wilhem Eyberg-Wertenegg (Sir John)—the whole giving *Me and My Girl* its widest, most fruitful career more than half a century after that tempestuous run in from Glasgow to London.

A wartime film version was made under the title *The Lambeth Walk* in which Lane was teamed with Seymour Hicks (Sir John) and soubrette Sally Gray, whilst a 1956 television version featured Lauri Lupino Lane alongside the Duchess of Marie Löhr.

USA: Marquis Theater 10 August 1986; Australia: State Theatre, Melbourne 3 January 1986; Hungary: József Attila Színház *Én és a kedvesem* 5 March 1988; Germany: Landestheater, Coburg 29 February 1992; Austria: Landestheater, Linz 15 November 1996

Film: CAPAD-Pinebrook *The Lambeth Walk* 1939

Recordings: London revival cast (EMI), Broadway cast (MCA), Mexican cast (private), Hungarian cast (Qualiton), Japanese cast (TMP), etc

MECCA *see* CAIRO

MÉDITERRANÉE Opérette à grand spectacle in 2 acts by Raymond Vincy. Music by Francis Lopez. Théâtre du Châtelet, Paris, 17 December 1955.

Plate 249. **Méditerranée.** *The scenery, and Tino Rossi serenading his Corsican belle.*

Corsican singing star Tino Rossi came late in his career from the screen to the stage to play Corsican singing star Mario Franchi, a dreamboatish tenor who becomes mixed up in some dangerous Mediterranean smuggling when he joins a holiday cruise around his home islands. The criminal turns out to be the yacht's captain; the lovely Paola (Dominique Rika) returns to her island and to the arms of the singer's rash but reformed brother (Henri-Jacques Huet); and all the comical folk who have enlivened the evening of Corsican revelry—from the jolly campers Juliette (Aglãé) and Mimile (Pierjac) to the priest Père Padovani (Fernand Sardou), the local gendarme Cardolacci (Ardisson) and the determinedly widowed innkeeper (Andrée Delavel) he pursues—are left to get on with their lives as Mario heads back to the big, bright world of showbusiness.

Vincy's colorful, comedy-filled book was illustrated by Lopez with a mixture of throbbing tenor solos for the star and sprightly comedy songs for the other folk. Rossi serenaded ''Les Filles d'Ajaccio'' and the ''Méditerranée,'' greeted the ''Campanella'' of his home town, and invited Paola to a party with ''Demain c'est Dimanche'' before bidding her farewell with the secret of their night out intact (''N'en dit rien à personne''), but he saved his biggest guns for one of the religious moments which had succeeded so well in Lopez's earlier *Andalousie,* as he prayed passionately for his smuggling brother's safety to the ''Vierge Marie.'' Mimile jollied about ''Un p'tit verre du p'tit vin du pays,'' Juliette swaggered about disguised as a moll with ''C'est mon mataf'' and the priest wondered over ''Les Paroissiens de mon village'' in some of the evening's lighter moments.

Méditerranée and Rossi won a fine success, and the piece played through 572 performances at the huge Théâtre du Châtelet before finding itself a secure place in the repertoire of French provincial theatres. A 1964 revival at the same house (11 July) starred Rossi's legitimate successor, Rudy Hirigoyen, through a further 181 performances.

Recordings: selection w Rossi (Pathé), selection w Hirigoyen (CBS/Odeon), etc

Plate 250. **Meet Me Victoria**

MEET ME VICTORIA Musical play in 2 acts by Lupino Lane and Lauri Wylie based on a story by H F Maltby. Additional dialogue by Ted Kavanagh. Lyrics by Frank Eyton. Music by Noel Gay. Victoria Palace, London, 8 April 1944.

Meet Me Victoria brought Lupino Lane back to the Victoria Palace, where he had triumphed in *Me and My Girl* and *Twenty to One* and done fairly well in *La-di-da-di-da,* with a fourth musical in which he exploited his chirpy cockney ''Bill'' character. Railwayman Bill Fish (Lane) needs cash and promotion to be able to wed his Dot (Phyllis Robins). He is befuddled into wedding a foreign strongwoman (Dorothy Ward) by a gang of traffickers in British citizenship, but he wins his stationmaster's cap and a happy ending when he brings them to justice. Gay's bundle of songs didn't include a ''Lambeth Walk,'' but Lane did well with the comical ''You're a Nice Little Baggage'' and a role which permitted all his favorite antics tucked inside a plot that was a mite more of a plot than those of his preceding shows. However, *Meet Me Victoria* was squeezed out of London by enemy action after 117 performances, and when it returned it managed only another 134 nights, suggesting that the line of shows Lane had produced in Victoria had seen its most popular days.

MEILHAC, Henri (b Paris, 21 February 1831; d Paris, 6 July 1897). Half of the most famous libretto-writing partnership of the heyday of opéra-bouffe.

Henri Meilhac began his working life behind the counter of a bookshop, and his writing career with humorous articles for magazines and newspapers. He took his first steps into the theatre as an author of vaudeville in 1855, and in 1861 made his first appearance on the bill of an opérette, when he wrote the text for a one-act piece composed by Louis Deffès and produced at the spa town

Plate 251. **Henri Meilhac.** *Half of one of the great libretto-writing teams of all time.*

of Bad Ems. *Le Café du roi* was a fine little success and moved swiftly to Paris, where it was played at first at the Théâtre Lyrique and a few years later at the Opéra-Comique itself. In 1863 Meilhac met up with Ludovic Halévy, a schooldays contemporary at the Lycée Louis le Grand, and the two combined on a little one-act vaudeville *Le Brésilien,* produced at the Palais-Royal (9 May) with a cast featuring the young Hortense Schneider. For this vaudeville Jacques Offenbach wrote the brief musical part, including an original song to Meilhac/Halévy words, ''Voulez-vous acceptez mon bras?,'' which, as sung by the rising star, became extremely popular.

This three-sided writing team continued their collaboration (Offenbach and Halévy had already worked episodically together for some eight years prior to this), and they had an immense success with their first full-length work together, the classical burlesque *La Belle Hélène* (1864). *La Belle Hélène* was followed by a whole series of opéras-bouffes and semi-bouffes of which *Barbe-bleue, La Vie parisienne, La Grande-Duchesse de Gérolstein, La Périchole* and *Les Brigands* all proved vastly popular, hoisting their writers to a preeminent theatrical position not only in France but, as these pieces led the invasion of the world's stages by French musical plays during the 1860s and 1870s, throughout the entire world.

Meilhac and Halévy now worked almost exclusively together, both for the musical stage and for the comic theatre where they were represented during the decade and a half of their collaboration by a long list of plays including *Frou-Frou* (Gymnase, 1869), *Tricoche et Cacolet* (Palais-Royal, 1871), *Le Réveillon* (Palais-Royal, 1872), *Le Roi Candaule* (1 act, Palais-Royal, 1873), *Toto chez Tata* (1 act, Variétés, 1873), *La Petite Marquise* (Variétés, 1874), *L'Ingénu* (1 act, Variétés, 1874), *La Mi-Carême* (Palais-Royal, 1874), *La Boule* (Palais-Royal, 1874), *La Cigale* (Variétés, 1877), *Le Mari de la débutante* (Palais-Royal, 1879) and *La Petite Mère* (Variétés, 1880). However, each did occasionally work with other partners and, after the rise of Charles Lecocq, also together but with a composer other than Offenbach.

For Lecocq they prepared the text for the most successful of his Théâtre de la Renaissance works, *Le Petit Duc,* as well as that for the internationally played *La Petite Mademoiselle* and the disastrous *Janot.* They also worked with Albert Millaud, to whom Halévy had allegedly supplied an uncredited part of the text for Offenbach's *Madame l'Archiduc,* on the book for the Théâtre des Variétés vaudeville *La Roussotte* (for which Lecocq supplied some of the music) and they made a memorable, rare venture into the opéra-comique when they adapted Prosper Mérimée's tale of *Carmen* as the libretto for Georges Bizet's celebrated work. Meilhac, alone, teamed again with Millaud on the text for Offenbach's *La Créole,* as he had with Nuitter on the text for the Opéra-Comique's *Vert-Vert* in his only two major musical ''infidelities'' to his partner.

La Roussotte, in 1881, marked the end of the partnership between ''Meil and Hal'' (as Offenbach apparently called them). Meilhac continued, with Millaud, to write two further vaudevilles for the Variétés and its star Anna Judic (Mme Millaud). One of these, *Mam'zelle Nitouche,* added to his already-long list of outstanding successes whilst the other, *La Cosaque,* which found the series fading, was nevertheless, in itself, as fine and funny (if not perhaps as protean) as its predecessors and won several productions beyond France. With Arnold Mortier he fabricated the tale of *Madame le Diable* which was set to music by Gaston Serpette for Paris and, a number of years later, by Adolf Müller for Vienna (*Des Teufels Weib* Theater an der Wien, 1890), and with Philippe Gille he worked on the version of Robert Planquette's British musical *Rip van Winkle* which has survived through a century in the French repertoire, as well as on the libretti for Massenet's opera *Manon* and Delibes's drame lyrique *Kassya.* After a decade away from the musical theatre, he was represented one final time, shortly before his death, by a collaboration with Albert de Saint-Albin on the book for Robert Planquette's successful *Panurge.*

For a man reputedly lazy, late-rising, and of a gadabout nature, Meilhac accomplished a vast amount of theatrical work of all kinds in the 20 years which comprised the main part of his career. Much of his best work came in that partnership with Halévy of which it was said that "Meilhac avait plus de cartouches mais Halévy avait un meilleur tir" ("Meilhac had more bullets, but Halévy was the better shot"), but he proved, when he moved on to work with other authors, that the esprit and ideas which he brought to his collaborations were no less effective when shaped by and with other partners. His range, too, was outstanding: from the extravagant bouffonneries of *La Belle Hélène* and *Barbe-bleue* to the crisp social comedy of *La Vie parisienne,* from the wildly comic vaudeville tones of a *Mam'zelle Nitouche* to the often delicate sentiment found in a piece such as *Le Petit Duc* or moments of *La Roussotte,* to the pathos of *Manon* and of the drama of *Carmen* and of some parts of works such as *Rip!,* he covered the whole gamut of the musical theatre. And it was notable that, in an age when the turnover of shows was fast and furious and authors were not scared to fail, very few of the pieces to which he contributed were short-lived.

As well as providing a crop of landmark shows to the Parisian stage, Meilhac also had a share in what have nowadays become accepted as being the most representative shows of both the 19th- and the 20th-century Viennese stage. His play *Le Réveillon* (w Halévy) was the basis for Richard Genée's libretto for Johann Strauss's *Die Fledermaus* (1874), whilst his earlier *L'Attaché d'Ambassade,* written solo in 1862 before his association with Halévy began, became, in the hands of Victor Léon and Leo Stein, the book for Franz Lehár's *Die lustige Witwe.* Many other of his works, particularly in the wake of these two successes, were also adapted as libretti for the Austrian stage, although not always with acknowledgment. *La Boule* (w Halévy) became the Posse *Von Tisch und Bett* written and composed by Julius Hopp (Theater an der Wien 7 September 1875); *Tricoche et Cacolet* (w Halévy) was given songs by Karl Treumann and Franz von Suppé (Carltheater, 1876) and more liberally musicalized as *Ein toller Geschaft* by Kren and Schönfeld for the Berlin stage (Thalia Theater 7 September 1901, mus: Einödshofer) and as *Spitzbub et Cie* by Wilhelm Ascher and Robert Pohl, with music by Josef Bayer, at the Lustspiel Theater (5 July 1907); *La Cigale* (w Halévy) was turned by H Osten and Julius Stern into *Bum-Bum* (Carltheater 24 October 1896); his 1888 play *Decoré* was set to music as *Der Sechs-Uhr-Zug* (1900) by Léon, Stein and Richard Heuberger (as well as being professedly borrowed from for a portion of the British musical *The Little Cherub*); and *La Petite Marquise* (w Halévy) became Felix Albini's chorusless musical comedy *Madame Troubadour* (1907). The delightfully comical *Le Mari de la débutante* was turned into two different Operetten at the Carltheater within eight months: Annie Dirkens played seven performances at both the home house and the Theater an der Wien in *Die Prima Donna* (Alfred Müller-Norden/Alexander Landesberg, Ludwig Fischl 31 January 1901) and Mizzi Günther played 10 nights as Nina in *Die Debutantin* (Alfred Zamara/A M Willner, Waldberg 4 October 1901). *La Roussotte,* in one of its hurly-burly series of international remakings, was adapted by Franz von Schönthan and given a new score by Carl Millöcker under the title of *Ein süsses Kind* (Theater an der Wien 1 April 1882) and the Offenbach opérette *La Diva* was rewritten by Zell and Genée into a piece called *Die Theaterprinzessin* (Theater an der Wien 30 December 1872).

1861 **Le Café du roi** (Louis Deffès) 1 act Ems 17 August; Théâtre Lyrique, Paris 16 November

1862 **Les Bourgignonnes** (Deffès) 1 act Ems 19 July; Opéra-Comique, Paris 16 July 1863

1864 **La Belle Hélène** (Offenbach/w Halévy) Théâtre des Variétés 17 December

1866 **Barbe-bleue** (Offenbach/w Halévy) Théâtre des Variétés 5 February

1866 **La Vie parisienne** (Offenbach/w Halévy) Palais-Royal 31 October

1867 **La Grande-Duchesse de Gérolstein** (Offenbach/w Halévy) Théâtre des Variétés 12 April

1868 **L'Elixir du docteur Cornélius** (Émile Durand/w Arthur Delavigne) 1 act Fantaisies-Parisiennes 3 February

1868 **Le Château à Toto** (Offenbach/w Halévy) Palais-Royal 6 May

1868 **La Pénitente** (Mme de Grandval/w William Busnach) 1 act Opéra-Comique 13 May

1868 **La Périchole** (Offenbach/w Halévy) Théâtre des Variétés 6 October

1869 **Vert-Vert** (Offenbach/w Charles Nuitter) Opéra-Comique 10 March

1869 **La Diva** (Offenbach/w Halévy) Théâtre des Bouffes-Parisiens 22 March

1869 **Les Brigands** (Offenbach/w Halévy) Théâtre des Variétés 10 December

1875 **La Boulangère a des écus** (Offenbach/w Halévy) Théâtre des Variétés 19 October

1875 **La Créole** (Offenbach/w Millaud) Théâtre des Bouffes-Parisiens 3 November

1876 **Berengère et Anatole** (Jules Massenet/w Paul Poirson) 1 act Cercle de l'union artistique January

1878 **Le Petit Duc** (Lecocq/w Halévy) Théâtre de la Renaissance 25 January

1879 **La Petite Mademoiselle** (Lecocq/w Halévy) Théâtre de la Renaissance 12 April

1881 **Janot** (Lecocq /w Halévy) Théâtre de la Renaissance 22 January

1881 **La Roussotte** (Hervé, Lecocq, Marius Boullard/w Halévy, Millaud) Théâtre des Variétés 28 January

1882 **Madame le Diable** (Gaston Serpette/w Arnold Mortier [and Millaud?]) Théâtre de la Renaissance 5 April

1883 **Mam'zelle Nitouche** (Hervé/w Millaud) Théâtre des Variétés 26 January

1884 **La Cosaque** (Hervé/w Millaud) Théâtre des Variétés 1 February

1884 **Rip!** French version w Philippe Gille (Théâtre des Folies-Dramatiques)

1895 **Panurge** (Planquette/w Albert de Saint-Albin) Théâtre de la Gaîté 22 November

MEINE SCHWESTER UND ICH Musical comedy in 2 acts, a Vorspiel and Nachspiel by Ralph Benatzky and Robert Blum based on the play *Ma soeur et moi* by Louis Verneuil and Georges Berr. Music and lyrics by Ralph Benatzky. Komödienhaus, Berlin, 29 March 1930.

A small-scale musical comedy with six principals and seven small-part players but with a full helping of songs, Benatzky's *Meine Schwester und ich* was adapted by its author-composer from a German version of Verneuil and Berr's 1928 comedy made by Robert Blum. A fine success on its first Berlin production, it traveled extensively thereafter.

Parisian Princess Dolly Saint-Labiche (Liane Haid) has fallen in love with the young professor Roger Fleuriot (Oskar Karlweis) who has been hired to catalogue her library. When he moves on to a job in Nancy, she disguises herself as her sister, and placing herself as a shopgirl in Filosel's (Felix Bressart) provincial shoe shop, she woos, wins and weds her man. However, when he discovers the truth he demands a divorce. The prologue and epilogue of the piece took place in court, framing the tale of the couple's courtship in a scene reminiscent of *Trial by Jury* or *Die geschiedene Frau,* and ended, of course, in reconciliation.

The score of the show featured the fashionable dance rhythms of the time, Dolly moving seductively into tango time (''Mein Freund!''), and joining Roger in a fox-trot (''Wie kommt der Mann zu den Frau'') and a shimmy (''Ich lade sie ein, Fräulein''), whilst he also took a turn through the slow fox (''Ich bin verliebt'') and waltz (''Ich bin diskret'') rhythms and scored his best as this last number moved into his catchy declaration that ''Mein Mädel ist nur ein Verkäuferin.'' Irma, the shopgirl whom Dolly pays off to go absent, uses the opportunity to go off to Paris to become—like every good shopgirl in German films, in particular—a revue star and, thus, she was given the chance at the second-act opening to demonstrate her revusical talents in a ''Tanz-Revue-Parodie'' and one-step.

Following its Berlin success, *Meine Schwester und ich* was produced by Rolf Jahn at Vienna's Die Komödie with Marita Streelen (Dolly), Karl Stepanek (Roger) and Josef Egger (Filosel) at the head of the cast of just ten, and it was later revived in a version revised by Benatzky as *Die Prinzessin auf der Leiter* (the princess on the ladder) at the Theater in der Josefstadt under Max Reinhardt (3 August 1934), the Scala Theater (4 September 1934) and at the Theater an der Wien (5 February 1935) with Gerda Maurus, Karlweis and Felix Bressart featured, for over one hundred performances. It returned to Berlin in 1939 (Renaissance Theater) with Johannes Heesters and Carola Hohn starring, and continued to be played throughout Germany and Austria in the decades that followed, returning to the Theater an der Wien once more in 1964 (20 November) and to Berlin's Theater des Wetens in 1974 (10 December, 36 performances).

The Shuberts hired Walter Slezak from Berlin for their quickly arranged American production of *Meet My Sister* (ad Harry Wagstaffe Gribble), apparently in a case of mistaken identity (they thought they were getting Karlweis), but he scored a personal success on Broadway, opposite the Dolly of Bettina Hall and George Grossmith as a comical Marquis, in a version which was recommended as a charming evening ''for folks weary of precision dancing and synthetic energy.'' It ran for 167 performances, and Grossmith swiftly persuaded his old ally Edward Laurillard to export the piece to England. Gribble's text was readapted as *My Sister and I* by a team of writers (Lauri Wylie, Brandon Fleming, Desmond Carter, Frank Eyton) and the piece mounted with Francis Lederer and Alexa Engstrom featured alongside Grossmith and aging star Joe Coyne as Filosel. A flop in town, it was put on the road after eight performances as *Meet My Sister* with Anne Croft and Roy Royston taking over alongside Coyne and Grossmith and with three additional songs by Billy Mayerl.

A 1954 film version, with Adrian Hoven, Rudolf Platte, Paul Hörbiger, Herta Staal and Sonja Ziemann featured, had Bentazky's score ''adapted'' by Friedrich Schröder, but a Swedish *Min syster och jag* (1950), which resituated the action in Scandinavia, seemingly kept the original music.

Austria: Theater ''Die Komödie'' 22 December 1930, Theater in der Josefstadt *Die Prinzessin auf dem Leiter* 3 August 1934; USA: Shubert Theater *Meet My Sister* 30 December 1930; UK: Shaftesbury Theatre *My Sister and I* (later *Meet My Sister*) 23 February 1931; Hungary: Andrássy-uti Színház *Exhercegnő* 28 January 1932

Films: *Min syster och jag* 1950, Paul Martin 1954

MELFORD, Austin [SMITH, Austin Alfred] (b Gosport, 24 August 1884; d London, 19 August 1971). Actor, writer and director for the musical stage between the wars in Britain.

An actor from childhood, Melford appeared for many years in provincial and West End plays and in the occasional touring musical (*The Talk of the Town, Faust Up-to-Date*) before making his first metropolitan musical appearances in revue and in the musical comedy *Mr Manhattan* (1916, Bobby Washington). In a long and fine subsequent career, which was shared equally between musical and non-musical comedies, he appeared in leading light-comedy roles at the Gaiety in *Theodore & Co* (1916, taking over from George Grossmith as Theodore), *Going Up* (1918, ''Hoppy'' Brown) and *The Kiss Call* (1919, Christopher Deare), and then as Maxime Paillard in Grossmith's production of *A Night Out* (1920) at the Winter Garden. After a first period as a member of the famous Co-Optimists concert party, operating as both a performer and a writer, he succeeded Grossmith as Otis in London's production of *Sally.*

Melford played further comic roles in *Whirled into Happiness* (*Der Tanz ins Glück,* 1922, Horace Wiggs), as Algernon Hozier in the Jack Buchanan boxing musical *Battling Butler* (1922, for which he also collaborated on the text), in *Up with the Lark* (1927, Jack Murray) and *Lucky Girl* (1928, replacing star Gene Gerrard as Hudson Greener), returning to the Co-Optimists in between times. In 1948 he appeared alongside Leslie Henson in his own musical *Bob's Your Uncle* (Mandeville). He later played Sir John in a revival of *Me and My Girl* and appeared, in his sixties, as Dudley Leake in *Blue for a Boy* (1950, the role he had created years previously in the play *It's a Boy* from which the musical was made), *Happy as a King* (1953, Count Domboli) and *Happy Holiday* (1955, Admiral Dallas-Buckingham).

In parallel to his career as a comic actor, Melford also worked both as a writer and a director. He fulfilled both functions in the successful *Yes, Uncle!, Bob's Your Uncle* and *Blue for a Boy;* directed *Lucky Girl* (1928), *Oh, Letty!* (1928) and *Here's How* (1934); and wrote or contributed to the texts of several other London plays and musicals. His other writing credits included the Prince's Theatre extravaganza *Magic Carpet,* the Fred Karno company's touring musical farce *French Beans* and a long list of film screenplays including the screen version of *A Southern Maid* (1933).

Melford's brother **Jack MELFORD** [John Kenneth George SMITH] (b London, 5 September 1899; d Poole, October 1972) also had a long and successful stage and film career, which included a regular dose of musical roles. In 1926 he appeared with the Astaires in *Stop Flirting* (Perry Reynolds) and in the juvenile role of the musical version of his uncle's hit play *Turned Up* (Frank Steadley). He paired with Basil Howes as Binnie Hale's exquisite ''ugly'' brothers in *Mr Cinders* (1929), played Hugh Posset in *Here's How!* (1934) and the titled hero of the ingenuous wartime *The Silver Patrol,* and toured in *Sunny, Tonight's the Night* and in the second tryout of *Happy Birthday* (1945). In 1950 he was seen at the Theatre Royal, Drury Lane, as the Heavenly Friend in *Carousel.*

Both performers were the sons of actor **Austin MELFORD** [Alfred SMITH] (b Fareham, 11 April 1855; d Twickenham, 23 January 1908), whose list of otherwise non-musical credits included the burlesque *Cruel Carmen* and the role of Yankee Thursby in *Hans the Boatman* (Strand Theatre, 1891) and actress Alice Gambra, and the nephews of actor and playwright **Mark MELFORD** [George SMITH] (b Fareham, ?1851; d Shepherd's Bush, 4 January 1914), whose works included, apart from the enormously successful *Turned Up,* the Leopolds' highly successful touring piece *Frivolity* (1883), Alice Atherton's musical comedy drama *Blackberries* (Prince of Wales Theatre, Liverpool 14 June 1886), the romantic comic opera *Jackeydora* (Theatre Royal, Leamington 26 December 1890) and the touring ''musical farcical comedy'' *Black and White* (Prince of Wales Theatre, Southampton 3 January 1898).

- 1917 **Yes, Uncle!** (Nat D Ayer/Clifford Grey/w George Arthurs) Prince of Wales Theatre 29 December
- 1921 **Yes, Papa** (Phil Braham/w Eric Blore) Coliseum, Cheltenham 21 February
- 1921 **French Beans** (Leslie Alleyne/w Blore, Fenton Mackay) Jubilee Hall, Weymouth 25 April
- 1922 **Battling Butler** (Braham/Douglas Furber/w Stanley Brightman) New Oxford Theatre 8 December
- 1924 **Patricia** (Geoffrey Gwyther/Dion Titheradge/w Denis Mackail, Arthur Stanley) His Majesty's Theatre 31 October
- 1928 **So Long, Letty!** (later *Oh, Letty!*) English version w Frank Eyton, Billy Mayerl, Theatre Royal, Birmingham 22 October
- 1930 **Nippy** (Mayerl/Eyton/w Arthur Wimperis) Prince Edward Theatre 30 October
- 1934 **Here's How!** (w Robert Nesbit, Eddie Pola, Robert Walker) Saville Theatre 22 February
- 1944 **Ring Time** revised *Battling Butler* w Noel Gay, Frank Eyton, Glasgow 28 August
- 1945 **Gay Rosalinda** (*Die Fledermaus*) English version w Rudolf Bernauer, Sam Heppner (Palace Theatre)
- 1947 **The Birdseller** (*Der Vogelhändler*) English version w Bernauer, Harry S Pepper (Palace Theatre)
- 1948 **Bob's Your Uncle** (Gay/Eyton) Saville Theatre 5 May
- 1949 **Roundabout** (aka *Hat in the Air*) (Edward Horan, Ken Attiwill, Eyton/w Attiwill) Saville Theatre 4 August
- 1950 **Blue for a Boy** (Harry Parr Davies/Harold Purcell) His Majesty's Theatre 30 November
- 1953 **Happy as a King** (Ross Parker/w Fred Emney) Princes Theatre 23 May

Autobiography: Melford, Mark: *Life in a Booth and Something More* (1913)

MELNOTTE, Violet [SOLOMON, Emma] (b Birmingham, 2 May 1855; d London, 17 September 1935). Producer and theatre manageress who launched one vast hit and one of her era's most important composers.

Throughout her life, ''Violet Melnotte,'' née Solomon, and known latterly to theatreland simply as ''Madame,'' covered up the facts of her early life and career with enormous diligence, telling a good few lies in a good few official documents on the way. But it appears that this daughter of a Birmingham cigar dealer and jewelry salesman was already a wife, probably a widow, and certainly a mother before ever beginning a theatrical career. Unless, that is, she was the ''Miss Melnotte'' whom I've noticed on the Birmingham stage back in 1868 nightly having her head cut off by conjurer ''Signor Philip Rubini.''

She allegedly first played as a professional actress as a minor member of the company in one of Sefton Parry's pantomimes at the Theatre Royal, Hull in the mid 1870s, and she made her first London appearance as Fezz in *Bluebeard* with Lydia Thompson's company at the Folly in 1876. She joined Kate Santley to play Ganymede in *Orphée aux enfers* and Selina in *A Quiet Family* at the Royalty in that same year, and subsequently appeared with the burlesque company at the Aquarium (Gnatbrain in *Black-eyed Susan,* 1877, ''decidedly conspicuous in an extraordinary dress''). She was a member of Alexander Henderson's opéra-bouffe company at the Globe in 1881 (Agio in *La Boulangère,* Miss Jones in *Seeing Frou-Frou*), acted with Tree in *Little Miss Muffit* (1882, Betsy), and appeared on two occasions at the Alhambra (Ousi in *The Bronze Horse* 1881, Ensign Rochoff in *The Beggar Student* 1884), before launching herself on a career as a producer.

With more than a little help from Henderson, she took his Avenue Theatre for a season in 1885 (14 March), mounting amongst other items a revival of the comic opera *Manteaux Noirs* and the one-act operettas *A Professional Beauty* (played Mrs Pearce Soapley) and *The Golden Wedding.* She was subsequently handed the lease of the Comedy Theatre on a plate by a now ill and exhausted Henderson and there, later the same year, she won what would be the singular success of her producing career with Paulton and Jakobowski's new comic opera *Erminie.* In her dual role of producer and second leading lady (Cerise Marcel) she saw *Erminie* through a good season in London before it moved on to enormous triumphs in America and on the touring circuits.

The following year she produced and played in Paulton's burlesque *Masse-e-yell-oh* (1886, Princess Elvira), and Ivan Caryll's first full-length musical *The Lily of Léoville* (1886, Turlurette), and in 1887 she fulfilled the same double role with a new piece by the now-celebrated authors of *Erminie, Mynheer Jan* (Camilla). A monetary disagreement with her authors during the run of the show resulted in *Mynheer Jan* being prematurely closed and the association between producer and writers ended. In 1889, Violet went off to Monte Carlo and, so the papers said, nearly broke the bank, coming home to Britain at the end of her holiday with a vast fortune in money in her bags.

In 1891 Miss Melnotte and her newest husband, Frank Wyatt [né Gunning] (the original Duke of Plaza Toro in Gilbert and Sullivan's *The Gondoliers* and the co-star of *Erminie*), built the Trafalgar Square Theatre, which Miss Melnotte ran, or leased to other producers, for most of the next 40 years, latterly under the names Trafalgar and Duke of York's Theatre. She produced and/or housed, and at various times appeared in, a long and sometimes eccentric list of plays and musicals at her theatre, a list which included, in the early days, revivals of *Dorothy* and *Mam'zelle Nitouche* (1893, Corinne), Toulmouche's *The Wedding Eve* (*La Veillée de noces*), Audran's *Baron Golosh* (*L'Oncle Célestin*), the successful *The Gay Parisienne,* the American musicals *Lost, Strayed or Stolen* and *The Girl from Up There,* and later, after a long succession of plays, J M Barrie's unfortunate musical attempt *Rosy Rapture, Toto, The Girl for the Boy, Nicolette,* such successful revues as *London Calling* and *The Punch Bowl* and many of Barrie's other works, notably the first production of *Peter Pan.* The Duke of York's was also the venue for the first production of Noël Coward's *Easy Virtue* and for the London version of *Daddy Long Legs.*

Right up until her death, at the fiercely denied age of 80, the forceful Miss Melnotte, resplendent in ''silver hair, wonderful fur coats and sparkling jewellery'' and known—by the polite—as one of the ''characters'' of London showbusiness, remained (with one gap of five years) at the helm of the theatre which sported her initials artistically linked in the pattern of its auditorium decor, and in her will she instructed that her trustees carry on its management ''so as to perpetuate my name and carry on the traditions thereof.'' When she died, after several rocky decades of management, it was more than half a century since she had been reponsible for producing, in *Erminie,* the most popular musical of the 19th-century American theatre, and for giving a start to an out-of-luck young Belgian musician and composer who called himself Ivan Caryll.

Several of Violet's family worked in her productions, including youngest sister **Delia MERTON** [Delia SOLOMON], who appeared for a number of years in *Erminie* (Clementine); brother **Henry BRANDON** [Daniel SOLOMON], who was her sometime company manager; brother-in-law **Arthur Douglas PIERPOINT,** who also played a small part in *Erminie* (Sergeant); and son **Frank Gunning WYATT** [Nevill Francis GUNNING]. Her daughter by an earlier marriage also appeared on the stage as **Nellie WYATT.**

MELVILLE, Alan [CAVERHILL, William Melville] (b Berwick-upon-Tweed, 9 April 1910; d Brighton, 27 December 1983).

Best known in the theatre as a witty sketch-writer and lyricist in revue (*Scoop, Sky High, Between Ourselves, À la Carte, At the Lyric, Going to Town, All Square,* etc) and most notably for the famous *Sweet and Low / Sweeter and Lower / Sweetest and Lowest* series, Melville also made several forays into the musical theatre. He supplied the lyrics to Ivor Novello for the author-composer's last show, *Gay's the Word,* a vehicle for Cicely Courtneidge (''Vitality,'' ''It's Bound to be Right on the Night,'' ''Bees are Buzzin''), wrote book and lyrics (''I Love Being in Love,'' ''I Want a Great Big Hunk of a Man,'' ''All on Account of a Guy'') for *Bet Your Life* to feature Arthur Askey and, less successfully, paired with his *Sweet and Low* colleague Charles Zwar on a musicalization of the romantic play *Marigold.*

1951 **Gay's the Word** (Ivor Novello) Saville Theatre 16 February

1952 **Bet Your Life** (Kenneth Leslie-Smith, Charles Zwar) London Hippodrome 18 February

1959 **Marigold** (Zwar) Savoy Theatre 27 May

Autobiographies: *Myself When Young* (Max Parrish, London, 1955), *Merely Melville* (Hodder & Stoughton, London, 1970)

MELVILLE, Emilie [TRETHEWAY, Emily] (b Philadelphia, 19 January 1851; d San Francisco, 19 May 1932). Round-the-world star of 19th-century opéra-bouffe.

The daughter of actor, playwight and director Robert JONES [né TRETHEWAY] (b 2 December 1817; d Boston, 24 August 1878), Emilie Melville was trained as an actress from toddling age by her mother, an actress-singer known as Julia MILES (d San Francisco, 25 October 1914), who had had a fine career in comedy, extravaganza and opera on the New York stage (Kitty in *New York as It Is,* Jenny in *Olympic at a Glance,* Jenny Bogert in *Mysteries and Miseries of New York,* Rosa in *Linda di Chamonix,* Fatemma in *Oberon,* Fetuah in *Ganem,* etc) and later as a member of Mrs Drew's Philadelphia company.

Emilie went on the stage as a child, making her debut aged four at Providence, RI, alongside Edwin Forrest as the little Duke of York in *Richard III.* By the age of eight she was already playing ingenue roles at Louisville and Baltimore, in 1863 she appeared in supporting roles at Laura Keene's Theatre, and she made her first star-billed appearance in New York, playing twice-daily in roaring melodrama and sentimental drama at Barnum's Museum in May–June of 1865. For her last week she performed *The Daughter of the Regiment* (with ''the entire music'') and as Jenny Leatherlungs in *Jenny Lind at Last.* She had

Plate 252. **Emilie Melville.** *The globe-trotting American soprano dressed to play Suppé's* Boccaccio.

well and truly made herself a name in Brooklyn, Philadelphia, Memphis, Indianpolis, St Paul and elsewhere before she appeared on Broadway, aged 16, as Brougham's *Po-ca-hon-tas* (1866) and as Columbia, the Goddess of Liberty, in his burlesque *Columbus Reconstructed* (1866). In 1868 she moved to San Francisco and there became the West Coast's first *La Grand-Duchesse* before going on to become soubrette in the stock company at the old California Theater. She played roles ranging from Shakespeare's Ophelia to Burnand's leggy Ixion before retiring to marriage as Mrs Thomas Derby. She was quickly back, however, to pick up a performing career which would ultimately stretch over three-quarters of a century.

Her youthful successes were in burlesque, opéra-bouffe and light opera, with which she toured indefatigably through America in the 1870s and early 1880s. She went with companies such as that run by C D Hess (1877–78, Arline, Serpolette, Zerlina in *Fra Diavolo* and creating the role of Queen Elizabeth I to the Shakespeare of William Castle in the ''romantic opera'' *A Summer Night's Dream*), often with the ''Emilie Melville Comic Opera Company,'' and sometimes with combinations such as the ''Hess-Melville Opera Company,'' playing regularly in New York in opéra-bouffe, in Gilbert and Sullivan (*HMS Pinafore, The Pirates of Penzance*) and in Operette (Fanchette Michel in *The Royal Middy,* Natalitza in *Apajune der Wassermann,* etc). At one stage she took over the management of San Francisco's Baldwin Theater. But mostly, through the 1870s and the 1880s, she was the preferred prima donna of the western seaboard, introducing many a new piece to Californian audiences at the head of various ''Emilie Melville'' companies owned and run by a variety of theatrical speculators.

Miss Melville did not, however, restrict her touring to America. She also toured both westward and southward, and made an enormous success when she appeared for the first time in Australia with W S Lyster's company in opéra-bouffe in 1875 (''the most successful vocalist that ever graced the Melbourne stage'' judged one commentator). She returned to Australia regularly thereafter, although she suffered a contretemps with producer J C Williamson and walked out of her position as prima donna in his 1882 season (*Giroflé-Girofla, Les Cloches de Corneville*) to launch one of her own Emilie Melville Opera Companies (*Fatinitza, The Royal Middy, La Périchole, Giroflé-Girofla*) in competition. In 1884–85 she took an extended tour of the orient with a vast baggage of musical shows (*Patience, La Mascotte, The Royal Middy, Fatinitza, La Périchole, La Belle Hélène, HMS Pinafore, The Pirates of Penzance, Maritana, Giroflé-Girofla, La Fille de Madame Angot, Les Noces d'Olivette, Madame Favart, Nell Gwynne,* etc) playing in such venues as Calcutta, Bombay, Rangoon, Burma, Shanghai, Yokohama, Kobe, Hong Kong, etc, but she found that the few thousand Europeans in these cities were not enough to fill her houses and abandoned the company to other managers.

She returned to Australia and appeared there in *Falka, La Périchole, La Fille de Madame Angot* (Clairette), *The Royal Middy* and as Planquette's *Nell Gwynne,* and in 1887, her voice now showing signs of a hole in the middle, began to ease herself into non-singing roles by playing *Masks and Faces.* But the non-singing did not last. The following year she was back as *The Grand Duchess,* and in 1889 she set off for South Africa where, billed as the ''Australian nightingale,'' she delivered *La Périchole* and others of her repertoire through two seasons, sometimes under the management of local managers and sometimes under her own banner.

Ultimately news filtered back that she had thrown up the stage, married her baritone, Signor Verdi (né George Green in the USA) and settled down to run an hotel in Capetown. Before long, however, the news was different: it reported that she was playing Rosalind in *As You Like It* in Johannesburg. However, she soon left South Africa and the hotel trade (and Mr Green?) and continued her career, now firmly on the straight stage, appearing in Australia (she played there with Nat Goodwin's company in 1896), on the West Coast (Aunt Priscilla in *The Moneymoon,* etc), on Broadway (notably as the original Mrs Chichester in *Peg o' My Heart*), in a wide variety of stock companies as both performer and director but, latterly, mostly back in San Francisco, where she became an important and highly respected member of the city's Alcazar company with which she played major character roles through into her seventies. At the age of nearly 80 she appeared in the film *Illusion* (1929), which must surely make her the only contemporary of Brougham to have been sound-and-sight recorded for posterity.

Julia Miles went with her daughter to San Francisco where she at first worked on the stage—now as Julia Melville—before becoming, as Julia Melville Snyder, one of the city's most effective dramatic teachers.

MENKEN, Alan (b New Rochelle, NY, 22 July 1949).

Theatre musician with a welcome sense of humor who submerged it in churning out movie ditties for the 1990s.

Menken came to international notice with his lively, clever score to the burlesque *Little Shop of Horrors* (1982), but thereafter his main contribution was not to the stage but to film. From 1989, he provided a considerable amount of music to the screen, including the songs for the popular series of Walt Disney animated features including *The Little Mermaid* (1989 w Ashman,) which won him an Academy Award for ''Under the Sea,'' *Beauty and the Beast* (1991 w Ashman), *Aladdin* (1993 w Ashman, Tim Rice, Academy Award), *Pocahontas* (1995 w Stephen Schwartz, Academy Award, ''Colors of the Wind''), *The Hunchback of Notre Dame* (1996 w Schwartz) and *Hercules* (1997).

He also provided the score for Disney's *Newsies* (1992 w Jack Feldman) and individual songs for a number of other films. *Beauty and the Beast* and *The Hunchback of Notre Dame* were subsequently adapted to the stage.

His other theatre credits have included the oratorical *King David* (w Tim Rice) performed as the opening attraction at the Disney organization's New Amsterdam Theater (15 May, 5 performances).

1979 **God Bless You, Mr Rosewater** (Howard Ashman/w Green) WPA Theater 17 May; Entermedia Theater 14 October

1982 **Little Shop of Horrors** (Ashman) WPA Theater 6 May; Orpheum Theater 27 July

1987 **The Apprenticeship of Duddy Kravits** (Austin Pendelton, Mordecai Richtler) Zellerbach Theater, Philadelphia 30 September

1992 **Weird Romance** (David Spencer) WPA 12 May

1994 **Beauty and the Beast** (Ashman, Tim Rice/Linda Woolverton) Palace Theater 18 April

1994 **A Christmas Carol** (Lynn Ahrens/Ahrens, Mike Ockrent) Madison Square Garden 1 December

1999 **The Hunchback of Notre Dame** (Stephen Schwartz/James Lapine ad Michael Kunze) Theater des Westens, Berlin 5 June

THE ME NOBODY KNOWS Musical based on the book of the same name edited by Stephen M Joseph. Lyrics by Will Holt. Music by Gary William Friedman. Orpheum Theater, New York, 18 May 1970; Helen Hayes Theater, 18 December 1970.

Based on a book compiled by a New York ghetto schoolteacher from the writings of his pupils, *The Me Nobody Knows* had no linear shape, but was simply a collection of scenes, songs and impressions developed from the children's stories and played by a group of 12 young people. It ran for six months at off-Broadway's Orpheum Theater, and subsequently reopened at the Helen Hayes Theater where it remained until it had reached a total of 587 performances. It was later seen on American television, in Hamburg and Munich in a German adaptation and was produced at London's subsidized Shaw Theatre, where it was played 20 times. In the 1980s a sequel was mooted, but did not appear.

Germany: Hamburg *Ich bin ich* May 1971; UK: Shaw Theatre 31 May 1973

Recordings: original cast (Atlantic), German cast (Global), etc

MERCENARY MARY Musical comedy in 3 acts by Isabel Leighton and William B Friedlander based on *What's Your Wife Doing?* by Herbert Hall Winslow and Emil Nyitray. Lyrics by Irving Caesar. Music by Con Conrad and William B Friedlander. Longacre Theater, New York, 13 April 1925.

A brightly typical 1920s musical comedy, *Mercenary Mary* was based on a 1923 play (in which authoress Leighton had appeared as an actress) full of the kind of marital and financial ins and outs that were overwhelmingly popular as subject matter for such shows at such a point in time. On the one hand, we have penniless Jerry (Allen Kearns) who can only marry millionaire's niece June Somers (Margaret Irving) if he earns a million and stays faithful. On the other we have Chris Skinner (Louis Simon) and his extravagant wife Mary (Winnie Baldwin), who was formerly engaged to Jerry, who stand to be disinherited by Chris's very rich grandfather (Sam Hearn) who disapproves of her. To earn his million, Jerry agrees to play the ''other man'' in the temporary Chris/Mary divorce which needs to be staged to get the money rolling but, when grandpa is slow to show up for the prepared scene of infidelity, Mary gets a little tipsy and takes Jerry's acting for revived romance. It is a whole other act before all ends happily with tills and marriage bells ringing.

The jazzy, dance-based score did not bring forth any deeply enduring numbers from amongst pieces such as ''I'm a Little Bit Fonder of You,'' ''Honey, I'm in Love with You,'' ''Charleston Mad'' and ''Beautiful Baby,'' and L Lawrence Weber's production of *Mercenary Mary* lasted only 17 weeks and 136 performances on Broadway before being shunted out of its producer's theatre and onto the road in duplicate. Before long even one of the touring companies had folded in disappointment.

However, *Mercenary Mary*'s life did not by any means end with this sort-of-semi-failure. Jack Waller and Herbert Clayton, who had scored an immense London hit with their production of *No, No, Nanette,* naturally wanted something in the same vein with which to follow up their big hit, and they selected *Mercenary Mary.* Produced at the London Hippodrome in an anglicized version by (non-English) Fred Jackson with June (June), Sonnie Hale (Jerry), Peggy O'Neil (Mary), A W Baskcomb (Chris) and Lew Hearn (Grandpa) featured, and with Vivian Ellis's ''Over My Shoulder'' and Vincent Youmans's ''Tie a String Around Your Finger'' (first heard in *Lollipop*) boosting June's role and the score, it was a great success with a public avid for the latest in transatlantic song-and-dance comedies. It was played for 446 performances and, if this was markedly less than the score notched up by *Nanette,* it was nevertheless the longest British run achieved by any other Broadway musical comedy of the time. It also prefaced first a good touring life (the show was still to be seen on the road during the second war) and then a production of the show, in its English version, in Australia under the management of Hugh J Ward. British soubrette Mai Bacon starred as Mary, alongside Jack Morrison (Chris), Florence Hunter (Joan), Sydney Smith (Harry) and Eddie Joyce (Grandpa) for two months in Melbourne before the company switched, with less success, to another Broadway import, *Betty Lee.* A Sydney season was sponsored by the Fullers in 1928 with Elsie Prince and Jimmy Godden starred (St James Theatre 11 February 1928).

Rather less expectedly, the show turned up next in another city anxious for more *No, No, Nanette*: Paris. Robert de Simone's production at the Théâtre des Bouffes-Parisiens (ad Yves Mirande, de Simone, Jean Bastia) starred Denise Grey as Mary alongside Bouffes regulars Sim-Viva (Jenny/June), René Koval (Charley/Jerry) and Edmond Roze (Christophe) and a large dancing chorus, all jazzily accompanied by Berson and Vauchant's Europa Ramblers. And they did just fine. However, more remarkable was yet to come for this show that Broadway only kind of liked. From Paris, *Mercenary Mary* continued on to Budapest.

Now, somehow, somewhere, someway, *No, No, Nanette* had apparently become sidetracked on its triumphant track through Europe, and had never (amazingly) found its way to Hungary, so, when *Mersz-e, Mary?* (ad Adorján Stella, Imre Harmath) arrived at Budapest's Király Színház towards the end of 1927, it was the first modern American musical comedy so to do. J C Piddock, the English ballet master of the Paris production was imported to stage the dances with 48 chorus girls equipped with 258 costumes, there were 48 orchestral players (one per chorus girl?), and there was a cast headed by acredited comics Márton Rátkai (Kristof) and Árpád Latabár sr (Harry), György Solthy (Charley), Erszi Péchy (Mary), Ilona Vaály (Souzy) and Vilma Orosz. Big guns. And the result? *Mersz-e, Mary?* proved the same kind of sensation in Hungary that *Nanette* had been elsewhere. Budapest's *Mary* had, however, clearly undergone some changes since Broadway. Firstly, it had been expanded and spectacularized. Secondly, it was textually an adaptation of the French adaptation of the British adaptation. But, most notably, the one Vincent Youmans song included in London, which had given way to a co-composing credit in Paris (obviously in an attempt to capitalize on the famous names of *Nanette*'s writers), had now become a sole credit: "music by Vincent Youmans and Irving Caesar." Had Friedlander and Conrad's songs really disappeared? And, if so, where had the Youmans/Caesar songs come from? Had Mr Piddock brought bits of *Nanette* from Paris with him? Did he, in fact, give Budapest a mélange of *Mary* and *Nanette*? This would explain why, in spite of the vast success of *Mersz-e, Mary?, Nanette* was never played in Hungarian. But the record book just shows that *Mercenary Mary,* rather than *No, No, Nanette,* became the megahit Broadway musical of the 1920s on Hungarian stages.

UK: London Hippodrome 7 October 1925; Australia: Princess Theatre, Melbourne 3 April 1926; France: Théâtre des Bouffes-Parisiens 5 April 1927; Hungary Király Színház *Mersz-e, Mary?* 5 November 1927

MERCER, Johnny [MERCER, John H] (b Savannah, Ga, 18 November 1909; d Los Angeles, 25 June 1976). Lyricist of many a popular song and filmland hit whose work for the stage musical was the less shining part of his career.

Having moved to New York in 1928, when the failure of the real-estate firm run by his lawyer father had brought down the shutters on the family's comfortable existence, Mercer at first made a living as a performer. He spent a period as a group vocalist with the Paul Whiteman band, but at the same time he was already writing song lyrics. He interpolated a number, "Out of Breath" (mus: Everett Miller), in *The Garrick Gaieties* (1930) and contributed to the score of George Lederer's out-of-town flop *The Pajama Lady* the same year, but his first successes came with non-theatre songs—"Lazybones" (Hoagy Carmichael, 1933), "I'm an Old Cowhand" (Mercer, 1936), "Goody Goody" (Matty Malneck, 1936), "Jeeper Creepers" (Harry Warren, 1938), "You Must Have Been a Beautiful Baby" (Warren, 1938), "Day in Day Out" (Rube Bloom, 1939), "Fools Rush In" (Bloom, 1939), etc.

Mercer wrote a number of lyrics for revue songs, including the whole score (mus: Bloom) for London's *Blackbirds of 1936,* and he supplied some words for Fred Astaire's tune to "I'm Building Up to an Awful Let-Down," performed in the Drury Lane flop *Rise and Shine* (1936), before collaborating with Hoagy Carmichael, composer of his first hit "Lazybones," on the score for the Shubert production *Walk with Music.* Six years and many hits later—"Tangerine," "Skylark," "Dearly Beloved," "You Were Never Lovelier," "I'm Old Fashioned," "That Old Black Magic," "Dream" and the Academy Award–winning "On the Atchison, Topeka and the Santa Fe" (1946, Harry Warren, The Harvey Girls)—he ventured a further theatre score in collaboration with Harold Arlen, his co-writer on "That Old Black Magic." Although the resulting show, *St Louis Woman,* did not have a long run on Broadway it added some superb songs and one major hit, "Come Rain or Come Shine," to Mercer's long list of successes.

The 1949 musical *Texas L'il Darlin'* and Mercer's one attempt to write and compose a full show-score on his own, *Top Banana* (1951), had much longer runs than *St Louis Woman* but brought forth no such single song successes. Ultimately, his biggest all-round theatre win came with the comic-strip musical *Li'l Abner* (1956) from which the song "Jubilation T Cornpone" emerged as the comical hit.

Although there were plenty of further song hits in the next part of his career ("Autumn Leaves," "Satin Doll," "Sobbin' Women," "Goin' Courtin'," "Blues in the Night," "Charade," "Somethin's Gotta Give," "Laura," "Hooray for Hollywood," etc) as well as three further Academy Awards for "In the Cool, Cool, Cool of the Evening" (1951, mus: Carmichael), "Moon River" (1961, mus: Henry Mancini) and "The Days of Wine and Roses" (1962, mus: Mancini), the handful of stage shows with which Mercer was subsequently involved did not equal the successes of his ventures in the 1940s and 1950s.

Since his death his film score (mus: Gene de Paul) for *Seven Brides for Seven Brothers* has been uncomfortably adapted to the stage (1982), and his songs have been regularly used in such theatre compilations as *A Day in Hollywood, A Night in the Ukraine* and *Dancin'.* A compilation show of Mercer songs entitled *Dream,* brought to Broadway from the Tennessee Repertory Theater in 1997 (Royale Theater 3 April), played 69 performances.

1930 **The Pajama Lady** (Phil Charig, Richard Myers/w Robert

B Smith/H B Smith, George Lederer) National Theater, Washington, DC 6 October

1930 **Paris in Spring** (*Das Veilchen vom Montmartre*) American lyrics, Curran Theater, San Francisco

1940 **Walk with Music** (ex- *Three After Three*) (Hoagy Carmichael/Parke Levy, Alan Lipscott) Barrymore Theater 4 June

1946 **St Louis Woman** (Harold Arlen/Arna Bontemps, Countee Cullen) Martin Beck Theater 30 March

1949 **Texas, L'il Darlin'** (Robert Emmett Dolan/John Whedon, Sam Moore) Mark Hellinger Theater 25 November

1951 **Top Banana** (Mercer) Winter Garden Theater 1 November

1956 **Li'l Abner** (Gene de Paul/Norman Panama, Melvin Frank) St James Theater 15 November

1959 **Saratoga** (Arlen/Morton da Costa) Winter Garden Theater 7 December

1964 **Foxy** (Dolan/Ian McLellan Hunter, Ring Lardner jr) Ziegfeld Theater 16 February

1974 **The Good Companions** (André Previn/Ronald Harwood) Her Majesty's Theatre, London 11 July

1982 **Seven Brides for Seven Brothers** (de Paul/Lawrence Kasha, David Landay) Alvin Theater 8 July

MERCIER, René [Yves Auguste] (d 1973).

Conductor and composer of dance and theatre music, Mercier contributed the scores to several Parisian musical comedies of the 1920s and 1930s, of which *Les Fifilles de Loth, Je t'veux* and *Déshabillez-vous* all had fine metropolitan careers and the second-named even got produced in Hungary. *Bégonia,* another piece which he illustrated, but in which the accent was firmly on comedy, also had a good run.

1920 **Le Béguin de la garnison** (Paul Murio) Théâtre des Capucines November

1922 **Les Fifilles de Loth** (Murio) Théâtre du Moulin-Bleu 4 February

1923 **Je t'veux** (w Fred Pearly, Gaston Gabaroche, Albert Valsien/Battaille-Henri/Wilned, Marcel Grandjean) Théâtre Marigny 12 February

1923 **Benjamin** (André Barde, Murio, Benjamin Rabier) Ba-ta-clan 11 April

1925 **Le Péché capiteux** (Pierre Veber) L'Étoile 18 September

1928 **Déshabillez-vous** (Barde) Théâtre des Bouffes-Parisiens 22 December

1930 **Bégonia** (René Pujol) Théâtre Scala 15 February

1934 **Elles font toutes l'amour** (Murio) Théâtre du Moulin-Bleu 7 May

1936 **Un p'tit bout de femme** (Daniel Normand, Charles Pothier, Belotti) Théâtre de la Gaîté-Lyrique

LA MÈRE DES COMPAGNONS Opérette in 3 acts by Henri Chivot and Alfred Duru. Music by Hervé. Théâtre des Folies-Dramatiques, Paris, 15 December 1880.

Juliette Simon-Girard appeared in *La Mère des compagnons* as Francine Thibault, the mascot of the local carpenter lads, who disguises herself as her aristocratic fiancé, Gaston (Simon-Max), while he escapes the agents of the republic. When he proves foolish and faithless, Francine returns to wed the solid carpenter lad, Marcel (Lepers), who has been sighing over her ever since the opening chorus. The comedy fell to Francine's outspoken mother (Mme Dharville), bumbling into the attempts of Gaston's family to make a lady of Francine, and to Édouard Maugé, as Marcel's impossible brother, venturing into extravagant disguises in his attempts to expose Gaston's shortcomings and ease his brother's aching heart. Hervé's lively score illustrated a thoroughly comical piece—which had more of the character of an old-fashioned ballad opera than of modern opéra-comique—most effectively and the show ran for 58 Parisian nights before going on to be seen at Budapest's Népszínház (ad Béla J Fái, Lajos Evva).

Hungary: Népszínház *Az ácslegények gazdasszonykája* 26 March 1881

MÉREI, Adolf [MERKL, Adolf] (b Hatvan, 7 February 1876; d Budapest, 12 March 1918).

Dramaturg and chief stage director at the Magyar Színház from 1899, Mérei wrote or, more often, translated and adapted libretti and lyrics for the brisk flow of French, Austrian and British musicals and comedies staged at that house, amongst which were included such major hits as the Hungarian versions of *Der Rastelbinder* and *Die lustige Witwe.* In 1907 he moved on to fulfill a similar position at the Népszínház-Vígopera, then to the Király Színház and, ultimately, to the Népopera.

Although the bulk of his writing work was in adapting opérettes and Operetten, and such plays as Bilhaud and Hennequin's *Nelly Rosier,* Rudyard Stone's *Lotty ezredesei* and Grenet-Dancourt and Vaucaire's *Le Fils surnaturel* for local versions that were equipped with added songs—and Conan Doyle's *The Hound of the Baskervilles* that was not—he also wrote a number of original pieces, combining on several operetts with popular song- and show-writer Béla Zerkovitz and writing the text for Huszka's little *Tilos a bemenet* and Szirmai's *A sárga dominó.*

1899 **Tilos a bemenet** (Jenő Huszka) Magyar Színház 2 September

1901 **Lotty ezredesei** Hungarian version w songs w Jenő Faragó (Magyar Színház)

1901 **A postásfiu** (*The Messenger Boy*) Hungarian version w Ernő Salgó (Magyar Színház)

1901 **A szerencsecsillag** (*The Lucky Star*) Hungarian version w Emil Makai (Magyar Színház)

1901 **A vesztaszüzek** (*Les Petites Vestales*) Hungarian version (Magyar Színház)

1901 **Svihákok** (*Die Landstreicher*) Hungarian version w Aurél Föld (Városligeti Színkör)

1901 **Florodóra** Hungarian version w Dezső Balint (Magyar Színház)

1902 **Herkules munkái** (*Les Travaux d'Hercule*) Hungarian version w Ernő Keszthelyi (Magyar Színház)

1903 **A szobalány** (*Nelly Rosier*) Hungarian version w songs (Magyar Színház)

1903 **A Drótostót** (*Der Rastelbinder*) Hungarian version w György Ruttkay (Magyar Színház)

1903 **Tavasz** (*Frühlingsluft*) Hungarian version (Magyar Színház)

1903 **Pesti nők** (later Pesti asszonyok) (*Wiener Frauen*) Hungarian version (Budai Színkör)

1904 **Sherry** (*Madame Sherry*) Hungarian version (Magyar Színház)

1904 **Hüvelyk Kató** (*La Petite Poucette*) Hungarian version (Magyar Színház)

1904 **A rikkancs** (*Das Marktkind*) Hungarian version w Ruttkay (Magyar Színház)

1904 **Pfefferkorn utazása** (*Pfefferkorns Reise*) Hungarian version (Magyar Színház)

1904 **Csak tréfa** (György Verő) Magyar Színház 10 September

1904 **A törvénytelen apa** (*Le Fils surnaturel*) Hungarian version w songs (Király Színház)

1904 **A próféta álma** (Jenő Márkus) Népszínház 25 November

1904 **Bebe hercegnő** (*Princesse Bébé*) Hungarian version (Magyar Színház)

1904 **Az ibolyáslány** (*Das Veilchenmädel*) Hungarian version (Magyar Színház)

1904 **Fecskefészek** (*Das Schwalbennest*) Hungarian version (Magyar Színház)

1904 **Huszárvér** (*Das Garnisonsmädel*) Hungarian version w Ruttkay (Magyar Színház)

1905 **A portugál** (Jenő Sztojanovits) Magyar Színház 3 January

1905 **A danzigi hercegnő** (*The Duchess of Dantzic*) Hungarian version (Király Színház)

1905 **Putifarné** (*Madame Potiphar*) Hungarian version (Magyar Színház)

1906 **A koldusgróf** (*Vergeltsgott*) Hungarian version (Magyar Színház)

1906 **Gyöngyélet** (*Tire-au-flanc!*) Hungarian version w Ferenc Molnár and music by Ferenc Békési, Magyar Színház 21 April

1906 **Cserelányok** (*Les Filles Jackson*) Hungarian version (Király Színház)

1906 **A milliárdoskisasszony** (*Frauenherz*) Hungarian version (Magyar Színház)

1906 **A víg özvegy** (*Die lustige Witwe*) Hungarian version (Magyar Színház)

1907 **A századik asszony** (Izsó Barna) Budai Színkör 7 June

1907 **A sárga dominó** (Albert Szirmai) Népszínház-Vígopera 4 October

1907 **Három feleség** (*Der Mann mit den drei Frauen*) Hungarian version (Népszínház-Vígopera)

1907 **Paris almája** (*Paris, ou le bon juge*) Hungarian version (Népszínház-Vígopera)

1907 **Víg nibelungok** (*Die lustigen Nibelungen*) Hungarian version (Király Színház)

1907 **A varázskeringő** (*Ein Walzertraum*) Hungarian version (Király Színház)

1907 **Fuzsitus kisasszony** (*Ein tolles Mädel*) Hungarian version (Fővárosi Nyári Színház)

1909 **A szerencsemalac** (*Das Glücksschweinchen*) Hungarian version (Fővárosi Nyári Színház)

1909 **Az erdészlány** (*Die Försterchristl*) Hungarian version (Városligeti Színkör)

1909 **Szinészvér** (*Künstlerblut*) Hungarian version (Fővárosi Nyári Színház)

1909 **Aranyhalacska** (*Der Goldfisch*) Hungarian version (Nagyvárad)

1911 **A muzsikus leány** (*Das Musikantenmädel*) Hungarian version (Fővárosi Nyári Színház)

1911 **A kék róka** (Béla Zerkovitz) Royal Orfeum 29 September

1912 **Az asszonyfaló** (*Der Frauenfresser*) Hungarian version (Budapesti Színház)

1912 **Az ártatlan Zsuzsi** (*Die keusche Susanne*) Hungarian version (Budai Színkör)

1912 **Tengerész Kató** (*Die Marinengustl*) Hungarian version (Népopera)

1912 **A régi Pest** (*Alt-Wien*) Hungarian version (Budapesti Színház)

1912 **A lila domino** (*Der lila domino*) Hungarian version (Népopera)

1912 **A kedves Augusztin** (*Der liebe Augustin*) Hungarian version (Népopera)

1912 **Ostromállapot** (*Ein Belagerungzustand*) Hungarian version (Royal Orfeum)

1913 **Finom familia** (Zerkowitz) Royal Orfeum 31 January

1913 **Aranyeső** (Zerkovitz/w Izor Béldi) Népopera 21 February

1913 **Budagyöngye** (*Hoheit tanzt Walzer*) Hungarian version (Népopera)

1913 **A nevető férj** (*Der lachende Ehemann*) Hungarian version (Népopera)

1913 **Katonadolog** (Zerkovitz/w Béldi) Népopera 25 October

1914 **Éjfélkor** (*Zwischen zwölf und eins*) Hungarian version (Népopera)

1914 **A mozitündér** (*Die Kino-Königin*) Hungarian version (Népopera)

1915 **Vándorfecskék** (Zerkovitz) Télikert 1 March; Royal Orfeum, Budapest 2 October

1915 **Kotnyeles naccsága** (*Botschafterin Leni*) Hungarian version (Népopera)

1916 **Marci** (Alfred Márkus/Engel, Horst ad) Fővárosi Nyári Színház 16 June

1917 **Az első feleség** (*Seine erste Frau*) Hungarian version (Budapesti Színház)

MERKÈS, Marcel (b Bordeaux, 7 July 1920).

MERVAL, Paulette [RIFFAUD, Paulette] (b La Roche Chalais, 3 November 1920).

Married during their student days at Bordeaux, baritone Merkès and soprano Merval subsequently led a large part of their careers in the musical theatre as a duo, appearing on Paris's larger stages as the stars of *Rêve de valse,* as Scotto's *Les Amants de Venise,* in *Les Amours de Don Juan* (1956), *Vienne chante et danse* (1967), *Rose-Marie, Michel Strogoff* and *Douchka* (1973). Merkès also created the hero of Scotto's *Violettes imperiales* and appeared as Frank Butler in France's *Annie du Far-West* and as Danilo in *La Veuve joyeuse.*

Freely recorded and re-recorded and regularly rereleased, constantly touring and/or televised in their later years in increasingly modest but spangled productions and, latterly, staged concerts, the couple known as the ''M et Mme Opérette'' of France were for decades the delight of their fans and the principal purveyors of the wrinkles, wobbles and glitter image of the opérette that became disastrously prevalent in France in the 1970s and 1980s.

Their son, **Alain Merkès,** followed his parents on to the musical stage.

Plate 253. **Ethel Merman.** *''I'm an Indian too . . . a Sioux . . .''*

MERMAN, Ethel [ZIMMERMAN, Ethel Agnes] (b Astoria, NY, 16 January 1908; d New York, 15 February 1984). Swingeing vocalist and queen-sized personality who moved smoothly from playing youthful wisecrackers to out-front mothers, taking her stardom with her all the way.

The young Miss Zimmerman worked first as a typist and a secretary and made her way into show business in her late teens singing in cabaret and in vaudeville and appearing in some short films. She came to the notice of the general public with a bang when she made her first Broadway musical-theatre appearance as the lusty, outwest Kate Fothergill in Aarons and Freedley's production of *Girl Crazy* (1930), introducing ''I Got Rhythm,'' ''Boy! What Love Has Done to Me'' and ''Sam and Delilah'' with all the oomph and vocal carrying-power that were to become her trademark. She appeared the following year in *George White's Scandals* (''Life Is Just a Bowl of Cherries'') and in 1932 in a De Sylva, Brown and Whiting piece which started out called *Humpty Dumpty* and which ultimately came to town as *Take a Chance* (Wanda Brill). Although the show was far from its writers' best, Miss Merman confirmed the effect of her first Broadway musical appearance with the help of the songs ''Eadie was a Lady'' and ''Rise 'n' Shine'' and helped *Take a Chance* to a good run. The role of chanteuse-cum-evangelist Reno Sweeney in Cole Porter's *Anything Goes* (1934) gave her her best opportunities to date. As she wisecracked and walloped her way through a nightclubby prayer meeting to the strains of ''Blow, Gabriel, Blow,'' and got appreciatively personal over William Gaxton in ''You're the Top'' and ''I Get a Kick Out of You,'' Miss Merman hoisted herself to a firm position amongst Broadway's favorite musical stars.

The built-to-bust-size roles of Nails Duquesne in Porter's *Red, Hot and Blue!* (1936, ''It's De-Lovely'') and Jeanette Adair in *Stars in Your Eyes* (1939) did less for the star than she did for the shows in question, but she found another fine, comic part as another nightclub singer, May Daly, who is dreamed into the character of Madame Dubarry, in *Dubarry Was a Lady* (1939, ''Friendship''). She had solo star-billing in two further Cole Porter shows, winning long-running success as nightclub owner Hattie Maloney in *Panama Hattie* (1940, ''Let's Be Buddies''), and rather less of a run as the chorus-girl-turned-munitions-worker heroine of *Something for the Boys* (1943, Blossom Hart).

Miss Merman moved out of her regular loud, jokey and loveable nightclub-singer/chorus-girl mold of roles when she was cast a little against type as the toughly innocent sharpshooter, Annie Oakley, in Rodgers and Hammerstein's production of *Annie Get Your Gun* (1946). If, as a result, Annie on the stage came out a bit different to Annie on the printed page, Miss Merman nevertheless triumphed in the part and in the songs with which Irving Berlin had supplied her: ''You Can't Get a Man with a Gun,'' ''Doin' What Comes Natur'lly,'' ''I

Got the Sun in the Morning,'' ''They Say It's Wonderful,'' ''Moonshine Lullaby.'' The star role of Berlin's next musical, *Call Me Madam,* was tailored perhaps better than any had yet been for its occupant. Miss Merman played the brash and bright, maddening and adorable Sally Adams, socialite turned ambassador, splashing cash and cheer around Ruritania (''You're Just in Love,'' ''The Hostess with the Mostes' on the Ball,'' ''The Best Thing for You'') and scored another major success.

Call Me Madam also marked the advance of Miss Merman—now in her forties—from playing girls to playing women and, if *Happy Hunting* (1956, Liz Livingstone), which actually cast her as a mother—even though she got the man in the final reel—proved one of her few unsatisfactory shows, her second older-woman role brought her another triumph. Cast as the rampaging stage-mother of Gypsy Rose Lee in a musical which, for all that it was called *Gypsy,* centered firmly on her parent, Miss Merman performed ''Everything's Coming Up Roses,'' ''Some People'' and an 11-o'clock act, Rose's Turn, which won itself a virtually legendary status, imitators (more male than female) and a consecration as the highlight of what has become regarded, more in hindsight than at the time, as the most popular and praised example of that peculiarly Broadway institution, the large lead role for a starry older woman with a scalding voice.

In fact, by this time Merman's voice was a little less scalding (its main quality had, apparently, never been actual volume, as the legend now has it, but a singular ability to project both notes and words with the utmost clarity to the last row of the gallery) and the artist a little less hungry. The star who had—unlike so many others—almost always stayed with her shows right throughout their often lengthy runs, began walking through performances of *Gypsy.* After 30 years at the very top of the tree, and as popular as ever, she had created her last Broadway role. Her final musical stage appearances were again as Annie, in her mid-fifties (with an extra song for the occasion), and as Dolly Gallagher Levi in Broadway's *Hello, Dolly!,* a role which she had originally turned down but which she finally took up, with two extra songs, for a period in the show's seventh Broadway year and her 62nd.

One of the most popular musical stage stars of her time, if not indeed the most popular, and certainly the one who aroused the most passionate following amongst her fans (and also amongst many who never ever saw her), Merman did not, however, manage to put herself across on the screen with the same success. She filmed versions of both *Anything Goes* (1936) and *Call Me Madam* (1953), but her other major roles—Annie and Rose, in particular—were filmed by other artists. As film guru Leslie Halliwell summarized ''Her style was too outsize for Hollywood.''

Autobiographies: w Martin, P: *Who Could Ask for Anything More?* (Doubleday, Garden City, 1955), w Eells, G: *Merman—An Autobiography* (Simon & Schuster, New York, 1978); Biographies: Thomas, B: *I Got Rhythm: The Ethel Merman Story* (Putnam, New York, 1985), Bryan, G: *Ethel Merman: A Bio-Bibliography* (Greenwood Press, New York, 1992)

MERRICK, David [MARGULOIS, David] (b St Louis, Mo, 27 November 1911; d London, 25 April 2000). Broadway's most up-front showman of the 1950s, 1960s, 1970s and 1980s and producer of a shower of hit shows.

At first a lawyer and subsequently on the staff of producer Herman Shumlin, Merrick moved into production in 1949 as associate producer on a comedy called *Clutterbuck* and entered the musical theater when he managed to get the rights to make Marcel Pagnol's celebrated trilogy of Marseillais novels/plays into a musical. The resultant piece, entitled *Fanny,* had an excellent Broadway run (888 performances) and was the starting point for a long series of Merrick productions of both plays and musicals. The latter included the Lena Horne vehicle *Jamaica* (1957), a second film adaptation with a score by *Fanny* composer Harold Rome, *Destry Rides Again* (1959), the highly successful *Gypsy* (1959) with Ethel Merman as the title-lady's mum, *Take Me Along* (1959), the English version of the French musical *Irma la Douce* (1960), the comedy musical *Do Re Mi* (1960), Michael Stewart and Bob Merrill's adaptation of the film *Lili* as *Carnival* (1961), the uncharacteristically unattractive *Subways Are for Sleeping* (1961), *I Can Get It for You Wholesale* (1962), the British musical successes *Stop the World—I Want to Get Off* (1962) and *Oliver!* (1962), and *110 in the Shade* (1963). This colorful and very largely successful selection came to its peak in 1964 with the record-breaking production of *Hello, Dolly!,* a musical version of the play *The Matchmaker* which Merrick had presented on Broadway a decade earlier.

The frenetic success rate sagged slightly in the mid-1960s, but amongst the Broadway failures of *Foxy* (1964) and *Pickwick* (1965), the pre-Broadway demises of *Hot September* (1965), *Breakfast at Tiffany's* (1966) and *Mata Hari* (1967) and the only average runs of *The Roar of the Greasepaint . . . the Smell of the Crowd* (1965), *How Now, Dow Jones* (1967) and *The Happy Time* (1968), Merrick still pulled out two further major hits with the two-handed *I Do! I Do!* (1966) and *Promises, Promises* (1968).

A reduced schedule in the reduced Broadway temperatures of the 1970s brought out an unprepossessing musical version of the screenplay *Some Like It Hot* (*Sugar*) which passed five-hundred performances on Broadway without establishing itself as a hit, the Hollywood tale of *Mack and Mabel* (1974) which lasted very much less long on stage but very much better off it, and a transfer of the Goodspeed Opera House production of a revamped *Very Good Eddie* (1975), whilst his production of another musicalized piece of Pagnol, *The Baker's Wife,* closed on the road. Merrick remarried success, however, in 1981, when he mounted a stage version of the famous film *42nd Street* which won him extended runs in both America and Britain.

The most loved, hated, feared, admired, but above all paragraphed producer on Broadway for many years, Merrick, in an era when musical-theatre production was steadily becoming an affair for syndicates and bankers, remained staunchly and loudly a one-man producing band with his own ideas on his shows (even down to the picking of a replacement chorus girl) and his own colorful ways of publicizing both them and himself. At a time when the ''show'' was falling rapidly out of ''showbiz'' on Broadway he stuck with some success to the (to the ''enlightened'') often corny and often transparent but eminently theatrical ways of the previous century.

A stroke, which left him with a severe speech impediment, depleted Merrick's energies only temporarily. In a saga worthy of a TV teatime mini-series, he fought off efforts to seize control of his affairs by having him declared incompetent to run them himself, kept his current productions running and before too long was back with a new one. If the transfer of a re-colored revival of Gershwin's *Oh, Kay!* (1990) proved an uncharacteristically gimmicky and unprofitable choice, it nevertheless allowed him to take on and severely stain the credibility of an over-powerful theatre critic, proving that he was still a presence to be counted on in the Broadway theatre. In 1996 he presented a stage version of the screen musical *State Fair,* and he formally announced his retirement from producing in 1999, less than a year before his death.

Biographies: Kissell, H: *David Merrick* (Applause, New York, 1993), Horn, B: *David Merrick: A Bio-Bibliography* (Greenwood Press, New York, 1992)

MERRIE ENGLAND Comic opera in 2 acts by Basil Hood. Music by Edward German. Savoy Theatre, London, 2 April 1902.

When William Greet took over the Savoy Theatre from the D'Oyly Carte family, he determined to continue to run it on the same diet of high-class comic opera on which it had always thrived. He commissioned his first show from the men who had proven themselves, in the Savoy's previous show, to be the natural successors to Gilbert and Sullivan—Basil Hood and Edward German—and in *Merrie England* they produced a piece noticeably better than their initial *The Emerald Isle.*

Queen Elizabeth (Rosina Brandram) has her romantic eye on young Sir Walter Raleigh (Robert Evett), but Raleigh is in love with her lady-in-waiting, Bessie Throckmorton (Agnes Fraser). The jealous queen plans to poison Bessie, but she is shamed from her design by an apparition of Herne the Hunter, engineered by the the Earl of Essex (Henry Lytton), himself ambitious for the queen's attention, the witch Jill-all-Alone (Louie Pounds) and her forester lover. The tale was set in the forests of Windsor, peopled with the folk of the town, and with a troupe of players which provided the principal if incidental comic roles of Walter Wilkins (Walter Passmore) and his sidekick Simkins (Mark Kinghorne).

Hood told his tale skillfully in a language amusingly redolent of ancient burlesque, full of puns and wordplay, of conceits and similes and three-quarter serious thee-ing and thou-ing, whilst German turned out a score full of beautiful ensembles and pluckable solos. Raleigh's tenor song ''The English Rose,'' Essex's baritone paean to ''The Yeomen of England,'' Bessie's soprano waltz song ''Oh Who Shall Say That Love Is Cruel?,'' her lost-letter song ''She Had a Letter from Her Love,'' and the Queen's contralto summoning of ''O Peaceful England'' all became concert and recording favourites over the half-century following.

However, *Merrie England,* in spite of comparing favorably with Sullivan's olde Englishe light opera *The Yeomen of the Guard,* did not find anything like the same degree of popularity as that piece at the Savoy. After 120 performances Greet took it on tour, and though it returned for a further 57 performances at the end of the year, its record remained a disappointment. Yet *Merrie England* remained staunchly in the repertoire. Provincial, amateur and concert performances were numerous through the following years, and the favorite songs were heard everywhere. Then, in 1934, a professional revival was mounted at the Prince's Theatre (6 September) with star tenor Joseph Hislop (Raleigh) and Enid Cruickshank (Elizabeth) featured. It topped the original production's total by running for a satisfying 187 performances. Another decade later, a second revival (Winter Garden Theatre 19 October 1944) was staged, and in 1945 a third, albeit of a rather badly adapted version (ad Edward Knoblock, Prince's Theatre 6 September). However, this last revival was produced by Jack Waller and cast to the hilt with Heddle Nash (Raleigh) and Dennis Noble (Essex) in the leading male roles. This time *Merrie England* lasted for 365 West End performances, bringing its all-time West End score up to 782 nights, a figure rather more in keeping with its off-stage popularity. Thereafter the show returned to London again briefly in 1951 (National Light Opera Co) and in 1960 when the Sadler's Wells Opera Company mounted another, less drastically revised, version (ad Dennis Arundell), proving itself one of the most solidly long-lived of latter day British comic operas.

If *Merrie England* was reluctant to take off in Britain, it was equally so in the colonies. Although South Af-

Plate 254. **Merrie England.** *''O Peaceful England'': Queen Elizabeth serenades her kingdom in rolling contralto tones.*

rica welcomed Sass and Nelson's company in 1905 (Standard Theatre, Johannesburg 10 January), Australia did not see a professional *Merrie England* until 1921 when, finally persuaded by the relentless popularity of its music, J C Williamson Ltd mounted a production with ex-Savoyard C H Workman as Wilkins, Strella Wilson (Bessie), Ethel Morrison/Pearl Ladd (Elizabeth), Ralph Errolle (Raleigh) and Howett Worster (Essex), as part of their Gilbert and Sullivan Company's season. It played brief seasons in Melbourne and Sydney (Theatre Royal 13 January 1922) but was not brought back.

Australia: Her Majesty's Theatre, Melbourne 18 November 1921

Recording: Sadler's Wells company (HMV/EMI)

MERRILL, Bob [LAVAN, Henry Robert Merrill] (b Atlantic City, NJ, 17 May 1921; d Beverly Hills, Calif, 17 February 1998). Songwriter of many a novelty hit of the 1950s who transferred his talents to the theatre with mixed results.

Merrill was introduced to the theatre through various jobs at the Bucks County Playhouse in his teens, but his first attempts at writing for the stage were made during a spell in the army. He subsequently spent periods working at NBC (1943–44) and at Columbia Pictures as an author of short and secondary movies, as a caster and ultimately as a director, before turning his attention to the popular-music world.

He had his first song hit in 1950 with the words for ''(If I Knew You Were Comin') I'd've Baked a Cake'' (w Al Hoffman, Clem Watts) and this was followed by a veritable rush of 1950s song successes, including many winning novelties, for which he mostly provided both music and words: ''Candy and Cake'' (1950), ''Me and My Imagination'' (1950 w Hoffman), ''Christopher Columbus'' (w Terry Gilkyson), ''Sparrow in the Treetop,'' ''A Beggar in Love,'' ''My Truly, Truly Fair,'' ''There's Always Room at Our House,'' ''Belle, Belle My Liberty Belle'' (all 1951), ''We Won't Live in a Castle,'' ''There's a Pawnshop on the Corner,'' ''Walkin' to Missouri,'' ''Feet Up,'' ''That's Why'' (all 1952), ''How Much Is That Doggie in the Window,'' ''All the Time and Everywhere,'' ''She Wears Red Feathers,'' ''Look at That Girl,'' ''If I Had a Golden Umbrella,'' ''Chick a Boom'' (all 1953), ''Mambo Italiano'' (1954), ''Where Will the Dimple Be,'' ''Make Yourself Comfortable'' (both 1955), ''Sweet Old Fashioned Girl,'' ''The Miracle of Love'' (both 1956) and ''In the Middle of a Dark, Dark Night'' (1957).

Merrill made his first appearance as a Broadway writer with the music and lyrics for the 1957 musical *New Girl in Town,* a version of Eugene O'Neill's *Anna Christie* which had a year's run on Broadway, and he followed up with a second piece of musical O'Neill, *Take Me Along* (based on *Ah, Wilderness*), which ran up an equivalent life. The 1961 show *Carnival,* a charming and catchy musical version of Paul Gallico's *Lili,* had not only a fine New York run but a wider appeal which brought it a good number of overseas productions. It also had a hit song in ''Love Makes the World Go Round'' which, with the help of Perry Como, became the highlight of a score which also included the wistful ''Mira,'' a swirling ''Grand Impérial Cirque de Paris'' and ''Sword, Rose and Cape,'' the pretty ''Yes, My Heart'' and ''A Very Nice Man'' for the show's little heroine and the misanthropic ''I've Got to Find a Reason'' for its anti-hero.

Merrill supplied the lyrics to Jule Styne's music for the highly successful Fanny Brice biomusical *Funny Girl* (''People,'' ''I'm the Greatest Star,'' ''You Are Woman,'' ''When a Girl Isn't Pretty,'' ''Don't Rain on My Parade''), which also earned him another pair of notches on his hit-parade tally, but subsequent ventures with music and lyrics (the unopened *Breakfast at Tiffany's,* 80 performances of *Henry, Sweet Henry*), book and lyrics (pre-Broadway closer *Prettybelle*) or all three (*The Prince of Grand Street*) were not successful. An adaptation of the screenplay *Some Like It Hot* under the title of *Sugar,* for which Merrill supplied the lyrics to another Styne score, did better than any of these with more than a year on Broadway and several foreign productions, but produced nothing in the way of memorable songs.

A television musical *The Dangerous Christmas of Little Red Riding Hood* was brought latterly to the off-Broadway stage, a compilation show of Merrill songs was produced at the Vineyard Theater in 1984 under the title *We're Home* (11 October), and in 1993 the veteran lyricist helped (under the pseudonym ''Paul Stryker'') in the unsuccessful doctoring of the flop musicalization of *The Red Shoes.*

Merrill committed suicide in 1998 following a long illness.

1957 **New Girl in Town** (George Abbott) 46th Street Theater 14 May

1959 **Take Me Along** (Joseph Stein, Robert Russell) Shubert Theater 22 October

1961 **Carnival** (Michael Stewart) Imperial Theater 13 April

1964 **Funny Girl** (Jule Styne/Isobel Lennart) Winter Garden Theater 26 March

1966 **Breakfast at Tiffany's** (*Holly Golightly*) (Nunnally Johnson, Abe Burrows, Edward Albee) Forrest Theater, Philadelphia 10 April; Majestic Theater previews only

1967 **Henry, Sweet Henry** (Johnson) Palace Theater 23 October

1971 **Prettybelle** (Styne) Shubert Theater, Boston 1 February

1972 **Sugar** (Styne/Peter Stone) Majestic Theater 9 April

1978 **The Prince of Grand Street** Forrest Theater, Philadelphia 7 March

1989 **The Dangerous Games of Red Riding Hood** (Styne) TADA Theater December

1990 **Hannah . . . 1939** Vineyard Theater 31 May

MERRILY WE ROLL ALONG Musical in 2 acts by George Furth based on the play by George S Kaufman and Moss Hart. Music and lyrics by Stephen Sondheim. Alvin Theater, New York, 16 November 1981.

A musical version of Kaufman and Hart's fairly successful play (Music Box Theater 29 September 1934, 155 performances), a piece which presented the particularity of telling its tale in reverse. The successful, shiny New York folk who are seen gathered together at the party that opens the evening are tracked back, through the events which have led them to their present point in life, to their college days where, full of ideas, ideals and promise, they are about to set out into the world. The point of the exercise is to emphasize that, to gain success both worldly and personal, it is usually necessary to compromise on shiny ideals: the only question seems to be, how much?

The musical version was updated to the present day and the central figure, Franklin Shepard (Jim Walton), became a songwriter and Hollywood producer. In reverse to the play, where adult actors played ''down'' in the final scenes, the show was cast with college-age performers who played ''up'' for the show's earlier scenes, thus allowing the young idealists to be still seen in the slick, disillusioned middle-aged characters they had become. Lonny Price played Charley Kringas, college friend and collaborator of Shepard until he falls by the hard wayside, Ann Morrison was Mary Flynn, best pal of always. The songs included a musical television interview (''Franklin Shepard Inc'') which was also a keystone in the tale, a hymn to ''Old Friends'' and a pretty ballad, ''Not a Day Goes By.''

Produced by Lord Grade, Martin Starger, Robert Fryer and director Hal Prince, the musical *Merrily We Roll Along* flopped in 16 Broadway performances. However, the reputation and name value of Stephen Sondheim ensured that it did not rest there. It has since received repeated performances (particularly in places where its young casting is an attraction) and some revisions—including three new musical pieces—as seen in a revival at California's La Jolla Playhouse. In 1994 it was seen for a season at off-Broadway's York Theater (26 May).

In Britain, the show caused a small stir when it was played by students at London's Guildhall School for Music and Drama, leading to its being played regionally in Britain. It did not, however, in spite of much talk, progress further.

UK: Manchester Library Theatre 28 September 1984

Recordings: original cast (RCA), English cast (Leicester Haymarket Theatre 1992) (TER), New York revival 1994 (Varese Sarabande)

THE MERRY DUCHESS Comic opera in 2 acts by George R Sims. Music by Frederick Clay. Royalty Theatre, London, 23 April 1883.

Kate Santley's continually brave production schedule included in 1883 a comic opera written by the respected journalist and playwright George Sims and composed by Frederic Clay, whose music she had introduced in *Cattarina* and *Princess Toto* some years previously. *The Merry Duchess* was a racing drama-comedy, transparently based on the love affair between the famous jockey Fred Archer and the Duchess of Montrose. This Duchess (Kate Munroe) has to surmount such problems as the villainous Brabazon Sikes (Henry Ashley) and his wife and fellow horse-doper, Rowena (Miss Santley), an accusation of doping her own horse (already, in 1883!) and a horrid bet which pledges her hand to the ghastly masher Lord Johnnie (R Martin) should her horse lose the St Leger, before she can get to the arms of the victorious Freddy Bowman (W E Gregory).

Robust and lively in its text, the show was musically agreeable in its ballads (''The Captive Bird,'' ''Love's Messenger''), brightly amusing in its comical numbers (''An English Jockey'') and particularly successful in its wealth of ensembles and concerted music, but it brought forth no songs that made it to the barrel organs. The combination, however, seemed to please and *The Merry Duchess,* in a move unusual for the time, sent out a second, touring company whilst the London production moved on towards its fine 177-performance total. America, too, opened its production, starring Selina Dolaro as the Duchess and Henry Dixey and Louise Lester as the villains, whilst London's ran on, and it played a respectable 46 performances in New York before heading for the regions.

Australia followed suit the next year with Gracie Plaisted (Rowena) and Phil Day (Brabazon) starred and Nellie Stewart (Duchess), Hans Phillips (Freddie) and Edwin Kelly (Sir Lothbury Jones) heading the rest of the Royal Comic Opera Company's cast for seasons in Sydney and Melbourne (Princess Theatre 1 November 1884), helping to give *The Merry Duchess* a wider coverage than most English comic operas of its era, the works of Messrs Gilbert and Sullivan, of course, apart.

USA: Standard Theater 8 September 1883; Australia: Theatre Royal, Sydney 23 August 1884

MERRY, MERRY Musical comedy in 2 acts by Harlan Thompson. Music by Harry Archer. Vanderbilt Theater, New York, 24 September 1925.

After the successes of *Little Jessie James* and *My Girl,* producer Lyle Andrews and writers Thompson and Archer followed up with a third piece in the same musical-comedy mold: limited settings (originally one, but it grew to take in an impressive opening scene in a subway), much farcical action, and lively songs in an up-to-date dancing mood. *Merry, Merry* proved as good, if not better, than the previous season's effort and it was whisked in from its tryout in Providence, RI, with a lot of fuss being made over its ingenue, 21-year-old Marie Saxon, who was advertised as having invented a new dance step—a ''diagonal high kick'' in which the right foot flirted with the left shoulder.

Miss Saxon featured as little Eve Walters who comes to New York to be a chorus girl in a Broadway show. She ends up sharing digs with one Sadie la Salle (Sacha Beaumont) who sets out to make enough money to wed her poor but favored boyfriend by tempting a wealthy admirer into a close embrace and then suing him royally for cracking one of her ribs. Eve ends up renouncing showbiz and folks like Sadie for a boy called Adam. Archer's 13 songs, which he conducted from the pit with his band, were in the same joyously modern vein as those from his earlier shows, and *Merry, Merry* lived up to its title through 176 Broadway performances and a happy touring life.

Four years later, it turned up in London. The story was still recognizable but the score was not. Only three of Archer's songs survived (''You're in Love,'' ''Little Boy, Little Girl,'' ''I Was Blue''), supplemented by seven numbers by producer Jack Waller and his team of Joe Tunbridge, Bert Lee and Bob Weston plus Weston's brother Harris, and one, ''Blue Shadows'' (a cue for a ballet in crinolines), by Louis Alter. There were now seven sets, a dance specialty and a chorus of 20 drilled by martial choreographer Ralph Reader. Gladys Cruickshank and Richard Dolman were Adam and Eve, A W Baskcomb cracked Peggy O'Neil's ribs, and W H Berry was chief comic. The show was given 131 performances with a transfer to the Lyceum in the middle.

UK: Carlton Theatre 28 February 1929

THE MERRY WIDOW *see* DIE LUSTIGE WITWE

LES MERVEILLEUSES (aka *The Lady Dandies*) Comic opera in 3 acts by Basil Hood based on the play by Victorien Sardou. Lyrics by Adrian Ross. Music by Hugo Felix. Daly's Theatre, London, 27 October 1906.

The popularity of his English version of *Les P'tites Michu* at Daly's Theatre had led George Edwardes to the belief that a new round of success for the theatre which had so long housed his English comic operas lay in the import of French pieces. However, on the principle that it was more sensible to build one's own French piece than to buy one, he took a libretto made up by Victorien Sardou from his 1873 play *Les Merveilleuses,* had it adapted by Basil Hood, and commissioned Hugo Felix, the Austrian composer whose *Madame Sherry* had caused him some embarrassment by its unexpected London failure, to provide the music.

Set in the *La Fille de Madame Angot* time of the Directoire (like the Lecocq hit, it introduced Citizen Barras into the plot), it dealt with the trials of the lovely Illyrine (Denise Orme), forced by the vicious regime to divorce her émigré husband (Robert Evett) and wed a vulgar Bulgar (W H Berry). Into this tale were introduced the merveilleuse Lodoiska (Evie Greene) and the ex-hairdresser Lagorille (Louis Bradfield) on the light comic/romantic hand, and two policemen (Fred Kaye, Fred Emney) on the low comic one. Felix's score, a well-crafted one with fine ensemble writing, if without the catchier strains of Jones and Monckton's music for the older Daly's shows, or the pure charm and class of Messager's work for more recent ones, included several pieces which were well noticed, including Illyrine's ''The Cuckoo'' and Lodoiska's ''Ring a Ring a Roses.''

Les Merveilleuses did not take off as it might have done. Edwardes changed the title to an English one (*The Lady Dandies*), and later brought old favorite Huntley Wright back, equipped with three Lionel Monckton songs, to attempt to add some of the appeal of earlier days, but the show had a run of only 196 performances. If this was more than fair in itself, it was disappointing when considered alongside the runs accumulated by the former Daly's musicals. However, Edwardes perservered with the Continental idea, and following the closure of *Les Merveilleuses* he tried another musical—already made, this time—by an Austrian composer. With *The Merry Widow* he did rather better.

Les Merveilleuses nevertheless did find an afterlife. It was played in Australia as *The Lady Dandies* with Florence Young (Lodoiska), Fanny Dango and, for a period, the young Rosina Buckman (both Illyrine), Reginald Roberts (Dorlis), Edmund Sherras (Lagorille) and W S Percy in the featured roles; it was toured through the Orient by Maurice Bandmann (1908); and was even later given a showing in Paris (ad Paul Ferrier), with Marthe Régnier and Juliette Méaly starred alongside a fine brochette of comics including Albert Brasseur and Guy.

Australia: Her Majesty's Theatre, Sydney *The Lady Dandies* 21 March 1908; France: Théâtre des Variétés 24 January 1914

MESDAMES DE LA HALLE Opérette bouffe in 1 act by Armand Lapointe. Music by Jacques Offenbach. Théâtre des Bouffes-Parisiens, Paris, 3 March 1858.

Mesdames de la Halle followed in the ''bouffe'' tradition of *Ba-ta-clan, Tromb-al-ca-zar* and *Croquefer* in the Offenbach opus but without taking advantage of their extravagant settings. It was a delicious piece of Parisian bouffonnerie, in which the burlesque was underlined by, and much of the comedy came from, the fact that the three aging market-ladies of the title were played by male comedians. Madame Poiretapée (Léonce), Madame Madou (Désiré) and Madame Beurrefondu (Mesmacre) all lust after the little kitchen-lad, Croûte-au-pot (played in travesty by Lise Tautin), who himself loves pretty orphaned Ciboulette (Mlle Chabert) who sings coloratura behind her fruit stall. The sixth principal character of the piece is the drum-major Raflafla (Duvernoy) who, in a parody of operatic coincidences to match that of *HMS Pinafore,* discovers (after a few false starts) that he is the long-lost husband of one of the Mesdames and the father of Ciboulette, all in time for the flourishingly happy ending. Offenbach's score accompanied the tale in typically glittering comic fashion through an arietta for Ciboulette (''Je suis la petite fruitière''), two lively numbers for Raflafla, a duo for the principal boy and girl and a burlesque septet in which the ladies battle in extravagantly motherly style for the privilege of owning the lost girl.

Produced at the Bouffes-Parisiens, *Mesdames de la Halle* proved a delightful addition to the rapidly growing Offenbach catalogue of short opéras-bouffes, and it was revived regularly until, in 1940 (4 May), it was given the consecration of being played at the Opéra-Comique. It made its way briskly to Vienna, being played at Karl Treumann's Theater am Franz-Josefs-Kai first by the Bouffes company on tour, with Lucille Tostée as Croûte-au-pot and Léonce, Désiré and Desmonts as the ladies; and then in German (ad Alois Berla), with Johann Nestroy himself donning skirts to play Jungfer Barbara alongside Wilhelm Knaack, Grois and Treumann as Raflafla. Knaack later played the long-lost mother in a different adaptation (*Die Damen der Halle*) at the Carltheater, with Karl Blasel and Röhring as his commères and Anna Grobecker as the boy. Budapest, too, saw the Bouffes company tour before the piece was adapted into Hungarian (ad Mihály Havi), and there, as well, other productions followed. In spite of the English travesty and burlesque traditions, however, and in spite of the successful production of a potted version of the show at London's Oxford Music Hall in 1865, there does not ever seem to have been either a contemporary or a later production in the English language.

Germany: Krolls Theater (Fr) 7 July 1859, *Die Damen der Halle* 6 August 1867; Austria: Theater am Franz-Josefs-Kai (Fr) 11 June 1861, *Die Damen von Stand* 22 February 1862; Hungary: Nemzeti Színház (Fr) 12 July 1861, Budai Népszínház *A kofák* 3 October 1863

Recording: complete (revised) (EMI)

MESSAGER, André [Charles Prosper] (b Montluçon, France, 30 December 1853; d Paris, 24 February 1929).

Composer and administrator whose favorite works largely held up the waning French opérette tradition in the early years of the 20th century.

The son of a civil servant, Messager entered the École Niedermeyer at an early age and completed his whole musical education there, both in Paris, and during the school's exile, in Switzerland in the time of the Franco-Prussian War, under Eugène Gigout (counterpoint), Adam Laussel (piano) and Clément Loret (organ). On leaving, aged 21, he became organist at Saint-Sulpice, a position he maintained until 1880 before moving on to the more expansive instruments at St-Paul-St-Louis (1881) and Sainte-Marie-des-Batignolles (1882–84). Whilst fulfilling these ecclesiastical duties, he began his wide-ranging career as a composer. A symphony was honored by the Society of Composers and performed at the Concerts Colonne (20 January 1878), a dramatic scena, *Prométhée enchaîné,* was awarded runner-up laurels in the Concours Musical de la Ville de Paris, a cantata, *Don Juan et Haydée,* was performed in 1877 by the Société Académique de Saint-Quentin and, at the same time that these works were being produced, Messager was also providing ballet music for and conducting at the Folies-Bergère (*Les Vins de France, Fleur d'oranger, Mignons et vilains*). Then, in 1880, he left Paris for a year to take an engagement as conductor at the Eden-Théâtre at Brussels. For that house, too, he composed and recomposed a number of ballet scores (*Insectes et fleurs,* etc).

Messager made his entry into the musical theatre through the aegis of his publishers, Messrs Enoch. When the young composer Firmin Bernicat died before completing the score for his opérette *François les bas-bleus* (1883), the publishers nominated Messager to provide the music needed to get the show into a state for production. *François les bas-bleus* was a great success, and the management of the Théâtre des Folies-Dramatiques offered Messager, whose work had more than stood up alongside Bernicat's, the opportunity to write the entire score for their next production. *La Fauvette du Temple* (1885) and, a month later, *La Béarnaise* confirmed the happy impression of the first work, without quite winning an equivalent international success.

In 1886 Messager composed what would be his most successful ballet, *Les Deux Pigeons,* for the Paris Opéra, but an 1887 opéra-comique *Le Bourgeois de Calais* failed, and the composer was hard put to find a librettist willing to confide a new text to him. When he did, that author was none less than Catulle Mendès and the result was the poetic fairy tale *Isoline,* a piece which, through a combination of circumstances, had but a short initial run but which has since found many champions amongst the lovers of light operatic music and which, in 1959, won itself a revival at the Opéra-Comique.

After an indifferent return to more standard opérette with *Le Mari de la reine* at the Bouffes-Parisiens, it was at the same Opéra-Comique that Messager's next piece, *La Basoche,* was staged. It won a considerable success, making the nearest approach that the composer had yet achieved to equalling the wide public popularity of *François les bas-bleus,* but it did not bring forth another similar opportunity for the composer. In the years that followed, suffering from a need to make himself a living, Messager was present on all fronts with a ballet, *Scaramouche* (1890 w Georges Street) for the opening of the Nouveau-Théâtre, the incidental music to Paul Delair's *Hélène* (1891), the Parisian opérette *Miss Dollar* which, although far from unsuccessful, could not be ranged amongst his best works, and *Mirette,* a piece written to order for D'Oyly Carte at London's Savoy Theatre. This comic opera, for which he insisted that his then wife, the English songwriter known as Hope Temple [Alice Maude DAVIS], had contributed a small (and uncredited) portion of the music, did not fulfill Carte's hopes as *The Nautch Girl* (an earlier and more successful alternative to Gilbert and Sullivan) had done, and in spite of the best Savoy casting, a withdrawal, a rewrite and representation, it failed to catch on. The most appreciable Messager work to emerge from this period was the Japanese-Parisian *Madame Chrysanthème* (1893), based on the novel by Pierre Loti and commissioned as the opening work for Détroyat's Théâtre-Lyrique de la Renaissance. It was another piece which, like *Isoline,* found more, and more expansive, admirers for its delicacy and musical intelligence in the years after, rather than during, its Paris run, and it has survived on the fringes of the played repertoire.

Messager returned to the Opéra-Comique in 1896 with *Le Chevalier d'Harmental,* a piece of which he was particularly proud, and he was devastated when it proved a total failure in Paris and did nothing to establish itself when mounted in the 1896–97 season at the Vienna Hofoper. A lighter piece, *La Fiancée en loterie,* produced at the Folies-Dramatiques (71 performances) and later at Munich's Theater am Gärtnerplatz (*Die Brautlotterie* 12 April 1902) and Berlin Theater des Westens (16 July 1902, 36 performances), did better, but the composer was now truly disheartened. He envisaged returning to Britain and abandoning composition, but the receipt of a delightful opérette libretto from Albert Vanloo and Georges Duval (a libretto which he was unaware had been refused by other composers) helped him to decide otherwise. His setting of that libretto with some of his most charming yet lively and melodious music ensured that *Les P'tites Michu* (1897) finally gave him the sizeable popular and international success that had so far eluded him in the musical theatre.

The same librettists followed up with another libretto which mixed refinement and gaiety in just the right proportions to appeal both to the general public and to the habitues of the Opéra-Comique. Messager's setting of *Véronique,* with its Swing Song and Donkey Duo (''Trot here, trot there'' to two generations of English-language vocalists), scored an even more remarkable success than *P'tites Michu,* helping materially to extend the borders of the great period of classic French opéra-bouffe and opéra-comique which, after half a century, was touching its end.

Véronique, however, had no comparable successor. Once again the Opéra-Comique intervened. Albert Carré, librettist of *La Basoche* and newly named as director of the Salle Favart, invited Messager to become his musical director and, as a result, the composer's output over the next 20 years was limited first by his activities at the Opéra-Comique, and subsequently by periods as director of both London's Royal Opera House (1901–7) and the Paris Opéra (1908–14), and throughout as a theatre and concert conductor. A German remake of *Le Mari de la reine* as *Der Prinz gemahl* (ad Théo de Gillert, Neues Königlichen Operntheater 24 July 1904), and the productions of *Les Dragons de l'Impératrice* (1905) and the opéra-comique *Fortunio,* pieces more in the vein of *La Basoche* than of his two great and happy hits, were his only contributions to his musical theatre oeuvre during this period, although he composed a ballet *Une aventure de la Guimard* (1900) for the Opéra-Comique to add to another, *Le Chevalier aux fleurs* (1897 w Raoul Pugno), written earlier for the Théâtre Marigny; incidental music for the Théâtre de la Porte-Saint-Martin's féerie *La Montagne enchantée* (1897 w Xavier Leroux); an opera, *Béatrice,* written to a text by de Flers and de Caillavet and produced both in Monaco (21 March 1914) and later at the Opéra-Comique; and a one-act opérette for the Concert Mayol.

After the war, however, Messager returned to the light musical theatre and, whilst the new-born rage for Jazz Age musical comedy whirled around him, he turned out the pieces that, after his two famous works of the previous decade, have proved the most enduring of his stage works. In the last decade of his life, he collaborated with the playwright Frederick Lonsdale on the English light opera *Monsieur Beaucaire* (1919, ''Philomel,'' ''Red Rose''); with Sacha Guitry on the exquisite musical play *L'Amour masqué* (''J'ai deux amants'') and the comedy *Deburau* (incidental music); and, finally, with Albert Willemetz, the librettist à la mode, on two modern opérettes, *Passionnément* (1926) and *Coups de roulis* (1928).

In descriptions of the works of Messager the words ''elegant'' and ''poetic'' recur the most frequently. His natural habitat was, perhaps, the area of light opera formerly cared for by the Opéra-Comique, an area which has steadily faded away in more recent years in favor of the extremes of operatic and popular musical theatre. However, he proved in such pieces as *Les P'tites Michu* that he was capable of the most delightfully sparkling gaiety and even comical effects in his music, and if he never quite let himself rip in the style of some of the more frankly popular composers of the different eras of the 45 years through which he was active, he succeeded in giving those eras and their musical theatre some of their most beautiful melodies and ensembles.

1883 **François les bas-bleus** (Firmin Bernicat, completed) Théâtre des Folies-Dramatiques 8 November

1885 **Le Petit Poucet** (Eugène Leterrier, Albert Vanloo, Albert Mortier) Théâtre de la Gaîté 28 October

1885 **La Fauvette du Temple** (Paul Burani, Eugène Humbert) Théâtre des Folies-Dramatiques 17 November

1885 **La Béarnaise** (Leterrier, Vanloo) Théâtre des Bouffes-Parisiens 12 December

1887 **Le Bourgeois de Calais** (Paul Burani, Ernest Dubreuil) Théâtre des Folies-Dramatiques 6 April

1888 **Isoline** (Catulle Mendès) Théâtre de la Renaissance 25 December

1889 **Le Mari de la reine** (Ernest Grenet-Dancourt, Octave Pradels) Théâtre des Bouffes-Parisiens 18 December

1890 **La Basoche** (Albert Carré) Opéra-Comique 30 May

1893 **Madame Chrysanthème** (Georges Hartmann, André Alexandre) Théâtre-Lyrique de la Renaissance 30 January

1893 **Miss Dollar** (Charles Clairville, Albert Vallin) Nouveau-Théâtre 22 December

1894 **Mirette** (Frederick E Weatherly/Michel Carré ad Harry Greenbank, revised by Adrian Ross) Savoy Theatre 3 July

1896 **La Fiancée en loterie** (w Paul Lacome/Camille de Roddaz, Alfred Douane) Théâtre des Folies-Dramatiques 13 February

1896 **Le Chevalier d'Harmental** (Paul Ferrier) Opéra-Comique 5 May

1897 **Les P'tites Michu** (Vanloo, Georges Duval) Théâtre des Bouffes-Parisiens 16 November

1898 **Véronique** (Vanloo, Duval) Théâtre des Bouffes-Parisiens 10 December

1905 **Les Dragons de l'Impératrice** (Vanloo, Duval) Théâtre des Variétés 13 February

1907 **Fortunio** (Robert de Flers, Gaston de Caillavet) Opéra-Comique 5 June

1916 **Cyprien, ôte ta main d'là** (Maurice Hennequin) 1 act Concert Mayol

1919 **Monsieur Beaucaire** (Ross/Frederick Lonsdale) Prince's Theatre, London 19 April

1921 **La Petite Fonctionnaire** (Antoine Capus, Xavier Roux) Théâtre Mogador 14 May

1923 **L'Amour masqué** (Sacha Guitry) Théâtre Édouard VII 15 February

1926 **Passionnément** (Albert Willemetz, M Hennequin) Théâtre de la Michodière 15 January

1928 **Coups de roulis** (Willemetz) Théâtre Marigny 29 September

1930 **Sacha** (completed by Marc Berthomieu/André Rivoire) Monte Carlo

Biographies: Augé-Laribé, M: *André Messager: Musicien de theatre* (Vieux Colombier, Paris, 1951), Fevrier, H: *André Messager: Mon maître, mon ami* (Amiot-Dumont, Paris, 1948), Wagstaff, J: *André Messager: A Bio-Bibliography* (Greenwood Press, New York, 1991)

THE MESSENGER BOY Musical comedy in 2 acts by James T Tanner and Alfred Murray. Lyrics by Adrian Ross and Percy Greenbank. Music by Ivan Caryll and Lionel Monckton. Gaiety Theatre, London, 3 February 1900.

The first of George Edwardes's Gaiety Theatre "girl" musicals to be a "boy," *The Messenger Boy* top-billed comedian Teddy Payne as Tommy Bang, entrusted by the villainous Tudor Pyke (John Tresahar) with a promissory note in disfavor of his rival in love, Clive Radnor (Lionel Mackinder), to be delivered to the father of their beloved Nora (Violet Lloyd) in Egypt. Pyke thus intends to discredit his rival, but Tommy must get to Lord Punchestown with his letter before Clive does. Only after the boy has set out does Pyke discover that he has actually given him another of his "useful" bits of paper by mistake: a compromising letter written by Lady Punchestown! So Nora, Lady Punchestown's maid, Rosa (Katie Seymour) and Pyke all set out to try to stop the messenger boy from delivering. Reorganization in the Gaiety's personnel meant that the star-billed old favorites were mostly not in the plot roles. Miss Seymour, Payne's partner since *The Shop Girl* more than five years earlier, and Connie Ediss, as Tommy's Mum who discovers her long-lost husband passing himself off as Hooker Pasha (Harry Nicholls), were the female stars, and there were character parts for such as dance captain Willie Warde, Fred Wright and former Gaiety burlesque star E J Lonnen.

The show's songs gave Payne a jolly title number and the expected duos with Miss Seymour, including one in which they imitated "Mummies," Miss Lloyd waxed patriotic in "When the Boys Come Home Once More" (it was Boer War time) and Miss Ediss scored with a comical "In the Wash," but it was a simple little piece called "Maisie," breathlessly sung in a non-existent role by the exquisite ex-chorus girl Rosie Boote, which proved the show's hit. It was scarcely an outstanding number, but it caught on rageously, and little Miss Boote's reward was a coronet. She left the show to become the Marchioness of Headfort.

The Messenger Boy was a tremendous Gaiety success (429 performances) and, as was now the norm with Gaiety shows, immediately began a long and wide career beyond Britain. Budapest's Magyar Színház mounted *A postás fiu* (ad Ernő Salgó, Adolf Mérei) whilst London's version still ran, Frank Wheeler produced *The Messenger Boy* in South Africa shortly after, and, as three touring companies worked their ways around Britain, Nixon and Zimmerman starred James T Powers, Georgia Caine (Nora) and May Robson (Mrs Bang) in a highly successful Broadway run (129 performances) of a localized version which featured such additional local songs as Pat Rooney's "Pansy" and two numbers in which Powers had a lyrical hand.

Australia and New Zealand saw J C Williamson's production in 1902 with Fred Graham playing Tommy alongside Lillian Digges (Nora) and Rose Musgrove (Rosa), and Vienna's Gabor Steiner, who had had considerable success with *The Circus Girl,* mounted the show for three weeks at his Danzers Orpheum (ad Carl Lindau, Leopold Krenn), with his Oberregisseur Karl Tuschl starring as Tommy, Franz Glawatsch as Cosmos Bey and Frlns Felsen and Huemer as Nora and Mrs Bang. The second act featured a tarantella and an interpolated song, by Karl Kappeller, for Helene Merviola, in the unfamiliar role of Anita, an Italian street-singer, and a "Frauen aus der ganzen Welt" display in which a waltz, "Die Wienerin," the work of Broadway's Ludwig Engländer, was displayed by "die gesammte Damenpersonal."

Having played its run, long or short, in each area, *The Messenger Boy* then moved aside to make way for the newest Gaiety offering.

Hungary: *A postás fiu* Magyar Színház 24 January 1901; USA: Daly's Theater 16 September 1901; Australia: Palace Theatre, Sydney 8 October 1902; Austria: Danzers Orpheum *Der Laufbursche* 31 October 1902

MESTÉPÈS, Eugène (b 1818; d Paris, 15 May 1878).

For two decades a supplier of mostly little libretti to the budding French musical theatre of the mid-19th century, Eugène Mestépès doubled in a "real job" as a theatrical administrator. He was in charge of the Théâtre des Bouffes-Parisiens from the little house's inception in 1855, and later ran the Théâtre de l'Ambigu. On the more substantial side of the musical theatre, he teamed with Victor Wilder to provide the libretto to Weber's *Sylvana* (1872).

1855 **Le Violoneux** (Jacques Offenbach/w Émile Chevalet) 1 act Théâtre des Bouffes-Parisiens 31 August

1855 **Le Duel de Benjamin** (Émile Jonas) 1 act Théâtre des Bouffes-Parisiens October

1856 **En revenant de la Pontoise** (Alfred Dufresne) Théâtre des Bouffes-Parisiens 20 February

1856 **En revenant de la revue** (Dufresne) Théâtre des Bouffes-Parisiens 20 March

1857 **Les Trois Baisers du Diable** (Offenbach) 1 act Théâtre des Bouffes-Parisiens 15 January

1857 **Le Roi boit** (Jonas/w Adolphe Jaime) 1 act Théâtre des Bouffes-Parisiens 9 April

1857 **Dragonette** (Offenbach/w Jaime) 1 act Théâtre des Bouffes-Parisiens 30 April

1857 **Maître Griffard** (Léo Delibes) 1 act Théâtre Lyrique 3 October

1857 **La Demoiselle d'honneur** (Théophile Semet/w A S Kaufmann) 1 act Théâtre Lyrique 30 December

1863 **Ondine** (Semet/w Lockroy) Théâtre Lyrique 7 January

1863 **Job et son chien** (Jonas) 1 act Théâtre des Bouffes-Parisiens 6 February

1864 **Le Manoir des Larenardière** (Jonas) 1 act Théâtre des Bouffes-Parisiens 29 September

1864 **La Fille du maître de chapelle** (Vauzanges/w Ventéjoul) Théâtre Déjazet 9 July

1865 **Avant la noce** (Jonas/w Paul Boisselot) 1 act Théâtre des Bouffes-Parisiens 24 March

1865 **Les Deux Arlequins** (Jonas) 1 act Fantaisies-Parisiennes 29 December

MEXICAN HAYRIDE Musical comedy in 2 acts by Herbert and Dorothy Fields. Music and lyrics by Cole Porter. Winter Garden Theater, New York, 28 January 1944.

The third successive collaboration and third successive long run (481 performances) for songwriter Cole Porter and librettists Herbert and Dorothy Fields, *Mexican Hayride* was a vehicle for popular comedian Bobby Clark, cast by the authors as a minor crook in a Mexican setting, pursued by the authorities through a series of disguises worthy of the most ebullient musical comedies of half a century earlier. June Havoc (Montana) portrayed a lady bullfighter, Wilbur Evans (David Winthrop) was her baritonic diplomat boyfriend, George Givot (Lombos Campos) the comic's comical partner in crime, and Corinna Mura was an extraneous lady called Lolita who sang Mexicanish songs.

The score brought forth no new Porter bonbons, although within the show ''Count your Blessings'' as comicked by the two crooks and the matadoress scored a popular success, and Evans sang an ''I Love You'' (allegedly as a result of a bet taken by Porter that he couldn't, or wouldn't dare, put out a piece with such a timeworn title) which became popular, on the one hand, and pulled out a Porter catalogue of names and rhymes for ''There Must be Someone for Me'' on another. Much of the musical material written for the show was, in fact, dropped on the way into town (notably Porter's latest dip into the celebrity telephone directory in ''It's Just Like the Good Old Days'') and Porter wasn't happy with what was finally heard on Broadway but, extravagantly produced by Mike Todd, with a large cast, crew, orchestra and publicity budget, *Mexican Hayride* proved popular wartime entertainment. The musical was not seen outside America, but its libretto (without the songs) was later made into an Abbott and Costello movie.

Recording: original cast (Decca/CBS)

MEYER, Joseph (b Modesto, Calif, 12 March 1894; d New York, 22 June 1987).

Songwriter Meyer flourished in the second half of the 1920s, supplying several major hit numbers to Broadway and London shows of which the most famous were ''California Here I Come'' (ly: B G De Sylva, Al Jolson), sung by Jolson in *Bombo* and again in *Big Boy;* ''A Cup of Coffee, a Sandwich, and You'' (w Billy Rose, Al Dubin), introduced by Gertrude Lawrence in *Charlot's Revue of 1926;* ''If You Knew Susie,'' which was originally part of the score for *Big Boy,* on which Meyer collaborated musically, but which was cut and handed over by Jolson to Eddie Cantor; ''Clap Hands, Here Comes Charlie'' and ''Tonight's My Night with Baby.''

Meyer supplied music to Gallagher and Shean's musical comedy *In Dutch,* which only played out of town, but he had major credits on four Broadway scores and placed songs in a number of other shows both in America (*Battling Butler, Ziegfeld Follies, Shuffle Along,* etc) and in Britain (*Happy Go Lucky, Lucky Girl*), where his work was used to make up part-scores for *Merely Molly* and for the Jack Buchanan vehicle *That's a Good Girl* (''Fancy Our Meeting''). One Meyer song, ''Crazy Rhythm'' (w Wolfe-Kahn, Caesar), originally played in Broadway's *Here's Howe,* actually appeared in both *That's a Good Girl* and *Lucky Girl* in London.

Although he continued to have occasional song successes (''Idle Gossip,'' ''I Wonder'') through into the 1950s, Meyer's connection with the musical theatre did not go beyond 1930.

1924 **In Dutch** (w others/William Cary Duncan, Irving Caesar) Newark, NJ 22 September

1925 **Big Boy** (w James F Hanley/B G De Sylva/Harold Atteridge) Winter Garden Theater 7 January

1926 **Merely Molly** (w Herman Finck/Harry Graham/J Hastings-Turner) Adelphi Theatre, London 22 September

1927 **Just Fancy** (w Phil Charig/Leo Robin/Joseph Santley, Gertrude Purcell) Casino Theater 11 October

1928 **Here's Howe** (ex- *And Howe!*) (w Roger Wolfe-Kahn/Irving Caesar/Fred Thompson, Paul Gerard Smith) Broadhurst Theater 1 May

1928 **That's a Good Girl** (w Charig/Douglas Furber, Desmond Carter, et al/Furber) London Hippodrome 5 June

1929 **Lady Fingers** (Edward Eliscu/Eddie Buzzell) Vanderbilt Theater 31 January

1930 **Jonica** (Moss Hart, Dorothy Heyward) Craig Theater 7 April

MEYERHOFF, Hermine (b Braunschweig, Germany, 26 March 1848; d Waltendorf, 24 February 1926). Leading lady of the 19th-century Vienna stage.

Hermine Meyerhoff began her career as a dancer at the ducal theatre in her native Braunschweig, before turn-

Plate 255. **Hermine Meyerhoff** *in the title role of Suppé's* Die schöne Galathee.

ing actress and then, after a very short course of vocal studies, singer. She made her debut as Ännchen in *Der Freischütz* at the age of 20, and went on to appear in opera at the Danzig Stadttheater and at Hamburg's Floratheater (Zerlina, Marie in *Der Waffenschmied,* Page in *Les Huguenots,* Zerlina in *Fra Diavolo, Zar und Zimmermann*) before winning herself notice in important places when she was cast in Pepi Gallmeyer's original role in *Wiener Geschichten* opposite the guesting Albin Swoboda.

In 1869 Meyerhoff moved to Vienna's Carltheater, making her debut there as Jeanne in Offenbach's *Toto* (*Le Château à Toto*), and over the following years she was seen in a series of further roles in shows by Offenbach—who expressed a particular liking for her work—and by other opéra-bouffe composers. She starred as Zanetta to the Regina of Gallmeyer in *Die Prinzessin von Trapezunt,* as Gabrielle in *Hundert Jungfrauen,* as the first Viennese Clairette in *Angot die Tochter des Halle,* as Rose Michon in *Schönröschen* and in the title roles of *Giroflé-Girofla* and *Prinz Conti* whilst also appearing in such roles as Oléander in *Tulipatan,* Laurette in *Fortunio,* Chloë in *Daphnis and Chloë,* Mimi in *Kakadu,* Ernestine in *Salon Pitzelberger,* Schamyl in *Schneeball,* Corraline in *Der Regimentzauberer,* Cannebas in *Cannebas,* Princess Girandole in *Confusius IX,* Mme Jobin in *Urlaub nach Zapfenstreich,* Billette in *Die schöne Bourbonnaise* and guesting at the Theater an der Wien as Rubin in *König Carotte.*

During this period, Meyerhoff also appeared in such early Viennese Operette roles as Lieschen in *Flotte Bursche,* Marianne in *Wein, Weib, Gesang,* Lisi in *In der Sackgasse,* Fanny in *Fitzliputzli,* Limonia in *Zehn Mädchen und kein Mann,* Galatea in *Die schöne Galathee* and Calumba in *Die Frau Meisterin.* As the Austrian tradition took off, she created the more significant role of Lydia in *Fatinitza* and played Pulcinella in *Prinz Methusalem* and Amanda in *Der Teufel auf Erden,* whilst still performing in such French pieces as *Jeanne, Jeannette et Jeanneton* (Jeanne) and *Der Kohlenhandler von Paris* (Thérèse).

In 1878, now established as one of Vienna's top Operettic performers, if without the star status of a Gallmeyer or a Geistinger, she moved—though long billed as a guest artist—to the Theater an der Wien. There she succeeded Gallmeyer as Gabrielle in *La Vie parisienne,* was the first Viennese Haiderose (ie, Serpolette) in *Die Glocken von Corneville* and starred as Marie in *Der letzte Mohikaner,* as Susanne to the Justine Favart of Geistinger in *Madame Favart,* and in the title role of Millöcker's *Gräfin Dubarry,* and appeared as Namuna in *Die hübsche Perserin,* Donna Irene in *Das Spitzentuch der Königin,* Palmyra in *Ein Schotte* (*L'Écossais de Chatou*) and Betsy in Strauss's short-lived *Blindekuh.*

Frln Meyerhoff then abandoned the Viennese theatre to star throughout Europe (Berlin, Hamburg, Dresden, Florence, Naples, Palermo, Moscow, St Petersburg, Odessa, Bucharest, etc) in a long series of Operettic productions. In 1886 she appeared as Strauss's Sáffi in Riga and then put a full stop to her career, retiring to married life as the Countess Tatischeff, the wife of a Russian aristocrat and diplomat.

MIAMI

Apparently a title which is considered more evocative outside America than in, *Miami* has been used as the name of musicals in Britain, France and Hungary, but not in the United States of America. In Britain it was used as the title for a melodramatic opera by John Hollingshead based on a popular drama, J B Buckstone's *The Green Bushes,* with lyrics by E Warham St Leger and music by J Haydn Parry. Produced at the Princess's Theatre, London on 16 October 1893 in an unfortunate production which used the name of the aging Hollingshead, the famous founder of the Gaiety Theatre (billed as manager, author and director), as a front, it folded in 11 performances. Violet Cameron played Buckstone's self-sacrificing Indian heroine (she was called ''Miami,'' thence the title) alongside Savoy Theatre stars Courtice Pounds, Jessie Bond and Richard Temple.

In Hungary the title was attached to an Operette in three acts by István Bródy and László Vajda, with music by Viktor Jacobi posthumously arranged by Zsigmond Vincze (Fővárosi Operettszínház 27 November 1925) and featuring Jacobi's successful waltz ''On Miami Shore'' (aka ''Golden Sands of Miami,'' ly: William Le Baron), a number which had already managed to get itself interpolated into not one but two Australian musical comedy productions—sung by Gladys Moncrieff in *Theodore & Co* and Cecil Bradley in *Yes, Uncle!*

The French *Miami* was a comédie-musicale by René Pujol with lyrics by Saint-Granier and a score credited to De Sylva, Brown and Henderson with additional numbers by Maurice Yvain (Théâtre des Ambassadeurs, Paris 20 December 1930), which starred Milton and Janie Marèse and which just may have been a version of *Follow Thru*'s ''musical slice of country club life,'' but may equally well not have been.

MICHAELIS, Robert [Armand René] (b ?St Petersburg, 22 December 1878; d Bristol, 29 August 1965). Handsome, French-bred baritone (some sources give his birthplace as Paris) who had a fine run as a musical-theatre leading man in his twenties and thirties in a career split by the First World War and more or less terminated with the coming of the all-dancing and very-little-singing shows of the mid-1920s.

Michaelis played in the British provinces in Serpette's *Amorelle (1798)* (1903, François), *The Gay Parisienne, The Belle of New York* and *Three Little Maids* before making his West End debut, succeeding Louis Bradfield as the hero of *The Girl from Kays.* In his twenties, he visited New York to appear in *The White Hen* (1907, Paul Blanche with a song called ''Edelweiss'') and followed up by succeeding William Percival as the hero of *Mlle Modiste* (1907, Étienne) opposite Fritzi Scheff, before returning to London where he succeeded Joe Coyne as Danilo to the Widow of Lily Elsie in London's *Merry Widow.* He played opposite Miss Elsie again as the hero of London's *The Dollar Princess* (1909, Freddy), beginning a series of romantic lead roles in George Edwardes's productions, both in London and on the road: *A Waltz Dream* (Niki), *The Count of Luxembourg* (René), *Gipsy Love* (Joszi), *The Marriage Market* (Jack Fleetwood), *A Country Girl* revival (Geoffrey Challoner).

After serving in the War, Michaelis returned to the London stage as James in *Who's Hooper?* (1919) and as J P Bowden in the British production of *Irene* (1920), appeared in *The Golden Moth,* Ivor Novello's rewrite of *Erminie* (1921, Pierre Caravan) and took a second turn on Broadway in *Orange Blossoms* (1922, Baron Roger Belmont). He then joined prima donna José Collins to provide her love interest in *Catherine* (1923, Mentschikoff), *Our Nell* (1924, Tom Miles) and *Frasquita* (1925, Armand), before moving on to his final West End appearances in the modern dance-and-comedy shows *Dear Little Billie* (1925, Harry Somerset) and *Up with the Lark* (1927, Baron Frétigny).

Michaelis was married to soprano **Phyllys Le GRAND** [Phyllis M Le GRAND] who played leading roles in town (t/o Diane in *The Quaker Girl* 1910, Alix Luttrell in *Autumn Manoeuvres* 1912, Nicolette in *Nicolette* 1925, etc) and on the road (Sonia in *The Merry Widow* 1909, Angèle Didier in *The Count of Luxembourg* 1911, Rosabel in *The Sunshine Girl* 1913, Lady Frayle in *My Lady Frayle* 1916, Madame Rabelais in *High Jinks* 1917, Diana Fairlie in *The Boy* 1918, Louise de Kérouailles in *Our Nell* 1924, etc) and appeared alongside her husband in Broadway's *Orange Blossoms* (1922, Hélène de Vasquez).

MICHELL, Keith [Joseph] (b Adelaide, 1 December 1927). Australian actor and singer who created and/or played several important roles in London musical productions.

Formerly an art teacher, Michell trained as an actor in Britain and made his earliest London appearance as King Charles to the Samuel Pepys of Leslie Henson in the musicalized *And So to Bed* (1951). He played for a number of seasons with the Shakespeare Company at Stratford-on-Avon, returning to the musical stage in 1958 in the role of Nestor in the long-running English-language version of *Irma la Douce* which he played in both London and in New York. The next of his liberally spaced musical roles, as Robert Browning to the Elizabeth Barrett of June Bronhill in London's *Robert and Elizabeth* (1964, ''I Know Now,'' ''The Moon in my Pocket''), gave him another major success, but in the following years only *Man of La Mancha* (1968) in which he took on the role created by Richard Kiley, first in London and later as a replacement on Broadway, brought him again to the musical stage during a period in which he became not only one of Britain's best-known and most-admired stage and television actors, but also the director of the Chichester Festival Theatre.

He returned once more, after over a decade away from the musical stage, to star with Julia McKenzie in the London production of *On the Twentieth Century* (1980, Oscar Jaffee) but, in the decades since, his only fresh appearances in the musical theatre, apart from a dressed concert staging of his own ''Captain Beaky'' poems, have been as Georges in *La Cage aux Folles* in America and Australia, and as George in *Aspects of Love* in Canada and America.

He appeared on the Brent-Walker set of Gilbert and Sullivan videos as Major General Stanley (*The Pirates of Penzance*) and Robin Oakapple (*Ruddigore*).

MICHEL STROGOFF Opérette à grand spectacle in 2 acts by Marc-Cab and René Richard based on the novel by Jules Verne. Music by Jack Ledru. Théâtre Mogador, Paris, 28 November 1964.

A popular and often-reprised Châtelet spectacular over the years, the 1880 stage adaptation by Jules Verne and Adolphe d'Ennery of Verne's novel was turned into an opérette à grand spectacle, equipped with no less than 25 sets, for Henri Varna's Théâtre Mogador in 1964. Marcel Merkès played Strogoff, riding across the wastes of Siberia, through the invading Tartar hordes, with his Nadia (Paulette Merval) ever near, suffering torture and imprisonment before finally delivering a vital letter to the Tsar of all the Russias. Accompanied by a romantico-scenic score very largely devoted to its hero and its heroine, *Michel Strogoff* ran for the best part of a year at the Mogador and has continued to win occasional provincial productions (with less than 25 sets) since.

Recording: original cast (CBS)

MIDAS Burletta (comic opera) in 2 acts by Kane O'Hara. Crow Street Theatre, Dublin, 22 January 1762; Theatre Royal, Covent Garden, London, 22 February 1764.

Variously described as a burletta or a comic opera, the extremely successful *Midas* was, in fact, a classical burlesque written in rhymed couplets and with its lyrical pieces set, in the style of the period, to borrowed music. It was asserted on occasion that it was a parody of a piece called *The Judgement of Midas* written by Sir Thomas Dale.

A marital squabble on Olympus results in Apollo (George Mattocks) being sent down to earth as punishment. There, disguised as a farmhand, he gets mixed up in the randy efforts of squire and justice Midas (Mr Shuter) and his pimp Damaetas (Mr Fawcett) to lay hands and things on the local maidens, Daphne (Miss Miller) and Nysa (Miss Hallam), both of whom complicate matters by falling for the pretty newcomer. When Midas crookedly backs his pal Pan (Mr Dunstall) in a singing competition with the disguised God of music, he brings down Apollo's godly wrath on his foolish head, and finds himself changed into an ass. The 20 to 30 musical items introduced into the action included a booming number for the jealous Juno (''Your favourite jades I'll plunge to the shades or into cows metamorphose them . . .''), a drinking song for Pan, a maypole number, a jealousy duet for the two sisters, several ensembles and the two competition songs, of which Apollo's was listed in the script as being ''introduced,'' and thus presumably of the performer's choice.

Produced at London's Theatre Royal, Covent Garden two seasons after its Dublin premiere, *Midas* was regularly revived thereafter. It was included in the touring baggage of dozens and dozens of road and repertoire companies, given revivals in London for well over a century and in the provinces for longer, at a time when only a very few burlesque pieces of former days (*The Beggar's Opera, Bombastes Furioso, Tom Thumb*) still found the stage. A notable revival was staged at the Haymarket Theatre in 1853 (3 October) with the future Mrs Howard Paul as Apollo, Mrs Caulfield as Nysa, Chippendale as Midas and Henry Corri as Silenus. In 1852 Rebecca Isaacs played Apollo at the Strand, succeeded in 1854 by Georgia Hodson. *Midas* was the most successful classical burlesque of its time, and stands historically as a forerunner to Planché, to *Orphée aux enfers,* to *Thespis* and to the other classic-based musical comedies which have so often been important landmarks in the musical theatre.

What may have been the first American performance was seen at New York's John Street Theater in 1773 with Mr Goodman (Midas), Mr Woolls (Apollo), Miss Stover (Nysa) and Mrs Morris (Daphne) on the bill.

Author O'Hara wrote several other pieces thereafter—the burletta *The Golden Pippin* mounted at Covent Garden (6 February 1773) with Anne Catley as Juno (''Push About the Jorum''), *The Two Misers* (mus: Dibdin, Covent Garden 21 January 1775), *April Day* (mus: Arnold, Haymarket 22 August 1777), and a version of *Tom Thumb* (Covent Garden 3 October 1780) amongst them—without finding again the same kind of success.

USA: John Street Theater 4 May 1773; Australia: Royal Victoria Theatre, Sydney 13 May 1839

MIDDLETON, Ray[mond] (b Chicago, 8 February 1907; d Panorama City, Calif, 10 April 1984). Broadway baritone who drew one outstanding role in 30 years of service.

Originally trained as an opera singer, Middleton made his first Broadway appearance as the giant in a version of *Jack and the Beanstalk* (1931) before taking a rather more conventional role as the all-American in Paris, John Kent, the juvenile leading man (surprisingly, without a song) of Jerome Kern's *Roberta* (1933). After a period which included some essays in opera, he returned to Broadway in 1938 as Washington Irving in *Knickerbocker Holiday,* then went through revue (*George White's Scandals, American Jubilee* at the

World's Fair), film (*Lady for a Night, The Girl from Alaska*) and a spell in the air force, before returning to create his most important musical-comedy role as Frank Butler in *Annie Get Your Gun* (1946, ''My Defences Are Down,'' ''The Girl That I Marry,'' ''Anything You Can Do,'' ''They Say It's Wonderful'').

Middleton subsequently starred on the musical stage as Samuel Cooper, the eternally married man of *Love Life* (1948), took over as Émile LeBecque in *South Pacific* from Ezio Pinza, and in his later years appeared in a character role in *Man of La Mancha* (1965, the Governor) and in *Purple Dust* at the Goodpeed Opera House. He was also seen in the film version of *1776* (McKean) and in the television version of *Damn Yankees* (Joe Boyd).

THE MIKADO, or The Town of Titipu Comic opera in 2 acts by W S Gilbert. Music by Arthur Sullivan. Savoy Theatre, London, 14 March 1885.

Of all the Gilbert and Sullivan musicals produced at the Savoy Theatre, it was *The Mikado* which succeeded in building the longest West End run (672 performances), the most extensive European reputation, and the widest and most enduring afterlife. After more than a century of repeated productions it remains as popular as ever, undoubtedly the most generally loved of the Gilbert and Sullivan canon and, many would argue, the best.

Gilbert chose an oriental setting for the show with which he and Sullivan followed their remake of his old burlesque *The Princess* as *Princess Ida.* The extravagant and quaintly burlesquable Orient had always been a popular and colorful choice of venue in comic opera, and since in the mid-1880s there was a new craze in Britain for ''all that's Japanese,'' Gilbert's decision to head east was a logical one. For his title he chose one announced and discarded nine years previously by Busnach and Liorat (they eventually gave the title of *Kosiki* to their *Le Mikado*), and for his plot he abandoned the direct burlesque typical of his previous pieces: the nautical and operatic burlesque of *HMS Pinafore,* the melodrama burlesque of *The Pirates of Penzance,* the aesthetic burlesque of *Patience,* the burlesque of faërie in *Iolanthe* or of Tennyson in *Princess Ida.* The story of *The Mikado* was in direct line of descent from previous British and French ''Japanese'' comic operas and opéras-bouffes and built not around any specific parody but, with the help of many familiar elements from the comic-opera tradition, around the company at the Savoy Theatre.

Leonora Braham was Yum-Yum, a Japanese schoolgirl (Gilbert said he made her a schoolgirl because she and her fellows Jessie Bond and Sybil Grey were all tiny) who is unwillingly engaged to Ko-Ko, the underworked Lord High Executioner of Titipu (George Grossmith). When Nanki-Poo (Durward Lely), the son of the Mikado (Richard Temple), comes to Titipu fleeing a forced marriage with the dragonistic Katisha (Rosina Brandram) and disguised as an itinerant trombonist, the little bride-to-be and the inept musician fall in love. Ko-Ko, finding himself forced to hold an execution to save his civic post from abolition, joins a plot to fake the death of Nanki-Poo only to find out, too late, that he is a royal, and that having ''executed'' him he is in a worse spot than before. Ko-Ko is obliged to wed Katisha himself before the young man agrees to come safely back to life for a happy ending. Rutland Barrington was cast as Pooh-Bah, a venal nobleman and ''Lord High-Everything-Else,'' and Jessie Bond was the conspiring Pitti-Sing.

If the various elements of the tale were far from original, Gilbert brought them all together in his inimitable style and language and combined them into their most celebrated incarnation in *The Mikado.* Sullivan, back to his lightest and most winning style after the more weighty moments of *Princess Ida,* supplied a score in his best opéra-bouffe vein. Yum-Yum pondered her own beauty in ''The Moon and I'' and joined her sisters in declaring themselves ''Three Little Maids (from school)'' in fluttering harmonies, Nanki-Poo tenorized fluently ''A Wandering Minstrel, I,'' and Katisha plumbed emotion with a slightly incongruous sincerity in the burlesque drawing-room ballad ''Hearts Do Not Break.'' On the more regularly humorous side, Grossmith detailed a topical series of public nuisances in ''I've Got a Little List'' and wrung hearts with his phony tale of dying for love, ''Tit Willow,'' and Temple described how, as supreme magistrate of Japan, he would ''make the punishment fit the crime'' (Mikado's Song). A jolly hymn to ''The Flowers that Bloom in the Spring'' and an unaccompanied madrigal ''Brightly Dawns our Wedding Day'' were amongst the most winning ensembles, while in a first-act finale of sub-operatic proportions, with the maddened Katisha riding dramatically over the voices of the massed company like a contralto Valkyrie on speed, Sullivan turned out one of his choicest massed musical moments.

The Mikado was a superb success at the Savoy, setting up a new long-run record for a British musical play in London and a worldwide record for a Gilbert and Sullivan production which would last almost a century until a Broadway revival of *The Pirates of Penzance* topped it in 1981. After the care D'Oyly Carte had taken to protect, in particular, the copy- and stage-rights of *The Pirates of Penzance* and *Iolanthe* in America, arrangements for *The Mikado* went rather curiously astray. The score and libretto were published, making them public domain, and several American impresarii promptly leaped into production with *Mikado*s. The irrepressible Sydney Rosenfeld opened his under-cast, under-rehearsed, under-exact and un-orchestrated production in Chicago,

Plate 256. *Katisha (Heather Begg) shows her affection for Nanki-Poo (Peter Cousens) in the Australian Opera's production of* **The Mikado.**

where it was reviewed as ''execrable' and deemed to be little more than an opportunity for the local importer of Japanese wares to display his entire stock on stage, and found himself arrested and imprisoned when he tried to bring it to New York's Union Square Theater. When rumors of the preparation of a proper, first-class New York production hit Carte in London, he acted swiftly, secretly transporting a company headed by American prima donna Geraldine Ulmar, tenor Courtice Pounds and comic George Thorne from London to New York and opening with them at the Fifth Avenue Theater (19 August 1885) before the opposition J C Duff version was ready. Duff opened hurriedly the next night and thus Broadway was given the sight of two rival *Mikado*s playing side by side for three months. Then Duff cried enough and took his company off on tour, whilst Carte's ran on to its 250th performance.

At the same time, while Carte's touring companies continued to carry the show to the regions of Britain, *The Mikado* was staged by J C Williamson's Royal Comic Opera Company at Sydney's Theatre Royal with Nellie Stewart (Yum-Yum), Howard Vernon (Ko-Ko) and the Savoy company's Alice Barnett (Katisha) featured. Australia later welcomed further Savoy members when Alfred Cellier conducted the Melbourne season, which ran for a remarkable 101 consecutive nights, and when Leonora Braham (dubbed by a down-under critic ''the yummiest Yum-Yum of them all'') repeated her original role, alongside the Broadway Mikado, Federici. In South Africa, Frank Wheeler starred himself as Ko-Ko.

Success for *The Mikado* in Britain, America and the other English-speaking areas was fairly forseeable. What was not forseeable was the success it would have on the Continent. It was by no means the first Gilbert and Sullivan work to be played in German or in Hungarian, but it was the first to become a success in those languages on the same scale that it had been on home territory. Dresden and Berlin first saw the piece in English when the Wallner-Theater was visited by one of Carte's companies, headed by several of his American cast (Pounds, Federici, Elsie Cameron) and by David Fisher (who went mad, allegedly from playing Ko-Ko for too long, thus prompting a debate on ''are long runs injurious to the brain''). The German version was produced, two years later, at the Friedrich-Wilhelmstädtisches Theater, following its splendid success in Vienna. It was again a notable hit, and established the piece as the second most popular English musical on 19th- and early-20th-century German stages (*The Geisha,* another oriental musical, was the number one). In 1900 Sullivan himself conducted *The Mikado* in Berlin before an audience including the German emperor.

Viennese theatregoers also saw the Carte Continental tour, in 1886, in advance of Camillo Walzel's production of his own adaptation (w Richard Genée) at the Theater an der Wien in 1888, in which Sebastian Stelzer (Ko-Ko), Karl Streitmann (Nanki-Poo), Ottilie Collin (Yum-Yum), Therese Biedermann (Pitti-Sing) and Carl Lindau (Mikado) headed the cast. The show was played regularly in the theatre's repertoire over the next six years, passing its 100th performance on 27 May 1894, and it was brought back again in a 1901 production which included ''Harry Delaney's genuine Japanese Geisha Girls from Tokio, Japan'' with four dance routines amongst its attractions. It was also played at the Theater in der Josefstadt in 1899 and produced at the Raimundtheater in 1909 with Franz Glawatsch (Ko-Ko) and Marthe Dorda-Winternitz as a rather bulky Yum-Yum.

The Hungarian stage received the show late—Carte's company, which had toured freely through Holland, Scandinavia, Germany and Austria, canceled its visit to Pest because of a cholera epidemic—but with the same vigor. First produced at the Népszínház (ad Jenő Rákosi, Jenő Molnár) with Aranka Hegyi playing Nanki-Poo in travesty to the Yum-Yum of Ilka Pálmay and Célia Márgo (Katisha), József Németh (Ko-Ko), Vidor Kassai (Pooh-Bah) and Nina Fehér as a Peep-Bo renamed Pep-Si at the head of its cast, it was revived there in 1891 and again in 1905. Played in all the principal musical theatres of Hungary, it appeared notably at the Városi Színház (25 September 1924) in a new translation by Ferenc Molnár.

Moscow, Brussels (the first French-language version by Charles Kufferath at the Alhambra 23 December 1889, even though the show had been announced at Paris's Eden Théâtre several months earlier), Prague, Bucharest, Riga, Buenos Aires, Stockholm, Zagreb, Copenhagen and Florence all hosted various translations of *The Mikado,* and it ingrained itself into the heart of the international repertoire in a way no British comic opera had previously done.

Inevitably, given the magnitude of its success, attempts were made to burlesque *The Mikado* (although many of these were the kind of ''burlesques'' which simply permitted variety houses to play as much as possible of the show's score in some kind of context). These appeared under such titles as the less-than-imaginative *Mickey-Do* (Haverly's Minstrels), *Mick-ah-Doo* (Thatcher & Primrose Minstrels) or *My-Card-Oh!* (Hallen and Hart). Koster and Bial's didn't try to burlesque the title, they just gave a plungingly low comic version of the original, whilst James J McCloskey turned out *The Mikado of Brooklyn* (Hyde & Behmans 16 November 1885) for the enjoyment of the citizens of that city. A parody produced in Philadelphia was credited to the Anglo-French star Marius and Hevrley's Minstrels later gave a *The Black Mikado* by Thomas Leary. In Germany a one-act *Der Mizekado, ein Tag in Pititu* (Otto Ewald/F Beier) was produced at Kassel (26 December 1886). However, the show, its characters and score were, from very early on, not so much burlesqued as squeezed into all kinds of improbable shapes, concepts and rhythms. Reports came back from America during the original London run of ''heartrending liberties'' being taken with the show in Boston, where Richard Mansfield played Ko-Ko as an English fop, eyeglass and all. In Sweden, a hybrid was made from *The Mikado* and Lecocq's *Kosiki,* the show which had originally been called *Le Mikado.* In later American days it suffered from being minstrelly blackened, with Chauncey Olcott appearing as a burnt-cork Nanki-Poo; swung (*The Swing Mikado,* Chicago, 1938); and hotted (*The Hot Mikado* 23 March 1939). In South Africa it was rearranged into a sort of an opéra-jigabouffe as another *The Black Mikado* for a successful London run (Cambridge Theatre 24 April 1975, 472 performances) and a season in Paris, whilst in Berlin the accredited librettists Bernauer and Österreicher remade the piece as something like a revue for the Grosses Schauspielhaus. Max Pallenberg starred as Ko-Ko in a witless version in which Nanki Poo became the son of an American sugar millionaire and filched Katisha's ''Hearts Do Not Break,'' relyricked as a love ballad. The lacerated score was reorchestrated for a ''modern'' band, and Erik Charell filled the stage with acrobats and charlestoning chorines to distract from the butchered content. In Austria, Franz Reinl decided to give Nanki-Poo a boost in his 1954 version for Salzburg's Landestheater, and the resultant piece was called *Der Sohn des Mikado.* A successful English National Opera production of 1986 copied Richard Mansfield's example of a century earlier by throwing out the Japanese element and resituating the action in Victorian England, whilst New Jersey's Paper Mill Playhouse produced a *Mikado Inc* (16 May 1990) which equated Japan with commerce rather than cherry blossoms. A remade *The Hot Mikado* was given a showing in Washington, DC, in 1994 (Ford's Theatre) and in London in 1995 (Queen's Theatre 24 May).

In between the oddities and the remakes, however, many a talented director has been found capable of making Gilbert's enduring fun and unstringent satire ring through without eccentric aids, and *The Mikado* continues into its second century with its head as firmly on its shoulders as Ko-Ko's victims. London, which in one season in the 1980s welcomed no less than three different *Mikado*s, has most recently seen a production by the new D'Oyly Carte company, whilst Broadway saw its latest *Mikado* in a production brought from Stratford, Ontario, and played at the Virginia Theater (2 April 1987) for 46 performances, and the 1990s even saw *The Mikado* break through for its first showings in France.

Amongst the numerous film and television *Mikado*s have been a 1960 NBC-TV Bell Telephone Hour encapsulation with a starry cast including Groucho Marx (Ko-Ko), Helen Traubel (Katisha), Stanley Holloway (Pooh-Bah) and Dennis King (Mikado); a 1939 film with Martyn Green (Ko-Ko) and Kenny Baker (Nanki-Poo); a 1967 British film with Valerie Masterson (Yum-Yum) and members of the D'Oyly Carte company; and a 1963 *Cool Mikado* made by Michael Winner, starring Frankie Howerd and with limited relevance to the original. The new D'Oyly Carte company put their production, with Jill Pert as Katisha, on video in 1993.

USA: Museum, Chicago 6 July 1885, Union Square Theater, New York 20 July 1885; Australia: Theatre Royal, Sydney 14 November 1885; Germany: Residenztheater, Dresden (Eng) 1886, Wallner Theater (Eng) 2 June 1886; Austria: Carltheater *Der Mikado, ein Tag in Titipu* 1 September 1886; Hungary: Népszínház *A Mikádó* 10 December 1886; France: Opéra, Toulon (Eng) 3 May 1991, Tours (Fr) 7 November 1992

Films: Victor Schertzinger 1939, D'Oyly Carte Co 1967, Brent-Walker video 1982, Stratford Festival video 1982, ENO video 1987, D'Oyly Carte video 1993, etc

Recordings: complete (Decca, HMV), selection (TER), *The Hot Mikado* (First Night), etc

MILHER [HERMIL, Ange Édouard] (b Marseille, 25 September 1833; d Aix-les-Bains, 13 August 1898).

A popular comic actor-singer on the French stage, from his Parisian debut at the Folies-Dramatiques in 1865, in the earliest days of opéra-bouffe, until his death just before the turn of the century, Milher had fine roles in many of Hervé's earliest works, creating parts in *L'Oeil crevé* (1867, Geromé), *Chilpéric* (1868, Doctor Ricin), *Le Petit Faust* (1869, Valentin) and *Les Turcs* (1869, Ababoum), as well as in the later *La Belle Poule* (1875, Baron de la Champignole) and *Alice de Nevers* (1875, Sire de Courbaril). He also created the role of duped van Ostebal in Jonas's triumphant *Le Canard à trois becs* (1869), played in the Folies-Dramatiques revival of *Les Chevaliers de la table ronde* (1872, Le Duc Rodomont) and alongside the underclad Blanche d'Antigny in the musicalised *Mazeppa* (1872), and got his come-ouchance as the villainous Fulbert in Litolff's *Héloïse et Abélard* (1872). He also appeared with Marie Desclauzas as the comical secret agent Grison in *La Belle Bourbonnaise* (1874), in Vasseur's *La Blanchissuese de Berg-op-Zoom* (1875), and created the roles of the Prince de Soubise in *Jeanne, Jeannette et Jeanneton* (1876), of Prince Ramollini in *La Foire St-Laurent* (1877), and, above all, the unusually pathetico-dramatic role of the miser, Gaspard, in *Les Cloches de Corneville* (1877) in which he was also seen in Belgium (1878).

Milher also played in such less successful pieces as *La Fiancée du roi de Garbe* (1874, Zaï), *Le Pompon* (1875, Don Melchior) and *Fleur de Baiser* (1876, boatswain) before switching from the Folies-Dramatiques to the Palais-Royal and, if that house provided little in the way of musical shows, he guested outside on occasions, repeating his most famous roles and appearing in such pieces as the spectacular *L'Arbre de Noël* (Porte-Saint-Martin, 1880, Oscar de Pulna). Milher continued to play on the musical stage up till his last days, being seen at the Palais Royal in *Le Commandant Laripète* (1892), at the Variétés as Tournesol XXIV in *Le Carillon* and in his old role in *L'Oeil crevé* in 1896 and as Le Commandant in *Le Pompier de Service* in 1897.

Alongside his career as an actor, Milher was also a prolific writer for the stage, under his real name of Hermil, providing a long run of mostly one-act entertainments—comedies, opérettes, revues, vaudevilles, many latterly written with his Palais-Royal confrere (and later Variétés director) Armand Numès—for the Folies-Saint-Antoine, the Théâtre Cluny, La Cigale and for a considerable number of other small Parisian and provincial houses.

1863 **Un mari qui fait des farces** (Eugène Moniot) Théâtre des Champs-Élysées 14 December

1864 **Un Troupier en bonne fortune** (Moniot) Théâtre des jeunes artistes 5 October

1866 **Encore un sapeur** (Camille Michel) 1 act Folies Saint-Antoine 1 September

1866 **Les Rendezvous interrompus** (Moniot) 1 act Théâtre du 19ème Siècle 6 May

1873 **La Fille de Dagobert** (Moniot) 1 act Folies-Bergère 19 October

1873 **Dans le bain** (w Gardel) 1 act Eldorado 7 April

1874 **Flon-flons et flic-flacs** (Moniot) Théâtre de la Tour d'Auvergne 20 February

1874 **La Noce à Briochet** (Hervé/w Gardel) Délassements-Comiques 26 April

1875 **Le Voyage du Prince Soleil** (Moniot/w Frantz Beauvallet, Henri Buguet) Théâtre du Parc 2 October

1879 **Un Concièrgicide** (Francis Chassaigne/w Armand Numès) 1 act Eldorado 23 August

1880 **Le Carnaval de Blizimard** (Charles Thony/w Numès) Alcazar 12 March

1880 **Atchi** (Frédéric Barbier/w Numès) 1 act Eldorado

1882 **Boum! Servi chaud!** (A de Villebichot/w Numès) 1 act Eldorado 20 June

1882 **Ma vieille branche** (Édouard Deransart/w Numès) 1 act Alcazar

1882 **Mon p'tit oncle** (Thony/Numès) 1 act Eldorado 9 September

1883 **Soupirs de coeur** (Jean Mitchell/w Paul Meyan, Numès) 1 act Eldorado 21 April

1883 **Politique en ménage** (Thony/w Numès) 1 act Dijon 21 July

1883 **La Cuisinière** (Thony/w Numès) 1 act Dijon 21 July

1883 **Le Nègre de la Porte-Saint-Denis** (Louis Desormes/w Numès) 1 act Eldorado 25 August

1884 **Malbrough** (Deransart/w Numès) Casino de Bougival 24 June

1885 **L'École de Tatété-les-Nèfles** (Thony/w Numès) 1 act Eden Concert 17 March

1885 **Suzette, Suzanne et Suzon** (Tac-Coën/w Numès) 1 act Eden Concert

1885 **Fièvre phyllaxérique** (Frantz Liouville/w Numès, Meyan) 1 act

1886 **Le Roi Mabouc** (''L Herpin'' [ie, L Perey]/w Numès) Scala 2 November

1889 **L'Étudiant pauvre** (*Der Bettelstudent*) French version w Numès (Théâtre des Menus-Plaisirs)

Other title attributed: *Tog* (Francis Chassaigne/w Numès)

MILK AND HONEY Musical play in 2 acts by Don Appell. Music and lyrics by Jerry Herman. Martin Beck Theater, New York, 10 October 1961.

The first book musical and first Broadway assignment of composer-lyricist Jerry Herman, after three off-Broadway revues, *Milk and Honey* had its starting point in its writers' decision to make a musical set in Israel. As a result, they spent several weeks in Israel but they came up with a script which, in fact, used the country only as a background to a main story of middle-aged romance which was wholly American and, of course, Jewish. The principals were widowed Ruth (Mimi Benzell) and separated Phil (Robert Weede) who fall in love in the Middle East whilst he is visiting his daughter and she is touring with a ladies' group. Ultimately, they separate, but with the hope that a divorce will soon leave Phil free. Alongside them, Phil's daughter Barbara (Lanna Saunders) and her husband (Tommy Rall) faced the wild-West challenge of making their home in a new land, whilst the comical widow Clara (Molly Picon) led her consoeurs in the search for a man.

The score was compiled of a combination of locally colored numbers—amongst which Phil's directions on the meaning of ''Shalom'' and the title song both proved highly successful—of thoroughly singable love songs for the two operatically experienced stars (''That Was Yesterday,'' ''As Simple as That'') and for the rich-voiced young Rall (''I Will Follow You''); and of what were virtual stand-up comic spots for Jewish-theatre star Molly Picon (''Chin Up Ladies'' and the pre–*Hello, Dolly!* monologue to her dead husband, ''Hymn to Hymie'').

Gerald Oestreicher's production ran for 543 performances on Broadway and toured thereafter, but *Milk and Honey* did not reach out to productions in the other main musical-theatre centers.

The show was revived by the American Jewish Theater in a revised version in May 1994 with Spiro Malas, Avi Hoffman and Chevi Colton featured.

Recording: original cast (RCA)

MILLAR, Gertie [MILLER, Gertrude] (b Manningham, Bradford, 20 February 1879; d Chiddingford,

Plate 257. *Gaiety star* **Gertie Millar** *in* The Girls of Gottenberg.

25 April 1952). Daintily pretty musical-comedy star who became the Gaiety Theatre's headliner in the early part of the 20th century.

The daughter of a Yorkshire millworker and an unknown father, Gertie Millar made her first stage appearances as a child, playing the girl babe in the pantomime *Babes in the Wood* at St James's Theatre, Manchester, in 1892. As a teenager she began touring in musical comedy, appearing as Dora in *The New Barmaid* for Alexander Loftus (1898), in Frank Carlyon's musical-comedy company as the ingenue in *The Silver Lining* (1898), as Sadie Pinkhose in *The Lady Detective* (1899) and then with a touring company playing *The Messenger Boy,* in which she was spotted by the show's composer Lionel Monckton. As a result, she was taken to London to play the role which would have gone to Rosie Boote had she not gone off to become a marchioness—the tiny part of the bridemaid, Cora (''Captivating Cora'') in *The Toreador* (1901).

Twenty-two-year-old Gertie stole the show, much as Miss Boote had done last time round, but she was not in such a hurry for her coronet. For the meanwhile, she simply saw her little role much enlarged as she set off on a road which would make her both a star and Mrs Lionel Monckton in double-quick time. She appeared at the Gaiety in increasingly important soubrette parts in *The Orchid* (1903, Violet Anstruther), *The Spring Chicken* (1905, Rosalie), *The New Aladdin* (1906, t/o Lally) and *The Girls of Gottenberg* (1907, Mitzi), then left temporarily to play Franzi in Edwardes's production of *A Waltz Dream* and to visit America to repeat her *Girls of Gottenberg* part, returning to star in the title roles of what would be two of her most memorable shows: Edwardes's productions of *Our Miss Gibbs* (1909, Mary Gibbs ''Moonstruck'') and *The Quaker Girl* (1910, Prudence ''The Quaker Girl,'' ''The Little Grey Bonnet''). She had a new role, Lady Babby, written for her in Edwardes's production of the otherwise too vocally hefty *Gipsy Love* (1912), starred in *The Dancing Mistress* (1912, Nancy Joyce), *The Marriage Market* (1913, Kitty Kent) and finally in a revival of *A Country Girl* (1914, Nan).

With the change of temperature that came over the musical theatre around wartime, Miss Millar tried her hand at revue in Monckton's *Bric à Brac* and *Airs and Graces* and ventured two musicals by revue producers, Cochran's *Houp-la!* and Charlot's *Flora.* Both the musicals were solid flops, the first real disasters (*A Waltz Dream* being only a half-disaster) that she had known in her career as London's favorite musical-comedy soubrette of more than a decade's standing. She and Monckton both renounced the new-style musical theatre, retired, and, after her husband's death, Gertie finally followed Rosie Boote into the peerage, for a seven-year run as the Countess of Dudley.

MILLAR, Ronald [Graeme] (Sir) (b Reading, 12 November 1919; d London, 16 April 1998).

Originally an actor and then a playwright, Millar had his first connection with the musical theatre when he was cast in the almost non-singing juvenile lead role of *Jenny Jones* (1944), a piece which he was later called upon to doctor (under the pseudonym John Jowett) on the road. He subsequently had considerable success as an author in the straight theatre (*Frieda, Waiting for Gillian, The Bride and the Bachelor, They Don't Grow on Trees, The Masters,* etc) and as a screenwriter (his Hollywood credits included the rewritten *Rose-Marie*), and found significant success on the musical stage in 1964 with his first attempt, an adaptation of *The Barretts of Wimpole Street,* the tale of the poets Browning and Barrett, as *Robert and Elizabeth* (libretto and lyrics). A second piece, *On the Level,* written in a very different idiom, was less successful, and when several proposed projects, including a musical version of Christopher Isherwood's Berlin stories, fell through he returned to the straight theatre, venturing back onto the musical stage only with a revusical biomusical, *Once More with Music* (Yvonne Arnaud Theatre, Guildford) for the aged Cicely Courtneidge and Jack Hulbert, and—in the same way that he had begun—as an uncredited play doctor on *Peg.*

He was knighted for services to politics after spending a number of years as speechwriter to Mrs Margaret Thatcher, PM, during which time he was responsible for coming up with many of the sometimes theatre-linked "catchphrases" and images which have entered everyday speech and everyday journalese as a result. Not to mention a campaign song to the melody of "Hello, Dolly."

1964 **Robert and Elizabeth** (Ron Grainer) Lyric Theatre 20 October

1966 **On the Level** (Grainer) Shaftesbury Theatre 19 April

Autobiography: *A View from the Wings* (Weidenfeld & Nicolson, London, 1993)

MILLAUD, [Arthur David Paul] Albert [Samuel] (b Paris, 13 January 1844; d Paris, 22 October 1892).

Alongside the famous "duos" of the French musical stage—Meilhac and Halévy, Chivot and Duru, Leterrier and Vanloo, and even those celebrated writers such as Nuitter, Tréfeu or Clairville who popped in and out of less wholly faithful collaborations as they collected their hits—the name of Albert Millaud remains one which has much less éclat. Yet Millaud, too, wrote internationally successful shows with Offenbach, Hervé and Lecocq, and for a solid half-dozen years had his name attached not only to the biggest musical hits in town, but to the biggest star of the musical theatre as well.

In the mid-1870s, with only one opéra-comique to his credit, journalist (*Figaro* as "Petit Nemesis"), travel writer and versifier (*Le Péché Veniel, Plutus*) Millaud became one of Offenbach's preferred collaborators. With, apparently, some uncredited help from Halévy he wrote the libretto and lyrics to *Madame l'Archiduc,* and in collaboration with Halévy's usual partner, Meilhac, he provided the composer with the text for *La Créole*—like the earlier piece starring Anna Judic. He subsequently worked with Eugène Grangé on the text for the revue *Les Hannetons* (Bouffes-Parisiens 22 April 1875), wrote the one-act *Tarte à la crème* (in which Offenbach supplied a little music), and contributed without credit to *Le Voyage dans la lune* after Offenbach had dragged him in, as the nearest handy writer, when he suddenly needed some words.

The couple of busy years of teaming with Offenbach past, Millaud found his future in the star they had shared. Between 1878 and 1884, in varying collaborations of which he was the continuing element, he provided the Théâtre des Variétés and its star, Anna Judic, with the series of vaudevilles which were the highlight of her career and also of that period of the French musical theatre. *Niniche, La Femme à papa, La Roussotte, Lili, Mam'zelle Nitouche* and *La Cosaque,* from the most flamingly successful (*Mam'zelle Nitouche*) to even the least long-lasting (*La Cosaque*), went around the world, played in a variety of languages whilst also becoming the bases for a number of other musicals and plays in Austria, Germany, Hungary, America and Britain. And Millaud compounded it all by becoming the second husband of the widowed Madame Judic.

When the famous run of vaudevilles was done, Millaud continued in the musical theatre, writing the Aristophanean libretto for Lecocq's *Plutus,* and two further—and this time not as successful—vaudevilles, *La Noce à Nini* and *La Japonaise* (15 performances) for the Variétés. The genre had done its dash, but much of the dashing had been done by author Millaud. And, of course, his wife. That wife, however, was to be his undoing. When Anna starting taking lovers, the devoted husband started taking morphia. His consolation killed him at the age of 48.

1873 **La Quenouille de verre** (Charles Grisart/w Henri Heugel ["Henri Moreno"]), Théâtre des Bouffes-Parisiens 7 November

1874 **Madame l'Archiduc** (Jacques Offenbach/[w Ludovic Halévy]), Théâtre des Bouffes-Parisiens 31 October

1875 **La Créole** (Offenbach/w Henri Meilhac) Théâtre des Bouffes-Parisiens 3 November

1875 **Tarte à la crême** (Offenbach) 1 act Théâtre des Bouffes-Parisiens 14 December

1878 **Niniche** (Marius Boullard/w Alfred Hennequin) Théâtre des Variétés 15 February

1879 **La Femme à papa** (Hervé/w Hennequin) Théâtre des Variétés 3 December

1881 **La Roussotte** (Hervé, Lecocq, Marius Boullard/w Henri Meilhac, Ludovic Halévy) Théâtre des Variétés 28 January

1882 **Lili** (Hervé/w Hennequin, Ernest Blum) Théâtre des Variétés 10 January

1883 **Mam'zelle Nitouche** (Hervé/w Meilhac) Théâtre des Variétés 26 January

1883 **Joséphine** (Louis Varney) 1 act Casino de Paramé (Trouville) 10 August; El Dorado 23 September; Théâtre des Variétés 16 March 1884

1884 **La Cosaque** (Hervé/w Meilhac) Théâtre des Variétés 1 February

1886 **Plutus** (Charles Lecocq/w Gaston Jollivet) Opéra-Comique 31 March

1887 **La Noce à Nini** (Hervé/w Émile de Najac) Théâtre des Variétés 19 March

1888 **La Japonaise** (Varney/w de Najac) Théâtre des Variétés 23 November

MILLER, Marilyn[n] [REYNOLDS, Mary Ellen or Marilynn] (b Evansville, Ind, 1 September 1898; d New

York, 7 April 1936). Diminutive, blonde dancing star of the Broadway 1920s.

Marilyn[n] Miller spent the earliest part of her career in vaudeville as part of a family act, billed at first as ''The Columbian Trio and Mdlle Sugarlump'' (she, aged four, was the sugarlump) and later the Columbian Five (mother, father, sisters Ruth and Claire and Marilynn), playing in America, Britain, Australia, the West Indies and on the Pacific circuit. She made her first Broadway appearances in 1914 and 1915 dancing and doing impressions (one of her ''targets'' was Clifton Crawford, another Adeline Genée) in the *Passing Show* series of revues.

Her first musical-comedy role, at the age of 20, was in the Shuberts' unremarkable *Fancy Free* (1918, Betty Pestlethwaite) alongside the same Clifton Crawford, but it was under the management of Florenz Ziegfeld (she dropped the extra ''n'' which she had originally sported on her Christian name at his suggestion) that she made her mark—first in two editions of his *Follies* and then in the title role of Jerome Kern's *Sally* (1920), where she introduced ''Look for the Silver Lining'' and ''Wild Rose'' in between her featured dance spots.

Miss Miller subsequently appeared on Broadway as J M Barrie's *Peter Pan* (1924), but had more success in the written-to-order title role of Kern's *Sunny* (1925, ''Who?''), a patent and pretty attempt to photocopy *Sally,* before going on to star in two more shows for Ziegfeld—Sigmund Romberg and George Gershwin's *Rosalie* (1928, Rosalie) and, alongside the Astaires, in the Vincent Youmans musical comedy *Smiles* (1930)—with rather less success. She then quit Broadway for Hollywood, where she starred in the screen versions of *Sally* and *Sunny* and in *Her Majesty Love* (1932), returning to Broadway for one final stage appearance in the revue *As Thousands Cheer* (''Easter Parade'') before her early death.

The leading character of the Jerome Kern musical comedy *The Cabaret Girl* (London 1922), revealingly named Marilynn Morgan, and played by Dorothy Dickson, was lightly based on Miss Miller, and in 1988 she was portrayed on the musical stage in the London extravaganza *Ziegfeld* by six-foot red-headed Australian dancer/actress Amanda Rickard who was physically as far away from the original as had been Judy Garland (*Till the Clouds Roll By,* 1946) and June Haver (*Look for the Silver Lining,* 1949) who had been the Marilyn[n] Millers on the screen.

Biography: Harris, W G: *The Other Marilyn* (Arbor House, New York, 1985)

MILLÖCKER, Carl (b Vienna, 29 April 1842; d Baden bei Wien, 31 December 1899). One of the trio of Viennese composers who were responsible for the bulk of the outstanding Operetten of the 19th-century Austrian stage.

The son of a goldsmith, Millöcker first worked, not very wholeheartedly, for his father whilst taking his first steps towards a career in music by studying the flute with a musician from the orchestra at the Theater an der Wien. He learned piano from books, and was given lessons in composition by an elderly city official with musical connections who tutored young musicians in his free time. He later took flute lessons at the Vienna Gesellschaft der Musikfreunde, and finally began a theatre-music career at the age of 16, playing in the woodwind section of the orchestra at the Theater in der Josefstadt.

During his time as an orchestral player, Millöcker wrote his first compositions, winning encouragement so it is said from no less an authority than Franz von Suppé, and over half a dozen years he turned out a regular stream of songs, orchestral music and theatre pieces. In 1864 Suppé was instrumental in getting him appointed as a conductor at the Thalia-Theater in Graz, and it was there that the young man's first stage works, the one-act burlesques *Der tote Gast* and *Die lustigen Binder,* were staged the following year. Towards the end of 1866 he left Graz, taking with him the theatre's leading lady, Fräulein Kling, who had become his wife, to go back to Vienna and employment at the Theater an der Wien, under the management of Friedrich Strampfer. This engagement, however, proved unproductive of the sort of opportunities for which he was looking as a composer and even as a conductor, and he moved on to a conducting job at the less up-market but more amenable Harmonietheater, a short-lived but enthusiastic establishment set up by the Countess von Pasqualati.

There Millöcker succeeded in getting a production for his first regular Operette, *Diana,* a medium-sized piece written to a mythological-satirical text by Josef Braun, the librettist of Suppé's *Flotte Bursche. Diana* was produced in January 1867, after its rather too daring libretto had at first led to its being postponed whilst it was sent back to the author for softening up. It was played for 13 successive nights, but then put away until a revised version was produced nearly a century later at Nuremberg (Städtische Bühnen 21 March 1959). Millöcker also supplied the music for several Possen and Singspiele—the local versions of musical comedies in the true sense of the words—for the Harmonietheater, and he worked on several pieces with the to-be-famous playwright Ludwig Anzengruber, at that stage an actor and house writer at the theatre. In 1868 he moved again, this time to Budapest, to take up a post as conductor at the Deutsches Theater, and it was there that he heard performed his first full-length score, a resetting of the Cogniard brothers' famous spectacular *Le Royaume des femmes* produced as

Die Fraueninsel. He returned to Vienna again the following year to take up a position as number-two conductor back at the Theater an der Wien and to place another full-length piece, *Der Regiments-Tambour,* at his youthful stamping ground, the Theater in der Josefstadt.

During the 14 years which he subsequently spent at the Theater an der Wien, where he was ultimately promoted to first conductor, Millöcker turned out original music and songs for a wide variety of pieces—revues, plays, many Singspiele and Possen, and pieces described as ''ländliche Gemälde'' (''local pictures'') or ''Lebensbilder'' (''life pictures''), but all variants of the comedy-with-songs-and-music genre, and mainly from the highly successful pens of Alois Berla, O F Berg and Karl Costa. Amongst the musical plays, the 1871 musical comedy *Drei Paar Schuhe* was a major success, being subsequently revived many, many times and giving Millöcker a pair of genuine hits with ''I und meine Bua'' and ''Bei Tag bin ich hektisch.'' Further successes, in Vienna and beyond, came with Berla's *Abenteuer in Wien* (1873), the revusical *Erinnerung an bessere Zeiten* (1874), which introduced Alexander Girardi to the Theater an der Wien, Berg's Possen *Der barmherzige Bruder* (1874) and *Der närrische Schuster* (1877) and Costa's *Ein Blitzmädel* (1875) and *Ihr Korporal* (1878).

In 1878, encouraged by the success of Strauss's *Die Fledermaus,* Millöcker ventured his nearest approach to date to a legitimate, full-sized Operette with the score for Berla's comical piece *Das verwunschene Schloss.* With Girardi and Gallmeyer in its starring roles, *Das verwunschene Schloss* and its songs ('' 'S is a Bisserl Liab' und a Bisserl Treu,'' ''Dalkata Bua!,'' ''O, du himmelblauer See!'') were first-rate and international successes and, although he produced further winners in the following years in the Posse genre, notably the 1880 *Die Näherin,* Millöcker devoted himself, from here on, principally to writing musically substantial Operetten. *Gräfin Dubarry* (1879) was only a moderate success (27 performances), but *Apajune, der Wassermann* (1880), seen 45 times at the Theater an der Wien before moving on, gave him another internationally played success, and *Die Jungfrau von Belleville* (1881) confirmed that success before in 1882, after nearly 20 years of composing for the theatre, Millöcker won his greatest triumph of all with the production of *Der Bettelstudent. Der Bettelstudent* not only proved the Theater an der Wien's most important hit since *Die Fledermaus,* but it also launched one of Viennese Operette's all-time greatest song hits, the loping baritone waltz ''Ach, ich hab' sie ja nur auf die Schulter geküsst,'' before moving on to enormous international success.

From *Der Bettelstudent* on, Millöcker's works almost all won productions around the world: the swashbuckling *Gasparone,* which has remained in the repertoire in Austria and Germany for the century since its production; *Der Feldprediger,* for a while highly popular (as *The Black Hussar*) in America; *Der Viceadmiral,* which suffered a little in the shadow of the production of Strauss's *Der Zigeunerbaron* and was played only 30 times first up; *Die sieben Schwaben;* and his most successful piece after *Der Bettelstudent,* the comical *Der arme Jonathan. Der arme Jonathan* provided a particularly happy role for the theatre's adored star, Alexander Girardi, but, in spite of worldwide success in the 1890s, it has not survived in the repertoire with the strength of the more physically picturesque and endlessly revamped *Gasparone.*

Das Sonntagskind (1892) was another success and *Der Probekuss* (1894) played 55 times in its first run, but, in the year of the latter's production, Millöcker suffered a stroke. He produced one more Operette thereafter, the indifferently received *Nordlicht* (1896)—a part of which was later reused to make up the score of a piece called *Der Damenschneider,* which topped a hundred straight nights in Berlin after the composer's death—but the long and brilliant career which had placed him alongside Suppé and Johann Strauss as one of the three pillars of the 19th-century Viennese school of Operette was at an end.

Two of a number of pasticcio Operetten made from his music, *Jung Heidelberg* (arr Ernst Reiterer/Leopold Krenn, Carl Lindau, Raimundtheater 9 July 1904, Neues Konigliches Opernhaus, Berlin 1905) and *Cousin Bobby* (arr L Sanger/Benno Jacobson, Franz Wagner, Theater des Westens, Berlin 29 December 1906) both found some success and productions in several countries.

Millöcker, as played by Paul Hörbiger, was the ''hero'' of the film *Operettenklänge* (1945) and also appeared as a character in the film *Operette* where, although subsidiary to theatre manager Franz Jauner in the text, he was played by Curd Jürgens.

1865 **Der tote Gast** (J L Harisch) 1 act Thalia-Theater, Graz 21 December

1865 **Die lustigen Binder** (Gustav Stolze) 1 act Thalia-Theater, Graz 21 December

1866 **Kleine Kinder** (Poly Henrion) 1 act Harmonietheater 20 October

1866 **Sachsen in Österreich** (Henrion) 1 act Harmonietheater 24 October

1866 **Wenn man Leben ins Haus bringt** 1 act Harmonietheater 3 November

1866 **Die Lehrbuben** (Josef Doppler) 1 act Harmonietheater 3 December

1866 **Stübenmädel-Geschichten, or Der junge Herr auf Nädeln** (Carl F Stix) 1 act Harmonietheater 8 December

1867 **(Die keusche) Diana** (Josef Braun) Harmonietheater 2 January

1867 **Die Neujahrstag** (Karl Elmar) 1 act Harmonietheater 5 January

1867 **Die Diamantengrotte** (Karl Riedl) Harmonietheater 7 January

1867 **Der Millionen-Bräutigam** (Doppler) Harmonietheater 19 January

1867 **Der Reformatürk** (Ludwig Anzengruber) Harmonietheater 26 January

1867 **Brave Stadtleute** (Henrion) Harmonietheater 6 February

1867 **Das Mädel aus Blitzblau** (Henrion) Harmonietheater 6 February

1867 **Die Eselshaut** (Eugen Sporck) Harmonietheater 10 February

1867 **Der Telegraphist in der Nacht** (Anzengruber) Harmonietheater

1867 **Der Sackpfeifer** (Anzengruber) 1 act Harmonietheater

1868 **Die Fraueninsel** (*Asszonyok szigete*) (Théodore Cogniard, Hippolyte Cogniard ad) Deutsches Theater, Budapest

1869 **Der Regiments-Tambour** Theater in der Josefstadt 23 October

1869 **Schottenfeld und Ringstrasse** (Alois Berla) Theater an der Wien 3 December

1870 **Bartelmanns Leiden** (Hugo Müller) Theater an der Wien 25 April

1870 **Wallach Menelaus** (Berla) Theater an der Wien 7 June

1870 **Die Kinder von Ungefahr** (Berla) Theater an der Wien 7 September

1870 **Grand Hotel** (Leopold Feldmann) Theater an der Wien 7 December

1871 **Drei Paar Schuhe** (Karl Görlitz ad Berla) Theater an der Wien 5 January

1871 **Die beiden Elfen** (Julius Feld) Theater an der Wien 19 March

1871 **In Paris** (Berla) Theater an der Wien 6 June

1871 **Gewonnen Herzen** (Müller ad Josef Böhm) Theater an der Wien 14 August

1871 **Der letzte Nationalgardist** (O F Berg) Theater an der Wien 23 September

1871 **Wähler und Quäler** (Berla) Theater an der Wien 21 October

1871 **Die Veilchendame** (Eduard Dorn) Theater an der Wien 26 December

1872 **Kläffer** (C Gärtner) Theater an der Wien 25 March

1872 **Ein nagender Wurm** (aka *Wechselbrief und Briefwechsel*) (Jules Moinaux ad Josef Weyl) Theater an der Wien 15 July

1872 **Das Haus Wiener und Sohn** (aka *Der Millionenschwindel*) (Dorn) Theater an der Wien 20 August

1873 **Abenteuer in Wien** (aka *Herr Bendels Abenteuer*) (Berla) Theater an der Wien 20 January

1873 **Theatralische Weltausstellungsträume** (Berla) Theater an der Wien 9 August

1873 **Die Tochter des Wucherers** (Anzengruber) Theater an der Wien 17 October

1873 **Gift** (J E Mand) Theater an der Wien 7 November

1874 **Die Prinzipien des Herrn Bezirksberger** (Julius Johann Krassnigg) Theater an der Wien 1 February

1874 **Durchgegangene Weiber** (Berla) Theater an der Wien 14 February

1874 **Erinnerung an bessere Zeiten** (Berg) Theater an der Wien 12 June

1874 **Die aufgeweckten Götter** (Berg) 1 act Theater an der Wien 12 July

1874 **Die Carlisten in Spanien** (Berla) Theater an der Wien 14 August

1874 **Der barmherzige Bruder** (Berg) Theater an der Wien 20 October

1874 **Die Frau von Brestl** (Berg) Theater an der Wien 25 December

1875 **Der Musik des Teufels** (Berla) Theater an der Wien 17 April

1875 **Dr Haslinger** (Berg) Theater an der Wien 1 November

1876 **Die schlimmen(de) Töchter** (Berg) Theater an der Wien 12 February

1876 **Der Confusionsrath** (Julius Rosen) Theater an der Wien 8 March

1876 **Der elegante Toni** (aka *Hass und Liebe*) (Alois Blank) 1 act Theater an der Wien 1 April

1876 **Die Reise durch Wien in 80 Stunden** (Hermann Salingré) Theater an der Wien 26 May

1877 **Ein Blitzmädel** (Karl Costa) Theater an der Wien 4 February

1877 **Der Löwe des Tages** (Heinrich Wilken) Theater an der Wien 1 April

1877 **Die Reise nach Sibirien** (Karl Bruno) Theater an der Wien 21 April

1877 **Hasemanns Tochter** (Adolphe L'Arronge) Carltheater 6 October

1877 **Ein Kassastück** (Costa) Theater an der Wien 21 October

1877 **Der närrische Schuster** (Berg) Theater an der Wien 31 October

1878 **Die Landpomeranze** (Alois Just) Theater an der Wien 12 January

1878 **Ihr Korporal** (Costa) Theater an der Wien 19 January

1878 **Das verwunschene Schloss** (Berla) Theater an der Wien 30 March

1878 **Die bezähmte Bisgurn** (Anton Langer) Theater an der Wien 10 April

1878 **Der Untaugliche** (Berg) Theater an der Wien 30 October

1878 **Die Trutzige** (Anzengruber) Theater an der Wien 8 November

1878 **Plausch net Pepi** (Berla) Theater an der Wien 23 November

1879 **Himmelschlüssel** (Costa) Theater an der Wien 15 March

1879 **Der Theaterteufel** (Berla) Theater an der Wien 29 March

1879 **Die umkehrte Freit** (Anzengruber) 1 act Theater an der Wien 4 April

1879 **Gräfin Dubarry** (F Zell, Richard Genée) Theater an der Wien 31 October

- 1879 **Aus'm g'wohnten Gleis** (Anzengruber) Theater an der Wien 25 December
- 1880 **Die Näherin** (Ludwig Held) Theater an der Wien 13 March
- 1880 **Vaterfreuden** (Theodore Taube) Theater an der Wien 12 November
- 1880 **Apajune, der Wassermann** (Zell, Genée) Theater an der Wien 18 December
- 1881 **Herz-Ass** (Karl A Görner) Theater an der Wien 29 January
- 1881 **Ihre Familie** (Berla) Theater an der Wien 12 February
- 1881 **Die Jungfrau von Belleville** (Zell, Genée) Theater an der Wien 29 October
- 1882 **Der Mann im Monde** (Costa, Eduard Jacobson) Theater an der Wien 16 February
- 1882 **Ein süsses Kind** (Franz von Schönthan) Theater an der Wien 1 April
- 1882 **Der Bettelstudent** (Zell, Genée) Theater an der Wien 6 December
- 1884 **Gasparone** (Zell, Genée) Theater an der Wien 26 January
- 1884 **Der Feldprediger** (Hugo Wittmann, Alois Wohlmuth) Theater an der Wien 31 October
- 1886 **Der Dieb** (Berla) 1 act Vaudeville Theater April
- 1886 **Der Viceadmiral** (Zell, Genée) Theater an der Wien 9 October
- 1887 **Die sieben Schwaben** (Wittmann, Julius Bauer) Theater an der Wien 29 October
- 1890 **Der arme Jonathan** (Wittmann, Bauer) Theater an der Wien 4 January
- 1892 **Das Sonntagskind** (Wittmann, Bauer) Theater an der Wien 16 January
- 1894 **Der Probekuss** (Wittmann, Bauer) Theater an der Wien 22 December
- 1896 **Nordlicht** (aka *Der rote Graf*) (Wittmann) Theater an der Wien 22 December
- 1898 **Der Maler Veri** (Bruno Hartl-Mitius) Theater an der Wien 5 February
- 1901 **Der Damenschneider** (Wittmann, Louis Hermann) Friedrich-Wilhelmstädtisches Theater; Carltheater 14 September

MILSTER, Angelika (b Neustrelitz, 9 December 1951).

One of the outstanding performers of the modern German musical theatre.

Angelika Milster made her debut at the Hamburg Thalia-Theater in 1971 and, in a career which has mixed theatre appearances with frequent film and television ones, was subsequently seen as Anna in *Feuerwerk* at Verden (1972), at the Berlin Schiller-Theater and at Düsseldorf as Gabrielle in *Pariser Leben* (1979, 1980) and at the Theater des Westens as Bianca in *Kiss Me, Kate* (1980). She played at the Zürich Opernhaus as Sally Bowles in *Cabaret* (1981) and in the title role of the musical *Eva Korngold* (1982), and in 1983 was the first German-language Grizabella in *Cats* at the Theater an der Wien. She followed up as the soloist in the German version of *Song and Dance* (1987) and in several revues before creating the role of Hilde Neumann in the musical *Blue Jeans* (1994) at the Theater des Westens, where she later played Rose in *Gypsy* (1997).

MILY-MEYER [MAYER, Émilie] (b 1852; d Paris, 8 July 1927). Impishly boyish, yet obviously feminine soubrette who became a major Parisian star.

The tiny, dark musical comedienne known as Mily-Meyer made her first Parisian appearances at the El Dorado and the Alcazar d'Hiver, but shot to fame in a barely comic role, as the petite Duchesse in Lecocq's hugely successful *Le Petit Duc* (1878, ''Je t'aime,'' ''Ah! Qu'on est bien'') and went on from there to build an oustanding career of some 30 years in the musical theatre. In, at first, often theoretically secondary soubrette roles she succeeded on a number of occasions in stealing a show before being confirmed herself as a top-billable name. She followed up her success in *Le Petit Duc* by creating other supporting roles at the Théâtre de la Renaissance: as the piquant little Colombe, with a tiny number in the second act of *La Camargo* (1878); as Jacqueline, the innkeeper's wife, in *La Petite Mademoiselle* (1879); and in breeches as the little sergeant Flambart in Planquette's *Les Voltigeurs de la 32ème* (1880). She played Aveline in the revived *La Marjolaine* (1880), introduced the comic washerwoman Marceline in Offenbach's posthumous *Belle Lurette* (1880), played soubrette roles in *Ninette* and *Janot* (1881, Suzon), created Offenbach's *Mademoiselle Moucheron* (1881), took a role specially introduced into a new version of *L'Oeil crevé* (1881) without great success, and appeared in the roles of Catherine in the play *La Cigale* and of Carmen in Jonas's opérette *La Bonne Aventure* (1882). In 1881 she was seen in London with the Renaissance company in *Le Petit Duc, Les Voltigeurs de la 32ème* and *Belle Lurette.*

She then moved from the Renaissance to the Théâtre des Nouveautés where she appeared as Lucinde in *Le Roi de carreau* (1883), and to the Folies-Dramatiques to play Kate in the French premiere of *Rip!,* stole the show as the unplotworthy Bagatella in *Babolin* (1884) and appeared in breeches again in *La Vie mondaine* (1885, Tom). She played at the Bouffes-Parisiens as the deceived Bianca in *La Béarnaise* (1885), as Mimosa in *Les Noces improvisées* (1886) and then, in the most successful role of her entire career, created the part of the youngest sister, Benjamine, in Ferrier and Carré's richly comical opéra-bouffe *Joséphine vendue par ses soeurs* (1886).

Now confirmed as a top-rank star, ''la plus petite, la plus mignonne, la plus frêle des étoiles d'opérette'' was seen in the years that followed in virtually all the principal musical theatres of Paris: at the Bouffes-Parisiens in *La Gamine de Paris* (1887, Baronne Tépida de la Roche-aux-mouettes) and a revival of *Les Petits Mousquetaires* (1887, Armide de Tréville); at the Variétés in *Nos bons jurés* (1887, Octavie) and a revival of *La Princesse de Trébizonde* (1888); at the Renaissance as Griotte in *La Gardeuse d'oies* (1888); at the Folies-Dramatiques in the title role of the French version of Millöcker's *La Demoiselle de Belleville* (1888, Virginie Troupeau); at the Bouffes again in Pugno's *Le Retour d'Ulysse* (1889, Calypso); in Messager's *Le Mari de la reine* (1889, Justine); at the Nouveautés in *Samsonnet* (1890, Esperanza), star-billed as *Cendrillonnette* and *La Petite Poucette* (1891), in *Le Petit Bois* (1893), as Clary to the Clara of Marie Nixau in *Clary-Clara* (1894), in *Fleur de vertu* (1894, Lucrèce), Serpette's *La Bonne de chez Duval* (1894) and the made-to-measure *L'Élève de conservatoire* (1894, Friquette); at the Eldorado in the spectacular *Le Royaume des femmes* (1896, Xéressa); at the Athénée-Comique in *Madame Putiphar* (1897, Lota); at the Châtelet as Catiche in *La Poudre de Perlinpinpin* (1898); and in the title role of the reprised *Les 28 Jours de Clairette* (1900)—all the while repeating her most successful creations, notably her Benjamine, which she played on the Paris stage as late as 1906, and all the time an adored favorite of public and critics. She retired from the stage in 1914, after the death of her son in the war.

MINNELLI, Liza [May] (b Los Angeles, 12 March 1946).

The daughter of film director Vincente Minnelli and film actress and vocalist Judy Garland, Miss Minnelli made appearances on the musical stage as a teenager in *The Fantasticks* and *Carnival* on the road, and off-Broadway in the 1963 Stage 73 revival of *Best Foot Forward.* She made her Broadway debut at the age of 19 in the title role of the short-lived Kander and Ebb musical *Flora, the Red Menace* (Tony Award), but thereafter her career blossomed in other directions, taking her away from the theatre to the variety and nightclub stages and to the recording and film studios. In 1972 she took the starring role of Sally Bowles in the film version of Kander and Ebb's *Cabaret* (Academy Award), transforming the girl of the book and of the stage musical into an altogether different character in one of the stage-to-screen's most memorable musical-play performances.

When she finally returned to the stage, it was in highly theatrical circumstances, deputizing for several weeks for the indisposed Gwen Verdon in Kander and Ebb's *Chicago.* She made a more regular return to the musical stage with two further pieces by the same team (*The Act, The Rink*), but neither provided the wheels that would carry her to the Broadway success on which the star has to date somehow missed out. Her latest musical-theatre appearance was again as a deputy deluxe, spelling Julie Andrews in the juvenile lead of *Victor/Victoria* (1997).

Among her television engagements, she appeared in the ABC musical *The Dangerous Christmas of Red Riding Hood* (1965) playing Red Riding Hood to the Wolf of Cyril Ritchard, and subsequently in *Sam Found Out* (1988), a program including a one-act Kander and Ebb musical.

Miss Minnelli was at one stage married to Australian vocalist and songwriter Peter Allen who appeared in the Broadway musical *Legs Diamond,* and whose life and career were celebrated in the successful Australian musical play *The Boy from Oz* (Her Majesty's Theatre, Sydney 5 March 1998, pasticcio/Nick Enright). Todd McKenney played Allen, and Miss Minnelli was impersonated by Angela Toohey.

Biographies: Parish, J R: *Liza!* (Simon & Schuster, New York, 1975), Petrucelli, A W: *Liza! Liza!* (Karz-Cohl, Columbus, 1983), Leigh, W: *Born a Star* (Dutton, New York, 1993)

MINNIE MOUSTACHE Comédie musicale in 2 acts by Jean Broussolle and André Hornez. Lyrics by Broussolle. Music by Georges van Parys. Théâtre de la Gaîté-Lyrique, Paris, 13 December 1956.

This spoofish Western about a donkey called Pittypat, which is to gold what a truffle hound is to truffles, featured Ginette Baudin in its title role as the keeper of a Nevada City saloon. However, the chief attraction of *Minnie Moustache* was the appearance in the cast of the favorite singing group Les Compagnons de la Chanson, who played nine Frenchmen wandering through the action in a variety of disguises, trying to rescue both the donkey and its little owner Calico (Thérèse Laporte) from the clutches of the outlaw Maguire. In the process, they sang "La Berceuse de l'inconnu," "Avant de nous embarquer," "L'Amour c'est de l'or," "Mariage Indien" and "San Francisco." One of them (Fred Mella) ended up with Calico, Minnie paired off with a singing coachman called Wells Fargo (Yves Thomas), and Germaine Roger-Montjoye's production ran for seven months.

Recording: original cast (Columbia)

MIRANDE, Yves [LE QUERREC, Anatole Charles] (b Lannion, Côtes-de-Nord, 8 March 1875; d Paris, 20 March 1957).

Parisian boulevardier, spinner of bons mots and the author of a long list of successful comedies, for 20 years in a nominal collaboration with theatre magnate Gustave Quinson (*Le Chasseur de chez Maxim* being "their" greatest hit), Mirande was also one of the most successful authors of libretti for the musical comedies of "les années folles," many of which Quinson mounted at his Théâtre des Bouffes-Parisiens.

Mirande's first dip into the musical theatre, in the earliest days of his career, was with a little thriller-sketch called *Ma gosse* (w Henri Cain), a tongue-in-cheek piece invented basically as a vehicle for the fashionable apache dance routine and introduced in Paris by Polaire. It sported, at various times, music by one van Oosternyck, a score composed and arranged by the Moulin-Rouge's Maurice Jacobi and, when played by Polly Goss at Vienna's Apollotheater (*Der schwarze Mali* 1909), interpolations by Béla von Ujj. *Ma gosse* was also seen at London's Palace Music-Hall (18 October 1909 ad J N Raphael), performed by Edmée Mollon and Gaston Silvestre, and for 48 nights at New York's American Music Hall (10 January 1910) and later at the Plaza Music Hall with the same partnership featured.

It was not, however, until more than a decade later, following his alliance with Quinson, and the production by his ally of the blockbusting *Phi-Phi,* that Mirande entered seriously into the manufacture of libretti and lyrics. When he did, his very first effort was a major hit. *Ta bouche,* with its tiny cast and no chorus, was built on the same proportions as *Phi-Phi,* but it was wholly French and wholly contemporary in its display of its subject matter—a perfect whirligig of sexual-cum-financial relationships—and its crisp, merrily sexphisticated dialogue helped set the tone for the musical theatre of the next decade. Mirande himself played a major part in that decade, for he followed *Ta bouche* with another hit, the Maurice Chevalier/Dranem show *Là-haut* and several other delightful musical comedies, of which *Trois jeunes filles . . . nues!* was probably the most successful, while continuing a heavy output as a writer of comedy for the Quinson theatres. His last contributions to the musical stage were an adaptation of his 1921 play *Simone est comme ça* for the Bouffes-Parisiens and the libretto for Nikola Bobrykine's opera *Inès.*

Mirande's *Le Chasseur de chez Maxim* was metamorphosed in 1922 into the Broadway musical *The Blue Kitten* (Rudolf Friml/Otto Harbach, William Cary Duncan), whilst his name also appeared on Budapest bills as source author for *Párizsi espress* (Márkus Park Színház, 1942, Béla Csanak/Andor Pünkösti) and the more recent *Uraim, cask egymás után* (Szabolcs Fényes/Adorján Stella, Városmajori Színpad 28 June 1984) and *Az utolsó bölény* (Gyula Bodrogi, József Vinkó, Vidám Színpad 1 June 1990).

Alongside his stage credits, Mirande also worked for film in both France and in Hollywood where he was responsible for the screenplays for some of the early Maurice Chevalier films.

1909 **Ma gosse** (various/w Henri Cain) 1 act Théâtre du Moulin-Rouge 20 August

1922 **Ta bouche** (Maurice Yvain/w Gustave Quinson) Théâtre Daunou 1 April

1923 **Là-haut!** (Yvain/Albert Willemetz/w Quinson) Théâtre des Bouffes-Parisiens 31 March

1923 **La Dame en décolleté** (Yvain/w Lucien Boyer) Théâtre des Bouffes-Parisiens 22 December

1924 **Troublez-moi** (Raoul Moretti) Théâtre des Bouffes-Parisiens 17 September

1925 **Ri-Ri** (Charles Borel-Clerc/w Willemetz, Quinson) Théâtre Daunou 4 November

1925 **Trois jeunes filles . . . nues!** (Moretti/Willemetz) Théâtre des Bouffes-Parisiens 3 December

1927 **Mercenary Mary** French version w Robert de Simone, Jean Bastia (Théâtre des Bouffes-Parisiens)

1930 **Arsène Lupin banquier** (Marcel Lattès) Théâtre des Bouffes-Parisiens 7 May

1936 **Simone est comme ça** (Moretti/Willemetz/w Alex Madis) Théâtre des Bouffes-Parisiens 5 March

Autobiography: *Souvenirs d'Yves Mirande* (Fayard, Paris, 1932)

LES MISÉRABLES Musical tragedy by Alain Boublil and Jean-Marc Natel based on the novel by Victor Hugo. Music by Claude-Michel Schönberg. Palais des Sports, Paris, 17 September 1980.

After the production of their first musical spectacular, *La Révolution Française* (w Raymond Jeannot, Jean-Max Rivière), mounted at the Palais des Sports in 1973, composer Claude-Michel Schönberg and librettist Alain Boublil, this time in collaboration with poet Jean-Marc Natel, attacked another oversized French subject for their second work: Victor Hugo's dramatic novel *Les Misérables.* Following the procedure successfully used with *Jesus Christ Superstar, Evita* and *La Révolution Française, Les Misérables* was at first performed as a recording (April 1980), and it was subsequently brought to the Paris stage, at the same Palais des Sports, in a staging by Robert Hossein, France's specialist in vast, popular theatrical productions. Many of the cast from the recording repeated their roles for the stage production in a version which followed fairly closely the layout which was presented on the record.

This musical reduction of *Les Misérables,* which took on the challenge of slimming Victor Hugo's novel, with its huge cast of characters, its wide time span and its momentous happenings and personal stories, into a few-hour spectacle, did not take the same line as that chosen for *La Revolution Française.* Whereas the earlier piece had skipped through its even wider span sketching most of its characters as extravagant near-caricatures in a comic-strip retelling of history, *Les Misérables* was played straight. Its characters and the events in which they were caught up were given their full dramatic import, and the music that illustrated the show was largely dramatic and romantic in tone.

Jean Valjean (Maurice Barrier) is released from prison, where he was long condemned for petty theft, on a

Plate 258. **Les Misérables.** *On the ramparts.*

ticket of leave, and over the years he struggles his way back to respectability and ultimately to the position of mayor in a provincial town. However, he has broken the terms of his ticket of leave, and the policeman Javert (Jean Vallée) has made it his mission to track the law-breaker down and return him to prison. When one of Valjean's employees, Fantine (Rose Laurens), is sacked, sinks into prostitution, and finally dies, the mayor takes on the responsibility of her child, Cosette (Fabienne Guyon). He rescues the girl from her crooked foster parents, the Thénardiers (Yves Dautin, Marie-France Roussel), and, keeping one pace ahead of the pursuing Javert, takes her to Paris.

Cosette is already in her teens by the time the stirrings of armed revolt begin in the capital. A band of students, amongst them the young Marius (Gilles Buhlmann), join the anti-government fighting. But Marius has met and fallen in love with Cosette, and she with him, and Valjean is determined that the boy shall come to no harm. When the barriers go up in the streets of Paris, Valjean joins the street-fighters and, as the scrappy revolt fails bloodily, he is able to carry the wounded Marius away to safety. But during the fighting he has also come up against the dogged Javert, still intent on capturing the escaped criminal. Circumstances put Javert in Valjean's power, and when the latter not only does not kill his ''enemy'' but sets him free, the uncomprehending policeman falls to pieces. Justice is on its head, the notions of right or wrong seem to have vainished in a world which Javert cannot any longer understand—there is nothing left but for him to leave it to its anomalies. Javert jumps from a bridge and drowns himself in the Seine.

Fantine is dead, Javert is dead, Marius's foolishly idealistic friends are all dead, and little Éponine (Marianne Mille), the Thénardiers' child, who was shot delivering a love letter for the Marius she herself loved, is dead. Even the urchin Gavroche is dead, killed scavenging for bullets for the empty guns of the street-fighters. But Cosette and Marius come at last to their joyful ending, and Valjean can himself die secure in the knowledge that he has made his child happy.

The sung-through score of the piece mixed a number of solo songs with musical scenes, as it moved from its beginnings in 1821, at the factory where Fantine is employed (chorus: ''La journée est finie'') through the various stages of its epic tale. Fantine sang her Air de misère (''J'avais des si joli défauts'') and tore her heart out thinking of what might have been (''J'avais rêvé d'une autre vie''), the little Cosette piped out her pauper's daydream ''Mon prince est en chemin,'' and Thénardier roughly pounded out his ''devise du cabaretier'' and, backed by his wife, waltzed insinuatingly through his bartering with Valjean for Cosette (La Valse de la fourberie). In the Paris scenes, Marius delivered a stinging paean to the ''Rouge et noir'' and his companion Enjolras hymned ''la volonté du peuple,'' before Marius and Cosette joined together in romance (''Dans ma vie''). There were also songs for Éponine (''L'un vers l'autre'') and for the boy Gavroche (''Bonjour Paris, c'est moi Gavroche,'' ''La Faute à Voltaire'') before the drama rose to its pre-fight height in the ensemble ''Demain.'' The final scenes featured Javert's final dilemma, powerfully expressed in the monologue ''Noir ou blanc.''

Hossein's production played for a predestined season of 105 performances in Paris, and closed. As in the case of *La Révolution Française,* things might have ended there, had not the piece come to the attention of Cameron Mackintosh, riding high as the London producer of *Cats.* Mackintosh took the piece up and joined together with *Cats* director Trevor Nunn, at that time chief of Britain's Royal Shakespeare Company, and his colleague John Caird—teamed initially with *Times* theatre critic James Fenton and later with Herbert Kretzmer as lyricist—to begin the process of turning the rather unwieldy piece of French-language spectacular entertainment into something more resembling an at least relatively conventional English stage musical in the tradition of *Evita.* The alterations were to be many, and the time long.

The Royal Shakespeare Company joined Mackintosh as co-producer of the new *Les Misérables,* with Nunn and Caird (who had teamed on the internationally successful *Nicholas Nickelby*) as joint directors, and the production had its first performances on the Shakespeare Company's stage at London's Barbican complex. Those performances ran nearer to four hours than to three in comparison with the two-and-a-half hour version played in Paris. Between the Palais des Sports and The Barbican well over an hour of new material had been dug from Hugo's text and eased into the telling of his story. The new *Les Misérables* concentrated rather less on skating almost filmically through the familiar (to the French) high spots of the famous tale and focused itself very much more firmly and deeply on the novel's central characters, almost all of whom had been given additional numbers in which to express themselves. Several scenes and characters originally omitted also now reappeared. The role of Jean Valjean (Colm Wilkinson) had been given some dramatic new music (''What Have I Done?,'' ''Who Am I?,'' the pianissimo ''Bring Him Home''); and Javert (Roger Allam) had a second solo, early in the piece (''Stars'')—as did Thénardier (Alun Armstrong), halting the action as he scavenged through the sewers of Paris to deliver a ''Dog Eats Dog''; and Marius (Michael Ball), achingly looking at the ''Empty Chairs and Empty Tables'' where his friends had joyously planned their little war. Éponine (Frances Ruffelle) had a replacement number (''On My Own,'' originally Fantine's Air de misère) for her original. Fantine (Patti LuPone) had versions of two numbers from the original score, and Cosette—the role split between a child and soprano Rebecca Caine as the grown-up girl—had English adaptations of her childish song (''My Castle in the Clouds'') and her love duo (''In My Life''). The production, too, took the same attitude, focusing on the individual stories and characters within the piece and, as a result, the whole piece became eminently more theatrical, rather than merely spectacular. It was, of course, too long. But where to cut? A 12-minute section detailing Javert's pursuit of Valjean and Cosette from Monfermeil to Paris had already been excised in preview—what else would go? One character who went for nothing to English audiences was the obvious target—but to make the French authors understand that Gavroche, almost the most loved and famous character of the novel, had little place in the proceedings and looked and sounded as if he'd wandered in from a production of *Oliver!,* was tough. Eventually almost all of Gavroche's original part went under the knife, leaving the gamin moments to the more attractive Éponine, and the comedy to Thénardier and his wife (Susan Jane Tanner) whose roles had been colored-up (though colored-down since Paris) into low-comedy relief, as the show was reduced by only a handful of minutes.

Les Misérables was not an instant success. More of the London critics had hard words for it than had encouragement following its opening, and the planned move to the West End's Palace Theatre was for a while in doubt. The cast recording was postponed, and those involved waited to hear whether they were to close at the end of the Barbican season. Ultimately, Mackintosh decided to go for it. The show transferred, with only a little in the way of alterations, and opened at the Palace Theatre on 4 December 1985. At the time of writing it is still there (6,000th performance, 24 May 2000) and promising to be so a while more.

The success that was won so slowly in London was won without the same suspense elsewhere as reproductions of Caird and Nunn's staging of the show appeared round the world in the years that followed. Broadway's production (Tony Awards Best Musical, book, score, directors, set, lighting), with Wilkinson and Miss Ruffelle (Tony Award) repeating their London performances, also featured Terrence V Mann (Javert), David Bryant (Marius), Judy Kuhn (Cosette), Michael Maguire (Enjolras, Tony Award), Randy Graff (Fantine) and Leo Burmester and Jennifer Butt as the Thénardiers in the first cast of a production which has held its place at the Broadway and then (16 October 1990) at the Imperial Theater ever since. A Los Angeles company (Shubert Theater 1 June 1988) ran simultaneously with the Broadway production, followed by a bus-and-truck touring company which took the show around America, whilst the Broadway production continued into its fourteenth year.

Australia's production, which opened in 1987 in Sydney, featured former pop singer Normie Rowe as Valjean and Philip Quast as Javert. Two years later, after a Sydney run which was one of the longest in that city's musical-theatre history, it progressed to Melbourne (Princess Theatre 9 December 1989) with Rob Guest and John Diedrich in the central roles. Vienna's Raimundtheater launched a German version (ad Heinz Rudolf Kunze) in 1988 with Reinhard Brussmann (Valjean), Norbert Lamla (Javert) and Felix Martin (Marius) in its principal roles, and in the same year Budapest's Rock Színház produced an Hungarian version (ad Miklos Tibor) with Gyula Vikidal (Valjean), Pal Makrai (Javert), Sándor Sasvári (Marius), Anikò Nagy (Éponine) and Zsuzsa Csarnóy (Cosette) featured. Germany came rather late on the scene, and *Les Misérables* got its first German showing only in 1996 when Jerzy Jeske (Valjean) and Hartwig Rudolz (Javert) played the protagonists in a production mounted at Duisburg.

In 1991, more than a decade after those first 105 performances at the Palais des Sports, *Les Misérables* finally arrived back where it had started when it was staged in Paris, at the Théâtre Mogador. It was, of course, the ''new'' *Les Misérables,* honed by thousands of performances around the world into something very different in tone and style from the version played initially, and some of the original pieces of the text that remained were not adapted back into the original French, but rewritten by the French authors. Michel Pascal (Valjean) and Patrick Rocca (Javert) starred alongside Jérome Pradon (Marius), Marie Zamora (Cosette) and Stéphanie Martin (Éponine) with Marie-France Roussel of the original cast repeating her Madame Thénardier, in a fine production which held up for but seven months in a Paris which, yet again, displayed its disinterest in modern musical theatre, even when essentially homemade.

Elsewhere round the world the Franco-English show found a much warmer welcome. As the original London and Broadway productions totted up their runs into the thousands of performances, versions of *Les Misérables* were seen in Japan (Imperial Theatre, Tokyo 17 July 1987), Israel (Cameri Theatre, Tel Aviv 9 August 1987), Iceland (National Theatre, Reykjavik 26 December 1987), Norway (Det Norske Teatre, Oslo 17 March 1988), Canada (Royal Alexandra Theatre, Toronto 15 March 1989), Poland (Teatr Muzyczny, Gdynia 30 June 1989), Sweden (Cirkus Theater 12 September 1990), Netherlands (Carré Theater, Amsterdam 28 February 1991), Denmark (Odense Theater 20 April 1991), New Zealand (Aotea Theatre, Auckland 29 May 1991), Czechoslovakia (Vnohrady Theatre, Prague 25 June 1992), Spain (Nuevo Apolo, Madrid 16 September 1992), the Philippines (Meralco Theatre, Manila 7 October 1993), through Asia (Arts Centre, Seoul 28 June 1996) and South Afriocs (Nico Opera, Cape Town 11 August 1996), and in Belgium (Stadsschouwburg, Antwerp 24 May 1998) as the show established itself as one of the great classics of the genre.

UK: Barbican Theatre 30 September (8 October) 1985; USA: Broadway Theater 12 March 1987; Australia: Theatre Royal, Sydney 27 November 1987; Austria: Raimundtheater 15 September 1988; Hungary: Rock Színház, Szeged *A Nyomorulták* 14 August 1987, Rock Színház, Budapest 14 September 1987; France: Théâtre Mogador 12 October 1991, Germany: Musical Theater, Duisburg 26 January 1996

Recordings: pre-production (Tréma, First Night), London cast (First Night), Broadway cast (Geffen), Japanese cast (Toshiba/ Pony Canyon), Austrian cast (Polydor), Hungarian cast (Radioton), Israeli cast (Hed-Arzi), Swedish cast (CBS), ''Complete Symphonic Recording'' (First Night), Dutch cast (Mercury), French cast (Tréma), Spanish cast (RCA), German cast (Polydor), Czech cast (Bonton), Danish cast (BMG),) Korean cast (Hanyang), Belgian cast (Arcade), London 10th anniversary concert (First Night), etc

Videos: *Stage by Stage: The Making of the Show* (Polygram), 10th anniversary concert performance (VCI)

Literature: Behr, E: *Les Misérables: History in the Making* (Pavilion, London, 1996)

MISS DUDELSACK Operette in 3 acts by Fritz Grünbaum and Heinz Reichert. Music by Rudolf Nelson. Neues Schauspielhaus, Berlin, 3 August 1909.

The most successful of Rudolf Nelson's stage works, *Miss Dudelsack* was based on a familiar operettic story, given a special color by a Scots setting. Sir Francis MacHumber's will leaves much of his estate to his nephew Lieutenant John Jack MacHumber on condition that he weds his cousin, Kitty Sommerset. John Jack prefers poor and pretty Mary (otherwise the titular ''Miss Bagpipes'') to riches, and his decision turns out to be right all round when Sir Francis turns up alive and turns out to be Mary's father.

Nelson's score gave most opportunities to Mary and her man, with John Jack's waltz song ''Eine dunkel Rose'' proving the favorite of the evening alongside his entrance number ''Reite, roter Leutnant,'' Mary's introduction ''Ich bin das Fräulein Dudelsack,'' their ''English'' duo ''Oh du my darling, du, du, du'' and their tale of the castle ghost (Das Schlossgespenst), but it also included two amusing sextets for the MacHumber relations and two substantial finales—a kind of writing which might have been less than expected from the pen of a man known mostly as a cabaret writer and performer.

Following a Berlin summer-season run, the piece went on to be played in Hungary (ad Jenő Faragó), in Vienna's summer theatre in the Prater with Annie Münchow as Mary, Grete Mayer as Kitty and Josef Victora as John Jack, and shortly after in America, where Louis F Werba and Mark A Luescher's production (ad Grant Stewart) featured Lulu Glaser as its heroine and Joseph Herbert at the head of the comedy as her unwanted suitor, Peter (ex- Patrick). Miss Glaser and her bagpipes failed to make it to Broadway.

Hungary: Városligeti Színkör *Dudakisasszony* 8 May 1910; Austria: Venedig in Wien 17 August 1911; USA: Boston Theater, Boston 16 October 1911

MISS ESMERALDA, or The Monkey and the Monk Melodramatic burlesque in 3 acts by ''A C Torr'' (Fred Leslie) and Horace Mills. Music by W Meyer Lutz. Additional songs by Robert Martin and Frederick Bowyer. Gaiety Theatre, London, 8 October 1887.

The third of the Gaiety ''new burlesques,'' following behind *Little Jack Sheppard* and *Monte Cristo Jr,* this loose-limbed parody of Victor Hugo's *Notre Dame de Paris* and its derivatives was written by the Gaiety's star comedian, Fred Leslie, who dragged in a city-gent chum from his local amateur theatre group to help. Leslie, in fact, didn't himself initially play in *Miss Esmeralda,* for he and his teammate, Nellie Farren, went on the road with their previous success and it was Edwin Lonnen who appeared at the Gaiety in the role of the mad monk, Claude Frollo, and Fannie Leslie who took the breeches part of Captain Phoebus. Marion Hood, the original Mabel of Gilbert and Sullivan's *Pirates of Penzance,* was Esmeralda, and another ex-Savoyard, Frank Thornton, played the lovelorn hunchback. Lutz composed a lively score which won approving notices, but the hit of the night was Bob Martin's interpolated Irish song ''Kilalloe'' as delivered by Lonnen, who played the star role Leslie had constructed for himself with an eccentric ghoulishness which confirmed his rise to the top of the Gaiety's B-team.

The show had a curiously cut-about run, as it was taken off as soon as Fred and Nellie were ready to return with their Christmas show, but was then restaged as an afternoon piece when the new show proved less popular. Lonnen led a company on the British road, whilst Leslie got to grips with the part of Frollo and Miss Farren with that of Phoebus in a Gaiety company tour through Australia and the United States in 1888–89. The piece continued to tour in Britain for some years thereafter (variety comic Little Tich appeared as Quasimodo in one tour) and it was also given a second Australian tour (with Lonnen starred). As a postscript, city-gent turned librettist Horace Mills ended up handing in his three-piece suit and becoming a comedian at the Gaiety!

Australia: Princess Theatre, Melbourne 1 August 1888; USA: Standard Theater 17 December 1888

MISS HELYETT Opérette in 3 acts by Maxime Boucheron. Music by Edmond Audran. Théâtre des Bouffes-Parisiens, Paris, 12 November 1890.

Miss Helyett gave composer Audran the greatest Parisian success of the second part of his career, a decade after his initial triumphs with *Les Noces d'Olivette* and *La Mascotte.* But although his score was written in his most charming vein, much of the credit for the show's success had to be given to the piece's librettist, Maxime Boucheron, for his delicately humorous if basically ''schocking'' book.

Miss Helyett (Biana Duhamel) is a pubescent little American Salvation Army lass whose pastor father (Montrouge) has inculcated her with a very firm morality. So when she goes walking in the mountains, slips over a cliff, is left hanging upside down from a branch with her skirts over her head, then tactfully left in a deep faint on the edge of the ravine by her rescuer, she simply has to find and promptly wed the unknown savior who has seen a portion of her anatomy that only a husband should see. She mistakenly lights at first on a cowardly bullfighter (Tauffenberger) who is already engaged to a dramatic Spanish lady (Mlle St-Laurent) with a fearsome mother (Mme Macé-Montrouge), then on her own dreary fiancé (Jannin), before discovering that the right man is the artist Paul (Piccaluga) for whom she had been demurely sighing all along. Musically, the role of the teenaged heroine was undemanding, though not short, and the principal singing moments fell to her baritone artist—notably in his duo d'album with his friend Bacarel (Desiré), sighing over the sketch he made of the young lady's predicament and portions before getting round to rescuing her (''Ah! ah! le superbe point de vue!'')—and particularly to the volatile trio of Spaniards.

Miss Helyett was a triumph at the Bouffes-Parisiens, making a star of the 21-year-old Mlle Duhamel, and playing there for virtually all of 1891 and 1892, topping its 700th night and setting up a new Parisian long-run record. It returned in 1893, in 1895 with Alice Favier in her debut as a very young Miss Helyett (900th performance, 11 January 1896), again later in 1896 with Mlle Favier, and yet again in 1901, whilst in the meanwhile having been played at the Théâtre des Menus-Plaisirs with Mariette Sully and by each of Duhamel, Mlle Deliane (1900–1901) and Evelyne Jeanney (1900) at the Renaissance. In 1905 Ève Lavallière improbably played the role of Helyett at the Variétés (''she can play anything *but* an ingenue''), whilst Juliette Méaly took her version round the Continent in 1893 and rare was the rising ingenue of the French turn-of-the-century stage who didn't have a *Miss Helyett* credit on her curriculum vitae before she turned 20.

In next to no time the piece went round the world, virtually all the main centers hastening the hit of the Parisian period on to the stage whilst its career in the French capital still continued. In Germany (ad Richard Genée) the show ''took [Berlin] by storm'' but had to be removed because of contracts. However, it was brought back to the bills briskly after the flop of *Des Teufels Weib.* Two years later Berlin got a further serving when the French version visited the Apollotheater with Mlle Aubert in the lead role, and the German version came back to the Theater Unter den Linden in 1895 with Frln Kramm as the little heroine.

Hungary (ad Lajos Evva, Viktor Rákosi) did not show quite the same delight in the adventures of *Miss Helyett,* and the Theater an der Wien, in spite of an acclaimed performance by Lilli Lejo in the star role and the featuring of Girardi as the bullfighter, played the piece only 16 times, but a British *Miss Decima,* directed by the Gallic Mons Marius, had a fine 191-performance run at London's little Criterion and then (when Charles Wyndham bumped it out to put on a play of his own) at the larger Prince of Wales Theatre. It was, however, as might have been expected, an Anglo-Saxonic deodorized version of Boucheron's play, F C Burnand having turned ''a scandalously suggestive French piece into a harmless but exceedingly amusing operatic comedy'' to feature the young French artist Juliette Nesville alongside David James as the pastor, Charles Conyers as Paul, Mary Ann Victor as the dragonistic Señora and American tenor Chauncey Olcott in a part called the Chevallier Patrick Julius O'Flanagan, fabricated on the bones of the bullfighter. When the show transferred, Decima Moore and Hayden Coffin took over the lead roles, and a comic duo for James and Miss Victor, composed by Teddy Solomon, was added to the score.

David Belasco and Charles Frohman's American production (ad Belasco, ly: Fred Lyster) took advantage of the fact that the vocal demands of the star role were limited, and cast the well-publicized, red-haired neophyte actress Mrs Leslie Carter (aged 30) as Miss Helyett alongside Mark Smith (Paul), Joseph Herbert (Jacques, ie, James) and British soprano Laura Clement as the fiery Manuela. It passed its 50th performance at the Star Theater (17 December), and since it was still running strongly when its preset season ended the producers moved it to the Standard (11 January) to complete what ended up as a run of 116 performances before the show went on to the rest of the country.

Australia chose the British adaptation for its production, and local soubrette Juliet Wray was teamed with a virtually all-British star cast: Jack Leumane (Chevallier), Henry Bracy (Marmaduke), Wallace Brownlow (Paul), Clara Thompson-Bracy (Señora) and George Lauri (pastor) for seasons in Sydney and Melbourne (Princess Theatre 16 May 1896).

Although the English-language productions fared well, and Germany proved partial, nowhere else in the world did *Miss Helyett* have the vast success it achieved in France. There it remained a favorite item in the repertoire for many years, until the arrival of the Viennese Operette and of the Jazz Age. The ''naughtiness'' of the 1890s and a few blushes over a bare bottom seemed altogether small beer compared to the modern level of theatrical comico-permissiveness. Even then, however, *Miss Helyett* continued to be revived, appearing in 1926 at the Gaîté and maintaining a presence in the provinces long after that.

Germany: Wallner-Theater 7 February 1891; Hungary: Népszínház *Miss Heliett* 25 April 1891; UK: Criterion Theatre *Miss Decima* 23 July 1891; USA: Star Theater 3 November 1891; Austria: Theater an der Wien 25 December 1891; Australia: Lyceum Theatre, Sydney *Miss Decima* 7 March 1896

Recording: complete (Gaîté-Lyrique)

MISS HOOK OF HOLLAND Dutch musical incident in 2 acts by Paul Rubens and Austen Hurgon. Music and lyrics by Paul Rubens. Prince of Wales Theatre, London, 31 January 1907.

One of the most likeable and certainly the most successful of Paul Rubens's musical comedies, *Miss Hook of Holland* was completed by writer-director Austen Hurgon when, as a result of Rubens's continual ill health, the show was not ready in time for rehearsals. The collaboration proved a fine one, for the resultant libretto avoided all the ''coy sallies of innuendo and dollops of bad taste'' which had infected most of Rubens's early shows, in a strong and entertaining ''Dutch musical incident'' set with a catchy series of what the songwriter called ''jingles and tunes.''

When the adorably vague distiller Hook (G P Huntley) loses his precious recipe for ''Cream of the Sky'' whilst taking it out for a walk, it is found by the professionally unemployed loafer Slinks (George Barrett), who sells it to Captain Papp (Herbert Clayton), the unfavored suitor of Sally Hook (Isabel Jay). However, after an actful of high jinks in the liquor factory at Amsterdam, Sally discomforts Papp, wins her beloved bandmaster Van Vuyt (Walter Hyde) and retrieves the missing formula. If comedy was high in *Miss Hook,* largely through the acclaimed creation of the elderly Hook by the not-elderly Huntley and the routines of the comic maid Mina (Gracie Leigh), Rubens supported it with some charming songs. Miss Leigh wondered why all the fellows give her underwear as a gift in ''A Pretty Pink Petty from Peter'' and explained why ''The Flying Dutchman'' (whose home life wasn't so hot) flew, Miss Jay sang ''Fly Away, Kite'' (apropos of very little) and joined operatic tenor Hyde in ''The Sleepy Canal,'' one of a series of lyrically Dutch songs (''Little Miss Wooden Shoes,'' ''Soldiers of the

Netherlands'') whilst Harry Grattan, in a supporting comedy role, had a good old-fashioned topical song, ''From Harwich to Hook.''

Frank Curzon's production of *Miss Hook of Holland* stayed at the Prince of Wales Theatre for 462 performances, and if it lost Huntley and Miss Jay during its run it gained matinée idol Maurice Farkoa for whom the role of the bandmaster was expanded by several extra songs. Curzon produced a concurrent Christmas season, played by a cast of children at matinées (Ida Valli was Mr Hook) and the piece set out on the first of countless tours, under the management of George Dance, as the overseas productions began.

Gabor Steiner played *Miss Hook* (ad Carl Lindau) at his Vienna summer theatre in both 1907 and 1908, for a total of over one hundred performances. His production boasted two outstanding stars, but in succession, for both Ilka Pálmay and Annie Dirkens preferred the fun of Gracie Leigh's role to the title part. The second act featured an ''Hollandisches Fest'' in which three songs and a routine called ''In Amsterdam'' danced by ''8 Original-Engländerinnen'' were featured. Having performed *Miss Hook* at 8 PM, most of the cast then proceeded to perform Lincke's *Frau Luna* at 11 for the later-night pleasure-seekers in the Prater. When Vienna was done, it was Hungary's turn, and Miksa Bródy's version of *A Hollandi lány* (the joke about the Hook of Holland was clearly untranslatable), worryingly described as a ''nagy oper'' or grand opera, had a good season at Budapest's Király Színház, where the latest novelties had been *Ein Walzertraum* and *Die Dollarprinzessin.*

Charles Frohman's Broadway production suffered an attempt to preempt its little bit of novelty, when Reginald De Koven's on-the-way-in *The Snowman* switched its title to *The Girls of Holland* under its nose, and also a sticky start when both the lead comedians were sacked on the road. However, with a cast which featured Christie MacDonald (Sally), Georgia Caine (Mina), Bertram Wallis (Papp) and Tom Wise as Hook it ultimately ran up 119 Broadway performances before going on to a fine road life. It went, however, under a different title. Star comic Frank Daniels was cast as Hook, and Miss Macdonald had to suffer having the title role of the show whisked from under her: it went out as *Hook of Holland.*

Australia welcomed Clarke, Meynell and Gunn's production, with husband and wife team Edwin Brett (Hook) and Emmeline Orford (Mina) and soprano Ruth Lincoln (Sally) from England starred, for an enormously successful run, in spite of the competition of *The Merry Widow.* It went on to a quick revival, and a tour of New Zealand. *Miss Hook* was also revived in London in 1914 for a wartime run, again in 1932 as part of a season of past glories, and in 1945 it was given a major tour in a revised version by producer Émile Littler which nevertheless did not follow his revamped *A Quaker Girl* into London. It also remained a great favorite with provincial houses and operatic societies for many more years.

Plate 259. *G P Huntley as Mr Hook, the daffy Dutch papa of* **Miss Hook of Holland.**

Austria: Venedig in Wien *Miss Hook von Holland* 22 June 1907; USA: Criterion Theater 31 December 1907; Australia: Theatre Royal, Melbourne 18 April 1908; Hungary: Király Színház *A Hollandi lány* 19 September 1908

Recording: Radio selection (AEI)

MISS LIBERTY Musical comedy in 2 acts by Robert Sherwood. Music and lyrics by Irving Berlin. Imperial Theater, New York, 15 July 1949.

Irving Berlin's follow-up to *Annie Get Your Gun* did not prove to be the same kind of success, in spite of being based on an amusing premise which was turned into a libretto by top-flight playwright Robert Sherwood (*Idiot's Delight, Reunion in Vienna*).

In the atmosphere of a newspaper circulation war, little photographer Horace Miller (Eddie Albert) goes off to France to find the original lady who modeled for the statue of Liberty. His publicity coup looks assured when he brings back pretty Monique Dupont (Allyn McLerie) but then it turns out he has the wrong girl. However, since he thus makes one newspaper magnate look foolish, Horace is assured of a job with the other. Mary McCarty played Horace's reporter helpmate, Maisie, and aged Ethel Griffies was the elderly and comical mother of the lassie who it turns out isn't ''Miss Liberty.'' Berlin's score did not bring forth any numbers to add to his list of standards, although Monique's final singing of the statue's motto ''Give Me Your Tired, Your Poor'' and the old lady's cynical and lively description of opportunism in ''Only for Americans'' both went down well in the show. It was an outcut, ''Mr Monotony'' (previously cut also from a film score), which was given the most enduring life when it was included in the retrospective compilation show staged as *Jerome Robbins' Broadway* (1989).

Moss Hart, Berlin and Sherwood's production, directed by Hart, choreographed by Robbins, and designed by Oliver Smith and Motley, was eagerly awaited and opened with a very large advance sale, but the show proved to have few of the attractions of *Annie Get Your Gun* for the theatregoing public and, although it ran on for 308 performances, *Miss Liberty* was generally voted a disappointment.

Recordings: original cast (Columbia), selections (RCA Victor, Decca)

MISS SAIGON Musical in 2 acts by Alain Boublil. Lyrics by Boublil and Richard Maltby jr. Music by Claude-Michel Schönberg. Theatre Royal, Drury Lane, London, 20 September 1989.

Miss Saigon is a modern version of the tale made famous as *Madam Butterfly* in the story by John Luther Long (1898), the play by David Belasco (5 March 1900) and the subsequent opera by Giacomo Puccini (1904), all of whom in their turn borrowed at least in part from a Pierre Loti tale previously utilized in the lighter musical theatre in André Messager's *Madame Chrysanthème* (1893). This newest incarnation of the story followed the fashion of the 1980s for anything that allowed a little safely distanced breast-beating over the Vietnam War by resetting the once-Japanese tale in the Saigon of the 1970s. Alain Boublil's text, however, made some significant changes to the best-known version of the romantic and tragic history of Loti's and Long's oriental bride, changes which were ultimately less in story line than in character and in motivation.

Kim (Lea Salonga) is an unenthusiastic tyro tart in a Saigon brothel run by a pimp known as the Engineer (Jonathan Pryce) when she is bought for a first night by GI Chris (Simon Bowman). During that night the two fall lickety-split in love, but the American army is being evacuated from Vietnam and Chris, although he had really intended to stay behind, is taken with it. He returns to America and weds Ellen (Claire Moore). Kim's cousin and promised husband, Thuy (Keith Burns), now powerful in the new regime, seeks her out and discovers that she has borne a son. When he tells her that this evidence of her past must be got rid of, she shoots him. From now on the girl's sole mission in life is simply to get United States citizenship for her son and, when Chris and Ellen go to Bangkok to find her, she deliberately kills herself to oblige the father to take his son home with him.

The authorial team of Schönberg and Boublil had, in their previous collaboration, taken the original French version of their *Les Misérables,* sharpened it and made it both more characterful and more theatrical for the English-language stage whilst always maintaining the strong forward-going storyline of the original. This process was missing in the case of *Miss Saigon,* which, commissioned for the English-language stage, had not been staged in the French in which Boublil had at first written it and the result was a piece much less coherent and effective than the earlier one. A curious piece of structuring had the scene of Chris's departure from Saigon, confusingly missing from its first-act place in the chronology, turning up—apparently for spectacular reasons, as it sported a particularly impressive practical helicopter—as a flashback in the middle of the second act; Kim's murder of Thuy had no apparent consequence; and the climax of the first part came on a piece of disconnected spectacle rather than on a moment of drama. In the inevitable comparison with *Madama Butterfly,* the imaginative transformation of the marriage-broker Goro into the Faginesque Engineer and the priestly Bonze into the vehement Thuy worked well, but the pushing-forward of the American wife (barely seen in the opera) served only to diffuse the principal story, and the metamorphosis of the heroine's motive for suicide from love and, above all, trust, to motherly and material ambition gave a tartly sour taste to the new piece, in contrast to the tragic romance of the earlier one. That taste was confirmed in the style of the English lyrics which were often coarse and ''realistic,'' particularly in the mouths of the American servicemen characters and the Engineer, and almost never in the vein of vaguely unreal lyricism which had served so well in *Les Misérables.*

Schönberg's score to the piece which, like the pair's two previous works, was virtually sung-through, took a similar turn and, as a result, the lyrical moments, headed by the repeated ''I Still Believe'' (Kim and Chris), proved to be less memorable than those of *Les Misérables,* and the main accent was placed on the incidental music and on such pieces as the Engineer's thumpingly cruel paean to ''The American Dream,'' played and staged in a harsh parody of Broadway, and his ''If You Want to Die in Bed''—a kind of bitter oriental version of Fagin's dilemma from *Oliver!*

Produced at London's Theatre Royal, Drury Lane (the first production of a new musical to be housed there in some 15 years), under the management of *Les Misérables* producer Cameron Mackintosh, *Miss Saigon* was received with some very fine notices, with Pryce, a former National Theatre leading actor, gaining particularly appreciative criticisms for his depiction of the pimp. It was a characterization which came over rather like a burlesque of 1960s musical-comedy star Anthony Newley, then appearing just down the road in a revival of *Stop the World—I Want to Get Off,* but Newley was soon gone, whilst *Miss Saigon* ran on. The harshness, all and any references to politics and the almost contemporary setting also pleased the papers, and, even without its songs making any particular impression on a chart world that was now used to show-music intrusions, *Miss Saigon* was quickly established as a success. It stayed at the Theatre Royal Drury Lane for 4,246 performances.

The London production was followed by a Broadway one in which the show itself almost went unnoticed under the swathes of newspaper-worthy side issues which it provoked. The one that gained the most column inches was over-casting. Mackintosh proposed to bring both Pryce and Miss Salonga from the original cast to repeat their roles in America, as he had done previously with the stars of *The Phantom of the Opéra.* However, egged on by a racist group within their ranks, Actors' Equity put a ban on the artists, claiming—in spite of the fact that their own president had been starring in a revival of *The Good Woman of Szechuan*—that it was immoral/illegal for a white actor to play a Eurasian. Mackintosh promptly responded that he would not cast his shows on racial considerations, canceled the production, and Equity, faced with putting their musical Asian members out of the best jobs they'd had since the last tour of *The King and I,* was forced into a shamed backdown. Broadway subsequently confirmed London's opinions of the performance which had largely caused all the kerfuffle by awarding Pryce the year's Tony Award for the best actor in a musical. *Saigon* stories became a wearisome feature of show-business columns in the months that followed, but in the meanwhile both London's and New York's *Miss Saigon* ran comfortably on, and—with Japan first off the mark (Imperial Theatre, Tokyo 23 April 1992)—further productions began to appear in other areas eager for the latest product from the *Cats/Les Misérables/Phantom of the Opéra* production house.

An Hungarian version (ad Tibor Miklós) was produced at Szeged, and later at Budapest's Rock theatre with Eszter Biró and Attila Csengeri at the head of its cast, a German version (ad Heinz Rudolf Kunze) with Uwe Kröger featured was mounted at Stuttgart, and Copenhagen's Ostre Gasvaerk Theater (3 October 1996) and Scheveningen's VSB Circustheater (10 November 1996) both hosted local versions, but an Australian mounting, with Peter Couzens and Joanna Ampil in the lead roles, proved disappointing. And meanwhile, as two touring companies took the piece around America, *Miss Saigon* worked its way steadily on into the top 10 long-run shows of all time on both sides of the Atlantic. The Broadway production ultimately totted up a run of more than nine and a half years (4,125 performances).

A slightly earlier musical-theatre version of the *Madam Butterfly* tale was produced at the Belvoir Street Theatre, Sydney (23 April 1987) under the title *Cho-Cho-San* (Dalmazio Babare, Boris Conley/Daniel Keene). A small-cast piece featuring mime and puppets, it was praised as ''visually splendid, musically exciting and . . . innovative'' but apparently went no further.

USA: Broadway Theater 11 April 1991; Germany: Musical Hall, Stuttgart 21 November 1994; Hungary: Szabadtéri Színpad, Szeged 12 August 1994, Rock Színház 2 September 1994; Australia: Capitol Theatre, Sydney 14 July 1995

Recording: original cast (Geffen), German cast (Polydor), Hungarian cast (Polygram), Japanese cast (Toho), Danish cast (Ostre Gasaverk), Dutch cast (Endemol), Swedish cast (GLC), ''Complete Recording'' (First Night), etc

Video: *The Heat Is On: The Making of Miss Saigon* (First Night)

Literature: Behr, E, Steyn, M: *The Story of Miss Saigon* (Jonathan Cape, London, 1991)

MITCHELL, Julian (b ?New York, 5 November 1852; d Long Branch, NJ, 24 June 1926). Ubiquitous director and choreographer of all types of musical plays through more than three Broadway decades.

A nephew of star actress Maggie Mitchell, Julian Mitchell got some of his earliest opportunities thanks to his aunt and her fame. After a youthful appearance at Niblo's in a *Black Crook* revival (1873, Skuldawelp), he went on the road with her in 1876, playing Gambrinus in *Mignon,* played in Ford's Baltimore Company (1876) and in Mrs Chanfrau's company as a blackface servant in *Parted* (1878) and again with his aunt in 1879–81. He subsequently became a dancer and actor with Willie Edouin's ''Sparks'' company (Charley Chaffaway in *Ripples* 1881–82, Gilly Spooner in *A Bunch of Keys* 1883).

He made his first steps as a director and choreographer in his early twenties and, from 1884, he doubled as an actor and stage director/choreographer for Charles Hoyt. As such, he directed the productions of such of Hoyt's musical shows as *A Rag Baby* (1884, Tony Jay), *The Maid and the Moonshiner* (1886), the long-running

A Trip to Chinatown (1891) and *A Black Sheep* (1896) and created roles in *A Hole in the Ground* (1887, The Tramp/League Base Umpire) and *A Texas Steer* (1890, Knott Initt). He also staged several outside pieces such as the farce comedies *Tuxedo* (1891) and *The Voodoo* (1892), *Boys and Girls* (1892), Frank Daniels's *Doctor Cupid* (1892), and *The Birth of Venus* (1895). Mitchell subsequently became stage director at Weber and Fields's Music Hall and there, between 1897 and 1902, he staged such revusical spectacles as *Pousse Café, Hurly-Burly, Helter Skelter, Whirl-I-Gig, Fiddle-dee-dee, Hoity-Toity* and *Twirly-Whirly* and their burlesque inserts. In between times, he also directed legitimate comic opera for Alice Nielsen (*The Fortune Teller, The Singing Girl*), less legitimate comic opera (*The Idol's Eye* with Frank Daniels, *The Princess Chic*) and Casino Theater musical comedy (*The Girl from Up There,* Ziegfeld's *Papa's Wife*).

Mitchell put a virtual end to his career on the boards after a tour of Australia with Hoyt's *A Milk White Flag* and *A Trip to Chinatown* in 1900 and thereafter he devoted himself wholly to directing, choreographing, and briefly producing for another 25 years. He scored an enormous success with his direction of the Fred Hamlin extravaganza *The Wizard of Oz* (1903) and it was on the heels of this success that he joined Hamlin to co-produce that show's follow-up, *Babes in Toyland* (1903). He then paired with Lew Fields to sponsor Victor Herbert's subsequent *It Happened in Nordland,* before going it alone as producer-director of the less successful *Wonderland* (1906). Its comparative failure convinced him to stick to directing.

Mitchell staged the revusical *About Town* (1906) and the imported musical comedy *The Girl Behind the Counter* (w J C Huffman) for Fields, and *The White Hen* (1907), *The Tattooed Man* (1907) and Joe Weber's *Hip Hip Hooray* and *Merry Widow Burlesque* (1908); choreographed *The Silver Star* (1909) and *The Red Mill* (the latter with *Wizard of Oz* stars Montgomery and Stone); staged the Chicago musical *The Alcayde* (1906); and rejoined Florenz Ziegfeld to direct Anna Held in *A Parisian Model* (1907). Thereafter he directed Ziegfeld's *Follies* between 1907 and 1914, as well as such of his musicals as *Miss Innocence* (1908), the unsuccessful *A Winsome Widow* (1912) and the Adeline Genée vehicle *The Soul Kiss* (w Herbert Gresham), for which the ballerina, however, supplied her own choreographer. Mitchell had his ''revenge'' by mounting a burlesque of her performance in the *Ziegfeld Follies* of the season. In 1910 he took briefly to the stage again to appear in that year's *Follies* and to dance ''The Dance of the Flirt'' and the part of the absinthe fiend in ''The Dance of the Vampire'' with Louise Alexander in *Miss Innocence* in Chicago.

In a kaleidoscope of shows which ranged from one end of the musical-theatre scale to the other, Mitchell acted as choreographer for the Ivan Caryll musicals *The Pink Lady, Oh! Oh! Delphine* (1912), *The Little Café* (1913) and *Papa's Darling* (1914) and choreographed and/or co-directed the same composer's *The Girl Behind the Gun* and *Little Miss Raffles.* He choreographed the American versions of the Continental Operetten *Eva* (1912), *Der Graf von Luxemburg* (1912), *Die Kino-Königin* (1914), *Zsuzsi kisasszony* (1916) and *Szibill* (1916) (although he did not direct a Viennese import until *The Yankee Princess* in 1922), and directed and/or choreographed *The Broadway Belles* (1910), Chicago's *The Girl in the Kimono* (1910), the Boston-born *The Merry Martyr* (1913), Hirsch's *The Rainbow Girl* (1918), Herbert's *The Velvet Lady* (1919) and George M Cohan's productions of the comic-opera burlesque *The Royal Vagabond* (1919), *Mary* (1920 w Sam Forrest), *The O'Brien Girl* (1921 w John Meehan), *Little Nellie Kelly* (1922) and *The Rise of Rosie O'Reilly* (1923).

Other directing and/or choreographing credits (the two were sometimes credited jointly with a collaborator without being more specific) included *Her Little Highness* (1913, w George Marion), *Forward March* (1914), *Some Night* (1918), *The Kiss Burglar* (1918), Ed Wynn's *The Perfect Fool* (1921), the black shows *In Bamville* (1923) and *The Chocolate Dandies* (1924), *Daffy Dill* (1922), *The Blue Kitten* (1922 w Leon Errol), and *Molly Darling* (1922), as well as the out-of-town flop *Lola in Love* (1922) and a number of other revues (*Fads and Fancies, Around the Map,* etc). Mitchell had his final Broadway assignment at the age of 71 when, as an ''old reliable,'' he was brought in to replace Julian Alfred as the choreographer on *Sunny,* providing the dances for star hoofer Marilyn[n] Miller.

One of the most important dance stagers of his day, Mitchell, along with such contemporaries as Edward Royce (jr), set the tone for the musical-theatre dance of the early years of the 20th century. It was not complex or highly technical choreography, nor did it rely on the drilling or the novelty dancing which would later become popular, but it did require some talent and teaching, and there was no place in Mitchell's shows for the old-time ''walker'' who filled the rows of the chorus simply to show off her figure. Whether for chorus or for principals, his dances were almost always energetic on the one hand or graceful on the other, with plenty of room kept for the comical, as so often used in his earliest work with Hoyt and as featured in his days with a Cohan who was quite capable of staging his own dances if he wished.

As a director, he naturally leaned towards the choreographer-director's eternal penchant for favoring the visual over the textual but, once again, early experiences in the Hoyt pieces, where comedy was nearly all, meant that he was able to stage such finely constructed comic pieces as *The Pink Lady* when occasionally called upon to do so. By and large, however, his directing assignments were on less tightly book-orientated pieces, and his principal groups of works were all in the loose-limbed area: the Hoyt shows, the Weber and Fields burlesques, the Ziegfeld revues and revusical musical comedies and his latter-day works for Cohan.

Mitchell was married first to Georgia Lake, a fellow member of the Hoyt company, and later to leggy dancer **Bessie CLAYTON** (b Philadelphia, 1 June 1875; d Long Beach, NJ, 16 July 1948), who played in *A Trip to Chinatown* (principal dancer), *A Black Sheep* and other Hoyt shows, in further farce comedies (*A Knotty Affair,* 1891), in burlesque (*Thrilby*), then at Weber and Fields's (*Helter Skelter, Fiddle-dee-dee, Hoity-Toity* and right up to the final *Roly Poly*), for Weber in *Hip Hip Hooray* (1907), in *The Ziegfeld Follies* (both as a player and a person impersonated), in such musical comedies as *It Happened in Nordland* (1905, Parthenia Schmitt), *The Belle of Mayfair* (1906, Pincott) and the *Merry Widow Burlesque* (1908, Kickette de Lingerie), and, finally, in *The Passing Show of 1913.*

1892 **A Mad Bargain** (various/w John J McNally) Bijou Theater 27 February

MITISLAW DER MODERNE Operette in 1 act by Robert Bodanzky and Fritz Grünbaum. Music by Franz Lehár. Hölle, Vienna, 5 January 1907.

One of the few short Operetten composed by Franz Lehár, *Mitislaw der moderne,* produced whilst Vienna was still in the throes of *Die lustige Witwe,* was a little bit of an in-joke. The character of Mitislaw, the prince whose mama always told him to be ''modern,'' was a burlesque on the Danilo of the more famous show, and he arrived on the scene—in the person of the original Danilo, Louis Treumann—accompanied by no less an escort than Lolo, Dodo, Joujou, Cloclo, Margot and Froufrou, the ladies from Maxims. In a little plot which hinged on virtue and the undoing of it, Mitislaw shared the limelight and the nine numbers which made up the show's musical part, with two leading ladies, Tina and Amaranthe, the professedly feeble Graf Jerzabinka, and the girls. Treumann delivered an entrance number (''Man sagte mir'') with his girls, and a Marschlied (''Ich schaff mir einen Musterstaat'') about being modern, and Amaranthe a mazurka and a minuet-cum-waltz.

First staged at the Theater an der Wien's little Hölle studio theatre, the piece proved to the liking not only of Vienna, but to the rest of the world. It was given in a proper theatre in Hungary, six months after the opening of *Die lustige Witwe,* but elsewhere it found itself a home in variety theatres such as Berlin's Apollotheater, and London's Hippodrome (ad J E MacManus) where it was mounted by Seymour Hicks with Maurice Farkoa (Mitislaw), Zena Dare (Amaranthe), Florence Wood (Tina) and John Le Hay (Graf).

Hungary: Király Színház *Miciszlav* 3 April 1907; Germany: Apollotheater 1 February 1908; UK: Hippodrome *Mitislaw, or The Love Match* 22 November 1909

MLLE MODISTE Comic opera in 2 acts by Henry Blossom. Music by Victor Herbert. Knickerbocker Theater, New York, 25 December 1905.

Operatic vocalist Fritzi Scheff was taken from the company at the Metropolitan Opera and introduced to the musical stage whilst still in her earliest twenties, starring first of all in Victor Herbert's comic opera *Babette* (1903). Neither that nor the *She Stoops to Conquer* musical *The Two Roses* brought her the kind of success that the other operatic refugee of the time, Emma Trentini, found with *Naughty Marietta* and *The Firefly,* but Herbert's second piece for the little prima donna ran these hits close, for *Mlle Modiste* turned out to be easily the best of the six new Broadway (and some pre-Broadway) musicals in which the star featured during her career.

Henry Blossom's libretto introduced Miss Scheff as Fifi, an industrious little milliner who is beloved by aristocratic Étienne (Walter Percival)—to the fury of his father (William Pruette)—and coveted by her employer Madame Cécile (Josephine Bartlett) as a useful wife for her fairly useless son Gaston (Leo Mars). A gift from a kindly American gentleman (Claude Gillingwater) who likes giving pretty girls gifts allows Fifi to quit millinery, and she goes off and becomes a singing star instead. When she returns to sing at a bazaar on the old Count's property she is so clever and so charming that he is wholly happy to hand over the son he had once forbidden her company.

Herbert's score gave Miss Scheff some splendid opportunities, from the *Fledermaus*-ish audition scene ''If I Were on the Stage'' with its extension waltz ''Kiss Me Again'' (taken from Herbert's bottom drawer), to the show-piece ''The Nightingale and the Star'' and the jaunty ''The Mascot of the Troop,'' whilst both Percival, with the delightful solo ''The Time, the Place and the Girl,'' and, above all, Pruette with his basso march-song ''I Want What I Want When I Want It,'' had hit material in their roles as well.

Charles Dillingham's production of *Mlle Modiste* had a very fine run of 202 performances on Broadway before going to the country for three years of touring. Miss Scheff returned to New York in her best vehicle on a number of occasions, both during that time—in 1906 (Knickerbocker Theater 1 September) and 1907 (Acade-

Plate 260. **The Mocking Bird**

my of Music 20 May, Knickerbocker Theater 9 September)—and after (Globe Theater 26 May 1913), and, almost a quarter of a century after her debut, for one final time (Jolson Theater 7 October 1929). However, in spite of the piece's popularity throughout America, no Broadway productions were played without the original star, and *Mlle Modiste* did not, apparently, travel into first-class productions outside the United States.

A film based on *Mlle Modiste* and using the title of its favorite song, ''Kiss Me Again,'' was produced in 1931. Bernice Claire appeared as Fifi alongside Walter Pidgeon as Paul St Cyr, Edward Everett Horton as René and original cast member Claude Gillingwater. The action was set in part in glamorous Algiers.

Film: *Kiss Me Again* (1931)

Recording: selections (part-record Reader's Digest, RCA)

THE MOCKING BIRD Musical play in 3 acts by Sydney Rosenfeld. Music by A Baldwin Sloane. Bijou Theater, New York, 10 November 1902.

The Mocking Bird's record of 64 New York performances and a brief return season at the same house in the following year (May 1903) was scarcely that of a major hit, but the piece, written by two men usually dismissed as hacks, contained some work that was very much better than a lot of the imported material which Broadway audiences were gobbling up eagerly in the turn-of-the-century years.

Rosenfeld's book prefigured those of *Naughty Marietta* and *A New Moon* with its tale of 18th-century romance and swashbuckling in New Orleans. Mabelle Gilman was Yvette Millet, the ward of the wealthy and importunate Maxime Grandpré (Robert Rogers); Frank Doane was Jean Villiers, otherwise ''a gentlemanly pirate'' called Jean Le Farge; and the plot was carried through some wholesome colonial rebellion (pro-France and anti-Spain) to a happy ending in which the heroine frees the heroic pirate and wins herself the Governor's tenor secretary, Eugèbe de Lorme (Sydney Deane), for a final duet. Sloane wove into his score the old minstrel song ''Listen to the Mocking Bird'' (written, as the critics didn't hesitate to point out, well after the 18th century!), here used by the pirate band as their rallying call, and by the composer as a delightful concerted finale to the second act, and came together with Rosenfeld on a kind of New Orleans coon song, ''What's the Matter with the Moon Tonight?,'' which, both in its irresistible melody and charmingly picturesque words, flew well above its authors' reputations. The rest of the score, ranging from a marching salute to ''France, Glorious France,'' to the waltzing love duet ''Just a Kiss,'' the saucy tale of ''Musette, Coquette'' and the tenor parlour ballad ''In Silence'' was a touch more conventional than the two top numbers, but as good as anything else of its kind and period. Yet Broadway rejected *The Mocking Bird* and, in the same season, Julian Edwardes's American Civil War musical *When Johnny Comes Marching Home,* whilst showing favor to the British fantasy *The Silver Slipper,* the vigorous low-comic fun of *The Sultan of Sulu,* the combination of fantasy and low comedy with large amounts of spectacle in *The Wizard of Oz,* and the tuneful mixture of Ruritania and jolly Dutch comedy in *The Prince of Pilsen.* The costume comic opera with a recognizable American setting had not yet found its day.

DAS MODELL Operette in 3 acts by Victor Léon and Ludwig Held. Music by Franz von Suppé. Carltheater, Vienna, 4 October 1895.

The little washergirl Coletta (Julie Kopácsi-Karczag) will not act as a model for the painter Tantini (Willi Bauer) any more, for she is being true to her promised Niccolo (Julius Spielmann), the peddler. But Niccolo finds a letter which has been dropped by Riccardo (Grinzenberger), the prospective husband of the lovely Stella (Betty Stojan), and he decides to return it to Stella's mother, Silvia (Adolphine Ziemaier), for whom he has a deep—and, for Coletta's taste, too deeply expressed—admiration. He turns up with the paper at a party where the piqued Coletta has agreed to pose in Tantini's living pictures, is mistaken for Riccardo and then, when the truth is discovered, ridiculed by all. Niccolo plots revenge on Tantini and on Silvia's husband Stirio (Karl Blasel), but he is finally soothed by a job in the latter's salami factory and the hand of the repentant Coletta.

Suppé's last major Operette, completed by Julius Stern and Alfred Zamara, *Das Modell* was produced by Blasel at the Carltheater, where it was played for seven straight weeks and thereafter remained in the repertoire for six years, under the management of Blasel and then Jauner, with Betty Stojan playing her original role throughout. It was also one of the earliest pieces brought into the repertoire at the new Johann Strauss-Theater (1908), where it was given occasional performances up to 1912. It won a certain popularity in Germany, being given in Berlin in 1901 with Julie Kopáci-Karczag as Coletta and Wellhof as Stirio and, similarly, played a respectable 29 times at Budapest's Népszínház (ad György Ruttkay, Emil Makai). It was also given briefly in the repertoire of the Ferenczy troupe at New York's German-language Terrace-Garten, just nine months after its premiere, with Edmund Löwe featured.

Another Operette of the same title with text by Kallenberg and music by Moritz (father of Leo) Fall was produced at Berlin's Theater Unter den Linden just shortly before Suppé's work appeared in Vienna (December 1892).

Germany: Carl-Schultze Theater, Hamburg 21 March 1896, Theater des Westens 8 February 1901; USA: Terrace-Garten *The Model* 2 July 1896; Hungary: Népszínház *A Modell* 1 February 1901

DIE MODERNE EVA Operette in 3 acts by Georg Okonkowski and Alfred Schönfeld, based on *Place aux femmes!* by Maurice Hennequin and Albin Valabrègue. Music by Jean Gilbert. Neues Operetten-Theater, Berlin, 18 October 1911.

A German musical version of the Palais-Royal comedy *Place aux femmes!* which had been produced in Paris 8 October 1898 with Jeanne Cheirel (Renée) and Charles Lamy (Courpstaux) amongst its leading players.

The modern ladies of the title of Okonkowski and Schönfeld's version are Niniche Cascadier, Doctor of Law (Poldi Augustin), and her daughters Renée, a painter (Mizzi Wirth), and Camille, a doctor (Lisa Weise). When Renée weds the rich young Pontgirard (Karl Pfann), her husband soon finds that her professional interests leave her insufficient time for him and so he begins to play around, taking the pseudonym of Count Castel-Bajour for the purpose. His long-subdued father-in-law takes to the idea too, but he adopts the same pseudonym for his adventures until, inevitably, there is a double-whammy backlash. Niniche's law firm takes both an action against the mysterious Castel-Bajour and then Renée's divorce case to court, and it takes a few twists and turns before a happy marital ending is arrived at. Camille's partner is the young lawyer Cibolet (Karl Bachmann).

Gilbert's score was topped by Renée's duo with her husband claiming ''Ich bin eine moderne Frau'' and the dance duo ''Liebchen, lass uns tanzen.''

Coming after its composer's *Polnische Wirtschaft* and *Die keusche Susanne* and before his *Autoliebchen* and *Puppchen*—all premiered in the space of three years and all very big hits—the slightly less appealing *Die moderne Eva* slipped a little from view after its original and well-received Berlin showing. Gilbert's own company took it on tour and it won several foreign productions, but comparatively little total exposure. Even Britain and George Edwardes, who leaped for Gilbert works until the First World War came, for some reason didn't take this one on. In Vienna it was produced by Karczag in a Viennezed version by E Rudy at the Raimundtheater, with Therese Tautenhayn as the renamed Sybilla, Rosa Mittermardi and Paula Zulka as the daughters, Franz Glawatsch as father and Robert Nästlberger as the philandering son-in-law. Gilbert billed himself under his Germanic wartime name as ''Max Winterfeld'' (but with Jean Gilbert still in brackets, just to be sure) and the show lasted one week.

America's Midwest however, showed a distinct taste for Okonkowski's up-to-date ladies. Mort Singer introduced an American version of the show (ad Will M Hough) in Chicago in 1912 with William Norris (Cascadier), Adele Rowlands (Camille) and Joseph Santley featured and with great success, winning a run of over 200 performances at the Garrick and Princess Theaters, but without a move east taking place. It was three years before John Cort picked up the rights and took a version of that version, with most of Gilbert's score replaced by tunes by Viktor Holländer and also a couple by Jerome Kern, to New York. Produced at the Casino Theater with Leila Hughes (Renée), Georgie Drew Mendum (Niniche) and William Norris (Cascadier) in the lead roles, it played 56 performances before going back on the road.

Britain had its *A Modern Eve,* in fact, but it was a different musical. Ada Reeve re-produced her made-to-measure vehicle *Winnie Brooke, Widow* in 1916 and put it out to tour under Okonkowski's title.

Austria: Raimundtheater 14 November 1914; USA: Elkhart, Ind *A Modern Eve* 4 April 1912, Garrick Theater, Chicago 21 April 1912, Casino Theater *A Modern Eve* 3 May 1915

MOINAUX, Jules [MOINAUX, Joseph Désiré] (b Tours, 29 October 1815; d Saint-Mandé, 4 December 1895).

A stenographer at the Paris law courts, Moinaux wrote comic pieces for Parisian magazines before venturing into the theatre. He was the partner of Offenbach on a number of his earliest short pieces, including the landmark *Les Deux Aveugles,* and later moved on to write several important full-scale musicals—the early musical comedy *Le Voyage de MM Dunanan père et fils* and the opéra-bouffe *Les Géorgiennes* with Offenbach, and the enjoyably ridiculous and long-popular *Le Canard à trois becs* with Émile Jonas.

Moinaux's *Le Ver rongeur* (Théâtre des Variétés 30 March 1870, w Henri Bocage, P Bocage) was used as the basis for the Singspiel *Ein nagender Wurm* (*Wechselbrief und Briefwechsel*) by Josef Weyl and Carl Millöcker, produced at the Theater an der Wien, 15 July 1872.

His son, under the nom de plume Georges Courteline (1860–1929), became one of the French theatre's most successful comic playwrights.

1853 **Pépito** (Jacques Offenbach/w Léon Battu) 1 act Salle Herz 27 February; Théâtre des Variétés 28 October

1855 **Les Deux Aveugles** (Offenbach) 1 act Théâtre des Bouffes-Parisiens 5 July

1855 **Oyayaie, ou la reine des Îles** (Offenbach) 1 act Théâtre des Folies-Nouvelles 4 August

1856 **Deux sous de charbon** (Léo Delibes) 1 act Théâtre des Folies-Nouvelles 9 February

1857 **La Demoiselle de la Hoche-Trombelon** (Laurent de Rillé) 1 act Théâtre des Folies-Nouvelles 20 October

1858 **Les Désespérés** (François Bazin/w Adolphe deLeuven) 1 act Opéra-Comique 26 January

1862 **Le Voyage de MM Dunanan père et fils** (Offenbach/w Paul Siraudin) Théâtre des Bouffes-Parisiens 23 March

1864 **Les Géorgiennes** (Offenbach) Théâtre des Bouffes-Parisiens 16 March

1864 **Le Joueur de flûte** (Hervé) 1 act Théâtre des Variétés 16 April

1869 **Le Canard à trois becs** (Émile Jonas) Théâtre des Folies-Dramatiques 6 February

1869 **L'Astronome du Pont-Neuf** (Émile Durand) 1 act Théâtre des Variétés 18 February

1871 **Le Testament de M Crac** (Charles Lecocq) 1 act Théâtre des Bouffes-Parisiens 23 October

1872 **L'Alibi** (Adolphe Nibelle) Théâtre de l'Athénée 10 October

1874 **Les Parisiennes** (Léon Vasseur/w Ernest Blum, Victor Koning) Théâtre des Bouffes-Parisiens 31 March

1875 **La Cruche cassée** (Vasseur/w Jules Noriac) Théâtre Taitbout 27 October

1877 **La Sorrentine** (Vasseur/w Noriac) Théâtre des Bouffes-Parisiens 24 March

MOINEAU Opérette in 3 acts by Henri Duvernois and Pierre Wolff based on their play *La Noce.* Lyrics by Guillot de Saix. Music by Louis Beydts. Théâtre Marigny, Paris, 13 March 1931.

The most successful work of the composer Beydts, a pupil and disciple of Messager, *Moineau* was a Parisian period piece which strove to follow the manner of Messager's *Véronique* even to the extent of setting its second act in the same Restaurant du Tourne-bride at Romainville as was featured in the middle act of the earlier piece, and to plugging the older composer's name in its lyrics.

A Montmartre layabout, Gaston Gilbert (Robert Burnier), makes it a rule to change his mistress each three months and in Act I he swaps Léontine (Nilda Duplessy) for little Moineau (Marcelle Denya), who makes wedding crowns for a living. His friends Chadec (Serjius) and Mme Froumentel (Nina Myral), thus cued, suggest an imitation wedding for the new lovers, and off they go to Romainville to celebrate. Moineau is a little sad that the "wedding" is not for real, but when the three months are up Gaston finds that he cannot let her go, so there is a happy ending after all.

Beydts's score was in his preferred Messager mode, with reminiscences of the more famous composer arising frequently, and with some attractive songs for Gaston ("Chaque souvenir d'amour"), Moineau ("De tous les voyages de noces") and the lively Madame Froumentel ("Ce petit coquin de printemps") set alongside some well-built concerted music and finales.

Produced by Léon Volterra at the Théâtre Marigny, the piece ran for a set season, but in spite of the appeal that it had for those who liked their opérette made in the soigné if not precisely popular mode, it was not brought back.

Beydts subsequently wrote an amount of orchestral and vocal music, including a considerable number of incidental theatre scores, film music (*La Kermesse héroïque, Le Diable boîteux, Valse de Paris,* etc), and the music for Yvonne Printemps to sing in her husband's little opéra-bouffe *La S.A.D.M.P.,* and in *Le Voyage de Tschoung-Li* and the little *Chagrin d'amour.* He was appointed Director of the Opéra-Comique in 1952 and held the post until his death the following year.

MOLLISON, Clifford [Lely] (b London, 30 March 1897; d Cyprus, 5 June 1986). Light-comedy leading man of the West End interwar stage.

The son of actor William Mollison, Clifford Mollison made his first West End musical appearance, after 15 years working in the straight theatre, as Adolar in Lehár's *The Blue Mazurka* (1927). Thereafter he played light-comedy leads in many British stage and screen musicals including *The Girl Friend* (1928, Richard Dennison), *Lucky Girl* (1929, King Stephan), *Here Comes the Bride* (1930, Frederick Tile) and opposite Binnie Hale in *Nippy*

(1931, Bob Deering). He played the role of Leopold in the British *White Horse Inn* (1931) in which he introduced Harry Graham's English version of Robert Stolz's added song "Goodbye," and during the 1930s featured in *Out of the Bottle* (1932, Peter Partridge), *The Gay Deceivers* (*Toi c'est moi,* 1935, Pat Russell), *Twenty to One* (1935, Timothy), *No, No, Nanette* (1936 rev, Billy Early) and *Balalaika* (1936, Nicki). On the screen he appeared in, amongst others, *A Southern Maid* (1933, Willoughby Rawdon) and in Bobby Howes's role of Jim in *Mr Cinders.*

After five years in the wartime army Mollison returned to the theatre and appeared in the Offenbach pasticcio *Can-Can* (1946, Paul Latour), but thereafter he appeared again largely in non-musical pieces. He returned to musical comedy in his sixties to play in *A Funny Thing Happened on the Way to the Forum* in Australia and Britain.

MOLLISON, [James] William (b London, 24 December 1893; d London, 19 October 1955). British director of a quarter of a century of interwar musicals.

After an early career as an actor and service during the First World War, Mollison spent a period in South Africa and Australia doubling as a jobbing actor and a when-I-can director. Another "ex-Australian," Jack Waller and Herbert Clayton hired him to direct the London production of *No, No, Nanette* (1925, also Paris 1926), and thus set in motion his long career as a director of London musical plays. The list of his credits in the later 1920s included *Mercenary Mary* (1925), *Princess Charming* (1926), The *Girl Friend, Hit the Deck* (1927), *Good News, Virginia* (1928), *Merry, Merry, Hold Everything!, Dear Love* (1929), *Silver Wings, Sons o' Guns* and *Little Tommy Tucker* (1930). He staged *Meet My Sister* for the Shuberts, Al Jolson's *Wonder Bar* and *Everybody's Welcome* on Broadway at the turn of the decade before returning to London for *The Cat and the Fiddle, Tell Her the Truth* (1932), *Jolly Roger, He Wanted Adventure, Give Me a Ring, Command Performance* (1933), *Lucky Break, Jill Darling* (1934), *Gay Deceivers, Seeing Stars* (1935), *Going Places* (1936), *The Laughing Cavalier* (1937), *Bobby Get Your Gun* (1938) and *Magyar Melody* (1939). He mounted wartime touring revivals of *No, No, Nanette, The Duchess of Dantzic* and *The Merry Widow* (1943), *Panama Hattie* (1943), reprises of *Irene* and *Merrie England* (1945), the pasticcio *Can-Can* (1946), *The Kid from Stratford* (1948) and in 1950 his last new musical, the touring *Caprice* for the same Jack Waller who had launched his London career 25 years earlier.

One of the most important and efficient musical-theatre directors in Britain between the wars, both with American musical comedies and with the new British pieces built around such comedy stars as Bobby Howes, George Robey, Flanagan and Allen and Leslie Henson, Mollison was increasingly bedeviled in his later days by persistent drunkenness and such postwar work as he found was largely for the faithful Waller.

MOLNÁR, Ferenc [NEUMANN, Ferenc] (b Budapest, 12 January 1878; d New York, 1 April 1952). Internationally successful Hungarian playwright whose career touched on the musical stage at each of its ends.

Journalist, editorialist, playwright (from 1902), dramatic translator and adapter, novelist, short-story writer and a war correspondent in the First World War, Molnár pursued an eclectic and all-embracing career through the years of his greatest early successes with the plays *Az Ördög* (the devil, 1907), *Liliom, egy csirkefogó é lete és halála* (Liliom, the life and death of a lout, 1909) and *Az testőr* (the guardsman, 1910). In his earliest years as a writer, he produced a flood of translations and adaptations of the plays of such authors as Maurice Hennequin, Georges Duval, de Flers and de Caillavet, Paul Gavault, Georges Berr and Jerome K Jerome for the Király Színház and the Magyar Színház, a list which included Hungarian versions of both French and German musical works as well as such musicalized French comedies as *Kati bácsi* (*Le Sursis*) and *Gyöngyélet* (*Tire-au-flanc!*).

His *The Phantom Lover* (*A farkas,* 1912) was used as the source for fellow Hungarian Victor Jacobi's 1921 Broadway musical *Love Letters,* but it was many years later, after Molnár had gone to live in America, before he had his next contact with the musical stage when others of his plays also became the bases for musical shows. If Billy Rose's commission to Rodgers and Hart to make a musical from his *The Play's the Thing* (*Színház*) was aborted when the work was only half complete, Rodgers more than compensated with his collaboration with Hammerstein on *Carousel* (1945), based on Molnár's *Liliom. Make a Wish* (Hugh Martin/Preston Sturges, Winter Garden Theater, New York 18 April 1951) was taken from his 1930 play *A jo tündér* (the good fairy), his 1929 one-act play *Egy, kettő, három* became the basis for a German musical *Eins, zwei, drei* (Theater des Westens 12 November 1989, Birger Heyman/Volker Kühn/Helmut Baumann) which dealt with the 1960s, and the outline of *Az testőr* was used as the book for the film version of *The Chocolate Soldier* after G B Shaw had effectively prevented the use of *Arms and the Man.* The piece was later more conventionally musicalized as *Enter the Guardsman* (Craig Bohmler/Marion Adler/Scott Wentworth Donmar Warehouse, London 11 September 1997).

Between 1922 and 1925 Molnár was the husband of the Hungarian musical-theatre star Sári Fedák from whom he was divorced with much noise and filling of newspaper front pages and a considerable and uncontested out-of-court settlement, made when Fedák threatened to ''tell the whole truth,'' whatever that might have been, before the Budapest divorce judge.

1900 **Veronka** (*Véronique*) Hungarian version (Magyar Színház)

1900 **Felfordult világ** (*Le Royaume des femmes*) Hungarian version w Emil Makai (Fővárosi Nyári Színház)

1901 **Az ikrek** (*Les Soeurs Gaudichard*) Hungarian version (Magyar Színház)

1901 **Korhelykirály** (*Le Roi frelon*) Hungarian version w Makai (Fővárosi Nyári Színház)

1903 **Makrancos hölgyek** (*Lysistrata*) Hungarian version w Jenő Faragó (Király Színház)

1905 **Kati bácsi** (*Le Sursis*) Hungarian version w songs Király Színház 20 January

1906 **Gyöngyélet** (*Tire-au-flanc!*) Hungarian version w songs by Adolf Mérei, Ferenc Békési Magyar Színház 21 April

1911 **A ferencvárosi angyal** (Alfred Szirmai/w Jenő Heltai) Royal Orfeum 31 December

1912 **Ábrahám a menyországban** (*Casimirs Himmelfahrt*) Hungarian version w Heltai (Fővárosi Nyári Színház)

1924 **Mikádo** (*The Mikado*) new Hungarian version (Városi Színház)

Autobiography: *Companion in Exile: Notes for an Autobiography* (Gaer, New York, 1950); Biography: Vécsei, I: *Ferenc Molnár* (Gondolat, Budapest,1966)

MONCKTON, [John] Lionel [Alexander] (b London, 18 December 1861; d London, 15 February 1924). Composer for the heyday of the Gaiety and Daly's Theatres musicals.

The son of London's town clerk, Sir John Braddick Monckton (1832–1902), and of Lady Monckton (née Maria Louisa Long), an enthusiastic amateur actress, Lionel Monckton was educated at Charterhouse and at Oxford University, where he took part in college theatricals and composed music for the dramatic society's productions. He began his working life in the legal profession, but worked on the side as a theatre and music critic on the *Pall Mall Gazette* and, subsequently, the *Daily Telegraph,* and all the time continued to write songs. He had his first stage piece, an operetta called *Mummies and Marriage* (lib: Alan M Mackinnon, J G Adderley) adapted from James Kenney's *An Illustrious Stranger,* produced by amateurs at Folkestone's Exhibition Palace in 1888 (6 December) under the nom de plume of ''Leslie Mayne.'' *The Era* commented ''The music, if not startlingly original, is at any rate tuneful and easy of performance.''

Monckton was 30 years old before he placed his first number in a professional musical show, the breakthrough occurring when George Edwardes put his ''What Will You Have to Drink?,'' with a lyric by no less a collaborator than Basil Hood, into the burlesque *Cinder-Ellen Up Too Late* (1891), to be sung by Edwin Lonnen. Monckton subsequently supplied interpolations for Edwardes's *Don Juan* (1893, ''Some Do It This Way'' w Horace Lennard), supplied some of the music for the burlesque *The Babble Shop,* contributed to the hotchpotch collection of songs which illustrated *King Kodak* (1894, ''We've Faith in the Old Flag Still,'' etc) and wrote half of the music for Arthur Roberts's burlesque *Claude Du-val* (1894)—before supplementing Ivan Caryll's score for the Gaiety Theatre's *The Shop Girl* (1894) with such successful pieces as George Grossmith's ''Beautiful Bountiful Bertie'' and Colin Coop's ''Brown of Colorado'' (w Adrian Ross).

The association with Edwardes and with Caryll (later the two were billed as co-composers rather than Monckton getting ''additional music by'') begun on *The Shop Girl* was to continue for 15 years—15 years in which the Gaiety Theatre was the world's center of musical comedy and Caryll and Monckton's songs for *The Circus Girl* (''A Simple Little String,'' ''The Way to Treat a Lady''), *A Runaway Girl* (''Soldiers in the Park,'' ''Society,'' ''The Sly Cigarette,'' ''The Boy Guessed Right'' also lyric, ''Not the Sort of Girl I Care About''), *The Messenger Boy* (''Maisie,'' ''In the Wash,'' ''When the Boys Come Home Once More'' also lyrics as ''Leslie Mayne''), *The Toreador* (''Captivating Cora,'' ''I'm Romantic,'' ''When I Marry Amelia,'' ''Keep Off the Grass,'' ''Archie''), *The Orchid* (''Liza Ann,'' ''Little Mary,'' ''Pushful,'' ''Fancy Dress''), *The Spring Chicken* (''I Don't Know, But I Guess,'' ''Alice Sat by the Fire,'' ''Under and Over Forty''), *The New Aladdin, The Girls of Gottenberg* (''Two Little Sausages'' also lyric, ''Rheingold,'' ''Berlin on the Spree'') and *Our Miss Gibbs* (''Moonstruck,'' ''Mary,'' ''In Yorkshire,'' ''Our Farm'') were amongst the most widely played and sung numbers of the contemporary light musical theatre.

Although, during this period, Monckton occasionally supplied single or multiple numbers for other producers and shows (*L'Auberge du Tohu-bohu, The Scarlet Feather, A Modern Don Quixote, Biarritz,* etc), his principal activity outside the Gaiety Theatre was in a similar capacity at Edwardes's other important musical house, Daly's Theatre, where the producer offered a more substantial, romantic-comic-opera kind of musical play than was presented at the Gaiety. At Daly's, rather than supplementing the work of Caryll, he operated in support of the other outstanding theatre composer of the contemporary London scene, Sidney Jones. They came together first on the score for Jones's greatest hit *The Geisha* (1896), for which Monckton provided the jaunty ''Jack's the Boy'' and Letty Lind's ''pop'' hit ''The Toy Monkey'' alongside Jones's beautiful romantic numbers, his more traditional comedy songs, and the finales and ensembles which were in any case musically outside Monckton's ''songwriting'' abilities. The mixture was repeated in *The Geisha's* successor, *A Greek Slave* (1898, ''I Want to Be Popular,'' ''I Should Rather Like to Try,'' ''What Will Be the End of It?''), and, with further international success, in *San Toy* (''Rhoda and Her Pagoda,'' ''Sons of the Motherland'').

Edwardes also put Monckton to work on one musical without Caryll or Jones, but still as an adept of the additional number, in the delightful *Kitty Grey* (1900/1, ''Little Zo-Zo,'' ''Kitty Grey'') but it was not until 1902 that the composer was given his first opportunity to write a full score himself. A little surprisingly, perhaps, this was not at the Gaiety, for which his lively and exceptionally catchy melodies seemed the best suited, and where he had for so long supplied his wife, the Gaiety's brightest star Gertie Millar, with her material, but for Daly's Theatre. With lyricist Harry Greenbank dead and composer Jones deployed elsewhere, Monckton teamed with librettist James Tanner, also more connected to date with the Gaiety, and with ubiquitous lyricist Adrian Ross to produce *A Country Girl.*

The piece proved an enormous success, launched several hit songs (''Molly the Marchioness,'' ''Try Again, Johnny,'' ''Under the Deodar''), both by Monckton and by Paul Rubens, who now filled the ''additional songs by'' line previously occupied by Monckton on the credits, and led to another Daly's musical from the same team, *The Cingalee.* However, although *The Cingalee* was fairly successful, the problems and palenesses he encountered in its production persuaded Edwardes to change his style at Daly's and, as Messager's *Les P'tites Michu,* Hugo Felix's *Les Merveilleuses* and ultimately *The Merry Widow* took over that stage, Monckton found, for the moment, no further outlet for his newly discovered vocation as principal composer. He had to content himself with working on more additional material—*The Girl from Kays* (''Papa''), *Les Merveilleuses* (''Publicity,'' ''A Lady with a Dowry,'' ''It's Only a Matter of Time'')—and part-scores, including more special material for his wife at the Gaiety. Then Edwardes decided to make a change at the Gaiety as well. He signed up Leslie Stuart, composer of *Florodora* and the 1908 Gaiety show *Havana,* as lead composer for the Gaiety musical to follow Caryll and Monckton's *Our Miss Gibbs,* and redirected Monckton (and his wife) down to the Adelphi Theatre, the latest addition to his chain of musical houses.

In the meanwhile, however, Monckton had found other collaborators. Before his first Adelphi show was seen, Robert Courtneidge had produced the first Lionel Monckton musical for many years not to have been

Plate 261. **Lionel Monckton**

mounted under the Edwardes banner. *The Arcadians* (1909), co-composed with his *Kitty Grey* colleague, Howard Talbot, was also the best Monckton musical—arguably the best musical of the whole Edwardian age—and it scored an enormous worldwide success. Monckton's ''The Pipes of Pan,'' ''The Girl with the Brogue'' and ''All Down Piccadilly'' became, in the age where the fashion was for ''anything one sees that's Viennese,'' as big hits as any of his previous show songs. When Edwardes produced Monckton's first Adelphi musical, *The Quaker Girl* (''The Quaker Girl,'' ''Come to the Ball,'' ''Tony from America'') with Miss Millar, who had followed her husband away from the Gaiety, starring in its title role, the composer—approaching 50, and with nearly two decades of almost unbroken success in the musical theatre behind him—found himself basking in his most outstandingly successful period of all.

However, it was a peak period which was not enduring. Monckton next combined with Talbot again on some enchanting music for another musical, *The Mousmé* (''I Know Nothing of Life,'' ''The Little Japanese Mamma,''

''The Temple Bell,'' ''The Corner of My Eye''), for Courtneidge, and repeated for the Adelphi, Edwardes and Miss Millar with *The Dancing Mistress.* Both pieces had respectable rather than outstanding runs, before the composer took part in one last huge success—the musical-comedy version of Pinero's *The Magistrate, The Boy* (''I Want to Go to Bye-Bye,'' ''The Game That Ends with a Kiss,'' ''Powder on Your Nose''), produced at the Adelphi by Alfred Butt during the war and after Edwardes's death. And then, having tried his hand, not unsuccessfully, at the newfangled revue in partnership with Herman Finck and others (*Bric à Brac, We're All in It, Airs and Graces*) he withdrew from the world of the musical theatre. Unable and unwilling to adapt his style of writing to the newly popular dance rhythms and ''noisy numbers'' which were invading the theatre, he simply stopped writing.

Monckton showed, through a quarter of a century of shows and songs, that, perhaps more than any other British songwriter of the great period of Gaiety and Daly's musical comedy, he had the ability to produce individual musical-comedy songs which stood out as hit singles in scores by the most appreciable composers of the time. But he also subsequently showed, in *A Country Girl* and *The Quaker Girl,* that he was capable of composing a complete, or quasi-complete score for a show with equal felicity and equal popular success, and even, in these latter days, of venturing occasionally into writing the concerted and ensemble music which had previously been the domain of his colleagues (though Monckton's arrangements and orchestrations were inevitably left to the useful Carl Kiefert). His contribution to the English-speaking musical theatre was vast, and his individual songs, from ''Soldiers in the Park,'' ''Jack's the Boy'' and ''Try Again, Johnny'' to ''Moonstruck,'' ''Come to the Ball'' and ''The Girl with the Brogue,'' lasted as favorites for many decades.

1893 **The Babble Shop, or Lord Wyndhamere's Fan** (w Arthur Godfrey/Edward Rose) Trafalgar Square Theatre 30 March

1894 **Claude Du-Val** (*Blend 1664–1894*) (w John Crook/Frederick Bowyer, ''Payne Nunn'' [Arthur Roberts]) Prince of Wales Theatre 25 September

1896 **The Circus Girl** (w Ivan Caryll/Adrian Ross, Harry Greenbank/James T Tanner, Walter Palings) Gaiety Theatre 5 December

1898 **A Runaway Girl** (w Caryll/Aubrey Hopwood, H Greenbank/Seymour Hicks, Harry Nicholls) Gaiety Theatre 21 May

1900 **The Messenger Boy** (w Caryll/Ross, Percy Greenbank/Tanner, Alfred Murray) Gaiety Theatre 3 February

1901 **The Toreador** (w Caryll, Paul Rubens/Ross, P Greenbank/Tanner, Nicholls) Gaiety Theatre 17 June

1901 **Kitty Grey** (w Howard Talbot, Augustus Barratt, Rubens/Ross, Rubens/J Smyth Piggott) Apollo Theatre 7 September

1902 **A Country Girl** (Ross, P Greenbank/Tanner) Daly's Theatre 18 January

1903 **The Orchid** (w Caryll/Ross, P Greenbank/Tanner) Gaiety Theatre 28 October

1904 **The Cingalee** (Ross, P Greenbank/Tanner) Daly's Theatre 5 March

1905 **The Spring Chicken** (w Caryll/Ross, P Greenbank/George Grossmith jr) Gaiety Theatre 30 May

1906 **The New Aladdin** (w Caryll/Ross, P Greenbank /Tanner, W H Risque) Gaiety Theatre 29 September

1907 **The Girls of Gottenberg** (w Caryll/Ross, Basil Hood/Grossmith, L E Berman) Gaiety Theatre 15 May

1909 **Our Miss Gibbs** (w Caryll/Ross, P Greenbank/''Cryptos,'' Tanner) Gaiety Theatre 23 January

1909 **The Arcadians** (w Talbot/Arthur Wimperis/Mark Ambient, Alexander M Thompson) Shaftesbury Theatre 28 April

1910 **The Quaker Girl** (Ross, P Greenbank/Tanner) Adelphi Theatre 5 November

1911 **The Mousmé** (w Talbot/Wimperis, P Greenbank/Thompson, Robert Courtneidge) Shaftesbury Theatre 9 September

1912 **The Dancing Mistress** (Ross, P Greenbank/Tanner) Adelphi Theatre 19 October

1914 **The Belle of Bond Street** revised *The Girl from Kays* ad Harold Atteridge (Shubert Theater, New York)

1917 **The Boy** (w Talbot/Ross, P Greenbank/Fred Thompson) Adelphi Theatre 14 September

MONCRIEFF, Gladys [Lillian] (b Bundaberg, Queensland, Australia, 13 April 1892; d Benowa, Queensland, 8 February 1976). Australia's favorite musical-comedy star between the wars.

A rangy, true-voiced soprano, Gladys Moncrieff worked at first in vaudeville before being signed at the age of 20 to a long-term contract by J C Williamson Ltd, Australia's most important producers of musical theatre. She began with ''the firm'' in the chorus, and worked as a small part player and understudy before progressing to larger roles (O Mimosa San in *The Geisha,* Yum-Yum, Sombra, the Merry Widow, etc) in Australia and on Williamsons' tours of New Zealand and South Africa. She made her first big personal success in the title role of *Katinka* (1918) and was featured thereafter as Delphine in *Oh! Oh! Delphine,* Ottilie in *Maytime,* Pansy in *Theodore & Co,* Diana in *The Boy* and Georgette in *Kissing Time* before, in 1921, she was starred in José Collins's famous role of Teresa in *The Maid of the Mountains. The Maid of the Mountains* was Gladys's greatest success, and she repeated her Teresa regularly for the rest of her career, becoming identified with the part even more strongly than Collins had in Britain. Whenever ''the firm'' was in trouble, they would call up Gladys (''Gladys, the ship is sinking . . .'') and remount the infallible *Maid of the Mountains.* She is said to have played Teresa 2,289 times and used up 18 different leading men.

Miss Moncrieff followed up in José Collins's other starring roles in *Sybil* and *A Southern Maid,* as well as appearing in *The Naughty Princess, The Merry Widow,* a revival of *Ma Mie Rosette* (Rosette), *The Lady of the Rose* (Mariana) and *The Street Singer* (Yvette). Then, her contract with Williamsons having expired, she decided to try her luck in London. She was given lead roles there in Künneke's disastrous *Riki-Tiki* and Lehár's indifferent *The Blue Mazurka* and returned to Australia disappointed. However, another gypsyish lady quickly put her right back on top. Her first new home engagement, for the Fuller Brothers, was to play the title role in *Rio Rita,* and as Rita she made a success second only to her *Maid of the Mountains* triumph.

In the years that followed, several attempts were made to create a native Australian musical around the country's biggest singing star, but *Collits' Inn* (1933), Dudley Glass's *The Beloved Vagabond* (1934, but 1927 in Britain) and *The Cedar Tree* (1934) did not prove any more successful than the half–New Zealand show *Jolly Roger* (1936). Otherwise, oddly starved by the all-powerful Williamsons of new shows and parts, she appeared largely in revivals of her most successful roles—Teresa, Rio Rita, the Merry Widow or as Viktória in Ábrahám's opérette of the same name—before putting an end to a career unequaled in the 20th-century Australian musical theatre where ''our Glad,'' as she was adoringly known, was a star like no other.

Autobiography: *My Life in Song* (aka *Our Glad*) (Rigby Ltd, Melbourne, 1971)

MONKHOUSE, Harry [McKIE, John Adolph] (b Newcastle-upon-Tyne, 17 May 1854; d London, 18 February 1901). British comedy star of the Victorian musical theatre.

Monkhouse appeared in concerts in his native Newcastle from childhood, and made his first appearance on the stage as a teenager at Blyth. He played with the companies at Choppington (1872, Roderigo in *Othello,* etc), South Shields (1873, Widow Mustapha in *Aladdin,* etc), West Hartlepool and Jersey (1875), and made his first London appearance in transpontine drama and trimmings at the suburban Elephant and Castle Theatre under Marie Henderson's management (Lady Concertina in *Little Tom Tucker* 1876, Baron Bloodhannebbonesho in *Jack the Valiant* 1877). He played thereafter at other secondary theatres, including the Victoria, the Marylebone and the Grecian (where he appeared in such rattlers as *The Black Flag* 1897, and *Australia, or The Bushrangers* 1881), before making his West End debut at the Alhambra as King Octopus in the 1882 revival of *Babil and Bijou.* From the Alhambra, he moved on to the Gaiety where in 1883 he played Tête de veau in *Blue Beard,* Prospero to the Ariel of Nellie Farren in the burlesque *Ariel* and in 1884 Ajax the First in the unsuccessful *Our Helen,* Blobbs in *Dick* and Lovel in a slightly musicalized version of *High Life Below Stairs.* He subsequently toured with Willie Edouin and Alice Atherton in their highly successful burlesque *The Babes* (1884, Bill Booty) and with Lizzie Coote in the burlesque *Cheribel* (1885, Conrad the Corsair), and in 1886 he made a winning debut as a producer with a farcical piece called *Larks* which he ran on the number-two circuits for several seasons.

In 1888 he launched another provincial musical comedy, this time of his own making: a jolly piece of Irishness called *Pat. Pat* was revised for a new production in 1891–92 and served several seasons on the British road and won a production in Sydney, Australia (Theatre Royal 21 December 1895), by which time the names of Sir Arthur Sullivan and Adrian Ross had become attached to the list of songwriting ''contributors.''

Monkhouse's career took a more permanent London turn when he was hired as principal comedian by the newly formed Carl Rosa Light Opera Company, and was featured as the old smuggler, Bouillabaisse, in their highly successful *Paul Jones* (1889) at the Prince of Wales Theatre. He remained at the Prince of Wales for lead comedy roles in *Marjorie* (1890, Gosric), *Captain Thérèse* (1890, Duvet), *The Rose and the Ring* (1890, Valoroso), and the British version of De Koven's *Robin Hood* (*Maid Marian,* Sheriff of Nottingham). By now established amongst the town's top musical comedians, he then proceeded to rack up a series of further London credits in *La Cigale* (1891, Matthew Vanderkoopen t/o), *The Mountebanks* (1892, Bartolo), *Incognita* (1892, Don Pedro), *The Magic Opal* (1893, Telemachus Ulysses Carambollas) and *Poor Jonathan* (1893, Jonathan). He also teamed with American soubrette Marie Halton to produce an unfortunate *La Rosière*—for which he himself was credited with the Frenchified libretto—at the Shaftesbury Theatre.

Monkhouse moved on to take the senior comic role in George Edwardes's musical comedy *A Gaiety Girl* (1893, Rev Montague Brierly), and thereafter he played for Edwardes in the Gaiety tour of Australia and America (1894–95), and in a series of important roles in important London shows: *The Shop Girl* (1895, t/o Hooley), *An Artist's Model* (1895, t/o Smoggins), *The Geisha* (1896, Marquis Imari), *A Circus Girl* (1896, Sir Titus Wemyss), *A Runaway Girl* (1898, Brother Tamarind), *The Messenger Boy* (1900, t/o Hooker Pasha) and *Kitty Grey* (1900, King of Illyria). He next succeeded Willie Edouin as Tweedlepunch in Tom Davis's *Florodora,* but died during his tenancy of the role, and just weeks after filing for bankruptcy.

1888 **Pat, the Irish Lancer** (various) Grand Theatre, Birmingham 18 June

1891 **Pat** (revised *Pat, the Irish Lancer*) (John Crook, Alfred Lee,

Plate 262. **Phyllis Monkman**

Edward Solomon, Fred Eplett/Mark Ambient, Frederic Wood/w George Roberts) Royal Artillery Theatre, Woolwich 16 November; revised version w add mus Edward Jakobowksi Aquarium, Yarmouth 1 August 1892

1893 **La Rosière** (Jakobowski) Shaftesbury Theatre 14 January

1899 **Larks in London** (aka *Larks Up to Date*) revised *Larks* (Jacques Greebe/ad J Wilton Jones ad) Lyric Theatre, Hammersmith 17 July

MONKMAN, Phyllis [HARRISON, Phyllis Ida] (b London, 8 January 1892; d London, 2 December 1976). Dancer and light-comedy actress who played several London leading roles in the 1920s and 1930s.

A teenaged dancer (a little girl in *Lady Madcap,* a Montezuma dancer, with her sister Dorothy, in *The Belle of Mayfair,* a soloist in *Butterflies*) and then a small-part player (*Dear Little Denmark, The Girl in the Train, The Quaker Girl, The Dancing Viennese*) in musical comedy, Miss Monkman made her mark during the 1910s in revue and with the Co-Optimists concert party. She appeared, during this time, in supporting roles in occasional musicals (*The Wild Geese,* as the naughty maidservant of *A Night Out*), but was given her first chance at leading roles in the productions of *Dear Little Billie* (1925, Billie), *Lady Luck* (1926, Jane Juste) and *So Long, Letty!* (1928, Letty Robbins), each produced by her husband, Laddie Cliff. In a later career which mixed musical appearances with some dramatic ones, she played Lucille in a revival of *No, No, Nanette* (1936), took over in *The Two Bouquets,* appeared in Noël Coward's *Operette* (1938, Maisie Welbey), played the leading female role in the wartime musical *Present Arms* (1942, Babette) and was seen in a West End musical for the last time as Lady Jane in a revival of *Rose Marie.*

MONNOT, Marguerite [Angèle] (b Decize, France, 28 May 1909; d Paris, 12 October 1961).

A student of Nadia Boulanger and a youthful concert pianist, Mlle Monnot won early laurels as a songwriter with ''L'Étranger'' and ''Mon Légionnaire'' (1935) and thereafter composed numerous successful songs, notably for Edith Piaf, several of which became international hits—''The Poor People of Paris,'' ''Milord,'' ''The Left Bank'' [''C'est à Hambourg''], ''If You Love Me'' [''Si tu m'aimes''], ''Un coin tout bleu,'' ''Hymne à l'amour,'' etc.

Monnot made her entry into the musical theatre with the score for a vehicle for Piaf and Eddy Constantine called *La P'tite Lili,* but she scored her greatest theatrical triumph with the songs for a musical which had more than a little of Piaf about its leading character. *Irma la Douce* (''Ah! dis-donc,'' ''Avec les anges,'' ''Y a que Paris pour ça'') proved the most internationally successful French musical play for decades. It was still playing in Paris, five years after its premiere, when its composer died.

1951 **La P'tite Lili** (Marcel Achard) Théâtre de l'ABC 3 March

1956 **Irma la Douce** (Alexandre Breffort) Théâtre Gramont 12 November

MONSIEUR BEAUCAIRE Romantic opera in 3 acts by Frederick Lonsdale founded on the story by Newton Booth Tarkington and the play by Tarkington and Evelyn Greenleaf Sutherland. Lyrics by Adrian Ross. Music by André Messager. Prince's Theatre, London, 19 April 1919.

The play *Monsieur Beaucaire* (1901), originally produced in America with Richard Mansfield in the starring role and since then a vehicle for many a matinée idol and romantic leading man, notably Britain's Lewis Waller, was a natural for transubstantiation into a romantic light opera. The men who took on the task, equally, seemed the natural choices: Freddie Lonsdale, the most literate of Britain's librettists and the author of the megahit *The*

Maid of the Mountains, and the 65-year-old leader of the French light opera tradition, André Messager, supported by lyricist Ross, director Pat Malone and designer Percy Anderson—each the doyen of his profession. The result came up to all but the most extravagant expectations.

Beaucaire (Marion Green), a French barber living in Bath, has been expelled from the Pump Rooms for presumptiousness. But he is determined to meet the beautiful Lady Mary Carlisle (Maggie Teyte), and when he catches the louche Duke of Winterset (Robert Parker) cheating at cards, the barber blackmails the aristocrat into taking him to a society ball, disguised as the Duc de Châteaurien. When Beaucaire and Lady Mary find a fast affinity, the furious Winterset first forces him into a duel, then exposes him. But Lady Mary holds to her love, and Winterset is confounded when Beaucaire turns out to be the exiled and incognito heir to the French throne.

The solos of Messager's score were written very largely for the two romantic leads, and that total was increased further when he added one more number for operatic diva Teyte, Debussy's admired Mélisande, between the Birmingham tryout and the London opening. The waltz-song "Philomel," learned by the prima donna in 24 hours, turned out to be the bonbon of a score in which she had several other fine romantic and dramatic pieces and duets with her baritone. Green, slightly overparted as a singing Lewis Waller, had several attractive ballads—"Under the Moon," "Red Rose," "English Maids"— whilst a soubrette couple, woven neatly into the main story (John Clarke, Alice Moffat), had two duos in Messager's lightest and brightest style.

Produced during the postwar rage for revue and ragtime, *Monsieur Beaucaire* put up a remarkable London run of 221 performances (no such light opera in memory had done so well) before Gilbert Miller handed over his entire production to Broadway's Abe Erlanger. Mme Teyte and one young supporting performer called Dennis King, who had been replaced during the run, did not go to Broadway, and Green starred in New York opposite Blanche Tomlin for a respectable 143 performances at the New Amsterdam Theater before the show was taken around America.

Six years after its London premiere, Messager's piece (ad André Rivoire, Pierre Veber), only slightly retouched, was produced in Paris with André Baugé and Marcelle Denya starred. Paris gave *Monsieur Beaucaire* its strongest welcome of all. The piece was played for more than two hundred performances in its initial season, revived for three and a half months at the Gaîté-Lyrique in 1929 with René Gerbert and Louise Dhamarys (1 October), again in 1935 (31 August), and was ultimately mounted at the Opéra-Comique, with Jacques Jansen and Denise Duval starred, in 1954. Britain hosted revivals in the West End in 1931 (Daly's Theatre 16 November) with Raymond Newell and Barbara Pett-Fraser, and on the road, under Tom Arnold's banner, in 1945 with Derek Oldham and Lisa Perli in the leading roles.

Like most other English light operas, *Monsieur Beaucaire* has slipped from the repertoire in its original language, but it still finds occasional plays in its French translation, the most recent of which was seen at the Grand Théâtre, Nancy with François Le Roux and Véronique Dietschy featured in 1980 (5 April).

USA: New Amsterdam Theater 11 December 1919; France: Théâtre Marigny 20 November 1925

Recordings: original cast (Opal/Pearl), French selection (EMI-Pathé)

MONSIEUR CHOUFLEURI RESTERA CHEZ LUI LE (24 JANVIER 1833) Opérette-bouffe in 1 act by Mr *** (Duc de Morny, et al). Music by Mr de St Rémy (Morny) and Jacques Offenbach. Privately, 31 May 1861; Théâtre des Bouffes-Parisiens, 14 September 1861.

A little piece, barely more than a sketch, originally evolved by Offenbach's friend-in-high-places, Charles Auguste Louis Joseph, Duc de Morny (1811–65), as a vehicle for some extravagant parody of the Italian opera, *Monsieur Choufleuri* was reorganized and, it would seem, largely composed by Offenbach and his friends (allegedly MM Meilhac, Halévy and Lepine) and, after a private production, ultimately put into the Offenbach company's repertoire and on to the stage at the Bouffes-Parisiens. It proved to be a thoroughly delightful piece of burlesque nonsense, and it has survived the 140 years since its first appearance through, at first, a rush of performances and, latterly, regular re-mountings, the most recent in Paris being as part of a three-part Offenbach evening inaugurated at the Salle Favart in December 1979 (w *Pomme d'api* and *Mesdames de la Halle*).

The bourgeois Monsieur Choufleuri (Désiré) has pretensions. He keeps a butler, even if he is only a Belgian (Marchand), and he won't let his daughter Ernestine (Lise Tautin/Mlle Auclair) wed anyone so unimpressive as her composer boyfriend Chrysodule Babylas (Potel). Monsieur Choufleuri decides to launch himself socially by giving a soirée to which he will invite the operatic stars Sonntag, Rubini and Tamburini. They will, of course, be expected to sing. The guests arrive, but of course the singers don't, and Ernestine, Babylas and Choufleuri are obliged to imitate them to save face. The guests, headed by Balandard (Bache) and his wife (Léonce in travesty) are as foolish as their host and go away thinking they have seen the real thing, whilst Babylas gets his reward for saving Choufleuri's face in the form of the hand of Ernestine. The musical part consisted of an overture and seven numbers of which the central burlesque Italian trio (''Italia la bella''), Choufleuri's lesson on how to fake Italian in the trio ''Babylas, Babylas,'' and a rollicking bolero for the two lovers (''Pedro possède une guitare'') were the highlights.

Monsieur Choufleuri proved as popular in other parts of Europe as it did at home. Offenbach's company introduced it to Vienna prior to its Bouffes opening (and with the same cast) as the highlight of an evening including *La Rose de Saint-Flour* and *Vent du soir,* and soon after Karl Treumann staged a German-language version as *Narren-Abend im Salon Pitzelberger* in which he himself played Baptist (ie, Babylas) to the Pitzelberger (Choufleuri) of Grois. Knaack was the Belgian butler, Anna Marek played Ernestine, there were no fewer than 84 guests, and a mazurka, a waltz, a quadrille, a ''magellone'' and a finale galoppade performed by the cast to music that was ''arranged by C F Stenzl'' were all included in this ''crazy evening at the Pitzelberger at-home.''

Berlin rechristened Choufleuri (whose jolly name seemed not to work in the German language) as the harsh-sounding Herr Jaschke, but Pál Tarnay allowed him to keep his name in the Hungarian version and, for his brief appearance at London's Gaiety Theatre, the English christened him Mr Nightingale. America saw *Choufleuri* regularly, but mostly in French. Tostée appeared as Ernestine in H L Bateman's production, Irma in James Fisk's, and Jacob Grau included *Choufleuri* in his company's repertoire as well, but Susie Galton (*Primadonna for a Night* ad Mary Ann Pyne Galton), Alice Oates (a version of ditto), Charles Drew (an ''elongated'' version called *Opera Mad* ad Drew) and other managers touring spectacles-coupés of short pieces gave various versions in English, and the little operetta-bouffe was also a favorite item on the bills of the Kelly and Leon Minstrels in both America and on the Australian/New Zealand circuit (*Mons Choufleuri at Home*). Female impersonator Leon tackled the stratospheric ''Sonntag'' soprano line allotted to Ernestine, Kelly was Choufleuri and his son, Edwin Lester, played Babylas. Leon kept the piece long in his repertoire and used it, or parts of it, under several titles, and as a burlesque of a whole range of contemporary prima donnas (*Her Majesty's Opera, or Patti's Visit to Vanderbilt,* etc). Broadway saw most of *Monsieur Choufleuri* again in 1884 at Koster & Bial's, and *Primadonna for a Night* in 1893 when it was played on the program at the Madison Square Amphitheatre (29 May). Most recently a new adaptation (ad James Stuart) was played at the Ohio Light Opera (*Regrets Only,* 1996, 1998).

NBC television broadcast a framed, fiddled-with version in 1951 (as *RSVP*) which was later issued on video.

Austria: Theater am Franz-Josef-Kai (Fr) 6 July 1861, *(Narren-Abend im) Salon Pitzelberger* 17 October 1861; Germany: *Salon Jaschke* 1862; Hungary: Budai Népszínház *Choufleuri úr otthon lesz* 18 April 1863, Budai Színkör *Salon Pitzelberger* 8 July 1868; USA: Théâtre Français (Fr) 5 March 1869, Chestnut Street Theater, Philadelphia *Primadonna for a Night* 17 June 1870, Olympic Theater *Primadonna for a Night* 20 October 1873; UK: St James's Theatre (Fr) 14 November 1871, Gaiety Theatre *Nightingale's Party* 27 March 1880; Australia: Queen's Theatre, Sydney *Primadonna for a Night* 16 February 1878

Video: NBC 1951

M[ONSIEUR] DE LA PALISSE Opérette in 3 acts by Robert de Flers and Gaston de Caillavet. Music by Claude Terrasse. Théâtre des Variétés, Paris, 2 November 1904.

Baron Placide de la Palisse (Albert Brasseur) has banned love amongst his tenants, since women in general and wives in particular only complicate your life and bring you problems and misery. Finally, however, he gives in and decides to marry his cousin, Heloïse de la Verdure (Léonie Laporte), who is safely aging and plain. But his plans go awry when his cousin Bertrand (Alberthal), who is scheduled to take part in a Congress at Seville, twists his ankle and calls upon Placide to take his place. The poor Baron, hastening away from the extravagantly amorous and anxious-to-be-wed Heloïse, heads for Spain and there he encounters an explosive little creature called Inésita (Ève Lavallière), the daughter of the Governor, Don Diego (Claudius). If the honor of the family is made safe by Placide's congressional mission accompli, the wife he brings home is a guarantee that his peace of mind is gone forever. The other principal female role was that of Dorette (Mlle Lanthelmy), the danseuse girlfriend of Bertrand, whilst the veteran Vauthier played Beni Zou-Zou.

Terrasse accompanied the piece with an opéra-bouffe score in the *Sire de Vergy* mold, from which the double-talk duo between Inésita and Palisse, ''Mon coeur est rempli d'un tendre tambour,'' which had the pair saying ''tambour'' when they meant ''amour'' and ''fauteuil'' instead of ''baiser,'' in order to get around Palisse's hang-ups; Dorette's waltz ''Ce sont des châteaux en Espagne''; and Inésita's saucy couplets ''Comm' ça,'' with their ''tra-la-la-la pfuut'' consummation, were the favorites—alongside the anti-hero's version of the old song of Monsieur de la Palisse (''La Palisse eût peu de bien pour soutenir sa naissance'') which had given the piece its title and its hero.

Produced by Fernand Samuel at the Théâtre des Variétés, *M de la Palisse* lasted only some 30 performances, in spite of the praise lavished on Terrasse's work and that of his highly admired and successful librettists. However, it was revived in 1913 and 1914 at the Apollo, on the first occasion with Henri Defreyn and Polaire (39 performances), on the second with Henri Fabert and Mlle

Docin, and it was brought back again, in 1930, at the Gaîté-Lyrique with Robert Allard and Janie Marèse top-billed, and with Duvaleix in the role of Don Diego.

A German production was staged in Munich, and Budapest saw 11 performances of Jenő Faragó's Hungarian version with a cast headed by Sári Petráss, but a version published in America under the title of *The Ambassador* (ad John Haliwell Hobbes) does not seem to have been produced on the professional stage.

Germany: Theater am Gärtnerplatz, Munich *Der Kongress von Sevilla* 21 April 1906; Hungary: Népszínház *Az erényes nagykövet* 12 January 1907

MONSIEUR ET MADAME DENIS Opérette in 1 act by Laurençin [Paul Aimé Chapelle] and Michel Delaporte. Music by Jacques Offenbach. Théâtre des Bouffes-Parisiens, Paris, 11 January 1862.

M et Mme Denis don't actually appear in this little piece. Their ward Gaston d'Amboise (Juliette Darcier) has taken advantage of their absence to whisk away their niece Lucile de Tondray (Mlle Pfotzer) from her pension, and the law, in the person of Sergeant Bellerose (Potel), has followed them to the Denis house. The maid, Nanette (Mlle Simon), dresses them up as M and Mme Denis, but the clumsy Gaston ruins the trick and it is left to Nanette to get the sergeant drunk to enable the runaways to run away further.

The short score which illustrated this tiny tale actually produced a hit number. Lucile's "Dansons la chacone," a showpiece waltz which tingled up to a top C before the rest of the cast joined in, turned out to be a show-stopper, did much to ensure the show's afterlife and was culled from its original place to make up the part of many pasticcio entertainments in the years that followed.

Successful enough in Offenbach's repertoire, *M et Mme Denis* proved even more popular in the German language. Karl Treumann produced it at his Kai-Theater (ad Alois Berla) with Anna Grobecker (Nanette), Helene Weinberger (Gaston), Anna Marek (Lucile) and himself as the Sergeant before Offenbach's own troupe visited with the French original, and the German version was later played at the Kärtnertor Theater (1870), the Hofoper (1881), the Raimundtheater (1881), at Ronacher (1883) and, in 1904, at a benefit at the Theater an der Wien with Elise Elizza as Lucile. Hamburg, Berlin and Prague all followed, whilst Budapest's Nemzeti Színház chose the piece (ad Kálmán Szerdahelyi) as one of the short list of opérettes which they introduced in Hungarian in the early 1860s. It was later played in Budapest in German, and this Berla version continued to be performed throughout central Europe for many years. It was also, apparently, the only version to be seen in America, where Louise Lichtenay featured as Nanette in a production at the German-language Terrace-Garten in 1873.

Plate 263. **Céline Montaland**

The only English-language sighting seems to have been a potted version introduced at London's Oxford Music Hall in 1867 (10 April) by a cast headed by Emily Soldene and Félix Bury.

Austria: Theater am Franz-Josefs-Kai *Monsieur und Madame Denis* 31 March 1862; Germany: Hamburg 22 May 1862, Friedrich-Wilhelmstädtisches Theater, Berlin 22 June 1862; Hungary: Nemzeti Színház *Denis úr neje* 31 July 1862, February 1963 (Ger); USA: Terrace-Garten *Herr und Madame Denis* 16 July 1873

MONTALAND, [Caroline Henriette Marie] Céline (b Ghent, 10 August 1843; d Paris, 8 January 1891). Handsome actress-who-sang, who appeared in opéra-bouffe in Europe and America.

The daughter of provincial actors, Céline Montaland began in the theatre as a very young child performer. She played at the Comédie-Française in Augier's *Gabrielle* and *Charlotte Corday* at the age of 6 and made herself a name ("la petite Montaland") at 7 in Labiche's *La Fille bien gardée* at the Palais-Royal. As a result she appeared in a number of tailor-made juvenile pieces around France, Italy and northern Africa. On her return to Paris in 1860 she was seen in *Le Pied de mouton* at the Porte-Saint-Martin, and at 20 at the Gymnase, before she rejoined the Palais-Royal where, in 1866, with the tag of "one of the most beautiful women in Paris" now attached to her, she created the role of the Baronne Gondremarck in *La Vie parisienne.* She disappeared from the boards for several years to live as the paramour of the Russian Prince Demidoff, but gave up the Prince in 1869 and returned to the stage. In 1870 she visited America with an opéra-bouffe company, starring as Marguerite in *Le Petit Faust,* the Duchess in *La Grande-Duchesse* (''she looked charmingly and sang well but her four-inch heels prevent her from dancing and give her a hobble in her walk'') and Fiorella in America's first *The Brigands.* She provoked enough interest to be burlesqued and paragraphed, but did not challenge the opéra-bouffe image established by Aimée, Tostée and Rose Bell and soon returned home.

She appeared in opérette at the Théâtre Taitbout (Javotte in *La Cruche cassée*) and the Nouveautés (Mme Durosel in *Fleur d'oranger, Les Deux Nababs*), in drama at the Odéon, in féerie at the Châtelet, and caused a small sensation when she visited St Petersburg, but she angled herself thereafter increasingly towards the non-musical theatre and in 1884, to surprise in some quarters, became a member of the Comédie-Française. She remained there until her death, from measles, six years later.

[GRISIER-]MONTBAZON, Marie [LIVERGNE, Marie Rose] (b Avignon, 29 January 1859; d Paris, 18 October 1922). ''The perfect all-rounder'' of the Parisian opérette of the 1880s.

The daughter of Montbazon, a popular provincial actor who went insane after breaking down in his Parisian debut in *Les Moucherons* at the Ambigu (1880), Marie Montbazon similarly began her career in regional theatres, making her debut at Lyon in 1879 in the role of Lecocq's Petit Duc. However, unlike her father, she not only made good in Paris, but scored a sensation in her very first metropolitan appearance. She had the good fortune, it must be said, to make her debut at the Théâtre des Bouffes-Parisiens in one of the best roles and opérettes of recent years—as the farmgirl Bettina in *La Mascotte*—but she soon confirmed the triumph of her first role, winning great praise for her pretty mezzo-soprano voice and delightful acting style as she guested at the Folies-Dramatiques as Suppé's *Boccaccio* (1882), then returned to the Bouffes to star as Audran's *Gillette de Narbonne* (1882). She took up the role of Simonne in the Bouffes' other current hit, *Les Mousquetaires au couvent,* and—now billed as Mme Grisier-Montbazon, following her marriage to playwright Georges Grisier (1853–1909, later to be manager of the Bouffes-Parisiens and the Ambigu)—revived *Madame Favart* and took the lead roles in such new pieces as *La Dormeuse éveillée* (1883, Suzette ''she is the gem of the piece'') and *Le Chevalier Mignon* (1884, Mignon).

In 1885 she performed *La Mascotte* at St Petersburg in Russian, and in 1886 she played in the spectacular féerie *Les Aventures de M Crac* (Anita) at the Châtelet and created the rôle à tirors which was the central part of *Madame Cartouche* (1886, Sylvine), but, although she repeated her early great roles and appeared in the classic repertoire (Serpolette, etc) with invariable success, pieces such as *Le Valet de coeur* (1888, Chloe de la Barbotière), *Les Délégués* (1887, Zoé), *Mam'zelle Crénom* (1888, Juliette) and *Le Mitron* (1891, Madelon) did not bring her any new triumphs. In 1893 she visited Vienna as the star of a company playing *Orphée aux enfers, La Belle Hélène, La Fille de Madame Angot, La Mascotte* and *La Périchole;* in 1894 she was spotted playing opposite Louise Théo in *La Timbale d'argent* at Monte Carlo, after which she seems to disappear from the world of the playbill.

MONTCHARMONT, Charles

Originally an actor, Montcharmont became the co-director (1906) and then the sole director (1912) of the Théâtre des Célestins at Lyon which, during 30 years at its head, he brought to a position as one of the most important provincial theatres in France. Simultaneously, he ran a play agency in Paris through which he obtained the rights to many of the foreign, and most particularly Viennese, Operetten of the 1910s and 1920s. Thus, pieces such as *Le Soldat de chocolat* (1911, *Der tapfere soldat*), *La Chaste Suzanne* (1913, *Die keusche Susanne*), *La Bayadère* (1925) and *Le Tsarewitsch* (1929) were presented at Lyon prior to being sold or transferred for Paris productions, and others, such as *Manoeuvres d'automne* (*Tatárjárás*) (1914) and Cuvillier's German Operette *Flora Bella* (1921), which were never played at Paris, were nevertheless seen in Lyon.

In an ever-adventurous program, Montcharmont mounted the revised Cuvillier/Barde *La reine s'amuse* (1912) which he had originally produced at Marseille, and sent it Paris-ward and, from there, to overseas productions. He produced the first French-language version of Lionel Monckton's *The Quaker Girl* (1913), the first French *Flup..!* (following its Belgian premiere), a number of major revivals of neglected classic works, the initial seasons of several of the Marseillais opérettes (*Un de la Canebière, Les Gangsters du Château d'If, Le Roi des galéjeurs*) and even an opérette by a local Lyonnais composer.

MONTE CARLO Musical comedy in 2 acts by ''Sydney Carlton'' (Harry Greenbank). Lyrics by Harry Greenbank. Music by Howard Talbot. Avenue Theatre, London, 27 August 1896.

A rare venture into libretto-writing by Daly's Theatre lyricist Harry Greenbank and a step up the ladder for the novice composer Howard Talbot, *Monte Carlo* arrived in London in the busiest year of the Victorian musical theatre (*The Geisha, The Circus Girl, My Girl, The Grand Duke, Shamus O'Brien* plus eight more new musicals in the West End), won fine reviews and folded after 76 performances.

Mrs Carthew (Lottie Venne) refound her former husband (E W Garden), while daughter Dorothy (Kate Cutler) paired off with her dashing Fred (Richard Green) and French soubrette Suzanne (Emmie Owen) with the whole male chorus, at the end of an evening of complex romancing on the Riviera which was enlivened by some common music-hall folk (Robb Harwood, the Belfrey sisters, Lalor Shiel) in what was little more than a superior variety musical. The entertainment included a representative array of songs from the ballad to the bouncing, and the hits of the evening were made by the diminutive Miss Shiel's music-hally ''I'm Jemima'' and the Belfrey sisters' imitation of ''The Sisters Gelatine.'' After the early closure, the show went on the road, but it was also picked up by E E Rice for Broadway. There, duly Americanized by the addition of some variety acts, an animated music sheet, an imitation of a striptease trapeze artist and some biograph pictures of a patriotic nature, and with a cast led by Marguerite Sylva (Dorothy) and including Marie Cahill as half of the Gelatine sisters, it lasted 48 performances.

Another musical by the same title was produced at the Neues Operetten-Theater, Leipzig (Ludwig Roman Ehmel/Carl Lindau, F Antony) on 7 April 1907.

USA: Herald Square Theater 21 March 1898

MONTE CRISTO JR Burlesque melodrama in 3 acts by ''Richard Henry.'' Music by Meyer Lutz, Ivan Caryll, Hamilton Clarke, G W Hunt, Henry J Leslie and Robert Martin. Gaiety Theatre, London, 23 December 1886.

Following the success of *Little Jack Sheppard* at the Gaiety Theatre, George Edwardes launched a series of what came to be called ''new burlesques,'' of which *Monte Cristo Jr* was the next in line. It was ''new'' in that it eased away a little from the old burlesque restrictions of rhyme and punning in its text (although both elements were still used here, they would soon largely vanish) and in that, like *Jack Sheppard,* it used custom-written songs for its score. The libretto, written by journalists Richard Butler and Henry Chance Newton as ''Richard Henry,'' burlesqued Dumas's *Le Comte de Monte Cristo.* Nellie Farren played Edmond Dantès, the imprisoned count, and Fred Leslie was Noirtier, the arch plotter with whom Dantès escapes from the Château d'If. In a plethora of disguises, the two set out to wreak vengeance on the bent policeman de Villefort (E J Lonnen), the nasty Danglars (George Honey) and the unpleasant Fernand (Fay Templeton), who has been sniffing around after Dantès's girl, Mercedes (Agnes de la Porte) during his enforced absence.

The plot took sufficient breaths for everyone to do his or her number: the unplotworthy Sylvia Grey danced gracefully, Lottie Collins danced vigorously, Mlle de la Porte sang a waltz and Miss Templeton gave a décolleté parlando number, whilst Nellie and Fred took the bulk of the evening's material, topical, comic and variety. Leslie's best ''spot'' came as he delivered a song called ''Imitations,'' an ever-changing series of impersonations which apparently ran, on a good night, to 22 verses. The hit songs of the show, however, proved to be two added during the run of this ever-mobile show. Robert Martin contributed a number for Lonnen about a phony temperance group called the Ballyhooley Blue Ribbon army (''Ballyhooley'') and a lively piece called ''I'm a Jolly Little Chap All Round'' for Nellie Farren, which pair became the take-away tunes of the night.

Monte Cristo Jr ran through till the end of the season, then went on the road—without Miss Templeton, who had been sacked for incessantly trying to expose more of herself than was permitted—whilst the Gaiety hosted its annual summer season of French plays. While on the road, the company began to prepare its next piece, but *Monte Cristo* was not forgotten. The following year the company, headed by Nellie, Fred, Charles Danby, Marion Hood and Letty Lind, took it to Australia and to America (including two visits to Broadway, during one of which James O'Neill was playing down the street in the serious *Monte Cristo*), following which several ''versions'' sprouted in America, including one (which professed not to stray too far from the original) that was toured for two seasons, by Jennie Kimball, with Corinne in Nellie Farren's role and Harry Brown as Noirtier. In fact, one ''version'' was put on the American stage even before Edwardes got his company across the ocean. Ripper-off-extraordinary M B Leavitt launched what he insisted was the Gaiety's show ''with a company engaged in London'' headed by British provincial comic Witty Watty Walton at New Haven two months ahead of the real thing. It bore more resemblance to Leavitt's usual legshows with specialities and it stayed well away from Broadway and the Gaiety company.

Another piece under the same title was mounted on Broadway in 1919. Charles Purcell starred as *Monte Cristo Jr* in a Harold Atteridge dream-sequence piece which whisked him, comedian Ralph Herz, and a bundle of variety acts back to Dumas's days, to the accompaniment of songs by Jean Schwartz and Sigmund Romberg, through 254 performances at the Winter Garden Theater (12 February).

USA: Hyperion Theater, New Haven 24 September 1888, Standard Theater 17 November 1888; Australia: New Princess Theatre, Melbourne 20 June 1888

MONTGOMERY, David [Craig] (b St Joseph, Mo, 21 April 1870; d Chicago, 20 April 1917). Star comedian of the Broadway musico-spectacular stage.

Paired with his partner of always, Fred Stone, Montgomery had a fine career in variety before the twosome turned to the musical theatre where their first engagement was in the Casino Theater musical comedy *The Girl from Up There.* A pair of grotesquely made-up, knockabout clowns in the style of an earlier era, Montgomery appeared as Solomon Scarlet to the Christopher Grunt of Stone in both New York and London. If *The Girl from Up There* did little for anyone but top-billed Edna May in its title role, the pair quickly found a vehicle that did. In 1903 Montgomery appeared as Mick Chopper, the Tin Man, to Stone's Scarecrow in Fred Hamlin's spectacular production *The Wizard of Oz,* and the team were immediately promoted to a major stardom which they confirmed in no small fashion when, in 1906, Montgomery created the role of Kid Connor—Stone was Con Kidder—in *The Red Mill* (''The Sidewalks of New York'').

Montgomery starred alongside Stone again in *The Old Town* (1909, Archibald Hawkins), in the modernized Cinderella tale *The Lady of the Slipper* (1912, Punks) and the updated *Aladdin, Chin-Chin* (1914, Chin Hop Lo), a series which combined to confirm them as Broadway's most popular musical-comedy funmakers, but in 1917, during the preparations for their next show, *Jack o' Lantern,* Montgomery died, leaving Stone to continue through five further Broadway musicals alone.

MONTGOMERY, James H (b USA, 27 April 1882; d New York, 17 June 1966).

Actor-turned-playwright James Montgomery wrote 12 Broadway plays of which he himself, alone or in collaboration, remade four as musicals, almost always with inverse results to those won on the straight stage. The first of his musicals, *Going Up,* based on his 1910 play *The Aviator,* scored an immense success both in America and overseas, but the second, *Oh, Look!,* taken from his hit play *Ready Money* (1912), had none of the same success, even if it had the consolation of producing Harry Carroll and Joseph McCarthy's ''I'm Always Chasing Rainbows'' from its score. Montgomery outpointed even his *Going Up* success in 1919 with the most winning of (Irish) Cinderella stories in *Irene,* which he extracted from his very short-lived play *Irene O'Dare* (1916), but an attempt to repeat the same formula with an original libretto for the same songwriting team of Tierney and McCarthy in *Glory* proved a flop. In 1925 he adapted *The Fortune Hunter,* a play which he had not written, but in which he had appeared during his acting days, under the title *The City Chap,* but neither this nor *Yes, Yes, Yvette,* a musical based on Montgomery's most enduring play of all, *Nothing But the Truth,* added to his total of two major musical hits.

Nothing But the Truth was also made over by others hands, becoming *Tell Her the Truth* in a British adaptation (Jack Waller, Joseph Tunbridge/R P Weston, Bert Lee) produced at London's Saville Theatre (14 June 1932) and briefly on Broadway. It was also later adapted by Michael Stewart, Mark Bramble and Cy Coleman, but this 1988 version remained unproduced.

Montgomery latterly worked as a writer for MGM, retiring as a playwright and as a producer in 1939.

1917 **Going Up** (Louis Hirsch/w Otto Harbach) Liberty Theater 25 December

1918 **Oh, Look!** (Harry Carroll/Joseph McCarthy) Vanderbilt Theater 7 March

1919 **Irene** (Harry Tierney/McCarthy) Vanderbilt Theater 18 November

1922 **Glory** (Tierney, Maurice de Packh/McCarthy, James Durenforth) Vanderbilt Theater 25 December

1925 **The City Chap** (Jerome Kern/Anne Caldwell/w William Cary Duncan) Liberty Theater 26 October

1927 **Yes, Yes, Yvette** (Phil Charig, Ben Jerome, Irving Caesar/w Duncan) Harris Theater 3 October

MONTI, Max (b Sopron, Hungary, 11 April 1859; d Vienna, 14 January 1929). Berlin producer of the early 20th century.

An actor and light baritone vocalist, Monti appeared as a performer at, among others, the Theater an der Wien (1884, Ein Hausirer in *Der Feldprediger,* etc), the Deutsches Theater in Budapest (1886–88), the Carltheater (briefly) and Berlin's Friedrich-Wilhelmstädtisches Theater. After seasons at Reichenberg and Linz, he played at Hamburg's Carl-Schultze Theater in 1893, toured America with the Ferenczy Operette company (1893–94, Stanislaus in *Der Vogelhändler, Lachende Erben*) and then, in 1897, became manager of Dresden's Tivoli Theater. He subsequently moved back to Hamburg to take over the management of the Carl-Schultze Theater, followed in 1904 by that of the Centralhallen-Theater, and in 1906 he made his happiest move of all when he secured the German rights to *Die lustige Witwe* which he produced at his Hamburg Neues Operetten-Theater and subsequently took to Berlin, for a guest season at the Theater des Westens, with huge success.

He followed up *Die lustige Witwe* with other Operetten including premieres of such as Fall's *Der liebe Augustin,* Winterberg's *Die Dame in Rot,* Jessel's *Die beiden Husaren* and Chantrier's *Gräfin Fifi,* establishing himself in the process firmly at the Theater des Westens and at the head of Berlin's musical theatre, and squeezing out his main competitor, Victor Palfi. He subsequently moved in to what had been the Neues Theater, renaming it Montis Operetten-Theater (1912) and producing there such pieces as Granichstaedten's *Die verbotene Stadt,* Fall's *Jung England* and Goetze's *Die liebe Pepi.* When the Theater des Westens was destroyed by fire in 1912, Monti moved his operations to the Theater am Nollendorfplatz, and later leased the rebuilt Westens to Carl Beese and Carl Bieber.

In 1916 he took the course that so few very impresarii have been able to take: successful and extremely wealthy, he sold up and got out of the business taking his profits with him. He was not rewarded for his acumen, alas, for he then lost his fortune in the shuddering inflation which ravaged postwar Germany.

MOODY, Ron [MOODNICK, Ronald] (b London, 8 January 1924).

After an early career in revue, Moody appeared on the musical stage in the brief London production of *Candide* (1959, Governor of Buenos Aires) before being cast in the role for which he is remembered, as the original Fagin in Lionel Bart's *Oliver!* (theatre 1960, film 1968).

He subsequently wrote and played the title role of a musicalized life of the famous historical clown in *The Great Grimaldi* (aka *Joey* and *Joey, Joey*), appeared as Aristophanes in a provincial musical based on *Lysistrata* which called her *Liz* (1968), and fell victim to the *Hair* syndrome with an effortfully trendy piece called *Saturnalia.* He took the lead in *The Showman* at the Theatre Royal, Stratford East, returned on several occasions to a broadening performance of his most famous part, and in 1989 created his first London musical part in 20 years in the title role in a short-lived London musical version of *Sherlock Holmes.* He subsequently appeared as Harry Ball, father to Vesta Tilley, in the musical *Bertie* (1993), Captain Hook in a musical version of *Peter Pan* (1994) and in a provincial production of *The Canterville Ghost* (1997).

1962 **Joey** Theatre Royal, Bristol 26 December

1966 **Joey, Joey** (aka *The Great Grimaldi*) revised *Joey* Saville Theatre 11 October

1971 **Saturnalia** Belgrade Theatre, Coventry 4 August

MOORE, [Lilian] Decima (b Brighton, 11 December 1871; d London, 18 February 1964).

The third daughter (''all sopranos, high sopranos'') of an analytical chemist, and a scholarship student at the Blackheath Conservatory, Decima Moore was discovered by D'Oyly Carte at the age of 16 and given the role of Casilda in the original production of *The Gondoliers.* She did not remain a member of the Savoy team, however, but moved on to succeed Juliette Nesville in the title role of *Miss Decima* (*Miss Helyett*) and Edith Chester as Violet Eaton-Belgrave in *A Pantomime Rehearsal,* before starring in the title role of a revival of *Dorothy* (1892). She top-billed as Yvonette in the short-lived *The Wedding Eve* (1892), returned to the Savoy to play the schoolgirl, Bab, in *Jane Annie* (1893) and played Clairette to the Lange of Amy Augarde in a revival of *La Fille de Madame Angot* before she came under George Edwardes's crook, and moved into the world of musical comedy to create the ingenue role of Rose Brierly in *A Gaiety Girl.*

In 1894 she went to Australia as the star of Edwardes's musical-comedy company to play Rose, Bessie Brent in *The Shop Girl,* Kitty Hetherton in *In Town* and Emma in *Gentleman Joe.* Back in Britain, however, she did not stay firmly in the Edwardes stable, but starred opposite Arthur Roberts in *The White Silk Dress* (1896), as Rose d'Été in the American musical comedy *Lost, Strayed or Stolen* (1897) and as Renée in George Musgrove's production of *The Scarlet Feather* (*La Petite Mademoiselle*). In between times, she toured as Winifred Grey in *A Runaway Girl* (1898). Covering the whole gamut of musical-theatre styles, she played Lucia in the burlesque *Great Caesar* (1899), succeeded to the roles of Scent-of-Lilies in Sullivan's *The Rose of Persia* and Angela in *Florodora,* played in the Christmas musical *The Swineherd and the Princess* (1901, Swineherd), toured in *The Gay Cadets* (1902, t/o Cara Luna) and created the ingenue to Sybil Arundale's *My Lady Molly* (Alice Coverdale) on the road, a role she repeated when the show came successfully to London in 1904. Then, after 15 years as a favorite singing ingenue, she effectively put her musical career to rest, turning to non-musical theatre for the remainder of her career.

Her sister **Eva MOORE** (b Brighton, 9 February 1868; d nr Maidenhead, 27 April 1955) began a career as an actress at the age of 17 in the chorus of *Dorothy.* She spent a considerable time touring with Johnnie Toole, but during her twenties also appeared in major roles in several musicals. She created the role of Minestra in Gilbert's *The Mountebanks,* succeeded to that of Violet Eaton-Belgrave (previously played by Decima) in *A Pantomime Rehearsal* at the Court, introduced the part of the dancer, Pepita, in *Little Christopher Columbus* and took over the title role of *The Shop Girl* at the Gaiety before going on to a substantial career as an actress. She also appeared in both British and American films, notably in the 1922 silent movie of *Chu Chin Chow.* She was the mother of actress Jill Esmond.

Another sister, **Jessie MOORE** (d London, 28 November 1910), also a member of the Savoy company, played Decima's *Gaiety Girl* role in the show's first tour, and succeeded Geraldine Ulmar in the lead role of *The Mountebanks.* She was the wife of the Savoy performer and teacher Lewis Cairns James.

Memoir: *We Two in West Africa* (Heinemann, London, 1909); Autobiography (Eva Moore): *Exits and Entrances* (Chapman & Hall, London, 1923)

MOORE, Grace (b Del Rio, Tenn, 5 December 1898; d nr Copenhagen, Denmark, 25 January 1947). Operatic vocalist who appeared in lighter fare on film and occasionally on the stage.

Grace Moore made her first Broadway appearance in the revue *Hitchy Koo of 1920* and performed in two editions of the *Music Box Revue* and as Jean Jones, the disguised film-star heroine of Joseph Gaites's musical comedy production *Up in the Clouds* / *Above the Clouds* (1922), before moving into the operatic world. She reemerged in 1932 to take the title role in Broadway's version of *The Dubarry,* but her non-operatic appearances were largely on film, where she starred in the screen version of *The New Moon* (1930), as Jenny Lind in *A Lady's Morals* (1930), in *One Night of Love* (1934), *Love Me Forever* (1935), *The King Steps Out* (1936), *When You're in Love* (1937), *I'll Take Romance* (1937), and *Louise* (1940). She was killed in an air crash in 1947.

A biographical film, *The Grace Moore Story* (*So This Is Love*), was made in 1953 with Kathryn Grayson impersonating Miss Moore.

Autobiography: *You're Only Human Once* (Doubleday, Doran, Garden City, 1944); Biography: Farrar, R R: *Grace Moore and Her Many Worlds* (Cornwall, New York, 1982)

MOORE, Victor [Frederick] (b Hammonton, NJ, 24 February 1876; d East Islip, NY, 23 July 1962). One of the great comic actors of the Broadway musical stage, blessed with a long list of fine roles in which to display his talents.

Ex-office boy Moore started out in the theatre as a teenaged super, and made his way through minor roles in plays and musicals (Percy Tooting in *The Girl from Paris* 1898, *The Real Widow Brown* 1899) and two years as a member of the New Century stock company in Newark, to a four-year stint in vaudeville, playing an Edward McWade act called "Change Your Act, or Back to the Woods" with a partner, Julia Blanc (later Pearl Hight inter alia). He moved straight from vaudeville to his first substantial Broadway role as the smart-talking Kid Burns, introducing the title song in George M Cohan's *Forty-Five Minutes from Broadway* (1905) to New York and, for two years thereafter, to the rest of the country. He followed up in the same character in the sequel, *The Talk of New York* (1907); then in a poor imitation of the same style of piece, a musical mounted by Frazee and Lederer called *The Happiest Night of His Life* (1910–11, Dick Brennan); and in the comedy *Shorty McCabe* (1911–12) before returning to his act and the vaudeville stage for several years.

Moore appeared in Chicago in the ex-French musical *See You Later* (*Loute*) in 1919, but his virtual second career in the musical theatre began when he was 50 years old, when he created the principal comedy role of Shorty McGee in *Oh, Kay!* After appearing in the 1927 revue *Allez Oop!,* he continued with a series of further Broadway roles, mostly in musical comedies, creating comic parts in several memorable shows and being himself memorable in several less durable ones. He appeared as the bungling burglar Herbert in *Funny Face* (1927), as Nosey Bartlett in the De Sylva, Brown and Henderson boxing musical *Hold Everything!* (1928), as the rum-running Skippy Dugan in Rodgers and Hart's *Heads Up!* (1929), as Irving Huff in the American version of Albert Szirmai's *Alexandra, Princess Charming* (1930), and as the wonderfully befuddled vice president, Throttlebottom, in *Of Thee I Sing* (1931).

This last piece paired him to enormous effect with William Gaxton, whose forthright, edgy comedy contrasted effectively with Moore's deceptively gentler, muddly style. The partnership was repeated in a sequel, *Let 'em Eat Cake,* and again in the production of *Anything Goes* (1934)—in which Moore created the role of Moon-face Mooney, the foolish and harmless public enemy number 13 (but with ambitions to rise in the rankings), and introduced "Be Like the Bluebird." He next created the part of the lost-lamblike Ambassador Alonzo P Goodhue (with Sophie Tucker as his wife and Gaxton as his rival) in Cole Porter's *Leave It to Me!* (1938); appeared as the investigative Senator Oliver P Loganberry, again pitted against Gaxton, in Irving Berlin's *Louisiana Purchase* (1940); and as Joseph W Porter to Gaxton's Dick Live-Eye in George S Kaufman's short-lived burlesque of *HMS Pinafore, Hollywood Pinafore* (1945).

His last Broadway appearance was in 1946, at the age of 70, when he was seen in the unsuccessful *Nellie Bly* as Phineas T Fogerty, racing the show's heroine around the world under the orders of Gaxton, although he was later seen as the Starkeeper in a City Center revival of *Carousel.*

Moore appeared in silent films and later in such musical movies as *Romance in the Rain* (1934), as a memorable Pop Cardetti in *Swing Time* (1936), in *Gold Diggers of 1937,* in his original roles in the screen versions of *Heads Up!* and of *Louisiana Purchase* (1941) and, at nearly 80, in *The Seven Year Itch* (1955).

A MOORISH MAID, or The Queen of the Riffs Comic opera in 2 acts by J Youlin Birch. Music by Alfred Hill. His Majesty's Theatre, Auckland, New Zealand, 26 June 1905.

Written by Auckland journalist Birch and composed by Hill, the most successful and considerable New Zealand composer of his generation, *A Moorish Maid* was produced for a week in Auckland, where, billed as a "romantic opera," and with Lillian Tree, Marion Mitchell and Frederick Graham heading the cast it won a fine success. It was repeated in Wellington, with the young Rosina Buckman in the title role and a company was then set up by George Stephenson to take the piece to Australia. The show was considerably rewritten for the occasion (the tenor part was cut out because there was no suitable singer available!) and Australia's version was labeled "a comic opera." Efforts to get *A Moorish Maid* staged in London failed, in spite of an audition in which the soon-to-be-famous Miss Buckman sang her role of La Zara, but it was repeated in both Australia (1910, ad David Souter) and New Zealand, and proved one of the few successful pieces to emerge from the prewar antipodean musical theatre.

Hill wrote a number of other theatre pieces including *Tapu, or The Tale of a Maori Pah* and *The Rajah of Shivapore* which won local productions but which did not bring him the same kind of success that his orchestral and vocal writings did.

Australia: Palace Theatre, Sydney 28 April 1906

Biography: (Alfred Hill) Thompson, J M: *A Distant Music* (OUP, Auckland, 1980)

MORE, Julian [Bensley] (b Llanelli, 15 June 1928). Author or co-author of several of the most successful musicals of the London 1950s.

Cambridge-educated More wrote material for the University Footlights shows before his first professional pieces, the adult pantomimes *Puss-in-Red-Riding-Breeches* (1952) and *Arabian Nightmare* (1953, mus: Geoffrey Beaumont), were produced at London's little Watergate Theatre. He collaborated on the revue *The World's the Limit* (1955) at the Theatre Royal, Windsor, and it was at that house that his first musical comedy, *Grab Me a Gondola,* was produced the following year, subsequently transferring to London for a good run. He had further successes, in collaboration with David Heneker and Monty Norman, on the English-language version of *Irma la Douce* and on the impressive *Expresso Bongo,* but a second teaming with *Grab Me a Gondola* composer James Gilbert was a swift flop.

His five subsequent musical shows did not play London, although *Quick, Quick, Slow,* an amusing tale of the competition ballroom-dancing world, teetered for many years on the brink of a West End showing and *R Loves J* was seen at Munich's Theater am Gärtnerplatz following its Chichester festival debut (ad Peter Goldbaum, Uwe Mund 4 May 1974). In 1979 More had a fresh success with *Songbook,* a burlesque of the flood of composer compilation shows at that time infesting the British theatre, but *Roza,* an adaptation of the Romain Gary screenplay *La Vie devant soi,* with a score by French songwriter Gilbert Bécaud, originally announced for London but subsequently produced on Broadway, did not take off.

Plate 264. **Victor Moore** *apparently dressed to go hunting in* Anything Goes.

- 1956 **Grab Me a Gondola** (James Gilbert) Lyric Theatre 26 December
- 1958 **Irma la Douce** English version w David Heneker, Monty Norman (Lyric Theatre)
- 1958 **Expresso Bongo** (w Heneker, Norman/Wolf Mankowitz) Saville Theatre 23 April
- 1960 **The Golden Touch** (Gilbert) Piccadilly Theatre 5 May
- 1963 **The Perils of Scobie Prilt** (w Norman) New Theatre, Oxford 12 June
- 1967 **The Man from the West** (David Russell) Adeline Genée Theatre, East Grinstead 25 March
- 1969 **Quick, Quick, Slow** (w Norman/David Turner) Birmingham Repertory Theatre 20 August
- 1971 **Good Time Johnny** (Gilbert) Birmingham Repertory Theatre 16 December
- 1973 **R Loves J** (Alexander Faris/Peter Ustinov) Chichester Festival Theatre 11 July
- 1974 **Bordello** (Al Frisch, Bernard Spiro) Queen's Theatre 18 April
- 1979 **Songbook** (w Norman) Globe Theatre 25 July
- 1987 **Roza** (Gilbert Bécaud) Royale Theater, New York 1 October

1988 **Can-Can** revised libretto (Strand Theatre)

MORENO TORROBA, Federico (b Madrid, 3 March 1891; d Madrid, 12 September 1982).

The successful composer of orchestral (''La Ajorca de oro,'' ''Caprichio romantico,'' ''Zoraida,'' ''Caudros castallanos,'' etc) and guitar music, as well as of the scores for some 80 zarzuelas, Torroba scored significant successes with his full-length musical plays *Luisa Fernanda* (Federico Romero, Guillermo Fernández Shaw, Teatro Calderón 26 March 1932) and *La Chulapona* (Romero, Fernández Shaw, Teatro Calderón 31 March 1934). He toured with his own zarzuela company in North and South America in the 1940s, and later became conductor at Madrid's Teatro de la Zarzuela.

His other stage works include *La virgen de la Mayo* (1925), *La mesonera de Tordesillas* (1925), *La marchenera* (1928), *Monte Carmelo* (1939), *Maravilla* (1941), *Caramba* (1928), *La ilustre moza* (1943), *Polonesa* (1944), *Siera morena* (1952), *Maria Manuela* (1957) and *Ella* (1965).

MORETTI, Raoul (b Marseille, 10 August 1893; d Venice, 6 March 1954). Songwriter who turned out the scores for a number of successful French musicals of the 1920s and 1930s.

Educated in Marseille before moving to Paris for his later studies, Moretti first became known in the world of the popular song, a field in which he was to find considerable success (''Le petit dactylo,'' ''Tu me plais,'' ''En parlant un peu de Paris,'' ''Ce sont des choses''). He won further success with the vast amount of dance music he turned out for the voracious orchestras and gramophones of the 1920s and 1930s, with music for the theatre and with such film scores as *Sous les toits de Paris, Il est charmant* and *Si tu veux.* The first of these gave him an international hit with its title song, ''Sous les toits de Paris'' (w René Nazelles, ad Irving Caesar, Bruce Sievier).

Gustave Quinson and Edmond Roze mounted Moretti's first stage piece, the medieval burlesque *En chemyse,* at the Bouffes-Parisiens, with a cast headed by Dranem and the heroine of *Phi-Phi,* Alice Cocéa, and then found a long-running success with a second Moretti musical, *Troublez-moi,* again starring Dranem, produced later in the same year. Well and truly launched by these two pieces, Moretti became one of the most popular Parisian theatre composers of the 1920s and early 1930s as he followed up his first big stage hit with several others: a third Bouffes piece with Dranem, *Trois jeunes filles . . . nues!* (1925, ''Est-ce que je te demande?,'' ''Quand on n'en a pas . . . on s'en passe,'' ''Quand on ne dit rien''), *Comte Obligado* (1927, ''La Caravane,'' ''Les artichauts,'' ''You-oo, ma Caroline,'' ''Un petit bout de femme,'' ''Si maman le veut''), produced at the Nouveautés with Milton at the head of the comedy, and the comical *Un soir de réveillon* (''Quand on est vraiment amoureux,'' ''Ninon,'' ''J'aime les femmes,'' ''Quand on perd la tête''). *Rosy,* played at the Folies-Wagram with a cast including Sim-Viva (''Quand j'ai promis, je tiens'') and Mireille Perrey (''C'est un rien, mais ça fait plaisir''), *La Femme de minuit,* with Urban (''Amour sauvage'') and soprano Danièle Brégis (''N'importe comment'') at its head, and *Six filles à marier,* again featuring Dranem as its overwhelming star (''T'as bonne mine,'' ''Tout va bien, bien, bien''), all added to the composer's list of well-played dance-era songs.

As the dance-era began to wane a little, Moretti's theatrical fortunes faded proportionately. *Les Soeurs Hortensia,* with Dranem yet again at the head of the comedy, did well enough without the accent being really on its songs, but *Les Joies du Capitole,* which cast Arletty as Agrippina and comedian Michel Simon as Claudius in some up-to-date Ancient Greek doings, did not succeed and *Simone est comme ça,* with a starry cast including film star Henri Garat, Duvaleix, René Koval and Davia, who had made so many Moretti (and other folk's) songs into favorites, lasted but seven weeks. Moretti's last musicals, *Destination inconnue,* with Réda Caire starred, *Le Mariage de Blanche-Neige, Monsieur Colibri* and *Mademoiselle Paris,* were played only in the provinces.

1924 **En chemyse** (Albert Willemetz, Cami) Théâtre des Bouffes-Parisiens 7 March

1924 **Troublez-moi** (Yves Mirande) Théâtre des Bouffes-Parisiens 17 September

1925 **Trois jeunes filles . . . nues!** (Mirande, Willemetz) Théâtre des Bouffes-Parisiens 3 December

1927 **Comte Obligado** (André Barde) Théâtre des Nouveautés 16 December

1930 **Rosy** (Barde) Folies-Wagram 1 March

1930 **Six filles à marier** (René Pujol/Jean Guitton) Scala 20 September

1930 **La Femme de minuit** (Barde) Théâtre des Nouveautés 11 December

1932 **Un soir de réveillon** (Paul Armont, Marcel Gerbidon, Jean Boyer) Théâtre des Bouffes-Parisiens 17 December

1934 **Les Soeurs Hortensia** (Barde) Théâtre des Nouveautés 11 April

1935 **Les Joies du Capitole** (Jacques Bousquet, Willemetz) La Madeleine 25 February

1936 **Simone est comme ça** (Willemetz/Mirande, Alex Madis) Théâtre des Bouffes-Parisiens 5 March

1936 **Figaro 36** (Pierre Varennes, Robert Diedonné) 1 act Théâtre de l'ABC 27 November

1939 **Destination Inconnue** (Pujol, Jean Baurel) Trianon, Bordeaux 17 November

1941 **Le Mariage de Blanche-Neige** (Maurice Bourbon) Annonay 2 March

1946 **Monsieur Colibri** (Raphael Derossi/Georges Brouens, Georges Chaillat) Opéra, Marseille 20 December

1951 **Mademoiselle Paris** (Max Raoul, Marcel Lamy, Pierre Jacon, G Lapeyronnie) Théâtre Municipal de Reims 31 March

MORGAN, Helen (b Danville, Ohio, 2 August 1900; d Chicago, 8 October 1941).

Pretty, bright-eyed Helen Morgan appeared in the chorus of a touring company of *Sally* (1924) and on Broadway in revue, but made her name as an extraordinarily effective singer of mostly despairing and/or dejected torch songs. She won Broadway stardom when she created the role of Julie La Verne in *Show Boat* (1927), introducing "Bill" and "Can't Help Lovin' Dat Man" in what Stanley Green has called her "tear-stained voice." Oscar Hammerstein II and Jerome Kern subsequently wrote *Sweet Adeline* (1929) to her measure, allowing her to pour out the negative sentiments and soaring melodies of "Why Was I Born?," "Here Am I" and "Don't Ever Leave Me" as the show's heroine rose to Broadway stardom with a broken heart. Thereafter, although she appeared in the *Ziegfeld Follies of 1931* and repeated her Julie in the 1932 *Show Boat* revival, she did not again visit Broadway in a new role before her alcohol-fueled death at the age of 41.

Miss Morgan appeared in several films, including *Applause* (1929), in which she appeared in the role of a sluttish, down-at-the-hem vaudeville performer, and *Go into Your Dance* (1936) and memorably re-created her *Show Boat* part in the 1936 movie version. A film loosely based on her life was made as *The Helen Morgan Story* in 1956, with Miss Morgan played by Ann Blyth.

Biography: Maxwell, G: *Helen Morgan, Her Life and Legend* (Hawthorn, New York, 1974)

MORILLA Operette in 3 acts with text by Julius Hopp based on a tale by Wieland. Music by Hopp. Theater an der Wien, Vienna, 13 November 1868.

One of the earliest full-length native Operetten to be produced in Vienna in the wake of the vast successes of Offenbach's opéras-bouffes, Julius Hopp's *Morilla* did not follow the burlesque mode, but instead stayed in the popular area of fairy-tale and chivalric romance. Its libretto, set in 15th-century Spain, told of a magic wishing-ring given to the peasant girl Morilla by a friendly fairy called Valida. It draws the Prince Leon from his bride to her, makes her beautiful, and summons up an army of Amazons to defeat his enemies. But when the Prince's foster brother Amarin gets her to wish for knowledge, Morilla realizes that only the ring makes Leon love her. Sadly, she hands the talisman over to the Prince, who happily finds that he loves her without the aid of magic.

Although played only four times at the Theater an der Wien on its initial production, *Morilla* proved to have a future. It was produced at Budapest's Budai Színkör with Kornelia Mindszenti starred in 1871, had its Berlin premiere the following year at the Viktoria Theater and was performed in America as late as 1890 at Gustav Amberg's German-language theatre with Carola Englander, Ernst Schütz and Carl Adolf Friese featured.

Hungary: Budai Színkör 3 June 1871; Germany: Viktoria Theater, February 1872; USA: Amberg Theater 2 May 1890

MORLET, [Louis] (d 1913). Star baritone/actor who had a fine career in the fin de siècle Parisian musical theatre.

At first a member of the company at the Opéra-Comique, where he made a considerable effect in his debut as Harlequin in Poise's *La Surprise de l'amour* (alongside Irma Marié and Galli-Marié), Morlet found that he was decidedly under-used at the Salle Favart thereafter. After appearing there in his first light opera, the premiere of Chabrier's one-act *Une Éducation manquée* (1879), he left and instead took over the role of Brissac in *Les Mousquetaires au couvent* (1880) at the Théâtre des Bouffes-Parisiens. The part, created by the actor Frédéric Achard, was reorganized and enlarged with two strong singing solos and Morlet, who proved to be as fine an actor as he was a baritone vocalist, became the star of the show.

As a result of this personal triumph, he was cast in the lead role of the piece that followed *Les Mousquetaires* at the Bouffes-Parisiens, and thus created the very contrasting light-comedy baritone role of Pippo in Audran's *La Mascotte* ("Glou Glou" duet) opposite the newly in-town Mlle Montbazon. After this second huge success, Morlet paired again with Mlle Montbazon in a third almost as great—Audran's *Gillette de Narbonne* (1882, Roger)—and he subsequently starred as a fine run of richly baritone leading men in the Parisian musical theatre, notably as Saverdy in Serpette's *Fanfreluche* (1883), as Lorenzo in Varney's *Babolin* (1884), le Comte in *Serment d'Amour* (1886) and in the piratical title role of Planquette's *Surcouf* (1887). He later created roles in *Miette* (1888), Messager's *Le Bourgeois de Calais* (1887, Duc de Guise) and *Isoline* (1888, Obéron), played the title role in Lecocq's *Ali Baba* (1889) and appeared in Planquette's *Le Talisman* (1893, Chevalier de Valpinçon)—as well as reappearing regularly in his first and most famous role of Brissac and other classic parts in between times.

Morlet was married to Mlle Gugot, a member of the Opéra-Comique company who appeared as Bettina in the 1883 revival of *La Mascotte*.

MOROCCO BOUND Musical farcical comedy in 2 acts by Arthur Branscombe. Lyrics by Adrian Ross.

Music by F Osmond Carr. Shaftesbury Theatre, London, 13 April 1893.

Poor Arthur Branscombe became the joke of theatrical London in the years around the turn of the century with his oft-repeated line ''when I invented musical comedy.'' The ex-Gaiety Theatre publicity man's claim was based on the fact that he was responsible for what passed for a libretto to the highly successful mixture of comedy and variety turns that was *Morocco Bound.* This ''musical farcical comedy'' followed and imitated George Edwardes's *In Town* to the extent of using the same composer and lyricist, whilst in other ways searching even further back in theatrical time for its inspiration. The result was a jolly, bright, topical, easily digestible piece of theatre which, whilst it affected to parody the music halls, was in fact compiled of material sufficiently like that purveyed by the ''halls'' to allow the polite Shaftesbury Theatre public, who would not even have considered going inside a music hall, to partake of the new society craze for the kind of songs and artists that might be seen there.

Spoofah Bey (John L Shine) is an Irish conman, out, with the aid of his phony countess sister (Jenny McNulty), to get the concession for music halls in Morocco. He takes nouveau-riche Squire Higgins (Charles Danby), his brother (Herbert Sparling), sons (Sydney Barraclough, Alfred C Seymour), sons' girlfriends (Violet Cameron, Letty Lind) and a lady journalist (Marie Studholme) out to Morocco, gets them all to do an act for the local Grand Vizier (Colin Coop) and, just when his concession looks safe, finds his plot blown apart by goofy Percy Pimpleton (George Grossmith) from the British Embassy. If the plot surfaced only intermittently, and vanished almost entirely in the second act when everyone lined up to do their ''turn'' in a veritable and unvarnished variety program, this structure did give each player in the cast the chance to perform the kind of item he or she did best. Some legitimacy was conferred on the ''musical farcical comedy'' by the fact that most of these items were actually written by Carr and Ross—at least to start with. Letty Lind scored best with her song and dance about ''Marguerite of Monte Carlo'' and imitated a society girl attempting the famous skirt dance (which Miss Lind had, to all intents and purposes, reinvented) and Shine had some jolly moments as he took the mickey out of Ireland's new parliament in ''The New Home Rule'' and duetted with Danby through a piece called ''The Music Hall'' which allowed them to impersonate favorite stars and their songs.

During the 295 performances for which the show ran at the Shaftesbury and later the Trafalgar Square Theatre, its musical content changed regularly and its cast underwent a number of changes, resulting in Savoyard Richard Temple (Vizier) and Minnie Palmer both joining the show for a period. Acts were also slipped in as required: the illusionist Hercat; Nini Patte en l'air and the quadrille dancers of the Moulin-Rouge; duettists A Nylsson Fysher and Maurice Farkoa; and two American artists, the as yet not famous Marie Cahill and the distinctly famous Loie Fuller with her tricked-up version of Letty Lind's skirt dance. When Miss Fuller moved on, Miss Lind returned to the cast and, according to *The Stage* newspaper, ''out-Fullered Fuller.''

After its London run, *Morocco Bound* toured and toured, first under Fred Harris's syndicate, which had concocted and produced the piece for town, then under Branscombe, whilst number-two and number-three companies were sub-licensed. *Morocco Bound*s were seen in South Africa and in Australia, where brother Wilfred Shine (Spoofah Bey) and William Elton (Squire) headed seasons in Sydney and Melbourne (Princess Theatre 6 October 1894); it was produced (after several abortive announcements) and toured in America by Adolphus H Chamberlyn (during one of his brief unbankrupt moments) with a cast headed by Dan Collyer, Herman West, Phil Branson and Tillie Salinger; and taken round the Continent by Harris, Chamberlyn, Gustav Amberg and Ernest Cavour in a company in which ''the remarkably clever songs and dance of the sisters Valli'' (future Broadway leading lady Valli Valli and her sister Lulu) won notice. Harry Braham (Spoofah Bey), Ruby Temple (Maude) and Ethel Newton (Ethel) featured. Full houses in Hamburg and Berlin applauded the songs and dances but sat stonily through the English dialogue, and the company had to wait for Amsterdam and Rotterdam to get their laughs back. The show was brought back to London in 1901 by William Greet with John Shine and Danby reappearing in their original roles and Branscombe, who had been unable to find himself another show, directing, and in 1914 it was brought out again to follow a newer fashion, compressed into a one-act entertainment to play in variety houses, under the title *I've Seen the 'arem.* It was revived in Boston in 1908 by Miner's Americans (Columbia Theater September).

Thus, while Branscombe, like most folk who make such claims, didn't ''invent'' anything, he did provide his part of a jolly variety musical which helped just a little to encourage the shift away from the dying ''new burlesque'' to Edwardesian musical comedy and, more particularly, to the kind of touring variety musical, with its first act of plot and its second act of virtual concert, which would be the joy of the British provinces and colonies in the 1890s.

Australia: Lyceum Theatre, Sydney 1 September 1894; Germany: Hamburg 2 February 1895, Theater Unter den Linden 11 March 1895; USA: Casino, Newport, RI 4 September 1900, Park Theater, Boston 11 January 1901

MOROSCO, Oliver [MITCHELL, Oliver] (b Logan, Utah, 20 June 1875; d Hollywood, Calif, 29 August 1945).

Protégé of circus acrobat turned theatre manager Walter MOROSCO (né BISHOP; b Guildford, Conn, 1846; d Fruitvale, Calif, 26 December 1901), one of the great personalitites of fin de siècle theatre on the American West Coast, Oliver worked with his ''father'' first as an acrobat, and subsequently in various theatrical management posts in California. He subsequently went out on his own, and in 1899 began producing largely in order to create product to fill his Morosco's Burbank Theater, Los Angeles, and later the half dozen other Californian theatres under his management. Amongst the shows which he produced and directed—and often co-wrote—on the West Coast, and mostly subsequently on the East as well, were the musical play *The Bird of Paradise* with which he made his New York debut as a producer (Daly's Theater 12 January 1912), *The Tik Tok Man of Oz* (Louis F Gottschalk/Baum Morosco Theater, Los Angeles 30 March 1913), *Pretty Mrs Smith, So Long, Letty, Canary Cottage, What Next, Merry Mary Brown, Linger Longer Letty* (Goodman/Grossman/Ann Nichols), *Letty Pepper,* the ''melody drama'' *Love Dreams, Lady Butterfly* and several highly successful plays including *Peg o' my Heart.* He was also involved in the construction of the Morosco Theater, New York, which was opened in 1917 with *Canary Cottage.*

1914 **Pretty Mrs Smith** (Alfred Robyn, Henry James/Earl Carroll/ w Elmer B Harris) Burbank Theater, Los Angeles 25 January; Casino Theater, New York 21 September

1915 **So Long, Letty** (Carroll/w Harris) Morosco Theater, Los Angeles 3 July; Shubert Theater, New York 23 October 1916

1916 **Canary Cottage** (Carroll/w Harris) Empress Theater, San Diego 18 March; Morosco Theater, New York 5 February 1917

1917 **What Next?** (Harry Tierney/Alfred Bryan/w Harris) Majestic Theater, Los Angeles 24 June

1919 **Merry Mary Brown** (Alfred Goodman/w Harris) Court Square, Springfield, Mass 10 November

1921 **Love Dreams** (Werner Janssen/Ann Nichols) Times Square Theater 10 October

[Auto]biography: Morosco, O ad Morosco, H, Dugger, L: *The Oracle of Broadway* (Caldwell, Idaho, 1944)

MORROW, Doretta [MARANO, Doretta] (b New York, 27 January 1928; d London, 28 February 1968). Broadway soprano who scored several times in a short career.

Pretty, dark Doretta Morrow took over and toured the role of Gretchen in the 1946 revival of *The Red Mill* at 18 years of age, played the heroine in the flop *Billy the Kid* musical *Shootin' Star* (Amy) in the same year, and subsequently created three major ingenue roles in Broadway musicals. The first of these was the part of Kitty in Frank Loesser's *Where's Charley?* (1948) in which she introduced ''My Darling, My Darling,'' the next Tuptim in Rodgers and Hammerstein's *The King and I* (1951) in which she teamed with Larry Douglas to sing ''I Have Dreamed'' and ''We Kiss in a Shadow'' and performed the narration to the Little House of Uncle Thomas ballet sequence, and the third and last was Marsinah in *Kismet* (1955) in which she introduced ''Baubles, Bangles and Beads,'' joined in ''And This Is My Beloved'' and shared ''A Stranger in Paradise'' with Richard Kiley.

Miss Morrow repeated her *Kismet* role in London and toured America in the title role of *Fanny* (1957), but when she returned to London to appear as the Princess in Cole Porter's *Aladdin* (1957), it became evident that she had for some reason utterly lost her stage confidence. She married soon after the show closed and did not perform again before her death from cancer at the age of 40. She appeared in 1950 as Tina in a TV version of *Knickerbocker Holiday,* in 1954 in CBS's *Once Upon an Eastertime* and in 1956 in a small-screen version of Elmer Rice's *The Grand Tour* entitled *Holiday.*

MORSE, Robert (b Newton, Mass, 18 May 1931).

After supporting roles in straight theatre and in the musicals *Say, Darling* (1958, Ted Snow) and *Take Me Along* (1959, Richard Miller), boyish, gap-toothed Morse shot to the forefront of the Broadway firmament with his Tony Award-winning performance as J Pierrepont Finch, the determinedly upwardly mobile window cleaner of *How to Succeed in Business without Really Trying* (1961, ''I Believe in You'') and its subsequent film (1967). He scored again on a return to Broadway as Jerry, the bass player who takes to a frock and attracts himself a millionaire, in *Sugar* (1972), the musical version of *Some Like It Hot.*

In a career embracing film, television and non-musical theatre, his last musical stage appearances have been in the short-lived *So Long, 174th Street* (1976), as Scooter Malloy in the Todd biomusical *Mike* (Philadelphia 26 March 1988) and on the road as Cap'n Andy in *Show Boat.*

MORSE, [Henry] Woolson (b Charleston, Mass, 24 February 1858; d New York, 3 May 1897). 19th-century Broadway composer.

Well-heeled Woolson Morse studied music at the Boston Conservatory and in Europe, and on his return—renouncing an at first expressed determination to become a carpet designer—he turned out the music for a whole swatch of musical shows (*Don Quixote,* Dexter Smith's *Alhambra,* etc), which got optioned (or so it seems) by a whole variety of managers . . . but not produced. He finally made it, after three or four years of constant writing and trying, with a piece that had started off as a straight musicalization of Tom Robertson's play *School* (*School, or The Charity Pupil*). This time, to ensure a production, the 22-year-old composer put his hand in his (father's) pocket and mounted his show himself, in an amateur production in Springfield, Massachusetts. There, somehow, it attracted the attention of Augustin Daly, and as a result, in March 1881, *Cinderella at School* was produced at Daly's Theater, New York, with May Fielding in the title role, James Lewis in the chief comedy role and such Daly luminaries as Laura Joyce, Digby Bell, Ada Rehan and Mrs Gilbert in supporting parts. It had undergone some change, however, and was now described as ''an adaptation of Kate Carrington's *Aschenbrödl* combined with a burlesque of Tom Robertson's play *School.*'' It was a genuine success, was swept happily away on to the touring circuits, was seen again, if briefly, on Broadway the following season, as performed by Rice's Surprise Party, and yet again in 1883.

Less prolific than most of his contemporaries, Morse turned out only four more Broadway scores in the next decade, of which a replacement for Chabrier's score to *L'Étoile* was the only one not to be given a quick exit visa from New York. However, the from-the-German variety musical *Hot Water* (in which his original music was supplemented by airs from *Der Feldprediger* and *The Mikado*) proved a useful touring vehicle for Alice Harrison.

In 1891 he teamed with his now-regular partner, Cheever Goodwin, to turn out the comical *Wang.* As played by De Wolf Hopper and his company, *Wang* became a major hit which served its star for a good many years and several returns to Broadway. A successor to *Wang,* in the same vein, cast the star as the *Panjandrum* (1893), but neither this nor a rewrite of *Cinderella at School,* rechristened *Dr Syntax* to give Hopper the title role, managed to approach the success of the earlier show.

The pair were, however, to find success again when Goodwin adapted and Morse musicalized the French comedy *Le Baptême du petit Oscar* under the title *Lost, Strayed or Stolen.* Broadway success was followed by a London production, a rare thing for an American musical at the time, but that success was to be Morse's last. He died the following year before his 40th birthday.

1880 **School, or The Charity Pupil** Springfield, Mass May

1880 **Dreams, or Fun in a Photograph Gallery** (w W A Rostetter, E E Rice, Harry Braham, et al/w Dexter Smith, Nat Childs, F T Robinson, et al/Willie Edouin, Childs) Park Theater, Boston 23 August; Bijou Theater, New York 30 August

1881 **Cinderella at School** (revised *School* w J Cheever Goodwin) Daly's Theater 5 March

1884 **Madam Piper** (w Goodwin) Wallack's Theater 5 December

1885 **Hot Water** (pasticcio arr/w Edward Holst) Opera House, Trenton, NJ 19 September; Arch Street Theater, Philadelphia 28 September

1887 **Circus in Town** (comp & arr Richard Stahl/w Holst) Bijou Theater 12 September

1889 **King Cole II** (Goodwin) (revised *Madam Piper*) Broad Street Theater, Philadelphia 24 April

1890 **The Merry Monarch** (*L'Étoile*) American version with new music w Goodwin (Broadway Theater)

1890 **Pippins** (Goodwin) revised version of Talfourd's burlesque *Atalanta* Broadway Theatre 26 November

1891 **Wang** (Goodwin) Broadway Theater 4 May

1893 **Panjandrum** (Goodwin) Broadway Theater 1 May

1894 **Dr Syntax** revised *Cinderella at School* Broadway Theater 23 June

1896 **Lost, Strayed or Stolen** (aka A *Day in Paris*) (Goodwin) McVicker's Theater, Chicago 15 June; Fifth Avenue Theater 21 September

MORTIER, Arnold [MORTJÉ, Arnold] (b Amsterdam, 1843; d Croissy-sur-Seine, 2 January 1885).

A prominent Parisian journalist and theatre critic (''Monsieur de l'orchestre'' of *Le Figaro*) for many years, Mortier also collaborated on a number of revues and several successful libretti for the French opérette stage. If the text for *Le Manoir du Pic-Tordu* was written in more the style of the later vaudeville-opérettes, his other pieces were all in the spectacular and féerie genre. Two of these, for his friend Offenbach, were more or less based on, or suggested by, the science-fiction novels of Jules Verne (*Le Voyage dans la lune, Le Docteur Ox*), the remainder included the three-act, 30-scene *L'Arbre de Noël* and the four-act, 25-scene tale of *Le Petit Poucet.* Mortier also co-wrote the scenarii for several ballets.

The libretti of *L'Arbre de Noël* (*Der Weinachtsbaum, Der Schatzgrüber*), *Le Petit Poucet* (*Der Daumling* ad Julius Stettheim, Viktoria Theater, Berlin 25 January 1886) and *Madame le Diable* (*Des Teufels Weib*) were all reused in Austria and/or Germany and/or Hungary, reset to scores by local composers.

Mortier authored a series of annuals on *Les Soirées Parisiennes* from 1874, looking at the theatrical season in a jokey and gossipy fashion, and is also credited with an uncredited hand in the libretto for Delibes' opera *Lakmé* (1883).

1875 **Le Manoir du Pic-Tordu** (Gaston Serpette/w Albert de Saint-Albin) Théâtre des Variétés 28 May

1875 **Le Voyage dans la lune** (Jacques Offenbach/w Albert Vanloo, Eugène Leterrier) Théâtre de la Gaîté 26 October

1877 **Le Docteur Ox** (Offenbach/w Philippe Gille) Théâtre des Variétés 26 January

1880 **L'Arbre de Noël** (Charles Lecocq/w Leterrier, Vanloo) Théâtre de la Porte-Saint-Martin 6 October

1882 **Madame le Diable** (Serpette/w Henri Meilhac) Théâtre de la Renaissance 5 April

1885 **Le Petit Poucet** (André Messager, et al/w Leterrier, Vanloo) Théâtre de la Gaîté 28 October

MOSS, Hugh (b Agra, India, 30 November 1855; d London, 23 July 1926). Director of Victorian musical comedy, operetta and burlesque.

Originally intended for the medical profession, Moss gave up his studies in 1880 to become an actor at West Hartlepool. He subsequently worked as a stage manager and stage director for such stars as Marie Litton, Wilson Barrett and Sarah Thorne and for producers Ben Greet and F R Benson. He entered the musical theatre when he directed the touring musical *The Punch Bowl* (1888) for Gilbert Tate, and followed this by staging *Gretna Green* (1890) and Luscombe Searelle's extravagant *The Black Rover* (*Isidora*) in London. He was reponsible for the direction of the original productions of Sullivan's opera *Ivanhoe* (1891) and of Messager's *La Basoche* (1891) at the English Opera House, and in the following decade directed a series of new musicals on the London stage. The burlesque *Blue-Eyed Susan* (1892), *La Rosière* (1893) and *The Bric-à-Brac Will* (for which he also took a cowriting credit) were less than wholly successful, but he scored a fine hit with Arthur Roberts's vehicle *Gentleman Joe* (1895) and he directed the comedian's *The White Silk Dress* the following year. His later credits included the touring *The Southern Belle* (1901) for which, though uncredited, he apparently had a share in the libretto, and the London production of the Laurence Housman/Liza Lehmann *The Vicar of Wakefield* (1906).

1895 **The Bric-à-Brac Will** (Emilio Pizzi/Harry Greenbank, W Sapte jr/w S J Adair Fitzgerald) Lyric Theatre 28 October

1901 **The Southern Belle** (F Osmond Carr/w Hugh Carson) Empire Theatre, Southend-on-Sea 7 March

MOSTEL, [Samuel Joel] Zero (b New York, 28 February 1915; d Philadelphia, 8 September 1977).

Moon-faced, pop-eyed comic actor Mostel did not make his first foray into the world of performing until he was in his late twenties. He began by working in cabaret before going on to appear in revue, musicals and plays, his first stage musical role on Broadway being as Hamilton Peachum in *Beggar's Holiday* (1946). His second, 16 years later, was as the rascally slave Pseudolus in the classical burlesque *A Funny Thing Happened on the Way to the Forum* (1962, Tony Award). In 1964 he created the role of the Russian-Jewish milkman Tevye in *Fiddler on the Roof* (''If I Were a Rich Man,'' ''Sunrise Sunset,'' ''Do You Love Me?''), a part which he repeated on a number of occasions thereafter and which brought him his second Tony Award from three Broadway musical appearances.

Mostel repeated his Pseudolus in the film based on *A Funny Thing,* and also appeared in the film version of *Dubarry Was a Lady* (1943, Paliostro), but his most famous screen role remains a non-musical one: as the improbable (?) musical-producing impresario of *The Producers* (1968).

Biographies: Mostel, K, Gilford, M: *170 Years of Show Business* (Random House, New York, 1978), Brown, J: *Zero Mostel* (Athenaeum, New York, 1989), Sainer, A: *Zero Dances: A Biography of Zero Mostel* (Limelight Editions, New York, 1998)

THE MOST HAPPY FELLA Musical in 3 acts by Frank Loesser based on the play *They Knew What They Wanted* by Sidney Howard. Imperial Theater, New York, 3 May 1956.

Frank Loesser's third musical, following behind the brittle British highjinks of *Where's Charley?* and the winning and warm New Yorkeries of *Guys and Dolls* was like neither of its predecessors. As with *Where's Charley?,* it was adapted from a successful play—Howard's Pulitzer Prize–winning *They Knew What They Wanted* had been a Theater Guild hit with Richard Bennett and Pauline Lord starred in 1924–25—and like *Guys and Dolls* it was a piece which was both set in America and peopled with a set of likeable American characters, but it still resembled neither of them, either textually or musically.

The Most Happy Fella, to which Loesser himself constructed the libretto, was not, like the two earlier shows, basically comic—it was inherently romantic, and the heart of its book was the unusual love story of the middle-aged Napa Valley winegrower, Tony Esposito. Hardworking Tony (Robert Weede) goes to town one day and is served in a restaurant by waitress Amy (Jo Sullivan) who catches his eye. In her he sees the kind of girl he would like to marry. He leaves her a note, addressed to ''Rosabella,'' and she writes back. A correspondance grows up between them and finally ''Rosabella'' asks Tony for his photo. Ashamed of being fat and fiftyish, Tony sends her a picture of his handsome foreman, Joe (Art Lund). When the correspondence culminates in an engagement and Rosabella comes to the Napa Valley to be married, the deception is bound to be uncovered. But tragedy strikes first. Tony's truck overturns on his way to pick his bride up at the station. Spurred on by a multitude of angers, Rosabella agrees to go through with the wedding, but that night she forgets her hurt in Joe's arms. As she nurses Tony back to health, however, real love grows between them only for her happiness to be shattered when Rosabella finds she is pregnant with Joe's child. She is at the bus station, leaving for New York, when Tony comes to find her and take her home. Susan Johnson as Cleo, Rosabella's comical waitress chum, and Shorty Long as the unshakably cheerful farm-worker,

Herman, with whom she pairs up, provided the lighter moments, with the Italian-American folk of the valley supplying the choruses and background color.

Loesser's music blended with the story in each of its parts. Tony laughed out his joy at being "The Most Happy Fella" in his postal love affair, whilst city Rosabella just plain wondered that "Somebody, Somewhere" actually cared about her, and when their love story rose to its first, happy peak their simple happiness filtered out in the silliness of an English lesson ("Happy to Make Your Acquaintance") and then poured out in one of the loveliest duets to have been written for a modern romantic operetta, "My Heart Is So Full of You." The straightforward Joe gave out with his wandering philosophy in "Joey, Joey, Joey" whilst Cleo wailed over her waitress's life in "Ooh, My Feet" and found a Texas friend in Herman who also comes from "Big D." Herman and his pals lilted out their fondness for the small-town pastime of "Standing on the Corner (watching all the girls go by)," whilst the farm folk provided some exuberant ensemble work ("Abbondanza").

The substantial musical values of the show were emphasized in Kermit Bloomgarden and Lynn Loesser's production by the casting of operatic baritone Robert Weede in the role of Tony, paired with the strong, straight young soprano of Miss Sullivan, and *The Most Happy Fella* was a substantial success. It played for 676 performances in its original Broadway run, and toured for six months. If that seemed rather less than its due, in comparison with other contemporary pieces, it was largely because the show was, in every way, substantial. It was a long evening in the theatre, an evening which never hastened through its action and which comprised no less than 30 musical pieces—many not slip-out songs—in its score. No matter how well it was done, it was more than many theatregoers were interested in taking.

This reasoning was behind the show's failure to travel at first. It was four years after the Broadway production before London saw the show and then it was H M Tennent Ltd, riding high on their production of *My Fair Lady,* who mounted the English *Most Happy Fella,* in association with Loesser's own Frank Productions. Another operatic bass-baritone, Inia te Wiata, played Tony, with Helena Scott (Rosabella), Libi Staiger (Cleo), Jack de Lon (Herman) and Lund in his original role in support, and the piece ran for 288 performances. The following year Australia also saw te Wiata in the role, supported by Barbara Leigh, Stella Moray and Myron Natwick for three months in Melbourne.

The Most Happy Fella has become one of those works that people talk about reviving much more often than they do it. However, Broadway saw its first return production of the show before it saw a proper repeat of *Guys and Dolls.* In 1979 Giorgio Tozzi starred in a Detroit-originated revival at Broadway's Majestic Theater (11 October) with Sharon Daniels (Rosabella), Richard Muenz (Joe), Louisa Flaningam (Cleo) and Dennis Warning (Herman) in the other main roles. It failed to run more than 53 performances.

It would seem that, in an age when a selection of musical theatre pieces have become fodder for the opera houses of the world, *The Most Happy Fella* would be a logical contender for such a home. Its logistics (cast and orchestra size), its length and its vocal demands all have an opera-house air to them. So, it was something of a surprise to find the show return to Broadway in 1992 (Booth Theater 13 February). The logistics question had been solved in an unexpected way: the Goodspeed Opera House's production had replaced Loesser's orchestra with two pianos. This rearrangement drew a mixed reaction, and the production, with Spiro Malas and Sophie Hayden featured, lasted only 229 performances.

UK: London Coliseum 21 April 1960; Australia: Princess Theatre, Melbourne 9 June 1961

Recordings: original cast (Columbia, 3 records), London cast (HMV), New York revival cast (RCA), selection (WRC), etc

MOUËZY-ÉON, André [MOUËZY, André Marie Joseph] (b Chantenay, Nantes, 9 June 1880; d Paris, 23 October 1967). Librettist for everything from vaudevilles to spectaculars in a long Parisian career.

Mouëzy-Éon had his first successful play produced in 1904, and he worked for more than a decade in the straight theatre, notably in the area of the military vaudeville (*Tire-au-flanc!, L'Enfant de ma soeur, L'Amour en manoeuvres, Les Dégourdis de la 11ème*), before becoming more than incidentally involved in the musical theatre. In the later part of the war years he wrote a handful of vaudevillesque pieces, mainly for the little Théâtre Édouard VII, scoring a distinct success with the first, the saucy *La Folle Nuit,* but it was to be a further decade before he devoted himself to what would be the main body of his musical work.

After the First World War he began a long association with the Théâtre du Châtelet, supplying the texts for the large, spectacular shows played there under the management of Alexandre Fontanes (*Malikoko, roi nègre, Capoulade de Marseille, Mam'zelle sans-peur*) and, later, of Maurice Lehmann, who favored a program of opérette à grand spectacle, original and imported, as the entertainment both at the Châtelet and at his Théâtre de la Porte-Saint-Martin.

Mouëzy-Éon worked frequently in tandem with lyricist Albert Willemetz on the original works which he wrote for the larger stages of Paris, combining musically in several cases with composers Maurice Yvain and

Tiarko Richepin, and on one occasion on an original opérette à grand spectacle, *Rose de France,* with Sigmund Romberg. From amongst these highly pictorial pieces it was the splenditious north-African *Sidonie Panache* and the gypsy-romantic *Chanson Gitane* which proved the most successful, but a number of his other opérettes à (very) grand spectacle, such as *Au temps des merveilleuses, Au soleil du Mexique, Venise* and *Pour Don Carlos,* had long runs on their initial productions and still receive occasional revivals in regional theatres.

Mouëzy-Éon also attempted rewritten versions of several classic opérettes—*Les Cent Vierges* with considerable success, *La Grande-Duchesse* and *Le Petit Faust* without—but his most successful adaptation was that of the Viennese Strauss pasticcio *Walzer aus Wien* for the French stage. The libretto as rewritten by him was a much more comically orientated version than either the original German or the subsequent English-language ones and, backed by a lavish production, established itself as a long-lasting favorite.

Mouëzy-Éon deputized for Lehmann at the head of the Châtelet's affairs for a period. His 1917 opérette *La Marraine de l'escouade* was adapted from his own play *Les Fiancés de Rosalie,* whilst his play *Le Loup dans la bergerie* was unsuccessfully adapted as an opérette, *Le Joly Jeu,* by other hands at Lyon in 1933. *Le Papa du régiment* (1909 w Jo Durieux) was turned into a Budapest musical comedy by Jenő Heltai and Károly Stephanides (*Az ezred apja* Vígszínház 13 May 1911) and his famous military vaudeville *Tire-au-flanc!* (w André Sylvane), adapted by no less an author than the young Ferenc Molnár, became *Gyöngyélet* (Ferenc Békési/Adolf Mérei, Magyar Színház 21 April 1906) on the Hungarian musical stage. As recently as 1984 he (w Yves Mirande) served as the source for another Hungarian musical comedy, *Uraim, csak egymás után* (mus: Szabolc Fényes), based on Adorján Stella's 1926 adaptation of one of his plays.

1906 **Monsieur Popotte** (Henry Moreau-Febvre) 1 act Théâtre Grévin 9 April

1917 **La Folle Nuit, ou Le Dérivatif** (Marcel Pollet/w Félix Gandéra) Théâtre Édouard VII 7 April

1917 **La Marraine de l'escouade** (Moreau-Febvre/w M Daveillans) Théâtre du Vaudeville 6 December

1917 **La Petite Bonne d'Abraham** (Pollet/w Gandéra) Théâtre Édouard VII 13 December

1918 **Daphnis et Chloë, ou la leçon d'amour** (Moreau-Febvre/w Gandéra) Théâtre Édouard VII 7 November

1919 **La Liaison dangereuse** (Pollet/w Gandéra) Théâtre Édouard VII 5 December

1919 **Malikoko, roi nègre** (Marius Baggers) Théâtre du Châtelet 10 December

1927 **Venise** (Tiarko Richepin/Albert Willemetz) Théâtre Marigny 25 June

Plate 265. **André Mouëzy-Éon**

1929 **Le Renard chez les poules** (Richepin/w Alfred Machard) Théâtre Michel 31 January

1929 **Olive** (Fred Pearly, Pierre Chagnon/w Pearly/w Alexandre Fontanes) Théâtre Ambigu October

1930 **Sidonie Panache** (Joseph Szulc/Willemetz) Théâtre du Châtelet 2 December

1931 **Nina Rosa** French version w Willemetz (Théâtre du Châtelet)

1932 **La Tulipe noire** (Richepin/Willemetz) Théâtre de la Gaîté-Lyrique 19 March

1933 **Rose de France** (Sigmund Romberg/Willemetz) Théâtre du Châtelet 28 October

1933 **La Dubarry** (*Die Dubarry*) French version (Théâtre de la Porte-Saint-Martin)

1933 **Valses de Vienne** (*Walzer aus Wien*) French libretto w Jean Marietti, Max Eddy (Théâtre de la Porte-Saint-Martin)

1934 **Le Petit Faust** revised version (Théâtre de la Porte-Saint-Martin)

1934 **Au temps des merveilleuses** (Richepin, Henri Christiné/Willemetz) Théâtre du Châtelet 25 December

1935 **Un coup de veine** (Yvain/Willemetz) Théâtre de la Porte-Saint-Martin 11 October

1935 **Au soleil du Mexique** (Maurice Yvain/Willemetz) Théâtre du Châtelet 18 December

1936 **Un de la Musique** (Roger Dumas/w Camille François) Théâtre de la Porte-Saint-Martin 12 March

1936 **La Margoton du bataillon** (C Oberfeld/René Pujol, Jacques Darmont) Théâtre de la Porte-Saint-Martin 22 December

1936 **Yana** (Richepin, Christiné/Willemetz/w Henri Wernert) Théâtre du Châtelet 24 December

1937 **Le Chant du Tzigane** (*Forbidden Melody*) French version w Henri Wernert (Théâtre du Châtelet)

1938 **Balalaika** French version w Maurice Lehmann (Théâtre Mogador)

1939 **Billy et son équipe** (*Roxy und ihr Wunderteam*) French adaptation w Willemetz (Théâtre Mogador)

1942 **Les Cent Vierges** revised version w Willemetz (Théâtre Apollo)

1945 **D'Artagnan** (''Bétove''/w André Mauprey, Robert de Mackiels, Maquet) Théâtre de la Gaîté-Lyrique 18 November

1946 **Les Chasseurs d'images** (Roger Dumas, Georges van Parys/Jean Manse) Théâtre du Châtelet 26 October

1946 **Chanson gitane** (Yvain/Louis Potérat) Théâtre de la Gaîté-Lyrique 13 December

1948 **La Grande-Duchesse de Gérolstein** revised version w Willemetz (Théâtre de la Gaîté-Lyrique)

1950 **Annie du Far-West** (*Annie Get Your Gun*) French libretto (Théâtre du Châtelet)

1950 **Pour Don Carlos** (Francis Lopez/w Raymond Vincy) Théâtre du Châtelet 17 December

1967 **Vacances au Tyrol** (*Saison in Salzburg*) French version w Henri Wernert (Belgium)

Autobiography: *Les Adieux de la troupe* (La Table Ronde, Paris, 1963)

MOUILLOT, Frederick [Charles Arthur] (b Dublin, 31 May 1864; d Brighton, 4 August 1911).

Frederick Mouillot worked for many years as a touring actor before moving into management where, in partnership with **H[enry] H[arvey] MORELL [MacKENZIE]** (d 8 January 1916), for many years he put out multiple companies of the popular musical comedies of the Gaiety/Daly's era in Britain and overseas. In 1904 he presented the successful touring musical *My Lady Molly* at Terry's Theatre for a 342-performance run and accomplished an unlikely feat by opening the same show the same night in South Africa where he also held extensive touring interests. First in partnership and later alone, he presented several original musicals including *The Little Duchess,* (1897) of which he was the part-author; the well-considered *The Transit of Venus* (1898), which had the top authorial names of James Tanner and Adrian Ross attached to its Napoleon Lambelet score; and *The Gipsy Girl* (1905), written by the brother of his *My Lady Molly* star, Sybil Arundale.

Mouillot was the owner of theatres in Dublin, Belfast, Cork, Jersey, Bournemouth, Boscombe, Southampton, Swansea, Margate, Leeds, Tunbridge Wells, Glasgow and the London suburbs.

1897 **The Little Duchess** (Frank Congden/w F W Marshall) Stockton-on-Tees 9 September

MOULAN, Frank (b New York, 24 July 1875; d New York, 13 May 1939). Broadway comedy star of the musical stage.

Originally a church choir singer, Moulan first took to the stage as a member of the Calhoun Opera Company and then, in 1897, joined the Castle Square Players. He appeared with them in their huge musical repertoire as Thorillière in *The Black Hussar* (*Der Feldprediger*), Jules le Meagre in Julian Edwards's *Madeleine,* Scalza in *Boccaccio,* Tuppit in *Dorothy,* Nakid in *A Trip to Africa* (*Die Afrikareise*), Major Murgatroyd in *Patience,* Paris in Gounod's *Romeo and Juliet,* Major General Stanley, Morales in *Carmen,* the Bailli in *Les Cloches de Corneville,* Alcindoro in *La Bohème,* Florestein in *The Bohemian Girl,* Baron Truenfels in *Lurline,* The Sheriff in *Martha,* Don Sancho in *The Queen's Lace Handkerchief,* Sir Joseph Porter in *HMS Pinafore,* Prince Paul in *La Grande-Duchesse,* Coquelicot in *Olivette,* The Mikado, Caius in Nicolai's *The Merry Wives of Windsor* and Figaro in *The Barber of Seville,* and in the first performances of Jakobowski's *La Tarentella* (1899, Philip Creek). In 1901 he played lead comic roles at St Louis's Delmar Gardens (Kibosh in *Wizard of the Nile,* Shrimps in *Princess Bonnie,* Bolero in *Giroflé-Girofla,* King Laurent in *La Mascotte, Boccaccio,* Coquelicot in *Olivette,* Muley Hassan in *The Tar and the Tartar,* etc). Then, in 1902, he followed his old employer, Castle Square producer Henry Savage, into the regular musical theatre in the starring role of Ki-Ram in *The Sultan of Sulu* (1902).

After the enormous and long-toured success of this piece, he moved on to appear in the Anna Held show *Mam'selle Napoleon* (1903, Flute) but was obliged to withdraw when his contractual obligations to Savage were hauled up in court. He subsequently starred for Klaw and Erlanger in *Humpty Dumpty* (1904, Little Mary), in the Chicago musical *The Winning Miss* (1906 t/o) and as George Washington Barker in *The Grand Mogul* (1907), and took a fresh turn at his old vehicle *The Sultan of Sulu* (1909) before taking up the chief comic part of Simplicitas/James Smith in the American production of *The Arcadians* (1910). During the craze for Viennese Operette, he starred first alongside Julia Sanderson as Baron Siegfried Bazilos in Leo Fall's *The Siren* (1911), then as the cut-out Grand Duke Rutzinov in *The Count of Luxembourg* (1912), and again as the thoroughly vamped Professor Josias Clutterbuck in *The Queen of the Movies* (1914, *Die Kino-Königin*). He then changed genre again to feature first in Joseph Santley's *About Town* (1915) and in the variety musical *Fads and Fancies* (1915, Professor Glum), then in Victor Herbert's *Her Regiment* (1917, Blanquet) and in *Little Miss Charity* (1920), in which he appeared as the crook ''Fingers'' Clay. His last Broadway creations were in the indifferent

Princess Virtue (1921, Hiram Demarest) and *Just Because* (1922, Mr Cummings), and though he returned in the early 1930s to play the chief comedy roles in several sets of Gilbert and Sullivan revivals (Ko-Ko, Sir Joseph Porter, Plaza Toro, Bunthorne, Major General, Lord Chancellor, Robin Oakapple, Point, Judge), he did not again find the opportunities his earliest Broadway roles had provided.

In 1937 he appeared in the Grand National film *The Girl Said No* alongside William Danforth and other members of this last Gilbert and Sullivan revival company, performing parts of his roles as part of a plot about a comic-opera company.

Moulan was for a period married to musical-theatre singer **Maud Lillian BERRI** (b 16 July), who appeared on Broadway in *The Little Corporal* (1898, Adèle de Tourville); alongside Moulan in *The Sultan of Sulu* (1902, Henrietta Budd) and as principal boy in *Humpty Dumpty* and in the leading lady's role of Ruth Walker in *The Grand Mogul* (1907); and alongside Kolb and Dill in *The Rich Mr Hoggenheimer* (1909, Flora Fair) and *A Peck of Pickles* (1914). She divorced Moulan after inheriting what was reported to be a million dollars.

LES MOULINS QUI CHANTENT Opérette in 3 acts by Frantz Fonson and Fernand Wicheler. Music by Arthur van Oost. Galeries Saint-Hubert, Brussels, 25 March 1911.

Les Moulins qui chantent was produced at Brussels's famous Galeries Saint-Hubert, then under the management of its co-author Frantz Fonson, and it gave him and his partner Wicheler, already the writers of the hit play *Le Mariage de Mlle Beulemans* (musicalized the following year as *Beulemans marie sa fille*), a second splendid success. Their little Dutch story, set amongst the mills of Zeeland, was stirred up by a bunch of silly men trying to win an infidelity from pretty Lisabeth (Angèle van Loo). When her loving husband Claes (Armand Franck) jokingly gives her a ''ticket'' permitting her a fling with any man, she uses it instead both to put the pretenders in their place and to win the pressing Parisian painter, Henry (Daniel Vigneau), for her niece, Nele (Gina Féraud). The most amusing characters of the piece, however, were two local children, Kate (Yvonne Arnold) and Petrus (Alice de Tender), professional Dutch postcard and biscuit-barrel models, whose tempestuous business association and romance ran alongside the ins and outs of Lisbeth's story. They also had a good share in the song and dance of a score in which the solos fell mostly to Lisbeth, Nele and Henry.

A London version (ad Leslie Stiles) produced as *The Love Mills* was a 24-performance failure.

UK: Globe Theatre *The Love Mills* 3 October 1911

THE MOUNTEBANKS Comic opera in 2 acts by W S Gilbert. Music by Alfred Cellier. Lyric Theatre, London, 4 January 1892.

Written and produced during Gilbert's estrangement from Sullivan and D'Oyly Carte, *The Mountebanks* was composed by Alfred Cellier (although Gilbert had wanted Arthur Goring Thomas, who turned the text down) and produced by Horace Sedger. It looked back to the author's pre-Savoy period in its style and subject matter, being more akin to such now-elderly pieces as Offenbach's *Les Brigands, Fra Diavolo* or *The Contrabandista* in its tale of comic-opera brigands than to the more sophisticated pieces the librettist had worked on with Sullivan. Its action centered on Gilbert's favorite ''lozenge'' plot, which Sullivan had so often rejected since its use in *The Sorcerer.*

Having gathered together some inefficient bandits (Frank Wyatt, Arthur Playfair, Cecil Burt, et al), some male (tenor J G Robertson) and female (prima donna Geraldine Ulmar) villagers, and a band of mountebanks (Lionel Brough, Aida Jenoure, Harry Monkhouse, et al), the author has them all take a magic potion by which everything becomes what it seems to be. Love affairs go awry and one village maiden (Miss Ulmar) who has pretended to be mad really does become so, until all is finally set back to normal. The construction of the piece was very close to that of *The Sorcerer,* there were clearly recognizable repeats of other Gilbert characters and motifs and, if there was still sufficient of the Savoy esprit in his writing, *The Mountebanks* did rather seem as if its author might have written it 15 years earlier.

Cellier supplied a score in a similar vein: attractive light-opera music of the kind heard in his *Dorothy,* but in the style of an earlier period and without the inherent humor of Sullivan's scores. A rousing song for Frank Wyatt as the brigand chief (''High Jerry, Ho!'') and a duo for the two mountebanks (Monkhouse, Miss Jenoure) who are turned into mechanical dolls (''Put a Penny in the Slot'') were the most popular numbers of a score which was left unfinished when Cellier died before the show's production. Musical director Ivan Caryll put the music in order, but the three numbers Cellier had not composed were simply cut.

London audiences, deprived of a genuine Savoy opera, supported *The Mountebanks* well, and Sedger's production played for eight months and 228 performances at the Lyric whilst no less than three touring companies took it on the road. Early the following year T Henry French produced the show in America with Lillian Russell's company, his star appearing in Miss Ulmar's role alongside sculptural baritone Hayden Coffin as her fellow villager and Laura Clement and Louis Harrison as the actor-dolls. Miss Russell, however, felt the need to enlarge her role, and to give herself a more prominent and personal first act curtain, so she added some extraneous and showy numbers to the score. San Francisco sniffed ''she is no more able to improve an opera by Gilbert than alter the ethics of Confucius.'' *The Mountebanks* was otherwise very well received and it played 47 Broadway performances as part of the company's touring repertoire schedule.

South Africa and Australia, where J C Williamson and George Musgrove's company played *The Mountebanks* through 1893–94, also both welcomed the latest work of Gilbert and the last of Cellier. However, it did not prove the kind of piece which, like the favorite works of either collaborator, would come back to the stage in the years that followed.

USA: Baldwin Theater, San Francisco 22 September 1892, Garden Theater 11 January 1893; Australia: Princess's Theatre, Melbourne 1 April 1893

THE MOUSMÉ Musical play in 3 acts by Robert Courtneidge and Alexander M Thompson. Lyrics by Arthur Wimperis and Percy Greenbank. Music by Howard Talbot and Lionel Monckton. Shaftesbury Theatre, London, 9 September 1911.

On the heels of the enormous success of *The Arcadians,* Robert Courtneidge attempted a follow-up with the same team of writers and performers. *The Mousmé* was, however, in a much less brightly comic and topically satirical vein than its predecessor, with its tale of oriental Hana (Florence Smithson) who sells herself to a geisha house to pay off the gambling debts of her beloved Fujiwara (Harry Welchman) so that he may take his honorable place in the army. The evil Yamaki (Eric Mathurin) takes credit for Fujiwara's heroic wartime deeds and dooms him to silence and disgrace by gaining Hana's indentures, but an earthquake kills the villain in time for a happy ending.

The composers supplied some lovely numbers for Miss Smithson—a temple bell song (Monckton), and a sweet song to ''My Samisen'' (Talbot) which allowed the singer to show off her exquisite E in alt—and some bouncy and humorous ones for Dan Rolyat as a comical fortune-teller (''In Toki-oki-o'') and Miss Courtneidge as the heroine's soubrette sister (''Honourable Jappy Bride,'' ''Little Japanese Mama''), whilst Courtneidge provided one of the most lavish productions seen in years, topped by an earthquake scene which won sighs of wonderment. Unfortunately, it also provoked vast deficits, for the running costs of *The Mousmé,* which was greeted enthusiastically all round, proved its undoing and, although it was played 209 times in London, the result was a £20,000 red figure. Henry Savage never used his American option, and the touring version which subsequently went out in Britain was cut down to a more realistic scale.

A French opérette of the same title, written by Michel Carré and Albert Acrémant and composed by Marius Lambert, was staged in Paris in 1920 (Théâtre Michel 11 July).

LES MOUSQUETAIRES AU COUVENT Opérette in 3 acts by Paul Ferrier and Jules Prével based on *Le Habit ne fait pas le moine* by Saint-Hilaire and Duport. Music by Louis Varney. Additional music by Achille Mansour. Théâtre des Bouffes-Parisiens, Paris, 16 March 1880.

A version of the successful comédie-vaudeville *Le Habit ne fait pas le moine,* produced at the Théâtre du Vaudeville in 1835, the libretto of *Les Mousquetaires au couvent* was entrusted by Bouffes-Parisiens director Louis Cantin, who had just had a splendid success with the first Paris work of one novice composer, Audran (*Les Noces d'Olivette*), to another, Louis Varney, a conductor and son of the well-known musician Alphonse Varney. The result was a success which outshone even that of *Les Noces d'Olivette* in the Parisian and French theatre, as the new composer's show established itself as one of the most enduring opérettes of its period.

Two soldiers, the lovelorn Gontran (Marcelin) and his energetic pal, Brissac (Frédéric Achard), steal the garb of some mendicant monks in order to fake their way into a convent to carry off Gontran's beloved Marie de Pontcourlay (Mlle Rouvroy) who, with her sister Louise (Élise Clary), is about to be forced to take the veil. Their plan goes awry amongst a festival of comical events, but they are saved and rewarded with the girls' hands when it turns out that the monks they left unclothed were not monks at all but a pair of plotters against Cardinal Richelieu. Although the principal story of the piece was theoretically the romance of Marie and Gontran, the more-incidental characters—best friend Brissac, naughty Louise, Gontran's comical tutor, the Abbé Bridaine (Paul Hittemans) and an innkeeper's wife, Simonne (Mme Bennati), who makes up with her feminine and soprano presence for the fact that the two girls don't get into the story until the action moves to the convent in the second act—take up the largest part of the action. This group was at the center of a plentiful supply of comedy scenes, highlighted by Brissac's drunken cavalcade through the convent, and was endowed with a barrelful of bright songs.

The score of *Les Mousquetaires au couvent* was a remarkable first major work, full of truly melodious and catchily lilting numbers—criticized at the time by some for being insufficiently ''original,'' they have by and large outlasted the pieces by which they were supposed to have been influenced—surrounded by some fine ensembles. There are repeated highlights, from the bouncy introduction of ''L'Abbé Bridaine,'' the disguised soldiers' monkish ''Nous venons de la Palestine'' and Louise's all-purpose confession (''Mon Père, je m'accuse'') to Gontran's lovely ''Il serait vrai, ce fut un songe'' and a superb trio for three male voices in Act I. Needed quickly, when Cantin's revival of *Fleur de thé* didn't last as long as was hoped, *Les Mousquetaires au couvent* had to be completed in a hurry, and apparently Varney—who later always seemed to compose at great speed—was not able to finish his last act in time. Two or three numbers of Act III are said to be the work of Mansour, musical director of the Bouffes-Parisiens.

In spite of the enormous success it won on its production, the show did not remain frozen. When the actor Achard was obliged to return to the Théâtre du Gymnase after the show's spring run, Cantin recast the role of Brissac with the former Opéra-Comique baritone Louis Morlet. The part, originally laid out for an actor-who-sings-a-bit, was now the property of a superb vocalist with notable acting talents. Varney promptly came up with two fine set-piece baritone numbers, the drunken ''Gris, je suis gris'' and the ringing ''Pour faire un brave mousquetaire'' which, as sung by Morlet, proved to be the hits of what became the definitive, if musico-dramatically lopsided, version of the show. A first run of 219 performances was followed by regular revivals at the Bouffes-Parisiens (1883, 1896, 1906 with the composer's daughter, Nina, featured) and the Folies-Dramatiques (1886, 1887, 1888, 1891, 1909), at the Menus-Plaisirs (1896–97), the Gaîté (1899, 1901, 1913, 1914, 1922, 1923, 1924, 1938, 1952, 1958) and at the Mogador (1940) as the piece established itself as one of the staples of the French opérette repertoire, regularly played in France up to this day. In 1992 it appeared in the now opérettic desert of Paris for a season at the Salle Favart (17 December) with Gabriel Bacquier as L'Abbé Bridaine, Michel Vassissère as Brissac and Patricia Jumelle as Marie.

Outside France, *Les Mousquetaires au couvent* was soon received in nearly all the main musical-theatre centres—as well as Brussels, Geneva, Cairo, Mexico, Buenos Aires, Madrid and Rome and a good few others—but with results which, although mostly good, did not reach the swingeing success of the French version. In London, H B Farnie's version, with Frank Celli (Brissac), Harry Paulton (Bridaine), Henry Bracy (Gaston) and Alice May (Simonne) featured, was played for a good three months, with only a brief hiccup when Celli got a fishbone stuck in his throat and had to be replaced by Guillaume Loredan. Budapest's production (ad Lajos Evva, Béla J Fái), played at the Népszínház with Pál Vidor (Brissac) and Vidor Kassai (Bridaine), was given a fine 37 times and revived there in 1897 (11 September) as well as on other Hungarian stages, but Vienna rejected its version of ''musketeers in frocks'' (*Die Musketiere in Damenstift* ad Julius Hopp, Eduard Mautner) at the Theater an der Wien after just 12 performances, in spite of a cast including Girardi (Brissac), Felix Schweighofer (Bridaine), Rosa Streitmann (Louise) and Karoline Finaly (Simonne). Maurice Grau's opéra-bouffe company introduced the show to America with Nigri (Brissac) and Duplan (Bridaine), and with Paola Marié choosing to play Simonne rather than the love interest; but whilst New York audiences were going wild over *Olivette* and *La Mascotte,* they rather overlooked the third of Cantin's great productions, and *Les Mousquetaires* did not get the kind of English-language showings the other two had won. However, even though the show was never given a Broadway run, it was widely seen outside New York, in several different English forms. One version was produced by the Bostonians in 1882 (New Haven, Conn 22 February) with George Frothingham (Bridaine) and W H MacDonald (Brissac) featured, and subsequently played in Boston and at Haverly's Theater in Brooklyn as a part of their repertoire; the Farnie version was mounted by Charles E Ford at Philadelphia Chestnut Street Opera House, 18 February 1882, as *The Musketeers*; another was given by H B Mahn's company at Chicago in January of the same year; and yet another remake, confusingly entitled *The Three Musketeers* or *The Three Guardsmen,* was given at the San Francisco Tivoli (30 November 1885) and in a number of summer seasons. Farnie's version of the piece was also played both at the Tivoli and regionally as *The Cavaliers.* Given the show's no-Broadway record, it was rather strange to find Tony Pastor's 14th Street Theater producing a Fred Intropidi burlesque of *Les Mousquetaires,* but May and Flora Irwin featured as Captain Slash and Miss Williams in a version reset at fashionable Vassar college and entitled *Riflemen at Vassar.*

In Germany the first performances were not seen until Mme Aubert's touring French company played *Les Mousquetaires au couvent* in their repertoire in 1893, and a vernacular version followed at Berlin's Alexanderplatz Theater in 1896.

Another *Musketiere in Damenstift,* by Charles Cassman and Fritz Baselt, was produced at the Königstadt Theater in Cassel (21 June 1896).

UK: Globe Theatre *Les Mousquetaires* 20 October 1880; Hungary: Népszínház *Tiszturak a sárdában* 11 February 1881; Austria: Theater an der Wien *Die Musketiere in Damenstift* 30 September 1881; USA: Grand Opera House, Chicago *The Musketeers* 20 January 1882, Fifth Avenue Theater (Fr) 25 April 1882; Germany: Apollotheater (Fr) 13 February 1893, Alexanderplatz Theater *Musketiere in Damenstift* 20 March 1896

Recordings: complete (Decca, EMI), selection (EMI-Pathé), etc

MOZART Comédie musicale in 3 acts by Sacha Guitry. Music by Reynaldo Hahn. Théâtre Édouard VII, Paris, 2 December 1925.

Guitry presented his wife, Yvonne Printemps, as the 23-year-old composer and himself as the Baron Grimm, the boy's nominal sponsor who finally sends him packing from Paris when his amours become embarrassing and irritating, in a blank verse piece to which Reynaldo Hahn supplied the score of 10 musical numbers, threaded through with Mozartian elements, which Messager had flatly refused to write. The hero did not have the entire score to herself for, alongside the Letter Song (''Depuis ton départ, mon amour''), which was, in the hands of Mlle Printemps, the musical highpoint of the show, and Mozart's final farewell to Paris and the woman with whom he has fallen in love (Air des adieux), the glamorous Countess d'Épinay, as portrayed by the beautiful soprano Germaine Gallois, was also given a chance to shine musically.

Mozart was a considerable success through some 200 performances at the Théâtre Édouard VII, and the Guitrys subsequently took it to London's Gaiety Theatre for a season—in French—before repeating their performances in America. In fact, America was treated to two versions of *Mozart* in little more than a month. Allegedly E Ray Goetz went to Paris to sign up the Guitrys for a Broadway season only to find that he had been forestalled by fellow producer A H Woods. He instead secured the English-language rights from Guitry and promptly staged the piece (ad Ashley Dukes, prologue: Brian Hooker) with his wife, Irene Bordoni, as the boy Mozart and Frank Cellier as the Baron von Grimm for a Broadway season of 32 performances, shortly before the French couple set foot in America. The Guitrys played their French *Mozart,* with Mlle Gallois supporting in her original role, 28 times before switching to *L'Illusioniste* for their last fortnight.

In France, *Mozart* has been revived on a number of occasions since Mlle Printemps's introduction of the piece: Graziella Sciutti appeared in the role at the Théâtre Marigny in 1952 (12 November) with considerable success and in 1985 the show was revived at the Théâtre des Variétés with Raphaëlle Ivéry in the starring role.

Other musical theatre pieces on Mozart's life include the one-act *Mozart und Schikanaeder* put together to the composer's music for the Theater in der Leopoldstadt in 1845, the Theater an der Wien's 1854 *Mozart* written by Alois Wohlmuth and with music by Suppé (23 September) and a 1923 Singspiel by H Duhan, Paul Frank and Julius Wilhelm (Volksoper 2 June). In 1873 Franz Jauner and Hermine Meyerhoff appeared at Vienna's Carltheater in a little ''Charakterstizze'' by Anton Langer as *Wolfgang und Constanze,* whilst one of the highlights of Vienna's Mozart celebrations of 1991 was the Wiener Kammeroper's production of a new play with Mozartean music, *Lacrymosa 91,* written and played by English actor Michael Heath. In 1999 Vienna got a new Mozart musical (Theater an der Wien 2 October, Sylvester Levay/Michael Kunze) written by the triumphant authors of the city's biggest postwar hit, *Elisabeth.* Unlike Guitry's piece, *Mozart!* concentrated not on the composer's fictional amours but on the psychology of child stardom, showing Wolfgang, the young man (Yngve Gasoy-Romdal), struggling to lead a normal and fulfilled young man's life whilst ever tied to the work and the worldly reputation imposed upon him by his everpresent and always-interfering genius. A dazzling and imaginative physical production, a luminous performance by Norwegian star-in-the-making Gasoy-Romdal supported by Uwe Kröger (Colloredo), Caroline Vasicek (Nannerl Mozart), Ruth Brauer (Constanze Weber), Thomas Bochert (Leopold Mozart) and Lenneke Willemsen (Baronin von Waldstatten), and a score which ranged from scalding modern tenor music for Mozart and Colloredo to gentler pieces for Nannerl (''Der Prinz ist fort''), Leopold, and the Baroness (''Gold von der Sternen''), and ensemble music humorous (''Eine ehrliche Familie'' for the grotesque traveling-player company of the Weber family), satirical (''Hier in Wien'') and beautiful (''Papa ist tot''), combined to give the *Elisabeth* team a new hit which, at the time of writing, has just begun its second season in Vienna and shows every sign of becoming as big a success as its predecessor.

UK: Gaiety Theatre 21 June 1926 (Fr); USA: Music Box Theater 22 November 1926 (Eng), 46th Street Theater 27 December 1926 (Fr)

Recording: complete (Gaîté-Lyrique)

MR CINDERS Musical comedy in 2 acts by Clifford Grey and Greatrex Newman. Additional lyrics by Leo Robin. Music by Vivian Ellis and Richard Myers. Opera House, Blackpool, 25 September 1928; Adelphi Theatre, London, 11 February 1929.

Originally commissioned from Grey and Newman by Leslie Henson as a vehicle in which to star himself as a male Cinderella, opposite Violet Loraine, *The Kid* (as it was then called) fell by the wayside when Henson went into London's production of *Funny Face.* It was sold instead to touring producer Julian Wylie, and a selection of second-hand songs which Grey had brought from his American collaboration with Richard Myers—a Philadelphia composer who racked up a remarkable percentage of pre-Broadway closures—were added to by Vivian Ellis. Bobby Howes and Binnie Hale were cast in the lead roles of poor, hard-done-by Jim and Jill, the rich man's daughter with whom he falls in love in her disguise as a maid. Well-produced, the piece had a fine 13-week tour

Plate 266. **Mr Cinders.** *Philip Bird and Graham Hoadly chaff their lowly half-brother (Denis Lawson) with the tales of all that they will get up to ''At the Ball.''*

and a Glasgow Christmas season, and was taken up for London by the trying-to-expand Australian firm of J C Williamson Ltd. Rearranged, redirected (twice, for original director Pat Malone died during rehearsals), rechoreographed, but with its two stars firmly in place, *Mr Cinders* scored a huge hit at the Adelphi Theatre. It ran there for five months, then shifted to the Hippodrome for another eight, closing only after a run of 529 West End performances.

Perhaps the most delightful musical comedy of its period, *Mr Cinders* gamboled through a succession of comical scenes filled with bright and bubbling banter as Jim was harassed by his booming stepmother (Eileen Redcott) and his grimly elegant stepbrothers (Jack Melford, Basil Howes), swanned around the ball given by Jill's father (Charles Cautley) disguised as the famous Amazonian explorer Lord Ditcham, or scrambled through the countryside on a motorbike with Jill on his pillion and a jewel thief in his baggage. The score, too, was a winner, with Ellis's charming encouragement to ''Spread a Little Happiness,'' as delivered by Miss Hale, proving a long-lived favorite, alongside the frenetic, revusical rhyming of Jim's description of life ''On the Amazon'' and the sweetly simple but affecting strains of such love songs as ''Every Little Moment'' and ''I Want the World to Know'' (by Myers, and originally heard in the very short-lived *You're Some Girl* and *Hello Yourself*) and the comical ''I've Got You.'' Myers's most successful contribution was the song ''One Man Girl,'' transplanted, like the attractive ''True to Two,'' from his *Brewster's Millions* musical *Bubbling Over* (1925) where it had been introduced, before the show folded out-of-town, by Jeanette MacDonald and Cecil Lean.

Following the London run, *Mr Cinders* quickly got back on the road, where Hindle Edgar and Marjery Wyn became a perennial Jim and Jill as the piece toured Britain year in and year out. Edgar also crossed the world to star in J C Williamson Ltd's hometown production, with the Australian star of *No, No, Nanette,* Elsie Prince, following Binnie Hale's example by taking up the role of Jill. Frank Leighton and Sonny Ray were the ugly brothers and veteran Maidie Hope boomed out her Lady Lancaster through a Sydney season followed by a disappointing month in Melbourne (Theatre Royal 11 October 1930) in which Edgar paired with another favorite local soubrette, *Sally* star Josie Melville.

In 1930 the show turned up in Germany as *Jim und Jill* (ad Hans Adler) and the following year it was seen both for 35 performances at Budapest's Vígszínház (ad István Zágon) and in Vienna, where Irene Palasty starred in what was now a ''grosse Tanz- und Ausstatungsoperette in 7 Bildern,'' with special dances inserted for the star (her Jim was down below the title whilst she had 80 percent billing above it) and the Palasty-Boys and Palasty-Girls in support. In 1934 *Mr Cinders* went into the film studio and emerged in a 70-minute version, starring Clifford Mollison and Zelma O'Neal, and with celebrated comic W H Berry as the policeman of the piece, which took the usual amount of liberties with the stage show.

In 1982 *Mr Cinders* was given a second life when, in the wake of a surprise hit-parade reappearance of ''Spread a Little Happiness'' (as crooned by pop vocalist Sting), American-born, London-based producer Dan Crawford exhumed it and presented a version, which kept pretty close to the original, on the pocket-handkerchief stage of London's King's Head Theatre Club. Denis Lawson was a Jim who had, billing oblige, appropriated the top song. Ellis's ''She's My Lovely'' was interpolated, one number was suppressed, the score was given a vivacious two-piano rearrangement and the evening, cast and staged with a wholly uncampy and unclichéd 1920s flavor, turned out to be the miniature delight of the London season. After three months the show transferred to the West End, where it continued until the total of the original run had been passed (587 performances). As a result *Mr Cinders* set off on a new round of touring and regional theatre productions as well as winning its first American performances at Metuchen, and subsequently at the Goodspeed Opera House (22 October 1988) and at New York's Mazur Theater. It also, temporarily, provoked a fresh look at an era of British musicals which had been thoroughly forgotten behind the mist of better-plugged shows from other countries.

Germany: Deutsches Künstlertheater *Jim und Jill* 16 September 1930; Austria: Wiener Bürgertheater *Jim und Jill* 6 February 1931; Hungary: Vígszínház *Jim és Jill* 4 April 1931; Australia: Her Majesty's Theatre, Sydney 5 July 1930; USA: Forum Theater, Metuchen, NJ 30 April 1986, Mazur Theater, New York 5 November 1992

Film: BFI 1934

MR MANHATTAN Musical play in 2 acts by Fred Thompson and C H Bovill. Additional lyrics by Ralph Roberts. Music by Howard Talbot. Prince of Wales Theatre, London, 30 March 1916.

Devised by London producers Grossmith and Laurillard as a British vehicle for the American comedian Raymond Hitchcock, *Mr Manhattan* featured its star as a foolishly rich young American in England. Melville (Hitchcock) has an apartment in London and is engaged to the lovely Evelyn (Peggy Kurton). In time-honored musical-comedy fashion, however, his valet has sublet his absent master's flat to a flashy tenor (Robert Cunningham) with a wife (Iris Hoey) who wears very thin negligees, and his friend Bobby (Austin Melford) has simultaneously decided to ''borrow'' it for a party with a lot of chorus girls. None of this impresses Evelyn's very strict papa. Harassed husbands, fathers and fiancé[e]s sweep through the apartment, and many farcical doings are the order of the day as the action gallops from London to France to a happy ending.

Howard Talbot's score was a slightly unusual one for, although it supplied its main characters with some top-notch songs—Hitchcock's recital of ''Things I Must Not Do,'' a winning solo for a lass on the make ''Remember, We Christened You Hope,'' and a male quintet about ''Man, Poor Man'' and his subjugation to woman—it also included what Talbot called scenas, virtual sung scenes in which the tenor and his wife quarreled to suitable music or a bunch of chorus girls greedily attacked their sugar daddy, chanting in ragtime rhythms their demands for money. A couple of borrowed American songs were interpolated, and of them ''All Dressed Up and No Place to Go'' (previously sung by Hitchcock in Broadway's *The Beauty Shop*) proved another success for the star, who won a delighted London reception and played to full houses for four and a half months before returning to America. He was replaced by another American comedian, Robert Emmett Keane, who did not have the same effect but who took the show through to the end of its 221-performance run.

Mr Manhattan proved that it could survive without the star for whom it had been created, however, when local comic Fred Duprez trouped it round the British provinces for several years with considerable success, Maurice Bandmann took it round the Far East circuits, and J C Williamson's musical-comedy company played Melbourne (four weeks) and Sydney (27 October 1917, five weeks) seasons with Louis Kimball as Mr Manhattan, supported by a fine cast including established London stars C H Workman, Carrie Moore (Lolotte) and Ethel Cadman (Evelyn).

Australia: Her Majesty's Theatre, Melbourne 15 September 1917

MR POPPLE [OF IPPLETON] Comedy with music in 3 acts by Paul Rubens. Apollo Theatre, London, 14 November 1905.

Mr Popple (of Ippleton) was, if not his most long-running, probably Paul Rubens's best work for the British musical stage. This was very largely thanks to a text which abandoned the coy English antics of so many of his libretti and, very largely, the schoolboyishly suggestive dialogue and songwords of such pieces as *Three Little Maids* or *Lady Madcap,* in a genuinely funny and farcical play which produced, in its title character, an endearing musical-comedy hero.

Freddy Popple (G P Huntley) comes up to London from very provincial Ippleton and, unable to find a hotel room, accepts the loan of an apartment from the actress La Boléro (Ethel Irving). In the second act, the two hopeful, bourgeois gentlemen (William Cheesman, Harold Eden) who have both leased the apartment for Boléro turn up, followed by their wives (one booming, one lachrymose) and by a bevy of other theatrical and society folk, and poor old Freddy finds himself temporarily declared as the actress's husband. He does his best obligingly to act up the part, but he is very happy when everybody is safely paired off where they belong and he can hurry back to uneventful Ippleton.

Huntley gave a wonderfully winning portrayal of the shy, gentle "country mouse," aided by such charming songs as "Rabbits" ("I'm not the least bit shy with rabbits"), and Ethel Irving stopped the show with the rousing exhibition of her profession in "Oh, la, la la!" and wooed Freddy comically with "You're Such a Dear, Sweet, Clumsy Old Thing." The show's very little concession to spectacle was made by edging in half-a-dozen girls in red satin as "the Scarlet Runners" and a final act set at the Kursaal at Bexhill, but *Mr Popple* didn't need spectacle—it was essentially a comedy in the best French style, illustrated by characterful and even plotful songs in their writer's most attractive style. A genuine small-house musical comedy of surprising quality.

Tom Davis's production of *Mr Popple* proved distinctly popular and the show cruised past its 100th performance on 21 February 1906, but after four months *Mr Popple* was obliged to move out of the Apollo Theatre because of a booking jam. Business was still booming, so Davis shifted his show to the Shaftesbury. After only seven weeks more, however, the County Council ordered the closure of the dilapidated Shaftesbury and, another transfer proving impracticable, the show had to shut down. Charles Macdona took over the management and put *Mr Popple* on the road with Huntley starring alongside Millie Legarde and with huge success, and he continued the tour in 1907, first with Huntley and then with Arthur Longley starred, through 1908 into 1909 (with

Plate 267. **Mr Popple of Ippleton.** *Freddy Popple (G P Huntley) has never had a lady straighten his tie in his life. And La Boléro (Ethel Irving) is . . . an actress!*

Huntley again, and then producer Macdona himself) until the piece had run more than three solid years around the country. Maurice Bandmann also introduced the show to India and the Eastern circuit from 1907.

Mr Popple was, however, not quite done. Almost a decade after its first production—and three years after a Werba and Luescher production, announced as a vehicle for comic Lionel Walsh, had been abandoned when its producers went bust—a version of the show turned up in New York. However, by the time it reached the stage, it had suffered more than most from the heavy rewriting invariably practiced in America on pieces purchased from overseas. What remained of *Mr Popple,* rechristened *Nobody Home* (20 April 1915), after Joseph Herbert, then Guy Bolton (book), Jerome Kern (music) and a variety of interpolaters had had a go at it, had less effect on Broadway-goers (135 performances) than the original (173 performances) had had on Londoners. Nevertheless, F Ray Comstock's production at the little Princess Theater was encouraging enough for the management to continue with more such unshowy, smallish-scale pieces, giving Bolton, Kern, and others the opportunity to turn out some happy comedy musicals on the same, well-proven and ever attractive French vaudeville lines.

MR PRESIDENT Musical comedy in 2 acts by Howard Lindsay and Russel Crouse. Music and lyrics by Irving Berlin. St James Theater, New York, 20 October 1962.

Following their successful teaming with Irving Berlin on *Call Me Madam,* Lindsay and Crouse supplied the composer with another libretto based on diplomacy and/or politics of which fictional United States President Stephen Decatur Henderson (Robert Ryan—although it is said the role was first offered to Ronald Reagan) and his wife (Nanette Fabray) and daughter (Anita Gillette) were the central characters. It followed the family's personal life through, most particularly, daughter Leslie's love affair with a high-up Turk (Jack Washburn), which is responsible for ruining her father's career and losing his party the next election. This, as everyone knows, is the most cardinal sin in politics. However, the now ex-President is apparently the sort of man the United States of America needs, for even the opposition invites him back into the charmed circle of his country's representatives before the curtain falls.

Mr President was a piece with a different flavor from the comically Ruritanian political shenanigans of *Call Me Madam,* and neither its book nor Berlin's agreeable score, which waved the flag rather less happily than George M Cohan had done decades earlier, produced anything to equal the highlights of the earlier show, or caught on in the same fashion. The performances of Ryan and Miss Fabray won plenty of praise, but the piece ran for only eight months and 265 Broadway performances, and didn't get inside any charmed circles.

Recording: original cast (Columbia)

MR WHITTINGTON Musical comedy in 2 acts by Clifford Grey, Greatrex Newman and Douglas Furber. Additional lyrics by Edward Heyman. Music by John W Green, Joseph Tunbridge and Jack Waller. London Hippodrome, 1 February 1934.

Grey and Newman's second musical-comedy version of a favorite pantomime tale, *Mr Whittington* was constructed on rather different lines than their earlier *Mr Cinders,* favoring an extravaganza style rather than that of musical farce. Without equaling the outsized success of its predecessor, it nevertheless proved a fine London and provincial success for the Moss' Empires circuit producing arm.

The show's tale had lad-about-town Dick Whittington (Jack Buchanan) ruined by the father of his sweetheart, Ena (Lalla Collins), so that she will have to marry fat and fatuous Lord Leatherhead (Fred Emney). His private (''there's nothing private about it'') secretary, Betty (Elsie Randolph), urges Dick to persevere, like his namesake, and, when he is knocked down by a cab, the modern Whittington dreams himself through a series of revusical situations—all ending in triumph—before waking up to find the stock market has reversed, his horse has won the Derby and the girl is still unwed. The ''dream'' scenes had Buchanan dancing with a bunch of policemen, riding the Derby winner, boxing for the Lonsdale belt, facing a county council made up of Christy Minstrels, and (on film) leading the scouts and guides of the nation, in a variety show which allowed the star to spread himself as never before.

Green's songs, topped by a gliding duo for Buchanan and Miss Randolph, ''Oceans of Time,'' and by the Buchanan-Collins ''Weep No More, My Baby'' (borrowed from his Broadway flop *Murder at the Vanities*), were the heart of an attractively dancing score, to which Tunbridge and Waller provided a burlesque ''Pipes of Pan'' number for the policemen's dance and the music for the minstrel show.

Produced for a Christmas season at Glasgow and Manchester (30 November 1933), with Buchanan directing and co-choreographing as well as starring, the show was taken to London in February and there played out 298 performances at the Hippodrome and the Adelphi before returning to the road.

MR WIX OF WICKHAM Musical comedy in 2 acts by Herbert Darnley. Music by Frank Seddon, George Everard, Frank E Tours and Herbert Darnley. Borough Theatre, Stratford East, London, 21 July 1902.

Conceived as a vehicle for music-hall star Dan Leno, *Mr Wix* had its hero mistaken for the descendant of a ducal family, fighting off African natives, getting arrested for going AWOL, court-martialed and finally acquitted by a female jury as part of a series of comic scenes which allowed Leno to display his talents, including the Lancashire clog dance which had originally made him famous, for three hours. When it was toured, however, the star's illness (he was going insane) forced the piece from the road after only six weeks. Although it never reached the West End, *Mr Wix* was played by William Walton in South Africa and was also taken up for Broadway. Rewritten by John Wagner, and with the name ''Jerome D Kern'' appearing alongside those of Darnley and Everard as composer, E E Rice's production, with Harry Corson Clark in Leno's role, played 41 performances in New York before going out on tour to ''popular-price houses,'' with Frank Lalor featured and a new title which showed up its burlesque-house kind of intentions: *The*

Merry Shop Girls. A second rewrite and relaunch, under the title *The Girl from London* was announced, but the end-of-career Rice finally renounced the project.

USA: Bijou Theater 19 September 1904

MR WONDERFUL Musical comedy in 2 acts by Joseph Stein and Will Glickman. Music and lyrics by Jerry Bock, Larry Holofcener and George Weiss. Broadway Theater, New York, 22 March 1956.

A musical play formed around the talents of the bright and youngish vocalist Sammy Davis jr and the act which he had successfully played in vaudeville with his uncle, Will Mastin, and his father, *Mr Wonderful* was the 1950s equivalent of the old variety musical, with its first act and plot existing principally to allow the performers to put a version of ''the act as known'' into the second. The billing read ''*Mr Wonderful* a new musical comedy with the Will Mastin Trio starring Sammy Davis jr'' (both in 80 percent of the title type).

Mr Wonderful simply presented Davis as young performer Charlie Welch who, supported by his girlfriend Ethel (Olga James) and his pals Fred (Jack Carter) and Lil Campbell (Pat Marshall), takes the course of the evening to get out of the showbusiness small time and into the showbusiness big time as represented by the ''Palm Club, Miami Beach.'' The piece gave Davis a fine Broadway showcase and also produced two numbers in its score which became standards, Davis's ''Too Close for Comfort'' and the title song as sung by Miss James. Chita Rivera, in a supporting role, had fun with ''I'm Available'' and Carter and Miss Marshall were the support act with three and a half numbers.

Jule Styne and George Gilbert's production had a 383-performance Broadway run, but, in spite of what seemed a reasonably sized production, the show failed to recoup its outlay and ended in the red.

Recording: original cast (Decca/MCA)

MÜLLER, Adolf (i) [SCHMID, Adolf] (b Tolna, Hungary, 7 October 1801; d Vienna, 29 July 1887). Prolific composer for the 19th-century Viennese stage.

Adolf Müller first appeared in the theatre at the age of 22 for a brief career as an actor and a singer before shifting his ground and becoming a conductor and a composer. He held an early position at the Vienna Hofoper, but in 1827 became a conductor at the Theater an der Wien where, apart from one period at the Theater in der Leopoldstadt and another, much later, at the Ringtheater, he spent the bulk of his more than half-a-century-long and hugely productive career.

Müller composed his first stage music for a short comic opera and a Posse in a spectacle-coupé at the Theater in der Josefstadt in 1825 and, over the next 60 years, wrote the music for more than 600 shows, mostly for the Theater an der Wien, ranging from Possen, Lebensbilder and every other kind of musical comedy, through children's shows, burlesques, vaudevilles, incidental music to dramas and comedies, ballets and a variety of spectaculars, as well as a handful of Operetten, only one of which, the latter-day *Der galante Vicomte* (1877, 5 performances)—announced as its composer's 615th stage work—was a regular, full-sized 19th-century Operette. It has been estimated that, in all, Müller composed over 5,000 individual numbers.

His earliest work staged at the Theater an der Wien was the enormously successful burlesque of Boïeldieu's opera *La Dame blanche* (*Die schwarze Dame*/Karl Meisl) and he followed up with other burlesque successes in *Othellerl der lustige Mohr von Wien* (on Rossini's *Otello*/Meisl) and *Robert der Teuxel* (*Robert le Diable,* 1833). He provided the original songs and scene music for Nestroy's Possen *Nagerl und Handschuh* (1832), *Der böse Geist Lumpacivagabundus* (1833), *Tritsch-Tratsch* (1833), *Eulenspiegel* (1835), *Zu ebener Erde und im ersten Stock* (1835), *Die beiden Nachtwandler* (1836), *Die verhängnisvolle Faschingsnacht* (1839), *Der Talisman* (1840), *Das Mädel aus der Vorstadt* (1841), *Einen Jux will er sich machen* (1842) and *Der Zerissene* (1844), as well as for many works by Karl Haffner, including *Therese Krones* (1854). The list of other authors with whom Müller worked included many of the Viennese theatre's writing royalty: Friedrich Hopp (*Hutmacher und Strumpfwirker*), Friedrich Blum, Julius Bittner (*Die Gefopten, Wiener Leben*), Alois Berla (*Zaunschlupferl*), Anton Langer (*Ein Wiener Freiwilliger, Die Aktien-Geissler, Ein Prater Wurstl*), Friedrich Kaiser (*Stadt und Land, Eine neue Welt*), Karl Elmar (*Paperl, Das Mädchen von der Spule*), O F Berg (*Die Probierenmamsell, An der schönen blauen Donau*), Julius Feld, Alois Blank (*Wiener G'schichten*) and Ludwig Anzengruber (*Der G'wissenwurm*).

He provided the music for Josef Böhm's parody *Die falsche Pepita* which introduced Marie Geistinger to Vienna in 1853, and for the Viennese versions of such successful French pieces as *Marie die Tochter des Regiments* (*La Fille du régiment*), the fairy-tale spectaculars *Schafhaxl* (*Pied de mouton*), *Die Eselshaut* (*Peau d'âne,* 1865) and *Prinzessin Hirschkuh* (*La Biche au bois,* 1866) and Dumas's vast *Napoléon* (1868), and for such Hungarian classics as the famous *A falu rossa* (*Der Dorflump,* 1879).

1825 **Wer andern eine Grube grabt** 1 act Theater in der Josefstadt 13 December

1827 **Die erste Zusammenkunft** 1 act Kärtnertör-Theater 29 March

1828 **Seraphine** (*Die Kriegsgefangene*) (M Schmid) Theater an der Wien 21 October

1856 **Der Liebeszauber** (*Barbier und Pächterin*) (Adolf Bahn) 1 act Theater an der Wien ?27 November

1864 **Die Fabriksmädeln** (Julius Findeisen) 1 act Theater an der Wien 3 December

1865 **Heinrich IV** (Schröder) 1 act Theater an der Wien 14 December

1877 **Der galante Vicomte** (aka *Der galante Abenteuer*) (K Plank) Theater an der Wien 30 November

MÜLLER, Adolf (ii) (b Vienna, 15 October 1839; d Vienna, 14 December 1901).

The son of the elder Müller, Adolf junior made a similar career as a conductor and composer. He worked from 1864 as a conductor in a series of provincial houses (at Posen, Magdeburg, Düsseldorf, Stettin, Bonn) as well as for periods at Pest's Deutsches-Theater and at Rotterdam's German-language opera house and, on two separate occasions, spent periods at the Theater an der Wien. He made his first theatrical composing venture with an opera, *Heinrich der Goldschmied,* produced in 1867 in Magdeburg (1 February). Three years later he had a short Operette produced at the Theater an der Wien, at a time when he had briefly taken up a conducting post alongside two celebrated house musicians, his father and Richard Genée, a team which was soon joined by the young Carl Millöcker. Although he had one more large-scale comic opera (*Waldmeisters Brautfahrt*) and one more opera (*Van Dyck* Rotterdam, 1877) produced, Müller then largely abandoned composing, and for some time concentrated on a career as a conductor.

When the fashion for Operette became established, however, he again began to compose for the stage. His first such piece, *Der kleine Prinz,* lasted only one week, but the second, *Der Hofnarr,* did altogether better. With Girardi, Friese, Carl Streitmann and Ottilie Collin featured, it played 85 performances at the Theater an der Wien, and was subsequently produced throughout Germany and Hungary (*Az udvari bolond*), around America, and in a Broadway season under the title *The King's Fool* (Niblo's Garden 17 October 1890). *Der Liebeshof* (13 performances) lasted but a short time, but there was further success waiting with *Des Teufels Weib,* a Viennese Operette version of Henri Meilhac and Arnold Mortier's libretto for *Madame le Diable,* originally set to music in France by Serpette (51 performances). Of his later works, *Der Millionen-Onkel* (34 performances), *Lady Charlatan,* produced at the Carltheater (34 performances) and given just one guest showing at Müller's own base, *General Gogo* (30 performances) and *Der Blondin von Namur* (31 performances) all had respectable runs, with *Lady Charlatan* coming the closest to repeating the success of *Der Hofnarr. Der Blondin von Namur* and *Lady Charlatan* were both played with some success in Germany. The only one of Müller's works which has survived into the classic repertoire, however, is a pasticcio reworking of Johann Strauss music into the score for the not very classic Operette *Wiener Blut* (1899).

Amongst his other theatre work, Müller supplied the score for Ludwig Anzengruber's highly successful *Der Pfarrer von Kirchfeld,* another successful Posse in *Eine Kleinigkeit,* and music for the German production of Mór Jókai's *Az arany ember* (*Der Goldmensch,* 1885). He also arranged a new score for the interminably traveling vaudeville *Le Voyage en Suisse,* contributed to the extremely successful Posse *Die Wienerstadt in Wort und Bild* (100 performances in two years) and rearranged his father's score, with other pasticcio elements, for a revised version of Nestroy's celebrated piece *Der böse Geist Lumpacivagabundus.*

1870 **Das Gespenst in der Spinnstube** (Julius Bacher) 1 act Theater an der Wien 20 August

1870 **Der Pfarrer von Kirchfeld** (Ludwig Anzengruber) Theater an der Wien 5 November

1870 **Der Glöckelpolster** (O F Berg) Theater an der Wien 22 December

1873 **Waldmeisters Brautfahrt** (Arthur Müller) Hamburg 15 February

1882 **Der kleine Prinz** (Julius Rosen) Theater an der Wien 11 January

1883 **Auf der Rax** (Eugène Labiche, Édouard Martin ad Theodore Taube) Theater an der Wien 1 February

1885 **Eine Kleinigkeit** (Heinrich Thalboth) Theater an der Wien 7 January

1886 **Der Reise in die Schweiz** (*Le Voyage en Suisse*) new pasticcio score (Theater an der Wien)

1886 **Der Hofnarr** (Hugo Wittmann, Julius Bauer) Theater an der Wien 20 November

1887 **Die Wienerstadt in Wort und Bild** (w Julius Stern, et al/ Bauer, Isidor Fuchs, F Zell) Theater an der Wien 10 April

1888 **Der Liebeshof** (Wittmann, Oskar Blumenthal) Theater an der Wien 11 November

1889 **Lumpaci** revised *Der böse Geist Lumpacivagabundus* new pasticcio score arr (Theater an der Wien)

1890 **Des Teufels Weib** (*Madame le Diable*) (Henri Meilhac, Arnold Mortier ad Theodor Herzl) Theater an der Wien 22 November

1892 **Der Millionen-Onkel** (Zell, Richard Genée) Theater an der Wien 5 November

1894 **Lady Charlatan** (Paul von Schönthan, Leo Stein) Carltheater 29 November

1896 **General Gogo** (Wittmann, Gustav Davis) Theater an der Wien 1 February

1896 **Der Pfiffikus** (Julius Horst, Stein) 1 act Raimundtheater 18 April

1898 **Der Blondin von Namur** (Horst, Stein) Theater an der Wien 15 October

1899 **Wiener Blut** (Johann Strauss arr/Victor Léon, Stein) Carltheater 26 October

1900 **Das Lied im Volke** (Richard Nordmann) Theater an der Wien 23 December

MÜLLER, Wenzel (b Tyrnau in Mähren, 26 September 1767; d Vienna, 3 August 1835).

Longtime musical director of the Theater in der Leopoldstadt and one of the most prolific and popular theatre composers of the late 18th- and early 19th-century Viennese stage, Müller composed a number of scores and songs which lasted well into the latter part of the 19th century as accompaniment to various successful Singspiele, Possen, Volksstücke, Zauberspiele, burlesques and plays ranging from the works of Shakespeare and Goldoni to those of the Viennese masters of the time.

Several of Müller's early works were billed as Operetten (*Je grösser der Schelm, je grösser das Glück* 1786, *Die Gräfin* 1786) or komische Oper (*Das Neusonntagskind* 1793, *Ritter Don Quixotte* 1802, *Die Bewöhner der Tukenschanze* 1804) and others as operas (*Jawina* 1807, *Die Prinzessin von Cacambo* 1814), but it was the various forms of musical comedy and fairy-tale spectaculars that made up such an important part of the theatre diet of his time which formed the bulk of his work.

Amongst his credits were included the music for Raimund's *Der Barometermacher auf der Zauberinsel* (1823), *Die gefesselte Phantasie* (1828) and *Alpenkönig und Menschenfeind* (1828), an 1800 Posse which was called *Der Bettelstudent* (already) and a comic-opera version of Shakespeare's *Tempest* (*Der Zauberinsel,* 1798).

Müller was the father of the "German Catalani," opera singer Therese Grünbaum (d Berlin, February 1876).

THE MULLIGAN GUARD[S]

The Mulligan Guards made their first ever appearance at the Chicago Academy of Music during the 1873 summer season given by John Hart's New York Theatre Comique Company, as represented by the vaudeville team of Harrigan and Hart in the course of a song and a sketch. Ned Harrigan and Dave Braham wrote the song "The Mulligan Guards" to be sung as part of an act which featured a marching band of two characters, the one based on a tailor called Dan Mulligan, the other on a Captain Jack Hussey, and which burlesqued the target-company exercises of the time, as the two volunteers spent their 10-minute sketch trying to master the maneuvers in their manual. Dressed in exaggerated military costumes, Tony Hart (as the captain) and Harrigan (as his troop of one) went through some ridiculous byplay to the strains of their custom-made song, and the sketch turned out a great success. When the company returned to their New York base, Harrigan and Hart repeated the sketch (8 September), along with another in which they played blackface (*Massa's Old Friend*) but it was the Mulligan routine which won the plaudits ("one of the best they have ever presented") and the song itself became all the rage. Publishers William Pond issued it in versions for piano, guitar, banjo, orchestra and brass band, and arranged as a waltz, galop, quickstep and quadrille, as well as in its pristine shape.

The partners repeated song and sketch regularly both in New York and around the country in the several years that followed, and the number was featured along with its companion "The Skidmore Guards" in their "three act drama with beautiful musical specialities," *The Doyle Brothers* (1875), where it was performed by a group of little boys, the Gallant 69th, who mimicked the adult maneuvers.

They did not, however, keep it to themselves, and the sketch was performed by other duos, even on Broadway, where the Arnold brothers appeared at the Parisian Varieties (January 1876) in the parts made famous by the author and his partner, and both the Reynolds Brothers and another English partnership (who performed the piece in English uniforms!) similarly helped themselves to "The Skidmore Guards." "The March of the Mulligan Guards" had been introduced to Londoners as early as Christmas 1874 by "Pony" Moore, of the Moore and Burgess Minstrels ("one of the best hits Mr Moore has made for a long time").

In 1878, with the Harrigan and Hart team now installed semi-permanently at New York's Theatre Comique, Ned Harrigan brought the Guards back for a more thorough exposure in his short farcical musical show *The Mulligan Guards' Picnic.* His Guards, now encountered in greater number, were a pseudo-military marching, parading, slogan-shouting, song-singing, dressing-up group of immigrant Americans, who liked nothing better than to get together flag-wavingly with ex-fellow countrymen to identify themselves loudly with the country they had abandoned, to drink as much as possible with them after the marching was over and, if possible, stir up a good fight with some other national and/or racial group. Hart this time played the Dan Mulligan whose name was given to the group.

The Mulligan Guards' Picnic was a singular success, and the Mulligan Guards and the characters Harrigan invented in and around them remained a feature of Harrigan and Hart's shows for many seasons. After the first piece, it was Harrigan who appeared as Dan Mulligan, whilst Hart was blacked and frocked-up to play the comical negress Rebecca Allup and/or Mulligan's son, Tommy, and there was usually a Germanic or a Jewish protagonist (or, rather, antagonist) somewhere to be found, as the series of shows ran through seven different titles in three years.

The pair tried out other shows and other characters, but Harrigan picked up the character of Dan Mulligan and Hart returned to Rebecca again regularly, notably in 1883 for one of their most successful shows, *Cordelia's Aspirations,* in which Annie Yeamans, the regular portrayer of Dan's hot-mouthed, pretentious wife, the aforesaid Cordelia, attempted—obviously, with no luck—to take the Mulligan family upmarket. They repeated one more time in the following *Dan's Tribulations* (1884) before letting go of their alter egos for good.

The plays drew their fun from all quarters of racist humor and lively, if clichéd, nationalist-immigrant characteristics—real, idealized and wished-for. The Irishman were stage Irishmen of the deepest hue, merry, boozy, impecunious, irresponsible, scrapping; the negro characters spoke in minstrel blackface dialect, with ''de'' for ''the'' and many a ''gwine,'' and were the Irishman's natural enemy; the German-Americans indulged in the ''Dutch'' comic dialect which was to grow into a valuable feature of the comedy industry in America. From these types, Harrigan drew some fine and funny characters whom he continued and even occasionally developed a little from show to show, giving his audiences a thrill of recognition equivalent to that found in the later film serials or television soap-operas. He also gave them some very clever, if not always very original, low-comic and farcical scenes. A bonus was added to the entertainment by musical director Dave Braham, who turned out a series of bristling songs (to Harrigan's lyrics) for the series, a number of which became popular and extractable standards. There was also, naturally, plenty of musical opportunity for the Guards to leap into displays of the costumed marching which always aroused the same type of enthusiasm in the theatre (why?) as it did out of it.

Played to an audience which reveled in the music halls and in farce-comedy, who identified with the characters and enjoyed seeing the opposition made fun of and/or beaten up, the Mulligan Guards series served Harrigan and Hart splendidly through the large part of their time as a team, and proved for many years one of the most successful popular entertainments on the American musical stage.

Literature: *Illustrated History of the Mulligan Guards* (Collin & Small, New York, 1874), Harrigan, E: *The Mulligans* (G W Dillingham, New York, 1901)

MUNROE, Kate [LISTER, Katherine] (b Cincinatti, 1846; d London, 17 October, 1887). Well-traveled American-born prima donna of the opéra-bouffe and -comique stage.

Daughter of a Brooklyn doctor, ''Kate Munroe'' left her native land in 1869 to go to Italy to study voice, and she made her first recorded stage appearance in Milan as Norina in *Don Pasquale.* Engaged as an opera singer in Paris, she soon found that her voice was not equal to operatic stresses and strains and she moved on to Britain where she entered the lighter musical theatre playing in *Pomme d'api* at the Gaiety Theatre in September 1874. She went on to play Prince to the principal girl of Connie Loseby in Hollingshead's production of *Cinderella* at Holborn (1874, Prince Felix), starred as Mlle Lange in *La Fille de Madame Angot* at the Gaiety and at the Philharmonic (1875), and then crossed to the Alhambra where, between 1875 and 1877, she was seen in a revival of *Chilpéric* (Galswinthe), in *Spectresheim* (Herminia), *Don Quixote* (Altissidora), *Le Voyage dans la lune* (Princess Fantasy), *Orphée aux enfers* (Eurydice) and as someone called Hilda in the house's so-so-successful version of *Die Fledermaus.* She then moved on to join the not-quite-yet-famous Alexander Henderson at the Folly Theatre to play Judic's role in *La Créole,* appeared as Dindonette in a version of *L'Oeil crevé* and was cast as the first British Serpolette in *Les Cloches de Corneville* (1878), a role which she retained for much of the show's record-breaking run.

She took time off from Planquette's piece to make an appearance in Paris in 1879, making a hit with a very blue ''Le Premier Cigare'' in Coedès's short-lived *Les Deux Nababs* at the Nouveautés and another in a role which was kindly made into that of an English girl in Hervé's *La Marquise des rues* (1879, Albina de Brignon) at the Bouffes-Parisiens. The critics noted that her French was better than her decidedly ''twangy'' Brooklyn English. She also visited New York for her only theatrical appearances in her home country, starring with the Comley-Barton Company as Serpolette. She returned to London to star in *La Belle Normande* (1881, Eglantine), *Boccaccio* (1882, Isabella), *The Merry Duchess* (1883, Duchess) and *Gillette de Narbonne* (1883, Rosita) before she married in 1885, but she was soon back on the stage at the Theatre Royal, Drury Lane, playing in *Frivoli* (1886, Marchioness de Piombino). This, however, was her last appearance. She died of jaundice in childbirth the following year.

MURPHY, Donna (b Corona, NY, 7 March 1958).

Rich-voiced American vocalist and actress who scored a dramatic hit in Broadwy's *Passion.*

Donna Murphy made her first Broadway appearance as one of the alter egos in the original production of *They're Playing Our Song* (1979), and was subsequently seen in *Zapata* (1980) at the Goodspeed Opera House, off-Broadway in *Francis* (1981), in the transferred *The Human Comedy* (1983) and in off-Broadway's *Little Shop of Horrors* as well as in several revues (*My Name is Alice, Showing Off*). In 1985 she played in *The Mystery of Edwin Drood,* succeeding Betty Buckley in the title role.

She subsequently mixed roles in plays (*Miss Julie, Privates on Parade, Twelve Dreams*) with such musical pieces as *Birds of Paradise* (1987), *Dangerous Music* (1988), *Song of Singapore* (1991, Rose), a Boston mounting of *Pal Joey* (Vera) and *Hello Again* (1994) before she exploded into prominence with her performance of a decade as the anguished Fosca in *Passion* (1994, Tony Award). She went on to star in the latest Broadway version of *The King and I* in 1996.

MURRAY, Alfred

British librettist of the Victorian stage.

After a promising showing with the burlesque *Little Carmen,* produced at a showcase matinée in 1884 by a striving Gaiety Theatre understudy, the team of Murray and composer Edward Jakobowski were commissioned to write a comic opera by the town's most active musical producer, John Hollingshead of the Gaiety Theatre. *Dick,* an enjoyable comic-opera version of the pantomime tale of Dick Whittington, won some success and several overseas productions. Whilst Jakobowski then went on to triumph with *Erminie,* Murray was taken up by *Erminie*'s producer Violet Melnotte, paired with the untried Belgian composer Ivan Caryll, and given the task of writing an English version of the original French libretto to which Caryll had composed what became his first full stage work, *The Lily of Léoville.* The show failed to repeat *Erminie*'s success, and although he won some runs with further French adaptations, and a veritable Broadway hit with *Nadgy,* for several years Murray drifted further and further from such success with such works as the complicated mythological-spectacle *The Palace of Pearl,* a provincial remake of *Le Grand Duc de Matapa* (*Glamour*) and *La Prima Donna,* an attempt at comic opera by the respected musician Tito Mattei, which used as its basis the same magazine story Gilbert later used for *The Grand Duke.*

He supplied some songwords for several further shows, including the Arthur Roberts *A Modern Don Quixote* and the long-running *A Chinese Honeymoon,* and finally had his name substantially connected to a genuine hit when he wrote the dialogue for the Gaiety musical comedy *The Messenger Boy* (1900).

1881 **Gibraltar** (aka *Madame Rose*) (*La Reine des Halles*) English version (Haymarket Theatre)
1883 **Lurette** (*Belle Lurette*) English version w Frank Desprez (Avenue Theatre)
1884 **Little Carmen** (Edward Jakobowski) Globe Theatre 7 February
1884 **Dick** (Jakobowski) Globe Theatre 17 April
1886 **The Lily of Léoville** English version (Comedy Theatre)
1886 **The Palace of Pearl** (Jakobowski, Frederic Stanislaus/w William Younge) Empire Theatre 12 June
1886 **Glamour** (William Hutchison/w H B Farnie) Edinburgh 30 August
1886 **La Béarnaise** English version (Prince of Wales Theatre)
1888 **Babette** (*La Grappe d'amour*) English version w J G Mosenthal (Strand Theatre)
1888 **Nadgy** (*Les Noces improvisées*) English version (Avenue Theatre)
1889 **La Prima Donna** (Tito Mattei/w Farnie) Avenue Theatre 16 October
1897 **La Périchole** English version (Garrick Theatre)
1899 **La Tarantella** (Jakobowski) Studebaker Theater, Chicago 17 July
1900 **The Messenger Boy** (Lionel Monckton, Ivan Caryll/Adrian Ross, Percy Greenbank/w James T Tanner) Gaiety Theatre 3 February

MUSGRAVE, Frank [BONNER, Francis Musgrave] (b Pimlico, c1834; d Bethnal Green, 11 May 1888).

A conductor and a composer of dance-music arrangements for publishing houses and of pasticcio songs and dances (''composed and arranged by'') for the burlesque stage, Musgrave, during his extended period as musical director of the old Strand Theatre, under the management of the Swanborough family, unwittingly assured himself a place in the history books when he composed a score of entirely original music for F C Burnand's 1865 burlesque *Windsor Castle.* Produced at the Strand, after a long series of the musical scissor-and-paste burlesques which were the norm at the time, and for many of which Musgrave had organized and sometimes composed more than the usual small original part of the score, *Windsor Castle* was justifiably claimed by Burnand as the ''first English opéra-bouffe.''

A member of the orchestra at Drury Lane as a young man, he became musical director at Liverpool's Theatre Royal in the late 1850s, and he was but 26 years of age when he took over from W H Montgomery at the head of the Strand orchestra for the winter season of 1860 (10 September). His first burlesque was a revival of Byron's successful Fra Diavolo; the first piece for which he supplied a ''composed and arranged'' score was Byron's outstanding *Cinderella* produced at Christmas the same year, followed at the Easter changeover by the writer's other most enduring burlesque piece, *Aladdin, or The Wonderful Scamp* (1861). After the *Windsor Castle* experiment in 1865, Musgrave composed an original score for a burlesque of *L'Africaine,* before the theatre returned to the old style of musical patchwork shows. He remained at the Strand, in all, for 11 years. In February 1868 he took a lease of the Prince of Wales Theatre in Liverpool, initially with William Swanborough as manager, and both the repertoire and company from the Strand Theatre were seen there. He gave up the theatre late in 1869 and returned to London to conduct the important London production of *Chilpéric* (1870) at the Lyceum.

He conducted several other opéra-bouffe productions thereafter, both in London and on the touring circuits, and took further turns into management at the Theatre Royal, Nottingham, the Theatre Royal, Margate and again for some not notably successful touring productions, including companies playing *Giroflé-Girofla, La Fille de Madame Angot* and his own *Prisoners at the Bar*. He was also engaged for a period as musical director at the Criterion Theatre. At the same time, without again venturing a complete London score, he continued to turn out the same sort of music and arrangements as before, mostly for touring burlesque companies such as those run by Emily Duncan (*The Miller and His Men, Sindbad* 1883, etc), but occasionally as interpolations in major musicals, such as H B Farnie's version of Offenbach's *La Vie parisienne* (''For Thee, My Love,'' ''The Tout''). He also visited America briefly in 1880 to conduct for Selina Dolaro in a combination grandiosely called M B Leavitt's Grand English Opera Burlesque Company, which staged a full-blooded *Carmen* burlesque with Musgrave's name on its music. However, the company and its management proved so iffy that Musgrave turned smartly around and went home.

In his fifties, Musgrave began to lose his sight, and in February 1886 a Benefit was mounted for him at the Comedy Theatre. He ''went away to rest,'' but a year later the ''inventor of English opéra-bouffe'' was discovered in the Bethnal Green lunatic asylum where, it was reported, he was ''too poor to buy winter clothes.'' He died there soon after.

1865 **Windsor Castle** (F C Burnand) Strand Theatre 5 June

1865 **L'Africaine** (Burnand) Strand Theatre 18 November

1873 **Nottingham Castle, or The Crusader, the Cruel Uncle and the Children of Sherwood** (F R Goodyer) Theatre Royal, Nottingham 22 September

1873 **Lothair, or Batti-Batti and the Shah-de-doo** (Frank W Green, Robert Soutar) Theatre Royal, Liverpool 13 October

1878 **Prisoners at the Bar** (C H Ross) 1 act Royal Alexandra Theatre, Liverpool 17 June

1879 **Sinbad the Sailor, or The Tar that was pitched into** (w Green) Princess's Theatre, Edinburgh 31 March; Royalty Theatre 10 April 1882 (mus arr Michael Connelly)

1880 **Carmen, or Soldiers and Seville-ians** (Green) Haverley's Theater, New York 13 September

MUSGROVE, George [Thomas] (b Surbiton, Surrey, 21 January 1854; d Sydney, Australia, 21 January 1916). Australian producer for both the colonial and London stage.

A nephew of the Australian opera and comic-opera producer William S Lyster, Musgrove originally worked in a solicitor's office before taking a job with his uncle, front-of-house at the Theatre Royal, Melbourne. In 1880–81 he had a considerable success with his own first producing venture, a more than usually lavishly staged Australian production of *La Fille du tambour-major* with imported stars Pattie Laverne and Alfred Brennir and a front line of long-legged British chorus-girls featured, and in 1882—now established as a producing power-to-be-reckoned-with—he joined with J C Williamson and Arthur Garner in a triumvirate (Williamson, Garner and Musgrove's Royal Comic Opera Company) which was to consolidate the foundations of Australia's most famous theatrical management.

Through the 1880s the partnership, with Musgrove very much an active element, imported shows and performers to Australia from around the world, but Musgrove then split from the firm to go on his own, mounting the Nellie Stewart Opera Company for his longtime de facto wife, and importing the Gaiety Theatre company (previously presented by Williamson) from London with their burlesques *Joan of Arc, Carmen Up-to-Data* and *Faust-Up-to-Date*. In 1893, however, he rejoined Williamson, and the partners continued through the next years to bring a flood of the most successful musical shows of the time to Australia.

From 1896 he based himself in London where he was intended to represent the partnership's interests. There he took a lease on the Shaftesbury Theatre and produced a version of Lecocq's *La Petite Mademoiselle* as a vehicle for Miss Stewart without success, but in 1898 he picked up an unlikely prospect in the Casino Theater's musical comedy *The Belle of New York,* which the American owners were touting around London. *The Belle of New York* proved to be the most successful American import the British theatre had ever hosted and it went on to a worldwide career from the Shaftesbury Theatre, making back all the money Musgrove had lost on his earlier London ventures and more, but also causing an irreparable split with Williamson, on whose company's name he had traded without consultation.

In 1900 Musgrove returned to Australia where, in rivalry with his former partner, he continued, through rather more downs than ups, for more than another decade as a force in the presentation of musical theatre, opera and plays.

Musgrove was the son of Fanny Hodson, and thus a nephew of the well-known Irish entertainer and burlesque actor **George [Alfred] HODSON** (b Dublin, 1822; d Bath, 28 June 1869), the vocalist **Georgia[na] HODSON** (Mrs W S Lyster), the original Po-ca-hon-tas of Brougham's famous burlesque and a longtime lead mezzo of Lyster's Australian opera companies, and a cousin of **Henrietta [Ellen] HODSON,** more famous for her liaison with the traitorous publisher and politician Labouchère, and for her public fights with W S Gilbert than for any talent as an actress.

MUSIC IN THE AIR Musical adventure in 2 acts by Oscar Hammerstein II. Music by Jerome Kern. Alvin Theater, New York, 8 November 1932.

A second calculated attempt by Jerome Kern, following his success with *The Cat and the Fiddle,* to write a Continental-style operetta, *Music in the Air* had, unlike the earlier piece, an Oscar Hammerstein libretto, but one that was made up of nothing more than a bundle of aging Viennese Operette clichés and characters. It was set in a picturesque Bavarian village and in Vienna, and its star characters were an operettic prima donna, her composer, and the ingenue who comes professionally and personally between them until she returns to her village lover for a chocolate-box happy ending (which, so the tale is told, Hammerstein insisted was an ''innovative'' unhappy one, apparently because the little lass didn't become a megastar).

Tullio Carminati played Bruno Mahler, the composer, Natalie Hall was the tempestuous Frieda, and Katherine Carrington the little Sieglinde Lessing whom Bruno decides to make his star and his lover until she turns out to have the temperament for neither. Walter Slezak was the village schoolmaster, Karl, who finally wins Sieglinde back and Al Shean (formerly of Gallagher and Shean) had an attractive role as her father, a ''merry peasant'' music-master with a village reputation as a composer who does not come up to scratch in the big city. Kern's score included a number of extremely winning pieces, the two most successful being the song written by Papa Lessing and sweetly sung into Mahler's heart by his little daughter, ''I've Told Every Little Star,'' and the tenor's rhapsodic love song ''The Song Is You.'' There were other highlights as well: the soprano's rendition of Mahler's operetta scena ''I'm Alone'' and, in particular, a charming little do-you-remember piece sung by a minor character, ''In Egern on the Tegern See.''

Music in the Air had a fine Broadway run, shifting from the Alvin to the 44th Street Theater to clock up a total of 342 performances. London's version, with Mary Ellis (Frieda), Arthur Margetson (Bruno), Eve Lister (Sieglinde) and Bruce Carfax (Karl) ran through 275 performances, a record which was better than those that such contemporary, and altogether less conventional, genuine Continental pieces as *Mother of Pearl* (*Eine Frau, die weiss, was sie will*) and *Ball at the Savoy* managed in the same London season, and more or less the equivalent of that put up by its nearest simulacrum, the vast combination of schmaltz and spectacle which made up London's version of *Wild Violets* (*Wenn die kleinen Veilchen blühen*).

In Australia, *Music in the Air* was given one of the most lavish and publicized productions of J C Williamson Ltd's long career, with local comedy favorite Cecil Kellaway starred as Dr Lessing, lovely down-under *Dubarry* star, Sylvia Welling, as Frieda and Shirley Dale, veteran Carrie Moore and Frank Sale in support. But Australia rejected the show wholly and Williamsons incurred both one of their biggest-ever losses and a real blow to their whole musical producing policy. In spite of this knock, the company did persevere, and *White Horse Inn* arrived at the right time to restore both finances and confidence.

In America, however, the show retained a public. It was filmed in 1934, with Gloria Swanson appearing as Frieda and Shean in his original role, toured briefly, and played in San Francisco first with Vivienne Segal starred, and again in the 1941–42 season with John Charles Thomas. It was mounted frequently in provincial houses, and returned to Broadway in 1951 in a revised version under the direction of Hammerstein, with Dennis King (Bruno), Jane Pickens (Frieda) and Charles Winninger (Lessing) for a run of 56 performances.

UK: His Majesty's Theatre 19 May 1933; Australia: Theatre Royal, Sydney 8 July 1933

Film: Fox 1934

Recordings: revival cast (RCA), film extracts (JJA), London cast items (WRC), selection (WRC), etc

THE MUSIC MAN Musical comedy in 2 acts by Meredith Willson based on a story by Willson and Franklin Lacey. Majestic Theater, New York, 19 December 1957.

''If *Guys and Dolls* is the most New York of Broadway musicals, *The Music Man* is surely the most American. There is more heart-warming truth in the Iowa folk of this tale of a tricksy traveling salesman finally shamed out of his shenanigans for the love of a good but difficult woman than in all the Ruritanian farmers and cowboys of *Oklahoma!* put together.''

The Music Man was a musical which was a long time a-borning, but it was one that proved worth waiting for. As early as 1949 Frank Loesser suggested to Meredith Willson that he make up a show out of his tales and reminiscences of his Iowa childhood, but it was another eight years, many writings and rewritings, and a false start with different producers (Feuer and Martin) before Kermit Bloomgarden's production of *The Music Man* opened on Broadway. In a tale perhaps a little reminiscent of George M Cohan's 1910 *Get-Rich-Quick Wallingford,* Robert Preston played ''Dr'' Harold Hill, a traveling salesman in musical instruments whose line of patter is good enough to lumber outback Americans with tubas and triangles which they only discover they have no use for, nor any manner of learning how to play, when Hill has moved safely on to the next state. But when he arrives to turn his chat onto the folk of River City, Iowa, he finds there not only his old comrade-in-charms, Marcellus

Plate 268. **The Music Man**

Washburn (Iggie Wolfington), but an inimical mayor (David Burns) and a young music teacher-cum-librarian, Marian Paroo (Barbara Cook), who doesn't seem to fall for his line. Harold gets the leading ladies of the town into Classical Dance and the bickering school board into barbershop harmonies, and he wins over Marian when she sees the joy a shiny cornet brings to her shy little brother, but he stays in town too long, falling in love. Exposure inevitably comes: Harold Hill is no ''Dr,'' no music teacher, the money the folk have been bamboozled into spending on instruments and band uniforms for their children is wasted. The Mayor is victorious, but Harold Hill has brought sunshine into many lives in River City: the once-bored ladies, the now harmonious school board, Marian and little Winthrop all rally to his side, and when the River City Boys Band marches in, bright and shiny and almost playing music, his case is won. The results pay for all, and Harold Hill has a right to his happy ending.

Willson's score had as much appeal as his tale. Hill's role was written to accommodate a limited voice, but it moved through a variety of styles from the platinum-tongued patter of ''Trouble'' as he persuades River City of its need for a band, to the swinging dream-description of ''Seventy-Six Trombones,'' the wry wish for ''A Sadder But Wiser Girl'' and the real romance of his duet with Marian, ''Till There Was You.'' Marian's other musical moment, in a strong but unshowy soprano role, came in her longing wish for a person to say ''Goodnight My Someone'' to, whilst the Buffalo Bills, as the harmonizing quartet, had some humorously barbershop moments in ''Lida Rose'' and ''Sincere,'' the town ladies niggled away hilariously in a ''Pick-a-Little'' ensemble, little Winthrop lisped out a joyous welcome to ''The Wells Fargo Wagon'' and the piece got off to a flying start with an imaginative, chanted salesmen's ensemble, battered out to the rhythms of the wheels of the train bringing Harold Hill to River City. If it was the marching ''Seventy-Six Trombones'' which became the take-away hit, virtually every part of the score of *The Music Man* was a winner.

Broadway's production ran for 1,375 performances. The first touring company went on the road nine months into the run, with Forrest Tucker in the starring role, and was still going strong when London's version opened and when the Broadway edition finally closed down. Harold Fielding's London production starred Van Johnson alongside Patricia Lambert (Marian) and a winsome Winthrop called Denis Waterman, who 20 years later would become one of Britain's biggest TV names. The piece played for 395 performances, surviving only a little Johnson's departure, but it did not catch on in the regions, where its very Americanness appeared to be a disadvantage.

Australia's Garnet Carroll featured Ted Scott and Carolyn Maye through five months in Melbourne and a fine Australian tour including a season at Sydney's Tivoli (12 December 1960), and a film version captured Preston's once-in-a-blue-moon performance in a musical in a film which retained virtually all of the show's original music. However, following its first runs all round, the show, whilst carrying on through a steady line of regional productions in America and occasionally elsewhere, took a long time to find itself a major revival. It was given a 1980 New York City Center season with Dick van Dyke starred (5 June) and a reprise at London's Open Air Theatre, Regent's Park in 1995 (31 July) with John Challis, Brian Cox and Liz Robertson in the leading roles, but only in 2000 did this most appealing of musicals get a fresh Broadway showing. Craig Bierko and Rebecca Luker featured in a primary-colored, high energy production which, at the time of writing, runs enthusiastically on.

UK: Adelphi Theatre 16 March 1961; Australia: Princess Theatre, Melbourne 5 March 1960

Film: Warner Bros 1962

Recordings: original cast (Capitol), London cast (HMV), New York revival cast (QVC), film soundtrack (Warner Bros), selection (Telare), composer (Capitol), etc

DAS MUSIKANTENMÄDEL Operette in 3 acts by Bernhard Buchbinder. Music by Georg Jarno. Theater in der Josefstadt, Vienna, 18 February 1910.

Jarno and Buchbinder's successor to the vastly successful *Die Förster-Christl* presented the composer Josef Haydn as one of its central characters in a curious love story which would seem to have no historical background. Whilst working as Kapellmeister to the womanizing Fürst Esterházy (Ferdinand Mayerhofer), Haydn (Kurt Lessen) takes time out to go and visit his nephew in a neighboring town. There, he is mightily taken with the boy's fancied maiden, the cowgirl Resel (Hansi Niese), and he ends up taking her back to Eisenstadt with him. There she falls under the eye of Esterházy, but she does the Fürst more harm than good when she innocently exposes his affair with the dancer Elena Montebelli (Käthe Krenn) to the Fürstin (Josefine Joseffy). Haydn is preparing himself to wed the young girl, when she discovers a song he once wrote which reveals that she is his illegitimate daughter. So nephew Karl (Leo Bünau) gets his girl after all.

Well, Haydn certainly did work for Esterházy, at Eisenstadt, as director of his concert and church orchestras, between 1760 and 1790. He was paid the equivalent of £36 a year, and had at his disposal a private theatre of 350 places. But the women . . . ? The theatre, incidentally, was still in action in the late 19th century.

Das Musikantenmädel played a regular 57 performances at Josef Jarno's Theater in der Josefstadt, with its central character tactfully described in the program simply as "the Kapellmeister." It was later played at the Raimundtheater (28 December 1913) and in Budapest (ad Adolf Mérei), but it was in Germany that it won its chief popularity, scoring a hit when played by Niese at Berlin's Berliner-Theater and going on to a mass of regional productions which combined to bring it to a place in the top 20 of Keller's up-to-1921 survey of 20th-century Operetten, ahead of such better-known pieces as *Zigeunerliebe, Herbstmanöver, Der tapfere Soldat, Der Rastelbinder* and *Die Kino-Königin.*

New York's German-speaking theatre mounted a production of the piece in 1910 with Siegfried Brook and Emma Malkowska featured, and later toured the show in repertoire with *Die Fledermaus* and Jean Gilbert's *Die Jungfernstift.*

Another Haydn sort-of-biomusical—this one portraying him as a boy of 15—was produced in Berlin in 1894 (Opernhaus 24 October). *Il piccolo Haydn* (Gaetano Cipollini/A Cipollini, ad Otto Eisenschütz) was played by Frln Krainz.

Germany: Berliner Theater 1 September 1910; USA: Irving Place Theater 15 November 1910; Hungary: Fővárosi Nyári Színház *A muzsikus leány* 4 June 1911

Plate 269. **Das Musikantenmädel.** *Kurt Lessen as the composer Haydn, and Hansi Niese as his country maiden.*

MY FAIR LADY Musical in 2 acts by Alan Jay Lerner based on *Pygmalion* by George Bernard Shaw. Music by Frederick Loewe. Mark Hellinger Theater, New York, 15 March 1956.

My Fair Lady is, probably deservedly, considered as the model amongst the scenes-and-songs shows that were the regular fare in the musical theatre in the 1940s and 1950s. An expertly adapted libretto based on an outstanding and outstandingly successful play in G B Shaw's bitter-sweet Cinderella tale, *Pygmalion,* is musically illustrated with a near-classic combination of the traditional elements of the merriest style of Operette—the soprano heroine, the light-comedy leading man, the romantic tenor and the music-hall–style low comedian (but no soubrets), each equipped with the type of songs suitable to their role—accompanied by spectacular and dance elements in perfectly dosed amounts, the whole treated in the tidiest style of contemporary Broadway.

Alan Jay Lerner's libretto slimmed Shaw's play tactfully whilst opening it out into more settings than previously, and in spite of combining or reorganizing some scenes and, above all, in spite of placing an emphasis on a romantic association between Professor Henry Higgins (Rex Harrison) and the cockney flower girl, Eliza Doolittle (Julie Andrews), whom he educates in speech and

Plate 270. **My Fair Lady.** *Eliza Doolittle (Julie Andrews) tries to get her twisted vowels right under the tutelage of Henry Higgins (Rex Harrison).*

manner until she passes for a princess—a romance Shaw specifically denied—the adaptation excels not only as a modern musical book, but also as a very fair representation in musical-theatre terms of Shaw's play.

The bulk of the score falls to the two principals, a mixture of the ingenue lyrical (''I Could Have Danced All Night,'' ''Wouldn't It be Loverly'') and the mixed-voiced characterful/soubrette (''Just You Wait,'' ''Show Me'') for Eliza and some crisp, wordful patter songs (''Why Can't the English,'' ''An Ordinary Man,'' ''A Hymn to Him'') topped by a wistfully semi-sung, semi-spoken ballad, ''I've Grown Accustomed to Her Face,'' for a Higgins coming, perhaps too late, to a realization of a dependency he would never have admitted in the presence of another. The low-comedy role of dustman Alfred Doolittle (Stanley Holloway), Shaw's philosopher of the lower classes, supports with a pair of cockney comedy numbers (''A Little Bit of Luck,'' ''Get Me to the Church on Time'') and Freddy Eynsford-Hill (John Michael King), Eliza's inept aristocratic suitor, completes the list of solo numbers with the starry-eyed, lilting hymn to just being ''On the Street Where You Live.''

Although the piece, in the American and musical-comedy style of its time, includes little in the way of ensemble work and no genuine duet in its score, such pieces as the choral Ascot Gavotte (Ascot having taken the place of Mrs Higgins's tea party as Eliza's first trial of her new vowels), the counter-melodied ''You Did It,'' and the gay, jubilant triologue ''The Rain in Spain,'' celebrating Eliza's triumph over her accent, provide the necessary variation to the series of solo numbers. Almost every song in the *My Fair Lady* score became individually successful outside the show, with the lyrical ''On the Street Where You Live'' and ''I Could Have Danced all Night'' finding particular popularity, but all, even the stand-up numbers for Doolittle, combined impeccably with the text, in a way increasingly deemed desirable at the time, in a smooth and extremely effective whole.

The idea of a musical *Pygmalion* had begun with Gabriel Pascal, the producer who had filmed the play—with Shaw's approval and the young Wendy Hiller starred—in 1938. However, Shaw refused his permission, and it was not until after the playwright's death that Pascal actively began to push the project. It was, apparently, turned down by a long list of potential adapters and composers from Coward to Porter to Rodgers and Hammerstein before Loewe and Lerner were approached, tried, gave up, and eventually came back for a second try which produced a piece that began its life under the title *My Lady Liza.* Pascal having died without seeing his idea come to fruition, producer Herman Levin took up the growing show, and it was under his management that *My Fair Lady*—a fairly flimsy title which has become honored with success and the years but which must, at the time, have been a desperation choice—opened in New Haven. There, before moving on to Broadway and a place in that street's history, it was slimmed of two songs, the cheekily titled ''Come to the Ball'' (had *The Quaker Girl*'s big hit been truly forgotten?) and Eliza's pre-ball ''Say a Prayer for Me'' (later reused in the film *Gigi*), and of an extraneous dance routine which, like the second-named song, held up Eliza's departure for the all-important ball.

Levin's production of *My Fair Lady* ran for 2,717 performances, establishing a long-run record for a musical play on Broadway which held for nearly a decade, until the advent of *Hello, Dolly!* A year into its run it sent out its first touring company, headed by Brian Aherne and Anne Rogers (like Miss Andrews, a *Boy Friend* Polly turned Eliza), and another year later the stars of the Broadway production (Miss Andrews, Harrison, Holloway and Robert Coote as Colonel Pickering) took themselves to London where the piece opened under the unlikely management of celebrated play-producers H M Tennent. It was a piece of cool action by Tennent director ''Binkie'' Beaumont which had secured the British rights before anyone else had had a chance to bid. Knowing Levin was desperate to have Rex Harrison to originate the lead role, he purposely kept his failing production of *Bell, Book and Candle* running, forcing Levin to ask him to give Harrison a release. In exchange for the release, Beaumont got a bit of the action, and *My Fair Lady* came to Tennent's. The show's fame was already thoroughly established by the time it reached London, where its Broadway triumph was repeated through a run of 2,281 performances. If this stopped just a few performances short of *Salad Days*' all-time long-run record, it clearly outvalued it by the size of the auditorium of the Theatre Royal, Drury Lane, as compared to that of the little Vaudeville Theatre.

The other principal English-language centers, headed by J C Williamson Ltd's first Australian production with Robin Bailey and Bunty Turner starred, soon followed on, but *My Fair Lady* went beyond that, to areas which Broadway and British musical shows had rarely penetrated in recent years. Robert Gilbert's German adaptation was mounted at Hans Wölffer's Theater des Westens with Karin Hübner and Paul Hubschmid as an agreeably youthful Higgins (774 performances), and in 1963 the once-again richly successful production moved south to play Vienna's Theater an der Wien with the same stars (112 performances). Vienna subsequently produced its own version (ad Gerhard Bronner) which translated Eliza's cockney caterwaulings into a broad Viennese (Theater an der Wien 11 November 1969) as played by Gabriele Jacoby alongside the Higgins of Josef Meinrad through two seasons totaling 148 performances. Vienna has most recently seen the show at the Volksoper where it was revived in 1993 (5 December) with Michel Heltau and Julia Stemberger featured.

Manolo Fabregas and Cristina Roja starred in Mexico's *Mi bella dama* (with a certain Plácido Domingo as one of Doolittle's pals), and Mogens Wieth and Gerda Gilboe top-billed in Denmark's *My Fair Lady,* Delia Scala and Gianrico Tedeschi in Italy's version and Zsuzsa Lehoczky and Lajos Básti in the Fővárosi Operettszínház's Budapest production (ad Tamás Ungvári, György Dénes), all of which maintained the now-famous English-language title. Rivka Raz and Shai Ophir starred in Israel and Bibi Ferreira and Paolo Autran in Buenos Aires, as *My Fair Lady* established itself as the most thoroughly international musical comedy in decades. Although a French-langauge version of the show was produced in Geneva (27 December 1968, ad Claude André Puget, Jean Valmy), France itself, as ever, stayed aloof and it was not until 1977 that a different version of *My Fair Lady* finally made its way to Lille (ad Bruno Tellenne, Pierre Carrel), there to be introduced by Claudine Coster and Dominique Tirmont.

In 1964 *My Fair Lady* was put on to film. Harrison and Holloway were called on to repeat their original roles but, with Hollywood worried at presenting a top-of-the-bill of all British names in their British story, Julie Andrews was replaced by proven film star Audrey Hepburn and the singing voice of Marni Nixon. There was little chance that any filmed *My Fair Lady* could get everything as right as the stage show had done, and so it proved. The obviously made-in-the-studio film did not become the classic its source had, and Miss Andrews went on to make exactly that kind of classic out of her first film, *Mary Poppins,* the same year.

My Fair Lady established itself as a worldwide perennial, both in the main centers and in regional theatres of innumerable languages, and it came round with unusual speed to its first major revivals. Broadway brought it back just a decade after its closure, with Ian Richardson and Christine Andreas starred (St James Theater 25 March 1976, 377 performances), and Cameron Mackintosh and Harold Fielding followed in London in 1979 when Tony Britton starred opposite Liz Robertson and Anna Neagle in the role of Mrs Higgins, a role which had been originated by another famous veteran, Cathleen Nesbitt, and first played in Britain by Zena Dare (Adelphi Theater 25 October). In 1981 Harrison took up his old role as a now-rather-aged Higgins with Miss Nesbitt as his extremely aged mother in a trouble-struck touring production which eventually camped at Broadway's Uris Theater (18 August) for 119 performances; in 1992 a British touring production with Helen Hobson and Edward Fox starred took the show around the main provincial houses once again, and the following year an American tour with Richard Chamberlain as Higgins was mounted. It visited Broadway's Virginia Theater (9 December 1993) for 156 performances, and was also seen in Europe, during which time it played the first Parisian performances of the show. Both these last productions made an interesting point about the show and the size of its classic status. Although classic operas have suffered all sorts of denaturization in the hands of dying-to-be-noticed directors in recent decades, classic musicals have—apart from a little rewrite or so, or a little restuffing with advisedly cut material—been largely spared ''re-thought'' and gimmicky stagings on the English-language stage. On the evidence of the 1990s, *My Fair Lady* is now—in advance of its fellows—becoming as fair game for egotistical stage-managers as *Rigoletto* or *Don Giovanni.*

Most regional productions in America and Britain have, like the London revival, shorn *My Fair Lady* of its principal piece of stage spectacle, the Embassy Ball scene, proving that *My Fair Lady* can be brought down to *Pygmalion*-size with no loss of effect, but in Europe, where *My Fair Lady* followed the ground-breaking *Kiss Me, Kate* into a prosperous and often-staged position in the German, Austrian and Hungarian Operette houses, it eventually and inevitably fell into the hands of the famous German ''Bearbeitung'' merchants, the ''improvers'' of classic pieces. And there, amongst 60-year-old Higginses and 50-year-old Elizas, it has been already proved that even as impeccably made a piece as *My Fair Lady* can be destructible.

UK: Theatre Royal, Drury Lane 30 April 1958; Australia: Her Majesty's Theatre, Melbourne 24 January 1959; Germany: Theater des Westens 25 October 1961; Austria: Theater an der Wien 19 September 1963; Hungary: Fővárosi Operettszínház 11 February 1966; France: Théâtre Sebastopol, Lille 8 October 1977, Théâtre Mogador, Paris (Eng) 12 December 1995

Recordings: original cast (Columbia), London cast (CBS), Austrian cast (Preiser), Danish cast (Philips), Israeli casts (Columbia, Acum), Italian casts (CBS), Mexican cast (Columbia), Netherlands cast (Philips), Swedish casts (Sonet, Stora Teatern), German casts (Fontana, Philips, Metronome), Japanese cast (King), Hungarian cast (Qualiton), American revival 1976 (Columbia), Netherlands revival 1994, Vienna revival 1993 (Reverso), film soundtracks in English, French, German (CBS), etc

Literature: Garebian, K: *The Making of My Fair Lady* (ECW, Toronto, nd), Jansen, W: *My Fair Lady* (Ger)

MY GIRL Domestic musical play in 2 acts by James T Tanner. Lyrics by Adrian Ross. Music by F Osmond Carr. Theatre Royal, Birmingham, as *The Clergyman's Daughter,* 13 April 1896; Gaiety Theatre, London, 13 July 1896.

For his successor to *The Shop Girl,* the first of his modern-dress ''musical comedies'' produced at the Gaiety Theatre, George Edwardes resorted to a practice which had not previously been his, the out-of-town try-out. *The Clergyman's Daughter* was opened at Birmingham, however, for a reason. It was very definitely much more of a musical play than had been the habit at the Gaiety—much more invested with such items as plot and character, whilst still full of Gaiety songs and dances written by the *In Town* team of Adrian Ross and Osmond Carr—and its producer needed to test the water.

Theo (Ernest Snow), son of the Rev Arthur Mildreth (Charles Ryley), has come to financial grief thanks to the devious doings of the financier von Fontein (Martin Adeson), who is now swanning around the town taking in the Mayor (Percy Paul) and his jumped-up wife (Connie Ediss) with a phony African Prince. With the help of the comical stock-jobber Alex McGregor (John Le Hay) the villain is unmasked, Theo gets his girl (Ethel Sydney) and his sister May (Kate Cutler), whose mining shares have opportunely rocketed, gets a Lord (Paul Arthur). The story was illustrated by some jolly songs which had jabs at lady cyclists, the music hall, the grenadier guards and a whole host of topical subjects, alongside such more plot-worthy pieces as ''Stocks and Shares'' and, the hit of the evening, a rewritten version of May Irwin's Broadway hit ''The Bully Song'' sung by Connie Ediss, drooling plumply over ''When My Husband Is Sir Tom.''

My Girl had been set up with the lead roles intended for Seymour Hicks and Ellaline Terriss, the husband and wife lead players of the latter days of *The Shop Girl,* but Hicks refused the part of Theo when the time for West End recasting came along and Miss Terriss played the role of May opposite Paul Arthur until Edwardes brought Louis Bradfield in. The piece was received by the Gaiety audiences with a mixed reaction. Some resented their frivolous fare being laden down with ''a number of facts about banks with limited liability and the different prices of shares''; others approved the principle and others, again, the result. Some newspapermen who had cried long and loud for more plot in musical entertainments recanted in the face of the evidence. Edwardes's confidence was not high and he started to prepare a new show. But *My Girl* prospered and Edwardes had to postpone the announced *The Circus Girl.* The second time he announced it, *My Girl's* figures promptly shot up again, so the producer transferred the hardy piece to the Garrick Theatre whilst *The Circus Girl* took over the Gaiety. Most of the Gaiety's stars, of course, stayed there, so it was a shadow of the original show which played out the final seven weeks of an 183-performance run its producer clearly hadn't expected. But *My Girl's* life continued much further. It played through no less than five provincial seasons and the show was seen in South Africa, where it had a considerable success, as late as 1903.

Another musical under the same title was mounted in America in 1924 (Vanderbilt Theater 24 November). Produced by Jules Hurtig and Lyle Andrews, it was Harry Archer and Harlan Thompson's successor to their hit musical comedy *Little Jessie James,* and it offered another set of lively, catchy dance songs set to a jolly, farcical book which was written this time around the popular theme of bootlegging. To the surprise of some theatrewatchers, who hadn't rated Archer and Thompson as repeaters (it got only the second-string critics on its first night), *My Girl* confirmed its authors' first success very nicely with a fine Broadway run of 291 performances.

MY LADY FRAYLE Musical play in 2 acts by Arthur Wimperis and Max Pemberton. Lyrics by Arthur Wimperis. Music by Howard Talbot and Herman Finck. Prince of Wales Theatre, Birmingham, as *Vivien,* 27 December 1915; Shaftesbury Theatre, London, 1 March 1916.

My Lady Frayle was a reversed-sex version of the Faust legend, in which Lady Frayle (Irene Browne) vows her soul and that of her ward, Dick Bassett (J V Bryant) to Lucifer (Cecil Humphreys) in exchange for the youth and beauty that will allow her to win Dick away from young Virginia Desborough (Anne Croft). The dramatic central story was shot through by a comical one involving the music hall's Miss Vera de Vere (Cicely Debenham), butler Wilcox (Arnold Richardson) and the Dean of Dorchester (Courtice Pounds). An unusually strong libretto was illustrated by a score which, at its best, was one of the finest London had heard in a long time, rising to a dramatic peak at the end of the first act as Lady Frayle cries out to Lucifer for her lost youth in Herman Finck's ''Just One Hour'' (one critic, already, compared the number to the work of Puccini). The comic side was well served too, with a jolly piece on ''Married Life,'' a speech lesson on ''Papa, Potato, Prisms and Prunes'' and a dissertation on that new phenomenon ''Flappers,'' as well as a ringing ''Song of the Bowl'' for aging D'Oyly Carte tenor Pounds, now in a second coming as the best singing character man in the business.

If Pounds was well cast, however, producer Courtneidge made a mess of his lead casting. He used up two Lady Frayles out of town and a third, 19-year-old Irene Browne, chosen to open in town, was so vocally underequipped that she lost her voice in rehearsal and the opening night was actually played by her understudy. Nevertheless, the show won a marvelous first-night reception and superlative notices, but not a run. It closed after 129 performances, and although it went out in three touring companies in 1916 and in 1917 (one with Dina North, one with Hilda Charteris, and one with certified vocalist Phyllys Le Grand) and again in 1918, 1919 and 1920, it never found itself the place in the repertoire that it might have been expected to.

My Lady Frayle was also seen in Australia, produced under the management of Hugh D McIntosh, with a fine singer, Vera Pearce, billed as ''Australia's own beauty actress,'' starred alongside ex-Savoyard Claude Flemming (Lucifer), Goodie—daughter of Ada—Reeve (Virginia) and Marie La Varre (Vera), but here again it struck bad luck. Announced to open on 1 February it saw its first night canceled when all Sydney's theatres were closed by the authorities because of an influenza epidemic. It was more than a month before the show could get on the stage and then, after a few weeks, it was closed down when the epidemic worsened again. Transferred to Melbourne (Tivoli 26 April) it finally got six uninterrupted weeks and was brought back later in the year for a second showing.

The ever-touring Maurice Bandmann company hawked *My Lady Frayle* as part of their repertoire throughout the Orient, but in spite of its wide showing, it did not succeed in leaving a mark in the southern hemisphere any more than in the northern. Its score was heard one last time when it was broadcast in 1936 by the BBC with Edith Day singing the role of Lady Frayle.

Australia: Tivoli Theatre, Sydney 8 March 1919

MY LADY MOLLY Comedy opera in 2 acts by George H Jessop. Additional lyrics by Percy Greenbank and Charles H Taylor. Music by Sidney Jones. Theatre Royal, Brighton, 11 August 1902; Terry's Theatre, London, 14 March 1903.

After Sidney Jones left Daly's Theatre, the site of his greatest successes, his first new work was a piece in a different mold from those he had written for George Edwardes's theatre. *My Lady Molly* was a ''comedy opera,'' a piece on the lines of *Dorothy* and classic English comic opera, with a libretto by George Jessop, recently the author of the dramatic *Shamus O'Brien,* which busied itself with marriages, disguises and rapier fights in 18th-century England. The score, whilst not neglecting the comic, was based largely on ballads in the classic English style and a full book of well-written ensembles. *My Lady Molly* used no Lionel Monckton, as Edwardes had done, to pop up-to-date point numbers into Jones's score.

The tale had Lady Molly Martingale (Sybil Arundale) getting into disguise as Harry Romney (Richard Green) to prevent that young man's marriage to Alice Coverdale (Decima Moore). The real Harry is imprisoned as an impostor, and ends up fighting a duel with and finally marrying the false Harry. The comedy was provided by the Irish servant of both Harrys, Mickey O'Dowd (Bert Gilbert), equipped with some fine comic songs (''Don't Whistle So Loud,'' ''Ballinasloe'').

Jones himself produced *My Lady Molly* and he put it out on the road with himself conducting and *Florodora* director-choreographer Sydney Ellison staging. It was a splendid success, and as a result the following year Frederick Mouillot took it over and produced it in London with the same leading players. It had an excellent run of 342 performances. The producer piled on four matinées a week to cope with the demand for seats, but when his lease of Terry's Theatre ran out he was obliged to close. The following season *My Lady Molly* was back on the road, its fine English record topped up by productions in South Africa and in Australia where Florence Young (Molly), Carrie Moore (Alice), Harold Thorley (Harry) and George Lauri (Mickey) were featured to considerable success. However, someone in America, doubtless sparked by the girl-in-man's-clothing plot of the show, came up with the idea of starring British music-hall star Vesta Tilley, the celebrated travesty ''Burlington Bertie from Bow,'' as Lady Molly. Miss Tilley naturally brought her own grindingly unsuitable material to interpolate in Jones's well-made score (''Algy,'' ''The Seaside Sultan'') and she and the show were encouraged to leave New York after 15 performances. Miss Tilley did not remain long with the show, and she was replaced by the slightly less unlikely Ethel Levey (who had already played the pre-Broadway Boston engagement) as *My Lady Molly* went around America.

Australia: His Majesty's Theatre, Melbourne 9 May 1903; USA: Daly's Theater 5 January 1904

MY MARYLAND Musical romance in 3 acts by Dorothy Donnelly. Music by Sigmund Romberg. Jolson's Theater, New York, 12 September 1927.

A musical version of Clyde Fitch's highly successful Civil War romance *Barbara Frietchie, My Maryland* presented the historically elderly Barbara (Evelyn Herbert) as a young and lovely adherent to the Union cause—and to the Union Captain Trumbull (Nathaniel Wagner)—in the Confederate stronghold of Frederick, Maryland. The jealous Jack Negly (Warren Hull) and his father, a colonel in the Confederate army (Louis Cassavant), try to kill Trumbull and then, when Barbara defiantly waves the Union flag before the advancing Confederate Colonel Stonewall Jackson (Arthur Cunningham), do their best to have her shot as a traitor. The girl is saved by Jackson's magnanimity. The musical did not, like the play, go on to include Barbara's murder by Negly and Negly's subsequent execution, but remained happily on an ending which brought the young folk together.

The work of the *Student Prince* team of author Dorothy Donnelly and composer Sigmund Romberg, in their first re-pairing in the three years since their great hit, the Shuberts' production of *My Maryland* was, from the first, marked out as a good thing. The fashion for romantic costume operetta was high, the tale was a dashing and respected one with opportunity not only for spectacle but for the massed male-voice choral effects that had been such a triumph in *The Student Prince,* and Romberg had written an attractive score, with the stirring Connecticut Marching Song, a choral hymn to ''Your Land and My Land,'' soon fingered as a big winner amongst a bookful of romantic music for Miss Herbert, Wagner and Hull. The rest of it (''familiar American airs worked into the texture of the European operetta form . . . a background of Offenbach with Viennese color and American decorations and flourishes'') included a strangely Irishy number called ''Mother'' for Barbara, waltz duos for her with Trumbull (''Silver Moon'') and the rejected Jack (''Won't You Marry Me?'') who, if he didn't get the girl, got marginally the better song, a sneezing song (''Ker-Choo!'') for Berta Donn in the supporting role of Sue Royce, and a touch of comedy and ragtimey music for George Rosener.

The show's reception in its pre-Broadway run in a Philadelphia in the throes of the Sesquiecentennial Exposition was sensational. There had been nothing quite like it in the proud and colorful history of the Philadelphia musical theatre. Business was so great that there was no question of moving the production onwards, and *My Maryland* simply stayed in Philadelphia. And stayed, and stayed. By the time that the Shuberts decided that enough was enough, and that it was time to take their newest hit to New York, it had played for no fewer than 40 weeks in Philadelphia, a record for a musical in the town and one which, three-quarters of a century later, still stands.

My Maryland was neither the first nor the last Philadelphia hit to find a less enthusiastic reception on Broadway. Not unenthusiastic, just less enthusiastic. Rom-

Plate 271. *A dramatic moment from* **My Maryland,** *the musical play which still holds the long-run record in the Philadelphia theatre.*

berg's score was much liked, particularly the now famous marching song, which nevertheless won some queries over its originality (''it starts out a bit like 'Le Sabre de mon père,' and swings by way of a German student song effect into 'John Brown's Body'[;] . . . none the less does it acquire a character of its own, a real 'lift' as well as a fine swing''), but the expected landslide didn't occur. However, Broadway was on a high in the later 1920s, business in general was grand, and the Shuberts had amortized their expenses thoroughly in Philadelphia, so, although it didn't provoke the interest of the season's other major musicals (*Good News, Show Boat, A Connecticut Yankee, The Three Musketeers, Funny Face*— although it had a longer run than the last-named), *My Maryland* ran through the season and closed with 312 Broadway performances to its credit. Although it subsequently toured, it was not exported in the way that each of those other pieces were, and its Philadelphia season remained its greatest achievement.

MYNHEER JAN Comic opera in 3 acts by Harry Paulton and ''Mostyn Tedde'' (Edward Paulton). Music by Edward Jakobowski. Comedy Theatre, London, 14 February 1887.

Paulton and Jakobowski's follow-up to the amazing *Erminie* was a piece dogged by what might have been bad luck, but might equally have been a case of a swollen head or two. Cleverly constructed on the *Erminie* plan, with Paulton and his *Erminie* sidekick, Frank Wyatt, this time cast as a pair of rebels in the Spanish-occupied Netherlands, *Mynheer Jan* had Hans (Paulton), disguised as Don Diego, the pretendent to the hand of the governor's daughter, Camilla (producer Violet Melnotte), with Wyatt as his servant, inveigling their way into the gubernatorial fortress in the same way the two thieves had done in the earlier play. Paulton's imitation of the Spanish grandee was the show's highlight and on a par with his Erminie performance as Cadeau/the Baron, and the company's new leading lady, Camille D'Arville, was well supplied with winning songs alongside the comical ones for Paulton and some quite stiff baritone music for Wyatt. A fine supporting cast included Kate Munroe, Madame Amadi in an older-lady role which was, for once, not a caricature, Marius as the Governor and the tenor Joseph Tapley.

The authors and producer were faced with competing with the reputation of their own great hit, but *Mynheer Jan* won a good London reception—notably better than that of Gilbert and Sullivan's *Ruddigore* a few weeks previously—and it looked set for a fine run, until authors and producer fell out, apparently over money. The show was closed after 35 performances, and the authors themselves then put it on tour . . . but without Wyatt who had recently become ''Mr Melnotte'' and without Miss Melnotte's business acumen. The tour lasted but eight weeks and, as a result, the prebooked production at Broadway's Casino Theater was canceled. The American success of *Erminie* nevertheless encouraged a production there by William T Carleton's reputable touring comic-opera company. The production, with Charles H Drew and Carleton paired in its featured roles, and with Clara Lane (Katrina), J K Murray (General Bombalo), Alice Vincent (Camilla) and Clara Wisdom in Madame Amadi's role, was toured in Carleton's repertoire through 1888–89 with considerable success, but did not get a Broadway showing.

USA: Chestnut Street Theater, Philadelphia 17 September 1888

MY ONE AND ONLY *see* FUNNY FACE

MYRTIL, Odette (b Paris, 28 June 1898; d Doylestown, Pa, 18 November 1978). French performer in mostly Broadway musicals.

At first a violinist in the music halls, Mlle Myrtil appeared in revue on both sides of the Atlantic, playing in two editions of Ziegfeld's *Follies* in New York, and in such pieces as *The Bing Boys Are Here, Tabs, Tails Up* and *Bubbly* in London. At the age of 21 she was seen as the French actress Cora Merville in the London musical farce *The Officers' Mess,* before returning to revue and cabaret. She made another musical-comedy appearance at the Paris Apollo, playing Venus in *La Ceinture de Vénus* in 1921, but in the mid-1920s, having moved definitively to America, she turned more to the musical stage and appeared on Broadway as Hortense Schneider to the Offenbach of Allan Prior in *Love Song* (1925), as the young gypsy Manja in *Gräfin Mariza,* and as George Sand opposite the Chopin of Guy Robertson in another biomusical pasticcio, *White Lilacs* (1928), and then created the role of the jealous Odette in Kern's *The Cat and the Fiddle* (1931).

During a period where she doubled her performing career with work as a dress designer, she took over from Lyda Roberti in *Roberta,* played Mrs van Dare in *The Firefly* in Los Angeles and, after more than a decade of absence from Broadway, returned to play the motoring Countess de la Fère in the 1945 revival of *The Red Mill* (equipped, as almost invariably, with her violin). After several years further playing in regional productions and nightclubs, she succeeded to the role of Bloody Mary in Broadway's *South Pacific* (1952). Her last Broadway appearances were as Madame Marstonne in the short-lived *Maggie* and as Belle Piquery in *Saratoga* (1959), after which she retired to run a restaurant in Pennsylvania.

Mlle Myrtil also appeared in the screen version of the Rodgers and Hart musical comedy *I Married an Angel.*

MY SON JOHN *see* RIQUETTE

THE MYSTERY OF EDWIN DROOD Musical in 2 acts suggested by Charles Dickens's novel of the same name. Book, lyrics and music by Rupert Holmes. Delacorte Theater, New York, 4 August 1985; Imperial Theater, 2 December 1985.

Billed as the ''solve-it-yourself Broadway musical,'' *The Mystery of Edwin Drood* took Charles Dickens's famously unfinished novel of the same name and presented it in a burlesque music-hall style up to the moment where Dickens's narrative ceased. At that point, the audience was asked both to vote as to the identity of the mysterious Dick Datchery and to nominate their choice as the murderer of Edwin Drood. The show finished in accordance with the chairman's opinion of the house's choices.

The entertainment was presented as the work of the ''Music Hall Royale'' company under their chairman Cartwright (George Rose), and the role of Edwin Drood was played in travesty by the company's ''leading lady'' Alice Nutting (Betty Buckley). Schizophrenic choirmaster John Jasper (Howard McGillin) lusts helplessly after the purer-than-pearls Rosa Bud (Patti Cohenour), the betrothed-since-birth of his nephew Edwin. She also attracts the attentions of the mysterious Singhalese Neville Landless (John Herrera), who has arrived in town with his sister, Helena (Jana Schneider). Add to the plot, amongst others, an opium-house keeper known as Princess Puffer (Cleo Laine), the curious Rev Crisparkle (George N Martin) and an enigmatic bit-part player with ambitions called Bazzard (Joe Grifasi), and when young Drood vanishes after a Christmas Eve storm, there are plenty of suspects on hand.

The score, like the libretto written by popular songster Rupert Holmes, was a winning mixture of pastiche music-hall songs for Puffer (''The Wages of Sin,'' ''The Garden Path to Hell'') and the Chairman and company (''Off to the Races''), some adventurous character solos for such as Jasper (''A Man Could Go Quite Mad''), Rosa (the beautiful soprano ''Moonfall'') and the peculiar Bazzard (''Never the Luck''), and several highly successful ensembles—a quartet with chorus about ''Ceylon,'' a warning pre-Christmas septet ''No Good Can Come from Bad'' and the passionate face-to-face of Rosa and Jasper which brought the first act to its climax (''The Name of Love'').

Following its original production at the New York Shakespeare Festival (25 performances), *The Mystery of Edwin Drood* moved to Broadway's Imperial Theater, gathering in the Tony Awards for the season's best musical, book, score and direction (as well as one for Rose) on its way. However, in spite of its attractions and the recognition given to them, the show did not take off as it might have. An effort to give it a snappier appeal was epitomized in a title change to the rather bald *Drood,* but ultimately *The Mystery of Edwin Drood* went the way of the majority of Broadway shows of the 1980s which favored wit and comic content over glitter, drama and/or spectacle. It found an audience for a respectable but barely blockbusting 608 performances.

A London production, mounted at the Savoy Theatre, had vaudeville straight man Ernie Wise (Chairman) and former pop star Lulu (Puffer) awkwardly top-billed alongside David Burt (Jasper), Julia Hills (Drood), Cohenour, Marilyn Cutts (Helena) and Paul Bentley (Bazzard), but the parody of music-hall styles still current in London's Players' Theatre and British provincial summer shows was no novelty for London, and the piece played to sparse houses (which nevertheless included a nub of hugely enthusiastic partisans who returned over and over again) for 68 performances.

The German premiere of *Drood* (ad Markus Weber) was given in Pforzheim in 1991 with Veit-Ulrich Kurth (Jasper), Tanja Hiller (Drood) and Lilian Huynen (Rosa) featured.

An earlier musical attempt to put an ending on *The Mystery of Edwin Drood* was given by T C de Leon in his *Jasper.* In this version Jasper turned out guiltless, and Drood was not dead but a druggie. A 1908 London play, *The Mystery of Edwin Drood,* by J Comyns Carr (His Majesty's Theatre 4 January) with Beerbohm Tree as Jasper, Adrienne Augarde as Rosa and Mrs Frederick Wright sr (mother of musical comedy star Huntley Wright) as Princess Puffer, which similarly had Drood not dead and which used its ''unwritten'' part to supply a dramatic madness-and-death scene for Tree, also included a number of songs.

UK: Savoy Theatre 7 May 1987; Germany: Pforzheim *Drood* 31 December 1991

Recording: original cast (Polydor)

MY SWEETHEART Operatic comic drama in 3 acts by William Gill. Music selected and arranged by R E Graham and Theo Bendix. Shattuck's Opera House, Hornellsville, NY, 27 August 1881; Haverley's 14th Street Theater, New York, 18 September 1882.

A vehicle for the little-girl-style personality performer Minnie Palmer, *My Sweetheart* was a combination of a heavily sentimental melodrama and a good deal of traditional ''Dutch'' low comedy, studded with songs, dances and any other ''turns'' the star felt like interpolating. Miss Palmer played Tina Hatzell, an angelic and very juvenile German-American who is the little sweetheart of the handsome Tony Faust (R E Graham). When Tony becomes rich and a German Count, the fawners and filchers crowd round and the adventuress Louisa Fleeter (May Davenport) wins his adoration, but Tina and good Doctor Oliver (Joseph J Dowling) expose the three-faced gold digger, and at the second-act curtain Tony goes blind from shock. He has regained his sight by the time the third act begins, cared for on the Hatzell farm, but Louisa and her crooked brother (L R Willard) return to try their hand again, only to be defeated a second time by purity, goodness and a timely song and dance. Louisa sweeps out, lamenting ''I have played high, and lost, and even you, Tina, cannot pity me! Farewell!,'' leaving Tony and his little sweetheart to waltz to the final curtain together. Some of the hither-and-yon collection of songs used in *My Sweetheart* became a popular and fixed part of the entertainment, whilst others were movable and were regularly moved and/or replaced.

Originally staged and toured in Miss Palmer's native America, this unsophisticated variety-show-cum-black-moustachioed-weepie decorated with songs ''so aged as to be rank'' was adapted for the British stage by Fred G Maeder. It proved both a novelty and an enormous success when the (as ever) heavily publicized Miss Palmer brought it to the British provinces. It was toured both with and later even without its star for many years. Miss Palmer went so far as to venture a London season with—for such a blatantly unsophisticated piece—outstandingly good results (163 performances), and she happily trouped her show as far afield as Australia, where she toured through Melbourne, Sydney (Opera House), Adelaide, Ballarat and Sandhurst for a total of 32 successful weeks, before moving on to New Zealand, Japan and to India. When she attempted new pieces (*My Brother's Sister, The School Girl*) she found that, in spite of a faithful following, *My Sweetheart* without her continued to do better than she did without *My Sweetheart,* and she returned time and again to her trusty vehicle.

My Sweetheart was still to be seen stalking around the American outerbacks, now credited to authors R A Roberts and Thomas Reilley and composer Alfred

Robyn, and with no less a leading man than Charles Winninger, as late as 1908.

In 1894 the British tour circuits which had welcomed the original show gave a fine welcome to a burlesque version as well. Arthur Alexander and A R Marshall's *Laughs, or Tina and Tony* was produced at the Theatre Royal Edinburgh (30 June) with Alexander playing Tina to the Tony of Julia Kent, and it toured vigorously through mostly smaller dates for two seasons.

UK: Royal Princess's Theatre, Glasgow 4 June 1883, Strand Theatre 14 January 1884; Australia: Princess Theatre, Melbourne 31 January 1886

N

EINE NACHT IN VENEDIG Operette in 3 acts by F Zell and Richard Genée based on *Le Château Trompette* by Eugène Cormon and Michel Carré. Music by Johann Strauss. Friedrich-Wilhelmstädtisches Theater, Berlin, 3 October 1883.

The zigzagging line of Johann Strauss's career as a theatrical composer followed the successes of *Das Spitzentuch der Königin* (1880) and the delicious *Der lustige Krieg* (1881) with a failure in *Eine Nacht in Venedig.* Theatrical myth has it that librettists Zell and Genée offered the composer the choice between their versions of *The Lady of Lyons* and the French comic opera text *Le Château Trompette,* previously set by François Gevaert (Opéra-Comique 23 April 1860), and kidded Strauss into taking the weaker of the two scripts, whilst Carl Millöcker made *Der Bettelstudent* of the other. That myth, for all that it made a good story, has now been discredited. Strauss—who had, in any case, a weakness for Italian-set texts—simply accepted and set the book of *Eine Nacht in Venedig* as he had those of his earlier works. It was only later that he vilified Zell and Genée's work and, claiming not to have read the dialogue prior to production, blamed it for not fitting the moods of his music. In fact, whilst the book for *Eine Nacht in Venedig,* with its conventional story of randy nobility and tricksy ladies and wenches paraded through an actful of disguises and now-you-bed-me-now-you-don'ts to a happy ending, was no masterpiece, it was no worse—and indeed even better—than many other Operette libretti of the era.

Old Senator Delacqua (Herr Binder) has plans to send his young wife, Barbara, to an out-of-the-way aunt when the philandering Duke of Urbino (Sigmund Steiner) comes to town. However, while the Duke's pimping barber, Caramello (Jani Szíka), is busy setting up a nice little enlèvement on his master's behalf, Barbara is organizing a trick or two of her own. She arranges for the fishergirl, Annina (Ottilie Collin), Caramello's sweetheart, to take her place in the Delacqua family gondola so that she—while her husband thinks her out of town—may spend the night, instead, with her young lover, Enrico. And so it is the disguised Annina who is duly lifted from the gondola as it glides towards Barbara's aunt's home and carried off to the ducal masked ball, which Delacqua is attending with a phony wife, the cook Ciboletta (Frln Grünfeld). As a result, both Caramello and Ciboletta's chap, the pastry cook Pappacoda, spend their entire evening trying to stop the Duke from getting their respective girls in a quiet corner. After a third act of little action, all ends happily with promotion and marriage for the two boys and their signorine, as the Duke covers his tracks.

If Strauss's score had neither the brilliance nor the warmth of the music of his *Der lustige Krieg,* it nevertheless included some winning ensembles—the swinging carnival ensemble ''Alle maskiert,'' the sweet soprano-voiced ''Die Tauben von San Marco'' and the pretty à propos of nothing serenade ''Ninana''—and, amongst its solos, a charming, unfishwifely soprano entrance for Annina (''Frutti di mare''), a gondola song for Caramello (''Komm in die Gondel'') and the Duke's featured Lagunen-Walzer (''Ach, wie so herrlich'').

Eine Nacht in Venedig was ill received on its Berlin production, and the authors put in some solid rewrites before the Theater an der Wien's subsequent production. One of the most notable of these was the transfer of the relyricked Lagunen-Walzer from the role of the Duke to that of Caramello, a part now in the hands of *Der lustige Krieg*'s triumphant Alexander Girardi, thoroughly turned into the star role of the piece. Josef Joseffy (Duke), Karoline Finaly (Annina), Felix Schweighofer (Pappacoda) and Rosa Streitmann (Ciboletta) headed the rest of a very fine cast, and this time the reception was better. The show was played a fair 35 times, with a guest season at the Carltheater. Maintained in the repertoire, *Eine Nacht in Venedig* was played in 1886–87 with Karl Streitmann as Caramello, Collin (whom the admiring Strauss had brought from Berlin to Vienna) in her original role and young Therese Biedermann making her Vienna debut as Ciboletta, again in 1892–93, passing its 100th performance in the process, and in 1896–98.

In spite of the improvements, however, the show did not excite international attention in the way Strauss's pre-

Plate 272. **Eine Nacht in Venedig.** *The Herzog von Urbino (Hans-Josef Kasper) and Annina (Monika Starke) unmasked in the Theater Trier production of 1986.*

vious shows had done. J C Duff ventured an English-language production (ad Marius Lazare ''an absolutely stupid libretto'') at New York's Daly's Theater with a cast headed by Louise Lester (Annina), Edward Connell (Pappacoda) and W H Fitzgerald (Caramello) and a featured pigeon ballet that won more notice from press and public than either music or players, and Gustav Amberg later ventured a three-week German-language season of what he called *Venetianische Nächte* with the visiting Streitmann (8 January 1890). Britain, France and Australia, however, all passed the piece by, and even the voracious Budapest theatre did not get around to trying it until several years on (ad Béla J Fái, Ferenc Reiner). The Népszínház finally played a version in 1890 and then only 12 times.

The name of Strauss on its billhead ensured that the piece reappeared occasionally in Austria, notably in a revival in 1912 at Ronacher with Grete Holm starred, but it did not ever find itself a real place in the general repertoire, until later writers latched on to the saleable Strauss name and, additionally encouraged by the picturesque setting of the show, started putting out their own versions of *Eine Nacht in Venedig.* Carl Hagemann seems to have started the process with his Baden-Baden production of 1918, before the Theater an der Wien staged an Ernst Marischka rewrite, with Strauss's score done over by E W Korngold, in 1923. The main effect of this musical remake, which pasted larger and smaller bits of other Strauss works into the composer's score, was to beef up the role of the Duke (played by Richard Tauber) with a couple of throbbingly romantic tenor bonbons, one (''Sei mir gegrüsst, du holdes Venezia'') fabricated from the song ''Der Frühling lacht, es singen die Vöglein'' from *Simplicius,* the other (''Treu sein—das liegt mir nicht'') made over from one of *Eine Nacht*'s own soprano songs. Betty Fischer (Annina) and Hubert Marischka (Caramello) co-starred through 32 performances, during which the show was further vulgarized by the addition of a piano concert, stuck into the second half to feature Pietro Mazzini in what now began to resemble an old-days variety musical.

However, Strauss, plus Venice, plus throbbing tenors were all definite pluses at this time, and versions of this version of the show began to appear elsewhere. The Vienna Staatsoper (1929) and the Berlin Opera (1931) took in *Eine Nacht in Venedig,* a new *Egy éj Velenceben* surfaced in Budapest (1924), Yvonne d'Arle starred in a St Louis Muny production in America (1924) and the Monte Carlo Opera House brought out a first French version (19 March 1930). Later, another inveterate adapter, Gustav Quedenfeldt, brought out his version (1936, w Eugen Rex, Karl Tutein), which subsequently surfaced at Vienna's Raimundtheater (31 December 1944), and, in 1948, conductor Anton Paulik brought out his version at the Volksoper, where the show returned in 1975 to mark Johann Strauss's 150th birthday. Britain finally heard *A Night in Venice* when it played briefly at London's Cambridge Theatre (ad Dudley Glass, Lesley Storm), with Dennis Noble and Daria Bayan heading the cast, before moving into the little Phoenix Theatre for a 433-performance run, by far the longest, in any-sized house, that the show had ever achieved. Another British version, based on Paulik's remake, but also taking in non-Strauss music, surfaced at the English National Opera in 1976, and in the new age of visual musical theatre Paris finally got an *Une Nuit à Venise* in 1997.

One planned revival, sponsored in America by the Shuberts, defied previous opinion by ultimately throwing out all the music and using just the despised libretto as the basis for what ultimately became Rudolf Friml's *Annina.* Since then, the show has found its niche—in varying versions—largely as a spectacular piece for specialist theatres: the vast American Jones Beach Marine Theater hosted a huge Mike Todd production of an alarmingly adapted version in 1952, and another version was given with great effect at the Seebuhne at Bregenz on several occasions. However, even without real water, gondolas and Venetian carnivals in support, *Eine Nacht in Venedig* seems to have been more liked, certainly by adapters and theatre directors, in the 1980s and 1990s than it was in the 1880s and 1890s, and it has indubitably outlasted the then more popular *Das Spitzentuch der Königin* and *Der lustige Krieg*—and that in spite of the fact that none of the many folk who have fiddled with Zell and Genée's libretto have come up with anything better than (or even anywhere near as good as) the text Strauss so disliked.

A 1953 film version, whose Rudolf Österreicher screenplay also stuck much closer to the original script than Operette films were inclined to do, featured Hans Olden (Duke), Jeannette Schultze (Annina), Hermann Thimig (Pappacoda), Peter Pasetti (Caramello) and Lotte Lang (Ciboletta), with Nico Dostal conducting his own arrangements of Strauss's music. Earlier, simultaneous Hungarian and German films had been made in Hungary, and Germany had issued a wartime remake with Harald Paulsen and Lizzi Waldmüller amongst its cast. Two German TV reductions, one with Erich Kunz and Sylvia Geszty, and a second featuring Wolfgang Brendel and Jeanette Scovotti, were produced in the 1970s.

Austria: Theater an der Wien 9 October 1883; USA: Daly's Theater 26 April 1884; Hungary: Budai Színkor *Egy éj Velenceben* 13 May 1887; UK: Cambridge Theatre *A Night in Venice* 25 May 1944; France: Opéra-Comique 4 December 1997

Films: Robert Wiene (Hun & Ger) 1933, Paul Verhoeven 1942, Universal Films 1953, German TV 1973, German TV 1975

Recordings: complete (EMI, HMV, CBS), etc

A NAGYMAMA Enekes vígjatek (musical comedy) in 3 acts by Árpád Pásztor adapted from the play by Gergely Csiky. Music by Raoul Mader. Népszínház-Vígopera, Budapest, 11 February 1908.

Csiky's play, first produced at the Nemzeti Színház on 6 March 1891 with Cornélia Prielle in the titular role of the grandmother, was made into a musical comedy for the Népszínház-Vígopera by experienced librettist Pásztor and the director of that short-lived theatre, composer Raoul Mader.

No less a star than Lujza Blaha played the Countess Szerémy, the grandmother of the musical's title, with Ferenc Pázmán as her grandson, Ernő. The Countess has arranged that her grandson should wed his beloved cousin, Marta (Olga Turchányi). Rather than cause the old lady pain, the girl has agreed to the betrothal even though she is in love with the young baron Kálmán Örkényi (Béla Balint). But the truth soon comes out. Then Ernő finds his affections engaged by Kálmán's sister, Piroska (Eugenie della Donna). The Countess—whose last thought was to make an unhappy match—now sees the prospect of a different unhappiness, for between the Szerémy family and the Örkényi family there is a shadow. In his youth, the senior baron Örkényi (Vince Horváth) asked for the hand of the Countess in marriage and was refused by her parents. Grandmother now takes matters in hand. She calls upon the Baron and tells him the old truth: she had been in love with him, but she had not been brave enough to defy her parents. She asks him to let the young folk wed, as their hearts will, and the Baron agrees.

Plate 273. **A nagymama.** *Lujza Blaha in the most famous role of the last part of her career, alongside Olga Turchanyi.*

A nagymama was far and away the most successful of the seven musical shows mounted at the Népszínház-Vígopera during its year of activity, passing its 50th night on 22 April 1908, and totaling 65 nights in the repertoire (more than twice as many as the next-best *The Catch of the Season, Der Mann mit den drei Frauen* or *Tündérszerelem*) before the theatre's closure. The show was then taken up by the Magyar Színház (22 September 1908), which had by now switched from musicals to an all-play schedule, but which kept this piece in its repertoire and included it in its program when it visited Vienna's Theater in der Josefstadt in 1912. The Király Színház followed just weeks behind, mounting its first musical *Nagymama* on 23 November 1908.

A film version was subsequently made, in which Blaha made her last film appearance.

A nagymama, stamped with Blaha's image, became a special classic of the Hungarian stage, reserved as a vehicle for other senior musical stars of special class. It was played by Lilly Berky—an operett soubrette before going on to an acting career—at the József Attila Színház, and later by Hanna Honthy, who appeared in a new production at the Fővárosi Operettszínház in 1964 (22 October). Another version mounted at the same house in 1990 (21 September), featuring Marika Németh in the title role, was an adaptation of Csiky's play by György Kardos with music by Szabolc Fényes. It was subsequently given at the Nemzeti Színház in 1996 (3 May).

Austria: Theater in der Josefstadt (Hun) *Die Grossmama* 13 June 1912

DIE NÄHERIN Posse mit Gesang in 4 acts by Ludwig Held. Music by Carl Millöcker. Theater an der Wien, Vienna, 13 March 1880.

Produced at the Theater an der Wien under the management of Maximilian Steiner, in a season in which the two old rivals Marie Geistinger and ''Pepi'' Gallmeyer were featured (Ludwig Held's musical comedy *Die Näherin* fell to the lot of Geistinger, whilst Gallmeyer got *Die Böhmin* and made do mostly with her previous year's hit *Die Gypsfigur*).

Geistinger played Lotti Griessmayer, the Näherin (seamstress) of the title, and made an ''unforgettable hit'' in the comical role of the girl who never stops talking. Alexander Girardi as Stefan Hoch, Carl Adolf Friese as Julius von Sombár and Herr Witte as Ferdinand supported the star. The show was played for 50 nights at the Theater an der Wien before settling in as part of Geistinger's regular repertoire. In 1881 she introduced it to America at New York's Thalia Theater, repeating the following season, only to discover that the opposition had brought Gallmeyer to America, and Gallmeyer, as well as playing her own famous roles, was playing *Die Näherin.* The show provoked sufficient interest in America for an English-language version (ad Sydney Rosenfeld) to be subsequently produced by John McCaull, first in Philadelphia in 1884, with John Howson and Mathilde Cottrelly starred, and the following year in New York as *Chatter.* Mme Cottrelly was again Lotti, De Wolf Hopper played Jeremiah Hackett (ex- Sombár), alongside Edwin Hoff (Frederick Hackett) and Harry Macdonough (Ganymede Gurgle). The production topped up Millöcker's score with the hit song from the theatre's previous production *The Black Hussar* (*Der Feldprediger,* also by Millöcker) and ran a regulation four weeks before going out to the rest of the country.

Die Näherin won further productions in Austria and Germany (ad Eduard Jacobson), in Prague and throughout central Europe following its Vienna premiere, but it remained always connected with Geistinger, who kept it in her repertoire for the rest of her career, playing it in America as late as 1897 and as part of her last seasons at the Carltheater and at Berlin's Thalia-Theater in 1898. In 1913 a revised version by Hugo Held, with additional music by Leo Held, was seen at Vienna's Theater in der Josefstadt (13 April).

Germany: Theater am Gärtnerplatz, Munich 7 May 1880, Friedrich-Wilhelmstädtisches Theater, Berlin 4 September 1880; USA: Thalia Theater (Ger) 8 April 1881, Haverly's Theater, Philadelphia *The Seamstress* 8 September 1884, Wallack's Theater *Chatter* 17 August 1885

DE NAJAC, Émile (b Lorient, 14 December 1828; d Paris, 11 April 1889).

A highly successful French playwright and vaudevillist, whose best-known work was his collaboration with Victorien Sardou on the international hit *Divorçons* (Palais-Royal 6 December 1880), de Najac also produced a number of opérette libretti without striking comparative success. It was said, however, that, although the names of Alfred Hennequin and Albert Millaud alone appeared on the bills, he had a fairly important but uncredited hand in the authorship of the hugely successful vaudeville-opérette *Niniche.* Several of his successful straight pieces were also subsequently turned into musical shows, notably the play *Bébé* (Gymnase 10 March 1877 w Albert Hennequin), produced in Britain as *Oh, Don't, Dolly!* (1919), the 1878 *Les Petites Correspondences* (w Hennequin), played in Vienna as *Kleine Anzeigen* (mus: Johann Brandl, Carltheater 25 September 1880), and, inevitably, *Divorçons,* which became *Frau Lebedame* in 1907 (Anselm Goetzl/Rudolf Bernauer, Alexander Pordes-Milo, Neue Deutsches Theater, Prague 31 December) and *Cyprienne* in 1966 (Gerhard Jussenhoven/Curt Flatow, Theater am Dom, Cologne, December).

His son, Raoul de Najac, also wrote for the stage (*Barbe-bleuette,* mus: Francis Thomé, 1891, etc).

1857 **La Momie de Roscoco** (Eugène Ortolan, Émile Jonas) 1 act Théâtre des Bouffes-Parisiens 27 July

1858 **Mam'zelle Jeanne** (Léonce Cohen) 1 act Théâtre des Bouffes-Parisiens 17 February

1860 **C'était moi** (Jean-Jacques de Billemont/w Charles Deulin) 1 act Théâtre des Bouffes-Parisiens 27 March

1861 **La Beauté du Diable** (Jules Alary/w Eugène Scribe) 1 act Opéra-Comique 28 May

1864 **Bégayements d'amour** (Albert Grisar/w Deulin) 1 act Théâtre Lyrique 8 December

1865 **Les Douze Innocents** (Grisar) 1 act Théâtre des Bouffes-Parisiens 19 October

1866 **Bettina** (Cohen) 1 act Fantaisies-Parisiennes 14 June

1868 **Petit Bonhomme vit encore** (Louis Deffès) 1 act Théâtre des Bouffes-Parisiens 19 December

1870 **Calonice** (Jules ten Brinck) 1 act Théâtre de l'Athénée 19 May

1872 **Le Docteur Rose** (Luigi Ricci) Théâtre des Bouffes-Parisiens 10 February

1872 **Au pied du mur** (Ricci) 1 act Théâtre des Bouffes-Parisiens 11 February

1872 **Un garçon de cabinet** (Adrien Talexy) 1 act Folies-Marigny 4 May

1872 **La Fête des lanternes** (Talexy) 1 act Folies-Marigny 2 October

1878 **Les Noces de Fernande** (Deffès/w Victorien Sardou) Opéra-Comique 19 November

1881 **Maître Grelot** (Talexy) 1 act Folies-Bordelaises, Bordeaux 1 September

1882 **La Bonne aventure** (Jonas/w Henri Bocage) Théâtre de la Renaissance 3 November

1882 **Ah! Le Bon billet** (Frédéric Toulmouche/w E Bureau, F Jattiot) 1 act Théâtre de la Renaissance 6 December

1883 **Le Premier baiser** (Jonas/w Raoul Toché) Théâtre des Nouveautés 21 March

1885 **La Vie mondaine** (Charles Lecocq/w Paul Ferrier) Théâtre des Nouveautés 13 February

1887 **La Noce à Nini** (Hervé/w Albert Millaud) Théâtre des Variétés 19 March

1887 **Le Roi malgré lui** (Emmanuel Chabrier/w Paul Burani) Opéra-Comique 18 May

1888 **La Japonaise** (Louis Varney/w Millaud) Théâtre des Variétés 23 November

NANON, die Wirthin vom ''goldenen Lamm'' Operette in 3 acts by F Zell based on the comédie-vaudeville *Nanon, Ninon et Madame de Maintenon* by Emmanuel Théaulon, Armand d'Artois and Lesguillon. Music by Richard Genée. Theater an der Wien, Vienna, 10 March 1877.

Zell and Genée's long-popular Operette was based on a comédie-vaudeville from the early part of the French century, and it told the story of Nanon, the hostess at the Inn of the Golden Lamb (Bertha Olma), and of her romance with the man she thinks is a drum major. He is actually the gaily philandering Marquis d'Aubigny (Jani Szíka) and as, when it comes to the point, he has no intention of marrying the innkeeper, he arranges opportunely to disappear by getting himself arrested for dueling. In order to try to win his release, Nanon goes to beg the court beauty Ninon de l'Enclos (Caroline Bendel) to use her influence with the King. Unfortunately for all concerned, Ninon is the merry Marquis's uptown lady. Ultimately, when d'Aubigny accidentally gets into genuine hot water and Nanon's pleas to the King himself save his head, he revises his behavior and makes her his Marquise. The chief comic role of the Marquis von Marsillac, master of the king's revels, was played by Carl Adolf Friese and the smaller role of his nephew Hector by the rising Alexander Girardi, whilst Bertha Steinher played Gaston, Ninon's page.

Genée's musical score was a catching one, with the usual mixture of waltzes (''Beim ersten Mal, wo er sich geschlagen'') and marches (Marsch der Wache, Marsch der Trommler und Pfeiffer), plus a minuet (''Nach diesem Intermezzo'') and a polka (''Man lernt's mit der Zeit'') topped off by a pretty lullaby and a lively entrance piece for the heroine. Nanon also had effective duos with both Ninon and d'Aubigny, and the second soprano, Ninon, some lively second-act couplets (''Was du nicht willst, das die geschehe''), which proved one of the evening's favorite numbers. There was a whole series of bright pieces for Marsillac, one teaching Hector how to behave (''Den Kopf jetzt in die Hoh''), another, and the most successful, a drinking song (''Ventre saint gris!''), a third theatrical (''Tritt man bei Ninon an''), and a fourth philosophical (''Wenn ich auch Philosoph bin''), which came to the conclusion ''Der Weiseste der Weisen ist wer zeitweise die ganze Weisheit vergisst.'' Alongside the comedian, d'Aubigny was rather less prominently served, his only solo being a little romanze in the first act.

Oddly, the show, which was to run to many hundreds of performances in all sorts of languages over the next 40 years or so, was given only a handful of showings on its original production in Vienna. Even when it was later revived at the Theater an der Wien (19 September 1885) with Paula Löwe (Nanon), Antonie Hartmann (Ninon), Girardi (Hector), Heinrich Thalboth (King Louis) and Josef Joseffy (d'Aubigny), its total exposure on that stage still came to only 28 performances, and a production at the Carltheater in 1909 with Mizzi Zwerenz (Nanon), Dora Keplinger (Ninon), Hubert Marischka (Hector) and Richard Waldemar (King Louis) added only another 18 nights to the tally.

Its short life in Vienna may have been the reason that it was slow to travel. Hungary's Népszínház, which had had such a success with Genée's previous *Der Seekadett,* mounted a production (ad Jenő Rákosi) in 1877 that played just a few performances, and Berlin's Walhalla-Theater, the next international house to pick up the piece, did not mount its production until 1883. When it did, however, the results were staggeringly different. In the 12 months following its first Berlin showing *Nanon* played more than three hundred performances, and the Operette was well and truly launched. It galloped through the houses of provincial Germany, was played in German-language theatres in Hungary and Russia, at Riga, Basel, Strasbourg, Prague and Brussels and at New York's Thalia Theater (2 January 1885), where it scored another big hit with Emmy Meffert (Nanon), Franziska Raberg (Ninon), Ferdinand Schütz (d'Aubigny) and Otto Meyer (King Louis) featured. Later, Emma Seebold took over the lead role, and the show reappeared regularly in the Thalia repertoire thereafter until the end of Gustav Amberg's tenancy in 1888.

In the meanwhile, *Nanon* had been picked up by New York's Casino Theater, where it was mounted with

Sadie Martinot, a very shapely lady who had climbed into the star system since being America's original Hebe in *Pinafore,* as Nanon and another singing beauty, Pauline Hall, as Ninon de l'Enclos. William T Carleton (d'Aubigny), Francis Wilson (Marsillac), Alice Vincent (Mme de Maintenon), W H Fitzgerald (Hector) and Gustavus Levick (King Louis) supported the two stars, and the show ran a superb four and a half months (152 performances), qualifying as a major hit. It was widely toured thereafter both by Carleton's own comic opera company and by Miss Hall's troupe and brought back to Broadway in 1892 (12 January), with Marie Tempest as the lady of the title, paired with Drew Donaldson (Ninon) and Schütz now playing d'Aubigny in English. *Nanon* remained one of the most popular of all Austrian Operetten in America for many years, thoroughly outpointing most of the works of such composers as Strauss and Suppé, as it was played regularly and widely throughout the country.

Nanon was also played all over Europe in the 1880s. It was adapted into Swedish, Polish, Croatian and Italian, revived at the Népszínház (as *Nanon, Ninon*) in 1892, at Berlin's Theater Unter den Linden in 1895 (23 March), and appeared at Berlin's Deutsches Opernhaus in 1917 in one of many productions throughout Germany, first in its original state and later in the inevitable adapted versions (Städtische Bühnen, Lubeck 6 February 1938 ad A Treumann-Nette).

In spite of its triumphs in other countries, the show never became part of the repertoire in Austria, nor was it ever staged in France, whilst a British production, mounted (well) in the wake of the American success, failed to reach the West End. Produced at Birmingham in an indifferent adaptation with two very capable vocalists in Laura Clement (Nanon) and Esme Lee (Ninon) featured as its central ladies, it toured discreetly and closed.

A 1938 UFA film entitled *Nanon* (scr: Georg Zoch, Eberhard Keindorff) used a fox-trotting musical score by Alois Melichar and Franz Baumann to illustrate the same tale (dutifully credited to Zell and Genée) for Erna Sack (Nanon), Dagny Servaes (Ninon) and Johannes Heesters (Aubigny).

Hungary: Népszínház *Nanon csaplarosné* 23 November 1877; Germany: Walhalla-Theater 30 October 1883; USA: Thalia Theater (Ger) 2 January 1885, Casino Theater (Eng) 29 June 1885; UK: Grand Theatre, Birmingham 16 September 1889

NAPIER, John [E] (b London, 1 March 1944).

A designer at Britain's principal subsidized theatres (*Nicholas Nickelby* RSC, *Equus* National Theatre, *Lohengrin, Macbeth* Royal Opera House, etc) over a number of years, Napier moved conspicuously into the musical theatre in the company of his Royal Shakespeare Company colleague, Trevor Nunn, as the designer of *Cats* (1980, Tony Award). He subsequently designed the mass of hydraulics and skating tracks on which *Starlight Express* (1984, Tony Award) was played, the atmospheric if less obviously intricate settings for *Les Misérables* (1985, Tony Award), *The Baker's Wife* (1989) and the moving mansion of *Sunset Boulevard* (1993) in further collaborations with Nunn, as well as masterminding the overwhelming space-age scenic effects for the vast Dominion Theatre's *Time,* the Creation in *Children of Eden* (1991), the helicopter and its accessory settings featured in *Miss Saigon* (1989), the 1997 revival of *Jesus Christ Superstar,* Canada's *Jane Eyre* (1997), the revised version of *Martin Guerre* (1998) and the National Theatre *Candide* (1999). Napier's early credits included the Galt MacDermot musical *Isabel's a Jezebel,* produced in London in 1970.

NAPLES AU BAISER DE FEU Opérette à grand spectacle in 2 acts by Henri Varna, Marc-Cab and René Richard. Music by Renato Rascel. Théâtre Mogador, Paris, 7 December 1957.

Continuing their series of opérettes à grand spectacle, which were the joy of the Théâtre Mogador in the 1950s, the team of manager Henri Varna and librettists Marc-Cab and René Richard followed up *Les Amants de Venise* and *Les Amours de Don Juan* with a new vehicle for star tenor Tino Rossi, fresh from his triumph in Francis Lopez's *Méditerranée* at the Châtelet. *Naples au baiser de feu,* loosely based on the singer's 1937 film hit, featured Rossi as an Italian singer who temporarily leaves his village love, Sylvia d'Andia (Jenny Marlaine), for a showier lady, Costanzella (Jacqueline Mille), but finally comes back to her only to find she has been blinded by the eruption of Mount Vesuvius. All comes right for the finale, which also brings together the soubret pair (Pierjac, Arlette Patrick), who have supplied the regular light relief. The tale allowed the Mogador stage to display the eruption of Vesuvius and 19 to 22 other picturesque scenes, while Rossi performed the bulk of a Napoli-flavored imitation of a Francis Lopez score by Italian songwriter Renato Rascel (''Serenade pour un ange,'' ''Te voglio bene tanto, tanto,'' ''Costanzella,'' Prière à San Gennaro, ''Sans toi,'' ''Naples au baiser de feu''), which replaced the Vincent Scotto numbers and Neapolitan standards that had illustrated the film. The Mogador lived up to its reputation for glamorous entertainment, and the show ran for 15 months. It has remained on the fringe of the French regional repertoire since and made a reappearance in 1990 at Rochefort.

Recordings: original cast (Columbia), studio cast (CBS)

NAPOLÉON UND DIE FRAUEN Singspiel in 3 acts by Heinrich Reinhardt. Volksoper (Kaiser-Jubiläums Stadttheater), Vienna, 1 May 1912.

Written and composed by the musician of *Das süsse Mädel, Napoléon und die Frauen* lived up thoroughly to its title. Its first act, set in 1790 and subtitled *Die Frau Oberst,* presented Napoléon (Herr Leonhardt) as a young sub-lieutenant in the Lafère Regiment becoming involved with his General's wife (Frln Engel), and the second act, subtitled *Die Putzmacherin,* set in 1804, with Napoléon now Emperor and married to the famous Josephine (Frln von Martinowska), found him face to face with charlady Madeleine Calot (Frln Sax), a part of his past who ends the act singing and dancing with the private secretary Vauban (Herr Markowsky) instead, as Napoléon moves on to the third act, *Die Wienerin.* In 1809, during his invasion of Vienna, he meets up with Lori ''die Gumpendorferin'' (Frln Ritzinger), in whose company he can at least try to pretend that he is still the carefree little corporal of his youthful days.

The role of Napoléon was liberally equipped with songs, from the ''heavy lies the head''–themed second-act solo ''Selig ist, wer des Herzens Zug,'' to the longing ''Es war ein kleiner Korporal'' of the last scenes, but, if Lori was a sweetly standard juvenile heroine with a song to fit (''Über Stock, über Stein''), the ripely enjoyable Frau Oberst, her comical husband and his seamstress-on-the side, the charlady and her secretary, and a couple of incidental Wiener-folk in the final act all provided the opportunity for plenty of song and dance in Reinhardt's most lively, singable and danceable style. Rainer Simons's production at the Volksoper was played in repertoire with such pieces as *Ernani, Der Kuhreigen* and *Carmen.*

The great success of Reinhardt's *The Spring Maid* (*Die Sprudelfee*) in America prompted a production of a version of *Napoléon* there. However, Reinhardt's neat tripartite story with its triple look at the love life of a man in power, went out the window, leaving Napoléon (Harrison Brockbank, replacing the celebrated vocalist Victor Maurel of the pre-town run) only one girl, Wanda (Valli Valli), with whom to wallow sentimentally, and the score was permeated with interpolations by William Frederick Peters, one of which, a pretty if worryingly reminiscent waltz song called ''The Mysterious Kiss,'' was plugged as the show's big number. However, Edward Martindel's performance of the booming ''Diplomacy,'' in the role of Colonel Stappe, was the show's highlight. Produced by Joseph Gaites as *The Purple Road,* with Eva Fallon (Kathi) and Clifton Webb (Bosco) in support of the two stars, the show was well received and ran for 138 Broadway performances.

Napoléon's attraction for Viennese girls was again celebrated in a piece called *Napoléon und die Wienerin* (Heinrich Strecker/Franz Gribitz), produced at the Breslau Schauspielhaus in 1934 (16 May), on one of the many occasions that the monarch has appeared on the musical stage. The internationally successful *The Duchess of Dantzic* and several other musicals—the most recent being the 1997 Aachen *Catharine*—presented him as the protagonist of Victorien Sardou and Émile Moreau's *Madame Sans-Gêne* tale, and Johannes Riemann played the emperor in Oscar Straus's *Teresina* (1925), where, as in *The Duchess of Dantzic,* he remained a dignifiedly non-singing character. In Richard Genée and Louis Roth's *Zwillinge* (1885), however, he seems to have been—as portrayed by one Herr Graselli—a dancing character. In France the ''little corporal'' has been seen portrayed in such diverse vehicles as Francis Lopez's *Viva Napoli!* and popular vocalist Serge Lama's spectacular vehicle [*De Bonaparte à*] *Napoléon* (Théâtre Marigny 20 September 1984, Yves Gilbert/Lama, Jacques Rosny), but an announced (by New York's Rudolf Aronson in 1890) Napoléon musical from the pen of Charles Lecocq did not materialize. Yet another Napoléon (Timothy Williams/ Andrew Sabiston) was mounted in Canada in 1994 (Elgin Theatre, Toronto) before moving on to try its luck in the West End in 2000, in one more effort at challenging the record of the finely made *The Duchess of Danzig,* still the champion amongst Napoléonic musicals.

Like the hero of *Viva Napoli!,* comedian Francis Wilson, in Broadway's *The Little Corporal* (1898), got himself disguised as Napoléon—if for rather different reasons, and in rather more low comic style—and the German musical comedy *Die Kino-Königin* included a let's-make-a-film scene in which the leading actor portrayed Napoléon. Perhaps the earliest musical-comedy Napoléon, however, was the one portrayed in the 1868 American extravaganza *The Great Ditch* (Opera House, Pittsburgh, June), where he was confronted with ''John Bull'' (rather than the feminine Queen Victoria) and with the latest American president in an early example of a singing-President show.

In Vienna, Hubert Marischka appeared as Napoléon junior in Petér Stojanovits's *Der Herzog von Reichstadt* and as Louis Napoléon in *Mariette* without graduating to their famous forebear. The Herzog von Reichstadt was seen again in the pasticcio Operette *Die Tänzerin Fanny Elssler* and, romancing the same ballerina, in August Pepöck's *Hofball in Schönbrunn,* whilst Louis Napoléon (ie, Napoléon III) put in an appearance in the Hungarian operett *Offenbach,* and was portrayed in the Viennese version of that show by Karl Althoff and on Broadway by Harrison Brockbank again. Napoléon's youngest brother had his moment on the Operette stage as the hero of Carl Michael Ziehrer's *König Jerome* (1878). None of these shows, however, was of the tone to deliver one of the most enjoyably off-the-wall Napoléon numbers of the musical theatre, E Ray Goetz and Vincent Bryan's ''Who Ate Napoleons with Josephine When Bonaparte Was Away?'' as delivered by Sam Bernard in Broadway's version of *As You Were* (1919).

Not to be outdone in the Napoléonic stakes, the ladies got in on the act as well, and Anna Held portrayed Jean Richepin's *Mam'selle Napoléon* (she was actually the actress Mlle Mars, and Arthur Laurence was himself) on Broadway. Oskar Nedbal provided the score for a piece of the same title in Europe.

USA: Liberty Theater *The Purple Road* 7 April 1913

NÄSTLBERGER, Robert (b Graz, 1887; d Hanover, 9 June 1942). Leading tenor-cum-choreographer for the interwar Viennese stage.

At first an army officer, Nästlberger exchanged his epaulets for the garb of an operettic tenor when his singing talent was discovered. He played in supporting roles at the Theater an der Wien in *Wenn zwei sich lieben* (1916, Agaston) and *Die Winzerbraut* (1916, Baron Bogdan Lukovac), then rose through larger to leading roles at Ronacher in *Liebe im Schnee* (1916, Gedeon von Rommler), at the Theater an der Wien in *Nimm mich mit!* (1919, Gregor Gregorowitsch), at the Raimundtheater in *Was Mädchen träumen* (1920, Fred von Emmerling Emmerling), *Zwölf Uhr nachts* (1920, Karl Hellmer) and *Der Tanz ins Glück* (1920, Fritz Wendelin), at the Apollotheater as Graf Leandro de Cavaletti in *Die Tangokönigin* (1921) and in *Indische Nächte,* and at the Stadttheater in *Die Siegerin* (1922, Alexander Mentschikoff) and *Ein Jahr ohne Liebe* (Hector von Fontenay).

He returned to the Theater an der Wien to replace Hubert Marischka in the star role of *Die gelbe Jacke* and subsequently appeared there opposite Fritzi Massary as Prinz Beladonis in *Die Perlen der Cleopatra,* at the Carltheater in the title role of *Hoheit Franzl* (1924), at the Johann Strauss-Theater as Caesar Christow in *Alexandra* (1926) and as Niki in a revival of *Ein Walzertraum,* and at the Bürgertheater in *Yvette und ihre Freunde* (1927, Rittmeister Marko Bajanescu). He starred as Murger in *Das Veilchen vom Montmartre* (1930) and Gabor Palffy in *Sisters* (1930) in Vienna, then opposite Gitta Alpár in Berlin's *Die Dubarry* (1931), before spending the latter years of his performing career in Berlin and in the German provinces, where he ultimately became manager of Hannover's Mellini Theater.

Nästlberger doubled his performing both with choreography (*Der Tanz ins Glück, Die Tangokönigin, Was Mädchen träumen, Eine Sommernacht, Die Tanzgräfin, General d'Amour,* the film *Operette* w Hedy Pfundmayr, Franz Bauer, etc) and, later, directing (Raimundtheater, etc) and also wrote the libretti for a wartime Operette, *Der Reiter der Kaiserin,* and the screenplays for several musical films.

1941 **Der Reiter der Kaiserin** (August Pepöck/w A von Czibulka) Raimundtheater 30 April

NATSCHINSKI, Gerd [Joachim] (b Chemnitz, 23 August 1928).

Conductor and composer of light music for film, television and the then East German theatre, Natschinski had a success with his first musical, *Messeschlager Gisela,* but his most popular work has been *Mein Freund Bunbury,* a piece ''freely'' based on Oscar Wilde's *The Importance of Being Earnest,* in which the original story is swamped under scenic considerations and alarming liberties are taken with the characters. Chasuble, for example, becomes a Salvation Army Major and opens the show leading the equivalent of ''Follow the Fold'' on Victoria Station.

Natschinski's later pieces *Terzett* and *Casanova* have also been played beyond their first runs. In 1978 he became, for a period, the director of the Berlin Metropoltheater.

1960 **Messeschlager Gisela** (Jo Schulz) Metropoltheater 16 October

1963 **Servus Peter** (Hans Hardt) Metropoltheater 27 October; revised version Eisleben 30 December 1972

1964 **Mein Freund Bunbury** (Helmut Bez, Jurgen Degenhardt) Metropoltheater 2 October

1974 **Terzett** (Bez, Degenhardt) Musikalische Komödie, Leipzig 15 June

1976 **Casanova** (Bez, Degenhardt) Metropoltheater 10 September

1979 **Das Dekameronical** (Heinz Kahlow) Halle 18 November; revised version (*Das neue Dekameronical*) Elbe-Ester-Theater, Wittenberg 4 June 1982

1982 **Ein Fall für Sherlock Holmes** (Degenhardt) Städtische Bühnen, Erfurt 10 April

1984 **Planet der Verlieben** (Kahlow) Metropoltheater 21 December

1988 **Caballero** (Degenhardt) Musikalische Komödie, Leipzig 16 December

NATZLER, Siegmund (b Vienna, 8 September 1865; d Vienna, 12 August 1913). Viennese singing comedian and stage director.

After a decade working in provincial theatres, Natzler moved up to play leading comedy roles at the Carltheater and at the Theater an der Wien in the last part of the 19th century and the early years of the 20th century, appearing in the regular Viennese repertoire and in a variety of foreign pieces both on the musical and non-musical stage. He also worked for a period as Oberregisseur at the Theater an der Wien, directing such pieces as *Befehl des*

Kaisers (1904), *Der rothe Kosak* (1904), *Der Juxheirat* (1904), *Pufferl* (1905), the 1905 revival of *Wiener Blut* and *Der Rebell.*

Amongst the roles in which he appeared at the Carltheater were the composer Lanner in the Festspiele *Sein erster Walzer* (1894), Papillon in *Die Königin von Gamara,* Dr Graham in *Lady Charlatan* (1894), Jules César in *Olympia* (*Les Forains*), Wasulko Okinski in *Die Lachtaube* (1895), Axel in Adolphe Ferron's *Sataniel,* Cheops in Victor Herbert's *Der Zauberer von Nil* (*The Wizard of the Nile*), Popolani in *Blaubart,* Siegbert in *König Chilpérich,* Dr Berndorf in *Bum-Bum* (1896), Harold in W S Gilbert's *Der Herr Gouverneur* (*His Excellency*), Bum in *Die Grossherzogin von Gérolstein,* Charles Rochou in *Der Cognac-König,* Wun Hi in *Die Geisha* (1897), Chrisostoms Barriolo-Schuyder in *Die Pariserin,* Graf Falconi in *Carneval in Rom,* Balthasar Groot in *Der lustige Krieg,* Klex in Ferron's *Das Krokodil* (1898), General des Ifs in *Die kleine Michus,* Mercury in *Adam und Eva* and Jacques Grognard in *Das kleine Korporal* (1899).

He was seen as Calchas in *Die schöne Helena* at the Theater an der Wien on the 70th birthday celebration of Karl Blasel in 1901, and played that role along with others such as Balthasar Groot and Frank in *Die Fledermaus* in repertoire when he joined the company there. In the years he spent at the Theater an der Wien he also created or introduced to Vienna such roles as Mister Archibald Handsome in *Die Dame aus Trouville,* Weisskopf in *Der Fremdenführer* (1902), Graf Tibor Korosi in *Der Lebemann,* Schwudler in *Bruder Straubinger,* Sir Archibald Slackett in *Der Toreador* (1903), von Karseboom in *Der neue Bugermeister,* Bartolomeo Sparaducci in *Der Generalkonsul,* Corporal la Galette in *Befehl des Kaisers,* Fürst Gavrile Lupasco in *Der rothe Kosak,* the detective Tom Clip in *Die Millionenbraut,* Major Baranyi in *Das Garnisonsmädel* (1904), Stampfl in *Pufferl,* Ypsheim-Gindelbach in the revised *Wiener Blut,* Sir Pomponius in *Prinz Bob,* Tobias Stephenson in *Vergeltsgott* and Schmulos in *Der Rebell,* before winning his most outstanding creation, in his last role there, as Baron Zeta in *Die lustige Witwe* (1905).

His brother, **Leopold NATZLER** (b Vienna, 17 June 1860; d Vienna, 3 January 1926), also led a career as a comedian in straight and musical theatre in Marburg, Oldenburg, Berlin (1884–86), Graz and Brünn and in Vienna at the Theater an der Wien—*Die indische Witwe,* Momo in *Capitän Fracassa* (1889), Mermeros in *Das Orakel,* Flink in *Drei Paar Schuhe,* Doux-Doux in *Die Jungfrau von Belleville,* Stefan Hoch in *Die Näherin,* Zsupán, Ajax I, etc—at the Theater in der Josefstadt and the Raimundtheater. He guested at the Carltheater in *Der liebe Schatz* (1902, Fabian Müller), at the Theater an der Wien as Tympanon in *Venedig in Paris* (1903) and, most

Plate 274. *Antje Rietz (Gisela) with her trade-fair mascot in the Neuköllner Oper's 1998 tongue-in-cheek revival of* **Natschinski's** *East German musical* Messeschlager Gisela.

memorably, alongside his brother as the conductor Klobuschitzky in *Der Toreador.* He subsequently became the manager of the 400-seat Hölle studio theatre, attached to the Theater an der Wien, in the early years of its activity. The brothers also, at one stage, ran a music publishing firm together, and Leopold contributed music of his own composition to the Vienna stage (*Ein kecker Schnabel* 1896, *Fräulein Stationschef* 1903).

Their sister, **Regine NATZLER** (b Vienna, 24 November 1866), played minor roles at the Theater in der Josefstadt and for six years at the Carltheater (Miss Grant in *Die Uhlanen,* Aline in *Das Fräulein vom Telephone,* Mary in *Lachende Erben,* Maud Palmer in *Goldland,* Filomena in *Die Brillantenkönigin,* etc).

NAUGHTON, James (b Middletown, Conn, 6 December 1945).

Naughton made his New York debut off-Broadway in *A Long Day's Journey into Night* in 1971, and in a subsequent career based largely in the non-musical theatre (*Whose Life Is It, Anyway?*) and television. He has made intermittent highly successful forays into the musical theatre, creating first the ''straight man'' role of Wally to Lenny Baker's clownish Alvin in *I Love My Wife* and scoring a major hit as the Bogartish gumshoe detective of fiction featured at the center of *City of Angels* (1989, Stone, Tony Award ''I'm Nothing without You''). He had a further musical-theatre success when he took the role of Billy Flynn in the enormously popular Roundabout revival of *Chicago* (1996, Tony Award).

Plate 275. **Leopold Natzler** *as the bandmaster in* The Toreador.

In 1998 Naughton appeared in a one-man musical revue, *Street of Dreams,* at the Manhattan Theatre Club, and subsequently at the Promenade (February 1999).

NAUGHTY MARIETTA Musical comedy in 2 acts by Rida Johnson Young. Music by Victor Herbert. New York Theater, New York, 7 November 1910.

Naughty Marietta was written as a commission from impresario Oscar Hammerstein, a transfuge from the world of opera, for a piece to feature the star members of his former opera company: the tiny, sparkling Italian prima donna Emma Trentini, the slightly portly ''little Caruso'' of America, Orville Harrold, French contralto Marie Duchêne and the tall, angular bass-baritone Edward Martindel. Mrs Young evolved a period story that cast Trentini as an Italian countess who impersonates a boy, Duchêne as a dramatic quadroon, Martindel as a colonial aristocrat and Harrold as a dashing American adventurer and, because Hammerstein also insisted on the introduction of some comedians from the variety stage to provide what was considered to be the necessary leavening to the operatic elements, she slipped in a couple of funny folk with some irrelevant scenes.

Captain Dick (Harrold), the head of a ranger band of new Americans, has sworn to track down the pirate Bras-Piqué, who has been harassing the colonies of the Louisiana coast. No one knows that the marauder is, in fact, the lofty Étienne Grandet (Martindel), whose foolish father has usurped the position of Governor in New Orleans. Marietta, Countess d'Altena (Trentini), who has hidden away on a bride ship to escape an unwanted marriage in Europe, arrives in New Orleans, and Dick helps her to hide, disguised as the son of a puppeteer. Marietta has sworn that she will marry only the man who can complete a melody that came to her once in a dream, but Étienne discovers her identity and determines to wed this profitable, high-born lady, much to the distress of his mistress, Adah (Duchêne), whom he, following the local tradition, puts up for auction at the Quadroon Ball. To Marietta's jealous annoyance, Dick saves Adah's reputation by buying her, but Adah repays her benefactor by betraying Étienne's piratical secret. Dick hurries to find Marietta, whom the Grandets have imprisoned, trying to force her into a marriage. Outside her window, he sings to her—it is her dream song, and he sings it all the way through. Blades flash, and a happy ending is achieved when Dick's followers march to the rescue.

Undoubtedly helped and even encouraged by the quality of the voices for which he was writing, Herbert turned out some of his best work in the score of *Naughty Marietta.* If the comic and choral numbers were unexceptional, Trentini (who complained originally that her songs were too high), Harrold and Duchêne were finely served. The dream song, ''Ah! Sweet Mystery of Life,'' had a quality that too many other songs that have been given such a key place in a plot have failed to achieve, and its romantic lyricism happily complemented the vigorous masculinity of Harrold's ''Tramp, Tramp, Tramp''—destined to become one of the world's most famous marching songs—his dreamy waltz ''I'm Falling in Love with Someone,'' and Trentini's brilliant Italian Street Song and vivacious title number. Perhaps the most impressive musical moments, however, came in less obvious places: the quadroon's somberly colored lament '''Neath the Southern Moon'' and the glorious second-act quartet ''Live for Today.''

Naughty Marietta underwent very little change on its way to town. Herbert stuck to his guns; all Trentini's high notes stayed in, and only one number, an irrelevant attempt at some local color called ''Boo, Mr Voodoo, Don't You Hoodoo Me,'' was dropped. When the show reached Broadway, it proved to be a fine success. It played 136 New York performances before moving on to Boston, then to the touring circuits under the management of Hammerstein's son, Arthur. It returned to Broadway in 1916, then again in 1929 and 1931 with Ilse Marvenga, another Continental star, as Marietta, and was played at San Francisco's Light Opera in 1941 and in 1948 with film star Susannah Foster featured. In 1955 Patrice Munsel and Alfred Drake starred in a television adaptation. In spite of its success in America, the show remained relatively unknown overseas until a 1935 film version, starring Nelson Eddy and Jeanette MacDonald (with a slightly different story, which no longer required the lady to get into short pants) popularized Herbert's songs internationally. ''Tramp, Tramp, Tramp,'' ''I'm Falling in Love with Someone,'' ''Ah! Sweet Mystery of Life,'' '''Neath the Southern Moon'' and the Italian Street Song became perhaps the best known of all Herbert's music outside America. Amateur societies took to the show that held them, and in 1945 British touring manager James Shirvell put out a road company with Lorely Dyer and Derek Oldham, directed by Edward Royce, and with a banderole ''prior to West End presentation'' attached. It didn't make it, and New York remains to this day the only theatrical capital to have hosted *Naughty Marietta,* most recently under the aegis of the New York City Opera (1978).

A further filmed version (ad Neil Simon) was made by NBC-TV in 1955, with Alfred Drake and Patrice Munsel in the leading roles.

UK: Ladbroke Hall (copyright) 24 October 1910, tour 1945

Films: MGM 1935, NBC-TV

Recordings: complete (Smithsonian Institution), selections (RCA Victor, MGM, Columbia, Capitol)

THE NAUTCH GIRL, or The Rajah of Chutneypore Indian comic opera in 2 acts by George Dance. Lyrics by George Dance and Fred Desprez. Music by Edward Solomon. Savoy Theatre, London, 30 June 1891.

Richard D'Oyly Carte, faced with a crisis when Gilbert split with Sullivan and with him after the production of *The Gondoliers,* turned to composer Teddy Solomon, hailed since his *Billee Taylor* more than a decade earlier as Sullivan's most likely rival, and to the clever if inexperienced young journalist and playwright George Dance. This pair were given the almost impossible task of providing the next new show for the Savoy Theatre while the living shades of Gilbert and Sullivan hovered over them. They were good choices, for Solomon, always supremely confident of his talent, would have no qualms, while Dance had nothing to lose and, as it turned out, the piece they supplied to their producer was well worthy of the Savoy and certainly comparable in quality with the works of their famous predecessors.

Indru (Courtice Pounds), son of Punka, the Rajah of Chutneypore (Rutland Barrington), falls in love with dancing girl Hollee Beebee (Leonore Snyder), but he cannot wed her because—for reasons too quaintly complex to explain—her family has gone and lost their Brahmin caste. Indru bravely renounces his own caste so that the wedding can take place, but then, after endless years of legal quiproquos, Beebee's appeal against her deprivation finally comes to court and she wins. She is a Brahmin again, and he is not, so their marriage is illegal. The Rajah is forced to condemn his law-breaking son to death, much to the delight of his ambitious relative, Pyjama (Frank Thornton), who has taken advantage of Punka's greatest failing, irrepressible nepotism, to become Grand Vizier. Punka's failing is so great it even stops him from arresting Pyjama for having stolen the diamond eye from Bumbo, the local idol (W H Denny), but the vile Pyjama has no such family compunctions. With the throne now in sight, he tries to get Punka deposed as being the father of a criminal. Bumbo himself descends from his shelf to administer letter-of-the-law justice, but then Hollee Beebee, who had fled the country and gone on tour with a dance group, returns—just in time—and around her neck is a diamond, a gift from a stage-door admirer. It is Bumbo's missing eye, and the delighted idol promptly condemns its thief before returning to his shelf accompanied by the amorous Chinna Loofah (Jessie Bond, in her most characterful Savoy role), who would rather be a wooden idol's bride than nobody's bride at all.

Carte's secretary, Frank Desprez, helped out on the lyrics for some songs that were Gilbertian enough without being imitations: a piece about fashionable ''Idols'' for Denny, a topical carmagnole for Denny and Miss Bond describing married life (''Vive la liberté''), a vast and vastly funny patter song for Thornton about avoiding bad luck, and some much-less-ordinary-than-usual romantic songs for Pounds.

The Nautch Girl was greeted by critics and public with surprise and relief. Gilbert and Sullivan were missed, but the Savoy could survive and supply the kind of entertainment its public loved without them. The show ran through two hundred performances at the Savoy and was taken on tour for the two following seasons. At a time when comic opera, even of a superior kind, was tumbling in popularity before the onslaught of new burlesque and similar entertainments, this was a considerable achievement, but the achievement ended there. Although Rudolf Aronson and John Stetson went into warring print, each claiming that Solomon had sold them the Broadway rights, only the title made it to America. While the warring went on, the downmarket Rentz-Santley company, snatching for the title of the moment, put out a burleycue piece called *The Nautch Girl, or The Beauty of Bengal.* The real *Nautch Girl* apparently, and rather curiously, was exported only to the eastern circuits, where

Plate 276. **Anna Neagle** *in* Charlie Girl: *''I Was Young, When This First Happened to Me . . .''*

a touring troupe played it to genuine Indian audiences, and, sadly, Dance and Solomon did not collaborate again.

NEAGLE, Anna (Dame) [ROBERTSON, Florence Marjorie] (b Forest Gate, Essex, 20 October 1904; d London, 3 June 1986). Much-loved star of the British screen and stage.

Originally a chorus dancer for Charlot and Cochran in revue and then in musicals (*Rose Marie, The Desert Song*), Miss Neagle played her first speaking role in a small part in the film *The Chinese Bungalow* before being promoted to partner Jack Buchanan as the ingenue of the 1931 musical *Stand Up and Sing.* She subsequently had a distinguished career as a film actress, mostly in stalwartly heroic roles but also in musical vehicles ranging from the film version of *Good Night, Vienna* (1932, w Buchanan) to *Bitter-Sweet* (1933), Hollywood's *No, No, Nanette* (1940) and *Sunny* (1941), and a version of *King's Rhapsody* (1956), which was reorganized to allow the by then important star to take a larger part in the action than the original Marta Karillos (Phyllis Dare) had done.

She appeared on stage in straight pieces ranging from *As You Like It* (Rosalind) and *Twelfth Night* (Olivia) to *Peter Pan* and *Emma* (opposite Robert Donat), and in the Coronation revue *The Glorious Days* in 1953 as a bevy of characters including Queen Victoria, but she had her only significant stage-musical success late in her career when she starred as Lady Hadwell throughout the seven-year run of *Charlie Girl* (1965) in Britain and then in Australia. *Charlie Girl* brought Miss Neagle back to the West End public's eye, and in 1973 she filled the role of Sue, remade for another dancer, Ruby Keeler, in the revised and revived *No, No, Nanette.* She made her last stage appearance, at the age of a failing 70-plus, as the fairy in pantomime at the London Palladium.

Autobiographies: *It's Been Fun* (1949), *There's Always Tomorrow* (W H Allen, London, 1974)

NEDBAL, Oskar (b Tabor, 26 March 1874; d Agram, 24 December 1930).

Nedbal studied at the Prague conservatory and worked at first as a viola player with the Bohemian String Quartet before moving on to a career as a conductor, initially with the Prague Philharmonic Orchestra and then, from 1906 to 1919, at the head of the Vienna Tonkünstlerorchester. His earliest compositions were in the field of chamber, orchestral and, in particular, ballet music (*Der faule Hans, Von Märchen zu Märchen, Prinzessin Hyazintha, Des Teufels Grossmütterchen, Andersen*), but his greatest success as a composer came when he moved into the field of Operette.

His first work, *Die keusche Barbara,* a piece set in 19th-century Britain, was originally produced in his native Czechoslovakia (*Cudná Barbara*), but it moved quickly to Vienna, Germany and later Hungary (*Az erénycsősz*), establishing its composer in the theatrical world in the process. Of the four full-length works that he then turned out for Viennese theatres between 1913 and 1918, the outstanding piece was his second work, *Polenblut* (1913). Produced at the Carltheater, it had a remarkable first run, was played throughout central Europe and, with Emma Trentini starring, on Broadway (*The Peasant Girl*), as it confirmed itself as a staple item in the ''Silver Age'' repertoire. However, Nedbal's other pieces were by no means unsuccessful. *Polenblut*'s successor, *Die Winzerbraut,* a piece set partly in Agram and the Slavonic countryside and mounted at the Theater an der Wien with Betty Fischer as its heroine and a cast including Ernst Tautenhayn, Robert Nästlberger, Karl Tuschl, Karl Pfann, Margit Suchy and Gustav Werner, also had a fine first run (137 performances) and later performances around Europe, while a second piece for the Carltheater, *Die schöne Saskia,* was played there 131 times and subsequently also produced in Hungary (*A szép Saskia* 8 November 1918 Városi Színház).

Nedbal returned enthusiastically to his homeland when the Czechoslovak republic was formed after the war, and he became widely involved in the musical and theatrical affairs of the country during the 1920s. His composing output, however, shrank, and only a comic opera, *Sédlak Jakub* (1922), and one last operetta score for Vienna were added to his work list during years that were often disillusioned and, altogether, less than happy ones. In 1930 he committed suicide by jumping from the window of the ballet room at the Agram theatre.

1910 **Die keusche Barbara** (Rudolf Bernauer, Leopold Jacobson) Theater Weinberge, Prague 14 September

1913 **Polenblut** (Leo Stein) Carltheater 25 October

1916 **Die Winzerbraut** (Stein, Julius Wilhelm) Theater an der Wien 11 February

1917 **Die schöne Saskia** (A M Willner, Heinz Reichert) Carltheater 16 November

1918 **Eriwan** (Felix Dörmann) Wiener Komodienhaus 29 November

1919 **Mam'selle Napoléon** (Emil Golz, Arnold Golz) 1 act Hölle 31 January

1925 **Donna Gloria** (Victor Léon, Reichert) Carltheater 30 December

Biography: Buchner, A: *Nedbal, Briefe und Dokumente* (1968; revised edition, Panton, Prague, 1986)

NEIDHART, August (b Vienna, 12 May 1867; d Berlin, 25 November 1934). All-purpose playwright and librettist of the Austrian and German stage.

Neidhart made his entry into the theatre as an actor, then moved to the Burgtheater to take up the post of prompter, and he did not begin writing for the stage until he was already in his thirties. His first pieces, mostly short comedies and adaptations, were staged in minor Viennese houses, and he provided the texts for a number of mostly modest musical plays in the first decade and a bit of the new century before being employed in 1916 as dramaturg and ''artistic advisor'' by Gustav Charlé at the Berlin Komische Oper. His first musical play for that theatre turned out to be Leon Jessel's triumphant *Das Schwarzwaldmädel,* which, even though its author was Viennese and its composer born in what is today Poland, may nevertheless be accounted one of the greatest successes of the German Operette stage. It was a kind of success that he did not repeat, although he combined with Jessel on six other musicals, several of which did well enough, and also partnered Leo Fall on *Die Strassensängerin* and Leo Ascher, an ally of earlier days, on an adaptation of the comedy *Im Klubsessel* (*Baronesschen Sarah*) and on *Ninon im Scheideweg* during a busy career that saw his works produced all around central Europe.

Neidhart committed suicide in Berlin in 1934.

1901 **Ein braver Ehemann** (Franz Wagner) Jantschtheater 10 May

1901 **Es ist erreicht** (Ludwig Gothov-Grüneke) Jantschtheater 6 July

1903 **Amor & Cie** (Paul Mestrozzi) Kaiser-Jubiläums Theater 11 September

1903 **Über Land und Meer** (Karl Rella) Jantschtheater 14 April

1904 **Die Praterfee** (Karl J Fromm) Jantschtheater 2 September

1904 **'s Zuckersgoscherl** (J Wolffsgruber/Jean Kren, Alfred Schönfeld ad w Carl Lindau) Carltheater 15 October

1905 **Friedl mit der Fidel** (Arthur von Henriques) Kleines Theater 10 October

1906 **Der Erste** (Richard Fronz) Bürgertheater 16 March

1906 **Der Triumph des Weibes** (Josef Hellmesberger) Danzers Orpheum 16 November

1907 **Wien bleibt Wien** (Josef Bayer) 1 act Venedig in Wien 11 June

1907 **Der Lebensretter** (F Kollmaneck/Ferdinand Korb) Lustspieltheater 20 August

1907 **Die schöne Griechin** (Max R Steiner/Lucien Boyer ad)1 act Danzers Orpheum 20 December

1908 **Die wilde Komtesse** (Adolf Ripka von Rechthofen) Stadttheater, Brünn 25 October

1909 **Ein Belagerungszustand** (Leo Ascher) 1 act Kabarett Fledermaus 1 November

1909 **Der junge Papa** (Edmund Eysler/w Alexander Engel) 1 act Apollotheater 3 February

1911 **Sein Herzensjunge** (Walter Kollo/w Rudolf Schanzer) Thalia-Theater, Elberfeld 1 April

1913 **Freddy und Teddy** (Digby la Touche/H L Melbourne ad w Lindau) Theater am Nollendorfplatz, Berlin 23 December

1914 **Schurzenmanöver** (Walter Goetze/w R von Gatti ad Hans Brennert) Neues Operettentheater, Leipzig 25 March

1914 **Komm, deutscher Bruder** (Eysler, Lehár/w Lindau) Raimundtheater 4 October

1915 **Die ledige Frau** (Karl Eibenschütz/w Lindau) Landestheater, Linz 3 December

1915 **Gri-gri** Viennese version (Wiener Stadttheater)

1917 **Liebessport** (Eibenschütz/w Lindau) Theater am Gärtnerplatz, Munich 26 May

1917 **Schwarzwaldmädel** (Leon Jessel) Komische Oper, Berlin 25 August

1918 **Ein modernes Mädel** (Jessel) Volkstheater, Munich 28 June

1918 **Ohne Mann kein Vergnügen** (Jessel) Komische Oper, Berlin

1920 **Die Schöne von Baden-Baden** (Hermann Beutten ad Eduard Künneke) Kurhaustheater, Baden-Baden 12 June

1920 **Die Strohwitwe** (Leo Blech) Stadttheater, Hamburg 16 June

1920 **Baronesschen Sarah** (Ascher) Komische Oper, Berlin 5 December

1921 **Die Postmeisterin** (Jessel) Centraltheater, Berlin 3 February

1921 **Die Strassensängerin** (Leo Fall) Metropoltheater, Berlin 24 September

1921 **Das Detektivmädel** (*Miss Nobody*) (Jessel) Centraltheater, Berlin 28 October

1923 **Süsse Susi** (Siegfried Grzyb/w Richard Bars) Schiller Theater

1923 **Die Abenteuerin**

1923 **Der unsterbliche Kuss**

1924 **Die Frau ohne Schleier** (Byjacco/Richard Rillo/w Lothar Sachs) Theater am Zoo, Berlin 24 November

1925 **Prinzessin Husch** (Jessel) Operettenhaus, Hamburg 22 December; Theater des Westens, Berlin 11 March 1926

1926 **Yvonne** (Hugo Hirsch/w Arthur Rebner) Theater am Kurfurstendamm 1 August

1926 **Der Trompeter vom Rhein** (Viktor Nessler arr Robert Winterberg/w Cornelius Bronsgeest) Centralhalle 23 December

1926 **Ninon am Scheideweg** (Ascher) Theater am Zoo 27 December

1928 **Die Männer von Manon** (Goetze/w Robert Gilbert) Kleines Haus, Düsseldorf 30 September

1929 **Prosit, Gipsy** (R Gilbert/w Henry) Deutsches Künstlertheater 19 April

1929 **Die Luxuskabine** (Jessel) Neues Operettentheater, Leipzig 20 October

1931 **Thron zu vergeben** (Bertram Wittmann) Komische Oper 29 August

1933 **Junger Wein** (Jessel) Theater des Westens, Berlin 1 September

NELL GWYNNE Comic opera in 3 acts by H B Farnie based on the musical comedy *Rochester, or King Charles the Second's Merry Days* by W T Moncrieff. Music by Alfred Cellier. Prince's Theatre, Manchester, 17 October 1876; revised as a comic opera in 2 acts by H B Farnie. Music by Robert Planquette. Avenue Theatre, London, 7 February 1884.

Following Cellier's considerable success with *The Sultan of Mocha,* his first and best musical for the Manchester theatre, he was commissioned to provide others. None of these proved, in fact, successful enough to move on from Manchester, but his score for the insufficiently well-received 1876 show *Nell Gwynne* (Pattie Laverne played the lady in question) was later adapted to become that of *Dorothy,* the most successful British musical of the century. Prior to this musical rebirth, however, librettist Farnie had withdrawn his text from the melded copyright of the show in order to have it reset by the hottest-name composer of the moment, Robert Planquette, just then at the peak of his popularity with the triumphs of *Les Cloches de Corneville* and Farnie's musical version of *Rip van Winkle.*

The enormous London success of *Rip* made the new *Nell Gwynne* a much awaited event. Produced by Alexander Henderson with Florence St John starring as Nell, D'Oyly Carte tenor Lyn Cadwaladr as Rochester, Giulia Warwick (the original Constance of *The Sorcerer*) as Jessamine and with two outstanding comic stars, Lionel Brough and Arthur Roberts, heading the comedy, it proved to be a pretty if slightly patchy piece, with Miss St John's "Only an Orange Girl" and Miss Warwick's little Song of the Clock more effective than the comical material of the score. The show lasted only a disappointing 86 performances in London, and though it was subsequently toured and produced in a number of other countries, it never established itself in the revivable repertoire in the way that *Rip van Winkle* had done or that *Dorothy* would.

As the latest work by the composer of *Les Cloches de Corneville,* the show quickly made its way to other centers and none more quickly than America, for, trusting to the fact that the libretto was an adaptation, and to the (lack of) copyright laws regarding published foreign material, the Uhrig's Cave summer theatre in St Louis leaped in (30 June 1884) and presented a *Nell Gwynne* that they claimed was Planquette's (non-copyright) music, attached not to Farnie's (copyright) text, but a fresh adaptation allegedly done by manager Charles Ford of the original *Rochester.* Blanche Champan played Nell, and advised parties of course noticed many a similarity with Farnie that was not in Moncrieff. The piece was picked up by some other summer troupes as *The Orange Girl.*

America's official Nell was Mathilde Cottrelly (but only for 38 performances), when John McCaull got *Nell Gwynne* on the stage in New York a few months later. Although the piece did not make a success on Broadway, it continued to win productions around the country and as late as 1901 (6 May), when the shoestring Maud Daniels Opera Company brought the show back to New York for a showing at Koster and Bial's.

Maurice Ordonneau and Émile André's French version simply dropped Mistress Gwynne (the French probably hadn't heard of her, anyway) from the show and called it and her, as played by Juliette Darcourt, *La Princesse Colombine* (19 performances). The Germans got even dizzier and made her into *Prinzessin Pirouette,* whilst the Hungarians—who obviously hadn't heard of Mistress Gwynne either, but who apparently liked her a little more—kept a touch closer to the original by calling Ilka Pálmay "The Countess of the Stage." However, by and large, it was India (Corinthian Theatre, Calcutta 20 March 1885) that seemed to like this particular piece the most, and that may have been because the Nell they got was the incisive American soprano and actress Emilie Melville. *Nell Gwynne* outdid more generally favored pieces in the large Melville touring-the-Orient repertoire, and it proved the hit of her otherwise very iffy eastern tour. She subsequently introduced her Nell to Australia.

All these switches of its heroine's identity came from the fact that the Farnie libretto had very little to do with even the more apocryphal details of the life of the semi-mythologized British actress and royal mistress. Her name was simply tacked on to the piece and its leading lady to give the show a nice, recognizably catchy title. The book followed the lines of Moncrieff's *Rochester* (Olympic Theatre, 1818), itself an adaptation from the French *L'Exil de Rochester* and already set to fresh music in America under the title *Fast Men of Olden Time* for the Boston Museum in 1860. This tale simply told of the discomforting of a couple of overbold courtly gentlemen who mistake a lady for an easy country lass and suffer her revenge.

Several other musicals that have portrayed Mistress Gwyn(ne) got little closer to what historical fact exists. José Collins starred as *Our Nell* (Gaiety Theatre 16 April 1924) in a piece that had originally been called *Our Peg* and originally presented her as Peg Woffington, and singer-songwriter Jackie Trent appeared as the sexy orange seller in a *Nell!* by John Worth and Philip Mackie produced at London's Richmond Theatre in 1970 (8 April). Cabaret vocalist Dorothy Squires threatened London with her own Nell Gwynne musical at one stage, but it got no further than a demonstration of its songs at the Dominion Theatre. Other briefly lived Nells included H T Arden and W H C Nation's ''new musical extravaganza'' *Nell Gwynne,* which survived 48 performances at its wealthy composer's expense at the Royalty Theatre, London, in 1871, and a one-act burlesque *Nell Go-In* composed by A Baldwin Sloane with Mabel Fenton as Nell, which was seen momentarily on Broadway in 1899 (New York Theater 31 October).

A highly successful character on the straight stage in the hands of Julia Neilson and others (*Sweet Nell of Old Drury*), Mistress Gwynne has singularly failed to appeal as the heroine of musical plays.

USA: Uhrig's Cave Garden, St Louis 30 June 1884; Casino Theater, New York 8 November 1884; Australia: Opera House, Melbourne 17 July 1886; France: Théâtre des Nouveautés *La Princesse Colombine* 7 December 1886; Hungary: Népszínház *Komedias hercegnő* 15 April 1887; Germany: Friedrich-Wilhelmstädtisches Theater *Prinzessin Pirouette* 7 December 1889

NELSON, Rudolf [LEWYSOHN, Rudolf] (b Berlin, 8 April 1878; d Berlin, 5 February 1960).

Pianist, accompanist and vocalist Nelson was a pioneering songs-at-the-piano performer in Berlin cabaret, composing much of his own material (''little Frenchified tunes'') as well as supplying a vast number of pieces to other performers. He continued throughout his life and career to perform in cabaret and later to run his own cabaret venues; at the same time he composed a considerable amount of music for revue, at first for for the Metropoltheater and later for his own house, as well as for musical comedies and for Operetten. One Operette, *Miss Dudelsack,* was well enough received in Berlin to later win productions not only in Austria and Hungary but also in America. His longest-running piece on home ground, however, was the wartime *Blaue Jungens,* which was played for six months at the Theater am Nollendorfplatz.

In 1914 Nelson opened his own Berlin theatre, the Nelson-Theater, where he was for a number of years director, author, composer and pianist, and he had a second spell as a Berlin manager in the early 1930s with a revue theatre. At the coming of National Socialism he moved to Zürich and to Amsterdam, still continuing to perform through his sixties and into his seventies, and even after his return to Berlin in 1949 he was seen on television and in his revue-concert ''Rudolf Nelson spielt,'' remaining active almost to the end of his days.

Nelson's music exported to mainly revue productions in other countries, but his name made an unaccustomed appearance on a southern-hemisphere playbill when it was writ large as the co-composer of a musical called *The Honeymoon Girl* mounted at Fuller's Theatre, Sydney (23 May) in 1925. Quite what of Nelson's music had been borrowed is unclear, for *The Honeymoon Girl* was a disguised version of the London show *Oh! Julie* of half a decade earlier, of which the nominal composers were Herman Darewski and H Sullivan Brooke. Originally, anyhow.

1903 **Die Herren Söhne** (Leo Walther Stein) Berliner Theater

1906 **Das bummelnde Berlin** (Benno Jacobson) Apollotheater 10 March

1908 **Principessa** (Fritz Grünbaum, Georg Burghard) Residenz-Theater, Frankfurt-am-Main 1 May

1909 **Miss Dudelsack** (Grünbaum, Heinz Reichert) Neues Schauspielhaus 3 August

1911 **Hoheit amusiert sich** (Julius Freund) Metropoltheater 29 April

1912 **Schwindelmeyer & Cie** (*The Arcadians*) new score for German version w Freund Metropoltheater 27 April

1914 **Der Krumel vor Paris** (Franz Cornelius) Residenz-Theater 13 October

1915 **Neueste Nachtrichten** (Cornelius, Willi Prager) Kristallpalast, Leipzig 1 January

1915 **Mufflick und Bimse** (Julius Winckelmann) Viktoria-Theater, Breslau 1 October

1915 **Verheiratet Junggesellen** (Arthur Lippschitz) Trianon-Theater 27 December

1916 **Blaue Jungens** (Hermann Frey/Hermann Haller, Kurt Kraatz) Theater am Nollendorfplatz 25 August

1917 **Neptune auf Reisen** (Franz Arnold, Ernst Bach) Apollotheater January

1918 **Inkognito** (*Der Damenkrieg*) (Kraatz, Richard Kessler) Berlin Kammerspiele 4 June; Theater des Westens 5 August

1921 **Das Prachtmädel** (Leo Walther Stein) Schillertheater, Berlin-Charlottenburg 10 July

1923 **Die Damen von Olymp** (Rudolf Schanzer, Ernst Welisch) Nelson-Theater May

1928 **Weisst du was?—wir heiraten!** (Franz Landry, Richard Rillo) Neues Theater am Zoo 21 December

NEMESIS, or Not Wisely But Too Well Bouffonnerie musicale by H B Farnie based on *Les Deux Noces de M Boisjoli* by Alfred Duru. Music selected and arranged by John Fitzgerald. Strand Theatre, London, 17 April 1873.

The most successful of the many pasticcio musicals expertly cobbled together from mostly French comic and music sources by the free-stealing Farnie for the London theatre, *Nemesis* combined a version of Alfred Duru's 1872 Palais-Royal comedy *Les Deux Noces de M Boisjoli* with a score borrowed from various stage works by Hervé, Delibes, Lecocq, Victor Robillard, Léon Vasseur, Émile Jonas and Adolphe Lindheim to make up what was really an equivalent of a French pasticcio vaudeville: a genuine "musical comedy."

The story of the piece dealt with the aptly named Calino (Edward Terry)—the Boisjoli of Duru's original—who determines on one last flirtation before settling down to the married life that is scheduled for him. The trouble is that he gets in a little deep, and he finds that he is "promised"—nay wed—to two ladies. Worse, the two ladies are the daughters of two neighbors, the retired butter maker Putiphar Patoche (Harry Cox) and the fire-breathing, oath-spouting military Major Roland de Ronceveaux Ramponneau (Claude Marius). And just to complicate things further, whilst he has wooed and wed Rosalie Ramponneau (Angelina Claude) under his real name, his amours with Praline Patoche (Nellie Bromley) have been conducted under the name of his friend Zidore de Filoselle (Maria Jones). Of course, it is this latter who, by the incontrovertible law of French farce, finally takes the spare wife off our hero's hands, but only after five scenes of bristling comedy and no less than 18 musical numbers from which Calino's "The Language of Love" and Rosalie's Tickling Song proved the pick. Sallie Turner featured as Praline's comically super-sentimental spinster aunt Turlurette.

Nemesis succeeded Farnie's version of *Geneviève de Brabant* as the musical hit of its time, and its only concession to the arrival of the all-conquering *La Fille de Madame Angot* was to begin advertising itself as an opéra-bouffe. An enormous run of 262 London performances was followed by revivals in 1874, 1875, 1876 and 1878, and the publishing house of J B Cramer made bold enough to publish all but two of the numbers that made up the pilfered score. The exceptions were two pieces with music "borrowed" from *La Fille de Madame Angot.*

By the time of an 1885 revival, with a cast including Arthur Roberts, Claude Marius and Lottie Venne, the score had, for the benefit of the first named, been augmented with the Geographical Love Song called "Grab," "Troubadour," what was called Tosti's "Goodbye and Go" and "S'm' Other Evening."

Tenor, director and would-be producer Henry Bracy purchased the overseas rights to *Nemesis* and took it in his baggage to the colonies, where it was produced at the Melbourne Opera House with Charles Lascelles, George Leopold, Alice Wooldridge and John Dunn featured. It served Bracy well enough on this first Australian visit for him to repeat it in 1878 and again as late as 1890. Bracy was also responsible for introducing the piece to America when he and his wife appeared in the musical under the direction of Fred Lyster in San Francisco in 1876. It was subsequently picked up by the local Tivoli Opera House, and a few years further down the line was given a further showing (advertised as "for the first time in this country") under the title *Calino* (Globe Theater, Boston 20 September 1880) in the repertoire of Edward Rice's touring New Extravaganza Company. Charles Groves was Calino, Pauline Hall Zidore, Louisa Searle Rosalie and George K Fortesque played Aunt Turlurette in skirts.

A Lebensbild mit Gesang also entitled *Nemesis,* written by O F Berg and composed by Adolf Müller, was produced at Vienna's Theater an der Wien, 23 October 1869, and ran for 20 performances. A Viennese adaptation of *Les Deux Noces de M Boisjoli* was mounted at the Carltheater (5 April 1873) under the title of *Zwei Hochzeiten und ein Brautigam* (mus: C F Conradin/ad Karl Treumann), with Karl Blasel as Boisjoli and Josef Matras as Quincampoix, just a fortnight before *Nemesis* appeared for the first time on the stage in London.

Australia: Opera House, Melbourne 2 February 1874; USA: Baldwin's Theater, San Francisco 4 September 1876

NESTROY, [Nepomuc] Johann (b Vienna, 7 December 1801; d Graz, 25 May 1862). Celebrated actor, playwright and producer of the mid-19th-century Viennese stage.

Nestroy made his debut as an actor in 1822, and appeared at a very young age as Sarastro in *Der Zauberflöte* at the Vienna Opera. He worked in Amsterdam, Brünn and Graz and from 1831 at the Theater an der Wien, where many of his most important works as a playwright were given their premieres. These included a long list of musical Possen such as *Tritsch-Tratsch* (20 November 1833), *Eulenspiegel* (22 April 1835), *Zu ebener Erde und im ersten Stock* (24 September 1835), *Die beiden Nachtwandler* (6 May 1836), *Der verhängnisvolle Faschingsnacht* (13 April 1839), *Der Talisman* (16 December 1840), *Das Mädel aus der Vorstadt* (24 November 1841) and *Der Zerissene* (9 April 1844), burlesques such as *Nagerl und Handschuh* (23 March 1832), *Zamperl der Tagdieb* (22 June 1832) and *Robert der Teuxel* (9 October

Plate 277. **Johann Nestroy's** Lumpacivagabundus, *remusicalized by Robert Stolz as* Drei von der Donau, *is seen here at the Dresden Staatsoperette, with Thomas Georgi (Leim), Frithjof Hoffmann (Knieriem), Werner Knodel (Zwirn) and Gottfried Neumann (Hausierer).*

1833) and Zauberspiele and Zauberpossen, including his famous [*Der böse Geist*] *Lumpacivagabundus* (11 April 1833). He subsequently supplied a number of pieces to the Theater in der Leopoldstadt, where his other most celebrated play, *Einen Jux will er sich machen* (15 January 1842), and his Wagner burlesque *Der fliegende Holländer zu Fuss* (4 August 1846) were both initially staged, and to other theatres (*Tannhäuser-Parodie,* etc), being eventually credited with a total of more than 60 works produced on the Viennese stage.

Between 1854 and 1860 Nestroy was the director of the Carltheater, where, with the collaboration of Karl Treumann, he mounted the first series of Offenbach productions to be seen in Vienna in the German language: *Die Hochzeit bei Laternenscheine, Das Mädchen von Elisonzo* (1858), *Schuhflicker und Millionär, Die Zaubergeige, Die Savoyarden, Der Ehemann vor der Türe* (1859) and *Tschin-Tschin* (1860), as well as the earliest attempt by a local writer and composer to follow in the same style—Conradin's *Flodoardo Wuprahall* (1859). In 1860 he adapted, mounted and starred in the first full-length opéra-bouffe production in Vienna, *Orpheus in der Unterwelt,* appearing in the show as a Jupiter written up like a meneur de revue, with a parade of topical jokes to hand.

After giving up the Carltheater, he appeared for a season at Treumann's little Theater am Franz-Josefs-Kai, where he played the part of Pan in a specially rearranged version of Offenbach's *Daphnis und Chloë,* and in his own adaptation of *Vent du soir* as *Häuptling Abendwind* (1 February 1862) in the last months before his death.

Many of Nestroy's works, virtually all of which were originally played with the accompaniment of music and songs, have been rearranged and remusicked over the years, but it is *Einen Jux will er sich machen* that has come down to modern times the most effectively, as an ancestor of the record-breaking musical *Hello, Dolly! Lumpacivagabundus* was also musicalized for the American stage, although with altogether less success, as *Gods and Men* (Academy of Music, Washington, DC 2 March 1891; J T Pratt/Max Knauer, Emil Wolff).

Nestroy himself became the hero of a couple of bio-musicals, one written by Bruno Zappert to a pasticcio score and produced at Graz, where Nestroy had had some of his earliest stage works played in the late 1820s (*Johann Nestroy* 17 January 1885), and the second a Singspiel mounted, even more aptly, at the Carltheater in 1918 (4 December). A M Willner and Rudolf Österreicher's libretto was set to an arrangement of old Viennese melodies made by Ernst Reiterer, and Willy Thaller portrayed Nestroy.

Biography: Preisner, M: *Johann Nepomuk Nestroy* (Hanser, Munich, 1968)

NESVILLE, Juliette [LESLE, Juliette] (b Paris, ?1870; d Paris, 26 July 1900). Heroine of several Paris, London and New York musicals during a very brief career.

Daughter of a Parisian restaurateur, Mlle Lesle was convent-raised in France and in Clapham before going on to study music. Shortly after graduating from the Paris Conservatoire, she was cast in the title role of the Parisian premiere of Paul Lacome's *Ma mie Rosette* (1890). She went on to appear at the Porte-Saint-Martin in *Jeanne d'Arc,* in revivals of *La Fille de l'air* (1890, Azurine) and *Gilette de Narbonne* and in *L'Égyptienne* (1890, Djemileh) and in 1891 was taken first to Brussels and then to London, where she starred as the modest, teen-aged heroine of the local versions of the Paris hit *Miss Helyett* (1891, *Miss Decima*). Mlle Nesville repeated her *Ma mie Rosette* role at London's Globe Theatre (1892) and at the Criterion in a revival of *La Fille de Madame Angot* (1893, t/o Clairette), before being signed up by George Edwardes.

She began with Edwardes in the London and Broadway original casts of *A Gaiety Girl* (1893), playing the French maid who causes the trouble that constitutes the plot (''When Your Pride Has Had a Tumble''), appeared as Nedda in the burlesque *A Pal o' Archies* (1893) at the Palace, took over as Madame Amélie in *An Artist's Model* (1895), and had the role of Juliette, the social-climbing French interpreter in *The Geisha* (1896, ''If That's Not Love, What Is?''). The following year a role—Juliette Belleville—was written into *In Town* when she was hired as a member of the company, which belatedly took this show to America, and in 1898 she played in the little vaudeville *An Old Muff* with her *Gaiety Girl* partner Maud Hobson at the Alhambra, and starred opposite Arthur Roberts in the tryout of *Campano,* before returning to Paris in 1899. She played in a revival of *Le Voyage de Corbillon* (1899) and took the title role in the vaudeville-opérette *Madame Pistache* at the Folies-Dramatiques (1899, Nina), revisited Brussels, and was rehearsing for her next role, in *Mariage Princier,* when she died suddenly at what seems to have been no more than 30 years of age.

THE NEW BARMAID Musical play in 2 acts by Frederick Bowyer and W Edwards Sprange. Music by John Crook. Opera House, Southport, 1 July 1895; Avenue Theatre, London, 12 February 1896.

Specially constructed for the British touring circuits, *The New Barmaid* was a musical comedy that told the twin tales of the reversal of the fortunes of two comical brothers (Arthur Alexander, J B Montague) and of the efforts of the aptly named Captain Lovebury (Wilfred Howard) to fend off a breach-of-promise suit from Brenda, the plotting ex-barmaid of his club (Reika Ronalds), so that he can wed her replacement, Ethel Joy (Amy Augarde). Ethel Joy, so it turns out, is actually a long-lost heiress.

The low comedy of the White brothers, the nice one rising from menial tasks to riches and the other not-so-nice one going the opposite way, and some lively musical numbers provided a very solid backbone for the entertainment, with the topical ''A Little Bit of Sugar for the Bird'' becoming a major hit, and other pieces such as ''Mother Was the Mother of Us Both,'' ''Just Bread and Cheese and Kisses'' and the satirical ''The Lady Journalist'' also proving very popular. Brought to town, and cast with Lottie Collins, J J Dallas and John Shine in its leading roles, *The New Barmaid* had a troubled run (138 performances) in two theatres before returning to its natural habitat on the road. There it trouped virtually nonstop for considerably more than a decade, playing thousands of performances through Britain and the colonies. One company, sent out by Alexander Loftus in 1904, with himself in the chief comic part, toured for 130 weeks with only one short break. The writers of *The New Barmaid* later potted their show as a music-hall item (Empire, Holloway 16 November 1903), and Loftus also manufactured another little variety musical from the show, which, as *Bill's Brother* (Bedford Music Hall 20 June 1910), he played in the music halls between continued stints as Bertie White in ''Miss Violet Osmund's company in the revised version'' of *The New Barmaid.*

The New Barmaid was introduced to Australia by John F Sheridan, who put aside the skirts of his famous Widow O'Brien and appeared as William White in seasons in Melbourne and Sydney (Lyceum 22 December 1900) before moving on to other frocked and unfrocked roles. But America, which at this period in time was snatching up even the most unlikely of British musical plays for importation, somehow, incomprehensibly, seems to have missed this hugely successful one.

Australia: Theatre Royal, Melbourne 3 February 1900, Criterion Theatre, Sydney *The Lady Barmaid* 31 January 1903

NEW GIRL IN TOWN Musical in 2 acts by George Abbott based on *Anna Christie* by Eugene O'Neill. Music and lyrics by Bob Merrill. 46th Street Theater, New York, 14 May 1957.

Eugene O'Neill's darkly dramatic play *Anna Christie* (Vanderbilt Theater 2 November 1921, 177 performances) had for its heroine a young woman who has known a parentless youth, rape by a relative and life as a prostitute before returning to New York to find her father and to doubtfully share with him his life as a bargee. She finds something cleansing in the sea, but when she meets a man she could love, and who would marry her, she has to complete that cleansing by revealing all her story to both her lover and her father. Then it is their turn to take once more to the sea, taking their thoughts with them, whilst Anna waits at home to see what will become of them all.

Highly praised, and the recipient of a Pulitzer Prize, *Anna Christie* might have been material for an operatic adaptation, but it seemed scarcely suitable as the source of a 1950s Broadway musical comedy. In fact, what became *New Girl in Town* began life trying to be a film, MGM having planned, shortly after O'Neill's death, to issue a musical version of the already twice-filmed (once with Garbo) piece with a Bob Merrill score. The film project—with Doris Day slated as its heroine—went the way of a lot of other film projects, but the idea stayed alive and found its way to George Abbott, who found his way to producers Freddie Brisson, Hal Prince and Robert E Griffith, who found the way to get the rights out of MGM and finally to get the show on to the stage.

They were, of course, playing with critical fire in putting a set of period pastiche songs and, above all, dances into what was still a recent dramatic success, but the show that eventuated, whilst sharing little with the original play but its main story line, was by no means incongruous to, at least, those who were not acquainted with O'Neill's play. The drama was recolored and reset amongst traditional musical-comedy elements and songs; Abbott and choreographer Bob Fosse were at the helm, and dancing actress Gwen Verdon, equipped with enough appeal to wow the O out of O'Neill and a rare pair of feet, played Anna. The result was a show with some considerable charms, most of which were dancing ones (''At the Check Apron Ball,'' ''There Ain't No Flies on Me''). The ones that weren't were in the hands of Thelma Ritter, who shared top-billing with Miss Verdon (the men were dumped below the title) in the low-comedy role of Anna's father's rough-and-tough mate (''Flings,'' ''Chess and Checkers''). *New Girl in Town* had sufficient attractions to run 432 performances, which was considerably more than *Anna Christie* had done on its first run, but it didn't win a Pulitzer Prize and there was no second run.

Recording: original cast (RCA)

NEWLEY, Anthony (b London, 24 September 1931; d Jensen Beach, Fla, 14 April 1999). Heavily mannered British actor and vocalist who later turned to mostly nightclub and cabaret entertaining.

Newley began his career as a juvenile actor, playing a memorable Artful Dodger in the 1948 film of *Oliver Twist,* and made his first adult stage appearance in the revue *Cranks.* In the 1950s he won success in all quarters, featuring in several successful British films and also finding fame as a popular vocalist as he reached the top of the hit parades with ''Why?'' and ''Do You Mind'' and placed three other numbers in the top 10 within a space of two years. He consolidated his success on British television (*The World of Gurney Slade*) and, then, at age 29, returned to the theatre as the star and director of the musical comedy *Stop the World—I Want to Get Off,* a little fable of one man's existence that he had himself written and composed in collaboration with Leslie Bricusse. *Stop the World* gave Newley, in what was almost a solo show, a grand success both in London and on Broadway, and launched several strong songs of the heartfelt variety towards the hit parades and cabaret circuits (''What Kind of Fool Am I,'' ''Once in a Lifetime''). In a career in which everything he attempted seemed to succeed, he also joined Bricusse in penning the title song for the James Bond film *Goldfinger* (1964).

A second show, *The Roar of the Greasepaint . . . the Smell of the Crowd,* written on similar lines to the first, closed on the road in Britain (with Norman Wisdom starring) to be remounted on Broadway with Newley featured in a role that echoed his *Stop the World* character through a fair 232 performances. However, if the show's stage life was limited, Newley and Bricusse's score again produced more than the usual quota of durable songs, and this time the tortured ballads (''Who Can I Turn To?,'' ''The Joker'') were complemented by the positive bounce of ''Nothing Can Stop Me Now'' and by ''On a Wonderful Day Like Today,'' a song destined to top the repertoire of what seemed like every holiday camp and pantomime artist for the next two decades.

Newley then disappeared from the theatre into the world of nightclubs, but he emerged again in 1972 as author, director and star of a third show, *The Good Old, Bad Old Days,* written on the same lines as the earlier ones.

The shallowly philosophizing style that had suited the 1960s seemed rather risible in the 1970s, Newley had turned himself into a braying caricature of his cockily abrasive old persona, and many of the new show's songs seemed like burlesques of their predecessors. *The Good Old, Bad Old Days* was shepherded through nine months in London before Newley returned to the cabaret circuits. He later reemerged to appear in an American musical based on the life of Charlie Chaplin, which stopped short of Broadway, to briefly bring *Stop the World* back to London (1989) and to feature in a stage musical version of *Scrooge* (Birmingham 1992, London 1996).

In 1978 a compilation show made up of Newley/Bricusse numbers was unsuccessfully produced in London under the title *The Travelling Music Show.*

1961 **Stop the World—I Want to Get Off** (w Leslie Bricusse) Queen's Theatre 20 July

1964 **The Roar of the Greasepaint . . . the Smell of the Crowd** (w Bricusse) Theatre Royal, Nottingham 3 August; Shubert Theater, New York 16 May 1965

1972 **The Good Old, Bad Old Days** (w Bricusse) Prince of Wales Theatre 20 December

1978 **The Travelling Music Show** (w Bricusse) Her Majesty's Theatre 28 March

1983 **Chaplin** (w Stanley Ross) Music Center Pavilion, Los Angeles 12 August

NEWMAN, [Herbert John] Greatrex (b Manchester, 3 July 1892; d Eastbourne, 27 January 1984).

The writer of sketches, scenarios and lyrics for many revues from 1914 onwards (*The Passing Show, Joy-Bells, The Punch Bowl* etc) and writer for and sometime proprietor of the long-flourishing concert parties The Co-Optimists and The Fol de Rols, Newman also wrote occasionally for the book musical stage. He supplied additional lyrics for the musicals *Patricia* (1924) and *The Blue Kitten* (1925), additional scenes in *Lady Luck* (1927), had his concert-party song ''Murders'' interpolated to fine effect in Broadway's and London's versions of *Tonight's the Night* and contributed to the remaking of an unspecified Arnold and Bach play and the 1912 Broadway musical *The Man from Cook's* as the short-lived *The Girl from Cook's* (1927) before scoring his major musical stage success as co-librettist and co-lyricist of *Mr Cinders* (1928). A second piece in similar vein, *Mr Whittington* (1933), also had a successful London run, but his last musical comedy, *Love Laughs—!,* was a failure.

Newman died at the age of 91 during the run of a successful revival of *Mr Cinders* (1982), for which he and composer Vivian Ellis had written an additional number.

1927 **The Girl from Cook's** (Raymond Hubbell, Jean Gilbert/w R H Burnside) Gaiety Theatre 1 November

1928 **Mr Cinders** (Vivian Ellis, Richard Myers/w Clifford Grey) Opera House, Blackpool 25 September; Adelphi Theatre 11 February 1929

1933 **Mr Whittington** (John Green, Joseph Tunbridge, Jack Waller/w Grey, Douglas Furber) Alhambra, Glasgow 30 November, London Hippodrome 1 March 1934

1935 **Love Laughs—!** (ex- *Leave It to Love*) (Noel Gay/w Grey) London Hippodrome 25 June

THE NEW MOON Romantic musical play in 2 acts by Oscar Hammerstein II, Frank Mandel and Laurence Schwab. Music by Sigmund Romberg. Chestnut Street Opera House, Philadelphia, 22 December 1927; Imperial Theater, New York (revised version), 19 September 1928.

The team responsible for that overwhelming hit of 1926, *The Desert Song,* mined a similar vein for their next collaboration, *The New Moon,* a romantic operetta set in the *Naughty Marietta* precincts of 18th-century New Orleans. In contrast to *Naughty Marietta,* this time it was the leading man, Robert Misson, rather than the heroine who was on the run from Europe, having sold himself into colonial servitude to escape arrest for the murder of a royal rapist. He is engaged as steward in the home of the Beaunoir family, where he falls in love with the aristocratic Marianne and where, eventually, the French policeman Ribaud tracks him down. Misson pirates the ship taking him back to France and trial, and he and his anti-Royalist followers sail it to an unoccupied island. There they establish a new colony where all men are equal, except, of course, Robert Misson. When the French invade, however, it turns out that things have changed. They now represent not the bad old King but the nice new Republic. Marianne is expediently converted to being Citizeness Misson, Ribaud, refusing to bow to the mob, is condemned, and Misson, named Governor of his island (since Kings are now not allowed), settles down for a happy ending with his men and his Marianne.

The show was produced in Philadelphia, which had given such a tremendous welcome to Romberg's *My Maryland* earlier the same year, with Robert Halliday as Misson, Desirée Tabor (quickly replaced by Jessie Royce Landis) as Marianne, and William O'Neal (Philippe), William Wayne (Alexander), Margaret Irving (Madame Duchêne) and Walter Brennan as Girard, supporting. *The New Moon* did not win the same response that *My Maryland* had, and Schwab and Mandel decided to close the production down rather than to fiddle with it on what looked like a rocky road to town. For seven months *The New Moon* went back into the workshop, and Romberg, with the five other musicals on which he had worked during 1927 finally out of the way, devoted himself to rewriting his score. Out went Julie and Alexander's ''When I Close My Eyes'' and Robert and Marianne's '''Neath a New Moon'' (leaving the show's title now referring only to the name of a ship!), Marianne's ''La, la, la, la'' and ''A Voice in the Dark,'' Besace's sea shanties and ''Women, Women, Women,'' Robert's ''I Love You,'' Mme Duchêne's praises of ''Paris,'' ''I'm Just a Sentimental Fool'' and ''Liar,'' leaving the stirring march ''Shoulder to Shoulder'' (later rechristened ''Stout hearted Men'') and the comical ''Try Them Out at Dancing'' [*sic*] from the original set of songs to be supplemented with more than half a score of new music. The additions included the heroine's waltz ''One Kiss'' and the love song ''Lover, Come Back to Me,'' the soaring duet ''Wanting You'' and one of Romberg's and, certainly, of Hammerstein's most beautiful songs, ''Softly as in a Morning Sunrise,'' sung not by either of the stars but by the tenor Philippe, an accessory to Misson's crime who has turned ''republican'' through sexual jealousy, sighing, in his American exile, over all that his foolishness has lost him.

On 27 August 1928 the producers reopened the much-altered show in Cleveland (even though they were opening *Hold Everything!* at virtually the same time in Newark), with Evelyn Herbert (Marianne), Robert Halliday (Misson), William O'Neal (Philippe) and Max Figman (Ribaud) in the dramatic roles and Gus Shy heading the incidental comedy. Former D'Oyly Carte tenor Pacie Ripple played Beaunoir. In a few weeks *The New Moon* was on Broadway, and Schwab and Mandel's decision to stop and rewrite was fully justified. *The New Moon* effaced the disappointments of Romberg's *My Princess* and *The Love Call,* scored a splendid success and finished by totting up an even longer Broadway run than *The Desert Song* with a total of 509 performances at the Imperial Theater.

Before even Broadway's production had closed, *The New Moon* was mounted at London's Theatre Royal, Drury Lane, following behind *Rose Marie, The Desert Song* and *Show Boat* at what had become the headquarters of the best of Broadway operetta in the West End. Howett Worster (Misson), Evelyn Laye (Marianne), Ben Williams (Philippe), Edmund Willard (Ribaud) and Gene Gerrard (Gus) headed the cast with Vera Pearce as Clotilde, but *The New Moon* proved not to have the same attractions for London as the previous pieces had had. It lasted only 148 performances and marked the theatre's first failure with an American musical spectacular play. Paris, which similarly saw the show in the wake of *Show Boat* (rechristened *Mississippi for France*), gave a warmer welcome to a version more explicitly retitled *Robert le Pirate* (ad Albert Willemetz). Here the figures were reversed, and *Robert le Pirate,* with the rising baritone André Baugé starred alongside the striking soprano Danielle Brégis and the comic Bach, played 237 times on the

Plate 278. **The New Moon.** *The French got it right; by the time the rewrites were done, ''Robert the Pirate'' was a much better title for the show.*

Châtelet's vast stage where the disappointing *Mississippi* had been seen just 115 times.

Like Britain, Australia reacted slightly disappointingly to *The New Moon,* especially given the huge local popularity of *The Desert Song.* J C Williamson Ltd's production, starring *The Desert Song*'s hero Lance Fairfax, Marie Bremner (Marianne), Frederick Bentley (Gus), Herbert Browne (Philippe) and Vera Spaull (Clotilde), played only a single Sydney season before it was replaced by a revival of *The Belle of New York.* Sydney Burchall took over as Misson for seven weeks in Melbourne (Theatre Royal 19 July 1930).

However, *The New Moon* and, most especially, its music were still destined to be received as classics throughout the English-speaking world, and, as in the case of *Naughty Marietta,* it was the cinema that was largely responsible for this. The first film version, with Grace Moore and Lawrence Tibbett starring, Adolphe Menjou as the Governor and Gus Shy, Roland Young and

Emily Fitzroy at the head of the comedy, used only a little of Romberg's score attached to a wholly different story that transported the action to the Caspian Sea and turned Marianne into yet another Princess and Robert into yet another hussar. She got to sing ''Lover Come Back to Me.'' However, a Nelson Eddy–Jeanette MacDonald movie of 1940 returned to a version much more like the stage show and found much more success. Eddy and Miss MacDonald imprinted their performances on the material and ensured *The New Moon* regular future productions—beginning with performances at Carnegie Hall (18 August 1942) and the New York City Center (17 May 1944)—which have continued, largely in regional and amateur circumstances, to the present day. The New York City Opera's production was televised in 1989.

The title *The New Moon* was previously used for an ''operatic fancy'' by R André and Isidor de Solla produced at the Savoy Hotel, London, 6 February 1893, with Richard Temple amongst the cast.

UK: Theatre Royal, Drury Lane 4 April 1929; France: Théâtre du Châtelet *Robert le Pirate* 20 December 1929; Australia: Her Majesty's Theatre, Sydney 4 January 1930

Films: MGM 1930, MGM 1940

Recordings: selections (Decca, RCA Victor, Columbia, Capitol, World Record Club), etc

NEWTON, H[enry] Chance [CHANCE, Henry] (b London, 13 March 1854; d London, 2 January 1931). Librettist for the Victorian burlesque stage.

After early experience as an actor, Newton became a journalist and for many years wrote slightly arch criticism and theatre gossip columns for, in particular, *The Referee* (as ''Carados''), *The Sketch* and *The New York Dramatic Mirror* (as ''Gawain''). Under the pseudonym ''Richard Henry,'' he collaborated with the editor of *The Referee,* Richard Butler, on the libretti for a number of burlesques, notably the Gaiety piece *Monte Cristo Jr,* which was amongst the earliest successes of the new burlesque era under George Edwardes. He also supplied the texts for several touring shows including vehicles for Vesta Tilley (*Cartouche & Co,* a burlesque of *Mam'zelle Nitouche*) and Marie Lloyd (*The ABC*), and later for sketches for the music halls, without ever equaling his first Gaiety success.

Alongside a book of memoirs, Newton wrote a music-hall history, *Idols of the Halls.*

1883 **Giddy Godiva, or The Girl That Was Sent to Coventry** (pasticcio) Astley's Theatre 13 October

1886 **Monte Cristo Jr** (W Meyer Lutz, et al/w Richard Butler) Gaiety Theatre 23 December

1887 **Jubilation** (Ivan Caryll, Henry J Leslie/w Butler) 1 act Prince of Wales Theatre 14 May

1887 **Frankenstein** (Lutz/w Butler) Gaiety Theatre 24 December

1889 **Lancelot the Lovely** (John Crook/w Butler) Avenue Theatre 22 April

1892 **Opposition** (Caryll/w Butler) 1 act Lyric Theatre 28 June

1892 **Cartouche & Co, or The Ticket of French Leave** (George Le Brunn) Theatre Royal, Birmingham 22 August

1893 **Weatherwise** (Ernest Ford) 1 act Lyric Theatre 29 November

1894 **Jaunty Jane Shore** (Crook/w Butler) Strand Theatre 2 April

1895 **The Newest Woman** (Georges Jacobi) 1 act Avenue Theatre 4 April

1895 **The House That Jack Built** (C E Howells) Opera Comique 24 December

1897 **The Maid of Athens** (F Osmond Carr/w Charles Edmund Pearson) Opera Comique 3 June

1898 **Much Ado About Something, or Beerbohm-Treelawney of the Wells** (sketch interpolated into *Dandy Dan, the Lifeguardsman*)

1898 **The ABC, or Flossie the Frivolous** (Granville Bantock, et al/w Butler) Grand Theatre, Wolverhampton 21 March

1901 **The Belle of Cairo** (F Kinsey Peile/revised libretto) Grand Theatre, Birmingham 25 November

1903 **His Fatal Beauty** (John Crook, Henry May, Jesse Williams/w Herbert Shelley, Walter Parke/Arthur Shirley) Metropole Theatre, Camberwell 27 April

1903 **Uncle Ned** (Clement Locknane/w Richard Coverley/Owen Trevine) Prince of Wales Theatre, Liverpool 11 May

1912 **Wellington** (John Neat/J P Harrington) 1 act Oxford Music Hall 22 January

Autobiography: *Cues and Curtain Calls* (John Lane/Bodley Head, London, 1927)

NICHOLAS, Paul [BEUSELINCK, Paul Oscar] (b Peterborough, 3 December 1944). Popular ever-young English performer turned producer through 30 years of musicals.

Paul Nicholas made his first appearance on the West End stage as Claude in London's production of *Hair* (1968) before being cast in the title role of the first British production of *Jesus Christ Superstar* (1972) and, in succession to Richard Gere, as Danny Zuko to the Sandy of Elaine Paige in London's version of *Grease* (1974). In a career that mixed stage appearances with film (*Tommy, Stardust, Lisztomania, Sergeant Pepper's Lonely Hearts Club Band*) and recording engagements (he made the British top 10 with ''Dancing with the Captain'' and ''Grandma's Party'' in 1976 and scored with ''Heaven on the Seventh Floor'' in America), Nicholas created his first musical roles as Talkative (and other characters) in *Pilgrim* (1975), a touring musicalization of Bunyan's *The Pilgrim's Progress,* and as the hero of the unfortunate successor to *The Rocky Horror Show, T Zee* (1976).

He had his most successful new role in 1981, when he created the part of the sleek, pop-singing puss, the Rum-Tum-Tugger, in *Cats,* and followed up as another

Plate 279. **Paul Nicholas** *as the Rum-Tum-Tugger.*

pop persona, the swinging minstrel with the ghastly girlfriend in Tim Rice and Stephen Oliver's *Blondel* (1983). However, a swelling television career that would establish him as one of the most popular adorable rogues of the British small screen meant that his stage appearances were, from then on, both more demanded and more limited. However, he appeared in Manchester and, later, in London as the Pirate King of *The Pirates of Penzance,* in London and in the provinces as Joe, the boyish hero of the revived *Charlie Girl,* as P T Barnum in a revival of the musical *Barnum* and as Don Lockwood in *Singin' in the Rain* (1995). In 1996 he appeared as Arthur in a Covent Garden festival revival of *Camelot,* and in 1998 featured in a Birmingham musical based on *A Tale of Two Cities.*

In 1992 Nicholas turned to producing and co-produced (w David Ian) a series of touring productions (*The Rocky Horror Show, Singin' in the Rain, Evita, Chess*) and, most notably, (w Robert Stigwood, David Ian) the 1993 London revival of *Grease* and the London Palladium mounting of *Saturday Night Fever* (1998), on the latter of which he, along with Stigwood and director/choreographer Arlene Phillips, took what appeared to be a co-libretto credit.

NICHOLLS, Harry [NICHOLLS, Henry Thomas] (b London, 1 March 1852; d Acton Hill, Mddx, 29 November 1926).

For many years a popular comedian and pantomime artist on the British stage, Nicholls spent the bulk of his acting career at the Theatre Royal, Drury Lane (''fourteen years principal comedian''), and at the Adelphi Theatre, but he had, in his early days on the stage, also appeared in burlesque (Frederick of Tellramund in *Little Lohengrin* 1881, Mrs Sinbad in *Sinbad* 1882, Gilbert Vaughan in *The Scalded Back* 1884, *Venus* 1890, etc) and played in comic opera on the London stage in Selina Dolaro's *La Périchole* (1879, Don Andrès). Alongside his performing career, Nicholls worked as a playwright, scoring a major hit with the comedy *Jane* (1890 ad w William Lestocq from his earlier little *Timson's Little Holiday* and allegedly from Desvallières *Prête-moi ta femme*) and further successes as the part-author of two of the most internationally played of the Gaiety Theatre musical comedies, *A Runaway Girl* and *The Toreador.* He also had a hand in a number of the Drury Lane pantomimes. In a busy and eclectic career, he also wrote a musical comedy played by the amateurs of the Bedford Park Club (*Another Girl,* mus: Cecil Cook 13 January 1904), composed many lyrics for both popular and show songs, and appeared at the Gaiety in the role of Hooker Pacha in *The Messenger Boy* (1900).

Jane was turned into a musical comedy in 1919 under the title *Baby Bunting* (Nat D Ayer/Clifford Grey/ Fred Thompson, Worton David) with some success, and it may very well have also been the basis of a pasticcio musical comedy called *Oh! Jemima,* which appeared in Melbourne, Australia, in 1913 with Nicholls's name attached to it and Carrie Moore as its star.

1898 **A Runaway Girl** (Ivan Caryll, Lionel Monckton/Aubrey Hopwood, Harry Greenbank/w Seymour Hicks) Gaiety Theatre 21 May

1901 **The Toreador** (Monckton, Caryll/Adrian Ross, Percy Greenbank/w James T Tanner) Gaiety Theatre 17 June

NIELSEN, Alice (b Nashville, Tenn, 7 June 1876; d New York, 8 March 1943). ''Winsome, mischievous, vivacious'' soprano star of 19th-century Broadway.

Alice Nielsen sang for several years as a church soloist in Kansas City and in various light-opera productions in California, appearing as Yum-Yum and La Périchole with Pike's Opera Company and in everything from *Satanella* to *Martha* at the San Francisco Tivoli (1895), before she joined joined the Bostonians (Boston Ideal Comic Opera Company) in 1896. She played Annabelle in *Robin Hood* and Nanette in Victor Herbert's *Prince Ananias* with the famous Boston-based company, and also created leading roles in Oscar Weil's *The Wartime Wedding* (1896), *Rip van Winkle* (1897, Minna) and, more significantly, in Herbert's *The Serenade* (1896, Yvonne). In *The Serenade,* however, she had to allow the center of attention to go to the Bostonians' much-loved contralto Jessie Bartlett Davis, and this did not fit with her ambitions. She swiftly split from the Bostonians, effectively if not immediately destroying a company that had been built up into America's finest light-opera troupe by taking a number of its performers with her, to form the Alice Nielsen Comic Opera Company.

With that company Miss Nielsen produced two new Victor Herbert works with herself in the starring roles. She played the dual lead role in *The Fortune Teller* (1898, ''she may not be the greatest soprano in the world, but she is the most fascinating'') successfully in both America and Britain, and if *The Singing Girl* (1899) was less popular, it still served her for a good season's touring in repertoire. Miss Nielsen then quit the light musical theatre to pursue a career in opera, where, under the aegis of impresario and inamorata Henry Russell, she found limited success in the lighter areas of the soprano repertoire (Zerlina, Norina, Susanna, Gilda, Mimi, Marguerite), apparently sharing a *Le nozze di Figaro* bill with Caruso on one occasion, appearing at San Carlo, Covent Garden and at the Metropolitan Opera House in 1909, but making the bulk of her operatic career under Russell in Boston.

She returned when that career was done to appear one last time on Broadway, under her own management, in the title role of the Rudolf Friml/Otto Harbach musical *Kitty Darlin'* in the 1917 season. The piece failed, and Miss Nielsen retired from the stage to a life as a doctor's wife.

NIESE, Hansi (b Vienna, 10 November 1875; d Vienna, 4 April 1934).

The most popular soubrette of the Viennese light comic stage for many years, the comical ''naïve'' Frln Niese was equally at home in straight or musical roles, which she mixed with considerable effect and great success during her years at the Raimundtheater (1893–98), at the Theater in der Josefstadt (1899 sq) and between times at other Viennese and Berlin houses run by her then husband, Josef Jarno.

She appeared in many musical Possen during her years at the Raimundtheater, mixing comedy and even occasionally drama with pieces such as the protean musical comedy *Das Blitzmädel* and co-starring on occasion with the visiting Girardi (*Der Schusterbub,* etc), but her most successful musical play creation was the part of Christl, the heroine of the Operette *Die Förster-Christl,* composed by her brother-in-law, Georg Jarno, and mounted by her husband at the Theater in der Josefstadt. She followed up in the Jarno brothers' *Das Musikantenmädel* (1910, Resel) and *Das Waschermädel* (1913, Betti), as well as in such other musical productions as *Die eiserne Jungfrau* (1911, Beate Binder), the oft-revived *Drei Paar Schuhe* (Leni), and Jarno's productions of Béla Zerkovitz's *Die Wundermühle* (1914, in a dual mother-and-daughter role as Josefa and Fritzi) and the Hungarian operett *Die Patronesse vom Nachtcafé* (1915, Marie Gangel). The musical part of her talent remained always an accessory to the comical, and in spite of her *Förster-Christl* success, she did not venture into the world of the Viennese Operette. In her second marriage Frln Niese became the Baroness Popper, whilst her daughter from her marriage to Jarno, Hansi Niese-Jarno, also took the stage for a small career prior to an early death.

THE NIGHT BOAT Musical comedy in 2 acts by Anne Caldwell based on *Le Contrôleur des wagons-lits* by Alexandre Bisson. Music by Jerome Kern. Liberty Theater, New York, 2 February 1920.

A light comedy, with touches of Kern's earlier *Very Good Eddie* in its shipboard setting and the duplicated names of its plotline, *The Night Boat* took its outline from Alexandre Bisson's internationally successful *Le Contrôleur des wagons-lits* (Théâtre des Nouveautés 11 March 1898), a piece that had been played in America in Madeleine Lucette Ryley's adaptation as *On and Off*

(Madison Square Theater 17 October 1898). John E Hazzard played the central Bob White who, in order to get a little respite from his wife's ever-present family, pretends that he is the captain of the Albany night boat (rather than the original's railway sleeping-car inspector), a ruse that allows him to get away ''to work'' in the evenings. Unfortunately, his wife's monstrous mother, Mrs Maxim (Ada Lewis), decides to check him out, and, accompanied by Mrs White (Stella Hoban) and her sister Barbara (Louise Groody), she books a ticket on the night boat. The second-act ride up the river—on which the real captain turns out to be called Robert White (Ernest Torrence)—provided a regulation ration of misunderstandings, flirtations and the opportunity for a jolly concert of favorite riverish songs from other musicals—Ivan Caryll's ''By the Saskatchewan'' (*The Pink Lady*), ''Congo Love Song'' (*Nancy Brown*), Paul Dresser's ''On the Banks of the Wabash'' (*Monte Carlo*), and Harry Tierney's ''M.I.S.S.I.S.S.I.P.P.I.'' (*Hitchy Koo, The Beauty Spot*)—as well as a round of speciality dances. These topped up effectively Kern's new first-act successes: the charming ''Whose Baby Are You?'' sung by the juvenile coupling of Miss Groody and Hal Skelly (Freddie), Miss Hoban's hit-worthy ''Left All Alone Again Blues'' and the pretty ensemble ''Good Night Boat.'' A melody that was later to be heard celebrating ''London, Dear Old London'' in Kern's British show *The Cabaret Girl,* here declared that ''Girls Are Like a Rainbow.'' An amusing novelty item had the chorus recapping the plot, some way into Act I, for the benefit of latecomers and rounding it off at the top of Act II for those who had to rush for early trains.

A splendid success through 38 weeks (313 performances) on Broadway, Charles Dillingham's production of *The Night Boat* was tumbled out of its New York home to let in the same producer's anticipated new hit, *The Half Moon.* Whilst *The Half Moon* flopped painfully, the ejected show moved on to several seasons of touring life in America. However, in spite of the announcement, in 1920, of a London production by Alfred Butt and William Boosey, *The Night Boat* did not cross either the Atlantic or the Pacific.

A NIGHT OUT Musical play in 2 acts by George Grossmith jr and Arthur Miller adapted from *L'Hôtel du Libre Échange* by Maurice Desvallières and Georges Feydeau. Lyrics by Clifford Grey. Music by Willie Redstone. Additional songs by Arthur Anderson and Melville Gideon, Cole Porter, R P Weston and Bert Lee, and Philip Braham. Winter Garden Theatre, London, 19 September 1920.

The Grossmith and Laurillard producing partnership continued with their successful recipe of turning French comedies into musicals (*Théodore & Cie, Les Dominos roses, Madame et son filleul*) by musicalizing the celebrated *L'Hôtel du Libre Échange* (aka *Hotel Paradiso* and, in its 1896 London production, *A Night Out*) for Leslie Henson and the rest of their Winter Garden Theatre team. Henson was the little Pinglet who takes his neighbor's neglected lady (Lily St John) out for the night and ends up in prison when their naughty hotel is raided. Fred Leslie (dupe), Davy Burnaby (heavy), Phyllis Monkman (maid) and Stella St Audrie (dragonistic wife) added to the essential comedy, assisted by some sparky songs (''The Hotel Pimlico,'' the Clifford Grey/Cole Porter ''Why Didn't We Meet Before?''), a burlesque of the then-popular Russian ballet, a caveman number about ''Bolshevik Love'' and some special material for Henson, through a highly successful 311-performance run prior to a three-year British and colonial touring life.

The Australian portion of that colonial life turned out to be quite a sensational one. *A Night Out* was first staged by J C Williamson Ltd in Melbourne with Maud Fane, Alfred Frith, Cecil Bradley, Cyril Ritchard and Madge Elliott featured in its cast, and there it ran a remarkable run of 18 weeks, a record second only to the all-time top recently set up there by *The Maid of the Mountains.* Moving on to Sydney (Her Majesty's Theatre 3 June 1922), the show confirmed its Melbourne run with a further three months of performances, and established itself as one of the most revivable in Williamson's repertoire of revivable pieces. As long as the fashion for comedy-based musicals lasted (and here it lasted longer than in most areas), *A Night Out* was regularly revived in Australia.

In spite of all this success, however, *A Night Out* flopped when it finally got to America. But the few Americans who saw it, saw it in a heavily remade form. Laurillard and Alex Aarons's production jettisoned almost the entire score (''Bolshevik Love'' and the Ragpickers Dance with its ballet burlesque remained) and replaced it with one by Vincent Youmans, freshly hot through *No, No, Nanette.* The producers imported British performers for the main roles, but the shine was taken off this when a visiting (unemployed) English actress sniffed in print—not without some justification—that she'd never heard of Mr Aarons's transatlantic ''stars.'' Norman Griffin, Henson's regular London cover, and Australian Toots Pounds were the principals, she getting to share ''Sometimes I'm Happy,'' the best song from the new score, with Frederick Lord in the two weeks before the show closed on the road.

Australia: Theatre Royal, Melbourne 21 January 1922; USA: Garrick Theater, Philadelphia 7 September 1925

NIMM MICH MIT! Operette in 3 acts by Heinrich von Waldberg and A M Willner based on the novel *His Offi-*

Plate 280. **A Night Out.** *It was all the maid's fault! Victorine (Phyllis Monkman) gets the pointed fingers of the police (E Graham), Mme Pinglet (Stella St Audrie), Pinglet (Leslie Henson), Matthieu (Davy Burnaby) and Maurice Paillard (Fred Leslie).*

cial Wife by Richard Henry Savage. Music by Hermann Dostal. Theater an der Wien, Vienna, 1 May 1919.

Nimm mich mit! was a Viennese musical-comedy remake of the tale related in Colonel Savage's vastly popular American spy novel, a book that had already been dramatized with great success for the German-language stage as a sensational drama by Hans Olden (*Die offizielle Frau,* Berliner Theater, but banned in Vienna) and by a number of others. This version starred Mizzi Günther as the seductive ''stranger'' who stands in for the stay-at-home wife of Franz Xaver Edelbrünner, President of the Society for Social Welfare in Vienna (Ernst Tautenhayn), on a trip to Russia, with all the expected complications and—given that the lady is actually a potential assassin—a few less expected ones too. Luise Kartousch appeared in breeches as Baron Boris Zofimov, a guards cadet, romancing sugar-magnate's daughter Sonia (Klara Karry), and Robert Nästlberger was the Russian Police Chief who gets caught up with the ''official wife'' both romantically and, when she turns out to be not what she seems, professionally. The title duet and Miss Günther's second-act waltz, ''Frauen aus Wien,'' were the principal musical successes of the piece, which was played 155 times at the Theater an der Wien and gave the elder Dostal his most significant success on the Viennese stage.

His Official Wife—which became *The Passport* in Britain, *Passe la grille!* in France, *Hivatalos feleség* in Hungary and so forth, in its dramatic form—was also used as the basis for the successful American musical *The Red Widow* (1911) and for Richard Kessler and Max Jungk's German musical comedy *Die offizielle Frau* (mus: Robert Winterberg), produced at Berlin's Theater am Nollendorfplatz on 23 December 1925.

NINA ROSA Musical play in 2 acts by Otto Harbach. Lyrics by Irving Caesar. Music by Sigmund Romberg. Forest Park Theater, St Louis, May 1930; Majestic Theater, New York, 20 September 1930.

A Peruvian love story in a fairly direct line of descent from *Rose Marie* and *Rio Rita, Nina Rosa* starred the original heroine of the latter show, Ethelind Terry (replacing Margaret Carlisle from the original St Louis open-air production), as the colorful foreigner of the title who ends up being paired off with the dashing American mining engineer Jack Haines (Guy Robertson) rather than a not-very-pleasant fellow South American called Pablo (Leonard Ceeley) at the end of a story of mining options and gold discovery, Inca ruins and horrid ambushes. Even the happier parts of Romberg's score, "Your Smiles, Your Tears" or "My First Love, My Last Love," were not in the same league as his previous year's *The New Moon* material, but they nevertheless provided an agreeable accompaniment to a huge 150-cast, 36-band, heavily scenic production.

Just fair runs on Broadway (137 performances)—where, once sufficient success had been established the producers' billing altered from "Milton I Shubert presents" to "the brothers Shubert present"—and in London (117 performances)—where Lee Ephraim teamed Miss Terry (later Helen Gilliland) with Geoffrey Gwyther and Robert Chisholm in his production at the Lyceum Theatre—were a prelude, however, to a considerable success in France (which had also liked *Rose-Marie* and, perhaps significantly, hadn't had *Rio Rita*). Staged with all the resources of Maurice Lehmann's Théâtre du Châtelet, the Paris production of *Nina Rosa* (ad André Mouëzy-Éon, Albert Willemetz) featured Sim-Viva, popular baritone André Baugé, comics Bach and Monique Bert, the Marche des Gauchos, 12 sets, 700 costumes, a car chase through the Andes in an LR4 Rosengart, and a vast amount of featured dances including a flamenco aux éventails, a marching drill, an exhibition rumba, a huge Inca ballet and even a children's dance. The production played no fewer than 710 performances, was brought back in 1936 (30 September) for a further 98 and established *Nina-Rosa* and such songs as "Les Femmes sont perfides," "Nina Rosa," "Toutes les roses" and "Un seul regard" in France in such a fashion that the show can still occasionally be seen or heard there today whilst it remains all but forgotten in its original language.

UK: Lyceum Theatre 7 July 1931; France: Théâtre du Châtelet 18 December 1931

NINE Musical in 2 acts by Arthur Kopit based on the screenplay *8 1/2* by Federico Fellini. Music and lyrics by Maury Yeston. 46th Street Theater, New York, 9 May 1982.

Guido Contini (Raul Julia) is a weakly macho Italian film director, a man who apparently has a sufficient reputation in his line of work for the fact that he has directed three successive failures not to prevent a producer from pursuing him to make a new movie. As the evening progresses, we see how the different sets of demands he encourages from the various women in his life allow him endlessly to postpone getting down to work. When he is finally forced to put up or ship out, he can come up with only a facile piece of screen spectacular that goes as wrong as his relationships with those women. Indecisive to the last, he is unable even to kill himself, but finally he accepts a useful bit of advice from his young self—"grow up."

The show's libretto compensated for the spinelessness of its central character and the non-action of its plot by following the example of the 1966 Italian musical *Ciao, Rudy* and surrounding its "hero" with a colorful collection of 21 variegated women that included his wife (Karen Akers), his current mistress (Anita Morris), his star (Shelly Burch), his producer (Liliane Montevecchi) and his mother (Taina Elg), and the score reflected that variety of color in a series of character numbers of which the wife's even "My Husband Makes Movies" and the star's admission that she loves the man "In an Unusual Way" proved coolly extractable.

On a one-set stage, tiled white to represent a spa, Miss Morris whispered suggestive nothings down the telephone in a mixture of chest and soprano tones whilst performing an ecstatic contortion act in what Guido tried to make his wife believe is "A Call from the Vatican," Kathi Moss recounted Contini's introduction to sex with booming exuberance ("Ti voglio bene"), Montevecchi displayed splendid legs in a pastichey piece about "Folies-Bergère" and Taina Elg reminisced gently over her son at "Nine" in a succession of revusical highlights, which were complemented by some appreciable choral part-writing in a sung "Overture di Donne" and a bristling introductory "The Germans at the Spa."

Nine was awarded the 1982 Tony Award as Best Musical in a season that also included *Dreamgirls* and the decade-old *Joseph and the Amazing Technicolor Dreamcoat,* and went on to a good Broadway run of 732 performances. In spite of a lot of announcements, however, it did not then travel, and a 1987 Australian production was the only one to appear in the other main centers in the years following the Broadway run. Cast to the hilt with some of the country's top female performers, it won sufficient local success for its producer to spread word of an international transfer that in the end did not take place. London got a concert performance, and then—in 1996—a brief season in a de-trappingsed version, featuring Larry Lamb, at the Donmar Warehouse.

On the other side of the Channel, however, the (almost) all-women piece went the same way as another (almost) all-women piece had done a century and more earlier. Like *An Adamless Eden, Nine* found the "all-women" aspect of the show taking the emphasis. The piece was produced at Paris's onetime showcase of femininity, the Folies-Bergère, in a version by Mario Fratti and Eric-Emmanuel Schmitt, with Jérôme Pradon playing gutless Guido for two months. Germany, which was at this time picking up and producing a number of the cultish musicals of Broadway's more recent past, gave this one (ad Ulf Dietrich) a run the following year, with Alfred Pfeifer in the central role of a production that had nothing of the cool white decoration and sophisticated style of the original, but instead went for as much colorful vulgarity as could be fitted on to a stage.

An earlier musical by the same name, libretto by Danam, Barthélémy and Marc-Cab and score by Vincent Scotto, was produced at the Eldorado, Nice, 10 January 1935.

Australia: Her Majesty's Theatre, Melbourne 5 March 1988; UK: Donmar Warehouse 6 December 1996; France: Folies-Bergère 16 September 1997; Germany: Theater des Westens 23 October 1998

Recordings: original cast (Columbia), Australian cast (Polydor), English concert (TER)

NINETTE Opérette in 3 acts by Charles Clairville. Music by Charles Lecocq. Théâtre des Bouffes-Parisiens, Paris, 28 February 1896.

The Ninette of the title of Lecocq's opérette is Ninon de l'Enclos, the same historical personage who battled for a man with Nanon of the Golden Lamb in Richarad Genée's *Nanon.* In Clairville's libretto she comes out better, scoring most of the hits in a lighthearted plot that matches her with the chevalier of the nose, Cyrano de Bergerac.

The aging Lecocq had originally intended the score of this piece as the material for a substantial *Cyrano de Bergerac,* which he hoped would be staged at the Opéra-Comique with Marcelle Dartoy as its Ninon, but, having failed to convince the gentlemen of the Salle Favart that Cyrano and/or Lecocq (who had failed there with *Plutus*) were suitable material for them, he transformed his score with a few lighter pieces into another and rather different kind of period piece. In spite of the then vogue for the "gentille" in musical theatre, the very well-made *Ninette* was played 107 times under Georges Grisier's management at the Bouffes-Parisiens with Germaine Gallois as the spirituelle Ninon and Piccaluga in the role of Cyrano. It won a production in Budapest and then, with fashion of the times thoroughly against it, slipped from the schedules.

Hungary: Népszínház 16 January 1897

NINICHE Vaudeville-opérette (pièce) in 3 acts by Alfred Hennequin and Albert Millaud [and Émile de Najac, uncredited]. Music composed and arranged by Marius Boullard. Théâtre des Variétés, Paris, 15 February 1878.

"Ask anyone of the thousands of English who flocked to Paris in 1867 what is his chief recollection of the first great Exhibition year, and he will certainly tell you 'the Variétés with Schneider in the *Grand Duchess,'* ask the same question of any visitor to Paris in the next Exhibition year of 1878 and you will get the same answer 'the Variétés,' again, only this time it is Judic in *Niniche*" (*Era*).

The first one of the most successful, and in some ways even the most successful—*Lili* and *Mam'zelle Nitouche* included—of the series of vaudeville-opérettes produced at the Théâtre des Variétés with Anna Judic as star, *Niniche* went a round the world several times after its huge initial success in Paris.

Judic was "Niniche," once a demi-mondaine, now the wife of the Polish Count Corniski. In her days in the demimonde, one of her admirers had been the heir to the Polish throne, and now, as his succession approaches, he is anxious to regain possession of some rather embarrassing letters that he once wrote to the lady. Unfortunately, the Countess left her old affairs in Paris in rather a dubious state when she vanished into the northern aristocracy, and her apartment and furniture have been seized by the bailiffs, sealed, and are about to be put up for auction. Everyone heads for Paris: the Countess, her diplomat husband (Baron), the friendly gommeux Anatole de Beaupersil (Lassouche) and the ambitious Grégoire (Dupuis), anxious to prove his abilities by being the one to bring back the letters. Alas, once on her old home ground, the Countess finds the urge to become "Niniche" again irresistible, a feeling and a fact that do not help matters during the two acts of farcical ins-and-outs, disguises and delicate situations that are gone through on the way to the ultimately modest and satisfactorily face-saving ending.

Judic caused a sensation in her role, not only with her virtuoso playing of the "double" part and her long-talked-about second-act entrance in a dazzling costume and toilette, transformed from the Countess Corniska back into "Niniche," but most particularly by appearing on the stage in a bathing costume. Dupuis, who had a fine role, also indulged in a bathing suit without creating a parallel sensation, and went through a comical scene of disguise as a waiter in the final act. In the other feminine roles, Paris's favorite "dragon," Aline Duval, played la veuve Sillery and Augustine Leriche appeared as Géorgina.

Although *Niniche* was, properly speaking, a vaudeville and thus not perhaps quite what the public normally expected to find in the way of entertainment at the theatre that had so long and well provided them with the best of Offenbach, Variétés director Eugène Bertrand had recognized when the piece was submitted to him for his consideration that it would make a fine vehicle for Judic, a star for the half-dozen years since *Le Roi Carotte* and *Le Timbale d'argent* and recently seen to advantage in Offenbach's *Le Docteur Ox.* He duly approached Offenbach to compose some music for the songs that were needed to make Judic's role into a sufficiently showy one, and was refused. The composer, apparently taken aback by the huge and recent success of Planquette's *Les Cloches de Corneville* and Lecocq's *Le Petit Duc,* was determined that his next work would be an important one, and he was not interested in writing vaudeville tunes. With his production already scheduled, Bertrand took the quickest way out: he asked former Variétés musical director Marius Boullard to supply the music for Judic's songs. Boullard, leaning in traditional fashion on ponts-neufs, the well and oft-used popular airs that were used and reused as melodies for vaudeville songs, provided just the straightforward, rhythmic and tuneful material that was required—music that allowed the actress to put across her songs rather than sing them too lyrically—to make up a score of eight numbers and some bits.

Judic opened with a swimsuited shivering song, complaining (though, of course, no one else did) ''Mon costume est si collant!'' and brrrr!-ing through a refrain that concluded ''Baigneur, viens me prendre, j'ai froid!,'' followed up with a rondo, and, in the second act, another as she looked longingly over her old Parisian haunt (''Nature supérieure''). She reminisced further, dressed in her grande toilette (''Avec ce costume, Anatole''), joined in a comic duo with Dupuis (''Il faut oser'') and tied up her vocal contribution with the Couplets du Commissaire of the final act. There was, of course, little space for anyone else in the music of the piece, and only Dupuis of the other leading players had his musical moments. He confided, in his Couplets du baigneur in the first scene, ''Si j'avais suivi les voeux de mon père, oui, j'aurais pu faire un bon sous-prefet,'' concluding ''Moi, je baigne!'' He teaches the ladies swimming, an occupation that, of course, involves putting his two hands . . . here! His hands and their occupation were also the subject of his second song, the Couplets du masseur, in the third act.

Niniche and Anna Judic turned out to be an enormous success together, quite able to compete and more with the Planquette and Lecocq triumphs at the Folies-Dramatiques and the Théâtre de la Renaissance, whilst Offenbach's ''substantial'' *Maître Péronilla* was a 50-performance flop at the Bouffes-Parisiens. The first run of Bertrand's production continued through the whole season at the Variétés (275 performances), and its amazing triumph persuaded the producer to continue with a policy of mounting similarly constructed and cast vaudeville-opérettes. It was a policy that turned out to be a paying one and one that, not unnaturally, included several revivals of *Niniche,* a piece and a role that Judic kept in her repertoire for more than two decades. Her last Paris appearance in the part was at the Variétés in 1901, nearly a quarter of a century after her first appearance in the famous maillot de bain. The maillot de bain was now a few sizes larger. So was Baron, still there in his original role alongside Petit and Simon.

Niniche was a great international success, but apart from the interminable tours made throughout Europe and America by Judic, and later by Jane Pierny, it was rarely seen outside France in the form in which it was played at the Théâtre des Variétés. Improvers were everywhere. In Vienna, the text (ad Richard Genée) was reset with new music by Josef Brandl for its production at the Carltheater. Josephine Zampa scored a huge personal success in Judic's role, alongside Wilhelm Knaack (Corniski), Karl Blasel (Beaupersil) and Franz Tewele (Grégoire), for a fine 28 straight performances before the show was put into repertoire (56 performances in 1878–79) and played throughout the country in provincial theatres. Its success was, indeed, so great that the Theater in der Josefstadt leaped promptly in with a soi-disant Bruno Zappert burlesque entitled *Ninischerl: Schwimmschul* (7 November 1878, mus: Ludwig Gothov-Grüneke). In Frankfurt and Berlin, however, it was banned by local censors as ''immoral.''

The Boullard music was performed by its original star at the Theater an der Wien in 1883 (16 November) and at the Carltheater when the Variétés company with Judic, Baron and Dupuis visited in 1889 (21 April). Judic repeated her role there again in 1895, before another version with the text of the piece (in a German version by Victor Léon and Heinrich von Waldberg, which made Niniche a South American princess), musically reset by Richard Heuberger as *Ihre Excellenz,* was performed at the Theater an der Wien, with Ilka Pálmay starred (28 January 1899). *Ihre Excellenz* was played later that same year in Germany (Nuremberg 14 July). However, the earlier ''Possenspiel mit Gesang,'' in its Brandl version, had already been played widely through Germany since its first production in Dresden, and *Ihre Excellenz* did not prove able to compete.

Budapest, in spite of following behind the Austrian and German premieres, did not take up Brandl's music, but, alone of the translated versions, stuck basically with Boullard's score for the production (ad Ferenc Csepreghy) at the Népszínház. Gerőffyné starred alongside István Együd (Korniszky), Elek Solymossy (Boperszil) and Miklós Tihanyi (Gregor) in a production that was a veritable hit (55 performances), resulting in a revival (9 September 1887) and a countrywide success, as the piece joined the other Judic shows, *Lili* and *Mam'zelle Nitouche,* in confirming an outstanding success for the family of Théâtre de Variétés vaudevilles in Hungary.

Although *Niniche* was ultimately played in America in its original state by Judic in the 1885–86 season, it had already been plundered for an American piece prior to the French star's visit. It was one that emphasized the swimsuit. *Newport; or, The Swimmer, the Singer and the Cypher* (ad Olive Logan Sykes, Daly's Theater 15 September 1879) was mounted by no less an impresario than Augustin Daly, with Catherine Lewis starring in Judic's role. Shortly after that, *Niniche* was seen in New

York in German, in the Brandl version, with Poldi Pietsch, Tewele (Grégoire) and Knaack (Corniski) starred. That version was also later remade in English, and the result was produced on Broadway as *The Merry Countess,* with Brandl's music intact. However, the first genuine English version of the piece seems to be that done by Colonel Milliken's company, with Madeleine Lucette starred, which visited Brooklyn the same week that Judic came to Broadway with the original. The whole thing was done over yet once more in 1901 as a vehicle for Anna Held—a performer aspiring to the Judic manner—as *The Little Duchess,* this time with a Reginald De Koven score. In between times, Judic came by and showed New York and the rest of America the real *Niniche.*

London, too, saw Judic play *Niniche* in its original form and language in her repertoire season (w *Lili*) in 1883 and (w *Mam'zelle Nitouche* and *La Cosaque*) in 1884, but an English version made by B C Stephenson for actress-manager Kate Santley was—in spite of that lady's haranguing the Examiner of plays at his home one 8 AM—refused a license. F C Burnand's highly successful English version, *Boulogne* (1879), was played—in spite of being introduced by the Gaiety Theatre's greatest musical comedy star, Nellie Farren—without any musical score. Since none of the American versions ever crossed the Atlantic, London ultimately never got a musical, English-language *Niniche.*

Niniche traveled to virtually every corner of the earth in one or another of its forms, more often than not gathering local music on the way. Thus Portugal's version picked up a musical score by Sgr Alvarenga, whilst in Italy a 1916 *Niniche* produced at Milan's Teatro Carcano (18 October) bore the names of Carlo Vizzotto and Angelo Bettellini under its title.

Austria: Carltheater (Brandl score) 12 October 1878; Germany: Dresden (Brandl score) 26 November 1878; Hungary: Népszínház *Niniss* 20 December 1878; London: Gaiety Theatre (Fr) 9 June 1883; USA: Thalia Theater (Ger, Brandl score) 31 October 1882, Wallack's Theater (Fr) 7 October 1885, Carll's Opera House, New Haven (Eng) 23 September 1885, Garrick Theater *The Merry Countess* 2 November 1895

NINI LA CHANCE Comédie musicale in 2 acts by Jacques Mareuil. Music by Georges Lifermann. Théâtre Marigny, Paris, 21 October 1976.

A vehicle for musical-comedy and popular-song star Annie Cordy, who started the show as a nurse in 1939 San Francisco and, by way of the phony war and the real war, ended up saving the life of an American colonel and becoming a Broadway star. Her love interest, Jimmy (author Mareuil), becomes a war hero, and his mate Tom (James Sparrow) gets to be a Hollywood film star. On the way, Mlle Cordy gave out with "Un gars comme ça," "Nini la Chance," "Y'a des moments" and "Ça ira mieux demain" in her inimitable style, and Sparrow declared himself fleet-footedly "Dingue de danse."

After a fine Paris season, *Nini la Chance* was toured through France and Belgium into 1978.

Recording: original cast (CBS)

NISIDA Comic Operette in 3 acts by Moritz West and F Zell. Music by Richard Genée. Carltheater, Vienna, 9 October 1880.

Another internationally played product of the early Viennese stage, *Nisida* was an up-to-date Cuban piece that mixed a standard romantic story, featuring Frln Klein in the title role as the soubrettey niece of a Spanish impresario called Barnacle (Wilhelm Knaack) and Karl Drucker as one Don Montiel de Caragui, who was apparently a spare-time buccaneer, with some showbiz jollity in which Barnacle was joined by a pair of theatrical agents (played by Franz Eppich and Müller) and the whole troupe of "Die lustigen Nigger," who have descended on Havana for the duration. Karl Blasel played the local potentate, Don Leonida Palestro, Corregidor in Havana and father of the buccaneering Montiel, Frau Benisch was his wealthy but unwed sister Micaëla, whilst Frln Bisca as their niece Mercedes and Josef Joseffy as the military Don Rodrigo Sandoval provided the secondary and more soulful love interest.

Nisida played only a few performances at the Carltheater, but they were by no means the end of its career. The piece promptly surfaced in the German-speaking theatre in New York, where Mathilde Cottrelly starred in the title role alongside Adolfi as the Corregidor, Schnelle (Montiel) and Lube (Barnacle), and it had a magnificent success, playing uninterruptedly for more than a month, a rare thing at that limited-audience theatre. Thus, it was not surprising that an English-language production soon followed. A fortnight after the end of the Thalia season—and only three months after the Viennese premiere—Daly's Theater opened *Zanina, or The Rover of Cambaye* billed as "Augustin Daly's adaptation [of] a musical comedy in 3 acts with an original East Indian Interlude by Harry W French, several original musical numbers by Mr E Mollenhauer, the words of the songs by Mr Fred Williams." Laura Joyce was Zanina, John Brand played Montiel, James Lewis was Lumlini Strakoschini Barnaco and Digby Bell was His Excellency Booma Poota, which was sufficient to show that the action no longer took place in Cuba. It had been shoved into the good old Orient, and decorated with a bundle of nautch girls with a dance performed "for the first time in the history of the world outside the confines of India," magicians who grew rice from grains of sand, transformed a rag baby into pigeons and did The Indian Basket Trick, snake charmers, a knife thrower and so forth, all of which the management insisted had been imported from India. There was also a hurricane to bring Act II to its peak. Ada Rehan played the small role of Muttra, ''a native with European tendencies but with the universal craving for rupees.''

Messrs Mollenhauer and Williams's contribution wasn't defined on the bills, but they were probably not responsible for the Cuban-flavored Smoking Duet, which insisted (already) ''Clearly smoking is annoying.'' There were solos for Montiel (''The Rover of Cambaye'') and Zanina (''I'm a Cherry Sweet to Taste,'' Song of the Czakik, Bolero)—who also joined in a pair of duos—Captain Trafalgar (ex- Sandoval, ''Love Is Made of Smiles and Tears'') and Numa (ex- Mercedes, ''Love with Doubt Can Never Dwell,'' ''Fragrant their perfume''), and the comics were equally well supplied, the three impresarii singing their self-praises and Booma Poota avoiding the usually unavoidable ''I am'' type of potentate song.

All Daly's trouble and expense, however, did not win him a hit. *Zanina* in English ran the same four weeks as the German version had done. In the meanwhile, however, that German version had been produced at Hamburg, and Berlin, Prague, Leipzig and many other central European theatres queued up to mount *Nisida* in the early 1880s. The show nevertheless remained well in the shadow of Genée's two major hits, *Der Seekadett* and *Nanon.*

A second and less extravagantly decorated American version of *Nisida* was produced almost simultaneously (3 February 1881) with Daly's version, under the original title, at San Francisco's Bush Street Theater, with Emilie Melville starred.

Another piece called *Nisida* (Carlo di Barbieri/Kruger) and subtitled *die Perle von Procida* was produced at Hamburg in 1852 (29 September).

USA: Thalia Theater (Ger) 7 December 1880, Daly's Theater *Zanina* 19 January 1881; Germany: Carl-Schultze Theater, Hamburg 15 January 1881, Friedrich-Wilhelmstädtisches Theater, Berlin 5 March 1881

LES NOCES DE JEANNETTE Opéra-comique in 1 act by Michel Carré and Jules Barbier. Music by Victor Massé. Opéra-Comique, Paris, 4 February 1853.

Massé's little opéra-comique was one of the mid-19th-century pieces which blended over the join between the Auber/Adam/Boïeldieu era of French opéra-comique and the newer, more frankly joyous style of musical play as composed by Hervé and Offenbach. Its libretto told of a young lad who takes fright for his liberty and runs off for a boozy spree when he should be getting married, only to be reconciled to his girl and to married life by her forbearance and charm. It was a book in the same vein as those that would characterize the little ''rural'' opérettes of Offenbach's early years (as opposed to the crazy burlesque ones), and Massé's score, whilst more vocally demanding in places than was later normal, rendered nothing to the later works in spirit and charm. Introduced at the Opéra-Comique (where much of Offenbach's work was refused) by Felix Miolan-Carvalho (Jeannette) and Couderc (Jean), it became a perennial item there (1,000th performance 10 May 1895) and quickly found its way into the repertoire of operatic troupes throughout the world and in a multitude of languages. Britain and America heard an English version from the Pyne and Harrison Opera Company, in an adaptation written by William Harrison in which Jeannette became Georgette, whilst Karl Treumann introduced the piece to Vienna at his Kai-Theater alongside the early works of Offenbach and such other survivors of the cross-over period as Poise's *Bonsoir voisin,* Caspers's *Ma tante dort,* Flotow's *Madame Bonjour* and Adam's *Les Pantins de Violette.* Another German version (ad Ida Schuselka-Brüning) was later played at the Vienna Hofoper, and, a witness to the durability of this little piece, a version of that adaptation was played in 1992 at the Dresden Staatsoperette. England, however, showed a rather cavalier attitude to Massé's music: an 1861 production at the Princess's Theatre (*Jeannette's Wedding* 10 October) simply omitted the score and played Carré and Barbier's libretto as a one-act play. Louisa Pyne later toured another version (ad Leicester Buckingham, Augustus Harris) as *Jeannette's Wedding.*

Australia, on the other hand, got the show in two stages. The first colonial *Jeannette's Wedding* was played at the Princess Theatre in Melbourne in 1858 (11 October), but again without Massé's music. The advertisement for the night stated that it had ''music composed expressly for this theatre by S D Nelson Esq.'' It was not, apparently, until 1906 that the ''Australian premiere'' took place, thus billed in a program given by singer Blanche Arrall (better known back home in France as Clara Lardinois) at the Sydney Town Hall, which, if it apparently included most of the music, does not seem to have otherwise been quite the whole piece.

A later English version (Crystal Palace 19 October 1880) was played under the title *Haste from the Wedding* (ad William Grist).

Germany: Dresden 9 January 1854, Berlin 30 October 1857; USA: New Orleans 1854, Niblo's Garden, New York *The Marriage of Jeannette* 9 April 1855; UK: Theatre Royal, Covent Garden *The Marriage of Georgette* 26 November 1860; Austria: Theater am Franz-Josefs-Kai 18 October 1862; Hungary: Nemzeti Színház *Jeannette menyegzője* 4 February 1879; Australia: Town Hall, Sydney *The Marriage of Jeannette* 29 September 1906

LES NOCES D'OLIVETTE Opérette in 3 acts by Henri Chivot and Alfred Duru. Music by Edmond Audran. Théâtre des Bouffes-Parisiens, Paris, 13 November 1879.

Having taken over the ailing Théâtre des Bouffes-Parisiens from Charles Comte (d Paris 13 August 1884), Louis Cantin took the first step towards restoring the house's popularity when he staged *Les Noces d'Olivette.* If the libretto was signed by two well-proven authors, the composer Edmond Audran was, on the other hand, unknown to Paris audiences. He had, however, had a significant success in Marseille with the delightful opérette *Le Grand Mogul,* a sufficient credential for Cantin to commission him to write a fresh piece for the Paris stage.

The text for *Les Noces d'Olivette* was one of the complex sexual-marital tales so popular at the time. Olivette (Élise Clary), the daughter of the seneschal of Perpignan, is in love with and due to be wed to Valentin (Marcelin). However, climbing up to a window he thinks is his soon-to-be bride's, Valentin instead breaks in upon the local potentate, Countess Bathilde de Roussillon (Mlle Bennati). Although the lady is far from displeased at the handsome lad's visit, his escapade leads to Valentin's ending up in prison. He escapes from his cell disguised as his uncle Merimac (Gerpré) and when Bathilde, now determined that Olivette will not wed Valentin, forces her instead to wed "Merimac," a curious marriage duly takes place, with Valentin having, in turn, to be both himself and his uncle. Since the truth is kept well hidden from all but the wedded pair, Bathilde still pursues Valentin, and things get even more complex when the real Merimac, taking advantage of the situation, tries to pretend that he is the legitimate husband of the heroine. However, after some local conspiring has led to the kidnapping of the Countess, all is ultimately untangled and a happy ending arrived at. Olivette's noces are clarified, and the Countess instead weds the chief conspirator, the Duc des Ifs (Alfred Jolly), to stop him from conspiring.

If Olivette had the title role of the piece, the two female parts were, in fact, of equal value, with the heroine being the soubrette role and Bathilde the more legitimate soprano. Olivette had her best moment in a jolly Chanson du mousse, Bathilde in the waltz "Pays du gai soleil," and the two joined together in the Act II farandole "Sous la tonnelle." A boléro for the Duc, the Couplets du Plongeon—a piece paralleling breaking up with a woman and overthrowing a government, which proved as pointed as it was no doubt intended to be—and a Chanson du vin de Roussillon for three supporting characters were the other musical high points.

Les Noces d'Olivette was a clear-cut success for Cantin, running an initial 89 nights at the Bouffes, and it followed its Parisian success by carrying its composer's name around the world. Alexander Henderson took up the show for London and produced it at the Strand Theatre (ad H B Farnie) with Florence St John, the sensational star of his *Madame Favart,* playing Olivette alongside Violet Cameron (Bathilde), Claude Marius (Merimac) and Henry Ashley (Duc des Ifs) and with tenor Knight Aston as Valentin. Amid accolades for its libretto "brimming with comic situations" and its score of "so much gaiety and liveliness," the show gave Henderson a second huge success, running through the whole of 1881 and into 1882 before closing after a remarkable 466 performances, which put it straight into the top-scoring handful of London musical shows of all time. It was later revived at the Avenue Theatre in the gap between *Manteaux Noirs* and *Belle Lurette* (1883), and it also proved a longtime touring proposition in Britain.

The reception given to *Olivette* in Britain was echoed thoroughly in the United States. Produced at the Bijou Theater by the Comley-Barton troupe, with a cast headed by the Welsh star of the recent hit *The Royal Middy,* soprano Catherine Lewis (Olivette), Britain's Hetty Tracy (Bathilde), Australian John Howson (Merimac), Milwaukee's Digby Bell (Coquelicot), Marie Jansen (Veloutine) and James Barton (Duc des Ifs), it was an instant hit. The tale of the "Torpedo and the Whale" challenged *Billee Taylor*'s "All on Account of Eliza" for the spot of show tune of the year as the company moved on from the Bijou to the Fifth Avenue Theater and other producers hurried to get themselves a version of *Olivette* on the stage. John Duff took just three weeks to get his *Olivette* up at the Park Theater (17 January 1881), the Bostonians brought their version to Booth's, Maurice Grau's French company gave the piece in its original French, Emilie Melville's company featured its manageress at the Standard Theater, J Fred Zimmerman starred Selina Dolaro in his version at the Metropolitan Alcazar and the burlesque merchants proffered an *All-of-it* and an *Oily-Vet, or The Wilful Maid and the Sad Sea-Dog* (Tony Pastor's 7 March 1881). While the *Olivette* craze raged on Broadway, dozens of more or less approximate and/or pirated versions sprouted up in every corner of the country, with stars ranging from virtually voiceless burleycue queens to patented vocalists Emily Soldene and Emma Abbott. It was a craze that was only partially extinguished by the arrival of *Olivette*'s successor from the pen of Audran, *La Mascotte,* and of the other megahit of the era, the English *Billee Taylor. Olivette* remained a favorite feature of the American musical-theatre circuits for many years.

Australia, too, welcomed *Olivette* enthusiastically as played by the J C Williamson troupe, featuring Elsa May (Olivette), Agnes Consuelo (Veloutine), Nellie Stewart (Bathilde), Edwin Kelly (Merimac) and E W Royce (Coquelicot), and the show was played in repertoire there for several seasons.

Europe was less swift to take the show up. Budapest's Népszínház did not play Lajos Evva's version until 1881, hard on the heels of the huge success in Hungary of *La Mascotte.* If the production with Mariska Komáromi (Olivette), Aranka Hegyi (Bathilde) and Vidor Kassai (Merimac) did not quite equal the run of the more famous piece, it was nevertheless played a fine 25 times and revived for a second run five years later (14 August 1886). Vienna, too, waited until *La Mascotte* had made Audran's name interesting, and Franz Tewele produced *Olivette* at the Carltheater in late 1881, with Antonie Schläger in the title role alongside Frln Horty (Bathilde), Karl Drucker (Valentin), Josef Joseffy (Duc des Ifs), Karl Blasel (Merimac) and Franz Eppich (Marvejol). This time, however, it didn't go. Tewele got just 17 performances out of the show. The piece was clearly not to German tastes either, for although it finally reached Munich in 1883, it was a further 12 years before a version of the show, played for some reason under the title of *Kapitän Caricciolo,* got to Berlin. There it rang no such bells as it had done in the French and English-speaking versions.

UK: Strand Theatre *Olivette* 18 September 1880; USA: Bijou Theater *Olivette* 25 December 1880; Australia: Theatre Royal, Sydney *Olivette* 13 August 1881; Hungary: Népszínház *Olivette lakodalma* 8 September 1881; Austria: Carltheater *Olivette* 29 October 1881; Germany: Theater am Gärtnerplatz, Munich *Olivettens Hochzeit* 4 November 1883, Theater Unter den Linden *Kapitän Caricciolo* 23 February 1895

LES NOCES IMPROVISÉES Opérette in 3 acts by Armand Liorat and Albert Fonteny. Music by Francis Chassaigne. Théâtre des Bouffes-Parisiens, Paris, 13 February 1886.

Delphine Ugalde's production of *Les Noces improvisées* (a last-minute change of title for *Les Noces de Nadjy,* previously *La Mariée d'un jour*) at the Bouffes-Parisiens did not have a notable career, playing just 35 performances before shutting down. But those 35 nights were to be the prelude to many hundreds more outside France.

Set in Hungary, the piece concerned itself with the folk hero Rákóczi (Alexandre) who, having been exiled, sneaks back into town, disguised as a wandering minstrel, to visit his beloved Nadgy (Jeanne Thibault). In Act II Nadgy is revealed as the heiress to the Hungarian throne who was carried off by the Austrian overlord as a child, and in Act III she and Rákóczi, disguised this time as glass vendors, make their way back into Hungary in time to lead their countrymen in a counterrevolt against the Austrian emperor. The marriage of the title referred to a union of convenience that Nadgy is forced to contract with a complaisant Austrian count (Paravicini, tenor) in Act I, presumably to make it decent for her to go cavalcading across Europe with a dangerous patriot in Acts II and III. The romance and rebellion were more than counterpointed by the show-stealing Mily-Meyer in the role of the helpful count's dancer-mistress, Mimosa, and chief comedian Édouard Maugé as one Bobinnrumkorff.

Chassaigne's score, occasionally tinted Hungarian (one csárdás), was topped off by the inclusion of the Berlioz march that had made the name of Rákóczi a peg to hang the action of the opérette on, made over into a song for Alexandre.

Following the exceptional success of Chassaigne's *Falka* in Britain, *Les Noces improvisées,* retitled *Nadgy* (ad Alfred Murray), was produced in 1888 with great pomp and promises by Henry Watkin at London's Avenue Theatre. The libretto, although its story remained fairly intact, had undergone some severe reorientation for the occasion. Arthur Roberts (Phelix Pharagas) and Marie Vanoni (Nadgy) were star-billed, he in an introduced comic role as a ''professor of deportment'' tagging on behind (or, more often, in front of) Rákóczi, she in the role originated by Mily-Meyer, now, confusingly, called by the name of the original romantic heroine. Tenor Joseph Tapley was Count Maximilien, comedian J J Dallas his uncle, the Marquis of Bobrumkoff, whilst Giulia Warwick (Princess Etelka) and Alec Marsh (Rákóczi) played the now rather submerged romantic roles but still ended up crowned king and queen of Hungary. The eagerly awaited piece, though faring well enough, did not, however, live up to its blockbusting predecessor in popularity, and it closed after 162 performances to go on the road.

The production of *Nadgy* in London was held up because of the long-running success at the Avenue Theatre of *The Old Guard;* consequently, Murray's adaptation was first seen on Broadway, mounted under the aegis of publisher Alfred Hays. With Marie Jansen (a last-minute replacement for Sadie Martinot as Nadgy), Isabelle Urquhart (Etelka), Mark Smith (Rákóczi), Henry Hallam (Maximilien), Fred Solomon (Marquis) and James T Powers as Pharagas in the lead roles, and staged by Richard Barker, it was singularly successful. It notched up a run of no fewer than five unbroken months before the Casino Theater decided to pull it in favor of their newest prize: *The Yeomen of the Guard.* Hays threatened to sue, as *Nadjy* [*sic*] had not fallen below its $4,500-per-week guaranteed figure. As a result, when Gilbert and Sullivan's piece ended its run, *Nadjy* was remounted at the Casino (21 January 1889), with Fanny Rice starring and Lillian Russell as Etelka, for a second run of a further three months, which brought its total run to a very fine 259 Broadway performances. This record, and London's perfectly respectable one, however, did not persuade the rest of the world to have a look at the show, but *Nadjy* or *Nadgy* nevertheless ended up with a very, very much better record to its credit than *Les Noces improvisées.*

Rákóczi got himself less over-imaginatively pictured in a native Hungarian operett, *Rákóczi,* written by Károly Bakonyi, with lyrics by Sándor Endrődi, Árpád Pásztor and Csaba Sassy, and music by Pongrác Kacsoh, produced with some success at Budapest's Király Színház 20 November 1906.

USA: Casino Theater *Nadjy* 14 May 1888; UK: Avenue Theatre *Nadgy* 7 November 1888

NOËL, Lucien [Charles Alexandre] (b Eghézée, Belgium, 14 March 1873; d La Varenne-St-Hilaire [St Maur], 11 April 1930).

For many years one of the most important lightish-baritone leading men on the French musical stage, Noël was condemned, by the lack of first-class new pieces appearing on the French stage in the early years of the 20th century, to have his most successful moments in revivals of such pieces as *Les Cloches de Corneville* (Marquis), *Le Petit Duc* (Montlandry), *La Fille de Madame Angot* (Ange Pitou), *Le Grand Mogol* (Joquelet), *Rip* (Rip), *Giroflé-Girofla* (Mourzouk), *La Petite Mariée* (Podestat), *François les bas-bleus* (François), *Surcouf* (Surcouf), *Fanfan la Tulipe* (Fanfan), *Boccace* (Tromboli), *Les Mousquetaires au couvent* (Brissac), *Les 28 Jours de Clairette* (Vivarel), *Les P'tites Michu* (Gaston), *La Mascotte* (Pippo) and *La Fauvette du Temple* (Pierre).

He created roles in such pieces as *Les Bicyclistes en voyage* (1893, Albéric), *Panurge* (1895, Pantagruel) and *La Poupée* (1896, Père Maximin), and after garnering a certain amount of publicity by an attempted amorous suicide in 1897, in *Le Maréchal Chaudron* (1898, D'Estillac), *Les Soeurs Gaudichard* (1899, Gontran), *Les Saltimbanques* (1899, Grand Pingouin), *Le Curé Vincent* (1901, Bernard), *Madame la Lune* (1904, *Frau Luna,* Karl) and *La Demoiselle du tabarin* (1910, Marcel) and played la Galette in *Ordre de l'Empereur,* Philippe de Bellegarde in the French premiere of *Capitaine Thérèse* (1901) and Brignol in Paris's *Les Hirondelles* (1907), as well as taking a turn as Danilo in Paris's *La Veuve Joyeuse.*

NO, NO, NANETTE Musical comedy in 3 acts by Frank Mandel, Otto Harbach and Irving Caesar based on *My Lady Friends* by Mandel and Emil Nyitray (and *Oh, James!* by May Edginton). Music by Vincent Youmans. Garrick Theater, Detroit, 23 April 1923; Harris Theater, Chicago, 7 May 1923; Globe Theater, New York, 16 September 1925.

The instigator of *No, No, Nanette* was Broadway producer Harry H Frazee. In 1919 he had, in collaboration with Dan V Arthur, produced a play called *My Lady Friends,* which had done decidedly well for him through 228 Broadway performances and after. Four years was quite a lapse in these times, when even the previous season's flop comedies served by the handful as the bases for the new annual crop of musicals, but *My Lady Friends* was a good property, and it had plenty of life to run through before it was ready to be remade. Composer Vincent Youmans thought it was a good property too, and he applied to Frazee for the job of composing the songs for the new musical version of the show. A sizeable production investment from the young man's mother convinced the producer that Youmans would be an ideal composer, and he duly became part of the new musical's team, along with the play's original author, Frank Mandel, and Otto Harbach, who had adapted Frazee's biggest musical success to date, *Madame Sherry.*

Jimmy Smith (Richard ''Skeets'' Gallagher) cannot get his careful wife, Sue (Juliette Day), to go out and spend the money his Bible-publishing firm makes, so instead he gives himself a little pleasure spending some of it on a row of cuties called Winnie and Betty and Flora. However, when the cuties start to get a bit pressing, Jimmy decides that they will have to go, and his lawyer friend Billy (Francis X Donegan) promises to help. He helps by arranging a showdown with all three lassies at one and the same time in the safely distant Atlantic City. It is actually a rotten choice, and one not nearly distant enough, for not only is Jimmy weekending down in Atlantic City with his ward, Nanette (Phyllis Cleveland), on that very date, but both Sue and Billy's suspicious wife, Lucille (Anna Wheaton), also turn up. The due actful of understandings and misunderstandings is gone through before wedded bliss is reestablished and Nanette safely proposed to by Billy's assistant, Tom. A dose of low comedy was injected into this jolly, harmless little tale in the person of a wisecracking maid (Georgia O'Ramey).

The tryout of *No, No, Nanette* started in Detroit. It began slowly, and the writers were pushed by their producer to come up with some fresh songs as the show moved on. Two of these, ''Tea for Two'' and ''I Want to Be Happy,'' were in place before the first major date, Chicago, was reached. The critics were pleased, but Frazee apparently was not. Within weeks he had sacked the director, E W Royce, and most of the lead players. With Louise Groody (Nanette), Charles Winninger (Jimmy), his wife, Blanche Ring (Lucille), and Bernard Granville (Billy) as replacements, and the two new songs already whistling through half of Chicago's teeth, Frazee got the critics in again, and this time he hit pay dirt. The show settled in for a record Chicago run of 12 months. Although *No, No, Nanette* had yet to get anywhere near Broadway (Frazee had booked his starry Chicago takeovers for New York, so New York had to wait until Chicago was done with them), other *Nanette*s were quick to follow.

Plate 281. **No, No, Nanette**

Neophyte British producers Jack Waller and Herbert Clayton, visiting America in search of novelties to launch them in London, picked up four musicals, one of which was the still-young *No, No, Nanette.* When the bigger boys came hunting, once the show had blossomed, they found they had been beaten to the game. London's *Nanette* was cast to the gunwales by its new boy producers, with Binnie Hale in the title role, *Merry Widow* hero Joe Coyne as Jimmy, George Grossmith as Billy, Irene Browne as Lucille and old-time comedienne Gracie Leigh as the maid. Equipped with a couple of fresh numbers (''I've Confessed to the Breeze,'' ''Take a Little One-Step''), it duly turned up West End trumps in a quite dramatic way. London's *No, No, Nanette* occupied the Palace Theatre for 665 performances. At the same time, Frazee branched out around America, opening a second company for a long run in Philadelphia whilst a third moved into Los Angeles for an extended stay—both companies cast up with such favorite performers as Donald Brian and Julia Sanderson, or Cecil Lean and Cleo Mayfield. And, whilst New York still waited for the show to end its run in Chicago, the Fullers and Hugh Ward opened their production in Melbourne, Australia. Elsie Prince was Australia's Nanette, with Jimmy Godden starred as Jimmy, and May Beatty, Madge White, Winifred Dalle and Charles Morton supported in a company that had a super four-and-a-half-month run in Melbourne—not too far behind the six-month record recently set by *Sally*—before moving on to Sydney's new St James Theatre (26 March 1926) and another fine season that both established the show as a favorite and led to a series of revivals.

Back in America, finally, the Chicago season ended, and *Nanette* moved into New York's Globe Theater with Miss Groody, Winninger and Miss O'Ramey (still there since the beginning) now teamed not with Fritzi Scheff, as had been at one stage promised, but with Josephine Whittell (Lucille), Wellington Cross (Billy) and Eleanor

Dawn (Sue). New York tried to be grumpy about not seeing the show everyone else had been raving about for more than a year until everyone else had seen it for more than a year, but the two now-enormous song hits—and that was not counting Lucille's ''Too Many Rings Around Rosie,'' ''Where Has My Hubby Gone'' blues and ''You Can Dance with Any Girl at All,'' the perky title song and Billy's lively appeal to his ''Telephone Girlie''—and the show's happy, dancing ladling of pure quality meant that it stayed on Broadway for 321 performances.

If New York hadn't turned out to be the show's best tour date, Frazee wasn't complaining. But now that he was in New York, he had another local hazard to look out for: the Broadway lawsuit. With *Nanette* such a big hit, it couldn't be long coming. Sure enough, old partner Dan Arthur now surfaced with a suit claiming an interest in the source material. There were 12 companies playing *Nanette* throughout America when a typical Broadway court awarded him a 25 percent stake in the royalty, which Frazee had allotted to *My Lady Friends.* Frazee fought back (after all, that royalty had presumably been his own perk), and presumably there was an end to it sometime.

In the meanwhile, *Nanette* made her dancing way through the cities of Europe. Paris was the first to take up the show, and what they took up was Waller and Clayton's London production. The Isola Brothers imported director William Mollison and musical director Percival Mackey (a white-gloved act in the pit all on his own), 20 English girl dancers and 10 boys (''the London Palace Boys and Girls'') and their captain and soloist Rita MacLean, and staged a fairly faithful French version (ad Roger Ferréol, Robert de Simone, Georges Merry, Paul Colline) of the London version of the show at the Théâtre Mogador. Plump-cheeked, bobbed and top-billed Loulou Hégoburu sang ''J'ai confessé à la brise'' and ''Thé pour deux'' with Adrien Lamy (Tom) and explained ''Vous marquez bien un temps'' with Cariel (Billy), whilst principal dancer Carlos Conte (who had previously had a charleston spot in the first act) danced illustratively. Félix Oudart (Jimmy) told his girls to ''Battez-vous pour moi,'' and dark and perky Gabrielle Ristori triumphed as Lucile with ''On tourne trop autour de Rose,'' ''Pourquoi suis-je triste quand tu pars?'' (ie, ''Where Has My Hubby Gone'') and ''Tu peux danser avec toutes les femmes.'' The comedy maid's role was reduced, the dances (both Miss MacLean and the dancer playing Winnie had solos as well as Conte) increased, the second-act setting was moved to ''Paris-Plage,'' and *No, No, Nanette* (the title was kept, even though the song went ''non, non, Nanette'') was an enormous success all over again. It passed its 400th performance and spurred the end-of-the-year revuists to the sort of parody titles reserved as a compliment to only the biggest hits—*Nu, nu, Nunette* (Concert Mayol, Vincent Scotto/Leo Lelièvre, Henri Varna, Deyrmon), *T'y fourre tout* (La Lune Rousse)—before the Isolas removed it to mount *Rose-Marie.* In the decades that followed, *No, No, Nanette* returned more frequently to the Paris stage (1930, 1935, 1946, 1965, all at the Mogador) than to the boards of any other musical theatre metropolis.

Germany's version (ad Hans Hellmut Zerlett, Arthur Rebner), which also followed the British version and set the action in London and the Isle of Wight (rather than New York and Atlantic City), and also for some reason rechristened Sue as Mary, was produced at the Metropoltheater with Irene Palasty as Nanette and Max Hansen giving an answer to the ''No, no'' of the title in an interpolated Shimmy-Lied by Rebner and Austin Eger, which insisted ''Jawohl! Jawohl! Jawohl!'' By the time this production arrived at Vienna's Bürgertheater 13 months later, it had gone past its 450th performance. Vienna added another 90 or so to the total, and the company then moved on to Budapest, where Miss Palasty (in German) starred for a fortnight at the Király Színház, where *Mersz-e, Mary?,* with a score attributed to Youmans, had triumphed five months earlier. But Budapest, apparently, stayed loyal to *Mercenary Mary,* which had got to them first (possibly with some of the *Nanette* music in it), and *Nanette* apparently got no Hungarian production.

London saw a *Nanette* revival in 1936 (Hippodrome 8 July), and film versions were produced in 1930 with Alexander Grey, Bernice Claire, Louise Fazenda and Lucien Littlefield featured in a ''Vitaphone sound film'' and in 1940 with Anna Neagle top-billed (another, entitled *Tea for Two,* used only two numbers of the score). But it was not until 1971 than *No, No, Nanette* made a return to Broadway (46th Street Theater 17 January 1971). Harry Rigby and Cyma Rubin's production top-billed old-time film star Ruby Keeler in an expanded version of Sue's role (she was given the Nanette/Billy ''Take a Little One-Step'' as a dance routine), alongside Susan Watson (Nanette), Jack Gilford (Jimmy), Bobby Van (Billy) and Helen Gallagher (Lucille), kept the comedy maid (Patsy Kelly) to her reduced proportions and ran for 861 performances. The success of this production gave the show a whole new impetus as it sent out road companies (one with June Allyson featured, another with Evelyn Keyes, Don Ameche and Swen Swensson), spawned a weakly done London copy of the production (Theatre Royal, Drury Lane 16 May 1973), with Anne Rogers (Lucille), Teddy Green (Billy) and Anna Neagle (Sue), that folded in 277 performances, an Australian revival with Yvonne de Carlo (later Cyd Charisse), and spurred *Nanette* on to making her way back into the regional theatres of the English-speaking world, still waving her credentials as the ultimate 1920s musical of the English-speaking stage. In 1982 she even made it back to the Berlin stage (Theater des Westens 21 May, 33 performances).

UK: Palace Theatre 11 March 1925; Australia: Princess Theatre, Melbourne 27 June 1925; France: Théâtre Mogador 29 April 1926; Germany: Metropoltheater 7 November 1926; Austria: Wiener Bürgertheater 23 December 1927; Hungary: Király Színház (Ger) 17 March 1928

Films: Vitaphone 1930, 1940

Recordings: London cast recordings (WRC, Stanyan), 1971 revival cast (Columbia), London revival cast (CBS), selections (Fontana, Saga, WRC, EMI, etc), selections in French (Pathé, CBS), etc

Literature: Dunn, D: *The Making of No, No, Nanette* (Citadel Press, Secaucus, NJ, 1972)

NORIAC, Jules [CAYRON, Claude Antoine] (b Limoges, 24 April 1827; d Paris, 2 October 1882).

A prominent figure in journalistic (*Le Figaro, Revue des Beaux-Arts, Monde illustré*) and literary circles, and in the French Société des Auteurs, Noriac ventured into the theatre both as a producer and as an author. He shared the directorship of the Théâtre des Variétés with the Cogniard brothers for a time and, in the late 1860s and early 1870s, was allied with Charles Comte at the Théâtre des Bouffes-Parisiens. It was at that theatre, which knew few profitable days during their management, that he co-authored his biggest opérette success with the particularly saucy libretto for *La Timbale d'argent,* the Léon Vasseur opérette, which, by its long and fruitful run, helped the Comte-Noriac management to hold up longer than it would otherwise have done. He had some further success with *La Branche cassée,* the first composition of another young composer, Gaston Serpette, and with another light blue piece, Vasseur's *La Cruche cassée,* produced at the little Salle Taitbout with Céline Chaumont as its chief attraction, but a collaboration with Offenbach brought little joy and his last piece with Vasseur, *La Sorrentine,* was a 40-performance failure.

He died at the age of 55 of ''smoker's cancer.''

1871 **Le Barbier de Trouville** (Charles Lecocq/w Adolphe Jaime) 1 act Théâtre des Bouffes-Parisiens 19 November

1872 **La Timbale d'argent** (Léon Vasseur/w Jaime) Théâtre des Bouffes-Parisiens 9 April

1873 **La Petite Reine** (Vasseur/w Jaime) Théâtre des Bouffes-Parisiens 9 January

1873 **Le Mouton enragé** (Paul Lacome/w Jaime) 1 act Théâtre des Bouffes-Parisiens 27 May

1874 **La Branche cassée** (Gaston Serpette/w Jaime) Théâtre des Bouffes-Parisiens 23 January

1875 **La Cruche cassée** (Vasseur/w Jules Moinaux) Théâtre Taitbout 27 October

1876 **Pierrette et Jacquot** (Jacques Offenbach/w Philippe Gille) 1 act Théâtre des Bouffes-Parisiens 13 October

1876 **La Boîte au lait** (Offenbach/w Eugène Grangé) Théâtre des Bouffes-Parisiens 3 November

1877 **La Sorrentine** (Vasseur/w Moinaux) Théâtre des Bouffes-Parisiens 24 March

1892 **Éros** (Paul Vidal/w Jaime, Maurice Bouchor) Théâtre des Bouffes-Parisiens 22 April

NORMAN, Monty (b London, 4 April 1928). Songwriter who worked on several highly successful British shows of the 1950s and one in the 1970s.

After beginning his working life as a barber's apprentice, Norman made his first moves into the music business as a singer and songwriter, appearing during the 1950s and early 1960s on stage, radio and television and as a band singer. He became involved in the musical theatre when he was brought in, as a potential leading man, to sing through the music of a show that never happened and he stayed to collaborate on its writing with the original authors, Julian More and David Heneker. The show that didn't happen did, however, result in a commission for another, and thus Norman, along with his two associates, became involved in two of the most interesting musicals of the late 1950s: as one of the adaptors of *Irma la Douce* for the English-speaking stage, and as a partner in the songs of the memorable *Expresso Bongo.* Further collaborations with *Expresso Bongo*'s librettist, Wolf Mankowitz, introduced him another success with *Make Me an Offer* and a failure, which nevertheless introduced a popular song (''The Dit-Dit Song''), in *Belle,* a piece that related the story of murderer Dr Crippen in music-hall terms.

Amongst film and television work in the 1960s, his stage shows included a spoof spy thriller, a Jewish fable, a humorous piece set in the world of competition ballroom dancing, a trendy 1970s version of the Jack Sheppard tale and the small-scale *So Who Needs Marriage?,* each played in provincial suburban theatres. However, nearly 20 years after his last West End venture Norman resurfaced in London with *Songbook,* a clever parody on the stream of so-and-so-and-his-music compilation shows that had been dampening British theatres since the Mermaid Theatre had ventured with *Cole* and *Cowardy Custard.* He subsequently supplied a score of humorous numbers for *Poppy,* a bitterer burlesque of Victorian British pantomime and breast-beating politics, which was drowned in production values at the Royal Shakespeare Theatre and the Adelphi Theatre in two attempts at making it to the big time. It was later played in a small-scale version to better effect.

His most recent stage musical was a 1930s piece fashioned from a Lope de Vega play as *Woman Overboard* and produced at Watford.

Norman's most important hit outside the theatre was his James Bond Theme, first heard as part of his score to the 1962 film *Doctor No.*

1958 **Expresso Bongo** (w David Heneker, Julian More/Wolf Mankowitz) Saville Theatre 23 April

1958 **Irma la Douce** English version w Heneker, More (Lyric Theatre)

1959 **Make Me an Offer** (w Heneker/Mankowitz) Theatre Royal, Stratford East 17 October; New Theatre 16 December

1961 **Belle** (Mankowitz) Strand Theatre 4 May

1963 **The Perils of Scobie Prilt** (w More) New Theatre, Oxford 12 June

1967 **Who's Pinkus, Where's Chelm?** (Norman/w C P Taylor) Jeannetta Cochrane Theatre 3 January

1969 **Quick, Quick, Slow** (w More/David Turner) Birmingham Repertory Theatre 20 August

1972 **Stand and Deliver** (Mankowitz) Royal Lyceum Theatre, Edinburgh 20 September

1975 **So Who Needs Marriage?** Gardner Centre, Brighton 8 May

1979 **Songbook** (w More) Globe Theatre 25 July

1982 **Poppy** (Peter Nichols) Barbican Theatre 25 September

1988 **Woman Overboard** (Adrian Mitchell) Palace Theatre, Watford November

NORTON, [George] Frederic[k] (b Broughton-in-Salford, 11 October 1869; d Holford, 15 December 1946). Singer turned songwriter for one huge hit.

Originally a clerk in insurance, Norton escaped and became instead a professional singer, touring as an operatic chorister with Carl Rosa and making occasional appearances in the musical theatre (Maximin in *La Poupée* tour, etc). He also tried his hand at writing parlor songs, turned out the music for a fairy play, and had the odd number interpolated in musical comedies (*The Beauty of Bath,* etc). In 1903 he was invited to Sandringham to entertain the British King and Queen with his songs at the piano (''Mama's Baby Boy,'' ''The Camel and the Butterfly,'' ''Madcap Marjorie,'' ''Tatters and Tucks,'' ''Oh Mr Moon,'' ''Naughty Little Maid,'' etc). In 1908, through the offices of a friend, he was brought together with author W Graham Robertson, and the result of their union was the charming little musical fairy tale *Pinkie and the Fairies* presented on the London stage by no less a personage than Beerbohm Tree with Ellen Terry and Stella Patrick Campbell in the cast. Tree subsequently recalled Norton to help with the messing-about-with of Offenbach's score for *Orpheus in the Underground* (1912). In 1913 he went on the road with Bertram Wallis's Musketeers concert party and, apart from a little revue called *What Ho, Daphne!* produced at the Tivoli music hall and a few songs for *The Passing Show of 1915,* Norton was heard little of as a composer until his Tree connection won him the opportunity to compose the score for Oscar Asche's fairy-tale spectacular *Chu Chin Chow.* The record-breaking success of that show, the popularity won by Norton's ''Any Time's Kissing Time'' and ''The Cobbler's Song,'' and the degree of skill apparent in such pieces as ''I Long for the Sun'' made it all the more strange that the composer failed utterly to follow up his one great hit. He turned out a rather pale score for the Lily Elsie musical *Pamela* the following year, before fading back into turning out just the odd interpolated number (''Rosie'' in Broadway's *The Man with Three Wives,* another in London's *Flora*). He ventured back onto the stage only with a little piece called *The Willow Pattern Plate* played by amateurs and a children's Christmas piece, *Teddie Tail.*

During the run of *Chu Chin Chow,* Norton occasionally stood in for Courtice Pounds in the chief comedy role of Ali Baba.

1908 **Pinkie and the Fairies** (W Graham Robertson) His Majesty's Theatre 19 December

1916 **Chu Chin Chow** (Oscar Asche) His Majesty's Theatre 31 August

1917 **Pamela** (Arthur Wimperis) Palace Theatre 10 December

1920 **Teddie Tail** (Charles Folkard) Duke of York's Theatre 26 December

NO SONG, NO SUPPER Comic opera in 2 acts by Prince Hoare. Music composed [and arranged] by Stephen Storace. Theatre Royal, Drury Lane, 16 April 1790.

One of the few 18th-century comic operas to have survived in production into the latter part of the 19th century, this humorous story of the lascivious lawyer Endless and his undoing over a supper of a leg of lamb was illustrated with an attractive score that featured not only some tidy solos but, most notably, a pretty ladies' trio (''Knocking at This Hour of Day'') and a quintet finale to the first act, all written in the French-flavored opéra-comique style of the time. However, although Storace's name alone was attached to the score, the old ballad-opera influences had not yet vanished, and the composer was quite content to borrow some of his music ''from the French''—notably from the oft-plundered Grétry—without bothering to acknowledge the fact.

No Song, No Supper was first performed at a benefit at Drury Lane with a celebrated cast, featuring Michael Kelly (the author of the famous *Reminiscences*), the concert vocalist Mr Dignum (Crop), the composer's sister Miss Storace (Margaretta, the mover of the plot) and Miss Romanzini (Dorothy Crop) in the featured singing roles, and Bannister and Suett, two noted comedians of the day, as Margaretta's jolly sailor and the discomforted lawyer. The leg of lamb, instead of being a prop, was genuine, and it remained a tradition in the years that followed, that for this particular opera a real piece of meat should always be used.

Widely played in the British provinces through many years, and a regular part of touring operatic companies' repertoires, *No Song, No Supper* was also given several major revivals in London, being staged at the Theatre Royal, Covent Garden, in 1820 with Frederick Pyne and Miss Stephens and again in 1827. In April 1853 the future Mrs Howard Paul appeared as Dorothy in a revival at the Strand, in 1870 it was played at Manchester and at the Haymarket and 1871 it was introduced at the Gaiety Theatre (13 May). In the late 1860s it was toured in America in the repertoire of the Susan Galton operetta company.

USA: Philadelphia 30 December 1792, New York 15 February 1793; Germany: Hamburg 20 February 1795

NO STRINGS Musical in 2 acts by Samuel Taylor. Music and lyrics by Richard Rodgers. 54th Street Theater, New York, 15 March 1962.

Richard Rodgers's first musical for the Broadway stage following the death of Oscar Hammerstein II was built around the talents of the young vocalist Diahann Carroll. Librettist Samuel Taylor cast her as Barbara Woodruff, an American model in Paris, who meets up with a successful but dropped-out novelist named David Jordan (Richard Kiley). Although she is profitably paired with the elegant Louis de Pourtal (Mitchell Gregg), Barbara is soon sharing intimate moments with David and encouraging him to throw over his indolent life and pick up his typewriter again. After an evening of American-in-Paris-isms, amatory swip-swaps and ups-and-downs among members of a supporting cast that included Alvin Epstein as a French fashion photographer, Noëlle Adam as his assistant, Jeanette, Ann Hodges as his infidelity, Gabrielle, Don Chastain as the loose-living Mike Robinson and Bernice Massi as a filthy-rich Europe-eater, and a trip through some other French locations, David heads back to America and a less unproductive life. It is 1962, so there is no happy ending. Barbara stays behind in Paris, where a black girl apparently has better opportunities than in America, and gets on with her work as well.

Rodgers's score mirrored its little tale to a degree, with love songs for the two central lovers and bright numbers for the other characters, and it got through the evening without a single song title mentioning Paris; in fact, the only number in praise of a place was Kiley's happy reminiscence of ''Maine.'' The score of *No Strings,* however, produced one number that would find itself a place on the bottom of the long list of Rodgers and Hart's and Rodgers and Hammerstein's hits: Kiley and Miss Carroll's introductory duet ''The Sweetest Sounds,'' which also served to close out the show. Alongside this winning piece, Barbara delivered ''Loads of Love'' and ''An Orthodox Fool,'' and paired with Kiley in further duos including a title number, ''You Don't Tell Me'' and ''Look No Further'' in what was the more appealing side of the score.

The handouts insisted that *No Strings* was not just another boy-meets-girl-by-the-Seine story, that it had an underlying theme that was ''yet another example of how Richard Rodgers has used his great skills to push out walls of the American musical theatre so that audiences today willingly accept meaningful, adult themes in works that still provide evenings of gaiety and enchantment'' and that it featured ''daring use of stagecraft and subject matter.'' The tricks of the evening were, in fact, mostly orchestral: a band with no strings, to go with the title of the show, which played not from the pit but onstage (a gimmick that was far from being the innovation that was suggested) or backstage, in a staging by Joe Layton which was simple and effective, and did not use the excuse of the French settings for vistas of scenery.

The simple (white) boy-meets-(black) girl-by-the-Seine tale, which eventually turned out to be less important than Rodgers's songs and name and the attractively spare mounting, all helped *No Strings* to a good Broadway run of 580 performances, and—in a season featuring *How to Succeed in Business* and *Carnival*—half-a-Tony Award each for Rodgers's music, Miss Carroll's performance and Joe Layton's dances. Then the show ran out of steam. An American tour company stayed on the road for five months, and a London production, mounted by Rodgers's own Williamson Music, with Art Lund (David) and Beverly Todd (Barbara) featured, and future Shakespearean star Geoffrey Hutchins as Luc, folded in 135 performances. Australia (and other countries) produced *Carnival* and *How to Succeed in Business,* but passed on *No Strings.*

Rodgers's own reputation and his string of romantic operetta hits with Hammerstein meant that whatever he had written at this stage of his career was bound to be placed in a difficult situation both with the public and the critics, and the pretentious announcements with which *No Strings* was launched cannot have helped. Opinions on the piece were widely divergent from the beginning (the Tony results mirror the problem), but the verdict of time has rejected the show just as it has favored the seductive melody of its hit song.

UK: Her Majesty's Theatre 30 December 1963

Recordings: original cast (Capitol), London cast (Decca/DRG), selections (Atlantic), etc

NOTRE DAME DE PARIS Musical, based on the work of the same name by Victor Hugo, by Luc Plamondon. Music by Riccardo Cocciante. Palais des Congrès, Paris, 16 September 1998.

A down-to-basics sketch of Victor Hugo's famous and (too?) often musicalized tale of ''the hunchback of Notre Dame,'' told in a score of Europop music of the kind that requires the performers to sport little head-microphones at 3 centimeters from their lips and to dose their performances with well-calculated ''popular'' vocal mannerisms, this *Notre Dame de Paris,* from the author of France's favorite modern musical *Starmania,* was produced at the 4,000-seat Palais des Congrès and followed—indeed took to its furtherest expression yet—the fin de siècle trend towards semi-staged pop-concert musicals.

The cast, made up largely of French-Canadian vocalists, included Hélène Ségara as Esmeralda, the gypsy girl who awakens lust in the heart of the monk Claude Frollo (Daniel Lavoie) and devotion in the poor hunchbacked bellringer, Quasimodo (Garou), who is his minion. The supporting juveniles of the piece were the duplicitious Captain Phoebus (the clear-voiced Patrick Fiori), his intermittently beloved Fleur de Lys (Julie Zenatti) and the ill-treated poet Gringoire (Bruno Pelletier), while Luck Mervil took the part of the Gypsy King, Clopin, represented here with political intent as the head of a band of ''sans papiers'' (illegal immigrants) crying one moment for refuge and the next making their demands on the city of Paris. Frollo and Phoebus, as the representatives of law and order, were here portrayed as the ''baddies.'' The story, recounted with the same kind of purposefully simplistic ingenuousness that had characterized *Starmania,* comes to its crises with Esmeralda's engineered condemnation to the gallows by the frustrated Frollo, and Quasimodo's revenge on the maddened monk.

The score, by the well-known vocalist Riccardo Cocciante, went for rhythm and repetition rather than for melody or lyric subtlety in a long schedule of musical numbers, which were linked by *Les Misérables*–style recitatives. The trio ''Belle,'' in which a longing Quasimodo, the panting Frollo and the confident Phoebus each express their desire for Esmeralda, turned out to be the public favorite, along with Phoebus's driving ''Déchiré'' (''entre deux femmes que j'aime''), Esmeralda's gentle prison-bound ''Vivre,'' and the most successful solo of the score, Gringoire's guitar-accompanied serenade to the ''Lune.'' Elsewhere the lyrics took simplicity over the edge of cliché, some rhymes provoked smiles (''Être prêtre et aimer une femme . . . ,'' ''Parlez-moi de Florence, et le Renaissance . . .'') from the over-15s, and the big moments lacked breadth. Frollo's centerpiece, ''Tu vas me détruire'' (the title phrase was repeated 21 times, which was one more than Phoebus had said ''Déchiré'' in his number), suffered largely in the obvious comparison with Javert's ''Stars'' (*Les Misérables*). The singers were accompanied not by an orchestra, but by a prerecorded electronic-music and backing tape, which the composer defensively claimed was ''the way of the future'' and in any case was necessary to provide the ''just like you hear it on a record'' sound which his audiences wanted to hear. Often, it seemed that not just the orchestra but the voices too came from the tapes, and that what was being given as ''live'' entertainment was nothing more than a *Black and White Minstrel*–type mime show.

The same Paris audience that had rejected *Les Misérables* and gone mad for *Starmania* found *Notre Dame de Paris* firmly to its taste. The show was played at the Palais de Congrès for a season of four and a half months, its songs became televisable favorites, Garou (without his hunchback guise) became established as a *Hello*!-featured star, and the show's recording sold by the million as *Notre Dame de Paris* established itself as an undoubted successor to *Starmania.* The piece was subsequently played in Canada and the French provinces, a second Parisian season began in October 1999, and it is clear that there will be many more. And laryngitis and winter colds will give the producers no problem.

An English adaptation of a slimmed down version (ad Will Jennings) was given in January 2000 at Las Vegas's Casino Hotel, and a full scale rendering, billed as ''the musical spectacular,'' was mounted by Michael White in the vastness of London's Dominion Theatre in May of the same year. It was greeted with derision, London's most thoughtful critic attacking ''[o]ne of the most stupefyingly awful musicals I have seen in two decades. . . . [T]his is not musical theatre but musical spectacle. . . . [T]he cast bellow relentlessly. . . . Acting? Forget it . . . garbage.'' At the time of writing, however, it still holds the stage in the West End.

USA: Casino Hotel 21 January 2000; UK: Dominion Theatre 23 May 2000

Recordings: pre-production (Sony), live performance original cast (Sony)

NOVELLO, Ivor [DAVIES, David Ivor] (b Cardiff, 15 January 1893; d London, 6 March 1951).

A matinée idol and silent-screen favorite as an actor, Ivor Novello (his nom de théâtre was borrowed from his well-known musician mother, Clara Novello Davies) led an equally successful parallel career as a writer and composer of both straight and musical plays.

His earliest single success as a writer and composer came in 1914 with the wartime song known popularly as ''Keep the Home Fires Burning,'' his first contribution to the theatre was a song included in the ex-French revue *The Bing Boys Are Here,* and his first full theatre credit came when, on the strength of his hit song, he replaced the ailing Paul Rubens as the basic composer of the highly successful Gaiety musical *Theodore & Co* (1916). He subsequently provided more or less music for several other book shows: C B Cochran's very considerable but successful remake of the Belgian musical play *Arlette* (1917), in which Novello's song ''On the Staff'' proved a hit for rising comedian Stanley Lupino, the romantic Harold Fraser-Simson operetta *A Southern Maid* (1917), with which José Collins confirmed her *Maid of the Mountains* hit, the long-running Pinero adaptation *Who's Hooper?* (1919) and Miss Collins's Nell Gwynne musical *Our Nell* (1924). He also contributed to several revues (*See-Saw, A to Z, Tabs, Puppets, The House That Jack Built*), had his comic song ''And Her Mother Came Too'' interpolated into Broadway's *Jack and Jill* (1923) and composed the whole score for the comic opera *The Golden Moth,* a new version of the *Erminie* story that ran for 281 performances at the Adelphi Theatre in 1921. At the same time, he was devoting increasing amounts of his time to the other areas of his high-profile career, and in the years that followed his name was absent from the bills of the musical stage.

When he returned in 1935, after a decade away, it was as a result of a lunchtime conversation with the head of the floundering Theatre Royal, Drury Lane. He found, at the end of the meal, that he had committed himself to write and star in a large-scale spectacular musical show. The success of the lush, romantic *Glamorous Night* led to a series of similar pieces, of which *Careless Rapture* (1936) was the first, and *The Dancing Years* (1939), produced like the two previous pieces, on the large Drury Lane stage, the three-generation tale of *Perchance to Dream* (1945) and *King's Rhapsody* (1949), each starring Novello in their non-singing lead role, were the most successful. They compiled long runs in the theatre and contributed a mass of richly sentimental and enduring songs (''Waltz of My Heart,'' ''I Can Give You the Starlight,'' ''We'll Gather Lilacs,'' ''Some Day My Heart Will Awake,'' ''Shine Through My Dreams,'' ''Love Is My Reason for Living'') to the concert stage. However, in spite of their large and long-lasting vogue in the British theatre, Novello's works remained staunchly ignored by the rest of the world. Even the British colonies and Dominions, which normally snapped up the hit products of the West End, ignored his pieces. It was not merely a case of their failing: they did not even get produced. Novello himself toured to South Africa with *Perchance to Dream,* and *The Dancing Years*—and it alone—was produced with unspectacular results in Australia. Broadway, itself floundering more than somewhat through much of the 1930s but scarcely in a financial state to host a Novello spectacular, passed, and the only productions of Novello's works in America have been in such bulwarks of romantic operetta production as St Louis's Municipal Opera.

In his final show, *Gay's the Word,* which he wrote as a vehicle for comedienne Cicely Courtneidge whilst he was performing in *King's Rhapsody,* Novello abandoned the Ruritanian tales of his large-scale pieces and returned with no little success to the brighter, musical-comedy style of his earliest days (''Vitality,'' ''It's Bound to Be Right on the Night''). However, he is almost entirely remembered today for his sentimental spectaculars and, particularly, for the broadly melodic and romantic songs that they produced.

1916 **Theodore & Co** (w Jerome Kern/Clifford Grey, Adrian Ross/H M Harwood, George Grossmith) Gaiety Theatre 19 September

1917 **Arlette** (w Guy Le Feuvre/Grey, Ross/ad Austen Hurgon, George Arthurs) Shaftesbury Theatre 6 September

1919 **Who's Hooper?** (w Howard Talbot/Grey/Fred Thompson) Adelphi Theatre 13 September

1921 **The Golden Moth** (Thompson, P G Wodehouse) Adelphi Theatre 5 October

1924 **Our Nell** (w Harold Fraser-Simson/Harry Graham/Reginald Arkell, Louis N Parker) Gaiety Theatre 16 April

1935 **Glamorous Night** (Christopher Hassall) Theatre Royal, Drury Lane 2 May

1936 **How Do, Princess** revised version of *Arlette* (Manchester)

1936 **Careless Rapture** (Hassall) Theatre Royal, Drury Lane 11 September

1937 **Crest of the Wave** (Hassall) Theatre Royal, Drury Lane 1 September

1939 **The Dancing Years** (Hassall) Theatre Royal, Drury Lane 23 March

1943 **Arc de Triomphe** (w Hassall) Phoenix Theatre 9 November

1945 **Perchance to Dream** (Novello) London Hippodrome 21 April

1949 **King's Rhapsody** (Novello) Palace Theatre 15 September

1951 **Gay's the Word** (Alan Melville) Saville Theatre 16 February

Biographies: Noble, P: *Ivor Novello, Man of the Theatre* (Falcon Press, London, 1951), Wilson, S: *Ivor* (Michael Joseph, London, 1975), MacQueen Pope, W: *Ivor* (Hutchinson, London, 1952), Harding, J: *Ivor Novello* (W H Allen, London, 1987), Webb, P: *Ivor Novello: A Portrait of a Star* (Stage Directions, London, 1999), Rose, R: *Perchance to Dream: The World of Ivor Novello* (Leslie Frewin, London, 1974), etc

NUITTER, Charles [TRUINET, Charles Louis Étienne] (b Paris, 24 April 1828; d Paris, 24 February 1899).

A Parisian lawyer who threw in the Bar for a career as a theatrical writer, ''Nuitter'' was the author of any number of farces, ballets (notably the scenarii for *Coppélia* and *La Source,* both w Saint-Léon) and vaudevilles and, for more than 40 years, a librettist for the opérette stage.

His earliest significant musical pieces were written for Offenbach: the adaptation of Cervantes' little tale *Los Habladores,* which ultimately became his first longer work as *Les Bavards,* the short pieces *Jeanne qui pleure et Jean qui rit* and *Le Soldat magicien,* the not very successful adaptation of de Leuven's vaudeville as the libretto for *Vert-Vert* and, the most often and internationally played of their collaborations, a comical variation on the doll-girl tale, *La Princesse de Trébizonde.* Nuitter collaborated on the French version of Émile Jonas's delightful retelling of the Cinderella tale as *Javotte* (*Cinderella the Younger*) and on the turning of Offenbach's *Whittington* into *Le Chat du Diable* for Paris, but his best and most successful original libretto, amongst a surprisingly large amount of minor work, was the sex-farcical tale set by Charles Lecocq as *Le Coeur et la main* (w Alexandre Beaumont).

Nuitter, who was employed subsequently as archivist at the Paris Opéra, also wrote a number of operatic texts (de Joncières's *Le Dernier Jour de Pompeii,* Boïeldieu's *La Halte du roi,* etc), without being associated with anything that became a standard, but he was also responsible, often in collaboration, for the French translations of a good number of the principal works of the operatic repertoire (*Der Zauberflöte, Abu Hassan, Preciosa, Oberon, I Capuletti e i Montecchi, Rienzi, Der fliegende Holländer, Tannhäuser, Macbeth, Crispino e la Comare, Lohengrin, La forza del destino, Aïda,* etc). He also wrote several books on classic opera.

His text (w Victorien Sardou) for the 1861 play *Piccolino* was subsequently used as the source for Johann Strauss's Operette *Carneval in Rom* and for Guiraud's opéra-comique *Piccolino* (Opéra-Comique, 1876).

1855 **Une nuit à Seville** (Frédéric Barbier/w Alexandre Beaumont) 1 act Théâtre Lyrique 14 September

1855 **Rose et Narcisse** (Barbier/w Beaumont) 1 act Théâtre Lyrique 21 November

1856 **Le Nid d'amour** (Édouard Montaubry/w Nerée Desarbres) 1 act Théâtre du Vaudeville 21 October

1858 **Le Pacha** (Barbier) 1 act Théâtre des Folies-Nouvelles 24 March

1861 **La Servante à Nicolas** (Jules Erlanger/w Desarbres) 1 act Théâtre des Bouffes-Parisiens 11 March

1861 **Flamberge au vent** (Barbier/w Georges Steaune) 1 act Théâtre du Chalet des Îsles 3 October

1862 **Bavard et Bavarde** (Offenbach) 1 act Bad Ems 11 June

1863 **Les Bavards** revised 2-act *Bavard et Bavarde* Théâtre des Bouffes-Parisiens 20 February

1863 **Il Signor Fagotto** (Offenbach/w Étienne Tréfeu) 1 act Ems 11 July; Friedrich-Wilhelmstädtisches Theater June 1864

1863 **Un Othello** (Isidore Legouix) 1 act Théâtre des Champs-Élysées 21 June

1864 **L'Amour chanteur** (Offenbach/w Ernest L'Épine) 1 act Théâtre des Bouffes-Parisiens 5 January

1864 **Die Rheinnixen** (Offenbach/w Tréfeu) Hofoper, Vienna 4 February

1864 **Jeanne qui pleure et Jean qui rit** (Offenbach/w Tréfeu) 1 act Ems 19 July; Théâtre des Bouffes-Parisiens 3 November 1865

1864 **Le Soldat magicien** (aka *Le Fifre enchanté*) (Offenbach/w Tréfeu) 1 act Ems 9 July; Théâtre des Bouffes-Parisiens 30 September 1868

1864 **Le Lion de Saint-Marc** (Legouix/w Beaumont) 1 act Théâtre Saint-Germain 24 November

1865 **Coscoletto** (Offenbach/w Tréfeu) Bad Ems 24 July

1865 **Une fantasia** (Hervé) 1 act Théâtre des Variétés 12 November

1865 **Les Mémoires de Fanchette** (Nicolo Gabrielli/w Desarbres) 1 act Théâtre Lyrique 22 March

1865 **Le Roi Midas** (Émile Jonas) 1 act privately

1866 **Les Oreilles de Midas** (Barbier/w Desarbres) 1 act Fantaisies-Parisiennes 21 April

1866 **Le Baron de Groschaminet** (Jules Duprato/w Charles Garnier) 1 act Fantaisies-Parisiennes 24 September

1867 **Cardillac** (Lucien Dautresme/w Beaumont) Théâtre Lyrique 11 December

1868 **Le Vengeur** (Legouix/w Beaumont) 1 act Théâtre de l'Athénée 20 November

1869 **Vert-Vert** (Offenbach/w Henri Meilhac) Opéra-Comique 10 March

1869 **La Princesse de Trébizonde** (Offenbach/w Tréfeu) Baden-Baden 31 July

1869 **La Romance de la rose** 1 act Théâtre des Bouffes-Parisiens 11 December

1870 **Le Kobold** (Ernest Guiraud/Louis Gallet) 1 act Opéra-Comique 26 July

1871 **Boule de Neige** (Offenbach/w Tréfeu) Théâtre des Bouffes-Parisiens 14 December

1871 **Javotte** (*Cinderella the Younger*) French version w Tréfeu (Théâtre de l'Athénée)

1872 **Der schwarze Korsar** (Offenbach/w Tréfeu) Theater an der Wien, Vienna 21 September

1874 **Les Dernières Grisettes** (Legouix/w Beaumont) Fantaisies-Parisiennes, Brussels 12 December

1875 **Amphitryon** (Paul Lacome/w Beaumont) 1 act Salle Taitbout 5 April

1877 **L'Oppoponax** (Léon Vasseur/w William Busnach) 1 act Théâtre des Bouffes-Parisiens 2 May

1878 **Pépita** (L Delahaye fils/w Jules Delahaye) 1 act Opéra-Comique 13 July

1878 **Maître Péronilla** (Offenbach/w Offenbach, Paul Ferrier) Théâtre des Bouffes-Parisiens 13 March

1880 **Monsieur de Floridor** (Théodore de Lajarte/w Tréfeu) 1 act Opéra-Comique 11 October

1882 **Le Coeur et la main** (Charles Lecocq/w Beaumont) Théâtre des Nouveautés 19 October

1888 **La Volière** (Lecocq/w Beaumont) Théâtre des Nouveautés 11 February

1888 **La Demoiselle de Belleville** (*Die Jungfrau von Belleville*) French version w Beaumont (Théâtre des Folies-Dramatiques)

1888 **Oscarine** (Victor Roger/w Albert Guinon) Théâtre des Bouffes-Parisiens 15 October

1890 **L'Égyptienne** (Lecocq/w Henri Chivot, Beaumont) Théâtre des Folies-Dramatiques 8 November

1893 **Le Chat du Diable** (*Whittington*) French version w Tréfeu (Théâtre du Châtelet)

1897 **La Gaudriole** (Albert Vizentini/w Tréfeu) Aix-les-Bains 12 September

1898 **Le Soleil à minuit** (Albert Renaud/w Beaumont) Théâtre des Bouffes-Parisiens 14 October

NUNN, Trevor [Robert] (b Ipswich, 14 January 1940). Royal Shakespeare Company and National Theatre director who spent a period, with wide and long success, in the spectacular musical theatre.

Nunn began his theatrical career on a directing bursary at the Belgrade Theatre, Coventry, where his early productions included a musical version of *Around the World in 80 Days.* In 1964 he joined the Royal Shakespeare Company and in 1968 was appointed its Artistic Director, a position he held until 1986. During his tenure at the Royal Shakespeare Company, Nunn ventured, in a regular directing schedule of classic plays, towards the musical theatre with a production of *The Comedy of Errors* (1976) into which sufficient song and dance elements (ch: Gillian Lynne) were introduced for it to be given a ''Best Musical'' award.

His first musical theatre directing assignment in the West End was the creation of the enormously successful Andrew Lloyd Webber musical *Cats* (1980 w Miss Lynne) from which he emerged not only with a directorial credit but also with a share in the lyric to the show's hit song, ''Memory,'' a number created from pieces and reminiscences of published and unpublished works of *Cats* ''librettist,'' T S Eliot. Nunn directed three further Lloyd Webber musicals in the songs-on-skates saga *Starlight Express* (1984) and the winningly atmospheric tale of love in warm places, *Aspects of Love* (1989), repeating his direction in each case in the American reproductions of the London stagings, and the 1993 *Sunset Boulevard.*

He joined *Cats* producer Cameron Mackintosh again to produce (under the name of, and in the theatre of, the Royal Shakespeare Company) and to direct (w John Caird) the enormously successful English adaptation of the French musical *Les Misérables* (1985), which won him awards both in Britain and America (Tony Award) and which was reproduced (sometimes by himself, sometimes by others) in most countries of the world where musical theatre is popular and in several where it isn't. In 1986 he took over the direction of the Tim Rice/Abba musical *Chess,* following the death of its intended director, Michael Bennett, and he staged two different versions of the show, the first in Britain with considerable success and a long run, and a revised one in America with little success and a short run.

In 1986 he quit the Royal Shakespeare Company to continue as a freelance director in theatre and film (*Hedda, Lady Jane*), and in 1989 he co-produced (Homevale Ltd) and directed a short-lived revival of the 1976 musical *The Baker's Wife* in his home town of Ipswich and at London's Phoenix Theatre. He subsequently directed an unsuccessful musical-play version of *The Blue Angel.*

In 1997 Nunn took over the management of Britain's National Theatre, where he subsequently produced and directed much admired revivals of *Oklahoma!* and *Candide* (w John Caird).

The director of two of the world's most successful musicals of the 1980s in *Cats* and *Les Misérables,* Nunn evinced both sense and sensitivity in his handling of large-scale modern musical theatre and its often large-scale stories and characters, human and other, whilst rejecting the gimmickry so many other directors of his generation have employed, in all fields from classic theatre to opera, in order to win themselves notice.

NYMPH ERRANT Play with music in 2 acts by Romney Brent adapted from the novel by James Laver. Music and lyrics by Cole Porter. Adelphi Theatre, London, 6 October 1933.

The novel *Nymph Errant,* written by James Laver, keeper of the theatrical collection at the Victoria and Albert Museum, was a triumphantly funny morsel of understated sexual frivolity and a piece of eminently natural fodder for the musical stage. The nymph of the title was a lass called Evangeline, gorgeous and comical and adored by men, and the ''errant'' qualification had nothing to do with a fall from purity. It referred, rather, to Evangeline's wanderings throughout all the most deliciously perilous and picturesque parts of Europe and Asia, passing from the lustful hands of one pretty potentate to another yet, to her despair, coming out at the end of a series of unforeseen and always masculine circumstances just as virginal as she had set out.

The book was dramatized by the actor Romney Brent, the songs written by Cole Porter, and C B Cochran's production mounted in London, under the direction of Brent, with revue star Gertrude Lawrence as the winsome Evangeline. The supporting cast included Hella Kürty (the original Mi of *Das Land des Lächelns*), Moya Nugent, Iris Ashley, Doris Carson, Elisabeth Welch, Austin Trevor, dancer Walter Crisham and American gangster-specialist David Burns. Doris Zinkeisen was the designer, and the young Agnes de Mille supplied the dances (subsequently redone by Barbara Newberry and Carl Randall). However, what should have been a spectacular and spectacularly funny extravaganza fell flat. The adaptation was considered weak, and the songs, many of them both amusing and attractive in their own right, were a revusical lot that often had little to do with the show.

Amongst those numbers that survived the production were ''The Physician,'' a remake of a 1930 number performed by Marie Cahill in the early stages of the production of *The New Yorkers,* and here put over by Miss Lawrence with a suggestiveness that led to its being banned by the BBC, a piece about mass adultery by the wives of ''Solomon'' introduced by Elisabeth Welch, and Moya Nugent's advice to the heroine to ''Experiment.'' The most fun, however, in what became a rather relentless, one-toned parade of not very wide variations on a sexual theme, came from Queenie Leonard, revusically complaining of being ''an annoyed, unemployed cocotte.'' One variation on the theme didn't please, however: Doris Carson's transvestite tale of ''Georgia Sands'' was dropped after the opening and replaced by a more conventional call to ''Cazanova'' [*sic*] to ''come ova.'' The show foundered in four months and 154 performances, and Cochran canceled his announced Broadway production. Although the favorite songs continued to find performances, the show was put sufficiently away for a fresh musicalization of Brent's script, unimaginatively titled *Evangeline,* to be mounted for the benefit of Frances Day in 1946 (George Posford, Harry Jacobson/Eric Maschwitz, Cambridge Theatre 14 March). It played 32 performances.

During the fashionable free-for-all that whirled around anything and everything written by Porter during the 1980s, *Nymph Errant* was played at New York's Equity Library Theatre (11 March 1982), given a concert performance in Britain and at various stages was mumbled about as a revival prospect without, however, reappearing on the metropolitan stage. It was given a production in a cut-down version at Britain's Chichester Festival in 1999.

Recordings: selection (EMI), concert 1989 (EMI)

NYPE, Russell (b Zion, Ill, 26 April 1924). Double Tony Award winner who won few other Broadway chances.

After an early career as a club singer, Nype played on Broadway in *Regina* (1949, Oscar Hubbard) and *Great to Be Alive* (1950) before creating the role of Kenneth Gibson, and the duet ''You're Just in Love'' with Ethel Merman, in *Call Me Madam* (1950, Tony Award). He won a second Tony for his portrayal of the hapless bridegroom George Randolph Brown in *Goldilocks* (1958, ''Shall I Take My Heart and Go'') and appeared at the New York City Center as Enoch Snow, Jeff Douglas (1967, *Brigadoon*) and Freddie Eynsford-Hill and on the road as Jimmy Smith in *No, No, Nanette.* He later succeeded to the role of Cornelius Hackl in *Hello, Dolly!* (1970), again alongside Miss Merman, 20 years after their more famous pairing.